INTRODUCTION TO THE LAW
OF
THE EUROPEAN COMMUNITIES

P.J.G. Kapteyn & P. VerLoren van Themaat

Introduction to the Law
of
the European Communities

From Maastricht to Amsterdam

Third Edition

Incorporating the Fifth Dutch edition

Edited and further revised by

LAURENCE W. GORMLEY

Barrister, Professor of European Law, Rijksuniversiteit Groningen

in cooperation with the editors of the Fifth Dutch Edition:
P.J.G. Kapteyn, P. VerLoren van Themaat, L.A. Geelhoed
and C.W.A. Timmermans

KLUWER LAW
INTERNATIONAL

LONDON-THE HAGUE-BOSTON

Published by
Kluwer Law International
Sterling House
66 Wilton Road
London SW1V 1DE
United Kingdom

Kluwer Law International incorporates
the publishing programmes of
Graham & Trotman Ltd.,
Kluwer Law & Taxation Publishers
and Martinus Nijhoff Publishers

Sold and distributed
in the USA and Canada by
Kluwer Law International
675 Massachusetts Avenue
Cambridge, MA 02139
USA

In all other countries, sold and distributed by
Kluwer Law International
P.O. Box 322
3300 AJ Dodrecht
The Netherlands

ISBN 90-411-9667-6 (Hardback)
ISBN 90-411-9666-8 (Student Edition)
© Kluwer Law International 1973, 1989, 1998
First published 1973
Second edition 1989 (ed. Gormley)
Reprinted 1991, 1992
Third edition 1998 (revision of the second English edition 1989 incorporating the 5th Dutch edition
with further revisions and material)

The moral rights of the authors and the editor have been asserted

British Library Cataloguing in Publication Data
A catalogue record for this book is available from the British Library

Library of Congress Cataloging-in-Publication Data is available

Learning Resources
Centre

Typeset in 11/12 pt Times by Acorn Bookwork, Salisbury, Wiltshire
Printed and bound in Great Britain by Antony Rowe Ltd, Reading, Berkshire

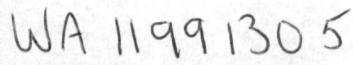

FOREWORD

The second edition of this work was based on the fourth Dutch edition and dealt with the state of the law of the European Communities after the first major amendment of the original treaties by the Single European Act (SEA) of 1987. It will be recalled that the most important, but not the only, objective of the SEA was to enable the Institutions of the EEC to complete the internal market after the lack of progress from 1965 to 1985.

The third English edition is based on the fifth Dutch edition which deals with the law of the European Communities following the entry into force of the Treaty of European Union (TEU) and the near completion of the internal market during the post-Maastricht period up to January 1995. For that Dutch edition we were lucky enough to get L.A. Geelhoed and C.W.A. Timmermans as co-editors and five other authors from a younger and equally highly qualified generation of Dutch European lawyers with great academic and practical national, as well as European, professional experience.

In the first footnote to each chapter of the new English edition the name of the author of the corresponding Dutch chapter is cited. Geelhoed, Kuyper and Timmermans, in addition to their wide academic experience, also have the benefit of having dealt with the problems of European integration in their present senior functions in either the national civil service (*e.g.* Geelhoed was formerly Secretary-General of the Dutch Ministry of Economic Affairs and is now Secretary General of the Office of the Dutch Prime Minister) or the legal service of the European Commission. Barents (as a Legal Secretary to the Dutch Judge in the European Court of Justice) and Lauwaars (as a member of the Dutch Council of State) are directly involved in respectively the European and the Dutch adminstration of justice involving European Community law. Finally, Mortelmans and Slot, now professors of European Community law at the Universities of Utrecht and Leiden respectively, have had and still have great practical experience in the field of Community law.

We were also lucky to find Laurence Gormley again willing to exhibit the high quality of his knowledge of the law and practice of the European Communities and his admirable ability to edit the Dutch edition (this time the 5th) into a pleasing English style. He also undertook the analysis of important further developments of the law from the beginning of 1995 (the cut-off date for the fifth Dutch edition) up to May 1998. In particular, he was able to benefit when faced with the enormous task of analysing the present state of implementation of the most spectacular achievement of the TEU, the detailed (perhaps too detailed) blue-print for Economic and Monetary Union, from the completely revised (to the beginning of 1998) Chapter IX of the Dutch edition by Geelhoed. This revised text also dealt with the European Investment Bank, the new Title VIa on employment in the Treaty of Amsterdam (the formal implementation of which has been anticipated in practice since the autumn of 1997), the further implementation of Title XIV of Part Three EC by the TEU on economic and social cohesion up to January 1998 and the implementation of the recent 'merger' (also anticipated) of the social policy provisions of the TEU in its new text of Title VIII EC with the 'Agreement on Social Policy' annexed to the Protocol on Social Policy, which at that time was not applicable to the United Kingdom. The close and important economic and social interrelations between these various parts of Chapter IX have been expansively discussed by Geelhoed, and Gormley has added a shorter analysis of the important developments between January and May 1998, including the decisions with regard to the start of the Third Stage of the EMU. This chapter may, therefore, be seen at the date of writing this Foreword, as probably the most up to date synthesis of the economic, monetary and social policies, and their necessary interrelations, of the European Community.

With regard to all the chapters of this work, we were mandated by the editors of the fifth Dutch edition to ensure consistency in the incorporation of the Dutch original texts into the English edition and to ensure that the expansion to incorporate analyses of new developments from the beginning of 1995 to May 1998 was in keeping with the structure and contents of the Dutch edition of 1995. The additional materials found by the editor of the English edition, in particular references to literature, case-law and secondary legislation, have led (as with the second English edition) to a spectacular growth in the number of footnotes compared with the Dutch edition.

Because of important new developments with regard to Chapters VII on the establishment of the internal market and VIII on competition policy in the broad sense as explained there, and *also* because of the special interest in Anglo-Saxon countries in particular in these two central objectives as a basis of a common market, we supported certain extensions to the text of these chapters by the editor. Even in the Dutch text these chapters made up one third of the whole book. It has also been necessary, of course, to take into account the many aspects of 'positive' or 'regulatory' or 'coordinating' elements of European integration in the three Community Treaties as well as their important institutional aspects. It was obviously also necessary to deal with these aspects in the remaining eleven chapters in both the Dutch and English editions of this work.

Taking note, as he also did with our more substantial observations on the other chapters of the book, of our suggestions concerning a stylistic updating of the first two sections of the Epilogue of the Dutch edition on the perspectives on and challenges for the future, the editor has also in cooperation with the author of the Dutch text, added a substantial new section 8 on the current state of play in meeting these challenges. The challenges were those already perceived in 1995 and discussed on the basis of the literature then available. The new section, as with Chapter IX (and to a lesser extent other chapters) also includes some references to the solutions for some of these challenges contained in the Treaty of Amsterdam.

This new English edition, like the fifth Dutch edition on which it is based, only briefly discusses Articles A-F and J-S of the TEU. This discussion may be found principally in Chapters I and II and in the Epilogue of this work.

The time-consuming character of our own mandate with regard to this third, further revised, edition was largely compensated for by the regard paid by the editor (despite his own much more time-consuming task) to our many suggestions on sometimes important details which – we hope – have increased the already high quality of the enormous amount of editing work undertaken by Gormley over a period of some 2½ years. We are grateful for his admirable work and we now trust that this third English edition (like its predecessor) will also find many interested readers, both in the various legal practicing professions and among teachers and students of European law. This time we hope that the interest will not only be in the present Member States of the European Union and the United States of America, but also in other European countries, whether candidates for membership of the Union or not (yet).

The fact that this edition, even more than the previous two editions, relates the law to economics and politics and the various policy areas to each other and to the institutional framework and therefore, in the words of the late British European veteran J.D.B. Mitchell (in his foreword to the first English edition) sets out 'to give the whole picture', contributes to our confidence in its future.

Luxembourg/Bilthoven
July 1998

P.J.G. Kapteyn
P. VerLoren van Themaat

PREFACE

Community law continues to be at once the most exciting and fast-moving area of law: so much has changed since the first edition appeared in 1973 and the second (which I edited) in 1989. In view of the foreword, my own comments as to the revisions which I have made in the course of preparing this edition can be brief. This edition reflects the myriad and substantial changes made in the fifth Dutch edition, published in 1995 in order to take account of the Treaty on European Union, with additional observations reflecting the traditions of Anglo-Saxon legal practice, and has been brought up to date to 9 May 1998, although sometimes it has been possible to take account of later developments at proof stage. It is, however, once again, as Kapteyn and VerLoren van Themaat noted in their part of the preface to the second English edition, 'much more than a translation' and again 'tries to combine the strengths of the continental and the English approach to this new important part of the law.' Indeed, as in the earlier Dutch and English editions of this work, more attention has again been paid to Dutch, French, German and Italian literature in the field than is usually found in English commentaries on Community law, and, as Kapteyn and VerLoren van Themaat also observed in relation to the second English edition, there are again more references in this new edition to cases and English literature and legal practice than in the fifth Dutch edition. Some of the comments which I was able to make in the preface to the second English edition still apply.

Kapteyn and VerLoren van Themaat rightly quote the late John Mitchell's foreword to the first edition, and it is worth recalling why he wrote about giving 'the whole picture.' This was because this work tried – and indeed still tries – 'to relate the law to economics and to relate the policies to each other and to the institutional framework.' Central to this approach is the reasoning by reference to the system of the Treaties. Thus, as in the Spaak Report itself, policy considerations form the key to the understanding of the Community system, which is viewed in relation to the aims which it seeks to achieve.

The first English edition appeared 25 years ago, and on this Silver Anniversary it is appropriate to note that its appearance, like the *Common Market Law Review* was a fruit of the discussions and friendships in the context of the London-Leiden meetings, which then, as now, attract so many distinguished participants, not merely from the United Kingdom and The Netherlands, but from far beyond, including the United States. The previous English editions have been received with particular interest in those Member States which (then) had recently and in those States which have since acceded to the European Communities (now to the European Union). I hope that this edition will be of particular interest for lawyers and law students from the present Member States, from those States now seeking to accede, and also for those from further afield. It is designed to be accessible for students and practitioners alike, and I hope that both will find it useful and even enjoyable. When I edited the second English edition, I was still at the Commission, and it was only when I took up the Chair in Groningen a year later that I was able to see how students at least reacted to that edition. Still at Groningen, I shall be most interested to hear the reactions of a new generation of students as well as of practitioners to this edition.

Kapteyn and VerLoren van Themaat have seen the drafts of this edition and their observations have again been incorporated as appropriate. I am grateful to them for the care and time they have taken in this regard. Kuyper (who revised Chapter XII in the Dutch edition) was also kind enough to let me have his observations on the draft of that Chapter in this edition.

I am grateful to a number of people who have facilitated in various ways the preparation of this edition. The present and former members of the Department of European and Economic Law at Groningen were most supportive and tolerant of the long time which had to be devoted to the preparation of this edition, with not inconsiderable external stress, which fortunately is unlikely to be repeated. Despite the fact that I have had to devote so much time to this work, my (now former) research assistants have themselves produced outstanding work in the fields of the free movement of goods and central bank independence and accountability, which has also inspired me to start writing in new areas of Community law. My physiotherapist kept the consequences of keyboard and computer activity under control, particularly in the last year. The student assistants in the Department have been, as ever, first-class. Susan Nicholas has been an outstanding legal editor and colleague, and I am so pleased that the publishers asked her to see this work through the press, which she has done with tolerance, patience, and good humour. The typesetters at Acorn Bookwork have been simply fantastic. Steven de Moel very kindly prepared the tables and I am particularly grateful to him for his willingness to perform this onerous task in such a short space of time. The publishers asked Alex Corrin to prepare the index, and I am likewise most grateful to her for her sterling work. Last, but most certainly not least, I am, as ever, heavily indebted to Rob Kroes for unstinting encouragement and support.

Groningen, 2 July 1998.   *Laurence W. Gormley*

CONTENTS

CHAPTER VII
The establishment of the internal market: the freedoms   575

GENERAL COMMENTARIES, COLLECTIONS OF SOURCE MATERIALS, ABBREVIATIONS AND PERIODICALS

1. THE MOST IMPORTANT GENERAL COMMENTARIES ON THE COMMUNITY TREATIES

Any list is necessarily heavily selective, as there are now so many books the market, catering for various needs. The following are particularly well-known. Two of the works (Slaughter *et al.* (ed) and Snyder (ed) offer perspectives from what may be called the Florence tradition of more critical legal analysis.

Barents, *Het Verdrag van Amsterdam* (Deventer, 1998)

Berman *et al.*, *Cases and Materials on European Community Law* (St. Paul, Minn, 1993, suppl. 1998)

Beutler *et al.*, *Die Europäische Gemeinschaft – Rechtsordnung und Politik* (4th. ed., Baden-Baden, 1993)

Boulouis and Darmon, *Contnetieux Communautaire* (Paris, 1997)

Bourgeois *et al.*, *Het Europees Gemeenschapsrecht* (Ghent, 1993)

Constantinesco *et al.* (eds.), *Traité instituant la CEE* (Paris1992)

Constantinesco *et al.* (eds.), *Traité sur l'Union européenne* (Paris, 1995)

Cartou, *L'Union européenne* (2nd. ed., Paris, 1996)

Craig and De Búrca, *EU Law: Text, Cases and Materials* (2nd ed., Oxford, 1998)

Dauses, *Handbuch des EG-Wirtschaftsrechts* (Munich, 1993)

Dinnage and Murphy, *The Constitutional law of the European Union* (Cincinnati, Oh., 1996)

Dehousse, *Europe after Maastricht, An Ever Closer Union?* (Munich, 1994)

Evans, *A Textbook on European Union Law* (Oxford, 1998)

Goldman *et al.*, *Droit Commercial Europé* (5th ed., Paris, 1994)

Grabitz (ed., continued by Hilf (ed.)): *Kommentar zum EWG-Vertrag* (Munich, loose leaf from 1984)

Hailsham of St. Marylebone (ed.): 52 *Halsbury's Laws of England* (4th. ed., London, 1986)

Hartley, *The Foundations of European Community Law* (3rd. ed., Oxford, 1994, 4th. ed., 1998)

Isaac, *Droit Communautaire général* (4th ed., Paris, 1994)

Lasok, *Law and Institutions of the European Union* (7th. ed., London, 1998)

Lenz (ed.), *EG-Vertrag Kommentar* (Cologne, 1994)

Micklitz and Weatherill, *European Economic Law* (Aldershot, 1997)

Mathijsen, *A Guide to European Union Law* (6th. ed., London, 1994)

Mégret *et al. (eds.), Le droit de la Communauti Economique Européenne* (15 vols., of which various have been published in a 2nd ed. since 1990,)

Monar *et al., The Maastricht Treaty on European Union, Legal Complexity and Political Dynamic* (Brussels, 1994)

Nugent, *The Government and Politics of the European Union* (3rd ed., London, 1994)

Rideau, *Droit institutionnel de l'Union et des Communautés européennes* (Paris, 1994)

O'Keeffe and Twomey (eds.), *Legal Issues of the Maastricht Treaty* (Chichester, 1994)

Slaughter *et al.* (eds.), *The European Courts and National Courts – Doctrine and Jurisprudence* (Oxford, 1997)

Shaw, *Economic and Social law and Policy of the European Union* (London, 1998)

Shaw, *The Law of the European Union* (2nd ed., London, 1996)

Snyder (ed.), *Constitutional Dimensions of European Economic Integration* (The Hague, 1996)

Smit and Herzog (eds., continued by Campbell (gen.ed.)), *The Law of the European Community* (loose leaf, New York, from 1976)

Toth, *The Oxford Encyclopedia of European Community Law* (Oxford, 1990)

Vaughan (ed.), *Law of the European Communities Service* (loose-leaf, London, from 1990)

Von der Groeben *et al. (eds.): Kommentar zum EU-/EG-Vertrag* (4th ed., Baden-Baden, 1991, 5th ed., Baden-Baden, 1997, in part awaiting publication, hence the references to both editions in this work)

Weatherill, *Law and Integration in the European Union* (Oxford, 1995)

Weatherill and Beaumont, *EC Law* (2nd ed., London, 1995, 3rd ed. in preparation)

Wyatt and Dashwood, *European Community Law* (3rd. ed., London,1993)

2. COLLECTIONS OF CASE-LAW

Reports of cases before the Court (usually abbreviated as ECR) Contains the case-law of the Court and is published, since 1986, in nine languages. Pagination is the same in all languages since 1970. The series starts with the case-law of the old Court of Justice of the ECSC and continues, since 1958 with the case-law of the Court of Justice of the European Communities. Since 1990 it appears in 2 volumes (Volume I contains case-law of the Court of Justice; Volume II case-law of the Court of First

Instance). Since 1994 staff cases have been hived off into a loose-leaf volume (ECR-SC); appeals to the Court of Justice from the Court of First Instance are also published in Volume I of the ECR, and judgments of the Court of First Instance in staff cases which are of more general interest may also be published in Volume II of the ECR. The gap between a judgment bing handed down and its appearance in the ECR has now narrowed considerably. Subscribers to the ECR may still find it useful also to subscribe to the roneoed texts which are available much quicker. Recent judgments are now available via the Court's home page (through the Europa.eu.int internet server), which means that access to judgments has now been greatly improved. The weekly summary of proceedings, issued by the Court's information service free of charge is also to be recommended; it too can be accessed via the Court's home page. The Court publishes its calendar of sittings. The registration of new cases, or the withdrawal of cases is noted in the 'C' series of the *Official Journal*, and the operative parts of the Court's judgments are also noted there.

Common Market Law Reports (usually abbreviated as CMLR) published by European Law Centre Ltd., London, contains some (but not all) judgments of the Court of Justice and of national courts (translated into English) and also contains other useful material, particularly in the volumes devoted to competition and trade law. In the early days they published their own translations of the Court of Justice's judgments (and many of the official translations in the ECR were subsequently based on the CMLR work) but the official translation is always that in the ECR.

The most valuable research tool remains *Celex* (the Community's legal database which is available in a number of languages, including English). It is available (on subscription) on line, and various commercial service providers offer gateway access. Various companies market information based on the *Celex* database in CD-ROM form (again, on subscription). *Lexis* also provides *Celex*-based information on line, in addition to its other services. *Celex* covers not only case-law and Community legislation and Union acts, it also embraces proposals from the Commission, lists national measures implementing Community law, and international treaties and Community soft law instruments (the latter are also to be found in the *Bulletin of the European Union*, which is issued monthly and is now also available in electronic form). The Community's SCAD database is a fruitful research tool for periodical literature in particular, and its RAPID database contains press releases and various other interesting documents. There is no doubt that since the Community's public databases have been accessible via the World Wide Web, the transparency of information has increased substantially. Progress in the adoption of Community legislation can be followed through the Parliament's OEIL server (accessible via the Parliament's home page through the Europa internet server). Legislation is also available for a limited period, free of charge, on the EUR-Lex facility through the Europa home page.

There are also now myriad case books on Community law, of varying merit, originality and added value: one or two have been included in the list of general commentaries, above.

3. COLLECTIONS OF LEGISLATIVE AND OTHER TEXTS

Official Journal of the European Communities

Published (now) in 11 languages, usually abbreviated in English as O.J. and in French as J.O. (for *Journal Officiel.* The O.J./J.O. has gone through various types of citation.

(a) Originally published in Dutch, French, German and Italian, as *the Journal Officiel de la Communauté Européenne du Charbon et de l'Acier,* the J.O. was published from 1952 to 19 April 1958. On 20 April 1958 the first issue of the *Journal Officiel des Communautis Européennes* appeared and its structure was unchanged until 1968. The **J.O.** between 1952 and 30 June 1967 is cited by the page number and the year *(e.g.* **J.O.** 154/66). From 1 July 1967 to 31 December 1967 each issue was paged separately.

(b) From 1 January 1968 the J.O. was divided into two separate series, the 'L' series contains legislation and the 'C' series contains notices, proposals and other information and communications. The 'L' series contains two parts, namely acts whose publication is obligatory and acts whose publication is not obligatory.

(c) From 1 January 1973 the Official Journal was also published in Danish and English.

(d) Most references to acts adopted before 1973 are to the English Special Edition which is the authentic English translation of the most important acts adopted by the Community Institutions.

(e) From 1 January 1981 the Official Journal has also been published in Greek and from 1 January 1986 also in Spanish and Portuguese, and from 1 January 1995 also in Finnish and Swedish.

Pagination is the same in all the editions (although the Special Editions have their own numbering but refer to the original J.O. page numbers). In the field of procurement, notices of invitations to tender and periodic indicative notices are published in a Supplement to the O.J. and are also available on the TED database. Twice a year a Directory of Community Legislation in force is issued, which is a useful hard copy reference source.

The most complete and updated collection of Community legislation in English is still Simmonds (ed.), *Encyclopedia of European Community Law* (Vols. B and C, loose leaf, London, from 1974), although Foster (ed.), *Blackstone's EC Legislation Handbook* (London, 1998) contains a useful selection of texts. More compact (if better suited to student pockets) is *e.g.* Rudden and Wyatt (eds.) *Basic Community Laws* (6th ed., Oxford, 1996), although other competing works are available. In addition to the on line research tools noted above, Butterworths' European *Communities Legislation Current Status* is very useful. The *Bulletin of the European Union* (abbreviated as Bull. EU, and available on line, as noted above) and supplements to it should also be consulted, as it gives a month-by-month overview of the activities of the European Union; the supplements often reproduce important COM documents or other major policy documents. The annual *General Report* is another useful source of information. The Court of Justice and the European Parliament produce regular bibliographic tools, including details of national judgments on Community law. European Depositaries or Documentation Centres are most helpful sources of information, as are the national Information Offices (or sub-offices) of the Commission and the European Parliament. *Europe* (published in English and French versions) is the well-known daily information service about European affairs. Finally, the Commission's library catalogue is available via the ECLAS database.

4. ABBREVIATIONS

Standard abbreviations have generally been used throughout this work (that is, the methods of citation used by the periodicals themselves, not the American standard citations which are somewhat different). COM refers to Commission documents (with explanatory memoranda) which set out proposed legislation or other policy papers; the proposed legislation is published in the O.J., without the accompanying memorandum. The O.J. will always give the COM number (*e.g.* COM (98) 1) which enables the memorandum to be traced. CMLR is the abbreviation for the *Common Market Law Reports*, **not** for the *Common Market Law Review* (which is CMLRev.). Not surprisingly, copious references are made to the Dutch-Belgian periodical SEW *(Sociáal-Economische Wetgeving)* and EuR *(Europarecht)* and other continental periodicals. Whilst most abbreviations will be obvious (see the list of major European law periodicals below) others are perhaps less frequently encountered by English readers. Thus *e.g.*: SMA *(Sociaal Maandblad Arbeid)*; ZfaöRuVR *(Zeitschrift für ausländisches öffentliches Recht und Völkerrecht)* and Rabel's Z. *(Rabel's Zeitschrift)*. Occasionally references are made to Stb. (the *Dutch Staatsblad*) and Trbl. (the Dutch *Tractatenblad*) when Dutch provisions are being considered.

5. PERIODICALS AND YEARBOOK

The most important periodicals and yearbook dealing with Community law are:

Cahiers de Droit Européen (CDE)
Columbia Journal of European Law (Columb. J. Eur. L.)
Common Market Law Review (CMLRev.)
Diritto Communitario e degli Scambi Internazionale
Europarecht (EuR)
Europäische Zeitschrift für Wirtschaftsrecht (EuZW)
European Business Law Review (EBLR)
European Competition Law Review (ECLR)
European Intellectual Property Review (EIPR)
European Law Journal (ELJ)
European Law Review (ELRev.)
Journal des Tribunaux (Droit Européen) (JdT Dr. Eur.)
Legal Issues of European Integration (LIEI)
Nederlandse Tijdschrift voor Europees Recht (NTER)
Revista de Instituciones Europeas (RIE)
Revue Héllenique de Droit Communautaire (RHDC)
Revue du Marché Commun (RMC)
Revue du Marché Unique Européen (RMUE)
Revue Trimestrielle de Droit Européen (RTDE)
Rivista di Diritto Europeo (RDE)
Sociaal-Economisch Wetgeving (SEW)
Yearbook of European Law (YBEL)

Most of these regularly contain commentaries on recent case-law and many of them also contain details of recent Community legislation and bibliographies of recent literature. The *Journal of Common Market Studies* also occasionally contains articles of legal interest. Myriad other specialist journals have now appeared in fields such as European Public Law, Private Law, and International Law, as well as European Foreign Affairs.

TABLES OF CASES

Opinions

Court of First Instance of the European Communities

INTERNATIONAL COURT OF JUSTICE

EUROPEAN COURT OF HUMAN RIGHTS

EFTA COURT

NATIONAL COURTS

Belgium

Denmark

France

Germany

Ireland

Italy

SpA BECA v. Amministrazione delle Finanze dello Stato (1985) RDI 338 553, 555
Fragd v. Amministrazione delle Finanze dello Stato (1989) 516
Frontini et al. v. Ministero delle Finanze [1974] 2 CMLR 386 554
SpA Granital v. Amministrazione delle Finanze dello Stato (1984) Il Foro Italiano 2062, (1986) CDE 185 553
Provincia di Bolzano v. Presidenti Consiglio Ministri (1989) RDI 404 553

United Kingdom

Allgemeine Gold- und Silberscheideanstalt v. H.M. Customs and Excise [1980] 2 WLR 555, [1980] 1 CMLR 488 591
Amies v. I.L.E.A. [1977] ICR 308, [1977] 2 All ER 100, [1977] 1 CMLR 336 89
An Bord Bainne Co-operative Ltd. v. Milk Marketing Board [1988] 1 CMLR 6 506
Bethell v. SABENA [1983] 3 CMLR 1 506
Blackburn v. Attorney-General [1971] 2 All ER 1380 83
Buttes Gas and Oil Co. v. Hammer (Nos. 2 and 3) [1982] AC 888 83
Doughty v. Rolls-Royce plc [1992] 1 CMLR 1045 549
Charles Early and Mariott (Witney) Ltd. [1977] 3 WLR 189 88
Chiron v. Murex (No. 3) The Times 14 October 1994 518
Concorde Express Transport Ltd. v. Traffic Examiner Metropolitan Area [1980] 2 CMLR 221 1191
Finnegan v. Clowney Youth Training Programme Ltd. [1990] 2 AC 407 525
Garland v. British Rail Engineering Ltd. [1983] AC 851 502
Handley v. Mono Ltd. [1979] ICR 47 88
Hasselblad (GB) Ltd. v. Orbison [1984] ECR 3 CMLR 540 161
Macarthys Ltd. v. Smith [1978] 1 WLR 849 88
Macarthys Ltd. v. Smith (CA) [1979] 3 All ER 325, [1979] 3 CMLR 44 86, 88
Macarthys Ltd. v. Smith [1981] 1 All ER 111 552
Magnavision v. General Optical Council (No. 2) [1987] 2 CMLR 262 518
Monckton v. Lord Advocate (1994) The Times 12 May 40
Polydor et al. v. Harlequin Record Shops Ltd. et al. [1980] 2 CMLR 403 506, 518
J.H. Rayner (Mincing Lane) Ltd. v. Department of Trade and Industry [1989] 3 WLR 969 [1989] 3 All ER 523 83, 102
R. v. Escauriaza [1989] 3 CMLR 281; R. v. Kraus (1982) 4 Cr. App. R. (S) 113 712
R. v. London Boroughs Transport Committee, ex parte Freight Transport Association Ltd. [1992] 1 CMLR 5 525
R. v. Manchester Crown Court, ex parte DPP [1994] 1 CMLR 457 (HL)157
R. v. Manchester Crown Court, ex parte DPP [1993] 1 WLR 693 (QBD), [1993] 1 WLR 1524 215
R. v. Marlborough Street Stipendiary Magistrate, ex parte Bouchereau [1977] 1 WLR 414 256
R. v. The Metropolitan Borough Council of Wirral, ex parte the Wirral Licensed Taxi Owners Association [1983] 3 CMLR 159 459
R. v. The Pharmaceutical Society of Great Britain, ex parte the Association of Pharmaceutical Importers [1987] 3 CMLR 951 520
R. v. Secretary of State for Foreign and Commonwealth Affairs, ex parte Rees-Mogg [1994] QB 552, [1994] 2 WLR 115, [1994] 1 All ER 457, [1993] 3 CMLR 101 40, 83
R. v. Secretary of State for the Home Department, ex parte Santillo [1980] 3 CMLR 212 (DC); [1981] 1 CMLR 569 (CA) 714
R. v. Secretary of State for Transport, ex parte Factortame Ltd. et al. (No. 1) [1990] 2 AC 85 552

United States

TABLE OF TREATIES

EC Treaty

Existing provisions

Article	Page

New Provisions (introduced by the Treaty of Amsterdam)*

* These tables covers wholly new provisions, or complete replacements; additions to existing provisions are included in the table of existing provisions. New Protocols are set out in the table of the Treaty of Amsterdam.

ECSC TREATY

Existing provisions

* This table covers wholly new provisions; additions to existing provisions are included in the table of existing provisions. New Protocols are set out in the table of the Treaty of Amsterdam.

EEC Treaty

EURATOM TREATY

Existing provisions

CONVENTION ON CERTAIN INSTITUTIONS COMMON TO THE EUROPEAN COMMUNITIES

FIRST BUDGETARY TREATY

*This table covers wholly new provisions; additions to existing provisions are included in the table of existing provisions. New Protocols are set out in the table of the Treaty of Amsterdam.

MERGER TREATY

SECOND BUDGETARY TREATY

SINGLE EUROPEAN ACT

TREATY ON EUROPEAN UNION

Existing Provisions

* Protocols 1-16 were annexed to the EC Treaty (*q.v.*); Protocol 17 to the TEU and to the
EC, ECSC and Euratom Treaties

New Provisions (introduced by the Treaty of Amsterdam)*

*This table covers wholly new provisions; additions to existing provisions are included in the table of existing provisions. New Protocols are set out in the table of the Treaty of Amsterdam.

TREATY OF AMSTERDAM

EEA AGREEMENT

Table of Treaties

TABLES OF EQUIVALENCES REFERRED TO IN ARTICLE 12 OF THE TREATY OF AMSTERDAM

A. TREATY ON EUROPEAN UNION

Previous numbering	New numbering
Title I	Title I
Article A	Article 1
Article B	Article 2
Article C	Article 3
Article D	Article 4
Article E	Article 5
Article F	Article 6
Article F.1 ()	Article 7
Title II	Title II
Article G	Article 8
Title III	Title III
Article H	Article 9
Title IV	Title IV
Article I	Article 10
Title V (***)	Title V
Article J.1	Article 11
Article J.2	Article 12
Article J.3	Article 13
Article J.4	Article 14
Article J.5	Article 15
Article J.6	Article 16
Article J.7	Article 17
Article J.8	Article 18
Article J.9	Article 19
Article J.10	Article 20
Article J.11	Article 21
Article J.12	Article 22
Article J.13	Article 23
Article J.14	Article 24
Article J.15	Article 25
Article J.16	Article 26
Article J.17	Article 27
Article J.18	Article 28

(*) New Article introduced by the Treaty of Amsterdam
(***) Title restructured by the Treaty of Amsterdam

Previous numbering	New numbering
Title VI (***)	Title VI
Article K.1	Article 29
Article K.2	Article 30
Article K.3	Article 31
Article K.4	Article 32
Article K.5	Article 33
Article K.6	Article 34
Article K.7	Article 35
Article K.8	Article 36
Article K.9	Article 37
Article K.10	Article 38
Article K.11	Article 39
Article K.12	Article 40
Article K.13	Article 41
Article K.14	Article 42
Title VIa (**)	Title VII
Article K.15 ()	Article 43
Article K.16 (*)	Article 44
Article K.17 (*)	Article 45
Title VII	Title VIII
Article L	Article 46
Article M	Article 47
Article N	Article 48
Article O	Article 49
Article P	Article 50
Article Q	Article 51
Article R	Article 52
Article S	Article 53

B. TREATY ESTABLISHING THE EUROPEAN COMMUNITY

Previous numbering	New numbering
Part One	Part One
Article 1	Article 1
Article 2	Article 2
Article 3	Article 3
Article 3a	Article 4
Article 3b	Article 5
Article 3c ()	Article 6
Article 4	Article 7
Article 4a	Article 8
Article 4b	Article 9
Article 5	Article 10

(*)   New Article introduced by the Treaty of Amsterdam
(**)   New Title introduced by the Treaty of Amsterdam
(***) Title restructured by the Treaty of Amsterdam

Previous numbering	New numbering
Article 5a (*)	Article 11
Article 6	Article 12
Article 6a (*)	Article 13
Article 7 (repealed)	–
Article 7a	Article 14
Article 7b (repealed)	–
Article 7c	Article 15
Article 7d (*)	Article 16
Part Two	Part Two
Article 8	Article 17
Article 8a	Article 18
Article 8b	Article 19
Article 8c	Article 20
Article 8d	Article 21
Article 8e	Article 22
Part Three	Part Three
Title I	Title I
Article 9	Article 23
Article 10	Article 24
Article 11 (repealed)	–
Chapter 1	Chapter 1
Section 1 (deleted)	–
Article 12	Article 25
Article 13 (repealed)	–
Article 14 (repealed)	–
Article 15 (repealed)	–
Article 16 (repealed	–
Article 17 (repealed)	–
Section 2 (deleted)	–
Article 18 (repealed)	–
Article 19 (repealed)	–
Article 20 (repealed)	–
Article 21 (repealed)	–
Article 22 (repealed)	–
Article 23 (repealed)	–
Article 24 (repealed)	–
Article 25 (repealed)	–
Article 26 (repealed)	–
Article 27 (repealed)	–
Article 28	Article 26
Article 29	Article 27
Chapter 2	Chapter 2
Article 30	Article 28
Article 31 (repealed)	–
Article 32 (repealed)	–

(*) New Article introduced by the Treaty of Amsterdam

Previous numbering	New numbering
Article 73 (repealed)	–
Article 73a (repealed)	–
Article 73b	Article 56
Article 73c	Article 57
Article 73d	Article 58
Article 73e (repealed)	–
Article 73f	Article 59
Article 73g	Article 60
Article 73h (repealed)	–
Title IIIa (**)	Title IV
Article 73i (*)	Article 61
Article 73j (*)	Article 62
Article 73k (*)	Article 63
Article 73l (*)	Article 64
Article 73m (*)	Article 65
Article 73n (*)	Article 66
Article 73o (*)	Article 67
Article 73p (*)	Article 68
Article 73q (*)	Article 69
Title IV	Title V
Article 74	Article 70
Article 75	Article 71
Article 76	Article 72
Article 77	Article 73
Article 78	Article 74
Article 79	Article 75
Article 80	Article 76
Article 81	Article 77
Article 82	Article 78
Article 83	Article 79
Article 84	Article 80
Title V	Title VI
Chapter 1	Chapter 1
Section 1	Section 1
Article 85	Article 81
Article 86	Article 82
Article 87	Article 83
Article 88	Article 84
Article 89	Article 85
Article 90	Article 86
Section 2 (deleted)	–
Article 91 (repealed)	–
Section 3	Section 2
Article 92	Article 87
Article 93	Article 88

(*)   New Article introduced by the Treaty of Amsterdam
(**)   New Title introduced by the Treaty of Amsterdam

Previous numbering	New numbering
Article 109l	Article 123
Article 109m	Article 124
Title VIa (**)	Title VIII
Article 109n (*)	Article 125
Article 109o (*)	Article 126
Article 109p (*)	Article 127
Article 109q (*)	Article 128
Article 109r (*)	Article 129
Article 109s (*)	Article 130
Title VII	Title IX
Article 110	Article 131
Article 111 (repealed)	–
Article 112	Article 132
Article 113	Article 133
Article 114 (repealed)	–
Article 115	Article 134
Article 116 (repealed)	–
Title VIIa (**)	Title X
Article 116 ()	Article 135
Title VIII	Title XI
Chapter 1 (***)	Chapter 1
Article 117	Article 136
Article 118	Article 137
Article 118a	Article 138
Article 118b	Article 139
Article 118c	Article 140
Article 119	Article 141
Article 119a	Article 142
Article 120	Article 143
Article 121	Article 144
Article 122	Article 145
Chapter 2	Chapter 2
Article 123	Article 146
Article 124	Article 147
Article 125	Article 148
Chapter 3	Chapter 3
Article 126	Article 149
Article 127	Article 150
Title IX	Title XII
Article 128	Article 151

(*)   New Article introduced by the Treaty of Amsterdam
(**)   New Title introduced by the Treaty of Amsterdam
(***) Title restructured by the Treaty of Amsterdam

Tables of Equivalences

(*)   New Article introduced by the Treaty of Amsterdam

Previous numbering	New numbering
Chapter 5	Chapter 5
Article 198d	Article 266
Article 198e	Article 267
Title II	Title II
Article 199	Article 268
Article 200 (repealed)	–
Article 201	Article 269
Article 201a	Article 270
Article 202	Article 271
Article 203	Article 272
Article 204	Article 273
Article 205	Article 274
Article 205a	Article 275
Article 206	Article 276
Article 206a (repealed)	–
Article 207	Article 277
Article 208	Article 278
Article 209	Article 279
Article 209a	Article 280
Part Six	Part Six
Article 210	Article 281
Article 211	Article 282
Article 212 (*)	Article 283
Article 213	Article 284
Article 213a (*)	Article 285
Article 213b (*)	Article 286
Article 214	Article 287
Article 215	Article 288
Article 216	Article 289
Article 217	Article 290
Article 218 (*)	Article 291
Article 219	Article 292
Article 220	Article 293
Article 221	Article 294
Article 222	Article 295
Article 223	Article 296
Article 224	Article 297
Article 225	Article 298
Article 226 (repealed)	–
Article 227	Article 299
Article 228	Article 300
Article 228a	Article 301
Article 229	Article 302
Article 230	Article 303
Article 231	Article 304
Article 232	Article 305
Article 233	Article 306
Article 234	Article 307

(*) New Article introduced by the Treaty of Amsterdam

Previous numbering	New numbering
Article 235	Article 308
Article 236 (*)	Article 309
Article 237 (repealed)	—
Article 238	Article 310
Article 239	Article 311
Article 240	Article 312
Article 241 (repealed)	—
Article 242 (repealed)	—
Article 243 (repealed)	—
Article 244 (repealed)	—
Article 245 (repealed)	—
Article 246 (repealed)	—
Final Provisions	Final Provisions
Article 247	Article 313
Article 248	Article 314

_____

(*)   New Article introduced by the Treaty of Amsterdam

CHAPTER I

The genesis of the European Communities and the accession of other European countries*

1. BACKGROUND TO THE SCHUMAN PLAN

On 9 May 1950 a press conference took place at the Quay d'Orsay to make public a proposal of the French government which was to have far-reaching importance for European integration. The French Foreign Minister, Robert Schuman, read a sensational declaration. It contained the proposal to place the whole of Franco-German coal and steel output under a common High Authority, in an organization open to the participation of the other countries of Europe.[1]

This proposal was sensational in two respects. In the first place it meant a turn of the tide in French policy with regard to Western Germany, a policy which had so far been directed at a continued tutelage by the Western Allies of the defeated enemy. Now, a proposal for a Franco-German partnership in a limited, but vital economic field, as the nucleus of a broader European co-operation, broke through this post-war policy. The form which would have to be given to this cooperation was equally revolutionary: a combination of coal and steel production under the direction of a common High Authority (composed of independent persons), capable of taking decisions binding on France, Germany, and any other participating countries. Thus a new element was introduced into the organizational pattern according to which the

---

* In the 5th Dutch edition of this work, this Chapter was revised by C.W.A. Timmermans. Sections 1–4 of this Chapter are revisions of the 2nd English edition by the editor, with minor linguistic changes, sections 5 and 6 are, after 1989, based on Timmermans's account but with additional material, until the end of 1994, thereafter the account is that of the editor.

1. See Diebold, *The Schuman Plan: A study in Economic Co-operation, 1950–1959* (New York, 1959). See also, more generally, on issues of interdependence and integration, Milward *et al.*, *The Frontier of National Sovereignty* (London, 1993).

promotion of common interests by states is wont to take place in international society.

The typical feature of this latter pattern had been an *intergovernmental* organization, commonly based on three principles. In the first place decisions of the organization are taken by organs composed of government representatives. Secondly, participating states are not legally bound by these decisions against their will. Even if the basic treaty provides for binding decisions, unanimity will be required to arrive at them. Decisions having no binding effect by virtue of the Treaty itself will only obtain this effect in relation to states accepting them. Thirdly, the implementation of decisions is reserved to the participating states themselves. There are, of course, exceptions to each of these three principles. But it is the abandonment of these principles as a starting point for the association of states in an international organization which justifies the *supranational* label which was later to be given to the form of organization which was developed on the basis of the Schuman Declaration.

1.1 The power vacuum in Europe and the tendency towards European integration

The background to this Declaration, which broke both with a main feature of post-war French foreign policy and with traditional views concerning the organization of cooperation between states is central to an understanding of the origins of the Communities. In the spring of 1950 the world presented a grim picture especially from the viewpoint of Western Europe.[2] The eastern part of Europe had finally been brought within the Russian sphere of influence. The *coup d'état* of 20 February 1948 in Czechoslovakia and the Berlin blockade from 24 June 1948 to 12 May 1949 had enhanced the fear of Russian expansionism. The explosion of the first Russian A-bomb in August 1949, three to four years earlier than the West had anticipated, and the strengthening of the monolithic communist block which was expected to result from the final victory of the party of Mao Tse Tung in China in the autumn of 1949 tended to foster even further the widely prevalent opinion in the West that the chances of a third world war had increased considerably.

The risk that Europe itself might once more be at the centre of a future conflict was recognized by many people. Indeed, armed forces of the two super-powers confronted each other there. The fuel for a conflict lay piled

2. See, generally, Haas, *The Uniting of Europe: Political, Social and Economic Forces 1950–1957* (2nd ed., 1968); Mayne, *The Community of Europe* (London, 1962); Milward, *The Reconstruction of Western Europe, 1945–51* (London, 1984); Van de Meerssche, *Europese integratie en disintegratie 1945–heden* (Antwerp/Amsterdam, 1978) and *Van Jalta tot Malta: politieke geschiedenis van Europa* (Utrecht, 1990).

high: the artificial division of Germany and the militarily weak position of the garrisons of the Western Allies in West Berlin. The countries of Western Europe, busily engaged in restoring their economy by means of the American financial aid under the Marshall Plan (1947), were involved in a first modest attempt to put up a co-ordinated defence of their territory against an attack from the East. Being helpless against superior Russian military power and without hope of ever being able to establish any adequate defence against it, they depended on the military and financial aid of the United States under the North Atlantic Treaty concluded on 4 April 1949. The impulse for this treaty had been given on the one hand by the Brussels Treaty of 17 March 1948, on the part of the United Kingdom, France and the Benelux countries, and on the other hand by the so-called Vandenberg Resolution. This Resolution had been adopted on 11 June 1948 by the U.S. Senate and had recommended an association of the United States with such regional and other collective arrangements as are based on continuous and effective self-help and mutual aid.

The international political situation which had developed after the war gave all the more impetus to a political trend which, by taking up pre-war plans and ideas, aimed at a firmly organized political and economic partnership of European nations. Europe on the basis of this partnership should muster enough strength to play once again its part in international politics instead of being at its mercy. The vacuum which had arisen in Europe had to be filled with a new political structure which would diminish the Russian menace and reduce the dependence on the United States. Winston Churchill was the first to give full publicity to the idea of European integration after the war. On 19 September 1946, in an address at Zurich University, he submitted that it was necessary to build a kind of United States of Europe for which he saw a partnership between France and Germany as the first step.

The year 1948 formed a climax for the numerous political groups which advocated a united Europe. On 7 May 1948 they jointly convened the Congress of Europe in the Knights' Hall at The Hague. A great many prominent parliamentarians, scholars and statesmen not in office at the time took part. In a series of resolutions they made an appeal for the formation of a political and economic union, the calling of a European Assembly whose members were to be appointed by the national parliaments, the framing of a Charter of Human Rights, and the creation of a Court of Justice for the supervision of the observance of the Charter.

At the instigation of the Belgian and French Governments these proposals were studied in the Council of the Brussels Treaty to ascertain to what extent they could be carried into effect. These discussions resulted in the Statute of the Council of Europe, signed on 5 May 1949, in which, in addition to the countries of the Brussels Treaty, Sweden, Norway, Denmark, Ireland, and Italy took part. The Statute was the result of a laboriously reached compromise, the British participants in particular having doggedly held out for an organization on purely intergovernmental lines. The British concession concerned the establishment of a Consultative Assembly in addition to the classical Committee of Ministers. This Assembly was composed of representatives of the Member States, who were to be designated in a way to be determined by each government. Although it was not expressly stated in the Statute, the intention of the framers was to pave the way for an organ in which the national parliaments might be represented, a novelty in the set-up of an international organization. It was not until 1951 that the logical consequence was drawn from this intention and the Statute was amended in the sense that henceforth each parliament, at least as a general rule, was to appoint the number of delegates in the Assembly assigned to the respective country.

For the rest, the Council of Europe turned out to be a disappointment for the champions of firm European partnership. The Consultative Assembly was only able to make recommendations to the Committee of Ministers, which in turn could do little more than frame recommendations to the Member States, in practically all important cases on a basis of unanimity. Nevertheless, the Consultative Assembly, a select group of parliamentarians, played a particularly important political role during the first few years. It was indeed from the midst of this body that the initiative came for the framing of a treaty which was eventually signed in Rome on 4 November 1950 as the European Convention for the Protection of Human Rights and Fundamental Freedoms and entered into force on 3 September 1953. In the Assembly the first great debates before the forum of public opinion concerning the form and substance of future European co-operation also took place. There the streams which had already manifested themselves at the Hague Congress became clearly apparent: the unionists, the federalists and the functionalists. The first desired a further development of intergovernmental co-operation between European countries. The federalists held that a European federation should be the ultimate aim. The boldest among them, the constitutionalists, wished to proceed to convene a *Constituante Européenne* which would draft and proclaim a constitution for a United States of Europe. The more prudent among the federalists, the functionalists, advocated a merger of sovereign national rights on concrete points *e.g.* heavy industries.[3]

1.2   The problem of Franco-German relations and the commitment of the German Federal Republic to Western Europe

It was this last approach which the French government followed up when making public its plan for establishment of a High Authority for coal and

3. See, generally, Brugmans *L'Idée Européenne, 1920–1970* (3rd ed., Bruges, 1970).

steel. It was not, however, only conceptions of the future political structure of Europe – although they were no doubt nursed by men such as Schuman and Monnet (the intellectual father of the plan) – which incited them to action. The central problem was that of Franco-German relations.

The aim of French European policy was to obtain effective guarantees against a revival of a German menace to French security. Such guarantees had been sought by successive French governments in a permanent restriction of the scope of development of German economic and political power after the collapse of the Third Reich in 1945. Especially after the final breach between the four Great Powers about the course of action to be taken with regard to Germany, this restrictive French policy appeared less and less feasible in an atmosphere of growing tension between East and West. The United States, in particular, followed by the United Kingdom, was bent on an early reconstruction of economic and political life in the Western zones of occupation. In Anglo-American circles a thriving Germany closely allied to the West was regarded more and more as an essential condition for the recovery of Europe and as an indispensable bulwark against the dreaded Russian expansionism. With many reservations therefore, French diplomats had to acquiesce in a series of preliminary measures which led to the establishment in May 1949 of the German Federal Republic. Within, as yet, fairly narrow limits the Occupation Statute introduced in May of that year made the Germans in the Western zones masters in their own house again.

Early in 1950 French policy was in an impasse. The negative attitude towards German economic and political recovery taxed relations with the new German state, which to an increasing degree was becoming a political and economic reality in Europe which had to be reckoned with. The position of the Saar, a politically autonomous area, but economically associated with France, bade fair to become a bone of contention. The German Federal Republic, in view of the inequality involved, took a very reserved attitude towards the Ruhr Statute, which was agreed by the end of 1948 particularly at the instigation of France and which ensured allied supervision over the coal and steel industry in this district by means of an international authority. The United States and the United Kingdom showed themselves less and less willing to give an effective shape to this supervision. Finally, the French government realized that with the aggravation of antagonism between East and West it would hardly be possible in the long run to resist American insistence on permitting the German Federal Republic play to the full its potential role in the economic, political and even military sphere among the nations of Europe.

The Schuman Plan constituted a brilliant attempt to break through this impasse. The policy aim remained the same: effective guarantees against a revival of a German menace to French security. But the means for achieving this aim were altered drastically. The former negative policy directed at a continued allied tutelage of Germany was replaced by a tendency towards a far-reaching partnership on a basis of parity of the two countries within a European setting. It was precisely the coal and steel sector, the traditional basis of every form of power politics, which seemed to be an excellent starting-point for such an association. The unilateral supervision over the German coal and steel industry, embodied in the Ruhr Statute, which had not proved viable, would make way for a coal and steel regime on a broader basis, which would subject this industry in France, Germany, and in any other European countries which wished to participate to supervision on an equal footing by a common High Authority. This arrangement would also place the Saar problem in a different perspective.

Thus the Schuman Plan formed a political answer to a series of political problems of the first order: the existence of a power vacuum in Europe, viewed by many people as one of the sources of the cold war, the more effective shaping of European integration which was widely deemed necessary, the settlement of Franco-German relations and finally the cementing of the German Federal Republic, which was again developing into a European power, into Western Europe on a basis of equality, but with maximum guarantees against independent German power politics, with all the dangers to Europe and world peace this could involve, particularly in view of the division of the former German territory into a Western and an Eastern sector.

1.3   Economic considerations

Conditions of a strictly economic character were not lacking, but they played a rather subsidiary part compared to the political considerations mentioned above, some of which were acute. Thanks to Marshall Aid, but also as a result of the activities of the Organization for European Economic Co-operation (OEEC), the economic prospects for the European countries at the beginning of 1950 were not unfavourable. At the instigation of the United States and in spite of initial objections, particularly on the part of the United Kingdom, the OEEC had been established on 16 April 1948 in connection with Marshall Aid as a continuous organization, meaning that after termination of this aid it would still have to give shape to economic co-operation between the participating countries of Europe. A Dutch suggestion that the OEEC be entrusted with the task of setting up a customs union on the model of the Benelux Treaty of 1944 and a French attempt to equip the organization with strong institutions had come to nothing, despite U.S. support. These ideas had been strongly opposed in particular by the United Kingdom, but with regard to the French proposal also by Benelux, which feared an excessive influence of the larger European countries.

Within the limits thus set to it, this intergovernmental organization of the traditional type had nevertheless taken the first important steps on the road towards the liberalization of trade and payments and towards a better mutual adjustment of national economic policies. However, aspirations for a far-reaching economic partnership based on abolition of common tariff frontiers, hopes widely cherished at least on the continent, could not be satisfied by the OEEC. Not only was there great difference of opinion among Member States about the nature of and the methods appropriate to a European economic partnership, but the institutional structure of the OEEC did not seem adapted to bear the load of the development and pursuance of a common policy in an economic union. Indeed, in view of many people this union would be the indispensable complement of the abolition of trade barriers between the countries of Europe.

Both in institutional respects and with regard to methods of European economic integration the Schuman Plan suggested new roads. A free movement of coal and steel products might be a first step on the road towards a series of sector markets which might finally lead to full economic integration. The production and sale of coal and steel seemed a good starting point also because this sector showed the striking inappropriateness of national frontiers, which cut up artificially the area where the greatest concentration of coal and iron ore in Western Europe was to be found.

2. THE ECSC TREATY OF 18 APRIL 1951

The French initiative, which was received with sympathy particularly by the United States, met with a favourable reception in several European capitals, especially in Bonn. On 20 June 1950 there was a conference in Paris of the six countries (the German Federal Republic, France, Italy and the three Benelux countries) which had subscribed to the principles of the Schuman Plan. An attempt to persuade the United Kingdom to join as well had failed. The fear of being impeded in the development of its own welfare state, then at the height of nationalized industry planning, and in the maintenance of the bonds with the Commonwealth, as well as an insufficient realization of the importance of the French proposal and the vistas it opened, caused the British government to cling to its standpoint that only a cooperation based on coordination of national policies within the framework of an intergovernmental organization like the OEEC was acceptable.

After nine months of negotiations the Treaty establishing the ECSC was signed in Paris on 18 April 1951. On 25 July 1952 it entered into force.[4] The basis of the common market for coal and steel thus called into being was formed within this market by the prohibition under Article 4 of the Treaty of:

4. It was concluded for 50 years, Art. 97 ECSC.

(i)   duties on importation or exportation or charges having equivalent effect and quantitative restrictions;
(ii)   measures and practices discriminating between producers, purchasers or consumers or interfering with the purchaser's free choice of supplier;
(iii) government subsidies, aids or special charges;
(iv)   restrictive practices tending towards the sharing or exploiting of markets.

According to the Schuman Plan the High Authority occupies a central place in the institutional structure of the Community. It is composed of independent persons jointly designated by the governments, has its own financial resources from a levy on coal and steel production and is provided with powers for binding the Member States and companies coming under the treaty regime. Thus it became a governmental authority operating in this new market instead of or side-by-side with the six national governments.

This breakthrough from the classical pattern of international organization, which in itself was quite revolutionary, was, however, attended by many safeguards. In the first place the powers of the High Authority are bound up strictly with the provisions of the Treaty.[5] In these provisions the policy to be pursued in the coal and steel sector is laid down fairly precisely. As the French delegation reported after the negotiations: 'la loi ici, c'est le Traité'. A Court of Justice was charged with ensuring the maintenance of law in the implementation of the Treaty.[6]

In the second place, the High Authority was obliged to consult governments and other interested parties frequently and co-operate closely with them. This was to be done either directly,[7] or in concert with the Special Council of Ministers,[8] or the Consultative Committee[9] as the case might be. The Council, which was created as a result of a Dutch initiative, is entrusted with the co-ordination between on the one hand the policy of the High Authority and on the other hand that of the governments responsible for the general economic policy of their countries,[10] a problem which indeed had to be provided for in a system of partial integration such as that in the ECSC system. It is only in exceptional cases that the Council of Ministers itself has the power to intervene in the coal and steel market (e.g. under certain conditions in crisis situations[11]). Its task consists chiefly in

5.   Art. 14 ECSC. See, generally, Reuter, La Communauté Européenne du Charbon et de l'Acier (Paris, 1953).
6.   Arts. 31–45 ECSC.
7.   Art. 46 ECSC.
8.   Arts. 26–30 ECSC.
9.   Arts. 18 and 19 ECSC.
10. Art. 26 ECSC
11. Arts. 58 and 59 ECSC.

giving its opinion – unanimously or by a qualified majority vote – to the High Authority on the decisions to be taken by the latter.[12] On a number of important issues the High Authority is obliged to obtain the prior consent of the Council to its decision by means of an assent.

Finally, the Treaty provided for a Common Assembly[13] originally composed of members of the national parliaments nominated by the latter, to which the High Authority is politically responsible for the implementation of the Treaty. This Assembly was given the right to dismiss the members of the High Authority collectively by the adoption of a motion of censure.[14]

The desire of the Contracting Parties not to give the High Authority too great a freedom of movement (and to this end obliging it to consult the governments and to respect democratic principles and the rule of law) only partly accounts for the heavy institutional structure of the Community. Indeed, considering the strong commitment to the detailed provisions of the Treaty, the High Authority was given only a modest scope for the development of a freely determined policy. The extensive institutional provisions were thus primarily justified by the political perspective, stated in the preamble of the Treaty, which was strongly influenced by the Schuman Declaration: namely the resolution 'to lay the foundations for institutions which will give direction to a destiny henceforward shared'.

3. THE FAILURE OF PLANS FOR A EUROPEAN DEFENCE COMMUNITY (EDC) AND A EUROPEAN POLITICAL COMMUNITY (EPC)

The Schuman Declaration of 9 May 1950 ushered in an era of ambitious attempts to give shape to European integration in a variety of other fields on this model. Two of these attempts reached the stage of elaborated texts: the Treaty establishing a European Defence Community (EDC) and the draft Statute for a European Political Community (EPC).

3.1 Background and content of these plans

The Treaty establishing the EDC originated in the Pleven Plan, which derived its name from the proposals of the then French Minister of Defence in October 1950. Shortly after the Schuman Declaration the Korean conflict had broken out, a conflict which created a deep impression in Europe. To many people in the West it seemed that convincing evidence

12. Art. 28 ECSC lays down special voting requirements relating to decisions and assents.
13. Arts. 20–25 ECSC.
14. Art. 24 ECSC.

had thus been produced of the aggressive designs of Moscow-directed international communism. What had happened in Korea, might be repeated in Europe. The future appeared gloomier than ever.

In August 1950 Winston Churchill (then in Opposition) launched, in the Consultative Assembly of the Council of Europe, the idea of a European army under a European Minister of Defence, although he left the British role in the dark. In September the North Atlantic Treaty Council met in New York. The U.S. Secretary of State announced that his country was going to station more armed forces in Western Europe. His government, however, regarded German rearmament as urgent and essential for the defence of that part of the world. The German forces would have to form part of an integrated Atlantic force to be set up, under a common supreme command, which was to receive political and strategic directives from NATO.

France vigorously opposed this proposal for German re-armament. In October Pleven submitted counter-proposals; these attempted to safeguard the objectives of French policy with regard to Germany by the methods of the Schuman Plan and at the same time to make possible the German re-armament stubbornly urged by the U.S. Government. A European army, composed of the smallest possible national units, would be placed under the control of a European Ministry of Defence, embedded in an institutional structure similar to that of the ECSC. As such, this European army would form part of the integrated Atlantic force which the North Atlantic Council had decided in September to proceed to form.

After a period of great confusion the French proposal was ultimately adopted in principle, partly under the influence of the recently appointed Atlantic commander-in-chief, the U.S. General Eisenhower, whose support had been enlisted for the idea. Laborious negotiations between the ECSC countries (with the United Kingdom again holding aloof) finally resulted on 27 May 1952 in the signing of the EDC Treaty, in which an institutional structure somewhat resembling that of the ECSC was provided for.

This new Treaty met with opposition from many quarters on widely different grounds, partly of a political, partly of a more pragmatic nature. One of the great political objections, which was also raised in the circles of those who wished to promote European integration, was the fact that a European army was being created without any provision for the framing of a European defence policy and military strategy and a European foreign policy bound up therewith. Another objection concerned the weak democratic character of the EDC.

In order to meet these objections, the six Foreign Ministers resolved on 10 September 1952 (anticipating ratification) already to implement Article 38 of the EDC Treaty. This Article had been included in the Treaty at the instigation of Italy and provided for proposals from the Parliamentary

Assembly of the EDC concerning institutional reform, *inter alia*, to ensure a stronger democratic character of this Community. These proposals were to be seen in the perspective of a later federal or confederal structure, founded on the principle of division of powers and containing especially a system of representation with two chambers. The Common Assembly of the ECSC, supplemented by co-opted persons so as to give it a composition similar to that of the Parliamentary Assembly provided for in the EDC Treaty, was requested by the Ministers to draft a Statute for a European Political Community, a request which went even further than the mandate contained in Article 38 of the EDC Treaty.

The invitation of the Ministers also spoke of the connection between on the one hand the establishment of such a Community and on the other hand the laying of common foundations for economic development and a fusion of essential interests of the Member States. This passage formed a response to a suggestion from the Dutch Foreign Minister, Beyen, who wanted to give the Latin tendency to set up institutional structures a firm starting-point in economic reality. His ideas about this were embodied in two Dutch memoranda, of December 1952 and February 1953, in which the outlines of a European common market were sketched. This so-called Beyen Plan, which broke with the then still prevalent idea of a progressive integration of the European economy by sectors, was later to form the basis of a successful Benelux initiative which in 1957 led to the conclusion of the EEC Treaty.[15]

The so-called '*ad hoc* Assembly' under the chairmanship of Paul Henri Spaak, the Belgian statesman, accomplished its task energetically. In March 1953 the Statute for a European Political Community, drafted by the Assembly and adopted by a very large majority, was handed to the six Ministers. This Community would be endowed with an institutional structure resembling that of the ECSC and the EDC, although a more important role than in either of these Communities was allotted to the independent policy-making institution and to the parliamentary element. The institutions of the EPC were to take over, on the basis of the respective treaties, the powers of those of the existing ECSC and the future EDC. Procedures had been provided to ensure the realization of a co-ordinated foreign policy of the participating countries, which might in course of time become a common policy, the introduction of a Community tax to defray Community expenses, and the establishment of a common market.

A solitary opponent, the French Gaullist Michel Debré, had vainly championed a different conception in the '*ad hoc* Assembly': that of a Political Union on purely intergovernmental lines, with a Conference of Heads of Government as the top organ.

15. See, generally, Grifftiths (ed.), *The Netherlands and the Integration of Europe 1945–1957* (Amsterdam, 1990).

3.2 Failure of these plans and 'relance européenne'

The draft Statue for an EPC was not to get beyond the phase of being an object of study. The chances of ratification of the EDC Treaty by France were gradually dwindling. On 30 August 1954 the French National Assembly finally resolved to adjourn the debate on the acceptance of the EDC Treaty *sine die*, with which the draft statute for an EPC also disappeared. Various factors led to this French attitude. A coalition of communists and Gaullists (whose numbers had greatly increased) had hotly opposed the EDC. The former resolutely rejected German re-armament. The latter turned against the abandonment of the instrument, *par excellence*, of national sovereignty: the French army. Moreover, in French circles there was a wide-spread fear of a confrontation with growing German power within an EDC without the United Kingdom.

The international situation, too, had changed. A political thaw in East–West relations appeared to set in after Stalin's death and the Korean Armistice in 1953. Besides, after the fall of Dien-Bien-Phu in August 1954, the French government of Pierre Mendès-France had some interest in giving the Soviet Government, which was carrying on a vehement campaign against acceptance of the EDC, as little cause for irritation as possible, because it badly needed its aid in an honourable liquidation of the French empire in Indo-China. To this should be added the French resentment of U.S. pressure to accept the EDC Treaty. The U.S.A. had far overshot the mark when in December 1953 the U.S. Secretary of State, Foster Dulles, had threatened an 'agonizing reappraisal of basic U.S. policy' if the EDC should fail to be established owing to French refusal.

The tendency towards European integration had been dealt a severe blow by the decision of the French Parliament. However, thanks to an initiative of the British Foreign Secretary, Anthony Eden, the essential matter which had formed the primary concern could be settled: the admission of the German Federal Republic as a partner on terms of equality in the Atlantic alliance. The so-called Paris Agreement of 23 October 1954, which had been reached at his instigation, provided, *inter alia*, for the creation of a Western European Union, equipped with a Parliamentary Assembly and an Agency for arms control, on the basis of a modification of the Brussels Treaty of 1948, to which Italy and the German Federal Republic now also became parties. In this looser European association the German Federal Republic, with due observance of certain restrictions, was allowed to proceed to rearmament and to make its contribution to the integrated Atlantic armed forces. The occupation regime of Western Germany, now to be admitted to NATO, was terminated, although the three Western occupying powers reserved to themselves their rights with regard to Berlin and to

Germany as a whole. An agreement between France and the German Federal Republic finally provided for a settlement of outstanding disputes between the two countries. With reference to the matter of the future position of the Saar the prospect of a plebiscite was offered, which in 1955 was to turn out in favour of confederation with the German Federal Republic.

The dismay in the circles of the champions of European integration about the rejection of the EDC treaty did not, however, last long. A *'relance européenne'* was started. A Benelux memorandum of 20 May 1955 resumed the thread of the Beyen Plan.[16] Economic integration should precede political integration. The memorandum proposed the convening of a conference for the purpose of working out texts for a treaty, which would give shape to far-reaching collaboration in the fields of transport infrastructure, co-ordination of energy policies, development of the peaceful use of atomic energy, and creation of a common market. In the two last-mentioned fields an important task was intended for a common Authority. The reaction of the other ECSC countries was not unfavourable, although the French government displayed an aversion to supranational institutions. The German government also showed some reserve in this field, possibly because it was apprehensive of the *dirigiste* tendency which it felt was already embodied in the ECSC in the powers of the High Authority. The main interest shown on the French side was in co-operation in the field of atomic energy. On 1–2 June 1955 the six Foreign Ministers of the ECSC countries met in Messina to discuss the Benelux memorandum. It was broadly approved, although in the resolution of the Ministers the institutional provisions relating to co-operation in the field of atomic energy and the establishment of a common market were discussed only in vague terms. It was decided to convene one or more conferences for working out treaties, and also to entrust the preliminaries for these conferences to a committee of government representatives. This was to be assisted by experts and to be presided over by a political personality who was to co-ordinate the activities. Paul-Henri Spaak was found willing to undertake the latter task. The United Kingdom, being a member of the WEU and a power allied with the ECSC in a somewhat superficial association (meant to keep a door open) was invited to take part in the activities. This invitation was accepted, although the United Kingdom government did not subscribe to the Messina Resolution. British participation in the work of the Intergovernmental Committee was to be only short-lived. Already in November 1955 it came to an end. The plans which had matured in the Committee could not be reconciled with the British preference for intergovernmental co-operation, preferably in the OEEC, and for a free-trade area rather than a customs union.

16. *Ibid.*

4. The Spaak Report and the Conclusion of the Treaties Establishing the European Economic Community (EEC) and the European Atomic Energy Community (EURATOM)

4.1 The contents of the Spaak Report

On the basis of the Messina Resolution the Intergovernmental Committee, led with great political imagination and dynamism by Paul Henri Spaak, had set to work on 9 July 1955. In April 1956 the Spaak report was completed in its final form.[17] Quite unlike the Schuman Plan, in which the matter of the institutions had taken priority, the Spaak Plan – particularly in the light of the widespread reticence about setting-up supranational structures after the *debacle* of the EDC – dealt with this question as a consequence of the substantive problems which had to be solved in the establishment of a common market and in the promotion of the peaceful use of atomic energy. In broad outline the measures required for the establishment of a common market and the underlying philosophy are traced. 'The purpose of a common market must be the creation of a large area with a common economic policy, so that a powerful unit of production is formed and continuous expansion is made possible, as well as an increased stability, an accelerated increase of the standard of living, and the development of harmonious relations between the Member States.'[18] For this, a fusion of the separate national markets was absolutely essential. A division of labour on a fairly large scale can put an end to the waste of economic resources. A greater certainty that the requisite sources of supply are permanently accessible makes it possible to abandon productive activities which pay no attention to costs.

This grand design is worked out further in the report around three topics. The *fusion of markets* involves the establishment of a customs union, the abolition of quantitative restrictions, free movement of services and a common agricultural policy. This fusion of markets should be accompanied by a *policy for a common market*. Indeed, in the present economic situation an expansion of markets and of competition *per se* would not yet be sufficient to ensure the more rational division of economic activities and the most favourable degree of expansion. A common competitive regime would be needed and also provisions for harmonization of laws and the development of a common transport policy. Another essential point was a co-ordination of national economic policies, so as to avoid difficulties with the balance of payments, if possible, and also common action for eliminating these difficulties, should they arise. *To ensure the development in this common market of European economic*

---

17. *Rapport des Chefs de Délégations aux Ministres des Affaires Etrangères* (Secretariat of the Intergovernmental Conference, Brussels, 21 April 1956).
18. *Ibid.*, p. 13 (our translation).

resources and their full use, financial aid for investments and retraining of workers would be necessary in order to promote the transformation of enterprises, the development of economically backward regions, and professional mobility. Freedom of movement should also be given to the production factors – labour and capital.

The report further contended that the realization of this ambitious programme could only take place during a transitional period divided into stages. A multiplicity of tasks embracing supervision, co-ordination, legislation, and administration would have to be carried out, which could not possibly all be regulated in detail in the text of the treaty. Moreover, it was felt essential to ensure that flexible methods could be used in working out the programme, because economic conditions are apt to change rapidly. A good deal therefore would have to be left to institutions, the powers of which would be clearly defined in the treaty, and to procedures, the diversity of which would match that of the problems which might arise.

With regard to the institutional structure and the division of powers the report subsequently developed four principles:

(1) pending a closer unity of monetary, budgetary, and social policies of the participating countries it would be necessary to make a distinction between:
   (*a*) matters of general policy, which would remain the reserved domains of the governments, and
   (*b*) problems involved in the functioning of the common market;
(2) the creation of an organ furnished with authority and Community responsibility would be inevitable, since:
   (*a*) the interest of producers and their legal certainty would demand a direct procedure (*i.e. not via* the governments) for the application and supervision of the rules concerning competition; the promptness required for enquiry and decision would not be compatible with '*la voie complexe des relations et des organisations intergouvernementales*';
   (*b*) the supervision of the fulfilment by the states of their obligations and the control of clauses which permit them to be temporarily relieved of these obligations under certain conditions (safeguard clauses) could hardly be subjected to '*un vote des gouvernements*': '*l'unanimité permettrait un veto ou des marchandages, la majorité pourrait traduire une coalition d'intérêts plutôt qu'une reconnaissance objective du droit*';
(3) the general policy measures falling within the competence of the governments have so decisive an effect on the functioning of the common market that agreement between the governments should be facilitated and the co-ordination of these measures more effectively ensured through the use of proposals from a common institution. Certain decisions are even so indispensable for the functioning and

development of the common market that, at the suggestion of this institution, acting objectively in the general interest, the rule of unanimity of the governments might be put aside, either in a strictly specified number of cases or after a given period had elapsed;
(4) it would be necessary to provide for appeal to a judicial body and for organization of parliamentary supervision.

On the basis of these principles the report reached the conclusion that four different institutions were needed: a Council of Ministers, a European Commission, a Court of Justice, and a Parliamentary Assembly. The functions of the two last institutions could be performed by the Court and the Common Assembly of the ECSC. A similar conclusion was drawn in the report with regard to an organization for the peaceful development of atomic energy. Highly varied and permanent responsibilities are involved in the promotion of research and the dissemination of scientific and technical information, the establishment and supervision of security norms, the encouragement of investment, the erection of common plants, safeguarding the supplies of ores and nuclear fuel, and the establishment and functioning of a common market for the atomic energy industry. Such responsibilities could rest only with a permanent institution, which was capable of reacting promptly; *i.e.* with a Commission incorporated in an institutional structure of the same kind as that proposed for promoting the common market.

By giving priority to the practical problems involved in the objectives to be reached over the problem of the institutional structure, the Spaak Report succeeded – and this is not the least of its numerous great merits – in demonstrating in a tactical but convincing way the opportuneness of an institutional structure co-ordinated with that of the ECSC. A Commission composed of independent persons and serving the Community interest was to be the pivot around which the institutional structure would revolve. It would be able to ensure an efficient discharge of functions of supervision and administration. It would have a task of stimulating and initiating common policies and common rules, and of stimulating the co-ordination of national policies and national laws. Thanks to the guarantee of impartiality implied in its composition and the formulation of its task, it would even be possible to break through the rule of unanimity in the collective determination of policy measures by the governments.

4.2   The conclusion of the EEC and Euratom Treaties

In 29 May 1956 the six Foreign Ministers met in Venice. At this conference they adopted the Spaak Report as basis for negotiations to frame the requisite treaties. An intergovernmental conference, again under the leadership of Paul-Henri Spaak, was convened for this purpose on 26 June

1956. The negotiations naturally did not proceed without difficulties. Formidable problems had to be solved. Fitting the weak French economy into a common market caused great concern. On the French side all sorts of guarantees were demanded on this point. Moreover, the French government wished its partners to share in the commercial and financial liabilities of France with regard to the overseas territories and countries associated with that country, particularly those in Africa. Nevertheless, on 25 March 1957 the Treaty establishing the European Economic Community and the Treaty establishing a European Atomic Energy Community were signed in Rome; unlike the ECSC Treaty, they were concluded for an indefinite period.[19] A successful ratification procedure followed. The long-standing fear that the French Parliament might ultimately refuse to accept the establishment of a common market was found to be unjustified. This fear had even helped to cause questions relating to the peaceful use of atomic energy (which after the Suez crisis of 1956 in the view of many people was of even greater importance than the common market) to be settled in a separate treaty. The partners wished to prevent the fate of cooperation in this field being dependent upon that of a common market.

The successful course of the negotiations and of ratification – the treaties entered into force on 1 January 1958 – was due primarily to the indefatigable efforts of the Action Committee for the United States of Europe, a very effective European pressure group set up by Jean Monnet.[20] He, who in 1952 had been appointed the first President of the High Authority, had tendered in his resignation from this office after the failure of the EDC Treaty in the French Parliament so that he might devote his full energy to the '*relance européenne*'. In the Action Committee he had managed to unite a large number of influential politicians and trade union leaders from the six countries who had declared themselves willing to make a joint effort to gain the support of their groupings for the federalist basic idea and for the specific resolutions of the Committee.

5. THE COMMUNITIES, THE UNITED KINGDOM, AND ENLARGEMENT TO INCLUDE OTHER DEMOCRATIC EUROPEAN COUNTRIES

As was to be expected, there was a reaction on the part of the other OEEC countries to the establishment of the EEC and Euratom. On a British

19. Arts. 240 EC and 208 Euratom. So far no state has ceased to be a member although Greenland (which forms part of Danish sovereign territory) decided by a referendum not to stay in the Community. Thus the application of the Community Treaties ceased as a result of a Treaty under Art. 236 EEC of 13 March 1984 (which entered into force on 1 February 1985) and Greenland now has the status of an associated territory under Art. 131 EC (see, generally, O.J. 1985 L 29/1 and Weiss (1985) 10 ELRev. 173).
20. See, generally, Monnet, *Memoirs* (London, 1978).

initiative an enquiry was started in the OEEC in the course of 1957 into the possibilities of bringing about an association in the form of a free-trade area between the OEEC countries, in which the Six would participate as an economic unit. Great differences of opinion appeared to exist on various issues about which the Six – who were apprehensive of the possibility that the integration process started by them might be watered down – were very much concerned. Some of the problems which worried them were the necessary degree of harmonization of economic and social policies, the settlement of the agricultural problem, the consequences of the lack of a common external tariff and of a common external trade policy, and the institutional form which would have to be given to such an association. The negotiations (started in the autumn of 1957, after the termination of the ratification procedure of the EEC Treaty) took place in the Inter-governmental Committee set up by the OEEC Council, under the leadership of the British Minister, Reginald Maudling. They came to an abrupt end in November 1958. The French Minister of Information, Jacques Soustelle, on behalf of the government of General De Gaulle, who had meanwhile come into power, informed the press (without any previous consultation with the five partners) that it was not possible to create a free-trade area without a common external tariff and without harmonization in the economic and social spheres. Thus, the door was closed to the other OEEC countries. Seven among them, *viz.* The United Kingdom, Denmark, Norway, Sweden, Austria, Switzerland and Portugal, decided in July 1959 to go their own way. On 4 January 1960, in Stockholm, the Treaty establishing a European Free Trade Association (EFTA) was concluded. Greece and Turkey associated themselves with the Community in agreements of 9 July 1961 and 12 September 1963 respectively, both based on Article 238 of the EEC Treaty.

However, after a few years a radical change took place in the British attitude towards the Communities. On 31 July 1961 Prime Minister Harold Macmillan informed the House of Commons that in the opinion of his government it would be right for the United Kingdom to make a formal application, under Article 237 of the EEC Treaty for negotiations with a view to joining the Community if satisfactory arrangements could be made to meet the special needs of the United Kingdom, the Commonwealth, and EFTA.[21] A solution of these problems, including, for the United Kingdom, those of British agriculture, would have to be found in conformity with the broad principles and purposes which inspired the concept of European unity and which were embodied in the Rome Treaty. The United Kingdom government subsequently submitted a request to the Council of Ministers of the EEC to open negotiations with a view to a possible accession. Denmark, Norway, and Ireland followed the British example. The other EFTA countries (Austria, Sweden, Switzerland, and Portugal) on the other

21. H.C Deb. Vol. 645, Col. 930.

hand made a request for negotiations with a view to the establishment of an association or some other economic arrangement.

The negotiations with the United Kingdom started in the autumn of 1961. After 16 months of laborious and often detailed negotiations, which did result in preliminary agreement on many points, the French government dramatically put an end to the negotiations. At his press conference of 14 January 1963 General De Gaulle plainly showed that he considered British membership of the Community premature and saw no purpose in continuing the negotiations. He alleged that the United Kingdom had not appeared ready to accept a genuine common external tariff, to renounce Commonwealth preferences, to abandon the claim that her agriculture must be privileged, and to cut her ties with the EFTA countries. If the United Kingdom (and with her inevitably the other EFTA applicant countries) were to join the Community, its character would change and its cohesion be lost. In the long run, General De Gaulle feared the Community would be swallowed up in a colossal Atlantic community, dependent on and controlled by the United States. In the General's view the Nassau Agreements of December 1962, according to which American aid to the development of the British Skybolt Missile was stopped and the British were to receive the American Polaris Missile as a substitute, had confirmed and reinforced the dependence of the United Kingdom on the United States. With the United Kingdom, the American horse would be dragged into the European Troy. Two weeks after this press conference, 29 on January 1963, it had to be stated in Brussels that the existing differences of opinion with France made any further negotiations impossible.

Rather more than five years after this failure, the Wilson government considered the time ripe for the United Kingdom to apply once again. On 2 May 1967 Harold Wilson declared in the House of Commons that his government had decided to make an application for membership of the EEC and parallel applications for membership of the ECSC and Euratom. He reported the readiness of his government 'to accept the Treaty of Rome, subject to the necessary adjustments consequent upon the accession of a new member and provided that we receive satisfaction on the points about which we see difficulty.'[22] These points concerned in particular the operation of the common agricultural policy of the Community: its potential effects on the cost of living and on the structure and well-being of British agriculture, the budgetary and balance-of-payments implications of its system of financing; and certain Commonwealth problems, in particular those of New Zealand and of the sugar-producing countries, whose needs were safeguarded by the Commonwealth Sugar Agreement. Other points about which questions arose were capital movements and regional policies. However, as Wilson stated, the government believed 'that there is nothing either in the Treaty of Rome or in the practical working

---

22. H.C Deb. Vol. 746, Col. 311.

of the Community which need make these problems insoluble'.[23] The
reactions of the countries of the Community to the British request for
accession, followed by those of Ireland, Denmark, and Norway,[24] were as
usual divided. From a communiqué of 19 December 1967, issued by the
Council of the European Communities, it finally became evident that
although no Member State had raised any fundamental objection to the
enlargement of the Community, nevertheless France, unlike the European
Commission and her five partners, was unwilling to start negotiations with
the four countries which had sought membership. The French government
considered it desirable that the re-establishment of the British economy
should be completed before the request of the United Kingdom could be
considered. The requests for accession presented by the four countries
remained on the Council's agenda.

The resignation of General De Gaulle and the coming into office of a
new French President, a confirmation of the United Kingdom's pledge to
Europe by the new Heath government and the definitive arrangement by
the Community of the financing of the common agricultural policy after
the expiry of the transitional period finally helped to create the conditions
for the re-opening of negotiations on the enlargement of the Communities.
The communiqué of the meeting of the Heads of State or government of
the Six at The Hague, on 1–2 December 1969,[25] in which a conception of
the future development of the Communities is set out, mentions as one of
the elements of agreement the opening of negotiations with the applicant
States in so far as they accept the Treaties and their political aims, the
decisions taken since the entry into force of the Treaties and the choices
made in the sphere of further development. After preliminary discussions
within the circle of the Six, negotiations started in the summer of 1970. In
the early summer of 1971 they resulted in general agreement between the
Six and the United Kingdom. On 22 January 1972 the Final Act embodying the instruments of accession was signed by the six Member States, the
United Kingdom, Ireland, Denmark and Norway. After the necessary
ratification procedures had been completed, the United Kingdom, Ireland
and Denmark acceded to the Communities on 1 January 1973.[26] Norway
did not accede, the referendum on accession having gone against
membership of the Communities. In the course of 1972 and 1973 free trade

23. *Ibid.*, Col. 313.
24. Sweden, too, intimated a desire to seek a form of participation in the Community
    which could be reconciled with its policy of neutrality.
25. Bull. EC. 1–1970 p. 11 at 16 (point 13 of the communiqué). See, generally, Von der
    Groeben, *The European Community: the formative years* (European Perspectives, Brus-
    sels, 1985).
26. For the United Kingdom see the European Communities Act 1972 (as amended). After
    various renegotiations conducted by the Labour government a referendum was held in
    the United Kingdom which indicated considerable majority support for Community
    membership (see Irving (1975–76) 1 ELRev. 1).

agreements principally relating to industrial products, were concluded with the remaining EFTA countries, Austria, Portugal, Sweden, Switzerland, Finland, Norway and Iceland.[27]

The enlargement of the Communities did not stop with the development of the Six into the Nine. Greece applied to accede in 1975 and became the tenth Member State on 1 January 1981.[28] In 1977 Spain and Portugal sought membership of the Communities and after long and difficult negotiations acceded on 1 January 1986.[29] Turkey made formal application for membership on 14 April 1987,[30] as did Morocco on 8 July 1987.[31] As will become apparent below, the enlargement process is continued and is set to continue apace, albeit at not the same speed for all applicants.

The already not inconsiderable problems relating to readiness and ability to take decisions apparent in a Community of nine increased substantially in a Community of twelve. Enlargement poses particular difficulties for the maintenance and expansion of a common market and Community policy, as the divergence in the level of development and economic structure within the Community is significantly increased.[32] In these circumstances it is understandable that attempts were resumed in the Eighties (having already been undertaken in the previous decade as part of efforts towards a European Union) to reform the Community in order to prevent a watering down of the integration process and give it, if possible, a new impulse. These efforts resulted in the Single European Act of 1986.[33]

27. For Austria see J.O. 1972 L 300/2; Portugal J.O. 1972 L 301/65 (this lapsed on Portuguese accession on 1 January 1986); Sweden J.O. 1972 L 300/98; Switzerland J.O. 1972 L 300/189; Finland O.J. 1973 L 328/2; Norway O.J. 1973 L 171/2 and Iceland J.O. 1972 L 301/2. These Agreements (and particularly the Protocols thereto) were amended from time to time; the agreements with Austria, Finland, Iceland, Norway and Sweden lapsed on the entry into force of the EEA Agreement on 1 January 1994
28. O.J. 1979 L 291.
29. O.J. 1985 L 302. See Sohier (1986) SEW 487.
30. Bull. EC 4–1987, points 1.3.1 and 1.3.2. On 27 April 1987 the Council opened the formal accession procedure, while noting that the assent of the European Parliament would be required. This was perhaps a polite way of noting that a speedy resolution of the application was unlikely.
31. Bull. EC 7/8–1987, point 2.2.35. This was put to one side on the ground that Morocco was not a European country (*Europa-Archiv* 1987, Z 207).
32. See Bull EC Supp. 1–3/78 as revised in COM (83) 116 final. The Committee of Three Wise Men set up as a result of the European Council's discussions in December 1978 in anticipation of a future enlargement to twelve Member States reported in October 1979 on the adaptations to the mechanisms and procedures of the Institutions which would be necessary (Report on European Institutions presented by the Committee of Three to the European Council). See, generally, VerLoren van Themaat (1980) SEW 144. As to two-speed integration see, *inter alia*, *Gedifferentieerde Integratie in de Europese Gemeenschappen* (14th session of the Asser Instituut Colloquium Europees Recht (1984), The Hague, 1985); Grabitz (ed.) *Abgestufte Integration* (Kehl, 1984); Ehlermann (1984) 82 Mich.L.Rev. 1274; Grabitz and Langeheine (1981) 18 CMLRev. 33, and Langeheine (1983) EuR. 227. With the flexibility provisions which are included in the Treaty of Amsterdam (not yet in force), adding a new Title VIa (Arts. K.15–K.17) to

The new dynamism in the continuation of the integration process in the late Eighties, with the completion of the internal market (the 1992 effect), made the Community more attractive to those outside it. Another contributory factor was the collapse of the Soviet hegemony in Central and Eastern Europe, first through the end of the tutelage imposed on the satellite states of Czechoslovakia, Hungary, Poland, Bulgaria and Romania, and later through the implosion of the Soviet Union itself. In the resulting turbulence, political unrest and economic insecurity, the European Community stood out as a beacon of economic prosperity and political stability.

The first territorial expansion eastward resulted from German unification on 3 October 1990. This took place without the need for a Treaty amendment as the new German *Länder* became part of the existing Federal Republic of Germany.[34] Immediately prior to unification, economic and monetary union was achieved between the old German Democratic Republic and the Federal Republic, which meant that the Community Treaties could be applied immediately in the new *Länder*.[35] The old German Democratic Republic achieved the necessary transformation of its legal system and legislation extremely quickly.

In response to the desire of the EFTA countries to strengthen their economic ties with the Community, not least on account of the dynamic programme for the completion of the internal market launched by the Commission in 1985,[36] the then President of the Commission, Jacques Delors, launched the concept of what became the European Economic Area[37] on 17 January 1989. This would involve the expansion of the Community's internal market and the relevant Community legislation to

the TEU and Art. 5a EC the way is set for a clear continuation of a multi-speed approach.
33. See section 6.2, *post*.
34. See Tomuschat (1990) 27 CMLRev. 415; Timmermans (1990) 27 CMLRev. 437, and Sinninghe Damsté and Wedekind (1991) SEW 455.
35. As to the package of transitional measures agreed in certain fields (*e.g.* agriculture, transport and the environment) see O.J. 1990 L 353.
36. COM (85) 310 final. See section 6.2, *post*.
37. In an address to the European Parliament, Bull. EC Supp. 1/89. This term in due course replaced the earlier notion of a European Economic Space which had been in currency since the meeting in April 1984 between the Foreign Ministers of the Community's Member States and those of the EFTA Member States. This was the first such multilateral meeting since the Free Trade Agreements had been signed in 1972, and took place against the background of the removal by both sides since 1 January 1984, of the last tariff barriers and quantitative restrictions in trade in industrial goods, see Bull. EC 4–1984, point 12.1 *et seq.* The change in terminology (from Space to Area) in English for linguistic reasons (the French and German names *Éspace* and *Wirtschaftsraum* were unchanged) was suggested by the Commission and accepted by the EFTA side at the opening of the formal negotiations on 20 June 1990. For discussion of the development of the EFTA-EC relationship, see Norberg *et al.*, *EEA Law* (Stockholm, 1993) 35–69.

embrace the EFTA countries. The negotiations which followed were difficult, as the highest possible degree of homogeneity of legislation and its adaptation in the future by the Community and the EFTA countries had to be reconciled with maintaining the independence of the Community system of decision-making and judicial protection.[38] On 2 May 1992 the EEA Agreement was signed in Oporto.[39] As a result of a referendum, Switzerland did not ratify the Agreement, which was then adapted by means of a Protocol.[40] The EEA Agreement thus entered into force on 1 January 1994, a year behind the original schedule.[41] The EEA Agreement meant that a large body of Community law was received into the laws of the participating EFTA countries, and, although they would be consulted, they did not attain any power of co-decision on future amendments of that body of law by the Community. It is thus understandable that the majority of the participating EFTA countries regarded the EEA as a step on the way to actual membership of the Communities.

Accession negotiations were opened with Austria, Finland, Norway and Sweden on 1 February 1993[42] and, given the preparatory work in the EEA Agreement and the high degree of affluence of the candidate countries, came to a very speedy resolution, so that the Treaty of Accession could be signed on 24 June 1994.[43] For a second time, however, the Norwegian people decided in a referendum against accession. On 1 January 1995 Austria, Finland and Sweden acceded to the European Union. The Treaty and Act of Accession and the Protocols attached thereto set out on the same basis as earlier accessions, namely acceptance by the new Member States of the *acquis communautaire*, but with technical adaptation of existing legislation on institutional as well as substantive aspects. Exceptions to the *acquis* are for a limited period only.

38. See Opinion 1/91 *EEA I* [1991] ECR I-6079, and Opinion 1/92 *EEA II* [1992] ECR I-2821. See also the contributions by Barents and Van Gerven in Stuyck and Looijestijn-Clearie (eds.) *The European Economic Area EC-EFTA* (Deventer, 1994) 57 and 33, respectively.
39. As to the text of the EEA Agreement, see O.J. 1994 L 1/3. See Norberg *et al.*, *op. cit.* (see note 37 *supra*); Blanchet *et al.*, *The Agreement on the European Economic Area (EEA)* (Oxford, 1994); Bright (ed.) *Business Law in the European Economic Area* (Oxford, 1994); Stuyck and Looijestijn-Clearie (eds.), *op. cit.* (see note 36, *supra*); Cremona (1994) 19 ELRev. 508; Norberg (1992) 29 CMLRev. 1171, and Steenbergen (1993) SEW 140. The EEA is a mixed agreement concluded between the EEC, the ECSC and their Member States on the one hand, and the participating EFTA countries on the other. Neither Euratom nor EFTA itself is a party to the EEA Agreement. As to mixed agreements, see Chapter 12, section 2.3, *post*.
40. Concluded on 17 March 1993, Bull. EC 3–1993, point 1.3.2. The Protocol contained special provisions permitting Liechtenstein to accede, and this took place on 1 May 1995, Bull. EC 3–1995, point 1.4.49, and 4–1995, point 1.4.59.
41. Bull. EU 1/2–1994, point 1.3.27.
42. Bull. EC 1/2–1993, point 1.3.1.
43. See O.J. 1994 C 241/9. See also Booß and Forman (1995) 32 CMLRev. 95 and Jorna (1995) 20 ELRev. 131.

Unlike with previous accessions, no general transitional period was necessary, as the legal arrangements of a transitional nature were already in place in the context of the EEA Agreement. The customs union and the Common Agricultural Policy apply in principle as from the date of accession. The reduction in agricultural prices in the new Member States resulting from accession is the subject of compensation through a special system of reducing national aid programmes. Environmental standards in the new Member States which were more stringent than the Community's harmonized standards formed a particular problem, which resulted in the new Member states being authorized to continue to apply their stricter standards for four years from accession, within which period Community legislation in the field is to be reviewed. Only after this revision will the question of the possible application of Article 100A(4) EC arise.[44] As far as institutional adaptations were concerned, the United Kingdom and Spain refused to agree to a mechanical adjustment of the provisions concerning qualified majority voting in the Council[45] and the resulting change in the number of votes required for a blocking minority. This problem was resolved in a somewhat unorthodox manner in the Ioannina Declaration.[46]

The remaining participants in the EEA from among the EFTA countries are Liechtenstein, Iceland and Norway. But the EEA idea is far from over, and it is still perhaps a potential halfway house towards membership of the European Union for some of the Central and Eastern European countries which are involved in accession negotiations.[47] These countries benefit from the Europe Agreements which are designed to promote a strengthening of close permanent relationships between the beneficiary countries and the Community.[48] Recognition of their ultimate aim of accession to the Union came at the Copenhagen European Council in June 1993, which agreed that the associated Central and Eastern

44. See Chapter VII, section 3.3.4, *post.*
45. Arts. 148 EC, 28 ECSC and 118 Euratom.
46. Bull. EU 3–1994, point 1.3.28, O.J. 1994 C 105/1, as adapted to take account of Norway not acceding, O.J. 1995 C 1/1. See further, Chapter IV, section 3.3, and Chapter V, section 3.2, *post.* The unorthodox character is reinforced by the fact that these decisions are published in the C Series of the O.J., although they are decisions of the Council. This reinforces the view that they have no legal force but represent a statement of intention by the Council to conduct its affairs in a certain manner. *Cf.* Case 68/86 *United Kingdom v. Council* [1988] ECR 855 at 898: 'A mere practice on the part of the Council cannot derogate from the rules in the Treaty. Such a practice cannot therefore create a precedent binding on Community institutions with regard to the correct legal basis.'
47. If accession is unrealistic because of political difficulties in relation to the European Union's Common Foreign and security Policy, the EEA model would at least permit these countries to have greater access to far-reaching economic benefits without tying their hands from the political perspective.
48. These Agreements are discussed in Chapter XII, section 4.2.3, *post.*

European countries that so desired should become members of the European Union as soon as they could satisfy the economic and political conditions required. These were that the candidate country had achieved stability of institutions guaranteeing democracy, the rule of law, human rights and respect for and protection of minorities, the existence of a functioning market economy as well as the capacity to cope with competitive pressures and market forces within the Union. Membership presupposed the candidate's ability to take on the obligations of member-ship including adherence to the aims of political, economic and monetary union. Another important consideration remains the Union's capacity to absorb new members while maintaining the momentum of European integration.[49] The Community proposed that the associated countries enter into a structured relationship with the institutions of the Union within the framework of a reinforced and extended multilateral dialogue and concertation on matters of common interest.[50] The Essen European Council in December 1994 agreed a comprehensive strategy to prepare these countries for accession to the European Union.[51]

Hungary and Poland submitted formal requests to accede to the Union in April 1994;[52] as did Romania and Slovakia in June 1995,[53] Latvia in October 1995,[54] Estonia, Lithuania and Bulgaria in December 1995,[55] the Czech Republic in January 1996,[56] and Slovenia in June 1996.[57] Besides these countries, Switzerland,[58] Malta[59] and

49. Conclusions of the Presidency, Bull. EC 6–1993, point I.13.
50. *Ibid.* As to the modalities, see *ibid.*, Annex II (point I.26). See also COM (94) 320 final; COM (9(4) 361 final; COM (95) 71 final, and COM (95) 163 final.
51. Conclusions of the Presidency, Bull. EU 12–1994, point I.13, see also the Council's Report (Annex IV to the Conclusions), *ibid.*, point I.39. Accession negotiations would not begin until after the conclusion of the 1996 Intergovernmental Conference, Corfu European Council, June 1994, Conclusions of the Presidency, Bull. EU 6–1994, point I.13. As to the political dialogue, see the Council's action on 7 March 1994 Bull. EU 3–1994, point 1.3.37.
52. Bull. EU 4–1994, points 1.3.18 and 1.3.19. On 18 April 1994 the Council formally set in motion the accession procedure under Art. O TEU in respect of these applications.
53. Bull. EU 6–1995, points 1.4.57 and 1.4.58. On 17 July 1995 the Council formally set in motion the accession procedure under Article O TEU in respect of these applications.
54. Bull. EU 10–1995, point 1.4.60. On 30 October 1995 the Council formally set in motion the accession procedure under Article O TEU in respect of this application.
55. Bull. EU 12–1995, points 1.4.59–1.4.61. On 4 December 1994 for Estonia, and 29 January 1996 for Lithuania and Bulgaria, the Council formally set in motion the accession procedure under Article O TEU in respect of these applications.
56. Bull. EU 1–1996, point 1.4.75. On 29 January 1996 the Council formally set in motion the accession procedure under Article O TEU in respect of this application.
57. Bull. EU 6–1996, point 1.4.49. On 16 July 1996 the Council formally set in motion the accession procedure under Article O TEU in respect of this application.
58. Bull. EU 5–1992, point 1.2.2. On 15 June 1992 the Council opened the formal accession procedure under Article O TEU in respect of this application.
59. Bull. EC 7/8–1990, point 1.4.24. On 17 September 1990 the Council opened the formal accession procedure under Article O TEU in respect of this application.

Cyprus[60] have applied to accede,[61] although only the application of Cyprus is actually active.[62] Despite the diverse situations of these applicants, there is every reason for the Union to develop its own policy relating to its enlargement. The presentation by the Commission at the Lisbon European Council in June 1992 of a number of general conditions for accession[63] has given a stimulus to such a development, although it is not on its own enough (as was in fact recognized by the fact that the Commission's paper was received and discussed, but not actually approved at that meeting). Institutional reform will be unavoidable if the Union is to undertake a new enlargement of any great order. This reform was one of the topics on the agenda of the 1996 Intergovernmental Conference.[64] The Essen European Council confirmed in December 1994 that the negotiations for new accessions could only be opened after the present 15 Member States had reached agreement on this thorny topic.[65]

Six months after the conclusion of the Treaty of Amsterdam, the Luxembourg European Council of 12–13 December 1997 agreed to launch the accession process with the 10 Central and Eastern European applicant countries and with Cyprus, as part of the implementation of Article O TEU.[66] That European Council meeting stressed that 'all these States are destined to join the European Union on the basis of the same criteria and that they are participating in the accession process on an equal footing.'[67] The accession process was launched on 30 March 1998 by a meeting of the Foreign Ministers of the 15 Member States and of the 11 applicant countries concerned. For 10 applicants the enhanced pre-accession strategy consists of accession partnerships and increased pre-accession aid; it is designed to enable all the applicant countries of Central and Eastern Europe eventually to become members of the European Union, and for this purpose to align themselves as far as possible on the Union *acquis* prior to accession.[68] In the case of Cyprus, a specific pre-accession strategy applies.[69]

60. Bull. EC 7/8–1990, point 1.4.25. On 17 September 1990 the Council opened the formal accession procedure under Article O TEU in respect of this application.
61. Turkey's application has already been noted, see note 30, *supra*.
62. The Maltese government suspended its application in October 1996, Bull. EU 5–1997, point 1.4.65, as corrected, Bull. EU 6–1997, point 2.5.1. Meng in Von der Groeben *et al.* (eds.), *Kommentar zum EU/EG-Vertrag* (5th ed., Baden-Baden, 1997) Vol. 5, 1155 reports that as a result of the Swiss referendum rejecting the EEA Agreement, the negotiations did not proceed.
63. See Bull. EC Supp. 3/92 and Conclusions of the Presidency, Bull. EC 6–1992, point I.4.
64. Art. N(2) TEU. The conference opened on 29 March 1996 in Turin. See also the Epilogue, sections 7 and 8.7, *post*.
65. Conclusions of the Presidency, Bull. EU 12–1994, point I.39.
66. Conclusions of the Presidency, Bull. EU 12–1997, point I.5 (point 10 of the communiqué).
67. *Ibid.*
68. *Ibid.* at para. 13.
69. *Ibid.* at para. 22. Of particular interest is the invitation (at para. 28) that the will-

Yet there is clearly a phased vision involved, as the European Council decided to convene bilateral intergovernmental conferences to begin negotiations with Cyprus, Hungary, Poland, Estonia, the Czech Republic and Slovenia.[70] These countries are seen as being in the first wave of accessions, whereas the European Council only undertook to speed up the preparation of negotiations with Romania, Slovakia, Latvia, Lithuania and Bulgaria.[71] As to Turkey, the European Council agreed a strategy, confirming Turkey's eligibility for accession, with the application being judged on the basis of the same criteria as the other applications. Even though the political and economic conditions allowing accession negotiations to be envisaged were not satisfied, the European Council considered it important for a strategy to be drawn up to prepare Turkey for accession by bringing it closer to the European Union in every field.[72] Thus the European Conference, which held its first session in London on 12 March 1998 is designed to 'bring together the Member States of the European Union and the European States aspiring to accede to it and sharing its values and internal and external objectives.'[73] Although the initial invitations were addressed to all of the 12 countries with active applications, Turkey declined to be present in London, clearly perceiving the exercise as scant consolation for lack of concrete progress in its application for accession.

6. EUROPEAN POLITICAL COOPERATION (EPC); THE EUROPEAN COUNCIL AND EUROPEAN UNION, THE SINGLE EUROPEAN ACT AND THE TREATY ON EUROPEAN UNION AND THE TREATY OF AMSTERDAM

6.1 EPC and the European Council

A solitary opponent, the French Gaullist Michel Debré had in vain at the beginning of 1953 championed a different idea in the '*Ad Hoc* Assembly' than the proposal for a supranational Political Community which it accepted.[74] He argued in favour of a Political Union on purely intergovernmental lines, with a Conference of Heads of Government as the top organ. Debré's proposal which was viewed sceptically by his fellow-members of the Assembly was revived in essence in 1960–1962

ingness of the government of Cyprus to include representatives of the Turkish Cypriot community in the accession negotiations delegation be acted upon.

70. *Ibid.* at para. 27 (1st sub-para.).
71. *Ibid.*, 2nd para.
72. *Ibid.*, point I.6 (see paras. 31–36 of the communiqué).
73. *Ibid.*, point I.4 (points 4–9 of the communiqué).
74. See section 3.1 (end) of this Chapter, *ante*. The *Ad Hoc* Assembly's draft was presented on 10 March 1953 (Information and Official Documents of the Constitutional Committee of the *Ad Hoc* Assembly (Paris, 1953) pp. 53 *et seq.*).

in General De Gaulle's proposals for the formation of a Political Union.[75]

In De Gaulle's perspective it was the states which were the only pillars on which Europe could be built. It was only the states which had the necessary legitimacy to exercise authority over the peoples of Europe. Political decisions could only be taken with the agreement of those in power in those states, *i.e.* national governments, although according to De Gaulle's concepts of political leadership this principally meant the Heads of State or government of all participating countries. Specialized organisms, such as the three Communities could do useful work relating to common problems but would be clearly subordinate to unanimous political decision-making by governments. The final version of the French proposals envisaged a Political Union with the aim of approximating, co-ordinating and unifying policies of the Member States in the spheres of foreign policy, the economy, culture and defence, under the general leadership of a Council of Heads of State or government.

De Gaulle's plans were discussed at two Summits, one in Paris on 10–11 January 1961 and the other in Bonn on 18 July 1961; the discussion continued thereafter in the so-called Fouchet Commission although this had to suspend its work in April 1962, without agreement having been reached. There were a number of stumbling-blocks: the intergovernmental framework, the fear of encroaching on the competence of the existing Communities, the still uncertain relations with the United Kingdom and the possible weakening of relations within NATO with the United States as a result of the proposed defence co-operation. The inflexible attitude of the Netherlands, supported by Belgium contributed substantially to the failure of the negotiations. These countries argued, in essence, that the principle of the supranational character of a political union could only be discussed if the United Kingdom participated from the outset (the negotiations on the first attempt by the United Kingdom to accede to the Communities had begun in Autumn 1961). France was resolutely opposed to this.

Often the word 'political' in relation to De Gaulle's proposed union is used to indicate that it concerned only external relations. This is not, however, the case; the French plans also envisaged the union laying down the powers of the governments acting by mutual agreement to take all important (*i.e.* political) decisions in the economic sphere. The Communities, acting under the supranational formula, would merely execute these decisions. Thus it was always inherent in the French view that there was no place in the Communities for qualified majority decisions on important matters, nor was there any room for an independent political role for the Commission.[76]

75. See *Le dossier de l'Union Politique* (Political Committee of the European Parliament, January 1964) and Nijenhuis (1986) *Internationale Spectator* 41.
76. See Kapteyn (1966) *Internationale Spectator* 51.

The rigour of the French position became apparent during the constitutional crisis provoked by France in 1965 as a result of certain agricultural financial proposals which the Commission had submitted to the Council and which were supported by the other members of the Council but were unacceptable to the French. The crisis took the form of a boycott by France of Council meetings (the empty chair policy) and only came to an end with the Luxembourg Accords of January 1966. These recorded French dissent from the views of the other Member States on majority voting and were thus in reality an agreement to disagree. As a result of these Accords the Council thenceforth avoided voting.[77]

After the failure of French plans for a Political Union and the French veto of the United Kingdom's application in January 1963, the three-monthly consultations on external policy which the Foreign Ministers had held since the end of 1959 were discontinued. To the great annoyance of the French government the *other* five Member States of the Communities wanted to discuss external policy only within the framework of the WEU Council (*i.e.* with the United Kingdom being involved).

Only after De Gaulle's resignation when the French position on United Kingdom accession changed were the conditions fulfilled for a closer co-operation between the Member States in foreign policy. At the Summit at The Hague on 1–2 December 1969, at which it was decided to open negotiations with the four countries which had applied to accede to the Communities, the Foreign Ministers were requested to study the best method of making progress in the field of 'political integration'.

This task resulted in a report of a committee of Directors-General for political affairs in the six foreign ministries under the chairmanship of Davignon (from Belgium). Six-monthly meetings of the Foreign Ministers to discuss matters of foreign policy were proposed, to be preceded by meetings of a political committee of Directors-General. The governments approved this report at the Luxembourg Summit on 27 October 1970 (hence it is often called the Luxembourg report). This laid the basis for European Political Cooperation (EPC). This was further expanded through the report approved at the Copenhagen Summit on July 23, 1973.[78] The report accepted by the Foreign Ministers in London on 13 October 1981 envisaged still further improvements in the EPC procedure.[79]

77. These Accords and their consequences are discussed further in Chapter V, section 3.2, *post*.
78. See *Seventh General Report on the activities of the European Communities* (Brussels, Luxembourg, 1973) p. 502 *et seq.*
79. See Bull. EC supp. 3/81 p. 14 *et seq.* These reports and the Solemn Declaration on European Union agreed at the Stuttgart Summit in 1983 (Bull. EC 6–1983 pp. 18–29) were confirmed and supplemented by Title III of the Single European Act which used to govern European Political Cooperation until Title III SEA was repealed by Art. P(2) TEU. Arts. 1 and 3(1) SEA, however, remain in force. See, generally, Nuttall, *European Political Co-operation* (Oxford, 1992) and his surveys in *Yearbook of Eur-*

The Foreign Ministers of the Member States and a member of the Commission used to meet at least four times a year within the framework of EPC; they could also discuss foreign policy within the framework of EPC on the occasion of meetings of the Council,[80] composed of the Foreign Ministers. The Commission was always fully associated with work carried out in this field.[81] The preparation of and follow-up to the ministerial meetings was in the hands of the Political Committee (composed of the Political Directors of the foreign ministries of the Member States);[82] it met ten to twelve times a year on a regular basis.[83]

A European Correspondents' Group, composed of officials of the twelve foreign ministries, was established to look after day-to-day matters.[84] Expert working groups carried out particular tasks; they discussed, for example, the policies which the Member States should pursue in different regions of the world. A direct telex network between the ministries facilitated mutual communication. In the twelve capitals the ambassadors consulted each other regularly (in the presence of the Foreign Minister of the country concerned if that Member State were President-in-office of EPC); this also happened in third countries and in representations to the main international organizations. In third countries in which there is a Commission Delegation the Head of the Delegation could well fulfil a political and commercial co-ordinating role for the Member States' interests and would convene meetings of the ambassadors of the Member States represented in those countries to discuss matters of mutual interest, a tendency which was reinforced by Article 30(9) SEA. The Presidency of EPC changed half-yearly on 1 January and 1 July along with the Presidency of the Council. The President-in-office was spokesman for the then Twelve Member States, representing their positions in relations with third countries in relation to EPC activities, and was responsible for initiating action and ensuring that the necessary consultation took place.[85]

Discussions which took place in EPC covered all important questions of foreign policy which are of concern to the Member States as a whole. The

opean Law (Oxford, annually), and Pijpers *et al.* (eds.) *European Political Co-operation in the 1980s* (Dordrecht, 1988).

80. Art. 30(3)(a) SEA.
81. Art. 30(3)(b) SEA. The Commission was always fully associated with work carried out in this field.
82. Art. 30(10)(c) SEA.
83. Art. 30(10)(d) SEA. It could be convened (as could a ministerial meeting) within 48 hours at the request of at least three Member States.
84. Art. 30(10)(e) SEA.
85. The Presidency was supported by a separate secretariat (based in Brussels, in the building which housed the Council) established under Article 30(10)(g) SEA. As part of the distinction between EPC and the Community institutional structure, the members of that secretariat were not Council or Commission Officials but were given the status of members of diplomatic missions based in Brussels, Art. 30(11) SEA.

aim was to make common policies possible through establishing and accepting common positions and common action. The co-ordination of the positions of the Member States concerning the political and economic aspects of security fell within the field of EPC.[86] Consultations took place before each Member State decided on its final position.

The European Parliament was associated with EPC, albeit often subject to restrictions because of the confidential nature of the discussions.[87] Once a year the president-in-office of EPC reported orally to a plenary session of the Parliament on progress in European political co-operation. After each ministerial meeting of EPC there was regularly a meeting between the presidency of EPC and the Political Affairs Committee of the Parliament. Since the end of 1974 the Parliament was able to ask questions of the Foreign Ministers meeting in political co-operation; these were answered by the Presidency.[88]

Cooperation in EPC (as in the present common foreign and security policy) was purely intergovernmental in nature. Yet despite the institutional separation in the days of EPC, cooperation in Community and EPC affairs inevitably occurred. Economic measures affecting the Community internally, the Community's commercial policy and the way in which relations with developing countries concerning development aid were and are handled affect the foreign policies of the Member States and are, in turn, influenced by them. Thus the Copenhagen report of 1973, with an eye to this point, envisaged the Commission being invited to give its views on subjects which could have an influence on Community activities. In practice the Commission was represented at all ministerial EPC meetings and all meetings of the Political Committee.[89] This was then put on a firm footing initially by the Single European Act which also emphasised the need to ensure that the European Community's external policies and the policies agreed in EPC were consistent.[90]

The connection between the activities of the Communities and the work on political co-operation was expressly recognized at the Paris Summit of 9–10 December 1974 in the setting up of the European Council. It was decided that the Heads of Government would meet at least three times a year, accompanied by their Foreign Ministers, as the Council of the Communities and in the context of political cooperation. The Foreign Ministers, in order to ensure consistency in Community activities and continuity of

86. Solemn Declaration on European Union adopted by the European Council, Stuttgart, 19 June 1983, para. 1.4.2 (Bull. EC 6–1983, point 1.6.1).
87. Art. 30(4) SEA.
88. Bull. EC 12–1974, p. 7 (point 1104, point 4, para. 2 of the communiqué). See, further, Nuttall (1987) 7 YBEL 211.
89. Bot (1977) *International Spectator* 788.
90. In the London report (1981) it was recognized that full involvement of the Commission within the framework of the rules and procedures laid down was essential in political co–operation at all levels.

work, were instructed to act as initiators and co-ordinators, meeting in the Council; at the same time they may hold political co-operation meetings. It was expressly provided that these arrangements did not affect the rules and procedures laid down in the Treaties or the provisions on political co-operation in the Luxembourg and Copenhagen reports. The Commission was to exercise its powers at all these meetings and play the part assigned to it in the various texts concerned.[91]

The setting up of the European Council institutionalized the Summit conferences which had taken place since December 1969, after De Gaulle's resignation, from time to time and with varying degrees of success.[92] At the same time these meetings, in so far as they related to questions falling within the competence of the Communities, were at least formally incorporated into the institutional scheme of the Communities. The European Council was at that time able to act in this field as the Council of the European Communities; it had no legal significance in Community law other than when it so acted, it was not a separate Institution of the Communities.[93]

The formation of the European Council with, on the one hand, EPC organized on an intergovernmental basis and, on the other hand, the Council's practice since the Luxembourg Accords, of not applying the qualified majority voting principle, at least in important matters, amounted to a recognition of the accuracy of some of De Gaulle's concepts. The thought of extending political co-operation into a more wide-ranging union was taken up again in the Seventies. At the Paris Summit in October 1972 the Heads of State and government 'assigned themselves the key objective of converting, before the end of this decade and in absolute conformity with the signed Treaties, all the relationships between Member States into a European Union.'[94] At the Paris Summit in December 1974 the then Belgian Prime Minister, Tindemans, was asked to prepare a report on the basis of reports from the Community Institutions and his discussions with governments and circles representative of public opinion in the Community. This report on European Union, presented in December 1975,[95] was neither accepted nor rejected by the European Council. It was

91. See Bull. EC 12–1974, p. 7 (point 3, 4th para., of the communiqué from the December 1974 Paris Summit).
92. The Hague (December 1969), Paris (October 1972), Copenhagen (December 1973) and Paris (December 1974). See, generally, Werts, *The European Council* (Amsterdam, 1992) and Glasener in Curtin and Heukels (eds.), *Institutional Dynamics of European Integration* (Essays in honour of Schermers, Vol. II, Dordrecht, 1994) 101.
93. Since the coming into force of the TEU it is no longer possible for the European Council to act as the Council, see, further, Chapter IV, section 2.2, *post*. The point about the European Council not being a Community body or Institution remains true.
94. Bull. EC 10–1972, p. 23. (point 16 of the communiqué).
95. Bull. EC Supp. 1/76. As to the reports from the Commission, the Parliament, the Court of Justice and the Economic and Social Committee, see Bull. EC Supps. 5/75 and 9/75.

simply agreed that the Foreign Ministers and the Commission would produce an annual report to the European Council about results achieved and the feasible advances in the short term which could be made in various fields of the Union.[96]

6.2 The Single European Act (1986)

Conversion of all the relations between the Member States into a European Union was impossible in the seventies. Only in 1981 was the thread taken up again. The German Foreign Minister, Genscher and his Italian colleague Colombo put forward a draft 'European Act' which envisaged an improvement of the institutional provisions and an intensification and expansion of co-operation, even in the field of foreign policy, on the way to a European Union. Although this was not the original intention, their initiative resulted not in an amendment of the Treaties but in the Solemn Declaration on European Union adopted by the European Council at Stuttgart on 19 June 1983 which largely broke down over intentions about the policy to be pursued and the procedures to be applied.[97] In the meantime there was a movement in circles in the European Parliament, led by the Italian member Spinelli, which sought to achieve a fundamental reform of European co-operation. This led to the drawing up of a Draft Treaty establishing the European Union which was adopted by the European Parliament on 14 February 1984 by a large majority.[98]

The Draft Treaty attracted much attention, not only in academic circles[99] but also in political circles in the Community. It was difficult for the governments not to react in some way. At its meeting in Fontainebleau on 25–26 June 1984 the European Council decided to set up an *ad hoc* Committee, composed of personal representatives of the Heads of State and government on the lines of the Spaak Committee. This *ad hoc* Committee, under the chairmanship of Dooge from Ireland was requested to make suggestions for improving European co-operation, in the Community field, in the field of political cooperation and in any other

96. Bull. EC 11–1976 point 2501 (p. 93).
97. Bull. EC 6–1983, point 1.6.1 (p. 24).
98. O.J. 1984 C 77/33; Bull. EC 2–1984, point 1.1.2 (p. 8).
99. *E.g.* Bieber *et al.* (eds.), *An Ever Closer Union* (European Perspectives, Brussels/Lux-embourg, 1985); Capotorti *et al.*, *The European Union Treaty* (Oxford 1986) (also pub-lished in French as *Le Traité d'Union Européenne* (Brussels, 1985) and in German as *Der Vertrag zur Grundung der Europäischen Union* (Baden–Baden, 1986)); Lodge (ed.), *The European Community in search of a Future* (London, 1986); Schwarze *et al.* (eds.), *Eine Verfassung für Europa* (Baden-Baden, 1984); Bos (1985) SEW 442; Capotorti (1985) CDE 512; Lauwaars (1985) SEW 398; Lodge, Freestone and Davidson (1984) 9 ELRev. 387; Louise (1985) CDE 530; Nickel (1984) CDE 511; Nickel and Corbett (1984) 4 YBEL 79; Pernice (1984) EuR 126, and Weiler and Modrall (1985) 10 EL Rev. 316.

field. In March 1985 the Committee produced its report, albeit not a unanimous one in all parts.[100] Partly as a result of this report the European Council at its meeting in June 1985 in Milan decided to convene a conference within the meaning of Article 236 EEC to draw up the text of a treaty on Community external and security policy and on amendments to the EEC Treaty. This conference commenced work in September 1985 and the candidate Member States (Spain and Portugal) were invited to participate. The conference had various materials before it: the report of the Dooge Committee; the report of the *ad hoc* Committee on a People's Europe (the Adonnino Committee which had also been established as a result of the Fontainebleau Summit);[101] the decisions of the Milan European Council on the realization of a single internal market by 1992,[102] and a draft revision of the treaties prepared by Luxembourg, then president-in-office of the Council. The result of the Committee's work, out of all the proposals before it, was the Single European Act which was signed on 17 February 1986 by nine Member States and on 28 February 1986 by Denmark (after a referendum), Greece and Ireland (also after a referendum).[103]

The Single European Act (SEA), which came into force on 1 July 1987[104] made on the one hand a number of amendments to the existing Community Treaties. On the other hand, it contained a number of independent provisions relating to the European Council[105] and EPC.[106]

100. See Bull. EC 3–1985, point 3.5.1.
101. Bull. EC supp. 7/85.
102. See the Commission's White Paper *Completing the Internal Market* COM (85) 310 Final, presented to the Milan European Council, June 28–29, 1985 (Bull. EC 6–1985, point 1.2.5).
103. Bull. EC Supp. 2/86. The Court of Justice has produced a collection of documents relating to the ratification process of the SEA (available in any European Documentation Centre).
104. See *e.g.* De Ruyt, *L'Acte Unique Européen* (2nd ed., Brussels, 1989); Arnull (1986) 11 ELRev. 358; Bieber *et al.* (1986) 23 CMLR 767; Campbell (1986) ICLQ 932; Edward (1987) 24 CMLRev. 19; Ehlermann (1987) 24 CMLRev. 361; Forman and Clough (1986) 11 ELRev. 383; Freestone and Davidson (1986) 23 CMLRev. 793; Glaesner (1986) EuR 119, (1986) 6 YBEL 283, and (1987) 10 Fordh. Int'l. L.J. 446; Gulman (1987) 27 CMLRev. 31; Krenzler (1986) EuR 384; Lodge (1987) XI *Journal of European Integration* 5; Mertens de Wilmars (1986) SEW 601; Pescatore (1986) EuR 153 and (1987) 24 CMLRev. 9; Toth (1986) 23 CMLRev. 803; VerLoren van Themaat (1986) SEW 464, and De Zwaan (1986) 23 CMLRev. 747. See also the 12th. Report of the House of Lords Select Committee on the European Communities, Session 1985–86 (HL 149). As to the SEA and environmental policy, see Krämer (1987) 24 CMLRev. 659 and Vandermeersch (1987) 12 ELRev. 407. As to the views of the Dutch government, see Kellermann (1987) 12 ELRev. 221.
105. Art. 2 SEA. See Capotorti in Capotorti *et al.* (eds), *Du droit international au droit de l'intégration* (*Liber Amicorum* Pescatore, Baden-Baden, 1987) 79 and Oppermann in *ibid.*, 537.
106. Arts. 1, 3rd para.; 3(2), and 30 SEA. See Frowein in Capotorti *et al.*, *ibid.*, 247 and Oppermann, *ibid.*

Article 2 of the SEA confirmed what has been the practice hitherto in recognizing that the President of the Commission has a place in the European Council. It continued to be assisted by the Foreign Ministers and a member of the Commission. It started to meet at least twice a year (rather than at least three times as established at the Paris Summit in December 1974). Thus existing practice was by and large confirmed, and the long-envisaged secretariat was set up in Brussels to assist the Presidency of EPC in preparing and implementing EPC's activities and in administrative matters.[107] Of the amendments made to the Community Treaties, the inclusion of the internal market concept in Article 8a EEC, and the envisaged completion of the internal market by 31 December 1992 were of particular significance. To facilitate this completion a new legal basis for harmonisation measures was introduced in Article 100a EEC, permitting decision-making by qualified majority. New policy areas, in which the Community was already active on the basis of Article 235 EEC were established, such as environmental protection and research and technological development. The cohesion policy, designed to strengthen economic and social cohesion between the Member States of the Community was strengthened. On the institutional side, the introduction of the co-operation procedure which gave the European Parliament more say in Community decision-making was particularly noteworthy, as was the attachment to the Court of Justice of a Court of First Instance, initially designed to deal with staff cases and to give first instance judgments on cases regularly involving complex assessment of factual issues, such as competition cases, but destined to see its jurisdiction expanded considerably.

6.3   The Treaty on European Union (1992)

After the entry into force of the Single European Act on 1 July 1987, and inspired by the progress of the market integration process, the drive towards an economic and monetary union (EMU), which had started in the early Seventies but had quickly appeared unattainable because of global monetary developments, was resumed. A completed internal market cannot continue to function without the keystone of an EMU. In a system of fixed, but adaptable exchange rates, to say nothing of a system of fluctuating exchange rates, so much uncertainty remains as to the results of cross-border investments, that the economic advantages of market integration cannot be optimally utilised. Moreover, an internal market without an EMU is never a safe haven, as the risk of unilateral intervention by a Member State disturbing the market remains. These economic realities caused the Hanover European Council in June 1988 to entrust to a committee of specialists, chaired by the President of the

107. *Cf.* note 85, *supra.*

Commission, Jacques Delors, the task of studying and proposing concrete stages towards EMU.[108] The Delors Committee Report was presented in April 1989[109] and, in December 1989, the Strasbourg European Council[110] decided that the first phase of EMU could begin on July 1, 1990 with the full liberalization of capital movements. At the same time it was decided to convene an intergovernmental conference before the end of 1990, for the purpose of amending the EEC Treaty with a view to the final stages of EMU.

At the same time the collapse of Soviet hegemony began. The breathtaking progress of German unification and the revolutions in the neighbouring Central and East European countries created a climate of hope, but also of considerable political and economic unrest and uncertainty. The German Chancellor, Kohl, strove to anchor a united Germany firmly in a strengthened European Community, strengthened into political unity in order to support the far-reaching restructuring in the former Eastern Bloc countries and to support an effective peace and security policy in Europe. Kohl linked German co-operation on EMU (which meant that Germany would have to surrender its much-prized monetary autonomy, as would the other participants) to a real strengthening of the Community in political terms. After initial hesitation, Mitterrand, then French President, supported this idea. In a joint initiative they presented to a special European Council in Dublin in April 1990 a proposal for the development of a common foreign and security policy.[111] In June 1990, during the regular Dublin European Council, it was agreed to convene a conference on political union to open on 14 December 1990, a day after the intergovernmental conference on EMU was to open.[112] The work of the two conferences was to run in parallel and to be concluded rapidly and at the same time.[113] The Dublin European Council thus confirmed the Franco-German linkage of these subjects.

In the event, both conferences opened on 15 December 1990, following on from the Rome European Council.[114] For the conference on EMU much preparatory work had been already undertaken, including a draft treaty drawn up by the Commission.[115] In the barely six months prior to

108. Bull. EC 6–1988, point 3.4.1.
109. Bull. EC 4–1989, points 1.1.1–1.1.9.
110. Bull. EC 12–1989, point 1.1.11.
111. Bull. EC 4–1990, point I.12 (alongside their paper on political union a paper from the Belgian government on the subject was also considered).
112. Bull. EC 6–1990, points I.11 and Annex I (political union); I.10 (EMU).
113. This point was specifically confirmed at the Rome European Council in December 1990, Bull. EC 12–1990, point I.10.
114. Bull. EC 12–1990, points 1.1.7 and 1.1.8. As to the problems of coherence between the two conferences, see the contributions by Louis and Maganza in Monar et al. (eds.), The Maastricht Treaty on European Union (Brussels, 1993) 163 and 173 respectively.
115. Bull. EC Supp. 2/91, 13–38, as to the draft treaty, see 39–62.

its opening, the conference on political union was much less well prepared; there was merely a list of subjects which had been drawn up on the basis of contributions by the Commission[116] and some Member States,[117] on the basis of which the Rome European Council requested the conference to pay particular attention to democratic legitimacy; common foreign and security policy; European citizenship; extension and strengthening of Community action, and the effectiveness and efficiency of the union.[118]

The negotiations proceeded pretty speedily, but at the expense of the ambitions of devotees of a Union concept, in which competence in more areas would be transferred to the Union level, at which the Community method would operate (rather than the intergovernmental method). The United Kingdom in particular maintained its strident opposition to such a development, reflecting a certain continuity in its distrust of supranational institutions, a factor which had kept it so isolated from Community developments, particularly in the 1950s. Thus the common foreign and security policy and co-operation in justice and home affairs, which are almost wholly intergovernmental in nature, remain outside the Community framework, even though a single institutional structure was to be developed. An attempt by the Dutch – at the time holding the Presidency – to bring the political union and the three Communities into a unitary structure, as had been intended with EMU all along, backfired dramatically. On 30 September 1991, apart from Belgium, the other Member States were not even prepared to accept the Dutch text as a basis for discussion. During the European Council at Maastricht on 9–10 December 1991 the negotiations were concluded, after certain concessions to a number of Member States, in particular to the United Kingdom in relation to social policy and EMU, and to the poorer Member States, which, led by Spain, forced a larger transfer of resources in their direction through a new cohesion fund.[119] The final text of the Treaty on European Union (TEU) was agreed and signed at Maastricht on 7 February 1992.[120]

116. See Bull. EC Supp. 2/91, 85–179. The Commission's Opinion of 21 October 1990 is set out in *ibid.*, 75–82.
117. See, generally, Cloos *et al.*, *Le Traité de Maastricht: genèse, analyse, commentaire* (Brussels, 1993) 59–83 (particularly at 75 *et seq.*).
118. Bull. EC 12–1990, points I.4–I.9. The Spanish Prime Minister Gonzales suggested the inclusion of European Citizenship. Looking, in the context of extension of Community action, at the possibility of bringing intergovernmental cooperation in matters such as immigration policy; organized crime; the fight against drugs, and cooperation in criminal matters within the ambit of political union, was included at the request of Chancellor Kohl.
119. Bull. EC 12–1990, points I.1 and I.3.
120. See Cloos *et al.*, *op. cit.* (see note 115, *supra*); Constantinesco *et al.* (eds.), *Traité sur l'Union Européenne* (Paris, 1995); Corbett, *The Treaty of Maastricht* (Longman, 1993); Dehousse (ed.), *Europe after Maastricht An ever closer union?* (Munich, 1994); O'Keeffe and Twomey (eds.), *Legal Issues of the Maastricht Treaty* (Chichester, 1994). See further, *e.g.* Constantinesco (1993) CDE 251; Curtin (1993) 30 CMLRev. 17;

The structure chosen for the Union is tripartite. The most important part, consisting of the three Communities, is strictly separated from the other two, common foreign and security policy (CFSP) and co-operation in the field of justice and home affairs (JHA), which operate in a much more intergovernmental framework, and in which parts the Commission, while it is fully associated with the work, does not have the sole right of initiative which is so central to its pivotal status in the Communities. This tripartite structure, often presented as resembling a temple facade with three pillars supporting the architrave and pediment of the Union,[121] is ambiguous and should be regarded as an interim phase in the development of the Union. Article N(2) TEU provided for a new intergovernmental conference to be convened in 1996, *inter alia* to review this structure. The Union established by the TEU does not itself have legal personality. It does not act in the place of the European Communities, but brings them, as a separately organised and still autonomous part, together with the two other parts into a relationship which in legal terms is extremely weakly set up. New Member States accede to the Union, rather than to the Communities. This differs from the approach of the Single European Act, as accessions were still to the Communities, involving accepting the original Treaties as modified and supplemented, and the *acquis communautaire*. The relationship between the three parts is made clear by the single institutional framework,[122] the purpose of which is to ensure the consistency and continuity of the activities carried out in order to attain the Union's objectives, while respecting and building upon the *acquis communautaire*.[123] Thus CFSP is determined by the Council, within the principles and general guidelines laid down by the European Council.[124] The Commission has a right of initiative, but not an exclusive one,[125] and the European Parliament is to be consulted by the Presidency on the main aspects and basic choices of CFSP.[126] The Court of Justice has been carefully excluded

Durand in Mégret *et al.* (eds.), *Le Droit de la CEE* Vol. 1 (2nd ed., Brussels, 1992) 357; Gosalbo Bono (1992) 12 YBEL 85; Harmsen (1994) NILQ 109; Hartley (1993) ICLQ 213; Lane (1993) 30 CMLRev. 939; Rideau (1992) *Rev. Aff. Eur.* No. 2, 21, and VerLoren van Themaat (1992) RMC 203. See also the contributions by Zuleeg, Jaqué and Beutler in Von der Groeben *et al.* (eds.), *op. cit.* (see note 62, *supra*) Vol. 1 46–133 and by Burghardt and Tebbe, Degen, Krück, Meng, Jacqué and Weber in *ibid.*, Vol. 5, 897–1183.

121. The image is frequently used, although classical temples had an even number of pillars.
122. But some connceptual uncertainties have appeared in practice, see Case C-170/96 *Commission v Council* [1998] ECR I-nyr (12 May 1998) on jurisdiction to review acts affecting the Community's powers.
123. Art. C TEU, 1st para.
124. Art. J.8 (1) and (2) TEU. See also Art. J.3 (1) TEU.
125. Art. J.8 (3) provides that any Member State or the Commission may refer questions or make proposals to the Council within the ambit of CFSP. The Commission must be fully associated with work in the field of CFSP, Art. J.9 TEU.
126. Art. J.7 TEU. The Presidency must ensure that the views of the European Parliament

from the picture.[127] As a whole, though, CFSP is somewhat more Community-orientated than was EPC, although the institutional model of CFSP is still essentially intergovernmental, not least because decision-making is based on unanimity.[128]

The TEU rebaptises the European Economic Community (EEC) into the European Community (EC), reflecting the long-standing reality that the Community's tasks are not solely economic in nature. The new provisions of the EC Treaty relating to EMU are set out in detail, so that this part of the Treaty in fact is a second *traité-loi*, like the ECSC Treaty, rather than a *traité-cadre*, like its other provisions. The separate preparation of the EMU and political union texts, which were integrated only in the final stages of the negotiations, has not led to clarity and transparency of the final version of the Treaty.[129] In addition to the inclusion of the principle of subsidiarity and the creation of a European citizenship, the major features of the TEU on the institutional side are the strengthening of the powers of the European Parliament, through the introduction of the co-decision procedure,[130] the right to set up temporary Committees of Inquiry,[131] the creation of a European Ombudsman,[132] the formalization of the right of petition to the Parliament,[133] the extension of the Assent procedure to certain categories of international agreements,[134] and participation in the appointment of members of the Commission.[135] All these points are discussed in detail in the relevant Chapters of this work.

The ratification of the TEU[136] met unexpectedly severe problems in certain Member States. The negative result of the first Danish referendum was followed by fierce discussions about the nature of the Community. In

must be taken into consideration; the Parliament must be kept regularly informed by the Presidency and the Commission of the development of CFSP, may ask questions of the Council or make recommendations to it, and holds an annual debate on progress in implementing CFSP, *ibid.*

127. See Art. M TEU. In JHA the only involvement of the Court is if Conventions adopted by the Member States confer jurisdiction upon it, Art. K.3(2)(c), 3rd para.

128. Save where the Council when adopting joint action and at any stage during its development decides (unanimously) that certain matters may be decided upon by a qualified majority (*i.e.* in accordance with Art. 148(2) EC, as most recently amended by the Adaptation Decision (Dec. 1/95 (O.J. 1995 L 1/1)), as action not based on a proposal from the Commission), Art. J.3(2) TEU. This in fact still applies even if the action taken as part of CFSP has been proposed by the Commission. It appears that in practice scant use is made of this possibility of qualified majority voting in CFSP.

129. *E.g.* Arts. 2, 3, and 3a EC.

130. Art. 189b EC.

131. Arts. 138c EC; 20b ECSC, and 107b Euratom.

132. Arts. 138e EC; 20d ECSC, and 107d Euratom.

133. Arts. 138d EC; 20c ECSC, and 107c Euratom.

134. Art. 228(3) EC.

135. Arts. 158 EC; 10, ECSC, and 127 Euratom.

136. See Laursen and Vanhoonacker (eds.), *The ratification of the Maastricht Treaty: Issues, Debates and Future Implications* (Dordrecht, 1994).

these discussions it became very apparent how weakly legitimised in the Member States Community action is, and just how much misunderstanding exists about the Community's structure and functioning. A second referendum in Denmark produced a positive result, after the Edinburgh European Council in December 1992 had given the Danish government support through a felicitous interpretation of certain parts of the TEU by means of a decision of the Heads of State or Government meeting within the European Council.[137] In France and the United Kingdom the ratification process proved extremely contentious, but was also ultimately successful.[138] After the German Federal Constitutional Court had ruled, albeit manifestly with scant enthusiasm, in an action brought by a former senior staff member of Commissioner Bangemann's office, that German ratification would not be incompatible with the Basic Law,[139] the Treaty on European Union finally struggled into force, nearly a year later than envisaged, on 1 November 1993.[140]

6.4   The approach to the Treaty of Amsterdam

Article N(2) TEU provides for an Intergovernmental Conference (IGC) to be convened during 1996 'to examine those provisions of this Treaty for which revision is provided, in accordance with the objectives set out in Articles A and B.' The fifth indent of Article B TEU specifies the objective of maintaining in full the *acquis communautaire* and building on it 'with a view to considering, through the procedure referred to in Article N(2), to what extent the policies and forms of cooperation introduced by this Treaty may need to be revised with the aim of

137. Bull. EC 12–1992, points I.34–I.39. See also *ibid.*, points I.33, the European Council's declarations, points I.40–I.41, and Denmark's unilateral declarations to be associated to the Danish act of ratification of the TEU, and of which the other 11 Member States took cognizance, points I.42–I.44. See, further, Howarth (1994) 31 CMLRev. 765; Curtin and van Ooik (1993) SEW 675 and, as to the Edinburgh European Council in general, VerLoren van Themaat (1993) SEW 423. On 6 April 1998 the Danish Supreme Court dismissed an action claiming that the implementation of the EC Treaty as amended by the TEU was incompatible with Article 20 of the Danish constitution, *Carlsen et al. v Rasmussen* (I361/1997, nyr).

138. As to England and Wales, see *R. v. Secretary of State for Foreign and Commonwealth Affairs, ex parte Rees Mogg* [1993] 3 CMLR 101 and as to Scotland, see *Monckton v. Lord Advocate* (1994) *The Times* 12 May; see also European Communities (Amendment) Act 1993, and Szyszczak (1993) 18 ELRev. 248. As to France, see the discussion by Cohen (1993) 18 ELRev. 233.

139. *Brunner* [1994] 1 CMLR 57. See *e.g.* Frowein (1994) ZaÖRV 1; Herdegen (1994) 31 CMLRev. 235; Ipsen (1994) EuR 1; Meyring (1997) 22 ELRev. 221; Tomuschat (1993) EuGRZ 489; Wieland (1995) EJIL 259; Weiler (1995) 1 ELJ 219, and Zuleeg (1997) 22 ELRev. 19.

140. The Court of Justice has produced a series of documents on the ratification of the TEU (available in any European Documentation Centre).

ensuring the effectiveness of the mechanisms and the institutions of the Community.'

A number of other specific references to revision on the occasion of the 1996 IGC are to be found: Article 189b(8) EC envisages consideration being given to extending the use of the cooperation procedure; Articles J.4(6) and J.10 TEU envisage review of the security aspects of CFSP (particularly in relation to the relationship with the WEU) and whether any other amendments to CFSP are necessary; the Decalaration on civil protection, energy and tourism, adopted on the occasion of signature of the Final Act adopting the TEU, places the possibility of introducing Titles into the EC Treaty dealing with these areas on the IGC's agenda, and Declaration on the hierarchy of Community acts, similarly adopted, agreed that the 1996 IGC would 'examine to what extent it might be possible to review the classification of Community acts with a view to establishing an appropriate hierarchy between the different categories of act.'

In addition to these programmed subjects, various other subjects were also on the table: in a *Modus Vivendi*[141] and an Interinstitutional Agreement,[142] the European Parliament, Council and the Commission agreed that the question of implementing acts and questions relating to budgetary discipline would be examined by the 1996 IGC; it was also agreed as part of the negotiations concerning Austrian, Finnish and Swedish accession that various institutional questions would be discussed by the IGC.[143]

A striking characteristic of the working of the 1996 IGC is undoubtedly the greater degree of transparency of the dialogue than was the case prior to the adoption of the TEU.[144] An important role was played by the input from a Reflection Group[145] and Reports from the Institutions and certain other bodies on the functioning of the TEU.[146] While the Reflection Group report chiefly set out the various divergent standpoints[147] and

141. O.J. 1996 C 102/1.
142. O.J. 1993 C 331/1.
143. Institutional reform in general, particularly as regards the weighting of votes in quali-fied majority voting in the Council,the number of members of the Commission, and any other measures felt necessary to facilitate the working of the Institutions in the perspective of their enlargement, Bull. EU 6–1994, point I.25
144. The availability of many documents on the Internet undoubtedly enabled a rather more informed discussion than was possible prior to the signature of the TEU.
145. *Reflection Group Report and other references for documentary purposes* (General Secre-tariat of the Council, Brussels, 1995).
146. The references are included in *ibid.* 89–90.
147. Expressed without actually naming names. *E.g.* (p. 22) 'Many of us think it important that the Treaty should clearly proclaim such European values as equality between men and women, non-discrimination on grounds of race, religion, sexual orientation, age or disability and that it should include an express condemnation of racism and xeno-phobia and a procedure for its enforcement. One of us believes that the rights and

contained few conclusions which were generally accepted by all participants, it set the scene for major dialogue, not least in academic circles, about the future shape of the Union.[148]

The actual mandate for the IGC was established at the European Council meeting in Turin in March 1996.[149] Three themes were evident. First, *bringing the Union closer to its citizens*: which involved in particular within the framework of defined objectives, better methods and instruments; ensuring better protection of the Union's citizens against international crime, in particular terrorism and drug trafficking; developing coherent and effective asylum, immigration and visa policies, and clearing divergent views on jurisdictional and parliamentary control of EU decisions in the field of justice and home affairs. Additionally, in view of the importance of the fight against unemployment, the IGC was to examine how the Union could provide the basis for better cooperation and coordination in order to strengthen national policies, and whether and how the efforts of governments and the social partners could be made more effective and better coordinated by the Treaty. Furthermore, a number of specific points were also mentioned: the compatibility between competition and universal access to essential services in the citizen's interest; the status of outer regions, overseas territories and island regions; how to make environmental protection more effective and coherent at the level of the Union, with a view to sustainable development, and, finally, better application and enforcement of the principle of subsidiarity, providing transparency and openness in the Union's work, and the possibility of simplifying and consolidating the Treaties. Secondly, *improving the institutions of the Union to ensure they function with greater efficiency, coherence and legitimacy*: this involved in particular looking at the most effective means of simplifying legislative procedures and making them clearer and more transparent; the possibility of widening the scope of co-decision in truly legislative matters; the question of the role of the European Parliament besides its legislative powers, its composition and the uniform procedure for its election. Other aspects to be examined within

responsibilities we have as citizens are a matter for our nation states: reaching beyond that could have the opposite effect to that intended.'
148. See, further, Dashwood (ed.), *Reviewing Maastricht – Issues for the 1996 IGC* (London, 1996); Duff, *Reforming the European Union* (London, 1997); Edwards and Pijpers (ed.), *The politics of European treaty reform – The 1996 Intergovernmental Conference and beyond* (London, 1997); Louis, *L'Union européenne et l'avenir de ses institutions* (Brussels, 1996); Winter *et al.* (eds.), *Reforming the Treaty on European Union* (The Hague, 1996); *Papers of the Symposium of Jean Monnet Chairs on the 1996 Intergovernmental Conference* (Brussels, 1996); Dehousse (1995) *Courrier hebdomadaire* No. 1499; Dehousse (1997) JdT 265; Lenaerts and De Smijter (1996) JTDE 217; De Witte (1996) SEW 253, and De Zwaan (1996) NTER 29. See also Dashwood and Ward (eds.) (1997) 22 ELRev. 395 (Cambridge EC Treaty project).
149. Bull. EU 3–1996, points I.3–I.6; see also point II.3. As to the formal convening of the IGC, see point II.4.

this theme were: how and to what extent national parliaments could, also collectively, better contribute to the Union's tasks; the functioning of the Institutions; the clarity and quality of legislation; methods of combating fraud, and the possibility of allowing certain Member States to develop a strengthened cooperation, while respecting the *acquis communautaire*, avoiding discrimination and distortions of competition and respecting the single institutional framework. Thirdly, *the strengthening of the Union's capacity for external action*. In this context, particular attention was to be paid to identifying the principles and areas of CFSP; defining the actions needed to promote the Union's interests in those areas and according to those principles; setting up procedures and structures designed to allow decisions to be taken in a more effective and timely manner, in a spirit of loyalty and mutual solidarity, and agreement on suitable budgetary provisions. The IGC was also invited to study whether and how the provision for a new specific function could give the possibility to the Union of expressing itself in a more visible and coherent way and with a more perceptible face and voice, and to address the question of a clearer definition of the Union's relationship with the WEU. Arrangements were also made to ensure that the European Parliament would be closely associated with the work of the IGC.[150] A particularly interesting aspect of this association was the undertaking that the Presidency of the Council would regularly provide oral or written information to the European Parliament and also provide information to the national parliaments through the Conference of bodies concerned with Community Affairs (COSAC).[151] The European Council envisaged the IGC finishing its work in about one year.[152]

At the European Council's meeting in Florence in June 1996 the Italian Presidency produced a report assessing the situation for the then incoming Irish Presidency, which latter was requested to prepare a general outline for a draft revision of the Treaties to be discussed at the European Council's meeting in Dublin in December 1996. The Florence European Council set out certain specific issues within the three themes identified at Turin,[153] and the Dublin European Council duly saw a general outline for draft revision presented.[154]

At the European Council meeting in Amsterdam in June 1997, political agreement was reached on the draft Treaty of Amsterdam,[155] with the IGC formally meeting at the level of Heads of State or Government. After final

150. Bull. EU 3–1996, point I.8.
151. *Ibid.* (para. 4 of the arrangements). See (prior to this) Schakleton in Laursen and Pappas (eds.), *The Changing Role of the Parliaments in the European Union* (EIPA Maastricht, 1995), 165).
152. Bull. EU 3–1996, point I.6, final para.
153. Bull. EU 6–1996, point I.7.
154. Bull. EU 12–1996, point I.7.
155. Bull. EU 6–1997, points I.3; II.1 and II.4.

legal editing and harmonization of the texts, the Treaty of Amsterdam (TOA) was signed on 2 October 1997.[156] As part of the exercise of simplification, Article 12 TOA provides that the EC Treaty and the TEU, as amended by the TOA, are to be renumbered in accordance with the tables of equivalence annexed to the TOA.[157] At the date at which this work states the law the TOA is still in the process of ratification, which, as the ratification process of the TEU demonstrated, should not be viewed as a mere formality. It is anticipated that a few Member States will have ratified the TOA by the time this work appears (August 1998), but in most the process may still take some time. In the Epilogue various observations are made about the structure and approach of the Treaty of Amsterdam.[158] In various places in this work an indication of the envisaged major changes has been given (mostly in the notes). In Chapter IX the discussion of social policy deals with the new situation as it will be after the Treaty of Amsterdam comes into force (reflecting the political reality that the Agreement and Protocol on Social Policy agreed at Maastricht have ceased to have any major significance as a result of the change in government in the United Kingdom).

156. Bull. EU 10–1997, point I.1. As to the text, see O.J. 1997 C 340/1.
157. As to the text of the renumbered treaties, see O.J. 1997 C 340/145 (consolidated TEU) and O.J. 1997 C 340/173 (consolidated EC Treaty). For ease of reference, the tables of equivalence are reproduced in the tables at the front of this work.
158. A number of major conferences on the TOA have already been held (e.g. in Groningen and Leiden in October 1997; Paris and New York in February 1998; in Edinburgh in March 1998, and in London in June 1998): most or all will result in books appearing in due course. In the meantime, apart from the observations in the Epilogue to this work, see Barents (1997) MJ 332; Blanchet (1997) RTDE 915; Blumann (1997) RTDE 721; Dehousse (1997) Courrier hebdomadaire No. 1565–1566 and (1997) CDE 265; Hilf (1997) EuR 347; Jacqué (1997) RTDE 903; Langrish (1998) 23 ELRev. 3; Manin (1998) Columb. J. Eur. L.1; Timmermans (1997) SEW 344; Wachsmann (1997) RTDE 883; and De Zwaan (1998) NTER 30.

CHAPTER II

General aspects of the European Communities and the European Union*

1. The European Union

1.1 Introduction and background

The Treaty on European Union (TEU), popularly called the Treaty of Maastricht, formally establishes the European Union[1] but does not endow it with legal personality. The European Union is 'founded on the European Communities, supplemented by the policies and forms of co-operation' which the TEU establishes, namely a common foreign and security policy (CFSP), and co-operation in the field of justice and home affairs (JHA). Although in the popular mind the European Union and the town of Maastricht in The Netherlands are inseparably linked, the concept of a European Union does not originate in Maastricht.[2] At the Paris Summit in October 1972, the Member States confirmed their intention to transform their common relations into a European Union,[3] although nothing was stated about what this would entail, and nothing came of nothing.[4] Fresh life was breathed into the idea with the European Parliament's Draft Treaty on European Union in 1984.[5] Prior to this, in June 1983, the European Council in Stuttgart had adopted a Solemn Declaration on European Union.[6] Subsequently, the concept of a Union

---

* In the 5th Dutch edition of this work, this Chapter was revised by C.W.A. Timmermans. Sections 2 to 5 of this Chapter are revisions of the 2nd English edition by the editor, with updating and minor linguistic corrections. Section 1 is based on Timmermans's account, with additional material and more extensive discussion of CFSP and JHA.
1. Art. A TEU, 1st para.
2. See Martinez Cuadrado in Schneider (ed.), *From Nine to Twelve: Europe's Destiny* (Alphen aan den Rijn, 1980) 179; Wellenstein (1992) 29 CMLRev. 205; Everling (1992) 29 CMLRev. 1053.
3. Bull. EC 10–1972, p. 23.
4. See Shakespeare, *King Lear*, I.i.
5. See Chapter 1, s. 6.2, *ante*, and the bibliography in note 99 thereto.
6. Bull. EC-6–1983, point 1.6.1.

was endowed with Treaty status in the Preamble to the Single European Act (SEA): through the reference to the Stuttgart Solemn Declaration, and the resolution to implement the European Union on the basis, firstly, of the Communities operating in accordance with their own rules and, secondly, of European Cooperation among the Signatory States in the sphere of foreign policy.[7] The European Communities and European Political Cooperation aimed to contribute together to making concrete progress towards European unity.[8] In this manner the SEA gives a foretaste of the concept of a Union which is developed in the TEU.

1.2   A hitchhiker's guide to the European Union under the TEU

1.2.1   The structure of the Union

An essential element in understanding the structure of the TEU, and thus the concept of the European Union which it establishes, is that the Treaty is the result of a hard fought-out compromise between, as always, proponents of the Community method (with its supranational institutions and in an increasing number of areas qualified majority voting) and proponents of the more classic intergovernmental form of interstate cooperation (in which the initiative remains very much with the Member States and decisions are almost invariably taken by unanimity).[9] There is sharp disagreement among the Member States about which of these approaches is more appropriate, and in which areas; they were unable to accept that the supplementary policies and forms of cooperation (CFSP and JHA) should be brought within the Community structure, even with their own procedures and a weakening of the Community method in those areas, as the Commission and later the Dutch Presidency had originally proposed.[10] On the other hand, the institutional structure of the CFSP and JHA does go rather further than the classic intergovernmental decision-making model would indicate, as the Commission is not left entirely to one side and there is some very limited provision for some matters to be decided by qualified majority rather than unanimity. The compromise is evident from this result.

The Union brings together the European Communities (the ECSC, the EEC which is rebaptised EC (for European Community) and Euratom) and the supplementary policies and forms of co-operation (CFSP and

7.   Preamble SEA, para. 3 (commencing 'RESOLVED to implement . . .'),
8.   Art. 1 SEA, 1st para.
9.   See Demaret in O'Keeffe and Twomey (eds.), *Legal Issues of the Maastricht Treaty* (Chichester, 1994) 3 at 4–7.
10.   As to the Commission's draft structure of the Treaty, see Bull. EC Supp. 2/91, p. 173. The Dutch Presidency's proposal was reproduced in *Europe* Documents No. 1746/1747 of 20 November 1991. See also VerLoren van Themaat (1991) SEW 436.

JHA). The Communities form a closed entity within this structure, retaining their own autonomy and legally independent organisation, as well as their own legal personality. Assumption into the Union has scant direct consequences for the Communities.[11] The Union offers first and foremost a home for the supplementary policies and forms of cooperation for which it creates institutional structures and brings them and the Communities under one roof.[12] The popular image of a temple with three pillars[13] is far too unnuanced,[14] as it ignores the fact that the Communities form the main load-bearing structure of the union, and yet at the same time disguises the independent nature of that pillar. Those familiar with the architecture of old cathedrals, with a main door and two side doors at the west end proclaiming the tripartite form of the Trinity leading to the one building[15] may see this as a rather more appropriate model with which to compare the Union. Be that as it may, the formula adopted in the TEU itself, of a Union founded on the European Communities, supplemented by the policies and forms of cooperation established by the TEU[16] makes the relationship between the three elements clear.

The construction of the Union is pretty weak. In part because the Union is not endowed with legal personality as such,[17] the role of the Member States in the Union's own policies and forms of co-operation remains decisive. In external actions the Union will have to call on its Member States, for example in order to conclude international agreements, as the Union has no power to conclude such agreements itself. The Member States declined to subject CFSP and JHA to supervision by the Court of Justice, as they dared not embark on the disciplining effect of such supervision of the fulfilment of the obligations entered into and the legal calibre of the policy pursued. This has not improved the solidity of the structure of the Union in these fields. In the field of JHA in particular this threatens to lead to problems in the maintenance of uniform law enforcement.

11. But see Art. 228a EC which provides for urgent action to be taken by the Community in accordance with a common position or joint action adopted under the common foreign and security policy. This provision confirms the practice of the Council hitherto, see Chapter XII, section 2.6, *post*.
12. Thus Art. C TEU provides that the Union shall be served by a single institutional framework, in which the Council and the Commission assure the consistency of its external activities.
13. See Chapter I, section 6.3, *ante*.
14. See Kapteyn (1992) SEW 667.
15. *Tria juncta in uno*. Weiler, in Monar *et al.* (eds.), *The Maastricht Treaty on European Union* (Brussels, 1993) 49 at 62, refers to 'a Trinity of Community, Justice and Home Affairs, and Common Foreign and Security Policy in which "oneness" and "separateness" co-exist simultaneously.'
16. Art. A TEU, 3rd para.
17. In the same sense, Eaton in O'Keeffe and Twomey (eds.), *op. cit.* (see note 9 *supra*) 215 at 224.

1.2.2   The 'constitution' of the Union

If the SEA in 1986 merely referred to a European Union, saying nothing about what it involved, the TEU does sketch out, albeit vaguely, the contours of a constitution of the Union. These are to be found in the Common Provisions in Title I and the Final Provisions in Title VII of the Treaty. Six points stand out in particular.

A Union of States and of Peoples. The task of the union is 'to organize, in a manner demonstrating consistency and solidarity, relations between the Member States and between their peoples.'[18] This gives an excellent picture of the nature of the Union as a form of international cooperation. It mixes largely classic forms of intergovernmental cooperation (particularly CFSP and JHA) with a far more ambitious integration model pursued by the Communities. Precisely because the Union is a context in which the peoples are directly involved, it is important that Article F(2) TEU requires the Union to respect fundamental rights, as guaranteed by the European Convention on Human Rights[19] and as they result from the constitutional traditions common to the Member States, as general principles of Community law. In the Preamble to the TEU the Member States reaffirm their commitment to the principles of liberty, democracy and respect for human rights and fundamental freedoms, and of the rule of law. However, the Union itself is scarcely equipped to realize these principles in its own (non-Community) policy areas. The peoples are left to rely on their own national structures. The requirement that the Union must respect the national identities of its Member States, whose systems of government are founded on the principles of democracy, makes it clear that satisfactory legitimacy of systems of government is a condition for membership of the Union.[20] However, these arrangements are scarcely satisfactory, particularly if the co-operation in CFSP and, in particular, in JHA reaches the intended degree of intensity. In the Community structure, which is the part of the Union in which the exercise of powers has the most far-reaching influence on the lives of citizens, there are rather firmer guarantees for the respect of the principles of democracy and the rule of law, although even there is still a considerable democratic deficit. The task of the Union does not affect the identity of the Member States as such: it

18. Art. A TEU, 3rd para.
19. The European Convention for the Protection of Human Rights and Fundamental Freedoms, Rome, 4 November 1950 (TS 71 (1953); Cmnd. 8969). However, as the Court of Justice has no jurisdiction to ensure compliance with Art. F TEU (see Art. L TEU), it will be impossible to test action under CFSP or JHA against the Convention, although action taken in the Community context could be challenged on the basis of failure to respect a rule of law relating to the application of the EC Treaty, see Art. 173 EC, Chapter IV, section 7.5.4 and Chapter VI, section 1.2, *post*.
20. Art. F(1) TEU. The Treaty of Amsterdam (not yet in force) strengthens this provision.

organises relations between them and between their peoples,[21] respecting the national identities of the Member States.[22] The perspective of a development in a federal direction (a *vocation fédérale*) which the Germans had insisted be included in the draft text of Article A EU was removed at British insistence at Maastricht (gaining notoriety as the 'F-word') and replaced by the more neutral phrase 'an ever closer union'.

Objectives of the Union. The first four objectives set out in Article B TEU concern and to a great extent correspond to the Union's three component parts: the Community; CFSP, and JHA. The introduction of a citizenship of the Union (the third objective) is realized in Articles 8–8e EC. The fifth objective, maintaining and building on the *acquis communautaire*, is of major significance for the relationship between the Union's component parts and their further development. The preference for the Community method as developed within the European Communities is evident. Thus the bringing together of the Communities with the more intergovernmental CFSP and JHA within the Union may not undermine what has been achieved in the Communities (the *acquis communautaire*) or the Community method itself. The Union has the express objective of building on the *acquis communautaire*, and the intergovernmental conference convened in 1996 to examine revisions of the Treaty will consider to what extent the policies and forms of cooperation introduced by the Treaty need to be revised with the aim of ensuring the effectiveness of the mechanisms and the institutions of the Community. This fifth objective refers to Article N(2) TEU which itself refers to the objectives of Articles A and B TEU. This somewhat cumbersome formulation gives a clear indication of a preference for a further expansion of the Community element in the Union. Read with a certain amount of goodwill, this points in the direction of a Union based on a single element, so that the divisions between the existing elements will be bridged and CFSP and JHA will be incorporated into the Community structure. While the Treaty of Amsterdam, when it enters into force, will make some improvements, there is still room for more.

Institutions of the Union. Article C TEU provides that the Union is to be served by a single institutional framework. This was necessary in order to ensure the requisite consistency of the Union's activities, particularly in view of the diversity of decision-making constructs. This requirement of consistency is specified in particular as regards the Union's external activities as a whole, in the context of its external relations, security, economic and development policies.[23] The single institutional framework consists

21. In a manner demonstrating consistency and solidarity, Art. A TEU, 3rd para.
22. Art. F(1) TEU.
23. Art. C TEU, 2nd para.

primarily of the European Council, which is composed of the Heads of State or Government of the Member States and the President of the Commission.[24] These persons are assisted by the Foreign Ministers of the Member States and by a member of the Commission.[25] The European Council provides the Union with the necessary impetus for its development and defines its general political guidelines.[26] This task also embraces the European Communities (as an integral part of the Union), although it is clear that in the implementation of any decisions taken by the European Council by the Communities, the appropriate decision-making procedures will have to be followed and the role of the Community Institutions therein will have to be respected, especially that of the Council and the European Parliament. The European Council as such is not an organ of the Communities: thus if, perhaps on an occasion on which the European Council met, the Heads of State or Government wish to act as the Council (and Article 109j EC provides for decisions to be taken by the Council in that composition, although the Council may meet in that composition on other occasions) the President of the Commission would remain at the table (as the Commission is always represented at Council meetings) but would be there as an observer, not, of course, being a member of the Council. Actions by the Council in these circumstances will be actions by most of the same people as the members of the European Council, but not all of them, and not in the same capacity, and they could only act in accordance with the provisions of the Community Treaties. The European Council is thus the only real organ of the Union as such. The other institutions which form the single institutional framework are those Institutions of the Community which are placed at the disposal of the Union: the European Parliament, the Council, the Commission and the Court of Justice.[27] However, these Community Institutions are not hereby transformed into institutions of the Union. Rather, in addition to their tasks and powers as Institutions of the Community, they are given supplementary tasks for the Union's own activities, although the involvement of the Court is dependent on Conventions conferring jurisdiction upon it.[28] The importance of this observation is that even in their activities solely in the context of the Union, the Parliament, Council and the Commission must·respect the institutional balance between themselves, as laid down in the Community Treaties, save to the extent that the TEU itself expressly otherwise provides.[29] The Council and the Commission in particular have responsibility for ensuring the con-

24. Art. D TEU, 2nd para.
25. Ibid.
26. Art. D TEU, 1st para.
27. Art. E TEU.
28. The Court's jurisdiction is limited to the Community Treaties (as amended), any jurisdiction which may be conferred by Conventions adopted in accordance with Art. K.3(2)(c) TEU, 3rd para., and to Arts. L-S TEU, see Art. L TEU.
29. Art. C TEU, 2nd para.

sistency of the Union's external activities, although the single institutional framework as a whole is to ensure consistency and continuity of the Union's activities while respecting and building upon the *acquis communautaire*.[30] This means that in so far as tension develops, particularly in relation to external policies, between the external policies of the Communities and CFSP, it is the latter which must be adapted to the former, not the other way round (otherwise this would jeopardize the *acquis communautaire*). In the exercise of their specific Union tasks, the institutions will naturally have to have regard to the principles and objectives set out in Title I TEU. Even though the Court's involvement in specific Union tasks is marginal in terms of jurisdiction[31] and the normal provisions concerning judicial protection do not apply to Title I TEU, it is likely that the Court will take account of the Union dimension in the exercise of its function to ensure that the law is observed.[32] This would be important particularly in respect of the requirement that the Union and its institutional framework respect and build upon the *acquis communautaire*.[33]

Powers of the Union. The most far-reaching powers of the Union are those attributed to the Communities. Decision-making power is also conferred on its institutions for the implementation of CFSP and JHA, although strictly speaking the competence thus conferred does not relate to powers of the Union, as that does not have legal personality as such. The definition and implementation of CFSP is in fact a matter for the Union and its Member States.[34] In the case of JHA the role of the Member States is even more significant, as this is not a common Union policy but a cooperation between the Member States, for which the Union is used as the framework.[35] Although Article F(3) TEU states that the Union shall provide itself with the means necessary to attain its objectives and carry through its policies, it is submitted that this somewhat obscure wording does not suffice to confer actual powers on the Union or its institutions. Rather this statement must be read as an instruction to the Union to furnish itself with the necessary means for an effective Union policy, using the powers and appropriate procedures otherwise conferred. This embraces in particular the necessary financial means.[36]

Subsidiarity and respect for fundamental rights. These principles must be respected as they form the limits which have to be respected in the exercise

30. *Ibid.*, 1st para.
31. See note 28 *supra*.
32. Arts. 164 EC, 31 ECSC, 136 Euratom.
33. Art. C TEU, 1st para.
34. Art. J.1(1) TEU.
35. This is evident from the beginning of Art. K.1 TEU, read in conjunction with Art. K.3(1) TEU (the Members States inform and consult one another within the Council).
36. *Cf.* Arts. J.11 and K.8 TEU.

of the powers of the Union.[37] For the European Community the principle of subsidiarity is defined in Article 3b EC, and that definition applies also in respect of Union powers.[38] Respect for fundamental rights already forms part of the *acquis communautaire* by virtue of the case-law of the Court of Justice.[39] In Article F(2) express reference is made to this case-law in terms of 'general principles of Community law.' The Court is thus indirectly accepted as the authority for the further development of the contents of at least this aspect of the constitution of the Union.

Amendment of the Treaty on European Union, and accession to the Union. The Final Provisions (Title VII) of the TEU set out in Article N the procedure by which amendments may be made to the TEU itself and the other Treaties on which the Union is founded. Article O TEU deals with the accession of European states to membership of the Union. These provisions replace the relevant provisions of the Treaties establishing the European Communities, which have been repealed.[40] These provisions demonstrate particularly clearly the unity of the Union structure, as applicants cannot accede to the Communities alone, nor may they accede to just one of CFSP and JHA. They become members of the Union and by virtue thereof accede to the various parts of it. To this extent the Communities in a certain way lose their independent character. But, on the other hand, these provisions start to bridge the gaps between the various elements of the Union. It is significant that it is the appropriate Community procedures which are applied to the Union as a whole, an approach which conforms completely to the objective of the Union to maintain in full and build on the *acquis communautaire*.[41] Thus, despite the decisive role that the Member States play in CFSP and JHA, new members can only be admitted to these elements of the Union with the assent of the European Parliament, the influence of which on these policy areas is otherwise extremely limited. Part of the compromise reached at Maastricht was to hold over various subjects which some Member States felt to be of significance, but on which it was then impossible to reach agreement, to be discussed at the intergovernmental conference in 1996 provided for in Article N(2) TEU. Those matters were to be re-examined to see if agreement on amendment of the Treaties could be reached. Thus the preliminaries leading to an intergovernmental conference set out in Article N(1) did not have to be followed in respect of the 1996 conference. The TEU itself placed the following subjects on the agenda of

37. Arts. A, 2nd para., B last para., F(2) TEU.
38. Art. B TEU, last para. See, further, Chapter III, section 5.1.1, *post*.
39. See Chapter VI, section 7.5.4, *post*.
40. The relevant provisions were Arts. 236 and 237 EC; Arts. 96 and 98 ECSC, and Arts. 204 and 205 Euratom, repealed by Arts. G(83); H(21); and I(28) TEU respectively.
41. Art. B TEU, 1st para., 5th indent.

that conference: the relationship between the Community, CFSP and JHA;[42] CFSP, including security policy;[43] the widening of the applicability of the co-decision procedure,[44] and various subjects mentioned in declarations annexed to the TEU.[45] Of these, certainly the first three are due to see considerable developments as a result of the Treaty of Amsterdam.[46]

1.2.3　Protection of the Communities

An important characteristic of the Union is the primacy of the Communities over the supplementary policies and forms of cooperation in CFSP and JHA. Those Member States, including the Netherlands, which advocate the Community method and fear its watering-down and infection by the predominantly intergovernmental method of CFSP and JHA, have ensured that the Communities are protected from the other elements of the Union structure. This has been achieved in three ways: first, by emphasising as an objective of the Union maintaining and building on the *acquis communautaire*;[47] secondly, by ensuring that provisions of the TEU which do not specifically amend the Community Treaties (particularly those provisions dealing with CFSP and JHA) do not affect those Treaties or subsequent Treaties and Acts modifying them,[48] and, finally, by envisaging the possibility of transferring certain matters presently reserved to JHA over to the European Community.[49] This interlink or *passerelle* provision operates in one direction only. Yet even in the changes made at Maastricht to the Community Treaties the Member States were somewhat flexible as regards the maintenance of the *acquis communautaire*, as is evidenced by the opt-out provisions for Denmark and the United Kingdom relating to the Third Stage of Economic and Monetary Union;[50] the Protocol and Agreement between the Member States except the United Kingdom on Social Policy;[51] The

42. Art. B TEU, 2nd para.
43. Arts. J.4(6) and J.10 TEU.
44. Art. 189b(8) EC.
45. Measures relating to civil protection, energy and tourism (Art. 3(t) EC and Declaration No. 1 annexed to the TEU), and the establishment of a hierarchy of Community acts (Declaration No. 16 annexed to the TEU).
46. Amsterdam, 2 October 1997 (O.J. 1997 C 340/1), not yet in force.
47. Art. B TEU, 5th indent. See also Art. C TEU, 1st para.
48. Art. M TEU. This approach had been used earlier in Art. 32 SEA.
49. Art. K.9 TEU provides for the application of Art. 100c EC to the areas covered by Arts. K.1(1)–(6) TEU.
50. Protocols 11 and 12 TEU.
51. Protocol 14 TEU, to which the Agreement is annexed. This has effectively been a dead letter since the election of the Labour government in the United Kingdom in 1997 and measures adopted under it have now been transposed through new Community direc-

so-called *Barber* Protocol,[52] and the Protocol on the acquisition of second homes in Denmark.[53]

1.2.4   The Union as an interim phase

The Union structure as established by the TEU can only be seen as a provisional structure. As is clear from the TEU itself, the Union in its present form is 'a new stage in the process of creating an ever closer union among the peoples of Europe'[54] The precise form of that ever closer union is not as yet predictable, although the TEU confirms that the character of the process of European integration embraces not only substantive but also institutional designs. No matter how inadequate the temporary accommodation of the Union may be, and it has been described it as resembling an emergency shelter,[55] the TEU sketches a cautious perspective for the further evolution of the Community model at the expense of intergovernmental cooperation.[56] The TEU provides an unmistakable impulse in that direction by scrounging the institutional structure of the Union from that of the Communities,[57] by referring to general principles of Community law formulated in the case-law of the Court of Justice as the criteria for the respect of fundamental rights by the Union,[58] by pre-programming the transfer of competence in various aspects of JHA to the European Community,[59] and, finally, by adopting the Community procedures for Treaty amendments and the accession of new Member States to the Union.[60]

tives, see Bull. EU 6–1997, point I.8; 7/8–1997, point 1.3.222, and 12–1997, point 1.2.267.

52. Protocol No. 2 TEU. The reference is to the effect in time of the operation of the judgment in Case C-262/88 *Barber v. Guardian Royal Exchange Assurance Group* [1990] ECR I-1889, [1990] 2 CMLR 513. See also *e.g.* Case C-200/91 *Coloroll Pension Trustees Ltd. v. Russell et al.* [1994] ECR I-4389, [1995] 2 CMLR 573.

53. Protocol No. 1 TEU. This was the second time that the Danes succeeded in safeguarding these rules, see also Dir. 88/31 (O.J. 1988 L 37/88). See, generally, on this piecemeal approach, Curtin (1993) 30 CMLRev. 17.

54. Art. A TEU, 2nd para. This recalls the first statement in the Preamble to the old EEC Treaty of 1957 which is still retained in the EC Treaty: 'Determined to lay the foundations of an ever closer union among the peoples of Europe' and the first statement in the Preamble to the TEU itself: 'Resolved to mark a new stage in the process of European integration undertaken with the establishment of the European Communities'.

55. VerLoren van Themaat (1991) SEW 436 at 454.

56. See Arts. B, C and N(2) TEU. The Treaty of Amsterdam (not yet in force) takes some steps forward in this evolutionary process towards more use of the Community method.

57. See in particular Arts. J.11 and K.8 TEU.

58. See Art. F(2) TEU.

59. Art. K.9 TEU.

60. Arts. N and O TEU.

1.3   The supplementary policies and forms of cooperation: CFSP and JHA

1.3.1   Common Foreign and Security Policy

Title V TEU, which governs the CFSP, contains provisions of a primarily procedural nature. A common foreign and security policy is created[61] but the substance of that policy has to be developed using the procedures and instruments set out in Title V, taking account of the general objectives formulated in Article J.1(2) TEU. These objectives reflect the Union's commitment to security and peace in the framework of various existing international commitments,[62] as well as to the development and consolidation of democracy and the rule of law, and respect for human rights and fundamental freedoms. The majority of the provisions of Title V finds its precursors in the old European Political Cooperation system set out in Article 30 SEA in 1986 and develops that system further.[63] The provisions of Title V are, however, more obligatory in nature.[64] CFSP covers all areas of foreign and security policy, although it does not extend to the external policy of the Communities.[65] A second limitation on the

61.   Art. J TEU.
62.   The preservation of peace and the strengthening of international security in accordance with the United Nations Charter (San Francisco 26 June 1945), as well as the principles of the Helsinki Final Act (1 August 1975; 14 ILM 1292 (1975)), and the objectives of the Charter of Paris for a New Europe (21 November 1990; Bull. EC 11–1990, point 2.2.1; 30 ILM 190 (1991)).
63.   See Chapter I, section 6.1, *ante*. See also Nuttall in Monar *et al.* (eds.), *op. cit.* (see note 15, *supra*) 133. See, further, Burghardt and Tebbe in Von der Groeben *et al.* (eds.), *Kommentar zum EU–/EG-Vertrag* (5th ed., Baden-Baden, 1997) Vol. 5, 891 *et seq.*
64.   Eaton, in O'Keeffe and Twouey (eds.), *op. cit.* (see note 9 *supra*) 220 describes the change as one from the language of *endeavour*, in EPC, to the language of *obligation*, in CFSP (emphasis in original). He opined that this might not amount to much in practice as the Member States had always regarded themselves as committed by common positions adopted under Art. 30(2)(c) SEA, 3rd para. and it remained the case that nothing would fall under cooperation (common position) or joint action unless agreed unanimously (save any matters which it had been agreed unanimously could be decided by qualified majority in accordance with Art. J.3(2) TEU).
65.   The latter primarily embraces external economic and monetary policy, development cooperation in so far as it falls under the EC Treaty, and external policy in other fields of Community activity such as environment, research and development and energy policy. The Council and the Commission are responsible for ensuring the consistency of the Union's external activities as a whole in the context of its external relations, security, economic and development policies, Art. C TEU, 2nd para. The requirement that the Union respect and build on the *acquis communautaire* and the express exclusion of implicit amendment of the Community Treaties (Art. M TEU) indicates that the Community policies remain a matter for the Community Institutions as such, although the consistency requirement clearly demands that the Union and its Member States take account of policies already pursued in the Community context, just as future developments in that context will have to take account of the CFSP factor. As to the implementation of consistency, see Neuwahl in O'Keeffe and Twomey (eds.), *op.*

broad drafting of Article J.1(1) TEU can be seen in relation to security matters. Article J.4(1) states that CFSP includes 'all questions related to the security of the Union, including the eventual framing of a common defence policy, which might in time lead to a common defence.' In this area the TEU is significantly more circumspect, as appears from the reservations relating to the specific character of the security and defence policy of certain Member States, NATO obligations and any development of closer cooperation between two or more Member States bilaterally, in the framework of the Western European Union (WEU) and NATO, although such cooperation must not run counter to or impede that provided for in Title V TEU.[66] The WEU, of which at the moment all Member States save Austria, Denmark, Finland, Ireland and Sweden are members, is designated as an integral part of the development of the European Union and is requested to elaborate and implement decisions and actions of the Union which have defence implications.[67] It is noteworthy that issues having defence implications dealt with under Article J.4 TEU are not subject to the procedures for adopting joint action set out in Article J.3 TEU, as the elaboration and implementation is left to the institutions of the WEU.[68]

Article J.1(3) sets out two means by which the objectives of CFSP are to be achieved. *First*, by establishing systematic cooperation between Member States in the conduct of policy. This takes place in accordance with Article J.2 TEU and involves the Member States informing and consulting one another within the Council on any matter of foreign and security policy of general interest. No criteria are however specified for determining when a matter is 'of general interest.' The systematic cooperation may result in the Council defining a common position if it deems it necessary[69] which is agreed unanimously[70] and binds the Member States.[71] This binding obligation also applies in international organizations and at international conferences, including those in or at which not all the Member States participate.[72] Common positions have been adopted on numerous

---

cit. (see note 9, *supra*) 227; as to the relationship between CFSP and the EC's external relations, see Cremona in *ibid.*, 247, and Monar in Monar *et al.* (eds.), *op. cit.* (see note 15, *supra*) 139.

66. Art. J.4(4) and (5) TEU. Thus variable geometry (or multi-speed integration) is permissible in relation to CFSP. As to the WEU and NATO, see Chapter I, sections 1.1 and 3.2, *ante*. See also the Declarations annexed as Declaration 30 to the TEU, and Eaton in O'Keeffe and Twomey (eds.), *op. cit.* (see note 9, *supra*) 215 at 218.

67. Art. J.4(2) TEU.

68. Art. J.4(3) TEU.

69. Art. J.2(2) TEU, 1st para.

70. Art. J.8(2) TEU, 2nd para.

71. Art. J.2(2) TEU, 2nd para. The Member States have to ensure that their national policies conform to the common position.

72. Art. J.2(3) TEU. Additionally, Member States must coordinate their action in such fora, *ibid.*, 1st para.

occasions in a variety of situations.[73] The *second* means is by gradually implementing, in accordance with Article J.3 TEU, joint action in the areas in which the Member States have important interests in common. This is a rather more far-reaching and closer form of cooperation than that provided for by the first of the two means. The Council, acting unanimously, decides, on the basis of general guidelines from the European Council, that a matter will be the subject of joint action.[74] When deciding on the principle of joint action, the Council lays down the specific scope, the general and specific objectives of the Union in carrying it out, if necessary its duration, and, finally, the means, procedures and conditions for its application.[75] A decision on joint action binds the Member States in the positions they adopt and in their joint activity.[76] Although unanimity is the general rule, the Council may, by unanimous vote, when adopting joint action or at any stage during its development, decide that certain matters will be decided by qualified majority.[77] The strength of the initial decisions on joint action is very great. Thus if there is a change in

73. See *e.g.* Dec. 93/614/CFSP (O.J. 1993 L 295/1) on economic relations with Libya, CP 96/697 (O.J. 1996 L 322/1) on Cuba and CP 97/826 (O.J. 1997 L 344/6) on Sierra Leone. See, further, Chapter XII, section 2.6, *post*.
74. Art. J.3(1) TEU, 1st para. (as to the voting requirement, see Art. J.8(2) TEU, 2nd para.). The principles of and general guidelines for CFSP are defined by the European Council (and set out in the Conclusions of the Presidency issued after every meeting of the European Council), see Art. J.8(1) TEU. The Conclusions are reproduced in the issue of Bull. EU (previously Bull. EC) for the relevant month(s). As to the methods by which the European Council acts, see Weerts, *The European Council* (Amsterdam, 1992) 95–104 and 120–137.
75. Art. J.3(1) TEU, 2nd para. As examples of joint action, see Dec. 93/603/ (aid to Bosnia O.J. 1993 L 286/1) and Dec. 93/604 (observers to parliamentary elections in Russia, O.J. 1993 L 286/1). See, further, Chapter XII, section 2.6, *post*.
76. Art. J.3(4) TEU. More generally, Art. J.1(4) imposes on the Member States the duty of active and unreserved support of the Union's external and security policy in a spirit of loyalty and mutual solidarity, as well as the duty not to undermine the Union's interests or effectiveness (broadly paralleling the provisions of Arts. 5 EC; 86 ECSC, 1st and 2nd paras., and 192 Euratom). The Council is to ensure that the principles set out in Art. J.1(4) TEU are complied with, *ibid.* If a Member State plans to adopt a national position or to take national action pursuant to joint action, it must provide information in time to allow, if necessary, for prior consultations within the Council, although if the measures merely transpose Council measures in the national system prior information is not obligatory, Art. J.3(5) TEU. However, there is no real sanction: if the problem relates to a joint action then discussion to seek an appropriate solution is prescribed, Art. J.3(7) TEU, otherwise the Commission or any Member State might refer the matter to the Council under Art. J.8(3) TEU.
77. Art. J.3(2) TEU, 1st para. In such cases the qualified majority is that applicable to acts not adopted on the basis of a proposal from the Commission (at least 62 votes in favour cast by at least 10 members), *ibid.*, 2nd para. (as amended by the Act of Austrian, Finnish and Swedish Accession, amended by the Adaptation Decision, Dec. 1/95 (O.J. 1995 L 1/1)). This rule applies in this case even if the proposal in fact emanates from the Commission (under Art. J.8(3) TEU the Commission or any Member State may refer questions relating to CFSP to the Council and may submit proposals to it).

circumstances having a substantial effect on the question subject to joint action, the Council is obliged to review the principles and objectives of the action and take the necessary decisions, but until it has acted the joint action stands. One Member State could frustrate the lifting of sanctions already agreed as joint action (unless it had previously been decided that such a decision may be taken by qualified majority). However, that need not mean that those Member States who wished to respond to a changed situation could not do so at all, as Article J.3(6) TEU provides that in cases of imperative need arising from changes in the situation and failing a Council decision, Member States may take the necessary measures as a matter of urgency having regard to the general objectives of the joint action.[78] Major difficulties in implementing joint action are referred by a Member State to the Council which must discuss them and seek appropriate solutions, although those solutions may not run counter to the objectives of the joint action or impair its effectiveness.[79] As has already been observed, issues having defence implications are not subject to these provisions concerning joint actions.

The decision-making procedures set out for CFSP are dominated by the intergovernmental method and the position of the typically Community institutions, the Commission and the Parliament is weak. It is the European Council which defines the principles of and general guidelines for the CFSP.[80] On the basis of such general guidelines the Council takes the decisions necessary for implementing the CFSP.[81] The fact that the Foreign Ministers assist the members of the European Council[82] ensures the necessary coordination between the European Council and the Council. In relation to CFSP it is the Council which is responsible for ensuring the unity, consistency and effectiveness of action adopted by the Union,[83] although the consistency of the Union's external relations as a whole has

The fact that the decision to permit qualified majority voting is taken in the context of a joint action means that it applies only in respect of that particular joint action: there is no power to specify generally that certain matters will always be decided by qualified majority: a provision could be included each time joint action is agreed so that a tradition might develop, but even if this were to occur, qualified majority voting could on any occasion be torpedoed as part of the price for agreeing to a joint action.

78. The Member State concerned must notify such measures to the Council immediately. A Member State which felt that the objectives had been achieved would in fact be free to lift sanctions in so far as they concerned matters within CFSP. However, trade sanctions imposed by Community decision could not be lifted unilaterally by one or more Member States. Zoller in Constantinesco et al. (eds.), Traité sur l'Union Européenne (Paris, 1995) 786 at 794 describes Art. J.3(6) TEU as little more than an 'opting-out' clause and suggests a comparison with Arts. 2(5), 49 and 50 of the United Nations Charter.

79. Art. J.3(7) TEU.
80. Art. J.8(1) TEU.
81. Art. J.8(2) TEU, 1st para.
82. Art. D TEU, 2nd para.
83. Art. J.8(2) TEU, 1st para.

to be ensured by both Council and Commission.[84] As has already been noted, the general rule is that the Council acts unanimously,[85] but Declaration 27 annexed to the TEU notes the agreement that Member States will, to the extent possible, avoid preventing a unanimous decision where a qualified majority exists in favour of that decision. The Commission shares the right of initiative with the Member States,[86] which means that the Council is not subject to the risk of withdrawal of the Commission's proposal leaving it unable to act, nor is it restricted to departing from the Commission's proposal only by unanimous vote.[87] The Parliament's position is remarkably weaker than it is within the structure of the Communities. Thus it is consulted by the Presidency on the main aspects and the basic choices of the CFSP and must ensure that the views of the Parliament are duly taken into consideration.[88] In addition, the President of the European Parliament is nowadays always received by the European Council, before it begins its deliberations, for an exchange of views about the subjects on its agenda.[89] Both the Presidency and the Commission must keep the Parliament regularly informed of the development of CFSP.[90] Codifying previous practice,[91] the Parliament may ask questions of the Council or make recommendations to it, and holds an annual debate on progress in implementing CFSP.[92] As has already been observed, decisions on common positions and joint actions bind the Member States, but compliance cannot be enforced by actions before the Court, which has no competence in this field. Thus political pressure by discussion is all that is available.[93] Eaton has observed that any attempt to adopt measures within the framework of CFSP which affected the Community Treaties (or implicitly Community measures) could be considered by the Court in the context of a ruling on the Community Treaties or measures, without the Court ruling on the internal validity of the CFSP decision involved.[94]

84. Art. C TEU, 2nd para.
85. Art. J.8(2) TEU. Procedural matters require a simple majority (on the basis that if neither unanimity nor a qualified majority is specified, a simple majority suffices). Qualified majority voting in the context of joint action has been discussed *ante*.
86. Art. J.8(3) TEU.
87. *Cf*. Arts. 189a EC; 119 Euratom.
88. Art. J.7 TEU, 1st para.
89. This has been standing practice since 1987, see Weerts, *op. cit.*, 159–160.
90. Art. J.7 TEU, 1st para. See European Parliament, Rules of Procedure (O.J. 1997 L 49/1), Rule 91.
91. See Weerts, *op. cit.*, 153–160.
92. Art. J.7 TEU, 2nd para. As to recommendations, see European Parliament, Rules of Procedure, Rule 92 and the Recommendation on improving the impact of joint actions (O.J. 1997 C 167/147).
93. Arts. J.3.(7) and J.8(3) TEU, in the context of joint actions generally, respectively. The Council's supervisory power is conferred by Art. J.1(4), last sentence.
94. Eaton in O'Keeffe and Twomey (eds.), *op. cit.*, 215 at 221–222.

The Presidency represents the Union in matters coming within CFSP;[95] it is responsible for the implementation of common measures, in which capacity it in principle expresses the Union's position in international organizations and international conferences,[96] and in these tasks it may be assisted by the other members of the troika, the previous and next Member States to hold the Presidency.[97] The representation of the Union in principle by the Presidency acknowledges that not all Member States may be represented in all international fora, and that the United Kingdom and France have permanent seats in the United Nations Security Council.[98] As has been noted above, the Presidency has consultation and information obligations *vis-à-vis* the European Parliament.[99] The Presidency may convene extraordinary meetings of the Council, either on its own motion or at the request of the Commission or a Member State, within 48 hours, or, in an emergency, within a shorter period.[100]

The Political Committee (usually referred to as PoCo), consisting of the Political Directors of the Member States' foreign ministries, originally governed by Article 30(10)(c) SEA is now governed by Article J.8(5) TEU. Its activities are expressly without prejudice to the status of *Coreper*[101] and its tasks are to monitor the international situation in the areas covered by CFSP, to contribute to the definition of policies by delivering opinions to the Council, either on its own initiative or at the Council's request, and to monitor the implementation of agreed policies, without prejudice to the responsibility of the Presidency or the Commission.[102] Clearly, it will provoke some difficulties if the advice

95. Art. J.5(1) TEU.
96. Art. J.5(2) TEU.
97. Art. J.5(3) TEU. As to the order in which the Presidency rotates, see Dec. 2/95 (O.J. 1995 L 1/220), in accordance with Arts. 146 EC, 27 ECSC and 116 Euratom (2nd para. in each case, as amended). As is explained in the text, *post*, the Commission is fully associated in these tasks.
98. The United Kingdom and France will, in the execution of their functions, ensure the defence of the positions and interests of the Union, without prejudice to their responsibilities under the provisions of the United Nations Charter; moreover, they, and any other Member States holding rotating seats in the Security Council, will concert and keep the other Member states fully informed, Art. J.5(4) TEU 2nd para. Without prejudice to the obligations under Article J.2(3) TEU to coordinate action and uphold common positions in international fora, or to the commitment under Article J.3(4) TEU as a result of joint actions, there is an obligation on Member States represented in international fora in which not all the Member States participate to keep the latter informed of any matter of common interest, Art. J.5(4) TEU 1st para.
99. Art. J.7 TEU, 1st para.
100. Art. J.8(4) TEU.
101. As to which, see Art. 151 EC, and Chapters IV, section 3.4, and V, section 3.3.3, *post*.
102. Art. J.8(5) TEU. As a Committee subordinate to the Council, PoCo votes (in so far as necessary) in the same way as the Council would on the matter concerned, thus usually by unanimity but by simple majority on procedural questions. As the Presidency of the Council rotates, so does the chairmanship of PoCo.

coming from the PoCo differs from that coming from *Coreper*, but proper internal coordination within each delegation should minimise the risks, and it is still *Coreper* which prepares the work of the Council, even in the field of CFSP.[103] Because of the single institutional framework, the old EPC Secretariat has been transformed into an integral directorate of the Council's secretariat.

The Commission is fully associated with the work carried out in the field of CFSP,[104] including representation of the Union by the Presidency and the responsibilities conferred on the Presidency in relation to the implementation of common measures and representation in principle in international fora.[105] The Commission shares responsibility with the Presidency for informing the European Parliament of the development of CFSP, with the Member States for initiating discussion of matters in the Council[106] and with them and the Presidency for convening extraordinary meetings of the Council.[107] However, its role is very clearly a subsidiary one, although Nuttall records that even under EPC the Commission did not hesitate to present views and even to suggest courses of action.[108] The existing cooperation between the diplomatic and Consular missions of the Member States and Commission delegations in third countries[109] is more fully developed by Article J.6 TEU, which imposes obligations on the missions and delegations to cooperate with one another in ensuring that the common positions and common measures adopted by the Council are complied with and implemented, and to step up cooperation by exchanging information, carrying out joint assessments and contributing to the implementation of the right conferred by Article 8c EC on citizens of the Union to diplomatic or consular protection by the relevant authorities of other Member States, on the same conditions as their nationals, if the Member State of which they are nationals is not represented in the third country concerned. The administrative expenditure entailed for the institutions in running CFSP is charged to the budget of the European Communities.[110] Operational expenditure may be charged to the budget of the Communities, in which case the budgetary procedure set out in the EC Treaty applies,[111] but a decision to

---

103. As to the relationship between PoCo and *Coreper*, see Galloway in Westlake, *The Council of the European Union* (London, 1995) 218–221.
104. Art. J.9 TEU.
105. Art. J.5(3) TEU.
106. Art. J.8(3) TEU. This is the shared or non-exclusive right of initiative.
107. Art. J.8(4) TEU.
108. Nuttall in Monar *et al.* (eds.), *op. cit.* (see note 15, *supra*) 133 at 134. The Commission's interventions were usually in areas related to the Community and even though eyebrows were sometimes raised by the delegations from the Member States, the practice has been on the increase, *ibid.*
109. See section 5.1 of this Chapter, *post.*
110. Art. J.11(2) TEU, 1st para.
111. See Chapter V, section 2, *post.* This would at least give the European Parliament a

do so must be unanimous.[112] Alternatively, the Council may determine that such expenditure will be charged to the Member States, where appropriate in accordance with a scale to be decided.[113] The cost of monitors in the former Yugoslavia was divided according to a GDP-based formula, with the Commission bearing the cost of its monitors.[114]

Eaton notes four main differences between EPC and CFSP: a strengthened commitment to common positions; the full coverage of security issues; the strengthening of cooperation to embrace joint action; the transition from the language of High Contracting Parties to the use of the EC institutions.[115] However, Zoller is entirely right to observe that just as CFSP has not been 'Communitarised', it has also not been democratised, and, like much of national foreign policy, it escapes real democratic control.[116]

1.3.2   Justice and home affairs

Unlike CFSP, Title VI of the Treaty on European Union restricts cooperation between Member States in the fields of Justice and Home Affairs to a number of areas expressed in Article K.1 TEU as being regarded as matters of common interest. These are asylum policy;[117] rules and controls on the crossing by persons of the external borders of the Member States;[118] certain aspects of immigration policy and policy regarding nationals of third countries;[119] combating drug addiction;[120]

---

lever with which to exert pressure on the Council in this field, a reason which may well cause the Council to opt for the alternative method of financing. See now, the Inter-institutional Agreement (Bull. EU 7/8–1997, point 2.3.1). The Treaty of Amsterdam (not yet in force) will make this the default situation (see the new Art. J.18(3) TEU).

112. Art. J.11(2) TEU, 2nd para, 1st indent.

113. *Ibid.*, 2nd indent.

114. Eaton in O'Keeffe and Twomey (eds.), *op. cit.* (see note 9, *supra*) 215 at 219.

115. *Ibid.* at 219–220.

116. Zoller in Constantinesco *et al.* (eds.), *op. cit.* (see note 78, *supra*) 786 at 799.

117. Art. K.1(1) TEU. See also Chapter VII, section 4.4, *post.*

118. Art. K.1(2) TEU. See also Chapter VII, section 4.4, *post.*

119. Art. K.1(3) TEU. The aspects concerned are: (a) conditions of entry and movement of such nationals on the territory of Member States; (b) conditions of their residence there, including family reunion and access to employment; and (c) combating unauthorized immigration, residence and work by such nationals there. Various aspects of these matters are presently the subject of Community legislation (such as the situation of spouses of Community nationals who are not such nationals), although Art. K.1 TEU makes it clear that cooperation in JHA is without prejudice to the powers of the European Community. Thus decisions agreed within JHA cannot derogate from rights which third country nationals may have as a result of Community legislation or agreements to which the Community and its Member States are parties, such as the EEA Agreement or the Europe Agreements.

120. Art. K.1(4) TEU, in so far as this is not covered by Art. K.1(7)–(9) TEU. See *e.g.* the Commission's Communication concerning a European Union action plan to combat

combating fraud on an international scale;[121] judicial cooperation in civil matters;[122] judicial cooperation in criminal matters;[123] customs cooperation;[124] police cooperation for certain purposes and the establishment of Europol.[125] Again, like in the case of CFSP, there is

drugs, COM (94) 234 Final. See also (within the Community structure) Dec. 102/97 (O.J. 1997 L 19/25) on a Community action programme on the prevention of drug dependence.

121. Art. K.1(5) TEU, in so far as this is not covered by Art. K.1(7)–(9). See the European Parliament's Resolution (O.J. 1994 C 20/185).

122. Art. K.1(6) TEU. See *e.g.* the Convention on the service in the Member States of the European Union of judicial and extrajudicial documents in civil and commercial matters (O.J. 1997 C 261/2; as to the Act drawing it up, see O.J. 1997 C 261/1). As to the Protocol on interpretation of this Convention by the Court of Justice, see O.J. 1997 C 261/18; as to the Act drawing up the Protocol, see O.J. 1997 C 261/17. See also the Commission's Communication *Towards greater efficiency in obtaining and enforcing judgments in the European Union* COM (97) 609 Final (O.J. 1998 C 33/3).

123. Art. K.1(7) TEU. See *e.g.* the Convention on the simplified extradition procedure between Member States of the European Union (O.J. 1995 C 78/2; as to the Act drawing up the Convention, see O.J. 1997 C 78/1; see also the Explanatory Report (O.J. 1996 C 375/4)) and the Convention on the improvement of extradition between Member States (O.J. 1996 C 313/12; as to the Act drawing up the Convention, see O.J. 1996 C 313/11; see also the Explanatory Report (O.J. 1997 C 191/13). See also the Convention on the protection of the Community's financial interests (O.J. 1995 C 316/49; as to the Act drawing up the Convention, see O.J. 1995 C 316/48; as to the explanatory report, see O.J. 1997 C 191/1; see further, the Protocol conferring jurisdiction on the Court of Justice to interpret the Convention (O.J. 1997 C 151/2, and the Act drawing it up (O.J. 1997 C 151/1), and the Second Protocol (O.J. 1997 C221/12, and the Act drawing it up (O.J. 1997 C 221/11), with the Explanatory Report (O.J. 1998 C 11/5)). See also the Convention on the fight against corruption involving Community officials or officials of the Member States (O.J. 1997 C 195/2; as to the Act drawing up the Convention, see O.J. 1997 C 195/1).

124. Art. K.1(8) TEU. Much customs cooperation takes place in the context of administrative cooperation in accordance with the Community Customs Code, as to which, see Chapter VII, section 2.4, *post*. Customs cooperation in the context of JHA does not affect the cooperation within the Community context, Art. K.1 TEU. See *e.g.* the CIS Convention on the use of information technology for customs purposes (O.J. 1995 C 316/34, as to the Act drawing it up, see O.J. 1997 C 316/33, and as to its provisional application, see O.J. 1995 C 316/58; see also the Protocol conferring jurisdiction on the Court of Justice to interpret it (O.J. 1996 C 151/2, and as to the Act drawing it up, see O.J. 1996 C 151/1)) and the Convention on mutual assistance and cooperation between the customs authorities of the Member States (O.J. 1998 C 24/2; as to the Act drawing up the Convention, see O.J. 1998 C 24/1).

125. Art. K.1(9) TEU. The purposes are: for preventing and combating terrorism, unlawful drug trafficking and other serious forms of international crime, including if necessary certain aspects of customs cooperation, in connection with the organization of a Union-wide system for exchanging information within a European Police Office (Europol). As to the Europol Convention, see O.J. 1995 C 316/2, and as to the Act drawing up the Convention, see O.J. 1995 C 316/1). See also the Protocol conferring jurisdiction on the Court of Justice to interpret the Europol Convention (O.J. 1996 C 299/2; as to the act drawing up the Protocol, see O.J. 1996 C 299/1). See also *e.g.* JA

express safeguarding of the powers of the European Community,[126] which implies that matters which are the subject of Community legislation will not be reopened in the context of JHA, although the dividing line is less than clear cut. Cooperation in JHA in the fields of common interest specified is solely for the purpose of achieving the objectives of the Union, in particular the free movement of persons.[127] A certain – albeit scarcely adequate – acknowledgement of concerns for individual liberty is provided for by Article K.2(1) TEU which requires cooperation in JHA to comply with the European Convention of Human Rights[128] and with the Convention relating to the Status of Refugees,[129] and to have regard to the protection afforded by Member States to persons persecuted on political grounds. Cooperation in JHA does not affect the exercise of the responsibilities incumbent on the Member States regarding the maintenance of law and order and the safeguarding of internal security.[130] The Member States must inform and consult one another within the Council with a view to coordinating their action in the areas falling within JHA, and collaboration has to be established between the relevant departments of their administrations to that end.[131]

The Council may use any of the three forms of cooperation which are envisaged. First, joint positions may be adopted and, using the appropriate forms and procedures, any cooperation contributing to the Union's objectives may be promoted.[132] Secondly, joint action may be adopted, but only in so far as the Union's objectives can be attained better by joint action than by the Member States acting individually on account of the scale or effects of the action envisaged.[133] Finally, the Council may,

95/73 (O.J. 1995 L 62/1, the ambit of which was extended by JA 96/748 (O.J. 1996 L 342/4)) on the Europol Drugs Unit; JA 97/827 (O.J. 1997 L 344/7), and JA 97/372 (O.J. 1997 L 159/1).

126. Art. K.1 TEU makes it clear that JHA operates without prejudice to the powers of the EC. See Case C-170/96 *Commission v. Council* [1998] ECR I-nyr (12 May 1998) in which the Court held it had jurisdiction to ascertain whether an act adopted within JHA should have been adopted within the Community framework. The case concerned an appeal against JA 96/197 (O.J. L63/8) relating to airport transport visas, and the Court concluded that adoption within JHA was correct.

127. See, generally, Monar and Morgan (eds.), *The Third Pillar of the European Union* (Brussels, 1994); Bieber and Monar (eds.), *Justice and Home Affairs in the European Union* (Brussels, 1995) which includes a useful bibliography; Degen in Von der Groeben *et al.* (eds.), *op. cit.* (see note 63, *supra*) Vol. 5, 999; Jessurun d'Olivera and Den Boer in O'Keeffe and Twomey (eds.), *op. cit.* (see note 9, *supra*) 261 and 279 respectively; Gautier in Constantinesco *et al.* (eds), *op. cit.* (see note 78, *supra*) 816.

128. See note 19, *supra*.

129. Geneva, 28 July 1951 (189 UNTS 150).

130. Art. K.2(2) TEU. See JA 97/339 (O.J. 1997 L 147/1) on cooperation on law, order and security.

131. Art. K.3(1) TEU.

132. Art. K.3(2)(a) TEU.

133. Art. K.3(2)(b) TEU. This develops the general commitment to subsidiarity in the

without prejudice to Article 220 EC,[134] draw up Conventions which it must recommend to the Member States for adoption in accordance with their respective constitutional requirements.[135] Measures implementing these Conventions must be adopted within the Council by a majority of two-thirds of the High Contracting Parties, unless the Convention concerned otherwise provides.[136] These Conventions may confer jurisdiction on the Court of Justice to interpret their provisions and to rule on any disputes relating to their application, in accordance with such arrangements as may be laid down in the Convention concerned.[137] In JHA the Council acts unanimously, except on matters of procedure, in which case a simple majority suffices,[138] and in relation to measures implementing joint action which it has unanimously decided are to be adopted by qualified majority, and also in relation to measures implementing Conventions (unless they in fact require unanimous adoption).[139] Where a qualified majority is provided for, it is that applicable to acts not adopted on the basis of a proposal from the Commission (at least 62 votes in favour cast by at least 10 members),[140] a rule which applies in this case even if the proposal in fact emanates from the Commission.[141]

The Commission is to be fully associated with the work in the areas covered by JHA.[142] It shares the right of initiative with the Member States, except for judicial cooperation in criminal matters, customs cooperation and police cooperation (including Europol), in respect of which only the Member States have the right of initiative.[143] Because of the obligation of full association, the lack of the right of initiative does not, though, mean that the Commission is kept out of those areas entirely. Indeed that would

second paragraph of Article B TEU and is phrased in partly similar terms to Art. 3b EC.

134. As to which, see Chapter VIII, section 2.5, *post*.
135. Art. K.3(2)(c) TEU, 1st subpara. Various examples have been mentioned in the footnotes in this section, *supra*.
136. *Ibid.*, 2nd subpara.
137. *Ibid.*, 3rd subpara. Hence under Art. L TEU the jurisdiction of the Court extends to this provision. The Commission's legal service has opined that there is a 'virtual obligation' to confer jurisdiction on the Court in cases where Conventions take over word for word a Community measure in a related field, see *Europe*, 6 July 1994, p. 11. See, further, Neuwahl in Bieber and Monar (eds.), *op. cit.* (see note 127, *supra*) 301 at 308 *et seq.* Sometimes jurisdiction is conferred by a Protocol to a Convention (reflecting an initial reluctance being overcome), on other occasions provisions conferring jurisdiction have been included in the Convention itself.
138. See note 89, *ante*.
139. Art. K.4(3) TEU.
140. *Ibid.*, 2nd para. (as amended by the Act of Austrian, Finnish and Swedish Accession, amended by the Adaptation Decision, Dec. 1/95 (O.J. 1995 L 1/1)).
141. Under Art. K.3(2) 1st indent in relation to the matters covered by Art. K.1(1)–(6).
142. Art. K.4(2) EC.
143. Art. K.3(2) TEU, 1st and 2nd indents respectively. These three areas are regarded as exceptionally sensitive by the Member States.

have been wholly unrealistic, given the Commission's right of initiative in relation to visa policy for third country nationals under Article 100c EC,[144] and that the Commission or a Member State may propose to the Council that Article 100c EC be applied to action in areas covered by Article K.1(1)–(6) TEU.[145] It is perhaps worth noting that much judicial and police cooperation takes place in the context of Conventions agreed in the wider forum of the Council of Europe, according to classic intergovernmental procedures;[146] moreover, much cooperation has in fact been bureaucratised, albeit that such a development is not always welcome in police circles.[147] Initiatives in JHA are effectively nationalised rather than 'Communitarised'.

Paralleling the approach in CFSP, within international organisations and international conferences in which they take part, Article K.5 TEU requires Member States to defend the common positions adopted in JHA.[148] The Presidency and the Commission must regularly inform the European Parliament of discussions in the areas covered by JHA,[149] and the Presidency is obliged to consult the European Parliament on the principal aspects of activities in cooperation in JHA, and, as the dialogue is two-way, it must ensure that the Parliament's views are duly taken into consideration.[150] As is the case with CFSP, the Parliament may ask questions of the Council or make recommendations to it on JHA matters, and it holds an annual debate on the progress made in implementing JHA.[151] In view of the

144. As to the Commission's role, see, generally, Meyers in Bieber and Monar (eds.), *op. cit.*, 277. As to visa requirements for entry into the EU by third country nationals, see Reg. 2317/95 (O.J. 1995 L 234/1).

145. *I.e.* the areas in which the Commission and the Member States share the right of initiative. At the same time as the Council so acts it determines the relevant voting conditions relating to such application, Art. K.9 TEU. The Council must recommend the Member States to adopt that decision in accordance with their respective constitutional requirements. This is the one-way interlink or *passerelle* procedure whereby measures in these areas may pass from the domain of cooperation in JHA to the Community sphere.

146. For a convenient collection of texts up to 20 November 1991, see Muller–Rappard and Bassiouni (eds.) *European Inter-State Co-operation in Criminal Matters* (2nd ed., Dordrecht, 1993).

147. Den Boer in Bieber and Monar (eds.), *op. cit.* (see note 127, *supra*) 191 at 192.

148. This is the only mention in the English version of Title VI TEU of the phrase 'common positions'. In the French text of Arts. K.3(2)(a) and K.5 TEU the words 'positions communes' are used in both cases, whereas the English text uses the words 'joint positions' and 'common positions' respectively. It is submitted that the English words should be treated as if they were also the same. Sometimes nomenclature is inconsistent, see in relation to negotiations within the Council of Europe and the OECD on combating corruption, CP 97/661 (O.J. 1997 L 279/1) and JP 97/783 (O.J. 1997 L 320/1), the first being expressed as a 'Common Position', the latter as a 'Joint Position'.

149. Art. K.6 TEU, 1st para.

150. *Ibid.*, 2nd para. See the contributions by Monar and Esders in Bieber and Monar (eds.), *op. cit.* (see note 127, *supra*) 243 and 259 respectively.

151. Art. K.6, 3rd para.

Schengen developments[152] and (now) of the Nordic Union,[153] Article K.7 TEU provides that the provisions governing cooperation in JHA do not prevent the establishment of closer cooperation between two or more Member States in so far as it that does not conflict with or impede cooperation in JHA.

The administrative expenditure entailed for the institutions in running cooperation in JHA is charged to the budget of the European Communities.[154] Operational expenditure may be charged to the budget of the Communities, in which case the budgetary procedure set out in the EC Treaty applies,[155] but a decision to do so must be unanimous.[156] Alternatively, the Council may determine that such expenditure will be charged to the Member States, where appropriate in accordance with a scale to be decided.[157] Detailed arrangements on financing have now been adopted.[158]

Almost last, but far from least, the perhaps notorious K.4 Committee deserves brief attention. This is the Coordinating Committee set up under Article K.4(1) TEU, consisting of senior officials. Its task is threefold: first, as the name suggests, it coordinates work in the sphere of JHA; secondly, it gives opinions for the attention of the Council, either on its own initiative or at the Council's request, and, thirdly, it contributes to the preparation of the Council's discussions within JHA and, in accordance with Article 100d EC, in the field of the common visa policy to be established under Article 100c EC for third country nationals entering a Member State of the Union.[159] Decisions (in the administrative rather than the legally binding sense) in the K.4 committee are made in principle unanimously, although on procedural questions a simple majority is sufficient.[160]

---

152. See, generally, Chapter VII, section 4.3, *post* and Nanz in Bieber and Monar (eds.), *op. cit.* (see note 127, *supra*) 29.

153. See, generally, Nordic Council, *Cooperation Agreements between the Nordic Countries* (Stockholm, 1978); Plender, *International Migration Law* (2nd ed., Dordrecht, 1988) 288. See also the Conventions on a common labour market and on passport control waiver (198 UNTS 47 and 322 UNTS 245 respectively) and Fode in Schermers, *et al.* (eds.), *Free Movement of Persons in Europe* (Dordrecht, 1993) 61.

154. Art. K.8(2) TEU, 1st para.

155. See Chapter V, section 2, *post*.

156. Art. K.8(2) TEU, 2nd para, 1st indent; JA 95/401 (O.J. 1995 L 238/1) and Dec. 95/402 (O.J. 1995 L 238/2). The Treaty of Amsterdam (not yet in force) will make charging operational expenditure to the Community budget the default situation (see the new Art. K. 13(3) TEU.

157. *Ibid.*, 2nd indent.

158. JA 95/401 (O.J. 1995 L 238/1) and Dec. 95/402 (O.J. 1995 L 238/2).

159. Art. K.4(1) TEU. The contribution to the preparation of the Council's discussions is without prejudice to the role of *Coreper* under Art. 151 EC (as to which, see Chapters IV, section 3.4, and V, section 3.3.3, *post.*), Art. K.4(1) TEU, 2nd indent.

160. This follows from the pattern of all committees or groups subordinate to the Council acting in accordance with the voting requirements of the Council itself. Similarly, the chair of the K.4 Committee rotates with the Presidency of the Council. See, generally, Niemeier, in Bieber and Monar (eds.), *op. cit.* (see note 127, *supra*) 321.

Finally, it should be noted that the Treaty of Amsterdam (TOA), which is not yet in force at the date at which this work states the law, will restructure the Third Pillar, redesignating JHA as Police and Judicial Cooperation in Criminal Matters, and that visa, asylum, immigration and other policies relating to the free movement of persons will move into the Community framework,[161] whereas the remaining areas will continue to be dealt with on a more intergovernmental basis.[162]

1.4   Concluding observations

The character of the present institutional model, as provisionally worked out in respect of the supplementary Second and Third Pillars discussed above, is not Community in nature, but also not wholly intergovernmental. A cautious opening for evolution in the direction of the Community method of decision-making has been provided, through the use of the Community Institutions for decision-making, so that most of them are involved, albeit that the Commission and the Parliament have still under-developed roles, and the Court's involvement is still very indirect. The almost total exclusion of the Court forms a handicap for the solidity and continuity of policies in the Second and Third Pillars.[163] The sole avenue of recourse for judicial supervision is to be found in the different national legal systems with their own procedures for judicial protection; this undoubtedly has disadvantages for the unity and uniform application of these policy areas. In view of the differences between the Community's autonomous legal order as described in the Court's case-law on the one hand, and the institutional model adopted for CFSP and JHA on the other, it is clear that these policy areas can lay no claim to the privileges of the Community legal order: supremacy in relation to national law and direct effect.[164]

2.   DIVERSITY AND UNITY OF THE COMMUNITIES AND COMMUNITY LAW

2.1   Differences in structure between the three Treaties

There are marked differences in structure between the ECSC Treaty and the EC Treaty (as the old EEC Treaty has now become[165]), owing to the

161. See the new Arts. 73i–73q EC, introduced by the TOA.
162. See, briefly, Chapter VII, section 4.4, *post.*
163. The changes made by the TOA will allow the Court's role to be increased, albeit with a major degree of variable geometry (see the new Art. K.7 TEU).
164. See section 3.2, *post.*
165. Art. G(1) TEU.

difference in method of integration. The ECSC is an example of integration by sectors, which, because of the indissoluble connection between the integrated sector and those sectors of the economy of the Member States which retained their national character, was called an *'opération contre nature'* by Reuter in his commentary of 1953.[166] The explanation for this unnatural operation lay in the political motives which had led to the establishment of the ECSC. It could only be economically justified in the perspective of a continued economic integration which was ultimately to embrace the whole economy of the Member States.

The rules governing the coal and steel market are laid down in detail in many parts of the Treaty (hence its description as a *'traité-loi'*). The resultant regime is aimed at a high degree of regulation of this market, a situation which can be accounted for by the oligopolistic market structure and the key position which the production of coal and steel was deemed to occupy in the early fifties in the economic, social and political spheres in the Member States. The core of the market regime is in two parts; a set of rules of conduct for the economic subjects of the Community concerning their competitive relations *inter se*, and also the grant of a number of powers, chiefly to the High Authority (replaced, since the Merger Treaty entered into force in 1967, by the Commission) enabling intervention in the market. In addition, in order to ensure the unimpeded functioning of the market, a number of prohibitions are imposed upon the national governments.

Far-reaching powers were accorded to the High Authority (now the Commission) in order to ensure the application of the rules of the market to the undertakings failing within it. By and large these powers have an executive character, because, even where they are regulatory powers (general decisions), the High Authority is considerably restricted in the freedom of its policy choices. In the marginal areas regulated in the Treaty, such as transport, social policy and external tariff and trade policy (which only fall within it in so far as they relate to the production of coal and steel or to those products themselves), the powers of the High Authority are limited in scope and are not very far-reaching. In such areas the main burden of implementing the Treaty, in contrast to the situation in the market regime proper, lies with those Member States which are obliged to take the necessary measures.

Both the approach to integration by sectors of industry and the determination of market policy in the Treaty itself have over the years been a constant source of difficulty in the ECSC. A proper functioning of the common market was hampered by considerable differences of opinion on the policy to be followed in neighbouring sectors which remained under national control. Adjustment of policies in the coal and steel sector to

---

166. *La CECA* (Paris, 1953) 32. See also Spierenburg and Poidevin, *Histoire de la Haute Autorité de la CECA, Une expérience supranationale* (Brussels, 1993).

changing economic conceptions and to structural changes in market relations involved serious problems, since revision of the Treaty in which those policies were laid down could only be achieved through a complicated and laborious procedure.

The ECSC Treaty, unlike the EC Treaty and the Euratom Treaty which were concluded for an unlimited period,[167] was concluded for a period of fifty years and expires at midnight on 24 July 2002.[168] The Commission's policy in recent years has been based on the assumption that the ECSC Treaty will not be extended; accordingly it is increasingly inclined to bring its ECSC activities into the sphere of the other two Communities so that they can take them over from that date.[169]

In contrast to the ECSC Treaty, the EC Treaty embraces practically the whole economy of the Member States and important sectors of national policy, such as social policy, environmental policy etc. Under the EC Treaty a common market, with free movement of goods, persons, services and capital, had to be set up and, while originally the economic policies of Member States had to be progressively approximated to each other, an economic and monetary union now has to be achieved. The emphasis here is on a free operation of the market mechanism under conditions ensuring effective and undistorted competition, or as Article 3a EC puts it, on an open market economy with free competition. Outside the sectors of transport and agriculture the possibility of market regulation was not provided for, but that does not exclude many forms of adjusting the market process.[170]

The EC is based on a customs union.[171] In this it differs from the ECSC, in which no common external tariff was provided for. The EC customs union found concrete shape in the Treaty in obligations imposed on Member States to take, according to a prescribed time-table, a series of clearly defined measures leading to the progressive elimination of mutual trade barriers and the creation of a common external tariff. Beyond this, the Treaty is principally a *traité-cadre*, a *traité de procédure*.[172] Objectives are formulated, principles are defined, but it is left to the Institutions to work out these principles and objectives in concrete measures. The most important exception to this approach is the timetable for the achievement

167. Arts. 240 EC and 208 Euratom.
168. Art. 97 ECSC (the ECSC Treaty entered into force on 25 July 1952).
169. See the Commission's Communications to the Council of 15 March 1991 (SEC (91) 407) and 18 November 1992 (SEC (92) 1889). This process is known as 'phasing in – phasing out.' See also Case C-128/92 *H.J. Banks & Co. Ltd. v. British Coal Corporation* [1994] ECR I-1209, [1994] 5 CMLR 30.
170. See Chapter III, *post* for more details.
171. There are two elements in a customs union: the abolition of internal barriers to trade and the creation of a common customs tariff towards the rest of the world. In a free trade area this second element is lacking. *Cf.* Art. XXIV(8) GATT.
172. Reuter: *Organisations européennes* (2nd ed., Paris, 1970) 188.

of Economic and Monetary Union, which is now the subject of detailed Treaty provisions. Time and adequate agreement to lay down a detailed set of rules in the Treaty were lacking. Moreover, it would have been unwise to do so, in some cases even inconceivable, because the measures taken would have to be appropriate to (and themselves allow adjustment to) varying circumstances.

In the EC Treaty a comprehensive policy-making and regulatory task has therefore been allotted to the Institutions. Considering the vital interests which are usually at stake and the high degree of freedom in the choice of policy that was accorded – such as in the development of a common policy in the sectors of transport, agriculture and external commercial relations – it is not surprising that this task was entrusted in the first instance to the Council of Ministers, although as a rule it could act only on proposals from the Commission. It is, however, striking that the Treaty provided that even in these fields the requirement of unanimity was in the course of time to be replaced by that of a qualified majority vote as the basis for Council decisions.

To a considerable extent the system created by the EC Treaty, even when fully worked out through Council decisions, consists of rules of conduct for the national governments in the form of instructions or prohibitions. Rules of conduct for enterprises are found among the provisions for a common competition policy, while such rules have also been frequently adopted in the few sectors in which market regulation (agriculture and transport) was intended. Powers of an executive character were included in the EC Treaty only to a fairly limited degree. This is not surprising in view of the character of this Treaty as a *traité de procédure*. In so far as such powers are granted in the Treaty, they are mostly allotted to the Commission and lie generally in the sphere of the control of safeguard clauses. Since the Council may delegate powers to the Commission for carrying into effect the rules it has laid down, a further evolution of the executive activity of the Commission has been made possible. Such an activity in direct relation to the economic subjects of the Community has been explicitly provided for only within the framework of rules laid down by the Council for implementing the Treaty as regards the prohibition of discrimination in the transport sector, and as regards competition between enterprises.

The structure of Euratom recalls that of the ECSC in several respects. Here again the integration concerns a sector of the economy. A common market is set up for nuclear basic materials, products and means of production. Ample scope is given in the Treaty to the planning of scientific, technological and economic activities in so far as they are related to the development of the peaceful use of nuclear energy. A striking feature is the strong emphasis which the Treaty lays on the control of these activities with the aid of modern methods of administration, such as planning, financial incentives and the use of private law structures.

Looking at the ECSC, EC and Euratom Treaties side-by-side raises the question of their inter-relationship. Article 232 EC expressly provides that the provisions of that Treaty shall not affect those of the ECSC Treaty (which was, of course, concluded prior to the EC Treaty); it also expressly provides that the provisions of the EC Treaty shall not derogate from those of the Euratom Treaty (concluded at the same time as the EC Treaty). It is generally accepted that the EC Treaty, which in principle embraces all economic activities, also applies to economic activities in the coal, steel and nuclear energy sectors, at least in so far as the ECSC Treaty does not govern a particular matter,[173] provided that the EC rules are not at variance with those of the ECSC or Euratom Treaties. This holds even though Article 232 EC does not compel such a conclusion, as a complete exclusion of the EC system in sectors covered by the ECSC Treaty and particularly in sectors covered by the Euratom Treaty would not be incompatible with the wording of that Article. The Court considers that the difference in the wording of Articles 232(1) and 232(2) EC justifies holding that the regulation of particular matters in the ECSC Treaty is exclusive. Thus there can be no question of supplementing measures under or by virtue of the EC Treaty in such cases.[174]

Even though the provisions of the sectorial integration Treaties take precedence as a *lex specialis* over the provisions of the EC Treaty as a *lex*

173. *Cf. Deuxième Rapport Général sur l'Activité des Communautés Européennes, 1968* (Brussels, Luxembourg, 1969) para. 655. See also Reg. 1612/68 (O.J. English Special Edition 1968 (II), p. 475, as amended) on the free movement of workers within the Community and the General Programmes on freedom of establishment (O.J. English Special Edition (2nd series) IX, p. 7) and the freedom to provide services *(ibid.,* p. 3). See further Simmonds (ed.), *Encyclopedia of European Community Law* (London, loose-leaf, 1974–94) Vol. B2, part B10, commentary on Art. 232 EEC, and Petersmann in Von der Groeben *et al.* (eds.), *op. cit* (see note 63, *supra*) Vol. 5, 545. See, in relation to the ECSC Treaty, Case 328/85 *Deutsche Babcock Handel GmbH v. Hauptzollamt Lübeck-Ost* [1987] ECR 5119 at 5139–5140.

174. Cases 188–190/80 *France et al. v. Commission* [1982] ECR 2545 at 2580. Probably already in the same sense Cases 27–29/58 *Compagnie des Hauts Fourneaux et Fonderies de Givors et al. v. High Authority* [1960] ECR 241. In Case 239/84 *Gerlach & Co. BV, Internationale Expeditie v. Minister for Economic Affairs* [1985] ECR 3507 at 3517 the Court observed that the rules of the ECSC Treaty and implementing provisions adopted thereunder remained in force as regards the functioning of the common market in coal and steel despite the adoption of the EEC Treaty. See also the Opinion of Van Gerven, Adv. Gen. in Case C-128/92 *H.J. Banks & Co. Ltd. v. British Coal Corporation* [1994] ECR I-1209 at 1218–1219 and contrast his view as to the direct effect of certain provisions of the ECSC Treaty with that of the Court (at 1236–1243 and 1274–1275 respectively.

175. Cf. Cases 27–29/58, *ibid.* at 255 which showed that the High Authority, in applying special internal carriage rates in the interest of coal or steel producers (Art. 70 ECSC, 4th para.) cannot take account of the principles of any appropriate regional policy, unlike in Art. 80(2) EC.

generalis,[175] in the interpretation of the *lex specialis* the Court may call on the *lex generalis*. Thus in Ruling 1/78 the Court held that in the light of the EC Treaty the provisions of the Euratom Treaty on the nuclear common market 'appear to be nothing other than the application, in a highly specialized field, of the legal conceptions which form the basis of the structure of the general common market.'[176] The provisions relating to the Institutions common to the Communities will, in particular, be interpreted by the Court in as far as possible a uniform manner and brought into harmony with each other.[177]

2.2   Common features of the three Treaties

In spite of these marked differences not only are the general objectives largely identical,[178] but the institutional structure and the legal order called into being by or under the three Treaties also display so many common features that it is justifiable to treat the Communities as a whole. In the discussion of the institutional and economic law of the Communities in the different chapters of the present work the emphasis will be on the law of the EC as the most comprehensive and most important part of Community law. In view of the mutual relationship between the three Treaties,[179] and with a view to any possible merger of the Treaties into one European Treaty (an objective which has been agreed to by the original six Member States), it would seem appropriate to deal with the law of the ECSC and of Euratom as branches of the economic law of the Communities in the same way as the branches relating to agriculture and transport in the EC. In this context it should be borne in mind that, especially in the ECSC, a number of rules of institutional law apply which sometimes differ substantially from the general rules of the EC. Thus, in the discussion of the institutional law of the EC attention will be drawn to a number of important differences of this kind.

The unity in the institutional structure of the three Communities is demonstrated in the Convention on certain institutions common to the

176. Ruling 1/78 [1978] ECR 2151 at 2172. *Cf.* also Case 13/60 *'Geitling' Ruhrkohlen Ver-kaufsgesellschaft mbH et al. v. High Authority* [1962] ECR 83 at 102 in which, in the interpretation of Art. 65 ECSC, reliance was placed on Art. 85(3) EC in the light of the common inspiration behind the two provisions. In Case 6/72 *Europemballage Cor-poration and Continental Can Company Inc. v. Commission* [1973] ECR 215 at 243 the Court refused to draw a comparison between Art. 86 EC and certain provisions of the ECSC Treaty.
177. Case 101/63 *Wagner v. Fohrmann et al.* [1964] ECR 195; see also Case 230/81 *Lux-embourg v. European Parliament* [1983] ECR 255 at 282–283.
178. Arts. 2 ECSC, 2 EC and 1 Euratom.
179. *Cf.* section 2.1. of this Chapter, *ante*.

European Communities and the Treaty establishing a single Council and a single Commission of the European Communities (the Merger Treaty). The Convention entered into force on the same date as the EC and Euratom Treaties. It provided for a single parliamentary Assembly (which called itself the European Parliament[180]) and laid down uniform rules for its composition. It also established a single Court of Justice. These bodies were to exercise the powers and jurisdiction conferred upon them by each of the three Treaties.[181] Further, a single Economic and Social Committee was to function in both EC and Euratom.[182]

The Merger Treaty of 8 April 1965, which entered into force on 29 July 1967 laid down similar rules with respect to the executive institutions. A single Council of Ministers[183] and a single Commission[184] thereafter exercised the powers and jurisdiction conferred upon the Council and the Commission respectively (in the case of the ECSC the single Commission exercised the powers conferred upon the High Authority) in each of the three Treaties. Under the Merger Treaty the composition of the Council and the Commission was regulated on identical lines for each of the three Treaties. Since 1 June 1977 a single Court of Auditors has served all three Communities.[185]

The structure of Community law and the way it is implemented can also be understood as a single internal system. The *primary* law of the Communities covers the law set up by the ECSC, EC and Euratom Treaties and agreements and Community decisions modifying these three Treaties, such as the decisions on the Community's own resources,[186] the First and Second Budgetary Treaties[187] and the Decision and Act on direct elections to the European Parliament;[188] it embraces the Single European Act[189] and the Treaty on European Union[190] in so far as they modify earlier Treaties.[191] It also embraces the decisions and Treaties concerning

180. The official designation of the Assembly as the European Parliament did not take place until the SEA referred to the European Parliament as such, Art. 3(1) SEA.
181. Convention, Arts, 1–4.
182. *Ibid.*, Art. 5. Both the Convention and the Merger Treaty leave the ECSC Consultative Committee intact; it remains as a special body of the ECSC Treaty (attached to the Commission) whose members are appointed by the Council.
183. Merger Treaty, Arts. 1–8.
184. *Ibid.*, Arts 9–19.
185. *Ibid.*, Art. 22 (as amended by the Second Budgetary Treaty, Art. 27).
186. Dec. 70/243 (O.J. English Special Edition 1970 (I) p. 224) replaced first by Dec. 85/257 (O.J. 1985 L 128/15) and then by Dec. 94/728 (O.J. 1994 L 293/9).
187. Of 21 April 1970 and 22 July 1975.
188. Of 20 September 1976.
189. O.J. 1987 L 169/1 (see Art. 32 SEA).
190. O.J. 1992 C 191/1, see Art. M.
191. It will also under the same conditions embrace the Treaty of Amsterdam (O.J. 1997 C 340/1) when that Treaty enters into force.
192. TS 16 (1979); Cmnd. 7461, O.J. 1972 L 73/5.
193. O.J. 1979 L 291/9.

the accession of the United Kingdom, Denmark and Ireland,[192] Greece,[193] Spain and Portugal[194] and Austria, Finland and Sweden,[195] as well as the Acts of Accession appended thereto in so far as they modify or supplement the earlier Treaties. The term 'Treaties' in the context of the ambit of primary Community law also covers the Annexes as well as the conventions and protocols appended to the Treaties.[196] *Secondary* Community law consists of the provisions adopted by the Community Institutions on the basis of the Treaties and in order to implement them. Agreements which the Member States conclude among themselves with a view to implementing the Treaties and the agreements which can be concluded by the Communities with third countries or international organisations form a separate category of rules of Community law.

Both the primary and the secondary law of the Communities consist of two groups of rules. The first group is formed by *institutional law*. These rules relate to the field of application of the Treaties and their revision, the legal personality of the Communities, their seat, language regime and immunities. These subjects will be dealt with in the present chapter as general aspects of the Communities. In addition, institutional law embraces the rules relating to the composition of the various Institutions and subsidiary bodies and the legal status of their members; the functions and powers of these Institutions and bodies, and the way in which they exercise them in relation to each other, to the Member States and their organs, or to third countries, international organisations or private persons subject to Community authority. These matters will be discussed in Chapters IV on the institutional structure, V on policy-making and administration, VI on the administration of justice, and partly also in Chapter XII on external relations.

The second group of rules of Community law consists of the *substantive law* of the Communities, which will be discussed in the remaining chapters of this work. In the present context discussion is confined to the treatment of some general aspects. The substantive law of the Communities can be classified according to its purposes into two categories of rules. The first category regulates the exercise of the powers of the national policy-making and administrative organs by means of Community prohibitions and injunctions. The Member States and their

---

194. O.J. 1985 L 302/9.
195. O.J. 1994 C 241/9.
196. Arts. 239 EC, 84 ECSC and 207 Euratom. See also Act of Accession (1972), Art. 158; Act of Greek Accession (1979), Art. 150, Act of Spanish and Portuguese Accession (1985), Art. 400, and Act of Austrian, Finnish and Swedish Accession (1994), Art.174. These are to be found, respectively in O.J. 1972 L 73/14; O.J. 1979 L 291/17; O.J. 1985 L 302/23, and O.J. 1994 C 241/21. The 1972 and 1994 Acts of Accession were adapted by Council decisions on account of Norway's non-accession: Adaptation Decision (O.J. 1973 L 2/1), and Dec. 95/1 (O.J. 1995 L 1/1) respectively.

organs are obliged either to abstain from certain measures or positively to take certain other measures in order to implement Community law. There can thus arise an obligation to abolish, to modify, or – if they are already in conformity with the obligation imposed – not to modify existing legislation, or to adopt new legislation (whether primary or secondary).[197] The second category of substantive law of the Communities consists of rules of conduct for private persons falling within Community law. These rules are to be found especially in the sphere of competition law.

The implementation of substantive Community law, which may ultimately lead to the application of this law in administrative acts or judicial decisions in concrete cases, may pass through many stages and has been entrusted in varying degrees to the Community Institutions and national bodies. At one end of the scale *e.g.* in the sphere of competition law, the Council and/or the Commission work out primary Community law and apply it up to the stage of decisions addressed to individual enterprises, in which case national bodies have only to intervene in its enforcement.[198] At the other end of the scale *e.g.* the abolition of internal tariffs in the EC, the whole elaboration and application of primary Community law may be entrusted to the states and their organs. The Commission and the Court will then chiefly have the task of exercising supervision over the way in which those obligations are executed.[199] Between these extremes of practically centralised Community administration and practically decentralised national administration there are many variations, according to the branch of Community law under consideration. The implementation will then be based on close co-operation between the Member States and the Community Institutions both performing on their own initiative their duties under Community law.[200] It is against this background that the importance of Article 5 EC should be understood; as the Court has indicated this is the expression of the more general rule imposing the Member States and the Community Institutions mutual duties of genuine co-operation and assistance.[201]

197. See Case 159/78 *Commission v. Italy* [1979] ECR 3247 at 3264: 'the maintenance of a provision incompatible with the Treaty gives rise to an ambiguous state of affairs by maintaining, as regards those subject to the law who are concerned, a state of uncertainty as to the possibilities available to them of relying on Community law.' This applies even if the national provision is in fact applied in a manner compatible with Community law (*e.g.* by not discriminating against nationals of other Member States) and even if the Treaty provision concerned has direct effect, see Case 16/73 *Commission v. France* [1974] ECR 359 at 372.
198. Arts. 192 EC, 92 ECSC and 164 Euratom.
199. Arts. 155 and 169–171 EC, 88 ECSC and 124 and 141–143 Euratom.
200. *Cf.* Case 76/70 *Ludwig Wünsche & Co. v. Hauptzollamt Ludwigshafen am Rhein* [1971] ECR 393 at 401.
201. *E.g.* Case 44/84 *Hurd v. Jones* [1986] ECR 29 at 81; Case C-2/88 Imm. *Zwartveld et al.* [1990] ECR I-3365 at 3372–3374 and 4405 at 4411.

3. Nature and Effect of Community Law

3.1 Nature of Community law

Community law can be distinguished from traditional public international law in (A) its content, (B) its instruments and (C) its sources of law.

A. Content

From the formal viewpoint, Community law belongs to international law. In fact, it is partly embodied in, partly based on treaties concluded between sovereign states. Community law, however, shows a number of properties which are foreign to traditional international law and which do not even occur in more advanced international law in this combination and intensity. *From the viewpoint of its content,* Community law is a common internal law in the Member States rather than a law between these states.

Indeed, the core of Community law is formed by the rules for the establishment and maintenance of a common market. The latter takes the place of the separate national markets and has a character analogous to that of the domestic market of one state.[202] The common market therefore is an internal market common to the Member States. Thus, in this market the difference between legal relations which in view of their subject-matter, persons, or place have an international or an internal character tends to become blurred, as does the distinction between, on the one hand what in principle is usually the potential domain of international law and, on the other hand, the reserved domain of national law. From the viewpoint of the common market all these relations have an internal character. The law regulating these relations is *internal law common to the Member States.*[203]

Further, those Community rules the object of which is the establishment and functioning of the common market cannot, upon closer analysis, be reduced exclusively to mutual rights and duties of the Member States, as is

---

202. See Chapter III, section 3.2, *post* and *e.g.* Case 270/80 *Polydor Ltd. et al. v. Harlequin Record Shops Ltd. et al.* [1982] ECR 329 at 348: 'the Treaty, by establishing a common market and progressively approximating the economic policies of the Member States, seeks to unite national markets into a single market having the characteristics of a domestic market.'

203. *Cf.* Lagrange, Adv. Gen. in Case 8/55 *Fédération Charbonnière de Belgique v. High Authority* [1954–1956] ECR 245 at 277 who spoke of the Treaty as being the charter of the Community, since the rules of law which derive from it constitute the *internal law of that Community* (italics in the original). In Opinion 1/91 *EEA Agreement I* [1991] ECR I-6079 at 6102 the Court held that 'the EEC Treaty, albeit concluded in the form of an international agreement, none the less constitutes the constitutional charter of a Community based on the rule of law.'

often the case in traditional international law.[204] The object of these Community rules is the regulation of the conduct of the national governments as well as private persons with respect to and in the common market. Community law regulates *a conglomerate of mutual rights and duties between the Community and its subjects, both Member States and private persons, and between these subjects amongst themselves.*

B.   Instruments

A characteristic feature of traditional international law is the primitive instruments of this law. Their creation, application and maintenance rest predominantly with the states, either collectively or individually. In classical intergovernmental organisation the task of the organs is generally limited to stimulating and registering agreement between states and to furthering the observance of the points agreed upon. Their task is directed to coordination and adaptation of the legislative and administrative activities of the participating states by means of organised persuasion and political pressure. Another striking point is the modest role of international adjudication, and consequently also of the judicial element in the functioning of these organisations, although there is now some evolution in this sphere: particularly in intergovernmental organisations in the economic, financial and social fields (WTO, ILO, OECD, the IMF, the World Bank and its associated organs) a tendency towards increasing justiciability can be detected, in the form of binding executive decisions, examination and dispute resolution procedures.

Characteristic features of Community law, on the other hand, are the extensive organisational and procedural provisions that have been made and the refined legal instruments available for supplementing, working out, amending, applying and maintaining this law. They will be discussed in detail in subsequent chapters. The discussion here is confined to a short characterisation, partly based on the Court's case-law.

As the Court emphasises, the Community is provided with its own Institutions and has legal personality, legal capacity and right of international representation. It is vested with real powers arising from a limitation of competence or a delegation of certain powers from the states to the Community.[205] Organs have been created which are to exercise sovereign rights derived from the states.[206] These organs may carry on autonomous legislative and administrative activities within the limits set by the Treaties.

204. *Cf.* Case 26/62 *NV Algemene Transport- en Expeditie Onderneming Van Gend en Loos v. Nederlandse administratie der belastingen* [1963] ECR 1 at 12.
205. Case 6/64 *Costa v. ENEL* [1964] ECR 585 at 593.
206. Case 26/62 *Van Gend en Loos* [1963] ECR 1 at 12.

The policy-making in this Community is not exclusively in the hands of a body composed of representatives of the Member States taking decisions by a unanimous vote. A Council of Ministers, which may take its decisions in a growing number of cases by a qualified majority, has to share this function with a Commission consisting of persons independent of the Member States. Moreover,[207] private persons who are affected as much as the Member States by the powers conferred upon the Institutions, are called upon to collaborate through the European Parliament and the Economic and Social Committee in the work of the Community. The extensive powers of the Court of Justice ensure that the law is respected, as regards the functioning of the Community, in a way that is without precedent in the law of international organisations.

C. Sources of law

Finally in its sources of law, too, Community law presents a picture that is unusual in traditional international law. International law finds its sources especially in inter-state treaties and in state practice generally accepted as the law. A striking feature of Community law is the importance of the acts of the Institutions and of general legal principles as a formal source of law. Fundamental rights form an integral part of Community law and in this respect Community law offers inhabitants of the Member States a protection comparable with that afforded by their own national law.[208] The Court thus regards the Communities as being a Community based on the rule of law.[209] Being, according to its nature, largely a system of internal law for the Community which is common to the Member States, Community law moreover employs legal constructions and legal concepts which also occur in national law to a much higher degree than in international law. In the definition of the content of those constructions and concepts according to Community law, therefore, national law will form a source of inspiration.[210]

207. *Ibid.*
208. *E.g.* Case 4/73 *J.Nold, Kohlen- und Baustoffgrosshandlung v. Commission* [1974] ECR 491 at 507; Case 265/87 *Hermann Schräder HS Kraftfutter GmbH & Co. KG v. Hauptzollamt Gronau* [1989] ECR 2237 at 2267–2268, and Case C-260/89 *Ellinki Radiophonia Tileorassi AE (ERT) v. Dimotiki Etairia Pliroforissis et al.* [1991] ECR I-2925 at 2963–2964, but see Chalmers (1992) 17 ELRev. 248 at 255. See also the Joint Declaration by the European Parliament, the Council and the Commission on Fundamental Rights, of 5 April 1977 (O.J. 1977 C 103/1), and Art. F(2) TEU. See, further, Chapter IV, section 3.3.4, *post.*
209. *E.g.* Case 294/83 *Parti écologiste 'Les Verts' v. European Parliament* [1986] ECR 1339 at 1365; Case C-2/88 Imm. *Zwartveld et al.* [1990] ECR I-3365 at 3372, and Opinion 1/91 *EEA Agreement I* [1991] ECR I-6079 at 6102.
210. See Chapter IV, section 3.3.1, *post.*

3.2   The Community legal order

It was partly on the strength of the properties described above that the Court found that the Treaties have called into being a new, distinctive legal order.[211] This legal order regulates the powers, rights and obligations of the Community and its subjects, and provides (an essential element of a legal order) for the procedures necessary for determining and adjudicating infringements of the law.[212]

The Community legal order created by the Treaty curtails the freedom of the Member States on certain points in ways other than those of traditional doctrines of international law. Thus, from the availability of the procedures necessary for determining and adjudicating infringements of the Treaty the Court has derived a prohibition of self-help for the Member States, except for those cases in which the Treaty expressly permits it.[213] In this context, however, it should be noted that the traditional international doctrine of self-help may be resuscitated again if these procedures, *e.g.* those of Articles 169 or 170 EC, have produced no result, since as the Treaties stand the Community cannot take proceedings against the Member States to enforce a judgment. Against the Member State which fails to fulfil its obligation under Article 171 EC and refuses to act upon a decision of the Court of Justice, the Court may impose a lump sum or penalty payment at the instance of the Commission.[214] If even that should fail to produce results, it is submitted that the Community or the Member States could then very well take reprisals, *i.e.* measures which *per se* are unlawful, but which are justified as a defence against the unlawful act of another state.[215]

211. Case 26/62 *Van Gend en Loos* [1963] ECR 1 at 12. See also Case 6/64 *Costa v. ENEL* [1964] ECR 585 at 593; Cases 90 and 91/63 *Commission v. Luxembourg and Belgium* [1964] ECR 625 at 631 (in which public international law is not mentioned); Case C-2/88 Imm. *Zwartveld et al.* [1990] ECR I-3365 at 3372; Cases C-6 and 9/90 *Francovich et al. v. Italy* [1991] ECR I-5357 at 5413–5414, and Opinion 1/91 *EEA Agreement I* [1991] ECR I-6079 at 6102. See generally on the Community legal order: Louis, *The Community Legal Order* (3rd ed., European Perspectives, Brussels, Luxembourg, 1993); Dagtoglou in Olmi *et al.*, *Thirty Years of Community Law* (European Perspectives, Brussels, Luxembourg, 1983) Chapter 11); De Witte (1984) RTDE 425; Pliakos (1993) RTDE 187; Schermers and Waelbroeck; *Judicial Protection in the European Communities* (5th ed., Deventer, 1992) Chapter 1 and literature cited there; Seidel (1992) EuR 125, and Wyatt (1982) 7 ELRev. 147.

212. Cases 90 and 91/63 *Commission v. Luxembourg and Belgium, ibid.*

213. *Ibid. Cf.* the special security safeguard clauses (Arts. 223 and 224 EC).

214. Art. 171(2) EC, 2nd and 3rd paras. See Chapter VI, section 1.1, *post.* See also the identically worded Art. 143(2) Euratom, 2nd and 3rd paras. Art. 88 ECSC, 3rd, 4th and 5th paras. makes rather different provision for reprisals to be taken by the Community, but it has never been applied.

215. It should be noted that the new Art. F.1 TEU, introduced by the Treaty of Amsterdam (not yet in force) permits the Council to take steps to suspend certain of the rights of a Member State under the TEU, when a serious and persistent breach of the principles

Self-help as a possible extension of the procedure of Articles 169 and 170 EC on the margin of the Community legal order does, however, form a more acceptable means for obtaining justice than is usually the case outside such an order in the weakly organised or unorganised society of states. In the first place, the Court will already have objectively established the infringement of the Treaty, so that the parties' subjective opinion about the facts no longer plays a part in the conflict. Moreover, the Court will also be in a position to examine the justice of the measures taken, in so far as they set aside EC law, and to ascertain whether they comply with the requirement of international law that the damage inflicted must bear a reasonable relation to the damage caused by the unlawful act of the other party (proportionality requirement). Indeed, as a Member State, the other party is entitled to lodge a complaint with the Court about alleged infringements of the Treaty due to reprisals of the Council, the Commission[216] or other Member States.[217]

The transfer of powers from the Member States to the Community is of an irreversible nature.[218] Given that the Member States agreed to establish a Community of unlimited duration, having permanent institutions invested with real powers, stemming from a limitation of authority or transfer of powers from the states to that Community, the powers 'thus conferred could not, therefore, be withdrawn from the Community, nor could the objectives with which such powers are concerned be restored to the field of authority of the Member States alone, except by virtue of an express provision of the Treaty.'[219] Thus it cannot be argued that a Treaty provision has lapsed if the Council fails to implement it. The Community does not lose its power; the Member States do not obtain the freedom to act at will in the field in question even if the Council is in default.[220]

mentioned in the new Art. F(1) TEU (liberty, democracy, respect for human rights and fundamental freedoms, and the rule of law) has been determined by the Council meeting in the composition of the Heads of State or Government. By virtue of the new Art. 236 EC (also so introduced) certain of the rights of the Member State concerned may also then be suspended. However, this does not authorise unilateral action by a Member State on its own. It will be a political determination (after the government of the Member State in question has been invited to submit its observations).

216. Under Arts. 173 EC, 33 ECSC, 146 Euratom, or under the special procedure of Art. 88 ECSC, 4th para.
217. Under Arts. 170 EC or 142 Euratom.
218. Case 7/71 *Commission v. France* [1971] ECR 1003 at 1018. See Mortelmans (1981) CDE 410 at 430–431 and Usher, *European Community Law and National Law: The Irreversible Transfer?* (London, 1981).
219. Case 7/71, *ibid.*
220. *Ibid.* See also Case 32/79 *Commission v. United Kingdom* [1980] ECR 2403 at 2434; Case 804/79 *Commission v. United Kingdom* [1981] ECR 1045 at 1073 and Cases 47 and 48/83 *Pluimveeslachterij Midden-Nederland BV et al.* [1984] ECR 1721 at 1738. See also Chapter III, section 5.2, *post.*

Community solidarity is one of the fundamental principles of the Treaty and, in accordance with the obligations under Article 5 EC, lies at the very foundation of the whole Community system.[221] If a Member State unilaterally breaks, according to its own conception of national interest, the equilibrium between advantages and obligations flowing from Community membership it infringes its duty of solidarity and thus strikes at the fundamental basis of the Community legal order.[222]

3.3   Effect of Community law in the internal legal sphere

In the view of the Court the traditional freedom of the state to decide for itself in what way it is going to comply with treaty obligations within its national legal order, provided it does fulfil them, has also been abolished by the Community legal order. Indeed, it is assumed fairly generally that international law does not require either that international rules of law should be applied directly and as such within the national legal order, or that these rules should take priority over national law within this legal order. The method followed in (the old) Articles 65, 66 and 67(2) of the Dutch Constitution[223] is not therefore prescribed imperatively by international law.

The view still prevalent particularly in Germany and in Italy, that according to constitutional law, written rules of international law can be applied within the domestic legal order only after their transformation into national rules, cannot therefore be deemed to conflict with general international law. In these countries the view is held that the transformation of the rules laid down in or under a treaty takes place in and by the act approving the treaty or authorising its ratification. The rules which are laid down under a treaty by international bodies created in this context[224] are generally assumed to be transformed into internal law by anticipation in the parliamentary act of approval. The transformation, in and by this national act, of rules laid down in the treaty and its implementing decisions leads to these rules obtaining the same force of law as this act itself has. In consequence, if there is a conflict between the rules transformed into national law and a later national law adopted by parliament, the latter will take priority on the basis of the adage *lex posterior derogat priori*.

---

221. Case 6 and 11/69 *Commission. v. France* [1969] ECR 523 at 540. See also Case 39/72 *Commission v. Italy* [1973] ECR 101 at 116; Case 128/78 *Commission v. United Kingdom* [1979] ECR 419 at 429. See, further, Chapter III, section 5.2, *post*.
222. Case 39/72 *Commission v. Italy* [1973] ECR 101 at 116; Case 128/78 *Commission v. United Kingdom* [1979] ECR 419 at 429.
223. See Van Dijk (1968–1969) 6 CMLRev. 283. See now Arts. 93–95 of the Dutch Constitution.
224. *Cf.* the regulatory powers conferred by Art. 189 EC.

This consequence of the transformation doctrine does not in itself conflict with general international law, although naturally the state can be fully called to account for a resultant infringement of its treaty obligations before an international forum and cannot evade its international liability by relying on its consitutional law ('a State cannot adduce as against another State its own Constitution with a view to evading obligations incumbent upon it under international law or treaties in force').[225] It should be noted that even in EC countries, such as France,[226] in which the transformation doctrine is not held, there is some doubt as to whether on the strength of constitutional law a national court can refuse to apply a national law of a later date in so far as it conflicts with written international law of an earlier date. In the United Kingdom treaty-making power is a prerogative of the Crown; it is thus beyond challenge in the courts.[227] Treaties have no effect on existing domestic law, such an effect can only be achieved through legislation (which alone can affect private rights).[228] From the point of view of the United Kingdom, if Parliament were to enact legislation inconsistent with a prior treaty obligation the courts would traditionally give effect to the legislation.[229]

The Court of Justice, however, on the basis of the Community legal order takes a quite different position from the current conception of international law, a conception which leaves the regulation of the internal effect of rules of international law to constitutional law. The case-law of the Court shows that Treaty provisions[230] (and sometimes even provisions

225. *Cf.* the Permanent Court of International Justice Advisory Opinion *Treatment of Polish nationals ... in the Danzig territory* Series A/B, No. 44, (1932); *c.f.* Vienna Convention on the Law of Treaties (1969), Art. 27.

226. The French Conseil d'Etat has now ceased to maintain its earlier negative attitude, see *Nicolo* [1990] 1 CMLR 173, noted by Manin (1991) 28 CMLRev. 499 and Kapteyn (1991) SEW 594. The doubt which previously existed in Belgium has been extinguished since the Cour de Cassation's judgment of 29 May 1971 in *Minister of Economic Affairs v. SA Fromagerie Franco–Suisse 'Le Ski'* [1972] 2 CMLR 330.

227. *E.g. Walker v. Bird* [1982] AC 491; *Buttes Gas and Oil Co. v. Hammer (Nos. 2 and 3)* [1982] AC 888 at 930; *Blackburn v. Attorney-General* [1971] 2 All ER 1380 at 1382 and 1383. See also *R. v. Secretary of State for Foreign and Commonwealth Affairs, ex parte Rees-Mogg* [1994] QB 552, [1994] 2 WLR 115, [1994] 1 All ER 457, [1993] 3 CMLR 101. The general position on treaties and the royal prerogative is well restated by Lord Oliver in *J.H. Rayner (Mincing Lane) Ltd. v. Department of Trade and Industry* [1989] 3 WLR 969 at 1002, [1989] 3 All ER 523 at 544–545. See also the attempt to fetter the Crown's power to make treaties in the European Parliament Elections Act 1978, s. 6(1) (15 *Halsbury's Statutes* 463).

228. *E.g. Attorney-General for Canada v. Attorney-General for Ontario* [1937] AC 326 at 347–348 (*per* Lord Atkin) and *British Airways Board v. Laker Airways Ltd.* [1984] QB 142 at 191.

229. This must be subject to the rule of construction in s. 2(4) of the European Communities Act 1972, explained in the text, *post*.

230. *E.g.* Case 26/62 *Van Gend en Loos* [1963] ECR I at 12–13 and (in the formulation given in the text) Case 28/67 *Firma Molkerei-Zentrale Westfalen Lippe GmbH v. Hauptzollamt Paderborn* [1968] ECR 143 at 152–154.

of decisions or directives addressed to Member States)[231] penetrate into the internal legal order without the aid of any national measure, to the extent that their character makes this appropriate. In other words, provisions of Community law may be directly applicable, they may produce direct effects. Provisions of Community law which impose clear and precise unconditional obligations and leave the Community Institutions and the Member States no discretionary freedom in their application or implementation will be directly effective in that the national courts can apply them, without stepping into the shoes of the legislature.[232] Such provisions, like regulations (which are by nature and function in the system of Community sources of law directly applicable),[233] must be applied by the national courts without the intervention of a legal measure designed to transpose Community law (as a whole or in respect of particular provisions) into domestic law.

The Court has made it clear that the fundamental principles and objectives of the Treaty demonstrate that 'the Community constitutes a new legal order, for the benefit of which the states have limited their sovereign rights, albeit within limited fields, and the subjects of which comprise not only the Member States but also their nationals'.[234] Community law has effect independently of the legislation of the Member States.[235] Thus there can be no question of the transformation doctrine applying in the field of Community law; the latter applies as such in the internal legal order of the Member States. In the United Kingdom the vehicle of the European Communities Act 1972 ensures that Community law is given effect through the combined operation of sections 2 and 3 of the Act; the Act is the means by which the concepts of the Community legal order are brought into the United Kingdom's system; the Community nature of those concepts remains clear and the method by which Community law is given effect in the United Kingdom is wholly orthodox.[236]

In its approach to the Community legal order the Court of Justice has

---

231. *E.g.* Case 9/70 *Grad v. Finanzamt Traunstein* [1970] ECR 825 at 837, Case 33/70 *SpA SACE v. Ministry for Finance of the Italian Republic* [1970] ECR 1213 at 1222–1223 and Case 41/74 *Van Duyn v. Home Office* [1974] ECR 1337 at 1348. see, further, Chapter VI, section 2.2.2, *post.*
232. See further, Chapter VI, section 2.2.1, *post.*
233. *E.g.* Case 43/71 *Politi S.A.S. v. Ministry for Finance of the Italian Republic* [1971] ECR 1039 at 1048–1049.
234. Case 28/67 *Firma Molkerei-Zentrale Westfalen Lippe GmbH v. Hauptzollamt Paderborn* [1968] ECR 143 at 152.
235. *Ibid.*
236. Collins, *European Community Law in the United Kingdom* (4th ed., London, 1984) 23. See, generally, Usher in 51 *Halsbury's Laws of England* (4th ed., London, 1986) paras. 3.01–3.05, 3.14 and 3.26–3.40, revised by Usher in Vaughan (ed.), *Law of the European Communities Service* (London, loose-leaf from 1990) Vol. 1, paras. 1–4 and 10–42.

clearly rejected the most important consequence of the transformation doctrine. Community provisions which are directly effective take priority over provisions of national law even when the latter are contained in subsequent statutes or even in a national constitution.[237] In its judgment in Case 6/64 *Costa v. ENEL*[238] the Court demonstrated that the essence of the common market stands or falls by ensuring a uniform effect of the relevant rules of Community law in every Member State. No domestic rule can be adduced before a national court against the law created by the Treaty (which springs from an original and autonomous source) lest the latter lose its Community character and the legal basis of the Community itself be impaired.[239] It may thus be concluded that the obligation to give priority in the internal legal sphere to Community law is a rule without which the rules forming the core of Community law would lose their significance or could not find any reasonable and useful application. This is an application of the 'principle of effectiveness' or *'effet utile'* in the interpretation of Community law. It is on this line of reasoning that the Court clearly based itself in a later judgment in stating that the EC Treaty had 'established its own system of law, integrated into the legal systems of the Member States, and which must be applied by their courts. It would be contrary to the nature of such a system to allow Member States to introduce or to retain measures capable of prejudicing the practical effectiveness of the Treaty. The binding force of the Treaty and of measures taken in application of it must not differ from one state to another as a result of internal measures, lest the functioning of the Community system should be impeded and the achievement of the aims of the Treaty placed in peril.'[240] Later in its celebrated judgment in *Simmenthal*[241] the Court put it thus: 'any recognition that national legislative measures which encroach upon the field within which the Community exercises its legislative power or which are otherwise incompatible with the provisions of Community law had any legal effect would amount to a corresponding denial of the effectiveness of obligations undertaken unconditionally and irrevocably by Member States pursuant to the Treaty and would thus imperil the very foundations of the Community.' The same principle was applied in the ruling on the reference from the House of Lords in *Factortame*,[242] so that the rule of English law that injunctions will not issue against the Crown could not

237. Case 11/70 *Internationale Handelsgesellschaft mbH v. Einfuhr- und Vorratsstelle für Getreide und Futtermittel* [1970] ECR 1125 at 1134.
238. [1964] ECR 585 at 594.
239. *Ibid.*
240. Case 14/68 *Wilhelm et al. v. Bundeskartellamt* [1969] ECR 1 at 14.
241. Case 106/77 *Amministrazione delle Finanze dello Stato v. Simmenthal SpA* [1978] ECR 629 at 643.
242. Case C-213/89 *R. v. Secretary of State for Transport, ex parte Factortame Ltd. et al.* [1990] ECR I-2433 at 2474.

be invoked to prevent the grant of interim relief by way of the disapplication of contested provisions of an Act of Parliament pending the outcome of the action.

It falls outside the jurisdiction of the Court of Justice to decree that the national court must assign internal effect and supremacy to rules of Community law within the national sphere of law in the face of national constitutional law as this law is interpreted in the national case-law. The Court can only pronounce on the effect which Community rules ought to have according to Community law within the domestic legal order. However, in its judgments, particularly in that in Case 6/64 *Costa v. ENEL*,[243] it made an attempt to lay the foundation for a theory which might enable a national court to take a different view of the effect of Community law from that which it thinks necessary on the basis of its constitutional law in the case of ordinary rules of international law. As the Court states, the Member States have limited their sovereign rights, though in a restricted area, in favour of the new Community legal order. The final limitation of their sovereign rights results from the transfer of the rights and duties corresponding to the Treaty provisions from the national legal order into the legal order of the Community. They are 'siphoned off' from the national legal order into the Community legal order.[244] Indeed, the duty of the national judge has now been clearly defined by the Court: 'every national court must, in a case within its jurisdiction apply Community law in its entirety and protect rights which the latter confers on individuals and must accordingly set aside any provision of national law which may conflict with it, whether prior or subsequent to the Community rule.'[245] It is thus unnecessary for the national court to request or await the prior setting aside of such a provision by legislative or other constitutional means.[246] In the United Kingdom the European Communities Act 1972, section 2(4) provides, *inter alia*, that any enactment passed or to be passed is to be construed and have effect subject to the recognition of rights and obligations flowing from Community law contained in the Act and section 3(1) of the Act makes it clear that the national courts must follow the principles laid down by and the decisions of the Court of Justice. In the absence of any clear intention in a subsequent statute to repudiate the European Communities Act 1972 in whole or in part the courts in the United Kingdom will have no hesitation in giving effect to Community law over a subsequent United Kingdom enactment.[247]

243. [1964] ECR 585 at 594.
244. *Ibid.*
245. Case 106/77 *Simmenthal* [1978] ECR 629 at 644. See also Case 14/68 *Wilhelm et al. v. Bundeskartellamt* [1969] ECR 1 at 14.
246. Case 106/77 *Simmenthal*, *ibid.* See also Case C-213/89 *Factortame* [1990] ECR I-2433 at 2474.
247. *Macarthys Ltd. v. Smith* [1979] 3 All ER 325 at 329 (*per* Lord Denning, MR); Lasok

Rules of Community law, therefore, have internal effect without reference to the national legal order, *viz.* in the area which has been created in consequence of the limitation of national sovereignty. In other words, national constitutional law with regard to the internal effect and the internal order of priority to be given to rules of international law does not apply with reference to rules of Community law, because it can apply only within the limits of sovereignty. Beyond these limits, *i.e.* within the Community legal order, the national court, without being hampered by consitutional restrictions, may give to the rules of Community law the effect desired by the Court of Justice. If the national court comes across legal measures conflicting with Community law, it must refrain from applying them, as has been indicated above, not because they are of a lower order than Community law, but because in such a case the national legislator has acted *ultra vires.*[248]

In the light of the Court's view, in which the Community legal order supersedes a part of the national legal order, it is unnecessary as far as Community law in the Netherlands is concerned, to rely upon the provisions of Articles 93, 94 and 95 of the Constitution. The question of whether a national judge may follow the Court's view is, from his point of view, a question of constitutional law. As has been observed, in the United Kingdom the position is clear.[249]

Private parties may rely on the application of directly effective provisions of Community law in their national legal order. They can rely on such provisions in national courts even in cases in which national legal provisions conflict with Community law.[250] This effect of Community law exists not only in the interests of the legal protection of private parties. It also serves the good maintenance of Community law in general. The Court has described the result as being that the 'vigilance of individuals concerned to protect their rights amounts to an effective supervision in addition to the supervision entrusted by Articles 169 and 170 to the diligence of the Commission and of the Member States.'[251] In the words of Hart, citizens acting as one-man lobbies seeking clarification and correction of the law,[252] can contribute through their vigilance to the

in 51 *Halsbury's Laws* (see note 236, *supra*) para. 1.23. See Gormley (1986) 23 CMLRev. 287 at 307; Bridge (1978) Denning L.J. 23 at 31 *et seq.*, and Usher in Vaughan (ed.), *op. cit.* (see note 236, *supra*) para. 43.

248. *Cf.* Lagrange in *Droit communautaire et droit national* (Semaine de Bruges, 1965, Bruges 1965) 21 at 24: '*Il ne s'agit pas d'une primauté dans le sens d'une ˆhiérarchieゝ entre un droit communautaire prééminent et les droits nationaux subordonnés, mais d'une substitution du droit propre de la Communauté au droit national dans les domaines où les transferts de competence ont été opérés...*'.

249. For further observations on this point see Chapter VI, section 2.2.4, *post.*

250. See the discussion in Chapter VI, section 2, *post.*

251. Case 26/62 *Van Gend en Loos* [1963] ECR 1 at 13.

252. (1954) 54 Columbia L.Rev. 489 at 493 (quoting Hurst).

complete and uniform application of the fundamental principles of the common market.

The extent to which they can make such a contribution depends in part on what legal procedures are available to them in order to enforce their claims and on the conditions under which they can use those procedures. Can a person who considers that another party (whether an authority or a private party) is treating him in a manner incompatible with a directly effective provision of Community law (*e.g.* relating to damages or a prohibition of trading) require the repayment to him of sums paid but not due or the annulment or suspension of the relevant administrative decision? Which is the competent judicial body for seeking redress, the ordinary courts or an administrative tribunal? In the United Kingdom there have been instances of tribunals refusing to apply Community law, claiming that as creatures of statute alone they can only give the remedies envisaged in the statute.[253] However, it has now been long clearly accepted that Community law is to be applied by administrative tribunals as well as by the courts.[254] The Court of Justice has made it clear that while the principle of cooperation laid down in Article 5 EC means that 'it is the national courts which are entrusted with ensuring the legal protection which citizens derive from the direct effect of the provisions of Community law',[255] it is the national legal system which, in the absence of Community rules on this subject, designates the courts or tribunals having jurisdiction and determines the procedural conditions governing actions at law intended to ensure the protection of rights which citizens have from the direct effect of Community law.[256] The Community as a whole has no uniform provisions concerning the availability or form of national procedures, or the legal results to which they may lead.[257] Nevertheless, the Court has always stressed, though, that these conditions cannot be less favourable than those relating to similar actions of a domestic nature, nor may they render virtually impossible or excessively difficult the exercise of

253. *Amies v. I.L.E.A.* [1977] ICR 308, [1977] 2 All ER 100, [1977] 1 CMLR 336; *Charles Early and Mariott (Witney) Ltd.* [1977] 3 WLR 189; *Snoxell and Davies v. Vauxhall Motors Ltd* [1978] 1 QB 11, *Macarthys Ltd v. Smith* [1978] 1 WLR 849.

254. *E.g. Shields v. E. Coomes (Holdings) Ltd.* [1977] 1 All ER 456 at 461–462 (*per* Lord Denning, MR); *Macarthys Ltd v. Smith* [1979] 3 CMLR 44 at 46; *Worringham and Humpherys v. Lloyds Bank Ltd.* [1980] 1 CMLR 293 at 300 and 308, and *Handley v. Mono Ltd.* [1979] ICR 47; see Gormley (1986) 23 CMLRev. 287 at 304.

255. Case 33/76 *Rewe Zentralfinanz eG et al. v. Landwirtschaftskammer für das Saarland* [1976] ECR 1989 at 1997; see also Case 45/76 *Comet BV v. Produktschap voor Sierge-wassen* [1976] ECR 2043 at 2053.

256. *Ibid.* and Case 13/68 *SpA Salgoil v. Italian Ministry for Foreign Trade* [1968] ECR 453 at 463.

257. See *e.g.* Case C-312/93 *Peterbroeck, Van Campenhout & Cie SCS v. Belgian State* [1995] ECR I-4599 at 4620–4621 and Cases C-430 and 431/93 *Van Schijndel et al. v. Stichting Pensioenfonds voor Fysiotherapeuten* [1995] ECR I-4705 at 4737 (reciting many earlier authorities).

rights conferred by Community law.[258] The important case-law on this subject which is still in the full thrust of development has had a certain harmonising effect on national procedural law.[259]

4.   SCOPE AND REVISION OF THE TREATY

4.1   Territorial scope of application, the Association system of Part IV of the EC Treaty, and Accession to the European Union

As to the territorial scope of application, Article 227(1) EC provides that the EC Treaty applies to the Contracting Parties mentioned there. Under general rules of international law it is clear that the Treaty is binding in relation to all the territory, including the non-European parts[260] falling under the sovereignty of the Parties,[261] at least in so far as the Treaty does not provide for exceptions or otherwise make special provision. An exception was made for the Netherlands by a Protocol to the EC Treaty (which the Dutch used at first) allowing ratification of the Treaty, notwithstanding Article 227, only in respect of its European territory and for what was then Dutch New Guinea (thus excluding Surinam and the Netherlands Antilles). Since 3 October 1990, the day of German unification, the Treaties have applied without more ado to the new *Länder* in Germany.[262]

Under Article 227(5) EC the Treaty does not apply to the Faroe Islands or to the Sovereign Base Areas of the United Kingdom in Cyprus.[263] Special rules are provided for the status of the Channel Islands and the Isle of Man.[264] Community law applies to the Canary Islands, Ceuta and Melilla, albeit with certain exceptions.[265] Given that Finland has deposited

---

258. See note 255, *supra* and *e.g.* Case 199/82 *Amministrazione delle Finanze dello Stato v. SpA San Giorgio* [1983] ECR 3595 at 3612.
259. See Chapter VI, section 2.3.2, *post*, and, generally Hartkamp (ed.), *Towards a European Civil Code* (2nd ed., The Hague, 1998).
260. The ECSC Treaty applies only to the European territories (Art. 79 ECSC), the Euratom Treaty on the other hand also applies to the non-European territories subject to the jurisdiction of the Member States (Art. 198 Euratom).
261. The territorial sea of the Member States of course is also covered by the Treaty, as being a part of their territory.
262. As to the package of transitional measures agreed in certain fields, see O.J. 1990 L 353.
263. Art. 227(5)(a) and (b) respectively.
264. Art. 227(5)(c) EC. See Act of Accession (1972), Protocol No. 3. See also WQ 1408/85 (Collins) O.J. 1986 C48/15–16.
265. See Act of Spanish and Portuguese Accession (1985), Arts. 25, 155 and Protocol No. 2. The Treaty of Amsterdam (not yet in force) will amend Article 227(2) EC so as to bring *inter alia* the Azores, Maderira and the Canary Islands fully within the scope of the EC Treaty, albeit that special provisions may be made relating those areas, placing them on a similar footing as the French overseas departments, see, further, Schröder

a declaration under Article 227(5)(d) EC, the Treaties also apply to the Åland Islands.[266] By virtue of Article 227(4) EC, the Treaty applies to the European territories for whose external relations a Member State is responsible: this now in fact only concerns Gibraltar, which is excluded from the scope of very significant parts of Community law, particularly secondary legislation relating to the common agricultural policy and the harmonisation of indirect taxation.[267] Gibraltar is also excluded from the customs territory of the Community.[268] While Monaco is part of the customs territory of the Community,[269] San Marino is now not.[270] They are both, like the Vatican City outside the scope of the EC Treaty.[271] Andorra is no longer a European territory covered by Article 227(4) EC.[272]

For non-European territories over which the contracting parties exercise sovereignty special rules are laid out in Articles 227(2) and (3) EC. Until 1960 only the general and the special rules specified in Article 227(2) EC applied to the French overseas departments. The Council has discretion, acting on a proposal from the Commission, to determine the conditions for the application of the other provisions of the Treaty to such departments.[273]

in Von der Groeben et al. (eds.), op. cit. (see note 63, supra) Vol. 5, 472–474. See also e.g. Decs. 91/315 (O.J. 1991 L 171/10) and 92/315 (O.J. 1992 L 248/74) on the Poseima programme for the Azores and Madeira. Cueta and Melilla are not part of the customs territory of the Community (Reg. 2913/92, Art. 3(1) (O.J. 1992 L 302/1, as amended).

266. See Act of Accession (1994), Protocol No. 2.
267. Act of Accession (1972), Art. 28. See Romeo and Smulders (1993) 13 YBEL 361.
268. Ibid., Annex I.1.4. See, generally, WQs. 1823–1825/84 (Ford, Lomas & Megahy) O.J. 1988 C 341/1; 2109/86 (Ford) O.J. 1987 C 112/45, and 566/87 (Caamano Bernal) O.J. 1987 C 331/30.
269. Reg. 2913/92, Art. 3(2) (O.J. 1992 L 302/1), as amended (by Reg. 82/97 (O.J. 1997 L 17/1).
270. By virtue of the amendment, ibid., in view of the Interim Agreement of 27 November 1992 (O.J. 1992 L 359/14). A customs union between the Community and San Marino has been proposed, COM (97) 8 Final (O.J. 1997 C 124/1).
271. See e.g. Cerhexe: Droit Européen, la libre circulation des personnes el des enterprises (Brussels, 1982) 37; also, impliedly, Thiesing in Von der Groeben et. al., Kommentar zum EWG-Vertrag (3rd ed., Baden-Baden 1983) Vol. 2, 1079, and Schröder in Von der Groeben et al. (eds.), op. cit. (see note 63, supra) Vol. 5, 455–456.
272. Since the entry into force of the Constitution of 4 May 1993. This change in status has clearly been accepted by France and Spain (see the Traité de bon voisinage, d'amité et de coopération between Andorra, France and Spain, reproduced in (1994) Rev. Gen. Dr. Int. Pub. 524).
273. Guadeloupe, French Guyana, Martinique, Reunion and (since 1976) Saint-Pierre and Miquelon (see WQ 400/76 (Lagorce) O.J. 1976 C 294/16). As to the EC system and these departments see Case 148/77 H. Hansen jun. & O. C. Balle GmbH & Co. v. Hauptzollamt Flensburg [1978] ECR 1787 at 1804–1805; Case C-163/90 Administration des douanes et des droits indirects v. Legros et al. [1990] ECR I-4625; Cases C-363/93 etc. René Lancry SA et al. v. Direction Générale des Douanes et al. [1994] ECR I-3978, and Case C-212/96 Chevassus-Marche v. Conseil Régional de la Réunion [1998] ECR I-nyr (19 February 1998). See also WQ 1839/84 (Poniatowski) O.J. 1985 C 263/1–3. The

Article 227(3) EC deals with the other non-European territories falling under other sovereignty of one of the Member States at the time of the conclusion of the Treaty or at the time of accession (the so-called overseas countries and territories (OCT)) listed in Annex IV to the Treaty and provides that only Part IV of the Treaty applies to them.[274] Part IV of the Treaty and implementing provisions[275] provide for an association arrangement in the field of commercial policy and finances for the benefit of the non-European countries and territories which have special relations with Belgium, Denmark,[276] France, Italy, the Netherlands and the United Kingdom.[277]

The applicability of Part IV of the EC Treaty to 18 associated overseas countries and territories in Africa and Madagascar came to an end – at least formally, for the arrangement was continued for the time being –

overseas territories, Saint Pierre and Miquelon and Mayotte do not form part of the customs territory of the Community, Reg. 2913/92, Art. 3(1) (O.J. 1992 L 302/1, as amended). The Treaty of Amsterdam (not yet in force) will revise Article 227(2) so as to make Community law clearly fully applicable there, although special arrangements may be made.

274. See Cases C-100 and 101/89 *Kaefer et al. v. French State* [1990] ECR I-4647, and Case C-260/90 *Leplat v. Territory of French Polynesia* [1994] ECR I-643. See, generally, Declaration No. 25 on the representation of the interests of the OCT, adopted on the signature of the Final Act of the Intergovernmental Conferences at Maastricht on 7 February 1992 (TEU Final Act). The Treaty of Amsterdam (not yet in force) sets out an updated list of Annex IV countries.

275. See Art. 136 EC, 2nd para. and, most recently, Dec. 91/482 (O.J. 1991 L 263/1, most recently amended by Dec. 97/803 (O.J. 1997 L 329/50)). Dec. 91/482 applies until 29 February 2000. See also Case C-430/92 *Netherlands v. Commission* [1994] ECR I-5197; Cases T-480 and 483/93 *Antillean Rice Mills NV et al. v. Commission* [1995] ECR II-2305; Case C-310/95 *Road Air BV v. Inspecteur der Invoerrechten en Accijnzen* [1997] ECR I-2229; Case C-110/97 R *The Netherlands v. Council* [1997] ECR I-1795; Case T-179/97 R *Government of the Netherlands Antilles v. Council* [1997] ECR II-1297; Case C-106/97 *Dutch Antilles Dairy Industry Inc. v. Rijksdienst voor keuringen van Vee en Vlees* (pending, O.J. 1997 C 142/12); Case C-301/97 *The Netherlands v. Council* (pending, O.J. 1997 C 318/8); Case T-310/97 R *Government of the Netherlands Antilles v. Council* [1998] ECR II-nyr (2 March 1998), and Case C-380/97 *Emesa Sugar (Free Zone) NV v. The Netherlands et al.* (pending, O.J. 1997 C 387/12).

276. Since 1 February 1985 (Treaty on Greenland, O.J. 1985 L 29/1). See Art. 136a EC and the Protocol on Special Arrangements for Greenland annexed to the EC Treaty; see Harhoff (1983) 20 CMLRev. 13 and Weiss (1985) 10 ELRev. 173.

277. Since 1 January 1973 (Art. 131 EC) as a result of the Act of Accession (1972), Art. 24(2) (as modified by the Adaption Decision (O.J. 1973 L 2/1). Association status applies to the Netherlands Antilles and to Aruba (which seceded from the former on 1 January 1986), see Dec. 91/482 (O.J. 1991 L 263/1, as amended) on the basis of an Agreement of 13 November 1962 between the then six Member States amending the Treaty; this came into force on 1 October 1964 (J.O. 2414/64). A supplementary enabling act would not suffice for this purpose (unlike in the case of Surinam) as the other Member States required certain guarantees relating to the importation into the Community of petroleum products refined in the Netherlands Antilles (this was done by adding a Protocol to the EC Treaty, see *ibid.*). Surinam is now a party to the Lomé Convention since its independence on 16 June 1974.

when in the years immediately succeeding the date of the conclusion of the Treaty (1958–1962) these countries gained their independence. Actually, according to Article 227 EC the legal basis of the application of the Treaty, in this case Part IV, to these countries was the fact that, at the date of signature, they formed part of the territory over which the Contracting Parties exercised sovereignty. The moment these countries were freed from the sovereignty of the Member States this basis (strictly speaking) ceased to exist. It has never been explicitly decided whether, on the strength of the rather vague doctrine of the succession of states, they could nevertheless claim certain rights to the continuation of the treaty regime established on their behalf before their independence.

In any event, the old association Implementing Convention entered into under Article 136 EEC was replaced after 1 July 1964 by the two successive Yaoundé Conventions. After 1 April 1976 this system was replaced by the Lomé Conventions, the fourth of which, signed on 15 December 1989, entered into force on 1 September 1991.[278] These Conventions embrace far more countries than those listed in Annex IV to the EC Treaty, covering the so-called ACP States (the African, Caribbean and Pacific States). Even though the Conventions do not speak of an 'association' they were concluded by the Community on the basis of Article 238 EC.[279] It should not be deduced from the wording of Article 227 EC that the sphere of application of the EC Treaty is restricted to territory falling under the sovereignty (*i.e.* complete jurisdiction) of a Member State.[280] The sphere of application can stretch beyond such territory in so far as a Member State exercises sovereign rights *(i.e.* a functionally limited jurisdiction) under general international law, *e.g.* in relation to the continental shelf,[281] fishing zones[282] and perhaps in the future exclusive economic zones. This is,

278. O.J. 1991 L 229/1. As to the predecessor regime, see Simmonds (1985) 22 CMLRev. 389.
279. Preamble to the Lomé Conventions.
280. The customs territory of the Community is not precisely the same as the territory of the Member States, see Reg. 2913/92, Art. 3 (O.J. 1992 L 302/1, most recently amended by Reg. 82/97 (O.J. 1997 L 17/1)).
281. The Commission is of the view that the Treaty applies to the continental shelf, see its Memorandum of September 1970, SEC (70) 3095 Final, and WQ 489/73 (O'Hagan) O.J. 1974 C 49/3. See also the settlement of the complaint about the Ninth round of offshore licensing, Commission Press Release IP(85) 303, *Financial Times*, 8 July 1985, p. 2. The Community Customs Code, Reg. 2913/92 (O.J. 1992 L 302/1, as amended), Art. 23(2)(h) includes in the definition of goods originating in a country (thus in a Member State in the case of export from the Community) 'products taken from the seabed or subsoil beneath the seabed outside territorial waters, if that country has exclusive rights to exploit that seabed or subsoil.'
282. Since 1 January 1977 the Member States in the North-East Atlantic and the North Sea have extended their fishing zones to 200 miles from their coast. See Reg. 101/76 (O.J. 1976 L 20/9) establishing a common fisheries policy (particularly Arts. 2 and 4 on the substantive scope). See also Cases 3, 4 and 6/76 *Kramer et al.* [1976] ECR 1279 at 1309. Regulations apply in principle to the same geographical area as the Treaty itself, Case 61/77 *Commission v. Ireland* [1978] ECR 417 at 446.

naturally, provided that the matter over which this functional jurisdiction extends falls within the substantive scope of the relevant provisions of the Treaty and that they do not contain any restriction of the ambit of their application to the territory of the Member States.[283]

Just as the SEA was silent as to the territorial scope of European Political Cooperation, so too the TEU is silent about the territorial scope of supplementary policies and forms of cooperation, CFSP and JHA. This is in fact unsurprising, as the interests covered by CFSP and JHA are not logically geographically limited: the interests of the Union may be affected by developments all over the world, not just in the obvious areas of commercial and economic relations, but also in general foreign and security policy terms and in relation to various aspects of cooperation in JHA. The very least, however, is that Article 227 EC applies by analogy.[284]

Accession to the European Union

The territorial scope of application of the Treaties may be enlarged by accession of states to the Union, and thereby to the Communities.[285] As new Member States accede to the Union as a whole, it is not possible for them to accede to the Communities alone or to only one or more of the supplementary policies and forms of cooperation. An application for accession will only be entertained if it is made by a European state. This application must be addressed to the Council, which, after obtaining the opinion of the Commission, and having received the Assent of the European Parliament,[286] takes a decision on it by a unanimous vote. As may be inferred from the context of these provisions, this decision concerns the question of whether the applicant state is acceptable as a member. Before the Council can take a decision, the conditions of admission and the resultant adjustments to the Treaties forming the subject of an agreement have to be negotiated between the fifteen

283. See Koers (1977) SEW 191. On the more general question of the extraterritorial application of Community law see Slot and Grabandt (1986) 23 CMLRev. 544 and Meng in Von der Groeben et al. (eds.), op. cit. (see note 63, supra) Vol. 5, 1207 and literature cited there.
284. Declaration No. 25 on the representation of the interests of the OCT, adopted on the signature of the Final Act of the Intergovernmental Conferences at Maastricht on 7 February 1992 (TEU Final Act) would seem to indicate that such a view is appropriate.
285. The procedure is set out in Art. O TEU, see Meng in Von der Groeben et al. (eds.), op. cit. (see note 63, supra) Vol. 5, 1138. The Treaty of Amsterdam (not yet in force) substitutes a new Art. O TEU which makes it clear that respect for the principles set out in the new Art. F(1) TEU (as to which, see note 215 supra) is a precondition for application.
286. Which acts by an absolute majority of its component members, ibid.

Member States and the state applying for accession. This agreement has to be ratified by all the Contracting States in accordance with their respective constitutional requirements. The conditions of admission usually cover in particular the transitional measures which have to be taken in order that the gradual integration of the new Member State in the Union in the economic and legal fields may proceed as smoothly as possible. Adjustments to the Treaties (and implementing measures, if any) will be necessary, even if only on the composition of the Institutions, voting rules and budgetary contributions. It is striking that, as regards the stage in which negotiations are conducted about the conditions of admission and the adjustment to the Treaties, there is no specific reference to the Community Institutions participating, although participation, particularly by the Commission, is not excluded. Indeed such participation is to be expected as a matter of principle (the Communities are greater than the sum of the Member States) and for the practical reason of the Commission's expertise.

In practice, both for the accessions to the Communities previously, and for accession to the Union now (Austria, Finland and Sweden acceded to the *Union* in 1995), a Community procedure is followed. Negotiations are conducted by the Community as such according to a uniform procedure at all levels and on all matters. The Council decides on a common position of the Community on all matters which arise in the negotiations and the Commission is invited to make the necessary proposals. Discussions in the Council are prepared by *Coreper*. The President-in-office of the Council puts forward the common position in the negotiations and defends it. If the Council so decides, particularly in relation to matters covered by existing Community policies, this task can be devolved to the Commission. Moreover, the Commission is sometimes entrusted with the discussion of a solution to specific problems with the applicant states and then reports back to the Council. Initially the Commission was disappointed about its modest role in accession negotiations, but it is clear that it can play an important part in the preparation of the Community's common position and in seeking solutions with the applicant states to specific problems. The introduction of the requirement of the Assent of the European Parliament[287] means that the Parliament is tempted to seek the inclusion of other amendments to the Treaties in the relevant Act of Accession, as a condition of its Assent, even though its Assent is not actually a requirement for the amendment of the Treaties under Article N TEU.[288]

---

287. Originally introduced by Art. 8 SEA into Art. 237 EEC (repealed by Art. G(83) TEU and replaced by Art. O TEU).
288. Although it must be consulted before an intergovernmental conference is convened, Art. N(1) TEU, 2nd para.

4.2 Scope of application *ratione temporis*, revision

As was noted above,[289] the EC and Euratom Treaties were concluded for
an unlimited period[290] whereas the ECSC Treaty was concluded for a
period of fifty years.[291] The Treaty on European Union is also concluded
for an unlimited period.[292] Just as accession is now uniformly regulated, so
too amendment of the Treaties on which the Union is founded is uniformly
regulated in Article N(1) TEU. This accords a right of initiative not only to
the Member States, but also to the Commission to propose amendments.
If, after consulting the European Parliament, the Commission where
appropriate, and (in the case of institutional changes in the monetary area)
the European Central Bank, the Council delivers an opinion[293] in favour
of convening a conference of the representatives of the governments of the
Member States, the President-in-office of the Council convenes the
requisite conference. This aims to lay down by common accord the
amendments to be made to the Treaty. The amendments enter into force
after being ratified by the Member States in accordance with their
respective constitutional requirements. However, by virtue of Article N(2)
TEU the procedure prior to the convening of a conference does not apply
to the Intergovernmental Conference convened on 29 March 1996.[294]
Apart from this revision procedure, and the specific simplified amendment
procedure for certain provisions of the Statute of the European System of
Central Banks and the European Central Bank set out in Article 106(5)
EC,[295] only the ECSC Treaty also recognises the procedure of a so-called
'small revision' which requires no ratification of the amendments by the
Member States. Such a simplified procedure is in keeping with a treaty
having to such a marked degree the character of a *'traité-loi'*. Paragraphs 3
and 4 of Article 95 ECSC, however, lay down strict requirements on the
scope of revisions as well as on the necessary institutional co-operation. In
practice these requirements have been found difficult to fulfil. On two
occasions the Court, to whose judgment the amendments proposed by the
Commission and the Council have to be subjected, rejected them as

289. In section 2.1, *ante*.
290. Arts. 240 EC and 208 Euratom.
291. Art. 79 ECSC, expiring at midnight on 24 July 2002.
292. Art. Q TEU.
293. By a simple majority (no other majority being specified).
294. See section 1.2.2., *ante*.
295. And in the ESCB and ECB Statute, Art. 41. The Council may act either on a quali-
    fied majority on a recommendation from the ECB and after consulting the Commis-
    sion, or unanimously on a proposal from the Commission and after consulting the
    ECB. In either case the assent of the European Parliament is required. If the Council
    choses the first of these routes, the qualified majority required will be 62 votes in
    favour, cast by at least 10 members; if the second route is chosen, only the normal
    qualified majority (62 votes in favour) applies, see Art. 148(2) EC, and, further,
    Chapter V, section 3.2, *post*.

conflicting with these provisions in relation to the scope of the revision.[296] On one occasion the Court was of opinion that a proposal[297] satisfied the relevant requirements[298] so that it could enter into force after having been approved by the European Parliament by the majority vote provided for at the end of Article 95 ECSC.

Many international treaties contain provisions with respect to their revision. It is generally assumed that such provisions do not require that amendment of such treaties is only permitted in conformity with the procedures laid down therein. The Contracting Parties retain the right to amend (or to terminate) the treaty in the same way as they brought it about, viz. by a later treaty. Does this also apply to the Community Treaties? The Dutch government, (relying on a generally accepted rule of international law), answered this question in the affirmative during the debates in the Lower Chamber of the States General on the Act approving the Treaty of 27 October 1957, for the amendment of the ECSC Treaty.[299] The Lower Chamber did not share the standpoint of the government. It adopted a resolution submitted by Van der Goes van Naters, in which it opined that revision of the Community Treaties 'could only take place in accordance with the amendment procedures laid down in these Treaties themselves'.[300] For its part, the government declared that in practice it would abide by the opinion contained in this resolution.[301] This is a not unimportant statement, because for an amendment of the Treaties by means of a non-Community procedure the co-operation of the governments of all Member States is of course necessary. This statement on policy was also supported in the Chamber with legal arguments,[302] arguments which, in the light of the case-law of the Court referred to in section 3.1 of this Chapter, above, have even gained in strength. In fact, it appears highly questionable whether reliance on a universally recognised rule of international law, according to which, notwithstanding the prescribed revision procedures, a treaty can always be amended by a later treaty, also applies to treaties which have called into being a new legal order which limits the sovereignty of the Member States and is binding on them as well as on their nationals. Treaties, moreover, which have created an institutional structure in which an institution independent of the Member States (the Commission) takes part in the exercise of sovereign powers derived from the Member States and in which a parliamentary institution (the European Parliament) embodies the

---

296. Opinion 1/59 ECSC Amendment [1959] ECR 259 at 268–274; Opinion 1/61 ECSC Amendment [1961] ECR 243 at 252–263.
297. Addition of a second para. to Art. 56 ECSC (J.O. 781/60).
298. Opinion 1/60 ECSC Amendment [1960] ECR 39.
299. Annexes to Proceedings of the Tweede Kamer, 1956–1957, 4763.
300. Ibid. 1957–1958, 4763.
301. Proceedings of the Tweede Kamer, 1957–1958, pp. 1088–1092.
302. Cf. Van der Goes van Naters (1959) NTIR (special issue) 120 et seq.

collaboration of citizens in the operation of the Communities. It is precisely the consultation of these Institutions which is prescribed by the Treaties in case of revision. Thus it is scarcely surprising that in Case 43/75 *Defrenne v. SABENA*[303] the Court indicated that 'apart from any specific provisions, the Treaty can only be modified by means of the amendment procedure carried out in accordance with Article 236'. The Court also considers that, as regards respecting prescribed procedures, the Treaties cannot be interfered with by the Member States willy nilly. Thus, in relation to the first draft EEA Agreement, the Court set its face against an informal modification of the Treaty which threatened significant aspects of the Community legal order,[304] and in Opinion 2/94 *Accession of the Community to the European Convention on Human Rights*[305] it found that although respect for human rights was 'a condition for the lawfulness of Community acts', accession to the Convention would 'entail a substantial change in the present Community system for the protection of human rights in that it would entail the entry of the Community into a distinct international institutional system as well as the integration of all of the provisions of the Convention into the Community legal order.' 'Such a modification of the system for the prevention of human rights in the Community, with equally fundamental institutional obligations for the Community and for the Member States, would be of constitutional significance and would therefore go beyond the scope of Article 235 [EC]. It could be brought about only by way of Treaty amendment.'[306]

5.   LEGAL PERSONALITY, PRIVILEGES AND IMMUNITIES, SEAT OF THE INSTITUTIONS AND LINGUISTIC REGIME OF THE UNION AND THE COMMUNITIES

5.1 Legal personality

Although legal personality is not conferred on the Union, it is conferred on the Communities on which the Union is based. 'The Community shall have legal personality'.[307] This reflects the intention of the Contracting Parties to confer on each of the Communities the capacity to have rights and obligations. Whether, to what extent, and in what legal sphere this is

303. [1976] ECR 455 at 478. See also Deliège-Sequarais (1980) CDE 539 and Louis (1980) CDE 553.
304. Opinion 1/91 *EEA Agreement I* [1991] ECR I-6079 at 6102–6103; 6105; 6107 and 6109–6111.
305. [1996] ECR I-1759 at 1789.
306. *Ibid.*
307. Arts. 210 EC; 6 ECSC, 1st para., and 184 Euratom. See Weber (1985) EuR 1 and Tomuschat in Von der Groeben *et al.* (eds.), *op. cit.* (see note 63, *supra*) Vol. 5, 17.

actually the case, is a question which has to be answered by reference to what the three Treaty provisions contain about the activities of the Communities in legal relationships. A clear distinction must be made in this context between the legal personality in the sphere of international law and the legal personality in the sphere of national law.

The private law legal personality of the Communities in the sphere of national law is established in the provision[308] that in each of the Member States they shall enjoy the most extensive legal capacity accorded to legal persons under their laws. They may, in particular, acquire or dispose of movable and immovable property and may be parties to legal proceedings. For this purpose the Commission is to represent the EC and Euratom. The latter addition does not occur in the ECSC Treaty. In that Treaty, therefore, the general clause applies according to which the ECSC is represented by its Institutions, each within the limits of its powers.[309] Finally, it should be noted that not only the Communities themselves, but also, for example, the European Central Bank;[310] the European Investment Bank,[311] and the Euratom Supply Agency[312] possess legal personality in the national law of the Member States.

International legal personality, however, is enjoyed principally by the Communities as such, although in practice the international legal personality of the European Investment Bank is also accepted.[313] The ECSC Treaty explicitly confers on the Community, in its international relationships, the legal capacity necessary to perorm its functions and to attain its objectives.[314] This is a formulation reminiscent of that by which the International Court of Justice described the international legal personality of the United Nations: '[w]hereas a State possesses the totality of international rights and duties recognised by international law, the rights and duties of an entity such as the Organisation must depend upon its purposes and functions.'[315] No provision like the one just referred to is to be found in the EC and Euratom Treaties. The latter confine themselves to merely developing the general clause concerning the legal personality of the Communities, occurring in all three Treaties, in so far as the legal

308. Arts. 211 EC; 6 ECSC, 3rd para., and 185 Euratom.
309. Art. 6 ECSC, 4th para.
310. Art. 106(2) EC; Protocol on the Statute of the ECSB and ECB, Art. 9.1. See Gormley and De Haan (1996) 21 ELRev. 95. The same applies in respect of the European Monetary Institute (the forerunner of the future ECB), Art. 109f(1) EC, Protocol on the EMI, Art. 14.
311. Art. 198d EC, 1st para.; Protocol on the EIB, Art. 28.
312. Art. 54 Euratom, 1st para.
313. In the Agreement establishing the European Bank for Reconstruction and Development (EBRD) the EIB was a party, alongside the EC and its Member States (O.J. 1990 L 372/4, see Dec. 90/674 (O.J. 1990 L 372/1)).
314. Art. 2 ECSC, 2nd para. See, generally, Groux and Manin, *The European Communities in the International Legal Order* (European Perspectives, Brussels, Luxembourg, 1985).
315. *Reparations for Injuries* Case [1949] ICJ Rep. 174 at 180.

personality in the national law of Member States is concerned. Nevertheless it is generally assumed that the Contracting Parties meant to confer an international 'functional personality' also on the EC and Euratom.[316]

The intention to confer international personality is substantiated by the Treaty provisions which envisage Community action in international legal relationships within the field of its functions and objectives. Curiously enough, it is precisely the ECSC Treaty, which sets forth its legal capacity in international relationships so elegantly in a general clause, which contains fewest provisions explicitly conferring on this Community its attribute *par excellence,* the power to conclude international agreements.[317] This is because the ECSC is not a customs union and the powers in the field of the commercial policy are reserved in principle to the Member States.[318] In the two other Treaties, on the other hand, many provisions are found which relate to the power of the Communities to conclude international agreements. The EC has power to conclude tariff and commercial agreements;[319] agreements in the field of monetary policy;[320] cooperation agreements in the field of research, technological development and demonstration;[321] agreements in the environmental field,[322] and development cooperation agreements.[323] In the Euratom Treaty, Chapter X is devoted to 'external relations', the Community being accorded, within the limits of its powers and jurisdictions, the general power to conclude agreements or contracts with a third state or an international organization (or a national of a third state).[324] In addition, both the EC and Euratom Treaties contain a series of provisions on the establishment and maintenance of relations with other international organizations[325] and on the conclusion of association agreements with a third state, a union of states, or an international organization.[326]

Initially it was generally assumed that the Community possessed treaty-

---

316. *Cf.* Case 6/64 *Costa v. ENEL* [1964] ECR 585 at 593 in which the Court spoke of the 'personality' and 'legal capacity' of the Community. This was confirmed in the ERTA/AETR judgment, Case 22/70 *Commission v. Council* [1971] ECR 263 at 274, in which the Court indicated that Art. 210 EC 'means that in its external relations the Community enjoys the capacity to establish contractual links with third countries over the whole field of objectives defined in Part One of the Treaty...'.

317. Arts. 52, 2nd para.; 93, and Art. 94 ECSC in conjunction with the Protocol on relations with the Council of Europe, Art. 6.

318. Art. 71 ECSC, 1st para.

319. Art. 113(3) EC.

320. Art. 109 EC.

321. Art. 130m EC.

322. Art. 130r(4) EC.

323. Art. 130y EC.

324. Art. 101 Euratom, 1st para.

325. Arts. 229–231 EC and 199–201 Euratom.

326. Arts. 238 EC and 206 Euratom.

making power only in those cases in which it was expressly conferred. Since the judgment in Case 22/70 *Commission v. Council*[327] which was of immense importance for the development of the Community's external powers, it is clear that the treaty-making power of the Community arises not only from express provisions of the EC Treaty (such as Articles 113 or 238) but may equally flow from other provisions of the Treaty and from measures adopted, within the framework of those provisions, by the Community Institutions.[328] The changes made to Article 228 EC by the TEU implicitly confirm this case-law.[329]

Given that international legal personality has not been conferred on the Union as such, it must be supposed that for the present it can manage without it. To the extent that it is felt desirable to conclude agreements with third countries or international organizations in the development of CFSP or JHA, it will be the Member States which will have to act. The Council can decide to act together in the context of common or joint positions or joint action.[330]

The *ius communicandi* of the Communities is not confined to relations with other international organizations. They also possess the right of legation, a typical attribute of the international legal personality. This is a right whose existence, in so far as the passive form is concerned, is referred to only indirectly, and this only in Article 17 of the Protocol on the privileges and immunities of the European Communities. This Protocol provides that the Member State in whose territory the Communities have their seat shall grant the customary diplomatic immunities and privileges to the missions of third countries accredited to the Communities. About 120 missions of third countries are so accredited; their credentials are presented to the President of the Commission and the President-in-office of the Council together. The Commission maintains delegations in various countries[331] which deal mainly with relations between the Community and certain third countries and organisations. Thus there are, for example, delegations in Washington, Ottawa, Tokyo, Caracas, Canberra, Belgrade, and Bangkok, besides those to the United Nations in New York, to UNESCO and OECD in Paris, to the WTO and the ILO in Geneva and to the IAEA in Vienna. There are also Commission delegates in a large number of ACP states.[332]

---

327. [1971] ECR 263 at 274. See Brinkhorst (1971) SEW 479; Waelbroeck (1971) *Viertel-jahreshefte zur Europaforschung* 79, and Winter (1971) 8 CMLRev. 550.
328. *Ibid.*
329. See in particular, Art. 228(1) and (2) EC.
330. See Arts. J.3 and K.3 TEU.
331. Their presence is acknowledged in Art. J.6 TEU.
332. As to the activities of these delegations see WQ 842/85 (Rogaila) O.J. 1985 C 87/34; Brinkhorst (1984/1) LIEI 23, Sobrino Heredia (1993) *Revista de Instituciones Europeas* 485, and Macleod *et al.*, *The External Relations of the European Communities* (Oxford, 1996) 215–222.

It may be concluded from the above that each of the Communities forms an international functional legal person and for this purpose is equipped with the requisite powers. This legal personality operates *vis-à-vis* the Member States because they have concluded the Treaties in which it was conferred on the Communities and developed. *Vis-à-vis* third states, however, these Treaties are *res inter alios acta*. In the case of a world-wide organization (the United Nations), the International Court of Justice reached the decision that this organisation possessed an objective international personality', not merely a legal personality with respect to its members. The argument advanced by that Court was that 'fifty States representing the vast majority of the members of the international community had the power, in conformity with international law, to bring into being an entity possessing objective international personality', *i.e.* a personality operating also *vis-à-vis* non-members of the United Nations.[333] This argument naturally does not apply to the Communities in this form.

It may therefore be assumed that the legal personality of the Communities *vis-à-vis* third states operates only after its existence has been recognised by these states. The recognition may be made expressly or tacitly. As has been noted above, many third states already maintain diplomatic relations with the Communities. From this as well as from the fact that several third states maintain treaty relations with the Communities it may be inferred that they have tacitly recognised their existence as a new international functional legal person. Problems in this respect caused by the former Soviet Union and its then satellite states have disappeared with the collapse of the Soviet hegemony. There has now been so universal a recognition of the legal personality of the Communities that it can safely be concluded that they have an objective international legal personality. The few states in the world which have not yet recognized the Communities will no longer be able to rely on this in international relationships to argue that for them the Communities do not exist as a legal entity.

5.2 Privileges and immunities

Since the entry into force of the Merger Treaty on 1 July 1967 the three Communities are subject to uniform rules on the privileges and immunities necessary for the performance of their tasks in the territories of the Member States. In accordance with Article 28 of the Merger Treaty[334] these rules are laid down in an annexed Protocol. This deals with the privileges and immunities of the Communities as such, of the members of their Institutions, their officials and other servants, the representatives of

---

333. *Reparations for Injuries* case [1949] ICJRep. 174. at 185.
334. Arts. 218 EEC; 76 ECSC, and 191 Euratom were thus replaced.

the Member States taking part in the work of their Institutions, and of the missions accredited to the European Communities. The provisions of the Protocol also apply in relation to the supplementary policies and forms of cooperation to the extent that the Community Institutions are entrusted with a decision-making role; to the European Investment Bank[335] and the European Central Bank[336] and its precursor, the European Monetary Institute.[337] The members of the Court of Auditors are placed on the same footing as members of the Court of Justice.[338] Articles 1 and 2 of the Protocol lay down rules concerning the inviolability of the premises, the buildings, and the archives of the Communities. They further provide that their property and assets may not be the subject of any administrative or legislative measure of constraint without the authorization of the Court of Justice.[339] The Court's authorization is required in order to prevent an untimely or inappropriate encroachment on the independent functioning of the Community in favour of private interests. Articles 3 and 4 of the Protocol contain rules on the exemption of the Communities from direct and indirect taxes or sales taxes and from customs duties or import or export prohibitions and restrictions. Article 6 relates to freedom of communication and to travel documents (*Laissez-passer*) for the members of the Institutions and officials and other servants. The orders of the Court in Case C-2/88 Imm. *Zwartveld et al.*[340] illustrate that the protection afforded by the Protocol is not absolute but functional in nature, and does not extend further than is necessary to avoid any interference with the functioning and independence of the Communities.

The immunity from jurisdiction normally granted to international organizations is lacking. In principle the Communities can also be summoned to appear before national courts in the Member States without their consent, at least in so far as the Court of Justice has not been declared competent in the matter by or in pursuance of the Treaties.[341] In view of the extensive competence of the Court this will only very rarely occur. The Court has jurisdiction in disputes concerning the Community's non-contractual liability.[342] Articles 179 EC and 152 Euratom declare that

335. Protocol on the EIB, Art. 28(1). This is annexed to the EC Treaty.
336. Protocol on the ESCB and ECB, Art. 40, annexed to the EC Treaty by the TEU Final Act; Protocol on Privileges and Immunities, Art. 23 (similarly inserted).
337. Art. 21, Protocol on the EMI (as so annexed, *ibid.*); Art. 23 Protocol on Privileges and Immunities (as so inserted, *ibid.*).
338. Arts. 188b(9) EC; 456(9) ECSC, and 1606(9) Euratom.
339. Case 4/62 *Application for authorisation to enforce a garnishee order against the High Authority* [1962] ECR 41 at 43.
340. [1990] ECR I-3365 at 3372–3373, and 4405 at 4409–4411. See also, Chapter III, section 5.2.4, *post*.
341. Arts. 183 EC; 40 ECSC, 3rd para., and 155 Euratom. See also *J.H. Rayner (Mincing Lane) Ltd. v. Department of Trade and Industry* [1989] Ch. 72, [1988] 3 All ER 257, CA; affd. on other grounds [1989] 3 WLR 969, [1989] 3 All ER 523, HL.
342. Arts. 178 EC; 40 ECSC, and 151 Euratom.

the Court also has jurisdiction in any dispute between the Communities and their servants.'[343] Moreover, in many contracts of a public law or private law nature, or in general conditions applicable thereto,[344] an arbitration clause confers jurisdiction on the Court to hear disputes relating to such contracts.[345] There have been occasional attacks on the privileges and immunities conferred by the Protocol but these have been stoutly resisted before the Court by individuals or by the Commission.[346]

5.3 Seat of the Institutions

The three founding Treaties contain identical provisions concerning the seat of the Community Institutions: it 'shall be determined by common accord of the governments of the Member States.'[347] For many years no final decision was taken (thus, for example, the Commission's notepaper always used to refer to its 'provisional address'). After repeated decisions on provisional working places, a decision was finally adopted at Edinburgh by common agreement of the Foreign Ministers as Representatives of the governments of the Member States.[348]

This decision largely confirmed the existing situation. Parliament has its seat in Strasbourg, where the 12 periods of monthly plenary sessions, including the budget session must be held. Periods of additional plenary sessions are held in Brussels, where the Parliament's Committees also meet. The Parliament's General Secretariat and its departments remain in Luxembourg. The Council has its seat in Brussels, but its meetings are held in Luxembourg during the months of April, June and October. The Commission also has its seat in Brussels, but certain departments are

343. *E.g.* Cases 43, 45 and 48/59 *Von Lachmuller et al. v. Commission* [1960] ECR 463; Cases 316/82 and 40/83 *Kohler v. Court of Auditors* [1984] ECR 641; Case 38/84 *J.K. v. European Parliament* [1985] ECR 1267; Case 141/84 *De Compte v. European Parliament* [1985] ECR 1951; Case T-497/93 *Hogan v. Court of Justice* [1995] ECR-SC I-A-77 (abstract; full text in Italian II-251), and Case T-273/94 *N v. Commission* [1997] ECR-SC I-A-97 (abstract; full text in French II 289). See Staff Regs. (as amended), Art. 91.
344. *E.g.* Case 220/85 *Fadex NV v. Commission* [1986] ECR 3387 (dispute under the Commission's General Terms and Conditions governing Supply Contracts, concerning work carried out laying a floor for a TV studio); Case C-299/93 *Bauer v. Commission* [1995] ECR I-839 (arbitration clause under a residential tenancy agreement), and Case C-42/94 *Heidemij Advies BV v. European Parliament* [1995] ECR I-1417 (arbitration clause under a contract for the extension of the Parliament's buildings in Brussels).
345. Arts. 181 EC; 42 ECSC, and 153 Euratom.
346. *E.g.* Case 23/69 *Klomp v. Inspectie der Belastingen* [19691 ECR 43; Case 152/82 *Forcheri et al. v. Belgian State et al.* [1983] ECR 2323; Case 85/85 *Commission v. Belgium* [1986] ECR 1149, and Case 260/86 *Commission v. Belgium* [1988] ECR 955.
347. Arts. 216 EC; 77 ECSC, and 189 Euratom.
348. O.J. 1992 C 341/1. The decision was adopted on the occasion of the Edinburgh European Council in December 1992, Bull. EC 12–92, points I.14 and I.32. See Chapter III, section 5.2.3, *post*, and VerLoren van Themaat (1993) SEW 423.

established in Luxembourg. The Economic and Social Committee (ECOSOC) and the Committee of the Regions (which shares an orgainisational structure with ECOSOC) also have their seat in Brussels. The Court of Justice and the Court of First instance, the Court of Auditors, and the European Investment Bank all have their seat in Luxembourg.

In October 1993, Frankfurt was designated as the seat of the European Monetary Institute and the future European Central Bank, and the seats of a number of other subsidiary bodies were determined.[349] By the same decision, The Hague was designated as the seat of Europol and the Europol Drugs Unit. It would have been possible to determine the seat of these bodies in the instruments establishing them, but the Member States preferred to undertake this task by intergovernmental decision-making in accordance with Article 216 EC.[350]

How this extremely complex and somewhat unhandy distribution of seats came about is still of interest. Originally, the High Authority with its services and the Special Council of Ministers of the ECSC with its secretariat as well as the Court (with its registry) and the Secretariat-General of the Parliament of the three Communities had their seats in Luxembourg. The Parliament as a rule met in Strasbourg; the Councils of Ministers, the Commissions and their staffs of the EEC and Euratom in Brussels. In consequence of the merger of the executives, the offices of the High Authority and the Council of the ECSC moved from Luxembourg to Brussels. In order to make compensation to Luxembourg for this loss, it was decided to accommodate there certain services of the new Commission of the three Communities as well as the European Investment Bank. Furthermore it was agreed, *inter alia*, that in future the Council of the three Communities was to meet in the months of April, June and October in Luxembourg and during the rest of the year in Brussels. For the rest the original arrangement was maintained. These agreements were laid down in a decision of the representatives of the governments of the Member States under Article 37 of the Merger Treaty and they entered into force on the same date as this Treaty.[351] The new Court of Auditors was established in Luxembourg in 1977[352] and the arrangements were confirmed by the European Council meeting in Maastricht on 23–24 March 1981.[353] Thus, the Institutions of the Communties remained distributed over Luxembourg, Brussels and Strasbourg. This situation,

---

349. Decision of the Representatives of the Governments of the Member States, meeting at Head of State or Government level, 29 October, 1993 (O.J. 1993 C 323/1), adopted at the time of the Brussels European Council, Bull. EC 10–1993, points I.10 and I.12–I.13. See also TOA, protocol 11 (not yet in force).
350. See also Arts. 77 ECSC and 189 Euratom. This was decided in Art. 2 of the Edinburgh decision (O.J. 1992 C341/1), see note 348, *supra*.
351. J.0. 1967 152/18 (decision of 8 April 1965, not published until July 1967).
352. O.J. 1977 L 104/40.
353. Bull. EC 3–1981, p. 9.

which is very unsatisfactory from the viewpoint of effective functioning and sound financial policy, can be explained by considerations of national and local prestige and, as far as Luxembourg is concerned, by financial and economic interests, which prevent a rational decision concerning the seat. In 1981 the Parliament decided, pending a final decison about the seat of the Community Institutions, to hold, as a rule, its plenary sessions in Strasbourg and its committee and group meetings in Brussels. Luxembourg contested this decision before the Court.[354] The Court held that although the Parliament was entitled, as part of its power to determine its own internal organisation, to fix its places of work, it had to respect the power of the governments to determine the seat of the Institutions and to respect the existing provisional decisions; it declined to hold that the Parliament's decision was incompatible with Article 37 of the Merger Treaty and the decision of 1965 based thereupon. It reached the opposite conclusion, though, on a decision by the Parliament in 1983 to move certain staff away from Luxembourg.[355] Two cases brought by France against moves to have supplementary or special sittings of the Parliament in Brussels failed,[356] as did two further challenges by Luxembourg to Parliament's decisions increasing the complement of its information staff in Brussels by transferring staff from Luxembourg.[357] That the tension has not yet disappeared is evident from the annulment (in 1997) of the Parliament's calendar of meetings for 1996 in so far as it failed to fix twelve periods of normal plenary sessions in that year.[358]

5.4   Linguistic régime

Finally, a few observations are appropriate about the Communities' linguistic régime. The texts of the EC and Euratom Treaties are equally authentic in twelve languages: Danish, Dutch, English, French, Finnish, German, Greek, Irish, Italian, Portuguese, Spanish and Swedish.[359] The

354. Case 230/81 *Luxembourg v. European Parliament* [1983] ECR 255, see Hartley (1984) 9 ELRev. 44 and Kapteyn (1984) SEW 9.
355. Case 108/83 *Luxembourg v. European Parliament* [1984] ECR 1945, see Hendry (1985) 10 ELRev. 126.
356. Cases 358/85 and 51/86 *France v. European Parliament* [1988] ECR 4821.
357. Cases C-213/88 and 39/89 *Luxembourg v. European Parliament* [1991] ECR 5643.
358. Case C-345/95 *France v. European Parliament* [1997] ECR I-5215. Thus the Parliament could only hold additional plenary sessions elsewhere if it held the 12 required sessions in Strasbourg in the calendar year concerned, *ibid.* at 5242.
359. Act of Accession (1994), Art. 176 (O.J. 1994 C 241/9, as substituted by the Adaptation Decision (Dec. 95/1 (O.J. 1995 L 1/1), Art. 38). The Treaty of Amsterdam (not yet in force) adds a new paragraph to Arts. 248 EC and 225 Eurotom to add the later languages to the original four languages mentioned there, pursuant to the Accession Treaties.

ECSC Treaty is, however, authentic only in the French text.[360] Various difficulties of interpretation may well arise. It will always have to be presumed that the texts have the same meaning in all the authentic languages. If upon comparison there is found to be a difference in meaning which cannot be eliminated by application of the usual methods of interpretation, the meaning to be adopted will have to be one which reconciles the texts with each other as much as possible.[361] In the ECSC and in the EC and Euratom 11 of the 12 languages mentioned above are also official and working languages (Irish being the exception).[362] The *Official Journal* appears in these 11 languages.[363] Although in European Political Cooperation English and French were used,[364] in CFSP and JHA the EC language régime applies.[365]

Around 15% of posts in the Commissions's services in 1997 related to translation or interpretation and of the A and LA category staff the ratio between policy staff and language staff is about 2:1; in the Parliament it is

360. Art. 100 ECSC (but it has been amended by Treaties authentic in all twelve languages).
361. *Cf.* Vienna Convention on the Law of Treaties (TS 58 (1980) Cmnd. 7964), Art. 33. See Case 29/69 *Stauder v. City of Ulm, Sozialamt* [1969] ECR 419 at 424–425; Case 30/47 *R. v. Bouchereau* [1977] ECR 1999 at 2010: 'The different language versions of a Community text must be given a uniform interpretation and hence in the case of divergence between the versions the provision in question must be interpreted by reference to the purpose and general scheme of the rules of which it forms a part.' In circumstances in which one or more of the texts involved may have to be interpreted in a manner at variance with the natural and usual meaning of the words it is preferable, in the interests of legal certainty, to explore the possibilities of solving the points at issue without giving preference to any one of the texts involved, Case 80/76 *North Kerry Milk Products Ltd. v. Minister for Agriculture and Fisheries* [1977] ECR 425 at 435. See also *e.g.* Case 283/81 *CILFIT Srl et al. v. Ministry of Health* [1982] ECR 3415 at 3430; Case 9/79 *Wersdorfer, née Koschniske v. Raad van Arbeid* [1979] ECR 2717 at 2724; Case C-449/93 *Rockfon A/S v. Specialarbejderforbundet i Danmark, acting on behalf of Nielsen et al.* [1995] ECR I-4291 at 4317, and Case C-72/95 *Aannemingsbedrijf P.J. Kraaijveld BV et al. v. Gedeputeerde Staten van Zuid-Holland* [1996] ECR I-5403 at 5443–5444.
362. The Treaty of Amsterdam (not yet in force) raises to Treaty level the right of every citizen of the Union to write to any of the Community Institutions or to the Ombudsman in any of the languages in which the EC Treaty is authentic and to have an answer in the same language (see the new para. to be added to Art. 8d EC). This means that the practical status of Irish is improved for the purposes of individual correspondence with the Community Institutions and the Ombudsman.
363. *Cf.* Arts. 217 EC and 190 Euratom; see also Reg. 1. of 1958 (O.J. English Special Edition 1952–1958, p. 59, most recently amended by the Act of Accession (1994), Annex I, Point XVIII, as substituted by the Adaptation Decision (Dec. 95/1 (O.J. 1995 L 1/1), Art. 39, and Annex I) on languages. See also the European Parliament's Resolution (O.J. 1995 C 43/91).
364. Appendix to Proceedings of the Tweede Kamer 1979–1980, 90; answer to a question by Brinkhorst.
365. Arts. J.11(1) and K.8(1) TEU apply the provisions of *inter alia* Art. 217 EC to CFSP and JHA respectively. See also Declaration No. 29, annexed to the TEU Final Act.

about 1:2 (excluding the staff in the political groups). A good third of the Commission's administration costs and over 60% of those of the Parliament arise from the linguistic régime. The amount of translation work is simply huge, and, with 11 working languages, simultaneous interpretation has to be provided in some 110 combinations in the Parliament.[366] The costs are high and delays in decision-making inevitably arise because of translation problems.

The question of the use of languages in the system of the European Union has major political and cultural implications, but also involves huge logistical problems and expense; these are undoubtedly going to increase further with future enlargements. The question whether it is not now time to apply more widely the practice of using one or two languages only becomes ever more pressing, and with the increasing importance of German, it is by no means certain that English and French should maintain unquestioned their present practical dominance in house. In so far as Community acts have legal effect, however, it is important that they be available to Community citizens in their own language. Similarly, it is important to safeguard the use of a person's own language in the European Parliament and, in so far as litigants are concerned, before the Court.[367]

The use of languages in the Court is laid down in the Rules of Procedure.[368] The official languages of the Court are the eleven languages mentioned above and Irish. Which of them is going to be the language of the proceedings depends upon the plaintiff's choice, with the reservation that if the defendant is a Member State or a natural or legal person from a Member State, the language shall be the official language of that Member State. If there is more than one official language in this Member State, as in the case of Belgium, the plaintiff may choose whichever suits him. Upon joint request of the parties the Court may authorise the use of another official language. In special cases the Court may further authorise the total or partial use of another official language as the language of the case. If a national court makes a request for a preliminary ruling[369] the language of the proceedings shall be that of this court. The publications of the Court of Justice appear in the eleven official languages.[370] However, only the text

---

366. See Corbett *et al.*, *The European Parliament* (3rd ed., London, 1995) 38–41.
367. In Case T-107/94 *Kik v. Council* [1995] ECR II-1717, and Case C-270/95 P *Kik v. Council* [1996] ECR I-1987 an appeal against the language regime at the Office for Harmonization in the Internal Market was rejected as manifestly inadmissible.
368. Rules of Procedure of the Court of Justice, Arts. 29–31 (O.J. 1991 L 176/7, most recently amended, O.J. 1997 L 103/3); and of the Court of First Instance, Arts. 35–37 (O.J. 1991 L 136/1, corr. O.J. 1991 L 317/34, most recently amended, O.J. 1997 L 103/6).
369. Arts. 41 ECSC; 177 EC, and 150 Euratom.
370. There have in the past been sometimes considerable delays (due to shortage of staff resources) in publication of the printed versions of the ECR (in all languages except French which always appears first), however, this now appears to have been resolved. But in order to reduce the translation load, many staff cases are now only printed in

of the Court's decision in the language of the proceedings is the authentic text. In fact most judgments of the Court are discussed in French, as the Court does not have interpreters present during its deliberations.[371] Administrative meetings of the Court (at which the Advocates General are present with the Judges) also take place in French. French was the only Community language which all members of the old ECSC Court spoke and it has become the *lingua franca* of the Court, although Chambers may sometimes discuss a case in another official language if this is more convenient.

---

summary form, or in full in the language of the case. Availability of recent judgments in full text on the Court's internet home page has been of considerable value in increasing ease of access to the judgments of the Court itself and of the Court of First Instance.

371. This means that a new Judge who does not speak French adequately or at all on appointment is, in deliberations, in the early days reliant on colleagues whispering in his or her ear to explain what is going on, and, in written discussions and drafts, very heavily reliant on good choices of Legal Secretaries (*référendaires*), not least because he or she may well be a specialist in areas other than Community law itself.

CHAPTER III

The basic principles of the European Community, and citizenship of the European Union*

1. THE STRUCTURE OF SUBSTANTIVE COMMUNITY LAW

1.1 Content and structure

The substantive law of the European Community sets out from the Principles contained in Part One of the EC Treaty. These are followed by the entirely new Part Two dealing with Citizenship of the Union. The new Part Three, which sets out Community policies, embraces five groups of provisions. First, the provisions designed to realize the free movement of goods, persons, services, capital and payments (and the exceptions to those provisions); secondly, the provisions on agriculture and transport from Part Two of the old EEC Treaty, thirdly, the provisions on competition, taxation and harmonization of laws now brought together in Title V of Part Three, and the important new Title VI which contains the provisions relating to economic and monetary policy, and, fourthly, the provisions on common commercial policy in Title VII. Finally, in Titles VIII–XVII, myriad provisions cover a range of other policy areas: revised provisions on social policy, education, vocational training and youth; new provisions on culture, public health, consumer protection, trans-European networks, and industry; and revised provisions on economic and social cohesion, research and technological development, and the environment, and, last but not least, a new Title XVII on development cooperation. The legal nature of Titles VI–XVII is not merely extremely diverse, but is also radically different from that of

* In the 5th Dutch edition of this work, this Chapter was revised by P. VerLoren van Themaat. The discussion has been completely rearranged by him there. In this third English edition that rearrangement has been followed by the editor, with the addition of various points not made in the Dutch work, extra footnoting, more extensive references to literature, and more use of case-law, also taking account of later developments.

the provisions of the first five Titles of the new Part Three of the Treaty.[1]

The substantive law of the European Community is constructed in the EC Treaty as follows. Articles 2, 3 and 3a EC set out in global terms the objectives of the Treaty and the means by which they are to be achieved. This is now done in a less clear-cut manner than was the case with the old Articles 2 and 3 EEC.[2] Some of the newly formulated objectives of the Community are clearly not economic in nature. Reflecting this Article G TEU rebaptizes the European Economic Community as the European Community throughout the old EEC Treaty, which consequently becomes the EC Treaty.

As has already been observed in Chapter II, Article A TEU, the first of the Common Provisions of the TEU, provides that the 'Union shall be founded upon the European Communities, supplemented by the policies and forms of cooperation established by this Treaty.' The term 'European Communities' embraces the ECSC and Euratom, along with the EC.[3] The policies and forms of cooperation, CFSP and JHA are primarily intergovernmental in nature, outside the three Communities. Thus decisions having legal consequences, based on CFSP and JHA and thus governed respectively by Titles V and VI TEU do not form part of the *acquis communautaire*. Article L TEU makes it clear that the Court of Justice has no powers in relation to CFSP and JHA, save potentially on one point which is not relevant for present purposes.[4] Similarly, the Court also has nothing to say about the substantive objectives and principles of the Union set out in the common provisions, Articles A-F TEU. The promotion of balanced and sustainable economic and social progress which is the first objective specified in Article B TEU is a differently formulated and incomplete summary of the objectives set out in Articles 2, 3 and 3a EC. As the Court is not empowered to apply Article B TEU, the different wording is of no legal significance for the interpretation of Article B. The principles and objectives of Titles I, V and VI TEU[5] do not form part of the substantive *legal* principles on which the European Community is based.

Each of the concrete activities of the Community set out in Articles 3 and 3a EC is subsequently developed more specifically in legal provisions in Part Three of the EC Treaty, save Article 3(q) on development cooperation, which is worked out in its own Part Four of the Treaty. Some of these provisions constitute directly effective rights (and in some

1. See, further, sections 3.3 and 3.5, and, more extensively, Chapters XI–XII, *post*.
2. See sections 1.2 and 2, *post*.
3. As to the ECSC and Euratom Treaties, see Chapter XI, *post*.
4. See Art. L(b) TEU (jurisdiction conferred by conventions adopted under Art. K.3(2)(c) TEU, 3rd subpara).
5. *I.e.* the Titles dealing with the common provisions, CFSP and JHA, respectively.

cases also obligations) for nationals and enterprises (or, in the language of Community competition law, undertakings) of the Member States, directly effective obligations for the Member States and also obligations or powers for in particular the Community Institutions[6] to adopt implementing or further regulatory measures. Setting the scene for these legal rules, which put flesh on the bones of Articles 2, 3, and 3a EC, are a trio of fundamental principles contained in Articles 3b and 5–6 EC. Article 6 EC somewhat confusingly[7] replaces the old Article 7 EEC, whereas the old Article 6 EEC has been repealed. Articles 7 and 7a–7c EC set out the timetable for the establishment of the common market, and its core component the internal market.[8] A further precursor of the rules in Part Three of the Treaty is the citizenship of the Union, set out in Part Two of the Treaty.

The actual institutional provisions, save those relating to Economic and Monetary Union, appear in Part Five of the EC Treaty, after the substantive legal principles and provisions, although the Community Institutions and other organs are actually created by Articles 4, 4a and 4b EC.[9] The place which these provisions occupy in the structure of the Treaty results from the approach in the Spaak Report that the nature and working methods of the institutions, and the division of powers between them would have to be adapted to the effective achievement of the substantive tasks which they were to carry out.[10] Thus in 1956 and 1957 they were dealt with at the end of the negotiations which led to the EEC Treaty, and not at the beginning. Following this approach, it is somewhat ominous that the European Council – which is purely intergovernmental in approach – is provided for in Title I of the TEU, prior to the provisions dealing with substantive Community matters. The European Council's political task, set out in Article D TEU to 'provide the Union with the necessary impetus for its development' and to 'define the general political

6.   Thus although the European Central Bank is not a Community Institution as such (it is not mentioned in Art. 4 EC), it will have important regulatory and executive powers. Moreover, Parts One and Three of the EC Treaty also contain other obligations and powers for the Member States.

7.   As the case-law and academic literature on Art. 6 EC will constantly have to refer to the existing extensive case-law and literature on Art. 7 EEC.

8.   These Arts. are identical to and replace the old Arts. 8 and 8a–8c EEC. Accordingly, the case-law referring to those Arts. applies in respect of the new Arts. On the legal effect of Art. 7a see section 4 of this Chapter, *post*.

9.   Art. 4(1) EC establishes the now five Institutions (the European Parliament, the Council, the Commission, the Court of Justice, and the Court of Auditors). Art. 4(2) provides for the Council and Commission to be assisted by an Economic and Social Committee and a Committee of the Regions, which have advisory status. Art. 4a establishes the European System of Central Banks and the European Central Bank, and Art. 4b establishes the European Investment Bank.

10. See Chapter I, section 4.1, *ante*.

guidelines' of the Union also embraces the substantive legal tasks of the Communities.

Although it may appear that the exclusively Community institutions and working methods are thus subordinated to the political guidelines of the European Council which are established in a purely intergovernmental fashion, it is submitted that this is merely a mirage. The European Council as such (which in any case is distinct from the Council meeting in the composition of Heads of State or Government)[11] is not subject to any parliamentary control, yet alone to judicial supervision. It is in any event not a Community Institution within the meaning of Community law. In accordance with Article C TEU, the European Council must respect and build upon the *acquis communautaire*. It cannot as such adopt any legally binding decisions, and, despite the general political guidelines which they may receive, the normal policy-making institutions of the Communities and the (future) European Central Bank remain fully legally responsible for their actions, according to the relevant substantive and institutional provisions of Community law.

The placing of the European Council at the head of the TEU confirms, though, what is well-known through experience, that in reality the relationship between the substantive and institutional aspects of Community law is dialectic in nature. The institutional structure and the procedures and legal instruments should indeed be appropriate for an effective achievement of the various tasks to be fulfilled, but the history of the last 40 years in fact demonstrates that the way in which the tasks are fulfilled is dependant on the institutional structure of the Communities. It has become increasingly apparent, as a result of *inter alia* constant expansion of the Communities, external factors and new insights, that there are substantial deficiencies in that structure. The discussion of the basic principles of Community law has been maintained in this Chapter as it is useful for a good understanding of the institutional Chapters which follow, while these Chapters in turn are important for a proper understanding of the substantive law Chapters which then follow, although the structure of the EC Treaty has not actually determined the structure of the approach in this book as a whole.

11. The European Council also includes the President of the Commission (on equal terms with the Heads of State or Government), and is assisted by the Foreign Ministers and a member of the Commission. Although the President of the Commission will invariably be present when the Council meets in the composition of the Heads of State or Government, he will not then be there on equal terms: he may participate in the meeting, but, as he is not a member of the Council, he has no vote.

1.2 The new Articles 2, 3 and 3a EC and their inter-relationship

1.2.1 The objectives of the European Community

Article 2 EC maintains the first objective of the old Article 2 EEC, the promotion throughout the Community of a harmonious and balanced development of economic activities. The other five previous objectives have, however, been replaced by a somewhat more detailed list, namely the promotion of 'sustainable and non-inflationary growth respecting the environment, a high degree of convergence of economic performance, a high level of employment and of social protection, the raising of the standard of living and quality of life, and economic and social cohesion and solidarity among Member States.'

All these matters are of fundamental importance. The harmonious and balanced development of economic activities, a high degree of convergence of economic performance, and economic and social cohesion and solidarity all reflect the new tasks of the Community relating to economic and social cohesion. Article 130a EC makes it clear that this aims in particular 'at reducing disparities between the levels of development of the various regions and the backwardness of the least-favoured regions, including rural areas.' The final objective rightly makes explicit the necessity for solidarity among the Member States.

The replacement of the old second objective (promoting a continuous and balanced expansion) by sustainable and non-inflationary growth respecting the environment clearly reflects the objective of 'sustainable growth' accepted at the UNCED Conference in Rio de Janeiro in 1992,[12] and this is rendered as 'sustainable economic and social development' in the new Title XVII of the EC Treaty dealing with development cooperation. The concept of sustainable growth embraces a form and rate of growth (in the whole world, including the developing countries) which is also sustainable for future generations. This growth must therefore not lead to an exhaustion of non-renewable raw materials and natural resources (including certain energy resources). Furthermore, it must not lead to environmental damage which destroys natural resources. This environmental component of the concept of sustainable growth is expressly emphasized *ex abundanti cautela*.[13] Through the words 'sustainable' and 'respecting the environment' the new terms of Article 2 EC emphasize that the desired economic growth must be sustainable in the long term, having regard to the availability of replacement natural resources and to what the physical and natural environment will support. The necessary reduction in the consumption of non-renewable or non-replaceable raw and natural

12. 31 ILM 876 (1992).
13. See, generally, Krämer, *E.C. Treaty and Environmental law* (2nd ed., London, 1995) 41–65.

materials and in environmental pollution does not however mean a reduction in the production of *all* goods and services. It is simply necessary to prevent both the exhaustion of non-replaceable raw and natural materials and environmental pollution. The formulation of the social dimension of Community policy in the fourth and fifth objectives set out in Article 2 appears to conform to this interpretation. If 'sustainable growth' does not necessarily need to lead to reduced growth but simply to differently directed growth of production and consumption and probably more part-time work, the fourth objective of 'a high level of employment is compatible with the concept of 'sustainable growth'. The changeover to more environmentally friendly investments can indeed lead to new employment opportunities. The fifth objective, which no longer speaks of 'an accelerated raising of the standard of living' but now of 'the raising of the standard of living and the quality of life' implies that material consumption (particularly of non-renewable raw and natural materials) cannot continue constantly increasing. On the other hand this sets a clear basis for the new objectives dealing with the quality of life included in Article 3 EC.

1.2.2   The means of achieving these objectives

The objectives of the Community are reasonably clearly formulated in Article 2 EC, consistent and adapted to the widely accepted new visions of society and its responsibilities. However, the formulation of the policy regulatory means of achieving the stated objectives of Article 2 EC is regrettably less clear than the formulation of the old Article 2 EEC. Two regulatory means are specified therein: the market ('the establishment of a common market') and steering mechanisms ('progressively approximating the economic policies of the Member States'). In the well-known terms of Tinbergen's doctrine these correspond to negative and positive integration respectively.[14] Tinbergen defines negative integration as measures consisting of the abolition of a number of impediments to the proper operation of an integrated area; positive integration he defines as the creation of new institutions and their instruments or the modification of existing instruments. The concept of the market is maintained in Article 2 EC as the first means of achieving the Community's objectives, and is reflected in six specific parts of Article 3

14. Tinbergen, *International Economic Integration* (2nd ed., Amsterdam, 1965) 76. Legal literature also makes a distinction between permanent rules (for maintaining a stable 'order') and flexible or temporary rules or measures (for 'steering' or 'regulating' the economy). See Pinder (1968) *The World Today* 88; Pelkmans, *Market Integration in the European Community* (The Hague, 1984) 4. See further the WRR Report No. 28: *De onvoltooide Europese integratie* (The Hague, 1986), published in English as *The unfinished European Integration* (The Hague, 1986).

EC[15] and in the basic principle of 'an open market economy' mentioned in Article 3a EC. But the second of the two original means was replaced by 'establishing ... an economic and monetary union and by implementing the common policies or activities referred to in Articles 3 and 3a'. Of the remaining fifteen means set out in those Articles, the establishment of the EMU is the second principal means of achieving the Community's objectives; the other fourteen means can be characterized as more specific forms of common policies or common activities.[16] These specific means are diverse in their regulatory character and extremely diverse in their practical importance.

Article 3 EC has thus at least in the first instance kept its character as a more specific development of the principal objectives specified in Article 2 EC into concrete job descriptions. These are then developed in Part Three of the EC Treaty in seventeen Titles into provisions which may, depending on their nature and content, be directly applicable.[17] In so far as the provisions are not directly applicable, they contain provisions for the development of secondary Community law in the form of regulations, directives, decisions, recommendations or opinions.[18] Thus in substance substantive Community law is constructed rather as a three-stage rocket: the first stage comprises Articles 2 and 3 (supplemented by 3a) EC; the second stage is Part Three of the EC Treaty (as restructured by the TEU), and the third stage is Community secondary legislation. Standing case-law[19] makes it plain that in the interpretation of each successive stage of the rocket, due account must be taken of the preceding stages, as well as of the general principles of law, which will be considered below. Article 3 EC, as the reference thereto in Article 2 EC makes plain, is also designed to supplement the two principal means mentioned in Article 2, by providing a large number of specific means for realizing those principal means.

Article 3a EC complicates still further the interpretation of Articles 2, 3 and 3a EC and their inter-relationship. It is submitted, though, that the correct interpretation of Article 3a is that it should be regarded primarily

15. Art. 3(a)–(d), (g), and (h) EC.
16. Art. 3(e), (f), and (i)–(t) EC.
17. This means that they are binding without any intervention by either the Community Institutions, or national parliaments or administrations, see Chapter VI, section 2.2, *post*.
18. *I.e.* the five legal instruments specified in Art. 189 EC whereby the tasks of the European Parliament and the Council together, the Council, and the Commission are to be carried out.
19. For an early example of this case-law, see Case 6/72 *Europemballage Corporation and Continental Can Company Inc. v. Commission* [1973] ECR 215 at 244–245, in which reference was made to the then Art. 3(f) EEC (now Art. 3(g) EC) in order to interpret Art. 86 EEC. See more recently, *e.g.* Case C-379/92 *Peralta* [1994] ECR I-3453 at 3495–3496 in which Arts. 3(f) and 7 EEC were discussed in addition to the answers to the questions on Arts. 30, 48, 52, 59, 62, 84 and 130r EEC.

as building upon the establishment of an economic and monetary union specified in Article 2 EC. It was after all for this important purpose that the Intergovernmental Conference on EMU was convened.[20] Article 2 EC refers also to Article 3a EC as one of the means by which the Community's objectives set out in Article 2 are to be achieved. To this extent Article 3a EC is a clear supplement to the other means specified in Article 3 EC for achieving those objectives. Those other means had already been largely rewritten and supplemented by that Intergovernmental Conference. Article 3a(1) EC, which deals with the adoption of a Community economic policy, refers only in very general terms to the other means mentioned in Article 3 EC, apart from the point specific to Article 3a(1) that the economic policy to be adopted is to be 'based on the close coordination of Member States' economic policies'.[21] In Article 3a EC, like in Article 3 EC, the objectives and means are mixed together. It is submitted, though, that even though Article 3a may at first sight appear incompatible with Articles 2 and 3, the interpretation advanced in this discussion means that there is in fact no incompatibility. At first sight it appears that Article 3a EC seeks to achieve the objectives specified in Article 2 EC solely through means of market forces ('conducted in accordance with the principle of an open market economy with free competition'), although in the interpretation advanced in this work that is the case only for the policy concerning economic and monetary union, as detailed in Title VI of Part Three of the EC Treaty. Article 3a EC leaves ample scope for other policy instruments, within the ambit of the Treaty provisions, in the policy fields mentioned in Article 3 EC which are not solely aimed at strengthening the market mechanism, such as the Common Agricultural Policy, social policy, and environmental policy. This raises the question to what extent the principle of an open market economy can be seen as a restatement of the first primary means of attaining the Community's objectives, the establishment of a common market.[22] The complexities in the working out of Articles 2, 3 and 3a EC are certainly primarily the result of the fact that they also take more express account of non-economic objectives than was the case in the old EEC Treaty. Building on this global characterization of the fundamental and legally relevant changes which Articles 2, 3 and 3a EC have made to the system of the

---

20. See Chapter I, section 6.3, *ante*.
21. This specific means, which no longer appears in Art. 3 EC owing to the replacement of the previous text, is worked out in more detail in Chapter 1 of Title VI of Part Three of the EC Treaty. The general and indeed only partial reference to the other means specified in Art. 3 EC is made by the reference in Art. 3a to the 'internal market ... the definition of common objectives' and principally to the economic policy being 'conducted in accordance with the principle of an open market economy with free competition' (which latter provision also appears *inter alia* in Art. 3a(2) EC).
22. This point is discussed further in section 3.2, *post*.

old Articles 2 and 3 EEC, the following sections expand on these provisions, and on their significance for the interpretation of the EC Treaty.

2. THE LINK BETWEEN THE PRINCIPAL MEANS SPECIFIED IN ARTICLE 2 EC AND ARTICLES 3 AND 3A EC

2.1 The link between Articles 2 and 3 EC

It is impossible to make a clear link between each of the seven objectives specified in Article 2 EC and certain policy areas specified in Article 3 EC which are all, save one,[23] dealt with in detail in Part Three of the EC Treaty. All of the twenty policy areas mentioned in Article 3, as the opening sentence of that provision makes plain, are designed to contribute to the achievement of the Community's objectives set out in Article 2. In some cases the link between the seven objectives of Article 2 and the policy areas specified in Article 3 is expressly underlined in the implementing provisions in Part Three. Article 130b EC, in Title XIV of Part Three provides *inter alia* that the Member States must conduct their economic policies and coordinate them in such a way as, in addition, to attain the objectives set out in Article 130a EC. Moreover, Article 130b further provides that the formulation and implementation of the Community's policies and actions and the implementation of the internal market must take into account the objectives set out in Article 130a and contribute to their achievement. Article 130b thereby in fact makes an explicit link between the sixth objective of Article 2 EC (economic and social cohesion) and all the other objectives mentioned therein. Statistics show, though, that so far the establishment of the internal market[24] has contributed more to the achievement of a harmonious and balanced development of economic activities, a high degree of convergence of economic performance, and economic and social cohesion[25] than have the measures specifically envisaged in Title XIV.[26]

Articles 130r(1) and 130u(1) EC are two other examples of the inter-relationship between the objectives in Article 2 EC and most of the policy areas recited in Article 3 EC. They develop the concept of growth[27] as concerns the aspects of sustainability and respecting the environment. Article 130r(1) expressly refers to the prudent and rational utilization of

23. Art. 3(t) EC.
24. *I.e.* liberalization of trade and investments, in accordance with Arts. 3(c) and 7a EC.
25. The first, third and sixth objectives mentioned in Art. 2 EC.
26. Only the development of Greenland is an exception. For statistical details, see Ver-Loren van Themaat and Schrijver in Chowdhury *et al.* (eds.), *The Right to Development in International Law* (Dordrecht, 1992) 89.
27. The second objective in Art. 2 EC, discussed in section 1.2.1, *ante*.

natural resources as one of the objectives of the environmental policy mentioned in Article 3(k) EC. Moreover, Article 130r(2) EC requires that environmental protection requirements be integrated into the definition and implementation of other Community policies. Article 130u(1) EC refers to fostering sustainable the economic and social development of developing countries as the first objective of the policy on development cooperation mentioned in Article 3(q), which is developed in the new Title XVII of Part Three of the EC Treaty. Thus Titles XVI (environment) and XVII build upon the UNCED concept of sustainable growth.[28] As will become apparent in Chapters VII–XII below, environmental policy in particular makes its influence felt on many of the policy areas mentioned in Article 3 EC. Article 130v EC requires – just like Article 130b prescribes in relation to internal economic and social cohesion within the Community – that in the policies which the Community implements which are likely to affect developing countries account be taken of the objectives referred to in Article 130u EC. On the basis that the greater includes the less, this clearly embraces each part of the policies, not merely the policies as a whole. These objectives include, in addition to sustainable economic and social development of the developing countries, the smooth and gradual integration of the latter into the world economy, just as Article 130b makes equivalent provision in relation to the internal economic and social cohesion within the Community. It is not yet apparent what consequences this will have in areas such as the Common Agricultural Policy, industrial policy, and the Common Commercial Policy of the Community.

These three examples do not detract from the strong inter-relationship between the other objectives in Article 2 EC and the other policy areas mentioned in Article 3 EC, which have already been discussed in the preceding section. Section 3 of this Chapter turns to the relationship concerning policy regulation (the very diverse means in Article 3 EC). Finally, in the last Chapter of this work attention will be paid to the demands which the link between the various substantive objectives and policy areas in general will place on the Commission and its services in the future.

2.2 The link between Articles 2 and 3a EC

As has already been observed,[29] Article 3a must primarily be seen as a more specific working out of one of the *means* mentioned in Article 2 EC for the achievement of the objectives of the Community, namely the establishment of an economic and monetary union. Just like Article 3 EC, Article 3a translates the objectives into more specific job descriptions. In

28. See section 1.2,1, *ante*.
29. In section 1.2.2, *ante*.

relation to the *economic* aspect of EMU, the description in Article 3a(1) is restricted to 'the adoption of an economic policy which is based on the close coordination of Member States' economic policies'. From the provisions implementing Article 3a(1), particularly Article 103 EC, it appears to follow that the economic policy is not primarily conceived in terms of the policy areas mentioned in Article 3a(1) but in terms of the general socio-economic policy of the Member States. Article 103 EC only mentions 'the broad guidelines of the economic policies of the Member States'. However the disappearance of the old Chapter heading 'Conjunctural Policy' for Article 103 EEC and of the possibility envisaged in the old Article 103(2) EEC for compulsory Community-level short-term economic policy measures does not mean that the broad guidelines may not cover short-term economic policy goals as well as more general structural policy objectives. Article 103a EC makes it clear that compulsory or other interventionist Community measures (such as the grant of Community financial assistance) can only be adopted exceptionally in the context of the Economic and Monetary Union: particularly in the case of severe difficulties in the supply of certain products, but not any more in the context of a general recession. Furthermore, Articles 104–104c EC offer the possibility of imposing in the final resort compulsory sanctions in order to avoid excessive government deficits in the Member States. However, since the coming into force of the TEU, specific stimulus measures, such as those designed to promote new or further employment opportunities[30] and specific Community measures in certain sectors or in specific policy areas outside the cases mentioned in Articles 103a and 104c EC, will have to be based on other Treaty provisions than those dealing with economic policy. Thus there appears to be a clear dividing line between the ambits of Articles 3 and 3a EC, which is consistent with the text of Article 2 EC: global economic policy falls within the scope of Economic and Monetary Union; specific economic and social policy in certain fields falls within the ambit of the policy areas enumerated in Article 3 EC or will have to be developed with a legal basis other than those expressly provided for in Articles 3 or 3a, such as Article 235 EC which has been retained from the old EEC Treaty. It cannot be deduced from the wording of Article 103 EC itself how far the broad economic policy guidelines may relate to specific forms of economic policy, although this point is addressed further in Chapter IX, below.

Article 3a(2) EC provides in the first instance for the irrevocable fixing of exchange rates leading to the introduction of a single currency, referred

---

30. Such as those decided on at the Edinburgh European Council (Bull. EC 12–1992 point I.30) and at the Brussels European Council (with the acceptance of the Commission's White Paper on Growth, competitiveness and employment (COM(93) 700 Final, Bull. EC Supp. 6/93), Bull. EC 6/93 point I.3.

to in the EC Treaty as the ECU, but which will be called the Euro.[31] Moreover, it provides for the definition and conduct of a single monetary policy and exchange-rate policy, the primary objective of both of which is to maintain price stability and, without prejudice to that objective, to support the general economic policies within the Community. This general economic policy has just as little legally binding force for the future European Central Bank as it has for the member States. At the end of the day the ECB, according to its Statute, decides independently of any global economic guidelines established either by the European Council or by the Council.[32]

Article 3a(3), referring to both monetary and economic policy, provides that these activities of the Member States and the Community entails compliance with the guiding principles of stable prices, sound public finances and monetary conditions, and a sustainable balance of payments. These principles are in fact lifted straight from the wording of the old Article 104 EEC, with the addition of 'sound public finances' and the deletion of 'a high level of employment'. As this latter concept is mentioned in Article 2 EC, the deletion most probably means that employment primarily belongs to the matters mentioned in Article 3 EC. Not all relevant aspects of employment opportunities will be able to be effectively dealt with by the Economic and Monetary Committee which will be established at the start of the third stage of EMU and which will play such a central role in that stage.[33] Concrete recommendations to certain Member States under Art. 103(4) EC may go further in this regard than the broad guidelines recommended to the Member States under Article 103(2) EC.

It appears, finally, from the last phrase of Article 3a(1) and (2) EC that both the (generally not legally binding but not therefore necessarily ineffective) obligation to adopt an economic policy based on the close coordination of that of the Member States' economic policies, and the monetary and exchange-rate policies must be implemented in accordance with the principle of an open market economy with free competition. This seems first of all to confirm that EMU will concern itself primarily with the general socio-economic policies of the Member States, including the avoidance of excessive government deficits, in addition to its monetary and exchange-rate policy functions. Secondly, the principle of an open

---

31. Decision of the Madrid European Council, Bull. EC 12–1995, point I.2.
32. See Arts. 4a and 107 EC; ECB Statute, Art. 7. However, without prejudice to the ECB's primary objective to maintain price stability, it is to support the general economic policies in the Community, Art. 105(1) EC and ECB Statute, Art. 2. See, generally, Gormley and De Haan (1996) 21 ELRev. 95.
33. The Committee will be established under Art. 109c(2) EC and will replace the present Monetary Committee provided for under Art. 109c(1). The Member States, the Commission and the ECB each appoint two members of the new Committee. As to the Committee's tasks, see Art. 109c(2) EC, 2nd para.

market economy can scarcely mean anything other than a market economy characterized by a liberal commercial policy, a principle which is noticeably lacking in Articles 2 and 3 EC, although it is fortunately maintained in Article 110 EC. Thirdly, the addition of the words 'with free competition' cannot be interpreted as declaring open season for policy competition between Member States which in fact distorts competition between them (in particular through State aids, fiscal and social policies), as Articles 3(g),[34] and 92–102 EC, which seek to combat such and other distortions of competition, make plain.

The concrete significance of involving the EMU as well in mentioning the purposes set out in Article 2 EC in the introductory words of Article 3a(1) EC is unclear. With the probable exception of the first objective in Article 2 (a harmonious and balanced development of economic activities) and the non-inflationary nature of the sustainable growth referred to in the second objective, the objectives in Article 2 would appear to have to be achieved primarily by means of the means set out in Article 3 EC and developed in Part Three of the EC Treaty, although this does not exclude a supplementary, supporting or adjusting role for Economic and Monetary Union. This is discussed further in Chapter IX.

3. THE MEANS FOR ACHIEVING THE OBJECTIVES OF ARTICLE 2 EC

3.1 The means

On the basis of the wording of Article 2 EC, the division of the means of achieving the objectives set out therein between Articles 3 and 3a EC and the concrete Treaty provisions based upon them is clear. Only the means of the establishment of an Economic and Monetary Union is actually developed in Article 3a itself, and then worked out in the concrete provisions of Title VI of Part Three of the EC Treaty. The two other means specified in Article 2 EC, the establishment of a common market, and implementing the common policies or activities, which are not covered by Article 3a are dealt with by Article 3 and the Titles of Part Three of the EC Treaty which are based thereupon.[35] It is useful both from the viewpoint of determining the type of policy regulation involved, and for legal practice, to distinguish which of the twenty means listed in Article 3 form part of the principal means of the establishment of a common market contained in Article 2. The value of the distinction is apparent because directly applicable Treaty obligations on the Member States and undertakings in Part Three of the Treaty, which can be relied upon by

34. To which Art. 2 EC refers (as part of Art. 3), as it does to Art. 3a EC.
35. *I.e.* all the Titles of Part Three except Title VI.

private individuals before their national courts,[36] occur (save for Article 119 EC) principally in Treaty provisions dealing with the establishment of a common market. In relation to the policy areas mentioned in Article 3a EC, Articles 104–104b EC contain directly effective (prohibiting) provisions as far as the Member States themselves are concerned. In the other policy areas enumerated in Articles 3 and 3a EC, directly effective rights and obligations for the Member States and their subjects are often achieved by means of implementing regulations and decisions. In other cases completely directly effective rights and obligations for the subjects of Member Sates can be achieved at the most by the transposition of Community *directives* into binding national law.[37] Finally Article 3 also includes policy areas in which legal instruments, without containing legal obligations to act in a certain manner, merely promote a certain course of conduct. Examples include the more or less strict recommendations and opinions, and conditional or unconditional financial incentives granted by the Community.[38] The following section attempts to achieve a systematic division and characterization of the means set out in Articles 3 and 3a EC to achieve the objectives specified in Article 2 EC.

3.2   The first principal means: the establishment of a common market

The concept of a common market is an essential part of countless obligations imposed by the Treaty.[39] The establishment of the common market embraces three aspects in particular: first, the establishment of 'an internal market characterized by the abolition, as between Member States, of obstacles to the free movement of goods, persons, services and capital;'[40] secondly, 'a system ensuring that competition in the internal market is not distorted,'[41] and, thirdly, a common commercial policy.[42] This triptych was already clear in the Commission's philosophy as long ago as 1965, and thus predates both the political vision of the Delors Commission and the

36. *I.e.* are directly effective. As to the distinction between direct applicability and direct effect, see Chapter VI, section 2.2, *post*.
37. As to the conditions for direct effect of directives, and the use which may be made of that direct effect, see Chapter VI, section 2.2.2, *post*.
38. See Zijlstra, *Politique économique et problèmes de concurrence dans la CEE et les États-membres* (CEE études: Série concurrence No. 2, Brussels, 1966) 39–44. For a brief summary of Zijlstra's planning typology, see note 80, *infra*.
39. See Arts. 3(h), 7(7), 38(2), 67(1), 85(1), 86, 92(1), 100–102, 105(2), 109h(l), 117, 223, 225, 226 and 235 EC.
40. Art. 3(a) and (c) EC, as further developed in Arts. 7a, 9–37, 48–73h, and 100–100b EC.
41. Art. 3(g) EC, further developed in Arts. 6 and 85–102 EC. The phrasing of Art. 3(g) represents a change from the old Art. 3(f) EEC which referred to 'the institution of a system ensuring that competition in the common market is not distorted'.
42. Art. 3(b) EC, further developed in Arts. 110, 112, 113 and 115 EC.

Single European Act.[43] The common commercial policy is the most important distinction between the concepts of a common market and a free trade area, and is necessary to guarantee *inter alia*, also in relation to imports from or exports to third countries, equal or equivalent conditions of competition for undertakings established within the common market. As the Court of Justice has made clear in myriad judgments,[44] the common market referred to in the EC Treaty is analogous in nature to the domestic market of a single state. More extensively defined, a common market is a market in which every participant within the Community in question is free to invest, produce, work, buy and sell, to supply or obtain services under conditions of competition which have not been artificially distorted[45] wherever economic conditions are most favourable. The internal aspect of this definition of a common market also embraces more than the concept of an internal market set out in Article 7a EC, which merely speaks of 'an area without internal frontiers in which the free movement of goods, persons, services and capital is ensured in accordance with the provisions of this Treaty.' The element of undistorted competition[46] is absent from that definition. However, in practice Community case-law and legislation on the implementation of Article 7a by Article 100a EC demonstrate that the latter provision may indeed be used for harmonization directives which are aimed at preventing distortions to competition resulting from differences between national legal or administrative provisions of the Member States.[47] This is made possible by the text of Article 100a(1) itself, which refers to measures approximating the laws, regulations or administrative action in Member States having as their object not merely the establishment of the internal market but also its functioning.

The emphasis on the fundamental instrumental significance of the common market is to be found not just in Article 2 EC, but also in the new Article 3a EC. Both economic and monetary policies have to be 'conducted in accordance with the principle of an open market economy with free competition.' The means of the common market is thus also a substantive principle for EMU which, unlike in Article 2 EC, is also proclaimed to be relevant for external economic and monetary policy, and

---

43. See von der Groeben, *Europa: Plan und Wirklichkeit* (Baden–Baden, 1967). Von der Groeben's speech to the European Parliament on June 16, 1965, reproduced in that book, already demonstrates this triptych in his summary of the principles of competition policy. Thus the abolition of internal frontiers and frontier controls was already part of the Commission's agenda.
44. *E.g.* Case 270/80 *Polydor Ltd. et al. v. Harlequin Record Shops Ltd. et al.* [1980] ECR 329 at 348–350 and Case 15/81 *Gaston Schul Douane–Expediteur BV v. Inspecteur der Invoerrechten en Accijnzen, Roosendaal* [1982] ECR 1409 at 1431–1432.
45. *I.e.* have not been rendered unequal.
46. Competition under equal conditions of competition as guaranteed by Arts. 6 and 85–102 EC.
47. *E.g.* Case C-300/89 *Commission v. Council* [1991] ECR I-2866 at 2899–2901.

embraces the whole tryptic of the elements of the common market concept set out above. One small blot on the landscape is that Article 3a EC erroneously speaks of 'free competition' without also specifying undistorted competition (competition under equal conditions). However, this error has no legal consequences, as Article 3a leaves Articles 2 and 3 EC intact.[48] It is submitted that after correcting this error the Court may well take the view that the principle of an open market economy with free and undistorted competition amounts to an abbreviated restatement of the common market concept,[49] thus embracing, as has already occurred in the case-law, 'a system ensuring that competition in the internal market is not distorted.'[50]

3.3   The second principal means: the establishment of an economic and monetary union

Article 3a EC and its implementing Title VI of Part Three EC[51] are to a certain extent bridges between the means of establishing a common market and the means of policy regulation (or steering) which are examined in section 3.4, below. Thus the Chapter on economic policy[52] contains, in addition to the non-legally binding policy steering mechanism of 'broad guidelines' referred to in Articles 102a and 103(2)–(4) EC, directly effective permanent prohibitory rules.[53] These rules relate to the financial policy of the national central banks and of the Community and central governments, regional, local or other public authorities, other bodies governed by public law, and public undertakings of the Member States. They are clearly of a market economy nature, and fit into the concept of a common market explained in section 3.2, above. Articles 103a(1) and 104c EC also provide for the possibility of compulsory temporary measures to remedy, respectively, severe supply difficulties and excessive government deficits. The steering mechanism of Community financial incentives can also be applied in exceptional cases in accordance with Articles 103a(2) and 104c(11) EC, in the form of positive or negative (sanctions) action respectively.

Article 3a makes the central role in monetary policy for the final stage of EMU of the irrevocable fixing of exchange rates, leading to the

48. Other differences in emphasis in the significance of the common market concept in various of the EC Treaty Arts. mentioned in this discussion are dealt with in the relevant parts of Chapters VII–IX, *post.*
49. *I.e.* of Art.3(a)–(d), (g) and (h) EC.
50. Art. 3(g) EC.
51. Arts. 102a–109m EC.
52. Arts. 102a–104c EC.
53. Just as is the case with the provisions of the EC Treaty dealing with the establishment and functioning of the common market.

introduction of a single currency, very clear. Both this central task and the definition and conduct of a single monetary policy and single exchange-rate policy, with as their primary objective the maintenance of price stability, may, in accordance with Article 108a EC also involve the application of steering measures in the form of regulations, decisions, recommendations or opinions adopted by the ECB. In appropriate cases these will take account of the provisions laid down by the Council under Article 106 EC. The primary objective of the European System of Central Banks (ECSB) is the maintenance of price stability.[54] The irrevocable fixing of exchange rates contributes to this primary objective by removing the influence on prices of alterations in exchange rates within the Community. The obligations to conduct general economic policy and monetary policy in accordance with the principle of an open market economy with free competition ensure that these policies will be in conformity with the market.

Economic and Monetary Union will thus assure greater stability of the common market economy, and will *inter alia* exclude exchange-rate risks in investment and trade within the Community, and help to prevent macro-economic disturbances of the balance within the Community. In legal terms it can be argued that monetary union in particular is already covered by the definition of a common market set out in section 3.2, above. Within a single domestic market there are no exchange-rate barriers with the inherent transaction costs in cross-border payments and risks of market disturbances.[55] Accordingly, it is no surprise that businessmen are extremely positive about EMU: it affords more certainty in planning investment, production and sales throughout the entire territory of the common market.

3.4   Policy regulation (steering mechanisms) in Article 3 EC

Numerous means specified in Article 3 EC also have a steering character to a greater or less extent.[56] However market economy principles are never entirely excluded in these areas and in, for example, the common transport policy they play an ever increasing part. In certain areas[57] this steering character may encompass compulsory intervention by means of regulations, directives or even implementing decisions; although in some cases this effect may at least result from the interaction with other policy areas.[58]

In respect of the areas covered by Article 3(l)–(n) EC only financial and

---

54. Arts. 3a(2) and 105(1) EC; Art. 2 ECSB Statute.
55. See, generally, VerLoren van Themaat (1991) 28 CMLRev. 291 (writing before the text of this part of the TEU was agreed).
56. Art. 3(d)–(f) and (h)–(s) EC.
57. Those covered by Art. 3(b), (d)–(f), (h)–(k) and (r)–(s) EC.
58. Art. 3(j) and (k) EC.

other measures which do not compel particular conduct but certainly act as an incentive to pursue certain conduct are available. Article 3(q) EC on development cooperation may additionally be implemented by multiannual programmes, for which express provision is made in Article 130w EC, by coordination of Community and Member States' policies, in accordance with Article 130x EC, and by cooperation with third countries and the competent international organisations, under Article 130y EC.

The provisions implementing Article 3(o) and (p) EC, dealing with the sensitive areas of education, vocational training and youth, culture, and public health,[59] seem primarily aimed at maintaining national sovereignty over non-commercial aspects of policy in those areas. Harmonization of national laws or regulations of the Member States is indeed expressly excluded.[60] Even the very weak instrument of recommendations in the fields of cultural policy and public health policy can only be adopted by unanimity;[61] only in relation to education is qualified majority voting permitted.[62] Only incentive measures are provided for:[63] these may include financial incentives and other facilities to assist in the achievement of the non-commercial objectives set out in these provisions.

All the policy regulation mechanisms set out in Article 3 are further developed in the relevant Titles of Parts Three and Four of the EC Treaty, save the matters covered by Article 3(t) EC, namely measures in the spheres of energy, civil protection and tourism. These are purely programmatic in nature, and according to the first Declaration attached to the Final Act of the Intergovernmental Conference which concluded the TEU, specific measures in these fields were to be dealt with in the Intergovernmental Conference which opened in Turin on March 29, 1996. Pending the resulting amendments, other areas of Part Three of the EC Treaty will be applied in these policy areas.[64]

3.5   The relationship between the establishment of a common market, the establishment of an economic and monetary union, and the policy regulation mechanisms set out in Article 3 EC

3.5.1   The nature of the policy areas

The aspects of Article 3 EC which were discussed in section 3.2, above, dealing with the establishment of a common market are predominantly of

59. Respectively, Arts. 126 and 127; 128 and 129 EC (the final part of each of these provisions makes this evident).
60. Arts. 126(4); 127(4); 128(5), and 129(4) EC (1st indent in each case).
61. Arts. 128(5) and 129(4) EC (2nd indent in both cases).
62. Art. 126(4) EC.
63. Arts. 126(4); 128(5), and 129(4) EC (1st indent in each case).
64. Commission's statement forming part of that Declaration. The 1996 IGC led to the

a market economy nature. While, as has been submitted in section 3.3, above, Article 3a EC and Title VI of part Three of the EC Treaty on the establishment of an economic and monetary union are primarily steering measures, they are designed to operate in accordance with the market. None of the economic and monetary policy instruments developed in those provisions may affect the principle of an open market economy with free competition. Thus the EMU has its own specific policy commitment.

It may well be, though, that the remaining steering mechanisms dealt with in section 3.4, above, may have a greater or less effect on the open market economy principle with free competition. The common commercial policy and immigration policy[65] may also involve restrictions on access from third countries to the common market.[66] As is well-known, the common agricultural and fisheries policies[67] embrace, very strongly, obligations restrictive of competition and aid measures which distort competition for market participants, in order to achieve the goals set out in Article 39 EC. Nevertheless, even here, Article 38(2) EC makes it clear that the rules for the establishment of a common market apply, unless there is an express derogation from them.[68] The common transport policy[69] has in practice become much more in conformity with the market, thus more liberal, partly on account of Article 75 EC and the action by the Parliament to force liberalization in the air transport sector.[70] The conditions of competition in the transport sectors in the various Member States can be extensively harmonized principally by means of harmonization measures in the social and fiscal spheres. There is not such a far-reaching market organization as in the agricultural and fisheries sectors. Unlike in the latter sectors, transport is not normally subject to malleable, repeatedly changing market conditions, but to more permanent rules of market conduct which are thus more in conformity with the

Treaty of Amsterdam of October 2, 1997, which is not yet in force, without producing concrete developments relating to energy, civil protection and tourism.

65. Art. 3(b) and (d) EC respectively.
66. This may well be done by the development of a degree of Community preference, which will be waived only in the event of the conclusion of bilateral or multilateral agreements guaranteeing access on a non-discriminatory basis for Community under-takings to the markets of the third countries concerned (an aspect which is particularly important in relations with the United States, where it is necessary to ensure, for example, access to contracts awarded at State or local level, not just at Federal level). See *e.g.* in the field of utilities procurement, Dir. 93/38 (O.J. 1993 L 199/84, corrigenda (O.J. 1994 L 82/39, 40) most recently amended by Dir. 98/4 (O.J. 1998 L 101/1)), Art. 36 and (before implementation of the new Agreement on Government Procurement), Dec. 95/215 (O.J. 1995 L 134/25).
67. Art. 3(e) EC.
68. See also Cases 80 and 81/77 *Société Les Commissionaires Réunis et al. v. Receveur des Douanes* [1978] ECR 927 at 945, and Case 61/86 *United Kingdom v. Commission* [1988] ECR 431 at 462.
69. Art.3(f) EC.
70. Case 13/83 *European Parliament v. Council* [1985] ECR 1513, [1986] 1 CMLR 138.

market, although there are temporary transitional arrangements for the transition to a more strongly liberalized transport market. Harmonization of laws, social policy, environmental policy, the association of overseas countries and territories, and consumer protection policy[71] may also lead to permanent binding rules of conduct, although in the latter three cases the steering measures are rather different in nature.

The remaining steering mechanisms in Article 3 EC[72] provide for either no or hardly any possibility of adopting binding rules: they are largely confined to the instruments of financial incentives and other facilities or incentive measures.

In the implementing provisions in Part Three of the EC Treaty relating to the policy ares which have clearly non-economic objectives, namely education, culture and public health protection, it is made clear that account must be taken of these non-economic objectives in other areas of Community policies.[73] The specific policies in these areas may not be achieved by harmonizing laws and regulations of the Member States.[74] To the extent that Article 3 EC also envisages steering mechanisms which are to a greater or less extent not in conformity with the market in order to achieve economic objectives, certain guarantees are always included in the implementing Treaty provisions to ensure that competition can never be entirely excluded by these steering mechanisms, and may not be more distorted than is necessary for the achievement of the relevant goals.[75] Binding rules of market conduct can certainly result in more restriction of competition than state aids, as the latter never completely exclude competition, even though they may considerably distort the conditions of competition for certain undertakings or groups of undertakings, and may artificially prolong the life of undertakings or industries which would be more or less unviable in a pure market economy. State aids will normally only obtain Community approval in very limited market circumstances, on the basis of the special grounds specified in Article 92 EC, which are mostly of a temporary nature, and subject to ever more stringent conditions. The Commission's express desire to maintain a level playing field for Community industry has however consistently run into conflict with the political interest of many Member States in shoring up faltering national prestige industries.

71. Art. 3(h),(k),(r) and (s) EC and the relevant implementing provisions in Parts Three and Four of the EC Treaty.
72. Art. 3(j) and (l)–(q) EC.
73. Art. 128(4) EC (culture); Art. 129(1) EC, last sentence (health protection).
74. Arts. 126(4); 128(5), and 129(4) EC (1st indent in each case).
75. As to the question of the extent to which the principle of proportionality set out in Art. 3b EC is of legal importance in examining the necessity for such distortion, see section 5.1.2, post.

3.5.2   The far-reaching economic neutrality of the Treaty as regards its economic system

Community policy regulation (steering) has gradually become more important over the years. Through the now virtually complete liberalization of free movement of goods, capital, labour and services, and of the right of establishment in other Member States for undertakings and the self-employed, it becomes ever more necessary to coordinate or even merge economic intervention by Member States. National market regulation becomes pointless if it can no longer be safeguarded by simultaneous regulation of imports and exports against disturbances originating abroad. The EC Treaty thus had to provide for a common policy in the two sectors, agriculture and transport, which are regulated in all the Member States. Autonomous application of incidental market-regulatory measures in other sectors of trade and industry[76] is possible only subject to considerable self-restraint, lest the measures infringe the Treaty or be simply ineffective. Even the effectiveness of broader autonomous economic or monetary policy measures will decrease sharply because of the spreading of their effects throughout the common market.[77] Thus the expansionist budgetary policy of Mitterrand's regime in France during 1981–82 led primarily to an increase in imports and with it a significant deficit in the balance of trade. Conversely, a successful counter-inflationary policy is partly dependent on the price of goods imported from other Member States. In the diminishing effectiveness of autonomous national economic and monetary policies and the increasing mutual dependence in an ever increasing number of policy areas lay the justification for, in turn: a common agricultural, transport and (external) commercial policy in the old EEC Treaty; the introduction of the European Monetary System in 1978; the gradual introduction of an economic and monetary union and the facilitation of a stronger Community social policy through the changes

---

76. *E.g.* ministerial validation of air transport tariffs, price regulations and restrictions on expansion or contraction of capacity adopted by regulatory bodies in the sectors concerned (in the Dutch system ministerial approval of *produktschap* decisions on such matters is required and similar arrangements can be found in France, *e.g.* Case 123/83 *Bureau National Interprofessionnel du Cognac v. Clair* [1985] ECR 391). See also *e.g.* Case C-185/91 *Bundesanstalt für den Güterfernverkehr v. Gebr. Reiff GmbH & Co. KG* [1993] ECR I-5801 at 5847–5848, and Case C-153/93 *Germany v. Delta Schiffahrts- und Speditionsgesellschaft mbH* [1994] ECR I-2517.
77. See Zijlstra, *op.cit.* (see note 38, *supra*) 39–44, in which the effects of the four freedoms on, successively, wages, prices, interest rates, taxation, budgetary, structural and competition policies are discussed. While the correctness of his conclusions was then not yet generally accepted, it is nowadays. The link between the achievement of the common market and the possibility of national policy regulation is more extensively discussed in the WRR report No. 28, *De onvoltooide Europese integratie* (The Hague, 1986) 34–38, published in English as *The unfinished European Integration* (The Hague, 1986) 34–38.

brought about by the TEU, and, a year later, at the European Council in Edinburgh in December 1992, the instigation of coordinated Community and national approaches to restoring growth and employment opportunities.[78] The increasing recognition of the importance of a coordinated environmental policy found its own justification in the cross-border nature of a large proportion of environmental questions. As the new text of Article 2 EC, the Title dealing with the environment, and the new Title on development cooperation recognize, environmental policy may also have a significant effect on internal and external economic policy.

Even after the amendments made by the TEU, it still follows from Articles 2, 3 and 3a EC and Part Three of the EC Treaty that the determination of the relative weight of market economy means on the one hand and policy regulation which may more or less conform to market principles is left to the political decision-making process in the European Council and the Community Institutions which shape Community policies, subject to review by the Court of Justice. Provided that the unity of the common market and the maintenance of sufficient effective competition are ensured, the steering measures taken by the Community Institutions for the attainment of the objectives laid down in Article 2 EC may very well be strengthened.[79] To this extent the Treaty remains neutral as far as the choice of economic system is concerned.

However, as a result of the TEU, there are a number of restricting points which have to be made about the Treaty remaining neutral as far as the choice of economic system is concerned. First, Article 3a clearly prescribes that (general) economic and monetary policy must conform to the market. Thus the general economic policy in the context of EMU will have to be confined to the lightest of Zijlstra's types of economic planning, types I and II, and possibly type III.[80] The use of financial incentives in the sense of his types IV and V will have to take place in the context of the policy areas mentioned in Article 3 EC. Monetary union may also result in

---

78. Bull. EC 12–1992, points I.8 and I.30.
79. See Mertens de Wilmars in *Miscellanea Ganshof van der Meersch* (Brussels, 1972) Vol. II 285 and VerLoren van Themaat, *Economic Law of the Member States of the European Communities in an Economic and Monetary Union* (EEC Studies: Competition Approximation of Legislation Series No. 20, Brussels, 1973).
80. Zijlstra, *op. cit.* (see note 38, *supra*) 32–33. For a summary of Zijlstra's planning types see VerLoren van Themaat (1970) 7 CMLRev. 311 at 311–314. Very briefly stated, planning type I contains only prognoses, type II quantitative assignments for macro-economic government policy, type III adds non-binding assignments for trade and industry. Type IV contains in addition unconditional and type V conditional incentives for trade and industry to act in accordance with the assignments. Planning type VI adds the instrument of coercive rules. Beyond a given degree of application this last type leads to a predominantly centrally planned economy. The A variants of Zijlstra's planning types apply the types to separate sectors of trade and industry. As to the very limited importance of Zijlstra's planning typology for monetary union, see Chapter IX, *post*.

binding provisions (economic planning type VI), which are necessary for its proper functioning. While the old list of more interventionist policy areas has been maintained, Article 3 has principally been expanded with policy areas in which lighter steering measures (recommendations, facilities and financial assistance measures) may be applied. The most important exceptions are the strengthening of the social dimension, environment policy and consumer protection policy. Just as in the areas in which there are common policies, so in these three areas binding measures can be adopted, as well as lighter steering measures, albeit that the binding measures, where Article 100a EC is unused in these contexts, are principally in the form of coordination directives which will be binding on citizens only after transformation into national law.

Secondly, and importantly, in practice the degree to which steering mechanisms can be employed will depend on the effectiveness of the composition, competence and working methods of the policy-making Community Institutions: the Commission, the Council and the Parliament. It will primarily depend on the Treaty amendments resulting from the Intergovernmental Conference which opened on March 29, 1996 whether the composition, competence and working methods of these institutions can be sufficiently adapted to enable them, even after further enlargement of the number of Member States, to adopt the adjustments necessary in view of the results of the open market economy to achieve the objectives specified in Article 2 EC. These results will be the inevitable consequences of the compulsory rules and measures laid down in or under the Treaty for the establishment of a common market. The adoption of the necessary adjustments, however, depends on an effective institutional structure and on the political will of the Member States. The challenges and risks which are involved are discussed in the final Chapter of this work.

Thirdly, the principles of subsidiarity and proportionality prescribed in the new Article 3b EC are of importance for the further development of the economic system of the Community. These matters are discussed in section 5, below.

In legal terms, the question of the desirable European economic system can be translated into the question of the desirable relationship between the substantive legal principles of freedom, equality and solidarity.[81] On a

81. See VerLoren van Themaat in Boes *et al.*, *Liber Amicorum Josse Mertens de Wilmars* (Antwerp/Zwolle, 1981) 355–383 and literature cited there. As explained there (at 379), the legal principles of freedom (*e.g.* the four freedoms) are supported within the Community by principles of equality (e.g. Arts. 6 and 95 EC) although some substantive variants of the principle of equality (such as reducing the differences in prosperity between the various regions) can only be realized on the basis of the principle of solidarity. See also VerLoren van Themaat in Hellingman (ed.) *Europa in de steigers: van Gemeenschap tot Unie* (Deventer, 1993) 121. As to the economic constitution of the Community, see, generally, Forschungsinstitut für Wirtschftsverfassung und Wettbewerb, *Weiterentwicklung der Europäischen Gemeinschaften und der marktwirtschaft* (Papers from the

global view, the five freedoms[82] and the freedom of competition guaranteed by Article 85 of the Treaty correspond to the principle of freedom. The various prohibitions of discrimination and other provisions of the Treaty which aim to ensure equal competitive conditions (such as the declaration of incompatibility of state aids with the common market under Article 92 EC, and the harmonization provisions in Articles 99–102 EC) correspond to the principle of equality. The provisions concerning positive integration are the most important expression of the principle of solidarity. The growth in mutual dependence caused by the five freedoms also requires solidarity and cooperation in the solution of problems which in the past would have been solved by the Member States separately. Since the completion of the common market even national measures to combat the backwardness of less-favoured regions (national regional policy which features in all the Member States) will often no longer be successful without contributions under the Community policy favouring economic and social cohesion (Community regional policy). Moreover, the policy of economic and social cohesion, in an analogous manner to national regional policy, also seeks to reduce the disparities between regions in the different Member States. Unlike the principles of freedom and equality, which are largely guaranteed in the EC Treaty itself, the principle of solidarity in fact has to be filled in by secondary legislation, even though that finds its legal basis in global principles in the Treaty itself.

4. THE TIMETABLE FOR THE ESTABLISHMENT OF THE COMMON MARKET

Save for the exceptions or derogations provided for in the Treaty, the expiry of the transitional period (which took place on 31 December 1969)

XXV FIW Symposium, Cologne, 1992); Gerber (1994) AJComp.L. 25; Götz, *Verfassungsschranken interventionistischer Regulierung nach europäischem Gemeinschaftsrecht im Vergleich mit dem Grundgesetz* (*Vorträge, Reden und Berichte aus dem Europa Institut, Universität des Saarlandes*, Nr. 166, 1989); Grimm (1995) 1 ELJ 282 with comment by Habermas at 303); Häberle (1992) EuGRZ 429; Joerges *Markt ohne Staat? Die Wirtschaftsverfassung der Gemeinschaft und die Renaissance der regulatieven Politik* (EUI Working Paper, Law 91/15 (Fiesole, 1991); Joerges in Dehousse (ed.) *Europe after Maastricht An ever closer Union?* (Munich, 1994) 29; Mestmäcker, *Die Wirtschftsverfassung in der Europäischen Union* (*Vorträge und Berichte des Zentrums für Europäische Wirtschaftsrecht*, Bonn, 1993); Padoa–Schioppa *Efficiency, Stability and Equity* (Oxford, 1987); Pescatore in *Miscellanea Ganshof van der Meersch* Vol. II (Brussels, 1972); Petersmann (1993) EuZW 593; Streit and Mussler (1995) 1 ELJ 5 (with Ehlermann's and Hancher's comments, and Streit and Mussler's reply at 84); VerLoren van Themaat in Mestmäcker *et al.* (eds.), *Eine ordnungspolitik für Europa* (*Festschrift* for von der Groeben, Baden–Baden, 1987) 425; Waelbroeck in Pérez González *et al.* (eds.), *Hacia un nuevo orden internacional y Europeo* (*Estudios en homenaje Díez de Velasco*, Madrid, 1993) 1297, and Weiler (1995) 1 ELJ 219. See, further, Allott (1997) 34 CMLRev. 439.

82. *I.e.* free movement of goods, persons, services, capital and payments, discussed in Chapter VII, *post.*

constituted, in accordance with the then Article 8(7)EEC (now Article 7(7) EC), the latest date by which all the rules laid down in the Treaty had to enter into force and all the measures required for establishing the common market had to be implemented. In the course of the Seventies and the beginning of the Eighties, it became ever more apparent, though, that the hundreds of measures of secondary legislation necessary to complete the common market could not be adopted without an improvement in the decision-making process in the context of a new tight time schedule. In particular there was a huge backlog in the liberalization of financial services and capital movements, as well as of transport, and in the myriad harmonization measures which were necessary in order to remove the barriers to trade which could, in the absence of such measures, be justified under Treaty exceptions relating to the classic four (in reality five) freedoms, such as Article 36 EC. On the basis of the Commission's White Paper *Completing the Internal Market*,[83] which envisaged the adoption of some 300 measures within a tight timetable, the old EEC Treaty was amended, in order to facilitate the completion of this most important element of the common market, by the SEA, which came into effect on July 1, 1987, which could be largely executed by the end of the period envisaged by the Commission, namely 31 December 1992.

The existing Article 8(7) EEC (now Article 7(7) EC) was supplemented by Articles 8a–8c EEC (which are now Articles 7a–7c EC) in order to anchor the new timetable firmly. The definition of the internal market which had to be completed was set out in the then Article 8a EEC as 'an area without internal frontiers in which the free movement of goods, persons, services and capital is ensured in accordance with the provisions of this Treaty.'[84] The first paragraph of Article 8a EEC provided that the measures to progressively establish the internal market were to be adopted over a period expiring on 31 December 1992 in accordance with the new and amended Treaty provisions[85] and without prejudice to the other provisions of the Treaty. As the measures which had to be taken were not clearly specified in advance, it would be difficult, if they were not to be adopted by that date, for automatic legal consequences to result, as had occurred in the case-law on primary Treaty provisions concerning the five freedoms, on the basis of the then Article 8(7) EEC.[86] In a

---

83. COM (85) 310 Final.
84. *I.e.* the then new Arts. 8b, 8c, 100a and 100b EEC and the amended Arts. 28, 49, 54(2), 56(2), 57(1) and (2), 59, 70(1), 84 and 99 EEC. In the TEU Arts. 49, 54, 56 and 57 EEC were again amended and the provisions of Part Three, Title 3, Chapter 4 on the movement of capital and payments were replaced on the entry into force of the TEU by Arts. 73b–73g EC.
85. *Ibid.*
86. *E.g.* Case 2/74 *Reyners v. Belgian State* [1974] ECR 631 at 651–652 (Art. 52 EEC); Case 33/74 *Van Binsbergen v. Bestuur van de Bedrijfsvereniging voor de Metaalnijverheid* [1974] ECR 1299 at 1311–1312 (Art. 59 EEC).

Declaration on Article 8a EEC by the Intergovernmental Conference attached to the Final Act noting the adoption of the SEA, it was stated that setting the date of 31 December 1992 did not create an automatic legal effect. However, the absence of automatic legal effect of the setting of the date could not exclude the possibility of an action for failure to act being brought under the then Article 175 EEC (now Article 175 EC) against the Council or the Commission, in respect of matters in which that deadline was not respected.[87] An additional reason why the setting of this date has no automatic legal effect can be found in Article 8c EEC (Article 7c EC), the text of which appears not to exclude that for certain Member States longer transitional periods may be fixed for certain measures.[88] In a number of measures implementing the completion of the internal market use has been made of this possibility of allowing certain Member States a longer period to meet the requirements of Community legislation. Accordingly, any action against failure to act would have to take account of such periods. In so far as the adoption of any adjustments was made a precondition in the Treaty for the establishment of the common market, they should have been adopted before the end of the transitional period at the end of 1969, in accordance with the last part of Article 8(7) EEC (Article 7(7) EC). This principally concerned the common agricultural, fisheries, transport, and external trade policies, as well as the programme of harmonization directives which should have been adopted by 31 December 1992, on the basis of the measures introduced into the Treaty by the SEA. The adjustment measures relating to these common policies, which are by their very nature versatile, will, unlike the internal market, never be complete. The same is true of other areas of intervention, such as environment and social policy, which are not expressed as preconditions for the establishment of a common market. They will continually have to be adjusted to take account of changing situations and perceptions. The Common Agricultural Policy is the clearest example of this. Of course, the Treaty provisions and secondary legislation relating to the establishment and proper functioning of the common market also have to be maintained and where necessary further developed even after the perceived completion of the internal market.

---

87. In the same sense, indicating this residual, not directly effective, possibility, Glaesner (1986) EuR 133, and Ehlermann (1987) 22 CMLRev. 372. The Declaration cannot derogate from the nature of a legal obligation which is apparent from the wording of Art. 8a EEC (now Art. 7a EC), even though the statement by the Intergovernmental Conference that no automatic legal effects were created by setting the date is acceptable.

88. On account of *e.g.* the transitional period agreed on accession not yet having expired, or the less developed state of the economy.

5. THE FUNDAMENTAL PRINCIPLES OF ARTICLES 3B, 5 AND 6 EC

5.1 The principles of subsidiarity and proportionality

5.1.1 The principle of subsidiarity

In the core second paragraph of Article 3b EC the principle of subsidiarity is mentioned as the general canon for the practical allocation of tasks in cases in which concurrent or parallel competence of the Community and its Member States exists, namely those areas in which the Community is not exclusively competent. This is remarkable in a number of respects. First, the subsidiarity principle originates in Catholic social doctrine, having been authoritatively laid down in the Papal Encyclicals *Quadragesimo Anno* in 1931 and *Pacem in Terris* in 1963. It is thus exclusively concerned with the relationship between the State and society, the relationship between the public authorities, citizens, families and intermediate organisations. In its origin it thus has no relevance to relationships between the different territorial administrative layers of a State, even within a federal State. Secondly, while in countries such as Italy and Portugal before the Second World War the principle justified the hold of the central authority on society in a corporatist State structure, experience in Germany[89] and in the United States shows that it does not hinder the gradual strengthening of central authority if this is justified by changed circumstances or perceptions.[90] Thirdly, and most importantly, in discussions about the relationship between States and international organisations, as here, the classic principle of sovereignty and its development is of far greater importance than the principle of subsidiarity, as above all the discussions in Denmark, France and the United Kingdom during the ratification procedure for the TEU made clear yet again. Weatherill has rightly opined that the principle reflects concern about the

---

89. Where Art. 72 of the *Grundgesetz* (Basic Law) served as an important positivist example in the drafting of Art. 3b EC.
90. As to the first two observations, see further, Kapteyn in Hellingman (ed.), *op. cit.* (see note 81, *supra*) 41–44, and Geelhoed (1991) SEW 422, who deals in particular with the German and American experiences. In the Netherlands, particularly during the preparation of the *Wet op de Bedrijfsorganisatie* (Law on Enterprise Organization), which aimed at creating a public law enterprise organization, this led to heated debates between Catholic proponents and protestant, liberal or socialist orientated political parties as opponents, as well as between a large number of academic economists. In the latter case the debates were inspired by arguments based on economics, as opposed to political dogma. On the political side many wholly differently oriented arguments were advanced, such as the principles of functional decentralization and sovereignty within individual groups, which primarily resist the integration approach which lies behind the principle of subsidiarity. As to these discussions, see further, VerLoren van Themaat and Muilwijk, *Handleiding bij de Wet op de Bedrijfsorganisatie* (2nd ed., Ijmuiden, 1956) 2–16 and 35–43.

scope of Community competence and its demarcation from national competence, but does little in practical terms to address that concern.[91] Even the European Communities are still to be regarded as international organisations *sui generis*.[92] Their individual nature is expressed *inter alia* in certain analogies with federal structures. On the basis, first, of the ideological origins of the principle of subsidiarity, which is not wholeheartedly accepted by the majority in all the present or even likely future Member States; secondly, of the completely different sphere of application of the principle, and, thirdly, of the experiences of federal States and international organisations, it must be concluded that the principle of subsidiarity as such is neither a useful new legal guarantee against an unreasonable expansion of Community competences,[93] nor an acceptable point of departure, with all the possible practical consequences, for all politicians.[94] This said, it is now appropriate to turn to a brief discussion of the legal significance of the wording of Article 3b EC.[95] It

91. Weatherill *Law and Integration in the European Union* (Oxford, 1995) 172. He regards the principle as an ill-defined counterweight to the expansion of Community competence agreed in the TEU (rather, though he does not say this, like Art. 100a(4) EEC was the price paid for Danish agreement to the use of qualified majority voting for harmonization measures for the completion of the internal market under Art. 100a(1) EEC) and apparent in the burst of legislative activity between the coming into force of the SEA and then. He views subsidiarity as intensifying the debate about Community competence rather than resolving it.

92. This is also true in the terminology of the Dutch Constitution (Art. 92) and of the constitutions of Belgium, Luxembourg, Portual and Spain, see Oberdorff, *Les Constitutions de l'Europe du Douze* (Paris, 1994). See also VerLoren van Themaat (1995) 32 CMLRev. 1319.

93. VerLoren van Themaat (in the 5th Dutch edition of this work, 90) has expressed surprise that Major and Thatcher were so enthusiastic about this integrative principle. The reason lies in the fact that the concept of federalism is widely misunderstood in the United Kingdom (as a centralizing principle, instead of as an allocation of competence) and the principle of subsidiarity was on the contrary portrayed as fundamentally decentralizing in nature. The irony is that, as is well-known, under the Thatcher and Major governments any idea of subsidiarity as a decentralizing force has stopped at Westminster. In actual fact they showed a marked tendency to agglomerate power to the centre at the expense of local authorities. What is sauce for the goose is clearly not always sauce for the gander!

94. Weatherill, *op. cit.* (see note 91, *supra*) 172–173, rightly observes that identifying the principle of subsidiarity as essentially fodder for a political talking-shop is not necessarily a point of criticism, and notes that 'if subsidiarity, as a question rather than an answer, has stimulated a more intensive, thoughtful examination of how the evolving European market should be regulated, then it will have fulfilled a valuable function.'

95. As to the background to and drafting of the principle of subsidiarity, see Cloos *et al.*, *Le Traité de Maastricht* (2nd ed., Brussels, 1994) 141–151. The volume of literature on subsidiarity is now enormous, see the Commission's Communication SEC (92) 1990 Final, reproduced in Bull. EC 10–1992, point 2.2.1; the agreement at the Edinburgh European Council in December 1992 on the overall approach by the Council to the principle of subsidiarity, Bull. EC 12–1992, point I.15; the Report of the House of Lords Select Committee on the European Communities, *Economic and Monetary Union*

might usefully be noted, as a preliminary point, that the principle of subsidiarity did not, before the entry into force of the TEU, constitute a general principle of law by reference to which the legality of Community acts should be reviewed, nor does it have retroactive effect.[96]

The first paragraph of Article 3b EC expressly provides that the Community 'shall act within the limits of the powers conferred on it by this Treaty and of the objectives assigned to it therein.' Given that the Community has long been held to operate on the basis of an attribution of powers, in accordance with the last sentence of Article 4(1) EC, the repetition of the concept of limited powers adds nothing to existing law,[97]

and Political Union (Session 1989–1990, 27th Report, HL 88–I), the Reports of the European Parliament's Committee on Institutional Affairs, July and October 1990, EP Docs. EN/RR/91692 and 98228. See, further, *e.g.* Adonis and Tyrie, *Subsidiarity* (IEA, London, 1990); Andriessen (1993) *De Naamlose Vennotschap* 282 (and other commentaries relating to specific areas which follow that article); Begg *et al.*, *Making Sense of Subsidiarity: How much centralization for Europe?* (CEPR, London, 1993); Bermann (1994) Columb. L.Rev. 331; Besselink *et al.* (1994) SEW 275; Cass (1992) 29 CMLRev. 1107; Constantinesco (1991) *Aussenwirtschaft* 439; Constantinesco (1991) YBEL 33; Constantinesco (1992) RMUE 227; Duff (ed.), *Subsidiarity within the European Community* (Federal Trust, London, 1993); Emiliou (1992) 17 ELRev. 383; Emiliou (1995) EPL 563; *Reports of the FIDE Congress, Lisbon, 1994*, Vol. 1; Geelhoed (1991) SEW 422; Kapteyn (1991) *Révue des Affaires Européennes* 35; Koopmans in Curtin and Heukels (eds.), *Institutional Dynamics of European Integration* (Essays in honour of Schermers, Vol. II, Dordrecht, 1994) 43; Lenaerts and van Ypersele (1994) CDE 3; Lenaerts (1994) 17 Fordh. Int'l. L. J. 848; Lenaerts (1995) 1 Columb. J. Eur. L. 1; Mackenzie Stuart in Curtin and O'Keeffe (eds.), *Constitutional Adjudication in European Community and National Law* (Essays in honour of O'Higgins, Dublin, 1992) 19; Müller–Graff (1995) ZHR 34; Palacio González (1995) 20 ELRev. 355; Pescatore in Due *et al.* (eds.) *Festschrift für Ulrich Everling* (Baden–Baden, 1995) Vol. II 1071; Schwarze (1991) RMC 615; Temple Lang (1995) 1 EPL 97; Toth (1992) 29 CMLRev. 1079; contributions by Toth, Steiner and Emiliou in O'Keeffe and Twomey (eds.), *Legal Issues of the Maastricht Treaty* (Chichester, 1994) 37 *et seq.*; contributions by Vignon and Kalbfleisch–Kottspier in Monar *et al.* (eds.) *The Maastricht Treaty on European Union* (Brussels, 1993) 69 *et seq.*; Wilke and Wallace, *Subsidiarity: approaches to power sharing in the European Community* (Discussion Paper No. 27, Chatham House, London, 1990); the *Proceedings of the Jacques Delors Colloquium, 1991: Subsidiarity: the Challenge of Change* (Maastricht, 1991); and Goucha Soares (1998) 23 ELRev. 132.

96. Case T-29/92 *Vereniging van Samenwerkende Prijsregelende Organisaties in de Bouwnijverheid et al. v. Commission* [1995] ECR II-289 at 331.

97. Durand in Mégret *et al.* (eds.) *Commentaire Mégret Le Droit de la CEE* Vol. 2 (2nd ed., Brussels, 1992) 429 concludes that, without ignoring the importance of the express insertion of this provision, it does not seem from the legal viewpoint that its introduction should lead to consequences which differ from those applicable prior to its introduction. Moreover, in any event, the Community always acts through its Institutions, *ibid.* at 428–429, although it might with respect be the case that the distinction is relevant in so far as bodies established by the EC Treaty (such as the European Investment Bank, which is not a Community Institution within the meaning of Art. 4(1) EC) or subsidiary bodies established under Community secondary legislation are caught by the obligation on the Community, even though they are not embraced by the last sentence of Art. 4(1), save to the extent that *delegatus non potest delegare.*

although Article 4(1) refers to the actions of each of the Community Institutions, whereas the first paragraph of Article 3b EC refers to the Community as a whole and adds the additional limiting factor of the objectives which the EC Treaty assigns to the Community. Unlike a Federal State, the Community has no *Kompetenz-Kompetenz*.[98] Thus, apart from the very limited possibilities envisaged in Article 235 EC,[99] the Community cannot create wholly new competences for itself without an amendment of the EC Treaty, even though Article F(3) TEU might create the contrary impression. This has been vividly emphasized by the Court in its recent negative Opinion on question of the possibility of the Community acceding to the European Convention on Human Rights.[100] The fact that the powers of the Community Institutions are expressly limited in Article 4(1) EC lays a clearer foundation for a political and, within the customary bounds, judicial review of secondary Community law against the relevant objectives concerned.[101]

The second paragraph of Article 3b EC is of crucial importance for the legal significance of the principle of subsidiarity: 'In areas which do not fall within its exclusive competence, the Community shall take action, in accordance with the principle of subsidiarity, only if and in so far as the objectives of the proposed action cannot be sufficiently achieved by the Member States and can therefore, by reason of the scale or effects of the proposed action, be better achieved by the Community.' As will be

---

98. *I.e.* it cannot itself determine the limits of its competence or extend them. See Case C-327/91 *France v. Commission* [1994] ECR I-3641 at 3676–3677, in which the Court annulled an Agreement concluded between the Commission and the United States on the application of Community and U.S. competition laws on the ground that the Commission had exceeded its competence. In view of that judgment a Joint Decision was adopted by the Council and the Commission, acting on behalf of the EC and the ECSC respectively approving the Agreement, with an exchange of interpretative letters with the U.S. government, on behalf of those two Communities, Dec. 95/145 (O.J. 1995 L 95/45). No single institution of the Community in fact has the power itself to increase the powers conferred on it by the EC Treaty. A suggestion has been advanced in German circles that, in order to keep an extension of competence through a broad interpretation of generally formulated powers (Arts. 100; 100a and 235 EC) within bounds, the grant of generally formulated 'functional' powers should be replaced by a clearer specification of the powers conferred, see further, Weidenfeld (ed.) *Europa '96, Reformprogramm für die Europäische Union* (Gütersloh, 1994) 14–30. In the context of discussions about the principle of subsidiarity such proposals will very likely frequently be raised, although there are very good reasons for not accepting these arguments, such as the dynamic nature of the Communities and the risks inherent in placing the Institutions within a straightjacket which will mean that they will be unable easily to adapt to new requirements of changed circumstances.
99. As to which, see Chapter IV, section 6.2, *post*.
100. Opinion 2/94 [1996] ECR I-1759, [1996] 2 CMLR 265.
101. Durand, in Mégret, *loc. cit.* (see note 97, *supra*), observes that the first sentence of Art. 3b EC is drafted positively, so that it involves an obligation to act, and that this should be understood as not simply involving the duty to act within the limits of the powers conferred but a duty to act in accordance with the objectives assigned.

apparent from the observations above, it is submitted that the reference to the principle of subsidiarity does not constitute a clarification of the other elements of this provision which is of use for judicial review. Indeed, Lord Mackenzie Stuart has described the definition of subsidiarity contained in the Treaty as 'a rich and prime example of gobbledygook'[102] and the principle of subsidiarity more generally as 'a busted flush'.[103] Subsidiarity is clearly a political principle: 'a political maxim, not a legal one'.[104] As such, it can be invoked as a justification for Community action, but also in opposition to it. In both instances, recourse must be had to the other elements in the second sentence of Article 3b EC in order to support the standpoint concerned.

Of these other elements, it is primarily the concept of 'exclusive competence' which lends itself to more precise definition through case-law. It is incontrovertible, on the basis of the EC Treaty itself and the case-law,[105] that such exclusive Community competence already exists primarily in the field of the common commercial policy and in relation to matters of external economic relations, where a transfer of competence has occurred in the internal Community sphere. It is submitted that the competence conferred on the Community in relation to Economic and Monetary Union and in the field of economic and social cohesion are also by their very nature exclusive in character. In the policy areas of agriculture, fisheries and transport the case-law appears to indicate that, despite the common policies provided for, there is an often far-reaching Community competence, but exclusivity is not wholly unlimited. Also in the fields of Community competition policy and harmonization of laws it is not always clear to what extent the undeniable powers conferred on the Community have a real exclusive effect, and to what extent they merely lead to the primacy of primary and secondary Community law over national laws which are incompatible with such Community law.[106] The Court of Justice (whether immediately, or on appeal from the Court of First Instance) will gradually have to shed light on the legal significance of the term 'exclusive competence' on the basis of the general and specific objectives of and conferments of competence in the EC

102. In a letter to *The Independent*, 15 June 1992.
103. In Curtin and O'Keeffe (eds.), *loc. cit.* (see note 95, *supra*). A 'busted flush', he explains, describes the situation in poker where an initially promising hand has been rendered worthless by the turn of the cards.
104. Mackenzie Stuart, *ibid.* at 23.
105. See Chapter XII, section 2, *post*.
106. Community competence in the field of merger control is at least in part clearly exclusive in nature, as is explained in Chapter VIII, section 4.5; the powers in relation to Arts. 85 and 86 EC, though, are more of a guaranteed competence which does not exclude the competence of the Member States (save in the application of Art. 85(3) EC), although Community law takes precedence over any incompatible national legal action. The Community power to control State aids, conferred by Arts. 92–94 EC is, however, exclusive in nature.

Treaty.[107] In practice it seems that the second paragraph of Article 3b EC will in the meantime be important in the areas of clear concurrent or parallel competence of the Community and the Member States. In areas in which the allocation of competence to the Community on the one hand or to the Member States on the other is, in the light of present or future case-law, clear, Article 3b EC is irrelevant: the principle of subsidiarity applies in the Community context only in areas in which competence is not clearly allocated to one level or the other.

The question remains, however, of the meaning of the limitation on Community competence in non-pre-allocated fields: 'the Community shall take action ... only if and in so far as the objectives of the proposed action cannot be sufficiently achieved by the Member States and can therefore, by reason of the scale or effects of the proposed action, be better achieved by the Community.' It may be recalled that the celebrated economist Tinbergen developed the invaluable theory of the optimal level of decision-making.[108] This involves decisions with external effects (*i.e.* decisions affecting third parties) being taken at sufficiently high level that external effects outside the sphere of legal competence of the decision-making level can be neglected. Kapteyn has observed that this doctrine is remarkably compatible with the provision in the German Basic Law[109] which is comparable with Article 3b EC.[110] In accordance with Article 72(II)(2) GG, the German Federation acts if the regulation of a particular matter by a *Land* could harm the interest of other *Länder* or the people as a whole ('*die Gesamtheit*'). Moreover, the Tinbergen theory rightly emphasizes that the Community must be able to act in matters of a cross-border nature or with important cross-border consequences, which the Member States cannot control, either because of the principle of territoriality, or because their policy is exclusively determined by their own national interests. Thus Belgium, France or Germany have less interest in acting to combat pollution of the Meuse, the Moselle or the Rhine caused within their frontiers to the extent that, because of the place of establishment of the polluter concerned, the pollution has serious consequences primarily for the Netherlands, whereas the Netherlands has no legal

107. See Lenaerts and van Ypersele (1994) CDE 3 at 13–28.
108. See Tinbergen, *International Economic Integration* (2nd ed., Amsterdam, 1965) 58 ('The fundamental problem of qualitative economic policy is to find the 'optimum order', that is, a set of institutions which maximizes national or social well-being.') and literature cited there. See also Tinbergen *et al.*, *Reshaping the International Order: A Report to the Club of Rome* (New York, 1976) 86.
109. The *Grundgesetz* (GG), Art. 72 deals with concurrent legislative competence. Art. 30 GG provides that: 'The exercise of governmental powers and the discharge of governmental functions shall be incumbent on the *Länder*, in so far as this Basic law does not otherwise prescribe or permit.' Thus, like the Community, the Federal level in Germany operates on the basis of attributed powers.
110. Kapteyn in Hellingman (ed.) *op. cit.* (see note 81, *supra*) 44.

possibility of effectively acting to combat such pollution. Similar observations can be made about cross-border cartel arrangements or mergers. In fact with the present degree of interdependence of the interests of the Member States, so many national laws and other policy measures have external effects for other Member States that a literal application of the theory of the optimal decision-making level would lead to such a centralization of powers at the Community level that at the end of the day less complete national regulations would better serve the objectives concerned than Community measures. Hence the importance of the words 'sufficiently' and 'better' in the text of the second paragraph of Article 3b EC: they make possible a political balancing of the interests and possibilities of the Member States individually on the one hand, and the Community as a whole on the other. The emphasis placed in that provision on not merely the effects of the proposed action but also on its scale make it plain that the financial or economic scale of a given operation will also be decisive, without the effects of the operation for other Member States having to be designated as co-decisive. The application criteria contained in Article 3b EC thus appear to leave a considerable freedom of discretion to the politically responsible Community Institutions. If in the reasoning of the positive or negative decision concerned it is stated that a Community objective is or is not involved, and moreover that Community action is or is not more effective than action by each of the Member States separately (or possibly by some of them acting together) it will be difficult to challenge successfully the result of that balancing of interests before the Court, at least as long as there is something in the way of evidence that the point has been considered.[111] Kapteyn has rightly

111. Weatherill and Beaumont, *EC Law* (2nd ed., London, 1995) 15 suggest that the Court will confine itself to a form of procedural, rather than substantive, review, *i.e.* requiring a reasoned statement in the Preamble to legislation as to how it is compatible with the Art. 3b EC, 2nd para. However, while a properly reasoned recital may well be sufficient to pass such review, it is submitted that a mere recital along the lines of 'Whereas the objective of [whatever] can by reason of the scale or effects of the proposed action, be better achieved by the Community' without more ado will be inadequate: see, for an analogous approach in relation to Art. 100a(4) EEC, Case C-41/93 *France v. Commission* [1994] ECR I-1829 at 1850, which would seem to be supported by the Court's approach to the reasoning in relation to subsidiarity in Case C-233/94 *Germany v. European Parliament and Council* [1997] ECR I-2405 at 2452–2453. The intention expressed in the Interinstitutional Agreement on procedures for implementing the principle of subsidiarity (Bull. EC 10–1993, point 2.2.2) is that the explanatory memorandum accompanying a Commission proposal (published as part of the COM document, but not in the 'C series' of the O.J.) is to include a justification of the proposal under the principle of subsidiarity, but this is hardly adequate, even though it may be the easiest place from the point of view of initial explanation. The COM documents are less readily accessible than the O.J., and a summary of the justification should be included in the Preamble. While reference to the Commission's proposal is always made in the final legislation, it is to the O.J. publication, rather than to the COM document (although the latter is always mentioned in the 'C series' publication).

observed[112] that on the basis of the words 'sufficiently' and 'better' due attention must be paid in the political balancing process to other values or interests than effectiveness in the technocratic sense, such as the interest of decision-making as close as possible to the citizen.[113] Accordingly, he rightly concluded that examination by the Court of the conclusions reached by the Community's political institutions in the light of the second paragraph of Article 3b EC will only be of a marginal nature.[114] In doing so the Court will, it is submitted, pay attention not merely to the meticulous respect of the appropriate decision-making process (including the care paid to the reasoning of the conclusion reached), but also to the consistency of the interpretation of the principle of subsidiarity in the various instances involved.

With a view to clarity of reasoning and the maintenance of consistency, it was agreed at the Edinburgh European Council, in December 1992, to seek an Interinstitutional Agreement on subsidiarity, on the basis of the basic principles and guidelines of the overall approach to the principle of subsidiarity by the Council which were also agreed on that occasion.[115] In

Amendments to the proposal made by the European Parliament or the Council will have to be accompanied by a justification if they involve more extensive or more intensive Community action than that proposed by the Commission, but this will only be really helpful if it is included when the amendments suggested or agreed upon are published in the O.J. In any event, use of the COM documents would not catch legislative action by the Commission under delegated powers. Accordingly, there is no real substitute for insisting on some clarity in the Preamble to the act concerned itself, and that appears to be the approached followed by the Community Institutions, at least in outline, see Case 233/94 *Germany v. European Parliament and Council, ibid.*

112. Kapteyn in Hellingman (ed.), *op. cit.* (see note 81, *supra*) 48.
113. Preamble TEU, Eleventh recital.
114. *Ibid.* In the same sense, *e.g.*: Weatherill and Beaumont, *loc. cit.* (see note 111, *supra*); Constantinesco in Constantinesco *et al.* (eds.), *Traité sur l'Union Européenne* (Paris, 1995), 114 (who bemoans like others the missed opportunity of allowing the Court to give an Opinion *ex ante* about the compatibility of a proposed measure with the principle of subsidiarity in the same way as is provided for in relation to the proposed conclusion of international agreements by the Community in Art. 228 EC), and Emiliou in O'Keeffe and Twomey (eds.), *op. cit.* (see note 95, *supra*) 65 at 80. In Case C-84/94 *United Kingdom v. Council* [1996] ECR I-5755 at 5811 the Court noted that an argument that the Community legislature had failed to establish that the aims of a particular directive would be better served at community level than at national level, really concerned the need for Community action. Once that had been demonstrated the Court was clearly unwilling to enter into an evaluation of whether Community action was better suited to achieving the aims than national action. As to the nature of judicial review of Community acts, see Chapter VI, section 1.1, *post.* Hartley, *The Foundations of European Community Law* (3rd ed., Oxford, 1994) 164 puts it rather sourly: 'Since the essence of subsidiarity is that it protects the rights of the Member States against encroachment by Brussels, it is doubtful whether the Court will want to give it any real bite.'
115. Bull. EC 12–1992, point I.15. As to the Interinstitutional Agreement, see Bull. EC 10–1993, point 2.2.2. As to the review of pending proposals and existing legislation in the light of the principle of subsidiarity, see Bull. EC 12–1992, point I.23, and the critical

accordance with the terms of Articles B and C TEU, the procedures for implementing the principle of subsidiarity do not call into question the *acquis communautaire*; nor do they call into question the Treaty provisions concerning the powers conferred on the Community Institutions or the institutional balance.[116] This guards against any temptation to misuse the principle of subsidiarity to resist use being made of Community powers on totally unrelated grounds. The overall approach also reflects the idea of subsidiarity in the drafting of a number of the more recent provisions of the EC Treaty, in which the subsidiary nature of Community action is expressly emphasized.[117] It further acknowledges that subsidiarity is a dynamic concept which should be applied in the light of the objectives set out in the EC Treaty, and (given the dynamic nature of those objectives) allows Community action to be expanded where circumstances so require, and thus, conversely, to be restricted or discontinued where it is no longer justified.[118]

The guidelines of the overall approach[119] are taken into account by the Commission in the drafting of its proposals, and by the European

discussion by Maher in Shaw and Moore (eds.), *New Legal Dynamics of European Union* (Oxford, 1995) 235. See further, *e.g. General Report 1997* (Brussels, Luxembourg, 1998) point 1104. A Protocol on the application of the principles of subsidiarity and proportionality is annexed to the EC Treaty by the Treaty of Amsterdam (not yet in force). This fleshes out the Edinburgh approach in more concrete terms, particularly making greater demands of the Commission in relation the justification of measures as complying with the two principles. The raising of the political approaches to the status of Treaty law in the form of a Protocol may perhaps cause more rigorous examination by the Court of the reasoning of legislation in relation to these principles.

116. Interinstitutional Agreement, *ibid.* The same sentiment was expressed in the approach agreed at Edinburgh: the principle of subsidiarity did not relate to or have the effect of calling into question the powers conferred on the Community by the EC Treaty, as interpreted by the Court of Justice; its application would respect the general provisions of the TEU, including the maintenance in full of the *acquis communautaire*, and it did not affect the primacy of Community law or call into question the principle set out in Art. F(3) TEU, which provides that the European Union is to provide itself with the means necessary to attain its objectives and carry through its policies: Bull. EC 12–1992, point I.15. In any event, mere practice cannot have the effect of altering the allocation of responsibilities or the other rules laid down by the EC Treaty, see *e.g.* Case 68/86 *United Kingdom* v. *Council* [1988] ECR 855 at 898 and 900.

117. Arts. 118a; 126–129b; 130, and 130g EC. Community action takes the form of minimum provisions (social policy); or has a supporting role in relation to policies which are in principle left to the Member States (education; vocational training; culture, and public health), or has a supporting or supplementary function (consumer protection, Trans-European Networks; industry, and research and technological development).

118. This demonstrates that Hartley's view of subsidiarity is somewhat one-sided (see note 114, *supra*) just as the pure application of Tinbergen's theory of the optimal level of decision-making has been shown above to be now somewhat unnuanced in its application to the Community.

119. Bull. EC 12–1992, point I.16.

Parliament and the Council in amendments to the Commission's text, where they entail more extensive or intensive intervention by the Community, and the three institutions regularly check, as part of the substantive examination of the action envisaged, both as regards the choice of legal instruments and the content of proposals, compliance with the provisions concerning subsidiarity.[120]

5.1.2 The principle of proportionality, or reasonableness

The third paragraph of Article 3b EC applies in fields in which the Community possesses merely concurrent powers (with the Member States) as well as in fields in which it has exclusive powers. It thus constitutes a supplement to the principle of subsidiarity developed in the second paragraph of Article 3b EC; a supplement which applies to each and every action of the Community, and which has a different character in each case. It is expressed bluntly: 'Any action by the Community shall not go beyond what is necessary to achieve the objectives of this Treaty.'[121]

The principle of proportionality, or reasonableness, has been developed as a general principle of law in the case-law of the Court of Justice, and as such is applied in ever-increasing measure by the Court of Justice.[122] It appears likely that the Court will, in the eminently cautious words of Kapteyn, proceed to 'a less marginal examination' of the policies pursued by the other Community Institutions.[123] They will have to respect the *acquis communautaire* developed – and developing – in the case-law, also in relation to proportionality, just as in relation to other aspects. The case-law of the Court in relation to proportionality in the field of free movement of goods[124] already caused the Commission and the Council to

120. Interinstitutional Agreement, Bull. EC 10–1993, point 2.2.2.
121. Lenaerts and van Ypersele (1994) CDE 3 at 67–68 rightly point out that the term 'objectives of this Treaty' means the *relevant* objectives of the Treaty for the action concerned. See also their discussion of the case-law on proportionality at 68–70. The most recent major work on proportionality is Emiliou, *The Principle of Proportionality in European Law* (London, 1996); see also Arnull, *The General Principles of EEC Law and the Individual* (London, 1990) Chapters 4, 9 and 14; de Búrca (1993) 13 YBEL 105; Jans (1992) SEW 751; Lenaerts (1994) 17 Fordh. Int'l. L.J. 846 at 882–893, and Schermers and Waelbroeck, *Judicial Protection in the European Communities* (5th ed., Deventer, 1992) 77–80.
122. For an impression, see the treatment of the concept in myriad places in this work, detailed under the heading 'proportionality' in the index.
123. Kapteyn in Hellingman (ed.), *op. cit.* (see note 81, *supra*) 49. This may well develop further in the light of the Protocol on the application of the principles of subsidiarity and proportionality annexed to the EC Treaty by the Treaty of Amsterdam (not yet in force).
124. *E.g.* Case 8/74 *Procureur du Roi v. Dassonville et al.* [1974] ECR 837, [1974] 2 CMLR 436; Case 120/78 *Rewe-Zentral AG v. Bundesmonopolverwaltung für Branntwein*

pursue a new, and less far-reaching approach to harmonization of laws,[125] which found further expression in the Single European Act.[126] That case-law had shown that 'the approximation of laws to the extent required for the proper functioning of the common market'[127] required in principle only sufficient equivalence rather than more or less total uniformity of national technical regulations or standards.[128]

According to its text, the principle of proportionality contained in the third paragraph of Article 3b EC primarily relates to the *degree of intervention* in national legislation or national policy. In addition, though, in the light of Articles 2, 3, and 3a EC it also concerns the legal nature of the *means* used to achieve the general or particular objectives of the Treaty.[129] Thus the principle could not merely lead more often to mutual recognition of legal acts of other Member States, and the establishment of minimum requirements; it could also justify the use of recommendations instead of legally binding Community measures, or of directives instead of regulations.[130] Moreover, the great emphasis which Articles 2, 3, and 3a

('*Cassis de Dijon*') [1979] ECR 649, [1979] 3 CMLR 494; Case 132/80 *NV United Foods et al. v. Belgian State* [1981] ECR 995, and Case 272/80 *Frans-Nederlandse Maatschappij voor Biologische Producten BV* [1981] ECR 3277, [1982] 2 CMLR 497.

125. See Gormley (1981) 6 ELRev. 454 and literature cited there.
126. With the introduction of Art. 100a EEC.
127. Art. 3(h) EC (unchanged).
128. As to which, see Chapter VIII, section 1.1., *post*.
129. In the same sense, Durand, in Mégret, *op. cit.* (see note 97, *supra*) 429–430.
130. Although given the problems which beset directives (implementation and their lack of horizontal direct effect (as to which, see Chapter VI, section 2.2.2, *post*), reasons of effectiveness may well plead for the use of regulations rather than directives in certain areas where there is a very clear Community policy or interest, as happened in the field of Community customs law, where old directives were replaced by regulations and then by a consolidated Community Customs Code (see Gormley in Emiliou and O'Keeffe (eds.), *The European Union and World Trade Law After the GATT Uruguay Round* (Chichester, 1996) 124). Emiliou, *op. cit.* (see note 121, *supra*) 140–141 usefully cites the views of the Lord Chancellor as expressed in a debate of the House of Lords, HL Deb. June 8, 1993, c. 713, which in spirit correspond with those expressed in the text, ('not a regulation if a directive would suffice; not a detailed directive if a frame-work directive would do') albeit that the learned Lord Chancellor's remarks demonstrate a mixing of the concepts of subsidiarity and proportionality, which, though related are in fact distinct (the Edinburgh overall approach (see note 115, *supra*) views the former dealing with whether the Community should act, the latter with the means by which it acts). As to criticism of that view, see Bermann (1994) Columb. L. Rev. 332 at 386–390. Emiliou, *ibid.* at 142, rightly sees proportionality not simply as a *judicial* doctrine for the Court to apply in reviewing the legality of Community action, but also as a *legislative* doctrine for the political institutions to observe in the exercise of their decision-making functions. Following Steiner in O'Keeffe and Twomey (eds.) *op. cit.* (see note 95, *supra*) 49 at 60, he concludes that subsidiarity and proportionality have a cumulative effect. Thus subsidiarity provides the initial justification for specific Community action, on efficiency grounds, determined by reference to the scale or effects of the action proposed, whereas proportionality ensures that the action taken does not exceed what is appropriate and necessary to achieve its proposed objective.

EC place on the market economy principle should justify an interpretation of Article 3b EC in the sense that no more far-reaching interference in the market mechanism is permissible than is necessary to achieve the objectives of the EC Treaty. In addition to giving priority to measures which do not compel a particular course of action, the principle of proportionality could lead to preference for Community financial contributions supporting national policies, rather than for steering measures of conditional financial assistance linked to a particular course of conduct, or even to preference for either of these means of assistance rather than either directives or regulations. Even in directives or regulations it would be possible to prefer less far-reaching intervention in the free market rather than more direct intervention in matters such as prices, production and investment. It may be useful to recall in this connection that Articles 5 and 57 ECSC already expressly provide for such an order of preference in favour of the least far-reaching measures of intervention in production and the market. In the EC Treaty too, as a result of the amendments to the old EEC Treaty introduced by the TEU a great many examples of such an approach are evident.[131] Both the more free-market developments in recent years in the field of transport policy, in which the text of the EC Treaty would permit a more interventionist approach, and the recent reforms in the Common Agricultural Policy demonstrate that a principle of less intervention is steadily gaining ground.[132] It is thus perfectly likely that the Court of Justice in its future case-law will interpret Article 3b EC as meaning that clear reasoning will usually be necessary in order to justify the necessity for more detailed legal instruments, or for stronger means of intervention in the market mechanism. Exceptions to this requirement would of course apply in the cases in which the EC Treaty itself already prescribes the use of specific means.

Finally, Article 3b EC also appears to be important for regulating the day-to-day implementation of Community policy. The principle of preference for directives rather than regulations, already applied in the implementation of Article 100a EC[133] means that the Community seeks to leave the implementation of the Community measures concerned to the Member States as much as possible, including the detailed legal or administrative details of that implementation. The execution of the common customs tariff and of the Common Agricultural Policy is also

---

Thus, in accordance with the view expressed in this work, proportionality serves to control the scope of legislation and to determine the least intrusive means for its implementation.

131. These matters are discussed in the various Chapters of this work dealing with substantive Community law.
132. Not for nothing was the emphasis laid on the principle of an open market economy, with free competition in Art. 3(a)(2) EC.
133. See the Declaration on Art. 100a EEC attached to the Final Act dealing with the SEA.

largely left to the Member States, to name but two areas in which Community law provides for detailed rules or intervention to a large degree in the operation of the market.

The most important areas of policy in which the Community Institutions themselves are charged with the day-to-day execution on the basis of the Treaty provisions are: competition law, on the basis of Articles 85–94 EC; anti-dumping policy, in the context of the common commercial policy, and a number of safeguard provisions in primary or secondary community law in various areas, which can only be applied at the request of Member states or interested private parties. In all these instances it is impossible to leave the administrative execution in the fields involved to the Member States, because of the cross-border nature of the facts concerned, or their cross-border consequences, or the cross-border nature of the objectives which have to be examined (such as cross-border distortions of competition). The unsatisfactory action so far to combat fraud and evasion in the areas of the Common Agricultural Policy and customs law make it clear that the criminal law territoriality principle, and the sometimes scant national financial loss as a result of fraud in the purely national execution of Community law, may endanger significant Community interests (including financial interests).[134] Even when the provisions to be implemented are extremely detailed, they do not always successfully prevent such risks.

It may be concluded that the principle of proportionality, or reasonableness, as set out in the third paragraph of Article 3b EC, can be seen as a general principle of law, the extent of which is now sufficiently clear, through myriad provisions of the EC Treaty and the case-law, to be confident that the Court of Justice will utilize it in the examination of Community action, always taking account of the margin of discretion permitted to the Community Institutions by primary or secondary Community law. With Jans[135] it is submitted that this admission makes it impossible for the balancing of interests to relate to anything other than the means by which it is sought to achieve the policy objectives which have been recognized. It is moreover submitted, on the basis of the analysis of Articles 2, 3 and 3a EC advanced in this Chapter, that both the principle of subsidiarity and the principle of proportionality relate solely to the means of achieving particular objectives, not to the evaluation of the

---

134. See Reg. 2988/95 (O.J. 1995 L 312/1); the Council Act of 26 July 1995 drawing up the Convention on the protection of the European Communities' financial interests (O.J. 1995 C 316/48), and the Convention itself, drawn up on the basis of Art. K.3 TEU (O.J. 1995 C 316/49). See further chapter II, section 1.3 (note 125) *ante* and Reg. 2185/96 (O.J. 1996 L 292/2) on-the-spot checks and inspections by the Commission, implemented, as regards financial control by the Member States of operations co-financed by the Structural Funds, by Reg. 2064/97 (O.J. 1997 L 290/1).
135. Jans (1992) SEW 751 at 765–770.

objectives themselves. In Articles 2 and 3a EC the market economy is also a means, not an objective. Even in the examination of policy measures in the light of contradictory policy objectives set out in the Treaties, which have to be achieved simultaneously, such as in the field of agriculture, or coal and steel policy, the Court has always been very reticent in its case-law, leaving the Community Institutions a wide margin of discretion in their evaluation of competing interests involving decisions on complex economic factors.[136]

5.1.3   Concluding observations on these principles

A general conclusion from the preceding analysis of Article 3b EC appears to be that, certainly from a legal viewpoint, the principle of proportionality expressed in that provision will potentially afford a more effective guarantee against too much and too detailed regulation from the Community level than will the principle of subsidiarity which occupies so central a place in Article 3b.

5.2   The principle of Community loyalty (or solidarity)

5.2.1   General observations

Article 5 EC contains two positive obligations for Member States and one negative: first, to take all appropriate measures, whether general or particular, to ensure fulfilment of the obligations arising out of the EC Treaty or resulting from action taken by the Community Institutions; secondly, to facilitate the achievement of the Community's tasks, and, thirdly, to abstain from any measures which could jeopardize the attainments of the objectives of the Treaty. It thus prohibits sins of commission and omission. The concrete effects of these three obligations are further developed in conjunction with other Articles of the Treaty or in secondary legislation.[137] The huge explosion in case-law in recent

---

136. *E.g.* Case 29/77 *SA Roquette Frères v. French State – Administration des Douanes* [1977] ECR 1835 at 1843–1844; Case C-311/90 *Hierl v. Hauptzollamt Regensburg* [1992] ECR I-2061 at 2081; Case C-280/93 *Germany v. Council* [1994] ECR I-4973 at 5057, and Case C-44/94 *R. v. Minister of Agriculture, Fisheries and Food, ex parte National Federation of Fishermen's Organisations et al.* [1995] ECR I-3115 at 3147–3149.

137. See *e.g.* Case 78/70 *Deutsche Grammophon Gesellschaft mbH v. Metro–SB Gross-markte GmbH & Co. KG* [1971] ECR 487 at 499; Case 31/74 *Galli* [19751 ECR 47 at 64; Case 229/83 *Association des centres distributeurs Édouard Leclerc et al. v. Sàrl 'Au blé vert' et al.* [1985] ECR 1 at 31–33 and Case 44/84 *Hurd v. Jones* [1986] ECR 29 at 83. See, generally, Constantinesco in Capotorti *et al.* (eds.), *Du droit international au*

years[138] indicates that obligations in Article 5 are thus largely supplementary in nature to the myriad more specific obligations contained in the EC Treaty. Only in conjunction with directly effective other provisions of Community law will the obligations of Article 5 sometimes create rights on which individuals can rely.[139] To this extent a parallel can be drawn with the specific obligation, phrased in similar terms, in Article 90(1) EC. Thus, for example, Article 5, or in this instance, the express terms of Article 90(1), prohibits Member States from enacting or maintaining in force any measure which would support infringements of Article 85 EC by undertakings. Moreover, case-law indicates that Article 5 links rights for individuals to the infringement by Member States of their obligations in other instances, such as infringements of the free movement of goods principle, the freedom of establishment, or the failure to transpose directives into national provisions on time or correctly.[140] Both Due and Durand have demonstrated that the extensive case-law on Article 5 EC can be better viewed than through the use of the three obligations specified in the Treaty.[141] Accordingly, in the following subsection the first positive obligation for the Member States may, like ancient Gaul, be divided into three parts:

(a) the obligation to take all appropriate measures necessary to ensure the effective application of Community law;

(b) the obligation to ensure the protection of rights stemming from primary and secondary Community law;

(c) the obligation to act (themselves) to achieve the objectives of the

droit de l'intégration (Liber Amicorum Pescatore, Baden–Baden, 1987) 97; Contributions by Bleckmann and Dauses in Bieber and Ress (eds.), Die Dynamik des Europäischen Gemeinschaftsrechts / The Dynamics of EC Law (Baden–Baden, 1987) 161 and 229; Due (1992) SEW 355; Garcia de Enterria (1993) 13 YBEL 19; Lück, Die Gemeinschaftstreue als allgemeines Rechtsprinzip im Recht der Europäischen Gemeinschaft (Baden–Baden, 1992); Schermers and Pearson in Baur et al. (eds.), Festschrift für Ernst Steindorff Berlin, 1990) 1359; Temple Lang (1987) 10 Fordham Int. L.J. 503; Temple Lang (1990) 27 CMLRev. 645; Temple Lang in Gormley (ed.) Current and Future Perspectives on Competition Law (London, 1996) 41; Van Gerven et al. (1990) Rechtskundig Weekblad 1158; Zuleeg in Von der Groeben et al., Kommentar zum EWG–Vertrag (5th ed., Baden–Baden, 1997) vol. 1, 262; and Temple Lang (1998) 23 ELRev. 109. For an example of a resolution making specific the duty of co-operation under Art. 5 EC see Case 141/78 France v. United Kingdom [1979] ECR 2923 at 2942.

138. The real explosion started in 1987, and between then and the date at which this work states the law, Art. 5 has featured in well over a hundred judgments.

139. As to the meaning of the term 'direct effect', see Chapter VI, section 2.2, post.

140. Cases C-6 and 9/90 Francovich et al. v. Italy [1991] ECR I-5357 at 5414 and Cases C-46 and 48/93 Brasserie du Pêcheur SA v. Germany [1996] ECR I-1029 at 1142–1155.

141. Due (1992) SEW 355; in greater detail, Durand in Mégret, op. cit. (see note 97, supra) 25 at 27. The discussion in the following subsections is based on their approach, adapted as necessary, in part in the light of recent case-law.

Treaty, in particular in the case of inaction by the competent Community Institution.

Thereafter, the following two subsections deal respectively with the abstention obligation contained in the second paragraph of Article 5, and the concept of Article 5 as an expression of the general principle of mutual cooperation.

5.2.2   The first positive obligation in Article 5 EC

(a) the obligation to take all appropriate measures necessary to ensure the effective application of Community law

It is unnecessary to allege an infringement of Article 5 EC in infringement proceedings under Articles 169 or 170 EC, where the primary infringement alleged relates to a specific provision of primary or secondary Community law.[142] In particular the far-reaching and complex common organizations of the agricultural markets require extensive supplementary general or particular national provisions, regulatory, budgetary, administrative and organizational, and provisions imposing sanctions and facilitating remedies, in order to ensure that the obligations arising from the EC Treaty or the Community action concerned are indeed fulfilled.[143] However, examples of

---

142. See *e.g.* Case C-35/88 *Commission v. Greece* [1990] ECR I-3125 at 3162. This also reflects Commission practice in infringement proceedings under Arts. 169 or 170 EC. Thus a failure to respond to letters from the Commission in relating to an alleged breach of Community law could be added to the substantive infringement complained of when the letter constituting formal notice is sent, and can be the subject of a specific finding of a failure by a Member State to fulfil its obligations, even if the substantive infringement alleged has not been proved, see *e.g.* Case 240/86 *Commission v. Greece* [1988] ECR 1835 at 1858. The Commission uses Art. 5 only exceptionally, as the Member State could terminate the infringement of Art. 5 EC by simply replying to that formal letter, and the general practice of the Commission is not to pursue further infringements which are brought to an end during earlier stages of the proceedings. The Commission is, however, certainly entitled to continue proceedings even if the Member State complies after the issue of the reasoned opinion, see *e.g.* Case 39/72 *Commission v. Italy* [1973] ECR 101 at 112; Case 103/84 *Commission v. Italy* [1986] ECR 1759 at 1771). Sometimes difficulties persist even at the judicial stage of the proceedings, see *e.g.* Case 272/86 *Commission v. Greece* [1988] ECR 4875 at 4902–4903; Case C-35/88 *Commission v. Greece* [1990] ECR I-3125 at 3161. See, further, Chapter VI, section 1.1, *post*.

143. From the myriad examples, including those cited by Due, Durand and by Zuleeg, *op. cit.* (notes 97 and 137, *supra*), see *e.g.* Case 39/72 *Commission v. Italy* [1973] ECR 101 at 115–116; Case 30/72 *Commission v. Italy* [1973] ECR 161 at 172; Case 394/85 *Commission v. Italy* [1987] ECR 2741 at 2752–2753; Case 10/88 *Italy v. Commission* [1990] ECR I-1229 (summary publication); Case C-8/88 *Germany v. Commission* [1990] ECR I-2321 at 2360–2361; Case 68/88 *Commission v. Greece* [1989] ECR 2965 at 2984–2985.

such requirements stemming from Community law are far from confined to the agricultural sector, and the case-law embraces examples from *inter alia* the sectors of equal treatment for men and women;[144] protection on the transfer of undertakings;[145] the free movement of workers and the right of establishment;[146] transport;[147] public procurement,[148] and the environment.[149]

The obligation applies to the legislative as well as to the executive and judicial organs of the State at whatever level, central, regional or local.[150] A particularly important example of the supplementary obligations for the national courts is the obligation to interpret national law (where possible) in conformity with the provisions of directives.[151] In so far as the State bears responsibility for its constitutionally independent organs, such as autonomous regions in Spain or Italy, or the German *Länder*, or the Belgian regions and communities, serious problems may arise in the practical enforcement of the respect for Community obligations.[152] The responsibility in Community law and in public international law of a Member State also embraces responsibility for the respect of Community law by any independent policy pursued by its various territorially decentralized authorities.[153] It remains, though, for the Member States to take the necessary legal, administrative, or even constitutional steps to ensure that internal liability is given effect; it is not for the Commission to rule on the

144. *E.g.* Case 14/83 *Von Colson and Kamann v. Land Nordrhein-Westfalen* [1984] ECR 1891 at 1909; Case 222/84 *Johnson v. Chief Constable of the Royal Ulster Constabulary* [1986] ECR 1651 at 1682; Case C-271/91 *Marshall v. Southampton and South West Hampshire Area Health Authority* [1993] ECR I-4367 at 4407–4408 and 4410.
145. *E.g.* Case C-382/92 *Commission v. United Kingdom* [1994] ECR I-2435 at 2475.
146. *E.g.* Case 222/86 *Union nationale des entraineurs et cadres techniques professionnels du football (Unectef) v. Heylens et el.* [1987] ECR 4097 at 4117; Case C-340/89 *Vlasso-poulou v. Ministerium für Justiz, Bundes- und Europaangelegenheiten Baden-Württemberg* [1991] ECR I-2357 at 2385.
147. *E.g.* Case C-326/88 *Anklagemyndigheden v. Hansen & Søn I/S* [1990] ECR I-2911 at 2935; Case C-7/90 *Vandervenne et al.* [1991] ECR I-4371 at 4387.
148. *E.g.* Case 31/87 *Gebroeders Beentjes BV v. The Netherlands* [1988] ECR 4635 at 4662.
149. *E.g.* Case C-56/90 *Commission v. United Kingdom* [1993] ECR I-4109 at 4138.
150. *E.g.* Case 103/88 *Fratelli Constanzo SpA v. Comune di Milano* [1989] ECR 1839 at 1871; Case C-8/88 *Germany v. Commission* [1990] ECR I-2321 at 2359; Case C-213/89 *R. v. Secretary of State for Transport, ex parte Factortame Ltd. et al.* [1990] ECR I-2433 at 2473; Cases C-6 and 9/90 *Francovich et al. v. Italy* [1991] ECR I-5357 at 5414, and Cases C-46 and 48/93 *Brasserie du Pêcheur SA et al. v. Germany et al.* [1996] ECR I-1029 at 1145.
151. See *e.g.* Case 125/88 *Nijman* [1989] ECR 3533 at 3546; Case C-106/89 *Marleasing SA v. La Commercial Internacional de Alimentación SA* [1990] ECR I-4135 at 4159; Case C-334/92 *Wagner Miret v. Fondo de garantía salarial* [1993] ECR I-6911 at 6932, and Case C-91/92 *Faccini Dori v. Recreb Srl* [1994] ECR I-3325 at 3357.
152. *E.g.* Case C-8/88 *Germany v. Commission* [1990] ECR I-2321 at 2359; Case C-2/90 *Commission v. Belgium* [1992] ECR I-4431.
153. *E.g.* Cases C-46 and 48/93 *Brasserie du Pêcheur SA et al. v. Germany et al.* [1996] ECR I-1029 at 1145, referring to the Opinion of Tesauro, A.G. at 1090.

division of competences or on the imposition of obligations between central and regional or local government in the Member States.[154]

(b) the obligation to ensure the protection of rights stemming from primary and secondary Community law

This obligation, ensuring judicial protection for individuals in the application of Community law, should, it is submitted, be distinguished from the obligation to take all appropriate measures necessary for the attainment of the substantive objectives of the Treaty. In relation to directly effective primary or secondary Community law, this obligation is principally directed at national courts.[155] The Court has now clarified the powers of the national courts to give additional or interim relief or to impose sanctions to reinforce protection of individuals.[156] The celebrated judgments in Cases C-6 and 9/90 *Francovich et al. v. Italy*[157] and Cases C-46 and 48/93 *Brasserie du Pêcheur SA et al. v. Germany et al.*[158] offer individuals a very effective means of judicial protection in the form of damages for loss suffered through the failure to transpose Community directives on time or correctly, and through the failure to comply with Community law the state of which is manifest.[159] This development offers a far more effective remedy than might have appeared possible from earlier case-law,[160] but the availability of damages for breach of Community law obligations by Member States was in fact foreshadowed, indeed expressly envisaged well before *Francovich*.[161] The long-established right of

---

154. *E.g.* Case C-8/88 *Germany v. Commission* [1990] ECR I-2321 at 2359. See, in relation to the recent reforms in Belgium, van Ingelaer (1994) SEW 67.
155. *E.g.* Case 68/79 *Hans Just I/S v. Danish Ministry for Fiscal Affairs* [1980] ECR 501, [1981] 3 CMLR 418; Case 265/78 *Ferwerda BV v. Produktschap voor Vee en Vlees* [1980] ECR 617, [1980] 3 CMLR 737; Case 61/79 *Amministrazione delle Finanze dello Stato v. Denkavit Italiana Srl.* [1980] ECR 1205, [1981] 3 CMLR 694. See also Case 199/82 *Amministrazione delle Finanze dello Stato v. San Giorgio SpA.* [1983] ECR 3595 at 3612 (and earlier authorities cited there).
156. See Case C-213/89 *R. v. Secretary of State for Transport, ex parte Factortame Ltd. et al.* [1990] ECR I-2433 at 2473–2474; Cases C-6 and 9/90 *Francovich et al. v. Italy* [1991] ECR I-5357 at 5414–5416; Cases C-46 and 48/93 *Brasserie du Pêcheur SA et al. v. Germany et al.* [1996] ECR I-1029 at 1153–1158; Case C-392/93 *R. v. H.M. Treasury, ex parte British Telecommunications plc* [1996] ECR I-1631 at 1668–1669; Case C-5/94 *R. v. Ministry of Agriculture, Fisheries and Food, ex parte Hedley Lomas (Ireland) Ltd.* [1996] ECR I-2553 at 2612–2614, and Cases C-178/94 *etc. Dillenkofer et al. v. Germany* [1996] ECR I-4845 at 4878–4880.
157. [1991] ECR I-5357, [1993] 2 CMLR 66.
158. [1996] ECR I-1029, [1996] 1 CMLR 889.
159. The conditions established in *Brasserie du Pêcheur* and applied in later judgments are discussed *in extenso* in Chapter VI, section 2.3.2, *post*.
160. In particular Case 33/76 *Rewe-Zentralfinanz EG et al. v. Landwirtschaftskammer für das Saarland* [1976] ECR 1989 at 1997–1998.
161. Case 39/72 *Commission v. Italy* [1973] ECR 101 at 112.

individuals to rely on unconditional and sufficiently clear provisions of directives which have not been transposed by Member States on time[162] was held to be in part founded on Article 5 EC only relatively recently.[163] As has now been stated in myriad cases, the obligation to ensure an adequate degree of judicial protection implies that the national legislatures must ensure the availability of proper rights of appeal (substantial and procedural rules).[164] Thus 'it is for the domestic legal system of each Member State to designate the courts having jurisdiction and determine the procedural conditions governing actions at law intended to safeguard rights which subjects derive from the direct effect of Community Law, it being understood that such conditions cannot be less favourable than those relating to similar actions of a domestic nature and that under no circumstances may they be so adapted as to make it impossible in practice to exercise the rights which the national courts have a duty to protect.'[165]

(c) the obligation to act (themselves) to achieve the objectives of the Treaty, in particular in the case of inaction by the competent Community Institution

Good examples of the effect of this obligation can be found, as both Durand[166] and Due observe,[167] in the case-law on the obligation on the Member States, in the absence of the Community directives envisaged in Article 57 EC, to take account of equivalent diplomas from other Member States when deciding on permitting nationals of another Member State to establish themselves in a professional capacity.[168]

This obligation also involves the obligation to take temporary national measures of positive integration,[169] where the competent Community

162. *E.g.* Case 148/78 *Pubblico Ministero v. Ratti* [1979] ECR 1629 at 1642.
163. Case 190/87 *Oberkreisdirektor des Kreises Borken et al. v. Handelsonderneming Moormann BV* [1988] ECR 4689 at 4722.
164. See note 155, *supra*, and, further, Chapter VI, section 2.3.2, *post*.
165. Case 811/79 *Amministrazione delle Finanze dello Stato v. Ariete SpA* [1980] ECR 2545 at 2554–2555. See also *e.g.* Case 68/79 *Hans Just I/S v., Danish Ministry for Fiscal Affairs* [1980] ECR 501; Case 199/82 *San Giorgio* [1983] ECR 3595 at 3612; Case 104/86 *Commission v. Italy* [1988] ECR 1799 at 1815–1816. See, further, Case C-312/93 *Peterbroeck, Van Campenhout en Cie GCV v. Belgian State* [1995] ECR I-4599 at 4620–4623; Cases C-430 and 431/93 *Van Schijndel et al. v. Stichting Pensioenfonds voor Fysiotherapeuten* [1995] ECR 4705 at 4737–4738, and Cases 46 and 48/93 *Brasserie du Pêcheur SA et al. v. Germany et al.* [1996] ECR I-1029 at 1153–1158.
166. *Op. cit.* (see note 97, *supra*) 32.
167. (1992) SEW 355 at 358.
168. *E.g.* Case 71/76 *Thieffry v. Conseil de l'ordre des avocats à la Cour de Paris* [1977] ECR 765 at 777; Case C-340/89 *Vlassopoulou v. Ministerium für Justiz, Bundes- en Europaangelegenheiten Baden-Württemberg* [1991] ECR I-2357 at 2383–2384, and Case C-55/94 *Gebhard v. Consiglio dell'Ordine degli Avvocati e Procuratori di Milano* [1995] ECR I-4165 at 4198. See, further, Chapter VII, section 6.6, *post*.
169. In Tinbergen's terms, see note 14, *supra*.

Institution has failed to act as it should have acted. Thus, in Case 804/ 79 *Commission v. United Kingdom*[170] the Court held that in a situation characterized by the inaction of the Council and by the maintenance, in principle, of the conservation measures in force, the Member States not only have an obligation to undertake detailed consultations with the Commission and to seek its approval in good faith but also a duty not to lay down national conservation measures in spite of objections, reservations or conditions which may be formulated by the Commission.[171] In its judgment in Case 41/76 *Criel, née Donckerwolcke et al. v. Procureur de la République et al.*[172] the Court had already reached an analogous, if less far-reaching conclusion relating to national measures of commercial policy. In Cases 47 and 48/83 *Pluimveeslachterij Midden-Nederland BV et al.*[173] the Council had failed to adopt measures designed in particular to improve quality and fix marketing standards for slaughtered poultry. These measures were necessary to ensure the proper functioning of the common organization in poultrymeat which had been set up in 1967.[174] The Court felt that in such a situation no objection could, in principle, be raised if a Member State maintained in force or introduced measures designed to achieve quality standards and thus sought to realize the aims of the common organization in its territory. However, as in the fisheries case,[175] the Court emphasized that such measures in these circumstances were not to be seen as an exercise of the competence of the Member State concerned but as compliance, in the *lacuna*, with the duty of co-operation imposed by Article 5 of the Treaty in order to achieve the aims of the common organization of the common market in poultrymeat. Thus the national measures could only be of a temporary and provisional nature and would have to cease to be applied as soon as the Community measures were introduced.[176] The use of Article 5 in this context was something of a master-stroke which allowed the Dutch measures to be upheld but struck down any argument about national competence as such; it emphasized the fiduciary nature of the Member States' obligations in

170. [1981] ECR 1045, [1982] 1 CMLR 543.
171. This is the Court's own summary of this judgment, see Case 269/80 *R. v. Tymen* [1981] ECR 3079 at 3091–3092.
172. [1976] ECR 1921, [1977] 2 CMLR 535.
173. [1984] ECR 1721.
174. Measures had to be adopted under Reg. 123/67 (O.J. English Special Edition 1967, p. 63), Art. 2, as codified in Reg. 2777/75 (O.J. 1975 L 282/77).
175. Case 804/79 *Commission v. United Kingdom* [1981] ECR 1045, [1982] 1 CMLR 543.
176. [1984] ECR 1721 at 1738. See, generally, on *lacunae*, Pescatore in Lüke *et al.* (eds), *Rechtsvergleichung, Europarecht und Staatenintegration* (*Gedächtnisschrift* for Constantinesco, Cologne, 1983) 559; Mortelmans (1981) CDE 410 and Lamoureux (1984) RMC 215. See also Case 48/74 *Charmasson v. Minister for Economic Affairs and Finance* [1974] ECR 1383, [1975] 2 CMLR 208 and Cases 3, 4 and 6/76 *Officier van Justitie v. Kramer et al.* [1976] ECR 1279, [1976] 2 CMLR 440.

these circumstances. They were effectively trustees for the benefit of the Community.[177]

5.2.3   The negative obligation on the Member States to abstain from any measure that could jeopardize the attainment of the objectives of the Treaty

As a general point, it should be noted that where criminal proceedings are brought under a national measure which is held to infringe Community law, a conviction in those proceedings is also incompatible with Community law.[178] It is convenient to adopt the tryptic approach of Durand in order to clarify the scope of this obligation.[179]

(a) The obligation to abstain from measures which could impede the effectiveness of Community law

In this connection both Durand[180] and, more extensively, Due[181] pay particular attention to what Due calls the 'corporatist tendencies' in a number of Member States, revealed through State measures which support

---

177. Gormley, *Prohibiting Restrictions on Trade within the EEC* (Amsterdam, 1985) 92, followed by Mortelmans in Van Dijk *et al.* (eds.), *Restructuring the International Economic Order: The Role of Law and Lawyers* (Deventer, 1987) 26. The Court expressed it as 'trustees of the common interest' [1981] ECR 1045 at 1075–1076. *Cf.* the situation in which there is no cooperation between the Commission and the Member State concerned, Case 325/85 *Ireland v. Commission* [1987] ECR 5041 at 5087–5088 (unilateral Commission proposals could not be regarded as Community rules), see also Case 326/85 *The Netherlands v. Commission* [1987] ECR 5091 at 5116, and Case 332/85 *Germany v. Commission* [1987] ECR 5143 at 5170.
178. Case 88/77 *Minister for Fisheries v. Schonenberg et al.* [1978] ECR 473 at 491; Case 179/78 *Procureur de la République v. Michelangelo Rivoira et al.* [1979] ECR 1147 at 1156; Case 269/80 *R. v. Tymen* [1981] ECR 3079 at 3093–3094. In Case 82/71 *Pubblico Ministero v. Società Agricola Industria Latte (SAIL)* [1972] ECR 119 at 135 the Court did not address the question specifically (despite saying in *Schonenberg* that it did) but dealt with a challenge to its jurisdiction, holding that Art. 177 drew no distinction between the nature, criminal or otherwise, of the national proceedings in the course of which the request for a preliminary ruling had been made. Thus 'the effectiveness of Community law cannot vary according to the various branches of national law which it may affect.' (*loc. cit.*) and the Court affirmed its jurisdiction and replied to the questions submitted. As to limits on penalties, see *e.g.* Case 41/76 *Criel, née Donckerwolcke et al. v. Procureur de la République et al.* [1976] ECR 1921 at 1938–1939; Case 203/80 *Casati* [1981] ECR 2595 at 2618–2619, and Case 199/82 *Amministrazione delle Finanze dello Stato v. SpA San Giorgio* [1983] ECR 3595 at 3612–3614. As to limits on the effect of directives in relation to penalties see Case 14/83 *Von Colson and Kamann v. Land Nordrhein–Westfalen* [1984] ECR 1891 at 1908–1909 and Case 80/86 *Kolpinghuis Nijmegen BV* [1987] ECR 3969 at 3986–3987, noted by Arnull (1988) 13 ELRev. 42.
179. Durand, *op. cit.* (see note 97, *supra*) 35–39.
180. *Ibid.*, at 35.
181. (1992) SEW 355 at 359–369.

agreements which are restrictive of competition and incompatible with Article 85(1) EC, such as measures declaring the provisions of an agreement generally binding, or equivalent measures. A spectacular example of this can be seen in Case 66/86 *Ahmed Saeed Flugreisen et al. v. Zentrale zur Bekämpfung unlauteren Wettbewerbs e.V.*[182] The Court found, in the context of tariff fixing in the air transport sector, that Article 5 EC (and, within its limited scope, Article 90 EC) precluded the national authorities from encouraging the conclusion of agreements incompatible with Articles 85 or 86 EC, as the case may be, and from approving the tariffs resulting from such agreements, unless[183] those measures were indispensable for the performance of a task of general interest which the air carriers were required to carry out, provided that the nature of that task and its impact on the tariff structure were clearly established.[184] However, such a link between Articles 5 and 85 or 86 cannot be made if there is no conduct by the undertakings involved which is itself incompatible with Articles 85 or 86. Thus the mere fact that the authorities themselves prescribe price regulations or other measures restrictive of competition will not infringe Article 5 EC,[185] even though the measures may well come into conflict with other provisions of the Treaty, such as Article 30 EC.[186]

(b) The obligation to abstain from measures which could hinder the internal functioning of the Community Institutions

A prerequisite for the proper functioning of the Community Institutions is protection from outside interference, by the Member States or otherwise. In some cases this independence is expressed in the Treaties in personal terms,[187] in other instances it is expressed in institutional terms as the right to determine their own organization.[188] In this latter context the European

---

182. [1989] ECR 803, [1990] 4 CMLR 102.
183. In the cases covered by Art. 90(2) EC.
184. [1989] ECR 803 at 854.
185. See *e.g.* Case C-2/91 *Meng* [1993] ECR I-5751; Case C-185/91 *Bundesanstalt für den Güternverkehr v. Gebr. Reiff GmbH & Co. KG* [1993] ECR I-5801; Case C-245/91 *Ohra Schadeverzekeringen NV* [1993] ECR I-5851, Case C-153/93 *Germany v. Delta Schiffahrts- und Speditionsgesellschaft mbH* [1994] ECR I-2517; Case C-96/94 *Centro Servizi Spediporto Srl v. Spedizioni Marittima del Golfo Srl* [1995] ECR I-2883; Cases C-140–142/94 *DIP SpA et al. v. Commune di Bassano del Grappa et al.* [1995] ECR I-3257, and Reich (1994) 31 CMLRev. 459. See further, Chapter VII, section 3 and Chapter VIII, section 4.1.1, *post*. See also Due, in Due *et al.* (eds.), *op. cit.* (see note 95, *supra*) Vol. I 273 at 277–278, and Edward and Hoskins (1995) 32 CMLRev. 157.
186. As to which, see Chapter VII, section 3, *post*.
187. Arts. 9(2) ECSC; 157(2) EC, and 126(2) Euratom (independence of the members of the Commission, see Chapter IV, section 4.1, *post*.
188. *E.g.* Arts. 25 ECSC; 142 EC, and 112 Euratom (adoption by the European Parliament of its Rules of Procedure). See, further, Chapter IV, section 5.1, *post*.

Parliament's efforts to move more of its activities to Brussels have given rise to some spectacular contortions. In Case 230/81 *Luxembourg v. European Parliament*[189] the Court stated that when the governments of the Member States made provisional decisions on the seats of the Community Institutions they were obliged, in particular by Article 5 of the Treaty, to 'have regard to the power of the Parliament to determine its internal organization.' As a result, the European Parliament has never accepted the decision made on the allocation of seats during the Edinburgh European Council meeting in December 1992,[190] which, by specifying where which plenary sessions of the Parliament will be held, and where the Parliament's committees will meet, would appear manifestly to interfere in the internal organization of the European Parliament's affairs. In other instances the Court has condemned national attempts to challenge the nature of payments to members of an Institution[191] or the special status accorded to Community officials or other servants.[192]

(c) The obligation to abstain from any measures which could hinder the development of the Community integration process

Durand[193] gives a number of illustrations of the effect of this obligation. First, Member States must abstain from acting in cases where a Community measure is in preparation.[194] This is certainly clear in instances in which a Commission proposal is being discussed in the Council in the context of implementing a common policy (such as agriculture, fisheries or transport);[195] it is also true in respect of the preparation of proposals under Directive 83/189,[196] although it is submitted that outside these areas

189. [1983] ECR 255 at 287. See also Case 108/83 *Luxembourg v. European Parliament* [1984] ECR 1945, [1986] 2 CMLR 507; Cases 358/85 and 51/86 *France v. European Parliament* [1988] ECR 4821, and Cases C-213/ 88 and 39/89 *Luxembourg v. European Parliament* [1991] ECR I-5643.
190. O.J. 1992 C 341/1, Bull. EC 12–1992, points I.14 and I.32. See Corbett *et al.*, *The European Parliament* (3rd ed., London, 1995) 36. See also Chapter II, section 5.3, *ante*.
191. Case 208/80 *Bruce of Donnington v. Aspden* [1981] ECR 2205, [1981] 3 CMLR 506. See also, as to the possibility of charging a former MEP for alleged fraud in relation to expenses claims, *R. v. Manchester Crown Court, ex parte D.P.P.* [1994] 1 CMLR 457 (HL).
192. *E.g.* Case 44/84 *Hurd v. Jones* [1986] ECR 29, [1986] 2 CMLR 1 (teachers at the European schools), and Case 186/85 *Commission v. Belgium* [1987] ECR 2029. See, further, Chapter II, section 5.2, *ante*.
193. Durand, *op. cit.* (see note 97, *supra*) 38.
194. Case 804/79 *Commission v. United Kingdom* [1981] ECR 1045 at 1075.
195. *E.g.* Case 804/79 *Commission v. United Kingdom* [1981] ECR 1045 at 1075, and Case C-195/90 *Commission v. Germany* [1992] ECR I-3141 at 3185–3186.
196. O.J. 1983 L 109/8, Art. 9(2) (Dir. 83/189 has been most recently amended by Dec. 96/ 139 (O.J. 1996 L 32/31)). See also Dec. 3052/95 (O.J. 1995 L 321/1) on information exchange.

the submission of a Commission proposal, or the mere commencement of the preparation of a proposal does not entail an obligation for the Member States.[197] Another example cited by Durand concerns the duty on Member states to abstain from entering into agreements with third countries which affect rules which the Community has already adopted on the matter in question.[198] Durand also speculates whether this obligation might be infringed if one or more Member States were to block decision-making in the Council on a matter in respect of which the Treaty or an existing Community act prescribes that action shall be taken a certain date. She acknowledges, though, that the most effective option in those circumstances would be an action on the ground of failure to act, under Article 175 EC. However, simply posing the question emphasizes that precisely because the final paragraph of Article 5 EC refers to the objectives of the Treaty, and not to concrete legal obligations, the case-law on this point may well evolve further.

   The Court has now made it clear that Member States must refrain from adopting, during the period between a directive's adoption and its entry into force, 'any measures liable seriously to compromise the result prescribed.'[199]

5.2.4   Article 5 EC as an expression of the general principle of mutual cooperation

This general principle has rightly been identified as a *leitmotif* in the case-law of the Court on Article 5 EC.[200] Durand has divided this into three specific elements: first, an obligation on national authorities and the Community Institutions to cooperate with each other; secondly, an mutual assistance obligation on the Member States, and, thirdly, an obligation on the Community Institutions to cooperate sincerely with the Member States.[201] There is, however, a fourth obligation which, though not expressed in Article 5 itself, has been derived from it by the Court: the duty on the Community Institutions to conduct the inter-institutional

197. Case 174/84 *Bulk Oil (Zug) AG v. Sun International Ltd. et al.* [1986] ECR 559 at 592–593. The Court has held that the fact that a Commission proposal before the Council would relieve a Member State of an existing obligation does not prevent the Commission from bringing infringement proceedings in respect of the failure to fulfil that existing obligation, nor is it a defence in such proceedings, see *e.g.* Case 220/83 *Commission v. France* [1986] ECR 3663 at 3705, and Case 306/84 *Commission v. Belgium* [1987] ECR 675 at 685–686.
198. Case 22/70 *Commission v. Council* [1971] ECR 263 at 275.
199. Case C-129/96 *Inter-Environnement Wallonie ASBL v. Région wallonne* [1997] ECR I-7411 at 7449.
200. See Durand, *op. cit.* (see note 97, *supra*) 39–42; Due (1992) SEW 355 at 363 *et seq.*, and Temple Lang in Gormley (ed.), *op. cit.* (see note , *supra*) 41 at 46–47.
201. Durand, *ibid.*

dialogue in terms of sincere cooperation.[202] While the mutual nature of these obligations, and the obligations on the Community Institutions, are not immediately apparent from the wording of Article 5 itself (which, after all, is addressed to the Member States), the case-law of the Court becomes logical if Article 5 is itself seen as a specific expression of a more general duty. The idea of mutuality and equivalence in the responsibilities also lies behind the approach to the conditions under which Member States may incur liability for damage caused to individuals by a breach of Community law.[203]

Durand has illustrated the first of her three elements by the obligations on the Member States to cooperate *bona fide* with the Commission in any inquiry which the latter undertakes, and to supply the Commission with all the information requested for that purpose;[204] to consult the Commission before adopting measures which could affect a Community field,[205] and to consult the Commission in the case of difficulties in implementing Community acts (particularly in relation to state aids).[206] Thus if, in giving effect to a decision, a Member State encounters unforeseen and unforeseeable difficulties, or perceives consequences which it feels the Commission has overlooked, it has to submit the problems to the Commission, with proposals for amendment of the decision concerned.[207] 'In such a case the Commission and the Member State concerned must respect the principle underlying Article 5 of the Treaty, which imposes a duty of genuine cooperation on the Member states and the Community institutions, and must work together in good faith with a view to overcoming difficulties whilst fully observing the Treaty provisions, and in particular the provisions on aid.'[208]

The second element is vividly illustrated by Durand using the judgment in Case 235/87 *Matteucci v. Communauté française of Belgium et al.*[209]

---

202. Case 204/86 *Greece v. Council* [1988] ECR 5233 at 5359 (expressly referring to Case 230/81 *Luxembourg v. European Parliament* [1983] ECR 255 at 287), and Case C-65/93 *European Parliament v. Council* [1995] ECR I-643 at 668.
203. This is particularly clearly expressed in Cases C-46 and 48/93 *Brasserie du Pêcheur SA et al. v. Germany et al.* [1966] ECR I-1029 at 1146–1148.
204. Case 192/84 *Commission v. Greece* [1985] ECR 3967 at 3979, although the Commission must specify the acts or omissions complained of when bringing infringement proceedings for failure to comply with Art. 5 EC, *ibid.* See also *e.g.* Case C-35/88 *Commission v. Greece* [1990] ECR I-3125 at 3160, and Case C-374/89 *Commission v. Belgium* [1991] ECR I-367 at 379.
205. *E.g.* Case 186/85 *Commission v. Belgium* [1987] ECR 2029 at 2057, and Case 141/78 *France v. United Kingdom* [1979] ECR 2923 at 2942.
206. *E.g.* Case 130/83 *Commission v. Italy* [1984] ECR 2849 at 2860; Case 52/84 *Commission v. Belgium* [1986] ECR 89 at 105; Case 94/87 *Commission v. Germany* [1989] ECR 175 at 192, and Case C-217/88 *Commission v. Germany* [1990] ECR I-2879 at 2907–2908.
207. Case 94/87 *Commission v. Germany* [1989] ECR 175 at 192.
208. *Ibid.* See also *e.g.* Case C-349/93 *Commission v. Italy* [1995] ECR I-343 at 357, and Case C-348/93 *Commission v. Italy* [1995] ECR I-673 at 694.
209. [1988] ECR 5589, [1989] 1 CMLR 357.

The Court interpreted Article 7 of Regulation 1612/68[210] as meaning that the Belgian authorities were not entitled, on the ground that scholarships under a Belgo–German cultural agreement were exclusively for Belgian nationals, to deny an Italian national, who had been born and educated in Belgium, where her father was employed, the benefit of a scholarship to pursue studies in Germany. Article 5 EC meant that if the application of a provision of Community law was likely to be impeded by a measure adopted pursuant to a bilateral agreement, even where that agreement fell outside the field of application of the Treaty, every Member State was under a duty to facilitate the application of the provision of Community law concerned, and, to that end, to assist every other Member State which was under an obligation in Community law.[211] The result is entirely understandable, as otherwise the equality of treatment required by Article 7 of the Regulation would be meaningless. Another clear recent example of this type of mutual assistance obligation in relation to social security payments to migrant workers can be seen in Case C-251/89 *Athanasopoulos et al. v. Bundesanstalt für Arbeit.*[212] In a wholly different field, the concepts of mutual assistance and mutual confidence have played an important role in the area of free movement of goods, so that Member States must, for example, take account of technical or chemical analyses or laboratory tests carried out in other Member States.[213] The obligation of mutual assistance among the Member States is also supported by the promotion of solidarity among Member States, which is the last of the Community's tasks specified in Article 2 EC.

The third element of Durand's analysis[214] results not from the wording of Article 5 EC itself, but from the general principle of mutual cooperation which underlies that provision. In an Order in Case C-2/88 Imm. *Zwartveld et al.*[215] the Court obliged the Commission to give its active assistance to national legal proceedings in which the national court, hearing a case on alleged infringements of Community rules, requested the production of Commission inspectors' reports and the attendance of Commission officials to give evidence. The duty of sincere cooperation imposed on the Community Institutions was of particular

---

210. O.J. English Special Edition 1968 (III) p. 475, most recently amended by Reg. 2434/92 (O.J. 1992 L 245/1).
211. [1988] ECR 5589 at 5611–5612.
212. [1991] ECR I-2797.
213. *E.g.* Case 123/80 *NV United Foods et al. v. Belgian State*[1981] ECR 995, [1981] 1 CMLR 273; Case 272/80 *Frans-Nederlandse Maatschappij voor Biologische Producten* [1981] ECR 3277. But as to the difficulties in the recognition of testing in the field of hallmarking, see Case C-293/93 *Houtwipper* [1994] ECR I-4249, and Gormley (1996) 21 ELRev. 59. The example of recognition of testing is also given by Due (1992) SEW 355 at 365. See, further, Chapter VII, section 1.1, *post.*
214. Like the fourth element (added by the editor).
215. [1990] ECR I-3365 at 3372–3373.

importance *vis-à-vis* the judicial authorities of the Member States, who had to ensure that Community law was applied and respected in the national legal system. In the absence of any imperative reasons relating to the need to avoid any interference with the functioning and independence of the Communities, the documents had to be made available.[216] Similarly, in the absence of any imperative reasons relating to the need to safeguard the interests of the Communities, the Commission officials had to be authorized to give evidence.[217] On the other hand, a Community Institution is bound to provide the police of a Member State with relevant information concerning an investigation into an alleged criminal offence involving one of its officials, but it is not entitled to supply information relating to the service, which as such is extraneous to the investigation.[218] In the competition field the duty of sincere cooperation has also been much in evidence: whereas in the past questions from national courts to the Commission met the response that the Commission would make its views known if a reference for a preliminary ruling[219] were to be made, but not otherwise, the attitude is now that the national courts are positively encouraged to ask the Commission for its views on problems before them.[220] The public interest that the Commission should not be frustrated in the enforcement of Community competition law has been recognized in the United Kingdom in the context of an attempt to bring defamation proceedings against a person who had given the Commission certain information about an undertaking.[221] The adoption of a legislative act by the Council will not infringe the obligation on the Member States to guarantee the impact and effectiveness of Community law, as the defence of its interests by

---

216. In a later Order in the same case, the Court added that legitimate grounds connected with the protection of the rights of third parties would also justify a refusal to produce documents, but concluded that there was not a shred of evidence to support refusal on any ground, Case 2/88 Imm. *Zwartveld et al.* [1990] ECR I-4405 at 4411.
217. In its later Order, *ibid.* the Court insisted that the officials be examined exclusively about the information contained in their reports. See also Case C-54/90 *Weddel & Co. BV v. Commission* [1992] ECR I-871.
218. Case 180/87 *Hamill v. Commission* [1988] ECR 6141 at 6156.
219. Under Art. 177 EC, see Chapter VI, section 2.1.1, *post*.
220. Case C-234/89 *Delimitis v. Henniger Bräu AG* [1991] ECR I-935 at 994, and Case T-24/90 *Automec Srl v. Commission* [1992] ECR II-2223 at 2279. See also the Commission's Notice on cooperation between national courts and the Commission in applying Arts. 85 and 86 EC (O.J. 1993 C 39/6). As to the working of this Notice, see Whish (1993) 5 EBLR 3 and (1994) ECLR 60 and Joris (1998) *Competition Policy Newsletter* No. 1, 47. See also the Commission's Notice on its cooperation with national competition authorities of the Member States (O.J. 1997 C 313/3) and the Notice on cooperation between national courts and the Commission in the field of state aids (O.J. 1995 C 312/7).
221. *Hasselblad (GB) Ltd. v. Orbison* [1985] 3 CMLR 540. As to the Commission's duty to its informants, see Case 145/83 *Adams v. Commission* [1985] ECR 3539, [1986] 1 CMLR 506.

each Member State within the Council forms no part of that obligation; nor will such adoption infringe the obligation of loyalty incumbent on the Council as an institution.[222]

5.2.5 The now repealed Article 6 EEC

It might be thought that Article 5 EC, as interpreted by the Court, also embraces the coordination of economic policies required by the old Article 6 EEC. However, the content of that former obligation appears to have been subsumed in the rather stronger language of the first sentence of Article 102a EC, and certainly in terms which are more clearly related to the objectives of the Community itself. This may well have been a reaction to Opinion 1/78 *International Agreement on Natural Rubber*,[223] in which the Court accepted that the economic policies of the Member States in the sense of Article 6 EEC were primarily matters of national concern, rather than Community concern.

5.2.6 Concluding observations on Article 5 EC

Article 5 EC has acquired an importance in the case-law of the Court far exceeding normal principles of public international law on the interpretation of treaties.[224] This importance would, though, appear to be more due to the decision to entrust the interpretation of the EC Treaty unreservedly to an independent Court of Justice, the task of which is to 'ensure that in the interpretation and application of this Treaty the law is observed',[225] than to the importance of a concept similar to the federal legal principle which is expressed in German constitutional law as *Bundestreue*.[226]

Teleological, systematic and *lacunae*-filling methods of interpretation are also regularly applied by courts in non-federal systems, and are indeed clearly envisaged in the EC Treaty itself.[227] To this extent it can even be argued that the case-law developed by the Court is also compatible with

222. Cases C-63/90 and 70/90 *Portugal and Spain v. Council* [1992] ECR I-5073 at 5156.
223. [1979] ECR 2871 at 2914. See also Durand, *op. cit.* (see note 97, *supra*) 43.
224. Due (1992) SEW 355 at 355 See the Vienna Convention on the Law of Treaties (1969), Arts. 26–33 (1155 U.N.T.S. 331).
225. Art. 164 EC, see also Arts. 31 ECSC (which also refers to rules laid down for the implementation of that Treaty) and 136 Euratom.
226. *I.e.* loyalty to the federal interest. Due (1992) SEW 355 at 366.
227. See *e.g.* Art. 2 EC (and myriad specific Titles of the Treaty); the reference in Art. 215 EC, 2nd para. to 'the general principles common to the laws of the Member States', and the very general drafting of Art. 164 EC itself. See also, as to methods of interpretation, Chapter IV, section 7.6, *post*.

the fundamental principle of Article 31 of the Vienna Convention on the Law of Treaties.[228] Now that other international organizations, such as the World Trade Organization have also opted for an independent dispute settlement procedure, it is quite likely that similar methods of interpretation will develop in these fora too. The influence of the rule of law, as interpreted by the Court on the basis of Article 164 EC is not only of importance for communities with a federal structure.[229]

5.3 The prohibition of discrimination on grounds of nationality: Article 6 EC

5.3.1 The concept of discrimination in general

Of much greater direct importance for nationals and enterprises of the Member States than the basic principle of Article 5 EC is Article 6 EC. This provision results from the deletion of Article 6 EEC and the consequent renumbering of Article 7 EEC as Article 6 EC.[230] The case-law dealing with the old Article 7 EEC discussed here still holds good for Article 6 EC.

As the clearly directly effective prohibition in Article 6 EC only applies to the extent that no more specific provisions of the Treaty with comparable effect are applicable,[231] any potential litigant seeking to invoke the prohibition of discrimination on ground of nationality will first have to ascertain whether the directly effective provisions relating to the free movement of goods, persons, services, and capital; the rules governing competition; the special non-discrimination provisions in the agricultural

228. 1155 UNTS 331.
229. See, in relation to the GATT, Brittan (1994) 31 CMLRev. 229 (guest editorial) and VerLoren van Themaat (1994) 31 CMLRev. 429 (book review). As to the WTO, see Dennin (ed.), *Law and practice of the World Trade Organization* (New York, loose-leaf, since 1995); Jackson, *Implementing the Uruguay Round* (Oxford, 1997); Querishi, *The World Trade Organization: implementing international trade norms* (Manchester, 1996), and Swacker *et al.*, *World Trade without barriers: the World Trade Organization (WTO) and dispute resolution* (Charlottesville, Va., 1995–1996).
230. Art. 6 EC 2nd para., permitting the Council to adopt rules designed to prohibit discrimination on ground of nationality, reflects redrafting to refer to Art. 189c EC (the cooperation procedure) but this is not a procedural change from the old Art. 7 EEC. The Treaty of Amsterdam will substitute the co-decision procedure for the adoption of such rules. See, generally, Durand, *op. cit.* (see note 97, *supra*) 45; Zuleeg in Von der Groeben *et al.* (eds.), *op. cit.* (see note 137, *supra*) Vol. 1, 277 (and bibliography cited there); and Weatherill (1990) 15 ELRev. 334. Measures to be adopted to combat discrimination based on sex, race, religion, age etc. under new Art 6a EC will have to be adopted by Council unanimously, on proposal from the Commission, after consulting EP.
231. See *e.g.* Case 305/87 *Commission v. Greece* [1989] ECR 1461 at 1477; Case C-179/90 *Merci convenzionali porto di Genova SpA v. Siderurgica Gabrielli SpA* [1991] ECR I-5889 at 5927; Case C-419/92 *Scholz v. Opera Universitaria di Calagri et al.* [1994] ECR

and transport fields[232] and in the field of taxation,[233] or Article 221 (which ensures non-discrimination with respect to participation in the capital of companies) do not provide a particular solution for the discrimination in question. If they do, it will be unnecessary to base a claim on Article 6 itself.[234]

Most of the cases in which reliance has been placed on the general non-discrimination on ground of nationality principle relate to admission of students to University or other vocational training in a Member State other than that of their own nationality.[235] The principal elements resulting from these cases have now been codified in Directive 93/96[236] which is the first directive adopted on the basis of the second paragraph of what was then Article 7 EEC. The third recital in the preamble to that directive makes the codification intention clear, stating without more ado that 'as the Court of Justice has held, Articles 128 and 7 of the Treaty prohibit any discrimination between nationals of the Member States as regards access to vocational training in the Community'. The directive rightly leaves the further development of the case-law concerning admission conditions (including provisions governing the tuition fees and maintenance grants) in the hands of the courts, as that case-law is heavily influenced by the individual circumstances of the students concerned, and does not lend itself to being frozen at the time of development of a directive.[237] Moreover, provisions under the second paragraph of Article 6 EC cannot restrict the scope of the first paragraph of that provision, (as the rules are designed to prohibit discrimination, not to determine or restrict the concept of

I-505 at 520; Case C-379/92 *Peralta* [1994] ECR I-3453 at 3495, and Case C-193/94 *Skanavi v. Chryssanthakopoulos* [1996] ECR I-929.

232. Arts. 40(3), 2nd para, and 79 EC respectively.
233. Art. 95 EC.
234. See note 231, *supra*, and *e.g.* Case C-19/92 *Kraus v. Land Baden-Württemberg* [1993] ECR I-1663 and Case C-55/94 *Gebhard v. Consiglio dell'Ordine degli Avvocati e Procuratori di Milano* [1995] ECR I-4165 (in relation to Arts. 48 and 52 EEC, and 52 and 59 EC, without reference to Arts. 7 EEC or 6 EC, respectively.
235. The first judgment based solely on Art. 7 EEC dealt with this issue: Case 152/82 *Forcheri et al. v. Belgium et al.* [1983] ECR 2323, [19841 1 CMLR 34. See also *e.g.* Case 293/83 *Gravier v. City of Liège* [1985] ECR 593, [1985] 3 CMLR 1; Case 24/86 *Blaizot et al. v. University of Liège et al.* [1988] ECR 379, [1989] 1 CMLR 57; Case 39/86 *Lair v. Universität Hannover* [1988] ECR 3161, [1989] 3 CMLR 545; Case 197/86 *Brown v. Secretary of State for Scotland* [1988] ECR 3205, [1988] 3 CMLR 403; Case 263/86 *Belgian State v. Humbel* [1988] ECR 5365, [1989] 1 CMLR 393; Case C-357/89 *Raulin v. Minister van Onderwijs en Wetenschappen* [1992] ECR I-1027, and Case C-109/92 *Wirth v. Landeshauptstadt Hannover* [1993] ECR I-6447.
236. O.J. 1993 L 317/59, which replaced Dir. 90/366 (O.J. 1990 L 180/30) which, as is explained in the text, *infra*, was annulled by the Court in Case C-295/90 *European Parliament v. Council* [1992] ECR I-4193, [1992] 3 CMLR 281.
237. Dir. 93/96, Art. 3 expressly provides that the directive does not establish any entitlement to the payment of maintenance grants on the part of students benefiting from the right of residence.

discrimination itself. For this reason the fifth and seventh recitals to the directive are also of interest, as they explain, respectively, that the right of residence for students forms part of a set of related measures designed to promote vocational training, and that in the present state of Community law, as established by the case-law of the Court, assistance granted to students did not fall within the scope of the then Article 7 EEC. Accordingly, in order to lay down conditions to facilitate the exercise of the right of residence and with a view to guaranteeing access to vocational training in a non-discriminatory manner, Directive 93/96 requires the Member States, to recognize the right of residence for any national of a Member State enrolled in a recognized educational establishment, who does not enjoy that right under other provisions of Community law, and for his or her spouse and dependent children if necessary.[238] However, the directive also took account of the need to ensure that beneficiaries of this right of residence did not become a burden on the public finances of the host Member State.[239]

As has been explained,[240] Directive 93/96 results from the annulment of Directive 90/366 by the Court of Justice. The Court found that the Council had wrongly based it on Article 235 EEC rather than on Article 7 EEC (as the Commission had proposed). The Court found that on the basis of the second paragraph of Article 7 EEC the Council could indeed take steps to prohibit discrimination on the ground of nationality in areas in which its competence was not based on one of the specific provisions governing the other fields of the Treaty; the acts adopted were not necessarily limited to governing the rights resulting from the first paragraph of Article 7 EEC but could embrace also aspects which it appeared necessary to regulate in order to make the exercise of the right to non-discrimination on ground of nationality effective.[241] Given that the

238. Dir. 93/96, Art. 1. A student who *e.g.* has already been exercising an economic activity (*cf.* Case 197/86 *Brown v. Secretary of State for Scotland* [1988] ECR 3205, [1988] 3 CMLR 403) or who is the child of a migrant worker will be exercising his or her rights under other provisions of Community law. Various specific provisions of Dirs. 68/360 (O.J. English Special Edition 1968 (II) p. 485 abolishing restrictions on movement and residence for workers, and 64/221 (O.J. English Special Edition 1963–64 p. 117) on grounds for expulsion or refusal of residence are incorporated by reference into Dir. 93/96.

239. Thus the student must demonstrate that he or she is covered by sickness insurance in respect of all risks in the host Member State. He or she must also assure the authority 'by means of a declaration or by such alternative means as the student may choose that are at least equivalent,' that he or she 'has sufficient resources to avoid becoming a burden on the social assistance system of the host Member State during the period of their residence', Dir. 93/96, *ibid*. The means of assurance is thus up to the student: what means are equivalent to a declaration is unclear, but the Member State is clearly not entitled to demand a particular means of assurance.

240. See note 236, *supra*.

241. Case C-295/90 *European Parliament v. Council* [1992] ECR I-4193 at 4235.

interest of the challenge by the European Parliament was inadequate participation in the legislative process[242] and the substance of the directive was not challenged by the Community Institutions or by the Member States, the Court upheld the effects of Directive 90/366 until the adoption of Directive 93/96.[243]

The application by the Court in myriad cases of the then Article 7 EEC in relation to conditions of access to vocational training in another Member States was possible because vocational training fell within the sphere of operation of the Treaty, albeit to a very limited extent, although it would have been impossible under Article 128 EEC to adopt compulsory Community rules on the matter. A spectacular example of the result of a situation falling within the scope of the Treaty, in which only Article 7 EEC was available to combat discrimination on the ground of nationality, can be seen in Case 186/87 *Cowan v. Trésor public*.[244] Cowan was a British tourist who was injured as a result of a mugging in Paris. He sought compensation from the French criminal injuries compensation scheme, as his assailants were never caught. As he was taking advantage of the freedom to receive services,[245] he could not be ruled ineligible for compensation on the ground that he was not French, or resident in France, or a national of a State which had a reciprocal agreement on compensation with France. The Court viewed the protection from harm of a Community national exercising the freedom to receive services, on the same basis as nationals or residents of the host Member State as the corollary of the right of free movement, and this involved equal right to compensation.[246] The fact that compensation was a charge on the public

242. Adoption under Art. 235 EEC was by unanimity in the Council, after consultation of the Parliament, adoption under Art. 7 EEC was by qualified majority in the Council, in cooperation with the Parliament (giving it two readings instead of one). These procedures still apply in respect of Arts. 235 and 6 EC respectively, although the Treaty of Amsterdam (not yet in force) will replace the cooperation procedure in Art. 6 EC by the co-decision procedure. As to the procedures, see Chapter V, section 3.4.2, *post*.

243. Art. 6 of Dir. 93/6 continued the effect of Dir. 90/366 until the date by which the Member States had to comply with Dir. 93/96 (December 31, 1993). As to precedents for the exercise of the Court's jurisdiction under Art. 174(2) EC, 2nd para. (which refers only in relation to regulations) by analogy, see Advocate General Jacobs's Opinion in Case C-295/90 *European Parliament v. Council* [1992] ECR 4193 at 4227.

244. [1989] ECR 195, [1990] 2 CMLR 613.

245. As to which, see Chapter VII, section 7, *post*. In Cases 286/82 and 26/83 *Luisi and Carbone v. Ministero del Tesoro* [1984] ECR 377 at 403 the Court had held that the freedom to provide services embraced the freedom to receive services, and that *inter alia* tourists from another Member State were recipients of services.

246. [1989] ECR 195 at 221. It is an established rule that reciprocity cannot be applied as a condition for the exercise of rights conferred by Community law by a national of another Member State, see *e.g.* Case 1/72 *Frilli v. Belgian State* [1972] ECR 457 at 466 and Case 270/83 *Commission v. France* [1986] ECR 273 at 307. See also Case C-20/92 *Hubbard v. Hamburger* [1993] ECR I-3777 at 3795.

purse made no difference whatsoever.[247] The French argument that rules of compensation for criminal injuries were part of the law of criminal procedure, which was an area wholly within the competence of the Member State and thus outside the scope of the prohibition of discrimination on ground of nationality received short shrift from the Court. The unspoken interest of the Community in rejecting such arguments is clearly that if they were to be accepted, a Member state could simply defeat the application of Community law to a given situation by classifying that situation within a certain area of its legislative or administrative provisions. Accordingly, while the Member States were indeed competent in principle in these areas, Community law set certain limits to the exercise of their power,[248] and that power could not be used to defeat one of the cornerstones of Community law, the principle of non-discrimination on ground of nationality.[249]

Just as in the cases on the admission of students to vocational training,[250] Cowan dealt with a situation covered by Community law, in this case as a beneficiary of the freedom to provide and receive services, for which no special prohibition of discrimination applied. Van Nuffel views the protection against the risk of assault and the right to obtain compensation, which are expressions of the right to equal protection of the integrity of Community nationals, as being a logical consequence of the free movement of persons.[251] Unlike the Commission's suggestion in its submissions in Cowan,[252] Van Nuffel does not regard such a right as being a constituent element of the specific prohibition of discrimination set out in Article 59 EC. In areas such as criminal law or criminal procedure, which the EC Treaty in principle leaves in the hands of the Member States, the distinction between the sphere of operation of Article 6 EC and Articles 48, 52 and 59 EC is understandable, as it does appear artificial to regard the discrimination in Cowan as being a hindrance to his ability to receive services as such. In other cases, such as the application of disproportionately high penalties to purely formal infringements of an

---

247. *Ibid.* See also Case 152/82 *Forcheri et al. v. Belgium et al.* [1983] ECR 2323 at 2336.
248. See Case 203/80 *Casati* [1981] ECR 2595 at 27. See also Warner Adv. Gen. in Case 30/77 *R. v. Bouchereau* [1977] ECR 1999 at 2025–2026.
249. Case 186/87 *Cowan v. Trésor public* [1989] ECR 195 at 222. See also Case 82/71 *Pubblico Ministero dell Repubblica Italiana v. Società Agricola Industria Latte (SAIL)* [1972] ECR 119 at 135: 'The effectiveness of Community law cannot vary according to the various branches of national law which it may affect.' See further, Case C-20/92 *Hubbard v. Hamburger* [1993] ECR I-3777 at 3795; Case C-43/95 *Data Delecta AB Aktiebolag v. MSL Dynamics Ltd.* [1996] ECR I-4661; Case C-323/95 *Hayes et al. v. Kronenberger GmbH* [1997] ECR I-1711, and Case C-122/96 *Saldanha et al. v. Hiross Holding AG* [1997] ECR I-5325 (security for costs). See also Case C-29/95 *Pastoors et al. v. Belgium* [1997] ECR I-285.
250. See note 235, *supra.*
251. (1991) SEW 794 798–799.
252. [1989] ECR 195 at 201–202.

administrative nature by nationals of other Member States, a different view is appropriate.[253]

A third important category of cases to which Article 6 EC applies relates to disguised discrimination which cannot be attacked on the basis of other provisions of the EC Treaty. Thus in various judgments the Court has expressly confirmed that Article 6 EC forbids not only overt discrimination by reason of nationality but also covert forms of discrimination, which by the application of other criteria of differentiation, in fact lead to the same result.[254] Of these, the most spectacular example is probably Case 61/77 *Commission v. Ireland*[255] which dealt with an attempt to use ostensibly objective criteria (vessel length and engine horsepower) to exclude large fishing boats (almost all of which were non-Irish) from a particular stretch of Irish maritime waters. The Court was willing to see through the ostensible argument to perceive that the Irish measures indeed breached the general non-discrimination rule.[256] In fact in that case the general non-discrimination rule was also specifically embraced in the Community secondary legislation involved,[257] so there are as yet no practical examples of disguised discrimination being found in circumstances involving Article 6 EC standing entirely alone. The judgment in Case 22/80 *Boussac Saint-Frères SA v. Gerstenmeier*[258] examined whether there was disguised discrimination on ground of nationality, but found that there was none.

5.3.2   The concept of discrimination more closely examined

As a result of the case-law discussed in the preceding subsection, Article 6 EC applies to discrimination on ground of nationality, whether it be barefaced or disguised, provided that the situation concerned falls within the sphere of operation of the EC Treaty, and to the extent that no other more specific provision of the Treaty covers the situation. The substantive content of discrimination covers not just treating similar situations differently, it also embraces treating different situations in the same

---

253. See *e.g.* Case 118/75 *Watson and Belman* [1976] ECR 1185 at 1199; Case C-265/88 *Messner* [1989] ECR 4209 at 4225, and Case C-193/94 *Skanavi v. Chryssanthakopoulos* [1996] ECR I-929.
254. Case 152/73 *Sotgiu v. Deutsche Bundespost* [1974] ECR 153 at 164; see, however, Case 143/87 *Stanton et al. v. INASTI* [1988] ECR 3877 at 3893–3894 and Cases 154 and 155/87 *Rijksinstituut voor de Sociale Verzekeringen der Zelfstandigen v. Wolf et al.* [1988] ECR 3897 at 3911–3912. See also Case 61/77 *Commission v. Ireland* [1978] ECR 417 at 450 and Case 22/80 *Boussac Saint–Frères SA v. Gerstenmeier* [1980] ECR 3427 at 3436.
255. [1978] ECR 417, [1978] 2 CMLR 466.
256. [1978] ECR 417 at 450–452.
257. Reg. 101/76 (O.J. 1976 L 20/19), Art. 2(1).
258. [1980] ECR 3427 at 3436–3437.

manner.[259] Hence, in Case 13/63 *Italy v. Commission*,[260] the Commission was held entitled to limit the safeguard measures which, on the basis of Article 226(1) EEC, it authorized France to take, to Italian refrigerators, given that the volume of imports of such products into France, and their price, when compared with the volume and price levels of imports from other Member States, justified such a measure. Moreover, that limitation was found to satisfy the requirements that such measures go no further than was strictly necessary to rectify the situation and adjust the sector concerned to the economy of the common market, and that priority be given to such measures as would least disturb the functioning of the common market.[261] In Case 106/83 *Sermide SpA v. Cassa Conguaglio Zucchero et al.*[262] the Court developed the principle expressed in Case 13/63 *Italy v. Commission* further: 'under the principle of non-discrimination between Community producers or consumers, which is enshrined in the second subparagraph of Article 40(3) of the EEC Treaty and which includes the prohibition of discrimination on grounds of nationality laid down in the first paragraph of Article 7 of the EEC Treaty, comparable situations must not be treated differently and different situations must not be treated in the same way unless such treatment is objectively justified.' The criteria for judging the objective justification of different treatment,[263] just like the concept of discrimin-

259. Case 13/63 *Italy v. Commission* [1963] ECR 165 at 178. The Court had already observed that an appearance of discrimination in form may correspond in fact to an absence of discrimination in substance, *ibid.*, at 177–178.
260. [1963] ECR 165, [1963] CMLR 289.
261. [1963] ECR 165 at 178. The provisions of Art. 226 EC are now spent (as the transitional period ended on 31 December 1969).
262. [1984] ECR 4209 at 4231 (referring to Arts. 40(3) and 7 EEC). See also *e.g.* Case C-217/91 *Spain v. Commission* [1993] ECR I-3923 at 3953; Case C-306/93 *Winzersekt GmbH v. Land Rheinland-Pfalz* [1994] ECR I-5555 at 5583–5584; Case C-309/89 *Codorniu SA v. Council* [1994] ECR I-1853 at 1887; Case C-56/94 *SCAC Srl v. Associazione dei Produttori Ortofrutticoli (ASIPO)* [1995] ECR I-1769 at 1788, and Cases C-296 and 307/93 *France et al. v. Commission* [1996] ECR I-795 at 847.
263. *In casu*, [1984] ECR 4209 at 4231–4234. A Member State will not be able to evade the prohibition by means of discriminatory acts on the ground of the place of establishment of the enterprise or the country of origin of a product unless such treatment is objectively justified. See, generally, Case 13/63 *Italy v. Commission* [1963] ECR 165 at 177–178; Case 14/68 *Wilhelm et al. v. Bundeskartellamt* [1969] 1 at 15–16; Case 152/73 *Sotgiu v. Deutsche Bundespost* [1974] ECR 153 at 164; Case 61/77 *Commission v. Ireland* [1978] ECR 417 at 450–451, and Case 22/80 *Boussac Saint–Frères SA v. Gerstenmeier* [1980] ECR 3427 at 3436. Case 147/79 *Hochstrass v. Court of Justice* [1980] ECR 3005, [1981] 2 CMLR 586 is an interesting example of the extremely detailed analysis which may sometimes be necessary in this field. More generally in relation to discriminatory treatment, see Cases 115 and 116/81 *Adoui and Cornuaille v. Belgian State et al.* [1982] ECR 1665, [1982] 3 CMLR 631 (noted by Gormley (1982) 7 ELRev. 399) and Case 121/85 *Conegate Ltd. v. H.M. Customs and Excise* [1986] ECR 1007, [1986] 1 CMLR 739 (noted by Gormley (1986) 11 ELRev. 443 and Millett (1987) 139 NLJ 39).

ation itself, have to be assessed in the light of the objectives of the particular provisions of Community or national law concerned.[264] While Zuleeg[265] has illustrated objective discrimination on the basis of cases involving the application of the second paragraph of Article 40(3) EC,[266] it is difficult to conceive of an objectively justified discrimination in relation to Article 6 EC *simpliciter*.

The application of Article 6 EC to cases of reverse discrimination (worse treatment of a Member State's own nationals than of nationals of other Member States) does not satisfy the definition of non-discrimination discussed above. It appears conceivable in relation to the limited scope of Article 6 EC only if a national of, say the United Kingdom, established in the Netherlands, on return to the United Kingdom, or in dealings or temporary stay there, in an area not covered by specific provisions of the EC Treaty,[267] is treated worse by a public authority, in an area falling within the scope of the Treaty, by reason of his nationality than nationals of other Member States.[268] Thus in the present state of Community law a

264. As examples of national provisions which have been held not to discriminate on grounds of nationality, see Case 22/80 *Boussac Saint–Frères SA v. Gerstenmeier* [1980] ECR 3427, [1981] 1 CMLR 202; Case 251/83 *Haug–Adrion v. Frankfurter Versicher-ungs–AG* [1984] ECR 4277, [1985] 3 CMLR 266; Case 143/87 *Stanton et al. v. INASTI (Institut national d'assurances sociales pour travailleurs indépendents)* [1988] ECR 3877 at 3893–3894; Cases 154 and 155/87 *Rijksinstituut voor de Sociale Verze-keringen der Zelfstandigen v. Wolf et al.* [1988] ECR 3897 at 3911–3912, and Case 31/87 *Gebroeders Beentjes v. The Netherlands State* [1988] ECR 4635. As to the difference between prohibited discrimination and permissible differentiation, see Timmermans (1982) SEW 426.
265. Zuleeg in Baur *et al.* (eds.) *Europarecht, Energierecht, Wirtschaftsrecht* (*Festschrift* for Börner, Cologne, 1992) 473
266. Zuleeg cites Cases C-267–285/88 *Wuidart et al. v. Laiterie coopérative eupenoise et al.* [1990] ECR I-435 at 480 and 484, and Case C-18/89 *Maizena GmbH v. Hauptzollamt Krefeld* [1990] ECR I-2587 (published in the ECR only in summary form). See further *e.g.* Case C-217/91 *Spain v. Commission* [1993] ECR I-3923 at 3953 (producers of brandy and liqueurs produce distinct products; different treatment of those products was objectively justified), and Case C-306/93 *Winzersekt GmbH v. Land Rheinland-Pfalz* [1994] ECR I-5555 at 5584 (entitlement to use a registered designation of origin was an objectively differentiating factor); Case T-493/93 *Hansa-Fisch GmbH v. Com-mission* [1995] ECR II-575 at 590–591 (citing myriad judgments of the Court of Justice; fishing activities in different zones are different situations), and Case C-315/93 *Flip CV et al. v. Belgian State* [1995] ECR I-913 at 935–936 (measures taken by certain Member States differing from those taken by others; compensation for owners of animals affected by some diseases but not for those affected by other diseases, both held not to infringe the requirements of non-discrimination).
267. As to the importance of the existence of Community legislation, see Case 115/78 *Knoors v. Secretary of State for Economic Affairs* [1979] ECR 399 at 410. See also Case 246/80 *Broekmeulen v. Huisarts Registratie Commissie* [1981] ECR 2311 at 2330, see Gormley (1982) 7 E.L.Rev. 37. This point is discussed further in Chapter VII, sections 1.2 and 6.2, *post*.
268. In similar vein, Zuleeg in von der Groeben *et al.* (eds.), *op. cit.* (see note 137, *supra*) 168–169.

Dutchman living in Belgium who committed a traffic offence in the Netherlands would not be able to invoke Article 6 EC, but a Dutch student living in Belgium who was denied access to a vocational education course in the Netherlands would indeed be able to rely on Article 6 EC.[269]

Any difference in treatment of nationals of the different Member States which is due to natural phenomena[270] will not infringe Article 6 EC. Nor does the fact that national legislation varies from one Member State to another amount to discrimination, as long as the legislation at issue affects all subject to it in accordance with objective criteria and without regard to their nationality.[271] In these cases it is correct to speak of a disparity, rather than a discrimination between national laws, which may give rise to a distortion of the conditions of competition between Member States which may be removed on the basis of Articles 100, 100a or 101 EC.[272] The conceptual confusion between discrimination and such distortions is regrettably still widespread.[273] The discrimination concept of the Treaty applies only to the unequal treatment of different persons by one legal subject, whereas distortions result from differences in legislation between *different* Member States.

Those who have never exercised their freedoms under Community law will not be able to rely on the prohibition of discrimination on ground of nationality: their situation falls outside the scope of Community law.[274]

269. This follows from Case 293/83 *Gravier v. City of Liège* [1985] ECR 593, [1985] 3 CMLR 1.
270. Case 52/79 *Procureur du Roi v. Debauve et al.* [1980] ECR 833 at 858. Natural phenomena in this instance embraced the fact that a prohibition on cable retransmission of television advertisements was largely ineffective as much if not all the territory of the Member States concerned (Belgium) was within the natural reception range of many foreign broadcasts.
271. See *e.g.* Case 14/68 *Wilhelm et al. v. Bundeskartellamt* [1969] ECR 1 at 16; Cases 185–204/78 *Van Dam en Zonen et al.* [1979] ECR 2345 at 2361; Case 223/86 *Pesca Valentia v. Minister for Fisheries and Forestry, Ireland et al.* [1988] ECR 83 at 109; Case 308/86 *Ministère public v. Lambert* [1988] ECR 4369 at 4392; Cases C-92 and 326/92 *Collins et al. v. Imtrat Handelsgesellschaft mbH et al.* [1993] ECR I-5145 at 5181, and Case C-177/94 *Perfili* [1996] ECR I-161 at 175–176.
272. Case 14/68 *Wilhelm et al. v. Bundeskartellamt* [1969] ECR 1 at 16.
273. *E.g.* the arguments advanced in Case 14/68 *Wilhelm et al v. Bundeskartellamt* [1969] ECR 1, [1969] CMLR 100 and more recently in Case 155/80 *Oebel* [1981] ECR 1993, [1983] 1 CMLR 390 and Case 126/82 *Smit Transport BV v. Commissie Grensoverschrijdend Beroepsgoederenvervoer* [1983] ECR 73, [1983] 3 CMLR 106.
274. For a good example of the practical significance of the restriction of the field of applicability of Art. 6 EC to areas in which Community law applies, see Case 35 and 36/82 *Morson and Jhanjan v. The Netherlands* [1982] ECR 3723, [1983] 2 CMLR 221. See also *e.g.* Case 175/78 *R. v. Saunders* [1979] ECR 1129; Case 44/84 *Hurd v. Jones* [1986] ECR 29 at 84–85, and Case C-332/90 *Steen v. Deutsche Bundespost* [1992] ECR I-341 at 356–357 (and on the internal consequences of that latter judgment, Case C-132/93 *Steen v. Deutsche Bundespost* [1994] ECR I-2715). These judgments and that in *Morson and Jhanjan*, show that the principle of non-discrimination now enshrined in Art. 6 EC, together with the specific expression of that principle in Art. 48 EC, cannot be applied

5.3.3   The addressees of Article 6 EC

Article 6 itself is silent as to whom it is addressed. As a fundamental legal principle it is clearly directed in any event to the Member States (including all their central or functionally or territorially decentralized organs or autonomous units). It also applies to the Community Institutions and other bodies themselves.[275] Three points may be made against the applicability of Article 6 EC to private parties, but, as will become apparent, they are less than wholly convincing. First, the general system of the EC Treaty is that the obligations or prohibitions which it contains are directed only to the Member States and/or the Community Institutions, unless expressly otherwise provided, as is the case with Articles 85 and 86 EC and with a number of implementing provisions in other fields. In these cases the provisions concerned – sometimes through Community secondary legislation – are expressly directed at undertakings; for systematic reasons this would seem to exclude the applicability of Article 6 EC. Secondly, Durand has opined[276] that the Commission would not be able to discharge its task of ensuring that the provisions of the Treaties and the measures taken by the institutions pursuant thereto are applied,[277] as it could only bring to the Court matter imputable to the Member States. Thirdly, she observes that the case-law so far does not support the horizontal direct effect of Article 6 EC.[278] Against the first of these arguments, it may be objected that precisely because this provision embraces a fundamental principle, which is rightly universally held also to apply to the Community Institutions, it is in principle impossible to conceive its being inapplicable

to situations which are wholly internal to a Member State and which are in no way connected to any situation envisaged by Community law. In the same sense in relation to Art. 52 EC see *e.g.* Case 204/87 *Bekaert* [1988] ECR 2029 at 2039. In relation to hairdressers and Dir. 82/489 (O.J. 1982 L 218/24), see Cases C-29-35/94 *Aubertin et al.* [1995] ECR I-301. See also Cases 281/85 *etc. Germany et al. v. Commission* [1987] ECR 3203, [1988] 1 CMLR 11 relating to non-EC migrants. It is, though, possible for a Member State to disadvantage its domestic industry in relation to the free movement of goods, see *e.g.* Case 86/78 *SA des Grandes distilleries Peureux v. Directeur des Services Fiscaux de la Haute-Saône et du Territoire de Belfort* [1979] ECR 897 at 914 (internal taxation); Case 178/84 *Commission v. Germany* [1987] ECR 1227 at 1268 (thus the German Government was free to continue to apply the *Reinheitsgebot* requirements to beer brewed in Germany for sale there (they did not apply to beer for export).

275. This is implicit from the judgment in Case 13/63 *Italy v. Commission* [1963] ECR 165, [1963] CMLR 289, although on the facts the Court held that the allegation of discrimination was not made out. See also on this point Cases 271/83 *etc. Ainsworth et al. v. Commission and Council* [1987] ECR 167, again, though, on the facts it was found that the allegation of discrimination was not made out (a somewhat unconvincing conclusion, now no longer relevant, see Chapter XI, section 5.7, *post*).

276. *Op. cit.* (see note 97, *supra*) 60.

277. Arts. 155 EC, 124 Euratom, 1st indent in each case. The phrasing of Art. 8 ECSC is slightly different.

278. *I.e.* reliance on Art. 6 EC by a private individual against another private individual.

to relationships between private parties (who could otherwise resurrect barriers which the Member States and the Community Institutions were required to abolish), in the fields covered by Community law. There can be no reason, for example, why a private vocational training institute should not be bound by the principle in Case 293/83 *Gravier v. City of Liège*.[279] There can be no reason why systematic discrimination by a private undertaking or a private law collective body against employees who are nationals of other Member States should not infringe the specific prohibition of discrimination contained in Article 48 EC. Moreover, there is clear authority in Case 36/74 *Walrave & Koch v. Association Union Cycliste Internationale et al.*[280] that discrimination on grounds of nationality by private parties in relation to areas covered by the Treaty is also prohibited: the second and third arguments have not prevented the Court from viewing the prohibition of discrimination on ground of nationality set out in Articles 48–51 and 59–66 EC as an expression of the more general prohibition now set out in Article 6 EC,[281] and thus applicable to employment relationships and to the provision of services.[282]

Accordingly, with Zuleeg,[283] it is submitted that the better view is probably that Article 6 EC is in principle applicable in relationships between private parties.[284] As Zuleeg suggested, this must take place taking account of a reasonable balance between the principle of freedom of the individual and the particular form of the principle of equality expressed in Article 6 EC. From the point of view of legal certainty, Durand has rightly recommended[285] that the applicability of Article 6 in relationships between private parties in specified fields should be defined in an implementing regulation or directive on the basis of the second paragraph of Article 6. It is submitted that such a measure should be based on the view that the

279. [1985] ECR 593, [1985] 3 CMLR 1.
280. [1974] ECR 1405, [1975] 1 CMLR 320. See also Case 13/76 *Donà v. Mantero* [1976] ECR 1333, [1976] 2 CMLR 578. These cases related to discriminatory terms for professional sportsmen (cyclists and football players respectively). See, further, Case C-415/93 *Union Royale Belge des Sociétés de Football Association ASBL et al. v. Bosman* [1995] ECR I-4921, [1996] 1 CMLR 645 (transfer rules for professional footballers).
281. [1974] ECR 1405 at 1420.
282. *Ibid.*, at 1418–1419.
283. In Baur *et al.* (eds.), *op. cit.* (see note 265, *supra*) 482–483. Durand, *op. cit.* (see note 97, *supra*) 60, thinks it unlikely that the Court will afford horizontal direct effect to Art. 6 EC. Zuleeg in von der Groeben *et al.* (eds.), *op. cit.* (see note 137, *supra*) 170 seems now perhaps more cautious on this point.
284. In view of the second argument against horizontal direct effect advanced by Durand, the Court will most likely encounter the problem through a reference under Art. 177 EC.
285. Durand, *op. cit.* (see note 97, *supra*) 61 and 63. She also sees two other means of enlarging the scope of Art. 6 EC: by developing further the notion of State responsibility; and by imposing on the State in a more systematic manner the obligation to ensure that within clearly defined areas the principle of non-discrimination between private parties is respected.

greater the dominant position of the individual or collective discriminating party or parties is, and thus the fewer the alternatives open to the victim of the discrimination,[286] the more likely a finding of discrimination will result. Moreover, if it were proven that a given Member State was jointly responsible with the private party concerned, particularly for collective discrimination against nationals of one or more Member States, this could be used as a reason for including the horizontal (private parties) as well as vertical (public authorities and bodies) effect of Article 6 EC in such a measure.[287] The Member States could be obliged in such a measure to ensure that sanctions were provided for and enforced for breach of the obligation of non-discrimination on ground of nationality. By basing such a provision also on other provisions of the EC Treaty which enable the specific prohibitions of discrimination in other Chapters of the Treaty to be developed further, a comparable horizontal effect could be added there too.

6. Citizenship of the Union: The New Part Two of the EC Treaty

6.1 The concept of 'citizenship of the Union'

The title of the new Part Two of the EC Treaty is a flag which fails to cover its cargo.[288] A separate Union citizenship appears not to exist in

---

286. As in Case 36/74 *Walrave and Koch* [1974] ECR 1405, [1975] 1 CMLR 320, and Case C-415/93 *Union Royale Belge des Sociétés de Football Association ASBL et al. v. Bosman* [1995] ECR I-4921.

287. This follows from the observations by Durand, *op. cit.* (see note 97, *supra*) 60.

288. As to how this political flag of the European Union came to find a home in the EC Treaty, see Cloos *et al.*, *op. cit.* (see note 95, *supra*) 162–166. They rightly note the difference between this political concept of citizenship rights and the individual citizen's rights (involving *inter alia* 'market rights') based even on the old EEC Treaty, which have been long recognised as fundamental: see *e.g.* the Adonnino Committee Report (Bull. EC Supp. 7/85) and Everson in Shaw and More (eds.), *op. cit.* (see note 115, *supra*) 73. See generally, *inter alia*, Meehan, *Citizenship and the European Community* (London, 1993); O'Leary, *The Evolving Concept of Community Citizenship* (London, 1996); Ackers (1994) JSWFL 391; Closa (1992) 29 CMLRev. 1137; Closa (1995) 32 CMLRev. 487; Duff (1995) 37 *Federalist* 191; Durand, *op. cit.* (see note 97, *supra*) 436–445; Evans (1984) 32 AJComp.L. 679; Garronne (1993) Schw. Z. Int. Eur. R. 251; Gamberale (1995) 1 EPL 417; Hall (1996) 21 ELRev. 129; Hobe (1993) *Staat* 245; contributions by Jessurun d'Olivera and Taschner in Monar *et al.* (eds.), *op. cit.* (see note 95, *supra*) 81 *et seq.*; Jessurun d'Olivera in Dehousse (ed.), *op. cit.* (see note 81, *supra*) 126; Koslowski(1994) JCMS 369; Mazzaferro (1993) 35 *Federalist* 63; Kovar and Simon (1993) CDE 285; Marias (1994) EIPA no. 4 1; Montani (1994) 36 *Federalist* 95; Meehan (1993) Pol. Quart. 172; O'Leary (1992) 12 YBEL 353; O'Leary (1995) 32 CMLRev. 519; contributions by O'Keeffe, Closa and Twomey in O'Keeffe and Twomey (eds.), *op. cit.* (see note 95, *supra*) 87 *et seq.*; Pinder (1995) Pol. Quart.

fact; moreover it is by no means a flag universally desired by the citizens it is supposed to embrace. Indeed, because of the confusion and indeed rejection of the concept of citizenship of the Union in various Member States, especially in Denmark, the Edinburgh European Council in December 1992 was obliged to clarify the meaning of the concept, entirely respecting Article 8 EC.[289] Thus, the provisions in Part Two of the EC Treaty regarding citizenship of the Union 'do not in any way take the place of national citizenship. The question whether an individual possesses the nationality of a Member State will be settled solely by reference to the national law of the Member State concerned.'[290] The European Council could have been even clearer had it said, in accordance with the definition in Article 8 EC, that citizenship of the Union would not embrace persons other than all persons holding the nationality of a Member State. Such citizenship has no independent content, and in particular it does not embrace nationals of third countries legally resident in a Member State.[291] Van Dijk in particular has regretted this narrow definition.[292]

But as Van Dijk himself admits,[293] not all the Member States would have accepted an extension of the concept to include all those legally resident. Moreover, it is unclear whether such an extension would have encountered objections in terms of public international law, particularly as regards relations with third countries. As he already indicates,[294] in the present state of international law, the granting of citizenship is solely a matter for the State concerned. At least as long as the European Union is not a federal State, the Union as such (a purely intergovernmental organization without even legal personality) and the Community remain

(supp.) 112; Preuß (1995) ELJ 267; Shaw (1997) 22 ELRev. 554; Taschner (1994) RMUE 13; Twomey (1994) EIPA no. 4 119; Van Dijk, Dutch Report in *Proceedings of the FIDE Congress Lisbon, 1992* Vol. 3, 285, also in (1992) SEW 277; Verhoeven (1993) *Annales de droit de Louvain* 165; Vincenzi (1995) Pub. L. 259, Weiler in Winter *et al.* (eds.), *Reforming the Treaty on European Union – The Legal Debate* (The Hague, 1996) and Wouters (1994) EIPA no. 4 25. See, further, *Report from the Commission on the Citizenship of the Union* (COM (93) 702 Final), and Chapter VII, section 4, *post.*

289. Bull. EC 12–1992 points I.33–I.44.
290. As to the position of Denmark, see Curtin and van Ooik (1993) SEW 675, especially at 681–683.
291. Although in many cases, such as in relation to nationals of the non-Community EEA States (Iceland, Liechtenstein and Norway) the principle of non-discrimination on ground of nationality applies to a greater or less extent (EEA nationals are treated in the same way as nationals of Member States; nationals of countries benefitting from one of the Europe Agreements benefit from the prohibition of discrimination on ground of nationality if they are lawfully resident in a Member State, but, they have no right to reside to seek work, unlike Community and EEA nationals).
292. Van Dijk, *op. cit.* (see note 288, *supra*) 292–293 and in Hellingman (ed.), *op. cit.* (see note 81, *supra*) 79.
293. *Ibid.* at 295 and 85, respectively.
294. (1992) SEW 277 at 290, referring to the Permanent International Court of Justice's Advisory Opinion on *Nationality Decrees in Tunis and Morocco* (PCIJ Series B Vol. 4, 24).

international organizations. International organizations tend not to have their own territory, with which they can do as they wish in many ways (such as expropriating property or imposing urban planning requirements); nor do they have 'subjects' of their own determination, on whom they, as sovereign authority, may confer rights and impose obligations in the same way as States. The absence of own territory does not however exclude the possibility of laying down in the treaties which establish such organizations the territorial scope of application of those Treaties.[295] Similarly, the absence of 'own subjects' does not prevent international treaties establishing international organizations from regulating the personal sphere of application of that body's actions. These may make also explicitly or implicitly it possible to apply its actions to subjects of third countries, on account of their presence on the territory of a Member State, or because their relevant actions take place within the territorial sphere of application of Community law, or have results there. Myriad examples of this will become apparent in subsequent chapters of this work.

6.2   The four special rights conferred by citizenship of the Union

Article 8a(1) EC confers on every citizen of the Union the right to move and reside freely within the territory of the Member States, albeit subject to the limitations and conditions laid down in the EC Treaty itself and by the measures adopted to give it effect. This new right was already conferred by Article 8a EEC, albeit without direct effect. What is more, existing case-law already made it clear that such a right was enjoyed for economic activities on the basis of directly effective provisions of primary or secondary Community law. Furthermore, case-law on the old Article 7 EEC (now Article 6 EC), in conjunction with Article 128 EC demonstrated that students who pursued a vocational training course also enjoyed this right.[296] Furthermore the freedom already conferred in Article 8a EEC had already been guaranteed for other groups of non-economically active people, such as the retired and others who did not already benefit from it under other provisions, through directives based on Article 235 EC.[297] One advantage of the new Article 8a EC is that implementing measures, at least as far as the non-economically active are concerned, will now have to be based on Article 8a(2) EC, which means obtaining the assent of the European Parliament. That provision also

---

295. See Arts. 227 EC, 79 ECSC, and 198 Euratom, which define the territorial scope of the Treaty (largely) in terms of the territory of the Member States.
296. See e.g. Case C-357/89 Raulin v. Minister van Onderwijs en Wetenschappen [1992] ECR I-1027.
297. Dir. 90/364 (O.J. 1990 L 180/26) deals with cases not covered by other provisions; Dir. 90/365 (O.J. 1990 L 180/28) deals with the retired. See also Dir. 93/96 (O.J. 1993 L 317/59) on students, discussed in section 5.3.1, supra.

makes it clear that such measures must facilitate the exercise of the right to move and reside freely. Following Durand,[298] it is submitted that this drafting presupposes that Article 8a(1) is directly effective, and can thus be relied upon by individuals before their national courts and administrations. The substantive question remains whether Article 8a in fact adds anything to the already existing provisions of primary and secondary community law.

The right to vote and stand as a candidate at municipal elections,[299] in the Member State where he resides and of which he is not a national, under the same conditions as nationals of that State, conferred by Article 8b(1) EC, and the right in the same circumstances and under the same conditions to vote and stand as a candidate for the European Parliament, conferred by Article 8b(2) EC, was certainly a major innovation in most of the Member States, requiring an amendment of the Constitution in some cases. The necessary implementing measures dealing with municipal elections are contained in Directive 94/80;[300] and those dealing with elections to the European Parliament are set out in Directive 93/109.[301]

Durand rightly observes[302] that Article 8b(2) EC ought to be a considerable stimulus to the adoption of a uniform electoral procedure in accordance with the new text of Article 138(3) EC. The fact that Article 138a EC recognizes the importance of political parties at European level as a factor for integration within the Union may well lead to candidates who are nationals of other Member States being included in party lists or being chosen for constituencies in proportion to the number of residents who are nationals of other Member States. There have already been instances of politicians from other Member States being candidates where national rules permitted it, even though they were non-residents, and one was even elected in Italy in 1989.[303] But only with a more systematic readiness to encourage candidates who are nationals of other Member States and with the use of a uniform electoral procedure will Article 8b(2) EC lead in reality to the basis for legitimacy of 'representatives of the peoples of the States, brought together in the Community' transcending national boundaries, which Article 138 EC manifestly symbolises.

Article 8c EC grants every citizen of the Union, in the territory of a third country in which the Member State of which he is a national has no representation, the right to protection by the diplomatic or consular

---

298. Durand, *op. cit.* (see note 97, *supra*) 441.
299. On the continent referred to as active and passive voting rights respectively.
300. O.J. 1994 L 368/38 (adopted on 19 December 1994, just meeting the deadline set by Art. 8b(1)). See also the Commission's proposal for amendment of this directive, COM (95) 499 Final. See further, Bull. EU 4–1995 point 1.1.1.
301. O.J. 1993 L 329/34 (again, adopted just within the deadline set out in Art. 8b(2) EC).
302. Durand, *op. cit.* (see note 97, *supra*) 442.
303. Corbett *et al.*, *op. cit.* (see note 190, *supra*) 17.

authorities of any Member State, on the same conditions as nationals of that State. Unlike the implementing measures envisaged by Articles 8a and 8b EC, the implementing measures for this right had to be adopted by December 31, 1993 under the intergovernmental model (*i.e.* by the Member States) rather than by the Council under the Community decision-making procedure.[304] It does not appear that this is meant to replace national diplomatic and consular representation by Community representation. In order to secure the protection set out in Article 8c international negotiations were in any event necessary, and that provision required that they too be started before the end of 1993. Cooperation between diplomatic missions of the Member States, and between them and the Commission Delegations in third countries was already an established phenomenon before the entry into force of the TEU, and the second paragraph of Article J.6 TEU expressly refers to stepping up cooperation *inter alia* by contributing to the implementation of the provisions of Article 8c EC. In reality, Article 8c adds relatively little to cooperation which was already in place, save that there are now formalised arrangements for the protection of unrepresented Community nationals (citizens of the union) in place.[305]

Article 8d EC and the new Article 138d make two important changes to the already existing, and continuing, right of citizens to petition the European Parliament. They are also important for Ombudsman established by Articles 8d and 138e EC, which the parliament, after great difficulty, finally managed to appoint.[306] On the basis of Article 138d and 138e EC the rights to petition and to apply to the ombudsman may be exercised not only by citizens of the Union, but by any natural or legal person residing in or having its registered office in a Member State. This means that unlike the other provisions of the new Part Two of the EC Treaty, non-citizens of the union benefit from these rights on equal terms with citizens of the Union. On the other hand, the rights conferred in both limbs of Article 8d EC are, by the reference to Articles 138d and 138e confined in their subject matter. In Chapter IV below this is discussed further, in the course of examination of the functions of the European Parliament.[307]

304. Guidelines for the protection of nationals of Member States unrepresented in third countries entered into force on July 1, 1993 (WQ E-822/94 (Kostopoulos) O.J. 1994 C 362/50). See Handoll, *Free Movement of persons in the EU* (Chichester, 1995) 300.
305. *Ibid.* See also Bull. EU 11–1995 point 1.1.1.
306. As to the difficulties, see Magliveras (1995) 20 ELRev. 401. As to the appointment of the first Ombudsman, see Bull. EU 7/8–1995 points 1.1.6–1.1.7; Dec. 94/114 (O.J. 1994 L 54/25); Dec. 95/376 (O.J. 1995 L 225/17) and the Parliament's Resolutions (O.J. 1994 C 91/60 and O.J. 1995 C 249/14, 28, 29, and 34). As to the right to petition, see, generally, Marias (1994) 19 ELRev. 169.
307. See Chapter IV, section 5, *post*.

6.3   The possibility of expanding the rights conferred by Article 8a–8d EC

On the basis of the Report required to be presented every three years[308] in accordance with the first paragraph of Article 8e EC, and without prejudice to the other provisions of the Treaty, the Council may, under the second paragraph of Article 8e, adopt provisions to strengthen or add to the rights laid down in this Part Two of the EC Treaty. The Council acts on the basis of a proposal from the Commission, after consulting the European Parliament, and recommends the provisions so adopted to the Member States for adoption in accordance with their respective constitutional requirements.

The wording of Article 8e does not appear to exclude the extension of the rights in Articles 8a–8c EC to persons other than citizens of the Union, as has occurred in Articles 138d and 138e EC. On the basis of the public international law considerations mentioned in the preceding section, it would appear difficult to envisage such an extension in respect of Article 8c EC. As regards Article 8b(1) EC, it appears that such an extension would founder on the rocks of the problem of general unacceptability of such an obligation, identified by Van Dijk.[309] The creation of a competence for the Member States in the matter would appear superfluous, as it can be accepted that Article 8b EC does not prevent a Member State which considers this desirable from the viewpoint of a general principle of equality and solidarity; indeed some already apply such principle.[310] In relation to elections to the European Parliament, such an expansion would falter on the terms of Article 137 EC ('representatives of the peoples of the States'), unless that phrase is deemed to embrace legally resident third country nationals. It may well be possible, though, to expand the right of movement and residence set out in Article 8a EC to the persons mentioned in Articles 138d and 138e EC, even though they come from third countries.[311]

Durand mentions[312] a much more interesting possible extension of the rights conferred under Part two of the EC Treaty: an express right for each citizen of the Union to invoke the rights protected by the European Convention for the protection of Human Rights and Fundamental Freedoms.[313] This had been proposed in the initial drafts leading to the TEU, but had not been accepted. As a *political* point of departure, this is already expressly mentioned in Article F(2) TEU and is inherent in Article F(1) TEU, although Article F TEU creates no rights for citizens. Cloos

---

308. For the Report required to be presented before December 31, 1993, see COM (93) 702 Final.
309. Van Dijk, *loc. cit.* (see note 292, *supra*).
310. *Inter alia* The Netherlands and Ireland.
311. But see Peers (1996) 21 ELRev. 150.
312. Durand, *op. cit.* (see note 97, *supra*) 445.
313. Rome, 4 November 1950 (TS 71 (1953); Cmnd 8986.

rightly observes[314] that within the Community the European Convention
on Human Rights does not only protect those possessing the nationality
of a Member State, although it has already been observed in the
preceding section, in relation to Article 8d EC in conjunction with Articles
138d and 138e EC, that the definition of citizenship of the Union in
Article 8 EC does not *per se* exclude the expansion of rights conferred on
such persons to embrace persons who are nationals of third countries.
There is thus no inherent reason why the suggestion to expand the rights
granted to embrace the right to rely on the European Convention could
not be accepted, albeit not limited to citizens of the Union but open to all
who reside in a Member State of the Community.

314. Cloos *et al.*, *op. cit.* (see note 95, *supra*) 164.

CHAPTER IV

Institutional structure*

1. INTRODUCTION

The European Union as such has only one organ of its own, the European Council.[1] To achieve its objectives, the Union makes use of four of the five Institutions of the European Communities: the European Parliament; the Council; the Commission, and the Court of Justice.[2] Together with the European Council they form the single institutional framework prescribed by Article C TEU, the task of which is to ensure the consistency and continuity of the activities carried out to attain the Union's objectives, while respecting and building upon the *acquis communautaire*.

In view of the separate status of the European Council, this body is examined first.[3] Thereafter the five Institutions of the Community (the fifth being the Court of Auditors) are examined in turn.[4] The institutional structure is of decisive importance for the balance of power within the Community, and the two most important actors are still undoubtedly the Council and the Commission, even after the changes introduced into the EC Treaty by the Treaty on European Union (TEU). It is on the co-operation of these two Institutions that the implementation of the Treaties is largely dependent. The discussion thus focuses on their composition, tasks and powers, including the tasks which they carry out in the context of the Union.

At the outset the European Parliament – the Institution which involves the peoples of the Member States in the activities of the Community[5] –

---

* In the Fifth Dutch edition of this work, this Chapter was revised by R. Lauwaars. In this edition this Chapter has been revised by the editor, taking Lauwaars's changes in the Dutch edition as the starting point, maintaining still relevant additions from the last English edition, and taking account of additional literature, case-law and practice, as well as of more recent developments.
1. Art. D TEU.
2. The use of these Institutions is facilitated by Art. E TEU.
3. See section 2 of this Chapter, *post*.
4. In sections 3–8, *post*.
5. See section 5, *ibid*. and Art. 137 EC.

played only a modest role in Community activities. Since 1979 the Parliament has been directly elected and its role has grown in importance, a trend which has been reinforced by the amendments made to the EC Treaty by the TEU. However, its role does not yet fully satisfy the standards which may be required of the Community and of the Union from the democratic point of view. After the examination of these three actors in the Community legislative process, attention turns to the scope of decision-making power of those actors.[6] The Court of Justice also plays a very important part in the institutional structure of the Community – but not of the Union – as it has to ensure the observance of the law in the implementation of the Treaty by the Institutions and the Member States.[7] Its jurisdiction enables the Court to contribute to the maintenance of the balance of rights and duties both amongst the Institutions themselves and between them and the Member States. The Court is also in the position of being able to ensure the legal protection of private parties, which is of great importance precisely because of the limited nature of parliamentary supervision of the behaviour of the Institutions. As far as direct actions by individuals are concerned, this jurisdiction is now exercised by the Court of First Instance, the establishment of which was made possible by the changes introduced by the Single European Act (SEA). Finally, attention turns to the Court of Auditors; to various independent Community bodies, and the myriad subsidiary bodies which assist the Council and the Commission in the discharge of many of their duties.[8]

2. EUROPEAN COUNCIL

2.1 Establishment and composition

As has already been mentioned,[9] the European Council was established at the second Paris Summit on 9–10 December 1974. According to the communiqué issued at the conclusion of that Summit, the Heads of State or Government announced that henceforth they would meet three times a year, accompanied by their Foreign Ministers, in the Council of the European Communities, and in the work on political cooperation.[10] Thus

6.   See section 6, *post*.
7.   See section 7, *ibid*.
8.   See section 9, *ibid*.
9.   See Chapter I, section 6.1., *ante*.
10. Bull-EC 12–1974 p. 7. See, generally, Weerts, *The European Council* (Amsterdam, 1992); Bulmer and Wessels, *The European Council: Decision-making in European Politics* (London, 1987), and the extensive literature cited therein, and Glaesner in Curtin and Heukels (eds.) *Institutional Dynamics of European Integration* (*Festschrift* for Schermers, Vol. II, Dordrecht, 1994) 101.

although the European Council was established outside the Community framework, and indeed remains outside that framework, it has in the meantime acquired an explicit basis in Treaty form. Thus Article D TEU provides that the European Council brings together the Heads of State or Government of the Member States and the President of the Commission, assisted by their Foreign Ministers and by a Member of the Commission, and that it shall meet at least twice a year.[11] It also formalizes the existing practice that the chairmanship of the European Council is held by the Head of State or Government which holds the Presidency of the Council. The only Head of State in the European Council initially was the French President (who has uncontested primary responsibility for foreign affairs), but the Finnish President has also attended since 1995.[12]

2.2. Tasks and powers

The establishment of the European Council in fact meant the institutionalization of the Summits which had been held hitherto. In its decision-making on Community matters, though, the European Council must take account of the provisions and procedures of the Treaties.[13] Formally, therefore, the Summit meetings could be incorporated into the Community's institutional system although in practice the European Council has remained distant from that system's rules.[14] Thus while it does not participate in the formal decision-making process, the European Council does make political pronouncements and lay down broad policy

11. Thus far Art. D TEU is identical to the old Art. 2 SEA. Note that the President of the European Council must invite the Economic and Finance Ministers to participate in European Council meetings when it is discussing matters relating to Economic and Monetary Union (Declaration No. 4 annexed to the Final Act on the occasion of signature of the TEU).
12. Westlake, *The Council of the European Union* (London, 1995) 22. Westlake also notes that the composition of the European Council reflects a compromise, taking account of the constitutional position of the French President; the differing status of Prime Ministers in the various Member States, and the interest of equitable and balanced political representation, *ibid*.
13. This point was already emphasized in the communiqué after the Paris Summit (Bull. EC 12–1974, p. 7). 'These arrangements do not in any way affect the rules and procedures laid down in the Treaties or the provisions on political cooperation in the Luxembourg and Copenhagen Reports. At the various meetings [both within and outside the Community structure] the Commission will exercise the powers vested in it and play the part assigned to it by the above texts.'
14. Westlake, *op. cit.*, 29 cites various reasons: a desire to avoid getting bogged down in technicalities; a determination to retain spontaneity and flexibility; and a generalized refusal by the Heads of State or Government to submit themselves to Community voting procedures (thereby avoiding being able to amend a proposal from the Commission only by unanimity). See, further, Weerts, *op. cit.*, 106–111.

lines whose implementation largely falls on the shoulders of the Council of the European Union.[15]

There was from the outset much uncertainty whether the European Council was in fact a purely intergovernmental body, or whether, in certain circumstances, particularly when exercising the powers of the Council, it was in fact a Council in a special composition and thus acting as an Institution. Initially it appeared that the European Council adopted the position of a purely intergovernmental body. On the one hand it distanced itself as much as possible from the Community decision-making process; on the other hand at its meeting in London on 29–30 June 1977 it drew up a list of tasks for itself in the so-called London Declaration[16] that is significantly different from the tasks of the Council set out in Article 145 EC. There was, that declaration stated, general agreement that the European Council should have both:

(I)   informal exchanges of view of a wide-ranging nature held in the greatest privacy and not designed to lead to formal decisions or public statements;

(II) discussions which are designed to produce decisions, settle guidelines for future action or lead to the issue of public statements expressing the agreed view of the European Council.

The declaration further recognized that the European Council would sometimes need to fulfil a third function, namely to settle outstanding issues from discussions at a lower level. To this extent the European Council was envisaged as having a sort of appellate function to resolve stalemates in the Council. Only in relation to this third function did the declaration state that 'In dealing with matters of Community competence the European Council will conform to the appropriate procedures laid down in the Community Treaties and other agreements.'

However, the Stuttgart Solemn Declaration on European Union[17] struck a rather different note. There the European Council clearly stated that when it acts in matters within the scope of the European Communities, it does so in its capacity as the Council within the meaning of the Treaties.[18]

---

15. As the Council of the European Communities (Merger Treaty, Art. 1) rebaptized itself, see Dec. 93/591 (O.J. 1993 L 281/18).
16. Bull. EC 6–1977, point 2.3.1.
17. Bull. EC 6–1983, point I.6.1. See also Chapter I, section 6.2, *ante*.
18. Point 2.1.3. of the Solemn Declaration, *ibid.* The role of the European Council was somewhat more philosophically formulated on that occasion (point 2.1.2 of the Solemn Declaration). 'In the perspective of European Union, the European Council:
    – provides a general political impetus to the construction of Europe;
    – defines approaches to further the construction of Europe and issues concerning general political guidelines for the European Communities and European political cooperation;

While this statement is certainly not included, yet alone repeated in the TEU, it is a foundation stone of that Treaty, albeit that the TEU reserves the name European Council for the sole body of the Union itself. This actually means that the European Council as such *cannot* exercise the powers of the Council concerning Community matters (the simple fact that the President of the Commission is a member of the European Council, but not of course of the Council makes the distinction plain). Accordingly, the TEU distinguishes between:

(i) the European Council as the body of the Union, consisting of the Heads of State or Government and the President of the Commission, assisted as mentioned above. This is the body whose task is now stated to be to provide the Union with the necessary impetus for its development and to define the general political guidelines thereof. It also defines the principles of and general guidelines for the CFSP;[19]

(ii) the Council in the composition of the Heads of State or Government. This special composition of the Council is provided for in Articles 109j(2)–(4) EC, dealing with the transition to the third stage of Economic and Monetary Union, and 109k(2) EC, dealing with discussions and decisions concerning Member States with a derogation as set out in Article 109k(3) EC. While the Heads of State or Government prefer to function as the European Council, the Treaty does not exclude the Council meeting in this composition to deal with matters other than those set out above;[20]

(iii) decisions of the governments of the Member States at the level of Heads of State or Government. These can be seen as top-level decisions of the representatives of the governments of the Member States,[21] and are provided for in Articles 109a(2) and 109f(1) EC which deal with appointment of the Executive Board of the European Central Bank and the President of the European Monetary Institute respectively.[22] Such decisions can also arise outside these contexts.[23]

– deliberates upon matters concerning European Union in its different aspects with due regard to consistency among them;
– initiates cooperation in new areas of activity;
– solemnly expresses the common position in questions of external relations.'
19. Art. J.8 TEU., see Chapter II, section 1.3.1, *ante*.
20. In these meetings the President of the Commission may well be present, with the Commissioner responsible for the economic and monetary portfolio, as the Commission is invariably present at Council meetings as an observer (see Art. 146 EC and section 3.1, *post*).
21. As to which, see Chapter V, section 1.6, *post*.
22. See section 9.2, *post*.
23. *E.g.* the Decision of the Heads of State or Government meeting within the European

It cannot be denied that the relations between the European Council and the Community Institutions, particularly the Commission and the Parliament (not to mention the Court) are particularly poor. The Commission's right of initiative and the co-decision powers of the European Parliament are diminished if the European Council takes a decision of principle without the Commission having presented a proposal and the Parliament having been consulted.[24] Westlake observes, though, that the existence of the European Council has actually encouraged rather than discouraged the Commission from embarking on major integrationist projects, and that in fact many of the major initiatives of the European Council find their origins in Commission initiatives.[25] Nevertheless, also in view of the numerous gordian knots which the European Council has cut over the years, such as the introduction of direct elections to the European Parliament; the expansion of the Communities, and the increase in the Communities' own resources, the overall evaluation of the European Council must be positive.

3. THE COUNCIL OF THE EUROPEAN UNION

3.1 Name, composition and character

The Council of the European Union is the rebaptised name of what was hitherto the Council of the European Communities,[26] and consists of a representative of each of the Member States at ministerial level, authorized to commit the government of that Member State.[27] For the first time it is specifically prescribed that the representative must be of ministerial level, a

Council concerning certain problems raised by Denmark on the Treaty on European Union (Bull. EC 12–1992 point I.34; O.J. 1992 C 348/1). While the Decision on the location of the seats of the Institutions was taken during the Edinburgh European Council, it is formally merely a Decision of the Representatives of the Governments of the Member States, not a Decision of the Heads of State or Government. See *ibid.*, point I.32 and O.J. 1992 C 341/1.

24. See Lauwaars (1977) 14 CMLRev. 25. A report on the outcome of each meeting, and a yearly written report on the progress achieved by the Union are presented to the European Parliament by the European Council. (Art. D TEU, previously point 2.1.4. of the Stuttgart Solemn Declaration). On the Commission's reports on these meetings see WQ 1730/83 (Van den Heuvel) O.J. 1984 C 148/10.

25. Westlake, *op. cit.* (see note 12, *supra*) 25–26. Westlake points out, *ibid.* at 26, that Delors, when President of the Commission was adept at recruiting the Member States to his causes in the European Council, which were then referred down to the Council for action.

26. See Dec. 93/591 (O.J. 1993 L 281/18).

27. Arts. 146 EC, 27 ECSC, and 116 Euratom, 1st para. in each case. This replaces the Merger Treaty, Art. 2 para. 1. See, generally, Westlake, *op. cit.* (see note 12, *supra*); Egger, *Das Generalsekretariat des Rates der EU* (Baden-Baden, 1994), and Dashwood in Curtin and Heukels (eds.), *op. cit.* (see note 10, *supra*) 117.

change motivated in part by the desire to enable ministers at regional level to represent a Member State, as long as they are authorized to commit the State as a whole, and in part by the desire to ensure that representation was not simply left to the level of officials.[28] Despite the confusion caused by rebaptism inspired by the desire to emphasize the single institutional framework serving the Union,[29] the Council is an Institution of the Communities, just like the Commission, the European Parliament, the Court of Justice and the Court of Auditors.[30] As an Institution it is bound by the Treaties and has to fulfil the duties which they entrust to it. In law it derives its powers exclusively from the Treaties and exercises them according to the procedure laid down therein. Its decisions have the legal effect stated in the Treaties and are subject to review of their legality by the Court of Justice.[31] The decisions of the Council, therefore, cannot be described as international agreements.[32]

The Council adopts its own Rules of Procedure[33] and the Presidency of the Council is held for a term of six months in the order decided by the Council acting unanimously.[34] The Council is the Institution of the Community in which the Member States are represented as such and by means of which they participate in the political and legal activities of the Communities. The members of the Council do not sit on it as persons, but as representatives of their Member State. Each of them acts on the instructions, and by a mandate, of his or her government. In this the Council differs from the Commission, whose members are independent.[35]

28. Macrae in O'Keeffe and Emiliou (eds.), *Legal Issues of the Maastricht Treaty* (London, 1994) 171 at 172; Cloos *et al.*, *Le Traité de Maastricht* (2nd ed., Brussels, 1994) 413–416. See also Westlake, *op. cit.* (see note 12, *supra*) 57, Constantinesco *et al.* (eds.) *Traité sur l'Union Européenne* (Paris, 1995) 528, and Lauwaars (1992) SEW 674 at 678–679. The question of being authorized to commit the Member State is a matter for the law and practice of each Member State, Cloos, *ibid.* 416.
29. Art. C TEU, 1st para.
30. See Arts. 4 EC, 7 ECSC, and 3 Euratom.
31. The Court has, however, no power to review decisions taken in the context of CFSP or JHA (Art. L TEU, subject to competence being conferred in the context of conventions drawn up under Art. K.3(2)(c) TEU, by virtue of the 3rd sub-paragraph of thereof). But questions of competence may be reviewed, Case C-170/96 *Commission v. Council* [1998] ECR I-nyr (12 May 1998).
32. Case 38/69 *Commission v. Italy* [1970] ECR 47 at 56 (see, Chapter V, section 1).
33. Dec. 93/662, O.J. 1993 L 268/1, as amended by Dec. 95/24, O.J. 1995 L 31/14). These Rules replaced the previous rules (O.J. 1979 L 268/1, as amended, O.J. 1987 L 291/7). See, generally, Westlake, *op. cit.* (see note 12, *supra*) 125–144, who conveniently also sets out all the previous Rules, including those of the Special Council of the ECSC (1952–58) and the provisional rules applied from 1958–1979.
34. Arts. 146 EC, 27 ECSC, and 116 Euratom, 2nd para. in each case (as amended by the Act of Accession (1994), Art. 12). The Presidency rotates according to the order laid down in Dec. 95/2 (O.J. 1995 L1/220) until the end of June 2003. The change takes place on 1 January and 1 July each year, but time has been known to overrun, see 51 *Halsbury's Laws of England* (4th ed., London, 1986) para. 1.81.
35. Arts. 157(2) EC, 9(2) ECSC, and 126(2) Euratom.

In the Council, therefore, the Community interest, which the Council as an Institution is as much required to protect as the Commission, will be viewed through the spectacles of national interests. According to the subject matter and the political climate in the Communities the colour of these spectacles will be more or less dark. A pure protection of national interests which encroaches upon essential interests of the Communities, however, conflicts with the responsibility which the Member States making up the Council bear for the protection of the interests of the Communities.[36] In a significant sense the Council is intergovernmental: it is composed of members of the governments of the Member States. Unlike the state of affairs in most international organizations having a 'Committee of Ministers' in one form or another, in the Communities no provision has been made for meetings of the Council at the level of official deputies of the members of the Council. By expressly limiting the composition of the Council to representatives at ministerial level, the contracting parties have given evidence of their intention to include those who bear direct political responsibility for national policies in the decision-making process of the Communities, in order thus to make the readiness and power of the Communities to take decisions as great as possible.

It must not be inferred from the obligation on governments to send someone of ministerial rank to the Council that the Council can only meet (and take decisions) in a valid way if all the governments have fulfilled this obligation. The Treaties provide for the possibility of voting by proxy.[37] From this it is evident that the Council can also function in the absence of one or more of its members.[38] In its Rules of Procedure, therefore, the Council has provided for the possibility of one of its members being represented if he is prevented from attending a session,[39] but it is clear, from the Treaty provisions concerning voting by proxy just referred to and from the Rules of Procedure, that such a representative, since he is not a member of a government, cannot himself validly give the vote of the member of the Council; this can only be done by another member of the Council.[40] The meetings of the Council are called by its

36. See Cases 2 and 3/60 *Niederrheinische Bergwerks-AG et al. v. High Authority* [1961] ECR 133 at 146–147 on this responsibility.
37. Arts. 150 EC, 28 para. 6 ECSC, and 120 Euratom.
38. The question whether the Council can validly meet in the absence of one of its members even if this member does not send a representative and does not authorize another member to vote for him is not a purely academic question. It arose during the constitutional crisis of the EEC in the years 1965–1966, when the French government followed an 'empty chair policy' for over six months and refused to participate in the meetings of the Council. See, further, in the context of the decision-making process, Chapter V, section 3.2., *post*.
39. Rules of Procedure, Art. 3 (see note 33, *supra*).
40. *Ibid.*, Art. 7(3). In practice nowadays it is extremely rare for a Member State to delegate its vote, see De Zwaan, *The Permanent Representatives Committee – its role in*

President, on his or her own initiative, or at the request of one of its members or of the Commission.[41]

It is left to the discretion of the governments to decide which minister they send to the Council. As a rule, the Foreign Ministers or their Ministers of State act as members of the Council. However, they will usually be accompanied or replaced by those of their colleagues under whose national competence particular questions come, so that in practice a 'multiple' member acts in the Council for each Member State. Usually the 'General Affairs' Council, composed of the Foreign Ministers, meets once a month; it was entrusted by the Paris Summit of December 1974 with the task of acting as initiator and coordinator in order to ensure consistency in Community activities and continuity of work.[42]

The wide-ranging nature of the Council's activities has led to the development of specialized Council sessions – sometimes between those of the General Affairs Council, sometimes simultaneously – in which the Council is composed of the ministers responsible for the area under discussions. These so-called sectoral or specialized Councils deal with budgetary matters, economic and financial affairs,[43] the internal market, fiscal affairs, energy policy, agricultural matters, fisheries policy, environmental policy, cooperation and development policy, health, social affairs, the Council of the Social Protocol (formally separate from but in practice indistinguishable from the social affairs Council), industry, consumer protection, transport matters, education, and research.[44] Thus, in recent years, the Council has held around 80 sessions each year (83 in 1997) and over 2,000 sessions of the Council have been held since the Merger Treaty came into force.[45] Outside the context of the Council, regular meetings are held, particularly by the several Finance, Justice and Education Ministers of the Member States, in the presence of members

European Union decision-making (Amsterdam, 1995) 43. As to earlier practice, see WQ 383/78 (Corrie) O.J. 1978 C 276/13 and WQ 600/74 (Patijn) O.J. 1974 C 56/10.

41. Arts. 147 EC, 27a ECSC, and 117 Euratom, Rules of Procedure, Art. 1 (see note 33, *supra*).

42. Bull. EC 12–1974, p. 7 (point 3 of the communiqué). On the related 'Marlia' procedure see WQ 730/79 (Van Miert) O.J. 1980 C 49/12. See, generally, Westlake, *op. cit.* (see note 12, *supra*) 164–179, and, as to the General Affairs Council's activities in CFSP, 211–233 (Galloway).

43. Usually known as the 'Ecofin' Council.

44. See Westlake, *op. cit.* (see note 12, *supra*) 164–210 and 252–284, in particular on the Budget Council 179–191 (Nicoll); on the Agriculture Council 191–210 (Culley); on the Ecofin Council and Economic and Monetary Union 252–275, and on the Council of the Social Protocol, 276–284.

45. The 2,000th meeting was of the agriculture ministers in Luxembourg, on 21 and 22 April 1997. Special meetings are not counted in the running total. Informal meetings are also often held (usually in an agreeable place in the Member State holding the presidency) for an exchange of views on issues of the moment or on more long-term perspectives.

of the Commission. As the Council stated in answer to questions asked by some members of the European Parliament,[46] these meetings are intended for 'the exchange of views and information of a general character' and may concern subjects coming under the competence of the Council. However, as soon as deliberations about decisions to be taken by the Community are necessary, these take place 'in accordance with the rules on Community competences and within the institutional framework'.

In relation to tasks which are specifically those of the Union, the members of the General Affairs Council constitute the Council as far as CFSP is concerned.[47] The Justice and Home Affairs Council is formally composed of representatives of the High Contracting Parties to the TEU (*i.e.* the ministers wearing a different hat).[48]

3.2 Tasks

In order to ensure that the objectives set out in the Treaty are attained the Council is to ensure, in accordance with the Treaty provisions, coordination of the general economic policies of the Member States;[49] it also has the power of decision.[50] As is evident from various provisions of the Treaty, this decision-making power lies generally[51] in the field of policy-making. This covers what can be called, in view of the Council's freedom of decision and the importance of the subject matter, Community legislation[52] and also covers the substantive regulation of relations with the outside world by means of the conclusion of Treaties.[53] In most areas governed by the Community Treaties, though, the Council can act only on the basis of a proposal from the Commission.

46. WQs 317/68 (Apel) J.O. 1969 C 65/5; 125/69 (Vredeling) J.O. 1969 C 94/21; 13/70 (Vredeling) J.O. 1970 C 97/2 and 284/70 (Vredeling) J.O. 1970 C 140/9 (our translation). See also WQ 516/73 (O'Hagan) O.J. 1974 C 22/32. On extra-mural meetings see Mortelmans (1974) 11 CMLRev. 62. On informal sessions see also WQs 1731/81 (Van Miert) O.J. 1982 C 129/11 and 2075 and 2076/82 (Cohen) O.J. 1983 C 118/27 and C 177/5. See Westlake, *op. cit.* (see note 12, *supra*) 116.
47. See note 42, *supra*.
48. See Westlake, *op. cit.* (see note 12, *supra*) 233–251.
49. Art. 145 EC, 1st indent. In the ECSC and Euratom Treaties, in view of the nature of partial integration, the emphasis of the coordinating function of the Council is placed on the mutual adjustment of, on the one hand, the action of these Communities and, on the other hand, the action of individual Member States (Arts. 26 ECSC, 1st para., and 115 Euratom, 2nd para.).
50. Arts. 145 EC, 2nd indent, 26 ECSC (implicit, but clear in view of Art. 28 ECSC), and 115 Euratom, 1st para.
51. But see Arts. 153, 154, 157(1), 2nd para., 165 para. 4, and 168a(2) EC for the Council's powers concerning a number of important points on the organization of the Communities.
52. See, *inter alia*, Arts. 43(2), 49, 75(1), 87, 113(1), (2) and (4) EC.
53. Arts. 109, 113, 130m, 130r(4), 228 (read with 113), and 238 EC.

The Council also has decision-making power in the overwhelmingly intergovernmental fields of the supplementary policies and forms of cooperation of the Union, CFSP and JHA. As far as CFSP is concerned, it takes the decisions necessary for defining and implementing the CFSP on the basis of the guidelines from the European Council, and ensures the unity, consistency and effectiveness of action by the Union.[54] It also decides, on the basis of general guidelines from the European Council, that a matter should be the subject of joint action.[55] In JHA the Council may adopt joint positions or joint action, as well as draw up conventions which it recommends to the Member States for adoption in accordance with their respective constitutional requirements.[56] This task in effect means the coordination of action by the Member States, and is a specific task of the Council as such. The Council's tasks in CFSP, though, are more in the nature of implementing, or putting flesh on the bones of the specific task of the European Council as a body of the Union, the defining of the principles and general guidelines of CFSP. The tasks of the Council in the composition of Heads of State or Government have already been addressed.[57]

3.3 Voting requirements

While the Treaties are silent on how many members of the Council constitute a quorum, the Council's Rules of Procedure indicate that the presence of eight members is required for the Council to vote.[58] The general rule under the Community Treaties is that the Council takes its decisions by simple majority of its members (eight), save as otherwise provided in the Treaties themselves.[59]

Mostly the Treaties prescribe unanimity or a qualified majority,[60] although the number of instances in which unanimity is required has been steadily declining over the years, particularly since the coming into force first of the Single European Act and then of the TEU.[61] In the case of qualified majority voting, the votes are weighted, and a qualified majority is attained with 62 out of the 87 votes.[62] If the Council

54. Art. J.8(2) TEU.
55. Art. J.3(1) TEU, 1st para.
56. Art. K.3(2) TEU.
57. See section 2.2, *ante*.
58. Rules of Procedure, Art. 7(4) (as amended, see note 33, *supra*); voting records are made public, Art. 7(5) and Annex.
59. Arts. 148(1), EC, and 118(1) Euratom. Special rules apply in the case of the ECSC Treaty, see Art. 28 ECSC (as most recently amended by Dec. 1/95 (O.J. 1995 L1/1).
60. See, further, Chapter V, section 3.2, *post*.
61. As to the SEA, see Chapter 1, section 6.2. The most important provisions still requiring unanimity are Arts. 99, 138(3), 168a(2), 201 and 235 EC.
62. Arts. 148(2) EC, 118(2) Euratom, and, for the purposes of Arts. 45b, 78 and 78b

is not adopting an act on a proposal from the Commission, the additional requirement is imposed that at least 10 members must vote in favour of the act, although there are very few instances when this occurs.[63] In practice this means that at least six of the smaller Member States must agree with all the larger Member States on these occasions. In cases in which the Council adopts an act on a proposal from the Commission, unanimity is required for an act constituting an amendment to that proposal.[64] As a matter of practical politics, a noteworthy decision of the Council at Ioannina on 29 March 1994[65] sought to resolve a crisis about the level of the blocking minority which would stop the qualified majority being achieved, but, as is explained below, it is submitted that it is of no legal effect.[66]

The expansion of qualified majority voting went hand-in-hand with revision of the Council's Rules of Procedure, so that, in addition to the old provision dating from 1979 that the Council votes on the initiative of its President, he or she has, since 1987, also been required to open voting proceedings on the initiative of a member of the Council or of the Commission, provided that a majority of the Council's members so decide.[67] The President draws up the provisional agenda for each meeting of the Council, and items on which a vote may be requested must be indicated thereon, subject to unanimous agreement during the adoption of the agenda at the meeting to the inclusion of items not on the provisional agenda; such items so included may be put to the vote.[68]

In the fields of CFSP and JHA the Council generally decides by unanimity (reflecting the consensus approach in classic intergovernmental decision-making); decisions by qualified majority can be taken only on matters for which the Council has already decided by unanimity that this will be permissible.[69]

ECSC only, Art. 28 ECSC, 4th para, as amended by Dec. 95/1 (O.J. 1995 L 1/1). Voting requirements are discussed in deatil in Chapter V, section 3.2, *post*. The blocking minority is 26 votes, see Westlake, *op. cit.* (see note 12, *supra*), 90–91. In the case of the Protocol on Social Policy, annexed to the EC Treaty by the Final Act on the signature of the TEU, the qualified majority is attained with 52 votes in favour (reflecting the absence of the United Kingdom), but the blocking minority remains at 26 votes, Westlake, *ibid.* 94 and 276–284.

63. As to the reasons for this variant (sometimes called a double majority), see Chapter V, section 3.2, *post*.
64. Arts. 189a EC (subject to the provisions of Art. 189b(4) and (5) EC) and 119 Euratom. See, further, the discussion in Chapter V, section 3.2, *post*.
65. O.J. 1994 C 105/1), as amended by a decision at Brussels on 1 January 1995 (O.J. 1995 C1/1).
66. See Chapter V, section 3.2, *post*.
67. Rules of Procedure (see note 33, *supra*), Art. 7(l).
68. Rules of Procedure (see note 33, *supra*), Art. 2. See Westlake, *op. cit.* (see note 12, *supra*) 63–65.
69. See Arts. J.3(2) and K.3(2) TEU.

In pursuit of greater openness and transparency[70] the Council and the Commission have now issued a Code of Conduct concerning public access to their documents[71] and the Council has adopted a decision on public access to Council documents,[72] The principle of greater access to Council documents relating to its acts in a legislative capacity is now recognized as being of major importance.[73] Voting in the Council is now made public in certain circumstances.[74]

3.4   The Committee of Permanent Representatives (*Coreper*)

While there is no provision for the Council to meet at the level of deputies,[75] a Committee of Permanent Representatives has been provided for as a subsidiary body of the Council.[76] The members of *Coreper* (as this body is habitually known after its name in French) are ambassadors who head the Permanent Representations of each of the Member States to the Communities.[77] The task of *Coreper* is to prepare the Council's work and to carry out the tasks, which the Council assigns to it.[78] It forms a permanent liaison body for the exchange of information between the national administrations and the Institutions of the Communities, and

70. See the Birmingham Declaration: Conclusions of the Presidency, Annex I (Bull. EC 10–1992 point I.8), and Bull. EC 12–1992 point I.5. See also the European Ombudsman's Special Report (O.J. 1998 C 44/10); Reg. 354/83 (O.J. 1983 L 43/1) on access to historic archives of the EEC and Euratom, and the Decision of the representatives of the governments of the Member States on access to archives on various negotiations (Dec. 94/271 (O.J. 1994 L 117/29).

71. Dec. 93/730 (O.J. 1993 L 340/41, corrig. O.J. 1994 L 23/34). See further, Case C-58/94 *Netherlands v. Council* [1996] ECR I-2169.

72. Dec. 93/731 (O.J. 1993 L 340/43, amended by Dec. 96/705 (O.J. 1996 L 325/19)), see Case T-194/94 *Carvel et al. v. Council* [1995] ECR II-2765; Case T-19/96 *Carvel et al. v. Council* [1996] ECR II-1519; Case T-610/97 R *Carlsen et al. v. Council* [1998] ECR II-nyr (3 March 1998) and Case T-174/95 *Svenska Journalistförbundet v. Council* [1998] ECR II-nyr (17 June 1998). See, as to fees, O.J. 1996 C 74/3.

73. Thus the Treaty of Amsterdam (not yet in force) will make further provision in this direction (amending Art. 151 EC and introducing a new Art. 191a EC).

74. See Chapter V, section 1, *post* (note 8).

75. Such a procedure is well-known elsewhere: in the Council of Europe decisions may be taken by Minister's Deputies, see Bowett, *The Law of International Institutions* (4th ed., London, 1982) 172 (who notes that the Deputies are in fact often the Permanent Representatives to the Council of Europe, but that they decisions on important questions of policy are reserved to the Ministers themselves).

76. *Coreper* was set up under the Merger Treaty, Art. 4, and is now governed by Arts. 151(1) EC, 30(1) ECSC, and 121(1) Euratom. See, generally, De Zwaan, *op. cit.*, (see note 40, *supra*) and Westlake, *op. cit.* (see note 12, *supra*) 285–307.

77. Third countries have missions to the Communities, the Member States have permanent representations.

78. Arts. 151(1) EC, 30(1) ECSC, and 121(1) Euratom. See also Rules of Procedure (see note 33, *supra*), Art. 19.

participates in the expression of the national standpoints and their co-ordination. *Coreper* does not, however, have independent powers of decision.[79] As a body preparing the decision-making of the Council it nevertheless plays an increasingly important part in the running of the Communities,[80] although in the field of agriculture the Special Committee for Agriculture tends to have a more important role than *Coreper*.[81] *Coreper* also plays a role in the field of CFSP and JHA, and while legally the special committees in this field, the Political Committee (*PoCo*) for CFSP and the Coordinating Committee (the K.4 Committee) for JHA, appear subordinate to *Coreper*,[82] Galloway makes it very clear that *PoCo* is not subordinate to *Coreper* in rank, or working at the latter's behest,[83] and Westlake notes that the relationship between the K.4 Committee and *Coreper* remains uneasy.[84]

The Presidency of *Coreper* rotates with that of the Council.[85] *Coreper* in fact operates at two levels, *Coreper I* and *Coreper II*. At the lower level (*Coreper I*) it usually consists of the deputy permanent representatives and deals with technical or routine matters. At the higher level (*Coreper II*) the permanent representatives themselves meet and discuss policy matters and questions of principle. The permanent representatives also fulfil an individual function in that they act (with their staff who form with them, the permanent representations) as letter-boxes in the sense that all official communications from the Community Institutions to the Member States pass through them, as negotiators within the Council structure and on individual problems with the Commission and its services, and as advocates in the sense that it is often the staff of the permanent representations who have to explain problems at the Community level to sometimes uncomprehending colleagues back home. An additional function has now been given to the Permanent Representatives, at the level of their deputies, as it is at this level that the Member States are invariably represented (with the Presidency of the Council sending a junior minister) if a Conciliation Committee with the European Parliament is activated under the co-decision procedure set out in Article 189b EC. The reason for

79. See Case C-25/94 *Commission v. Council* [1996] ECR I-1469 at 1505. Treaty of Amsterdam (not yet in force) will amend the relevant Treaty provisions so as to permit *Coreper* to adopt procedural decisions in cases provided for in the Council's Rules of Procedure.
80. See, further, Chapter V, section 3.3.3.
81. See Culley in Westlake, *op. cit.* (see note 12, *supra*) 201–204.
82. The function of *Coreper* as set out in the Treaties (in particular, Art. 151(1) EC) and that Arts. J.8(5) and K.4(1) make it clear that *PoCo* and the K.4. Committee respectively operate without prejudice to Art. 151 EC.
83. Galloway in Westlake, *op. cit.* (see note 12, *supra*) 220, although he notes that *Coreper* guards its right to decide how matters should be prepared and presented for ministerial discussion. This usefully demonstrates the distinction between legal status and political realities. See, generally, *ibid.* 218–221.
84. In Westlake *ibid.* 239.
85. Rules of Procedure (see note 33, *supra*), Art. 19(3).

putting this at the level of *Coreper I* is that most matters to be decided under the co-decision procedure concern the internal market or other technical fields which fall within the remit of *Coreper I*.[86]

4. THE COMMISSION OF THE EUROPEAN COMMUNITIES

4.1 Composition and character of the Commission

The Commission of the European Communities is the formal title of what is more generally referred to as the European Commission.[87] It consists of 'twenty members, who shall be chosen on grounds of their general competence and whose independence is beyond doubt'.[88] Members of the Commission have to be nationals of a Member State and at least one national (but no more than two) of each Member State is to be appointed.[89] In practice this means that two nationals of each of the five larger countries are appointed whereas one national of each of the smaller countries is appointed. The governments of the Member States attempt to ensure that the composition of the Commission reflects a balanced representation of European political tendencies.[90]

Strictly speaking, the attention devoted to the division of the seats of the Commission according to nationality ought to be unnecessary, for these nationals are not representatives of the states. On the contrary, they have the duty and the right to perform their tasks with complete independence in the general interest of the Communities, and they are forbidden to seek or take instructions from any government or other body.[91] They are to

86. Westlake, *op. cit.* (see note 12, *supra*) 300.
87. Merger Treaty, Art. 9.
88. Arts. 157(1) EC, 9(1) ECSC, 126(1) Euratom (1st para., as last amended by Dec. 95/1 (O.J. 1995 L 1/1)). A unanimous decision of the Council is necessary in order to alter the number of members of the Commission, *ibid.*, 2nd para.
89. *Ibid.*, 3rd para.
90. Thus from the United Kingdom so far a Conservative and a Labour party figure has been appointed each time by common accord of the governments of the Member States (although the United Kingdom government has not always accepted the suggestion of the Leader of the Opposition as to whose name should be put forward). A breach with precedent relating to the members of the Commission of German nationality occurred in 1987 after the death of Pfeiffer (a Social Democrat); he was replaced by Schmidhuber (a Christian Socialist) despite the fact that the other incumbent of German nationality (Narjes) was a Christian Democrat. See, further, Donnelly and Ritchie in Edwards and Spence (eds.), *The European Commission* (2nd ed., London, 1997) 33–36.
91. Arts. 157(2) EC, 9(2) ECSC, and 126(2) Euratom, 1st and 2nd subparas. in each case. The Commission swears an oath (or affirmation) of office before the Court of Justice, usually on the day before its first formal meeting, see *e.g. General Report on the activities of the European Union, 1995* (Brussels, Luxembourg, 1996) point 1053. The independence question can sometimes be thorny, see the refusal of the discharge in respect of the 1992 budget, O.J. 1994 C 128/332.

refrain from any action incompatible with the nature of their duties.[92] The Member States have undertaken to respect this principle and not to seek to influence the members of the Commission in the performance of their tasks.[93] During their term of office Commissioners may not engage in any other occupation,[94] and even after they have ceased to hold office they are required to behave with integrity and discretion as regards the acceptance of certain appointments or benefits.[95] Privileges and immunities ensure undisturbed performance of their duties.[96] For obvious reasons, the Member States are anxious that in the performance of their duties the Commissioners bear in mind the various national ways of thinking, the sometimes divergent national aspirations and the very real problems which beset various parts of the Community. At least at this stage of European integration a certain degree of proportionality is exercised in practice by the *a priori* reservation of more seats in the Commission for nationals of the large countries than for those of the smaller ones. A reduction in the number of commissioners appears, however, desirable both from the point of view of internal cohesion and to ensure a more even distribution of

92. *Ibid.*, 2nd subpara. in each case. The Commission feels that its members are free, in the exercise of their political responsibility, to conduct personal discussions with parliamentarians or members of government of their own or other countries if they wish to do so. It is convinced that during such discussions each of its members will adhere strictly to the obligations laid down in Art. 10(2) of the Merger Treaty, see WQ 10/71 (Vredeling) J.0. 1971 C 61/1.

93. An old example of a flagrant breach of this obligation was a statement to the press by the then French agriculture minister, Chirac, after the Council meeting on 16 July 1973 in which he accused Commissioner Cheysson (who was of French nationality) of betraying the interests of the French government, see WQ 298173 (Taverne) O.J. 1973 C 110/30. If members of the Commission stand in national elections the practice has been that they refrain from exercising their functions as Commissioners during the campaign (and resign if elected). In 1972 the then President of the Commission, Malfati, resigned in order to participate in national elections and in 1982 O'Kennedy was granted leave on personal grounds to stand in the Irish general election and resigned upon being elected. In 1998 Thilbaut de Silguy eventually decided not to stand as a candidate in regional elections in France while remaining a Commissioner.

94. *Ibid.* As an example of the unpleasant position in which a member of the Commission can find himself if this provision is not scrupulously observed, see WQ 657/73 (Laban) O.J. 1974 C 39/26 concerning the payment of a contested subsidy from the Community budget to a municipal slaughterhouse in which a Commissioner had managerial responsibility. Andriessen was appointed a Special Professor at Utrecht University towards the end of his final term as a Commissioner, but that is clearly not incompatible with a Commissioner's independence, see WQs 32–34, J.O. 1960, 1105, 1107 and 1108. See, for controversy over diary plans, *Europe* nos. 6591 pp. 4a–b and 6592 p. 5 (25 and 26 October 1995). See, generally, Lasok (D.) in Vaughan (ed.) *Law of the European Communities Service* (London, loose-leaf from 1990) Part 1, para. 1101–1106.

95. Arts. 157(2) EC, 9(2) ECSC, and 126(2) Euratom, 3rd para. in each case. See WQs 1941/84 and 652/85 (Dankert) O.J. 1985 C 176/12 and 272/12 respectively.

96. Protocol on Privileges and Immunities of the European Communities, Arts. 20 and 12–15 (the Protocol is annexed to the Merger Treaty).

portfolios, not least because there is only a limited number of 'real jobs' to go round.[97]

While it is the duty of the Commission to serve the general interest of the Communities as a whole, this does not mean that it has to neglect national interests in performing its duties. It will, however, have to consider all matters from the viewpoint of the Community interest. Thus, in making its contribution to the policy-making in the Council, where national interests are very much to the fore and frequently clash with each other, it will have to try to find, for these antitheses, solutions which do justice to the Community interest. It should be noted, though, that just as the Council, as the natural representative of the various national interests, has nevertheless to protect the essential interests of the Community, the Commission for its part has also to take account of the vital interests of a Member State. The Commission, therefore, should never help to outvote a Member State if the latter's vital interests might – in the opinion of the Commission – be prejudiced. The Commission bears this responsibility because in most cases under the EC and Euratom Treaties qualified majority decisions of the Council can only be reached with its cooperation.[98]

The members of the Commission are appointed by common accord of the governments of the Member States, nowadays for a term of five years; they may be re-appointed.[99] The European Parliament plays an important role in this process. Only after first consulting the Parliament do the governments of the Member States nominate, by common accord, the person they intend to appoint as President of the Commission.[100] In

97.   As to earlier suggestions for reform of the Commission's services and of the Commis-
      sion itself see the Spierenburg Report (Brussels, 1979) although the opportunity to
      implement its proposals was not taken up on the occasion of revisions of the Treaties
      caused by Spanish and Portuguese accession and the adoption of the Single European
      Act. See further, the Dooge Committee Report (Bull. EC 3–1985, point 3.5.1) and
      Declaration 15 annexed to the Final Act on signature of the TEU. The present
      number of Commissioners results from the Act of Accession (1994) as adapted follow-
      ing Norway's non-accession (Dec. 95/1, O.J. 1995 L 1/1).
98.   See Chapter V, section 3.2, post.
99.   Arts. 158(1) EC, 10(1) ECSC, and 127(1) Euratom (subject, if necessary to the provi-
      sions of Arts. 144 EC, 24 ECSC, and 114 Euratom on the vote of censure by the Eur-
      opean Parliament, as to which, see section 5.2.2, post). The term of office used to be
      four years, but a five-year term now permits the term of office of the Commission to
      run closer to that of the Parliament (which is also five years). Thus one of the first
      major functions of a newly-elected Parliament will now be to participate in the
      appointment of a new Commission to hold office from the following January.
100. Arts. 158(2) EC, 10(2) ECSC, and 127(2) Euratom, 1st subpara. in each case.
      However, although the nomination of Santer was formally made after the Parliament
      was consulted, it was preceded by a very public row at the level of Heads of State or
      Government, with Major vetoing the candidature of Dehaene, and other candidates
      withdrawing, somewhat wounded. Thus the intention to nominate Santer was in fact
      clear before Parliament was formally consulted (politicians are wary about making

consultation with that nominee, the governments of the Member States then nominate the other persons whom they intend to appoint as Members of the Commission.[101] The President and other nominees are then subject as a body to a vote of approval by the European Parliament, and only after receiving that approval can they be appointed by common accord of the governments of the Member States.[102] Before Parliament takes the vote on the motion of confidence, the nominees appear before confirmation hearings held by the committee of the Parliament appropriate to their intended area of responsibility.[103] This new method of appointment was applied for the first time to the President and other Members of the Commission whose term of office began on 7 January 1995, and the appointments beginning on 7 January 1993 (the third Delors Commission) were accordingly made for two years only.[104] Each year the Commission always presents its programme of activities to Parliament and a debate and vote ensues.[105]

This method of appointment still involves the risk that one of the governments may prevent the appointment or reappointment of a member of the Commission it does not like, a risk that is now perhaps very slightly lessened by the need to propose someone whose nomination will pass parliamentary scrutiny. A government has, of course, the right to refuse its

their candidature for the Presidency entirely obvious before they know that their political chickens are hatched at least as regards the other Member States, so it is perhaps understandable that there is no practice of, say, submitting two or three names to the Parliament for that body to express its views). Parliament now votes in plenary session on the intended candidate, see Corbett *et al.*, *The European Parliament* (3rd ed., London, 1995) 247–250 (who also discuss previous practice). The Treaty of Amsterdam (not yet in force) *ibid.*, 1st subpara. in each case so as to involve the Parliament after the nomination, removing the requirement of consultation before nomination: the nomination will have to be approved by the Parliament.

101. *Ibid.*, 2nd subpara. in each case. This gives the nominee for President some influence, but nothing like the final say. Before this influence was formalized there had been the occasional incident in the past when a nominee for President found that he was forced to work with a (continuing) Member of the Commission about whom he had made unflattering remarks. See, generally, Donnelly and Ritchie in Edwards and Spence (eds.), *op. cit.* (see note 90, *supra*) 33–36. The Treaty of Amsterdam (not yet in force) will amend Art. 158(2) EC, 2nd subpara. so that the nomination of the other members of the Commission will be by the governments of the Member States by common accord with the nominee for President. The latter will thus for the first time be able to veto a suggested person.

102. *Ibid.*, 3rd subpara. in each case. This formalizes a practice which had developed since 1981 with a vote of confidence after the Thorn Commission took office. The vote in the prospective Commission *en bloc* is appropriate in view of the Commission's collegiate responsibility.

103. Rules of Procedure of the European Parliament (O.J. 1997 L 49/1), Rule 33. As to the procedure on the nomination of the President, see Rule 32.

104. Arts. 158(3) EC, 10(3) ECSC, and 127(3) Euratom.

105. As to the 1998 programme (and the implementation of the 1997 programme), see Bull. EU 12–1997, point 1.9.14. See also Bull. EU Supp. 1/98.

co-operation in re-appointing a member of the Commission in whose impartiality, competence, or administrative ability it has lost confidence.[106] If, however, such a government avails itself of this right solely on the basis of a difference of opinion on the policy advocated by the member in question, it fails to fulfil its obligation not to seek to influence the members of the Commission in the performance of their duties.[107] In practice such a tendency by a Member State to repress a policy it does not like by refusing to co-operate in the re-appointment of the member concerned can, at least potentially, have an inhibiting effect on the conduct of members, an effect which is tantamount to an unlawful attempt to influence them in the performance of their duties. On the other hand, a five-year term may well mean that it is more likely that a different government will be in power at home when possible renomination is in issue than when the initial appointment was made, so the maintenance of too close links to a home government may be something of an unruly horse.

While governments appoint the members of the Commission, they cannot discharge them during their five-year term of office. The Court of Justice alone, on the application of the Council or the Commission, may compulsorily retire an individual member of the Commission from office if he no longer fulfils the conditions required for the performance of his duties or if he has been guilty of serious misconduct.[108] Only the European Parliament can compel the Commission to resign as a body, by means of a motion of censure on its activities,[109] although Parliament may wish to pass a resolution criticizing an individual Commissioner, or even calling on him or her to resign, if necessary backed up with a threat to censure the Commission en bloc on the ground that the person concerned is one of its members.[110]

The fact that members of the Commission are obliged to perform their duties in complete independence, in the general interest of the Communities, forbids their being prejudiced in favour of or against particular national standpoints or interests, but it does not imply that they

106. Although some people are not proposed for re-appointment for the simple reason that they are perceived as having 'gone native' (having done their job too well, and too independently), both Lord Richard (Ivor Richard) and Lord Cockfield are cases in point.
107. Arts. 157(2) EC, 9(2) ECSC, and 126(2) Euratom, 2nd subpara. in each case, although the likelihood of anyone bringing infringement proceedings on this ground is remote.
108. Arts. 160 EC, 12a ECSC, and 129 Euratom. So far there has been only one instance of this provision being used. Borschette was removed from office after it became clear that he was not going to recover from a coma. He died shortly after having been replaced by Vouel. The Centre Borschette (where various meetings take place) in Brussels is named after him. See Dec. 76/619 (O.J. 1976 L 201/31).
109. There have been several attempts to censure the Commission but none has so far succeeded, see Corbett et al., op. cit. (see note 100, supra) 246–247; see, further, note 242, infra.
110. See, further, section 5.2.2, post.

also have to practise political neutrality and to refrain from making statements that may be regarded as interference in the domestic affairs of a Member State.[111] It is a typical obligation for an *official* to refrain from interference in political questions in the performance of his duties.[112] The Commission, however is not a body of officials which is hierarchically subordinate to the Council. It is not subject to instructions from the Council, but is a body bearing its own political responsibility. This is made clear by the provision that it must resign *en bloc* if a political body, the European Parliament, censures it. Moreover it is entrusted, particularly under the EEC Treaty, with a task which has not only an administrative, but also a political content, as appears from the role entrusted to in the formulation of Community *policies*. It is entirely incorrect, therefore, to equate the Commission with a kind of many-headed Secretary-General in the service of the body representing the Member States of the organization.[113] The Commission is a body having its own political responsibility, its own political task and its own accountability to an elected Parliament. If there is a sort of international secretariat in the Communities, it is the civil service structure of the various Community Institutions and other bodies.[114]

111. See the letter of 20 July 1968 from Mansholt, then Vice-President of the Commission, to Debré, then French foreign minister, which was reproduced in (1968) *Agenor* No. 8, pp. 67–68. The Commission regards its members as being permitted to engage in national politics as long as they are not involved in specific political controversies: see WQs 1175/81 (Radux) O.J. 1981 C 345/22 and 1682/85 (Vandemeulebroucke) O.J. 1986 C 55/12. Under certain circumstances, *e.g.* if the free democratic system in the Communities were in issue, there could even be an obligation on members of the Commission to comment (according to the German Secretary of State, Moersch, answering a question by a German Parliamentarian: (1971) *Agenor* No. 21, p. 10). When Lord Cockfield was appointed to the Commission, the European Parliament adopted a resolution requesting him not to sit in the House of Lords during his mandate (O.J. 1985 C 12/97).
112. Indeed in some Member States (such as the United Kingdom), civil servants (at least in the policy grades) may not even be passive members of a political party. Other Member States have different approaches, in some cases civil servants find themselves appointed to ministerial or junior ministerial office.
113. See also Sidjanski's criticism (1964–65) 3 *JMCS* 47 *et seq.* of the views of Siotis (1963–64) 2 *JCMS* 222 *et seq.* Even today many newspapers speak erroneously of the Community's Executive Commission (even Dutch newspapers are known to talk about the Community's *dagelijks bestuur* or day-to-day management board), or of the Commissioners as civil servants (which is just as inaccurate as British weather forecasters speaking about Europe when they mean the Continent). See also Schermers and Blokker, *International Institutional Law* (3rd ed., The Hague, 1995) 375.
114. As to the structure of the Community civil service, see Spence in Edwards and Spence (eds.), *op. cit.* (see note 90, *supra*) 62–116 (on the Commission), Corbett *et al.*, *op. cit.* (see note 100, *supra*) 179–185 (on the European Parliament), and (on the Council) Westlake, *op. cit.* (see note 12, *supra*) 321–335 and Egger, *op. cit.* (see note 27, *supra*). The Council's General Secretariat, and the position of its Secretary-General, is now specifically recognized in Arts. 151(2) EC, 30(2) ECSC, and 121(2)

4.2. Internal organization

The Commission's President is very much *primus inter pares*, although his[115] personal authority within the college of Commissioners has varied over the years.[116] The Commission itself may appoint one or two Vice-Presidents from among its members.[117] While it is the Commission itself which decides on the allocation of portfolios amongst its members, the President has considerable influence in the initial allocation, although no power to shift responsibilities or reshuffle the team.[118] The Commission adopts its own rules of procedure so as to ensure that both it and its services operate in accordance with the provisions of the Treaties.[119] Each member of the Commission has a personal staff – his *cabinet* – which assists him, not least by enabling him to keep abreast of matters falling within his colleagues' portfolios and thus participate in the collegiate

Euratom. The Treaty of Amsterdam (not yet in force) will amend those provisions to make the Secretary-General High Representative for CFSP; he will be assisted by a Deputy Secretary-General who will be responsible for the running of the General Secretariat.

115. There has not yet been a female President of the Commission; the first female members served in the second Delors Commission (1989–93) and the present Commission (appointed in 1995) has five female members.

116. As to the collegiate nature of the Commission's responsibilities, see Donnelly and Ritchie in Edwards and Spence (eds.), *op. cit.* (see note 90, *supra*) 41–42. See also Rules of Procedure (Dec. 93/942, Art. 1 (O.J. 1993 L 230/15) and *e.g.* Case 5/85 *AKZO Chemie BV et al. v. Commission* [1986] ECR 2585 at 2614, and Case C-137/92 P *Commission v. BASF et al.* [1994] ECR I-2555 at 2650–2652.

117. Arts. 161 EC, 11 ECSC, and 130 Euratom. This departs from the previous practice of a number of Vice-Presidents, which had given rise on occasions to a Member being upgraded to Vice-President for the remaining mandate of the Commission (in one instance with less than two working weeks to go, see *Eighteenth General Report on the Activities of the European Communities 1984* (Brussels, Luxembourg, 1985) point 24), with the appropriate pension and severance package consequences of the higher salary. The Vice-President(s) deputize for the President, chairing the weekly meeting of the Commission in his absence.

118. See Donnelly and Ritchie in Edwards and Spence (eds.), *op. cit.* (see note 90, *supra*) 41–42. The stories of the in-fighting during meetings in the infamous Val Duchesse chateau in Brussels when the portfolios have been allocated are legion, not to say notorious, see Tugendhat, *Making Sense of Europe* (New York, 1986) 140–141, and (in relation to a meeting of the nominated but not yet appointed Commission in Luxembourg in October 1994) *The Times*, 31 October 1994. The Treaty of Amsterdam (not yet in force) will undoubtedly strengthen the President's hand through the insertion into Arts. 163 EC, 13 ECSC, and 132 Euratom of a new paragraph: 'The Commission shall work under the political guidance of its President.'

119. Arts. 162(2) EC, 16 ECSC, final para., and 131 Euratom, 2nd para. As to the Rules of Procedure, see Dec. 93/492 (O.J. 1993 L 230/15), amended by Dec. 95/148 (O.J. 1995 L 97/82) as a result of the annulment of various decisions in the competition field, see Case C-137/92 P *Commission v. BASF AG et al.* [1994] ECR I-2555 (the PVC case). The present rules replace the long-standing provisional rules dating from 1967 (J.O. 1967 147/1, last amended O.J. 1986 L 72/34).

responsibility for the Commission's policies.[120] The *chefs de cabinet* or their representatives meet weekly to prepare the Commission's meetings; at these preparatory meetings the points which do not need to be discussed by the Commissioners (and whose adoption will be a formality) are ascertained – these points are known as 'A' points. Every so often there are additional meetings of the *chefs* or their representatives to discuss complaint dossiers and infringement proceedings and to make concrete proposals as to the action which should be taken by the Commission. As with other items, the Commission will effectively only discuss those dossiers on which no agreement has been reached at the level of the *chefs* – known as 'B' points. The *chefs* also have very regular meetings devoted to state aids questions and less frequent meetings on infringements of directives.

Urgent cases can, of course, be brought up at any time. The *Spierenburg Report*[121] noted that the *cabinets* have steadily enhanced their role at the expense of the senior officials of the directorates-general and recommended a strengthening of the role of Directors-General.[122] The Commission's services are divided into at present 26 directorates-general and a number of horizontal services, such as the secretariat-general, the spokesman's service and the legal service. Each Commissioner has responsibility (sometimes shared) for one or more directorates-general, directorates or other services.

4.3   The Commission's tasks

4.3.1   Participation in policy formation by the Council

The Commission's key position in the process by which the Council reaches decisions is particularly apparent in the adoption of Community legislation. In practically all cases in which decision-making power is conferred on the Council, it can act only on the basis of a proposal from the Commission.[123] The Commission thus has the right of initiative. This is exclusive – no Commission proposal, no act by the Council.[124] The right of

---

120. See Donnelly and Ritchie in Edwards and Spence (eds.), *op. cit.* (see note 90, *supra*) 42–51.
121. Submitted on 24 September 1979, see Bull. EC 9–1979, points 1.3.1 *et seq.*
122. See Donnelly and Ritchie in Edwards and Spence (eds.), *op. cit.* (see note 90, *supra*) 49–50 for a balanced view of the *cabinets* and administrative liaison. The *cabinet* system has many advantages, but certainly increases the politicization of the treatment of dossiers and sometimes enables shoddy deals to be done while Commissioners parade with clean hands (with varying degrees of credibility).
123. This describes the situation in the Community sphere.
124. There is an exception to this exclusivity: Art. 106(6) EC permits the Council to adopt certain provisions relating to the European Central Bank on the basis of a proposal from the Commission or a recommendation from the ECB. See also Art. 106(5) EC. The European Parliament has a quasi-right of initiative, see section 5.2.4, *post*.

initiative is given greater significance because normally the Council may amend such a proposal only by unanimous vote[125] and as long as the Council has not yet taken a decision the Commission may alter its proposal;[126] indeed, in some cases, when it has been apparent that the Council intended to adopt an emasculated version of a Commission proposal, the Commission has even withdrawn the proposal at the last minute rather than accept its emasculation, although this technique is not uncontroversial.[127] Because of its right of participation and also because of its undisputed competence and impartiality, the Commission fulfils an extremely important function in the decision-making process in the Council; this function stamps it as a body which helps to decide policy and is discussed further in the examination of the decision-making process in section 3.3 of Chapter V, below.

The Commission's participation in the shaping of measures taken by the Council, and by the European Parliament in the manner provided for in the EC and Euratom Treaties[128] does not always take the form of a proposal. It may be that the Commission may only be empowered to adopt non-binding recommendations or opinions.[129] The Commission has

125. Arts. 189a(1) EC and 119 Euratom. The exception (Art. 189b(4) and (5) EC) concerns decisions of the Council adopting a joint text agreed in the Conciliation Committee with the European Parliament, which can be taken by qualified majority without the Commission having altered its proposal to reflect that joint text.
126. Arts. 189a(2) EC, see also Art. 119 Euratom, 2nd para.
127. Dashwood argues that withdrawing a proposal which is on the point of being adopted by the Council, in order to prevent the Council from amending it contrary to the Commission's wishes would be an abuse of power, Wyatt and Dashwood, *European Community Law* (3rd ed., London, 1993) 48. In the same sense, Dewost in Mégret *et al.* (eds.) *Le droit de la Communauté économique européenne* Vol. 9 (Brussels, 1979) 135–136. Harnier in Von der Groeben *et al.* (eds.) *Kommentar zum EWG-Vertrag* (4th ed., Baden-Baden, 1991) Vol. 3, 4296 notes that the Council could avail itself of Art. 152 EC, or it or any other party entitled to bring an action could seek the annulment of the decision to withdraw the proposal, using Art. 173 EC. This point is not repeated by Schoo in Von der Groeben *et al.* (eds.), *Kommentar zun EU-/EG-Vertrag* (5th ed., Baden-Baden, 1997) Vol. 4, 1071–1072. Certainly withdrawal at the last minute has caused fury in the Council on occasions, but there is no case-law as yet on the point. See, further, Chapter V, section 3.3.1, *post*.
128. Arts. 155 EC and 124 Euratom, 3rd indent in each case.
129. Opinions are provided for in Arts. 104c(5) (excessive deficits); 109i(3) (protective measures in balance of payments crises); 118 (social policy) and 203(2) EC (Community budget). The Commission is also consulted on applications for membership of the European Union, Art. O TEU, 1st para. It delivers its views in the form of an opinion.
    Recommendations forming the basis for action by the Council are provided for in Arts. 103(2) and (4) (broad guidelines of economic policies of the Member States and of the Community); 109 (exchange-rate system for the ECU in relation to non-Community countries, and the conclusion of international agreements in this sphere); 109d (various economic and monetary matters); 109h (difficulties in relation to balance of payments); 109j (fulfilment of the necessary conditions for the adoption of a single currency); 109k (derogations relating to the 3rd stage of EMU; 113(3) (negotiation of international agreements in the field of the common commercial policy) and 228(1)

in any event a general power to make recommendations and to adopt opinions.[130] The Commission's right of initiative is also recognized in the supplementary policies and forms of cooperation, CFSP and JHA, although this right is in these cases not exclusive.[131]

4.3.2   The Commission's administrative function

The original administrative function of the Commission is based on 'its own power of decision ... in the manner provided for in this Treaty.'[132] Its delegated administrative function is based on 'the powers conferred on it by the Council for the implementation of the rules laid down by the latter.'[133] The administration to be performed by the Commission on the basis of these powers is wide-ranging. Thus, for example, it gives effect to the budget and to the maintenance of the Community's external relations.[134] In the EC Treaty an original administrative function has only rarely been given to the Commission contrary to what is the case in the ECSC and Euratom Treaties. This is an obvious consequence of the difference between a framework treaty (*traité-cadre*) on the one hand and a treaty-law (*traité-loi*) or management treaty (*traité de gestion*) on the other. The administrative activities of the Commission which are directly based on the EC Treaty are mainly in the fields of the customs union, competition policy and safeguard clauses. These are in fact the main areas in which the EC Treaty exhibits the characteristics of a treaty-law or management treaty.[135] The

(negotiations leading to international agreements). The recommendations under Art. 109d may be requested by the Council or by a Member State. This is a specific instance of the more general power conferred on the Council by Arts. 152 EC, 26 ECSC, 3rd para., and 122 Euratom to request the Commission to undertake any studies which the Council considers desirable for the attainment of the common objectives, and to submit to it any appropriate proposals. As to the meaning of 'proposals' in this context, see Chapter V, section 3.3.1 on the function of the Commission.

130. Art. 155 EC, 2nd indent, 14 ECSC, 1st para., and 124 Euratom, 2nd indent. The EC and Euratom provisions do not confine the Commission's powers here to specific instances; if the Commission considers it necessary to issue recommendations or deliver opinions, it may do so.
131. In CFSP the right to refer to the Council any question relating to CFSP and to submit proposals may be exercised by any Member State or the Commission, Art. J.8(3) TEU. In JHA the Member States have the right of initiative in all matters, which is shared with the Commission in the areas covered by Art. K.1(1)–(6) TEU, Art. K.3(2) TEU. The right of initiative is also shared under Art. K.9 TEU.
132. Arts. 155 EC and 124 Euratom, 3rd indent in each case. *Cf.* Art. 14 ECSC.
133. Arts. 155 EC, and 124 Euratom, 4th indent in each case. *Cf.* Art. 145 EC, 3rd indent.
134. See Chapters V, section 2.3 and XI, section 2.5, *post*, respectively.
135. Note the Commission's original administrative function in adopting safeguard measures in the event of delays in the annual decision-making process in the Council con-

The Commission of the European Communitites 205

Court has observed[136] that the Commission's own power of decision in the manner provided for in the Treaty, set out in Article 155 EC is expressed in almost identical terms to those used in Article 145 EC to describe the same function of the Council; thus there can be no question of inferring any inherent restriction of the Commission's power of decision from the wording of Article 155 EC. Commission proposals may, in certain circumstances, in the case of a failure by the Council to act, have certain legal consequences where they form the basis of a process of cooperation between the Commission and the Member States to enable the Community to meet its responsibilities, but in the absence of such process of cooperation, unilateral proposals by the Commission cannot be regarded as Community rules.[137]

The administration of safeguard clauses deserves special attention.[138] In certain circumstances specified in the Treaty the Member States may temporarily deviate from their Treaty obligations, although this requires the authorization of the Community Institutions.[139] If, in urgent cases, the autonomous resort to protective measures is permitted exceptionally, these Institutions have the right to intervene *a posteriori*. In these latter cases the Commission does not have the monopoly position that was proposed for it, on convincing grounds, in the *Spaak Report*.[140] Sometimes the Council takes the necessary decisions on the basis of a proposal[141] or an opinion[142] from the Commission. In other cases, it exercises a control *a posteriori* over the Commission.[143]

While the original, Treaty-based, administrative function of the Commission has a narrow scope, the delegated administrative function assigned to it by the Council under the EC Treaty system for the implementation of the rules laid down by the Council is very wide-ranging indeed. Implementing powers for the Commission are provided for not only in those cases where the Treaty expressly lays down such a delegated administrative task,[144] but also in practically all decisions of the Council

   cerning agricultural prices. This is based on Arts. 5 and 155 EC. See WQ 1169/85 (Debatisse) O.J. 1986 C 29/9 and Schwarze (1982) EuR 133 *et seq.*
136. Cases 188–190/80 *France, Italy and United Kingdom v. Commission* [1982] ECR 2545 at 2573.
137. Case 325/85 *Ireland v. Commission* [1987] ECR 5041; see also Case 804/79 *Commission v. United Kingdom* [1985] ECR 1045 and the discussion in Chapter III, section 5.2.3, *ante.*
138. The Commission also administers safeguard clauses in the course of its delegated administrative function in the field of the common agricultural policy; see Sack (1983) 20 CMLRev. 757, and *e.g.* Reg. 1766/92 (O.J. 1992 L 181/21, most recently amended by Reg. 923/96 (O.J. 1996 L 126/37)), Art. 17 (cereals).
139. *E.g.* Arts. 25 and 109h(3) EC.
140. See Chapter 1, section 4.1, *ante.*
141. Art. 25(1) EC.
142. Art. 109i(3) EC.
143. Art. 109h(3) EC, 2nd para.
144. *E.g.* Arts. 79(4) and 87(2)(d) EC.

which are of any importance.[145] If, however, these powers are considered from the viewpoint not of quantity but of quality, it must be observed that the Council usually displays an extremely narrow view of the administrative task to be entrusted to the Commission. Despite the fact that the new third indent of Article 145 EC requires the Council to confer implementing powers on the Commission,[146] the Council is still very much inclined to exercise its power under that provision to reserve implementing measures to itself in sensitive areas or where it has been unable to impose the 'safety-net procedure'.[147] Wherever it does delegate power to adopt implementing measures, it invariably tries to ensure that the Commission's powers are subject to strict conditions, even though this clearly goes against the express desire of the Member States, as expressed on the occasion of the adoption of the SEA, that preference should be given to advisory committees (as opposed to regulatory or management committees) in the interests of speed and efficiency in the decision-making process.[148]

4.3.3   The Commission's supervisory function

In accordance with the proposals of the *Spaak Report* the Commission has been directed to ensure 'that the provisions of this Treaty and of the measures taken by the institutions pursuant thereto are applied.'[149] This supervision extends in the first place to ensuring the observance by the Member States of their obligations under the Treaty. If the Commission considers that a Member State has failed to fulfil its obligations, it may institute proceedings which may ultimately lead to a judgment of the Court

145. See the impressive list in the Jozeau–Marigé Report (European Parliament Session Documents 1968–1969, No. 115) Until the end of 1989 the Commission had power to settle disputes about bracket or obligatory transport tariffs see Reg. 2831/77, Arts. 7 and 13 (O.J. 1977 L 334/22, replaced by Reg. 3568/83 (O.J. 1983 L 359/1, which was extended until 31 December 1989 by Reg. 1991/88 (O.J. 1988 L 176/5)) and *e.g.* Dec. 78/559 (O.J. 1978 L 188/24). See also Dec. 82/595 (O.J. 1982 L 244/32) based on Reg. 517/72 (O.J. English Special Edition 1972(l), p. 143).
146. See section 6.4, *post*. See also COM (98) 380 Final.
147. *Ibid.*, see Docksey and Williams in Edwards and Spence (eds.), *op. cit.* (see note 90, *supra*) 137 and 143–146.
148. Declaration on the powers of implementation of the Commission, annexed to the Final Act on the adoption of the SEA. See *e.g.* the *General Reports* for 1993–1995 (Brussels, Luxembourg, 1994–1996) points 1003, 1174, and 1032 respectively. As to measures implementing acts of the European Parliament and the Council, see the *modus vivendi* O.J. 1996 C 102/1. As to further proposals in this area, see COM (98) 380 Final.
149. Arts. 155 EC and 124 Euratom, first indent in each case. No equivalent general enabling provision is to be found in the ECSC Treaty, although the Court clearly acknowledged the supervisory role of the High Authority (now the Commission) as a general principle in Case 20/59 *Italy v. High Authority* [1960] ECR 325.

of Justice.[150] The supervisory function of the Commission also extends to ensuring the observance by private parties of their Community obligations. This appears from its powers in relation to violations of the principle of non-discrimination in transport[151] or of breach of the rules of competition by undertakings.[152] In the regulations of the Council in these fields,[153] control by the Commission has taken the form of a series of specific powers, particularly those by which it can oblige an undertaking to put an end to an infringement[154] and those by which it can impose, administrative, fines and/or periodic penalty payments for breaches of the rules.[155]

In order to exercise its supervisory function the Commission must of course possess the necessary information.[156] For this purpose, in addition to the data which it obtains through complaints by Member States or private parties, or through questions asked by members of the European Parliament,[157] it can always request the Member States to provide it with the requisite information. The Member States are obliged by virtue of Article 5 EC to comply with such requests.[158] Many implementing acts of the Council, particularly harmonization directives, impose a duty on Member States to provide information as a result of which the Commission can judge whether or not they are fulfilling their obligations.[159] An obligation to provide information to the Commission and a right of investigation by it may also arise in relation to undertakings[160] or procedures may be set up which give the Commission the requisite data[161]

---

150. Arts. 169 and 171 EC, see also Arts. 88 ECSC and 141 and 143 Euratom. See further, Chapter VI, section 1.1.
151. Arts. 79(3) and (4) EC.
152. Arts. 89 and 87(2)(d) EC.
153. Reg. 11 (O.J. English Special Edition 1959–1962, p. 60) and Reg. 17 (*ibid.*, p. 87) as amended.
154. Reg. 17, *ibid.*, Art. 3.
155. *Ibid.*, Arts. 15 and 16; Reg. 11 (see note 153, *supra*). Arts. 17 and 18.
156. See, generally, Audretsch, *Supervision in European Community Law* (2nd ed., Amsterdam/New York/Oxford, 1986) Chapter 3.
157. *E.g.* WQ 1558/84 (Rogalla) O.J. 1985 C 161/21.
158. See also Arts. 86 ECSC and 192 Euratom. Thus when the Commission writes asking for details of national legislation in a particular field it writes to the Permanent Representations; delay in answering usually elicits a reminder citing Art. 5 EC (or Art. 86 ECSC or Art. 192 Euratom, as the case may be). It is possible to use these provisions to pursue a failure to supply information but all a Member State would have to do to terminate the infringement is supply the information. Sometimes Art. 5 EC (*etc.*) is used in conjunction with other Articles of the Treaty in infringement proceedings as a subsidiary head of infringement.
159. *E.g.* Dir. 75/439 (O.J. 1975 L 194/23, most recently amended by Dir. 91/692 (O.J. 1991 L 377/48)).
160. *E.g.* Reg. 11, Arts. 11 and 13, and Reg. 17, Arts. 12 and 14 (see note 153, *supra*).
161. *E.g.* notification of agreements *etc.* in accordance with Reg. 17, Arts. 4 and 5 (see note 153, *supra*).

in some other way. Article 213 EC[162] contains a general provision according to which the Commission (within the limits and under the conditions laid down by the Council in accordance with the provisions of the Treaty) may collect any information and carry out any necessary checks. This provision has not so far led to a general regulation of the Commission's powers in this field, and initially only formed the basis for decisions of the Council relating to a series of statistical enquiries to be carried out by the Commission.[163] This last example makes it equally clear that the Commission's rights of enquiry and verification, arising under general or particular provisions of Community law, may also be essential to its policy determination function. For that function to be properly performed the necessary information must be at the Commission's disposal. Finally, it should be mentioned that an obligation of secrecy with regard to information which is by nature confidential has been imposed on the members of the Commission as well as on members of the other Community Institutions, members of committees, and officials and other servants of the Community.[164] The obligation of secrecy is not absolute as far as the Commission is concerned. Thus, in cases before it the Commission must weigh the interest of secrecy against interests such as the proper course of investigation proceedings, the rights of the defence and the duty to state reasons for Commission decisions.[165] In pursuit of greater openness and transparency[166] the Council and the Commission have now issued a Code of Conduct concerning public access to their documents[167]

---

162. See also Art. 187 Euratom and, without intervention by the Council, Art. 47 ECSC, 1st para. See also the extensive powers of the Commission concerning inspections for safeguard controls under Title II, Chapter VII Euratom.

163. Art. 213 EC does not prevent the Commission from imposing a duty on the Member States to provide information on the basis of specific provisions: Cases 188–190/80 *France et al. v. Commission* [1982] ECR 2545 at 2754; Case C-426/93 *Germany v. Commission* [1995] ECR I-3723 at 3756–3758.

164. Arts. 214 EC, 47 ECSC, 2nd para., and, extensively, 24–27 and 194 Euratom. See Case 145/83 *Adams v. Commission* [19851 ECR 3539 at 3587–3590.

165. See Case 53/85 *AKZO Chemie BV et al. v. Commission* [1986] ECR 1965, [1987] 1 CMLR 231 and Cases 296 and 318/82 *Netherlands and Leeuwarder Papierwarenfabriek BV v. Commission* [1985] ECR 809 at 825. See also the Notice on internal rules of procedure for processing requests for access to the file in various competition fields (O.J. 1997 C 23/3). In some cases the 'chinese walls' system operates, as in the anti-dumping field, where information obtained in the course of a proceeding cannot be used for any other purposes, Reg. 384/96, Art. 19(6) (O.J. 1996 L 56/1). This in particular means that it cannot be used for the purposes of competition proceedings.

166. See the Birmingham Declaration: Birmingham European Council, Conclusions of the Presidency, Annex I (Bull. EC 10–1992 point I.8). See also Bull. EC 12–1992 point I.5. See also the European Ombudsman's Special Report (O.J. 1998 C 44/10); Reg. 354/83 (O.J. 1983 L 43/1) on access to historic archives of the EEC and Euratom, and the decision of the representatives of the governments of the Member States on access to archives on various negotiations (Dec. 94/271 (O.J. 1994 L 117/29).

167. Dec. 93/730 (O.J. 1993 L 340/41, corrig. O.J. 1994 L 23/34). See also the Commis-

and the Commission has adopted a decision on public access to Commission documents.[168]

5. EUROPEAN PARLIAMENT

5.1 Composition and character of the Parliament

The European Parliament (which was originally called the Assembly but soon rebaptised itself long before its name was formally changed)[169] consists of 'representatives of the peoples of the States brought together in the Community.'[170] Thus the members of the European Parliament are representatives of the peoples and this body itself represents the peoples of the Community collectively and independently. As representatives of the peoples the members of the European Parliament are not bound by instructions of their governments, or of the national parliaments.[171] As representatives of the peoples they exercise their duties without any specific instructions or obligation to consult. By the use of the words 'representatives of the peoples' the modern concept of representation, as laid down in the constitutional law of the Member States, has also been incorporated in the Treaties. The undisturbed discharge of their function is guaranteed by the arrangements in their favour contained in the Protocol on the Privileges and Immunities of the European Communities.[172]

sion's Communications (O.J. 1993 C 156/5 and 166/4). See further, Case C-58/94 *Netherlands v. Council* [1996] ECR I-2169.

168. Dec. 94/90 (O.J. 1994 L 46/58, amended by Dec. 96/567 (O.J. 1996 L 247/45). See Case T-105/95 *WWF UK (World Wildlife Fund for Nature) v. Commission* [1997] ECR II-313; Case T-156/97 *Berge v. Commission* [1997] ECR II-2097; Case T-124/96 *Interporc Im- und Export GmbH v. Commission* [1998] ECR II-231, and Case T-83/96 *Van der Wal v. Commission* [1998] ECR II-nyr (19 March 1998).

169. See the Resolutions of 20 March 1958 (J.O. 6/58) and 30 March 1962 (J.0. 1045/62). Art. 3(1) SEA brought the name 'European Parliament' into the Treaties where it changed or supplemented them, and that provision was not repealed by the TEU. In the United Kingdom the European Communities (Amendment) Act 1986, s. 3 provides that references to the 'European Parliament' shall be substituted for any reference (however worded) to the Assembly of the European Communities.

170. Arts. 137 EC, 20 ECSC, and 107 Euratom.

171. See the Act concerning the election of the representatives of the Assembly by direct universal suffrage, annexed to Dec. 76/787 (O.J. 1976 L 278/1 and 5), Art. 4(1). This is henceforth referred to as the Act on direct elections.

172. Act on direct elections, Arts. 8–10 (see also Art. 4(2)). The Court interprets the period of immunity mentioned in the Protocol on Privileges and Immunities of the European Communities (annexed to the Merger Treaty), Art. 10 in a wide sense: it is valid 'during the sessions' (and while travelling to and from the place of meeting of the Parliament). Thus in Case 149/85 *Wybot v. Faure et al.* [1986] ECR 2391 the Court held that 'during the sessions' must be interpreted as meaning that the European Parliament is in session, even if it is not actually sitting, until the decision

The representatives form part of a body which itself represents not one people, but a plurality of peoples, although in a collective sense. By the use of the plural 'peoples' the Treaties do justice to reality, reflecting the diverse peoples who together are Community citizens. However, by substituting for the short term 'Member States', commonly used in the Treaties, the phrase 'States brought together in the Community',[173] the Treaties emphasise not their individual, but their collective character. The members of the European Parliament represent not only their own people, but also the other peoples of the Community.

The formation of European political party-groups[174] which already took place in the old Common Assembly of the ECSC, clearly demonstrates this notion, and indeed the importance of political parties at European level has now been formally recognized.[175] It is the groups rather than the national parties which put their stamp on the work of the Parliament. This is evident in debates as well as in the composition of the various parliamentary bodies. The conditions for official recognition of groups are laid down in the Parliament's Rules of Procedure.[176] Currently the minimum number of members necessary to form a group is 29 if all come from one Member State, 23 if they come from two Member States, 18 if they come from three, and 14 if they come from four or more.[177] In the Parliament elected in the direct elections held in June 1994, and taking the accessions in January 1995 and the direct elections in Austria and Finland in 1996, and Sweden in 1995 into account, there now 626 members,[178] at present divided into eight groups: the Party of European Socialists (PSE) are the largest with 215 members; then come the European Peoples Party (PPE, Christian Democrats) who have 181 members; the Union for Europe Group (UPE) with 55; the Liberal, Democratic and Reformist Group (ELDR) with 41; the Confederal European United Left (GUE)/ Nordic Green Left (NGL) with 33 (Communists and regionalists); the EP Green

---

is taken closing its annual or extraordinary sessions. As to jurisdiction in relation to actions for non-contractual liability for acts committed on the European Parliament's premises, see Case C-201/89 *Le Pen et al. v. Puhl et al.* [1990] ECR I-1183.

173. Arts. 137 EC, 20 ECSC, and 107 Euratom.
174. Usually referred to simply as the political groups.
175. Art. 138a EC.
176. Parliament's Rules of Procedure (O.J. 1997 L 49/1), Rule 29.
177. *Ibid.*, Rule 29(2).
178. Act on direct elections, Art. 2, as last substituted by Dec. 95/1, Art. 3 (O.J. 1995 L1/1), amending Act of Accession (1994), Art. 11 (O.J. 1994 C 241/21). In the period prior to the autumn 1996 direct elections in Austria, Finland and Sweden the MEPs from those countries were nominated from among member of their national parliaments. The Treaty of Amsterdam (not yet in force) will add a new paragraph to Arts. 137 EC, 20 ECSC, and 107 Euratom, so that the number of MEPs may not exceed 700. This is clearly designed to limit the growth of the Parliament on future enlargements. It will also incorporate Arts. 1–3(1) of the Act on direct elections into Article 138 EC, with various consequential amendments.

Group (*Les Verts*) with 28; the European Radical Alliance (ARE) with 19, and the Group of Independents for Europe of the Nation States (I-END) who have 18 members. There are also 36 non-affiliated members.[179]

Until 1979 members of the European Parliament were appointed by and from the national parliaments in accordance with the procedure laid down by each Member State, the number of delegates per country being specified in the Treaty.[180] This method of appointing members was envisaged as being only temporary, as was clear from the old Article 138(3) EEC (and the equivalent provisions in the ECSC and Euratom Treaties) which required the Parliament to draw up proposals for elections by direct universal suffrage in accordance with a uniform procedure in all Member States. It also provided that the Council, acting unanimously, was to lay down the appropriate provisions which it would 'recommend to Member States for adoption in accordance with their respective constitutional requirements.'

As long ago as 1960 the European Parliament had already drawn up proposals for direct general elections.[181] However, the Council never adopted provisions on the basis of those proposals as at least one Member State felt that the introduction of direct elections was inopportune. After the first enlargement in 1973 the Parliament reviewed the matter, and after extensive preparation Patijn, the *rapporteur* of the political committee, succeeded in having the text of a draft Treaty adopted, with some modifications, on 14 January 1975.[182] These new proposals formed the basis of action by the Council which on 20 September 1976 decided to recommend to the Member States provisions in the form of an Act concerning the election of the representatives of the Assembly by direct universal suffrage.[183] After the Act had been accepted by all the Member States in accordance with their respective constitutional requirements[184] and the necessary implementing measures had been adopted,[185] the first

---

179. Source: *General Report 1997* ((Brussels, Luxembourg, 1998) point 1124 (situation at 31 December 1997).
180. Arts. 138 EEC, 21 ECSC, and 108 Euratom. These provisions lapsed on 17 July 1979 in accordance with Act on direct elections, Art. 14. The Treaty of Amsterdam (not yet in force) will incorporate Articles 1–3(1) of that Act into Art. 138 EC with consequential amendments.
181. Resolution of 17 May 1960 (J.O. 834/60) approving a draft convention on the introduction of direct elections (Dehousse report, EP Session 1960–1961, no. 22).
182. O.J. 1975 C 32/15 (for the Patijn report see EP session documents 1974–1975 no. 368/74).
183. Dec. 76/787 and the Act on direct elections, O.J. 1976 L 278/1 and 5.
184. For the United Kingdom, see the European Parliamentary Elections Act 1978, and now the European Parliamentary Elections Act 1993; for The Netherlands see Trb. 1976, 175 and Stb. 1977, 407, now the Kieswet 1989 Stb. 423, most recently amended 1996 Stb. 623 (see Part V, Chapter Y).
185. For the United Kingdom see *ibid.* For the Netherlands see now the Kieswet 1989 Stb. 423 as amended, Part V and the Wet Incompatibiliteiten Staten-Generaal en Europees Parlement Stb. 1994, 295.

direct elections were held between 7–10 June 1979.[186] The first directly elected European Parliament met for the first time on 17 July 1979.[187] The second elections were held between 14–17 June 1984;[188] the third elections between 15–18 June 1989,[189] and the fourth elections between 9–12 June 1994.[190]

The Act on direct elections does not prescribe a uniform electoral procedure for all the Member States and national views on this point are still diverse. The preference for a particular electoral system, whether of proportional representation or 'first past the post' is deeply ingrained in national traditions and political power relationships. Had it been necessary to decide on a uniform electoral procedure the introduction of direct elections would certainly have been still further delayed. The task of finding a consensus on a uniform procedure falls upon the Parliament and the Council with the former having now the right of veto, as its assent is required before the Council may act.[191] Until a uniform electoral procedure enters into force, elections are governed in each Member State by its national provisions[192] although there are a few Community provisions relating to timing and the count.[193]

186. Dec. 78/639 (O.J. 1978 L 205/75).
187. On which day under the Act on direct elections, Art. 14 the first and second parts of Arts. 138 EEC, 21 ECSC, and 108 Euratom ceased to have effect.
188. Dec. 83/285 (O.J. 1983 L 155/11).
189. Dec. 88/435 (O.J. 1988 L 210/25), altering the date from the Parliament's original proposal.
190. This took place at the normal five-year interval, so no decision (altering the date) was necessary.
191. See Arts. 138(3) EC, 21(3) ECSC, and 108(3) Euratom, strengthening the Parliament's right of initiative under Act on direct elections, Art. 7(l). The Council acts unanimously after having obtained the assent of the Parliament, which acts by a majority of its component members (which means that absences or abstentions count as votes against the proposal), Art. 138(3) EC (etc.). As to more recent proposals on steps towards a uniform procedure see O.J. 1993 C 115/67 (Resolution of 10 March 1993). As to the principal issues involved in drawing up a uniform electoral system, see Corbett et al., op. cit. (see note 100, supra) 19–30. See also Case C-41/92 The Liberal Democrats v. European Parliament [1993] ECR I-3153, and Bradley and Feeney (1993) 13 YBEL 383 at 391–392 (where they rightly describe the judgment in The Liberal Democrats as 'curious') and 422–423. As to the earlier proposal and background, see O.J. 1982 C 87/61 and Sasse et al.: The European Parliament: towards a uniform procedure for direct elections (Florence, 1981) and Van de Berghe (1979) 4 ELRev. 331. The Treaty of Amsterdam (not yet in force) will replace the existing Art. 138(3), 1st subpara. to provide for the Parliament to 'draw up a proposal for elections by universal suffrage in accordance with a uniform procedure in all Member States or in accordance with principles common to all Member States.'
192. Act on direct elections, Art. 7(2): i.e. national provisions established or declared applicable for the elections.
193. Ibid., Art. 9. The elections are held on dates fixed by the Member States within a particular period beginning on a Thursday morning and ending on the following Sunday.

Fixing the number of seats and dividing them up according to nationality proved most problematical. In order to ensure a satisfactory representation on the basis of population of the Member States as well as ensuring a reasonable cross-section of political movements, it was felt necessary to expand the number of members and to distribute seats more proportionately than had been done in relation to the old Parliament, always bearing in mind that the smallest Member State, Luxembourg, had to have a certain minimum number of seats. The end result was a compromise arrived at by the European Council. After Spanish and Portuguese accession, there were 518 seats,[194] which rose to 567 as a result of the increased number of seats allocated to Germany as a result of unification, and the rebalancing in favour of various Member States agreed on that occasion.[195] As a result of the accession in 1995, of the 626 seats in the European Parliament, the number of seats attributed to Germany is 99; France, Italy and the United Kingdom each elect 87 members, Spain 64, the Netherlands 31, Belgium, Greece and Portugal each elect 25, Sweden 22, Austria 21, Denmark 16, Ireland 15, and Luxembourg elects 6 members.[196] The envisaged capping of the number of members has already been noted.[197]

The Act on direct elections makes provision relating to incompatibility of functions. It is significant that a dual mandate (being a member of a national as well as the European Parliament) is expressly permitted by Article 5 of the Act.[198] However, Article 6 of the Act specifically declares certain functions to be incompatible with membership of the European

194. Act of Accession (1985), Art. 10 (amending the Act on direct elections, Art. 2 accordingly).
195. The political decision was agreed at the Edinburgh European Council, December 1992 (Bull. EC 12–1992 point I.13) and the Act on direct elections, Art. 2 was amended accordingly by Dec. 93/81 (O.J. 1993 L 33/15). Prior to the 1994 direct elections, 18 observers from the former German Democratic Republic had been initially selected from the former East German Parliament, but were later selected by the German *Bundestag*, although they had only limited internal rights, see Corbett *et al.*, *op. cit.* (see note 100, *supra*) 25; Bull. EC 7/8–1990 point 1.2.4 and 10–1990 point 1.8.7, and *24th General Report on the Activities of the European Communities 1990* (Brussels, Luxembourg, 1991) point 19. See also Case C-25/92 *Miethke v. European Parliament* [1993] ECR I-473.
196. Dec. 95/1 (O.J. 1995 L 1/1), Art. 5 amends the Act on direct elections, Art. 2 accordingly.
197. See note 178, *supra*. The Treaty of Amsterdam (not yet in force) will amend the Act on direct elections, Art. 2 to prescribe that in the event of amendments to that provision 'the number of representatives elected in each Member State must ensure appropriate representation of the peoples of the States brought together in the Community.'
198. In the Netherlands, a dual mandate is prohibited, Wet Incompatibiliteiten Staten-Generaal en Europees Parlement, Stb. 1994, 294. In the United Kingdom it is not prohibited. Given the express permissibility as a matter of Community law of a dual mandate, the prohibition in various Member States may be open to question, although many political parties have excluded a dual mandate, either in their rules or in practice, Corbett *et al.*, *op. cit.* (see note 100, *supra*) 22.

Parliament, *e.g.* members of the government of a Member State, member of the Commission, Court of Justice, Court of Auditors, the Economic and Social Committee, the Consultative Committee of the ECSC, active officials or servants of any of the Community Institutions or specialised body attached to them, or the Registrar of the Court.[199] Until the entry into force of a uniform electoral procedure the Member States may declare, at national level, other positions to be incompatible with membership of the European Parliament.[200] Members of the European Parliament are elected for five years.[201] Their credentials are verified by the Parliament pending the entry into force of a uniform electoral procedure; for this purpose it takes note of the results declared officially by the Member States.[202] Evaluation of whether members elected satisfy the conditions laid down in national legislation takes place under national provisions, again, pending the entry into force of a uniform electoral procedure.[203] Until that moment the filling of seats falling vacant during the Parliament's term of office occurs according to national procedures.[204]

The Act on direct elections contained no provisions relating to active and passive voting rights; the modalities remain matters for the Member States, subject now to the obligations resulting from Directive 93/109[205] which implements the right conferred by Article 8b EC for every citizen of the Union residing in a Member State of which he is not a national to vote and to stand as a candidate in elections to the European Parliament in that Member State under the same conditions as nationals of that State.

199. Act on direct elections, Art. 6(1) gives the full list. The Treaty of Amsterdam (not yet in force) will add membership of the Committee of the Regions to that list.

200. *Ibid.*, Arts. 6(2) and 7(2). For the United Kingdom see the European Parliamentary Elections Act 1978, Sch. 1, para. 5 and for the Netherlands see the Wet Incompatibiliteiten Staten-Generaal en Europees Parlement Stb. 1994, 295, most recently amended 1997 Stb. 789. The Treaty of Amsterdam (not yet in force) will amend the act on direct elections, Art. 7(2) so as to read 'pending the entry into force of a uniform electoral procedure or a procedure based on common principles...' (rest unchanged).

201. Act on direct elections, Art. 3(1), which the Treaty of Amsterdam (not yet in force) will incorporate into the revised Art. 138 EC (as Art. 138(3), with consequential renumbering).

202. *Ibid.*, Art. 11. See Case C-25/89 *Miethke v. European Parliament* [1993] ECR I-473. The Treaty of Amsterdam (not yet in force) will amend the Act on direct elections, Art. 11 so as to read 'pending the entry into force of the uniform electoral procedure or a procedure based on common principles...' (rest unchanged).

203. *Ibid.* In the Netherlands the Second Chamber (of the Dutch Parliament) decides: Kieswet, Art. Y 25, Stb. 1989, 423 (as amended) and Rules of Procedure of the Second Chamber, Art. 138. In the United Kingdom there is provision for judicial proceedings relating to disqualification: European Assembly Elections Act 1978, Sch. 1. para. 6.

204. Act on direct elections, Art. 12, which will be similarly amended as indicated *supra* by the Treaty of Amsterdam (not yet in force). As to some of the difficulties in this regard, see Bradley and Feeney (1993) YBEL 383 at 412–413, and (1994) 14 YBEL 428–429.

205. O.J. 1993 L 329/34. See Chapter III, section 6.2, *ante*. See the Resolutions of the European Parliament O.J. 1994 C 44/159 and C 128/316.

Article 13 of the Act on direct elections permits the Council, acting unanimously on a proposal from the Parliament after consulting the Commission, to adopt measures to implement the Act after endeavouring to reach agreement with the Parliament in a conciliation committee consisting of the Council and representatives of the Parliament.[206] Regrettably, the first attempt to set up a Community system, based on this provision,[207] concerning the salaries and tax liability of members of the European Parliament failed through lack of unanimity. As a result each Member State has adopted the necessary financial rules for members which it returns,[208] as long as Parliament has not adopted any rules on the matter in the exercise of its budgetary powers. The present differences in salaries and other financial arrangements according to nationality scarcely fit in with membership of an Institution which represents the peoples of the Community assembled. Moreover, there is a real danger that financial dependence on national rules or their application could be abused in order to put pressure on members. The Parliament appears to have attempted to compensate for the difference in salaries to some extent by granting members generous expenses on a lump-sum basis.[209]

In the long term the introduction of direct elections may bring about significant changes in the institutional balance within the Community. Voters can air their views directly on Community policy and thus their representatives are better placed than were their indirectly elected predecessors to make the Council and the Commission aware of those views (although invariably politicians will – at present perhaps understandably – say that elections to the European Parliament offer an opportunity for voters to express their dissatisfaction with their own

206. On the procedure, see point 5, 6 and 7 of the Joint Declaration of the European Parliament, the Council and the Commission (O.J. 1975 C 89/1). In French this procedure is referred to as '*concertation*' rather than conciliation, which emphasizes the distinction from the conciliation procedure (in French '*conciliation*') within the context of Art. 189b EC; as to both procedures, see Chapter V, section 3.4.2, *post*. See also Annex III to the Act on direct elections.

207. It may be doubted whether this provision can be used for this purpose: see Maas (1979) SEW 686 at 696–697.

208. For the United Kingdom see the European Assembly (Pay and Pensions) Act 1979; for the Netherlands see the Wet Schadeloosstelling, uitkering en pensioen leden Europees Parlement, Stb. 1979, 379.

209. As an internal organization measure under Arts. 142 EC, 25 ECSC, and 112 Euratom which empower the Parliament to adopt rules of procedure (and thus measures of internal organization). In Case 208/80 *Rt. Hon. Lord Bruce of Donnington v. Aspden* [1981] ECR 2205 at 2219–2221 the Court held that although there was no specific exemption from national taxation for members of the European Parliament no national taxation could be levied on the lump-sum expense allowance as this would be tantamount to exercising an administrative restriction on the free movement of members of the European Parliament. See Van Hecke (1982) SEW 642 and *R. v. Manchester Crown Court, ex parte DPP* [1993] 1 WLR 693 (QBD), reversed on other grounds, [1993] 1 WLR 1524.

national parties, particularly with those in government). The distribution of seats reflects the relative size of the peoples of the Member States more satisfactorily.[210] The removal of the link between membership of the European Parliament and membership of national parliaments allows the members of the European Parliament to pursue their European activities on a full-time basis and the presence of members from opposition parties as well as from parties in government emphasises the fact that the European Communities are not purely intergovernmental but are essentially autonomous in character. These factors may well lead to a significant increase in the authority of the Parliament's pronouncements.[211]

The way in which the Parliament carries out its tasks will be of considerable importance in establishing its authority. It will need to strengthen its internal organization and working methods, particularly through group formation and committee work, in order that the process of formation of political will leads to well-founded and clear pronouncements which will be sufficiently convincing to mobilise public opinion in the Member States, and indeed the recent improvements in its procedure have been designed to streamline its procedures with this in mind.[212] From the point of view of organization and influence, a single seat, preferably at the same place as the Council and the Commission would undoubtedly be of considerable benefit. The European Parliament will have to use to the full all the means made available in the Treaties in order to bring the influence of its political will to bear on Community policies. A European Parliament which appeals to voters by setting itself up as the pacemaker, direction finder and guardian of the integration process can contribute significantly to changing the still heavily national-orientated thoughts and actions of voters and political parties. Such a change would open the way for closer collaboration of national parties in the European context if not for the formation of European parties, the importance of which has explicitly been recognized in Article 138a EC.

A strengthening and expansion of the powers of the Parliament in isolation is less essential than may be thought. The realisation of a significant Community power centre,[213] based on a clear transparent separation of national and Community competences and responsibilities in

210. See note 197, *supra*.
211. This is by no means certain, however, as the participation in direct elections has shown. An average turnout of 55–60% of the electorate is not unsatisfactory, but it is somewhat less than overwhelming, and in some Member States the turnout has been significantly less, although in Belgium, Greece, Ireland, Italy and Luxembourg the turnout has been markedly greater, see *e.g.* Bull. EU 6–1994 point 1.7.6 (table 9).
212. The procedural changes made during 1993 to take account of the changes introduced by the TEU are now incorporated in the current version of the Rules of Procedure (O.J. 1997 L 49/1).
213. *Cf.* Chapter II, section 1.2.4, *ante*.

which the Parliament can exercise its powers, is of rather more importance. If the Parliament develops into a political force it will be essential for the Community power centre to take account of the Parliament's views and to assure itself of the Parliament's support. Even the development of the national systems of government into parliamentary democracies came about principally by means of a change in the manner in which the Head of State and ministers exercised their constitutional powers, and owed far less to the grant of new powers to national parliaments.

5.2 Powers and duties

The European Parliament exercises the powers conferred on it by the Treaties.[214] It has a general power to discuss any matter concerning the Communities, to adopt resolutions thereupon and to invite the governments of the Member States to act.[215] Particularly because it has been granted powers of decision, especially concerning legislative measures of the Council, and concerning the budget, the European Parliament differs from the parliamentary bodies of other European organizations such as the Council of Europe, the Western European Union and Benelux which are endowed with almost exclusively advisory functions.

5.2.1 The Parliament's role in the decision-making process

The way in which the Parliament is involved in the decision-making process has developed remarkably since the coming into force of the EEC and Euratom Treaties in 1958. While the decision-making process is discussed fully below,[216] a brief explanation of the Parliament's role here is appropriate. Apart from special cases, the EC Treaty envisages four general ways in which the European parliament participates in decision-making by the Council, which are most conveniently discussed chronologically. The original, and least far-reaching involvement is the *consultation* procedure, whereby the Council consults the Parliament to ascertain its views on a proposal from the Commission. There was no general rule requiring such consultation: the obligation to consult existed

214. Arts. 137 EC and 107 Euratom. Note that Art. 20 ECSC speaks only of 'supervisory' powers. The previous limitation in Arts. 137 EEC and 107 Euratom to 'advisory and supervisory powers' – in the French text *'pouvoirs de délibération'* which was a wider function than a purely advisory function – has thus been removed.
215. See Case 230/81 *Luxembourg v. European Parliament* [1983] ECR 255 at 287. See also the Stuttgart Solemn Declaration on European Union (Bull. EC 6–1983, point I.6.1, p. 24 at p. 26).
216. See Chapter V, section 3, *post.* See also Ress in Curtin and Heukels (eds.), *op. cit.* (see note 10, *supra*) 153.

only where specifically laid down in the Treaty provision which conferred competence on the Council to act in relation to the matter concerned. In practice, however, the Council often sought the opinion of the Parliament even where it was not required by the Treaties. Moreover, the Parliament itself sometimes addresses opinions to the Council on its own initiative.[217] When consultation of the Parliament is required but the Parliament's opinion has not been taken into account, the measure taken can be annulled by Court of Justice on the ground of infringement of an essential procedural requirement.[218]

From the formula used in many of the specific provisions of the Treaties, *viz.* on a proposal from the Commission and after consultation of the European Parliament', it is clear that it is the Council, not the Commission, which is required to consult the Parliament, although the additional possibility of consultation by the Commission before it submits its proposal to the Council is not excluded, since it is also accountable to the Parliament for the proposals submitted by it. The proposal from the Commission is the subject of the consultation of the Parliament as it constitutes, both in form and substance, the basis for the decision to be taken by the Council. The Commission may alter its proposal, as long as the Council has not acted.[219] The fact that the Commission may decide to alter its original proposal in the sense desired by the Parliament or even withdraw it[220] confirms that the opinion of the Parliament is also important for the Commission, in view to its parliamentary accountability,

---

217. *E.g.* Resolution of 11 May 1979 on measures to promote the development of fish farming (O.J. 1979 C 140/117) which it accompanied by a draft proposal for a Council regulation (O.J. 1979 C 140/120) which it invited the Commission to submit to the Council. As to the development of invitations to the Commission to act, see Corbett *et al.*, *op. cit.* (see note 100, *supra*) 217–219. Parliament now has the express right to request the Commission to submit appropriate proposals, see the end of this section, *infra*.

218. Case 138/79 *SA Roquette Frères v. Council* [1980] ECR 3333 at 3360; Case 139/79 *Maizena GmbH v. Council* [1980] ECR 3393 at 3424. See Beutler (1981) EuR 55, Hartley (1981) 6 ELRev. 181, Jacobs (1981) 18 CMLRev. 219, and Lenaerts (1981) SEW 397. See also *e.g.* Case 817/79 *Buyl et al. v. Commission* [1982] ECR 245 at 261–264 in relation to examination to see if this essential requirement had been met. As to the Parliament's strategy, see Corbett *et al.*, *ibid.* at 192–193.

219. Arts. 189a(2) EC and 119 Euratom, 2nd para.

220. *E.g.* the two proposals relating to origin-marking, first for a Directive (see O.J. 1980 C 294/3; 1981 C 185/32 and 1981 C 101/49) and then for a Regulation (see O.J. 1982 C 93/11 and 1983 C 211/46) were withdrawn as a result of the adverse reaction which they received. The old Art. 149 EEC, 2nd para. and the text of Art. 119 Euratom, 2nd para. (which is still in force) make it clear that the right to amend a proposal may be exercised 'in particular when the Parliament has been consulted on that proposal.' The dropping of this statement in Art. 189a(2) EC in no way diminishes the Parliament's role, but is merely a consequence of the new procedures introduced by the TEU, which are discussed *post*. As to withdrawal of proposals, see section 4.3.1, *ante*, and Chapter V, section 3.3.1, *post*.

which has if anything increased since the Parliament has a clear say in the appointment of the Commission.[221] The consultation procedure, and thus the advisory role of the Parliament is still significant and has been maintained in a number of policy areas which pre-date the coming into force of the TEU.[222] It is also prescribed in various new areas of Community policy.[223] Moreover the Parliament is also consulted on the most important aspects of CFSP and JHA, albeit in these two areas about policy and activities rather than about proposed legislation as such.[224]

With the coming into force of the SEA on 1 July 1987, a second procedure was established, the cooperation procedure,[225] This procedure is designed to permit the Parliament a second reading of a proposed act in the Council, often called a 'second bite at the cherry.' Thus in the first reading the Parliament expresses its opinion on the Commission's proposal,

221. See section 4.1, *ante*.
222. Arts. 43(2) (agriculture); 54(1) (freedom of establishment); 75(3) (transport); 99 (tax harmonization); 100 (harmonization of laws); 130b (economic and social cohesion); 130i(4) (specific research and development programmes); 130o (joint undertakings for research, technological development and demonstration programmes); 130s(2) (specified environmental measures); 209 (financial regulations and control), and 228(3) EC, 1st subpara. (international agreements save those excluded or subject to the assent procedure). The Treaty of Amsterdam (not yet in force) will repeal the existing Art. 54(1) EC, with consequential renumbering.
223. Arts. 8b and 8e, 2nd para. (citizenship of the Union); 100c(1) and (3) (visas); 104(c)(14) (rules and application of the Protocol on the excessive deficit procedure); 106(6) (various implementing measures provided for under the Statute of the ECSB); 108a(3) (conditions for fines or penalties imposed by the ECB); 109a(2)(b) (appointments to the Executive Board of the ECB); 109f(1),(6) and (7) (various matters relating to the EMI); 109j(2)–(4) (transition to the third stage of EMU); 109k(2) (abrogation of derogation); 109l(1) (action immediately after the decision on the date for the beginning of the third stage of EMU has been set; 130(3) (industry); 130s EC (certain specific types of environmental measures), and the Agreement attached to the Protocol on Social Policy, Art. 2(3). The Treaty of Amsterdam (not yet in force) will repeal Art. 100c EC and the Protocol and Agreement on Social Policy. It will provide for consultation in the new Arts. 73o (in relation to Arts. 73j, 73k, 73m and 73n on visa, asylum, immigration and other policies related to free movement of persons (subject to Art. 73o(4)), 109q (guidelines in relation to employment policies), 109s (establishment of an Employment Committee), 113(5) (extension of common commercial policy to international negotiations and agreements on services and intellectual property in so far as they are not already within that policy), and 118(3) (certain social policy areas).
224. Arts. J(7), 1st para. (CFSP), and K.6, 2nd para. (JHA) TEU. The Treaty of Amsterdam (not yet in force) provides for consultation in the new Arts. J.1, 1st para., K.11(1) and K.14 TEU, and imposes various other obligations to inform the Parliament.
225. Art. 6 SEA. The procedure was contained in the new Art. 149 EEC (introduced by Art. 7 SEA), and is now contained in Art. 189c EC. Unlike the consultation procedure, the mechanics of the cooperation procedure are set out in great detail. Although Art. 6 SEA did refer to the 'cooperation procedure', the substantive provisions of the EC Treaty now simply mention 'in accordance with the procedure referred to in Article 189c'. See, further, Chapter V, section 3.4.2, *post*.

whereas on the second reading it expresses its opinion on the Council's common position adopted after examining the Commission's proposal (which the latter may have been amended) and the Parliament's opinion given on the first reading. Another difference between the consultation and the cooperation procedures is that in the latter the Parliament can reject the common position of the Council, which means that the Council can only act on a second reading by unanimity. Moreover, the cooperation procedure emphasises that the Council can only deviate from amendments put forward by the Parliament[226] by unanimity if these proposals are taken on board by the Commission in its re-examined proposal.[227] The cooperation procedure originally applied to all the decisions specified in Article 6(1) SEA, but a number of matters have since been moved over to fall under the new co-decision procedure, discussed below. Accordingly, of the original matters only four remain,[228] although a number of new provisions using the cooperation procedure have been introduced.[229] The cooperation procedure does not apply in relation to the ECSC and Euratom Treaties.

With the changes made by the TEU, a third procedure was introduced, the co-decision procedure, whereby legislation is adopted by the European Parliament and the Council.[230] The two characteristic elements in this procedure are the convocation of a Conciliation Committee and the Parliament's right to veto legislation.[231] The co-decision procedure applies

226. Parliament uses the term 'amendments', but Art. 189c(c) makes it clear that these are proposed amendments.
227. The Council can by unanimity adopt Parliament's proposed amendments which have not been so taken over. The logic is consistent with the (general) requirement of unanimity for the Council to depart from a Commission proposal, see Art. 189a(1) EC (a principle which had previously been absolute, see the old Art. 149(1) EEC).
228. Arts. 6, 2nd para. (prohibition of discrimination); 118a(2) (minimum provisions concerning health and safety of workers); 130e (implementing decisions concerning the ERDF), and 130o (implementing multiannual framework programmes) EC. With the extension of co-decision (see *post*) by the Treaty of Amsterdam (not yet in force) the cooperation procedure in these areas will disappear.
229. Arts. 75(1) and 84 (transport); 103(5) (economic policy multilateral surveillance); 104a(2) (definitions for application of prohibition of privileged access to financial institutions); 104b(2) (definitions for application of prohibition of overdraft or other credit facilities or assumption of commitments); 105a(2) (denominations and technical specifications of coinage); 125 (European Social Fund); 127(4) (vocational training); 129d, 3rd para. (other measures relating to Trans-European networks); 130s(1) and (3) (environment); 130w(1) (development cooperation) EC, and Agreement annexed to the Protocol on Social Policy, Art. 2(2). With the extension of co-decision by the Treaty of Amsterdam (not yet in force) the cooperation procedure will exist only in the area of Economic and Monetary Union (Arts. 103(5), 104a(2), 104b(2) and 105a(2) EC).
230. Art. 189b EC. The various substantive Treaty provisions simply refer to 'in accordance with the procedure referred to in Article 189b' as the term 'co-decision procedure is not actually used in the EC Treaty. This procedure will become the most generally used form (and considerably simplified) when the Treaty of Amsterdam comes into force.
231. See, further, Chapter V, section 3.4.2, *post*.

principally in relation to acts necessary to complete the internal market in the Community, including free movement of persons, and a number of new policy areas.[232] Acts which are adopted under the co-decision procedure are signed by the Presidents of the Council and the Parliament[233] and are referred to as being 'adopted jointly by the European Parliament and the Council'.[234] The co-decision procedure does not apply in relation to the ECSC and Euratom Treaties.

Finally, there is a number of cases in which the Council needs the assent of the European Parliament before it may act. The assent procedure had already been introduced by the SEA, and initially only concerned the accession of new Member States[235] and the conclusion of association agreements.[236] It has now been extended to embrace the adoption of a uniform electoral procedure,[237] certain specific types of international agreements,[238] and a number of diverse other matters.[239] The rearrange-

232. Arts. 49 (measures to achieve free movement of workers); 54(2) (directives achieving the right of establishment); 56(2), 2nd sentence (directives on limitations on the right of establishment); 57 (mutual recognition of qualifications); 66 (applying *in casu* Arts. 56(2) and 57 to the freedom to provide services) 100a(1) and 100b (internal market harmonization); 126(4) (education, except in respect of recommendations); 128(5) (culture, except recommendations); 129d, 1st para. (guidelines relating to trans-European networks); 129(4) (public health, except recommendations); 129a(2) (consumer protection); 130i (multiannual framework programmes for research and technological development), and 130s(3), 1st subpara. (residual general action programmes concerning the environment) EC. The Treaty of Amsterdam (not yet in force) will considerably expand the use of the co-decision procedure, so that it will become the normal method of decision-making, save in those relatively few areas where consultation or co-decision are prescribed, or the assent procedure (see *post*) applies.
233. Art. 191(1) EC.
234. Art. 190 EC. See also Art. 173 EC, 1st para. But the Court considers that these acts are acts of the Council, Case C-259/95 *European Parliament v. Council* [1997] ECR I-5303 at 5322. This is certainly not how they are presented in the O.J.
235. Originally Art. 237 EEC, 1st para., see now Art. O TEU, 1st para.
236. Originally Art. 238 EC, 2nd para., see now Art. 228(3) EC, 2nd subpara. (agreements falling within Art. 238 EC).
237. Art. 138(3) EC, 2nd subpara. Note that the Treaty of Amsterdam (not yet in force) will amend Art. 138(3), 1st subpara. to refer not only to 'a uniform procedure' but also to permit the alternative of 'in accordance with principles common to all Member States'. The assent procedure remains unchanged, although other amendments to Art. 138 result in renumbering of the paras.
238. Art. 228(3) EC, 2nd subpara. (in addition to association agreements already covered: agreements other than commercial policy agreements; agreements having important budgetary implications for the Community, and agreements entailing the amendment of acts adopted under the co-decision procedure).
239. Arts. 8a(2) (facilitation of the rights of movement and residence of citizens of the Union, save where the EC treaty otherwise makes specific provision); 105(6) (prudential supervision by the ECB); 106(5) (amendment of certain provisions of the Statute of the ECSB), and 130d (structural funds and Cohesion Fund) EC. The Treaty of Amsterdam (not yet in force) will change the Parliament's involvement under Art. 8a(2) EC to co-decision rather than assent. As to the mechanics of the procedure, see Chapter V, section 3.4.2, *post*.

ment of the provisions on decision-making means that they now form part of the 'Provisions common to several Institutions' rather than part of the provisions dealing solely with the Council. This emphasises that Community decision-making is no longer primarily a matter of interplay between the Commission and the Council, but is truly a tripartite affair, involving the Parliament, the Council and the Commission. In a sense the improvements have proceeded through a salami approach, so that at each major revision of the Treaties Parliament's position has been strengthened. But the need for clearer involvement of the national parliaments in scrutiny and discussion of consultation documents and proposals for legislation is now increasingly recognized.[240]

5.2.2 Political control by the Parliament

The European Parliament is required to supervise the activities of the Commission in the three Communities. The power to dismiss the Commission *en bloc* by the adoption of a motion of censure forms the ultimate weapon in the right of supervision. Such a motion can only be carried by open vote by a two-thirds majority of the votes cast, which at the same time must represent a majority of the number of members. In view of the serious character of such a motion a 'period of reflection' of at least three days must elapse between the motion being tabled and the vote being taken.[241]

Although a censure motion has occasionally been tabled,[242] no such

---

240. To this end the Treaty of Amsterdam (not yet in force) will attach to the TEU and the EC, ECSC and Euratom Treaties a Protocol on the role of national parliaments in the European Union which, *inter alia* is designed to give them an opportunity to discuss such matters (and thus to make their views known to their governments). It will also permit the Conference of European Affairs Committees (COSAC) to make various contributions. See, generally, Laursen and Pappas (eds.), *The Changing Role of Parliaments in the European Union* (EIPA Maastricht, 1995); Pappas (ed.), *National Administrative Procedures for the Preparation and Implementation of Community Decisions* (EIPA Maastricht, 1995), and Smith (ed.), *National Parliaments as Cornerstones of European Integration* (London, 1996).

241. Arts. 144 EC, 24 ECSC, and 114 Euratom. As to the further modalities, see the Parliament's Rules of Procedure, Rule 34 (see note 176, *supra*).

242. Prior to the first direct elections in 1979 there were four motions presented: relating to budgetary powers in November 1972 (Bull. EC 12–1972, pp. 110–112); the milk product surplus in May 1976 (Bull. EC 5–1976, p. 76, point 2403); export premiums for malt in December 1976 (Bull. EC 12–1976, p. 81, point 2403), and export of butter to Soviet Russia in March 1977 (Bull. EC 3–1977, p. 83, point 2.3.32.). Since 1979 there have been three motions presented: on the Commission's policy in general (Bull. EC 1/2–1990 p. 111 point 1.6.6); on the Commission's external relations policy (Bull. EC 7/8–1991 p. 123, point 1.7.1., and (with the highest level of support) on the Commission's negotiation tactics in the GATT Uruguay Round discussions on agriculture (Bull. EC 12–1992 p. 162 point 1.7.2).

motion has ever been approved. Nevertheless, the fact that the possibility of censure exists makes it clear that the Commission must pay some attention to members' views, just as national governments do in national parliaments, even though the latter only rarely pass motions of no confidence. When a censure motion has been seriously threatened the Commission has backed down or sought a compromise on the issue at stake. The adoption of a censure motion has long been seen as a leap in the dark because until recently the appointment of the new members of the Commission rested entirely with the governments collectively, and it is only since the nomination of the Santer Commission that the Parliament has had a say in the appointment.[243] As long as the European Parliament was not consulted there was (or, indeed, still as long as it does not actually elect the Commission there is) no formal guarantee that the policy of a newly appointed Commission will in fact conform to the wishes of the Parliament, although given that the new Commission has since 1981 submitted itself to a vote of confidence in the Parliament,[244] and that this procedure is now formalized as part of the appointment procedure,[245] it is now much more likely that the Commission will take due account of the Parliament's wishes, while of course reserving its right of initiative. If the Parliament were to adopt a censure motion the members of the Commission are obliged to resign as a body, although they continue to deal with current business until they are replaced.[246] Their replacements are appointed, for the remainder of the term for which the censured Commission was appointed, by the normal procedure for appointment of the Commission.[247] It is still the case that there is nothing to stop the Member States from renominating the censured Commission, which would as likely as not fail to gain approval in the Parliament. It is, however, difficult to imagine serious politicians agreeing even to stand for office in such circumstances, and if such a stalemate were to occur the Member States would be politically obliged to put forward other candidates. While it is true that the Member States enjoy more political authority than even the directly elected European Parliament, politicians, particularly candidates to be President of the Commission, are mostly unwilling to risk

---

243. Arts. 158 EC, 10 ECSC, and 127 Euratom (the Santer Commission took up office for a period of five years beginning 23 January 1995 (a few days later than originally scheduled), Dec. 95/12 (O.J. 1995 L19/51).
244. In 1989 and 1993 (the 2nd and 3rd Delors Commissions) it delayed swearing the oath before the Court of Justice until it had received the vote of confidence. The Treaties call this a "vote of approval" rather than a vote of confidence, but it is invariably referred to by the latter term.
245. Arts. 158(2) EC, 10(2) ECSC, and 127(2) Euratom, 3rd para. in each case. See EP Rules of Procedure (O.J. 1997 L 49/1), Rule 33. The Commission also presents its annual work programme to the Parliament.
246. Arts. 144 EC, 24 ECSC, and 114 Euratom, 2nd para. in each case.
247. *Ibid.* in conjunction with Arts. 158(1) and (2) EC, 10(1) and (2) ECSC, and 127(1) and (2) Euratom.

repeated rebuffs at the hands of elected representatives. In such circumstances the force of *noblesse oblige* would be immense, and a Parliament which backed down in the face of renomination by the Member States would be seen to lack any semblance of a backbone.

The censure motion has thus remained an ultimate weapon, but one which the Commission need not be too afraid of because it is a weapon not readily taken up, the procedure is difficult, and involves great risks for the Parliament which wields it. In the European Communities, even after the amendments made by the TEU, the Council of Ministers still has a greater share of legislative power than either the Parliament or the Commission.[248] This means that the Commission's dependence on the Council is significant, and that a censure motion against the Commission because of its role in the legislative process relating to a particular matter would often be addressed to the wrong Institution. In the circumstances it is understandable that the Commission can permit itself much greater political freedom *vis-à-vis* the European Parliament than would be the case in a normally functioning parliamentary system. All the same, the mere existence of the right to dismiss the Commission, however unlikely its exercise may be, profoundly influences relations between the Commission and the European Parliament.[249] These relations are determined by the political accountability of the Commission to the Parliament, which gives the latter a typically parliamentary and the former a typically governmental appearance. It is always possible for the Parliament to adopt a resolution critical of a particular Commissioner, even if necessary calling on him or her to resign; the threat that ignoring such a resolution would lead to a motion of censure on the Commission as a whole may be sufficient to concentrate the mind of the person concerned. Another possible way of expressing displeasure would be the adoption of a resolution that the Commission's salary (or that of a member of the Commission) should be reduced by a specified amount. Although such a resolution would not be enforceable without the cooperation of the Council[250] it might perhaps have the necessary moral force.

---

248. This will still be the case even after the considerable simplification of the co-decision procedure which the Treaty of Amsterdam will introduce when it comes into force.
249. This is true even though not infrequently the Commission and the Parliament are in fact natural allies against the Council.
250. Such a proposal was mooted by Brinkhorst, *NRC Handelsblad* 11 October 1996, p. 12. The obvious precedent is known *e.g.* in the United Kingdom, where the adoption by the House of Commons of a resolution 'that the salary of x be reduced by one penny' would oblige the minister concerned to resign. The difficulty is that the Council, rather than the Parliament fixes the Commissioners' remuneration (it is expressed in terms of a percentage of a top-of-scale Director General's salary, the percentages for the President and any Vice-Presidents being higher). Thus even though the salary might not in fact be reduced, a motion saying that it ought to be should carry home the necessary political message.

This political accountability is confirmed and supported in a series of Treaty provisions and in procedures developed by parliamentary practice which enable the European Parliament to supervise the policy and activities of the Commission and engage it in a pretty well continual dialogue, reviewing Community affairs. The procedure of oral and written parliamentary questions forms a particularly important means of supervision. Other examples of supervisory mechanisms include the public deliberations on the obligatory general report produced annually by the Commission,[251] the statutory annual session[252] which is distributed over the whole year by means of a series of adjournments,[253] the participation of members of the Commission in debates,[254] the right to put questions,[255] and the system of parliamentary committees[256] (of which there are at present 20) which have to prepare the decisions of the Parliament and maintain regular contact with the Commission in the periods during which the Parliament is not actually meeting; these committees regularly hear members of the Commission and officials in the course of their deliberations. The Parliament also uses its budgetary powers to hold the Commission accountable if it does not approve of the way in which the Commission fulfils its executive tasks in a particular field requiring the spending of non-compulsory expenditure – it can freeze the appropriation in Chapter 100 of the Budget (the reserve) until it is satisfied that the Commission will take account of its wishes; this also permits bargaining over how policies are to be carried out.[257]

251. As to the General Report, see Arts. 156 EC, 17 ECSC, and 125 Euratom; as to the debate thereupon in the European Parliament, see Arts. 143 EC, 24 ECSC, 1st para., and 113 Euratom. See also the Parliament's Rules of Procedure (O.J. 1997 L 49/1), Rule 43.

252. Arts. 139 EC, 22 ECSC, and 109 Euratom, 1st para. in each case (as amended by Merger Treaty, Art. 27(1). Without prejudice to these provisions, the Parliament meets, without requiring to be convened, on the first Tuesday after expiry of one month from the end of the period during which direct elections are held, Act on direct elections, Art. 10(3).

253. See Case 149/85 *Wybot v. Faure et al.* [1986] ECR 2391.

254. Arts. 140 EC, 23 ECSC, and 110 Euratom, 2nd para. in each case; see also the Parliament's Rules of Procedure, Rules 37 and 41–44.

255. Arts. 140 EC, 23 ECSC, and 110 Euratom, 3rd para. in each case; see the Parliament's Rules of Procedure, Rules 40–42. Questions may be oral or in writing. The institution of Question Time (Rule 41 and Annex II) is also particularly effective, although having ascertained the likely answer through informal contacts with Commission officials beforehand certainly enables MEPs to ask the right questions. 'Does the Commission think...' questions have been known to elicit one-word answers. There is no tradition of House of Commons style pro-forma questions followed by the real issue as a supplementary question of which the minister may or may not have an inkling beforehand (although even that tradition is presently less in vogue).

256. Rules of Procedure, Rules 135–152 and Annex VI. See Corbett *et al., op. cit.* (see note 100, *supra*) 105–149 and 257.

257. This means that the Commission has to return to the Parliament to seek release of the appropriations concerned.

Unlike the Commission, the Council is not responsible to the European Parliament in any formal sense, although, it does have certain obligations towards the Parliament, and a certain degree of political responsibility.[258] The individual members of the Council are still responsible to their own national parliaments for their individual part in Community decision-making, which means that a minister who has voted for a measure which is unpopular at home, or who has blocked or opposed a measure enjoying considerable support at home, will have some explaining to do. Nevertheless, the Council and the Parliament have developed a number of formal contacts outside the legislative process which mean that the Council is prepared to answer written and oral questions from members of the European Parliament[259] and to inform Parliament about its intended programme and the progress in its activities.[260] In relation to CFSP and JHA specific provision is made for the Parliament to be informed and consulted, and for it to ask questions of the Council or make recommendations to it.[261] Parliament also holds an annual debate on progress in implementing CFSP and the areas covered by cooperation in JHA.[262] The European Council is obliged by Article D TEU to submit a report to the Parliament after each of its meetings and to submit a yearly written report on the progress achieved by the Union, and the Parliament can hold a debate on the report.

258. As is explained, *infra*. The Presidency is in fact responsible for these matters and indeed Ludlow has suggested that it should become an Institution in its own right, and, moreover, that the Parliament should have the power to censure the Presidency, thus forcing the resignation of the Member State concerned from the office of President, see Ludlow, *Preparing for 1996 and a Larger European Union* (CEPS Special Report No. 6, Brussels, 1995) 38–39.

259. In 1973 the Council agreed to participate in Question Time (which had been introduced under pressure from the new British MEPs) and then agreed to reply to written and oral questions (*Seventh General Report 1973* (Brussels, Luxembourg, 1974) p. 64; Bull. EC 10–1973 p. 89), although in so far as matters fell within the sphere of what was to become European Political Cooperation the answers were for many years invariably that the matter was one for the foreign ministers, not for the Council. The situation was put on a firmer footing in the Stuttgart Solemn declaration on European Union (Bull. EC 6–1983 point 1.6.1. (point 2.3.3 of the Declaration). The Council is heard by the Parliament in accordance with the conditions which the Council lays down in accordance with its Rules of Procedure (Arts. 140 EC and 110 Euratom, 4th para. in each case; the phrasing in Art. 23 ECSC, 4th para. is different – the members of the Council are entitled to attend all meetings of the Parliament and to be heard at their request). See also the Council's Rules of Procedure (see note 33, *supra*), Rule 25, and the Parliament's Rules of Procedure (see note 176, *supra*), Rules 40–42. See, further, including as to the role of the General Affairs Group (rather unfortunately abbreviated as GAG), Westlake, *op. cit.* (see note 12, *supra*) 343–344 and Corbett *et al.*, *op. cit.* (see note 100, *supra*) 266–269.

260. The Council produces its own annual report on its activities.

261. Arts. J.7 and K.6 TEU. The Treaty of Amsterdam (not yet in force) will make such provision in the new Arts. J.11, K.11, K.14 and K.17 TEU (see also the new Art. K.12(2) TEU).

262. *Ibid.*

5.2.3 Adopting the budget

As a result of the First Budgetary Treaty[263] the European Parliament obtained from 1975 the right for its President to declare the adoption of the budget and the last word on non-compulsory expenditure. As a result of the Second Budgetary Treaty[264] it also obtained from 1 June 1977, the right to reject the entire draft budget 'if there are important reasons'[265] and also the right to grant the Commission discharge in respect of the implementation of the budget.[266] The Parliament's powers in this field are discussed in more detail elsewhere.[267]

5.2.4 The Parliament's other powers

The European Parliament possesses a number of deliberative powers which are not directly connected with its supervisory, consultative or budgetary functions. Primarily these relate to its own power of internal organization such as laying down its Rules of Procedure[268] and the power to adopt appropriate measures to ensure the due functioning and conduct of its proceedings.[269] In addition the Parliament also has always had three special powers:

(i)   to approve amendments of the Treaty in the case of the so-called 'small revision' of the ECSC Treaty;[270]

263. 22 April 1970, Simmonds (ed.) *Encyclopedia of European Community Law* Vol. B (London, loose-leaf 1974–1995) para. B 8–103.
264. 22 July 1975, Simmonds, *ibid.*, para. B 8–222.
265. Arts. 203(8) EC, 78(8) ECSC, and 177(8) Euratom. For examples of this happening see Bull. EC 12–1979, pp. 93 and 120, 12–1982 p. 7 (supplementary and amending budget) and 12–1984, p. 28. As to quick footwork to enable policies to be implemented even when they were not originally envisaged, see *23rd General Report 1989* (Brussels, Luxembourg, 1990) points 84–88.
266. Arts. 206 EC, 78g ECSC, and 180b Euratom.
267. Chapter V, section 2.4, *post*.
268. Arts. 142 EC, 25 ECSC, and 112 Euratom. As to the Rules, see note 176, *supra*. As to public access to Parliament's documents, see Dec. 97/632 (O.J. 1997 L 263/27), and as to fees, Dec. 98/306 (O.J. 1998 L 135/46).
269. On its powers in this respect and the limits thereof see Case 230/81 *Luxembourg v. European Parliament* [1983] ECR 255 at 287 and Case 208/80 *Rt. Hon. Lord Bruce of Donnington v. Aspden* [1981] ECR 2205 at 2219–2221; Case 108/83 *Luxembourg v. European Parliament* [1984] ECR 1945 at 1960; Case 78/85 *Group of the European Right v. European Parliament* [1986] ECR 1753 at 1757; Case 190/84 {*arti écologiste 'Les Verts'. v. European Parliament* [1988] ECR 1017 at 1035; Cases 358/85 and 51/86 *France v. European Parliament* [1988] ECR 4821 at 4851–4857, and Case C-68/90 *Blot et al. v. European Parliament* [1990] ECR I-2101 at 2104–2105. See also Case 149/85 *Wybot v. Faure et al.* [1986] ECR 2391 and Cases C-213/88 and 39/89 *Luxembourg v. European Parliament* [1991] ECR I-5643.
270. Art. 95 ECSC, 4th para. (most recently amended by Dec. 1/95 (O.J. 1995 L1/1), Art. 7).

(ii)   to draw up proposals for the uniform electoral system for elections to it;[271]

(iii) to refer matters to the Court of Justice if the Council or the Commission, in infringement of the EC or Euratom Treaty, fails to act.[272]

to which the amendments made by the TEU have added:

(iv)   to bring actions for annulment for the purpose of protecting its prerogatives;[273]

(v)   to set up a temporary Committee of Inquiry to investigate alleged contraventions or maladministration in the implementation of Community law;[274]

(vi)   to receive petitions from any citizen of the Union, and any natural or legal person residing or having its registered office in a Member State, whether individually or in association with other citizens or persons, on a matter coming within the Community's fields of activity and which affects him, her or it directly;[275]

(vii) to appoint an Ombudsman empowered to receive complaints from any citizen of the Union, and any natural or legal person residing or having its registered office in a Member State concerning instances of maladministration in the activities of the Community Institutions or bodies, apart from the Court of Justice and the Court of First instance acting in their judicial role.[276]

---

271. Arts. 138(3) EC, 21(3) ECSC, and 108(3) Euratom. The Treaty of Amsterdam (not yet in force) will provide for the altternative of proposals 'in accordance with principles common to the Member States.' It will also renumber the parts of Arts. 138 EC, 21 ECSC, and 108 Euratom.

272. Arts. 175 EC and 148 Euratom.

273. Arts. 173 EC, and 146 Euratom, 3rd para. in each case, and 33 ECSC, 4th para. This in effect codifies the result of Case C-70/88 *European Parliament v. Council* [1990] ECR I-2041 at 2072–2073.

274. Arts. 138c EC, 20b ECSC, and 107b Euratom. As to the modalities, see the decision of the European Parliament, the Council and the Commission, Dec. 95/167 (O.J. 1995 L 78/1). See, further, Corbett *et al.*, *op. cit.* (see note 100, *supra*) 139 and 276–278. This places the Parliament's practice developed since the first direct elections in 1979 on a firm footing. Arts. 130c EC *etc.* provide that the right to set up such a committee may not be exercised 'where the alleged facts are being examined before a court and while the case is still subject to legal proceedings.' *I.e.* the *sub judice* rule applies. As to the first two temporary Committees of Inquiry set up under the new framework, see O.J. 1996 C7/1 and C 239/1.

275. This is the counterpart of the right of such citizens or persons to present such a petition, Arts. 138d EC, 20c ECSC, and 107c Euratom, building on Art. 8d EC, 1st para. Again, this merely puts the existing practice on a firm footing, see Corbett *et al.*, *ibid.* at 290–292 and has existed in the European Parliament's Rules of Procedure since 1953, presently see Rules 156–158 (see note 176, *supra*).

276. Arts. 138e EC, 20d ECSC, and 107d Euratom, building on Art. 8d EC, 2nd para. As

Of these last four powers the first three merely enshrine prevailing rights or practice. The Parliament has no formal right of initiative in the field of Community legislation other than that mentioned under (ii) above; apart from this the right of initiative belongs to the Commission, although the Parliament now has what may be called a right of quasi-initiative: acting by a majority of its members, it may request the Commission to submit any appropriate proposal on matters which it considers that a Community act is required for the purpose of implementing the EC, ECSC or Euratom Treaties.[277] By the means of political control at its disposal (such as freezing appropriations in Chapter 100 of the budget) the Parliament may give additional weight to such a request.

5.3   The Parliament and the Court of Justice

The extent to which legal remedies can be used instead of political techniques by, but also against the Parliament is a sign of the limited development of the principles of parliamentary democracy in the Community system in comparison with the development therein of the principles of the *Rechtsstaat*. The Parliament has used the possibility of declaring the Council to be in default through failure to act in order to obtain a judgment of the Court on whether the Council was in breach of its obligations under the Treaty because it had failed to adopt a common transport policy.[278] The Court was prepared to pronounce on the question, albeit not in so far-reaching a manner, and confined itself to the provisions which were to be laid down by the Council under Article 75(1)(a) and (b) EEC. The Court had to confine itself to holding that the Council should have acted – the Court has no power to decide what provisions have to be adopted.[279] Nevertheless, the Parliament's armoury was supplemented with

to the regulations and general conditions governing the performance of the Ombudsman's tasks, see Dec. 94/262 (O.J. 1994 L 113/15) which was adopted after the Parliament's previous decision (O.J. 1993 C 329/136) had been approved by the Council in Dec. 94/114 (O.J. 1994 L 54/25). As to the appointment of the first Ombudsman (Jacob Söderman), see Dec. 95/376 (O.J. 1995 L 225/17). See the Parliament's Rules of Procedure (see note 176, *supra*), Rules 159–161 and Parliament's Resolution on the role of the Ombudsman (O.J. 1995 C 249/200). See also Corbett *et al.*, *op. cit.* (see note 100, *supra*) 292–293 and Magliveras (1995) 20 ELRev. 401.

277.   Arts. 138b EC, 2nd para., 20a ECSC, and 107a Euratom. Again, this enshrines the existing practice whereby the Parliament could make suggestions to the Commission, which could always adopt it in the form of a concrete proposal to the Council.

278.   Case 13/83 *European Parliament v. Council* [1985] ECR 1513, [1986] 1 CMLR 138. See Fennel (1985) 10 ELRev. 264, Erdmenger (1985) EuR 375 and Schermers and Slot (1985) SEW 786 at 800.

279.   *Ibid.* [1985] ECR 1513 at 1600–1601, see WQ 2294/87 (Musso) O.J. 1988 C 93/75. As to action by the Institution concerned after the action was brought but before judgment, see Case 377/87 *European Parliament v. Council* [1988] ECR 4017 at 4048, but *cf.* Case

a weapon which, used sparingly and after reflection, forms a not insignificant means of putting pressure on the Council and its members to come to a decision. The Parliament also avails itself of the right conferred on the Community Institutions to intervene in cases pending before the Court (something which the Commission does as a matter of standing practice). Thus, for example, in the isoglucose cases[280] Parliament intervened when undertakings were seeking to challenge the legality of a Council regulation on the ground of failure properly to fulfil the requirement of consultation of the Parliament, and in relation to rules concerning transparency in access to documents the Parliament intervened in an action brought by the Netherlands before the Court of Justice[281] and an action brought by a journalist and *The Guardian* newspaper before the Court of First instance.[282]

The Parliament can be the defendant as well as plaintiff; this has been clear for years in staff cases. More recently, the Parliament has had to defend its decisions against challenge by other Community Institutions or other litigants. Several cases concerned decisions relating to the working places of the Parliament which were challenged by Luxembourg[283] or France.[284] The ecologists party '*Les Verts*' challenged decisions of the Bureau of the Parliament[285] relating to the apportionment and use of

C-41/92 *The Liberal Democrats v. European Parliament* [1993] ECR I-3153 at 3175–3176, and see the discussion by Bradley and Feeney (1993) 13 YBEL 383 at 392–393.
280. Case 138/79 *SA Roquette Frères v. Council* [1980] ECR 3333; Case 139/79 *Maizena GmbH v. Council* [1980] ECR 3393.
281. Case 58/94 *The Netherlands v. Council* [1996] ECR I-2169.
282. Case T-194/94 *Carvel and Guardian Newspapers Ltd. v. Council* [1995] ECR II-2765.
283. Case 230/81 *Luxembourg v. European Parliament* [1983] ECR 255, [1983] 2 CMLR 726, Case 108/83 *Luxembourg v. European Parliament* [1984] ECR 1945 (see Kapteyn (1984) SEW 427 at 436, Hartley (1984) 9 ELRev. 44, Hendry (1985) 10 ELRev. 126 and Masclet (1984) RTDE 538), and Cases C-213/88 and 39/89 *Luxembourg v. European Parliament* [1991] ECR I-5643, see Brown (1993) 30 CMLRev. 599 and Minor (1992) 17 ELRev. 517 (Case 15/86 *Luxembourg v. European Parliament* was withdrawn (O.J. 1986 C 280/8)). Standing to bring the action in the first of these cases was founded on Art. 38 ECSC, which was also the basis of the second action. It was not until after the judgment in Case 294/83 *Parti écologiste 'Les Verts' v. European Parliament* [1986] ECR 1339 at 1366 that the Court acknowledged that an action for annulment could lie under Article 173 EEC against measures adopted by the Parliament intended to have legal effect *vis-à-vis* third parties. This has now been incorporated into Arts. 173 EC and 146 Euratom, 1st para. in each case (standing under Art. 38 ECSC is conferred on Member States and the Commission only).
284. Cases 358/85 and 51/86 *France v. European Parliament* [1988] ECR 4821 and C-345/95 *France v. European Parliament* [1997] ECR I-5215 (Case 18/86 *France v. European Parliament* was withdrawn (O.J. 1986 C 280/8)); Case C-267/96 *France v. European Parliament* (O.J. 1996 C 269/21) is still pending at the date at which this work states the law). As to the continuing sensitivities, despite the settlement of the issue of the seats of the Institutions (see Chapter II, section 5.3, *ante*), see Bradley and Feeney (1994) 14 YBEL 401 at 430.
285. The Bureau of the Parliament consists of the President and the 14 Vice Presidents.

credits destined to reimburse political groups' expenditure to be incurred in the 1984 direct elections.[286] Even though Article 173 EEC spoke only of review of the legality of acts of the Council and the Commission, the Court saw no objection to considering an appeal against acts of the Parliament. Indeed, any other interpretation would have been incompatible with the spirit of the Treaty as expressed in Article 164 EC as well as with the system whereby an appeal may lie against all decisions of the Institutions which are intended to produce legal effects.[287] In Case 34/86 *Council* v. *European Parliament*[288] the Council, supported by three Member States obtained a ruling that the decision of the President of the Parliament declaring the 1986 budget adopted was illegal.[289]

As far as the Parliament's right to bring annulment proceedings is concerned, the Court's case-law, initially ostrich-like approach in the comitology judgment,[290] was quickly reversed in the Chernobyl judgment.[291] The main objection to the Court's initial denial of standing for the Parliament to bring an action under Article 173 EEC was that this left the Parliament entirely powerless in the face of a failure to take its interests into account or apply the proper procedure. Simply expecting the

The Quaestors are members of the Bureau in an advisory capacity, EP Rules of Procedure (see note 176, *supra*), Rule 21. As to the functions of the Bureau, see Rule 22.

286. Case 294/83 *Parti écologiste 'Les Verts'* v. *European Parliament* [1986] ECR 1339, [1987] 2 CMLR 343.

287. Case 294/83, *ibid.*, [1986] ECR 1339 at 1366, [1987] 2 CMLR 343 at 371–372. See also Case 190/84 *Parti écologiste 'Les Verts'* v. *European Parliament* [1988] ECR 1017; Case 78/85 *Group of the European Right* v. *European Parliament* [1986] ECR 1753; Case 221/86R *Group of the European Right et al.* v. *European Parliament* [1986] ECR 2579 and 2969, [1986] 3 CMLR 462; Case C-68/90 *Blot et al.* v. *European Parliament* [1990] ECR I-2101 and Case C-68/90R *ibid.* at 2177; Case C-314/91 *Weber* v. *European Parliament* [1993] ECR I-1093 (discussed by Bradley and Feeney (1993) 13 YBEL 383 at 394–395) and Case C-25/92 *Miethke* v. *European Parliament* [1993] ECR I-473. As to the Parliament as defendant under Art. 181 EC, see Case C-338/92 *Compagnie d'Enterprise CFE SA* v. *European Parliament* [1993] ECR I-5237 and Case C-42/94 *Heidemij Advies BV* v. *European Parliament* [1995] ECR I-1417.

288. [1986] ECR 2155, [1986] 3 CMLR 94, see Arnull (1986) 11 ELRev. 431 and Audretsch (1987) SEW 740. However, the annulment of the budget was not allowed to affect the validity of payments made and commitments entered into in implementation of the 1986 budget prior to the date of delivery of the judgment: [1986] ECR 2155 at 2212, [1986] 3 CMLR 94 at 152.

289. See also Case 23/86R *United Kingdom* v. *European Parliament* [1986] ECR 1085; Case C-284/90 *Council* v. *European Parliament* [1991] ECR I-2277, and Case C-41/95 *Council* v. *European Parliament* [1995] ECR I-4411. See further, Chapter V, section 2.1.1 (part D), *post*.

290. Case 302/87 *European Parliament* v. *Council* [1988] ECR 5615. See Boulouis (1989) RMC 119, Bradley (1988) 8 YBEL 27, Dashwood in Whyte and Smythe (eds.), *Current Issues in European and International Law* (London, 1990) 73, Jaqué (1989) RTDE 225 at 239; Thill (1989) CDE 367, and Weiler (1989) 14 ELRev. 334.

291. Case C-70/88 *European Parliament* v. *Council* [1990] ECR I-2041, [1992] 1 CMLR 91. See Bradley (1991) 16 ELRev. 245, Chambault (1991) RMC 40, Hilf (1990) EuR 273, Jacqué (1990) RTDE 617, Kortmann (1991) SEW 163, and Schoo (1990) EuGRZ 525.

Commission to act (ensuring under Article 155 EEC that the provisions of the Treaty were applied) was hardly a realistic expectation, particularly since it was the Commission that proposed the legal basis for action by the Council, and only if the latter changed the legal basis might the Commission be expected to seek the annulment of the measure concerned. Moreover, as individuals have very limited standing to challenge acts of the Institutions, and the chance that the Court might receive a reference from a national court for a preliminary ruling was very uncertain, the other possibilities for obtaining judicial review appeared too ineffective or uncertain. The Court was unable to rewrite the Treaties to give the Parliament an unfettered standing to bring an action for annulment. However, in view of the Court's duty to ensure that the Treaties' provisions on the institutional balance were applied, and that the Parliament's prerogatives, like those of the other Institutions should not be breached without an effective legal remedy being available from among those provided for in the Treaties, the Court concluded that the fundamental interest of maintaining and observing the institutional balance prevailed over the niceties of a procedural *lacuna*. Accordingly, it held that provided the action for annulment sought only to safeguard its prerogatives, and founded only on submissions alleging their infringement, such an action brought by the Parliament was admissible.[292]

These prerogatives included participation in the drafting of legislative measures, in particular participation in the cooperation procedure,[293] but the Court has held that an alleged inadequacy of reasoning is not an infringement of the Parliament's prerogatives.[294] Perhaps unsurprisingly, much use has been made of this possibility to challenge the choice of legal base for action,[295] failure to consult the Parliament,[296] and the Council's action in making substantive amendments to Commission proposals without reconsulting the Parliament.[297] It has also been invoked to

292. Case C-70/88, *ibid.* [1990] ECR I-2041 at 2073.
293. *Ibid.*
294. Case C-156/93 *European Parliament v. Commission* [1995] ECR I-2019 at 2045; Case C-303/94 *European Parliament v. Council* [1995] ECR I-2943.
295. *E.g.* Case C-295/90 *European Parliament v. Council* [1992] ECR I-4193 (right of residence for students); Case C-187/93 *European Parliament v. Council* [1994] ECR I-2857 (waste shipments); Case C-360/93 *European Parliament v. Council* [1996] ECR I-1195 (public procurement), and Case C-271/94 *European Parliament v. Council* [1996] ECR I-1689 (Edicom – telematic networks).
296. *E.g.* Case C-65/93 *European Parliament v. Council* [1995] ECR I-643 (generalized tariff preferences); Case C-156/93 *European Parliament v. Commission* [1995] ECR I-2019 (genetically modified micro-organisms in organically produced agricultural products), and Case C-303/94 *European Parliament v. Council* [1996] ECR I-2943 (marketing of plant protection products).
297. See *e.g.* Case C-65/90 *European Parliament v. Council* [1992] ECR I-4593 on access for non-resident carriers to national road haulage ('*cabotage*'); Case C-388/92 *European Parliament v. Council* [1994] ECR I-2067 (operation by non-resident carriers of

challenge a specific Council directive (on which the Parliament did not have to be consulted on the ground of incompatibility with a basic Council directive which had been the subject of consultation.[298] The Court has found that an act adopted by the co-decision procedure (thus by the Parliament and the Council acting together) could be amended by a decision of the Council alone acting in pursuance of power granted in an Act of Accession to adapt acts of the Institutions to the circumstances;[299] acts adopted by co-decision are considered to be acts of the Council.[300]

This result has now been expressly incorporated into Article 173 EC. Thus actions for annulment may be brought against acts of the Parliament intended to produce legal effects *vis-à-vis* third parties.[301] As far as the Parliament's right to bring actions for annulment is concerned, the phrasing used by the Court has been taken over literally: jurisdiction is conferred on the Court in actions brought by the Parliament for the purpose of protecting its prerogatives.[302] Parliament is now clearly in a position to enforce repect of its rights through bringing the necessary legal proceedings, most of which will be concerned with drawing the line between the myriad decision-making procedures. Viewed as a whole, judicial supervision forms an important supplement to the still manifestly unsatisfactory system of parliamentary supervisory and (co-)legislative functions in the Community and in the Union.

6.   SCOPE OF DECISION-MAKING POWERS

6.1   Principle of attributed powers

The Council, acting alone or with the European Parliament, and the Commission have been granted powers of decision, *i.e.* powers to take decisions which are legally binding upon the subjects of the

national road passenger transport services); Case C-417/93 *European Parliament v. Council* [1995] ECR I-1185 (technical assistance to the independent States of the former Soviet Union and to Mongolia); Case C-21/94 *European Parliament v. Council* [1995] ECR I-1827, and Case C-392/95 *European Parliament v. Council* [1997] ECR I-3213 (visas for nationals of third countries).

298. Case C-303/94 *European Parliament v. Council* [1995] ECR I-2943 (marketing of plant protection products). As to revision of a directive without consultation, see Case C-417/93 *European Parliament v. Council* [1995] ECR I-1185 at 1219 (citing earlier case-law on implementing powers), see further, section 6.4.1, *post*.
299. Case C-259/95 *European Parliament v. Council* [1997] ECR I-5303 at 5321–5322.
300. *Ibid.* at 5322 (citing Arts. 56(2), 100a(1) and 129a(2) EC. This is at odds with the practice in the O.J. of presenting acts adopted by co-decision as acts of both Institutions, signed by the Presidents of both.
301. Arts. 173 EC and 146 Euratom, 1st para. in each case. The original provisions of Art. 38 ECSC still apply in respect of that Treaty (see note 283, *supra*).
302. Arts. 173 EC, 146 Euratom, 3rd para. in each case, Art. 33 ECSC, 4th para.

Communities.[303] This has not been done by way of a general authorization
to decide within the scope of application of the Treaty, but by the grant of
a plurality of specific powers of decision (attributed powers) which are
defined as accurately as possible in the various Treaty articles according to
their nature and subject-matter. Article 3b EC sets out the general
limitation that the Community must act within the limits of the powers
which the Treaty confers upon it, and of the objectives assigned to it.[304]
This general principle of division of competence between the Community
and the Member States[305] is developed in the Treaties, so that each
Institution may act only within the limits of the powers conferred upon it
by the Treaties.[306] Each decision taken by an Institution must therefore be
based directly or indirectly on one or more[307] specific provisions of the
Treaties.[308]

303. Such powers are not conferred on these bodies in respect of CFSP or JHA.
304. Art. 3b EC, 1st para.
305. See Chapter III, section 5.1, *ante*.
306. Arts. E TEU; 4(1), 2nd subpara, 145, 155 and 189 EC; 5, 1st para., 8, 14, and 26, 1st
     para. ECSC, and 3, 2nd para., 115, 124 and 161 Euratom. *Cf.* Art. 3(1) SEA which,
     like Art. E TEU also refers specifically to parts of the instrument of which it forms
     part. See, generally, Cases C-327/91 *France v. Commission* [1994] ECR I-3641 and C-
     426/93 *Germany v. Council* [1995] ECR I-3723, and, further, Dashwood (1996) 21
     ELRev. 113; Dashwood in Dashwood (ed.), *Reviewing Maastricht – Issues for the IGC*
     (London, 1996) 6, Hilf's comments 23, the report of the debate, 37, and Slynn's
     summing up 64; papers by VerLoren van Themaat and Petersmann in Winter *et al.*
     (eds.), *Reforming the Treaty on European Union* (The Hague, 1996) 249 and 265
     respectively.
307. Sometimes the Council bases its acts on two specific Articles of the Treaty as a com-
     promise in the event of a dispute amongst its members as to which Article provides
     the correct legal basis. This can be of importance, particularly in relation to the voting
     procedure and to the extent of any involvement of the European Parliament or other
     bodies required to be consulted. One well-known example is directives harmonizing
     veterinary legislation which were invariably based on Art. 43 EC as well as on Art.
     100 EC. As an example of litigation on this point see Case 45/86 *Commission v.
     Council* [1987] ECR 1493, [1988] 2 CMLR 131, Steenbergen (1987) 24 CMLRev. 731
     and Arnull (1987) 12 ELRev. 448. See also internal market measures in the environ-
     mental field (*cf.* Arts. 100a and 130s EC) and Forwood and Clough (1986) 11 ELRev.
     383; Kramer (1987) 24 CMLRev. 659 and Vandermeersch (1987) 12 ELRev. 407. See
     further, *e.g.* Case 68/86 *United Kingdom v. Council* [1988] ECR 855, [1988] 2 CMLR
     543; Case 131/86 *United Kingdom v. Council* [1988] ECR 905, [1988] 2 CMLR 364;
     Case C-300/89 *Commission v. Council* [1991] ECR I-2867; Case C-155/91 *Commission
     v. Council* [1993] ECR I-939; Case C-187/93 *European Parliament v. Council* [1994]
     ECR I-2857 and Somsen (1992) 29 CMLRev. 140.
308. The grant by the Court of Justice to the High Authority (Commission) of a general
     power to make recommendations to the Member States to remind them of their
     Treaty obligations, notwithstanding the opening words of Art. 14 ECSC is a curious
     departure from this principle. However, in view of the limited force of recommenda-
     tions under the ECSC Treaty (they are binding only as to the aims to be pursued,
     which in this case means the Treaty provisions) this power does not amount to much:
     see Case 25/59 *Netherlands v. High Authority* [1960] ECR 355 (see also [1960] ECR
     386). Barents (1993) SEW 5 at 26 denies the validity of this principle, submitting that

The principle of action within the limits of an Institution's powers was an important factor in the judgment of the German Federal Constitutional Court in the notorious judgment on the compatibility with the German constitution of the TEU.[309] That court noted that even after the changes introduced by the TEU, the EC Treaty adheres to the principle of specific empowerment[310] and then discussed whether this requirement was in fact respected by Article F(3) TEU;[311] by the possibility of attributing new tasks and powers to the Union and the Community;[312] and the provisions concerning Economic and Monetary Union.[313] While the Federal Constitutional Court answered these points positively, it expressly reserved the right to examine whether legal acts taken by the Community Institutions or other bodies were within the limits of the powers conferred upon them by the Community Treaties and the TEU.[314] This judgment, often referred to as *Solange III*, controversially reasserts the right of the German courts to examine the validity of Community acts, a point of view which is certainly not accepted by the Court of Justice, which alone claims the right to review the legality of acts of the Community Institutions or other bodies.[315]

6.2   Filling in the *lacunae* in the system of powers: Article 235 EC

The framework of powers granted in the manner just set out reflects the desire of the contracting parties to restrict as much as possible the inroads which would be made on their sovereignty. The system of attributed powers means that there may well be cases in which the Communities have to act in order to ensure the achievement of their objectives but lack the requisite specific powers. Thus, in the three Treaties special provision exists designed to cover such an eventuality.[316] It is the Council, acting unanimously on a proposal from the Commission and after consulting the European Parliament, which then takes the appropriate measures in the

---

all legal provisions in the internal market sphere which do or may affect intra-Community trade are a Community matter.

309. *Brunner* [1994] 1 CMLR 57. See *e.g.* Frowein (1994) ZaÖRV 1; Herdegen (1994) 31 CMLRev. 235; Ipsen (1994) EuR 1; Kokott (1996) 2 EPL 237; Meyring (1997) 22 ELRev. 221; Tomuschat (1993) EuGRZ 489; Wieland (1995) EJIL 259; Weiler (1995) 1 ELJ 219, and Zuleeg (1997) 22 ELRev. 19.
310. *Prinzip der beschränkten Einzelermächtigung* (points A.I.1(b) and C.II.1(a) of that judgment).
311. Which provides that the Union shall provide itself with the means necessary to attain its objectives and carry through its policies.
312. Art. B TEU, 1st para., 5th indent.
313. See points C.II.2(a)–(f) of the judgment.
314. Point C.1.3 of the judgment, *in fine*.
315. *E.g.* Case 314/85 *Foto-Frost v. Hauptzollamt Lübeck-Ost* [1987] ECR 4199 at 4231.
316. Arts. 235 EC, 95, 1st para. ECSC, and 203 Euratom.

EC and Euratom. In the ECSC the decision is taken by the Commission, but with the unanimous assent of the Council and after consultation of the Consultative Committee.[317]

The significance of Article 235 EC for effective Community action justifies a closer examination of its interpretation and application. Article 235 itself contains the conditions for its use. First, action by the Community must be 'necessary to attain, in the course of the operation of the common market, one of the objectives of the Community'. Thus it is clear that the *lacuna* must be in the powers granted, not in the sum of objectives of the Community. As far as objectives are concerned, these are not merely the general objectives in Article 2 EC as amplified in Article 3 EC, but also the objectives mentioned in the various specific Articles of the Treaty, even when they simply boil down to the general objectives. However, Article 235 cannot be used to enlarge the scope of Community competence beyond the general framework resulting from the provisions of the Treaties as a whole, and in particular from those defining the Communities' objectives and tasks.[318] The meaning of the phrase 'in the course of the operation of the common market' is not to be understood in the geographical sense; not as restricting the operation of Article 235 to the strict field of the attainment of one of the two means by which the Community's objectives are to be achieved, namely the establishment of a common market. Rather, the application of Article 235 is designed to ensure that the common market, as defined in the Treaty, may function more effectively.

The second condition which Article 235 sets out for its use is that the Treaty has not provided the necessary powers. That does not mean that no powers exist at all; it may be that powers do exist but that they do not provide for a satisfactory and effective solution. An good example can be seen in the field of harmonisation of laws under Article 100 EC which provides for the adoption of directives whereas it may be that in a particular case a single global regulation is really necessary.[319] A narrow interpretation of the ambit or reach of the powers conferred by a particular Article of the Treaty, rather than a wide interpretation will lead to the conclusion that recourse must be had to Article 235. It used to appear that even when a wide interpretation of the powers conferred by the Treaty was justified, the Court would leave the Council a certain liberty to invoke Article 235 in the interests of legal certainty; this is clearly no longer the case, as the Court has now stated that 'it follows from the very wording of

317. Art. 95 ECSC, 1st para.
318. Opinion 2/94 *Accession to the European Convention on Human Rights* [1996] ECR I-1759 at 1788.
319. *E.g.* in the field of customs law, see Case 8/73 *Hauptzollamt Bremerhaven v. Massey-Ferguson GmbH* [1973] ECR 897 at 908 relating to the old Reg. 803/68 (O.J. English Special Edition 1968, p. 170) on the valuation of goods for customs purposes.

Article 235 that its use as the legal basis for a measure is justified only where no other provision of the Treaty gives the Community institutions the necessary power to adopt the measure in question.'[320]

Provided that these two conditions are met, 'appropriate measures' may be taken by the Council, acting unanimously on a proposal from the Commission and after consulting the European Parliament. 'Appropriate measures' covers not merely the forms of action set out in Article 189 EC,[321] but also any other form of action which may be appropriate. On the basis of the difference in wording between Article 84(2) EC and Article 235[322] it has been argued that Article 235, unlike Article 84(2), does not permit the Council to adopt provisions under which it either retains the power to adopt implementing measures in a particular field itself or delegates such power to the Commission under Article 155 EC.[323] The Council's practice in applying Article 235 shows, however, that this restrictive interpretation is misconceived.[324] Accepting that Article 235 does not oblige the Council, when there is no specific power conferred in the Treaty, to take appropriate measures in every case, but rather allows the Council the freedom to take such measures and to decide whether to entrust implementation to the Commission or in specific cases[325] to implement them further itself, it appears acceptable in principle that Article 235 can be the basis for creating new bodies and endowing them with legal personality.[326] The utility of doing so is, however, heavily circumscribed by the restrictive criteria which the Court has laid down concerning the lawfulness of delegating powers of decision to bodies other than the Commission.[327]

320. Case 45/86 *Commission v. Council* [1987] ECR 1493 at 1520 (generalized tariff preferences); Case 242/87 *Commission v. Council* [1989] ECR 1425 at 1452 (Erasmus programme), and Case C-350/92 *Spain v. Council* [1995] ECR I-1985 at 2012.
321. *I.e.* regulations, directives, decisions, recommendations or opinions.
322. Art. 84(2) EC provides that the 'Council may, acting by a qualified majority, decide
whether, to what extent and by what procedure, appropriate provisions may be laid
down for sea and air transport.' Art. 235 EC provides that if 'action by the Community should prove necessary to attain, in the course of the operation of the common
market, one of the objectives of the Community and this Treaty has not provided the
necessary powers, the Council shall, acting unanimously on a proposal from the Commission and after consulting the Assembly, take the appropriate measures.'
323. Gericke: *Allgemeine Rechtssetzungsbefügnisse nach Artikel 235 EWG-Vertrag*
(Hamburg, 1970) 86–87; see also Ipsen: *Europäisches Gemeinschaftsrecht* (Tübingen,
1972) 4/32 and 20/41.
324. See Gericke, *ibid.* 87–90.
325. *Cf.* Art. 145 EC, 3rd indent, 3rd sentence.
326. Thus *e.g.* the Council set up the European Centre for the Development of Vocational
Training (Cedefop) (by Reg. 337/75, O.J. 1975 L 39/1); the European Foundation for
the Improvement of Living and Working Conditions (by Reg. 1365/75, O.J. 1975 L
139/1), and the European Agency for the Evaluation of Medicinal Products (by Reg.
2309/93, O.J. 1993 L 214/1).
327. See section 6.4. of this Chapter, *post.*

Within the limits laid down in Article 235 itself[328] the Council can indeed use that provision in order to supplement the Treaty provisions to a certain extent and it is interesting to see how this power compares with other means of supplementing the law of the Treaty. One of these is the system of decisions of the representatives of the governments of the Member States meeting within the Council.[329] In the *ERTA* judgment[330] the Court did not regard the Council as being obliged to use Article 235 in every case in which it could use it. This appeared to leave the door wide open for the use of decisions of the representatives of the governments of the Member States meeting within the Council as an alternative to 'appropriate measures' under Article 235. Such an approach would be objectionable because it would mean that the governments could take action outside the competence and procedures of the Community. However, the Court appears to have placed an important restriction on its remarks in the *ERTA* judgment. In Case 8/73 *Hauptzollamt Bremerhaven* v. *Massey-Ferguson GmbH*[331] it stated that no objection could be raised to the application of Article 235 in the interests of legal certainty when it was not perhaps entirely clear that various specific Articles of the Treaty did confer the necessary powers because, in the light of the specific requirements of Article 235, 'the rules of the Treaty on the forming of the Council's decisions or on the division of powers between the institutions are not to be disregarded.'[332] From this it can be deduced that using a decision of the representatives of the governments of the Member States meeting within the Council would not have been upheld, as using such a decision would have been to disregard the rules of the Treaty. These decisions always come about without reference to the Commission's right of initiative or consultation of the European Parliament. Indeed, it may be concluded that the use of such decisions is always impossible if Article 235 itself could be used. The procedures of that Article are part of 'the rules of the Treaty on the forming of the Council's decisions or on the division of powers between the institutions' which the Court will not permit to be disregarded. In relation to the demarcation between Article 235 EC and Article N TEU, it should be noted that the procedure for amendment of the Treaty, now laid down in Article N TEU, must be used whenever the conditions for the use of Article 235 are not fulfilled.[333] This is particularly the case if it is necessary to confer powers for the achievement of objectives

328. *I.e.* action by the Community has to be necessary to achieve, in the course of the operation of the common market, one of the objectives of the Community and the Treaty has not provided the necessary powers.
329. See Chapter V, section 1.6, *post*.
330. Case 22/70 *Commission v. Council* [1971] ECR 263 at 283.
331. [1973] ECR 897.
332. *Ibid.* at 908 (but see Case 45/86 *Commission v. Council* [1987] ECR 1493, [1988] 2 CMLR 131).
333. See note 318, *supra*.

not mentioned in the Treaty or if changes in the institutional structure of the Community are to be made. The latter would also involve a change in the institutional structure of the Union itself.[334] Considerations of a change in the institutional arrangements lay behind the Court's conclusion that, in the present state of Community law, the Community was not competent to accede to the European Convention on Human Rights.[335]

Originally the Council was pretty restrained in using Article 235.[336] This provision was principally used to integrate trade in processed agricultural products into the system of the common agricultural policy and to achieve uniform regulation of customs law.[337] Post-1972 this approach changed significantly. The final communiqué of the Paris Summit in October 1972 showed a clear preference for the use of Article 235 as the basis of the achievement of economic and monetary union and the development of complementary policies such as a common regional and social policy, a common policy for science and technology and common environmental and energy policies.[338] A series of decisions in these sectors, based on Article 235 followed in the succeeding years; at the same time more widespread use was made of Article 235 even in the traditional sectors of agriculture, the customs union, establishment and services and commercial policy.[339]

The need to fall back on Article 235 has now significantly diminished since the coming into force of the SEA on 1 July 1987. This introduced various specific powers in relation to monetary capacity, social policy, economic and social cohesion, research and technological development and the environment which have now been further developed by the changes made through the TEU. Accordingly, action in matters such as environmental policy will no longer normally have to be based on Article 235. At the same time these developments have gone hand in hand with an

334. *Cf.* Arts. C and E TEU.
335. Opinion 2/94 *Accession to the European Convention on Human Rights* [1996] ECR I-1759 at 1789 (insertion of the Community in a separate international institutional system and integration of the whole of the Convention's provisions into the Community legal order).
336. See the Council's answer to WQ 204/67 (Vredeling) O.J. 1968 C 17/2 – Art. 235 EEC would not be applicable whenever it was intended to give rise to new obligations going beyond those set out in the Treaty.
337. *E.g.* Reg. 1059/69 (J.O 1969 L 141/1) on trade arrangements applicable to certain goods resulting from the processing of agricultural products and Reg. 803/68 (see note 319, *supra*).
338. Bull. EC 10–1972, pp. 14–20.
339. See Lauwaars (1976) EuR 100 *et seq.* In the period to 30 March 1977 Art. 235 EEC had been used 120 times, of which 86 had been since 1 January 1973: WQ 168/77 (Maigaard) O.J. 1977 C 180/18. See, further, WQs 18/92 (Marcelino *et al.*) O.J. 1992 C 235/29; 1130/92 (Christensen) O.J. 1992 C 285/28; E-1627/96 (Howitt) O.J. 1996 C 356/69; E-3131/95 (Cabezón Alonso) O.J. 1996 C 79/52, and E-2858/96 (Cabezón Alonso) O.J. 1997 C 60/121.

express limitation of the use of Article 235: The old Article 102a EEC[340] required institutional changes necessary for the establishment of Economic and Monetary Union to be undertaken by means of the procedure for amendment of the Treaties. A similar type of restriction is also apparent in Articles 126–129 EC in the fields of education, vocational training and youth; culture, and public health, as those provisions expressly exclude any harmonization of laws and regulations of Member States.[341] On this basis the Edinburgh European Council concluded that the use of Article 235 EC for these purposes is also excluded.[342] Moreover the European Council declared that the principle of subsidiarity must also be respected in the application of Article 235 EC.[343]

Apart from the restrictive interpretation of Article 235 set out above, there remains the inherent objection to the use of this provision that it provides for the European Parliament only to be consulted. Even a wide interpretation should not lead to decisions being taken on the basis of Article 235 EC which should properly be exposed to full involvement of the European Parliament. As long as there is no full decision-making authority for the Parliament, or at the very least co-decision, which would lend real parliamentary democratic legitimacy to the use of Article 235,[344] fundamental decisions should, it is submitted, preferably be taken using the amendment procedure of Article N TEU. This latter procedure requires ratification by all the Member States in accordance with their respective constitutional requirements.

6.3 Application of the theory of implied powers

It may be thought, and indeed has repeatedly been argued that the existence of Article 235 EC to cover unforeseen developments means that the theory of implied powers, which is a theory particularly well-known in the laws of federal states and international organizations, has no place in Community law. Such a view rests on scarcely convincing foundations. In the system of the European Community Treaties, which is based on an

340. Subsequently amended by the TEU, removing this limitation, in view of the specific provisions introduced by the TEU.
341. Arts. 126(4); 127(4); 128(5), and 129(4) EC.
342. Bull. EC 12–1992 point I.15 (final sub-point, p. 14, note 1. However, this did not mean that the pursuit of other Community objectives through Treaty articles other than Arts. 126–129 might not produce effects in these areas, *ibid*. In *Brunner* [1994] 1 CMLR 47 the German Constitutional Court expressly referred to this aspect of the European Council's declaration (point C.II.2.a (end)).
343. Bull. EC 12–1992 point I.15, (p. 13, basic principles on the implementation of Art. 3b EC).
344. The Vedel Report envisaged parliamentary cooperation on, *inter alia*, the use of Art. 235 EEC as one of the first steps in the expansion of the Parliament's powers (Bull. EC 1972 Supp. 4/72) but nothing came of it.

attribution of a series of specific powers to the Council and the Commission, provisions like Article 235 EC have a different scope of application than the theory of implied powers. As each case arises the Treaties confer the powers required for the activities of the Communities. Article 235 grants the power to act in a case where such action is necessary to attain, in the course of operation of the common market, one of the objectives of the Communities, but this power is lacking. A new, independent power of action is created alongside the existing ones.[345]

On the other hand the application of the theory of implied powers in the system of the Treaties can only relate to existing powers of action. It cannot fill a gap in the totality of the specific powers conferred on the Institutions for the activities of the Communities – for this purpose a provision like Article 235 has been created – but it can only supplement a specific power to act, explicitly conferred on the Communities, which shows a gap.[346] In fact the theory is an outcome of 'a rule of interpretation generally accepted in both international and national law, according to which the rules laid down by an international treaty or a law presuppose the rules without which that treaty or law would have no meaning or could not be reasonably and usefully applied,[347] and it has been adopted as such by the Court of Justice in the interpretation of the ECSC Treaty. When adapted to the system for specific powers in the European Treaties, this 'principle of effectiveness' (*effet utile*) implies that such power without which an explicitly conferred specific power either would not make sense or would not permit of a reasonable application must be deemed to be included in the power that has been explicitly conferred. It is, therefore, a matter not of an independent, but a derived power, which is necessary to attain the objectives for which the main specific power is intended.

Article 235 and the corresponding Articles in the Euratom and ECSC Treaties, therefore, do not in principle form an obstacle to an application of the theory of implied powers in the context of a rational interpretation of a Treaty provision. The significance of this theory for the institutional law of the Communities, however, must not be overestimated. The implied powers of decision will seldom be very wide because, first of all, they can only result from one of the specific powers which the Council and the Commission already have and, secondly, because these specific powers have been carefully defined and delimited in the Treaties. Save in the field of external relations even the cautious case-law of the Court[348] does not

---

345. Subject to the conditions explained in section 6.2, *ante* (see especially pp. 236–237, *supra*).
346. Art. 235 EC cannot in itself vest exclusive competence in the Community at international level, see Opinion 1/94 *WTO – GATS and TRIPs* [1994] ECR I-5267 at 5414.
347. Case 8/55 *Fédération Charbonnière de Belgique v. High Authority* [1954–1956] ECR 292 at 299.
348. *Ibid.*; Case 25/59 *Netherlands v. High Authority* [1960] ECR 355 at 374–377; Cases 281, 283–285 and 287/85 *Germany et al. v. Commission* [1987] ECR 3203 at 3253–

justify an assumption that the theory of implied powers will play a great part in the development of the powers of the Community. In the field of external relations, however, it has been clear since the *ERTA* judgment[349] that the Community's power to conclude international agreements can arise not merely from an explicit grant of power in the Treaty[350] but also from other Treaty provisions and from decisions taken by the Community Institutions in connection with those provisions.[351]

6.4 Delegation of powers

The Council, acting alone or in conjunction with the European Parliament, and the Commission may exercise their powers of decision to lay down provisions or to apply provisions laid down in the Treaties or in implementing acts. The extent to which they may delegate their powers to other Institutions, agencies or other bodies is a matter of considerable importance, as is the distinction between various types of delegation.

6.4.1 Delegation by the Council to the Commission

Delegation of powers by the Council to the Commission is expressly envisaged in the EC and Euratom Treaties.[352] The Commission exercises the powers conferred on it by the Council 'for the implementation of the rules laid down by the latter.'[353] Such delegation has now acquired a tighter character since the addition of a third indent to Article 145 EC by the SEA. This parallels Article 155 EC and makes it plain that the circumstances in which the Council reserves the right to exercise specific implementing powers itself are to be the exception, not the rule.[354] As a safeguard against proliferation of procedures and *ad hoc* horse-trading on the extent of delegation in any particular case, the Council was required

---

3254, and Case C-295/90 *European Parliament v. Council* [1992] ECR I-4193 at 4235–4236 (right of residence for students).

349. Case 22/70 *Commission v. Council* [1971] ECR 263 at 274–276. See also Cases 3, 4 & 6/76 *Kramer el al.* [19761 ECR 1279 and Opinion 1/76 [1977] ECR 741.

350. As in Arts. 113 and 238 EC.

351. See, most recently, Opinion 2/91 *ILO Convention on safety in the use of chemicals at work* [1993] ECR I-1061 at 1076; Opinion 1/94 *WTO – GATS and TRIPs* [1994] ECR I-5267 at 5416, and Opinion 2/94 *Accession to the European Convention on Human Rights* [1996] ECR I-1759 at 1787.

352. Arts. 145, 3rd indent, and 155, 4th indent EC, and 124, 4th indent Euratom.

353. Arts. 155 EC and 124 Euratom (4th indent in each case).

354. This is apparent from the limitation of the Council's right to specific cases (although these are not further defined). In Case 16/88 *Commission v. Council* [1989] ECR 3457 at 3485 the Court confirmed this view, adding that the Council would have to state in detail the grounds for such a decision.

to decide unanimously in advance on a proposal from the Commission and after obtaining the opinion of the European Parliament the principles and rules which were to be observed in relation to the delegation of powers and its exercise.[355] Delegation to the Commission is of great importance in the case of the EC Treaty, because as a framework Treaty it gives the Council regulatory powers in wide fields. The concept of 'implementation' has been held to comprise 'both the drawing up of implementing rules and the application of rules to specific cases by means of acts of individual application.'[356] The rules laid down by the Council, therefore, may have a rather general character. It is sufficient that the Council decides upon the essential elements of the matter which has to be regulated,[357] as happens for example in the regulations concerning the common organizations of the market for agricultural products 'which are intended to give concrete shape to the fundamental guidelines of Community policy.'[358] If the Council derives a regulatory power from the Treaty, the Council may not delegate this *in toto* to the Commission. The implementation by the Commission, if that were done, would not really be an implementation of the rules laid down by the Council, but rather of those laid down by the Treaty itself.

---

355. Art. 145 EC, 3rd indent. These have been laid down in Dec. 87/373 (O.J. 1987 L 197/ 33), For the statements entered in the minutes when this decision was adopted see *Europe* No. 1477 of 28 October 1987 (documents annexed to that day's issue). See, generally, Blumann (1988) RTDE 23; Bradley (1992) 29 CMLRev. 693; Ehlermann (1988) RMC 152; Kalbheim and Winter in Winter (ed.), *Sources and Categories of European Union Law* (Baden-Baden, 1996) 583, and the Commission's Reports *Delegation of Executive Powers to the Commission* SEC (89) 1591 Final and SEC (90) 2589 Final. See further, COM (98) 380 Final. As to implementing measures for acts adopted by the European Parliament and the Council jointly under the co-decision procedure, see the *Modus Vivendi* adopted by those Institutions and the Commission (O.J. 1996 C 102/1). See also Case 417/93 *European Parliament v. Council* [1995] ECR I-1185 at 1219. As to Interinstitutional Agreements generally, see Monar (1994) 31 CMLRev. 693 and Snyder in Winter (ed.), *op. cit.* 453.
356. Case 16/88 *Commission v. Council* [1989] ECR 3457 at 3485.
357. Case 25/70 *Einfuhr- und Vorratsselle für Getreide und Futtermittel v. Köster, Berodt & Co.* [1970] ECR 1161 at 1170. See also Case 41/69 *ACF Chemiefarma NV v. Commission* [1970] ECR 661 at 688 which makes it clear that Art. 155 EC does not restrict the Commission's powers to non-regulatory powers. In Case 23/75 *Rey Soda v. Cassa Conguaglio Zucchero* [1975] ECR 1279 at 1300 the Court expressly stated that the structure of the Treaty and practical requirements indicated that a wide meaning should be given to the concept of 'implementation'. The Court avoided using the term 'delegation' in its judgment but rather spoke of 'conferring of powers'; this was clearly intended to avoid any thoughts of supervision or subservience which are inherent in some concepts of 'delegation', see Louis (1978) SEW 803. See, futher, Cases C-296 and 307/93 *France et al. v. Commission* [1996] ECR I-795 at 840.
358. Case C-240/90 *Germany v. Commission* [1992] ECR I-5383 at 5434. That judgment (at 5435) also shows that the Council may leave it up to the Commission to oblige the Member States to impose specific penalties on the basis of a delegating provision drafted in general terms.

The third indent of Article 145 EC in fact gives an express basis in the Treaty for a practice dating from the Sixties by which, in conferring implementing powers on the Commission, the Council in the provision conferring the delegation sets out the conditions under which the Commission could exercise its powers, effectively trying to tie the Commission's hands (or at least keep an eye on what it was doing) by the comitology procedure.[359] Even in those days, the Council in its decisions was frequently wont to reserve certain powers to itself,[360] but, as has been shown above, it now has to justify itself if it does so.[361]

6.4.2 Delegation to third parties

The question of the extent of permissible delegation of powers to third parties was considered in a pair of important judgments in cases brought by an Italian company, Meroni, against the old High Authority.[362] These judgments, the importance of which stretches way beyond the individual facts, show that in principle delegation is possible, even if this is not expressly provided for in the Treaties, provided that the exercise of the delegated powers is subject to the same rules as are laid down in the Treaties concerning the exercise of the powers by the delegating Institution itself – particularly as far as the obligation to state reasons for acts and subjection to judicial review are

359. As to the comitology decision, see note 355, *supra*. See, further, Chapter V, section 3.1, *post*, and Falke and Winter in Winter (ed.), *op. cit.* (see note 355, *supra*) 541. The second sentence of Art. 145 EC, 3rd indent expressly permits the Council to impose certain requirements in respect of the exercise of the powers delegated to the Commission.

360. Sometimes the Council tends to declare a simplified decision-making procedure applicable in relation to the exercise of powers which it has granted itself – simplified in comparison with the procedures laid down in the Treaty for the exercise of the basic enabling provision (*e.g.* no proposal is needed from the Commission, other voting provisions or no need to consult the European Parliament; see also Case C-417/93 *European Parliament v. Council* [1995] ECR I-1185 at 1219). In such cases the same conditions should apply as apply in the case of delegation to the Commission: according to the procedure laid down in the Treaties the Council has to prescribe the essential elements of the matter to be regulated. Any blanket self-empowering which did not respect the Treaty procedures would distort the institutional balance. *Cf.* Ehlermann (1970) EuR 250 at 252 who opined that even in cases in which the Council confers powers on itself the Commission's right of initiative cannot be excluded as, in the application of the global regulation to individual cases the Council is bound by that regulation and cannot deviate from the rules which it has laid down. See the ball-bearings cases, *e.g.* Case 119/77 *Nippon Seiko KK et al. v. Council and Commission* [1979] ECR 1303 at 1331.

361. See note 354, *supra*.

362. Case 9/56 *Meroni & Co., Industrie Metallurgiche SpA v. High Authority* [1957 and 1958] ECR 133; Case 10/56 *Meroni and Co., Industrie Metallurgiche SAS v. High Authority* [1957 and 1958] ECR 157.

concerned.[363] What is not permitted, however, is the delegation of broad discretionary powers to institutions different from those set up by the Treaties for the purpose of ensuring and controlling the exercise of powers within the field of their respective functions. Such a delegation would amount to a breach of a basic guarantee which the Treaties afford to the subjects of the Communities (including individuals) and which is implied in the balance of powers which is characteristic of the institutional structure of the Communities.[364] The only delegation which is permitted, therefore, is that of clearly defined executive powers, the use of which can be strictly controlled by reference to objective criteria which have been imposed by the delegating authority.[365]

The significance of this ECSC case-law for the question of delegation of powers in relation to the EC Treaty lies in the principle of the balance of powers, part of which is the supervision of legality by the Court; this balance may not be disturbed. The question arises whether this case-law forms the basis for a complete prohibition of the delegation of discretionary powers in the functioning of the EC. In the ECSC system, which is characterized by strong powers conferred on the Commission by the Treaty (which, however, the Treaty narrowly defines), the strict test for permissible delegation is justified because if the Commission were to transfer its powers to other bodies this would be tantamount to a *carte blanche* delegation. The EC system often confers very broad powers on the Council and the emphasis of the test lies on the clear and precise delimitation of the powers transferred, on the resulting restriction of free decision making powers and not on the exclusion of all freedom.[366] Thus, in Case 98/80 *Romano v. Institut National d'Assurance Maladie-Invalidité*[367] the Court indicated that it followed from Article 155 EEC and from the judicial system created by the EEC Treaty – in particular by Articles 173 and 177 – that a body such as the Administrative Commission on Social Security for Migrant Workers[368] could not be empowered by the Council

363. *Cf.* the provisions of Art. 53 Euratom, 2nd para., relating to the activities of the Euratom Supply Agency.
364. Case 10/56 *Meroni* [1957 and 1958] ECR 157 at 173. *Cf.* on this criterion Case 25/70 *Köster* [1970] ECR 1161 at 1171; see Ehlermann (1971) EuR 250 *et seq.*
365. Case 10/56 *Meroni*, *ibid.*
366. The relative nature of the concept of implementation was indicated by the Court in Case 25/70 *Koster, loc. cit.* (see note 357, *supra*). The criterion of a clear and precise delimitation of powers was applied in Opinion 1/76 *European Laying-up Fund for Inland Waterway Vessels* [1977] ECR 741 at 759–760 even though it did not relate in that instance to an internal delegation but to the attribution of powers to an international organization under a Treaty concluded by the Community with a third country. See Kapteyn (1978) SEW 360 at 366–367.
367. [1981] ECR 1241 at 1256.
368. See Reg. 1408/71, Arts. 80 *et seq.* (O.J. English Special Edition 1971 (II), p. 416) as substituted by Reg. 118/97 (O.J. 1997 L 228/1), most recently amended by Reg. 1290/97 (O.J. 1997 L 176/1).

to adopt acts having the force of law. Delegation of powers to the new independent Community bodies[369] and to management bodies such as the Socrates Bureau[370] will also have to respect the boundaries set out in this case-law.[371]

6.4.3 Internal delegation

On a strict view, it would not be permissible for the Commission to delegate its power of decision to one of its members as this would conflict with its collective responsibility before the European Parliament and with the requirement that the Commission take decisions by a majority of the number of its members.[372] However, such a rigorous prohibition of delegation is impossible in view of the enormous number of Commission decisions which have to be taken, particularly in the agricultural sector. Accordingly, the Commission authorises its individual members to exercise its powers; this is done in the name of the Commission, under its supervision and taking account of the principle of collective responsibility;[373] the procedure is referred to as *habilitation*. The Court has been willing to accept this type of public law power of execution because no power of own decision is conferred on the person mandated and his or her power is limited to the area of administration and management and does not permit him or her to take decisions of principle in the matters concerned.[374] However, it is now clear that certain types of decision cannot be left to the *habilitation* procedure: in Case C-137/92 P *Commission* v. *BASF AG et al.*[375] the Court of Justice

369. See section 9.3, *post*.
370. See Dec. 95/819 (O.J. 1995 L 87/20).
371. See, generally, Everson in Winter (ed.), *op. cit.* (see note 355, *supra*) 601 and, more extensively, (1995) ELJ 180.
372. Art. 163 EC, 1st para., Rules of Procedure (see note 119, *supra*), Art. 1.
373. Rules of Procedure, *ibid.*, Art. 11 (as amended). Such delegated powers may be sub-delegated (usually to senior officials) only if the enabling decision so provides, *ibid.* Separate rules provide for delegation in respect of financial matters, the powers conferred on the appointing authority (recruitment, appointment, dismissal and terms of service of officials) and the authority empowered to conclude contracts of employment, and the general rule on delegation is expressly without prejudice to those separate rules.
374. Case 5/85 *AKZO Chemie BV et al.* v. *Commission* [1986] ECR 2585 [1987] 3 CMLR 716, although this was implicit in earlier judgments: see Case 48/69 *Imperial Chemical Industries Ltd.* v. *Commission* [1972] ECR 619 at 649–650; Case 8/72 *Vereeniging van Cementhandelaren* v. *Commission* [1972] ECR 977 at 989; Cases 43 and 63/82 *Vereniging ter Bevordering van het Vlaamse Boekwezen, VBVB et al.* v. *Commission* [1984] ECR 19 at 56–57 and Case 8/83 *Officine Fratelli Berioli SPA* v. *Commission* [1984] ECR 1649 at 1662–1663. See also Cases 46/87 and 227/88 *Hoechst AG* v. *Commission* [1989] ECR 2859 at 2930–2931.
375. [1994] ECR I-2555 at 2652, upholding, on this point, on appeal, the view of the Court of First Instance in Cases T-79/89 *etc. BASF AG et al.* v. *Commission* [1992] ECR II-

made it plain that decisions finding an infringement of the competition rules of the EC Treaty may not be the subject of delegation to the holder of the competition portfolio. At the end of the day such decisions represent (subject to review by the Court of First Instance and/or the Court of Justice as appropriate) the final conclusion of proceedings affecting individuals which alter their legal position and can impose hefty fines or result in their having to repay state aid received contrary to Community law; they must therefore be adopted in accordance with the collegiate nature of the Commission and be authenticated as prescribed in the Commission's Rules of Procedure. The administrative or management decisions taken on behalf of the Commission by the member responsible for competition prior to the conclusion of the proceedings thus resemble a public law mandate rather than a real delegation of powers.

6.4.4 'Delegation' to Member States

Many Community acts provide for the adoption of implementing measures by the Member States and in these situations the national authorities may be seen as agents of the Community – even as bodies exercising a type of delegated power.[376] Thus, particularly in the regulation of common organizations of the market in agricultural products and in the collection of agricultural levies, customs duties and (to an extent) Value Added Tax, as well as in the payment of agricultural refunds, national authorities often appear as administrative extensions of the Community.[377] In these circumstances the Court is not afraid to speak of power delegated to the Member States.[378] However, the Court declines to attach any consequences to such delegation, maintaining the separation of responsibility strictly.[379] The close intertwining of Community and

315 at 348. The latter Court concluded that the procedural defects in the *PVC* saga were such as to render the purported decision non-existent. On appeal, though, the Court of Justice took the view that there had indeed been a decision (and consequently set aside the judgment of the Court of First Instance), but annulled that decision for breach of an essential procedural requirement (failure to authenticate the decision in the prescribed manner).

376. See Maas (1976) SEW 2 and Louis (1978) SEW 802–814.
377. See, generally, Barents, *The Agricultural Law of the EC* (Deventer, 1994) 62–64 and Louis, *The Community Legal Order* (3rd ed., Brussels, Luxembourg, 1995) 206 *et seq.*
378. Cases 213–215/81 *Norddeutsches Vieh- und Fleischkontor Herbert Will et al. v. Bundesanstalt für landwirtschaft-liche Marktordnung* [1982] ECR 3583 at 3599 on management of tariff quotas by the Member States. See the more general observations relating to the action of the Member States in the Community interest in areas in which the Community alone is competent in Case 804/79 *Commission v. United Kingdom* [1981] ECR 1045, [19821 1 CMLR 529 and Cases 47 and 48/83 *Pluimveestachterij Midden-Nederland BV et al.* [1984] ECR 1721 (see Chapter III, section 5.2.2, *ante*).
379. *Cf.* Cases 178–180/73 *Belgium and Luxembourg v. Mertens et al.* [1974] ECR 383 and

national administrations gives rise to unsatisfactory circumstances for litigants, particularly in relation to actions for damages, as they may be uncertain whether to sue (first of all) the national authorities or the Community or, indeed, both.[380]

6.4.5 Delegation to new international organs

The more the Community participates in international activities the more it will have to face the question of how far it can accord decision-making powers to international bodies established by agreements with third countries when Community law confers these powers in the internal sphere upon the Community Institutions. It appears from Opinion 1/76 *European Laying-up Fund for Inland Waterway Vessels*[381] that the Court regards this as lawful in so far as the powers accorded to the international body are clearly and precisely defined and limited.[382] In Opinion 1/91 *EEA I*[383] the Court confirmed that the Community is competent to conclude an international agreement providing for a system of courts whose decisions would be binding on the Contracting Parties, including the Community and its Institutions – including, therefore the Court of Justice itself. However, the Court found that the first draft of the EEA Agreement was incompatible with Article 164 EEC, and, more generally, with the very foundations of the Community as the proposed EEA Court would have had power to determine the interpretation not merely of provisions of the EEA Agreement itself but also, because of the proposed homogeneity between EEA rules and Community rules, of the corresponding rules of Community law.[384] The subsequent abandonment of the idea for an EEA Court and the assurance of the inviolability of the Court of Justice's case-law led the Court of Justice to find the revised draft agreement compatible with Community law.[385]

Case 110/76 *Pretore of Cento v. A person or persons unknown* [1977] ECR 851, [1977] 2 CMLR 515.
380. As to this point, see Chapter VI, section 1.3.3, *post*.
381. [1977] ECR 741, [1977] 2 CMLR 279.
382. [1977] ECR 741 at 759–760.
383. [1991] ECR I-6079 at 6106.
384. *Ibid.* at 6106–6107. The envisaged organic links (partial overlap of judges between the EEA Court and the Court of Justice was also found unacceptable (*ibid.* at 6108) as was the option of courts from EFTA States seeking purely advisory answers to requests for a preliminary ruling from the Court of Justice (*ibid.* at 6109–6110). There was, though, no objection to an international agreement conferring jurisdiction on the Court of justice to interpret provisions of such an agreement for the purpose of its implementation in non-Member States of the Community, nor did the Court of Justice object to the proposed variable geometry solution of allowing EFTA States to decide for themselves whether to authorize their courts or tribunals to make a reference, and if so whether there should be a power or an obligation to make a reference (*ibid.* at 6109).
385. See Opinion 1/92 *EEA II* [1992] ECR I-2821 at 2840 and 2843–2844.

7. THE COURT OF JUSTICE

7.1 One Institution, two bodies

Judicial supervision in the Community is exercised by one Institution, the Court of Justice.[386] The powers and tasks of this Institution are nowadays exercised by two bodies: the original Court of Justice of the European Communities,[387] and the Court of First Instance subsequently attached thereto.[388]

This means that the expression 'Court of Justice' means different things at different places in the Treaties. It may refer to the Institution as such, in which case the division of competence between the two bodies deals with the question which of the two is meant in any concrete case, or it may refer to the Court of Justice as body (as opposed to the Court of First Instance). Given that the division of competence between the two bodies has already changed, and may well evolve still further,[389] the discussion below uses the expression 'Court of Justice' to refer to the Court of Justice as a body, save where expressly otherwise stated, so that the Court of First Instance is separately discussed.

7.2 The Court of Justice

7.2.1 Composition, structure and procedure

The Court of Justice consists of fifteen Judges, assisted now by nine Advocates General.[390] It is the duty of the Advocates General 'acting with

386. Arts. 4(1) EC, 7 ECSC, and 3 Euratom (4th indent in each case).
387. The old ECSC Court was in effect taken over, and its membership adjusted (the criteria for appointment were brought into line with those specified in Arts. 167 EEC and 139 Euratom (1st para. in each case), which meant that a number of members of the old ECSC Court, who had a background in economics rather than law, were ineligible for appointment to the new Court), see Convention on certain Institutions common to the European Communities (signed on the occasion of the signature of the EEC and Euratom Treaties, 25 March 1957), Arts. 3 and 4.
388. By virtue of Arts. 168a EC, 32d ECSC, and 140a Euratom (originally added by the SEA and amended by the TEU). The original version of these provisions empowered the Council, acting unanimously at the request of the Court of Justice, after consulting the Commission and the European Parliament, to establish a Court of First Instance, which establishment was duly effected by Dec. 88/591 (O.J. 1988 L 319/1, corrected version in O.J. 1989 C 215/1), which was amended so as to enlarge the Court of First Instance's jurisdiction, by Dec. 93/350 (O.J. 1993 L 144/21, in turn amended by Dec. 94/149 (O.J. 1994 L 66/29)).
389. *E.g.* in relation to Art. 171 EC. See Lauwaars (1992) SEW 681; Van Gerven in Winter *et al.* (eds.) *Reforming the Treaty on European Union – The Legal Debate* (The Hague, 1996) 221; Hunnings, *The European Courts* (London, 1996) 159–175; and *The Role and Future of the European Court of Justice* (British Institute of International and Comparative Law Report, London, 1996).
390. Arts. 165 and 166 EC, 32 and 32a ECSC, and 137 and 138 Euratom (as amended by

complete impartiality and independence, to make, in open court, reasoned submissions on cases brought before the Court of Justice.'[391] The function of the Advocates General is modelled on that of the *commissaire du gouvernement* in the French *Conseil d'Etat*.[392] The task of the Advocates General is of great importance, particularly as their impartial submissions on law and on the facts form an extremely valuable basis on which the Court can arrive at its judgment.[393] The appointment of Judges and Advocates General has been uniformly regulated in the Treaties: they are appointed by common accord of the governments of the Member States,

Dec. 1/95 (O.J. 1995 L 1/1, which adjusted the Act of Austrian, Finnish and Swedish Accession (1994), as a result of Norway's non-accession to the Union). These provisions also enable the number of Judges and Advocates General to be increased by the Council, acting unanimously on a request from the Court of Justice, and the appropriate adjustments may be made to those provisions and to Arts. 167 EC, 32d ECSC, and 139 Euratom. The number of Advocates General is in fact eight, but provision was made for a ninth Advocate General to be appointed from the date of accession (1 January 1995) until 6 October 2000, as La Pergola, who had been appointed in October 1994 as the second Judge of Italian nationality (when there were twelve Member States there were thirteen judges, so that the full Court could sit with an uneven number of Judges), was appointed Advocate General (thereby ensuring an uneven number of Judges from the date of accession). While the Treaties use the hyphenated form (Advocates-General), usage since 1982 has preferred the unhyphenated form, see Brown and Kennedy, *The Court of Justice of the European Communities* (4th ed. (with 1995 suppl.), London, 1995) 60.

391. Arts. 166 EC, 32a ECSC, and 138 Euratom (2nd para. in each case).
392. See Barav (1974) 26 RDIC 809, Brown and Kennedy, *op. cit.*, (see note 390, *supra*) 60–69. See also Dashwood (1982) 2 LS 202; Gori (1976) CDE 375, Warner (1975) *Journal of the Law Society of Scotland* 47, and Hunnings, *op. cit.* (see note 389, *supra*) 56–59. Wyatt and Dashwood, *European Community Law* (3rd ed., London, 1993) 106 rightly note the widely held view that in the light of its development in the Community context the office of Advocate General must be regarded as *sui generis*.
393. Sometimes the Advocate General's Opinion will contain considerations entirely different from those raised by the parties, which are in fact then adopted by the Court. See *e.g.* Case 17/74 *Transocean Marine Paint Association v. Commission* [1974] ECR 1063 at 1079–1080 (Court) and 1088–1090 (Warner, Adv. Gen.), and Warner (1976) 14 JSPTL 15 at 18–19. Until the 1990s the Court made a practice of not referring to the Opinion, although this practice has now clearly been abandoned. Thus on occasions the Court has even expressly adopted the reasoning of the Advocate General entirely (*e.g.* Case C-284/91 *Belgian State v. Suiker Export NV* [1992] ECR I-5473 at 5483; Case C-59/92 *Hauptzollamt Hamburg-St. Annen v. Ebbe Sönnischsen GmbH* [1993] ECR I-2193 at 2210, and Case C-377/92 *Felix Koch Offenbach Couleur und Karamel GmbH v. Oberfinanzdirektion München* [1993] ECR I-4795 at 4810) or in part (*e.g.* Case Case C-36/92 P *Samenwerkende Elektriciteitsproduktie-bedrijven NV (SEP) v. Commission* [1994] ECR I-1911 at 1938), and it now quite frequently specifically adopts certain points made by the Advocate General (*e.g.* Case C-27/90 *Société industrielle de transformation de produits agricoles (Sipta) v. Office national inter-professionnel des fruits, des légumes et de l'horticulture (Oniflhor)* [1991] ECR I-133 at 158; Case C-426/93 *Germany v. Council* [1995] ECR I-3723 at 3753, and Case C-275/94 *Van der Linden v. Berufsgenossenschaft der Feinmechanik und Elektrotechnik* [1996] ECR I-1393 at 1413).

for a period of six years, and are chosen from 'persons whose independence is beyond doubt and who possess the qualifications required for appointment to the highest judicial offices in their respective countries or who are jurisconsults of recognized competence.'[394] Provisions relating to the taking of the oath, privileges and immunities, incompatible secondary functions, and deprivation of office are intended to ensure the independence of both Judges and Advocates General.[395] On the other hand the relatively short term of office which has been provided for is of doubtful wisdom, as is the fact that the appointment of Judges and Advocates General has been placed entirely in the hands of the governments. This forms far too small an institutional guarantee of their independence. Very great confidence indeed is thus placed both in the disinterestedness of the governments with respect to their appointment and in the moral qualities of the persons appointed, a confidence which so far has fortunately not been misplaced.[396] The limited tenure of the Judges is often used as the major reason for maintaining the practice of giving one single judgment, no matter how small the majority in favour of it, nor how contorted or conspicuous by absence the resulting reasoning, as looming reappointment might perhaps influence a Judge or incite a Member State to exert pressure upon a Judge. If dissenting judgments are ever introduced (and the arguments for and against are often discussed), this would have to be accompanied by a revision in the terms of tenure for the Judges. In this respect, the precedent of an eight-year non-renewable term for the

---

394. Arts. 167 EC, 32b ECSC, and 139 Euratom (1st para. in each case). Retiring Judges and Advocates General are eligible for reappointment, *ibid.* (4th para. in each case), and every three years there is a partial replacement of Judges (eight and seven judges alternately) and Advocates General (four on each occasion), *ibid.* (2nd and 3rd paras. in each case). Non-renomination has on occasions led to considerable controversy, see Everling), *Verhandlungen des 60. Deutschen Juristentags* (Munich, 1994) Vol. II N 9 at N 20–21, and if the Member States give no timely indication of their intentions the efficient planning of the Court's workload becomes well-nigh impossible. On one occasion the appointment of a Judge has even given rise to a petition being presented, see *Europe* No. 6565, p. 10 (18/19 Sept. 1995) and to a Written Question, both of which were somewhat unceremoniously brushed aside, see WQ P-2529/95 (Vandemeulebroucke) O.J. 1996 C 56/24. The European Parliament has called for its Legal Affairs Committee to 'meet with prospective members of the Court of Justice prior to their appointment' (O.J. 1994 C 61/126). As to the meaning of the word 'jurisconsults', see Lasok (K.P.E.), *The European Court of Justice, Practice and Procedure* (2nd ed., London, 1994) 14–15.
395. They are incorporated in the Statutes of the Court of Justice annexed as separate protocols to each Treaty (*cf.* Arts. 188 EC, 45 ECSC, and 160 Euratom, 1st para. in each case, and Arts. 2–4, 7 and 13 ECSC Statute, Arts. 2–4, 6 and 8 EC and Euratom Statutes) and in the Protocol on the Privileges and Immunities of the European Communities (Art. 21 with Arts. 12–15 and 18), annexed to the Merger Treaty. No use has been made of the procedure for removal from office (ECSC Statute, Art. 7; EC and Euratom Statutes, Art. 6).
396. Although see note 394, *supra.*

President, Vice-President and other members of the Executive Board of the European Central Bank is of interest.[397]

The Judges appoint from among their number a President for a period of three years; this appointment is renewable.[398] The Court appoints its Registrar.[399] In principle the Court sits in plenary session, but it may form Chambers, each consisting of three, five or seven judges, either to undertake certain preparatory enquiries or to adjudicate on particular categories of cases.[400] This means that the Court may now assign any case to a Chamber, including actions brought by Member States and appeals from the Court of First Instance, unless a Member State or a Community Institution which is a party to the proceedings requests that the case be decided in plenary session.[401] If a Chamber feels that a case should be decided by the full Court then it may refer the case to be heard in plenary session; this possibility is particularly useful if different Chambers have adopted different approaches (which has happened occasionally in staff

397. See Art. 109a(2)(b) EC, and Gormley and De Haan (1996) 21 ELRev. 95. In its Initial Contribution to the Intergovernmental Conference (*Proceedings of the Court of Justice and the Court of First Instance* No. 15/95) the Court, noting the interest of ensuring judicial independence, voiced no objection to extended, non-renewable tenure, but put no figure on what number of years might be appropriate. The *Reflection Group Report* for the 1996 Intergovernmental Conference (Council Secretariat-General, Brussels, 1995) noted that a majority of representatives favoured a nine-year term with no possibility of reappointment (point 121).

398. Arts. 167 EC, 32b ECSC, and 139 Euratom (5th para. in each case). The Advocates General choose one of their number to serve as First Advocate General for the year (which runs from October to October).

399. Arts. 168 EC, 32c ECSC, and 140 Euratom. So far there have been only four Registrars since the foundation of the ECSC Court: Albert van Houtte; Paul Heim; Jean-Guy Giraud, and the current Registrar, Roger Grass.

400. Arts. 165 EC, 32 ECSC, and 137 Euratom (2nd para. in each case), as amended by the Act of Austrian, Finnish and Swedish Accession, Art. 18). As to the rules laid down for these purposes, see *ibid.*, Art. 19, and Rules of Procedure (O.J. 1991 L 176/7, most recently amended, O.J. 1997 L 103/1 and 3), Art. 95. As to the determination of which judges will sit when cases are assigned to Chambers with a larger number of judges than seats for any given case (the First and Second Chambers currently have four members rather than three, and the Fifth and Sixth Chambers have seven judges, but the Court has decided that the latter will in fact sit as Chambers of five judges, see the Court's decisions of 25 January 1995 (O.J. 1995 C 54/2). As to the background, see Brown and Kennedy, *op. cit.* (see note 390, *supra*), 37–39 and update 3–4. See also Case C-7/94 *Landesamt für Ausbildungsförderung Nordrhein-Westfalen v. Gaal* [1995] ECR I-1031 at 1044–1045 (a manifestly ill-founded attack on the Court's autonomy of internal organization, *per* Adv. Gen. Tesauro, *ibid.* at 1034).

401. For the purposes of Rules of Procedure, Art. 95, *ibid.*, the expression 'a party to the proceedings' covers Member States or Community Institutions which are parties, interveners, or which have submitted written observations in any reference for a preliminary ruling or a reference under Art. 41 ECSC, see Rules of Procedure, Art. 103. Previously, the competence of Chambers was much more restricted, see Brown and Kennedy, *ibid.*

cases).[402] Judgments of Chambers have the same authority as judgments of the full Court.[403] The quorum for the full Court, sitting in plenary session, is now nine Judges[404] and the full Court often sits with 11 or 13 Judges, but less frequently with all 15. The Court of Justice is not formally bound by its own previous judgments[405] but it nevertheless tries to take steps to ensure uniformity and consistency in its approach, and increasingly it cites its earlier rulings in the reasoning of its judgments. That is not to say that it is not on occasion capable of spectacular about-turns and manifest deviations from earlier lines of authority.[406]

Since there are no Treaty provisions on the subject, the nationality of Judges and Advocates General has no legal relevance to their candidature for appointment.[407] In practice, though, the governments of the Member

402. See Case 110/75 *Mills v. European Investment Bank* [1976] ECR 955 and 1613. As examples of a Chamber referring a case to the full Court after having heard the Advocate General see Case 192/85 *Newstead v. Department of Transport et al.* [1987] ECR 4753, [1988] 1 CMLR 219 and Case 20/85 *Roviello v. Landesversicherungsanstalt Schwaben* [1988] ECR 2805, and after the hearing, Case C-370/89 *Société générale d'enterprises électro-méchaniques v. European Investment Bank* [1992] ECR I-6211. The decision to refer back may be made at any stage, Rules of Procedure (see note 400, *supra*), Rule 95(3). *Cf.* Cases T-177 and 377/94 *Altmann et al. v. Commission* [1996] ECR-SC IA-533; II-1471 with Cases 271/83 *etc. Ainsworth et al. v. Council* [1987] ECR 167 (in which the Court of First Instance was able to depart from an earlier judgment of the Court of Justice because of a changed situation, see, further, Chapter XI, section 5.8, *post*).

403. In the sense that a judgment of a chamber is as effective as a judgment of the full Court. The cases referred to chambers tend to be ones in which there is an already established body of case-law or in which the legal points are less fundamental. It is unthinkable, though, that a chamber would decide a case in a manner which was inconsistent with previous judgments of the full Court: it would refer the case to the full Court (which might pronounce only on certain points and refer the rest back to the chamber, as happened in Case 110/75 *Mills, ibid.*). On the authority of judgments generally, see Toth (1984) 4 YBEL 1.

404. ECSC Statute, Art. 18; EC and Euratom Statutes, Art. 15 (as amended by the Act of Accession (1994)). The EC Statute was subsequently amended, but not on this point, by Dec. 94/993 (O.J. 1994 L 379/1). See also rules of Procedure (see note 400, *supra*), Rule 26 (as amended in 1997).

405. See Koopmans in O'Keeffe and Schermers (eds.): *Essays in European Law and Integration* (Deventer, 1982) 11 and literature cited there; Arnull (1993) 30 CMLRev. 247; Brown and Kennedy, *op. cit.* (see note 390, *supra*) 343 *et seq.*, and Hunnings, *op. cit.* (see note 389, *supra*) 133–151.

406. *E.g.* Case C-10/89 *SA CNL-SUCAL NV v. HAG GF AG* [1990] ECR I-3711, [1990] 3 CMLR 571 reached a contrary result to that in Case 192/73 *Van Zuylen Frères v. Hag AG* [1974] ECR 731, [1974] CMLR 127 (rightly bowing to the chorus of criticism of the latter judgment). In Cases C-267 and 268/91 *Keck and Mithouard* [1993] ECR I-6097 at 6131 the Court controversially stood the analysis in a long line of cases on its head, see *e.g.* Gormley (1995) 5 EBLR 63 and (1996) 19 Fordh. J. Int'l. L. 866; Mattera (1994) RMUE 117, and (seeking to justify this) Joliet (1995) 1 Columb. J. Eur. L. 436. See, further, Chapter VII, section 3.2.1, *post*.

407. As to the interesting question of a Member State nominating someone who was a national of another Member State, see Lasok, *loc. cit.* (see note 394, *supra*).

States do look to nationality, there usually being one national of each Member Sate, and, unlike the unseemly situation which has on occasions surrounded the appointment of Presidents of the Commission (or, less often, of Members of the Commission), there is an informal understanding that Member States do not block each other's candidates. Nationality also plays a role in relation to the Advocates-General – the practice is that there is one each from the United Kingdom, Germany, Italy, France and now Spain, and three from the smaller Member States in turn.[408] Unlike in many international jurisdictions there is no system of appointing an *ad hoc* judge from a State which is party to proceedings but has no judge of its nationality on the tribunal.[409] The three Statutes of the Court of Justice prevent any party seeking a change in the composition of the Court or its Chambers on the ground of the nationality of a Judge or the absence of a Judge of the same nationality as that party.[410] In this manner the internal Community nature of the Court's jurisdiction in the Communities is emphasised.

The provisions governing procedure in the Court are to be found partly in the Statutes[411] and partly in the Rules of Procedure.[412] The Council may, at the Court's request and after consulting the Commission and the European Parliament, amend the provisions of the Statute relating to procedure (Title III) by unanimous vote.[413] The Rules of Procedure are laid down by the Court but they require the unanimous approval of the Council.[414] The procedure consists of three stages:

408. See the Joint Declaration on Dec. 95/1, Art. 31 (O.J. 1995 L 1/221). The list in the text, of course, totals eight, but, as already explained (see note 390, *supra*), Mr. La Pergola (an Italian) is presently in office as ninth Advocate General.
409. *Cf.* Statute of the International Court of Justice, Art. 31.
410. ECSC Statute, Art. 19; EC and Euratom Statutes, Art. 16 (4th para. in each case). See also ECSC and EC Statutes, Art. 44, Euratom Statute, Art. 45. See, further, in relation to the Court of First Instance, Case T-47/92 *Lenz et al. v. Commission* [1992] ECR II-2523 at 2531.
411. Annexed to the EC, ECSC and Euratom Treaties respectively, as amended by Dec. 88/591 (as to which, see note 388, *supra*). The EC Statute was subsequently amended by Dec. 94/993 (O.J. 1994 L 379/1).
412. See note 400, *supra*.
413. Arts. 188 EC, 45 ECSC, and 160 Euratom (2nd para. in each case, inserted by Arts. 5, 12, and 27 SEA).
414. Arts. 188 EC and Art. 160 Euratom (2nd para. in each case); ECSC Statute, Art. 55 (as renumbered by Dec. 88/591 (see note 388, *supra*), Art. 8). See, generally, Barents, *Procedures en Procesvoering voor het Hof van Justitie en het Gerecht van Eerste Aanleg van de Europese geneenschappen* (Deventer, 1996); Brown and Kennedy, *op. cit.* (see note 390, *supra*); Lasok, *op. cit.* (see note 394, *supra*); Edward (1995) 20 ELRev. 539; Lasok and Millett in Vaughan (ed.), *Law of the European Communities Service* (London, loose-leaf, since 1990, being a revision of what was originally the relevant part of 51 *Halsbury's Laws of England* (4th ed., London, 1986) Vol. I, Part 2 by Slynn, Lasok and Millett); Usher, *European Court Practice* (London, 1983, 2nd ed. in preparation); Slynn, *Introducing a European Legal Order* (43rd Hamlyn Lecture Series, London, 1992) 1–40, and Vandersanden and Barav: *Contentieux Communautaire* (Brussels, 1979).

(a) *written procedure*, starting with a request which is served on the defendant, followed by a statement of defence and a reply and a rejoinder, and finally the preliminary report of the Judge acting as *rapporteur* on whether the case requires investigation;[415]

(b) if the Court so decides, a stage of *investigation*, in connection with which witnesses and experts may be summoned and heard;[416]

(c) *oral procedure*, ending with submissions.[417]

Parties may only address the Court through their agents, legal advisers, or lawyer.[418] Member States and Institutions must be represented by an agent, who may be assisted by a legal adviser or by a lawyer who is a member of the bar of one of the Member States or of another state which is a party to the European Economic Area Agreement; other parties must be represented by a lawyer who is a member of such a bar.[419] Intervention by Member States or by other Institutions, including the Parliament,[420] is permitted.[421] Any other person who establishes that he or she has an interest in the result of any case submitted to the Court may be allowed to intervene in the proceedings, but individuals are not permitted to intervene in cases between Member States *inter se*, between Member States and the Community Institutions, or between the Community Institutions themselves.[422] The submissions contained in the application for intervention must be limited to supporting the form of order sought by one of the parties.[423]

---

415. Court's Rules of Procedure (see note 400, *supra*), Arts. 37–34. As to written procedure in references for preliminary rulings, see EC Statute (as amended by Dec. 94/993 (O.J. 1994 L 379/1)), Art. 20; Euratom Statute, Art. 21, and Rules of Procedure, Art. 103.

416. Rules of Procedure, *ibid.*, Rules 45–54.

417. *Ibid.*, Arts. 55–62. The oral procedure may be dispensed with in exceptional circumstances, *ibid.*, Art. 44a, see Lasok, *op. cit.* (see note 394, *supra*) 78–80.

418. EC Statute, Art. 29, ECSC Statute, Art. 28, 3rd para. and Euratom Statute, Art. 30. However, where, in references for preliminary rulings, national law permits litigants to appear in person, they may do this before the Court of Justice (as the proceedings are steps in the national proceedings), see Rules of Procedure (see note 400, *supra*), Art. 104(2).

419. EC Statute, Art. 17 (as amended by Dec. 94/993 (O.J. 1994 L 379/1), Art. 1. ECSC Statute, Art. 20 and Euratom Statute, Art. 17 still only refer to the bar of a Member State. An unpublished proposal to amend the rules of procedure to bring them into line with the EC Statute after the changes relating to the EEA States foundered in the Council (on the use of languages). It should be noted that the Court is very firm on deadlines, see *e.g.* the cases cited on time-limits in Chapter V, section 1.2, *post*.

420. Case 138/79 *SA Roquette Frères v. Council* [1980] ECR 3333 at 3357; Case 139/79 *Maizena GmbH v. Council* [1980] ECR 3393 at 3420.

421. EC Statute, Art. 37 (as amended by Dec. 94/993 (O.J. 1993 L 379/1). That amendment permits non-member States who are parties to the EEA Agreement, and the EFTA Surveillance Authority to intervene in cases before the Court where one of the fields of application of the Agreement is concerned.

422. EC Statute, Art. 37 (amended, *ibid.*, but not on this point), and Euratom Statute, Art. 38. The wording of ECSC Statute, Art. 34 is somewhat different.

423. EC Statute (as amended), Art. 37. The ECSC Statute, Art. 34, and Euratom Statute,

On references for a preliminary ruling the parties in the main proceedings before the national court[424] may submit a statement of case or written observations; there is, however, no obligation on them to do so. In any event, the parties may not change the tenor of the questions referred by the national judge, nor may they have them declared to be without purpose – it is the court or tribunal, not the parties, which refers the case to the Court of Justice.[425] While normally there will be an oral part in the proceedings on a reference, the Court may decide to dispense with that part, provided that no oral hearing has been requested by any person entitled to do so.[426] In order to cope with the sometimes wayward tendencies of national courts to refer questions manifestly identical to those on which the Court of Justice has already ruled, the Rules of Procedure provide for the possibility of making a reasoned order, referring to the previous judgment.[427]

The ever-increasing number of cases and the resulting prolongation of the length of time taken for a case to come to judgment have not made good administration of justice any easier. Indeed, in direct actions, improvements made inside the Commission in attempting to streamline procedures are to little avail if it is now going to take the Court on average some 19 months[428] to decide a case – by this time a complainant whose products are being kept out of a particular Member State because of national rules or practices may well have decided to sell his or her products elsewhere. While it is true that it is possible for interim measures to be

Art. 38 still provide that submissions on intervention must be limited to supporting the submissions of one of the parties. As to the rules on the language of the case see Chapter 2, section 5.4, *ante*.

424. The Court of Justice sees a reference for a preliminary ruling as being a step in the national proceedings, see Rules of Procedure (see note 400, *supra*), Art. 104(2) and *e.g.* Case 62/72 *Bollmann v. Hauptzollamt Hamburg Waltershof* [1973] ECR 269 at 275 and Case 313/82 *NV Tiel-Utrecht Schadeloosverzekering v. Gemeenschappelijk Motorwaarborgfonds* [1984] ECR 1389 at 1402, which mean that due account is taken of the rules of procedure of the referring court, Rules of Procedure, Art. 104(2). As such, national legal aid is available for references, see *R. v. Marlborough Street Stipendiary Magistrate, ex parte Bouchereau* [1977] 1 WLR 414 (Div. Ct, QBD). See, further, Usher, *op. cit.* (see note 414, supra) 328–329. The Court of Justice can grant legal aid under Rules of Procedure, Art. 76 (contentious proceedings) or Art. 104(5) (references for a preliminary ruling), see Lasok, *op. cit.* (see note 394, *supra*) 143–152.

425. See Case 44/65 *Hessische Knappschaft v. Maison Singer et Fils* [1965] ECR 965 at 970.

426. Rules of Procedure (see note 400, *supra*), Art. 104(4). See *e.g.* Case C-79/91 *Knüfer et al. v. Buchmann* [1992] ECR I-6895 at 6907–6908 (Jacobs, Adv. Gen.).

427. *Ibid.*, Art. 104(3). A national court is free to refer an identical question, see Cases 28–30/62 *Da Costa en Schaake NV et al.v. Nederlandse Belastingadministratie* [1963] ECR 31 at 38, but it may be that a flood of identical references arrives, which can best be dealt with by a brief judgment to which is annexed a copy of the earlier judgment: see *e.g.* Case 168/86 *Procureur général v. Rousseau* [1987] ECR 996 at 1002.

428. In 1996 the average was 19.6 months, in 1997 19.7 months (see the Court's *Annual Report* for those years).

requested, it is only occasionally done at present and the results are unpredictable.[429] It is also true that a complainant can go to a national court to seek redress, but it is unfortunately still the case that he or she may not always find that the national court is receptive to Community law points. If a national court makes a reference – and the number of references is increasing – it now takes on average some 21 months before the Court of Justice gives its ruling.[430] Such a long delay endangers a satisfactory system of judicial protection which requires speedy legal process; it also risks endangering good cooperation between national courts and the Court of Justice in ensuring the uniform interpretation and application of Community law. Even appeals against judgments of the Court of First Instance are taking now on average some 17 months to be dealt with.[431] There are, though, a number of major problems which the Court has had to cope in recent years: numerous new judges have been appointed, either at the end of their predecessors' mandates, or on the accession of new Member States, or to replace judges who have deceased; there has been a real explosion not only in the number of cases, but also in their complexity; the procedural time-scales and delays caused by interventions also impose constraints, and, finally, the translation resources have been ever-more hard-pressed to cope with the increased workload (caused *inter alia* by the greater complexity and volume of pleadings in cases coming to the Court of First Instance), not least because the budgetary authority has not always been wholly supportive in permitting an increased allocation of resources.

7.2.2   Duties and powers of the Court of Justice

The Court, under Articles 164 EC, 31 ECSC and 136 Euratom, ensures the observance of law in the interpretation and application of the treaties and their implementing rules. To this end, a number of powers have been expressly conferred on the Court, and its powers are limited to those conferred upon it.[432] These are mainly intended to enable the Court to

---

429. See *e.g.* Case 154/85 R *Commission v. Italy* [1985] ECR 1753; Case 45/87 R *Commission v. Ireland* [1987] ECR 783 and 1369, [1987] 2 CMLR 197 and 563, and Case C-120/94 R *Commission v. Greece* [1994] ECR I-3037; although see also case 194/88 R *Commission v. Italy* [1988] ECR 5647 and Case C-195/90 *Commission v. Germany* [1990] ECR I-3351. An action for interim measures may sometimes be withdrawn on a Member State's undertaking, see Case C-243/89 *Commission v. Denmark* [1993] ECR I-3353 at 3360. See, further, section 7.4, *post*.
430. In 1996 an average of 20.8 months, in 1997 21.4 months.
431. In 1996 an average of 14 months, in 1997 17.4 months.
432. In accordance with the concept of attribution of powers in Community law. But the Court is perfectly capable of taking a specific power and applying it by analogy, where it appears eminently sensible to do so, *e.g.* Case C-295/90 *European Parliament*

judge the acts and omissions of the Institutions and the Member States in accordance with Community law, and to ensure uniformity of interpretation of Community law in the application of this law by national courts. The conditions under which and the manner in which the Court is required to exercise the powers which form part of this heart of its jurisdiction will be discussed more fully in Chapter VI, below. The present discussion concentrates on a broad survey of the various powers of the Court and a number of aspects of its jurisdiction and of the functions which it performs within the Communities. This discussion deals mainly with the relevant provisions of the EC Treaty.

The powers of the Court can be divided into three categories: the settling of disputes, the giving of binding opinions,[433] and the giving of preliminary rulings. An examination of the first and most extensive category of these powers shows that the jurisdiction of the Court extends to disputes about the interpretation and application of Community law between the Institutions, between Member States, and between Institutions and Member States or private parties. It is a hallmark of the Court of Justice of the European Communities that it is relatively widely accessible to private persons who wish their Community rights to be upheld. In this it differs from most international courts, before which (apart from the case of administrative tribunals settling disputes between international organizations and their officials) private parties cannot as a rule appear as parties to the proceedings.

In the domain of settling disputes the Court acts in the first place as the administrative court (in the continental sense) for the Communities, whose duty it is to protect the legal subjects, Member States as well as private persons, against the illegal acts or omissions of the Institutions. The Court usually exercises this administrative jurisdiction[434] when it is seised of:

(1) an action for annulment of the legal acts of the European Parliament and the Council acting jointly, the Council, the Commission and the European Central Bank (ECB)[435] (see also judgments on the

---

v. Council [1992] ECR I-4193 at 4237 (maintaining the effects of an annulled directive for important reasons of legal certainty, until it was replaced by a directive adopted on the correct legal basis, whereas Art. 174 EC (and Art. 147 Euratom) confer this power only in relation to regulations).

433. This happens only occasionally, although the frequency has increased recently as the Community becomes active in ever-increasing spheres of activity on the international plane.

434. As to the rules on execution of judgments of the Court so far as private parties are concerned see the final part of Chapter V, section 1.5, post.

435. Arts. 173 EC, 33 ECSC, and 146 Euratom. In actions brought by private parties this jurisdiction is now exercised by the Court of First Instance, subject to appeal to the Court of Justice itself on a point of law only. For a special form of appeal see Art. 37 ECSC. The Court of Justice also has jurisdiction under Art. 180(b) EC in actions brought by any Member State, the Commission or the board of Directors of the European Invest-

validity of acts of the Community Institutions given in rulings on references for preliminary rulings[436] and in relation to the plea of illegality concerning regulations of the European Parliament and the Council acting jointly, the Council, the Commission and the ECB);[437]

(2) an action for a declaration that, in infringement of the Treaty, the Council or the Commission has failed to act;[438]

(3) an action against administrative penalties – an instance of unlimited jurisdiction;[439]

(4) a claim for damages on the basis of the non-contractual liability of the Communities;[440]

(5) an action based on an arbitration clause in a contract concluded by or on behalf of the Communities;[441]

---

ment Bank (EIB) against decisions adopted by the Board of Governors of the EIB (the grounds are those specified in Art. 173 EC). It further has jurisdiction under Art. 180(c) EC in actions brought by Member States or by the Commission against measures adopted by the Board of Directors of the EIB, under the conditions laid down in Art. 173 EC, solely on the grounds of non-compliance with the procedure provided for in Statute of the EIB (annexed to the EC Treaty), Art. 21(2), (5), (6) and (7).

436. Arts. 177 EC and 150 Euratom (1st para., point (b) in each case), and 41 ECSC.

437. Arts. 184 EC, 36 para. 3rd ECSC (decisions or recommendations), and 156 Euratom.

438. Arts. 175 EC, 35 ECSC, and 148 Euratom. In actions brought by private parties this jurisdiction is now exercised by the Court of First Instance, subject to appeal to the Court of Justice itself on a point of law only.

439. Arts. 172 EC, 36 ECSC and 144(b) Euratom. In actions brought by private parties this jurisdiction is now exercised by the Court of First Instance, subject to appeal to the Court of Justice itself on a point of law only. The unlimited jurisdiction under Art. 144(a) Euratom still rests entirely with the Court of Justice itself. This means that the relevant Court may raise, lower or annul such penalties. The Court of Justice as an Institution has thus a certain penal jurisdiction (but not in the sense of criminal law).

440. Arts. 178 EC, 40 ECSC (as amended by Merger Treaty, Art. 26), and 151 Euratom. In actions brought by private parties this jurisdiction is now exercised by the Court of First Instance, subject to appeal to the Court of Justice itself on a point of law only.

441. Arts. 181 EC, 42 ECSC, and 153 Euratom. The jurisdiction applies whether the contract is governed by public or private law, *ibid.* See *e.g.* Case 23/76 *Pellegrini v. Commission* [1976] ECR 1807, [1977] 2 CMLR 77; Case 426/85 *Commission v. Zoubek* [1986] ECR 4057, [1988] 1 CMLR 257, and Case C-42/94 *Heidemij Advies BV v. European Parliament* [1995] ECR I-1417. In actions brought by private parties this jurisdiction is now exercised by the Court of First Instance, subject to appeal to the Court of Justice itself on a point of law only, but, if the action is brought by a Community Institution, it goes straight to the Court of Justice itself. Contracts concluded before the date of entry into force of Dec. 93/350 (O.J. 1993 L 241/21, *i.e.* 1 August 1993) still fall within the purview of the Court of Justice itself, irrespective of which side initiates the action, *ibid.*, Art.3, 2nd para. (unaffected by Dec. 94/149 (O.J. 1994 L 66/29)). See *e.g.* Case C-76/95 *Commission v. Royale Belge SA* [1996] ECR I-5501; Case C-114/94 *Intelligente Systemen, Database toepassingen, Elektronische diensten BV (IDE) v. Commission* [1997] ECR I-803, and Case C-224/96 *SA Promotion Léopold v. European Parliament* (pending, O.J. 1996 C 269/6).

The Court acts more like an international court in the following types of cases:

(6) disputes between the Commission and Member States or between Member States themselves about a Member State's failure to fulfil its obligations under one of the Treaties;[442]
(7) disputes between Member States in connection with the subject-matter of the Treaties, which are submitted to the Court under a special agreement.[443]

The Court acts as a constitutional court if it has to deliver an opinion[444] on whether:

(8) amendments in the so-called 'small' revision of the ECSC Treaty[445] conform to the provisions laid down by the Treaty thereon;
(9) agreements concluded by the EC[446] or by Member States within the

---

442. Arts. 169 and 170 EC, 88 ECSC, and 141 and 142 Euratom. The Court also has jurisdiction under Art. 180(a) EC in disputes brought concerning the fulfilment by the Member States of obligations arising under the EIB Statute, in which case the Board of Directors of the EIB enjoy the powers conferred on the Commission under Art. 169 EC. Further, the Court has jurisdiction under Art. 180(d) EC in disputes concerning the fulfilment by national central banks of obligations under the EC Treaty and the Statute of the European System of Central Banks (ESCB) annexed to the EC Treaty. In this connection the powers of the Council of the European Central Bank (ECB) are the same as those conferred on the Commission in respect of Member States under Art. 169 EC. If the Court of Justice finds that a national central bank has failed to fulfil an obligation under the EC Treaty, that bank is required to take the necessary measures to comply with the judgment of the Court of Justice, Art. 180(d) EC. The Treaty of Amsterdam (not yet in force) will introduce, in the new Art. K.7(7) jurisdiction in certain disputes between the Member States about the interpretation of acts adopted under the new Art. K.6 TEU, or between Member States and the Commission on the interpretation or application of Conventions adopted under the new Art. K.6(2)(d) TEU.

443. Arts. 182 EC, 89 ECSC, 2nd para., and 154 Euratom.

444. The EC Treaty uses the term 'opinion' and it seems from the context of Art. 228 EC that this has the same force as a binding judgment. The terms 'ruling' and, 'adjudicating' are used in Art. 103 Euratom. See Van Dijk (1979) SEW 190.

445. Art. 95 ECSC, 4th and 5th paras.

446. Art. 228(6) EC. The Court considers that an 'agreement' for these purposes is 'any undertaking entered into by entities subject to international law which has binding force, whatever its formal designation': Opinion 1/75 *OECD Understanding on a Local Cost Standard* [1975] ECR 1355 at 1360. This concerned a binding resolution of the OECD Council: the Understanding covered export credits and guarantees. In giving its opinion on the proposed agreement the Court allowed itself room to opine on the division of competence between the Member States on the one hand and the Community on the other, a subject on which there was a clear difference of opinion. See Maas (1976) SEW 322–324. There need not actually be a draft agreement already prepared: it may well be that a Community institution seeks the opinion of the Court on the general competence to accede to an existing agreement, see Opinion 2/94 *Accession*

field of application of Euratom[447] are compatible with the respective Treaties.

In the case of the so-called small revision of the ECSC Treaty the Court judges the amendments by reference to the rules laid down in the 3rd paragraph of Article 95 ECSC. This provides in particular that these amendments should not affect Articles 2, 3 and 4 ECSC (which, along with Article 5 ECSC, are considered by the Court to be essential to that Treaty) nor upset the institutional balance. Thus they may not change the relationship between the powers conferred respectively on the High Authority (*i.e.* the Commission) and the other Institutions of the Community. This rule was supplemented by the Court itself when it added the prohibition against modifying the division of powers between the High Authority (the Commission) on the one hand and the Member States on the other as embodied in the ECSC Treaty.[448] In numerous opinions given under Article 228(6) EC (or its predecessor, Article 228(1) EEC) and in a ruling under Article 103 Euratom the Court has expanded its constitutional function through making important observations on the ambit of the Community's external competence.[449] This point is discussed further in Chapter XI, below.

The function of the Court as a constitutional court is not, however, exhausted by these heads of jurisdiction. In contentious proceedings, chiefly in an action for annulment or in an action to have an infringement of a Treaty provision by a Member State established,[450] the Court helps to safeguard the maintenance of the basic structural provisions of the Treaties as well as the complicated balance of powers which they establish between the Institutions and between the Communities and the Member States. Moreover, an action for annulment in certain cases creates a particular opportunity to examine whether the Community

by the Communities to the European Convention on Human Rights [1996] ECR I-1759 at 1785–1786.

447. Art. 103 Euratom, 3rd para.
448. Opinion 1/60 *Revision of the ECSC Treaty II* [1960] ECR 39.
449. Opinion 1/75 *OECD Understanding on a Local Cost Standard* [1975] ECR 1355, [1976] 1 CMLR 75; Opinion 1/76 *Laying-Up fund for Inland Waterway Vesels* [1977] ECR 741, [1977] 2 CMLR 278; Opinion 1/78 *International Agreement on Natural Rubber* [1979] ECR 2871, [1979] 3 CMLR 639; Ruling 1/78 *Draft IAEA Convention on the Physical protection of Nuclear Materials, Facilities and Transports* [1978] ECR 2151; Opinion 1/91 *EEA Agreement I* [1991] ECR I-6079, [1992] 1 CMLR 245; Opinion 2/91 *ILO Convention 170 on Safety in the use of Chemicals at Work* [1993] ECR I-1061, [1993] 3 CMLR 800; Opinion 1/92 *EEA Agreement II* [1992] ECR I-2821, [1992] 2 CMLR 217; Opinion 2/92 *Third Revised Decision of the OECD on National Treatment* [1995] ECR I-521, [1996] 2 CMLR 325; Opinion 1/94 *WTO – GATS and TRIPs* [1994] ECR I-5267, [1995] 1 CMLR 205; Opinion 2/94 *Accession by the Communities to the European Convention on Human Rights* [1996] ECR I-1759, [1996] 32 CMLR 265, and Opinion 3/94 *Framework Agreement on Bananas* [1995] ECR I-4577.
450. Heads (1) and (6) above.

legislation concerned is compatible with the Treaties. This examination deals, as the Court has indicated,[451] with the constitutionality of quasi-legislative acts emanating from a public authority and which have a normative effect *erga omnes*. It is on this very ground that the right to seek the annulment of such acts has been virtually refused to private persons under the Treaties.[452] Although, looked at from the point of view of their form, the activities of the Court in the contentious proceedings mentioned here more or less resemble those of an administrative or international court, looked at from the viewpoint of their content they resemble a 'constitutional' jurisdiction.[453]

In the majority of the cases discussed above the jurisdiction of the Court is based directly on the European Treaties. This can be described as an obligatory jurisdiction, *i.e.* a jurisdiction which is exercised by the Court to the exclusion of national[454] or international[455] judicial bodies. In a number of cases, however, the Treaties also provide for an optional jurisdiction of the Court, *i.e.* a jurisdiction the compulsory character of which depends on the existence of a particular unilateral or multilateral legal act other than a Treaty provision, which then forms the legal basis for jurisdiction.[456]

A unilateral legal act as the legal basis for jurisdiction is found, for instance, in Regulation 11[457] and in a host of regulations in the

---

451. Case 8/55 *Fédération Charbonnière de Belgique v. High Authority* [1954–56] ECR 245 at 258. See also Case 18/57 *J. Nold KG v. High Authority* [1957 and 1958] ECR 121 at 123–124.

452. See Chapter VI, section 1.3, *post*.

453. See, generally, Curtin and O'Keeffe (eds.), *Constitutional Adjudication in European Community Law and National Law* (Dublin, 1992).

454. Arts. 183 EC, 40 3rd para. ECSC, and 155 Euratom.

455. Arts. 219 EC, 87 ECSC, and 193 Euratom.

456. Jurisdiction is conferred on the Court, outside the framework of the Treaties, to give preliminary rulings on the Conventions (concluded on the basis of Art. 220 EC) on the mutual recognition of companies and legal persons (Bull. EC Supp. 7/71) and jurisdiction and enforcement of judgments (O.J. 1978 L 304/50 (as subsequently amended), see the latest consolidated version of the Convention and the Protocol in O.J. 1998 C 27/1 *et seq.*). Similar jurisdiction was conferred on the Court by two protocols of 19 December 1988 (O.J. 1988 L 48/1 and 17) in respect of the Rome Convention on the Law applicable to Contractual Obligations (O.J. 1980 L 266/1, in force from 1 April 1991, although the Protocols are not yet in force; see the consolidated version of the Convention and the Protocols in O.J. 1998 C 27/34 *et seq.*). Art. 111(3) EEA (O.J. 1994 L 1/1 at 27, in force since 1 January 1994) confers jurisdiction on the Court to give a ruling, at the request of the Contracting Parties to a dispute, on the interpretation of the provisions of the EEA Agreement which are in substance identical to corresponding rules of the EC or ECSC Treaties and acts adopted in pursuance thereof. Certain powers are also conferred on the Court under the Community Patent Convention (O.J. 1989 L 401/1), which is not yet in force. See, further, Chapter VI, section 2.1, *post*.

457. O.J. English Special Edition 1959–62, p. 60 (Art. 25). This deals with the elimination of discrimination in relation to freight prices and transport conditions.

competition field,[458] in which by virtue of Article 172 EEC[459] the Council conferred unlimited jurisdiction on the Court with reference to the administrative penalties laid down therein. A similar basis is also found in the Staff Regulations adopted by the Council[460] in which the settlement of disputes between the Communities and their servants is entrusted to the Court by virtue of the relevant Treaty articles.[461] The Court has also recently been entrusted with appeals against decisions of a Board of Appeal of the Office for Harmonization in the Internal Market (trade marks and designs) or of the Community Plant Variety Office.[462]

Jurisdiction based on a multilateral legal act can be derived by the Court from an arbitration clause in contracts,[463] from a special agreement between Member States in the matter of a dispute connected with the subject-matter of the Treaties,[464] or from a convention in accordance with Article K.2(c) TEU.[465]

---

458. Regs. 17 (O.J. English Special Edition 1959–62, p. 87 (Art. 17)); 1017/68 (O.J. English Special Edition, 1968 (II), p. 301 (Art. 24)); 4056/86 (O.J. 1986 L 378/4 (Art. 21)); 3975/87 (O.J. 1987 L 374/1 (Art. 14)), and 4064/89 (as corrected, O.J. 1990 L 257/14 (Art. 16)).

459. Now Art. 172 EC (embracing also regulations adopted by the European Parliament and the Council jointly).

460. Reg. 259/68 (O.J. English Special Edition 1968 (1), p. 30 (as subsequently amended) (Arts. 22 and 91). See head (3), *supra.*

461. See Arts. 179 (and 215, 4th para.) EC, 40 ECSC, 2nd para. (as amended by Merger Treaty, Art. 26), and 152 (and 188, 3rd para.) Euratom. This jurisdiction is now exercised by the Court of First Instance, subject to appeal to the Court of Justice on a point of law only. Under Art. 43 ECSC, 2nd para., the Court may also rule in cases relating to the subject matter of that Treaty where jurisdiction is conferred upon it by the law of a Member State. There is no equivalent provision in the EC and Euratom Treaties.

462. For the Office for Harmonisation in the Internal Market, see Reg. 40/94 (the Community Trade Mark Regulation, O.J. 1994 L 11/1), Art. 63, which provides for appeal by any party to the proceedings adversely affected by a decision of a Board of Appeal. The grounds of appeal and time limits are the same as those applicable for appeals against acts of the Community institutions. Unlike those appeals, though, the Court has plenary jurisdiction in that it can not merely annul a decision of a Board of Appeal but can alter the decision, Art. 63(3). *Cf.* Chapter VI, section 1.3.1, *post.* Appeals will in fact come before the Court of First Instance, subject to appeal on a point of law only to the Court of Justice itself. The same applies in respect of the Community Plant Variety Office, see Reg. 2100/94 (the Community Plant Variety Rights Regulation, O.J. 1994 L 227/1), Arts. 73 and 74, save that the Court does not there have such plenary jurisdiction, and is confined to the marginal examination which normally applies in respect of appeals against acts of the Community Institutions. Under *ibid.*, Art. 73(3) the Commission and the Plant Variety Office are also entitled to appeal (which in the case of the Commission would be heard by the Court of Justice, not the Court of First Instance).

463. See Head (5) above and note 441, *supra.*

464. See Head (7), above.

465. *E.g.* the Protocol on the Europol Convention (O.J. 1996 C 299/2), attached to the Act of the Council, recommending that the Member States ratify that Protocol, in accor-

The jurisdiction of the Court discussed so far does not cover all cases in which there may be a question of judicial application of Community law. In disputes between Member States and private persons or between private persons themselves[466] questions relating to the interpretation and application of Community law may arise before a national court. In this field, too, a specific type of jurisdiction has been conferred on the Court. It is competent:

(10) to pronounce by way of a preliminary ruling on the interpretation of the Treaty provisions and on the validity and the interpretation of acts of the Institutions of the Communities if a question on this subject is raised before a national court or tribunal.[467]

Such a court or tribunal may, or (if it functions as a jurisdiction from which there is no appeal, which need not be a court of final instance) must request such a ruling from the Court.[468] Thanks to this jurisdiction the Court is able to promote the uniformity of interpretation of Community law in the legal practice of the Member States. In the discussion of references for a preliminary ruling[469] it will become apparent that as a consequence of this jurisdiction the Court can, in co-operation with national courts, make a real contribution to the judicial control of the observance of Community law by the Member States, and thus to the legal

dance with their respective constitutional requirements (O.J. 1996 C 299/1), see, further, Chapter II, section 1.3.2, *ante*. The Treaty of Amsterdam (not yet in force) will introduce in the new Art. K.7 TEU an optional acceptance of the jurisdiction of the Court of Justice to give preliminary rulings, under the conditions set out in that provision (which include the option to limit the right to make references to courts against whose judgment there is no appeal).

466. Or in disputes between the Communities and private persons on contracts concluded by them or on their behalf if they do not entrust their settlement to the Court. The practical importance of this national jurisdiction is, though, very small (see Chapter II, section 5.2., *ante*).

467. Arts. 177 EC and 150 Euratom (and, rather more restrictively, Art. 41 ECSC). As to Art. 177 references generally, see Andenas (ed.), *Article 177 References to the European Court – Policy and Practice* (London, 1994); Anderson (1994) 14 YBEL 179; Chevalier and Maidani, *Guide Pratique Article 177 CEE* (Luxembourg, 1982); Daig in Grewe *et al.* (eds.), *Europäische Gerichtsbarkeit und nationaler Verfassungsgerichtsbarkeit* (*Festschrift* for Kutscher, Baden-Baden, 1981) 135; Pescatore, References for preliminary rulings under Article 177 of the EEC Treaty and cooperation between the Court and national courts (Luxembourg, 1986), and Schermers *et al.* (eds.), *Article 177 EEC: Experiences and Problems* (Amsterdam, 1987). The Treaty of Amsterdam (not yet in force) will provide for the limited application of Art. 177 EC in respect of the new Title on visa, asylum, immigration and other policies related to the free movement of persons, so that only a national court against the decision of which there is no judicial remedy will make a reference, see the new Art. 73p EC.

468. Unlike under Art. 41 ECSC which concerns only rulings on the validity of acts of the Commission and the Council; there the reference is obligatory.

469. See Chapter VI, section 2.1, *post*.

protection of individuals against acts of those Member States which infringe Community law.

The Court of Justice itself, finally, has jurisdiction:

(11) to hear appeals on points of law only from the Court of First Instance.[470]

7.3 The Court of First Instance

7.3.1 Composition, structure and procedure

The composition of the Court of First Instance is determined by the Council at the request of the Court of Justice, and after consulting the European Parliament and the Commission.[471] The Court of First Instance consists of 15 members, who elect their President from among their number for a period of three years; he or she is eligible for re-election.[472] It has no permanent Advocates General: a Judge may be called upon to perform the task of an Advocate General in a particular case,[473] and in such circumstances his or her function in that case is identical to that of an Advocate General of the Court of Justice.[474] The method of appointment of Judges of the Court of First Instance is also identical to that of Judges

---

470. Arts. 168a(1) EC, 32d(1) ECSC, and 140a(1) Euratom; ECSC and EC Statutes, Art. 49; Euratom Statute, Art. 50. See, further, section 7.3.1, *post*.

471. Arts. 168a(2) EC, 32d(2) ECSC, and 140a(2) Euratom. See, generally, Biancarelli (1990) RTDE 1; Brown and Kennedy, *op. cit.* (see note 390, *supra*) 70–100 and 1995 update 10–13; Cruz Vilaça (1990) 10 YBEL 1; Due (1988) 9 YBEL 1; Hunnings, *op. cit.* (see note 389, *supra*) 184–229; Kirschner, *Das Gericht erster Instanz der Europaäischen Gemeinschaften* (Cologne, 1995); Kennedy (1989) 14 ELRev. 7 and (1990) 15 ELRev. 54; Lasok, *op. cit.* (see note 394, *supra*) 8–21, 57–62, 94–97 and 472–488; Lenaerts (1990) SEW 527; Joliet and Vogel (1989) RMC 423; Millett (1989) 38 ICLQ 811; Millett, *The Court of First Instance of the European Communities* (London, 1990); Tizzano and Capponi (1990) *Il Foro Italiano* 438, and Vesterdorf (1992) 29 CMLRev. 897.

472. Dec. 88/591 (O.J. 1988 L 319/1, corrected version in O.J. 1989 C 215/1) Art. 2(1) and (2), as amended on this point by Dec. 1/95 (O.J. 1995 L 1/1), Art. 10, which amended Act of Austrian, Finnish and Swedish Accession (1994), Art. 17(2).

473. Dec. 88/591, *ibid.*, Art. 2(3). The Judge called upon so to act then takes no part in the judgment of the case, *ibid*. The Court of First Instance has only sparingly made use of this possibility: see Cases T-51/89 *Tetra Pak Rausing SA v. Commission* [1990] ECR II-309 at 312; Cases T-1/89 *Rhône-Poulenc SA v. Commission* [1991] ECR II-867 at 869; Case T-120/89 *Stahlwerke Peine-Salzgitter v. Commission* [1991] ECR II-279 at 282, and the single Opinion given in Case T-24/90 *Automec srl v. Commission* and Case T-28/90 *Asia Motor France SA et al. v. Commission* [1992] ECR II-2223 at 2226 (2285 at 2287 refers to 2226). As to the selection of who is to act as Advocate General and the criteria for deciding when to designate one, see Rules of Procedure (see note 476, *infra*), Arts. 17–19.

474. See section 7.2.1, *ante*.

and Advocates General of the Court of Justice, save that the qualification for appointment is less stringent.[475] The provisions as to the oath of office, privileges and immunities and so on are also identical.[476] The Court of First Instance sits in Chambers of three or five Judges[477] (a five Judge Chamber is referred to as a Chamber in extended composition), although in certain circumstances the Court may sit in plenary session.[478] Thus whenever the legal difficulty or the importance of the case or special circumstances so justify, a case may be heard in plenary session, or by a Chamber composed of a different number of Judges.[479]

The regulation of procedure before the Court of First Instance is to be found in part in the Statutes[480] and in part in the Rules of Procedure,[481] the latter being established by the Court of First Instance, in agreement with the Court of Justice and requiring the unanimous approval of the Council.[482] This procedure is designed to be as close as possible to that of the Court of Justice itself, and is thus largely similar to that followed by the Court of Justice in direct actions for annulment or actions against failure to act.[483] The major innovation, compared with procedure before the Court of Justice, is that the Court of First Instance plays a much more

475. Judges of the Court of First Instance must possess the ability required for appointment to judicial office, Arts. 168a(3) EC, 32d(3) ECSC, and 140a(3) Euratom (as opposed to the highest judicial office). The requirement further differs from that for Judges and Advocates General of the Court of Justice in that there is no link between the judicial office and their respective countries, nor are jurisconsults of recognized competence eligible for appointment.

476. Save as otherwise provided by the Council, the provisions of the Treaties relating to the Court of Justice, and in particular those of the Protocols on the Statutes of the Court of Justice, apply to the Court of First Instance, Arts. 168a(2) EC, 32d(2) ECSC, and 140a(2) Euratom. Dec. 88/591 (as amended, see note 472, *supra*), Art. 2(5) provides that the Protocol on Privileges and Immunities, Art. 21, and Merger Treaty, Art. 6 apply to the members of the Court of First Instance and its Registrar. But the procedure as to deprivation of office, pension or other benefits first involves deliberation by the Court of First Instance, before the matter is considered by the Court of Justice, see Rules of Procedure of the Court of First Instance (O.J. 1991 L 136/1, corrigendum, O.J. 1991 L 317/34, most recently amended O.J. 1997 L 103/6), Rule 5. The Court of First Instance appoints its Registrar, EC and ECSC Statutes, Art. 45; Euratom Statute, Art. 46, and Rules of Procedure, Art. 20.

477. Dec. 88/591 (as amended, *ibid.*), Art. 2(4). As to the detailed rules governing the assignment of cases to the various Chambers, see O.J. 1994 C 304/14.

478. *Ibid.* In this case the quorum is nine judges, Rules of Procedure, Art. 32(2), as amended.

479. Rules of Procedure, Art. 14.

480. EC and ECSC Statutes, Arts. 44–54 (see particularly Art. 46); Euratom Statute, Arts. 45–55 (see particularly, Art. 47).

481. See note 476, *supra*.

482. Arts. 168a(4) EC, 32d(4) ECSC, and 140a(4) Euratom. See also EC and ECSC Statutes, Art. 46, and Euratom Statute, Art. 47. See also the Guidelines for lawyers and agents for the written procedure in the Court of First Instance (O.J. 1994 C 120/16).

483. Under Arts. 173 EC, 33 or 38 ECSC, or 146 Euratom (annulment), or 175 EC, 35 ECSC, or 148 Euratom (failure to act).

active role in steering the proceedings: thus it may prescribe any 'measure of organization of procedure'[484] designed to promote the efficiency and clarification of the proceedings, and to facilitate an amicable settlement of the dispute. Thus the aim is to ensure that cases are prepared for hearing, procedures carried out and disputes resolved under the best possible conditions.[485]

Appeal against judgments of the Court of First Instance lies to the Court of Justice on a point of law only.[486] Such an appeal against final decisions of the Court of First Instance and its decisions disposing of the substantive issues in part only, or disposing of a procedural issue concening lack of competence or inadmissibility, must be brought within two months of the notification of the decision appealed against.[487] Thus appeal lies against decisions on myriad interlocutory matters as well as final judgments. The appeal may be brought by any party which has been unsuccessful, in whole or in part, in its submissions, although interveners other than Member States or Community Institutions may bring such an appeal only if the decision of the Court of First Instance directly affects them.[488] The grounds of appeal are limited to lack of competence of the Court of First Instance, a breach of procedure before it which adversely affects the interests of the applicant, as well as infringement of Community law by the Court of First Instance.[489] If the appeal is well-founded, the Court of Justice quashes the decision of the Court of First Instance; it may itself give final judgment in the matter, where the state of proceedings so permits, or it may refer the case back to the Court of First Instance for judgment.[490] An interesting aspect of the Court of Justice's appellate

484. Rules of Procedure (see note 476, *supra*), Arts. 49 and 64.
485. *Ibid.*, Art. 64(1).
486. Arts. 168a(1) EC, 32d(1) ECSC, and 140a(1) Euratom; EC and ECSC Statutes, Art. 51; Euratom Statute, Art. 52. As to the condidtions under which appeals may be lodged, see EC and ECSC Statutes, Arts. 49–54; Euratom Statute, Arts. 50–55, and Rules of Procedure of the Court of Justice (see note 400, *supra*), Arts. 110–123. An appeal does not have suspensory effect, EC and ECSC Statutes, Art. 53; Euratom Statute, Art. 54 (1st para. in each case). As to the special circumstances applicable to the effect of a judgment of the Court of First Instance annulling a regulation, see *ibid.* (2nd para. in each case).
487. EC and ECSC Statutes, Art. 49; Euratom Statute, Art. 50 (1st para. in each case). In the case of appeals against dismissal of requests to intervene, the period is two weeks, and in the case of appeals against judgments relating to suspension of acts, interim measures, or the enforcement of pecuniary penalties (see Arts. 185, 186 and 192, 4th para. EC, 39 and 92, 3rd para. ECSC, and 157, 158, and 164, 3rd para. Euratom); the period is two months, EC and Statutes, Art. 50; Euratom Statute, Art. 51.
488. *Ibid.*, (2nd para. in each case).
489. EC and ECSC Statutes, Art. 51; Euratom Statute, Art. 52. If the grounds of a judgment of the Court of First Instance reveal an infringement of Community law but the operative part appears well-founded on other legal grounds, the appeal will be dismissed, Case C-20/91 P *Lestelle v. Commission* [1992] ECR I-3755 at 3786; Case C-32/92 P *Moat v. Commission* [1992] ECR I-6379 at 6384.
490. EC and ECSC Statutes, Art. 54; Euratom Statute, Art. 55 (1st para. in each case). As

jurisdiction concerns appeals (other than in Staff cases) brought by a Member State or a Community Institution which did not intervene in the proceedings before the Court of First Instance; they are placed in the same position as Member States or Community Institutions which did intervene at first instance.[491] In all these cases, if an appeal is well-founded, the Court of Justice may, if it considers this necessary, state which of the effects of the decision of the Court of First Instance which has been quashed are to be considered definitive in respect of the parties.[492]

7.3.2 Tasks and powers

The Court of First Instance's task is to determine at first instance, subject to appeal as set out immediately above, certain classes of action or proceeding defined by the Council, acting unanimously, at the request of the Court of Justice, after consulting the European Parliament and the Commission.[493] The Court of First Instance is expressly debarred from hearing and determining questions referred for a preliminary ruling.[494] It now hears:

(1) Staff cases;[495]
(2) Actions for annulment, for failure to act, or for compensation for damage brought by legal or natural persons;[496]

to the procedure on referral back, see Rules of Procedure of the Court of First Instance (see note 476, *supra*), Arts. 117–121. See *e.g.* Case C-360/92 P *Publishers Association v. Commission* [1995] ECR I-23 (Court of Justice deciding the case itself) and Case C-19/93 P *Rendo NV et al. v. Commission* [1995] ECR I-3319, corrected, [1996] ECR I-1997 (partial annulment and reference back, partial dismissal of the appeal).

491. EC and ECSC Statutes, Art. 50; Euratom Statute, Art. 51.
492. EC and ECSC Statutes, Art. 54; Euratom Statute, Art. 55 (3rd para. in each case). This is in part inspired by Arts. 174 EC and 147 Euratom, but permits a belated action by a Member State or Community Institution which may have been caught unawares by a judgment of the Court of First Instance which is not appealed by the parties, so that the Court of Justice could preserve the some or all of effects of the first instance judgment, while denying it wider application. *Cf.* the exceptional review permitted by way of third party proceedings: EC Statute, Art. 39; ECSC Statute, Art. 36, and Euratom Statute, Art. 40; Rules of Procedure of the Court of Justice (see note 400, *supra*), Art. 97), and of the Court of First Instance (see note 476, *supra*), Art. 97.
493. Arts. 168a(1) and (2) EC, 32d(1) and (2) ECSC, and 140a(1) Euratom. Any category of direct action may now be transferred to the Court of First Instance (including, although this has not yet been done, actions brought brought by or against Member States) under this procedure.
494. Arts. 168a(1) EC, 32(d)(1) ECSC, and 140a(1) Euratom (last sentence in each case).
495. *I.e.* disputes referred to in Arts. 179 EC and 152 Euratom between the Community and its Officials or other servants.
496. Under, respectively, Arts. 173 EC, 33 ECSC, and 146 Euratom (2nd para. in each case); 175 EC, 3rd para., 35 ECSC, 2nd para., and 148 Euratom, 3rd para., and 178

(3) Actions brought by legal or natural persons under an arbitration clause contained in a contract (whether governed by private or public law) concluded by or on behalf of the Community.[497]

The present jurisdiction of the Court of First Instance was not conferred all at once: the transfer was phased and subject to much reluctance on the part of some Member States and on the part of the Commission, particularly in relation to the field of appeals against anti-dumping regulations, in which the likelihood of the Court of First Instance being much more concerned with an investigation of the Commission's factual evaluation caused flutters in certain dovecotes.[498] The Court of First Instance commenced work on 31 October 1989,[499] and the first transfer of pending cases took place by an Order of the Court of 15 November 1989,[500] with subsequent transfers on 27 September 1993[501] and 18 April 1994.[502] Certainly the Court of First Instance seems to be taking its task of conducting thorough investigations into the facts, and thereby promoting judicial protection very seriously, even though its sometimes over-formalistic approach has given rise to controversy.[503] There is no doubt, though, that the establishment of the Court of First Instance has contributed significantly to an improvement in the workload of the Court of Justice; given that there have been few appeals to the Court of Justice, and that of those, the overwhelming majority have been rejected, it appears that the Court

EC, 40 ECSC, 1st and 2nd paras., and 151 Euratom. The Court of First Instance also exercises the at first instance the jurisdiction of the Court of Justice under the Community Trade Mark Regulation and the Community Plant Variety Rights Regulation (see note 462, *supra*). The Court of First Instance also exercises at first instance the unlimited jurisdiction under Arts. 172 EC, 36 ECSC, and 144(b) Euratom (see note 439, *supra*).

497. Under Arts. 181 EC, 42 ECSC, and 153 Euratom. See note 441, *supra*.
498. Initially, the Court of First Instance was given competence in staff cases; ECSC cases, and competition cases (Dec. 88/591, O.J. 1989 L 319/1, corrected version in O.J. 1989 C 215/1), Art. 3. Dec. 93/350 (O.J. 1993 L 144/21) transferred all cases brought by legal or natural persons, but excluded anti-dumping cases, and these were eventually transferred by Dec. 94/149 (O.J. 1994 L 66/29) which amended Dec. 93/350 accordingly. In the meantime, the old Arts. 168a EEC, 32d ECSC, and 140a Euratom, originally introduced by the SEA, were revised by the Treaty on European Union to facilitate the expansion of jurisdiction of the Court of First Instance.
499. See O.J. 1989 L 317/48, in accordance with Dec. 88/591 (O.J. 1988 L 319/4, corrected version in O.J. 1989 C 215/1) Art. 13 (unaffected by subsequent amendments).
500. O.J. 1989 C 317/10.
501. O.J. 1993 C 303/6. Since 2 August 1993 new cases brought by private parties (other than anti-dumping cases) have been lodged with the Court of First Instance.
502. See O.J. 1994 C 146/5 (14 anti-dumping actions). New anti-dumping cases have been lodged with the Court of First Instance since 15 March 1994 (Dec. 94/149 (O.J. 1994 L 66/29), Art. 1).
503. *E.g.* the *PVC Cartel* judgment, see note 375, *supra*.

of First Instance is rightly commanding the confidence of those who come before it.

Obvious problems which had to be sorted out were what to do if a document was lodged before the wrong Court, or if it becomes apparent that the other Court is in fact competent, or if both Courts are seized of cases relating to the same subject-matter. As to the first of these, if an application or other procedural document addressed to the one Court is lodged by mistake with the Registrar of the other, it is immediately transmitted to the correct destination.[504] If the Court of First Instance finds that it does not have jurisdiction to hear and determine an action which falls within the jurisdiction of the Court of Justice, it refers the action to the Court of Justice; in the reverse situation the Court of Justice refers the action to the Court of First Instance, which may not then decline jurisdiction.[505] This avoids a situation arising in which both Courts decline jurisdiction and a litigant is left empty-handed. The third problem of parallel proceedings is particularly apparent in state aid cases: a competitor of a beneficiary undertaking may seek the annulment of the Commission's decision (addressed to the Member State concerned) approving the aid, which action will come to the Court of First Instance; another Member State might also challenge that decision before the Court of Justice, and a competitor might challenge the national decision to grant the aid, which action before the national court would, if the subject of a reference for a preliminary ruling, come before the Court of Justice. If the Member State concerned were to grant the aid in the face of an adverse Commission decision, the Commission might commence infringement proceedings against that State before the Court of Justice, whereas the beneficiary undertaking might seek the annulment of the Commission's adverse decision by the Court of First Instance, and, again, a competitor might obtain a reference from a national court to the Court of Justice. Particularly where there is no reference for a preliminary ruling, if the Court of Justice were to decide on the direct action before it while the Court of First Instance simply suspended the proceedings pending the Court of Justice's judgment, the private parties would find that the Court of Justice had pronounced without taking any account of their arguments

---

504. EC and ECSC Statutes, Art. 47; Euratom Statute, Art. 48 (1st para. in each case).
505. *Ibid.* (2nd para. in each case). See Case T-78/91 *Moat et al. v. Commission* [1991] ECR II-1387, and Case C-322/91 *Association of Independent Officials for the Defence of the European Civil Service (TAO/AFI) v. Commission* [1992] ECR I-6373, with Case T-65/91 *White v. Commission* [1994] ECR-SC II-23. However, the Court of First Instance may decide to decline jurisdiction for other reasons, unrelated to the reasons which led the Court of Justice to refer the case to it, as happened in Case T-42/91 *Koninklijke PTT Nederland NV et al. v. Commission* [1992] ECR II-273 (as to the earlier referral to the Court of First Instance, see Case C-66/90 *Koninklijke PTT Nederland NV et al. v. Commission* [1992] ECR I-2723; as to the final result, see Cases C-48 and 66/90 *The Netherlands et al. v. Commission* [1992] ECR I-565).

(as they cannot intervene in direct actions between the Member States and the Community Institutions).[506] Accordingly, where both Courts are seized of cases in which the same relief is sought, the same issue of interpretation is raised or the validity of the same act is called into question, the Court of First Instance may, after having heard the parties, stay the proceedings before it until after the Court of Justice has delivered judgment.[507] But if applications are made for the same act to be declared void (actions for annulment), the Court of First Instance may also decline jurisdiction, so that the Court of Justice may rule on the applications.[508] In all these cases of parallel proceedings the Court of Justice may also decide to stay the proceedings before it, in which case the proceedings before the Court of First Instance continue.[509]

7.4 Interim measures

Bringing an action before the Court does not have suspensory effect,[510] although the Court of Justice does have the power to order suspension of the operation of the contested act if it considers that circumstances so require.[511] In cases before it the Court may prescribe any necessary interim measures.[512] The procedure for doing so is set out in detail in the Statutes

506. EC Statute, Art. 37; Euratom Statute, Art. 38 (2nd para. in each case). Nor can they intervene in disputes between Member States or between the Community Institutions, *ibid*. ECSC Statute, Art. 34 permits intervention by any natural or legal person establishing an interest in the result of any case submitted to the Court (either one).
507. EC and ECSC Statutes, Art. 47; Euratom Statute, Art. 48 (3rd para. in each case).
508. *Ibid*. See Case T-42/91 *Koninklijke PTT Nederland NV et al. v. Commission* [1992] ECR II-273; Case T-488/93 *Hanseatische Industrie-Beteiligungen GmbH v. Commission* [1995] ECR II-469, and Case T-490/93 *Bremer Vulkan Verbund AG v. Commission* [1995] ECR II-477. See further, Brown and Kennedy, *op. cit.* (see note 390, *supra*) 87–90 and Lasok, *op. cit.* (see note 394, *supra*) 57–62.
509. EC and ECSC Statutes, Art. 47; Euratom Statute, Art. 48 (3rd para. in each case).
510. An exception to this rule is made for appeals against Commission decisions imposing sanctions for infringement of security provisions in the nuclear field (Art. 83(2) Euratom). The lodging of an appeal has suspensory effect although the Court can, on application by the Commission or any Member State concerned, order the immediate enforcement of the decision concerned.
511. Arts. 185 EC, 39 ECSC, and 157 Euratom. See, generally, Borchardt (1985) 22 CMLRev. 19; Gray (1979) 4 ELRev. 80; Lasok, *op. cit.* (see note 394, *supra*) 230–299; Mertens de Wilmars (1986) SEW 32, and Oliver (1992) 29 CMLRev. 7. in this section separate references to the Rules of Procedure are given for the Court of Justice and the Court of First Instance. Decisions on interim measures are now given by the appropriate President or Court as the case may be, and no further distinction is made in this discussion between the two Presidents or Courts.
512. The competence of the Court to suspend the enforcement of decisions of the Council or the Commission imposing pecuniary obligations on persons other than states (Arts. 192 EC, 92 ECSC, and 162 Euratom – final para. in each case) which is also covered by the Court's Rules of Procedure of the Court of Justice (see note 400, *supra*), Rules

of the Court and the Rules of Procedure.[513] Under Article 36 of the EC Statute the President (or the Judge who takes his place) adjudicates on applications to suspend execution or to prescribe interim measures. The President has the right to decide the application himself or to refer it to the Court. Referral to the Court used to happen on applications for interim measures in the context of Article 169 EC proceedings against a Member State, although lately the President seems to be deciding on these applications himself. If such an application is referred to the Court then all other cases are postponed and the Court gives its decision after having heard the Advocate-General.[514]

The difference between an application for suspension of the act of an Institution and an application for the grant of some other form of interim relief[515] is relevant to the question of who can apply. Only the person who is challenging the measure in proceedings before the Court may apply for the operation of the measure to be suspended. In relation to other forms of interim relief any party to a case before the Court may apply as long as the application relates to that case; thus a defendant may apply for interim measures other than suspension.[516]

Articles 185 and 186 EC leave no doubt that interim measures can only be prescribed in connection with a case pending before the Court.[517] Thus while an application for interim measures or suspension may effectively be made at the same time as the application commencing the action, it should be made in a separate document and and should be handed in after application commencing the action![518] The application must seek to

83–89, and the Court of First Instance's Rules of Procedure (see note 476, *supra*), Rules 104–110 is not discussed here (but as an example of a case on this see Case 213/86 R *Montedipe SpA v. Commission* [1986] ECR 2623).

513. EC Statute Art. 36; ECSC Statute, Art. 33, Euratom Statute, Art. 37; as to the Rules of Procedure, see note 512, *supra*.

514. Rules of Procedure of the Court of Justice, Art. 85. *Mutatis mutandis*, Rules of Procedure of the Court of First Instance, Art. 106 (without reference to the Advocate General), (see note 512, *supra*).

515. Rules of procedure of the Court of Justice, Art. 83(1) treats an application for suspension (or enforcement) as a species of the genus interim measures, as does Art. 104(1) of the Rules of Procedure of the Court of First Instance.

516. It has been submitted that Art. 83(1) of the Rules of Procedure of the Court of Justice does not restrict the possibility of seeking interim relief to cases involving review of the legality of acts: see Mertens de Wilmars (1986) SEW 32 at 37–38 who does not totally exclude suspension being used in references for a preliminary ruling under Art. 177 EC (and equivalents) at least in so far as an act of a Community Institution is concerned (*ibid.* at 40).

517. Rules of Procedure of the Court of Justice, Art. 83(1), of the Court of First Instance, Art. 104(1), (see note 512, *supra*).

518. Rules of Procedure of the Court of Justice, Art. 83(3), and of the Court of First Instance, Art. 104(3), provide that the application for interim measures must be made separately (see note 512, *supra*). The point is that documents are registered in the order in which they arrive; if the application for interim measures is handed in first,

limit or avoid the disadvantage which would result from the infringement alleged in the main action. As a consistent line of decisions of the Court makes clear, interim measures may be adopted by the judge hearing the application for such measures 'if it is established that their adoption is *prima facie* justified in fact and in law, if they are urgent in the sense that it is necessary, in order to avoid serious and irreparable damage, that they should be laid down, and should take effect, before the decision of the Court on the substance of the action and if they are provisional in the sense that they do not prejudge the decision on the substance of the case, that is to say that they do not at this stage decide disputed points of law or of fact or neutralize in advance the consequences of the decision to be given subsequently on the substance of the action.'[519] This is the framework within which the balance of interests must be weighed. The extent to which these criteria have to be satisfied varies as they can only be evaluated as a whole. The criteria of urgency and necessity are thus less stringent when it appears that there is a high probability that the applicant in the main proceedings will succeed.[520] Indeed, it is significant that the balance of convenience[521] and the likelihood of legality have been described by Mertens de Wilmars, a former President of the Court of Justice, as being the heart of interim measures proceedings.[522]

Interim measures are by definition temporary; if the decision prescribing them does not specify the date on which they are to lapse they lapse on delivery of the final judgment.[523] No appeal lies from a decision on the application for interim measures by the Court of Justice,[524] although appeal to the Court of Justice from a decision of the (President of the) Court of First Instance is possible.[525] The enforcement of such a

there is no action already registered, and thus the application for interim measures is inadmissible.

519. Case 20/81R *Arbed SA et al. v. Commission* [1981] ECR 721 at 731 (correcting the obvious misprint). See also *e.g.* Case 231/86R *Breda-Geomineraria v. Commission* [1986] ECR 2639, and Case T-228/95 *S. Lehrfreund Ltd. v. Council et al.* [1996] ECR II-111. See also, as to the extent of the link between admissibility of the main action and the application for interim measures, Case T-219/95 R *Danielsson et al. v. Commission* [1995] ECR II-3051 (a case with a controversial background, providing a useful summary of earlier case-law).

520. The so-called *fumus boni juris*. For an example of a hopeless case see Case 160/88 R *Fédération Européenne de la Santé Animale el al. v. Council* [1988] ECR 4121.

521. A balancing of interests always takes place, *e.g.* Case 293/85 R *Commission v. Belgium* [1985] ECR 3251 and Case 45/87 R *Commission v. Ireland* [1987] ECR 783 and 1369, [1987] 2 CMLR 197 and 563.

522. (1986) SEW 32 at 48.

523. Rules of Procedure of the Court of Justice, Art. 86(3), of the Court of First Instance, Art. 107(3), (see note 512, *supra*).

524. Rules of Procedure of the Court of Justice, Art. 86(1), (see note 512, *supra*).

525. EC and ECSC Statutes, Art. 50; Euratom Statute, Art. 51 (2nd para. in each case). See *e.g.* Case C-268/96 P(R) *Stichting Certificatie Kraanverhuurbedrijf (SCK) et al. v.*

decision may be made conditional on the lodging of security by the applicant; the amount and nature of which is fixed in the light of the circumstances.[526] This possibility is repeatedly used in cases appealing against the imposition of fines.[527] Interim measures can be granted *ex parte*[528] and are sometimes granted in order to preserve the *status quo* in the interests of the good administration of justice in anticipation of the final outcome in order to ensure that proceedings seeking interim relief do not become otiose.[529]

A decision on interim measures can be given very quickly, even on a Sunday.[530] In that case a decision was taken at the request of the German government in relation to the decision adopted by the Commission four days earlier on protective measures to be taken by the German government relating to the import and export of agricultural products connected with the floating exchange-rate of the D-Mark.[531] From the same decision of the Court it appears that the Court handles the power to take provisional measures in a very cautious way, so as not to be forced to take policy decisions. Interim measures can also be ordered against the Member States. Thus, having first given all other interested parties and the Commission the opportunity to find a solution to the dispute, the Court ordered Ireland on 13 July 1977 to suspend, until judgment was given in the main action, the application to fishing boats registered in any of the Member States of the two Sea Fisheries orders challenged by the Commission; these Orders were intended to drastically reduce fishing by foreign-flag boats in Irish waters.[532] Likewise, in the Dundalk water pipeline contract case, Ireland was ordered not to take any steps which would alter the *status quo,* in particular by awarding the contract, until the application for interim measures had been decided upon after a hearing *inter partes.*[533] Again, in

---

     Commission [1996] ECR I-4971. An appeal to the Court of Justice does not have sus-
     pensory effect, Arts. 53 and 54 respectively.

526. Rules of Procedure of the Court of Justice, Art. 86(2), and of the Court of First
     Instance, Art. 107(2).

527. *Eg.* Case 392/85 R *Finsider v. Commission* [1986] ECR 959.

528. Rules of Procedure of the Court of Justice, Art. 84(2), and of the Court of First
     Instance, Art. 105(2), (see note 512, *supra*).

529. *E.g.* Case 61/77 R *Commission v. Ireland* [1977] ECR 1411 at 1413; Case 45/87 R
     Commission v. Ireland [1987] ECR 783 (then refused after a hearing *inter partes*, 1369),
     [1987] 2 CMLR 167 (and 563).

530. Case 50/69 R *Germany v. Commission* [1969] ECR 449, [1971] CMLR 724.

531. J.O. 1969 L 250/29.

532. Case 61/77 R *Commission v. Ireland* [1977] ECR 1411 (for the final judgment in Case
     61/77 see [1978] ECR 417, [1978] 2 CMLR 466). See also Timmermans (1978) SEW
     235, Wainwright (1977) 2 ELRev. 349, Churchill (1979) 4 ELRev. 391, Winkel and
     Von Borries (1978) 15 CMLRev. 494 and Marston (1978) JWTL 461

533. Case 45/87 R *Commission v. Ireland* [1987] ECR 783 and 1369, [1987] 2 CMLR 197
     and 563.

Case 246/89 R *Commission* v. *United Kingdom*,[534] the Commission obtained an order requiring the British government to suspend the application of nationality requirements designed to attack the problem of quota-hopping by fishermen from other Member States, pending delivery of judgment in the main proceedings.[535] In recent years the significance of interim measures proceedings has increased; by the end of 1964 there had been just 21 decisions, by the end of 1974 there had been 40, by the end of 1987 there had been 182. The stream in nowadays fairly stable: in 1995 there were 10 and in 1997 there were 13 in all. The number of applications is slightly more but some do not actually result in a decision being handed down. Not surprisingly, most applications are now to the Court of First Instance.[536]

7.5 Application of the law

7.5.1 Unwritten law

In the exercise of its jurisdiction the Court has to interpret and apply Community law. This law also embraces the unwritten Community law which has been moulded by the case-law of the Court itself. In its case-law there are regular references to general principles of law, such as good faith, legal certainty, due diligence, the principle of equality, legitimate expectation and the principle of proportionality.[537] Unwritten law also affords solutions to numerous problems for which no answer is to be found in written Community law. The possibility of relying on general principles of law in order to fill *lacunae* in Community law is not, however, unlimited. Thus these principles cannot be invoked to exclude double jeopardy of fines, particularly for breach of national and Community competition law, at least as long as the Council has not adopted a regulation under Article 87(2)(e) EC on the matter.[538] Similarly, no limitation period for infringements of Community competition law can be

---

534. [1989] ECR 3125, [1989] 3 CMLR 601.
535. Case C-246/89 *Commission v. United Kingdom* [1991] ECR I-4585, [1991] 3 CMLR 706.
536. But the Court of Justice still receives high-profile applications, *e.g.* Case C-180/96 R *United Kingdom v. Commission* [1996] ECR I-3903.
537. See, Arnull, *The General principles of EEC Law and the Individual* (Leicester, 1990); Prechal and Heukels (1986) SEW 287; Schermers (1983) SEW 514; Schermers and Waelbroeck: *Judicial Protection in the European Communities* (5th ed., Deventer, 1992) 27–94 and literature cited therein, and Usher, *General Priciples of EC Law* (London 1998). See also *Reports of the FIDE Congress, Paris, 1986*, Vol. 1, and Emiliou, *The Principle of Proportionality in European Law* (London, 1996). The principle of proportionality is now made generally applicable to Community action, Art. 3b EC (final para.), see Chapter III, section 5.1.2, *ante*.
538. Case 14/68 *Walt Wilhelm et al. v. Bundeskartellamt* [1969] ECR 1 at 15.

deduced from these principles,[539] although the Court subsequently indicated that, in the absence of any provisions on the matter, the principle of legal certainty prevented the Commission from indefinitely delaying the exercise of its power to impose fines.[540] The Court made it clear that, in order to fulfil their function of ensuring legal certainly, limitation periods must be fixed in advance; a task which was a matter for the Community legislator.[541] An illustration of the application of unwritten law can be seen in the Court's formulation of the conditions under which an administrative act conferring rights on people could be withdrawn. Rules on this matter exist in the administrative law of various Member States, but no specific rules on this matter are to be found in the ECSC Treaty. In the case in question the Court considered itself compelled (lest it deny justice) to solve the problem by reliance on rules recognized in the legislation, learned writings, and case-law of the Member States.[542] Since the judgment in Case 29/69 *Stauder* v. *City of Ulm* it has been clear that fundamental human rights are enshrined in the general principles of Community law and protected by the Court.[543]

It is understandable that the Court, in order to 'find' these general legal principles and rules of unwritten law, consults the national legal systems of the Member States.[544] In classical international law as well 'the general principles of law recognized by civilized nations' form a source of law.[545] This source, however, flows less copiously in the international administration of justice than in that of the Communities. Indeed, in many sectors Community law, much more so than classical international law, shows a marked affinity in its tenor as well as in its legal technique and procedures with national legal systems, and above all with national

539. Case 41/69 *ACF Chemiefarma NV* v. *Commission* [1970] ECR 661 at 683.
540. Case 48/69 *Imperial Chemical Industries Ltd.* v. *Commission* [1972] ECR 619 at 653.
541. See notes 539 and 540, *supra, loc. cit.* Limitation periods were laid down by Reg. 2988/74 (O.J. 1974 L 319/1). As examples of the requirement of legal certainty see the judgments of 15 December 1987, *e.g.* Case 239/86 *Ireland* v. *Commission* [1987] ECR 5271 and Case 325/85 *Ireland* v. *Commission* [1987] ECR 5041.
542. Cases 7/56 and 3–7/57 *Algera et al.* v. *Common Assembly* [1957–1958] ECR 39 at 55. Mortelmans (1981) CDE 410 discusses how *lacunae* in general which appear as a result of the case-law are dealt with other than by action by the Court in areas in which the Community is competent to act.
543. [1969] ECR 419 at 425. For an overview of the earlier case-law on this point see the Opinion of Mischo, Adv. Gen., in Case 15/85 *Consorzio Cooperative d'Abruzzo* v. *Commission* [1987] ECR 1005 at 1014 *et seq.* This point is discussed further in section 7.5.4., *post.*
544. See the Opinion of Lagrange, Adv. Gen., in Case 8/55 *Fédération Charbonnière de Belgique* v. *High Authority* [1954–1956] ECR 245 at 269. Arts. 215 EC and 188 Euratom (2nd para. in each case) specifically provide for this procedure to be followed. This concerns the obligation 'to make good any damage caused' by the Community Institutions or their servants in the performance of their duties 'in accordance with the general principles common to the laws of the Member States.'
545. Statute of the International Court of Justice, Art. 38c.

administrative and economic law. The Court's finding of law, therefore, is largely an exercise in comparative law. This use of the comparative technique is not governed by an *a priori* intent to find the highest common denominator; rather is it governed by an intent to trace elements from which Community legal principles and rules can be built up which will offer an appropriate, fair and viable solution for the questions with which the Court is confronted. Comparative law in this sense also forms the source of inspiration for the determination of the autonomous meaning of many legal terms occurring in written Community law.[546] This comparative exercise is sometimes performed by the Advocates General in their submissions, as happened in relation to the meaning of the term 'misuse of power' – in French, *détournement de pouvoir* – in Article 33 ECSC.[547] But as a rule it will naturally take place *in camera* during the deliberations between judges who, each of them educated and initiated in their own national legal system and way of thinking, together have to give effect to written and unwritten Community law.

Apart from the above principles, which are common to the legal systems of the Member States, there are also other principles which the Court of Justice derives from the EC Treaty itself. Thus already in Case 78/70 *Deutsche Grammophon Gesellschaft mbH* v. *Metro-SB-Großmärkte GmbH & Co. KG*[548] the Court found that the second paragraph of Article 5 EC laid down 'a general duty for the Member States, the actual tenor of which depends in each individual case on the provisions of the Treaty or on the rules derived from its general scheme.' Other principles which the Court has derived in particular from Article 5 include the principle of sincere cooperation which creates obligations not merely for the Member States but also for the Community Institutions themselves,[549] and the principle of State liability in damages for loss suffered by individuals as a

546. Although the meaning of such a term in Community law 'must be determined on the basis of the legal framework within which it is intended to take effect': Case 4/68 *Firma Schwarzwaldmilch GmbH* v. *Einfuhr- und Vorratsstelle für Fette* [1968] ECR 377 at 385 concerning the concept *of force majeure* in Arts. 6(2)–(4) of Reg. 136/64 (J.O. 1964, p. 601). In Case 59/85 *State of the Netherlands* v. *Reed* [1986] ECR 1283 the Court considered the term 'spouse' in Art. 10 of Reg. 1612/68 (O.J. English Special Edition 1968 (11), p. 475 (as amended)) in the light of social evolution as a provision which had effects in all Member States; thus the situation in the whole Community had to be considered, not just the situation in one Member State. The term 'public policy' in Community law also has a Community meaning and is not simply beholden to an individual national interpretation: Case 36/75 *Rutili* v. *Minister for the Interior* [19751 ECR 1219 at 1231.
547. See the Opinion of Lagrange, Adv. Gen., in Case 3/54 *ASSIDER* v. *High Authority* [1954–1956] ECR 63 at 74–89. The phrase also occurs in Arts. 173 EC and 146 Euratom.
548. [1971] ECR 487 at 499.
549. Case C-2/88 Imm. *Zwartveld et al.* [1990] ECR I-3365 at 3372; see also Case C-54/90 *Weddel & Co. BV* v. *Commission* [1992] ECR I-871 at 894–895 (consideration of the Commission's proper relations with national administrations).

result of a failure by the State to fulfil its obligations under Community law.[550]

The Court of First Instance also applies unwritten law. Apart from the myriad staff cases, general principles of law have been particulaly important in competition cases, in particular the principles of the rights of the defence. Thus in its Order in Case T-30/89 *Hilti AG* v. *Commission*[551] the Court of First Instance took account of 'certain general principles of law and certain essential principles such as that of the protection of confidentiality of written communications between lawyer and client.'

7.5.2 Public international law

Finding and creating law, the Court applies Community law but it also has the right to apply public international law.[552] As far as international law is concerned, the Community legal order is an open system. Various distinct types of case can be distinguished. The first type are the cases in which the Community as such is bound by norms of international law *vis-à-vis* third parties. This can result from treaties which it has concluded with third parties.[553] It may also occur, based on norms of international law which bind all the Member States, whenever the application of these norms is actually transferred to the Community and this transfer is recognized by third countries; this is the application of the principle of substitution.[554] In such cases the legal norms by which the Community as such is bound will be directly applied by the Court of Justice in the Community legal order if they lend themselves to such direct application.[555]

550. This principle was also found to be inherent in the system of the Treaty, Cases C-6 and 9/90 *Francovich et al.* v. *Italy* [1991] ECR I-5357 at 5414.
551. [1990] ECR II-163 at 168.
552. See Schermers and Waelbroeck, *op. cit.* (see note 537, *supra*) 99–107 and literature cited therein. In view of their special character, the possible application by the Court of the 'acts of the representatives of the governments of the Member States' is considered in Chapter V, section 1.6.
553. Such as association agreements. On the interpretation of provisions of these see *e.g.* Case 181/73 *Haegeman* v. *Belgian State* [1974] ECR 449, [1975] CMLR 515; Case 87/75 *Bresciani* v. *Amministrazione Italiana delle Finanze* [1976] ECR 129, [1976] 2 CMLR 62, and Case 65/77 *Razanatsimba* [1977] ECR 2229, [1978] 1 CMLR 246. As to free trade agreements see *e.g.* Case 270/80 *Polydor Ltd. et al.* v. *Harlequin Record Shops et al.* [1982] ECR 329, [1982] 1 CMLR 677; Case 104/81 *Hauptzollamt Mainz* v. *Kupferberg & Cie. KG a.A.* [1982] ECR 3641, [1983] 1 CMLR 1, and Case C-207/91 *Eurim-Pharm GmbH* v. *Bundesgesundheitsamt* [1993] ECR I-3723.
554. See Cases 21–24/72 *International Fruit Company NV et al.* v. *Produktschap voor Groenten en Fruit* [1972] ECR 1219 at 1226–1227 which dealt with provisions of the GATT to which all Member States were Contracting Parties, although the reasoning would seem to apply to customary international law as well.
555. See *ibid.* and in the light thereof also Art. 228(7) EC. The Court concluded that the

The second type of case covers cases in which the Community as such is not involved but one or more of the Member States has international obligations towards third parties which are incompatible with the obligations resulting from provisions of Community law. It is clear in any event from the first sentence of the first paragraph of Article 234 EC[556] that the provisions of the Treaty do not affect rights and obligations arising from agreements concluded before the entry into force of the EC Treaty between one or more Member States on the one hand and more or more third countries on the other.[557] An analogous application of the principle set out in that sentence would appear reasonable in cases in which the Member States, after entry into force of the Treaty, have entered into oligations with third countries whilst still being empowered to do so in Community law, and these obligations subsequently become incompatible with Community secondary legislation.[558]

The third type of case covers situations in which norms of public international law have to be invoked in order to define legal relationships within the Community. The EC Treaty only once makes express reference to decisions of an international body.[559] The application of unwritten international law appears to be the obvious course if and in so far as the Treaties do not cover any typical problem of international law which may arise.[560] Thus in its judgment in Case 41/74 *Van Duyn v. Home*

Community as such was bound by the GATT, but that the provisions of the GATT in issue were not capable of conferring rights on Community citizens which they could invoke before the courts. See also *e.g.* Cases 267–269/81 *Amministrazione delle Finanze dello Stato v. Società Petrolifera Italiana SpA el al.* [1983] ECR 801 at 803. However, in its judgment in Case 87/75 *Bresciani* [1976] ECR 129 at 142 the Court interpreted a provision of the First Yaoundé Convention (J.O. 1964, p. 1430) as having direct effect from 1 January 1970; likewise in relation to the old Free Trade Agreement with Portugal in Case 104/81 *Kupferberg* [1982] ECR 3641 at 3662–3666. See also Chapter VI, section 2.2.3, *post.*

556. See also Act of Accession; Act of Greek Accession; Act of Spanish and Portuguese Accession, and Act of Austrian, Finnish and Swedish Accession (Art. 5 in each case). See, further, Arts. 105 and 106 Euratom.

557. As to the use of prior agreements in attempts to justify barriers to trade between Member States see Case 121/85 *Conegate Ltd. v. H.M. Customs and Excise* [1986] ECR 1007. See also Case 235/87 *Matteucci v. La Communauté Française de Belgique et al.* [1988] ECR 5589.

558. On the other hand Art. 234, 1st para. does not apply if the obligations contained in the first agreement are repealed by a later agreement between the same parties, see Case C-158/91 *Ministère public et al. v. Levy* [1992] ECR I-4287, and Case C-13/93 *Office National de l'Emploi v. Minne* [1994] ECR I-137.

559. Arts. 31, 2nd para., and 33(6) EC; the reference is to the OEEC (now the OECD).

560. The Court rejected an appeal based on the international law principle of self-help in Cases 90 and 91/63 *Commission v. Luxembourg and Belgium* [1964] ECR 625 (see Chapter II, section 3.2, *ante*) and an appeal based on the international law 'local remedy' rule in a case concerning the ECSC Protocol on Privileges and Immunities of the Community in Case 6/60 *Humblet v. Belgian State* [1960] ECR 559.

Office[561] the Court explained that 'it is a principle of international law, which the EEC Treaty cannot be assumed to disregard in the relations between Member States, that a State is precluded from refusing its own nationals the right of entry or residence.' In the second judgment in the *Foglia* v. *Novello* saga[562] the Court indicated that 'in the absence of provisions of Community law in the matter, the possibility of taking proceedings before a national court against a Member State other than that in which that court is situated depends both on the laws of the latter and on the principles of international law.' In *Wood Pulp*[563] the Court noted that 'the Community's jurisdiction to apply its competition rules [to anti-competitive conduct outside the Community implemented within it] is covered by the territoriality principle as universally recognized in public international law.' Finally, it should be noted that the Court sometimes employs international law as an auxiliary (not as an independent) source of law for the interpretation and definition of Community rules.[564] The Court tends to do so relatively sparingly, since in most cases, reliance on principles and rules of national law as an auxiliary source of law may yield a more appropriate, fair and viable result.

7.5.3   National law

With respect to national law, the primary rule is that the Court does not apply this directly. The Court bases this primary rule on the distinctiveness

561. [1974] ECR 1337 at 1351.
562. Case 244/80 *Foglia* v. *Novello* [1981] ECR 3045 at 3064. See Wyatt (1982) 7 ELRev. 186 and Bebr [1982] 19 CMLRev. 421. For the earlier judgment in this saga see Case 104/79 *Foglia* v. *Novello* [1980] ECR 745 and, generally, Barav (1980) 5 ELRev. 443, Bebr (1980) EuR 244, Tizzano (1981) RGDIP 514 and Lipstein in Capotori *et al.* (eds.): *Du droit international au droit de l'intégration* (*Liber amicorum* Pescatore, Baden-Baden, 1987) 373. For a case which went the other way see Case 261/81 *Walter Rau Lebensmittelwerke* v. *De Smedt PvbA* [1982] ECR 3961, [1983] 2 CMLR 496 in which Belgian legislation was effectively condemned on a reference from a German court. See also Case 140/79 *Chemial Farmaceutici SpA* v. *DAF SpA* [1981] ECR 1, [1981] 3 CMLR 350.
563. Cases 89/85, *etc. A. Åhlström Oskeyhtio et al.* v. *Commission* [1988] ECR 5193 at 5243.
564. *E.g.*, in relation to Art. 234 EC, Case 10/61 *Commission* v. *Italy* [1962] ECR 1 at 10 (the Commission's submission was approved by the Court) and, in relation to Art. 88 ECSC, Case 20/59 *Italy* v. *High Authority* [1960] ECR 325 at 339. For reference to the European Convention on Human Rights in relation to the restrictions which Community law places on Member States' powers to control aliens see Case 36/75 *Rutili* v. *Minister for the Interior* [1975] ECR 1219 at 1232. See also Case 44/79 *Hauer* v. *Land Rheinland-Pfalz* [1979] ECR 3727 at 3745–3746 in relation to the right to property. See also Case 14/70 *Deutsche Bakels GmbH* v. *Oberfinanzdirektion München* [1970] ECR 1001 at 1009, and Cases 69 and 70/76 *Firma Rolf H. Dittmeyer* v. *Hauptzollamt Hamburg-Waltershof* [1977] ECR 231 at 238 (opinions of Nomenclature Committee of the Customs Cooperation Council and of the Committee on Common Customs Tariff Nomenclature, respectively, valid aids to interpretation, even though non-binding).

of its mandate, which is limited to the interpretation and application of Community law[565] and on the principle (which it considers to be contained in the Treaties) of a strict separation between the powers of the Institutions and those of the organs of the Member States, and consequently also between those of the Court and of national judicial bodies. Accordingly, the Court has considered it inappropriate to pronounce on the validity of the acts of the Community Institutions under national legislation or constitutional rules.[566] The Court has equally refused to proceed on its own authority 'to annul or repeal legislative or administrative acts of a Member State.'[567] In the former case the Court even held that in general it ought to abstain from pronouncements on rules of national law.[568] This is an approach to which there is a well-known exception if the Court is required, in accordance with Article 169 EC,[569] to pronounce on whether particular internal rules of a Member State do or do not infringe obligations of that State under the Treaty. In such cases the Court does pronounce on such rules, although, if they conflict with the Treaty provisions, it cannot itself render them inoperative.[570]

There are, though, a number of exceptions to the basic rule that the Court does not apply national law as such. The Treaty provisions refer, sometimes implicitly and often expressly, to the relevant national law of a Member State.[571] When Community rules contain terms like 'representatives of Member States at ministerial level,'[572] 'undertakings,'[573] 'legal persons,'[574] 'companies or firms constituted under civil or commercial law,'[575] or 'workers'[576] the Court is faced with the question

---

565. Arts. 164 EC, 31 ECSC, and 136 Euratom.
566. Case 1/58 *Friedrich Stork & Co. v. High Authority* (1959) ECR 17 at 26; Cases 36–38 and 40/59 *President Ruhrkohlen-Verkaufsgesellschaft mbH v. High Authority* [1960] ECR 423 at 438.
567. Case 6/60 *Humblet v. Belgian State* [1960] ECR 559 at 568.
568. Case 1/58 *Stork, loc. cit.*
569. See also Arts. 88 ECSC and 141 Euratom.
570. As to the effect of judgments see Lasok and Millett, *op. cit.* (see note 414, *supra*) para. 146. See also Cases 314–316/81 and 83/82 *Procureur de la République et al. v. Waterkeyn et al.* [1982] ECR 4337 at 4360–4361.
571. *E.g.* EC Statute, Art. 17 refers to the relevant national law when dealing with those entitled to plead before the Court: 'A lawyer entitled to practice before a court of a Member State or of another State which is party to the Agreement on the European Economic Area' and 'University teachers being nationals of a Member State whose law accords them a right of audience.' The Court may also be confronted with questions of national law even in the absence of any express or implied reference to it in Community texts, *e.g.* Case 18/57 *Nold v. High Authority* [1959] ECR 41 at 48–49 (powers of representation and bar disciplinary measures).
572. *E.g.* Art. 146 EC.
573. *E.g.* Art. 85(1) EC.
574. *E.g.* Art. 173 EC.
575. *E.g.* Art. 58 EC, 2nd para.
576. *E.g.* Art. 48(1) EC.

whether the reference is to the relevant national law or to a concept of Community law. If the former be the case the question whether 'a person' or 'a thing' is covered by the term used is a question which must be judged according to the rules of the national law governing that 'person' or 'thing.' In some cases this may lead to differences in the application of rules of Community law which prejudice their objectives or are detrimental to the persons or things concerned. In its judgments, therefore, the Court, in the absence of a reference to the national law of the Member States,[577] prefers to create Community legal concepts.[578] Finally, it should be noted that by virtue of its optional jurisdiction under an arbitration clause in a contract concluded by or on behalf of the Communities the Court can be required to apply the law of a given State.[579]

7.5.4 Fundamental rights[580]

Written Community law contains no specific provisions dealing with respect for fundamental rights in the Community authorities' dealings with Community citizens. As the Communities expanded their field of activities

---

577. Case 154/80 *Staatssecretaris van Financiën v. Coöperatieve Aardappelenbewaarplaats GA* [1981] ECR 445 at 453.

578. *E.g.* The term 'bought' in ECSC Dec. 22/54 (O.J. English Special Edition 1952–1958, p. 16), Art. 3 in Case 14/63 *Forges de Clabecq v. High Authority* [1963] ECR 357 at 372–373; the term 'wage-earner or assimilated worker' in Reg. No. 3 (J.O. 1958 p. 561), Art. 19(1) in Case 75/63 *Hoekstra, née Unger v. Bestuur der Bedrijfsvereniging voor Detailhandel en Ambachten* [1964] ECR 177 at 185; the term 'self-employed person' in Reg. 1408/71 (O.J. English Special Edition 1971 (II), p. 416, as amended and consolidated), Art. 1(a)(iv) in Case 300/84 *Van Roosmalen v. Bestuur van de Bedrijfsvereniging voor de Gezondheid Geestelijke en Maatschappelijke Belangen* [1986] ECR 3097 at 3122–3124; the term 'services' in Art. 60 EC in Case C-159/90 *Society for the Protection of the Unborn Child Ltd. v. Grogan et al.* [1991] ECR I-4685 at 4739; the term 'legal person' in Case 135/81 *Groupement des Agences de Voyages Asbl v. Commission* [1982] ECR 3799 at 3808, and the term 'undertaking' in competition law in Case C-41/90 *Höfner and Elser v. Macrotron GmbH* [1991] ECR I-1979 at 2016–2017.

579. Arts. 181 with 215 EC, 42 ECSC, and 153 with 188 Euratom. See section 7.2.2, *ante* (under head (5) of the heads of jurisdiction). For an example of the application of Belgian law in a dispute between the Commission and a contractor see Case 318/81 *Commission v. CO.DE.MI. SpA* [1985] ECR 3693.

580. See, among the more recent works, Betten, *The Right to Strike in Community law: the incorporation of fundamental rights in the legal order of the European Communities* (Amsterdam, 1985) 25–45; Clapham *et al.*, *Human Rights and the European Communities* (Baden-Baden, 1991); Schwemer, *Die Bindung des Gemeinschaftsgesetzgebers an die Frundfreiheiten* (Frankfurt, 1995); Coppel and O'Neill (1992) 29 CMLRev. 669; the contributions by Gaja and Jacobs in Curtin and O'Keeffe (eds.), *op. cit.* (see note 10, *supra*) 549 and 561; Dauses (1985) 10 ELRev. 398; Schermers and Waelbroeck, *op. cit.* (see note 537, *supra* 37–42; Schwarze (1986) 23 CMLRev. 401, and Weiler and Lockhart (1995) 32 CMLRev. 51 and 579.

this *lacuna* gave rise to serious objections, first of all in Germany. It was scarcely surprising that it was in Germany that objections were first raised as there legal protection of fundamental rights is the most developed in the Community and these rights also play an important part in the socio-economic sphere. Thus it was German appellants who challenged various decisions of the Community Institutions before the Court of Justice, alleging that they were incompatible with national constitutionally-guaranteed rights. In these cases the Court was content to observe (not unjustifiably) that it was not competent to review decisions of the Institutions in the light of national constitutional provisions.[581]

Partly under the influence of discussions in German legal circles about the relationship between Community law and national constitutional law and the view of many participants in those discussions that German judges were entitled to review Community decisions in the light of their own constitutional rights,[582] at the end of the Sixties the Court revised its passive stance on the matter of fundamental rights in the Community. Thus in the celebrated judgment in Case 29/69 *Stauder* v. *City of Ulm*[583] the Court confirmed that fundamental human rights were enshrined in the general principles of Community law and were protected by the Court. In doing so the Court took a view consistent with its case-law on general principles of Community law which already offered guarantees affecting the sphere of human rights. This was amplified in the celebrated judgment in Case 11/70 *Internationale Handelsgesellschaft mbH* v. *Einfuhr- und Vorratsstelle für Getreide und Futtermittel*[584] when the Court, noting that respect for fundamental human rights formed an integral part of the general principles of law protected by the Court of Justice, indicated that whilst the protection of such rights was inspired by the constitutional traditions common to the Member States, it had to be ensured within the framework of the structure and objectives of the Community. The Court went a step further in the second *Nold* judgment,[585] noting that it flowed from the inspiration from the constitutional traditions of the Member States that the Court could not uphold measures which were incompatible with fundamental rights recognized and protected by the constitutions of

581. See note 566, *supra*.
582. See Chapter VI section 2.3.1, *post*.
583. [1969] ECR 419 at 425.
584. [1970] ECR 1125 at 1134.
585. Case 4/73 *J. Nold Kohlen- und Baustoffgrosshandlung* v. *Commission* [1974] ECR 491 at 507–508. This judgment was pronounced only very shortly after France had become the last of the then Member States to recognize the right of individual petition under the European Convention on Human Rights (with effect from 3 May 1974). See also Case 44/79 *Hauer* v. *Rheinland-Pfalz* [1979] ECR 3727 at 3744 and the criticism by Geelhoed (1986) SEW 690; see, more recently, Case 234/85 *Stadtanwaltschaft Freiburg* v. *Keller* [1986] ECR 2897 at 2912, and Cases 46/87 and 227/88 *Hoechst AG* v. *Commission* [1989] ECR 2859 at 2924.

those States. In accordance with the approach in the Member States, the protection of fundamental rights is always subject to limitations laid down in accordance with the public interest; accordingly, it was appropriate, the Court felt, to subject these rights, if necessary, 'to certain limits justified by the overall objectives pursued by the Community, on condition that the substance of these rights is left untouched.'[586]

The protection of fundamental rights is not restricted to those specified in national constitutions or constitutional law.[587] It also embraces the fundamental rights guaranteed in the European Convention on Human Rights.[588] Even though the Comunity itself is not a party to the Convention, the Court did observe in the second *Nold* judgment that 'international treaties for the protection of human rights on which the Member States have collaborated or of which they are signatories, can supply guidelines which should be followed within the framework of Community law.'[589] Later, in its judgment in Case 36/75 *Rutili* v. *Minister for the Interior*[590] the Court concluded that the limitations which Regulation 1612/68[591] placed on the powers of the Member States to control aliens were a specific manifestation of a more general principle enshrined in various provisions of the Convention.[592] In various other judgments the Court has cited provisions of the Convention in support of its reasoning,[593] and has now started to refer directly to the provisions of the Convention themselves.[594]

Through this case-law of the Court of Justice, which is followed by the

586. Case 4/73 *Nold, ibid.*
587. The present discussion leaves to one side the issue whether a principle has to feature in all the constitutions of the Member States, or whether a fundamental right recognized specifically in only one or a few Member States can also be recognized as a Community fundamental right.
588. Convention for the Protection of Human Rights and Fundamental Freedoms (Rome, 4 November 1950 (TS 71 (1953); Cmnd 8969)).
589. [1974] ECR 491 at 507.
590. [1975] ECR 1219 at 1232.
591. O.J. English Special Edition 1968 (II), p. 475 (as amended).
592. See also Case 130/75 *Prais* v. *Council* [1976] ECR 1589 at 1599; Case 44/79 *Hauer* v. *Land Rheinland-Pfalz* [1979] ECR 3727 at 3745–3750 and, in relation to the European Social Charter and Convention No. 111 of the ILO, Case 149/77 *Defrenne* v. *SABENA* [1978] ECR 1365 at 1378.
593. *E.g.* Cases 209–215 and 218/78 *Van Landewyck et al.* v. *Commission* [1980] ECR 3125 at 3248 (Art. 6 of the Convention); Case 136/79 *National Panasonic (UK) Ltd.* v. *Commission* [1980] ECR 2033 at 2056–2057 (Art. 8 of the Convention) and Case 63/83 *R.* v. *Kirk* [1984] ECR 2689 at 2718 (Art. 7 of the Convention). See also Case 222/84 *Johnston* v. *Chief Constable of the Royal Ulster Constabulary* [1986] ECR 1651 and Case 222/86 *Union Nationale des Entraineurs et Cadres Techniques et Professionnels du Football (Unectef)* v. *Heylens et al.* [1987] ECR 4097 at 4117.
594. *E.g.* Cases 46/87 and 227/88 *Hoechst AG* v. *Commission* [1989] ECR 2859 at 2924; Case 85/87 *Dow Benelux NV* v. *Commission* [1989] ECR 3150 at 3157; Cases 97–99/87 *Dow Chemical Ibérica SA et al.* v. *Commission* [1989] ECR 3165 at 3185–3186, and Case C-404/92 P *X* v. *Commission* [1994] ECR I-4737 at 4789.

Court of First Instance,[595] a reasonable protection of the fundamental
rights and freedoms of citizens has been ensured in the functioning of the
Community. Examples of rights which are thus protected include the rights
of property, freedom to exercise a profession or trade, protection of private
life, the right to a fair trial, equal treatment and as in staff cases – the right
to free exercise of religious beliefs and the right of association.[596] There
nevertheless remains a need for a more systematic and express system of
guarantees in this field than can be offered by judge-made law. The void
has not been filled despite benediction of this case-law by the Joint
Declaration by the Parliament, Council and Commission[597] that they will
respect fundamental rights stemming from the constitutions of the Member
States and the European Convention. From the legal point of view, more
important steps were the determination, expressed in the Preamble to the
SEA 'to work together to promote democracy on the basis of the
fundamental rights recognized in the Convention for the Protection of
Human Rights and Fundamental freedoms and the European Social
Charter, notably freedom, equality and social justice' and the requirement
in Article F(2) TEU that the European Union respect the fundamental
rights resulting from the Convention from and those resulting 'from the
constitutional traditions common to the Member States, as general
principles of Community law.' A major shortcoming, however, remains the
lamentable fact that the Court of Justice is not yet competent to decide on
compliance with Article F(2) TEU.[598] To that extent, and it is a serious
shortcoming, critics of the Union structure are certainly justified in
pointing to the inadequacy of the protection of fundamental rights within
the Union.

All Member States are parties to the European Convention on Human
Rights – indeed respect for fundamental rights has become a *conditio sine
qua non* for membership of the Union.[599] It appeared at one time possible

---

595. *E.g.* Case T-19/91 *Société d'Hygiène Dermatalogique de Vichy v. Commission* [1992]
     ECR II-415 at 429–431 and 463–466 (various rights of the defence).
596. See, generally, on general principles of law, Arnull, *op. cit.* (see note 537, *supra*);
     Lasok and Millett, *op. cit.* (see note 414, *supra*) paras. 1209 *et seq.*; Schermers and
     Waelbroeck, *op. cit.* (see note 537, *supra*) 27–943; Wyatt and Dashwood, *European
     Community Law* (3rd ed., London, 1993) 88–103, and Brown and Kennedy, *op. cit.*
     (see note 390, *supra*) 323–342.
597. O.J. 1977 C 103/1, On the legal significance of this Declaration see WQ 129/77 (Don-
     delinger) O.J. 1977 C 168/23 and Forman (1977) 2 ELRev. 210.
598. Although the Treaty of Amsterdam (not yet in force) will permit the Court to exercise
     its powers in relation to Art. F(2) TEU insofar as it has jurisdiction under the EC,
     ECSC and Euratom Treaties and under the TEU itself, see the new Art. L(d) TEU.
599. So much so that the Treaty of Amsterdam (not yet in force) will introduce specific
     mention of *inter alia* respect for human rights and fundamental freedoms in the new
     Art. F(1) TEU, and mechanism will be created for suspending certain of the rights of
     Member States in respect of the conduct of which 'the existence of a serious and per-
     sistent breach' of the principles mentioned in Art. F(1) is determined, see the new Art.
     F.1 TEU. See also the new Arts. 236 EC, 96 ECSC, and 204 Euratom.

to argue that on the principle of substitution[600] the Community is itself
bound by the Convention in so far as it exercises authority in the place of
the Member States,[601] and indeed the Commission has in the past
proposed that the European Communities should accede to the European
Convention on Human Rights.[602] This would mean not merely that the
Communities would be formally bound by the catalogue of rights
enshrined in the Convention but also, if the right of individual petition
were accepted, that citizens would be able, after judicial remedies in the
Communities were exhausted, to bring a complaint to the European
Commission of Human Rights in Strasbourg on the ground that the
behaviour of the Community Institutions violated their rights.[603] Accession
to the Convention would require not merely the agreement of all parties to
the Convention but also the solution of a number of procedural and
substantive points which would be raised by the special nature of the
Communities and which would have to be resolved in an accession
protocol.[604] In order to shed some light on the question whether
Community accession would be compatible with the EC Treaty as it
stands, the Council sought the opinion of the Court of Justice under
Article 228(6) EC. In Opinion 2/94 *Accession by the Communities to the
European Convention on Human Rights*[605] the Court concluded that in
the present state of Community law the Community had no competence
to accede to the European Convention, as no provision of the Treaty
conferred in a general way the power on the Community Institutions
to enact rules concerning human rights or to conclude international
agreements in that field; moreover, Article 235 EC could not be used to

---

600. See section 7.5.2, *ante.*
601. In the same sense Schermers, *Judicial Protection in the European Communities* (3rd ed.,
     Deventer, 1983) 85 (although this view is not repeated in the 4th or 5th eds. (1987 and
     1992)). See, posing the question, the Commission's *Memorandum on the Accession of
     the European Communities to the European Convention on Human Rights and Funda-
     mental Freedoms* Bull. EC Supp. 2/79. However, such a substitution would require
     recognition by third countries (and would require amendment of the Convention or
     an additional Protocol as the Convention is only open to signature by Member States
     of the Council of Europe).
602. See the Commission's Memorandum, *ibid.*, and Bull. EC 10–1990 point 1.3.218. As to
     the views of the European Parliament, see Bull. EU 1/2–1994 point 1.1.6. It appears
     that the Commission was at one time of the view that accession was unnecessary: see
     The Protection of Fundamental Rights in the European Community Bull. EC Supp. 5/76.
603. The European Commission of Human Rights held on 10 July 1978 that a complaint
     by the Confédération Française Démocratique du Travail was inadmissible because
     legal acts of the Council could not be viewed as acts attributable to the jurisdiction of
     the Member States within the meaning of Art. 1 of the Convention, See also Case 66/
     76 *Confédération Française Démocratique du Travail v. Council* [1977] ECR 305, [1977]
     1 CMLR 589, and WQ 911/77 (Patijn) O.J. 1977 C 60/1.
604. See the Commission's Memorandum cited in note 375, *supra,* and, further Golsong
     (1978) EUGRZ 346 and (1979) EUGRZ 70 and Schermers (1978/1) LIEI 1.
605. [1996] ECR I-1759, [1996] 2 CMLR 265.

in effect widen the scope of the Treaty without amending it.[606] The Court held that respect for fundamental rights was a condition of the lawfulness of Community acts,[607] but the conclusion was that accession would require an amendment of the Treaties under the procedure prescribed by Article N TEU.

A different approach had long found favour in the European Parliament. In the past it appeared to favour the drawing-up of a charter of fundamental rights, specially adapted to the exercise of Community competence which would also cover economic and social rights.[608] However, instead of such a charter, the European Parliament adopted on 10 February 1994 a draft Constitution for the European Union, which includes provisions concerning the protection of fundamental rights.[609]

The protection of fundamental rights in the Community legal order binds not merely the Community Institutions themselves; the Court will also use general principles of law, and in particular those concerning fundamental rights where a Member State relies on the provisions of the Treaty (such as Article 56 EC) in order to justify national rules which are likely to obstruct the exercise of a freedom guaranteed by Community law.[610] However fundamental rights are not unfettered prerogatives, and the Court recognizes that they 'may be restricted, provided that the restrictions in fact correspond to objectives of general interest pursued by the Community and that they do not constitute, with regard to the objectives pursued, a disproportionate and intolerable interference which infringes upon the very substance of the rights guaranteed.'[611] The Court of Justice has no power to examine the compatibility with the European Convention of national rules which do not fall within the scope of Community law.[612] But if such rules do fall within the scope of

---

606. [1996] ECR I-1759 at 1787–1788.
607. *Ibid.* at 1789.
608. See the proceedings of the Round Table Conference on Special Rights and the Charter of Rights of Citizens of the European Community (Florence, 26–28 October 1978) and annexed documentation (European Parliament, Luxembourg, 1979). See also the Parliament's Resolution of 27 April 1979 (O.J. 1979 C 127/68–70), the De Gucht Report (EP Docs. A3–0025/93 and A3–0025/ANN/93 and the Parliament's Resolutions of 11 March 1993 (O.J. 1993 C 115/78) and 18 January 1994 (O.J. 1994 C 44/32).
609. See the Herman Report (EP Doc. A3–0064/94 and the Parliament's Resolution (O.J. 1994 C 61/155). The draft Constitution was not itself put to the vote, but was annexed to the Resolution (Bull. EU 1/2–1994 point 1.7.10).
610. See Case C-260/89 *Elliniki Radiophonia Tileorassi – AE (ERT) v. Dimotiki Etairia Pliroforissis et al.* [1991] ECR I-2925 at 2964; Case 5/88 *Wachauf v. Germany (Bundesamt für Ernährung und Forstwirtschaft* [1989] ECR 2609 at 2640.
611. Case 265/87 *Hermann Schräder HS Kraftfutter GmbH & Co. KG v. Hauptzollamt Gronau* [1989] ECR 2237 at 2268; Case C-62/90 *Commission v. Germany* [1992] ECR I-2575 at 2609. Objectives which may justify such restrictions include the protection of public health and human life (Case C-62/90, *ibid.*).
612. *E.g.* Cases 60 and 61/84 *Cinéthèque SA et al. v. Fédération nationale des cinémas fran-*

Community law, and a national court seeks a preliminary ruling, then the Court will give the necessary criteria of interpretation to the national court to enable it to determine whether the national rules concerned are compatible with the fundamental rights the observance of which the Court ensures, and which derive in particular from the Convention.[613]

7.6 Role of the Court of Justice in the process of integration

From the observations made above about the powers and functions of the Court it is clear that a vital place has been accorded to the legal element in the functioning of the Communities, something which does not tend to be the case in traditional international organizations. The Court has used this opportunity in an effective manner in order to give legal support and direction to the process of integration.[614] The most spectacular examples of this are in the fields of the relationship between Community law and national law,[615] the competence of the Community to conclude

çais [1985] ECR 2605 at 2627; Case 12/86 *Demirel v. Stadt Schwäbisch Gmünd* [1987] ECR 3719 at 3754; Case C-260/89 *Elliniki Radiophonia Tileorassi – AE (ERT) v. Dimotiki Etairia Pliroforissis et al.* [1991] ECR I-2925 at 2964, and Case C-159/90 *Society for the Protection of the Unborn Children Ireland Ltd. v. Grogan et al.* [1991] ECR I-4685 at 4741, and Case C-299/95 *Kremzow v. Austrian State* [1997] ECR I-2629 at 2645–2646. As to the judgment in *Grogan*, see O'Leary (1992) 17 ELRev. 138. The Court's reasoning in that case has led Chalmers, (1992) 17 ELRev. 248 at 255, to opine that 'there are disturbing signs … that the Court will avoid striking down measures of acute national sensitivity on the grounds of their incompatibility with the European Convention by reshaping Community rules, so that the enjoyment of many of the rights contained in the Convention falls outside the Treaty.' See also Biesheuvel (1988) SEW 659. In Case C-60/92 *Otto BV v. Postbank BV* [1993] ECR I-5683 at 5712–5713 the Court refused to transpose the restrictions on the Commission's investigative powers in competition matters requiring respect for the rights of the defence into the forum of a civil law dispute between private parties about the application of Community competition law: this concerned solely relationships between private parties and could not lead to the impostiton of any sanctions imposed by a public authority.

613. Case C-260/89 *ERT, ibid.*
614. See, generally, Green, *Political Integration by Jurisprudence* (Leiden, 1969) and Rasmussen, *On Law and Policy in the European Court of Justice* (Dordrecht, 1986). The latter should be read with the reviews by Cappelletti (1987) 12 ELRev. 3 and Weiler (1987) 24 CMLRev. 555 but see also Rasmussen (1988) 13 ELRev. 28. See further, Cappelletti *et al.* (eds.), *Integration through Law* (Berlin & New York, 1986); Easson (1989) RIE/JEI 101; Ehlermann (1984) 82 Mich.LR 1274; Hartley (1986) 34 AJComp.L 229; Kapteyn in *Mélanges Fernand Dehousse* (Paris, Brussels, 1979) Vol. II 45; Koopmans (1986) 35 ICLQ 925; Lenaerts (1992) 12 YBEL 1; Mertens de Wilmars and Steenbergen (1984) 82 Mich. LR 1377; Mouly (1985) RDIC 895; Sandalow and Stein (eds.), *Courts and Free Markets* (Oxford, 1982); VerLoren van Themaat (1984) Mich.LR 1422 and in Mestmäcker *et al.* (eds.), *Eine Ordnungspolitik für europa* (*Festschrift* for Von der Groeben, Baden-Baden, 1987) 425. See also Bengoetxea, *The Legal Reasoning of the European Court of Justice* (Oxford, 1993).

agreements[616] and the validity of fundamental rights in the Community legal order.[617]

In a less spectacular way, though, the Court has also made an important contribution to the establishment and proper functioning of the common market. It has given concrete form to the Community rules and powers in this area and has extended and refined them by always systematically co-ordinating them and relating them to the general and the specific objectives of Community law and its component branches. With the aid of this systematic teleological interpretation,[618] Community law has been endowed with the maximal effect where this has been possible and permitted; it has been moulded into a consistent legal system which can be managed in a supple manner to seek solutions for the varied and ever-changing legal questions which arise in the process of integration.

There are, though, certain limits to the Court's activities; these are linked to the special nature of Community law and to the judicial function as such. Community law is predominantly economic law. This means that in many cases Community law must allow the Institutions sufficient discretion in the exercise of the economic management entrusted to them to take appropriate measures in the varying and varied circumstances of economic life. This discretion may concern the opportuneness of their action or the means to be chosen or both.[619] But even if action is obligatory, or action is limited as to the means to be applied, this obligation as a rule will depend on, or the means to be applied will be determined by, an appreciation of a particular set of economic facts which have been defined in Community law in an objective sense, but which presuppose a certain subjective discretion in favour of the Community Institutions (or in some cases also in favour of the Member States on which the obligation has been

615. See Chapter II, section 3.3., *ante*, and Chapter VI, section 2.2, *post*.
616. See Chapter XII, section 2, *post*.
617. See section 7.5.4., *ante*.
618. See Bredimas, *Methods of Interpretation and Community Law* (Amsterdam, 1978); Brown and Jacobs, op. cit. (see note 390, *supra*) 299–322; Geelhoed in Schermers *et al.*, *Rechtsbescherming in de Europese Gemeenschappen* (Deventer, 1975) 129 at 148; Lasok and Millett, *op. cit.* (see note 414, *supra*) paras. 1105–1208; Mathijsen: *Teleologische interpretatie der Europese verdragen* (Inaugural Lecture, Nijmegen, 1970); *Reports of the Judicial and Academic Conference 27–28 September 1976* (Luxembourg, 1976), and Mertens de Wilmars (1986) CDE 5. See also Gormley in Krämer *et al.* (eds.), *Law and diffuse Interests in the European Legal Order* (*Festschrift* for Reich, Baden-Baden, 1997) 11.
619. See Case 78/74 *Deuka, Deutsche Kraftbutter GmbH B.J. Stolp v. Einfuhr- und Vorratsstelle für Getreide und Futtermittel* [1975] ECR 421 at 432. See also Case C-350/88 *Société française des Biscuits Delacre et al. v. Commission* [1990] ECR I-395 at 424–427 on the Commission's margin of dicretion in relation to common organizations of markets requiring continual adaptation depending on changes in the economic situation; in these circumstances there can be no legitimate expectation on the part of traders that the *status quo* will be maintained by the Community Institutions.

imposed).[620] Such *unbestimmte Rechtsbegriffe* (indeterminate legal concepts) are found, for instance, in Article 226 EC.[621]

Restrictions have, of course, been imposed on the Court's control of this discretion.[622] In this, the Court models its action on the national judicial control of the exercise of discretionary powers of government: judging according to principles of 'good government' and 'confining itself to an examination of the relevance of the facts and of the legal consequences' deduced from them[623] and examining whether or not the choice made in the exercise of discretion is of an arbitrary nature[624] and 'whether the evaluation of the comvetent authority contains a patent error or constitutes a misuse of power.'[625] In order to ensure a reasonable level of supervision, the Court generally tends to set high standards for fulfilment of the obligation to state reasons laid down in the Treaties.[626]

Whilst Community law is largely economic law, it is economic law in the making. It is law which in many ways has to be developed by 'Community legislation' and continually adapted to changing circumstances and views. The Community legislator is in principle the Council but this body in all too many cases fails to fulfil its functions as a result of failure to achieve unanimity on points where unanimity is not legally necessary but is in practice nevertheless doggedly insisted upon, even down to fine details.[627] Yet another problem is posed by the Council's reluctance to devolve further legislative power to the Commission.[628]

620. See *e.g.* (in relation to Art. 95 EC 2nd para.) Case 27/67 *Fink-Frucht GmbH v. Haupt-zollamt München-Landsbergerstrasse* [1968] ECR 223 at 232–233.
621. 'Difficulties which are serious and liable to persist in any sector of the economy or which could bring about serious deterioration in the economic situation of a given area', 'protective measures in order to rectify the situation and adjust the sector concerned to the economy of the common market' and 'priority to such measures as will least disturb the functioning of the common market' (the effect of Art. 226 EC is now spent). The various Acts of Accession usually contain similar provisions for safeguard measures for a limited period. See also Case 13/63 *Italy v. Commission* [1963] ECR 165, [1963] CMLR 289.
622. In Art. 33 ECSC, 1st para., 2nd second sentence, an attempt has been made to define the restriction on the Court's control of this discretion; in the other two Treaties it has been left to the Court itself to fix the limits.
623. Cases 56 and 58/64 *Ets. Consten SARL and Grundig- Verkaufs-GmbH v. Commission* [1966] ECR 299 at 347. See also Case 42/84 *Remia BV v. Commission* [1985] ECR 2545 at 2575.
624. Case 5/67 *W.Beus GmbH v. Hauptzollami München* [1968] ECR 83 at 96.
625. Case 78/74 *Deuka, loc. cit.* (see note 619, *supra*): 'When examining the lawfulness of the exercise of the Commission's freedom of discretion, the courts cannot substitute their own evaluation of the matter for that of the competent authority.' See also *e.g.* Case 324/85 *Boutellier v. Commission* [1987] ECR 529 and Case 233/85 *Bonino et al. v. Commission* [1987] ECR 739.
626. Art. 190 EC. See also Arts. 15 ECSC and 162 Euratom. See, further, Chapter V, section 1.5, *post*.
627. See Chapter V, sections 3.2, *post*.
628. See section 6.4.1, *ante*.

In these circumstances the Court has sometimes been obliged with the aid of the systematic teleological method of interpretation to deduce solutions from Community law for concrete problems which should have been dealt with by the Community legislator.[629] This has led to the Court being accused of indulging in judicial policy-making. Geelhoed has rightly observed, though, that the systematic teleological method of interpretation binds the judges to the system and aims of Community law and thus limits their freedom of policy choice.[630]

However, the systematic teleological approach seems to bind the judges less in some areas than in others with the result that the Court's case-law acquires a stronger aspect of judicial creativity than lawyers are used to seeing from national judges. Van Gerven even goes so far as to speak of the legislative activity of the Court, adducing support for this view from the case-law on competition in particular.[631] He considers this justified as long as the content of the given rule corresponds to a balance of interests about which there is a consensus in broad societal circles.

Such a strongly acentuated judicial creativity is open to objection on the ground of the lack of legal certainty.[632] Moreover, precisely because Community society is so heterogeneous in many ways, there is a danger that the Court may be mistaken in relation to the consensus although this can only appear finally in the light of reactions to its judgments. After well over 40 years' experience, though, there is less reason to fear such a mistake.

In the Report on 'The Unfinished European Integration,'[633] it was remarked that the Court's 'great' judgments concern the interpretation of

---

629. See *e.g.* Case 804/79 *Commission v. United Kingdom* [1981] ECR 1045, [1982] 1 CMLR 529, and the discussion in Chapter III, section 5.2.2, *ante*. See also Pescatore in Lüke *et al.* (eds.) *Rechtsvergleichung, Europarecht und Staatenintegration* (*Gedächtnisschrift* for Constantinesco, Cologne, 1983) 559.

630. See Geelhoed, *op. cit.* (see note 618, *supra*) 151.

631. In VerLoren van Themaat *et al.*, *Europees Kartelrecht Anno 1973* (Deventer, 1973) 175 *et seq.* In this sense he sees (at 211) the judgment in Case 6/72 *Europemballange Corporation and Continental Can Company Inc. v. Commission* [1973] ECR 215, [1973] CMLR 199 as being a high point of 'legislative activity'. See also Baardman (1973) *Ars Aequi* 315 and Chapter VIII, section 4.4, *post*.

632. Perhaps with a view to this point, in its judgments in Case 22/70 *Commission v. Council* [1971] ECR 263, [19711] CMLR 335 and Case 6/72 *Continental Can, loc. cit.* (see note 631, *supra*), in which it developed a 'new' rule, the Court concluded that on the facts the 'new' rule was inapplicable. Similarly, in exceptional circumstances the Court may limit in time the effect of its judgments, particularly, but not only, when it gives an interpretation going well beyond what was generally expected, *e.g.* in the application of the principle of equal pay for men and women (Art. 119 EC) in Case 43/75 *Defrenne v. SABENA* [1976] ECR 455 at 480–481. See, further, Chapter VI, sections 1.2.1 and 2.1.1, *post*.

633. WRR Report No. 28 (The Hague, 1986) p. 153 (161 in the Dutch version). This observation is based on the judgments in Case 26/62 *NV Algemene Transport- en Expeditie Onderneming Van Gend en Loos v. Nederlandse Administratie der Belastingen*

negative integration provisions.[634] The Court can explain the inter-
relationships of the unconditional obligations which the Treaty places on
Member States but, as has been shown above, it cannot substitute its
own judgment for that of the Council and the Commission in cases in
which the realisation of aims laid down in the Treaty requires positive
action by the Institutions. As the years advance and the emphasis is
placed more on positive integration, so the Court's role in the
integration process will become more modest. The Court also appears –
more so than in the past – to be impressed by the limits placed on its
task of judicial creativity. Nevertheless, it must be said that the Court
has often acted as the motor of integration, applying at once a carrot
and a stick to ensure that the Community Institutions and the Member
States comply with the obligations imposed upon them. Against the
background of a changing intellectual climate, Koopmans saw a
reversion to a more minimalist role, that of conflict-resolver. 'The Court
tries, more than it did, to identify areas in which a judicial approach
may be helpful, and it then applies strict minimum standards to matters
like discrimination on grounds of nationality or sex, the treatment of
aliens, or technical requirements for commodities.'[635] That view is not
universally shared, and in the Nineties the Court has not been afraid to
make huge strides forward in various areas, such as a Member State's
liability for damges for loss caused by its breaches of Community law,[636]
even if sometimes judgments have been criticised for less than convincing
reasoning.[637]

8. THE COURT OF AUDITORS

Since the coming into force of the Second Budgetary Treaty on 1 June
1977, the European Communities have been equipped with a Court of
Auditors, and this body was raised to the status of a Community

---

[1963] ECR 1, [1963] CMLR 105; Case 8/74 *Procureur du Roi v. Dassonville* [1974]
ECR 837, [1974] 2 CMLR 436; Case 2/74 *Reyners v. Belgian State [1974]* ECR 631,
[1974] 2 CMLR 305 and Cases 286/82 and 26/83 *Luisi and Carbone v. Ministero del
Tesoro* [1984] ECR 377, [1985] 3 CMLR 52.

634. On the difference between positive and negative integration see Chapter III, section
1.2.3, *ante*; see, further, Mertens de Wilmars (1982/1) LIEI 1.

635. (1986) 35 ICLQ 925 at 931. He points to the judgment in Case 293/83 *Gravier v. City
of Liège* [1985] ECR 593, [1985] 3 CMLR 1; see Timmermans (1986) SEW 86.

636. See Chapter VI, section 2.3.2, *post*.

637. *E.g.* Cases C-267 and 268/91 *Keck and Mithouard* [1993] ECR I-6079, [1995] 1 CMLR
105. See, generally (referring to other literature and the *Keck* debate) Gormley (1996)
19 Fordh. Int'l. LJ 866; Joliet (1995) 1 Columb. J. Eur. L. 436, Ross in Caiger and
Floudas (eds.), *1996 Onwards: Lowering the barriers further* (Chichester, 1996) 45, and
VerLoren van Themaat (1996) SEW 398. As to some other examples, see Gormley in
Krämer *et al.* (eds.), *op. cit.* (see note 618, *supra*).

Institution by the amendments made by the Treaty on European Union,[638] and the provisions of the Treaties governing the Court of Auditors have been revised accordingly.[639] Originally the audit function was carried out internally but then an Audit Board was established for all three Communities.[640] This was then replaced by the Court of Auditors which is now composed of fifteen members, chosen 'from among persons who belong or have belonged in their respective countries to external audit bodies or who are especially qualified for this office' and their independence 'must be beyond doubt.'[641] They are appointed for a term of six years by unanimous vote of the Council after having consulted the European Parliament and are eligible for reappointment.[642] In the general interest of the Communities they are to be completely independent in the performance of their duties[643] and in this their task resembles that of the members of the Commission and the Court of Justice; indeed, their general legal position is pretty well the same.[644] Even before the Treaties conferred on the Court of Auditors the status of an Institution of the Communities, it was effectively treated as if it already had such status.[645]

The Court of Auditors examines the revenue and expenditure of the Communities.[646] It examines whether all revenue has been received and all expenditure incurred in a lawful and regular manner and whether the financial management has been sound.[647] The control is based on records and, if necessary, can be performed on the spot in the Community

638. Arts. 4(1) EC, 7 ECSC, and 3(1) Euratom.
639. See Arts. 188a–188c EC, 45a–45c ECSC, and 160a–160c Euratom, replacing the old Arts. 206 EEC, 78e ECSC, 180 Euratom, and Merger Treaty, Art. 22 (as amended). The effect was to move the old provisions from among the financial provisions to the institutional provisions of the Treaties, and to specify that the Court of Auditors carries out the audit (Arts. 188a EC, 45a ECSC, and 160a Euratom).
640. Merger Treaty, Art. 22 (as originally adopted).
641. Arts. 188b(1) and (2) EC; 45b(1) and (2) ECSC, and 160b(1) and (2) Euratom.
642. Arts. 188b(3) EC; 45b(3) ECSC, and 160b(3) Euratom (1st and 3rd paras. in each case). A phased retirement was assured, *ibid.* (2nd para. in each case). The European Parliament has begun to flex its muscles in regard to the approval of nominees, refusing to approve the nomination of a new Portuguese member in 1994 (O.J. 1994 C 44/68). See Bradley and Feeney (1994) 14 YBEL 401 at 423. As to the procedure, see the European Parliament's Rules of Procedure (O.J. 1997 L 49/1), Rule 35.
643. Arts. 188b(4) EC; 45b(4) ECSC, and 160b(4) Euratom. In the performance of their duties they are prohibited from seeking or taking instructions from any government or any other body, and they must refrain from any action incompatible with their duties, *ibid.*
644. See Arts. 188b(5)–(9) EC, 45b(5)–(9) ECSC, and 160b(5)–(9) Euratom.
645. See, generally, Price (1982) 2 YBEL 239. See also Case 828/79 *Adam v. Commission* [1982] ECR 269 at 290–291.
646. Arts. 188c(1) EC, 45c(1) ECSC, and 160c(1) Euratom. The Court also examines the accounts of all revenue and expenditure of all bodies set up by the Community in so far as the relevant constituent instrument does not preclude such examination, *ibid.*
647. Arts. 188c(2) EC, 45c(2) ECSC, and 160c(2) Euratom. The Treaty of Amsterdam (not yet in force) will add the obligation to report in particular on any irregularity (putting existing practice on a firm legal basis).

Institutions and in the Member States; in the latter cases this is done in liaison with the audit bodies or competent national departments.[648] The annual report drawn up at the close of each financial year is forwarded to the Institutions and is published, with their replies, in the Official Journal.[649] The Court of Auditors is empowered to submit observations at any time, particularly in the form of special reports, on specific questions and to deliver opinions at the request of any Community Institution.[650] The annual report of the Court of Auditors and the Institutions' replies thereto form an important part of the procedure leading to the discharge which the Parliament grants to the Commission in respect of the implementation of the budget.[651] In a Declaration annexed to the Final Act on the occasion of signature of the TEU, the Conference of the Representatives of the Governments of the Member states emphasized the special importance attached to the work of the Court of Auditors, and requested the other Community Institutions to consider, together with the Court of Auditors, all appropriate ways of enhancing the effectiveness of its work.[652] See, further, section 2.2.5 of Chapter V, below.

9. INDEPENDENT COMMUNITY ORGANS

9.1 The European Investment Bank

Article 129 EEC set up the European Investment Bank (EIB) and gave it legal personality, and its establishment is now effected by Article 4b EC.[653] The members of the EIB are the Member States.[654] Its organization, tasks and methods of working are now set out in Articles 198d and 198e EC and in the Protocol on the Statute of the European

---

648. Arts. 188c(3) EC, 45c(3) ECSC, and 160c(3) Euratom. The other Community Institutions, the national audit bodies and other national departments are obliged to forward to the Court of Auditors, at its request, any document or information necessary to carry out its tasks, *ibid.* The Treaty of Amsterdam (not yet in force) will amend Art. 188c(3) EC so as to improve considerably the effectiveness of the audit.
649. Arts. 188c(4) EC, 45c(4) ECSC, and 160c(4) Euratom.
650. *Ibid.* Additionally, under Art. 45c(5) ECSC the Court of Auditors draws up a separate annual report stating whetherthe accounting other than that for expenditure otherwise covered, and the financial management by the Commission relating thereto have been effected in a regular manner. This report is drawn up within 6 months of the end of the financial year involved and is presented to the Commission and the Council; it is forwarded to the Parliament by the Commission, *ibid.*
651. Arts. 206 EC, 78g ECSC, and 180b Euratom. The Court of Auditors assists the European Parliament and the Council in exercising their powers of control over the implementation of the budget, Arts. 188c(4) EC, 45c(4) ECSC, and 160c(4) Euratom.
652. Declaration No. 21.
653. Legal personality is now conferred by Art. 198d EC, 1st para.
654. Art. 198d EC, 2nd para.; Protocol on the EIB, Art. 3.

Investment Bank which is annexed to the Treaty.[655] The direction and management of the Bank is entrusted to three bodies. The Board of Governors is composed of ministers designated by the Member States, and lays down general directives for the credit policy of the EIB;[656] the Board of Directors decides on the various operations undertaken by the Bank and ensures that it is properly run; its 25 members and 13 alternates are nominated by the Member States and the Commission according to a formula laid down in Article 11 of the EIB Statute;[657] the Management Committee consisting of a President and six Vice-Presidents is appointed for a period of six years by the Board of Governors, acting on a proposal from the Board of Directors and is responsible for the day-to-day running of the Bank.[658] The members of the Board of Directors and of the Management Committee, and the staff of the EIB, are independent in the performance of their duties and are responsible only to the EIB itself.[659] In accordance with the scheme of Article 4 of the Statute the Member States subscribe the capital of the Bank. The latter may grant loans and guarantees to its members (the Member States) or to private or public undertakings to facilitate the financing of investment projects in all sectors of the economy of the types listed in Article 198e EC. The projects must be in the European territories of the Member States and finance is available to the extent that funds are not available from other sources on reasonable terms; the territorial restriction applies unless a derogation is authorised by unanimous vote of the Board of Governors on a proposal from the Board of Directors.[660] Various agreements concluded by the Communities with third countries or groups of third countries by the Bank envisage the grant of loans for projects in these countries.[661]

655. Last revised by Dec. 95/1 (O.J. 1995 L 1/1), Art. 42. As to the activities of the EIB, see Chapter IX, section 5.4, *post*. As to public access to documents, see O.J. 1997 C 243/13.
656. EIB Statute, Art. 9. The measures taken by the Board of Directors may be subject to actions for annulment, under Art. 180(b) EC, at the instance of any Member State, the Commission, or the Board of Directors.
657. As most recently amended by Dec. 95/1 (O.J. 1995 L 1/1). The Board of Directors exercises the infringement proceedings powers conferred on the EIB under Art. 180(a) EC. Measures adopted by the Board of Directors may be subject to annulment proceedings, under Art. 180(c) EC, at the instance of Member States or the Commission, on the limited grounds set out in that provision.
658. *Ibid.*, Art. 13.
659. EIB Statute, Arts. 11(2), last para. (Board of Directors chosen from persons whose independence and competence is beyond doubt), and 13(8), as expressed in the text.
660. *Ibid.*, Art. 18(1).
661. See *e.g.* the Lomé Agreements (the latest is the Fourth, signed on 15 December 1989, which entered into force on 1 September 1991 (Dec. 91/400, O.J. 1991 L 229/1)), the Association Agreement with Turkey; the Agreements with the Mediterranean countries, and the Europe Agreements with the Central and Eastern European Countries.

9.2   The European Monetary Institute; European Central Bank, and European System of Central Banks

From 1 January 1994, the starting date of the second stage of Economic and Monetary Union,[662] the European Monetary Institute (EMI) came into being and started work;[663] it has a number of tasks aimed at preparing for the transition to the third stage, and specifically monitors the functioning of the European Monetary System.[664] It replaced the Committee of Governors of Central Banks of the Member States, established in 1964, and the European Monetary Co-operation Fund, set up by the Council in 1973. The Fund had been established in the context of the then current plans to achieve an economic and monetary union, and performed certain important technical financial functions relating to the exchange rate system set up by the Communities, first known as 'the snake' and since 1 January 1979 called the European Monetary System. Both of these bodies were dissolved on 1 January 1994.[665] The EMI has legal personality and is directed and managed by a Council, consisting of a President, and the Governors of the national central banks, one of whom is Vice-President.[666] The EMI 's activities and functioning are further detailed in the EMI Statute, which is contained in a Protocol annexed to the EC Treaty.

The EMI is empowered to formulate, or submit opinions and formulate, submit or make recommendations on various aspects of exchange rate and monetary policy pursued by the Member States, and on the functioning of the European Monetary System.[667] On the basis of bilateral contracts with the national central banks, the EMI may hold and manage foreign exchange reserves as agent for, and at the request of those banks.[668] The seat of the EMI, and of its impending successor, the European Central

662. Art. 109e(1) EC.
663. Art. 109f(1) EC.
664. See Art. 109e(2) and (3).
665. Art. 109f(1), final subpara., and (2), 5th indent, respectively.
666. Art. 109f(1) EC, 1st subpara. The President is appointed by common accord of the governments of the Member States, acting at the level of Heads of State or Government, acting on a recommendation, (for the initial appointment) from the Committee of Governors of the central banks of the Member States, and thereafter from the Council of the EMI itself, and after consulting the European Parliament and the Council; as to the procedure in the Parliament, see European Parliament's Rules of Procedure (O.J. 1997 L 49/1), Rule 36. The President is selected from among persons of recognized standing and professional experience in monetary or banking matters, and must be a national of a Member State. The Vice-President is appointed by the Council of the EMI itself, Art. 109f(1) EC, 2nd subpara.
667. Art. 109f(4). In these cases it acts by a majority of two-thirds of the members of its Council, ibid., but a decision to publish its opinions and recommendations must be taken unanimously, Art. 109f(5). See also EMI Statute, Arts. 4–7.
668. EMI Statute, Art. 6.4. Profits and losses regarding these reserves fall to the national central banks, ibid.

Bank, is in Frankfurt am Main.[669] The Protocol on Privileges and Immunities of the European Communities applies to the EMI.[670]

With effect from the start of the third and final stage of Economic and Monetary Union, the EMI will be dissolved and replaced by a European Central Bank (ECB),[671] which is part of a European System of Central Banks (ESCB).[672] The primary objective of the ESCB is to maintain price stability, and without prejudice to that objective, the ECSB will support the general economic policies in the Community with a view to contributing to the achievement of the Community's objectives as laid down in Article 2 EC.[673] The provisions governing the ESCB and the ECB are split (with some duplication) between the body of the EC Treaty itself and the ESCB and ECB Statute, annexed to that Treaty.[674] Like its precursor, the EMI, the ECB does have legal personality,[675] although the ESCB as such does not. The ECB's governing bodies are the Governing Council and the Executive Board.[676] The Governing Council consists of the members of the Executive Board and the Governors of the national central banks.[677] The Executive Board comprises the President, the Vice-President, and four other members, and is appointed for a non-renewable term of 8 years.[678] The Governors of the national central banks are

---

669. See Chapter II, section 5,3, *ante.*
670. Protocol on Privileges and Immunities, Art. 23 (added by a Protocol annexed to the EC Treaty). As to public access to administrative doucments of the EMI, see Dec. 9/ 97 (O.J. 1998 L 90/43).
671. Arts. 4a and 109l(2) EC. It is operational since 1 July 1998.
672. Art. 106(1) EC.
673. Art. 105(1) EC; ESCB and ECB Statute, Art. 2.
674. Arts. 105–109b EC; Statute, Arts. 3–25. See, generally, Amtenbrink, *The Democratic Accountability of Central Banks: the European Central Bank in the light of its peers* (Diss., Groningen, 1998); Andenas *et al.* (eds.), *European Economic and Monetary Union: The Institutional Framework* (London, 1997); Gormley and de Haan (1996) 21 ELRev. 95; Harden in Gretschmann (ed.), *Economic and Monetary Union: Implications for National Policy-makers* (Dordrecht, 1993) 149; Louis in Stuyck (ed.), *Financial and Monetary Integration in the European Economic Community: Legal, Institutional and Economic Aspects* (Deventer, 1993) 13; Slot in Curtin and Heukels (eds.), *op. cit.* (see note 10, *supra*) 229, and Smits (1992) SEW 702 and (1996) 45 ICLQ 319.
675. Art. 106(2) EC; ESCB and ECB Statute, Art.9.1.
676. Art. 106(3) EC. Exceptionally, as long as there are Member States with a derogation, a third decision-making body will exist, the General Council of the ECB, ESCB and ECB Statute, Art. 45 (see also *ibid.*, Art. 53).
677. Art. 109a(1) EC; ESCB and ECB Statute, Art. 10.1. As to voting, see Statute, Art. 10(2) and (3).
678. Art. 109a(2) EC; Statute, Art. 11. The appointments are made, from among persons of recognized standing and professional experience in monetary or banking matters, by common accord of the governments of the Member States, acting at the level of Heads of State or Government, on a recommendation from the Council, after the Council has consulted the European Parliament and the Governing Council of the ECB, and only nationals of Member States may be members of the Executive Board,

appointed unde the normal national procedures, but they enjoy considerable security of tenure.[679] It is a hallmark of the ECB that it enjoys identical guarantees of independence, and non-interference, to those enjoyed by the Judges and Advocates General at the Court, the members of the Commission, and the members of the Court of Auditors.[680]

The ESCB is a system involving sixteen banks: the fifteen national central banks, and the ECB itself. As has already been observed, the ESCB as such has no legal personality; it also has no organs of its own. It is governed by the decision-making bodies of the ECB, namely the Governing Council and the Executive Board.[681] In order to carry out the tasks entrusted to the ESCB, the ECB will, in accordance with the various provisions of the EC Treaty and under the conditions laid down in the ESCB and ECB Statute, make regulations, take decisions, and issue recommendations and opinions.[682] Binding acts of the ECB will be open to review by the Court of Justice in actions for annulment under Article 173 EC, and the ECB itself is entitled to bring actions for annulment under that provision for the purpose of defending its prerogatives. The ECB can also be the subject of, or bring an action for failure to act under Article 175 EC. Moreover, the ECB may bring infringement proceedings on account of failures by national central banks to fulfil their obligations under the EC Treaty or the Statute.[683] In the second stage of Economic and Monetary Union, these actions may be taken by, or brought against the EMI.[684] The Protocol on Privileges and Immunities of the European Communities applies to the ECB.[685] See, further, section 3.3.3 of Chapter IX, below.

---

ibid. As to the initial appointment of the members, see Statute, Art. 50, which will ensure that not everyone retires at the same time, and permits the initial membership of the Executive Board to be less than six, but not less than four people.

679. ESCB and ECB Statute, Art. 14. The Member States are obliged to ensure that their national legislation, including the Statutes of their national central banks, is compatible with the EC Treaty and the Statute, Art. 108 EC, Statute, Art. 14.1.

680. Art. 107 EC, ESCB and ECB Statute, Art. 7.

681. Art. 106(3) EC. ESCB and ECB Statute, Art. 8 does not repeat the specification of the two bodies, as the General Council will have some functions as long as it exists, see Statute, Art. 47.

682. Art. 108a(1) EC. Such instruments have the usual effects, see Art. 108a(2) EC; regulations and decisions must be reasoned, regulations must, and decisions, recommendations and opinions may be published, Art. 108a(3) EC. The ECB may under certain conditions impose fines or periodic penalty payments on undertakings for failure to comply with its regulations and decisions, Art. 108a(3) EC, and these fines and payments are enforceable, Art. 192 EC, in conjunction with Art. 108a(2) EC.

683. Art. 180(d) EC.

684. Art. 109e(9) EC; EMI Statute, Art. 19.

685. Protocol on Privileges and Immunities, Art. 23 (added by a Protocol annexed to the EC Treaty).

9.3 Other independent Community bodies

Besides the bodies discussed above, a number of independent bodies have been established or are in the process of being established. These Agencies or Offices all have specific and important functions, but their activities are not considered further in this work.[686] In chronological order, these bodies are:

(1) The European Centre for the Development of Vocational Training (CEDEFOP);[687]
(2) The European Foundation for the Improvement of Living and Working Conditions;[688]
(3) The European Environment Agency;[689]
(4) The European Training Foundation;[690]
(5) The European Monitoring Centre for Drugs and Drug Addiction;[691]
(6) The European Agency for the Evaluation of Medicinal Products;[692]
(7) The Office for Harmonization in the Internal Market (trade marks, designs and models);[693]
(8) The European Agency for Safety and Health at Work;[694]

---

686. The Euratom Supply Agency (set up under Art. 53 Euratom) and the Joint Under-takings to be established by Council Decision under Art. 49 Euratom also have legal personality on the basis of the Treaty provisions. See, further, Chapter XI, section 5, *post*. Europol and the Europol Drugs Unit are Union bodies rather than Community bodies, see Chapter II, section 1.2.3, *ante*.

687. Reg. 337/75 (O.J. 1975 L 39/1, most recently amended by Reg. 3541/95 (O.J. 1995 L 41/1)), established originally in Berlin, subsequently in Thessaloniki.

688. Reg. 1365/75 (O.J. 1975 L 139/1, most recently amended by Act of Austrian, Finnish and Swedish Accession (1994) as adapted), established in Dublin.

689. Reg. 1210/90 (O.J. 1990 L 120/1), established in Copenhagen, see Davies (1994) 14 YBEL 313. As to proposed amendments, see COM (97) 282 Final (O.J. 1997 C 255/9, amended by COM (98) 191 Final (O.J. 1998 C 123/6)) and COM (97) 489 Final (O.J. 1997 C 335/16). As to public access to documents, see O.J. 1997 C 282/5.

690. Reg. 1360/90 (O.J. 1990 L 131/1, amended by Reg. 2063/94 (O.J. 1994 L 216/90), established in Turin. As to proooposed amendments, see COM (97) 489 Final (O.J. 1997 C 335/18). As to public access to documents, see O.J. 1997 C 369/10.

691. Reg. 302/93 (O.J. 1993 L 214/1), established in Lisbon. As to proposed amendments, see COM (97) 489 Final (O.J. 1997 C 335/17).

692. Reg. 2309/93 (O.J. 1993 L 214/1), established in London, see Gardner (1996) 2 ELJ 48. As to proposed amendments, see COM (97) 489 Final (O.J. 1997 C 335/15).

693. Reg. 40/94 (O.J. 1994 L 11/1, amended by Reg. 3288/94 (O.J. 1994 L 349/83) and implemented by Reg. 2868/95 (O.J. 1995 L 303/1)), established in Alicante (popularly known as the European Trade Mark Office). As to proposed amendments, see COM (96) 372 Final (O.J. 1996 C 300/11) and COM (97) 489 Final (O.J. 1997 C 335/13).

694. Reg. 2062/94 (O.J. 1994 L 216/1), established in Bilbao. As to proposed amendments, see COM (97) 489 Final (O.J. 1997 C 335/17). See, generally, the Decision on seats (O.J. 1993 C 323/1). The Community's Veterinary and Phytosanitary Office (OICVP) mentioned therein is not an independent body, it works within the Commission, Bull. EC 12–1991 point 1.2.201.

(9)   The Community Plant Variety Office;[695]
(10)   The Translation Centre for bodies of the European Union;[696]
(11)   The European Monitoring Centre on Racism and Xenophobia.[697]

10.   SUBSIDIARY BODIES

10.1   The Consultative Committee of the ECSC; the Economic and Social Committee of the EEC and Euratom

Within the Communities provision has been made for an institutionalised representation of economic and social life, the organization and duties of which are laid down by the Treaties.[698] The ECSC Treaty provides for a Consultative Committee, in which three categories of interested parties in this sector are equally represented, *viz.* producers, workers, and consumers and dealers.[699] All sectors of economic and social life, including the liberal professions and the 'general interest', are represented in the Economic and Social Committee of the EC and Euratom (ECOSOC).[700] An adequate representation of these sectors has to be ensured. In practice three groups of approximately equal size can be distinguished in the ECOSOC: employers in the field of industry, trade, and agriculture (with the exception of the small-scale trades), workers and a residual group made up of representatives of consumers' interests and experts in matters of general interest.

As regards the number of seats to be allotted to each nationality, no rules have been laid down in the ECSC Treaty for the 84–108 members of the Consultative Committee. The division of the 222 seats in ECOSOC, on the other hand, has been fixed in the Treaties.[701] The members of both Committees are appointed by the Council (for the ECOSOC this is by

---

695. Reg. 2100/94 (O.J. 1994 L 227/1), established in Angers (O.J. 1996 C 36/1).
696. Reg. 2964/94 (O.J. 1994 L 314/1, amended by Reg. 2610/95 (O.J. 1995 L 268/1). This is a somewhat unusual construction, established in Luxembourg, operating independently (having its own legal personality) within the Commission's translation services, providing translation facilities to various other independent Community bodies. As to proposed amendments, see COM (97) 489 Final (O.J. 1997 C 335/19). As to public access to documents, see O.J. 1998 C 46/5.
697. Reg. 1035/97 (O.J. 1997 L 151/1, corrig. O.J. 1997 L 230/19), established in Vienna (O.J. 1997 C 194/4). As to proposed amendments, see COM (97) 489 Final (O.J. 1997 C 335/19).
698. Arts. 193–198 EC, 165–170 Euratom. See also the Convention on Certain Institutions common to the European Communities (concluded on the signing of the EEC and Euratom Treaties, Rome, 25 March 1957), Art. 5, and Arts. 18–19 ECSC.
699. Art. 18 ECSC (as amended by Dec. 95/1 (O.J. 1995 L 1/1)), Art. 16. As to the functioning of this Committee, see Art. 19 ECSC.
700. As to the appointment, functioning, and consultation of ECOSOC, see Arts. 193–198 EC and 165–170 Euratom. The Convention on Certain Institutions (see note 698, *supra*), Art. 5(2) provides for a section specializing in nuclear energy questions.
701. Arts. 194 EC and 166 Euratom.

unanimous vote) and sit in their personal capacity. The procedure of appointment of members of the ECOSOC is less democratic than is the ECSC procedure of appointment to the Consultative Committee. In the former the Member States have the right to nominate candidates. In the ECSC this right is possessed by representative (national) organizations designated by the Council, at least as far as groups of producers and workers are concerned. The Council hardly ever avails itself of the possibility, provided in the EC and Euratom Treaties, to obtain the opinion of the European bodies which are representative of the various economic and social sectors to which the activities of the Communities are of concern, although such organizations exist in many sectors.[702] An element of Community procedure is provided for in the EC and Euratom Treaties by the requirement to consult the Commission.[703] ECOSOC members may not be bound by any mandatory instructions, and are completely independent in the performance of their duties, in the general interest of the Community.[704]

In the Treaties the two Committees are not given the status of Community Institutions in the formal sense.[705] The Consultative Committee assists the Commission. The latter is sometimes required to consult it and may always do so. Moreover, the Committee may give its opinion to the Commission without being asked. This possibility can be inferred from its right to be called together not only at the request of the latter Institution, but also at the request of a majority of its members, for the purpose of discussing a given question.[706] ECOSOC used not to have such a right but now does.[707] It addresses opinions to the Council as well as to the Commission.[708] These Institutions may, if they so which, proceed to consult ECOSOC; they are required to do so in those cases where this is prescribed by Treaty provisions. Under the Euratom Treaty it is invariably the Commission which is required to consult ECOSOC. Under the EC

---

702. See Arts. 195(2) EC and 167(2) Euratom. There are many hundreds of interest group organisations operating at the European level; they include the free and Christian trade unions, UNICE (the industrial lobby), COPA (the agricultural lobby) BEUC (the consumers loby) and the CCBE (the lawyers' lobby).
703. Arts. 195(2) EC and 167(2) Euratom. On the appointment of members of ECOSOC see Case 297/86 *Confederazione Italiana Dirigenti di Azienda (CIDA) et al. v. Council* [1988] ECR 3531, and Case T-381/94 *Sindacato Pensionati Italani et al. v. Council* [1995] ECR II-2741.
704. Arts. 194 EC and 166 Euratom (3rd para. in each case).
705. See Arts. 4(2) EC, 7 ECSC, and 3(2) Euratom.
706. Art. 19 ECSC, 4th para.
707. Arts. 196 EC and 168 Euratom (3rd para. in each case), codifying earlier practice which had developed since a decision of the Paris Summit of October 1972 (Bull. EC 10-1972, p. 23). ECOSOC may now adopt its own Rules of Procedure, Arts. 196 EC and 168 Euratom (2nd para. in each case), as to which, see O.J. 1996 L 82/1. As to public access to ECOSOC documents, see Dec. 97/1210 (O.J. 1997 L 339/18).
708. See Arts. 4(2) EC and 3(2) Euratom.

Treaty, on the other hand, this obligation rests (with one exception)[709] with the Council. As regards this compulsory consultation, just as for that of the European Parliament,[710] no distinct system has been followed in the Treaty.[711] It is, for instance, striking that the EC Treaty does not provide for obligatory consultation of ECOSOC on decisions of the Council in the field of the rules of competition (Articles 85 *et seq.* EC).

The possibility of consulting ECOSOC without being obliged to do so has been widely used by the Council and the Commission, either of their own motion or at the request of the chairman of ECOSOC. The Commission in particular has made great efforts to involve ECOSOC as much as possible, and informally, in the execution of its tasks, so as to gain understanding and support for its policies, thus members of the Commission participate in the various ECOSOC meetings. The influence of ECOSOC on Community policy is, however, on the whole not as great as it might be, owing to lack of homogeneity of ECOSOC itself. The great variety of interests represented, which still show a strong national trend, makes it difficult to find majorities for making clear pronouncements.[712] For their concrete desires concerning the content of Community policy the various interest groups have the opportunity of lobbying their governments individually in a national context and the Commission in the European context.

10.2   The Committee of the Regions

The Committee of the Regions assists the Council and the Commission in an advisory capacity.[713] It consists of representatives of regional and local bodies, and consists of 222 members, identical to the number of members of ECOSOC, and distributed among the Member States according to the same pattern.[714] Members of the Committee may not be bound by any mandatory instructions, and are completely independent in the performance of their duties, in the general interest of the Community.[715] The consultation of the Committee also largely follows that applicable to ECOSOC, although whenever ECOSOC is consulted the Committee is to

709. Under Art. 43(2) EC.
710. As to which, see section 5.2.1, *ante.*
711. But the Council or Commission may now, if it considers it necessary, set a time limit of not less than one month for ECOSOC to submit its Opinion, and upon the expiry of the time-limit the absence of an opinion will not prevent further action, Arts. 198 EC and 170 Euratom (2nd para. in each case).
712. ECOSOC does not always accept that the Commission's proposals are sensible, and sometimes they are withdrawn or substantially amended on account of the adverse reaction they receive in *inter alia* ECOSOC.
713. Art. 4(2) EC; see, further, Arts. 198a–198c EC.
714. Art. 198a EC.
715. Art. 198a EC, 3rd para.

be informed by the Council or the Commission of the request for an opinion; where the Committee considers that specific regional interests are involved, it may issue an opinion on the matter; it may also issue own initiative opinions.[716] The Committee adopts its own Rules of Procedure, but they require the unanimous approval of the Council.[717]

10.3 Other Committees

A very important subsidiary body of the Council is the Committee of Permanent Representatives already referred to in section 3.4. of this Chapter, above.[718] In view of its influential function in the decision-making process of the Council the role of *Coreper* will be discussed more fully in section 3.3 of Chapter V, below.

Particularly in the EC structure there are a great many consultative committees, the institution of which is sometimes provided for in the Treaties,[719] but mainly in decisions of the Council.[720] According to their composition, two types of committees can be distinguished; those whose members are representatives of the Member States or national experts and those in which the interested parties in a given sector are represented. A tripartite composition (governments, workers and employers) is provided for *inter alia*, in the case of the Committee for the European Social Fund set up under Article 124 EC.

According to their tasks these committees can be divided into those which assist the Council, the Commission and the Member States in the preparation of a common or co-ordinated policy (policy-making committees) and those which provide the Commission with opinions in the performance of its delegated administrative duties (advisory committees).[721] A whole series of policy-making committees usually composed of senior officials or other highly qualified experts has been set up by the Council in the field of co-ordination of economic policies (in the wide sense of this

---

716. Art. 198c EC. The Committee's opinion and the record of its proceedings are forwarded to the Council and to the Commission, *ibid.* As it does with ECOSOC, the Commission takes the Committee very seriously and its members brief the Committee on key relevant policies.

717. Art. 198b EC, 2nd para. See O.J. 1994 L 132/49, amended O.J. 1995 L 69/47. As to public access to the Committee's Reports, see O.J. 1997 L 351/70. The *General Report 1997* ((Brussels, Luxembourg, 1998) points 1166–1174 gives a good overview of the increasing activities of this Committee.

718. Arts. 151(1) EC, 30(1) ECSC, and 121(1) Euratom.

719. Arts. 83, 109c(1) and 124 EC, see also Art. 134 Euratom.

720. See the overview in Bull. EC 1980 Supp. 2/80 and COM (84) 93 final. See also Dec. 98/235 (O.J. 1998 L 88/59) on various advisory committees set up by the Commission in the agricultural sector. The annex to Art. 251 of the Budget (annually) lists the committees involved. As to the types of committee by category, see Docksey and Williams in Edwards and Spence (ed.), *op. cit.* (see note 90, *supra*) 141–143 and literature cited there.

term), and they have been charged in particular with the promotion of co-operation between the Member States in this field. A Monetary Committee was already provided for in Article 109c EC, although it will be dissolved at the beginning of the third stage of Economic and Monetary Union when it is replaced by the Economic and Financial Committee provided for in Article 109c(2) EC. Under Article 145 EC, the Council set up a Committee on Economic Policy;[722] on the same basis it also established a Committee of Governors of Central Banks, which has now been dissolved.[723] A coordination group was set up to ensure permanent mutual information concerning co-ordination of short-term economic and financial policy in the context of a European Monetary Union;[724] the Member States and the Commission are each represented by a senior official. Under Article 145 EC the Council has also set up a Permanent Committee for Labour Problems of the European Communities,[725] consisting of representatives of the Council (or the governments of the Member States), the Commission and all but one of the European employers' and trade union organizations. A Committee on Employment and the Labour Market has also been established.[726]

There is hardly any field of administration delegated by the Council to the Commission in which the Commission is not required to consult committees, specially established for the purpose, in which the official services of the Member States working in that field are represented. The opinions issued sometimes have legal consequences, as in the case of the management committees for the organization of the markets for various agricultural products, and the regulatory committees in the field of public health and customs regulations.[727] In addition to these committees of officials there are also in many cases consultative committees, in which directly interested parties are represented, particularly, for instance, in the field of market organizations for various agricultural products,[728] agricultural structure policy,[729] social problems of agricultual workers[730], and the opening-up of public procurement.[731] Thus, even at the executive

---

721. See WQ 188/76 (Noè) O.J. 1976 C 203/6.
722. Dec. 74/122 (O.J. 1974 L 63/21), replacing earlier committees.
723. Dec. 64/300 (O.J. English Special Edition 1963–1964, p. 141) established the Committee; Art. 109f(1) EC, final para. dissolved it (with effect from 1 January 1994).
724. Council Resolution of 21 March 1972 (O.J. English Special Edition (2nd Series) IX, p. 65).
725. Dec. 70/532 (O.J. English Special Edition 1970 (II), p. 863) and Dec. 75/62 (O.J. 1975 L 21/17)
726. Dec. 97/16 (O.J. 1997 L 6/32).
727. See Chapter V, section 3.1, post.
728. See Dec. 98/235 (O.J. 1998 L 88/59).
729. Dec. 87/83 (O.J. 1987 L 45/40).
730. Dec. 74/442 (O.J. 1974 L 243/22, most recently amended by Dec. 87/445 (O.J. 1987 L 240/24).
731. Dec. 87/305 (O.J. 1987 L 152/22, amended by Dec. 87/560 (O.J. 1987 L 388/37)).

level, by means of these two kinds of committees national governments and interest groups generally participate in the work of the Community. Whilst committee procedures afford a means of ensuring that the Commission takes account of national views, they are also a means of tying down its freedom to act in the wider Community interest and it is against this background that the Council decision laying down the standard procedures for the exercise of implementing powers conferred on the Commission[732] must be viewed as being less than satisfactory.

10.4   Community staff

Each of the Institutions, as well as the Economic and Social Committee and the Court of Auditors, has its own staff of officials. Some 27,300 staff (including those employed at research centres) are employed on a permanent or temporary basis by the Communities. The vast majority (almost 18,800) are employed in the Commission's services which presently comprise 26 Directorates-General and a number of smaller services.[733] Irrespective of the Institution for which they work, other servants form part of a single Community administration in the sense that they are subject to the same set of legal rules, namely the Staff Regulations and Conditions of Employment of Servants.[734]

Under the Staff Regulations an official is a person who, in accordance with the Staff Regulations, has been appointed to an established post on the staff of one of the Institutions or of the Economic and Social Committee by a written decision of the appointing authority designated by the Institution or body concerned. The legal status of officials is governed entirely by public law (*i.e.* by the Treaties and the Staff Regulations and rules made thereunder) and is not a contractual relationship. In this it is inspired by the concept of *der Beamte* or *fonctionnaire* (office-holder) in the German and French administrative traditions. Other members of staff (referred to as 'Other Servants') are employed on a contractual basis[735]

732. Dec. 87/373 (O.J. 1987 L 197/33). See, further, section 6.4, *ante* and COM (98) 380 Final.
733. See section 4.2, *ante*. See also (though now, of course, dated) the *Proposals for reform of the Commission of the European Communities and its services* (Brussels, 24 September 1979 – the Spierenburg report) and on the Commission's reaction to it WQ 100/82 (Welsh) O.J. 1982 C 198/8. See also, generally, the *Report on European Institutions* (Brussels, October 1979 – the 'Report of the Three Wise Men'). See, further, Epilogue, sections 7 and 8.7, *post*.
734. On the basis of Merger Treaty, Art. 24(1), Reg. 259/68 (O.J. English Special Edition 1968 (1), p. 30, as amended on myriad occasions). See, generally, Rogalla, *Dienstrecht der Europäischen Gemeinschaften* (Cologne, 1981) (in French as *La fonction publique européenne* (Brussels, 1982)).
735. See Cases 66–68 and 136–140/83 *Hattet et al. v. Commission* [1985] ECR 2459; Cases 87, 77 *etc. Salerno et al. v. Commission et al.* [1985] ECR 2523; Case 123/84 *Klein v.*

and the majority of these are employed as local agents performing manual labour or auxiliary services. The long-felt need for modernization of the approach to staff policy in particular within the Commission now seems to be meeting tangible responses.[736]

It is the duty of every official, just as of any national official, to be loyal to the authority which has appointed him and the public interest of the Community for the benefit of which he is working.[737] For an international official this duty takes on a special dimension because it means that he must also show himself independent of the government of the state whose nationality he possesses and that he must not be guided by considerations of national interest. It has, therefore, been laid down that the Community official, in discharging his functions and in determining his conduct, should keep in mind solely the interests of the Communities, without seeking or accepting instructions from any government or from any authority, organization or person outside his Institution.[738] The Dutch government used to insist that the principle of independence meant that any Dutch civil servants recruited by the Community Institutions had to resign from the national civil service although this view has since been revised in view of the fact that various other Member States simply place such civil servants on non-active status with a guaranteed right of return (sometimes to a rank reflecting promotion). This latter approach may have been defensible in the early days of the Community when its future was uncertain but is less so now. In any event, recruitment is now more frequent from a range of backgrounds and lawyers in particular often come from the academic world or private practice and now less frequently from a civil service background.

As a rule, two criteria which are not always easy to combine are applied in recruiting officials of international organizations; they have to satisfy the most exacting demands as to ability, efficiency, and integrity, and at the same time the filling of these posts should be spread over as wide a geographical area as possible. In several organizations the latter requirement is in practice a euphemistic expression covering a system of strict national quotas for the division of the posts at every level on the basis of criteria such as the size of population or the amount of contributions of the participation countries. Such a system, according to which vacancies fall to a given nationality, is in the interest neither of the

    Commission [1985] ECR 1907 at 1916–1918 and Case 232/84 *Commission v. Tordeur et al.* [1985] ECR 3223 at 3233–3235.

736. See *e.g. General Report 1997* ((Brussels, Luxembourg, 1998) points 1097–1101 and, generally, Spence in Edwards and Spence (eds.), *op. cit.* (see note 90, *supra*) 68–124.

737. See Case T-203/95 *Connolly v. Commission* (pending), and Case T-203/95 R *Connolly v. Commission* [1995] ECR II-2993. See also European Parliament Debates No. 475, p. 192 (Commission's answer to a question by Bondé concerning Connolly, *The Rotten Heart of Europe* (London, 1995)).

738. Staff Regs., Art. 11.

service nor of the officials already working in the organization, because the possibilities of selection for the filling of such posts are thus seriously restricted and the chances of advancement for the officials appointed are very slim. These two criteria are also applied in the recruitment of Community officials by virtue of Article 27 of the Staff Regulations. Each Institution attempts to maintain a broad reasonable balance of nationalities across the range of posts.[739] Unlike in most international organizations the quota system is of subsidiary importance, although it is no secret that the Member States take an active interest in senior appointments. However, the career principle is laid down in Articles 29–31 of the Staff Regulations, which also provide in Article 7(1) that an official is to be appointed solely in the interests of the service and irrespective of his nationality, and in Article 27 that no single post may be reserved for nationals of a particular Member State.[740] Not unnaturally, the Community staff organizations have reacted unfavourably to the 'parachuting' of people into senior positions from outside the Community civil service as this is seen as being incompatible with the career concept of a European civil service acting solely in the interests of the Communities (although this brings in new blood).[741] Part of the price for being able to be appointed without having passed a competition, though, is that officials in grades A1 and A2 (the most senior grades) can be retired in the interests of the service;[742] they do not have the same security of tenure as other officials.

The Court has concluded, on the basis of the Staff Regulations, that only where the merits and qualifications of the various candidates are equal may the appointing authority take into consideration the nationality of a candidate as one fact of amongst others in its choice.[743] In other judgments the Court has pointed out that 'the fulfilment of the obligation to secure the recruitment of officials on the broadest geographical basis must not be limited to a small number of posts within a

---

739. For statistics relating to the Commission and the Council see WQs 1193/86 (Lagakos) O.J. 1986 C 337/30 and 1524/84 (Wieczorek–Zeul) O.J. 1985 C 83/31. See also WQ 585/86 (Pearce) O.J. 1986 C 299/72 and, for more recent discussion and figures, Spence in Edwards and Spence (eds.), *op. cit.* (see note 90, *supra*) 81–89.
740. Perhaps unsurprisingly, this provision is sometimes regarded as being more honoured in the breach, and the Court of Justice and the Court of First Instance are regularly confronted with fixed competitions (*concours bidons*) or other irregularities, see *e.g.* Case 85/82 *Schloh v. Council* [1983] ECR 2105 at 212–2128 and 2131 (reservation of a particular post for a particular nationality), and Cases 44/85 *etc. Hochbaum and Rawes v. Commission* [1987] ECR 3259 (but see Case T-38/89 *Hochbaum v. Commission* [1990] ECR II-43 (summary publication).
741. As to *parachutage, pistons* and *sousmarins*, see Spence in Edwards and Spence, *op. cit.* (see note 90, *supra*) 80–82 and 84–89.
742. Under the Staff Regs., Art. 50 (which results in few financial tears being shed).
743. Case 282/81 *Ragusa v. Commission* [1983] ECR 1245 at 1258. See also Case 15/63 *Lassale v. European Parliament* [1964] ECR 31, [1964] CMLR 259.

single Directorate-General,'[744] and has decided in favour of priority for the career principle over the principle of the broadest possible geographical spread.[745]

The privileges and immunities of the officials and other servants are regulated in the Protocol on the Privileges and Immunities of the European Communities, annexed to the Merger Treaty.[746] They are almost identical with those which had been accorded to them in the Protocols previously applying to each individual Community. The reason behind the grant of these privileges and immunities to categories of servants determined by the Council[747] is the interest of the Communities, not their own personal interest.[748] It is, therefore, in this spirit that the Court has invariably interpreted the respective provisions, in particular those regulating the most important immunities: the immunity from suit and legal process[749] and the exemption from national taxes.[750] The immunity from suit and legal process relates to acts performed by the officials in their official capacity, including their spoken and written words and does not, of course, apply to cases that may be brought before the Court of Justice,[751] such as those relating to their personal accountability to the Communities.[752] According to the Court, a limited meaning is to be given to the words 'in their official capacity.' This immunity, therefore, covers only acts which, by their nature, represent a participation of the person entitled to the immunity in the performance of the tasks of the institution to which he belongs.[753] The privileges and immunities have a 'functional character, inasmuch as they are intended to avoid any interference with the functioning and independence of the Communities.'[754]

Community officials and other servants are exempt from national taxes on salaries, wages and emoluments paid by the Communities but are, however, liable to a tax levied by the Communities themselves which goes into the general budget.[755] The combination of exemption from national

744. Case 17/68 *Reinarz v. Commission* [1969] ECR 91 at 72. The case concerned posts at A2 level (Director).
745. See also Case 85/82 *Schloh v. Council* [1983] ECR 2105 at 212–2128 and 2131 (reservation of a particular post for a particular nationality).
746. See Chapter II, section 5.2, *ante*.
747. See Protocol on Privileges and Immunities, Art. 16.
748. *Ibid.*, Art. 18.
749. *Ibid.*, Art. 12(a).
750. *Ibid.*, Art. 13 2nd para.
751. *Ibid.*, Art. 12(a).
752. *Ibid.*, Art. 22.
753. Case 5/68 *Sayag et al. v. Leduc et al.* [1968] ECR 395 at 402.
754. *E.g.* Case C-2/88 Imm. *Zwartveld et al.* [1990] ECR I-3365 at 3372; see also Case C-54/90 *Weddel & Co. BV v. Commission* [1992] ECR I-871 at 894–895
755. The tax is levied on the basis of Protocol on Privileges and Immunities, Art. 1, 1st para., by Reg. 260/68 (O.J. English Special Edition 1968 (II), p. 37, as amended). See Case 3/83 *Abrias et al. v. Commission* [1985] ECR 1995.

taxation but subjection to a Community tax prevents the effective remuneration of Community officials and other servants 'firstly and chiefly, ... from differing according to their nationality or fiscal domicile as a result of the assessment of different national taxes, and secondly ... from being inordinately taxed as a result of double taxation.'[756] The fact that a Community official does not pay tax on his salary to the national Treasury is not a valid reason for differentiating the case of an official and his family from that of a migrant worker whose income is liable to taxation by the State in which he resides.[757]

Community officials and other servants are subject to disciplinary rules[758] and can also be held financially liable for any losses suffered by the Communities through gross negligence on their part in the exercise of their function or in connection with it.[759] The Court of Justice has unlimited jurisdiction over disputes, which arise in this respect. Indeed, Article 91 of the Staff Regulations provide that the Court has exclusive jurisdiction on the legality of a decision affecting any person to whom the Staff Regulations apply.[760] In disputes of a financial nature the Court has unlimited jurisdiction: *i.e.* it may annul the decision but can also award damages or grant other means of redress. The term 'legality' should be interpreted broadly in the sense of lawfulness as decisions are examined in the light of unwritten as well as written Community law (in other words, general principles of law apply to staff cases as well). It should be noted that whilst the Court has construed its powers broadly to cover matters dealing with trade union representation,[761] a direct action by a staff association under the procedure of Articles 90 and 91 of the Staff Regulations will not be entertained.[762] Staff cases now come before the Court of First Instance, subject to appeal to the Court of Justice on a point of law only.[763]

756. Case 32/67 *Van Leeuwen v. City of Rotterdam* [1968] ECR 43 at 48. See further on national taxation and Community officials see also Case 23/68 *Klomp v. Inspektieder Belastingen* [1969] ECR 43; Case 85/85 *Commission v. Belgium* [1986] ECR 1149 and Case 260/86 *Commission v. Belgium* [1988] ECR 955. On European Schools and national taxation see Case 44/84 *Hurd v. Jones* [1986] ECR 29.

757. Case 152/82 *Forcheri et al. v. Belgian State et al.* [1983] ECR 2323 at 2337.

758. Staff Regs., Arts. 86–89.

759. *Ibid.*, Art. 22.

760. Which includes an unsuccessful candidate: Case 130/75 *Prais v. Council* [1976] ECR 1589, [1976] 2 CMLR 708, an employee of the EIB: Case 110/75 *Mills v. European Investment Bank* [1976] ECR 955 and an employee of the Court itself: Case 15/60 *Simon v. Court of Justice* [1961] ECR 115; Case 2/80 *Dautzenberg v. Court of Justice* [1980] ECR 3107.

761. Case 175/73 *Union Syndicale v. Council* [1974] ECR 917, [1975] 1 CMLR 131; Case 18/74 *Syndicat Général des Organismes Européens v. Commission* [1974] ECR 933, [1975] 1 CMLR 144.

762. Case 18/74 *Syndicat Général* [1974] ECR 933 at 944–945.

763. See section 7.3.1, *ante*.

11. CONCLUDING OBSERVATIONS

11.1 The distinction between Institutions and other bodies

With the use of the concept 'Community Institution',[764] the framers of the Treaties desired to express that those bodies of the Communities possessed far-reaching powers of their own, and, in particular, the power to enact measures which would bind the citizens of the Community directly.[765] In the course of the years, though, there have been a number of developments which have blurred the distinction between the Institutions and other bodies in the sense of customary organs of a public international organization. In this context, the following developments may be noted. First, the Council has set up a number of independent Community bodies, as was noted in section 9.3, above; it has delegated to them the power of decision.[766] Secondly, the setting up of the European Council is another case in point. The TEU expressly reserves the denomination European Council for the sole organ of the Union itself, so that the European Council cannot itself exercise the competence of the Council of the European Union, although that does not mean that it might not sucumb to the temptation to intervene in matters falling within the remit of the Council of the European Union.

Unlike under the TEU, that was not possible under the Stuttgart Solemn Declaration on European Union.[767] In the latter the European Council stated that when it acts on a matter within the scope of the Communities, it did so in its capacity as the Council within the meaning of the Treaties.[768] That meant that in such a case it would have to follow the Community decision-making procedure, and that its decisions in that capacity would be open to review by the Court of Justice. But the TEU ensures that the European Council is never as such subject to the Community decision-making procedure, and thus its acts are not subject to such review. Its tasks as set out in Article D TEU are also not a watertight barrier against the tasks and powers of the Council of the European Union, which means that the European Council can in fact intervene, without sanctions, in the sphere of activities of the Community Institutions, without having to transform itself into the Council *simpliciter*.

---

764. Arts. 4(1) EC, 7 ECSC, and 3(1) Euratom.
765. Herzog in Smit and Herzog, *The Law of the EEC* (New York, loose-leaf since 1976) Vol. I, para. 4.03, p. 1030.1. This must now be read as citizens of the Union, Art. 8(1) EC.
766. See also section 6.4, points (b) and (e), *ante*. Thus, *e.g.* Reg. 337/75 (O.J. 1975 L 39/1, as amended), Art. 7, and Reg. 1365/75 (O.J. 1975 L 139/1, as amended), Art. 9 expressly envisage decisions being adopted by CEDEFOP and the European Training Foundation, respectively, and Reg. 1210/90 (O.J. 1990 L 120/1), Art. 8(3), makes similar provision in relation to the European Environment Agency.
767. See note 13, *supra*, (section 2.2, *ante*).
768. *Ibid.*

Although the Council of the European Union may meet in the composition of the Heads of State or Government (and in certain matters relating to Economic and Monetary Union must do so), as was observed in section 2.2, above, the Council of the European Union even in that composition is not the same thing as the European Council.

Thirdly, Article 4a EC, which establishes the European System of Central Banks, consisting of the European Central Bank and the national central banks[769] does not fit in the institutional system established by Article 4 EC. While the ESCB is not a body in the sense discussed here, a new entity has been created in the context of Economic and Monetary Union, which does not belong to the institutional structure of the Treaties.[770] Fourthly, the essentially intergovernmental role of the Institutions in relation to CFSP and JHA should be remembered. Despite the safeguarding of the Community system,[771] it cannot be excluded that the (intergovernmental) working methods in these areas will have a negative effect on the functioning of the institutional system of the Communities, which would transform the Institutions into mere organs.[772]

11.2   The Agreement on Social Policy

This is an Agreement between 11 Member States, without the United Kingdom, adopted among themselves, and annexed to a Protocol on Social Policy, which, by virtue of Article 3 thereof, is annexed to the EC Treaty.[773] Although shortly after the signature of the TEU, doubts were expressed by some authors whether the Protocol and the Agreement belonged to the Community legal order at all,[774] it is now generally accepted that the Protocol is an agreement between the then 12 Member States that only 11 of them will be bound by the new social provisions, and that as the Protocol is annexed to the EC Treaty, and the Agreement to the Protocol, by virtue of Article 239 EC the Protocol is an integral part

---

769. See section 9.2, *ante*, and Chapter IX, section 3.4.3, *post*.
770. Barents has called the ESCB a sub-organization with a wholly separate and independent status, Barents and Brinkhorst, *Grondlijnen van Europees Recht* (6th ed., Alphen a/d Rijn, 1994) 83.
771. See Chapter II, section 1.2.3, *ante*.
772. See the political agreement within the Council on the summoning of cooperation councils with ministers from the Central and Eastern European countries, *Europe* No. 6329 (October 5, 1994), p. 6.
773. See section 1.2.3, *ante*. See further, Chapter IX, section 6.1, *post*.
774. See in particular, Barnard (1992) 8 IJCLLIR 15; Curtin (1993) 30 CMLRev. 17 at 52–61; Vogel-Polsky, *Evaluation of the Social Provisions of the Treaty on European Union* (Report prepared for the Committee on Social Affairs of the European Parliament (DOC. EN-CM-202155), cited by Watson (1993) 30 CMLRev. 481 at 491), and Weiss (1992) IJCLLIR 15.

of the EC Treaty and thus of the Community legal order.[775] The 11 Now 14) Member States are authorized by Point 1 of the Protocol to have recourse to the Institutions, procedures and mechanisms of the EC Treaty, and by virtue of Point 2 the United Kingdom plays no part in the deliberations and the adoption of Commission proposals made on the basis of the Protocol and the Agreement. Accordingly, Point 2, as amended[776] provides that where a qualified majority is required for acts of the Council adopted under the protocol, it is achieved with 52 out of the 77 votes (unanimity involves all 14 of the Member States voting in favour). It is the clear intention, as the amendment provision shows, that the Protocol now applies to 14 out of the 15 Member States, and in fact forms part of the *acquis communautaire* accepted by the new Member States on accession.

The Protocol and its annexed Agreement were adopted, as were all the amendments made by the TEU, according to the provisions then applicable for amendment of the Treaties.[777] In Opinion 1/91 *EEA Agreement I*[778] the Court indicated that an amendment could not cure an incompatibility with the very foundations of the Community. It may well be questioned whether the boundary line has not in fact been crossed by the Protocol, particularly as the applicability of acts adopted by the Council and any financial consequences (other than administrative costs for the Community Institutions) to the United Kingdom is excluded.[779] This provision is certainly incompatible with the fundamental principle of the uniform application of Community law (and is also logically incompatible with a common market in which conditions of competition are not artificially distorted). On the other hand, in so far as the Member States remain masters of the Treaties[780] when acting unanimously to revise them, and in view of the fact that at least transitional measures are agreed on new accessions, and the phased applicability of much Community legislation (particulaly in the environmental field) was agreed for the new German *Länder*, the policy objection to the pragmatic nature of the Protocol is less dramatic. The first measure under taken under provisions of the Agreement annexed to the Protocol was Directive 94/5.[781] Perhaps

---

775. Barents (1992) SEW 691–694; Watson (1993) 31 CMLRev. 481 at 488; Whiteford (1993) 18 ELRev. 202. See, further, Barnard, *EC Employment Law* (Chichester, 1995) 65–67.
776. Dec. 95/1 (O.J. 1995 L1/1), Art. 8 (amending Act of Austrian, Finnish and Swedish Accession, Art. 15(4)).
777. Arts. 236 EEC, 96 ECSC, and 204 Euratom (see now Art. N TEU).
778. [1991] ECR I-6079 at 6111–6112.
779. Protocol, point 2, last para.
780. See Everling in Beyerlin *et al.* (eds.), *Recht zwischen Umbruch und Bewahrung (Festschrift for Bernhardt*, Berlin, 1995) 1161, and literature cited there.
781. O.J. 1994 L 254/64 on the establishment of European Works Councils or a procedure in Community-scale undertakings and Community-scale groups of undertakings for

somewhat ironically, many British multinationals set up works councils very quickly, although it has to be observed that this was often more motivated by a desire to have a mechanism in place by 22 September 1996.[782]

The election of a Labour government in the United Kingdom in May 1997 made it clear that the days of second-class social protection in the United Kingdom were numbered: at the Amsterdam European Council in June 1997 the United Kingdom announced its intention to accede to the Protocol and satisfaction was expressed at its intention to accept the directives deriving from the Agreement which had already been adopted or which might be adopted before the Treaty of Amsterdam entered into force.[783] In the light of this intention, the Council and the Commission agreed to give effect both to the directives in question and to any other instrument which might be adopted in the lifetime of the Agreement on Social policy by the adoption of directives under Article 100 EC, in respect of which the Commission was to put forward proposals.[784] The first of these was presented in September 1997 and the proposals were adopted at the end of 1997.[785] Further proposals and measures have now been presented or adopted.[786] The Treaty of Amsterdam (not yet in force) will see the repeal of the Protocol and Agreement on Social Policy, and the revision of Articles 117–120 EC: social protection will then take its proper place in Community law as a whole. Community social policy is discussed in more detail in section 6 of Chapter IX, below.

the purposes of informing and consulting employees; now extended to include the United Kingdom and Ireland by Dir. 97/74 (O.J. 1998 L 10/22).

782. As if they had a voluntary scheme in place on that date, the directive would be inapplicable, Dir. 94/45, Art. 13.

783. Bull. EU 6–1997, points I.8 and 1.3.255.

784. Bull. EU 7/8–1997, point 1.3.222. This was felt to be the most elegant way of enabling application of the measures even though the Agreement on Social Policy was still in force.

785. Dir. 97/74 (O.J. 1998 L 10/22) on works councils, and Dir. 97/75 (O.J. 1998 L 10/24) extending Directive 96/34 (O.J. 1994 L 145/4) on the framework agreement reached by the social partners on parental leave.

786. COM (1998) 84 Final to extend the scope of Dir. 97/80 (O.J. 1998 L 14/6) on the burden of proof in sex discrimination cases (O.J. 1998 C 123/13), Dir. 98/23 (O.J. 1998 L 131/10) extends the scope of Dir. 97/81 (O.J. 1998 L 14/9) on the framework agreement on part-time work.

CHAPTER V

Policy-making and administration[*]

1. LEGAL INSTRUMENTS

The principal legal instruments for the development and application of Community law are of course the *acts of the European Parliament and the Council acting jointly; acts of the Council, and acts of the Commission*. It is to these instruments that the greater part of the present section will be devoted. A second group of legal instruments which are of importance is formed by *international treaties, conventions, agreements* or international legal transactions by whatever other name they may be referred to. Legal instruments handled by the Communities themselves consist of treaties which can be concluded with states and international organizations, in the fields in which they are competent to do so, such as external trade policy and associations and third countries. They will be discussed in connection with the external relations of the Communities in Chapter XII, below.

Other legal instruments relevant to the Communities are the treaties concluded by the Member States among themselves concerning questions connected with the subject-matter of the Community Treaties. They may be very important for the attainment of the objectives of the Communities and may be concluded with a view to these very objectives. Sometimes Community law requires the Member States to regulate collectively a given subject.[1] But even if there is no connection with a specific provision of Community law, the Member States are naturally free to regulate by mutual consent, with a view to the common implementation (or at least with due observance) of the general basic obligations of Article 5 EC,[2] certain questions connected with the subject-matter of the Treaties and essential for the attainment of their objectives. They can do this only to

---

[*] In the Fifth Dutch edition of this work, sections 1 and 3 of this chapter were revised by P.J.G. Kapteyn; section 2 was revised by L.A. Geelhoed. This edition has been further revised by the editor, incorporating the revisions made by Kapteyn and Geelhoed in the Dutch edition, but taking substantial additional account of literature, case-law and practice, as well as of more recent developments.

1. *E.g.* Art. 50 EC and 'so far as is necessary' Art. 220 EC.
2. See also Arts. 86 ECSC and 192 Euratom.

the extent to which Community law has left them the power to regulate these questions. This limitation can be overcome only by a modification of the Treaties according to the procedure of revision laid down therein.[3] In the conclusion of such treaties the Institutions of the Communities, in particular the Commission, will often have an initiating or advisory function. They may also be involved in the implementation and application of these treaties, in accordance with the provisions laid down therein.

In so far as such treaties bear the name and outward signs of ordinary international treaties *i.e.* of an instrument signed by representatives of the Member States and, if necessary, subject to a ratification procedure, no special problems will present themselves. Such problems will, however, arise with regard to the legal construction of the so-called 'acts of the representatives' which have developed in practice in the margin of the Community legal order. In such 'acts' the points agreed upon by the Member States for the implementation or completion of Community law are often laid down. These instruments, which are generally referred to as *'acts of the representatives of the governments of the Member States meeting within the Council'* give rise to a number of questions concerning their legal character and their relation to Community law, which justify a discussion in a separate sub-section.

It should be particularly noted that such 'acts of the representatives' must be clearly distinguished from acts of the Council. Indeed, the latter, characterized as Community acts on account of both their object and the institutional framework within which they have been agreed, do not have the character of an international agreement, even though unanimity may be required for their conclusion. The scope and effects of acts of the Council, therefore, are determined by their content, and they cannot, as in the case of international agreements, be limited by reservations or statements made in the course of the adoption of the measure concerned.[4]

It is not unknown for declarations to be included in the minutes of meetings of the Council, relating to acts which have been adopted. As far as they contain declarations or reserves on the part of one or more members of the Council, they have no significance in the eyes of the Court of Justice.[5] If such declarations are declarations of the Council itself, they cannot be used for the purpose of interpreting a provision of Community

3. See Chapter II, section 4.2, *ante*.
4. See Case 38/69 *Commission v. Italy* [1970] ECR 47 at 56–57 in which the Court refused to classify a Council decision based on Art. 235 EEC as an international agreement, even though the measures taken supplemented the Treaties in certain respects. See also, relating to directives, Case 91/79 *Commission v. Italy* [1980] ECR 1099 at 1105; Case 39/72 Commission v. Italy [1973] ECR 101 at 115; Case 143/83 *Commission v. Denmark* [1985] ECR 427 at 436 and Case 237/84 *Commission v. Belgium* [1986] ECR 1247 at 1256.
5. See Case 38/69 *Commission v. Italy* [1970] ECR 47 at 57. See, further, WQ 151/85 (Toksvig) O.J. 1985 C241/14; Nicoll (1993) JCMS 559, and Nicoll in Westlake, *The Council of the European Union* (London, 1995) 120–125.

secondary legislation where no reference is made in the wording of the provision involved to the content of the declaration; accordingly such declarations also have no legal significance.[6] 'The Court has consistently held that the true meaning of rules of Community law can only be derived from those rules themselves, having regard to their content.'[7] Thus the Court has set its face against any temptation to secret quasi-legislation (as such declarations are usually not published). To have held otherwise would have been to reinforce the already secretive nature of Council decision-making;[8] as Nicoll rightly observes, unpublished entries in the Council minutes do not sit easily with the agreement on measures to secure greater transparency, adopted at the Edinburgh European Council,[9] but, perhaps more seriously, they are not available to the European Parliament, which is crucial when that Institution acts jointly with the Council.[10] It is of course possible that a declaration or other statement in the minutes may be an aid, albeit not the only one, to interpretation of a provision which is unclear or equivocal.[11]

6.   Case C-292/89 *R. v. The Immigration Appeal Tribunal, ex parte Antonissen* [1991] ECR I-745 at 778; see also Case C-25/94 *Commission v. Council* [1996] ECR I-1469 at 1508 and Case C-329/95 *VAG Sverige AB* [1997] ECR I-2675 at 2694.

7.   Case 237/84 *Commission v. Belgium* [1986] ECR 1247 at 1256. Thus their meaning cannot be affected by a statement inserted into the Council's minutes, *ibid.*

8.   Although, since late 1993 the record of voting is made public in the following circumstances: (i) when the Council acts as legislator (explained, *infra*), including when it adopts a common position under Arts. 189b or 189c EC; (ii) when votes are cast by members of the Council or their representatives on the Conciliation Committee set up under Art. 189b EC; (iii) when the Council acts in CFSP or JHA by a unanimous Council decision taken at the request of one of its members, and (iv) in other cases, by Council decision taken at the request of one of its members (this is by simple majority), Rules of Procedure, Dec. 93/662 (O.J. 1993 L 268/1, amended, but not on this point, by Dec. 95/24 (O.J. 1995 L 31/14)), Art. 7(5). The Annex to *ibid.* explains that the Council acts as legislator for the purpose of (i) when it adopts rules which are legally binding in or for the Member States, whether by means of regulations, directives or decisions, on the basis of the relevant provisions of the Treaties, in particular on the basis of Arts. 43 EC, or in the framework of Arts. 189b and 189c EC, with the exception of discussions leading to the adoption of internal measures, administrative or budgetary acts, acts concerning inter-institutional or international relations or non-binding acts such as conclusions, recommendations or resolutions. Votes will not be made public in the case of discussions leading to indicative votes or the adoption of preparatory acts. Votes cast in the Council are published in press releases. The Treaty of Amsterdam (not yet in force) will raise the present practice to a Treaty-level transparency requirement through the revised Art. 151(3) EC (which will actually require such provisions to be in the Council's Rules of Procedure).

9.   Bull. EC 12–1992 point I.25.

10. Nicoll, in Westlake, *op. cit.* (see note 5, *supra*) 124–125. Westlake observes, *ibid.* at 125, that the Parliament has started to make unilateral statements in the minutes of the Conciliation Committee, but those are not, of course, the same as the minutes of the Council itself.

11. See Darmon, Adv. Gen. in Case C-292/89 *R. v. The Immigration Appeal Tribunal, ex parte Antonissen* [1991] ECR I-745 at 765. But in view of the Court's decision in that

Both the Council,[12] and the European Council,[13] tend to adopt resolutions, especially when setting up Community action programmes in a particular area and a timetable for the realization of the programme. Such resolutions can generally only have binding force if they are intended to have legal effects and, more over, if the power to attach such legal effects is conferred by or through the Treaties.[14] Usually it will be clear simply from the name 'resolutions' that the first of these two conditions is not

case, it seems that this will only be possible where reference is made to the content of the declaration in the provision in question, *ibid.* at 778. See also Case 136/78 *Ministère public v. Auer* [1979] ECR 437 at 450.

12. *E.g.* the Declaration by the Council and the representatives of the governments of the Member States meeting within the Council and the representatives of the governments of the Member States meeting within the Council on the EC action programme on the environment (O.J. 1973 C 112/1) and the resolutions on its continuation and implementation (O.J. 1977 C139/1, O.J. 1983 C46/1 and O.J. 1987 C328/1), and the Council resolution on energy and the environment (O.J. 1975 C 168/2). For an earlier list of such resolutions see Annex II to the Burger Report, E.P. Session Documents 1968–69, no. 215. See also WQ 785/84 (Maij-Weggen) O.J. 1985 C 39/7 for an overview of the number of directives, resolutions and recommendations 1979–1983. See also the resolution adopted at The Hague on 3 November 1976 on the introduction of a 200 mile fishing zone (O.J. 1981 C 105/1). Sometimes a resolution will be adopted jointly by the Council and the representatives of the governments of the Member States meeting within the Council (in other words the same people wearing two hats, coping with issues which in part fall within, and in part outside Community competence), *e.g.* the Resolution of 23 October 1995 on the response of educational systems to the problems of racism and xenophobia (O.J. 1995 C 312/1). The Council also sometimes publishes its conclusions on a particular issue, *e.g.* on social participation as a factor for quality in education prior to university education (O.J. 1995 C 312/3), and the Ecofin Council's conclusions on the comparative analysis of the reports supplied by the Member States on national measures taken to combat wastefulness and the misuse of Community resources (Bull. EU 12–1995 point I.61. In relation to action taken under JHA, see *e.g.* O.J. 1996 C 274/1 *et seq.*

13. *E.g.* the resolution of 5 December 1978 on the setting-up of the European Monetary System (Bull. EC 12–1978 p. 10 *et seq.*), and the Declaration on Democracy (Bull. EC 3–1978 p. 5).

14. In Case 22/70 *Commission v. Council* [1971] ECR 263 at 276–279 (the ERTA judgment) the Court dealt with conclusions of the Council relating to establishing a negotiating position and to the negotiating procedure for the European Road Transport Agreement (often referred to by its French acronym AETR but it is known in English as ERTA). The Court concluded that the conclusions had definite legal effects both on relations between the Community and the Member States and on the relationship between Institutions. See also the binding force attributed to the Hague Resolution (see note 12, *supra*) in Case 141/78 *France v. United Kingdom* [1979] ECR 2923 at 2941–2942, and Case 32/79 *Commission v. United Kingdom* [1980] ECR 2403 at 2432–2433; 2437–2439; 2445 and 2449. Resolutions of the European Parliament may also have such legal effects, in particular when based on its power to regulate its own internal affairs, see Cases C-213/88 and 39/89 *Luxembourg v. European Parliament* [1991] ECR I-5643 at 5699 (contrasting the situation in which a resolution of the Parliament (as an opinion) is merely a step in the procedure for drawing up Community rules, *ibid.* at 5642–5643, referring to earlier case-law).

fulfilled.[15] The Court of Justice regards these resolutions as expressions of the Council's political will.[16] The failure to comply with such a resolution cannot in itself give rise to an infringement of Community law;[17] thus private parties cannot rely on such a resolution,[18] nor can it be invoked against them.[19] Such a resolution does not modify Treaty provisions.[20] It can, though, be an aid to the interpretation of legal acts of the Institutions[21] designed to give effect to it.

Resolutions and declarations by which the Institutions agree with each other to exercise their powers in a certain way have a particular significance. Examples of these include the Joint declaration of the European Parliament, the Council and the Commission on a conciliation procedure;[22] the Interinstitutional Agreement of 29 October 1993 on budgetary discipline and the improvement of the budgetary procedure;[23] the Interinstitutional Declaration of 25 October 1993 on democracy, transparency and subsidiarity;[24] the Interinstitutional Agreement (annexed thereto) on procedures for implementing the principle of subsidiarity,[25] and the Interinstitutional Agreement of 20 December 1994 on an accelerated working method for official codification of legislative texts.[26] It is submitted, and there is support in the case-law of the Court for this proposition, that a legal obligation has thus been created which can be relied upon by the Community Institutions and, in appropriate cases, even by the Member States and private parties.[27] The legal significance of the

15. *E.g.* Cases 90 and 91/63 *Commission v. Luxembourg and Belgium* [1964] ECR 625 at 631–632 (the dairy products case).
16. Case 59/75 *Pubblico Ministero v. Manghera* [1976] ECR 91 at 102. See also Wqs 451/83 and 452/83 (Rogalla) O.J. 1983 C 227/15, and 246/82 and 2215/82 (Eisma) O.J. 1983 C 212/4.
17. Cases 90 and 91/63 *Commission v. Luxembourg and Belgium* [1964] ECR 625 at 631–632
18. Case 9/73 *Schlüter v. Hauptzollamt Lörrach* [1973] ECR 1135 at 1161.
19. Case 59/75 *Pubblico Ministero v. Manghera* [1976] ECR 91 at 102.
20. *Ibid.* See also Case 43/75 *Defrenne v. Sabena* [1976] ECR 455 at 478.
21. Case 43/72 *Merkur–Aussenhandels GmbH v. Commission* [1973] ECR 1055 at 1071.
22. O.J. 1975 C 89/1, see section 3.4.2, *post.*
23. O.J. 1993 C 331/1. See also the Declaration by the European Parliament, the Council and the Commission of 6 March 1995 on the incorporation of financial provisions into legislative acts (O.J. 1996 C 102/4).
24. Bull. EU 10–1993 point 2.2.1 (approved by the European Parliament O.J. 1993 C 329/132, draft C 329/133).
25. Bull. EU 10–1993 point 2.2.2, approved by the European Parliament O.J. 1993 C 331/132, draft C 329/133).
26. O.J. 1996 C 102/2 (with the declarations annexed thereto). See also the *modus vivendi* of 20 December 1994 between the European Parliament, the Council and the Commission on implementing measures for acts adopted under the co-decision procedure (Art. 189b EC), O.J. 1996 C 102/1.
27. The Commission's view (WQ 170/77 (Maigaard) O.J. 1977 C 180/18) was that the Joint Declaration amounted merely to a statement of intention of a political nature and is thus only politically and morally binding, without there being any legal obliga-

Joint Declaration of the European Parliament, the Council and the Commission of 5 April 1977 on fundamental rights'[28] is different again; it supports the case-law of the Court on the subject and enables, in cases of doubt, an interpretation to be given by the Court which is in conformity with fundamental rights, now that the Institutions have committed themselves to attach prime importance to the protection of fundamental rights.[29]

1.1 Acts of the Institutions in general

The EC and Euratom Treaties contain a set of general provisions relating to the principal categories of acts of the Community Institutions which are in practically identical terms[30] and specify the nature and the legal effects of such acts; they also contain rules relating to the reasoning, publication, entry into force an enforcement of these acts. Articles 189 EC and 161 Euratom provide that regulations, directives and decisions of the European Parliament and the Council acting jointly, the Council and the Commission are to have binding force (although this varies depending on which of these is concerned). Under these Treaties recommendations[31] and opinions[32] have no binding force. Regulations, decisions, recommendations and opinions of the European Central Bank will have identical effect.[33]

tion as such misunderstands the legal nature of this arrangement. The Council was of the view that in the final resort it is only the Court which can determine the legal scope of the political commitments contained therein (WQ 169/77 (Maigaard) O.J. 1977 C 259/4). The Court is prepared to decide whether or not it was right to dispense with the conciliation procedure: see Case 262/80 *Andersen et al.* v. *European Parliament* [1984] ECR 195 at 207–208 and Case 260/80 *Andersen et al.* v. *Council* [1984] ECR 177 at 193. See, further, Monar (1994) 31 CMLRev. 693; Klabbers (1994) 31 CMLRev. 997, and Snyder in Winter (ed.), *Sources and Categories of European Union Law* (Baden-Baden, 1996) 453, and the discussion in section 3.4.2, *post*.

28. O.J. 1977 C 103/1. See Chapter IV, section 7.5.4, *ante*.
29. *Cf.* the Commission's position: WQ 129/77 (Dondelinger) O.J. 1977 C 168/23.
30. Arts. 189–192 EC and 161–164 Euratom; see also Arts. 14–15 and 92 ECSC.
31. Although recommendations can under certain circumstances form an aid to the interpretation of Community and national provisions, see Case C-322/88 *Grimaldi v. Fonds des maladies professionnelles* [1989] ECR 4407 at 4421.
32. Although a reasoned opinion issued by the Commission under Art. 169 EC will have legal effects in the sense that non-compliance may lead to the matter being brought to the Court of Justice.
33. Art. 108a(1) EC. In a sense remarkably, in view of the principle of subsidiarity in Art. 3b EC, the ECB will have no power to issue directives. The most likely explanation is that there have been so many problems with the non-implementation of directives by Member States – and with the absence of horizontal effect of directives (as to which, see Chapter VI, section 2.2.4, *post*) that no risk could be taken, either in relation to exchange rate and monetary policy, or banking supervision that acts of the ECB would be ignored and be virtually practically unenforceable pending litigation. While the Dutch text of Art. 108a(1) speaks of a regulation being '*van algemene toepassing*'

Decisions and recommendations of the Commission (which replaced the old High Authority) under the ECSC Treaty have binding force by virtue of Article 14 ECSC. In the ECSC system only opinions have no binding force.

The difference is less great than it would appear to be at first glance. In fact, the ECSC Treaty distinguishes between 'decisions which are individual in character' and 'general decisions',[34] a distinction which has been defined more precisely in the case-law of the Court and which is comparable to that between regulations and decisions in the EC and Euratom systems. Moreover, recommendations in the ECSC system (which should be clearly distinguished from non-binding recommendations in the EC and Euratom systems) are by their nature practically identical to a directive,[35] although, unlike a directive, they may be addressed not only to the Member States, but also to enterprises. Wherever in the present section, therefore, regulations, directives, and decisions are referred to, the relevant observations will also apply to general decisions, recommendations, and individual decisions respectively under the ECSC Treaty.

The general provisions of the Treaties[36] only contain a *legal definition* of the various categories of acts. It appears from the text of these Articles that the European Parliament and the Council acting jointly (in the EC); the Council and the Commission (in the EC and Euratom), and (in the ECSC) the Commission alone, may adopt these acts for the achievement of their tasks 'in accordance with this Treaty.' These Institutions cannot therefore derive from these provisions any general authorization to adopt such acts. The question whether, and in what form, they may adopt acts will depend on the definition of the powers conferred upon them in specific Articles of the Treaties.[37] This principle

rather than having '*algemene strekking*,' there is no difference in the English or French texts, and it is submitted that there was no intention that ECB regulations should have an effect different from those of regulations adopted by the Community Institutions empowered to adopt them.

34. Arts. 15 and 33 ECSC (2nd para. in each case).
35. Case C-221/88 *ECSC v. Acciaierie e ferriere Busseni SpA (in liquidation)* [1990] ECR I-495 at 525–526.
36. Arts. 189 EC, 14 ECSC, and 161 Euratom.
37. The concept of attributed powers. *Cf.* Chapter IV, section 6.1 and the exception to this rule in the ECSC case-law (mentioned in note that Chapter). In highly exceptional cases, in which it is completely clear that the global framework of the Treaties apply, yet it is difficult to find a basis in a specific provision, the Commission will make do with a general reference to the Treaty as a legal basis for a measure. See WQ 348/76 (Patijn) O.J. 1976 C 251/17. Advisory committees tend to be set up on the basis of a general reference to the Treaty, *e.g.* Dec. 98/235 (O.J. 1998 L88/59) setting up agricultural advisory committees. The warning in Case 45/86 *Commission v. Council* [1987] ECR 1493 at 1520 should, though, be borne in mind for the future: 'in the context of the organization of the powers of the Community the choice of the legal basis for a measure may not depend simply on an institution's conviction as to the objective pursued but must be based on objective factors which are amenable to judicial review.'

of attributed powers has now been firmly anchored in Article 3b EC, the first paragraph of which expressly requires the Community to act within the limits of the powers conferred on it by the Treaty and of the objectives assigned to it therein.

If the specific Articles in the Treaties or in regulations do not mention one or more of the three legal instruments by name, the interpretation of those Articles will be the basis for determining whether an act adopted thereunder may have the character of a regulation, a directive, or a decision. Thus 'measures' within the meaning of Article 100a EC embrace not merely directives, but also in any event regulations,[38] and 'appropriate measures' in Article 235 EC embraces all legal instruments at the Council's disposal, provided that they are appropriate to the objective to be attained. There are, however some cases in which certain acts to be adopted show various features which make it impossible to place them in one of these categories as such. The catalogue of acts given in the general provisions, therefore, is not exhaustive.[39] There is a residual category of acts which, for lack of a better term, are usually taken together under the denomination acts 'sui generis'.

These acts *sui generis* are encountered, for instance, in the internal management of the Communities such as in laying down rules of procedure or setting up committees. The adoption of the budget also follows a special form,[40] and Council decisions approving international agreements, while often taken in the form of decisions or regulations, do not really fall under any one of the three categories of instruments discussed above. Other acts deserving special attention are those by which the Treaty is modified in certain aspects,[41] or rules are laid down which take place of Treaty rules the validity of which has come to an end, such as acts under Article 136 EC in respect of the application and procedure of association with overseas countries and territories. These

See also *e.g.* Case 68/86 *United Kingdom v. Council* [1988] ECR 855 at 898 and Case C-271/94 *European Parliament v. Council* [1996] ECR I-1689 at 1711.

38. Even though the Commission is (at least politically) obliged to give precedence to the use of directives if harmonization involves the amendment of legislative provisions in more than one Member State, Declaration on Art. 100a EEC, annexed to the Final Act on the occasion of the signature of the Single European Act. See also the Conclusions of the Presidency, Edinburgh European Council, Bull. EC 12–1992 point I.19: 'Other things being equal, directives should be preferred to regulations, and framework directives to detailed measures.' The Protocol on the application of the principles of proportionality and subsidiarity annexed to the EC Treaty by the Treaty of Amsterdam (not yet in force) will make this latter approach a clear requirement.

39. See Cases 90 and 91/63 *Commission v. Luxembourg and Belgium* [1964] ECR 625 at 631.

40. See Arts. 78 and 78a–c ECSC, 203–205 EC and 177–179 Euratom. See, further, Von der Vring in Winter (ed.), *op. cit.* (see note 27, *supra*) 467.

41. *E.g.* Art. 166 EC, 3rd para. (Council's power, at the Court's request, to increase the number of Advocates General and to make the necessary adjustments to Art. 167 EC, 3rd para.).

acts regulate the subject-matter after the expiry of the Implementing Convention annexed to the Treaty which applied during the first five years of the Community's existence. The legal effect which acts *sui generis* have must always be determined by reference to the tenor of the provisions on which they are based. Thus, an act amending Article 166 EC will have the same binding force as the Treaty. The same applies to an act under Article 136 EC, which, however, cannot in itself alter the principles of Part IV of the EC Treaty, on which it must be based. Sometimes the Council adopts declarations or resolutions which do not produce any legal effects, but only contain an agreement on, for instance, the time-limit within which the adoption of a given regulation based on the Treaty must be achieved, or the principles on which such a regulation must be based. The non-legally binding notices and other policy statements issued by the Commission in which it announces the criteria for examining individual cases of competitive behaviour and state aids or describes the sort of cases which it feels to be incompatible with Community law, form a particular category of acts.[42]

The distinction between these categories is relevant in several respects. The legal effect varies according to the category and there may be a difference in rules concerning, for example, their publication and entry into force. Moreover, the distinction is relevant in those cases where the exercise of a given power is bound up with acts of a specific kind. Thus at the same time the power of the Institutions is delimited. Finally, the distinction also entails a difference in judicial protection. In general, a private person cannot appeal directly to the Court against regulations, directives, and acts *sui generis*, while the plea of illegality can only be invoked in respect of regulations.[43] In the context of judicial protection, the Court has already ruled several times that the distinction between the various categories of acts is of a substantive rather than a formal nature. It is not the form or name by which an Institution calls a measure, but rather its object and content which are decisive for the determination of its legal status and effects.[44]

---

42. On this pseudo-legislation see Kapteyn in *Liber Amicorum Mr J van der Hoeven* (Zwolle, 1985) 80–82 and, more generally, Mortelmans (1979) SEW 25 *et seq.* and Lauwaars (1992) NTB 18. As an example of Commission Communications, see the Communication on the *Cassis de Dijon* case (O.J. 1980 C 256/2), with comments by Barents (1981) 18 CMLRev. 271, Slot (1981) SEW 174, Timmermans (1981) SEW 381, Gormley (1981) 6 ELRev. 454 and Mattera (1980) RMC 505. As an example of notices, see the Notice on Minor Agreements (O.J. 1997 C 372/13).
43. See Chapter VI, section 1.3.2, *post*.
44. See Case 20/58 *Phoenix-Rheinrohr AG v. High Authority* [1959] ECR 75 at 82; Cases 16 and 17/62 *Confédération nationale des producteurs des fruits et légunes et al. v. Council* [1962] ECR 471 at 478; see, more generally, Cases 22 and 23/60 *Elz v. High Authority* [1961] ECR 181 at 188 'it is for the Court to classify legal measures according to their nature rather than according to their form'.

1.2 Regulations

The three characteristic elements of a regulation are:

(a) its general application,
(b) its binding character in all respects, and
(c) its direct applicability in each Member State.[45]

The general application of a regulation concerns the impersonal, non-individualized character of the situation to which it applies as well as legal effects it entails for the legal subjects to whom it is addressed. A measure has general application provided that 'it is applicable ... to objectively determined situations and involves legal consequences for categories of persons viewed in a general and abstract manner.'[46] By its general application a regulation differs from a decision. It will not always be easy to decide, by reference to the formulation of the Court, whether a provision of what purports to be a regulation actually has the character of a regulation. However, the 'pathology' of a regulation and the way in which the Court draws the line will be dealt with later, in the discussion of the judicial protection of private parties, in which context the distinction between a regulation and a decision has such great importance.[47]

A regulation not only has general application, but it is also binding in every respect; thus it differs from a directive which is only binding as to the result to be achieved. Moreover, a regulation is directly applicable in all Member States.[48] The system established by a regulation must therefore 'be applied with the same binding force in all the Member States within the context of the Community legal system which they have set up and which, by virtue of the Treaty, has been integrated into their legal systems'.[49]

Thus the Member States may not adopt measures applying the regulation which modify its scope or add provisions to it, unless this is provided for in the regulation itself.[50] Likewise, the Member States are not permitted to transform the contents of a regulation into national legislative

---

45. Arts. 189 EC and 161 Euratom, 2nd para. in each case.
46. Case 6/68 *Zuckerfabrik Watenstedt GmbH v. Council* [1968] ECR 409 at 415. *Cf.* earlier, in a somewhat different formulation Cases 16 and 17/62 *Confédération nationale des producteurs des fruits et légumes et al. v. Council* [1962] ECR 471 at 478.
47. See Chapter VI, section 1.3, *post.*
48. This does not mean that a regulation cannot contain rules concerning the situation in one of the Member States or even in a part of its territory. This is implicit in the judgment in Case 30/67 *Industria Molitoria Imolese SpA et al. v. Commission* [1968] ECR 115 at 121. Despite the limited territorial field of application such a regulation has Community-wide validity.
49. Case 17/67 *Firma Max Neumann v. Hauptzollamt Hof/Saale* [1967] ECR 441 at 453.
50. Case 40/69 *Hauptzollamt Hamburg-Oberelbe v. Firma Paul G. Bollmann* [1970] ECR 69 at 79 (the 'turkey tail' case); Case 74/69 *Hauptzollamt Bremen-Freihafen v. Waren-Import- Gesellschaft Krohn and Co.* [1970] ECR 451 at 459–460.

provisions as otherwise uncertainty would be created about the legal nature of the applicable provisions and the time of their entry into force. Such implementing measures would have the result of creating an obstacle to the direct effect of Community regulations and of jeopardizing their simultaneous and uniform application in the whole of the Community.[51]

Where national authorities are responsible for the implementation of a Community regulation, the forms and procedures of national law apply, provided that they are compatible with Community law[52] and provided that the uniformity of application of Community law, which is necessary to avoid unequal treatment of economic subjects, is not endangered. In general, the Member States are empowered, if not obliged under Article 5 EC, to lay down the necessary administrative and procedural rules to enforce compliance with the Community provisions and to prescribe sanctions for non-compliance. The Member States are, however, not permitted to issue binding rules of interpretation of Community regulations.[53]

In so far as a regulating power in a given field has been conferred on the Community and this power has been exercised by it, the Member States are no longer entitled to issue regulations in this field without being authorized by the Community rules, or to enter into engagements with third countries affecting these rules.[54] In these circumstances both internal and external regulatory competence has, according to the case-law of the Court, become the exclusive competence of the Community. The question of to what

51. Case 39/72 *Commission v. Italy* [1973] ECR 101 at 114. See also Case 50/76 *Amsterdam Bulb BV v. Produktschap voor Siergewassen* [1977] ECR 137 at 146–147 and Case 94/77 *Fratelli Zerbone Snc v. Amministrazione delle Finanze dello Stato* [1978] ECR 99 at 116: 'Accordingly Member States must not adopt or allow national institutions with a legislative power to adopt a measure by which the Community nature of a legal rule and the consequences which arise from it are concealed from the persons concerned.' However, in the special circumstances in which the application of the system depends on a combination of a number of provisions adopted at Community, national and regional level, it will be permissible for regional laws to incorporate some elements of the Community regulations involved, for the sake of coherence, and in order to make them comprehensible to those to whom they apply, Case 272/84 *Commission v. Italy* [1985] ECR 1057 at 1074. The same must logically apply at national level: the essential mischief is that the Community nature of the regulations, their direct applicability, and their direct effect are not disguised or otherwise compromised.
52. Case 39/70 *Norddeutsches Vieh- und Fleischkontor GmbH v. Hauptzollamt Hamburg-St. Annen* [1971] ECR 49 at 58–59. See also Cases 205–215/82 *Deutsche Milchkontor GmbH et al. v. Germany* [1983] ECR 2633 at 2665.
53. Case 94/77 *Fratelli Zerbone Snc v. Amministrazione delle Finanze dello Stato* [1978] ECR 99 at 116. See also Case 54/81 *Firma Wilhelm Fromme v. Bundesanstalt für landwirtschaftliche Marktordnung* [1982] ECR 1449 at 1463. See Lauwaars (1983/1) LIEI 41 *et seq.* and Adam and Winter in Winter (ed.), *op. cit.* (see note 27, *supra*) 507.
54. Case 22/70 *Commission v. Council* [1971] ECR 263; [1971] CMLR 335; Opinion 2/91 *ILO Convention 170 on Safety in the Use of Chemicals at Work* [1993] ECR I-1061 at 1077. See Chapter XII, section 2.1, *post.*

extent a regulation covers a particular field and thus has exclusive effects is a question of interpretation which has raised a good many problems, particularly in the area of common organizations of the markets for various agricultural products. An example of such problems is the extent to which Member States may adopt national price-regulatory measures covering products subject to price formation provisions of a scheme of common organization, particularly when such national measures are designed with another purpose in mind, such as counter-inflation. The dividing line between the area in which the Member States have lost their powers and that in which they have retained them but are required not to jeopardize the aims or functioning of the common organization is not always easily drawn into practice.[55]

The direct applicability of regulations is discussed in section 2.2.2. of Chapter VI, below.

1.3   Directives

A directive has binding force in relation to the result to be achieved for each Member State to which it is addressed but it leaves the Member States free to choose the form and methods for implementing it.[56] This brief definition of the nature and effect of this legal instrument, for which there is no clear parallel in national or international law, raises questions which have given rise to differences of opinion in legal writings and which have received, so far, only signpost answers from the Court of Justice. It is unclear, in particular, whether the legal definition of the nature and effect of a directive implies a limitation of the competence of the Community Institutions over and above that already contained in the specific Treaty Article which authorized the adoption of the directive and, if so, the extent of this limitation. It can, though, hardly be denied that a limitation of competence is implied, bearing in mind that a comparison of the legal

---

55. In Case 218/85 *Association comité économique agricole régional fruits et légumes de Bretagne (Cerafel) v. Le Campion* [1986] ECR 3513 at 3532 the Court made it clear that there are three grounds on which national measures will be prohibited because of the existence of a Community regulation: the national rules affect a matter exhaustively dealt with in the common organization of the market concerned; the national rules are contrary to the provisions of Community law, or they interfere with the proper functioning of the common organization of the market concerned. See Cross (1992) 29 CMLRev. 447; Timmermans, *Het recht als multiplier in het Europese integratie proces* (Deventer, 1978) 13 *et seq.*; Waelbroeck in Sandalow and Stein (eds.), *Courts and Free Markets* (Oxford, 1982) Vol. II 548; Furrer in Winter (ed.), *op. cit.* (see note 27, *supra*) 521, and, in relation to the free movement of goods, Gormley, *Prohibiting Restrictions on Trade within the EEC* (Amsterdam, 1985) 73–95, 111–121 and 253–254.
56. Arts. 189 EC and 161 Euratom (3rd para. in each case). See also, in relation to Recommendations, Art. 14 ECSC.

definitions makes it clear that a directive is less far-reaching than a regulation or a decision (although this view is nuanced below). The comparable terms of Article 14 ECSC which empower the Commission to adopt decisions also empower it to confine itself, if it so wishes, to making recommendations. It may thus be inferred that if a specific Treaty Article, such as Article 100 EC, empowers the Institutions to adopt directives, their competence is more limited than is the case when they are empowered to adopt regulations or decisions. However, this does not mean that the provisions of a directive have less binding effects than those of any other rule of Community law. Indeed, the correct implementation of directives is all the more important because the implementing measures are a matter for the Member States.[57]

The real problems arise, however, in considering the extent of the limitation of the competence of the Institutions. A comparison of the legal definitions of these acts show that a directive, unlike a regulation, can impose obligations only on Member States.[58] It is, like a decision addressed to Member States, a means of fettering the powers of Member States by obligations and prohibitions, as is evident from its name. Furthermore, a directive differs from regulations and decisions by the fact that its binding force is limited to the result to be achieved. In so far as it also concerns the form and the methods, it has no binding force. The distinction, however, between 'result' on the one hand and 'form and method' on the other raises many questions which so far have received no answer in the case-law. What is to be understood by these terms? Where does the limit of the binding force lie? Can a directive go into details? Can it impose the introduction of uniform rules on the twelve Member States? The many different views on these and other questions in legal literature[59] cannot be discussed within the scope of this section; the following observations are thus restricted to a few general remarks.

It should be stated at the outset that the answers to these questions must not be confined to abstract speculations on the meaning of the vague terms used in the legal definition of a directive but account should also be taken of the Treaty provisions in which the directive is the only instrument prescribed and of the subject-matter to which those provisions relate. On closer examination of those provisions it appears that a directive serves to

---

57. Case 79/72 *Commission v. Italy* [1973] ECR 667 at 672 and Case 52/75 *Commission v. Italy* [1976] ECR 227 at 284. This is, as is made clear in this section, subject to the requirement that the implementation be by means which are legally certain and effective, so that mere circulars or expressions of pious intention, which reflect simply the current whim of a national administration, will not be good compliance.
58. That does not exclude a directive addressed to all Member States being found to be an act of general application, see Case 70/83 *Kloppenburg v. Finanzamt Leer* [1984] ECR 1075 at 1086.
59. See, generally, Prechal, *Directives in European Community Law* (Oxford, 1995), and Winter in Winter (ed.), *op. cit.* (see note 27, *supra*) 487.

fetter the law-making power of one or more Member States individually or collectively on certain points. As a rule a directive is an instrument of Community intervention, often with a view to harmonization of laws,[60] in a given complex of interrelated legislative provisions, such as the right of establishment[61] or in other legislative areas, certain provisions of which directly affect the establishment or functioning of the common market[62] or the internal market.[63] Examples of the latter include food and drugs legislation. Because of divergent national legislation on the requirements which such products have to satisfy, trade in these products within the common market is impeded (as even a cursory glance at the Court's case-law on the free movement of goods will show). One of the numerous other examples is legislation concerning indirect taxation.

In all these cases Community intervention is limited; not in the sense that the consequences of intervention may not be very considerable, but in the sense of a limitation of the aspects which may be subject to Community intervention. The Community may oblige the national legislator to do justice to a given Community interest when regulating a given field. The national legislator remains competent, for example, to regulate the right of establishment, but is obliged by Community law to remove legal provisions which discriminate against nationals of other EC countries.[64] It is moreover obliged to modify those provisions in such a way that, through co-ordination of legislative and administrative provisions of the Member States, factual (not simply formal) discrimination which prejudices nationals of other Member States is removed.[65] The obligation to modify national food and drugs legislation as well as legislation in the field of indirect taxation applies only to the extent necessary for the functioning of the common market.[66]

Directives are binding as to the 'result to be achieved,' which may be defined as a legal or factual situation which does justice to the Community interest which, under the Treaty, the directive is to ensure. This may be, for instance, the equal treatment, both in law and in fact, of nationals of all EC countries upon establishment in a given industrial or professional sector in one of these countries, or the free movement of food and drugs in

60. See Chapter VIII, section 2, *post*.
61. Arts. 54(2), 56(2) and 57(2) EC.
62. Art. 100 EC.
63. Art. 100a EC (which also permits the use of other measures, see note 38, *supra*, and text thereto).
64. The Community acts through measures adopted under Art. 54(2) EC.
65. This obligation arises in pursuit of measures adopted under Art. 57(2) EC.
66. See Art. 3(h) EC. So far the restricting wording of Art. 3(h) EC has not been inter-preted as a restriction on the competence to harmonize on the basis of Art. 100 EC and other provisions. It may be that this will change now that Art. 3b EC, 3rd para., has prescribed the principle of proportionality as a limitation on Community action. See, more generally, Mortelmans and Van Rijn (1991) SEW 279, who also point to the role of the principle of subsidiarity in this regard.

the common market, unimpeded by national technical or administrative rules. Further, the result to be achieved by virtue of a directive will practically always necessitate amendment of national law unless it already confirms with the directive. A directive will thus have to contain instructions as to the content of such an amendment: if not the actual 'form', at least the 'methods' by which the result should be achieved. To that extent a directive will impose constraints on the power of the national authorities to choose form and methods. The legal definition of a directive makes it clear that this power must be left with the national authorities in so far as the result to be achieved permits, although it is equally clear that they cannot be deprived of this power altogether.

The relationship between 'result' and 'form and methods' is thus a fluctuating one, although there is a limit to the fluctuation: a directive can never oblige a Member State to introduce an exhaustive set of rules entirely unconnected with the national legislation in the context of which the field concerned was regulated. If it were otherwise the national authorities would not retain any freedom to incorporate the result to be achieved into their national legislation. As the Court has recognized,[67] the answer to the question of whether a directive may contain binding instructions on details of amendments to national legislation or whether it may even, in the case of harmonization, oblige the Member States to introduce uniform rules, depends on whether the result to be achieved calls for this, in view of the specific nature of the field being regulated. In any event, the limit mentioned above applies.

It has been submitted above that the legal definition of a directive implies a limitation of the competence of the Institutions over and above that already contained in the specific Treaty provision under which the directive was adopted. In the light of the conclusion just drawn this statement deserves some qualification. It appears that the competence-limiting effect of the legal definition of a directive has no significance of its own but is significant only in conjunction with the substantive enabling Treaty provisions which define the fields in which, and the interest on behalf of which the Community may intervene by adopting a directive. Because the legal definition of a directive takes the result to be achieved as the measure of a directive's binding force, it provides a criterion for the delimitation of the substantive enabling provisions according to the subject-matter being regulated. This delimitation may be important particularly where the drafting of the Treaty is rather vague, as in the case of the provisions on harmonization of laws.

67. See Case 38/77 *Enka BV v. Inspecteur der Invoerrechten en Accijnzen* [1977] ECR 2203 at 2212 in which the Court concluded that harmonization in the customs field could necessitate ensuring the absolute identity of provisions governing the treatment of goods imported into the Community whatever the Member State across whose frontier they are imported.

Directives must be implemented within the period prescribed therein.[68] Each Member State has the freedom to delegate powers to its domestic authorities as it considers fit and to implement directives by means of measures adopted by regional or local authorities, but that internal division or allocation of powers will not release the State from the obligation to ensure that the provisions of the directive concerned are properly implemented in national law.[69] While the implementation of social policy objectives pursued by a directive may be left by the Member States in the first instance to management and labour, to be regulated, say, by collective agreements, that possibility will not discharge the Member States from their obligation to ensure that all workers in the Community are afforded the protection required by the directive (by, for instance declaring collective agreements to be binding in all cases), so that the State guarantee forms a residual guarantee of effective protection where this is not ensured by other means.[70] The form and methods of implementation of the result to be achieved must be chosen in a manner which ensures that the directive functions effectively, account being taken of its aims.[71] A firm line of case-law makes it clear that each Member State is obliged to implement directives in a manner which satisfies the requirements of clarity and legal certainty and thus to transpose the provisions of the directive into national provisions having binding force.[72] Transposition need not necessarily require enactment in precisely the same words in an express legal provision; thus a general legal context (such as appropriate already existing measures) may be sufficient, as long as the full application of the directive is assured in a sufficiently clear and precise manner.[73] So mere circulars, official

68. On the importance of this see Case 52/75 *Commission v. Italy* [1976] ECR 277 at 284; during the period prescribed for implementation Member States must not adopt measures liable seriously to compromise the result prescribed, Case C-129/96 *Inter-Environnement Wallonie ASBL v. Région Wallonne* [1997] ECR I-7411 at 7449. There are countless instance of cases in which the deadline has not been respected. See, generally, the Commission's annual reports on monitoring the application of Community law: COM (84) 181 Final (for 1983); COM (85) 149 Final (for 1984); O.J. 1986 C 220/1 (for 1985); O.J. 1987 C 338/1 (for 1986); O.J. 1988 C 310/1 (for 1987); O.J. 1989 C 330/1 (for 1988); O.J. 1990 C 232/1 (for 1989); O.J. 1991 C 338/1 (for 1990); O.J. 1992 C 250/1 (for 1991); O.J. 1993 C 233/1 (for 1992); O.J. 1994 154/1 (for 1993); O.J. 1995 C 254/1 (for 1994); O.J. 1996 C 303/1 (for 1995), and O.J. 1997 C 332/1 (for 1996).
69. Case 96/81 *Commission v. The Netherlands* [1982] ECR 1791 at 1804; Case 97/81 *Commission v. The Netherlands* [1982] ECR 1819 at 1833, and Cases 227–230/85 *Commission v. Belgium* [1988] ECR 1 at 11.
70. Case 143/83 *Commission v. Denmark* [1985] ECR 427 at 434–435; Case 235/84 *Commission v. Italy* [1986] ECR 2291 at 2302–2303.
71. Case 48/75 *Royer* [1976] ECR 497 at 518.
72. Case 239/85 *Commission v. Belgium* [1986] ECR 3645 at 3659. See also Case 300/81 *Commission v. Italy* [1983] ECR 449 at 456.
73. Case 29/84 *Commission v. Germany* [1985] ECR 1661 at 1673 (The existence of general principles of constitutional or administrative law may render implementation by specific legislation superfluous, provided that those principles guarantee full application of the

instructions or administrative practices, which by their nature can always be changed as and when the authorities please and which are not publicized enough, will not be sufficient to constitute proper fulfilment of the obligation to implement directives.[74] Particularly if a directive creates rights on which individuals can rely, high demands are made for the transposition into the national legal order, so that beneficiaries may be aware of their rights and can exercise them before their national courts if necessary.[75] The fact that in specific circumstances a provision of a directive may be relied upon before a national court does not exempt a Member State from the obligation to adopt appropriate implementing measures within the period prescribed in the directive.[76]

The direct effect of provisions of directives and their application in general by national courts is discussed in detail in section 2.2.2. of Chapter VI, below.

directive by national authorities, and that, where the directive creates rights for individuals, the legal position resulting from those principles is sufficiently clear and precise and the persons concerned are made fully aware of their rights and, where appropriate, are afforded the possibility of invoking them before the national courts. This last point is of particular importance where the directive is intended to afford rights to nationals of other Member States, as they are not normally aware of such principles.); Case 252/85 *Commission v. France* [1988] ECR 2243 at 2263 (But faithful transposition becomes particularly important when the management of the common heritage is entrusted to the Member States in their respective territories.); Case C-360/87 *Commission v. Italy* [1991] ECR I-791 at 814; Case C-131/88 *Commission v. Germany* [1991] ECR I-825 at 867; Case C-361/88 *Commission v. Germany* [1991] ECR I-2567 at 2600–2601, and Case C-190/90 *Commission v. The Netherlands* [1992] ECR I-3265 at 3309.

74. Case 239/85 *Commission v. Belgium* [1986] ECR 3645 at 3659; Case 300/81 *Commission v. Italy* [1983] ECR 449 at 456, and *e.g.* Case 102/79 *Commission v. Belgium* [1980] ECR 1473 at 1486; Case 147/86 *Commission v. Greece* [1988] ECR 1637 at 1656; Case C-361/88 *Commission v. Germany* [1991] ECR I-2567 at 2602; Case C-381/92 *Commission v. Ireland* [1994] ECR I-215 at 221, and Case C-242/94 *Commission v. Spain* [1995] ECR I-3031 at 3039. It is not sufficient to seek to implement by issuing a circular declaring an earlier law or decree unenforceable: implementation must be at least by the same level of instrument as the rules previously applicable and must be transparent. See Hilf (1983) YBEL 79 and Beyerlin (1987) EuR 126. The fact that a Member State's practice is consistent with the protection afforded under a directive will not justify a failure to implement the directive concerned in the national legal order by means of provisions capable of creating a sufficiently clear and precise situation permitting individuals to be aware of and enforce their rights; this means that full implementation in law is required, implementation in fact alone will not be good compliance, as a legal framework is required, Case C-339/87 *Commission v. The Netherlands* [1990] ECR I-851 at 885; Case C-131/88 *Commission v. Germany* [1991] ECR I-825 at 868, and Case C-361/88 *Commission v. Germany* [1991] ECR I-2567 at 2603–2604. This parallels the position with regard to fundamental freedoms conferred by the Treaties, see Case 167/73 *Commission v. France* [1974] ECR 359 at 372–373.

75. *E.g.* Case C-361/88 *Commission v. Germany* [1991] ECR I-2567 at 2601–2602. See Heukels (1993) NTB 59. As to the legal framework for implementation in the United Kingdom, see Usher in Daintith (ed.), *Implementing EC Law in the United Kingdom* (Chichester, 1995) 91.

76. Case 102/79 *Commission v. Belgium* [1980] ECR 1473 at 1487.

1.4 Decisions

Decisions are binding in all respects on their addressees.[77] They can be addressed to Member States[78] as well as to private parties and are the means by which the Community adopts individual administrative acts. In other words, they are the means by which Community law is applied in specific cases. As in national administrative law, there are many types of decisions. Some decisions authorize the Member States or undertakings to do things. Examples of this type include decisions granting undertakings an exemption from the cartel prohibition by a declaration that Article 85(1) EC is inapplicable to the cartel in question.[79] Other decisions may impose obligations. Examples of this type include decisions requiring a Member State to abolish or modify a particular state aid measure because it infringes the prohibition contained in Article 92 EC[80] and decisions requiring undertakings to put an end to an infringement of the cartel prohibition.[81] Yet another type of decision is a declaratory decision granting 'negative clearance' in competition cases in which, at the request of the undertaking concerned, the Commission certifies that 'on the basis of the facts in its possession, there are no grounds under Article 85(1) or Article 86 EC for action on its part in respect of an agreement, decision or practice'.[82] A formal and express refusal to take a decision also amounts to a decision in Community law.

The case-law of the Court of Justice has frequently dealt with the problem of how to distinguish a decision from non-binding communications, opinions or recommendations. A decisive point is the Court's definition of a decision as 'a measure emanating from the competent authority, intended to produce legal effects and constituting the culmination of procedure within that authority, whereby the latter gives its final ruling in a form from which its nature can be identified.'[83] The judgments relating to whether these conditions have been met is strongly

---

77. Arts. 189 EC and 161 Euratom (4th para. in each case). *Cf.* Art. 14 ECSC, 2nd para.
78. In which case they are binding on all organs of the Member States concerned, including, therefore, national courts, Case 249/85 *Albako Margarinefabrik Maria von der Linde GmbH and Co. KG v. Bundesanstalt für landwirtschaftliche Marktordnung* [1987] ECR 2345 at 2360.
79. Reg. 17 (O.J. English Special Edition 1959–62, p. 87 (as amended), Art. 6, applying Art. 85(3) EC. Reg. 17, Art. 8(1) permits the exemption to be granted for a limited period, and subject to conditions.
80. Art. 93(2) EC.
81. Reg. 17 (see note 79, *supra*), Art. 3.
82. *Ibid.*, Art. 2. See, as an example of such a purely declaratory decision in which the Court treated a letter from the High Authority confirming an undertaking from a company as a decision, Case 14/59 *Société des Fonderies de Pont-à-Mousson v. High Authority* [1959] ECR 215 at 224–225.
83. Case 54/65 *Compagnie des Forges de Châtillon, Commentry et Neuves-Maisons v. High Authority* [1966] ECR 185 at 195.

casuistic in nature and it appears that the Court is heavily influenced by the importance which a positive or negative answer may have for the legal protection of private parties.

Considerable problems have arisen over the years regarding the status of letters signed by senior Commission officials, particularly (but not only)[84] in the field of Community competition law. The status of such letters varies, according to the addressee and the subject-matter. In a group of competition cases known for convenience as the perfumes cases[85] the Court discussed the status of so-called 'comfort letters' which are sent by the Commission, usually signed by the Director-General for Competition and form part of its informal application of competition policy.[86] The Court concluded that these letters could not be characterized as decisions granting negative clearance or decisions granting an exemption under Article 85(3) EC, within the meaning of Articles 2 and 6 of Regulation 17.[87]

Acts which do not in themselves have legal effects, but which are steps in proceedings leading to a decision, will not be open to review;[88] thus a statement of objections in competition proceedings does not amount to a decision.[89] A letter communicating to a complainant in the competition or anti-dumping fields a decision to close the file on a complaint will be open to review, as it communicates a decision of the Commission which has legal effects.[90] There is, however, no entitlement as such to a decision in

---

84. *E.g.* Cases C-199 and 200/94 P *Pesquería Vasco-Montañesa SA (Pevasa) et al. v. Commission* [1995] ECR I-3709 at 3717–3719; Case T-5/96 *SAbout Betodlares Centralförening et al. v. Commission* [1996] ECR II-1299 at 1309–1311, and Case T-137/96 R *Valio Oy v. Commission* [1996] ECR II-1327 at 1338–1341. See in staff cases, *e.g.* Case 56/72 *Goeth-Van der Schueren v. Commission* [1973] ECR 181 at 186–187 and Case 806/79 *Gerin v. Commission* [1980] ECR 3515 at 3524; see also on oral decisions in staff cases, Cases 316/82 and 40/83 *Kohler v. Court of Auditors* [1984] ECR 641 at 656.

85. Cases 253/78 and 1–3/79 *Procureur de la République et al. v. Giry et al.* [1980] ECR 2327; Case 37/79 *Anne Marty SA* [1980] ECR 2481; Case 99/79 *SA Lancôme et al. v. Etos BV et al.* [1980] ECR 2511 and Case 31/80 *NV L'Oréal et al. v. PVBA De Nieuwe AMCK* [1980] ECR 3775. See, generally, Korah (1981) 6 ELRev. 14.

86. As opposed to formal application by means of a decision, see, further, Chapter VIII, section 4.2.3, *post.*

87. *E.g.* [1980] ECR 2327 at 2373–2374; [1980] ECR 2481 at 2499. As to Reg. 17, see note 79, *supra.*

88. See, citing earlier case-law, *e.g.* Case T-64/89 *Automec Srl v. Commission* [1997] ECR II-367 at 381–388 (*Automec I*); Case T-90/96 *Automobiles Peugeot SA v. Commission* [1997] ECR II-663, and Case T-9/97 *Elf Atochem SA v. Commission* [1997] ECR II-909. The remedy is to raise the point as one of the reasons for seeking the annulment of the final decision. But see, as to irreversible consequences, *e.g.* Case 53/85 *AKZO Chemie BV et al. v. Commission* [1986] ECR 1965 at 1990. As to delegation of powers by the Commission to one of its members see Chapter IV, section 6.4.3, *ante.*

89. *E.g.* Case 60/81 *International Business Machines Corporation v. Commission* [1981] ECR 2639 at 2654 and Case C-282/95 P *Guérin Automobiles v. Commission* [1997] ECR I-1503 at 1542.

90. Case 210/81 *Demo-Studio Schmidt v. Commission* [1983] ECR 3045 at 3063–3064

either of these fields, nor in relation to complaints which may lead to proceedings against a Member State under Article 169 EC.[91]

While a decision is distinguished from mere communications, opinions, and recommendations by its binding character, it differs from a regulation by its individual character. As already observed during the discussion of regulations, this difference, too, has received ample attention from the Court. In fact, Article 173 EC makes it plain that private parties do not, in principle, have a direct right of appeal against a regulation. The Court considers the limitation of the persons to whom the decision 'is addressed' as a characteristic feature; it applies to a limited number of specified or identifiable natural or legal persons.[92] Although this does not appear to be

(citing earlier case-law); Case 298/83 *Comité des industries cinématographiques des Communautés européennes (CICCE) v. Commission* [1985] ECR 1105 at 1122; Cases 142 and 156/84 *British American Tobacco Company Ltd. et al. v. Commission* [1987] ECR 4487 at 4571; Case 53/85 *AKZO Chemie BV et al. v. Commission* [1986] ECR 1965 at 1990; Case T-24/90 *Automec Srl v. Commission* [1992] ECR II-2223 at 2274–2276 (and, as to the Commission's obligations generally, see *ibid.* at 2274–2280); Case C-39/93 P *Syndicat français de l'Express international et al. v. Commission* [1994] ECR I-2681 at 2710–2711 (A letter closing the file would only be viewed as a preliminary or preparatory statement of position if the Commission had clearly indicated that its conclusion was valid only subject to the submission by the parties of supplementary observations, *ibid.* at 2711.), and Case C-19/93 P *Rendo NV et al. v. Commission* [1995] ECR I-3319 at 3357, corrected, but not on this point, [1996] ECR I-1997 (both these latter judgments reveal the different approaches of the Court of Justice and the Court of First Instance to this problem). But the Courts accept that a decision to reject a complaint which does not definitively rule on whether there is a breach of Art. 85(1) EC, and does not grant an exemption under Art. 85(3) is merely an assessment by the Commission of the agreements and practices concerned (see *e.g.* Case C-282/95 P *Guérin Automobiles v. Commission* [1997] ECR I-1503 at 1542), and as such has the same legal status as comfort letters; see, further, Chapter VIII, section 4.6.4, *post.* See also *e.g.* Case T-504/93 *Tiercé Ladbroke SA v. Commission* [1997] ECR II-923 at 944–945 (appeal pending in Case C-300/97 *Tiercé Ladbroke SA v. Commission* (O.J. 1997 C 318/7). In relation to anti-dumping, see Case 191/82 *EEC Seed Crushers' and Oil Processors' Federation (Fediol) v. Commission* [1983] ECR 2913 at 2935–2936.

91. *E.g.* Case 125/78 *GEMA v. Commission* [1979] ECR 3173 at 3189–3190; Case C-19/93 P *Rendo NV et al. v. Commission* [1995] ECR I-3319 at 3357, and Case T-575/93 *Koelman v. Commission* [1996] ECR II-1 at 18 (upheld on appeal in Case C-59/96 P *Koelman v. Commission* [1997] ECR I-4809 at 4838). But if comments have been submitted in response to a letter announcing a provisional intention to reject a complaint and giving a period for the submission of observations, the Commission then has to make up its mind, see Case C-282/95 P *Guérin Automobiles v. Commission* [1997] ECR I-1503 at 1542–1543. In relation to anti-dumping, see Case 191/82 *EEC Seed Crushers' and Oil Processors' Federation (Fediol) v. Commission* [1983] ECR 2913 at 2935–2936. As regards Art. 169 EC proceedings, see *e.g.* Case 48/65 *Alfons Lütticke GmbH et al. v. Commission* [1966] ECR 19 at 27; Case 247/87 *Star Fruit Company SA v. Commission* [1989] ECR 291 at 301, and Case T-575/93 *Koelman v. Commission* [1996] ECR II-1 at 31–32 (upheld on appeal in Case C-59/96 P *Koelman v. Commission* [1997] ECR I-4809 at 4842) .

92. Cases 16 and *17/62 Confédération Nationale des Producteurs des fruits et légumes et al. v. Council* [1962] ECR 471 at 478.

prescribed as a formal requirement in the legal definition ('addressed' need not mean 'specified'), as a rule a decision will be recognizable by the fact that it mentions by name the persons to whom it 'is addressed'. If this is not the case, the identifiability of the persons bound when a decision is taken will usually be sufficient to qualify it as a decision.

A special problem arises in the case of a decision addressed to a Member State. It may contain an authorization, a prohibition or a refusal to grant an authorization which leads to the adoption, abolition, or non-adoption of national legislative rules. The question may arise whether such a decision should not be considered as an act of general application in view of the legislative character of the acts to which it leads. The Court answered this question in the negative when it was raised by the Commission (as one of the arguments against the admissibility of the case) in connection with an action by a private person against a decision taken by the Commission, in which it had refused a request by Germany for authorization (under Article 25(3) EC) partially to suspend certain customs duties. This amounted to a refusal to allow Germany to enact rules of national law. The Court took the view that the decision was addressed to a particular party and had legal effects only in respect of this party.[93] The Court did not consider any legal consequences which may have resulted in national law.

The question of the extent to which decisions are directly effective is discussed in section 2.2.2. of Chapter VI, below.

1.5 Statement of reasons, publication, entry into force and enforcement

Regulations, directives and decisions adopted by the Council or the Commission have to state the reasons on which they are based and refer to any proposals or opinions which were required to be obtained in accordance with the Treaties.[94] The requirement to refer to proposals or opinions makes it possible to check whether the decision-making procedure required by the Treaties has been followed. A consistent line of authority shows that 'the extent of the duty to provide a statement of reasons prescribed in Article 190 of the Treaty depends on the nature of the measure in question and on the circumstances in which it was adopted.'[95]

93. Case 25/62 *Plaumann and Co. v. Commission* [1963] ECR 95 at 107.
94. Arts. 190 EC, 15 ECSC, and 162 Euratom. Art. 190 EC also applies to regulations and decisions adopted by the European Central Bank, Art. 108a(2) EC, 4th para.; ESCB and ECB Statute, Art. 34.2, 4th para.
95. *E.g.* Cases 142 and 156/84 *British–American Tobacco Company Ltd. et al. v. Commission* [1987] ECR 4487 at 4585; Case 250/84 Case 250/84 *Eridania zuccherifici nazionali SpA et al. v. Cassa conguaglio zucchero et al.* [1986] ECR 117 at 146, and Case C-156/87 *Gestetner Holdings plc v. Commission* [1990] ECR I-781 at 844. See, generally, Schermers and Waelbroeck, *Judicial Protection in the European Communities* (5th ed. Deventer, 1992) 204–213.

The Community authority adopting the act concerned must state its reasoning clearly and unambiguously so that interested parties are in a position to know the reasons for the measure involved and so that the Court is in a position to exercise its supervisory function.[96] If no reasons or inadequate reasons are given this is an infringement of an essential procedural requirement which is one of the grounds for annulment of a contested act.[97]

It appears from the case-law of the Court, which is very detailed as regards the demands made of the requirement to give reasons, that the facts on which the measure is based have to be mentioned, as well as the arguments which were decisive for the adoption of the measure.[98] The basic elements of the train of thought of the Institution which adopted the measure should be present in the statement of reasons.[99] Both the nature of the power exercised and the nature of the measure adopted are relevant to the degree of accuracy with which the statement of reasons must be formulated. It is settled case-law that the reasoning 'must show clearly and unequivocally the reasoning of the institution which enacted the measure so as to inform the persons concerned of the justification for the measure adopted and to enable the Court to exercise its powers of review.'[100] In view of the limitation of judicial control of the exercise of discretionary powers,[101] it is precisely in these cases that rigorous demands will have to be made as to accuracy.[102] The statement of reasons of a regulation need not be as detailed as that of a decision. It may be confined to a statement

---

96. *E.g.* Case 250/84 *Eridania zuccherifici nazionali SpA et al. v. Cassa conguaglio zucchero et al.* [1986] ECR 117 at 146; Case C-156/87 *Gestetner Holdings plc v. Commission* [1990] ECR I-781 at 844, and Case 24/62 *Germany v. Commission* [1963] ECR 63 at 68–69.

97. Arts. 173 EC, 33 ECSC and 146 Euratom. As to corrections by the Council's secretariat see *e.g.* Case 131/86 *United Kingdom v. Council* [1988] ECR 905 at 934–935; and by Commission officials see Cases T-79/89 *etc. BASF AG et al. v. Commission* [1992] ECR II-315 at 343–346 (to be read with the appeal which quashed the judgment of the Court of First Instance but annulled the Commission's decision on other grounds, partly involving subsequent action by officials finalizing wording, Case C-137/92 P *Commission v. BASF AG et al.* [1994] ECR I-2555 at 2650–2651).

98. *Eg.* Case 2/56 *Geitling selling agency for Ruhr coal et al. v. High Authority* [1957–58] ECR 3 at 15.

99. *E.g.* Case 14/61 *Koninklijke Nederlandsche Hoogovens en Staalfabrieken NV v. High Authority* [1962] ECR 253 at 275. See also Case 41/69 *ACF Chemiefarma NV v. Commission* [1970] ECR 661 at 690, in which the Court considered the statement of reasons sufficient 'if it indicates clearly and coherently the considerations of fact and law on the basis of which the fine has been imposed on the parties concerned, in such a way as to acquaint both the latter and the Court with the essential factors of the Commission's reasoning.'

100. Case C-353/92 *Greece v. Council* [1994] ECR I-3411 at 3444; Case C-478/93 *The Netherlands v. Commission* [1995] ECR I-3081 at 3011.

101. See Chapter IV, section 7.6, *ante.*

102. *E.g.* Cases 36–38 and 40/59 *President Ruhrkohlen-Verkaufsgesellschaft mbH. et al. v. High Authority* [1960] ECR 423 at 439–445.

about the overall situation which led to the adoption of the regulation on the one hand and, on the other hand, about the general objectives it proposes to achieve. A specific enumeration of the sometimes numerous and complicated facts which led to its adoption together with a more or less complete opinion on these facts is, however, not required.[103] A specific statement of reasons in support of all the details in general measures is unnecessary provided such details fall within the general scheme of the measures as a whole.[104] Thus the assessment of the adequacy of reasoning will have regard not only to the wording but also to the context of the act concerned and all the legal rules governing the matter in question.[105] In relation to decisions, the obligation to state the reasons for an individual decision is imposed in order that the Court may be in a position to review the legality of the decision and that the addressees of the decision and others affected by it may be able to ascertain the basis on which the decision was taken and challenge its legality should they wish to do so.[106] It is thus necessary to mention all the various details which are relevant in law or as facts: thus attention is paid not merely to the text of the decision, but also to the context in which it is adopted and the corpus of legal rules governing the matter in question. Moreover, the required degree of precision of the statement of reasons for a decision will also be weighed against practical realities and the time and technical facilities available for making the decision.[107] The actual circumstances under which measures have to be adopted may sometimes be relevant in that they may lead to a reduction of the pretty rigorous demands which the Court usually makes of the reasoning of decisions. In particular, if the appellant Member State or undertaking concerned has been closely involved in the process leading to the adoption of the decision, the reasoning may be less detailed.[108] A

---

103. Case 5/67 *W. Beus GmbH and Co. v. Hauptzollamt München* [1968] ECR 83 at 95. See also Case 166/78 *Italy v. Council* [1979] ECR 2575 at 2597 and Case 167/88 *Association générale des producteurs du blé et autres céréales (AGPB) v. Office national interprofessionnel des céréales (ONIC)* [1989] ECR 1653 at 1686.

104. *E.g.* Case 166/78 *Italy v. Council, ibid.*

105. *E.g.* Case C-478/93 *The Netherlands v. Commission* [1995] ECR 3081 at 3111 (citing earlier case-law) and Case C-22/94 *The Irish Farmers Association et al. v. Minister for Agriculture, Food and Forestry, Ireland et al.* [1997] ECR I-1809 at 1843.

106. *E.g.* Case 16/65 *Firma C. Schwarze v. Einfuhr- und Vorratsstelle für Getreide und Futtermittel* [1965] ECR 877 at 889; Case 8/83 *Officine Fratelli Bertoli SpA v. Commission* [1984] ECR 1649 at 1660, and, referring to further case-law, Case C-350/88 *Société française des Biscuits Delacre et al. v. Commission* [1990] ECR I-395 at 422.

107. *E.g.* Case C-350/88 *Société française des Biscuits Delacre et al. v. Commission* [1990] ECR I-395 at 422 (citing earlier case-law).

108. *E.g.* Case 13/72 *The Netherlands v. Commission* [1973] ECR 27 at 39; Case 9/83 *Eisen und Metall AG v. Commission* [1984] ECR 2071 at 2085, and Case 347/85 *United Kingdom v. Commission* [1988] ECR 1749 at 1797. The same applies where the Member States have been closely associated with the process of drafting other types of Community acts, see *e.g.* Case C-54/91 *Germany v. Commission* [1993] ECR I-3399 at 3424; Case C-478/93 *The Netherlands v. Commission* [1995] ECR I-3081 at 3111.

decision which follows a well-established line of decisions may be less fully reasoned and may simply refer to the standing administrative practice of the Commission, although if it goes appreciably further than previous decisions the Commission must give an explicit account of its reasoning.[109] The extent of the duty to state reasons also depends on the subject matter to which the measure relates; on this point see Chapters VII (competition policy and state aids) and XI (agriculture), below.

All Regulations and (since the coming into force of the TEU) directives addressed to all Member States, as well as decisions adopted by the European Parliament and Council acting jointly, are to be published in the *Official Journal*.[110] They take effect on the date appointed by them or, failing this, on the twentieth day following their publication.[111] Limits have been set on the freedom of the Institutions to fix the date of entry into force. Entry into force on the date of publication,[112] and *a fortiori* on an earlier date, is permitted only if reasons for this are present.[113] The Court has emphasized on several occasions that 'in general the principle of legal certainty ... precludes a Community measure from taking effect from a point in time before its publication, it may exceptionally be otherwise where the purpose to be achieved so demands and where the legitimate

---

109. Case 73/74 *Groupement des fabricants de papiers peints de Belgique et al. v. Commission* [1975] ECR 1491 at 1514; Cases 142 and 156/84 *British–American Tobacco Company Ltd. et al. v. Commission* [1987] ECR 4487 at 4585, and Case C-350/88 *Société française des Biscuits Delacre et al. v. Commission* [1990] ECR I-395 at 422.

110. Arts. 191 EC and 163 Euratom (1st and 2nd paras. in each case). Since the Council Decision of 15 September 1958 (O.J. English Special Edition 1952–58, p. 60) there is a single Official Journal (O.J.) for the three Communities, currently published in eleven languages. Before that there was an ECSC *Official Journal* in which, *inter alia*, general Decisions and Recommendations of the ECSC were published (*cf.* Art. 15 ECSC). previously, it was not compulsory to publish directives in the O.J., although this was invariably done, under a heading 'Acts whose publication is not obligatory.' Regulations made by the European Central Bank are also covered by the obligation to publish, Art. 108a(2) EC, 4th para.; ESCB and ECB Statute, Art. 34.2, 4th para.

111. Arts. 191 EC and 163 Euratom.

112. In the absence of evidence to the contrary a regulation is regarded as being published throughout the Community on the date appearing on the relevant issue of the Official Journal: Case 98/78 *Firma A. Racke v. Hauptzollamt Mainz* [1979] ECR 69 at 84; Case 99/78 *Weingut Gustav Decker KG v. Hauptzollamt Landau* [1979] ECR 101 at 109. Particularly at the end of the year issues of the O.J. may well be published later than the date of the issue, see Case C-65/93 *European Parliament v. Council* [1995] ECR I-643 at 670 (publication on a later date than than the date borne by the O.J. did not affect the assesment of the legality of the regulation on the date of its adoption).

113. Case 17/67 *Firma Max Neumann v. Hauptzollamt Hof/Saale* [1967] ECR 441 at 456. In a case in which the entry into force of a regulation was fixed as the date of the O.J. in which it was published, but in fact it had not been effectively published and distributed, the Court refused to allow retroactive effect to the date of the O.J., Case 88/76 *Société pour l'exportation des sucres SA v. Commission* [1977] ECR 709 at 726.

expectations of those concerned are duly respected.'[114] Clearly established case-law shows moreover that substantive rules of Community law must, in order to ensure respect for the principles of legal certainty and the protection of legitimate expectation, be interpreted as applying to situations which existed before their entry into force only in so far as it clearly follows from the terms, objectives or general scheme of those rules that such an effect must be given to them.[115] The principle that penal provisions may not have retroactive effect is one of the general principles of law whose observance the Court of Justice ensures.[116]

Directives (other than those adopted by the European Parliament and the Council acting jointly) which are not addressed to all Member States and decisions (other than those adopted by the European Parliament and the Council acting jointly) must be notified to their addressees and take effect upon such notification.[117] Irregularities in the notification procedure are extraneous to the measure and cannot therefore invalidate it.[118] Notification in accordance with the Treaty takes place on communication of the measure to the addressee and the latter being put on a position to take cognisance of it.[119] In view of the importance which directives and decisions may have for parties other than their addressees, the fact that the Community Institutions now generally publish these in the *Official Journal* even when this is not obligatory is to be welcomed as promoting the transparency of Community law. Finally, it should be mentioned that decisions of the Council and the Commission which contain pecuniary obligations for private persons,[120] such as those by which the Commission imposes a fine or a penalty,[121] have the enforceability of a court judgment.

---

114. *E.g.* Case 114/81 *Tunnel Refineries Ltd. v. Council* [1982] ECR 3189 at 3206 (citing some earlier authorities).

115. Case 21/81 *Openbaar Ministerie v. Bout et al.* [1982] ECR 381 at 390 (citing earlier case-law). See, generally, Heukels, *Intertemporales Gemeinschaftsrecht* (Baden-Baden, 1990).

116. Case 63/83 *R. v. Kirk* [1984] ECR 2689 at 2718.

117. Arts. 191 EC and 163 Euratom (3rd para. in each case). The same applies to ECSC individual decisions and recommendations, Art. 15 ECSC, 2nd para. Decisions made by the future European Central Bank are also covered by the obligation to publish, Art. 108a(2) EC, 4th para.; ESCB and ECB Statute, Art. 34.2, 4th para.

118. Case 48/69 *Imperial Chemical Industries Lid. v. Commission* [1972] ECR 619 at 652.

119. Case 6/72 *Europemballage Corporation and Continental Can Company Inc. v. Commission* [1973] ECR 215 at 241.

120. Arts. 192 EC and 92 ECSC EC. The restriction to pecuniary obligations is not contained in Art. 164 Euratom. Art. 192 EC applies to regulations and decisions adopted by the European Central Bank, Art. 108a(2) EC, 4th para.; ESCB and ECB Statute, Art. 34.2, 4th para. As to the conditions under which the Council may authorize the ECB to impose fines or periodic penalty payments on undertakings for failure to comply with obligations under its regulations and decisions, see Art. 108a(3) EC; ESCB and ECB Statute, Art. 34.3. As to the procedure, see Art. 106(6) EC; ESCB and ECB Statute, Art. 42.

121. *E.g.* Reg. 17 (see note 79, *supra*), Arts. 15 and 16.

They are enforced by virtue of the rules of civil procedure in each of the Member States.[122] The order for their enforcement is issued by the national authority designated for this purpose by each government.[123] No other verification takes place except the verification of the authenticity of the document.[124] This procedure also applies to judgments of the Court of Justice.[125]

1.6   Acts of the representatives of the governments of the Member States meeting within the Council

The so-called 'acts of the representatives' do not, unlike decisions of the Council, originate from an Institution of the Communities, but from a diplomatic conference, although the latter has the same composition as the Council. This formal distinction between decisions of government representatives as members of an Institution (decisions of the Council) and decisions taken by these representatives as such by general agreement ('acts of the representatives') has great legal importance. In fact, because of this distinction, the rules in the Treaties concerning the way in which decisions of the Community Institutions are taken, their legal effects, implementation and judicial review cannot apply to 'acts of the representatives'. The question which may arise in this connection will largely have to be answered, as far as the 'acts of the representatives' are concerned, by general international law.

Broadly speaking, two categories of cases may be distinguished, which in practice have led to the use of 'acts of the representatives'. The *first* category concerns cases in which Treaty provisions direct the governments to adopt a collective legal act of an administrative nature for the implementation of those provisions, such as the appointment of the members of the Commission[126] or the framing of a joint programme for the exchange of young workers.[127] The *second* category relates to cases in which the governments make use collectively of the discretion allowed, or allowed for the present, by the Treaties to each individual Member State to regulate a given subject-matter on its own initiative, with a view to a proper implementation of the Treaties or the realization

122. Arts. 192 EC, 92 ECSC, and 164 Euratom.
123. For the United Kingdom see the European Communities (Enforcement of Community Judgments) Order 1972 (S.I. 1972 No. 1590). The order for enforcement is appended by or under the authority of the Secretary of State. The competent authority in the Netherlands is the Registrar (*Griffier*) of the *Hoge Raad* but requests are addressed to the Minister of Justice.
124. Arts. 192 EC, 92 ECSC, and 164 Euratom.
125. Arts. 187 EC, 44 ECSC, and 159 Euratom.
126. Arts. 158 EC, 10 ECSC, and 127 Euratom.
127. Art. 50 EC.

of their objectives. A well-known example is the so-called acceleration decisions of 12 May 1960 and 15 May 1962.[128] On these dates the representatives of the governments decided by general agreement to develop the customs union more rapidly than had been provided for in the EEC Treaty.[129]

The legal device of the 'acts of the representatives' was created in order to establish a simple and informal method for laying down the points agreed upon between the government representatives in the margin of Council sessions in all those cases where an act of the Council was not considered possible or opportune. This desire for simplicity and informality was frequently inspired by the motive of avoiding time-consuming and laborious Community or national decision-making procedures. These would be necessary if the Institutions themselves (if at all possible[130]) were to take decisions on the subjects concerned, or the agreement reached were to be laid down in a treaty which would have to be approved by the national parliaments.[131]

It is generally held that 'acts of the representatives' are to be treated as international agreements, although two exceptions have to be made to this view. *First*, for those cases where the Treaties direct the governments to enact collectively particular legal acts which are indissolubly linked with the functioning of the institutional system of the Communities, such as the nomination of members of the Commission, Judges of the Court of Justice and Advocates-General and the fixing of the seat of the Institutions. Thus, the governments act together as an *ad hoc* Community organ, which exercises a power based on the Treaties and clearly defined therein; for these nominations they act as an electoral college. The decisions taken on the basis of such a power, although not originating from an Institution within the meaning of the Treaties, form part of Community law and as such are not subject to any rules of national constitutional law on the conclusion of international agreements.

The *second* exception concerns those 'acts of the representatives' where it may be assumed, on the basis of the parties' intention, that they did not contemplate creating a legal obligation between the Member States, but the governments wished to confine themselves to making each other

128. J.O. 1217/60 and 1284/62.
129. See now Arts. 15(2) and 24 EC.
130. If specific Articles on competence afford no basis for such decisions, they might, for instance, be taken in the EC system on the basis of Art. 235 EC, at least if the requirements of that Article are satisfied. See Chapter IV, section 6.2, *ante*. As to an example in the ECSC system of a combined decision of the representatives of the Governments of the Member States meeting within the Council and of the Commission see Dec. 87/603 (O.J. 1987 L 389/61).
131. Internal agreements made between representatives of the Member States for the implementation of association agreements do contain a ratification clause, albeit in a more simplified form than is internationally customary.

promises concerning the policy which they would follow, promises which are legally binding neither on future governments nor on the Member States as such. Such 'acts of the representatives' are not international agreements, but legally non-binding policy agreements (gentlemen's agreements). It is often difficult to ascertain the intention of the parties to such acts. There is sometimes a tendency to assume all too readily that such an act is no more than a policy agreement when in national constitutional law it is doubtful whether a government is really entitled to enter into the obligation resulting from the decision without the co-operation of the national parliament. Dutch law contains strict provisions on this point.[132] The intention of the fifteen parties, however, must not be judged only by what is permitted to one or some of them by their Constitution. Many of these 'acts of the representatives' are of the greatest importance for the functioning of the Communities and are applied without any doubt arising among the parties involved as to whether they should also be applied in law. It is therefore advisable to take as a starting-point that 'acts of the representatives' are aimed at creating a legal obligation for the Member States, unless there is clear evidence to the contrary.[133]

Opinions differ widely as to whether 'acts of the representatives' do or do not form part of the system of Community law. Some writers answer this question in the affirmative, others in the negative; many others confine themselves to observing that such acts are in the no man's land between Community law and international law. A question of greater practical importance concerns the relationship between Community law (proper) and the acts in question. It is generally assumed that these acts cannot alter the obligations for Member States under the Treaties and the decisions of the Institutions based thereon. Such an alteration can be effected only by a formal amendment of the Treaties or Community decisions. In the case, of Treaty amendments the revision procedure required by the Treaties will have to be observed.[134] If an 'act of the

132. See the Rijkswet goedkeuring/bekendmaking verdragen, Stb. 1994, 542.
133. Thus, the 'Decision of 29 January 1966 of delegations of the Member States assembled in an extraordinary session of the Council', better known as the 'Luxembourg Accords' (Bull. EC 12–1966 p.5), is not even largely a policy agreement. Indeed, it merely contains a statement on the desirable modalities of an arrangement to be made with the Commission for its relations with the Council, and a statement to the effect that there was no agreement between the delegations on the application of the procedure for majority decisions in the Council. A remarkable act of the representatives is the 'Decision of the Heads of State or Government, meeting within the European Council, concerning certain problems raised by Denmark on the Treaty on European Union (O.J. 1992 C 348/1; Bull. EC 12–1992 point I.34), as to the legal status of which, see Curtin and Van Ooik (1993) SEW 675.
134. Case 43/75 Defrenne v. SABENA [1976] ECR 455 at 478. See Chapter II, section 4.2, ante.

representatives' or its implementation by Member States is contrary to their obligations under the Treaties, the Commission may bring an action against them for infringement of the Treaty.[135] An action for annulment of the act in question, however, will not be successful, since such an action lies only in the case of acts of the European Parliament and the Council acting jointly, acts of the Council, of the Commission and of the ECB, and acts of the European Parliament intended to produce legal effects *vis-à-vis* third parties.[136] The Court, pointing out that it made no difference whether an 'act of the representatives' was entitled 'Act of the Member States meeting within the Council' or 'Act of the representatives of the governments of the Member States meeting within the Council,' is willing to investigate whether what purports to be an 'act of the representatives' is in fact a Council decision, and in doing so the Court will take note of whether the Community has exclusive competence in the matter concerned.[137] It may be deduced from this that the Member States as a whole cannot simply detach themselves from judicial supervision by adopting 'acts of the representatives' in a field in which the Community is exclusively competent.

Although the use of the legal device of 'acts of the representatives' can contribute to the effectiveness of the Community Institutions and facilitate the achievement of their tasks, such acts are not part of the Community primary or secondary legal order, at least in so far as they do not find their legal basis in the Treaties (which the first category of acts discussed above clearly does). The Court does not regard itself as competent to interpret in any event the second category of acts discussed above.[138]

On the accession of new Member States the *acquis communautaire* which the new Member States accept by virtue of accession is extended to all decisions and agreements adopted by the representatives of the Member States, meeting within the Council, and the new Member States are placed in the same situation as the existing Member States in relation to 'declarations or resolutions or other positions ... concerning the European Communities adopted by common agreement of the Member States.'[139] But this provision does not attach any additional legal effects to the measures to which it applies, and it leaves unanswered the question whether or not they have legal effects.[140]

---

135. Arts. 169 EC, 88 ECSC, and 141 Euratom.
136. Art. 173 EC. *Cf.* Arts. 33 and 38 ECSC and 146 Euratom.
137. Cases C-181 and 248/91 *European Parliament v. Council and Commission* [1993] ECR I-3685 at 3717–3718.
138. Case 44/84 *Hurd v. Jones* [1986] ECR 29 at 76–77.
139. *E.g.* Act of Accession (1972), Art. 3(1) and (3).
140. Case 44/84 *Hurd v. Jones* [1986] ECR 29 at 79.

2. FINANCES

2.1 The Budget of the European Communities[141]

2.1.1 Historical development prior to the Delors I package decisions of 1988

The financial system of the Community has an eventful history, in which four strands of development can be distinguished: the development from budgetary diversity to unity; the development of the Community's financial autonomy; the development of financial mechanisms supporting Community policies, and the evolution of the budgetary authority. These strands are discussed in turn.

(A) The development from budgetary diversity to unity. Initially the ECSC budget was divided into two budgets; one for operational expenditure, the other for administrative expenditure. There was a similar division for Euratom: an operating budget and the budget for research and development. The then EEC had one single budget from the start. Since the Merger Treaty of 1965 entered into force on 1 July 1967 there has been one general budget, which includes the administrative expenditure and the related revenue of the ECSC and the revenue and expenditure of the EEC and Euratom, in so far as they were previously entered in their operating budgets. The First Budgetary Treaty of 22 April 1970 added to this the revenue and expenses of the research and investment budget of Euratom.[142]

There are, however, four exceptions to the uniformity of the budget of the Communities, which principle is nowadays enshrined in Article 199 EC.[143] *First*, the operational expenditure and the revenue of the ECSC form the subject of a separate budget, as they display a number of characteristics which make it impossible to integrate them into the general budget. They are financed out of ECSC levies,[144] and can cover expenditure on the promotion of technical and economic research and the readaptation of the workforce.[145] In respect of this budget the Commission

---

141. As to the budget generally see Strasser, *The Finances of Europe* (European Perspectives, Brussels, Luxembourg, 7th ed. (3rd English ed.), 1991) and the Commission's publication *European Union Public Finance* (Edition 1995, Brussels, Luxembourg, 1995), which latter has been extensively used by the editor in revising this section. See also Corbett *et al.*, *The European Parliament* (3rd ed., London, 1995) 224–244 and Nicoll in Westlake, *op. cit.* (see note 5, *supra* 179–191.
142. Merger Treaty, Art. 20(l) as amended by the First Budgetary Treaty, Art. 10.
143. Indeed, in Case C-284/90 *Council v. European Parliament* [1992] ECR I-2277 at 2329 the Court noted that the unity of the budget was one of two fundamental principles in budgetary matters (the other is the annual nature of the budget).
144. Art. 49 ECSC.
145. Art. 50 ECSC contains the general proposition, as to the details, see Arts. 54, 1st and 2nd paras., 55 and 56 ECSC.

alone is the budgetary authority. *Secondly*, the decentralized bodies (satellites) have their own budgets in order to guarantee them a certain measure of autonomy. Their precise relationship with the general budget of the Community varies considerably.[146]

The *third* exception is the European Development Fund. Its revenue comes from contributions by the Member States, and the Fund is subject to separate financial rules.[147] The Member States desire to maintain influence on its activities by a separate management procedure. The *fourth* exception concerns borrowing and lending operations and guarantees of

146. Four categories can be identified:

(1) Bodies based on an organizational measure internal to the Commission, which are Commission departments subject to special operating regulations. The Statistical Office of the European Communities (Eurostat) and the European Community Humanitarian Office (ECHO) are in fact integrated in the general budget. The appropriations to cover the Joint Research Centre's activities are entered in a special subsection of Part B of the general budget and special financial rules govern its expenditure (Title VII of the Financial Regulation (O.J. 1977 L 356/1, most recently amended by Reg. 2444/97 (O.J. 1997 L 340/1).

(2) Interinstitutional bodies (the Office for Official Publications) providing services to the various institutions, keeping their own accounts.

(3) Bodies established by the Treaties or by Community legislation. Of these, the Euratom Supply Agency, despite the autonomy by virtue of the Euratom Treaty, is in reality a Commission department, and is the only satellite body established directly by the Treaty. Initially only the European Centre for the Development of Vocational Training (Cedefop) and the European Foundation for the Improvement of Living and Working Conditions were the only two satellites of the Community and its budget established by legislation. They have a separate budget which principally comes by means of a subsidy from the general budget. The Joint European Torus (JET), established by the Council under Chapter V of the Euratom Treaty, has wider autonomy than the above bodies, drawing only 80% of its resources from the Community budget. The newer generation of satellites (the European Environment Agency, the European Training Foundation, the European Health and Safety at Work Agency and the European Drugs and Drug Addiction) Centre operate in a similar way to Cedefop, but have more autonomy as regards financial rules. The newest form of satellites (such as the European Medicinal Products Evaluation Agency, the Office for Harmonization in the Internal Market (Trade Marks, Designs and Models), and the Community Plant Variety Office, are meant to be self-financing, with a subsidy from the Community budget to balance their budgets on an exceptional or temporary basis. See also, as to the Translation Centre for bodies of the European Union, the report in O.J. 1997 C 393/47. As to these satellites, see Chapter IV, section 9.3, *ante*.

(4) Finally, the European Schools, and the European University Institute in Florence, established by intergovernmental agreements have their own financial arrangements, even though they derive most of their financing from the Community budget.

As in the case of all beneficiaries of Community funds, these bodies are subject to control by the Court of Auditors.

147. Reg. 86/548 (O.J. 1986 L 325/42).

Community loans. The Community is expressly empowered to borrow and lend by virtue of Articles 49 ECSC and 172(4) Euratom. The EC Treaty made no provision for such powers. Borrowing and lending is based on instruments adopted under Article 235 EC. Thus loans have been granted by the Council to Member States finding themselves in balance of payments difficulties, a facility originally set up in 1975 as a result of the first oil crisis;[148] macroeconomic assistance has now also been accorded to various Central and Eastern European countries and the republics of the former Soviet Union, and the New Community Instrument, originally called the Ortoli Facility, established on 16 October 1978 by the Council, authorized the Commission to raise loans to support projects and investments contributing to greater convergence and integration of the economic policies of the Member States.[149] Euratom borrowed funds from the Export–Import Bank (Eximbank) in 1959 enabling it to finance Community loans for European unclear power plants, but while the Community is presently authorized to contribute to the financing of nuclear power plants within the Community, and indeed the ceiling for such loans was raised to 4 billion ECU in 1990, no operation of this type has been undertaken since 1989.[150] Euratom loans may now also be contracted to improve the efficiency and safety of nuclear power plants in Central and Eastern Europe and in certain Independent States of the former Soviet Union.[151] The field of action for ECSC loans was extended in 1990 to Poland and Hungary, where they have been used principally to promote the sale of Community steel and industrial products which could be implemented within joint ventures.[152] However, with the expiry of the ECSC Treaty due on 24 July 2002, the ECSC's financial activities are now being scaled down.[153] Various European Investment Bank (EIB) own resources loans outside the Community are now covered by a Community guarantee underwritten by the general budget against possible default by the beneficiary countries.[154] While the lending activities of the Community

148. See now Reg. 1969/88 (O.J. 1988 L 178/1). The current ceiling is 14 billion ECU. In recent years examples of this type of medium-term financial assistance include grants to Greece in 1986, 1987 and 1991, and to Italy in 1993, although it has not always been necessary for the amounts granted to be drawn down.
149. Originally established under Dec. 78/870 (O.J. 1978 L 298/9), see further, Decs. 82/169 (O.J. 1982 L 78/19), 83/200 (O.J. 1983 L 112/26), 87/182 (O.J. 1987 L 71/34). There have been no new lending operations since 1991.
150. Dec. 77/271 (O.J. 1977 L 88/11) was most recently amended by Dec. 90/212 (O.J. 1990 L 112/26). See also Dec. 77/270 (O.J. 1987 L 88/9), most recently amended by Dec. 94/179 (O.J. 1994 L 84/41).
151. Dec. 94/179 (O.J. 1994 L 84/41). These loans are examined and administered by the European Investment Bank.
152. Bull. EC 3–1990, point 1.2.5; 5–1990, point 1.3.6.
153. See *General Report on the activities of the European Union 1994* (Brussels, Luxembourg, 1995) point 1160 and COM (97) 506 Final.
154. These concern loans to various countries in Central and Eastern Europe and the inde-

Institutions and the EIB are quite considerable, they are not included in the general budget, although the Commission is obliged to give detailed information on borrowing and lending operations.[155]

(B) The development of the Community's financial autonomy. The ECSC has had financial autonomy right from the beginning, as a result of the power to raise levies conferred by Article 49 ECSC. Because, when the Merger Treaty entered into force on 1 July 1967, the administrative expenditure of the ECSC was taken into the general budget, it partially lost that autonomy. Between 1958 and 1970 the EEC and Euratom budgets, and the ECSC administrative expenses were principally financed by a system of contributions from the Member States, although an extension of the Community's own resources was envisaged in the old Articles 201 EEC and 173 Euratom. However, that state of affairs was changed by the first own resources decision of 21 April 1970 which was duly ratified by the Member States in accordance with their respective national requirements.[156] This system was gradually applied with effect from 1 January 1971, and applied fully from 1 January 1980, by which time all Community expenditure was to be financed from its own resources. These comprised, most importantly,[157] customs duties,[158] agricultural levies,[159] and percentage of the Value Added Tax levied by the Member States.[160]

Until the full application of the first own resources decision, the Member States paid transitional and declining contributions to balance the general budget of the Community. Already in the early Eighties the budgetary ceiling, which stemmed from the revenue arising out of own resources (as the Community budget has to be in balance[161]) began to loom

      pendent states of the former Soviet Union, various Mediterranean countries, various Latin American countries, and South Africa. See, further, Dec. 97/256 (O.J. 1997 L 102/33) and *European Union Public Finance* (see note 141, *supra*.) 144–146. See also Reg. 2728/94 (O.J. 1994 L 293/1).

155. An annual report is presented, see *European Public Finance, ibid.*, 145. As to the report for 1996, see COM (97) 312 Final, Bull. EU 6–1997, point 1.6.6.
156. Dec. 70/243 (O.J. English Special Edition 1970(I), p. 224). The present system is governed by Dec. 94/728 (O.J. 1994 L 293/8).
157. Other own resources included (and still include) a series of smaller items such as the proceeds of fines and penalties and the tax levied on the salaries of Community officials together with income from the sale of discarded furniture and so on. More important initially, however, were the ECSC's own financial resources from the levies on coal and steel products, but this resource has become substantially less important in recent years.
158. These were transferred to the Community in a gradual process between 1971 and 1975.
159. These have been collected by the Member States on behalf of the Community since 1971.
160. This was initially limited to a 1% ceiling calculated on a uniform basis, and was gradually applied as progress was made in harmonization of the VAT basis.
161. See Arts. 199 EC and 171(1) Euratom.

uncomfortably close. That was related to the declining revenue from customs duties as a result of the Tokyo Round of tariff reductions within the GATT, and from the agricultural levies as a result of the increasing Community self-sufficiency for most agricultural products. The revenue from VAT turned out to show relative stagnation in relation to economic activity because of the declining share of the gross national product (GNP) accounted for by consumer expenditure in the economies of the Community's Member States. On the other hand, the Community's expenditure continued to grow, particularly as it was unable to contain agricultural expenditure. Here too, the continual growth in Community self-sufficiency was a contributory factor. On top of these factors, three relatively less prosperous Member States, Greece, Spain and Portugal, had acceded to the Community, making greater calls on the existing Funds, such as the European Social Fund and the European Regional Development Fund, but contributing proportionally less. New policies involving intensive expenditure, and the strengthening of existing policies contributed in the Eighties to the growth in the tension between the growing expenditure and the relatively stagnating revenue. Already during late 1983 it was clear that the VAT resources available within the 1% limit would be insufficient for real needs in 1984, and it became necessary for the Member States to agree to provide additional financing 'outside the own resources ceiling' for the 1984 and 1985 budgets, in the former case through repayable advances, in the latter case through non-repayable advances. While political agreement was reached at the European Council meeting in Fontainebleau in June 1984 that the VAT ceiling should be raised to 1.4%, this was not given legal form until the second own resources decision in May 1985,[162] and took effect from 1 January 1986. This reform too bore scant fruit. The 1986 budget was kept in balance only by deferring certain items of agricultural expenditure to 1987, and the problem of exhaustion of the 1.4% VAT Ceiling became acute in 1987, when two months' agricultural payments had to be deferred. While in 1979 and in 1984 attempts had been made to restrict the growth of non-compulsory expenditure, and to limit agricultural guarantee expenditure, these attempts failed owing to growing disputes between the two arms of the budgetary authority in the Community, the Parliament and the Council, and because of the fragmentation of the decision-making process in the Council, with that body in the composition of the agricultural ministers in particular being reluctant to accept the budgetary discipline arrangements for the agricultural sector laid down by their colleagues, the finance ministers, in the Ecofin Council.

The introduction of a system of own resources had created a troublesome apportionment problem between the Member States. On the one hand that was connected with the composition of the own resources

162. Dec. 85/257 (O.J. 1985 L 128/15).

package. Member States which import a relatively large quantity of agricultural products from outside the Community and themselves have a relatively small agricultural sector, end up contributing proportionately more to the Community and receive comparatively little benefit from the Community's agricultural spending in return. This discrepancy may become even greater if a very large proportion of the Member State's GNP is accounted for by the VAT base.

As early as 1974 this structural imbalance in the United Kingdom's financial relationship with the Community became a major political headache for the latter. Thrice attempts were made to agree some form of corrective mechanism in the forum of various European Council meetings between 1975 and 1984. The first mechanism was set out in Regulation 1172/76:[163] compensation would be provided from the Community budget to any country facing an unacceptable situation because of the unfair financial burden it was carrying, based on the partial repayment of the United Kingdom's VAT own resources payments, provided that certain relatively stringent indicators were triggered. While the mechanism stayed in place until 1980, it was never triggered, even though the United Kingdom was a net contributor during that period, except in 1977. The second attempt was finalized in October 1980, and permitted a reduction in the United Kingdom's net contribution to the Community budget, which went hand-in-hand with supplementary measures to reduce regional disparities in the United Kingdom.[164] The third attempt led to what has so far been a definitive solution to this British problem, which was originally embodied in the second own resources decision in 1985,[165] and has been repeated in the own resources decisions since.[166] Three key elements are involved in this settlement: first, 66% of the difference between on the one hand the United Kingdom's share of VAT payments and its percentage share of allocated Community expenditure, and on the other hand the total allocated Community expenditure;[167] secondly, the reduction in the United Kingdom's contribution was made up by all the other Member States (except Germany), in accordance with their respective percentage share of VAT payments, and, thirdly, the

163. O.J. 1976 L 131/7 (amended in 1980).
164. See Reg. 2743/80 (O.J. 1980 L 284/1) which applied until the end of 1982; Reg. 2744/80 (O.J. 1980 L 284/4, replaced by Reg. 624/83 (O.J. 1983 L 73/6) which latter instrument applied until at the latest the end of 1983) and Bull. EC 10–1980, point 2.3.46.
165. Dec. 85/257 (O.J. 1985 L 128/15), later amended by Art. 29 SEA As is explained in sections 2.1.2. and 2.1.3, *post*, certain adaptations were made to this system in 1988 and 1994.
166. Dec. 88/376 (O.J. 1988 L 185/24) and the present decision, Dec. 94/728, Arts. 4 and 5 (O.J. 1994 L 293/9). The text above sets out the arrangements presently in force.
167. The figures take into account that the United Kingdom does not participate in financing its own compensation, and that the German contribution is reduced by one-third, as is explained in the text hereto.

special position of Germany which requested that its position as the main contributor to the Community budget should be taken into account, and so was made liable for only two-thirds of the payment it would otherwise make, the shortfall thus arising being proportionately redistributed among the remaining Member States. A number of objections may be made to this complex and artificial settlement, both as matters of principle and as practical objections. What is perceived as a solution in fact merely stimulates the *juste retour* mentality of the Member States in relation to the Community,[168] which fails to recognize the many indirect advantages of the process of European integration. Moreover, on the Community's revenue side, such a compensation leads to a disappearance of the incentive to remove the causes of the undesired imbalances in the distribution of the direct benefits and burdens of the integration process on the expenditure side. The most important practical objection against such an apparently beneficial manoeuvre for the Member State concerned is that it becomes a permanent and sacrosanct arrangement, not least for the so-called Euro-sceptics.

(C) The development of financial mechanisms supporting Community policies. As in national economic policy, since the end of the Fifties financial steering instruments have gradually assumed more importance in which the Community is competent. From the outset the ECSC and Euratom had powers anchored directly in the Treaties to administer Funds. The EEC Treaty only provided for the establishment of special Funds in relation to agricultural guidance and guarantee policies[169] and the training and retraining of workers.[170] Since the beginning of the Seventies Community policy orientation through financial instruments has blossomed, even outside areas specifically envisaged in the then EEC Treaty. These activities, which were based on Article 235 EEC, included the establishment of the European Regional Development Fund;[171] the New Community Instrument;[172] the first framework programmes for Community research, development and demonstration activities, adopted in the form of a Council resolution,[173] and the Integrated Mediterranean Programmes (IMPs).[174] The extent of this phenomenon of expansion from the mid-

168. In the 2nd ed. of this work (p. 219) it was noted that the 'housewife' approach might have its virtues, but an understanding of the wider aspects of European integration did not appear to be one of them.
169. Art. 40(4) EEC (unchanged as Art. 40(4) EC).
170. Art. 123 EEC (the retraining objectives were evident in Art. 125 EEC, but have now been brought into Art. 123 EC).
171. Originally by Reg. 724/75 (O.J. 1975 L 73/1), see now Reg. 4254/88 (O.J. 1988 L 374/15) as integrally amended by Reg. 2083/93 (O.J. 1993 L 193/34).
172. See note 149, *supra*.
173. O.J. 1983 C 208/1.
174. Reg. 2088/85 (O.J. 1985 L 197/1).

Seventies can be deduced from the myriad decisions, mostly on the basis of Article 235, in which the changed composition of the Community was reflected, particularly in relation to regional economic policy, while in the field of scientific and technological research the scale and composition of the Community's administration of Funds largely parallels the intensification of the technological race between the United States, Japan and Europe. The growing influence of the Parliament was expressed principally in the smaller programmes for specific social and regional objectives.

(D) The evolution of the budgetary authority. In the original EEC and Euratom Treaties the Council was the sole budgetary authority. Until 1971 the Parliament's role in relation to the budget was purely consultative; it was the Council which adopted the budget. Unlike in normal procedures, the Council did not act on a formal proposal from the Commission as the basis for its decision-making. The Council consulted the Parliament on the draft budget which it had drawn up, after preparatory work by the Commission. The First Budgetary Treaty of 22 April 1970 made various changes to the budgetary procedure and the power of decision, besides incorporating the Euratom research and investment budget into the general budget: first, it introduced a distinction between compulsory and non-compulsory expenditure;[175] secondly, it conferred on Parliament the power to adopt the budget, but did not yet give it the final say on non-compulsory expenditure, and, thirdly, it provided that the discharge in respect of the budget would be given by a joint decision of the Parliament and the Council. It is remarkable that there was no strengthening of the role of the Commission, although it had proposed to the Council that its co-responsibility should be more strongly expressed. But neither the Council nor the Parliament was willing to support such a development. This was a significant mistake, as the institution which was to play a key role in the legislative process, which in the Seventies would become ever more relevant for the Community's expenditure, was kept in a subservient, administrative function. This already made it more difficult to attune substantive and financial policy.

The Second Budgetary Treaty of 22 July 1975, which came into force on 1 June 1977[176] made some important changes, the most important of which were: first, changes to Article 203 EEC meant that decision-making powers on budgetary matters would henceforth be shared between the Council and the Parliament, which became the two arms of the budgetary authority, so that Parliament obtained the last word over non-compulsory

---

175. Compulsory expenditure is expenditure necessarily resulting from the Treaties or from acts adopted in accordance therewith, Arts. 203(4) EC, 78(4) ECSC, and 177(4) Euratom. Non-compulsory expenditure is thus all other expenditure.
176. O.J. 1977 L 359/1. See, further, section 2.2, *post*.

expenditure and the power to reject the budget in its entirety, and the Council retained the power of decision on compulsory expenditure; secondly, the power to grant the discharge in respect of the budget was placed solely in the hands of the Parliament, acting on a recommendation from the Council, under Article 206b EEC; thirdly, by Articles 206 and 206a EEC a Court of Auditors was established, replacing the old Audit Board, to exercise budget control, and, finally, while the Commission remained the sole budgetary authority for the operating budget of the ECSC, budgetary control powers were assigned to the new Court of Auditors under the final paragraph of Article 7 ECSC.

After the coming into force of the Second Budgetary Treaty, serious tension developed between the Parliament and the Council, at the root of which were four causes. First, the asymmetry between the powers of the Council as legislator and joint budgetary authority on the one hand, and the powers of the Parliament as joint budgetary authority on the other. Parliament took the view that the budget itself was a sufficient legal basis for the use of the appropriations entered in it, and thus sought to compensate its limitations in the sphere of policy-making and legislation by inserting many new budget headings and entering appropriations which could be used to commence new actions. It was able to do this by using its power of decision on non-compulsory expenditure under Article 203(4) EEC. That the Council did not share the Parliament's view about the budget being itself a sufficient legal basis for using appropriations, was hardly a big surprise.[177]

The second problem was the difference in views between the Parliament and the Council on the substantive distinction between compulsory and non-compulsory expenditure; here too, the Parliament took a broad view as to the interpretation of non-compulsory expenditure, the Council a narrow one. The third cause of tension was the restriction, provided for in Article 203(9) EEC, laid down by the Commission of the maximum rate of increase in non-compulsory expenditure. Increases in such expenditure were in principle limited by that maximum rate, and although there was a certain degree of flexibility, depending on what the Council did with the draft budget, or if the Parliament and the Council were to agree a different maximum rate, the existence of the maximum rate provision was an important limitation on the Parliament's freedom of action. Finally, the expansion in compulsory expenditure, particularly in the sphere of agricultural guarantee expenditure, in the second half of the Seventies and the first half of the Eighties, was an additional cause of friction. Given that the revenue from own resources was more or less stagnating, and given the requirement of Articles 199 EEC and 171 Euratom that the Community budget be in balance, this expansion in agricultural

---

177. The Commission took a middle line between the two extremes, see *European Union Public Finance* (see note 141, *supra*) 17–18 and the discussion in section 2.2.2, *post*.

expenditure could not take place other than to the detriment of non-compulsory expenditure.

Thus the budgetary procedure between 1980 and 1987 was characterized by recurring friction between the Parliament and the Council, which repeatedly culminated in litigation before the Court of Justice, which in one instance in that period got as far as final judgment.[178] Although the Commission attempted to mediate in these conflicts (which affected the budgets for 1980, 1982, 1985, 1986, 1987 and 1988), within the limits of its rather subordinate role in the budgetary process, these efforts booked scant success. Even the Joint Declaration of the Council, Parliament and Commission of 30 June 1982[179] which dealt with the distinction between the two types of expenditure and saw recognition that a separate legal basis was required for the utilization of appropriations for any 'significant action'[180] did not lead to more harmonious collaboration. While other efforts to improve the Parliament's involvement in financial questions were also undertaken,[181] 1988 began with an fundamental impasse relating to the budget.

2.1.2   The Delors I package (1988–1992)

The coming into force of the SEA and the enlargement to embrace Spain and Portugal led to major differences in the prosperity of the Member States of the Community, which strengthened the demand for an extensive vertical financial balancing of the Community in the direction of the less prosperous regions. At the same time it appeared that controlling the compulsory agricultural expenditure was posing an ever-increasing problem. The proportion of such expenditure in an already over-stretched

178. Case 34/86 *Council v. European Parliament* [1986] ECR 2155 (in respect of the 1986 budget). The actions in respect of the 1982 budget were removed from the register on 14 July 1982 and in respect of the 1988 budget the Court ruled in Case 377/87 *European Parliament v. Council* [1988] ECR 4017 and Case 383/87 *Commission v. Council* [1988] ECR 4051 that there was no need for it to proceed to give judgment. There is still friction, see *e.g.* Case C-284/90 *Commission v. European Parliament* [1992] ECR I-2277 and Case C-41/95 *Council v. European Parliament* [1995] ECR I-4411.
179. O.J. 1982 C 194/1, see Dankert (1983) 20 CMLRev. 701 and Dewost and Lepoivre (1982) RMC 514.
180. Joint Declaration, *ibid.*, point IV.3(c). If such appropriations were entered in the budget before a proposal had been presented, the Commission undertook to present a proposal, and the other parties undertook to endeavour to adopt it as soon as possible. This, of course, as the Joint Declaration recognized, could provide fertile ground for disputes about when action was significant, as oppose to a one-off or specific action.
181. The conciliation procedure (*concertation*) in legislative proposals is discussed in section 3.4.2, *post*. The SEA also had consequences for certain basic instruments (such as the adoption of certain specific research and development programmes, and the vertical implementing regulation relating to the ERDF) which directly affect the budget.

Community budget rose to more than 70%. The differences in the views of the Council and the Parliament discussed in the preceding section meant that the annual budgetary procedure, laid down in Article 203 EEC, was taking longer and longer to complete, all the more because the gap between the resources available and the demands made upon them was continually increasing. An additional factor in the size of this gap was the manifest ambitions of the Commission and the Parliament to increase the administration of Funds by the Community.

In February 1987 the Commission presented a package of comprehensive proposals for the reform of the Community's public finances, in the form of a triptych, consisting of a new system of own resources, improved budgetary discipline, and a reform of the Community's structural funds.[182] This Delors I package found political agreement in the European Council in Brussels in February 1988[183] and culminated in decision-making in June and July 1988, as set out below.

(A) A new system of own resources. The third own resources decision, Decision 88/376, changed the composition of the Community's own resources and extended their scope.[184] *First*, in order to ensure a stable stream of revenue, the total amount of own resources was no longer linked to a single item of revenue (VAT), but to Community GNP, so that for each of the years 1988–1992 overall ceilings were set for total own resources at a percentage of the Community's total GNP, rising from 1.15% in 1988 to 1.2% in 1992, with a further overall ceiling of 1.3% of total Community GNP being set for 1992 in terms of commitment appropriations.[185] *Secondly*, an adjustment was made to VAT-based own resources, to allow for the disparity in economic structures (the differences in the proportion of Member States' GNP accounted for by consumption). Thus VAT resources were henceforth established by applying a 1.4% rate to the uniform VAT base for all Member States, as determined by Community rules. However this was capped, so that a Member State's VAT base could not exceed 55% of its GNP at market prices.[186]

The *third* change was to rationalize the system of traditional own resources (customs duties, agricultural levies, and the levies on sugar and isoglucose). The 10% collection costs, charged by the member states, who

---

182. These were set out in two communications: *The Single European Act: A new frontier for Europe* (COM (87) 100 Final), and *Report on the financing of the Community Budget* (COM (87) 101 Final). These were then given concrete shape in various proposals culminating in the package of measures agreed in June 1988.
183. Bull. EC 1/2–1988, points 1.1.1–1.1.10.
184. O.J. 1988 L 185/24. See also Reg. 1552/89 (O.J. 1989 L 155/1, most recently amended by Reg. 1355/96 (O.J. 1996 L 175/3)). See also COM (98) 209 Final and COM (97) 652 Final. Dec. 88/376 and Reg. 1552/89 are still transitionally relevant.
185. *Ibid.*, Art. 3.
186. *Ibid.*, Art. 2(1)(c).

act on behalf of the Community, were henceforth to be deducted at source, before the revenue was passed on to the Community, instead of being separately reimbursed and charged to the expenditure side of the budget. This led to considerable administrative simplification. Moreover, customs duties on products falling under the ECSC Treaty were added to the Common Customs tariff duties.[187] *Fourthly*, and most importantly, a new 'fourth resource' was introduced, based on the Member States' GNP.[188] This fourth resource is a balancing item, and is calculated by applying to a base made up of the sum of the Member States' GNP at market prices a rate to be determined during the budgetary procedure in the light of the total of all other revenue.[189] This is designed to ensure that there is balance in the Community budget, and is therefore often called an 'additional resource' in budget documents. The most important side-effect of the fourth resource is to match each Member State's payments more closely to its ability to pay. The *fifth* alteration, as a result of these changes, was to make the necessary adjustments to the compensation mechanism which had been agreed for the United Kingdom.[190] In reality this amounted to ensuring that the United Kingdom was in the same position as if the previous arrangements had continued. The amount of compensation is calculated on the basis that the budget is fully financed by non-capped VAT, from which amount the saving accruing to the United Kingdom by the capping of the VAT base at 55% and the introduction of the fourth resource is deducted. The resulting correction is accorded to the United Kingdom in the form of a reduction in its VAT payments. The other Member States no longer finance this compensation in proportion to their VAT payments, but in proportion to their GNP. Germany still benefits from its reduced participation in the compensation, and Spain and Portugal were accorded a refund of a declining share of their payments of compensation until 1991 (which was the remaining transitional period accorded to them on accession).

(B) Budgetary discipline. The greatest threats to budgetary discipline which existed in the budgetary procedure of Article 203 EEC were threefold. *First*, the tendency of the Parliament to increase the non-compulsory expenditure, in respect of which it had the most to say, as much as possible; secondly, the virtually autonomous continual increase in the agricultural guarantee expenditure, and, finally, the price (in the form of greater expenditure than was permitted) of the annual conflict between the Parliament and the Council. Thus inevitably the achievement of budgetary discipline formed the central panel of the triptych structure of the Delors I

187. *Ibid.*, Arts. 2(3) and 2(1)(b).
188. *Ibid.*, Art. 2(1)(d).
189. See also *ibid.*, Art. 2(5).
190. *Ibid.*, Art. 4.

package. On the one hand it took shape in Decision 88/377[191] on budgetary discipline, and on the other hand in the Interinstitutional Agreement on budgetary discipline and improvement of the budgetary discipline signed five days later.[192] In both measures it is confirmed that the Council, the Commission and the Parliament have a shared responsibility for budgetary discipline, without encroaching on the powers conferred on each of them by the Treaties. The Interinstitutional Agreement entered into force on 1 July 1988 and contains rules for a pragmatic cooperation between the three Institutions involved in the budgetary procedure, in order to avoid conflicts during that procedure.[193] The Financial Regulation was also further amended.[194] The most important five elements of these arrangements will now be discussed.

First, at the core of budgetary discipline lies the financial perspective. It is intended to result in harmonious and controlled development in the broad sectors of budget expenditure, and to establish a new balance in the allocation of expenditure by the guarantees established for the development of policies connected with the SEA, such as economic and social cohesion envisaged in Articles 130a–130e EEC. It was accepted that the financial perspectives should be regarded as binding expenditure ceilings (subject to agreed technical adjustment and revision procedures) both for payment appropriations and commitment appropriations.[195]

Six separate headings of expenditure were identified in the Interinstitutional Agreement:

- European Agricultural Guidance and Guarantee Fund (Guarantee section) expenditure;
- structural operations , including those under the ERDF and the ESF;
- policies with multiannual allocations, such as IMPs and research and development programmes;
- other policies, such as environment, transport and third countries;
- repayments and administration, including financing of agricultural stock disposal, and
- a monetary reserve in order to absorb consequences for agricultural expenditure of significant and unforeseen movements in the exchange rate of the ECU against the U.S. dollar.

According to the 1988 projections, the first two headings would account for some 80% of total Community expenditure, amounting to some 53 billion ECU. The relationship between compulsory and non-compulsory

191. O.J. 1988 L 185/29).
192. O.J. 1993 L 185/33. the importance attached to this Agreement can be gauged from the fact that it was published in the 'L series' of the O.J.
193. On Interinstitutional Agreements in general, see section 1, *ante*.
194. By Reg. 2730/94 (O.J. 1994 L 293/7). As to the latest amendment, see 146, *supra*.
195. As to the difference between these, see section 2.2.3, *post*.

expenditure would be about 65% to 35%. The financial perspective 1988–1992 formed for the first time in the Community's history a reference framework which would have to be respected in the annual budgetary procedure. This was intended to reduce enormously the risk of clashes between legislative power and budgetary power, between the two arms of the budgetary authority, as they exercised their powers under Article 203 EEC. A further factor intended to ensure a balanced interpretation of the existing institutional arrangements was the terms of Article 16 of Decision 88/377, according to which: '[t]he financial implementation of any Council decisions exceeding ... the appropriations provided for in the financial estimates may not take place until ... the financial estimates have been suitably amended.' This obliged the Council as legislator to acknowledge that the exercise of that power could interfere with the powers of the Parliament as joint budgetary authority. The financial perspective would be adjusted annually by the Commission, taking account of movements in GNP and prices in the Community. If the allocations provided in the financial perspective for multiannual programmes could not be used in full during a given year, their transfer would be authorized, and the perspectives adjusted accordingly. Finally, the commitment appropriations could be revised in the light of developments in the international situation which were unforeseen at the time the Interinstitutional Agreement was signed, such as German unification. Thus the financial perspective did not amount to a multiannual budget; the annual budgetary procedure remained necessary, in accordance with the principle of the annuality of the Community budget, to determine the actual level of expenditure, and its distribution over the various budget lines. The global division into 6 headings served primarily to safeguard the main priorities agreed between the institutions involved.

Secondly, all the good intentions to maintain budgetary discipline would, though, come to nothing if the seemingly autonomous growth in agricultural guarantee expenditure were not contained. Controlling this expenditure was a central element in Decision 88/377. Article 1 of that decision set out the principle of the agricultural guideline, the maximum progression for EAGGF Guarantee Section expenditure, which had to be respected each year, and formed the ceiling for the first heading in the financial perspective. Five points played a role in this agricultural guideline:

- the annual rate of growth of EAGGF Guarantee Section expenditure was limited to a maximum of 74% of the annual rate of growth of the Community's GNP;
- mechanisms were adopted for the systematic depreciation of existing and future agricultural stocks, so that their value became more realistic. The disposal of such stocks had been one of the biggest setbacks to the Community budget prior to 1988;

- the existing stabilization mechanisms were reinforced and extended to other production sectors, and additional measures were introduced aimed at limiting supply directly by the set-aside scheme, with the possibility of direct income support to farmers;
- an early warning system on the development of EAGGF Guarantee Section expenditure was introduced, monitoring expenditure budget chapter by budget chapter (as opposed to aggregate expenditure previously);
- the introduction of the monetary reserve mentioned above.[196]

The *third* element of budgetary discipline was the adoption by the Council, in accordance with Article 14 of Decision 88/377, of a reference framework, taking account of the financial estimates of the Interinstitutional Agreement, for compulsory expenditure other than EAGGF guarantee expenditure. This obliged the Council to consider whether the development of expenditure required revision of the rules on the basis of which it was incurred.

The *fourth* element is that the Parliament and the Council agreed in the Interinstitutional Agreement to accept, for the financial years 1988–1992 the maximum rates of increase for non-compulsory expenditure deriving from the budgets established within the ceilings set by the financial perspective. The Parliament thus committed itself not to use its powers under Article 203(9) EEC to increase the maximum rate of increase set by the Commission. Making use of that power could infringe the limits of the expenditure ceiling. Within that maximum rate of increase, the allocations of commitment appropriations provided for the policies with multiannual allocations were to be respected.

Finally, the *fifth* element was that in order to improve the Community's budget management so as to strengthen the principle of annuality, the Financial Regulation of 21 December 1977[197] was amended.[198] Differentiated appropriations were no longer carried over automatically, although the Commission was empowered to authorize carry-overs under duly substantiated conditions, and appropriations corresponding to commitments cancelled could, exceptionally, be made available again by a decision of the Commission, in both cases on the basis of specific criteria set out in the Financial Regulation.

(C) The reform of the Structural Funds. The third panel in the triptych of the Delors I package was the reform of the Structural Funds. With the accession of Greece, Spain and Portugal the differences in regional pros-

196. Dec. 88/377, Arts. 1–13 (O.J. 1988 L 185/29).
197. O.J. 1977 L 356/1.
198. By Reg. 2049/88 (O.J. 1988 L 185/33). As to the latest amendment, see note 146, *supra*.

perity in the Community had increased in the Eighties. The Member States on the Community's periphery and the economically less strong Member States feared that the completion of the internal market in the Community would further strengthen those differences. This was the main reason for the introduction of Articles 130a–130e EEC by the SEA. In February 1988 the European Council at Brussels drew the political consequences and decided to double the commitment appropriations for the structural funds in real terms by 1993, as compared with 1987. This meant that the management of the proper functioning of these Funds, which already accounted for 27% of the Community budget in 1992, became still more essential. Thus a framework measure, Regulation 2052/88 on the tasks, effectiveness and coordination of the Structural Funds, was adopted.[199] In this context, it may be observed that as a result of that regulation the financial resources for structural measures in the various Community areas covered by the objectives set out were laid down for the whole period covered by the financial perspective. In the annual budgetary procedure, the budgetary authority was thus bound by the considerable allocations to the various Member States. Thus the budgetary rights of the Parliament were limited to a certain extent, as a binding allocation of non-compulsory expenditure had already been made. Although Parliament was consulted in the decision-making resulting in the framework regulation, by virtue of Article 130d EEC, and was, as a party to the Interinstitutional Agreement, involved in the fixing of the expenditure ceiling for the relevant heading 2 of the financial perspective, it incontestably lost a certain room for manoeuvre. This erosion of the Parliament's formal competence under Article 203 EEC has to be balanced against the gain in terms of stability and efficiency which the Delors I package produced. In the evaluation of this balance, it should be added that Parliament had obtained a number of new powers concerning some of the expenditure-intensive legislative or programming Community acts, under the cooperation procedure, then set out in Article 149(2) EEC.[200]

2.1.3   After Maastricht and Edinburgh (1992–1994), and beyond: the Delors II package

The TEU made certain changes to Title II of Part Five of the EC Treaty.[201] The most important change concerns the control of the

---

199. O.J. 1988 L 185/9, subsequently amended by Reg. 2081/93 (O.J. 1993 L 193/5); Act of Accession (1994), Annex I.XVII, and Reg. 3193/94 (O.J. 1994 L 337/1). See also the other measures in those issues of the O.J. See, further, Chapter IX, section 4.3, *post*.
200. *E.g.* Arts. 130e and 130q(2) EEC (now Arts. 130e and 130o, 2nd para. EC). As to the cooperation procedure (now under Art. 189c EC), see section 3.4.2, *post*.
201. See Cloos *et al.*, *Le Traité de Maastricht* (Brussels, 1994) 437–446.

Community's financial management. The Court of Auditors was raised to the status of a Community Institution.[202] Accordingly, the provisions relating to its composition, powers and methods of working were moved from Title II of Part Five to Title I of that Part (provisions governing the Institutions).[203] This change, largely the result of British pressure, was intended to place more emphasis than hitherto on the formal legality, regularity and soundness of the Community's financial management, and thus to sharpen the responsibilities of the Parliament as well as of the Court of Auditors.[204] The greater emphasis on sound financial management and control is also reflected in the rules relating to the implementation of the budget by the Commission and to the grant of the discharge by the Parliament.[205] The changes in the actual budgetary procedure[206] have been kept to a minimum, although both the Dutch delegation to the Intergovernmental Conference which led to the TEU and the Commission pressed for an amendment of these provisions to bring them more into line with the current practice since 1988. These changes involved including provision to charge administrative expenditure occasioned for the Community Institutions by the provisions in the TEU relating to CFSP and JHA to be charged to the Community budget;[207] the existence of the Community's own resources was finally taken into account,[208] and the introduction into the Treaties of the concept of budgetary discipline.[209] Articles 202 and 203 EEC remained unchanged as Articles 202 and 203 EC.

Attempts by various delegations to the Intergovernmental Conference leading to the TEU to include the own resources system in the Treaties themselves, in order to increase the unity of the budget further, to strengthen the role of the Parliament in the determination of the Community's own resources, to abolish the distinction between compulsory and non-compulsory expenditure, and to introduce a Community tax, came to nothing. A majority of the delegations did not want to burden a strongly institutionally-orientated Intergovernmental Conference with a financial debate, which could have arisen as a result of these proposals. A

202. Arts. 4 EC, 7 ECSC, and 3 Euratom.
203. Thus Arts. 206 and 206a EEC, 78e and 78f ECSC, and 180 and 180a Euratom were revised and then moved to become Arts. 188a–188c EC, 45a–45c ECSC, and 160a–160c Euratom.
204. See especially Arts. 189c(1) EC, 45c ECSC, and 160c Euratom (2nd para. in each case).
205. Arts. 205 and 206 EC, 78c and 78g ECSC, and 179 and 180b Eurotom, respectively.
206. Arts. 199–203 EC, 78–78a ECSC, and 173–177 Euratom.
207. Art. 199 EC. Operational expenditure occasioned by the implementation of those provisions may be charged to the budget under the conditions set out in Arts. J.11(2) and K.8(2) TEU, respectively.
208. By the repeal of Arts. 200 EEC and 172 Euratom and the revision of Arts. 201 EEC and 173 Euratom.
209. Arts. 201a EC and 173a Euratom.

further important change was the introduction of the concept of the protection of the Community's financial interests,[210] which is considered in section 2.2.6, below.

During the European Council in Edinburgh in December 1992, general agreement was reached on the Delors II package.[211] This was necessary for three reasons: the timetable imperative, as the instruments of the 1988 reform only made provision until the end of 1992, so that in any event decisions on the financial perspective and priorities for the next 5 years were necessary, and the gradual increase in the own resources ceiling was coming to an end; a further expansion and redeployment of Community finances resulted from the changes made by the TEU, as in the negotiations leading to that Treaty it had appeared that the institutional and substantive deepening of the integration process through Economic and monetary union would be politically impossible without an expansion of the transfers from the more prosperous Member States to the economically weaker regions or Member States; finally, the experiences with the implementation of the Delors I package made a reassessment or sharpening of the financial managements essential. The conclusions of the Edinburgh European Council related to own resources, budgetary discipline, and a further reform of the Structural Funds.

(A) Own resources, the 1994 settlement. The conclusions of the European Council emphasize that the Community needs adequate resources to finance its expanding policies, while taking account of the ability of the individual Member States to pay and of the commitments already made (such as the doubling of the allocations to the Structural Funds). However, it was not until 31 October 1994 that the Council was able to adopt the fourth own resources decision, Decision 94/728,[212] which replaced the third one agreed in 1988.

The main points of the 1994 own resources decision are as follows:

- a gradual rise in the own resources ceiling will take place, from 1.2% of GNP in 1993 to 1.27% in 1999;
- the uniform rate applied to the VAT assessment base will decline,

210. Arts. 209a EC, 78i ECSC, and 183a Euratom.
211. Bull. EC 12–1992, points I.45 et seq. As to the working of the 1988 Interinstitutional Agreement during its currency, see COM (92) 82 Final; as to the Commission's report on own resources, see COM (92) 81 Final.
212. O.J. 1994 L 293/9 (corrigenda O.J. 1994 L 299/32 and L 303/62), which, like all the other resources was recommended to the Member States for adoption in accordance with their respective constitutional requirements (Arts. 201 EC and 173 Euratom). The predecessor decision remains for the moment of transitional interest (see Dec. 94/728, ibid., Art. 11(2)). Although not all Member States had ratified the decision by 1 January 1995, it in fact entered into force (with retroactive effect where necessary) from that date. See also Dec. 97/245 (O.J. 1997 L 97/12) and COM (97) 652 Final.

from 1.32% in 1995 to 1% in 1999. Moreover, Member States whose *per capita* GNP in 1991 was less than 90% of the Community average (the cohesion beneficiaries) have their VAT assessment base capped at 50% from 1995. For the other Member States this reduction in capping takes place gradually, from 54% in 1995 to 50% in 1999). This implies that the importance of the VAT resource will decrease and that will be a shift to the fourth, or additional, resource, In this way the burden is allocated more according to ability to pay; in the cohesion beneficiaries (Ireland, Greece, Spain and Portugal) the share of consumption is greater and the GNP lower, and thus effect is given to the concept of cohesion;

– the confirmation, in Article 4, of the compensation previously agreed for the United Kingdom, even though there was less reason for it after the changes which had been made and are being made in the Common Agricultural Policy. This confirms that privileges in the institutional context, once conceded to a Member State, become self-perpetuating;

– it was agreed that before the end of 1999 the Commission would present a report on the functioning of the system of own resources, including a re-examination of the correction of the compensation arrangement for the United Kingdom, and a feasibility report on the creation of a new own resource[213] and arrangements for the possible introduction of a fixed uniform rate applicable to the VAT base.

(B) Budgetary discipline. The system for ensuring budgetary discipline agreed in 1988 was to a large extent continued and renewed, a choice which reflected the fact that experiences with the 1988 system had been positive, as well as the fact that the Community was still confronted with excess expenditure, in particular in relation to agricultural guarantee payments. After a year of tough negotiations,[214] a new Interinstitutional Agreement[215] was agreed on 29 October 1993, but it was another year

213. This would be a tax, levied within the framework of common policies and introduced by new own resources decision, which would be recommended for ratification in the normal way (Arts. 201 EC and 173 Euratom). But the Commission recognizes the delicacy of such a development, see *European Union Public Finance* (see note 141, *supra*) 47.

214. The European Parliament was dissatisfied with the financial framework agreed at the Edinburgh European Council, feeling it was too restrictive, so it made its agreement to the figures in the financial perspective subject to significant progress at institutional level.

215. O.J. 1993 C 331/1. This Interinstitutional Agreement was thus not published in the 'L series' of the O.J. See also O.J. 1996 C 102/4. In Case C-41/95 *Council v. European Parliament* [1995] ECR I-4411 at 4427 La Pergola, Adv. Gen. rightly noted the vital instrumental function of interinstitutional agreements, which, although they do not supplement the basic Treaty provisions, certainly serve to implement them. He also noted the importance of the principle of agreement in the balance between the Parliament and the Council in the establishment of the budget (at 4426–4427).

before a new decision on budgetary discipline[216] was agreed on 31 October 1994 (the same day as the adoption of the 1994 own resources decision). Five main features characterize these arrangements:

- the adoption of a new financial perspective for the period 1993–1999, which, as adapted to take account of the enlargement in 1995,[217] now ranges from some commitment appropriations of some 81 billion ECU at 1995 prices in 1995 to some 92 billion ECU, again at those prices, in 1999. The highest priority is given to structural actions in the Community, which initially were to see an increase of roughly 50%, from some 21 billion ECU to 30 billion ECU, at 1992 prices, over this period, which became some 26 billion in 1995 at 1995 prices, rising to some 33 billion in 1999, again at 1995 prices. The division into headings has seen some changes compared with 1988.[218] The role of the Parliament has also been somewhat strengthened in the budgetary procedure agreed in Annex II to the Interinstitutional Agreement, as it is now involved at an earlier stage in the establishment of the draft budget.[219] Moreover, an *ad hoc* conciliation procedure has been established for compulsory expenditure, although the Council still retains the last word on such matters.[220] It is remarkable that in this manner the Institutions make arrangements between themselves in relation to the budgetary procedure which depart from the provisions regulating that procedure;[221]

- the revision of the budgetary discipline decision primarily concerns

216. Dec. 94/729 (O.J. 1994 L 293/14).
217. See O.J. 1995 C 18/37–38 and Bull. EU 12–1994, point 1.5.2.
218. Structural operations are broken down into the Cohesion Fund and the Structural Funds, and the reserves are expanded to earmark specific provision for emergency aid and loan guarantees, under the heading of external action. Further alterations were made to provide for the EEA financial mechanism (under the EEA Agreement), and as a result of the alterations made in the light of Austrian, Finnish and Swedish accession, various ceilings were raised, and a new heading 7 was added, to accommodate the compensation to be received by the new Member States in accordance with the Act of Accession (1994), see O.J. 1995 C 18/37–38.
219. This trialogue meeting between the President of the Council (in its composition for budgets), the Chairman of the Parliament's Committee on Budgets, and the member of the Commission responsible for budgets discusses the possible priorities for the budget for the forthcoming year, with due account being taken of the powers of the Institutions.
220. Interinstitutional Agreement 1993, Annex II. Conciliation also takes place on the results of the trialogue meeting, *ibid.*
221. Arts. 203 EC, 78 ECSC, and 177 Euratom. See Monar (1994) 31 CMLRev. 693 at 714–715. Indeed, the Court has stressed that Art. 203(10) EC (and thus by extension the ECSC and Euratom equivalents) require each Institution to exercise its powers in budgetary matters with due regard for the provisions of the Treaty; courteous behaviour will not modify Council positions duly adopted, Case C-41/95 *Council v. European Parliament* [1995] ECR I-4411 at 4438–4439.

improvement of the management of agricultural expenditure. The agricultural guideline first established in 1988 remains, but its scope has been extended. The rules relating to the monitoring of agricultural expenditure have been strengthened, and the Council is to take appropriate measures if the expenditure threatens to exceed the guideline. As the reforms in the Common Agricultural Policy should lead to expenditure being less sensitive to movements in the exchange rate between the ECU and the U.S. dollar, the monetary reserve has been reduced to 500 million ECU from 1995;

- revision of the Financial Regulation was necessary in the light of the revision of the EC Treaty and the entry into force of the European Economic Area, as well as in order to improve the presentation of borrowing and lending operations and the new reserves;[222]
- in accordance with the conclusions the Edinburgh European Council,[223] a Guarantee Fund for external action[224] has been established to cover the risks incurred as a result of guarantees granted under the general budget for loans granted to third countries. These loans are examined and administered by the EIB on behalf of the Community, and the target size of the Fund is set at 10% of the outstanding liability of the Community arising from external loans and guarantees;
- the Edinburgh conclusions place separate emphasis on the role of the EIB in financing projects and programmes by loans raised on the capital markets and other market-based means outside the Community budget.[225] The role of the EIB in achieving cohesion within the Community was also noted.[226]

(C) Further reform of the Structural Funds. In the TEU and in the conclusions of the Edinburgh European Council an obligatory further reform was implied, and this has largely been achieved. The substantive consequences are discussed in section 5 of Chapter IX, below. Although in both the 1988 and the 1993 Interinstitutional Agreements the expenditure on the Structural Funds was classified as non-compulsory expenditure, Parliament will have to respect the allocations made in the framework Regulation[227] in the

222. The amendments were made by Reg. 2333/95 (O.J. 1995 L 240/1). See also Regs. 2334/95 and 2335/95 (O.J. 1995 L 240/9 and 12) relating respectively first to the treatment of fines, the role of the Financial Controller, recovery of debts and late adjustment, and, secondly, to special provisions applicable to research and technological development appropriations. Further amendments have been made by Reg. 244/97 (O.J. 1997 L 340/1) and been proposed in COM (98) 206 Final.
223. Bull. EC 12–1992, point I.72.
224. Reg. 2728/94 (O.J. 1994 L 293/1).
225. *Ibid.*, point I.71.
226. *Ibid.*
227. *I.e.* Reg. 2052/88 (O.J. 1988 L 185/9, as amended *inter alia* to take account of Austrian, Finnish and Swedish accession (see Reg. 3193/94 (O.J. 1994 L 337/1) and the Act of Austrian, Finnish and Swedish Accession (1994)). A new Structural Fund in

annual budgetary procedure. Here too a shift or implicit restriction of the Parliament's express powers under the Treaties is apparent.[228]

2.2 Legal aspects

2.2.1 The unity of the budget (Article 199 EC)

From the overview of the course of developments in Community finances, it may be deduced that the principle of budgetary unity expressed in Article 199 EC still has some remarkable *lacunae*, principally relating to the Community's borrowing and lending operations, although the most remarkable omission is undoubtedly the fact that the European Development Fund's activities still remain outside the Community budget.[229] The increasing lending activities of the Community, to *inter alia* the countries of Central and Eastern Europe is becoming steadily more visible in the budget in terms of *pro memoriam* headings relating to loans and guarantees granted. Not inconsiderable risks for a responsible budgetary and management policy result. If, for example, the debtors default, in whole or in part on the loans, the consequences will have to be absorbed in the general budget of the Community. It is against this background that it was decided, first, that the Guarantee Fund for external action[230] should stand apart from the budget. While the Council actually authorizes the lending operation, it is the budgetary authority (thus the Council and the Parliament) which authorizes the grant of the guarantee. This 'performance guarantee' is granted by the inclusion of the *p.m.* token entry referred to above for each of the categories of operations concerned, so that when the guarantee is activated, appropriations are allocated to the relevant headings in the budget through transfer or by means of a supplementary or amending budget. Secondly, as a buffer against the possible activation of the guarantee, the Interinstitutional Agreement of 1993 provided for provision to be made against default by the entry of a reserve in the budget to guarantee the loans to non-member countries. This reserve, currently some 320 million ECU at 1995 prices, is entered in the budget each year, but is only called upon from the Member States if there is a default. In addition to this buffer function, the gradual constitution of

the fisheries and aquaculture (FIFG) was also established by Reg. 2080/93 (O.J. 1993 L 193/1).
228. Arts. 203 EC, 78 ECSC, and 177 Euratom.
229. In Case C-316/91 *European Parliament v. Council* [1994] ECR I-625 at 663–664 the Court rejected the Parliament's submission that EDF expenditure in the context of the Fourth Lomé Convention (O.J. 1991 L 229/3) was Community expenditure which had to be entered in the budget, and to which Art. 209 EC (and thus the Financial Regulation) applied.
230. Established by Reg. 2728/94 (O.J. 1994 L 293/1).

the Guarantee Fund for external action by payment of a percentage of each new loan granted to non-member countries, acts as a means of budgetary discipline, so that the evaluation of the risk is improved. Thus, a considerable proportion of the Community's lending activities comes by this means within the reach of the Community's budgetary authority.[231] A Statement was also annexed to the Interinstitutional Agreement of 1993 in which the Council undertook to examine, on the basis of a report from the Commission, the detailed arrangements and possibilities for entering the eighth EDF in the budget from 1995 onwards,[232] and on 12 July 1995, Parliament passed a resolution calling for the EDF to be incorporated in the general budget and for EDF expenditure to be classified as non-compulsory expenditure.[233]

So far the most important reason for the Council to resist bringing borrowing and lending operations into the budget has been its desire to maintain exclusive control over decisions concerning such operations, and thus not to share control with the Parliament, It may well be, though, that the positive experiences with the 1988 and 1993 Interinstitutional Agreements will finally lead to consolidation of all activities into one single budget. Although it seemed unlikely even a few years ago that this would also mean that the operational expenditure for CFSP and JHA would come within the budget (as administrative expenditure in those areas already does),[234] such this has now become the general rule.[235] This also implies that activities within these pillars of the Union structure fall within the purview of the budgetary authority (and thus, as the expenditure is classed as non-compulsory expenditure, the Parliament).

2.2.2   The Community's own resources (Articles 201 and 201a EC)

It may be concluded from the history of the Community budget since 1970 that the extent and composition of the Community's own resources is to a large extent determined by the dynamics of the integration process, as

231. See *European Union Public Finance*, (see note 141, *supra*) 144–146.
232. The report was presented in April 1994, Bull. EU 4–1994, point 1.5.1. but concluded that while a certain flexibility could be retained if the EDF were budgetized, it was unlikely that the Council would approve budgetization under the present system of own resources. The Commission envisaged a transitional solution of financing the EDF by specific revenue being entered in the budget, with the contributions continuing to be based on an *ad hoc* scale.
233. O.J. 1995 C 249/68, Bull. EU 7/8–1995, point 1.6.1.
234. Art. 199 EC, 2nd para.
235. As to CFSP, see Interinstitutional Agreement of 16 July 1997, Bull. EU 7/8–1997, point 2.3.1. The Treaty of Amsterdam (not yet in force) will incorporate this approach into the new Art. J.18 TEU. As to JHA, see JA 95/401 (O.J. 1995 L 238/1) and Dec. 95/402 (O.J. 1995 L 238/2). Again, the Treaty of Amsterdam will incorporate this approach into the new Art. K.13 TEU.

expressed in the Community's tasks and activities, by the differences in the ability of the various Member States to pay, and the financial conse-quences for the Member States of Community policies. This made a revision of the provisions on own resources almost inevitable. Practice, as it seems to have developed, since the Brussels European Council of February 1988 offers a responsible balance between the stability in the development of the Community's revenues which is necessary for its budgetary programming in the medium term, and the equally necessary adaptation of the financial space to the changed requirements made of the Community. Accordingly, Articles 201 EC and 173 Euratom provide for a system of own resources.[236] The requirement that the decision on own resources must be adopted by unanimity and be recommended to the Member States 'for adoption in accordance with their respective constitutional requirements' forms on the one hand a barrier against a too matter-of-course expansion of own resources, but on the other hand makes possible the necessary medium-term flexibility.

The many positive results of the Delors I package were the reasons behind the suggestion from some delegations to the Intergovernmental Conference leading to the TEU that the most important provisions of the then own resources decision (of 1988) should be taken into the Treaties themselves. The suggestion was rightly not taken up, as it could have led to undesirable institutional rigidity. It would be better, on the revision of the Treaties, to include a provision whereby the Council would determine the provisions on own resources every five years.

The terms of Articles 201a EC and 173a Euratom logically complement Articles 201 EC and 173 Euratom respectively. In its policy development the Community must ensure that it remains within the financial limits imposed by the own resources decision in force from time to time. It is unlikely that this instruction in Articles 201a and 173a applies solely to the development of new policies, as serious dangers for the prescribed financial framework may flow from the application of existing open-ended rules. Thus it is strange that only the Commission is the addressee of these provisions, an inert Council or a too ambitious Parliament acting under its powers to increase non-compulsory expenditure[237] may be just as threatening to the boundaries set by the own resources decision.

2.2.3 The implementation of the budget (Arts. 202, 205 and 205a EC)

From the legal point of view the budget has the same significance in Community law (in so far as the expenditure side is concerned) as that of

---

236. As to the present system, see Dec. 94/729 (O.J. 1994 L 293/14), and the discussion of the evolution of the own resources decisions in the immediately preceding sections of this Chapter.
237. Arts. 203(9) EC, 78(9) ECSC, and 177(9) Euratom.

the Member States. It contains both an estimate of the various expenses and an authorization of these expenses (or of obligations to enter into these expenses) in the financial year concerned, which coincides with the calendar year.[238] This is one of the three means by which the *principle of annuality* is ensured; the other two flow from Article 1 of the Financial Regulation.[239] Thus budgetary operations relate to a specific financial year in order to facilitate control of the activities of the Community executive. It is still difficult to reconcile the rule of annuality with the need to engage in multiannual operations, which now play an increasingly important role in the budget. A solution to this problem has been found with the device of differentiated appropriations,[240] *viz.* commitment appropriations and payment appropriations.[241] Commitment appropriations cover in the financial year the total cost of the legal obligations entered into in respect of operations to be carried out over a period of more than one financial year. Payment appropriations cover expenditure, up to the amount entered in the budget, resulting from the commitments entered into during the financial year and/or previous financial years. The risk with this in itself sensible division is that there is a 'time-lag' between commitments being entered into and payments being made, so that it is not always possible to determine precisely when the latter must occur. In order to remedy this problem the Commission purged dormant commitments in 1986 and 1987, and proposed that in future both arms of the budgetary authority should ensure both an orderly increase in commitment appropriations and the maintenance of a strict relationship between commitment appropriations and payment appropriations. These proposals were formally enshrined in Article 3 of both the 1988 and 1994 own resources decisions.[242]

Owing to management constraints, it is not always possible to make the use of appropriations coincide with the calendar year, so Article 202

---

238. Arts. 203(1) EC, 78(1) ECSC, and 177(1) Euratom.
239. See note 146, *supra*. All items of revenue and expenditure are included in estimates drawn up for each financial year (Financial Regulation, *ibid.*, Art. 1(1)). Expenditure shown in the budget is authorized for one financial year (*ibid.*, Art. 1(2)). The terms of Art. 203(1) EC *etc.* are repeated in Financial Regulation, Art. 6, 1st para. In Case C-284/90 *Council v. European Parliament* [1992] ECR I-2277 at 2329 the Court noted that the annuality of the budget was one of two fundamental principles in budgetary matters (the other is the unity of the budget).
240. Presently, only administrative expenditure, EAGGF Guarantee Section expenditure, repayments to Member States and loan guarantees are normally entered in the budget as non-differentiated appropriations, as other categories of expenditure consist of wholly or partly differentiated appropriations.
241. The distinction can be traced to Art. 176(1) Euratom, and was widely applied by Art.1(4) of the Financial Regulation.
242. As well as in the accompanying Interinstitutional Agreements (point 16 in that of 1988, point 18 in that of 1993). See also Arts. 1(4), 1(7), 7(2) and 7(6) of the Financial Regulation.

EC[243] provides an extremely pragmatic solution by authorizing carry-over to the next financial year only, except in the case of staff expenditure. Article 202 EC, also enshrines the *rule of specification*.[244] This means that each appropriation has to have a given purpose and be assigned to a specific objective, so that there is no confusion between appropriations, whether on authorization or at implementation. This also guarantees transparency at the control stage. It may be, though, that there is a need to transfer appropriations from one heading to another. Accordingly, in order to ensure sufficient flexibility in implementation, Article 205 EC,[245] in conjunction with Article 26 of the Financial Regulation, permits budgetary transfers within very clearly defined margins. A distinction is made between transfers between different chapters of the budget[246] and transfers within the same chapter.[247] Special rules apply in relation to research and development appropriations.[248]

The *rule of equilibrium* applies strictly to the Community budget, so it

---

243. And Arts. 78a ECSC and 175 Euratom. See Art. 7 of the Financial Regulation.

244. See also Arts. 78a ECSC and 175 Euratom, and Arts. 15, 19 and 20 of the Financial Regulation. See, further, *European Union Public Finance* (see note 141, *supra*) 68–73.

245. And Arts. 78c ECSC and 179 Euratom. (3rd para. in each case).

246. For transfers between chapters in the Commission's operating appropriations, proposals are prepared by the Commission, and a further distinction is drawn between compulsory and non-compulsory expenditure (the Council by qualified majority or the Parliament by a simple majority respectively decide on the request, after consulting the other, but if no decision is taken within 6 weeks the Commission's proposals are deemed accepted). If such proposals involve mixed appropriations (thus both types) they are deemed approved unless one of the two arms of the budgetary authority vetoes the request, but if the amount requested is reduced by one arm or the other, the transfer is deemed approved at the lower amount. Article 26(6) of the Financial Regulation now expressly permits transfers between differentiated and non-differentiated appropriations.

The key role of the Parliament in relation to transfers of non-compulsory expenditure is the reason for its use of the technique of freezing appropriations in chapter 100 of the budget (the reserve), so that they cannot be used without reference to the Parliament. This clearly gives the Parliament a significant lever on policy direction in the fields concerned.

As far as the Commission's administrative appropriations are concerned, it may make the transfer itself, on giving the budgetary authority 2 weeks' notice (3 weeks' notice is given by the Management Committee of the Office for Official Publications). The Council and the Parliament take their own decisions as masters in their own house, after informing the Commission. The Court of Justice and the Court of Auditors send their proposals to the Commission which transmits them to the budgetary authority, and may express its opinion on the proposals.

247. The Commission takes decisions on such transfers within its own section of the budget. The Parliament and the Council are again masters in their own house, after informing the Commission. The Court of Justice and the Court of Auditors decide on their own transfers in their own sections of the budget, after informing the budgetary authority and the Commission 3 weeks beforehand.

248. Arts. 91–95 of the Financial Regulation.

must balance, and, thus, unlike the Member States, the Community may not borrow to cover its expenditure.[249]

The budget is the necessary legal basis for Community expenditure. The Commission, which is responsible for the implementation of the budget,[250] may not expend any moneys unless the necessary appropriations are contained in the budget. The other Institutions have their own powers in relation to their own administrative expenditure, subject to the detailed rules in the Financial Regulation.[251] The Commission's power to implement the budget has caused two severe differences of opinion between the Institutions concerned. The first concerned the question whether, and, if so, in which cases the budget forms an adequate legal basis for expenditure. Is in addition a decision by the Council (or now in appropriate cases by the Parliament and the Council acting jointly) as Community legislator necessary to provide a legal basis for such expenditure? This question was of particular currency between 1975 when the European Parliament obtained an increased function in the adoption of the Community budget, and 1988, a period in which there were considerable policy differences between the two arms of the budgetary authority, the Parliament and the Council. In view of the asymmetry between the Parliament's powers in relation to Community legislation and its powers in relation to the budget, it was obvious that the European Parliament should attempt by means of the budgetary procedure to increase its say in Community affairs as much as possible and thus be inclined to view the budget as a sufficient legal basis for operational expenses by the Commission. The Council, on the other hand, tended to the opposite view, *viz.* that the provision of an appropriation in the budget was a book-keeping exercise and that all operational expenditure by the Commission required a particular legal basis.[252]

The Treaties themselves offer no guidance for a resolution of the legal question involved in this dispute. However, two aspects are important. The first is the division of competence between the Community and the Member States. The budget can never be a legal basis for expenses which go beyond the context of the provisions of the Treaties. There is no doubt,

---

249. Arts. 199 EC and 171(1) Euratom. This principle was also incorporated in all the own resources decisions (1970, 1985, 1988 and 1994).

250. Under Arts. 205 EC, 78c ECSC, and 179 Euratom (1st para. in each case). The 1st para. of these provisions will be amended by the Treaty of Amsterdam (not yet in force) so as to require the Member States to cooperate with the Commission to ensure that the appropriations are used in accordance with the principles of sound financial management.

251. Arts. 205 EC, 78c ECSC and 179 Euratom (2nd para. in each case). See Arts. 21–26 of the Financial Regulation, and notes 246 and 247, *supra*.

252. As Tugendhat (then a member of the Commission, observed in a debate in the Parliament on 23 October 1979, see the Aigner Report, EP session documents 1–463/79, p. 106.

though, about the general proposition that the Community may use financial means even if the Treaties do not either expressly[253] or impliedly[254] so provide. In areas in which the Community is given power to act on the basis of provisions of the Treaties (*i.e.* to co-ordinate the behaviour of legal subjects by means of lasting provisions with a view to the achievement of particular policy objectives deemed to be socially desirable), it is also free to bring about a co-ordination of behaviour by financial means in place of, or in order to support such lasting provisions. This starting-point offers a solution for cases in which the Community has a more heavyweight regulatory competence, although if, as in Article 118 EC, the Community competence is more lightly based, the legal basis remains uncertain. This is one of the reasons why the administration of Funds by the Community has been so strongly anchored in Article 235 EC, either alone or in conjunction with other provision, in cases in which another adequate specific legal basis was not to be found. The steady advance of the use of financial means by the Community administration has been one of the reasons why in sensitive areas such as education and training the Community's use of financial instruments has been so precisely delimited.[255]

The second aspect relates to the division of competence between the Institutions as such. In Case 242/87 *Commission v. Council*[256] the Court observed that 'under the scheme of the Treaty the conditions under which legislative and budgetary powers are exercised are not the same.' Thus care is required in the exercise of these respective powers, as the one set has implications for the other.[257] Given that in the Treaties there is no basis for the legislative powers to take precedence over the budgetary powers, or *vice versa*, the Institutions concerned must exercise their powers in such a way that they respect each other's sphere of competence as much as possible. In practice this boils down to meaning that the Parliament may not, acting as budgetary authority, formulate Community policy with normative provisions, while the Council may not, in the exercise of its legislative powers, so develop its normative provisions in financial terms that the Parliament's margin of discretion as budgetary authority in reality completely disappears. This applies irrespective of the practical detail that a dual legal basis (inclusion in the budget and a measure adopted by the Council on the basis of specific Treaty provisions) cannot therefore be required for all expenditure. Indeed, this would be inconsistent with long-standing budgetary practice. Expenditure on a whole series of items such as aid to victims of disasters within and outside the Community, pilot

---

253. *E.g.* Art. 130 EC.
254. *E.g.* Art. 103 EC.
255. See Chapter IX, section 6.2 (point D), *post.*
256. [1989] ECR 1425 at 1454 (concerning the Erasmus Programme).
257. *Ibid.*

projects, undertaking studies, and expenses for administrative purposes, and so on, is based solely on being included in the budget,[258] and continues to be so based. The Commission's line on this question offers sufficient guidance, even though the boundary line is undoubtedly difficult to draw, and the sums concerned are relatively small and the expenditure is of an accessory or incidental nature. The Commission distinguished between budget lines which authorize expenditure for measures which form part of a Community policy but which cannot be precisely described and specified in the budget, and appropriations destined for clearly defined and specific measures, in French known as *actions ponctuelles*.[259] In the case of the former, another legal basis besides inclusion in the budget is necessary (*viz.* a measure based on Article 205 EC); in the latter case inclusion in the budget is deemed sufficient.

This view is consistent with the nature of financial instruments as a substitute for or supplement to the exercise of Community powers by legal instruments. Community competence for financial management is then determined and delimited by its power of regulatory management. However, such a power cannot be derived without more ado from the right to adopt the budget. The requirement of a legal basis which anchors the power to manage with financial resources will almost always involve the legislative competence of the Council.

The above leads to the conclusion that the budget is not the place for the determination of requirements relating to cases described in the abstract in which expenditure can or must take place. It also indicates how possible conflicts between the Council and the Parliament over the substance of their competence as to the budget should be resolved. In the meantime, the difference of opinion between the Council and the Parliament on this issue has lost much of its edge because of a number of developments. First, the Council, Commission and Parliament have long since agreed to make spending of budgetary appropriations for substantial new Community activities dependent upon the prior adoption of a basic regulation.[260] Secondly, they recognized in the Interinstitutional Agreements of 1988 and 1993[261] that the financial perspectives contained therein constituted binding expenditure ceilings for the Community. Thirdly, it has been agreed that the financial implementation of any Council decision or of any decision of

---

258. *Cf.* the Cointat report, EP session documents 150/78, pp. 59–60.
259. It will be recalled that on the basis of its implementing powers concerning the budget (Arts. 205 EC, 78c ECSC, and 179 Euratom) the Commission is entitled to use appropriations for specific activities within the limits of the relevant budget line and its explanatory notes. See WQ 769/80 (Poniatowski) O.J. 1980 C 288/6 on the decision-making procedure for the grant of emergency aid.
260. Joint Declaration by the European Parliament, the Council and the Commission on various measures to improve the Budgetary Procedure (O.J. 1982 C 194/1), para. IV. 3.c.
261. See sections 2.1.2 and 2.1.3, *ante* (under the discussion of budgetary discipline).

the European Parliament and the Council exceeding the appropriations available in the budget or the amounts specified in the financial perspective may not take place until the budget, and, where appropriate, the financial perspective have been suitably amended according to the procedure applicable for each.[262] Finally, the Parliament has become more involved in legislation having financial implications.[263]

The second controversy between the Council and the Parliament relates to whether the power of implementation of the budget conferred on the Commission[264] is exclusive, or whether it must be shared if the implementation of the budget is inseparable from the implementation of Council decisions having financial implications. This concerns in particular Council decisions the implementation of which involves committees of national experts.[265] The Commission has long maintained that the Treaties confer on it the exclusive competence in budgetary matters. Thus as Article 145 EC left no room for co-decision by or on behalf of the Council in the implementation of the budget, in view of the Commission's exclusive right to implement the budget under Article 205 EC, individual decisions on spending budgetary resources on the basis of rules laid down in a measure adopted by the Council were matters for the Commission alone, unfettered by committee procedures. This systematic interpretation is, however, untenable.[266]

It was demonstrated above that the budgetary authority may not unilaterally arrogate to itself the power of policy-making which is the province of the Community legislator. Consequentially in Community policy having financial implications the budget and the relevant policy instruments are inseparably linked. The practical complement between budgetary authority and Community legislator has a consequence for the implementation of the budget.[267] Thus the Court has noted that the Commission's power to implement the budget is not such as to modify the Treaty division of powers whereby the general or individual measures may be adopted within certain areas; this led it to conclude that even though an individual measure might almost inevitably entail the commitment of expenditure, the measure and the commitment had to be distinguished, particularly since the power to adopt the administrative decision and the power to commit the expenditure might be entrusted,

---

262. Dec. 94/729 (O.J. 1994 L 293/14), Art. 18. (Dec. 88/377 (O.J. 1988 L 185/29), Art. 16 was in similar terms (without joint decisions)). As an example of flexibility through immediate revision of the financial perspective in order to achieve desired political objectives (immediate aid to Poland and Hungary), see Bull. EC 12–1990, point 2.5.1.
263. Under *E.g.* Arts. 129d and 130d EC.
264. Arts. 205 EC, 78c ECSC, and 179 Euratom.
265. See section 3.1, *post*.
266. *Contra* Bieber in Von der Groeben *et al.* (eds.), *Kommentar zum EWG-Vertrag* (5th ed., Baden-Baden, 1997) Vol. 4, 1516.
267. See Case 16/88 *Commission v. Council* [1989] ECR 3457 at 3486–3487.

within the internal organization of each Institution, to different officials.[268]

On the revenue side, the principle of annuality also applies, subject to the possibility of paying own resources for January in advance (they are paid monthly to the Community) and a supplementary or/or amending budget adopted at the end of the following year to adjust the entries of own resources from VAT and the additional (fourth) resource.[269]

2.2.4   The budgetary procedure (Articles 203 and 204 EC)

Article 203 EC appears at first sight to have a central function in Title II of Part Five of the Treaty.[270] It sets out in detail the roles of the Council and the Parliament as component parts of the budgetary authority. The conflicts during the years 1975 to 1988 between the two arms of the budgetary authority primarily relate to the interpretation and application of this provision. However, while Article 203 EC and its sister provisions appear formally to govern the budgetary procedure, the substantive practice since the coming into effect of the Interinstitutional Agreement of 1988, and its successor Agreement of 1993 appears to have altered drastically. Thus Article 203 EC and its sister provisions may be characterized as a mask, behind the very stylized appearance of which a different, even virtual reality lurks. Only if the Council and the Parliament are no longer *ad idem* in and about that virtual reality will they step out from behind the mask into the role-play of Article 203 EC, the function of which in the virtual reality is that it is held in reserve.[271] Thus it is no longer sufficient merely to explain the formal situation and the points of dispute between the two arms of the budgetary authority which are normally set against each other, it is necessary to bear in mind also the practice in relation to the budget, in so far as it differs from the formal scheme.

(A) Article 203 EC; the divided budgetary authority. As set out in Article 203 EC, the budgetary procedure has four stages. In the *first stage* of the new budgetary procedure[272] the Commission consolidates the estimates of the expenditure of each of the Institutions in a preliminary draft budget,

---

268. *Ibid.*
269. See Art. 6 of the Financial Regulation.
270. As does Art. 177 Euratom in Title IV of that Treaty; Art. 78 ECSC is but one of many key provisions in Title IV of that Treaty.
271. See on possible legal objections to the practice of virtual reality, Bieber in Von der Groeben *et al.* (eds.), *op. cit.* (see note 266, *supra*) 1496–1497.
272. See Arts. 203(1)–3 and (4), 1st sentence EC, 78(1)–(3) and (4), 1st sentence ECSC, and 177(1)–(3) and (4), 1st sentence Euratom.

which it lays before the Council.[273] To this it attaches an opinion which may contain divergent estimates. After consultation with the Commission, the Parliament, and, where appropriate, other Institutions, the Council by qualified majority establishes the draft budget and transmits it to the Parliament. Both the draft budget and the preliminary draft will also comprise an estimate of revenue.

In the *second* stage,[274] the Parliament then has a time-limit of 45 days within which to pronounce on the draft submitted. It has the right to amend the draft budget as far as these amendments do not relate to the expenditure necessarily resulting from the Treaty or the acts adopted in accordance therewith. In respect of such 'compulsory' expenditure it may only propose modifications to the Council. The introduction of amendments in respect on non-compulsory expenditure is subject to a more rigorous voting procedure: the Parliament can only adopt them by a majority of its members.[275] For the adoption of proposed modifications the ordinary voting procedure applies: an absolute majority of the votes cast is required. The draft budget as amended and with the proposed modifications is sent to the Council.

If, on the other hand, the Parliament approves the draft budget, the budget has been finally adopted. If the draft budget is not approved within 45 days after it was submitted to the Parliament, or if the Parliament has neither amended it nor proposed modifications within this period, the budget is considered to be finally adopted. It is the President of the Parliament who declares the budget adopted.[276]

A third stage commences when an amended draft budget or one in which modifications have been proposed (or usually both) is laid before the Council.[277] The Council, after having discussed the draft budget with the Commission and, where appropriate, the other Institutions concerned, is then free to alter the amendments of the Parliament. As far as the proposed modifications are concerned, a distinction must be drawn between proposals which do not increase the total amount of expenditure of an Institution (*e.g.* by compensating for an increase in one budget line

273. It should be noted that by virtue of a gentlemen's agreement the Council and the Parliament do not amend each other's estimates; thus the Parliament is master of its own internal budget.
274. Arts. 203(4) EC, 78(4) ECSC and 177(4) Euratom. See the Parliament's Rules of Procedure (O.J. 1997 L 49/1), Rule 85 and Annex IV. The numbering of the stages in the Rules corresponds to the stages within Parliamentary deliberation, not to the numbering used in the present discussion.
275. This requirement is always interpreted by the Parliament as the majority of its current members: Rules, *ibid.*, Annex IV (*i.e.* vacant seats are not counted).
276. Arts. 203(7) EC, 78(7) and 177(7) Euratom. The declaration by the President of the Parliament is open to judicial review, *e.g.* Case 34/86 *Council v. European Parliament* [1986] ECR 2155, [19861 3 CMLR 94, and Case C-41/95 *Council v. European Parliament* [1995] ECR I-4411.
277. Arts. 203(5) EC, 78(5) ECSC, and 177(5) Euratom.

by a decrease in another) and those which do result in such an increase. In
the first case, these proposals are deemed to be accepted unless the Council
rejects them. In the second case, the reverse is true: they are deemed to be
rejected unless the Council accepts them. Council decisions regarding the
Parliament's amendments and those regarding its proposed modifications
are taken by a qualified majority of votes.[278] If within 15 days the Council
does not alter the amendments and does not reject or (as the case may be)
accept the proposed modifications, the budget is deemed to be finally
adopted. The Council informs the Parliament of this. The President of the
Parliament will thereupon declare that the budget has been finally
adopted.[279]

If, on the other hand, within the time-limit of 15 days the Council has
altered one or more of the amendments made by the Parliament, or if the
Council has rejected (or as the case may be) not accepted the modifications
proposed by the Parliament, the draft budget is again sent to the latter. In
doing so, the Council informs the Parliament of the results of its
deliberations. A *fourth* stage thus commences.[280] The procedure then is
that within 15 days of the draft budget being placed before it, the
Parliament (which will have been notified of the action taken on its
proposed modifications) may, acting by a majority of its members and
three-fifths of the votes cast, amend or reject the alterations to its
amendments made by the Council and shall adopt the budget accordingly.
If within that period the Parliament has not acted the budget shall be
deemed to be finally adopted. The Parliament may cancel the alterations
made to its *amendments* by the Council or may adopt compromises. It has
not been accorded the right to change the budget in accordance with its
proposals for modification. This right is only possessed by the Council in
the third stage. When this procedure has been concluded, the President of
the Parliament declares that the budget has been finally adopted.[281]

The Parliament does have the right, though, acting by a majority of it
members and two-thirds of the votes cast, if there are important reasons,
to reject the draft budget and ask for a new draft to be submitted to it.[282]

Both the Parliament and the Council are bound in two ways as regards
the establishment of the budget, as was noted in section 2.1, above. The
first restriction is one of a general nature, deriving from two factors: the
requirement that revenue and expenditure must be balanced;[283] the
requirement that each institution concerned in the budgetary procedure

278. This rule applies since the Second Budgetary Treaty of 22 July 1975 (Arts. 203(5) EC,
     78(5) ECSC, and 177(5) Euratom (point (b) in each case).
279. See note 276, *supra*.
280. Arts. 203(6) EC, 78(6) ECSC, and 177(6) Euratom.
281. See note 276, *supra*. This applies except where the result of the vote is that a new
     maximum rate of increase in non-compulsory expenditure has to be set.
282. Arts. 203(8) EC, 78(8) ECSC, and 177(8) Euratom.
283. Arts. 199 EC and 171(1) Euratom.

exercise its powers under that procedure with due regard in particular to measures adopted relating to the Community's own resources and the balance between revenue and expenditure.[284] Given the weight of the decision-making process for own resources decisions,[285] and in view of the fact that since 1988 the development of own resources has been set down in five-year programmes, the resulting financial space for the budgetary authority is pretty well fixed.[286]

The second way in which the Parliament and the Council are bound applies only in relation to non-compulsory expenditure.[287] While this restriction also binds the Council, it has always been intended primarily to curtail the right of amendment of the Parliament, a right which, in any case, only relates to such expenditure. The maximum rate of increase in non-compulsory expenditure is fixed annually by the Commission on the basis of:

– the trend, in terms of volume, of the gross national product within the Community;
– the average variation in the budgets of the Member States; and
– the trend of the cost of living during the previous financial year.[288]

This quantitative restriction on the growth of non-compulsory expenditure is mitigated to some extent for the Parliament by the provision that in any case it may, in exercising its right of amendment, increase this expenditure by up to half of the maximum rate of increase, even if the draft budget established by the Council already requires more than half of the amount available according to the maximum rate of increase prescribed by the Commission. Furthermore it is possible, if the Parliament, the Council or the Commission so propose[289] to exceed the prescribed maximum rate; in this case another rate can be fixed by agreement between the Council (acting by a qualified majority) and the Parliament (acting by

284. Arts. 203(10) EC, 78(10) ECSC, and 177(10) Euratom.
285. Arts. 201 EC and 173 Euratom.
286. The 1994 own resources decision (Dec. 94/728, O.J. 1994 L 293/9) reflects the agreement at the Edinburgh European Council in December 1992 (Bull. EC 12–1992, point I.47) that there should again (as with the 1988 decision) be only a gradual increase in the maximum own resources, so that they will rise from a ceiling of 1.21% of total GNP in 1995 to 1.27% of total GNP of all the Member States with an orderly rise in commitment appropriations to a maximum of 1.335% of total GNP by 1999.
287. I.e. 'expenditure other than that necessarily resulting from this Treaty or from acts adopted in accordance therewith' (Arts. 203(9) EC, 78(9) ECSC, and 177(9) Euratom (1st para. in each case).
288. Arts. 203(9) EC, 78(9) ECSC, and 177(9) Euratom. All the Institutions are informed of this rate each year before 1 May. They are obliged to respect this rate during the whole of the budgetary procedure. Accordingly, they will have to take it into account from the moment they draw up their estimates.
289. The earlier limitation of this right to 'exceptional cases' was removed as a result of the Second Budgetary Treaty.

a majority of its members and three-fifths of the votes cast). Although the
Court has rightly observed that no criterion has been laid down for the
modification of the maximum rate of increase,[290] on the basis of the link
between Articles 199, 201 and 203(9) EC it must be accepted that even if
the budgetary authority were to agree a new maximum rate of increase, the
requirements of a balanced budget and the currently applicable own
resources decision would have to be respected.[291]

The experience with the budgetary procedure between 1975 and 1988
demonstrate that the complex budgetary procedure of Article 203 EC
and its sister provisions cannot properly work if the Council and the
Parliament do not maintain good contacts and do not attempt to devise
a solution for continually recurring problems with the procedure. Already
in a Resolution recorded in the minutes of the Council meeting on 22
April 1970 (the date of the signature of the First Budgetary Treaty) the
Council undertook to take the necessary steps to ensure close cooperation with the European Parliament on this matter. On the basis of
this Resolution, numerous arrangements, most of which are now included
in the Financial Regulation, were established which promote mutual
communication in the various phases of the budgetary procedure; they
are still applied.[292] The conciliation (*concertation*) procedure set up in
1975, which is discussed in section 3.4.2 of this Chapter, below, also
provides an appropriate framework for the resolution of such problems.
The Joint Declaration of 30 June 1982 relating to various measures to
ensure the better functioning of the budgetary procedure[293] is still
relevant in part, although to the extent to which it sought to resolve the
classification of expenditure as compulsory or non-compulsory it has

290. Case 34/86 *Council v. Parliament* [1986] ECR 2155 at 2208–2209.
291. In *ibid.* and in Case C-41/95 *Council v. European Parliament* [1995] ECR I-4411 at
     4436–4437 the Court stressed the importance of any agreement, noting in the latter
     judgment that there has to be agreement on the total amount of expenditure to be
     classified as non-compulsory in order for there to be an agreement on a new rate of
     increase. For each of the years 1993–1999 both arms of the budgetary authority have
     agreed to accept the maximum rates of increase for non-compulsory expenditure
     deriving from the budgets established within the ceilings set by the financial perspec-
     tive (see the Interinstitutional Agreement 1993, point 17).
292. Thus the President-in-office of the Council or another Council member is present at
     the first and second readings of the draft budget. The preliminary draft budget which
     the Commission sends to the Council is also sent to the Parliament. Before the
     Council draws up the draft budget on the basis of the preliminary draft there are dis-
     cussions between the Council and a delegation from the Parliament at which the
     Commission is also present. Such discussions also take place before the Council
     decides on Parliament's amendments and proposed modifications to the draft budget.
     Indeed the President-in-office of the Council frequently attends meeting of the Parlia-
     ment's Budget Committee. If there are particularly thorny problems then discussions
     tend to take place even before the plenary session of the Parliament in the final phase
     of the budgetary procedure.
293. O.J. 1982 C 194/1.

been overtaken by later developments discussed in the preceding sections, above.

(B) Restrictions on Parliament's budgetary powers. The asymmetry in the division of competence in the exercise of regulatory and budgetary power between the Institutions concerned has worked its way through into Article 203 EC and its sister provisions. A budgetary procedure in which the Council has to share its powers with the parliament, which ultimately has the last word on non-compulsory expenditure, has inevitably created tension between the Council, as the Community legislator (albeit in some instances now jointly with the Parliament) and primary policy-maker on the one hand, and the Parliament, in the exercise of its budgetary functions. on the other. As has been shown above, this tension may lead to Parliament being able to obtain certain powers of policy-determination through a wide interpretation of its budgetary powers, through opening new 'budget lines' without the requisite legal basis for their implementation. The reverse is also conceivable, through the Parliament being unwilling to vote resources for the implementation of Community legislation with financial implications. In order to avoid this occurring, Article 203(4) EC[294] make the distinction between compulsory and non-compulsory expenditure, with the differing powers of the Council and the Parliament respectively. With the benefit of hindsight, it has to be observed that this handiwork of the framers of the revisions to the Treaties, when introducing this distinction which was meant to safeguard the powers of the Council as legislator and policymaker, has been somewhat infelicitous from the point of view of that objective. The same can be said in relating to the drafting of the maximum rate of increase provision in Article 203(9) and its sister provisions. By subjecting the powers of the Parliament to such a two-part limitation, there is almost an open invitation to a permanent discussion about the demarcation between compulsory and non-compulsory expenditure, and over the room which the maximum rate of increase leaves for the space for political evaluation by the Parliament as joint budgetary authority.

The formulation of the distinction between compulsory and non-compulsory expenditure[295] is less than wholly clear. It clearly stems from the days when agricultural guarantee expenditure swallowed up the vast majority of the Community expenditure (it now accounts for less than half in the present financial perspective 1995–1999). Because of the extensive political weight of the Common Agricultural Policy the Community legislator clearly sought to protect that area from the consequences of giving the Parliament a joint say in the determination of the Community budget. The uncertainties about the difference between compulsory

---

294. Arts. 78(4) ECSC and 177(4) Euratom.
295. See note 175, *supra*.

expenditure and non-compulsory expenditure appear from the history of the application of Article 203(9) and its sister provisions. It appears that the Council initially interpreted the formula in the sense that the right of amendment applies principally to administrative expenditure. In an unofficial document from the President-in-office of the Council, dated 3 February 1970[296] a distinction was made relating to the budget for 1970. In a Declaration entered in the Council's minutes on the signing of the First Budgetary Treaty it was stated that the Council was guided by the classification of budgetary expenditure laid down in this document, but that it recognized that 'this classification may change in the light of the operational requirements of the Communities'.[297] In the then current budgetary terms that would mean that the right of amendment of the Parliament related to only 3.6 per cent of the total expenditure of the Community. Moreover, it has rightly been observed that over 80% of this 3–4% of expenditure is already fixed, because it has an compulsory character (salaries of the existing staff of officials, rent for buildings, telephone and other expenses, etc.),[298] which means that the Parliament's right of amendment was perceived as being only marginal.

In the course of preparing the budget for 1975, Parliament agreed with the Council's view that expenditure could only be regarded as compulsory if no one budgetary authority – whether Council or Parliament could freely fix appropriations relating to it.[299] But even this formula was unable to resolve the differences of opinion between the two Institutions, as it lacked a clear differentiating capacity. In the Joint Declaration of 30 June 1982[300] the Institutions tried again, even attaching in an annex to that Declaration a classification of then existing budget lines into compulsory or non-compulsory expenditure and establishing a procedure to deal with differences of opinion on new budget lines. But even this Joint Declaration could not remove the friction between the Council and the Parliament, despite the trialogue dispute resolution mechanism envisaged in part II of that Joint Declaration.

A satisfactory legal distinction between the two types of expenditure can be constructed, treating expenditure necessarily resulting from the Treaties

296. The Harmel list, published by the Dutch government in Annexes to the proceedings of the Tweede Kamer, 1970–1971, 10915 no. 7.
297. This declaration related to what then became 203(8) EEC (and corresponding ECSC and Euratom provisions) relating to the maximum amount of non-compulsory expenditure (see now Art. 203(9) EC and corresponding provisions). The same formula was used there as in Art. 203(4) EC.
298. E.P. Doc. no. 42/1970–1971 (Spenale), Annex 1, paras. 36 and 42.
299. Resolution of November 1974, para. 13 (O.J. 1974 C 155/34).
300. O.J. 1982 C 194/1. See point 1. 1. of the Declaration: 'The three Institutions consider compulsory expenditure such expenditure as the budgetary authority is obliged to enter in the budget to enable the Community to meet its obligations, both internally and externally, under the Treaties and acts adopted in accordance therewith.'

or from acts adopted in accordance therewith as being only expenditure in respect of which, in the implementation of the budget under Article 205 EC and its sister provisions, the Commission has no right to refuse to meet its obligation to pay. In other words, cases in which third parties have a legal right, on the basis of a rule of one of the Treaties or of provisions adopted thereunder,[301] to performance which gives rise to expenditure. Thus on this view the simple fact that a Council measure has expressly allocated the necessary financial resources for the implementation of the measure is insufficient to render the expenditure compulsory. The decisive element is thus whether or not the Commission has a discretionary power.

This legal distinction, which in itself is maintainable, would not, however, suffice to solve the tension between the Parliament and the Council, as the dispute is not primarily legal in nature but political. Thus there are certain rules in the Common Agricultural policy which do indeed leave the Commission a certain margin of evaluation as to the question whether there is an obligation to pay, and, if there is, to how much. Nevertheless, the Council has always maintained that the expenditure for such purposes is compulsory expenditure. For the provisions in the various Structural Funds regulations, the reverse is true, so that even though the appropriations are classified as non-compulsory appropriations, there are provisions which leave the Commission very little margin of discretion, if the conditions for the application of the provisions are met. At the end of the day tensions about political policy-driven differences of interpretation can only be resolved by political arrangements between the Institutions concerned. Indeed this has proved to be the appropriate route, as the Joint Declaration of 1982 showed. It is a route along which the parties continue to travel, as is demonstrated by the 1988 and 1993 Interinstitutional Agreements.[302]

The result of the 1993 Interinstitutional Agreement[303] is that only EAGGF Guarantee section expenditure covered by the agricultural guideline,[304] certain external expenditure,[305] and expenditure on pensions for former officials or other staff of the Institutions[306] are treated as

301. Including agreements concluded by the Communities with third countries.
302. See Case 204/86 *Greece v. Council* [1988] ECR 5323 at 5339: the Court, having noted that the interinstitutional dialogue had to be conducted on the basis of mutual duties of sincere cooperation, observed that as far as classification of expenditure was concerned, the Community Institutions possessed a discretionary power which was limited by the separation of powers, as laid down in the [EC] Treaty, between the Institutions. The Court had to ensure that in the context of the dialogue the Institutions do not ignore the rules of law and do not exceed their discretionary power in a manifestly wrong or arbitrary way.
303. O.J. 1993 C 331/1, point 16.
304. *Ibid.*, heading 1 in the financial perspective.
305. Fisheries agreements and subscriptions to the capital of international financial institutions, *ibid.*, heading 4.
306. *Ibid.*, heading 5.

compulsory expenditure.[307] Expenditure on structural action and internal policies are specifically categorized as being non-compulsory expenditure.[308] A Statement annexed to the Agreement makes it clear that the parties have agreed to classify expenditure on financial protocols with non-member countries which are concluded (in the future) or renewed will be regarded as non-compulsory expenditure.[309] The result will be that in due course compulsory expenditure will virtually entirely relate to agriculture.

The much debated distinction between compulsory and non-compulsory expenditure seems now to be well past its zenith. To summarize the discussion as a whole, the reasons are: first, the increasing voice of the Parliament in Council decisions having financial implications; secondly, the arrangement, made initially in 1988 and strengthened in the 1993 Agreement, that the agreed financial perspective applied to both categories of expenditure, to which the 1993 Agreement added the rider that a revision of the compulsory expenditure in the financial perspective should not lead to a reduction in the amount available for non-compulsory expenditure;[310] thirdly, the introduction of the agricultural guideline in the decisions on budgetary discipline,[311] which forms the basis for the control of compulsory agricultural expenditure; and, finally, the agreement between both arms of the budgetary authority to respect the allocations in the financial perspective for, in particular, the Structural Funds and the Cohesion Fund which are important parts of non-compulsory expenditure.[312] The Statement annexed to the 1993 Interinstitutional Agreement that the parties considered that the budgetary procedure provisions of the Treaties, including the arrangements relating to compulsory and non-compulsory expenditure should be reviewed at the 1996 Intergovernmental Conference confirmed that further evolution in this area was likely, but the only major effects will be the changes which the Treaty of Amsterdam will make to the provisions dealing with operational expenditure in CFSP and JHA (or as it will become, Police and Judicial cooperation in criminal matters), which raise existing arrangements to Treaty level.[313]

The complex rules of Article 203(9) EC for the determination of the maximum rate of increase for non-compulsory expenditure have lost

307. This represented some 55% of the total Community budget, even in 1995, but is due to decline relatively to about 50% of the financial perspective for 1999.
308. *Ibid.*, headings 2 and 3 (see point 16, 3rd para.).
309. Thus expenditure under current financial protocols, until extension, is still treated as compulsory, *European Union Public Finance* (see note 141, *supra*) 109.
310. Point 13, 4th para. of the agreement.
311. Originally in Dec. 88/377 (O.J. 1988 L 185/29), Art. 1, now replaced by Dec. 94/729 (O.J. 1994 L 293/14), Art. 2, which strengthens the guideline considerably.
312. *Ibid.*, point 21. The Cohesion Fund was established under Reg. 1164/94 (O.J. 1994 L 130/1).
313. See note 235, *supra*.

much of their practical importance since the 1998 Interinstitutional Agreement. The limitation which the maximum rate posed for the Parliament's right of amendment as joint budgetary authority, which was the cause of numerous conflicts between the Parliament and the Council in the Eighties has in practice been replaced by the programmed ceilings of the financial perspective, set out in the Interinstitutional Agreements.[314] Indeed, the parties actually agreed that if necessary, they would, following the voting rules of Article 203(9) EC, agree to lower the ceilings of the financial perspective in order to ensure compliance with the ceiling on own resources.[315] This raises the question whether the Parliament may further restrict its powers under the Treaty by means of an Interinstitutional Agreement. Strictly speaking, this question must be answered in the negative, as the Community Institutions are bound by the division of powers laid down by the contracting parties to the Treaty in the treaty itself. This is even more the case as the division of powers is closely linked to the institutional balance between the different Institutions. The contrary argument, that the Parliament by concluding an Agreement is in fact exercising its powers over the medium term is less than wholly convincing, given that Article 203(9) EC envisages an annual determination of the maximum rate of increase, quite independently of the question whether the available own resources actually permit such a maximum increase in expenditure.[316] A solution may well be offered by the fact that the Interinstitutional Agreements of 1988 and 1993 expressly do not alter the respective budgetary powers of the various Institutions as laid down in the Treaties.[317] This makes it possible to interpret the Agreements as political arrangements between the Institutions concerned, which expressly leave it open to the Parliament, should sufficient support exist among its members, to fall back on the formal division of powers as prescribed in the Treaties.[318] In this interpretation, Article 203(9) EC continues to fulfill a not unimportant reserve function, as the possibility of using it can be a means of concentrating minds in the negotiation process between Parliament and the Commission and the Council. The concentration of minds is more effective according to the degree to which

314. But problems as to agreeing a new maximum rate of increase and the total amount of non-compulsory expenditure may still occur, see Case C-41/95 *Council v. European Parliament* [1995] ECR 4411. This led the Parliament to adopt a resolution on 18 July 1996 to which was annexed a list of budget lines considered to be non-compulsory expenditure and a list of mixed budget lines (involving both types of expenditure). As to the Interinstitutional Agreement on the financing of CFSP, see Bull. EU 7/8–1997, point 2.3.1.
315. Interinstitutional Agreement 1993, point 8, 2nd para.
316. Bieber in Von der Groeben *et al.* (eds.), *op. cit.* (see note 266, *supra*) 1497. Case 204/86 *Greece v. Council* [1988] ECR 5323 at 5359 also offers some support for this proposition.
317. Point 3 in both Agreements.
318. Monar (1994) 31 CMLRev. 693 at 700–703.

non-compulsory expenditure will form a larger part of the total Community budget.

Finally, it should be noted that the budget is denominated in ECU, which is the weighted average of the currencies of all the Member States, and is calculated daily.[319] On 30 June 1998 the the equivalent of 1 ECU in Sterling was 65.7130 pence and in Guilders 2.22993.

(C) The budgetary procedure in practice. Since the adoption of the Delors I package the budgetary procedure in the Community can be seen as a means of financial framework programming as to the major points, in which the programming takes place every 5 years, combined with an annual fleshing out of the programme within the agreed global framework. The medium-term financial programming is based on the political agreement achieved in the European Council on the basis of proposals from the Commission. This political consensus has a clearly intergovernmental character. It relates to the global financial space of the Community, the development of the most important heads of expenditure, and the space available for agricultural expenditure. The political orientation from the European Council is developed in a legal framework in three forms. First, the own resources decision which, in accordance with Articles 201 EC and 173 Euratom, determine the Community's revenue (its financial space); secondly, the decision on budgetary discipline, with its agricultural guideline and the procedures for controlling agricultural guarantee expenditure, and, thirdly, the Interinstitutional Agreements which prescribe the margins for the Parliament and the Council for the development of expenditure by (mostly global) headings and sub-headings.

The annual budgetary procedure laid down in Article 203 EC and its sister provisions tends to operate within the limits of these three instruments, and takes account of them. As has been explained above, these instruments are important for an accurate evaluation of the conduct of the Parliament and the Council in the exercise of their powers as the joint budgetary authority. The still increasing gulf between the letter of the Treaties and the actual operation of the budgetary dialogue in practice makes a thorough revision of the budgetary provisions of the Treaties an urgent necessity. A clear place needs to be given in those provisions to medium-term financial programming, as well as to the relationship between that programming and the annual budgetary procedure, by giving a clear legal basis to the decision on budgetary discipline and the Interinstitutional Agreement. As the distinction between the two types of expenditure has lost much of its significance. The different consequences of the distinction for the powers of the two arms

---

319. See Arts. 207 EC, and the Financial Regulation (see note 146, *supra*), Art. 11. The latter regulates in detail many technical aspects of the budgetary procedure.

of the budgetary authority do not yet reflect the new practical
developments discussed above. This provision should therefore be
adjusted accordingly.

(D) Absence of a budget. If at the beginning of the financial year no
budget has yet been adopted, the provisions of Articles 78b ECSC, 204
EC and 178 Euratom come into play. These set up the system of the
provisional twelfths. Not more than the equivalent of one-twelfth of the
preceding financial year's budget appropriations may be spent in respect
of any chapter or sub-division of the budget in any one month, in accordance with the Financial Regulations. This system cannot, though, have
the effect of placing at the Commission's disposal appropriations in
excess of one-twelfth of those contained in the draft budget in the course
of preparation. Acting by a qualified majority, the Council may authorize
additional expenditure as long as the other conditions are observed. If,
however, such a decision relates to non-compulsory expenditure the decision is sent to the Parliament which may adopt a different decision on
the excess over one-twelfth, acting by an absolute majority of its
members and three-fifths of the votes cast. During a thirty-day period
the Council's decision relating to non-compulsory expenditure is suspended until the Parliament has taken a decision. If it fails to do so or
takes a decision which does not differ from that of the Council, the latter's decision is deemed to be finally adopted. The decisions lay down the
necessary measures relating to resources to ensure that the three Articles
concerned are applied. There have been several occasions, on which a
budget has not been adopted by the beginning of the relevant financial
year. The precise political reasons vary from year to year, it may be that
Parliament has exercised its power to reject the budget, as happened in
December 1979, when the first directly elected Parliament flexed its
muscles, in relation to the 1980 budget, in December 1982 in respect of
the supplementary and amending budget for that year, and in December
1984 in respect of the 1985 budget. At the end of 1987, when the
Copenhagen Summit failed to offer a solution to the differing views of
Council members on (particularly agricultural) spending, the Parliament
decided to bring the Council's failure to act to the Court of Justice.[320] If
the budget is annulled at a very late stage in the financial year concerned, the Court tends to maintain in force the effects of the annulled

320. See *e.g.* Case 377/87 *Parliament v. Council* [1988] ECR 4017; Case 383/87 *Commission
v. Council* [1988] ECR 4051. As to the absence of a budget and the resulting legal
consequences see Pipkorn (1981) 18 CMLRev. 141. See also, on difficulties resulting
from the one-twelfths rule, Forman (1985) 8 *Journal of European Integration* 139.
Note the effect of the absence of a budget on the calculation of the uniform rate of
VAT and the rate applicable to Member States' GNP for own resources: Dec. 94/728
(O.J. 1994 L 293/9), Art. 2(6). See, further, the Financial Regulation (see note 146
supra), Art. 9.

budget,[321] although the budget procedure must be resumed at the appropriate point in order to lead to the adoption of a valid budget.[322]

2.2.5 Control and accountability (Arts. 205a and 206 EC)

As has been noted in the preceding discussion, the Commission is responsible for the implementation of the budget,[323] Just as in national budgetary and accounting law, this responsibility also embraces care for the legality and effectiveness of the expenditure. There is provision for discharge of this responsibility to be given by the Parliament.[324]

Prior to the coming into force of the TEU this took place on the basis of a report from the Court of Auditors, the Parliament acting on a recommendation, adopted by the Council by qualified majority.[325] The discharge procedure was scarcely satisfactory. It was concluded far too late. The final report of the Court of Auditors tended to appear only in the November of the year following the relevant financial year. The Council then made its recommendation in the Spring of the following year (thus in the second year after the end of the relevant financial year), and only then did the Parliament get a chance to decide whether to grant the discharge. Moreover, the discharge procedure was in practice not strict enough. The consideration of the report of the Court of Auditors seldom resulted in stringent recommendations, even where they were palpably necessary. Mostly the Council tied to exonerate itself in cases in which the practical implementation of Community provisions with financial implications was involved. The weak points in the implementation of the Community budget, namely the susceptibility of much Community legislation to fraudulent transactions, the lack of sufficient powers of control for the Court of Auditors and for the Commission (which has its own Financial Controller) at the national level, and plain old administrative mismanagement in various Member States (for most of the expenditure decisions are taken by national administrations) were left largely undiscussed by the Council. This meant little for the discharge

321. *E.g.* Case C-41/95 *Council v. European Parliament* [1995] ECR I-4411 at 4441.
322. *Ibid.* at 4410.
323. Arts. 205 EC, 78c ECSC, and 179 Euratom. In June 1995 the Commission commenced the introduction of the SEM 2000 Programme (Sound and Efficient Management) designed to improve the Commission's administrative and financial management. As to developments, see Bull. EU 12–1996, points I.4 and 1.6.2; Bull. EU 11–1997, point 1.6.1, and *General Report 1997* ((Brussels, Luxembourg, 1998) points 1050–1052.
324. Arts. 206 EC, 78g ECSC, and 180b Euratom. The Treaty of Amsterdam (not yet in force) will amend these provisions so as to ensure that the statement of assurance provided for in Arts. 188c(1) EC, 45c(1) ECSC, and 160c(1) Euratom (2nd subpara. in each case, likewise amended) is taken into account.
325. Arts. 206b EEC, 78g ECSC, and 180b Euratom (the last two in the version then applicable).

powers of the Parliament, it was the Commission after all which was being discharged.

In the modifications introduced by the TEU the control provisions have been significantly strengthened. The Court of Auditors, which was raised to the status of a Community Institution[326] has seen its powers significantly extended.[327] It not only obliged to examine the accounts of all revenue and expenditure of the Community and of all bodies set up by the Community (unless the instruments establishing them provide otherwise),[328] it is now also obliged to provide the Parliament and the Council with a statement of assurance as to the reliability of the accounts and the legality and regularity of the underlying transactions.[329] This overcomes the most important defect in the financial control in the Community, the lack of imperative consequences of the Court of Auditors' report. There is now the threat of a negative declaration by the Court of Auditors, which would should result in the Parliament refusing to grant the discharge.[330] A further improvement is the new specific power for the Court of Auditors to present special reports.[331]

Parliament's powers on the discharge[332] which were not really compelling under the previous procedure, have also been significantly strengthened, as the Commission is not only required to comply with any requests for information from the Parliament,[333] but it is required to take all appropriate steps to act on the observations in the discharge decisions and any other observations made by the Parliament concerning the execution of expenditure, as well as on comments accompanying the Council's recommendation to the Parliament about the discharge.[334] Further, it can also be required by the Parliament or the Council to report

---

326. Arts. 4 EC, 7 ECSC, and 3(1) Euratom.
327. Arts. 188c EC, 45c ECSC, and 160c Euratom.
328. The Commission submits annually to the Council and the Parliament the accounts of the preceding financial year relating to the implementation of the budget, together with a statement of the Community's assets and liabilities, Arts. 205a EC, 78d ECSC, and 179a Euratom. But the audit by the Court of Auditors is not confined to accounts which have already been closed (see Art. 188c(2) EC and corresponding provisions).
329. Arts. 188c(1) EC, 45c(1) ECSC, and 160c(1) Euratom (2nd subpara. in each case. The Treaty of Amsterdam (not yet in force) amends these provisions so as to require the statement of assurance to be published in the *Official Journal*.
330. Refusal to grant a discharge does happen, *e.g.* O.J. 1994 C 128/322 (in respect of the 1992 budget, see Bradley and Feeney (1994) 14 YBEL 401 at 427–428; discharge was eventually granted O.J 1995 L 141/51); O.J. 1996 L 148/56 (in respect of the EDF activities in 1994, following the Court of Auditors' report (O.J. 1995 C 352/97)), and O.J. 1996 C 141/125 (in respect of Cedefop's activities in 1994). See also COM (97) 48 Final, as to action taken.
331. Art. 188c(4) EC (and corresponding provisions).
332. See Rules of Procedure (O.J. 1997 L 49/1) Rule 86, and Annex V.
333. Arts. 206(2) EC, 78g ECSC, and 180b Euratom.
334. Art. 206(3) EC, 1st para., and corresponding ECSC and Euratom provisions.

on the follow-up to the observations and comments, and in particular on the instructions given to the departments responsible for the implementation of the budget.[335] In the past, conflicts between Council and the Commission related to the Parliament's power to authorize expenditure as joint budgetary authority; these reporting obligations open up the possibility for the Parliament to make its presence felt in the exercise of its supervisory powers. Because the problems in the exercise of the Community budget are to a large extent thanks to the lack of transparency and the susceptibility to fraudulent transactions of the relevant Community legislation, Parliament will be able to exercise indirect influence on Community legislation and its application at national level if it exercises its supervisory powers percipiently.

2.2.6 Prevention of fraud

The Community is extremely vulnerable to fraud, as myriad reports of the Court of Auditors have demonstrated.[336] On the revenue side, customs duties and agricultural import levies are very vulnerable to avoidance and evasion,[337] while on the expenditure side the same is especially true of refunds on the export of agricultural products and the ever more important expenditure of the Structural Funds. Against this background various attempts have been taken in the past to ensure effective protection of the community's financial interests. It must, though, be remembered that on the revenue side as well as on the expenditure side responsibility for control, prosecution and punishment lies with the Member States. The principle of Community loyalty or solidarity laid down in Article 5 EC applies to compliance in this field, as elsewhere.[338] The control of that compliance is a matter for the Commission. It regularly exercises this supervisory power in relation to the annual clearance of EAGGF accounts. The tension which has arisen in this context as a result of the Commission's action explains why attempts to ensure better protection of the Community's financial interests met with such little success in the past.[339]

---

335. *Ibid.*, 2nd para. in each case.
336. See *e.g.* O.J. 1994 C 53/1 on fraud in the agricultural sector and O.J. 1998 C 121/1. See, generally, the *General Reports 1995–1997* ((Brussels, Luxembourg, 1996–1998) points 1007–1011, 1009–1015, and 1084–1090 respectively, and the Commission's annual reports on the fight against fraud, *e.g.* COM (96) 173 Final (for 1995), and COM (97) 200 Final (for 1996). See, generally, Vervaele, *Fraud against the Community: the Need for European Fraud Legislation* (Deventer, 1992); White, Protection of the Financial Interests of the European Communities (The Hague, 1998; Michiels (1996) SEW 362, and White (1996) 21 ELRev. 465
337. *E.g.* Case 68/88 *Commission v. Greece* [1989] ECR 2965; see also COM (95) 108 Final.
338. See, generally, Chapter III, section 5.2, *ante.*
339. See Van Rijn in Vervaele (ed.), *Bestuursrechtelijke toepassing en handhaving van gemeenschapsrecht in Nederland* (Deventer, 1993) 155.

Moreover, a majority of the Member States deny the Community any competence in the field of criminal law.[340] Even the fairly modest Dutch proposal in the negotiations prior to the signature of the TEU foundered because it would have given the Commission supervisory powers on the policy pursued on this matter by the Member States, in addition to providing for cooperation between the competent national authorities in the criminal and administrative fields. The final text of Article 209a EC[341] comes from a British proposal. The first paragraph of that provision is a specific expression of the principle of Community loyalty or solidarity, whereas the second paragraph primarily creates a legal basis for the coordination of action by the Member States to protect the financial interests of the Community against fraud. The novel element in this is that the Commission's role therein is very expressly a subordinate, supporting role.

The Commission did not hesitate to use its new competence, and in the spring of 1994 it published its working programme for the protection of the financial interests of the Community.[342] This has now resulted in the adoption of Regulation 2988/95[343] which seeks to establish homogenous controls and administrative measures (which must be effective, proportionate, and dissuasive) relating to irregularities with regard to Community law. Further action has also been taken in the context of JHA with the adoption of the Convention on the protection of the Community's financial interests.[344]

3. DECISION-MAKING PROCEDURE

This section examines in further detail the rules and practice of decision-making in the Council and the Commission, the Institutions which are concerned (to an extent with the European Parliament) with policy determination and administration in the Communities.[345] Special attention

---

340. But the Court permits the Community a substantial power to prescribe that penalties must be imposed by the national authorities (but it is up to them to decide whether they shall be administrative or penal in nature), see Case C-240/90 *Germany v. Commission* [1992] ECR I-5383 at 5434.
341. And Arts. 78i ECSC, and 183a Euratom.
342. COM (94) 92 Final. This is now revised annually, for 1997–98, see COM (97) 199 Final.
343. O.J. 1995 L 312/1, corrigendum O.J. 1998 L 36/16. See Case C-354/93 *R. v. Minister for Agriculture, Fisheries and Food, ex parte National Farmer's Union* [1997] ECR I-4559 at 4606. See also Reg. 2185/96 (O.J. 1996 L 292/2) as to on-the-spot inspections.
344. O.J. 1995 C 316/48 and 49; see the explanatory report (O.J. 1997 C 191/1). See, further, the various Protocols (O.J. 1996 C 313/1 and 2 (with the explanatory report (O.J. 1998 C 11/5) on corrupt officials); O.J. 1997 C 151/1 and 2 conferring jurisdiction on the Court of Justice, and O.J. 1997 C 151/1 and 2, and O.J. 1997 C 221/11 and 12 on money laundering.
345. As to the Institutions see Chapter IV, section 1, *ante*. See, generally, Raworth, *The Legislative Process in the European Community* (Deventer, 1993).

will be paid to the position of the Commission and the European Parliament with regard to the decision-making procedure in the Council, and the influence they can exercise thereon. The special procedures leading to the adoption of the budget and the conclusion of treaties by the Communities are not discussed here. The former has already been discussed in the preceding section; the procedure for the conclusion of treaties will be dealt with in the discussion of external relations of the Communities.[346]

3.1 Decisions of the Commission and 'comitology'

The Commission takes decisions by a majority of its members, *viz.* eleven out of twenty votes;[347] the quorum for its meetings is also a majority of its members[348] and decisions are adopted only when at least eleven votes are in favour.[349] In many cases the Commission will not be able to take legally binding decisions before complying with the requirement of consultation with the Council or other bodies, imposed on it by the Treaties or by implementing decisions. Consultation with the Council in the exercise of its powers derived from the Treaty is frequently prescribed in the ECSC Treaty. In many cases consultation is obligatory and in certain cases the assent of the Council is required.

In ECSC practice the Commission is accustomed to exercise its powers of decision in close consultation with the Council, even when it is not formally obliged to do so.[350] The old High Authority was so much alive to the necessity of reaching agreement with the members of the Council about the decisions to be taken by it, even if no assent was required, that the character of its decisions has sometimes been referred to as *décisions*

346. See Chapter XII, *post.*
347. Arts. 163 EC, 13 ECSC, and 132 Euratom (1st para. in each case).
348. *Ibid.* (2nd para. in each case); Commission's Rules of Procedure (Dec. 93/492, O.J. 1993 L 230/15, amended, but not on this point by Dec. 95/148, O.J. 1995 L 97/82), Art. 5.
349. Commission's Rules of Procedure, *ibid.*, Art. 6. The effect is that even if the number of Commissioners is less than twenty (through resignation or death, there not yet being a replacement appointed) or if a number of Commissioners are away, the requirement of eleven votes is maintained. However, agreement by a majority of members present is sufficient to permit discussion of an item not on the agenda or for which the necessary working documents have been distributed late, *ibid.*, Art. 4, 5th para, 1st sentence (in conjunction with Art. 6, 3rd para., final sentence). In fact most decisions, particularly in the agricultural sphere, are taken by written procedure: WQ 469/76 (Keersmaeker) O.J. 1976 C 294/33. As to the written procedure and *habilita-tion*, see Chapter IV, section 6.4.3, *ante* and Case C-137/92 P *Commission v. BASF AG et al.* [1994] ECR I-2555 (the *PVC* saga).
350. The ECSC Treaty lays down no detailed provisions for co-operation in cases in which an assent is required. See Case 244/81 *Klöckner-Werke AG v. Commission* [1983] ECR 1451 at 1477.

négociées. Several principal factors contributed to the development of this practice. In the first place, in this integration by sectors there is a close connection between the subjects on which the old High Authority (now the Commission) takes decisions without consulting the Council and those on which it is required to consult the Council or obtain its assent. These subjects in turn are closely connected with matters of which the separate Member States have kept control. A harmonious co-operation between the two Institutions in all fields was therefore required, the more so because with the passing of the years the co-operation of the Member States became evermore important for the resolution of problems which the authors of this *traité-loi* had not foreseen in 1951. Secondly, the High Authority was confronted with a relatively small number of powerful bodies, the coal and steel enterprises. Any action against them would have chances of success only if the High Authority could gain the support of the governments, or at least would not be faced with their open opposition.

In the EC and Euratom the term 'opinion' or 'assent' of the Council is not known as such. On the whole the Commission exercises independently its original administrative task, derived from the Treaty. In the exercise of most of its other administrative tasks, however, particularly in the 'exercise of powers conferred on it by the Council for the implementation of rules laid down by the latter,'[351] the Commission is obliged in its decision-making to consult other bodies. Decision-making by the Commission is thus tied down by myriad procedures for consultation with the Council, with the several Member States, and with committees consisting of representatives of the Member States, experts, or representatives of interested parties; the brand name for these diverse bodies is comitology.[352]

On the whole these consultations do not result in legal effects, although in many cases of course the opinions given will have a certain impact. However, legal effects do flow from the so-called 'management committee procedure' and from the 'regulatory committee procedure'. The former procedure derives its name from the committees whose consultation is required in the Commission's management of common organizations of the market under the common agricultural policy. It has, however, also been applied, with certain variations, in other fields. A characteristic of the management committee procedure is the fact that the Commission is not obliged to follow the opinion of the committee consulted (which is delivered by the same qualified majority voting system as provided for in Article 148 EC), but the Council itself may within a given time-limit

351. Arts. 155 EC and 124 Euratom.
352. There are presently some 200 committees in existence, and a list is annexed to the budget each year, see WQs E-3505–3516, 3536 and 3537/95 (Cassidy) O.J. 1996 C 109/52. See, generally, Bradley (1992) 29 CMLRev. 693 and (1997) 3 ELJ 230, the contributions by Falke and Winter, and by Kabelheim and Winter in Winter (ed.), *op. cit.* (see note 27, *supra*) 541 and 583 respectively, and literature cited there; Joerges and Neyer (1997) 3 ELJ 273, and Vos (1997) 3 ELJ 210.

substitute a measure for the measure taken by the Commission, if the latter
is not in conformity with the opinion. If, however, the committee agrees
with the Commission's draft or cannot come to an opinion, the Council
cannot decide to set aside the decision of the Commission.[353] The Court
upheld this system in Case 25/70 *Einfuhr-und Vorratsstelle für Getreide und
Futtermittel v. Köster, Berodt & Co.*[354] A special, rather widely divergent
variant of the management committee procedure is the regulatory
committee procedure, a rather inelegant name, which is intended to
indicate that the opinions to be sought relate to the Commission's exercise
of its delegated regulatory powers. This procedure has been used in a
number of regulations and decisions of the Council since 1968.[355] While in
the management committee procedure departure from the opinion of a
management committee is the condition under which the Council may
intervene repressively, in the regulatory committee procedure there is a
conditional delegation of powers to the Commission. In the first instance
the Commission can only lay down provisions if a consenting opinion has
been given. If no opinion or a negative one is given, the Commission must
submit a proposal to the Council, which must then take a decision within
a given time-limit on the basis of this proposal. If no such Council decision
is forthcoming, the power of decision of the Commission becomes
operative again: it lays down the proposed provisions itself. This is known
in Community jargon as the *filet* procedure.[356]

The Commission has a generally favourable view of the working of these
procedures in practice.[357] However, it like the European Parliament, has
serious objections to a variant of the regulatory committee procedure
which gives the Council the right to veto, by a simple majority,
Commission proposals, without being obliged to adopt other measures in
their place (this is the so-called *contrefilet* or safety net procedure);[358] the

---

353. This was expressly confirmed by the Court in Case 35/78 *N.G.J. Schouten BV v.
Hoofdproduktschap voor Akkerbouwprodukten* [1978] ECR 2543 at 2558 and in Case
95/78 *Dulciora SpA v. Amministrazione delle Finanze dello Stato* [1979] ECR 1549 at
1568.
354. [1970] ECR 1161 at 1171 and Case 30/70 *Scheer v. Einfuhr-und Vorratsstelle für
Getreide und Futtermittel* [1970] ECR 1197 at 1208–1209. See also Chapter IV, section
6.4.1, *ante.*
355. Particularly in the field of customs law, see now the Community Customs Code, Reg.
2913/92 (O.J. 1992 L 302/1, as amended, but not on this point, Arts. 247–249). *Cf.*
also various directives on the elimination of technical barriers to trade and *e.g.* Case
C-263/95 *Germany v. Commission* [1998] ECR I-465.
356. This is the net which guarantees that a decision will be taken, as if the Council fails to
act on a matter, competence returns to the Commission.
357. *Second General Report* (1968) (Brussels, Luxembourg, 1969) para. 640; SEC (90) 2589
para. 34, cited by Bradley (1992) 29 CMLRev. 693 at 721; *Commission Report for the
Reflection Group, Intergovernmental Conference 1996* (Brussels, Luxembourg, 1995) 31
(para. 52).
358. Thus the Commission has consistently refused to propose this type of committee

Standing Veterinary Committee was shackled in this way.[359] The Commission's proposals to scrap this variant have not found favour in the Council's eyes.[360] The Commission's objections are not legal but political as it is possible for no decision to be taken even though a decision is in fact necessary.[361] Remarkably, many years ago the Court appeared to see no legal objection, precisely on the ground that the Commission is always free to submit a new proposal, so that there is no question of the decision-making process being paralysed.[362] It may, however, happen that no qualified majority is obtainable in the committee or in the Council for any particular solution but a simple majority in the Council is obtainable to thwart the Commission's proposals.[363]

For the Council these procedures mean a way out of the dilemma with which it is faced when laying down rules, either reserving their implementation entirely to itself (which is impractical and sometimes impossible) or entrusting the implementation completely to the Commission, which in many cases it considers politically inopportune. The expansion of the independent administrative task of the Commission and the resulting significant development of the administrative power of the Community, however, are not assisted by the constantly increasing application of such procedures, while the ability of the Communities to take decisions may also be jeopardized by the *contrefilet* regulatory Committee procedure. The Commission's dissatisfaction with the Council's approach is evident.[364]

An exercise of the Commission's administrative task in close concert with the Council and national administrations would appear inevitable, because the centre of gravity of the application of Community law lies with the national governments and official apparatus rather than with the Community Institutions and their services. But this may actually lead to

procedure, which it considers illogical since it can lead to a situation in which no decision is taken, *Commission Report for the Reflection Group, ibid.*; *General Report on the activities of the European Union 1995* (Brussels, Luxembourg, 1996) point 1032.

359. *Second General Report* (see note 357, *supra*), paras. 641 and 642. The objection relates to the procedure on consultation of the Standing Veterinary Committee set up under Dec. 68/361 (O.J. English Special Edition 1968 (II), p. 473), see *Second General Report, ibid.* para. 200. Similar procedures apply to the Standing Committee for Feedingstuffs (Dec. 70/372, O.J. English Special Edition 1970 (II), p. 534) and the Standing Committee on Plant Health (Dec. 76/894, O.J. 1976 L 340/25). See, further, WQ 77/24 (Patijn) O.J. 1975 C 108/28 in which the Commission indicated that the Standing Veterinary Committee was functioning satisfactorily.

360. *E.g.* O.J. 1981 C 102/2.

361. See WQ 760/74 (Jahn) O.J. 1975 C 108/26, and the Commission Report for the Reflection Group (see note 357, *supra*), *loc. cit.*

362. Case 5/77 *Tedeschi v. Denkavit Commerciale Srl* [1977] ECR 1555 at 1580.

363. *Cf.* Maas (1979) SEW 695.

364. See *E.g. General Report 1995* (Brussels, Luxembourg, 1996) point 1032, and *General Report 1997* ((Brussels, Luxembourg, 1998) point 1097.

a confusion of national and Community responsibilities, which hampers control of the administration by the European Parliament and national parliaments. This is a serious objection to the regulatory committee procedure. The special procedures described above involve the risk of lack of clarity as to responsibilities. Indeed, the Commission may be tempted to choose the easiest way out and adapt the content of its decisions to the ideas of the Committee consulted, so as to avoid complications and delay. Furthermore, majority decisions of the Council not based on a proposal from the Commission largely escape parliamentary control, as will be shown presently. Such procedures are therefore objectionable from a democratic point of view as well. Now that various acts are adopted by the European Parliament and the Council acting jointly, parliamentary concerns about the lack of democratic input in relation to implementing measures have for the time being been assuaged by the adoption of a *Modus Vivendi* between the European Parliament, the Council, and the Commission on implementing measures in relation to such acts,[365] pending examination of the problem by the Reflection Group working in relation to the Intergovernmental Conference 1996. This means that in practice the appropriate committee of the European Parliament will be consulted at the same time as the committee which has to be consulted under the parent legislation prior to the adoption of an act by the Commission; the Commission informs the appropriate parliamentary committee if the measures adopted or envisaged by the Commission are not in accordance with the other committee's opinion, or if, in the absence of such an opinion, the Commission must submit a proposal to the Council regarding the action to be taken. The Council has agreed to adopt a draft implementing act referred to it under an implementing procedure only after informing the European Parliament, setting a reasonable time-limit for the delivery of its opinion, and, in the event of an unfavorable opinion, taking due account of the European Parliament's point of view without delay, in order to seek a solution in the appropriate framework. In any case, the act must be adopted within the deadlines specified in the parent act. For its part, the Commission undertakes to take account as far as possible of any comments from the European Parliament, and to keep it informed at every stage of the procedure of its intended action, to enable the Parliament to assume its responsibilities in full knowledge of the facts. This represents a pragmatic involvement of the Parliament, at the same

---

365. O.J. 1996 C 102/1 (replacing the text published in 1995). See Corbett *et al., op. cit* (see note 141, *supra*) 255–257. As to other implementing measures, the Parliament is informed under the Plumb–Delors procedure, agreed in an exchange of letters in 1988, as to which, see *ibid.* 254–255. Implementing measures in the area of the Structural Funds are covered by the Klepsch–Millan agreement of 13 July 1993 (which seems to be unpublished, it is not referred to in Bull. EC).

time as an implicit recognition by the other parties that there is a need for a clearer legal framework.

Involvement of committees of some type, of whatever composition, in the Commission's decision-making is one of the conditions which the Council can prescribe for the implementation by the Commission of the powers which the Council confers on it. The text of Article 145 EC, reflecting the modification by the Single European Act (SEA), envisages the Council deciding in advance, acting unanimously on a proposal from the Commission after obtaining the opinion of the European Parliament, the principles and rules for the exercise of implementing powers which it confers on the Commission in acts which it adopts. The Council is also permitted to reserve the right, in specific cases, to exercise directly implementing powers itself. In its proposal on comitology[366] the Commission proposed the adoption of the three tried and tested procedures, advisory committees, management committees and regulatory committees (with streamlined procedures and without the *contrefilet* procedure mentioned above).[367] However, in Decision 87/373 on comitology,[368] which was – controversially – unsuccessfully challenged by the European Parliament,[369] the Council adopted the three standard procedures discussed above (and a procedure on safeguard measures) but with a number of variants. The comitology decision does not affect procedures for the exercise of implementing powers conferred by the Commission before its entry into force, although where acts establishing such procedures are amended or extended the Council will have the choice of adapting them to the comitology decision procedures or retaining the existing procedures. It is evident from the wording of the third indent of Article 145 EC and of Article 1 of the comitology decision that the instances in which the Council reserves the right to exercise directly implementing powers itself are meant to be the exception, not the rule. Article 2 of the decision sets out the three procedures:

Procedure 1 (advisory committees). The Commission is assisted by an advisory committee composed of representatives of the Member States and

366. O.J. 1986 C 70/6. See the European Parliament's Opinion O.J. 1986 C 297/94. See also *Europe* Documents No. 1447/1448, 3 April 1987 (comments by Ehlermann in evidence to the House of Lords Select Committee on the European Communities) and that Committee's Report, Session 1985–86, 19th Report (HL 228).
367. *Twentieth General Report* (1986) (Brussels, Luxembourg, 1987) p. 35, point 4.
368. O.J. 1987 L 197/33. See Domestici-Met (1987) RMC 556; Ehlermann (1988) RMC 232; Nicholl (1987) RMC 703, and literature cited in note 352, *supra*.
369. Case 302/87 *European Parliament v. Council* [1988] ECR 5615 (the negative effect of which was subsequently undone in the Chernobyl judgment, Case C-70/88 *European Parliament v. Council* [1990] ECR I-2041, [1992] 1 CMLR 91); the result in the latter judgment, that the Parliament may challenge acts in order to protect its prerogatives, is now codified in Art. 173 EC.

chaired by the representative of the Commission who submits draft measures to the committee which delivers its opinion within a time limit laid down by the chairman according to the urgency of the matter, if necessary by taking a vote. The opinion is recorded in the committee's minutes and each Member State may also have its position so recorded. The Commission has to 'take the utmost account of the opinion delivered by the committee' and inform the committee of the manner in which its opinion has been taken into account.

Procedure 2 (management committees). The Commission is assisted by a committee composed of the representatives of the Member States and chaired by the representative of the Commission who submits draft measures to the committee which delivers its opinion within a time limit laid down by the chairman according to the urgency of the matter. The opinion is adopted by a qualified majority as provided for in Article 148 (2) EEC (with at least 54 votes in favour of the Commission's proposal); the chairman does not have a vote. The Commission then adopts the measures which apply immediately. If, though, they are not in accordance with the committee's opinion the Commission is obliged to communicate them to the Council forthwith. If this happens there are two variants to the procedure.

– *variant (a)*

The Commission may defer application of the measures which it has decided for a period of up to one month from the date of their communication to the Council which may, within this time limit, take a different decision by a qualified majority.

– *Variant (b)*

The Commission is obliged to defer application of the measures which it has decided for a period to be laid down in each act adopted by the Council but which may not exceed three months from the date of their communication to the Council which may, within this time limit, take a different decision by a qualified majority.

Procedure 3 (regulatory committees). The Commission is assisted by a committee composed of the representatives of the Member States and chaired by the representative of the Commission who submits draft measures to the Committee which delivers its opinion within a time limit laid down by the chairman according to the urgency of the matter. The opinion is adopted by a qualified majority as provided for in Article 148(2) EC (with at least 62 votes in favour of the Commission's proposal); the chairman does not have a vote. The Commission adopts the measures envisaged if they are in accordance with the opinion of the committee. If they are not, or if no opinion is delivered then the Commission submits to the Council without delay a proposal on the measures to be taken. The Council then acts by a qualified majority on the proposal. There are then two variants in the procedure.

– *variant (a) (the* filet *procedure)*

If, on the expiry of a period to be laid down in each act to be adopted by the Council using this variant, but which may not exceed three months from the date of referral to the Council, the Council has not acted, the proposed measures are to be adopted by the Commission.

– *variant (b) (the* contrefilet *procedure)*

If, on the expiry of a period laid down in each act to be adopted by the Council using this variant, but which may not exceed three months from the date of referral to the Council, the Council has not acted, the proposed measures are to be adopted by the Commission, save where the Council has decided against them by a simple majority.

Article 3 of the comitology decision sets out the procedure which may be applied where the Council gives the Commission power to decide on safeguard measures. The Commission is to notify the Council and the Member States of any decision regarding safeguard measures and the Council, in the enabling act, may stipulate that before adopting its decision the Commission must consult the Member States in accordance with procedures to be determined in each case. Any Member State may refer the Commission's decision to the Council within a time limit to be determined in the act in question. There are two variants of what may happen next. Under *variant (a)* the Council may take a different decision by a qualified majority within a time limit to be determined in the act in question; under *variant (b)* the Council may confirm, amend or revoke the Commission's decision but if the Council has not taken a decision within a time limit to be determined in the act in question, the decision of the Commission is deemed to be revoked. *Variant (b)* caused the Commission to express and maintain reservations as there is no guarantee that a decision of some sort will be taken; in its view the retention of the right to use this formula would not facilitate its conduct of the day-to-day aspects of the common commercial policy.[370] Various other observations relating to the functioning of the comitology decision's provisions were also entered in the minutes of the Council on the adoption of that decision.[371]

The Court has now had the opportunity to pronounce on certain aspects of the scope of the third indent of Article 145 EC.[372] This provision applies

370. Statement entered in the Council minutes (*Europe* documents, No. 1477, 28 October 1987).
371. *Ibid.*
372. Case 16/88 *Commission v. Council* [1989] ECR 3457 (which concerned the making of the Commission's authorization to adopt certain measures with financial implications in the fisheries sphere subject to the management committee procedure).

unless the EC Treaty expressly[373] or implicitly[374] provides that the Commission is empowered to take the necessary individual decisions in particular circumstances. On the basis of the third indent of Article 145 EC, the Council may reserve the right, in specific cases, to exercise directly implementing powers itself, and it must state in detail the reasons for such a decision.[375] The exercise by the Commission of the powers conferred on it by the Council may be made subject only to the procedures which have been set out in the comitology decision, and the concept of implementation for the purposes the third indent of Article 145 EC 'comprises both the drawing up of implementing rules and the application of rules to specific cases by means of acts of individual application.'[376] The Court made it very plain that the Commission's power to implement the budget was not such as to modify the division of powers resulting from the various institutional[377] or substantive[378] provisions of the Treaty.[379] However, the Court has not yet formally pronounced on the legality of the regulatory committee procedure in the light of the third indent of Article 145 EC.[380]

While the Council was to review the procedures laid down in the comitology decision on the basis of a report submitted by the Commission before the end of 1990,[381] no changes to the comitology decision resulted. In that report the Commission made plain its deep concern at what it saw as a regression rather than progression in the practice of comitology, a

373. Art. 79(4) EC.
374. Art. 87(2)(d) EC.
375. Case 16/88 *Commission v. Council* [1989] ECR 3457 at 3485. While the Court gave no specific authority for demanding the statement of reasons, reasoning is a general requirement for Community legislation, see Arts. 190 EC and 162 Euratom.
376. *Ibid.* See further the *Modus Vivendi* (O.J. 1996 C 102/1).
377. *E.g.* Arts. 145 and 155 EC.
378. *E.g.* Art. 43 EC (in the field of agriculture).
379. Case 16/88 *Commission v. Council* [1989] ECR 3457 at 3486.
380. This issue surfaced in Case C-155/91 *Commission v. Council* [1993] ECR I-939, being raised by the European Parliament which had intervened in the action, but the Court found the point inadmissible as the grounds on which the Parliament claimed the directive concerned should be annulled were different from those on which the Commission sought annulment (*ibid.* at 969: at that time applications to intervene were limited to supporting the submissions of one of the parties; now the point would be considered, as EC Statute, Art. 37 has been amended to provide that applications to intervene are limited to supporting the form of order sought by one of the parties, Dec. 94/993 (O.J. 1994 L 379/1)). In Case C-359/92 *Germany v. Council* [1994] ECR I-3681 the point was not addressed, as the delegation was not contested if the legal base of the directive concerned were Art. 100a EC (*ibid.* at 3712). See, further, Bradley (1992) 29 CMLRev. 693 at 716–717. The express reference in Case 16/88 *Commission v. Council* [1989] ECR 3457 at 3486 to the earlier judgment in Case 25/70 *Köster* [1970] ECR 1161 at 1171 appears to confirm the legality of the management committee procedure, although the Court expressly noted that the latter judgment related to the system as it was prior to the coming into force of the Single European Act.
381. The report was submitted in January 1991 (SEC (90) 2589 Final).

view which it has consistently maintained in the annual *General Reports* on the Union's activities.[382] Thus there has been a clear tendency on the Council's part to use regulatory committees rather than advisory committees, contrary to what the Commission proposed, and a marked preference for the *contrefilet* procedure, although sometimes the Council has found it easier not to confer implementing powers than to agree to confer powers subject to the *contrefilet* procedure. The 1996 IGC has not as such resulted in any changes to the delegation of powers to the Commission; the Conference simply adopted a Declaration (No. 31) at the time of the signature of the Final Act of the Treaty of Amsterdam calling on the Commission to submit a proposal by the end of 1998 to amend the comitology decision; the Commission has submitted its proposal, aiming for simplification and greater transparency and democracy.[383]

3.2 Decisions of the Council; voting requirements

The Council takes decisions by an absolute majority of its members, except where otherwise provided in the Treaties.[384] As a rule, the Treaties require unanimity[385] or a qualified majority. In the latter case the voting rules of Article 148(2) EC or Article 118(2) Euratom apply. A qualified majority is obtained with 62 out of 87 weighted votes. The weighting is ten votes each for France, Germany, Italy and the United Kingdom, 8 for Spain, 5 votes each for Belgium, Greece, the Netherlands and Portugal, 4 votes each for Austria and Sweden, 3 votes each for Denmark, Finland and Ireland, and 2 for Luxembourg. The background to and problems of the Ioannina compromise in relation to qualified majority voting are discussed at the end of this section, below.

382. *E.g.* the 1995 *General Report* (Brussels, Luxembourg, 1996) point 1032 and the 1997 *General Report* (*ibid.*, 1998) points 1097. See, further, Docksey and Williams in Edwards and Spence (eds.), *The European Commission* (2nd ed., London, 1997) 125 *et seq.* (especially at 143–146).
383. COM (98) 380 Final.
384. The special voting rules under Art. 28 ECSC are not discussed here. On qualified majority voting see WQs E-2479/95 and E-318/96 (Moorhouse) O.J. 1995 C 56/20 and 1996 C 280/20; Dashwood in Schwarze (ed.), *Legislation for Europe 1992* (Baden-Baden, 1989) 79; Dewost in Capotorti *et al.* (eds.), *Du droit international au droit de l'intégration* (*Liber amicorum* Pescatore, Baden-Baden, 1987) 167; Nicoll (1986) RMC 135, and Westlake, *op. cit.* (see note 5,*supra*) 87 *et seq.*
385. Although when the SEA came into force on 1 July 1987, the requirement of unanimity was replaced by a requirement of a qualified majority in a number of instances (Arts. 28, 49, 57, 70, 75 and 84 EC) or was introduced as a derogation (Art. 100a EC) in addition to being used for myriad new areas. The new powers conferred by amendments introduced by the TEU also make use of qualified majority voting in many instances. It is quite remarkable in how many instances the provisions relating to economic and monetary policy use qualified majority voting. The extension of qualified majority voting which will be achieved when the Treaty of Amsterdam enters into force will be modest.

If the decision is not being taken on the basis of a proposal from the Commission it is further required that 10 members must vote in favour (this is sometimes referred to as a double qualified majority). In practice this means that a qualified majority supported by the five largest Member States cannot be obtained without the co-operation of at least three of the smaller Member States. The explanation for this requirement is that the interests of the smaller countries are safer in the hands of the Commission than in those of a Council majority principally made up of the larger Member States. In fact, if the Council takes a decision on a proposal from the Commission it may only amend the proposal by unanimous vote.[386] If no proposal from the Commission is required for the Council to be able to act, the safeguard for the smaller countries inherent in such a proposal is lacking. Until the entry into force of the TEU, the budgetary procedure[387] was the prime example of the use of double qualified majority voting. Since then, in the context of Economic and Monetary Union, a number of provisions in which the Council acts, not on the basis of a proposal from the Commission, but on the basis of a recommendation from the Commission make use of this mechanism.[388] In some instances the Council is empowered to act on the basis of a recommendation from either the Commission or the European Central Bank.[389]

During the transitional period the rule of unanimity was replaced in a growing number of fields by that of a qualified majority (and in doing so the Community followed the pattern prescribed in the *Spaak Report* of renouncing the unanimity rule normally found in classic models of intergovernmental organizations). It is, therefore, not without reason that the application of qualified majority voting formed one of the crucial points at issue during the constitutional crisis which broke out in 1965 in connection with the Commission's agricultural proposals. In fact, on 1 January 1966 the third stage of the transitional period began, which meant that matters of great political importance, such as the agricultural policy, the transport policy, and the external trade policy could henceforth be regulated by the Council by a qualified majority. The French Government, anticipating developments, opposed an unlimited application of qualified majorities. In its view it should not be applied if vital interests of one or more partners are at stake.

The other governments were not prepared to accept this view. This is apparent in the second part of the Luxembourg Accords of 28–29 January

386. Art. 189a(1) EC, subject to the provisions of Art. 189b(4) and (5) EC, which make it plain that this rule does not apply when, in the co-decision procedure voting takes place by the Council's representatives in the Conciliation Committee, or by the Council itself on the basis of a joint text approved by such a Committee, see, futher, the discussion in section 3.4.2, point (iii), *post*.
387. Art. 203(3) and (5) EC.
388. Arts. 103(2) and (4), 104c(6) and (13), 109j(2) and (3), and 109k(1) and (2) EC.
389. Arts. 106(5) (proposal and recommendation, respectively) and 109 EC.

1966, which for the time being put an end to the crisis.[390] The governments were unanimously prepared to accept the idea that, whenever very important interests of one or more of them were at issue, the members of the Council would try within a reasonable time-limit to find a solution acceptable to all of them 'while respecting their mutual interests and those of the Community, in accordance with Article 2 of the Treaty.'[391] However, they did not agree with the French standpoint 'that when very important interests are involved, the discussion must be continued until unanimous agreement is reached.'[392] However, the Accords also specified that this difference of opinion did not bar the resumption of activities according to normal procedures.[393] In so far as the 'normal' procedure includes the application of the qualified majority rule in matters of great importance, this statement seems rather too optimistic. If one of the members of the Council takes the firm position that in such matters, if his or her interests are at stake, he or she will never acquiesce in a decision taken by qualified majority and moreover will not be a party to outvoting other members of the Council if their interests are at stake, this will inevitably make its impact on Community decision-making.

Under these circumstances the significance of the qualified majority rule is seriously undermined. Indeed, its significance resides in the fact that its application is not a foregone conclusion, rather than in its relentless application. The mere existence of the rule, even if it were to be applied only rarely, promotes the attainment of an acceptable compromise, because it calls for an accommodating and reasonable attitude on the part of the members of the Council as long as they are in doubt whether the rule will or will not be applied. Those who contend that the French point of view in the Luxembourg Accords was acceptable, because after all decisions on politically important questions will always be taken by unanimous vote, fail, with respect, to appreciate the real significance of the qualified majority rule.

The Luxembourg Accords – often called, more accurately, an agreement to disagree – reinforced the already present tendency in the Council to avoid voting and to achieve decisions by means of a consensus, even on matters in which no important interests are at stake. Only rarely was there a vote in the Council, even on unimportant matters, save in the budgetary field. In 1969 the President-in-office of the Council was led to observe that the proceedings of his Institution all too often assumed the character of inter-governmental negotiations which threatened to make the essential difference between the Community and inter-governmental organizations

---

390. Bull. EC 3–66, p. 8.
391. *Ibid.*, point b(1). It appears that a reasonable time is interpreted as the next meeting of the Council (at least in the relevant composition).
392. *Ibid.*, (2).
393. *Ibid.* (4).

disappear. He wondered if the world really would come to an end if each member of the Council in turn were to feel obliged to accede to the view of the majority.[394]

There was no improvement as a result of this complaint. The readiness and ability to take decisions declined still further with the first enlargement from six to nine Member States, it being even more difficult to obtain agreement among the Nine than it was among the Six. The participants at the Paris Summit in 1974 considered it 'necessary to renounce the practice which consists of making agreement on all questions conditional on the unanimous consent of the Member States, whatever their respective positions may be regarding the conditions reached in Luxembourg on 28 January 1966.'[395] A certain improvement occurred in that voting in the Council, particularly in agricultural management affairs, became a less exceptional phenomenon. In such cases Council members who do not agree with a measure tend to abstain rather that vote against it.[396] In the Solemn Declaration of the European Council in Stuttgart on 12 June 1983, the Council was called upon to utilize every opportunity to promote decision-making, including – in cases in which unanimity was required – abstention.[397]

It had become apparent in May 1982 that the Council would occasionally not be afraid to take important decisions in these circumstances. Then, for the very first time in the history of the Community, the Council fixed agricultural prices for the new marketing year by a qualified majority, with the United Kingdom, Denmark and Greece abstaining.[398] In contrast, in May 1985, the German government successfully invoked its 'very important interests' to prevent a decision being reached on cereal prices; only the Benelux countries and Italy appeared ready to cast their votes in these circumstances and the other Council members joined the German member in refraining from voting.[399] A further nail in the coffin of the Luxembourg Accords appeared with the further extension of qualified majority voting, by the amendments made by the SEA and the TEU, and Teasdale has noted that the Luxembourg Compromise (as the

---

394. Cited in WQ 343/69 (Burger) J.O. 1970 C 38/5.
395. Bull. EC 12–1974, p. 8 (point 1104, para. 6 of the communiqué).
396. As to the effect of abstention, see the discussion, *post*.
397. Bull. EC 6–1983 point 1.6.1. (point 2.2.2. of the Solemn Declaration).
398. *Sixteenth General Report* (1982) (Brussels, Luxembourg, 1983) paras. 12 and 404. The attempted veto was in fact being used for bargaining purposes rather than to defend real vital national interests, see Howe's explanation to the House of Commons, HC Deb. 1986 Vol. 96, cols. 320–321 and Campbell (1986) 35 ICLQ 932 at 937–938.
399. *Nineteenth General Report* (1985) (Brussels, Luxembourg, 1986) para. 544. Vasey (1988) 25 CMLRev. 725 at 727 and 730–731 records that the Commission used its emergency powers to adopt interim measures which reflected the measures desired by the majority of Member States.

Accords are often called) effectively died with the entry into force of the SEA.[400]

On 20 July 1987 the Council adopted a not insignificant change to its Rules of Procedure.[401] It is now expressly provided that the Council votes on the initiative of its President who is, furthermore, required to open voting proceedings on the invitation of a member of the Council or of the Commission, provided that a majority of the Council's members so decide.[402] The provisional agenda for each meeting is sent by the President-in-office to other members of the Council and to the Commission at least fourteen days before the beginning of the meeting and includes items which the Council's General Secretariat has been requested by a member of the Council or by the Commission to include thereupon, the request having been received at least sixteen days before the beginning of the meeting concerned. The provisional agenda also indicates the items on which the Presidency, delegations or the Commission may request a vote. If a request for inclusion of an item on the agenda or an indication concerning voting is received out of time, it is still circulated but it will only be included on the agenda (the Council formally adopts its agenda at the beginning of each meeting in traditional continental style) if all members agree. Items put on the agenda in this manner may be put to the vote.[403]

In 1988 the Greek government unsuccessfully attempted to invoke the Luxembourg Accords over the size of the devaluation of the green drachma as part of the otherwise agreed annual revision of agricultural prices.[404] Finally, in 1996, without specifically invoking the Luxembourg Accords, the United Kingdom government manifestly failed to cover itself in glory with a short-lived policy of ceasing to cooperate normally in decision-making, even regarding measures which it actually supported, the result of which was to delay the adoption of numerous measures.[405]

---

400. Teasdale in Westlake, *op. cit.* (see note 5, *supra*) 109. Wyatt and Dashwood, *European Community Law* (3rd ed., London, 1993) 46 state that the question whether the Compromise still exists does not have a legal answer; it depends on whether in a given case enough of the Member States to constitute a blocking minority can be persuaded by the Member State claiming a vital interest to refrain from voting. Hartley, *European Community Law* (3rd ed., Oxford, 1994) 22 and 106 takes a similar view (the effects are political, not legal). See, further, Weatherill and Beaumont, *EC Law* (2nd ed., London, 1995) 78–81.
401. O.J. 1987 L 291/27 (there had been a move in this direction with the change made in December 1986). As to the present Rules of Procedure, see Dec. 93/662 (O.J. 1993 L 268/1, as amended by Dec. 95/24, O.J. 1995 L 31/14).
402. Rules of Procedure, *ibid.*, Art. 7(1).
403. The above discussion reflects the Council's Rules of Procedure, *ibid.*, Art. 2.
404. Teasdale in Westlake, *op. cit.* (see note 5, *supra*) 109–110.
405. Bull. EU 5–1996 point 1.10.10. The policy lasted about one month, and normal business resumed (though this does not appear in Bull. EU) after the Florence European Council in June 1996.

It now appears that the taboo, since the Luxembourg Accords, on majority voting in the Council has clearly been broken, although this should not disguise the fact that it may still exist politically, at least in so far as one Member State (especially if it is a large one) invokes important interests,[406] and Westlake has stressed the strength of what may be called a *de facto* veto, citing the example of the Union respecting Spain's specific interest in the outcome of a fishing dispute with Canada in 1995.[407]

It appears that first the prospect and then the achievement of the enlargement of the Community first to 12 and now 15 Member States has substantially contributed to the greater tendency to vote in the Council, with the members preferring to abstain when a qualified majority or unanimity is being sought, rather than to vote against. It is widely acknowledged that the extension of qualified majority voting makes for greater efficiency in the decision-making process of an enlarged European Union, even though considerations such as the acceptability of Union decisions will have to be borne in mind, and the precise means of extending further the use of qualified majority voting is still the subject of controversy.[408]

During the constitutional crisis in 1965, in consequence of the French boycott of Council meetings, the question arose whether the Council had the right to take decisions without French participation. Since the Council is an Institution of the Community, this question should be answered in accordance with the rules on decision-making laid down in the Treaties. Articles 148(1) and (2) EC (the equivalent provisions of the Euratom Treaty are in identical terms) regulate the requirements for decisions by majority votes. In this context it is not the votes cast, but a given majority of the votes of the members of the Council which is at issue. There was, until the Rules of Procedure were modified in 1993, no provision about a quorum.[409] If the required number of votes has been secured, the decision has been accepted. Even without French

---

406. Thus it seems that the suggestion by the 'three wise men' in October 1979 on this point could well become a reality: *Report on European Institutions* (Brussels, October 1979) 58. See, generally, Dashwood in Schwarze, *op. cit.* (see note 384, *supra*) 79, and in Curtin and Heukels (eds.), *Institutional Dynamics of European Integration* (Essays in honour of Schermers Vol. II, Dordrecht, 1994) 117. In debates in the French parliament on the constitutional amendment necessary to permit ratification of the TEU, the then French Foreign Minister proclaimed that not one government would accept, in a Community debate, that a vital interest could be sacrificed in any way whatsoever, *Le Monde* 14 May 1992, p. 8.

407. Westlake, *op. cit.* (see note 5, *supra*) 103–104. As to the background to and resolution of this dispute, see the 1995 *General Report* (Brussels, Luxembourg, 1996) point 578.

408. Bull. EU 6–1996 point I.101 (Presidency's progress report to the Florence European Council, June 1996, on the Intergovernmental Conference).

409. The present quorum for a vote to be taken is eight, Rules of Procedure, Art. 7(4) (see note 8, *supra*).

participation in the vote, therefore, the Council could have taken majority decisions. If this were not the case, a right of veto would have been conferred indirectly on a Member State in those very cases where the Treaty meant to refuse it.

Article 148(3) EC contains a provision on decisions by unanimity: abstentions by members of the Council either present or represented (by proxy under Article 150 EC) do not prevent the adoption of such decisions. Unanimity is to be understood not as unanimity of the votes cast, but of the members of the Council. The provision on abstentions, therefore, should be regarded as an exception, which must be interpreted restrictively. It will not do, therefore, in the case of Article 148(3) EC to equate 'abstentions by members either present or represented' with 'non-participation in the vote by a member of the Council, who also is not present by proxy.' However paradoxical it may sound, in the context of unanimous decisions taken according to Article 148(3) EC Treaty, abstention also constitutes the casting of a vote: he or she who abstains does not wish to resist the realization of a decision by using the right to veto, to which he or she is entitled. A member of the Council who is not present, either in person or by proxy, does not cast his or her 'vote'. In that case, therefore, the Council is unable to take decisions for which unanimity is required.[410] In fact, though, decisions of the Council, other than procedural decisions, were restricted during the constitutional crisis to what was strictly necessary for the functioning of existing rules. They were taken with French co-operation according to the written procedure provided for in the Council's Rules of Procedure.[411]

The drawing up of new rules relating to voting requirements prior to and consequent on the accession of Austria, Finland and Sweden in 1995 gave rise to problems on account of the fear by the larger Member States of the increasing influence of the smaller Member States in the decision-making process. Hitherto, even as a result of the earlier accessions, the weighting of votes required for a qualified majority had always stayed virtually the same (at about 71% of the total number of votes).[412] The application of the formula producing the same weighting with effect from 1 January 1995 foundered on strong resistance from the United Kingdom and Spain, and, initially but only briefly, Italy. They found a decrease in the possibility for the larger Member States to block the adoption of

410. In the same sense Wohlfarth *et al.*: *Die Europäische Wirtschaftsgemeinschaft* (Berlin/Frankfurt-am-Main, 1960) 449, *contra* Quadri *et al. Commentario CEE* (Milan, 1965) 1103. The counter-argument is basically that the Treaty should not be interpreted in such a way that one Member State could obstruct its functioning by non-attendance.
411. Under the Council's then Provisional Rules of procedure, Art. 6. Those Provisional Rules were never formally published, but are conveniently reproduced in Westlake, *op. cit.* (see note 5, *supra*) 130. As to the present rule governing written procedure, see Rules of Procedure (see note 8, *supra*), Art. 8.
412. For a good overview of the history of weighting of votes, see Westlake, *ibid.* 91 *et seq.*

measures by qualified majority unacceptable. In a Community of the Twelve it had always been possible for the United Kingdom and Spain (which had eighteen votes together), aided by one of the smaller Member States having five votes to block a decision, as the blocking minority was 23 votes.[413] On the other hand, a variety of coalitions could also thwart the ambitions of the four largest Member States.[414] The British and Spanish proposal would have kept the blocking minority at 23, which would have meant that it would have reduced from 30% to 25%, translating into a situation in which two large Member States and one smaller one with at least three, or, if Spain were one of the two larger Member States involved, at least five votes could still block decision-making by qualified majority.

However, the demand that there be no mechanical application of the weighting formula to maintain the 71% figure for a qualified majority was to no avail, and it was proposed (on the basis that Norway would also accede) to fix the qualified majority at 64 out of 90 votes, which would have made the blocking minority 27 votes. In Ioannina, in Greece, on 29 March 1994, the Council adopted a decision on qualified majority decision-making with effect from the accessions envisaged for 1995.[415] As modified[416] on account of Norway's decision not to accede to the European Union, the qualified majority was reduced to 62 out of 87 votes, and the blocking minority thus became 26 votes. Consequently, this Ioannina Compromise now provides that 'if members of the Council representing a total of 23 to 25 votes indicate their intention to oppose the adoption by the Council of a decision by qualified majority, the Council will do all within its power to reach, within a reasonable time and without prejudicing the obligatory time-limits laid down by the Treaties and by secondary legislation, such as those in Articles 189b and 189c of the Treaty establishing the European Community, a satisfactory solution that can be adopted by at least 65 votes. During this period, and always respecting the Rules of Procedure of the Council, the President undertakes, with the assistance of the Commission, any initiative necessary to facilitate a wider basis of agreement in the Council. The

413. See Westlake, *ibid.* 90–91. He notes 3 basic purposes of a blocking minority. First, it can be used simply to prevent the adoption of a measure; secondly, it can be used to force the Commission to amend its proposal, even if it is impossible to achieve unanimity in the Council to enable the latter to amend the proposal, and, thirdly, if the Commission refuses to amend its proposal where there is a division of views in the Council, with some finding the proposal unacceptable, and some being strongly in favour, a blocking minority can be used to oblige the Council to modify the Commission's proposal unanimously.

414. *E.g.* Spain, with Belgium, the Netherlands and Portugal could together muster twenty-three votes (8 + (3 x 5)).

415. O.J. 1994 C 105/1, Bull. EU 3–1995, point 1.3.27, which refers to point 1.2.28. See, however, the Commission's statement, Bull. EU 3–1995, point 1.3.29.

members of the Council lend him their assistance. The mention of the Council's Rules of Procedure is important, as it respects the provisions whereby the Council votes on the initiative of its President, who is required to open a voting procedure on the initiative of a member of the Council or of the Commission, provided that a majority of the Council's members so decide.[417] A vote on the question whether to proceed to a vote is thus always decided by a simple majority.

While the Ioannina Compromise, which is objectionable from the point of view of effective decision-making in an enlarged Community, appears to recall the Luxembourg Accords, it has a different purpose than the latter, namely to achieve a stronger qualified majority than that required by the Treaties,[418] but it does not seek to impose unanimity. In view of the fact that the Ioannina Compromise expressly respects obligatory time-limits, it may be thought that the expression 'within a reasonable time' means by the next Council meeting (at least in the relevant composition). Not the least of the curious features of the Council's decision at Ioannina is its publication in the 'C series' of the *Official Journal* (Information and Notices) as opposed to the 'L series' (Legislation), which indicates that the Council was conscious of the fact that the decision was not legally binding. This means that the Council's decision is not open to legal challenge, but it also appears to exclude reliance on the decision. Thus the decision merely formalizes the declaration of intent by the representatives of the then 12 Member States at the end of the Intergovernmental Conference concerning the envisaged accession,[419] of which the decision in fact forms an integral part. Another curious feature of the decision is that the Council took a decision in March 1994 about how it would operate after the accession of the new Member States, before that the latter could formally agree, although the declaration of the Twelve (and thus the decision) were incorporated in a declaration of the Member States and the (then) four applicant countries, in which the latter expressed their agreement with the declaration of the Twelve and the decision.[420] The Commission, however, recalled its earlier warning that to proceed to enlargement of the Community in a way which

416. O.J. 1995 C 1/1, Bull. EU 1/2–1995, point 1.8.1.
417. Rules of Procedure (see note 8, *supra*), Rules 7(1) and (2).
418. This idea is not wholly novel. The German government during the 1991 Intergovern-
    mental Conference (which led to the TEU) proposed a reinforced qualified majority
    requirement in the field of social policy as a last-ditch attempt to persuade the United
    Kingdom to accept the Social Chapter in what became the TEU. The weightings and
    categories of Member States would have been the same as in other respects, but the
    number of votes to reach a qualified majority would have been 66 (as opposed to 54)
    out of the 76 votes, or 89%, with the blocking minority being 11 (so that *e.g.* the
    United Kingdom and Luxembourg could have blocked a measure (10 + 1)). See Wes-
    tlake, *op. cit.* (see note 5, *supra*) 93.
419. Bull. EU 3–1994, point 1.3.28.
420. Bull. EU 3–1994, point 1.3.28 (final para.).

reduced its effectiveness would be an error.[421] Furthermore, the Commission reminded the Member States of its right to call for a vote in the Council at any time, in particular when it believed, on a case-by-case basis, that a reasonable time-limit to find a wider majority than that required by the Treaties had elapsed.[422] The Ioannina Compromise had, by 11 June 1996, been invoked only once; the Council noted that the experience showed that the Compromise had not formed an obstacle to its functioning.[423]

At the 1996 IGC no agreement was reached about what to do on the question of qualified majority voting, as is explained in section 8.7 of the Epilogue, below: this is reflected in the Protocol on the Institutions with the prospect of enlargement of the European Union which will be annexed to the EC, ECSC and Euratom Treaties and to the TEU, and a Declaration (No. 50) adopted by the IGC, annexed to the Final Act on the occasion of the signature of the Treaty of Amsterdam. This Declaration extends the Ioannina Compromise until the entry into force of the next enlargement, and notes that a solution for Spanish interests is to be found by that date.

3.3   Decision-making in the Council; the function of the Commission; the Committee of Permanent Representatives (*Coreper*)

3.3.1   The Commission's function

The important function which the Commission usually fulfills in the decision-making process in the Council[424] is based on three principles:

(1) Without a proposal from the Commission the Council cannot take a decision whenever, as in most cases, such a proposal is required (thus within the Community pillar the Commission has the exclusive right of initiative[425]);

421. Bull. EU 3–1994, point 1.3.29, referring to its report on *Europe and the challenge of enlargement* Bull. EC supp. 3/92 (which had been received (but significantly without express endorsement) at the Lisbon European Council in June 1992 (Bull. EC 6–1992, point I.4 (final para.).

422. Bull. EU 3–1994, point 1.3.29.

423. WQ E-316/96 (Moorhouse) O.J. 1996 C 280/19.

424. Save in the case of provisions relating to economic and monetary policy (as to which, see note 389, *supra*; in the very few other cases in which the Council does not act on the basis of a proposal from the Commission (typically in the case of appointments to specific functions), and when the Council acts, whether or not on the basis of a proposal from the Commission, in the fields of CFSP and JHA.

425. This is still the case (save where the Council does not decide on the basis of a proposal from the Commission, or where the right to make recommendations is shared with the European Central Bank).

(2) so long as the Council has not yet taken its decision, the Commission may amend its proposals;[426]

(3) the Council may only amend the proposal by unanimous vote.[427]

The proposal from the Commission, therefore, is a draft measure which forms not only the formal starting-point, but also the substantive basis on which the Council takes a decision.

The Commission's exclusive right of initiative also entitles it to determine whether and at what time it will submit a proposal. This of course applies only to the extent to which the specific Treaty provision which its proposal is intended to implement leaves it free to do so. If, for instance, this provision lays down a binding time-limit within which it must be implemented, the Commission is of course obliged to submit the appropriate proposals in good time. The fact that the Council may request the Commission to undertake any studies the Council considers desirable for the attainment of the common objectives, and to submit to it any appropriate proposals[428] does not detract from the Commission's right of initiative. Various other provisions confer on not only the Council but also on any Member State the right to request the Commission to make a recommendation or a proposal as appropriate.[429] In response to pressure from the European Parliament, that Institution has now been accorded a quasi-right of initiative, in that it may, acting by a majority of its members, request the Commission to submit any appropriate proposal on matters which it considers that a Community act is required for the purposes of implementing the ECSC, EC or Euratom Treaties.[430] Even

426. Arts. 189a(2) EC and 119 Euratom, 2nd para. As to political withdrawals see note 457, *infra* and Chapter IV, section 4.3.1, *ante*. See also the debate on the exercise of the right of withdrawal in relation to the cooperation procedure (note 507, *infra*) and the co-decision procedure (at the end of the discussion) in section 3.4.2, *post*. If the Commission amends its proposal during the decision-making process (which happens frequently) the amended proposal does not have to be in writing, even though it often will be, Case C-280/93 *Germany v. Council* [1994] ECR I-4973 at 5054. The Commission has undertaken to give the Parliament and the Council prior notification before withdrawing its proposals (Code of Conduct agreed between the Parliament and the Commission (O.J. 1995 C 89/69), point 3.9).

427. Arts. 189a(1) EC and 119 Euratom, 1st para. (*Cf.* the general rule on unanimity in the ECSC system, all must vote in favour, although there are exceptions, *e.g.* Art. 28 ECSC, 3rd para., second sentence). This applies to the substance of the proposal as well as to its legal basis: the choice of the latter may affect the determination of the content of the proposed measure, Case 131/86 *United Kingdom v. Council* [1988] ECR 905 at 929.

428. Arts. 152 EC and 122 Euratom (*cf.* Art. 26 ECSC, 3rd para.).

429. Arts. 109d EC (relating to various matters concerning economic and monetary union); 100c(4) EC (visa policy relating to third country nationals), see also Art. 32 Euratom (revision of basic health and safety standards relating to ionizing radiation at the request of the Commission or of a Member State).

430. Arts. 20a ECSC; 138b EC, 2nd para., and 107a Euratom. See Parliament's Rules of

before this specific right was conferred, it was possible for the Parliament to address such requests to the Commission and to call it to account if no action resulted. Now that there is a specific legal basis for such requests, if there is no response from the Commission the way would appear open for the Parliament to bring an action for failure to act.[431]

Can the Council convert the *right* of initiative of the Commission into an *obligation* to take the initiative, by inviting it under Article 152 EC[432] to submit proposals? This question arose in 1962, when the Council, obviously also referring to this Article, required the Commission to submit a proposal for withdrawing transport from the application of the general regime of competition of the (then) EEC Treaty, an issue on which the Commission disagreed with the Council. In the end the Commission yielded to the pressure from the Council, perhaps partly influenced by the invocation of Article 152.[433] Certainly the majority of writers take the view that the Commission is indeed obliged to accede to such a request and present a proposal, although it maintains the freedom to determine itself the contents of such a proposal.[434] The duty of interinstitutional cooperation imposed by Article 5 EC lies behind this obligation,[435] and the fact that in other instances the Commission is expressly obliged to examine the request[436] does not detract from the force of this general duty to respond to requests to present a proposal. If the Commission fails to submit a proposal in response to a request, the Council could, on this view, institute proceedings for failure to act.[437] If, on the basis of these provisions, the Council can oblige the Commission to submit a proposal in a field in which the Treaties themselves do not oblige the Commission to act but only confer the right to submit a proposal, the right of initiative might be degraded to a formality, especially if the members of the Council unanimously want to adopt a certain decision. Indeed, in this way the Commission might be compelled to give exclusively formal cooperation to the realization of Council decisions which it does not regard as consonant

Procedure (O.J. 1995 L 293/1), Rule 50 (this point is unaffected by subsequent amendments).

431. Under Arts. 175 EC or 148 Euratom (the Parliament does not have this power under Art. 35 ECSC). See also the Code of Conduct agreed between the Parliament and the Commission (O.J. 1995 C 89/69), point 3.3.

432. *Cf.* Arts. 20a ECSC and 122 Euratom.

433. See Samkalden (1962) SEW 697–700. WQ 865/82 (Radoux) O.J. 1982 C 298/5 indicates that the Commission feels that Art. 152 is a legal basis for compliance with such a request from the Council.

434. See Harnier in Von der Groeben *et al.* (eds.), *op. cit.* (see note 266, *supra*) Vol. 4, 255–256, and literature cited there, *contra* Louis (1992) CDE 251 (at para. 46).

435. *Cf.* Chapter III, section 5.2.4, *ante.*

436. Art. 109d EC further obliges the Commission to submit its conclusions to the Council without delay; Art. 32 Euratom merely obliges the Commission to examine any request made by a Member State.

437. Under Arts. 35 ECSC; 175 EC or 148 Euratom, as the case may be.

with the interests of the Community. In fact, in that case, the draft to be submitted by it would merely enable the Council to take a divergent decision, already established in advance.

The Commission may (and this is the second principle of the relationship between the Council and Commission in the decision-making process) amend its proposal after submission. It may do so, for instance, in the light of the opinion delivered by the European Parliament.[438] This is a useful reminder of the parliamentary accountability of the Commission. But practice shows that this power serves primarily to enable the Council to reach a decision. In fact, as a rule governments will lack the requisite qualified majority or unanimity respectively to decide either to adopt the proposal or to depart from it. Negotiations (sometimes lengthy and often laborious) between the members of the Council are needed before a decision can be taken. The good offices of the Commission, as an expert and impartial agency involved in the whole procedure of decision-making in the Council, are of great importance for bringing about a compromise which may do justice to the different points of view. Such a compromise must, depending on the voting requirements, be agreed by all the members of the Council or by a qualified majority. The cooperation of the Commission is indispensable, not only *de facto* but also (as regards reaching decisions by a qualified majority) *de jure* in view of the third principle set out above concerning the relationship between the Council and the Commission in the decision-making process (*i.e.* unanimity being required for departures from the Commission's proposals). In practice, therefore, the position of the Commission during the decision-making process of the Council is that of the sixteenth party in the negotiations leading to a decision of the Council: a sixteenth party fulfilling the important role of a mediator between the fifteen national standpoints and also putting forward its own views, prompted by the Community interest, on the decision to be taken. If qualified majority decisions are possible, this mediating function may develop into that of an arbitrator, whose voice may be decisive.

If it appears that there is no readiness in the Council to apply the qualified majority rule if necessary, the role of arbitrator is not reserved to the Commission. Even its mediating function is endangered when the narrow promotion of national interests is to the fore and the concept of the Community interest, propagated by the Commission, pushed into the background. It is gradually more often the case that it is not the Commission which amends its proposals in order to break a deadlock, but the Council, acting unanimously, on the basis of a compromise worked out by the Presidency.

---

438. Art. 119 Euratom, 2nd para. mentions reaction to consultation of the European Parliament as a specific circumstance for alteration of the Commission's original proposal.

Even the right of initiative has often seemed to slip from the Commission's hands, particularly in the development of policies in new fields in which the Treaties contain no guidelines on which the Commission can develop proposals. Before making proposals in these fields the Commission tends to set out possible premises, objectives and instruments in communications, Green Papers, or in reports to the Council in order to gain a better insight, by discussions with the Council and also with the European Parliament, into the views of the Institutions. Indeed, this approach also serves to promote a broad discussion, in which the social partners and other interested parties (such as environmental, consumer and other pressure groups) may make their views known. As long as the Commission in so doing makes its own preferences clear and is also willing to put forward proposals on its own responsibility after this dialogue, without being too led by what can obtain the prior agreement of all members of the Council, such a procedure is probably inevitable. If, though, as repeatedly occurs, the European Council or the Council develops policy lines and leaves to the Commission simply the formal making of the necessary proposals, the exclusive right of initiative given to the Commission by the Treaties is infringed.

This development has in fact been strengthened by the changes introduced by the TEU. First, the role of the European Council has been considerably strengthened, as the first paragraph of Article D TEU makes plain: the European Council provides not only the necessary impetus for the development of the European Union but also defines the general political guidelines of such development. These political guidelines clearly also embrace the areas in which the Commission is granted the exclusive right of initiative in the sense set out above. It is true that these political guidelines do not legally bind the Community institutions, as Article M TEU provides that, save as regards the amendments made by the TEU to the Community Treaties, and the final provisions of the TEU itself, nothing in the TEU affects the Community Treaties, or the subsequent Treaties or acts modifying or supplementing them. Thus there is no escaping the political accountability of the Commission towards the European Parliament, or the legal accountability of the Council (alone or jointly with the Parliament) and the Commission by invoking the general political guidelines laid down by the European Council, although the latter cannot itself be brought to account. Yet in fact a practice of transferring the right of initiative in important questions to the European Council is settled. However, depending on the competence and political weight of the President and other members of the Commission, that Institution may well be able to influence the general political guidelines which the European Council defines.

Secondly, the provisions of the EC Treaty relating to economic and monetary policy[439] which have been placed into the EC Treaty by the

439. Arts. 102a–109m EC.

TEU, sit not unlike a cuckoo in the nest of the decision-making system of the rest of the EC Treaty, as they pretty well wholly remove decision-making by the Council from the fundamental rule of acting on the basis of a proposal from the Commission, from which the Council may depart only by unanimity. As has been noted above,[440] the Council usually acts in this sphere on the basis of a recommendation, rather than a proposal, from the Commission,[441] and this right to make recommendations is in many cases shared with the European Central Bank. Finally, as will be explained below[442] the fundamental rule of departing from a Commission proposal only on the basis of unanimity is not maintained in relation to texts approved by a Conciliation Committee established under the co-decision procedure introduced by Article 189b EC.

3.3.2 *The decision-making process*

It is largely on the ground of the basic principles discussed above that a decision-making procedure has developed which usually takes the following stages when decisions of the Council on important matters are involved.[443] In the *first stage* the Commission's proposal is prepared by its services. As a rule national experts appointed for the purpose by the national governments at the Commission's request will participate in this. These experts, who are generally national officials, are consulted in their personal capacity. They are not, therefore, subject to specific instructions from their governments, neither can they commit the latter. The Commission, too, retains full freedom to act or not to act on their opinion. However, the working meetings held with them enable the Commission to gauge the view of national administrations and to benefit from their expert knowledge. The Commission is also free to consult any parties it wishes

---

440. See section 3.2, *ante* (2nd para.).
441. For an exception, see the Council's powers to amend certain provisions of the Statute of the European System of Central Banks (ESCB) and the European Central Bank (ECB), Art. 106(5) EC (paralleled in ESCB and ECB Protocol, Art. 41.1). If the Council acts on a proposal from the Commission, and after consulting the European Parliament and the ECB, the Council must decide by unanimity, but if the Council is deciding on a recommendation from the ECB, and after consulting the European Parliament and the Commission, only a qualified majority is needed. Thus more weight is clearly accorded to the ECB's recommendation. Most of the provisions of the Statute can only be changed by the procedure for amendment of the Treaty (Art. N(1) TEU). Note that the independence and primary objective of the ECB (price stability) have also been constitutionalized in the German Basic Law, see Gormley and De Haan (1996) 21 ELRev. 95 at 101.
442. See section 3.4.2, *post* (in the part dealing with the co-decision procedure).
443. See, generally, Dashwood (1994) 19 ELRev. 343 and in Winter *et al.* (eds.), *Reforming the Treaty on European Union* (The Hague, 1996) 147; Piris (1994) 19 ELRev. 449, and Westlake, *op. cit.* (see note 5, *supra*) 77–85.

and particularly professional, industrial or commercial organizations interested in the relevant field; it may choose to consult and promote discussion more widely by presenting ideas or the problems involved in the form of a Green Paper,[444] and sometimes a framework for action, involving discussion and decisions, may be set out in the form of a White Paper.[445] The Commission will often be lobbied by interested parties, frequently with diametrically opposed views.[446]

The second stage starts with the Commission's decision adopting the proposal which has been prepared by its services after wide-ranging internal and external consultations (sometimes in the light of discussions with the Council and the Parliament on the basis of Green Papers, White Papers or other Communications presented to the Council concerning the main points of a prospective policy). This proposal is submitted to the Council.[447] In the *third stage* consultations, if any are required by virtue of the legal basis proposed, with the European Parliament, the Economic and Social Committee, the Committee of the Regions, or the European Central Bank, on the Commission's proposal take place. The Council sends this proposal to these bodies.[448] After having heard the Commission on the proposal, they report to the Council.[449] Then follows the *fourth stage*, the preparation of the decision of the Council (acting alone, or jointly with the European Parliament under the co-decision procedure) on the basis of the Commission's proposal and the opinions received. This takes place in the Committee of Permanent Representatives *(Coreper)* which thus fulfills its first task of 'preparing the work of the Council.'[450] *Coreper* sets up

444. *E.g.* The Green Paper on Public Procurement in the European Union (COM (96) 583 Final). The Commission has undertaken to forward to the European Parliament and the Council, on an absolutely equal footing, all its strategic initiatives, such as Green or White papers in areas in which the Community could be required to act; if these strategic intitatives are accompanied by a draft resolution, that will also be submitted to the Parliament, Code of Conduct agreed between the Parliament and the Commission (O.J. 1995 C 89/69), point 3.1.

445. *E.g.* the White Paper on Completing the Internal Market (COM (85) 310 Final) and the White Paper on Preparation of the associated countries of Central and Eastern Europe for entry into the Internal Market of the Union (COM (95) 163 Final).

446. See Mazey and Richardson in Edwards and Spence (eds.), *op. cit.* (see note 382, *supra*) 178–198 and the Commission's documents reproduced at 199–212 (O.J. 1993 C 63).

447. Or, in cases in which the co-decision procedure applies (as to which, see section 3.4.2, point (iii), *post*), to the Parliament and the Council. See, generally, WQ 773/74 (Bertrand) O.J. 1985 C 151/6, and, as to the Commission's role, section 3.3.1, *supra*.

448. Save under the co-decision procedure, *ibid.*, when the proposal is sent to the Parliament and the Council by the Commission.

449. For the more technical proposals in the agricultural policy field the Special Committee for Agriculture acts in place of *Coreper*. See, further, Culley in Westlake, *op. cit.* (see note 5, *supra*) 201–203, and De Zwaan, *The Permanent Representatives Committee – its Role in European Union Decision-Making* (Amsterdam, 1995) 154–160.

450. Arts. 30(1) ECSC; 151(1) EC, and 121(1) Euratom. The second task is 'carrying out the tasks assigned to it by the Council,' *ibid.* As to *Coreper* generally, see Westlake,

working groups consisting of national officials, who study the Commission's proposal and report on it. The discussions in these working groups and, in connection with their reports, in *Coreper* are in practice always attended by officials representing the Commission.[451] The chairmanship of these working groups (and of *Coreper*) always rotates with the rotation of the Presidency of the Council.[452] In the fourth stage amendments to the proposal will usually be submitted by national administrations, which may or may not induce the Commission to amend its proposals. *Coreper* concludes the deliberations at this level with the decision[453] to submit the amended or unamended proposal to the Council, appending any amendments proposed by the national representatives and any opinions of the Institutions consulted.

The *fifth stage* takes place in the Council, in practice always in the presence of members of the Commission.[454] When full agreement has been reached at the level of *Coreper* between the governments and the Commission, the draft measure is placed on the agenda of the Council as a so-called A-item *i.e.* an item of the agenda on which no further discussion in the Council takes place. The Council then confines itself to adopting the draft measure without debate, unless objections are raised during the meeting.[455]

If no agreement has been reached in *Coreper* the matter is put on the Council's agenda as a B-item; it is then discussed by the members of the Council in order to find a common viewpoint. Such a discussion is of a negotiating nature and, in cases in which it proves impossible to proceed to a vote either through a lack of readiness to do so or because unanimity is required, can well be lengthy and exhausting, as witness the so-called marathon sessions which were required to give shape to the common agricultural policy, an area which still sees such sessions all too frequently, particularly on the fixing of agricultural prices and fishing quotas. The

op. cit. (see note 5, *supra*) 285; De Zwaan, *op. cit.* (see note 449, *supra*), and, further, Chapter IV, section 3.4, *ante*.

451. This stems from the Council's Rules of Procedure (see note 8, *supra*), Art. 4(2) and (3).
452. Rules of Procedure (*ibid.*), Art. 19(3). See, generally, Rometsch and Wessels in Edwards and Spence (eds.), *op. cit.* (see note 382, *supra*) 213–238 and Westlake, *op. cit.* (see note 5, *supra*) 336–339.
453. This is not a decision in the sense of the Treaties, as *Coreper* has no independent power of decision, see Case C-25/94 *Commission v. Council* [1996] ECR I-1469 at 1505. But the Treaty of Amsterdam will revise Art. 151 EC (and the corresponding ECSC and Euratom provisions) so as *inter alia* to permit *Coreper* to adopt procedural decisions in accordance with the Council's Rules of Procedure.
454. Rules of Procedure (see note 8, *supra*), Arts. 4(2) and (3).
455. Sometimes a matter which is really an 'A-item' is put on the agenda as a 'false B-item.' These are matters of considerable importance on which political agreement has been reached, but it is felt unseemly, from the point of view of public relations for them to 'go through on the nod'(see Westlake, *op. cit.* (see note 5, *supra*) 114 (quoting an unpublished paper by Spence).

members of the Council have to make concessions on both sides, a difficult process, which on politically important issues can often be resolved only under the pressure of the circumstances: either the objective necessity to reach a decision[456], or the creation of an atmosphere of crisis by means of a time-limit in terms of an ultimatum, set by a government which can afford to do so.

In the decision-making process several subjects are often combined, so as to meet the desire of certain Member States that concessions required from them in, say, the field of the agricultural policy, be compensated by concessions from other Member States, in, say, the field of the customs union for industrial products. In the preparation of a set of measures which is balanced from the viewpoint of mutual concessions and which is acceptable to the members of the Council and to the Commission ('package deal') the knowledge of the subject and the political insight of the Commission may be of decisive importance. The most effective time to influence the shape of proposed legislation undoubtedly remains the initial stages: influencing the direction of the Commission's proposal is a most effective manner of steering the subsequent discussion.

From the above broad description of the decision-making procedure of the Council in the EC system, it is obvious to what an extent policy-making in the Communities takes place in close co-operation and in a constant dialogue between the Member States and the Commission. Community administration also involves such co-operation and dialogue, albeit in a different manner. The Commission has to uphold Community interest in policy-making, though in a great many cases this cannot happen to the extent which may be considered desirable. Frequently the Commission, when confronted with the dilemma of taking no decision or taking a decision which is imperfect from the Community point of view, will give preference to the latter. This will then find expression either in the formulation of its original proposal or sometimes in essential amendments made subsequently. There have been instances, however, of the Commission withdrawing a proposal rather than accepting its emasculation by the Council.[457] The more modest the Commission's role in the decision-making process becomes, so the importance of the presidency of the Council increases. Either with the support of the Council secretariat or in

---

456. Sometimes the Agriculture Council has been known to 'stop the clock' at midnight on the day before the deadline and continue negotiating in a marathon session. As Westlake points out, few people are up between midnight and six in the morning to worry about a legal vacuum through the absence of a decision (Westlake, *ibid.* at 117).

457. *E.g.* the Erasmus programme (Dec. 87/327 O.J. 1987 L 166/20) proposal was withdrawn by the Commission and then resubmitted: WQ 2421/86 (Herman) O.J. 1987 C 157/40. Sometimes proposals are withdrawn because of opposition in the European Parliament *e.g.* the chocolate/'vegelate' proposal: WQ 145/86 (Cottrell) O.J. 1987 C 31/5. As has been observed in Chapter IV, section 4.3.1, *ante*, this technique is not uncontroversial.

co-operation with the Commission, the President-in-office often tends to lay compromise proposals on the table which can break a deadlock.[458]

It should not be surprising that with such a complicated and time-consuming decision-making process the Community often lacks the ability to take decisions appropriate to its expanding internal and external responsibilities in the socio-economic field. As long as the practice of preferring consensus – reluctance to seek a qualified majority – prevails in the Council, there is scant inclination at the level of officials in the working groups to conclude discussions on Commission proposals whenever there is too much divergence in views to hold out the prospect of agreement in *Coreper* or in the Council. The result has been that some proposals remain in the air in an atmosphere in which political vision does not get the chance to bridge opposition.[459] Sometimes there has been the somewhat bizarre spectacle of ministers making speeches at home saying what a good idea a proposal from the Commission is, whilst at the same time their civil servants are doing their best to obstruct agreement on the proposal in the relevant working group. A letter from a Commissioner to the minister drawing attention to the divergent approaches may well produce results.

3.3.3   The Committee of Permanent Representatives

The constantly increasing importance over the years of the function of the Committee of Permanent Representatives in the decision-making process is not without some danger to the position of the Commission and to the institutional equilibrium in general. It should be stated at the outset, though, that, at the present stage of integration, *Coreper* forms an indispensable link between the national capitals and the Community capital, Brussels.[460] Moreover, it fulfills a key role in the preparation of the multi-faceted and extensive activities of the Council.

The members of *Coreper* (in contrast to the national ministers and officials, who appear in Brussels intermittently) are permanently posted at the point of intersection of national and Community politics and are able to make an important contribution to better mutual understanding among

458. As to the Presidency, generally, see De Zwaan, *op. cit.* (see note 449, *supra*) 106–121 and Westlake, *op. cit.* (see note 5, *supra*) 37–54. Westlake, *ibid.* at 337, notes that Delors regarded the Commission's two most important functions as being its right of initiative, and its consensus-building, mediating function.

459. The days when a large number of Commission proposals simply lay on the table in Council without anything happening now appear to be over, particularly as a result of the Commission pursuing a more active withdrawal policy. There is nowadays a reasonable annual balance between proposals and measures adopted. The Commission rightly indicated some time ago that a large proportion of the proposals and measures concern decisions of ongoing management or of a highly technical nature, WQ 153/85 (Toksvig) O.J. 1985 C 255/24.

460. As to literature on *Coreper*, see Chapter IV, section 3.4, *ante*.

the sixteen participants in the decision-making process and to create a reasonable negotiating climate. It is precisely this favourable position which involves the risk of a shifting of the centre of gravity of the decision-making process to *Coreper*. A bureaucratization of the decision-making process threatens to occur if negotiations on the essential substance of the Commission's proposals take place in *Coreper* so that the political decision has already been taken by the time the proposal appears on the agenda of the Council in the form of an A-item. Theoretically, everything may be in due order, for the Council takes the decision; but in actual fact the political decision-making no longer takes place in the Institution which the Treaty designates for it, namely the Council.[461] Indeed, it is the Council which consists of those who bear political responsibility and who have to reach a decision in joint deliberations with the politically responsible members of the Commission.[462]

3.4   Decisions of the Council: the influence of the European Parliament

The possibilities for the European Parliament to influence the decision-making process in the Council as such procedure has been described and analyzed above, rest on two elements: the direct involvement in this decision-making process; and the parliamentary responsibility of the Commission to account for its share in the decision-making of the Council.

   The direct involvement of the Parliament in decision-making in the Council may take various forms.[463] The basic form is simple consultation by the Council, which is discussed in section 3.4.1, below. Departing from the basis of consultation, over the years special procedures have been introduced in a (so far) ever-increasing number of fields, with the aim of increasing the influence of the Parliament on Community decision-making. These are, in turn, the conciliation (or *concertation*) procedure; the

461. It will be recalled that the Court of Justice has recently confirmed that *Coreper* itself has no independent power of decision, Case C-25/94 *Commission v. Council* [1996] ECR I-1469 at 1505; and, moreover, that the Treaty of Amsterdam (not yet in force) will confer on *Coreper* the power to adopt procedural decisions in accordance with the Council's Rules of Procedure.

462. Westlake, *op. cit.* (see note 5, *supra*) 300 notes that in fact the Council decides in most cases without actually moving to a vote. If the member of the Council is absent, and the Permanent Representative is left holding the fort, Westlake submits that his or her silent acquiescence in a decision is as valid as any minister's, as long as the Council is quorate. As to the *esprit de corps* within *Coreper*, see Westlake, *ibid.*, 301.

463. See, generally, Corbett *et al.*, *op. cit.* (see note 141, *supra*) 188–223, and Westlake, *op. cit.* (see note 5, *supra*) 340–344. Once a request for an opinion has been received, the proposal is referred by the President to the appropriate committee for consideration, which later reports to the Parliament in plenary session, in which the resolutions embodying Parliament's opinion are adopted. As to the procedure in the Parliament on the various readings of proposals, see Rules of Procedure (O.J. 1997 L 49/1), Rules 51–79 and 83.

cooperation procedure, and the co-decision procedure. In addition the Parliament's assent is required in a limited (but important) number of instances. These special procedures are discussed in section 3.4.2, below.

3.4.1 Consultation by the Council

The basic rule of consultation remains[464] that the Council consults the Parliament on the Commission's proposal and does so on that proposal in its original form. This latter point follows from the terms of Article 119 Euratom and from the (less specific) text of what is now Art. 189a EC which permit the Commission to alter its original proposal, particularly where the Parliament has been consulted on it.[465] It would be contrary to this rule if the Council were to refer the original proposal back to the Commission without having consulted the Parliament.

A reasonable application of this basic rule, moreover, leads to the observance of two other rules: the original proposal must not reflect a compromise already achieved in negotiations between the government representatives[466] and the Commission should keep the Parliament regularly

The simplifications in respect of consolidation of existing legislation are not separately discussed, but see *ibid.*, Rule 82 and the Interinstitutional Agreement of 20 December 1994 (O.J. 1996 C 102/2) with the Joint Declarations annexed thereto (O.J. 1996 C 102/3). See, further, COM (93) 261 Final; the Council Resolution of 8 June 1993 (O.J. 1993 L 166/1); the Declaration (No. 39) adopted by the IGC annexed to the Final Act on the occasion of signature of the Treaty of Amsterdam) Barents (1994) 1 MJ 101; Gormley in Emiliou and O'Keeffe and Emiliou (eds.), *The European Union and World Trade Law* (Chichester, 1996) 124; the Molitor Group Report COM (95) 288; Kellermann *et al.* (eds.), *Improving the Quality of Legislation in Europe* (The Hague, 1998) and Timmermans (1997) 34 CMLRev. 1229.

As to consultation of and provision of information to the Parliament in the context of CFSP and JHA, see Rules of Procedure, *ibid.*, Rules 91 and 93 respectively, and as to recommendations from the Parliament to the Council in these fields, see Rules 92 and 94, respectively. The debates provided for under Arts. J.7 and K.6 TEU are held in accordance with the procedure for laid down in Rule 37(2)–(4), see Rules 92(4) and 94(2), respectively.

464. The basic rule of consultation used to be contained in the now repealed Article 149(2) EEC and in Article 119 Euratom. The Euratom provision has survived the changes made first by the SEA and then by the TEU unscathed, but the text of Article 149(2) EEC had been amended by the SEA, Art. 7. Although the co-operation and co-decision procedures have been introduced in certain areas the old consultation procedure remains in other areas. The European Parliament's participation in the legislative process is generally set out in Art. 138b EC, 1st para.

465. This last particularization, and the specific reference to the original proposal are expressed in Art. 119 Euratom, and were also expressed in the original Art. 149 EEC, 2nd para. (before the amendments introduced by the SEA which reformulated the right of withdrawal in what became Art. 149(3) EEC). However, Art. 189a EC makes no specific mention of the original proposal or of the consultation of the Parliament.

466. The idea laid down in point a(1) of the Luxembourg Accords (as to which, see section 3.2, *ante*) that the Commission should not approve any proposals of particular impor-

informed of the progress of the proposal in the Council.[467] If these rules are not observed, the opinion would lose a good deal of its meaning. The Parliament, therefore, will have to exercise close supervision over the application of the basic rule as well as the rules derived from it. If the submission of a Commission proposal to the Council has been preceded at an earlier stage by a Green or White Paper or other Communication then the Parliament, as well as the Council, will have made its views known. Proposals which are merely the result of policy lines developed in the European Council or in the Council on the initiative of Member States constitute serious infringements not just of the Commission's right of initiative but also of the Parliament's right to opine.

The content of the measure adopted by the Council must be clearly related in the essentials to the content of the Commission's original proposal on which the Parliament has been consulted. The duty to consult includes the requirement to reconsult whenever the text finally adopted, viewed as a whole, departs substantially from the text on which the Parliament has already been consulted, save where the amendments essentially correspond to the Parliament's wishes.[468] The Council has in fact developed the habit of

tance without first having taken up appropriate contacts with the governments of the Member States, would, if it were put into practice, constitute a development of doubtful wisdom.

467. See the Code of Conduct agreed between the Parliament and the Commission (O.J. 1995 C 89/69). This replaces the Code agreed in 1990 stemming from Delors's 7 points mentioned in a debate in the Parliament on 13 December 1990 (EP Debates 1990, no. 3–286/32–33). See, further, Case C-417/93 *European Parliament v. Council* [1995] ECR I-1185 at 1214 in which the Court upheld the Council's practice of considering the proposal actively while awaiting the opinion of the Parliament, as making good use of the intervening period and as long as the Council did not definitively adopt its position before receiving the opinion. In the 2nd ed. of this work it was suggested that the Council should not initiate the decision-making process (or at any rate put the matter to a vote) before it had received the opinion of the Parliament (259–260). The Council's practice of reaching informal agreement in some cases runs the risk of marginalizing the influence of the Parliament, and has rightly been deprecated by the latter (see Bradley (1990) 10 YBEL 367 at 378–379), although the Court's point that it is sensible for the Council to proceed with its examination in the intervening period makes administrative good sense. There is a fine line between making progress in considering a proposal and ensuring that it has become a fried egg by the time the opinion has been received. See, further, criticizing the Court's view of administrative realities, particularly in Case C-65/93 *European Parliament v. Council* [1995] ECR I-643 at 668–669, Boyron (1996) 21 ELRev. 145 at 417 *et seq.* The Commission has undertaken to remind the Council's bodies (working groups, *Coreper* or other committees) in good time not to reach political agreement on its proposals before Parliament has given its opinion, and to request discussion to be concluded at ministerial level after a reasonable time has been given to the members of the Council to examine the opinion, Code of Conduct, *ibid.*, point 3.4.

468. Case C-65/90 *European Parliament v. Council* [1992] ECR I-4593 at 4621. See also Case 41/69 *ACF Chemiefarma NV v. Commission* [1970] ECR 661 at 689; Case 138/79 *SA Roquette Frères v. Council* [1980] ECR 3333 at 3360; Case 139/79 *Maizena GmbH*

taking informal decisions before the opinion of the Parliament has actually been adopted, then simply confirming them by formally adopting the measure on which it had already reached political agreement. This can be seen as giving the impression that the Parliament's opinion counts for little in the consultation procedure. Not surprisingly, this practice had attracted academic comment[469] and eventually the Parliament decided to test the waters on this point. The Court found in Case C-417/93 *European Parliament v. Council*[470] that as long as the Council did not definitively adopt its position before being appraised of Parliament's opinion, there was nothing to stop the Council from using the time between requesting the opinion and its being received to consider the Commission's proposal or to search for a general approach or even a common position.[471] The Court does appear ready to examine whether the opinion has been validly taken into account in the decision of the Council: this can be ascertained from the dossier put before the Council by *Coreper*.[472] But it is clear that a claim that the Council has in fact pre-cooked the matter will not be entertained in the absence of clear evidence.[473]

Even in urgent cases, if the Council fails to obtain an opinion which must be obtained, it has no power to take a decision,[474] although the

---

v. Council [1980] ECR 3393 at 3424; Case 817/79 *Buyl et al. v. Commission* [1982] ECR 245 at 262 and 264–265; Cases C-13–16/92 *Driessen en Zonen vof et al. v. Minister van Verkeer en Waterstaat* [1993] ECR I-4751 at 4789; Case C-388/92 *European Parliament v. Council* [1994] ECR I-2067 at 2085; Case C-280/93 *Germany v. Council* [1994] ECR I-4973 at 5054–5055; Case C-417/93 *European Parliament v. Council* [1995] ECR I-1185 at 1215–1218 (which is particularly interesting as to what constitutes a substantial amendment), and Case C-21/94 *European Parliament v. Council* [1995] ECR I-1827 at 1852 and 1854. As to reconsultation, see the Parliament's Rules of Procedure (see note 463, *supra*), Rule 62. Reconsultation will in particular be necessary when the Council changes the legal basis of a proposal, so as to alter the decision-making procedure applicable; in these cases the Council frequently reconsults only on the amended legal basis, rather than on the whole proposal as revised. The Commission has agreed to ensure that the Council adheres to the rules evolved by the Court of Justice requiring Parliament to be reconsulted if the Council substantially amends a Commission proposal; it has also undertaken to inform the Parliament of any reminder to the Council of the need for reconsultation, see the Code of Conduct agreed between the Parliament and the Commission (O.J. 1995 C 89/69), point 3.6.

469. See Weatherill and Beaumont, *op. cit.* (see note 400, *supra*) 113 and Bradley (1990) 10 YBEL 367 at 378–379.

470. [1995] ECR I-1185 at 1214. See Boyron (1996) 21 ELRev. 145 and De Búrca (1996) 33 CMLRev. 1051.

471. The Court noted, *ibid.*, that the Parliament did not object to the Council's starting work in parallel with it after referring the matter to the Parliament, but merely claimed that the Council had in fact definitively adopted its position before requesting an opinion.

472. Case 262/80 *Andersen v. European Parliament* [1984] ECR 195 at 207 and Case 260/80 *Andersen v. Council* [19841 ECR 177 at 193.

473. See Case C-417/93 *European Parliament v. Council* [1995] ECR I-1185 at 1214–1214.

474. Case C-65/93 *European Parliament v. Council* [1995] ECR I-643 at 668. But see the

Parliament will not be able to complain if the absence of the opinion is due to its failure to fulfil its duty of sincere cooperation with the Council when the latter has used the special procedures designed to cope with urgent situations.[475] There are two such procedures. First, the Council (or the Commission or the President, a committee or 29 members of the European Parliament) can apply to the Parliament for a consultation to be treated as urgent under Rule 97 of the Rules of Procedure of the Parliament, and thus for a debate to take place.[476] Secondly, under Article 139 EC[477] the Council or the Commission may request the Parliament to convene an extraordinary session (this may also happen at the request of a majority of members of the European Parliament).

In its judgments in the isoglucose cases[478] the Court emphasized that consultation of the Parliament 'is the means which allows the Parliament to play an actual part in the legislative process of the Community. Such power represents an essential factor in the institutional balance intended by the Treaty. Although limited, it reflects at Community level the fundamental democratic principle that the peoples should take part in the exercise of power through the intermediary of a representative assembly. Due consultation of the Parliament in the cases provided for by the Treaty therefore constitutes an essential formality disregard of which means that the measure concerned is void.'[479] The Council was thus obliged to use all the means at its disposal in order to obtain the opinion of the Parliament, viz. to avail itself of one off the two special procedures, which it had manifestly failed to do.

However, in those judgments the Court left open the consequences of a refusal by the Parliament to give an opinion. It was often submitted that in such circumstances the Council could validly adopt the measure involved as there cannot have been an intention to confer a veto right on the Parliament in this manner.[480] It might perhaps be thought that such an

discussion in the text, *post*. See also the discussion of the co-decision and assent procedures in section 3.4.2, *post*.

475. *Ibid.* at 668–669. See the critical observations of Boyron (1996) 21 ELRev. 145 at 146 and 147–148.
476. O.J. 1995 L 293/1 (the subsequent amendments do not relate to this provision).
477. Or Art. 109 Euratom. *Cf.* Art. 22 ECSC.
478. Case 138/79 *Roquette* [1980] ECR 3333; Case 139/79 *Maizena* [19801 ECR 3393. See further, Case 114/81 *Tunnel Refineries Ltd. v. Council* [1982] ECR 3189 at 3208–3210. See also Corbett *et al.*, *op. cit.* (see note 141, *supra*) 192–193.
479. Case 138/79 *Roquette Frères* and 139/79 *Maizena*, *ibid.*, at 3360 and 3424 respectively. The principle is constantly repeated, *e.g.* Case C-65/90 *European Parliament v. Council* [1992] ECR I-4593 at 4621 and Case C-65/93 *European Parliament v. Council* [1995] ECR I-643 at 668. The problems arose because of the end of the period of office of the last non-directly elected Parliament in 1979. As to the Parliament's present rules governing unfinished business see Rules of Procedure (O.J. 1997 L 49/1, Rule 167.
480. *Cf.* Beutler (1984) EuR, 143 at 149–150, although views were divided on this question.

intention could not be so extraordinary in a system in which both the Commission (by declining to make a proposal or even by withdrawing it[481]) and the Council itself are able to prevent decision-making.[482] The Court has now resolved this question, while upholding the observations above about the importance of the Parliament's role, by finding that 'the institutional dialogue, on which the consultation procedure in particular is based, is subject to the same mutual duties of sincere cooperation as those which govern relations between Member States and the Community institutions.'[483] Accordingly, if the Council has made a justified request that the Parliament bear in mind the need for the proposed measure to be adopted by a certain date, and the Parliament, notwithstanding assurances given then decides for wholly unconnected reasons to adjourn its plenary session without having debated the proposal, in circumstances in which the Council simply cannot avail itself of the possibility of under Article 139 EC of requesting an extraordinary session, the Court will regard the Parliament as the author of its own misfortune.[484] This approach by the Court has found an elegant balance between protecting the Parliament's prerogatives on the one hand and preventing unconscionable stagnation in decision-making on the other.

It is understandable that the European Parliament would like to know why the Council has not followed its opinion, as usually tends to be the case. If the Council were always prepared to state its reasons before the Parliament for a departure from the parliamentary opinion, this would compel it to devote some attention to these opinions. After initial resistance,[485] the Council has become more ready to provide information

---

Bieber in Von der Groeben *et al.* (eds.) *Kommentar zum EWG-Vertrag* (4th ed., Baden-Baden, 1991) Vol. 3, 4134–4135 submitted that 'self-help' by the Council was not permitted as it is for the Court to decide whether an Institution has acted lawfully or not.

481. Although, as has been noted, this is controversial, see Chapter IV, section 4.3.1, *ante.*

482. As an older example of a case in which the Council did decide to act even though Parliament had refused to give its opinion, see the preamble to Reg. 1992/83 (O.J. 1983 L 196/1) on food aid. See further, Beutler, (1984) EuR 143 at 149–150 and Bieber (1984) EuR 185 at 191–192. See also Reg. 3917/93 (O.J. 1992 L 396/1) which was the subject of the Parliament's unsuccessful action in Case C-65/93 *European Parliament v. Council* [1995] ECR I-643, discussed in the text, *post.* See also Boyron (1996) 21 ELRev. 145 and Heukels (1995) 32 CMLRev. 1407.

483. Case C-65/93 *European Parliament v. Council* [1995] ECR I-463 at 668 (citing Case 204/86 *Greece v. Council* [1988] ECR 5323 at 5359).

484. Case C-65/93 *European Parliament v. Council* [1995] ECR I-463 at 669.

485. The Council regarded explanations as very much exceptional, and was keen to safeguard its collegiality and the secrecy of its deliberations, see WQ 55/67 (Vredeling) J.O. 1967 178/1. The Council was at pains in this reply to state that the Commission also had to observe these matters when supplying information to the Parliament. However, the absurdity of this reluctance was evident as the motives for adopting standpoints in the Council can be extraordinarily divergent, and anything but collegiate, and the Council had no objection to its members indicating their own positions in the discussions with their national Parliaments, and many ministers spilled the beans

about what has happened to opinions from the Parliament.[486] The Council is nowadays ready to exchange views on this matter during the periodic meetings with the President of the European Parliament, and has also agreed to explain orally or in writing on request the reasons for decisions which are not in line with opinions of the Parliament.[487]

3.4.2 Special procedures (conciliation (concertation), cooperation, co-decision and assent)

Since 1975 the involvement of the European Parliament in the legislative process in the Communities has been considerably extended.[488] In that year the conciliation procedure (nowadays referred to as the *concertation* procedure) was established by mutual agreement of the Presidents of the Parliament, the Council and the Commission, which aimed, along with the increased budgetary powers granted in 1971, to give the Parliament greater influence in the adoption of Council decisions having financial implications. Then, with the coming into force of the SEA on 1 July 1987,

anyway to the press outside the Council's meeting rooms. *Cf.* WQ 429/74 (O'Hagan) O.J. 1975 C 19/8. The Council for many years refused to hold any sessions in public, *e.g.* WQ 677/4 (O'Hagan) O.J. 1975 C 56/17, and even now the public sessions which do take place are largely devoted to set piece exchanges of views.

486. When the decision was taken in 1970 to enlarge the Parliament's budgetary powers, the Council became more accommodating about giving information on the fate of the Parliament's opinions: it undertook to explain to the Parliament the reasons which caused it to depart from the opinions submitted by the Parliament, not only in the case of decisions having financial consequences, but also in any matter of special importance. With respect to parliamentary opinions delivered in other cases the Council was prepared to pronounce in each case, on the basis of the nature of the question asked, on the desirability as well as the substance and the form of the answer to be given. *Cf. Dix-huitième Aperçu des activités du Conseil* 1969–70 (Brussels, 1971) para. 407. See also on measures involving financial consequences, *Twentieth Review of the Council's work,* 1972 (Brussels, 1973) para. 396. See further, Patijn, *De uitbreiding van de bevoegdheden van het Europees Parlement* (Diss., Rijksuniversiteit Utrecht, 1973) 111–113 and WQ 2277/83 (Elles) O.J., 1984 C 173/17. See now the European Parliament's Rules of Procedure (O.J. 1997 L 49/1), Rule 61. The question has diminished in importance since the introduction of the cooperation and co-decision procedures (Arts. 189c and 189b EC, respectively).

487. This means that the Presidency will explain on behalf of the Council, and this may well take place in the regular monthly meetings between the Presidents of the European Parliament, the Commission and the Council, or when the Presidency next appears before the Parliament. As to older material explaining the practice, see the Council's note of 10 October 1973, reproduced in Grabitz and Läufer, *Das Europäische Parlement* (Bonn, 1980) 646–648, and the letter from the President-in-office, Bull. EC 11–1982, p. 53 *et seq.* See, further, Corbett *et al., op. cit.* (see note 141, *supra*) 190–191.

488. See the contributions by Bieber, Corbett and Schmuck, and Wessels in Engel and Wessels (eds.), *From Luxembourg to Maastricht, Institutional Change in the European Community* (Bonn, 1992), and Ress in Curtin and Heukels (eds.), *op. cit.* (see note 406, *supra*) 153.

the so-called cooperation procedure was introduced[489] which then only applied to a number of provisions of importance for the completion of the internal market within the Community. In the light of the experience of the working of that procedure, it still features in the scheme of the EC Treaty after the coming into force of the TEU on 1 November 1993, although its significance is less prominent since the introduction of the co-decision procedure on that date. This co-decision procedure, provided for in Article 189b EC, strengthened the Parliament's influence on the decision-making process still further, but remains several sandwiches short of a picnic as regards giving the Parliament full, or even principal legislative responsibility in the Community, yet alone the Union. The TEU also further expanded the assent procedure which had been introduced by the SEA. These procedures are now considered in turn.

(i) The conciliation (*concertation*) procedure. On 4 March 1975 the Presidents of the Parliament, Council and the Commission signed a Joint Declaration on a conciliation procedure.[490] This Joint Declaration established a conciliation procedure between the Parliament and the Council with the active assistance of the Commission.[491] As explained above, this is nowadays referred to as the *concertation* procedure.[492] Under point 2 of the Joint Declaration the procedure may be followed if three conditions are fulfilled: the subject matter must be Community acts of general application; they must have appreciable financial implications[493] and, thirdly, their adoption must not be required by virtue of existing acts. This last condition is clearly designed to exclude agricultural prices decisions from the conciliation procedure.

Under point 3 of the Joint Declaration the Commission, when submitting its proposal, indicates whether it thinks that the act in question is capable of being the subject of the procedure. Both the Parliament when giving its opinion and the Council may request that the procedure be opened. They are clearly not bound by the Commission's view. If the three

---

489. Now Art. 189c EC, previously Art. 149(2) EEC.
490. O.J. 1975 C 89/1. *Cf.* Parliament's Rules of Procedure, (see note 486, *supra*), Rule 63. The Parliament's efforts to persuade the Council to accept a broader formulation were unsuccessful, see, generally, Forman (1979) 16 CMLRev. 77–108 and Nicoll (1986) RMC 11, and, further, Corbett *et al.*, *op. cit.* (see note 141, *supra*) 193–195.
491. Point 1 of the Joint Declaration.
492. The French term *Concertation* has thus been included in the heading to this discussion. It makes plain the distinction between a Conciliation Committee meeting under the co-decision procedure (*Conciliation*), and a Conciliation Committee meeting under this procedure, although the Parliament's delegation is composed in the same manner in both instances (see the Parliament's Rules of Procedure (see note 486, *supra*), Rule 75 (which applies by virtue of Rule 63(3)). In German the term *Konzertierung* is used, with the Conciliation Committee under the co-decision procedure being known as the *Vermittlungsauschuß*).
493. The preamble makes it clear that this means giving rise to important expenditure or revenue to be charged or credited to the budget.

conditions referred to are fulfilled and the Council intends to depart from the Parliament's opinion then, under point 4 of the Joint Declaration, the procedure is opened.[494] In practice the Parliament tends to reserve the right in giving its opinion in such cases to open the procedure if it appears that the Council intends to depart from the opinion.[495] If this transpires, the Council does not adopt a formal decision but assumes a 'common position' which it presents to the Parliament.

Concertation takes place in a committee composed of members of the Council and a corresponding number of representatives of the Parliament; the Commission participates in the work of this Committee.[496] The parliamentary delegation thus consists of 15 members, including in principle the chairmen and the *rapporteurs*[497] of the relevant committees of the Parliament; it is led by the President or one of the Vice-Presidents of the Parliament, and care must be taken in its composition to ensure balanced representation of political tendencies.[498] Point 6 of the Joint Declaration states that the aim of the procedure is to seek agreement between the Parliament and the Council and thus should normally take place within three months unless the act in question has to be adopted before a specific date or the matter is urgent (in these cases the Council may fix an appropriate time limit). Point 7 of the Joint Declaration provides that when the positions of the two Institutions are sufficiently close the Parliament may give a new opinion[499] after which the Council shall take definitive action. If the *concertation* procedure fails the Council naturally still has the right to decide.

Since 1975 the *concertation* procedure has been applied in a series of cases, although with success in only a few instances.[500] Often the Council

494. Parliament's Rules of Procedure (see note 486, *supra*), Rule 63(2). The procedure is initiated by the Parliament, either on its own initiative, or on that of the Council, *ibid.* As to the Court's supervision of the taking into account of the Parliament's views in the context of conciliation see Case 262/80 *Andersen v. European Parliament* [1984] ECR 195 at 207–208. The dialogue is subject to the same mutual duties of sincere cooperation which governs relations between the Member States and the Community Institutions (on the basis of Art. 5 EC), see Case 204/86 *Greece v. Council* [1988] ECR 5323 at 5359.

495. Rules of Procedure, *ibid.*, Rule 63(1).

496. Point 5 of the Joint Declaration; Parliament's Rules of Procedure (*ibid.*), Rule 63(1). As to the representation of the Council, see Council's Rules of Procedure (see note 8, *supra*), Art. 25(1). Members of the Council have turned up in person under this procedure (whereas the practice in Conciliation committees under the co-decision procedure is to leave the matter to deputy permanent representatives, led by a junior minister from the Member State holding the Presidency).

497. The *rapporteur* drafts the report of the committee.

498. Parliament's Rules of Procedure (see note 486, *supra*), Rule 75(3) and (6), which apply by virtue of Rule 63(3).

499. The appropriate parliamentary committee produces a report on the results of the conciliation.

500. See Forman, *op. cit.* and Corbett, *op. cit.* (see note 490, *supra*) and Oosterman–Meu-

is unable to move from its position, which has probably been arrived at with not undue difficulty.[501] There is scarcely any question of an open dialogue between the members of the Council and the parliamentary delegation; and the Presidency of the Council simply expresses that institution's viewpoint.[502] The introduction in broad fields of the cooperation and co-decision procedures seems to have diminished the significance of the *concertation* procedure, but it is not impossible to envisage its being applied at least on the first reading in the cooperation procedure in order to investigate at that early stage the possibility of reconciling the positions of the Parliament and the Council.[503] The fact that the result of such an informal *concertation* might lead to avoiding the need to go through the whole complexity of the cooperation procedure (consensus during the first reading would in turn facilitate Parliament's approval of the Council's common position) could well lead to the Council's being more flexible than it has tended to be when conciliation has taken place in the context of the simple consultation of the Parliament. Informal *concertations* have also been held, and the Council has interpreted the notion of legislation 'with appreciable financial implications' flexibly, but an extension of the procedure in the context of simple consultation has always been resisted.[504]

(ii) The Cooperation procedure. Article 189c EC now governs the co-operation procedure,[505] the application of which has been considerably extended.[506] In some of these provisions decisions were to be taken by a

lenbeld (1986) NJB 742. Successes include the conciliations on the Financial Regulation in 1977, the restructuring of the European Social Fund in 1983, the Food Aid Regulation in 1986, the New Community Instrument authorizing the Commission to raise loans to support certain types of projects and investments; the reform of agricultural structures in June 1987, the budgetary discipline introduced in 1988, the reform of the Structural and Social Funds in 1989, and the collection of own resources, also in 1989.

501. *E.g.* the proposal for a regulation on financial and technical assistance to non--associated developing countries (O.J. 1977 C 54/5, opinion EP O.J. 1977 C 118/60) which became Reg. 442/81 (O.J. 1981 L 48/8).
502. *Report on European Institutions* (Brussels, October 1979) 37–38. Council's Rules of Procedure (see note 8, *supra*), Art. 25(1).
503. In the same sense, De Zwaan, *op. cit.* (see note 449 *supra*) 230. See also Haag in Von der Groeben *et al.* (eds.), *op. cit.* (see note 266, *supra*) Vol. 4, 123–124. According to point 5 of a resolution adopted on 12 December 1992 (O.J. 1993 C 21/138–141) the Parliament also regards the application of an informal *concertation* procedure as being desirable during the first reading in the co-decision procedure.
504. See Corbett *et al.*, *op. cit.* (see note 141 *supra*) 195.
505. The procedure was provided for in Art. 6 SEA, and introduced by Art. 7 SEA which amended Art. 149 EEC. The present provision results from the amendments made by the TEU. As to the procedure in the Parliament, see Rules of Procedure (see note 486, *supra*), Rules 53–73.
506. The cooperation procedure applies in relation to measures adopted on the basis of the

qualified majority, in other amendments made by the SEA introduced the qualified majority system.

When the cooperation procedure is applicable, the first reading starts, as in the case of *concertation*, with the Council coming to a common position (by a qualified majority) on a Commission proposal after having consulted the Parliament in same way as under the ordinary consultation procedure set out above. Given that the Council is acting on the basis of a proposal from the Commission, Article 189a(1) EC applies, so that the Council may amend that proposal only by unanimity. The Council then communicates its common position to the Parliament[507] and the Council and the Commission inform the Parliament fully of the reasons which led the Council to adopt its common position;[508] the Parliament is also to be fully informed of the Commission's position. The Parliament then has three

following provisions of the EC Treaty: Arts. 6, 2nd para. (rules to prohibit discrimination on ground of nationality); 75(1) (rules relating to transport, save in the exceptional cases envisaged in Art. 75(3)); 84(2) (sea and air transport); 103(5) (multilateral surveillance of economic policies); 104a(2) (prohibition of public sector privileged access to financial institutions); 104b(2) (prohibition of Community and Member States' liability for public sector commitments and overdraft facilities of (other) Member States); 105a(2) (harmonization of the denominations and technical specifications of coins); Art. 118a (social policy measures concerning health and safety, especially in the working environment); Art. 125 (implementing decisions relating to the European Social Fund); 127(4) (vocational training); 129d (implementing measures and financial support for Trans-European Networks); 130e (implementing decisions on economic and social cohesion relating to the European Regional Development Fund); 130o, 2nd para. (implementation of the multiannual framework programme for research and technological development); 130s(1) and (in certain cases) (3) (action to achieve the Community's objectives concerning the environment), and 130w (measures to further the Community's objectives concerning development cooperation). The cooperation procedure also applies in relation to the Protocol on Social Policy, Art. 2, as between the fourteen participating Member states, with the consequent adjustment of the qualified majority, laid down in the Agreement on Social Policy, Art. (2). Once the Treaty of Amsterdam enters into force the cooperation procedure will remain relevant only for the provisions in the field of Economic and Monetary Union.

507. As to the formalities for establishing when the common position has been communicated see the Parliament's Rules of Procedure (see note 486, *supra*), Rule 64(l). See, generally, on the cooperation procedure, *ibid.* Rules 44–52. Wyatt and Dashwood, *op. cit.* (see note 400, *supra*) 48) argue that the Commission has no right to withdraw its proposal once the Council has adopted a common position, as it is for the European Parliament to make up its mind thereupon, and the consequences of its actions are clearly set out in Art. 189c(c) *et seq.* Weatherill and Beaumont, (see note 400, *supra*) 120 take the view that the freedom to withdraw the proposal is available as long as the Council has not adopted the proposal definitively, basing this view on the wording of Art. 189a(2) EC, which certainly appears to support that conclusion.

508. The Council agreed, during the Interinstitutional Confrence at Luxembourg on 25 October 1993 that it would take steps to publish the common positions and the accompanying statement of reasons, Bull. EC 10–1993, point 2.2.1. See also Corbett *et al.* (see note 141, *supra*) 209.

months (or up to four if it and the Council agree to the extension[509]) in which to react, and this phase is known as the second reading in the Parliament. If, within this period, the Parliament approves the common position or has not taken a decision, the Council definitively adopts the act in question in accordance with the common position. Thus inaction by the Parliament cannot block action by the Council.

Within this period, though, the Parliament may propose amendments to the Council's common position or even reject it, in each case by an absolute majority of its members. However, given that the cooperation procedure is 'a second bite at the cherry,' no new amendments are proposed by the Parliament in its second reading;[510] essentially the second reading serves as an opportunity for dialogue about why the Council did not take up amendments proposed by the Parliament in its first reading, or why the Commission has amended its proposal (other than to meet the wishes of the Parliament already expressed) in between the first reading in the Parliament and the adoption of the common position, or as an opportunity to include further amendments agreed as a compromise between the Council and the Parliament. If the common position is rejected, the Council can act in its second reading of the proposed measure only by unanimous vote.[511] The Parliament transmits the result of its proceedings to the Council and the Commission. Thus it is possible for the Council to override the rejection by the Parliament.

If amendments were proposed then further developments depend on the Commission. It re-examines its proposal and decides within one month whether to accept any or all of the Parliament's proposed amendments (in whole or in part) and incorporate them into its proposal. It will be remem-

509. Art.189c(g) EC, see the Parliament's Rules of Procedure (see note 486, *supra*), Rule 65.
510. An amendment to the common position is admissible if it seeks to restore wholly or partly the position adopted by the Parliament in its first reading, or if it is a compromise amendment representing an agreement between the Council and the Parliament, or it seeks to amend a part of the text of a common position which was not included in – or differs in content from – the proposal submitted in first reading and does not amount to a substantial change justifying reconsultation of the Parliament afresh, Parliament's Rules of Procedure (see note 486, *supra*), Rule 72 (amendments may only be proposed by the committee responsible, a political group, or at least 29 members, and must in any event comply with *ibid.*, Rules 124 (on procedure) and 125 (on admissibility), *ibid.*, Rule 72; the same applies in respect of a proposal to reject the Council's common position, *ibid.*, Rule 71). The Commission has undertaken to take the utmost account of amendments proposed by the Parliament, and to explain any decision, taken at the level of the Colege of Commissioners (the Commission as a body), not to support or include amendments adopted by the Parliament, Code of Conduct agreed between the Parliament and the Commission (O.J. 1995 C 89/69), point 3.7.
511. If it gets the opportunity, as the Commission has undertaken to withdraw, where appropriate, a proposal which the Parliament has rejected, or to explain why not, if, for important reasons, and after consideration by the College, it decides to maintain its proposal, Code of Conduct, *ibid.*, point 3.8.

bered that as long as the Council has not acted the Commission can always amend its proposal by virtue of Article 189a(2) EC.[512] The Commission then forwards the re-examined proposal to the Council, along with any of the proposed amendments which it has been unable to accept, accompanied by its opinion on them.

The Council then has three months (or up to four if it and the Parliament agree to the extension) in which to act. If no decision has been reached within this period the Commission's proposal is deemed not to have been adopted. The normal decision-making rules apply in this second reading of the re-examined Commission proposal in the Council, both in relation to that proposal and in relation to the amendments which the Commission did not accept: the Council needs a qualified majority to adopt the re-examined proposal, but it can only adopt the unaccepted amendments and vary the re-examined Commission proposal by unanimous vote. This also means, for example, that if the Council wished to reject an amendment made by the Parliament which the Commission had accepted, it would have to do so by unanimity.

Despite some somber predictions by many writers that the complicated nature of the cooperation procedure could lead to aggravation, delay and even paralysis in decision-making,[513] it is now generally acknowledged that the procedure has worked satisfactorily, particularly in carrying out the programme for the completion of the internal market.[514]

(iii) The Co-decision procedure. This entirely new procedure, which aims to respond to the Parliament's desire to become (at least) an equal partner in the Community legislative process, is of a complexity which threatens to confuse not least those who participate in it. The co-decision procedure is set out in Article 1896 EC and applies, since the coming into force of the TEU on 1 November 1993,[515] in myriad aspects of the establishment and

---

512. Schoo in Von der Groeben et al. (eds.), op. cit. (see note 266, supra) Vol. 4, 1117 does not specifically deal with the point about withdrawal at this stage (although he points out that the English and the German texts of Art. 189c EC give more support than does the German text for the view that the Commission's right to amend the proposal is limited in function of what the Parliament has proposed.

513. Including in the 2nd ed. of this work (p. 266).

514. E.g. the Commission's positive assessment, Twenty-seventh General Report, 1993 (Brussels, Luxembourg, 1994) point 1001. Corbett et al. (see note 141, supra) 199 notes that the procedure meant that the Parliament entered further into the traditional Commission-Council dialogue, devoted time and energy to it and had a considerable impact, and that in the first six years of operation of this procedure (since 1 July 1987) some 2,000 parliamentary amendments had been incorporated into Community legislation under this procedure, and in only one instance had the Council been able to overturn on second reading a rejection by the Parliament of the common position.

515. As to problems relating to proposals in the pipeline on this date (when in various instances the applicable procdure changed from cooperation to co-decision), see Corbett et al., ibid., 203–204 and Bradley and Feeney (1993) 13 YBEL 404.

functioning of the Community's internal market (there replacing the cooperation procedure introduced by the SEA),[516] and in a number of other
specific instances involving new or expanded policy areas.[517] In all except

516. The procedure applies to proposals based on the following provisions of the EC
Treaty: Art. 49 (measures achieving free movement of workers); Art. 54(2) (directives
promoting the freedom of establishment); Art. 56(2), 2nd sentence (directives on
national safeguard measures on grounds of public policy, public security or public
health restricting the right of establishment); Art. 57(1) (mutual recognition of diplomas *etc.*); Art. 57(2),3rd sentence (taking up and pursuit of self-employed activities in
professions which are not regulated, as regards individuals, in any of the Member
States); Art. 66 (application *mutatis mutandis* of the last three provisions mentioned
above, in relation to the freedom to provide services); Art. 100a(1) (harmonization for
the establishment and functioning of the internal market), and 100b (recognition of
equivalence of unharmonized provisions).
    The Treaty of Amsterdam (not yet in force), apart from simplifying the co-decision
procedure, as explained in the notes, moves the areas presently using the cooperation
procedure (see note 506, *supra*) over to the co-decision procedure (save for the provisions in the area of Economic and Monetary Union); it also redrafts Art. 56(2) EC.
517. The procedure thus also applies to proposals based on the following provisions of the
EC Treaty: Arts. 126(4) (incentive measures, not involving harmonization, in the field
of education, vocational training and youth (but not recommendations in this field,
which are adopted by the Council acting solely on a recommendation from the Commission)); 128(5) (incentive measures not involving harmonization, in encouraging
cooperation between the Member States and, if necessary, supporting and supplementing their action in certain cultural areas); 129(4) (incentive measures, excluding
harmonization, encouraging cooperation between the Member States, and, if necessary, lending support to their action (although coordination is the responsibility of the
Member States in liaison with the Commission, and any recommendations in this field
are adopted by the Council acting solely on a proposal from the Commission));
129a(2) (specific action supporting and supplementing the policy pursued by the
Member States to protect the health, safety and economic interests of consumers and
to provide adequate information to consumers); 129d, 1st para. (guidelines governing
the objectives, priorities and broad lines of measures envisaged in the sphere of Trans-
European Networks); 130i(1) (multiannual framework programmes concerning Community activities in research and technological development (the specific programmes
are adopted under the consultation procedure, Art. 130i(4)), and 130s(3) (general
action programmes setting out priority objectives relating to the environment, other
than the action governed by the cooperation procedure or the primarily fiscal provisions, town and country planning, certain land use and energy choice measures
covered by the consultation procedure).
    The Treaty of Amsterdam (not yet in force) will also apply the co-decision proce-
dure in the following provisions of the EC Treaty: the new Art. 73o(4) (measures on
procedures and conditions for issuing visas for up to three months by Member States
and rules on a uniform visa); the new Arts. 109r (employment incentive measures) and
116 (customs cooperation); the revised Arts. 118(2) and 119(3) (in the fields of social
policy and equal pay (the existing Arts. 117–120 are integrally repealed and replaced);
the expanded and revised Arts. 129(4); 129a(3); 129d, 1st para.; 130i(1) (removing the
previous requirement of unanimity in the Council); the new Art. 191a (general principles and limits relating to access to documents); the revised Art. 209a (countering
fraud affecting the Community's financial interests), and the new Arts. 213a (measures
for the production of statistics); and 213b (establishment of an independent super-

two cases a qualified majority applies as far as the Council is concerned.[518] The results of the 1996 Intergovernmental Conference which was charged with examining whether the scope of the co-decision procedure should be widened[519] have led to significant streamlining by the Treaty of Amsterdam (not yet in force); for the sake of clarity in this discussion these changes are simply reflected in the notes at appropriate places below.

The equality of the Parliament and the Council is expressed at the beginning and at the end of the procedure.[520] Whenever the co-decision procedure applies, the Commission submits its proposal to the European Parliament and the Council.[521] Regulations, directives and decisions adopted in accordance with this procedure are signed by the President of the European Parliament and by the President of the Council.[522] The substance of the procedure combines elements of the conciliation (*concertation*) and co-decision procedures with the right of the Parliament at the end of the day to reject the text adopted against its wishes by the Council.[523] As will be explained below, the procedure also eats into the fundamental principle of the Commission's exclusive right of initiative, and

visory body responsible for montoring the application to Community Institutions and bodies of Community acts on the protection of individuals with regard to the processing of personal data and the free movement of such data). After five years from the date of entry into force of the Treaty of Amsterdam the Council will also be able to decide unanimously that all or parts of the new provisions on visa, asylum, immigration and other policies related to the free movement of persons may be governed by the co-decision procedure, see the new Art. 73o(2) EC, from which the new Art. 73o(4) EC mentioned above derogates.

518. The exceptions at present are Art. 128(5) and 130i(1) EC, where the Council has to act by unanimity. The Treaty of Amsterdam (not yet in force) will replace the requirement of unanimity by qualified majority in Art. 130i(1) EC. It will also introduce the co-decision procedure with the Council acting by unanimity in the following revised provisions of the EC Treaty: Arts. 8a(2) (provisions facilitating the exercise of rights of citizens of the Union); 51 (social security for migrant workers), and 57(2), 2nd sentence (directives to facilitate the taking up and pursuit of activities as self-employed persons which involve in at least one Member State amendment of existing principles laid down by law governing the professions with respect to training and conditions of access for natural persons (previously the consultation procedure and unanimity applied; for directives not involving such amendment the normal co-decision procedure applies, as at present)).

519. Art. 189b(8) EC. The amendments would be effected in accordance with Art. N(2) TEU on the basis of a report to be submitted to the Council by the Commission by the end of 1996. As to the Commission's view on the application of the co-decision procedure, see SEC (96) 1225 Final.

520. But see Case 259/95 *European Parliament v. Council* [1997] ECR I-5303 at 5321–5322.

521. Art. 189b(2) EC; Parliament's Rules of Procedure (see note 486, *supra*), Rule 79. As to the detailed procedure in the Parliament, see Rules of Procedure (*ibid.*), Rules 51–79 and 83.

522. Art. 191(1) EC (the President of the Council means the president-in-office of the Council in the relevant composition).

523. Art. 189b(6) EC. This parallels the Parliament's right to reject the draft budget, Art. 203(8) EC.

the associated requirement of unanimity in the Council to amend a proposal from the Commission.

After the proposal has been submitted to the Parliament and the Council, the first reading in each of these Institutions takes place. This culminates in the Council adopting a common position by qualified majority, after having obtained the opinion of the Parliament; this common position may well reflect the Parliament's opinion, it may also incorporate changes which the Commission has made to its proposal during the deliberations in the Council, its working groups or *Coreper*.[524] While there is no express reference in Article 189b(2) EC to the common position being adopted on the basis of the Commission's proposal (unlike in the case of the cooperation procedure in Article 189c(a) EC), there is no reason to suppose that the normal rule of modifications to that proposal being adopted by unanimity is inapplicable at this stage.[525] This common position is communicated to the Parliament, which must also be informed fully by the Council of the reasons which led it to adopt the common position;[526] the Commission must also inform the Parliament fully of its position on the common position of the Council.

The Parliament then has three months (or up to four if it and the Council agree to the extension[527]) in which to react, and this phase is known as the second reading in the Parliament. If, within this period, the Parliament approves the common position or has not taken a decision, the Council definitively adopts the act in question in accordance with the common position. Thus inaction by the Parliament cannot block action by the Council.

Within this period, though, the Parliament may reject the common position, or propose amendments to it, in each case by an absolute majority of its members. However, unlike in the case of the cooperation procedure, rejection cannot simply take place without more ado.[528] If Parliament indicates, by an absolute majority of its component members, that it intends to reject the common position, it must immediately inform the Council, which

524. The Treaty of Amsterdam will simplify this stage, so that if the Council approves all the amendments contained in the Parliament's opinion, or if the Parliament proposes no amendments, the Council may then adopt the act (where appropriate as so amended) without more ado. Otherwise the Council adopts a common position.
525. Art. 189a(1) EC. The only exceptions specified therein are Art. 189b(4) and (5) EC, which deal with a later stage in the co-decision procedure, as is explained, *infra*.
526. In the cooperation procedure this obligation is imposed on the Commission as well, see Art. 189c(b), 1st subpara. The common position and the accompanying explanation are published, see note 508, *supra*. As to the formalities for establishing when the common position has been communicated see the Parliament's Rules of Procedure (see note 486, *supra*), Rule 64(l).
527. Art. 189b(7) EC, see the Parliament's Rules of Procedure (see note 486, *supra*), Rule 65.
528. The Treaty of Amsterdam will simplify matters by removing the requirement that the Parliament announce its intention to reject; thus Parliament will be able to reject the common position without more ado, and the proposed act will be deemed not adopted.

may convene a meeting of the Conciliation Committee[529] to explain further its position. Depending on the result of this explanation, the Parliament may then confirm, by an absolute majority of its component members, its rejection of the common position.[530] In this case the proposed act is deemed not to have been adopted.[531] Alternatively, the Parliament may propose amendments to the common position.[532] Whether as a result of retreat from the threat of rejection or not, the right to propose amendments in second reading is (as was noted above in relation to the cooperation procedure) 'a second bite at the cherry,' thus no new amendments are proposed by the Parliament in its second reading,[533] although the opportunity can be used to include further amendments agreed as a compromise between the Council and the Parliament in the Conciliation Committee.[534]

The ball is then in the court of the Council. In its second reading, it has three months (or up to four if it and the Parliament agree to the extension) to approve by qualified majority all the amendments of the Parliament. If it does so, it amends the common position accordingly and adopts the act in question. In this respect the rule of unanimity in the Council for alterations to a Commission proposal is somewhat sacrificed, although the sacrifice is mitigated by the requirement of unanimity in respect of any amendments on which the Commission delivers a negative opinion. This treatment of the Parliament's amendments which find favour with the Commission formally differs significantly from that in the cooperation procedure,[535] and means that a qualified majority has to be found for each

529. The working of which is explained, *infra*. Note that if the Conciliation Committee is convened at this stage the three month period for the second reading in the Parliament is automatically extended by two months, Art. 189b(7). Conciliation at this stage is sometimes called a minor conciliation, as there are no formal negotiations, only an explanation from the Council, see Corbett *et al.*, *op. cit.* (see note 141, *supra*) 204. As to the procedure in the Parliament, see Rules of Procedure (see note 486, *supra*), Rules 69 and 70.

530. As to the procedure in the Parliament, see *ibid.*, Rule 71. The Commission has agreed to withdraw proposals rejected by the Parliament, or explain why, if for important reasons, it decides at the level of the College of Commissioners (the Commission as a body), not to accept or support amendments adopted by the Parliament, Code of Conduct agreed between the Parliament and the Commission (O.J. 1995 C 89/69), point 3.8.

531. Thus, unlike in the cooperation procedure, Parliament's rejection of the common position cannot be overridden by the Council acting unanimously.

532. Art. 189b(2)(b) mentions only these two possibilities; it is submitted that the Parliament could still decide, after all, to approve the common position, but it is politically extremely unlikely that this would occur. The Commission has agreed to take the utmost account of such amendments, and to explain why, if for important reasons, it decides at the level of the College, not to accept or support amendments adopted by the Parliament, Code of Conduct, *ibid.*, point 3.7.

533. As to admissibility of amendments in second reading, see note 510, *supra*, and text thereto *et seq*.

534. The possibility of a Conciliation Committee at this stage will disappear when the Treaty of Amsterdam comes into force (but there is nothing to prevent an informal *concertation*).

535. There the Commission determined which amendments it would accept and incorpo-

and every one of such amendments individually. If the Council does not approve the act in question, unlike in the cooperation procedure, it does not fall without more ado. The President of the Council, in agreement with the President of the European Parliament forthwith convenes a meeting of the Conciliation Committee.

The Conciliation Committee is composed of members of the Council or their representatives[536] and an equal number of representatives of the Parliament.[537] Its task is to reach agreement on a joint text, by qualified majority on the Council's side,[538] and by majority on the Parliament's side.[539] The Commission takes part in the Committee's proceedings – effectively as a kind of honest broker – and takes all the necessary initiatives with a view to reconciling the parties' positions.[540] Corbett et al.[541] explain that given the number of civil servants accompanying each participant on the Council's side, the number of advisers accompanying the parliament's own delegation, and the Commission's representation, there may well be over a hundred people in the room during conciliation. Thus preliminary contacts are established between the

rated them into a re-examined proposal, which meant that the Council could only overturn them by unanimity, or threaten not to take a decision within the requisite period of three (or four) months, which would lead to the act being deemed not to have been adopted, see Art. 189c(d)–(g) EC. However, in practice, at the same time as the Commission presents its opinion on the Parliament's amendments it actually presents the Council with a revised proposal, taking on board those amendments which it can accept. Thus the Commission appears to act in fact in the same way as it would during the cooperation procedure.

536. It will be recalled from the discussion in preceding sections that usally the Council is represented at deputy permanent representative level (*Coreper I*), headed by a junior minister on behalf of the presidency. If the subject-matter is particularly important, though, some ministers may attend in person.

537. The parliamentary delegation thus consists of fifteen members, including in principle the chairmen and the *rapporteurs* of the relevant committees of the Parliament; it is led by the President or one of the Vice-Presidents of the Parliament, and care must be taken in its composition to ensure balanced representation of political tendencies, see Parliament's Rules of Procedure (see note 486, *supra*), Rule 75. See, further, Foster (1994) 19 ELRev. 185.

538. Thus in the Conciliation Committee the Council may agree variations from its common position by qualified majority, irrespective of whether the Commission agrees with those variations or not, Art. 189a(1) EC, in conjunction with Art. 189b(4) EC.

539. The Treaty of Amsterdam will introduce the requirement that the Conciliation Committee address the common position on the basis of the amendments proposed by the European Parliament.

540. Art. 189b(4) EC. As to the procedure, see the arrangements agreed during the Inter-institutional Conference at Luxembourg on 25 October 1993, Bull. EC 10–1993, point 2.2.3. The Commission's function switches from that of protagonist (with a clear effect on whether amendments will have a chance of going through) to facilitator (and thus a more service-orientated capacity).

541. *Op. cit.* (see note 141, *supra*) 206. This explanation of the working of the Committee is based on his account.

participants,[542] although full conciliation meetings tend to be lengthy affairs, given the need to break to allow for consideration of offers made, and the preliminary meetings which are held. The meetings are alternatively chaired by the leaders of each side's delegation, and take place alternatively on each side's premises (alternating within each conciliation if more than one meeting of the Committee takes place). The Committee must conclude its activities within six weeks (or up to eight weeks if the Parliament and the Council agree).[543]

If the Conciliation Committe approves a joint text within this period, there follows the third reading in both the Parliament[544] and the Council. Within six, or as the case may be, eight, weeks, both Institutions must have approved the joint text, otherwise it is deemed not to have been adopted. The Parliament this time acts by an absolute majority of the votes cast;[545] the Council by qualified majority.[546]

If the Conciliation Committee fails to approve a joint text, the default position is that the proposed act is deemed not to have been adopted.[547] If, however, within six weeks (or eight weeks if the Parliament and the Council agree) of the expiry of the peroiod granted to the Conciliation Committee, the Council, acting by a qualified majority, confirms its common position which it adopted prior to the start of the conciliation procedure, the default position then becomes that the act is finally adopted. In this confirmation the Council is entitled to vary that common position to take account of amendments proposed by the Parliament.[548] If,

542. On the Parliament's side usually the chairman and/or the *rapporteur* of the relevant committee; on the Council's side, the Presidency.

543. Time runs from the time at which the Committee first meets, Parliament's Rules of Procedure (see note 486, *supra*), Rule 74. As to extension, see *ibid.*, Rule 76. But clearly these time periods have not always worked. Thus a Declaration (No. 34) adopted by the Conference on the occasion of the signature of the Final Act of the Treaty of Amsterdam calls on the European Parliament, the Council and the Commission 'to make every effort to ensure that the co-decision procedure operates as expeditiously as possible.' It moreover recalls the importance of strict respect for the deadlines in Art. 189b EC, and confirms that recourse to extension of those deadlines should be considered only where strictly necessary, and states that in no case should the period between the second reading in the European Parliament and the outcome of the Conciliation Committee exceed nine months.

544. As to the procedure, see *ibid.*, Rule 77.

545. No amendments may be tabled, and the joint text is voted on as a whole, *ibid.*, Rule 77(3) and (4). Parliament on 1 March 1995 thus failed to approve the joint text agreed in by the Conciliation Committee for a directive on the legal protection of biotechnological inventions, Bull. EU 3–1995, points 1.3.17 and 1.10.2, and the proposal fell.

546. This also corresponds to its functioning in the Conciliation Committee; accordingly it matters not whether the Commission agrees with the joint text or not, Art. 189a(1) EC, in conjunction with Art. 189b(4) EC.

547. The Treaty of Amsterdam will make this final, so that the text of the rest of this paragraph will no longer apply.

548. It may well be that conciliation foundered on one or more items, but that the Council had indicated that it could accept some of the Parliament's amendments, hence provi-

though, within six weeks (or eight if the Parliament and the Council agree) of the confirmation by the Council, the Parliament, this time by an absolute majority of its component members, rejects the Council's text, the proposed act is deemed not to have been adopted.[549] At the end of the day, therefore, the Parliament has a right of veto to override unilateral action by the Council, but it can exercise this only if it can muster sufficient support among its members.[550]

Despite the complexity of this procedure, it has undoubtedly led to an significant increase in Parliament's involvement in the legislative process. Thus, although the Council can in practice make its will prevail if conciliation fails, unless the Parliament is indeed able to muster the necessary majority,[551] experience with the budgetary procedure, in which the Parliament has a similar right of veto already showed that the mere existence of the right forces the Council to treat the Parliament with the requisite respect.[552] This right of veto is available on three occasions in this procedure: in the second reading with rejection of the common position, and in the third reading with the failure to approve the joint text agreed by the Conciliation Committee (a negative veto) and with the rejection of the Council's unilateral text adopted after the failure of the Conciliation Committee to agree a joint text. As has been noted in this discussion, the Parliament has made it clear that it is no paper tiger in this (or indeed any) respect. The changes which will be introduced by the Treaty of Amsterdam will in fact make the Parliament a far more equal partner in the co-decision procedure.[553]

Particular controversy surrounds the extent to which the Commission may still exercise its right to withdraw its proposal, as has already been noted in relation to the cooperation procedure.[554] If the Council and the Parliament agree a joint text, that becomes the basis for further action,

sion is made for the Council to give effect to compromises so agreed, or to amendments with which it decides after all to take on board.

549. The Council is invited to justify its decision to the Parliament in plenary session; no amendments may be proposed, and the vote to reject is taken on the text as a whole, Parliament's Rules of Procedure (see note 486, *supra*), Rule 78.

550. *E.g.* on 21 July 1994 the Parliament rejected the Council's confirmation of its common position on the proposed Directive on the application of open network provision (ONP) to voice telephony (Bull. EU 7/8–1994, points 1.2.101 and 1.6.3).

551. But see *ibid.*, Parliament has now shown that it can indeed do this. See, further, Ver-Loren van Themaat (1991) SEW 436 at 447, and the critical observations of Curtin on this procedure (1993) 30 CMLRev. 17 at 41. Dashwood has noted that the name 'co-decision' is not ideal for a procedure which does not give an equal right of final approval to both parties, Wyatt and Dashwood, *op. cit.* (see note 400, *supra*) 42 and (1994) 19 ELRev. 343 at 349. See also the Parliament's Resolution A3–285/92 of 17 December 1992 (O.J. 1993 C 21/138).

552. See section 2.2.4, *ante*.

553. Thus the Council will no longer be able to seek to force through a text on which the Conciliation Committee has been unable to reach agreement.

554. See note 507, *supra*.

and Wyatt and Dashwood take the view that in those circumstances, and also if the Council seeks to push its text through unilaterally after failure of conciliation, the Commission's proposal ceases to be relevant, as the proposal is no longer the basis for action.[555] That is a position at one end of the debate, but, with respect, its merit is certainly less than wholly evident: any act will always in its preamble include the phrase 'having regard to the proposal from the Commission' and, if there is no Commission proposal on the table, there is no basis on which an act can be adopted. But it might be argued that it would amount to a breach of the duty of sincere cooperation if the Commission were to withdraw its proposal after a joint text had been agreed, as this would frustrate the result of the conciliation procedure.[556] On the other hand, a different line might be taken in relation to the Commission's withdrawing a proposal to prevent unilateral action to adopt the Council's text, especially if the Parliament were to request the Commission to withdraw the proposal.[557] On the face of it, though, the wording of Article 189a(2) EC does indeed appear wide enough to support the view that the Commission's right to withdraw a proposal is unfettered.[558] It remains to be seen whether the Court will have an opportunity to consider this matter.

Another unclear matter is the applicable voting requirement if the Council, acting unilaterally following a failure of conciliation, wishes to incorporate amendments proposed by the Parliament. The wording of Article 189b(6) (confirmation by qualified majority of the previously agreed common position prior to conciliation, possibly with amendments

555. *Op. cit.* (see note 400, *supra*) 50. This view is unsurprising in view of Dashwood's experience in the legal service of the Council, and it is understood that this represents the line taken by the Council's legal service.

556. If the Parliament and the Council went ahead and purported to adopt the joint text, with which the Commission disagreed (*e.g.* because in its view it was incompatible with the Treaties), the Commission would undoubtedly consider taking both Institutions to the Court, seeking to annul the act, or, particularly if it had formally withdrawn its proposal on the adoption of the joint text, even, at least in the alternative, to have what purported to be an act declared non-existent. If the Council has approved the joint text adopted after conciliation but the Parliament still has to meet (within the 6 or 8 week period), it is submitted that it would at that stage be impossible for the Commission to withdraw its proposal, as the Council had acted to adopt the act. If the Commission wished to challenge the measure, it would have to take the two Institutions to Court after Parliament had also adopted the measure concerned.

557. At one stage the Parliament wanted the Commission to withdraw its proposal automatically if conciliation failed, but that view now appears to have been modified; the Commission would, though consider any specific request seriously, see Westlake in Edwards and Spence (eds.), *op. cit.* (see note 382, *supra*) 239 at 251. It might be argued against this proposition that it should be left to the Parliament to see if it can muster the requisite majority to reject the Council's text.

558. Usher in Edwards and Spence (*ibid.*) 155 at 156–157 also appears to accept the Commission's view that the wording of Article 189a(2) means withdrawal may take place at any time during the procedure, as long as the Council has not acted.

proposed by the Parliament) supports the view that they may be incorporated by qualified majority, irrespective of whether the Commission were to opine unfavourably on them. But if this were the case, and unanimity were not required for the Council to modify its common position in third reading against the wishes of the Commission, the omission of Article 189b(6) EC from the exceptions specified in Article 189a(1) EC is extraordinary. This time Commission would not have Parliament to throw it the political lifeline of a request to withdraw a proposal, as Parliament would naturally wish to see as many of its amendments incorporated as possible. The Commission's ultimate remedy would seem to be to withdraw the proposal, take the matter to the Court, or both. As a reult of the amendments which the Treaty of Amsterdam will introduce upon its entry into force, the issues discussed in this paragraph will cease to be relevant.

(iv) The Assent procedure. Initially, the changes introduced by the SEA included provision for the assent of the Parliament to be obtained prior to the accession of new Member States[559] and prior to the conclusion of association agreements with third countries.[560] The TEU extended the use of the assent procedure in this latter sphere, so that the requirement of assent specifically for association agreements was replaced by a more wide-ranging requirement of the Parliament's assent to agreements establishing a specific institutional framework by organizing cooperation procedures, agreements having important budgetary implications for the Community, and agreements entailing amendment of acts adopted under the new co-decision procedure.[561] The assent of the Parliament is also required if the Council wishes to adopt provisions with a view to facilitating the exercise of the rights of movement and residence within the territory of the Member states by citizens of the Union;[562] or to confer upon the European Central Bank specific tasks relating to prudential supervision;[563] or to amend certain provisions of the Statute of the European System of Central Banks;[564] to define the tasks, priority objectives and the organization of the Structural Funds or to set up the Cohesion Fund,[565] or, finally, if the

---

559. Now Art. O TEU, previously Art. 237 EEC.
560. Art. 238 EEC.
561. Art. 228(3) EC, 2nd para. As to the development of the Parliament's role in the field of international agreements, see Chapter XII, *post*, and Corbett *et al.*, *op. cit.* (see note 141, *supra*) 212–217. See further, Westlake in Edwards and Spence (eds.), *op. cit.* (see note 382, *supra*) 239 at 252–253.
562. Art. 8a(2) EC. When the Treaty of Amsterdam enters into force these measures will be adopted under the co-decision procedure, with the Council acting unanimously.
563. Art. 105(6) EC (prudential supervision of credit institutions and other financial institutions, except for insurance undertakings).
564. Art. 106(5) EC; Protocol on the Statute of the ESCB and the ECB, Art. 41.1.
565. Art. 130d EC.

Council wishes to lay down the appropriate provisions, which it will recommend to the Member States for adoption in accordance with their respective constitutional requirements, concerning a uniform procedure for direct elections to the European Parliament in all Member States.[566] The assent of Parliament is normally give by a simple majority, although in respect of the accession of new Member States and the uniform procedure for direct elections, Parliament acts by a majority of its component Members.[567] The assent procedure will also apply, once the Treaty of Amsterdam enters into force, if a determination is to be made that a Member State is in 'serious and persistent breach' of the principles mentioned in the revised Article F(1) TEU.[568] Finally, a special form of assent applies in respect of the so-called small amendments of the ECSC Treaty, where the approval of the Parliament, by three-quarters of the votes cast and two-thirds of the members, is required.[569]

3.4.3   The Commission's parliamentary accountability

The Commission is accountable to the Parliament for it's part in decision-making by the Council (as well as for the exercise of its executive powers). Thus the Parliament has an important instrument at its disposal in order to influence such decision-making, to the extent to which the Commission's role therein is substantial. That will be the case if the three essential principles relating to the Commission's function in the decision-making process discussed at the beginning of section 3.3.1, above, are applicable both in theory and in reality. If they are not respected adequately or at all, there is a corresponding restriction of the possibility for the Parliament to exercise influence on the the process of decision-making in the Council through the mechanism of holding the Commission accountable.

Certainly the three principles are not respected in relation to decision-making in the field of economic and monetary policy, as the Council almost always acts on the basis of a recommendation from the Commission, as opposed to a proposal, and the Commission's right of initiative is frequently shared with the European Central Bank.[570] The

---

566. Art. 138(3) EC. In the same terms, Arts. 21(3) ECSC and 108(3) Euratom. The Treaty of Amsterdam will amend these provisions so as to permit the proposal may be for a uniform procedure in all Member States or in accordance with principles common to all Member States.

567. As to the assent procedure in the Parliament, see Rules of Procedure (see note 486, *supra*), Rule 80; in relation to accession treaties, see Rule 89, and as to international agreements requiring Parliament's assent, see Rule 90.

568. See the new Art. F.1(1) TEU, which will be introduced by the Treaty of Amsterdam.

569. Art. 95 ECSC, 4th para. As to the procedure in the Parliament, see Rules of Procedure (see note 486, *supra*), Rule 88.

570. *Cf.* section 3.3.1, *ante*.

principles will not be fully respected if in practice the Commission's right of initiative degenerates into simply giving effect to the political guidelines of the European Council.[571]

The Commission's parliamentary responsibility extends to:

(1) its original proposal to the Council;
(2) the adoption or otherwise of amendments to the proposal suggested in Parliament's opinion to the Council;
(3) the amendments which it makes to its original proposal during Council deliberations in order to facilitate a decision being taken (including taking accepting or rejecting Parliament's amendments at the appropriate stages);
(4) the decision taken by the Council, if, and in so far as this is identical to the proposal, and
(5) the role which it plays during the conciliation process (whether under the conciliation (*concertation*) procedure, or under the co-decision procedure, or in any informal conciliations).

In practice, procedures have gradually developed which, though in some respects still imperfect, do reasonable justice to the Commission's parliamentary responsibility with regard to the first two points. During the preparation of politically important proposals members of the Commission (or its staff) in many cases explain the Commission's intentions in the appropriate parliamentary committees.[572] The Commission always used to send its proposals to the Parliament for information, a few days after they had gone to the Council, but since 1991 it has ensured strict parallelism in the transmission of documents to both of these Institutions, both in content and in timing.[573] Whenever the Council asks Parliament for its opinion on the Commission's proposals (or memoranda) members of the Commission or its staff appear before parliamentary committees to explain and defend the proposals, and this presence continues whenever Parliament is discussing a proposal; the level of representation in the Parliament's committees has, since 1986, been the same as that in the Council's bodies.[574] Since 1970 the Commission informs the Parliament as soon as possible (and if possible during the meeting, but in any case in writing afterwards) of its position on the Parliament's proposed amendments.[575] The Commission has undertaken to explain its refusal to accept amendments proposed by the Parliament and, in so far as it accepts those

---

571. *Ibid.*
572. *Cf.* WQ 157/83 (Pearce) O.J. 1983 C 177/29.
573. This is also expressed in the Code of Conduct agreed between the Parliament and the Commission (O.J. 1995 C 89/69), point 1.
574. Westlake in Edwards and Spence (eds.), *op. cit.* (see note 382, *supra*) 242.
575. *Cf.* WQ 1135/82 (Jackson) O.J. 1982 C 298/18 and the Code of Conduct agreed between the Parliament and the Commission (O.J. 1995 C 89/69), point 3.5.

amendments, to modify its proposal to the Council accordingly.[576] Since 1988, an Annual Legislative Programme has been drawn up; this is agreed by the Presidents of the Parliament and the Commission, on behalf of their respective Institutions; the President of the Council is also invited to take part on behalf of that Institution.[577]

3.4.4   Summarizing remarks

In the reality of institutional power one of the two elements on which the Parliament's ability to influence the decision-making process in the Council is based, identified in section 3.4, above, namely the direct involvement of the Parliament in that process, has been significantly increased in the last two decades. The budgetary powers conferred on the Parliament in 1971 obliged the Council to treat the Parliament as a serious interlocutor, and led to the introduction of the conciliation (*concertation*) procedure in 1975. In contrast to experience with the latter, the cooperation procedure introduced from 1 July 1987, with the coming into force of the SEA has in practice worked very satisfactorily. The co-decision procedures introduced by the TEU, which will be expaned in scope and simplified in application when the Treaty of Amsterdam enters into force have led to new opportunities for the Parliament to influence decision-making in the Council. Finally, the assent procedure, introduced by the SEA, and expanded by the TEU has also significantly increased Parliament's influence.[578]

However, the second element on which the Parliament's influence is based, the accountability of the Commission for its role in the decsion-making process in the Council, has been damaged during the same period. It was never a very secure foundation. The precise influence of the Commission in any negotiations in the Council is still difficult to ascertain. Moreover, the motion of censure as a sanction weapon to call the Commission to account is of limited value in situations in which, as is often the case, the Community interest in having at the end of the day a decision from the Council, however unsatisfactory, prevails over considerations of the actual content of such a decision.

It should be observed, though, that the political links between the Parliament and the Commission, and thus also the political prestige of the Commission have been somewhat strengthened by the TEU, given the

---

576. As to the consequences of the Commission's failure to honour its commitments, see the Parliament's Rules of Procedure (see note 486, *supra*), Rules 61 and 73.
577. See Rules of Procedure, *ibid.*, Rule 49. See also the Code of Conduct agreed between the Parliament and the Commission (O.J. 1995 C 89/69), point 3.2; as to legislative planning, see point 8.
578. The further extension of the assent procedure by the Treaty of Amsterdam will be modest.

structural involvement of the Parliament in the nomination of the person whom the Member States intend to nominate by common accord as President of the Commission, and in the requirement that that person and the nominees for appointment as other members of the Commission receive a vote of approval as a body before they may be appointed.[579] The successful adoption of a motion of censure is thus nowadays less likely than it was in the days when the appointment of a new Commission was exclusively a matter for the common accord of the Member States. Reliance by the Commission on its parliamentary acountability during the negotiations in the course of decision-making by the Council may also thereby attain a more realistic significance.

But in contrast to this latter positive development, stands the erosion of the basis of this second element. More serious than the danger noted in section 3.3.1, above, of a hedging in of the Commission's exclusive right of initiative by intergovernmental political guidelines, on which it is difficult for the Parliament to exert an influence, is the fact that in the field of economic and monetary policy the Council acts under many provisions by qualified majority not on the basis of a proposal from the Commission, but only on the basis of a recommendation, and it may well be that a recommendation from the European Central Bank has already been placed on the Council's table. The Commission cannot be called to account by the Parliament for decisions taken by the Council by qualified majority on the latter basis. Only in two instances is the assent of the Parliament required,[580] the co-decision procedure is not used at all, and in four instances the cooperation procedure is used.[581] In all other instances in the field of economic and monetary policy, a qualified majority in the Council is sufficient to determine that policy, in many cases even without consultation of the Parliament at all, or only on the basis of informing the Parliament, so that there is no parliamentary accountability at Community level, and, as far as the Member States who have been outvoted are concerned, there is no parliamentary accountability possible at national level either. In the system which, prior to the coming into force of the TEU, formed the basis of decision-making in the Council there was, in pretty well all areas, at least a fragmented, albeit only national parliamentary accountability for each member of the Council for Council decisions taken by unanimity. In respect of such decisions adopted by

---

579. Arts. 138(2) EC, 10(2) ECSC, and 127(2) Euratom.
580. Arts. 106(5) EC; Protocol on the Statute of the ESCB and ECB, Art. 41.1 (technical modifications of the Statute of the ESCB and ECB) and Art. 105(6) EC (prudential supervision).
581. Arts. 103(5) (multilateral surveillance of economic policies); 104a(2) (prohibition of public sector privileged access to financial institutions); 104b(2) (prohibition of Community and Member States' liability for public sector commitments and overdraft facilities of (other) Member States), and 105a(2) EC (harmonization of the denominations and technical specifications of coins).

qualified majority, Parliament could always call the Commission to account, as cooperation by the latter was essential for such decisions to be taken. Clear inroads have now been made into this system as a result of the changes made by the TEU. This is to be regretted, not merely from the viewpoint of parliamentary democracy, but also because the interests of the Member States which have been out-voted may come under pressure. The principle that the Council could only deviate from a Commission proposal by unanimity forms a reasonable guarantee for the minority in the Council, as the Commission is obliged to take account of the interests of all the Member States in its proposal (and it is thus logical that a stronger or double qualified majority, based on at least 10 Member States is required when the Council acts by qualified majority where no proposal from the Commission is involved). But when, as the amendments made by the TEU permit, qualified majority decisions are possible despite the Commission's views, this departs from the principle laid down in the *Spaak Report*, of putting the rule of unanimity of governments aside when action was taken at the suggestion of the Commission acting objectively in the general interest.[582] This principle is also neglected in the co-decision procedure, in which qualified majority decisions may be adopted which depart from the Commission proposals which form the basis of the decision-making. In this respect, the strengthening of the Parliament's position is at the expense of that of the Commission, although clearly the Commission has not found this objectionable.[583]

The developments in the SEA and the TEU leading to the greater involvement of the Parliament in the decision-making process of the Community, which it has so long sought, have resulted in the Parliament becoming a real negotiating partner, in addition to the Council and the Commission. It remains highly questionable, though, whether a further development in this process can remove the democratic deficit which is widely perceived to exist within the Community. A number of problems can be identified in this respect. First, no solution is offered for the policy to be pursued by the Council in the context of Economic and monetary Union. This area is, though, not typically legislative in character, and it does not lend itself to the Parliament being continually involved in the decision-making process. But there has been an extremely regrettable regression in this area, now that decisions in this field can be adopted by a qualified majority, without the Commission bearing any responsibility at all for those decisions. Secondly, a parliamentary democracy can only function optimally if important decisions are taken in public, or at the very least if there is clarity about who can be called to account for such

---

582. See Chapter I, section 4.1, *ante*.
583. The observations of the Parliament's committees and the resolution based thereon on the results of the intergovernmental Conferences which culminated in the TEU are silent on this point, see O.J. 1992 C 125/81.

decisions. In that respect, the greater involvement of the Parliament as a negotiating partner founders on the defect of an untransparent decision-making process, in which the Council, uniquely among legislative bodies in at least the western systems, acts to a great extent behind closed doors.

Various crumbs have been thrown in the direction of greater transparency, but it is submitted that they fall several sandwiches short of a picnic, as far as transparent decision-making is concerned. The Inter-institutional Declaration on Democracy, Transparency and Subsidiarity adopted at the Interinstitutional Conference in Luxembourg on 25 October 1993[584] demonstrates that some progress, albeit political, more than legal, is being made. The revised Code of Conduct agreed between the Parliament and the Commission[585] will also help to ensure that the Parliament is better informed about what transpires in the Council. The Council has also agreed to a greater degree of openness as to voting within that Institution.[586] Further steps, of a more legally tangible nature, have been taken in relation to public access to documents.[587] However, the half-hearted nature of the steps so far (even the much-vaunted televised debates in the Council have been decidedly stage-managed discussions of the programme for the forthcoming months, or have been confined to set-piece speeches), while less than wholly satisfactory, is perhaps understandable given the frontiers of the negotiating nature of the decision-making process as presently conceived. It remains the case that little is added to the openness and transparency of the discussions themselves.[588] As is explained in section 8.7 of the epilogue, below, further developments in the direction of transparency have now been agreed at Amsterdam in 1997.

Finally, it may rightly be wondered whether the social and political integration in the Community is sufficiently advanced to offer a basis for a widespread acceptance of decisions based on qualified majority voting in the Council, which have received the acceptance of clear majority of

584. Bull. EC 10–1993, point 2.2.1. See also the Birmingham Declaration (Bull. EC 10–1992, point I.8) and the Conclusions of the Presidency after the Edinburgh and Copenhagen European Councils (Bull. EC 112–1992, points I.24–I.29 and Bull. EC 6–1993, point I.22 respectively). This point also received attention in the Florence European Council (Bull. EU 6–1996, points I.73–I.75).
585. O.J. 1995 C 89/69.
586. Council's Rules of Procedure (see note 8, *supra*), Art. 7(5) and Annex. See, generally, Westlake, *op. cit.* (see note 5, *supra*) 144–154 and 162–163 (and, as to the voting on the proposal to make votes public, the correspondence quoted at 157–158).
587. See the Code of Conduct (O.J. 1993 L 340/41) and, as to the Council, see Dec. 93/731 (O.J. 1993 L 340/43), on which see Case T-194/94 *Carvel et al. v. Council* [1995] ECR II-2765; Case C-58/94 *Netherlands v. Council* [1996] ECR I-2169 Case T-19/96 *Carvel et al. v. Council* [1996] ECR II-1519; Case T-610/97 R *Carlsen et al. v. Council* [1998] ECR II-nyr (3 March 1998), and Case T-174/95 *Svenska Journalist förbundet v. Council* [1998] II-nyr (17 June 1998). As to the Commission, see Dec. 94/90 (O.J. 1994 L 46/58, amended by Dec. 96/567 (O.J. 1996 L 247/45)).
588. See Curtin and Meijers (1995) NJB 158.

members of the European Parliament, as is possible under the co-decision procedure, without the Commission being able to offer the guarantee of a balanced promotion of the reasonable interests of *all* the Member States.[589] As the Court has noted long ago in the context of agriculture, the very idea of the Community means that 'the Member States should emphasize their interests, whilst it falls to the Commission to arbitrate, through the measures taken by it, between possible conflicts of interest from the point of view of the general interest.'[590] If it is desired to reduce the democratic deficit, attention will have to be paid, not only to making the Parliament a real Community co-legislator (which may be less politically opportune in the eyes of national interests at least at present), but also (and these steps are perhaps more urgently needed) to strengthening the position of the Commission in the process of decision-making in the Council, ensuring that the Commission is indeed accountable to the Parliament for its then enlarged role in that decision-making process, ensuring broad support in the Parliament for the policy which the Commission pursues, and introducing an exclusive right of initiative for the Commission in the context of economic and monetary policy, although this in latter case the Commission will have to take account of the independence of the European Central Bank and its right to make its views known.[591]

---

589. As to the legitimacy of such decisions, see Weiler (1991) YLJ 2403, especially at 2466–2474.
590. Case 57/72 *Westzucker GmbH v. Einfuhr- und Vorratsstelle für Zucker* [1973] ECR 321 at 341 (actually in the context of the management committee procedure).
591. See Gormley and De Haan (1996) 21 ELRev. 95, and literature cited there.

CHAPTER VI

Administration of Justice*

1. THE COURT OF JUSTICE

As has been explained in section 7.1 of Chapter IV, above, the powers of the Court as an Institution are now exercised by two bodies, the original Court of Justice itself and the Court of First Instance which was subsequently attached to it. In the discussion in this chapter, references to the Court embrace the Court of First Instance in respect of those matters in which it exercises at first instance the jurisdiction of the Court, in accordance with the allocation of competence under the decision taken in pursuance of Article 168a(2) EC.[1]

In the context of a general introduction only limited space can be given to the discussion of the conditions under which and the way in which the Court exercises its multifarious jurisdiction, as outlined in section 7.2.2 of Chapter IV, above. The present discussion deals only with those procedures which concern the core of the Court's jurisdiction and which require the Court to judge whether the acts and omissions of the Member States (section 1.1) and the Institutions (section 1.2) are in conformity with Community law. Special attention will be devoted to the right of action of private parties against Community measures (section 1.3), including a brief examination of the possibilities for individuals to bring actions for damages before the Court on the ground of the Community's non-contractual liability (section 1.3.3). The activities of the Court in the field of preliminary rulings, which also belong to the core of its jurisdiction, will be

---

* In the Fifth Dutch edition of this work, this chapter was revised by P.J.G. Kapteyn. This edition has been further revised by the editor, taking on board those revisions by Kapteyn and maintaining relevant additions from the last English edition, but taking substantial additional account of literature, case-law and practice, as well as of more recent developments.
1. And Arts. 32d ECSC and 140a Euratom. See Dec. 88/591 (O.J. 1988 L 319/1, corrected version in O.J. 1989 C 215/1), amended by Dec. 93/350 (O.J. 1993 L 144/21), which latter decision was in turn amended by Dec. 94/149 (O.J. 1994 L 66/29). As to literature, see Chapter IV, section 7.2, *supra*. See also Plender (ed.), *European Courts Practice and Precedents* (London, 1997).

discussed in the next section of this Chapter, in the context of the co-operation between the Court and the national courts (section 2.1).

1.1 Supervision of the acts of Member States: actions for infringement of the Treaty

In the procedures which may lead to a pronouncement of the Court on the question whether a Member State has failed to fulfil one of its obligations under the Treaty a very important function has been assigned to the Commission.[2] Although, at least in the EC and Euratom systems, the Member States themselves may also take the initiative for such a procedure,[3] in practice they have tended to leave this initiative almost entirely to the Commission, which, being an impartial body, is preeminently suited for this.[4]

2. Arts. 169–170 EC, 88 ECSC, and 141–142 Euratom. Individuals cannot force the Commission to bring Art. 169 EC proceedings, see *e.g.* Case 48/65 *Alfons Lütticke GmbH et al. v. Commission* [1966] ECR 19 at 27; Case 247/87 *Star Fruit Company SA v. Commission* [1989] ECR 291 at 301; Case T-13/94 *Century Oils Hellas AE v. Commission* [1994] ECR II-431 at 437–438 and Case T-47/96 *Syndicat Départemental de Défense du Droit des Agriculteurs (SDDDA) v. Commission* [1996] ECR II-1559 at 1575. The Commission thus has a discretion whether or not (and, if so, when) to open proceedings (and against whom and in what order), see Case 7/68 *Commission v. Italy* [1968] ECR 423 at 428; Case 7/71 *Commission v. France* [1975] ECR 1003 at 1016; and Evans (1979) 4 ELRev. 442. As to possible liability as a result of such conduct by the Commission see Case 9/75 *Meyer-Burckhardt v. Commission* [1975] ECR 1171 at 1189 (Warner, Adv. Gen.) and Case 14/78 *Denkavit Srl et al. v. Commission* [1978] ECR 2497 at 2505. As to the distinction between infringement proceedings and Commission action suspending or removing assistance under the Structural Funds, see Case T-461/93 *An Taisce – The National Trust for Ireland et al. v. Commission* [1994] ECR II-733 at 749–750 (appeal dismissed as clearly unfounded, Case C-325/94 P *An Taisce – The National Trust for Ireland et al. v. Commission* [1996] ECR I-3727).
   The Council of the European Central Bank (until 1 January 1999, the Council of the European Monetary Institute, Art. 109(f)(9) EC) exercises identical powers to those of the Commission under Art. 169 EC, in infringement proceedings brought under Art. 180(d) EC relating to the fulfillment by national central banks of their obligations; the Board of Directors of the European Investment Bank enjoys similar powers in respect of the fulfillment by Member States of their appropriate obligations, Art. 180(a) EC.
3. Before a procedure under Arts. 170 EC or 142 Euratom can get to Court the complaining Member State must bring the matter before the Commission which has to deliver a reasoned opinion after each of the States involved has had the opportunity to submit both oral and written observations on its own case and the other party's; if no reasoned opinion has been delivered within three months of the matter being brought before the Commission the matter may go directly to the Court notwithstanding the absence of the reasoned opinion.
4. These complaints do not normally get as far as the Court but for one which did see Case 141/78 *France v. United Kingdom* [1979] ECR 2923. The specific supervisory task of ensuring that the Treaty provisions and the measures taken by the Institutions pursuant thereto are applied is the first of the Commission's tasks, Arts. 155 EC and 124

In the first stage the procedure initiated by the Commission has an administrative character[5] and is intended to give the Member State the opportunity of justifying its behaviour or legislation and to give the Commission, in appropriate cases, the chance of persuading the Member State to comply with the provisions of the Treaty of its own volition.[6] Although no less an authority than Advocate General Roemer has pointed out that the object of the procedure is not to attach moral blame but to clarify the legal position to enable the state concerned to stay on the path of legality[7] it has to be said that some Member States do not regard infringement proceedings in this light, and that the degree of national sensitivity is not infrequently high. If the Commission, in the light of the information it has received and gathered[8] is of the view that a Member State has failed to fulfil the obligations imposed on it by the Treaties themselves or the measures for their implementation, it must give this state a prior opportunity to submit its observations. This is done in a letter designed to set out the points at issue and to put the state in a position in which it can prepare its defence.[9] The fact that the Member State is given

Euratom. The Commission's sole duty under Art. 8 ECSC is to ensure that the objectives set out in that Treaty are attained in accordance with the provisions thereof.

5. Under Arts. 93(2), 100A(4) and 225 EC the Commission may bring the matter directly to the Court of Justice without going through the normal Art. 169 or 170 EC procedure (the right is also available to any interested Member State under Art. 93(2) and to any Member State under Arts. 100A(4) and 225 EC; see also Arts. 38 and 92 Euratom). For the procedure under Art. 93(2) EC applicable when the Commission (or an interested Member State) regards a national state aid measure as being incompatible with the common market, see Chapter VIII, sections 3.2.2 and 2.2.3, *post*. The powers of the Council of the European Central Bank (ECB) under Art. 180(d) EC are exercised during the second stage of Economic and Monetary Union by the European Monetary Institute (EMI), Art. 109f(9) EC. These powers are those of the Commission under Art. 169 EC. The Board of Directors of the European Investment Bank (EIB) also enjoys these powers under Art. 180(a) EC.
6. *E.g.* Cases 142 and 143/80 *Amministrazione delle Finanze dello Stato v. Essevi SpA et al.* [1981] ECR 1413 at 1432–1433.
7. Case 7/71 *Commission v. France* [1971] ECR 1003 at 1034, see also Gand, Adv. Gen. in Case 77/69 *Commission v. Belgium* [1970] ECR 237 at 247, and, generally, Audretsch, *Supervision in European Community Law* (2nd ed., Amsterdam, 1986) 110–112. It has been observed that infringement procedures are brought in the interest of the public order of the Communities (Louis in *Miscellanea W.J. Ganshof van der Meersch* (Brussels, 1972) Vol. II 225 at 237). See, further, Brown and Kennedy, *The Court of Justice of the European Communities* (4th ed., London, 1995, with 1995 suppl.) 105–122; Lasok and Millett in Vaughan (ed.), *Law of the European Communities Service* (London, loose-leaf, since 1990) Part 2, paras. 82–161, and Timmermans and Van Rijn in Curtin and Heukels (eds.), *Institutional Dynamics of European Integration* (Essays in honour of Schermers, Vol. II, Dordrecht, 1994) 391 and 409 respectively.
8. See Chapter IV, section 4.3.3, *ante*. The overwhelming majority of complaints to the Commission or of the dossiers opened on the Commission's own initiative (*cas décélé d'office*) are in fact resolved without the need for formal action.
9. Case 211/81 *Commission v. Denmark* [1982] ECR 4547 at 4557. In practice the Art. 169 letter (*lettre de mise en demeure*) is signed by a Commissioner (after the Commission has

such an opportunity is considered an essential guarantee by the Court. Non-observance of it constitutes an infringement of an essential procedural requirement.[10] The Commission, therefore, is not free to request the Court in the later (judicial) stage of the procedure to pronounce on a failure of the Member State which has not been or could not be mentioned in the administrative stage of the procedure.[11] In complicated cases from the viewpoint of the interpretation of law and facts the dialogue between Commission and Member State on the question whether an infringement has or has not occurred may take a good deal of time. In a great many cases the deliberations tend to lead to the Member State either convincing the Commission that it is mistaken or remedying its failure in a way that is satisfactory to the Commission. The procedure has then achieved its purpose.

If the Member State refuses to put an end to the infringement and the Commission adheres to its original view, the Commission then decides on

decided to open proceedings) but it need not be and a satisfactory letter which puts the Member State in a position in which it can set out its defence will do. The draft letter is prepared by the directorate general responsible, and sent to the legal service for its opinion; and any other services which may be involved are also consulted, as is the *cabinet* of the member of the Commission responsible. On receipt of the favourable opinion or comments of the legal service and the replies to the other consultations, the draft (as amended if necessary) is sent to the *cabinet*; a copy is sent to the secretariat general, which prepares the letter for signature. The letter is addressed to the Foreign Minister of the Member State concerned and is delivered to its permanent representation in Brussels, which then sends it on.

10. *E.g.* Case 293/85 *Commission v. Belgium* [1988] ECR 305 at 352 and Case C-306/91 *Commission v. Italy* [1993] ECR I-2133 at 2158–2159.

11. Case 31/69 *Commission v. Italy* [1970] ECR 25 at 33; Case 7/69 *Commission v. Italy* [1970] ECR 111 at 117; Case 51/83 *Commission v. Italy* [1984] ECR 2793 at 2804. See also Case C-47/88 *Commission v. Denmark* [1990] ECR I-4509 at 4534 (the Court will not deal with a possible infringement of a different provision than that which is the subject-matter of the action). It is possible (if it later becomes apparent that the alleged infringement is more extensive, or if new aspects emerge which have not been dealt with in the Art. 169 EC letter, or if on reflection it is felt that the letter was not detailed enough) to send a supplementary Art. 169 letter and then to continue on that basis, although if a reasoned opinion was already sent in the meantime, a new reasoned opinion, taking account of the reply, if any, to the supplementary letter, will be necessary before the action so extended can be brought to the Court, see *e.g.* Case 211/81 *Commission v. Denmark* [1982] ECR 4547 at 4558.

Deadlines for replying may be short but they must be reasonable, taking account of all the circumstances of the case, Case 293/85 *Commission v. Belgium* [1988] ECR 305 at 352. Thus very short periods may be justified, particularly where there is an urgent need to remedy a breach, or where the Member State concerned is fully aware of the Commission's views before the procedure starts, *ibid*. The attention paid to this point must be seen in the light of the fact that the Court gave judgment on the same day on two references for a preliminary ruling dealing with the same problem, thus it could give a remedy and at the same time remind the Commission of the need to be reasonable in its dealings with national administrations (see Case 309/85 *Barra v. Belgian State et al.* [1988] ECR 355 and Case 24/86 *Blaizot v. University of Liège et al.* [1988] ECR 379).

its final position. In the EC and Euratom systems this is done by means of a (non-binding) reasoned opinion which serves to define the dispute.[12] The Commission sets out its views, giving the reasons for them[13] and invites the Member State to take the appropriate measures[14] within a period which the Commission fixes[15] to remedy its default. A reasoned opinion has legal consequences only in relation to bringing the matter to the Court in the context of the proceedings which have been initiated.[16] If the Member State does not comply with the reasoned opinion within the given period the Commission may bring the matter before the Court. It is for the Commission to decide at which moment it wishes to do this.[17] The

12. Cases 142 and 143/80 *Amministrazione delle Finanze dello Stato v. Essevi et al.* [1981] ECR 1413 at 1432–1433. The reasoned opinion is drafted by the Legal Service (often heavily drawing on the Art. 169 letter) and sent to the directorate general responsible for its agreement. In the light of the observations made by it and any other services consulted, the agreed draft is forwarded by the directorate general to the *cabinet* of the member of the Commission responsible, and a copy is sent to the secretariat general. The latter then prepares the formal version for signature by the relevant member of the Commission, and the reasoned opinion, duly signed and addressed to the Foreign Minister of the Member State concerned, is sent to its permanent representation for onward transmission. In Case C-191/95 *Commission v. Germany* (pending, O.J. 1995 C 208/15) the German government has argued that procedural deficiencies in the decision-making process should lead to the proceedings being ruled inadmissible (see the opinion of Cosmas, Adv. Gen., 17 February 1998).
13. *I.e.* the reasoned opinion must contain 'a coherent statement of the reasons which led the Commission to believe that the state in question has failed to fulfil an obligation under the Treaty', Case 7/61 *Commission v. Italy* [1961] ECR 317 at 327.
14. These may, in appropriate cases, be specified, Case 70/72 *Commission v. Germany* [1973] ECR 813 at 828–829; however the Commission is not obliged to indicate what specific action should be taken, Case C-247/89 *Commission v. Portugal* [1991] ECR I-3659 at 3689.
15. As to deadlines, see note 11, *supra*. In practice, the Commission will usually give two months, although a period of one month or even less is not unknown in urgent cases. Similar practice applies in respect of the Art. 169 EC letter. As to the difficulties which breakdowns in communication may cause, see the order in Case C-266/94 *Commission v. Spain* [1995] ECR I-1975.
16. Any temporary indulgence granted by the Commission in the course of Art. 169 EC proceedings (or otherwise) cannot change the obligations of the Member States under the Treaty and cannot preclude individuals from relying on rights conferred upon them by the Treaty in order to challenge any legislative or administrative measures of a Member State which may be incompatible with Community law, Cases 142 and 143/80 *Amministrazione delle Finanze dello Stato v. Essevi et al.* [1981] ECR 1413 at 1433.
17. Case 7/68 *Commission v. Italy* [1968] ECR 423 at 428; Case 7/71 *Commission v. France* [1971] ECR 1003 at 1016. The time between the infringement taking place or commencing and being brought to the Court can vary enormously: anything from one month in Case 61/77 *Commission v. Ireland* [1978] ECR 417, [1978] 2 CMLR 466 to five years in Case 7/71 *Commission v. France* [1971] ECR 1003, [1972] CMLR 453 and even more than six years in Case C-422/92 *Commission v. Germany* [1995] ECR I-1097 (a fact which did not go unremarked, at 1130–1131). The average time is between four and 12 months. The Court has noted that the excessive duration of the pre-litigation procedure may make it more difficult for the Member State concerned to rebut the Com-

Commission does not have to show the existence of a legal interest 'since, in the general interest of the Community, its function is to ensure that the provisions of the Treaty are applied by the Member States and to note the existence of any failure to fulfil the obligations deriving therefrom, with an view to bringing it to an end.'[18] The Commission must always ensure that its reasoned opinion and its application to the Court for a finding that a Member State has failed to fulfil its obligations under a particular provision of Community law are based on the same grounds, arguments and submissions.[19]

In the ECSC system, on the other hand, the Commission itself establishes in a binding form the Member State's failure in a 'reasoned decision'[20] in which the Member State is required to fulfil its obligations within a given period. The Member State may appeal to the Court, but the latter does not automatically suspend the period within which the decision has to be executed.[21] The decision by which the Commission establishes a failure in the ECSC system has a declaratory character.[22] It cannot impose on a Member State any obligations other than those already incumbent on it by virtue of the Treaty. The Commission cannot derive from Article 88 ECSC any implied power to create new obligations, since the procedure involved here is 'a procedure far exceeding the rules heretofore recognized in classical international law to ensure that obligations of States are fulfilled', so that this Article must be strictly interpreted.'[23]

mission's arguments, and may thus infringe the rights of the defence, see Case C-96/89 *Commission v. The Netherlands* [1991] ECR I-2461 at 2492, although in that instance, and in Case C-422/92, *loc. cit.*, it upheld the Commission's discretion, in the latter case holding that it was not for the Court to review that discretion. This appears to represent a return to absolutism, as opposed to the small chink which Case C-96/89 appeared to offer (albeit requiring a very heavy burden of proof). The Commission may well wish to use salami tactics, taking proceedings first against one or two Member States, and starting proceedings against others when the first group is at a more advanced stage, as it can be difficult to persuade the *chefs de cabinet* to support taking action against most or all of the Member States at the same time, see, generally, Case C-235/89 *Commission v. Italy* [1992] ECR I-777 at 797 and 799–804, and Case C-30/90 *Commission v. United Kingdom* [1992] ECR I-829 at 850–855. See, further, Schermers and Waelbroeck, *Judicial Protection in the European Communities* (5th ed., Deventer, 1992) 284–286.

18. Case 167/73 *Commission v. France* [1974] ECR 359 at 368–369.
19. *E.g.* Case C-217/88 *Commission v. Germany* [1990] ECR I-2879 at 2902; Case C-347/88 *Commission v. Greece* [1990] ECR I-4747 at 4784; Case C-52/90 *Commission v. Denmark* [1992] ECR I-2187 at 2213–2215, and Case C-243/89 *Commission v. Denmark* [1993] ECR I-3353 at 3389–3391.
20. Art. 88 ECSC. The Court has also recognized the power of the Commission to remind Member States of their obligations by means of a recommendation. If they fail to heed the recommendation then Art. 88 ECSC proceedings may be commenced: Case 25/59 *Netherlands v. High Authority* [1960] ECR 355 at 374.
21. Case 3/59 *Germany v. High Authority* [1960] ECR 53 at 58–59.
22. *Ibid.* at 60.
23. Case 25/59 *The Netherlands v. High Authority* [1960] ECR 355 at 374–375.

It is relatively seldom that such cases will lead to a lawsuit. The procedure is clearly intended to avoid rather than obtain a condemnation of the defaulting state. The number of actual judgments of the Court on infringement proceedings is considerably smaller than the number of cases in which the Commission deals with matters relating to the failure of Member States to fulfil obligations under the Treaty. The judgments of the Court form the tip of an iceberg: in most cases an amicable settlement is reached before the matter goes to the Court.[24] Sometimes a Member State climbs down after a case has gone to the Court but before judgment; in such circumstances the Commission usually withdraws its application, asking for the Court to remove the case from its register.[25] It should be noted that although an order as to costs is always requested in infringement proceedings the Commission and the Member States do not in practice claim costs from each other; the effect is more psychological than real and in cases in which each of the parties may have 'won' various points the Court frequently decides that each party will bear its own costs. In infringement proceedings the order as to costs is purely academic. In the

24. Up to the end of 1978 there had been some 750 infringement proceedings commenced of which some 6% resulted in judgment by the Court, but the number of proceedings has on trend seen an increase of substantial proportions. Thus in 1982 335 proceedings were commenced, rising to 572 in 1987, 1,217 in 1992, 1,016 in 1995, and 1142 in 1996. Although the figures as such are not strictly comparable (proceedings commenced in one year do not necessarily go to the next stage in the same year) the figures for reasoned opinions in these years were 157, 197, 248, 192 and 435 respectively (with a peak in 1994 of 546 reasoned opinions). For cases brought to the Court for infringement the figures were 45, 61, 64, 72 and 92 respectively (again, there was a peak in 1994 of 89) and for judgments handed down the figures were 31, 42, 50, 39 and 46 respectively. In the *General Report 1995* (Brussels, Luxembourg, 1996) the Commission noted that the fact that 1,336 infringement proceedings had been terminated during that year bore witness 'to the effectiveness of the pre-litigation procedure, the aim of which is to remedy the infringement without the need for full contentious proceedings. See, generally, Schermers and Waelbroeck, *op. cit.* (see note 17, *supra*) 255 and the annual Reports to the European Parliament on Commission monitoring of the application of Community law (see Chapter V, note 68, *ante*). For 1997 the figures given in the *General Report 1997* ((Brussels, Luxembourg, 1998) point 1106 and Table 24 were 1,422 infringement proceedings opened; 331 reasoned opinions and 121 cases brought to the Court of Justice; 46 judgments were handed down in Art. 169 EC actions in that year. See further, Ehlermann in Grewe *et al.* (eds.), *Europäische Gerichtsbarkeit und nationale Verfassungsgerichtsbarkeit* (*Festschrift* for Kutscher, Baden-Baden, 1981) 135; Everling (1984) 9 ELRev. 215, and the contributions by Ehlermann and Louis in Capotorti *et al.* (eds.) *Du droit international au droit de l'intégration* (*Liber Amicorum* Pescatore, Baden-Baden, 1987) 205 and 387.

25. *E.g.* Case 301/84 *Commission v. United Kingdom* (O.J. 1985 C 40/4, removed from the register, O.J. 1985 C 275/6) on 'buy-British' preferential car purchase loan schemes applied by local authorities. Some had climbed down before the case was taken to Court but the last was recalcitrant and did not climb down until later. As to the sensitivities which may be involved, see the order in Case C-120/94 *Commission v. Greece* [1996] ECR I-1513 at 1537–1540 (withdrawal after the Adv. Gen. had given his opinion).

past the Commission appeared to bring infringement proceedings on a specimen basis although in the mid to late Eighties and in the early Nineties they have were pursued rather more systematically. In particular in the field of the free movement of goods the major cases were almost always the result of references under Article 177 EC until the end of the Seventies. The pursuit of failure to implement directives has also tightened up considerably.[26] It is unfortunately true that one of the defects in the Article 169 EC procedure is that swift action is not assisted by the procedural steps which have to be gone through before a case can be brought to the Court. There is a need for a procedure to be set up which would allow rapid intervention, if necessary *ex parte*, without prior formalities by the Commission to remedy problems encountered by persons seeking to use their rights under Community law. There has in the last few years been a noticeable cooling in the enthusiasm of the Commission to act in effect as a free representation unit for all and sundry who complain.[27] A greater selectivity in pursuing complaints has been accompanied by greater encouragement of complainants to seek their remedy in national courts, even though their approach to remedies for breach of Community law may on occasions resemble an unguided missile. In a climate in which the 'big stick' approach to supervision is less politically popular than ever, complainants faced with reluctance on the part of the Commission to take up a case (sometimes reflecting political pressure or even deals) may also be faced by misunderstanding or little sympathy in national fora, particularly when challenging national sacred cows. It may be thought that this scarcely promotes confidence in the business community and among individuals in the much-vaunted opening up of the common or even internal markets. It is respectfully submitted that a strengthening of the Commission's guardian role in the Community interest by a rapid intervention mechanism is not merely desirable but also essential.

The action which, in the EC and Euratom systems, the Commission may lodge with the Court of Justice when its reasoned opinion is not complied

26. See the various annual Reports mentioned in note 24, *supra*. See, generally Ciavarini Azzi (ed.) *L'Application du Droit Communautaire par les États Membres* (Maastricht, 1985) and, for the United Kindgom, the general observations in Gormley (1986) 23 CMLRev. 287 at 312 *et seq.* (in German (1987) EuR 359 at 374 *et seq.*); see, further, Barnard and Greaves (1994) 31 CMLRev. 1055; the frequent surveys by Dutheil de la Rochère and Grief, *e.g.* (1993) RTDE 65 and 665 and (1995) RTDE 805; Dutheil de la Rochère, Grief and Jarvis (1996) 32 RTDE 717 and (1998) RTDE 93, and Daintith (ed.), *Implementing EC Law in the United Kingdom* (Chichester, 1995). As to France, see also Roseren (1994) 31 CMLRev. 315. See also Curtin and Mortelmans in Curtin and Heukels (eds.), *op. cit.* (see note 7, *supra*) 423 and literature cited there.

27. In part this reflects the greater focus on the business of getting legislation through the decision-making procedures. But the same tendency is also true in the way the Commission's approach to competition law has developed, see the Commission's *Notice on Cooperation between National Courts and the Commission in applying Articles 85 and 86 of the EEC Treaty* O.J. 1993 C 39/6.

with, and the appeal which in the ECSC system a Member State may bring against the decision of the Commission, both fall under the Court's 'unlimited' jurisdiction.[28] This means that the Court must judge the behaviour of the Member State as a whole and, in so doing, must take into account all relevant facts, such as the question of whether in the given circumstances the State has been given sufficient time to take the appropriate measures for remedying its failure.[29] The question as to whether the State has failed to fulfil its obligations is of course decided by the Court in accordance with the strict standards of law. The conciliatory administrative stage of the procedure is then at an end: even if the Member State ultimately fulfil its obligation in accordance with the opinion of the Commission, the judicial procedure is continued if the Commission, for instance with a view to the risk of recidivism, has an interest in 'obtaining a declaration by the Court whether the failure has or has not occurred.'[30] However, sometimes there may well be an interest in pursuing the action, particularly if the Commission knows that individuals will be able to claim damages, invoking the judgment, before their national courts, or if the point of law involved is of more general application.[31]

If the action is directed against a decision of the Commission (in the ECSC system) the Court, depending on its findings, may either dismiss the action or annul the decision or, if the latter specifies the measures to be taken by the State, annul or modify it on this point.[32] If the action is brought by the Commission (in the EC and Euratom systems) and is not dismissed by the Court, the latter will rule in its judgment that the Member State has failed to fulfil its obligations. In that case the State is obliged to take the necessary measures to comply with the judgment.[33] The process of compliance must, in the interest of the immediate and uniform

28. See Schermers and Waelbroeck, *op. cit.* (see note 17, *supra*) 281. Unlimited jurisdiction means that the Court can look at all the arguments and replace the decision by another one; the applicant does not have to demonstrate a specific head of illegality.
29. See Case 293/85 *Commission v. Belgium* [1988] ECR 305 at 352.
30. Case 7/61 *Commission v. Italy* [1961] ECR 317 at 326; see also Case 26/69 *Commission v. France* [1970] ECR 565 at 575–576 (although most of the time the Commission will withdraw the action (see note 25, *supra*)).
31. The interest of this point was recognized as long ago as 1973 in Case 39/72 *Commission v. Italy* [1973] ECR 112 at 112. See also *e.g.* Case 240/86 *Commission v. Greece* [1988] ECR 1835 at 1855–1856 and Case C-263/88 *Commission v. France* [1990] ECR I-4611 at 4623. As to damages in national courts for breach of Community law, see section 2.3.2, *post*. In Cases C-46 and 48/93 *Brasserie de Pêcheur SA et al. v. Germany et al.* [1996] ECR I-1029 at 1159–1160 the Court stated (citing the judgment in Cases 314–316/81 and 83/82 *Procureur de la République et al. v. Waterkeyn et al.* [1982] ECR 4337 at 4361) that '[r]ights arising for individuals out of Community provisions cannot depend on the Commission's assessment of the expediency of taking action against a Member State pursuant to Art. 169 of the Treaty or on the delivery by the Court of any judgment finding an infringement'.
32. Case 3/59 *Germany v. High Authority* [1960] ECR 53 at 60.
33. Arts. 171(1) EC and 143(1) Euratom.

application of Community law, be initiated immediately and must be completed as soon as possible.[34] For the competent national authorities (a term which includes national courts) this entails a prohibition 'against applying a national rule recognized as incompatible with the Treaty and, if the circumstances so require, an obligation on them to take all appropriate measures to enable Community law to be fully applied.'[35] The Court's judgments do not themselves have direct effect but if the Court finds that a Member State has failed to fulfil its obligations under a directly effective provision of Community law, it is the duty of a national court to draw the necessary inferences from that judgment, for example by refusing to apply national provisions incompatible with those obligations.[36] A judgment can, moreover, form the basis for 'a responsibility that a Member State can incur as a result of its default, as regards other Member States, the Community or private parties.'[37] It should be noted that an order of a national court may constitute a measure incompatible with Articles 30 or 34 EC,[38] although it is unlikely that the Commission would commence infringement proceedings against a Member State because of a ruling of a national court as this would be likely to prejudice judicial co-operation in relation to Community law; the one exception (at least in recent years) has been in relation to the Hoechst inspection affair in which the order of the national court effectively attacked the Commission's own powers.[39]

---

34. See Case 169/87 *Commission v. France* [1988] ECR 4093 at 4118; Case C-328/90 *Commission v. Greece* [1992] ECR I-425 at 437, and Case C-101/91 *Commission v. Italy* [1993] ECR I-191 at 206.

35. *E.g.* Case 48/71 *Commission v. Italy* [1972] ECR 527 at 532; Cases 24 and 97/80R *Commission v. France* [1980] ECR 1319 at 1333, and Case C-101/91 *Commission v. Italy* [1993] ECR I-191 at 205–206. See also, more generally, Case 249/85 *ALBAKO Margarinefabrik Maria von der Linde GmbH & Co. KG v. Bundesanstalt für landwirtschaftliche Marktordnung* [1987] ECR 2345 at 2359–2360. See (earlier) Nicolaysen (1985) EuR 368 and Temple Lang, *The duties of national courts under the constitutional law of the European Community* (Dominik Lasok Lecture 1987, Exeter, 1987), and more recently, Temple Lang (1997) 22 ELRev. 3.

36. Cases 314–316/81 and 83/82 *Procureur de la République et al. v. Waterkeyn et al.* [1982] ECR 4337 at 4360–4361.

37. Case 39/72 *Commission v. Italy* [1973] ECR 101 at 112. See section 2.3.2, *post*.

38. Case 58/80 *Dansk Supermarked A/S v. A/S Imerco* [1982] ECR 181 at 194; Case 6/81 *BV Industrie Diensten Groep v. J.A.Beele Handelmaatschappij BV* [1982] ECR 707 at 716, and Case C-313/94 *F.lli Graffione SNC v. Ditta Fransa* [1996] ECR I-6039 at 6057.

39. As to the application for interim measures attacking the decision ordering Hoechst to submit to inspection see Case 46/87R *Hoechst AG v. Commission* [1987] ECR 1549, [1988] 4 CMLR 430. The Commission's case against Germany went to the reasoned opinion but the proceedings were then effectively suspended pending the outcome of Case 46/87 *Hoechst* [1989] ECR 2859, [1991] 4 CMLR 410 and then not taken any further, as the Commission felt that the point had been made. The question of the advisability of commencing proceedings in such cases has been raised on various occasions in reaction to judgments of the French Conseil d'État. The Commission always took the view that proceedings were possible but inopportune. See WQs 100/67

In practice the implementation of the judgments of the Court of Justice has never been downfaced by a categorical and definitive refusal to comply by the Member State concerned. However, the number of instances in which the procedure for failure to take measures to comply with a judgment of the Court has had to be initiated has dramatically increased in recent years.[40] It has been repeatedly necessary for the Court to hand down a second judgment in which the failure to comply with Article 171 EC is established.[41] The cause of the failure by the Member States to fulfil its obligations is often to be found in the need for long drawn-out and difficult legislative procedures involved.[42]

If, in the ECSC system, a Member State does not fulfil its obligations within the period laid down in the decision, or if its appeal against the decision is dismissed, the Community may take sanctions against it.[43] The old EEC Treaty made no provision for organized sanctions, which was widely regarded as one of the fundamental weaknesses in the Community system.[44] In fact no sanctions were ever applied in the ECSC system. It is perhaps one of the most remarkable achievements of the TEU that Article 171 EC now makes provision for the imposition by the Court of Justice of a lump sum or penalty payment on the defaulting Member State, if the latter is indeed found not to have taken the necessary measures to comply with the earlier judgment. The hope is that this will act as a yet further incentive against non-compliance.[45] If the administrative phase of the

(Westerterp) O.J. 1967 276/12; 28/68 (Deringer) O.J. 1968 C71/1; 349/69 (Westerterp) O.J. 1970 C20/4; 608/78 (Krieg) O.J. 1979 C28/8 and, further, WQs 414/74 and 23/75 (Cousté) O.J. 1975 C54/1 and 161/11. See also Lauwaars in Schermers et al., *Rechtsbescherming in de Europese Gemeenschappen* (Deventer, 1975) 37 at 63–64 and Audretsch, *op. cit.* (see note 7, *supra*) 100–103 for a more extensive discussion of the general point. The main concern appears to be a desire not to endanger the judicial cooperation between the Court of Justice and national courts which has developed in the context of Art. 177 EC. The independence of the judiciary has also been borne in mind, although the binding nature of Community law applies in respect of judicial activities, just as it does in respect of other actions by or attributable to the State, see (recently restating the already firmly established proposition) Cases C-46/93 and 48/93 *Brasserie du Pêcheur SA et al. v. Germany et al.* [1996] ECR I-1029 at 1145.

40. The details can be traced in the annual Reports on the application of Community law (see note 24, *supra*).

41. Spectacular examples include Cases 227–230/85 *Commission v. Belgium* [1988] ECR 1, [1989] 2 CMLR 797; Case 169/87 *Commission v. France* [1988] ECR 4093; Case C-75/91 *Commission v. The Netherlands* [1992] ECR I-549, and Case C-291/93 *Commission v. Italy* [1994] ECR I-859.

42. Particular efforts have been made in Italy (a regular client of the Court in Art. 169 proceedings in particular) by the introduction of the 'La Pergola Law' which aimed to improve the effective implementation of Community law (not simply compliance with judgments), see Gaja (1990) 27 CMLRev. 83, although the expectations appear to have been underwhelmed by the results.

43. Art. 88 ECSC (3rd–5th paras.).

44. For an analysis of the problem, and possible solutions, see Bull. EC Supp. 2/91, 151 *et seq.*

45. In addition to the earlier steps taken by the Court, relating to the principle of the

infringement procedure under Articles 171(2) EC or 143(2) Euratom for infringement of Articles 171(1) or 143(1) respectively goes to the reasoned opinion,[46] continued non-compliance after the deadline set out in the reasoned opinion may result in the Commission bringing the matter to the Court of Justice. Here, as with other infringement proceedings, the Commission has a discretion. If it exercises that discretion to go to the Court, the Commission is now obliged to specify, in its application to the Court, the amount of the lump sum or periodic penalty payment to be paid by the Member State concerned which it considers appropriate in the circumstances.[47] The Court's jurisdiction here too is unlimited, and, if it finds the alleged infringement proved, it decides what amount will have to be paid. In June 1996 Commission adopted a memorandum in which it stated the criteria according to which it would fix the amount which it would specify,[48] and it sought financial penalties for the first time in January 1997.[49]

The Court considers the power of the Commission to make use of the above procedures to induce Member States to fulfil their obligations as an 'essential power'.[50] It has, therefore, repudiated any attempts by defaulting Member States to frustrate these procedures by means of other procedures, or to mix up the matter dealt with therein with matters that ought to have been dealt with in other procedures.[51] Thus it will be to no avail that a Member State seeks to defend itself in infringement proceedings with an argument that the directive or decision which it is alleged to have failed to implement adequately or at all is tainted by illegality.[52] A line of cases also demonstrates that a Member State may not rely on the alleged failure by another Member State in order to justify its own failure to fulfil its

supremacy of Community law, the development of the concept of direct effect, particularly in relation to directives, the general duty to interpret national law in conformity with Community law, and the development of liability of the Member States in damages for infringement of Community law. These developments are discussed in section 2 of this chapter, *post*.

46. The procedure followed is identical to the normal Art. 169 EC or 141 Euratom proceedings described above.
47. Arts. 171(2) EC and 143(2) Euratom (2nd para. in each case).
48. O.J. 1996 C 242/6. As to the method of calculation, see O.J. 1997 C 63/2.
49. Commission press release IP[97]63 (against Germany and Italy), although the proceedings were later terminated, IP[97]568. As to other instances of proceedings being initiated, see IP[97]571 (Greece); IP[97]1109 (Greece); IP[97]1115 (Belgium), and IP[98]331 (France).
50. Cases 2 and 3/62 *Commission v. Luxembourg and Belgium* [1962] ECR 425 at 430 (the 'gingerbread' case).
51. *E.g. ibid.*; Case 7/61 *Commission v. Italy* [1961] ECR 317 at 326–327; Cases 90 and 91/63 *Commission v. Luxembourg and Belgium* [1964] ECR 625 at 631; Cases 6 and 11/69 *Commission v. France* [1969] ECR 523 at 544; Case 31/69 *Commission v. Italy* [1970] ECR 25 at 32–33, and Case 3/59 *Germany v. High Authority* [1960] ECR 53 at 61.
52. *E.g.* Cases 6 and 11/69 *Commission v. France* [1969] ECR 523 at 544; Case 226/87 *Commission v. Greece* [1988] ECR 3611 at 3623–3624, Case C-74/91 *Commission v.*

obligations under Community law.[53] It has also rejected any attempt by a Member State to justify its failure to implement provisions of Community law on the ground that the provisions have direct effect.[54] The Court is prepared to guarantee effective use of the Commission's power to initiate proceedings against Member States involved in infringements of obligations under the Treaties.

Finally, it should be noted that the Court has expressly stated that a Member State is responsible for a failure under Article 169 EC irrespective of the question of which national agency is actually responsible for the failure, even if this agency be independent according to national constitutional law.[55] Thus, for example, action by local authorities incompatible with Articles 30 or 34 EC can be attacked by infringement proceedings against the state concerned[56] or by individuals in national proceedings in actions against the local authority.[57] As has been mentioned above, even decisions of national courts can give rise to a breach of a Member State's obligations, although, the use of the infringement procedure will be largely inopportune, save where there is a systematic breach of Community law which can really only be brought to an end through legislation, or save where the competence of the Community Institutions themselves is in issue.[58] A Member State may not rely on national provisions or practices to justify its failure to fulfil its obligations or to comply with time-limits laid down in Community acts.[59] The Member States are obliged to take the necessary steps to fulfil their Community obligations by the due date, even in circumstances of political crisis.[60]

Germany [1992] ECR I-5437 at 5466. The position could be different if there were such particularly serious and manifest defects that it could be deemed non-existent, see *e.g.* Case 226/87, *ibid.* at 3624 and Case C-74/91, *ibid.*, but the Court is extremely reluctant to find that a measure is in fact non-existent, see Case C-137/92 P *Commission v. BASF AG et al.* [1994] ECR I-2555. Member States may be able to plead the absolute impossibility of implementing a Community decision properly, *e.g.* Case 213/85 *Commission v. The Netherlands* [1988] ECR 281 at 300 and case C-74/91, *ibid.*, although such arguments do not have a track record of success on the facts.

53. *E.g.* Case 52/75 *Commission v. Italy* [1976] ECR 277 at 284; Case 78/76 *Firma Steinike und Weinlig v. Germany* [1977] ECR 595 at 612, and Case C-38/89 *Ministère public v. Blaguernon* [1990] ECR I-83 at 92–93.
54. Case 168/85 *Commission v. Italy* [1986] ECR 2945 at 2960–2961.
55. Case 77/69 *Commission v. Belgium* [1970] ECR 237 at 243.
56. *E.g.* Case 301/84 *Commission v. United Kingdom* (O.J. 1985 C40/4, withdrawn after the local authorities had put an end to the infringement, O.J. 1985 C275/6).
57. *E.g. R. v. The Metropolitan Borough Council of Wirral, ex parte the Wirral Licensed Taxi Owners Association* [1983] 3 CMLR 159 (see Gormley (1983) 8 ELRev. 41).
58. See the discussion above, and notes 38 and 39, *supra*. See also Warner, Adv. Gen. in Case 9/75 *Meyer-Burckhardt v. Commission* [1975] ECR 1171 at 1187.
59. Case 30/72 *Commission v. Italy* [1973] ECR 161 at 172. See also *e.g.* Case 215/85 *Commission v. Belgium* [19851 ECR 1039 at 1054.
60. Case 79/72 *Commission v. Italy* [1973] ECR 667 at 671–672; Case 52/75 *Commission v. Italy* [1976] ECR 1359 at 1365 and Case 123/76 *Commission v. Italy* [1977] ECR 1449 at 1458–1459.

1.2   Supervision of the acts of the Institutions: action for annulment; action against failure to act

The action for annulment occupies in practice a central place amongst the judicial remedies provided for in the Treaties.[61] At the time at which the ECSC Treaty was concluded this procedure was clearly modelled on the *recours pour excès de pouvoir* in French administrative law. In one form or another, however, it is also found in the legal systems of the other Member States in the supervision of the legality of administrative acts; in the continental Member States this is done by the administrative courts.[62]

1.2.1   Action for annulment

An action for annulment can be brought to the Court of Justice against regulations, directives, decisions and ECSC recommendations. Furthermore, in the EC system, any acts of the European Parliament and the Council jointly, the Council, the Commission, and the European Central Bank are subject to appeal (in so far as they are not recommendations or opinions), as are acts adopted by the European Parliament which are intended to have legal effects *vis-à-vis* third parties.[63] An action can also lie against *sui generis* acts of these Institutions.[64] The ECSC system provides only for a separate right of action, limited as to the

61. Arts. 173 EC, 33 ECSC, and 146 Euratom. See, generally, Albors-Llorens, *Private Parties in European Community Law* (Oxford, 1996); Brown and Kennedy, *op. cit.* (see note 7, *supra*) 125–149; Lasok and Millett in Vaughan (ed.), *op. cit.* (see note 7, *supra*) paras. 162–224; Micklitz and Reich (eds.), *Public Interest Litigation before European Courts* (Baden-Baden, 1996); Schermers and Waelbroeck, *op. cit.* (see note 17, *supra*) 157–247; Arnull (1992) ECLR 73 and (1995) 32 CMLRev. 7; Craig (1994) 14 OJLS 507; Harding (1992) 17 ELRev. 105; Harlow (1992) 12 YBEL 213; Neuwahl (1996) 21 ELRev. 17; Nihoul (1994) 30 RTDE 171; Usher (1994) 19 ELRev. 636; Waelbroeck and Verheyden (1994) CDE 399. Among older literature, see Audretsch, *op. cit.* (see note 7, *supra*) 240–247; Bebr, *Development of Judicial Control of the European Communities* (Dordrecht, 1981) 19–155; Toth, *Legal Protection of Individuals in the European Communities* (Amsterdam, 1978) Vol. II, chapter 5, and Rasmussen (1980) 5 ELRev. 112.
62. *Cf.* in The Netherlands appeal on the basis of Chapter 8 of the *Algemene Wet Bestuursrecht* (1992 Stb. 315).
63. The present text of Arts. 173 EC and 146 Euratom (1st para. in each case) codifies the earlier case-law of the Court of Justice, see Case 294/83 *Parti écologiste 'Les Verts' v. European Parliament* [1986] ECR 1339 at 1365–1366. See also Case 190/84 *Parti écologiste 'Les Verts' v. European Parliament* [1988] ECR 1017, [1989] 2 CMLR 880. Because the old EEC and Euratom Treaties contained no provision relating to the annulment of acts of the European Parliament, Art. 38 ECSC was used in Case 230/81 *Luxembourg v. European Parliament* [1983] ECR 255, [1983] 2 CMLR 726.
64. *E.g.* Case 22/70 *Commission v. Council* [1971] ECR 263 at 276–278; in this judgment at action by the Commission contesting a Council resolution was held admissible because the resolution had definite legal effects both on relations between the Community and the Member States and on the relationship between Institutions. See also

grounds to be advanced,[65] against acts of the Council and the European Parliament, which are *sui generis* by definition, since *a priori* they do not fall within the legal definitions of Article 14 ECSC.

No action lies against non-binding opinions, recommendations, communications and acts of an internal character. In Case 60/81 *International Business Machines Corporation v. Commission*[66] the Court noted that 'According to the consistent case-law of the Court any measure the legal effects of which are binding on, and capable of affecting the interests of, the applicant by bringing about a distinct change in his legal position is an act or decision which may be the subject of an action under Article 173 for a declaration that it is void.' It added, however, that 'the form in which such acts or decisions are cast is, in principle, immaterial as regards the question whether they are open to challenge under that article.'[67] It is equally clear, the Court said, that in principle an act is open to review only if it is a measure definitively laying down the position of the Commission or the Council on the conclusion of the procedure concerned and not a provisional measure intended to pave the way for the final decision.[68] In the earlier discussion of the difference between decisions and non-binding

Case 2/71 *Germany* v. *Commission* [1971] ECR 669 at 676, and Cases C-213/88 and 39/89 *Luxembourg* v. *European Parliament* [1991] ECR I-5643 at 5696–5699. An Act of Accession negotiated between the Member States and an applicant state is not an act of the Council susceptible to judicial review under Art. 173 EC: Cases 31 and 35/86 *Levantina Agricola Industrial SA (Laisa) et al.* v. *Council* [1988] ECR 2285 at 2319.

65. Art. 38 ECSC.

66. [1981] ECR 2639 at 2651. If the act is one of general application appeal will lie irrespective of the nature or form concerned, in so far as the act is intended to have legal effects, Case 22/70 *Commission* v. *Council* [1971] ECR 263 at 277 (the *ERTA/AETR* case). For these purposes the Court will look to see whether such acts, although adopted in the form of internal instructions to Community officials or codes of conduct for the Member States, aim to impose obligations which do not flow from Community law, see Case C-366/88 *France* v. *Commission* [1990] ECR I-3571 at 3598–3599 and Case C-325/91 *France* v. *Commission* [1993] ECR I-3283 at 3308–3311.

67. *Ibid.*

68. *Ibid.* at 2652. The Court went on to say that it 'would be otherwise only if acts or decisions adopted in the course of the preparatory proceedings not only bore all the legal characteristics referred to above but in addition were themselves the culmination of a special procedure distinct from that intended to permit the Commission or the Council to take a decision on the substance of the case.' (*Ibid*). The Court also noted 'that whilst measures of a purely preparatory character may not themselves be the subject of an application for a declaration that they are void, any legal defects therein may be relied upon in an action directed against the definitive act for which they represent a preparatory step.' (*Ibid*). Cf. Case 54/65 *Compagnie des Forges de Châtillon, Commentry et Neuves-Maisons* v. *High Authority* [1966] ECR 185 at 195. See also Case 53/85 *AKZO Chemie BV et al.* v. *Commission* [1986] ECR 1965 at 1989–1990. See further, Case T-175/96 *Berthu* v. *Commission* [1997] ECR II-811 and Case C-180/96 *United Kingdom* v. *Commission* [1998] ECR I-nyr (5 May 1998). As an *e.g.* of an unsuccessful attempt to attack an act of a purely internal character, not producing legal effects see Case 190/84 *Parti écologiste 'Les Verts'* v. *European Parliament* [1988] ECR 1017, [1989] 2 CMLR 880. The complications relating to letters

acts[69] it was observed that in drawing the line between legally assailable and non-assailable acts the Court is largely guided by the interest which the Community's subjects have in legal protection against the act at issue. The Court is willing to investigate whether what purports to be an 'act of the representatives' is in fact a Council decision, and in doing so the Court will take of whether the Community has exclusive competence in the matter concerned.[70] The Court's attitude to letters has been considered elsewhere.[71]

It is primarily the Member States, the Council and the Commission which have a right of action,[72] They form a class of privileged applicants.[73] The right of action has also been extended to the European Parliament and to the European Central Bank for the purpose of protecting their prerogatives,[74] and to that limited extent they are semi-privileged

from the Commission in the competition sphere are well illustrated in Case C-39/93 P *Syndicat Français de l'Express international (SFEI) et al v. Commission* [1994] ECR I-2681.

69. In Chapter V, section 1.4, *ante*.
70. Cases C-181 and 248/91 *European Parliament v. Council et al.* [1993] ECR I-3685 at 3717–3718. But if it finds that the act is an act of the representatives, the action for annulment will be inadmissible. See also, as to acts under JHA, Case C-170/96 *Commission v. Council* [1998] ECR I-nyr (12 May 1998).
71. See Chapters V, section 1.4, *ante* and VIII, section 4.2.3, *post*.
72. In the ECSC system, under Art. 38 ECSC, only the Member States and the Commission may bring an action against an act of the Council or the European Parliament. Note the Court's special jurisdiction in relation to the EIB, Art. 180(b) and (c) EC.
73. The fact that the minister representing the Member State voted in favour of a Council act is no bar to the Member State challenging it, Case 166/78 *Italy v. Council* [1979] ECR 2575 at 2596. As to the privileged position of the Member States, the Commission and the Council see Case 45/86 *Commission v. Council* [1987] ECR 1493, [1988] 2 CMLR 131. Decentralized organs of the Member States do not enjoy the status of privileged applicants (they must be able to demonstrate direct and individual concern if they are not the addressees of a decision), Case 222/83 *Municipality of Differdange et al. v. Commission* [1984] ECR 2889 at 2896; Cases 62 and 72/87 *Exécutif régional wallon et al. v. Commission* [1988] ECR 1573 at 1591–1592 (implicitly); see now expressly Case C-95/97 *Région Wallonne v. Commission* [1997] ECR I-1787 at 1792 (the action was thus transferred to the Court of First Instance, and was found there to be inadmissible, Case T-70/97 *Région Wallonne v. Commission* [1997] ECR II-1513 at 1521.
74. Art. 173 EC. This codifies, in respect of the European Parliament, the case-law of the Court of Justice, see Case C-70/88 *European Parliament v. Council* [1990] ECR I-2041, [1992] 1 CMLR 91. A challenge based on inadequacy of reasons has been held not to be a challenge for the purpose of protecting prerogatives, see Case C-156/93 *European Parliament v. Commission* [1995] ECR I-2019 at 2045 (although the right to be consulted is a prerogative of the Parliament, *ibid.* and Case C-316/91 *European Parliament v. Council* [1994] ECR I-625 at 658). See also Case C-303/94 *European Parliament v. Council* [1996] ECR I-2943 at 2968. During the second stage of Economic and Monetary Union the right of the ECB to bring an action in order to protect its prerogatives is exercised by the EMI, Art. 109f(9) EC. Arts. 33 ECSC, 4th para. and 146 Euratom, 3rd para. confer standing for the purpose of those treaties on the European Parliament. The Treaty of Amsterdam (not yet in force) will add the Court of Auditors to these lists of semi-privileged applicants.

applicants. It is true that the right of action has also been granted to private parties, but only with certain restrictions which are connected with the character and the effect of the contested act. In general their right of action is virtually confined to decisions addressed to them or, under certain conditions, other acts of an individual character. These conditions are less stringent in the ECSC system than in the EC system. Because of the importance of the subject the details of the right of action of private parties and the problems involved are discussed separately in section 1.3. of this chapter, below.

All those who are entitled to bring an action are obliged to do so within a given period of time: in the EC system within two months, in the ECSC system within the (very short) period of one month, dating, as the case may be, either from the publication of the act concerned or from its notification to the applicant[75] or (in the EC system), failing that, from the day on which the applicant had knowledge of that act.[76]

There are four grounds of action:[77]

(1) lack of competence;[78]
(2) infringement of an essential procedural requirement;[79]

---

75. Arts. 33 ECSC and 146 Euratom.
76. See Art. 173 EC. As to the details, see Rules of Procedure of the Court of Justice (O.J. 1991 L 176/1, most recently amended O.J. 1997 L 103/1), Arts. 80 and 81; Rules of Procedure of the Court of First Instance (O.J. 1991 L 136/1, corrigendum O.J. 1991 L 317/34, most recently amended O.J. 1997 L 103/6), Arts. 101 and 102. See *e.g.* Case 152/85 *Misset v. Council* [1987] ECR 223 (with the comparative survey by Mancini, Adv. Gen. at 229 and 231–232); Cases 281/85 *etc. Germany et al. v. Commission* [1987] ECR 3203; [1988] 1 CMLR 11, and (referring to earlier case-law), Cases T-432–434/93 *Socurte et al. v. Commission* [1995] ECR II-503 at 519–520. See also *e.g.* Cases T-452 and 453/93 *Pesquería Vasco-Montañesa SA (Pevasa) et al. v. Commission* [1994] ECR II-229 at 243–244; Case T-85/97 *Interprovinciale des Fédérations d'Hoteliers, Cafetiers et Enterprises Assimilées de Wallonie ASBL (Féd. Horeca-Wallonie) v. Commission* [1997] ECR II-2113 at 2121–2122, and Case C-239/97 *Ireland v. Commission* [1998] ECR I-nyr (7 May 1998). In staff cases the time-limit is three months. Annex II of the Court's of Justice's Rules of Procedure provides for extension on account of distance (it applies to both courts). In an ECSC case the Court did not regard an action lodged before publication of the contested decision as being premature: Cases 172 and 226/83 *Hoogovens Groep BV v.Commission* [1985] ECR 2831 at 2845–2846.
77. Arts. 173 EC and 146 Euratom (2nd para. in each case). Art. 33 ECSC, 2nd para. restricts the grounds on which undertakings may challenge *general* decisions and recommendations; they may only invoke misuse of powers. Art. 38 ECSC, 3rd para. permits actions against acts of the Council or the European Parliament on grounds of lack of competence of infringement of an essential procedural requirement.
78. *E.g.* Cases 281/85 *etc. Germany et al. v. Commission* [1987] ECR 3203, [1988] 1 CMLR 11; Case C-327/91 *France v. Commission* [1994] ECR I-3641, [1994] 5 CMLR 517, and Case C-267/94 *France v. Commission* [1995] ECR I-4845.
79. *E.g.* Case 138/79 *SA Roquette Frères v. Council* [1980] ECR 3333; Case 61/86 *United Kingdom v. Council* [1988] ECR 431, [1988] 2 CMLR 98; Case 131/86 *United Kingdom*

(3) infringement of the Treaty or of any rule of law relating to its application;[80]
(4) misuse of powers.[81]

The first ground is self-explanatory, and does not call for further discussion. Examples justifying reliance on the second ground have been mentioned before: failure to give adequate reasons or to obtain the required proposals or opinions.

The ground which has the widest scope and which in practice is the most important is undoubtedly the third, which (if the other three were not mentioned separately) might well embrace those as well. The term any rule of law relating to the application of the Treaty includes provisions of international agreements by which the Community itself is bound.[82] Rules of law relating to the application of the Treaty also encompass rules of unwritten law.[83]

The fourth ground, misuse of powers (*détournement de pouvoir*), refers to a concept known in the law of each of the Member States, although its content varies rather widely in the different legal systems. From the case-law of the Court it appears that in its interpretation of the concept, with the various national systems of law as sources of inspiration, the Court has pursued its own course, finding that 'a decision may amount to a misuse of powers only if it appears, on the basis of objective, relevant and consistent factors, to have been taken with the exclusive purpose, or at any rate the main purpose, of achieving an end other than that stated or evading a procedure specifically prescribed by the Treaty for dealing with the circumstances of the case.'[84]

    v. Council [1988] ECR 905, [1988] 2 CMLR 364; Case C-49/88 *Al-Jubail Fertilizer Company et al. v. Council* [1991] ECR I-3187, [1991] 3 CMLR 377; Case C-353/92 *Greece v. Council* [1994] ECR I-3411, and Case C-263/95 *Germany v. Commission* [1998] ECR I-441.

80. E.g. Case 18/62 *Barge v. High Authority* [1963] ECR 259; Case 27/63 *Raponi v. Commission* [1964] ECR 129; Case 325/85 *Ireland v. Commission* [1987] ECR 5041, and Case T-42/96 *Eyckeler & Malt AG v. Commission* [1998] ECR II-401.

81. E.g. Cases 18 and 35/65 *Gutmann v. Commission (Euratom)* [1966] ECR 103; Case 105/75 *Giuffrida v. Council* [1976] ECR 1395; Cases 59 and 129/80 *Turner v. Commission* [1981] ECR 1883; Case 69/83 *Lux v. Court of Auditors* [1984] ECR 2447; Cases 140, 146, 221 and 226/82 *Walzstahl-Vereinigung et al. v. Commission* [1984] ECR 951; Case C-156/93 *European Parliament v. Commission* [1995] ECR I-2019; and Case C-89/94 *United Kingdom v. Council* [1996] ECR I-5755. See Bleckmann in Grewe, *op. cit.* (see note 24, *supra*) 25.

82. E.g. Cases 21–24/72 *International Fruit Company NV et al. v. Produktschap voor Groenten en Fruit* [1972] ECR 1219 at 1227. See also (as regards good faith and legal certainty), Case T-115/94 *Opel Austria GmbH v. Council* [1997] ECR II-39 at 71 and 82. *Cf.* Chapter IV, section 7.5.2, *ante*.

83. Cf. Chapter IV, section 7.5.1, *ante*.

84. Case C-331/88 *R. v. Minister for Agriculture, Fisheries and Food et al., ex parte Fedesa*

If the Court reaches the conclusion that the action for annulment is justified on one of the above-mentioned grounds, the act concerned will be declared wholly or partly void in the Court's judgment.[85] The act is then void from the moment it originated and with respect to everyone (effect *ex tunc* and *erga omnes*). It is, therefore, important that in the EC and Euratom systems express provision has been made for the jurisdiction of the Court to state, in cases of annulled regulations, which of the effects thereof shall be considered as definitive.[86]

Thus severance of offending provisions of a regulation is possible. This is particularly important in relation to the maintenance in force of acts which have been adopted in the meantime in implementation of the annulled regulation and the maintenance in force of the consequences of a regulation in the interests of legal certainty until it is replaced. This avoids the risks of an annulment causing unreasonable damage to the interests of the Community or others. Accordingly, in Case 59/81 *Commission v. Council*,[87] the Court decided that in order to avoid any lack of continuity in the system of remuneration the provisions in the annulled regulations concerning the adjustment of remuneration of Community officials should continue to have effect until such time as the Council had adopted the measures incumbent upon it in order to ensure compliance with the judgment. Although the power to maintain the effects of an annulled act is only expressly conferred in relation to regulations, the Court has applied it by analogy in relation to directives[88] and decisions,[89] and has also applied it by analogy in respect of rulings on

---

    et al. [1990] ECR I-4023 at 4065 (summarizing earlier case-law). See also *e.g.* Case C-84/94 *United Kingdom v. Council* [1996] ECR 5755 at 5814 and Case C-180/96 *United Kingdom v. Council* [1998] ECR I-nyr (5 May 1998). The Court observed in Case C-157/96 *R. v. Ministry of Agriculture, Fisheries and Food et al., ex parte National Farmers' Union et al.* [1998] ECR I-nyr (5 May 1998) that although 'the objective of a decision is to be determined by an analysis of the recitals in its preamble, that analysis must relate to the whole of the text, and not to a single element taken in isolation.'

85. Arts. 174 EC and 147 Euratom (expressly), and 34 ECSC, 1st para. (implicitly).
86. Arts. 174 EC and 147 Euratom (2nd para. in each case). See *e.g.* Case 264/82 *Timex Corporation v. Council et al.* [1985] ECR 849 at 870 (aim of the action being not to have the anti-dumping duty removed but increased and its scope extended), and Case 45/86 *Commission v. Council* [1987] 1493 at 1522 (in which no explanation was given by the Court, but Lenz, Adv. Gen. observed (at 1515) that the substantive rules involved (on the Community's Generalized System of Preferences) were not being called into question by either party.
87. [1982] ECR 3329 at 3359; see also Case 81/72 *Commission v. Council* [1973] ECR 575 at 586.
88. *E.g.* Case C-295/90 *European Parliament v. Council* [1992] ECR I-4193 at 4236–4237;
89. *E.g.* Case 34/86 *Council v. European Parliament* [1986] ECR 2155 at 2212; Case C-284/90 *Council v. European Parliament* [1992] ECR I-2277 at 2331, and Case C-41/95 *Council v. European Parliament* [1995] ECR I-4411 at 4441 (all involving budgets), and Case C-271/94 *European Parliament v. Council* [1996] ECR I-1689 at 1719 (effects of decisions adopted pursuant to an annulled decision).

the validity of acts of the Community Institutions in preliminary rulings on references from national courts.[90] The Court will be extremely reluctant to reach a conclusion that what purports to be an act of an institution is so defective that it must be characterized as non-existent; the main reason for this reluctance being legal certainty, thus there must be 'particularly serious and manifest defects' before non-existence will be established.[91]

The Institution whose act has been declared void is required to take the necessary measures to comply with the judgment.[92] The illegality of the annulled act may, if the relevant requirements have been met, give rise to a claim for damages to be paid by the Communities to the party injured by the act. In the ECSC system special conditions apply on this point,[93] which diverge from those of the general rule.[94] In the EC and Euratom systems the injured party may bring an action for damages before the Court in accordance with the general principles of the noncontractual liability of the Community.[95] As to this, see section 1.3.3, below.

1.2.2 Action against failure to act

Apart from the action for annulment, the Treaties also provide for an action against failure to act where such failure is contrary to Community law.[96] This action is meant to induce action by the Institution which failed

90. *E.g.* Case 112/83 *Société des Produits de Maïs v. Administration des douanes et des droits indirects* [1985] ECR 719 at 747–748; Case 41/84 *Pinna v. Caisse d'Allocations Familiales de la Savoie* [1986] ECR 1 at 26–27, and C-38/90 and 151/90 *R. v. Lomas et al.* [1992] ECR I-1781 at 1816–1818. See, further, section 2.1.2, *post.*
91. See Case 15/85 *Consorzio Cooperative d'Abruzzo v. Commission* [1987] ECR 1005 at 1036; for a particularly notorious example, see the *PVC saga*, Cases T-79/89 *etc. BASF AG et al. v. Commission* [1992] ECR II-315 at 352 *et seq.*, quashed on appeal in Case C-137/92 P *Commission v. BASF AG et al.* [1994] ECR I-2555 (but the Court of Justice then annulled the decision). An action will formally be brought seeking the annulment of the act, albeit that the argument will point to non-existence; if the act is found by the Court not to exist, the action is dismissed (as there is no act which can be annulled) and the applicants are awarded their costs.
92. Arts. 176 EC, 34 ECSC, and 149 Euratom. See also *e.g.* Case 44/81 *Germany v. Commission* [1982] ECR 1855 at 1874; Cases 97/86 *etc. Asteris a.e. et. al. v. Council* [1988] ECR 2181 at 2208–2209; Case T-84/91 *Meskens v. European Parliament* [1992] ECR II-2335 at 2357–2359; Cases C-15 and 108/91 *Josef Buckl und Söhne OHG et al. v. Commission* [1992] ECR I-6061 at 6097, and C-56/91 *Greece v. Commission* [1993] ECR I-3433 at 3458–3460.
93. Art. 34 ECSC.
94. Art. 40 ECSC.
95. Art. 215 EC, 2nd para. in conjunction with Art. 178 EC; Art. 188 Euratom, 2nd para. 2 in conjunction with Art. 151 Euratom. As to remedies for unsuccessful tenderers for contracts financed by the European Development Fund see the judgments discussed by Brown (1985) 10 ELRev. 421 and (1986) 11 ELRev. 435.
96. In French often called an *action en carence*; Arts. 175 EC, 35 ECSC, and 148 Euratom. See, generally, Schermers and Waelbroeck, *op. cit.* (see note 17, *supra*) 247–261; Lasok and Millett, *op. cit.* (see note 7, *supra*) paras. 225–250; Shaw (1983) 18

to act. In the EC and Euratom systems this is the European Parliament, the Council or the Commission, in the ECSC on the other hand only the Commission, (which can be explained by its dominant position in the implementation of that Treaty). The Institution in question must first be called upon to act. This should be done within a reasonable period of it[97] having become clear that the Institution is not going to act. If it has not defined its position within two months, an action may be brought before the Court.[98] Actions may also be brought by the European Central Bank in the areas falling within its field of competence, and actions or proceedings may also be brought against the ECB for failure to act.[99] There are, however, considerable differences between the ECSC system and the EC system (not only of a terminological nature) in the rules governing this action; a few of these are discussed here.

In the ECSC system an action against failure to act is directed against the implied refusal of the Commission to issue a decision or a recommendation within two months of being called upon to act. If the Commission refuses expressly, the usual action for annulment against such a decision may be brought.[100] The Court regards the action against the implied refusal of the Commission as a special kind of action for annulment, i.e. against an implied decision of refusal.[101] The Member States, the Council or the undertakings are entitled to bring such an action, 'as the case may be.' As it is, in the opinion of the Court, a special form of action for annulment, this means that the conditions of Article 33 ECSC must be satisfied. Whether an undertaking may lodge an action against a failure to act and, if so, under what conditions depends, therefore, on the nature of the act required; as to this see section 1.3.1, below.

In the EC system the action is meant to cause the Court to establish an infringement of the Treaty by the European Parliament, the Council, the

ELRev. 427; Toth, *op. cit.* (see note 48, *supra*) Vol. II Chapter 6, and Bebr, *op. cit.* (*ibid.*) 158–189.

97. *Cf.* Case 59/70 *Netherlands v. Commission* [1971] ECR 639 at 653. The Court deduced this from the common purpose of Arts. 33 and 35 ECSC from which it follows that the requirements of legal certainty and continuity of Community action underlying the time-limits laid down in Art. 33 ECSC bearing in mind also exercise by interested parties of the rights conferred by Art. 35 ECSC.

98. The time limit for this is also two months in the Euratom system but only one month in the ECSC system.

99. During the second stage of Economic and Monetary Union this applies in respect of the EMI, Art. 109f(9) EC.

100. In earlier ECSC case-law an action against failure to act under Art. 35 ECSC was also regarded as applying also to an express refusal to act, despite the clear wording of the last paragraph of that Article. See, though, now Case 30/59 *De Gezamenlijke Steenkolenmijnen in Limburg v. High Authority* [1961] ECR 1 at 15–16. As an *e.g.* of a successful challenge to an implied refusal see Cases 167 and 212/85 *ASSIDER et al. v. Commission* [1987] ECR 1701, [1988] 2 CMLR 783.

101. Cases 7 and 9/54 *Groupement des Industries Sidérurgiques Luxembourgeois v. High Authority* [1954–1956] ECR 175 at 192.

Commission or the ECB, on account of their failure to act. Such failure is involved if the Institution, after having been called upon to act, 'has not defined its position' within two months. The Member States, the Institutions,[102] the ECB in the areas falling within its competence, and private parties (natural and legal persons) may bring such an action. The right of action of a private party, however, is subject to a double restriction: the failure must concern an act of a binding character (*i.e.* other than a recommendation or an opinion),[103] and the act must be addressed to him or her or would have concerned him or her directly and individually.[104] The Court regards Articles 173 and 175 EC as expressions of one and the same method of recourse,[105] and the possibility for individuals to assert their rights does not depend upon whether the Community Institution concerned has acted or failed to act.[106] This very logical conclusion comes after various twists in the earlier case-law.[107]

Any action using Article 175 EC or Article 148 Euratom aimed at obtaining from the Court a ruling that the Commission has failed to fulfil its obligations by not commencing infringement proceedings under Articles 169 EC or 141 Euratom will be inadmissible.[108] This is otherwise in the

102. It is remarkable that, as an Institution, the Court of Auditors may bring an action for failure to act, although, in view of the wording of Arts. 173 EC and 148 Euratom, it has no *locus standi* to seek the annulment of an act.

103. E.g. Case 15/70 *Chevalley v. Commission* [1970] ECR 975 at 980 and Cases 6/70 *Borromeo Arese et al. v. Commission* [1970] ECR 815 at 819.

104. Case C-107/91 *Empresa nacional de Urânio SA (ENU) v. Commission* [1995] ECR I-599 at 630 (in relation to Art. 148 Euratom); Case C-68/95 *T. Port GmbH & Co. KG v. Bundesanstalt für Landwirtschaft und Ernährung* [1996] ECR I-6065 at 6105. In the same sense, Dutheillet de Lamothe, Adv. Gen. in Case 15/71 *Mackprang v. Commission* [1971] ECR 797 at 808.

105. Case 15/70 *Chevalley, ibid.* at 979; Case C-68/95 *T. Port GmbH & Co. KG v. Bundesanstalt für Landwirtschaft und Ernährung* [1996] ECR I-6065 at 6105. This does not mean, however, that Art. 175 EC can be used to evade the conditions laid down in Art. 173 EC, particularly in relation to the time-limit for bringing an action (*cf.* Cases 10 and 18/68 *Società 'Eridania' Zuccherifici Nazionali et al. v. Commission* [1969] ECR 459 at 482–483).

106. Case C-68/95 *T. Port GmbH & Co. KG v. Bundesanstalt für Landwirtschaft und Ernährung* [1996] ECR I-6065 at 6105.

107. See *E.g.* Case 15/71 *Mackprang v. Commission* [1971] ECR 797 at 804; Case 134/73 *Holtz & Willemsen GmbH v. Council* [1974] ECR 1 at 11; Case 246/81 *Nicholas William, Lord Bethell v. Commission* [1982] ECR 2277 at 2291; Case 90/78 *Granaria BV v. Council et al.* [1979] ECR 1081 at 1091–1092; Case 60/79 *Fédération Nationale des producteurs de Vins de table et vins de pays v. Commission* [1979] ECR 2429 at 2433; Case C-371/89 *Emrich v. Commission* [1990] ECR I-1555 at 1557 and Case C-72/90 *Asia Motor France v. Commission* [1990] ECR I-2181 at 2184.

108. *E.g.* Case C-371/89 *Emrich,* Case C-72/90 *Asia Motor France, loc. cit.* This parallels the approach already evident in Case 48/65 *Alfons Lütticke GmbH et al. v. Commission* [1966] ECR 19 at 27 (seeking to annul a refusal to bring infringement proceedings). In Case 247/87 *Star Fruit Company SA v. Commission* [1989] ECR 291 at 301 the Court reached the same result on the reasoning that the applicant was seeking the adoption of acts which were not of direct and individual concern to it within the meaning of Art. 173 EEC and

ECSC system. Article 88 ECSC provides for a binding act of the Commission: the reasoned decision, adopted after the Member State concerned has been given an opportunity to submit its comments, imposes an obligation of compliance on the Member State, which, as was noted above, may appeal to the Court. The Commission is in fact obliged to adopt the decision recording the failure by the Member State concerned to fulfil its obligations (in contrast to the discretion to adopt a non-binding reasoned opinion in the EC and Euratom systems). Furthermore, the right of individuals to appeal against decisions which are not addressed to them is more extensive in the ECSC system than in the EC and Euratom systems, as is explained in section 1.2, below. This combination of factors has led to the Court finding in the ECSC system that an appeal by a private party against an implied decision refusing to adopt a reasoned decision under Article 88 ECSC was indeed admissible.[109]

It is noteworthy that in the EC system an action against failure to act is open to all the Institutions, *i.e.* also to the European Parliament. Probably this right was accorded to the latter to enable it to lend force to its own rights under the Treaty: the right to be consulted by the Council in the cases provided for in the Treaty, and the right to dismiss the Commission by means of a motion of censure. However, the possibility is not excluded that the Parliament might use this procedure for other purposes. Given a reasonable use of it, a means has thus been given to the Parliament for compelling the Council to define its position,[110] for embarking on a dialogue with it, and for aiding the Commission in its efforts to induce the Council to take decisions on the basis of the proposals the Commission has submitted. Thus this procedure was used by the Parliament in its efforts to force the Council to remedy its failure to take the necessary measures in the field of transport policy.[111]

An action against failure to act is inadmissible in the EC system if the Institution has *defined its position* within two months of being requested to do so. Article 175 EC does not lay down any formal conditions on this definition of position. It is sufficient that the applicant knows where he stands, whether the Institution will act on his application or not. This can

which it could therefore not challenge by means of an action for annulment. That line of argument was advanced, but not examined by the Court of Justice in Cases C-15 and 108/91 *Josef Buckl und Söhne OHG et al. v. Commission* [1992] ECR I-6061 at 6096–6097. See also, discussing earlier case-law, Case T-47/96 *Syndicat Départemental de Défense du Droit des Agriculteurs (SDDA) v. Commission* [1996] ECR II-1559 at 1574–1575. In any event, the Commission's discretion in the matter is clearly recognized, *e.g. ibid.* at 1575.

109. Cases 7 and 9/54 *Groupement des industries Sidérurgiques Luxembourgeoises v. High Authority* [1954–56] ECR 175 at 191.
110. Art. 175 para. 2 EC
111. Case 13/83 *European Parliament v. Council* [1985] ECR 1513, [1986] 1 CMLR 138 (see Chapter IV, section 5.3., *ante*). However, the effectiveness of this procedure should not be over-estimated, see Case C-17/90 *Pinaud Wieger GmbH Spedition v. Bundesanstalt für den Güterfernverkehr* [1991] ECR I-5253 at 5282–5283.

occur by addressing an act to the applicant,[112] by means of a communication which makes the refusal to act clear or, it may be concluded, by definite promises which can be called in later by those who have called upon the Institution to act, in so far at least as action in the short term cannot reasonably be requested under Community law. This takes account of the fact that sometimes complex and time-consuming procedures have to be set in motion.[113] It is also sufficient if the Institution acts in relation to the object of the request. Acting in a different manner from that in which the requesting party regards as desirable or necessary is also a definition of a position.[114] If the requesting party disagrees with such action it is open to him or her to bring an action for annulment.

Once an Institution has defined its position within the prescribed period the Court will not look further into the question of whether the request could be submitted under Article 175 EC or even whether the action against failure to act is inadmissible on the ground of want of *locus standi* to bring the action.[115] This question arises only when the Institution has not defined its position, by, for example, not replying to the request within the deadline[116] or by stating that it will not react to the request because the Article 175 EC procedure is not applicable.[117] If the act, of which the failure to adopt led to the action, is in fact adopted between the action being brought and the judgment being given, the action becomes devoid of purpose. This is because the remedy in Articles 175 EC and 148 Euratom is based on the premise that a declaration can be obtained from the Court that the failure to act is contrary to the Treaty, in so far as it has not been repaired by the Institution(s) concerned or the ECB. The effect of such a declaration is that the Institution(s) concerned or the ECB must take

112. Such a definition of a position may consist of issuing a particular procedural measure in the context of competition law, *cf*. Case 8/71 *Deutscher Komponistenverband e.V. v. Commission* [1971] ECR 705 at 710 and Case 125/78 *GEMA v. Commission* [1979] ECR 3173 at 3190.

113. The importance of deadlines and the complexity of issues involved is well illustrated in Case C-107/91 *Empresa nacional de Urânio SA (ENU) v. Commission* [1995] ECR I-599 (under Arts. 53 and 148 Euratom) and Case T-195/95 *Guérin Automobiles v. Commission* [1996] ECR II-171.

114. *E.g*. Case 8/71 *Deutscher Komponistenverband, ibid.*; Cases C-15 and 108/91 *Josef Buckl und Söhne OHG et al. v. Commission* [1992] ECR I-6061 at 6097; Case C-25/91 *Pesqueras Echebastar SA v. Commission* [1993] ECR I-1719 at 1758–1759; Case T-126/95 *Dumez v. Commission* [1995] ECR II-2863 at 2878, and (in relation to Art. 148 Euratom) Case C-107/91 *Empresa nacional de Urânio SA (ENU) v. Commission* [1993] ECR I-624 at 629.

115. *Eg*. Case 48/65 *Alfons Lütticke GmbH et al. v. Commission* [1966] ECR 19 at 27–28 and Case 42/71 *Nordgetreide GmbH & Co. KG v. Commission* [1972] ECR 105 at 110–111.

116. *E.g*. Case 90/78 *Granaria BV v. Commission* [1979] ECR 1081.

117. *E.g*. Case 15/70 *Chevalley v. Commission* [1970] ECR 975; Case 15/71 *Mackprang v. Commission* [1971] ECR 797 and Case 6/70 *Borromeo Arese et al. v. Commission* [1970] ECR 815.

the necessary measures to comply with the judgment,[118] without prejudice to any actions in respect of non-contractual liability which may result from the judgment.[119] Such a declaration by the Court has no further point if the result has, in effect, already been achieved.[120] It is, of course, open to the requesting party to whom a definition of position has been addressed to attack it under Article 173 EC; in this case the Court will look at the admissibility of that action under the criteria of that Article.[121]

Finally, one point should be made about the judgment of the Court. In the ECSC system the Court may annul the implied decision of refusal; the Institution is then, under Article 34 ECSC, required to take the necessary steps to comply with the judgment, *i.e.* to issue the decision or recommendation requested. In the EC and Euratom systems, on the other hand, the Court decides that the failure to act consitutes an infringement of the Treaty. Here too the Institution is obliged to take the necessary measures to comply with the judgment,[122] *i.e.* to take a decision or at the very least to define its position. As to the possibility of bringing an action for damages in the event of an unlawful failure to act see section 1.3.3, below.

1.3 Supervision of acts of the Institutions: the restricted right of action by private parties; the plea of illegality and actions for damages

1.3.1 The restricted right of action by private parties[123]

It has already been observed above that the Member States form a class of privileged applicants among the Community's subjects. The admissibility of

118. Arts. 176 EC and 149 Euratom.
119. Under Arts. 215, 2nd para. in conjunction with 178 EC (Arts. 188, 2nd para. and 151 Euratom).
120. See Cases 377/87 *European Parliament v. Council* [1988] ECR 4017 at 4048; Case 383/87 *Commission v. Council* [1988] ECR 4051 at 4064. See also Cases C-15 and 108/91 *Josef Buckl und Söhne OHG et al. v. Commission* [1992] ECR I-6061 at 6097.
121. *Cf.* the judgments cited in note 114, *supra*. See further, Case T-64/89 *Automec Srl v. Commission* [1990] ECR II-367 at 387. Not every letter from an Institution or from the ECB in response to a request under Art. 175 EC will amount to a decision for the purposes of Art. 173 EC, 2nd para. Thus a letter from the President of the European Parliament, written as a matter of courtesy, in a case in which that Institution had no power to act on the request, was not a decision, see Case C-25/92 *Miethke v. European Parliament* [1993] ECR I-473 at 478. As to letters, generally, see Chapter V, section 1.4, *ante*.
122. Arts. 176 EC and 149 Euratom (1st para. in each case). But the Court will not, in proceedings under Art. 175 EC, direct a Community Institution to make a payment of financial aid, Case C-25/91 *Pesqueras Echebastar SA v. Commission* [1993] ECR I-1755 at 1759. See further, Case T-84/91 *Meskens v. European Parliament* [1992] ECR II-2335 at 2357–2359.
123. See the literature cited in note 61, *supra*, (which in turn refers to earlier literature) and

their action for annulment of the acts of the Institutions or the ECB is subject to no conditions other than those with respect to the period within which the action must be brought and the grounds to be advanced. They do not need to prove that they have a direct interest in an action, any more than the Council or the Commission. Their interest in the strict application of Treaty law and in the maintenance of the balance of power, laid down in the Treaty, between the Institutions and between the Communities and themselves is presumed. An action by private parties, on the other hand, is only admissible if a number of other conditions have also been fulfilled, conditions which are connected with the nature and with the effects of the contested acts.

For private parties, an action against decisions (and ECSC recommendations) addressed to them is always open in the system of all three Communities. Private parties can bring an action *de pleine juridiction* (unlimited jurisdiction) against decisions by which a fine or periodic penalty payment is imposed on them; in these actions they do not have to limit themselves to advancing the four grounds of appeal. The Court has full discretion to judge the facts which led to the application of the sanction, and may substitute its decision for that of the Institution which applied the sanction (or for the decision of the ECB imposing the sanction); it may cancel, lower, or increase the fine or the penalty. In the ECSC the sanctions are provided for in the Treaty itself.[124] An action in unlimited jurisdiction against them is always open to the parties.[125] In the EC sanctions can be included in Council regulations.[126] An action in unlimited jurisdiction against them is open only if the Council in its regulations expressly confers unlimited jurisdiction on the Court.[127] In the Euratom system the Court has unlimited jurisdiction in proceedings to have the appropriate terms fixed for the granting by the Commission of licences or sub-licences,[128] and in proceedings instituted by persons or undertakings against sanctions imposed on them by the Commission.[129]

An action by private parties against *sui generis* acts and, in the EC and Euratom systems, against regulations *stricto sensu* and directives, is entirely impossible. Their right of action is limited in the case of decisions (or, in the ECSC system individual recommendations) addressed to parties other

Van Dijk, *Judicial Review of Governmental Action and the requirement of an interest to sue* (Alphen aan de Rijn, 1980) 241–309.
124. *E.g.* Art. 65(5) ECSC.
125. Art. 36 ECSC, 2nd para.
126. *E.g.* Reg. 17 (O.J. English Special Edition 1959–62, p. 87, as amended), Arts. 15 and 16.
127. Art. 172 EC, *cf.* Reg. 17, *ibid.*, Art. 17 and Reg. 11 (O.J. English Special Edition 1959–62, p. 60), Art. 25(2).
128. Art. 144(a) Euratom; the proceedings are instituted under Art. 12 Euratom.
129. Art. 144(b) Euratom; the sanctions are imposed under Art. 83 Euratom for infringement of the safeguard obligations.

than themselves. In the ECSC system they also have a very limited right of action against general decisions and recommendations. It is to these limiting conditions that this subsection will be largely devoted. Wherever decisions in ECSC context are referred to below, they must be deemed to include recommendations, which, in relation to the right of action, are governed by the same rules.

The preceding discussion has already dealt with the restricted right of private parties to lodge an action against failure to act; the present discussion therefore leaves this out of account. It will be recalled that in the ECSC system the restrictions on the right of private parties to bring an action for failure to act parallel those on their right to seek the annulment of an act of a Community Institution. The limitation in the EC and Euratom systems is more extensive.

A. Actions against decisions addressed to other parties. The wording used to set out the limitations on the right of appeal by private parties reveals the more extensive restriction applicable in the EC and Euratom systems than in the ECSC system. The wording is unmistakably more restrictive than in that used in the ECSC Treaty and stands in the way of the application in those newer systems of the broader interpretation which the Court has given to the ECSC provisions.[130]

In the ECSC system undertakings[131] have the right of action 'against decisions or recommendations concerning them which are individual in character.'[132] The interpretation of the words 'concerning them which are individual in character' governs whether, and if so to what extent, undertakings may also challenge decisions not addressed to themselves. The Dutch text (which is not authentic as Article 100 ECSC provides that only the French text is authentic) appears to support a narrow interpretation. In the event it will in most cases only be the undertaking to whom the decision is addressed which will be concerned by it. However, the Court opted for a wide interpretation which the French text ('*les décisions individuelles les concernant*') permitted. In the case-law it refused to link the concepts of 'individual' on the one hand and 'concerning' on the other; it interpreted 'concerning' in the sense of interests being affected by an individual decision; thus a decision which may affect the competitive relationship between undertakings can be challenged by a competitor of the addressee.[133]

---

130. *Cf.* Cases 16 and 17/62 *Confédération nationale des producteurs de fruits et légumes et al. v. Council* [1962] ECR 471 at 498: the Court admitted that the newer systems were more restrictive but felt it inappropriate for it to pronounce on the merits of the system. See the critical comments by Rasmussen (1980) 5 ELRev. 112.
131. Having legal personality, Case 50/84 *Srl Bensider et al. v. Commission* [1984] ECR 3991 at 3997.
132. Art. 33 ECSC, 2nd para.
133. An undertaking is concerned by a Commission decision addressed to a Member State

In the EC and Euratom systems an action is open to a private party (whether a natural or a legal person)[134] against a decision 'which, although in the form of a regulation or a decision addressed to another person, is of direct and individual concern' to the applicant.[135] Thus it is not enough that a private party is affected by a decision addressed to someone else, as in the ECSC system; the decision must also be 'of direct and individual concern' to the applicant. The Court has on myriad occasions in its case-law pronounced on the requirements for the admissibility of actions against decisions addressed to others in connection with actions by private parties against Commission decisions addressed to Member States,

In Case 25/62 *Plaumann Co. v. Commission*[136] the Court rejected the Commission's argument that the words 'another person' could not refer to Member States 'in their capacity as sovereign authorities' and that thus individuals should not be allowed to challenge decisions of the Council or the Commission addressed to a Member State. The Court held that as Article 173 EEC neither defined nor limited the scope of 'another person' the words and the natural meaning of that provision justified the broadest interpretation, particularly since 'provisions of the Treaty regarding the right of interested parties to bring an action must not be interpreted restrictively.'[137] This principle had also been a feature of the case-law of the ECSC Court. However, the Court evidently felt obliged to take a narrow view because of the terms of the Treaty when, in the same case, it had to define the meaning of 'of individual concern.' It concluded that a decision could only be of individual concern to persons other than the addressee if it affects third parties 'by reason of certain attributes which are peculiar to them or by reason of circumstances in which they are differentiated from all other persons and by virtue of these factors distinguishes them individually just as in the case of the person addressed.'[138]

which permits benefits to be granted to one or more undertakings which are in competition with it: Cases 24 and 34/58 *Chambre syndicale de la sidérurgie de l'est de la France v. High Authority* [1960] ECR 281 at 292; see also Cases 172 and 226/83 *Hoogovens Groep BV v. Commission* [1985] ECR 2831 at 2847.

134. It should be noted that the concept of a legal person in Art. 173 EC does not necessarily coincide with that concept in the various national legal orders, *cf.* Case 135/81 *Groupement des Agences de Voyages asbl v. Commission* [1982] ECR 3799 at 3808 (referring to earlier judgments).

135. Arts. 173 EC and 146 Euratom (4th para. in each case). As to interim measures and objections of inadmissibility for want of *locus standi* see *e.g.* Case 376/87R *Distrivet SA v. Council* [1988] ECR 209, [1988] 2 CMLR 436; Case T-203/95 R *Connolly v. Commission* [1995] ECR II-2919 and Case T-219/95 R *Danielsson et al. v. Commission* [1995] ECR II-3051 (citing previous orders). As a call for nominations is by its nature addressed to an unspecified number of persons, a person concerned merely by being a citizen of the Union has no standing to challenge it, Case T-146/95 *Bernardi v. European Parliament* [1996] ECR II-769.

136. [1963] ECR 95; [1964] CMLR 29.

137. [1963] ECR 95 at 107.

138. *Ibid.*

It appears from this formula, which was repeated by the Court in later judgments,[139] that private parties, if they wish to bring an action against decisions addressed to other persons, find a formidable barrier in their way in the form of the fourth paragraph of Article 173 EC. The issue is not only, as in the ECSC system, that such parties are affected by the consequences of a decision, but also *how* they are affected: because of certain characteristics which are particular to them or by reason of a specific situation, by reference to which they are individually described in a way similar to that of the addressee of the decision.[140]

A decision is also the appropriate means by which the Commission authorizes, or refuses to authorize, Member States to take certain measures by virtue of a safeguard clause.[141] By a decision the Commission also determines for the Member States, with binding effect, the c.i.f. prices on the basis of which they are to fix the levies and export subsidies (refunds) for particular agricultural products. Importers or exporters, for instance, may have an interest in the annulment of decisions of this type addressed to Member States. In the light of the formula used by the Court the chances that an action bought by one of them will be admissible are, however, very small. In fact such a party will be affected by these decisions in his or her capacity as an importer or exporter. Thus in *Plaumann* the Court classed the applicant, an importer of clementines, as a person affected 'by reason of a commercial activity which may at any time be practised by any person and is not therefore such as to distinguish the

---

139. *E.g.* Case 11/82 *Piraiki-Patraiki et al. v. Commission* [1985] ECR 207 at 242; Case 231/82 *Spijker Kwatsen BV v. Commission* [1983] ECR 2559 at 2566; Case 282/85 *Comité de Developpement et de Promotion du Textile et de l'Habillement (DEFI) v. Commission* [1986] ECR 2469 at 2480; Case 97/85 *Union Deutsche Lebensmittelwerke GmbH et al. v. Commission* [1987] ECR 2265 at 2286–2287 (see Arnull (1987) 12 ELRev. 451); Case C-198/91 *William Cook plc v. Commission* [1993] ECR I-2487 at 2527–2528, and Case C-321/95 P *Stichting Greenpeace Council (Greenpeace International) et al. v. Commission* [1998] ECR I-nyr (2 April 1998). See also, before the Court of First Instance, *e.g.* Cases T-481 and 484/93 *Vereniging van Exporteurs in levende Varkens et al. v. Commission* [1995] ECR II-2941 at 2961, and Case T-219/95 R *Danielsson et al. v. Commission* [1995] ECR II-3051 at 3071–3072.

140. There is no problem in cases such as those involving a Commission decision addressed to a Member State concerning a state aid to a particular undertaking, see *e.g.* Case 730/79 *Philip Morris Holland BV v. Commission* [1980] ECR 2671 at 2687, and Cases 296 and 318/82 *The Netherlands et al. v. Commission* [1985] ECR 809 at 821. If a number of persons seek to challenge a decision (or, in appropriate cases, a regulation) and only some of them have a real chance of satisfying the *Plaumann* formula, they would often be well advised to bring one single action together, as even if only one applicant in a single case actually satisfies the formula, all will be able to make their views known, see *e.g.* Case C-313/90 *Comité internationale de la rayonne et des fibres synthétiques (CIRFS) et al. v. Commission* [1993] ECR I-1125 at 1185, and Case T-442/93 *Association des Amidonneries de Céréales de la CEE (AAC) et al. v. Commission* [1995] ECR II-1329 at 1354.

141. *E.g.* Under Art. 115 EC, although this has now become virtually a dead letter with the removal of systematic customs formalities at the community's internal frontiers.

applicant in relation to the contested decision as in the case of the addressee.'[142] The capacity as an importer of a given product is not particular to him or her, but to all members of a group which can be described only in an abstract way, because, at least potentially, anyone may belong to this group. Even if the number and identity of the importers affected by the consequences of such a decision could be determined, this still does not constitute a factual situation which is, as compared with all other persons, particularly relevant to them, if this results from purely fortuitous circumstances.[143]

Only in a few cases so far could the barrier of the individual concern be overcome. In those cases there was no question of *fortuitous* circumstances on the basis of which certain importers, the number and identity of whom could be determined, were affected by a decision; the number and identity of these importers were determined and could be determined at the moment at which the decision was taken and the Commission was in a position to know that its decision affected only the interests and the legal position of these importers. In these circumstances they were characterized and individualized, as compared with all other persons, in a way similar to that of the addressee of the decision.[144] There are no fortuitous circumstances when the number and identity of those who will be affected by a decision can be determined if the adoption of the decision is in any way influenced by their identity or their actual or probable conduct; there is then a causal link between the acquaintance with the specific situation in which those persons find themselves and the decision taken.[145]

The explanation for the Court's traditionally strict interpretation of the concept of individual concern is most probably to be found in the fact that the early cases concerned challenges to agricultural safeguard measures

142. Case 25/62 *Plaumann & Co. v. Commission* [1962] ECR 95 at 107.
143. Case 38/64 *Getreide-Import Gesellschaft mbH. v. Commission* [1965] ECR 203 at 208. See, *inter alia*, Case 1/64 *Glucoseries Réunies v. Commission* [1964] ECR 413 at 417 and Case 97/85 *Union Deutsche Lebensmittelwerke GmbH et al. v. Commission* [1997] ECR 2265 at 2286–2287. Even if a party is the only importer affected by a Commission decision addressed to a Member State, that party will not be found individually concerned (unless he or she forms part of a closed class, as is explained in the text), see, in this very restrictive sense, *e.g.* Case 231/82 *Spijker Kwatsen BV v. Commission* [1983] ECR 2559 at 2566 and Case 11/82 *Piraiki-Patraiki et al. v. Commission* [1985] ECR 207 at 243–244.
144. Cases 106 and 107/63 *Alfred Toepfer & Co. et al. v. Commission* [1965] ECR 405 at 411–412. See also Case 62/70 *Bock v. Commission* [1971] ECR 897 at 907–908. See, further, *e.g.* Case 92/78 *Simmenthal SpA v. Commission* [1979] ECR 777 at 798; Case 112/77 *August Töpfer & Co. GmbH v. Commission* [1978] ECR 1019 at 1030; Case 88/76 *Société pour l'exportation des sucres SA v. Commission* [1977] ECR 709 at 725; Case 11/82 *Piraiki-Patraiki et al. v. Commission* [1985] ECR 207 at 244, with the overview of previous case-law by VerLoren van Themaat, Adv. Gen., *ibid.* at 213–217, and Case 1/84 R *Ilford SpA v. Commission* [1984] ECR 423 at 428.
145. *Cf.* Waelbroeck in *e.g.* (1978) Rev. Crit. de Jur. Belge. 105–106 and in Mégret *et al.* (eds.), *Le Droit de la CEE* Vol. 10 (2nd ed., Brussels, 1993) 132. See also Cases T-480 and 483/93 *Antillean Rice Mills NV et al. v. Commission* [1995] ECR II-2305.

which had major implications for the sectors concerned; in these circumstances the Court seems to have been concerned to set its face against an *actio popularis* or general attempts to torpedo Community administration in pursuit of individual interests.[146] However, particularly in view of the singularly unsatisfactory results in the environment and public interest fields of the application of the *Plaumann* interpretation of individual concern,[147] the merit of the continued universal application of that criterion has been the subject of much debate.[148]

The decision addressed to other persons must *affect* a third party not only individually, but also *directly* for the action to be admissible.[149] When does a decision addressed to Member States affect a private party directly? As a rule it is characteristic of such decisions that for private parties their consequences manifest themselves indirectly, *i.e.* in the national measures which have been taken or maintained under these decisions. If the national authorities have no discretion whatever in this connection, these measures may be equated to Community decisions, which accordingly may affect private parties directly.[150] But even if the national measures have a discretionary character, private parties may be affected directly by the

146. Bebr, *op. cit.* (see note 61, *supra*) 21.
147. *E.g.* Case T-585/93 *Stichting Greenpeace Council (Greenpeace International) et al. v. Commission* [1995] ECR II-2205, upheld on appeal in Case C-321/95 P *Stichting Greenpeace Council (Greenpeace International) et al. v. Commission* [1998] ECR I-nyr (2 April 1998) and Case T-219/95 R *Danielsson et al. v. Commission* [1995] ECR II-3051. See also Cases T-481 and 484/93 *Vereniging van Exporteurs in Levende Varkens et al. v. Commission* [1995] ECR II-2941.
148. See, generally, Micklitz and Reich (eds.), *op. cit.* (see note 61, *supra*). See also the discussion under point C, *post*.
149. As to direct concern in the context of assistance to the states formerly part of the Soviet Union, see Case C-386/96 P *Société Louis Dreyfus & Cie v. Commission* [1998] ECR I-nyr, Case C-403/96 P *Glencore Grain Ltd. v. Commission* [1998] ECR I-nyr and Case C-404/96 P *Glencore Grain Ltd. v. Commission* [1998] ECR I-nyr (all 5 May 1998).
150. Cases 41–44/70 *NV International Fruit Company et al. v. Commission* [1971] ECR 411 at 422–423 (see Kapteyn (1972) SEW 589). In this judgment the Court regarded the challenged regulation as a bundle of decisions; the question was whether they were of individual concern to the applicant. *Cf.* also the ball bearings cases, Case 113/77 *NTN Toyo Bearing Company Ltd. et al. v. Council* [1979] ECR 1185 at 1205; Case 118/77 *Import Standard Office v. Council* [1979] ECR 1277 at 1293–1294; Case 119/77 *Nippon Seiko KK et al. v. Council and Commission* [1979] ECR 1303 at 1327; Case 120/77 *Koyo Seiko Co. Ltd. et al. v. Council and Commission* [1979] ECR 1337 at 1353 and Case 121/77 *Nachi Fujikoshi Corporation et al. v. Council* [1979] ECR 1363 at 1379; see also Case 100/74 *Société C. A. W. SA v. Commission* [1975] ECR 1393 at 1402–1403. In Case 92/78 *Simmenthal SpA v. Commission* [1979] ECR 777 at 798 in which the Court held an action against a decision addressed to a Member State admissible, it nevertheless stressed that the subject-matter of the application was restricted to the effect the contested decision may have been able to have on those to whom it was addressed and those who were directly and individually concerned by it; any disputes about the activities of the intervention agencies in carrying out their duties (or in disregarding Community legal provisions) in so far as they had a discretion were a matter for the national courts.

Community decisions on which these measures are based, particularly if it is certain or highly probable what the effect of the measures will be.[151] The following celebrated judgment illustrates this well.

The circumstances in Cases 106 and 107/63 *Alfred Toepfer & Co. et al. v. Commission*[152] were quite extraordinary. In fixing a free at frontier price for maize from 1 October 1963 the Commission forgot to take account of the new harvest; the price was fixed at a level such that the import levy was reduced to zero; not surprisingly 14 importers applied for import licences for large quantities of maize. Concerned by this, the German government suspended the issue of all the licences and sought approval from the Commission of its safeguard measures. Under the relevant regulation such safeguard measures could be amended, abolished or authorised by a directly applicable decision. The Commission fixed a new free at frontier price for 2 October 1963 and retroactively authorised the German government to maintain the safeguard measures until and including 4 October 1963. The Court took the view[153] that the authorising decision had the same effect *vis-à-vis* interested parties as a decision amending or abolishing the national measures. Like such a decision, an authorising decision directly affected the interested parties in exactly the same way as the measures which it replaced. In practice, though, more attention is frequently paid to the question of individual concern rather than of direct concern.

The view that the Court would not apply the strict test for direct and individual concern with the same strictness is considering actions brought by private parties against decisions addressed not to Member States but to *other private parties* received a certain amount of support in the judgment in Cases 10 and 18/68 *Société 'Eridania' Zuccherifici Nazionali et al. v. Commission.*[154] It is true that the actions brought by a number of Italian sugar refiners against decisions addressed to the Italian Government and certain other Italian sugar refiners were declared inadmissible because the

151. Case 62/70 *Bock v. Commission* [1971] ECR 897 at 908 (see Kapteyn (1972) SEW 596). See also *e.g.* Case 11/82 *Piraiki-Patraiki et al. v. Commission* [1985] ECR 207 at 242; Cases T-435/93 *Association of Sorbitol Producers within the EC (ASPEC) v. Commission* [1995] ECR II-1281 at 1306; Case T-442/93 *Association des Ammidonneries de Céréales de la CEE (AAC) v. Commission* [1995] ECR II-1329 at 1351; Cases T-480 and 483/93 *Antillean Rice Mills NV et al. v. Commission* [1995] ECR II-2305 at 2331–2335 (under appeal in Case C-350/95 P *Antillean Rice Mills NV et al. v. Commission* (pending, O.J. 1996 C 46/6)), and Case T-380/94 *Association Internationale des Utilisateurs de Fils de Filaments Artificiels et Synthétiques et de Soie Naturelle (AIUFFAS) et al. v. Commission* [1996] ECR II-2169 at 2187 (appeal dismissed in Case C-55/97 P *Association Internationale des Utilisateurs de Fils de Filaments Artificiels et Synthétiques et de Soie Naturelle (AIUFFAS) et al. v. Commission* [1997] ECR I-5383). *Cf.* these judgments with those in Case 69/69 *SA Alcan Aluminium Raeren et al. v. Commission* [1970] ECR 385 at 393 and Case 123/77 *Unione Nazionale Importatori e Commercianti Motoveicoli Esteri et al. v. Council* [1978] ECR 845 at 852.
152. [1965] ECR 405.
153. *Ibid.* at 411.
154. [1969] ECR 459.

applicants were not directly and individually concerned. However the formulation which the Court tends to use in examining an action by a private party against a decision addressed only to a Member State is not to be found in this judgment. The Court looked at whether there were 'specific circumstances' which could enable a private party to bring an action but did not develop the concept of 'specific circumstances' in any general definition. It did observe, though, that the 'mere fact that a measure may exercise an influence on the competitive relationships existing on the market in question cannot suffice to allow any trader in any competitive relationship whatever with the addressee to be regarded as directly and individually concerned by that measure.'[155]

Particularly in the field of competition law, interested third parties will have to be given ample possibilities of contesting Commission decisions before the Court (such as exemption decisions under Article 85(3) EC). In comparable situations within national legal systems they will also have such a right of action. Moreover, in these cases the reason behind the limitation of the right of action by private parties against decisions addressed to Member States does not apply. There is no question of an application of law where weighty collective national and Community interests are at issue and where individual interests can only play a minor part. The long-awaited judgment in a competition case came in 1977 in Case 26/76 *Metro SB-Grossmärkte GmbH & Co. KG v. Commission*.[156] The Court declared an appeal by an interested third party (Metro) against a decision addressed by the Commission to another undertaking (SABA) admissible. However, it refrained from formulating any general criteria. The circumstances which differentiated the applicant from all other persons and distinguished it individually just as in the case of the addressee were that the contested decision was adopted in particular as a result of a complaint from Metro relating to the provisions of a selective distribution system operated by SABA, which were relied upon to justify a refusal to deal with Metro or to appoint it a wholesaler for SABA products. The Court concluded that it was 'in the interests of a satisfactory administration of justice and of the proper application of Articles 85 and 86 that natural or legal persons who are entitled, pursuant to Article 3(2)(b) of Regulation No. 17, to request the Commission to find an infringement of Articles 85 and 86 should be able, if their request is not complied with either wholly or in part, to institute proceedings in order to protect their legitimate interests.'[157]

The starting point remains the *Plaumann* formula;[158] differentiating

155. *Ibid.* at 481.
156. [1977] ECR 1875 at 1898–1901, see van Empel (1978) SEW 422–424, Korah (1979) JBL 177 and Dinnage (1979) 4 ELRev. 15.
157. [1977] ECR 1875 at 1901.
158. See note 136, *supra*.

circumstances in the sense of that judgment are present, according to a line of judgments,[159] if a regulation, such as Regulation 17[160] in the competition field or now Regulation 384/96[161] on anti-dumping, affords procedural guarantees to undertakings which enable them to request the Commission to find an infringement of Community rules. In such cases undertakings must have a right of action in order to protect their legitimate interests.[162] If they have not lodged the complaint themselves then it will be relevant to examine their role in the pre-contentious procedure, *e.g.* to see if they have been concerned in the development of the complaint which led to the opening of the investigation procedure or if they have been heard or if their observations have substantially determined the conduct of the procedure; their position on the market to which the contested legislation applies can also be taken into account.[163] A similar approach to the question of admissibility is also involved when the Commission investigates state aids, given that Article 93(2) EC gives in general terms undertakings the right to submit their comments to the Commission. In such cases undertakings must be able to show that their position on the market is substantially affected by the state aid which is the subject of the decision challenged.[164] The more substantive aspects of judicial protection in these fields are discussed in sections 3.2.4 and 4.6.4 of

159. See note 162, *infra.*
160. See note 126, *supra.*
161. O.J. 1996 L 56/1, most recently amended by Reg. 905/98 (O.J. 1998 L 128/18). Anti-dumping duties are established by regulation, see the discussion on this instrument, *post.*
162. Case 169/84 *Compagnie Française de l'Azote (COFAZ) SA at al. v. Commission* [1986] ECR 391 at 414–415 referring to Case 26/76 *Metro SB-Grossmärkte GmbH & Co. KG v. Commission* [1977] ECR 1875; Case 191/82 *EEC Seed Crushers' and Oil Processors' Federation (Fediol) v. Commission* [1983] ECR 2913 and Case 210/81 *Schmidt, trading as Demo-Studio Schmidt v. Commission* [1983] ECR 3045. See also *e.g.* Case C-358/89 *Extramet Industrie SA v. Council* [1991] ECR I-2501 at 2531–2532 (with the rather more different analysis of Jacobs, Adv. Gen. at 2508–2523).
163. *E.g.* Case 264/82 *Timex Corporation v. Council et al.* [1985] ECR 849 at 865–866, and Case 75/84 *Metro SB-Grossmärkte GmbH & Co. KG v. Commission* [1986] ECR 3021.
164. Case 169/84 *Compagnie française de l'azote (Cofaz) SA et al. v. Commission* [1986] ECR 391 at 416; 'may adversely affect their legitimate interests by seriously jeopardiz-ing their position on the market in question.' See also, among more recent case-law relating to lobbies or organizational frameworks, Case C-198/91 *William Cook PLC v. Commission* [1993] ECR I-2487 at 2528; Cases T-447–449/93 *Associazione Italiana Tecnico Economica del Cemento et al. v. Commission* [1995] ECR II-1971; Case T-442/93 *Association des Amidonneries de Céréales de la CEE (AAC) et al. v. Commission* [1995] ECR II-1329 at 1352, and Case T-435/93 *Association of Sorbitol Producers within the EC (ASPEC) et al. v. Commission* [1995] ECR II-1281 at 1307; Case T-442/93 *Association des Ammidonneries de Céréales de la CEE (AAC) v. Commission* [1995] ECR II-1329 at 1351, and Case T-380/94 *Association Internationale des Utilisateurs de Fils de Filaments Artificiels et Synthétiques et de Soie Naturelle (AIUFFAS) et al. v. Commission* [1996] ECR II-2172 at 2188 (appeal dismissed in Case C-55/97 P *Associa-tion Internationale des Utilisateurs de Fils de Filaments Artificiels et Synthétiques et de*

Chapter VIII and in section 3.3.3 of Chapter XII, below. See also the discussion of the direction of recent case-law on admissibility under point C of this section, below.

B. Actions against general decisions and against improper regulations.[165] In the ECSC system private parties have been accorded a right of action against general decisions and recommendations although the grounds of action have been limited: they can only attack a general decision or recommendation if it involves a misuse of powers affecting them.[166] To ensure the admissibility of the action it is sufficient to advance pertinent arguments supporting the contention of misuse of powers.[167] Once the action is admissible the applicant may attack the general decision or recommendation only on the ground of misuse of powers. He or she cannot therefore obtain the annulment of the general decision or recommendation on any of the other grounds of action mentioned in Article 33. In practice it appears very hard to prove misuse of powers.[168] The Court has never upheld an appeal by a private party against a general decision.

In the EC and Euratom systems an action by private parties against regulations *stricto sensu* is impossible. They may only institute proceedings against decisions which, 'although in the form of a regulation..., are of direct and individual concern to them.'[169] The regulation must therefore in reality be a decision or a similar act of an individual nature, and this decision or act must be of direct and individual concern to the applicant. The purpose of this provision, according to the Court, 'is in particular to prevent the community institutions, merely by choosing the form of a regulation, from being able to exclude an application by an individual against a decision of direct and individual concern to him and thus to make clear that the choice of form may not alter the nature of a measure.'[170] In dealing with the question of whether what purports to be a regulation is indeed one or not the Court does not take a very formalistic

---

Soie Naturelle (AIUFFAS) et al. v. Commission [1997] ECR I-5383). See, further, Gormley in Micklitz and Reich (eds.), *op. cit.* (see note 61, *supra*) 159.

165. The Court appears prepared to treat directives, as acts of general application, in the same way as regulations, as far as the right of appeal by private parties is concerned, see, referring to earlier authorities, Cases C-298/89 *Government of Gibraltar v. Council* [1993] ECR I-3603 at 3654–3655.

166. Art. 33 ECSC, 2nd para.

167. Case 8/55 *Fédération Charbonnière de Belgique v. High Authority* [1965] ECR 441 at 454–455, and Cases 55/63 etc. *Acciaiere Fonderie Ferriere di Modena et al. v. High Authority* [1964] ECR 211 at 228.

168. But for an example of a successful challenge see Cases 140/82 etc. *Walzstahl-Vereinigung et al. v. Commission* [1984] ECR 951.

169. Arts. 173 EC and 146 Euratom (4th para. in each case).

170. *E.g.* Case 307/81 *Alusuisse Italia SpA v. Council et al.* [1982] ECR 3463 at 3471–3472; Case T-476/93 *Fédération régionale des syndicats d'exploitants agricoles (FRSEA) et al. v. Council* [1993] ECR II-1187 at 1194–1195, and Case T-70/94 *Comafrica SpA et*

view. In the first place it considers that the aim and content of the purported regulation is decisive, not its form or name.[171] It is therefore necessary to examine the nature of the contested measures and in particular the legal effects which they are intended to produce or in fact produce.[172] Thus a regulation may actually be a bundle of decisions.[173] Secondly, the Court recognises the possibility that measures, even if as a whole they are of a regulatory nature, 'may nevertheless contain provisions addressed to specific persons in such a way as to distinguish them individually in the sense of the second paragraph of Article 173 of the Treaty.'[174]

Two questions are relevant for the admissibility of the action by a private party against a regulation (or a part thereof):

(1) is it either a regulation *strico sensu* or a decision or a similar act, and, if the latter,
(2) is this decision of direct and individual concern to the applicant?

Since a decision will by definition be of direct and individual concern to a given party (a Member State or an individual), the two questions are closely linked,[175] although it is of course conceivable that a regulation must be qualified as a decision or a similar act, but that an applicant is not directly and individually affected by it, for instance because it is actually addressed to Member States. The difference between a regulation

al. v. Commission [1996] ECR II-1741 at 1760 (under appeal in Case C-73/97 P *France v. Comafrica SpA et al.* (pending, O.J. 1996 C 131/5).

171. See Chapter V, section 1.1, *ante.*
172. Case 370/81 *Alusuisse* [1982] ECR 3463 at 3472.
173. Cases 41–44/70 *NV International Fruit Company et al.* [1971] ECR 411 at 422; see also the ball bearings cases (see note 150, *supra*) *loc. cit.*
174. Case 30/67 *Industria Molitoria Imolese et al v. Council* [1968] ECR 115 at 121; see also Cases 16 and 17/62 *Confédération nationale des producteurs des fruits et légumes et al. v. Council* [1962] ECR 471 at 478–479, and Case 112/77 *August Töpfer & Co. GmbH. v. Commission* [1978] ECR 1019 at 1030.
175. The Court sometimes tends to pass over the first question, see *e.g.* Case 40/64 *Sgarlata et al. v. Commission* [1965] ECR 215 at 226 and Case 123/77 *Unione Nazionale Importatori e Commercianti Motoveicoli Esteri et al. v. Council* [1978] ECR 845 at 851; Case 333/85 *Mannesmannrohren-Werke AG et al. v. Council* [1987] ECR 1381 (challenge to a regulation restricting the export of steel pipes and tubes to the USA), and Cases C-232 and 233/91 *Odette Nikou Petridi Anonymos Kapnemporiki Eteria AE et al. v. Commission* [1991] ECR I-5351 at 5355. See Storme and Maresceau: *Europese Rechtspleging en Rechtspraak* (2nd ed., Ghent, 1979) 65–66, *contra* Lauwaars, in O'Keeffe and Schermers (eds.), *Essays in European Law and Integration* (Deventer, 1982) 29 at 37–38. As to the rights of defence, generally, see Due (1987) CDE 383 and *Due Process in the administrative procedure* (FIDE Congress Reports Copenhagen, 1978, Vol. 3). See also *Procedures and sanctions in economic administrative law* (FIDE Congress Reports Berlin, 1996, Vol. 3).
176. Case 307/81 *Alusuisse* [1982] ECR 3463 at 3473. The Court observed, *ibid.*, that this

and a decision lies exclusively in the nature of the measure itself and the legal effects which it produces and not in the procedures for its adoption.[176] The decisive factor for the regulatory character of an act is its general import, and this implies that it 'is applicable to objectively determined situations and involves legal consequences for categories of persons viewed in a general and abstract manner.'[177] a decision, on the other hand, is characterised by the fact that the category of those to whom it is addressed is limited. It applies to a limited number of natural or legal persons that are identified or can be identified.[178] The difficulty is, however, that regulations, too, may sometimes actually apply to a limited number of identifiable persons.

According to the case-law of the Court, however, the regulatory character of an act is not lost merely because it is possible to determine with a greater or lesser degree of accuracy the number or even the identity of the persons to whom it applies at any given time, provided that the measure clearly applies 'as a result of an objective situation of fact or law which it specifies and which is in harmony with its ultimate objective.'[179] If, therefore, it appears from the context of a regulation that it is of purely secondary importance that a provision of that regulation applies to legal subjects whose number and identity can be determined, that provision keeps its regulatory character. It retains the objective character which is the essential element of a regulation. Likewise, provisions which restrict the application of a regulation for a particular period or by reference to a particular area or territory do not in doing so lose their normative character.[180]

A considerable body of case-law has developed in the field of anti-

solution conformed with the system of Community law as importers could contest individual measures taken by national authorities in application of the Community regulations. See also Case 143/77 *Koninkijke Scholten-Honig NV v. Council and Commission* [1979] ECR 3583 at 3626.

177. Case 6/68 *Zuckerfabrik-Watenstedt GmbH v. Council* [1968] ECR 409 at 415. See also *e.g.* Cases 789 and 790/79 *Calpak SpA et al. v. Commission* [1980] ECR 1949 at 1961 and, further, Chapter V, section 1.2, *ante*.

178. Cases 16 and 17/62 *Confédération nationale des producteurs des fruits et légumes et al. v. Council* [1962] ECR 471 at 498, see Chapter V, section 1.4, *ante*.

179. Case 6/68 *Zuckerfabrik Watenstedt* [1968] ECR 409 at 415. See also *e.g.* Case 64/69 *La Compagnie Française Commerciale et Financière SA v. Commission* [1970] ECR 221 at 226–227; Case 64/80 *Guiffrida et al. v. Council* [1981] ECR 693 at 703; Case 242/81 *SA Roquette Frères v. Council* [1982] ECR 3213 at 3230; Cases 87/83 *etc. Salerno et al. v. Commission and Council* [1985] ECR 2523 at 2535; Cases 9/86 *etc. Asteris AE et al. v. Commission* [1988] ECR 2181 at 2205–2206; Cases C-15 and 108/91 *Josef Buckl & Söhne OHG et al. v. Commission* [1992] ECR I-6061 at 6099.

180. See Case 6/68 *Zuckerfabrik Watenstedt*, *loc. cit.*, *ibid.* and Case 64/69 *La Compagnie Française Commerciale et Financière SA v. Commission*, *loc. cit.*, *ibid.* See further *e.g.* Cases 103–109/78 *Société des usines de Beauport et al. v. Council* [1979] ECR 17 at 24–25; Case 26/86 *Deutz und Geldermann, Sektkellerei Breisach/Baden GmbH v. Council* [1987] ECR 941 at 951–952, and Case C-168/93 *Government of Gibraltar et al. v. Council*

dumping, in relation to attempts to challenge anti-dumping duties definitively imposed by the Council, often preceded by provisional duties imposed by the Commission, after an investigation proceeding conducted by the Commission. This case-law well illustrates the difficulties in the application of the criteria developed by the Court and set out above. In a sense the Court wants to have its cake and eat it, as it accepts the possibility that a regulation may be of direct and individual concern to a particular person or group, but at the same time retain its general normative character in respect of all other persons. The case-law concerns which persons may appeal against anti-dumping regulations (or against countervailing duties imposed to compensate for export subsidies granted by third countries),and under which circumstances such an action will be admissible. Despite the normative character of anti-dumping duties, it is not only the complainant which is directly and individually concerned by the relevant regulation,[181] certain producers and exporters accused of dumping may also be able to challenge the regulation, if they can show that they are identified in the regulation or that they were involved in the administrative proceeding leading to the adoption of the measure concerned.[182] If they had not been allowed to challenge the regulation, they would effectively have been left without a remedy, as it is normally the importer concerned who would actually pay the duty. Importers have, though, found *locus standi* requirements something of an unruly horse. Associated importers (*i.e.* if there is an association between the exporter and the importer and the export price determination or the calculation of the anti-dumping duty itself is made by reference to the importer's resale price) will be able to challenge the regulation concerned.[183] Independent importers are normally given no

[1993] ECR I-4009 at 4014. The same applies in relation to a directive temporarily exempting a particular area from the scope of application of another directive, see Case C-298/89 *Government of Gibraltar et al. v. Council* [1993] ECR I-3605 at 3654–3655.

181. Case 191/82 *EEC Seed Crushers' and Oil Processors' Federation (FEDIOL) v. Commission* [1983] ECR 2913 at 2935–2936 (complainants) and Case 264/82 *Timex Corporation v. Council and Commission* [1985] ECR 849 at 866. Timex had lodged a complaint which had been rejected on the ground that only one Community producer had complained. When an association of producers then lodged an identical complaint which resulted in the imposition of an anti-dumping duty which did not satisfy Timex, the Court found Timex's challenge to the regulation concerned admissible in view of the determining role it had played in the proceeding and its market position.

182. See *e.g.* Cases 239 and 275/82 *Allied Corporation et al. v. Commission* [1984] ECR 1005 at 1030; Cases C-133 and 150/87 *Nashua Corporation v. Commission and Council* [1990] ECR I-719 at 772–773, and Case C-16/87 *Gestetener Holdings plc v. Council and Commission* [1990] ECR I-781 at 833–834. These parties are individually concerned only by the anti-dumping duties imposed on their products, not on those imposed on the products of other parties, see *e.g.* Case 240/84 *NTN Toyo Bearing Company Ltd. et al. v. Council* [1987] ECR 1809 at 1851–1852 and Case 258/84 *Nippon Seiko KK v. Council* [1987] ECR 1923 at 1960–1961.

183. *E.g.* Case 118/77 *Import Standard office (ISO) v. Council* [1979] ECR 1277 at 1292, Cases 239 and 275/82 *Allied Corporation et al. v. Commission* [1984] ECR 1005 at 1031,

standing to challenge anti-dumping regulations, as they are found merely to be part of a general group objectively affected within the meaning of the *Plaumann* formula, although it is open to them to attack in the national courts the actual decision of the national customs authorities (whereby the duty is collected in pursuance of the regulation).[184] In doing so, they would invariably submit that the regulation was invalid, and ask the national court to refer that question to the Court of Justice under Article 177 EC.[185] An exception to the normal approach was made by the Court in Case C-358/89 *Extramet Industrie SA v. Council*[186] owing to the exceptional circumstances involved.[187] In anti-dumping cases nowadays no specific attention appears to be paid to the question whether litigants are directly concerned by the imposition of duties.[188]

and Cases C-305/86 and 160/87 *Neotype Techmashexport GmbH v. Commission et al.* [1990] ECR I-2945 at 2998.

184. *E.g.* Case 307/81 *Alusuisse Italia SpA v. Council et al.* [1982] ECR 3463 at 3472–3473; Cases 239 and 275/82 *Allied Corporation* [1984] ECR 1005 at 1031, and Case 205/87 *Nuova Ceam Srl v. Commission* [1987] ECR 4427 at 4431–4432. See, generally, Inama (1994) 28 JWT 67.

185. See *e.g.* Case C-16/90 *Nölle v. Hauptzollamt Bremerhaven-Freihafen* [1991] ECR I-5163. As to the disadvantages of this route, see Advocate General Jacobs in Case C-358/89 *Extramet Industrie SA v. Council* [1991] ECR I-2501 at 2524–2525. See also (in relation to State aids decisions and the relationship between references and the possibility of seeking the annulment of an act) Case C-188/92 *TWD Textilwerke Deggendorf GmbH v. Germany* [1994] ECR I-833 and (in relation to a decision refusing exemption from liability to pay a special contribution to a scrapping fund) Case C-178/95 *Wiljo NV v. Belgian State* [1997] ECR I-585.

186. [1991] ECR I-2501 at 2532.

187. Extramet was the largest importer of calcium metal and also the end-user of the product. Moreover, its business activities were to a very large extent dependent on those imports and were seriously affected by the contested regulation: there were very few manufacturers of the product and Extramet had been refused supplies from the sole Community producer which was at the same time its main competitor for the processed product. It would have been maifestly unjust to deny Extramet standing. Jacobs, Adv. Gen., pointed out that Extramet did not fall within the *Plaumann* criteria as hitherto applied by the Court and proposed that 'an undertaking should in principle have standing to challenge an anti-dumping regulation where it is identified, even if only implicitly, by the regulation or where it played an important part in the procedure leading to the adoption of the regulation, at least where its position on the relevant market has been significantly affected.' [1991] ECR I-2501 at 2523. This proposed criterion may offer greater certainty than the prospect that the Court might simply pull an equitable rabbit out of the hat by concluding (as it did) that the existing recognition of standing for certain categories of traders did not prevent other traders from also claiming to be individually concerned within the meaning of *Plaumann*. The learned Advocate General's criterion would not so be easy to apply more generally outside the fields of competition, anti-dumping and state aids.

188. The duties are collected by the national customs authorities who have no discretion in carrying out the instruction to collect the duties the regulation imposes. Initially the Court did consider the matter, see Case 113/77 *NTN Toyo Bearing Company Ltd. et al. v. Council* [1979] ECR 1185 at 1205 (and the other ball-bearings cases decided on the same day).

C. Towards new approaches? The slightly more flexible approach that the Court has appeared to follow in relation to actions against anti-dumping regulations has not percolated into a more general reappraisal of the *Plaumann* formula in respect of regulations, nor does it as yet seem to herald any general revisitation of the Court's seemingly hybrid approach to the question how a regulation can at the same time be of general normative application and of direct and individual concern to certain persons.[189] In Case C-309/89 *Codorniu SA v. Council*[190] the Court of Justice with little ceremony accepted that the proprietor of a registered trade mark who was prevented from continuing to use that mark by a Council regulation was individually concerned within the *Plaumann* fomula. It did not address the question whether Codorniu was directly concerned, presumably on the ground that there was no element of discretion involved in the contested regulation. It may be that it really concluded that the facts in *Codorniu* were directly comparable with those in Cases 106 and 107/63 *Alfred Toepfer Co. et al. v. Commission*[191] (which concerned a decision) and that the applicant was part of an already certain closed class of persons whose interests would be adversely affected at the time the regulation concerned was adopted, or it may be that it simply silently, without attribution, followed the approach of the Advocate General.[192] Arnull has suggested[193] that the message of *Codorniu*, 'read in the light of the Advocate General's Opinion, seemed to be that the approach embodied in the early case-law was liable to cause injustice and that the Community's political institutions were now sufficiently robust to withstand more intense judicial scrutiny of their activities.' Indeed, fears of such increased scrutiny of the arguments and evaluation of the facts lay behind the initial refusal on the part of some Member States to allow the Court of First Instance jurisdiction in actions challenging anti-dumping regulations, a position which perhaps unsurprisingly found support among certain Commission officials.

189. Despite the invitation to do so by Jacobs, Adv. Gen., in Case C-358/89 *Extramet* [1991] ECR 2501 at 2525 (following his extensive discussion of the various approaches, *ibid.* at 2515–2520). See, generally, Nettesheim in Micklitz and Reich, *op. cit.* (see note 61, *supra*) 225.
190. [1994] ECR I-1853 at 1886.
191. [1965] ECR 405. Usher (1994) 19 ELRev. 636 at 637–638 cites Case 100/74 *Société C.A.M. SA v. Commission* [1975] ECR 1393 at 1403 as an isolated example of the Court applying the more flexible approach later found in the anti-dumping cases.
192. The difficulty the Court had in reaching a decision may be gauged from the fact that the case was lodged in October 1989, Lenz, Adv. Gen., gave his Opinion in October 1992 and the judgment was not handed down until May 1994. The learned Advocate General drew parallels with the *Extramet* situation, noting that Codorniu was the largest producer of the type of sparkling wine involved, its economic activity was largely dependent on business transactions adversely affected by the contested regulation, and that activity was severely affected by that regulation, [1994] ECR I-1853 at 1870–1871. Arnull, in Micklitz and Reich (eds.), *op. cit.* (see note 61, *supra*) 39 at 46 has described the reasoning in *Codorniu* as 'terse, in places even incoherent.'
193. *Ibid.*

But any reports of the death of the *Plaumann* formula appear, like reports of Mark Twain's death, to be as yet greatly exaggerated. The Court of First Instance did not perceive any lead from *Cordorniu* towards a more flexible approach to *locus standi*, whether in relation to regulations[194] or decisions.[195] Indeed it now clear, given the judgment in Case C-321/95 P *Stichting Greenpeace Council (Greenpeace International) et al. v. Commission*[196] that the Court of Justice will not revisit the *Plauman* criteria. Arnull has suggested[197] that the reason for the reluctance on the part of the Court of First Instance might be in part managerial: a fear of being flooded out with appeals. He opined that 'it seems wrong in principle that a litigant's right to invoke the jurisdiction of a court of law should depend on factors which are unrelated to the circumstances of his claim and which may vary with the passage of time.'[198] It may seem strange that the requirements for admissibility should vary according to the area of Community law involved, and it might be thought that Community law is now sufficiently robust to permit a more generous

194. See *e.g.* Case T-489/93 *Unifruit Hellas EPE v. Commission* [1994] ECR II-1201 at 1212–1216; Case T-472/93 *Campo Ebro Industrial SA et al. v. Council* [1995] ECR II-421 at 434–436 (appeal in Case C-138/95 P *Campo Ebro Industrial SA et al. v. Council* [1997] ECR I-2027 dismissed) in which the Court of First Instance seems not to have been impressed by the emphasis in *Extramet* on the competitive position of the applicant, and Case T-107/94 *Kik v. Council et al.* [1995] ECR II-1717 at 1730–1731 (appeal dismissed as manifestly unfounded in Case C-270/95 *Kik v. Council et al.* [1996] ECR I-1987). See also Case T-183/94 *Cantina Cooperativa fra Produttori Vitivinicoli di Torre di Mosto et al. v. Commission* [1995] ECR II-1941 at 1963–1968, in which the Court of First Instance was unmoved by arguments about the diligence of the applicants and the problems which they perceived at the national level, the proper forum for judicial protection being the national courts. But in Case T-70/94 *Comafrica SpA et al. v. Commission* [1996] ECR II-1741 at 1761 the Court of First Instance rightly found that the contested regulation could in reality be characterized as a bundle of decisions (see the pending appeal in Case C-73/97 P *France v. Commission* (O.J. 1997 C 131/5).
195. *E.g.* Case T-117/94 *Associazione Agricoltori della provincia di Rovigio et al. v. Commission* [1995] ECR II-455 at 464–467 (appeal dismissed in Case C-142/95 P *Associazione Agricoltori della provincia di Rovigio et al. v. Commission* [1996] ECR I-6669); Case T-96/92 *Comité Central d'Enterprise de la Société Générale des Grandes Sources et al. v. Commission* [1995] ECR II-1213 at 1231–1237; Case T-12/93 *Comité Central d'Enterprise de la Société Anonyme Vittel et al. v. Commission* [1995] ECR II-1247 at 1266–1277; Case T-585/93 *Stichting Greenpeace Council (Greenpeace International) et al. v. Commission* [1995] ECR II-2205 (appeal dismissed in Case C-321/95 P *Stichting Greenpeace Council (Greenpeace International) et al. v. Commission* [1998] ECR I-nyr (2 April 1998)) and Case T-219/95 R *Danielsson et al. v. Commission* [1995] ECR II-3051. See also Cases T-481 and 484/93 *Vereniging van Exporteurs in Levende Varkens et al. v. Commission* [1995] ECR II-2941.
196. [1998] ECR I-nyr (2 April 1998), dismissing the appeal from the judgment of the Court of First Instance in Case T-585/93 *Stichting Greenpeace Council (Greenpeace International) et al. v. Commission* [1995] ECR II-2205.
197. In Micklitz and Reich (eds.), *op. cit.* (see note 61, *supra*) 39 at 51. He was, of course, writing well before the Court of Justice's ruling in the Greenpeace case.
198. *Ibid.*

standing for private litigants. The test of 'an act adversely affecting an applicant's interests' is a possible reformulation of the fourth paragraph of Article 173 EC which could be adopted on revision of the Treaty.[199] Frivolous or vexatious claims can to a cetain extent be deterred by the order as to costs. Furthermore, a streamlined procedure would enable the Court of First Instance or the Court of Justice as appropriate to dispatch mere mischief-making and posturing speedily, so as to ensure that examination of serious issues is not delayed.[200] It is certainly clear that any expansion of *locus standi* would be a matter for a Treaty amendment.

There are, however, a number of arguments which can be raised against a wider interpretation of general standing for non-addressees. First, as was noted at the beginning of heading A in this section, above, the wording of Article 173 EC is clearly less extensive than the wording of Article 33 ECSC: this reflects a conscious decision by the Member States as contracting parties to those two treaties that access to the Court for private individuals should be less extensive in the EC system. Secondly, the judicial architecture of the EC system is much less centralized than it is in the ECSC system: the former involves an allocation of tasks between the Community judiciary and national courts. In that context the case-law of the Court of Justice has in relation to first and second generation problems created a framework within which also judicial decisions are taken as close to the citizens as possible. This approach is consistent with the wording of the second paragraph of Article A TEU. Finally, a formula such as 'an act adversely affecting an applicant's interest' risks undermining this judicial architecture by having a centralizing effect through opening the flood-gates for unrestrained appeals for annulment of decisions addressed to Member States, as well as of regulations and directives, particularly given that the interests of a great many persons may be adversely affected by myriad acts of the Community Institutions. It is true that *Extramet* and *Cordorniu* demonstrate that the Article 173 EC case-law is unsatisfactory in cases in which private parties have no possibility to seek redress in front of their national courts, although the Court of Justice is certainly now taking this problem more into account.[201]

---

199. Advocated by Arnull, *ibid.* at 53–54. But as is explained below, this is not without problems.

200. Considerations of space prevent a full discussion of the various possibilities, see, generally, the contributions of the Court of Justice and the Court of First Instance to the Intergovernmental Conference 1996 (published in the *Proceedings of the Court of Justice and Court of First Instance of the European Communities* No. 15/95); Grévisse (1995) RMC 11; Kapteyn in Curtin and Heukels (eds.), *op. cit.* (see note 7, *supra*) 135; Micklitz and Reich (eds.), *op. cit.* (see note 61, *supra*); Scorey (1996) 21 ELRev. 224, and Van Gerven (1996) 21 ELRev. 211.

201. See *e.g.* Case C-395/95 P *Geotronics v. Commission* [1997] ECR I-2271 at 2295–2297.

1.3.2 The plea of illegality

It will be apparent from the above that a private party is deprived, in the ECSC system almost entirely and in the EC system completely, of the right to lodge a direct action for annulment of an act of the Council or the Commission which has general effect. If, however, in an action before the Court for some other reason a regulation or (in the ECSC) a general decision or recommendation is in issue a private party may plead the illegality thereof, on the same grounds as those applying to an action for annulment and notwithstanding the expiration of the time limit for appeal.[202] Thus, a private party may raise this plea if he or she institutes an action for annulment against a decision addressed to him or her which is based, for instance, on a regulation or a general decision.[203] If the plea is admitted, the Court in a specific case will not apply the regulation or general decision; it will thus annul the decision based on the regulation or general decision.[204] The regulation or general decision itself, however, cannot be annulled,[205] although the Institution which issued it will of course draw the appropriate conclusions and take measures to replace the illegal act; the effect is that the regulation or general decision is rendered unenforceable.

In the ECSC Treaty the possibility of pleading the illegality of the parent measure would at first sight seem to be limited to the case where a private party attacks a decision by which a fine or periodic penalty payment has been imposed on him or her. He or she may then plead the illegality of the decision or recommendation (of a general, not of an individual nature),[206] with the breach of which he or she has been accused. The Court, however, gave a wider scope to this rule. It does not regard the provision of the third paragraph of Article 36 ECSC as a special provision, but as the

---

202. Arts. 184 EC, 36 ECSC, 3rd para., and 156 Euratom. This plea of illegality is often called 'the exception of illegality' (after the French). See, generally, van Rijn, *Exceptie van onweittigheid en prejudiciele procedure inzake geldigheid van gemeenschapshandelingen* (Deventer, 1978); Barav (1974) 11 CMLRev. 366; Behr (1966) 4 CMLRev. 7; Schermers and Waelbroeck, *op. cit.* (see note 17, supra) 261–265; Dubois (1978) CDE 407; van Rijn (1980) CDE 177; Bebr, op. *cit.* (see note 48, *supra)* 192–218 and Lasok and Millett, *op. cit.* (see note 7, *supra*) paras. 467–483.
203. The decision addressed to the private party must be based on the rules alleged to be illegal; see Cases 275/80 and 24/81 *Krupp Stahl AG v. Commission* [1981] ECR 248 at 2517–2518. See also Cases 140/82 etc. *Walzstahlvereinigung et al. v. Commission* [1984] ECR 951 at 983 for the conditions which the Court requires to be fulfilled in a concrete case.
204. See Case 9/56 *Meroni & Co., Industrie Metallurgiche SpA v. High Authority* [1957 and 1958] ECR 133 at 140.
205. See Cases 31 and 33/62 *Milchwerke Heinz Wöhrmann & Sohn KG et al. v. Commission* [1962] ECR 501 at 507 and Cases 15–33/73 etc. *Schots, née Kortner et al. v. Council et al.* [1974] ECR 177 at 191–192.
206. See Case 3/59 *Germany v. High Authority* [1960] ECR 53 at 61.

application of a general principle, which Article 36 declares applicable to the special case of an action in which the Court has unlimited jurisdiction.[207] In one form or another this principle can be found in the national law of the Member States.[208]

The wide scope of this principle received express recognition in the EC system,[209] although exclusively for regulations, not for directives.[210] The Court regards Article 184 EC as covering all acts of the Institutions which, even though they are not in the form of a regulation, nevertheless produce similar legal effects and on those grounds may not be challenged under Article 173 EC by natural or legal persons other than Community Institutions and Member States.[211] Thus the plea of illegality can be invoked against all acts which have general effect which form the legal basis for the individual measures attacked by the applicant. The Court justified this wide interpretation on the ground that it was necessary to protect those who were precluded by the second paragraph of Article 173 EEC (now the fourth paragraph of Article 173 EC) from challenging general acts; they should have the benefit of a judicial review of those acts at the time when they are affected by implementing decisions which are of direct and individual concern to them.[212] It should be noted that the contested general act on which the individual decisions are based can be reviewed by the Court under written as well as unwritten Community law[213] on the same grounds as in the case of a direct action for annulment of Community acts.[214] It is important to understand that Article 184 EC does not create an independent right of action; the plea of illegality may only be raised indirectly in proceedings against an implementing measure, the validity of the regulation is challenged in so far as it constitutes the legal basis of the implementing measure.[215]

Any party may invoke the plea of illegality in connection with a dispute concerning a regulation adopted by the European Parliament and the Council acting jointly, the Council, the Commission, or the ECB. The

---

207. See Case 9/56 *Meroni, loc. cit.*
208. See the opinion of Lagrange, Adv. Gen. in Case 15/57 *Compagnie des Hauts Four- neaux de Chasse v. High Authority* [1957 and 1958] ECR 211 at 235–236.
209. Arts. 184 EC and 156 Euratom.
210. *Cf.* the ECSC system, in which the plea of illegality may be invoked against general recommendations as well as general decisions.
211. Case 92/78 *Simmenthal SpA v. Commission* [1979] ECR 777 at 800; see also (already) van Rijn, *op. cit.* (1978, see note 202, *supra*) 172 and 261.
212. *Ibid.* Barav, in Constantinesco *et al.* (eds.), *Traité instuant la CEE* (Paris, 1992) 1158 notes that this had been anticipatd by Morand, *La législation dans les Communautés européennes* (Paris, 1968) 41 and Pescatore, *L'Ordre juridique des Communautés eur- opéennes* (Liège, 1973) 158.
213. See Chapter IV, section 7.5.1, *ante.*
214. Arts. 184 EC and 156 Euratom; in relation to the ECSC Treaty Case 9/56 *Meroni* [1957 and 1958] ECR 133 at 141.
215. *E.g.* Case 33/80 *Albini v. Council et al.* [1981] ECR 2141 at 2157; Cases 87/77 *etc.*

question has arisen whether the term 'dispute' also refers to proceedings concerning a Community regulation before a national court. The Court answered this question in the negative when private parties to national proceedings applied directly to it, pursuant to Article 184, holding that this provision concerned only a plea for inapplicability of a regulation in a dispute pending before the Court of Justice on the basis of another Article of the Treaty, and then only incidentally and with limited effect.[216] The Court did refer in this context to the possibility that the national court might ask for a preliminary ruling. Indeed, such a request may concern 'the validity ... of the acts of the Institutions of the Community.'[217]

The question arises whether Member States too may invoke Article 184 EC by way of defence in infringement proceedings brought by the Commission under Article 169 EC or the ECB under Article 180(d) EC. The majority view in the literature is that they may,[218] although the Court, which in the light of the case-law discussed above, seems to have sought the ratio of Article 184 EC in the limited right of direct appeal for private parties, has yet to pronounce on the point. In the context of an action against non-compliance with a Commission decision under Article 93(2) EC in the state aids field, however, the Court has refused to allow a Member State, which has let the time-limit for challenging the decision expire, then to plead the illegality of that decision in its defence to the non-compliance proceedings.[219]

1.3.3 Actions for damages on the ground of the Community's non-contractual liability

At first sight the provisions on non-contractual liability in the ECSC Treaty on the one hand and the EC and Euratom Treaties on the other

Salerno et al. v. Commission et al. [1985] ECR 2523 at 2536, and Case C-64/93 *Donatab Srl et al. v. Commission* [1993] ECR I-3595 at 3602. See also Case 216/82 *Universität Hamburg v. Hauptzollamt Hamburg Kehrwieder* [1985] ECR 2771 at 2788 which confirms that the principle underlying Art. 184 EC can be pleaded in national proceedings against a national measure based on a Community decision (*in casu* on non-exemption of apparatus from customs duty).

216. Cases 31 and 33/62 *Wöhrmann* (see note 205, *supra*), *loc. cit.* The judgments cited in note 215, *supra*, are the logical consequence of this approach.

217. Art. 177 EC, *cf.* section 2.1, *post.*

218. See Waelbroeck (M. and D.) and Vandersanden in Mégret *et al.* (eds.), *Le Droit de la CEE* (Vol. 10, 2nd ed., Brussels, 1993) 132–133 and Barav in Constantinesco *et al.* (eds.), *loc. cit.* (see note 212, *ante*).

219. Case 156/77 *Commission v. Belgium* [1978] ECR 1881 at 1896–1897. See, in relation to private parties, Case C-188/92 *TWD Textilwerke Deggendorf GmbH v. Germany* [1994] ECR I-833 at 853, and Cases T-244 and 486/93 *TWD Textilwerke Deggendorf GmbH v. Commission* [1995] ECR II-2265 at 2302 (appeal dismissed in Case C-355/95 P *TWD Textilwerke Deggendorf GmbH v. Commission* [1997] ECR I-2549).

hand appear different. Article 40 ECSC is clearly inspired by French administrative law. The Community[220] can be sued in the Court of Justice for injury caused in carrying out the ECSC Treaty by a wrongful act or omission on the part of the Community in the performance of its functions or caused by a personal wrong by a servant of the Community in the performance of his duties.[221] These two headings reflect the concepts *'faute de service'* and *'faute personnelle'* in the French system; the distinction determined whether the administrative courts or the civil courts dealt with the matter.[222] The concept of fault covers the objective illegality as well as the concrete reprehensibility of the conduct.[223]

These terms are wholly absent in the second paragraphs of Articles 215 EC and 188 Euratom. The damage which the Institution or its servants (or the ECB or its servants) have caused in the performance of their duties must be made good 'in accordance with the general principles common to the laws of the Member States.'[224] Two general questions arise in relation to this. First, what is meant by general principles common to the laws of the Member States? The second question is whether Community liability under the second paragraphs of Articles 215 EC and 188 Euratom rests on another and clearly different basis than that under Article 40 ECSC?

The first question can be dealt with in the light of what has been said in

220. In Cases 63–69/72 *Wilhelm Werhahn Hansamühle et al. v. Council and Commission* [1973] ECR 1229 at 1247 the Court observed that the interests of good administration of justice required that where Community liability was involved the Community be represented by the Institution or Institutions whose action has allegedly given rise to liability. Art. 211 EEC (now Art. 211 EC), which deals with the legal capacity and representation of the Community in the legal systems of the various Member States, was inapplicable because it concerned legal capacity and representation only in the national legal systems.

221. Art. 34 ECSC makes special provision for the Commission to take steps to ensure equitable redress for the harm resulting directly from a decision or recommendation declared void, and, where necessary, to pay appropriate damages. As to the relationship between Arts. 34 and 40 ECSC, see Cases C-363 and 364/88 *Finanziaria Siderurgica Finsider SpA et al. v. Commission* [1992] ECR I-359 at 415–418 and Case C-220/91 P *Commission v. Stahlwerke peine-Salzgitter AG* [1993] ECR I-2393 at 2443–2445.

222. *Cf.* Vegting, *Het Algemene Nederlands Administratiefrecht* Vol. II (Alphen aan de Rijn, 1954–1957) 176 *et seq.*

223. Thus the Court found that the concept of fault covered 'inexcusable mistakes' in Cases 14/60 *etc. Meroni & Co et al. v. High Authority* [1961] ECR 161 at 171; 'grave neglect of the duties of supervision required by a normal standard of care' in Cases 19 and 21/60 and 2–3/61 *Société Fives Lille Cail et al. v. High Authority* [1961] ECR 281 at 297, and 'an increasingly obvious lack of care' in Cases 19/63 *etc. Société Anonyme des Laminoirs, Hauts Fourneaux, Forges, Fonderies et usines de la Providence et al. v. High Authority* [1965] ECR 911 at 937.

224. Arts. 215 EC and 188 Euratom (2nd para. in each case). See generally, Schermers *et al.* (eds.), *Non-contractual Liability of the European Communities* (The Hague, 1988); Schermers and Waelbroeck, *op. cit.* (see note 17, *supra*) 328–364; Heukels and McDonnell (eds.), *The Action for Damages in Community Law* (The Hague, 1997); Bronkhorst (1983/1) LIEI 99; Cornelis (1984) SEW 5; Goran Lysen (1985/2) LIEI 86;

section 7.5.1 of Chapter IV about the Court and unwritten law. The Court is not obliged to seek the highest common denominator in the Member States' laws on administrative liability, but should focus on tracking down the elements from which Community legal principles and rules can be constructed which yield an appropriate, fair and viable solution to the problem of Community liability. The provisions of Article 215 EC should be understood 'in the sense of an orientation on the underlying principles whereby the *measure* of the responsibility of the administration is assessed in the national sphere.'[225]

On the second question, it is clear that the case-law of the Court relating to liability of the EC continues the line of that relating to the ECSC liability; there is no question of a split. The Court was able to pursue its general efforts towards as close an integration as possible of the law of the three Communities in this field precisely because in framing the Community liability of the ECSC it pursued its own path. In doing so it implicitly (albeit not expressly) based itself on the most important principles of administrative liability in the various national legal systems, thus clearly not merely on the French system.[226] However, the continuity in the case-law on Community liability does not mean that the liability is identical in all three Treaties. Thus the EC and Euratom Treaties (unlike the ECSC Treaty through the restriction requiring fault) do not exclude no-fault liability, something which is principally of interest in the case of Euratom. The continuity does mean that whenever there is a wrongful act or omission in the performance of functions or duties (a '*faute de service*') within the meaning of the ECSC case-law this will also result in liability for resulting damage in the EC system.

In a general formula in Case 4/69 *Alfons Lütticke GmbH* v. *Commission*[227] the Court laid down certain conditions, based on the second paragraph of Article 215 EC and the general principles to which it refers, which must be satisfied in order for the Community to be liable. These conditions relate to:

(1) the existence of actual damage;

Hermann-Rodeville (1986) RTDE 5; Heukels (1992) SEW 151 and 317; Lasok and Millett in Vaughan (ed.), *op. cit.* (see note 7, *supra*) paras. 282–346; Mackenzie Stuart (1975) 12 CMLRev. 495; Rudden and Bishop (1981) 6 ELRev. 243; Sack (1986) 241; Schockweiler *et al.* (1990) RTDE 27; Van Gerven (1996) MJ 6, and Wils (1992) 17 ELRev. 191. As an example of Community liability for acts of its servants see Case 145/83 *Adams* v. *Commission* [1985] ECR 3539 at 3585–3590 and, in relation to duties of the Community under free trade agreements see Case 53/84 *Adams* v. *Commission* [1985] ECR 3595 at 3400–3401.

225. *Per* Roemer, Adv. Gen. in Case 25/62 *Plaumann & Co.* v. *Commission* [1963] ECR 95 at 116 (italics in the original).

226. *Cf.* Goffin in Schermers, *op. cit.* (see note 39, *supra*) 75 at 101. For an example *vis-à-vis* officials and the police see Case 180/87 *Hamill* v. *Commission* [1988] ECR 6141.

227. [1971] ECR 325.

(2) a causal link between the damage claimed and the conduct alleged against the Institution;
(3) the illegality of such conduct.[228]

Conduct does not just cover purely substantive acts but also the execution (or non-execution) of legal measures. This last point is of interest here in relation to the legal protection of private parties. To what extent and subject to what conditions does an action for damages against the Community, as a result of or in conjunction with an action for annulment or against failure to act, offer redress to legal subjects aggrieved by unlawful action or inaction by the Community Institutions?

Certainly a suit will have a chance of success if annulment of the act or condemnation of the inaction on which the suit is based has taken place. As has been shown in section 1.2.1. of this Chapter, above, Article 34 ECSC imposes a specific obligation on the Commission to take steps to ensure equitable redress for the harm resulting directly from the decision or recommendation declared void and, if necessary, to pay appropriate damages. Articles 176 EC and 149 Euratom refer expressly to Articles 215 EC and 188 Euratom respectively, thus the obligation to take the necessary measures to comply with a judgment of the Court annuling or condemning a failure to act does not affect any obligation resulting from the Community's non-contractual liability. But even if an act has not previously been annulled (or a failure to act condemned) an action for damages on the ground of the unlawfulness of the act or failure to act may be able to succeed.

At first it did not appear that this would be the case. It appeared to follow from the judgment in Case 25/62 *Plaumann Co. v. Commission*[229] that only an annulled act or a condemned failure to act could give rise to a claim for damages. Given that the right of private parties to appeal in the EC and Euratom systems is extremely limited the same restrictions would have in fact applied to bringing an action for damages. Plaumann's action against a decision addressed to a Member State was held inadmissible because the decision did not concern him individually. Thus the Court did not address the lawfulness or otherwise of the decision. In later judgments the Court reconsidered this unsatisfactory position.

Both in the case of an allegedly unlawful failure to act[230] and in the case of an allegedly unlawful act[231] the Court has expressly stated that

---

228. *Ibid.* at 337. See also Case 50/86 *Société des Grands Moulins de Paris SA v. EEC* [1987] ECR 4833 at 4856–4857. The concept of illegality should be understood in the more general sense of unlawfulness; breach of unwritten Community law can also give rise to liability.

229. 'An administrative measure which has not been annulled cannot of itself constitute a wrongful act on the part of the adminstration inflicting damage upon those whom it affects.' [1963] ECR 95 at 108.

230. Case 4/69 *Lütticke* [1971] ECR 325 at 336.

231. Case 5/71 *Aktien-Zuckerfabrik Schöppenstedt v. Council* [1971] ECR 975 at 983–984.

the 'action for damages provided for by Article 178 and the second paragraph of Article 215 was established by the Treaty as an independent form of action with a particular purpose to fulfil within the system of actions and subject to conditions for its use, conceived with a view to its specific purpose.'[232] The independent nature of this form of action means that even though the action for damages may in certain circumstances lead to a result comparable to that achieved by an action against a failure to act, this will not be a ground for its inadmissibility. The action for damages differs from an action for annulment 'in that its end is not the abolition of a particular measure but compensation for damage caused by an institution in the performance of its duties.'[233] Although the form of action is independent it should be borne in mind that actions for damages will be declared inadmissible if they are clearly simply designed to escape the consequences of a dismissal of an action for annulment, in other words if they are in substance a disguised action for annulment or for failure to act.[234] The mere fact that some of the conditions for an action for damages coincide with those for an action for annulment will not, however, be a sufficient reason to describe the former as a misuse of the procedure.[235]

Since the judgment in Case 5/71 *Aktien-Zuckerfabrik Schöppenstedt v. Council*[236] it is clear that injury resulting from normative acts of the Institutions which involve particular economic policy choices[237] can give rise to Community liability only if 'a sufficiently flagrant violation of a

232. See notes 230 and 231, *supra, loc. cit.*
233. *Ibid.* Private parties cannot be forced to seek a judgment from the Court of Justice on the validity of a measure through the Art. 177 EC mechanism in national courts before they pursue a claim for damages in the Court of Justice. Although initially Case 96/71 *Sprl R. and V. Haegeman v. Commission* [1972] ECR 1005 indicated otherwise, in the judgment in Case 43/72 *Merkur-Aussenhandels GmbH v. Commission* [1973] ECR 1055 at 1069 the Court rejected the separate pursuit argument as 'not being in keeping with the proper administration of justice and the requirements of procedural efficiency.'
234. *Cf.* Roemer, Adv. Gen. in Case 5/71 *Schöppenstedt* [1971] ECR 975 at 992–993, referring to earlier cases. See also Case 175/84 *Firma Krohn & Co. Import–Export GmbH and Co. KG v. Commission* [1986] ECR 753.
235. Cases 197/80 *etc. Ludwigshafener Walzmühle Erling KG et al. v. Council and Commission* [1981] ECR 3211 at 3243. See also Case 153/73 *Holtz & Willemsen GmbH v. Council and Commission* [1974] ECR 675 at 692.
236. [1971] ECR 975 at 984.
237. The case-law has always dealt with economic policy choices but there is no reason to think that this is a restrictive definition of policy choices; see (citing earlier judgments) Cases 279/84 *etc. Walter Rau Lebensmittelwerke et al. v. EEC* [1987] ECR 1069 at 1122 in which although the Court noted that the Community Institutions had a permanent duty to reconcile the individual aims laid down in Art. 39 EEC and could not pursue any single aim in isolation, the Community Institutions could 'allow one of them a temporary priority in order to satsify the demands of the economic or other conditions in view of which their decisions are made.' See also Arnull (1987) 12 ELRev. 451; Van Gerven (1979) SEW 2 at 10, and Case 50/86 *Société des Grands Moulins de Paris SA v. EEC* [1987] ECR 4833.

superior rule of law for the protection of the individual has occurred.'[238] Given that in the EC system an action challenging genuine regulations is completely excluded, this constitutes a welcome extension of judicial protection of private parties against Community 'legislation', even though the chances of success in such actions must not be over-rated.[239]

In referring to superior rules of law it seems that the Court had in mind Treaty provisions or provisions of a superior rank than legislative acts, as well as general principles of law. In examining the lawfulness of a legislative act in actions for damages in the light of superior rules of law the Court adopts the same approach as in the case of an action for annulment. What is meant by a sufficiently flagrant violation has become clearer since the judgment in Cases 83/76 *etc. Bayerische HNL Vermehrungsbetriebe GmbH & Co. KG et al. v. Council et al.*[240] The Court had declared a Council regulation void in three preliminary rulings.[241] When a number of undertakings sought damages from the Council and the Commission as a result of the annulment of the regulation the Court considered that the violation of a superior rule of law was insufficiently flagrant. Liability for legislative measures (normative acts) in fields in which the Community Institutions have wide discretionary powers, will not be incurred unless the Institution concerned 'has manifestly and gravely disregarded the limits on the exercise of its powers.[242]

Later case-law shows that the Court will look at the seriousness of the transgression of the limits of powers itself[243] as well as the seriousness of the consequences thereof as revealed in the number of persons affected and the scale of the injury in the light of normal economic risks in the activities in the sectors concerned.[244] The view which the Court has adopted since

238. [1971] ECR 975 at 984.
239. But as a very important example of a successful action, see Cases C-104/89 and 37/90 *Mulder et al. v. Council and Commission* [1992] ECR I-3061 and the Commission's Communication (O.J. 1992 C 198/4). See further, the unsuccessful arguments in Case T-246/93 *Bühring v. Council et al.* [1998] ECR II-171.
240. [1978] ECR 1209 at 1224–1225.
241. Mentioned at [1978] ECR 1209 at 1223.
242. [1978] ECR 1209 at 1224. In this case there was no question of this having happened because of repercussions affected very wide categories of traders so that their effects on individual undertakings were very much lessened. The Court based its restrictive approach on the principles governing the liability of public authorities for damage caused to individuals by legislative measures. Although they varied considerably from one Member State to another it was clear that public authorities only exceptionally and in special circumstances incurred liabilty for legislative measures which were the result of economic policy choices.
243. See *e.g.* Cases 116 and 124/77 *G.R. Amylum NV et al. v. Council et al.* [1979] ECR 3497 at 3561 (the defendants' behaviour was held not to verge on the arbitrary and the actions for damages were dismissed).
244. See *e.g.* Case 238/78 *Ireks-Arkady GmbH v. Council et al.* [1979] ECR 2955 at 2973. See, generally, Rudden and Bishop (1981) 6 ELRev. 243.

Schöppenstedt[245] appears to confirm that the Court regards the relativity principle (*Schutznormtheorie*) as applicable in relation to Community liability.[246] The superior rules of law must be *for the protection of the individual*.[247] It is not, however, required that those superior rules of law must be of direct and individual concern to private parties.[248]

National and Community administrations often act in a complex interwoven pattern in the field of Community law. Thus in certain circumstances both can be held liable for the same injury; the national authorities in the national courts in the sphere of national law, the Community authorities in the Court of Justice in the Community legal order. After a long period of uncertainty about the Court's line, recent case-law can be summarized by reference to Case 175/84 *Firma Krohn Co Import–Export GmbH Co. KG v. Commission*.[249] If the measure involved[250] is taken by a national body in implementation of Community rules the Court (now the Court of First Instance) will only be competent to consider an action for damages if the alleged unlawfulness on which the action is founded emenates from a Community Institution and cannot be attributed to the national body. If the national body acts under instructions of a Community Institution then the unlawfulness is attributed to the latter. But the matter does not end there as the admissibility of proceedings before the Court of First Instance may in certain circumstances depend on national procedures available for the annulment of the national decision having been exhausted. It is a condition that these procedures effectively ensure the protection of interested parties through permitting redress for injury suffered. Only the existence of an effective form of action in the national courts can prevent private parties from pursuing the procedure of Article 215 EC; if there is no effective remedy open to them in the

---

245. See note 236, *supra*.
246. See van Gerven (1976) SEW 2 and, generally, the literature cited in note 224, *supra*.
247. Case 5/71 *Schöppenstedt* [1971] ECR 975 at 984 see also *e.g.* Case 281/84 *Zuckerfabrik Bedburg AG et al. v. EEC* [1987] ECR 49 at 90; Case T-120/89 *Stahlwerke Peine-Salzgitter v. Commission* [1991] ECR II-279 at 388–389 (citing earlier case-law), and Cases T-480 and 483/93 *Antillean Rice Mills NV et al. v. Commission* [1995] ECR II-2305 at 2366–2367. As examples of earlier judgments, see Cases 9 and 12/60 *Société Commerciale Antoine Vloeberghs SA v. High Authority* [1961] ECR 197 and Cases 5/66 *etc. Firma E. Kampffmeyer et al. v. Commission* [1967] ECR 245 at 262–263.
248. Cases 5/66 *etc. Kampffmeyer, ibid.*
249. [1986] ECR 753, [1987] 1 CMLR 231 which clarifies the earlier judgments in Case 12/79 *Hans-Otto Wagner GmbH Agrarhandel KG v. Commission* [1979] ECR 3657; Case 133/79 *Sucrimex SA et al. v. Commission* [1980] ECR 1299 and Case 217/81 *Compagnie Interagra SA v. Commission* [1982] ECR 2233. See also *e.g.* Case 50/86 *Les Grands Moulins de Paris v. EEC* [1987] ECR 4833 and Cases 279/84 *etc. Firma Walter Rau lebensmittelwerke et al. v. EEC* [1987] ECR 1069.
250. The situation is completely different if it is the Community measure itself which is in issue, see Case 59/83 *SA Biovilac NV v. EEC* [1984] ECR 4057 at 4074 and Case 126/76 *Firma Gebrüder Dietz v. Commission* [1977] ECR 2431 at 2441.

national legal system their failure to bring an action in the national courts is not a ground for holding an action before the Court of First Instance inadmissible.[251] The case-law would not have appeared to have met all the objections on the ground of judicial protection of private parties which flow from the division of competence for declarations for annulment or invalidity of Community legislative acts and actions for damages resulting from the application of those acts between the Court of Justice or Court of First Instance on the one hand and national courts on the other, in a system in which Community and national administrations are so intertwined.[252]

2. THE COURT OF JUSTICE AND NATIONAL COURTS

Not only the Court of Justice, but also national courts are required to ensure observance of Community law. In disputes arising between private parties, or between private parties and national administrative authorities, the question will arise whether rules of Community law are applicable to the dispute, and whether these rules, if they belong to secondary Community law, are legally valid. This question is presented in particular with respect to EC law as a result of three factors.

In the first place, a good deal of space has been given in this law (unlike that of the ECSC and Euratom) to rules containing instructions and prohibitions addressed to Member States.[253] If certain conditions have been met (which will be discussed separately below) private parties can invoke such Community rules before the national court against national authorities.

Secondly, the application of EC law in respect of individuals has for the most part been placed in the hands of national authorities. This is the case, for instance, in a broad field of such as activities the collection of Community customs duties and levies. If a private person wishes to contest the legal validity under Community law of the acts of these national bodies, he or she cannot apply to the Court of Justice, but only to the national court. In the other two Communities, on the contrary, particularly in the ECSC, the application of Community law in respect of individuals has mainly been entrusted to the Community authorities, and a private person affected thereby may appeal against acts of the Community to the Court of First Instance, which has exclusive jurisdiction (subject to appeal

251. See in this sense also Cases 197/80 *etc. Ludwigshafener Walzmühle Erling KG et al. v. Council* [1981] ECR 3211 at 3244 and Case 281/82 *Srl Unifrex v. Commission et al.* [1984] ECR 1969 at 1982–1983.
252. See Wils (1992) 17 ELRev. 191, who regards joint and several liability as the only satisfactory solution. See also Meij (1993) NTB 75.
253. *Cf.* Chapter II, section 2.1, *ante.*

on a point of law only to the Court of Justice), so that the national courts are not involved.

Thirdly, EC law assigns a less exclusive role than ECSC law to the Community authorities with a view to ensuring compliance with the obligations imposed on private persons by Community law. Unlike the ECSC Treaty,[254] the EC Treaty has assigned a task not only to the national administration[255] but also to the national courts[256] in the field of competition law.

The effect of these factors is strengthened even further by the wide scope of application of EC law and the fact that in principle the number of its legal subjects is unlimited. The chances that EC law may be relied on in national proceedings are accordingly much greater than for the law of the two other Communities. It is, therefore, justifiable to state that national courts fulfil a very important function in ensuring the maintenance of EC law, that of judge of the common law of Community law. This section discusses in turn judicial cooperation between the Court of Justice and national courts by means of preliminary rulings and problems connected with the application of Community law by national courts, referring to various provisions of the EC Treaty and some examples from national case-law.

2.1 Cooperation between the Court of Justice and national courts: preliminary rulings

2.1.1 Powers of the Court and national courts, division and coordination

In general. Under Article 177 EC[257] the Court of Justice has jurisdiction to give preliminary rulings relating in particular to the interpretation of the Treaty, acts of the Community Institutions and the validity of those acts.

---

254. See Art. 65(4) ECSC, 2nd para. See also Case C-128/92 *H.J. Banks Ltd. v. British Coal Corporation* [1994] ECR I-1209 at 1275 and Case C-18/94 *Hopkins et al. v. National Power plc et al.* [1996] ECR I-2281 at 2319–2321.
255. See Art. 88 EC, read with Reg. 17 (see note 126, *supra*), Art. 9(3).
256. See Art. 85(1) and (2) EC read with Reg. 17, *ibid.*, Art.l. See also Case C-234/89 *Delimitis v. Henninger Bräu AG* [1991] ECR I-935 at 991–994 and Case T-24/90 *Automec srl v. Commission* [1992] ECR II-2223 at 2278–2280.
257. See also Art. 150 Euratom. Art. 41 ECSC provides for preliminary rulings only on the validity of acts of the Commission or the Council when their validity is in issue in national proceedings; see Case 172/84 *Celestri and C SpA v. Ministry of Finance* [1985] ECR 963 at 969–970; see also Case C-128/92 *H.J. Banks Ltd. v. British Coal Corporation* [1994] ECR I-1209, [1994] 5 CMLR 30 and Case C-18/94 *Hopkins et al. v. National Power plc et al.* [1996] ECR I-2281, [1996] 4 CMLR 745. In Case C-221/88 *ECSC v. Acciaierie e ferriere Busseni SpA (in liquidation)* [1990] ECR I-495 at 523–524 the Court held that the competence conferred on it by Art. 41 ECSC covered not merely the validity of Community acts but also their interpretation. As to Art. 177 EC, generally, see Andenas (ed.), *Article 177 References to the European Court: Practice and*

There would appear to be no reason to interpret the word 'acts' restrictively. They include regulations, directives, decisions and *sui generis* measures irrespective of whether they have direct effect.[258] They also cover, at least as far as interpretation is concerned, treaties concluded by the Community with third countries or international organisations[259] or which are binding on the Community in other ways,[260] as in the case of mixed agree-

Procedure (London, 1994); Anderson, *References to the European Court* (London, 1995); Bebr, *op. cit.* (see note 61, *supra*) Chapters 9–12; Brown and Kennedy, *op. cit.* (see note 7, *supra*) Chapter 10; Caranta in Micklitz and Reich (eds.), *op. cit.* (see note 61, *supra*) 95; Chevallier and Maidani: *Guide Pratique Article 177* (Luxembourg, 1982); Lasok and Millett, *op. cit.* (see note 7, *supra*) paras. 583–706; Schermers *et al.* (eds.), *Article 177 EEC. Experiences and Problems* (Amsterdam, 1987); Schermers and Waelbroeck, *op. cit.* (see note 17, *supra*) 390–446, and Usher in Plender (ed.), *European Courts Practice and Procedure* (London, 1997) Chapter 31. See also the Court's guidance note on references, reproduced in (1997) 22 ELRev. 55. Among more recent periodical literature, see Alexander (1988) 8 YBEL 11; Arnull (1988) 13 ELRev. 40, (1989) 52 MLR 622, (1990) 15 ELRev. 375 and (1993) 18 ELRev. 129; Bebr (1988) 25 CMLRev. 667; Mancini and Keeling (1991) 11 YBEL 1; Joliet (1993) JdT (Dr. Eur.) 2; Kennedy (1993) 18 ELRev. 121; Tesauro (1993) 13 YBEL 1; Walsh (1993) 56 MLR 881, and Anderson (1994) 14 YBEL 179. See also Lenaerts and Ter Kuile in Curtin and Heukels (eds.), *op. cit.* (see note 7, *supra*) 355 and 381 respectively; Mattli and Slaughter, *Constructing the European Community Legal System from the ground up: The role of individual litigants and national courts* (Harvard Jean Monnet Working Papers, No. 6/96) and Strasser, *The Development of a Strategy of Docket Control for the European Court of Justice and the Question of Preliminary References* (*ibid.* No. 3/95). Two protocols of 3 June 1971 confer jurisdiction on the Court of Justice to interpret the two Conventions concluded under Art. 220 EC, namely the Convention on the Mutual Recognition of Companies and Bodies Corporate (29 February 1968, Bull. EC Supp. 2/69) and the Convention on Jurisdiction and the Enforcement of Civil and Commercial Judgments (29 September 1968 (see the consolidated version, O.J. 1998 C 27/1). Art. 177 EC was the model for both protocols. The protocol dealing with the latter Convention differs from Art. 177 EC in relation to the bodies competent to request a preliminary ruling. See Mok (1971) 8 CMLRev. 485–494, and Case C-346/93 *Kleinwort Benson Ltd. v. City of Glasgow District Council* [1995] ECR I-615 at 641. The Convention of 19 June 1980 on the Law Applicable to Contractual Obligations (see the consolidated version, O.J. 1998 C 27/34) contains no equivalent provision but the Contracting Parties in a Joint Declaration agreed to examine the possibility of making an equivalent agreement, as to which, see Chapter IV, *ante*, note 456 and Usher in Plender, *op. cit.* 770–801. As to Art. 111 EEA and Protocol 34 to that Agreement, see Usher, *ibid.* 801–804. Various Conventions adopted in the context of JHA confer similar jurisdiction on the Court (see Chapter II, section 1.3.2, *ante*) and the Treaty of Amsterdam (not yet in force) will make further provision in this regard in the new Art. K.7 TEU as regards matters falling under the revised Third Pillar and in the new Art. 73p EC a differentiated application of Art. 177 EC is provided for in respect of the new Title IIIa of Part Three of the EC Treaty.

258. See, in so many words, Case 111/75 *Impressa Costruzioni Comm. Quirino Mazzali v. Ferrovia del Renon* [1976] ECR 657 at 665.

259. See particularly Case 181/73 *R. and V. Haegeman v. Belgian State* [1974] ECR 449 at 459–460. Implementing rules adopted by a Joint Committee on the basis of such agreements also form part of the Community law and, even though they are not directly effective, they can be interpreted by the Court under Art. 177 EC, see Case C-

ments to which the Community and the Member States are parties, even covering, in these mixed agreements, obligations of the Member States thereunder.[261] The Court can also interpret acts which do not produce legal effects, even if only to decide whether they do produce legal effects.[262] It is difficult to raise questions as to the validity of these latter acts because the question of their validity arises after the question of whether or not the acts produce legal effects. Questions of interpretation can also relate to the clarification of unwritten legal principles inherent in Community law.[263] Even if a provision of Community law, as a result of being referred to in a national law[264] or in an agreement concluded between the parties,[265] is in substance used to determine the rules applicable in a situation not governed by Community law (being a purely domestic matter within the Member State involved), the Court will regard itself as competent to respond to questions relating to provisions of Community law posed by a national court or tribunal.

The national court is entitled, and, if a court of last instance in the case

188/91 *Deutsche Shell AG v. Hauptzollamt Hamburg-Harburg* [1993] ECR I-363 at 388.
260. See, *inter alia*, Cases 21–24/72 *International Fruit Company NV et al. v. Produktschap voor Groenten en Fruit* [1972] ECR 1219 at 1227–1228 and, further, Cases 267–269/81 *Amministrazione delle Finanze detio Stato v. Società Petrolifera Italiana SpA (SPI) et al.* [1983] ECR 801 at 827–832 and Cases 290 and 291/81 *Compagnia Singer SpA et al. v. Amministrazione delle Finanze dello Stato* [1983] ECR 847 at 861–862. In this type of judgment no act of an Institution is involved.
261. This appears to follow from Case C-18/90 *Office national de l'emploi (Onem) v. Kziber* [1991] ECR I-199 at 225–227. Tbe Court has no jurisdiction under Art. 177 EC 'to give a ruling on the interpretation of provisions of international law which bind Member States outside the framework of Community law.': Case 130/73 *Magdalena Vandeweghe et al. v. Berufsgenossenschaft für die Chemische Industrie* [1973] ECR 1329 at 1333. As to mixed agreements generally, see O'Keeffe and Schermers (eds.), *Mixed Agreements* (Deventer, 1983).
262. See Case 9/73 *Schlüter v. Hauptzollamt Lörrach* [1973] ECR 1135 at 1161 (the Economic and Monetary Union resolution of 22 March 1971) and Case 113/75 *Frecassetti v. Amministrazione delle Finanze dello Stato* [1976] ECR 983 at 993 (a recommendation).
263. *E.g.* Case 11/70 *Internationale Handelsgesellschaft mbH. v. Einfuhr- und Vorratsstelle für Getreide und Futtermittel* [1970] ECR 1125 (respect for human rights) and Case 84/78 *Angelo Tomandini Snc v. Amministrazione delle Finanze dello Stato* [1979] ECR 1801 (protection of legitimate expectation).
264. Cases C-297/88 and 197/88 *Dzodzi v. Belgian State* [1990] ECR I-3763 at 3793–3794 and Case C-231/89 *Gmurzynska-Bscher v. Oberfinanzdirektion Köln* [1990] ECR I-4003 at 4018. See also Case C-28/95 *Leur-Bloem v. Inspecteur der Belastingdienst / Ondernemingen Amsterdam 2* [1997] ECR I-4161 at 4201–4202 and Case C-130/95 *Giloy v. Hauptzollamt Frankfurt am Main-Ost* [1997] ECR I-4291 at 4301–4304.
265. See Case C-88/91 *Federazione Italiana dei Consorzi Agrari (Federconsorzi) v. Aziend di stato per gli Interventi nel mercato Agricolo (AIMA)* [1992] ECR I-4035 at 4064.
266. On this last point see Case 166/73 *Rheinmühlen-Düsseldorf v. Einfuhr- und Vorratsstelle für Getreide und Futtermittel* [1974] ECR 33 at 38. See further Cases C-87–89/90 *Verholen et al. v. Sociale Verzekeringsbank* [1991] ECR I-3757 at 3788–3789. The question whether the *ex officio* application of Community law could be restricted by

concerned, even obliged, to ask the Court for a preliminary ruling if a
question of interpretation or validity is raised before it either by the parties
or by the court itself *ex officio*.[266] Further, it must consider that a decision
on such a question is necessary to enable it to give judgment. If these
conditions are satisfied, the national court will suspend and proceedings
and will on its own initiative notify the Court of the decision to refer the
matter.[267] The preliminary ruling of the Court 'is binding on the national
court hearing the case in which the decision is given.'[268]

The judgment is declaratory, even if it concerns an interpretation. The
interpretation given clarifies and defines the meaning of the rule of
Community law which should have been applied and understood since its
coming into force. Thus the national court ought to apply the rule as so
interpreted even to legal relationships which commenced before the
preliminary ruling was handed down.[269] It is only in very exceptional cases
that the Court of Justice restricts the retroactive effect of its judgment for
interested parties.[270]

national law was considered in Case C-312/93 *Peterbroeck, Van Campenhout & Cie
SCS v. Belgian State* [1995] ECR I-4599 at 4621–4623 and Cases C-430 and 431/93
Van Schijndel et al. v. Stichting Pensioenfonds voor Fysiotherapeuten [1995] ECR I-
4705 at 4736–4738. The different rules involved in fact led to divergent results, but the
effect is the national rules apply (*Van Schijndel*) unless the Court finds the impossibility for a national court to raise a Community law point 'not reasonably justified by
principles such as the requirement of legal certainty or the proper conduct of procedure'(*Peterbroeck* at 4623). Community law does not require national courts to raise
Community law points of their own motion where examination of such points would
go beyond the ambit of the dispute and force them to rely on other facts or circumstances than those on which the party with an interest in those points being taken has
based his or her claim (*Van Schijndel* at 4738). See Prechal (1998) 35 CML Rev. 595.

267. Statute of the Court of Justice (EC), Art. 20: see also *ibid.* (Euratom) Art. 21 and, in
relation to proceedings referred to the Court under Art. 41 ECSC, the Court's Rules
of Procedure, Art. 103(3) (O.J. 1991 L 176/1, most recently amended O.J. 1997 L
103/1).

268. Case 29/68 *Milch- Fett- und Eierkontor GmbH. v. Hauptzollamt Saarbrücken* [1969]
ECR 165 at 180; it is, though, also for the national court to decide 'whether it is sufficiently enlightened by the preliminary ruling given or whether it is necessary to make
a further reference to the Court.' (*ibid.*) See also Case 52/76 *Benedetti v. Munari F.lli
s.a.s.* [1977] ECR 163 at 183. As to national reactions see Schermers and Waelbroeck,
op. cit. (see note 7, *supra*) 439–442. It is submitted that whilst a preliminary ruling is
not formally binding on courts other than the court to which it is addressed, it should
be regarded as highly persuasive authority and should be followed (although a new
reference can always be made). In the United Kingdom section 3 of the European
Communities Act 1972 should be borne in mind; for this reason the problem is unlikely to cause difficulties in the United Kingdom; see, further, *Garland v. British Rail
Engineering Ltd.* [1983] AC 851 at 771–771 (Lord Diplock) and Lasok and Millett in
Vaughan (ed.), *op. cit.* (see note 7, *supra*) para. 705.

269. See *e.g.* Case 61/79 *Amministrazione delle Finanze dello Stato v. Denkavit Italiana srl*
[1980] ECR 1205 at 1233 and Cases 66, 127 and 128/79 *Amministrazione delle Finanze
v. Srl Meridionale Industria Salumi et al.* [1980] ECR 1237 at 1260.

270. *E.g.* Case 43/75 *Defrenne v. SABENA* [1976] ECR 455 at 480–481; Cases 66/79 *etc.*

Judicial co-operation. In the words of the Court, Article 177 EC establishes 'a special field of judicial co-operation which requires the national court and the Court of Justice, both keeping within their respective jurisdiction, and with the aim of ensuring that Community law is applied in a unified manner, to make direct and complementary contributions to the working out of a decision.'[271]

This definition clearly shows the relationship between the Court of Justice and the national courts as well as the main function of Article 177. The Court of Justice has not been placed hierarchically as the highest court above the national courts, but co-operates with them, each exercising its own jurisdiction. The main function of Article 177 is set out in the above definition. The object is to ensure uniform application of Community law in all Member States, both as regards the interpretation of this law by the national courts and in relation to the validity or invalidity of the Community acts. As will appear from the following subsections, Article 177 also fulfils an important function in the maintenance of law and in legal protection. It fosters the inclusion of Community law in the national legal orders, having direct effect and priority over national law. As the Court put it in the celebrated judgment in Case 166/73 *Rheinmühlen-Düsseldorf v. Einfuhr- und Vorratsstelle für Getreide und Futtermittel,*[272] 'Article 177 is essential for the preservation of the Community character of law established by the Treaty and has the object of ensuring that in all circumstances this law is the same in all States of the Community.' Any gap in the system set up could undermine the effectiveness of the provisions

Amministrazione delle Finanze v. Srl Meridionale Industria Salumi [1980] ECR 1237 at 1261; Case 309/85 *Barra v. Belgian State et al.* [1988] ECR 355 at 375–376; Case 24/86 *Blaizot et al. v. University of Liège* [1988] ECR 379 at 405–406; Case C-262/88 *Barber v. Guardian Royal Exchange Group* [1990] ECR I-1889 at 1955–1956 (see also the so-called *Barber* Protocol (concerning Art. 119 EC) added to the EC Treaty by the TEU, as to which see Hervey in O'Keeffe and Twomey (eds.), *Legal Issues of the Maastricht Treaty* (Chichester, 1994) 329); Case C-109/91 *Ten Oever v. Stichting Bedrijfspensioenfonds voor het Glazenwassers en schoonmaakbedrijf* [1993] ECR I-4879 at 4944–4945; Case C-200/91 *Coloroll Pension Trustees Ltd. v. Russell et al.* [1994] ECR I-4389 at 4417–4418 (and other judgments handed down on the same day). See, generally, Waelbroeck (1981) 1 YBEL 115 and (1983) CDE 363; Bebr (1981) 18 CMLRev. 475; Brown (1981) 18 CMLRev. 590; Schermers (1986) 23 CMLRev. 473; Isaac (1987) CDE 444; Simon in Capotorti, *op. cit.* (see note 24, *supra*) 651; Mertens de Wilmars in Grewe, *op. cit.* (see note 24, *supra*) 283; Alexander (1988) 8 YBEL 11; Hudson (1992) 17 ELRev. 163 and (on the substantive consequences of *Barber* and its sequels) Moore (1995) 20 ELRev. 159. See also Chapter IV, section 7.6, *ante*. In relation to the effect in time of declarations of invalidity, see the end of the present section, *post*.

271. Case 16/65 *Firma C. Schwarze v. Einfuhr- und Vorratsstelle für Getreide und Futtermittel* [1965] ECR 877 at 886. See also Case 244/80 *Foglia v. Novello* [1981] ECR 3045 at 3062–3063 on the mutual duty to have regard to each others responsibilities. See, further, Caranta (1995) 32 CMLRev. 703.
272. [1974] ECR 33 at 38.

of both primary and secondary Community law.[273] The Court has also indicated that 'Article 177 is to be applied regardless of any domestic law, whenever questions relating to the interpretation of the Treaty arise.'[274] Subsequently, the Court used these points to declare that a lower court is entitled to refer to the Court of Justice a point of law covered by a ruling of a higher court, even though the lower court may in national law be bound by the ruling of the higher court; the mere existence of such a rule in national law cannot deprive the lower court of its right to make a reference.[275] While this case concerned a German procedural rule, it is clearly of importance for other jurisdictions, particularly for the Member States with (in whole or in part) a common law tradition of binding precedents. Clearly if the answer of the Court of Justice to the request for a preliminary ruling is incompatible with the earlier judgment of the higher national court the lower court must follow and apply the ruling of the Court of Justice, not the disapproved view of the higher national court. It is clear that there can be no fetters on the discretion of a national court or tribunal to refer a question to the Court of Justice,[276] As Mitchell elegantly put it '*Rheinmühlen*, not *Bulmer*, must rule.'[277]

The different functions of the Court of Justice and national courts. According to a consistent line of case-law, Article 177 EC is based 'on a clear separation of functions between national courts or tribunals and the Court of Justice.'[278] The jurisdiction of the Court based on Article 177 EC is confined to a decision on the interpretation of Community law and on the validity of Community acts; it does not enable the court to investigate the facts.[279] In particular it does not pronounce on the application of Community law to the facts of the case referred to in the proceedings before the national court.[280] It does not, therefore, consider itself competent to

273. *Ibid.*
274. Case 6/64 *Costa v. ENEL* [1964] ECR 585 at 594.
275. See Case 146/73 *Rheinmühlen-Düsseldorf v. Einfuhr- und Vorratsstelle für Getreide und Futtermittel* [1974] ECR 139 at 147.
276. Case 166/73 *Rheinmühlen* [1974] ECR 33 at 38–39.
277. (1974) 11 CMLRev. 351 at 355. Thus the infamous guidelines of Lord Denning, M.R. in *H.P. Bulmer Ltd. v. J. Bollinger SA* [1974] Ch. 401 which have (at least in the early years) had a significant impact on the attitude of English Courts (see, *e.g.* Dashwood and Arnull (1984) 4 YBEL 255; Gormley (1986) 23 CMLRev. 287 (in German (1987) EuR 359); Collins, *European Community Law in the United Kingdom* (4th ed., London, 1990) 172–214; Usher in Vaughan, *op. cit.* (see note 7, *supra*) paras. 507 *et seq.*, and Weatherill and Beaumont, *EC Law* (2nd ed., London, 1995) 294–300) must be regarded, with the greatest respect, as binding on nobody. For the Irish approach see *Campus Oil Ltd. et al. v. Minister for Industry and Energy et al.* [1984] 1 CMLR 479 (Irish Supreme Court).
278. See *e.g.* Case 20/64 *Sàrl Albatros v. Société des pétroles et des Combustibles liquides (Sopéco)* [1965] ECR 29 at 34.
279. Case 6/64 *Costa v. ENEL* [1964] 585 at 593.
280. See, *inter alia,* Cases 28–30/62 *Da Costa en Schaake NV et al. v. Nederlandse Belastingadministratie* [1963] ECR 11 at 38. Sometimes the Court does, however, go pretty

examine whether, for instance, a given contractual obligation between certain parties is prohibited and consequently void in accordance with Article 85(1) and (2) EC, but confines itself to answering the questions of interpretation of that Article raised by such an obligation.[281] Nor does it have jurisdiction to pronounce on the question whether particular laws or administrative acts of a Member State are compatible with Community law.[282]

It can, though, give the national court all those criteria for the interpretation of Community law which may enable it to judge the issue of compatibility of the national laws or acts with Community law,[283] and in doing so it will not be afraid to reformulate the questions asked.[284] It has to be said, though, that although the Court in an Article 177 ruling will not declare a national law or act incompatible with Community law but leaves this to the national court concerned the Court of Justice's rulings are frequently couched in such terms that the conclusion that the national law cannot be upheld is glaringly obvious. If a Member State does not

far along the road, particularly when its interpretation is requested of terms in Community law classifying products for customs purposes, *e.g.* Case 40/69 *Hauptzollamt Hamburg-Oberelbe v. Firma Paul G. Bollman* [1970] ECR 69 at 81 and Case 200/84 *Driber v. Hauptzollamt Reutlingen* [1985] ECR 3363 at 3381–3384. The Court has also on occasions given its views in such clear terms that the national court has little left to do but mechanically apply the ruling; this sometimes appears to stem from apparent frustration at the inability of national courts to come to a clear conclusion as a result of earlier rulings, although the risk is that litigants then seek to obtain resolution by the Court of their problems however thin the integrationist merit of the question, see *e.g.* Case C-312/89 *Union départementale des syndicats CGT de l'Aisne v. SIDEF Conforama et al.* [1991] ECR I-997 at 1025, in which a much clearer view was taken than in Case C-145/88 *Torfaen Borough Council v. B & Q PLC (formerly B & Q (Retail) Ltd.* [1989] ECR 3851 at 3888–3889, in which the determination was clearly left in the hands of the national court; see further, the backlash reaction in Cases C-267 and 268/91 *Keck and Mithouard* [1994] ECR I-6097 at 6131 which in fact raised as many questions as it attempted to solve, see, further, Chapter VII, section 3.2.1, *post*. See also, for a very concrete answer to a question on the interpretation of Reg. 17 (O.J. English Special Edition 1959–62, p. 87), Art. 4(2) Case 43/69 *Braueri A. Bilger Söhne GmbH v. Jehle et al.* [1970] ECR 127 at 135.

281. See Case 13/61 *Kledingverkoopbedrijf de Geus en Uitdenbogerd v. Robert Bosch GmbH et al.* [1962] ECR 45, [1962] CMLR 1.

282. See, *inter alia*, Case 20/64 *Albatros* [1965] ECR 29 at 34; Case 823/79 *Carciati* [1980] ECR 2773 at 2778–2779; Case 249/84 *Ministére Public et al. v. Profant* [1985] ECR 3237 at 3254, and Case 227/82 *Van Bennekom* [1983] ECR 3883 at 3899.

283. See Case 112/75 *Directeur régional de la sécurité sociale de Nancy v. Hirardin et al.* [1976] ECR 553 at 560; Case 227/82 *Van Bennekom, loc. cit.*

284. *E.g.* Case 1/71 *SA Cadillon v. Firma Höss, Maschinenbau KG* [1971] ECR 351 at 356; Case 78/70 *Deutsche Grammophon Gesellschaft mbH v. Metro-SB-Großmärkte GmbH & Co. KG* [1971] ECR 487 at 498; Case 12/82 *Ministère Public v. Trinon* [1982] ECR 4089 at 4100; Case 28/85 *Deghillage v. Caisse primaire d'assurance maladie de Maubeuge* [1986] ECR 991 at 1003; Case 83/78 *Pigs Marketing Board v. Redmond* [1978] ECR 2347 at 2366–2367; Case C-199/90 *Italtrade SpA v. Azienda di stato per gli Interventi nel Mercato Agricolo (AIMA)* [1991] ECR I-5545 at 5564–5565; Case C-179/90

then take steps to change its national law or practices the Commission may well bring infringement proceedings under Article 169 EC. It should be noted that it is not enough that the national law becomes effectively unenforceable; there is a clear duty to repeal or amend the offending provisions in the interests of transparency and legal certainty.[285]

The strict separation between interpretation on the one hand and application of Community law *in concreto* on the other hand tends of course to give rise to considerable difficulties in practice. The process of thought leading to a judicial decision cannot be readily separated into two independent parts: the interpretation of general rules and the subsequent application of the rules thus interpreted to the facts. The interpretation given by a court is also determined by the facts. This means that it is of the greatest importance to the Court of Justice that the national court in asking for a preliminary ruling should inform it of the facts of the case.[286] A study of the various judgments given by the Court pursuant to Article 177, makes it quite obvious that the Court was inspired by the facts of the case in its interpretation of Community law and has given an interpretation *in concreto*.[287]

The Court has repeatedly emphasized that national courts must explain on what grounds they consider an answer to their questions to be necessary for judgment of the main proceedings if those grounds are not unequivocally evident from the file on the case. Moreover, the need to give an interpretation of Community law which will be of use to the national

Merci convenzionali porto di Genova SpA v. Siderurgica Gabrielli SpA [1991] ECR I-5889 at 5926–5927; Case C-320/91 *Corbeau* [1993] ECR I-2533 at 2566–2567, and Cases C-171 and 172/94 *Merckx et al. v. Ford Motors Company Belgium SA* [1996] ECR I-1253 at 1272–1273. However, in Case 247/86 *Société alsacienne et lorraine de télécommunications et d'électronique (Alsatel) v. SA Novasam* [1988] ECR 5987 at 6007 the Court declined to answer a question not posed by the national court but to which the defendant and the Commission had invited it to reply.

285. See *e.g.* Case 167/73 *Commission v. France* [1974] ECR 359 at 372–373 (by analogy); Cases 314/81 *etc. Procureur de la République et al. v. Waterkeyn et al.* [1982] ECR 4337 at 4360–4361, and Case 104/86 *Commission v. Italy* [1988] ECR 1799 at 1817.

286. See *e.g.* Case 56/65 *Société Technique Minière v. Maschinenbau Ulm GmbH* [1966] ECR 235 at 247–248; Cases 36 and 71/80 *Irish Creamery Milk Suppliers Association v. Ireland* [1981] ECR 735 at 748, although there is no restriction on the discretion to refer, see Case 72/83 *Campus Oil Ltd. et al. v. Minister for Industry and Energy et al.* [1984] ECR 2727 at 2745 and Case 14/86 *Pretore di Salo v. X* [1987] ECR 2545 at 2568–2569; see Arnull (1988) 13 ELRev. 40. In the United Kingdom this advice is generally, but not always followed, *e.g. Bethell v. SABENA* [1983] 3 CMLR 1; *An Bord Bainne Co-operative Ltd. v. Milk Marketing Board* [1988] 1 CMLR 6 and, exceptionally, *Polydor et al. v. Harlequin Record Shops Ltd. et al.* [1980] 2 CMLR 403.

287. On the connection between interpretation and application in the context of the Court's jurisdiction under Art. 177 EC see Donner in *Miscellanea W.J. Ganshof van der Meersch* (Brussels, 1972) Vol. II, 103.

288. Cases 141–143/81 *Holdijk et al.* [1982] ECR 1299 at 1311 (citing earlier judgments). See also *e.g.* the English cases cited in note 286, *supra*; Dashwood and Arnull (1984) 4 YBEL 255 at 265–268; Gormley (1986) 23 CMLRev. 287 at 291, and Collins, *op. cit.*

court makes it essential to define the legal context in which the interpretation requested should be placed. The Court has also indicated that it might be convenient, if circumstances permit, for the facts in the case to be established and for questions of purely national law to be settled at the time when the reference to the Court of Justice is made.[288] If it is not apparent what the factual problem is, the Court tends nowadays to find the reference either inadmissible or to conclude that there is no need to answer the questions posed.[289]

The national court in turn will often be inclined to make its request in very concrete terms.[290] Entirely in the spirit of co-operation provides for in Article 177, the Court of Justice in this respect will exercise a minimum of formality. From the request of the national court, even if it is loosely phrased,[291] it selects those questions of interpretation or validity with respect to which it has jurisdiction. Even if the questions of interpretation asked by a national court should in reality concern the validity of Community acts, 'it is appropriate for the Court to inform the national court at once of its view without compelling the national court to comply with purely formal requirements which would uselessly prolong the procedure under Article 177 and would be contrary to its very nature.'[292]

The jurisdiction of the Court of Justice is subject solely to the existence of a request within the meaning of Article 177, without it being required to examine whether the decision of the national court has become *res judicata* under the provisions of the latter's domestic law.[293] Article 177 EC does

(see note 277, *supra*) 186–189. In relation to the necessity of explaining why a judgment is felt to be necessary by the national court, see *e.g.* Cases 98/85 etc. *Bertini et al. v. Regione Lazio* [1986] ECR 1885.

289. *E.g.* Cases C-320–322/90 *Telemarsicabruzzo SpA et al. v. Circostel et al.* [1993] ECR I-393 at 426–427; Case C-157/92 *Pretore di Genova v. Banchero* [1993] ECR I-1086 at 1090; Case C-386/92 *Monon Automobiles – Maison du deux-Roues* [1993] ECR I-2047 at 2053–2054; Case C-307/95 *Max Mara Fashion Group Srl v. Ufficio del Registro di Reggio Emilia* [1995] ECR I-5083 at 5087–5088; Case C-257/95 *Bresle v. Préfet de la Région Auvergne et al.* [1996] ECR I-133 at 240–241; Case C-2/96 *Sunino et al.* [1996] ECR I-1543 at 1547–1548; Case C-191/96 *Modesti* [1996] ECR I-3937 at 3941–3942, and Case C-196/96 *Lahlou* [1996] ECR I-3945 at 3949–3950. The Court seems much more critical than on some occasions in the past, which increases the interest in establishing the factual context of the dispute before making a reference. See, further, the discussion of misuse of the Art. 177 EC procedure, *post.*

290. *E.g.* in Case 13/61 *Bosch* (see note 281, *supra*).

291. See *e.g.* Case 251/83 *Haug-Adrion v. Frankfurter Versicherungs-AG* [1984] ECR 4277 at 4287 and (more generally) Case 82/71 *Pubblico Ministero della repubblica Italiana v. Società Agricola Industria Latte (SAIL)* [1972] ECR 119 at 135. The latter judgment is also authority for the proposition that Art. 177 references can be made irrespective of the nature (criminal or otherwise) of the proceedings. 'The effectiveness of Community law cannot vary according to the various branches of national law which it may affect.' (*Ibid.*)

292. Case 16/65 *Firma C. Schwarze v. Einfuhr- und Vorratsstelle für Getreide und Futtermittel* [1965] ECR 877 at 886.

293. Case 13/61 *Bosch* (see note 281, *supra*) [1962] ECR 45 at 50.

not prevent a decision to make a reference from being subject to the normal appeal procedure of national law;[294] the preliminary ruling procedure will continue, however, 'as long as the request of the national court has neither been withdrawn nor become devoid of object.'[295] The Court is seised of a request within the meaning of Article 177 if the questions posed evidently relate to an interpretation of Community law or the validity of a Community measure.[296] The request must originate from the national court itself, not from the parties to the action pending before it.[297] The distribution of functions between the Court of Justice and the national court means that it is not for latter to determine whether the decision to make the reference was in accordance with the rules of national law on court organization and procedure.[298]

The strict division of powers between the Court of Justice and national courts is mandatory. It cannot be altered, nor may the exercise of those powers be impeded, in particular by agreement between private parties aiming to compel national courts to request a preliminary ruling by depriving them of their discretion under the second paragraph of Article 177.[299] The Court is not there to be used as a tool for political purposes

294. Case 146/73 *Rheinmühlen-Düsseldorf v. Einfuhr- und Vorratsstelle für Getreide und Futtermittel* [1974] ECR 139 at 147; *contra* Warner, Adv. Gen. [1974] ECR 33 at 44–45.
295. See Case 127/73 *Belgische Radio en Televisie et al. v. SV SABAM et al.* [1974] ECR 51 at 62; in Case 106/77 *Amministrazione delle Finanze dello Stato v. Simmenthal SpA* [1978] ECR 629 at 642 the Court refers to this as 'its unvarying practice.' On the operation of Order 114 of the Rules of the Supreme Court (England and Wales) see Collins, *op. cit.* (see note 277, *supra*) 194–203 (and particularly on the suspension of the transmission of the reference pending expiry of the period for appeal, 197 with reference to other writers). In the Chanel case in the Netherlands, the Rotterdam Rechtbank informed the Court that an appeal had been lodged against its decision to refer the case and that the effect of the appeal was to defer execution of the decision to refer. The Court suspended judgment until the appeal had been decided. The case was removed from the register of the Court as the reference had lost its purpose after the Rechtbank notified the Court that the appeal to the Gerechtshof been successful, see the orders of 3 June 1969 and 16 June 1970 in Case 31/68 *SA Chanel v. Copeha Handelsmaatschappij NV* [1970] ECR 403. It appears that it was only by quick footwork that the Court of Justice was able to ensure that it handed down the judgment in Case C-10/89 *SA CNL-SUCAL NV v. HAG GF AG* [1990] ECR I-3711, [1990] 3 CMLR 571 just before the parties were due to ask the Bundesgerichtshof to withdraw the reference as there was no longer any interest in pursuing the dispute, the trade marks involved having in the meantime returned into one pair of hands. Sometimes the Court may ask the referring Court if it wishes to withdraw the reference in the light of intervening case-law.
296. This has been clear ever since Case 26/62 *Van Gend en Loos* [1963] ECR 1 at 11.
297. See Statute of the Court of Justice (EC), Art. 20 and Cases 31 and 33/62 *Milchwerke Heinz Wöhrmann & Sohn KG et al. v. Commission* [1962] ECR 501 at 507.
298. Case 65/81 *Reina et al. v. Landeskreditbank Baden-Württemberg* [1982] ECR 33 at 42–43 and Cases C-332/92 *etc. Eurico Italia Srl et al. v. Ente Nazionale Risi* [1994] ECR I-726 at 733–734.
299. Case 93/78 *Mattheus v. Doego Fruchtimport und Tiefkühlkost eG* [1978] ECR 2203 at 2210.

by private parties.[300] The division of powers also means that the Court of Justice does not regard itself competent to criticise the grounds or purpose of the referring court.[301] The Court will not enquire into the relevance of the reference even if it is difficult to imagine how its answers to the questions posed could affect the resolution of the main proceedings.[302] It is for the national court to judge whether interpretation of Community law is necessary to enable it to give judgment in the action.[303] That does not, however, prevent the Court investigating of its own motion the circumstances in which the national court has referred a case to it. In Case 244/80 *Foglia v. Novello*[304] the Court was at pains to point out that it could not remain indifferent to the assessments made by national courts in the exceptional cases in which those assessments may affect the proper working of the Article 177 procedure. It had to take account not only of the interests of the parties to be proceedings but also of the interests of the Community and the Member States. In Article 177 proceedings the Court does not consider that its function is to deliver advisory opinions on general or hypothetical questions; rather its duty is to assist in the administration of justice.[305] Thus it does not have jurisdiction to reply to questions of interpretation submitted to it in the framework of procedural devices set up by the parties to obtain a pronouncement from the Court on problems of Community law which do not correspond to an objective requirement inherent in the resolution of a dispute.[306] Thus there must be a real dispute involved, not simply one set up in order to get a pronouncement from the Court of Justice.[307] Sometimes cases come close

300. Or to resolve particular theories advanced by comentators, see Case C-83/91 *Meilicke v. ADV/ORGA AG* [1992] ECR I-4919 at 4934–4935 (but *cf.* the view of this action adopted by Tesauro Adv. Gen., *ibid.* at 4902–4905).
301. *E.g.* Case 6/64 *Costa v. ENEL* [1964] ECR 585 at 593.
302. See Cases 98/85 *etc. Bertini et al. v. Regione Lazio et al.* [1986] ECR 1885 and Cases 2–4/82 *SA Delhaize Frères 'Le Lion' et al. v. Belgian State* [1983] ECR 2973 at 2986.
303. *E.g.* Case 56/65 *Société Technique Minière v. Maschinenbau Ulm GmbH* [1966] ECR 235 at 247–248; Case 13/68 *SpA Salgoil v. Italian Ministry for Foreign Trade* [1986] ECR 453 at 459; Case 180/83 *Moser v. Land Baden-Württemberg* [1984] ECR 2539 at 2545; Cases 209–213/84 *Ministère Public v. Asjes et al.* [1986] ECR 1425 at 1460–1461 and Case 14/86 *Pretore di Salo v. X* [1987] ECR 2545 at 2568.
304. [1981] ECR 3045 at 3062–3064.
305. *E.g.* (citing earlier judgments) Case C-415/93 *Union Royale Belge des Sociétés de Football Association ASBL et al. v. Bosman et al.* [1995] ECR I-4921 at 5060–5061, and Case C-291/96 *Grado et al.* [1997] ECR I-5531 at 5540.
306. See *e.g.* Case 93/78 *Mattheus v. Doego* [1978] ECR 2203 at 2210–2211; Case 338/85 *Fratelli Pardini SpA v. Ministero del commercio con l'estero et al.* [1988] ECR 2041 at 2074–2075; Case C-83/91 *Meilicke v. ADV/ORGA AG* [1992] ECR I-4871 at 4933, and Case C-326/95 *Banco de Fomento e Exterior SA v. Pechim et al.* [1996] ECR I-1385 at 1390–1391.
307. Case 104/79 *Foglia v. Novello* [1980] ECR 745 at 759–760; see Bebr (1980) 17 CMLRev. 525 and Barav (1980) 5 ELRev. 443; see also Lipstein in Capotorti *et al.*, *op. cit.* (see note 24, *supra*) 373. See further, *e.g.* Case C-286/88 *Falciola Angelo SpA v.*

to the bounds of acceptability[308] but the Court has given a ruling even when the effect of a ruling on a reference from a German court was that it become clear that Belgian legislation was incompatible with Community law.[309]

Questions of validity, specific problems. There has been uncertainty as to the extent of the Court's competence to pronounce on the validity of Community acts. The Court put an end to this uncertainty by examining first implicitly, and later expressly in connection with the validity of decisions addressed to Member States, not only the formal validity but also the substantial validity of the latter.[310] Subsequently it appears that the fact that an applicant has no reasonable chance of attacking such decisions before the Court was a major consideration in the Court's approach.[311] If it is clear that a party could have challenged an act under Article 173 EC but failed to do so within the prescribed period, the Court will not entertain a challenge to the validity of the measure by that party in the context of Article 177 EC proceedings.[312] The Court has also held that its jurisdiction cannot be limited by the grounds upon which the validity of the measures at issue in the Article 177 proceedings may be contested, thus it has

Commune di Pavia [1990] ECR I-191 at 195; Cases C-297/88 and 197/89 *Dzodzi v. Belgian State* [1990] ECR I-3763 at 3794; Case C-67/91 *Dirección General de Defensa de la Competencia v. Asociación Española de Banca Privada (AEB) et al.* [1992] ECR I-4785 at 4829, and Case C-343/90 *Lourenço Dias v. Director da Alfândega do porto* [1992] ECR I-4673 at 4708–4710.

308. *E.g.* Case 140/79 *Chemial Farmaceutici SpA v. DAF SpA* [1981] ECR 1, [1981] 3 CMLR 350 and Case 46/80 *Vinal SpA v. Orbat SpA* [1981] ECR 77, [1981] 3 CMLR 524, see Wyatt (1981) 6 ELRev. 447 (and on the substance Gormley (1982) 7 ELRev. 49).

309. Case 261/81 *Walter Rau Lebensmittelwerke v. De Smedt PvbA* [1982] ECR 3961, [1983] 2 CMLR 496. In Case C-150/88 *KG in Firma Eau de Cologne & Parfümerie-Fabrik Glockengasse No 4711 v. Provide Srl* [1989] ECR 3891 at 3913 the Court expressly noted that the provision of criteria for the interpretation of Community law which would enable the national court to solve the legal problem with which it was faced also covered situations in which it was to be determined whether the provisions of a Member State other than that of the court requesting the ruling were compatible with Community law.

310. Cases 73 and 74/63 *NV. Internationale Credit- en Handelsvereniging 'Rotterdam' et al. v. Minister van Landbouw en Visserij* [1964] ECR 1 (implicitly) and Case 16/65 *Schwarze* [1965] ECR 877 at 886 (explicitly).

311. Case 216/82 *Universität Hamburg v. Hauptzollamt Hamburg-Kehrwieder* [1983] ECR 2771 at 2788.

312. See Case C-188/92 *TWD Textilwerke Deggendorff GmbH v. Germany* [1994] ECR I-833 at 852–853. This concerned a decision addressed to the German government requiring it to ensure that unlawful state aid be repaid. The government brought the decision to the attention of the applicant. As to the sequel to this case, see Cases T-244 and 486/93 *TWD Textilwerke Deggendorff GmbH v. Commission* [1995] ECR II-2265 at 2302 (appeal dismissed in Case C-355/95 P *TWD Textilwerke Deggendorff GmbH v. Commission* [1997] ECR I-2549). *Cf.* Case 730/79 *Philip Morris Holland BV v. Commission* [1980] ECR 2671 at 2689.

jurisdiction to examine all grounds capable of invalidating those measures, including examining their compatability with rules of international law.[313] However, that provision of international law must bind the Community and be be capable of conferring rights on citizens of the Community which they can invoke before the courts.[314]

The Court has expressly held in Case 16/65 *Firma C. Schwarze v. Einfuhr- und Vorratsstelle für Getreide und Futtermittel*[315] that although in Article 177 EC proceedings it can decide on the validity of a measure (*i.e.* it can declare a measure invalid), it has no jurisdiction in such proceedings to declare a measure void. While a preliminary ruling in which the Court declares a measure of an Institution invalid is addressed only to the referring court, it is a sufficient legal basis for any other court to regard the measure as invalid. Indeed this results from the particularly imperative requirements of legal certainty in addition to those of the uniform application of Community law.[316] No doubt the Community Institution which adopted the measure concerned, would, faced with its clear unenforceability, take the necessary steps to remedy the situation.

Yet another problem concerns the reference of questions on the validity of Community acts. The lower national courts have no obligation under Article 177 to refer a question to the Court (unless, of course, they are last instance courts in the case), and for many years it was wondered whether they could declare a Community measure invalid. The Court has now expressly confirmed in Case 314/85 *Foto-Frost v. Hauptzollamt Lübeck-Ost*[317] that national courts do not have jurisdiction to declare Community measures invalid and that if they have any doubts about such measures a reference must be made. A number of key and indeed obvious considerations were involved in this finding. The uniformity of Community

---

313. Cases 21–24/72 *International Fruit Company NV v. Produktschap voor Groenten en Fruit* [1972] ECR 1219 at 1226.
314. *Ibid.*
315. [1965] ECR 877 at 886. As to declarations that an act is void and declarations of invalidity, see Daig, *Nichtigkeits-und Untätigkeitsklagen im Recht der Europäischen Gemeinschaften* (Baden-Baden, 1985).
316. Case 66/80 *International Chemical Corporation v. Amministrazione delle Finanze dello Stato* [1981] ECR 1191 at 1215; see also Case 112/83 *Société des produits de maïs SA v. Administration des Douanes et droits indirects* [1985] ECR 719 at 747. As an *e.g.* of the effects of a ruling finding a regulation invalid see Case 199/86 *Raiffeisen Hauptgenossenschaft e.G. v. Bundesanstalt für landwirtschaftiche Marktordnung* [1988] ECR 1169. As to annulment and declaration of invalidity going hand-in-hand, see Case 162/86 *Livestock Sales Transport Ltd. et al. v. Intervention Board for Agricultural Produce* [1988] ECR 489 and Case 61/86 *United Kingdom v. Commission* [1988] ECR 431, [1988] 2 CMLR 98; see also Cases C-122/95 *Germany v. Council* [1998] ECR I-973 and C-364 and 365/95 *T. Port GmbH & Co. v. Hauptzollamt Hamburg-Jonas* [1998] ECR I-1023.
317. [1987] ECR 4199 at 4231. See also (1988) 13 ELRev. 1. The Court did add that the general rule might need to be qualified in certain circumstances relating to interim measures (*ibid.* at 4232) but it did not as yet elaborate on this point.

law was particularly important when its validity was involved: divergences between national courts in different Member States as to the validity of Community acts would be liable to jeopardize the unity of the Community legal order and detract from the fundamental requirement of legal certainty. Moreover, the necessary coherence of the complete system of legal remedies established by the Treaties would be undermined. Further, the Court of Justice was the only body empowered to annul Community acts and the coherence of the system required that it alone should pronounce on the validity of such acts. Last, but not least, it was best placed to pronounce, as it was only before the Court of Justice that the Community Institutions (and now the ECB) would be able to submit observations on the validity of the act under attack; Member States could also participate in the proceedings or be required to furnish the Court with all the necessary information. All these considerations militated against national courts being permitted to declare Community acts invalid. There was, of course, no objection to a national court finding that a Community act was indeed valid, as that did not threaten the Community system.

The Court's exclusive competence to declare a Community act invalid does not however prevent a national court, in interlocutory proceedings, from suspending the enforcement of a national measure based on a Community act, such as a regulation, if it has serious doubts about the validity of the community act involved.[318] However, the suspension must retain the character of an interim measure, and may last only until such time as the Court has delivered its ruling on validity of the Community act concerned. If the question has not yet been referred to the Court, the national court must make a reference itself, setting out why it beleives the regulation concerned to be invalid. Moreover, the uniform application of Community law requires that identical conditions apply in all Member States with regard to the granting of suspensory relief (even though the making and examination of the application for such relief was a matter for national law). The Court found that the conditions which apply to the grant of interim relief by the Court itself in actions for annulment should apply to the grant of interim relief by national courts. This means that the criterion of urgency has to be satisfied: it must be necessary for the suspensory measures to be adopted and take effect before the decision on the substance of the case, in order to avoid serious and irreparable damage to the party seeking such measures. Thus the national court has to have

318. Cases C-143/88 and 92/89 *Zuckerfabrik Süderdithmarschen AG et al. v. Hauptzollamt Itzehoe et al.* [1991] ECR I-415 at 540–544. Referring to Case C-213/89 *R. v. Secretary of State for Transport, ex parte Factortame Ltd. et al.* [1990] ECR I-2433, [1990] 3 CMLR 1, the Court observed ([1991] ECR I-415 at 541) that the interim legal protection which Community law ensured for individuals before national courts had to remain the same, irrespective of whether they were contesting the compatibility of national provisions with Community law or the validity of secondary Community law itself, as the dispute in both cases was in fact based on Community law.

regard to whether such damage is likely to materialize before the Court pronounces on the reference.[319] Furthermore, it must bear in mind the Community interest, particularly its financial interest, so that Community regulations should not be set aside without guarantees. The Community interest thus involved considering, first, whether the act would be deprived of all effectiveness if it were not immediately implemented, and, secondly, if there was likely to be a financial risk to the Community through suspension of a regulation, the national court would have to be able to require the applicant to provide adequate guarantees, such as a deposit or a bank guarantee.[320]

These conditions were further clarified in the highly politically charged banana saga, in Case C-465/93 *Atlanta Fruchthandelsgesellschaft mbH et al. (I) v. Bundesamt für Ernährung und Forstwirtschaft*[321] in which the Court first considered whether a national court could positively disapply a regulation so as to render it provisionally inapplicable as regards a particular individual. The Court saw no difference between such disapplication and mere suspension of enforcement of the national measures adopted on the basis of the regulation concerned. Repeating much of *Zuckerfabrik Süderdithmarschen*, it examined further the final point in that judgment, dealing with the Community interest. It found on the first limb of that aspect that a national court had to take account of the damage which the interim measure might cause the legal regime established by the regulation for the Community as a whole, and had to consider, on the one hand, the cumulative effect which would result if a large number of courts were also to adopt interim measures for similar reasons, and, on the other hand, those special features of the applicant's situation which distinguished it from the other operators concerned. The Court then added a criterion, applicable to the assessment of all the *Zuckerfabrik Süderdithmarschen* conditions, developed in the light of the obligation on the national court, flowing from Article 5 EC, to respect what the Court of Justice has decided on the questions at issue before it. Thus if on the merits an action for annulment of a regulation has been dismissed by the Court of Justice, or that Court has found, in a preliminary ruling on validity that there was no reason to find the regulation invalid, a national court could no longer order interim measures, or would have to revoke existing measures, unless the grounds of illegality advanced differed from the pleas in law or grounds of illegality rejected by

---

319. The Court regards purely financial damage as not irreparable. The examination of all the circumstances is a matter for the national court, which must decide whether irreversible damage to the applicant would result which could not be made good if the Community act were to be declared invalid, [1991] ECR I-415 at 543.

320. *Ibid.* at 543–544.

321. [1995] ECR I-3761 at 3788–3795. In Case C-466/93 *Atlanta Fruchthandelsgesellschaft mbH et al. (II) v. Bundesamt für Ernährung und Forstwirtschaft* [1995] ECR I-3799 the Court found no factor disclosing that the contested regulation was invalid.

the Court in its judgment. The same applied in respect of a final and binding judgment of the Court of First Instance dismissing on the merits an action for annulment or a plea of illegality.[322] The Court then noted that it had upheld, in the same factual situation as that involved in *Atlanta*, that Member States bringing an action for annulment of a regulation were entitled to take judicial proceedings to defend interests, especially economic and social interests, regarded as general interests at national level.[323] The national court, callled upon to protect the rights of individuals, could indeed assess the extent to which refusal to order an interim measure might have a serious and irreparable effect on important individual interests, but in the absence of any demonstration by the applicant of a specific situation which distinguished it from other operators in the relevant sector, the national court had to accept any findings already made by the Court of Justice relating to the serious and irreparable nature of the damage. The obligation to respect a decision of the Court applied in particular to its assessment of the Community interest and the balance between that interest and that of the economic sector concerned.

This remarkable case-law clearly demonstrates a concern to find a balance between on the one hand defending the Community interest, both in financial terms, and in terms of the uniform application of Community law (with the resulting uniform conditions of competition or allocation of priorities, and level of judicial protection), and, on the other, keeping the national judiciary on board, so as not to remove entirely any national level protection for individual cases which, in effet, satisfy a criterion seemingly not unduly dissimilar to individual concern as used in relation to Article 173 EC. The balancing act involved is a judicial version of a high-wire act in the most difficult of circumstances. In Case C-68/95 *T. Port GmbH & Co. KG v. Bundesanstalt für Landwirtschaft und Ernährung*[324] the Court took the question of the possibility of national courts awarding interim measures a step further: where a Council regulation empowered the Commission to adopt particular implementing measures to adjust banana quotas, national courts were not authorized to order provisional measures in interim relief proceedings until such time as the Commission had adopted the measures it deemed necessary. There was, thus, no possibility of national interim measures pending action by a Community Institution: the existence and scope of traders' rights had not yet been established by a measure adopted by the Commission, and there was no possibility for a national court to ask the Court of Justice for a declaration that a

322. Case C-465/93 *Atlanta* [1995] ECR I-3761 at 3794.
323. Case C-280/93 R *Germany v. Council* [1993] ECR I-3667 at 3677. They were thus entitled to invoke damage affecting a whole sector of their economy, in particular when the contested regulation could entail unfavourable consequences on the level of employment and the cost of living, *ibid.*
324. [1996] ECR I-6065 at 6104.

Community Institution had failed to act. Only the Court of Justice or the Court of First Instance, as the case might be, could ensure judicial protection for the persons concerned.

Sometimes there is little point in declaring an act invalid because the unlawfulness does not lie so much in what is in the text as in what is not. In such cases the Court contents itself with a declaration that the relevant provision is incompatible with Community law and that the competent Community Institution is obliged to adopt the necessary measures to correct the incompatability.[325] Thus the Court implicitly recognized that a declaration of invalidity in Article 177 proceedings brings into operation the duty laid down in Article 176 EC to take the necessary measures to comply with the judgment; this analogous application of the terms of Article 176 (which applies on the annulment of an act or condemnation of a failure to act) is justified, as the Court later expressly indicated,[326] by the necessary consistency between the preliminary ruling procedure and the procedure of an action for annulment as two mechanisms for reviewing the legality of acts of the Community Institutions.

In a series of judgments on 15 October 1980[327] the Court proceeded in preliminary rulings to apply the second paragraph of Article 174 EC (which permits the Court to uphold the effects (or some of them) of a regulation which it has annulled) in relation to a Commission regulation concerning monetary compensatory amounts for dependent products. Because a declaration of invalidity operates retroactively (*ex tunc*), on the ground of considerations of legal certainty the Court declined to allow the fact that the regulation had been found invalid to enable the charging or payment of monetary compensatory amounts relating to periods before the date of the judgment to be challenged.[328] The operation from the date of

325. *E.g.* Cases 124/76 and 20/77 *SA Moulins et Huileries de Pont-à-Mousson v. Office National Interprofessionnel des Céréales* [1977] ECR 1795 at 1813; Cases 117/76 and 16/77 *Albert Ruckdeschel & Co. et al. v. Hauptzollant Hamburg-St. Annen et al.* [1977] ECR 1753 at 1771.
326. Case 112/83 *Société des produits de maïs SA v. Administration des Douanes et droits indirects* [1985] ECR 719 at 747.
327. Case 4/79 *Société Co-opérative 'Providence Agricole de la Champagne' v. Office National Interprofessionnel des Céréales (ONIC)* [1980] ECR 2823; Case 109/79 *Sàrl Maiseries de Beauce v. ONIC* [1980] ECR 2883 and Case 145/79 *SA Roquette Fréres v. French State – Customs Administration* [1980] ECR 2917.
328. *E.g.* Case 145/79 *Roquette*, *ibid.* at 2946. The referring courts declined to follow the judgment on this point, taking the view that only the national court had jurisdiction to determine the consequences of a declaration of invalidity, a view upheld on appeal by the Cour d'Appel, Douai (1993) Gaz. du. Pal. 292; see Van Rijn (1982) SEW 628 and WQ 1549/82 (Geurtsen) O.J. 1983 C34/17. Subsequently the Cour de Cassation Cass. Comm. 10 December 1985 (1986) RTDE 195 followed the approach of the Court of Justice, unlike the Conseil d'État (1985) Rec. Lebon 233, (1985) AJDA 615. See Errera in Schermers *et al.*, *op. cit.* (see note 257, *supra*) 78 at 97–100; Desmazières de Séchelles in *ibid.* 148 at 161–162, and Van Rijn (1986) SEW 264 *et seq.* See also Servan Schreiber (1986) 11 ELRev. 158 at 176–177 who notes that it has been

the judgment (*ex nunc*) of the declaration of invalidity thus resulting, which affected everyone concerned (effect *erga omnes*), attracted much criticism,[329] and the Court in other proceedings subsequently made it plain that, in the interests of a uniform application of Community law throughout the Community, any determination of a temporal limitation on the effect of a declaration of invalidity is a matter exclusively for it; not, therefore, a matter for the national court.[330] But the criticism was clearly taken to heart, as where the Court decides to limit the temporal effect of a declaration of invalidity, it will now consider whether an exception to that temporal limitation may be made in favour of the party to the main proceedings which brought the action before the national court against the national measure taken in pursuance of the regulation, or whether a declaration of invalidity applicable only to the future is an adequate remedy even for that party.[331] A limitation of past effects would mean that the litigant, having obtained a declaration of invalidity, would in fact find his or her claim in the naional court dismissed, which would undermine the practical effect of Article 177 EC and deprive the litigant of its right to effective judicial protection. Thus the Court permits the following to rely on its judgment: the litigant concerned, other traders who prior to the Court's judgment had commenced proceedings in a national court challenging the national measure taken in pursuance of the regulation concerned, and other traders who had submitted an administrative complaint seeking reimbursement of the sums already paid in response to that national measure.[332] This parallels the approach taken in relation to limitations in time of the effect of interpretation of Treaty provisions.[333]

suggested that the Conseil d'État's erratic behaviour might be explained by its willingness to oppose the Court of Justice's judgments in every possible way, for lack of a better explanation (M.A.F. (1980) RTDE 594). See, further, note 329, *infra*.

329. See, generally, Alexander in Alexander *et. al.*, *In Orde* (*Liber Amicorum* VerLoren van Themaat, Deventer, 1982) 1; Koopmans (1980) CLJ 287; Waelbroeck (1981) 1 YBEL 115; Bebr (1981) 18 CMLRev. 475; Brown (1981) 18 CMLRev. 509; Masclet (1986) RTDE 161; Isaac (1987) CDE 444, and Paulis (1987) CDE 243. Much of the criticism is conveniently discussed by Darmon Adv. Gen. in Case C-228/92 *Roquette Frères SA v. Hauptzollamt Geldern* [1994] ECR I-1445 at 1451–1463. See also on this problem the judgment of the Corte Costituzionale in Italy in *Fragd v. Amministrazione delle Finanze dello Stato* (1989) Riv. Dir. Int. 103 (discussed by Darmon at 1456–1457).

330. Case 112/83 *Société des produits de maïs SA* [1985] ECR 719 at 747–748; the Court was giving judgment on a reference from the Tribunal d'Instance, Paris concerning the consequences of invalidity of Community measures and designed to resolve the uncertainty resulting from the national judgments in the earlier litigation (see note 328, *supra*). See, further, Case 41/84 *Pinna v. Caisse d'Allocations Familiales de la Savoie* [1986] ECR 1 at 26–27; Cases C-38 and 151/90 *Lomas et al.* [1992] ECR I-1781 at 1816–1818, and Case C-222/92 *Roquette Frères SA v. Hauptzollamt Geldern* [1994] ECR I-1445 at 1471–1473 (noted by Alexander (1995) SEW 51).

331. See *e.g.* Case C-228/92 *Roquette* [1994] ECR I-1445 at 1472.

332. *Ibid.* at 1473.

333. See note 270, *supra*.

2.1.2 National courts and tribunals: power and obligation to refer

Which courts or tribunals are entitled or obliged to ask the European Court for a preliminary ruling, and under what conditions are they obliged to refer the matter? These questions relate to the interpretation of Article 177; they are, therefore, questions which may or must themselves be the subject of a request for a preliminary ruling when a national court or tribunal is confronted with them.

First of all, what is to be understood by the term 'any court or tribunal of a Member State'? It clearly covers those bodies which according to the commonly used terminology in each of these Member States belong to the judiciary in the wide sense; thus in the continental Member States it includes administrative courts. It embraces even courts in associated countries and territories to which only part of the EC Treaty applies.[334] It also covers tribunals set up under Acts of Parliament having particular jurisdiction.[335] Administrative bodies which decide on administrative appeals against decisions of bodies to which they are organizationally linked will not be considered 'courts or tribunals' for the purposes of Article 177 references, even if in the national system they are regarded as exercising an appellate function, as they are not acting as third parties in relation to the authority which adopted the decision under appeal.[336] Moreover, it is clear that it is not necessary to wait until the substantive trial of the action, a court or

---

334. Cases 100 and 101/89 *Kaefer and Procacci v. French State* [1990] ECR I-4647 at 4670 and Case C-260/90 *Leplat v. Territory of French Polynesia* [1992] ECR I-643 at 668 (French Polynesia). See Arnull (1993) 18 ELRev. 129 at 132. Thus the courts of the Netherlands Antilles and Aruba could also refer questions to the Court of Justice. As to the Isle of Man, see Case C-355/89 *Department of Health and Social Security v. Barr et al.* [1991] ECR I-3479 at 3500–3501 (and in particular the opinion of Jacobs Adv. Gen., *ibid.* at 3489–3491 and 3492–3494). As to Jersey, see Case C-171/96 *Pereira Roque v. H.E. The Lieutenant Governor of Jersey* [1998] ECR I-nyr (16 July 1998) and Case C-199/97 *Rios v. H.E. The Lieutenant Governor of Jersey* (O.J. 1997 C 212/22).

335. *Worringham and Humphreys v. Lloyds Bank Ltd.* [1980] 1 CMLR 293 at 308 (*per* Lord Denning, M.R.). For a brief outline of the problem see Gormley (1986) 23 CMLRev. 287 at 303–304 and 51 *Halsbury's Laws of England* (4th ed., London, 1986) para. 3.75.

336. Case C-24/92 *Corbiau v. Administration des Contributions du Grand-Duché de Luxembourg* [1993] ECR I-1277 at 1304. In the Netherlands the Crown Requests (Administrative Litigation Section of the Raad van State) were answered by the Court without bothering to enquire whether the reference came from a 'court or tribunal' within the meaning of Art. 177 EC, see Case 36/73 *NV Nederlandse Spoorwegen v. Minister van Verkeer en Waterstaat* [1973] ECR 1299 (in particular the Opinion of Mayras, Adv. Gen., *ibid.* at 1318–1320) and Case 126/82 *D.J. Smit Transport BV v. Commissie Grensoverschrijdend Beroepsgoederenvervoer* [1983] ECR 73. *Cf.* the judgment of the European Court of Human Rights in *Benthem v. The Netherlands* (23 October 1985, (Series A, No. 97; [1986] 8 EHHR 1)) in which it considered that the concept of 'tribunal' in Art. 6(1) ECHR embraced the 'power of decision.' See further, Case C-54/96 *Dorsch Consult Ingenieurgesellschaft mbH v. Bundesbaugesellschaft Berlin mbH* [1997] ECR I-4961 at 4992–4996.

tribunal seised of an interlocutory point may made a reference.[337] The nature of the case before a court does not restrict the right to refer; thus Article 177 can be used in non-contentious proceedings.[338] The corollary of a national court not being empowered to make a reference unless there is a case pending before it is that the Court of Justice has no jurisdiction to hear a reference when at the time it is made the referring court is not in a position to take the ruling on the reference into account, for instance when the procedure before the referring court has terminated.[339]

A body dealing with litigation not set up by the state requires to be sufficiently closely linked with the general system of judicial protection established in the state if a reference from it is to be admissible. Recent case-law indicates that two factors are significant. First, the question whether in law or in fact the parties are obliged to submit their disputes to the body concerned or whether they may bring the matter to the ordinary courts instead. Secondly, the Court attaches weight to the question whether or not dispute settlement occurs in the framework of a system by which the State confers on or leaves to private parties or their professional organisations the responsibility for implementing Community obligations in a given field.[340]

337. Case 107/76 *Hoffmann-La Roche v. Centrafarm Vertriebsgesellschaft Pharmazeutischer Erzeugnisse mbH* [1977] ECR 957 at 971–973; see also Cases 35 and 36/82 *Morson and Jhanjan v. State of the Netherlands et al.* [1982] ECR 3723 at 3734–3735. Indeed a reference has even been made by the English Court of Appeal at a time at which no pleadings were before it: *Polydor Ltd. et al. v. Harlequin Record Shops Ltd. et al.* [1980] 2 CMLR 413, as Case 270/80 [1982] ECR 329, [1982] 1 CMLR 677.

338. Case 199/82 *Amministrazione delle Finanze dello Stato v. SpA San Giorgio* [1983] ECR 3595 at 3611 (referring to earlier judgments); see also Case 32/74 *Friedrich Haaga GmbH* [1974] ECR 1202 at 1205/1206. But see Case C-111/94 *Job Centre Coop. arl* [1995] ECR I-3361 at 3387 (as to voluntary jurisdiction). For a reference by an Examining Magistrate at the Tribunal de Grande Instance Nanterre, see Case 65/69 *Procureur de la République v. Chatain* [1980] ECR 1345. See further, *e.g.* Case 14/86 *Pretore di Salo v. X* [187] ECR 2545 at 2568–2569; Case C-10/92 *Balocchi v. Ministero delle Finanze* [1993] ECR I-5105 at 5138; Cases C-332, 333 and 335/92 *Eurico Italia Srl et al. v. Ente Nazionale Risi* [1994] ECR I-711 at 733, and Case C-18/93 *Corsica Ferries Italia Srl v. Corpo dei Piloti del Porto di Genova* [1994] ECR I-1783 at 1818. Although the Parliamentary Commissioner for Administration in the United Kingdom is not technically a court, there have been several instances (reported in CMLR) of his having considered the administration of Community law by the United Kingdom authorities, *e.g. Re Health Care Form E 111* [1983] 1 CMLR 739.

339. Case 338/85 *Fratelli Pardini SpA v. Ministero del commercio con l'estero et al.* [1988] ECR 2041 at 2074–2075; Case C-159/90 *Society for the Protection of Unborn Children Ltd. v. Grogan et al.* [1991] ECR I-4685 at 4737–4738. The difficulties arising in situations relating to leave to appeal in which an English court may find itself *functus officio* are well illustrated in *Chiron v. Murex (No. 3) The Times* 14 October 1994 and *Magnavision v. General Optical Council (No. 2)* [1987] 2 CMLR 262 at 265–266, see Anderson, *op. cit.* (see note 257, *supra*) 157–161.

340. Case 246/80 *Broekmeulen v. Huisarts Registratie Commissie* [1981] ECR 2311 at 2326–2327; Case 102/81 *Nordsee Deutsche Hochseefischerei GmbH v. Reederei Mond Hochseefischerei Nordstern AG & Co. KG* [1982] ECR 1095 at 1110 (and the opinion of

The Court has thus accepted a reference from a medical appeals committee[341] and rejected a reference from the Paris Bar Council.[342] The Court has also, not uncontroversially, refused to rule on a reference from an arbitrator to whom the parties had agreed to submit their dispute.[343] This judgment is of particular interest in countries such as the Netherlands and the United Kingdom. In the Netherlands in particular a not insignificant proportion of administration of justice is conducted entirely by arbitration; this may involve the application of Community law, particularly in the competition field. The effect of refusing references from arbitrators is that the Court's scope for using its influence to ensure the uniform application and maintenance of Community law for, *inter alia*, the benefit of the judicial protection of those affected by Community law is restricted.

Classification problems arise particularly for tribunals which lie on the border between private and public law. In Case 61/65 *Vaassen (née Goebbels) v. Bestuur van het Beamtenfonds voor het Mijnbedrijf*[344] the Court treated the arbitration tribunal of the miners' fund as being a tribunal within the meaning of Article 177 even though the tribunal itself considered that it was not a court within the meaning of Dutch legislation; the Court of Justice looked at the functions of the arbitration tribunal and laid much emphasis on their public law character, completely ignoring the point that formally the arbitration tribunal only gave binding opinions; they were in practice always followed but if they had to be enforced this could only be done through the civil courts.[345]

The next question which arises is which courts or tribunals are not only entitled to refer questions to the Court but are also under an obligation to do

Reischl, Adv. Gen., *ibid.* at 2335–2338). See also Alexander and Grabandt (1982) 19 CMLRev. 413.

341. Case 246/80 *Broekmeulen, ibid.*
342. Case 138/80 *Borker* [1980] ECR 1975 at 1977. The Bar Council had no case before it which it was under a legal duty to try but a request for a declaration relating to a dispute between a member of the Bar and the courts or tribunals of another Member State.
343. Case 102/81 *Nordsee*, [1982] ECR 1095 at 1110–1111. The Court was concerned that there was an insufficiently close link between the arbitration procedure and the organization of legal remedies through the German courts for the arbitrator to be considered a 'court or tribunal of a Member State' within the meaning of Art. 177, *ibid.* See Lasok and Millett in Vaughan (ed.), *op. cit.* (see note 7, *supra*) para. 629, Bebr [1985] 22 CMLRev. 489 and Hepting (1982) Eur 315. The English courts have been willing to give leave to appeal against an arbitrator's award in order that a reference may be made in the course of court proceedings, see Case 174/84 *Bulk Oil (Zug) AG v. Sun International Ltd. et al.* [1984] 1 All ER 386, [1986] ECR 559. It is clear though, that an arbitrator remains bound to apply Community law just as he or she is bound to apply the law in general (see 51 *Halsbury's Laws*, para. 3.76). A court deciding on an appeal from an arbitrator's award is a 'court or tribunal' for the purposes of art. 177 EC, Case C-393/92 *Gemeente Almelo et al. v. Energiebedrijf IJsselmij NV* [1994] ECR I-1477 at 1515, even when it must give judgment 'according to what appears fair and reasonable.'
344. [1966] ECR 261 at 273; see Haardt (1966–1967) 4 CMLRev. 440.
345. See the observations of the defendant [1966] ECR 261 at 266.

so. The obligation to refer binds all courts or tribunals of a Member State
'against whose decisions there is no judicial remedy under national law.'[346]

In the Netherlands it is clear that the following bodies are bound by the
obligation: the Hoge Raad, the Centrale Raad van Beroep (to the extent that
no appeal to the Hoge Raad is possible), the College van Beroep voor het
Bedrijfsleven, the administrative litigation section (Afdeling bestuursrecht-
spraak) section of the Raad van State (Council of State), the Tariefcommissie
(which deals with *inter alia* customs matters) and the Crown.[347]

In the United Kingdom the obligation is not confined to the House of
Lords.[348] Thus it is submitted that the obligation to refer binds the highest
court in the case rather than simply the highest court in the hierarchy;
whilst this point has been the subject of divergent views (the debate
between advocates of the 'concrete' theory who favour the standpoint just
advanced and the advocates of the 'abstract' theory who would restrict the
obligation to the highest courts in the hierarchy) it is submitted that the
'concrete' theory is to be preferred in the interests of good administration
of justice. Indeed the 'concrete' theory finds implicit support in the case-
law of the Court of Justice.[349]

The obligation to refer does not apply, however, if a question of
Community law is raised in interlocutory proceedings and the decision be
taken does not bind the court or tribunal which later has to deal with the
substance of the case. This is provided, however, that each of the parties
can institute proceedings on the substance of the cases (or require them to
be instituted) even before the courts or tribunals of another jurisdictional
system and that during such proceedings any question of Community law
provisionally decided in the earlier proceedings may be re-examined and be
the subject of a reference.[350]

---

346. Arts. 177 EC and 150 Euratom (para. 3 in each case). See, generally, Lieber, *Über die
     Vorlagepflicht des Artikel 177 EWG Vertrag und deren Missachtung* (Munich/Florence,
     1986).
347. As to the Benelux Court of Justice, see Case C-337/95 *Parfums Christian Dior SA et
     al. v. Evora BV* [1997] ECR I-6013 at 6043–6045.
348. 51 *Halsbury's Laws* para. 2.183 (see also in more detail para. 3.82); see further Brown and
     Kennedy, *op. cit.* (see note 7, *supra*) 214–215; Hartley: *The Foundations of European
     Community Law* (3rd ed., Oxford, 1994) 281–283 ('This view seems preferable, though
     the matter cannot be regarded as settled.'); Collins, *op. cit.* (see note 277, *supra*) 113–115;
     Jacobs (1977) 2 ELRev. 119, and Usher in Vaughan, *op. cit.* (see note 7, *supra*) 543.
     Collins, *ibid.* 153 has rightly described Lord Denning's view that only the House of Lords
     is obliged to refer (in *H.P. Bulmer Ltd v. J.A. Bollinger SA* [1974] Ch. 401 at 420) as
     'plainly wrong.' *Contra*, Parry and Hardy, *EEC Law* (2nd ed., London, 1981) 126. See
     also the views of Kerr, L.J. in *R. v. The Pharmaceutical Society of Great Britain, ex parte
     the Association of Pharmaceutical Importers* [1987] 3 CMLR 951 at 969–970.
349. In Case 6/64 *Costa v. ENEL* [1964] ECR 585 the Milan magistrate had first and last
     instance jurisdiction (because of the small sum involved in the contested electricity bill)
     and the Court clearly felt that the magistrate was indeed bound to make the reference.
350. Cases 35 and 36/82 *Morson and Jhanjan v. State of the Netherlands et al.* [1982] ECR

2.1.3   Relevance, 'acte éclairé' and acte clair

Is the court of highest instance in the case always obliged to refer as soon as the requirement has been satisfied that a question of Community law is being submitted to it? At first sight the third paragraph of Article 177 would seem to lead to an affirmative answer. The Court, too, in principle does not consider that there is any limitation on the obliation to refer, as soon as such a question has been raised.[351] This statement, however, can be reconciled with the theory that a second requirement must also be satisfied, *i.e.* the one mentioned in the second paragraph of Article 177, which deals with the possibility of referring the matter to the Court: the national court (also one which is obliged to refer) must consider that a decision on the point of Community law is necessary to enable it to give judgment. In fact, in order to be obliged to refer, a court or tribunal against whose decision there is no judicial remedy will first have to be entitled to do so in accordance with the provision of the second paragraph of Article 177. If this were not the case unacceptable consequences would result. The mere fact that a question of Community law is raised, however irrelevant or absurd, would oblige the court of highest instance in the case to refer to the Court of Justice. This would open wide the door to chicanery.[352]

The relevance of the question raised is therefore a prerequisite for the right, and consequently the obligation, to refer to the Court. Article 177 leaves it to the discretion of the national court (including one which is obliged to refer) to decide whether application of Community law is necessary to enable it to give judgment in the dispute before it. It is of the greatest importance that national courts should use this discretion in the proper way. It implies that a national court cannot be (or, as the case may be is not) obliged to refer to the Court of Justice if it is able to settle the dispute exclusively on grounds of national law.

Even if the highest court in the case considers a decision on a question raised before it necessary to enable it to settle a dispute, it need not always

---

3723 and Case 107/76 *Hoffmann-La Roche v. Centrafarm Vertriebsgesellschaft Pharmazeutischer Erzeugnisse mbH.* [1977] ECR 957 at 973.

351.   Cases 28–30/62 *Da Costa en Schaake NV et al. v. Nederlandse Belastingadministratie* [1963] ECR 31 at 38.

352.   *Cf.* Protocol of 3 June 1971 on the interpretation of the Convention of 28 September 1968 on jurisdiction and the enforcement of civil and commercial judgments (concluded under Art. 220 EC, consolidated version O.J. 1998 C 27/1), Art. 3(1). The report, annexed to the Protocol, of the working group of experts makes it clear that this provision is to be considered as conforming to the hitherto generally accepted interpretation of Art. 177 EC; see, criticising this view, Dumont (1972) SEW 225 *et seq*. See also Case 283/81 *Srl CILFIT et al. v. Ministry of Health* [1982] ECR 3415 at 3428–3429. As to the attitude of the English Courts to when a reference can be said to be necessary, see, generally, Dashwood and Arnull (1984) 4 YBEL 255 at 283–286; Gormley (1986) 23 CMLRev. 287 at 296–296 and Collins *op. cit.* (see note 257, *supra*) 176–189.

be obliged to refer. The Court itself made an exception to this obligation. The 'authority of an interpretation under Article 177 already given by the Court may deprive this obligation of its purpose and thus empty it of its substance. Such is the case especially when the question raised is materially identical with a question which has already been the subject of a preliminary ruling in a similar case.'[353] This situation is often described as 'acte éclairé.' The Court took the opportunity in Case 283/81 Srl CILFIT et al. v. Ministry of Health[354] to take this rather further, noting that the same effect (i.e. that the obligation to refer becomes devoid of purpose) 'may be produced where previous decisions of the Court have already dealt with the point of law in question, irrespective of the nature of the proceedings which led to those decisions, even though the questions at issue are not strictly identical.' Thus it is clear that the previous decisions need not have been given in Article 177 rulings. The Court went on to stress, though 'that in all such circumstances national courts and tribunals, including those referred to in the third paragraph of Article 177, remain entirely at liberty to bring a matter before the Court of Justice if they consider it appropriate to do so.'[355] The Court always retains the possibility of reconsidering its case-law.[356]

The Court in CILFIT also added another exception to the obligation to refer, an exception which in practice was being made by the highest national courts even before the judgment in CILFIT. This follows French legal practice known as the 'théorie de l'acte clair' in relation to references. This theory holds that the obligation to refer does not apply if the highest court concerned is of opinion that there can be no reasonable doubt about the answers to the questions raised. Put in the words of the Court in CILFIT 'the correct application of Community law may be so obvious as to leave no scope for any reasonable doubt as to the manner in which the

353. Cases 28–30/62 Da Costa [1963] ECR 31 at 38.
354. [1982] ECR 3415 at 3429.
355. Ibid. at 3430. Sometimes the Court has been flooded out with references on a point identical to one decided earlier; in almost sheer exasperation it responded with a terse judgment saying that the case raised an issue identical to that in an earlier judgment, a copy of which was annexed (e.g. Cases 79 and 80/84 Procureur de la République v. Chabaud and Rémy [1985] ECR 2953 and Cases 271–274/84 and 6 and 7/85 Procureur de la République et al. v. Chiron et al. [1986] ECR 529). If a reference arrives on a point already decided, the Court's registry will draw the attention of the referring court to the earlier judgment and ask it if it wishes to maintain the reference; usually the national court then withdraws the reference, although it is, of course, perfectly entitled not to do so.
356. Thus the concept of direct effect has been broadened since its initial development and the Court has reconsidered its initial view that an act had to be annulled before a claim for damages could be considered, see Brown and Kennedy, op. cit. (see note 7 supra) 345–347. See, generally, Arnull (1993) 30 CMLRev. 247. Sometimes the reversal of earlier approaches is spectacular, e.g. Cases C-267 and 268/91 Keck and Mithouard [1993] ECR I-6097, [1995] 1 CMLR 101 and Case C-10/89 SA CNL-SUCAL NV v. HAG GF AG [1990] ECR I-3711, [1990] 2 CMLR 55.

question raised is to be resolved.'[357] But the Court has warned that it is not enough that the highest court concerned thinks that the answer is evident. Before it comes to a conclusion that there is no reasonable doubt on the point 'the national court or tribunal must be convinced that the matter is equally obvious to the courts of the other Member States and to the Court of Justice.'[358] The national court or tribunal must assess this 'on the basis of the characteristic features of Community law and the particular difficulties to which its interpretation gives rise.'[359] The Court then proceeded to indicate what should be borne in mind, namely:

- Community legislation is drafted in several languages, the different language versions being equally authentic; interpretation of a provision of Community law thus involves a comparison of the different language versions;
- even when the different language versions completely agree, Community law uses its own terminology; moreover, legal concepts do not necessarily have the same meaning in Community law and in the law of the various Member States;[360]
- every provision of Community law must be placed in its context and interpreted in the light of the provisions of Community law as a whole, in the light of the objectives of Community law and its state of evolution at the date on which the provision involved is to be applied.[361]

However, the freedom not to refer in such a case to the Court of Justice will have to be used with great circumspection by the highest national court. Thus Donner, himself then a judge of the European Court warned: 'One should be suspicious of the apparent clarity of the texts. Experience shows that the same technical term may have different meanings for lawyers coming from different countries. This is a specific danger of Community law, for the very reason that on the one hand the juridical

357. [1982] ECR 3415 at 3430. For a powerful critique of the *acte clair* doctrine see Capotorti, Adv. Gen., *ibid.* at 3435 *et seq.* See Rasmussen (1984) 9 ELRev. 242, Bebr (1983) 20 CMLRev. 439 and Wyatt (1983) 8 ELRev. 179. *Cf.* Art. 6(4) of the Treaty concerning the establishment and the Statute of a Benelux Court ((1965) 13 *European Yearbook* 259–266), which, however, prohibits reference to this court in such a case.
358. [1982] ECR 3415 at 3430.
359. *Ibid.*
360. The concept of 'public policy' in Arts. 36, 48 and 56 EC (also Art. 69 ECSC) is just such an example: it is not a concept determined by national law alone, even though it may vary from time to time and from situation to situation. It is thus not simply an excuse for whatever the authorities wish and its application is certainly subject to constraints imposed by Community law, so that its exercise becomes a Community law concept, even if its content is (at least primarily) a matter for national law, Case 36/75 *Rutili v. Minister for the Interior* [1975] ECR 1219 at 1231.
361. Case 283/81 *CILFIT* [1982] ECR 3415 at 3430.

vocabulary of the six countries is practically identical, whilst on the other hand the terms have acquired a slightly, and sometimes even profoundly, different connotation under the influence of six independent sets of case-law.'[362]

It must be recognised that the *acte clair* exception to the obligation to refer is necessary; it is neither in the interest of the satisfactory administration of justice nor conducive to proper co-operation between the Court of Justice and the highest judicial bodies in Member States if the latter are subjected so strongly to the control of the Court that they are automatically obliged to refer, even if there cannot be the slightest doubt on the interpretation of the text of Community law.

It has been suggested that it might be advisable to provide for a corrective to the right to apply the theory of *acte clair*, a right that cannot be denied to the highest judicial bodies. Such a corrective might at the same time prevent abuse of the freedom given to them to judge the relevance of Community law to the decision in the dispute before them. In the literature various suggestions in this direction are to be found.[363] The proposal to confer on the Commission, the Member States, the Council, or the Advocates General the right to lodge an appeal to the Court 'in the interest of the law'[364] is least apt to interfere with the system of Article 177. This would parallel the system of Attorney General's references in English law. The contested national decision would stand, but the Court would have an opportunity to make a ruling on the legal question at issue, which would have the authority of a binding interpretation for future cases. In

362. *Les rapports entre la compétence de la Cour de Justice des Communautés Européennes et les tribunaux internes* Rec. des Cours A.D.I., 1965. II, 45 (our translation). This is even more true with 15 Member States.

363. *E.g.* Lauwaars (1968) SEW 396, the *Merchiers Report*, European Parliament session documents 1969/1970 no. 94, and the Court of Justice's *Report on European Union* Bull. EC Supp. 9/75, p. 18. See also, generally, the *Report of the Court of Justice on certain aspects of the application of the Treaty on European Union, Proceedings of the Court of Justice and the Court of First Instance of the European Communities* No. 15/1995.

364. *Cf.* the system of the Protocol of 3 June 1971 concerning the interpretation of the Convention of 27 September 1968 on jurisdiction and the enforcement of civil and commercial judgments (concluded under Art. 220 EC, consolidated version O.J. 1998 C 27/1), Art. 4. In this case the competent authorities of a Contracting State may ask the Court for a preliminary ruling on a question of interpretation of the Convention if decisions taken by courts or tribunals of that state are in conflict with the interpretation given either by the Court of Justice itself or by a decision of a court or tribunal of another Contracting State. The interpretation given by the Court does not affect the decisions in respect of which the interpretation was requested. The Treaty of Amsterdam (not yet in force) will provide in the new Art. 73p(3) EC that rulings given by the Court in response to requests from the Council, the Commission or a Member State on the new Title IIIa of Part Three of the EC Treaty or on acts adopted thereunder shall not apply to judgments of courts or tribunals of the Member States which have become *res judicata*.

this way the main function of Article 177 could be reasonably safeguarded: ensuring uniformity of application of Community law in the Member States. If the Community's legal subjects are to be guaranteed as complete a legal protection as possible, this corrective would of course be inadequate and it would be necessary to look at other possible remedies, such as the possibility of an appeal to the Court by parties to the basic proceedings against a refusal to refer.[365] Even apart from the opposition which such a fundamental modification of the relationship between the Court of Justice and the highest national courts would arouse in this stage of European integration, it may be doubted whether such a solution would do justice to another important interest which ought to be legally protected, *viz.* that of a prompt and not too complicated judicial procedure.[366] It must always be borne in mind that the Article 177 EC procedure works because of the mutual confidence which has been fostered between the Community and national judiciaries; cooperation is essential and the Court has always been at pains to stress that the national courts and it have a joint role in ensuring that Community law is upheld; the Court of Justice is there more as a concerned godfather than as a sergeant-major.[367]

2.2 National courts and Community law

In its celebrated judgment in Case 26/62 *NV Algemene Transport- en Expeditie Onderneming Van Gend en Loos v. Nederlandse administratie der belastingen*[368] the Court observed that 'the task assigned to the Court of Justice under Article 177, the object of which is to secure uniform interpretation of the Treaty by national courts and tribunals, confirms that the states have acknowledged that Community law has an authority which

---

365. There is always the risk of national courts going off on frolics of their own, *e.g.* in the United Kingdom: *R. v. London Boroughs Transport Committee, ex parte Freight Transport Association Ltd.* [1992] 1 CMLR 5 at 20–21 (HL), a questionable example of the national court finding the first *CILFIT* criterion (irrelevance) applicable (see Weatherill (1992) 17 ELRev. 299); *Finnegan v. Clowney Youth Training Programme Ltd.* [1990] 2 AC 407 at 416–417 (HL), refusal to interpret national legislation in conformity with a directive, and *In re Sandhu The Times*, 10 May 1985 (HL, transcript on *Lexis*), no reference, relying on a judgment decided between the hearing and the speeches which was of questionable relevance. These undoubtedly isolated incidents should not detract from the usually satisfactory approach in the Judicial Committee of the House of Lords.
366. The Bundesverfassungsgericht regards the Court as the 'lawful judge' in the sense of Art. 101 of the German Basic Law. If a German court against whose judgment there is no remedy under national law fails in its duty to refer, it causes an infringement of this *jus non evocando*, see *Kloppenburg* [1988] 3 CMLR 1, 75 BVerfGE 223.
367. See, *e.g.* Kutscher in *Reports of the Judicial and Academic Conference 27–28 September 1976* (Luxembourg, 1976) 1–14 and Case 283/81 *CILFIT* [1982] ECR 3415 at 3428.
368. [1963] ECR 1 at 12.

can be invoked by their nationals before those courts and tribunals.' If individuals are to be able to rely on provisions of Community law the provisions concerned must be (in the language of public international law) self-executing; in other words they must lend themselves by their very nature to direct application by, in this case, a court in the national legal system (in the language of Community law they must be capable of producing direct effects). The direct applicability of Community law deals, it is submitted, with the question whether Community law has to be transformed into domestic law;[369] a question which, as has been seen in section 3.3. of Chapter II, above, received a negative answer from the Court.

In the early days of Community law there was a tendency to use the terms 'direct applicability' and 'direct effect' interchangeably,[370] but this is no longer generally done, even in Leiden.[371] Much confusion can be avoided if it is remembered that the question of direct applicability deals with whether action by national bodies (in effect by Parliament, regional bodies, or the administration under delegated powers) is necessary to give effect to a provision of Community law. The question of direct effect relates to whether an individual can rely on a particular provision of Community law before national courts.[372]

The question whether provisions of Community law apply as such (*i.e.* without transformation) in the national legal system is not always indentical with the question whether provisions of Community law may be relied upon before national courts. This is evident from the fact that even if the view were taken that the validity of Community law in the national legal system rested on the approval of the Treaty by a law – a view which the Court has rejected[373] – that would not answer the question of whether

369. Winter (1972) 9 CMLRev. 425 first made the distinction plain; see also Usher in Vaughan (ed.), *op. cit.* (see note 7, *supra*) paras. 189–202

370. A tendency still found at the Court, even in later years, *e.g.* Case 43/75 *Defenne v. SABENA* [1976] ECR 455 at 474. See Maresceau, *De direkte werking van het Europese Gemeenschapsrecht* (Deventer, 1978) 46 (and 118–123 on the distinction between direct applicability and direct effect which was then found only in Dutch discussions). See also Brown (1986) 23 CMLRev. 905.

371. To adapt Heuston's famous phrase: Heuston, *Essays in Constitutional Law* (2nd ed., London, 1964) 1.

372. All organs of the administration, national, regional and local (and including national courts) are obliged to respect the direct effect of those provisions of Community law which are directly effective, Case 103/88 *Fratelli Constanzo SpA v. Comune di Milano* [1989] ECR 1839 at 1870–1871. The obligation on such authorities applies irrespective of whether they act in a public law or in a private law capacity, Case 152/84 *Marshall v. Southampton and South-West Hampshire Area Health Authority (Teaching)* [1986] ECR 723 at 749. The obligation also covers organizations and bodies subject to the authority or control of the state or which have special powers going beyond those resulting from the normal rules applicable to relations between individuals, Case C-188/89 *Foster et al. v. British Gas plc* [1990] ECR I-3313 at 3348–3349 (citing earlier case-law).

373. See Chapter II, section 3.3, *ante.*

a provision of Community law having the force of national law could be relied upon before the national courts. This latter question clearly depends on whether the provision lends itself to being so relied on.

It is generally assumed, as the Permanent Court of International Justice has stated, 'that, according to a well-established principle of international law an international agreement cannot, as such, create direct rights and obligations for private individuals. But it cannot be disputed that the very object of an international agreement, according to the intention of the contracting parties, may be the adoption by the parties of some definite rules creating individual rights and obligations and enforceable by the national courts.'[374] Under the influence of this idea national courts will not readily assume that a Treaty provision which is expressly addressed to the contracting states can be invoked by a private party in an action pending before that court. Rather they will be inclined to consider a Treaty provision as self-executing on the basis of the intention of the contracting parties if it is clearly addressed to private parties, *i.e.* imposes an obligation on them or grants them a subjective right.

Whereas in an ordinary treaty the national court itself will ascertain the intention of the contracting parties in this respect by means of an interpretation of the text of the relevant provision, in the EC Treaty this is a question of interpretation which can or must be referred by the national court to the Court of Justice under Article 177. On the very first occasion on which the Court could pronounce on this point by means of a preliminary ruling it took a much wider view of the self-executing character of provisions addressed to Member States than might have been expected from national courts in the light of the case-law relating to ordinary treaties; it did this on the basis of the special character of the EC Treaty. In *Van Gend en Loos*[375] the Court interpreted the criteria on the basis of which the provisions must be deemed to be directly effective in a wide sense. Article 12 EC was held to be confer rights on individuals even though it does not refer to rights of private parties, but only imposes a so-called 'standstill' obligation on Member States in the field of customs duties and charges having equivalent effect in intra-Community trade.

According to the Court in *Van Gend en Loos*, the answer to the question whether a provision of an international treaty is self-executing and accordingly has direct effect depends on its spirit, its general scheme and its wording. In the light of the spirit of the Treaty there is clearly a favourable predisposition towards direct effect. In *Van Gend en Loos* the

---

374. *Jurisdiction of the Courts of Danzig*, Advisory Opinion 1928, Series B. No. 15. pp. 17–18.
375. [1963] ECR 1 at 12. (The Court actually spoke of the provisions being directly applicable.)
376. *Ibid.* See, further, Chapter II, sections 3.2 and 3.3, *ante.*
377. See note 374, *supra, loc. cit.*
378. Case 26/62 *Van Gend en Loos* [1963] ECR 1 at 12.

Court, having found that 'the Community constitutes a new legal order of international law for the benefit of which the states have limited their sovereign rights, albeit in limited fields' concluded that independently of the legislation of Member States 'Community law therefore not only imposes obligations on individuals but is also intended to confer upon them rights which become part of their legal heritage. These rights arise not only where they are expressly granted by the Treaty, but also by reason of obligations which the Treaty imposes in a clearly defined way upon individuals as well as upon the Member States and upon the institutions of the Community.'[376]

The 'very object' of the EC Treaty, to use the words of the Advisory Opinion of 1928 of the Permanent Court of International Justice,[377] is 'the adoption of some definite rules creating individual rights and obligations and enforceable by national courts,' provided that the term 'rights' is taken in a wide sense, *i.e.* as embracing also the right to rely on generally binding Community rules before national courts. The EC Treaty, therefore, contains self-executing provisions to which direct effect must be assigned. Considering the special character of the Community legal order, there is evidently no reason for the Court of Justice to take a narrow view in giving its opinion on the question whether a provision has direct effect: these rights for private parties are created 'not only where they are expressly granted by the Treaty, but also by reason of obligations which the Treaty imposes in a clearly defined way upon individuals as well as upon the Member States and upon the Community institutions.'[378]

The general scheme of the Treaty and the place therein of the relevant provision are also of importance.[379] Thus in *Van Gend en Loos* the Court pointed out that Article 12 EC was a more specific application of Article 9 EC which was one of the essential provisions of the customs union on which the Community was based.[380] Again, in its examination of the direct effect of the first paragraph of Article 95 EC in Case 57/65 *Alfons Lütticke GmbH v. Hauptzollamt Saarlouis*[381] the Court noted that that provision 'constitutes in fiscal matters the indispensable foundation of the Common Market.'

Finally, the wording of the provision concerned is naturally of importance. As has already been observed, the fact that a Treaty provision takes the form of an obligation on the Member States is not an obstacle to its having direct effect. In myriad cases since *Van Gend en Loos* the Court has confirmed this viewpoint. Thus, for example, in Case 28/67 *Firma Molkeri-Zentrale Westfalen/Lippe GmbH v. Hauptzollamt Paderborn*[382] it

379. See Kuipers (1968) SEW 574–576.
380. [1963] ECR 1 at 12.
381. [1966] ECR 205 at 210.
382. [1968] ECR 143 at 152.

repeated that directly effective 'rights arise not only where they are expressly granted by the Treaty but also by reason of obligations which the Treaty imposes in a clearly defined way upon individuals as well as upon the Member States and upon the institutions of the Community.' It added that 'it is necessary and sufficient that the very nature of the provision of the Treaty in question should make it ideally adapted to produce direct effects on the legal relationship between Member States and those subject to their jurisdiction.'[383] Thus the wording of the provisions indicates whether their *very nature* is such that they produce direct effects.

2.2.1 Specific conditions for direct effect[384]

The case-law of the Court on the specific conditions for direct effect developed up to 1970 in the context of references from national courts requesting a ruling on whether private parties could rely on various provisions of the EEC Treaty in those courts against the national authorities. Only after 1970 did the Court have to look at the direct effect of Community measures (regulations, directives and decisions as well as international agreements binding the Community) and at the question of to what extent provisions of Community law could be relied upon by private parties against other private parties (this is often called horizontal direct effect). The special aspects of the case-law on these two points are examined in sections 2.2.2 and 2.2.3 of this Chapter, below. The present discussion deals with the case-law which particularly concerns Treaty provisions which impose obligations on the Member States. This discussion is also of importance for other provisions of Community law as the conditions developed in the Court's case-law also apply *mutatis mutandis* to other provisions.

A consistent line of case-law shows that a provision can have direct effect if the obligation imposed on Member States is (A) clear and precise and (B) unconditional and, if implementing measures are provided for, (C)

---

383. *Ibid.* at 152–153.
384. As to direct effect in general, see Prechal, *Directives in European Community Law* (Oxford, 1995) Chapter 11; Schermers and Waelbroeck, *op. cit.* (see note 7, *supra*) 138–154; De Búrca (1992) 55 MLR 215; Coppel (1994) 54 MLR 859; Craig (1992) OJLS 453; Curtin (1990) 27 CMLRev. 709 and (1990) 15 ELRev. 195; Eleftheriadis (1996) 16 YBEL 205; Maltby (1993) 109 LQR 301; Steiner (1990) 106 LQR 144 and (1993) 18 ELRev. 3, and Tridimas (1994) 19 ELRev. 621. For older, but still important literature, see Winter (1972) CMLRev. 425; Van Gerven in Jacobs (ed.), *European Law and the Individual* (Amsterdam, 1976) 4–9; Dashwood (1978) 16 JCMS 229; Easson (1979) 4 ELRev. 67; Timmermans (1979) 16 CMLRev. 533; Eassson (1981) 1 YBEL 1; Steiner (1982) 98 LQR 229 (on direct applicability); Wyatt (1982) 7 ELRev. 147; Pescatore (1983) 8 ELRev. 155; Wyatt (1983) 8 ELRev. 241; Bebr (1983) 20 CMLRev. 35, and Green (1984) 9 ELRev. 295.

the Community Institutions or the Member States are not allowed any margin of discretion.[385] These conditions are now discussed in turn.

A. The content of the obligation must be clear and precise. This condition need not exclude the direct effect of provisions whose interpretation causes difficulties. Neither the complexity of the wording of a provision[386] nor the fact that a provision involves the evaluation of economic factors[387] need be an obstacle to the provision having direct effect. In Case 27/67 *Firma Fink-Frucht GmbH v. Hauptzollamt München-Landsbergerstrasse*[388] the Court had to consider indefinite legal concepts such as 'similar products' and 'indirect protection' in interpreting and applying Article 95 EC.[389] If, however, the concepts contained in a provision leave the Member States a certain discretion in their application then such a provision will not have direct effect.[390] The distinction between indefinite legal concepts and concepts which imply a policy discretion is discussed under (C) below.

B. The wording of the provision must make the obligation unconditional and unqualified. A provision is conditional as long as it is inapplicable for a certain period. On the expiry of this period the condition has been satisfied and on this point there is no further obstacle to direct effect.[391] It is, however, necessary that the Member States are left with no discretion as to the date by which the obligation must be fulfiled.[392] This requirement results from the condition discussed at (C) below. The fact that the Treaty recognises exceptions to a given rule is not regarded as making the

---

385. See Mayras, Adv. Gen. in Case 41/74 *Van Duyn v. Home Office* [1974] ECR 1337 at 1354, see also, more recently, Case 44/84 *Hurd v. Jones* [1986] ECR 29 at 83.
386. Case 6/64 *Costa v. ENEL* [1964] ECR 585 at 597–598.
387. Case 27/67 *Firma Fink-Frucht GmbH v. Hauptzollamt München Landsbergerstrasse* [1968] ECR 223 at 232.
388. *Ibid.*
389. See Brinkhorst (1969) *Arts Aequi 230.*
390. In Case 13/68 *SpA Salgoil v. Italian Ministry for Foreign Trade* [1968] ECR 453 at 461 the Court concluded that a number of concepts used in Art. 33(1) and (2) EC ('national production' and 'total value') contained a certain margin of discretion because as the Treaty gave no indication of the data to be used in calculating these concepts or of the methods to be applied several solutions could be envisaged. The national court is, of course, able to examine whether the margin of discretion has been exceeded; see Case 51/76 *Verbond van Nederlandse Ondernemingen v. Inspecteur der Invoerrechten en Accijnzen* [1977] ECR 113 at 125–127 in relation to the margin of discretion relating to the term 'capital goods' in Art. 17 of the Second VAT Directive (O.J. English Special Edition 1967, p.16). See also Keur (1982) SEW 653.
391. This occurred at the end of the transitional period in relation to Arts. 52, 59 1st para. and 60 3rd para. EC, see Case 2/74 *Reyners v. Belgian State* [1974] ECR 631 at 651–652 and Case 33/74 *Van Binsbergen v. Bestuur van de Bedrijfsvereniging voor de Metaalnijverheid* [1974] ECR 1299 at 1309–1310.
392. Case 57/65 *Lütticke* [1966] ECR 205 at 210.

fulfilment or effect of the obligation contained in that rule subject to a condition. Even if the exception embraces vague concepts such as 'public policy, public security or public health' in Article 48(3) EC this will not deprive the relevant rule (in this case of free movement of workers) of direct effect since the application of the exception is subject to judicial control.[393]

If a provision provides for the adoption of implementing measures by the Community Institutions or by the Member State this is regarded as a condition, albeit one which is satisfied when the implementing measures are adopted. As soon as the Member States or the Community Institutions as the case may be have adopted the required measures the relevant provision acquires direct effect.[394] Provisions may depend on further Community or national measures as regards part of their scope, but this does not prevent the rest of the provisions having direct effect or having direct effect in particular respects.[395]

It is important to emphasise that the mere fact that a provision contains an obligation to adopt implementing measures need not necessarily mean that the obligation is dependent on such measures for its execution or effect. This will only be the case if the Member States are given a discretion in the matter (on which point see (C) below). The presence of a link between the Community rule and its application does not consitute in itself an insurmountable obstacle to the direct effect of the rule.[396]

393. Sec Case 41/74 *Van Duyn v. Home Office* [1974] ECR 1337 at 1347.
394. See Case 13/68 *Saigoil* [1968] ECR 453 at 460–461 (standstill provision of Art. 31 para. 2 EC) once the lists of liberalised products had been supplied or at the latest once the time-limit for supplying them had expired; Case 77/72 *Capolongo v. Azienda Agricola Maya* [1973] ECR 611 at 621–622 – when the provisions of Art. 92(1) EEC 'have been put in concrete form by acts having general application provided for by Art. 94 or by decisions in particular cases envisaged by Article 93(2).' In Case 2/74 *Reyners* and Case 33/74 *Van Binsbergen* (see note 391, *supra*) the Court expressly viewed the direct effect after the end of the transitional period of Arts. 52, 59, 1st para. and 60, 3rd para. EC as not depending on the adoption by the Council during the transitional period of the directives envisaged in Arts. 54, 57 and 63 EC. The directives relating to preservatives or antioxidants authorised for use in foodstuffs intended for human consumption contain an interesting approach to the Member States' powers under harmonisation directives; whilst they are left with a considerable freedom to permit or prohibit the use of certain substances in such foodstuffs, they may not totally prohibit the use of these substances, nor may they impose a general prohibition on the marketing of foodstuffs containing these substances. This prohibition has been held to be 'unconditional and sufficiently precise' and thus to be capable of being relied upon before the national courts, Case 88/79 *Ministère Public v. Grunert* [1980] ECR 1827 at 1837.
395. Thus Art. 119 EC (on equal pay for men and women for equal work) has direct effect as far as direct and overt discrimination is concerned but not in respect of indirect and disguised discrimination: Case 43/75 *Defrenne v. SABENA* [1976] ECR 455 at 473–474.
396. Mertens de Wilmars (1969) SEW 78. See *e.g.* Case 28/67 *Firma Molkerei-Zentrale Westfalen/Lippe GmbH v. Hauptzollamt Paderborn* [1968] ECR 143 at 152.

C. The absence of a discretion in the implementation of obligations. Originally, so it appears in hindsight, this criterion hid behind the Court's finding that a provision had direct effect because it 'contains a clear and unconditional prohibition which is not a positive but a negative obligation.'[397] In such cases there is no question of the Member States having any discretion. In its later case-law the Court took the opportunity of developing this more fundamental criterion when it had to deal with the question of the direct effect of provisions which could not (or not completely) be reduced to negative obligations.[398] The criterion of the absence of discretion was clearly indicated in the judgments in Case 28/67 *Molkerei-Zentrale*[399] and Case 13/68 *SpA Salgoil v. Italian Ministry for Foreign Trade.*[400] In the latter judgment, the Court considered the direct effect of the last sentence of Article 32, Article 33(1) and the first sub-paragraph of Article 33(2) EC and looked, as these provisions consisted of positive obligations, at 'the question whether the Member States may in performing them exercise any discretion such as to exclude the above mentioned effects wholly or in part.' Daig has observed[401] that in using the words 'wholly or in part' the Court clearly left open the possibility that a provision or set of provisions could leave no discretion and thus could have direct effect in some respects but in other respects could not have direct effect as discretion was left in its implementation to the Member States.

Difficulties can arise in the consideration of provisions which use vague concepts. Are these indicative of discretion or are they indefinite legal concepts whose content must be defined by the courts in the light of the facts of the case? As has already been observed, in Case 27/67 *Fink-Frucht*[402] the Court found that the concepts of 'similar products' and 'indirect protection' in Article 95 EC did not imply any discretion. It found the contrary in relation to the concepts of 'total value' and 'national production' in Article 33 EC in *Salgoil*.

Theoretically it is correct to speak of indefinite legal concepts if several views on interpretation are possible but only one is right. Discretion, on the other hand, only exists if not only is a choice of different views possible but also it is lawful to follow any of them. The application of this distinction will in practice present difficulties of interpretation.

397. *E.g.* the standstill provision of Art. 12 EC, Case 26/62 *Van Gend en Loos* [1963] ECR 1 at 13.
398. A first pointer in this direction can be seen in Case 57/65 *Lütticke* [1966] ECR 205 at 210.
399. [1968] ECR 143 at 156.
400. [1968] ECR 453 at 461.
401. (1970) EuR. 26.
402. [1968] ECR 223 at 232.

Conclusions on the specific conditions. It is clear from the three conditions just discussed that the central condition is the *absence of discretion* of the Member States or Community Institutions relating to the coming into force or application of the Treaty rule concerned. As is apparent from the above discussion this element is also involved in the discussion of each of the other criteria. Ipsen summarized the central question in examining direct effect as the presence of 'a change in the legal order applicable in the Member States brought about by Community law,'[403] of an '*Alternativ-Normierung*' in Community law which can be applied by the national courts. If this is not present then the national court should not take the place of the legislator acting as if it itself were laying down provisions on the basis of Community law.

Finally, it is important to note that the direct effect of Community law can be relative in nature. Thus provisions may be dependent in some respects on further elaboration in Community or national measures. That does not prevent them having direct effect to the extent that they are not so dependent.[404] If a provision sets clear limits on the freedom of discretion of the Member States, individuals will be able to rely on the provision concerned if the measures adopted by the Member States exceed the bounds of the permitted discretion.[405] If the concrete meaning of certain concepts, such as 'similar products' and 'indirect protection' in Article 95 EC depends on the evaluation of economic facts, the Court will regard the national court as competent and obliged to ensure the rules of the Treaty are observed, whenever *it* can ascertain, in the light of the Court's case-law, that the conditions necessary for the application of the provision concerned are fulfilled.[406]

2.2.2 Reliance before national courts on secondary Community law and on international agreements binding on the Community

Regulations, as the Court has said on myriad occasions 'by reason of their nature and their function in the system of Community law, ... have direct effect and are as such, capable of ceating individual rights which national

---

403. (1966) EuR 359 (our translation).
404. Case 13/68 *Salgoil* [1968] ECR 453 at 461. See Daig (1970) EuR 26.
405. This is partticularly the case in the implementation of directives, see Case 51/76 *Verbond van Nederlandse Ondernemingen v. Inspecteur der Invoerrechten en Accijnzen* [1977] ECR 113 at 125–127 and Case 88/79 *Ministère Public v. Grunert* [1980] ECR 1827 at 1837.
406. Case 27/67 *Fink-Frucht* [1968] ECR 223 at 232. *Cf.* Case 43/75 *Defrenne* [1976] ECR 455 at 473 in which the Court considered that the concepts of indirect and disguised discrimination could 'only be identified by reference to more explicit implementing provisions of a Community or national character' rather than by the national court alone.

courts must protect.[407] The Court reached this conclusion on the basis of Article 189 EC which provides that regulations 'shall have general application' and 'shall be directly applicable in all Member States.' They need, therefore, no transformation into national law and, as has been seen in section 3.3. of Chapter II, above, their Community character may not be disguised; implementing measures or detailed rules adopted by the Member States in pursuance of regulations are lawful only to the extent to which they are provided for in the regulations themselves. Sometimes regulations provide for implementing or further measures to be taken by the Community Institutions, sometimes by the Member States or by the national administrations through administrative measures; these clearly involve a certain discretion for the body which adopts them.[408] Sometimes it is necessary to indicate which bodies are entrusted with implementation on a national basis. Unlike in the case of provisions of the Treaties themselves and in relation to decisions and directives, the national courts do not need to ask the initial question of whether a regulation satisfies the conditions for direct effect.[409]

The nature and function of a regulation mean that it has direct effect. When a national court is faced with the application of a provision in the case before it it is evident whether, and, if so, to what extent, the provision can be applied without exceeding the court's judicial function. Thus the national court's task is no different from that which confronts it in applying provisions of national law. These too may contain provisions which require further rules of a substantive or organisational nature which leave a certain discretion in the hands of the administration. If a regulation

407. *E.g.* Case 43/71 *Politi SAS v. Ministry of Finance of the Italian Republic* [1971] ECR 1039 at 1048; Case 84/71 *SpA Marimex v. Ministry of Finance of the Italian Republic* [1972] ECR 89 at 96; Case 93/71 *Leonesio v. Ministry for Agriculture and Forestry of the Italian Republic* [1972] ECR 287 at 295–296; Case 34/73 *F.lli Variola SpA v. Amministrazione Italiano delle Finanze* [1973] ECR 981 at 990; Case 50/76 *Amsterdam Bulb BV v. Produktschap voor Siergewassen* [19771 ECR 137 at 146, and Case 94/77 *Fratelli Zerbone Snc v. Amministrazione delle Finanze dello Stato* [1978] ECR 99 at 115–116.

408. See Case 230/78 *SpA Eridania-Zuccherifici nazionali et al. v. Minister of Agriculture and Forestry et al.* [1979] ECR 2749 at 2771. In such cases the detailed rules for the exercise of that power are governed by the public law of the Member State concerned although it is for the national courts to judge whether the national measures taken are in accordance with the regulation. See Lauwaars (1983/1) LIEI 41 *et seq.*

409. The fact that in Case 9/73 *Schlüter v. Hauptzollamt Lörrach* [1973] ECR 1135 at 1158 the Court exceptionally decided to state that a provision of a regulation was 'itself clear and precise' and did 'not leave any margin of discretion to the authorities by whom it is to be applied' can probably be explained by the fact that this provision made an exception to a GATT obligation of the Community which the Court found not to have direct effect as such. In Case 87/82 *Rogers v. Darthenay* [1983] ECR 1579 at 1591 the Court found a provision of a regulation 'independent and perfectly clear' and thus directly effective and not dependent upon the adoption of detailed implementing rules provided for.

does not prescribe any national implementing measures the national court may not in any event take account of national provisions or practices which would require such implementing measures. Otherwise 'the fundamental rule requiring the uniform application of regulations throughout the Community' would be disregarded.[410]

Decisions addressed to Member States[411] and *directives* may contain directly effective provisions. Thus in Case 9/70 *Grad v. Finanzamt Traunstein*[412] the Court regarded a prohibition on introducing or re-introducing certain taxes, addressed to Member States in a decision as essentially mandatory and general in nature which was 'unconditional and sufficiently clear and precise to be capable of producing direct effects in legal relationships between the Member States and those subject to their jurisdiction.' The fact that the date of entry into force of the prohibition contained in the decision was contained in a directive did not detract from the binding force of the decision.

The reasoning which the Court used in relation to the possible direct effect of provisions of decisions caused it to be thought that provisions of directives which stood alone (*i.e.* not in direct combination with other directly effective provisions of Community law[413]) might also have such an effect. The Court confirmed this view in its judgment in Case 41/74 *Van Duyn v. Home Office*[414] in the context of a provision of Directive 64/221[415] which particularised the powers laid down in Article 48(3) EC, which is directly effective.

The reasoning used in relation to the possible direct effect of decisions was repeated in *Van Duyn* in relation to directives. There were four points. First, it could not be argued on the basis that Article 189 EC spoke about direct applicability only in relation to regulations that the other categories

---

410. Case 93/75 *Leonesio* [1972] ECR 287 at 295. In this judgment the Court held that national budgetary provisions formed no obstacle to the direct applicability of a Community provision and the realisation of the individual rights created thereby.

411. Community decisions addressed to individuals define the scope of application of directly effective provisions of Community law in concrete and specific cases. It is inadvisable to use the term 'direct effect' for such decisions but to reserve it for the effect of legislative measures which have legislative effect in the domestic legal systems of the Member States, *e.g.* some of the decisions addressed to Member States.

412. [1970] ECR 825 at 838. See also Case 20/70 *Transports Lesage & Cie v. Hauptzollamt Freiburg* [1970] ECR 861 at 874 and Case 23/70 *Haselhorst v. Finanzamt Düsseldorf-Altstadt* [1970] ECR 881 at 893. Contrast the situation in these cases with that in Case 249/85 *ALBAKO Margarinefabrik Maria von der Linde GmbH & Co. KG v. Bundesan-stalt für landwirtschaftliche Marktordnung* [1987] ECR 2345 (see Arnull (1987) 12 ELRev. 451).

413. Even Case 33/70 *SpA SACE v. Ministry for Finance of the Italian Republic* [1970] ECR 1213; [1971] CMLR 123 (like the cases cited in note 412, *supra*) dealt with com-bined effect.

414. [1974] ECR 1337 at 1348. See also Case 71/85 *State of The Netherlands v. Federatie Nederlandse Vakbeweging* [1986] ECR 3855, [1987] CMLR 767.

415. O.J. English Special Edition 1963–64, p. 117.

of acts mentioned in that Article could never have a similar effect. Secondly, it would be incompatible with the binding effect of directives (and, for that matter of decisions) to exclude in principle the possibility of those concerned invoking the obligation which they impose. Thirdly, in particular in cases in which the Community authorities have imposed an obligation on Member States by a directive (or, indeed, by a decision) to pursue a particular course of conduct, the useful effect ('*effet utile*') of such an act would be weakened if private parties were to be unable to rely on it before their national courts and if the courts could not take the act into consideration as an element of Community law. Fourthly, and lastly, Article 177 EC implied that Community acts could be invoked by private parties in their national courts, although the Court reiterated that on this last point it was 'necessary to examine, in every case, whether the nature, general scheme and wording of the provision in question are capable of having direct effects on the relationship between Member States and individuals.'[416] The Court found that 'legal certainty for the persons concerned requires that they should be able to rely on this obligation even though it has been laid down in a legislative act which has no automatic direct effect in its entirety.'[417] This judgment demonstrates that the Court applies the same conditions for direct effect in these cases as it did in relation to the direct effect of Treaty provisions (on which see section 2.2.1. above). Subsequently the Court indicated that 'the right of an individual Community citizen to rely on an unconditional and sufficiently precise provision of a directive against a Member State which has failed to implement it or has not correctly implemented it is based on the combined provisions of the third paragraph of Article 189 and Article 5 of the [EC] Treaty.'[418]

In two later judgments[419] the Court dealt with the question of whether a national implementing measure could be examined against the provisions of directives. Having observed, as it had done in *Van Duyn*, that the useful effect of directives would be weakened if private parties were to be prevented from relying on them before their national courts and if the latter were to be unable to take directives into consideration as an element of Community law, the Court pointed out that this was 'especially so when

416. [1974] ECR 1337 at 1348.
417. *Ibid.*
418. Case 190/87 *Oberkreisdirektor des Kreises Borken et al. v. Handelsonderneming Moorman BV* [1988] ECR 4689 at 4722.
419. Case 51/76 *Verbond van Nederlandse Ondernemingen v. Inspecteur der Invoerrechten en Accijnzen* [1977] ECR 113, [1977] 1 CMLR 413 and Case 38/77 *Enka BV v. Inspecteur der Invoerrechten en Accijnzen* [1977] ECR 2203, [1978] 2 CMLR 212. See further, as to interpretation in cases of inconsistency between language versions, *e.g.* Case C-72/95 *Aannemersbedrijf P.K. Kraaijeveld BV et al. v. Gedeputeerde Staten van Zuid-Holland* [1996] ECR I-5403 at 5443–5444 (interpretation by reference to the purpose and general scheme of the rules of which the provision in question forms part).

the individual invokes a provision of a directive before a national court in order that the latter shall rule whether the competent national authorities, in exercising the choice which is left to them as to the form and methods for implementing the directive, have kept within the limits as to their discretion set out in the directive.'[420]

Case 148/78 *Pubblico Ministero v. Ratti*[421] provided the Court with an important opportunity to consider a situation in which national implementing measures had not been adopted in due time. In such a case examination of existing national provisions against the terms of a directive can result in the national provisions not being applied. A Member State which has failed to adopt the implementing measures required by a directive in due time cannot rely, as against individuals who act in conformity with that directive, on its own failure to perform the obligations which the directive entails. Nobody many rely on his own wrongful act or failure to act; the Member State is in effect estopped from claiming that individuals may not rely on the directive (if, of course, the directive fulfil the conditions for direct effect).[422]

In Case 8/81 *Becker v. Finanzamt Münster-Innenstadt*[423] the Court considered a provision in the Sixth VAT Directive[424] which permitted the Member States to exempt certain activities from VAT. Neither the general scheme of this harmonising directive nor the margin of discretion which it left to Member States in the implementation of some of its other provisions could be relied upon to deny any effect to those provisions which fulfil the conditions for direct effect, even though the directive as a whole had not been implemented.[425]

Since the judgment in *Becker* the case-law on direct effect of provisions of directives can best be summarized in the words of the Court in Case 152/84 *Marshall v. Southampton and South West Hampshire Area Health Authority (Teaching)*:[426] 'wherever the provisions of a directive appear, as far as their subject-matter is concerned, to be unconditional and sufficiently precise, those provisions may be relied upon by an individual against the State where that State fails to implement the directive in national law by the end of the period prescribed or where it fails to

---

420. [1977] ECR 113 at 127 and [1977] ECR 2203 at 2212.
421. [1979] ECR 1629, [1980] 1 CMLR 96. As against private parties acting in accordance with a directive national provisions (including those prescribing penalties) which are incompatible with the directive cannot be applied in cases in which they have not been brought into line with the directive by the date prescribed by the directive as long as the obligation imposed by the directive is sufficiently clear and precise.
422. [1979] ECR 1629 at 1642. The Court has not used the term 'estopped' but it is clear that the Court's position is the language of estoppel, *e.g.* Pescatore (1983) 8 ELRev. 155 at 169 and Easson (1981) YBEL 1 at 38 (see also Green (1984) 9 ELRev. 295 at 302–309 and 313–315).
423. [1982] ECR 53, [1982] 1 CMLR 499.
424. O.J. 1977 L145/1 (modified on myriad occasions).
425. [1982] ECR 53 at 72.

implement the directive correctly.' This case-law is based on the point that it would be incompatible with the binding nature which Article 189 EC confers on directives to hold as a matter of principle that the obligation thereby imposed cannot be relied upon by those concerned.[427] From this the Court has drawn the conclusion that 'a Member State which has not adopted the implementing measures required by the directive within the prescribed period may not plead, as against individuals, its own failure to perform the obligations which the directive entails.'[428]

Even if provisions of directives do not fulfil the conditions laid down in the case-law for being relied upon by private parties they need not be deprived of all effects. Case 14/83 *Von Colson and Kamann v. Land Nordrhein-Westfalen*[429] shows that the obligation on Member States to achieve a particular result envisaged by a directive as well as the obligation on them to take all general or particular measures to ensure fulfilment of that obligation (Article 5 EC) is binding on *all* the authorities of Member States including, for matters wthin their jurisdiction, the courts. It follows that in applying national law, particularly the provisions of a law specifically introduced to comply with a directive, national courts are required to interpret national law in the light of the wording and purpose of the directive in order to achieve the result required by the third paragraph of Article 189 EC. In the light of any interpretation of the pro-vision of the directive concerned given by the Court it will be for the national court to interpret and apply the national legislation adopted to implement the directive in conformity with the requirements of Community law in so far as the national court is given discretion to do so under

426. [1986] ECR 723 at 748.
427. This approach is also well summarized in Case C-236/92 *Comitato di Coordinamento per la Difesa della Cava et al. v. Regione Lombardia et al.* [1994] ECR I-483 at 502
428. *Ibid.* at 748–749. If the case-law in which one and the same provision was held on its wording to have direct effect in some respects but not in others is borne in mind (see the end of section 2.2.1 of this chapter, *ante*, *in fine*, it will be apparent that this does not not necessarily mean that the Court has gone back on its judgment in Case 51/76 *Verbond van Nederlandse Ondernemingen* [1977] ECR 113 at 127 which tended towards an objective control of legality. If a Member State, in working out a provision of a directive, exceeds the limits of the margin of discretion left to it, it may already be implicit in the concept of those limits that such a provision may be clear and precise enough to lend itself to producing direct effect, see *e.g.* the carefully constructed rea-soning in Case 222/84 *Johnston v. The Chief Constable of the Royal Ulster Con-stabulary* [1986] ECR 1615 [1986] 3 CMLR 240 follows this approach.
429. [1984] ECR 1891 at 1909. The Court also took the opportunity to point out that if Member States chose to penalise breaches of the prohibition of discrimination (the directive concerned having left them free to choose which sanctions to impose) by the award of compensation 'then in order to ensure that it is effective and that it has a deterrent effect, that compensation must in any event be adequate in relation to the damage sustained and must therefore amount to more than purely nominal compen-sation such as, for example, the reimbursement only of the expenses incurred in con-nection with the application.' (*Ibid.*)

national law.[430] This approach was further developed but at the same time nuanced in Case C-106/89 *Marleasing SA v. La Comercial Internacional de Alimentación SA*[431] when the Court found that 'in applying national law, whether the provisions in question were adopted before or after the directive, the national court called upon to interpret it is required to do so, as far as possible, in the light of the wording and the purpose of the directive in order to achieve the result pursued by the latter and thereby comply with the third paragraph of Article 189 of the Treaty.' The development is in the clear ruling that the obligation to interpret national law in conformity with a directive applies irrespective of when the national law was adopted, disposing therefore of any argument that the national law had nothing to do with the directive. The nuancing is that the words 'in so far as the national court is given discretion to do so under national law' in *Von Colson* have given way to the phrase 'as far as possible' in *Marleasing*.[432]

More generally, the national court would do well to examine first of all whether it can interpret the national provisions in a manner which is consistent with the relevant provision of the directive concerned before looking at whether the latter provision can or cannot be relied upon as against the national provisions.[433] It is clear that the duty to interpret national law in conformity with a directive is not absolute.[434] First, as has been shown above, directives cannot of themselves impose obligations on individuals.[435] Secondly, in Case 80/86 *Kolpinghuis Nijmegen BV*[436] the Court added an important gloss to the principle in *Von Colson*, namely that the duty to interpret and apply national legislation in conformity with the directive is subject to the general principles of legal

---

430. *Ibid.*

431. [1990] ECR I-4135 at 4159. See Stuyck and Wytinck (1991) 28 CMLRev. 205.

432. See, generally, Curtin in Curtin and O'Keeffe (eds.), *Constitutional Adjudication in European Community and National Law* (Essays in honour of O'Higgins, Dublin, 1992) 33 at 39–41.

433. According to the view of the Dutch Hoge Raad, see Koopmans (interview) (1987) *Ars Aequi* 138 at 142.

434. As an *e.g.* of the obligation to interpret national law in conformity with the EC Treaty's provisions, see Case C-165/91 *Van Munster v. Rijksdienst voor Pensioenen* [1994] ECR I-4661 at 4698: 'When applying domestic law, the national court must, as far as is at all possible interpret it in a way which accords with the requirements of Community law' and 'when, for the purpose of applying a provision of domestic law, a national court has to characterize a social security benefit awarded under the statutory scheme of another Member State, it should interpret its own legislation in the light of the aims of Arts. 48 to 51 of the Treaty and, as far as is at all possible, prevent its interpretation from being such as to discourage a migrant worker from actually exercising his right to free movement.'

435. Case 152/84 *Marshall v. Southampton and South-West Hampshire Area Health Authority (Teaching)* [1986] ECR 723 at 737.

436. [1987] ECR 3969 at 3986, see also Case 14/86 *Pretore di Salò v. X* [1987] ECR 2545 at 2570.

certainty, so a directive could not on its own, and independently of national implementing measures, determine or aggravate the criminal liability of people who acted in breach of its provisions. The Court also indicated that the national court's power or duty to interpret provisions of national law in the light of the relevant directives was unaffected by the question whether or not the deadline for implementing the directives had expired.[437] Finally, as has been shown above, the duty applies 'as far as possible' which excludes any obligation to interpret national law *contra legem*.[438] The remedy for a litigant who finds that he or she is unable to obtain redress because of the impossibility of interpreting national law in conformity with a directive is simply to seek redress in a separate action against the Member State for damages.[439] This matter is discussed in section 2.3.2 of this Chapter, below, but it might perhaps be noted at this stage that forcing litigants to commence further litigation simply lines the pockets of lawyers, although joining the State as third party to a claim could mitigate the burden on litigants to some extent. In any event, the situation is less than wholly satisfactory, although the message from the Court's case-law in this area, like that rejecting the horizontal direct effect of directives which is discussed in section 2.2.4 of this Chapter, below, appears to be that if the Community legislator is serious about creating rights for individuals on which they can rely against other individuals as well as against the State, it must either extend the use of regulations rather than directives (which will in certain instances require amendments to the EC Treaty) or it must support the Commission taking much firmer teps to ensure the proper transposition of directives into national law.

The case-law of the Court on reliance on directives has met with incomprehension and opposition in some national courts. In Germany, the Bundesfinanzhof's resistance to accepting the direct effect of provisions of the Sixth VAT Directive was finally overcome through the intervention of the Bundesverfassungsgericht.[440] In France the Conseil d'État had already in 1978 decided that that incompatibility with provisions of a directive

---

437. It is submitted that Arnull (1988) 13 ELRev. 42 at 45 was correct to opine that the duty to interpret national provisions in accordance with any relevant directive does not apply in cases dealing with incidents which took place before the adoption of the directive but which come to trial afterwards; the interests of non-retroactivity and legal certainty mentioned in *Kolpinghuis Nijmegen* favour this interpretation. See also Case C-316/93 *Vaneetveld et al. v. Le Foyer SA et al.* [1994] ECR I-763 at 784–785.

438. Van Gerven (1994) 1 MJ 6 at 10.

439. See Case C-334/92 *Wagner Miret v. Fondo de garantía salarial* [1993] ECR I-6911 at 6932 and Case C-91/92 *Faccini Dori v. Recreb Srl* [1994] ECR I-3325 at 3357.

440. Bundesfinanzhof 25 April 1985 BFHE 143, 383, see Tomuschat (1985) EuR 346 and Magiera (1985) DOV 937, quashed on appeal by the Bundesverfassungsgericht, *Kloppenburg* [1988] 3 CMLR 1, see Hilf (1988) EuR 1. See also WQ 880/85 (Rothley) O.J. 1985 C 276/23. As to the Court of Justice's approach, see Case 70/83 *Kloppenburg v. Finanzamt Leer* [1984] ECR 1075 at 1085–1086.

could not be relied upon as against individual decisions of the French administration, even if the directive's provisions laid down clear, precise and unconditional obligations on the Member States.[441] This approach still holds,[442] even though there are certain signs that the Conseil d'État is becoming more *communautaire* in its general approach to Community law.[443] It is remarkable that the Conseil d'État has opened the way for private parties to attack French legislation[444] on the ground of incompatibility with the objectives of a directive,[445] which, according to the legal definition of a directive in Article 189 EC, involves examination based on the result to be achieved by the directive. Thus in the French administrative courts an individual is unable to obtain the annulment, on the ground of incompatibility with a directly effective provision of a directive, of an administrative decision addressed to him or her. But he or she can obtain its annulment if the national legislation on which the decision is based is incompatible with the objectives of the directive. This so-called '*invoquabilité d'exclusion*' (the objectives of the directive exclude application of the national rule) in fact makes directives more effective than they are under the case-law of the Court of Justice.[446] The case-law of the Conseil d'État is however less far-reaching in that withholds the so-called '*invoquabilité de substitution*' (application of the provision of a directive in place of the national rule) from provisions of directives, even if the national court is obliged, in accordance with standing case-law of the Court, to give effect to those provisions.[447]

441. Conseil d'État (Assemblée) 22 December 1978 (*Cohn-Bendit*) (1979) RDTE 157.
442. *Compagnie Générale des Eaux* [1994] 2 CMLR 373.
443. See Pollard (1990) 15 ELRev. 267; Cohen (1991) 16 ELRev. 144; Manin (1991) 28 CMLRev. 499; Errera (1992) PL 340, and Roseren (1994) 31 CMLRev. 315 at 326–336.
444. Initially only subordinate legislation, *e.g. Compagnie Alitalia* [1990] 1 CMLR 248, subsequently also primary legislation, *Nicolo* [1990] 1 CMLR 173 (see Pollard (1990) 15 ELRev. 267 and Manin (1991) 28 CMLRev. 499) and *Boisdet* [1991] 1 CMLR 3. Damages were awarded for loss sustained through enforced compliance with legislation incompatible with a directive (from 1972) in *SA Rothmans International France et al.* [1993] 1 CMLR 253 (see Errera (1992) PL 340). See also *Rassemblement des Opposants à la Chasse* [1990] 2 CMLR 831.
445. *Union des Transporteurs en commun des Voyageurs des Bouches-de-Rhône (UTCV) et al.* [1994] 3 CMLR 121 and *Association Force ouvrière Consommateurs* [1994] 1 CMLR 721. Various provisions of the French Tax Code were disapplied on the ground of incompatibility with a directive in *Groupement pour le Developpement de la Coiffure (GDC)* [1993] Les Petites Affiches No. 81, p. 19.
446. See *e.g.* Case C-435/92 *Association pour la Protection des Animaux Sauvages et al. v. Préfet de Maine-et-Loire et al.* [1994] ECR I-67 at 93–94 in which the Court responded to a request from a the administrative court in Nantes for a ruling on the interpretation of Art. 7(4) of Directive 79/409 (O.J. 1979 L 103/1) which at first sight is not directly effective, in order to enable it to evaluate the fixing of closing dates for hunting wild birds.
447. See, on the difference between these two *invoquabilités*, Galmot and Bonichot (1988) Rev. Fr. Dr. Admin. 1.

A criticism which is sometimes made (and a favourite examination question for students) is that the difference between the effect in the national legal order of a regulation and that of a directive has not well nigh disappeared. This is not, with respect, the case. Regulations are directly applicable and by reason of their nature have direct effect as the Court has repeated on myriad occasions. The direct effect of provisions of a directive depends on the question of whether the content of such provisions satisfy certain conditions, *viz.* unconditionality and sufficient precision. Thus, as the Court made clear in Case 102/79 *Commission v. Belgium*[448] it is only 'in specific circumstances, in particular where a Member State has failed to take the implementing measures required or has adopted measures which do not conform to a directive' that the Court has recognized the right of a person who is affected by such conduct to rely on a directive as against a defaulting Member State.[449] This reveals a second difference from regulations and also a difference from directly effective provisions of the Treaties. A regulation does not need to be and may not be transformed into national law unless it specifically requires or empowers Member States to adopt implementing measures. A directly effective provision of the Treaties needs by very definition no transformation into national law,[450] whilst a directly effective provision of a directive has this effect despite the fact that it needs such transformation by definition. (It is, of course, given direct effect precisely because the transformation which should have taken place has not occurred adequately or at all.) A third difference between regulations and directives is, as has been noted above, that the provisions of directives do not on their own impose obligations on individuals and a provision of a directive cannot be relied upon as such against individuals. It may well be that the Court itself chose to avoid the term 'direct effect' in the case of directives and instead to speak of 'similar effects' precisely in order to keep the distinction between regulations and directives apparent.[451]

448. [1980] ECR 1473 at 1487.
449. Maresceau (1980) SEW 655 at 662–664 criticises this description as being narrow.
450. This also explains why in the conditions for direct effect of Treaty provisions the Court requires, besides unconditionality and sufficient precision, that the provisions be not subject to implementing measures of a discretionary nature being adopted, a condition which is not required in the case of directives. *Cf. e.g.* Case 44/84 *Hurd v. Jones* [1986] ECR 29 at 83 with Case 152/84 *Marshall v. Southampton and Southwest Hampshire Area Health Authority (Teaching)* [1986] ECR 723 at 748.
451. Case 8/81 *Becker* [1982] ECR 53 at 70: 'It follows from well-established case-law of the Court ... that whilst under Art. 189 regulations are directly applicable and, consequently, by their nature capable of producing direct effects, that does not mean that other categories of measures covered by that Article can never produce similar effects.' Yet in Case C-188/89 *Foster et al. v. British Gas plc* [1990] ECR I-3313 at 3348–3349 the Court spoke of 'the provisions of a directive capable of having direct effect may be relied upon.' The term 'direct effect' does not, however, feature in any of the subsequent major judgments (even though it is used extensively by Advocates General).

2.2.3 Reliance before national courts on agreements binding the Community

Provisions of international agreements which are binding on the Community form part of the Community legal order.[452] This also applies in respect of agreements concluded by all the Member States before the entry into force of the EEC Treaty which are binding on the Community, in so far as it has assumed the rights and obligations of the Member States on the basis of the principle of substitution (as was the case with the GATT).[453] If questions of the validity or interpretation of international agreements binding the Community arise before national courts, they may (or must, as appropriate) refer them to the Court of Justice under Article 177 EC. The question of the direct effect of provisions of such an agreement is one of those questions.

If such a provision is directly effective, it may be relied upon before national courts to attack the validity of Community measures.[454] Article 177 EC does not limit the grounds on which the validity of acts of the Institutions may be contested, thus those grounds include incompatibility with a rule of international law.[455] Litigants are also free to allege that a national measure is incompatible with one of these agreements.[456]

In various cases relating to the GATT[457] the Court held that provisions

---

452. This has been the standing approach since Case 181/73 *Sprl R. & V. Haegeman v. Belgian State* [1974] ECR 449 at 459–460 in which the Court found that an international agreement concluded by the Council (on behalf of the Community) was an act of an Institution within the meaning of point (b) of the 1st para. of Art. 177 EC (see also *e.g.* Case 12/86 *Demirel v. Stadt Schwäbisch Gmünd* [1987] ECR 3719 at 3750). This in itself somewhat unfortunate classification could not of course be used in the case of international agreements binding the Community under the principle of substitution, see the reasoning used for such agreements in Case 226/81 *Società Italiana per l'Oleodotte Transalpino (SIOT) v. Ministero delle Finanze et al.* [1983] ECR 731 at 780 and Cases 267–269/81 *Amministrazione delle Finanze dello Stato v. Società Petrolifera Italiana SpA (SPI) et al.* [1983] ECR 801 at 830–831.
453. See Chapter IV, section 7.5.2, *ante*. See Cases 21–24/72 *International Fruit Company NV et al. v. Produktschap voor Groenten en Fruit* [1972] ECR 1219 at 1226.
454. Cases 21–24/72 *International Fruit Company* [1972] ECR 1219 at 1226. Before invalidity can be relied upon before a national court the provision of international law concerned must also be capable of conferring rights on citizens of the Community which they can invoke before the courts, *ibid.* See, generally, Schermers (1982) 19 CMLRev. 563; Bebr (1983) 20 CMLRev. 35; Petersmann (1983) 20 CMLRev. 397; Groux (1983) CDE 203; Bebr (1983) EuR 128 and Tagaras (1984) CDE 15. See, further, McGoldrick, *International Relations Law of the European Union* (Harlow, 1997) Chapter 7; Macleod *et al.*, *The External Relations of the European Communities* (Oxford, 1996) Chapter 5; Cheyne (1994) 18 ELRev. 581; Hancher (1994) NYIL 259; Groux and Manin, *The European Communities in the International Order* (Brussels, European Perspectives, 1985).
455. Cases 21–24/72 *International Fruit Company, ibid.*
456. Implicit in Case 65/77 *Razanatsimba* [1977] ECR 2229, [1978] 1 CMLR 246.
457. Cases 21–24/72 *International Fruit Company* [1972] ECR 1219 at 1228; Case 9/73 *Schlüter v. Hauptzollamt Lörrach* [1973] ECR 1135 at 1158; Case 226/81 *Società Italiana per l'Oleodotte Transalpino (SIOT) v. Ministero delle Finanze et al.* [1983] ECR

of the GATT did not have direct effect on the ground of the general
consideration that the GATT 'is characterized by the great flexibility of its
provisions, in particular those conferring the possibility of derogation, the
measures to be taken when confronted with exceptional difficulties and the
settlement of conflicts between the contracting parties.'[458] The Court found
that there was no context which excluded the direct effect of provisions of
the Second Yaoundé Convention,[459] the Association Agreements with
Greece,[460] and Turkey,[461] the Free Trade Agreement with Portugal,[462] and
the Cooperation Agreement with Morocco.[463] Certain provisions of the
Lomé Convention may also have direct effect,[464] as may certain provisions
of the EEA Agreement.[465] The meaning of a term in a free trade agreement
and an identically phrased term in the EC Treaty is not necessarily the
same[466] but the interpretation will depend on the objectives of an

731 at 780; Cases 267–269/81 *Amministrazione delle Finanze dello Stato v. Società Petrolifera Italiana SpA (SPI) et al.* [1983] ECR 801 at 830–831, and Cases 290–291/81
Compagnia Singer SpA et al. v. Amministrazione dello Finanze dello Stato [1983] ECR
847. More recent authorities include Case C-469/93 *Amministrazione delle Finanze
dello Stato v. Chiquita Italia SpA* [1995] ECR I-4533 at 4565.

458. *E.g.* Cases 21–24/72 *International Fruit Company* [1972] ECR 1219 at 1227–1228
(criticised by Petersmann (1983) 20 CMLRev. 397) and Case C-469/93 *Amministrazione delle Finanze dello Stato v. Chiquita Italia SpA* [1995] ECR I-4533 at 4565. In
Cases C-364 and 365/95 *T. Port GmbH & Co. v. Hauptzollamt Hamburg-Jonas* [1998]
ECR I-1023 the Court found that it did not need to address the issue of direct effect
of the GATT; it in fact declared partially invalid the Community regulation concerned
on the ground of a difference in treatement of certain operators which was not the
automatic consequence of differences in treatment accorded to third countries under
in this case the GATT Framework Agreement on Bananas (and partly annulled the
same regulation in Case C-122/95 *Germany v. Council* [1998] ECR I-973).

459. Case 87/75 *Conceria Daniele Bresciani v. Amministrazione Italiana delle Finanze* [1976]
ECR 129 at 141–142. This Convention has since been replaced by the successive
Lomé Conventions.

460. Case 17/81 *Pabst & Richarz KG v. Hauptzollamt Oldenburg* [1982] ECR 1331 at 1350–
1351. The agreement lapsed on Greek accession.

461. See *e.g.* Case 12/86 *Demirel v. Stadt Schwäbisch Gmünd* [1987] ECR 3719 at 3751;
Case C-192/89 *Sevince v. Staatssecretaris van Justitie* [1990] ECR I-3461 at 3503–3504,
and Case C-355/93 *Eroglu v. Land Baden-Württemberg* [1994] ECR I-5113 at 5137–
5138 and 5140.

462. Case 104/81 *Hauptzollamt Mainz v. C.A. Kupferberg Cie. KG a.A.* [1982] ECR 3641 at
3662–3665. The application of the strict criteria applied in the cases on the GATT
should have led to the opposite conclusion, see van Houtte (1983) SEW 429 and
Bourgeois (1984) 82 Mich.L.Rev. 1250. The agreement lapsed on Portuguese accession.

463. Case C-18/90 *Office national de l'emploi (Onem) v. Kziber* [1991] ECR I-199 at 225–
227.

464. Case C-469/93 *Amministrazione delle Finanze dello Stato v. Chiquita Italia SpA* [1995]
ECR I-4533 at 4567–4568.

465. Case T-115/94 *Opel Austria GmbH v. Commission* [1997] ECR II-39 at 73–74.

466. Case 270/80 *Polydor Records Ltd. et al. v. Harlequin Record Shops Ltd. et al.* [1982]

agreement as well as on the context of the provision concerned.[467] In this way the Court has actually managed to ensure that a significant number of rights conferred (particularly on non-Community nationals) by international agreements to which the Community is a party are not simply made dead letters by national authorities whose motivation may perhaps be less than wholly transparent.[468] It has also prevented wholly unmeritorious barriers to trade arising which would jeopardize the aim of the international agreement concerned.[469]

The question whether individuals can rely before national courts on provisions of international agreements binding the Community should be distinguished from the question whether they can rely on such provisions in direct actions before the Court of First Instance under, say, Articles 173 or 175 EC. It still appears controversial whether the doctrine of direct effect should apply in such direct actions. The doctrine is historically explicable as a means of ensuring in all circumstances the effectiveness of Community law in the national legal systems of the Member States. In view of the very diverse rules and traditions in the Member States relating to the direct application of provisions of international agreements by national courts, it was necessary for Community law to develop a doctrine that could be applied by national courts in all Member States and which could be absorbed into the corpus of the divergent rules and traditions without too much difficulty.

It appears difficult to understand why the doctrine of direct effect should play a part in direct actions relating to reliance on provisions of international agreements binding the Community, while there has never been any question of its playing a part when provisions of the EC Treaty itself are involved in such actions. There are some indications in the case-law of the Court that in direct actions the doctrine of direct effect of agreements has no role to play.[470] From the case-law the consequence

ECR 329 at 349. The justification is the different degree of integration sought to be achieved by the EC Treaty and the agreement concerned.

467. Opinion 1/91 *EEA Agreement I* [1991] ECR I-6079 at 6103–6104; Case C-163/90 *Administration des Douanes et des Droits Indirects v. Legros et al.* [1992] ECR I-4625 at 4668. See also Case T-115/94 *Opel Austria GmbH v. Council* [1997] ECR II-39 at 74–77.

468. *E.g.* the judgments in *Sevince*, *Eroglu* and *Kziber*, *supra*. See also Case C-237/91 *Kus v. Landeshauptstadt Wiesbaden* [1992] ECR I-6781 at 6816 and Case C-171/95 *Tetik v. Land Berlin* [1997] ECR I-329 at 348, but *cf.* Case C-434/93 *Bozkurt v. Staatssecretaris van Justitie* [1995] ECR I-1475 at 1503 and 1506 (the Court noted in *Tetik* at 354 that the situation there was different from that in *Bozkurt*).

469. Case C-163/90 *Administration des Douanes et des Droits Indirects v. Legros et al.* [1992] ECR I-4625 at 4668 and Case C-207/91 *Eurim-Pharm GmbH v. Bundesgesundheitsamt* [1993] ECR I-3723 at 3748.

470. Case C-69/89 *Nakajiima All-Precision Co. Ltd. v. Council* [1991] ECR I-2069 at 2178 (GATT Anti-Dumping Code), and Case 53/84 *Adams v. Commission* [1985] ECR 3595 at 3600–3601 (Joint Committee). See, however, if the Community intended to implement a particular obligation under the GATT or if the Community act expressly

should then follow that the question of the validity of an act of a Community Institution in the light of an alleged breach of an international agreement should be answered in the same manner, which has not happened in existing case-law.[471] The Court of First Instance has found that an applicant could rely on Article 10 EEA in a challenge to a regulation (withdrawing a tariff concession concerning gearboxes produced in Austria) adopted between the date of deposit of the Communities' instrument of ratification of the EEA Agreement, as the last of the Contracting Parties, and the date of entry into force of that Agreement.[472] In reaching this conclusion the Court was clearly influenced by the manifest breach of the principle of good faith, the corollary of which in Community law is the protection of legitimate expectation,[473] but its findings go further than that aspect and directly address the interpretation of the EEA Agreement as well.[474] Accordingly, particularly where agreements into which the Community enters seek to achieve a high degree of integration and homogenity, or where the Community itself relies on an agreement to justify its actions, there can be no policy consideration militating against giving relief to individuals demonstrating that the Community has breached its obligations.

2.2.4   The so-called horizontal effect of provisions of Community law

How far may private parties rely on provisions of Community law not just against the national authorities but also against other private parties? It is beyond doubt that provisions of the Treaties or of regulations can impose obligations on individuals if they are clear from their very nature and scope, as, for example, is the case for undertakings in the field of competition.[475] However, directives cannot of themselves impose

refers to specific provisions of the GATT, Case 70/87 *Fédération de l'industrie de l'huilerie de la CEE (Fediol) v. Commission* [1989] ECR 1781 at 1831; Case C-69/89 *Nakajiima All-Precision Co. Ltd. v. Council* [1991] ECR I-2069 at 2178 and Case C-280/93 *Germany v. Council* [1994] ECR I-4973 at 5073–5074. See the critical observations of Scott in Shaw and More (eds.), *New Legal Dynamics of European Union* (Oxford, 1996) 147 at 164.

471. Cases 21–24/72 *International Fruit Company* [1972] ECR 1219 at 1228; Case 9/73 *Schlüter v. Hauptzollamt Lörrach* [1973] ECR 1135 at 1158. See further, Kapteyn in González et al. (eds.) *Hacia un nuevo orden internacional y europeo* (Essays in honour of Díez de Velasco, Madrid, 1993) 1007.

472. Case T-115/94 *Opel Austria GmbH v. Council* [1997] ECR II-39.

473. *Ibid.*, paras. 90–95.

474. Direct effect for the fundamental principles of the EEA Agreement was ensured by extending the ambit of myriad provisions of Community secondary legislation to benefit nationals of the non-member States which are parties to the EEA Agreement.

475. *Cf.* Cases 56 and 58/64 *Ets. Consten SARL and Grundig-Verkaufs-GmbH v. Commission* [1966] ECR 299 at 345–346 in which the Court spoke of 'Community rules on

obligations in such a vertical manner on individuals, as they impose obligations only on 'each Member State to which it is addressed.'[476]

The issue has in practice come to a head in relation what is known as horizontal direct effect: can private parties in their legal relationships with other private parties rely on provisions of Community law which are addressed only to the Member States? The implication that the Court did not exclude reliance on Treaty provisions in such circumstances was already apparent from the Court's case-law on the free movement of goods under Articles 30–36 EC in conjunction with the second paragraph of Article 5 EC. This always involved actions in national courts between private parties about the limits which Article 36 EC placed on the exercise of exclusive rights under national legislation on the protection of industrial and commercial property, as proprietors of such rights may only rely on such legislation within these limits.[477]

The Court has expressly held that the prohibition of discrimination on grounds of nationality contained in Articles 6, 48 and 59 EC has horizontal direct effect. Thus the prohibition in Articles 48 and 59 EC does not merely apply to actions of public authorities but also covers other types of provisions including collective agreements or rules in the employment field and in the field of the supply of services.[478] The non-discrimination provisions of the Treaty thus impose obligations on private parties as well as on the Member States.

The judgment of the Court in Case 43/75 *Defrenne v. SABENA*[479] caused more of a stir,[480] given that Article 119 EC is addressed specifically to each Member State and deals with a principle. In that judgment the principle of equal pay for men and women for equal work was declared applicable not only to the action of public authorities but also 'to all

competition which have immediate effect and are directly binding on individuals.' In Case 127/73 *Belgische Radio en Televisie et al. v. SV SABAM et al.* [1974] ECR 51 at 62: 'As the prohibitions of Articles 85(1) and 86 tend by their very nature to produce direct effects between individuals, these Articles create direct rights in respect of the individuals concerned which the national courts must safeguard.' See also Case 37/79 *Anne Marty SA v. Estée Lauder SA* [1980] ECR 2481 at 2500.

476. Art. 189 EC, 3rd para. Case 80/86 *Kolpinghuis Nijmegen BV* [1987] ECR 3969 at 3985. See also the discussion in relation to a number of Dutch cases before the Hoge Raad, Timmermans (1985) TVVS 135 and Lauwaars (1985) SEW 590.

477. *E.g.* Case 78/70 *Deutsche Grammophon Gesellschaft mbH. v. Metro-SB- Großmärkte GmbH & Co. KG* [1971] ECR 487 at 499–500, although in this case and in subsequent cases this area the question of direct effect was not expressly discussed.

478. *E.g.* Case 36/74 *Walrave and Koch v. Association Union Cycliste Internationale et al.* [1974] ECR 1405 at 1418–1419; the same applies for Art. 52 EC, see Case 90/76 *Srl Ufficio Henry van Ameyde v. Srl. Ufficio Centrale Italiano di Assistenza Assicurativa Automobilisti in Circolazione Internazionale (UCI)* [1977] ECR 1091 at 1127, and to Art. 48 EC, see Case C-415/93 *Union Royale Belge des Sociétés de Football Association ASBL et al. v. Bosman et al.* [1995] ECR I-4921 at 5063–5066.

479. [1976] ECR 455 at 475–476.

480. See VerLoren van Themaat (1977) SEW 90 and Van Gerven (1977) CDE 131.

agreements which are intended to regulate paid labour collectively, as well as to contracts between individuals'[481] in so far as in all these cases direct and overt discrimination is involved rather than indirect and disguised discrimination.

The fact that Treaty provisions impose obligations on Member States need not be an obstacle to horizontal direct effect. What is decisive is whether national courts can apply these provisions without national law having conformed with them. The national courts are clearly an arm of the state bound by the obligations. Thus in Case 43/75 *Defrenne* the Court found that in referring to Member States Article 119 EC was 'alluding to those states in the exercise of all those of their functions which may usefully contribute to the implementation of the principle of equal pay.'[482] The Court added that Article 119 EC was far from merely referring to the powers of the national legislative authorities and thus the intervention of the Courts in direct application of that provision could not be excluded.[483]

In its judgment in Case 43/75 *Defrenne* the Court attached to a provision which unmistakably imposed an obligation on the Member States an obligation on private parties, namely to pay men and women equally for equal work. Giving a direct horizontal effect, *i.e.* creating obligations for private parties, to what was clearly a duty of the Member States under the Treaty gave rise to the question whether horizontal direct effect could result from directives which, *per se*, impose obligations on the Member States.[484] In Case 152/84 *Marshall v. Southampton and South West Hampshire Area Health Authority (Teaching)*[485] the Court firmly stated that it cannot. The Court emphasized that under Article 189 EC the binding nature of a directive, which constitutes the basis for the possibility of being able to rely on a directive before a national court, exists only in relation to 'each Member State to which it is addressed.' Thus the Court concluded that 'a directive may not of itself impose obligations on an individual and a provision of a directive may not be relied upon as against such a person.'[486]

---

481. [1976] ECR 455 at 476.
482. *Ibid.* at 475.
483. *Ibid.*
484. In addition to the literature cited in note 384, *supra*, see Barents in O'Keeffe and Schermers, *op. cit.* (see note 175, *supra*) 97.
485. [1986] ECR 723 at 749. Despite the chorous of criticism, referred to, *post*, the Court has maintained this stance, see Case C-91/92 *Faccini Dori v. Recreb Srl* [1994] ECR I-3325 at 3355–3356 and Case C-192/94 *El Corte Inglés SA v. Blázquez Rivero* [1996] ECR I-1281 at 1303–1304. A certain indirect effect on the position of third parties is, however, not to be excluded when direct effect in favour of a private party is found. See the not entirely successful attempt by the Court in Case 8/81 *Becker* [1982] ECR 53 at 75 and the criticisim by Mok (1983) SEW 273 at 276. See also Usher (1982) 7 ELRev. 193 and Case 78/70 *Deutsche Grammophon* [1971] ECR 487.
486. [1986] ECR 723 at 749.

The result for Miss Marshall was, however, that she could rely on sufficiently precise and unconditional provisions of the directive against an organ of the State; it is immaterial in this context whether the organ concerned acts *qua* employer or *qua* public authority.[487] The Court was very concerned to avoid Member States being able to benefit from their own failure to comply with Community law, in particular by failing adequately or at all to transpose directives into national law.[488] Thus the concept of the State was broadly interpreted: in addition to health authorities (*Marshall*) and other authorities,[489] it also embraces 'a body, whatever its legal form, which has been made responsible, pursuant to a measure adopted by the State, for providing a public service under the control of the State and has for that purpose special powers beyond those which result from the normal rules applicable in relations between individuals.'[490]

This approach in *Foster* is not without difficulties.[491] The borderline beyond which a body will not be regarded as the State acting as an employer is unclear, and remains so after *Foster*. There remains a distinction, which is in itself difficult to justify, between companies who are assimilated to the State and other companies who are not affected by directly effective provisions of directives.[492]

It is scarcely surprising that calls on the Court to allow hoizontal direct effect for provisions of directives which confer on individuals sufficiently precise and unconditional rights are heard ever more loudly,[493] although

487. *Ibid.* The case concerned Dir. 76/207 (O.J. 1976 L 39/40) on equal treatment for men and women in *inter alia* access to employment. See, for further developments in the saga, Case C-271/91 *Marshall v. Southampton and South West Hampshire Area Health Authority* [1993] ECR I-4367, [1993] 3 CMLR 293. See also Case 222/84 *Johnson v. The Chief Constable of the Royal Ulster Constabulary* [1986] ECR 1651 at 1691 (Chief Constable part of the State) and Case 103/88 *Fratelli Constanzo SpA v. Comune di Milano* [1989] ECR 1839 at 1870–1871 (local authority part of the State).
488. Case 152/84 *Marshall* [1986] ECR 723 at 749.
489. See note 487, *supra*.
490. Case C-188/89 *Foster et al. v. British Gas plc* [1990] ECR I-3313 at 3348–3349. (British Gas was a nationalized industry at the relevant time.)
491. See Van Gerven, Adv. Gen., *ibid.* at 3332–3336 and 3339–3340. The House of Lords found little difficulty in applying the test when *Foster* returned to it, [1991] 2 AC 306, but in *Doughty v. Rolls-Royce plc* [1992] 1 CMLR 1045 the Court of Appeal felt that control was only one of several criteria, all of which had to be satisfied, an approach which, with the utmost possible respect, seems to ignore the sensible approach in Lord Templeman's speech in *Foster*, [1991] 2 AC 306 at 315.
492. The Court in *Marshall* dismissed this point with the observation that correct implementation would have removed any inequality, thus putting the ball firmly back in the camp of the national authorities, [1986] ECR 723 at 749. See Curtin (1990) 27 CMLRev. 709 and Prechal (1990) 27 CMLRev. 451.
493. *E.g.* Emmert and Perreira de Azevedo (1993) RTDE 503 and Boch and Lane (1992) Leiden J. Int'l. L. 171; Van Gerven, Adv. Gen. in Case C-271/91 *Marshall* [1993] ECR I-4367 at 4387–4388; Jacobs, Adv. Gen. in Case C-316/93 *Vaneetveld et al. v. Le Foyer et al.* [1994] ECR I-763 at 772–776 (in a particularly powerful opinion), and

they are calls so far firmly resisted by the Court.[494] It appears in part to be afraid of blurring the distinction between regulations and directives and of creating obligations for persons who are not the addressees of directives.[495] There is clearly a now package of remedies, the more recent developments of which are clearly designed to mitigate the absence of horizontal direct effect of directives, namely direct effect for appropriate provisions of directives against the State in whatever form, the obligation to interpret national law whenever possible in confomity with the provisions (and objectives) of a directive, and the development of liability of the Member States in damages for loss suffered by individuals for breach of Community law.[496] As has been suggested above,[497] the present situation is not entirely satisfactory and according horizontal direct effect to directives has obvious attractions from the point of view of disappointed claimants. However, given that certain national courts have demonstrated certain difficulties in accepting that even vertical direct effect of directives remains wihin the bounds of acceptable judicial creativity,[498] it is unsurprising that the Court of Justice is unwilling to stretch national judicial tolerance to an unlimited extent. It may well be that the sort of approach evident from the more recent case-law of the French Conseil d'État discussed in section 2.2.2, above, would offfer an appropriate solution to a number of the present problems. Thus national law should not stand in the way of achieving the result which the directive prescribes; such an approach manifestly flows from Article 5 EC. While this would not solve every problem, it would at least facilitate an improvement in the legal position of private parties in their dealings with other private parties concerning compliance with unimplemented directives. Indeed, this approach of using the obligation not to hinder the achievement of the prescribed result has also been used by the Court in another context.[499] It is evident, though, that such a system stands or falls on the shoulders of the national courts, in terms of the extent to which they are prepared to grant fast, effective and genuine remedies for breach of Community law. It is to these problems that the following section now turns.

Lenz Adv. Gen. in Case C-91/92 *Faccini Dori* [1994] ECR I-3325 at 3338–3345 (in a comprehensive survey of the competing arguments).

494. Case C-91/92 *Faccini Dori v. Recreb Srl* [1994] ECR I-3325 at 3355–3356 and Case C-192/94 *El Corte Inglés SA v. Blázquez Rivero* [1996] ECR I-1281 at 1303–1304

495. Case C-91/92 *Faccini Dori* [1994] ECR I-3325 at 3356.

496. *Ibid.* at 3356–3357.

497. See the discussion on p. 540 of this Chapter, *ante*.

498. See the discussion on pp. 540–541, *ante*, in relation to the French Conseil d'État and the judgment of the Bundesverfassungsgericht in Germany in *Kloppenburg* [1988] 3 CMLR 1. See also section 2.3.1, *post*.

499. See Case C-129/96 *Inter-Environnement Wallonie ASBL v. Région wallonne* [1997] ECR I-7411 at 7449 in the context of the Member State's powers in the period between a directive being adopted and the latest date for its implementation (referring at 7448–7449 to the general obligation to achieve the prescribed result).

2.3 National courts: Community law and national law

2.3.1 Priority of provisions of Community law; Community law and national constitutional law

The position which the Court had adopted in earlier celebrated cases[500] concerning the priority of directly effective (applicable) Community law over national law was strengthened and its logical consequences were set out in a manner which could not be misunderstood in Case 106/77 *Amministrazione delle Finanze dello Stato v. Simmenthal SpA.*[501] The Court stated that 'in accordance with the principle of the precedence of Community law, the relationship between provisions of the Treaty and directly applicable measures of the institutions on the one hand and the national law of the Member States on the other is such that those provisions and measures not only by their entry into force render automatically inapplicable any conflicting provisions of current national law but – in so far as they are an integral part of, and take precedence in, the legal order applicable in the territory of each of the Member States – also preclude the valid adoption of new national legislative measures to the extent to which they would be incompatible with Community provisions.'[502] Thus it followed that 'every national court must, in a case within its jurisdiction, apply Community law in its entirety and protect rights which the latter confers on individuals and must accordingly set aside any provision of national law which may conflict with it, whether prior or subsequent to the Community rule.'[503]

This judgment concerned directly effective provisions of Community law. It should be remembered, though, that, apart from the question of whether such provisions are involved, the principle of the priority of Community law can also arise when a national court, in examining national rules in a field in which the national legislator is charged with implementation of Community law, does not apply such rules to the extent to which they exceed any limits of discretion (in so far as the limits are prescribed in sufficiently clear and precise and unconditional provisions) permitted in such implementation; the principle also arises in the absence of any discretion, in which case the provisions of Community law must prevail over incompatible rules of national law.[504]

The principle of the priority of Community law is a principle of

---

500. Case 26/62 *Van Gend en Loos* [1963] ECR 1, [1963] CMLR 105 and Case 6/64 *Costa v. ENEL* [1964] ECR 585, [1964] CMLR 425.
501. [1978] ECR 629, [1978] 3 CMLR 263.
502. [1978] ECR 629 at 643.
503. *Ibid.* at 644. See also Case 249/85 *ALBAKO Margarinefabrik Maria von der Linde GmbH & Co. KG v. Bundesanstalt für landwirtschaftliche Marktordnung* [1987] ECR 2345 at 2360.
504. On this point see section 2.2.2 of this Chapter, *ante*.

Community law itself. Thus it is Community law and not national law which decrees such priority. Thus, for example, a Dutch judge, in the event of a conflict with rules of Community law, would refuse to apply the relevant national provisions not on account of incompatability with Article 94 of the Dutch Constitution but on account of their incompatibility with Community law. In the United Kingdom, although the European Communities Act 1972 was the vehicle for the entry of Community law into the national legal systems, the priority which Community law has occurs by virtue of Community law.[505] If a national court accepts this construction then it cannot arrive at judgments like that of the French Conseil d'État[506] which (then) refused on constitutional grounds to decline to enforce a French decree (which had the force of a law) which was incompatible with an earlier EEC regulation. It is true that Article 55 of the French Constitution expressly gives priority to norms of written international law but clearly the Conseil d'État, unlike the Cour de Cassation[507] did not consider that it had jurisdiction to consider the issue, on the basis that it would then have to consider the compatability of the decree with the Constitution, *i.e.* with Article 55 itself! Considering questions of compatability is outside the jurisdiction of judges in France as well as in the Netherlands. In the meantime the Conseil d'État has revised its standpoint and has accepted the primacy of the law of international agreements, thus including Community law, even above subsequent national law.[508]

Another view which does not fit in with the Court of Justice's construction is the view which the Italian Corte Costituzionale demonstrated in the *Simmenthal* case. The latter court took the view that it alone

505. *Contra*, Lord Denning, MR in *Macarthy's Ltd. v. Smith* [1981] 1 All ER 111 at 120. With respect to the learned Master of the Rolls, his observation appears to confuse two points. The priority of Community law is a principle of that law; that law (including the principle) is recognised by the European Communities Act 1972 but priority is not (as such) given by the Act. The substitution of the word 'recognised' for the word 'given' would have rendered the remarks unobjectionable. See, further, *R. v. Secretary of State for Transport, ex parte Factortame Ltd. et al. (No. 1)* [1990] 2 AC 85 at 140 (Lord Bridge of Harwich, in a speech in which the other noble Lords concurred), *R. v. Secretary of State for Transport, ex parte Factortame Ltd. et al. (No. 2)* [1991] 1 AC 603 at 659 (Lord Bridge of Harwich), and *Webb v. EMO Air Cargo (UK) Ltd.* [1992] All ER 929 at 939.
506. In *Syndicat Général de Fabricants de Semoules de France* [1970] CMLR 395, see Brinkhorst (1968) SEW 519 and, for cases prior to more recent developments, Olmi (1981) RMC 242 at 245; see, further, Genvois (1985) EuR 355.
507. In *Administration des Douanes v. Société 'Café Jacques Vabre' et al.* [1975] CMLR 367, see March Hunnings (1975) JBL 326; Kovar (1975) CDE 631 and Simon (1976) 92 LQR 85.
508. In *Nicolo* [1990] 1 CMLR 173, [1989] RFD Admin. 824, concerning international treaties in general, see Manin (1991) 28 CMLRev. 499, Pollard (1990) 15 ELRev. 267, and Reestman (1990) *RM Themis* 420; in *Boisdet* [1991] 1 CMLR 3, concerning Community law in particular, see Cohen (1991) 16 ELRev. 144.

– and no other Italian court – was competent to decide whether a national provision was incompatible with Community law, on the ground that only it had jurisdiction in constitutional questions. The conflict between national law and Community law was 'translated' into an infringement of constitutional law,[509] just as happened in the old case referred to above before the Conseil d'État in France, albeit with a difference on one point, namely that in France no court is empowered to examinelaws against the Constitution whereas in Italy the Corte Costituzionale is so empowered.

The judgment of the Court of Justice in Case 106/77 *Simmenthal*[510] makes it clear that it rejects these views out of hand. Thus 'a national court which is called upon, within the limits of its jurisdiction, to apply provisions of Community law is under a duty to give full effect to those provisions, if necessary refusing of its own motion to apply any conflicting provisions of national legislation, even if adopted subsequently, and it is not necessary for the court to request or await the prior setting aside of such provision by legislative or other consitutional means.'[511] It would be incompatible with the requirements which are the very essence of Community law, in the event of conflict between a provision of Community law and a subsequent national law 'if the solution of the conflict were to be reserved for an authority with a discretion of its own, other than the court called upon to apply Community law, even if such an impediment to the full effectiveness of Community law were only temporary.'[512] The Corte Costituzionale has now accepted the approach of the Court of Justice on this point, even though its reasons for accepting it may be less than wholly orthodox.[513]

The principle of the priority (supremacy) of Community law also excludes review of Community law against national constitutional law. This is not only implicit from the judgment of the Court in *Simmenthal*, it was also expressly stated in the celebrated judgment in Case 11/70 *Internationale Handelsgesellschaft mbH v. Einfuhr- und Vorratsstelle für getreide und Futtermittel*[514] when the Court held that community law could not, 'because of its very nature, be overridden by rules of national law, however framed,

---

509. *In casu* whether the incompatability with Community law created a breach of Art. 11 of the Italian Constitution which permits limitations of sovereignty in favour of international organisations.
510. See note 394, *supra*.
511. [1978] ECR 629 at 644.
512. *Ibid.*
513. In *SpA Granital v. Amministrazione delle Finanze dello Stato*, 8 June 1984, (1984) *Il Foro Italiano* 2062, (1986) CDE 185. See Petriccione (1986) 11 ELRev. 320. See also Gaja (1984) 21 CMLRev. 756; Barav (1985) RTDE 313; Menis (1983) CDE 320; La Pergola and Del Duca (1985) 79 AJIL 598, and Gori (1981) 6 ELRev. 222. See, further, *SpA BECA v. Amministrazione delle Finanze dello Stato* (1985) RDI 338; *Provincia di Bolzano v. Presidenti Consiglio Ministri* (1989) RDI 404; Gaja (1990) 27 CMLRev. 83 and Daniele (1990) CDE 3.
514. [1970] ECR 1125 at 1134.

without being deprived of its character as Community law. Therefore the validity of a Community measure or its effect within a Member State cannot be affected by allegations that it runs counter to either fundamental human rights as formulated by the constitution of that state or the principles of a national constitutional structure.' It was, however, willing to examine whether any analogous guarantee inherent in Community law itself had been disregarded.[515] This made it clear that written and unwritten Community law affords guarantees comparable with those found in national constitutions and constitutional law, and that the Court of Justice itself is entrusted with the task of ensuring that such guarantees (in particular respect for fundamental rights) are protected in the Community legal order, particularly in proceedings under Article 177 EC.

Problems on this point have arisen in Germany and Italy where laws can be reviewed against the Constitution. As has been observed in section 3.3. of Chapter II, above, the case-law in these Member States has gradually accepted, at least for regulations, the theory developed by the Court of Justice of the restriction of national sovereignty *vis-à-vis* the Community legal order operating within the national legal sphere on its own authority and entirely independently, not transformed into Community law. Support for this could be found in Article 24(1) of the German Grundgesetz which permits the transfer of sovereignty to a supranational organisation and in Article 11 of the Italian Constitution which permits the limitation of sovereign powers aimed at encouraging international organisations having the aim of assuring peace and justice between nations. It should be noted that with a view to the ratification of the TEU, the entirely revised version of Article 23 of the German Grundgesetz now contains a number of conditions for and limitations on the transfer of sovereign powers to the European Union.

In both countries, the Constitutional Courts have continually held that their Constitutions place limits on such transfer. Thus the essential elements of the constitutional order, particularly fundamental rights, may not be affected by any such transfer.[516] In 1973 the Corte Costituzionale regarded this as rather a theoretical problem. While it reserved the right to intervene if the EEC, contrary to its expectations were to be given an unacceptable power to violate the fundamental principles of the Italian constitutional order or the inalienable rights of man, the Corte Costituzionale declined to control the constitutionality of each individual Community regulation.[517] In Germany the Bundesverfassungsgericht in

---

515. *Ibid.*
516. Judgments of the Bundesverfassungsgericht of 29 May 1974: *International Handelsgesellschaft* BVerfGE 37, 271; [1974] 2 CMLR 551, see Ipsen (1975) EuR 1; Hilf, Klein and Bleckmann (1975) ZaöRV 51, and Feige (1975) AöR 530), and of the Corte Costituzionale of 27 December 1973 *Frontini et al. v. Ministero delle Finanze* [1974] 2 CMLR 386, see Gori (1981) 6 ELRev. 222 and Bebr (1974) 11 CMLRev. 408.
517. [1974] 2 CMLR 386 at 389, see Petriccione (1986) 11 ELRev. 320.

1974, on the contrary, regarded itself as having jurisdiction to review regulations against the fundamental rights laid down in the German Constitution as long as (hence the popular name '*Solange* judgment') the process of integration in the Community had not developed far enough so that Community law contained a codified catalogue of fundamental rights decided upon by a democratically legitimate and elected parliament which offered the same guarantees as those afforded by the German Constitution.[518] If the judgment of the Corte Costituzionale was reasonably satisfactory, the same cannot be said of that of the Bundesverfassungsgericht.

However, in a judgment of 22 October 1986[519] the Bundesverfassungsgericht reversed the thrust of its earlier judgment as it was convinced that the aims expressed in 1974 had been achieved. Satisfactory durable guarantees existed that the European Communities, particularly through the case-law of the Court, ensured an effective protection of fundamental rights against action by the Community authorities, a protection which in essence was the same as that required as a minimum by the German Constitution, particularly because it guaranteed the essential core of fundamental rights. The Bundesverfassungsgericht based this conclusion on an exhaustive analysis of the Court's case-law on the protection of fundamental rights, the Joint Declaration by the European Parliament, the Council and the Commission on Fundamental Rights, of 5 April 1977 and the Declaration of the European Council of 7 and 8 April 1978 on Democracy.[520] As long as this guarantee is present (and hence the name *Solange II* for this judgment) it would not hear cases seeking to challenge the constitutionality of secondary Community law. Thus the Bundesverfassungsgericht has followed the approach of the Corte Costitutionale on this point.[521]

It is a cause for concern that the Bundesverfassungsgericht regards it as a matter for it to ensure that the Community Institutions, including the Court, do not exceed the sovereign powers transferred by the German

---

518. [1974] 2 CMLR 511 at 552.

519. *Wünsche Handelsgesellschaft* BVerfGE 73, 339; [1987] 3 CMLR 225; (1987) EuR 51 (with note by Ipsen); (1988) 25 CMLRev. 201 (with note by Frowein), see further, judgment of 10 April 1987 2 BvR 1236/86 (1987) EuR 269 (this judgment was a unanimous judgment of the First Chamber of the Second *Senat*).

520. See Chapter IV, section 7.5.4, *ante*.

521. Indeed the Corte Costituzionale in its judgment of 23 April 1985 *SpA BECA v. Amministrazione delle Finanze* (1985) RDI 338 (see Petriccione (1986) 11 ELRev. 320) now apppears to recognise more fully the authority of the Court of Justice. For the Court's rejection of Italian arguments that the development of the case-law of the Corte Costituzionale meant that as Italian legislation contrary to Community law was unenforceable, the maintenance of such legislation on the statute book did not rise to an infringement of Community law, see Case 104/86 *Commission v. Italy* [1988] ECR 1799 at 1817.

enabling (ratification) law. Thus in *Kloppenburg*[522] it examined whether, in according vertical direct effect to certain provisions of directives, the Court of Justice had remained within the bounds of what it regarded as acceptable judicial creativity. Thus the clear confirmation in *Brunner*[523] on the constitutionality of the TEU in terms of the Grundgesetz, that legal acts of the Community Institutions and other bodies of the European Union which, in its opinion,were no longer covered by the Treaty in the form which constituted the basis of the German law approving it would not be binding on German territory[524] is also scarcely a great surprise. The Bundesverfassungsgericht has become, as the self-appointed 'highest' judge in Europe, the guardian of the boundaries of Community competence.[525]

The view of the Bundesverfassungsgericht that the direct effect and supremacy of Community law can only be recognized within the boundaries of the powers conferred on the Community is in itself correct. But whether these boundaries have been respected is a matter for the Court of Justice, as it is a question of interpretation of Community law. By claiming to reserve to itself the final determination of this matter, the Bundesverfassungsgericht has created the possibility of conflicts between the two highest courts, that in the Community and that in Germany, which could seriously threaten the uniform interpretation and application of Community law. It is to be hoped that the Bundesverfassungsgericht will itself take seriously the relationship of cooperation with the Court of Justice, by which it claims to lay such store, and, before reaching a definite judgment on a question, make a reference to the Court of Justice under Article 177 EC.[526]

Directly effective provisions of Community law will, if they are relevant, always be applied by national courts to the concrete dispute before them. Moreover, in appropriate cases national courts will have to examine rules emanating from national authorities in the field of national implementation of such provisions of Community law against the terms of those provisions themselves.[527] The question whether the duty of the national courts to apply directly effective provisions of Community law of their own motion[528] also applies to procedural rules governing the right of parties to

---

522. 2BvR 687/85 [1988] 3 CMLR 1, 75 BVerfGE 223, see Hilf (1988) EuR 1.
523. 2 BvR 2134 and 2159/92 [1994] 1 CMLR 57, 89 BVerfGE 155; (1993) EuGRZ 429, see Everling (1994) 14 YBEL 1 (and literature cited there) and Zuleeg (1997) 22 ELRev. 19.
524. End of Part C.I.3 of the judgment.
525. See Tomuschat (1993) EuGRZ 489.
526. In its judgment in *Brunner* (part B.2(b)), the Bundesverfassungsgericht notes that it exercises its jurisdiction over the applicability of secondary Community law in a relationship of cooperation with the Court of Justice. Because the latter guarantees the protection of basic rights in each individual case for the entire Community territory, the Bundesverfassungsgericht states that it is able to confine itself to providing a general guarantee of the unalterable standard of basic rights.
527. See section 7.5.4 of Chapter IV, *ante*. See, generally, Temple Lang (1997) 22 ELRev. 3.
528. Case 166/73 *Rheinmühlen* [1974] ECR 33 at 38–39; Case 33/76 *Rewe-Zentralfinanz eG*

advance new legal arguments and to limitation periods has been effectively left in the hands of national law,[529] subject to what is justified for the requirements of legal certainty and the proper conduct of proceedings.[530]

In this way national courts play an important part in ensuring the judicial protection of private parties against measures taken by the Member States which are incompatible with Communtiy law. This function was expressly confirmed by the Court of Justice in Case 26/62 *Van Gend en Loos*.[531] Three governments had argued in their observations that only the Commission or another Member State could act against an infringement of Community law by a Member State under Articles 169 and 170 EC. This argueuent was rejected by the Court partly because it 'would remove all direct legal protection of the individual rights of their nationals.' The Court added that there was 'the risk that recourse to the procedure under these Articles would be ineffective if it were to occur after the implementation of a national decision taken contrary to the provision of the Treaty.'[532] Without diminishing the essential and practical importance of the standpoint of the European Court, it is nevertheless to be noted that a conflict between a rule of Community law and a national statutory rule of a later date will in practice usually not present itself in an acute form. As a rule national courts will try to avoid an outright choice of one rule or the other by intepreting them in such a way that they do not conflict with each other. Indeed, national courts will not readily assume that the national legislature has acted contrary to the international obligations of the State. In this context it will hardly be relevant whether the courts concerned to or do not consider themselves obliged to give priority to the rule of Community law in accordance with national constitutional law or in accordance with Community law.[533] It is, though, very important that national courts, especially those against whose decision there is no judicial

---

et al. v. Landwirtschaftskammer für das Saarland [1976] ECR 1989 at 1997–1998, and Cases C-87–89/90 *Verholen et al. v. Sociale Verzekeringsbank* [1991] ECR I-3757 at 3788 and 3790–3791.

529. Cases C-430 and 431/93 *Van Schijndel et al. v. Stichting Pensioenfonds voor Fysiotherapeuten* [1995] ECR I-4705 at 4737–4738.

530. Case C-312/93 *Peterbroeck, Van Campenhout & Cie SCS v. Belgian State* [1995] ECR I-4599 at 4622–4633. The requirements of equal treatment and not rendering the exercise of Community rights conferred by Community law either virtually impossible or extremely difficult also apply, *ibid.* at 4620–4621; Cases C-430 and 431 *van Schijndel* [1995] ECR I-4705 at 4737. See Prechal (1998) 35 CML Rev. 681.

531. [1963] ECR 1 at 13. See Stein (1981) AJIL 1.

532. *Ibid.* The fact that national legal remedies may be used by interested parties to rely on directly effective provisions of Community law is no bar to Art. 169 EC proceedings being brought by the Commission, see Case 31/69 *Commission v. Italy* [1970] ECR 25 at 32. A reference under Art. 177 EC and an Art. 169 EC case may well run in parallel, *e.g.* Case 118/78 *C.J. Meijer BV v. Department of Trade et al.* [1979] ECR 1387, [1979] 2 CMLR 427 and Case 231/78 *Commission v. United Kingdom* [1979] ECR 1447, [1979] 2 CMLR 427.

533. Petriccione, (1986) 11 ELRev. 320 at 327.

remedy, should refer the interpretation of the rule of Community law to the Court of Justice under Article 177 EC. The intervention of the Court of Justice by means of a preliminary ruling ensures that this rule will not be interpreted in a narrow sense in order to prevent conflict with the rule of national law. If the national court wishes to avoid such a conflict, it will not be able to do so at the expense of the content or the scope of application of the Community rule, but only by means of a narrow interpretation of the national rule.[534]

It must, therefore, be considered very important that the application of Article 177 should not be barred to the national court. Thus, it is not surprising that the Court opposed in such a vigorous and broad argumentation the contention of the Italian Government in Case 6/64 *Costa v. ENEL* that the request of the Milan magistrate for a preliminary ruling was 'absolutely inadmissible.' According to the Italian Government this national judge was obliged to apply the later national law, irrespective of the question whether it was contrary to the provisions of the EEC Treaty. The Milan judge could not and should not decide the question of how to interpret those provisions. Consequently, the Court of Justice found itself obliged to argue forcefully, on the basis of an exhaustive explanation of the supremacy of Community law, that 'Article 177 is to be applied regardless of any domestic law whenever questions relating to the interpretation of the Treaty arise.'[535]

2.3.2   National courts and the application of Community law

The application of Community law takes place, at least in the decentralised structure within which EC law is given effect in vast areas, principally in the day-to-day legal activities within the Member States. The national courts thus occupy a central role in this process. Informed, if necessary, by the Court of Justice by a preliminary ruling under Article 177 EC, it is their task to decide whether national rules and administrative acts are compatible with Community law, and whether individuals have acted in accordance with the obligations incumbent on them under Community law, and to give effect to the consequences of that decision in national law or, in some cases,[536] in Community law itself. The national courts may also be faced with the question whether decisions of the Community Institutions are compatible with the Community law on which they are

---

534. See the question of interpreting community law in conformity with directives, discussed in section 2.2.2 of this Chapter, *ante*. As to interpreting in conformity with treaty provisions, see Case C-165/91 *Van Munster v. Rijksdienst voor Pensioenen* [1994] ECR I-4661 at 4697–4698.
535. [1964] ECR 585 at 594.
536. *E.g.* nullity of agreements under Art. 85(2) EC, or the award of damages for breach of Community law, discussed *post*.

based. The national judge can thus be portrayed as the judge of the common law of the Community.

As has been explained in the previous section, the national court is obliged to interpret national law as far as possible in conformity with Community law, to apply directly effective provisions of Community law, and, in the case of conflict between the latter and national provisions, to disapply national law. However, the degree to which the national court, thus equipped, can apply Community law is actually dependent on the possibilities offered by its national legal order for this purpose. Thus Keus has described national law as being the vehicle on which Community law must ride.[537] Whether Community law can actually be enforced depends on what legal means are afforded by the national legal system, and under what conditions these legal means may be used. Thus a number of questions arise. Can someone who feels that another, whether a an authority or an individual, has acted in breach of a directly effective provision of Community law seek damages for loss suffered, or an injunction restraining the conduct concerned, or the repayment of sums paid but not due, or the quashing or suspension of the relevant decision of an authority? Which appeal or limitation periods apply? And in front of which court must he or she then appeal – the civil courts or the administrative courts, does the action lie in public or private law, by way of writ or judicial review?

Given that the various national legal systems may display great divergence in the remedies available and in the requirements which have to be fulfilled, the complete and uniform application of Community law may actually be crowded out, despite its direct effect and supremacy. The effectiveness of direct effect, as Mertens de Wilmars has put it[538] may thus be limited. He has called the resulting problems, second generation problems, which loom up after a number of fundamental problems of the first generation (the special, independent character of the Community legal order, direct effect, and the primacy of Community law) had been solved.[539]

These second generation problems raise the question whether there are any framework limits to the manner in which Community law is received into national law. The Court has found that there are.[540] Community rules relating on the one hand to fixing and collection of the financial charges which the Community is empowered to levy as own resources, such as customs duties, agricultural levies, and monetary compensatory amounts

537. Keus, in Hendius et al. Europees Privaatrecht, Naareen (Lelystad, 1993) 33.
538. 'L'effet utile de l'effet direct', Reports of the FIDE Congress, London, 1980, Vol. I, p. 1.2.
539. Ibid. (Cited by Koopmans in Boes et al., Liber Amicorum Josse Mertens de Wilmars (Antwerp, 1982) 119 at 121).
540. E.g. Case 265/78 H. Ferwerda BV v. Produktschap voor Vee en Vlees [1980] ECR 617 at 627–630.

are extremely important, as are, on the other hand, the conditions for the granting and payment of financial benefits such as agricultural export refunds and other subsidies which are for the account of the Community budget. It is thus not surprising that the case-law on these second generation problems initially developed primarily in this field.[541] These charges and benefits are applied and granted by the Community in indirect administration, by means of decisions of the national authorities. Disputes about the lawfulness of those decisions thus arise within the national legal orders and are decided there, they are settled under national law in so far as no provisions of Community law are relevant.[542]

The requirement of cooperation, laid down in Article 5 EC, means that the national courts must provide 'the legal protection made available as a result of the direct effect of the Community provisions both when such provisions create obligations for the subject and when they confer rights on him. It is, however, for the national legal system of each Member State to determine the courts having jurisdiction and to fix the procedures for applications to the courts intended to protect the rights which the subject obtains through the direct effect of Community law but such procedures may not be less favourable than those in similar procedures concerning internal matters and may in no case be laid down in such a way as to render impossible in practice the exercise of the rights which the national courts must protect.'[543]

This passage from the judgment in *Ferwerda*, which embraces earlier case-law,[544] contains three elements which apply whenever a national court is faced with a dispute involving directly effective Community provisions. The first concerns its duty to afford judicial protection. This duty is deduced from Article 5 EC, which obliges the Member States and their organs, including national courts, to ensure compliance with the obligations resulting from Community law. The second element is the procedural autonomy of the Member States' legal systems. The concept of procedure covers all substantive and organizational rules and principles applicable to actions brought to obtain such judicial protection. It only applies, of course, to the extent to which no provisions of Community law

---

541. See Hubeau (1980) SEW 601; Tatham (1994) 19 ELRev. 146, and, more generally, Bridge (1984) 9 ELRev. 28.
542. Case 265/78 *H. Ferwerda BV v. Produktschap voor Vee en Vlees* [1980] ECR 617 at 629.
543. *Ibid.*
544. Case 33/76 *Rewe-Zentralfinaz eG et al. v. Landwirtschaftskammer für das Saarland* [1976] ECR 1989 at 1997–1998; Case 45/76 *Comet BV v. Produktschap voor Sierge-wassen* [1976] ECR 2043 at 2053, and Case 26/74 *Société Roquette Frères v. Commission* [1976] ECR 677 at 686–687. This is the Court's standing approach to these second generation problems, see *e.g.* Case C-312/93 *Peterbroeck, Van Campenhout & Cie SCS v. Belgian State* [1995] ECR I-4599 at 4620–4621 and Cases C-430 and 431/93 *Van Schijndel et al. v. Stichting Pensioenfonds voor Fysiotherapeuten* [1995] ECR I-4705 at 4738.

deal with the point or harmonize national provisions.[545] The third element is the two conditions laid down: there must be no distinction between claims brought under community law and claims brought purely under national law (requirement of equal treatment), and the exercise of the rights must not be made virtually impossible or otherwise illusory (requirement of effectiveness),[546] even when such a situation would be in conformity with the equal treatment requirement.[547]

The requirement of effectiveness, in the form of affording effective judicial protection (remedies) to individuals whose fundamental rights conferred by Community law are at issue has played an increasingly important role in the case-law in the last ten or so years.[548] The principle of effective judicial control reflects 'a general principle of law which underlies the constitutional traditions common to the Member States.'[549] It is also laid down in Articles 6 and 13 of the European Convention on Human Rights, the principles of which have been recognized as having to be taken into consideration in Community law.[550] Fundamental Community rights do not only embrace the right to equal treatment of

545. Such provisions apply in relation to the Community Customs Code (see Title VII of Reg. 2913/92 (O.J. 1992 L 302/1, most recently amended by Reg. 82/97 (O.J. 1997 L 17/1)). See also in relation to remedies in the procurement field, Dirs. 89/665 (O.J. 1989 L 395/33) and 92/13 (O.J. 1992 L 76/14), see Gormley (1992) 1 PPLR 259.

546. As to the consequences of these requirements for national law, see *e.g.* Case 68/79 *Hans Just I/S v. Danish Ministry for Fiscal Affairs* [1980] ECR 501 at 522–523; Case 170/84 *Bilka-Kaufhaus GmbH v. Weber von Hartz* [1986] ECR 1607 at 1628; Case 222/84 *Johnston v. Chief Constable of the Royal Ulster Constabulary* [1986] ER 1651 at 1682–1683 and 1690–1691; Case 109/88 *Handels- og Kontorfunktionærernes Forbund i Danmark v. Dansk Arbejdsgiverforeningg, acting on behalf of Danfoss* [1989] ECR 3199 at 3226 (burden of proof); Case 130/79 *Express Dairy Foods Ltd. v. Intervention Board for Agricultural Produce* [1980] ECR 1887 at 1899–1900 (in which the Court regretted the absence of Community provisions harmonizing procedures and time-limits), and Case 54/81 *Firma Wilhelm Fromme v. Bundesanstalt für landwirtschaftliche Marktordnung* [1982] ECR 1449 at 1462–1464 (calculation of interest). See also Case C-312/93 *Peterbroeck, Van Campenhout & Cie SCS v. Belgian State* [1995] ECR I-4599 at 4620–4621 and Cases C-430 and 431/93 *Van Schijndel et al. v. Stichting Pensioenfonds voor Fysiotherapeuten* [1995] ECR I-4705 at 4738.

547. See Case 199/82 *Amministrazione delle Finanze dello Stato v. SpA San Giorgio* [1983] ECR 3595 at 3612–3614. Requirements as to the burden and standard of proof (rules of evidence), even if equally applicable, must not make it virtually impossible or excessively difficult to secure repayment of charges levied contrary to Community law (*ibid.* at 3613). But if the burden of the charges has indeed been passed on and has caused no quantifiable loss, see *ibid.*; Case 68/79 *Hans Just* [1980] ECR 501 at 522–523, and Cases C-192–218/95 *Société Comateb et al. v. Direction Générale des douanes et des droits indirects* [1997] ECR I-189–190.

548. See Curtin and Mortelmans in Curtin and Heukels (eds.), *op. cit.* (see note 7, *supra*) 423.

549. Case 222/84 *Johnston v. Chief Constable of the Royal Ulster Constabulary* [1986] ECR 1651 at 1682; see also Case 222/86 *Union nationale des entraîneurs et Cadres techniques professionnels du football (Unectef) v. Heylens et al.* [1987] ECR 4097 at 4177.

550. *E.g. ibid.*

men and women, they in any event also cover rights such as the free movement of persons and the freedom to provide services. Not only must an appeal be possible against a decision of a national authority refusing a person the exercise of those rights, but the judicial control must also be effective.[551]

The obligation on the national court to assure effective judicial protection is based in Article 5 EC. The consequences which may result are well demonstrated from the application of Directive 76/207.[552] Article 6 of that directive obliges the Member States to 'introduce into their national legal systems such measures as are necessary to enable all persons who consider themselves wronged by failure to apply to them the principle of equal treatment within the meaning of Articles 3, 4 and 5 to pursue their claims by judicial process after possible recourse to other competent authorities.'[553] While the Court has concluded that the Member States are free to choose between the different solutions suitable for achieving the objective of the directive, they are required to adopt measures which are sufficiently effective to achieve that objective and to ensure that the measures may be relied upon by individuals before national courts: this means that if Member States choose to make a remedy in damages available, they may not simply offer a nominal sum (or reimbursement of expenses), but the remedy has guarantee real and effective judicial protection and have a deterrent effect, thus it must in any eventbe adequate in relation to the damage sustained.[554] Article 6 of the directive thus means that 'reparation of the loss and damage sustained by a person injured as a result of discriminatory dismissal may not be limited to an upper limit fixed *a priori* or by excluding an award of interest to compensate for the loss sustained by the recipient of the compensation as a result of the effluxion of time until the capital sum awarded is actually paid.'[555] As against the State and authorities emanating from the State, a person who has suffered loss or damage may, before the national courts, rely on Article 6, in combination with Article 5(1) of the directive, which prohibits discriminatory dismissal.[556]

---

551. *Ibid.* and Case 36/75 *Rutili v. Minister for the Interior* [1975] ECR 1219 at 1232–1233, which means that a person must be clearly notified of why a decision has been taken, be allowed to take effective steps to prepare his or her defence, and thus have a right of appeal to an authority having no organizational links with the authority which took the decision, see also Case C-175/94 *R. v. Secretary of State for the Home Department, ex parte Gallagher* [1995] ECR I-4253 at 4276–4278 (summarizing earlier case-law).
552. O.J. 1976 L 39/40 on equal treatment of men and women as regards access to employment, vocational training and promotion, and working conditions.
553. *Cf.* Dir. 89/665 (O.J. 1989 L 395/33), Arts. 1 and 2; Dir. 92/13 (O.J. 1992 L 76/14), Arts. 1 and 2 (in the field of procurement).
554. Case 14/83 *Von Colson and Kamann v. Land Nordrhein-Westfalen* [1984] ECR 1891 at 1907 and1909.
555. Case C-271/91 *Marshall v. Southampton and South West Hampshire Area Health Authority* [1993] ECR I-4367 at 4409.
556. *Ibid.* at 4410.

Moreover, if the Member State has chosen to apply the sanction in terms of the employer's civil liability, any breach of the prohibition of discrimination must, in itself, be sufficient to make the employer liable, and the emplyer will not be able to escape liability by invoking grounds of exception envisaged by national law.[557]

The duty of the national courts to afford effective judicial protection means that they must disapply national legal rules in order to ensure that the protection is effective. A classic example of this in action can be seen in Case C-213/89 *R. v. Secretary of State for Transport, ex parte Factortame Ltd. et al.*[558] The Court found that a national court in interlocutory proceedings, awaiting a ruling from the Court of Justice, was obliged to set aside a national rule which was the sole obstacle preventing it from granting interim relief in order to ensure the full effectiveness of the judgment to be given on the existence of the rights claimed under Community law, which were alleged to be breached by national provisions.[559] The rules involved were the presumption that national measures were compatible with Community law unless and until it they are declared incompatible, combined with the common law rule that an interim injunctionwould not lie against the Crown to suspend the effect of an Act of Parliament. It may well be asked whether as a result of *Factortame* the national court derives its power to suspend the operation of an Act from Community law itself, or whether it simply makes use of its power to issue interim injunctions under national law but with a wider sphere of application than that envisaged by national law.

In *Factortame* the Court did not pronounce as to the conditions under which interim relief had to be granted. From the reference to the national rule as 'the sole obstacle' it may be deduced that the normal conditions for the grant of interim relief apply, save that this obstacle is left to one side. Such conditions were prescribed in Cases C-143/88 and 92/89 *Zuckerfabrik Süderdithmarschen AG et al. v. Hauptzollamt Itzehoe et al.*[560] This involved the question whether a national court in interlocutory proceedings could order the suspension of enforcement of a national administrative measure based on a Community regulation. According to that judgment, the national court is not, as is the case with the approach in *Factortame*, obliged to leave to one side national rules which would prevent it from granting relief on the basis of Community law, rather the Court of Justice found that the national court could grant interim relief only subject to the specific conditions which the Court prescribed.[561] These

---

557. Case C-177/88 *Dekker v. Stichting Vormingscentrum voor Jong Volwassenen (VJV-Centrum) Plus* [1990] ECR I-3941 at 3976. The Hoge Raad did not ask about the (horizontal) direct effect of the directive.
558. [1990] ECR I-2433, [1990] 3 CMLR 1.
559. [1990] ECR I-2433 at 2474.
560. [1991] ECR I-415 at 540–544. See section 2.1.1 of this Chapter, *ante*.
561. *Ibid.* at 542–544.

conditions are analogous to those applicable when the Court itself grants interim relief.[562] If uniform conditions did not apply in this situation, the uniform application of Community law would be jeopardized, given the very divergent national rules involved.

The failure to transpose directives into national law, on time, adequately or at all, is a frequently encountered problem which serioussly weakens the rights which the directives seek to grant to individuals. A number of developments have already been discussed in the preceding sections of this Chapter, through which the Court is making it steadily less attractive an option for the Member States to fail to fulfil their obligations in this respect, such as the development of the concept of direct effect for sufficiently precise and unconditional provisions capable of conferring rights on individuals, and the duty to interpret national law as far as possible in conformity with Community law. In this line, there are two other important developments, relating to the use of limitation periods, and the availability of a remedy in damages.

The first of these is founded in the judgment in Case C-208/89 *Emmott v. Minister for Social Welfare et al.*[563] Until a directive has been properly transposed, a Member State which is in default may not rely on an individual's delay in commencing proceedings against it to protect rights which the directive confers on him or her: thus a limitation period for commencing proceedings cannot start running before the date of proper transposition.[564] However, this does not prevent a Member State from limiting retrospective invalidity claims, as the Court has drawn a distinction between the possibility of bringing an action and the period in respect of which a retroactive claim for benefit may be made.[565] The failure to transpose a directive into national law was also the background against which the Court found the opportunity to lay the basis for State liability for failure to comply with its obligations under Community law.

Already in older case-law the Court had noted that if damage had been caused through an infringement of Community law the state was liable to the injured party for the consequences in accordance with national law on state liability.[566] The question remained whether, and, if so, under what conditions, national law permitted liability for actions of the legislator,

---

562. See section 2.1.1 of this Chapter, *ante* (under Questions of validity, specific problems).
563. [1991] ECR I-4269 at 4298–4299.
564. *Ibid.* at 4299.
565. Case C-338/91 *Steenhorst-Neerings v. Bestuur van de Bedrijfsvereinging voor Detailhandel, Ambachten en Huisvrouwen* [1993] ECR I-5475 at 5503–55504. See also Case C-410/92 *Johnson v. Chief Adjudication Officer* [1994] ECR I-5483 at 5511–552 (in which, with the utmost possible respect, the Court's dismissal of the alleged distinction between Johnson's case and that of Steenhorst-Neerings was summary in the extreme and does not satisfy even the standards of reasoning which the Court demands of the Comission).
566. Case 60/75 *Russo v. Azienda di stato per gli Interventi sul Mercato Agricolo (AIMA)* [1976] ECR 45 at 56. This had been signalled in earlier case-law, *e.g.* Case 39/72 *Commission v. Italy* [1973] ECR 101 at 112.

particularly in relation to primary legislation of a normative character. It was thus extremely important that in its celebrated judgment in Cases C-6 and 9/90 *Francovich et al. v. Italy*[567] the Court anchored the principle of State liability for damage suffered by individuals through breach of Community law attributable to the State firmly in Community law itself.[568] Two bases were given for the principle of state liability. First, the Court found that it was inherent in the system of the EC Treaty itself, because of the requirements of the full effectiveness of Community rules and the particular indispensibility of obtaining redress where the full effectiveness of Community rules is subject to prior action on the part of the State and without such action individuals are unable to enforce in national courts the rights conferred on them by national law.[569] Secondly, the Court noted that the Member States were obliged, by virtue of Article 5 EC, to nullify the unlawful consequences of a breach of Community law.[570]

The conditions under which liability will give rise to a remedy in damages depends on the nature of the breach of community law giving rise to the loss and damage. In *Francovich* the Court considered the failure adequately or at all to transpose a directive into national law, setting out three conditions which, if fulfilled would give rise to a right founded directly on Community law for individuals to obtain reparation:

(1) The result prescribed by the directive must entail the grant of rights to individuals;
(2) It must be possible to identify the content of those rights on the basis of the provisions of the directive; and
(3) There must be a causal link between the breach of the state's obligations and the loss and damage suffered by the injured parties.[571]

Further the Court confirmed its traditional approach discussed above, that reparation had to be made on the basis of national law on liability, that in the absence of Community legislation it was for the national legal order in each Member State to designate the competent courts and lay down the detailed procedural rules for legal proceedings intended to safeguard fully the rights individuals derived from Community law; and that the requirements of no less favourable treatment than domestic claims and of not making obtaining reparation virtually impossible or excessively difficult also applied.[572] The principles of equal treatment and effectiveness were thus upheld.

---

567. [1991] ECR I-5357, [1993] 2 CMLR 66. See, *inter alia*, Curtin (1993) SEW 87; Schockweiler (1992) RTDE 27, and Steiner (1993) 18 ELRev. 3.
568. [1991] ECR I-5357 at 5414.
569. [1991] ECR I-5357 at 5414.
570. *Ibid.*
571. [1991] ECR I-5357 at 5415.
572. *Ibid.* at 5416. For the sequel, see Case C-479/93 *Francovich v. Italy* [1995] ECR I-3843.

Francovich left many questions unanswered, particularly whether any breach of Community law would automatically give rise to liability in damages, and whether the Court was not perhaps imposing on the Member States liability for breach of Community law in circumstances in which, if the action involved had been that of a Community Institution, the Court would not have held it liable in view of the case-law on the interpretation of the second paragraph of Article 215 EC. During 1996 the Court took the opportunity to expound further on this subject and to clarify matters considerably, and its approach is sufficiently important to merit detailed examination.

In Cases C-46 and 48/93 *Brasserie du Pêcheur SA et al. v. Germany et al.*[573] it commenced by rejecting the argument that liability in damages arose only when the provisions infringed were not directly effective, holding that direct effect of Treaty provisions was a minimum guarantee and not in itself sufficient to ensure the full and complete implementation of the Treaty; it was in fact to ensure that Community law prevailed over national provisions. It could not in every case secure the benefits of Community rights for individuals, hence the approach in *Francovich* of founding a remedy in damages in the need to ensure the full effectiveness of Community law. In the case of non-implementation or incorrect implementation of a directive, the purpose of reparation was to redress the injurious consequences for beneficiaries of the directive of the failure on the part of the Member State.[574] This was all the more true of infringement of directly effective rights conferred by provisions of Community law, where the right to reparation was 'the necessary corollary of the direct effect of the Community provision whose breach caused the damage sustained.'[575] As the Treaty was silent on the consequences of a breach of Community law by the Member States, the Court had recourse to generally accepted methods of interpretation, referring especially to the fundamental principles of the Community legal system, and, where necessary, to the general principles common to the legal systems of the Member States. This latter point of reference is expressly referred to in Article 215 EC where the principle of Community non-contractual liability is an expression of the general principle known to the legal systems of the Member States that an unlawful act or omission gives rise to an obligation to make good the damage caused. Article 215 EC also reflected the obligation on public authorities to make good damage caused in the performance of their duties.

---

573. [1996] ECR I-1029, [1996] 1 CMLR 889, [1996] All ER (EC) 684. See Craig (1997) 113 LQR 67.
574. [1996] ECR I-1029 at 1142–1143.
575. *Ibid.* at 1143. The Court then dismissed the argument that a general right for individuals to repartion had to be created by legislation rather than by case-law, noting that the the existence and extent of state liability were questions of Treaty interpretation which fell within the Court's jurisdiction and had been referred to it by national courts.

Moreover the courts in many national legal systems had developed the essentials of the legal rules governing state liability.

As state liability had been found in *Francovich* to be inherent in the system of the Treaty, that liability attached whatever the organ of the state responsible for the act or omission: Community law had to be uniformly applied, which meant that liability could not be made dependent on domestic rules as to the division of powers between constitutional authorities;[576] moreover, in international law state liability was viewed in terms of the state as a single entity, irrespective of whether the breach giving rise to the damage was an act of the legislature, the judiciary or the executive. This approach applied *a fortiori* in the Community legal order. Thus the fact that a breach complained of was an act of the legislature could not affect the right of individuals to obtain redress.[577] Two considerations then led the Court to look at its case-law on Article 215 EC. First, although only Article 215 EC expressly refers to the general principles common to the laws of the Member States, in the absence of written rules the Court also draws inspiration from those principles in other areas of Community law. Secondly there it should make no difference for the protection of rights of individuals whether the responsibility for the damage suffered as a result of a breach of Community law could be laid at the feet of the Community Institutions or the national authorities.

In view of this the Court drew a distinction between those areas in which the national legislature had a wide margin of discretion and those where it did not. Taking the second of these first, the Court noted that the obligations imposed on the national legislature to achieve a particular result, to act, or to refrain from acting could reduce, sometimes considerably, the margin of discretion. The failure to transpose a directive on time to achieve the result required was one such instance. In cases in which a wide discretion was left to the it was appropriate that they should incur liability in principle in the same circumstances as the Community Institutions would incur liability. Thus where policy choices were permitted by Community law, a right to reparation would exist if three conditions were satisfied:

(1) The rule of law infringed was intended to confer rights on individuals;
(2) The breach was sufficiently serious; and

576. Otherwise national authorities could escape liability by their own internal allocation of tasks. The Court has also rejected attempts to exclude the application of fundamental Community rights on the ground of classification of national laws (*e.g.* Case 186/87 *Cowan v. Trésor publique* [1989] ECR 195 at 221–222) as well as attempts to make the division of powers within a Member State the touchstone for the division of powers within the Community (*e.g.* Case C-359/92 *Germany v. Council* [1994] ECR I-3681 at 3712).

577. *Brasserie de Pêcheur* [1996] ECR 1029 at 1145.

(3) There was a direct causal link between the breach of the state's obligations and the damage sustained by the injured parties.[578]

Directly effective Treaty provisions, such as Articles 30 and 52 EC which were involved in the instant cases, clearly satisfied the first of these conditions. As to the second condition, the decisive test both as concerns Community liability under Article 215 EC and Member State liability for breach of Community law, for finding a breach sufficiently serious was 'whether the Member State or Community Institution concerned had manifestly and gravely disregarded the limits on its discretion.'[579] In the case of the Member States this was clearly a matter for the national courts, but the Court of Justice gave clear indications of the factors which they could take into account. These include 'the clarity and precision of the rule breached, the measure of discretion left by that rule to the national or Community authorities, whether the infringement and the damage caused was intentional or involuntary, whether any error of law was excusable or inexcusable, the fact that the position taken by a Community institution may have contributed towards the omission, and the adoption or retention of national measures or practices contrary to Community law.'[580] 'On any view', added the Court, 'a breach of Community law will clearly be sufficiently serious if it has persisted despite a judgment finding the infringement in question to be established, or a preliminary ruling or settled case-law of the Court on the matter from which it is clear that the conduct in question constituted an infringement.'[581] The third condition was a matter which the national court had to determine itself.

---

578. *Ibid.* at 1149. These conditions satisfied the requirement of full effectiveness of the rules of Community law and of effective protection of the rights conferred by those rules, and corresponded in substance to the rules for liability of the Community Institutions for unlawful legislative measures, *ibid.* As to the rules for such liability, see section 1.3.3 of this Chapter, *ante.*
579. *Ibid.* at 1150.
580. *Ibid.*
581. *Ibid.* The Court then pointed out that the situation in relation to the designation of products marketed (in *Brasserie de Pêcheur*, beer) was clear in the light of existing case-law, but in relation to additives was less clear until the Court's judgment on the *Rein-heitsgebot* in Case 178/84 *Commission v. Germany* [1987] ECR 1227, [1988] 1 CMLR 780. In relation to the second of the two joined cases, the damages claim by *Factor-tame*, the Court suggested that the national court might take account matters such as the legal disputes relating to particular features of the common fisheries policy, the Commission's attitude (which was made plain to the United Kingdom in good time), and the assessments as to the state of Community law made by the national courts in the interim proceedings which had been brought by those affected by the legislation concerned. Moreover, if the allegation that the United Kingdom had failed immediately to adopt the measures needed to comply with an Order of the President of the Court, and that this failure needlessly increased the loss sustained, were proved correct, the national court should regard this as constituting in itself a manifest, and thus sufficiently serious breach of Community law, [1996] ECR I-1029 at 1151–1152.

However, while these three conditions were necessary and sufficient to found a right to redress for individuals, if national law imposed liability under less strict conditions, only those less strict conditions could be impose in respect of breach of Community law.[582] Restrictions in national law applicable where a law is in breach of higher-ranking national provisions, or holding misfeasance in public office to be inconceivable on the part of the legislature were rules could not be applied, however, as they would in practice make it impossible or extremely difficult for effective reparation to be obtained.[583] The Court finally dealt with three practical points. First, reparation of loss or damage could not be made subject to any concept of fault, whether intentional or negligent, on the part of the organ of the state concerned, going beyond that of a sufficiently serious breach of Community law.[584] Secondly, the quantum and basis of damages. Here, the systematic approach of starting out from the principle of equal treatment and prohibition of making remedies in practice impossible or excessively difficult to obtain was applied. Thus reasonable diligence in mitigating the extent of loss or damage could be required, as could evidence that the claimant had availed himself or herself in time of all the available legal remedies. Exemplary damages also had to be available if they would be avilable in equivalent claims or actions unde domestic law. However, the total exclusion of loss of profit in particular was found incompatible with Community law, as it would make reparation practically impossible.[585] Finally, the Court rejected the argument that a prior judgment of the Court should be required before liability would start to run, finding that a prior judgment would be determinative, but not essential to satisfy the condition that a breach of Community law was sufficiently serious.[586]

The criterion of what is a sufficiently serious breach clearly leaves a great deal of room for the national courts, if they so desire, to dismiss even the most meritorious claims. Happily, further guidance has now been given in a number of judgments at Community level.[587] In Case 392/93 *R. v. H.M. Treasury, ex parte British Telecommunications plc*[588] the Court dealt with the transposition of the utilities procurement directive.[589] Incorrect transposition (as opposed to failure to transpose) would be tested by the conditions applicable in the case of situations in which a wide

582. *Ibid.* at 1153.
583. *Ibid.*
584. *Ibid.* at 1156.
585. *Ibid.* at 1157–1158.
586. *Ibid.* at 1159.
587. See also Barav (1996) 16 YBEL 87 and Waelbroeck in Heukels and McDonnell (eds.), *op. cit.* (see note 224, *supra*) 311.
588. [1996] ECR I-1631, [1986] 2 CMLR 217.
589. Dir. 90/531 (O.J. 1990 L 297/1), subsequently replaced by Dir. 93/38 (O.J. 1993 L 199/84).

discretion was left to the Member States. In circumstances in which a provision of a directive was imprecisely worded and reasonably capable of bearing the interpretation given to it by the national authorities, as well as the different construction applied by the Court, an interpretation applied in good faith on the basis of reasonable arguments, shared by other Member States and not covered by case-law or a challenge from the Commission, the Court found that the conduct of the Member State was not a sufficiently serious breach of Community law as to found libility.[590] In Case C-5/94 *R. v. Ministry of Agriculture, Fisheries and Food, ex parte Hedley Lomas (Ireland) Ltd.*[591] the Court noted that when a Member State was not called upon to make any legislative choices and only had considerably reduced discretion, or even no discretion at all, the mere infringement of Community law could be sufficient to establish the existence of a sufficiently serious breach.[592]

Finally, in Cases C-178/94 etc. *Dillenköfer et al. v. Germany*[593] the Court held that where the Member State had taken no action at all to implement a directive, and the result required by the directive entailed the grant of rights to individuals, the content of those rights being identifiable on the basis of its provisions, and a causal link could be shown between the breach of the obligation to implement the directive and the loss suffered by an individual, the Member State was liable for such loss, without any other conditions having to be taken into consideration. Thus in *Dillenkoffer* the Court clearly placed the facts of *Francovich* clearly within this framework: non-implementation is plainly a sufficiently serious breach of Community law for these purposes.

The message from this case-law is clearly that there is now no hiding place for Member States which manifestly flout their obligations under Community law to respect the rights which individuals are granted under Community law. Individuals are now assured of a means of enforcing their actual rights, as well as rights which they should have had if the Member State had complied with its obligations. Much still remains in the hands of the national courts, and if it becomes clear that they are simply finding every excuse in the book to deny litigants an adequate remedy, the Court will have to express itself in strong terms, as it has done in *Dillenköfer*, in order to offer a realistic hope that national courts will in fact start to

---

590. [1996] ECR I-1631 at 1669 (the Court felt that it had all the necessary elements to assets itself whether there was a sufficiently serious breach of Community law, even though the assessment was in principle a matter for the national court, *ibid.* at 1668. In the circumstances this approach is sensible, as it reduces costs for the parties by ensuring that no time needs to be wasted fighting the issue of seriousness further in the national litigation. See also Cases C-283, 291 and 292/94 *Denkavit International BV et al. v. Bundesamt für Finanzen* [1996] ECR I-5063.
591. [1996] ECR I-2553.
592. *Ibid.* at 2613.
593. [1996] ECR I-4845, [1996] 3 CMLR 469.

award damages without insisting on sending each and every claim to the Court of Justice.

Certainly, it should be remembered that the duty on the national courts to afford effective judicial protection to individual claimants forms part of their general duty to ensure as far as possible the effective application of Community law within their own legal order. Thus, within the limits permmitted by their judicial function, they must ensure that infringements of Community law are penalized under the same substantive and procedural conditions as comparable and equally serious infringements of purely national law (in accordance with the principle of equality). This is, of course subject to the requirement that the remedy must not be practically impossible or extremely difficult to obtain, and if the domestic conditions are less stringent than the Court's criteria, the former must be applied. The penalties must be effective, proportionate and dissuasive in effect (in accordance with the principle of effectiveness). National authorities must also be equally energetic in the pursuit of infringements of Community law as they are in the pursuit of similar national provisions.[594] The duty of the Member States to take the same measures to counter fraud affecting the financial interests of the Community as they take to counter fraud affecting their own financial interests is now specifically expressed in the first paragraph of Article 209a EC.[595]

While in some circumstances the Court's case-law means that restrictions on claims under national law cannot be invoked in respect of Community law claims as they are felt by the Court to make remedies virtually impossible or excessively difficult to obtain (which may perhaps cause the national legislator or judiciary to reassess the merit of persisting with such restrictions in purely domestic situatons), the requirement of effectiveness may sometimes lead to the restriction of the application of rules and principles which tend to protect individual interests. If, for example, the actual application of Community law requires that national measures to safeguard the Community's financial interests have to be enforced within a certain period of time, a Member State may not in infringement proceedings rely on the fact that a decision ordering immediate implementation would have probably have been appealed in the national courts, which might have suspended its operation.[596] The national courts must take account of this.

594. Case 68/88 *Commission v. Greece* [1989] ECR 2965 at 2985. Although this judgment dealt with the duty of a Member State, on the basis of Art. 5 EC the same applies to national courts, on the basis that the national principles of the rule of law permit this. See Widdershoven (1993) NTB (Special issue) 47 and Guldenmond, *Strafrechtelijke Handhaving van Gemeenschapsrecht* (Arnhem, 1992).
595. See, generally, Vervaele, *Fraud against the Community: The Need for European Fraud Legislation* (Deventer, 1992).
596. Case C-217/88 *Commission v. Germany* [1990] ECR I-2879 at 2906. Moreover, a reference for a preliminary ruling could have been made by the national courts.

A good illustration of the tension which can arise in the interaction of Community and national law can be seen in the question of whether, and if so to what extent, general principles of law in national law can be applied if the result would be that insufficient account would be taken of the complete effect of Community law. In so far as such principles, like the protection of legitimate expectations and legal certainty also form part of Community law, there can be scant objection to their being applied by the national court.[597] The case-law of the Court however requires that in the application of these principles the national courts take full account of the Community interest.[598] The case-law of the Court on requiring the repayment of state aids to undertakings granted in breach of Community law is an excellent concrete example of the clash between general principles of national law and ensuring respect of the Community interest. The Court has stated that the recovery of aid unlawfully paid must in principle take place in accordance with the relevant procedural provisions of national law, subject, though, to those provisions being applied in such a way that the recovery which community law requires is not rendered practically impossible.[599] The Member State which has paid the unlawful aid cannot rely on the legitimate expectations of the recipients in order to escape from the duty to take the necessary steps to give effect to a Commission decision ordering it to obtain the repayment of the aid. If it were otherwise, the prohibition on state aids incompatible with the common market, contained in Article 92 EC and the surveillance regime of Article 93 EC would be rendered hopelessly ineffective, shutting the stable door after the horse has bolted, with the Member States in effect able to rely on their own unlawful conduct to deprive Commission decisions of their effectiveness. It remains possible in principle for a recipient undertaking to invoke the legitimate expectation that the aid is lawful, but it will only be very exceptionally that such a claim will have any chance of success, given that the Commission has given widespread publicity to the consequences of accepting unlawful State aid.[600] A prudent undertaking will normally be in a position to ascertain whether the procedure prescribed in Article 93 EC has been followed in respect of state aid granted to it.[601]

597. As to the application of national legal principles in relation to the application of Community law, see the contributions of Kapteyn and Widdershoven (1993) NTB (Special Issue) 38 and 47, and of Kapteyn, De Moor-Van Vugt and Brenninkmeyer in Vervaele (ed.), *Bestuursrechtelijke toepassing en handhaving van Gemeenschapsrecht in Nederland* (Deventer, 1993), and Keus, in Hondius *et al. op. cit.* (see note 537, *supra*).

598. Cases 205–215/82 *Deutsche Milchkontor GmbH et al. v. Germany* [1983] ECR 2633 at 2669. See also Case C-366/95 *Landbrugsministeriet – EF-Direktoratet v. Steff-Houlberg Export I/S et al.* [1998] ECR I-nyr (12 May 1998).

599. This is a long-standing principle, see *e.g.* Case 94/87 *Commission v. Germany* [1989] ECR 175 at 192 and Case C-142/87 *Belgium v. Commission* [1990] ECR I-959 at 1019.

600. O.J. 1983 C 318/3, [1984] 1 CMLR 214. See also O.J. 1995 C 156/5. See, further, Chapter VIII, section 3.2, *post*.

601. For a good overview of the case-law, see Case C-5/89 *Commission v. Germany* [1990]

The application of Community law means that the procedural autonomy of the Member States is far from absolute, as the case-law discussed in this section well demonstrates. The principles of equality and effectiveness require the national courts, informed by the case-law of the Court of Justice, particularly in the context of Article 177 EC, to apply the rules and principles of national law in such a way as to ensure the full application of Community law. Of course, this is subject to the requirement that the national court must not step beyond its judicial function.[602] The national court cannot create new national rules like rabbits pulled out of a hat; what it can and must so is simply apply Community law, as interpreted by the Court of Justice, if necessary setting aside any obstacles arising from national law.[603]

ECR I-3437 at 3456–3458. See also Case C-188/92 *TWD Textilwerke Deggendorf GmbH v. Germany* [1994] ECR I-833 at 852–855; Cases T-244 and 486/93 *TWD Textilwerke Deggendorf GmbH v. Commission* [1995] ECR II-2265 at 2290–2293 (appeal dismissed in Case C-355/95 P *TWD Textilwerke Deggendorf GmbH v. Commission* [1997] ECR I-2549), and Case C-25/95 *Land Rheinland-Pfalz v. Alcan Deutschland GmbH* [1997] ECR I-1591.

602. See Cases C-430 and 431/93 *Van Schijndel et al. v. Stichting Pensioenfonds voor Fysiotherapeuten* [1995] ECR I-4705 at 4738.

603. See, generally, Szyszczak (1996) 21 ELRev. 351; Hoskins (1996) 21 ELRev. 365, and Temple Lang (1997) 22 ELRev. 3.

CHAPTER VII

The establishment of the internal market: the freedoms*

1. INTRODUCTION

The establishment of the internal market and of the common market are fundamentally important for the achievement of the objectives of the EC Treaty, as is apparent from the initial provisions of the EC Treaty itself.[1] In section 4 of Chapter III, above, the establishment of the internal market was placed in the context of the substantive principles; this Chapter examines that phenomenon itself. Article 7a EC describes the internal market as 'an area without internal frontiers in which the free movement of goods, persons, services and capital is ensured in accordance with the provisions of this Treaty.' It thus forms part of the concept of a common market, but is logically distinct from that concept.[2] The Treaty provisions and case-law dealing with these four freedoms, and with the free movement of payments, which forms a fifth freedom, are systematically discussed in the sections that follow below. The emphasis is on the case-law of the Court of Justice, although there is also some discussion of Community secondary legislation, particularly in relation to the free movement of workers and the rights of residence. The central role of the case-law reflects the explosion in the number of judgments interpreting and applying central provisions of the Treaty, such as Articles 30 and 59 EC. While it is trite law that the Court does not hand down academic opinions or deal with hypothetical questions,[3] certain clear lines of approach can be drawn, even

---

* In the fifth Dutch edition this Chapter was revised by K.J.M. Mortelmans. The editor has further revised this Chapter, taking on board those revisions, and taking account of still relevant additions from the last edition, new case-law, literature and developments, as well as adopting a more critical standpoint on certain issues (any difference of views is indicated in the relevant places) or giving a more detailed discussion.
1. As to the internal market, see Arts. 3(c) and 7a–7c EC; as to the common market, see Arts. 2 and 7 EC.
2. See Chapter III, section 4, *ante*.
3. See *e.g.* Case C-83/91 *Meilicke v. ADV/ORGA AG* [1992] ECR I-4871 at 4933–4935.

though it will become apparent that the Court's approach is not always clearly explained in its reasoning and that sometimes it does not even respect its own rules of interpretation of Community legislation.[4] While it is impossible within the confines of this work to deal with the myriad facets of this abundance of judgments, the major principles and issues can certainly be explored.

1.1 The achievement of the internal market

The area without internal frontiers is established through the effect of the principle of freedom, through the principle of mutual acceptance and through harmonized or uniform rules.[5]

The Five Freedoms

As explained above, in addition to the four fundamental freedoms mentioned in Articles 3 and 7a EC, Article 73b EC provides for a fifth freedom, the free movement of payments, in order to achieve the internal market in practice. The five freedoms were realised during the transitional period on the basis of the procedural provisions contained in the Treaty and through directly effective prohibitions on the introduction of new restrictions on these freedoms. The procedural provisions are now of only historical significance since the end of the transitional period on at midnight on 31 December 1969. Since that date all the freedoms (except the free movement of capital which was phrased in different terms in the old Article 67 EEC until the amendments made by the TEU brought it into line with the other freedoms) were guaranteed by Treaty provisions binding on the Member States[6] which are directly effective and can thus be

---

4. This is particularly the case in relation to Arts. 30–36 EC, and sometimes also in relation to the free movement of persons, as will become apparent in the discussion below. A very good insight into the inconsistencies and often clear insights into the approach of the Court can be gained from the opinions of the Advocates General, sometimes involving radical new lines of analysis, see *e.g.* Van Gerven, Adv. Gen. in Case C-145/88 *Torfaen Borough Council v. B & Q plc* [1989] ECR 3851 at 3869 *et seq.* or criticizing the Court's previous stance, see *e.g.* Jacobs, Adv. Gen. in Case C-10/89 *SA CNL-SUCAL NV v. HAG GF AG* [1990] ECR I-3711 at 3727 *et seq.* and Case C-412/93 *Société d'Importation Édouard Leclerc-Siplec v. TF1 Publicité SA et al.* [1995] ECR I-179 at 194 *et seq.*

5. As to the political economy background to these techniques, see Pelkmans in Cappelleti *et al.* (eds.), *Integration through Law* (Vol. 1, Book 1, Berlin, 1986) 318; Pelkmans, *De interne EG-markt voor industriële produkten, Voorstudies en achtergronden* (WRR, V 48, The Hague, 1984) and *ibid.*, *Market Integration in the European Community* (The Hague, 1984).

6. Sometimes complemented by implementing measures adopted during and after the transitional period.

relied upon by private parties in their national courts.[7] Sometimes these provisions can also affect private collective rules.[8] They also apply in principle to the Community itself.[9] Thus the Community Institutions may derogate from the free movement of goods principle only to the extent expressly or implicitly authorized in the Treaty.[10] It is submitted that the same rule must apply in relation to the free movement of persons, the freedom to provide services and the freedom of payments.

In the case of the free movement of persons, a distinction is made between the free movement of workers and the freedom to exercise a trade or profession, the latter being designed to embrace both natural and legal persons. The introduction in Article 8 EC of the concept of citizenship of the Union makes it plain that not only economically active persons fall within the scope of the EC Treaty: every citizen of the Union has as a rule the right to reside freely in the territory of another Member State, and to travel within the Community.[11]

The exceptions to free movement

There are a number of exceptions to the Treaty provisions on the five freedoms; these can be conveniently grouped in three types, of which the first two are economic in nature, and the third as a rule is non-economic in nature. The first group embraces provisions which were of interest only during the transitional period, such as Articles 26 and 226 EC. As has been noted above, these provisions are of historical interest only.

7.   As to the concept of direct effect, see Chapter VI, section 2.2.1, *ante*.
8.   Case 36/74 *Walrave and Koch v. Association Union Cycliste Internationale et al.* [1974] ECR 1405 at 1418–1419.
9.   *E.g.* Cases 80 and 81/77 *Société Les Commissionnaires Réunis Sàrl et al. v. Receveur des Douanes* [1978] ECR 927 at 946–947; Case 37/83 *Rewe-Zentral AG v. Director of the Landwirtschaftskammer Rheinland* [1984] ECR 1229 at 1248–1249; Case 218/82 *Commission v. Council* [1983] ECR 4063 at 4075 and Case 61/86 *United Kingdom v. Commission* [1988] ECR 431 at 462.
10. Cases 80 and 81/77 *Les Commissionnaires Réunis, ibid.* For an example of the Court accepting a barrier to trade (the system of Monetary Compensatory Amounts) as being less damaging to the interests of the Community than diversion of trade caused by monetary factors see Case 9/73 *Schlüter v. Hauptzollamt Lörrach* [1973] ECR 1135 at 1152, 1158 and 1159. Health inspections prescribed under Community provisions are not barriers to trade but are measures designed to remove national inspections which could otherwise be justified under Art. 36 EC, see Case 35/76 *Simmenthal SpA v. Italian Minister for Finance* [1976] ECR 1871 at 1885–1887.
11. In fact this right had been effectively achieved through Community legislation (the so-called June 1990 package of directives, see section 4.1, *post*) and greatly stimulated by judgments such as those in Cases 286/82 and 26/83 *Luisi and Carbone v. Ministero del Tesoro* [1984] ECR 377, [1985] 3 CMLR 52 and Case 186/87 *Cowan v. Trésor public* [1989] ECR 195, [1990] 2 CMLR 613, but Art. 8 EC can be regarded as to a certain degree codifying this case-law.

Analogous provisions have been included in the various Acts of Accession: these too have or will become otiose with the passage of time. The second group comprises economic safeguard clauses and has been revised as a result of the amendments made by the TEU. It covers Article 73e EC dealing with the free movement of capital; Article 103a which deals with economic policy,[12] and denial of Community treatment to goods originating in third countries.[13] The third group comprises provisions the restrictive effect on free movement of which should be limited as much as possible through harmonization or uniform legislation.[14] In addition to these three groups of exceptions, there are a number of specific exceptions relating to public undertakings[15] or certain specific sectors.[16]

Harmonization and uniform legislation

The negative integration provisions which aim to achieve the free movement of goods[17] go in a number of instances hand in hand with acts adopted by the Community Institutions. The abolition of obstacles by one Member State (direct and indirect discrimination) will in many cases be insufficient to achieve an area without internal frontiers. Quality rules for goods (health requirements) and for persons (diplomas) will remain necessary in a number of instances. Dissimilar legislation between Member States causes restrictions or distortions of free movement[18] The Community Institutions are granted powers to adopt harmonization measures or to adopt uniform measures, as in the case of the Community trade mark.[19] Many proposals for Community measures failed to be adopted prior to the coming into force of the SEA on 1 July 1987 because of the maintenance of the requirement of unanimity. To cope with this problem, Article 100a EC permitted harmonization measures for the completion of the internal market to be adopted by qualified majority,

12. As to economic policy, see Chapter IX, section 3.2, *post*. This chapter also deals with temporary balance of payment difficulties (Arts. 109h and 109i EC).
13. Art. 115 EC. As is noted in Chapter XII, *post*, this provision has become something of a dead-letter since the abolition of systematic customs controls at the internal frontiers within the Community.
14. Arts. 36, 48, 56, 66, 73d and 222–224 EC.
15. Arts. 37 and 90(2) EC.
16. Arts. 44 and 46 EC in relation to agriculture; Art. 80 EC in relation to transport.
17. Note the words 'elimination' in Art. 3(a) EC and 'abolition ... of obstacles' in Art. 3 EC.
18. As to distortions of competition, see Chapter VIII, *post*. As to the difference between distortion and discrimination, see Case 14/68 *Walt Wilhelm et al. v. Bundeskartellamt*. [1969] ECR 1, [1969] CMLR 100; Case C-379/92 *Peralta* [1994] ECR I-3453 and Case C-384/93 *Alpine Investments BV v. Minister van Financiën* [1995] ECR I-1141.
19. Reg. 40/94 (O.J. 1994 L 11/1, amended by Reg. 3288/94 (O.J. 1994 L 349/83), implemented by Reg. 2868/95 (O.J. 1995 L 303/1).

although the price for this was the inclusion of Article 100a(4). The more supple approach in Article 100a(4) meant that by the target date of the end of 1992 most of the some 300 proposals presented by the Commission as part of its internal market programme[20] had been approved by the Council. As a result of this legislative operation a number of exceptions may no longer be relied upon, or relied upon only in very limited circumstances.[21] In many cases, though, harmonization is still incomplete, so that Community law has not completely occupied the field, and primary Community law in terms of the free movement principle and the recognized exceptions to it may still be invoked in the unoccupied areas.[22] The most important Community measures (positive integration) in the different policy areas are mentioned in the course of this Chapter, but reference should be made to section 2 of Chapter VIII, below, for a systematic discussion of harmonization.

The mutual acceptance principle

The far-reaching failures in the years 1970–1986 of the attempts to adopt Community measures were partially compensated by the case-law of the Court of Justice on the mutual recognition of national rules, in which the celebrated judgment in *Cassis de Dijon* is something of a landmark.[23] While it is often mistakenly opined that the Court in that judgment *introduced* the 'rule of reason' in the form of case-law exceptions to the principle of Article 30 EC[24] as a counterbalance to the broad interpretation

20. *Completing the Internal Market* (COM (85) 310 Final).
21. *E.g.* Art. 36 EC, see Case 5/77 *Tedeschi v. Denkavit Commerciale srl* [1977] ECR 1555 at 1576–1577; Case 148/78 *Pubblico Ministero v. Ratti* [1979] ECR 1629 at 1644; Case 815/79 *Cremoni and Vrankovich* [1980] ECR 3583 at 3607; *cf.* Art. 100a(4) EC.
22. *I.e.* in the areas not covered by Community action, see *e.g.* Case 72/83 *Campus Oil Ltd. et al. v. Minister for Industry and Energy et al.* [1984] ECR 2727 at 2749–2751 and Case 227/82 *Van Bennekom* [1983] ECR 3883 at 3904–3905. In such cases there is an additional duty, by virtue of Art. 5 EC, to abstain from any action which would jeopardize the effectiveness of such Community measures as have been adopted. See, further, section 3.6, *post*.
23. Case 120/79 *Rewe-Zentral AG v. Bundesmonopolverwaltung für Branntwein* [1979] ECR 649, [1979] 3 CMLR 337. See the Commission's Communication (O.J. 1980 C 256/2) and Mattera (1980) RMC 505; Slot (1981) SEW 174 at 176; Timmermans (1981) SEW 381; Barents (1981) 18 CMLRev. 271 at 296; Gormley (1981) 6 ELRev. 454; Capelli (1981) RMC 421, and Mattera (1992) RMUE 13. The mutual recognition principle was also formulated a month before the judgment in *Cassis* in Cases 110 and 111/78 *Ministère Public et al. v. Van Wesemael and Follachio* [1979] ECR 35 at 52–53.
24. The term 'mandatory requirements' was new, but the 'rule of reason' by way of case-law (as opposed to exceptions by way of Treaty provisions) was not, see Case 8/74 *Procureur du Roi v. Dassonville et al.* [1974] ECR 837 at 852. (*Contra*, apparently, Mortelmans in the 5th Dutch edition of this work (1995) 349). As to the rule of reason exceptions, see section 3.3.3, *post*.

of Article 30 EC,[25] the central novelty in that judgment is in fact the development of the concept of mutual acceptance (mutual recognition) of goods as a positive gloss upon the wording of Article 30 EC itself. This mutual acceptance principle means that Member State A must admit goods or services coming from Member State B to its territory, if those goods or services have been lawfully produced or marketed according to the rules applicable in Member State B.[26] Member State A may hinder the free movement of such goods only on the grounds of overriding public interest requirements, being either those recognized in the rule of reason case-law or expressly in the EC Treaty itself. While the mutual acceptance principle has played an essential role in achieving free movement without the need for harmonization, and has undoubtedly led to a lightening of the legislative burden, it is not without problems. Thus the limits of mutual recognition have been signalled occasionally in the case-law,[27] and it appears that this home state (or origin) principle[28] leads to competition between legal systems.[29] In sensitive areas, such as health protection, the Community still adopts harmonization measures, but dealing with the essential requirements which have to be protected.[30] In these areas there is a danger that too broad an interpretation of the mutual acceptance principle would lead to a reduction in the national standards.[31] In its internal market programme[32] the Commission consciously presented the mutual acceptance principle as a new strategy.[33] Depending on the subject-

25. See Case 8/74 *Dassonville, ibid.*
26. See Gormley, *Prohibiting Restrictions on Trade within the EEC* (Amsterdam, 1985) 48 and Chalmers (1994) 19 ELRev. 385 at 395–396, and Case 59/82 *Schutzverband gegen Unwesen in der Wirtschaft v. Weinvertriebs GmbH* [1983] ECR 1217, Case 27/80 *Fietje* [1980] ECR 3839 at 3855 and Case 220/81 *Robertson* [1982] ECR 2349 at 2361. Yet the Court still often speaks, as it did in *Cassis* [1979] ECR 649 at 664 of goods 'lawfully produced and marketed.' See also O'Connor (1993) EFLR 177.
27. See Case 188/84 *Commission v. France* [1986] ECR 419 and Case C-293/93 *Houtwipper* [1994] ECR I-4249.
28. See Roth (1995) ZHR 78 at 85 and 91.
29. See Koopmans (1992) SEW 446 and Reich (1992) 29 CMLRev. 861.
30. This was signalled in the Commission's Communication (see note 23, *supra*) and again in the White Paper COM (85) 310 Final, para. 39. See Chapter VIII, section 2.1, *post.*
31. This view surfaced principally in the German literature (and indeed the fear was expressed by many consumer groups, although they later generally accepted that this resembled reports of Mark Twain's death), see Steindorff (1984) ZHR 338; Sedemund in Schwarze (ed.), *Der Gemeinsame Markt Bestand und Zukunft in wirtschaftlicher Perspektive* (Baden-Baden, 1987) 37. But particularly in the field of medicinal products the genuine nature of this concern was acknowledged by the Court, see Case C-320/93 *Lucien Ortscheit GmbH v. Eurim-Pharm Arzneimittel GmbH* [1994] ECR I-5243 at 5265.
32. See note 20, *supra.*
33. See, generally, Bardenhewer and Pipkorn in Von der Groeben *et al.* (eds.), *Kommentar zum EU-/EG-Vertrag* (5th ed., Baden-Baden, 1997) Vol. I 295–343; Bieber *et al.* (eds.), *1992: One European Market?* (Baden-Baden, 1988); Behrens, *Rechtsfragen der grensü-berschreitenden Umstrukturierung von Unternehmen im Binnenmarkt* (Bonn, 1993), and

matter involved, the internal market is achieved through mutual acceptance or through harmonized or uniform rules.[34]

1.2 The incomplete internal market

While 1992 was undoubtedly an important milestone in the history of the Community, and the old Article 8a EEC (now Article 7a EC) required the completion of the internal market by 31 December 1992, it was neither in law nor in fact completed by that date.[35] The growing pains examined below are still evident

Domestic market and reverse discrimination

If all relevant aspects of an economic activity occur within one Member State and there are no relevant provisions of Community secondary legislation which are applicable, the Court of Justice will find that the matter concerns a purely internal situation, which means that the provisions of Articles 48, 52 and 59 EC may not be relied upon.[36] In such

Gormley (1989/1) LIEI 9. See also Stuyck, *De Europese Interne Markt, de Lid-Staten, de Marktdeelnemers en de Burgers* (Brussels, 1988); Schwarze and Schermers (eds.), *Structure and Dimensions of European Community Policy* (Baden-Baden, 1988); Pelkmans, *The Internal EC-market for Industrial Products* (WRR, The Hague, 1985) (in Dutch as *De interne EG-markt voor industriële produkten*); the WRR report No. 28, *The Unfinished European Integration* (The Hague, 1986) (in Dutch as *De onvoltooide Europese Integratie*); Cecchini, *The European Challenge, 1992* (Aldershot, 1988) and associated reports and COM (88) 650 final. See, further, the Sutherland Report, *The Internal Market after 1992 – meeting the challenge* SEC (92) 2277, and the Commission's Communications COM (93) 256 Final, COM (93) 361 Final, COM (96) 520 Final, and the *Action Plan for the Single Market* CSE (97) 1 Final.

34. Progress may be traced through the internal market rubric in the monthly Bull. EU and in the annual reports on the internal market (for 1995 see COM (96) 51 Final). See also, more generally, COM (96) 520 Final. In respect of Cassis de Dijon, Community legislation now governs the matter, see Reg. 1576/89 (O.J. 1989 L 160/1, most recently amended by the Act of Austrian, Finnish and Swedish Accession (1994) and by Reg. 3378/94 (O.J. 1994 L 366/1)).

35. See Koopmans (1989) *RM Themis* 472 and (1994) ZHR 149.

36. See *e.g.* Case 175/78 R. v. *Saunders* [1979] ECR 1129 at 1135 (Art. 48 EC); Cases C-29–35/94 *Aubertin et al.* [1995] ECR I-301 at 316; Case C-60/91 *Batista Morais* [1992] ECR I-2085 at 2105 (Arts. 52 and 59 EC); Case 52/79 *Procureur du Roi v. Debauve et al.* [1980] ECR 833 at 855 (Art. 59 EC), and Case C-134/95 *Unità Socio-Sanitaria Locale No 47 di Biella (USSL) v. Instituto Nazionale per l'Assicurazione contro gli Infortuni sul Lavoro* [1997] ECR I-195 at 210 (in relation to Arts. 48, 52 and 59 EC). In relation to taxation and Art. 52 EC, see Case C-112/91 *Werner v. Finanzamt Aachen-Innenstadt* [1993] ECR I-429 at 470, which is, it is submitted, highly unsatisfactory from the viewpoint of Community nationals who may wish to reside in another Member State while working in their home Member State, and should be revisited in

situations a person or product may well suffer from reverse discrimination, but the Court has consistently found that Community law does not prevent a Member State from treating national products or its own citizens less favourably than imported products or persons who make use of their rights of free movement.[37]

U-turn constructions

A person or a product in Member State A may benefit from the rules on free movement if he or she has performed activities in Member State B or if the product was in circulation in Member State B. If a Dutch national exercises his or her right of free movement by, say, exercising his profession in Belgium, and later wishes to exercise that profession in The Netherlands, he or she is a beneficiary of Community rights. This is not an internal situation and he or she may exercise his or her profession in The Netherlands under the same conditions as a Belgian who wishes to exercise that profession in The Netherlands.[38] This case-law gave rise to the application of U-turn constructions. In many cases a product returns to its home Member State after 'residence' in another. The purpose of this operation is to escape stricter national rules on matters such as minimum prices or establishment requirements by using Articles 30 EC (goods) or 59 EC (services). The Court will not permit these provisions to be relied upon if it appears from objective circumstances that the goods or services were

view of the clear expansion of rights of residence for Community nationals (through the June 1990 package of directives, discussed in section 4.1, *post*), although the Court has held that Art. 8 EC, establishing citizenship of the Union, does not extend the scope *ratione materiae* of the Treaty to embrace purely internal situations having no link with Community law, see Cases C-64 and 65/96 *Land Nordrhein-Westfalen v. Uecker* [1997] ECR I-3171 at 3190. As to Art. 30 EC, see now Cases C-321–324/94 *Pistre et al.* [1997] ECR I-2343 at 2374, and Jarvis, *The Application of EC Law by National Court: The Free Movement of Goods*, Oxford, 1998) Chap. 5. For a rather broader interpretation, see Case C-41/90 *Höfner and Elser v. Macrotron GmbH* [1991] ECR I-1979 at 2020 and Cases C-363 and 407–411/93 *René Lancry SA et al. v. Direction Générale des Douanes et al.* [1994] ECR I-3957 at 3991–3992.

37. See *e.g.* Case 86/78 *SA des Grandes Distilleries Peureux v. Directeur des Services Fiscaux de la Haute Saône et du Territoire du Belfort* [1979] ECR 897 at 914; Cases 35 and 36/82 *Morson et al. v. State of the Netherlands et al.* [1982] ECR 3723 at 3735–3736; Case 355/85 *Driancourt v. Cognet* [1986] ECR 3231 at 3242; Case 308/86 *Ministère public v. Lambert* [1986] ECR 4369 at 4392. See further, Kewenig (1990) JZ 20; König (1993) AöR 591; Meier (1987) RIW 841; Mortelmans (1979) SEW 654; Pickup (1986) 23 CMLRev. 135; Schilling (1994) JZ 8, and Schöne (1989) RIW 450. But see also Cases C-321–324/94 *Pistre et al.* [1997] ECR I-2343 at 2374.

38. Case 115/78 *Knoors v. Secretary of State for Economic Affairs* [1979] ECR 399 at 409–410; Case 246/80 *Broekmeulen v. Huisarts Registratie Commissie* [1981] ECR 2311 at 2329–2330. In both of these cases there was a Community act facilitating mutual recognition of the qualifications concerned.

exported simply in order to be reimported and thereby to escape a legal requirement with which they would otherwise have had to comply.[39] There have, though, been instances of United Kingdom nationals who wished to marry third country spouses circumventing the Home Office's traditionally distrustful attitude to what it saw as often 'arranged' marriages designed to obtain residence rights for the spouse in question, by going to The Netherlands to work or practise a profession for a reasonable period (such as six months), marrying there and returning with the spouse to the United Kingdom. As they were now persons who had exercised their Community rights, the spouse could not be denied residence in the United Kingdom.[40]

EC market participants

For persons there is a specific problem as to whether the internal market concept means that a national of Member State A who works in Member State B has a right of residence in Member State C. The Court has not as yet answered this question, but it may be approached in two ways. On the one hand the right of residence may be linked to the place of work. A Portuguese national working in the United Kingdom could obtain a residence permit in the United Kingdom but not in The Netherlands.[41] On the other hand a teleological approach may be taken. Thus the purpose of the EC Treaty is to create an internal market without internal frontiers, and market participants should not be punished for taking advantage of the possibilities which are thus presented. On this approach the Portuguese national would be entitled to a residence permit in The Netherlands. In fact the general right of residence would now make this possible under certain conditions,[42] but even without that directive there

39. Case 229/83 *Association des Centres distributeurs Édouard Leclerc et al.* v. *Sàrl 'Au blé vert' et al.* [1985] ECR 1 at 35; Case C-370/90 *R.* v. *Immigration Appeal Tribunal and Singh, ex parte Secretary of State for the Home Department* [1992] ECR I-4265 at 4295, and Case C-23/93 *TV 10 SA* v. *Commissariaat voor de Media* [1994] ECR I-4795 at 4832–4833.
40. See Case C-370/90 *R.* v. *Immigration Appeal Tribunal and Singh, ex parte Secretary of State for the Home Department* [1992] ECR I-4265 at 4293–4295 which explains the Community provisions concerned. Clearly the burden of proving that any marriage is a sham must, as a matter of Community law, fall on the immigration authorities who seek to argue that there is an abuse of the rights conferred by Community law. See also the Council's Resolution (O.J. 1997 C 382/1) and Case C-336/94 *Dafeki* v. *Landesversicherungsanstalt Württemberg* [1997] ECR I-6761.
41. This approach was taken by the Dutch Hoge Raad (1994) NJ no. 743.
42. Dir. 90/364 (O.J. 1990 L 180/26), Art. 1(1). This directive applies to those nationals of Member States who do not enjoy the right of residence under other provisions of Community law; they and their families must be covered by sickness insurance in respect of all risks in the host Member State and have sufficient resources to avoid becoming a burden on that State's social assistance system during their period of residence, *ibid.*

are certain pillars to support such an interpretation in the case-law of the Court of Justice.[43]

1.3 The concept of freedom

The term 'free movement' for the achievement of the internal market in Article 7a EC begs the general question of what the concept of freedom implies. In the present context of state regulation of inter-state movements of goods, persons or services the freedom concept can have three main connotations.[44] The practical importance of this distinction is enormous. With acceptance of the first freedom concept the Member States are far more restricted in what they may do than is the case with the other two concepts. With acceptance of the second freedom concept, for example, restrictions on imports can be prohibited which, because no domestic production exists, do not give rise to discrimination in the sense of the third freedom concept. The distinction is also important for the right of the Member States to invoke exceptions to those prohibitions. As a rule of thumb, a broad scope of the principle of freedom opens the possibility that more exceptions will be permissible than in the case of a limited scope of the prohibition involved in that principle. The rule of reason case-law is an example of this.[45]

Discriminatory and equally applicable measures (first concept of freedom)

First, freedom is sought to be achieved by prohibiting, at least in principle, the Member States from adopting (or maintaining in force) any measure which, whether exclusively or not, touches on inter-state trade and makes inter-state trade more difficult or distorts it. In this sense – a sense which greatly restricts the law-making powers of the Member States – the freedom concept is found in the American Constitution in the Commerce Clause.[46] In this widest sense it is immaterial whether the measures

43. Case C-113/89 *Rush Portugesa Lda v. Office national d'immigration* [1990] ECR I-1417 at 1444–1445; Case C-308/89 *Di Leo v. Land Berlin* [1990] ECR I-4185 at 4208–4209; Case C-419/92 *Scholz v. Opera Universitaria di Cagliari et al.* [1994] ECR I-505 at 521–522, and Case C-43/93 *Vander Elst v. Office des Migrations Internationales* [1994] ECR I-3803 at 3823–3826.
44. As to the distinction between discrimination and permissible differentiation, see Timmermans (1982) SEW 426; Lenaerts (1991) CDE 14, and Schockweiler (1991) *Rivista di Diritto Europeo* 12.
45. See section 1.4, *post*.
46. See, generally, Tribe, *American Constitutional Law* (2nd ed., Mineola, 1988) 305–317 and Chapter 6 and Sandalow and Stein (eds.), *Courts and Free Markets* (Oxford, 1982).

concerned affect only inter-state commerce (discriminatory measures) or both domestic and inter-state commerce (equally applicable measures). Even prohibition of the sale of already imported products or prohibition of transport by out-of-state (foreign) lorries is caught by this wide concept of freedom. The same is true even when these prohibitions are applied to comparable domestic situations. The question whether only discriminatory measures fall under the 'free movement' concept, or whether that concept also embraces equally applicable measures[47] is of major importance in the interpretation and application of the prohibitions on measures having equivalent effect to quantitative restrictions on imports[48] and on restrictions on the freedom to provide services.[49]

Measures exclusively affecting movement in or out of national territory (second concept of freedom)

In the second concept the principle of free movement may mean that the Member States may not adopt (or maintain in force) freedom-restricting provisions which exclusively concern importation or exportation (or, in relation to nationals of other Member States, immigration or emigration). The difference from the first concept of freedom is that, for example, measures which affect imports and exports as well as the domestic market are not caught. This second concept plays an important part in the interpretation and application of the prohibitions of customs duties on imports and exports[50] and of measures having an equivalent effect on exports.[51]

National treatment (third concept of freedom)

Finally, the freedom principle may be a pure and simple application of the principle of non-discrimination on grounds of nationality of origin of destination.[52] The general principle of the prohibition of discrimination on ground of nationality, contained in Article 6 EC, can only be applied autonomously in situations covered by Community law in respect of which the EC Treaty does not provide for specific prohibitions of discrimination.[53] This is the case in relation to the prohibition of fiscal discrimination in

47. Sometimes called indistinctly applicable measures.
48. Art. 30 EC, see section 3.3.3, *post*.
49. Art. 59 EC, see section 7.4.2, *post*.
50. Arts. 12 and 16 EC, see section 2.4.1, *post*.
51. Art. 34 EC, see section 3.2.3, *post*.
52. See Chapter III, section 5.3, *ante*.
53. *E.g.* Case C-179/90 *Merci convenzionali porto di Genova SpA v. Siderurgica Gabrielli SpA* [1991] ECR I-5889 at 5927 and Case 18/93 *Corsica Ferries Italia Srl v. Corpo dei Piloti del Porto di Genova* [1994] ECR I-1783 at 1819–1820.

Articles 95–97 EC and the free movement of persons in Articles 48 and 52 EC. This national treatment concept now appears to be rather more broadly interpreted in the case-law concerning Articles 48, 52 and 95 EC, so that it is moving in the direction of the First Concept set out above.[54]

1.4   Types of barriers to free movement

The obstacles caused by actions of the Member States are of various types: those discussed in this Chapter are tariff and non-tariff barriers and fiscal barriers.[55] Other obstacles, such as state aids and those arising through private anti-competitive behaviour, are discussed in Chapter VIII, below. The obstacles examined here are dealt with in various places in the EC Treaty. In general there is a stricter system in Articles 9–29 EC for tariff barriers and in Articles 30–37 EC for non-tariff barriers than there is in Articles 95–99 EC for fiscal barriers: the first two types of barriers have to be removed, save where an exception may be relied upon; but fiscal systems have to be applied in a non-discriminatory manner.

These various approaches work through into the case-law of the Court of Justice. If cattle are subjected to veterinary checks and a fee is charged for the examination, the examination and the fee fall within the ambit of different provisions of the Treaty. Examinations on export are considered under Article 34 EC, but the fee is considered under Article 16 EC. Examination on importation is assessed under Article 30 EC but the fee is examined under Article 12 EC. An examination fee cannot be justified on the basis of an exception which justifies the examination itself, although if both result from Community measures (as opposed to unilateral national measures) they will both be governed in the first instance by those Community measures.[56]

1.5   External aspects of the internal market

In the analysis of the various obstacles to free movement a distinction should be drawn between intra-Community movement and movement between a Member State and a third country.[57] The rules which apply in

---

54. See sections 2.5.1, 5.3.1 and 6.5.1, *post*.
55. As to a systematic analysis and comparison between EC law and GATT rules, see Tumlir in Hilf *et al.* (eds.), *GATT und die Europäische Gemeinschaft* (Baden-Baden, 1986) 87.
56. Case 46/76 *Bauhuis v. The Netherlands State* [1977] ECR 5 at 15, 17–18 and 20.
57. The free movement of goods principle benefits goods originating in the Community and goods from third countries placed in free circulation in a Member State, Art. 9(2) EC. As to the meaning of free circulation, see Art. 10(1) EC.

respect of the European Economic Area (EEA) are very similar to those applicable within the Community itself.[58] Individual rules govern the freedom of movement between the Community and other third countries: they are connected with *inter alia* the characteristics of the freedoms themselves (a service is more moveable than most persons) and with the international arrangements (such as the GATT or the GATS), which vary according to the factor of production concerned. The WTO and the agreements it administers in any case only embrace goods and services, not the movement of persons.

Now that the internal market has in legal terms been achieved, and in theory controls at the internal frontiers of the Member States within the Community are no longer possible, the Community's external frontier has become of crucial importance. It is thus of major significance to indicate which persons, goods, services and capital are permitted in the Community's internal market and subject to what conditions. This Chapter examines this dimension briefly, although reference should also be made to Chapter XII, below, for a more detailed discussion.[59]

1.6 Main themes of this Chapter

There are a number of main themes running through this Chapter, which are more or less visible at different points, but it may be useful to note them here.

Crucial role of the Court of Justice

In fact the achievement of the internal market is based in the first instance on the effect of a number of pivotal negative integration provisions[60] and their interpretation by the Court of Justice. An increasing number of market participants have been relying on these provisions, so that in myriad preliminary rulings on references under Article 177 EC the Court had to give an (indirect) answer to the question whether a particular national provision was incompatible with the directly effective prohibition provisions of the EC Treaty or fell under one of the exceptions known to Community law, even in circumstances in which the rules at first sight had nothing to do with obstacles to the free movement of goods or services.[61] The Court has interpreted the free movement rules widely (so that equally applicable

---

58. As to the EEA, see Chapter XII, section 4.2.2, *post.*
59. See also Eekhout, *The European Internal Market and International Trade: A Legal Analysis* (Oxford, 1994).
60. Arts. 12, 30, 48, 52, 59, 67, 73b and 95 EC.
61. *Cf.* Cases C-267 and 268/91 *Keck and Mithouard* [1993] ECR I-6097 at 6131.

measures also fall under the prohibitions) and the exceptions narrowly.[62] Yet this case-law is continually in movement and may be expected to develop further.[63] Indeed the Court has sought to place a number of national rules which are not intended to govern trade between Member States but do have an impact on it outside the scope of Article 30 EC.[64] It is possible to see this in terms of a judicial application of the principle of subsidiarity.[65]

The assimilation of the freedoms and exceptions

Under the influence of the case-law of the Court there has been a growing unity in the effect of the prohibitions as well as of the exceptions.[66] However, important differences continue to exist, as will become apparent from an analysis of the different freedoms. The qualification of a situation as involving establishment or the provision of services, and the question whether a measure is discriminatory or equally applicable are just two of the issues in respect of which it is important to know which article of the Treaty applies and which line of case-law is applicable in a given case. The judgment in Case C-384/93 *Alpine Investments BV v. Minister van Financiën*[67] illustrates this well: through a wide interpretation of Article 59 EC, confirming that measures applicable irrespective of the destination of the service fell under the prohibition, the case-law on goods in such circumstances developed under Article 34 EC[68] has been brought into question.

The starting point for the assimilation of the prohibitions is certainly the Court of Justice's case-law on Article 30 EC. The wide equally-applicable definition (corrsponding to the first concept of freedom explained in

62. Art. 36 EC is thus not expanded to embrace matters other than those expressly mentioned, and the proportionality principle is applied, see section 3.1, *post*.
63. *E.g.* the case-law on measures applicable irrespective of the destination of a product under Art. 34 EC following and that on local regulation of socio-economic life (selling practices) following Cases C-267 and 268/91 *Keck and Mithouard* [1993] ECR I-6097, [1995] 1 CMLR 101.
64. *E.g.* Cases C-267 and 268/91 *Keck and Mithouard* [1993] ECR I-6097, [1995] 1 CMLR 101. This point was also mentioned in a number of earlier judgments, but the intention to regulate inter-state trade is not a necessary condition for a measure to be capable of hindering trade between Member States; if intention had been necessary the Commission could never have won the *Reinheitsgebot* judgments (Case 176/84 *Commission v. Greece* [1987] ECR 1193, [1988] 1 CMLR 813 and Case 178/84 *Commission v. Germany* [1987] ECR 1227, [1988] 1 CMLR 780).
65. Lendaerts and Van Ypersele (1994) CDE 3 at 18–19, *cf.* Müller-Graf (1995) ZHR 34.
66. See Behrens (1992) EuR 145.
67. [1995] ECR I-1141, [1995] 2 CMLR 209.
68. Case 15/79 *P.B. Groenveld BV v. Produktschap voor Vee en Vlees* [1979] ECR 3409, [1981] 1 CMLR 207.

section 1.3, above) of *Dassonville*[69] and *Cassis de Dijon*[70] has gradually been taken over in the interpretation of Article 59 EC. So far the approach to the prohibitions contained in Articles 48 and 52 EC has been more limited.[71] The same applied to Article 67 EEC in relation to the free movement of capital. The changes introduced by the SEA, particularly in what is now Article 7a EC, which gives the definition of the internal market, and the new provisions on the free movement of capital,[72] introduced by the TEU, provide incitations to a further assimilation of the prohibitions. Article 30 EC has also acted as a catalyst for the assimilation of the exceptions, as the rule of reason exceptions formulated in *Cassis de Dijon*[73] for the free movement of goods have been accepted also in relation to the freedom to provide services.[74] They are also gradually finding their way into the free movement of persons.[75] Article 73d EC, inserted by the TEU, shows similarities with Articles 48(3) and 56 EC.

1.7 Plan of this Chapter and its place in the scheme of this work

The various freedoms are systematically discussed in separate sections. First, the prohibition is discussed, then the exceptions. Attention then turns to measures of positive integration in the field concerned, discussing the most important secondary legislation, and, finally, there follows a brief discussion of the external dimension.

In relation to the free movement of goods, tariff and non-tariff barriers are separately examined in sections 2 and 3 below respectively. The treatment of free movement of persons sets out from the concept of citizenship in section 4, moving on to the free movement of workers in section 5, and the freedom of establishment of legal and natural persons in section 6, below. The freedom to provide services is examined in section 7 and the free movement of capital and payments in section 8, below.

This Chapter develops a number of substantive principles which were examined in Chapter III, above. The emphasis lies on tariff and non-tariff

---

69. Case 8/74 *Procureur du Roi v. Dassonville et al.* [1974] ECR 847 at 852.
70. Case 120/78 *Rewe Zentral AG v. Bundesmonopolverwaltung für Branntwein* [1979] ECR 649 at 664.
71. See Moitinho de Almeida in Rosenløv *et al.* (eds.), *Festskrift til Ole Due* (Copenhagen, 1994) 241.
72. Art. 73b EC.
73. [1979] ECR 649 at 662.
74. *Cf. ibid.* with Case C-353/89 *Commission v. The Netherlands* [1991] ECR I-4069 at 4094.
75. *E.g.* Case C-379/87 *Groener v. Minister for Education et al.* [1989] ECR 3967 at 3993–3994; Case C-340/89 *Vlassopoulou v. Ministerium für Justiz, Bundes- und Europaangelegenheiten Baden-Württemberg* [1991] ECR I-2357 at 2384–2385, and Case C-19/92 *Kraus v. Land Baden-Württemberg* [1993] ECR I-1663 at 1696–1698.

obstacles to trade between Member States stemming from national authorities or other bodies for whose acts they are in Community law responsible. Distortions of competition by undertakings, which the EC Treaty combats in Articles 85–89 EC, or by Member States in favour of certain undertakings, which are dealt with in Articles 92–94 EC, are discussed in Chapter VIII, below.

There is a clear link between this Chapter and Chapters XI on sectoral policy and XII on horizontal and flanking policies. Goods, services and persons falling under a special regime are as a rule also covered by the system of the internal market. Specific rules also often apply. In the horizontal and flanking policies the rules on free movement are also applicable in a number of instances. Given that those areas are non-economic policy areas, the Member states will continually seek to invoke exceptions on grounds such as the protection of the environment, of culture, health and so on. These national rules are in many instances simply disproportionate to the non-economic policy objective concerned, and will have to be adjusted to the prohibitions laid down.

2. FREE MOVEMENT OF GOODS: TARIFF BARRIERS AND FISCAL BARRIERS

2.1 The concept of goods

Articles 9–37 EC use the terms 'goods' and 'products' interchangeably, and these terms are not themselves defined in the EC Treaty.[76] In Case 7/68 *Commission v. Italy*[77] the Court defined goods as 'products which can be valued in money and which are capable, as such, of forming the subject of commercial transactions.' However, it is not necessary that goods should be imported in a commercial context in order that they may benefit from the principle of free movement.[78] In Case C-2/90 *Commission v. Belgium*[79] the Court examined whether recyclable or non-recyclable waste constituted 'goods' for the purposes of the EC Treaty. It had no difficulty in accepting the undisputed view that recyclable and reusable waste had 'an intrinsic commercial value, possibly after being treated' and thus was covered. In relation to non-recyclable and non-reusable waste the Court noted that 'objects which are shipped across a frontier for the purposes of commercial

---

76. This distinction is also found in *e.g.* the Dutch, French, Italian, Portuguese and Spanish texts, but in the German and Danish texts the same word (*Waren* and *varer*, respectively) is used.
77. [1968] ECR 423 at 428 (the *First Art. Treasures* judgment).
78. Case 34/79 *R. v. Henn and Darby* [1979] ECR 3795 at 3827, *per* Warner, Adv. Gen.; Gormley, *op. cit.* (see note 26, *supra*) 2; Case 215/87 *Schumacher v. Hauptzollamt Frankfurt-am-Main-Ost* [1989] ECR 617.
79. [1992] ECR I-4431 at 4478–4479.

transactions are subject to Article 30, whatever the nature of those transactions.[80] This definition is wider as there 'valued in money' is no longer mentioned. The Court treats electricity as falling within this wide concept of goods.[81]

Specific rules govern drugs,[82] counterfeit money,[83] weapons and strategic goods.[84] There are special rules for agricultural products falling within the scope of Article 38(1) EC.[85] Save as otherwise provided in the Agriculture Title of the EC Treaty, the rules on the establishment of the common market apply to agricultural products just as to all other products.[86] Annexes to the ECSC and Euratom Treaties state the products which fall within the ambit of those treaties.[87] The Europol Drugs Unit has been charged with the exchange of information and analysis of data and intelligence on illegal trade in drugs, motor vehicles and radioactive and nuclear materials.[88]

There are demarcation problems with the other freedoms. In Case 7/78 *R. v. Thompson et al.*[89] The Court found that coins which were legal tender in a Member State or which were treated as being equivalent to currency on the money markets of those member States which allowed dealings in them were not goods, although coins which were no longer legal tender but which could still be exchanged at the national Central Bank were goods.[90] There have also been demarcation problems between

80. The Court thus followed the approach taken by the American Supreme Court in *Philadelphia v. New Jersey* 437 US 617, 98 S.Ct. 2531 (1978), affirmed in *Chemical Waste Management Inc. v. Hunt* 504 US 334 (1992). See also Case C-324/93 *R. v. Secretary of State for the Home Department, ex parte Evans Medical Ltd. et al.* [1995] ECR I-563 at 604.
81. Case 6/64 *Costa v. ENEL* [1964] ECR 585 at 597–598; Case C-393/92 *Gemeente Almelo et al. v. Energiebedrijf Ijsselmij NV* [1994] ECR I-1477 at 1516. See Andersen (1994/2) LIEI 49
82. Case 50/80 *Horvath v. Hauptzollamt Hamburg-Jonas* [1981] ECR 385, [1982] 2 CMLR 522; Case 294/82 *Einberger v. Hauptzollamt Freiburg* [1984] ECR 1177, [1985] 1 CMLR 765; Case 289/86 *Vereniging Happy Family v. Inspecteur der Omzetbelasting* [1988] ECR 3655, [1989] 3 CMLR 743.
83. Case C-343/89 *Witzemann v. Hauptzollamt München-Mitte* [1990] ECR I-447.
84. See Art. 223 EC and Gormley in Vaughan (ed.), *Law of the European Communities Service* (London, loose-leaf since 1990) Vol. 3, Part 12, para. 562. See further, Case C-367/89 *Richardt et al.* [1991] ECR I-4621.
85. Which extends the common market to agriculture and trade in agricultural products.
86. Art. 38(2) EC.
87. See Case C-128/92 *H.J. Banks & Co. Ltd. v. British Coal Corporation* [1994] ECR I-1209 and Case 36/83 *Mabanaft GmbH v. Hauptzollamt Emmerich* [1984] ECR 2497 at 2523.
88. Joint Action 95/73 (O.J. 1995 L 62/1), adopted on the basis of Art. K.3(2)(b) TEU. See WQs E-1971/94 and E-1977/94 (Smith) O.J. 1995 C 81/3.
89. [1978] ECR 2247, [1979] 1 CMLR 47.
90. [1978] ECR 2247 at 2274–2275. The coins treated as currency were Krugerrands, which were legal tender in South Africa. As to the sequel to this case, see *Allgemeine Gold- und Silberscheideanstalt v. H.M. Customs and Excise* [1980] 2 WLR 555, [1980] 1

the concepts of 'goods' and 'services' in relation to roadworthiness tests,[91] lotteries,[92] and in the media sector. In this latter area, the Court found in Case 155/73 *Sacchi*[93] that transmissions of television signals, including advertising fell under the ambit of services, but that 'trade in material sound recordings, films, apparatus and other products used for the diffusion of television signals' fell within the definition of 'goods.'[94] Demarcation problems may also arise between the free movement of goods and the free movement of persons, particularly in the case of movement of human mortal remains.[95]

2.2   The customs union as the foundation of the Community

Article 9 EC provides that the Community is based upon a customs union covering all trade in goods and comprising the prohibition, as between Member States, of customs duties on imports and exports and all charges having equivalent effect as well as the adoption of a common customs tariff for their relations with third countries. The principle of a customs union, as expressed in Article 9(2) EC, requires that free movement of goods within that union be ensured across the whole spectrum, embracing also movement between the regions of the Community and not merely trade between the Member States.[96] As will become apparent, a common customs tariff also necessitates on a number of points a common, and on other points a harmonized customs law. As regards customs duties of course it also entails the necessity of a common commercial policy vis-à-vis third countries.

Although the right of free transit of goods within the Community is not expressly conferred in the EC Treaty, the Court has always acknowledged the existence of such a principle. The Member States are prohibited from imposing transit dues or other levies in connection with transit on goods transported through their territory.[97]

CMLR 488. See, further, Cases C-358 and 416/93 *Bordessa et al.* [1995] ECR I-361 at 383 (coins, banknotes and bearer cheques are not goods but means of payment).
91. Case C-55/93 *Van Schaik* [1994] ECR I-4837. See also Case 50/85 *Schloh v. Auto Contrôle Technique Sprl* [1986] ECR 1855.
92. Case C-275/92 *H.M. Customs and Excise v. Schindler et al.* [1994] ECR I-1039, see Gormley (1994) 19 ELRev. 644.
93. [1974] ECR 409 at 427.
94. See Hunnings (1975) JBL 72.
95. See WQ E-3966/93 (Kostopoulos) O.J. 1994 C 340/60.
96. Cases C-363/93 *etc. René Lancry SA et al. v. Direction Générale des Douanes et al.* [1994] ECR I-3957 at 3991. See also Cases C-37 and 38/96 Sodiprem SARL v. Direction générale des Douanes [1998] ECR I-nyr (30 April 1998), referring to earlier caselaw. See, Vaulont in Von der Groeben *et al.* (eds.), *op. cit.* (see note 33, *supra*) Vol. I 407 *et seq*, and Vandersanden in Mégret *et al.* (eds.), *Le Droit de la CEE* (2nd ed., Brussels, 1992) Vol. 1 67 *et seq*.
97. Case 266/81 *Società Italiana per l'Oleodotto Transalpino (SIOT) v. Ministero delle*

According to the definition in Article XXIV of the GATT the concept of a customs union, subject to the permitted exceptions, also embraces the abolition of all non-tariff trade barriers in inter-state trade.[98] The non-tariff aspects of the customs union are discussed in section 3 of this Chapter, below. The Court has interpreted Articles 12 and 16 EC in extensive case-law, and has paid particular attention to the distinction between charges having equivalent effect to a customs duty and fiscal measures caught by Article 95 EC.

The customs union is the essential foundation stone of the Community because it forms the first important step towards achieving an optimum division of labour within the Community. In fact, in such a situation, except for differences in transport rates and for possible distortion of competition, the producer with the lowest cost of production gets in all Member States the same potential outlets as local producers with a higher cost of production. Thus the customs union tended to stimulate enlargement of the scale and growth of production of the most efficient enterprises, encouraging concentration and specialization, and at the same time the selection of the most economic locations for new production plants or trade centres. Thus the customs union has already made an indirect contribution to the development of the inter-state movement of persons, services and capital. At the same time it has made the economies of the Member States mutually interdependent, thereby laying a good basis for an economic and monetary union.

2.3   The origin of goods

Free movement of goods applies to products originating in the Community and to products originating outside it which are placed in free circulation in a Member State.[99] Article 10(1) EC provides that products coming from

Finanze et al. [1983] ECR 731 at 778–779; Case C-16/94 *Édouard Dubois et Fils SA et al. v. Garonor Exploitation SA* [1995] ECR I-2421 at 2437–2438.

98. In 1931 the Permanent Court of International Justice gave an even stricter definition (Series A/B no. 41, 1931, p. 18).

99. Art. 9(2) EC. As to the definition of origin of goods, see the Community Customs Code, Reg. 2913/92 (O.J. 1992 L 302/1, most recently amended by Reg. 82/97 (O.J. 1997 L 17/1)), Arts. 23–26. See, generally, Gormley in Vaughan (ed.), *op. cit.* (see note 84, supra) paras. 29–43. This Regulation applies to the free movement of all goods within the Community and to non-preferential trade with third countries. All the preferential trade agreements also contain rules on the determination of the origin of goods. See further *e.g.* Case 10/61 *Commission v. Italy* [1962] ECR 1, [1962] CMLR 187; Case 32/64 *Italy v. Commission* [1965] ECR 365, [1965] CMLR 207, and, as examples of the importance of origin, Case 100/84 *Commission v. United Kingdom* [1985] ECR 1169, [1985] 2 CMLR 199; Case 68/88 *Commission v. Greece* [1989] ECR 2965, and Case C-432/92 *R. v. Minister of Agriculture, Fisheries and Food, ex parte S.P. Anastasiou (Pissouri) Ltd. et al.* [1994] ECR I-3087, noted by Emiliou (1995) 20 ELRev. 202.

a third country are considered as being in free circulation in a Member State 'if the import formalities have been complied with and any customs duties or charges having equivalent effect which are payable have been levied in that Member State and if they have not benefited from a total or partial drawback of such duties or charges.'[100] This rule applies to agricultural products and to industrial products alike.[101] Article 9(2) EC makes it plain that, as far as the right to free movement within the Community is concerned, products in free circulation are definitively and wholly assimilated to products originating in a Member State, a point which means that the provisions of Article 30 EC cover both types of products without distinction.[102] This assimilation may only have full effect if the same customs duties and commercial import conditions apply to the goods irrespective of the Member State in which they are placed in free circulation. The incomplete nature of the Community's common commercial policy does cause certain deflections in trade, and in certain circumstances Article 115 EC may be invoked to permit denial of Community treatment to goods originating from third countries. This has, though, become something of a dead letter since the abolition of customs controls at the Member States' internal Community frontiers.[103]

2.4 Intra-Community customs duties and charges having equivalent effect

All customs duties in inter-state trade within the Community have been abolished between the original six Member States since the end of 1969 (most having already gone at the end of June 1968) in accordance with the obligations of Articles 13–15 EC, and the same is true since the end of the various transitional periods agreed on the various accessions, so

100. See, generally, Case 16/65 *Firma C. Schwarze v. Einfuhr- und Vorratsstelle für Getreide und Futtermittel* [1965] ECR 877 at 889 and, in relation to interpretation problems in this field, Case 34/78 *Yoshida Nederland BV v. Kamer van Koophandel en Fabrieken voor Friesland* [1979] ECR 115, [1979] 2 CMLR 747 and Case 114/78 *Yoshida GmbH v. Industrie- und Handelskammer Kassel* [1979] ECR 151, [1979] 2 CMLR 747. The fact that a customs union benefits goods from third countries is the major difference between a customs union and a free trade area (in the latter each Member State applies its own customs tariff to third country goods coming from another Member State).
101. Case 69/84 *Padovani et al. v. Amministrazione delle Finanze dello Stato* [1985] ECR 1859 at 1869–1870.
102. Case 41/76 *Criel, née* Donckerwolcke et al. v. *Procureur de la République au Tribunal de Grande Instance, Lille et al.* [1976] ECR 1921 at 935; Case 119/78 *SA des Grandes Distilleries Peureux v. Directeur des Services Fiscaux de la Haute-Saône et du Territoire de Belfort* [1979] ECR 975 at 98, and Case 125/88 *Nijman* [1989] ECR 3533 at 3547. See further, Gormley, *op. cit.* (See note 26, *supra*) 4 and Oliver, *Free Movement of Goods in the European Community* (3rd ed., London, 1996) 17–22.
103. See Chapter XII, section 3.2.2, *post*.

that by the end of 1992 (the date by which the internal market was to be achieved) there has been a complete customs union between all the Member States, which was maintained on Austrian, Finnish and Swedish accession on 1 January 1995. The result is a complete customs union throughout the Community of 15.

The prohibition in Article 12 EC on the introduction of new import or export duties or charges having equivalent effect remains of importance as it is directly effective and can thus be relied upon before national courts.[104] Import and export duties and charges having equivalent effect which were still permissible during the transitional period became prohibited as from the end of that period; this follows from Articles 13 and 16 EC read in conjunction with Article 7(7) EC.[105] The Court has held that the prohibition of charges having equivalent effect is the logical and natural complement of the prohibition of customs duties in trade between Member States.[106] The prohibitions have the same meaning in respect of imports and exports.[107] The following two sections examine the scope of the prohibition and the exceptions in more detail.

2.4.1 Charges having equivalent effect to customs duties: definition

The Court of Justice has clarified the scope of charges having equivalent effect to an import or export duty in a number of cases.[108] Such charges may be defined as 'any pecuniary charge, however small and whatever its designation and mode of application, which is imposed unilaterally on domestic or foreign goods by reason of the fact that they cross a frontier, and which is not a customs duty in the strict sense.'[109] In this broad

104. *E.g.* Case 26/62 *NV Algemene Transport- en Expeditie Ondememing Van Gend en Loos v. Nederlandse administratie der belastingen* [1963] ECR 1 at 13.
105. See Case 33/70 *SpA SACE v. Ministry for Finance of the Italian Republic* [1970] ECR 1213, [1971] CMLR 123 and Case 18/71 *Eunomia di Porro e C. v. Ministry of Education of the Italian Republic* [1971] ECR 811, [1972] CMLR 4.
106. See Cases 52 and 55/65 *Germany v. Commission* [1966] ECR 159 at 169.
107. *Cf.* Case 7/68 *Commission v. Italy* [1968] ECR 423 at 428–429 and Cases 2 and 3/69 *Sociaal Fonds voor de Diamantarbeiders v. SA Ch. Brachfeld and Sons et al.* [1969] ECR 211 at 221–223.
108. For a general list of examples of charges caught see Gormley in Vaughan (ed.), *op. cit.* (see note 84, *supra*) paras. 330–340. See also, generally, Barents (1978) 15 CMLRev. 415 and Beschel and Vaulont in Von der Groeben *et al.* (eds.), *op. cit.* (see note 33, *supra*) Vol. I 458 *et seq.*
109. Case 24/68 *Commission v. Italy* [1969] ECR 193 at 201; see also *e.g.* Cases 2 and 3/69 *Sociaal Fonds voor de Diamantarbeiders v. SA Ch. Brachfeld and Sons et al.* [1969] ECR 211 at 222; Case 29/72 SpA *Marimex v. Italian Finance Administration* [1972] ECR 1309 at 1318–1319; Case C-266/91 *Celulose Beira Industrial (CELBI) SA v. Fazenda Pùblica* [1993] ECR I-4337 at 4361 and Case C-272/95 *Bundesanstalt für Landwirtschaft und Ernährung v. Deutsches Milch-Kontor GmbH* [1997] ECR I-1905 at

definition the emphasis lies on the hindering effect on the free movement of goods. The prohibition is also to be found repeated in secondary legislation as interpreted in that context in the same way as in the EC Treaty itself.[110] The fact that the charge is not imposed for the benefit of the state, or has no discriminatory or protectionist effects, or that because of its small amount does not lead to an increase in price, or that the goods involved are not in competition with domestic products makes no difference to the Court's view: a charge falling within the definition is prohibited.[111] It also makes no difference at what point the charge is levied, whether on actual crossing of a border or subsequently.[112] As will be evident, there is no *de minimis* rule. In any event, a charge together with the administrative formalities to which it gives rise already forms an obstacle to the free movement of goods[113] It makes no difference whether the charge is imposed for the general benefit of the public purse, or for an autonomous fund, likewise it matters not in what manner the pecuniary charge is levied (by the national authorities or an independent body) or for what purpose the charge is levied.[114] It should be noted that Articles 12 and 16 EC will not apply at the same time as the prohibition of fiscal discrimination against imports and exports contained in Articles 95 and 96 EC.[115]

1926. As to the link between unilateral charges and alternative solutions, see Case 39/ 82 *Donner v. The Netherlands State* [1983] ECR 19 at 34–36. The fact that a charge had a protective effect and that the imported product caught by it competed with a domestic product was regarded as relevant in older case-law, but this is no longer the case, *cf.* Cases 2 and 3/62 *Commission v. Luxembourg and Belgium* [1962] ECR 425 at 432 with Cases 2 and 3/69 *Sociaal Fonds voor de Diamantarbeiders v. SA Ch. Brachfeld and Sons et al.* [1969] ECR 211 at 221–223.

110. Case 34/73 *F.lli Variola SpA v. Amministrazione italiana delle Finanze* [1973] ECR 981 at 989; Case 21/75 *Firma I. Schroeder KG v. Oberstadtdirektor der Stadt Köln* [1975] ECR 905 at 913. The terms of Arts. 12 and 16 EC, like those of Arts. 30–36 EC were repeated in the texts of early agricultural regulations, to ensure that the prohibitions would be directly effective in the spheres concerned even before the end of the transitional period at the end of 1969.

111. Case 24/68 *Commission v. Italy* [1969] ECR 193 at 201; See also *e.g.* Cases 2 and 3/69 *Sociaal Fonds voor de Diamantarbeiders v. SA Ch. Brachfeld and Sons et al.* [1969] ECR 211 at 222; Case 29/72 SpA *Marimex v. Italian Finance Administration* [1972] ECR 1309 at 1318–1319; Case C-266/91 *Celulose Beira Industrial (CELBI) SA v. Fazenda Pùblica* [1993] ECR I-4337 at 4361 and Case C-272/95 *Bundesanstalt für Landwirtschaft und Ernährung v. Deutsches Milch-Kontor GmbH* [1997] ECR I-1905 at 1926.

112. Case 78/76 *Firma Steinike und Weinlig v. Germany* [1977] ECR 595 at 613.

113. Case 34/73 *F.lli Variola SpA v. Amministrazione italiana delle Finanze* [1973] ECR 981 at 989.

114. *E.g.* Case 7/68 *Commission v. Italy* [1968] ECR 423 at 429; Case 29/72 *SpA Marimex v. Italian Finance Administration* [1972] ECR 1309 at 1318–1319; Case 78/76 *Firma Steinike und Weinlig v. Germany* [1977] ECR 595 at 613; Case 158/82 *Commission v. Denmark* [1983] ECR 3573 at 3585–3586, and Case C-426/92 *Germany v. Deutsches Milch-Kontor GmbH* [1994] ECR I-2757 at 2784–2785. In relation to private contracts, see Case C-16/94 *Édouard Dubois et Fils SA et al. v. Garonor Exploitation SA* [1995] ECR I-2421 at 2437–2438.

115. *E.g.* Cases 2 and 3/69 *Sociaal Fonds voor de Diamantarbeiders v. SA Ch. Brachfeld and*

Although the words 'charge ... which is imposed unilaterally' may create the impression that charges imposed by the Community Institutions are not caught by the prohibition, the case-law of the Court demonstrates that they are caught.[116] Yet the prohibition as regards acts of the Community Institutions does not have the same prohibitive character for the them as for acts of the Member States.[117] Charges imposed by Community legal acts, such as in the past Monetary Compensatory Amounts in the agricultural sphere, were not considered by the Court to fall under Article 12 EC, but on the contrary as measures designed to facilitate the unity of the market by avoiding distortions which would otherwise have occurred, and thus being devoid of protectionist effect.[118]

2.4.2   The exceptions to the prohibition

The only exceptions mentioned in Title I of Part Three of the EC Treaty, dealing with the free movement of goods, are those in Article 36 EC, which may be relied upon by the Member States (or in certain instances private individuals). However, these only relate to Articles 30 and 34 EC and cannot be relied upon to justify charges falling under Articles 12 or 16 EC.[119] Thus a single economic operation, such as inspection and the fee charged fall under two different systems, so that in respect of both there will be an examination of which regime is applicable and, if appropriate, whether a justification known to Community law exists.[120] In such situations the obvious first step is to decide whether the inspection is justified, as if it is not the fee cannot stand in any event, and if it is then to look to the question whether the fee can be justified.[121] There are three grounds of justification on which a charge will escape the prohibition in Articles 12 and 16 EC, namely that it forms part of a general system of

Sons et al. [1969] ECR 211 at 222–223; Case 94/74 *Industria Gomma Articoli Vari, IGAV v. Ente Nazionale per la Cellulosa e per la carta, ENCC* [1975] ECR 699 at 710, and Cases C-149 and 150/91 *Sanders Adour SNC et al. v. Directeur des Services Fiscaux des Pyrénées-Atlantiques* [1992] ECR I-3899 at 3923.

116. *E.g.* Cases 80 and 81/77 *Société Les Commissionnaires Réunis Sàrl et al. v. Receveur des Douanes* [1978] ECR 927 at 946–947.
117. See section 3.2.2, *post* and Barents (1978) 15 CMLRev. 415 at 419.
118. *E.g.* Case 5/73 *Balkan Import-Export GmbH v. Hauptzollamt Berlin-Packhof* [1973] ECR 1091 at 1108–1109 and Case 9/73 *Schlüter v. Hauptzollamt Lörrach* [1973] ECR 1135 at 1152; see the distinction drawn in Cases 80 and 81/77 *Société Les Commissionnaires Réunis Sàrl et al. v. Receveur des Douanes* [1978] ECR 927 at 947.
119. Case 46/76 *Bauhuis v. The Netherlands State* [1977] ECR 5 at 15.
120. As was observed in section 1.4, *ante.*
121. See *e.g.* Case 50/85 *Schloh v. Auto Contrôle Technique Sprl* [1986] ECR 1855; any fee for any justified test of roadworthiness must be the same for imports as for domestic products, *ibid.*

internal taxation;[122] the second is that the charge is a recompense for a service actually rendered, and the third is that the fees are permitted under a Community provision. The recognition of the first ground is on the basis of the EC Treaty itself, the second and third grounds are creatures of case-law creation, and are examined below.

Recompense for a service actually rendered. A recompense for a service actually rendered to the importer can fall outside the scope of the prohibitions of Articles 12, and 16 EC but the case-law makes it clear that this exception will be strictly interpreted.[123] It therefore became abundantly clear that no recompense could be charged for compulsory frontier formalities since the Court has held that statistical fees and levies for health inspections applied on criteria other than those on which they are applied to domestic goods are prohibited.[124] The case-law shows that the recompense demanded may not exceed the actual cost of the service provided and that the service must be a specific service actually rendered and individually conferred.[125] In Case C-111/89 *Staat der Nederlanden v. P. Bakker Hillegom BV*[126] the Court observed that the condition relating

122. And thus falls to be considered under Articles 95 or 96 EC, as to which, see section 2.5, *post.*
123. *E.g.* Case 251/78 *Denkavit Futtermittel GmbH v. Minister für Ernährung, Landwirtschaft und Forsten des Landes Nordrhein-Westfalen* [1979] ECR 3369 at 3394; Case 132/78 *Denkavit Loire Sàrl v. France* [1979] ECR 1923 at 1934–1935; Case 39/73 *Rewe-Zentralfinanz e GmbH v. Direktor der Landwirtschaftskammer Westfalen/Lippe* [1973] ECR 1039 at 1044 and Case 39/82 *Donner v. Netherlands State* [1983] ECR 19 at 34. See also *e.g.* Case 314/82 *Commission v. Belgium* [1984] ECR 1543 at 1555.
124. For further developments see *e.g.* Case 39/73 *Rewe, ibid.;* Case 63/74 *W. Cadsky SpA v.* Instituto nazionale per il Commercio Estero [1975] ECR 281, [1975] 2 CMLR 246; Case 4/75 *Rewe-Zentralfinanz e GmbH v. Landwirtschaftskammer* [1975] ECR 843, [1977] 1 CMLR 599; Case 21/75 *Firma L. Schroeder KG v. Oberstadtdirektor der Stadt Köln* [1975] ECR 905, [1975] 2 CMLR 312; Case 87/75 *Conceria Daniele Bresciani v. Amministrazione Italiana delle Finanze* [1976] ECR 129, [1976] 2 CMLR 62; Case 35/76 *Simmenthal SpA v. Italian Minister for Finance* [1976] ECR 1871, [1977 2 CMLR 1 and Case 46/76 *Bauhuis v. Netherlands State* [1977] ECR 5. More recent examples (applying the principles laid down in these judgments) include Case 32/80 *Officier van Justitie v. Kortmann* [1981] ECR 251, [1982] 3 CMLR 46, Case 314/82 *Commission v. Belgium* [1984] ECR 349, [1985] 1 CMLR 453; Case 158/82 *Commission v. Denmark* [1983] ECR 3573, [1984] 2 CMLR 658.
125. *E.g.* Case 24/68 *Commission v. Italy* [1969] ECR 193 at 201; Case 39/82 *Donner v. The Netherlands State* [1983] ECR 19 at 34; Case 46/76 *Bauhuis v. Netherlands State* [1977] ECR 5 at 15; Case 132/78 *Denkavit Loire Sàrl v. French State (Customs Authorities)* [1979] ECR 1923 at 1934; Case 132/82 *Commission v. Belgium* [1983] ECR 1649 at 1658–1659; Case 158/82 *Commission v. Denmark* [1983] ECR 3753 at 3586; Case 340/87 *Commission v. Italy* [1989] ECR 1483 at 1511–1512, and Case C-209/89 *Commission v. Italy* [1991] ECR 1575 at 1595–1596.
126. [1990] ECR I-1735 at 1751.
127. *Ibid.* at 1752. See also Case C-209/89 *Commission v. Italy* [1991] ECR I-1575 at 1595–1596.

to not exceeding the actual cost of the operations in respect of which the fee was charged required there to be 'a direct link between the amount of the fee and the actual inspection in respect of which the fee is charged.' Otherwise it would be impossible to ensure that the amount did not exceed the actual cost. Accordingly, if the calculation basis were the duration of the inspection, the number of persons required, the cost of materials, overheads or similar factors, it would be legitimate, even if this were expressed in a fixed hourly rate. However, if the calculation were based on the weight or invoice value of the goods concerned, that would infringe the prohibition in Articles 12 or 16 EC as appropriate.[127] Duties paid by way of fees or dues within the meaning of Article 12(1)(e) of Directive 69/335[128] are not caught by the prohibition.[129]

The narrow nature of the exceptions to the prohibition is well illustrated by the finding that the placing of imported products in temporary storage in special stores of public warehouses clearly represented a service to traders, and that commensurate charges were permissible, but this would not be the case if the storage charges were equally payable when goods were presented at the public warehouse solely for the purpose of completing customs formalities, even though they had been exempted from storage and the importer had not requested that they be put into temporary storage. In this latter case the charge could not be regarded as a charge for a service actually rendered to the importer.[130] Charging fees in return for customs services performed on private premises will also be impermissible, as will fees applied on an *ad valorem* basis.[131] Charges levied in respect of quality controls or health inspections on crossing a frontier are unacceptable (a service for traders in general does not constitute a service as specified above).[132] Thus the Court requires that the costs occasioned by inspections prescribed in the public interest must be

128. O.J. English Special Edition 1969 (II) 412, most recently amended by Dir. 85/303 (O.J. 1985 L 156/23).
129. Cases C-71 and 178/91 *Pontente Carni SpA et al. v. Amministrazione delle Finanze dello Stato* [1993] ECR I-1915 at 1958 (as to the link with a service provided, see 1959). See also, in relation to Art. 10(c) of Dir. 69/335, Case C-2/94 *Denkavit Internationaal BV et al. v. Kamer van Koophandel en Fabrieken voor Midden-Gelderland et al.* [1996] ECR I-2827 at 2865–2866.
130. Case 132/82 *Commission v. Belgium* [1983] ECR 1649 at 1659–1660; see also Case 340/87 *Commission v. Italy* [1989] ECR 1483 at 1511–1512 .
131. Case 340/87 *Commission v. Italy* [1989] ECR 1483 at 1511–1512; see also Case 170/88 *Ford España SA v. Estado español* [1989] ECR 2305 at 2308 (summary publication).
132. E.g. Case 29/72 *SpA Marimex v. Italian Finance Administration* [1972] ECR 1309 at 1318–1319; Case 39/73 *Rewe-Zentralfinanz e GmbH v. Direktor der Landwirtschaftskammer Westfalen Lippe* [1973] ECR 1039 at 1044; Case 63/74 *W. Cadsky SpA v. Instituto nazionale per il Commercio Estero* [1975] ECR 281 at 290–291; Case 87/75 *Conceria Daniele Bresciani v. Amministrazione Italiana delle Finanze* [1976] ECR 129 at 138–139; Case 46/76 *Bauhuis v. Netherlands State* [1977] ECR 5 at 15, and Cases C-277, 318 and 319/91 *Ligur Carni Srl et al. v. Unità Sanitaria Locale No. XV di Genova et al.* [1993] ECR I-6621 at 6659–6660.

financed from the public purse.[133] If services are rendered to several undertakings at the same time, and the whole fee for an individual service is levied on each undertaking, this will be unacceptable if it results in more being charged than the actual costs per undertaking.[134]

Community provisions. Where the charges are for inspections carried out in accordance with Community provisions or international agreements, they will be acceptable, provided that they do not exceed the cost of carrying out the inspection (although this may vary from Member State to Member State in the absence of a harmonized charging system).[135] Fees for inspections prescribed by Community legislation in domestic and inter-state situations fall within the ambit of Articles 95 or 96 EC.[136] The explanation given by the Court is that such inspections replace the myriad unilateral national inspections which might otherwise be justifiable under Article 36 EC and thus contribute to the free movement of goods rather than hinder it.

2.5 Fiscal barriers: national taxation and harmonization[137]

A separate problem is posed by the demarcation between Article 12 EC and the fiscal non-discrimination provisions of Articles 95–97 EC. The practical importance of this demarcation consists of course in the fact that Article 12 prohibits the charges on imported goods referred to therein, whilst Article 95 on the contrary permits the imposition of taxes on imported products, provided similar domestically-produced products are subjected to the same taxes. The Court of Justice has rightly observed as

133. Case 87/75 *Conceria Daniele Bresciani v. Amministrazione Italiana delle Finanze* [1976] ECR 129 at 138–139.
134. Case C-209/89 *Commission v. Italy* [1991] ECR I-1575 at 1595–1597.
135. Case 46/76 *Bauhuis v.* Netherlands State [1977] ECR 5 at 17–18; Case 89/76 *Commission v. Netherlands* [1977] ECR 1355 at 1365, and Case 70/77 *Simmenthal SpA v. Amministrazione delle Finanze dello Stato* [1978] ECR 1453 at 1472–1473 and 1475. See also Barents (1979) SEW 218. The exception has been criticized by Lauwaars and Timmermans, *Europees Gemeenschapsrecht in kort bestek* (4th ed. Groningen, 1997) 169–170. It is clear that if differences resulting from the varying charges are to be eliminated, Community legislation will have to provide either for the fee to be absorbed by the public purse (national or the Community budget) or for a set fee which could be reviewed at Community level from time to time.
136. See *e.g.* Case 50/85 *Schloh v. Auto Controle Technique Sprl* [1986] ECR 1855; fee for justified test of roadworthiness must be same for imports as for domestic products, *ibid.*
137. See, generally, Easson, *Taxation in the European Community* (London, 1993); Farmer and Lyall, *EC Tax Law* (Oxford, 1994); Lier *et al., Tax and Legal Aspects of EC Tax Harmonisation* (Deventer, 1993); Mégret *et al.* (eds.), *Le Droit de la CEE* Vol. 5 (2nd ed., Brussels, 1993); Terra and Wattel, *European Tax Law* (Deventer, 1993); De Wit, *Nationale milieubelastingen en het EG-Verdrag* (Deventer, 1997); Williams, *EC Tax Laws* (London, 1998); Barents (1983) SEW 239, (1986) 23 CMLRev. 641 and (1991) SEW 767, and Wattel (1997) SEW 424. See also Burgers and Gormley (eds.), *Europees Belastingrecht* (Lelystad, 1997).

early as in Case 57/65 *Alfons Lütticke GmbH v. Hauptzollamt Saarlouis*[138] that Articles 12 and 95 EC cannot be applied at the same time to one and the same situation; a charge falls under one heading or the other but not both. From this viewpoint, Article 95 EC is at the same time both a complement to the prohibition of customs duties and charges having equivalent effect on imports and exports and an exception to that prohibition.[139] Article 95 does not affect the fiscal sovereignty of the Member States as such.[140] Thus a Member State is free, providing it respects Articles 95–97 EC, to establish its system of taxation and to determine the level of fiscal tariffs until such time as harmonization of fiscal legislation has taken place.[141] Following Barents,[142] the following distinctions are drawn in the examination of the tax provisions of the EC Treaty in the next three sections below: first, the various elements of the prohibition of fiscal discrimination are considered;[143] secondly certain derogations from the prohibition;[144] and, thirdly, tax harmonization is briefly examined.

2.5.1 The prohibition of fiscal discrimination in Article 95 EC

The first paragraph of Article 95 EC prohibits the Member States from imposing, 'directly or indirectly, on the products of other Member States any internal taxation of any kind in excess of that imposed directly or indirectly on similar domestic products.' In the second paragraph of Article 95 EC the ambit of the prohibition is extended to embrace any internal taxation of such a nature as to afford indirect protection to other products. These prohibitions are directly effective since the end of the first stage of the transitional period.[145]

If products for export are more heavily taxed than products for the

---

138. [1966] ECR 205 at 211; see also *e.g.* Case 25/67 *Firma Milch- Fett- und Eierkontor GmbH v. Hauptzollamt Saarbrücken* [1968] ECR 207 at 220; Case 27/74 *Demag AG v. Finanzamt Duisburg-Süd* [1974] ECR 1037 at 1046; Case 15/81 *Gaston Schul Douane-Expediteur BV v. Inspecteur der Invoerrechten en Accijnzen, Roosendaal* [1982] ECR 1409 at 1428–1429 (which also shows that VAT is not a charge having equivalent effect to a customs duty), and Case C-266/91 *Celulose Beira Industrial (CELBI) SA v. Fazenda Pùblica* [1993] ECR I-4337 at 4361.
139. Cases 2 and 3/62 *Commission v. Luxembourg and Belgium* [1962] ECR 425 at 433; Cases 2 and 3/69 *Sociaal Fonds voor de Diamantarbeiders v. SA Ch. Brachfeld and Sons et al.* [1969] ECR 211 at 221–223.
140. Case 127/75 *Bobie Getränkevertrieb GmbH v. Hauptzollamt Aachen-Nord* [1976] ECR 1079 at 1087–1088; Case 15/81 *Gaston Schul Douane-Expediteur BV v. Inspecteur der Invoerrechten en Accijnzen, Roosendaal* [1982] ECR 1409 at 1431.
141. On the basis of Arts. 99 or 100 EC.
142. (1983) SEW 438 and (1991) SEW 767.
143. Section 2.5.1, *post*.
144. Section 2.5.2, *post*.
145. Case 57/65 *Alfons Lütticke GmbH v. Hauptzollamt Saarlouis* [1966] ECR 205 at 210–211 (*i.e.* since 1 January 1962).

domestic market and the tax concerned is part of an internal fiscal system in the sense of Article 95 EC, that provision may be applied by analogy.[146]

It is the first paragraph of Article 95 which states the main principle, setting out from a comparison of fiscal burdens on imported and national products which are considered to be similar. The second paragraph is directed at all forms of sideways protectionism of products which, although not similar, are indirectly or potentially in a competitive relationship with some domestic products.[147]

Article 95 EC consists of three elements, each of which are examined in turn, below: 'internal taxation'; 'products', and 'of other Member States'. On the basis of these elements two comparisons take place for the purpose of the application of the prohibition. First, a product comparison, whether, as the case may be, the domestic products on which the tax is levied are either similar to or merely competing with imported products. Then there takes place a fiscal comparison in order to ascertain whether the tax on the imported product is, as the case may be, higher or protective in its effects. In each of these two comparisons, the first option covers the first paragraph of Article 95 EC, the second involves the second paragraph of that provision.[148]

By virtue of Article 96 EC, for products exported to the territory of any Member State, any repayment of internal taxation may not exceed that which has been directly or indirectly imposed on them.[149] This provision is linked to the destination country principle of taxation, according to which tax should be charged in the country in which the product is used or consumed. On exportation internal taxation borne by the products should be repaid and on arrival in the country of destination they should be taxed there according to the applicable system. It should be noted, though,[150] that the Community has in respect of Value Added Tax modified this approach in the transitional arrangements presently applicable, pending agreement on a definitive system.

Internal Taxation. The concept of 'internal taxation' owes its origins to Article III(2) of the GATT[151] and does not refer to domestic tax law, but

---

146. Case 142/77 *Statens Kontrol med Ædle Metaller v. Larsen* [1978] ECR 1543 at 1588. See Barents (1979) SEW 128 and Rasmussen (1979) 4 ELRev. 485. In its answer to WQ 170/71 (Westerterp) J.O. 1972 C 1/1 the Commission appeared to believe that this *lacuna* in the system could be filled by the application of Arts. 13 or 16 EC. See Farmer and Lyall, *op. cit.* (see note 137 *supra*) 52–56.
147. Case 168/78 *Commission v. France* [1980] ECR 347 at 359–360.
148. Barents (1991) SEW 767 at 768.
149. See Case 45/64 *Commission v. Italy* [1965] ECR 857, [1966] CMLR 97 and [1969] ECR 453; Case C-152/89 *Commission v. Luxembourg* [1991] ECR I-3141, and Case C-153/89 *Commission v. Belgium* [1991] ECR I-3171.
150. See section 2.5.3, *post.*
151. See, generally, Case C-469/93 *Amministrazione delle Finanze dello Stato v. Chiquita Italia SpA* [1995] ECR I-4533.

is a collective term embracing all charges which are imposed on imports as well as domestic products, irrespective of their nature or purpose. The application of Article 95 EC is concerned with guaranteeing the complete neutrality of internal taxation as regards competition between imports and domestic products.[152] The tax concerned may be based on legislation, international agreements (as in the case of the Benelux countries)[153] or in administrative instructions.[154]

If a fiscal charge falls to be considered as forming part of a system of internal taxation the application of the principle of non-discrimination will ensure that the principle of competitive neutrality is respected. If such a charge is discriminatory then the amount by which the charge on imports exceeds that on domestic products will still be treated as being part of the internal taxation system, albeit incompatible with Article 95 EC, and will not be treated as a charge having equivalent effect to a customs duty.[155] The concept of a tax must be widely interpreted,[156] a conclusion which was already supported by the reference to 'internal taxation of any kind' in the first paragraph of Article 95 EC. It covers not merely taxes in the technical sense, such as consumption taxes,[157] but also parafiscal charges,[158] monopoly levies,[159] inspection fees,[160] surcharges on general loading or landing duties,[161] sealing and stamp duties,[162] weights and measures fees;[163] and environmental levies.[164]

152. *E.g.* Case 356/85 *Commission v. Belgium* [1987] ECR 3299 at 3323; Case 252/86 *Bergandi v. Directeur général des impôts* [1988] ECR 1343 at 1374; Case 323/87 *Commission v. Italy* [1989] ECR 2275 at 2300.
153. Cases C-367–377/93 *F.G. Roders BV et al. v. Inspecteur der Invoerrechten en Accijnzen* [1995] ECR I-2229 at 2257–2259.
154. Case 17/81 *Pabst & Richarz KG v. Hauptzollamt Oldenburg* [1982] ECR 1331 at 1344 (administrative circulars).
155. Case 25/67 *Firma Milch-, Fett- und Eierkontor GmbH v. Hauptzollamt Saarbrücken* [1968] ECR 207 at 220, see also *e.g.* Case C-72/92 *Herbert Scharbatke GmbH v. Germany* [1993] ECR I-5509 at 5529. In Case 28/67 *Firma Molkerei-Zentrale Westfalen/Lippe v. Hauptzollamt Paderborn* [1968] ECR 143 at 154 the Court held that it was for the national court to decide in accordance with rules of national law whether the illegality affected the whole tax or merely the discriminatory excess. See also Case 34/67 *Firma Gebrüder Lück v. Hauptzollamt Köln-Rheinau* [1968] ECR 245 at 251.
156. Case 20/76 *Schöttle & Söhne OHG v. Finanzamt Freudenstadt* [1977] ECR 247 at 258.
157. *E.g.* Case 112/84 *Humblot v. Directeur des Services Fiscaux* [1985] ECR 1367, [1986] 2 CMLR 338.
158. *E.g.* Case 77/72 *Capolongo v. Azienda Agricola Maya* [1973] ECR 611, [1974] 1 CMLR 230, see section 2.5.2, *post.*
159. *E.g.* Case 45/75 *Rewe-Zentrale des Lebensmittel-Großhandels GmbH v. Hauptzollamt Landau/Pfalz* [1976] ECR 181.
160. *E.g.* Case 46/76 *Bauhuis v. The Netherlands State* [1977] ECR 5 at 17.
161. Case C-90/94 *Haahr Petroleum Ltd. v. Åbenrå Havn* [1997] ECR I-4085; see also Cases C-114 and 115/95 *Texaco A/S et al. v. Middelfart havn et al.* [1995] ECR I-4263 and Case C-242/95 *GT-Link A/S v. De Danske Statsbaner (DSB)* [1997] ECR I-4449.
162. Case 77/69 *Commission v. Belgium* [1970] ECR 237.
163. Case 142/77 *Statens Kontrol med Ædle Metaller v. Larsen* [1978] ECR 1543.
164. Implicit in Case 21/79 *Commission v. Italy* [1980] ECR 1. See further, Sevenster, *Mili-*

Products. The term 'products' in Article 95 EC has the same meaning as that term has in Article 9 EC.[165] Thus Article 95 also applies to agricultural products.[166] Special rules which are broadly similar to Article 95 EC apply in respect of ECSC products[167] Those financial charges which involve a restriction of the cross-border supply of services will have to be examined in the light of Article 59 EC.[168] Article 95 EC is also inapplicable to monetary and capital transactions.[169] In the transport field, the Commission has argued in relation to road tolls that a unilateral discriminatory national measure primarily infringed Article 76 EC, and in the second place Article 95 EC.[170]

The production stage at which the tax is imposed is irrelevant, as can be deduced from the term 'directly or indirectly'.[171] Thus the first paragraph of Article 95 EC 'refers to all taxation which is actually and specifically imposed on the domestic product at all earlier stages of its manufacture and marketing or which corresponds to the stage at which the product is imported from other Member states, it nevertheless being understood that the effect of this taxation diminishes in proportion to the previous stages of manufacture and of marketing become more remote and that this burden tends rapidly to become negligible.[172]

Of other Member States. In this respect too, the comparison with Article 9 EC is appropriate, so that Article 95 also applies to products originating in a third country which are in free circulation in a Member State.[173] A

eubeleid en Gemeenschapsrecht (Deventer, 1993) 310. However, a fiscal differentiation in the environmental sector which does not discriminate against producers from other Member States and is compatible with various Community provisions, such as Art. 95 EC, does not thereby *per se* become compatible with other provisions of the various Community noise and emission directives. The particular provisions of those directives are a complement to the non-discrimination provisions of Art. 95 and afford an appropriate framework for the grant of fiscal stimulus measures, see WQ E-127/93 (Metten) O.J. 1994 C 317/1.

165. See section 2.1, *ante.*
166. *E.g.* Cases 36 and 71/80 *Irish Creamery Milk Suppliers Association et al. v. Government of Ireland et al.* [1981] ECR 735, [1981 2 CMLR 455.
167. See Dec. 30–53 O.J. English Special Edition 1952–58, p. 9. This decision of the old High Authority was based on Art. 60(1) ECSC.
168. Cases 62 and 63/81 *Seco SA et al. v. Établissements d'Assurance contre la Veillesse et l'Invalidité* [1982] ECR 223 at 235.
169. Case 267/86 *Van Eycke v. ASPA NV* [1988] ECR 4769 at 4794.
170. But the Court declined to examine whether there was a breach of Art. 95 EC, finding that any discriminatory effects would only be the direct consequence of the infringement of Art. 76 EC, see Case C-195/90 *Commission v. Germany* [1992] ECR I-3141 at 3185.
171. Case 45/64 *Commission v. Italy* [1965] ECR 857 at 866; Case 28/67 *Molkerei-Zentrale Westfalen/Lippe GmbH v. Hauptzollamt Paderborn* [1968] ECR 143 at 155.
172. Case 28/67, *ibid.* See also Case 78/76 *Firma Steinike und Weinlig v. Germany* [1977] ECR 595 at 613.
173. See section 2.3, *ante,* and Case 193/85 *Cooperativa Co-Frutta Srl v. Amministrazione*

charge in the framework of a general system of taxation on imports of goods coming directly from third countries is permitted, to the extent that its imposition is not incompatible with the application of the common commercial policy or with international agreements between the Community and the third countries from which the product comes.[174] National taxes which treat domestic products more severely than imports are not affected by the prohibition in Article 95 EC.[175]

Product comparison. In the comparison of products attention is paid to the definition of the relationship between the products on which the tax to be compared is imposed. Although Article 95 EC does not prevent the Member States from imposing taxation on imports even if there is no domestic production of similar products, any such tax must not be of such an amount that imports of the products concerned are thereby hindered.[176] In the absence of any discriminatory or protective effect (which would cause Article 95 to be applicable), the only means of challenging the level of such a tax would be Article 30 EC.[177]

The first paragraph of Article 95 EC covers 'similar' products; once similarity is found, the tax must be equal, although there are certain exceptions to this non-discrimination principle which can be found in the case-law.[178] The Court interprets the term 'similar' in a wide sense, thus products are considered to be similar, if they 'have similar characteristics and meet the same needs from the point of view of consumers.'[179] The concept of similarity is a Community legal concept, and the first consideration is 'certain objective characteristics' of both products (or categories of products) concerned, such as their composition and method of manufacture, and, in the case of products such as alcoholic beverages,

delle Finanze dello Stato [1987] ECR 2085 at 2112, confirming the view advocated in 52 Halsbury's laws of England (4th ed., 1986) para. 20.07 (note 1).

174. Cases C-228/90 etc. Simba SpA et al. v. Ministero delle Finanze (Dogane di Savona e della Spezia) [1992] ECR I-3713 at 3751; Case C-130/92 OTO SpA v. Ministero delle Finanze [1994] ECR I-3281 at 3299. See also Case 469/93 Amministrazione delle Finanze dello Stato v. Chiquita Italia SpA [1995] ECR I-4533 at 4571. Thus Art. 95 EC is inapplicable to goods imported into a Member State from a third country, see e.g. Simba at 3750; OTO, loc. cit. and Case C-284/96 Tabouillot v. Directeur des services fiscaux de Meurthe-et Moselle [1997] ECR I-7471.

175. Case 86/78 SA des Grandes Distilleries Peureux v. Directeur des Services Fiscaux de la Haute-Saône et du Territoire de Belfort [1979] ECR 897 at 913.

176. Case 31/67 Firma August Stier v. Hauptzollamt Hamburg-Ericus [1968] ECR 235 at 241; Case C-47/88 Commission v. Denmark [1990] ECR I-4509 at 4533–4534.

177. Case C-47/88 Commission v. Denmark [1990] ECR I-4509 at 4533–4534.

178. See section 2.5.2, post.

179. E.g. Case 45/75 Rewe-Zentrale des Lebensmittel-Großhandels GmbH v. Hauptzollamt Landau/Pfalz [1976] ECR 181 at 194; Case 169/78 Commission v. Italy [1980] ECR 385 at 400; Case 216/81 Cogis (Compagnia Generale Interscambi) v. Amministrazione delle Finanze dello Stato [1982] ECR 2701 at 2712, and Case 106/84 Commission v. Denmark [1986] ECR 833 at 870.

taste and alcohol content; secondly, consideration is given to whether or not they 'are capable of meeting the same needs from the point of view of consumers.'[180] National law, customs or consumer habits cannot be advanced in order to ascertain the similarity of products, and Community law may well provide indications as to similarity: the products may fall under the same common customs tariff classification heading, or under the same system of common organization of the market.[181] The Court has also held that 'the tax policy of a Member State must not therefore crystallize given consumer habits so as to consolidate an advantage acquired by national industries concerned to comply with them.'[182]

In the second paragraph of Article 95 EC, product comparison is concerned with indirect protection. The decisive element in this instance is whether the products concerned are competing with domestic products.[183] Although the case-law of the Court indicates that the first paragraph of Article 95 is the main approach,[184] Barents has pointed out that from the viewpoint of the objectives the relationship between the two limbs of Article 95 is inverted.[185] The purpose of Article 95 is to place imported products in a fiscally neutral position on the domestic market, for which the determination of the competitive position is a necessary condition. In this view, the second paragraph of Article 95 appears to be more general in character, and the first paragraph more particular. Thus the latter can be regarded as a *lex specialis* in relation to the former. Even if an internal tax satisfies the requirements of the first paragraph, it may well still fall foul of the second. In deciding whether there is indirect protection, ascertaining the relevant market is important. Competition embraces not merely actual competition, but also indirect or potential

180. Case 243/84 *John Walker & Sons Ltd. v. Ministeriet for Skatter og Afgifter* [1986] ECR 875 at 881.
181. *E.g.* Case 168/78 *Commission v. France* [1980] ECR 347, [1981] 2 CMLR 631; Case 169/78 *Commission v. Italy* [1980] ECR 385, [1981] 2 CMLR 673; Case 170/78 *Commission v. United Kingdom* [1980] ECR 417, [1980] 1 CMLR 716; Case 171/78 *Commission v. Denmark* [1980] ECR 447, [1981] 2 CMLR 688; Case 55/79 *Commission v. Ireland* [1980] ECR 481; Case 356/85 *Commission v. Belgium* [1987] ECR 3299, [1988] 3 CMLR 277, and Case C-230/89 *Commission v. Greece* [1991] ECR I-1909, [1993] 1 CMLR 869. See also the second judgment in Case 170/78, [1983] ECR 2265, [1983] 3 CMLR 512. As to the point about customs classification, see also *e.g.* Case 178/84 *Commission v. Germany* [1987] ECR 1227 at 1271.
182. Case 170/78 *Commission v. United Kingdom* [1980] ECR 417 at 434. This idea has also been taken up in relation to Arts. 30–36 EC, see *e.g.* Case 178/84 *Commission v. Germany* [1987] ECR 1227 at 1270–1271.
183. Case 27/67 *Firma Fink-Frucht GmbH v. Hauptzollamt München-Landsbergerstraße* [1968] ECR 223 at 232.
184. *E.g.* Case 168/78 *Commission v. France* [1980] ECR 347, [1981] 2 CMLR 631 (the Court in fact avoided giving a ruling on similarity as it concluded that the products were in competition with each other, [1980] ECR 347 at 369); Case 184/85 *Commission v. Italy* [1987] ECR 2013 at 2026.
185. Barents (1983) SEW 438 at 445.

competition.[186] Thus the Court has denied that bananas are similar to other sorts of table fruit, but found that they are in competition with each other, so that the amount of internal taxation on bananas could not be such as to afford indirect protection to domestically produced table fruit.[187]

Fiscal comparison. Fiscal comparison only involves the fiscal burdens on the products concerned. Article 95 EC provides no basis for arguments for compensating by the fiscal route an advantage or disadvantage of an economic nature.[188] The comparison takes place on the basis of the national system of internal taxation concerned, and within that framework the non-discrimination principle must be respected.[189] The comparison involves not only the rate of the tax but also the basis of assessment: 'the decisive criterion of comparison for the purposes of Article 95 is the actual effect of each tax on national production on the one hand and on imported products on the other, since even where the rate of tax is equal the effect of that tax may vary according to the detailed rules for the basis of assessment and levying thereof applied to national production and imported products respectively.'[190] The application of any preferences and the methods of payment,[191] as well as penalties[192] will also be relevant.

2.5.2   The exceptions to the prohibition

In a number of instances the prohibition of discrimination in Article 95 does not produce a satisfactory result according to the case-law of the Court, namely in the areas of parafiscal charges, double taxation, fiscal preferences and differentiated taxation of products. Barents, following Pescatore, has submitted that the prohibition of discriminatory internal taxation has in fact been extended by the case-law to prohibit even non-discriminatory internal taxation which hinders imports or disadvantages them or, as Everling has put it, conflicts with the competitive neutrality of

---

186. Case 168/78 *Commission v. France* [1980] ECR 347 at 360; Case 170/78 *Commission v. United Kingdom* [1980] ECR 417 at 432.
187. Case 184/85 *Commission v. Italy* [1987] ECR 2013 at 2026; Case 193/85 *Cooperativa Co-Frutta Srl v. Amministrazione delle Finanze dello Stato* [1987] ECR 2085 at 2110. In the context of Art. 86 EC the Court had reached a different conclusion in Case 27/76 *United Brands Company et al. v. Commission* [1978] ECR 207 at 272–273. See Barents (1991) SEW 767 at 778.
188. Case 45/75 *Rewe-Zentrale des Lebensmittel-Großhandels GmbH v. Hauptzollamt Rheinland-Pfalz* [1976] ECR 181 at 195.
189. Case 127/75 *Bobie Getränkevertrieb GmbH v. Hauptzollamt Aachen-Nord* [1976] ECR 1079 at 1088.
190. Case 55/79 *Commission v. Ireland* [1980] ECR 481 at 491.
191. Case 171/78 *Commission v. Denmark* [1980] ECR 447 at 466 and 471–472.
192. Case 299/86 *Drexl* [1988] ECR 1213 at 1233–1235.

taxation by distorting competition.[193] These unsatisfactory areas are now examined in turn.

Parafiscal charges. The prohibition of fiscal discrimination does not operate satisfactorily in relation to parafiscal charges which are destined to function as state aids which benefit only national products or production. The policy is usually the same: a public law body levies the charge without discrimination as to the origin of the product concerned and uses the revenue raised for its own purposes, such as promotion or research, to the benefit of national production. Article 95 EC appears not to be infringed as the charge itself does not discriminate against imported products in any manner. The discriminatory effect, and thus the obstacle to trade, occurs later, namely at the time that the revenue from the charge is applied as selective aid. It might be thought that this would be examined in the light of Articles 92 and 93 EC, which is the policy followed by the Commission in a number of agricultural cases.[194] However, the Court very early on adopted another approach,[195] departing from Article 95 EC, looking at the selective state aid aspect and placing such a measure firmly in the realm of Articles 12, 13 and 16 EC, thus treating such parafiscal charges as being in reality equivalent to a customs duty: this is often called the *Capolongo* approach.[196]

The conditions for this 'back to square one' approach were amplified in subsequent case-law. Thus 'if the advantages stemming from the use of revenue from a contribution which constitutes a parafiscal charge fully offsets the burden borne by the domestic product when it is placed on the

193. (1983) SEW 438 at 461 (referring to Pescatore's speech) and 477 (see Everling (1982) EuR. 301 at 307). See also Case 15/81 *Gaston Schul Douane-Expediteur BV v. Inspecteur der Invoerrechten en Accijnzen, Roosendaal* [1982] ECR 1409, [1982] 3 CMLR 229.
194. *E.g. XXIIIrd Report on Competition Policy 1993* (Brussels, Luxembourg, 1994) point 551.
195. See Barents (1983) SEW 438 at 450.
196. Case 77/72 *Capolongo v. Azienda Agricola Maya* [1973] ECR 611 at 623. See also *e.g.* Case 94/74 *Industria Gomma Articoli Vari, IGAV v. Ente Nazionale per la Cellulosa e per la Carta, ENCC* [1975] ECR 699 at 710; Case 78/76 *Firma Steinike und Weinlig v. Germany* [1977] ECR 595 at 612–613; Case 77/76 *Fratelli Cucchi v. Avez SpA* [1977] ECR 987 at 1005; Case 105/76 *Interzuccheri SpA v. Ditta Rezzano e Cavassa* [1977] ECR 1029 at 1041–1042; Cases C-78–83/90 *Compagnie commerciale de l'Ouest et al. v. Receveur principal des douanes de La Pallice-Port* [1992] ECR I-1847 at 1880–1882; Case C-149 and 150/91 *Sanders Adour Snc v. Directeur des Services Fiscaux des Pyrénées-Atlantiques* [1992] ECR I-3899 at 3923–3925; Case C-17/91 *Georges Lornoy en Zonen NV et al. v. Belgian State* [1992] ECR I-6523 at 6551–6553; Case C-266/91 *Celulose Beira Industrial (CELBI) SA v. Fazenda Pùblica* [1993] ECR I-4337 at 4361–4362, and Case C-72/92 *Herbert Scharbatke GmbH v. Germany* [1993] ECR I-5509 at 5529–5531. See also Case 222/78 *I.C.A.P. v. Benevetti* [1979] ECR 1163, [1979] 3 CMLR 475 and Cases C-228/90 *etc. Simba SpA et al. v. Ministero delle Finanze (Dogane di Savona e della Spezia)* [1992] ECR I-3713. See, further, Barents (1978) 15 CMLRev. 415 at 425.

market, that contribution constitutes a charge having equivalent effect to customs duties, contrary to Articles 9 and 12 of the Treaty. If those advantages only partly offset the burden borne by domestic products, the charge would be incompatible with Article 95 of the Treaty and is therefore prohibited to the extent to which it discriminates against imported products, that is to say to the extent to which it partially offsets the burden borne by the taxed domestic product.'[197] It is a matter for the national court to decide on the question of whether the charge is wholly or partially offset.[198]

Fiscal preferences and differentiated taxation of products. In the case of taxes, the purpose plays a more limited role than in the case of non-tariff barriers. The purpose of fiscal measures is to obtain revenue for the state, but on the expenditure side, such as in the grant of state aid, the objectives of a measure may well be divided.[199] Yet certain fiscal preferences are accorded, and differential taxation is levied. These national policy objectives have to conform to the non-discrimination principle of Article 95 EC.[200] As is the case with Articles 30 and 34 EC, the starting point of the analysis is the absence of a Community rule on the matter concerned. The preference or differentiation must be based on objective criteria, such as the engine size of motor vehicles, or the type of raw materials involved, and the advantages must serve legitimate economic or social purposes.[201] The difference may not lead to direct or indirect discrimination against the imported products

197. Case C-72/92 *Herbert Scharbatke GmbH v. Germany* [1993] ECR I-5509 at 5529, summarizing earlier case-law, see also Case C-28/96 *Fazenda Pública v. Fricarnes SA* [1997] ECR I-4939 at 4950–4953. As an example of partial offset, see Case 105/76 *Interzuccheri SpA v. Ditta Rezzano e Cavassa* [1977] ECR 1029. The taxed product and the domestic product benefiting must be the same, Case 77/76 *Fratelli Cucchi v. Avez SpA* [1977] ECR 987 at 1005–1006.

198. E.g. Cases C-78–83/90 *Compagnie commerciale de l'Ouest et al. v. Receveur principal des douanes de La Pallice-Port* [1992] ECR I-1847 at 1882; Case C-17/91 *Georges Lornoy en Zonen NV et al. v. Belgian State* [1992] ECR I-6523 at 6553.

199. As in the case of some parafiscal charges, see e.g. Case 45/75 *Rewe-Zentrale des Lebensmittel-Großhandels GmbH v. Hauptzollamt Rheinland-Pfalz* [1976] ECR 181 at 195. See Barents (1983) SEW 438 at 455.

200. E.g. Case 21/79 *Commission v. Italy* [1980] ECR 1 at 12; Case 26/80 *Schneider-Import-Export GmbH & Co. KG v. Hauptzollamt Mainz* [1980] ECR 3469 at 3484–3486.

201. E.g. Case 148/77 *H. Hansen jun. & O.C. Balle GmbH & Co. v. Hauptzollamt Flensburg* [1978] ECR 1787 at 1826–1827; Case 112/84 *Humblot v. Directeur des services fiscaux* [1985] ECR 1367 at 1378–1379; Case 433/85 *Feldain v. Directeur des services fiscaux du département du Haut-Rhin* [1987] ECR 3521 at 3540–3542; Cases 76/87 etc. *Seguela et al. v. Adminisitration des impôts* [1988] ECR 2397 at 2409; Case C-132/88 *Commission v. Greece* [1990] ECR I-1567 at 1592–1593; Case C-47/88 *Commission v. Denmark* [1990] ECR I-4509 at 4535–4536; Case C-327/90 *Commission v. Greece* [1992] ECR I-3033 at 3055–3058; Case C-343/90 *Lorenço Dias v. Director da Alfândega do Porto* [1992] ECR I-4673 at 4715–4716 and case C-375/95 *Commission v. Greece* [1997] ECR I-5981.

concerned, nor to protection of competing national products.[202] The distinction which the Court has drawn in some isolated older judgments between prohibited discrimination and permitted differentiation on grounds of economic policy in fiscal matters has been controversial.[203]

Double taxation. As long as there is no or no complete fiscal harmonization, there is a risk of double taxation. Because of the general use of the destination country principle, double taxation problems remained very much the exception. When the Court had to deal with such problems, it concluded that there was no infringement of Article 95 EC if the exported products and the products which were processed domestically were treated equally in fiscal terms: although the double taxation did indeed constitute an obstacle to trade, it could only be removed through harmonization.[204]

In Case 15/81 *Gaston Schul Douane-Expediteur BV* v. *Inspecteur der Invoerrechten en Accijnzen, Roosendaal*,[205] which must rank as potentially one of the most important judgments of the Court from the point of view of the man in the street, the Court found that it was incompatible with Article 95 EC for a Member State to charge VAT on the importation of second-hand goods from another Member State by a private party whilst the sale of such goods within the Member State was not liable to VAT, in so far as no account was taken of the residual element of VAT paid in the Member State from which the goods had been exported which was still contained in the value of the goods on importation. The burden of proving facts which justify the taking into account of the tax already paid falls on the importer; in order to take advantage of the *Gaston Schul* principle importers must have all their paperwork in order. In Case 47/84 *Staatssecretaris van Financiën* v. *Gaston Schul Douane-Expediteur BV*[206] the Court gave clear guidelines on the calculation of the amount of tax to be taken into account.

2.5.3 Harmonization of taxation

For the abolition of fiscal frontiers within the Community, more is necessary than the mere application of the prohibition of fiscal

---

202. Cases 142 and 143/80 *Amministrazione delle Finance dello Stato* v. *Essevi SpA & Salego* [1981] ECR 1413 at 1434.
203. Case 140/79 *Chemial Farmaceutici SpA* v. *DAF SpA* [1981] ECR 1, [1981] 3 CMLR 350 and Case 46/80 *Vinal SpA* v. *SpA Orbat* [1981] ECR 77, [1981] 3 CMLR 524, see Timmermans (1982) SEW 426 and Gormley (1982) 7 ELRev. 49. See Kellermann in Alexander *et al., In Orde (Liber Amicorum* VerLoren van Themaat, Deventer, 1982) 143.
204. Case 142/77 *Statens Kontrol med Ædle Metaller* v. *Larsen* [1978] ECR 1543 at 1559.
205. [1982] ECR 1409, [1982] 3 CMLR 229, see Gormley (1982) 7 ELRev. 323 and the Commission's Communication O.J. 1986 C 13/2. See also Case 299/86 *Drexl* [1988] ECR 1213 at 1232..
206. [1985] ECR 1491, [1986] 1 CMLR 559.

discrimination contained in Article 95 EC.[207] Article 99 EC gives the Council the power to adopt provisions for the harmonization of legislation concerning turnover taxes, excise duties and other forms of indirect taxation to the extent such harmonization is necessary to ensure the establishment and functioning of the internal market.[208]

The most important tax in this context is undoubtedly Value Added Tax (VAT). This is based on the principle that on goods and services a general consumer tax is imposed which is strictly proportional to their price, regardless of the number of transactions involved in the process of production and distribution prior to the stage of imposition. On every transaction VAT is calculated by application of the respective turnover tax tariff to the sales price, but the seller, when handing the VAT over to authorities, may deduct the tax he or she has paid upon purchase of the goods or services concerned. VAT is applied right the way down to the retail stage.[209] This deduction ensures that each stage of production or distribution pays a tax only on the value added at that stage. The system of VAT is thus economically neutral, applying irrespective of whether goods or services have come from one single producer or have passed through several hands before reaching the consumer. Thus in relation to imports and exports the rules of Articles 95 and 96 EC apply to VAT.[210]

In various judgments the Court has dealt with the question of the extent of the direct effect of the VAT directives.[211] Part of the revenue from VAT is also an element in the Community's own resources, and VAT is also important in the calculation of those resources.[212]

---

207. Indeed, the Court recognized many years ago that one of the few remaining reasons for having customs formalities in intra-Community trade was the collection of taxes, see Case 159/78 *Commission v. Italy* [1979] ECR 3247 at 3258.

208. This version of Art. 99 EC differs from the original version: as to this difference, see VerLoren van Themaat (1986) SEW 464 at 477. The obligation was to adopt the necessary provisions by 31 December 1992, see Art. 99 EC in conjunction with Art. 7a EC. See Dec. 888/98 (O.J. 1998 L 126/1) on the Fiscalis programme.

209. So that the final burden is in fact borne by the ultimate consumer or user, as the case may be, see Dir. 67/227 (O.J. English Special Edition 1967, p. 14), Art. 2 (as amended).

210. See Case 54/72 *Fonderie Officine Riunite FOR v. Vereinigte Kammgarn-Spinnereien VKS* [1973] ECR 193; Case 15/81 *Gaston Schul Douane-Expediteur BV v. Inspecteur der Invoerrechten en Accijnzen, Roosendaal* [1982] ECR 1409, [1982] 3 CMLR 229; Case 47/84 *Staatssecretaris van Financiën v. Gaston Schul Douane-Expediteur BV* [1985] ECR 1491, [1986] 1 CMLR 559, and Case 299/86 *Drexl* [1988] ECR 1213.

211. Case 9/70 *Grad v. Finanzamt Traunstein* [1970] ECR 825 at 838–839; Case 20/70 *Transports Lesage & Cie v. Hauptzollamt Freiburg* [1970] ECR 861 at 874; Case 23/70 *Haselhorst v. Finanzamt Düsseldorf-Altstadt* [1970] ECR 881 at 893–894; Case 8/81 *Becker v. Finanzamt Munster-Innenstadt* [1982] ECR 53, [1982] 1 CMLR 499; Case 255/81 *R.A. Grendel GmbH v. Finanzamt für Körperschaften in Hamburg* [1982] ECR 2301, and Case 70/83 *Kloppenburg v. Finanzamt Leer* [1984] ECR 1075, [1985 1 CMLR 205. See also Chapter VI, section 2.2.2, *ante*.

212. See Chapter V, section 2, *ante*.

VAT harmonization commenced during the 1960s, and the cumulative multi-stage turnover tax systems, which distorted competition and created barriers to trade between Member States, were abolished.[213] By 1977 the Council was able to adopt the Sixth VAT Directive, Directive 77/388,[214] which establishes a common system of VAT with a uniform basis of assessment. In order to facilitate the completion and proper functioning of the internal market, the Council was to adopt the necessary measures by the end of 1992,[215] but disagreement about the nature of the appropriate system led to the adoption of an interim solution in Directive 91/680.[216] While this directive still takes the destination country principle as the basis for trader-to-trader transactions, in such cross-border transactions the customer now accounts for the tax on his or her internal VAT return on acquisition, so that although goods are still exempted from VAT on exportation, they are no longer subject to a charge on their importation into another Member State. This effectively privatises the system. In respect of retail sales to individuals, though, the origin system applies, so that VAT is paid in the Member State in which the goods are purchased and the goods concerned may be freely imported into any other Member State without further ado. However, the Council was clearly aware of the need to combat fiscal deflections of trade resulting from the differences in rates applied in the various Member States.[217] Thus special arrangements have been included in the transitional provisions, so that the destination principle applies in relation to certain categories of trade, especially cross-border purchases by public authorities and other institutional purchasers, mail order sales to individuals, new means of transport, and goods subject to excise duties.[218] The provisions applicable to the cross-border supply of services remain largely the same, as they were already covered by the internal

213. By the First and Second VAT Directives, Dirs. 67/227 and 67/228 (O.J. English Special Edition 1967, pp. 14 and 16 respectively). As to the nature of this distortion or restriction of inter-state trade (which *inter alia* heavily distorted competition between vertically-integrated and non-integrated undertakings and enabled the Member States to abuse Art. 97, 1st para. for protectionist purposes), see the 2nd ed. of this work (ed. Gormley, Deventer, 1989) 373–374 and the 1st ed. (London, 1973) 196–200.
214. O.J. 1977 L 145/1, most recently amended by Dir. 96/95 (O.J. 1996 L 338/89).
215. Art. 99 EC, in conjunction with Art. 7a EC.
216. O.J. 1991 L 376/1. This system was to apply until 31 December 1996, but has been automatically extended until such time as the Council decides on the definitive system of VAT, Dir. 77/388, Art. 28l.
217. This problem has in fact been more prevalent in relation to differences in excise duties, as is explained, *post*, but will remain a problem as long as there is no clearer willingness on the part of the Member States to align their tax rates. As long as this unwillingness persists, consumers (and others with no right of deduction) will rightly take advantage of a more favourable climate elsewhere, particularly in areas adjacent to the Member States' internal Community frontiers.
218. Dir. 77/388, Arts. 28a and 28b.

systems of the Member States.[219] Special arrangements now govern second-hand goods, works of art, antiques and collectors' items.[220] The Commission has now presented proposals for the move to an origin system as the definitive VAT arrangements, but these were still under discussion at the date at which this work states the law.[221] A particular more general fiscal problem being addressed is tax competition between the Member States, an end to which is seen as essential for the achievement of undistorted conditions of competition, a concept which lies at the very heart of the common market.[222] The sale of duty-free goods in intra-Community sea and air travel is set to continue only until 30 June 1999.[223]

The question of excise duties has led to the most spectacular fiscal deflections of trade.[224] The general arrangements for products subject to excise duty are contained in Directive 92/12[225] which retains a destination system for commercial transactions, but applies the origin system in relation to personal imports for private use. The guidelines as to what quantities constitutes private use are generous, and it is only for imports above the guideline amounts that persons may be requested to provide evidence that they are indeed for private use. As has been explained above, market forces have been particularly active as a result. Specific measures deal with tobacco,[226] alcohol and alcoholic drinks,[227] petroleum products,[228]

---

219. Special arrangements exist covering small undertakings, travel agents and farmers, see Dir. 77/388, Arts. 24–26, see *e.g.* Case C-260/95 *Commissioners of Customs and Excise v. DFDS A/S* [1997] ECR I-1005.

220. Dir. 77/388, Arts. 26a and 28o.

221. See COM (96) 328 Final. See also COM (98) 374 Final (electric commerce).

222. See COM (97) 495 Final and COM (97) 564 Final. See, further, the Conclusions of the ECOFIN Council (O.J. 1998 C 2/1) and the Code of Conduct for Business Taxation (O.J. 1998 C 2/2). See also O.J. 1998 C 99/1.

223. Dir. 77/388, Art. 28k, see Case C-408/95 *Eurotunnel SA et al. v. Sea France* [1997] ECR I-6315.

224. In the past, one of the most celebrated examples was Martelange, which on one side of the road is in Belgium and on the other is in Luxembourg, where it consisted of garages and shops selling alcoholic beverages, perfumes and the like, excise duty and VAT being lower in Luxembourg than in Belgium. Perhaps the most economically important present example is cross-Channel private imports of wine, spirits and beer (as well as tobacco) from France to the United Kingdom. The novel approach of the then Chancellor of the Exchequer, Clarke, was to raise excise duties on alcoholic beverages, to the bemusement of traders in the South-East of England.

225. O.J. 1992 L 76/1, amended by Dir. 92/108 (O.J. 1992 L 390/124). See Case C-408/95 *Eurotunnel SA et al. v. Sea France* [1997] ECR I-6315 and Case C-269/95 *R. v. Commissioners of Customs and Excise, ex parte EMU Tabac SARL et al.* [1998] ECR I-nyr (2 April 1998).

226. Dirs. 92/78 (O.J. 1992 L 316/5); 92/79 (O.J. 1992 L 316/8), and 92/80 (O.J. 1992 L 316/10). See also Dir. 95/59 (O.J. 1995 L 291/40).

227. Dirs. 92/83 (O.J. 1992 L 316/21) and 92/84 (O.J. 1992 L 316/29).

228. Dirs. 92/81 (O.J. 1992 L 316/12) and 92/82 (O.J. 1992 L 316/19). See also Dec. 92/510 (O.J. 1992 L 316/16) and (still relevant for Greece and Portugal) Dec. 93/697 (O.J. 1993 L 321/29).

and road tax.[229] A proposal for a tax on carbon dioxide emissions has aroused controversy.[230]

Harmonization of direct taxes, which has so far remained very limited,[231] is based on Article 100 EC, as Article 100a(2) EC excludes fiscal provisions from the qualified majority voting system for internal market legislation. Unless the conditions for application of Article 101 are fulfilled, this means that such harmonization has to be on the basis of unanimity in the Council, a matter which gives rise to problems particularly in relation to progress on witholding taxes.[232] So far only two directives have been adopted in this area: the parent-subsidiary directive[233] and the merger directive.[234] However, a Tax Arbitration Convention[235] has also been adopted, and important proposals for future action were submitted in the Ruding Committee Report.[236] The Commission's proposals as a result of this Report are still under discussion at the date at which this work states the law.[237]

Article 73d(1)(a) EC permits the Member States to apply the relevant provisions of their tax law which distinguish between taxpayers who are not in the same situation with regard to their place of residence or with regard to the place where their capital is invested.[238] This provision was included in the EC Treaty because the larger Member States desire to retain as much sovereignty as possible in the field of direct taxation,[239] and can be seen as a codification of case-law in this field.[240] These measures

229. Dir. 93/89 (O.J. 1993 L 279/32).
230. COM (97) 30 Final (O.J. 1997 C 139/14).
231. See Wattel (1994) SEW 395 and Wouters (1994) MJ 179.
232. See the Commission's proposal (O.J. 1991 C 53/26, and Bull. EC supp. 4/91), amended COM (93) 196 Final (O.J. 1993 C 178/18). See, further, COM (98) 295 Final (O.J. 1998 C212/13). As to the conditions for the application of Article 101 EC, see Chapter VIII, section 2.1, *post* and the recently adopted Code of Conduct for Business Taxation (O.J. 1998 C2/2).
233. Dir. 90/435 (O.J. 1990 L 225/6). See Vanistendal (1997) 34 CMLRev. 1279 on the first cases on this directive.
234. Dir. 90/434 (O.J. 1990 L 225/1).
235. O.J. 1990 L 225/10, originally proposed in the form of a directive, but was adopted as a Convention under Art. 220 EC. See Hinnekens (1992) EC Tax Rev. 70.
236. *Report of the Committee of Independent Experts on Company Taxation* (Brussels, Luxembourg, 1992). See Vanistendael (1992) EC Tax Rev. 3 (and McLure, *ibid.* at 13; Knobbe-Keuk, *ibid.* at 22, and Darolles and Tucci, *ibid.* at 39) and *The Ruding Committee Report: a personal view* (Inst. Fiscal Stud., *Fiscal Studies*, London, 1992); De Buitlier (1993) *European Taxation* 15 and Messere (1993) *European Taxation* 2.
237. SEC (92) 1118 Final.
238. See the Commission's Recommendation on taxation of certain income of non-residents obtained in another Member State (O.J. 1994 L 39/42).
239. Vermeend, *Staatscourant*, 27 May 1993, p. 10.
240. *E.g.* Case 270/83 *Commission v. France* [1986] ECR 273, [1987] 1 CMLR 401; Case C-175/88 *Biehl v. Administration des contributions du grand-duché de Luxembourg* [1990] ECR I-1779; Case C-204/90 *Bachmann v. Belgian State* [1992] ECR I-249; Case C-300/90 *Commission v. Belgium* [1992] ECR I-305. See also Case C-112/91 *Werner v. Finan-*

may not, however, constitute a means of arbitrary discrimination or a disguised restriction on the free movement of capital and payments as defined in Article 73b EC.[241]

2.6 Customs duties and charges having equivalent effect in relation to third countries

Levying customs duties and charges having equivalent effect in relation to trade between the Community and third countries is part of the Community's common commercial policy, a policy which is discussed *in extenso* in Chapter XII, below, as part of the Community's external relations. In relation to agricultural products subject to a common organization of the market, a special regime is applicable: this is considered in Chapter XI, below. The discussion in this section examines the external dimension of the free movement of goods, emphasizing two aspects: the common customs tariff and the rules on the levying of charges having equivalent effect to customs duties in external trade. The discussion is confined to the general system, and does not take account of particular product regimes, such as agriculture or textiles; nor does it deal with preferential arrangements or association arrangements for particular countries.[242]

In Articles 18 and 110 EC the Member States have declared their intention to follow a liberal tariff policy *vis-à-vis* third countries on a basis of reciprocity. This provision has not remained a dead letter. Even before

zamt Aachen-Innenstadt [1993] ECR I-429; Case C-330/91 *R. v. Inland Revenue Commissioners, ex parte Commerzbank AG* [1993] ECR I-4017; Case C-1/93 *Halliburton Services BV v. Staatssecretaris van Financiën* [1994] ECR I-1137; Case C-279/93 *Finanzamt Köln-Innenstadt v. Schumacker* [1995] ECR I-225; Case C-80/94 *Wielockx v. Inspecteur der Directe Belastingen* [1995] ECR I-2493; Case C-151/94 *Commission v. Luxembourg* [1995] ECR I-3685; Case C-107/94 *Asscher v. Staatssecretaris van Financiën* [1996] ECR I-3089, and Case C-250/95 *Futura Participations SA et* al. v. *Administration des Contributions* [1997] ECR I-2471.

241. Art. 73d(3). This is clearly inspired *mutatis mutandis* by the second sentence of Art. 36 EC. See, further, section 8.3, *post*.

242. See Chapter XII, *post*. See also *e.g.* Case 17/81 *Pabst & Richarz KG v. Hauptzollamt Oldenburg* [1982] ECR 1311, [1983] 3 CMLR 11; Case 104/81 *Hauptzollamt Mainz v. Kupferberg & Cie. KG a.A.* [1982] ECR 3641, [1983] 1 ECR 1; Case 430/92 *The Netherlands v. Commission* [1994] ECR I-5197; Cases T-480 and 483/93 *Antillean Rice Mills NV et al. v. Commission* [1995] ECR II-2305 (under appeal in Case C-390/95 P *Antillean Rice Mills NV et al. v. Commission* (O.J. 1996 C 46/6); Case T-26/97 *Antillean Rice Mills NV v. Commission* (O.J. 1997 C 108/22); Case T-41/97 R *Antillean Rice Mills NV v. Council* [1997] ECR II-447, and Case T-179/97 R *Government of the Netherlands Antilles v. Council* [1997] ECR II-1297. See further Case C-207/91 *Eurim-Pharm GmbH v. Bundesgesundheitsamt* [1993] ECR I-3723 and Cases C-114 and 115/95 *Texaco A/S et al. v. Middelfart Havn et al.* [1997] ECR I-4623.

the common customs tariff entered into force, on 1 July 1968, very considerable tariff reductions were allowed via the framework of the GATT, first in the Dillon Round, but particularly later on, in the Kennedy Round (1964–1967), and further reductions were later agreed in the Tokyo Round (1973–1979). The common customs tariff was first introduced by Regulation 950/68[243], but with effect from 1 January 1988 the new integrated tariff and statistical nomenclature system introduced by Regulation 2658/87[244] has replaced the old system of Regulation 950/68. This new Combined Nomenclature is based on the International Convention on the Harmonized Commodity Description and Coding System and forms the basis of the integrated tariff, with Community subdivisions, known as the 'Taric'. The Combined Nomenclature together with the rates of duty and other relevant charges and the tariff measures included in the Taric or in other Community arrangements now constitute the common customs tariff referred to in Article 9 EC. The applicable duties and levies are fixed annually through an amendment of the Annex to Regulation 2658/87.[245] Two columns of duty are shown: the autonomous duty and the conventional duty. The former applies when it is less than the conventional duty or when there is no conventional duty. Since 1995 the common customs tariff reflects the results of the multilateral agreements entered into in the Uruguay Round.

Because application of the common customs tariff is actually undertaken by the national customs administrations, there being as yet no Community customs administration, the unity and correctness of interpretation of the tariff have to be ensured through references under the procedure of Article 177 EC.[246] The same procedure is used in cases in which the Commission uses it power to determine a classification question by regulation and interested parties seek to challenge the classification made. Challenge by way of an action under Article 173 EC is impossible as the Court does not regard interested importers as being directly and individually concerned by such a regulation. This is clear from the judgment in Case 40/84 Casteels PVBA v. Commission,[247] the background to which shows that the tariff classification can be important in relation to the applicability of non-tariff import restrictions. The correct method to challenge a classification is thus to attack the concrete decision of the national customs authorities based on the classification made at Community level; the plaintiff should request the national court to refer the matter to the Court of Justice. On the

---

243. O.J. English Special Edition 1968(I), p. 275.
244. O.J. 1987 L 256/1. See also the Commission's Communication O.J. 1994 L 342/1.
245. For 1998, see Reg. 2086/97 (O.J. 1997 L 312/1 (see also Reg. 1048/98 (O.J. 1998 L 151/1)).
246. See e.g. Gormley in Vaughan (ed.), op. cit. (see note 84, supra) para. 27 and Possen (1973) SEW 371 and (1984) SEW 511.
247. [1985] ECR 667 (see also the opinion of VerLoren van Themaat, Adv.-Gen., ibid. at 668–669).

successive accession of new Member States their national customs tariffs were progressively brought into line with the Community's tariff which now applies throughout the Community.

Under Article 25 EC (which applies even now that the transitional period has ended) the Member States are given, subject to the substantive and the procedural safeguards contained in Article 25 EC itself, a certain title to tariff quotas at a reduced rate or duty-free if the production of the products concerned in the Community is insufficient and tariffs raised by the introduction of the common customs tariff would entail harmful consequences for their traditional supplies from third countries. It appears, however, from the text of the Treaty and the case-law of the Court that this does not constitute an automatic right. On the contrary, the situation is that according to this case-law the basic rules of Articles 2 and 3 EC and the guidelines mentioned in Article 29 EC form the framework within which the Commission is to exercise the power conferred on it by Article 25 EC to submit proposals to the Council or to act on its own initiative (according to the products involved).[248]

Under Article 28 EC the Council, acting (since the end of the transitional period) by a qualified majority on a proposal from the Commission, may autonomously alter or suspend any duties in the common customs tariff. The present text of this Article is the simplified form substituted by the Single European Act. The powers of Article 25 and 28 EC have been repeatedly exercised. Article 28 EC can also be used to establish Community tariff quotes to replace national tariff quotas established under Article 25 EC; it can also be used to change or clarify the nomenclature. This latter use can occur, for example, to take account of new technological developments. In the light of the Community's obligations towards third countries, autonomous changes in duties will normally only amount to reductions. Article 29 EC contains guidelines for the Commission in carrying out its policy in relation to Articles 20–22 and 25–28 EC.

The Commission has established a Customs 2000 programme with a view to improving the controls at the Community's external frontiers and making the fight against fraud more effective.[249]

The EC Treaty contains no provisions on charges having equivalent effect to customs duties in trade with third countries. The concept is indeed referred to in Article 10(1) EC, but that provision, which deals with goods

---

248. Case 24/62 *Germany v. Commission* [1963] ECR 63, [1963] CMLR 347; Case 34/62 *Germany v. Commission* [1963] ECR 131, [1963] CMLR 369.
249. Dec. 210/97 (O.J. 1997 L 33/24). See also the Mattheus Programme involving the retraining and adaptation of customs officers in view of the abolition of systematic customs controls at the Community's internal frontiers, Dec. 91/341 (O.J. 1991 L 187/41), implemented by Dec. 93/23 (O.J. 1993 L 16/13). Equivalent measures have been taken with regard to indirect taxation (the Mattheaus Tax Programme), Dec. 93/588 (O.J. 1993 L 280/27).

in free circulation in a Member State, contains no obligations or prohibitions as such. The Court was first confronted with charges having equivalent effect in external trade in 1973,[250] after it had already dealt with such charges in internal trade in 1969.[251] It considered that even though no mention was made in Articles 18–29 EC of charges having equivalent effect to customs duties, that did not mean that such charges could be maintained, let alone introduced. In answering this problem, the requirements of the common customs tariff and the common commercial policy would have to form the starting point of the approach. Although the common customs tariff regulation did not in so many words require the repeal or equalization of such charges, it appeared from the objectives of Regulation 850/68 that it involved a prohibition of the levying by the Member States of charges additional to the customs duties for which it provided, and thus of creating changes to the level of protection provided for in the common customs tariff itself. Even in the absence of protectionist characteristics, such charges could be incompatible with the common commercial policy of the Community. Accordingly, since the coming into force of the common customs tariff, the Member States are forbidden to introduce unilateral new charges or to increase the level of existing charges. As to the latter, it was up to the Commission or the Council to decide whether they were compatible with the EC Treaty. The common customs tariff thus involved 'the elimination of national disparities, whether in the field of taxation or commerce, affecting trade with third countries.[252]

2.7 Community customs legislation

The regulation which first established the common customs tariff that entered into force on 1 July 1968 also contained a beginning of a common customs legislation. On this point Article 27 EC only recognises a procedure of recommendations for harmonization during the first stage of the transitional period, but during 1968, it became apparent that the Council felt that Article 27 EC did not exclude the possibility that after the first stage, and specifically after the common customs tariff had come into

---

250. Cases 37 and 38/73 *Sociaal Fonds voor de Diamantarbeiders v. NV Indiamex et al.* [1973] ECR 1609. See also Case 70/77 *Simmenthal SpA v. Amministrazione delle Finanze dello Stato* [1978] ECR 1453, [1978] 3 CMLR 670, and Case 30/79 *Land Berlin v. Wigei, Wild-Geflügel-EierImport GmbH & Co. KG* [1980] ECR 151. See further, Barents (1979) SEW 218.

251. Cases 2 and 3/69 *Sociaal Fonds voor de Diamantarbeiders v. SA Ch. Brachfeld and Sons et al.* [1969] ECR 211; see also Case C-130/93 *Lamaire NV v. Nationale Dienst voor Afzet van Land- en Tuinbouwprodukten (NDALTP)* [1994] ECR I-3215.

252. Cases 37 and 38/73 *Sociaal Fonds voor de Diamantarbeiders v. NV Indiamex et al.* [1973] ECR 1609 at 1623.

force, the necessary unification of customs duties could be realised by regulations or directives.[253] Accordingly, myriad regulations were adopted, concerning, for example, the common definition of the origin of goods; a common scheme for the calculation of the customs value of goods; the definition of the customs territory of the Community; processing under customs control; temporary importation of goods, Community transit, relief from duties and the repayment or remission of duties. Directives were adopted where, provided a certain degree of harmonization was achieved, the national authorities could be permitted a certain amount of discretion. Thus directives were adopted relating, for example, to inward and outward processing, customs warehouses, free zones, presentation of goods to customs, release of goods for free circulation and the deferred payment of import or export duties (including, in the context, charges having equivalent effect and agricultural levies). However, particularly in the mid-Eighties, the trend was to transform Community provisions in this field from directives to regulations.[254] This enabled tighter control of the use of special procedures and the integration of such control into a firmer and more coherent common commercial policy; it also put some restraint on competition between Member States in the field of favourable customs regimes. Community legislation acts as a means of pursuing commercial policy ends as well as of controlling commercial activities as such.

The removal of formalities and other obstacles to intra-Community trade, external pressures, and the desire for simplification of Community legislation all contributed to the development of the Community Customs Code, which is contained in Regulation 2913/92.[255] The Code, which was further implemented by Regulation 2454/93[256] has replaced the labyrinth of legislation which preceded it by a relatively clear and largely self-contained set of rules.[257] It builds on the tightening of the Community customs regime established by the earlier movement towards the

253. Regulations under Arts. 28, 111 (now repealed), or 235 EC; Directives under Art. 100 EC.
254. E.g. Dir. 69/73(O.J. English Special Edition 1969(I), p. 75) on inward processing was replaced by Reg. 1999/85 (O.J. 1985 L 188/1) from 1 January 1987.
255. O.J. 1992 L 302/1, most recently amended by Reg. 82/97 (O.J. 1997 L 17/1). See, generally, Gormley in Vaughan (ed.), *op. cit.* (see note 84, *supra)* paras. 1–323, and Gormley in Emiliou and O'Keeffe (eds.), *The European Union and World Trade Law* (Chichester, 1996) 124; Case C-130/95 *Giloy v. Hauptzollamt Frankfurt am Main-Ost* [1997] ECR I-4291 and Case C-334/95 *Krüger GmbH & Co. KG v. Hauptzollamt Hamburg-Jonas* [1997] ECR I-4517. See also Terra, *Community Customs Law* (The Hague, 1995).
256. O.J. 1993 L 253/1, most recently amended by Reg. 75/98 (O.J. 1998 L 7/3).
257. As to the legislation repealed, see Regs. 2913/92, Art. 251 and 2454/93, Art. 913. These two provisions repeal 105 measures between them. These lists also enables research for case-law dealing with the previously applicable provisions, which, in so far as the new provisions are identical, will still be relevant.

replacement of directives by regulations. The core of the Code is mostly contained in Title IV which deals with customs-approved treatment or use, but the Code also contains myriad provisons dealing with all aspects of customs matters; it undoubtedly represents a major improvement in Community customs legislation.

3. FREE MOVEMENT OF GOODS: NON-TARIFF ASPECTS

Apart from customs duties and charges having equivalent effect, inter-state trade could also be restricted by quota systems and other quantitative restrictions or measures having equivalent effect, as well as by exchange control. With the exception of the latter kind of control, for which the Treaty contains separate rules,[258] these measures are discussed in this section.[259]

The EC Treaty distinguishes between restrictions on imports[260] and those on exports,[261] but Article 36 EC also refers to goods in transit, although there is no doubt that Articles 30 and 34 EC, including the exceptions thereto, apply also to goods in transit.[262] Since the end of the transitional period the prohibition of existing or new quantitative restrictions on imports and exports and all measures having equivalent effect has had direct effect and can thus be relied upon before national courts.[263] The judgment in Case 48/74 *Charmasson v. Minister for*

---

258. See section 8, *post*.
259. The literature on Arts. 30–36 EC is extensive, see Gormley, *op cit.* (see note 26, *supra*); Allfeld, Zwingende Erfordernisse im Sinne der Cassis-Rechtsprechung des Eurōpaischen gerichtshof zu Art. 30 EGV (Baden-Baden, 1997); Gulman, *Handelshindringer i EF-Retten* (Copenhagen, 1980); Mattera, *Le Marché Unique Européen – Sès règles, son fonctionnement* (2nd ed., Paris, 1990); Oliver, *op cit.* (see note 102, *supra*); Poiares Maduro, *We, the Court* (Oxford, 1998); Quitzow, *Fria varurörelser I den Europeiska gemenskapen* (Stockholm, 1995); Müller-Graff in Von der Groeben *et al.* (eds.), *op. cit.* (see note 33, *supra*) Vol. I, 602–846 all of which contain extensive bibliographies; Defalque in Mégret *et al.* (eds.), *op. cit.* (see note 96, *supra*) 210 *et seq.*; Friedbacher (1996) 2 ELJ 226; Gormley in Vaughan (ed.), *op. cit.* (see note 84, *supra*) paras. 347–541; Gormley (1990) 27 CMLRev. 825 and (1996) 19 Fordh. Int'l. L.J. 866; Matthies in Due *et al.* (eds.), *Festschrift für Ulrich Everling* Vol. I (Baden-Baden, 1995) 803; Mattera (1994) RMUE 117; Mortelmans (1991) 28 CMLRev. 115, and (1998) SEW 226 with further references; Schilling (1994) EuR 50;, and Weatherill (1996) 33 CMLRev. 885; see also Jarvis, *op cit.* (see note 36, *supra*). Further literature is cited at relevant places in the discussion, *post*.
260. Art. 30 EC.
261. Art. 34 EC.
262. In Case 2/73 *Riseria Luigi Geddo v. Ente nazionale* Risi [1973] ECR 865 at 879 the Court stated that quantitative restrictions also covered 'measures which amount to a total or partial restraint of ... goods in transit.' See also Case 266/81 *Società Italiana per l'Oleodotto Transalpino (SIOT) v. Ministero delle Finanze et al.* [1983] ECR 731 at 778–779; Case C-367/89 *Richardt et al.* [1991] ECR I-4621 at 4650.
263. Arts. 30–32 EC for restrictions on imports; in relation to Arts. 31 and 32(1) EC, see

Economic Affairs & Finance[264] shows that this also applies to agricultural products not yet subject to a system of common organization. Since the end of the transitional period the directly effective prohibition also applies to products subject to common organisation. In many instances in respect of these latter products the relevant national rules will also (or only) be incompatible with the system of the common organization of the market in question.[265]

Article 30 EC, or Articles 3(g), 5, 85 and 86 EC?

Certain economic law instruments, such as price-regulatory measures, may be adopted by the public authorities, by the private sector, or by both acting together. If the public authorities act, this action may fall within the scope of Article 30 EC;[266] even if the public authority concerned is more of a public body than an authority as such.[267] If the prices are fixed by one or more undertakings, Articles 85 or 86 EC may be applicable.[268] There remains though a broad field covered by measures taken by both public and private sectors together, such as in those areas where the authorities have power to declare arrangements reached in particular branches of commerce and industry generally binding on all market participants: examples include competition arrangements[269] and measures by which the action of one market participant makes action by another superfluous.[270] It is in this context that the growing case-law on Articles

Case 13/68 *SpA Salgoil v. Italian Ministry of Foreign Trade* [1968] ECR 453 at 461; in relation to Art. 30 EC, see Case 74/76 *Iannelli & Volpi SpA v. Ditta Paola Meroni* [1977] ECR 557 at 575 and Case 251/78 *Firma Denkavit Futtermittel GmbH v. Minister für Ernährung, Landwirtschaft und Forsten des Landes Nordrhein-Westfalen* [1979] ECR 3369 at 3384; in relation to Art. 34 EC, see Case 83/78 *Pigs Marketing Board v. Redmond* [1978] ECR 2347 at 2373 and Case C-47/90 *Éts. Delhaize Frères et Compagnie Le Lion SA v. Promalvin SA et al.* [1992] ECR I-3669 at 3711.

264. [1974] ECR 1383, [1975] 2 CMLR 208. For a useful discussion of the effect of this judgment see Pescatore in Lüke *et al.* (eds.), *Rechtsvergleichung, Europarecht und Staatenintegration* (*Gedächtnisschrift* for Constantinesco, Cologne, 1983) 559 at 562–563. See also Case 232/78 *Commission v. France* [1979] ECR 2729, [1980] 1 CMLR 418.

265. See Gormley, *op. cit.* (see note 26, *supra*) 73–95 and 111–121. In fact this latter specific incompatibility nowadays adds nothing, as Arts. 30, 34 and 36 are directly effective, see Case 251/78 *Denkavit Futtermittel GmbH v. Minister für Ernährung, Landwirtschaft und Forsten des Landes Nordrhein-Westfalen* [1979] ECR 3369 at 3384; Case C-131/93 *Commission v. Germany* [1994] ECR I-3303 at 3319.

266. *E.g.* Cases 88–90/75 *Società SADAM et al. v. Comitato Interministeriale dei Prezzi et al.* [1976] ECR 323, [1977] 2 CMLR 183.

267. Such as *produktschappen* in The Netherlands; see *e.g.* Case 82/77 *Openbaar Ministerie v. Van Tiggele* [1978] ECR 25, [1978] 2 CMLR 528.

268. *E.g.* Cases 177 and 178/82 *Van de Haar et al.* [1984] ECR 1797, [1985] 2 CMLR 566.

269. *E.g.* Case 123/83 *Bureau National Interprofessional du Cognac v. Clair* [1985] ECR 391, [1985] 2 CMLR 430.

270. *E.g.* Case 229/83 *Association des Centres Distributeurs Édouard Leclerc et al. v. Sàrl 'Au*

3(g), 5, 85 and 86 EC must be situated.[271] It is important for several reasons whether Article 85 or Article 30 is applicable. First, the exceptions to the prohibition of Article 30 are more numerous and extensive than, and different in character (non-economic) from those to Article 85(1) set out in Article 85(3); secondly, Article 85 embraces measures which are confined to national territory but which create barriers to entry for imports,[272] whereas Article 30 does not embrace purely internal situations involving no real link to inter-state trade, in particular local regulation of socio-economic life.[273] Thirdly, Article 85(3) EC is not directly effective, in view of the Commission's exclusive power of exemption, whereas Article 30 is. Finally, there is no *de minimis* rule in relation to Article 30 EC,[274] whereas there is in relation to the application of Article 85 EC.[275]

blé vert' et al. [1985] ECR 1 at 31–32. See *e.g.* VerLoren van Themaat in Gutzler *et al.* (eds.), *Wettbewerb in Wandel (Festschrift* for Gunther, Baden-Baden, 1976) 373; Werthei- mer and Barents in Alexander, *op. cit.* (see note 203, *supra*) 353; Waelbroeck in Capotorti *et al.* (eds.), *Du droit international au droit de l'intégration (Liber Amicorum* Pescatore, Baden-Baden, 1987) 781; Pescatore (1987) 10 Fordham Int'l. L.J. 373; Marenco, *ibid.* 420 (and Pescatore's reply, *ibid.* 444); Pappalardo in Mestmäcker et al. (eds.), *Eine Ordnung- spolitk für Europa (Festschrift* for Von der Groeben, Baden-Baden, 1987) 303; Van der Esch (1988) 11 Fordham Int'l. L.J. 409; Verstrynge (1988) *Fordham Corporate law Insti- tute* (Irvington-on-Hudson, 1989) Chap. 17; Gyselen (1989) 26 CMLRev. 33; Joliet (1989) 12 Fordham Int'l. L.J. 163; Ehricke (1990) 14 *World Competition* 79; Hoffman (1990) 10 ECLR 11; Bright (1993) ECLR 263; Reich (1994) 31 CMLRev. 459 Chung (1995) 16 ECLR 87, and Fenger and Broberg (1995) 16 ECLR 364.

271. See Chapter III, section 5.2.3, *ante*, and Chapter VIII, section 4.1.1, *post*. See also Steinberger, *Staatliche Wirtschaftsinterventionen als Verstoss gegen die Wettbewerbsre- geln des EG-Vertrages* (Cologne, 1994). See further *e.g.* Case C-96/94 *Centro Servizi Spediporto Srl v. Spedizioni Marittima del Golfo Srl* [1995] ECR I-2883 (citing earlier case-law).

272. Case 8/72 *Vereniging van Cementhandelaren v. Commission* [1972] ECR 977 at 991.

273. See section 1.2, *ante* and section 3.2.1, *post*. See also Cases C-241 and 242/91 P *Radio Telefis Eireann (RTE) et al. v. Commission* [1995] ECR I-743 at 828. See, also, though, Cases C-321–324/94 *Pistre et al.* [1997] ECR I-2343 at 2374: 'Article 30 cannot be considered inapplicable simply because all of the facts of a specific case before a national court are confined to a single Member State.' This may well be intended to deflect part of the criticism heaped on Cases 267 and 268/91 *Keck and Mithouard* [1993] ECR I-6097, [1995] 1 CMLR 101 as to the absence of evidence that the products in the specimen charges were in fact foreign products.

274. Case 16/83 *Prantl* [1984] ECR 1299 at 1326; Cases 177 and 178/82 *Van de Haar et al.* [1984] ECR 1797 at 1812–1813; Case 269/83 *Commission v. France* [1985] ECR 837 at 846; Case 103/84 *Commission v. Italy* [1986] ECR 1759 at 1773. In Case C-412/93 *Société d'Importation Édouard Leclerc-Siplec v. TF1 Publicité SA et al.* [1995] ECR I-179 at 194–197 Jacobs, Adv. Gen. pleaded for a *de minimis* approach, but this found no response from the Court. In Art. 30 EC, it is submitted, a *de minimis* approach is wholly unworkable, (not least in the case of minimum price controls or other measures which clearly are also aimed at or affect imports) as any threshold would be simply an invitation to set a limit to protectionist tenden- cies of the public authorities, whereas the approach of the Treaty is to prohibit them altogether.

275. See *e.g.* Case 5/69 *Völk v. Ets. J. Vervaecke* [1969] ECR 295 at 302.

Approach in this section

The discussion is divided, unlike ancient Gaul, into six parts. In section 3.1, the prohibition of quantitative restrictions is briefly discussed; then in section 3.2 attention turns to measures having equivalent effect. In section 3.3 the exceptions to Articles 30 and 34 EC are considered, both those stemming from the case-law (the 'rule of reason' otherwise referred to as 'mandatory requirements') and those contained in the EC Treaty itself. State monopolies of a commercial character are considered in section 3.4, before attention turns briefly in section 3.5 to the relationship between Articles 30–36 EC and trade with third countries, and, finally, in section 3.6, to the effect of Community legislation occupying the field.

3.1 Quantitative restrictions

Quantitative restrictions are 'measures which amount to a total or partial restraint of, according to the circumstances, imports, exports or goods in transit.'[276] Quantitative import or export restrictions thus include all legislative or administrative rules or administrative measures restricting the importation or exportation of one or more products according to quantitative norms. So, for instance, fixing a ceiling at a given percentage of imports or exports in a basic year or of national production in that basic year, or prescribing for every import or export a licence which is restricted each time to fixed quantities is prohibited, save only to the extent to which such action may be justified under Community law.

A quota system proper never formed a serious obstacle in the Community, since it had already been largely abolished in 1958 within the framework of the Organisation for European Economic Co-operation. For industrial products the last quantitative restrictions within the Community were abolished on 31 December 1961. For agricultural products abolition was achieved during the transitional period as common organisation regulations were adopted for the market in various products.[277] The concept of a quantitative restriction features very rarely in the case-law of

---

276. Case 2/73 *Riseria Luigi Geddo v. Ente nazionale Risi* [1973] ECR 865 at 879.
277. The terms of Art. 30 *et seq.* EC were reproduced as an integral part of the regulations setting up common organizations before the end of the transitional period. This was done because Arts. 30 and 34 EC were not yet directly applicable and did not create rights on which individuals could rely before national courts; including an equivalent provision in regulations got round this problem. Since the end of the transitional period repetition is unnecessary, see Warner, Adv. Gen. in Case 5/79 *Procureur Général v. Buys et al.* [1979] ECR 3203 at 3243, specifically approved by the Court in Case 251/78 *Denkavit Futtermittel GmbH v. Minister für Ernährung, Landwirtschaft und Forsten des Landes Nordrhein Westfalen* [1979] ECR 3369 at 3384.

the Court.[278] In many instances national measures which belong under the heading of quantitative restrictions are simply brought under the heading of measures having equivalent effect.[279] Since the end of the transitional period at midnight on 31 December 1969, as far as the original Member States were concerned, and since the end of the transitional periods allowed under various Acts of Accession in respect of newer Member States, the distinction is now viewed as immaterial,[280] although it may not always be devoid of practical significance, at least in the hands of national courts.[281]

3.2   Measures having equivalent effect

This discussion is divided into a number of headings: in section 3.2.1 the evolution of the case-law from *Dassonville* to *Keck and Mithouard* and beyond is sketched; then in the next two sections the prohibitions of measures having equivalent effect are considered in relation to imports and then to exports. Finally, the relationship between Article 30 EC and other provisions of the EC Treaty is very briefly noted. The grounds of exception to the prohibitions are considered in the next major section, section 3.3, below. Accordingly, particularly in sections 3.2.2 and 3.2.3, below, it should be borne in mind that one or more of the grounds mentioned in section 3.3, below, may be applicable.

3.2.1   Searches for conceptual clarity? From Dassonville through *Keck und Mithouard* and beyond

If the definition of quantitative restrictions proved easy enough, the same cannot be said of measures having equivalent effect. In a reply to a parliamentary question the Commission summarized its expressed the view that this concept covered all 'legislative rules and administrative provisions as well as administrative practices forming a barrier to importation or

278. Case 118/78 *C.J. Meijer BV v. Department of Trade et al.* [1979] ECR 1387, [1979] 2 CMLR 427; Case 231/78 *Commission v. United Kingdom* [1979] ECR 1447, [1979] 2 CMLR 427 and Case 34/79 *R. v. Henn and Darby* [1979] ECR 3795, [1980] 1 CMLR 246. A refusal to issue an export licence is a quantitative restriction on exports, see Case C-5/94 *R. v. Ministry of Agriculture, Fisheries and Food, ex parte Hedley Lomas (Ireland) Ltd.* [1996] ECR I-2553 at 2611.
279. Case 40/82 *Commission v. United Kingdom* [1982] ECR 2793, [1982] 3 CMLR 497; Case 261/85 *Commission v. United Kingdom* [1988] ECR 547, [1988] 2 CMLR 11; Case C-131/93 *Commission v. Germany* [1994] ECR I-3303. In Cases 194 and 241/85 *Commission v. Greece* [1988] ECR 1037 the Court found it unnecessary to find whether the Greek banana import licensing system constituted a quantitative restriction or a measure having equivalent effect.
280. Oliver, *op. cit.* (see note 102, *supra*) 68.
281. See Jarvis, *op. cit.* (see note 36, *supra*) 17–20.

exportation that might otherwise take place, including those provisions and practices which render the importation or the exportation more expensive or difficult in comparison with the sales of home production on the domestic market.'[282] The Commission added, though, that provisions which apply indiscriminately to imports and home products do not as a rule constitute measures having an equivalent effect to quantitative restrictions.

In reaction to this answer,[283] VerLoren van Themaat advocated a much wider definition of measures having equivalent effect, so that all measures of public authorities which had a restrictive effect on cross-border movement of goods (other than macro-economic policy measures) would be caught by the probibition and only capable of being saved by specific provisions of the EC Treaty itself.[284] Primarily in German academic literature a rather more narrow view was taken, advocating discrimination as the touchstone criterion (in some cases accepting that indirect or disguised discrimination would also be caught).[285] The Commission sat on the fence somewhat, and in a set of directives adopted as a Christmas package in December 1969 to coincide with the ending of the transitional period developed its views.[286] Thus it considered that provisions and administrative practices restricting imports or exports which particularly affected imports or exports amounted in principle to measures having equivalent effect to a quantitative restriction, but measures which applied equally to imports and domestic products did not. Maintaining both limbs of this approach, the Commission gave, however, in Directive 70/50[287] a number of concrete cases in which equally applicable measures could fall within the concept of measures prohibited by Article 30 *et seq.* EC. Put in general terms, the Commission felt that such measures would be caught if a Member State were to misuse its freedom, which the Commission in principle recognized, to regulate internal trade by making imports either impossible or more difficult or expensive than the sale of domestic products, without this being necessary to achieve an aim falling within the ambit of the powers left to the Member States by the Treaty.[288]

282. WQ 64/67 (Deringer) J.O. 1967 169/12 (editor's translation). See, for a discussion of the early approaches to Arts. 30–36 EC, Gormley, *op. cit.* (see note 26, *supra*) Chapter 2.
283. See also WQ 118/67 (Deringer) J.O. 901/67.
284. VerLoren van Themaat (1967) SEW 632.
285. See, for an overview of the debate, Gormley, *op. cit.* (See note 26, *supra*) 8; Meij and Winter (1976) 13 CMLRev. 79.
286. The full package can be found in J.O. 1970 L 13, and is based on Art. 33(7) EC.
287. O.J. English Special Edition 1970(I), p. 17 (the second of the package of directives, not all of which are in the English Special Edition).
288. Thus in Dir. 70/50, Art. 2, the Commission indicated that measures which distinguished between domestic products and those imported from other Member States fell within the prohibition of Art. 30 EC: thus checks applicable only to imported products were caught. In Art. 3 of the directive, the Commission brought a well-

Some of the examples mentioned in Directive 70/50 remain of interest because the Court sometimes refers to them in its judgments, and indeed traces of the influence of the directive can be seen in many cases even when the Court does not specifically refer to it. However, it has rightly been observed that the quotation of Directive 70/50 by the Commission in its submissions and references to it by the Court merely serve to show that the condemnation of such measures has been consistent.[289]

Dassonville. The leading judgment, both from the point of view of the basic principle and the application of provisos or exceptions on the basis of case-law, is still that in Case 8/74 *Procureur du Roi v. Dassonville et al.*[290] In that judgment the Court laid down the basic principle in the following terms: '[a]ll trading rules enacted by Member States which are capable of hindering, directly or indirectly, actually or potentially, intra-Community trade are to be considered as measures having an effect equivalent to quantitative restrictions.'[291] This definition was certainly closer to that advocated by VerLoren van Themaat than to the other views explained above. The main thesis of the Commission that measures which applied equally to domestic and imported products did not, in principle, fall under the prohibitions of Articles 30 *et seq.* was not followed by the Court of Justice, a standpoint which has been confirmed on many occasions.[292] Whilst the Commission accepted equally applicable measures, save in cases of misuse, despite any hindering effect on imports, the Court sets out from the premise that even equally applicable measures are in principle prohibited if they are capable of restricting imports. Thus the Court applies the first concept of freedom,[293] although it immediately made it plain that measures in principle prohibited could be accepted in certain circumstances: '[i]n the absence of a Community system guaranteeing for

---

defined category of equally applicable measures under the prohibition, namely provisions concerning the placing on the market of products, such as rules governing shape, weight and composition, which have a more restrictive influence on the free movement of goods than is envisaged in the framework of such measures. See, further, VerLoren van Themaat (1970) SEW 258 and Gormley, *op. cit.* (see note 26, *supra*) 11–12 and 14–15.

289. VerLoren van Themaat (1970) SEW 258 at 260; Gormley *op. cit.* (see note 26, *supra*) 12 citing earlier authorities; Capotorti, Adv. Gen. in Case 249/81 *Commission v. Ireland* [1982] ECR 4005 at 4028–4029.

290. [1974] ECR 837, [1974] 2 CMLR 436.

291. [1974] ECR 837 at 852. See, further, section 3.2.2, *post*.

292. *E.g.* Case 120/78 *Rewe-Zentrale AG v. Bundesmonopolverwaltung für Branntwein* [1979] ECR, [1979] 3 CMLR 494; Case 82/77 *Openbaar Ministerie v. Van Tiggele* [1978] ECR 25, [1978] 2 CMLR 528; Case 132/80 *NV United Foods et al. v. Belgian State* [1981] ECR 995 at 1023; Case 207/83 *Commission v. United Kingdom* [1985] ECR 1201, [1985] 2 CMLR 259; Case 182/84 *Miro BV* [1985] ECR 3831, [1986] 3 CMLR 545 and Case 178/84 *Commission v. Germany* [1987] ECR 1227, [1988] 1 CMLR 813.

293. See section 1.3, *ante*.

consumers the authenticity of a product's designation of origin, if a Member State takes measures to prevent unfair practices in this connexion, it is however subject to the condition that these measures are reasonable and that the means of proof required should not act as a hindrance to trade between Member States and should, in consequence, be accessible to all Community nationals.'[294] The Court then added: '[e]ven without having to examine whether or not such measures are covered by Article 36, they must not, in any case, by virtue of the principle expressed in the second sentence of that Article, constitute a means of arbitrary discrimination or a disguised restriction on trade between Member States.'[295] This was the rule of reason, later referred to by the Court as the 'mandatory requirements' which has excited so much discussion over the years. It can be seen as the counterpart to the wide basic principle, and in fact became a significant means of judicial supervision outside the pure Articles of the EC Treaty, reflecting an equitable approach to the legitimate interests or values which, though not covered by Article 36 EC, were nevertheless felt worthy of protection pending Community action in the fields concerned.

Cassis de Dijon. This rule of reason was developed further in Case 120/78 *Rewe-Zentral AG v. Bundesmonopolverwaltung für Branntwein,*[296] more often referred to as *Cassis de Dijon.* Perhaps the most important condition in the rule of reason case-law was not clearly stated in *Dassonville* or *Cassis,* but was made explicit subsequently, namely that national measures had to be equally applicable, in law and in fact, if they were to benefit from the rule of reason justifications.[297] Such measures may thus benefit from the rule of reason as well as from Article 36 EC, whereas only the latter may also benefit measures which differentiate between domestic and imported products.[298] As will become clear below, there is now a category of measures which the Court formerly would have evaluated under the rule of reason, but now regards as not being caught by Article 30 at all, an approach which to say the least has been dogged by controversy, as much about the reasoning as about the concrete result. But the most important aspect of *Cassis* is that it laid the foundations of the positive aspect of Article 30, namely that it

---

294. [1974] ECR 837 at 852.
295. *Ibid.* See section 3.3.3, *post.*
296. [1979] ECR 649, [1979] 3 CMLR 494.
297. *E.g.* Case 113/80 *Commission v. Ireland* [1981] ECR 1625 at 1639; Case 207/83 *Commission v. United Kingdom* [1985] ECR 1201 at 1212. It is submitted that the bizarre approach in Case 2/90 *Commission v. Belgium* [1992] ECR 4431 at 4480 does not affect the generality of the statement in the text. See, further, Gormley in Krämer *et al.* (eds.), *Law and Diffuse Interests in the European Legal Order* (*Festschrift* for Reich, Baden-Baden, 1997) 11 at 22.
298. *E.g.* Case 4/75 *Rewe-Zentralfinanz GmbH v. Landwirtschaftskammer* [1975] ECR 843 at 860.

involved not merely the prohibition of restrictions on trade between Member States, it also involved the idea of the mutual acceptance of goods. That in turn was a substantial element in the revision of the Commission's approach to harmonization of laws and formed the central tenet of the White Paper *Completing the Internal Market* in particular as regards technical harmonization and the approach to financial services.[299]

Groenveld – an export peculiar. Logically, a reader of the EC Treaty would assume that the *Dassonville* approach would be applied *mutatis mutandis* to exports, but, as will be explained in more detail in section 3.2.3, below, that has not been the case since the judgment in Case 15/79 *P.B. Groenveld BV v. Produktschap voor Vee en Vlees.*[300] The *Dassonville* approach is still applied to measures solely applicable to exports, but measures applicable irrespective of the destination of the products will now only fall foul of Article 34 EC if they have as their 'specific object or effect the restriction of patterns of exports and thereby the establishment of a difference in treatment between the domestic trade of a Member State and its export trade in such a way as to provide a particular advantage for national production or for the domestic market of the State in question at the expense of the production or the trade of other Member States.'[301] The result of this limitation of the prohibition and the application of the second variant of the freedom concept[302] is that non-discriminatory measures which hinder exports, a phenomenon regularly seen in environmental cases, do not need any specific justification.[303] Those export restrictions which are caught by Article 34 EC will not be able to benefit from the case-law based exceptions of the rule of reason, they will stand or fall according to the criteria of Article 36 EC.[304]

299. See section 1.1, *ante*.
300. [1979] ECR 3409 at 3415, confirmed in Case 155/80 *Oebel* [1981] ECR 1993 at 2009 and in myriad judgments subsequently. The judgment in *Groenveld* reflects a fear that exports of Dutch meat products would have reduced had the Court found the measure incompatible with Art. 34 EC, but it would have been open to the Court to uphold the measure on the ground of consumer protection or prevention of unfair commercial practices. This judgment is perhaps a classic example of hard cases making bad law: an approach which might be defensible in its original context is simply repeated willy nilly in subsequent judgments.
301. *Ibid.*
302. See section 1.3, *supra*.
303. But see the approach in relation to Community directives in *e.g.* Case 172/82 *Syndicat national des fabricants raffineurs d'huile de graissage et al v. GIE 'Inter-Huiles' et al.* [1983] ECR 555, [1983] 3 CMLR 485; Case 173/83 *Commission v. France* [1985] ECR 491 at 507, and Case 240/83 *Procureur de la République v. Association de défense des Brûleurs d'uiles Usagées (ADBHU)* [1985] ECR 531 at 549–550.
304. See, further, sections 3.2.3 and 3.3, *post*.

Local regulation of socio-economic life: licensing laws, Sunday trading and sales techniques. The application of the *Dassonville* approach, with its wide basic principle and its case-law approach of a rule of reason in particular began to run into some difficulties in the early Eighties, which magnified with a series of attacks on various aspects of what may be termed the local regulation of socio-economic life. Thus the Court was confronted with challenges to café licensing laws;[305] bans on nightwork in bakeries;[306] flour-milling quotas;[307] sex shop licensing bye-laws,[308] powers of tax collectors to seize goods;[309] obligations on sellers to divulge all relevant information;[310] and, most significantly, Sunday trading laws.[311] In fact there was little consistency in these judgments, with most of these areas being held to fall outside the scope of Article 30 EC, save in the cases dealing with Sunday trading. In the first of the Sunday trading cases, Case C-145/88 *Torfaen Borough Council v. B & Q PLC*[312] the Court clearly accepted that a Sunday trading measure was caught by Article 30 EC, but left the question of the assessment of the justification of the measure firmly in the hands of the national court. Subsequently, the Court indicated that in its view Sunday trading measures were reasonable and justified, at least in the absence of any discrimination against foreign products.[313] It might have been thought that this approach was then clear enough: the Court did not want to know about Sunday trading. After the judgment in *Torfaen* a

---

305. Case 75/81 *Blesgen* [1982] ECR 1211, [1983] 1 CMLR 431. In the 2nd ed. of this work (ed. Gormley, Deventer, 1989) 380 this judgment and that in Case 155/80 *Oebel* [1981] ECR 1993, [1983] 1 CMLR 390 were described as being instances 'in which the final result may well have been correct but the reasoning, with the greatest respect, was not.'

306. Case 155/80 *Oebel* [1981] ECR 1993, [1983] 1 CMLR 390.

307. Case 148/85 *Directeur Général des Impôts v. Forest* [1986] ECR 449, [1988] 2 CMLR 577.

308. Case C-23/90 *Quietlynn Ltd. v. Southend Borough Council* [1990] ECR I-3059; Case C-350/89 *Sheptonhurst Ltd. v. Newham Borough Council* [1991] ECR I-2387.

309. Case C-69/88 *H. Krantz GmbH & Co. v. Ontvanger der Directe Belastingen et al.* [1990] ECR I-583.

310. Case C-93/92 *CMC Motorradcenter GmbH v. Baskiciogullari* [1993] ECR I-5009.

311. Case C-145/88 *Torfaen Borough Council v. B & Q PLC Torfaen Borough Council v. B & Q PLC* [1989] ECR 3851, [1990] 1 CMLR 337; Case C-312/89 *Union départementale des syndicats CGT de l'Aisne v. SIDEF Conforama et al.* [1991] ECR I-997; Case C-332/89 *Marchandise et al.* [1991] ECR I-1027; Case C-169/91 *Council of the City of Stoke-on-Trent et al. v. B & Q PLC* [1992] ECR I-6635, [1993] 1 CMLR 4287; Case C-306/88 *Rochdale Borough Council v. Anders* [1992] ECR I-6457, and Case C-304/90 *Reading Borough Council v. Payless DIY Ltd. et al.* [1992] ECR I-6493. See further, Barnard (1994) 57 MLR 449, and Jarvis (1995) 44 ICLQ 451.

312. [1989] ECR 3851, [1990] 1 CMLR 337, see Arnull (1991) 16 ELRev. 112; Gormley (1990) 27 CMLRev.141, and Oliver (1991) ILJ 298.

313. E.g. Case C-312/89 *Union départementale des syndicats CGT de l'Aisne v. SIDEF Conforama et al.* [1991] ECR I-997 at 1025; Case C-332/89 *Marchandise et al.* [1991] ECR I-1027 at 1041; Case C-169/91 *Council of the City of Stoke-on-Trent v. B & Q PLC* [1992] ECR I-6635, [1993] 1 CMLR 4287.

considerable discussion took place in academic literature over the scope of Article 30 EC.[314] While the Commission's agent in *Torfaen*[315] and Advocate General Van Gerven in *Torfaen* both sought to restrict the breadth of the basic principle in *Dassonville*, the Court did not follow this approach. Indeed it did not follow that approach in any of the other Sunday trading cases, but followed by and large orthodox reasoning (finding the measure capable of hindering trade between Member States and then looking at the justification advanced). There remained the fact, though, that the approach to the other types measures mentioned above was different: the Court found that they fell outside the scope of Article 30. Indeed, in some of these judgments the Court even noted that the measures were not designed to hinder trade between Member States.[316]

However, there was another line of case-law which dealt with methods of sales properly so-called (sales techniques).[317] Here the approach of traders was greeted with far more success in general than was the case with the type of 'social order' measures discussed above. This type of measures entered into the heart of the consumer protection field, and it was not surprising that the Court treated them as being effectively rule of reason questions of consumer protection or the prevention of unfair commercial practices. Indeed, the judgment in Case C-362/88 *GB-INNO-BM v. Confédération du Commerce Luxembourgeois*[318] may be described as the high water mark of the cross-border consumer as a beneficiary of Community law. The line coming from these judgments was very clearly that restrictions on the use of certain sales techniques could indeed

314. White (1989) 26 CMLRev. 235; Gormley (1989) 9 YBEL 197; Gormley (1989/1) LIEI 9; Mortelmans (1991) 28 CMLRev. 115; Steiner (1992) 29 CMLRev. 749; Chalmers (1993) 42 ICLQ 269, and Wils (1993) 18 ELRev. 475.

315. White. Not surprisingly, the argument presented followed that in his article, *ibid.* After the judgment in *Torfaen* the Commission returned to a more orthodox approach in its observations.

316. But, as was mentioned in note 64, *supra*, it is the effect which is decisive (although intention may very well be relevant in particular to deciding whether the measure is justified or infringes the second sentence of Art. 36 EC, or to deciding whether an infringement is sufficiently serious to give rise to liability on the part of the Member State in damages).

317. Case 286/81 *Oosthoek's Uitgeversmaatschappij BV* [1982] ECR 4575, [1983] 3 CMLR 428; Case 382/87 *Buet v. Ministère public* [1989] ECR 1235, [1993] 3 CMLR 659; Case 362/88 *GB-INNO-BM v. Confédération de Commerce Luxembourgeois* [1990] ECR I-667, [1991] 2 CMLR 801; Case C-369/88 *Delattre* [1991] ECR I-1487; Case C-60/89 *Monteil et al.* [1991] ECR I-1547; Case C-239/90 *SCP Boscher, Studer et Fromentin v. SA British Motors Wright et al.* [1991] ECR I-2023; Cases C-1 and 176/90 *Aragonesa de Publicidad Exterior SA et al. v. Departmento de Sanidad y Seguridad Social de la Generalitat de Cataluña* [1991] ECR I-4151; Case C-126/91 *Schutzverein gegen Unwesen in der Wirtschaft eV v. Yves Rocher GmbH* [1993] ECR I-2361, and Case C-271/92 *Laboratoire de Prothèses Oculaires (LPO) v. Union Nationale des Syndicats d'Opticiens de France (UNSOF)* [1993] ECR I-2899.

318. [1990] ECR I-667, [1991] 2 CMLR 801.

constitute measures having equivalent effect under Article 30; the Court then went on to discuss whether the alleged justification appeared to be made out. In fact the Court's examination of the alleged justifications became so detailed that the referring national court had little to do but apply the judgment of the Court mechanically. This was also true in the Sunday trading judgments after *Torfaen*. It was thus scarcely surprising that traders began to see the Court of Justice as the market deregulator *par excellence*.[319]

Keck and Mithouard. In the remarkable judgment in Cases C-267 and 268/91 *Keck and Mithouard*[320] the Court purported to clarify its case-law in the areas considered immediately above. This judgment has been described as 'arrogant',[321] 'reasoning renounced',[322] 'inexplicable', 'impudent', and the 'wrong answer to the right question'[323] by its critics, although Mortelmans has opined that it came as no surprise.[324] As an attempt to clarify the law it has been recognized as being underwhelming, not to say a qualified success.[325] It is no accident that perhaps the two most strident critics of *Keck and Mithouard* have considerable experience in dealing with Article 30 complaints in the Commission, particularly during its very active pursuit of Article 30 enforcement in the Eighties.[326] The core criticism in fact

319. In fact even in instances in which attacks through case-law did not always succeed, the pressure of public opinion, combined with a more deregulatory approach on the part of the administration achieved the results desired by traders (*e.g.* in the United Kingdom in respect of Sunday trading). It will, though, be remembered that in principle socio-economic policy choices are matters for the Member States, subject to compliance with Community law; the Court of Justice is rightly not in the business of setting the socio-economic agenda of the Community or of the Member States – that is the businesss of elected politicians. But the Court can and does face the Member States and the Community Institutions with the consequences in Community law of the obligations into which they have entered.

320. [1993] ECR I-6097, [1995] 1 CMLR 101, see (from the vast array of annotations and discussions) Ackermann (1994) RIW 189; Becker (1994) EuR 162; Capelli (1996) RMC 678; Chalmers (1994) 19 ELRev. 385; Gormley (1994) 5 EBLR 63 and (1996) 19 Fordh. Int'l. L.J. 866; Joliet (1995) 1 Columb. J. Eur. L. 436 (in French in (1994) JT (Dr. Eur.) 145, in German in (1994) GRURInt. 979); Mattera (1994) RMUE 117; Mortelmans (1994) SEW 120 and 236; Reich (1994) 31 CMLRev. 459; Ross in Craiger and Floundas (eds.), *1996 Onwards – Lowering the Barriers Further* (Chichester, 1996) 45; Roth (1994) 31 CMLRev. 845; Sack (1994) WRP 281 and (1994) EWS 37; Schilling (1994) EuR 50; Stuyck (1994) CDE 431, and Weatherill (1996) 33 CMLRev. 885.

321. Biesheuvel in *NRC Handelsblad*, 17 December 1993, p. 14.

322. Gormley (1994) 5 EBLR 63.

323. Mattera (1994) RMUE 117 at 118.

324. (1994) SEW 115 at 120.

325. *E.g.* Jacobs, Adv. Gen. in Case C-412/93 *Société d'Importation Édouard Leclerc-Siplec v. TF1 Publicité SA et al.* [1995] ECR I-179 at 194; Tesauro (1995) 15 YBEL 1 at 7, and Due in Due *et al.* (eds.), *op. cit.* (see note 259, *supra*) 273 at 281.

326. Mattera (for years head of the Article 30 unit in the old DG III (now a director in DG XV) with unrivalled experience in the field) and Gormley.

centres more around the paucity of reasoning than the concrete result for the traders concerned, and reflects concern at the hands-off signal which it sent to the Member States.[327] The following discussion sets out the reasoning advanced by the Court and then examines case-law since *Keck and Mithouard*.[328]

Keck and Mithouard draws a distinction between product requirements and selling arrangements. It clearly does not alter the basic principle in *Dassonville*, as it expressly repeats that principle. The positive approach of mutual acceptance of goods stemming from *Cassis de Dijon* is clearly maintained and equally applicable provisions concerning the conditions with which products must comply are still evaluated under Article 30 with application of the rule of reason or Article 36 EC as appropriate. The illustrative list of types of measures covered by Article 30 which the Court borrowed from *Cassis de Dijon* (requirements as to designation, form, size, weight, composition, presentation, labelling and packaging) bears a distinct resemblance to the list of measures presented by the Commission in Directive 70/50.[329] The result clearly follows the line taken in relation to the local regulation of socio-economic life in the cases discussed above dealing with matters other than Sunday trading or sales techniques.

Expressly stating that it was finding '[c]ontrary to what has previously decided,'[330] but without indicating what case-law was thus overruled, the Court held that 'the application to products coming from other Member States of national provisions restricting or prohibiting certain selling arrangements is not such as to hinder directly or indirectly, actually or potentially, trade between Member States within the meaning of the *Dassonville* judgment, provided that those provisions apply to all afffected traders operating within the national territory and provided that they affect in the same manner, in law and in fact, the marketing of domestic products and of those from other Member States.'[331] The Court concluded

327. They have attempted to invoke the *Keck and Mithouard* approach in cases in other areas than Art. 30 EC, so far to no avail, as was noted by Tesauro (1995) 15 YBEL 1 at 7. Criticism of the reasoning (but also not the result) was advanced by Jacobs, Adv. Gen. in Case C-412/93 *Société d'Importation Édouard Leclerc-Siplec v. TF1 Publicité SA et al.* [1995] ECR I-179 at 194.

328. Reference should be made to the literature cited for full treatment of the *Keck and Mithouard* debate. That the judgment was less than a model of clarity seems virtually universally accepted. As to the background to *Keck and Mithouard*, see the opinions of Tesauro, Adv. Gen. in Case C-292/92 *Hünermund v. Landesapothekerkammer Baden-Württemberg* [1993] ECR I-6787 at 6800–6815 (delivered before the judgment in *Keck and Mithouard*) and Van Gerven, Adv. Gen. in Cases C-401 and 402/92 *Tankstation 't Heuske vof et al.* [1994] ECR I-2199 at 2212–2221.

329. See section 3.2.1, *ante*. It also effectively takes on board much of White's approach (1989) 29 CMLRev. 235.

330. [1993] ECR I-6097 at 6131.

331. *Ibid*.

that if 'those conditions are fulfilled,the application of such rules to the sale of products from another Member State meeting the requirements laid down by that State is not by nature such as to prevent their access to the market or to impede such access any more than it impedes the access of domestic products. Such rules therefore fall outside the scope of Article 30 of the Treaty.'[332]

What was clearly absent was any definition of the term 'selling arrangements'. Clearly this would be necessary to determine precisely which equally applicable measures would infringe Article 30 in the new vision. But measures which discriminate against imports, whether on the face of the measures or otherwise, will still be caught by Article 30 EC, as discrimination is a sufficient but not a necessary criterion for infringement of Article 30.[333] In Case C-320/93 *Lucien Ortscheit GmbH v. Eurim-Pharm Arzneimittel GmbH*[334] the Court spoke of 'marketing' rather than 'selling arrangements', which reflects that transactions may involve lease or hire-purchase rather than simply sales.

The approach in *Keck and Mithouard* was confirmed soon afterwards in Case C-292/92 *Hünermund v. Landesapothekerkammer Baden-Württemberg*[335] which dealt with rules of professional conduct prohibiting pharmacists from advertising para-pharmaceutical products outside their pharmacies and in various judgments dealing with Sunday trading or shop-closing legislation.[336] Thus it is plain that in *Keck and Mithouard* the Court was seeking to head off not merely challenges to sales techniques legislation but also to other types of non-discriminatory local regulation of socio-economic life. The Court has also found that national legislation restricting the sale of infant formula processed milk to pharmacists' shops is not caught by Article 30 EC.[337] A similar conclusion was adopted in respect of national legislation prohibiting the televising of advertisements for the distribution sector,[338] the sale of products at extremely small profit

332. *Ibid.*
333. Case C-317/92 *Commission v. Germany* [1994] ECR I-2039; Case C-320/93 *Lucien Ortscheit GmbH v. Eurim-Pharm Arzneimittel GmbH* [1994] ECR I-5243.
334. [1994] ECR I-5243 at 5261–5262, a point picked up by Van Gerven, Adv. Gen. in Cases C-401 and 402/92 *Tankstation 't Heuske vof et al.* [1994] ECR I-2199 at 2212, originally pointed out by Mortelmans (1994) SEW 115 at 122.
335. [1993] ECR I-6787. This would have been a better case in which to shut off attempts to challenge equally applicable local regulation of socio-economic life.
336. *E.g.* Cases C-401 and 402/92 *Tankstation 't Heukske vof et al.* [1994] ECR I-2199; Cases C-69 and 258/93 *Punto Casa SpA et al. v. Sindaco del Commune di Capena et al.* [1994] ECR I-2355; Cases C-418/93 *etc. Semeraro Casa Uno Srl et al. v. Sindaco del Commune di Ebrusco et al.* [1996] ECR I-2975, and Cases C-140-142/94 *DIPSpA et al. v. Commune di Basso del Grappa et al.* [1995] ECR I-3257.
337. Case C-391/92 *Commission v. Greece* [1995] ECR I-1621.
338. Case C-412/93 *Société d'Importation Édouard Leclerc-Siplec v. TF1 Publicité SA et al.* [1995] ECR I-179. See also Cases C-34–36/95 *Konsmentombudsmannen (KO) v. De Agostini (Svenska) Förlag AB et al.* [1997] ECR I-3843 at 3890–3891.

margins,[339] and reserving the retail sale of manufactured tobacco products to authorized distributors.[340] Thus the earlier case-law relating to channelling of sales through certain types of traders[341] would certainly seem to be undone by the *Keck and Mithouard* approach,[342] yet, with the utmost possible respect, the Court seems to have forgotten that the basic principle in *Dassonville* struck a fundamental blow against channelling of sales through certain types of traders.[343]

But if some of these judgments seem to neglect the interest of the consumer in parallel import channels, in cases since *Keck and Mithouard* dealing with rules which clearly affect products as such or how they are presented the Court has made it clear that the *Dassonville* basic principle and the evaluation of rule of reason arguments will continue. Thus in Case C-315/92 *Verband Sozialer Wettbewerb eV v. Clinique Laboratories SNC et al.*[344] the Court upheld the right of the trade-mark owner to sell its cosmetics under the name 'Clinique', noting that nobody was likely to believe that he or she was buying a pharmaceutical product, particularly as in Germany cosmetics were sold in beauty parlours or department stores rather than in pharmacies.[345] Similarly, in Case C-470/93 *Verein gegen Unwesen in Handel und Gewerbe, Köln eV v. Mars GmbH*[346] the Court, as so often in the past, refused to accept 'nannying' of consumers, holding that the standard of consumer protection had to reflect 'reasonably circumspect consumers'[347] and thus that Mars could not be forced to repackage its products for the German market because the mention of increased weight for the same price took up proportionately greater space of the packing than the percentage of free increased weight. In Case C-320/93 *Lucien Ortscheit GmbH v. Eurim-Pharm Arzneimittel GmbH*[348] it was easy for the Court to bring the prohibition of advertising within the scope of Article 30 EC as it applied solely to imported products,[349] and in Case

339. Case C-63/94 *Groupement national des négociants en pommes de terre de Belgique v. ITM Belgium SA et al.* [1995] ECR I-2467.
340. Case C-387/93 *Banchero* [1995] ECR I-4663.
341. Case C-369/88 *Delattre* [1991] ECR I-1487; Case C-60/89 *Monteil et al.* [1991] ECR I-1547 and Case C-271/92 *Laboratoire de Prothèses Oculaires (LPO) v. Union Nationale des Syndicats d'Opticiens de France (UNSOF)* [1993] ECR I-2899.
342. Unless the obligation is a 'local grab' measure, see Cases C-277/91 *etc. Ligur Carni Srl et al. v. Unità Sanitaria Locale no XV di Genova et al.* [1993] ECR I-6621 at 6661 (obligation to use a municipal slaughterhouse).
343. [1974] ECR 837 at 852.
344. [1994] ECR I-317.
345. On the continent retail pharmacies have not gone in the same direction as in the United Kingdom, but even in the latter cosmetics are always presented separately from any pharmaceutical or para-pharmaceutical products.
346. [1995] ECR I-1923.
347. *Ibid.* at 1944.
348. [1994] ECR I-5243 at 5261–5262.
349. Cases C-34–36/95 *Konsumentombudsmannen (KO) v. De Agostini (Svenska) Förlag AB et al.* [1997] ECR I-3843 at 3890–3891 show the importance of the need to

C-368/95 *Vereinigte Familiapress Zeitungsverlags- und vertriebs GmbH v. Heinrich Bauer Verlag*[350] the Court found that while prize games in magazines constituted a method of sales promotion, they were an integral part of the magazine in which they appeared, thus the application of national legislation prohibiting prize games did not constitute a 'selling arrangement' within the meaning of *Keck and Mithouard*, but clearly jeopardized the access of the product concerned to the market of the importing Member State. Finally, the Court has rejected attempts to import the *Keck and Mithouard* approach wholesale into the freedom to provide services,[351] although a particularly important feature of that judgment was that it concerned restrictions imposed by the exporting Member State rather than the importing Member State.[352]

Clearly if a measure which is considered by the Court to be a 'selling arrangement' or 'marketing arrangement' under the *Keck and Mithouard* approach is to escape the ambit of Article 30 EC, two conditions must be satisfied: it must be applicable to all traders, and it must apply equally to domestic and imported products, both in law and in fact. The first of these seems to recall the statement in *Dassonville* that the means of proof had to be accessible to all Community nationals, but it may be wondered what the added value of the statement is.[353] As to equal applicability in law and in fact, this simply reflects one of the criteria already applied in relation to the rule of reason.[354] Again, this represents nothing new.

demonstrate that an ostensibly equally applicable advertising ban in fact has a greater effect on imported than on domestic products if Art. 30 EC is to be invoked (although the rule of reason or Art. 36 EC may very well save an advertising ban).

350. [1997] ECR I-3689 at 3714.
351. Case C-384/93 *Alpine Investments BV v. Minister van Financiën* [1995] ECR I-1141 at 1177–1178. Similarly, an attempt to apply the *Keck and Mithouard* approach to the free movement of workers in Case C-415/93 *Union Royale Belge des Sociétés de Football Association ASBL et al. v. Bosman et al.* [1995] ECR I-4921 at 5070–5071 received short shrift.
352. It certainly seems unlikely that the Court will fall to the temptation to extend the scope of the *Keck and Mithouard* approach (a view which appears to be shared by Tesauro (1995) YBEL 1 at 7). In any event, in *Alpine Investments* the Court concluded that the measure was justifiable in the interests of protecting consumers against 'cold calling' in the field of financial services.
353. See Jans (1995) SEW 205, *cf.* Mortelmans (1994) SEW 124. The prohibition of discrimination on ground of nationality contained in Art. 6 EC surely covers the point, and in any event, Art. 30 EC benefits goods as such, irrespective of the nationality of their owner, consignor, consignee or transporter.
354. See Van Gerven, Adv.Gen. in Cases C-401 and 402/92 *Tankstation 't Heukske VOF et al.* [1994] ECR I-2199 at 2216–2217. As to discrimination on the face of a measure, see *e.g.* Case 152/78 *Commission v. France* [1980] ECR 2299, [1981] 2 CMLR 743; as to discrimination in fact, see Case 177/83 *Theodor Kohl KG v. Ringelhahn & Rennett SA* [1984] ECR 3651, [1985] 3 CMLR 340; Case 207/83 *Commission v. United Kingdom* [1985] ECR 1201, [1985] 2 CMLR 259, and Case C-275/92 *H.M. Commissioners of Customs and Excise v. Schindler et al.* [1994] ECR I-1039, [1995] 1 CMLR 4.

Since *Keck and Mithouard*, while the Court has mostly shown itself keen to consider measures as 'selling arrangements' or as 'marketing arrangements', it has not always addressed the issue.[355] Nor has the Court contributed to the clarity of its case-law by still referring to some of the judgments which *Keck and Mithouard* appears to overrule.[356] However, the answer to the latter point is that these cases are still good law for certain issues, such as the relationship between the rule of reason and Article 36 EC for the purposes of health protection;[357] the proposition that 'a national measure having limited territorial scope cannot escape being characterized as discriminatory or protective for the purposes of the rules on the free movement of goods on the ground that it affects both the sale of products from other parts of the national territory and the sale of products imported from other Member States',[358] or as illustrations of the assessment of the proportionality of a measure,[359] but no longer for the more general point of the ambit of Article 30 EC itself.

Jarvis has rightly opined that the impact and importance of *Keck and Mithouard* should not be overstated,[360] although his welcome of that approach as being a rule-based approach which is better for legal certainty[361] is perhaps too optimistic: the Court in fact was unwilling to offer certainty with regard to which of its earlier case-law it was overturning and if anything made matters less clear, even if it was attempting to bring a semblance of system into what was certainly an inconsistent and unsystematic body of case-law. Tesauro has stated that the Court 'has merely pointed out that the ruling in *Dassonville*, given in relation to a measure concerning imported products and impairing their access to the market of the importing country, cannot be extended to marketing arrangements of products which, once they have gained

See also Cases C-34–36/95 *Konsumentombudsmannen (KO) v. De Agostini (Svenska) Förlag AB et al.* [1997] ECR I-3843 at 3890–3891.

355. *E.g.* Case C-277/91 *Ligur Carni Srl et al. v. Unità Sanitaria Locale No XV di Genova et al.* [1993] ECR I-6621 at 6660–6661; Case C-323/93 *Société Civile Agricole du Centre d'Insémination de la Crespelle v. Coopérative d'Élevage et d'Insémination Artificielle du Département de la Mayenne* [1994] ECR I-5077 at 5106–5109, pointed out by Lenz, Adv. Gen. in Case 391/92 *Commission v. Greece* [1995] ECR I-1621 at 1630.

356. *E.g.* the reference to *Buet* in Case C-315/92 *Verband Sozialer Wettbewerb eV v. Clinique Laboratories SNC et al* [1994] ECR I-317 at 336 and the reference to *Aragonesa* in Case C-277/91 *Ligur Carni Srl et al. v. Unità Sanitaria Locale No XV di Genova et al.* [1993] ECR I-6621 at 6661 and Case C-189/95 *Franzén* [1997] ECR I-5909. In all instances the references were to propositions which are clearly unaltered by the *Keck and Mithouard* approach.

357. Cases C-1 and 176/90 *Aragonesa de Publicidad Exterior SA et al. v. Departmento de Sanidad y Seguridad Social de la Generalitat de Cataluña* [1991] ECR I-4151 at 4183–4184.

358. *Ibid.* at 4186.

359. Case 382/87 *Buet et al. v. Ministère public* [1989] ECR 1235 at 1251.

360. Jarvis, *op. cit.* (see note 36, *supra*) 120.

361. *Ibid.* at 119–120.

unhindered access to the market, are subject to such arrangements in the same way as domestic products.'[362] Although he also claims that the Court has clarified matters, he has to pray in aid judgments subsequent to those in *Keck and Mithouard* and *Hünermund* in aid in support of that claim.[363] But certainly, any sounding of the death-knell of the internal market is, like reports of Mark Twain's death, greatly exaggerated.

3.2.2 The prohibition of measures having equivalent effect and imports: Article 30 EC

After the overview in the preceding section which has traced the development of the Court's approach to the local regulation of socio-economic life and selling or trading arrangements as such, and noted the new approach which excludes them from the ambit of Article 30 EC, the basic principle in *Dassonville*, which is still the point of departure for the Court, is now examined in more concrete detail. It is convenient to repeat that principle: '[a]ll trading rules enacted by Member States which are capable of hindering, directly or indirectly, actually or potentially, intra-Community trade are to be considered as measures having an effect equivalent to quantitative restrictions.'[364] This principle has been repeated on countless occasions, and, as has been observed in the preceding section, is still cited in and after *Keck and Mithouard*. The various elements of this definition are now discussed.

Trading rules. The phrase 'trading rules' in the basic principle in *Dassonville* is not restrictive; in various judgments the Court has simply spoken of the measures in question being capable of acting as a hindrance to imports between Member States.[365] In other cases the Court has condemned restrictions on production or investment as being incompatible with the prohibition on measures having equivalent effect to quantitive restrictions.[366] Thus the phrase should be understood in the sense of

362. Tesauro (1995) 15 YBEL 1 at 6.
363. *Ibid.* At 7.
364. [1974] ECR 837 at 852. See, further, section 3.2.2, *post.*
365. *E.g.* Case 4/75 *Rewe-Zentralfinanz GmbH v. Landwirtschaftskammer* [1975] ECR 843 at 858; Case 65/75 *Tasca* [1976] ECR 291 at 307–308; Case 72/83 *Campus Oil Ltd et al. v. Minister for Industry and Energy et al.* [1984] ECR 2727 at 2746, and Case 75/81 *Blesgen v. Belgian State* [1982] ECR 1211 at 1228–1229. Sometimes the Court does mention 'trading rules' (*e.g.* Case 41/76 *Criel, née Donckerwolcke et al v. Procureur de la République et al.* [1976] ECR 1921 at 1935 and Case C-189/95 *Franzén* [1997] ECR I-5909) but it is clear that the ambit of Article 30 is wider than purely trading rules.
366. Case 190/73 *Officier van Justitie v. Van Haaster* [1974] ECR 1123, [1974] 2 CMLR 521 and Case 111/76 *Officier van Justitie v. Van der Hazel* [1977] ECR 901. But see the reasoning relating to quotas for milling of flour in Case 148/85 *Direction Générale des Impots v. Forest et al.* [1986] ECR 3449 at 3475. In this latter judgment the English

'rules'[367] or 'measures'.[368] Obstacles affecting suppliers or consumers (such as patients) are covered.[369] The case-law of the Court shows that in a number of instances even non-binding decisions or acts may be regarded as measures having equivalent effect within the meaning of Article 30 EC.[370] Indeed, the concept of a prohibited measure extends to cover 'full and fair opportunity' clauses and criteria (such as the contribution which a tenderer intends to make to the development of the economy of a Member State) which a public body intends to take into account when awarding exploration and exploitation licenses.[371] An intention to take a decision or measure does not, it is submitted, itself constitute a prohibited measure.[372] It will be recalled that there is no *de minimis* rule in Article 30 EC.[373] The term 'measures' is wide enough to embrace judicial acts,[374] decisions of

text is at variance with the French, the French being the language of the case. The conclusion in French was '*une telle mesure de contingentement au niveau de la production de fairine n'a, en réalité, pas de lien avec l'importation de blé et n'est pas de nature à entraver le commerce entre Etats membres.*' In English this is rendered as 'such a system of quotas at the level of flour production in fact has no effect on wheat imports and is not likely to impede trade between Member States.' In view of what has been discussed in the preceding section, *Forest* must now be placed, along with *Blesgen* in the line of judgments culminating in *Keck and Mithouard.*

367. Case 190/73 *Van Haaster* [1974] ECR 1123 at 1133–1134; Cases 177 and 178/82 *Van de Haar et al.* [1984] ECR 1797 at 1812–1813.
368. Case C-324/93 *R. v. Secretary of State for the Home Department, ex parte Evans Medical Ltd. et al.* [1995] ECR I-563 at 604–605.
369. Case 215/87 *Schumacher v. Hauptzollamt Frankfurt am Main-Ost* [1989] ECR 617 at 639–640; Case C-362/88 *GB-INNO-BM v. Confédération du Commerce Luxembourgeois* [1990] ECR I-667 at 688–689.
370. Case 249/81 *Commission v. Ireland* [1982] ECR 4005, [1983] 2 CMLR 104 (the buy-Irish case); Case 21/84 *Commission v. France* [1985] ECR 1355 at 1364 (Pitney Bowes postal franking machines). The latter judgment is an example of an administrative practice being caught by Art. 30. For this to occur the Court required (at 1364–1365) 'a certain degree of consistency and generality. That generality must be assessed differently according to whether it is a market, such as that in postal franking machines, on which only a few undertakings are active. In the latter case, a national administration's treatment of a single undertaking may constitute a measure incompatible with Article 30.' Oliver, *op. cit.* (See note 102, *supra*) 78 is rightly critical of the narrowness of this criterion.
371. 52 *Halsbury's Laws of England* (4th ed., London, 1986) paras. 12.69 and 12.80; Gormley in Vaughan (ed.), *op. cit.* (see note 84, *supra*) paras. 382–384 and 408.
372. See Mortelmans (1995) SEW 65 (discussing a Dutch case). An announcement of an intention, just like a Ministerial speech inciting people to buy national products may well give rise to a letter from the Commission reminding the Member State of the relevant Treaty provisions, and of Art. 5 EC in particular, but it is thought unlikely that the Commission would commence infringement proceedings solely on the basis of such (however undesirable) action of a political nature.
373. See note 274, *supra*.
374. Case 58/80 *Dansk Supermarked A/S v. A/S Imerco* [1981] ECR 181 at 194; Case 6/81 *BV Industrie Diensten Groep v. J.A. Beele Handelmaatschappij* [1982] ECR 707 at 716. The likelihood of infringement proceedings because of judicial infringement of Art. 30 EC is, though, in practice nil (on the basis of experience so far). Again, a

professional bodies having a public regulatory function,[375] and national practices resulting from international agreements.[376] All these examples concerned specific measures. Global measures such as a restrictive budgetary or credit policy do not fall under the concept of measures caught by Article 30 EC; they must now be examined in the context of the EC Treaty's provisions dealing with Economic and Monetary Union.[377]

Member States: the addressees of Articles 30 and 34 EC. The prohibition contained in Article 30 EC is directed not only to Member States, it is also directed to the Community Institutions themselves.[378] It applies to measures of the public authorities at whatever level (national, regional or local) and to public bodies or institutions for whose acts the state is responsible in Community law.[379] Thus it embraces measures which apply only in part of a Member State, and a measure will not escape the ambit of Article 30 EC because it also affects products coming from another part of the Member State concerned as well as products imported from other Member States.[380] Thus the question whether a measure applies to imported and domestic goods alike is irrelevant in deciding whether it is capable of hindering, directly or indirectly, actually or potentially, trade

letter may wing its way from the Commission to the authorities of the Member State concerned, although that is scant comfort for victims of judicial misconception.

375. Cases 266 and 267/87 *R. v. The Royal Pharmaceutical Society of Great Britain, ex parte Association of Pharmaceutical Importers et al.* [1989] ECR 1295 at 1327; Case C-292/92 *Hünermund v. Landesapothekerkammer Baden-Württemberg* [1993] ECR I-6787 at 6821–6822.

376. Case C-324/93 *R. v. Secretary of State for the Home Department, ex parte Evans Medical Ltd. et al.* [1995] ECR I-563 at 605–607.

377. See Chapter IX, *post.*

378. Cases 80 and 81/77 *Société Les Commissionnaires Réunis Sàrl et al. v. Receveur des Douanes* [1978] ECR 927 at 946–947; Case 37/83 *Rewe-Zentral AG v. Director of the Landwirtschaftskammer Rheinland* [1984] ECR 1229 at 1248–1249; Case 218/82 *Commission v. Council* [1983] ECR 4063 at 4075 and Case 61/86 *United Kingdom v. Commission* [1988] ECR 431 at 462.

379. *E.g.* Case 77/69 *Commission v. Belgium* [1970] ECR 237 at 243; Case 249/81 *Commission v. Ireland* [1982] ECR 4005 at 4023. Case 45/87 R *Commission v. Ireland* [1987] ECR 1369 at 1376; Case 45/87 *Commission v. Ireland* [1988] ECR 4929 at 4962; Cases C-1 and 176/90 *Aragonesa de Publicidad Exterior SA et al. v. Departmento de Sanidad y Seguridad Social de la Generalitat de Cataluña* [1991] ECR I-4151 at 4183, and Case C-302/88 *Hennen Olie BV v. Stichting Interim Centraal Orgaan Voorraadvorming et al.* [1990] ECR I-4625 at 4643–4644. See, generally, Curtin (1990) 15 ELRev. 195 and Case C-188/89 *Foster et al. v. British Gas plc* [1990] ECR I-3313 at 3348–3349, and Van Gerven, Adv. Gen. at 3332–3336. As was noted above, even judicial acts may give rise to infringements of Art. 30 EC.

380. *E.g.* Case C-21/88 *Du Pont de Nemours Italiana SA v. Unità Sanitaria Locale No 2 di Carrara* [1990] ECR I-889 at 920; Cases C-1 and 176/90 *Aragonesa de Publicidad Exterior SA et al. v. Departmento de Sanidad y Seguridad Social de la Generalitat de Cataluña* [1991] ECR I-4151 at 4183–4184, and Cases C-277/91 *etc. Ligur Carni Srl et al. v. Unitarià Sanitaria Locale No XV di Genova et al.* [1993] ECR I-6621 at 6661.

between Member States. The fact that a measure is equally applicable will open the possibility of the application of the rule of reason,[381] but it is logically irrelevant to the question whether the measure is caught by the basic principle in *Dassonville*. Agreements concluded between various Member States may also fall within Article 30. EC.[382]

As far as the Community Institutions are concerned, the Court has occasionally applied the prohibition somewhat less stringently,[383] but it will have no hesitation in taking a strict view if it feels that they have not genuinely acted in the Community interest.[384] It is not yet wholly clear to what extent the Community Institutions themselves may rely on the exceptions to the free movement of goods principle.[385] It now seems decided that Articles 30–36 EC do not apply to the conduct of private parties in the sense that they would not catch a 'buy-British' policy of a chain of stores or a decision by an individual to boycott, say, French perfumes[386] on the ground of nuclear testing in the South Pacific, but that does not mean that these Articles do not have an effect on the conduct of private parties; thus the Court has placed limits on the extent to which a private party may rely on rights granted under national industrial and commercial property

381. As to which, see section 3.3.3, *post*.
382. Case 144/81 *Keurkoop BV v. Nancy Kean Gifts BV* [1982] ECR 2853, [1983] 2 CMLR 47; Case 286/86 *Ministère Public v. Deserbais* [1988] ECR 4907; Case C-3/91 *Exporteur SA v. LOR SA et al.* [1992] ECR I-5529; Case C-324/93 *R. v. Secretary of State for the Home Department, ex parte Evans Medical Ltd. et al.* [1995] ECR I-563. As to the relationship between Art. 30 EC and Art. 234 EC, see section 3.3.5, *post*.
383. See Case 46/76 *Bauhuis v. The Netherlands State* [1977] ECR 5 at 16–18 (on the basis that the Community provisions replaced otherwise justifiable diverse national provisions with a single set of rules); Case 37/83 *Rewe-Zentral AG v. Director of the Landwirtschaftskammer Rheinland* [1984] ECR 1229 at 1249; Case 15/83 *Denkavit Nederland BV v. Hoofdakkerbouwproduktschap voor Akkerbouwprodukten* [1984] ECR 2171 at 2184; Case C-39/90 *Denkavit Futtermittel GmbH v. Land Baden-Württemberg* [1991] ECR 3069 at 3108–3109; Case C-51/93 *Meyhui NV v. Schott Zwiesel Glaswerke AG* [1994] ECR I-3879 at 3898–3901, and Case C-114/96 *Kieffer and Thill* [1997] ECR I-3629 at 3655–3657. See also Tesauro, Adv. Gen. in Case C-41/93 *France v. Commission* [1994] ECR I-1829 at 1834. The controversial judgment in Case 106/81 *Kind v. Commission and Council* [1982] ECR 2885 was somewhat nuanced by Case 61/86 *United Kingdom v. Commission* [1988] ECR 431, [1988] 2 CMLR 98.
384. See note 378, *supra* and Case C-363/93 *Lancry v. Direction Générale des Douanes* [1994] ECR I-3957 at 3990–3992 (in relation to Arts. 9, 12 and 13 EC).
385. See section 2.4.1, *ante*; Currall (1985) 5 YBEL 191, and Oliver (1979) CDE 245. Clearly, the Court is prepared to take account of the Community interest of a measure (as in *Bauhuis*), which would suggest that a no less stringent examination of the justification for a barrier to trade between Member States resulting from Community legislation is appropriate than that applied to national justifications.
386. Case 311/85 *Asbl. Vereniging van Vlaamse Reisbureaus v. Asbl. Sociale Dienst van de plaatselijke en gewestlijke overheidsdiensten* [1987] ECR 3801 at 3830 (in relation to undertakings) states the proposition somewhat blandly, a line supported by Cases 177 and 178/82 *Van de Haar* [1984] ECR 1797 at 1812–1813. See the discussion of the various views in Gormley, *op. cit.* (see note 26, *supra*) 259–262, and Quinn and McGowan (1987) 12 ELRev. 163.

legislation or unfair competition legislation to prevent the importation of goods from another Member State or the sale of goods so imported.[387] Moreover, the Court has held that agreements between private parties may not derogate from the mandatory provisions of the Treaty on the free movement of goods.[388] The Court has confirmed that the Member States are obliged to adopt the necessary measures to ensure the free movement of goods, which means in particular that they may not stand idly by in the face of public disorder venting local anger at imports of, say, Welsh lamb into France, or Irish beef into the United Kingdom.[389]

Directly or indirectly, actually or potentially. The words 'indirectly' and 'potentially' indicate that the prohibition has a wide scope and is not limited to actually quantifiable barriers to trade between Member States. The term 'directly' is also now used in the case-law relating to Article 59 EC.[390] The term 'directly or indirectly' also occurs in the first paragraph of Article 95 EC.[391] The basic principle in *Dassonville* is very close to the definition applied to prohibited cartel agreements under Article 85 EC 'which may affect trade between Member States'. Thus in Cases 56 and 58/64 *Éts. Consten Sàrl and Grundig-Verkaufs-GmbH v. Commission*[392] the Court noted that 'what is particularly important is whether the agreement is capable of constituting a threat, either direct or indirect, actual or potential, to freedom of trade between Member States in a manner which might harm the attainment of the objectives of a single market between States.' This is an excellent example of the inter-relationship between the prohibitions on the conduct of Member States and the prohibitions on the conduct of undertakings. The EC Treaty, which seeks the removal of barriers to trade between Member States, cannot be regarded as permitting undertakings themselves to maintain or erect such barriers.[393] There are, however, important differences which should be recalled: there is no *de minimis* rule in Article 30, but there is in Article 85, and the Court has

---

387. *E.g.* Case 15/74 *Centrafarm BV et al. v. Sterling Drug Inc.* [1974] ECR 1147, [1974] 2 CMLR 480 and Case 187/80 *Merck & Co. Inc. v. Stephar BV et al.* [1981] ECR 2063, [1981] 3 CMLR 463.
388. Case 58/80 *Dansk Supermarked A/S v. A/S Imerco* [1981] ECR 181 at 195; Case 78/70 *Deutsche Grammophon Gesellschaft mbH v. Metro-SB-Großmärkte GmbH & Co. KG* [1971] ECR 487 at 499–500.
389. Case C-265/95 *Commission v. France* [1997] ECR I-6959. The same is obviously true in relation to official inaction in the face of lorry drivers' disputes blocking access or egress for foreign lorry drivers. See also Elworthy in Holder (ed.), *The Impact of EC Environmental Law in the United Kingdom* (Chichester, 1997) 303.
390. Case C-384/93 *Alpine Investments BV v. Minister van Financiën* [1995] ECR I-1141 at 1176 and 1178.
391. See section 2.5.1, *ante.*
392. [1966] ECR 299 at 340. See also Case 5/69 *Völk v. Éts. J. Vervaecke* [1969] ECR 295 at 302.
393. *Ibid.*

found that the criterion 'may affect trade between Member States' in Articles 85 and 86 EC refers to conduct affecting 'patterns of trade between Member States'[394] whereas Article 30 deals, as expressed in the basic principle in *Dassonville*, with measures which may 'hinder' intra-Community trade.[395]

Intra-Community trade. Article 30 EC applies not only to trade between Member States in goods originating within the Community, but also, by virtue of Article 9(2) EC, to goods originating in third countries which are in free circulation in a Member State.[396] Thus Article 30 does not apply to goods which for one reason or another are not already in free circulation, such as those which are undergoing inward processing or which are directly imported from a third country.[397] Nor is Article 30 applicable to wholly internal situations having noting to do with intra-Community trade.[398]

Examples of measures having equivalent effect. Over the years the case-law on Article 30 EC has gone from a steady trickle through a stream, to a flood and even a small sea of authority. It is in fact striking just how much of the case-law has been in the form of Article 177 EC references. Particularly until after the Commission's Communication on the consequences of the *Cassis de Dijon* judgment,[399] infringement proceedings were fairly thin on the ground. Certainly in the Eighties the Commission became extremely active in pursuing infringements; not necessarily because the Member States had become more protectionist (although during the recession years the kites of protectionism were ceratinly being flown in many circles), but because people simply became more aware of their rights under Community law. This was true of private individuals, small and medium-sized enterprises and large companies and multinationals alike. So much so that the unit dealing with Article 30 EC infringements in the Commission at times seemed like a free legal advice centre for the whole Community. Since the Eighties the pursuit of infringement proceedings in this field continues, albeit that the pace is perhaps less robust, in part

394. Case 56/65 *Société Technique Minière v. Maschinenbau Ulm GmbH* [1966] ECR 235 at 249; Case 22/78 *Hugin Kassaregister AB et al. v. Commission* [1979] ECR 1869 at 1899–1901.
395. See, further, VerLoren van Themaat (1996) SEW 398.
396. In accordance with Art. 10(1) EC. See Case 41/76 *Criel, née Donckerwolke et al. v. Procureur de la République et al.* [1976] ECR 1921 at 1935; Case 119/78 *SA des Grandes Distilleries Peureux v. Directeur des Services Fiscaux de la Haute-Saône et du Territoire de Belfort* [1979] ECR 975 at 986. See also Tegeder (1994) 19 ELRev. 86.
397. *E.g.* Case 51/75 *EMI Records Ltd. v. CBS United Kingdom Ltd.* [1976] ECR 811, [1976] 2 CMLR 235, and Case C-355/96 *Silhouette International Schmied GmbH & Co. KG v. Hartlauer Handelsgesellschaft mbH* [1998] ECR-nyr (16 July 1998).
398. See section 1.2, *ante.*
399. O.J. 1980 C256/2, see Mattera (1980) RMC 505; and Gormley (1981) 6 ELRev. 454 and literature cited there.

reflecting a desire to allocate resources more to getting legislation through the Council, in part perhaps reflecting the growing importance of Article 177 EC references. In any event, the approach of the Court has been very much on a case-by-case basis, rather than on a wholly systematic basis, as is evident from the criticisms voiced in section 3.2.1, above.

A complete discussion of the case-law and the various types of measures having equivalent effect to quantative restrictions is impossible in the space available here[400] but the following list gives some examples of the most important types of provisions, actions or administrative practices which are caught by the concept of measures having equivalent effect. Many of these measures had already been identified by the Commission in Directive 70/50.[401] In using these examples, it should be remembered that the Court may impliedly or even expressly decide that a measure is in fact justified and thus acceptable in the circumstances.[402] Account has been taken of the developments in the case-law referred to in section 3.2.1, above, in this list, so that some clarity as to the extent of the *Keck and Mithouard* approach may be afforded.

Accordingly, the following are classic examples of measures which will be caught by Article 30 EC: the promotion of particular import channels[403] or of particular products;[404] maximum or minimum price-regulatory measures (if a maximum price is fixed at such a low level that importing is simply not worthwhile, or if a minimum price is fixed at such a high level that the cheaper cost of imports cannot be reflected in the resale price, a price-regulatory measure will infringe Article 30 EC, even if it applies to domestic and imported products alike);[405] restrictions on production (in so

---

400. See, generally, Gormley in Vaughan (ed.), *op. cit.* (see note 84, *supra*), paras. 362–421, and Oliver, *op. cit.* (see note 102, *supra*) 130–171. Overviews of the case-law include those by Barents (1981) 18 CMLRev. 271; Gormley (1985) 10 ELRev. 431; Oliver (1986) 23 CMLRev. 325; Van Rijn (1988) 25 CMLRev. 593, and Gormley (1990) 27 CMLRev. 825. Weatherill has written regular overviews of the case-law in recent years in ICLQ.

401. O.J. English Special Edition 1970 (I), p. 17.

402. See section 3.3, *post.* Although in rulings on Art. 177 EC references the final say is in the hands of the national court, not infrequently the Court of Justice will make its view so clear that the national judge has little left to do but to apply the ruling concerned.

403. *E.g.* Case 8/74 *Procureur du Roi v. Dassonville et al.* [1974] ECR 837, 2 CMLR 436; Case 104/75 *Officier van Justitie v. De Peijper* [1976] ECR 613, [1976] 2 CMLR 271, and Case C-359/93 *Commission v. The Netherlands* [1995] ECR I-157. But no longer, it would appear, the obligation to sell through particular types of traders, see notes 337 and 341, *supra.* As to the obligation to go through a particular local operator, see Cases C-277/91 *etc. Ligur Carni Srl et al. v. Unità Sanitaria Locale no XV di Genova et al.* [1993] ECR I-6621 at 6661.

404. *E.g.* Case 269/83 *Commission v. France* [1985] ECR 837, [1985] 2 CMLR 399; Cases 266 and 267/87 *R. v.The Royal Pharmaceutical Society of Great Britain, ex parte Association of Pharmaceutical Importers et al.* [1989] ECR 1295, and Case C-18/88 *Régie des télégraphes et des téléphones v. GB-INNO-BM SA* [1991] ECR I-5941.

405. *E.g.* Case 13/77 *NV GB-INNO-BM v. Vereniging van de Kleinhandelaars in Tabak*

far as they lead to a reduction in the possibility of exporting);[406] legislation on the origin, packaging or presentation, composition or designation of goods;[407] buy-national policies or obligations to use national products;[408] 'local grab' measures;[409] duplicate checks or inspections,[410] and admini-

(*ATAB*) [1977] ECR 2115 [1978] 1 CMLR 283; Case 82/77 *Openbaar Ministerie v. Van Tiggele* [1978] ECR 25, [1978] 2 CMLR 528; Case 78/82 *Commission v. Italy* [1983] ECR 1955; Case 181/82 *Roussel Laboratoria BV v.The Netherlands State* [1983] ECR 3849, [1985] 1 CMLR 834; Case 238/82 *Duphar BV et al. v. The Netherlands State* [1984] ECR 523, [1985] 1 CMLR 256; Case 301/82 *SA Clin-Midy et al. v. Belgian State* [1984] ECR 251; Case 229/83 *Association des Centres distributeurs Édouard Leclerc et al. v. Sàrl 'Au blé vert' et al.* [1985] ECR 1 at 35 (which indicates that import transactions must be genuine, so exporting books for the purpose of reimporting them in order to escape from fixed prices will not constitute a genuine import transaction); Case 231/83 *Cullet et al. v. Centre Leclerc Toulouse et al.* [1985] ECR 306, [1985] 2 CMLR 524, Cases 80 and 159/85 *Nederlandse Bakkerij Stichting v. Edah BV* [1986] ECR 3359, [1988] 2 CMLR 113; Case 56/87 *Commission v. Italy* [1988] ECR 2919; Case C-249/88 *Commission v. Belgium* [1991] ECR I-1275; Case C-287/89 *Commission v. Belgium* [1991] ECR I-2233, and Case C-306/91 *Commission v. Italy* [1993] ECR I-2133. As to price controls in the pharmaceutical sector, see also the Commission's Communication (O.J. 1986 C 310/7), its general Communication on the pharmaceutical industry (COM (93) 718 Final), and the transparency directive, Dir. 89/105 (O.J. 1989 L 40/8). In relation to price-regulatory measures in sectors in which a common organization of the market exists see Gormley, *op. cit.* (see note 84, *supra*) 77–85 and *e.g.* Case 65/75 *Tasca* [1976] ECR 291, [1977] 2 CMLR 183; Cases 88–90/ 75 *Società SADAM et al. v. Comitato Interministeriale dei Prezzi et al.* [1976] ECR 323, [1977] 2 CMLR 183; Case 154/77 *Procureur du Roi v. Dechmann* [1978] ECR 1573, [1979] 2 CMLR 1; Cases 16–20/79 *Openbaar Ministerie v. Danis et al.* [1979] ECR 3327, [1980] 3 CMLR 492; Case 116/84 *Roelstraete* [1985] ECR 1705; Case 216/ 86 *Antonini v. Prefetto di Milano* [1987] ECR 2919; Case 127/87 *Commission v. Greece* [1988] ECR 3333, and Case 188/86 *Ministère public v. Lefevre* [1987] ECR 2963. It is clear that a price control measure which on its face discriminates against imported products will be incompatible with Art. 30 EC on that basis.

406. *E.g.* Case 190/73 *Officier van Justitie v. Van Haaster* [1974] ECR 1123, [1974] 2 CMLR 521 and Case 111/76 *Officier van Justitie v. Van der Hazel* [1977] ECR 901.

407. *E.g.* Case 113/80 *Commission v. Ireland* [1981] ECR 1625, [1982] 2 CMLR 706; Case 207/83 *Commission v.United Kingdom* [1985] ECR 1202, [1985] 2 CMLR 259 (on origin marking); Case 27/80 *Fietje* [1980] ECR 3839; Case 261/81 *Walter Rau Lebensmittel-werke v. De Smedt PvbA* [1982] ECR 3961, [1983] 2 CMLR 496; Case 16/83 *Prantl* [1984] ECR 1299, [1985] 2 CMLR 238 (on packaging); Case 94/82 *De Kikvorsch Groo-thandel-Import-Export BV* [1983] ECR 947, Case 176/84 *Commission v. Greece* [1987] ECR 1193 and Case 178/84 *Commission v. Germany* [1987] ECR 1227, [1988] 1 CMLR 813 (beer); Case 12/74 *Commission v. Germany* [1975] ECR 181, [1975] 1 CMLR 350 (*Sekt* and *Weinbrand*); Case 13/78 *Joh. Eggers Sohn & Co. v. Freie Hansestadt Bremen* [1978] ECR 1935, [1979] 1 CMLR 562 (*Weinbrand*); Case 788/79 *Gilli and Andres* [1980] ECR 2071, [1981] 1 CMLR 146 and Case 193/80 *Commission v. Italy* [1980] ECR 3019 (vinegar); Case 182/84 *Miro BV* [1985] ECR 3731, [1986] 3 CMLR 545 (*Jenever*); Case 179/85 *Commission v. Germany* [1986] ECR 3879 (*Pétillant de raisin*); Case 298/87 *Smanor SA* [1988] ECR 4489 (yoghurt); Case 407/85 *Drei Glocken GmbH. et aL v. U.S.L. Centro-Sud & Provincia Autonoma di Bolzano* [1988] ECR 4233 and Case 90/86 *Zoni* [1988] ECR 4285 (pasta, with a particularly exciting opinion by Mancini, Adv. Gen. at 4246); Case 286/86 *Ministère public v. Deserbais* [1988] ECR 4907 (cheese

strative practices disadvantaging imports.[411] Grandfather clauses (such as the exclusive use of national standards) are also caught by Article 30 EC,[412] as are import licences and prior authorization requirements, even if mere formalities;[413] certificates;[414] inspections on importation;[415] customs

names); Case C-47/90 *Éts. Delhaize Frères et Compagnie Le Lion SA v. Promalvin SA et al.* [1992] ECR I-3669 (wine of designated origin); Case C-3/91 *Exportur SA v. LOR SA et al.* [1992] ECR I-5529 (indications of provenance and designations of origin); Case C-315/92 *Verband Sozialer Wettbewerb eV v. Clinique Laboratories SNC et al.* [1994] ECR I-317 (name under which cosmetics are sold); Case 220/81 *Robertson* [1982] ECR 2349 and Case C-293/93 *Houtwipper* [1994] ECR I-4249 (hallmarking), and Case C-368/95 *Vereinigte Familiapress Zeitungsverlags- und vertriebs GmbH v. Heinrich Bauer Verlag* [1997] ECR I-3689 (advertisements forming integral part of magazines). See also the Commission's Communication on the names under which foodstuffs are sold (O.J. 1991 C 270/2), and Lister (1993) 18 ELRev. 179.

408. *E.g.* Case 119/78 *SA des Grandes Distilleries Peureux v. Directeur des Services Fiscaux de la Haute-Saône et du Territoire de Belfort* [1979] ECR 975; Case 152/78 *Commission v. France* [1980] ECR 2299, [1981] 2 CMLR 743; Case 249/81 *Commission v. Ireland* [1982] ECR 4005, [1983] 2 CMLR 99; Case 72/83 *Campus Oil Ltd. et al v. Minister for Industry and Energy et al.* [1984] ECR 2727, [1984] 3 CMLR 544; Case 103/84 *Commission v. Italy* [1986] ECR 1759 and Case C-137/91 *Commission v. Greece* [1992] ECR I-2032. As to 'full and fair opportunity' policies, see note 371, *supra*. In the specific context of public or utilities procurement, see Case 45/87 *Commission v. Ireland* [1988] ECR 4929; Case 263/85 *Commission v. Italy* [1991] ECR I-2457; Case C-21/88 *Du Pont de Nemours Italiana SA v. Unità Sanitaria Locale No 2 di Carrara* [1990] ECR I-889; Cases C-277/91 *etc. Ligur Carni Srl et al. v. Unitarià Sanitaria Locale No XV di Genova et al.* [1993] ECR I-6621, and Case C-359/93 *Commission v. The Netherlands* [1995] ECR I-157. As to the promotion of agricultural products, see Case 222/82 *Apple and Pear Development Council v. K.J. Lewis Ltd et al.* [1983] ECR 4083, [1983] 3 CMLR 733; Case 237/82 *Jongeneel Kaas BV v. The Netherlands State* [1984] ECR 483, [1985] 2 CMLR 53, and the Commission's guidelines on the promotion of agricultural products (O.J. 1986 C 272/3). In this last sector the problem has always been to draw a distinction between promotion of a product because of its specific qualities or its suitability for specific purposes, and promotion of a product because of its national origin. Policy considerations have also played a role in the Commission's approach in this sector, as (not only) agricultural products from third countries are under no constraints about emphasizing their national origin.

409. *E.g.* Case 18/84 *Commission v. France* [1985] ECR 1339, [1986] CMLR 605 (preferential tax treatment encouraging industry to locate in France); Case C-235/89 *Commission v. Italy* [1992] ECR I-777 and Case C-30/90 *Commission v. United Kingdom* [1992] ECR I-829, [1992] 2 CMLR 709 (incitement to locate production on of patented products or products covered by plant breeder's rights on national territory on pain of grant of a compulsory licence), and Case C-277/91 *etc. Ligur Carni Srl et al. v. Unità Sanitaria Locale no XV di Genova et al.* [1993] ECR I-6621 at 6661 (obligation to go through a local slaughterhouse). See also Case C-105/95 *Paul Daut GmbH & Co. KG v. Oberkreisdirektor des Kreises Gütersloh* [1997] ECR I-1877 at 1899–1900 (the most appropriate establishment may well be in another Member State), see, further, in relation to exports, the waste oils cases, note 434, *infra*.

410. *E.g.* Case 104/75 *Officier van Justitie v. De Peijper* [1976] ECR 613, [1976] 2 CMLR 271; Case 251/78 *Denkavit Futtermittel GmbH v. Minister für Enrährung, Landwirtschaft und Forsten des Landes Nordrhein-Westfalen* [1979] ECR 3369, [1980] 3 CMLR 513; Case 32/80 *Officier van Justitie v. Kortmann* [1981] ECR 251 and Case 132/80 *NV*

formalities and delays,[416] and the imposition of fines or penalties.[417] An obligation to appoint a representative in the importing Member State;[418] requirements of deposits, cautions, payments in cash or or discriminatory credit conditions;[419] stock restrictions;[420] requirements as to the use of a

United Foods et al. v. Belgian State [1981] ECR 995, [1982] 1 CMLR 273. On equivalence and mutual recognition of tests and the duty of Member States to co-operate with each other see Case 272/80 *Frans-Nederlandse Maatschappij voor Biologische Producten* [1981] ECR 3277, [1982] 2 CMLR 497; Case C-373/92 *Commission v. Belgium* [1993] ECR I-3107; and see the summary of the case-law on questions of doubt about the scientific evidence in relation to additives in Case 178/84 *Commission v. Germany* [1987] ECR 1227, [1988] 1 CMLR 813. In cases involving a Community system see *e.g.* Case 42/82 *Commission v. France* [1983] ECR 1013, [1984] 1 CMLR 160 (and Case 42/82R, [1982] ECR 841); Case 35/76 *Simmenthal SpA v. Italian Minister for Finance* [1976] ECR 1871, [1977] 2 CMLR 1; Case 46/76 *Bauhuis v. The Netherlands State* [1977] ECR 5; Case 227/82 *Van Bennekom* [1983] ECR 3883, [1985] 2 CMLR 692; Cases 2–4/82 *SA Delhaize Frères 'Le Lion' et al. v. Belgian State* [1983] ECR 2973, [1985] 1 CMLR 561, and Case C-5/94 *R. v. Ministry of Agriculture, Fisheries and Food, ex parte Hedley Lomas (Ireland) Ltd.* [1996] ECR I-2553 at 2611. On mutual recognition and roadworthiness tests see Case 406/85 *Procureur de la République v. Gofette et al.* [1987] ECR 2525, [1988] 2 CMLR 907.

411. Case 21/84 *Commission v. France* [1985] ECR 1355.
412. Case 45/87 *Commission v. Ireland* [1988] ECR 4929, [1989] 1 CMLR 225, relating to the obligatory use of asbestos cement pipes certified as conforming to a particular Irish Standard. See, generally, Mohr, *Technische Normen und freier Warenverkehr in der EWG: deutsche übertriebliche technische Normen und ihre staatliche Rezeption als massnahmen gleicher Wirkung wie mengenmässige Einfuhrbeschränkungen gemäss Art. 30, 36 EWG-Vertrag* (Cologne, 1990). A 'grandfather clause' is a term of art developed from American case-law and refers to the protection or privileging of one group of people or a product. The term originates from the attempt by some of the southern states to make the right to vote dependent (by means of a literacy test) upon, in effect, a person's grandfather having had that right, a criterion which would have excluded blacks for ever; scarcely surprisingly such attempts to privilege or 'grandfather' the white population were struck down as being incompatible with the Constitution see *Guinn v. United States* 238 U.S. 347 (1915) and *Myers v. Anderson* 238 U.S. 368 (1915).
413. *E.g.* Cases 51–54/71 *International Fruit Company NV et al. v. Produktschap voor Groenten en Fruit* [1971] ECR 1107; Case 41/76 *Criel, née Donckerwolke et al. v. Procureur de la République, Lille et al.* [1976] ECR 1921, [1977] 2 CMLR 535, and Case C-249/92 *Commission v. Italy* [1994] ECR I-4311. See also Case C-120/95 *Decker v. Caisse de maladie des employés privés* [1998] ECR I-nyr (28 April 1998). They may well, though, be justifiable under Art. 36 EC, *e.g.* Case 40/82 *Commission v. United Kingdom* [1984] ECR 283 at 301, and Case 74/82 *Commission v. Ireland* [1984] ECR 317 at 346.
414. Case 8/74 *Procureur du Roi v. Dassonville et al.* [1974] ECR 837, [1974] 2 CMLR 436 (certificates of authenticity); Case 52/77 *Cayrol v. Giovanni Rivoira e Figli* [1977] ECR 2261, [1978] 2 CMLR 253 (certificates of origin), and Case 251/78 *Denkavit Futtermittel GmbH v. Minister für Ernährung, Landwirtschaft und Forsten des Landes Nordrhein-Westfalen* [1979] ECR 3369, [1980] 3 CMLR 513; Case 272/80 *Frans-Nederlandse Maatschappij voor Biologische Producten BV* [1981] ECR 3277; Case 25/88 *Bouchara, née Wurmser, et al.* [1989] ECR 1105, [1991] 1 CMLR 173, and Case C-205/89 *Commission v. Greece* [1991] ECR I-1361 (certificate attesting the health status of goods).
415. *E.g.* Case 4/75 *Rewe Zentralfinanz GmbH v. Landwirtschaftskammer* [1975] ECR 843,

particular language;[421] requirements that imported products must conform to the requirements of the exporting country;[422] difficulties in rebutting presumptions in respect of imports;[423] obstacles to deliveries;[424] and negative lists[425] will likewise fall foul of Article 30 EC. Recipe laws[426]

[1977] 1 CMLR 599; Case 50/83 *Commission v. Italy* [1984] ECR 1633, [1985] 1 CMLR 777; Cases C-277/91 etc. *Ligur Carni Srl et al. v. Unità Sanitaria Locale No XV di Genova et al.* [1993] ECR I-6621, and Case C-80/92 *Commission v. Belgium* [1994] ECR I-1019.

416. Case 159/78 *Commission v. Italy* [1979] ECR 3247, [1980] 3 CMLR 446; Case 132/80 *United Foods NV v. Belgian State* [1981] ECR 995, [1982] 1 CMLR 273, and Case 42/82 *Commission v. France* [1983] ECR 1013, [1984] 1 CMLR 160.

417. Case 41/76 *Criel, née Donckerwolke et al. v. Procureur de la République, Lille et al.* [1976] ECR 1921, [1977] 2 CMLR 535; Case 52/77 *Cayrol v. Giovanni Rivoira e Figli* [1977] ECR 2261, [1978] 2 CMLR 253; Case 179/78 *Procureur de la République v. Rivoira* [1979] ECR 1147, [1979] 3 CMLR 456.

418. Case 247/81 *Commission v. Germany* [1984] ECR 111, [1985] 1 CMLR 640, and Case 155/82 *Commission v. Belgium* [1983] ECR 531, [1983] 2 CMLR 566.

419. Case 95/81 *Commission v. Italy* [1982] ECR 2187; Cases 206/80 etc. *Orlandi Italo e Figlio v. The Ministry for Foreign Trade* [1982] ECR 2147 (cautions); Case 53/83 *Commission v. Greece* [1984] ECR 2027, [1986] 1 CMLR 673 (payment in cash), and Case 192/84 *Commission v. Greece* [1985] ECR 3967, [1988] 1 CMLR 420.

420. Case 13/78 *Joh. Eggers Sohn & Co. v. Freie Hansestadt Bremen* [1978] ECR 1935, [1979] 1 CMLR 562; Case 192/84 *Commission v. Greece* [1985] ECR 3967, [1988] 1 CMLR 420, and Case C-323/93 *Société Civile Agricole du Centre d'Insémination de la Crespelle v. Coopérative d'Élevage et d'Insémination Artificielle du Département de la Mayenne* [1994] ECR I-5077.

421. Case 27/80 *Fietje* [1980] ECR 3839, [1981] 3 CMLR 722; Case C-369/89 *Piageme et al. v. BVBA Peeters* [1991] ECR I-2971; Case C-85/94 *Groupement des producteurs, Importateurs et Agents Généraux d'Eaux Minérales Étrangères, VZW (Piageme) et al. v. Peeters NV* [1995] ECR I-2955. See also the Commission's Communication (O.J. 1993 C 345/3); Albers and Swaak (1996) 21 ELRev. 71; Gormley (1997) EFLR 1 at 6–8, and González Vaqué and Pirotte (1994) RMUE 25. As to the Court's reaction to Community legislation dealing with labelling of crystal, see Case C-51/93 *Meyhui NV v. Schott Zwiesel Glasswerke AG* [1994] ECR I-3879.

422. Case 59/82 *Schutzverband gegen Unwesen in der Wirtschaft v. Weinvertriebs GmbH* [1983] ECR 1217, [1984] 1 CMLR 319.

423. Cases 89/74 etc. *Procureur Général près la Cour d'Appel, Bordeaux v. Arnaud et al.* [1975] ECR 1023, [1975] 2 CMLR 490 (and the judgments on this point handed down on the same day).

424. Case 155/80 *Oebel* [1981] ECR 1993, [1983] 1 CMLR 390 (at least in so far as they prevent market access for the products) but it would appear that a restriction on deliveries between certain times (*e.g.* designed to contain the flow of heavy goods traffic in a town centre) which applied equally to all-comers would be unlikely to found incompatible with At. 30 EC, see Weatherill (1992) 17 ELRev. 299 (critical discussion of *R. v. London Boroughs Transport Committee, ex parte Freight Transport Association Ltd.* [1991] 3 All ER 915, [1992] 1 CMLR 5 (HL)).

425. Case 238/82 *Duphar BV et al. v. The Netherlands State* [1984] ECR 523, [1985] 1 CMLR 256.

426. *E.g.* liqueurs: Case 120/78 *Rewe-Zentrale AG v. Bundesmonopolverwaltung für Branntwein* [1979] ECR 649, [1979] 3 CMLR 494 ('*Cassis de Dijon*'); Jenever: Case 182/84 *Miro BV* [1985] ECR 3731; beer: Case 94/82 *De Kikvorsch v. Groothandel Import–*

have been particularly frequently examined in the light of Article 30 EC.[427]

In the light of the discussion of recent case-law in section 3.2.1, above, it is submitted that the prohibition of particular sales techniques, and rules which can properly be classified as concerning to the local regulation of socio-economic life (such as shop closing legislation) will not now be found to fall within the scope of Article 30 EC in the absence of any discrimination against imported products or traders; similarly, unless advertising restrictions are discriminatory, or actually affect the imported product integrally (such as restrictions on newspaper advertisements, or advertisements in magazines), they will not now be found to fall within Article 30 EC.

3.2.3 The prohibition of measures having equivalent effect to quantitative restrictions on exports: Article 34 EC

As has been noted in section 3.2.1, above, the application of a consistent view of measures having equivalent effect has run into certain problems in relation to exports, even though Article 34 EC is formulated in the same way as Article 30 EC. It is clear that the Court applies the basic principle

Export BV [1983] ECR 947; Case 176/84 *Commission v. Greece* [1987] ECR 1193, [1988] 1 CMLR 813, and Case 178/84 *Commission v. Germany* [1987] ECR 1227, [1988] 1 CMLR 780; yoghurt: Case 298/87 *Smanor SA* [1988] ECR 4489; pasta: Case 407/85 *Drei Glocken GmbH et al. v. Unità Sanitaria Locale Centro-Sud et al.* [1988] ECR 4233 and Case 90/86 *Zoni* [1988] ECR 4285; cheese: Case 53/80 *Officier van Justitie v. Koninklijke Kaasfabriek Eyssen BV* [1981] ECR 429, [1982] 2 CMLR 20; Case 286/86 *Ministère public v. Deserbais* [1988] ECR 4907; Case C-196/89 *Nespoli and Crippa* [1990] ECR I-3647, and Case C-210/89 *Commission v. Italy* [1990] ECR I-3697; milk substitutes: Case 216/84 *Commission v. France* [1988] ECR 793 and Case 76/86 *Commission v. Germany* [1989] ECR 1021; meat products: Case 247/87 *Commission v. Germany* [1988] ECR 4607; Case 52/88 *Commission v. Belgium* [1989] ECR 1137, and Case C-269/89 *Bonfait BV* [1990] ECR I-4169; bread: Case 130/80 *Fabriek voor Hoogwaardige Voedingsprodukten Kelderman BV* [1981] ECR 527; Case C-17/93 *Van der Veldt* [1994] ECR I-3537 and Case C-358/95 *Morellato v. Unità Sanitaria Locale (USL) No 11, Pordenone* [1997] ECR I-1431; and *sauce hollandaise* and *sauce béarnaise*: Case C-51/94 *Commission v. Germany* [1995] ECR I-3599. See, generally, the Commission's Communication on foodstuffs (O.J. 1989 C 271/3); Brouwer (1988) 25 CMLRev. 237 and (1990) *Tijdschrift voor Consumentenrecht* 324; Wils (1990) EFLR 92; Von Heydebrand u. d. Lara (1991) 16 ELRev. 391; Streinz (1991) ZfRV 357; O'Connor (1993) EFLR 169, and Gormley (1997) EFLR 1.

427. Case 104/75 *Officier van Justitie v. De Peijper* [1976] ECR 613, [1976] 2 CMLR 271; Case 32/80 *Officier van Justitie v. Kortmann* [1981] ECR 251; see also Case 174/82 *Officier van Justitie v. Sandoz BV* [1983] ECR 2445, [1984] 3 CMLR 43; Case 227/82 *Van Bennekom* [1983] ECR 3883, [1985] 2 CMLR 692; Case 247/81 *Commission v. Germany* [1984] ECR 1111, [1985] 1 CMLR 640 and Cases 87 and 88/85 *Société Cooporative des Laboratoires de Pharmacie Legia et al. v. Minister for Health, Luxembourg* [1986] ECR 1707.

in *Dassonville* when dealing with measures applicable only to exports.[428] The Court also applies it when looking at equally applicable measures in agricultural sectors covered by common organization at the Community level,[429] pehaps because of a desire to preserve the unity of the agricultural market.

However, in relation to measures which apply, outside such sectors, irrespective of the destination of the goods, the Court has departed from the *Dassonville* approach. Thus in Case 15/79 *P. B. Groenveld BV v. Produktschap voor Vee en Vlees*[430] and in Case 155/80 *Oebel*[431] the Court stated that 'Article 34 concerns national measures which have as their specific object or effect the restriction of patterns of exports and thereby the establishment of a difference in treatment between the domestic trade of a Member State and its export trade, in such a way as to provide a particular advantage for national production or for the domestic market of the state in question' (in *Groenveld* adding 'at the expense of the production or of the trade of other Member States.'). It opted for a discrimination criterion, departing in so doing from the clear and logical reasoning suggested by Advocate General Capotorti.[432] At first it appeared that the sensitive nature of the product in *Groenveld* (horsemeat) and the interest involved in *Oebel* (protection of night workers in bakeries) might explain the Court's reluctance to find that the measures concerned were capable of hindering trade between Member States (even though it could have then applied the rule of reason). However, subsequent judgments

428. Case 53/76 *Procureur de la République de Besançon v. Bouhelier et al.* [1977] ECR 197, [1977] 1 CMLR 436.
429. Case 190/73 *Officier van Justitie v. Van Haaster* [1974] ECR 1123, [1974] 2 CMLR 521; Case 111/76 *Officier van Justitie v. Van der Hazel* [1977] ECR 901; Case 94/79 *Vriend* [1980] ECR 327, [1980] 3 CMLR 473; Case 237/82 *Jongeneel Kaas BV v. The Netherlands State* [1984] ECR 43, [1985] 2 CMLR 53; Case C-426/92 *Germany v. Deutsches Milch-Kontor GmbH* [1994] ECR I-2757 (and Case C-272/95 *Bundesanstalt für landwirtschaftliche Marktordnung v. Deutsches Milch-Kontor GmbH* [1997] ECR I-1905). However, in Case 15/83 *Denkavit Nederland BV v. Hoofdproduktschap voor akkerbouwprodukten* [1984] ECR 2171 at 2184 the *Groenveld* approach (see *post*) was referred to, but found to be inapplicable to the Community measures involved; the same approach was adopted in relation to Community fisheries legislation in Case C-9/89 *Spain v. Council* [1990] ECR I-1383 at 1411. The different approach in the case of common organizations was discussed in Case C-44/94 *R. v. Minister of Agriculture, Fisheries and Food, ex parte National Federation of Fishermen's Organizations et al.* [1995] ECR I-3115 at 3151 but the Court merely stated that the obligation to refrain from jeopardizing a system of common organization did not prevent a Member State from adopting national measures on the terms provided for by the relevant Community legislation (obviously side-stepping any investigation as to whether that Community legislation was compatible with Art. 34 EC).
430. [1979] ECR 3409 at 3415.
431. [1981] ECR 1993 at 2009.
432. The learned Advocate General treated Arts. 30 and 34 EC in the same way in *Groenveld* and again in *Oebel*, applying the basic principle in *Dassonville* and then examining possible justifications. As to discrimination, see section 1.3, *ante*.

show that the Court has now made this test the general test for measures applicable irrespective of the destination of the product (save for products subject to a common organisation).[433]

The Court's criterion is certainly wide enough to catch 'local grab' measures affecting exports,[434] but it appears to leave no room for an application of the rule of reason.[435] While VerLoren van Themaat has explained the distinction between the prohibition in Article 30 EC and that in Article 34 EC on the ground that the chance of protectionist measures concerning exports is less,[436] the *Groenveld* approach has come in for considerable criticism.[437] It might be noted that in Case C-384/93 *Alpine Investments BV v. Minister van Financiën*[438] the Court found that a measure which applied to services irrespective of their destination was

433. *E.g.* Cases 141–143/81 *Officier van Justitie v. Holdijk et al.* [1982] ECR 1299 at 1313; Case 237/82 *Jongeneel Kaas BV v. The Netherlands State* [1984] ECR 43 at 54; Case 286/81 *Oosthoek's Uitgeversmaatschappij BV* [1982] ECR 4575 at 4587; Case 238/82 *Duphar BV et al. v. The Netherlands State* [1984] ECR 523 at 543; Case 251/83 *Haug-Adrion v. Frankfurter Versicherungs-AG* [1984] ECR 4277 at 4289; Case 174/84 *Bulk oil (Zug) AG v. Sun International Ltd.* [1986] ECR 559 at 589; Case C-9/89 *Spain v. Council* [1990] ECR I-1383 at 1411; Case C-302/88 *Hennen Olie BV v. Stichting Interim Centraal Orgaan Voorraadvorming et al.* [1990] ECR I-4625 at 4644; Case C-332/89 *Marchandise et al.* [1991] ECR 1027 at 1041, and Case C-80/92 *Commission v. Belgium* [1994] ECR I-1019 at 1035.

434. See, in the context of a Community directive, Case 172/82 *Syndicat national des fabricants raffineurs d'huile de graissage et al. v. GIE 'Inter-Huiles' et al.* [1983] ECR 555, [1983] 3 CMLR 485; Case 295/82 *GIE 'Rhône Alpes Huiles' et al. v. Syndicat national des fabricants raffineurs d'huile de graissage et al.* [1984] ECR 575; Case 240/83 *Procureur de la République v. Association de Défense des Brûleurs d'Huiles Usagées (ADBHU)* [1985] ECR 531, and Case 173/83 *Commission v. France* [1985] ECR 491 at 507 (the waste oils cases). The most appropriate establishment may well be located in another Member State, see (in relation to Art. 30 EC) Case C-105/95 *Paul Daut GmbH & Co. KG v. Oberkreisdirektor des Kreises Gütersloh* [1997] ECR I-1877 at 1899–1900. See also Case 118/86 *Openbaar Ministerie v. Nertsvoederfabriek Nederland BV* [1987] ECR 3883, [1989] 2 CMLR 436. As to requirements of bottling at source, see Case C-47/90 *Éts. Delhaize Frères et Compagnie Le Lion SA v. Promalvin SA et al.* [1992] ECR I-3669, and Case C-3/91 *Exporteur SA v. LOR SA et al.* [1992] ECR I-5529; Stuyck (1993) 30 CMLRev. 847, and Brouwer (1993) 30 CMLRev. 1209. As to consideration of 'local grab' measures in the United States, see *Foster-Fountain Packing Co. v. Haydel* 278 US 1 (1928) and *New England Power Co. v. New Hampshire* 455 US 331 (1982).

435. Oliver (1982) 19 CMLRev. 217 at 241. See, section 3.3.3 (note 618, *infra*), *post.*

436. VerLoren van Themaat (1980) R.M. Themis 378 at 391.

437. *E.g.* Gormley, *op. cit.* (see note 26, *supra*) 108–111; Mattera, *op. cit.* (see note 259, *supra*) 516 *et seq.*, and Roth (1995) ZHR 78. See also the discussion by Müller-Graff in Von der Groeben *et al.* (eds.), *op. cit.* (see note 33, *supra*) Vol. I 772–773. Oliver, *op. cit.* (see note 102, *supra*) 121 suggests that the formula (as expressed in *Oebel* and subsequently) should be slightly reworded so as to cover any measure having the object or effect of singling out exports for less favourable treatment than goods intended for the domestic market, even where the discrimination is not apparent on the face of the measure.

438. [1995] ECR I-1141.

caught by Article 59 EC. With the utmost possible respect, revisiting *Groenveld* is long overdue in the interests of consistency and clarity.

3.2.4   Articles 30 and 34 EC and other provisions of the EC Treaty

At the beginning of section 3, above, reference was made to demarcation problems with certain other provisions of the Treaty. The main demarcation problems have arisen with Articles 12 and 95 EC[439] on the one hand, and Article 92 EC[440] on the other, but the Court has been careful to point out that even a state aid must be compatible with Article 30 EC.[441] Articles 12 or 95 will apply in preference to Article 30 (as they deal with the more specific type of barrier to trade), but the legality of an inspection is a distinct issue from the legality of a charge for it, although obviously if an inspection is unjustified, any fee charged will also be unjustified.[442]

3.3   Measures having equivalent effect: the exceptions

Both the drafters of the EC Treaty and the Court, which has to interpret its provisions, have attempted to find a balance between the interest in achieving the common market on the one hand and the need to take into account on the other hand general interests such as human health and a sustainable environment.[443] In the Treaty itself, particularly as originally framed, the balance lay between the prohibitions contained in Articles 30 and 34 on the one hand and the exceptions contained in Article 36 on the other. In what can be seen as a second period of development, the Court compensated for the aplication of Article 30 to equally applicable measures by the development of the rule of reason initially in Case 8/74 *Procureur du*

---

439. *E.g.* Case 74/76 *Ianelli & Volpi SpA v. Meroni* [1977] ECR 557 at 574; Case C-47/88 *Commission v. Denmark* [1990] ECR I-4509 at 4534; Cases C-78–83/90 *Compagnie commerciale de l'Ouest et al. v. Receveur principal des douanes de La Pallice-Port* [1992] ECR I-1847 at 1880; Case 17/91 *Georges Lonroy en Zonen NV et al. v. Belgian State* [1992] ECR I-6523 at 6554, and Case C-266/91 *Celulose Beira Industrial (CELBI) SA v. Fazenda Pública* [1992] ECR I-4337 at 4365.
440. *E.g.* Case 249/81 *Commission v. Ireland* [1982] ECR 4005 at 4021; Case 18/84 *Commission v. France* [1985] ECR 1339 at 1348; Case 103/84 *Commission v. Italy* [1986] ECR 1759 at 1774; Case C-21/88 *Du Pont de Nemours Italiana SpA v. Unità sanitaria locale No 2 di Carrara* [1990] ECR I-889 at 922, and Case C-351/88 *Laboratoiri Bruneau v. Unità sanitaria locale RM/24 di Monterotondo* [1991] ECR I-3641 at 3656–3657.
441. *Ibid.* See, further, Chapter VII, section 3.2.2, *post.*
442. *E.g.* Case 46/76 *Bauhuis v. The Netherlands State* [1977] ECR 5 at 15; Case 50/85 *Schloh v. Auto contrôle technique SPRL* [1996] ECR 1855 at 1870.
443. See section 1.4, *ante.*

Roi v. Dassonville et al.[444] The amendments to the Treaty introduced by the SEA heralded a third period of development, so that the emphasis came to be placed less on case-law developments but on the activities of the Commission and the Council which have adopted measures, mostly on the basis of Article 100a EC, designed to make recourse to Articles 30–36 EC superfluous in many cases.[445] The price for such harmonization with the use of qualified majority voting was the inclusion of Article 100a(4) EC.[446]

It is against this background that the exceptions to Articles 30 and 34 EC must be viewed. Those exceptions have a number of conditions in common, which are examined in section 3.3.1, below. The parting of the ways occurs in that Article 36 EC can benefit measures whether they are equally applicable or not, whereas the case-law rule of reason exceptions benefit only equally applicable measures.[447] The effect of Articles 100a and 100b EC is considered in section 3.3.4, below, and the other exceptions contained in the EC Treaty itself are discussed in section 3.3.5, below.

3.3.1   Conditions applicable to exceptions to Articles 30 and 34 EC

'Article 36 EC is not designed to reserve certain matters to the exclusive jurisdiction of Member States, but permits national laws to derogate from the principle of the free movement of goods to the extent to which such derogation is and continues to be justified for the attainment of the objectives referred to in that article.'[448] Thus where, in application of Articles 100 or 100a EC, Community directives provide for the harmonization of the measures necessary to ensure the protection of one of the objectives mentioned in Article 36, recourse to that provision is no longer justified: the harmonization directive becomes the framework within which those objectives must be realized, as the Community is then regarded as having occupied the field to the exclusion of unilateral national measures.[449] If however, the harmonization has taken place on the basis of

444. [1974] ECR 837 at 852.
445. In pursuance of the Commission's White Paper *Completing the Internal Market* (COM (85) 310 Final).
446. The phases referred to here follow Mertens de Wilmars (1986) SEW 601. See, further, Chapter VIII, section 2.2, *post*.
447. See, respectively, sections 3.3.2 and 3.3.3, *post*.
448. Case 35/76 *Simmenthal SpA v. Italian Minister of Finance* [1976] ECR 1871 at 1886; Case 5/77 *Tedeschi v. Denkavit Commerciale Srl* [1977] ECR 1555 at 1576. See also (in relation to both Arts. 30 and 36 EC) Case 182/84 *Miro BV* [1985] ECR 3731 at 3744.
449. *E.g.* Case 5/77 *Tedeschi, ibid.* at 1576–1577; Case 148/76 *Pubblico Ministero v. Ratti* [1979] ECR 1629 at 1644; Case 251/78 *Firma Denkavit Futtermittel GmbH v. Minister für Ernährung, Landwirtschaft und Forsten des Landes Nordrhein-Westfalen* [1979] ECR

Article 100a EC, this proposition is clearly modified, although only in so far as a Member State justifiably invokes Article 100a(4) EC.[450] In fact very little use has been made of that latter provision.[451]

Narrow (strict) interpretation. This term in fact has various meanings. First, already in the Sixties the Court held that the list of exceptions contained in the first sentence of Article 36 EC was exhaustive.[452] However, the rule of reason exceptions are not exhaustive, they do not constitute a closed class.[453] Secondly, in Case 46/76 *Bauhuis v. The Netherlands State*[454] the Court held that Article 36 could not be understood as authorizing measures of a different nature from those referred to in Articles 30–34 EC. It is submitted that the same must be true of the rule of reason. It may be possible to invoke Article 36 if Article 37 EC is applicable.[455] Finally, the application in a given case of the rule of reason or the first sentence of Article 36 is by no means automatic, as the national measure concerned must be necessary and proportionate, as is explained below.

Absence of Community measures. For Article 36 EC or the rule of reason to apply, there must be no Community measures occupying the field concened.[456] The blocking effect of the Community measures on the possibility of invoking Article 36 or the rule of reason applies from the date by which the Community measures had to be transposed into national law[457] or from the date on which those measures entered into

3369 at 3388, and Case C-52/92 *Commission v. Portugal* [1993] ECR I-2961 at 2978–2979. See also Case 815/79 *Cremonini and Vrankovich* [1980] ECR 3583 at 3607 and Case 72/83 *Campus Oil Ltd. et al. v. Minister for Industry and Energy et al.* [1984] ECR 2727 at 2749–2751.

450. Mertens de Wilmars (1986) SEW 601 at 610.
451. See Chapter VIII, section 2.2, *post*, and Case C-41/93 *Commission v. France* [1994] ECR I-1829.
452. *E.g.* Case 7/68 *Commission v. Italy* [1968] ECR 423 at 431; Case 46/76 *Bauhuis v. The Netherlands State* [1977] ECR 5 at 15; Case 113/80 *Commission v. Ireland* [1981] ECR 1625 at 1638; Case 95/81 *Commission v. Italy* [1982] ECR 2187 at 2204, and Case 229/83 *Association des Centres distributeurs Édouard Leclerc et al. v. Sàrl 'Au blé vert' et al.* [1985] ECR 1 at 35.
453. See *e.g.* Case 120/78 *Rewe-Zentral AG v. Bundesmonopolverwaltung für Branntwein* [1979] ECR 649 at 664, and Capotorti, Adv. Gen. in Case 788/79 *Gilli and Andres* [1980] ECR 2071 at 2082.
454. [1977] ECR 5 at 15. See also Case 32/80 *Officier van Justitie v. Kortmann* [1981] ECR 251 at 267.
455. Case C-347/88 *Commission v. Greece* [1990] ECR I-4747 at 4790–4791 (although the Court dealt with Art. 36 in relation to Art. 30, not Art. 37), see, further, section 3.4, *post*.
456. As to Art. 36 Ec, see *e.g.* Case 35/76 *Simmenthal SpA v. Italian Minister for Finance* [1976] ECR 1871 at 1887 and Case 5/77 *Tedeschi v. Denkavit Commerciale Srl* [1977] ECR 1555 at 1576; as to the rule of reason, see *e.g.* Case 8/74 *Procureur du Roi v. Dassonville et al.* [1974] ECR 837 at 852 and Case C-39/90 *Denkavit Futtermittel GmbH v. Land Baden-Württemberg* [1991] ECR I-3069 at 3107.
457. Case 35/76 *Simmenthal SpA v. Italian Minister for Finance* [1976] ECR 1871 at 1887;

force.[458] An international agreement to which all the Member States are parties is treated in the same way as a Community measure for these purposes.[459] If, however, the Community measures are incomplete, not therefore wholly occupying the field, or are not binding, the Member Sates may invoke Article 36 or the rule of reason in relation to aspects not covered by the Community measures.[460] Thus in the case of minimum harmonization and other forms of incomplete harmonization the Court will look to see whether the national measures indeed remain within the area left to the Member States or whether they have strayed into the area occupied by Community legislation.[461] Although the justifications in Article 36 EC (and the rule of reason) have a fundamentally interim character in so far as they give way in the face of Community legislation, it is unlikely that recourse to Article 36 at least will disappear altogether given the unlikelihood of any move to harmonise public morality!

Interests of a non-economic nature. Already at an early stage the Court found that Article 36 EC protects non-economic interests,[462] and thus a Member State will not be permitted to plead economic difficulties resulting from the removal of obstacles to intra-Community as a pretext for avoiding measures provided for in the Treaty[463] and thus failing to respect the free movement of goods. This means that the Court will reject a justification based on the need to ensure the survival of a particular undertaking,[464] although if the justification is the need to ensure that a country has reliable supplies of a product for essential medical

Case C-320/93 *Lucien Ortscheit GmbH v. Eurim-Pharm Arzneimittel GmbH* [1994] ECR I-5243 at 5263.

458. If no transposition is required (as in the case of regulations).

459. Case 89/76 *Commission v. The Netherlands* [1977] ECR 1355, [1978] 3 CMLR 630.

460. See *e.g.* Case 251/78 *Firma Denkavit Futtermittel GmbH v. Minister für Ernährung, Landwirtschaft und Forsten des Landes Nordrhein-Westfalen* [1979] ECR 3369 at 3389–3390; Case 227/83 *Van Bennekom* [1983] ECR 3883 at 3904; Case 190/87 *Oberkreisdirektor des Kreises Borken v. Handelsonderneming Moormann BV* [1988] ECR 4689 at 4720, and Case C-39/90 *Denkavit Futtermittel GmbH v. Land Baden-Württemberg* [1991] ECR I-3069 at 3107. This is also subject to the additional obligation (on the basis of Art. 5 EC) not to jeopardize the effectiveness of the Community measures which have been adopted. See also Case 72/83 *Campus Oil Ltd. et al. v. Minister for Industry and Energy et al.* [1984] ECR 2727 at 2749–2751 (the Community measures were regarded as not offering an absolute guarantee of security of supplies).

461. *E.g.* Case C-11/92 *R. v. Secretary of State for Health, ex parte Gallaher Ltd. et al.* [1993] ECR I-3545 at 3563–3566. See Temmink (1995) SEW 79.

462. *E.g.* Case 7/61 *Commission v. Italy* [1961] ECR 317 at 329; Case 95/81 *Commission v. Italy* [1982] ECR 2187 at 2204; Case 238/82 *Duphar BV v. The Netherlands State* [1984] ECR 523 at 542, and Case 288/83 *Commission v. Ireland* [1985] EC 1761 at 1776.

463. Case 72/83 *Campus Oil Ltd. et al. v. Minister for Industry and Energy et al.* [1984] ECR 2727 at 2752.

464. Case C-324/93 *R. v. Secretary of State for the Home Department, ex parte Evans Medical Ltd. et al.* [1995] ECR I-563 at 608.

purposes,[465] or that the essential services of the state can keep running,[466] it will be accepted provided that it satisfies the proportionality test.[467] The Court has accepted in one remarkable instance a 'local grab' measure to ensure that a refinery survived which was justified on the ground of public security, holding that once a justification on a ground recognized in Article 36 EC had indeed been made out the fact that economic aims could also be achieved by the measure would not exclude the application of Article 36 EC.[468] It is submitted that the limitation to interests of a non-economic nature also applies in respect of the rule of reason justifications. If economic difficulties arise, recourse must be had to the specific procedures contained in the EC Treaty itself, such as those in Articles 103a, 109h, 109i or 115 EC.

Justification: necessity and proportionality. The first sentence of Article 36 EC links the exceptions to the prohibition through the term 'justified'. In Case 8/74 *Procureur du Roi v. Dassonville et al.*[469] the Court spoke of measures having to be 'reasonable' and in Case 120/79 *Cassis de Dijon*[470] they had to be 'necessary'. It is thus manifestly evident that it is one thing for a Member State to invoke a justification, it is quite another for it to do so successfully. The criteria of the necessity for and proportionality of a measure have to be satisfied.[471]

These criteria have been the subject of much discussion in academic writings.[472] In particular Van Gerven, both extra-judicially[473] and in his opinions[474] has approached these matters systematically, drawing a distinction between necessity and proportionality. This is logical since it

465. *Ibid.*
466. Case 72/83 *Campus Oil* [1984] ECR 2727 at 2752.
467. See also Case C-347/88 *Commission v. Greece* [1990] ECR I-4747 at 4790 (measures disproportionate).
468. Case 72/83 *Campus Oil* [1984] ECR 2727 at 2752.
469. [1974] ECR 837 at 852.
470. [1979] ECR 649 at 662.
471. See also Chapter III, section 5.1.2, *ante*.
472. See, generally, Emiliou, *The Principle of Proportionality in European Law* (London, 1996) 227–265; De Búrca (1993) 13 YBEL 105 at 126 *et seq.*; De Moor-van Vugt, *Maten en gewichten, het evenredigheidsbeginsel in Europees perspectief* (Zwolle, 1995); Jans (1992) SEW 751 and (1995) SEW 205, and Van Gerven in Neskens-Ipshording (ed.), *In het nu, wat worden zal* (*Festschrift* for Schoordijk, Deventer, 1991) 75 and (1991–1992) *Rechtskundig Weekblad* col. 1244. Various Dutch case-law impliedly or expressly applying the proportionality principle is reported in (1995) SEW 444 and (1995) SEW 540. See also Gormley, *op. cit.* (see note 84, *supra*) 359–360 (note 27) and literature and case-law cited there. See also Case 42/82 *Commission v. France* [1983] ECR 1013 at 1047–1050 (an example of the Court initially mentioning necessity and then both necessity and proportionality (at 1047)).
473. Van Gerven, *ibid.*
474. Case C-169/89 *Gourmetterie Van den Burg BV* [1990] ECR I-2143 at 2156–2159, and the joint opinion in Cases C-312/89 *Union départementale des syndicats CGT de l'Aisne v. SIDEF Conforama et al.* and Case C-332/89 *Marchandise et al.* [1991] ECR I-997 at 1012 and 1016–1017.

may well be necessary to protect a particular interest but the means chosen may be unreasonable.

However, the Court is, with respect, not always systematic in its approach. In most of the judgments in which Article 36 EC or the rule of reason is applied, the Court applies the necessity and/or proportionality test implicitly or expressly, but in view of the fact that much of the case-law consists of rulings on Article 177 EC references the concrete evaluation is frequently effectively in the hands of the national court, although the Court of Justice sometimes makes that evaluation a merely mechanical process by clearly expressing its own assessment.[475] Nevertheless, certain guiding principles are apparent from the case-law. The heads of justification in Article 36 cannot assist measures which are not essential for the achievement of the justifiable non-economic objectives; in other words the measures which it is sought to justify must be essential for the non-economic purpose involved.[476] This means first that they must be necessary for the effective protection of the interest concerned.[477] There thus has to be a causal link between the national measure and the interest which it seeks to protect. Secondly, the measures must be proportionate to their purpose. Thus, if the legitimate objective could be effectively achieved by means less restrictive of trade between Member States the measure under review will not be upheld.[478]

The principle of proportionality has been particularly frequently applied in the foodstuffs sector,[479] in which the attitude of the Court to the nannying of consumers has been particularly dismissive: thus appropriate labelling has been found to offer a sufficient degree of consumer protection;[480] after an initially shaky start[481] the case-law on additives

---

475. *E.g. Cf.* Case C-145/88 *Torfaen Borough Council v. B & Q PLC* [1989] ECR 3851 with Case C-312/89 *Union départementale des syndicats CGT de l'Aisne v. SIDEF Conforama et al.* [1991] ECR I-997.

476. *E.g.* Case 104/75 *Officier van Justitie v. De Peijper* [1976] ECR 613 at 636; Case 124/81 *Commission v. United Kingdom* [1983] ECR 203 at 206; Case 42/82 *Commission v. France* [1983] ECR 1013 at 1047–1048, and Case 261/85 *Commission v. United Kingdom* [1988] ECR 547 at 574. See in relation to the freedom to provide services, *e.g.* Case C-76/90 *Säger v. Dennemeyer & Co. Ltd.* [1991] ECR I-4221 at 4244–4245 and Case C-384/93 *Alpine Investments BV v. Minister van Financiën* [1995] ECR I-1141 at 1179–1181.

477. *Ibid.*

478. *E.g.* Case 104/75 *Officier van Justitie v. De Peijper* [1976] ECR 613 at 636; Case 155/82 *Commission v. Belgium* [1983] ECR 531 at 543–544, and Case 261/85 *Commission v. United Kingdom* [1988] ECR 547 at 574.

479. See, in relation to wholly excessive customs controls, Case 42/82 *Commission v. France* [1983] ECR 1013 at 1047–1050.

480. *E.g.* Case 120/78 *Cassis de Dijon* [1979] ECR 649 at 664; Case Case 178/84 *Commission v. Germany* [1987] ECR 1227 at 1271–1272; Case 274/87 *Commission v. Germany* [1989] ECR 229 at 254–255, and Case C-51/94 *Commission v. Germany* [1995] ECR I-3599 at 3628–3630.

481. Case C-53/80 *Officier van Justitie v. Koninklijke Kaasfabriek Eyssen BV* [1981] ECR 409, [1982] 2 CMLR 20.

seems finally to have settled down with the Court distinctly more sceptical about certain Member States' reluctance to accept international scientific research.[482] A procedural twist has added to the proportionality test in that market participants must have access to procedural and judicial protection if a Member State decides to prohibit certain products, foodstuffs or additives.[483]

Burden of proof. On the basis of the presumption in favour of free movement and the principle of the mutual acceptance of goods, market participants will be able to invoke the directly effective prohibitions of Articles 30 and 34 EC before their national courts. In such cases it is for the national judicial authorities to determine whether the national measure concerned is caught by those prohibitions and, if so, whether it can stand the scrutiny of Article 36 EC or the rule of reason. While the burden of proof that a measure is justified under Article 36 or the rule of reason lies on the Member State concerned (or, in the case of actions seeking to protect industrial and commercial property rights, on the person seeking to restrain trade),[484] the national authorities may, in so far as they do not have it themselves, ask an importer to produce all the information in its possession needed to assess the facts, but they themselves must make the assesment in the light of all the relevant information.[485] Since the judgment in Cases C-267 and 268/91 *Keck and Mithouard*[486] rather more attention has been focused on the interpretation of the prohibition (whether Article 30 applies) than was the case in the past, before turning to interpret the exceptions (justifications advanced for the measures involved).

Conflicting general interests and extra-territorial protection. It is possible in certain specific cases that the interests to be protected will conflict. For example, environmentally friendly packing may in fact afford the consumer less information, and questions of health protection will arise if it appears that the packing involved is in fact less hygenic. There has not

---

482. *E.g.* Case C-174/82 *Sandoz BV* [1983] ECR 2445, [1984] 3 CMLR 43; Case C-247/84 *Motte* [1985] ECR 3887; Case 176/84 *Commission v. Greece* [1987] ECR 1193, [1988] 1 CMLR 813; Case 178/84 *Commission v. Germany* [1987] ECR 1227, [1988] 1 CMLR 780, and Case C-42/90 *Bellon* [1990] ECR I-4863.

483. Case 178/84 *Commission v. Germany* [1987] ECR 1227 at 1274; Case C-18/88 *Régie des télégraphes et des téléphones v. GB-INNO-BM SA* [1991] ECR I-5941 at 5984, and Cases C-46/90 and 93/91 *Procureur du Roi v. Lagauche et al.* [1993] ECR I-5267 at 5328–5329.

484. *E.g.* Case 251/78 *Firma Denkavit Futtermittel GmbH v. Minister für Ernährung, Land-wirtschaft und Forsten des Landes Nordrhein-Westfalen* [1979] ECR 3369 at 3392, and Case 174/82 *Sandoz BV* [1983] ECR 2445 at 2464 and 2465.

485. *E.g.* Case 174/82 *Sandoz BV* [1983] ECR 2445 at 2464. In particular they may not make authorization subject to proof that the marketing of the product concerned meets a market demand, *ibid.* at 2465.

486. [1993] ECR 6097, [1995] 1 CMLR 101.

yet been any judicial pronouncement from the Court on how such conflicts should be resolved, but it appears convenient that it is for the national authorities to determine which of these interests deserves priority, although Community law may well lay down certain conditions. The Court has indicated that the protection of the health and life of humans rank first among the interests protected by Article 36 EC,[487] and in the case of any possible overlap between the application of Community rules on pharmaceuticals and those on cosmetics, the pharmaceutical rules will take precedence.[488]

The extent to which a Member State may adopt measures hindering trade between Member States not to protect its own legitimate interests but those of another Member State or third country has been somewhat unclear. This problem is primarily relevant in relation to product-oriented environmental policy.[489] A number of judgments throw light on this problem, albeit sometimes indirectly, and it appears that as long as a measure is necessary and proportionate on grounds known to Community law, a Member State will be entitled, in the absence of Community legislation occupying the field, or if authorized under such legislation, to protect the interests of a Member State of destination, and thus to insist that products be treated in accordance with its requirements.[490]

3.3.2 The main Treaty-based exception: Article 36 EC

As an exception to the fundamental rule of the free movement of goods, Article 36 EC is interpreted strictly,[491] and thus does not extend to

---

487. Case 104/75 *Officier van Justitie v. De Peijper* [1976] ECR 613 at 635; Case C-320/93 *Lucien Ortscheit GmbH v. Eurim-Pharm Arzneimittel GmbH* [1994] ECR I-5243 at 5264.
488. Case C-112/89 *The Upjohn Company et al. v. Farzoo Inc. et al.* [1991] ECR I-1703 at 1744–1745. See also, generally, Case C-290/90 *Commission v. Germany* [1992] ECR I-3317 at 3347–3348 and Case C-315/92 *Verband Sozialer Wettbewerb eV v. Clinique laboratories SNC et al.* [1994] ECR I-317 at 334–337.
489. As to the various views, see Jans *et al.*, *Zo sterk als de zwakste schakel: Nederlands productgericht milieubeleid in Europees- en internationaal verband* (Amsterdam, 1993) 158. See also, Jans, *European Environmental law* (London, 1996) and Gormley in Holder (ed.), *op. cit.* (see note 389, *supra*) 289 at 295–297.
490. See Case 118/86 *Openbaar Ministerie v. Nertsvoederfabriek Nederland BV* [1987] ECR 3883, [1989] 2 CMLR 436; Case C-3/91 *Exporteur SA v. LOR SA et al.* [1992] ECR I-5529, and, in relation to services, Case C-55/93 *Van Schaik* [1994] ECR I-4837. See also, in the context of Community legislation, Case 172/82 *Syndicat national des Fabricants Raffineurs d'Huile de Graissage et al. v. GIE 'Inter-Huiles' et al.* [1983] ECR 555 (and the other 'local grab' judgments relating to waste oils, see note 434, *supra*); Case 46/76 *Bauhuis v. The Netherlands State* [1977] ECR 5. See further, Case 2/90 *Commission v. Belgium* [1992] ECR I-4431, [1993] 1 CMLR 365.
491. E.g. Case 7/68 *Commission v. Italy* [1968] ECR 423 at 430; Case 46/76 *Bauhuis v. The Netherlands State* [1977] ECR 5 at 15, and Case 113/80 *Commission v. Ireland* [1981] ECR 1625 at 1638.

justifications not mentioned therein.[492] The development of the rule of reason has shown that there are other grounds not mentioned in the EC Treaty on which barriers to trade between Member States may be justified, which may be felt to sit uncomfortably with this strict approach to Article 36 EC.[493] Unlike the rule of reason, though, the justifications enumerated in the first sentence of Article 36 will be available to benefit measures which do distinguish between imports and domestic products, as long of course as the measures, including the difference in treatment, are necessary, proportionate and do not infringe the requirements of the second sentence of Article 36 itself. The strict interpretation of Article 36 also means that it cannot be invoked to justify measures of another type than those mentioned in Articles 30 or 34 EC.[494] The strict approach taken to attempts to rely on Article 36 is not, though, designed to remove the margin of discretion which is left to the Member States by that provision;[495] rather the Court can be seen as examining whether the Member State concerned has remained within that margin of discretion.

In order for an interest or value mentioned in the first sentence of Article 36 EC to avail a Member State (or an individual in appropriate cases) seeking to restrain importation or the sale of imported products, a number of conditions must be satisfied, as was demonstrated in section 3.3.1, above. Thus there must be no Community legislation occupying the field; the measure must be necessary for the protection of one or more of those interests or values, and it must be proportionate. Furthermore, it must satisfy the requirement of the second sentence of Article 36 EC, namely it must not 'constitute a means of arbitrary discrimination or a disguised restriction on trade between Member States.' These conditions, like various of the heads of justification mentioned in the first sentence of Article 36, are inspired by Article XX GATT.[496] Unfortunately these conditions are not systematically applied by the Court, often being mentioned hand-in-hand.[497] It is appropriate though to examine the second sentence of Article 36 EC after the first sentence.

492. *Ibid.*
493. See section 3.3.3, *post*. But the distinction between Art. 36 exceptions and those under the rule of reason is clear, see *e.g.* Case 25/88 *Bouchara, née Wurmser, et al.* [1989] ECR 1124 at 1127–1128. See also Mortelmans (1997) SEW 182.
494. See note 454, *supra*, and text thereto. Thus, *e.g.* Art. 36 EC will not justify a charge for an inspection, even if the inspection is justified.
495. *E.g.* Case 53/80 *Officier van Justitie v. Koninklijke Kaasfabriek Eyssen BV* [1981] ECR 409 at 422423; Case 174/82 *Sandoz BV* [1983] ECR 2445 at 2463–2464; Case 97/83 *CMC Melkunie BV* [1984] ECR 2367 at 2386, and Case 178/84 *Commission v. Germany* [1987] ECR 1227 at 1273–1276.
496. See, generally, *GATT Law and Practice 1947–1994* (6th ed., Geneva, 1994) which discusses GATT theory and practice in this area.
497. *E.g.* Case 27/80 *Fietje* [1980] ECR 3839 at 3855, and Case 42/82 *Commission v. France* [1983] ECR 1013 at 1047–1050.

The interests or values mentioned in Article 36 EC, first sentence. The specific grounds mentioned are a diverse collection and have given rise to a wealth of case-law, although inevitably some headings have seen more activity than others. In view of the abundance of case-law, simply the principal points arising are discussed here,[498] although all the headings are covered. In view of the assimilation of exceptions to the various freedoms, reference should also be made to the relevant case-law.[499] In many cases, although reliance was placed on Article 36, the purported justification was clearly rejected by the Court; these cases demonstrate the limits of attempts to invoke the heads of justification.

Public morality is the first head, but it is clear that a two-level approach to public morality will not be accepted by the Court.[500] Public policy, the second ground, is not simply an excuse for whatever suits the government, and it is not defined by national concepts of the term; the limits on its use are set by Community law (given that its use is subject to strict control as a result of the case-law of the Court) and it is submitted that the interpretation developed (in relation to the free movement of workers) of the same term in Article 48(3) is applicable, *mutatis mutandis*, here.[501]

498. See, further, the literature cited in note 259, *supra*.
499. See, generally, section 1.6, *ante*, and the relevant discussion as to workers, establishment and services, and capital and payments, *post*.
500. Case 121/85 *Conegate Ltd v. H.M. Customs and Excise* [1986] ECR 1007, [1986] 1 CMLR 739, noted by Gormley (1986) 11 ELRev. 443 and Millett (1987) 137 NLJ 39. See also Case 34/79 *R. v. Henn and Darby* [1979] ECR 3795, [1980] 1 CMLR 246 (on which see Gormley, *op. cit.* (see note 26, *supra*) 126–128 and literature cited there).
501. The concept of public policy has been considered in a few cases; on the protection of the integrity of coinage see Case 7/78 *R. v. Thompson et al.* [1978] ECR 2247, [1979] 1 CMLR 47; on speculative transactions see Case 95/81 *Commission v. Italy* [1982] ECR 2187 (and *cf.* Cases 206/80 etc. *Orlandi Italo e Figlio v. The Ministry for Foreign Trade* [1982] ECR 2147); see also Warner, Adv. Gen. in Case 30/77 *R. v. Bouchereau* [1977] ECR 1999 at 2025–2026. The ambit of public policy has nothing to do with the rule of reason: Case 113/80 *Commission v. Ireland* [1981] ECR 1625 at 1638, and Case 177/83 *Theodor Kohl KG v. Ringelhan & Rennett SA* [1983] ECR 3651 at 3663. The Court has refused to accept the argument that a measure is justified on public policy grounds simply because it was reinforced by penal sanctions: Case 16/83 *Prantl* [1984] ECR 1299 at 1329. In keeping with the general rule that Art. 36 does not benefit economic interests, public policy may not be relied upon to protect such interests, Case 188/83 *Commission v. Ireland* [1985] ECR 1761 at 1776, nor is it pertinent if reliance is placed on the public security heading, Case 72/83 *Campus Oil Ltd. et al. v. Minister for Industry and Energy et al.* [1984] ECR 2727 at 2751. There has been a divergence of academic opinion on a possibility of invoking the need to quell public unrest (as a result of imports of, say, Italian wine into France) as a ground for restricting imports; for a brief summary of views see Gormley, *op. cit.* (see note 26, *supra*) 133. In Case 42/82 *Commission v. France* [1983] ECR 1013, [1984] 1 CMLR 160 the French government did not attempt to justify its actions on the ground of public policy; in Case 231/83 *Cullet et al. v. Centre Leclerc Toulouse et al.* [1985] ECR 305 at 324 the Court merely stated in response to an argument about public order and security that the French government had not shown that it would be unable, using the means at its disposal, to deal with the con-

Public security, the third ground, is a somewhat nebulous concept, and what is still the leading judgment was, it is respectfully submitted, characterized by less than wholly convincing reasoning and conclusions.[502]

The fourth ground, the protection of health and life of humans, animals or plants has given rise to a royal abundance of case-law,[503] with particular problems arising in relation to pharma-

sequences which an amendment of the rules in question in accordance with the prin-ciples of Community law would have upon public order and security; see also the opinion of VerLoren van Themaat Adv. Gen. *ibid.* at 312. In Case C-265/95 *Commission v. France* [1997] ECR I-6959 the Court, dealing with an infringement pro-ceeding concerning failure to take action to combat violent incidents arising from protests at imports, confirmed that the Member States are obliged to adopt the necessary measures to ensure the free movement of goods. Interestingly enough, it did not go into a discussion of Article 36 EC, finding that whatever reasons there might be for not intervening on a particular occasion, there was no justification for a global non-intervention policy. There is as yet no judicial view on the general pro-position about an equivalent interpretation of the concept throughout Arts. 36, 48(3), 56(1), 66 and 73(d)(2) EC.

502. Case 72/83 *Campus Oil Ltd et al. v. Minister for Industry and Energy et al.* [1984] ECR 2727, [1984] 3 CMLR 544, see Gormley, op. *cit.* (see note 84, *supra*) 134–139. However, it is now clear that public security will not be a *carte blanche* heading for the Member States, see Case C-347/88 *Commission v. Greece* [1990] ECR I-4747. The concept of public security cover both the internal and external security of a Member State, see Case C-367/89 *Richardt et al.* [1991] ECR I-4621 at 4652. As to public security in the sense of disturbances of public order, see public policy (note 501, *supra*). See also Case 174/84 *Bulk Oil (Zug) AG v. Sun International Ltd et al.* [1986] ECR 559; [1986] 2 CMLR 732, and Case 231/83 *Cullet et al v. Centre Leclerc Tou-louse et al.* [1985] ECR 305 at 324. See further, Case 222/84 *Johnston v. Chief Con-stable of the Royal Ulster Constabulary* [1986] ECR 1651 at 1683–1688 (in the context of equal treatment of men and women). As to roadworthiness (type-approval or safety) tests, see Case 50/83 *Commission v. Italy* [1984] ECR 1633, [1985] 1 CMLR 777; Case 50/85 *Schloh v. Auto contrôle technique Sprl* [1986] ECR 1855 at 1868–1869 (treated as relating to the health and life of humans, rather than public secur-ity); Case 406/85 *Procureur de la République v. Gofette and Gilliard* [1987] ECR 2525 at 2542 (road safety under Art. 36 without further specification); and Case C-55/93 *Van Schaik* [1994] ECR I-4837 at 4858 (in the context of services: road safety an overriding public interest).

503. *E.g.* as to straightforward bans, Case 153/78 *Commission v. Germany* [1979] ECR 2555, [1980] 1 CMLR 198; Case 152/78 *Commission v. France* [1980] ECR 2299, [1981] 2 CMLR 743; Case 124/81 *Commission v. United Kingdom* [1983] ECR 203, [1983] 2 CMLR 1; Case 40/82 *Commission v. United Kingdom* [1982] ECR 2793, [1982] 3 CMLR 497 and [1984] ECR 283, and Case C-131/93 *Commission v. Germany* [1994] ECR I-3303. As to licensing, see *e.g.* Case 251/78 *Firma Denkavit Futtermittel GmbH v. Minister für Ernährung, Landwirtschaft und Forsten des Landes Nordrhein-Westfalen* [1979] ECR 3369 at 3392; Case 124/81 *Commission v. United Kingdom* [1983] ECR 203 at 234; Case 40/82 *Commission v. United Kingdom* [1983] ECR 283 at 301, and Case 74/82 *Commission v. Ireland* [1984] ECR 317 at 346. See, generally, Cases 141–143/81 *Officier van Justitie v. Holdijk et al.* [1982] ECR 1299, [1983] 2 CMLR 635; Case 118/86 *Openbaar Ministerie v. Nertsvoederfabriek Neder-land BV* [1987] ECR 3883, and Case C-323/93 *Société Civile Agricole du Centre d'In-sémination de la Crespelle v. Coopérative d'Élevage et d'Insémination Artificielle du*

ceuticals;[504] additives;[505] health inspections,[506] and mutual recognition of tests and certificates,[507] and the application of the mutual recognition concept in the field of technical standards and other technical regulations.[508] The Court has made it clear that even if the interests

Département de la Mayenne [1994] ECR I-5077. The mere fact that a product has crossed a border does not in itself increase any risk to health, Case 153/78 *Commission v. Germany* [1979] ECR 2555 at 2566. A requirement that a representative be established in the importing Member State is not justified under Art. 36, see Case 155/82 *Commission v. Belgium* [1983] ECR 531 at 544 (although *cf.* Case 25/88 *Bourcara, née Wurmser, et al.* [1989] ECR 1105 at 1129–1130).

504. In relation to marketing authorisations for parallel imports, the definition of medicinal products and national requirements allegedly justified in the interests of health protection. Celebrated examples include Case 104/75 *Officier van Justitie v. De Peijper* [1976] ECR 613, [1976] 2 CMLR 271; Case 32/80 *Officier van Justitie v. Kortmann* [1981] ECR 251, [1982] 3 CMLR 46; Case 247/81 *Commission v. Germany* [1984] ECR 1111, [1985] 1 CMLR 640; Case 155/82 *Commission v. Belgium* [1983] ECR 531, [1983] 2 CMLR 536; Case 181/82 *Roussel Laboratoria BV v. The Netherlands State* [1983] ECR 3849, [1985] 1 CMLR 834; Case 227/82 *Van Bennekom* [1983] ECR 3883; Case 238/82 *Duphar BV v. The Netherlands State* [1984] ECR 523, [1985] 1 CMLR 256; Cases 87 and 88/85 *Société Coopérative des Laboratoires de Pharmacie Legia et al. v. Minister for Health, Luxembourg* [1986] ECR 1707; Case C-347/89 *Freistaat Bayern v. Eurim-Pharm GmbH* [1991] ECR I-1747; Case C-62/90 *Commission v. Germany* [1992] ECR I-2575; Case C-290/90 *Commission v. Germany* [1992] ECR I-3317; Case C-320/94 *Lucien Ortscheit GmbH v. Eurim-Pharm Arzneimittel GmbH* [1994] ECR I-5243; Case 266/87 *R. v. Royal Pharmaceutical Society of Great Britain, ex parte the Association of Pharmaceutical Importers et al.* [1989] ECR 1295; Case 125/88 *Nijman* [1989] ECR 3533; Case C-440/93 *R. v. Licensing Authority of the Department of Health et al., ex parte Scotia Pharmaceuticals Ltd.* [1995] ECR I-2851; Case C-324/93 *R. v. Secretary of State for the Home Department, ex parte Evans Medical Ltd. et al.* [1995] ECR 563 (which is important in relation to arguments as to security of supplies), and Case C-201/94 *R. v. The Medicines Control Agency, ex parte Smith & Nephew Pharmaceuticals Ltd.* [1996] ECR I-5819. See the Commission's Communication O.J. 1982 C 115/5. As to importation by an individual for his or her own use, see Case 215/87 *Schumacher v. Hauptzollamt Frankfurt am Main-Ost* [1989] ECR 617. See also Case C-120/95 *Decker v. Caisse de maladie des employés privés* [1998] ECR I-nyr (28 April 1998). As to Community legislation in the field, see Chapter VIII, section 2.7, *post.* As to the cases on reserving the right to sell certain products to certain professionals, see the discussion of the local regulation of socio-economic life in section 3.2.1, *ante*; it is submitted that such rules will now fall outside Art. 30 EC as long as they are equally applicable to all comers. See, reaching an analogous result to that in Case 104/75 *De Peijper, supra,* in relation to parallel imports from a country with which the Community has a free trade agreement, Case C-207/91 *Eurim-Pharm GmbH v. Bundesgesundheitsamt* [1993] ECR I-3723.

505. *E.g.* Case 53/80 *Officier van Justitie v. Koninklijke Kaasfabriek Eyssen BV* [1981] ECR 409, [1982] 2 CMLR 20; Case 94/83 *Albert Hein BV* [1984] ECR 3263; Case 174/82 *Officier van Justitie v. Sandoz BV* [1983] ECR 2445; Case 247/84 *Motte* [1985] ECR 3887; Case 304/84 *Ministère public v. Muller et al.* [1986] ECR 1511; Case 176/84 *Commission v. Greece* [1987] ECR 119, [1988] 1 CMLR 813; Case 178/84 *Commission v. Germany* [1987] ECR 1227, [1988] 1 CMLR 780; Case C-95/89 *Commission v. Italy* [1992] ECR I-4545; Case C-293/89 *Commission v. Greece* [1992] ECR I-4577; Case C-344/90 *Commission v. France* [1992] ECR I-4791, and Case C-42/90 *Bellon* [1990] ECR I-4863. See also Case 97/83 *CMC Melkunie BV* [1984] ECR 2367, [1986] 2 CMLR

of health protection specified in the Article 36 EC can in principle justify controls or inspections on goods imported from another Member State, the principle of proportionality means that the authorities concerned must take account of equivalent standards and similar controls or inspections in force or carried out in the exporting Member State.[509]

The fifth ground, the protection of national treasures possessing artistic, historical or archaeological value, has given rise to no case-law directly on the point, although the issue of heritage protection for works of art is something of which policy-makers have now taken steps to protect at Community level;[510] which points in the direction of consciousness developing of the patrimony of the Community as a whole (as opposed to merely local patrimony); in any event, Duquesne's observation should be

318; Case 216/84 *Commission v. France* [1988] ECR 793, and Case 76/86 *Commission v. Germany* [1989] ECR 1021. See also Case C-293/94 *Brandsma* [1996] ECR I-3159. As to Community action see section 3.3.1, *ante*.

506. *E.g.* Case 4/75 *Rewe Zentralfinanz GmbH v. Landwirtschaftskammer* [1975] ECR 843, [1977] 1 CMLR 599; Case 35/76 *Simmenthal SpA v. Italian Minister for Finance* [1976] ECR 1871, [1977] 2 CMLR 1; Case 46/76 *Bauhuis v. The Netherlands State* [1977] ECR 5; Case 132/80 *NV United Foods et al. v. Belgian State* [1981] ECR 995, [1982] 1 CMLR 273; Case 272/80 *Frans-Nederlandse Maatschappij voor Biologische producten BV* [1981] ECR 3277, [1982] 2 CMLR 497; Cases 2–4/82 *SA DElhaize Frères 'Le Lion' et al. v. Belgian State* [1983] ECR 2979; Case 50/83 *Commission v. Italy* [1984] ECR 1633, [1985] 1 CMLR 777; Case 73/84 *Denkavit Futtermittel GmbH v. Land Nordrhein-Westfalen* [1985] ECR 1013, [1986] 2 CMLR 482; Cases C-277/91 etc. *Ligur Carni Srl et al. v. Unità Sanitaria Locale No XV di Genova et al.* [1993] ECR I-6621, and Case C-80/92 *Commission v. Belgium* [1994] ECR I-1019.

507. *E.g.* Case 104/75 *Officier van Justitie v. De Peijper* [1976] ECR 613, [1976] 2 CMLR 271; Case 251/78 *Firma Denkavit Futtermittel GmbH v. Minister für Ernährung, Landwirtschaft und Forsten des Landes Nordrhein-Westfalen* [1979] ECR 3369, [1980] 3 CMLR 513; Case 132/80 *NV United Foods et al. v. Belgian State* [1981] ECR 995, [1982] 1 CMLR 273, Case 272/80 *Frans-Nederlandse Maatschappij voor Biologische Producten BV* [1981] ECR 3277, and Case 50/83 *Commission v. Italy* [1984] ECR 1633.

508. *E.g.* Case 188/84 *Commission v. France* [1986] ECR 419, and Case C-293/93 *Houtwipper* [1994] 1 CMLR 4249, see Gormley (1996) 21 ELRev. 44. It may be very difficult to decide objectively what is equivalent to what. The International Standardization Organisation (ISO) definition of equivalent standards is limited to identicality save for minor editorial changes. In the Court's case-law relating to the mutual recognition of testing in the health field (*e.g.* Case 272/80 *Frans-Nederlandse Maatschappij voor Biologische Producten* [1981] ECR 3277) the concept of equivalence is used in the rather different sense of offering equivalent guarantees of safety and reliability. See also Case 45/87 *Commission v. Ireland* [1988] ECR 4929. See, further, Chapter VIII, section 2.1, *post*.

509. *E.g.* Case 104/75 *Officier van Justitie v. De Peijper* [1976] ECR 613 at 636–638; Case 132/80 *NV United Foods et al. v. Belgian State* [1981] ECR 995 at 1025 and Case 272/80 *Frans-Nederlandse Maatschappij voor Biologische Producten* [1981] ECR 3277 at 3291–3292. The same principle is applied in relation to services, see *e.g.* Case 279/80 *Webb* [1981] ECR 3305 at 3326.

510. The only case involving art treasures involved a tax, rather than a measure falling under Arts. 30–36, see Case 7/68 *Commission v. Italy* [1968] ECR 423, [1969] CMLR

borne in mind: '*certaines oeuvres sont culturelles par nature et ... tous les autres peuvent le devenir.*'[511]

The final head of justification is the protection of industrial and commercial property. This head has seen important developments in the case-law which have major significance for the commercial behaviour of undertakings; accordingly the main thrust of the case-law is discussed below.

Industrial and commercial property rights. Because national laws enable holders of, for example, patent, trade mark or plant breeder's rights to oppose by means of infringement proceedings the marketing by others of products covered by their rights, the possibility of conflict between the free movement of goods principle and industrial and commercial property rights was inevitable.[512] To the extent to which national law permitted such proceedings without any restriction against all imports of the products involved then holders of rights would be given the possibility of using court orders to divide up the common market[513] and consequently, for

1. As to the ambit of this heading, see Gormley, *op. cit.* (see note 26, *supra*) 182–184 and Oliver, *op. cit.* (see note 259, *supra*) 221–224. See also Mattera (1993) RMUE 9 and Margue (1992) RMC 905. As to Community action in this field, see Dir. 93/7 (O.J. 1993 L 74/74) and Reg. 3911/92 (O.J. 1992 L 395/1, implemented by Reg. 752/93 (O.J. 1993 L 77/24)), and De Ceuster (1993) RMUE 33; Margue (1993) RMUE 89; Siehr in Immenga *et al.* (eds.), *Festschrift für Ernst-Joachim Mestmäcker* (Baden-Baden, 1996) 483 and (1996) Z.Ver.RW 170, and Biondi (1997) 34 CMLRev. 1173. See further, the UNIDROIT Convention (Rome, 24 June 1995).

511. In Vanden Abeele (ed.): *Le Marché Commun et le marché de l'art* (Brussels, 1982) 35 at 37.

512. The literature in this field is vast, but much is now very dated. As to more recent work, see, generally, Bellamy and Child, *Common Market Law of Competition* (4th ed., London, 1993) Chap. 8 and 1st supp. (London, 1996); Ebenroth, *Gewerblicher Rechtsschutz und europäische Warenverkehrsfreiheit: ein Beitrag zur Erschöpfung Gewerblicher Schutzrechte* (Heidelberg, 1992); Govaere, *The Use and Abuse of Intellectual Property Rights in E.C. Law* (London, 1996, with useful bibliography); Groves *et al.*, *Intellectual Property and the Internal Market of the European Community* (London, 1993); Tritton, *Intellectual Property in Europe* (London, 1996); Beier (1990) IIC 131 and (1991) I.I.C. 157; Gormley in Vaughan (ed.), *op. cit.* (see note 84, *supra*) paras. 504–529 (and, in relation to competition, Cooper *et al.* in *ibid.* Part 19, paras. 1903–2348); Oliver, *op. cit.* (see note 102, *supra*) 247–300, and Jarvis, *op. cit.* (see note 36, *supra*) 282–327 (as to practice in various national courts). As to the tension between market participants established in the Community and those from developing countries, see Alexander, *De betrekkelijke waarde van de intellectuele eigendom* (Zwolle, 1993). See also the TRIPs Agreement, within the framework of the WTO (O.J. 1994 L336/214).

513. See Case 58/80 *Dansk Supermarked A/S v. A/S Imerco* [1981] ECR 181 at 194; Case 6/81 *BV Industrie Diensten Groep v. J.A. Beele Handelmaatschappij* [1982] ECR 707 at 716. See further, Koopmans (1983) RMT 342, Wichers-Hoeth (1984) RMT 356, and Koopmans (1994) *Informatierecht/AMI* 107. As to the difference between national and international trade, see Opinion 1/94 *WTO-GATS and TRIPs* [1994] ECR I-5267 at 5405.

example, to pursue different pricing policies on the different national markets. Even if a product covered by, say, a patent or trade mark were to be marketed in a Member State by the patentee or trade mark owner (or with his consent by, for example, a licensee) he could always oppose the importation of the product into another Member State. Given that intellectual propety infringement proceedings were primarily based on national legislation, it was obvious that national courts would make references under Article 177 EC to the Court of Justice about the extent of this head of justification.[514]

From the economic standpoint these are practices of undertakings restricting competition. Moreover, they are often linked to agreements between undertakings restricting competition. Hence it is scarcely surprising that these problems first arose in judgments relating to Article 85 EC.[515] It rapidly became apparent, though, that such infringement proceedings could be brought against traders who imported products lawfully marketed in another Member State, even though the proceedings did not stem from any agreement restrictive of competition. Given that the Court has repeatedly stated that the possession of a patent or trade mark right does not in itself necessarily lead to an economically dominant position there could often be no recourse to Article 86 EC either to resist such proceedings.[516] Refusal to provide information about forthcoming

514. The Berne Convention 1886 (UKTS 14 (1897)), most recently revised, Paris, 24 July, 1971 (Cmnd. 5002 (1974)) has also been considered, see Cases C-241 and 242/91 P *Radio Telefis Eireann (RTE) et al. v. Commission* [1995] ECR 743 at 829–832; See also the submissions in Cases C-92 and 362/92 *Collins et al. v. Imtrat Handelsgesellschaft mbH et al.* [1995] ECR I-5145, [1993] 3 CMLR 773; Opinion 1/94 *WTO-GATS and TRIPs* [1994] ECR I-5267. In Case T-56/92 *Koelman v. Commission* [1993] ECR II-1267 the Court of First Instance dimissed summarily a complaint based in part on the Convention. The Paris Union Convention 1883 (most recently revised, Stockholm, 14 July 1967 (828 UNTS 306)) was considered in Case 6/81 *BV Industrie Diensten Group v. J.A. Beele Handelsmaatschappij BV* [1982] ECR 707 at 717; Cases 43 and 63/82 *Vereniging ter Bevordering van het Vlaamse Boekwezen, VBVB et al. v. Commission* [1984] ECR 19 at 63; Case 182/84 *Miro BV* [1985] ECR 3731 at 3745; Case 130/85 *Groothandel in, Im- en Export van Eieren en Eierenprodukten Wulro BV* [1986] ECR 2035 at 2044–2045; Case C-235/89 *Commission v. Italy* [1992] ECR I-777 at 826; Case C-30/90 *Commission v. United Kingdom* [1992] ECR I-829 at 867, and in the submissions in Opinion 1/94, *supra.*

515. See Cases 56 and 58/64 *Éts. Consten SARL and Grundig-Verkaufs-GmbH v. Commission* [1966] ECR 299, [1966] CMLR 418; Case 24/67 *Parke, Davis & Co. v. Probel et al.* [1968] ECR 55, [1968] CMLR 47; Case 40/70 *Sirena Srl v. Eda Srl et al.* [1971] ECR 69, [1971] CMLR 260; Case 125/78 *GEMA v. Commission* [1979] ECR 3173, [1980] 2 CMLR 177, and Case 35/83 *BAT Cigaretten-Fabrieken GmbH v. Commission* [1985] ECR 363, [1985] 2 CMLR 470. More recently, see *e.g.* Case 395/87 *Ministère public v. Tournier* [1989] ECR 2521, [1991] 4 CMLR 248, and Cases 110/88 etc. *Lucazeau et al. v. Société des auteurs, compositeurs et éditeurs de musique (Sacem) et al.* [1989] ECR 2811, [1991] 4 CMLR 248.

516. See Case 24/67 *Parke, Davis & Co. v. Probel et al.* [1968] ECR 55, [1968] CMLR 47; Case 40/70 *Sirena Srl v. Eda Srl et al.* [1971] ECR 69, [1971] CMLR 260; Case 78/70

television programmes may well constitute an abuse of a dominant position.[517] This case-law is dealt with elsewhere in this work.[518]

In a series of judgments the Court developed a clear doctrine on the points which have just been discussed. Article 36 leaves industrial and commercial property rights granted by national legislation intact as such, thus the *existence* of these rights cannot be incompatible with Articles 30–34 EC, but the *exercise* of those rights may well be.[519] The case-law boils down to the delimitation in various situations between rights which form part of the *specific object* (or specific subject matter) of patents, trade marks and similar rights, and the exercise or disposal of rights which do not form part of that specific object. The Court has held that the specific object of a patent is 'the guarantee that the patentee, to reward the creative effort of the inventor, has the exclusive right to use an invention with a view to manufacturing industrial products and putting them into circulation for the first time, either directly or by the grant of licences to third parties, as well as the right to oppose infringements.'[520]

In Case 16/74 *Centrafarm BV et al. v. Winthrop BV* the Court defined the specific object of a trade mark as 'the guarantee that the owner of the trade mark has the exclusive right to use that trade mark, for the purpose of putting products protected by the trade mark into circulation for the first time.'[521] Thus it was 'intended to protect him against competitors wishing to take advantage of the status and reputation of the trade mark by selling products illegally bearing that trade mark.'[522]

Deutsche Grammophon Gesellschaft mbH v. Metro-SB-Großmärkte GmbH & Co. KG [1971] ECR 487, [1971] CMLR 631; Case 127/73 *Belgische Radio en Televisie et al. v. SV SABAM et al.* [1974] ECR 313, [1974] 2 CMLR 238; Case 51/75 *EMI Records Ltd. v. CBS Schallplatten GmbH* [1976] ECR 913, [1976] 2 CMLR 235 (and associated cases decided on the same day); Case 22/79 *Greenwich Film Production v. SACEM et al.* [1979] ECR 3275, [1980] 1 CMLR 629; Case 262/81 *Coditel SA et al. v. Ciné-Vog Films SA et al.* [1982] ECR 3381, [1983] 1 CMLR 49, and Case 395/87 *Ministère public v. Tournier* [1989] ECR 2521, [1991] 4 CMLR 248.

517. Cases C-241 and 242/91 P *Radio Telefis Eireann (RTE) et al. v. Commission* [1995] ECR 743, [1995] 4 CMLR 718.
518. See Chapter VIII, section 4.2.4, *post.*
519. Case 40/70 *Sirena Srl v. Eda Srl* [1971] ECR 69 at 81; Case 78/70 *Deutsche Grammophon Gesellschaft mbH v. Metro-SB-Großmärkte GmbH. & Co. KG* [1971] ECR 487 at 499–500, and Case 15/74 *Centrafarm BV et al. v. Sterling Drug Inc.* [1974] ECR 1147 at 1162.
520. Case 15/74 *Centrafarm BV et al. v. Sterling Drug Inc.* [1974] ECR 1147 at 1162. The specific subject matter of a patent may cover a clause in a patent licensing agreement requiring components protected by the patent to be marked with a notice indicating the fact of a licence, Case 193/83 *Windsurfing International Inc.* [1986] ECR 611 at 660.
521. [1974] ECR 1183 at 1194.
522. As to imports from third countries see Case 51/75 *EMI Records Ltd. v. CBS United Kingdom Ltd* [1976] ECR 811, [1976] 2 CMLR 235 (and the parallel litigation decided on the same day), and Case C-355/96 *Silhouette* (see note 397, *supra*).

More extensive rights recognised by national legislation or case-law on the exercise of patents or trade marks (or analagous rights) such as the right to object to the importation of goods which have been marketed in another Member State by or with the consent of the patentee or trade mark owner, are not saved by the terms of the first sentence of Article 36 EC. In these circumstances the rights are said to have been exhausted.[523] An analogy may be drawn here with Article 222 EC on property rights in general.[524]

Particular problems have arisen with repackaging of trade-marked goods,[525] as well as with the initial application[526] and later rejection[527] of the so-called common origin doctrine, whereby the originally the Court

523. If marketing has first taken place within the Community in a Member State which does not recognize patent protection for the products concerned, the exhaustion rule still applies, see Case 187/80 *Merck & Co. Inc. v. Stephar BV et al.* [1981] ECR 2063, [1981] CMLR 463; see, further, Cases C-267 and 268/95 *Merck & Inc. et al. v. Primecrown Ltd. et al.* [1996] ECR I-6285, [1997] 1 CMLR 83; Castillo de la Torre (1997) EIPR 304; McKnight (1996) EIPR 271; Shea (1997) EIPR 103, and Torremans and Stamatoudi (1997) 22 ELRev. 248. See, further, as to exhaustion generally, Case C-352/95 *Phytheron International SA v. Jean Bourdon SA* [1997] ECR I-1729; and as to the submission of samples in an application for registration, where the samples are manufactured in accordance with a patented process without the consent of the patentee, Case C-316/85 *Generics BV v. Smith, Kline & French Laboratories Ltd.* [1997] ECR I-3929. Products manufactured under a compulsory licence have not been marketed with the consent of the patentee, and thus national rights in other Member States may be relied upon to stop imports of such products, Case 19/84 *Pharmon BV v. Hoechst AG* [1985] ECR 2281, [1985] 3 CMLR 775; see, further, Case C-191/90 *Generics (UK) Ltd. et al. v. Smith, Kline and French Laboratories Ltd.* [1992] ECR I-5335, [1993] 1 CMLR 89. As to licences of right, see Case 434/85 *Allen and Hanbury Ltd. v. Generics (U.K. Ltd.)* [1988] ECR 1245, [1988] 1 CMLR 701. As to the threat of grant of a compulsory licence because of failure to work a patent (or plant breeder's right), see Case C-259/89 *Commission v. Italy* [1992] ECR I-777, and Case C-30/90 *Commission v. United Kingdom* [1992] ECR I-829, [1992] 1 CMLR 70978. As to relative novelty, see Case 35/87 *Thetford Corporation v. Fiamma SpA et al.* [1988] ECR 3585.
524. See Case 30/90 *Commission v. United Kingdom* [1992] ECR I-829, [1992] 1 CMLR 709 and Case C-350/92 *Commission v. Spain* [1995] ECR I-1985. See Bartels, (1995) *Ars Aequi* 243.
525. See Case 102/77 *Hoffmann-La Roche & Co. AG et al. v. Centrafarm Vertriebsgesellschaft Pharmazeutischer Erzeugnisse mbH* [1978] ECR 1139, [1978] 3 CMLR 217; Case 3/78 *Centrafarm BV v. American Home Products Corporation* [1978] ECR 1823, [1979] 1 CMLR 326; Case 1/81 *Pfizer Inc. v. Eurim-Pharm GmbH* [1981] ECR 2913, [1982] 1 CMLR 406; Cases C-427/93 *etc. Bristol-Myers Squibb et al. v. Paranova A/S* [1996] ECR I-3457; Cases C-71–73/94 *Eurim-Pharm Arzneimittel GmbH v. Beiersdorf AG et al.* [1996] ECR I-3603; Case C-232/94 *MPA Pharma GmbH v. Rhône-Poulenc Pharma GmbH* [1996] ECR I-3671. These more recent judgments now set out clearly the conditions under which repackaging is permissible. See also Case C-349/95 *Loendersloot v. George Ballantine & Son Ltd. et al.* [1997] ECR I-6227 on relabelling of Scotch Whisky.
526. Case 192/73 *Van Zuylen Frères v. Hag AG* [1974] ECR 731, [1974] CMLR 127. Contrast Mann (1975) 24 ICLQ 31 and Jacobs (1975) 24 ICLQ 643, and the latter with the opinion of Jacobs, Adv. Gen. in Case C-10/89 *SA CNL-CNL-Sucal NV v. Hag AG* [1990] ECR I-3711 at 3725 *et seq.*
527. Case C-10/89 *SA CNL-CNL-Sucal NV v. Hag AG* [1990] ECR I-3711, [1990] 3 CMLR

gave priority to the unity of the market (and, silently, the non-continuation of the consequences of wartime reparations) over the more consumer-related aspect of the name and reputation of the mark.[528] In fact the appropriate vehicle to tackle market division through trade mark assignment is Article 85 EC.[529]

The specific object of copyright and related rights, as governed by national legislation, 'is to ensure the protection of the moral and economic rights of their holders. The protection of moral rights enables authors and performers, in particular, to object to any distortion, mutilation or other modification of a work which would be prejudicial to their honour or reputation.'[530] The economic aspect to these rights is 'that they confer the right to exploit commercially the marketing of the protected work, particularly in the form of licences granted in return for payment of royalties.'[531] Particular problems have

571, see Cornish (1990) 10 YBEL 469; Joliet (1991) GRUR Int. 177; (191) 22 IIC 303, and (1991) 27 RTDE 169.

528. See, further, Case C-9/93 *IHT Internationale Heiztechnik GmbH et al. v. Ideal Standard GmbH et al.* [1994] ECR I-2789, [1994] 3 CMLR 857, see Alexander (1995) 32 CMLRev. 327; Jarvis (1995) 20 ELRev. 195, and Tritton (1994) EIPR 422. But Oliver, *op. cit.* (see note 102, *supra*) 284, following the opinion of Gulman, Adv. Gen. [1994] ECR I-2789 at 2818–2820, observes that the consumer has been made a pretext for a ruling which may well not be in his or her interests at all. As to identical or confusingly similar trade marks which have arisen independently for similar products, and where there are no legal or economic ties between the undertakings concerned, see Case 119/75 *Terrapin (Overseas) Ltd. v. Terranova CA Kapferer & Co.* [1976] ECR 1039, [1976] 2 CMLR 482 and Case C-317/91 *Deutsche Renault AG v. Audi AG* [1993] ECR I-6227. See further, the cases cited in note 545, *infra*. As to consumer confidence and intellectual property in relation to pharmaceuticals, see Cases 266 and 267/87 *R. v. Royal Pharmaceutical Society of Great Britain, ex parte Association of Pharmaceutical Importers et al.* [1989] ECR 1295, [1989] 2 CMLR 751. As to the relationship between trade marks and copyright, see Case C-337/95 *Parfums Christian Dior SA et al. v. Evora BV* [1997] ECR I-6013.

529. Case C-9/93 *IHT Internationale Heiztechnik GmbH et al. v. Ideal Standard GmbH et al.* [1994] ECR I-2789 at 2855, in which case the context, the commitments underlying the assignment, the intention of the parties and the consideration for the assignment would all be relevant.

530. Cases C-92 and 326/92 *Collins et al. v. Imtrat Handelsgesellschaft mbH et al.* [1993] ECR I-5145 at 5179. As to the relationship between copyright and taxation, see Case 90/79 *Commission v. France* [1981] ECR 283, [1981] 3 CMLR 1. As to the relationship between trade marks and copyright, see Case 58/80 *Dansk Supermarket A/S v. A/S Imerco* [1981] ECR 181, [1991] 3 CMLR 590 and Case C-337/95 *Parfums Christian Dior SA et al. v. Evora BV* [1997] ECR I-nyr (4 November 1997). As to importation of infringing products from countries associated with the Community, see Case 270/80 *Polydor Ltd. v. Harlequin Record Shop Ltd.* [1982] ECR 329 at 349. Art. 36 EC was raised in Cases 60 and 61/84 *Cinéthèque SA et al. v. Fédération nationale des cinémas français* [1985] ECR 2605, [1986] 1 CMLR 365 but the case was decided on grounds relating to the rule of reason, see section 3.3.3, *post*.

531. *Ibid.* See also Cases 55 and 57/80 *Musik-Vertrieb membran GmbH v. GEMA* [1981] ECR 147 at 162.

arisen in relation to the hiring of works and performing rights, as well as the collection of royalties.[532]

Plant breeder's rights are treated in the same way as other industrial and commercial property rights,[533] and a similar view has been taken in respect of registered designs.[534] The case-law on the protection of indications of origin has undergone considerable clarification,[535] although reactions have been mixed.[536] Industrial and commercial property rights may not be relied upon by traditional user of a particular shape of packaging, such as a bottle, for their product to restrain the importation or sale of products in similar shaped packaging from other Member States lawfully and traditionally marketed there.[537] Unfair competition and precise imitation

532. See Case 78/70 *Deutsche Grammophon Gesellschaft mbH v. Metro-SB-Großmärkte GmbH & Co. KG* [1971] ECR 487, [1971] CMLR 631; Case 62/79 *Compagnie Générale pour la Diffusion de la Télévision, Coditel SA v. Ciné Vog Films SA* [1980] ECR 881, [1981] 2 CMLR 362; Cases 55 and 57/80 *Musik-Vertrieb membran GmbH v. GEMA* [1981] ECR 147, [1981] 2 CMLR 44; Case 262/81 *Coditel SA v. Ciné Vog Films SA* [1982] ECR 3381, [1983] 1 CMLR 49; Case 402/85 *Basset v. Sacem et al.* [1987] ECR 1747, [1987] 3 CMLR 173; Case 158/86 *Warner Brothers Inc. v. Christiansen* [1988] ECR 2605; Case 341/87 *EMI Electrola GmbH v. Patricia Im- und Export Verwaltungs-gesellschaft mbH et al.* [1989] ECR 79, [1989] 2 CMLR 413; Case 395/87 *Ministère public v. Tournier* [1989] ECR 2521; Cases 110/88 etc. *Lucazeau v. Sacem et al.* [1989] ECR 2811, [1991] 4 CMLR 248, and Case C-270/86 *Cholay et al. v. Sacem* [1990] ECR I-4607 (summary publication only). See WQ E-2137/94 (McNally) O.J. 1995 C 75/21.
533. Case 258/78 *LC Nungesser KG et al. v. Commission* [1982] ECR 2015; Case 27/87 *Louis Erauw-Jacquery Sprl v. La Hesbignonne Société Coopérative* [1988] ECR 1919, [1988] 4 CMLR 576. See also Case C-259/89 *Commission v. Italy* [1992] ECR I-777 (in which the original complaint concerned plant breeder's rights).
534. Case 144/81 *Keurkoop BV v. Nancy Kean Gifts BV* [1982] ECR 2853, [1983] 2 CMLR 47; Case 53/87 *Consorzio italiano della componentistica di ricambio pe il autoveicoli et al. v. Régie nationale des usines Renault* [1988] ECR 6029, [1990] 4 CMLR 265, and Case 238/87 *AB Volvo v. Erik Veng (UK) Ltd.* [1988] ECR 6211, [1994] 4 CMLR 122.
535. The Court's approach in Case 12/74 *Commission v. Germany* [1975] ECR 181, [1975] 1 CMLR 350 was heavily criticized by Beier in Cohen Jehoram (ed.), *Protection of Geographic Denominations of Goods and Services* (Alphen aan den Rijn, 1980) 183. See further, Case 16/83 *Prantl* [1984] ECR 1299, [1985] 2 CMLR 238; Case C-47/90 *Éts. Delhaize Frères et Compagnie Le Lion SA v. Promalvin SA et al.* [1992] ECR I-3669; Case C-3/91 *Exporteur SA v. LOR SA et al.* [1992] ECR I-5529, and Cases C-321-324/94 *Pistre et al.* [1997] ECR I-2343. See further, Case C-317/95 *Canafane Cheese Trading AMBA et al. v. Ministries of Commerce, Finance etc.* (O.J. 1995 C 333/16), pending. Other cases were dealt with under the rule of reason, see Case 8/74 *Procureur du Roi v. Dassonville et al.* [1974] ECR 837[1974] 2 CMLR 436; Case 2/78 *Commission v. Belgium* [1979] ECR 1761, [1980] 1 CMLR 216 (a wholly misconceived judgment at odds with the rest of the case-law); Case 207/83 *Commission v. United Kingdom* [1985] ECR 1201, [1985] 2 CMLR 259, and Case 179/85 *Commission v. Germany* [1986] ECR 3879, [1988] 1 CMLR 135.
536. See Beier (1993) GRUR Int. 76; Cornish (1992) 12 YBEL 635 at 637; Stuyck (1993) 30 CMLRev. 847, and Brouwer (1993) 30 CMLRev. 1209. See also the discussion in Oliver, *op. cit.* (see note 102, *supra*) 291–300.
537. Case 16/83 *Prantl* [1984] ECR 1299 at 1339, see also Case 179/85 *Commission v. Germany* [1986] ECR 3879 at 3898.

(which embraces the English concept of 'passing off') have been dealt with under the rule of reason rather than Article 36 EC.[538]

In order to simplify matters and to provide for much-needed Community level rules, a number of instruments of positive integration have been adopted in this field.[539] In so far as the measures merely involve harmonization, Community competence is based on Articles 100 or 100a EC, but it may create new rights on the basis of Article 235 EC.[540] In relation to patents, progress has in fact been most marked in a wider European framework than the Community;[541] but Regulation 1768/92 has established a supplementary protection certificate for medicinal products;[542] Regulation 1610/96 makes equivalent provision for plant protection products,[543] and the Commission has presented a Green Paper on the Community Patent and the patent system in Europe.[544]

Trade mark law has been a rather more successful area for Community action, with the adoption of the first directive on trade mark law[545] and

538. Case 58/80 *Dansk Supermarked A/S v. A/S Imerco* [1981] ECR 181, [1981] 3 CMLR 590; Case 6/81 *BV Industrie Diensten Groep v. J.A. Beele Handelmaatschappij* [1982] ECR 707, [1982] 3 CMLR 102.

539. See WQ E-2536/94 (Quisthoudt-Rowohl) O.J. 1995 C 88/22; the Green Paper on copyright COM (88) 172 Final, and the Commission's Work Programme on copyright and neighbouring rights COM (90) 584 Final.

540. As to competence, see Opinion 1/94 *WTO – GATS and TRIPs* [1994] ECR I-5267 at 5405–5409 and 5418–5419.

541. See the European Patent Convention (Munich, 5 October 1973) T.S. 20 (1978), Cmnd. 7090, see Brinkhof, *Europees octrooirecht* (Zwolle, 1989) and (1994) BIE 188; Singer, *The European Patent Convention: A Commentary* (ed. Lunzer, London, 1995); Cook (1997) EIPR 367; Cornish (1976) JBL 112, and Ullrich (1991) GRURInt. 1. The Community Patent Convention (O.J. 1976 L 17/1, as revised, O.J. 1989 L 401/1) is not yet in force, see McClellan (1978) CDE 202, but this has not prevented parties from basing arguments on it or the Court from citing it, *e.g.* Case C-235/89 *Commission v. Italy* [1992] ECR I-777, 795–797 and 826–827, and Case C-316/95 *Generics BV v. Smith Kline & French Laboratories Ltd.* [1997] ECR I-3929 at 3962.

542. O.J. 1992 L 182/1, see Case 350/92 *Spain v. Council* [1995] ECR I-1985; Case C-181/95 *Biogen Inc. v. Smithkline Beecham Biologicals SA* [1997] ECR I-357, and Case C-110/95 *Yamanouchi Pharmaceutical Co. Ltd. v. Comptroller-General of Patents, Designs and Trade Marks* [1997] ECR I-3251.

543. O.J. 1996 L 1610/96.

544. COM (97) 314 Final.

545. Dir. 89/104 (O.J. 1989 L 40/1, amended by Dir. 92/10 (O.J. 1992 L 6/35)). See Cases C-427/93 etc. *Bristol-Myers-Squibb et al. v. Paranova A/S* [1996] ECR I-3457; Cases C-71–73/94 *Eurim-Pharm Arzneimittel GmbH v. Beiersdorf AG et al.* [1996] ECR I-3603; Case C-232/94 *MPA Pharma GmbH v. Rhône-Poulenc Pharma GmbH* [1996] ECR I-3671; Case C-313/94 *Fratelli Graffione SNC v. Fransa* [1996] ECR I-6039; Case C-352/95 *Phytheron International SA v. Jean Bourdon SA* [1997] ECR I-1729; Case C-337/95 *Parfums Christian Dior SA et al. v. Evora BV* [1997] ECR I-6013; Case C-251/95 *SABEL BV v. Puma AG, Rudolf Dassler Sport* [1997] ECR I-6191, and Case C-349/95 *Loendersloot v. George Ballantine & Son Ltd. et al.* [1997] ECR I-6227. See also Case C-355/96 *Silhouette International Schmied Gesellschaft mbH & Co. KG v. Hartlauer Handelsgesellschaft mbH* ([1998] ECR I-nyr (16 July 1998); Case C-39/97 *Canon*

the Community Trade Mark Regulation.[546] In relation to copyright and related rights, the Community has taken steps to deal with the legal protection of computer programs,[547] the protection of rental and lending rights,[548] satellite broadcasting and cable retransmission,[549] the term of copyright protection,[550] and the legal protection of databases.[551] The Commission once proposed that the Community accede to the Berne Convention,[552] and it has presented a proposal for a directive on artists' resale right;[553] it has presented a Green Paper on copyright and related

---

Kabushiki Kaisha v. Pathe Communications Corporation (O.J. 1997 C 94/11); Case C-63/97 *Bayerische Motorenwerke AG et al. v. Deenik* (O.J. 1997 C 107/14); Cases C-108 and 109/97 *WSC Windsurfing Chiemsee Produktions- und Vertriebs GmbH v. Boots-und Segelzubehör Walter Huber* (O.J. 1997 C 166/4), and Case C-278/97 *Wrangler Germany GmbH v. Metro Seblstbedienungs-Grosshandel GmbH* (O.J. 1997 C 295/19). Before the EFTA Court, see Case E-2/97 *Mag Instrument Inc. v. California Trading Company Norway, Ulsteen* (O.J. 1997 C 209/24), pending. See, Gotzen, *Algemene problemen van merkenrecht* (Brussels, 1994); Holzhauer (ed.), *Eurobrands: het eerste standaardwerk over Europese merkenbeleid* (Deventer, 1994); Schweer, *Die erste Markenrechts-Richtlinie der Europäischen Gemeinschaft und der Rechtschutz bekannter Marken* (Baden-Baden, 1992); Gielen (1992) EIPR 262; Huet (1994) JDInt. 623; Eeckman (1995) SEW 23, and Tilman (1994) ZHR 371.

546. Reg. 40/94 (O.J. 1994 L 11/1, amended by Reg. 3288/94 (O.J. 1994 L 349/83)), implemented by Reg. 2868/95 (O.J. 1995 L 303/1). See Gielen (1996) EIPR 83. Amendments have been proposed, COM (96) 372 Final (O.J. 1996 C 300/11) and COM (97) 489 Final (O.J. 1997 C-353/13, amended COM (98) 289 Final (O.J. 1998 C 194/5)). This does not replace national trade marks but superimposes the Community trade mark on national marks, see Case C-9/93 *IHT Internationale Heiztechnik GmbH et al. v. Ideal-Standard GmbH et al.* [1994] ECR I-2789 at 2853–2854. As to the linguistic regime applicable at the Office for Harmonization in the Internal Market, established by that regulation, see WQ E-1684/94 (Thyssen) O.J. 1995 C 30/5 and Case C-270/95 P *Kik v. Council et al.* [1997] ECR I-1987. The Community is a party to the Treaty on Trade-Mark Law (Geneva, 27 October 1994), *General Report 1995* (Brussels, Luxembourg, 1996) point 717.

547. Dir. 91/250 (O.J. 1991 L 122/42, amended by Dir. 93/98 (O.J. 1993 L 290/9).

548. Dir. 92/100 (O.J. 1992 L 346/61, amended by Dir. 93/98 (O.J. 1993 L 290/9). See Case C-200/96 *Metronome Musik GmbH v. Music Point Hohkamp GmbH* (O.J. 1996 C 233/6) and Case C-61/97 *Foreningen af danske Videogramdistributorer v. Laserdisken* (O.J. 1997 C 108/14), pending. See further, Dommering (1994) *Informatierecht/AMI* 187 and Reinbothe and Von Lewinski, *The EC Directive on Rental and Lending Rights and on Piracy* (London, 1994). As to royalties, see COM (98) 67 Final (O.J. 1998 C 123/9).

549. Dir. 93/83 (O.J. 1993 L 248/15), see Hugenholtz (1994) *Informatierecht/AMI* 87. As to the wider Europen context, see Bull. EU 4–1996, point 1.3.13.

550. Dir. 93/98 (O.J. 1993 L 290/9), see Jorna and Martin-Prat (1994) EIPR 145; Quadflieg (1995) *Informatierecht/AMI* 3, and Verkade and Visser, *ibid.* 47 and (1995) *Mediaforum* 2.

551. Dir. 96/9 (O.J. 1996 L 77/20).

552. As to which, see note 514, *supra*. The proposal has been withdrawn (O.J. 1997 C 2/2). See also the WIPO Copyright Treaty (1997) EIPR 176 and Performances and Phonographs Treaty (1997) EIPR 179, see Reinbothe *et al.* (1997) EIPR 171 and Vinje (1997) EIPR 230.

553. COM (96) 97 Final (O.J. 1996 C 178/16), amended COM (98) 78 Final (O.J. 1998 C 125/8).

rights in the information society[554] and proposed a directive on legal protection for encrypted services in the internal market.[555]

On the basis of Article 113 EC, Regulation 3295/94 deals with counterfeit and pirated goods.[556] Regulation 2100/94 deals with plant variety rights.[557] While the proposal for a directive on designs has made progress,[558] that for a Community regulation in the field has not.[559] The Commission has presented a Green Paper on utility models.[560] The proposal for a directive on the legal protection of biotechnological inventions[561] came to grief[562] but has been revived in another form.[563] Directive 87/54 provides *sui generis* legal protection for semiconductor topographies.[564] Finally, Regulation 2081/92 deals with the protection of geographical indications and designations of origin for agricultural products and foodstuffs[565] which has been not uncontroversially received.[566]

Article 36 EC, second sentence. The second sentence of Article 36 EEC contains a most important limitation on the first sentence of that Article; even if measures capable of hindering imports or exports can in principle be justified under the first sentence of Article 36, they may not constitute a means of arbitrary discrimination or a disguised restriction on trade between Member States. The same condition also applies to

554. COM (95) 382 Final, as to the follow-up, see COM (96) 568 Final.
555. COM (97) 356 Final (O.J. 1997 C 314/7), amended COM (98) 332 Final (O.J. 1998 C 203/12). This follows the Green Paper COM (96) 76 Final.
556. O.J. 1994 L 341/8, implemented by Reg. 1367/95 (O.J. 1995 L 133/2).
557. O.J. 1994 L 227/1, amended by Reg. 2506/95 (O.J. 1995 L 258/3), implemented by Regs. 1238/95 (O.J. 1995 L 121/36) and 1239/95 (O.J. 1995 L 121/59), see van der Kooi (1995) *Agrarisch Recht* 54.
558. See the Common Position (O.J. 1997 C 237/1); currently in the third reading. See Cohen Jehoram (1994) NJB 1298.
559. COM (93) 342 Final (O.J. 1994 C 29/20), see Horton (1994) EIPR 51. By the end of 1995 it had become politically clear that a new proposal would be needed.
560. COM (95) 370 Final.
561. COM (88) 496 Final, amended COM (92) 589 Final.
562. Rejected by the European Parliament, Bull. EU 3–1995, point 1.3.17.
563. The Common Position (O.J. 1998 C 110/17) was approved without amendment, publication of the directive is expected.
564. O.J. 1987 L 24/36. The benefit of this directive has been extended to various countries by numerous individual decisions.
565. O.J. 1992 L 208/1, amended by Regs. 535/97 (O.J. 1997 L 83/3 and 1068/97 (O.J. 1997 L 156/10), and implemented by Regs. 2037/93 (O.J. 1993 L 185/5, amended by Reg. 1428/97 (O.J. 1997 L 196/39)) and 1107/96 (O.J. 1996 L 148/10, most recently amended by Reg. 1065/97 (O.J. 1997 L 156/6)). See Cases C-321–324/94 *Pistre et al.* [1997] ECR I-2343. Myriad cases were pending before the Court of Justice and the Court of First Instance at the date at which this work states the law.
566. Beier and Knaak (1992) GRURInt. 411 (in English, (1994) IIC 1) and (1993) GRURInt. 602; Tilman (1993) GRURInt. 610, and Salignon (1994) RMUE 107, see also Oliver, *op. cit.* (see note 102, *supra*) 299–300.

measures in respect of which the rule of reason is invoked.[567] The Court has on various occasions tended to speak of the principle of proportionality as being the basis of the second sentence of Article 36[568] but in relation to the first sentence of that Article the second sentence is more in the nature of a 'notwithstanding' provision or, as Brändel has suggested, an 'emergency brake' in Community law.[569] A good example of arbitrary discrimination being found in the application of ostensibly justifiable inspections can be seen in Case 42/82 *Commission v. France*[570] which arose out of the Franco-Italian wine war. More generally, typical examples include import prohibitions which are sometimes applied and sometimes not,[571] controls on compliance by imports with provisions which also apply to domestic products but which are carried out more rigorously on imports[572] and an injunction issued against an importer in circumstances which would not justify its issue, against a purely domestic party.[573] Case 152/78 *Commission v. France*[574] shows that the Court will sometimes treat unequal treatment of imports *vis-à-vis* domestic products as a prohibited arbitrary discrimination *per se*. In such cases, though, it is submitted that the Court should rather apply the proportionality test in the evaluation under the first sentence of Article 36 EC.[575] Not every difference in treatment amounts to arbitrary discrimination, though, but any difference must be objectively and genuinely justified.[576] Thus any suspicion that products are dangerous or that health rules have not been complied with must be a genuine suspicion based on reasonable grounds and may not be

567. *E.g.* Case 8/74 *Procureur du Roi v. Dassonville et al.* [1974] ECR 837 at 852.
568. *E.g.* Case 174/82 *Officier van Justitie v. Sandoz BV* [1983] ECR 2445 at 2463; Case 227/82 *Van Bennekom* [1983] ECR 3883 at 3905, and Case 247/84 *Motte* [1985] ECR 3887 at 3905. The second sentence is clearly designed to prevent misuse of health justifications just as it is designed to prevent the misuse of other justifications, see *e.g.* Case 144/81 *Keurkoop BV v. Nancy Kean Gifty BV* [1982] ECR 2853 at 2872–2873; Case 34/79 *R. v. Henn and Darby* [1979] ECR 3795 at 3815, and Case 40/82 *Commission v. United Kingdom* [1982] ECR 2793 at 2825. See the discussion in Gormley, *op. cit.* (see note 26, *supra*) 210–218 and literature cited there.
569. [1980] GRUR Int. 512.
570. [1983] ECR 1013 at 1048–1049.
571. As in the case of discrimination between direct imports and parallel imports in Case 8/74 *Procureur du Roi v. Dassonville et al.* [1974] ECR 837, [1974] 2 CMLR 436. See also Case 104/75 *Officier van Justitie v. De Peijper* [1976] ECR 613, [1976] 2 CMLR 271.
572. *E.g.* Case 42/82 *Commission v. France* [1983] ECR 1013, [1984] 1 CMLR 160, or when there are no controls at all on domestic products, *e.g.* Case 4/75 *Rewe-Zentralfinanz GmbH v. Landwirtschaftskammer* [1975] ECR 843, [1977] 1 CMLR 599..
573. Case 434/85 *Allen and Hanburys Ltd. v. Generics (U.K.) Ltd.* [1988] ECR 1245, [1988] 1 CMLR 701.
574. [1980] ECR 2299 at 2316.
575. See also Case 121/85 *Conegate Ltd v. H.M. Customs & Excise* [1986] ECR 1007, [1986] 1 CMLR 739.
576. Case 4/75 *Rewe-Zentralfinanz GmbH v. Landwirtschaftskammer* [1975] ECR 843 at 860.

simply an excuse for interfering systematically or in an arbitrary manner with inter-state trade.[577] As has been explained earlier in this section, the burden of showing that a restriction on trade is justified lies on the Member State or person seeking to restrain importation or the sale of an imported product.

The intention of the prohibition of disguised restrictions on trade between Member States is to prevent reliance on the justifications contained in Article 36 (or the rule of reason) from leading to artificial partitioning or fragmentation of markets within the common market. Such risks are particularly evident in the use of industrial and commercial property rights, and it is unsurprising that it is in that context that much attention has been paid to the concept of a disguised restriction.[578] The first judgment in Case 40/82 *Commission v. United Kingdom*[579] demonstrates that in any event intentional protection of domestic products will render reliance on the first sentence of Article 36 impossible. It is submitted more generally that the view of Advocate-General Capotorti in Case 1/81 *Pfizer Inc. v. Eurim-Pharm GmbH*[580] correctly states the law, *viz.* that the application of the second sentence of Article 36 depends on the *effect* of artificially dividing the market and that proof of the subjective intention to misuse the heads of justification mentioned in the first sentence of Article 36 does not need to be adduced.[581] The Commission has interpreted the term 'disguised restriction' in the context of Article 100a(4) EC.[582]

3.3.3 The rule of reason: case-law based justifications

The rule of reason (or, as the Court refers to it, 'mandatory requirements') is a creation of case-law, thus in Case 8/74 *Procureur du Roi v. Dassonville et al.* the Court phrased the rule of reason in the following words: 'In the absence of a Community system guaranteeing for consumers the authenticity of a product's designation of origin, if a Member State takes measures to prevent unfair practices in this connexion, it is however subject

---

577. Case 42/82 *Commission v. France* [1983] ECR 1013 at 1043 (see also 1048–1049).
578. *E.g.* Case 15/74 *Centrafarm BV et al. v. Sterling Drug Inc.* [1974] ECR 1147, [1974] 2 CMLR 480; Case 102/77 *Hoffmann-La Roche & Co. AG v. Centrafarm Vertriebsgesellschaft Pharmazeutischer Erzeugnisse mbH* [1978] ECR 1139, [1978] 3 CMLR 217; Case 144/81 *Keurkoop BV v. Nancy Kean Gifts BV* [1982] ECR 2853, [1983] 2 CMLR 47, and Case C-9/93 *IHT Internationale Heiztechnik GmbH et al. v. Ideal Standard GmbH et al.* [1994] ECR I-2789, [1994] 3 CMLR 857.
579. [1982] ECR 2793, [1982] 3 CMLR 497 (the second judgment is at [1984] ECR 283).
580. [1981] ECR 2913 at 2935.
581. See, in the same sense, Cases C-427/93 *etc. Bristol-Myers Squibb et al. v. Paranova A/S* [1996] ECR I-3457 at 3536.
582. Dec. 94/783 (O.J. 1994 L 316/43 at 47).

to the condition that these measures be reasonable and that the means of proof required should not act as a hindrance to trade between Member States and should, in consequence, be accessible to all Community nationals.'[583] The Court then added that 'Even without having to examine whether or not such measures are covered by Article 36, they must not, in any case, by virtue of the principle expressed in the second sentence of that Article, constitute a means of arbitrary discrimination or a disguised restriction on trade between Member States.'[584]

The rule of reason is essentially a temporary acceptance of state regulation of the interest or value concerned pending Community regulation which will replace the need (and thus the justification) for unilateral national measures.[585] It has been submitted that the development of the rule of reason is essentially an equitable development, acknowledging that the strict application of the basic principle may in certain circumstances lead to an unconscionable *result*.[586] The rule of reason can also be seen as the reverse side of the coin in relation to the wide basic principle in *Dassonville*[587] and the development in *Cassis de Dijon*[588] (and more clearly subsequently)[589] of the principle of the mutual acceptance of goods.[590] It is now clear that the rule of reason is available only to assist measures which apply to domestic and imported products alike[591] and that the Court will look behind the face of measures to see if this really is the case.[592] It is

583. [1974] ECR 837 at 852. The means of proof must be open to anyone, as goods which are in free circulation in a Member State have a right to move irrespective of the nationality of their owner, consignor, consignee or transporter.
584. *Ibid.*
585. Just as reliance on Art. 36 EC becomes otiose when Community measures occupy the field. See, generally, Gormley in Vaughan (ed.), *op. cit.* (see note 84, *supra*) paras. 422–445.
586. Gormley, *op. cit.* (see note 26, *supra*) 52–53. This took account of the fact that interests such as consumer protection (and later environmental protection) were not major concerns at the time the original EEC Treaty was drafted, but they were concerns the *prima facie* legitimacy of which could not be ignored.
587. [1974] ECR 837 at 852.
588. [1979] ECR 649 at 664.
589. *E.g.* Case 27/80 *Fietje* [1980] ECR 3839 at 3853–3855; Case 261/81 *Walter Rau Lebensmittelwerke v. De Smedt PvbA* [1982] ECR 3961 at 3973 and the literature cited in note 23, *supra*.
590. The point made in section 1.1, *ante*, was that the rule of reason was not *introduced* in *Cassis de Dijon* but in *Dassonville*. The coin approach analogy itself does not give rise to difficulties.
591. *E.g.* Case 788/79 *Gilli and Andres* [1980] ECR 2071 at 2078; Case 113/80 *Commission v. Ireland* [1981] ECR 1635 at 1639; Case 16/83 *Prantl* [1984] ECR 1299 at 1327; Case 177/83 *Theodor Kohl KG v. Ringelhan & Rennett SA et al.* [1984] ECR 3651 at 3662–3663; Case 207/83 *Commission v. United Kingdom* [1985] ECR 1201 at 1212; Case 25/88 *Bouchara, née Wurmser, et al.* [1989] ECR 1105 at 1127–1128, and Cases C-1 and 176/90 *Aragonesa de publicidad Exterior SA et al. v. Departamento de Sanidad y Seguridad Social de la Generalitat de Cataluña* [1991] ECR I-4151 at 4184.
592. *E.g.* Case 177/83 *Theodor Kohl KG v. Ringelhan & Rennett SA et al.* [1984] ECR 3651

submitted that the quite extraordinary reasoning in relation to environmental protection in Case 2/90 *Commission v. Belgium*[593] does not detract from the generality of this proposition (which was clearly acknowledged by the Court).

The rule of reason is not an application of the public policy provision in the first sentence of Article 36 EC[594] nor is it an expansion of the heads of the first sentence of Article 36.[595] The interests or values covered by the rule of reason do not constitute a closed class[596] but the case-law has given a clear indication of the sort of non-discriminatory national provisions which it will accept, provided that the conditions for acceptance are fulfilled. The Court has accepted only non-economic justifications as falling within the rule of reason,[597] although the remarkable thing is just how few of the Member States' arguments have been accepted on the facts; in the overwhelming majority of cases the Court has indicated that certain justifications are admissible but has then gone on to find that the national measures involved were unreasonable, disproportionate or even protectionist (albeit disguised).[598] In view of the assimilation principle,[599] a number of headings which owe their origin to the freedom to provide services have to an extent permeated the headings recognized in relation to the free movement of goods.[600] So far the Court has indicated that national measures justified in the interests of consumer protection;[601] the

at 3662–3663 and Case 207/83 *Commission v. United Kingdom* [1985] ECR 1201 at 1212. See also (in the context of services) Case C-275/92 *H.M. Customs and Excise v. Schindler et al.* [1994] ECR I-1039 at 1094–1095, and Gormley (1995) 20 ELRev. 644.

593. [1992] ECR I-4431 at 4480. See also (in relation to Arts. 48 and 59 EC) the unconvincing reasoning in Case C-204/90 *Bachmann v. Belgian State* [1992] ECR I-249 at 281–285.

594. Case 113/80 *Commission v. Ireland* [1981] ECR 1625 at 1638.

595. This follows from the Court's insistence on a strict interpretation of the provisions of the first sentence of Art. 36 EC, see section 3.3.1, *ante*, even though a certain tension can be felt between saying on the one hand that there is no extension of Art. 36 and yet on the other hand recognizing the legitimacy of other interests or values.

596. Case 120/78 *Rewe-Zentrale AG v. Bundesmonopolverwaltung für Branntwein (Cassis de Dijon)* [1979] ECR 649 at 664; Capotorti, Adv. Gen. in Case 788/79 *Gilli and Andres* [1980] ECR 2071 at 2082; Barents (1979) SEW 746 at 750 and *e.g.* VerLoren van Themaat (1980) *R.M. Themis* 378 at 384. This is clear from the fact that the Court has accepted other interests or values than those mentioned in *Dassonville* or *Cassis de Dijon*, as the illustrations, *post*, demonstrate.

597. Barents (1981) 18 CMLRev. 271 at 289; VerLoren van Themaat (1982) CDE 124 at 131, and Gormley, *op. cit.* (see note 26, *supra*) 67.

598. *E.g.* Case 120/78 *Cassis de Dijon* [1979] ECR 649 at 662–664; Case 16/83 *Prantl* [1984] ECR 1299 at 1327–1328; Case 177/83 *Theodor Kohl KG v. Ringelhan & Rennett SA et al.* [1984] ECR 3651 at 3662–3663, and Case C-407/93 *Verein gegen Unwesen in Handel und Gewerbe Köln e.V. v. Mars GmbH* [1995] ECR I-1923 at 1941–1944. Notable exceptions include Case 302/86 *Commission v. Denmark* [1988] ECR 4607, [1989] 1 CMLR 619 and Case C-2/90 *Commission v. Belgium* [1992] ECR I-4431, [1993] 1 CMLR 365.

599. See section 1.6, *ante*.

600. These are mentioned in the notes, *infra*, but see further, section 7.4.2, *post*.

601. *E.g.* Case 8/74 *Dassonville* [1974] ECR 837 at 852; Case 120/78 *Cassis de Dijon* [1979]

prevention of unfair commercial practices (sometimes expressed as the promotion of fair trading or the prevention of unfair competition)[602]; the effectiveness of fiscal supervision[603]; environmental protection;[604] improvement of working conditions;[605] the promotion of culture in

ECR 649 at 662 and 664; Case 130/80 *Fabriek voor Hoogwaardige Voedingsprodukten Kelderman BV* [1981] ECR 527 at 536; Case 193/80 *Commission v. Italy* [1981] ECR 3019 at 3035–3036; Case 6/81 *BV Industrie Diensten Group v. J.A. Beele Handelmaatschappij BV* [1982] ECR 707 at 716–718; Case 179/85 *Commission v. Germany* [1986] ECR 3879 at 3897–3898; Case 25/88 *Bouchara, née Wurmser, et al.* [1989] ECR 1105 at 1127–1128; Case C-196/89 *Nespoli* [1990] ECR I-3647 at 3666; Case C-293/93 *Houtwipper* [1994] ECR I-4249 at 4267–4268; Case C-312/92 *Verband Sozialer Wettbewerb eV v. Clinique Laboratories SNC et al.* [1994] ECR I-317 at 337; Case C-51/93 *Meyhui NV v. Schott Zwiesel Glaswerke AG* [1994] ECR I-3879 at 3900–3901 (in relation to Community legislation), and Case C-490/93 *Verein gegen Unwesen in Handel und Gewerbe Köln eV v. Mars GmbH* [1995] ECR I-1923 at 1941 (but the standard is that of 'reasonably circumspect consumers' (*ibid.* at 1944). See also Case C-240/95 *Schmidt* [1996] ECR I-3179. The Court has frequently examined consumer protection in relation to advertising (and in the past in relation to sales techniques, see the case-law discussed in section 3.2.1, *ante*), as a recent example, see Cases C-34–36/95 *Konsumentombudsmannen (KO) v. De Agostini (Svenska) Förlag AB et al.* [1997] ECR I-3843 at 3891 (*cf.* Case C-412/93 *Société d'Importation Édouard Leclerc-Siplec v. TF1 Publicité SA et al.* [1995] ECR I-179 at 217). Technical specifications for connection to public networks may be justified in the interests of protecting users as consumers of services and of the protection of the network, if decisions refusing permission to connect are open to challenge before national courts, Case C-18/88 *Régie des télégraphes et téléphones v. GB-INNO-BM SA* [1991] ECR I-5941 at 5983–5984 and Cases C-46/90 and 93/91 *Procureur du Roi v. Lagauche et al.* [1993] ECR I-5267 at 5328. As far as language requirements are concerned, the case-law is in some disarray, as the indications from the case-law are unclear as to the extent of the interests of the consumer, see note 421, *supra*. As to wide-ranging advertising campaigns and point-of-sale information, see Case C-85/94 *Groupement des producteurs, Importateurs et Agents Généraux d'Eaux Minérales Étrangères, VZW (Pigeme) et al. v. Peeters NV* [1995] ECR I-2955 at 2978 (in the context of Community legislation).

602. *E.g.* Case 8/74 *Dassonville* [1974] ECR 837 at 852; Case 58/80 *Dansk Supermarket A/S v. A/S Imerco* [1981] ECR 181 at 194–194; Case 6/81 *BV Industrie Diensten Group v. J.A. Beele Handelmaatschappij BV* [1982] ECR 707 at 716–718; Case 182/84 *Miro BV* [1985] ECR 3731 at 3746–3747; Case 179/85 *Commission v. Germany* [1986] ECR 3879 at 3897–3898; Case C-196/89 *Nespoli* [1990] ECR I-3647 at 3666; Case C-238/89 *Pall Corp. v. P.J. Dahlhausen & Co.* [1990] ECR I-4827 at 4848–4849, and Case C-293/93 *Houtwipper* [1994] ECR I-4249 at 4267.

603. *E.g.* Case 120/78 *Cassis de Dijon* [1979] ECR 649 at 662; Case 823/79 *Carciati* [1980] ECR 2773 at 2780, and Case 90/82 *Commission v. France* [1983] ECR 2011 at 2030. See also, Case 134/83 *Abbink* [1984] ECR 4097, [1986] 1 CMLR 579 and Case 127/86 *Ledoux* [1988] ECR 3741. See further, Wattel (1997) SEW 424.

604. *E.g.* Cases 3/76 *etc. Kramer et al.* [1976] ECR 1279 at 1313 (biological marine resources); Case 240/83 *Procureur de la République v. Association de défense des brûleurs d'huiles usagées (ADBHU)* [1985] ECR 531 at 549, and Case 302/86 *Commission v. Denmark* [1988] ECR 4607 at 4630. See, generally, Jans, *European Environmental Law* (London, 1995); Krämer (1993) 30 CMLRev. 111; De Sadeleer (1994) RMUE 71; Von Wilmowsky (1993) 30 CMLRev. 541, and Gormley in Holder, *op. cit.* (see note 389, *supra*) 289. In Case C-18/93 *Corsica Ferries Italia Srl v. Corpo dei Piloti del Porto di*

678   The establishment of the internal market: the freedoms

general,[606] and the plurality of the media[607] may be accepted, even though they are capable of affecting trade between Member States. Although the protection of public health was included among the examples of rule of reason justifications in *Cassis de Dijon*[608] it has now recognized that public health protection falls exclusively under Article 36 EC itself.[609] The Court also referred to working and non-working hours reflecting national or regional socio-cultural characteristics,[610] but it is unclear whether it intended to add a new head to the list of justifications or was merely thinking of working conditions.[611] It is unclear whether safety in general

Genova [1994] ECR I-1783 at 1823 the Court (dealing with the provision of pilotage services) noted that even if the objectives of navigational safety, national transport policy or environmental protection justified intervention by the public authorities in the transport sector, they did not justify discriminatory tariffs.

605. Case 155/80 *Oebel* [1981] ECR 1993 at 2008; Case C-312/89 *Union départementale des syndicats CGT de l'Aisne v. Conforama et al.* [1991] ECR I-997 at 1025, and Case C-332/89 *Marchandise et al.* [1991] ECR I-1027 at 1040–1041.

606. This head was advanced in Case 229/83 *Association des Centres distributeurs Édouard Leclerc et al. v. Sàrl 'Au blé vert' et al.* [1985] ECR 1 at 35 but rejected on the ground that 'the protection of creativity and cultural diversity in the realm of publishing' was mentioned in Art. 36 EC, and as the measures discouraged imports the rule of reason could not apply (confirmed in Case 95/84 *Boriello et al. v. Darras et al.* [1986] ECR 2253). In Cases 60 and 61/84 *Cinéthèque SA et al. v. Fédération nationale des cinémas français* [1985] ECR 2605 at 2626 the Court found that a policy to encourage the creation of cinematographic works irrespective of their origin was legitimate. The interest must clearly be culture in general (not just a particular national culture). See (also in the context of services), Case C-17/92 *Federación de Distribuidores Cinematográficos (FEDICINE) v. Spanish State* [1993] ECR I-2239, and the heading plurality of the media, *post*.

607. Case C-368/95 *Vereinigte Familiapress Zeitungsverlags- und Vertriebs GmbH v. Heinrich Bauer Verlag* [1997] ECR I-3689 at 3715. In relation to services (frequently linked to cultural policy), see *e.g.* Case C-154/89 *Commission v. France* [1991] ECR I-659 at 686–687; Case C-198/89 *Commission v. Greece* [1991] ECR I-727 at 741–742; Case C-288/89 *Stichting Collectieve Antennevoorziening Gouda et al. v. Commissariaat voor de Media* [1991] ECR I-4007 at 4043–4044; Case C-353/89 *Commission v. The Netherlands* [1991] ECR I-4069 at 4094; Case C-148/91 *Vereniging Veronica Omroep Organisatie v. Commissariaat voor de Media* [1993] ECR I-487 at 518, and Case C-23/93 *TV 10 SA v. Commissariaat voor de Media* [1994] ECR I-4795 at 4832.

608. [1979] ECR 649 at 663, and in several other judgments, *e.g.* Case 788/79 *Gilli & Andres* [1980] ECR 2071 at 2078, and Case 193/80 *Commission v. Italy* [1981] ECR 3019 at 3036.

609. Cases C-1 and 176/90 *Aragonesa de Publicidad Exterior SA et al. v. Separtamento de Sanidad y Seguridad Social de la Generalitat de Cataluña* [1991] ECR I-4151 at 4184. Mertens de Wilmars (writing extra-judicially) acknowledged that it was a slip of the pen to include public health in the list of rule of reason measures, (1984–85) *Rechtskundig Weekblad* Col. 16, note 2.

610. Case C-145/88 *Torfaen Borough Council v. B & Q plc* [1989] ECR I-3851 at 3889 and Case C-169/91 *Council of the City of Stoke-on-Trent et al. v. B & Q plc* [1992] ECR I-6635 at 6658.

611. As appears from Case C-145/88 *Torfaen, ibid.* In any case, matters such as non-discriminatory local regulation of socio-economic life now fall outside Art. 30 itself, thus rule of reason analysis has no part to play (see section 3.2.1, *supra*).

(road safety or otherwise) more properly falls under the rule of reason or under Article 36 EC.[612]

Some of the heads of justification (previously) recognized in the rule of reason (health, safety, environmental protection and consumer protection) obtained a Treaty-based status in relation to proposals for harmonization under Article 100a EC,[613] although the grounds of major needs for the application of national measures under Article 100a(4) EC only specify Article 36 EC, the protection of the environment and the working environment.[614] A number of specific essential requirements, such as the safety of consumers, personnel and the public telecommunications network have been included in Directive 91/263 on telecommunications terminal equipment.[615] Specific grounds of protection are also included in various directives in the foodstuffs sector.[616]

As has been explained in section 3.3.1, above, in order to be justified under the rule of reason, measures must be non-discriminatory, necessary, and are subject to the proportionality test. Further, there must be no Community measures occupying the field. Additionally, the measures concerned must not constitute a means of arbitrary discrimination or a disguised restriction on trade between Member States.[617] Oliver has rightly opined that as long as the Court takes the view that the rule of reason is open only to equally applicable measures yet continues to propound its discrimination test under Article 34 EC for such measures it is difficult to see how the rule of reason can be used in relation to measures capable of hindering exports.[618]

3.3.4 Articles 100a and 100b EC

Article 100a EC is not only now the most important legal basis for harmonization measures in order to achieve the free movement of goods in

612. See, as to roadworthiness tests in relation to public security or health, note 502, *supra*. In Case 188/84 *Commission v. France* [1986] ECR 419 at 435–436 safety arguments relating to woodworking machines were examined under Art. 36 EC.
613. Art. 100a(3).
614. See, generally, Mortelmans (1997) SEW 182.
615. O.J. 1991 L 217/21, most recently amended by Dir. 93/68 (O.J. 1993 L 220/1), Art. 4. See also Case C-18/88 *Régie des télégraphes et téléphones v. GB-INNO-BM SA* [1991] ECR I-5941 at 5983–5984; Cases C-46/90 and 93/91 *Procureur du Roi v. Lagauche et al.* [1993] ECR I-5267 at 5328, and Case C-314/93 *Rouffeteau et al.* [1994] ECR I-3257 at 3278. The present directive replaces the earlier measure, partly annulled in Case C-202/88 *France v. Commission* [1991] ECR I-1223, [1992] 5 CMLR 552.
616. *E.g.* Dir. 79/112 (O.J. 1979 L 33/1, most recently amended by Dir. 97/4 (O.J. 1997 L 43/21)), Art. 15.
617. Case 8/74 *Dassonville* [1974] ECR 837 at 852.
618. Oliver (1982) 19 CMLRev. 217 at 241. See, however, Case C-203/96 *Chemische Afralstoffen Dusseldorp et al. v. Ministerie van VROM* [1998] ECR I-nyr (25 June 1998).

the internal market, it also contains a number of substantive and procedural rules. The substantive rules are important as they contain a development and adaptation of the exceptions contained in Articles 36 EC and the rule of reason.

Article 100a(4) permits a Member State, if it deems it necessary, 'to apply national provisions on grounds of major needs referred to in Article 36 EC, or relating to protection of the environment or the working environment'.[619] With this list of protected interests, it appears to place the exceptions of Article 36 EC on all fours with those of the rule of reason, but, given that Article 100a(3) EC refers to health, safety, environmental protection and consumer protection in connection with proposals for harmonization, it is submitted that the grounds of exception in Article 100a(4) are not illustrative biut limitative in nature, an approach confirmed by the case-law on the narrow interpretation of the exceptions to Articles 30 and 34 EC, discussed in section 3.3.1, above.

In Case C-41/93 *France v. Commission*[620] the Court pointed out that it is only after the Member State has obtained a decision from the Commission confirming the measures which the former intends to apply that the measures may be applied. The Commission has to satisfy itself that all the conditions for reliance on Article 100a(4) are fulfilled. In particular, it must establish whether the national provisions concerned are justified on the grounds specified in that article and that the measures are not a means of arbitrary discrimination or a disguised restriction on trade between Member States.[621]

The most important departure from the case-law on the consequences of the existence of Community measures[622] resulting from Article 100a(4) is that even after a complete system of harmonisation has been set up recourse to Article 36 EC and to certain of the grounds of the rule of reason will still be possible. This will, of course, only be the case when the Community measures have been adopted by a qualified majority under Article 100a(1); it does not apply when the measures have been adopted unanimously under Article 100 EC. The Court has not answered the question whether recourse to Article 100a(4) will only be possible for Member States which have voted against the measures.[623]

As for harmonization on the basis of other Treaty provisions[624] there is no limitation of the standing case-law on the effect of Community action. In a number of instances, such as the working environment[625] and the

619. See, generally, Flynn (1987) 24 CMLRev. 696.
620. [1994] ECR 1829 at 1848–1849.
621. *Ibid. Cf.* VerLoren van Themaat (1986) SEW 479.
622. See section 3.3.1, *ante*.
623. See Chapter VII, section 2.2, post (note 40).
624. *E.g.* Arts. 57, 99, 100 and 235 EC.
625. Art. 118a EC.

environment[626] the Member States are permitted to introduce more stringent measures compatible with the EC Treaty.

The Court has dealt with the question whether 'apply' in Article 100a(4) refers to existing or only new measures by noting in Case C-41/93 *France v. Commission* that Germany in that case intended to apply existing measures.[627] In any event, experience shows that the Member States have been retiscent about invoking Article 100a(4), a provision which is indeed, it is submitted both as to substance and as to legislative technique, bad for the development of the Community.[628]

Decision 3052/95 provides for the exchange of information on national measures derogating from the free movement of goods.[629] It should enable the Community to address in a transparent and pragmatic manner the problem of mutual recognition of the remaining unharmonized national rules.[630]

The second sentence of Article 100b(1) EC permits the Council to apply the principle of mutual recognition by the legislative route.[631] To date this opportunity for the Council to codify the mutual acceptance principle in the interests of legal certainty has been left unseized, but that does not mean that the Court will be unable to apply the concept in individual cases.

3.3.5 Other exceptions

The nature of goods (as strategic goods), the third country origin of goods, and the economic situation of a Member State may be such that the normal rules of the free movement of goods must give way to exception clauses. The Council may still adopt measures to cope with severe economic difficulties or the consequences of exceptional occurrences in accordance with Article 100a EC.[632] Under the transitional provisions relating to Economic and Monetary Union, if a Member State experiences a sudden crisis in the balance of payments, action may be taken by the Commission, and, if necessary by the Council through mutual assistance, under Article 109h EC, or, in the absence of an immediate decision, a Member State may take the necessary protective measures as a precaution.[633]

Member States which have entrusted undertakings with the operation of

---

626. Arts. 130s and 130t EC.
627. [1994] ECR I-1829 at 1848. See Temmink (1995) SEW 77.
628. See Mertens de Wilmars (1986) SEW 610; Ehlermann (1987) 24 CMLRev. 389.
629. O.J. 1995 L 321/1.
630. *Cf.* Art. 100b(1) EC, first sub-para.
631. See the Commission's Communication COM (93) 669 Final (O.J. 1993 C 353/4), point 30, and Mortelmans (1994) SEW 236.
632. See Chapter IX, section 3.2, point E, *post.*
633. Under the conditions of Art. 109i EC. See, further, Chapter IX, section 3.3.1, *post.*

services of general economic interest or having the character of a revenue-producing monopoly may, on the basis of Article 90(2) EC be able to insist on an exceptional position under certain conditions for such undertakings.[634]

There is also a certain degree of tension between market integration and regional policy.[635]

Article 223 contains two safeguard clauses in the interest of the security of the Member States themselves. The first exempts Member States from the obligation to supply information the disclosure of which they consider contrary to the essential interest of their security. On the strength of the second clause any Member State may take such measures as it considers necessary for the protection of the essential interests of its security which are connected with the production of, or trade in, arms, munitions, and war material. On 15 April 1958 the Council, in accordance with Article 223(2) EC drew up a list of products to which the provisions of this second safeguard clause apply. This list has not been officially published and it has not been revised since.[636] Modern weapons would thus fall under the ordinary rules on the free movement of goods, and thus under a more liberal regime than that applicable to the products in the 1958 list. There is, however, a proviso in Article 223(1) that the measures taken by the Member States may not adversely affect the conditions of competition in the common market regarding products which are not intended for specifically military purposes. Examples of the latter could be, for instance, import restrictions and subsidies for national industry producing sporting-guns.[637] Specific rules have been adopted in relation to dual-use goods.[638] It must be inferred from this proviso (aimed at preventing abuse) as well as from Article 92 EC, that a Member State may not subsidise the production of non-military material by the producers in question through the purchase of military material at an excessive price.

Like Article 223 EC, Article 224 EC is connected with the security of the state. This concept is rather different from the concept of 'public security'

---

634. See Case 72/83 *Campus Oil Ltd. et al. v. Minister for Industry and Energy et al.* [1984] ECR 2727, [1984] 3 CMLR 544. See, further, Chapter VIII, section 4.7.2, *post.*
635. Case C-21/88 *Du Pont de Nemours Italiana SpA v. Unità sanitaria locale No 2 di Carrara* [1990] ECR I-889, [1991] 3 CMLR 25; Case C-351/88 *Laboratori Bruneau v. Unità sanitaria locale RM/24 di Monterondo* [1991] ECR I-3641. See further, Fernández Martín (1991) 16 ELRev. 216 and Chapter IX, section 5, *post.*
636. It has, however, been included in *Towards a Stronger Europe* (Independent European Programme Group (within NATO), Brussels, 1987) Vol. 2, 152. See further, Colijn and Rusman, *Het Nederlandse wapenexportbeleid 1963–1988* (The Hague, 1989).
637. Particular problems arise in relation to items such as jeeps or uniforms as well as in the area of compensatory purchase arrangements designed to offset the cost by other (not necessarily linked) stimuli to the economy. In general such arrangements in intra-Community trade will be unacceptable, see Mattera (1976) RMC 252 at 262).
638. See, further, Chapter XII, section 3.1.2, *post.*

found in Articles 36, 48, and 56 EC.[639] It requires Member States to consult each other with a view to taking together the steps needed to prevent the functioning of the common market being affected by measures which a Member State may be called upon to take in the event of serious internal disturbances affecting the maintenance of law and order, in the event of war or serious international tension constituting a threat of war, or in order to carry out obligations it has accepted for the purpose of maintaining peace and international security.

On the one hand, therefore, Article 224 contains a safeguard clause which in the circumstances indicated may go beyond the concept of public policy in Article 36 EC. In these circumstances the measures needed in a situation of serious shortage in the economy can be taken, such as rationing measures, hoarding prohibitions, prohibitions of price rises, requisitioning measures, and the like. Such measures are never permitted by Article 36 and in the event of supply difficulties due to other causes they can only be permitted under Article 103a EC. On the other hand Article 224 contains an obligation for Member States to consult each other with a view to taking the steps needed to prevent interference with the functioning of the common market by such measures. It is submitted that effect must be given to this obligation as soon as one or more Member States by way of precaution provide a legal basis for measures of this kind (which has already happened) and, moreover, it is submitted that the Commission must ensure the observance of this obligation.

Article 225 EC prescribes that even within the scope of the safeguard clauses of Articles 223 and 224 conditions of competition may not be distorted. To the extent that importation of military material is not prohibited on grounds of security, the conditions of competition in case of such importation may not, therefore, be distorted by discrimination based on nationality, by subsidies, or otherwise. If such an effect occurs nevertheless, the Commission, together with the Member State concerned, in accordance with Article 225 examines how these measures can be adjusted to the rules laid down in the Treaty. As far as Article 224 EC is concerned this particular obligation on the Commission is, it is submitted, additional to the task which it already has under Article 155 EC to ensure that the consultation procedure laid down in Article 225 is observed. There is provision for direct access to the Court (by way of derogation from the normal procedures of Articles 169 or 170 EC) so that the Commission or another Member State may challenge any alleged misuse of Articles 223 or 224 speedily.[640] In such

---

639. In the Dutch version of the EC Treaty, the same word is used for security and safety (see Arts. 100a and 118a EC), but in the English version the two concepts are rightly distinct.

640. See Case C-120/94 R *Commission v. Greece* [1996] ECR I-3037. As to similar procedures, see also Art. 93 EC (interested Member States have this right as does the Com-

cases the Court's judgment is given *in camera*. The security policy of the Member States is the (joint) subject of Title V TEU in the form of CFSP.[641]

The fact that a measure results from an international agreement predating the original EEC Treaty or the accession of a Member State, and that the Member State on the basis of Article 224 maintains the measure, even though it hinders trade between Member States, does not mean that the measure escapes the ambit of Article 30 EC, as Article 234 EC is applicable only if the agreement places an obligation on the Member State concerned which is incompatible with the EC Treaty.[642]

3.4 State trading monopolies

A separate problem is posed by state trading monopolies. For these, Article 37(1) EC provides that they should be progressively adjusted so as to ensure that when the transitional period has ended no discrimination regarding the conditions under which goods are procured and marketed exists between nationals of Member States. Any organisation through which a Member State, *de jure* or *de facto*,[643] either directly or indirectly, supervises, determines, or appreciably influences imports or exports between Member States is equated with a state trading monopoly. Article 37 EC also applies to delegated monopolies. Classic monopolies for specific products include those found in various Member States relating to alcohol, tobacco, or petroleum products. The term 'adjust' does not mean that all these monopolies have to be lifted.[644] However, exclusive

mission) and Art. 100a(4) EC. See also, in the context of an Art. 177 EC reference, Case C-273/97 *Sirdar v. The Army Board et al.* (O.J. 1997 C 295/17), pending.

641. See, further, Chapter II, section 1.3.1, *ante*, and Chapter XII, sections 2.6 and 3.3.5, *post*.

642. Case C-324/93 *R. v. Secretary of State for the Home Department, ex parte Evans Medical Ltd. et al.* [1995] ECR I-563 at 605. See also Case 34/79 *R. v. Henn and Darby* [1979] ECR 3795, [1980] 1 CMLR 246; Case 121/85 *Conegate Ltd. v. H.M. Customs and Excise* [1986] ECR 1007, [1986] 1 CMLR 739; Case 286/86 *Ministère public v. Deserbais* [1988] ECR 4907; Case C-158/91 *Levy* [1993] ECR I-4287, and Cases C-241 and 242/91 *Radio Telefis Eireann (RTE) et al. v. Commission* [1995] ECR I-743, [1995] 4 CMLR 718. See further, in other contexts, Case C-13/93 *Office national de l'Emploi v. Minne* [1994] ECR I-371; Case C-124/95 *R. v. H.M. Treasury et al., ex parte Centro-Com Srl* [1997] ECR I-81; Case C-182/95 *Firma T. Port GmbH & Co. v. Hauptzollamt Hamburg-Jonas* (1995 O.J. C 208/12), and Cases C-364 and 365/95 *Firma T. Port GmbH & Co. v. Hauptzollamt Hamburg-Jonas* [1998] ECR I-1023.

643. Art. 37(1) EC, 2nd subpara.

644. *E.g.* Case 59/75 *Pubblico Ministero v. Manghera et al.* [1976] ECR 91 at 100; Case 91/75 *Hauptzollamt Göttingen et al. v. Wolfgang Miritz GmbH & Co.* [1976] ECR 217 at 229; Case 91/78 *Hansen GmbH & Co. v. Hauptzollamt Flensburg* [1979] ECR 935 at 952, and Case C-189/95 *Franzén* [1997] ECR I-5909. Art. 37 EC remains applicable wherever,

rights to import must be abolished,[645] as, it must be concluded, must exclusive rights to export. Non-discriminatory taxation is compatible with Article 37(1)[646] and with Article 37(2).[647]

It can be deduced from Article 37(1) that two conditions must be satisfied for Article 37 to apply. First, there has to be an action by the state, such as a law, which (whether in combination with a production monopoly or not) grants exclusive purchase or sales rights or the possibility of control of imports or exports;[648] and, secondly, the grant must be *either* to a state service or state enterprise which is given exclusive purchase or sales powers (state monopolies),[649] *or* to an institution of the state which has the power to hinder imports or exports between Member States within the meaning of Articles 30 or 34 EC,[650] *or* to one or more private bodies (delegated monopolies to particular undertakings).[651]

Article 37 EC applies only to goods; thus it does not cover the free movement of services, nor does it cover capital movements.[652] It reaches

even after the required adjustment, the exercise by a State monopoly of its exclusive rights entails a discrimination or restriction prohibited by Art. 37, Case 91/78 *Hansen GmbH & Co. v. Hauptzollamt Flensburg* [1979] ECR 935 at 956.

645. *E.g.* Case 59/75 *Pubblico Ministero v. Manghera et al.* [1976] ECR 91 at 101 (expressly); Case 91/75 *Hauptzollamt Göttingen et al. v. Wolfgang Miritz GmbH & Co.* [1976] ECR 217 at 230 (impliedly).

646. Case 233/83 *Sektkellerei C.A. Kupferberg & Cie KG a. A. v. Hauptzollamt Mainz* [1985] ECR 157 at 184–185.

647. Case 13/70 *Francesco Cinzano & Cia GmbH v. Hauptzollamt Saarbrücken* [1970] ECR 1089 at 1096–1097.

648. Case 30/87 *Bodson v. Pompes funèbres des régions libérées SA* [1988] ECR 2479 at 2511; Case C-393/92 *Gemeente Almelo et al. v. Energiebedrijf Ijsselmij NV* [1994] ECR I-1477 at 1516–1517. See also case C-189/95 *Franzén* [1997] ECR I-5909.

649. Art. 37(1) EC, 1st subpara.

650. Art. 37(1) EC, 2nd subpara. Case 30/87 *Bodson v. Pompes funèbres des régions libérées SA* [1988] ECR 2479, [1989] 4 CMLR 984 concerned the powers of local authorities to make provision for funeral services. The requirement is that the national authorities must be in a position to control, direct or appreciably influence trade between Member States through a body established for that purpose or a delegated monopoly, [1988] ECR 2479 at 2511.

651. Art. 37(1), 2nd subpara., last sentence. This heading was included with the French mineral oil delegated monopolies of state and private undertakings in mind. See Cases C-46/90 and 93/91 *Procureur du Roi v. Lagauche et al.* [1993] ECR I-5267 at 5329–5330 as to type-approval requirements. As to concession contracts, see Case 30/87 *Bodson v. Pompes funèbres des régions libérées SA* [1988] ECR 2479 at 2511–2513 and Case C-393/92 *Gemeente Almelo et al. v. Energiebedrijf IJsselcentrale NV* [1994] ECR I-1477 at 1517.

652. Case 155/73 *Sacchi* [1974] ECR 409 at 427–428; Case 271/81 *Société Coopérative d'Amélioration de l'Élevage et d'Insémination artificielle du Béarn v. Mialocq et al.* [1983] ECR 2057 at 2072 (although the Court pointed out, *ibid.*, that it might be possible for a monopoly over the provision of services to have an indirect influence on trade in goods between Member States). See, generally, Hochbaum in Von der Groeben *et al., op. cit.* (see note 33, *supra*) Vol. I 846; see also Druesne and Kremlis: *La Politique de Concurrence de la CEE* (Paris, 1986) 113–122. Literature in English

'only activities intrinsically connected with the specific business of the monopoly'[653] and is 'irrelevant to national provisions which have no connexion with such specific business.'[654] Thus general national provisions which apply in the sector irrespective of whether the products concerned are covered by the monopoly involved are outside the ambit of Article 37.[655]

For a long time after the end of the transitional period, though, there was a great deal of uncertainty about the scope of Article 37(1)[656] and it was not until the judgment in Case 59/75 *Pubblico Ministero v. Manghera et al.*[657] that this was resolved. In this judgment the Court not only held that Article 37(1) was directly effective since the end of the transitional period, it also found that Article 37(1) EC had to 'be interpreted as meaning that as from 31 December 1969 every national monopoly of a commercial character must be adjusted so as to eliminate the exclusive right to import from other Member States.'[658] This judgment thus disowned the Council resolution of 21 April 1970 which had provided for a longer adjustment period.[659]

New state trading monopolies which may give rise to the possibility of discrimination may not be introduced; this prohibition, contained in Article 37(2) EC is absolute and is also directly effective.[660] Article 37(2) also means that no new measures may be taken relating to state trading monopolies which interfere with the principle of progressive adjustment or which restrict the ambit of the Articles of the Treaty concerning the abolition of customs duties and quantitative restrictions.[661]

Article 37 EC covers only goods in intra-Community movement; it does not affect products imported directly from a third country.[662] Production

includes Oliver (1980) 17 CMLRev. 251; Kon (1981) 6 ELRev. 75 at 96–101; Ross (1982) 7 ELRev. 281, and Burrows (1983) 3 YBEL 25.

653. Case 86/78 *SA des Grandes Distilleries Peureux v. Directeur des Services Fiscaux de la Haute-Saône et du Territoire de Belfort* [1979] ECR 987 at 913.

654. *Ibid.*

655. Case 120/78 *Cassis de Dijon* [1979] ECR 649 at 662; Case 17/81 *Pabst & Richatz KG v. Hauptzollamt Oldenburg* [1982] ECR 1331 at 1349; Case C-78–83/90 *Compagnie commerciale de l'Ouest et al. v. Receveur principal des douanes de La Pallice-Port* [1992] ECR I-1847 at 1883–1884. It may well be that Art. 30 EC will be applicable (as in *Cassis de Dijon* and in Case C-189/95 *Franzén* [1997] ECR I-5909).

656. For the different views see *e.g.* Colliard (1964) *Rec. Dalloz (Chron.)* 263–272.

657. [1976] ECR 91, [1976] 1 CMLR 557.

658. [1976] ECR 91 at 101.

659. J.O. 1970 C50/2. See further, the various Reports on Competition Policy.

660. Case 6/64 *Costa v. ENEL* [1964] ECR 585 at 597; Case 59/75 *Manghera, infra*; Case 120/78 *Cassis de Dijon*; Case 86/78 *Peureux*, both *supra*, and Case 90/82 *Commission v. France, infra.*

661. See *e.g.* Case 59/75 *Pubblico Ministero v. Manghera et al.* [1976] ECR 91 at 100; Case 90/82 *Commission v. France* [1983] ECR 2011, [1984] 2 CMLR 516, See also Case 161/82 *Commission v. France* [1983] ECR 2079, [1984] 2 CMLR 296.

662. Case 91/78 *Hansen GmbH & Co. v. Hauptzollamt Flensburg* [1979] ECR 935 at 956.

monopolies have not yet been the subject of clear case-law:[663] some writers submit that under certain circumstances they may be caught by Article 37,[664] although others opine that Article 222 prevents this.[665] If they are not covered by Article 37, they must be judged on the basis of other provisions on free movement, such as Articles 52 and 59 EC,[666] or on the basis of the competition provisions.[667]

On the basis of its powers under Article 37(6) EC, the Commission has over the years addressed recommendations to various Member States relating to the adjustment of various monopolies. Scarcely surprisingly, these were mainly directed at the tobacco, alcohol and mineral oils sectors.[668] More recently attention has turned primarily to the electricity and telecommunications sectors,[669] but Article 37 EC remains something of an unruly horse, as the Commission rediscovered to its cost in October 1997.[670]

Goods from third countries which are in free circulation in a Member State are, it will be recalled, assimilated to goods originating inside the Community (see Arts. 9 and 10(1) EC).

663. In Case C-347/88 *Commission v. Greece* [1990] ECR I-4747 the Court noted (at 4787–4788) that the Commission had expressly refrained from challenging a refining monopoly which was indissociable from the state's right to import crude oil for refining.

664. See Defalque in Mégret *et al.* (eds.), *op. cit.* (see note 96, *supra*) Vol. 1, 331 and literature cited there.

665. Mattera, *op. cit.* (see note 259, *supra*) 51 *et seq.*

666. See Case 271/81 *Société Coopérative d'Amélioration de l'Élevage et d'Insémination Artificielle de Béarn v. Mialocq et al.* [1983] ECR 2057 at 2072; Cases C-46/90 and 93/91 *Procureur du Roi v. Lagauche et al.* [1993] ECR I-5267 at 5329.

667. Arts. 85, 86 and 90 EC. See Case 30/87 *Bodson v. Pompes funèbres des régions libérées SA* [1988] ECR 2479 at 2512; Case C-393/92 *Gemeente Almelo et al. v. Energiebedrijf IJsselmaatschappij NV* [1994] ECR I-1477 at 1517–1518. See Akyürek–Kievits (1993) SEW 326 and, generally, Stuyck and Vossestein (eds.), *State Entrepreneurship, National Monopolies and European Community Law* (Deventer, 1993). If state trading monopolies have been transformed into public undertakings without exclusive import or export rights then the general rules of the Treaty and the specific rules of Article 90 EC applicable to public undertakings come into play, see, further, Chapter VIII, section 4.7, *post*.

668. Hochbaum, *op. cit.* (see note 652, *supra*) 910–912 lists the various recommendations, which latterly have been made on the basis of the relevant provisions of the various Acts of Accession.

669. See also Dir. 88/301 (O.J. 1988 L 131/73) on competition in the markets in telecommunications terminal equipment (based on Art. 90(3) EC). In part as a result of Case C-202/88 *France v. Commission* [1991] ECR I-1223, Dir. 88/301 was amended by Dir. 94/46 (O.J. 1994 L 268/5).

670. Case C-157/94 *Commission v. The Netherlands* [1997] ECR I-5699; Case C-158/94 *Commission v. Italy* [1997] ECR I-5789; Case C-159/94 *Commission v. France* [1997] ECR I-5815; Case C-160/94 *Commission v. Spain* [1997] ECR I-5815. See also Case C-189/95 *Franzén* [1997] ECR I-5909. As to all these judgments, see Mortelmans (1998) SEW 30. Earlier examples of difficulties include Case 78/82 *Commission v. Italy* [1983] ECR 1955; Case 90/82 *Commission v. France* [1983] ECR 2011, [1984] 2 CMLR 516, and Case 161/82 *Commission v. France* [1983] ECR 2079, [1984] 2 CMLR 296.

The question whether Article 36 EC may be invoked in connection with Article 37 EC has not yet been clearly answered. While the wording of Article 36 would seem to militate against invocation in this context, there are indications in the case-law that Article 36 is applicable if quantitative restrictions or measures having equivalent effect are concerned, even if they relate to products which are the subject of the monopoly.[671] If, though, the restrictions fall solely under Article 37 EC, or are not covered by Articles 30 or 34 EC, then Article 36 may not be invoked.

The relationship between Article 37 EC and the other parts of the Treaty is not yet fully worked out. The special provisions of Article 37(4) for state trading monopolies for agricultural products may not be relied upon since the end of the transitional period to justify the maintenance or introduction of exclusive import or export rights or discriminatory charges or other discriminatory provisions.[672] The special provisions establishing common organizations of the market take precedence over Article 37 EC.[673] As has been implied above, service monopolies fall exclusively within the scope of Article 59 EC,[674] although they may well have an effect on mopolies as to goods.[675] The relationship between Article 37 EC and the fiscal provisions of the Treaty has been judicially considered,[676] as has that between Article 37 EC and the state aids provisions.[677]

3.5 Third countries

The prohibitions in Articles 30, 34 and 37 EC relate to the movement of goods between Member States.[678] Quantitative restrictions and measures

671. Case C-347/88 *Commission v. Greece* [1990] ECR I-4747 at 4789–4790 (security of supplies). See also Case C-189/95 *Franzén* [1997] ECR I-5909 at 5968-5974 (public interest aim of protecting public health against the harm caused by alcohol).

672. See *e.g.* Case 45/75 *Rewe-Zentrale des Lebensmittel-Großhandels GmbH v. Hauptzollamt Landau/Pfalz* [1976] ECR 181, [1976] 2 CMLR 1; Case 91/75 *Hauptzollamt Göttingen v. Wolfgang Miritz GmbH & Co.* [1976] ECR 217.

673. Case 83/78 *Pigs Marketing Board v. Redmond* [1978] ECR 2347 at 2368.

674. See section 7.5, *post.* See also note 652, *supra.*

675. See note 652, *supra.*

676. Case 45/75 *Rewe-Zentrale des Lebensmittel-Großhandels GmbH v. Hauptzollamt Landau/Pfalz* [1976] ECR 181, [1976] 2 CMLR 1; Case 91/75 *Hauptzollamt Göttingen v. Wolfgang Miritz GmbH & Co.* [1976] ECR 217; Case 148/77 *H. Hansen jun. & O.C. Balle GmbH & Co. v. Hauptzollamt Flensburg* [1978] ECR 1787, [1979] 1 CMLR 604; Case 86/78 *SA des Grandes Distilleries Peureux v. Directeur des Services Fiscaux de la Haute-Saône et du Territoire de Belfort* [1979] ECR 987, [1980] 3 CMLR 337; Case 17/81 *Pabst & Richatz KG v. Hauptzollamt Oldenburg* [1982] ECR 1331, [1983] 3 CMLR 11, and Cases C-78–83/90 *Compagnie commerciale de l'Ouest et al. v. Receveur principal des douanes de La Pallice-Port* [1992] ECR I-1847.

677. Case 91/78 *Hansen GmbH & Co. v. Hauptzollamt Flensburg* [1979] ECR 935, [1980] 1 CMLR 162.

678. *E.g.* Case 51/75 *EMI Records Ltd. v. CBS United Kingdom Ltd.* [1976] ECR 811,

having equivalent effect in trade between the Community and third countries are thus regarded as forming part of the Community's common commercial policy.[679] In some instances agreements between the Community and third countries contain specific provisions,[680] but even if they are phrased identically to Articles 30–36 EC, they do not *necessarily* produce have the same result, as the objective of such agreements (such as the establishment of a free trade area between the Community and the country concerned) is less far-reaching than the objective of the EC Treaty itself, which *inter alia* is to establish a common market, and the activities which the Community undertakes to that end, such as harmonization of laws.[681]

3.6 Community regulatory measures

The internal market within the Community is achieved not only through Articles 30 and 34 EC, but also through the myriad measures of positive integration which have been adopted in order to achieve an area without internal frontiers.[682] During the Sixties various efforts were made to adopt all the necessary directives for this purpose prior to the end of the transitional period at midnight on 31 December 1969. These efforts were less than resoundingly successful. On the one hand, the Community sought to achieve too much, such as complete harmonization of product legislation for many foodstuffs; on the other hand, the member States wanted too little. For diverse reasons, ranging from the protection of legitimate interests, such as health protection, to pure protectionism, continually changing coalitions in the Council blocked agreement on Community measures at a time when unanimity was still required.

Certainly the Court showed the way forward with the development in *Cassis de Dijon*[683] of the mutual acceptance of goods and thus of national legislation.[684] This principle was adopted by the Commission as a key

---

[1976] 2 CMLR 235; Case Case 91/78 *Hansen GmbH & Co. v. Hauptzollamt Flensburg* [1979] ECR 935, [1980] 1 CMLR 162; Case 190/87 *oberkreisdirektor des Kreises Borken et al. v. Handelsonderneming Moormann BV* [1988] ECR 4689, [1990] 1 CMLR 656, and Case C-191/90 *Generics (UK) Ltd. et al. v. Smith, Kline and French Laboratories Ltd.* [1992] ECR I-5335, [1993] 1 CMLR 89.

679. As to which, see Chapter XII, section 3, *post*.

680. See *e.g.* Case 174/84 *Bulk Oil (Zug) AG v. Sun International Ltd.* [1986] ECR 559, [1986] 2 CMLR 732.

681. *E.g.* Case 270/80 *Polydor Ltd. et al. v. Harlequin Record Shops Ltd. et al.* [1982] ECR 329 at 348–349; Case 104/81 *Hauptzollamt Mainz v. C.A. Kupferberg & Cie. KG a. A.* [1982] ECR 3641 at 3665, and Case C-207/91 *Eurim-Pharm GmbH v. Bundesgesundheitsamt* [1993] ECR I-3723 at 3745–3748 (useful effect of the agreement).

682. See section 1.1, *ante*.

683. Case 120/78, [1979] ECR 649, [1979] 3 CMLR 494.

684. See section 1.1, *ante*.

element of its celebrated White Paper *Completing the Internal Market* in 1985,[685] and it achieved Treaty status through the amendments to the old EEC Treaty made by the SEA. The latter resulted from recognition that the only way to cut through the 'Eurosclerosis' which had developed in the field of harmonization was by means of qualified majority voting. Thus Article 100a EC permits the necessary measures to be adopted for the achievement of the internal market objectives set out in Article 7a EC, although the price paid for this was Article 100a(4) which can be seen as a balancing factor in the advantage of the Member States. These measures – principally directives – are examined in the discussion of harmonization of laws in section 2 of Chapter VIII, below.[686] At the end of 1992 the Sutherland Report *The Internal market after 1992 – meeting the challenge*[687] prompted the Commission to propose a *Strategic Programme for the Internal Market*[688] which subsequently bore fruit in the 1996 Report on *The Impact and Effectiveness of the Single Market.*[689] This in turn led to the adoption of the *Action Plan for the Single Market*[690] by the Commission in June 1997.[691] This plan identifies four strategic targets: making the rules more effective; dealing with key market distortions; removing sectoral obstacles to integration, and delivering a Single Market for the benefit of all citizens. An important part in this is undoubtedly played by the SLIM initiative[692] The Newsletter of DG XV provides a regular overview of progress towards these targets and the results of the SLIM initiative.[693] The *Single Market Review* provides the most far-reaching analysis to date of the effectiveness of measures taken in creating the single market.[694]

Gradually a system of various legal instruments (regulations, directives and recommendations) has been put in place in the various areas in which Community action was necessary. Depending on the extent of the Community action, a distinction may be drawn between the mutual acceptance principle;[695] notification procedures;[696] the new strategy and the

685. COM (85) 310 Final (point 60 *et seq.*).
686. A good overview of the state of transposition of these measures is to be found in the annual *Report on the Application of Community Law*: for 1996, see COM (97) 299 Final (O.J. 1997 C 332/1).
687. SEC (92) 2277 Final. The Report was also published in a non-standard citable form as a small booklet with a foreword by Bangemann and Van Miert. As to legislative consolidation, see COM (93) 261 Final.
688. COM (93) 256 Final, see WQ E-3170/93 (Beumer) O.J. 1993 C 350/48.
689. COM (96) 520 Final.
690. CSE (97)1 Final. The draft was presented in COM (97) 184 Final.
691. Bull. EU 6–1997, point 1.3.41.
692. Simpler Legislation for the Internal Market. This programme is now in its second phase, see COM (97) 618 Final. As to the first and pilot phases, see COM (96) 204 and 559 Final.
693. *Single Market News* (published five times a year, free of charge, by the Commission).
694. This is a series of 38 reports and a business survey, (Luxembourg, 1997).
695. See section 1.1, *ante*.
696. *E.g.* under Dir 83/189 (O.J. 1983 L 109/8, as amended), see Chapter VIII, section 2.5,

new approach;[697] various methods of harmonization, such as minimum harmonization,[698] optional harmonization and total harmonization;[699] and uniform Community rules which are primarily used in the agricultural field.[700] In the first two of these cases in particular there are no substantive Community rules, but procedures are established; particularly where there is harmonization the Community itself adopts substantive rules.[701] The classification according to the type of legal instrument and the type of economic instrument increases in importance as the Community itself adopts these aspects as points of departure in the context of discussions about subsidiarity.[702]

4. FREE MOVEMENT OF PERSONS AND CITIZENSHIP OF THE UNION

Only a very few years after their nationals had been at war with each other, the Franco-German initiative which led to the ECSC Treaty in 1951 achieved free movement for workers in the coal and steel sectors between those two countries as well as with the other Member States. 44 years later, in 1995, citizenship of the European Union exists from the north of Sweden to the south of Italy, from Greece to Portugal. Article 69(1) ECSC enabled workers who were nationals of Member States and had recognized qualifications in a coalmining or steelmaking occupation to exercise such an activity in another Member State; thus restrictions based on nationality had to be removed, subject to limitations imposed by the basic requirements of public policy, public health and public security. Article 69(2) ECSC required the establishment of common definitions of skilled trades and qualifications therefor, and the determination by common accord of the limitations referred to above.[703] The Member States also undertook to endeavour to work out job-seeker and vacancy matching arrangements, and in the case of workers from the coal and steel industries who could no longer be employed there, the Member States undertook facilitate their re-employment; in the case of shortage of suitable labour to

post. See also (as examples of non-compliance with the obligation to notify) Case C-52/93 *Commission v. The Netherlands* [1994] ECR I-3591 and Case C-C-61/93 *Commission v. The Netherlands* [1994] ECR I-3607.

697. See the Council Resolution of 7 May 1985 (O.J. 1985 C 136/1 and Chapter VIII, section 2.1, *post*.
698. See Chapter VIII, section 2.6, *post*, and Temmink (1995) SEW 79.
699. See Chapter VIII, section 2.1, *post*, and literature cited there.
700. See Case C-204/88 *Ministère public v. Paris* [1989] ECR 4361.
701. Mortelmans and Van Rijn (1991) SEW 279.
702. Which have led *inter alia* to the SLIM initiative. See the Conclusions of the Presidency after the Edinburgh European Council, Bull. EU 12–1992, point I.15 *et seq.* (particularly at point I.23). See, further, Chapter III, section 5.1.1.
703. See the Decision of the Representatives of the Governments of the Member States, O.J. 367/57 *et seq.*

cope with growth of coal or steel production they undertook to adjust their immigration rules to the extent necessary to remedy such a situation.[704] Moreover, discrimination in remuneration and working conditions between nationals and migrant workers was to be prohibited, and the Member States undertook to endeavour to settle among themselves steps to ensure that social security arrangements did not hinder labour mobility.[705]

The EC Treaty took over the basic provisions of the ECSC Treaty for free movement of persons and developed them, so that free movement was no longer restricted to workers in specific sectors but embraced all occupations, although a distinction was drawn between the free movement of workers, dealt with in Articles 48–51 EC, and the self-employed, who are covered by Articles 52–58 EC (as are legal persons). Free movement was to be achieved by the end of the transitional period for the achievement of the common market.[706] This deadline was not fully met as for many occupations the secondary provisions, such as diplomas and secondary working conditions constituted a then insurmountable obstacle.

In the course of time there has been a change of emphasis in the importance of the various freedoms. The first phase of migration largely benefited Italian workers who moved to coalfields of Northern continental Europe (some of their children later played in the Belgian football team), but over the years the freedom to provide (and receive) services and the freedom of establishment (of both legal and natural persons) assumed greater importance. Thus Dutch skiing holidays might be arranged by a company established in the United Kingdom through its subsidiary, a Dutch company which it had taken over. An internal market was surely developing apace, but the questions remained, for whom, and subject to what conditions? Moreover, the question arose whether non-economically-active persons (such as those who have always worked in one Member State but wish to spend their retirement in another Member State, or those of independent means) could also benefit from the freedoms afforded by the EC Treaty.

Citizenship of the Union is established by Article 8(1) EC, and according to Article 8a(1) EC every citizen of the Union has the right to move and reside freely within the territory of the Member States, subject to the limitations and conditions laid down in the EC Treaty itself and by the measures adopted to give it effect. According to the Commission and

---

704. Art. 69(3) ECSC.
705. Art. 69(4) ECSC. These steps culminated in the adoption of the European Convention on Social Security for Migrant Workers 1957 (Dutch *Tractatenblad* 1958, no. 54). This was later replaced by Regs. 3/58 and 4/58 (O.J. 561/58 and 597/58 respectively). These were in turn replaced by Regs. 1408/71 (O.J. English Special Edition 1971 (II), p. 416 and 574/72 (O.J. 1972 English Special Edition (I), p. 159). The text of both these regs. was most recently integrally replaced by Reg. 118/97 (O.J. 1997 L 28/1), and that version has been most recently amended by Reg. 1223 (O.J. 1998 L 168/1).
706. 31 December 1969.

(then) 11 of the (then) 12 Member States, Article 8a EC is aimed at the abolition of controls of all persons at the Community's internal frontiers, irrespective of their nationality, but the United Kingdom took – and indeed still takes – the view that the abolition of controls only relates to nationals of Member States (and now of nationals of the other States of the EEA who are assimilated to nationals of Member States for these purposes).[707] Thus the United Kingdom takes the view that it is entitled to maintain checks to establish whether a person is or is not a national of an EC or EEA State. The question whether a person possesses the nationality of a Member State or of another EEA State is one which is solely a matter for the national law of the State concerned.[708]

The concept of citizenship of the Union has been examined in section 6 of Chapter III, above. In the present chapter the emphasis is placed on the economic activities of market participants, and reference should be made to Chapter VI, above, in relation to litigation for the enforcement of these rights. Before attention here turns to examining the legal contours of the various freedoms on a freedom-by-freedom basis, the scope of the free movement of persons is examined below.

4.1   From the exercise of economic activities to a general right of residence

Case-law from the Seventies shows that persons only fall within the scope of Articles 48, 52 (or 59) EC if they are nationals of a Member State who exercise economic activities.[709] If a person has the status of being a privileged employee or self-employed person because he or she exercises (or indeed has exercised) his or her Community rights, certain members of his or her family also derive rights of entry and residence under Community law, irrespective of their own nationality.[710] Community law also provides

---

707. WQ E-2692/92 (Rogalla) O.J. 1994 C 349/2. There does not appear to have been a formal view expressed by or on behalf of Austria, Finland and Sweden since their accession.

708. Case C-369/90 *Micheletti et al. v. Delegación del Gobierno en Cantabria* [1992] ECR I-4239 at 4262. 'Under international law, it is for each Member State, having due regard to Community law, to lay down the conditions for the acquisition and loss of nationality. However, it is not permissible for the legislation of a Member State to restrict the effects of the grant of the nationality of another Member State by imposing an additional condition for the recognition of that nationality with a view to the exercise of the fundamental freedoms provided for in the Treaty.' See also the Declaration (No. 2) on nationality of a Member State, attached to the Final Act on the occasion of signature of the TEU, and O'Leary (1992) 12 YBEL 353. As to citizenship of the Union, generally, see O'Leary, *The Evolving Concept of Community Citizenship* (London, 1996).

709. Case 36/74 *Walrave and Koch v. Association Union Cycliste Internationale et al.* [1974] ECR 1405 at 1417.

710. Reg. 1612/68 (O.J. English Special Edition 1968 (II), p. 575, most recently amended by Reg. 2434/92 (O.J. 1992 L 245/1)).

for the continuation of the right of residence after termination of the economic activity concerned.[711]

During the Eighties case-law brought tourists, those travelling to other Member States to receive medical treatment, and those so travelling for the purpose of education or business under the beneficiaries of Article 59 EC as recipients of services.[712] Indeed, the Court has been at pains to point out that as students enjoy the right to receive educational services in other Member States they therefore enjoy the right of residence for that purpose.[713]

A package of directives was adopted in June 1990 in order to confer a right of residence on those nationals of Member States who did not already possess it on a specific basis: the package covered three categories of persons: employees and self-employed persons who have ceased their occupational activity;[714] students;[715] and nationals of Member States who do not enjoy a right of residence under other provisions of Community law.[716] Again, certain members of the beneficiary's family also enjoy the benefit of the rights conferred. Unlike in the case of workers,[717] the beneficiaries under this package have to show that they have sickness insurance in respect of all risks in the host Member State and that they have sufficient resources to avoid becoming a burden on the social assistance system of the host Member State during their period of residence.[718]

711. Art. 48(3)(d), implemented by Reg. 1251/70 (O.J. English Special Edition 1970 (II), p. 402.
712. Cases 286/82 and 26/83 *Luisi and Carbone v. Ministero del Tesoro* [1984] ECR 377 at 403; Case 186/87 *Cowan v. Trésor public* [1989] ECR 195 at 220–221.
713. Case C-357/89 *Raulin v. Minister van Onderwijs en Wetenschappen* [1992] ECR I-1027 at 1065; Case C-295/90 *European Parliament v. Council* [1992] ECR I-4193 at 4234–4235.
714. Dir. 90/365 (O.J. 1990 L 180/28).
715. See now Dir. 93/96 (O.J. 1993 L 317/59) which replaced Dir. 90/366 (O.J. 1990 L 180/30) after the latter was annulled by the Court of Justice in Case C-295/90 *European Parliament v. Council* [1992] ECR I-4193, [1992] 3 CMLR 281 (although its effects were preserved by the Court until it was so replaced). As will be apparent from the text above, in between the adoption of Dir. 90/366 and shortly before its annulment the Court clearly stated that for the purpose of following a course of vocational training students had the right of residence on the basis of the EC Treaty itself.
716. Dir. 90/364 (O.J. 1990 L 180/26).
717. See section 5.2, *post*.
718. Dirs. 90/364 and 90/365, Art. 1(1), 1st para. in each case; Dir. 93/96, Art. 1. In the latter case the student simply has to assure the relevant national authority 'by means of a declaration or by such alternative means as the student may choose' that he or she has sufficient resources; the student must also be enrolled in a recognized vocational educational establishment for the principal purpose of following a vocational training course there. Thus a Member State may not make the grant of a residence permit to a student who is following a course conditional on the student having a bank account in the Member State concerned with a minimum balance. See, generally, Van Nuffel (1990) SEW 903.

In Part Three of the EC Treaty, free movement of workers and freedom of establishment are covered by Chapters 1 and 2 respectively. Workers are natural persons, whereas the freedom of establishment covers both natural and legal persons. There are clear links between the provisions for workers and those for the self-employed: thus the social security provisions which under Article 51 EC were designed for workers were extended to the self-employed on the basis of Article 235 EC;[719] the initial directives concerning establishment requirements and mutual recognition of diplomas for medical doctors were also applied to such doctors in employment through the same method,[720] and Directive 64/221,[721] which is based on Article 56(2) EC, applies to all nationals of Member States who reside in or travel to another Member State, for whatever purpose. Nevertheless, the case-law demonstrates that each of the various freedoms still has its own characteristics which justify a separate system. These differences are examined in the discussion of these freedoms below.

4.2 Free movement of persons within the internal market

Free movement of persons applies within the territory of the Member States of the European Union;[722] this internal market is the area in which free movement applies. However, the non-discrimination rules have to a certain extent extra-territorial effect, as, if legal relationships can be located within the territory of the Community either by the place where they are entered into or the place where they take effect, those rules will be applicable.[723] Similarly, as with the free movement of goods, account must

---

719. Thus Reg. 1408/71 (see note 705, *supra*) was so extended by Reg. 2001/83 (O.J. 1983 L 230/6).
720. Dirs. 75/362 (O.J. 1975 L 167/1) and 75/365 (O.J. 1974 L 167/14). These have since been replaced by Dir. 93/16 (O.J. 1993 L 165/1, most recently amended by Dir. 98/21 (O.J. 1998 L 119/15)).
721. O.J. English Special Edition 1963–64, p. 117.
722. See Chapter II, section 4.1, *ante*. By virtue of the EEA Agreement (Oporto, 2 May 1992 (O.J. 1994 L 1/1), Arts. 28–39, equivalent treatment extends to nationals of all states which are members of the EEA. See, generally, Garrone, *La libre circulation des personnes: liberté de mouvement, égalité, liberté économique; étude de droit communautaire et suisse* (Zurich, 1993); Handoll, *Free movement of Persons in the EU* (Chichester, 1995); Plender in Vaughan (ed.), *Law of the European Communities Service* (London, looseleaf since 1990) Part 15; Schermers *et al.* (eds.), *Free Movement of Persons in Europe* (Dordrecht, 1993); Daniele (1997) 22 ELRev. 191; Hilf in Hailbronner *et al.* (eds.), *Staat und Völkerrechtsordnung* (*Festschrift* for Doehring, Berlin, 1989) 339; O'Keeffe (1992) 17 ELRev. 3 and in O'Reilly (ed.), *Human Rights and Constitutional Law* (Essays in honour of Walsh, Dublin, 1992) 263, and Schweitzer and Streinz (1991) ZfR 82.
723. Case 36/74 *Walrave and Koch v. association union Cycliste Internationale et al.* [1974] ECR 1405 at 1420.

be taken of what is often referred to as purely internal situations: thus nationals of a Member State who do not leave their own Member State cannot invoke the rules on free movement.[724] It really must be wondered whether this case-law deserves to survive in a single internal market: in other words whether reverse discrimination should really be permitted within an internal market without internal frontiers. This question will certainly have to be addressed by the Court in the coming years, although there seem to be somewhat mixed signals coming from the case-law.[725]

The free movement of persons provisions also benefit those who have availed themselves of their right of free movement[726] as well as those possessing dual nationality.[727] Nationals of a Member State employed in another Member State by an international organization may also invoke the free movement provisions.[728] In certain circumstances nationals of a Member State who are posted to a third country may also be able to invoke Articles 48–51 EC.[729]

4.3   Free movement of persons and the Schengen Agreement

Since 11 April 1960 free movement of persons has been liberalized between the Benelux countries to a greater extent than the liberalization achieved in the EC context.[730] This state of affairs is expressly permitted by Article 233

---

724. *E.g.* Case 175/78 *R. v. Saunders* [1979] ECR 1129 at 1135; Cases 35 and 36/82 *Morson and Jhanjan v. State of the Netherlands et al.* [1982] ECR 3723 at 3736; Case 180/83 *Moser v. Land Baden-Württemberg* [1984] ECR 2539 at 2547; Cases C-297/88 and 197/89 *Dzodzi v. Belgian State* [1990] ECR I-3763 at 3791–3792; Case C-332/90 *Steen v. Deutsche Bundespost* [1992] ECR I-341 at 356–257; Cases C-64 and 65/96 *Land Nordrhein-Westfalen et al. v. Uecker et al.* [1997] ECR I-3171 at 3188–3189.

725. On the one hand, the internal situation approach is upheld in *e.g.* Cases C-64 and 65/96 *Land Nordrhein-Westfalen et al. v. Uecker et al.* [1997] ECR I-3171 at 3188–3189; on the other hand Cases C-321–324/94 *Pistre et al.* [1997] ECR I-2343 may indicate (in relation to Art. 30 EC at least) a somewhat different approach. See also section 1.2, *ante* and Handoll, *op. cit.* (see note 722, *supra*) 74–75.

726. Case 246/80 *Broekmeulen v. Huisarts Registratie Commissie* [1981] ECR 2311 at 2329; Case 235/87 *Matteucci* [1988] ECR 5589 at 5611, and Case C-370/90 *R. v. Immigration Appeal Tribunal and Singh, ex parte Secretary of State for the Home Department* [1992] ECR I-4265 at 4293–4295.

727. Case 292/86 *Gullung v. Conseils de l'ordre des avocats du barreau de Colmar et de Saverne* [1988] ECR 111 at 136.

728. Cases 389 and 390/87 *Echternach and Moritz v. Netherlands Minister for Education and Science* [1989] ECR 723 at 759.

729. Case 237/83 *Prodest v. Caisse Primaire d'Assurance Maladie de Paris* [1984] ECR 3153 at 3162. See also Case 9/88 *Lopes de Veiga v. Staatssecretaris van Justitie* [1989] ECR 2989; Case C-60/93 *Aldewereld v. Staatssecretaris van Financiën* [1994] ECR I-2991, and Case C-214/94 *Boukhalfa v. Bundesrepublik Deutschland* [1996] ECR I-2253.

730. As to the provisions, (the Benelux Convention on Establishment and the Convention on the Transfer of Entry and Exit Controls to the External frontiers of the Benelux Territory), see, respectively (1960) VIII *European Yearbook* 169 and 175, or (in Dutch) *Tractatenblad* 1960 nos. 40 and 102.

EC. On 14 June 1985 the Benelux countries, Germany and France concluded an agreement at Schengen (in Luxembourg) which involved *inter alia* the abolition of border controls between those Member States.[731] The objective of this agreement was to achieve an internal market for the free movement of persons between the signatory countries pending the establishment of the Community internal market in respect of the movement of persons.[732]

Article 134 of the Schengen Convention of 1990 provides that the Convention is to apply only in so far as it is compatible with Community law. The Agreement (with the Convention) is an example of two-speed integration whereby a number of Member States proceed at a faster pace than others[733] (the clear exceptions now being the United Kingdom and Ireland which have their own common travel area). The Treaty of Amsterdam makes provision for the Schengen *acquis* adopted before that Treaty's entry into force to be absorbed into the structure of the European Union, although the *acquis* will be regarded as acts based on Title VI TEU until the Council (in the composition of the 13 Member States involved) determines, in accordance with the relevant provisions of the Treaties, the legal basis for each provision or decision which constitutes the Schengen *acquis*.[734] The two-speed approach is now clearly anchored in the EC and EU systems.[735]

In the Netherlands in particular the Schengen arrangements have been much criticized, on account of the manner in which they have come into being, their lack of a democratic element, and their substance.[736] One of the most difficult points has been the relocation of controls on persons to the external frontiers, a point which has also arisen in the wider EC context since the achievement of the Community's internal market since

---

731. Agreement on the Gradual Abolition of Controls at the Common Frontiers (1986) XXXII *European Yearbook* 17 (unofficial English translation, also in Schermers *et al.* (eds.), *op. cit.* (see note 722, *supra*) 547 and HL Paper 90 (1989), Session 1988–1989 22nd Report 35) and in Dutch *Tractatenblad* 1985, No. 102. See also the Convention of 19 June 1990 applying the 1985 Agreement (in Dutch, French and German in *Tractatenblad* 1990 No. 145; an unofficial English translation is to be found in Schermers *et al.* (eds.), *op. cit.* 552 and in [1991] 1 CLE 33 and (1991) 30 ILM 73. See also O'Keeffe (1991) 11 YBEL 185 and literature cited there. The following countries are now parties to the Schengen Agreement: the original signatories, Italy, Spain, Portugal, Greece, Austria, Denmark, Norway, Sweden, Finland and Iceland. As to the application of the Schengen Agreement in respect of Member States which are not signatories to it, see WQ E-1837/94 (Megahy) O.J. 1995 C 55/10).
732. See Boeles (1990) SEW 686; Donner (1990) SEW 766 and Pauly, *Schengen en panne* (Maastricht, 1994).
733. See WQ 413/89 (Glinne) O.J. 1990 C 90/11.
734. Protocol integrating the Schengen *acquis* into the EU framework, annexed to the TEU and EC Treaty by the TOA, Art. 2(1).
735. See the new Arts. 5a EC and K.12 TEU, which are to be inserted by the TOA.
736. See Meijers (1992) NJCM-Bull. 356 and Jesserun d'Oliveira (1990) NJB 129. See also Van Arum (1996) SEW 12.

the end of 1992. This point is discussed further in the following section below.

4.4　Movement of persons at the Community's external frontiers

The achievement of the internal market, the expansion of the scope of the European Union from market participants to citizens, and the political and economic situation elsewhere in Europe caused provisions on cooperation in Justice and Home Affairs to be included in the TEU. These provisions in Title VI TEU confer on the Member States the power to act in an intergovernmental manner in relation to a number of subjects, *inter alia* asylum policy,[737] rules governing the crossing by persons of the external borders of the Member States and the exercise of controls thereon,[738] immigration policy,[739] and customs cooperation.[740] As a general rule the Council acts unanimously.[741] The role of the European Parliament and the Commission is extremely limited.[742] These provisions are altogether different in content and spirit from the provisions on free movement of

737. The Dublin Convention (15 June 1990) determining the state responsible for examining asylum applications lodged in a Member State entered into force on 1 September 1997 (O.J. 1997 C 254/1). See Hailbronner and Thiery (1997) 34 CMLRev. 957; the Council's conclusions of 27 May 1997 (O.J. 1997 C 191/27); Dec. 1/97 of the Committee set up by Art. 18 of the Dublin Convention (as Dec. 97/662 (O.J. 1997 L 281/ 1)); Jas 97/477 (O.J. 1997 L 205/3) and 97/478 (O.J. 1997 L 205/5); Decs 97/340 (O.J. 1997 L 147/3) and 97/420 (O.J. 1997 L 178/6) and the Resolution of 26 June 1997 on unaccompanied minors who are nationals of third countries (O.J. 1997 C 221/23). As to refugees, see JP 96/196 (O.J. 1996 L 63/2). As to older initiatives, reference should be made to the annual *General Report* which in more recent years includes a discussion of the Union's asylum, external frontiers and immigration activities. See also COM (94) 23 Final.

738. *Cf.* the Commission's proposals COM (93) 684 Final (O.J. 1994 C 11/6) with the Council's Conclusions (O.J. 1996 C 274/49) and Reg. 2317/95 (O.J. 1995 L 234/1, but see note 744, *infra*). See, further, the Commission's proposal for a Convention on rules for admission of third-country nationals to the Member States COM (97) 387 Final (O.J. 1997 C 337/9). See also JA 96/197 (O.J. 1996 L 63/8) on airport transit arrangements and JP 96/622 (O.J. 1996 L 281/1) on pre-frontier assistance at third-country airports.

739. *Ibid.* As to residence permits issued to third country nationals by Member States, see JA 97/11 (O.J. 1997 L 7/1). See also Dec. 96/749 (O.J. 1996 L 342/5) on monitoring the implementation of Council acts on illegal immigration, readmission, the unlawful employment of third country nationals and cooperation in the implementation of expulsion orders.

740. *E.g.* Jas 96/698 (O.J. 1996 L 322/3) and 96/750 (O.J. 1996 L 342/6). Art. K.1 TEU sets out the full list of matters falling under JHA.

741. Art. K.4(3) TEU. See *E.g.* Dec. 94/795 (O.J. 1994 L 327/1) on the admission of third country nationals for study purposes, and the package of resolutions and recommendations agreed at the same time (O.J. 1996 C 274/7 *et seq.*).

742. See Arts. K.4(2) and K.6 TEU.

persons in the EC Treaty: the latter confer rights on individuals directly and are implemented through the Community method, involving the Commission, the Parliament and the Council), both as regards the rights conferred and the exceptions thereto.

Article K.1 TEU provides that cooperation in JHA is without prejudice to the powers of the EC.[743] The so-called *passerelle* provision in Article K.9 TEU permits the Council, acting unanimously on the initiative of the Commission, to apply Article 100c EC in *inter alia* the fields of asylum policy, external borders policy and immigration.[744] There is a clear tension between the rights of persons, including nationals of third countries, which are conferred by the EC Treaty and the intergovernmental system of the Third Pillar of the Union.[745] Article K.2(1) TEU, which requires the matters covered by Article K.1 to be dealt with in compliance with the European Convention on Human Rights provides some guarantee of the protection of the interests of those affected by the decisions taken under J.H.A.

The restructuring of the Third Pillar (redesignated Police and Judicial Cooperation in Criminal Matters) provided for in the Treaty of Amsterdam will bring a significant improvement in the involvement of the European Parliament and a less significant involvement of the Court, in relation to the new framework decisions involving harmonization (which will operate in the same way as Community directives), binding decisions not having direct effect and not involving harmonization, and conventions recommended for adoption by the Member States in those areas still within this intergovernmental approach.[746] Visas, asylum, immigration and other policies relating to the free movement of persons will move into the Community framework in order to establish progressively an area of freedom, security and justice within the Community.[747]

4.5 Rights and obligations of persons

Free movement of persons involves three aspects. First, rights of migration. These concern the rules on the entry, admission, establishment and residence of persons. Natural persons physically pass an (external) border and are obliged to prove their identity on so doing. After admission they may establish themselves and reside in the territory of the Member State

---

743. See Müller-Graf (1994) 31 CMLRev. 493.
744. But not in the fields covered by Art. K.1(7)–(9) TEU. See Regs. 1683/95 (O.J. 1995 L 164/1) and 2317/95 (O.J. 1995 L 234/1). The latter was annulled in Case C-392/95 *European Parliament v. Council* [1997] ECR I-3213 (but its effects were maintained in force).
745. See O'Keeffe (1995) 20 ELRev. 20 and Evans (1994) EJIL 199.
746. See the new Art. K.11(1) TEU in conjunction with the new Art. K.6(2)(b)–(d) TEU.
747. See the new Arts. 73i–73q EC, introduced by the TOA.

concerned. Legal persons are subject to a system adapted to their separate legal situation.[748] The rights of migration are achieved by the directly effective prohibitions of obstacles to free movement which apply for the various categories of persons concerned, and in which the principle of non-discrimination on the ground of nationality forms an essential element. These substantive rules are linked to procedural rules.[749] Thus the persons concerned must be able to appeal against adverse administrative decisions affecting them,[750] and in particular the European Convention on Human Rights must be respected.[751]

The second aspect is rights of access to the market. These secondary rights give the person concerned access to the various markets, provided that a number of conditions are fulfilled. Very few specific conditions are in fact laid down for workers, but for the self-employed there are qualifications requirements and establishment requirements in respect of many professions. Although these national rules apply without distinction to nationals of the host Member State and nationals of other Member States alike, in many cases they have the effect of being less easy for persons moving to another Member States to satisfy. These market access conditions which lead to distortions are overcome, either by the mutual recognition principle, or by harmonization of laws, or by Community-wide uniform rules.[752]

Finally, there are ancillary rights. On the basis of the first two types of rights set out above an internal market for persons can be achieved and market competition is present. An employee or a self-employed person who wishes to migrate will only exercise their rights if a number of guarantees are afforded, such as the portability of their social security rights, such as pension periods. An undertaking which wishes to establish itself, or employ employees or provide services will also look to the social legislation and the fiscal climate in a Member State. Establishment burdens for undertakings, which may lead to policy competition (particularly fiscal competition) fall outside the scope of this discussion of free movement of persons,[753] save in relation to social security rights; they have been mentioned in the discussion of fiscal matters in section 2.5.3, above, and are also mentioned in the discussion of social policy in Chapter IX, below.

---

748. Art. 52 EC, 2nd para.
749. *E.g.* Case 36/75 *Rutili v. Minister for the Interior* [1975] ECR 1219 at 1230–1233.
750. *E.g.* Case 222/86 *Union national des entraîneurs et Cadres techniques professionnels du football (Unectef) v. Heylens et al.* [1987] ECR 4097 at 4117.
751. *E.g.* Case 36/75 *Rutili v. Minister for the Interior* [1975] ECR 1219 at 1232.
752. See section 1.1, *ante*.
753. See Case 81/87 *R. v. H.M. Treasury et al., ex parte Daily Mail and General Trust PLC* [1988] ECR 5483, [1989] 3 CMLR 713 and *e.g.* Case C-204/90 *Bachmann v. Belgian State* [1992] ECR I-249 and Case C-330/91 *R. v. Inland Revenue Commissioners, ex parte Commerzbank AG* [1993] ECR I-4017, [1993] 3 CMLR 357. See also O.J. 1998 C 2/2 and Wattel (1998) NTER 17.

5. FREE MOVEMENT OF WORKERS

European workers are bound to their residence and their country by numerous ties to a much greater extent than American workers are. The free movement of workers has thus in practice been far less important than the free movement of goods and, more recently, the freedom to provide (and receive) services. Whether the internal market and the citizenship of the Union will result in major developments in this field will only become apparent with the course of time.

The provisions of Articles 48–51 EC principally concern the political and economic aspects of free movement: residence, establishment and market access. The social aspects are visible in Article 51 EC concerning social security matters. The employment market and working conditions policies of the Member States and the Community are governed by the terms of Articles 117–123 EC and (although this has now effectively ceased to be important) the Protocol on Social Policy annexed to the TEU.[754] Articles 123–125 EC on the European Social Fund and Articles 130a–130e EC on the Structural Funds set out the conditions for financial stimuli for the creation of employment opportunities for certain groups or regions. These matters are discussed in Chapter IX, below.[755]

The present discussion now examines first the beneficiaries of the freedom of movement for workers, in section 5.1, before turning to migration rights in section 5.2; proceeds to rights of market access in section 5.3, and finishes with social security rights, in section 5.4, below.[756]

5.1   The concept of a worker and Articles 48–51 EC

The EC Treaty itself does not define the concept of a 'worker' or the concept of employment, so these concepts had to be defined through case-law. The Court has sought to give these concepts as wide an interpretation as possible, on the basis that the free movement of workers is one of the foundations of the Community, and thus the provisions conferring those freedoms must be widely interpreted.[757] In practice this means that these

---

754. As to developments in this area, see Chapter IX, section 6, *post*.
755. See Pelkmans in Muysken and Soete (eds.), *Maastricht kritisch bechouwd* (Utrecht, 1993) 135.
756. In the 5th Dutch edition of this work, Mortelmans based his approach on Denys in *Praktijkboek EG-recht* section B2 (Deventer, 1992). See, generally, note 722, *supra* and Feik, *Die Freizügigkeit der Arbeitnehmer nach EG-Recht* (Vienna, 1993); Hervey in Shaw and More (eds.), *New Legal Dynamics of European Union* (Oxford, 1995); Wölker in Von der Groeben *et al.* (eds.) *Kommentar zum EU-/EG-Vertrag* (5th ed., Baden-Baden, 1997) Vol. 1 1047–1204; Johnson and O'Keeffe (1994) 31 CMLRev. 1313; Laske (1993) 30 CMLRev. 515, and Mattera (1993) RMUE 47.
757. *E.g.* Case 53/81 *Levin v. Staatssecretaris van Justitie* [1982] ECR 1035 at 1049–1050

concepts are given a Community law meaning and are not determined by reference to national legislation of the Member States.[758] '[T]he principle of cooperation in good faith requires the competent authorities in the Member States to use all the means at their disposal to achieve the aim of Article 48 of the Treaty'[759] and thus to overcome problems resulting from differences in legislation between Member States.[760]

These concepts 'must be defined in accordance with objective criteria which distinguish the employment relationship by reference to the rights and duties of the persons concerned.'[761] Thus the essential feature of an employment relationship 'is that for a certain period of time a person performs services for and under the direction of another person in return for which he [or she] receives remuneration.[762] This means that the nature of the legal relationship between the employer and the employee is not decisive for the applicability of Article 48 EC.[763] Activities which are non-economic in nature, such as purely amateur sport or appearances in national teams do not fall under the concept of employment.[764] A traineeship which is used as practical preparation directly related to the actual pursuit of the occupation concerned may well be sufficient for the

and Case C-357/89 *Raulin v. Minister van Onderwijs en Wetenschappen* [1992] ECR I-1027 at 1059.

758. Case 75/63 *Hoekstra, née Unger v. Bestuur der Bedrijfsvereniging voor Detailhandel en Ambachten* [1964] ECR 177 at 184; Case 53/81 *Levin v. Staatssecretaris van Justitie* [1982] ECR 1035 at 1049–1050, and Case 139/85 *Kempf v. Staatssecretaris van Justitie* [1986] ECR 1741 at 1750.

759. Case C-165/91 *Van Munster v. Rijksdienst voor Pensioenen* [1994] ECR I-4661 at 4697.

760. *Ibid.*

761. Case 66/85 *Lawrie-Blum v. Land Baden-Württemberg* [1986] ECR 2121 at 2144; Case C-3/87 *R. v. Ministry of Agriculture, Fisheries and Food, ex parte Aggregate Ltd.* [1989] ECR 4459 at 4505.

762. *E.g. ibid.*; Case 197/86 *Brown v. Secretary of State for Scotland* [1988] ECR 3205 at 3244; Case C-357/89 *Raulin v. Minister van Onderwijs en Wetenschappen* [1992] ECR I-1027 at 1059. See also Case 196/87 *Steymann v. Staatssecretaris van Justitie* [1988] ECR 6159 at 6173 (activities performed by members of a religious or philosophical community as part of the latter's commercial activities are economic activities in so far as the services which the community provides to its members may be regarded as the indirect quid pro quo for genuine and effective work), and Case 344/87 *Bettray v. Staatssecretaris van Justitie* [1989] ECR 1621 at 1645 (activities matched to the individual in a rehabilitation or reintegration programme do not constitute a means of effective and genuine economic activity).

763. *E.g.* Case 152/73 *Sotgiu v. Deutsche Bundespost* [1974] ECR 153 at 163, and Case 344/87 *Bettray v. Staatssecretaris van Justitie* [1989] ECR 1621 at 1645.

764. Case 36/74 *Walrave and Koch v. Association Union Cycliste Internationale et al.* [1974] ECR 1405 at 1418, and Case 13/76 *Donà v. Mantero* [1976] ECR 1333 at 1340. But professional or semi-professional sport is within the scope of the EC Treaty, *ibid.*, and restrictions on participation in matches or events (by limiting the number of foreign players who may be fielded) are not permitted, as they restrict the chances of employment of players because participation is the essential purpose of a professional player's activity, Case C-415/93 *Union Royale Belge des Sociétés de Football Association ASBL et al. v. Bosman et al.* [1995] ECR I-4921 at 5074–5075.

trainee to be regarded as a worker.[765] The test which must be satisfied is whether effective and genuine work is being undertaken, so that part-time work or casual work on the basis of a call-up contract may well satisfy that test, but purely marginal and ancillary work will not be enough, although a Member State is not entitled to require that the remuneration received be at least the national minimum wage.[766] The question whether a person is engaged in effective and genuine work is a question of fact for the national court to decide; thus the irregular nature of work actually performed and the length of time for which the activity may be taken into account.[767]

The free movement of workers benefits workers who are nationals of a Member State[768] or of the European Economic

765. Case 66/85 *Lawrie-Blum v. Land Baden-Württemberg* [1986] ECR 2121 at 2144–2145. See also Case C-3/90 *Bernini v. Minister van Onderwijs en Wetenschappen* [1992] ECR I-1071 at 1105 (the national court may examine whether the person concerned has completed a sufficient number of hours in order to familiarize him or herself with the work).

766. Case 53/81 *Levin v. Staatssecretaris van Justitie* [1982] ECR 1035 at 1049–1050; Case 344/87 *Bettray v. Staatssecretaris van Justitie* [1989] ECR 1621 at 1645; Case C-357/89 *Raulin v. Minister van Onderwijs en Wetenschappen* [1992] ECR I-1027 at 1059, and Case C-3/90 *Bernini v. Minister van Onderwijs en Wetenschappen* [1992] ECR I-1071 at 1105.

767. Case C-357/89 *Raulin v. Minister van Onderwijs en Wetenschappen* [1992] ECR I-1027 at 1060. See also Case C-3/90 *Bernini v. Minister van Onderwijs en Wetenschappen* [1992] ECR I-1071 at 1105.

768. Art. 48(2) EC; Reg. 1612/68 (O.J. English Special Edition 1968 (II) 475, most recently amended by Reg. 2434/92 (O.J. 1992 L 245/1)), Art. 1. See Case 238/83 *Caisse d'Allocations Familiales de la Région Parisienne v. Meade et al.* [1984] ECR 2631 at 2638. See also Case C-355/89 *Department of Health and Social Security v. Barr et al.* [1991] ECR I-3479 at 3502–3504 (in relation to the Isle of Man). As to the status of the Channel Islands and the Isle of Man, see Art. 227(5)(b) EC and Act of Accession (1972), Protocol 3 (which latter expressly excludes the Channel Islanders and Manxmen from the benefit of the free movement of persons and services), and *Barr*, *loc. cit.* As to the Channel Islands, see also Case C-171/96 *Pereira Roque v. H.E. The Lieutenant Governor of Jersey* [1998] ECR I-nyr (16 July 1998). The EC Treaty does not apply to the United Kingdom's Sovereign Base Area in Cyprus, Art. 227(5)(c) EC, nor does it apply to the Faroe Islands. Freedom of movement does extend to Gibraltar, Art. 227(4) EC, and to the Åland Islands (as the Finnish Government has given notice in accordance with Art. 126(2) EEA (O.J. 1995 L 75/18) but the provisions listed in Art. 126(2) apply. The free movement of persons no longer applies to Greenland (which is now an Annex IV country), Greenland Treaty (O.J. 1985 L 29/1), see also the Protocol on Greenland annexed to the EC Treaty. Monaco and San Marino appear to be more in the nature of independent states than European territories for whose external relations France and Italy respectively are responsible, Jennings and Watts (eds.), *Oppenheim's International Law* (9th ed., London, 1992) Vol. 1, 271. It appears that the free movement of persons does not extend to Andorra, Plender in Vaughan (ed.), *op. cit.* (see note 722, *supra*) para. 302. The same applies in respect of the Vatican City. The special status of Mount Athos was recognized in a Joint Declaration annexed to the Final Act on the occasion of the signature of the Act of Greek Accession (1979). As to Cueta and Melilla, see Act of Spanish and Portuguese

Area.[769] It does not apply to employees from the Overseas Countries and Territories mentioned in Annex IV to the EC Treaty, such as The Netherlands Antilles and Aruba; as those countries are covered by Article 135 EC.[770] The benefits of free movement also do not apply in respect of nationals of third countries.[771] In a number of association agreements with European[772] and non-European countries[773] special provisions concern the free movement of workers. The Commission has established a procedure providing for prior communication and consultation on policies in relation to migration by third country nationals.[774]

The difference between a person's situation as an employee of a company providing services and a person's own individual movement as a worker was very clearly highlighted in Case C-113/89 *Rush Portugesa Lda*

Accession (1985), Art. 25 (the freedoms apply without derogations). That provision also covers the Canary Islands, but there are no provisions on free movement of persons or services included in Community legislation applicable there, see Reg. 1911/91 (O.J. 1991 L 171/1, amended by Reg. 284/92 (O.J. 1992 L 31/6)). Free movement applies in full to Madeira and the Azores.

769. EEA Agreement, Art. 28 and Annex V.

770. See also Reg. 1612/68, Art. 42. See further, Mortelmans and Temmink (1991) *Tijdschrift voor Antiliaans Recht-Justicia* (Spec. Nr. Nov. 1991) 51.

771. Case 65/77 *Razanatsimba* [1977] ECR 2229 at 2239 (no interpretation of the Lomé Convention in the same way as the EC Treaty provisions on the right of establishment; no requirement that nationals of one ACP State be treated in the same way as nationals of another ACP State provided that the difference results from the provisions of an international agreement comprising reciprocal rights and advantages). See also Chapter IX, section 6.1, *post*.

772. *E.g.* Turkey, see O.J. 1977 L 361/29 and *e.g.* Case 12/86 *Demirel v. Stadt Schwäbisch Gmünd* [1987] ECR 3719; Case C-192/89 *Sevince v. Staatssecretaris van Justitie* [1990] ECR I-3461; Case C-237/91 *Kus v. Landeshauptstadt Wiesbaden* [1992] ECR I-6781; Case C-355/93 *Eroglu v. Land Baden-Württemberg* [1994] ECR I-5116; Case C-434/93 *Bozkurt v. Staatssecretaris van Justitie* [1995] ECR I-1475; Case C-171/95 *Tetik v. Land Berlin* [1997] ECR I-329; Case C-351/95 *Kadiman v. Freistaat Bayern* [1997] ECR I-2133; Case C-386/95 *Eker v. Land Baden-Württemberg* [1997] ECR I-2697; Case C-285/95 *Kol v. Land Berlin* [1997] ECR I-3069; Case C-36/96 *Günaydin et al. v. Freistaat Bayern* [1997] ECR I-5143, and Case C-98/96 *Ertanir v. Land Hessen* [1997] ECR I-5179. See, further, Lichtenberg *et al.* (eds.) *Gastarbeiter – Einwander – Bürger?* (Baden-Baden, 1996). See also Case C-58/93 *Yousfi v. Belgian State* [1994] ECR I-1353 and Case C-277/94 *Taflan-Met et al. v. Bestuur van de Sociale Verzekeringsbank* [1996] ECR I-4085. The Europe Agreements (as to which, see Chapter XII, section 4.2.3, *post*) offer non-discriminatory treatment to nationals of beneficiary countries lawfully employed in a Member State, but do not confer the right to go to look for a job. See, further, Plender in Vaughan (ed)., *op. cit.* (see note 722, *supra*) paras. 55–81.

773. Such as the Lomé Convention countries (see Chapter XII, section 4.2.5, *post*), see *e.g.* Case 65/77 *Razanatsimba* [1977] ECR 2229 and Plender in Vaughan (ed.), *op. cit.* (see note 722, *supra*) paras. 82–83. See also Case C-103/94 *Kid v. Caisse Nationale d'Assurance Vieillesse des Travailleurs Salariées (CNAVTS)* [1995] ECR I-719.

774. Dec. 88/384 (O.J. 1988 L 183/35, corrigenda O.J. 1988 L 277/43 and 320/35) which replaced Dec. 85/381 (O.J. 1985 L 217/25) which was annulled in Cases 281/85 *etc. Germany et al. v. Commission* [1987] ECR 3203. See Lanfranchi, *Droit communautaire et travailleurs migrants des états tiers* (Paris, 1994) 75–122, and section 4.4, *ante*.

v. *Office national d'immigration.*[775] At that time free movement of workers
was not yet achieved between Portugal and the other Member States,
although in almost all sectors there were no transitional restrictions on the
freedom of establishment or the freedom to provide services. Rush
Portugesa used its own Portuguese employees in the performance of a sub-
contract relating to work on several *TGV Atlantique* sites in France. It
appealed against an administrative fine imposed because it was using its
Portuguese staff rather than persons having a work permit, and because it
infringed the defendant's monopoly on the recruitment and bringing into
France of foreign workers. The Court had no difficulty in holding that
Rush Portugesa was in fact providing services, and that to penalize it for
using its own staff would be an obstacle to its ability to provide those
services. Its staff did not as such enter the French labour market, as they
simply returned home on completion of the contract. The situation would
have been different if it had been an undertaking engaged in the making
available of labour, as the temporary derogation whereby the free
movement of workers was not immediately achieved would be undermined.
In fact the feared disruption of the labour market in other Member States
(especially Luxembourg which had a derogation for a longer period) failed
to materialize, not least because of the less favourable economic
circumstances in many Member States in the late Eighties; thus the
derogation was in fact terminated early so that there was full free
movement of workers in the Community on 1 January 1992.[776] On future
accessions transitional provisions on the free movement of workers may
well be agreed, which would again make questions of entry to the labour
market relevant. The whole question of Community provisions concerning
posted workers proved controversial, and it was not until December 1996
that Directive 96/71 was finally adopted.[777]

5.2 Migration rights (exit, entry and residence)

Every national of a Member State, irrespective of his or her place of
residence, has the right to take up an activity as an employed person, and
to pursue such activity, within the territory of another Member State
under the same conditions as nationals of the host Member State.[778]

---

775. [1990] ECR I-1417, [1991] 2 CMLR 818. See also Case 9/88 *Lopes da Viega v. Staatssecretaris van Justitie* [1989] ECR 2989, and (in relation to third-country nationals
  employed in one Member State sent to another Member State in the course of the
  performance of services by their employer) Case C-43/93 *Vander Elst v. Office des
  Migrations Internationales* [1994] ECR I-3803.
776. Reg. 2194/91 (O.J. 1991 L 206/1).
777. O.J. 1997 L 18/1.
778. Reg. 1612/68, Art. 1(1). The same rights enure to nationals of EEA States in Member
  States and to nationals of the latter in EEA States which are not Member States of

Article 1 of Directive 68/360[779] requires Member States to abolish restrictions on the movement and residence of nationals of the Member States and of certain members of their families.[780] A national of a Member State who has worked in another Member State may only derive a right of residence under the EC Treaty on that basis if he or she was already a national of a Member State at the time at which he or she was employed in the host Member State, so that a person who has never been employed in the host Member State since the accession of his own country to the European Union (but was beforehand) cannot derive a right of residence on the basis of Article 48(3)(c) EC.[781]

The logical corollary to the right of entry and residence is the right for nationals and their dependent families to leave the territory of a Member State in order to take up or pursue employment in another Member State.[782]

The right of entry may be exercised simply on production of a valid passport or identity card.[783] Thus a Member State is not entitled to demand that other formalities be satisfied,[784] or that a person state his or her purpose and duration of stay and the financial means at his or her disposal as a condition of entry.[785] Somewhat controversially, the Court refused to condemn general controls on the possession of a residence permit being carried out sporadically and unsystematically even if this were done at the frontier, where a Member State obliged those enjoying a right of residence under Community law to carry their residence or establishment permit at all times and there was an identical obligation on the host Member State's own nationals in relation to their identity cards.[786]

---

the EU. This point is henceforth taken as read and not repeated further in the discussion.

779. O.J. English Special Edition 1968 (II), p. 485. A proposal to amend this directive has been presented, COM (95) 348 Final (O.J. 1995 C 307/18).
780. *I. e.* those to whom Reg. 1612/68 applies, see *ibid.*, Art. 10.
781. Case C-171/91 *Tsiotras v. Landeshauptstadt Stuttgart* [1993] ECR I-2925 at 2956. The person is thus deemed never to have been employed in a Member State, and is thus outside the scope of Dir. 68/360.
782. Dir. 68/260, Art. 2(1). The right may be exercised simply on production of a valid identity card or passport, *ibid.* The Member State which issued the identity card or passport must allow the holder to re-enter its territory without any formality, even if the card or passport is no longer valid or the nationality of the holder is in dispute, *ibid.*, Art. 3(4).
783. *Ibid.*, Art. 3(1).
784. Case 157/79 *R. v. Pieck* [1980] ECR 2171 at 2184–2185.
785. Case C-68/89 *Commission v. The Netherlands* [1991] ECR I-2637 at 2655 (the case arose when Dutch border officials refused admission to a German lawyer who was on his way from Aachen via The Netherlands to dinner with an official of the European Parliament in Antwerp).
786. Case 321/87 *Commission v. Belgium* [1989] ECR 997 at 1011. Certainly if these controls at point of entry were carried out in a systematic, arbitrary or unnecessarily restrictive manner, the Court would have been prepared to find them incompatible

The right of residence must be granted to nationals and their dependent families who are able to produce specified documents.[787] The right of residence is proved by a specific residence permit for a national of a Member State, which is declaratory in nature, rather than constitutive.[788]

with Community law, *ibid.* Where there is no such general obligation on a Member State's own nationals, such controls will clearly be unacceptable. One of the downsides of the achievement of the abolition of systematic border controls (in the Schengen countries at least) has been that they have been replaced by so-called spot checks on identity papers a few kilometers away from the border. As to the (il)legality of these, see Van Arum (1996) SEW 12.

787. Dir. 68/360, Art. 3(1). For the worker, these are the document with which he or she entered the territory of the host Member State and either a confirmation of engagement from the employer concerned or a certificate of employment. Thus (unlike in the case of those enjoying the right of residence under what is referred to as the June 1990 package of directives, as to which, see section 4.1, *ante*) no requirement may be made as to evidence of registration with the social security system, see Case C-363/89 *Roux v. Belgian State* [1991] ECR I-273 at 291–292. As to the members of the worker's family, the document with which they entered the country, a document issued by the competent authority of the state of origin or the state whence they came, proving their relationship, and, in the case of dependents, a document so issued testifying that they are dependent on the worker or that they live under his roof in such country, Art. 4(3). As long as a worker possesses a valid identity card, his or her right of residence must be recognized, even if the card did not allow the holder to leave the territory of the issuing Member State, Case C-376/89 *Giagoundis v. Stadt Reutlingen* [1991] ECR I-1069 at 1091–1092. As a worker might no longer have the document with which he or she entered the country, production of either a valid identity card or a valid passport will suffice to claim the right of residence, *ibid.* at 1093. A member of the family who is not a national of a Member State must be issued with a residence document having the same validity as that of the worker upon whom he or she is dependent, Dir. 68/360, Art. 4(4). As to family (or ex-family) members who are not themselves nationals of a Member State, see Oliver (1985) 5 YBEL 57; Reg. 1612/68, Arts. 10 and 11; and (more generally) Cases 35 and 36/82 *Morson and Jhanjan v. State of the Netherlands et al.* [1982] ECR 3723, [1983] 2 CMLR 720; Case 94/84 *Office national de l'emploi v. Deak* [1985] ECR 1873; Case 59/85 *State of the Netherlands v. Reed* [1986] ECR 1283, [1987] 2 CMLR 448; Case 131/85 *Gül v. Regierungspräsident Düsseldorf* [1986] ECR 1573, [1987] 1 CMLR 501; Case 147/87 *Zaoui v. Caisse régionale d'assurance-maladie de l'Île- de-France (Cramif)* [1987] ECR 5511; Cases C-297/88 and 197/89 *Dzodzi v. Belgian State* [1990] ECR I-3763; Case C-370/90 *R. v. Immigration Appeal Tribunal and Singh, ex parte Secretary of State for the Home Department* [1992] ECR I-4265, [1992] 3 CMLR 358, and Cases C-64 and 65/96 *Land Nordrhein-Westfalen et al. v. Uecker et al.* [1997] ECR I-3171. *Cf.* Case C-18/90 *Office national de l'emploi (Onem) v. Kziber* [1991] ECR I-199.

788. Case 48/75 *Royer* [1976] ECR 497 at 513; Cases 389 and 390/87 *Echternach and Moritz v. Netherlands Minister for Education and Science* [1989] ECR 723 at 762. The permit must state that it is issued pursuant to Reg. 1612/68 and measures taken to implement Dir. 68/360, *ibid.*, Art. 4(2); the text of such statement is annexed to Dir. 68/360. The present Dutch residence permit issued to the editor fails to comply with this requirement. The residence period must be valid throughout the territory of the issuing Member State, and must be issued for five years, *ibid.*, Art. 6(1). As to the possibility of shorter periods, see *ibid.*, Arts. 6(3) and Case C-344/95 *Commission v. Belgium* [1997] ECR I-1035.

The decision to grant or refuse a residence permit must be taken as soon as possible, and in any event within six months from the date of application for the permit.[789] Any failure to obtain or renew the residence permit may only be the subject of reasonable sanctions, reflecting the administrative nature of the offence.[790] With a view to protecting the migrant worker against economic misfortune, Article 7 of Directive 68/360 afford the worker considerable protection against the withdrawal or non-renewal of his or her residence permit solely on the ground of not being in employment.[791] The residence permit must be issued free of charge or on payment of a fee which may not be higher than the dues and taxes charged for the issue of identity cards to nationals.[792] Article 8(1) of the directive deals with special situations: residence for short-term employment of up to three months (for which no permit is needed), those who live in one Member State and work in another, returning at least weekly, and seasonal workers; in all these cases the person concerned may be required to report his or her presence in the territory of the host Member State.[793]

The question of the right of residence for the purpose of seeking employment has given rise to spectacular case-law. In a declaration by the Council which was entered in the minutes at the time of the adoption of Directive 68/360 and Regulation 1612/68, but which was unpublished in the *Official Journal*, a right to look for work for a period of at least three months was recognized, the stay having to be terminated if they had found no work at the end of that period. If during that period the person became dependent on public support (social assistance) in the host Member State, he or she could be requested to leave that State's territory. In Case C-292/

789. Dir. 64/221 (O.J. English Special Edition 1963–64, p. 117), Art. 5(1). The applicant (logically, but not stated, also his spouse and dependent family) must be allowed to remain temporarily in the territory of the Member State concerned pending the decision, *ibid.* In exceptional cases, and not as a matter of routine, the host Member State may request the applicant's home Member State, and if need be other Member States to provide information concerning any previous police record; the Member State(s) concerned must reply within two months, *ibid.*, Art. 5(2).

790. Case 48/75 *Royer* [1976] ECR 497 at 513–514 (these do not include expulsion or imprisonment, *ibid.* at 514–515 and Case 157/79 *R. v. Pieck* [1980] ECR 2171 at 2187); although there may be differences compared with infringement of a national obligation to carry an identity card, Case 8/77 *Sagulo et al.* [1977] ECR 1495 at 1506, the sanctions must be comparable, Case C-363/89 *Roux v. Belgian State* [1991] ECR I-273 at 294 (citing earlier authorities).

791. If the cause is temporary incapacity as a result of illness or accident, or because of involuntary unemployment, this being duly certified by the competent employment office, Dir. 68/360, Art. 7(1). On first renewal the period of residence may be restricted to no less than 12 months if the worker has been involuntarily unemployed in the host Member States for more than 12 consecutive months, *ibid.*, Art. 7(2).

792. Dir. 68/360, Art. 9(1). See Case C-344/95 *Commission v. Belgium* [1997] ECR I-1035. Thus if there are no compulsory identity cards, the residence permit must be issued free of charge. See also WQ E-2333/94 (Ribeiro) O.J. 1995 C 88/9.

793. Dir. 68/360, Art. 8(2). See Case C-265/88 *Messner* [1989] ECR 4209.

89 *R. v. The Immigration Appeal Tribunal, ex parte Antonissen*[794] the Court held that 'such a declaration cannot be used for the purpose of interpreting a provision of secondary legislation where, as in this case, no reference is made to the content of the declaration in the wording of the provision in question.'[795] The declaration accordingly had no legal significance.[796] Given, though, that there was no Community provision prescribing the period during which a person might look for work, the United Kingdom's period of six months did not appear in principle insufficient to enable a person to seek and obtain appropriate employment. The sting in the tail of this acceptance, though, was the reversal of the burden of proof if a person sought to stay longer without yet having found work: the Court held that he or she must in that case produce evidence that he or she is continuing to seek employment and has genuine chances of being engaged. If this were provided, he or she could not be required to leave the host Member State.[797] The conceptual difficulty is in the second part of the proof: quite how anyone can prove that he or she has genuine chances of being engaged is surely beyond the imagination of most job-seekers. Accordingly, this second condition should, it is respectfully submitted, be seriously reconsidered.

The Member States may not derogate from the provisions of Directive 68/360, except on grounds of public policy, public security or public health, grounds which are also found in Article 48(3) EC. These grounds are worked out in Directive 64/221.[798] This directive applies not only to the free movement of workers; it also covers nationals of Member States who are self-employed, providing services, or entering or residing under the celebrated June 1990 package of directives.[799] Its scope was also extended by Directive 72/194[800] to cover employees who exercise their right to remain in the territory of another Member State after having been employed there. Measures taken on grounds of public policy or public security have to be justified on grounds of the individual conduct of the person concerned;[801] the mere existence of a criminal conviction is not enough.[802]

The diseases and disabilities which justify restrictions on the exercise of

794. [1991] ECR I-745, [1991] 2 CMLR 373.
795. [1991] ECR I-745 at 778.
796. *Ibid.*
797. *Ibid.* at 779.
798. O.J. English Special Edition 1963–64, p. 117. The directive is in fact based on Art. 56(2) EC.
799. See sections 6.5.2 and 7.4.2, *post*, and 4.1, *ante*, respectively.
800. O.J. English Special Edition 1963–64, p. 474.
801. Dir. 64/221, Art. 3(1), see, further, *post*. Expiry of the identity card or passport used to enter the host Member State and obtain the residence permit does not justify expulsion, *ibid.*, Art. 3(3).
802. Previous criminal convictions are not in themselves grounds for denying a person the right of entry or residence, *ibid.*, Art. 3(2), see, further, *post*.

the right of free movement are contained in the Annex to Directive 64/221.[803] 'The right to restrict freedom of movement on grounds of public health is intended not to exclude the public health sector, as a sector of economic activity and from the point of view of access to employment, from the application of the principles of freedom of movement but to permit Member States to refuse access to their territory or residence there to persons whose access or residence would in itself constitute a danger for public health.'[804] Diseases or disabilities occurring after a first residence permit has been issued do not justify refusal to renew the permit or expulsion from the host Member State.[805]

Article 2(2) of the directive provides that the grounds of public policy, public security or public health 'shall not be invoked to service economic ends.' This provision is particularly important as it prevents Member States from expelling Community citizens in times of economic recession. Besides the definition of the exceptions the directive also prescribes procedural guarantees for those affected by the application of its provisions.

Since 1974 the number of cases concerning the application of Directive 64/221 and Article 48(3) EC has been significant.[806] Neither the EC Treaty

---

803. The Annex specifies two categories. Category A covers the following diseases which might endanger public health: (1) diseases subject to quarantine listed in International Health Regulation No. 2. of the World Health Organization of 25 May 1951; (2) Tuberculosis of the respiratory system in an active state or showing a tendency to develop; (3) Syphilis; (4) other infectious diseases or contagious parasitic diseases if they are the subject of provisions for the protection of nationals of the host country. Category B lists diseases and disabilities which might threaten public policy or public security; (1) drug addiction; (2) profound mental disturbance; manifest conditions of psychotic disturbance with agitation, delirium, hallucinations or confusion. As to AIDS/HIV, see Dworkin and Steyger (1989) Tex. Int'l.L.J. 295; Dispersyn (1990) Rev. Belge de Dr. Int. 232, and Van Overbeek (1990) 27 CMLRev. 791. The Annex reflects the circumstances of 1964 and has not been revised since. A new *infectious* disease could be covered if the conditions of point (4) of category A are fulfilled.
804. Case 131/85 *Gül v. Regierungspräsident Düsseldorf* [1986] ECR 1573 at 1589.
805. Dir. 64/221, Art. 4(2).
806. Case 41/74 *Van Duyn v. Home Office* [1974] ECR 1337, [1975] 1 CMLR 1, [1975] Ch, 358, [1975] 3 All ER 190; Case 67/74 *Bonsignore v. Oberstadtdirektor der Stadt Köln* [1975] ECR 297, [1975] 1 CMLR 472; Case 36/75 *Rutili v. Minister for the Interior* [1975] ECR 1219, [1976] 1 CMLR 140; Case 48/75 *Royer* [1976] ECR 497, [1976] 2 CMLR 619; Case 118/75 *Watson and Belmann* [1976] ECR 1185, [1976] 2 CMLR 552; Case 8/77 *Sagulo et al.* [1977] ECR 1495, [1977] 2 CMLR 85; Case 30/77 *R. v. Bouchereau* [1977] ECR 1999, [1977] 2 CMLR 800, [1978] QB 732, [1981] 2 All ER 924; Case 98/79 *Pecastaing v. Belgian State* [1980] ECR 691, [1980] 3 CMLR 685; Case 131/79 *R. v. Secretary of State for the Home Department, ex parte Santillo* [1980] ECR 1585, [1980] 2 CMLR 308, [1981] 2 All ER 897; Case 98/80 *Romano v. Institut National d'Assurance Maladie-Invalidité* [1981] ECR 1241, [1983] 2 CMLR 698; Cases 115 and 116/81 *Adoui and Cornuaille v. Belgian State et al.* [1982] ECR 1665, [1982] 3 CMLR 631; Cases C-297/88 and 197/89 *Dzodzi v. Belgian State* [1990] ECR I-3763; Case C-292/89 *R. v. The Immigration Appeal Tribunal, ex parte Antonissen* [1991] ECR

itself nor Directive 64/221 attempts to define what is meant by the concepts of public policy, public security and public health. While these concepts may be recognized by the case-law as being primarily defined by national law, the application thereof is so hedged about by limitations demanded by Community law that it becomes a question of Community law itself; hence, for example, the concept of public policy in Community law does not simply correspond to the English law use of the term.

Like all exceptions in the Treaty, the grounds in Article 48(3) EC and Directive 64/221 must be strictly construed.[807] In the first place this means that Community law places limits on the freedom of national law to interpret the grounds.[808] Because the Treaty requires that restrictions be *justified* (as is the case also in relation to Article 36 EC) on the grounds specified, it is possible to challenge the use which a Member State makes of its powers in a particular case; redress is thus available against misuse or actions which go beyond the margin of freedom left to the Member States. Additionally the terms of Directive 64/221 (which co-ordinates national provisions) form a clear boundary for that margin of freedom. More general policy considerations (such as *décourager les autres*) may not be adduced and discrimination between a Member State's own nationals and nationals of other Member States is not permitted.[809] Thus a Member State may not simply determine that because a national of another Member State is, say, a prostitute or a lesbian or has green hair that person may not stay in its territory.[810] In Case 36/75 *Rutili v. Minister for the Interior*[811] the Court held that 'restrictions cannot be imposed on the right of a national of any Member State to enter the territory of another Member State, to stay there and to move within it, unless his presence or conduct constitutes a genuine and sufficiently serious threat to public policy.' That judgment also made it clear that restrictions on the freedoms laid down in the European Convention on Human Rights could not go

---

I-745, [1991] 2 CMLR 373; Case C-363/89 *Roux v. Belgian State* [1991] ECR I-273; Case C-175/94 *R. v. Secretary of State for the Home Department, ex parte Gallagher* [1995] ECR I-4253, [1996] 1 CMLR 557, and Cases C-65 and 111/95 *R. v. Secretary of State for the Home Department, ex parte Shingara et al.* [1997] ECR I-3343. See also Case C-171/96 *Periera Roque v. H.E. The Lieutenant Governor of Jersey* [1998] ECR I-nyr (16 July 1998). Among older literature, see, generally, Boonk, *De openbare orde als grens aan het vrije verkeer* (Alphen aan den Rijn, 1977) 136–148; Lauwaars (1978) SEW 829; Evans (1986) 102 LQR 510; O'Keeffe (1982) 19 CMLRev. 35; Hubeau (1981) CDE 207, and Barav (1981) 6 ELRev. 139.

807. *E.g.* Case 41/74 *Van Duyn* [1974] ECR 1337 at 1350.

808. *E.g.* Cases 115 and 116/81 *Adoui and Cornuaille* [1982] ECR 1665 at 1707–1708.

809. See Case 67/74 *Bonsignore* [1975] ECR 297 at 306–307 and Cases 115 and 116/81 *Adoui and Cornuaille* [1982] ECR 1665 at 1708–1709.

810. This follows from the requirement of the individual's conduct giving rise to the threat, Dir. 64/221, Art. 3(1), see *e.g.* Case 115 and 116/81 *Adoui and Cornuaille*, [1982] ECR 1665 at 1708–1709.

811. [1975] ECR 1219 at 1231.

further than was necessary in the interests of public order in a democratic society.[812] The measures taken must be proportionate to the nature of the offence committed against a public order provision[813] and, on the procedural side, the enjoyment of the legal protection ensured by Directive 64/221 must be guaranteed.[814] The existence of a criminal conviction of the person concerned can 'only be taken into account in so far as the circumstances which gave rise to that conviction are evidence of personal conduct constituting a present threat to the requirements of public policy.'[815] The classic restatement of the criterion for justifiable refusal to permit a Community citizen to exercise his right to free movement in another Member State is contained in the Court's dictum in Case 30/77 *R. v. Bouchereau*: '[i]n so far as it may justify certain restrictions on the free movement of persons subject to Community law, recourse by a national authority to the concept of public policy presupposes, in any event, the existence, in addition to the perturbation of the social order which any infringement of the law involves, of a genuine and sufficiently serious threat to the requirements of public policy affecting one of the fundamental interests of society.'[816] It is now clear that a Member State cannot claim that an individual's conduct fulfills this test if it takes no repressive measures against similar conduct by its own nationals.[817]

The procedural safeguards contained in Articles 5–9 of Directive 64/221 are particularly important and have received considerable attention in the case-law.[818] Thus apart from the time limit within which the residence

812. *Ibid.* at 1232. The Court referred to the European Convention in the context of national security or public safety, but public order (or the prevention of disorder) is also referred to in the Convention (in the Articles cited by the Court).

813. This will in many cases exclude arrest or deportation (in *R. v. Bouchereau* [1977] 2 CMLR 800 at 801 the Marlborough Street Stipendiary Magistrate decided not to recommend the deportation of Bouchereau).

814. As is explained further, *post*.

815. Case 30/77 *R. v. Bouchereau* [1977] ECR 1999 at 2012–2013. In relation to past conduct, this will not generally be enough to constitute a present threat. Although the Court recognized that it may be evidence of a propensity to act in the same way in the future the evaluation must be made 'in each individual case in the light of the particular legal position of persons subject to Community law and of the fundamental nature of the principle of the free movement of persons.' *Ibid.* at 2013).

816. [1977] ECR 1999 at 2014. Yet the United Kingdom courts interpret 'a genuine and sufficiently serious threat' as simply meaning that a person's continued presence would be to the detriment of the United Kingdom, *R. v. Escauriaza* [1989] 3 CMLR 281; *R. v. Kraus* (1982) 4 Cr. App. R. (S) 113.

817. Cases 115 and 116/81 *Adoui and Cornuaille* [1982] ECR 1665 at 1708, somewhat nuancing the approach in Case 41/74 *Van Duyn* [1974] ECR 1337 at 1350 (which approach was understandable in view of the impossibility of refusing admission to the United Kingdom to those scientologists who were United Kingdom nationals; the United Kingdom government discouraged people from becoming scientologists, but could not prevent its own nationals (or in fact anyone else) from doing so).

818. Case 48/75 *Royer* [1976] ECR 497, [1976] 2 CMLR 619, Case 118/75 *Watson and*

permit must be issued, noted above, the applicant is entitled to be informed of the grounds of public policy, public security, or public health on which the decision taken in his or her case is based, unless this is contrary to the interests of the security of the state involved.[819] Official notification of a decision refusing the issue or renewal of a residence permit, or to expel a person from the territory of the host Member State.[820] The person concerned must have the same legal remedies as are available to nationals of the host Member State in respect of acts of the administration, in order that he or she may challenge any decision concerning entry, or refusing the issue or renewal of a residence permit, or ordering his or her expulsion from the host Member State.[821] If there is no appeal possible in the sense of Article 8 of the directive, if any appeal may only be as to the legal validity of the decision, or if the appeal cannot have suspensory effect, a special procedure is prescribed, which has given rise to considerable case-law.[822]

Bellmann [1976] ECR 1185, [1976] 2 CMLR 552; Case 8/77 Sagulo et al. [1977] ECR 1495, [1977] 2 CMLR 85, Case 98/79 Pecastaing [1980] ECR 691, [1980] 3 CMLR 685; Case 131/79 Santillo [1980] ECR 1585, [1980] 2 CMLR 308, [1981] 2 All ER 987; Cases 115 and 116/81 Adoui and Cornuaille [1982] ECR 1665, [1982] 3 CMLR 631; Cases C-297/88 and 197/89 Dzodzi v. Belgian State [1990] ECR I-3763; Case C-292/89 R. v. The Immigration Appeal Tribunal, ex parte Antonissen [1991] ECR I-745, [1991] 2 CMLR 373; Case C-363/89 Roux v. Belgian State [1991] ECR I-273; Case C-175/94 R. v. Secretary of State for the Home Department, ex parte Gallagher [1995] ECR I-4253, [1996] 1 CMLR 557 (see White (1996) 21 ELRev. 241) and Cases C-65 and 111/95 R. v. Secretary of State for the Home Department, ex parte Shingara et al. [1997] ECR I-3343.

819. Dir. 64/221, Art. 6. In particular this means that, when notifying an individual of a restrictive measure adopted in his case, the state concerned must give him or her a sufficiently precise and comprehensive statement of the grounds for the decision, to enable him or her to take effective steps to prepare his or her defence, Case 36/75 Rutili v. Minister for the Interior [1975] ECR 1219 at 1233; it is sufficient if the notification is made in such a way as to enable the person concerned to comprehend its content and effect, Cases 115 and 116/81 Adoui and Cornuaille v. Belgian State et al. [1982] ECR 1665 at 1709. This must therefore be in a language which the person understands.

820. Dir. 64/221, Art. 7. The person concerned must be given a period of not less than 15 days if a residence permit has not been granted, and not less than one month in other cases within which to leave. However, in cases of urgency this period may be less. This exception is clearly relied upon to deport summarily the likes of unruly football fans or to refuse them admission, although this appears often to occur without regard to rights to remedies, explained below.

821. Ibid., Art. 8. This means the same remedies as against acts of the administration generally in that state (as opposed to specific remedies available to nationals of the host Member State refused entry, see Cases C-65 and 111/95 R. v. Secretary of State for the Home Department, ex parte Shingara et al. [1997] ECR I-3343 at 3387–3388 (also discussing earlier case-law). As to limitations on movement within the host Member State, see Case 36/75 Rutili v. Minister of the Interior [1975] ECR 1219 at 1234–1235. See also Case 175/78 R. v. Saunders [1979] ECR 1129 at 1135.

822. Dir. 64/221, Art. 9(1) provides that refusal of renewal of a residence permit or expul-

A particularly interesting example of the operation of Article 48(3) EC and Article 9 of Directive 64/221 can be seen in Case 131/79 *R. v. Secretary of State for the Home Department, ex parte Santillo*.[823] Santillo was convicted of various sexual offences and at the time of sentence a recommendation for deportation was made. While Santillo was in prison a deportation order was served on him (just over four and a half years after he had been sentenced). He challenged the order on the basis that the opinion of the court at the time of sentencing could not reasonably be said to be an opinion on his conduct (and any likely danger to society) almost five years later. The reason why he had been a model citizen since the opinion was given was, of course, at least in part the result of enjoying Her Majesty's hospitality. The Court of Justice gave pretty clear guidance in its ruling, holding that the opinion of the competent authority had to be 'sufficiently proximate in time to the decision ordering expulsion to ensure that there are no new factors to be taken into consideration.'[824] It went on to say that a lapse of time amounting to several years between the recommendation for deportation and the decision by the administration was likely to deprive the recommendation of its function as an opinion within the meaning of Article 9 of the directive; indeed, the Court considered it essential that the social danger resulting from the foreigner's presence should be assessed at the very time of the making of the expulsion decision, as the factors to be taken into account, particularly concerning the person's conduct, would be likely to change in the course of time.[825] The reaction of the English Courts to this seemingly clear signal – they rejected his appeal against the order[826] – has been described as

sion of the holder of such a permit by the administrative authority is not permitted (save in cases of urgency) until an opinion has been obtained from a competent authority of the host country before which the person has the right of defence and of assistance or representation as that country's domestic law provides for. As to this competent authority, see Case C-175/94 *R. v. Secretary of State for the Home Department, ex parte Gallagher* [1995] ECR I-4253 at 4278–4279 (citing earlier case-law). A decision cannot be taken until the opinion has been obtained (otherwise the procedure is a farce), *ibid.* at 4276–4277. In the case of a decision relating to the issue of a first residence permit or to expel a person before such permit is issued, Dir. 64/221, Art. 9(2) provides that if the person concerned so requests that decision must be referred to the competent authority provided for under Art. 9(1), and the person concerned is entitled to submit his or her defence in person, save where this would be contrary to the interests of national security. Thus this procedure is distinct from that of Art. 9(1), see *Gallagher* [1995] ECR I-4253 at 4277–4278 and Cases C-65 and 111/95 *R. v. Secretary of State for the Home Department, ex parte Shingara et al.* [1997] ECR I-3343 at 3389–3390. As to subsequent applications for a fresh residence permit, see Cases 115 and 116/81 *Adoui and Cornuaille* [1982] ECR 1665 at 1709 and *Shingara* [1997] ECR I-3343 at 3391–3392.

823. [1980] ECR 1585, [1980] 2 CMLR 308, [1981] 2 All ER 897.
824. [1980] ECR 1585 at 1600.
825. *Ibid.* at 1601.
826. [1980] 3 CMLR 212 (Divisional Court, Queen's Bench Division); [1981] 1 CMLR 569

questionable to say the least[827] and represents a serious, but thankfully isolated, instance of clear misinterpretation and misapplication of a ruling of the Court of Justice. The record of prostitutes is perhaps better in Community law than that of their clients.[828]

5.3   Rights of market access

Just as in the case of the other freedoms, the EC Treaty contains a key prohibition provision in order to achieve the free movement of workers; this is discussed in section 5.3.1, below. In a number of cases the Treaty provides for certain exceptions on the basis of which the Member States may refuse access to their market; these are discussed in section 5.3.2, below. In both areas there has been substantial case-law examination of the ambit of the relevant provisions.

5.3.1   The prohibition of discrimination, and other measures

In accordance with Article 48(1) EC the free movement of workers was secured by the end of the transitional period at the latest. The Court has held that Article 48 is directly effective since then.[829] The achievement of free movement for workers was ensured during the transitional period by Regulation 1612/68[830] which, like Directive 68/360[831] was adopted on the basis of Article 49 EC and replaced earlier provisions.[832] Regulation 1251/70[833] supplements the basic Regulation 1612/68 with rules relating to the right of workers to stay on in the territory of another Member State after having been employed there. Article 48(2) provides that freedom of

(CA). The English courts chose to interpret the Court of Justice's ruling as meaning that a lapse of time between the opinion and the deportation order only invalidates the former if it can be shown that new factors favourable to the prospective deportee, which ought to have been taken into consideration have arisen in the meantime. Santillo's deportation order was upheld (in fact he had gone back to Italy sometime beforehand on the basis that he would be allowed back into the United Kingdom if his appeal were successful).

827. Gormley (1986) 23 CMLRev. 287 at 302.
828. See Cases 115 and 116/81 *Adoui and Cornuaille* [1982] ECR 1665, [1982] 3 CMLR 631.
829. *E.g.* Case 167/73 *Commission v. France* [1974] ECR 359 at 372 and Case 41/74 *Van Duyn v. Home Office* [1974] ECR 1337 at 1347.
830. O.J. English Special Edition 1968 (II). p. 475, most recently amended by Reg. 2434/92 (O.J. 1992 L 245/1).
831. O.J. English Special Edition 1968 (II), p. 485.
832. Reg. 15 (J.O. 1961, p. 1073) was replaced by Reg. 38 (J.O. 1964, p. 965) which was in turn replaced by the present Regulation 1612/68.
833. O.J. English Special Edition 1970 (II), p. 402.

movement entails the abolition of any discrimination based on nationality between workers of Member States as regards employment, remuneration and other conditions of work and employment. The prohibition applies not merely to action by the authorities, it also applies to legal relationships governed by private law, such as collective bargaining agreements.[834] This embraces not merely visible forms of discrimination,[835] but also disguised and indirect forms of discrimination, which, by the application of other criteria of differentiation, lead in fact to the same result.[836] But discrimination will not be found if there are objective differences in the situations concerned.[837] The basic right under the free movement of workers is still seen in terms of equal treatment, (unlike the free movement of goods and the freedom to provide (and receive) services, in which equal treatment is an aspect of the rights but they extend much further than a mere non-discrimination principle). Thus the Court has not yet interpreted Article 48 EC so extensively as also to embrace systematically measures which do not distinguish (in law or in fact) between migrant workers and those of the host Member State, although there are older judgments which provide an opening in this direction[838] and the possibility of an approach not requiring a distinction between migrants and nationals of the host Member State is heralded more clearly in more recent judgments concerning the equivalence of qualifications and concerning education.[839]

834. Case 36/74 *Walrave and Koch v. Association Union Cycliste Internationale et al.* [1974] ECR 1405 at 1419; Case 13/76 *Donà v. Mantero* [1976] ECR 1333 at 1340, and Case C-415/93 *Union Royale Belge des Sociétés de Football Association ASBL et al. v. Bosman et al.* [1995] ECR I-4921 at 5063–5067.

835. Even if the obstacle is secondary (*e.g.* a legal provision which is not in fact applied, as this creates uncertainty), Case 167/73 *Commission v. France* [1974] ECR 359 at 373. See also *e.g.* Case 225/85 *Commission v. Italy* [1987] ECR 2625 at 2639.

836. *E.g.* Case 152/73 *Sotgiu v. Deutsche Bundespost* [1974] ECR 153 at 164; Case 41/84 *Pinna v. Caisse d'allocations familiales de la Savoie* [1986] ECR 1 at 25; Case 33/88 *Allué et al. v. Università degli Studi di Venezia* [1989] ECR I-1591 at 1610; Case C-175/88 *Biehl v. Administration des contributions du grand-duché de Luxembourg* [1990] ECR I-1779 at 1792; Case C-27/91 *Union de Recouvrement des Cotisations de Sécurité Sociale et d'Allocations Familiales de la Savoie (URSSAF) v. Hostellerie Le Manoir Sàrl* [1991] ECR I-5531 at 5541–5542; Case C-300/90 *Commission v. Belgium* [1992] ECR I-305 at 317–318; Case C-279/93 *Finanzamt Köln-Altstadt v. Schumacker* [1995] ECR I-225 at 259, and Case C-90/96 *Petrie et al. v. Università degli Studi di Verona et al.* [1997] ECR I-6527.

837. *E.g.* Case 152/73 *Sotgiu v. Deutsche Bundespost* [1974] ECR 153 at 164–165, and Case C-279/93 *Finanzamt Köln-Altstadt v. Schumacker* [1995] ECR I-225 at 259–260.

838. Case 96/85 *Commission v. France* [1986] ECR 1475; Case 143/87 *Stanton et al. v. Inasti* [1988] ECR 3877; Cases 154 and 155/87 *Rijksinstituut voor de Sociale Verzekering der Zelfstandigen v. Wolf et al.* [1988] ECR 3897; Case C-33/88 *Allué et al. v. Università degli Studi di Venezia* [1989] ECR I-1591 at 1610; Case C-204/90 *Bachmann v. Belgian State* [1992] ECR I-249, and Case C-300/90 *Commission v. Belgium* [1992] ECR I-305.

839. *E.g.* Case C-19/92 *Kraus v. Land Baden-Württemberg* [1993] ECR I-1663; Cases C-259, 331 and 332/91 *Allué et al. v. Università degli Studi di Venezia et al.* [1993] ECR I-

Thus in Case C-19/92 *Kraus v. Land Baden-Württemberg*[840] the Court held that in principle Articles 48 and 52 EC precluded a national rule, even though it applied without distinction, concerning the right to use an academic title which was 'liable to hamper or to render less attractive the exercise by Community nationals, including those of the Member State which enacted the measure, of fundamental freedoms guaranteed by the Treaty.'

The prohibition of discrimination on the ground of nationality is worked out in considerable detail in Regulation 1612/68. The most important provisions of the regulation, which have been the subject of considerable judicial scrutiny, are those concerning the employment, equality of treatment and rights of members of a worker's family. Quotas restricting employment of foreigners in any undertaking, branch of activity or region, or at a national level are inapplicable to nationals of other Member States.[841] Article 7(1) of the regulation, which requires equal treatment in respect of any conditions of employment and work, and in particular regarding remuneration, dismissal and, in the event of unemployment, reinstatement or re-employment, has been broadly interpreted, covering, for example, absence for military service[842]; special protection granted on social grounds to specified categories of workers,[843] and separation allowances.[844] The concepts of social advantages[845] and tax

4309; Case C-272/92 *Spotti v. Freistaat Bayern* [1993] ECR I-5185, and Case C-90/96 *Petrie et al. v. Università degli Studi di Verona et al.* [1997] ECR I-6527).

840. [1993] ECR I-1663 at 1697.
841. Reg. 1612/68, Art. 4(1). Thus a 'grandfather clause' requiring employers to hire local labour will infringe this provision. But in Case 31/87 *Gebroeders Beentjes BV v. State of the Netherlands* [1988] ECR 4635 at 4659 (in the context of a public procurement contract) the Court noted that the obligation to employ long-term unemployed persons could *inter alia* infringe what is now Art. 6 EC if only tenderers from the state concerned could satisfy that requirement or tenderers from other Member States would have difficulty in complying with such a condition; otherwise it was acceptable (obviously in the absence of discrimination against those on the unemployment register who are nationals of other Member States). Reg. 1612/68, Art. 5 requires job seekers from other Member States to be given the same assistance by employment offices as that which the latter offer to job seekers from the host Member State.
842. Case 15/69 *Württembergische Milchverwertung-Südmilch-AG v. Ugliola* [1969] ECR 363, [1970] CMLR 194. See further, Case C-315/94 *De Vos v. Stadt Bielefeld* [1996] ECR I-1417 and Case C-248/96 *Grahame et al. v. Bestuur van de Nieuwe Algemene Bedrijfsvereniging* [1997] ECR I-6407.
843. Case 44/72 *Marsman v. Rosskamp* [1972] ECR 1243 at 1248.
844. Case 152/73 *Sotgiu v. Deutsche Bundespost* [1974] ECR 153 at 163-164.
845. As to social advantages, see *e.g.* Case 32/75 *Christini v. SNCF* [1975] ECR 1085 at 1094-1095 (fare reduction cards for large families); Case 63/76 *Inzirillo v. Caisse d'Allocations Familiales de l'Arondissement de Lyon* [1976] ECR 2057 at 2068 (allowance for the handicapped); Case 207/78 *Ministère public v. Even et al.* [1979] ECR 2019 at 2033-2034 (war veteran's benefits not social advantages within the meaning of Reg. 1612/68, Art. 7(2)); Case 65/81 *Reina et al. v. Landeskredietbank Baden-Württemberg*

advantages,[846] which Article 7(2) of the regulation requires to be available on equal terms has also given rise to considerable case-law. These provisions apply solely to a worker and his or her family;[847] but they do not benefit descendants of a worker who have reached the age of 21 and are no longer dependent on that worker, if they themselves do not have the status of workers;[848] nor do they benefit those moving in search of employment, as they qualify for equal treatment only in relation to access to employment in accordance with Article 48 EC and Articles 2 and 5 of Regulation 1612/68.[849] On myriad occasions the Court has had to consider social advantages in relation to the admission to and equal treatment at education facilities of children of migrant workers.[850] Students and those

[1982] ECR 33 at 44–45 (childbirth loans, even where the grant was discretionary); Case 249/83 *Hoeckx v. Openbaar Centrum voor Maatschappelijk Welzijn, Kalmthout* [1985] ECR 973; Case 137/84 *Ministère public v. Mutsch* [1985] ECR 2681 at 2696 (right to use another language in court proceedings when nationals of the host Member State could also exercise that right); Case 59/85 *State of the Netherlands v. Reed* [1986] ECR 1283 at 1303 (possibility for an unmarried companion to reside with the worker); Case 39/86 *Lair v. Universität Hannover* [1988] ECR 3161 at 3196–3197, Case 197/86 *Brown v. Secretary of State for Scotland* [1988] ECR 3205 at 3245, Case C-357/89 *Raulin v. Minister van Onderwijs en Wetenschappen* [1992] ECR I-1027 at 1061–1062 (maintenance and training grant for University studies leading to a professional qualification (although the non-discrimination requirement of Art. 6 EC only applies to enrolment and other fees, such as tuition fees, charged for access to the course)), Case C-3/90 *Bernini v. Minister van Onderwijs en Wetenschappen* [1992] ECR I-1071 at 1105–1107 (*ibid.*, particularly in relation to continuing parental support); Case C-326/90 *Commission v. Belgium* [1992] ECR I-5517 at 5527 (diverse allowances); Case C-315/94 *De Vos v. Stadt Bielefeld* [1996] ECR I-1417 (military service allowances); Case C-237/94 *O'Flynn v. Adjudication Officer* [1996] ECR I-2617 (funeral payment), and Case C-278/94 *Commission v. Belgium* [1996] ECR I-4307 (special employment programmes). The emphasis has moved over the years from merely facilitating the mobility of workers to positively promoting the integration of workers in the host Member State (this is particularly evident in *Mutsch* and *Reed, supra*). See O'Keeffe (1985) 5 YBEL 93 and Peers (1997) 22 ELRev. 157.

846. See Case C-175/88 *Biehl v. Administration des contributions du grand-duché de Luxembourg* [1990] ECR I-1779, [1990] 3 CMLR 143; Case 204/90 *Bachmann v. Belgian State* [1992] ECR I-249; Case C-300/90 *Commission v. Belgium* [1992] ECR I-305 at 317–318; Case C-112/91 *Werner v. Finanzamt Aachen-Innenstadt* [1993] ECR I-429; Case C-279/93 *Finanzamt Köln-Altstadt v. Schumacker* [1995] ECR I-225 at 259, and Case C-336/96 *Gilly et al. v. Directeur des Services Fiscaux du Bas-Rhin* [1998] ECR I-nyr (12 May 1998). See also p. 737, *post*.

847. *E.g.* Case 261/83 *Castelli v. Office National des Pensions pour Travailleurs Salariés (ONPTS)* [1984] ECR 3199 at 3213; Case 157/84 *Frascogna v. Caisse des dépôts et consignations* [1985] ECR 1739 at 1749; Case 94/84 *Office national de l'emploi v. Deak* [1985] ECR 1873 at 1886, and Case C-3/90 *Bernini v. Minister van Onderwijs en Wetenschappen* [1992] ECR I-1071 at 1106–1108.

848. Case 316/85 *Centre public d'aide sociale de Courcelles v. Lebon* [1987] ECR 2811 at 2836.

849. *Ibid.* at 2839.

850. *E.g.* Case 9/74 *Casagrande* [1974] ECR 773, [1974] 2 CMLR 423; Case 39/86 *Lair v. Universität Hannover* [1988] ECR 3161, [1989] 3 ECR 545; Case 197/86 *Brown v.*

in private education are regarded as falling under the freedom to receive services, as they are recipients of educational services.[851] Article 7(3) of the regulation specifically requires equal treatment in access to training in vocational schools and retraining centres.[852] The case-law in this area has been further developed through the interpretation of what is now Article 127 EC.[853] Article 7(4) makes any clause of collective or individual agreements or any other collective regulation concerning eligibility for employment, employment, remuneration and other conditions of work or dismissal null and void in so far as it lays down discriminatory conditions concerning workers who are nationals of other Member States.[854] Trade union and representation rights are set out in Article 8 of the regulation.[855] Equal treatment in access to housing, ownership of housing which the worker needs, and in the right to put his or her name down on a housing list is guaranteed by Article 9 of Regulation 1612/68.[856]

The members of a worker's family are covered by Articles 10–12 of Regulation 1612/68. The spouse[857] and the descendants of him or her and the worker who are under the age of 21 or are dependents, and dependent

---

Secretary of State for Scotland [1988] ECR 3205, [1988] 3 CMLR 403; Case 235/87 *Matteucci* [1988] ECR 5589, [1989] 1 CMLR 357, and Case C-3/90 *Bernini v. Minister van Onderwijs en Wetenschappen* [1992] ECR I-1071.

851. See section 7, *post*, and Chapter section 5.3.1, *ante*.

852. A 'vocational school' means solely establishments which provide only instruction interposed between periods of employment or else closely connected with employment, during apprenticeship, thus university studies which prepare for a qualification for a particular profession, trade or employment or which provide the necessary training and skills for such a profession, trade or employment constitute vocational training, but universities are not vocational schools for the purposes of Reg. 1612/68, Art. 7(3), Case 197/86 *Brown v. Secretary of State for Scotland* [1988] ECR 3205 at 3242 (see also the general discussion of university education at 3241–3142, citing earlier case-law). See further, Case 39/86 *Lair v. Universität Hannover* [1988] ECR 3161 at 3200 (the right of access under Art. 7(3) does not depend on the continued existence of an employment relationship, thus migrant workers are guaranteed certain rights linked to the status of a worker even when they are no longer employed).

853. Previously Art. 128 EEC. See Case 39/86 *Lair v. Universität Hannover* [1988] ECR 3161 at 3200, and Case C-357/89 *Raulin v. Minister van Onderwijs en Wetenschappen* [1992] ECR I-1027 at 1065. See further, pp. 1077–1080.

854. See Case C-15/96 *Schöning-Kougebetopoulou v. Freie und Hansestadt Hamburg* [1998] ECR I-47.

855. See Case 149/79 *Commission v. Belgium* [1980] ECR 3881 at 3902; Case C-213/90 *ASTI (Association de Soutien aux Travailleurs Immigrés) v. Chambre des Employés Privés* [1991] ECR I-3507 at 3530–3531, and Case C-118/92 *Commission v. Luxembourg* [1994] ECR I-1891 at 1897–1898. See also Case 36/75 *Rutili v. Minister for the Interior* [1975] ECR 1219 at 1232.

856. See Case 305/87 *Commission v. Greece* [1989] ECR 1461 at 1478; see also Case 63/86 *Commission v. Italy* [1988] ECR 29 at 32 (Commission's claim admitted by Italy), and 50 (proceedings on this point discontinued after amendment of Italian legislation).

857. As to unmarried partners, see Case 59/85 *State of the Netherlands v. Reed* [1986] ECR 1283 at 1303. It is submitted that 'unmarried companion' is not confined to a companion of the opposite sex.

relatives in the ascending line of the worker and his or her spouse have the right, irrespective of their nationality, to install themselves with a worker who is a national of one Member State and who is employed in another Member State.[858] In fact it is not only in relation to education that myriad cases deal with social advantages for workers or indeed for members of their families.[859] If a national of a Member State is a worker or is self-employed in the territory of another Member State, the spouse and those of the children who are under 21 or dependent on the former are entitled to take up an activity as an employed person throughout the territory of that Member State, even if they are not nationals of any Member State.[860] The family of the worker also falls within the personal scope of the coordination arrangements relating to social security rights.[861] Both in

858. Reg. 1612/68, Art. 10(1). The Member States are obliged to facilitate the admission of any member of the family not falling within Art. 10(1) if that person is dependent on the worker or living under his or her roof in the country whence he or she comes, Art. 10(2). As to the meaning of 'dependant', see Case 316/85 *Centre public d'aide sociale de Courcelles v. Lebon* [1987] ECR 2811 at 2838–2839. See further *e.g.* Case 131/85 *Gül v. Regierungspräsident Düsseldorf* [1986] ECR 1573, [1987] 1 CMLR 501; Case 235/87 *Matteucci* [1988] ECR 5589, [1989] 1 CMLR 357; Case 249/86 *Commission v. Germany* [1989] ECR 1263, [1990] 3 CMLR 540, and Cases C-64 and 65/96 *Land Nordrhein-Westfalen et al. v. Uecker et al.* [1997] ECR I-3171.

859. *E.g.* Case 63/76 *Inzirillo v. Caisse d'Allocations Familiales de l'Arrondissement de Lyon* [1976] ECR 2057; Case 107/78 *Ministère public v. Even et al.* [1979] ECR 2019 at 2034 (the advantages extended to nationals of other Member States who are migrant workers 'are all those which, whether or not linked to a contract of employment, are generally granted to national workers primarily because of their objective status as workers or by virtue of the mere fact of their residence on the national territory and the extension of which to workers who are nationals of other Member States therefore seems suitable to facilitate their mobility within the Community'); Case 65/81 *Reina et al. v. Landeskredietbank Baden-Württemberg* [1982] ECR 33 at 45 (the concept of 'social advantage' in Reg. 1612/68, Art. 7(2)), encompasses not only the benefits accorded by virtue of a right but also those granted on a discretionary basis'); Case 249/83 *Hoeckx v. Openbaar Centrum voor Maatschappelijk Welzijn, Kalmthout* [1985] ECR 973; Case 261/83 *Castelli v. ONPTS* [1984] ECR 3199: Case 122/84 *Scrivner et al. v. Centre public d'aide sociale de Chastre* [1985] ECR 1027; Case 94/84 *Office national de l'emploi v. Deak* [1985] ECR 1873; Case 157/84 *Frascogna v. Caisse des dépôts et consignations* [1985] ECR 1739 and Case 137/84 *Ministère public v. Mutsch* [1985] ECR 2681, [1986] 1 CMLR 648; Case 63/86 *Commission v. Italy* [1988] ECR 29, [1989] 2 CMLR 601; Case 263/86 *Belgian State v. Humbel* [1988] ECR 5365; [1989] 1 CMLR 393; Case 235/87 *Matteucci v. Communauté française of Belgium et al.* [1988] ECR 5589, [1989] 1 CMLR 357, and Case C-57/96 *Meints v. Minister van Landbouw, Natuurbeheer en Visserij* [1997] ECR I-6689.

860. Reg. 1612/68, Art. 11. See *e.g.* Case 131/85 *Gül v. Regierungspräsident Düsseldorf* [1986] ECR 1573, [1987] 1 CMLR 501; Case 235/87 *Matteucci v. Communauté française de Belgique et al.* [1988] ECR 5589, [1989] 1 CMLR 357; Case 249/86 *Commission v. Germany* [1989] ECR 1263, [1990]3 CMLR 540, and Cases C-64 and 65/96 *Land Nordrhein-Westfalen et al. v. Uecker et al.* [1997] ECR I-3171.

861. Reg. 1408/71 (O.J. English Special Edition 1971 (II), p. 416, most recently consolidated and substituted by Reg. 118/97 (O.J. 1997 L 28/1), and most recently amended by Reg. 1223 (O.J. 1998 L 168/1)), Art. 2(1).

relation to rights under Regulation 1612/68 and under the social security arrangements, family rights are derived rights, thus they depend on the worker having the status of a worker, and they cease if the worker ceases to enjoy that status.[862] Finally, Article 12 of Regulation 1612/68 requires equal treatment in admission to the host Member State's general educational, apprenticeship and vocational training courses, if the children are residing in the territory of the host Member State.[863] This provision also embraces University education.[864]

A key requirement of Regulation 1612/68 is the prohibition of national rules or practices which limit application for and offers of employment, or the right of foreign nationals to take up and pursue employment, or subject these to conditions not applicable to the host Member State's own nationals, or of rules or practices which, though applicable irrespective of nationality, have the exclusive or principle aim or effect of keeping nationals of other Member States away from the employment offered.[865] Sometimes specific requirements are prescribed for the exercise of a particular profession in employment, such as in the case of employed medical doctors. Article 6(1) of the regulation prohibits the engagement and recruitment of a national of one Member State in another being made dependent on medical, vocational or other criteria which are discriminatory on grounds of nationality by comparison with those criteria applied to nationals of the host Member State wishing to pursue the same activity.[866]

Article 45 of Regulation 1612/68 obliges the Commission to submit proposals to the Council for measures seeking to abolish obstacles to the free movement of workers resulting from the absence of mutual recognition

---

862. See Case 40/76 *Kermaschek v. Bundesanstalt für Arbeit* [1976] ECR 1669 at 1676–1677. As to the right of workers and their families to remain after the worker has been employed, see Reg. 1251/70 (O.J. English Special Edition 1970 (II), p. 402). See further, Cases C-297/88 and 197/89 *Dzodzi v. Belgian State* [1990] ECR I-3763 and Case C-171/91 *Tsiotras v. Landeshauptstadt Stuttgart* [1993] ECR I-2925. See also, as to Reg. 1251/70 more generally, Case C-279/89 *Commission v. United Kingdom* [1992] ECR I-5795; Case C-334/94 *Commission v. France* [1996] ECR I-1307, and Case C-151/96 *Commission v. Ireland* [1997] ECR I-3327.

863. See *e.g.* Case 76/72 *S. v. Fonds national de reclassement social des handicapés* [1973] ECR 457; Case 9/74 *Casagrande v. Landeshauptstadt München* [1974] ECR 773; Case 197/86 *Brown v. Secretary of State for Scotland* [1988] ECR 3205, [1988] 3 CMLR 403; Case 263/86 *Belgian State v. Humbel et al.* [1988] ECR 5365, [1989] 1 CMLR 393; Case C-308/89 *Di Leo v. Land Berlin* [1990] ECR I-4185, and Case C-7/94 *Landesamt für Ausbildungsfördeung Land Nordrhein-Westfalen v. Gaal* [1995] ECR I-1031.

864. Cases 389 and 390/87 *Echternach and Moritz v. Netherlands Minister for Education and Science* [1989] ECR 723, [1990] 2 CMLR 305.

865. Reg. 1612/68, Art. 3(1). The linguistic knowledge exception is considered in section 5.3.2, *post*.

866. Although Art. 6(2) permits an employer in a Member State other than that in which a person to whom an offer is made is a national to insist that the person concerned undergo a vocational test, if the request is expressed when the offer of employment is made.

of diplomas, certificates or other evidence of formal qualifications. To this end two general systems of mutual recognition have been adopted[867] which have resolved problems in the many areas not already governed by specific provisions.[868] In other instances the obligation to compare diplomas obtained in the Member State of origin with the requirements in the host Member State is sufficient. The mutual recognition and acceptance concept developed in relation to the freedom to provide services and the freedom of establishment applies also in appropriate cases to the free movement of workers.[869]

5.3.2   Exceptions to market access

In a number of situations a host Member State may invoke exceptions which have the effect of preventing a migrant worker who is admitted to its territory from exercising a particular activity; these concern individual cases. Employment market policy in general, as a part of social policy, falls under the system of Article 118 EC.[870]

Article 48(4) EC provides that the provisions of Article 48 EC 'shall not apply to employment in the public service.'[871] This exception has been narrowly interpreted by the Court of Justice, in line with its approach of interpreting fundamental freedoms broadly and exceptions narrowly.[872] Thus it 'cannot justify discriminatory measures with regard to remuneration or other conditions of employment against workers once they have been admitted to the public service.'[873] The nature of the

---

867. Dir. 89/48 (O.J. 1989 L 19/16) concerning higher education diplomas awarded on completion of professional education and training of at least three years' duration, and Dir. 92/51 (O.J. 1992 L 209/25, most recently amended by Dir. 97/38 (O.J. 1997 L 184/31)) for the recognition of professional education and training. As to further proposed amendments to both of these directives, see COM (97) 638 Final (O.J. 1998 C 28/1). As to Dir. 89/48, see Case C-164/94 Arantis v. Land Berlin [1996] ECR I-135 and Case C-225/95 Kapasakalis v. Greece [1998] ECR I-nyr (2 July 1998).
868. As to which, see section 6.6, post.
869. See Case 222/86 Union national des entraîneurs et Cadres techniques professionnels du football (Unectef) v. Heylens et al. [1987] ECR 4097 at 4116.
870. See Chapter IX, section 6, post.
871. See the Commission's Communication (O.J. 1988 C 72/2) and inter alia Everling (1990) Deutsches Verwaltungsblatt 225; Handoll (1988) 13 ELRev. 223; Groenendijk (1989) NILRev. 107; Lenz (1989/2) LIEI 75, and O'Keeffe in Curtin and O'Keeffe (eds.), Constitutional Adjudication in European Community and National Law (Essays for O'Higgins, Dublin, 1992) 89. Cf. the different wording of Art. 55 EC in relation to the self-employed, as to which, see section 6.5.2, post.
872. E.g. Case 66/85 Lawrie-Blum v. Land Baden-Württemberg [1986] ECR 2121 at 2146.
873. Case 152/73 Sotgiu v. Deutsche Bundespost [1974] ECR 153 at 162; Case C-248/96 Grahame et al. v. Bestuur van de Nieuwe Algemene Bedrijfsvereniging [1997] ECR I-6407. See also Case C-187/96 Commission v. Greece [1998] ECR I-1095.

employment relationship with the administration is immaterial[874] as otherwise the Member States would in practice be able to extend at will the number of posts covered by Article 48(4) EC.[875] Article 48(4) EC applies to 'a series of posts which involve direct or indirect participation in the exercise of powers conferred by public law and duties designed to safeguard the general interests of the State or of other public authorities.' Such posts in fact presume on the part of those occupying them the existence of a special relationship of allegiance to the state and reciprocity of rights and duties which form the foundation of the bond of nationality.[876] Thus Article 48(4) does not, for example, cover railway workers, gardeners or painters;[877] teachers;[878] general careers in the utilities sectors,[879] or nurses.[880] It does on the other hand cover certain supervisory or security functions (including even that of night watchman) or a position as a municipal architect,[881] as well as management and state advisory functions in public research bodies.[882]

The broad interpretation given to the prohibition in Article 48 EC, which points in the direction of a prohibition also covering measures which apply without distinction, is somewhat counterbalanced by the acceptance of rule of reason type exceptions.[883] Thus an exception in the interest of the coherence of the fiscal system has been introduced by the Court.[884]

874. *Ibid.* at 163. See also Case 307/84 *Commission v. France* [1986] ECR 1725 at 1738.
875. Case 307/84 *Commission v. France* [1986] ECR 1725 at 1738.
876. Case 149/79 *Commission v. Belgium* [1980] ECR 3881 at 3900. Work experience in the public service of another Member State must be taken into account on an equal footing with experience in that of the host Member State, see Case C-419/92 *Scholz v. Opera Universitaria di Cagliari et al.* [1994] ECR I-505 at 521–522, and Case C-15/96 *Schöning-Kougebetopoulou v. Freie und Hansestadt Hamburg* [1998] ECR I-47 at 68.
877. Case 149/79 *Commission v. Belgium* [1982] ECR 1845 at 1852 (2nd judgment).
878. *E.g.* Case 66/85 *Lawrie-Blum v. Land Baden-Württemberg* [1986] ECR 2121 at 2147 (trainee teachers); Case 33/88 *Allué et al. v. Università degli Studi di Venezia* [1989] ECR 1591 at 1609–1610 (foreign language assistants); Case C-4/91 *Bleis v. Ministère de l'Éducation Nationale* [1991] ECR I-5627 at 5641 (secondary school teachers), and Case C-473/93 *Commission v. Luxembourg* [1996] ECR I-3207 at 3257–3258 (primary school teachers). The same clearly applies in respect of University teachers.
879. Case C-473/93 *Commission v. Luxembourg* [1996] ECR I-3207 at 3257; Case C-173/94 *Commission v. Belgium* [1996] ECR I-3265 at 3282, and Case C-290/94 *Commission v. Greece* [1996] ECR I-3285 at 3327–3328.
880. Case 307/84 *Commission v. France* [1986] ECR 1725 at 1739.
881. Case 149/79 *Commission v. Belgium* [1982] ECR 1837 at 1851 (2nd judgment).
882. Case 225/85 *Commission v. Italy* [1987] ECR 2625 at 2639, (but see the situation of research workers, *ibid.* at 2639–2640).
883. See section 1.1, *ante.*
884. Case C-204/90 *Bachmann v. Belgian State* [1992] ECR I-249 at 282–284; Case C-300/90 *Commission v. Belgium* [1992] ECR I-305 at 319–320. This had the effect of upholding the national system. See also Case C-336/96 *Gilly et al. supra* note 846. But see Case C-175/88 *Biehl v. Administration des contributions du grand-duché de Luxembourg* [1990] ECR I-1779 at 1793 and Case C-279/93 *Finanzamt Köln-Altstadt v. Schumacker* [1995] ECR I-225 at 261–262.

The Court has found that the provisions of the EC Treaty do not preclude legitimate measures, such as those intended to ensure the proper management of universities, but the principle of proportionality required that they be necessary and appropriate to the objective pursued.[885] In similar vein, the general interest of ensuring compliance with legitimate professional rules of conduct will be acceptable, provided that the rules are objectively necessary and account is taken of guarantees offered by professional supervision in the home Member State.[886] The protection of the public against the abuse of academic titles has been recognized as being in principle a legitimate interest, subject to the proportionality of the authorization requirements.[887] Thus the Court is not inclined to allow the free movement rules to be used as a rogues' charter. Accordingly, U-turn constructions simply designed to escape from legitimate national requirements in a person's home Member State will not be supported by the Court, at least in the absence of specific Community legislation conferring rights on the basis of possession of a particular qualification.[888]

Finally, Community secondary legislation may provide for exceptions in certain circumstances. Thus the linguistic knowledge exception to the key requirement of Article 3(1) of Regulation 1612/68 mentioned at the end of section 5.3.1, above, must be borne in mind. That exception permits 'conditions relating to linguistic knowledge required by reason of the nature of the post to be filled.' As it is an exception to a general rule, it should have been interpreted narrowly, so as to apply in respect of the specific post concerned. However, in Case C-379/87 *Groener v. Minister for Education et al.*[889] the Court accepted a policy requiring a knowledge of Irish, even though it was being enforced in the instant case in respect of an

885. Cases C-259/91 *etc. Allué et al. v. Università degli Studi di Venezia et al.* [1993] ECR I-4309 at 4334. See also Case 33/88 *Allué et al. v. Università degli Studi di Venezia* [1989] ECR 1591 at 1610–1611 and Case C-272/92 *Spotti v. Freistaat Bayern* [1993] ECR I-5185 at 5208, in which somewhat specious arguments that special treatment of particular categories was necessary to ensure that knowledge is up to date found no favour with the Court.
886. Case C-106/91 *Ramrath v. Ministre de la Justice* [1992] ECR I-3351 at 3384–3385 (building on earlier case-law, and paralleling the approach taken in relation to risks of circumventing legitimate requirements, explained further in sections 6.5.2 and 7.4.2, *post*).
887. Case C-19/92 *Kraus v. Land Baden-Württemberg* [1993] ECR I-1663 at 1697–1699.
888. Case C-19/92 *Kraus v. Land Baden-Württemberg* [1993] ECR I-1663 at 1696–1697. As to the situation where there is specific Community legislation, see Case 115/78 *Knoors v. Staatssecretaris voor Economische Zaken* [1979] ECR 399, [1979] 2 CMLR 357; Case 246/80 *Broekmeulen v. Huisarts Registratie Commissie* [1981] ECR 2311, [1982] 1 CMLR 91, and Case C-61/89 *Bouchoucha* [1990] ECR I-3551, [1992] 1 CMLR 1033. This principle was originally developed in relation to the self-employed, but is also applicable to workers, see *Kraus, loc. cit.*
889. [1989] ECR 3967, [1990] 1 CMLR 401.

appointment at a college in Dublin which functioned entirely in English. The policy was directed at the promotion of the first official language in Ireland (English being recognized as a second official language). The somewhat novel and controversial approach in this case was only partly mitigated by the ruling that the level of knowledge required should not be disproportionate and the insistence that there could be no requirement that the linguistic knowledge required should have been acquired within the national territory.[890]

5.4 The scheme of social security

There would be little point in enabling workers to move freely from one Member State to another if in doing so they were to lose the right to social security benefits such as unemployment benefit and old-age pension rights. Thus Article 51 EC provides for measures to be taken coordinating national social security systems.[891] The main objective of these measures as well must be to remove one of the most important obstacles to the free movement of workers.[892] In Case 92/63 *Nonnenmacher v. Bestuur der Sociale Verzekeringsbank*[893] the Court found that this meant that legislative restrictions which would put migrant workers at a disadvantage had to be

---

890. [1989] ECR 3967 at 3993–3994.
891. Case 1/67 *Ciechelski v. Caisse Régionale de Sécurité Sociale du Centre d'Orléans et al.* [1967] ECR 181 at 188. See, generally, Eichenhofer (ed.), *Reform des Europäischen koordinierenden Sozialrechts* (Berlin, 1993); Pennings, *Introduction to European Social Security Law* (Deventer, 1994); Schoukens and Cornelissen, *Social Protection of the Self-Employed in the European Union* (Deventer, 1994); Wilms in Von der Groeben et al. (eds.), *op. cit.* (see note 756, *supra*) Vol. 1 1209; Cornelissen (1989) SEW 126; Eichenhofer (1991) EuZW 171 and (1992) JZ 269; Gosseries (1993) *Journal des Tribunaux de Travail* 265, and Séché (1993) 509. Clearly, in the scope of this work the present discussion is but a bare outline; reference should be made to the literature cited above for a more extensive discussion. At present the Council acts unanimously on a proposal from the Commission, and the European Parliament does not have to be consulted. The Treaty of Amsterdam (not yet in force) will amend Art. 51 EC so as to apply the co-decision procedure of Art. 189b EC instead.
892. *Ibid.*; Case 2/67 *De Moor v. Caisse de Pension des Employés Privés* [1967] ECR 197 at 206; Case 19/68 *De Cicco v. Landesversicherungsanstalt Schwaben* [1968] ECR 473 at 479, but in the present state of Community law a Member State is entitled to treat its own nationals who have worked in a third country and return home where they no longer work more favourably than their own nationals who have worked in another Member State and likewise return home where they no longer work, Case C-297/92 *Istituto Nazionale della Previdenza Sociale (INPS) v. Baglieri* [1993] ECR I-5211 at 5233. As to interesting examples of the interaction between social security and Arts. 48 and 52 EC in general, see Cases 154 and 155/87 *Rijksinstituut voor de Sociale Verzekeringen der Zelfstandigen v. Wolf et al.* [1988] ECR 3987 and Case 143/87 *Stanton et al. v. Institut National d'Assurances sociales pour Travailleurs Indépendants* [1988] ECR 3877.
893. [1964] ECR 281 at 288.

abolished. Both in this judgment and even more clearly in Case 100/63 *Kalsbeek (née van der Veen) v. Bestuur der Sociale Verzekeringsbank*[894] the Court found that measures implementing Article 51 may not result in workers who exercise their right to free movement losing rights already acquired in any given Member State.[895] The migrant worker may in certain circumstances actually find him or herself in a more favourable position than a national worker.[896]

Initially Article 51 EC was implemented by Regulations 3 and 4 adopted in 1958;[897] the former dealt with the substantive principles and the latter with administrative implementation. In 1971 and 1972 the original regulations (which had in the meantime been subject to numerous modifications) were replaced by Regulations 1408/71[898] and 574/72.[899] Since then both regulations have been changed on so many occasions; the latest codification dates from 1997.[900] In 1981 the scope of the regulations was extended to cover the self-employed and members of their families.[901] The substance of the Community measures does not harmonize national social security systems, but coordinates their application.[902] There was no automatic harmonization at the end of the period envisaged in Article 7a

894. [1964] ECR 565 at 573–574.
895. See also *e.g.* Case 3/70 *Caisse de compensation pour allocations familiales des Charbonnages du Couchant de Mons v. Beninato (née Di Bella)* [1970] ECR 415 at 421; Case 24/75 *Petroni et al. v. Office national des pensions pour travailleurs salariés (ONPTS)* [1975] ECR 1149 at 1160; Case 254/84 *De Jong v. Bestuur van de Sociale Verzekeringsbank* [1986] ECR 671 at 682; Case C-168/88 *Dammer v. VZW Securex Kinderbijslagfonds et al.* [1989] ECR I-4553 at 4576, and Case C-227/89 *Rönfeldt v. Bundesversicherungsanstalt für Angestellte* [1991] ECR I-323 at 343. See further, Case 807/79 *Gravina et al. v. Landesversicherungsanstalt Schwaben* [1980] ECR 2205 at 2218–2219.
896. Case 27/71 *Keller v. Caisse Régionale d'Assurance Vieillesse des Travailleurs Salariés de Strasbourg* [1971] ECR 885 at 891.
897. J.O. 1958, p. 561 and J.O. 1958, p. 597 respectively.
898. In its original version, O.J. English Special Edition 1971(II), p. 416.
899. *Ibid.* 1972(1), p. 159.
900. In Reg. 118/97 (O.J. 1997 L 28/1) which substitutes a new integral text in both original regs. The most recent amendments are contained in Reg. 1223/98 (O.J. 1998 L68/1).
901. Reg. 1390/81 (O.J. 1981 L 143/1). See *e.g.* Case C-15/90 *Middelburgh v. Chief Adjudication Officer* [1991] ECR I-4655 and Case C-121/92 *Staatssecretaris van Financiën v. Zinnecker* [1993] ECR I-5023.
902. Case 9/67 *Colditz v. Caisse d'Assurance Vieillesse des Travailleurs Salariés de Paris* [1967] ECR 229 at 234. See also Case 41/84 *Pinna v. Caisse d'allocations familales de la Savoie* [1986] ECR 1 at 24–25 ('Community rules must refrain from adding to the disparities which already stem from the absence of harmonization of national legislation', *ibid.* at 25). Thus bilateral treaties remain particularly relevant in so far as they are more favourable than the Community system, see Case C-227/89 *Rönfeldt v. Bundesversicherungsanstalt für Angestellte* [1991] ECR I-323 at 343–344. See also Case 21/87 *Borowitz v. Bundesversicherungsanstalt für Angestelte* [1988] ECR 3715 (treaties with third countries).

EC for the completion of the internal market:[903] any harmonization must thus take place on the basis of another provision of the Treaty, such as Articles 100 or 235 EC.

The structure of Regulation 1408/71 is as follows. Title I sets out the definitions of the beneficiaries of the arrangements (such as employed and self-employed persons, refugees, and survivors) and of the key concepts, such as place of residence, competent state, periods of insurance, benefits and pensions, legislation, and admission to voluntary or optional continued insurance.[904] The persons and matters covered are also set out in that Title. As far as the applicability of social security legislation is concerned, the Member States apply different (territorial) starting points: this may in cross-border movements mean that a migrant falls under the legislation of more than one Member State (positive conflict of laws) or even under the legislation of no Member State at all (negative conflict of laws). Given that Regulation 1408/71 does not contain any provision as to its territorial scope, the provisions of Article 227 EC apply. Title I also deals with the most important principles on which the coordination of the national systems is based, namely equality of treatment of persons resident in the territory of a Member State;[905] the relationship between benefits and residence;[906] and the prevention of overlapping of benefits.[907] It also covers certain international agreements which remain unaffected.[908] The treatment

903. Case C-297/92 *Istituto Nazionale della Previdenza Sociale (INPS) v. Baglieri* [1993] ECR I-5211 at 5233.
904. As to the latter, see Case C-297/92 *Istituto Nazionale della Previdenza Sociale (INPS) v. Baglieri* [1993] ECR I-5211.
905. Reg. 1408/71 (as substituted), Art. 3. See *E.g.* Case 41/84 *Pinna v. Caisse d'allocations familales de la Savoie* [1986] ECR 1, [1988] 1 CMLR 350; Case C-105/89 *Haji v. Institut national d'assurances sociales pour travailleurs indépendants* [1990] ECR I-4211; Case C-18/90 *Office national de l'emploi (Onem) v. Kziber* [1991] ECR I-199; Case C-10/90 *Masgio v. Bundesknappschaft* [1991] ECR I-1119; Case C-326/90 *Commission v. Belgium* [1992] ECR I-5517; Case C-165/91 *Van Munster* [1994] ECR I-4611; Case C-308/93 *Bestuur van de Sociale Verzekeringsbank v. Cabanis-Issarte* [1996] ECR I-2097; Case C-126/95 *Hallouzi-Choho v. Bestuur van de Sociale Verzekeringsbank* [1996] ECR I-4807; Cases C-245 and 312/94 *Hoever et al. v. Land Nordrhein-Westfalen* [1996] ECR I-4895, and Case C-131/96 *Romero v. Landesversicherungsanstalt Rheinprovinz* [1997] ECR I-3659. As to workers residing in one Member State but working in another, see Case C-160/96 *Molenaar et al. v. Allgemeine Ortskrankenkasse Baden-Württemberg* [1998] ECR I-880.
906. Case 300/84 *Van Roosmalen v. Bestuur van de Bedrijfsvereniging voor de Gezondheid, Geestelijke en Maatschappelijke Belangen* [1986] ECR 3097.
907. *E.g.* Case 1/67 *Ciechelski v. Caisse Régionale de Sécurité Sociale du Centre d'Orléans et al.* [1967] ECR 181; Case 2/67 *De Moor v. Caisse de Pension des Employés Privés* [1967] ECR 197; Case 238/81 *Raad van Arbeid v. Van der Bunt-Craig* [1983] ECR 1385; Case 296/84 *Sinatra v. Fonds national de retraite des ouvriers mineurs (FNROM)* [1986] ECR 1047; Case C-335/93 *Union Nationale des Mutualités Socialistes v. Del Grosso* [1995] ECR I-939, and Case C-98/94 *Schmidt v. Rijksdienst voor Pensioenen* [1995] ECR I-2561.
908. Reg. 1408/71 (as substituted), Art. 7. See *e.g.* Case C-23/92 *Grana-Nova v. Land-*

of a person as 'employed' or 'self-employed' for social security purposes is determined by the legislation of the Member State in which the activity concerned takes place.[909]

Title II of Regulation 1408/71 deals with the legislation applicable. Article 13 ensures that the persons to whom the regulation applies are subject to the legislation of a single Member State only, without prejudice to their rights under the rules concerning the coordination of the social security systems. The idea behind this approach 'is to avoid any plurality or purposeless overlapping of contributions and liabilities which would result from the simultaneous or alternate application of several legislative systems, and moreover, preventing those concerned, in the absence of legislation applying to them, from remaining without protection in the matter of social security.'[910] This Title also covers rules dealing with conflicts for certain special categories of persons, such as mariners.

The very extensive provisions of Title III set out the special provisions relating to various categories of benefits, such as sickness[911] and maternity;[912] invalidity[913] and old age[914] pensions; accidents at work and occupational diseases; death grants, and unemployment benefits;[915] family

esversicherungsanstalt Hessen [1993] ECR I-4505 and Case C-305/92 Hoorn v. Landesversicherungsanstalt Westfalen [1994] ECR I-1525.

909. This was clearly controversial, see the extensive discussion in Case C-340/94 De Jaeck v. Staatssecretaris van Financiën [1997] ECR I-461 and Case C-221/95 Institut National d'Assurances Sociales pour Travailleurs Indépendants (Inasti) v. Hervein et al. [1997] ECR I-609.

910. Case 50/75 Caisse de pension des employés privés v. Massonet [1975] ECR 1473 at 1482 (correcting the obvious misprint).

911. E.g. Case 22/86 Rindone v. Allgemeine Ortskrankenkasse Bad Urach-Münsingen [1987] ECR 1339; Case C-196/90 Fonds voor Arbeidsongevallen v. De Paep [1991] ECR I-4815; Case C-45/90 Paletta et al. v. Brennet AG [1992] ECR I-3423, and Case C-425/93 Calle Grenzshop Andresen GmbH & Co. KG v. Allgemeine Ortskrankenkasse für den Kreis Schleswig-Flensburg [1995] ECR I-269.

912. E.g. Case 75/63 Hoekstra, née Unger v. Bestuur der Bedrijfsvereniging voor Detailhandel en Ambachten [1964] ECR 177, [1964] CMLR 319; Case C-214/90 Chief Adjudication Officer v. Twomey [1992] ECR I-1823, and Case C-451/93 Delavant v. Allgemeine Ortskrankenkasse für das Saarland [1995] ECR I-1545.

913. E.g. Case 232/82 Baccini v. Office National de l'Emploi (ONEM) [1983] ECR 583; Case C-108/89 Pian v. Office national des pensions [1990] ECR I-1599; Case C-342/88 Rijksdienst voor Pensioenen v. Spits [1990] ECR I-2259; Case C-287/92 Toosey v. Chief Adjudication Officer [1994] ECR I-279, and Case C-12/93 Bestuur van de Nieuwe Algemene Bedrijfsvereniging v. Drake [1994] ECR I-4227.

914. These provisions have been the subject of myriad judgments, most of which are more of individual than general interest. Some, however, are of more general concern, e.g. Case 24/75 Petroni et al. v. Office national des pensions pour travailleurs salariés (ONPTS) [1975] ECR 1149; Case C-165/91 Van Munster [1994] ECR I-4611, and Cases C-31–33/96 Naranjo Arjona et al. v. Instituto Nacional de la Seguridad Social (INSS) et al. [1997] ECR I-5501.

915. E.g. Case 126/77 Frangiamore v. Office National de l'Emploi [1978] ECR 725; Case 388/87 Bestuur van de Nieuwe Algemene Bedrijfsvereniging v. Warmerdam-Steggerda [1989] ECR 1203; Case C-272/90 Van Noorden v. Association pour l'Emploi dans l'Industrie et

and child benefits,[916] and benefits for dependent children of pensioners[917] and for orphans.

Titles IV and V establish two bodies. Without prejudice to the task of competent national courts and tribunals and of the Court of Justice in interpreting Regulation 1408/71, an Administrative Commission on Social Security for Migrant Workers has been established; it can deal with administrative questions and questions of interpretation.[918] Its decisions are non-binding.[919] An Advisory Committee on Social Security for Migrant Workers has also been set up under Article 82 of Regulation 1408/71 and its membership includes representatives of various interested bodies.

Although many of the judgments in this complex and detailed field are more of individual than general importance, some have a general social importance, such as the judgments on the place of residence principle and child benefits.[920] Other judgments have acquired a political flavour because of overt criticism of the judgments by and in certain Member States.[921] Both for migrant workers and for the Member States the problems surrounding social security questions remain somewhat labyrinthine. The

le Commerce (ASSEDIC) de l'Ardèche et de la Drôme [1991] ECR I-2543; Case C-62/91 Gray v. Adjudication Officer [1992] ECR I-2737, and Case C-131/95 Huijbrechts v. Commissie voor de Behandeling van Administratieve Geschillen ingevolge Artikel 41 van de Algemene Bijstandswet in de Provincie Noord-Brabant [1997] ECR I-1409.

916. As a result of the judgment in Case 41/84 Pinna v. Caisse d'allocations familales de la Savoie [1986] ECR 1, [1988] 1 CMLR 350, Reg. 1408/71 was amended by Reg. 3427/89 (O.J. 1989 L 331/1 (since silently repealed by the latest consolidation).) In Pinna the Court had declared what was then Art. 73(2) of the regulation, permitting the place of residence principle to be applied in relation to family members living in another Member State (the approach followed in France) to be incompatible with Community law. See also Case 114/88 Delbar v. Caisse d'allocations familales de Roubaix-Tourcoing [1989] ECR I-4067; Case C-228/88 Bronzino v. Kindergeldkasse [1990] ECR I-531; Case C-78/91 Hughes v. Chief Adjudication Officer, Belfast [1992] ECR I-4839; Cases C-4 and 5/95 Stöber et al. v. Bundesanstalt für Arbeit [1997] ECR I-511; Case C-266/95 Merino Garcia v. Bundesanstalt für Arbeit [1997] ECR I-3279, and Case C-194/96 Kulzer v. Freistaat Bayern [1998] ECR I-895.

917. See Case C-194/96 Kulzer v. Freistaat Bayern [1998] ECR I-895.

918. Reg. 1408/71 (as amended), Arts. 80 and 81. As to the Rules of the Administrative Commission see O.J. 1992 C 61/3. The Administrative Commission publishes reports on its activities annually.

919. See e.g. Case 98/80 Romano v. Institut Nationale d'Assurance Maladie-Invalidité [1981] ECR 1241 at 1256.

920. E.g. Case 41/84 Pinna v. Caisse d'allocations familales de la Savoie [1986] ECR 1, [1988] 1 CMLR 350.

921. This is particularly the case in relation to the case-law on incapacity for work and declarations by a doctor in the country of origin, see Case C-45/90 Paletta et al. v. Brennet AG [1992] ECR I-3423 and Case C-360/90 Arbeiterwohlfahrt der Stadt Berlin Ev v. Bötel [1992] ECR I-3589, as to which, see the editorial comments in (1993) 30 CMLRev. 899 and, more polemically, Bötel in Handelsblatt 13 October 1992; Blum in Der Spiegel 30 November 1992 and Spruch als hebel in Der Spiegel No. 43, 1992. See further, Case C-206/94 Brennet AG v. Paletta [1996] ECR I-2357.

Commission has recently adopted a proposal for a directive to ensure that employees and the self-employed retain supplementary pension rights on migration within the European Union.[922] It has also proposed that the scope of Regulation 1408/71 be extended to embrace third-country nationals resident in a Member State.[923]

6. THE RIGHT OF ESTABLISHMENT

The free movement of persons mentioned in Article 3(c) EC is not restricted to those in employment. The self-employed and undertakings are also offered the opportunity of exercising economic activities within the internal market. The right of establishment, provided for in Articles 52–58 EC sets out the framework within which this takes place. The freedom of establishment has much in common with the freedom to provide (and receive) services. Both involve the free exercise of a trade or profession. The framers of the EC Treaty dealt with them successively, linking them by means of an incorporation by reference of certain provisions applying to establishment.[924] The linkage was made more permanent by the SEA. Besides this linkage within the provisions on free movement of persons,[925] the influence of the market (particularly the increase in invisible transactions) and the development of the mutual recognition or acceptance principle in the case-law of the Court of Justice have over the years caused a closer relationship to develop between the provisions on the freedom to provide services and those on the free movement of goods. This has been particularly evident in the telecommunications sector. Yet despite this apparent tendency towards a uniform approach, there are divergences which will become apparent over the following sections. Thus section 6.1 examines the meaning of establishment, and section 6.2 deals with the beneficiaries of that right, below. Sections 6.3 and 6.4 below then turn to an analysis of substantive provisions, and a distinction is drawn between the primary and secondary scope of the right of establishment in sections 6.5 and 6.6, below. Harmonization of company law is examined separately in section 6.7, below.

---

922. COM (97) 486 Final (O.J. 1998 C 5/4, amended COM (98) 325 Final).
923. COM (97) 561 Final (O.J. 1998 C 6/15).
924. Art. 66 EC incorporates Arts. 55–58 EC into the provisions on services.
925. A good example of how the principles relating to the free movement of persons inter-act can be seen in Case C-415/93 *Union Royale Belge des Sociétés de Football Association ASBL et al. v. Bosman et al.* [1995] ECR I-4921, [1996] 1 CMLR 645. Earlier judgments in which the legal position of the persons concerned was less clear, were based on Arts. 6, 48, 52 and 59 EC, *e.g.* Case 36/74 *Walrave and Koch v. Association Union Cycliste Internationale et al.* [1974] ECR 1405, [1975] 1 CMLR 320 and Case C-370/90 *R. v. Immigration Appeal Tribunal and Singh, ex parte Secretary of State for the Home Department* [1992] ECR I-4265, [1992] 3 CMLR 358.

6.1 The concept of establishment[926]

The concept of establishment embraces activities other than in the course of employment, on the part of natural and legal persons. The decisive criterion in deciding whether a particular activity falls under the heading of establishment is whether the presence of the person or undertaking in the host Member State is on a permanent basis or not.[927] Thus, in Case 205/84 *Commission v. Germany*[928] the Court concluded that an undertaking of one Member State which maintains a permanent presence in another Member State falls within the scope of the provisions on establishment (rather than the provision of services), even if the presence were not in the form of a branch or agency, but merely of an office managed by the undertaking's own staff or by an independent person authorized to act on a permanent basis for the undertaking. In those circumstances, such an undertaking could not avail itself of Articles 59 and 60 EC with regard to those activities.[929] Subsequently, the Court stated that the concept of establishment involved 'the actual pursuit of an economic activity through a fixed establishment in another Member State for an indefinite period.'[930] This latter statement clearly applies to natural and legal persons alike. But the scope of establishment is not limited to economic activities as such. Thus '[u]nder Community law every national of a Member State is assured of freedom both to enter another Member State in order to pursue an employed or self-employed activity and to reside there after having pursued

926. Recent writings in this area have been principally in German. See, generally, contributions by Everling and Roth in Schoen (ed.), *Gedächtnisschrift Brigitte Knobbe-Keuk* (Cologne, 1997) 607 and 729 respectively; Troberg in Von der Groeben *et al.* (eds.), *op. cit.* (see note 756, *supra*) Vol. 1 1261; Everling (1990) *Der Betrieb* 1853; Knobbe-Keuk (1990) *Der Betrieb* 2573; Moitinho de Almeida in Rosenlv *et al.* (eds.), *Festskrift til Ole Due* (Copenhagen, 1994) 241; Nachbaur (1991) EuZW 470; Ress (1990) EuZW 521; Roth (1997) ZBB 373; Steindorff (1988) EuR 19, and Wägenbaur (1991) EuZW 427

927. See in particular Case C-55/94 *Gebhard v. Consiglio dell'Ordine degli Avvocati e Procurati di Milano* [1995] ECR I-4165 at 4195. There the Court made it clear that the temporary nature of the provision of services did not mean that the service provider could not equip him or herself with some form of infrastructure in the host Member State, including as an office, chambers or consulting rooms, in so far as that was necessary for the purposes of performing the services concerned.

928. [1986] ECR 3755 at 3801.

929. *Ibid.*

930. Case C-221/89 *R. v. The Secretary of State for Transport, ex parte Factortame Ltd. et al.* [1991] ECR I-3905 at 3965. In Case C-55/94 *Gebhard v. Consiglio dell'Ordine degli Avvocati e Procurati di Milano* [1995] ECR I-41656 at 4194 the Court stated that the provisions on services are subordinate to those on establishment in two respects: the wording of the 1st para. of Art. 59 EC assumes that the provider and the recipient of services are established in two different Member States; and the 1st para. of Art. 60 EC specifies that the provisions on services apply only if those on establishment do not.

such an activity. Access to leisure activities is a corollary to that freedom of movement.'[931]

6.2   Beneficiaries of the right of establishment

It can be deduced from the first paragraph of Article 52 EC that all nationals of Member States enjoy the right of establishment. This also embraces those who are nationals of a Member State and a third country;[932] it even applies if the persons concerned reside outside the Community.[933]

Natural persons may have a secondary place of establishment in such forms as agencies, subsidiary undertakings or branches. The right to set up an secondary establishment remains limited to nationals of a Member State who are established in the territory of a Member State.[934] Nationals of Member State A who have exercised an activity in another Member State may exercise freely their right to (re-)establish themselves in their home Member State. This extensive interpretation of the freedom of establishment is principally of importance for those activities in respect of which no harmonization of laws has yet been adopted. Member State A may however prevent its nationals misusing this right by simply seeking to escape from the scope of application of national legislation by means of the so-called 'U-turn' constructions.[935] Nationals who do not leave their

931. Case C-334/94 *Commission v. France* [1996] ECR I-1307 at 1341 and Case C-151/96 *Commission v. Ireland* [1997] ECR I-3327 at 3339–3340.
932. Case C-369/90 *Micheletti et al. v. Delegación del Gobierno en Cantabria* [1992] ECR I-4239 at 4262–4263.
933. As to requirements of a single place of establishment, see Case 107/83 *Ordre des Avocats au Barreau de Paris v. Klopp* [1984] ECR 2971, [1985] 1 CMLR 99 and Case C-106/91 *Ramrath v. Ministre de la Justice* [1992] ECR I-3351, [1992] 3 CMLR 173. See also, more generally, Case C-55/94 *Gebhard v. Consiglio dell'Ordine degli Avvocati e Procurati di Milano* [1995] ECR I-4165. External residence makes no difference, as the criterion is the nationality of the person concerned, not his or her place of residence. Thus a Belgian doctor residing in the United States may establish him or herself in the United Kingdom, but an American doctor residing in Belgium would not be able to claim a right of establishment under Community law.
934. Art. 52 EC, 1st para., 2nd sentence. Thus a Greek doctor residing and practising in Lebanon may not open a subsidiary practice in Italy. This requirement of establishment is also to be found in Art. 59 EC on the freedom to provide services, as to which, see section 7, *post*.
935. The freedoms conferred by Community law are not a charter for charlatans. If, though, Community legislation as such permits access on the basis of a qualification, irrespective of the Community nationality of the person concerned, the right conferred by that qualification applies, irrespective of whether the national of Member State A acquired the qualification in Member State B in order, say, to circumvent a national *numerus clausus* rule. See *e.g.* Case 115/78 *Knoors v. Secretary of State for Economic Affairs* [1979] ECR 379, [1979] 2 CMLR 357; Case 246/80 *Broekmeulen v. Huisarts*

own Member State, and thus do not exercise activities in another Member State, do not fall within the ambit of Article 52 EC, as they are in a purely internal situation.[936]

As to companies or firms, they are treated on the same footing as natural persons for the purposes of the right of establishment.[937] For this they must satisfy two conditions. The first concerns their form and the profit motive: the second paragraph of Article 58 EC defines 'companies or firms' as those 'constituted under civil or commercial law, including cooperative societies, and other legal persons governed by public or private law, save for those which are non-profit-making.' Thus they do not need to have the form of a company as such, and the decisive criterion is clearly the profit motive.[938] The second condition concerns the nationality of the entity: the first paragraph of Article 58 EC provides that they must be formed in accordance with the law of a Member State and have their registered office, central administration or principal place of business within the Community. The registered office 'serves as the connecting factor with the legal system of a particular State, like nationality in the case of natural persons.'[939] This means that companies and other legal persons from third countries cannot rely on Articles 52–58 EC.[940] The Community may, however, enter into agreements with third countries in this field.

Registratie Commissie [1981] ECR 2311, [1982] 1 CMLR 91; Case C-61/89 *Bouchoucha* [1990] ECR I-3551, [1992] 1 CMLR 1033, and Case C-370/90 *R. v. Immigration Appeal Tribunal and Singh, ex parte Secretary of State for the Home Department* [1992] ECR I-4265, [1992] 3 CMLR 358. As to the general concern about enforcement of legitimate rules on matters such as professional ethical conduct, see *e.g.* Case 33/74 *Van Binsbergen v. Bestuur van de Bedrijfsvereniging voor de Metaalnijverheid* [1974] ECR 1299, [1975] 1 CMLR 298; Case 71/76 *Thieffry v. Conseil de l'Ordre des Avocats à la Cour de Paris* [1977] ECR 765, [1977] 2 CMLR 373; Case 107/83 *Ordre des Avocats au Barreau de Paris v. Klopp* [1984] ECR 2971, [1985] 1 CMLR 99; Case 292/86 *Gullung v. Conseils de l'ordre des avocats au barreau de Colmar et de Saverne* [1988] ECR 111, [1988] 2 CMLR 57; Case C-76/90 *Säger v. Dennemeyer & Co. Ltd.* [1991] ECR I-4221, [1993] 3 CMLR 639; Case C-19/92 *Kraus v. Land Baden-Württemberg* [1993] ECR I-1663; Case C-55/94 *Gebhard v. Consiglio dell'Ordine degli Avvocati e Procurati di Milano* [1995] ECR I-4165, [1996] 1 CMLR 603, and Case C-3/95 *Reisebüro Broede v. Sandker* [1996] ECR I-6511.

936. *E.g.* Case 20/87 *Ministère public v. Gauchard* [1987] ECR 4879, [1989] 2 CMLR 489; Case 204/87 *Bekaert* [1988] ECR 2029; Cases C-54 and 91/88 and 14/89 *Nino et al.* [1990] ECR I-3537, [1992] 1 CMLR 83; Case C-147/91 *Laderer* [1992] ECR I-4097, and Case C-152/94 *Van Buynder* [1995] ECR I-3981.

937. Art. 58 EC, 1st para.

938. See Case C-70/95 *Sodemare SA et al. v. Regione Lombardia* [1997] ECR I-3395.

939. Case 270/83 *Commission v. France* [1986] ECR 273 at 304; Case 79/85 *Segers v. Bestuur van de Bedrijfsvereniging voor Bank- en Verzekeringswezen, Groothandel en Vrije Beroepen* [1986] ECR 2375 at 2387.

940. See also Lauwaars and Timmermans, *op cit.* (see note 135, *supra*) 201 and 204. *Cf.* Opinion 1/94 *WTO – GATS and TRIPs* [1994] ECR I-5267 at 5412.

The freedom of establishment only entails a right to transfer their registered office after the Member States have made an arrangement for the problems of company law involved therein within the framework of Article 220 EC.[941] So long as this is not the case, the right of establishment entails for companies in particular the right to set up and manage agencies, branches, or subsidiaries in other Member States on the same footing as nationals or companies from that country. This has already taken place on a large scale. From the second paragraph of Article 52 EC the right to participate in the foundation of joint ventures in other Member States must also be inferred.

Title 1 of the General Programme concerning the right of establishment[942] develops these Treaty provisions further. As regards the setting up of agencies, branches, or subsidiaries there is the additional requirement that the activities of a company which has only registered office within the Community must show an effective and permanent link with the economy of one of the Member States if it is to benefit from the right of establishment in other Member States. Despite this restriction, undertakings from third countries, once they have established a real and actual subsidiary in one of the Member States (not thus a subsidiary which primarily exists in name only), may also participate via that subsidiary in this important part of the right of establishment. This is an extremely important matter for the open character of the common market. Undertakings from third countries can thus leap over the fence of the external tariff by, in particular, providing employment, contributing to the Community's economic and technological development and paying taxes. It is at the discretion of each Member State to permit the first leap towards its territory and this opportunity has been made use of widely. The agreements on establishment concluded by the various Member States with third countries have also played a part in this.[943] An undertaking which has its registered office in say the United Kingdom and pursues no economic activities there, but has a subsidiary in another Member State, such as The Netherlands, where all company activities are concentrated, is free to establish where it will, relying on the freedom of establishment in

---

941. *Contra*, 52 *Halsbury's Laws of England* (4th ed., London, 1986) para. 16.04. The view advanced in the text (maintaining the view in previous editions) has been confirmed by Case 81/87 *R. v. H.M. Treasury et al., ex parte Daily Mail and General Trust PLC* [1988] ECR 5483 at 5512. See also Van Solinge (1991) TVVS 169 and Bellingwout (1995) TVVS 29 (the latter referring to the KPMG study *Étude sur le transfert de siège d'une société d'un état membre à un autre* (KPMG European Business Centre, Brussels, 1993).

942. O.J. English Special Edition (2nd Series) IX, p. 7.

943. As to national treatment concerning the conditions under which undertakings under foreign control participate in economic activities within the Member States in which they are active, see Opinion 2/92 *OECD Third Revised Decision on National Treatment* [1995] ECR I-521.

The Netherlands.[944] This case-law is diametrically opposite to that on 'U-turn' constructions considered above, and it has opened the door for 'Delaware practices.'[945]

6.3 The scope of the right of establishment

As was seen in relation to the free movement of workers, in section 5, above, a distinction may be drawn between migration rights and rights of market access; these are examined in sections 6.4 and 6.5, below. Rights of access to markets for the liberal professions and for undertakings are subject to more rules than is the case for workers. For this reason, a distinction is drawn between the primary scope of the right of establishment and the secondary scope thereof: the former dealing with discriminatory measures; the latter with equally-applicable measures, such as professional and commercial provisions and their possible harmonization. The second paragraph of Article 52 EC expressly refers to 'the right to take up and pursue activities as self-employed persons and to set up and manage undertakings, in particular companies or firms...'

6.4 Migration rights (exit, entry and residence)

Directive 73/148[946] deals with the abolition of restrictions on the movement and residence within the Community for nationals of Member States with regard to establishment and the provision of services, and Directive 75/34[947] contains provisions dealing with the right to remain in the territory of another Member State after having pursued an activity there in a self-employed capacity. These directives involve equivalent rights to those outlined in section 5.2, above, provided for in Directive 68/360 for workers. Directive 73/148 only applies to natural persons and thus does not benefit legal persons.[948]

---

944. Case 79/85 *Segers v. Bestuur van de Bedrijfsvereniging voor Bank- en Verzeker-ingswezen, Groothandel en Vrije Beroepen* [1986] ECR 2375 at 2387.
945. See Timmermans in Christiaanse (ed.), *Tot vermaak van Slagter* (Deventer, 1988) 324.
946. O.J. 1973 L 172/14 (a proposal to amend this directive has been presented, COM (95) 348 Final (O.J. 1995 C 307/18). See Case C-363/89 *Roux v. Belgian State* [1992] ECR I-273, [1993] 1 CMLR 3, and Case C-370/90 *R. v. Immigration Appeal Tribunal and Singh, ex parte Secretary of State for the Home Department* [1992] ECR I-4265, [1992] 3 CMLR 358. By virtue of Arts. 31–35 and Annex VIII EEA, the right of establish-ment also benefits nationals of those non-Member States who are parties to the EEA Agreement. As to the French overseas departments, see Dec. 64/350 (O.J. English Special Edition 1963–64, p. 144).
947. O.J. 1975 L 14/10.
948. Case 81/87 *R. v. H.M. Treasury et al., ex parte Daily Mail and General Trust PLC* [1988] ECR 5483 at 5513.

By virtue of Directive 75/35[949] the scope of Directive 64/221 on public policy, public security and public health, which was examined in section 5.2, above, has been extended to cover those who exercise the rights conferred by Directive 75/34; it already embraced those who migrate for the purpose of establishment.[950] In relation to establishment however, there is substantially less case-law than there is in relation to workers, even though sensitivities in relation to the fishing sector and the question of registration of vessels have latterly led to major disputes.[951]

6.5 The primary scope of the right of establishment

As with the other freedoms, the EC Treaty contains a general prohibition provision, here Article 52 EC, and various exceptions. It is primarily in recent years that the Court has had the opportunity to interpret and develop these opinions.

6.5.1   The prohibition of discriminatory and other measures

The freedom of establishment involves, as does the freedom to provide services, in the first instance a prohibition of discrimination on the ground that a person possesses the nationality of another Member State,[952] or of both another Member State and a third country.[953] This covers not merely

949. O.J. 1975 L 14/14. This directive is based on Arts. 56(2) and 235 EC, whereas Dir. 64/221 was based solely on the former provision.
950. Dir. 64/221, Art. 1(1).
951. See, e.g. Case 79/85 Segers v. Bestuur van de Bedrijfsvereniging voor Bank- en Verzekeringswezen, Groothandel en Vrije Beroepen [1986] ECR 2375; Case C-3/88 Commission v. Italy [1989] ECR 4035; Case C-221/89 R. v. The Secretary of State for Transport, ex parte Factortame Ltd. et al. [1991] ECR I-3905, [1991] 3 CMLR 589; Case C-93/89 Commission v. Ireland [1991] ECR I-4569, [1991] 3 CMLR 97; Case C-246/89 Commission v. United Kingdom [1991] ECR I-4585, [1991] 3 CMLR 706; Case C-334/94 Commission v. France [1996] ECR I-1307, and Case C-151/96 Commission v. Ireland [1997] ECR I-3327.
952. E.g. Case 2/74 Reyners v. Belgian State [1974] ECR 631 at 651–652 (holding Art. 52 to be directly effective since the end of the transitional period at midnight on 31 December 1969); Case 90/76 Srl Ufficio Henry van Ameyde v. Srl Ufficio Centrale Italiano di Assistenza Assicurativa Automobilisti in Circulazione Internazionale (UCI) [1977] ECR 1091, [1977] 2 CMLR 478; Case 197/84 Steinhauser v. City of Biarritz [1985] ECR 1819, [1986] 1 CMLR 53; Case 63/86 Commission v. Italy [1988] ECR 29, [1989] 2 CMLR 601; Case 198/86 Conradi et al. v. Direction de la concurrence et des prix des Hauts-de-Seine et al. [1987] ECR 4469; Case 38/87 Commission v. Greece [1988] ECR 4415; Case 147/86 Commission v. Greece [1988] ECR 1637, [1989] 2 CMLR 845; Case C-61/89 Bouchoucha [1990] ECR I_3551, [1992] 1 CMLR 1033; Case 334/94 Commission v. France [1996] ECR I-1307, and Case C-151/96 Commission v. Ireland [1997] ECR I-3327.
953. Case C-369/90 Micheletti et al. v. Delegación del Gobierno en Cantabria [1992] ECR I-4239 at 4262–4263.

direct or manifest discrimination, it also embraces indirect restrictions, whether in the host Member State or in the home Member State[954] which may relate *inter alia* to the right to establish in two Member States;[955] the recognition of a driving licence;[956] the manner in which a name is written;[957] exemption from tax on taxation on transactions,[958] or other discriminatory fiscal treatment.[959] While the second paragraph of Article 52 EC takes 'the law' as the reference point for equal treatment, it is clear from the General Programme adopted on the basis of Article 54(1) EC[960] that administrative measures also fall within the scope of the prohibition of discrimination.[961]

Although the provisions concerning establishment, unlike those dealing with non-tariff obstacles to the free movement of goods, do not make any express distinction between restrictions on imports and exports, there are indications in the case-law of the Court that the prohibition in Article 52 EC applies also to restrictions on outward movement from one Member State to another.[962] Over the years the prohibition has acquired a wider scope, so that for example the Court found that even though Article 222 EC did not call into question a Member State's right to establish a system

---

954. Case 81/87 *R. v. H.M. Treasury et al., ex parte Daily Mail and General Trust PLC* [1988] ECR 5483 at 5510.

955. *E.g.* Case 107/83 *Ordre des Avocats au Barreau de Paris v. Klopp* [1984] ECR 2971, [1985] 1 CMLR 99; Case 96/85 *Commission v. France* [1986] ECR 1475; Case 221/85 *Commission v. Belgium* [1987] ECR 719; Case 143/87 *Stanton et al. v. Inasti* [1988] ECR 3877; Cases 154 and 155/87 *Rijksinstituut voor de Sociale Verzekering der Zelfstandigen v. Wolf et al.* [1988] ECR 3897; Case C-106/91 *Ramrath v. Ministre de la Justice* [1992] ECR I-3351, [1992] 3 CMLR 173; Case C-55/94 *Gebhard v. Consiglio dell'Ordine degli Avvocati e Procurati di Milano* [1995] ECR I-4165, and Case C-53/95 *Inasti v. Kemmler* [1996] ECR I-703.

956. Case 16/78 *Choquet* [1978] ECR 2293, [1979] 1 CMLR 535. See also Case C-193/94 *Skanavi et al.* [1996] ECR I-929 (which is of major importance in relation to the proportionality of penalties), and now Dir. 91/439 (O.J. 1991 L 237/1, most recently amended by Dir. 97/26 (O.J. 1997 L 150/41)).

957. Case C-168/91 *Konstantinidis v. Stadt Altensteig* [1993] ECR I-1191, [1993] 3 CMLR 410.

958. Case C-1/93 *Halliburton Services BV v. Staatsecretaris van Financiën* [1994] ECR I-1137, [1994] 3 CMLR 377, see Keeling and Shipwright (1995) 20 ELRev. 580.

959. *E.g.* Case 80/94 *Wielockx v. Inspecteur der Directe Belastingen* [1995] ECR I-2493, [1995] 3 CMLR 85; Case C-107/94 *Asscher v. Staatssecretaris van Financiën* [1996] ECR I-3089, [1996] 3 CMLR 61, and Case C-118/96 *Safir v. Skattemyndighat i Dalarnas Län* [1998] ECR I-nyr (28 April 1998).

960. See note 942, *supra*.

961. Case 71/76 *Thieffry v. Conseil de l'ordre des avocats à la Cour de Paris* [1977] ECR 765 at 777.

962. Case 81/87 *R. v. H.M. Treasury et al., ex parte Daily Mail and General Trust PLC* [1988] ECR 5483 at 5510–5511. See also Lenz, Adv. Gen. in Case C-381/93 *Commission v. France* [1994] ECR I-5145 at 5157–5159 (primarily in relation to services). See further, section 7.4.1, *post*. See, as to the Community's obligations in this context, Case C-233/94 *Germany v. Parliament and Council* [1997] ECR I-2405 and Roth (1997) ZBB 373.

of compulsory acquisition by public bodies in the general interest, it was bound to respect the non-discrimination requirement of Article 52 EC.[963]

As far as the freedom of movement for companies is concerned, a similar extension of the prohibition is evident.[964] However, there remains an essential difference between the scope of Articles 30 and 59 EC on the one hand and Article 52 EC on the other: in the case of establishment, in the absence of specific provisions at Community level the presumption is in favour of the permissibility of the national rule, whereas this is not the case for the free movement of goods and is also much less the case for the freedom to provide services.[965]

According to Article 221 EC the Member States were obliged by the end of 1960 to 'accord nationals of the other Member States the same treatment as their own nationals as regard participation in the capital of companies or firms within the meaning of Article 58, without prejudice to the application of the other provisions of this Treaty.' It is against this background that the bitter disputes about ownership of vessels in particular have been played out.[966] In this context the question arises whether, and, if so, to what extent, when nationalized industries are being privatized different conditions may be imposed if undertakings from other Member States take over the concerns involved than those for a takeover by a Member State's nationals or companies established there. In its evaluation of French privatization in 1986 the Commission rightly answered this

---

963. Case 182/83 *Robert Fearon and Co. Ltd. v. The Irish Land Commission* [1984] ECR 3677, [1985] 2 CMLR 228. A similar approach applies in relation to direct taxation, which likewise falls within the competence of the Member States, see *e.g.* Case 80/94 *Wielockx v. Inspecteur der Directe Belastingen* [1995] ECR I-2493 at 2514 and Case C-107/94 *Asscher v. Staatssecretaris van Financiën* [1996] ECR I-3089 at 3124. The non-exclusion of an area of law from compliance with the fundamental principles of the EC Treaty is a general principle, see *e.g.* Case 186/87 *Cowan v. Trésor public* [1989] ECR 195 at 221–222.

964. *E.g.* Case 270/83 *Commission v. France* [1986] ECR 273; Case 79/85 *Segers v. Bestuur van de Bedrijfsvereniging voor Bank- en Verzekeringswezen, Groothandel en Vrije Beroepen* [1986] ECR 2375; Case C-221/89 *R. v. The Secretary of State for Transport, ex parte Factortame Ltd. et al.* [1991] ECR I-3905, [1991] 3 CMLR 589; Case C-211/91 *Commission v. Belgium* [1992] ECR I-6757 (also in relation to Art. 59 EC); Case C-330/91 *R. v. Inland Revenue Commissioners, ex parte Commerzbank AG* [1993] ECR I-4017, [1993] 3 CMLR 457, and Case C-250/95 *Futura Participations SA et al. v. Administration des Contributions* [1997] ECR I-2492.

965. See Van Gerven, Adv. Gen. in Case C-340/89 *Vlassopoulou v. Ministerium für Justitz, Bundes- und Europaangelegenheiten Baden-Württemberg* [1991] ECR I-2357 at 2368–2373. See also Cases C-277/91 etc. *Ligur Carni Srl et al. v. Unità Sanitaria Locale No XV di Genova et al.* [1993] ECR I-6621.

966. *E.g.* Case C-221/89 *R. v. The Secretary of State for Transport, ex parte Factortame Ltd. et al.* [1991] ECR I-3905, [1991] 3 CMLR 589; Case C-93/89 *Commission v. Ireland* [1991] ECR I-4569, [1991] 3 CMLR 97; Case C-246/89 *Commission v. United Kingdom* [1991] ECR I-4585, [1991] 3 CMLR 706; Case C-334/94 *Commission v. France* [1996] ECR I-1307, and Case C-151/96 *Commission v. Ireland* [1997] ECR I-3327. See also Case C-211/91 *Commission v. Belgium* [1992] ECR I-6757.

question in the negative.[967] It has even been known for Member States to seek to reserve a certain percentage of the shares on a privatization for its own nationals.[968] Given that the case-law is somewhat unruly on this matter, it is surprising that there has not yet been any judicial consideration of the point.[969]

6.5.2   Exceptions to the prohibition of Article 52 EC

Article 56(1) EC permits Member States to deny or restrict the exercise of the right of establishment on the grounds of public policy, public security or public health. These grounds have already been examined in relation to Article 48(3) EC in section 5.2, above, and their exercise in the case of establishment is subject to the same rules.[970] There are a number of other grounds of exception to the exercise of the right of establishment. Because, unlike in the cases of the free movement of goods[971] and the freedom to provide services,[972] there is still a lack of clarity as to the scope of the prohibition, particularly as to the extent to which measures which are equally-applicable are caught by Article 52 EC, the division into Treaty-based exceptions and case-law based exceptions cannot be as systematically made as in the case of the free movement of goods (under Articles 30–36 EC) and the freedom to provide services (under Article 59 EC). Yet in a number of judgments there are indications of 'rule of reason' exceptions. Article 73d EC provides that the provisions of the Chapter of the EC Treaty on capital and payments 'shall be without prejudice to the applicability of restrictions on the right of establishment which are compatible with this Treaty.' The latter part of that provision embraces rule of reason exceptions developed by the Court and the general interests expressed in Community secondary legislation.

Treaty-based exceptions. The first paragraph of Article 55 EC provides that the provisions relating to freedom of establishment are inapplicable, 'so far as any given Member State is concerned, to activities which are connected, even occasionally, with the exercise of official authority.' No use has yet been made of the power provided for in the second paragraph of that article for the Council to rule that the provisions on establishment shall not apply to certain activities. The first paragraph of Article 55 EC has been the subject of considerable judicial consideration, which parallels the approach to Article 48(4) EC, considered in section 5.3.2, above.

---

967. WQ 1226/87 (Crawley) O.J. 1988 C 325/3. See WQs E-291/87 (Dell'Alba) O.J. 1997 C 319/53 and E-417/97 (Caccavale *et al.*) O.J. 1997 C 319/54.
968. *E.g.* WQ 488/87 (Cassidy) O.J. 1988 C 189/1.
969. See Turrini (1993) Rev. Dr. Aff. Int. 813.
970. Thus, as was noted in section 5.2, *ante*, Dir. 64/221 is based on Art. 56(2) EC.
971. See sections 3.3.2 and 3.3.3, *ante*.
972. See section 7.4.2, *post*.

Unsurprisingly, the interpretation of the first paragraph of Article 55 EC is strict (as an exception to a fundamental principle) and it may not be invoked further than is strictly necessary to safeguard the interests which the Member States are permitted to protect.[973]

Article 222 EC may also be considered to be an exception provision[974] in the form of a genuine reservation of sovereignty. It provides that the 'Treaty shall in no way prejudice the rules in Member States governing the system of property ownership'. This provision (again like all exceptions in Community law) is to be strictly interpreted. It does not, therefore, affect rules about the disposal or use of property rights. Special control provisions for subsidiaries or agencies of undertakings from other Member States are thus prohibited. Article 222 EC permits in particular the nationalization of undertakings, subject to the prohibition of discrimination on grounds of nationality contained in Article 6 EC and specific prohibitions of discrimination (such as Articles 54(3)(e) and 221 EC); it also permits, for example, expropriation of land[975] and requisition on forfeiture of goods.[976] Article 90(2) EC permits the Member States under certain conditions to make an exception to the prohibition of Article 52 EC.[977]

Rule of reason exceptions. The interest of measures to combat fraud has been recognized in a number of company law judgments,[978] and the Court has also recognized the interest of effective fiscal supervision.[979] These exceptions appear related to the public policy criterion in Article 56(1) EC itself. In various directives dealing with banking and insurance a number

---

973. *E.g.* Case 2/74 *Reyners v. Belgian State* [1974] ECR 631 at 654; Case 147/86 *Commission v. Greece* [1988] ECR 1637 at 1654; Case C-3/88 *Commission v. Italy* [1989] ECR I-4035 at 4060, and Case C-306/89 *Commission v. Greece* [1991] ECR I-5863 at 5883. See also Case 166/85 *Bullo et al.* [1987] ECR 1583; Case C-42/92 *Thijssen v. Controledienst voor de Verzekeringen* [1993] ECR I-4047, and Case C-272/91 *Commission v. Italy* [1994] ECR I-1411 at 1433–1436. In Case C-55/96 *Job Centre Coop. arl* [1997] ECR I-7119 the Court did not need to rule on the exercise of official authority issue.

974. See Bartels (1995) *Ars Aequi* 243.

975. See Case 182/83 *Robert Fearon and Co. Ltd. v. The Irish land Commission* [1984] ECR 3677, [1985] 2 CMLR 228.

976. See Kovar in Schwarze (ed.), *Discretionary Powers of the Member States in the Field of Economic Policies and their Limits under the EEC Treaty* (Baden-Baden, 1988) 97.

977. See *e.g.* Case C-49/89 *Corsica Ferries France v. Direction générale des douanes françaises* [1989] ECR 4441, [1991] 2 CMLR 227; Case C-179/90 *Merci convenzionali porto di Genova SpA v. Siderurgica Gabrielli SpA* [1991] ECR I-5889, [1994] 4 CMLR 422; Case C-18/93 *Corsica Ferries Italia Srl v. Corpo dei Piloti del porto di Genova* [1994] ECR I-1783; Case C-70/95 *Sodemare SA et al. v. Regione Lombardia* [1997] ECR I-3395, and Case C-55/96 *Job Centre Coop. arl* [1997] ECR I-7119.

978. Case 270/83 *Commission v. France* [1986] ECR 273 and Case 79/85 *Segers v. Bestuur van de Bedrijfsvereniging voor Bank- en Verzekeringswezen, Groothandel en Vrije Beroepen* [1986] ECR 2375.

979. *E.g.* Case C-250/95 *Futura Participations SA et al. v. Administration des Contributions* [1997] ECR I-2471 at 2501. As to unsuccessful attempts to rely on the coherence of the tax system (which in principle is also accepted), see Case 80/94 *Wielockx v. Inspec-*

of general interests are specified, such as controls for statistical purposes and appropriate measures in the case of irregularities.[980] These exceptions relate to the same matters as various Treaty-based exceptions to the free movement of capital and payments set out in Article 73d EC.

There have been attempts to invoke the interests of the local population in order to justify restrictions in relation to fishing,[981] but the Court did not touch on the argument and the learned Advocate General took the view that if such interests were deserving of protection the residence requirement was in any event disproportionate.[982]

The Court has on occasion considered 'mandatory requirements' justifying exceptions, a phrase which recalls that used in Cassis de Dijon,[983] but it has avoided using that term specifically in relation to Article 52 EC, instead referring to 'an overriding requirement of general interest capable of justifying a restriction on the exercise of fundamental freedoms guaranteed by the Treaty'[984] or requirements 'justified by the general good'[985] or 'justified in the general interest.'[986] These cases mostly concerned professional ethical rules or the recognition of academic titles. While the cultural policy objectives have been pleaded in the context of access to cable television networks, the argument was rejected on the ground of the discriminatory nature of the measure.[987] Not surprisingly, this case-law is closely linked to that concerning case-law-based exceptions to Articles 30 and 59 EC. It is evident here too that these exceptions may be invoked only if the rule is equally applicable (in law and in fact) and meets the requirements of necessity and proportionality.[988] On the procedural side, adverse decisions must be reasoned and open to judicial proceedings.[989]

teur der Directe Belastingen [1995] ECR I-2493, [1995] 3 CMLR 85 and Case C-107/94 Asscher v. Staatssecretaris van Financiën [1996] ECR I-3089, [1996] 3 CMLR 61.

980. E.g. Dir. 89/646 (O.J. 1989 L 386/1, as subsequently amended), Art. 21.
981. Case C-3/87 R. v. Ministry of Agriculture, Fisheries and Food, ex parte Aggregate Ltd. [1989] ECR 4459, [1990] 1 CMLR 366 and Case C-221/89 R. v. The Secretary of State for Transport, ex parte Factortame Ltd. et al. [1991] ECR I-3905, [1991] 3 CMLR 589.
982. Mischo, Adv. Gen. in both cases, see e.g. Case C-221/89 R. v. The Secretary of State for Transport, ex parte Factortame Ltd. et al. [1991] ECR I-3905 at 3951–3952.
983. Case 120/78 Rewe [1979] ECR 649 at 662.
984. Case C-250/95 Futura Participations SA et al. v. Administration des Contributions [1997] ECR I-2471 at 2501.
985. E.g. Case 71/76 Thieffry v. Conseil de l'ordre des avocats à la Cour de Paris [1977] ECR 765 at 776 and Case C-55/94 Gebhard v. Consiglio dell'Ordine degli Avvocati e Procurati di Milano [1995] ECR I-4165 at 4197.
986. E.g. Case C-106/91 Ramrath v. Ministre de la Justice [1992] ECR I-3351 at 3384. In Case C-19/92 Kraus v. Land Baden-Württemberg [1993] ECR I-1663 at 1697 the Court spoke of measures pursuing a legitimate objective compatible with the Treaty and justified by pressing reasons of public interest.
987. Case C-211/91 Commission v. Belgium [1992] ECR I-6757 at 6776–6777.
988. Case C-19/92 Kraus v. Land Baden-Württemberg [1993] ECR I-1663 at 1697.
989. E.g. ibid. at 1698; Case 222/86 Union national des entraîneurs et Cadres techniques professionnels du football (Unectef) v. Heylens et al. [1987] ECR 4097 at 4117; Case C-

6.6 Secondary scope of the right of establishment

Even non-discriminatory rules with reference to the exercise of a trade or profession may form a greater obstacle for aliens than for the state's own nationals. An example of this can be seen in the Dutch rules governing the establishment of businesses (*e.g.* in retail trade), which contain requirements with respect to commercial knowledge and professional skill which aliens have great difficulty in meeting.[990] Other instances include the diplomas which are required for the exercise of certain liberal professions, such as that of a medical practitioner, a Barrister, or an architect.

The case-law in this area has evolved over time, as is well-evidenced by a number of judgments concerning the right of establishment for lawyers.[991] Thus the Court has moved from the simple application of the non-discrimination principle and ascertaining that Article 52 EC had become directly effective,[992] to the possibility of freedom of establishment in cases in which the person concerned did not possess the requisite 'national' qualification but a comparable one.[993] Yet these individual

---

340/89 *Vlassopoulou v. Ministerium für Justitz, Bundes- und Europaangelegenheiten Baden-Württemberg* [1991] ECR I-2357 at 2385; Case C-104/91 *Colegio Oficial de Agentes de la Propiedad Inmobiliaria v. Borrell et al.* [1992] ECR I-3003 at 3029. See also, in relation to the free movement of goods, Case 178/84 *Commission v. Germany* [1987] ECR 1227 at 1274.

990. This policy has now been much simplified, see De Wilde (1994) SEW 775.

991. See now Dir. 98/5 (O.J. 1998 L 77/36) on establishment of lawyers. See also Dir. 77/249 (O.J. 1977 L 78/17, most recently amended by the Act of Austrian, Finnish and Swedish Accession as adapted) on the provision of services by lawyers, and, further, Case 292/86 *Gullung v. Conseils de l'ordre des avocats au barreau de Colmar et de Saverne* [1988] ECR 111, [1988] 2 CMLR 57; Case 427/85 *Commission v. Germany* [1988] ECR 1123, [1989] 2 CMLR 677; Case C-294/89 *Commission v. France* [1991] ECR I-3591, and Case C-55/94 *Gebhard v. Consiglio dell'Ordine degli Avvocati e Procurati di Milano* [1995] ECR I-4165. See, generally, Foster (1991) 40 ICLQ 607; Lonbay (1993) 18 ELRev. 408; Siskind (1992) *International Lawyer* 899, and Stuyck and Geens (1993) SEW 111.

992. Case 2/74 *Reyners v. Belgian State* [1974] ECR 631, [1974] 2 CMLR 305.

993. Case 71/76 *Thieffry v. Conseil de l'Ordre des Avocats à la Cour de Paris* [1977] ECR 765, [1977] 2 CMLR 373 and Case C-340/89 *Vlassopoulou v. Ministerium für Justitz, Bundes- und Europaangelegenheiten Baden-Württemberg* [1991] ECR I-2357, [1993] 3 CMLR 221. The Court founded this approach on the General Programme for establishment, as to which, see note 942, *supra*. See further, Case 107/83 *Ordre des Avocats au Barreau de Paris v. Klopp* [1984] ECR 2971, [1985] 1 CMLR 99; Case 292/86 *Gullung v. Conseils de l'ordre des avocats au barreau de Colmar et de Saverne* [1988] ECR 111, [1988] 2 CMLR 57; Case C-19/92 *Kraus v. Land Baden-Württemberg* [1993] ECR I-1663; Case C-55/94 *Gebhard v. Consiglio dell'Ordine degli Avvocati e Procurati di Milano* [1995] ECR I-4165, [1996] 1 CMLR 603, and, in relation to debt collecting, Case C-3/95 *Reisebüro Broede v. Sandker* [1996] ECR I-6511. As to estate agents, see Case C-104/91 *Colegio Oficial de Agentes de la Propiedad Inmobiliaria v. Borrell et al.* [1992] ECR I-3003 and Case C-147/91 *Laderer* [1992] ECR I-4097. As to football trainers, see Case 222/86 *Union national des entraîneurs et Cadres techniques professionnels du football (Unectef) v. Heylens et al.* [1987] ECR 4097, [1989] 1 CMLR 901.

cases are in fact atypical as the persons concerned either possessed the qualification (as in *Reyners*) or an equivalent qualification and training. While much has been achieved in many Member States for lawyers wishing to advise on their own legal systems or on Community or international law, the possibility of practising under the professional title of the host Member State has only recently been opened up.[994]

In order to make the right of establishment a practical proposition for the self-employed, particularly, but not only in the liberal professions, Article 57(1) EC makes provision for the adoption of directives on the mutual recognition of diplomas, certificates and other evidence of formal qualifications.[995] Article 57(2) EC provides for the adoption of directives coordinating the provisions laid down by law, regulation or administrative action concerning the taking-up and pursuit of activities as self-employed persons.[996]

The content of these directives has changed over the years. In the Seventies and early Eighties, much later than required,[997] mutual recognition of diplomas was agreed for a wide variety of professions such as doctors,[998] veterinary practitioners,[999] dentists,[1000] nurses,[1001] midwives,[1002] hairdressers,[1003] architects,[1004] and pharmacists.[1005]. Various advances were also

994. By the adoption of Dir. 98/5 (O.J. 1998 L 77/36).
995. The co-decision procedure of Art. 189b EC applies. These directives are known as recognition directives.
996. The co-decision procedure of Art. 189b EC applies, but the Council for its part acts unanimously if the implementation of a directive will involve 'in at least one Member State amendment of the existing principles laid down by law governing the professions with respect to training and conditions of access for natural persons.' These directives are known as coordination directives.
997. See Art. 57(2) EC. The Treaty of Amsterdam (not yet in force) removes this now otiose reference to the end of the transitional period.
998. See now Dir. 93/16 (O.J. 1993 L 165/1, most recently amended by Dir. 98/21 (O.J. 1998 L 119/15)) which replaces measures from 1975. See further, Cases C-69–79/96 *Garofalo et al. v. Ministero della Sanità et al.* [1997] ECR I-5603.
999. Dir. 78/1026 (O.J. 1978 L 362/1, most recently amended by Dir. 90/568 (O.J. 1990 L 353/73)). See Case 136/78 *Ministère public v. Auer* [1979] ECR 437, [1979] 2 CMLR 373; Case 271/82 *Auer v. Ministère public* [1983] ECR 2727, [1985] 1 CMLR 123; Case 5/83 *Rienks* [1983] ECR 4233, [1985] 1 CMLR 144, and Case C-17/94 *Gervais et al.* [1995] ECR I-4353.
1000. Dir. 78/686 (O.J. 1978 L 233/1, likewise so amended). See Case C-154/93 *Tawil-Albertini v. Ministre des Affaires Sociales* [1994] ECR I-451.
1001. Dir. 77/452 (O.J. 1977 L 176/1, likewise so amended).
1002. Dir. 80/154 (O.J. 1980 L 33/1, likewise so amended).
1003. Dir. 82/489 (O.J. 1982 L 218/24). See Cases C-29/94 *etc. Aubertin et al.* [1995] ECR I-301.
1004. Dir. 85/384 (O.J. 1985 L 223/15, likewise so amended). See Case C-310/90 *Nationale Raad van de Orde van Advocaten v. Egle* [1992] ECR I-177; Case C-166/91 *Bauer v. Conseil National de l'Ordre des Architectes* [1992] ECR I-2797, and Case C-447/93 *Dreessen v. Conseil National de l'Ordre des Architectes* [1994] ECR I-4087. See also Case 11/77 *Patrick v. Ministre des Affaires Culturelles* [1977] ECR 1199, [1977] 2 CMLR 523.
1005. Dir. 85/432 (O.J. 1985 L 253/34, likewise so amended).

made in the field of financial services.[1006] All these vocational measures concern the mutual recognition of qualifications obtained in a Member State; other specific provisions apply to the recognition of qualifications obtained in third countries.[1007]

The emphasis has now shifted, however, to the general principle of the mutual recognition of qualifications. This was in response to the scant progress which was being made on the basis of a profession-by-profession approach (the time taken to negotiate the architects directive had been particularly excessive). Following the recommendations of the Adonnino Committee,[1008] the Commission announced a proposal for a general system for the recognition of higher education diplomas awarded on completion of vocational courses of at least three years duration.[1009] As was noted in section 5.3.1, above, this idea eventually resulted in the adoption of two important general system directives.[1010]

The so-called '1992 effect' and the support of the Court[1011] led to the adoption of further coordination directives in the banking and insurance sectors[1012] which set out from the principles of mutual recognition and supervision by the home Member State.[1013] In some cases account is taken of two-speed problems through means of an express reference to Article 7c EC.[1014]

Primarily in the Sixties and early Seventies there were two other types of

1006. See section 7.6, post.
1007. Case C-154/93 Tawil-Albertini v. Ministre des Affaires Sociales [1994] ECR I-451 at 463. See the Resolution of 18 June 1992 (O.J. 1992 C 187/1).
1008. Bull. EC supp. 7/85.
1009. See the White Paper Completing the Internal Market COM (85) 310 Final, point 91. As to the recognition of teaching qualifications in England and Wales, see Hopkins (1996) 21 ELRev. 435. See also, generally, Lonbay (1989) 14 ELRev. 363 and Shaw (1992) Journal of Law and Education 415.
1010. Dir. 89/48 (O.J. 1989 L 19/16) concerning higher education diplomas awarded on completion of professional education and training of at least three years' duration, and Dir. 92/51 (O.J. 1992 L 209/25, most recently amended by Dir. 97/38 (O.J. 1997 L 184/31)) for the recognition of professional education and training. See also the Commission's Communication COM (94) 596 Final. As to further proposed amendments to both of these directives, see COM (97) 638 Final (O.J. 1998 C 28/1).. As to Dir. 89/48, see Case C-164/94 Arantis v. Land Berlin [1996] ECR I-135 and Case C-225/95 Kapasakalis v. Greece [1998] ECR I-nyr (2 July 1998). The difficulties experienced by lawyers with Dir. 89/48 resulted in Dir. 98/5 (O.J. 1998 L 77/3).
1011. Case 205/84 Commission v. Germany [1986] ECR 3755, [1987] 2 CMLR 69 (and the other insurance cases decided on the same day).
1012. As to which, see section 7.6, post. See also Case C-63/89 Les Assurances du crédit et al. v. Council and Commission [1991] ECR I-1799.
1013. E.g. the 2nd Banking Directive, Dir. 89/646 (O.J. 1989 L 386/1, most recently amended by Dir. 92/30 (O.J. 1992 L 110/52)), Preamble, recital 8.
1014. The old Art. 8c EEC, e.g. in the second Direct Insurance Directive, Dir. 88/357 (O.J. 1988 L 172/1, most recently amended by Dir. 92/49 (O.J. 1992 L 228/1), preamble, final point.

directives which were adopted in this field: directives requiring restrictions to be removed, and transitional directives. The former were designed to remove existing restrictions on the ground of nationality.[1015] The direct effect of Article 52 EC since the end of the transitional period has already been noted above. Transitional measures were designed to deal with those occupations for which no mutual recognition or coordination directives had yet been adopted: thus measures were adopted for the wholesale trade and middlemen,[1016] industry and handicrafts,[1017] and the retail trade.[1018] In fact with the coming into force of the second of the two general system directives, the practical importance of these older directives has diminished substantially[1019] and the Commission has proposed that the myriad older directives be substantially revised.[1020]

6.7 Harmonization of company law

Article 54(3)(g) EC contains a special co-ordination obligation relating to the safeguards which the Member States require of companies or firms within the meaning of the second paragraph of Article 58 EC for the protection of members and others, so that these safeguards may be made equivalent throughout the Community.[1021] It is submitted that the term 'others' is wide enough to cover not merely the interests of creditors but also those of employees. If the Council were continually to refuse to take account of those interests it is submitted that proceedings for failure to act could be initiated under Article 175 EC.

1015. *E.g.* Dir. 68/365 (O.J. English Special Edition 1968 (II), p. 505, amended by the Act of Accession (1972) as adapted) covering various food manufacturing and beverage industries.
1016. Dir. 64/222 (O.J. English Special Edition 1963–64, p. 120). See Case 115/78 *Knoors v. Staatssecretaris voor Economische Zaken* [1979] ECR 399, [1979] 2 CMLR 357 and Case 130/88 *Van der Bijl v. Staatssecretaris voor Economische Zaken* [1989] ECR 3039.
1017. Dir. 64/427 (*ibid.* p. 148).
1018. Dir. 68/364 (O.J. English Special Edition 1968 (II), p. 501). See Case 20/87 *Ministère public v. Gauchard* [1987] ECR 4879, [1989] 2 CMLR 489 and Case 204/87 *Bekaert* [1988] ECR 2029.
1019. But there have been problems in practice, see WQs E-1689/94 (Van Velzen) O.J. 1995 C 30/6 and 1754/94 (Ewing) O.J. 1995 C 30/13. See also the Commission's report COM (96) 46 Final.
1020. COM (96) 22 Final (O.J. 1996 C 115/16), amended by COM (97) 363 Final (O.J. 1997 C 264/5). Some 35 older directives will be affected.
1021. See Wachter and Van Hulle, *Harmonisatie van het vennootschaps- en effectenrecht* (Deventer, 1988); Lubbers and Westbroek (eds.), *Vennootschapsrecht in EG-per-spectief* (Deventer, 1993); Wouters and Schneider, *Current Issues of Cross-Border Establishment of Companies in the EU* (Antwerp, 1995); Timmermans (1984) Rabels Z 12; Werlauff (1992) 17 ELRev. 207, and Wouters (1991) *Tijdschrift voor Rechtspersoon en Vennootschap* 456. EuZW, JBL, BLR, NV, TVVS and equivalent journals in other Member States regularly monitor developments in this field.

Directive 68/151[1022] (the First Company Law Directive) initiated the co-ordination required by Article 54(3)(g) and deals with the publication of documents and particulars concerning companies (including the annual report and accounts), the capacity of companies and their directors and the nullity of companies. The Second Directive[1023] relates to the formation of public limited companies and the maintenance and altera-tion in their capital. The Third Directive[1024] covers internal mergers between joint stock companies. Some months later the Fourth Directive[1025] dealt with the annual accounts of limited liability companies and to certain extent is an extension of the First Directive, it is itself complemented by the Seventh Directive[1026] on consolidated accounts. The old draft Fifth Directive concerned the structure of limited liability companies and the powers and obligations of their organs.[1027] Its progress foundered on the stumbling-back of employee participation, but eventually, in the context of social policy, Directive 94/45[1028] on European Works Councils or other employee information and consultation procedures was adopted. The Sixth Directive[1029] deals with the division of public limited liability companies and complements the Third Directive. The Seventh Directive has already been mentioned. The Eighth Directive[1030] deals with the qualifications of company auditors. A draft Ninth Directive was intended to deal with the behaviour of groups of companies.[1031] The

1022. O.J. English Special Edition 1968 (1), p. 41, most recently amended by Act of Aus-trian, Finnish and Swedish Accession (as adapted). See Case 136/87 *Ubbink Isolatie BV v. Dak- en Wandtechniek BV* [1988] ECR 4665 and Case C-106/89 *Marleasing SA v. La Comercial Internacional de Alimentación SA* [1990] ECR I-4135, [1992] 1 CMLR 305.

1023. Dir. 77/91 (O.J. 1977 L 26/1, likewise so amended). See Cases C-19 and 20/90 *Karella et al. v. Minister of Industry, Energy and Technology et al.* [1991] ECR I-2691; Case C-381/89 *Sindesmos Melon tis Eleftheras Evangelikis Ekklisias et al. v. Greek State et al.* [1992] ECR I-2111; Cases C-134 and 135/91 *Kerafina -Keramische und Finanz-Holding AG et al. v. Greek State et al.* [1992] ECR I-5699, and Case C-441/93 *Panagis Pafitis et al. v. Trapeza Kentrikis Ellados AE et al.* [1996] ECR I-1347.

1024. Dir. 78/855 (O.J. 1978 L 295/36, likewise so amended).

1025. Dir. 78/660 (O.J. 1978 L 222/11, likewise so amended). See Case C-38/89 *Ministère public v. Blangueron* [1990] ECR I-83 and Case 234/94 *Tomberger v. Gebrüder von der Wettern GmbH* [1996] ECR I-3133 (corrigendum issued in [1997] ECR Part 7, I-XXXIII).

1026. Dir. 83/349 (O.J. 1983 L 193/1, likewise so amended).

1027. Originally submitted in 1972 (J.O. 1972 C 131/49), amended in 1983 (O.J. 1983 C 240/2). As to the background, see the Gundelach report on Employee Participation and Company Structure (Bull. EC supp. 8/75) and also the Vredeling Draft Direc-tive, originally submitted in 1980 (O.J. 1980 C 297/3), amended in 1983 (O.J. 1983 C 217/3).

1028. O.J. 1994 L 254/64, extended to embrace the United Kingdom by Dir. 97/74 (O.J. 1998 L 10/22).

1029. Dir. 82/891 (O.J. 1982 L 378/47).

1030. Dir. 84/253 (O.J. 1984 L 126/20).

1031. See Wooldridge (1983) JBL 272. This was in fact never presented formally.

draft Tenth Directive concerns cross-border public limited liability company mergers.[1032] The Eleventh Directive[1033] concerns disclosure requirements in respects of branches set up in one Member State by companies established in another. The Twelfth Directive[1034] deals with single member private limited companies. The proposal for a Thirteenth Directive concerning takeover bids is currently going through the legislative process.[1035] A proposal for a Fourteenth Directive on transfers of the registered office was expected in the near future.[1036] Further action relating to the proposal for a European Company[1037] is expected in the course of 1998.[1038]

Much work is currently concentrating on international harmonization of accounting standards[1039] and on the question of statutory auditors' liability.[1040] A number of directives have also been adopted in the field of securities regulation[1041] and fiscal aspects of company law.[1042] However, the Council has not confined itself to coordination directives, thus a new creature, inspired by the French *Groupement d'Intérêt Economique*, called the European Economic Interest Grouping was brought into being by Regulation 2137/85.[1043] Other fruits of activities in this field include the Convention on the Mutual Recognition of Companies and Bodies Corporate[1044] (although this is not yet in force having been particularly sabotaged by the Dutch).[1045]

1032. At the date at which this work states the law, a revised proposal is still anticipated. As to the original proposal, see COM (84) 727 Final (O.J. 1985 C 23/11). See Van Solinge, *Grensoverschrijdende juridische fusie* (Deventer, 1994).

1033. Dir. 89/666 (O.J. 1989 L 395/36).

1034. Dir. 89/667 (O.J. 1989 L 395/40, amended by the Act of Austrian, Finnish and Swedish Accession (1994).

1035. As to the amended proposal, see COM (97) 565 Final (O.J. 1997 C 378/10).

1036. But has not yet appeared.

1037. See the various proposals for different types of associations contained in COM (91)273 Final (O.J. 1992 C99/1 *et seq.*, amended in COM (93) 252 Final (O.J. 1993 C 236/1 *et seq.*)). The legal basis is Art. 100a EC rather than Art. 54(3)(g) EC. See, further, Huiskes, *De Europese Vennootschap* (Zwolle, 1993) and Jaeger, *Die Europäische Aktiengesellschaft* (Baden-Baden, 1994).

1038. Depending on the progress made in the Davignon Group. See COM (95) 184 Final.

1039. COM (95) 508 Final.

1040. See the Green Paper, COM (96) 338 Final, and O.J. 1998 C 143/12.

1041. See Andenas and Kenyon-Slade, *EC Financial Market Regulation and Company Law* (London, 1993).

1042. Dir. 90/434 (O.J. 1990 L 225/1, most recently amended by Act of Austrian, Finnish and Swedish Accession as adapted), see Case C-28/95 *Leur-Bloem v. Inspecteur der Belastingdienst/Ondernemingen Amsterdam 2* [1997] ECR I-4161, and Dir. 90/435 (O.J. 1990 L 225/6, likewise so amended).

1043. O.J. 1985 L 199/1. As to participation by EEIGs in publicly financed public procurement contracts, see COM (97) 434 Final (O.J. 1997 C 285/17).

1044. Bull. EC supp. 2/69.

1045. By the withdrawal of the proposal for ratification, see *Kamerstuk* 11 790 (R 852), no. 7.

7. FREEDOM TO PROVIDE SERVICES

Article 3(c) EC lists the abolition of restrictions on the freedom to provide services as between Member States as one of the characteristics of the internal market. This declaration of principle is developed in Articles 59–66 EC.[1046] Although these provisions working this freedom out are primarily addressed to persons, and in particular to providers of services,[1047] over the years this freedom has seen spectacular developments. Thus it covers not simply matters such as the provision of services by lawyers, it embraces matters such as procurement (of works and supplies as well as of services), banking and insurance services, invisible transactions by telecommunications,[1048] and cross-border provision of services in relation to lotteries.[1049]

In some invisible transactions, particularly those by telecommunications, the movement of goods and the movement of services are closely related.[1050] The relationship between establishment and services is so close that Article 66 provides that various of the provisions on establishment shall also apply in respect of the provision of services. As far as the link with free movement of capital is concerned, Article 61(2) EC provides that the liberalization of banking and insurance services connected with movements of capital are to be effected in step with the former.[1051] Article 61(1) provides that the freedom to provide services in the transport field[1052] is to be governed by the provisions of the Title relating to

1046. See Annabolis (1994) RMUE 173; Hailbronner (1992) EuZW 105; Hoekman and Sauvé (1994) JCMS 283; Lasok and Thompson in Vaughan (ed.), *op cit.* (see note 84, *supra*) Part 16; Marenco (1992) 12 YBEL 111; Reich (1989) ZHR 571; Roth (1987) EuR 7; Speyer (1991) EuZW 588; Steindorff (1988) Fordham Int'l. L.J. 347 and Troberg in Von der Groeben *et al.* (eds.), *op. cit.* (see note 756, *supra*) Vol. 1 1441.

1047. Arts. 59 EC, 1st para. and Art. 60 EC.

1048. See Case C-353/89 *Commission v. The Netherlands* [1991] ECR I-4069.

1049. Case C-275/92 *H.M. Customs and Excise v. Schindler et al.* [1994] ECR I-1039, [1995] 1 CMLR 4, see Gormley (1994) 19 ELRev. 644.

1050. *Cf.* the approach in Case 155/73 *Sacchi* [1974] ECR 409, [1974] 2 CMLR 177; Case 352/85 *Bond van Adverteerders et al. v. The Netherlands State* [1988] ECR 2085, [1989] 3 CMLR 113 and Cases C-34–36/95 *Konsumentombudsmannen (KO) v. De Agostini (Svenska) Förlag AB et al.* [1997] ECR I-3843 (televised advertisements falling under services) with that in Cases 60 and 61/84 *Cinéthèque SA et al. v. Fédération nationale des cinémas français* [1985] ECR I-2605, [1986] 1 CMLR 365 (distribution of films on video). See also Case C-412/93 *Société d'Imporatation Édouard Leclerc-Siplec v. TF1 Publicité SA et al.* [1995] ECR I-179, [1995] 3 CMLR 422.

1051. See Case 205/84 *Commission v. Germany* [1986] ECR 3755, [1987] 2 CMLR 69 (and the other related judgments decided on that day). See also Cases C-358 and 416/93 *Bordessa et al.* [1995] ECR I-361 and Jarvis (1995) 20 ELRev. 514.

1052. See Case 13/83 *European Parliament v. Council* [1985] ECR 1513, [1986] 1 CMLR 138; Case 4/88 *Lambregts Transportbedrijf v. Belgian State* [1989] ECR 2583; Case C-49/89 *Corsica Ferries France v. Direction générale des douanes françaises* [1989] ECR 4441, [1991] 2 CMLR 227; Case C-17/90 *Pinaud Wieger GmbH Spedition v. Bunde-*

transport.[1053] The relationship between movement of capital, payments and the provision of services has been the subject of judicial consideration,[1054] as has that between Article 59 EC and Articles 85 and 86 EC.[1055]

This section first examines in section 7.1 the concept of a service, before turning to examine the beneficiaries of the freedom in section 7.2, below. Section 7.3 deals with migration rights and market access rights are considered in section 7.4, below. Finally, attention turns to service monopolies in section 7.5 and harmonization in the field of services is examined in section 7.6, below.

7.1 The concept of a service

Article 60 EC provides that services within the meaning of the EC Treaty are those services 'normally provided for remuneration' in so far as they are not governed by the provisions relating to the free movement of goods, capital and persons. It also provides an illustrative list of what is covered by the term services. Not surprisingly, there has been considerable case-law on this point. Services must thus be economic activities[1056] which are normally provided for remuneration.[1057] On the basis of these criteria, publicly-financed education in another Member State is not regarded as

     sanstalt für den Güterfernverkehr [1991] ECR I-5253, and Case C-18/93 Corsica Ferries Italia Srl v. Corpo dei Piloti del porto di Genova [1994] ECR I-1783.

1053. See Opinion 1/94 WTO – GATS and TRIPs [1994] ECR I-5267 at 5402. See further, Chapter XI, section 3, post.

1054. Cases 286/82 and 26/83 Luisi and Carbone v. Ministero del Tesoro [1984] ECR 377, [1985] 3 CMLR 52.

1055. E.g. in relation to intellectual property rights, Case 22/79 Greenwich Film Production v. Société des Auteurs, Compositeurs et Editeurs de Musique (SACEM) et al. [1979] ECR 3275, [1980] 1 CMLR 629; Case 7/82 Gesellschaft zur Verwertung von Leistungsschutzrechten mbH (GWL) v. Commission [1983] ECR 483, [1983] 3 CMLR 645, and Cases C-92 and 326/92 Phil Collins et al. v. Imtrat Handelsgesellschaft mbH et al. [1993] ECR I-5145, [1993] 3 CMLR 773.

1056. Case 36/74 Walrave and Koch v. Association Union Cycliste Internationale et al. [1974] ECR 1405 at 1417; Case 13/76 Donà v. Mantero [1976] ECR 1333 at 1340; Case 15/78 Société Générale Alsacienne de Banque SA v. Koestler [1978] ECR 1971 at 1979–1980; Case 196/87 Steymann v. Staatssecretaris van Justitie [1988] ECR 6159 at 6172, and Case C-275/92 H.M. Customs and Excise v. Schindler et al. [1994] ECR I-1039 at 1089. See also Case C-70/95 Sodemare SA et al. v. Regione Lombardia [1997] ECR I-3395.

1057. Case C-275/92 H.M. Customs and Excise v. Schindler et al. [1994] ECR I-1039 at 1089. The absence of an economic link between the service provider and the person about whose activities information was being provided free of charge was crucial in Case C-159/90 Society for the Protection of Unborn Children Ireland Ltd. v. Grogan et al. [1991] ECR I-4685, [1991] 3 CMLR 849. The person who receives the service provided does not have to be the same as the person paying for the provision, see Case 352/85 Bond van Adverteerders et al. v. The Netherlands State [1988] ECR 2085 at 2131.

falling under the freedom to provide services.[1058] The activity concerned must not be confined in all its aspects to one single Member State: there has to be a cross-border element.[1059] A service is also provided within the meaning of Articles 59 and 60 EC if an undertaking has established itself in another Member State in order to escape either from the legislation applicable in the Member State in which the service is received or from the legislation applicable to undertakings in the home Member State of the undertaking concerned.[1060] However, the home Member State may adopt measures in reaction to such a move,[1061] provided always that those measures are necessary and justified in Community law.[1062] These 'U-turn' constructions have already been examined in section 1.1, above, and at various earlier stages in the analysis in this Chapter. It may not be required that the recipient of the service be ascertained in advance.[1063]

Undoubtedly the key demarcation between the provision of services and the right of establishment is to be found in the word 'temporary' in Article 60 EC. As was demonstrated in section 6.1, above, establishment is more permanent in nature, requiring a permanent presence in the territory of the Member State where the economic activity is being exercised,[1064] but permanent presence, on a stable and continuous basis from an established professional base or at least presence for an indefinite period will be found even if the presence is in the form of an office managed by an

1058. Case 263/86 *Belgian State v. Humbel et al.* [1988] ECR I-5365 at 5387–5388 and Case C-109/92 *Wirth v. Landeshauptstadt Hannover* [1993] ECR I-6447 at 6469.

1059. *E.g.* Case 52/79 *Procureur du Roi v. Debauve et al.* [1980] ECR 833 at 855; Case C-41/90 *Höfner and Elser v. Macrotron GmbH* [1991] ECR I-1979 at 2020; Case C-159/90 *Society for the Protection of Unborn Children Ireland Ltd. v. Grogan et al.* [1991] ECR I-4685 at 4740; Cases C-330 and 331/90 *López Brea et al.* [1992] ECR I-323 at 336; Case C-60/91 *Batista Morais* [1992] ECR I-2085 at 2105–2106; Case C-20/92 *Hubbard v. Hamburger* [1993] ECR I-3777 at 3794; Case C-134/95 *Unità Socio-Sanitaria Locale No 47 di Biella (USSL) v. Instituto Nazionale per l'Assicuriazione contro gli Infortuni sul Lavoro (INAIL)* [1997] ECR I-195 at 211, and Case C-70/95 *Sodemare et al. v. Regione Lombardia* [1997] ECR I-3395 at 3435–3436. See also Case 186/87 *Cowan v. Trésor public* [1989] ECR 195 at 221. See also section 1.1, *ante*.

1060. See Case 23/93 *TV 10 SA v. Commissariaat voor de Media* [1994] ECR I-4795 at 4831. See also Case C-56/96 *VT4 Ltd. v. Vlaamse Gemeenschap* [1997] ECR I-3143 at 3167–3168.

1061. Case 33/74 *Van Binsbergen v. Bestuur van de Bedrijfsvereniging voor de Metaalnijverheid* [1974] ECR 1299 at 1309–1310; Case 205/84 *Commission v. Germany* [1986] ECR 3755 at 3801, and Case C-148/91 *Vereniging Veronica Omroep Organisatie v. Commissariaat voor de Media* [1993] ECR I-487 at 519.

1062. See section 7.4.2, *post*.

1063. Case C-384/93 *Alpine Investments BV v. Minister van Financiën* [1995] ECR I-1141 at 1174.

1064. *E.g.* Case 196/87 *Steymann v. Staatssecretaris van Justitie* [1988] ECR 6159 at 6173–6174; Case C-211/89 *R. v. The Secretary of State for Transport, ex parte Factortame Ltd. et al.* [1991] ECR I-3905 at 3965; Case C-294/89 *Commission v. France* [1991] ECR I-3591 at 3613–3634, and Case C-55/94 *Gebhard v. Consiglio dell'Ordine degli Avvocati e Procurati di Milano* [1995] ECR I-4165 at 4194–4197.

undertaking's own staff or by an independent person permanently authorized to act.[1065] If any supply or physical involvement of goods is merely incidental to the provision of services, Articles 59 and 60 EC will apply, rather than Article 30 EC.[1066] The Court will not allow any moral view of a particular type of activity legally practised in a Member State to cloud its view as to whether or not it is to be characterized as a service.[1067]

7.2   Beneficiaries of the freedom to provide services

The first paragraph of Article 59 EC requires the progressive abolition during the transitional period of restrictions on the freedom to provide services within the Community in respect of nationals of Member States who are established in a Member State other than that of the person for whom the services are intended. Unlike the first establishment,[1068] for the provision of services by natural persons, establishment within the Community is thus required in addition to the requirement of nationality of a Member State. This combined requirement is only made in relation to the provider of services; it does not apply to the recipient of services. Thus third-country nationals who are established within the Community may benefit from the freedom to provide services in their capacity as recipients of services.[1069]

The Council is empowered under the second paragraph of Article 59 EC to extend the provisions on services to nationals of third countries who

---

1065. Case 205/84 *Commission v. Germany* [1986] ECR 3755 at 3801. But the existence of some form of infrastructure (such as an office, chambers or consulting rooms) which is necessary for the performance of the services in question will not automatically take a person out of the realm of the provision of services and into that of establishment, Case C-55/94 *Gebhard v. Consiglio dell'Ordine degli Avvocati e Procurati di Milano* [1995] ECR I-4165 at 4195. It will depend on the facts in the particular case. See also Case C-221/89 *R. v. The Secretary of State for Transport, ex parte Factortame Ltd. et al.* [1991] ECR I-3905 at 3965.

1066. Case C-275/92 *H.M. Customs and Excise v. Schindler et al.* [1994] ECR I-1039 at 1088-1089; see also Case C-55/93 *Von Schaaik* [1994] ECR I-4837 at 4857.

1067. Case C-159/90 *Society for the Protection of Unborn Children Ireland Ltd. v. Grogan et al.* [1991] ECR I-4685 at 4739; Case C-275/92 *H.M. Customs and Excise v. Schindler et al.* [1994] ECR I-1039 at 1090 (neither the chance element, nor the recreational character of lotteries take them out of the ambit of services, *ibid.* at 1091, but the Court may well have regard to perceived moral aspects in looking at alleged justifications, *ibid.* at 1096–1097). Subsequent to the judgment in *Grogan*, a Protocol (No. 17) was annexed to the TEU and the ECSC, EC and Euratom Treaties providing that nothing therein or in modifications or supplements thereto would affect the application in Ireland of Art. 40.3.3 of the Irish Constitution. See, further, O'Leary (1992) 17 ELRev. 138 and Quigley (1992) 3 EBLR 62.

1068. Art. 52 EC, see section 6.2, *ante*.

1069. Lauwaars and Timmermans, *op. cit.* (see note 940, 942, *supra*) 205. See also Case C-180/89 *Commission v. Greece* [1991] ECR I-709 at 738–739.

provide services and who are established within the Community, but as yet it has not availed itself of this power.[1070]

Although Articles 59 and 60 EC refer to natural persons, Article 66 EC in conjunction with Article 58 EC make it clear that legal persons also benefit from the freedom to provide services. But they must, as a provider of services have an economic link with at least one Member State.[1071]

The case-law on the freedom to provide services has examined myriad situations involving the cross-border provision of services, and it is clear that the ambit of Articles 59 and 60 EC has become very wide indeed, as the emphasis has developed over the years.[1072] Four situations can be distinguished: the first is where the service provider moves from one Member State to another to provide the service; the second is where it is not the provider who moves but the recipient, so that the recipient goes to another Member State to receive services there; in the third situation, neither the provider nor the recipient moves, the service being provided and received by means of telecommunication (telephone, fax, internet or other data traffic, particularly in the field of financial transactions) or mail; lastly, the fourth scenario is that both the service provider and the recipient move from their respective Member States to a third Member State so that the performance of the service takes place there.

Initially the accent clearly lay on the provider of the service moving, a situation expressly envisaged in Article 60 EC. Indeed, early case-law still saw the Court too only thinking of this scenario.[1073] The spectacular expansion to the second situation arrived when the Court made it clear that those who were travelling abroad as tourists, or to receive educational services, medical treatment or for business purposes were beneficiaries of Articles 59 and 60 EC.[1074] Thus on a trip from Luxembourg to Trier for

1070. *Cf.* Opinion 1/94 *WTO – GATS and TRIPs* [1994] ECR I-5267 at 5412. It has, though, accorded equal treatment in a number of areas on the basis of reciprocity, *e.g.* Dec. 95/215 (O.J. 1995 L 134/25) on procurement (United States) pending more global resolution of questions (such as through the Agreement on Government Procurement (GPA) negotiated in the Uruguay Round, see Chapter XI, section 3.2.2, *post*). See also section 7.6, *post*.

1071. See the General Programme for the removal of restrictions on the freedom to provide services (O.J. English Special Edition (2nd Series) IX, p. 3), Title I.

1072. The approach set out here demonstrates great similarities to GATS, Art. I(2) (Marrakesh, 15 April 1994). See also Opinion 1/94 *WTO – GATS and TRIPs* [1994] ECR I-5267 at 5401.

1073. Case 33/74 *Van Binsbergen v. Bestuur van de Bedrijfsvereniging voor de Metaalnijverheid* [1974] ECR 1299 at 1309. See also Case 16/78 *Choquet* [1978] ECR 2239, [1979] 1 CMLR 535; Case 279/80 *Webb* [1981] ECR 3305, [1982] 1 CMLR 406, and Case 76/81 *SA Transporoute et Travaux v. Minister of Public Works* [1982] ECR 417, [1982] 3 CMLR 382; Case 205/84 *Commission v. Germany* [1986] ECR 3755, [1987] 2 CMLR 69 (and the other insurance judgments decided on that day).

1074. Cases 286/82 and 26/83 *Luisi and Carbone v. Ministero del Tesoro* [1984] ECR 377 at 401. See also Case 186/87 *Cowan v. Trésor public* [1989] ECR 195 at 220–221; Case C-159/90 *Society for the Protection of Unborn Children Ireland Ltd. v. Grogan et al.*

tea, a Community (or EEA) national benefits from the freedom to receive services.[1075] There are now myriad instances of the third situation arising in the case-law.[1076] The fourth situation is typified by the situation of tourist guides, a driver and holidaymakers on a coach trip or guided tour in another Member State, who are faced with a requirement that local guides or drivers must be used.[1077]

7.3 Migration rights (entry, exit and residence)

Migration rights have already been examined in relation to the free movement of workers and in relation to the right of establishment.[1078] Given that both the service provider and the service recipient may benefit from the freedom, regard must be had to both the demand and the supply sides of the market. Thus not only a medical doctor but also his or her patient may encounter the public health exception if he or she takes advantage of the freedom to provide or receive services.[1079]

7.4 Market access rules

Article 59 EC is directly effective since the end of the transitional period[1080] and prohibits restrictions on the free provision of services.[1081] Article 62 EC contains a standstill provision[1082] which has the same scope of application as Article 59 EC.[1083] The addressees of this prohibition are

[1991] ECR I-4685 at 4739–4740, and Case C-55/93 *Van Schaik* [1994] ECR I-4837 at 4856. As to educational services, the Court clearly had in mind those for which fees are paid, see note 1058, *supra*.

1075. As to EEA nationals, see Arts. 36–39 EEA, and for particular types of services, Annexes IX–XI EEA.

1076. *E.g.* Case C-353/89 *Commission v. The Netherlands* [1991] ECR I-4069; Case C-76/90 *Säger v. Dennemeyer & Co. Ltd.* [1991] ECR I-4221, [1993] 3 CMLR 639, and Case C-384/93 *Alpine Investments BV v. Minister van Financiën* [1995] ECR I-1141, [1995] 2 CMLR 209.

1077. Case C-154/89 *Commission v. France* [1991] ECR I-659 at 685; Case C-180/89 *Commission v. Italy* [1991] ECR I-709 at 721, and Case C-198/89 *Commission v. Greece* [1991] ECR I-727 at 739. See also Case C-20/92 *Hubbard v. Hamburger* [1993] ECR I-3777 at 3794.

1078. See sections 5.2 and 6.4, respectively.

1079. Dir. 64/221, discussed in *ibid.*, also applies to those providing services (see Art. 1(1). Dir. 73/148 (discussed in section 6.4, *ante*) also covers the abolition of restrictions and movement for nationals of Member States with regard to the provision of services. See, further, the General Programme (see note 1071, *supra*), Title III.

1080. Case 33/74 *Van Binsbergen v. Bestuur van de Bedrijfsvereniging voor de Metaalnijverheid* [1974] ECR 1299 at 1311–1312.

1081. See the Commission's interpretative Communication (O.J. 1993 C 334/3).

1082. Case 48/75 *Royer* [1976] ECR 497 at 517.

1083. Case C-159/90 *Society for the Protection of Unborn Children Ireland Ltd. v. Grogan et*

not only national or local authorities[1084] or bodies for whose acts the State is responsible in Community law;[1085] Article 59 EC also affects rules of a private law nature.[1086]

Article 60 EC also has direct effect.[1087] According to the last sentence of the third paragraph of that provision, a service provider may temporarily pursue his or her activity in the host Member State under the same conditions as that state imposes on its own nationals. This provision is limited to non-discrimination, but 'it does not follow from that paragraph that all national legislation applicable to nationals of that state and usually applied to the permanent activities of undertakings established therein may be similarly applied to the permanent activities of undertakings which are established in other Member States.'[1088]

7.4.1   The prohibition

Article 59 implies first of all the abolition of all discrimination, even of a minor nature[1089] against the provider or the recipient of services on the grounds of his, her or its nationality[1090] or establishment in another Member State.[1091] Fiscal measures which may constitute an obstacle to the

al. [1991] ECR I-4685 at 4741 (Art. 62 EC cannot prohibit restrictions which do not come within the scope of Art. 59 EC). See also Case C-55/93 *Van Schaik* [1994] ECR I-4837 at 4857–4858.

1084. *Cf.* Art. I(3) GATS.

1085. The principle follows *mutatis mutandis* from the case-law on Art. 30 EC, see section 3.2.2, *ante*, but has been expressly confirmed in Case 63/86 *Commission v. Italy* [1988] ECR 29 at 52.

1086. Case 36/74 *Walrave and Koch v. Association Union Cycliste Internationale et al.* [1974] ECR 1405 at 1419 (which also shows the extraterritorial effect of Art. 59 EC, at 1420); Case 13/76 *Donà v. Mantero* [1976] ECR 1333 at 1341, and Case 90/76 *Srl Ufficio Henry van Ameyde v. Srl Ufficio Centrale Italiano di Assistenza Assicurativa Automobilisti in Circulazione Internazionale (UCI)* [1977] ECR 1091 at 1127.

1087. Case 205/84 *Commission v. Germany* [1986] ECR 3755 at 3802. See also Case 33/74 *Van Binsbergen v. Bestuur van de Bedrijfsvereniging voor de Metaalnijverheid* [1974] ECR 1299 at 1311–1312.

1088. Case 204/84 *Commission v. Germany* [1986] ECR 3755 at 3802.

1089. Case C-49/89 *Corsica Ferries France v. Direction générale des douanes français* [1989] ECR I-4441 at 4456.

1090. *E.g.* Case 168/85 *Commission v. Italy* [1986] ECR 2945 at 2960–2961; Case 63/86 *Commission v. Italy* [1988] ECR 29 at 52; Case C-154/89 *Commission v. France* [1991] ECR I-659 at 685; Case C-180/89 *Commission v. Italy* [1991] ECR I-709 at 721, and Case C-198/89 *Commission v. Greece* [1991] ECR I-727 at 739; Case C-260/89 *Elliniki Radiophonia Tileorassi AE v. Dimotiki Etairia Pliroforossis et al.* [1991] ECR I-2925 at 2959 (hereafter *ERT*); Case C-353/89 *Commission v. The Netherlands* [1991] ECR I-4069 at 4093; Case C-58/90 *Commission v. Italy* [1991] ECR I-4189 at 4202; Case C-17/92 *Federación de Distribuidores Cinematográficos (FEDICINE) v. Spanish State* [1993] ECR I-2239 at 2271, and Case C-45/93 *Commission v. Spain* [1994] ECR I-911 at 920.

1091. *E.g.* Case 33/74 *Van Binsbergen v. Bestuur van de Bedrijfsvereniging voor de Metaal-*

freedom to provide and receive services fall within the scope of Article 59 EC.[1092] The right to equal treatment does not depend on the existence of a reciprocal agreement between the host Member State and the Member State of which the service provider or recipient is a national.[1093] A Member State may not, as was seen in section 7.4, above, make the provision of services in its territory subject to compliance with all the rules applicable in the case of establishment, as otherwise the useful effect of the freedom to provide services would be negated.[1094] As powers and rights pertaining to the exercise of state authority cannot be extended beyond national territory, their exercise does not fall within Article 59 EC.[1095]

Article 59 EC is a *lex specialis* in relation to Article 6 EC.[1096] It also applies so that a service provider may use his or her own personnel in the course of the provision of services.[1097] In order for Article 59 EC to be applicable it is not necessary that all undertakings in one Member State be

nijverheid [1974] ECR 1299 at 1311; Case 39/75 *Coenen et al. v. Sociaal-Economische Raad* [1975] ECR 1547 at 1555; Cases 62 and 63/81 *Seco SA et al. v. Établissement d'Assurance contre la Vieillesse et l'Invalidité* [1982] ECR 223 at 235; Case 76/81 *SA Transporoute et Travaux v. Minister of Public Works* [1982] ECR 417 at 427–428, and Case 205/84 *Commission v. Germany* [1986] ECR 3755 at 3802. But mere differences in laws between Member States do not themselves infringe Arts. 6, 52 or 59 EC if they apply to all-comers in accordance with objective criteria and irrespective of their nationality, see *e.g.* Case C-164/94 *Arantis v. Land Berlin* [1996] ECR I-135 at 175–176 (citing earlier authorities).

1092. Implicitly in Case 127/86 *Ministère public et al. v. Ledoux* [1988] ECR 3741 at 3758; explicitly in Case C-49/89 *Corsica Ferries France v. Direction générale des douanes français* [1989] ECR I-4441 at 4455–4456 (in which the Court referred to *Ledoux*, although the equivalent idea expressed there in fact refers to frontier workers, not to services).

1093. Case 1/72 *Frilli v. Belgian State* [1972] ECR 457 at 466 (in relation to workers); Case 186/87 *Cowan v. Trésor public* [1989] ECR 195 at 220, and Case C-20/92 *Hubbard v. Hamburger* [1993] ECR I-3777 at 3795.

1094. *E.g.* Case 205/84 *Commission v. Germany* [1986] ECR 3755 at 3802; Case C-180/89 *Commission v. Italy* [1991] ECR I-709 at 722.

1095. Case C-55/93 *Van Schaik* [1994] ECR I-4837 at 4857–4858. This case concerned non-recognition in The Netherlands of German garages as authorized issuers of road-worthiness certificates in respect of a vehicle registered The Netherlands. As to the many questions which arise in the exercise of enforcement jurisdiction, see Slot (1995) SEW 130.

1096. Case 90/76 *Srl Ufficio Henry van Ameyde v. Srl Ufficio Centrale Italiano di Assistenza Assicurativa Automobilisti in Circulazione Internazionale (UCI)* [1977] ECR 1091 at 1126; Case C-41/90 *Höfner and Elser v. Macrotron GmbH* [1991] ECR I-1979 at 2020, and Case C-92 and 326/92 *Phil Collins et al. v. Imtrat Handelsgesellschaft mbh et al.* [1993] ECR I-5145 at 5180.

1097. Case C-113/89 *Rush Portugesa Lda v. Office national d'immigration.* [1990] ECR I-1417, [1991] 2 CMLR 818. See also Case 9/88 *Lopes da Viega v. Staatssecretaris van Justitie* [1989] ECR 2989, and (in relation to third-country nationals employed in one Member State sent to another Member State in the course of the performance of services by their employer) Case C-43/93 *Vander Elst v. Office des Migrations Internationales* [1994] ECR I-3803.

preferred at the expense of undertakings from other Member States; it is sufficient that a preferential system works in favour of even only one domestic undertaking.[1098]

A number of judgments, already in the Seventies gave indications that the ambit of the prohibition of Article 59 EC went further than simply the prohibition of direct or indirect discrimination.[1099] More recent case-law has confirmed these indications, stating unequivocally that Article 59 also concerns non-discriminatory national measures which form an obstacle to the freedom to provide services.[1100] The prohibition falls therefore not merely within the third concept of freedom, it also falls within the first concept.[1101] The prohibition applies whenever the application of the national rules concerned to foreign service-providers 'is not justified by overriding reasons relating to the public interest or if the requirements embodied in that legislation are already satisfied by the rules imposed on those persons in the Member State in which they are established.'[1102]

Certainly the impression that the prohibitions in Articles 30 and 59 EC, the Treaty-based exceptions of Articles 36 and 56 EC, and the case-law based rule of reason exceptions appear to display great similarities.[1103] Yet the lines are not entirely parallel. To be sure, the general approach and exceptions ought to be interpreted in a similar manner – the unity of the market should be the same for goods and services – but so far the Court has resisted invitations to apply the *Keck and Mithouard*[1104]

1098. Case C-353/89 *Commission v. The Netherlands* [1991] ECR I-4069 at 4095. This parallels the approach in relation to 'local grab' measures under Art. 30 EC, see section 3.2.2, *ante*. Cf. Case 6/64 *Costa v. ENEL* [1964] ECR 585 at 597 (concerning establishment).

1099. Case 33/74 *Van Binsbergen v. Bestuur van de Bedrijfsvereniging voor de Metaalnijverheid* [1974] ECR 1299 at 1309; Cases 100 and 111/78 *Ministère public et al. v. Van Wesemael and Follachio et al.* [1979] ECR 35 at 52, and Case 279/80 *Webb* [1981] ECR 3305 at 3324–3325. See Leenen (1985) SEW 549.

1100. This is clear from Case 205/84 *Commission v. Germany* [1986] ECR 3755 at 3802–3803; Case C-154/89 *Commission v. France* [1991] ECR I-659 at 685–686; Case C-180/89 *Commission v. Italy* [1991] ECR I-709 at 721–723; Case C-198/89 *Commission v. Greece* [1991] ECR I-727 at 740–741, and Case C-353/89 *Commission v. The Netherlands* [1991] ECR I-4069 at 4093–4094 but is most celebratedly proclaimed in Case C-76/90 *Säger v. Dennemeyer & Co. Ltd.* [1991] ECR I-4221 at 4243 ('also the abolition of any restriction, even if it applies without distinction to national providers of services and to those of other Member States, when it is liable to prohibit or otherwise impede the activities of a provider of services established in another Member State where he lawfully provides similar services.'), see also Case C-275/92 *H.M. Customs and Excise v. Schindler et al.* [1994] ECR I-1039 at 1093.

1101. See section 1.3, *ante*.

1102. *E.g.* Case C-353/89 *Commission v. The Netherlands* [1991] ECR I-4069 at 4093–4094 (citing earlier case-law).

1103. See section 1.4, *ante* and the Commission's Communication on the scope of the freedom to provide services (O.J. 1993 C 334/3).

1104. Cases C-267 and 268/91 *Keck and Mithouard* [1993] ECR I-6097, [1995] 1 CMLR 101, as to which, see section 3.2.1, *ante*.

approach developed in relation to Article 30 in the domain of Article 59.[1105] A key element in the Court's consideration in *Alpine Investments* may well have been that the restriction was imposed by the home Member State: it was found to affect directly access to the market in services and thus to be capable of hindering trade in services between Member States.[1106] Thus while the Court has not formally stated that the *Keck and Mithouard* approach does not apply to services, the clear resistance to the invitations would suggest that the Court is not prepared to extend its scope in such a direction.

The provisions concerning services apply to obstacles to the export of services as well as to obstacles to their importation.[1107] Unlike Article 34 EC, it appears that Article 59 EC is also applicable in full force to measures applicable irrespective of the destination of the service.[1108] The perceived assimilation of the freedoms is certainly less than wholehearted.[1109]

7.4.2   The exceptions to the freedom to provide services

The general conditions for the interpretation and application of the exceptions to Article 30 EC, discussed in section 3.3.1, above, are gradually finding their way into the provisions on services. The exceptions are narrowly interpreted,[1110] they are non-economic in nature,[1111] and are subject to the

1105. In Case C-275/92 *H.M. Customs and Excise v. Schindler et al.* [1994] ECR I-1039 the Court did not deal with this issue; in Case C-384/93 *Alpine Investments BV v. Minister van Financiën* [1995] ECR I-1141 at 1177–1178 the Court rejected the view that the prohibition on cold calling was analogous to a trading rule within the *Keck and Mithouard* sense. In Cases C-34–36/95 *Konsumentombudsmannen (KO) v. De Agostini (Svenska) Förlag AB et al.* [1997] ECR I-3843 the Court considered *Keck and Mithouard* in relation to Art. 30 EC, but not in relation to Art. 59 EC. See also Case C-415/93 *Union Royale Belge des Sociétés de Football Association ASBL et al. v. Bosman et al.* [1995] ECR I-4921 at 5070–5071 and, extra-judicially, Tesauro (1995) 15 YBEL 1 at 7.

1106. Case C-384/93 *Alpine Investments BV v. Minister van Financiën* [1995] ECR I-1141 at 1178.

1107. Case 49/89 *Corsica Ferries France v. Direction générale des douanes françaises* [1989] ECR 4441, [1991] 2 CMLR 227; Case C-379/92 *Peralta* [1994] ECR I-3453; Case C-381/93 *Commission v. France* [1994] ECR I-5145, and Case C-384/93 *Alpine Investments BV v. Minister van Financiën* [1995] ECR I-1141, [1995] 2 CMLR 209. See section 6.5.1, *ante*.

1108. See Case C-384/93 *Alpine Investments* [1995] ECR I-1141 at 1178.

1109. See section 1.6, *ante*.

1110. *E.g.* Case 325/85 Case 352/85 *Bond van Adverteerders et al. v. The Netherlands State* [1988] ECR 2085 at 2135.

1111. *E.g.* Cases 62 and 63/81 *Seco SA et al. v. Établissement d'Assurance contre la Vieillesse et l'Invalidité* [1982] ECR 223 at 236–237; Case 325/85 Case 352/85 *Bond van Adverteerders et al. v. The Netherlands State* [1988] ECR 2085 at 2135; Case C-353/

requirements of necessity and proportionality.[1112] The fact that in one Member State less strict rules are applied than in others does not mean that the rules in the latter are unreasonable.[1113] The exceptions may only be invoked if there is no Community legislation on the matter.[1114] The complicating factor of Article 100a(4) EC which plays a part in a number of cases in relation to Article 30 EC does not apply to the movement of services, if the directives concerned are based on Article 57 EC in conjunction with Article 66 EC. The Court has determined that in the interpretation of a number of the exceptions the European Convention on Human Rights is of importance.[1115]

The Treaty-based exceptions. Articles 55 and 56 EC, which have already been examined,[1116] also apply in relation to the provision of services. The justifications of exercise of official authority,[1117] and public policy[1118] have been invoked on occasion, so far unsuccessfully. Exceptions such as public policy and public security also occur in Community secondary legislation in the field of services.[1119]

Case-law-based rule of reason exceptions. These exceptions may only be invoked to justify equally-applicable measures.[1120] In various Community

89 *Commission v. The Netherlands* [1991] ECR I-4069 at 4093, and Case C-17/92 *Federación de Distribuidores Cinematográficos (FEDICINE) v. Spanish State* [1993] ECR I-2239 at 2272.

1112. *E.g.* Case 205/84 *Commission v. Germany* [1986] ECR 3755 at 3802–2803; Case C-353/89 *Commission v. The Netherlands* [1991] ECR I-4069 at 4094 (citing myriad authorities), and Case C-384/93 *Alpine Investments BV v. Minister van Financiën* [1995] ECR I-1141 at 1179 (with an extensive discussion of proportionality).

1113. Case C-384/93 *Alpine Investments BV v. Minister van Financiën* [1995] ECR I-1141 at 1181.

1114. *E.g.* Case 205/84 *Commission v. Germany* [1986] ECR 3755 at 3805; Case C-353/89 *Commission v. The Netherlands* [1991] ECR I-4069 at 4093, and (in relation to goods, rather than services) Case C-37/92 *Vanacker et al* [1993] ECR I-4947 at 4978.

1115. Case C-260/89 *ERT* [1991] ECR I-2925 at 2964, and Case C-353/89 *Commission v. The Netherlands* [1991] ECR I-4069 at 4097. But contrast the situation when the national rule falls outside the scope of Community law, see Case C-159/90 *Society for the Protection of Unborn Children Ireland Ltd. v. Grogan et al.* [1991] ECR I-4685 at 4741 and Case C-164/94 *Aranitis v. Land Berlin* [1996] ECR I-135 at 177. See also Chalmers (1992) 17 ELRev. 248 at 255.

1116. See Sections 6.4 and 6.5.2, *ante.* See also section 5.2, *ante.*

1117. Case C-3/88 *Commission v. Italy* [1989] ECR 4035 at 4060 and Case C-306/89 *Commission v. Greece* [1991] ECR I-1637 at 5583; Case C-272/91 *Commission v. Italy* [1994] ECR I-1409 at 1435–1436, and Case C-114/87 *Commission v. Spain* (pending, O.J. 1997 C 166/5). See also Case 147/86 *Commission v. Greece* [1988] ECR 1637 at 1654.

1118. Case 352/85 *Bond van Adverteerders et al. v. The Netherlands State* [1988] ECR 2085 at 2135 and Case C-260/89 *ERT* [1991] ECR I-2925 at 2960.

1119. *E.g.* Dir. 90/388 (O.J. 1988 L 298/23, most recently amended by Dir. 96/19 (O.J. 1996 L 74/13)) on competition in market for telecommunications services (Art. 6).

1120. Case 353/89 *Commission v. The Netherlands* [1991] ECR I-4609 at 4093–4094.

directives rule of reason interests such as culture,[1121] protection of the public telecommunications network from harm,[1122] and professional rules of conduct[1123] have featured. Myriad heads of justifications have so far been discussed in the case-law. Thus, again, without the rule of reason being presented in any way as a closed class,[1124] the Court has recognized consumer protection;[1125] the fairness of commercial transactions;[1126] observance of professional rules of conduct connected, in particular with the administration of justice and with respect for professional ethics (including protection of the recipient of services);[1127] the prevention of

1121. See the approach in the 'Television without Frontiers Directive', Dir. 89/552 (O.J. 1989 L 298/23, most recently amended by Dir. 97/36 (O.J. 1997 L 202/60)). As to this directive, see Case C-412/93 *Société d'Importation Édouard Leclerc-Siplec v. TF1 Publicité SA et al.* [1995] ECR I-179, [1995] 3 CMLR 422; Case C-222/94 *Commission v. United Kingdom* [1996] ECR I-4025; Case C-11/95 *Commission v. Belgium* [1996] ECR I-4115; Cases C-320/94 etc. *Reti Televisive Italiane SpA (RTI) et al. v. Ministero delle Poste e Telecommunicazioni* [1996] ECR I-6471; Case C-14/96 *Denuit* [1997] ECR I-2785; Case C-56/96 *VT4 Ltd. v. Vlaamse Gemeenschap* [1997] ECR I-3143, and Cases C-34–36/95 *Konsumentombudsmannen (KO) v. De Agostini (Svenska) Förlag AB et al.* [1997] ECR I-3843.
1122. Dir. 91/263 (O.J. 1991 L 128/1, amended by Dir. 93/68 (O.J. 1993 L 220/1)), Art. 4 (implemented by myriad measures).
1123. Dir. 77/249 (O.J. 1977 L 78/17, most recently amended by the Act of Austrian, Finnish and Swedish Accession (as adapted). See Case 292/86 *Gullung v. Conseils de l'ordre des avocats au barreau de Colmar et de Saverne* [1988] ECR 111, [1988] 2 CMLR 57; Case 427/85 *Commission v. Germany* [1988] ECR 1123, [1989] 2 CMLR 677, and Case C-55/94 *Gebhard v. Consiglio dell'Ordine degli Avvocati e Procurati di Milano* [1995] ECR I-4165, [1996] 1 CMLR 603.
1124. There is a good list of justifications in Case C-353/89 *Commission v. The Netherlands* [1991] ECR I-4069 at 4094.
1125. *E.g.* Case 220/83 *Commission v. France* [1986] ECR 3663 at 3709; Case 252/83 *Commission v. Denmark* [1986] ECR 3713 at 3748–3749; Case 205/84 *Commission v. Germany* [1986] ECR 3755 at 3803–3804; Case 206/84 *Commission v. Ireland* [1986] ECR 3817 at 3850; Case C-180/89 *Commission v. Italy* [1991] ECR I-709 at 723, and Case C-198/89 *Commission v. Greece* [1991] ECR I-727 at 741–742. See also Case C-275/92 *H.M. Customs and Excise v. Schindler et al.* [1994] ECR I-1039 at 1096, and Case C-384/93 *Alpine Investments BV v. Minister van Financiën* [1995] ECR I-1141 at 1179-1180.
1126. *E.g.* Case C-384/93 *Alpine Investments BV v. Minister van Financiën* [1995] ECR I-1141 at 1179–1180 and Cases C-34–36/95 *Konsumentombudsmannen (KO) v. De Agostini (Svenska) Förlag AB et al.* [1997] ECR I-3843 at 3893. This clearly also embraces protection in relation to advertising, *ibid.*
1127. *E.g.* Case 33/74 *Van Binsbergen v. Bestuur van de Bedrijfsvereniging voor de Metaalnijverheid* [1974] ECR 1299 at 1309–1310; Cases 100 and 111/78 *Ministère public et al. v. Van Wesemael and Follachio et al.* [1979] ECR 35 at 52, and Case 279/80 *Webb* [1981] ECR 3305 at 3324–3325–3326; Case 292/86 *Gullung v. Conseils de l'ordre des avocats au barreau de Colmar et de Saverne* [1988] ECR 111 at 137–138; Case C-76/90 *Säger v. Dennemeyer & Co. Ltd.* [1991] ECR I-4221 at 4244; Case C-106/91 *Ramrath v. Ministre de la Justice* [1992] ECR I-3351 at 3384; Case C-19/92 *Kraus v. Land Baden-Württemberg* [1993] ECR I-1663 at 1697, and Case C-3/95 *Reisebüro Broede v. Sandker* [1996] ECR I-6511 at 6540.

fraud, the social order, and legitimate social policy objectives[1128] as being in principle legitimate justifications. It has also recognized the interests of ensuring the good repute of the national financial sector;[1129] protection of workers and the labour market;[1130] the protection of intellectual property rights;[1131] the effectiveness of fiscal supervision (including the coherence of the tax system);[1132] control of wagering contracts or gambling;[1133] cultural policy objectives,[1134] including the conservation of the national historical and archaeological heritage,[1135] and discussed the preservation of artistic heritage by promotion of the use of a particular language.[1136] Moreover, it has recognized or discussed the interest of road safety[1137] and of marine safety,[1138] as well as environmental protection[1139] as possible justifications. However, as in the case of the rule of reason justifications advanced in relation to the free movement of goods, on many occasions these justifications have been pleaded to no avail, as the measures were either unnecessary or disproportionate, or the alleged justifications were even merely pretexts.

1128. Case C-275/92 *H.M. Customs and Excise v. Schindler et al.* [1994] ECR I-1039 at 1096–1097.
1129. Case C-384/93 *Alpine Investments BV v. Minister van Financiën* [1995] ECR I-1141 at 1179.
1130. Case 279/80 *Webb* [1981] ECR 3305 at 3325–3326; Cases 62 and 63/81 *Seco SA et al. v. Établissement d'Assurance contre la Vieillesse et l'Invalidité* [1982] ECR 223 at 236–237; Case C-113/89 *Rush Portugesa Lda v. Office national d'immigration.* [1990] ECR I-1417 at 1445, and Case C-43/93 *Vander Elst v. Office des Migrations Internationales* [1994] ECR I-3803 at 3826.
1131. Case 62/79 *SA Compagnie Générale pour la Diffusion de la Télévision Coditel et al. v. SA Ciné Vog Films et al.* [1980] ECR 881 at 903–904; Case 395/87 *Ministère public v. Tournier* [1989] ECR 2521 at 2571, and Cases C-92 and 326/92 *Phil Collins et al. v. Imtrat Handelsgesellschaft mbh et al.* [1993] ECR I-5145 at 5180.
1132. Case C-204/90 *Bachmann v. Belgian State* [1992] ECR I-249 at 282–285 and Case C-300/90 *Commission v. Belgium* [1992] ECR I-305 at 319–321.
1133. Case 15/78 *Société Générale Alsacienne de Banque SA v. Koestler* [1978] ECR 1971 at 1981 and Case C-275/92 *H.M. Customs and Excise v. Schindler et al.* [1994] ECR I-1039 at 1089. See also Case C-272/91 *Commission v. Italy* [1994] ECR I-1409.
1134. *E.g.* Case C-353/89 *Commission v. The Netherlands* [1991] ECR 4069 at 4097; Case C-154/89 *Commission v. France* [1991] ECR I-659 at 687; Case C-180/89 *Commission v. Italy* [1991] ECR I-709 at 723, and Case C-198/89 *Commission v. Greece* [1991] ECR I-727 at 741–742, and Case C-211/91 *Commission v. Belgium* [1992] ECR I-6757 at 6776–6777.
1135. Case C-180/89 *Commission v. Italy* [1991] ECR I-709 at 723.
1136. Case C-211/91 *Commission v. Belgium* [1992] ECR I-6757 at 6777.
1137. Case C-55/93 *Van Schaik* [1994] ECR I-4837 at 4858.
1138. Case C-18/93 *Corsica Ferries Italia Srl v. Corpo dei Piloti del porto di Genova* [1994] ECR I-1783 at 1823, although in weak terms.
1139. *Ibid.*, although in weak terms. In Case C-37/92 *Vanacker et al.* [1993] ECR I-4947 at 4972–4974 (one of the waste oils cases concerning goods) Lenz, Adv. Gen. also came to this conclusion (on the basis of earlier cases on that subject).

7.5 Service monopolies and Article 90 EC

There is no provision relating to services which is comparable to Article 37 EC.[1140] With the development of telecommunication markets the question arose whether the principle laid down in Case 59/75 *Pubblico Ministero v. Manghera et al.*[1141] that exclusive import rights are incompatible with the EC Treaty also applied in relation to the importation of reports by means of telecommunication. In relation to a telecommunications monopoly the Court has found that although the existence of a service monopoly is not in itself incompatible with Community law, 'the manner in which such a monopoly is organized and exercised must not infringe the provisions of the Treaty on the free movement of goods and services or the rules on competition.'[1142] Service monopolies have also been considered in the areas of harbour facilities,[1143] employment placement,[1144] and veterinary services.[1145] Monopolies in the sector of waste oils disposal have in fact been dealt with as monopolies concerning goods rather than services.[1146] In many of these cases the Member States concerned have sought to rely in their observations before the Court on Article 90(1) and (2) EC, but to no avail.[1147] The Commission thus adopted Directive 90/388 on competition in the markets for telecommunications services.[1148]

1140. As to Art. 37, see section 3.4, *ante*. See, generally, Emmerich in Forstmoser (ed.), *Festschrift für Max Keller zum 65. Geburtstag* (Zurich, 1989) 685 and Hailbronner (1991) NJW 593.

1141. [1976] ECR 91, [1976] 1 CMLR 557.

1142. Case C-260/89 *ERT* [1991] ECR I-2925 at 2957. See also Cases C-271/90 *etc. Spain et al. v. Commission* [1992] ECR I-5833, [1993] 4 CMLR 110; Case C-17/94 *Gervais et al.* [1995] ECR I-4353, and Case C-55/96 *Job Centre Coop. arl* [1997] ECR I-7119. See further, Case C-55/93 *Van Schaik* [1994] ECR I-4837; Case C-37/92 *Vanacker et al* [1993] ECR I-4947, and Case C-163/96 *Raso et al.* [1998] ECR I-533.

1143. Case C-179/90 *Merci convenzionali porto di Genova SpA v. Siderurgica Gabrielli SpA* [1991] ECR I-5889. See also case C-163/96 *Raso et al.* [1998] ECR I-533, where a company which was itself established in a port and provided dock labour there could not also have a monopoly on the supply of temporary labour to other undertakings who were active in that port. See further, Case C-266/96 *Corsica Ferries France SA v. Groupo Antichi Ormeggiatori del Porto di Genova Coop.arl* [1998] ECR I-nyr (18 June 1998).

1144. Case C-41/90 *Höfner and Elser v. Macrotron GmbH* [1991] ECR I-1979, [1993] 4 CMLR 306 and Case C-55/96 *Job Centre Coop. arl* [1997] ECR I-nyr (11 December 1997). See also Case C-163/96 *Raso et al.* [1998] ECR I-533.

1145. Case C-17/94 *Gervais et al.* [1995] ECR I-4353.

1146. See Case C-37/92 *Vanacker et al* [1993] ECR I-4947 (referring also to other waste oils judgments).

1147. See, further, Chapter VIII, section 4.7, *post*.

1148. O.J. 1990 L 192/10, most recently amended by Dir. 96/19 (O.J. 1996 L 74/13). The directive largely survived a challenge in Cases C-271/90 *etc. Spain et al. v. Commission* [1992] ECR I-5833, [1994] 4 CMLR 110 (the directive was annulled to the extent to which it purported to govern special rights). As to subsequent developments, see Chapter VIII, section 4.7.3, *post*. See, generally, the Commission's Green paper on

7.6 Harmonization and freedom to provide services

In its White Paper *Completing the Internal Market*[1149] in 1985 the Commission observed that although free movement had been directly applicable[1150] since 1970, firms and individuals had not yet succeeded in taking full advantage of that freedom. Thus it considered that swift action should be taken to open up the whole market for services.

Prior to 1970, in implementation of the General Programmes on Establishment and Services,[1151] myriad transitional directives were adopted, primarily in the commercial and industrial and handicrafts sectors.[1152] They were intended to remove the obstacles which existed because of various establishment requirements as to skill and professional knowledge, by regarding actual exercise of a trade or managerial activities in the branches of trade or industry concerned as evidence of the requisite commercial knowledge and professional skill. Later attention[1153] turned to activities in the insurance,[1154] and banking[1155] sectors, the stock exchange sector,[1156]

telecommunications services (O.J. 1988 C 257/1) and Motesteshar, *European Community Telecommunications Regulation* (London, 1993).

1149. COM (85) 310 Final, points 98–99.
1150. Clearly what the Commission meant was that the right had been directly effective.
1151. See notes 942 and 1071 respectively, *supra*.
1152. See, generally, section 6.6, *ante*.
1153. See, generally, Campbell (ed.), *Financial Services in the New Europe* (London, 1993); Dassesse *et al.*, *EC Banking Law* (London, 1994); Dixon, *Banking in Europe: The Single Market* (London, 1991); Hoffmann, *Banken- und Börsenrecht der EWG* (Baden-Baden, 1990); Ferrarini (1994) 31 CMLRev. 1283; Van Gerven (1991) *Revue de la Banque* 39; Ottow (1992) 29 CMLRev. 511; Roth (1990) *Rabels Z.* 63, and Strivens (1992) 29 CMLRev. 283.
1154. The First Life Assurance Directive, Dir. 79/267 (O.J. 1979 L 63/1, most recently amended by Dir. 95/26 (O.J. 1995 L 168/7)), the Second Life Assurance Directive, Dir. 90/619 (O.J. 1990 L 330/50, likewise so amended), and the Third Life Assurance Directive, Dir. 92/96 (O.J. 1992 L 360/1, likewise so amended); the First Non-Life Directive, Dir. 73/240 (O.J. 1973 L 228/3, likewise so amended), the Second Non-Life Directive, Dir. 88/357 (O.J. 1988 L 172/1) which was most recently amended by the Third Non-Life Directive, Dir. 92/49 (O.J. 1992 L 228/1, also amended by Dir. 95/26, *supra*). See also Dir. 78/473 (O.J. 1978 L 151/25) on co-insurance.
1155. See Dir. 73/183 (O.J. 1973 L 194/1, corrig. O.J. 1975 L 45/21) self-employed activities of banks and other financial institutions; the First Banking Directive, Dir. 77/780 (O.J. 1977 L 322/30, most recently amended by Dir. 96/13 (O.J. 1996 L 66/15)), and the Second Banking Directive, Dir. 89/646 (O.J. 1989 L 386/1, corrig. O.J. 1990 L 83/128, most recently amended by Dir. 92/30 (O.J. 1992 L 110/52)). A further amendment to Dir. 79/780 has been agreed and publication is awaited. (Common Position (O.J. 1998 C 135/32) approved unamended).
1156. Dir. 79/279 (O.J. 1979 L 66/21, most recently amended by Dir. 88/627, *infra*) on admission to listing; Dir. 89/390 (O.J. 1980 L 100/1, most recently amended by Dir. 94/18 (O.J. 1994 L 135/1)) on listing particulars of securities for which admission has been applied; Dir. 82/121 (O.J. 1981 L 48/26) on information which listed companies must regularly publish; Dir. 88/627 (O.J. 1988 L 348/62) on information to be published on the acquisition or disposal of major interests in listed companies; Dir. 89/

and investment services in securities.[1157] Measures have also been taken in the interests of investor protection[1158] and with regard to capital adequacy requirements and the like.[1159] Two Green Papers indicate future policy orientations in this area: *Financial Services: meeting consumers' expectations*,[1160] and *Financial Services: enhancing consumer confidence*.[1161] In this vein, Directive 97/5 deals with cross-border credit transfers,[1162] and the Green Papers on *Commercial Communications in the Internal market*[1163] and *Legal Protection for Encrypted Services*,[1164] and the proposal for a directive relating to conditional access services[1165] reflect the growing importance of the internet and electronic services in general. The Commission has also adopted a Communication on electronic means of payment and a Recommendation to increase consumer confidence in this area.[1166] An interpretative Communication on services and the general good in the banking sector has been published,[1167] as has a draft of a similar interpretative Communication for the insurance sector.[1168] The Commission has also published a Green Paper on supplementary pensions in the internal market.[1169]

Another major area of Community activity relates to the procurement

298 (O.J. 1989 L 124/8) on prospectuses to be published when transferable securities are offered to the public. See also the Unit Trusts Directive, Dir. 85/611 (O.J. 1985 L 375/3, most recently amended by Dir. 95/26 (O.J. 1995 L 168/7)), and Dir. 89/592 (O.J. 1989 L 334/30) on insider dealing.

1157. Dir. 93/22 (O.J. 1993 L 141/27, most recently amended by Dir. 97/9 (O.J. 1997 L 84/22)). Proposals to amend Dir. 93/22 further foundered when conciliation failed in April 1998.

1158. Dir. 94/19 (O.J. 1994 L 135/5) on Deposit-Guarantee Schemes, and Dir. 97/9 (O.J. 1997 L 84/22) on Investor Compensation Schemes, the latter instrument being based on Art. 100a EC.

1159. Dir. 89/299 (O.J. 1989 L 124/16, most recently amended by Dir. 92/30, *infra*) on credit institutions' own funds; Dir. 89/647 (O.J. 1989 L 286/1, most recently amended by Dir. 96/10, *infra*) on their solvency ratio; Dir. 92/30 (O.J. 1992 L 110/52) on the their supervision on a consolidated basis, which was amended by Dir. 93/6 (O.J. 1993 L 141/1) on capital adequacy requirements for investment firms and credit institutions; and Dir. 92/121 (O.J. 1992 L 29/1, amended by the Act of Austrian, Finnish and Swedish Accession (as adapted)). A further amendment to Dirs. 89/647 and 93/6 has been agreed and publication is awaited (Common Position (O.J. 1998 C 135/32) approved unamended).

1160. COM (96) 209 Final; see also COM (97) 309 Final..

1161. COM (97) 309 Final.

1162. O.J. 1997 L 43/25. This directive is based on Art. 100a EC.

1163. COM (96) 192 Final.

1164. COM (96) 76 Final.

1165. COM (97) 356 Final (O.J. 1997 C 314/7).

1166. COM (97) 353 Final. See also the Communication on a European initiative in electronic commerce COM (97) 157 Final.

1167. O.J. 1997 C 209/6.

1168. O.J. 1997 C 365/7.

1169. COM (97) 283 Final.

of works, supplies and services.[1170] The initial directives from the Seventies[1171] were being widely ignored and enforcement seemed scarcely a priority. All that changed with the identification of procurement as a priority area in the White Paper *Completing the Internal Market*.[1172] The present public procurement provisions are contained in Directives 92/50 for services;[1173] 92/36 for supplies,[1174] and 93/37 for works.[1175] Procurement by the utilities is governed by Directive 93/38.[1176] The extension of procurement rules to the utilities was in fact one of the major achievements in this field. Two directives also lay down requirements as to the availability of remedies in relation to public and utilities procurement.[1177] For various reasons (such as the desire not to disrupt commercial relationships) companies are sometimes reluctant to bring actions before their national courts when they feel themselves unfairly excluded from a procurement procedure, so much case-law has taken the form of infringement proceedings brought by the Commission,[1178] many of which demonstrate the major problems which

1170. See, generally, Arrowsmith, *The Law of Public and Utilities Procurement* (London, 1996); Fernández-Martin, *The EC Procurement Rules: a Critical Analysis* (Oxford, 1996); Gormley (ed.), *Gordian Knots in European Public Procurement Law* (Cologne, 1997); Van Marissing, *De regelgeving voor overheidsopdrachten op het niveau van de EG en de GATT, alsmede de gevolgen hiervan voor de Nederlandse regelgeving* (Deventer, 1995); Trepte, *Public Procurement in the EEC* (Bicester, 1993); Van der Horst and Van Weele, *Overheidsaanschafbeleid in Europees perspectief: de invloed van de EG-regelgeving op de inkopende overheid* (Deventer, 1992); Van der Meent, *Overheidsaanbestedingen: de EG-rechtelijke context* (Deventer, 1995); Weiss, *Public Procurement in European Community Law* (London, 1993); Brown (1993) 30 CMLRev. 721, and Winter (1991) 28 CMLRev. 741. See further, generally, *Public Procurement Law Review*, and the *Reports of the FIDE XIV Congress* (Madrid, 1990), Vol. I.
1171. Dirs. 71/305 (O.J. English Special Edition 1971 (II), p. 682) and 77/62 (O.J. 1977 L 13/1).
1172. COM (85) 310 Final, points 81–87. See, further, COM (98) 143 Final.
1173. O.J. 1992 L 209/1, most recently amended by Dir. 97/52 (O.J. 1997 L 328/1) to take account of the Agreement on Government Procurement (GPA) negotiated in the Uruguay Round.
1174. O.J. 1993 L 199/1, likewise so amended.
1175. O.J. 1993 L 199/54, likewise so amended.
1176. O.J. 1993 L 199/84, most recently amended by Dir. 98/4 (O.J. 1998 L 101/1) as a result of the Uruguay Round.
1177. Dirs. 89/665 (O.J. 1989 L 395/33) covering public procurement, and 92/13 (O.J. 1992 L 76/14, amended by the Act of Austrian, Finnish and Swedish Accession (as adapted)). See Gormley (1992) PPLR 259 and Gormley in Lonbay and Biondi (eds.), *Remedies for Breach of EC Law* (Chichester, 1997) 155.
1178. *E.g.* Case 45/87 *Commission v. Ireland* [1988] ECR 4929, [1989] 1 CMLR 225, see Gormley (1989) 14 ELRev. 156; Case 194/88 R *Commission v. Italy* [1988] ECR 4547; Case C-3/88 *Commission v. Italy* [1989] ECR 4035; Case C-243/89 *Commission v. Denmark* [1993] ECR I-3353; Case C-247/89 *Commission v. Portugal* [1991] ECR I-3659; Case C-24/91 *Commission v. Spain* [1992] ECR I-1989; Case C-362/90 *Commission v. Italy* [1992] ECR I-2353; Case C-360/89 *Commission v. Italy* [1992] ECR I-3401; Case C-272/91 *Commission v. Italy* [1994] ECR 1409; Case C-328/92 *Commission v.*

still exist in this field, but some references for preliminary rulings are now being made in this area by the national courts.[1179]

8. FREE MOVEMENT OF PAYMENTS AND CAPITAL

Unlike in the cases of the free movement of goods, persons and services, the emphasis in the field of the fourth freedom, that of movement of capital, and the fifth freedom, that of payments, lies more in the field of legislation than in contribution of case-law. Until the entry into force of the TEU, freedom of movement of capital was governed by Articles 67–73 EEC and the directives based thereon.[1180] The free movement of payments was governed by Articles 67(2) and 106 EEC. Globally the Treaty system amounted to freedom for payments and partial freedom for capital movements, with the definition of these concepts and their inter-relationship being judicially considered on several occasions,[1181] particularly in the

Spain [1994] ECR I-1569; Case C-87/94 *Commission v. Belgium* [1996] ECR I-2043; Case C-359/93 *Commission v. The Netherlands* [1995] ECR I-157; Case C-79/94 *Commission v. Greece* [1995] ECR I-1071; Case C-57/94 *Commission v. Italy* [1995] ECR I-1249; Case C-433/93 *Commission v. Germany* [1995] ECR I-2303; Case C-314/94 *Commission v. Germany* [1996] ECR I-1949; Case C-234/95 *Commission v. France* [1996] ECR I-2415; Case C-253/95 *Commission v. Germany* [1996] ECR I-2423; Case C-311/95 *Commission v. Greece* [1996] ECR I-2433; Case C-231/95 *Commission v. Greece* [1996] ECR I-4459; Case C-311/96 *Commission v. France* [1997] ECR I-2939; Case C-312/96 *Commission v. France* [1997] ECR I-2947, and Case C-43/97 *Commission v. Italy* [1997] ECR I-4671.

1179. Cases 27–29/86 *SA Constructions et Enterprise Industrielles (CEI) et al. v. Fonds des Routes et al.* [1987] ECR 3347; Case 31/87 *Gebroeders Beentjes BV v. Staat der Nederlanden* [1988] ECR 4635, [1990] 1 CMLR 287; Case 103/88 *Fratelli Constanzo SpA v. Comune di milano* [1989] ECR I-1839, [1990] 3 CMLR 239; Case C-21/88 *Società Du Pont de Nemours Italiana SpA v. Unità Sanitaria Locale No 2 di Carrara et al.* [1990] ECR I-889, [1991] 1 CMLR 25; Case C-351/88 *Laboratori Bruneau Srl v. Unità Sanitaria Locale No R/M 24 di Monterotondo* [1991] ECR I-3641; Case C-295/89 *Impresa Donà Alfonso di Donà Alfonso & Figli v. Consorzio per lo sviluppo industriale del comune di Monfalcone et al.* [1991] ECR I-2967 (summary publication); Case C-331/92 *Gestión Hotelera Internacional SA v. Comunidad Autónoma de Canarias et al.* [1994] ECR I-1329; Case C-389/92 *Ballast Nedam Groep NV v. Belgian State* [1994] ECR I-1289; Case C-324/93 *R. v. Secretary of State for the Home Department, ex parte Evans Medical Ltd. et al.* [1995] ECR I-563; Case C-143/94 *Furlanis Costruzioni Generali SpA v. Azienda Nazionale Autonoma Strade (ANAS) et al.* [1995] ECR I-3633; Case C-392/93 *R. v. H.M. Treasury, ex parte British Telecommunications plc* [1996] ECR I-1631, [1996] 2 CMLR 217; Case C-54/96 *Dorsch Consult Ingenieursgesellschaft mbH v. Bundesbaugesellschaft mbH Berlin* [1997] ECR I-4961; Case C-5/97 *Ballast Nedam Groep NV v. Belgian State* [1997] ECR I-7549, and Case C-44/96 *Mannesmann Anlagebau Austria AG et al. v. Strohal Rotationsdruck GesmbH* [1998] ECR I-73.

1180. Most recently Dir. 88/361 (O.J. 1988 L 178/5). See Cases C-358 and 416/93 *Bordessa et al.* [1995] ECR I-361.

1181. Case 7/78 *R. v. Thompson et al.* [1978] ECR 2247, [1979] 1 CMLR 47; Case 203/80 *Casati* [1981] ECR 2595, [1982] 1 CMLR 365; Cases 286/82 and 26/83 *Luisi and Carbone v. Ministero del Tesoro* [1984] ECR 377, [1985] 3 CMLR 352; Case 157/85

context of the direct effect of the provisions involved and the degree of liberalization achieved at the relevant times. The somewhat tardy liberalization of capital movements when compared with the other freedoms was undoubtedly due to the close relationship between capital movements, balance of payments questions and monetary policy. Articles 108 and 109 EEC thus served as interim solutions in the event of balance of payments difficulties.

Since the entry into force of the TEU, Title VI of the EC Treaty contains the legal development of the model for Economic and Monetary Union, within which the freedom of movement of payments and of capital plays an important role. This is discussed further in Chapter IX, below. On the basis of Article 73a EC the old EEC regime has been replaced since 1 January 1994 by the new system which is set out in Articles 73b–73g EC. Given the long period of delay before the TEU actually entered into force, the transitional system of Article 73h EC, the text of which is identical to that of Article 106 EEC, lasted a mere two months, thereby forming an example of a short-term Treaty provision. The new Chapter on capital and payments is structured according to the scheme of first setting out the prohibition, found in Article 73b EC; then Articles 73c–g EC deal with various exceptions. This structure is followed in the discussion below.[1182]

8.1 The beneficiaries

Notwithstanding the exceptions discussed in section 8.3, below, free movement of capital and payments, both within the Community and between Member States and third countries is not restricted in terms of categories of beneficiaries, unlike the free movement of persons and services. This means that, as with the free movement of goods, third-country nationals may also rely on Article 73b EC.[1183]

> *Brugnoni et al. v. Cassa di Risparmio di Genova e Imperia* [1986] ECR 2013; Case 143/86 *East et al. v. Cuddy et al.* [1989] ECR 625; Case 308/86 *Ministère public v. Lambert* [1988] ECR 4369; Case C-148/91 *Vereniging Veronica Omroep Organisatie v. Commissariaat voor de Media* [1993] ECR I-487, and Cases C-358 and 416/93 *Bordessa et al.* [1995] ECR I-361.

1182. See, also following such a structure, Buijs in *Praktijkboek EG-recht* (Deventer, loose-leaf since 1992) Part B4, and Smits (1992) SEW 702 (the approach of these authors was used in the preparation of the Dutch edition of this work). See further, Cranston (ed.) *The Single Market and the Law of Banking* (London, 1991); Kiemel in Von der Groeben *et al.* (eds.), *op. cit.* (see note , *supra*) Vol. 1 1524 (with extensive bibliography); Stuyck (ed.), *Financial and Monetary Integration in the European Economic Community* (Deventer, 1993); Usher, *The Law of Money and Financial Services in the European Community* (Oxford, 1994); Dourado (1994) *EC Tax Law Review* 176; Lelakis (1991) RMUE 47, and Weber (1992) EuZW 561.

1183. In the same sense as regards capital and payments, Lauwaars and Timmermans, *op. cit.* (see note 135, *supra*) 214.

8.2 The rule: prohibition of restrictions on movement

Save as far as the specific exceptions are concerned, all restrictions on movement of capital and on payments within the Community and between the Member States and third countries are prohibited.[1184] The word 'all' indicates that it is not merely discriminatory measures which are prohibited, but also other measures. It remains to be seen whether the case-law will make the same distinction in these areas (at least as regards justifications) between discriminatory and equally-applicable measures as has been developed in relation to the free movement of goods and of services.[1185]

The legal distinction between capital and payments in Community law has now disappeared, and the restrictions on payments have also gone, so that Annex III EC, referred to in Article 73h EC, no longer has any significance.[1186] As far as payments are concerned, Directive 97/5 deals with cross-border credit transfers[1187] and the Commission has issued a draft notice on the application of the competition rules in that sector.[1188]

Given that Article 73b(2) EC refers to the prohibition on restrictions on payments operating '[w]ithin the framework of the provisions set out in this Chapter' it might be argued that such a prohibition only related to payments concerning movements of capital (the other subject of the Chapter in addition to payments), but such a restrictive view is wholly at odds with the objectives of the internal market. It is submitted that the prohibition relates, as was expressly mentioned in the old Article 106(2) EEC, not merely to movements of capital but also to the movement of goods and services.[1189] Moreover, as can be deduced from Article 73h EC, it also relates to matters such as salary transfers and to the movement of people. Even with this broad interpretation, the question arises whether all payments are liberalized, or only those which are linked to the other freedoms. In the latter case restrictions could still exist in relation to cross-border donations or money-laundering. It is submitted that these types of financial transactions may not be combated by restrictions on movements of capital or payments. In the case of money-laundering operations, these certainly may be caught at source – rather than by means of inter-state (border) controls – without constituting an indirect restriction of movements of capital or

1184. Art. 73b EC.
1185. See *ibid.* 207.
1186. Smits (1992) SEW 702 at 706.
1187. O.J. 1997 L 43/25. This directive is based on Art. 100a EC.
1188. SEC (95) 1403 Final. The ECB may make regulations to ensure efficient and sound clearing and payment systems within the Community and with other countries, Statute ESCB/ECB, Art. 22.
1189. See Cases C-358 and 416/93 *Bordessa et al.* [1995] ECR I-361 at 383.

payments.[1190] The Court has however held that Member States are entitled to make the export of coins, banknotes or bearer cheques subject to prior declaration, although they are not entitled to require prior authorization.[1191]

Article 73b EC is directly effective.[1192] The Court has so far been seized of a number of cases, most of which are still pending at the date at which this work states the law.[1193] Unlike the other freedoms, the prohibition also extends to movements between Member States and third countries,[1194] although this additional liberalization is somewhat tempered by three additional exceptions, considered in section 8.3, below.

8.3   The exceptions to the prohibition

The Treaty structure makes an implicit distinction between exceptions which apply in intra-Community movements and those applicable to movements involving third countries. The intra-Community exceptions, specified in Article 73e EC, are addressed to the Member States. The exceptions relating to movements involving third countries may be invoked by the Community and the Member States. Article 73d EC contains general exceptions applicable to all financial movements.

General exceptions. Article 73d(1)(b) EC envisages for all financial transactions, within the Community and between the Member States and third countries, an exception on the grounds of public policy or public security. Thus measures to ensure effective fiscal supervision and to prevent illegal activities such as tax evasion, money-laundering, drug trafficking or terrorism are covered by Article 73d(1)(b),[1195] and they justify a prior declaration requirement but they do not justify a requirement of prior authorization.[1196] Article 73d(1)(b) thus permits declaration requirements

---

1190. See Art. 73d(1)(b) EC. See also WQs E-204/93 (Kostopoulos) O.J. 1994 C 219/1 on offshore banking and E-2251/93 (Ribeiro) O.J. 1994 C 385/5 on money-laundering of drugs money. As to money-laundering, see Dir. 91/308 (O.J. 1991 L 166/77).

1191. Cases C-163/94 etc. Sanz de Lera et al. [1995] ECR I-4821 at 4837–4839.

1192. Cases C-163/94 etc. Sanz de Lera et al. [1995] ECR I-4821 at 4841–4843.

1193. See ibid. and Case C-118/96 Safir v. Skattemyndighet i Dalarnas Län [1998] ECR I-nyr (28 April 1998), and the following cases: Case C-178/96 Serbini v. Ministero del Commercio con l'Estero (O.J. 1996 C 197/16); Case C-410/96 Ambry (O.J. 1997 C 74/12), and Case C-222/97 Trummer v. Mayer (O.J. 1997 C 228/12).

1194. See, generally, Dec. 96/412 (O.J. 1996 L 167/23) as to the results of negotiations within the WTO on financial services and on movement of natural persons. See also Reg. 2271/96 (O.J. 1996 L 309/1, corrig. O.J. 1997 L 309/1).

1195. Cases C-163/94 etc. Sanz de Lera et al. [1995] ECR I-4821 at 4837.

1196. Ibid. at 4838–4839.

for administrative or statistical purposes. Indeed, such provisions are also to be found in various of the banking and insurance directives.[1197] However, the exercise of this power must be proportionate.[1198]

Finally, Article 73d(1)(a) permits the Member States to apply relevant provisions of their tax laws which distinguish between taxpayers who are not in the same situation with regard to their place of residence or with regard to the place where their capital is invested. Declaration No. 7 attached to the Final Act on the occasion of the signature of the TEU states that this right of the Member States 'will apply only with respect to the relevant provisions which exist at the end of 1993.' It further provides that the declaration only applies to capital movements between Member States and to payments effected between Member States.

Somewhat hidden in Article 73d(2) EC is that the provisions of this Chapter of the Treaty are without prejudice to the applicability of restrictions on the right of establishment which are compatible with the Treaty. The exceptions in Article 73d are thus well tied-in to the exceptions to the other freedoms, and the necessity and proportionality requirements are made manifest in Article 73d(3) EC, which clearly draws on Article 36 EC, *mutatis mutandis*. Thus the measures and procedures permitted by Article 73d(1) and (2) may not constitute a means of arbitrary discrimination or a disguised restriction on the free movement of capital and payments as defined in Article 73b EC. The interest of the coherence of the fiscal system, recognized by the Court in Case C-204/90 *Bachmann v. Belgian State*[1199] is clearly reflectd in Article 73d(1)(a) EC.

As has been suggested in section 8.2, above, the broad formulation of Article 73b EC may probably permit rule of reason exceptions in respect of equally-applicable measures, but this will have to await judicial consideration.[1200]

Exceptions applicable only to intra-Community movements

The exceptions in respect of movements of capital in Article 73e were applicable only until the end of 1995 at the latest, and in fact applied only

1197. *E.g.* the Second Banking Directive, Dir. 89/646 (O.J. 1989 L 386/1, as amended), Art. 21.
1198. See Cases C-163/94 *etc. Sanz de Lera et al.* [1995] ECR I-4821 at 4838–4841 (citing earlier case-law).
1199. [1992] ECR I-249 at 282–284; see also Case C-300/90 *Commission v. Belgium* [1992] ECR I-305 at 319–320.
1200. It might be possible to argue that restrictions could be justified in the interest of, say, the pluriformity of the media, or even consumer protection or the good reputation of a financial centre, see *e.g.* Case C-148/91 *Vereniging Veronica Omroep Organisatie v. Commissariaat voor de Media* [1993] ECR I-487 and Case C-384/93 *Alpine Investments BV v. Minister van Financiën* [1995] ECR I-1141, [1995] 2 CMLR 209.

for the benefit of Greece.[1201] On 16 May 1994 Greece abolished its last remaining restrictions, which means that there are no more restrictions on the movement of capital within the European Union.[1202]

Only in the Second Stage of Economic and Monetary Union (which now means until the end of 1998) may the Member States rely on the provisions of Articles 109h or 109i EC (which largely repeat the old Articles 108 and 109 EEC) where they are in difficulties or are seriously threatened with balance of payments difficulties, or face a sudden crisis in the balance of payments. By virtue of Article 109k(6) EC, Member States with a derogation in the Third Stage of Economic and Monetary Union may continue to avail themselves of Articles 109h and 109i EC.[1203]

Exceptions applicable only to movements between Member States and third countries

Article 73c(1) EC permits the application to third countries of any restrictions existing on 31 December 1993 under national or Community law adopted in respect of the movement of capital to or from third countries involving direct investment, including in real estate, establishment, the provision of financial services or the admission of securities to capital markets. This means that the reciprocity provisions of the Second Banking Directive could remain intact.[1204] Restrictions in the field of current payments for transactions in goods and services are thus excluded.[1205] Article 73c(2) EC permits the Council, while endeavouring to achieve the objective of free movement of capital between Member States and third countries to the greatest extent possible and without prejudice to the other Chapters of the EC Treaty, to adopt measures on the movement of capital to or from third countries involving direct investment, including in real estate, establishment, the provision of financial services or the admission of securities to capital markets. It acts by qualified majority on the basis of a proposal from the Commission; thus, as in the case of the common commercial policy, the European Parliament is not consulted. If, however, such measures constitute a step back in Community law as regards the liberalization of the movement of capital to or from third countries, unanimity in the

---

1201. On the basis of Dir. 92/122 (O.J. 1992 L 409/33).

1202. *General Report 1994* (Brussels, Luxembourg, 1995) point 138. (Save for requirements based on Art. 73d, *ante*.)

1203. As to the meaning of 'Member States with a derogation', see Art. 109k(3) EC. As from 1 January 1999, this will mean Denmark, Greece, Sweden and the United Kingdom (the four Member States not (yet) moving to the third stage of EMU).

1204. Dir. 89/646 (O.J. 1989 L 386/1, as amended), Art. 9. See Smits (1992) SEW 702 at 707.

1205. Buijs, *op. cit.* (see note 1182, *supra*) B4–33.

Council is required. The Council has now approved the results of the negotiations in the WTO on financial services and the movement of natural persons.[1206] It has also adopted, on the basis of Articles 73c, 113 and 235 EC, Regulation 2271/96 on protection against the extraterritorial application of third countries' laws and acts based on or resulting therefrom.[1207]

The Council, acting by qualified majority on a proposal from the Commission and after consulting the ECB may adopt safeguard measures with regard to third countries for a period not exceeding six months if such measures are strictly necessary to combat, in exceptional circumstances, serious difficulties or threats thereof for the operation of Economic and Monetary Union.[1208] The Council may also take urgent measures on the movement of capital and on payments as regards third countries if Community action is deemed necessary in the cases envisaged in Article 228a EC.[1209] Without prejudice to the obligation to consult each other imposed by Article 224 EC, until the Council adopts such measures, Member States are free 'for serious political reasons and on grounds of urgency' to take unilateral measures against a third country with regard to capital movements and payments. The Commission and the other Member States must be informed of the measures at the latest by the date of their entry into force.[1210] However, the Council may require that the Member State concerned amend or abolish such measures.[1211]

1206. Dec. 96/412 (O.J. 1996 L 167/23).
1207. O.J. 1996 L 309/1, corrig. O.J. 1997 L 179/10. See also JA 96/668 (O.J. 1996 L 309/7).
1208. Art. 73f EC.
1209. *I.e.* when a Common Position or Joint Action adopted within CFSP provides for an interruption or complete or partial reduction in economic relations with one or more third countries. The Council acts by qualified majority on a proposal from the Commission.
1210. Art. 73g(2) EC, 1st para.
1211. *Ibid.*, 2nd para. The Council acts by qualified majority on a proposal from the Commission.

CHAPTER VIII

The competition policy of the European Community*

1. INTRODUCTION

Competition policy is here taken in the wide sense.[1] Thus it embraces all the matters covered by Articles 85–102 EC, provisions which principally relate to the functioning of the common market established by the five freedoms discussed in Chapter VII, above. These matters, competition rules applicable to undertakings (including public undertakings), state aids, and provisions relating to the harmonization of laws, allow a considerable discretion to the Community, unlike the five freedoms. This policy discretion can primarily be used to supplement and reinforce negative integration. It is also possible, though, to use the diverse powers comprised in these provisions in a more interventionist direction. In cartel and competition policy the Commission may only pursue the promotion of actual competition or it may approach collaboration between undertakings also, under certain strict conditions, as an instrument of economic policy coordination or of other policies. In the application of the provisions concerning state aids the Commission principally aims to achieve the elimination of distortion of competition to ensure a level playing-field within the Community, but it can also attempt to give shape to coordinated regional, sectoral and flanking policies. Finally, harmonization

---

* In the Dutch edition of this work, sections 1, 2, and 4 were revised by R. Barents, section 3 by L.A. Geelhoed. This edition has been further revised by the editor, taking on board those revisions and maintaining relevant additions from the last English edition, but taking additional account of literature, case-law and practice, as well as of more recent developments.

1. In which the old Commission of the European Economic Community used it – including for the purpose of organizing its services – until 1967. On this, see the fundamental address by Von der Groeben, the member of the Commission in that period responsible for competition, to the European Parliament on June 16, 1965: *La politique de concurrence: partie intégrale de la politique économique dans le Marché Commun* (Brussels, 1965).

of laws can be primarily regarded as supplementing the five freedoms (*e.g.* by eliminating distortion of competition resulting from disparities in national legislation), but also as an instrument of positive integration. Article 100a EC is a good illustration of the different gradations which the relationship between negative and positive integration can assume. In the case-law on the position of that provision as the legal basis in relation to other provisions of the EC Treaty the practical consequences of the relationship between both forms of integration chosen by the Community legislator become apparent.[2] In the broad sense described above, competition policy, as set out in the scheme of the EC Treaty and in this work, forms the bridge between the five freedoms and the coordination or making common of Community economic policy, and the Community's flanking and sectoral policies.[3]

2.   HARMONIZATION OF LAWS

2.1   Functions of harmonization[4]

In Chapter VII, above, it was seen that on a number of points of great practical importance the five freedoms have to be supplemented by harmonization of laws.[5] This makes it clear that the first function of

2. See Barents (1993) SEW 5.
3. As to the terms 'negative and positive integration', see Chapter III, section 1.2.3, *ante*. There is scant literature on the relationship between negative and positive integration. For an approach from the standpoint of liberalization, see Von der Groeben and Mestmäcker, *Ziele und Methoden der europäischen Integration* (Frankfurt, 1972) 60. The need for positive integration is particularly stressed in the WRR Report No. 28, *De onvoltooide Europese integratie* (The Hague, 1986), published in English as *The Unfinished European Integration* (The Hague, 1986).
4. For a more extensive analysis (and bibliography) see Taschner in Von der Groeben et al. eds.), Kommentar zum EWG-Vertrag (4th ed., Baden-Baden, 1991) Vol.II 2785 (and, on tax harmonization, Reicherts, *ibid.* 2749). Specifically on technical and administrative obstacles see Slot, *Technical and Administrative Obstacles to Trade in the EEC* (Leiden, 1975) and Farr, *Harmonization of Technical Standards in the EC* (2nd ed., Chichester, 1996). Older but still useful literature on harmonization under Art. 100 EC includes Beuve-Méry (1967) RTDE 845, Leleux (1968) CDE 129 and Timmermans (1980) *R.M. Themis* 406. See further, 51 *Halsbury's Laws of England* (4th ed., London, 1986), paras. 6.01–6.85; Gormley, *Prohibiting Restrictions on Trade within the EEC* (Amsterdam, 1985) 174–181 and 234–238; Close (1978) 3 ELRev. 461; Currall (1984) 4 YBEL 169; McMillan (1985) RMC 284; Schwartz in Mestmäcker *et al.* (eds.), *Eine Ordnungspolitik für Europa* (*Festschrift* for Von der Groeben, Baden-Baden, 1987) 333 and Taschner in *ibid.* 407; Langeheine (1988) EuR 235; Waelbroeck (1988) CDE 243; Vignes (1990) 15 ELRev. 358 and Slot (1996) 21 ELRev. 378. See also Lauwaars and Marleveld, *Harmonisatie van Wetgeving in Europese organisaties* (Deventer 1987) and further literature mentioned in this section, *post*.
5. In accordance with the prevailing views in academic literature, no distinction is drawn between the expressions 'harmonization', 'coordination' and 'approximation of legislation'.

harmonization of laws relates to the *establishment* of a common market. In relation to the free movement of goods, customs frontiers and associated controls in internal trade,[6] fiscal barriers and associated controls resulting from the divergent legislation relating to the basis and tariffs of turnover taxes and excise duties could and can only be removed by far-reaching harmonization.[7] The exception clause of Article 36 EC means that so-called technical obstacles to inter-state trade, resulting from technical rules on the composition, quality, presentation, packaging, *etc.* of products, can likewise be largely removed only by harmonization of laws in so far as they can be justified under Article 36 or the rule of reason case-law on essentially non-economic grounds.[8] Finally, public services still tend to discriminate on grounds of nationality in purchasing goods; this tradition will really only be brought to an end by harmonized legislative safeguards against discrimination. To this end various directives have been adopted[9] in order to ensure that the public procurement sector and regulated procurement by the utilities – which represents a substantial sector of the economy – is opened up to genuine competition in accordance with the philosophy of ensuring that the conditions of competition prevailing within the Community are characteristic of those in a single domestic market. The provisions for the free movement of persons from the outset provided for some harmonization (coordination) of laws, which was to complete the respective prohibitions against discrimination *vis-à-vis* nationals and undertakings from other Member States in order to achieve real equality of access to the various professions and trades in each of the Member States. The intended and still incomplete harmonization of company law is also based on these provisions. Again, the liberalization of the free movement of services and capital provided for in the EC Treaty had to be completed by harmonization of laws if the aim of establishing a

6. See the Commission's White Paper on completing the internal market COM (85) 310 final. See also Case 159/78 *Commission v. Italy* [1979] ECR 3247 at 3258.
7. To the extent that such controls and formalities are still permitted by the provisions of the EC Treaty, in particular Arts. 36, 56 and 66 EC and the rule of reason case-law (as to which, see Chapter VII, Section 3.3.3 *ante.*). As to the Commission's recent proposals relating to tax law, see COM (96) 328 Final.
8. See Chapter VII, section 3.3.3, *ante.*
9. As to the public sector, see Dirs. 93/36 (O.J. 1993 L 199/1) on public supply contracts; 93/36 (O.J. 1993 L 199/54, corrigendum O.J. 1994 L 111/115) on public works contracts; 92/50 (O.J. 1992 L 209/1) on public service contracts. These measures have been amended to take account of the Agreement on Government Procurement (Marrakesh, 15 April 1994) by Dir. 97/52 (OJ 1997 L 328/1). See also Dir. 89/665 (O.J. 1989 L 395/33, corrigendum O.J. 1990 L 34/30) on remedies. As to the utilities (which may be public or private sector), see Dir. 93/38 (O.J. 1993 L 199/84, corrigenda O.J. 1994 L 82/39–40, amended by Dir. 98/4 (O.J. 1998 L 101/1)) and, as to remedies, see Dir. 92/13 (O.J. 199⁓ L 76/14). See, generally, Trepte, *Public Procurement in the EEC* (Bicester, 1993) and ⌐ nández Martín, *The EC Public Procurement Rules: A Critical Analysis* (Oxford, 19⁰

common market, comparable to a domestic internal market, was to be achieved.[10] As far as services were concerned, harmonization of legislation was particularly necessary in the financial services sectors (banking, insurance and securities) as well as in relation to the procurement of services and the execution of public works. The harmonization already achieved in relation to the free movement of capital has now been codified at treaty level in Arts. 73a *et seq.* EC. Each of the five freedoms thus needed to be complemented by harmonization, although the harmonization was of a facilitating nature, or to remove barriers arising from divergent justified unilateral requirements of the Member States; the Court did not allow the delay in harmonization to defeat the direct effect of the fundamental freedoms for individuals.

According to Article 7(7) EC the necessary harmonization should have been achieved by the end of the transitional period at midnight on 31 December 1969. However, as a result of cumbersome decision-making procedures, particularly the requirement of unanimity in Article 100 EC, and the extremely detailed and wide-ranging scope of the harmonization initially undertaken, this was not to be the case.[11] In view of the manifest failure of the initial approach the Commission, in its White Paper *Completing the Internal Market*[12] the Commission set out a detailed scheme of some 300 legislative proposals to remove the remaining barriers to a complete internal market by 31 December 1992. With a similar aim, the changes in the then EEC Treaty which came into effect through the SEA from 1 July 1987, included the same target date for completion of the internal market[13] and the introduction of a more supple procedure for the harmonization needed for that goal in Article 100a EC. As will be noted in section 2.2, below, the flexibility was not without a price.

---

10. See Chapter VII, sections 1.1–1.6, *ante* and literature cited there. The remarks above concerning Art. 36 EC apply also in respect of Arts. 56 and 66 EC. As a useful example of reasons for harmonization see the preamble to Dir. 72/166 (O.J. English Special Edition 1972 (II), p. 360) on insurance against civil liability in respect of the use of motor vehicles and compulsory insurance against such liability.
11. See the still relevant Council resolutions on the harmonization programme for technical barriers to trade and the adaptation of directives to technical progress, J.O. 1969 C 76/1 and 8. An overview of the situation at the end of the transitional period is contained in Bull.EC Supp. 6/70. The number of proposals adopted by that date was far too small. It should not be thought that there were no proposals between 1970 and 1985, very much the contrary is the case. The difference lies largely in the new impetus developed after 1979 in the light of the Court's lead.
12. COM (85) 310 final. See, generally, Bieber, *et al.* (eds.), *1992: One European Market?* (Baden-Baden, 1988) and (1989/1) LIEI (whole issue). See, further, Chalmers in Shaw and More (eds.), *New Legal Dynamics of European Union* (Oxford, 1996) 55 and Caiger and Floudas (eds.), *1996 Onwards: Lowering the Barriers Further* (Chichester, 1996).
13. Art. 7a EC (previously Art. 8a EEC).

Particularly since the judgment in Case 120/78 *Rewe Zentral AG v. Bundesmonopolverwaltung für Branntwein*[14] (more popularly known as the *Cassis de Dijon* judgment), and extensively in the White Paper mentioned above, the Commission has rethought its entire policy in the harmonization field. Two strands characterize its present policy; the new strategy and the new approach. The new strategy was made possible by the positive gloss put on Articles 30–36 EC by the case-law of the Court of Justice based on the mutual acceptance of goods (also called mutual recognition). Departing from the principle that goods lawfully produced or marketed in one Member State must be accepted in all other Member States save where refusal is justified on grounds known to Community law,[15] the need to harmonize everything in sight disappears.[16] Accordingly, the new strategy concentrates on harmonizing national measures which create barriers to trade which are justified; it is these barriers which have to be removed by Community action occupying the field and guaranteeing the health and safety concerns involved.[17] The new approach deals with how this is done. No longer will detailed technical provisions need to be incorporated in Community directives. With the development of European standards being entrusted to the European standardization bodies such as CEN and CENELEC[18] the European standards can be incorporated by reference into Community directives: this has the advantages of removing technical details from the legislative field, lessening the workload of the Council and ensuring that no new legislation is needed to take account of technical progress (the change in the terms of the European standard takes place at the technical level).[19] Measures have also been taken to

---

14. [1979] ECR 649, [1979] 3 CMLR 494. See the Commission's Communication (O.J. 1980 C 256/2), discussed by Mattera (1980) RMC 505; Slot (1981) SEW 174 at 176; Timmermans (1981) SEW 381; Barents (1981) 18 CMLRev. 271 at 296 and Gormley (1981) 6 ELRev. 454.

15. See Chapter VII, section 3.2.2, *ante*.

16. Although the limits of the mutual recognition approach are well demonstrated by the judgments in Case 188/84 *Commission v. France* [1986] ECR 419 and Case C-293/93 *Houtwipper* [1994] ECR I-4249. As to the latter, see Gormley (1996) 21 ELRev. 44.

17. See, generally, the White Paper, COM (85) 310 final 17–19.

18. The European Committees for Standardization and Electrotechnical Standardization respectively (they share a building in Brussels). In telecommunications matters the competent body is ETSI (the European Telecommunications Standards Institute).

19. Criticisms of this approach in terms of a consequent absence of judicial control and the lack of a clear delimitation between the roles of public authorities and private industry have on occasion been voiced but, are, it is submitted, misplaced, see, discussing these concerns, Gormley (1989/1) LIEI 9 at 13. See, generally, Council Resolution of 18 June 1992 on the role of European standardization in the European economy (O.J. 1992 C 173/1). As to the broader use of standardization in Community policy, see the Commission's Communication, COM (95) 412 final, and as to standardization and intellectual property rights, see COM (92) 445 Final. See, generally, Nicolas with Repussard, *Common Standards for Enterprises* (2nd ed., Brussels, Luxembourg, 1994).

avoid a proliferation of new barriers to trade in the standards and technical regulations area in the meantime.[20]

Two other pieces of jargon are frequently encountered, namely the terms total and optional harmonization. Total harmonization means that the Community measures occupy the field and deprive the Member States of the power to maintain rules at variance with the Community measures.[21] Optional harmonization describes the situation in which the Community has adopted a set of measures and products complying with them must be accepted throughout the Community but the Member States are free to maintain their own rules as well. This form of harmonization has particularly been used in the automobile type-approval sector.[22] Although the optional approach is claimed to offer flexibility (so that, for example, a manufacturer who did not intend to sell its products abroad could continue to manufacture to local standards) it is not without difficulties and in the long term is scarcely satisfactory.[23]

The significance of harmonization is not limited to the *establishment* of the common market. Article 3(h) EC makes it clear that harmonization is also prescribed whenever these provisions directly affect the *functioning* of the common market. In the first place this includes provisions which, whilst they do not hinder access to the market, do determine and may distort the conditions of competition in the market. In principle this is particularly the case for all legislative and administrative provisions which directly concern market behaviour, particularly behaviour towards competitors (*e.g.* patent and trade mark law and provisions relating to

20. By the adoption of Dir. 83/189 (O.J. 1983 L 109/8, as subsequently extended and amended), see section 2.5, *post*.
21. Sometimes the Community harmonized totally only certain aspects of activity (*e.g.* in the pharmaceutical sector), in which case the approach is one of partial harmonization. In these circumstances the Member States remain free to regulate non-harmonized matters subject to compliance with the normal rules of Community law (*e.g.* Arts. 30–36 EC, see Case 227/82 *Van Bennekom* [1983] ECR 3883 at 3904–3905 and Case C-315/92 *Verband Sozialer Wettbewerb eV v. Clinique Laboratories SNC et al.* [1994] ECR I-317 at 334–335) and subject to the requirement that their measures do not jeopardize the objectives or functioning of the Community measures. The latter condition follows by analogy with the case-law on Arts. 30–36 EC and common organization of the market, on which see Gormley, *op. cit.* (see note 4, *supra*) 73–95 and 111–121 and Waelbroeck in Sandalow and Stein (eds.), *Courts and Free Markets* (Oxford, 1982) Vol. II 548–577.
22. See 51 *Halsbury's Laws* (see note 4, *supra*) paras. 6.45–6.60. However, Community type approval has become mandatory since 1 January 1996, with Dir. 92/53 (O.J. 1992 L 225/1) amending Dir. 70/156 (O.J. English Special Edition 1970 (I), p. 96) and marking the transition from optional to total harmonization in this field. See, generally, the Comission's Notice on the procedures for type-approval and registration of vehicles previously registered in another Member State (O.J. 1996 C 143/4).
23. A point recognized by its abandonment in relation to automobile type approval, *ibid.* For further discussion of the problems, see Gormley, *op. cit.* (see note 4, *supra*) 234–238.

unfair competition), workers (many directives have already been adopted dealing with the labour market, conditions of work and workers' protection), consumers (particularly consumer protection) or buyers or sellers in general (*e.g.* many parts of private commercial law). There is also direct influence on the functioning of the common market whenever the provisions concerned, such as fiscal and environmental provisions, influence the *market position* (competitive position) of the undertakings involved, even though they do not directly concern *market behaviour*.[24]

2.2 Articles 100, 100a and 100b EC

The general harmonization provisions of the EC Treaty are to be found in Article 100 EC and, since the amendments made by the SEA, Article 100a EC. Procedurally the most important difference between the two provisions is that whereas Article 100 EC requires unanimity in the Council for the adoption of directives, Article 100a now makes possible the adoption of measures by the co-decision procedure, thus with a qualified majority in the Council.[25] The price which had to be paid for this improvement, in decision-making, the safeguard provision of Article 100a(4) EC is discussed below. The second, instrumental, difference is that the measures to be adopted under Article 100a are not confined to directives; regulations in particular may be used. However, the practical effect of this is somewhat weakened by the fourth declaration annexed to the Final Act signed on the adoption of the SEA which states that in its proposals pursuant to Article 100a(1) 'the Commission shall give precedence to the use of the instrument of a directive if harmonization involves the amendment of legislative provisions in one or more Member States.' Legally this declaration cannot fetter the Commission's discretion but politically it is in such cases a powerful disincentive to the use of instruments other than directives.[26]

In the last edition of this work, extensive attention was devoted to the distinction between the concept of an internal market, now to be found in Article 7a EC, to which Article 100a EC refers, and that of a common

24. Harmonization in the context of EMU, social policy, sectoral policies and other areas is discussed in the various specific Chapters, *post.*
25. Art. 100 EEC provided for simple consultation of the European Parliament and the Economic and Social Committee in the case of directives whose implementation would involve the amendment of legislation in one or more Member States. This limitation, which meant nothing in practice, has now been dropped.
26. The vast majority of measures adopted under Art. 100a EC are directives, there are a couple of dozen or so regulations, largely in the customs field, where as part of the process of removing internal border controls and tightening the common commercial policy the previous Community directives have been replaced by regulations. As to this process, see Gormley in Emiliou and O'Keeffe (eds.), *The European Union and World Trade Law After the GATT Uruguay Round* (Chichester, Wiley, 1996) 124. Very few decisions have also been based on Art. 100a EC.

market which is expressed in Article 100 EC.[27] The Court seems to treat these concepts as synonymous, even though the latter is in fact logically more wide-reaching than the former.[28] Thus in the first judgment on the application of the safeguard clause in Article 100a(4) EC the Court confirmed this synonymous approach.[29] Already in the titanium dioxide judgment[30] the Court made it plain that harmonization under Article 100a could deal with the removal of distortions of competition resulting from divergent national rules on the discharge of environmentally harmful waste.[31] Thus Article 100a EC, like Article 100 EC, concerns the establishment as well as the functioning of the Community market as a whole. This interpretation flows from Article 3(h) EC, from which both Articles 100 and 100a EC flow, which speaks of 'approximation of laws to the extent required for the functioning of the common market.' Given that the words 'as directly affect' in Article 100 EC are absent in Article 100a(1) EC, it can even be argued that scope of Article 100a is actually wider than that of Article 100, at least to the extent that the exceptions in Article 100a(2) are inapplicable.[32] Article 100a has thus evolved into a general provision for the management of the common or internal market which is certainly increasing in importance now that the European Parliament has the power of co-decision. Legislative practice also

27. Kapteyn and VerLoren van Themaat, *Introduction to the Law of the European Communities* (2nd ed., ed. Gormley, Deventer, 1989) 473.
28. See Chapter III, section 3.2, *ante*, particularly in view of the definition of the internal market in Art. 7a EC. However, well before the time the White Paper was adopted in 1985 it had become more usual in political and business circles to speak of a single market, or of the internal market, and less of a common market, although both phrases are now used in the EC Treaty. It may well be that the Court's mingling of the concepts merely reflects the modified political usage.
29. Case C-41/93 *France v. Commission* [1994] ECR I-1829 at 1847. The apparent mingling of the two concepts was apparent from earlier judgments, *e.g.* Case 15/81 *Gaston Schul Douane-Expediteur BV v. Inspecteur der Invoerrechten en Accijnzen, Roosendaal* [1982] ECR 1409 at 1431–1432.
30. Case 300/89 *Commission v. Council* [1991] ECR I-2867, see Barnard (1993) 17 ELRev. 127 and Somsen (1992) 29 CMLRev. 149.
31. *Ibid.* at 2899. The Court treated the establishment of the common market predicated in Arts. 2 and 3 EEC as a precondition for the existence of an internal market as then defined in Art. 8a EEC (now Art. 7a EC). It will be recalled that disputes on the legal basis really centre around the voting requirements and the degree of involvement of the European Parliament: Art. 100a EEC required a qualified majority in the Council and cooperation with the European Parliament, Art. 130s EEC required unanimity in the Council after merely consulting the Parliament.
32. Art. 100a(2) EC declares that Art. 100a(1) 'shall not apply to fiscal provisions, to those relating to the free movement of persons nor to those relating to the rights and interests of employed persons.' These matters were already covered by specific provisions. The term 'fiscal provisions' in the system of the Treaty only embraces Arts. 95–99 EC. Harmonisation of direct taxation and harmonisation of indirect taxation for objectives other than those specified in the new text of Art. 99 EC will only be possible on the basis of Art. 100 EC, in so far as Arts. 92, 95–98 or 101–102 cannot be used.

demonstrates that Article 100 EC has now really only a residual function, *e.g.* in relation to any proposals concerning harmonization of direct taxation.

The procedural improvements introduced in Article 100a EC are to a great extent undermined by the safeguard clause of Article 100a(4) which was the political price paid for majority voting in various areas of harmonization. It enables a Member State, after a harmonization measure has been adopted with a qualified majority in the Council, to derogate from that measure if it 'deems it necessary to apply national provisions on grounds of major needs referred to in Article 36, or relating to the protection of the environment or the working environment' and has notified such provisions to the Commission, which has confirmed them. Both in terms of substance and procedure this safeguard clause raises a number of questions, some of which have been answered in Case C-41/93 *France v. Commission*,[33] in which France (under the third paragraph of Article 100a(4) EC) sought review of the Commission's decision under the second paragraph of Article 100a(4) confirming the measures Germany had notified to it. The Court explained that as Article 100a(4) permitted a derogation from a common Community measure designed to achieve one of the fundamental objectives of the Treaty, *in casu* the free movement of goods, its application had been specifically made subject to review by the Commission and the Court.[34] Although a literal interpretation of Article 100a(4) might seem to indicate otherwise, that provision is thus not a unilateral safeguard clause which the Member States can use at will for the protection of the interests specified therein.[35] The Court found that the procedure of Article 100a(4) was 'intended to ensure that no Member State may apply national rules derogating from the harmonized rules without obtaining confirmation from the Commission.'[36] This confirmation by the Commission under the second paragraph of Article 100a(4) is an act capable of review in the sense of Article 173 EC, and a measure of the importance attached to ensuring that no improper use is made of Article 100a(4) can be seen in the fact that the third paragraph of that provision permits the Commission or any Member State to bring the matter directly to the Court, without going through the stages prescribed in Articles 169 or 170 EC. The Court also explained the Commission's duties in evaluating national measures for which confirmation is sought. The Commission, after provisions have been notified to it, must be satisfied that all the conditions for reliance on Article 100a(4) are fulfilled, in particular whether the measures are

33. See note 29, *supra.*
34. [1994] ECR I-1829 at 1848.
35. *Ibid.* at 1849.
36. *Ibid.* Otherwise harmonizing measures designed to remove hindrances to intra-Community trade would be rendered ineffective, *ibid.*

justified on the grounds specified in that provision and whether they are not a means of arbitrary discrimination or a disguised restriction on trade between Member States.[37] Compared with Article 36 EC the Commission's controlling task goes clearly further, on the basis that unlike Article 36 EC, Article 100a(4) deals with a situation in which Community legislation exists.[38] The Court also subtly answered the question whether Article 100a(4) could cover only new or also existing measures, by noting that in the instant case Germany intended to continue to apply national provisions.[39] It did not, however, answer the question whether a Member State would have to have voted against the Community measure in the Council in order for it to be able to avail itself of Article 100a(4).[40] Even though, in view of the background of the unity of the common market, the Court has firmly chosen a restrictive interpretation of Article 100a(4), that provision is still rightly regarded as a clearly regressive step, as even in the face of total harmonization a Member State may retain its existing more far-reaching measures. Moreover, it creates an imbalance in that the products concerned coming from a Member State which has invoked Article 100a(4) must be accepted by the other Member States. However, given the very limited use which has so far been made of this provision, there is no real threat to the common market.[41] The possibility of invoking Article 100a(4) will rather have an influence during the negotiations leading to the adoption of Community legislation, so that the requirements of Member States which would be likely to make use of that provision can be already taken into account. If that provision is in fact invoked then total harmonization is in fact replaced by a geographically determined partial harmonization which

37. This reflects the principles of necessity, proportionality and the second sentence of Art. 36 itself and is also applied in the Court's rule of reason case-law in relation to Art. 30 (ever since the judgment in Case 8/74 *Procureur du Roi v. Dassonville et al.* [1974] ECR 837 at 852.
38. See note 36, *supra*.
39. [1994] ECR I-1829 at 1848.
40. Clearly the Court expressly did not wish to answer this question, as it noted, *ibid.* at 1845 that *inter alia* Germany had voted against the adoption of the directive, but did not then go on to say that because it had done so it could indeed invoke Art. 100a(4). While it might logically be expected that a vote against would be a precondition (see Mertens de Wilmars (1986) SEW 601), the situation is unclear. A Member State may seek to introduce derogations subsequently in the light of, say, new information relating to environmental dangers. Moreover, the Court has permitted a Member State to seek the annulment of a Community act even though it voted in favour of the act in the Council, see Case 166/78 *Italy v. Council* [1979] ECR 2575 at 2596.
41. The Commission has adopted two decisions (other than that addressed to Germany (O.J. 1992 C 334/8) annulled in Case C-41/93 *France v. Commission* [1994] ECR I-1829) confirming prohibitions or restrictions of PCP, derogating from Dir. 91/173 (O.J. 1991 L 85/34), see Dec. 94/783 (O.J. 1994 L 316/43) addressed to Germany and Dec. 96/211 (O.J. 1996 L 68/32) addressed to Denmark). The Netherlands has for some time being trying to obtain confirmation for its measures but so far to no avail.

may in the future still become total harmonization by an amendment raising the level of protection prescribed by the measure concerned.[42] In appropriate cases a safeguard procedure must be incorporated in harmonization measures based on Article 100a, subject to a Community control procedure, in accordance with Article 100a(5) EC.[43] The weak elements of Article 100a (4) EC will be largely eliminated when the Treaty of Amsterdam enters into force by the substitution of the new text of Article 100a (3)–(6) EC and the repeal of Articles 100c and 100d EC.

Article 100b EC permits the Council, acting in accordance with Article 100a EC, to decide that the provisions in force in a Member State must be recognized as being equivalent to those applied by another Member State. The intention was to remove any barriers still remaining on 31 December 1992. Apart from the fact that the Commission, together with each Member State, still has not drawn up the inventory of national laws, regulations and administrative action which fall under Article 100a and had not been harmonized pursuant thereto, it may very seriously be doubted whether the procedure of Article 100b EC would in reality reduce the need for harmonization under Article 100a EC.

2.3 Specific harmonization provisions

The EC Treaty contains a series of provisions concerning harmonization of laws concerning specific subjects and sectors which are not extensively discussed here.[44] In relation to agriculture, Article 43 EC confers power on the Community to proceed to harmonize veterinary, health and plant health, zootechnical and botanical legislation.[45] Harmonization in the

42. It should be noted that as a result of case-law, harmonization in the agricultural sector is exclusively based on Art. 43 EC (see Case 68/86 *United Kingdom v. Council* [1988] ECR 855 at 894–896 and Case 131/86 *United Kingdom v. Council* [1988] ECR 905 at 929–931), which means that many directives which concern the interests or values specified in Art. 36 EC will escape the potential scope of Art. 100a(4) EC. Harmonization in the transport sphere is a matter for Arts. 75–84 EC. Similarly, Arts. 56 and 66 are also outside the scope of Art. 100a(4). See Barents (1993) SEW 5 and Everling (1991) EuR 1991.
43. E.g. Dir. 92/59 (O.J. 1992 L 228/4) on general product safety, see Case C-359/92 *Germany v. Council* [1994] ECR I-3681, noted by Gormley (1996) 21 ELRev. 59.
44. See *inter alia* Arts. 27 (customs), 49(b) (eligibility restrictions for available employment), 54(2) (implementation of the general programme for the abolition of restrictions on freedom of establishment), 54(3)(g) (company law safeguards), 56(2) (restrictions on freedom of establishment), 57(1) and (2) (mutual recognition of qualifications), and 63(2) EC (implementation of the general programme for the abolition of restrictions on the freedom to provide services), discussed in Chapter VII, *ante*.
45. See Case 68/86 *United Kingdom v. Council* [1988] ECR 855 at 896–897; Case 131/86 *United Kingdom v. Council* [1988] ECR 905 at 931–932; Case C-131/87 *Commission v. Council* [1989] ECR 3743 at 3770–3771, and Case C-11/88 *Commission v. Council* [1989] ECR 3799 (summary publication only).

transport sector, including its social aspects, takes place on the basis of Articles 75 and 84 EC. In the field of the common commercial policy, Article 113 is the appropriate instrument. Harmonization for the achievement of liberalization in relation to the free exercise of professional activities and the freedom to provide services is based on Articles 57 or 63 EC as appropriate, whereas the harmonization of company law is based on Article 54(3)(g) EC. The role of directives under Article 90(3) EC, dealing with public undertakings or undertakings having special or exclusive rights is examined in section 3.10, below. The harmonization of indirect taxation and excise duties takes place on the separate legal basis of Article 99 EC. This was first changed by the SEA, replacing the initial 'can be harmonized in the interest of the common market' by 'to the extent that such harmonization is necessary to ensure the establishment and the functioning of the internal market' by the end of 1992. Given the development of the case-law on Article 100a EC, it would now appear that initial fears that the effect of that change would be to make it impossible to tackle distortions of competition in the fiscal sphere, were less than wholly justified.[46] Finally, specific provisions were introduced by the SEA for harmonization measures dealing with health and safety of workers and the environment, in Articles 118a and 130s EC respectively.

2.4 Article 100a and the other harmonization provisions

It has already been noted in section 2.2 of this Chapter, above, that Article 100a EC has evolved, both in law and in fact, into virtually a general power to enact rules relating to the establishment and functioning of the internal market. Indeed the wording of Article 100a itself points in this direction. On the one hand, Article 100a(3) indicates that the power to harmonize also covers health, safety, environmental protection and consumer protection, even though all those subjects are dealt with in separate provisions of the Treaty. On the other hand, Article 100a(2) specifically excludes fiscal provisions, provisions dealing with the free movement of persons,[47] and provisions dealing with the rights and interests of employees from the ambit of harmonization under Article 100a(1). All three latter areas deal with matters on which a considerable area of disagreement exists among the Member States about the direction and

46. Expressed in the 2nd ed. of this work, see note 27, *supra*, 476.
47. Dir. 91/477 (O.J. 1991 L 256/51) on the control of the acquisition and possession of weapons is in fact designed to promote the free movement of persons by removing police controls at the Community's internal frontiers, but because it was phrased in terms of the acquisition and possession of weapons the directive could be adopted under Art. 100a EC.

degree of further progress towards common rules. Article 100a can be seen as a synthesis of the two functions of harmonization discussed in section 2.1 of this Chapter, above, which clearly reflects the fact that the establishment and proper functioning of the internal or common market is a matter for negative as well as positive integration. Given that the concept of 'establishment and functioning of the internal market' embraces more than the lifting of the Community's internal frontiers, and that the restriction to national measures which 'directly affect the establishment and functioning of the common market' does not apply to Article 100a EC, the Community legislator has a much wider margin of discretion as to where it draws the line in concrete cases between competition and intervention.[48] In other words, Article 100a EC may be used for liberalizing measures, but also, and even primarily, for regulating measures in order to realize a specific sectoral or flanking policy.[49] This also appears from the instruction in Article 100a(3) to the Commission to take as a base for its proposals in specified fields a high level of protection. Moreover the new powers in those fields expressly refer to Article 100a, certainly as far as binding measures are concerned.[50]

As a result of the wide concept of 'establishment and functioning of the internal market' the scope of Article 100a EC is extensive. The only general limitations for the exercise of the power to harmonize laws flow from Articles 2, 3, 3a and 3b EC; there are also more specific limitations through the terms of Article 100a(2) and through the existence of other provisions of the Treaty which envisage specific powers of harmonization. The wide scope of Article 100a has a number of important consequences.[51] First, it can be used for measures concerning matters which are only very indirectly linked with the internal market.[52] Secondly, the concept of harmonization can have a relative meaning.[53] In some cases the actual

48. This was already recognized by the Court in Case 240/83 *Procureur d la République v. Association de défense des brûleurs d'huiles usagées (ADBHU)* [1985] ECR 531 at 549–550.
49. It may be noted that the old DG III (Internal Market and Industrial Affairs) has split into two, leaving industrial affairs with DG III and hiving off the internal market to DG XV, where they were combined with financial services. This is not the first time that industrial affairs and the internal market have been under separate leadership.
50. Express reference to measures adopted pursuant to Art. 100a EC is found in Art. 129a EC (consumer protection). The provisions on education, vocational training and youth (Arts. 126 and 127 EC), culture (Art. 128 EC) and public health (Art. 129 EC) do not create a basis for harmonization of laws.
51. As to the relationship between the wide scope of Art. 100a EC and the system of attribution of specific competence in the Treaty, see Barents (1993) SEW 3; Crosby (1991) 16 ELRev. 451, and Everling (1991) EuR 179.
52. *E.g.* Dirs. 94/21 (O.J. 1994 L 164/1) and 97/44 (O.J. 1997 L 206/62) on Summer Time and Dec. 92/264 (O.J. 1992 L 137/21) on a single access number (OO) for international telephone traffic in the Community. Dec. 91/396 (O.J. 1991 L 217/31) on a single emergency call number (112) was adopted on the basis of Art. 235 EC.
53. *E.g. ibid.*

harmonization of national laws is extremely limited and the measure really concerns an individual specific action.[54] Legislative practice confirms that the old discussion in academic literature about whether harmonization of laws was correctly involved in matters which were not yet covered by legislation in the Member States has now become obsolete.[55] Thirdly, harmonization directives relating to certain flanking policies do not always have to be based on the specific powers relating to those policies,[56] but if the emphasis of the measure is on the removal of distortions of competition, Article 100a will be an adequate legal basis.[57] There have recently been a number of challenges to the legal basis of measures involving the role of Article 100a, which demonstrate that the dividing line between that provision and the specific harmonization provisions of the Treaty is less than wholly clear-cut, although the central issue is undoubtedly what the main purpose of the measure is.[58] The existence of Article 100a EC certainly cannot be used to restrict the scope of more specific provisions.[59] Article 100a is even being used in cases in which Article 235 EC would previously have been used because of the (correctly or incorrectly) perceived absence of a specific legal basis. Thus Article 100a has an actual and potential significance as an instrument of energy policy,[60] of telecommunications policy,[61] for the prevention of money laundering,[62] for

54. *E.g.* the Mattheus Programme on Community action for vocational training for customs officers, Dec. 91/341 (O.J. 1991 L 187/41).
55. See *e.g.* Dir. 90/220 (O.J. 1990 L 117/15, most recently amended by Dir. 97/35 (O.J. 1997 L 169/72)) on the deliberate release into the environment of genetically modified organisms (further amendment proposed COM (98) 85 Final (O.J. 1998 C 139/1)), and the proposal relating to the protection of biotechnological inventions (O.J. 1989 C 10/ 3, which attracted much controversy and has been replaced, see O.J. 1996 C 296/4, amended O.J. 1997 C 311/12).
56. *E.g.* Arts. 118a (see the Commission's original proposal on atypical work (O.J. 1990 C 224/6, amended O.J. 1990 C 305/8) and 130s EC (see the Commission's original proposal on the possession of and trade in wild flora and fauna (O.J. 1992 C 26/1).
57. Case C-300/89 *Commission v. Council* [1991] ECR I-2867 at 2901, see also Case C-350/ 92 *Spain v. Council* [1995] ECR I-1985 at 2014–2015.
58. See Case C-155/91 *Commission v. Council* [1993] ECR I-939 at 968 (waste management); Case C-187/93 *European Parliament v. Council* [1994] ECR I-2857 at 2882–2883; Case C-426/93 *Germany v. Council* [1995] ECR I-3743 at 3753–3754, and Case C-271/ 94 *European Parliament v.* Council [1996] ECR I-1689 at 1716–1717. See also Case C-360/93 *European Parliament v. Council* [1996] ECR I-1195 at 1218. It certainly appears that the Court has retreated to an extent from the case-law cited in note 57, *supra*.
59. Case C-271/94 *European Parliament v. Council* [1996] ECR I-1689 at 1716–1717.
60. See Dir. 96/92 (O.J. 1997 L 27/20) on common rules for the internal market in the electricity sector; and Dir. 98/30 (O.J. 1998 L 204/1, in the gas sector.
61. In addition to the directives adopted on the basis of Art. 90(3) EC, see *e.g.* Dirs. 87/ 372 (O.J. 1987 L 196/85) on digital cellular mobile communications; 90/544 (O.J. 1990 L 310/28) on semaphore services, and 91/287 (O.J. 1991 L 144/45) on frequency bands for digital cordless telecommunications (DECT).
62. Dir. 91/308 (O.J. 1991 L 166/77).

combatting the drugs trade,[63] and for the protection of privacy.[64] The wide scope of Article 100a EC means, finally, that conflicts regularly arise between the Community Institutions themselves, or between the Member States and the Council or Commission in particular, when preference is for political reasons given to a legal basis which requires unanimity or a lesser degree of involvement for the European Parliament.

2.5 Character and contents of harmonization under Articles 100 and 100a EC

The numerous general legal problems involved in the harmonization of laws cannot be discussed extensively in the space available here. For the determination of the content of harmonization directives the objective set out in Article 3(h) EC, namely a properly functioning common market (or, in the case of the use of Articles 99 or 100a a properly functioning internal market) is decisive. This means that the way in which the mutual adjustment is achieved is by no means immaterial. Thus in the case of the harmonization of turnover tax, even a cumulative cascade system with equal rates, completely identical in all Member States, would not have resulted in abolition of fiscal barriers. Nor would it have excluded commercial policy manipulations of the amount of countervailing charges and repayments at the frontiers. Nor would it have meant abolition of the artificial competitive advantage of integrated as against specialized and horizontally differentiated undertakings. The goal of a properly operating and undistorted market economy without internal frontiers called for a neutral system (uni-stage taxation or VAT). The ultimate goal is here abolition of all compensations at the frontiers.

In many cases, particularly concerning technical obstacles to the free movement of goods, free movement could initially only be guaranteed if the harmonization directives went into very great detail, and in borderline cases even required partial or complete uniformity of national provisions. Only in the post-*Cassis de Dijon*[65] phase did it become possible in most cases to catch up with the backlog of harmonization directives using less detailed measures. Further legal problems were also apparent in the adaptation of existing directives to technical progress, with the accompanying comitology and delegation of powers questions (as far as non-EC bodies were involved), harmonization of conformity assessment, certification and testing,[66]

---

63. Dir. 92/109 (O.J. 1992 L 370/76).
64. Dir. 95/46 (O.J. 1995 L 281/31).
65. See note 14, *supra* (with the discussion in the text of section 2.1 of this Chapter, *ante*).
66. See COM (89) 290 Final; Council Resolution of 21 December 1989 (O.J. 1990 C 10/1) on a global approach to this problem, following on from that of 7 May 1985 (O.J. 1985 C 136/1); Dec. 90/683 (O.J. 1990 L 380/3) on conformity assessment procedures; Dec. 93/465 (O.J. 1993 L 220/23) on CE marks and Council Resolution of 18 June 1992 on the role of European standardization in the European economy (O.J. 1992 C

penalties, and the extent to which citizens could rely on directly effective provisions of these directives before their national courts, if the directives were not transposed correctly or at all.

A particularly important vehicle for preventing the erection of new barriers to trade between Member States or distortions of competition arising from a proliferation of divergent national standards and technical regulations has been Directive 83/189[67] which sets up a whole new notification and standstill procedure[68] in the field of standards and technical regulations. The Court has now confirmed the Commission's long-held view that breach of the obligation to notify technical regulations in draft renders them inapplicable, so that they are unenforceable against individuals.[69]

A special complex of problems arises out of the territoriality principle in the variety of ways in which it crops up either in the application or in the maintenance of rules, particularly those of public law. For rules of private law the problem of the 'linking' of different national systems of law with regard to international legal facts has been solved to a far-reaching extent by private international law, although this is still capable of improvement. In the field of public law, however, in the first place the territorial scope of the application of the law is as a rule more limited than it is in the field of civil or commercial law. Secondly, governmental acts for carrying out, supervising, or maintaining rules of public law are generally not possible outside the state's own territory. Thirdly, generally speaking, no national

173/1). See also the Commission's Communication on the broader use of standardization in Community policy COM (95) 412 Final. As to benchmarking, relating quality improvement to improvement in the competitive position of Community industry, see COM (96) 463 Final, Bull. EU 11–1996, point 1.3.68 and 12–1996, point I.5. See further, McMillan (1991) RMUE 181; Waelbroeck (1988) CDE 243, and Carle and Johnsson (1998) ECLR 74.

67. O.J. 1983 L 109/8, extended by Dirs. 88/182 (O.J. 1988 L 81/75), 90/230 (O.J. 1990 L 128/15), 92/400 (O.J. 1992 L 221/55), 94/10 (O.J. 1994 L 100/30), Act of Austrian, Finnish and Swedish Accession, and Dec. 96/139 (O.J. 1996 L 32/31), and see Fronia and Casella (1995) RMUE 37; Lecrenier (1985) RMC 6 and (1988) RMC 121; McMillan (1985) RMC 93; Mattera, *Le Marché Unique Européen: ses règles, son fonctionnement* (2nd ed., Paris, 1990) 147, and Weatherill (1996) YBEL 129. For the most recent report on the application of Dir. 83/189, see COM (96) 286 Final. The Commission has proposed that the scope of Dir. 83/189 be further expanded, see COM (96) 392 Final (O.J. 1996 C 307/11) and has presented a proposal for a codified version of the directive, COM (96) 642 Final. The annual *General Reports* indicate the growing number of notifications under Dir. 83/189 (in 1985, several dozen; in 1990, 386; in 1995, 438; in 1996, 523, and in 1997, 900).

68. The standstill obligation in Art. 31 EC does not apply to measures covered by Art. 36 EC. See further, Case C-13/96 *Bic Benelux SA v. Belgian State* [1997] ECR I-1753.

69. Case C-194/94 *CIA Security International SA v. Signalson SA et al.* [1996] ECR I-2201 at 2248. See Slot (1996) 33 CMLRev. 1035. But see Case C 226/97 *Lemmens* [1998] ECR I-nyr (16 June 1998). In 1997 the revelation that many Dutch measures had not been notified gave rise to major controversy.

legal system attributes legal effects within its own territorial limits either to foreign rules of public law or to the governmental acts of foreign states.[70] The fact that the territoriality principle applies in these ways may give rise to serious restrictions of inter-state trade. In the first place double 'charges' or 'burdens' in a wide sense may result from it. Thus, if a product is to be sold in all Member States, it will be subject simultaneously to the technical rules and the procedures of supervision of all fifteen Member States,[71] or an undertaking must pay taxes to different states on the profits it has made in international trade. Secondly, even if the substantive rules are completely harmonized, the non-assignment of internal legal effects to implementing or supervisory acts of other Member States may in practice obstruct the importation of particular products, as also may the maintenance of national rules under criminal law. These two difficulties will present themselves most clearly in those cases where supervision must take place in the territory where the product is produced, whilst access to the market or criminal prosecution takes place in the country importing the product. Thus, if Germany were not to recognize the rules of meat inspection in French slaughterhouses, even if the rules of inspection were harmonized, French meat could not be imported into Germany without renewed inspection. Directives on harmonization, therefore, also have to entail an obligation of mutual recognition of certain state acts, and in the example of meat inspection this has already occurred.[72] On 28 May 1969 the Council adopted a resolution in which the principle of mutual recognition of acts of supervision in the field of technical obstacles to trade was generally accepted, provided that the substantive rules are sufficiently similar.[73] However, the case-law examined in Chapter VII, above, on Articles 30–36 EC, shows that problems still arise regularly in this field.

70. Like all rules, these three rules admit certain exceptions which prove them. The exceptions may be based on public international law treaties or custom or on European Community law and, in the case of the first and third rules, also on national legal concepts. Inside the Community mutual assistance in the recovery of financial claims resulting from the system of financing agricultural organisations, customs duties and VAT is provided for by Dir. 76/308 (O.J. 1976 L 73/18, most recently amended by Dir. 92/12 (O.J. 1992 L 76/1), which deals with excise duties and itself is most recently amended by Dir. 96/99 (O.J. 1997 L 8/12) and the Act of Austrian, Finnish and Swedish Accession); mutual assistance in the levying of direct taxation is dealt with by Reg. 218/92 (O.J. 1992 L 24/1); see also (on direct and indirect taxation) Dir. 77/799 (O.J. 1977 L 336/15, most recently amended by Dir. 92/12 and by the Act of Austrian, Finnish and Swedish Accession). The mutual recognition of tests of products is ensured in various agricultural regulations.
71. If the provisions are mutually incompatible then various production runs become necessary. On the aspect of the expense of this see the opinion of VerLoren van Themaat, Adv. Gen. in Case 188/84 *Commission v. France* [1986] ECR 419 at 422–430.
72. For an example of the Court's attitude to such Community measures see Case 35/76 *Simmenthal SpA v. Italian Minister for Finance* [1976] ECR 1871, [1977] 2 CMLR 1.
73. J.O. 1969 C 76/7.

In two categories of cases difficulties arising out of the territoriality principle will not be completely solved even then. The first category concerns those cases where linking of national systems of law requires an adequate redistribution of the fields of application of national laws (excluding both overlaps and gaps), or uniform rules for changing over to another system of law, or a careful regulation of co-operation between the different administrative or judicial authorities. In Chapter VII the solutions found for problems of this type in the field of social security have already been discussed.[74] Article 220 EC provides for further treaties between Member States to solve such problems in the following fields: abolition of double taxation within the Community (in the narrow fiscal sense); mutual recognition of companies within the meaning of the second paragraph of Article 58 EC, the retention of legal personality in the event of transfer of their seat from one country to another and the possibility of mergers between companies governed by the national laws of different Member States; simplification of formalities governing the reciprocal recognition and enforcement of judgments and of arbitration awards.[75] Three such Conventions provided for in the Treaty have since been signed,[76] although other draft Conventions have been prepared but came to nothing[77] and further work is under way.[78]

74. Under Art. 51 EC.
75. See the Declaration of the Representatives of the Governments of the Member States of 17 December 1973 on the removal of legal obstacles to the linking-up of undertakings (O.J. 1973 C 117/15).
76. A Convention on the mutual recognition of companies and bodies corporate was signed on 29 February 1968 (Bull.EC Supp. 2/69) but is not yet in force. A Convention on jurisdiction and the enforcement of civil and commercial judgments was signed on 27 September 1968 (Bull.EC Supp. 2/69 and J.O. 1972 L 299/32) see now O.J. 1998 C 27/1. See also the various accession conventions (O.J. 1978 L 304/77, O.J. 1982 L 388/1; O.J. 1989 L 285/1, and O.J. 1997 C 15/1) and the *Jenard Report* (O.J. 1979 C 59/1), the *Schlosser Report* (O.J. 1979 C 59/71), the *Evrigenis and Kerameus Report* (O.J. 1986 C 298/1) and the *Almeida Cruz, Desantes Real and Jenard Report* (O.J. 1990 C 189/33). A protocol to the Judgments Convention confers jurisdiction on the Court to apply it, see now O.J. 1998 C 27/1. The Commission has proposed an entirely new convention, based on Art. K3(2)(c) TEU, COM (97) 609 Final (O.J. 1998 C 33/20). Notes on the case-law concerning the Convention may be found regularly in ELRev. and in the YBEL. *Cf.* the Lugano Convention (O.J. 1988 L 319/9). A Convention on the abolition of double taxation in connection with the adjustment of profits of associated enterprises was signed on 23 July 1990 (O.J. 1990 L 225/10).
77. The draft Convention on international mergers (Bull. EC Supp. 13/1973 (now obsolete), the draft Bankruptcy Convention (Bull. EC 2/1982, see the Commission's Opinion O.J. 1981 C 391/23 and the *Tizzano Report* O.J. 1990 C 219/1 at 4). However, the Member States of the Council of Europe have signed a European Convention on Certain International Aspects of Bankruptcy (Istanbul, July 1990 (ETS No. 136)), see Güneysu (1991) 11 YBEL 295. A draft Convention on insolvency proceedings was initialled on 25 September 1995 (Bull. EU 9–1995, point 1.5.7).
78. On family matters, see Beaumont and Moir (1995) 20 ELRev. 268, although whether Art. 220 will be the legal basis is as yet uncertain. The Rome Convention on Con-

The second category of cases for which directives cannot offer a satisfactory solution arises when the facts themselves have a transnational character. In this case the national territoriality principle has to be excluded. A regulation of the facts in question by Community law is desirable. This category embraces international liquidations, European patents, trade marks, designs, and the concept of the European Company. Legislative practice indicates that Article 100a EC offers interesting possibilities here too.

Thus Article 100a EC has served as the legal basis for the creation of a supplementary protection certificate for medicinal products[79] and for plant protection products,[80] the first directive on trade mark law,[81] the data protection directive,[82] the legal protection of databases,[83] the legal protection of computer programs,[84] the term of copyright protection,[85] and the protection of rental and lending rights.[86] Proposals relating to a regulation on the Statute for the European company[87] and regulations on the Statute for, respectively, a European cooperative society, a European mutual society, and a European association,[88] as well as for a directive on the legal protection of designs[89] are under consideration, with varying prospects of success.

Outside this framework, under the European Patent Convention,[90] to which myriad European States are parties, one application to the European Patent Office, the headquarters of which are in Munich, can lead to the

tractual Obligations (O.J. 1980 L 266/1, consolidated version O.J. 1998 C 27/1) is *not* based on Art. 220 EC but is regarded as a natural sequel to the Judgments Convention (see the *Giuliano and Lagarde Report* (O.J. 1980 C 282/1 at 5).

79. Reg. 1768/92 (O.J. 1992 L 182/1 (amended by the Act of Austrian, Finnish and Swedish Accession (1994))).

80. Reg. 1610/96 (O.J. 1996 L 198/30).

81. Dir. 89/104 (O.J. 1989 L 40/1, amended by Dir. 92/10 (O.J. 1992 L 6/35). See Kur (1997) IIC 1. The Community Trade Mark Regulation (Reg. 40/94 (O.J. 1994 L 11/1)) is based on Art. 235 EC.

82. Dir. 95/46 (O.J. 1995 L 281/31).

83. Dir. 96/9 (O.J. 1996 L 77/20).

84. Dir. 91/250 (O.J. 1991 L 122/42, amended by Dir. 93/98 (O.J. 1993 L 290/9). Arts. 57 and 66 were also used as the legal basis of this directive.

85. Dir. 93/98 (O.J. 1993 L 290/9). Arts. 57 and 66 were also used as the legal basis of this directive.

86. Dir. 92/100 (O.J. 1992 L 346/61, amended by Dir. 93/98 (O.J. 1993 L 290/9).

87. O.J. 1989 C 263/41, amended proposal O.J. 1991 C 176/1). This replaces much earlier proposals, see Bull. 7/8–1989, point 1.2.1. See also the proposal (based on Art. 54 EC) complementing the Statute with regard to the involvement of employees (O.J. 1989 C 263/69, amended O.J. 1991 C 138/8). See further, COM (95) 547 Final and Bull. EC 11–1995, point 1.3.189.

88. O.J. 1992 C 99, amended proposals O.J. 1993 C 236. See also COM (95) 547 Final and Bull. EU 11–1995, point 1.3.189.

89. O.J. 1993 C 345/14, amended proposal COM (97) 622 Final.

90. The Convention on the Grant of European Patents was signed in Munich in October 1973 (T.S. 20 (1978): Cmnd. 7090).

grant of a patent in all the signatory states.[91] In contrast, the Community Patent Convention[92] is not yet in force. The long-awaited Community Trade Mark Regulation was finally adopted, on the basis of Article 235 EC, at the end of 1993.[93]

2.6   Methods of harmonization and the scope of directives

In relation to harmonization a distinction should be drawn between the method of harmonization which is adopted, usually by a directive, and the scope of a harmonizing directive. The distinction between total and optional harmonization has already been noted.[94] In the case of total harmonization the Member States may not derogate from the provisions of the directive, save to the extent permitted by the directive itself.[95] Free movement of all products covered by such a directive is assured, as it is no longer possible for Member States to invoke Article 36 EC, although Article 100a(4) could be used if the conditions for its application were satisfied.[96] In such (rare) cases the total Community harmonization is transformed into a geographically differentiated harmonization. For products covered by an optional harmonization directive, free movement is in any event assured for products conforming with its requirements, so that undertakings operating on a common market scale or who otherwise engage in intra-Community trade may simply manufacture to one set of requirements, whereas those operating merely locally are not obliged to take the Community measure into account. The choice is thus left to the manufacturer.[97] In the case of minimum harmonization, the Member States, as the name implies, must comply with the minimum requirements of the directive concerned, but are free to apply stricter or more far-reaching requirements.[98] Article 118a EC expressly requires this method of

91. The first such groups of patents were issued in 1978.
92. O.J. 1976 L 17/1, amended by the Agreement on Community Patents (O.J. 1989 L 401/1). The protocol relating to judicial interpretation of this Convention has not yet been drawn up. See, generally, Jung in Plender (ed.), *European Courts Practice and Precedents* (London, 1996) Chap. 38.
93. Reg. 40/94 (O.J. 1994 L 11/1, amended by Reg. 3288/94 (O.J. 1994 L 349/83), implemented by Reg. 2868/95 (O.J. 1995 L303/1). A further amendment has been proposed, see now COM (98) 289 Final.
94. See section 2.1 of this Chapter, *ante*.
95. See *e.g.* Case 5/77 *Tedeschi v. Denkavit Commerciale srl* [1977] ECR 1555, [1978] 1 CMLR 1, and Case 228/87 *Pretura unificata di Torino v. X* [1988] ECR 5099 at 5120. The same applies *a fortiori* in relation to regulations.
96. See section 2.2 of this Chapter, *ante*.
97. Whereas in the case of partial harmonization the Community measures are binding in all cases in the matters which they cover, see note 21, *supra*. See Currall (1984) 4 YBEL 169.
98. As long as they do not form a disproportionate or unjustified barrier to trade between Member States and do not amount to a means of arbitrary discrimination or a disguised restriction on trade between Member States.

harmonization to be used in the fields which it covers. This method is also used in the consumer protection field,[99] where it may also involve a horizontal approach to harmonization, permitting the Commission in urgent cases to require the Member States to take certain specific measures, such as the withdrawal of a particular product or batch of products.[100] Other methods of harmonization include the mutual recognition of national standards and the mutual recognition of controls.

The question of the scope of a directive is relevant for the examination of national measures against the terms of the directive itself and against primary community law. If the directive exhaustively occupies the field, thus harmonizing all relevant provisions on the matter concerned, there is no possibility for Member States to rely on Article 36 EC or the rule of reason justifications recognized in relation to the free movement of goods.[101] In such cases the matters are governed entirely by Community law itself, so that the directive means that any national measures incompatible with it are in fact *ultra vires* the Member States.[102] In the case of non-exhaustive Community provisions, in which the Community provisions only occupy certain areas of the field, the Member States remain free to maintain or introduce national measures in the non-harmonized areas, subject to their being compatible with Community law.[103] Such partial harmonization is often the beginning of a process which in time will culminate in total harmonization. The Court has expressly approved the legality of such an approach.[104] It should be remembered, however, that all Community harmonization directives, like all Community secondary legislation must be interpreted in the light of the Treaty rules on the free movement of goods,[105] and national rules implementing such directives will

---

99. It is implicit in Art. 129a(3) EC.
100. See *e.g.* Dir. 92/59 (O.J. 1992 L 228/24), Art. 9, and Case C-359/92 *Germany v. Council* [1994] ECR I-3681 at 3706–3712, noted by Gormley (1996) 21 ELRev. 59. The fact that national law may make regional authorities responsible for carrying out such instructions is no bar to the Commission's being entitled to issue such instructions to the national authorities, [1994] ECR I-3681 at 3712.
101. *E.g.* Case 148/78 *Pubblico Ministero v. Ratti* [1979] ECR 1629 at 1644.
102. See Case 123/76 *Commission v. Italy* [1977] ECR 1449 and Case 815/79 *Cremonini and Vrankovich* [1980] ECR 3583, [1981] 3 CMLR 49 (on Dir. 73/23 (O.J. 1973 L 77/29), the low voltage directive).
103. See note 21, *supra.* New technical regulations will have to be notified under Dir. 83/189 (see note 67, *supra*).
104. Case 37/83 *Rewe-Zentrale AG v. Director of the Landwirtschaftskammer Rheinland* [1984] ECR 1229 at 1249.
105. *E.g.* Case C-47/90 *Ets. Delhaize Frères et Compagnie le Lion SA v. Promalvin SA et al.* [1992] ECR I-3891 at 3711, Case C-315/92 *Verband Sozialer Wettbewerb eV v. Clinique Laboratories SNC et al.* [1994] ECR I-317 at 335. Only express or implicit authorization in the EC Treaty itself will permit the Community Institutions to derogate from Arts. 30–36 EC, see *e.g.* Cases 80 and 81/77 *Société Les Commissionnaires Réunis Sàrl et al. v. Receveur des Douanes* [1978] ECR 927 at 945.

be similarly interpreted.[106] Poor quality legislation with vague provisions resulting from political compromises sometimes make it difficult to ascertain what the precise character of a harmonization directive really is. In many cases the determination of the precise scope of a directive will require a close analysis of its objectives and the system involved.[107]

2.7   The present state of harmonization of laws[108]

Most of the directives adopted on the basis of the general harmonization provisions of the EC Treaty by the Council and the Commission are aimed at removing barriers to trade justified under Article 36 EC or under the rule of reason doctrine espoused first in Case 8/74 *Procureur du Roi v. Dassonville et al.*[109] and subsequently in the *Cassis de Dijon* line of authority.[110] As has been explained in section 2.1 of this Chapter, above, the present policy of the Community legislator is largely based on the new approach, the principal elements of which were set out in a Council Resolution of 7 May 1985[111] and worked out in the White Paper on *Completing the Internal Market*[112] These four elements were also visible in some earlier directives.[113] First, harmonization is confined to the adoption of essential safety requirements (or other requirements in the general interest) to which products placed on the market must conform in order to enjoy free movement throughout the Community. Secondly, the task of drawing up the technical specifications to ensure manufacture and marketing of products meeting those essential requirements was entrusted to the standardization bodies, taking due account of technological progress. Thirdly, those technical specifications would be voluntary as opposed to mandatory (this is the key distinguishing feature of standards as opposed to technical regulations). Finally, national administrations are obliged to presume that products manufactured to harmonized standards (or, provisionally, with national standards) conform to the essential requirements laid down in the directives. This means that there is a positive incentive for a manufacturer to produce to the harmonized standards, as such products automatically enjoy a presumption of conformity. He or she

---

106. Case C-315/92 *Clinique, ibid.* at 336.
107. *E.g.* Case 249/84 *Ministère public et al. v. Profant* [1985] ECR 3237 and Case C-392/93 *R. v. H.M. Treasury, ex parte British Telecommunications plc* [1996] ECR I-1631.
108. This section examines the most important directives based on Art. 100a EC. The *Directory of Community Legislation in force*, published every 6 months by the Community's Office for Official Publications gives a comprehensive listing, as does the *Celex* database.
109. [1974] ECR 837 at 852.
110. See section 2.1 of this Chapter, *ante.*
111. O.J. 1985 C 136/1.
112. COM (85) 310 Final.
113. Particularly in the low voltage directive, Dir. 73/23, see note 102, *supra.*

remains free to manufacture to other standards if desired, but in such a case the burden of demonstrating conformity with the essential requirements of the relevant directive shifts to the manufacturer.[114]

The new approach has been used for directives on simple pressure vessels,[115] toys,[116] machinery safety,[117] electromagnetic compatibility,[118] gas appliances,[119] personal protective equipment,[120] lifts,[121] active implantable medical devices,[122] medical devices,[123] equipment and protective systems for use in potentially explosive atmospheres,[124] footwear,[125] and pressure equipment.[126] Proposed directives on the safety of cableways[127] and on medical devices for *in vitro* diagnosis[128] are presently under consideration.

In relation to foodstuffs,[129] harmonization is as yet still incomplete, although considerable progress has been made. The main

114. See the Commission's Communication O.J. 1989 C 267/3. The new approach is also conveniently summarized in *Nineteenth General Report on the activities of the European Communities 1985* (Brussels, Luxembourg, 1986) points 210–212. On the basis of Art. 113 EC, Reg. 339/93 (O.J. 1993 L 40/1) on conformity checks for products from third countries permits customs authorities to suspend the release into free circulation of goods imported from third countries where those goods pose a serious and immediate threat to health or safety.
115. Dir. 87/404 (O.J. 1987 L 220/48), amended by Dirs. 90/488 (O.J. 1990 L 270/25) and 93/68 (O.J. 1993 L 220/1).
116. Dir. 88/378 (O.J. 1988 L 187/1), amended by Dir. 93/68, *ibid.*
117. Dir. 89/392 (O.J. 1989 L 183/9, amended by Dirs. 91/368 (O.J. 1991 L 198/16), 93/44 (O.J. 1993 L 175/12) and 93/68, *ibid*). The Commission has presented a proposal for a codified version of the directive, COM (96) 667 Final.
118. Dir. 89/336 (O.J. 1989 L 139/19), amended by Dirs 92/31 (O.J. 1992 L 126/11) and 93/68, *ibid.*
119. Dir. 90/396 (O.J. 1990 L 196/15), amended by Dir. 93/68, *ibid.* See also Dir. 92/42 (O.J. 1992 L 167/17) on efficiency requirements for certain types of new hot water boilers, likewise so amended.
120. Dir. 89/686 (O.J. 1989 L 399/18), amended by Dirs. 93/95 (O.J. 1993 L 276/11), 93/68, *ibid.*, and 96/58 (O.J. 1996 L 236/44).
121. Dir. 84/529 (O.J. 1984 L 300/72), amended by Dirs. 86/312 (O.J. 1986 L 196/56) and 90/486 (O.J. 1990 L 270/21) and replaced with effect from 1 July 1999 by Dir. 95/16 (O.J. 1995 L 213/1).
122. Dir. 90/385 (O.J. 1990 L 189/17), amended by Dirs. 93/42 (O.J. 1993 L 169/1) and 93/68, *ibid.*
123. Dir. 93/42 (O.J. 1993 L 169/1).
124. Dir. 94/9 (O.J. 1994 L 100/1).
125. Dir. 94/11 (O.J. 1994 L 100/37).
126. Dir. 97/23 (O.J. 1997 L 181/55).
127. O.J. 1994 C 70/8, amended proposal COM (95) 523 Final (O.J. 1996 C 22/12).
128. O.J. 1995 C 172/21, amended proposal COM (96) 643 Final (O.J. 1997 C 87/9).
129. See the still relevant Council Resolution of 28 May 1969 (J.O. 1969 C 76/5) containing the harmonization programme in this field. In relation to future action on labelling and consumer protection, see the Council Resolution of 5 April 1993 (O.J. 1993 C 110/1), and the Commission's Green Paper COM (97) 176 Final. See also the latest proposals on ionising radiation in food, COM (98) 188 Final.

point of departure is the principle of mutual acceptance in other Member States of products lawfully produced or marketed in a Member State, enshrined in the *Cassis de Dijon* judgment,[130] so that only the protection of, *in casu*, health (under Article 36 EC) or consumer protection (under the rule of reason) will justify a refusal to accept such goods. Two types of directives can be identified: so-called vertical directives relating to specific products, and framework directives of the Council which are then worked out in detailed measures adopted by the Commission under powers delegated in the framework directives. Vertical directives embrace products as diverse as cocoa and chocolate,[131] certain sugars intended for human consumption,[132] honey,[133] fruit juices and certain similar products,[134] dehydrated preserved milk for human consumption,[135] coffee and chicory extracts,[136] and fruit jams, jellies, marmalades and chestnut purée.[137] Simplification of all these directives has now been proposed in accordance with the subsidiarity principle as applied by the European Council at Edinburgh in December 1992.[138] Other vertical directives cover natural mineral water,[139] milk proteins,[140] and quick-frozen foodstuffs.[141] Framework directives cover *inter alia* additives,[142] erucic acid in oils and

130. See note 14, *supra*. The Court in fact spoke of goods lawfully produced and marketed, but that is clearly an oversight, in view of the requirements of Arts. 9 and 10(1) EC, see Gormley, *op. cit.* (see note 4, *supra*) 47–48.
131. Dir. 73/241 (O.J. 1973 L 228/23), most recently amended by Dir. 89/344 (O.J. 1989 L 142/19).
132. Dir. 73/747 (O.J. 1973 L 356/71), most recently amended by the Act of Spanish and Portuguese Accession (1985).
133. Dir. 74/409 (O.J. 1974 L 221/10), most recently amended by *ibid.*
134. Dir. 93/77 (O.J. 1993 L 244/23).
135. Dir. 76/118 (O.J. 1976 L 24/49), most recently amended by the Act of Spanish and Portuguese Accession.
136. Dir. 77/436 (O.J. 1976 L 172/20), most recently amended by Dir. 85/573 (O.J. 1985 L 372/20).
137. Dir. 79/693 (O.J. 1979 L 205/5), most recently amended by Dir. 88/593 (O.J. 1988 L 318/44).
138. As to the proposals, see COM (95) 722 (O.J. 1996 C 231/1 *et seq.*), and as to cocoa and chocolate, COM 97 682 Final (O.J. 1998 C 118/10). As to the European Council conclusions, see Bull.EC 12–1992, points I.4 and I.15.
139. Dir. 80/777 (O.J. 1980 L 229/1), most recently amended by Dir. 96/70 (O.J. 1996 L 299/26).
140. Dir. 83/417 (O.J. 1983 L 237/25) on lactoproteins, most recently amended by the Act of Spanish and Portuguese Accession.
141. Dir. 89/108 (O.J. 1989 L 40/34), amended by the Act of Austrian, Finnish and Swedish Accession (1994).
142. Dir. 89/107 (O.J. 1989 L 40/27), amended by Dir. 94/34 (O.J. 1994 L 237/1). See further, Dirs. 94/35 (O.J. 1994 L 237/3) on sweeteners, 94/36 (O.J. 1994 L 237/13) on colours, and 95/2 (O.J. 1995 L 61/1), amended by Dir. 96/85 (O.J. 1997 L 86/4), on food additives other than colours and sweeteners. A further amendment to Dir. 95/2 has been proposed, COM (96) 303 Final (O.J. 1997 C 76/34). See also Dec. 292/97 (O.J. 1997 L 48/13) on the maintenance of national laws prohibiting the use of certain additives in certain specific foodstuffs.

fats or foodstuffs containing them,[143] foodstuffs for particular nutritional use,[144] flavourings,[145] extraction solvents,[146] and products which come into contact with foodstuffs, such as regenerated cellulose film,[147] ceramic articles,[148] and plastic materials and articles.[149] Other important measures include Regulation 258/97 on novel foods and food ingredients,[150] Regulation 315/93 on contaminants,[151] Directive 96/738 on maximum levels of pesticide residues,[152] Directive 93/43 on hygiene of foodstuffs,[153] Directive 92/52 on infant formulae and follow-on formulae intended for export to third countries,[154] Directive 93/5 on assistance provided by the Member States to the Commission in the scientific examination of foodstuffs,[155] Directive 89/397 on official controls,[156] various measures on labelling and presentation of foodstuffs,[157] and Directive 89/396 on indications or marks identifying the lot to which a foodstuff belongs.[158] Regulations have also been adopted under Article 100a EC establishing a virtually complete system for the definition, description and presentation of spirits[159] and aromatized wines and similar products.[160]

143. Dir. 76/621 (O.J. 1976 L 202/35), most recently amended by the Act of Spanish and Portuguese Accession.
144. Dir. 89/398 (O.J. 1989 L 186/27), amended, so as to establish the innovation procedure, by Dir. 96/84 (O.J. 1996 L 48/20).
145. Dir. 88/388 (O.J. 1988 L 184/61), amended by Dir. 91/71 (O.J. 1991 L 42/25). See also Reg. 2232/96 (O.J. 1996 L 199/1).
146. Dir. 88/344 (O.J. 1988 L 157/28), most recently amended by Dir. 94/52 (O.J. 1994 L 331/10, which in turn has been amended by Dir. 96/21 (O.J. 1996 L 88/5), further amendment proposed COM (96) 375 Final, revised COM (97) 467 Final.
147. Dir. 93/10 (O.J. 1993 L 93/27), amended by Dir. 93/111 (O.J. 1993 L 310/41). See also Dir. 78/142 (O.J. 1978 L 44/15) on materials and articles containing vinyl chloride monomer.
148. Dir. 84/500 (O.J. 1984 L 277/12).
149. Dir. 90/128 (O.J. 1990 L 75/19), most recently amended by Dir. 96/11 (O.J. 1996 L 61/26).
150. O.J. 1997 L 43/1.
151. O.J. 1993 L 37/1.
152. O.J. 1996 L 335/54.
153. O.J. 1993 L 175/1.
154. O.J. 1992 L 179/129.
155. O.J. 1993 L 52/18.
156. O.J. 1989 L 186/23, amended by Dir. 93/99 (O.J. 1993 L 290/1). Various other directives provide for specific controls. See also Recommendations 97/77 (O.J. 1997 L 22/77) and 96/738 (O.J. 1996 L 335/54).
157. Dir. 79/112 (O.J. 1979 L 33/1), most recently amended by Dir. 97/4 (O.J. 1997 L 43/21), a further amendment has been proposed, COM (97) 20 Final, and Dir. 94/54 (O.J. 1994 L 300/14), amended by Dir. 96/21 (O.J. 1996 L 88/5).
158. O.J. 1989 L 186/21), most recently amended by Dir. 92/11 (O.J. 1992 L 65/32).
159. Reg. 1576/89 (O.J. 1989 L 160/1), most recently amended by Reg. 3378/94 (O.J. 1994 L 366/1), and implemented by Reg. 1014/90 (O.J. 1990 L 105/9), most recently amended by Reg. 2626/95 (O.J. 1995 L 269/5).
160. Reg. 1601/91 (O.J. 1991 L 149/1), most recently amended by Reg. 2061/96 (O.J. 1996 L 277/1), implemented by Reg. 122/94 (O.J. 1994 L 21/7). Reg. 2081/92 (O.J. 1992 L

Similarly, harmonization of laws in the field of cosmetics is achieved through various Commission directives which in turn have their legal basis in a general framework directive adopted by the Council.[161] In the pharmaceuticals field, the very open definition of medicinal products in Directive 65/65[162] led to myriad judgments.[163] The free movement of medicinal products for human use has been greatly enhanced by the adoption of a series of measures dealing with their wholesale distribution, classification, labelling, packaging and advertising.[164] The establishment of the European Agency for the Evaluation of Medicinal Products[165] makes it possible to obtain a single Community-wide authorization for pharmaceuticals for human or veterinary use under a centralized procedure, in addition to the decentralized procedure available through the relevant agencies in the individual Member States. It may be anticipated that the benefits of the single application route will be of considerable interest to the pharmaceutical industry. The harmonization of legislation relating to veterinary medicinal products is also extensive.[166]

208/1) on the protection of geographical indications and designations of origin for agricultural products and foodstuffs was adopted on the basis of Art. 43 EC.

161. Dir. 76/768 (O.J. 1976 L 262/169), last amended by Dir. 93/35 (O.J. 1993 L 151/32). There have been some 20 adaptations by the Commission of Dir. 76/768 to technical progress, e.g. Dir. 97/1 (O.J. 1997 L 16/85). See the particularly important judgments in Case C-112/89 *The Upjohn Company et al. v. Farzoo Inc. et al.* [1991] ECR I-1703 and Case C-315/92 *Verband Sozialer Wettbewerb eV v. Clinique Laboratories SNC et al.* [1994] ECR I-317.

162. O.J. English Special Edition (1965–66), p. 20, most recently amended by Dir. 93/39 (O.J. 1993 L 214/22). See also Dirs. 75/318 (O.J. 1975 L 147/1) and 75/319 (O.J. 1979 L 147/13), likewise most recently amended see COM (97) 369 Final (O.J. 1997 C 306/ 9. See, further, Dirs. 92/73 (O.J. 1992 L 297/8) as regards homeopathic medicinal products. See, generally, Bogaert, *EC Pharmaceuticals Law* (London, later Chichester, loose-leaf, since 1992), and, in relation to good manufacturing practice, Gormley in Smit Sibinga *et al.* (eds.), *Good Manufacturing Practice in Transfusion Medicine* (Dordrecht, 1994) 59. See also COM (97) 369 Final (O.J. 1997 C 306/9).

163. *E.g.* Case 227/82 *Van Bennekom* [1983] ECR 3383, [1985] 2 CMLR 692; Case C-369/ 88 *Delattre* [1991] ECR 1487, [1993] 2 CMLR 445; Case C-60/89 *Monteil et al.* [1991] ECR I-1547; Cases 266 and 267/87 *R. v. Royal Pharmaceutical Society of Great Britain, ex parte the Association of Pharmaceutical Importers et al.* [1989] ECR 1295, [1989] 2 CMLR 751, and Case 215/87 *Schumacher v. Hauptzollamt Frankfurt-am-Main-Ost* [1989] ECR 617, [1990] 2 CMLR 465. See also Case C-112/89 *Upjohn* (see note 161, *supra*).

164. Dirs. 92/25–28 (O.J. 1992 L 113/1, 5, 8 and 13).

165. Established by Reg. 2309/93 (O.J. 1993 L 214/1), see also Reg. 1662/95 (O.J. 1995 L 158/4). See further, Regs. 540/95 (O.J. 1995 L 55/5) on notification of possible unexpected side-effects; 542/95 (O.J. 1995 L 55/15) on changes in authorizations, 2141/96 (O.J. 1996 L 286/6) on transfers of authorizations, and 1662/95 (O.J. 1995 L 158/4) on Community decision-making procedures on Community authorizations (O.J. 1995 L 158/4). See, generally, Gardner (1996) ELJ 48.

166. Dirs. 81/851 (O.J. 1981 L 317/1), most recently amended by Dir. 93/40 (O.J. 1993 L 214/31).

In relation to motor vehicles, already in 1970 the Community began to harmonize national provisions in this field, and myriad directives now deal with pretty well all technical, safety and environmental protection aspects of automobiles. The optional harmonization which characterized this sector has now given way to total harmonization, so that a single type-approval attesting to conformity with the Community provisions is valid throughout the Community.[167] This facilitates Community-scale thinking on the part of the manufacturers, as well as the activities of parallel importers who seek to take account of the still widespread price differences throughout the Community.[168] Myriad measures also cover agricultural and forestry tractors.

Measurements have also necessitated steps at the Community level, with directives being adopted on measuring instruments and methods of meteorological control,[169] weights,[170] automatic and non-automatic weighing machines,[171] as well as on myriad specific measuring instruments.[172] Directives have also been adopted covering specific products, including crystal glass,[173] aerosols,[174] pressurized steel and aluminium gas cylinders,[175] paints,[176] lawnmowers,[177] and explosives for

167. See note 22, *supra*.
168. See the Commission's Notice on the procedures for the type approval and registration of vehicles previously registered in another Member State (O.J. 1996 C 143/4).
169. Dir. 71/316 (O.J. English Special Edition 1971 (II), p. 707, most recently amended by the Act of Austrian, Finnish and Swedish Accession (1994). See also Dirs. 73/362 (O.J. 1973 L 335/56) on measurements for materials, most recently amended by Dir. 85/146 (O.J. 1985 L 54/29); 75/107 (O.J. 1975 L 42/14) on bottles used as measuring containers, and 80/181 (O.J. 1981 L 39/40) on units of measurement, most recently amended by Dir. 89/617 (O.J. 1989 L 357/28).
170. Dirs. 71/317 (O.J. English Special Edition 1971 (II), p. 721 and 74/148 (O.J. 1974 L 84/3). See also Dirs. 75/106 (O.J. 1976 L 42/1) on prepackaged liquids, most recently amended by Dir. 89/676 (O.J. 1989 L 398/18), 76/211 (O.J. 1976 L 46/1) on prepackaged goods, most recently amended by Dir. 78/891 (O.J. 1978 L 311/21), and 80/232 (O.J. 1980 L 51/1) on ranges of nominal quantities and capacities, most recently amended by Dir. 87/356 (O.J. 1987 L 192/48).
171. Dirs. 78/1031 (O.J. 1978 L 364/1) on automatic weighing machines and 90/384 (O.J. 1990 L 189/1) on non-automatic weighing machines, amended by Dir. 93/68 (O.J. 1993 L 220/1). Dir. 90/384 was one of the new approach directives.
172. *E.g.* gas and electricity meters, cold and hot water meters, liquid meters, taxi meters and manometers.
173. Dir. 69/493 (O.J. English Special Edition 1969 (II), p. 599, most recently amended by the Act of Spanish and Portuguese Accession. See Case 51/93 *Meyhui NV v. Schott Zwiesel Glaswerke AG* [1994] ECR I-3879.
174. Dir. 75/324 (O.J. 1975 L 147/40), most recently amended by Dir. 94/1 (O.J. 1994 L 23/28).
175. Dirs. 84/525–527 (O.J. 1984 L 300/1, 20 and 48).
176. Dir. 77/728 (O.J. 1978 L 303/23), most recently amended by Dir. 92/32 (O.J. 1992 L 154/1).
177. Dir. 84/538 (O.J. 1984 L 300/71), most recently amended by Dir. 88/181 (O.J. 1988 L 81/71).

civil uses.[178] An important framework directive deals with the classification, packaging and labelling of dangerous substances,[179] and there are myriad directives dealing with waste.[180] The free movement of tobacco products has required not merely action in relation to excise duties, but also in relation to composition[181] and labelling requirements.[182]

Harmonization of national provisions on consumer protection was originally intended to remove the need for producers to have multiple production runs as a result of differences in national requirements on packaging, presentation and labelling. Subsequently consumer protection has acquired a more independent significance.[183] Harmonization in this sphere is of particular importance for national private law.[184]

In addition to harmonization relating to products, myriad measures cover matters such as the labelling, presentation and advertising of

178. Dir. 93/15 (O.J. 1993 L 121/20).
179. Dirs. 67/548 (O.J. English Special Edition 1967, p. 234), most recently amended by Dir. 96/56 (O.J. 1996 L 236/35); 88/379 (O.J. 1988 L 187/14), most recently amended by Dir. 95/65 (O.J. 1996 L 263/15), and 76/769 (O.J. 1976 L 262/201), most recently amended by Dir. 96/55 (O.J. 1996 L 231/20). A further amendment to Dir. 76/769 has been proposed, see the amended proposal COM (95) 531 (O.J. 1996 C 12/12). A number of individual directives deal with specific dangerous substances, e.g. Dir. 78/631 (O.J. 1978 L 206/13), most recently amended by Dir. 92/32 (O.J. 1992 L 154/1) covers pesticides; Dir. 73/404 (O.J. 1973 L 347/51), most recently amended by Dir. 86/94 (O.J. 1984 L 80/51) covers detergents; Dirs. 82/883 (O.J. 1982 L 378/1), most recently amended by the Act of Austrian, Finnish, and Portuguese Accession, and 92/112 (O.J. 1992 L 409/11) cover titanium dioxide; Dir. 84/156 (O.J. 1984 L 74/49), most recently amended by Dir. 91/692 (O.J. 1991 L 372/48) covers mercury discharges, and Dir. 91/157 (O.J. 1991 L 78/38) deals with batteries and accumulators.
180. The general measures are Dirs. 75/442 (O.J. 1975 L 194/39), most recently amended by Dec. 96/350 (O.J. 1996 L 135/32), on waste; 91/689 (O.J. 1991 L 377/20), most recently amended by Dir. 94/31 (O.J. 1994 L 168/28) on hazardous waste; Dir. 94/62 (O.J. 1994 L 365/10) on packaging waste, and Dir. 94/67 (O.J. 1994 L 365/34) on incineration of hazardous waste. See also Reg. 259/93 (O.J. 1993 L 30/1), most recently amended by Reg. 120/97 (O.J. 1997 L 22/14), on waste shipments within, into and out of the Community, and Dir. 93/75 (O.J. 1993 L 247/19), most recently amended by Dir. 97/34 (O.J. 1997 L 158/40), on vessels carrying dangerous or polluting goods. A further proposal for amendment of Reg. 259/93 is under consideration, see COM (96) 515 Final. See further, Chapter X, section 3, post.
181. Dir. 90/239 (O.J. 1990 L 137/36) on the maximum tar content of cigarettes.
182. Dir. 89/662 (O.J. 1989 L 359/1), amended by Dir. 1992 L 158/30.
183. See further, Chapter X, section 4, post.
184. See, generally, e.g. Micklitz (ed.), Rechtseinheit oder Rechtsvielfalt in Europa? (Baden-Baden, 1996 (many of the contributions are in English, the rest in German)); Hondius et al., Naar een Europees burgelijk recht: een bonte lappendeken (Lelystad, 1993); Hartkamp et al., Towards a European Civil Code (2nd ed., The Hague, 1998); De Ly, Europese gemeenschap en privaatrecht (Zwolle, 1993), and Müller-Graff (1993) NJW 13.

foodstuffs for sale to the ultimate customer;[185] specific products;[186] specific objectives,[187] and packaging.[188] Other more wide-ranging measures deal with misleading advertising,[189] contract negotiated away from business premises (doorstep selling),[190] product liability,[191] consumer credit,[192] package holidays and package tours,[193] general product safety,[194] unfair terms in consumer contracts,[195] and timesharing;[196] comparative advertising,[197] contracts negotiated at a distance (distance selling),[198] product price indication,[199] and injunctions for the protection of consumers' interests.[200]

Legal liability insurance for motor vehicles has been the subject of specific measures which are important in relation to the free movement of persons and the removal of border controls within the Community.[201] Article 100a EC has also been used as the legal basis of measures on the return of cultural objects unlawfully removed from the territory of a Member State.[202] Harmonization directives based on specific provisions of the Treaty are discussed in the relevant chapters of this work.

185. Dir. 79/112 (O.J. 1979 L 33/1), most recently amended by Dir. 93/102 (O.J. 1993 L 291/14). See Case C-83/96 *Provincia Autonoma di Trento et al. v. Dega di Depretto Gino Snc* [1997] ECR I-5001. See also Dir. 94/54 (O.J. 1994 L 300/14), most recently amended by Dir. 96/21 (O.J. 1996 L 88/5).

186. Dir. 71/307 (O.J. English Special edition 1971 (II), p. 694), most recently amended by the Act of Austrian, Finnish and Swedish Accession, deals with textiles; Dir. 87/250 (O.J. 1987 L 113/57) deals with alcoholic beverages, and Dir. 89/662 (O.J. 1989 L 359/1), most recently amended by Dir. 92/41 (O.J. 1992 L 158/30) deals with tobacco products.

187. Dirs. 79/530 (O.J. 1979 L 145/1) and 92/75 (O.J. 1992 L 297/16) cover energy consumption of household appliances, and Dir. 90/496 (O.J. 1990 L 276/40) deals with nutrition labelling of foodstuffs.

188. See note 170, *supra.* See also Dir. 90/35 (O.J. 1990 L 19/14) on child-resistant fastenings.

189. Dir. 84/450 (O.J. 1984 L 250/17 amended by Dir. 97/55 (O.J. 1997 L 290/18), see Case C-373/90 *Complaint against X* [1992] ECR I-131.

190. Dir. 85/577 (O.J. 1985 L 372/31).

191. Dir. 85/374 (O.J. 1985 L 210/29) an amendment has been proposed, COM (97) 478 Final (O.J. 1997 C 337/54).

192. Dir. 87/102 (O.J. 1987 L 42/48), amended by Dir. 90/88 (O.J. 1988 L 61/14).

193. Dir. 90/314 (O.J. 1990 L 158/89). See Cases C-178/94 *etc. Dillenkofer et al. v. Germany* [1997] ECR I-4845 and Case C-364/96 *Verein für Konsumenteninformation v. Österreichische Kreditversicherungs AG* [1998] ECR I-nyr (14 May 1998).

194. Dir. 92/59 (O.J. 1992 L 228/24), see Case C-359/92 *Germany v. Council* [1994] ECR I-3681, noted by Gormley (1996) 21 ELRev. 59.

195. Dir. 93/13 (O.J. 1993 L 95/29).

196. Dir. 94/47 (O.J. 1994 L 280/83).

197. Dir 97/55 (O.J. 1997 L 290/18) which amends Dir. 84/450 (see note 189, *supra*), accordingly.

198. Dir. 97/7 (O.J. 1997 L 144/27).

199. Dir. 98/6 (O.J. 1998 L 80/27).

200. Dir. 98/27 (O.J. 1998 L 166/51).

201. Dirs. 72/166 (O.J English Special Edition 1972 (II), p. 360), 84/5 (O.J. 1984 L 8/17), and 90/232 (O.J. 1990 L 129/33).

202. Dir. 93/7 (O.J. 1993 L 74/74, amended by Dir. 96/100 (O.J. 1997 L 60/59)).

3.　Distortion of Conditions of Competition

3.1　Articles 101 and 102 EC

The direct significance of Articles 101 and 102 EC for administrative practice and case-law has not been great, although the founding fathers of the Treaty clearly expected otherwise.[203] Nevertheless, it is desirable to devote some attention to these provisions, as they cast further light on the question of what degree of distortion of competition through disparities in national policy and provisions is still compatible with the common market, a question which has become very current since the introduction of Articles 3b, 100a(4), 118a and 130t EC. Furthermore, an analysis of Articles 101 and 102 EC provides a useful introduction to Articles 92–94 EC, which are far more important in terms of administrative practice and case-law.

Articles 101 and 102 EC were really intended as a *lex specialis* in relation to Article 100 EC, in the sense that in the case of particularly flagrant distortions of competition the Community would have a more stringent and more useable instrument at its disposal.

In Article 101 EC this more stringent character is marked by the fact that the necessary directives or other measures can, since the second stage of the transitional period, be adopted by the Council acting by a qualified majority on a proposal from the Commission, when consultation has not resulted in elimination of the distortion of competition. Unlike directives adopted under Article 100, these directives may even be addressed to one State only. Articles 101 and 102 EC make no provision for the European Parliament or the Economic and Social Committee to be involved. Given that the European Parliament's influence has been significantly increased since the introduction of Article 100a EC (originally by the SEA) and that qualified majority decision-making has been strengthened by that provision, the dividing line between Articles 101 and 100a has in fact become especially important, as is made clear under point B, below.

A.　Conditions for the applicability of Articles 101 and 102 EC

For Articles 101 and 102 to be applicable, two substantive conditions must be satisfied. In the first place there must be difference between the legislative or administrative rules of Member States. In the second place this difference must interfere with the conditions of competition in the common market and thus cause distortion which should be eliminated.

---

203. See the Spaak Report *(Rapport des Chefs de Délégations aux Ministres des Affaires Etrangères* (Secretariat of the Intergovernmental Conference, Brussels, April 21, 1956). See, further, Sprung (1959–60) *Finanzarchiv* 201. In contrast, the equivalent provision in the ECSC Treaty (Art. 67 ECSC) has been frequently applied.

The concept of distortion is as such neutral. In economic literature it is described as a noticeable influence of the market allocation of production and the factors of production through public intervention. Many distortions of the market place are express result of public policy, such as the taxation of alcohol, tobacco and motor vehicles, and the selective unburdening of merit goods or services, such as education and lead-free petrol.

The vast majority of market distortions, however, is the more or less unintended result of fiscal or administrative measures which are adopted for other than economic policy reasons. Thus the costs of income taxation and social security in Western Europe bear mostly on the factor of labour and, depending on the organization of the national social security system concerned, more or less on low-productive labour. The implementation and compliance costs of complex health, quality and environmental legislation are usually more easily absorbed by larger companies than by smaller ones. Depending on the health, safety and environmental risks involved in particular economic activities, the compliance costs may also vary. In the national sphere the question whether a distortion should be eliminated or on the contrary strengthened, is a policy question *par excellence*, the answer to which will depend on the balancing of the interests concerned.

In policy practice a distinction is made, according to the scale on which they occur, between global, generic and specific distortions. Global distortions occur at macro level, *e.g.* as a result of differences in the average level of the collective tax and social security burdens, developments in labour costs, in the development of interest rates and relative movements in exchange rates. Not every difference in the development of these costs results immediately in a distortion. If, for example, an increase in collective tax and social security burdens is compensated by restrained wages growth, the macro-economic competitive position of the economy concerned is globally unchanged, at least in the short term. The same is true if relatively high labour costs growth is compensated by an at least as high growth in productivity. In times of stable exchange rates the best indicator for global distortions is the occurrence of differences in the rate of inflation. If such differences, as will be the case in the final stage of Economic and Monetary Union (EMU), can no longer be corrected by adjustments in exchange rates, they must be remedied by adjustments in the global level of costs in the economy concerned.[204]

Generic distortions occur at the meso level of sectors, regions or categories of the economy. Sectoral generic distortions occur if one sector is relatively advantaged or disadvantaged in relation to other sectors. Thus the Common Agricultural policy consciously creates a cluster of sectoral distortions in the agricultural sector, the burdens of which fall on other

204. See further, Chapter IX, section 3, *post*.

sectors of the economy. In the Netherlands until recently the relatively low excise duty on diesel caused sectoral distortion in favour of freight transport by road. Regional generic distortions are generally the desired result of fiscal and budgetary infrastructure facilities for the economically less prosperous regions. In the 1970s attempts were made in France, the Netherlands and the United Kingdom to influence the geographical spread of investment in industry through generic regional tax measures (tax holidays and the like).[205] Generic distortions by category result from disparities in the burden for categories of undertakings on account of their size, or other functional characteristics, such as their orientation towards export markets, or intensity of labour, capital or energy. Thus the so-called 'red tape burden' forms an unintended distortion disadvantaging small and medium-sized industries, whereas various generic measures in the fiscal sphere are precisely intended to create positive distortions in favour of small-scale undertakings. Regulating energy levies, such as eco-taxes intentionally aims to influence competitive relationships to the disadvantage of activities which damage the environment.

Specific distortions at the micro level of the individual undertaking are pretty well never the intended or unintended result of targeted public measures designed to raise tax and social security burdens or costs. The principle of equality before the law, constitutionally anchored in most Member States prevents this. There are, though, specific distortions on quite a large scale as a result of individual aid measures in whatever form and under whatever name. This phenomenon is most widespread in those Member States where the state plays a relatively large role in the market economy, such as France, Italy and Spain, but even other Member States tend to support national undertakings which they regard as of vital importance for industrial or technology policy reasons.[206]

Global distortions have by definition cross-border effects, as they become visible in the competitive relationships between national economies. Articles 102a–109m EC regulate in detail how these global distortions must be redressed with a view to the formation of EMU, which national measures are permissible, and how, in a completed EMU

---

205. Particularly in the United Kingdom this policy was accompanied by an active inward investment policy, encouraging companies from third countries to set up production (or assembly) facilities in certain areas. This not infrequently gave rise to concerns about 'local content' requirements, real value-added products and jobs, and, on at least one occasion, to attempts by another Member State to consider goods produced as not having Community origin (Nissan Bluebirds).

206. Sometimes these may be a cover for political reasons, where the 'fall-out' from an undertaking closing is considered to be too great. In the United Kingdom, in the Eighties and most of the Nineties lame ducks have been left to their fate. Sometimes millions are effectively poured down the drain in order to keep an undertaking open a little longer in the (as with Fokker, sometimes forlorn) hope that a White Knight will appear.

such distortions must be prevented and managed.[207] Generic and specific distortions as a result of disparities between national measures can in principle be remedied in three ways. First, by a communitarization or, as the case may be, harmonization of the national measures which are the source of the distortions. Examples of this approach are the Common Agricultural Policy, the extensive harmonization of national measures on the basis of Articles 99, 100 and 100a EC, and the partial communitarization of regional economic policy in the context of Articles 130a–130e EC.[208]

The second method of attacking generic and specific distortions, which is particularly effective in relation to generic distortions resulting from relatively high national tax and social security burdens, involves the effects of the market forcing the necessary adaptations to be made. As deeper penetrating market integration occurs and the allocation processes of production and the factors of production become more responsive to relative differences in tax and social security burdens, the pressure on the Member States concerned spontaneously to adapt their policies will increase.

The third method is elimination of the national measures which give rise to the distortion concerned. This approach is desirable if the distortion has serious consequences in the common market, spontaneous policy adaptation is unlikely, and the risks of undesired policy imitation by other Member States are high. This occurs normally in the case of state aids: they can seriously distort market allocation; the beneficiary undertaking is strengthened by the maintenance of its competitive advantage, which puts pressure on other Member States to advantage their undertakings too. The result is an expensive and counterproductive subsidy race, and any hope of a level playing field disappears. Thus Article 92 EC, which is particularly directed to state aids, declares such measures to be in principle incompatible with the common market.

The requirement of a difference between the legal and administrative provisions of the Member States makes it possible to draw a dividing line between the scope of Article 101 EC and the scope of the numerous prohibitions of discrimination in the EC Treaty discussed in Chapter VII, above. In fact, discrimination implies unequal treatment by one Member State of subjects or objects in equal circumstances, or equal treatment by this Member State of subjects or objects in unequal circumstances. The essential point for Article 101, on the contrary, is that the unequal treatment of subjects or objects moving within the common market is the result of difference between the legislative or administrative rules of two or more Member States.

The term 'distortion of competition' occurs in the EC Treaty both in a

207. See Chapter IX, section 3, *post*.
208. See Chapter IX, section 4, *post*.

very general meaning, which comprises discrimination as well as restrictions of competition and other 'distortions'[209] and in a narrower
sense.[210] From the cumulation of the two elements, *i.e.* that the difference,
owing to its interference with the conditions of competition, must cause a
distortion, it appears that Article 101 (like Article 92 EC) has a more
limited meaning in view. On the strength of the Spaak Report[211] and of a
systematic interpretation of the Treaty it will have to be assumed that, in
any event, a distortion in this narrow sense of the word is involved if the
following three criteria are met. In the first place one group of
undertakings in a Member State must be subject to higher or lower charges
than other groups of undertakings in the same Member State.[212] Secondly,
in the other Member States there must not be an equal deviation for the
same group of undertakings as compared with other groups of undertakings (the national intervention must, as has been explained above, have
a cross-border influence on competitive relationships, thus an external
effect). Thirdly, the deviation in question must not be compensated by
other targeted charges or benefits.

Careful use of this balancing criterion is essential, as a broad
interpretation could give rise to untenable comparisons of the total tax and
social security burdens to which the persons concerned are subject in the
various Member States. The compensating burdens or benefits must
therefore be targeted and have a substantive link with the measures for
which they are designed to compensate.

If, on the basis of these criteria, it is found that there exists a distortion
which is relevant for the application of Article 101 EC, the balancing
contained in the phrase 'the resultant distortion needs to be eliminated'
takes place.[213] In the evaluation, it is submitted, the decisive factor should
be the risk that the distortion poses to the functioning of the common
market, irrespective of the motive which led the Member State concerned
to adopt the measure causing the distortion. In this evaluation the intensity
and scope of the actual or potential distortion of market forces has to be

209. Art. 3(g) EC.
210. In Arts. 101 and 92 EC.
211. See note 203, *supra*.
212. It is submitted that this criterion should not be restrictively interpreted. Because specific distortions are rare in the field of application of Art. 101 EC, that provision is of
significance primarily for generic distortions which affect groups of undertakings
defined on the basis of sectors, regions or categories. The restrictive interpretation
apparently maintained by the Commission's legal service (see Van Grinsven (1991)
SEW 173 at 188) is, it is submitted, untenable. It makes the use of Art. 101 EC
impossible from the start, and is the main reason why Art. 101 has been a dead-letter
provision so far.
213. The margin of discretion accorded to the Commission and the Council means that
Art. 101 is not directly effective, see, in relation to Art. 102, but the reasoning is identical, Case 6/64 *Costa v. ENEL* [1964] ECR 585 at 595 and Case C-134/94 *Esso Española SA v. Comunidad Autónoma de Canarias* [1995] ECR I-4223 at 4249.

examined, as well as the likelihood of spontaneous policy adaptation by the Member State concerned in response to market forces.

The motives of the Member State concerned for adopting the measure causing the distortion may well play a part in the choice of measures which the Council takes, acting on a proposal from the Commission. If, for example, the relevant measure was adopted in order to protect significant public interests, which are also accepted elsewhere in the Community as deserving protection, an initiative towards harmonization is the most obvious approach. In such circumstances, in cases when Article 100a EC is applicable, the use of that provision as the legal basis is in principle preferable (in view of its more democratic and flexible provisions). A solution in this direction may well gain more currency than hitherto. With a far-reaching market integration the Member States will after all be faced with the prisoner's dilemma: generic interventions which are in themselves desirable will not take place or will have sub-optimal effect because the resulting distortions operate unilaterally to the detriment of parts of a Member State's own industry. Examples of this phenomenon are presently to be seen in environmental policy (regulating and targeting levies) and in transport policy (road pricing). Articles 101 and 102 EC offer the possibility, without prejudice to other legal bases in the Treaty, to cut through such prisoner's dilemmas.

In other cases a more obvious solution is a measure obliging the Member State concerned to eliminate its distorting measure, particularly if other Member States threaten to proceed to policy imitation and the final result is negative for the functioning of the common market. The Council's measures may also be limited to certain Member States, if the distortion involved only affects those Member States. Distortions affecting only part of the common market may well occur particularly in the sphere of environmental policy.

Article 102 EC includes an obligation for Member States to consult the Commission in case of introduction of new provisions when there is objective reason to fear that these may cause distortion. Since the criterion has not been left to the discretion of Member States, the Commission must ensure compliance with the obligation.[214] If the distortion is only to the detriment of the state's own industries, Article 101 cannot apply if a Member State does not comply with a recommendation of the Commission.

B.   Articles 101 and 102 EC and other provisions of the EC Treaty

The relationship between Articles 101 and 102 EC and Articles 92–94 has already been discussed in A above by implication. The latter provisions are

214. See Case 6/64 *Costa v. ENEL, ibid.* on the obligation to consult the Commission.

exclusively applicable to distortions arising through state aids. Thus a separate regime governs this quantitatively and qualitatively very important category of distortions.

A more difficult demarcation problem occurs between Article 101 EC on the one hand and Article 100a EC on the other. As has been suggested in section 1, above, Article 100a EC can also be used to remove distortions of competition. Where the substantive scope of both provisions overlaps to a significant extent, the question immediately arises whether there is any significant room left for the maintenance of Article 101 EC. This question is even more pressing as it appears that the involvement of the European Parliament in the application of Article 100a EC in principle forces that provision to be used as the legal basis in cases in which it overlaps with provisions in which the Parliament has less extensive powers.[215]

It is submitted that in any event room will remain for the use of Article 101 EC in the areas in which the harmonization procedure of Article 100a EC is by virtue of Article 100a(2) inapplicable. The recently adopted Code of Conduct for Business Taxation corresponds, as a voluntary basis for the elimination of distortions in this field, to the consultation phase of Article 101 EC.[216] In addition, irrespective of the policy area involved, Article 101 is still applicable where its use is preferable on functional grounds, as in the case of distortions which occur between only some Member States, distortions which must be eliminated in the short term, and distortions the removal of which should occur not through harmonization of legislation or policy but through unilateral adaptation of its policy by the Member State which causes the distortion. If there is a functional reason for using Article 101 EC, neither the content of the policy area concerned nor the nature of the public interest involved, nor the other motives which may be behind the national measures causing a distortion will be a ground for excluding the applicability of Articles 101 and 102 EC.[217] Since the coming into force of the TEU the legal and perhaps even the practical consequences of the above have become potentially important. Thus any reliance on the principle of subsidiarity contained in Article 3b EC will not prevail if Community action objectively satisfies the criteria for such action specified in Article 101 EC. This is logical, as it cannot be maintained that national measures which cause distortions in the common market fall outside the ambit of Community competence.[218] The margin of discretion to decide

---

215. Case C-300/89 *Commission v. Council* [1991] ECR I-2867.
216. See Wattel, (1998) NTER 17. A mandatory implementation of this Code, as announced in its text, might then well be based on the second step provided for in Art. 101 EC, *ibid.* As to the Code, see O.J. 1998 C2/2.
217. Certainly as far as legal reasons are concerned, although the political reality may determine otherwise.
218. Thus the viewpoint of the Commission's legal service (see note 212, *supra*) that the concept of distortion should be restrictively interpreted is untenable on systematic grounds and is, with the utmost possible respect, functionally counterproductive.

whether, and, if so, how a particular distortion must be removed clearly falls within Community competence.

More specifically, the Member States may not base arguments against Community action on the exceptional safeguard clauses of Articles 100a(4), 118a(3) and 130t EC if the use which they make of their powers under those provisions leads to distortions which justify the application of Article 101 EC. The more such exception provisions are inserted into the EC Treaty, their possible consequences for the functioning of the common market become more important, and a more stringent application of Articles 101 and 102 EC, with all their possibilities for positive and negative intervention by the Community is appropriate. In extreme circumstances it is not impossible that a more far-reaching degree of policy harmonization is achieved by the application of Article 101 EC than is possible under the social provisions in Articles 117–122 EC. If a significant distortion in the common market should result from an initiative of the overwhelming majority of the Member States under the Agreement on Social Policy annexed to the Protocol on Social Policy, the Council may, by qualified majority, 'issue the necessary directives' or, and it appears from the absence of any other specific requirement, by simple majority, 'take any other appropriate measures' provided for in the EC Treaty. Such directives or other measures include harmonization for the Community as a whole. Neither in the Protocol nor in the Agreement is there any basis for declaring Article 101 EC inapplicable.[219]

Global distortions between the economies of the Member States will have to be removed through the coordination of general economic policy, as envisaged in Articles 103, 104a and, with a view to the final stage of EMU, 109e and 109j EC. In such coordination the principles set out in Articles 3a and 102a EC must be taken into account, including 'the principle of an open market economy with free competition, favouring an efficient allocation of resources'. From this it can be deduced that in the execution of their economic policy coordinated in the Community context Member States confronted with a looming overheating of their economies may not take any measures which cause generic or specific distortions, such as selective levies imposed on particular products. If they were nevertheless to adopt such measures and generic distortions were to result, Articles 101 and 102 EC would again be applicable. Here too, the policy considerations leading to the national measures concerned form no obstacle to the application of these provisions.

C. Policy in practice

Although over the years the various consultation procedures provided for in Articles 101 and 102 EC have been invoked, those provisions have so

219. See further, Chapter IX, section 5, *post.*

far not played an important role in policy practice. But, as has been submitted above, this may well change in the future. Much will depend on how much attention the Commission devotes to compliance with the obligation to consult imposed by Article 102 EC. A number of reasons explain why the legal and practical importance of Articles 101 and 102 EC has lagged behind the expectations of the *Spaak Report*.[220] First, the wide interpretation given by the Court to the prohibitions in Articles 30, 52 and 59 EC, discussed in Chapter VII, above, have meant that Articles 100 and later also 100a EC came to be applied in such a way that myriad possible distortions as a result of differences in national legislation could already be eliminated by those means. Secondly, the substantive scope of Article 101 was further limited through the wide interpretation which the Court gave to the concept of state aids in Article 92 EC, as is explained in section 3.2, below. Thirdly, the EC Treaty provides for a number of specific legal bases for harmonization of those national laws which result in burdens for market participants, particularly in the fiscal sphere,[221] and in relation to sectoral policies.[222] Fourthly, targeted increases in burdens as instruments of economic steering have gradually fallen into disuse, in part under the influence of the increasing pressure of market integration in Western Europe. The fifth factor is that many of the generic distortions which initially still existed have been removed through spontaneous processes of adaptation, whether through adaptation of national legislation to European requirements or through compensating relatively heavy national burdens through measures elsewhere in the fiscal or social security legislation. Finally, the supervision by the Commission of compliance with Articles 92 and 93 EC has been significantly stricter than that of compliance with Articles 101 and 102 EC.

220. See note 203, *supra*. Art. 102 EC is mentioned in Rec. 69/14 (J.O. 1969 L 18/13) dealing with the draft German wine law, in the Commission's Communication on the Environmental Policy Programme (O.J. 1972 C 52/1), and in Dec. 96/542 (O.J. 1996 L 231/23) on Italian aid to the footwear industry. Art. 101 has been referred to in Rec. 69/14, *supra*; the European Energy Charter (O.J. 1994 L 380/3 and 24); exchanges of letters with Hungary relating to transit traffic and road transport infrastructure (O.J. 1993 L 347/269 and 271); Dec. 96/305 (O.J. 1996 L 117/9), based on the Euratom Treaty and concerning the JET Joint Undertaking; Dec. 96/369 (O.J. 1996 L 146/42) on aid to German airlines; Dec. 96/542 (O.J. 1996 L 231/23) on aid to the Italian footwear industry, and in the proposal for approval of an Agreement with Kazakhstan on nuclear safety (COM (96) 572 Final). The possibility of the Commission finding the existence of a distortion is mentioned in Cases 181 and 229/78 *Ketelhandel P. van Paassen BV et al. v. Staatssecretaris van Financiën et al.* [1979] ECR 2063 at 2078. Two cases are presently pending involving *inter alia* Art. 101 EC: Case C-46/96 *Germany v. Commission* (O.J. 1996 C 108/4) and Case C-182/96 *Germany v. Commission* (O.J. 1996 C 210/8).

221. Art. 99 EC.

222. Arts. 43 and 75 EC.

3.2 Articles 92–94 EC: state aids[223]

3.2.1 General significance of Articles 92–94 EC

A weapon against distortions of competition that is much sharper and more important in practice than Articles 101 and 102 is created by Articles 92 and 93 EC. These Articles form a special set of rules for the particular case of aids granted by Member States or paid in any way whatever by means of state resources which distort or threaten to distort competition by favouring certain undertakings or the production of certain goods.[224] Such aids are declared to be incompatible in principle with the common market to the extent to which they affect trade between Member States. The aim of these provisions is clear, and the Court has confirmed that they

223. See, generally, Wenig in Von der Groeben, *op. cit.* (see note 4, *supra*) Vol. II 2631 (and literature cited there); *Reports of the FIDE Congress, Paris, 1986* (Paris, 1986) Vol. II; Bellamy and Child, *Common Market Law of Competition* (4th ed., London, 1993, and 1st supp., 1996) Chapter 18; Evans, *EC Law of State Aids* (Oxford, 1997) and (1997) ECLR 259; Hancher *et al.*, *EC State Aids* (Chichester, 1993, 2nd Ed. announced, London, 1998); Harden (ed.), *State Aid: Community Law and Policy* (Cologne, 1993); Joris, *Nationale Steunmaatregelen en het Europees Gemeenschapsrecht* (Antwerp, 1994); Ross, *Supervision of State Aids and Public Undertakings under EC Law* (Leicester, 1994); Schina, *State Aids under the EEC Treaty Articles 92 to 94* (Oxford, 1987); Winter: *Nationale steunmaatregelen en het gemeenschapsrecht* (Deventer, 1981); Pappalardo in Bates *et al.* (eds.), *In Memoriam J. D. B. Mitchell* (London, 1983) 184; Muffat-Jeandet (1983) RTDE 1; Flynn (1983) 8 ELRev. 297; Mortelmans (1984) 21 CMLRev. 405; Schramme (1985) RTDE 487; Dominick (1985) 22 CMLRev. 591; Ottervanger (1985) SEW 2; Van den Oosterkamp (1985) SEW 719; Lasok (1986) ECLR 53; Vogelaar (1985) *Swiss Review of International Competition Law* 31; Hellingman (1986) 23 CMLRev. 111; Ross (1986) 23 CMLRev. 867; Cownie (1986) 11 ELRev. 247; 51 *Halsbury's Laws* (see note 4, *supra*) paras. 7.01–7.39; Barents (1988) SEW 352; Quigley (1988) 13 ELRev. 242; Bentley (1990) 1 EBLR 91; Slot (1990) 27 CMLRev. 741; Evans (1991) 16 ELRev. 79; Fernández Martín (1991) 16 ELRev. 216; Faber (1992) DVBl. 1346; Magiera in Baur *et al.* (eds.), *Europarecht, Energierecht, Wirtschaftsrecht* (*Festschrift* for Börner, Cologne, 1992); Bast (1993) WuW 181; Struys (1993) RTDE 17; Winter (1993) 30 CMLRev. 311; Gyselen (1993) CDE 417; Hancher (1994) ECLR 134; Ehlermann (1994) Fordham Int'l. L.J. 410 and (1995) *ibid.* 1212; Hancher and Slot (1995) SEW 307; Ross (1995) 15 YBEL 79; Balfour (1995) 15 YBEL 157; Schütte and Hix (1995) 32 CMLRev. 215; Slotboom (1995) 20 ELRev. 289; Evans (1996) 21 ELRev. 263; Gormley in Micklitz and Reich (eds.), *Public Interest Litigation before European Courts* (Baden-Baden, 1996) 159; Nordberg (1997/1) LIEI 35; Priess (1996) 33 CMLRev. 69; Stuart (1996) ECLR 226, and Bishop (1997) ECLR 84. See also the annual *Report on Competition Policy* published by the Commission, and the *Fifth Survey on State Aid in the European Union in the Manufacturing and Certain Other Sectors* (COM (97) 710 Final). As to UNICE's suggestions for reform of state aid control, see *Modernising EU Competition Policy – Reform of State Aid Control* (Brussels, September 1995), summarized in Stuart (1996) ECLR 226 at 238. Recent developments may also be traced in the Commission's quarterly *Competition Policy Newsletter*.
224. The English text speaks of 'goods'. The Dutch text speaks of '*producties*' which would be wide enough to embrace services.

form an essential complement of the free movement provisions.[225] Thus the free movement of goods and services made possible by those provisions and the optimum division of labour would be seriously undermined if Member States were to confer on their trade and industry an artificial advantage over their competitors in other Member States through means of state aids.[226]

There is a connection between supervision of national aid measures and the coordination of national economic policy[227] which is of increasing importance as the realization of Economic and Monetary Union comes in sight. If the total volume of aid which the richer Member States grant to their industries is higher than that granted by the poorer Member States the result will be global distortions to the disadvantage of the latter. Effective control of state aids will therefore involve not merely the intensity of the aid (scope and terms), but also the (total) volume. Such control may well take place in the context of the Ecofin Council, possibly using the procedure envisaged in Article 101 EC.[228]

Both the content of Article 92 EC and its link with Article 93 EC make it plain that the former provision does not contain a directly effective prohibition of state aid.[229] Article 92(1) EC sets out from the principle that aid 'which distorts or threatens to distort competition by favouring certain undertakings or the production of certain goods' is incompatible with the common market in so far as such aid affects trade between Member States. Article 92(2) then explains what types of aid are nevertheless compatible with the common market, and Article 92(3) sets out what types of aid may be considered compatible with the common market. Article 93 EC deals with the Commission's tasks of supervising compliance with Article 92 EC and in fact deals with the lawfulness of the aid. The distinction between the two provisions is important, as the categories of lawfulness and compatibility do not completely overlap. Thus aid is incompatible with the common market within the meaning of Article 92 EC if it falls within Article 92(1) but fails to satisfy the criteria for in either Article 92(2) or (3). Aid is unlawful, and thus prohibited, if it is granted in breach of the obligations and procedural requirements of Article 93 EC. Thus aid which

---

225. See *e.g.* Case 18/84 *Commission v. France* [1985] ECR 1339 at 1347–1348; Case 103/84 *Commission v. Italy* [1986] ECR 1759 at 1774, and Case C-21/88 *Du Pont de Nemours Italiana SpA v. Unità sanitaria locale No 2 di Carrara* [1990] ECR I-889 at 922.
226. See Case C-21/88 *Du Pont de Nemours, ibid.*
227. Art. 103 EC *et seq.*
228. See section 3.1 of this Chapter, *ante.*
229. Case 78/76 *Firma Steinike und Weinlig v. Germany* [1977] ECR 595 at 609. The contrary was primarily argued in older German literature. If, though, the provisions of Art. 92 EC have been applied by the general provisions provided for in Art. 94 EC or by specific decisions under Art. 93(2) EC, the compatibility of an aid may be challenged before national courts, *ibid.* This is in addition to any right which may be available to challenge a Community measure under Art. 173 EC, as to which, see section 3.2.4, *post.*

is in itself compatible with the common market may well be unlawful.[230] Article 94 EC confers power on the Council to prescribe appropriate regulations for the application of Articles 92 and 93 EC, in particular determining the conditions of application of the discretionary compatibility envisaged in Article 92(3) and the categories of aid exempted from the procedure.[231]

3.2.2 Substantive aspects of Articles 92–94 EC

Given the major threat which state aids pose to the unity of the common market, it is not surprising that the Court has interpreted the concept of an aid widely. In Case 61/79 *Amministrazione delle Finanze dello Stato* v. *Denkavit Italiana Srl*[232] the Court found that the concept of an aid 'refers to the decisions of Member States by which the latter, in pursuit of their own economic and social objectives, give, by unilateral and autonomous decisions, undertakings or other persons resources or procure for them advantages intended to encourage the attainment of the economic or social objectives sought.' This definition is entirely in line with modern legal views of subsidies as instruments of economic policy.[233] This definition also makes it clear that the essential element of the concept of state aid in Article 92(1) EC is the creation of an artificial advantage of whatever nature which costs the state money. Such advantages may lower the costs of investment, production or distribution and thereby distort existing or potential competition.[234] The decisive factor is the effect of the envisaged aid for the common market; thus economic or social objectives, no matter how justified or worthy, will not as such suffice to permit an aid measure to escape the ambit of Article 92 EC.[235] Case-law and the Commission's

230. See Case C-354/90 *Fédération Nationale du Commerce Extérieur des Produits Alimentaires et al.* v. *French State* [1991] ECR I-5505 at 5529.
231. This power also means, according to the judgment in Case 77/72 *Capolongo* v. *Azienda Agricola Maya* [1973] ECR 611 at 621–622, that the criteria of discretionary compatibility set out in Art. 93(3) can be further worked out, which permits direct effect for Art. 92(1) EC in respect of existing systems of aid. See Reg. 994/98 (O.J. 1998 L 142/1) and the proposal for detailed rules, COM (98) 73 Final (O.J. 1998 C 116/13).
232. [1980] ECR 1205 at 1228.
233. See Geelhoed (1983) TVVS 81 and 111. The concept of an aid is, though, wider than that of a subsidy, see Case 30/59 *De Gezamenlijke Steenkolenmijnen in Limburg* v. *High Authority* [1961] ECR 1 at 19 (in relation to Art. 4 ECSC which contains *inter alia* an express prohibition of subsidies or aids).
234. Case 102/87 *France* v. *Commission* [1988] ECR 4067 at 4087–4088. But not all differences in treatment automatically mean that there is a benefit in the sense of Art. 92 (1) EC: see Case C-353/95 P *Tiercé Ladbroke SA* v. *Commission* [1997] ECR I-7007 at 7036–7037.
235. Case 310/85 *Deufil GmbH & Co. KG* v. *Commission* [1987] ECR 901 at 926. The Commission has a discretion in the application of Art. 92(3) and the evaluation of economic and social assessments must be made in a Community context, *ibid.* and Case 730/79 *Philip Morris Holland BV* v. *Commission* [1980] ECR 2671 at 2691. See also Cases T-

practice show that advantages caught by Article 92 may take the form of direct financial payments, loan guarantees, loans at lower than commercial rates of interest, deferred loans, exemptions, reduction or remission of direct or indirect taxation,[236] or social security contributions;[237] lower charges for goods or services delivered by the State;[238] export aid;[239] preference in the placing of public contracts, distribution guarantees, participation in equity capital if private investors would not have made capital available in such market conditions or on similar terms;[240] or sales

244 and 486/93 *TWD Textilwerke Deggendorf GmbH v. Commission* [1995] ECR II-2265 at 2296 (confirmed on appeal in Case C-355/95 P *TWD Textilwerke Deggendorf GmbH v. Commission* [1997] ECR I-2549 at 2576 citing earlier case-law).

236. In Case 70/72 *Commission v. Germany* [1973] ECR 813 the German government did not actually contest the Commission's allegation that its tax breaks constituted aid, but contested the matter on procedural grounds: this case is thus formally only implicit authority for the proposition in the text (though it is often cited as explicit authority); firm authority can be found in Case C-387/92 *Banco de Crédito Industrial SA now Banco Exterior de España SA v. Ayuntamiento de Valencia* [1994] ECR I-877 at 908. See further, *e.g.* Decs. 92/389 (O.J. 1992 L 207/47) and 92/35 (O.J. 1992 L 14/35). As an example of the Commission's attitude to loan guarantees, see the partial final decisions on EFIM (O.J. 1993 C 267/11 and C 349/2), *XXIIIrd Report on Competition Policy 1993* (Brussels, Luxembourg, 1994) points 387 and 401.

237. Case 173/73 *Italy v. Commission* [1974] ECR 709 at 719–720; Case 203/82 *Commission v. Italy* [1983] ECR 2525 (uncontested acceptance that the measure condemned in Dec. 80/932 (O.J. 1980 L 264/28) was an aid).

238. By Dec. 85/215 (O.J. 1985 L 97/49) the Commission condemned preferential natural gas tariffs for Dutch horticulture, see Cases 67, 68 and 70/85 *Kwekerij Gebroeders van der Kooy BV et al. v. Commission* [1988] ECR 219, [1989] 2 CMLR 804 and Case 213/85 *Commission v. Netherlands* [1988] ECR 281, [1988] 2 CMLR 287. But if the preferential tariff, in the context of the market concerned, is objectively justified by economic considerations such as the need to withstand competition on the same market, it will not constitute an aid, see *Van der Kooy* [1988] ECR 219 at 270–271 and Case C-56/93 *Belgium v. Commission* [1996] ECR I-723 at 772. The observation, *ibid.* that the fact that other objectives can thereby also be achieved will not diminish the justification made out reflects the approach in relation to Art. 36 EC in Case 72/83 *Campus Oil Ltd. et al. v.* for Industry and Energy *et al.* [1984] ECR 2727 at 2752.

239. Cases 6 and 11/69 *Commission v. France* [1969] ECR 523 at 540 (preferential rediscount rate for exports); Case 57/86 *Greece v. Commission* [1988] ECR 2855 at 2871 (interest rebates for loans to exports).

240. *Fourteenth Report on Competition Policy* (Brussels, Luxembourg, 1985) 124–125 (point 198); Case 323/82 *SA Intermills v. Commission* [1984] ECR 3809 at 3830; Cases 296/82 and 318/82 *Netherlands and Leeuwarder Papierwarenfabriek BV v. Commission* [1985] ECR 809 at 823–824 (even though the actual decisions were struck down on other grounds). The Commission was more successful in other cases dealing with this such as Case 234/84 *Belgium v. Commission* [1986] ECR 2263, [1988] 2 CMLR 331, see also Case 40/85 *Commission v. Belgium* [1986] ECR 2321, [1988] 2 CMLR 301 and Pappalardo (1988) 11 Fordham Int'l. L.J. 310. Further examples include (on capital participation by public bodies) Case C-305/89 *Italy v. Commission* [1991] ECR I-1433 at 1474 and Case C-305/89 *Italy v. Commission* [1991] ECR I-1603 at 1639–1641. See also Cases C-278–290/92 *Spain v. Commission* [1994] ECR I-4103 at 4153–4155.

at lower prices or gifts of land.[241] Improvements in infrastructure which wholly or largely benefit one undertaking or a specific group of undertakings may also be characterized as aid.[242] All these cases concern economic advantages which the undertakings concerned could not have obtained in similar circumstances or on the same terms on the open market. In the evaluation of the incompatibility of an aid regard is had not merely to the advantage created as such but also to the context within which that advantage is created. Thus, because of its method of financing, an aid, although acceptable as to its purpose, may be incompatible as a whole with the common market, as happened, to a French levy on textile goods which was raised on imports as well as domestic products, in Case 47/69 *France v. Commission*.[243]

Article 92 EC also clearly covers not merely state aid but also aid financed out of the public purse. It thus reaches aids granted by public or private bodies (whether or not specially established for the purpose),[244] deconcentrated or decentralized public authorities such as regional executives (as in Belgium), autonomous regions (as in Spain or Italy) or the *Länder* in Germany[245] or *produktschappen* or *bedrijfschappen* in the Netherlands.[246] In certain circumstances even aid measures which are not actually financed through state resources but which are granted as a result of pressure from the public authorities on the body concerned will fall foul of Article 92 EC.[247] Competitive advantages for a particular

241. *E.g.* Dec. 91/390 (O.J. 1991 L 215/11) on St. Gobain; Dec. 92/11 (O.J. 1992 L 6/36) on Toyota, and Dec. 94/827 (O.J. 1994 C 21/4) on Fresenius.
242. Case C-225/91 *Matra SA v. Commission* [1993] ECR I-3203 at 3257.
243. [1970] ECR 487 at 496. For further application of this view see Dec. 74/8 (O.J. 1974 L 14/23) and Case 78/76 *Firma Steinike und Weinlig v. Germany* [1977] ECR 595, [1977] 2 CMLR 688. See also Case 249/81 *Commission v. Ireland* [[192] ECR 4005 at 4021.
244. Case 78/76 *Firma Steinike und Weinlig v. Germany* [1977] ECR 595 at 611; Case 290/83 *Commission v. France* [1985] ECR 439 at 449; Case 57/86 *Greece v. Commission* [1988] ECR 2855 at 2872, and Cases 67, 68 and 70/85 *Kwekerij Gebroeders Van der Kooy BV et al. v. Commission* [1988] ECR 219 at 722.
245. *E.g.* Case 77/69 *Commission v. Belgium* [1970] ECR 237 at 243 and (on the general point) Cases 51–54/71 *International Fruit Company NV et al. v. Produktschap voor Groenten en Fruit* [1971] ECR 1107 at 115–116. As an example of aid granted by a regional body see Cases 62 and 72/87 *Exécutif Régional Wallon et al. v. Commission* [1988] ECR 1573, [1989] 2 CMLR 771.
246. In the same sense already, Winter, *op. cit.* (see note 223, *supra*) 223–226. As to the general point (as opposed to the specific examples in the text), see *e.g.* Case 290/83 *Commission v. France* [1985] ECR 439 at 449 and Case 57/86 *Greece v. Commission* [1988] ECR 2855 at 2872.
247. Case 290/83 *Commission v. France* [1985] ECR 439 at 449 (although the Commission's application was held inadmissible on the ground that the procedure laid down in Art. 93(2) had not been followed). State resources do not need to be transferred for a measure to constitute an aid, thus tax exemptions are also covered, see Case C-387/92 *Banco de Crédito Industrial SA now Banca Exterior de España SA v. Ayuntamiento de Valencia* [1994] ECR I-877 at 909 and Dec. 93/337 (O.J. 1993 L 134/25) on aid for investment in the Basque country. See also the *XXIIIrd Report on Competition Policy*

branch of industry which result from legal or administrative measures but are not directly quantifiable in money terms probably fall outside the concept of an aid.[248] Article 92 EC does not reach aid measures from Community resources.[249] Although the Court has held that Articles 92 and 30 do not overlap,[250] the distinction between the two provisions has not always been consistently applied,[251] and the Court has now firmly stated that even if a measure can be classified as an aid, Article 92 EC could not be used to frustrate the free movement of goods.[252]

1993, point 391, and the extension of the fiscal investment premium to West Berlin, Dec. 97/551 (O.J. 1997 L 228/9).

248. Cases C-72 and 73/91 *Sloman Neptun Schiffarts AG v. Betriebsrat Bodo Ziesemer der Sloman Neptun Schiffarts AG* [1993] ECR I-887 at 933–934. The disturbing element in this judgment is not so much that it seeks to confine the concept of state aid to specific advantages, as the conclusion that the measures involved conferred no specific advantage on the employers. The Court found that the partial relief from social security contributions did not seek to create an advantage amounting to an additional burden for the state or for public or private bodies appointed by or set up by the state. But a tax holiday in relation to a uniform business rate or a local tax on property is a specific (if not in advance entirely quantifiable) advantage, as is a tax holiday in relation to corporation tax. The judgment is, with all due respect, scarcely supportable and makes a nonsense of any attempt to maintain an effects doctrine in relation to state aids. Damages which national authorities are ordered to pay to individuals as compensation for loss do not constitute state aid, Cases 106–120/87 *Asteris a.e. et al. v. Greece et al.* [1988] ECR 5515 at 5539–5540, nor does a national provision exempting only one undertaking from complying with generally applicable legislation concerning fixed-term employment contracts, Cases C-52–54/97 *Viscido et al. v. Ente Poste Italiane* [1998] ECR I-nyr (7 May 1998).

249. Such as waiver of a levy in the context of the Common Agricultural Policy, see Cases 213–215/81 *Norddeutsches Vieh- und Fleischkontor Herbert Will et al. v. Bundesanstalt für landwirtschaftliche Marktordnung* [1982] ECR 3583 at 3602, or the grant of assistance under the Structural Funds or in pursuance of the Community's research and development policy. Such measures can distort competition on the common market and unfavourably affect trade between Member States. In such cases the Community measure concerned can be examined in the light of the principle of non-discrimination. See, generally, Frazer (1995) 20 ELRev. 3.

250. Case 74/76 *Iannelli & Volpi SpA v. Meroni* [1977] ECR 557 at 574–575.

251. Case 249/81 *Commission v. Ireland* [1982] ECR 4005 at 4021; Case 18/84 *Commission v. France* [1985] ECR 139 at 1347–1348, and Case 103/84 *Commission v. Italy* [1986] ECR 1759 at 1774. See Barents (1988) SEW 353.

252. See *ibid.* and Case C-21/88 *Du Pont de Nemours Italiana SpA v. Unità sanitaria locale No 2 di Carrara* [1990] ECR I-889 at 922. This latter judgment (in the context of an obligation to obtain at least 30% of supplies from undertakings established in the Mezzogiorno) has been the subject of criticism for further confusing the relationship between Articles 30 and 92 EC (Winter (1991) 28 CMLRev. 741 at 779–781) and for taking insufficient weight of the policy interest of addressing regional disparities (Fernández Martín and Stehmann (1991) 16 ELRev. 216 at 245, a view repeated in Fernández Martín, *op. cit.* (see note 9, *supra*) 72–79 who gives an excellent defence of his position and a review of the debate over the years) but the Court confirmed its approach in Case C-351/88 *Laboratori Bruneau v. Unità sanitaria locale RM/24 di Monterotondo* [1991] ECR I-3641 at 3656–3657. In fact if it is borne in mind that

Delimitation problems can also occur between Article 92 EC on the one hand and Articles 12, 16 and 95, 37, 85, 86 and 90 on the other.[253] Separate regimes govern state aids to agriculture under Article 42 EC[254] and in the transport sector under Article 77 EC.[255]

Article 92(1) thus applies to the concept of state aid as defined above if, first, the advantages involved benefit for one or several undertakings,[256]

reserving a set percentage of contracts for undertakings from a given area is an open invitation to continue the cosy relationships in procurement which the directives in that field seek to abolish, the Court's approach is entirely justified. It may well be that the initial severability test in Case 74/76 *Ianelli & Volpi SpA v. Meroni* [1977] ECR 557 at 575–576 (separating conditions or factors not necessary for the attainment of the object of the aid or for its proper functioning, evaluating them under other appropriate articles of the EC Treaty, leaving the core within the scheme of Arts. 92 and 93 EC) has been jettisoned (although in Case C-225/91 *Matra SA v. Commission* [1993] ECR I-3203 at 3260 the Court did note that in *Ianelli* it had observed that some aspects of the aid which are incompatible with other articles of the Treaty may be so indissolubly linked that it is impossible to evaluate them separately). In view of the difficulties the Court has had in applying that test, such a move is in fact to be welcomed rather than criticized. See note 253, *infra*.

253. See, further, Hancher *et al.*, *op. cit.* (see note 223, *supra*) 39–51 (also covering the relationship between Arts. 92 and 93 EC and the ECSC and Euratom Treaties). As to Art. 90 EC, see also Case T-106/95 *Fédération française des sociétés d'assurances (FFSA) et al. v. Commission* [1997] ECR II-229 (appeal dismissed in Case C-174/97 P *FFSA et al. v. Commission* [1998] ECR I-1303. As to consistency between Arts. 92 and 93 EC and other articles of the Treaty, particularly those seeking to ensure undistorted competition, see Case 225/91 *Matra SA v. Commission* [1993] ECR I-3203 at 3260–3261 and Case T-49/93 *Société internationale de diffusion et d'édition (SIDE) v. Commission* [1995] ECR II-2501 at 2528.

254. See, generally, Barents, *The Agricultural Law of the EC* (Deventer, 1994) 197–202. As to state aids for the advertising of agricultural products, see Case 222/82 *Apple and Pear Development Council v. K.J. Lewis Ltd.* [1983] ECR 4083 at 4120 and the Commission's Communication, O.J. 1987 C 302/6, [1988] 1 CMLR 545.

255. As to the intermingling of law and politics in relation to air transport, see Balfour (1995) 15 YBEL 157.

256. As with Arts. 85 and 86 EC, the concept of an undertaking is broadly interpreted, as is evidenced by the addition of the term 'production' in Art. 92(1) EC. Public undertakings can also fall under the definition of undertakings, see Case 118/85 *Commission v. Italy* [1987] ECR 2599 at 2621–2622. See also Case C-39/94 *Syndicat français de l'Express international (SFEI) et al. v. La Poste et al.* [1996] ECR I-3547 at 3595–3596 and Case T-106/95 *Fédération française des sociétés d'assurances (FFSA) et al. v. Commission* [1997] ECR II-229 at 279–280 (appeal dismissed, see note 253, *supra*). See also the Commission's Communication on state aids and financial transparency concerning public undertakings in the manufacturing sector (O.J. 1993 C 307/3) which replaced the earlier communication (O.J. 1991 C 273/2); see also Dir. 80/723 (O.J. 1980 L 195/35), amended by Dir. 93/84 (O.J. 1993 L 254/16). The replacement and amendment respectively resulted from the annulment of the first Communication in Case C-325/91 *France v. Commission* [1993] ECR I-3283. In relation to formally untargeted social assistance where a wide margin of discretion is available to the financing body, notably as to the choice of beneficiaries, the amount of and conditions attached to assistance, see Case C-241/94 *France v. Commission* [1996] ECR I-4551 at 4576.

and, secondly, the grant of the aid distorts or threatens to distort competition and inter-State trade is thereby affected.[257] The first of these requirements is generally referred to as the specificity or selectivity criterion; it embraces the demarcation line between the applicability of the general provisions on distortions of competition found in Articles 101 and 102 EC and the state aids provisions.[258] In accordance with the objective of the latter provisions the Court interprets this criterion widely; thus selectivity will be found not merely in relation to aid which benefits one branch of industry, it will also be found if the beneficiary undertakings are distinguished from industry as a whole by other means, such as through aid to exports,[259] labour-intensive production,[260] and regional aid schemes.[261] The second requirement requires an analysis of the effects of the aid on competition and inter-State trade, even if it appears from the case-law that this analysis does not have to be as deep as in the case of Articles 85 and 86 EC.[262] This is understandable given that aid creates a competitive advantage by very definition.[263] Against this background it is also explicable that the Court has not created any *de minimis* rule in whether as to the amount of the aid or the size of the beneficiary undertaking relation to Article 92(1) EC.[264] Thus the Court looks more to

257. The Commission must not merely consider the effect on intra-Community trade at the time of the grant of the aid but also the likely effect in the future, see Cases T-447– 449/93 *Associazione Italiana Tecnico Economia del Cemento et al. v. Commission* [1995] ECR II-1971 at 2021–2022. The Commission may not simply look to the domestic market of the Member State concerned, *ibid.* at 2020, referring to earlier case-law. A good discussion of the concept of aid can be found in the *XXVth Report on Competition Policy 1995* (Brussels, Luxembourg, 1996) points 156–162.

258. Thus *e.g.* the tax deductibility of investment costs from income and corporation tax liability which is generally applicable for industry as a whole will not be caught by Art. 92 EC. Specificity is the more widely used international term (*cf.* GATT 1994 Agreement on Subsidies and Countervailing Measures, Art. 2), whereas the Commission tends to use the term selectivity.

259. See Cases 6 and 11/69 *Commission v. France* [1969] ECR 523 at 540 and Case 57/86 *Greece v. Commission* [1988] ECR 2855 at 2871–2872. As to the Commission's policy in relation to short-term export credit insurance, see O.J. 1997 C 281/4.

260. See Case 173/73 *Italy v. Commission* [1974] ECR 709 at 719–720.

261. These are considered, *post*.

262. Case 730/79 *Philip Morris Holland BV v. Commission* [1980] ECR 2671 at 2688–2689.

263. See Case 102/87 *France v. Commission* [1988] ECR 4067 at 4087–4088 in which the Court rejected the argument that Art. 92(1) EC was inapplicable as the undertaking concerned did not itself export its products. (The undertaking competed on its domestic market with beers from other Member States.) See also Case C-305/89 *Italy v. Commission* [1991] ECR I-1603 at 1642 (Alfa Romeo/Fiat) and Cases C-278–280/92 *Spain v. Commission* [1994] ECR I-4103 at 4158.

264. Case 730/79 *Philip Morris Holland BV v. Commission* [1980] ECR 2671 at 2688–2689; Case 234/84 *Belgium v. Commission* [1986] ECR 2263 at 2285; Case 259/85 *France v. Commission* [1987] ECR 4393 at 4418–4419; Case C-142/87 *Belgium v. Commission* [1990] ECR I-959 at 1015 (Tubemeuse); Cases 278–280/92 *Spain v. Commission* [1994] ECR I-4103 at 4159. See also Case C-303/88 *Italy v. Commission* [1991] ECR I-1433

the effect of the aid on intra-Community trade,[265] although the Commission has recently revised its *de minimis* policy for aid to small and medium-sized enterprises[266] and its Guidelines on state aid to such enterprises.[267] The Court does demand that the Commission clearly explain why competition threatens to be distorted and intra-Community trade affected.[268]

Two groups of exceptions apply to the incompatibility with the common market proclaimed in Article 92(1) EC. The first group is aids for the purposes specified in Article 92(2) EC, these aids are *de jure* compatible with the common market.[269] The second group is formed by aids for the purposes listed in Article 92(3) EC, which involve a discretionary evaluation by the Commission in the framework of the supervision procedure set out in Article 93 EC; the Commission may declare such aids compatible with the common market. The four initial heads of Article 92(3) EC have, since the coming into force of the TEU, been joined by what is now Article 92(3)(d), the fourth of the now five heads: aid promoting culture and heritage conservation.[270] This is in fact heavily circumscribed with the condition that it must not affect trading conditions and competition in the Community to an extent that is contrary to the common interest. Article 92(3)(e) empowers the Council

at 1477–1478 (ENI-Lanerossi). It can be deduced from Case 248/84 *Germany v. Commission* [1987] ECR 4013 at 4041 that there must be an appreciable advantage to recipients in relation to their competitors when individual decisions under in themselves compatible aid programmes are concerned.

265. Case C-225/91 *Matra SA v. Commission* [1993] ECR 3203 at 3259.
266. In a Notice (O.J. 1996 C 68/9).
267. O.J. 1996 C 213/4 (replacing earlier guidelines from 1992 (O.J. 1992 C 213/2). Council Regulation 994/98 (O.J. 1998 L 142/1) permitting the Commission to adopt group exemptions for certain categories of horizontal aid permits *de minimis* categorization.
268. Simply repeating the text of the Treaty in a decision is insufficient, see Cases 296/82 and 318/82 *Netherlands and Leeuwarder Papierwarenfabriek BV v. Commission* [1985] ECR 809 at 824–825; as the extent of reasoning in an aid programme, see Case 248/84 *Germany v. Commission* [1987] ECR 4013 at 4041.
269. Even these aids have to be notified (in the same sense, Hancher *et al.*, *op. cit.* (see note 223, *supra* 55), *contra* Bellamy and Child, *op. cit.* (see note 223, *supra* 920) and are subject to supervision by the Commission under Art. 93 EC, because it is the Commission, subject to review by the Court, which must be satisfied that the aid does indeed fall within the categories of Art. 92(2) EC. As to the aids mentioned in Art. 92(2)(a), see Case 52/76 *Benedetti v. Munari F.lli s.a.s.* [1977] ECR 163 at 190 (Reischl, Adv. Gen.) and the *XXIVth Report on Competition Policy 1994* (Brussels, Luxembourg, 1995) point 354. The 'German clause' (Art. 92(2)(c)) is interpreted by the Commission as still permitting certain aid since unification directly related to circumstances prior to unification (*e.g.* Dec. 92/465 (O.J. 1992 L 263/15)); aid to the new German *Länder* will fall to be considered under the discretionary terms of Art. 92(3)(a) EC.
270. The judgment in Case T-49/93 *Société internationale de diffusion et d'édition (SIDE) v. Commission* [1995] ECR II-2501 at 2533–2534 deals with a decision taken before the entry into force of the TEU.

to extend the grounds on which aid may be approved as being compatible with the common market.[271] Article 92(3)(a) relates to the underdeveloped areas of the Community. In relation to the concepts of an abnormally low standard of living and serious underemployment mentioned in that provision, the Court has held that these indicate that Article 92(3)(a) 'concerns only areas where the economic situation is extremely unfavourable in relation to the Community as a whole.'[272] The compatibility heading of Article 92(3)(c) which deals with regional aid – which in practice is the most important heading – is interpreted in the case-law, following the text of that provision, more widely, 'as it permits the development of certain areas without being restricted by the economic conditions laid down in Article 92(3)(a), provided such aid 'does not adversely affect trading conditions to an extent contrary to the common interest'. That provision gives the Commission power to authorize aid intended to further the economic development of areas of a Member State which are disadvantaged in relation to the national average.'[273] The objectives mentioned in Article 92(3)(b) in practice nowadays principally permit aid in the wake of natural disasters (earthquakes and so on).[274]

271. This has taken place in relation to aid to shipbuilding (the current scheme is that of the 7th directive adopted partly in the context of Art. 113 EC, Dir. 90/684 (O.J. 1990 L 380/27), most recently amended by Dir. 94/73 (O.J. 1994 L 351/10) which is due to be replaced on the entry into force of the OECD Agreement on aid to shipbuilding by Reg. 3094/95 (O.J. 1995 L 332/1), the entry into force of which has been postponed until then (and at the latest 31 December 1998) by Reg. 2600/97 (O.J. 1997 L 351/18)). See also Reg. 1013/97 (O.J. 1997 L 148/1). The effect of using this possibility is not to declare aid *a priori* compatible with the common market but to confer discretion on the Commission to evaluate the compatibility with the common market of proposed aid, which involves not only examining whether the OECD criteria are satisfied but also verifying the particular development content of the proposed aid, see Case C-400/92 *Germany v. Commission* [1994] ECR I-4701 at 4731–4732.

272. Case 248/84 *Germany v. Commission* [1987] ECR 4013 at 4042. See also Cases C-278–280/92 *Spain v. Commission* [1994] ECR 4103 at 4161–4164.

273. Case 248/84 *Germany v. Commission* [1987] ECR 4013 at 4042.

274. But matters such as research and technological development (see the framework, O.J. 1986 C 82/2, amended Bull. EU 12–1995, point 1.3.57, *XXVth Report on Competition Policy 1995* (Brussels, Luxembourg, 1996) point 201 and Bull. EU 7/8–1996, point 1.3.69); environmental protection improvements (*e.g.* O.J. 1994 C 72/3) 103–106) , non-fossil fuel arrangements (*XXIst Report on Competition Policy 1991* (Brussels, Luxembourg, 1992) point 268; privatization programmes to promote economic recovery (*ibid.*, point 251); Eureka projects such as High Definition Television (*ibid.*, point 180) and the manufacture of aircraft and aircraft parts (*Second Report on Competition Policy* (Brussels, Luxembourg, 1973) point 100) have also been covered by Art. 92(3)(b). In Cases 62 and 72/87 *Exécutif Régional Wallon et al. v. Commission* [1988] ECR 1573 at 1594–1595 the Court approved the Commission's argument that a project could only be of common European interest if it formed part of a transnational European programme supported jointly by a number of governments of Member States, or if it arose from concerted action by a number of Member States to combat a common threat such as environmental pollution. If an aid leads to the transfer of investment which would otherwise have taken place in another Member State which is

Article 92(3) EC is clearly phrased so as to give the Commission a discretion.[275] In this context the Commission enjoys a wide discretion, the exercise of which involves assessments of an economic and social nature in a Community context, although the reasoning which it follows must remain consistent.[276] In the evaluation of the compatibility of a proposed aid with the common market, significant weight attaches to the question whether the impact on the proper functioning of the common market (which in principle excludes state aids) is compensated by the positive contribution which the aid may deliver to the achievement of certain community objectives.[277]

On the basis of its discretionary powers in declaring aid compatible with the common market, the Commission has been in a position to develop a policy relating to myriad types of aid. In general terms a distinction may be drawn between four major groups of aid measures: regional aid; sectoral aid (both in general and in relation to specific sectors); flanking policies aid (environment and research and development); and other areas (such as export aid, rescue aid; aid to individual companies and so on). Given the absence of general regulatory powers for the Commission, its policy in relation to state aids is still somewhat fragmentarily set out in the annual *Report on Competition Policy* and in myriad publications of Notices or Guidelines in the 'C' Series of the *Official Journal*.[278] In the evaluation of aid the Commission is obliged to comply with the rules which it has laid down in this way.[279]

The criteria for the evaluation of regional aid were laid down in a Resolution of the representatives of the Member States meeting within the

in a less favourable situation Art. 92(3)(b) will not apply, Case 730/79 *Philip Morris Holland BV v. Commission* [1980] ECR 2671 at 2691–2692. See also Cases T-447–449/ 93 *Associazione Italiana Tecnico Economica del Cemento et al. v. Commission* [1995] ECR II-1971 at 2107–2018.

275. Case 730/79 *Philip Morris Holland BV v. Commission* [1980] ECR 2671 at 2690.
276. Cases C-278–280/92 *Spain v. Commission* [1994] ECR 4103 at 4162. See also Case T-380/94 *Association Internationale des utilisateurs de Fils de Filaments Artificiels et Synthéthiques et de Soie Naturelle (AIUFFAS) v. Commission* [1996] ECR II-2169 (appeal dismissed in Case C-55/97 P *Commission v. AIUFFAS* [1997] ECR I-5383).
277. See, generally, *ibid.* at 4166–4167, and Mortelmans (1984) 21 CML Rev. 405.
278. A detailed discussion of the Commission's policy is beyond the scope of this section, see, further, Hancher *et al.*, *op. cit.* (see note 223, *supra*). See also the *XXIVth Report on Competition Policy 1994* (Brussels, Luxembourg, 1994) points 337–398, the *XXVth Report 1995* (*ibid.*, 1996) points 148–219, the *XXVIth Report 1996* (*ibid.*, 1997) points 158–228, and the *XXVIIth Report 1997* (*ibid.*, 1998) points 195–320 which give an excellent combination of a discussion of the annual activities in the field and the principles applied. The Court strictly ensures that the Commission does seek to create legal obligations by means of communications, see Case C-325/91 *France v. Commission* [1993] ECR I-3283 at 3311–3312. As to the EFTA Surveillance Authority's Guidelines on state aids, see O.J. 1994 L 231/1. As to the Commission's proposals for detailed rules, see COM (98) 73 Final (O.J. 1998 C 116/13).
279. Cases C-278–280/92 *Spain v. Commission* [1994] ECR 4103 at 4164.

Council on 20 October 1971[280] and are applied in accordance with various Communications from the Commission.[281] The general principles of this policy are as follows: in principle the Commission will only approve aid for initial investment, not operating aid.[282] State aid arrangements are coordinated under five aspects which form one whole: ceilings of aid intensity (the proportion of aid to total costs) differentiated according to the nature and gravity of the regional problems; transparency; regional specificity (except in the cases of Luxembourg and Ireland the aid must be targeted to a region, not to the whole Member State); the sectoral repercussions of regional aids (for example regional aid in sectors in which there is overcapacity is in principle not approved, and there are rules against cumulation of regional and sectoral aid), and a system of supervision. The differentiated ceilings are fixed in net grant equivalents (sometimes also called net subsidy equivalents) expressed either as a percentage of initial investment or in ECUs per job created by the initial investment. There is now significantly greater coordination of the objectives of economic and social cohesion and the Community's policy towards regional aids.[283]

Guidelines dealing with sectoral aid were laid down in a Communication from the Commission to the Council in May 1978,[284] in which it reiterated its long-standing view that sectoral aid can be permitted in order to facilitate the development of sunset industries – straggling sectors (or sectors which have run into difficulties as a result of external causes) – by means of a defined restructuring programme (modernization or reduction in capacity) or in order to facilitate the development of whole new technological sectors with future prospects (sunrise industries in fields such as energy and information technology). Production or marketing aids as well as aid for an expansion of capacity are in principle seen as inadmissible. In case of serious difficulties necessitating restructuring, temporary aid (or if necessary even aid to reduce production costs) is regularly permitted subject to strict conditions, particularly as to the restructuring undertaken. Specific sectoral criteria apply in relation to

280. J.O. 1971 C 111/1.
281. See the *Fifth Report on Competition Policy* (Brussels, Luxembourg, 1976) points 85–87, and the Communications in O.J. 1979 C 31/9; O.J. 1986 C 3/3; O.J. 1988 C 212/2; O.J. 1989 C 78/5; O.J. 1990 C 163/5; O.J. 1992 C 114/4; O.J. 1994 C 364/8; O.J. 1996 C 232/10, and O.J. 1998 C 74/9. See also the Multisectoral Framework on regional aid for large investment projects (O.J. 1998 C108/7).
282. This policy is approved by the Court, see Case C-86/89 *Italy v. Commission* [1990] ECR I-3891 at 3909–3910 and by the Court of First Instance in Case T-459/93 *Siemens SA v. Commission* [1995] ECR II-1675 at 1696–1697 and 1705–1706 (appeal dismissed in Case C-278/95 P *Siemens SA v. Commission* [1997] ECR I-2507).
283. See the Commission's Communication (O.J. 1988 C 212/2); the *XXIst Report on Competition Policy 1991* (Brussels, Luxembourg, 1992), point 56, and the *XXIVth Report 1994* (*ibid.*, 1995) point 362. See also O.J. 1994 C 364).
284. *Eighth Report on Competition Policy* (Brussels, Luxembourg, 1979) points 172 *et seq.*, and Bull. EC 5-1978, point 2.1.29.

shipbuilding;[285] synthetic fibres, textiles and clothing;[286] and the motor vehicle industry.[287] Other specific sectoral coordination frameworks have been developed for transport,[288] coal and steel,[289] and numerous decisions have been taken in relation to energy.[290] In relation to flanking policies, new framework rules deal with aid to small and medium-sized industries;[291] aid for environmental protection,[292] and research and development.[293] The last two of these primarily concern the interpretation of Article 92(3)(b) EC. Important other guidelines deal with rescuing and restructuring firms in difficulty;[294] aid in the fisheries and aquaculture sector;[295] aid for the promotion of employment;[296] aid for the reduction of labour costs;[297] aid to undertakings in deprived urban areas,[298] and aid for the sale of land by public bodies.[299] Regulation 994/98 will permit the Commission to adopt group exemptions which would declare various types of horizontal aid (including approved regional aid) compatible with the common market and exempt them from notification.[300]

285. See note 271, supra.
286. First Report on Competition Policy (Brussels, Luxembourg, 1972) point 171, and Seventh Report (ibid., 1978) point 202. As to the present framework for synthetic fibres, see O.J. 1996 C 94/11 and Bull. EU 1/2–1996, point 1.3.58.
287. The framework of 1988 (O.J. 1989 C 123/3) was extended (O.J. 1991 C 81/4) and then prolonged for what the Commission thought was indefinitely until the next review (O.J. 1993 C 36/17), but the Court held that the prolongation was only until the end of 1994, Case C-135/93 Spain v. Commission [1995] ECR I-1651 at 1683–1684. As to subsequent events, see the XXVth Report on Competition Policy 1995 (Brussels, Luxembourg, 1996) point 166, and Case C-292/95 Spain v. Commission [1997] ECR I-1931. A new framework has been established (O.J. 1997 C 279/1).
288. See, generally, Hancher et al., op. cit. (see note 223, supra) 137–148 and e.g. the guidelines for air transport (O.J. 1994 C 350/5) and the guidelines on aid to Community shipping companies (O.J. 1997 C 205/5).
289. On the basis of the ECSC Treaty, as to coal, see Dec. 3632/93 (O.J. 1993 L 329/12); as to steel, see Dec. 2496/96 (O.J. 1996 L 338/42). See Case T-239/94 Association des Aciéries Européennes Indépendents (EISA) v. Commission [1997] ECR II-1839; Case T-243/94 British Steel plc v. Commission [1997] ECR II-1887, and Case T-129/96 Preussag Stahl AC v. Commission [1998] ECR II-nyr (31 March 1998).
290. Also on the basis of the ECSC and Euratom Treaties, see, generally, Hancher, et al., op. cit. (see note 223, supra) 193; the XXIst report on Competition Policy 1991 (Brussels, Luxembourg, 1992) points 265–268; the XXnd Report 1992 (ibid., 1993) points 443–437, and the XXIIIrd Report (ibid., 1994) points 532–533.
291. O.J. 1996 C 213/4.
292. O.J. 1994 C 72/3.
293. O.J. 1996 C 45/5.
294. O.J. 1994 C 368/12, see also O.J. 1998 C 74/31.
295. O.J. 1994 C 189/5 and C 260/3; O.J. 1996 C 29/4, C 44/2, and Dec. 94/173 (O.J. 1994 L 79/29).
296. O.J. 1995 C 334/4.
297. O.J. 1997 C 1/10.
298. O.J. 1997 C 146/6.
299. O.J. 1997 C 209/3.
300. O.J. 1998 L 142/1. This will considerably lighten the administrative burden on the Commission, just as the block exemptions have done in the context of Article 85 EC.

An examination of the development of the evaluation policy briefly outlined above leads to the conclusion that this policy lies more and more in the transitional area between negative (liberalizing) and positive (directing) integration. The evaluation policy pursued by the Commission reflects a gradual movement within the economic systems pursued at national level. Aid measures are becoming an even more normal instrument of economic policy as a response to new short term economic problems and particularly to structural problems at national, Community and world levels. If aid measures with in themselves laudable objectives are taken in a large number of Member States or even in all of them, then distortions of competition should preferably be tackled through coordination of the national aid measures involved. Such coordination will then most likely be fitted into the Community's own policy in the fields concerned (such as regional policy, industrial policy relating to research and technological development, environmental policy, small and medium-sized industries policy) which have their own objectives and their own instruments.[301] Competition policy will have to ensure that on the one hand the amount, competition-distorting means of implementation and the period of national aid measures do not exceed that which is necessary on the grounds of the objectives permitted under Article 92(2) and (3) EC.[302] On the other hand competition policy will only permit differences amongst national aid measures to undertakings competing with each other in the common market to the extent to which these differences are justified from the Community standpoint. The good illustration of this evaluation criterion is the different ceilings for regional aid measures. Meantime the movement from prohibition to coordination must not lose sight of the fact that aid measures are very expensive and that the resulting burden falls either on other sectors of industry or on private consumption or collective facilities. In particular, aid to uncompetitive undertakings will frequently not only weaken the competitive position of stronger undertakings in the sector concerned but also weaken the position of other sectors and hinder the development of new investment affording better prospects. In other words, aid measures will not constitute a hindrance to an optimal allocation of production factors only if and to the extent that a demonstrable and quantifiable socio-economic need is present which is greater than the costs which the aid measures place on the Community. To that observation must be added that the maintenance of these frameworks and principles requires high standards of political independence on the part of the Commission, which raises the question whether it is at present (or in the last fifteen years or so has been) able to guarantee an acceptable trade-off between the principles of an open market economy and industrial policy

301. Indeed, the common agricultural policy provides good examples of such coordination, see Barents, *loc. cit.* (see note 223, *supra*).
302. See the various annual *Reports on Competition Policy*.

on the one hand and laudable aid measures of the Member States on the other.[303]

3.2.3 Procedural aspects

In section 3.2.1, above, it was noted that Article 92(1) EC does not contain a directly effective prohibition.[304] Compliance with the rule that no aid may be granted which is incompatible with the common market is ensured by decisions of the Commission under the procedure of Article 93(2) EC, which are directly effective,[305] by the directly effective obligation under the first sentence of Article 93(3) EC to notify in advance plans to grant or alter aid, and by the also directly effective obligation under the blocking effect of the third sentence of Article 93(3) not to put proposed measures into effect until the procedure set out in Article 93(2) EC has resulted in a final decision (approving those measures).[306] In relation to these procedures and related problems the Council could adopt appropriate regulations (such as exemptions from the requirement of notification, conditions for requiring repayment of aid and so on). So far this has occurred only very rarely,[307] with the result that recourse must be had to the case-law of the Court and the various communications from the Commission.[308]

303. Le Monde, 20 July 1994 and Agence Europe, 28 July 1994 reported that the Commission had approved a complete recapitalization aid to Air France (Dec. 94/662 (O.J. 1994 L 258/26)) inter alia on the ground that a negative decision would not be respected by France. See Case T-358/94 Compagnie Nationale Air France v. Commission [1996] ECR II-2109. See also Cases T-371 and 394/94 British Airways plc et al. v. Commission [1998] ECR II-nyr (25 June 1998), annulment of Dec. 94/653 (O.J. 1994 L254/73).
304. Case 78/76 Steinike und Weinlig v. Germany [1977] ECR 595 at 609.
305. Ibid. and Case 77/72 Capolongo v. Azienda Agricola Maya [1973] ECR 611 at 621–622.
306. See Case 120/73 Gebr. Lorenz GmbH v. Germany et al. [1973] ECR 1471; Case 84/82 Germany v. Commission [1984] ECR 1451, [1985] 1 CMLR 153, and Cases C-278–280/92 Spain v. Commission [1994] ECR 4103.
307. Reg. 1107/70 (O.J. English Special Edition 1970 (II), p. 360), most recently amended by Reg. 2255/96 (O.J. 1996 L 304/3), dealing with aids for transport by rail, road, and inland waterway was based on inter alia Art. 94 EEC. A number of regs. dealing with Community aid in the agriculture have also seen Art. 94 EC used as their legal basis. Reg. 3094/95 (O.J. 1995 L 332/1), amended by Reg. 1904/96 (O.J. 1996 L 251/5) on aid to shipbuilding is also in part based on Art. 94 EC. Reg. 994/98 (O.J. 1998 L 142/1) and the procedural rules proposed by the Commission, COM (98) 73 Final (O.J. 1998 C 116/13) should improve matters considerably. Aids declared compatible with the common market under such group exemptions will then not have to be notified.
308. Slot has rightly submitted that the Commission's view that such measures are unnecessary is misguided, (1990) 27 CMLRev. 741 at 759. In view of the recent developments set out in note 305, supra, the Commission's view has clearly changed.

A clear distinction is made between existing aids and new aids in the procedure under Article 93 EC. Existing aids are those which were in operation when the EC Treaty came into force on 1 January 1958, or when new Member States acceded to the Community (now to the Union), as well as those subsequently implemented in accordance with the provisions of the Treaty, *i.e.* which have been notified to the Commission and which it has then approved or raised no objection. The latter group are thereby transformed into existing aids.[309] The distinction is important as Article 93 provides for a system of preventive supervision, based on the obligation to notify new aids under the first sentence of Article 93(3), whereas existing aids are subject to repressive supervision through the system of constant review set out in Article 93(1) EC, and do not need to be notified. The Commission is entitled, as part of that ongoing review, to propose to the Member States 'any appropriate measures required by the progressive development or by the functioning of the common market'.[310] An existing aid may be implemented as long as the Commission has not, in the process of constant review, found it to be incompatible with the common market,[311] which forms a second difference between the treatment of existing and new aids.

309. Case 120/73 *Gebr. Lorenz GmbH v. Germany et al.* [1973] ECR 1471 at 1482; see also Case C-313/90 *Comité International de la Rayonne et des Fibres Synthétiques (CIRFS) et al. v. Commission* [1993] ECR I-1125 at I-1186. The question whether an aid is an existing aid, a new aid, or an alteration to an existing aid is to be determined by reference to the provisions, legislative or otherwise, providing for it, and not to its scale or amount, Case C-44/93 *Namur – Les Assurances du Crédit SA v. Office National du Ducroire et al.* [1994] ECR I-3829 at 3874–3875. Measures to grant or alter aid, where the alteration relates to existing aid or to initial plans notified to the Commission, are regarded as new aid subject to the notification procedure of Art. 93(3) EC, Cases 91 and 127/83 *Heineken Brouwerijen BV v. Inspecteurs der Vennootschapsbelasting, Amsterdam and Utrecht* [1984] ECR 3435 at 3453. Information about modifications to initial plans may be supplied during consultations following initial notification, *ibid.* Unnotified alterations to a planned aid to which, in its notified form, the Commission has not objected, will preclude the putting into effect of the aid in its entirety, *ibid.* at 3454. The position may be different only if the alteration is in fact a separate aid measure which should be separately assessed, and which would not influence the Commission in the assessment which it had already made of the original proposal, *ibid.*

310. Art. 92(1) EC.

311. Case C-312/90 *Spain v. Commission* [1992] ECR I-4117 and Case C-47/91 *Italy v. Commission* [1992] ECR I-4145: precisely because of this difference, in both these cases, the Court regarded the decision to open the procedure under Art. 93(2) as an act capable of review under Art. 173 EC, as is explained, *post*. See, in the context of the compatibility of individual aid with a previously authorized aid scheme, Case C-47/91 *Italy v. Commission* [1994] ECR I-4635 at 4654–4655, and Cases T-447–449/93 *Associazione Italiana Tecnico Economia del Cemento et al. v. Commission* [1995] ECR II-1971 at 2015–2019. The decision in such cases is not a management or administrative matter and may not be taken by the *habilitation* procedure (as to which, see Chapter IV, section 6.4.3, *ante*), see Case T-435/93 *Association of Sorbitol Producers within the EC (ASPEC) et al. v. Commission* [1995] ECR II-1281 at 1319–1323, and

The obligation to notify 'any plans to grant or alter aid'[312] is designed to enable the Commission to undertake a preliminary examination of the plans.[313] However, the Commission has announced that aid which falls to be considered as *de minimis* need not be notified.[314] The preliminary examination may result in the conclusion that the plans do not involve state aid within the meaning of Article 92(1) EC, or that although they do, the aid is compatible with the common market on the basis of the criteria in Article 92(2) or (3) EC. In either of these cases the Commission is not obliged to issue a formal decision within the meaning of Article 189 EC.[315] If the Commission does have doubts as to the compatibility of the proposed aid with the common market, it must open the contentious

Case T-442/93 *Association des Amidonneries de Céréales de la CEE (AAC) et al. v. Commission* [1995] ECR II-1329 at 1363–1367.

312. Art. 93(3) EC, 1st sentence.
313. The Commission has now introduced standard notification forms and annual reports, see *XXIIIrd Report on Competition Policy 1993* (Brussels, Luxembourg, 1994) 418 and 426 respectively. As to public undertakings, see Dir. 80/723 (O.J. 1980 L 195/35) amended by Dirs. 85/413 (O.J. 1985 L 229/20) and 93/84 (O.J. 1993 L 254/15) and the reissued Communication (O.J. 1993 C 307/3). See also Reg. 994/98 (O.J. 1998 L 142/1).
314. See initially O.J. 1990 C 40/2, later O.J. 1992 C 213/2 (guidelines for SMEs) and O.J. 1992 C 213/13 (accelerated clearance), and now O.J. 1996 C 68/9 and the new guidelines for SMEs, O.J. 1996 C 213/4. Aid falling within the limits thus established is considered to fall outside Art. 92(1) EC, and is thus automatically regarded as being compatible with the common market.
315. Case 120/73 *Gebr. Lorenz GmbH v. Germany et al.* [1973] ECR 1471 at 1482. It is in the interests of good administration for the Commission to inform the Member State concerned of its view, *ibid*. Given that the Commission's conclusions either way have legal consequences, as the new aid concerned is transformed into existing aid and may be granted (and is then subject to review of existing aid), it would seem obvious to categorize such an act as a decision capable of review under Art. 173 EC. In the preliminary examination there is no obligation to consult anyone other than the Member State granting the aid (this is implicit from Case 84/82 *Germany v. Commission* [1984] ECR 1451 at 1488), so if that examination leads to a decision not to raise objection to the proposed aid, and thus not to initiate the contentious procedure, third parties may very well remain wholly ignorant of developments. Some decisions not to open proceedings are published in the 'C series' of the *Official Journal*, others are the subject of press releases, but many are not publicized in either form, although they are all listed in the annual *Report on Competition Policy*. In Case T-95/94 *Chambre Syndicale National des Enterprises de Transport de Fonds et Valeurs (Sytraval) v. Commission* [1995] ECR II-2651 at 2671–2673 and 2677–2678 the Court of First Instance found that the Commission had to consult a complainant who had complained about an unnotified state aid, about the information it had obtained during the investigation. In view of the above view about there being no obligation to consult more widely than with the Member State concerned, the Commission appealed against this judgment: see Case C-367/95 P *Commission v. Chambre Syndicale National des Enterprises de Transport de Fonds et Valeurs (Sytraval)* [1998] ECR I-nyr (2 April 1998); although the appeal was dismissed the Court of Justice did make important qualifications to the Court of First Instance's statements (see paras. 46–47 and 57–62 of the judgment). See also Case T-16/96 *Cityflyer Express Ltd. v. Commission* [1998] ECR II-nyr (30 April 1998).

procedure set out in Article 93(2) EC without delay.[316] The Court has held that the expression 'without delay' means within two months.[317] If within that period the Commission has not made its view known, the aid may be granted[318] and then becomes an existing aid.[319] The two month period may not be terminated unilaterally by the Member State concerned.[320]

The decision to open the contentious procedure under Article 93(2) EC is a decision capable of review under Article 173 EC.[321] This procedure is used for notified aid, as well as for aid which has not been notified;[322] the Commission is obliged to respect the rights of the defence in all respects,[323] particularly the right to be heard, and the obligation not to rely on any information against a party if that party has not been given an opportunity to comment on it.[324] The first sentence of Article 93(2) itself in fact makes this obligation clear, by requiring the Commission first to give notice to the parties concerned to submit their comments.[325] The Member States and interested undertakings are thus given the chance to make comments, usually through a notice in the 'C series' of the *Official Journal*. If the Commission comes to the conclusion that the proposed aid is compatible with the common market, the procedure is terminated by summary

316. Art. 93(3) EC, 2nd sentence. Other procedures may not be used as the judicial protection of interested parties would then be undermined: such parties can only make their views known in the context of an Art. 93(2) procedure, see Case 84/82 *Germany v. Commission* [1984] ECR 1451 at 1488–1489 and Case C-198/91 *William Cook plc v. Commission* [1993] ECR I-2487 at 2529–2530.
317. By analogy with Arts. 173 and 175 EC, see Case 120/73 *Gebr. Lorenz GmbH v. Germany et al.* [1973] ECR 1471 at 1481.
318. On condition that the Commission is notified in advance, *ibid.* and Case 171/83 R *Commission v. France* [1983] ECR 2621 at 2628.
319. The Commission is of opinion that the period of 2 months begins to run from the moment that it has all the relevant information in order to commence the preliminary examination, a viewpoint which finds some support in Case 84/82 *Commission* [1984] ECR 1451 at 1489 (the Commission's view is summarized at 1487), and Case C-301/87 *France v. Commission* [1990] ECR I-307 at 358.
320. Case 120/73 *Gebr. Lorenz GmbH v. Germany et al.* [1973] ECR 1471 at 1481.
321. Case C-312/90 *Spain v. Commission* [1992] ECR I-4117 and Case C-47/91 *Italy v. Commission* [1992] ECR I-4145. The Court noted that the effects of a decision to open the contentious procedure differed, according to whether the aid was new aid or (had become) existing aid, in the former case the Member State may not implement the proposed aid, in the latter case it may, *ibid.* at 4141–4143 and 4161–4162 respectively, (until it has been established that the aid is incompatible with the common market).
322. Case 173/73 *Italy v. Commission* [1974] ECR 709 at 716–717.
323. Case 84/82 *Germany v. Commission* [1984] ECR 1451 at 1488–1490.
324. Case C-301/87 *France v. Commission* [1990] ECR I-307 at 358–359 (citing earlier case-law). However, if the communication of the information to the party concerned would not have led to a different outcome of the contentious procedure, the decision concerned will not be annulled, *ibid.* at 359. See also Case C-142/87 *Belgium v. Commission* [1990] ECR I-959 at 1016.
325. As to the significance of this requirement in relation to the admissibility of an action against a decision or communication from the Commission, see Case 169/84 *Compagnie française de l'azote (Cofaz) SA et al. v. Commission* [1986] ECR 391 at 414–415.

decision, of which informal announcement is made in the 'C series' in due course.[326] If, on the other hand, it concludes that the proposed aid is incompatible with the common market, the contentious procedure results in a decision prohibiting the aid, or approving it only subject to certain conditions.[327]

The distinction between aid which is incompatible with the common market and unlawful aid, drawn in section 3.2.1, above, is important in order to ascertain the correct legal consequences of non-compliance with the obligations in the context of proceedings under Article 93 EC. These may be summarized as follows. First, aid which is notified, but in respect of which the Commission has not yet concluded the preliminary examination within the prescribed period or has not yet concluded the contentious procedure of Article 93(2) EC may not be granted. This direct blocking effect is clear from the final sentence of Article 93(3) EC. The blocking effect also applies to the grant of non-notified aid,[328] even if such aid may in itself be compatible with the common market.[329] If unnotified aid comes to the Commission's attention, it may open the contentious procedure under Article 93(2) EC,[330] take an interim decision requiring the Member State concerned to suspend the payment of the aid,[331] and require the latter to furnish it with all information and documents necessary to

326. Such a decision is taken by a formal decision, even though the publication of the fact that a decision is taken is only summary, cf. Case 120/73 *Gebr. Lorenz GmbH v. Germany et al.* [1973] ECR 1471 at 1482.
327. Art. 93(2) EC is silent as to the period within which the Commission must conclude the investigation in a contentious procedure. While the Court has indicated that the Commission must have a reasonable time within which to arrive at its findings (Case 59/79 *Fédération Nationale des Producteurs de Vin de Table et Vins de Pays v. Commission* [1979] ECR 2425 at 2428), it has annulled a decision taken over 2 years after the initiation of the contentious procedure, citing the company's reasonable grounds for believing that there would be no objection to the aid (Case 223/85 *Rijn-Schelde-Verolme (RSV) Maschinenfabrieken en Scheepswerven NV v. Commission* [1987] ECR 4617 at 4659). This may be useful in attacking a requirement that the aid must be repaid, although, as is explained, *post*, legitimate expectation is an unruly horse as an argument contesting such requirements. In Cases T-244 and 486/93 *TWD Textilwerke Deggendorf GmbH v. Commission* [1995] ECR II-2265, [1996] 1 CMLR 332 the Court of First Instance upheld a condition imposed for the approval of aid in Decs. 91/391 (O.J. 1991 L 215/6) and 92/330 (O.J. 1992 L 183/36) that payment of the aid be suspended until earlier aid previously declared unlawful in Dec. 86/509 (O.J. 1986 L 300/34) had been recovered. This judgment was upheld on appeal, Case C-355/95 P *TWD Textilwerke Deggendorf GmbH v. Commission* [1997] ECR I-2459.
328. Case 6/64 *Costa v. ENEL* [1964] ECR 585 at 595–596.
329. Case C-142/87 *Belgium v. Commission* [1990] ECR I-959 at 1009–1110.
330. But it is not obliged to do so, case C-198/91 *William Cook plc v. Commission* [1993] ECR I-2487 at 2529–2530.
331. The first example of this being done in Dec. 92/35 (O.J. 1992 L 14/35), *France/PMU*. The Commission is of opinion that requiring suspension is often inadequate, and will now be willing, in appropriate cases, to order by way of an interim decision that the aid be recovered, see O.J. 1995 C 156/5.

enable it to examine the compatibility of the aid concerned with the common market.[332] If the Member State concerned does not comply, the procedure may be concluded in appropriate cases by way of a final decision prohibiting the aid.[333] If the information is supplied, the procedure runs its normal course.[334] The grant of aid in breach of a final or interim decision under Article 93(2) is, of course, prohibited, and if a beneficiary of the aid concerned, having been informed in writing of the Commission's decision by the Member State concerned, fails to bring an action for annulment against it in due time, a national court will be bound by that decision.[335] If the Member State concerned carries on with the aid regardless of the Commission's decision, the Commission (or any other interested Member State) may refer the matter direct to the Court of Justice.[336] If the aid is granted in breach of conditions prescribed by the Commission in the Article 93(2) EC decision approving it, the Commission may adopt a new decision finding that action to be aid incompatible with the common market, but if it does so, it must commence the contentious procedure under Article 93(2) again, in order to permit the parties concerned to submit their comments.[337]

The doctrine that the obligation in the first paragraph of Article 93(2) EC to abolish or alter within a period of time to be determined by the Commission aid which is incompatible with the common market or which is being misused 'may include an obligation to require repayment of aid granted in breach of the Treaty' is of long standing.[338] Thus it was that in 1983 the Commission issued a communication reminding Member States and undertakings of the risks attaching to aid granted

332. Case C-301/87 *France v. Commission* [1990] ECR I-307 at 356; Case 142/87 *Belgium v. Commission* [1990] ECR I-959 at 1009. See the policy principles on non-notified state aids, *Xxth Report on Competition Policy 1990* (Brussels, Luxembourg, 1991) point 172. As to recovery of illegally paid state aid, see O.J. 1995 C 156/5, and *post*.

333. Case C-301/87 *France v. Commission* [1990] ECR I-307 at 357; Cases C-324 and 342/90 *Germany et al. v. Commission* [1994] ECR I-1173 at 1206.

334. Cases C-324 and 342/90 *Germany et al. v. Commission*, ibid.

335. Case C-188/92 *TWD Textilwerke Deggendorf GmbH v. Germany* [1994] ECR I-833 at 852–855. This means that in these circumstances a challenge to a national decision implementing a decision of the Commission requiring aid to be recovered cannot invoke any argument alleging illegality of the Commission's decision. In an interesting judgment, the French *Cour de Cassation* has found that there is no professional negligence where a lawyer fails to make an application in time for aid which had been declared incompatible with the common market but which the French government still carried on paying to others, *Lener Ignace SA v. Beauvois* [1994] 2 CMLR 419.

336. Thus without having first to go through the administrative requirements of Arts. 169 or 170 EC, as appropriate. This is logical, as the defaulting Member State will have had the opportunity to argue its case prior to an Art. 93(2) decision being taken.

337. Case C-294/90 *British Aerospace plc et al. v. Commission* [1992] ECR I-493 at 522. Non-compliance with the original conditions could indeed have been met with a direct reference of the matter to the Court, *ibid*.

338. Case 70/72 *Commission v. Germany* [1973] ECR 813 at 829.

illegally.[339] It announced that it would henceforth systematically oblige recipients of illegally granted aid to refund it. It was subsequently made clear that this policy would also be applied to aid which was illegal only for procedural reasons, *i.e.* where the aid was not notified prior to being given or was paid before the Commission had taken a final decision on its compatibility with the common market.[340] The requirement that aid be recovered is normally prescribed in an Article 93(2) EC decision, and the obligation is on the Member State concerned to comply with that decision and obtain repayment of the illegally granted aid. Separate reasoning is not required for the requirement of repayment.[341] Repayment can only be required for aid which the Commission has found incompatible with the common market in accordance with the contentious procedure, thus a requirement of repayment relating solely to non-notified aid will not be possible unless that procedure is first followed;[342] it will also not be possible for the Commission to order repayment if it has taken an excessive time to draw up its decision under Article 93(2) EC.[343] Despite wily endeavours on the part of various Member States, the Court has refused to allow them to escape from the obligation to secure repayment by pleading rules or principles of national law.[344] While recovery takes place according to the procedural provisions of national law,[345] this is subject to the proviso that those provisions

339. O.J. 1983 C 318/3. See, further, O.J. 1995 C 156/5, and *XXVth Report on Competition Policy 1995* (Brussels, Luxembourg, 1996) point 154.

340. *Fifteenth Report on Competition Policy, 1985* (Brussels, Luxembourg, 1986) point 171. See also the *Sixteenth Report* (*ibid.*, 1987) point 203, and the *XXVth Report* (*ibid.*, 1996) point 154.

341. Case C-303/88 *Italy v. Commission* [1991] ECR I-1433 at 1484; Cases C-278–280/92 *Spain v. Commission* [1994] ECR I-4103 at 4170. This could already be deduced from the judgment in Case 70/72 *Commission v. Germany* [1973] ECR 813 at 829. But the Commission is not required to order recovery of the aid, Case T-49/93 *Société internationale de diffusion et d'édition (SIDE) v. Commission* [1995] ECR II-2501 at 2533.

342. Case C-301/87 *France v. Commission* [1990] ECR I-307 at 357. The Court refused to accept the Commission's argument that non-notification rendered aid unlawful, *ibid.* at 354–357. See also Case T-49/93 *Société internationale de diffusion et d'édition (SIDE) v. Commission* [1995] ECR II-2501 at 2533–2534. If the Commission were simply to be able to require repayment of non-notified aid without first having had to go through the contentious procedure, it would, in effect, be taking a decision ignoring the rule *audi alteram partem*.

343. Case 223/85 *Rijn-Schelde-Verolme (RSV) Maschinenfabrieken en Scheepswerven NV v. Commission* [1987] ECR 4617 at 4658–59, at least in the absence of a convincingly valid explanation why it has taken so long.

344. This flows from the general principle that national legal obstacles may not hinder the application and enforcement of Community obligations, see *e.g.* Case C-5/89 *Commission v. Germany* [1990] ECR I-3437 at 3457–3458 (Case C-74/89 *Commission v. Belgium* [1991] ECR I-491 and Case C-383/89 *Commission v. Belgium* [1991] ECR I-383 are reproduced only in summary form in the ECR) and Case C-24/95 *Land Rheinland-Pfalz v. Alcan Deutschland GmbH* [1997] ECR I-1591 at 1617 and 162–1621.

345. Case C-142/87 *Belgium v. Commission* [1990] ECR I-959 at 1019.

must not be applied in such a way as to make the recovery required by Community law practically impossible.[346] Thus only the complete impossibility of obtaining recovery will be an acceptable reason for non-compliance with a Commission decision requiring recovery;[347] the fact that repayment might lead to the insolvency of the undertaking[348] involved or other financial problems[349] will be to no avail. Similarly, a Member State may not rely on any alleged legitimate expectation on the part of the beneficiary undertaking, as otherwise Article 93(3) would be deprived of useful effect.[350]

346. *Ibid.* and Case C-5/89 *Commission v. Germany* [1990] ECR I-3437 at 3456. The same principle applies in respect of recovery of Community aid, Cases 205–215/82 *Deutsche Milchkontor GmbH et al. v. Germany* [1983] ECR 2633 at 2669. In particular, the Community's interests must be fully taken into account in the application of any national provision requiring a balancing of competing interests before a defective administrative measure is withdrawn, *ibid.* and Case 94/87 *Commission v. Germany* [1989] ECR 175 at 192. Recovery may sometimes be ordered not from the beneficiary company itself but from a holding company which had itself aided a beneficiary, see Case C-305/89 *Italy v. Commission* [1991] ECR I-1603 at 1644–1645. Repayment may take the form of payment to a public body which manages state funds, as the result to be achieved is that the beneficiary undertaking should be deprived of its benefit, Case C-348/93 *Commission v. Italy* [1995] ECR I-673 at 696; Case C-350/93 *Commission v. Italy* [1995] ECR I-699 at 716. As to the incidence of tax and questions of interest, see Case T-459/93 *Siemens SA v. Commission* [1995] ECR II-1675 (upheld on appeal in Case C-278/95 P *Siemens SA v. Commission* [1997] ECR I-2507). See also the Commission's Press Release IP (95) 87 (1 February 1995).
347. *E.g.* Case 52/84 *Commission v. Belgium* [1986] ECR 89 at 104; Case 94/87 *Commission v. Germany* [1989] ECR 175 at 191. If the Member State concerned encounters unforeseen and unforeseeable consequences in giving effect to the Commission's decision, or perceives certain consequences which the Commission has overlooked, it may place those problems before the Commission, with proposals to amend the decision involved, and, in accordance with Art. 5 EC efforts to reach a solution, respecting the Treaty provisions in full, must be made, *ibid.* at 105 and 192 respectively.
348. Case 52/84 *Commission v. Belgium* [1986] ECR 89 at 104;
349. Case 63/87 *Commission v. Greece* [1988] ECR 2875 at 2892; Case C-142/87 *Belgium v. Commission* [1990] ECR I-959 at 1019–1020. National time-bars for the revocation of a decision granting the aid (in order to give effect to the Commission's decision) may not stand in the way of the revocation of the decision granting the aid, see *e.g.* Case C-24/95 *Land Rheinland-Pfalz v. Alcan Deutschland GmbH* [1997] ECR I-1591 at 1619.
350. Case 94/87 *Germany v. Commission* [1989] ECR 175 at 191; Case C-5/89 *Commission v. Germany* [1990] ECR I-3437 at 3457; Case C-169/95 *Spain v. Commission* [1997] ECR I-nyr (14 January 1997), and Case C-24/95 *Land Rheinland-Pfalz v. Alcan Deutschland GmbH* [1997] ECR I-1591 at 1620–1621. Particularly in view of the Commission's long-standing policy (see note 337, *supra*) and its practice of drawing attention, usually at the start of the contentious procedure under Art. 93(2) EC, to the risks in accepting (and spending) unlawful aid, it is understandable that the Court finds that a prudent businessman would normally be able to determine whether the correct procedure had been followed, see Case 5/89, *loc. cit.* Thus the circumstances leading to annulment of the decision in Case 223/85 *Rijn-Schelde-Verolme (RSV) Maschinenfabrieken en Scheepswerven NV v. Commission* [1987] ECR 4617 at 4659 are exceptional. As will be evident from the above judgments, the legitimate expectation

3.2.4 Aspects of judicial protection

The procedural rules summarized in the preceding section and the legal consequences of them which the case-law has demonstrated already contain judicial protection for the Member States, the undertaking benefiting from the aid and the undertakings disadvantaged thereby. In relation to the examination of the Commission's actions, as far as the question of the applicability of Article 92(1) EC is concerned, it may be taken, on the basis of the case-law, that the Commission has as little discretionary power on that point as it has in the examination of agreements under Article 85(1) EC.[351] The situation in the examination of the Commission's action under Article 92(3) is different: here the Commission has a discretion which will be only marginally examined by the Court, so that annulment will follow primarily if there are procedural errors or if the reasoning is inadequate.[352]

As far as the judicial protection of the Community is concerned, Article 93(2) permits the Commission to bring actions directly to the Court, without following the normal procedure of Article 169 EC, if a Member State fails to comply with a decision under Article 93(2) EC.[353] This also applies in case of non-compliance with a decision requiring recovery of unlawful aid. The Commission may also require that the payment of non-notified aid, or aid which has been notified but not yet been approved be suspended.[354] Non-compliance with such a decision may also be brought

argument has been particularly strongly pleaded in Germany, see Steindorff (1988) ZHR 474. Any plea of legitimate expectations will be a matter for the national courts, if necessary after a reference to the Court of Justice, see, citing earlier case-law, Cases T-244 and 486/93 *TWD Textilwerke Deggendorf GmbH v. Commission* [1995] ECR II-2265 at 2292–2293 (upheld on appeal in Case C-355/95 *TWD Textilwerke Deggendorf GmbH v. Commission* [1997] ECR I-2549) and Case T-459/93 *Siemens SA v. Commission* [1995] ECR II-1675 at 1714, upheld on appeal in Case C-278/95 P *Siemens SA v. Commission* [1997] ECR I-2507).

351. This appears to follow from the analysis of Art. 92 EC in Case 730/79 *Philip Morris Holland BV v. Commission* [1980] ECR 2671 at 2688–2689; Case 323/82 *SA Intermills v. Commission* [1984] ECR 3809 at 3830–3831, and Cases 296 and 318/82 *The Netherlands et al. v. Commission* [1985] ECR 809 at 823–824.

352. *E.g.* Cases 296 and 318/82 *The Netherlands et al. v. Commission* [1985] ECR 809 at 824–8254; Case 310/85 *Deufil GmbH & Co. KG v. Commission* [1987] ECR 901 at 926, and Case 248/84 *Germany v. Commission* [1987] ECR 4013 at 4041–4042; Case C-169/84 *Société CdF Chimie azote et fertilisants SA et al. v. Commission* [1990] ECR I-3083 (manifest errors of assessment); Case C-313/90 *Comité International de la Rayonne et des Fibres Synthétiques (CIRFS) et al. v. Commission* [1993] ECR I-1125 at 1188 (measure of general scope establishing an aid discipline in a given sector cannot be amended by a subsequent individual decision), and Case C-56/93 *Belgium v. Commission* [1996] ECR I-723 at 772.

353. Another interested Member State may do likewise, without having to follow the procedure in Art. 170 EC.

354. Case C-301/87 *France v. Commission* [1990] ECR I-307 at 356. If a general aid scheme has been approved but the Commission wishes to obtain suspension of individual aid

before the Court, if necessary also using an application for interim measures.[355] Decisions prohibiting aid, or approving subject to conditions, may be challenged by all Member States on the grounds specified in Article 173 EC.[356] An action may also be brought against a decision to open the contentious procedure under Article 93(2) EC, in relation to the question whether the aid is new aid or existing aid.[357] If a Member State fails to challenge a decision addressed to it within the prescribed time-limit, it will be unable to challenge that decision in proceedings for non-compliance brought under the second paragraph of Article 93(2) EC.[358] The third paragraph of Article 93(2) EC permits the Council, on application by a Member State, to decide unanimously that a particular aid which a Member State is granting or intends to grant is to be considered compatible with the common market, despite the fact that it does not satisfy the normal conditions, if such decision is justified by exceptional circumstances.[359] An application to the Council under this provision has the effect of suspending a contentious procedure already started by the Commission, until the Council has made its attitude known, although if this has not occurred within three months of the application being made, the Commission gives its decision.[360]

granted under the scheme, it must first conclude that the individual aid is in fact new aid, subject to Art. 93(3), falling outside the scheme, Case C-47/91 *Italy v. Commission* [1994] ECR I-4635 at 4658–4659.

355. Cases 31 and 53/77 R *Commission v. United Kingdom* [1977] ECR 921 at 924. See also Case C-301/87 *France v. Commission* [1990] ECR I-307 at 357.

356. See Case 84/82 *Germany v. Commission* [1984] ECR 1451, [1985] 1 CMLR 153 on approval of aid to the Belgian textile industry. More frequently, an interested government will intervene in support of another action. As to regional authorities, see *e.g.* Case T-214/95 *Het Vlaamse Gewest v. Commission* [1998] ECR II-nyr (30 April 1998, discussing (at para. 28) earlier case-law).

357. Case C-312/90 *Spain v. Commission* [1992] ECR I-4117 at 4140–4143, and Case C-47/91 *Italy v. Commission* [1992] ECR I-4145 at 4160–4162.

358. Case 156/77 *Commission v. Belgium* [1978] ECR 1881 at 1897, and Case 93/84 *Commission v. France* [1985] ECR 829 at 834. In an exceptional instance, Cases 6 and 11/69 *Commission v. France* [1969] ECR 523 at 539–541 the Court agreed to look at the legal basis of a decision which was alleged, out of time, to have been taken in a sphere which belonged exclusively to the jurisdiction of the Member States.

359. Whether set out in Art. 92 itself, or under regulations adopted under Art. 94 EC. The procedure of approval by the Council has been invoked on a number of occasions in the agricultural sector in order to permit certain aid measures, despite the fact that the regulations on the common organizations of the markets for various agricultural products prescribe that Art. 92 is applicable in those spheres. Particularly important examples concern temporary income support in the form of a reduction in VAT rates to compensate for losses of income through the abolition or reduction of positive Monetary Compensatory Amounts. See, generally, Case C-122/94 *Commission v. Council* [1996] ECR I-881 at 926 (in which the Court simply fell back on the Council's discretion to evaluate complex economic factors, and did not attempt to determine what constituted 'exceptional circumstances').

360. In Case 70/72 *Commission v. Germany* [1973] ECR 813 at 835 Mayras, Adv. Gen.

Beneficiary undertakings (including potential beneficiaries of proposed aid) are directly and individually concerned, within the meaning of the fourth paragraph of Article 173 EC, and may bring an action for annulment of a decision prohibiting an aid, authorizing it subject to conditions, or requiring them to repay the aid received.[361] An undertaking which fails to take advantage of the possibility of bringing an action for annulment in time may not attempt to challenge the validity of a decision through an action in a national court leading to a reference under Article 177 EC, as the national court is bound by the decision.[362] Undertakings whose competitive position is substantially disadvantaged by the aid measure will be able to challenge a decision approving it (whether subject to conditions or not), or declining to open the contentious procedure under Article 93(2) EC, before the Court under Article 173 EC.[363]

submitted that the application to the Council had to be made 'either before the Commission had put in motion the procedure for abolishing or altering the aid in question or, in any event, before the Commission has made its decision.'

361. Case 730/79 *Philip Morris Holland BV v. Commission* [1980] ECR 2671 at 2687; Case 323/82 *SA Intermills v. Commission* [1984] ECR 3809 at 383824, and Cases 296 and 318/82 *The Netherlands et al. v. Commission* [1985] ECR 809 at 821. In Cases 67, 68 and 70/85 *Kwekerij Gebroeders van der Kooy BV et al. v. Commission* [1988] ECR 219 at 267–268 the Court found that Van der Kooy was merely one of a number of horticulturalists affected by a general measure granting preferential gas tariffs, and thus was not individually concerned. In the light of subsequent case-law on the right of action of competitor undertakings (as to which, see *post*), it is uncertain whether the same conclusion would be reached today.

362. Case C-188/92 *TWD Textilwerke Deggendorf GmbH v. Germany* [1994] ECR I-833 at 853, see Ross (1994) 19 ELRev. 640.

363. Case 169/84 *Compagnie française de l'azote (Cofaz) SA et al. v. Commission* [1986] ECR 391 at 415–416. VerLoren van Themaat, Adv. Gen. observed that the undertaking had to demonstrate that a substantial proportion of its activities were in competition with a substantial proportion of the activities of the beneficiary undertaking, *ibid.* at 406. That standard was described by Tesauro, Adv. Gen. in Case C-198/91 *William Cook PLC v. Commission* [1993] ECR I-2487 at 2511 as a minimum threshold of admissibility, so that standing should be denied only to those who are not active competitors of the beneficiary and are thus only marginally concerned. See also Case C-313/90 *Comité international de la rayonne et des fibres synthétiques (CIRFS) et al. v. Commission* [1993] ECR I-1125 at 1185; the judgment in *William Cook* [1993] ECR I-2487 at 2527–2528 and Case C-225/91 *Matra SA v. Commission* [1993] ECR I-3202 at 3254–3255. However, the *Cofaz* criteria do not mean that an undertaking unable to demonstrate the existence of those circumstances could never be found to be individually concerned for the purposes of Art. 173 EC, Case T-442/93 *Association des Amidonneries de Céréales de la CEE (AAC) et al. v. Commission* [1995] ECR II-1329 at 1352 and Case T-435/93 *Association of Sorbitol Producers within the EC (ASPEC) et al. v. Commission* [1995] ECR II-1281 at 1307. See, in particular on public interest aspects of *locus standi* in relation to state aids, Gormley in Micklitz and Reich (eds.), *loc. cit.* (see note 223, *supra*). The Court of First Instance is understandably less flexible in finding standing in relation to general, as opposed to individual aids, see Case T-398/94 *Kahn Scheepvaart BV v. Commission* [1996] ECR II-477 at 490–495, finding that the undertaking was in fact only marginally concerned (at 495). As to interven-

Disadvantaged competitors may also challenge the national measure actually granting the aid before their national courts, seeking to restrain the implementation of non-notified or not yet approved aid,[364] or the grant of aid in breach of the terms of a decision under Article 93(2) EC.[365]

4.   COMPETITION RULES FOR UNDERTAKINGS

4.1   General observations

Articles 85–90 EC have been the subject of countless commentaries solely devoted to them, whether in book or loose-leaf form, in the form of monographs or theses or in reports, addresses, articles in learned periodicals or case-notes.[366] National and Community case-law, and the

tion, Case T-330/94 *Salt Union Ltd. v. Commission* [1996] ECR II-2281.

364. Case C-354/90 *Fédération Nationale du Commerce Extérieur des Produits Alimentaires et al. v. French State* [1991] ECR I-5505 at 5528–5529. See also Case C-39/94 *Syndicat français de l'Express international (SFEI) et al. v. La Poste et al.* [1996] ECR I-3547 at 3597–3598.

365. As to the role of national courts in state aid proceedings, see *ibid.* and the Commission's Communication (O.J. 1995 C 312/8). See also Case C-24/95 *Land Rheinland-Pfalz v. Alcan Deutschland GmbH* [1997] ECR I-1591.

366. See, generally, from amongst this vast array: Amato, *Antitrust and the Bounds of Power: the Dilemma of Liberal Democracy in the History of the Market* (Oxford, 1997); Bellamy and Child, *op. cit.* (see note 223, *supra*); Cooper *et al.* in Vaughan (ed.) *Law of the European Communities Service* (London, loose-leaf, since 1990) Part 19; Fierstra, *Europees Mededingingsrecht* (Deventer, 1993); Freeman and Whish (eds.), *Butterworths' Competition Law* (London, loose-leaf since 1991); Green and Robertson, *Commercial Agreements and Competition Law: Practice and Procedure in the U.K. and EC* (2nd ed., London, 1997); Gormley (ed.), *Current and Future Perspectives on EC Competition Law* (London, 1997); Goyder (D.), *EC Competition Law* (3rd ed., Oxford, 1998); Goyder (J.), *EC Distribution Law* (2nd ed., Chichester, 1996); Hawk, *Common Market and International Antitrust: A Comparative Guide*, Vol. II, *Common Market Competition Law* (New York, loose-leaf, since 1986); Kerse, *EC Antitrust Procedure* (4th ed., London, 1998); Korah, *An Introductory Guide to EC Competition Law and Practice* (6th ed., Oxford, 1997); Lonbay (ed.), *Frontiers of Competition Law* (Chichester, 1994); Mégret *et al.* (eds.), *Le Droit de la CE* (Vol. 4, 2nd ed., by Waelbroeck and Frignani, Brussels, 1997) Ortiz Blanco, *EC Competition Procedure* (Oxford, 1996); Ritter *et al.*, *EEC Competition Law – A Practitioner's Guide* (Deventer, 1991); Sauter, *Competition Law and Industrial Policy in the EU* (Oxford, 1997); Schröter *et al.* in Von der Groeben, *op. cit.* (see note 4, *supra*) Vol. II 1299 (with an extensive bibliography); Slot and McDonnell (eds.), *Procedure and Enforcement in E.C. and U.S. Competition Law* (London, 1993); Van Bael and Bellis, *Competition Law of the European Community* (3rd ed., Bicester, 1994); Van Gerven *et al.*, *Kartelrecht Europese Economische Gemeenschap* (2nd ed., Zwolle, 1997), and Whish, *Competition Law* (3rd ed., London, 1993 (4th ed. in preparation)). The annual proceedings of the *Fordham Corporate Law Institute* invariably contain papers of high quality. Recent developments may be traced in the Commission's quarterly *Competition Policy Newsletter* and in the annual surveys in ELRev. and YBEL. An excellent reference source is Jones, Van der Woude and Lewis, *EC Competition Law Handbook* (London, annually). Among many older

Commission's practice in decision-making in this field is steadily growing year by year. They present an ever more precise but also ever more complicated picture of this field of Community law which is so important for industry and commerce. Nevertheless, the legal developments do demonstrate a number of principal themes which are discussed below. Merger control is discussed in section 4.5, below, and Article 90 EC is dealt with separately, in section 4.7, below.

4.1.1 Function of the rules on competition

Articles 85(1) and 86 EC contain directly effective prohibitions, addressed to undertakings, of the prevention, restriction or distortion of competition within the common market, subject to the conditions laid down in those provisions.[367] Both provisions are thus expressions of a system of prohibition. Constant case-law of the Court shows that the function of Articles 85 and 86 EC is to guarantee the system of undistorted competition laid down in Article 3(g) EC,[368] which system in its turn serves the establishment and functioning of the common market expressed in Article 2 EC.[369]

This perspective explains why the function of Articles 85 and 86 EC in relation to the five freedoms discussed in Chapter VII, above, is primarily complementary. This is particularly true in relation to the free movement of goods and the freedom to provide services; but it in principle also holds true in relation to the other freedoms.[370] This complementary function is expressed in a trio of mutually related aspects. *First,* Articles 85 and 86 EC too are aimed at the removal of existing and the prevention of new

---

works, see: Joliet, *The Rule of Reason in Antitrust Law, American, German and Common Market Laws in Comparative Perspective* (The Hague, 1967); Mestmäcker, *Europäisches Wettbewerbsrecht* (Munich, 1974, a 2nd ed. has been announced), and VerLoren van Themaat *et al., Europees Kartelrecht, Anno 1980* (Deventer, 1980).

367. Case 127/73 *Belgische Radio en Televisie et al. v. SV SABAM et al.* [1974] ECR 51 at 62.

368. Previously in Art. 3(f) EEC.

369. Case 32/65 *Council and Commission* [1966] ECR 389 at 405 (The Court's language was, with respect, slightly misleading in that, as has been seen in Chapter III, *ante,* establishing the common market is one of the means of achieving the Community's tasks; it is not simply an objective in itself.); see also Case 6/72 *Europemballage Corporation and Continental Can Company Inc. v. Commission* [1973] ECR 215 at 244–245.

370. *E.g.* in relation to services, Case 172/80 *Züchner v. Bayerische Vereinsbank AG* [1981] ECR 2021, [1982] 1 CMLR 313 (banking); Case 45/85 *Verband der Sachversicherer e. v. v. Commission* [1987] ECR 405, [1988] 4 CMLR 264 (insurance); Case 311/85 *VZW Vereniging van Vlaamse Reisbureaus v. VZW Sociale Dienst van de Plaatselijke en Gewestelijke Overheidsdiensten* [1987] ECR 3801, [1989] 4 CMLR 213 (travel agencies); Cases 209–213/84 *Ministère public v. Asjes et al.* [1986] ECR 1425, [1986] 3 CMLR 173 (air travel), and Case C-41/90 *Höfner and Elser v. Macrotron GmbH* [1991] ECR I-1979, [1993] 4 CMLR 306 (executive recruitment consultants). See, in relation to the link between competition and the free movement of capital, Case 267/86 *Van Eycke v. ASPA NV* [1988] ECR 4769, [1990] 4 CMLR 330.

obstacles to free movement. What is prohibited for the Member States, namely the maintenance or adoption of measures which protect national markets, cannot be permitted to undertakings.[371] *Secondly*, distortions of competition have to be prevented within the common market once it is established. In relation to measures taken by the Member States themselves this is sought to be attained by means of Articles 92–102 EC; in relation to actions of undertakings this is done through Articles 85 and 86 EC. Thus the Treaty expresses that the coordination of economic decisions of the market participants should primarily take place through the proper functioning of the market mechanism. A properly functioning market mechanism may not be thwarted by anti-competitive agreements or by the abuse by undertakings of their dominant positions.

Thirdly, the complementary function of Articles 85 and 86 EC means that there is an interaction between these provisions and those relating to the free movement of goods and the freedom to provide services. Initially the provisions on the free movement of goods had a clear influence on the formation of competition policy (the first complementary function of Articles 85 and 86 EC referred to above). That which is forbidden to Member States must also be forbidden to undertakings. Particularly since 1974 the interpretation of Articles 85 and 86 (and more recently also of Article 90 EC) has had a clear inverse influence on the application and interpretation of Articles 30–37 and 59 EC.[372] Particularly in cases in which barriers to trade arise through the active or passive interplay of public measures and action by undertakings, Community or national proceedings must sometimes cover both groups of provisions, or it may well be difficult for a litigant to decide on which group of provisions to base an action, or for a national court to decide how to formulate a reference under Article 177 EC. This is particularly true in respect of the conduct of public undertakings. In any event, this interaction demonstrates that the provisions relating to the establishment and proper functioning of the common market are more and more acquiring the character of an inter-connected unity. This explains the express recognition by the Court

---

371. Cases 56 and 58/64 *Établissements Consten SARL and Grundig-Verkaufs-GmbH v. Commission* [1966] ECR 299 at 340. As a good *e.g.* of how arrangements between private parties can regulate and divide a market, see Case 246/86 *Belasco et al. v. Commission* [1989] ECR 2117, [1991] 4 CMLR 96.

372. *E.g.* Case 8/74 *Procureur du Roi v. Dassonville et al.* [1974] ECR 837, [1974] 2 CMLR 436; Case 15/74 *Centrafarm BV et al. v. Sterling Drug Inc.* [1974] ECR 1147, [1974] 2 CMLR 480, Case 16/74 *Centrafarm BV et al. v. Winthrop BV* [1974] ECR 1183, [1974] 2 CMLR 480; Case 59/75 *Pubblico Ministero v. Manghera et al.* [1976] ECR 91, [1976] 1 CMLR 557; Case 13/77 *NV GB-INNO-BM v. Vereniging van de Kleinhandelaars in Tabak* [1977] ECR 2115, [1978] 1 CMLR 283 and Case 229/83 *Association des Centres distributeurs Edouard Leclerc et al. v. Sàrl 'Au blé vert' et al.* [1985] ECR 1, [1985] 2 CMLR 286. For the limits of this mutual influence see, though, Cases 177 and 178/82 *Officier van Justitie v. Van de Haar et al.* [1984] ECR 1797. [1985] 2 CMLR 566. See further, VerLoren van Themaat (1996) SEW 398.

of the significance of Articles 30 *et seq.* for the system of Article 3(g) EC.[373] This does not, though, mean that Articles 30–37 and 59 on the one hand, and Articles 85 and 86 on the other hand can be applicable at the same time to the same set of facts: the former provisions do not concern the conduct of undertakings,[374] whereas the latter do not concern legal, administrative and other public measures.[375] Articles 85 and 86 do mean that the Member States may not adopt any measures which would detract from the effectiveness of those provisions, *e.g.* by requiring, favouring or reinforcing the effects of agreements which are contrary to Article 85 EC,[376] or by depriving legislation of its official character by delegating responsibility for taking decisions affecting the economic sphere to private traders.[377]

Similarly, competition policy has made clear the connection between the application of competition rules for undertakings and the co-ordination of economic policy, in the sense that competition policy too can contribute to positive integration. This follows in general terms from the text of Article 85(3) and already became evident at an early stage in the agricultural sector.[378] The Commission's practice also demonstrates the existence of a

373. Case C-18/88 *Régie des télégraphes et des téléphones v. GB-Inno-BM SA* [1991] ECR I-5941, (the Court examined first the competition aspects, and then the Art. 30 EC aspects, but the approach in relation to the problem is clearly complementary).

374. Save that Arts. 30–36 do limit the use which may be made of national industrial and commercial property rights, and Art. 59 EC does affect the conduct of at least private regulatory bodies. As to the latter, see Case 36/74 *Walrave and Koch v. Association Union Cycliste International et al.* [1974] ECR 1405, [1975] 1 CMLR 320.

375. Case 24/67 *Parke, Davis & Co. v. Probel, Reese, Beintema-Interpharm and Centrafarm* [1968] ECR 55 at 71–72; Case 5/79 *Procureur Général v. Buys et al.* [1979] ECR 3203 at 3230–3231; Case 30/87 *Bodson v. Pompes funèbres des régions libérées SA* [1988] ECR 2479 at 2511–2512, and Case C-339/89 *Alsthom Atlantique SA v. Compagnie de construction méchanique Sulzer SA* [1991] ECR I-107 at 123. The Commission cannot address decisions to Member States on the basis of Art. 85 EC, see Case T-113/89 *Nederlandse Associatie van de Farmaceutische Industrie 'Nefarma' et al. v. Commission* [1990] ECR II-797 at 817–818.

376. Case 136/86 *Bureau national interprofessionnel du cognac v. Aubert* [1987] ECR 4789 at 4815; Case 267/86 *Van Eycke v. ASPA NV* [1988] ECR 4769 at 4791; Case C-2/91 *Meng* [1993] ECR I-5751 at 5797–5798; Case C-185/91 *Bundesanstalt für den Güterfernverkehr v. Gebrüder Reiff GmbH & Co. KG* [1993] ECR I-5801 at 584; Case C-245/91 *Ohra Schadeverzekeringen NV* [1993] ECR I-5851 at 5878; Case C-153/93 *Germany v. Schiffahrts- und Speditionsgesellschaft mbH* [1994] ECR I-2517 at 2530, and Cases C-140–142/94 *DIP SpA et al. v. Commune di Bassano del Grappa et al.* [1995] ECR I-3257 at 3293–3294.

377. Case 267/86 *Van Eycke v. ASPA NV* [1988] ECR 4769 at 4791 and Cases C-401 and 402/92 *Tankstation 't Heuske vof et al.* [1994] ECR 2199 at 2236. See also Case 13/77 *NV GB-INNO-BM v. Vereniging van de Kleinhandelaars in Tabak* [1977] ECR 2115 at 2144–2146; Case 66/86 *Ahmed Saeed Flugreisen et al. v. Zentrale zur Bekämpfung unlauteren Wettbewerbs e.V.* [1989] ECR 803 at 852–853; Case 229/83 *Association des Centres distributeurs Edouard Leclerc et al. v. Sàrl 'Au blé vert' et al.* [1985] ECR 1 at 31–32, and Case 231/83 *Cullet et al. v. Centre Leclerc Toulouse et al.* [1985] ECR 305 at 320.

378. Cases 40/73 etc. *Coöperatieve vereniging 'Suiker Unie' UA v. Commission* [1975] ECR 1663, [1976] 1 CMLR 295.

link between competition law and the process of positive integration in the fields of the common commercial policy,[379] energy policy,[380] employment policy,[381] environmental policy,[382] industrial policy,[383] and Community research and development policy.[384] This part of competition policy too reflects the mixed economic order which the Community strives to attain.

4.1.2   Article 85 EC as an expression of the first concept of freedom

As has been indicated in the preceding section, it appears from the case-law that the system of undistorted competition guaranteed by Articles 85 and 86 EC forms the core of the common market which the EC Treaty seeks to establish. This system must not, however, be confused with a normative *laissez-faire* system which excludes any intervention at all on the part of undertakings or of the national or Community authorities.[385]

In order to guarantee this system, in the first instance all commercial practices of undertakings which create trade barriers or channels between different national markets have to be prohibited. Such practices embrace in particular market sharing agreements, collective exclusive dealing agreements between national producers and their distributors, agreements to adapt import prices to national price levels, collective rebate or discount agreements concerning the total turnover within one Member State, as well as import or export restrictions or bans in whatever form. In this context it is sufficient to point to the parallel with Articles 30 and 34 EC.

But a prohibition of horizontal (*e.g.* between producers, or between distributors) cartels is insufficient. Channels and barriers between national markets can also flow from vertical agreements, such as exclusive distribution or purchasing agreements between one producer and one

379. Dec. 74/634 (O.J. 1974 L 343/19) on the Franco–Japanese ball-bearings cartel.
380. Decs. 76/248 (O.J. 1976 L 51/7) *United Reprocessors* and 76/249 (O.J. 1976 L 51/15) *KEWA*.
381. Case 26/76 *Metro SB-Großmärkte GmbH & Co. KG. v. Commission* [1977] ECR 1875, [1978] 2 CMLR 1.
382. See the reports of the Commission's action in *Disma* (*XXIIIrd Report on Competition Policy 1993* (Brussels, Luxembourg, 1994) points 223–224, and *Oliebranchens Fllesrad XXIVth Report 1994* (*ibid.*, 1995) Annex II, A.2.j (pp. 368–369).
383. Decs. 84/380 (O.J. 1984 L 207/17) and 84/387 (O.J. 1984 L 212/21) on restructuring in the synthetic fibres and petrochemicals industries respectively. See also Dec. 83/671 (O.J. 1983 L 376/30) addressed to the International Energy Agency, permitting allocation of supplies in an emergency, and Dec. 94/153 (O.J. 1994 L 68/35).
384. *E.g.* Reg. 240/96 (O.J. 1996 L 31/2) on technology transfer agreements.
385. Constant case-law demonstrates that the various economic fundamental rights do not exclude every specific intervention by the Community or national authorities, see Case 230/78 *SpA Eridania-Zuccherifici nazionali et al. v. Minister for Agriculture and Forestry et al.* [1979] ECR 2749 at 2768 and 2771; Case 139/79 *Maizena GmbH v. Council* [1980] ECR 3393 at 3421–3422, and Case 84/87 *Erpelding v. Secrétaire d'État à l'Agriculture et à la Viticulture* [1988] ECR 2647 at 2673–2674.

distributor, particularly when they are combined with absolute territorial protection (a prohibition on active sales outside the contract territory, and also a prohibition on passive sales within that territory to persons from outside it) or relative territorial protection (a prohibition on active sales outside the contract territory[386]). Market-sharing effects may also result from agreements concerning industrial or commercial property rights, although in its case-law on Articles 30–36 EC, considered in section 3.3.2 of Chapter VII, above, the Court has imposed very heavy restrictions on the possibility of dividing up the common market by the use of such rights without such agreements. Indeed it is precisely in the field of industrial and commercial property rights that the Court's attempts to ensure consistency between the provisions on the free movement of goods and those on competition law appear.

The wording of Article 85 EC also makes it apparent that it is not certain conduct of undertakings which is restrictive or distortive of competition that is prohibited, but rather all forms of restriction of competition within the common market by means of an agreement between undertakings, a decision of an association of undertakings, or a concerted practice of undertakings. Thus Article 85 EC not only prohibits market-sharing and restrictions on imports or exports, it also catches competition arrangements in respect of which market-sharing or such restrictions cannot be demonstrated. Thus Article 85 can be regarded as an expression of the first concept of freedom explained in Chapter VII, above. The effects of such restrictions on competition must be 'appreciable' and have cross-border effects (which may well be in the form of barriers to entry for foreign undertakings). Examples include international price agreements, international agreements on other trading conditions, and production or distribution cartels, as mentioned by way of example in Article 85(1) EC.[387] Even intrinsically useful agreements on co-operation in the field of specialization, joint purchase or sale, sales-promoting agreements, and joint research or technical cooperation, etc. with competition restricting side-effects are covered by the prohibition. Such intrinsically useful cooperation agreements, however, which do not appear in the list of examples of prohibited agreements in Article 85(1), will qualify more easily for exemption from the prohibition under Article 85(3) than the other examples mentioned.[388]

---

386. Although, as will become apparent, *post*, various block exemption regulations permit bans on active sales outside the contract territory, but not bans on passive sales.

387. See also Case 41/69 *ACF Chemiefarma NV v. Commission* [1970] ECR 661 at 693 *et seq.* (even a gentlemen's agreement falls under Art. 85) and Case 48/69 *Imperial Chemical Industries Ltd. v. Commission* [1972] ECR 619, [1972] CMLR 557.

388. For a number of forms of cooperation the Commission is of the opinion that they do not need an exemption, since they do not tend to restrict competition and for that reason fall by law outside Art. 85(1), even if they relate to importation or exportation as between Member States (Communication from the Commission concerning agree-

In the light of the first concept of freedom, of which Article 85 EC is an expression, it is understandable that in Case 8/72 *Vereeniging van Cementhandelaren* v. *Commission*[389] the Court held that even an agreement 'extending over the whole of the territory of a Member State by its very nature has the effect of reinforcing the compartmentalization of markets on a national basis, thereby holding up the economic interpenetration which the Treaty is designed to bring about and protecting domestic production.' Thus potentially all significant national cartels, national vertical price fixing systems and, if collectively they hinder imports, even groups of national exclusive dealing agreements fall within the ambit of Article 85 EC. Agreements with or between undertakings from third countries which restrict or distort competition within the Community also fall under Article 85.[390] In short, Article 85 covers all significant national and international cartels which restrict or distort competition within the common market.

4.1.3   Other forms of distortion of competition

Mergers. In its celebrated judgment in Case 6/72 *Europemballage Corporation and Continental Can Company Inc.* v. *Commission*[391] the Court held that the concept of an abuse of a dominant position within the meaning of Article 86 EC could occur 'if an undertaking in a dominant position strengthens such position in such a way that the degree of dominance reached substantially fetters competition, *i.e.* that only undertakings remain in the market whose behaviour depends on the dominant one.' Thus the basis was laid for a system of merger control at the Community level. Already in the summer of 1973 the Commission proposed a draft merger control regulation; this was modified on numerous occasions since but was not in fact adopted by the Council until 1989. The present merger control system is discussed in section 4.5, below.

Prohibited Discrimination. The distortion of competition against which Articles 85 and 86 EC are directed embraces, in addition to restrictions of competition in inter-state trade, discrimination based on nationality but is not restricted to such discrimination. Discrimination based on nationality is already prohibited under Article 6 EC even without cartel agreements or

ments, decisions, and concerted practices in the field of cooperation between undertakings, J.O. 1968, C 75/3 with corrections in C 84/14 Dutch and French texts – and C 93/3 – German and Italian texts).
389. [1972] ECR 977, [1973] CMLR 7.
390. See Case 22/71 *Béguelin Import Co. et al.* v. *SAGL Import Export et al.* [1971] ECR 949, [1972] CMLR 81 and Dec. 85/202 (O.J. 1985 L 85/1); on appeal (as to the extraterritoriality point) Cases 89/85 *etc. Ahlström Osakeijhtö et al.* v. *Commission* [1988] ECR 5193, [1988] 4 CMLR 901.
391. [1973] ECR 215 at 245 (hereafter '*Continental Can*').

the need for a dominant economic position.[392] The distortion of competition also covers forms of discrimination based on grounds other than nationality, country of origin, or country of destination,[393] if parties to commercial transactions are thus placed at a competitive disadvantage.[394] A special form of price discrimination based on nationality, *viz.* dumping within the Community, is referred to in Article 91 EC. This provision, unlike Articles 85 and 86, does not contain a self-executing prohibition, but a procedure of recommendations by the Commission, followed, if necessary, by an authorization to the injured Member State to take protective measures. Article 91 also provides for an automatic possibility of re-exportation to the exporting country free of all customs duties, quantitative restrictions, or measures having equivalent effect. In the early years of the existence of the Community this procedure worked properly and also reasonably promptly. In later years the number of complaints decreased; probably for reasons connected with the growing liberalization of interstate trade. Since the special procedure of Article 91 was provided only for the transitional period, from the end of the transitional period only Articles 6, 85 and 86 are applicable under the conditions provided therein. The experience gained with Article 91 regained relevance for trade between the Community of Ten and Spain and Portugal[395] and may again become relevant on future accessions.[396]

Apart from restrictions of competition and discrimination, Articles 85 and 86 also prohibit other forms of distortion of competition, where the undertakings concerned abuse their power, particularly by tie-in

---

392. Given that Arts. 48 and 59 EC also apply to discrimination on ground of nationality by private parties, the same must be true of Art. 6 EC, as the case-law treats the former provisions as a specific development of the latter, see Chapter III, section 5.3, *ante*.

393. One example of price discrimination can be seen in Dec. 72/403 (O.J. 1972 L 272/35) addressed to Pittsburgh Corning (concerning differential prices agreed between the manufacturer and Dutch and Belgian distributors in order to protect the German market). In Cases 6 and 7/73 *Instituto Chemioterapico Italiano SpA & Commercial Solvents Corporation v. Commission* [1974] ECR 223, [1974] 1 CMLR 309 the Court considered discrimination through refusal to supply. As examples of discrimination by undertakings with a dominant economic position see also, *inter alia*, Case 155/73 *Sacchi* [1974] ECR 409, [1974] 2 CMLR 177; Cases 40/73 *etc. Coöperatieve vereniging 'Suiker Unie' UA et al. v. Commission* [1975] ECR 1663, [1974] 1 CMLR 295; Case 27/76 *United Brands Company et al. v. Commission* [1978] ECR 207, [1978] 3 CMLR 83; Case 85/76 *Hoffmann-La Roche & Co. AG v. Commission* [1979] ECR 461, [1979] 3 CMLR 211; Case 77/77 *Benzine en Petroleum Handelsmaatschappij BV et al. v. Commission* [1978] ECR 1513, [1978] 3 CMLR 174 and Case 226/84 *British Leyland plc v.Commission* [1986] ECR 3263, [1987] 1 CMLR 185.

394. Arts. 85(1)(d) and 86(c) EC.

395. See Act of Spanish and Portuguese Accession (O.J. 1985 L 302/23), Art. 380.

396. AntI-dumping duties were prohibited in relations between the Contracting Parties to the EEA Agreement (Art. 26 and Protocol 13 EEA, save as otherwise provided in the EEA), hence the lack of significance of the experience of Art. 91 EC after Austrian, Finnish and Swedish Accession.

requirements or by charging excessive prices, or by exercising coercion on other undertakings to induce them to pursue a given line of conduct, and the like. An accurate distinction between restrictions of competition, discrimination and other forms of distortion of competition has little legal importance since Article 85 lumps them together. Article 86 does not make such a distinction explicitly. Moreover, a specific practice will often fall simultaneously within more than one of the categories in question.

4.1.4   The protected minimum of competition

It is decidedly not true that Articles 85 and 86 EC are intended to realize perfect or even maximum competition. This appears particularly from the fact that Article 85(3) permits, under conditions which in themselves are stringent, certain useful forms of co-operation restricting competition. Again, not all mergers and other forms of concentration are prohibited by Article 86.[397] However, Article 85(3) does guarantee in its last condition that even the most useful form of co-operation should leave a substantial degree of competition intact. As has already been seen, the same applies in relation to concentrations.[398] In Case 6/72 *Continental Can*[399] the Court noted that 'the restraints on competition which the Treaty allows under certain conditions because of the need to harmonize the various objectives of the Treaty, are limited by the requirements of Articles 2 and 3. Going beyond this limit involves the risk that the weakening of competition would conflict with the aims of the common market.' Thus the Court regarded Articles 85 and 86 as seeking to achieve the same aim, the maintenance of effective competition within the common market, and thus both provisions had to be interpreted in a mutually coherent manner in the light of the requirements of Article 85(3) EC.[400]

In Case 26/76 *Metro SB-Großmärkte GmbH & Co. KG v. Commission*[401] the Court observed that the requirement in Articles 3(g)[402] and 85 EC that competition shall not be distorted 'implies the existence on the market of workable competition, that is to say the degree of competition necessary to ensure the observance of the basic requirements and the attainment of the objectives of the Treaty, in particular the creation of a single market achieving conditions similar to those of a domestic market.' The

397. See also Art. 90(2) EC.
398. See section 4.5, *post* on merger control.
399. [1973] ECR 215 at 244.
400. *Ibid.* at 244–245.
401. [1977] ECR 1875 at 1904. See also Case 75/84 *Metro SB-Großmärkte GmbH & Co. KG v. Commission* [1986] ECR 3021, [1987] 1 CMLR 118, and Case C-376/92 *Metro SB-Großmärkte GmbH & Co. KG v. Cartier SA* [1994] ECR I-15, [1994] 5 CMLR 331.
402. Then Art. 3(f) EEC.

importance of this statement is that it relates to Article 85 as a whole, with the consequence that Article 85(1) does not only apply where there is an interference with workable competition as defined by the Court. It thus reinforces the conclusion that even in the exemption policy under Article 85(3) workable competition as described must be maintained, which also appears true in respect of Article 86 EC as a result of the *Continental Can* judgment. The requirement of workable competition is thus a minimum requirement which must be satisfied in all cases.

4.2 Article 85(1) EC

Article 85(1) contains a directly applicable prohibition of all agreements between undertakings, all decisions by associations of undertakings, and all concerted practices[403] meeting two criteria. If they are to fall within the prohibition, they must in the first place have as their object or effect the prevention, restriction or distortion of competition within the common market. Secondly, they must tend to have an adverse effect on inter-state trade. The wording of Article 85(1) mentions some examples of agreements which – at least as a rule – meet the first criterion.

The two criteria are mentioned in Article 85 in the opposite order, but the order here given is more logical, and accordingly is invariably followed by the Commission in its decisions. As a matter of fact, the 'adverse nature' of the possible effect of an agreement on inter-state trade cannot be viewed as being independent of whether an agreement does or does not restrict competition. It is precisely because an agreement prevents, restricts, or distorts competition in inter-state trade that it may have an adverse effect thereon.

Undertakings. In view of the objectives and type of the competition provisions, the concept of an 'undertaking'[404] embraces all entities engaged in an economic activity, regardless of their legal status and the way in which they are financed.[405] Thus while an employee does not fall within the

403. The term 'agreements' is used hereafter as shorthand for all three of these forms of cooperation.
404. As to the concept of an 'association of undertakings', see Cases 209–215 and 218/78 *Van Landewyck Sàrl et al. v. Commission* [1980] ECR 3125 at 3249–3251 (*FEDETAB*); Case 45/85 *Verband der Sachversicherer e.V. v. Commission* [1987] ECR 405 at 454–455; Dec. 94/815 (O.J. 1994 L 343/1), *Cement*, under appeal in Case T-25/95 *SA Cimenteries CBR v. Commission* (O.J. 1995 C 101/10), and Cases T-39 and 40/92 *Groupement des Cartes Bancaires 'CB' et al. v. Commission* [1994] ECR II-49 at 80–81.
405. Case C-41/90 *Höfner and Elser v. Macrotron GmbH* [1991] ECR 1979 at 2016. Thus sickness funds, and organizations engaged in the management of the public social security system do not constitute undertakings, as their function is social, not economic in nature, based on the principle of solidarity and being non-profit-making; the statutory benefits bear no relation to the contributions, see Cases C-159 and 160/91

concept,[406] a self-employed person may well.[407] To the extent that he or she is economically dependent on his or her principal and assumes no entrepreneurial risks other than the usual *del credere* guarantee, a commercial agent will not be regarded as an undertaking.[408] A group of companies will be regarded as a single undertaking if its component parts form an economic unit within which the subsidiary has no real freedom to determine its activities within the common market, thus an agreement between a parent and its subsidiaries solely concerning the internal distribution of tasks among them will fall outside the scope of Article 85(1) EC.[409]

Activities of public authorities. The result of the interpretation of the concept of an 'undertaking' is that certain activities of public authorities may also come, within the scope of Articles 85 and 86 EC. This is not

Poucet and Pistre v. Assurances Générales de France (AGF) et al. [1993] ECR I-637 at 670. Clearly, commercial insurers would not fall under this exception; in relation to an optional non-profit-making scheme with limited aspects of solidarity, where the benefits depended solely on the contributions paid and the investment results, operating in competition with commercial insurers, the Court has found that a public scheme was an undertaking, Case C-244/94 *Fédération Française des Sociétés d'Assurance et al. v. Ministère de l'Agriculture et de la Pêche* [1995] ECR I-4013 at 4028–4030. The question of the status of professional mutual schemes, participation in which was made obligatory by ministerial decree, was raised, but did not need to be answered, in Cases C-430 and 431/93 *Van Schijndel et al. v. Stichting Pensioenfonds voor Fysiotherapeuten* [1995] ECR I-4705 (see the discussion by Jacobs, Adv. Gen. at 4724–4727).

406. Cases 40/73 *etc. Coöperatieve vereniging 'Suiker Unie' UA et al. v. Commission* [1975] ECR 1663 at 2007.

407. *E.g.* Dec. 76/743 (O.J. 1976 L 254/40) *Reuter/BASF* (Reuter was a controlling shareholder and exploited his own research results, as well as a commercial adviser to third parties) and Dec.78/516 (O.J. 1978 L 157/39) *RAI/Unitel* (world class opera singers). The Commission expects that there will be a growing number of cases concerning the liberal professions, *XXVth Report on Competition Policy 1995* (Brussels, Luxembourg, 1996) point 88.

408. See the Commission's Notice on Exclusive Agency Contracts made with Commercial Agents (J.O. 2921/62). Revision of this Notice has been under consideration for some time, and at the end of 1990 and beginning of 1991 a draft of a new Notice was widely circulated, proposing a broader definition of the risks that a commercial agent could accept, and a broader range of permissible restrictions in agreements between 'integrated' agents and their principals, without coming within the scope of Art. 85(1). It was expected that a new Notice might be adopted in 1996 but this had still not happened by May 1998. See further, Cases 56 and 58/64 *Consten and Grundig v. Commission* [1966] ECR 299 at 340; Dec. 72/403 (J.O. 1972 L 272/45) *Pittsburg Corning Europe*; Cases 40/73 *etc. Suiker Unie* [1975] ECR 1663 at 2005–2010 (see also 1994–2000); Case 311/85 *VZW Vereniging van Vlaamse Reisbureaus v. VZW Sociale Dienst van de Plaatselijke en Gewestelijke Overheidsdiensten* [1987] ECR 3801 at 3828; Dec. 91/562 (O.J. 1991 L 306/22) *Eirpage*; Case C-266/93 *Bundeskartellamt v. Volkswagen AG et al.* [1995] ECR I-3477 at 3516–3518, and Case T-14/93 *Union Internationale des Chemins de Fer v. Commission* [1995] ECR II-1503 at 1523–1524, appeal dismissed in Case C-264/95 P *Commission v. Union Internationale des Chemins de Fer* [1997] ECR I-1287. See also Dir. 86/653 (O.J. 1986 L 382/17).

new, as Article 90(1) EC confirms that the activities of public undertakings and undertakings to which Member States grant special or exclusive rights are also subject to the competition rules of the Treaty. However, the case-law does not afford complete clarity as to the dividing line between the activities which do fall under the competition provisions and those which do not. On the one hand, it could be argued on the basis of the judgment in Case C-41/90 *Höfner and Elser v. Macrotron GmbH*[410] that many more activities of public authorities could be considered those of an undertaking than was previously supposed,[411] on the other hand the judgment in Cases C-159 and 160/91 *Poucet and Pistre* v. *Assurances Générales de France (AGF) et al.*[412] makes it clear that the concept of 'economic activities' may not be extended so widely as to bring every public activity which could also be exercised by a private undertaking within the scope of Articles 85 and 86 EC. The approach in Case C-244/94 *Fédération Française des Sociétés d'Assurance et al.* v. *Ministère de l'Agriculture et de la Pêche*[413] and in Case C-343/95 *Diego Cali & FigliSrl* v. *Servizi ecologici porto di Genova SpA (SPEG)*[414] demonstrates, though, that regard must be had to the type of commercial activities,and, in particular to whether the body concerned is acting *qua* official authority or as a market participant.[415] An optimal coordination between the competition provisions on the one hand and the provisions addressed to the Member States on the other militates against a structural overlap of the scope of provisions addressed to the public

409. Dec. 70/332 (J.O. 1970 L 147/24) *Kodak*; Case 48/69 *Imperial Chemical Industries Ltd. v. Commission* [1972] ECR 619 at 662; Case 22/71 *Béguelin Import Co. et al. v. SA G.L. Import Export et al.* [1971] ECR 949 at 959; Case 15/74 *Centrafarm BV et al. v. Sterling Drug Inc.* [1974] ECR 1147 at 1167; Case 170/83 *Hydrotherm Gerätebau GmbH v. Compact del Dott. Ing. Mario Andreoli & C. sas* [1984] ECR 2999 at 3016, and Case T-102/92 *Viho Europe BV v. Commission* [1995] ECR II-17 at 33–36, upheld on appeal in Case C-73/95 P *Viho Europe BV v. Commission* [1996] ECR I-5457. See also Dec. 91/335 (O.J. 1991 L 185/23) *Gosme/Martell-DMP*.
410. [1991] ECR I-1979 at 2016–2019.
411. See Wilmowsky (1991) ZHR 545.
412. [1993] ECR I-637 at 670.
413. [1995] ECR I-4013 at 4028–4030.
414. [1997] ECR I-1547 at 1587–1589.
415. See also Case C-364/92 *SAT Fluggesellschaft mbH v. European Organization for the Safety of Air Navigation (Eurocontrol)* [1994] ECR I-55 at 63–64. The point is also supported by Case 2/73 *Geddo v. Ente nazionale Risi* [1973] ECR 865 at 879, in which the Court found that the imposition of a levy for the financing of a state aid did not amount to an abuse under Art. 86 EC; in Case 52/76 *Benedetti v. Munari F.lli s.a.s.* [1977] ECR 163 at 191 it considered it very doubtful whether a national intervention agency entrusted with tasks flowing from the regulations on the common organization of agricultural markets could be regarded as a public undertaking to which the competition provisions applied. Thus the applicability of the competition provisions does not follow the principle of vertical direct effect, which applies irrespective of whether the State or a public body acts *qua* authority or *qua* market participant, see Case 152/84 *Marshall v. Southampton and South-West Hampshire Area Health Authority (Teaching)* [1986] ECR 723 at 749.

authorities and those addressed to undertakings through a wide interpretation of the concept of an undertaking.

Agreements and concerted practices. The concept of an 'agreement' concerns the 'existence of elements of concerted practice'[416] irrespective of the applicable national law.[417] It matters not whether an agreement is a horizontal or vertical agreement,[418] oral or in writing.[419] Non-binding agreements and so-called 'gentlemen's agreements' are also caught.[420]

While normally Article 85 catches bilateral or multilateral conduct and Article 86 abusive unilateral conduct, unilateral measures restricting competition can be prohibited under Article 85 EC if they are the object or result of an agreement between undertakings and expressly or tacitly are accepted by the parties.[421] A refusal to admit a distributor to a selective distribution system will also be caught if the refusal is intended to consolidate the agreements between the manufacturer and its distributors.[422]

The concept of concerted practices was more closely defined in the *Dyestuffs* cases.[423] In general terms the Court defined this concept as 'a form of co-ordination between undertakings which, without having reached the stage where an agreement properly so called has been concluded, knowingly substitutes practical co-operation between them for the risks of

416. Case 51/75 *EMI Records Ltd. v. CBS United Kingdom Ltd.* [1976] ECR 811 at 849. 'It is sufficient if the undertakings in question have expressed their joint intention to conduct themselves on the market in a specific way,' Case T-7/89 *SA Hercules Chemicals NV v. Commission* [1991] ECR II-1711 at 1804 (citing earlier case-law).
417. Case 123/83 *Bureau national interprofessionnel du cognac v. Clair* [1985] ECR 391 at 424.
418. Case 56/65 *Société Technique Minière v. Maschinenbau Ulm GmbH* [1966] ECR 235 at 248–249; Cases 56 and 58/64 *Consten and Grundig* [1966] ECR 299 at 339; Case 32/65 *Italy v. Council and Commission* [1966] ECR 389 at 407.
419. Case 28/77 *Tepea BV v. Commission* [1978] ECR 1391 at 1413–1417;
420. Case 41/69 *ACF Chemiefarma NV v. Commission* [1970] ECR 661 at 693, and Case T-141/89 *Tréfileurope Sales SARL v. Commission* [1995] ECR II-791 at 830–831. No-challenge agreements relating to industrial property licensing may under certain circumstances be caught, Case 65/86 *Bayer AG et al. v. Süllhöfer* [1988] ECR 5249 at 5286–5287.
421. Cases 32 and 36–82/78 *BMW Belgium SA et al. v. Commission* [1979] ECR 2435 at 2476–2478; Case C-277/87 *Sandoz prodotti farmaceutici SpA v. Commission* [1990] ECR I-45 (summary publication, mentioning an export ban on the invoices). See, further, Dec. 96/478 (O.J. 1996 L 201/1) *ADALAT*, under appeal in Case T-41/96 *Bayer AG v. Commission* (O.J. 1996 C 145/13), see Case T-41/96 R *Bayer AG v. Commission* [1996] ECR II-381, [1996] 5 CMLR 290.
422. Case 107/82 *Allgemeine Elektricitäts-Gesellschaft AEG-Telefunken AG v. Commission* [1983] ECR 3151 at 3194–3196. See also Cases 25 and 26/84 *Ford-Werke AG et al. v. Commission* [1985] ECR 2725 at 2743 (implicit acceptance by dealers of manufacturer's decision as to which models will be supplied).
423. E.g. Case 48/69 *Imperial Chemical Industries Ltd. v. Commission* [1972] ECR 619, [1972] CMLR 557.

competition.'[424] The co-ordination must be apparent from the behaviour of the participants. While parallel behaviour does not automatically mean a concerted practice, as any undertaking is entitled to adapt its behaviour to its competitors' present or foreseeable behaviour, it may 'amount to strong evidence of such a practice if it leads to conditions of competition which do not correspond to the normal conditions of the market, having regard to the nature of the products, the size and number of the undertakings, and the volume of the said markets.'[425] Thus in various of the *Polypropylene* judgments,[426] the Court of First Instance upheld the Commission's conclusion that there was a concerted practice where, having participated in meetings at which price and sales volume targets were set and information was exchanged, an undertaking not only pursued 'the aim of eliminating in advance uncertainty about the future conduct of its competitors but also, in determining the policy which it intended to follow on the market it could not fail to take account, directly or indirectly, of the information it obtained during the course of those meetings. Similarly, in determining the policy which they intended to follow, its competitors were bound to take into account the information disclosed to them by the applicant about the course of conduct which the applicant itself had decided upon or which it contemplated adopting on the market.'[427] The examples of the Commission attacking concerted practices are legion, although there have on occasions been problems with the burden of proof, so that if there are other plausible explanations for the parallel conduct,[428] it may well be accepted that it merely reflects a reaction to moves in the market place, rather than pre-baked conduct. If, though, there have been contacts at which price behaviour was discussed, it will in fact be pretty easy for the Commission to demonstrate the

424. [1972] ECR 619 at 655. See also Case 49/69 *Badische Anilin- und Soda-Fabrik AG v. Commission* [1972] ECR 713 at 733.
425. *Ibid.* See also Cases 40/73 *etc. Coöperatieve Vereniging 'Suiker Unie' UA et al. v. Commission* [1975] ECR 1663 at 1942–1943 and 1944–1945 and Cases 100–103/80 *SA Musique Diffusion Française et al. v.* Commission [1983] ECR 1825 at 1897–1899.
426. Three batches of judgments were handed down, the first on 24 October 1991, *e.g.* Case T-1/89 *Rhône-Poulenc SA v. Commission* [1991] ECR II-867, the second on 17 December 1991, *e.g.* Case 6/89 *Enichem Anic SpA v. Commission* [1991] ECR II-1623, and the third on 10 March 1992, *e.g.* Case T-9/89 *Hüls AG v. Commission* [1992] ECR II-299. A number of these judgments are under appeal (*e.g.* Case T-4/89 *BASF AG v. Commission* [1991] ECR II-1523 as Case C-225/92 P *BASF AG v. Commission* (O.J. 1992 C 187/10), Case 6/89 *Enichem* as Case C-49/92 P *Commission v. Enichem Anic SpA* (O.J. 1992 C 77/5), and Case T-10/89 *Hoechst AG v. Commission* [1992] ECR II-629 as Case C-227/92 P *Hoechst AG v. Commission* (O.J. 1992 C 167/9)).
427. This is repeated in a number of the polypropylene judgments, *e.g.* Case T-1/89 *Rhône-Poulenc SA v. Commission* [1991] ECR 867 at 1074, and Case T-7/89 *SA Hercules Chemicals NV v. Commission* [1991] ECR II-1711 at 1805–1806.
428. *E.g.* Cases 89/85 *etc. A. Åhlström Osakeyhtiö et al. v. Commission* [1993] ECR I-1307 at 1599 and 1603–1614 (*Wood Pulp*), and Cases 29 and 30/83 *Compagnie Royale Asturienne des Mines SA et al. v. Commission* [1984] ECR 1679 at 1702.

existence of a cartel.[429] If dates of price movements are very close,[430] and if there is an absence of competitive trading, or if commercially competitive information has been exchanged,[431] the scent of prohibited practices will be strong. The nature of a concerted practice will always require a careful analysis of the relevant market and the conduct of the undertakings concerned.[432]

Restriction of competition. If it appears from the content of the agreement that it is apt to restrict competition between the parties and/or third parties,[433] according to the Court in the judgments in Cases 56 and 58/64 *Établissements Consten SARL and Grundig-Verkaufs-GmbH v. Commission*[434] and Case 56/65 *Société Technique Minière v. Maschinenbau Ulm GmbH*,[435] its practical effect on competition need not be examined. In the

429. The Commission will not have to show that parallel behaviour occurred or that the price movements were implemented, *Polypropylene, e.g.* Case T-6/89 *Enichem Anic SpA v. Commission* [1991] ECR II-1623 at 1662–1663 (under appeal, see note 426, *supra*).
430. *E.g.* Case 48/69 *Imperial Chemical Industries Ltd. v. Commission* [1972] ECR 619 at 657–661; Cases T-68/89 *etc. Società Italiano Vetro SpA v. Commission* [1992] ECR II-1403 at 1468–1476. In Cases C-89/85 *etc. Wood Pulp* [1993] ECR I-1307 at 1604 the Court did take note of the effect of rapid means of communication and of well-informed trade buyers on the widespread and rapid availability of information throughout the sector concerned on price movements.
431. *E.g.* Case 172/80 *Züchner v. Bayerische Vereinsbank AG* [1981] ECR 2021 at 2033; Case 86/82 *Hasselblad (GB) Ltd. v. Commission* [1984] ECR 883 at 903–904.
432. Which may require the Court to appoint experts to advise it, as happened in *Dyestuffs* and *Wood Pulp*. The complex analysis required often leads to lengthy litigation. Two sets of litigation stemmed from aspects discovered by the Commission in the course of the *Polypropylene* proceedings. In the *PVC* litigation, the Court of Justice annulled Dec. 89/190 (O.J. 1989 L 74/1) in Case C-137/92 P *Commission v. BASF AG et al.* [1994] ECR I-2555 on procedural grounds (quashing the earlier judgment of the Court of First Instance in Cases T-79/89 *BASF AG et al. v. Commission* [1992] ECR II-315). The Commission then adopted Dec. 94/599 (O.J. 1994 L 239/14) which repeated the substantive findings in the earlier decision, reflecting a stricter policy, as in earlier years the Commission tended not to take new decisions in this field where earlier ones had been annulled for procedural reasons. Dec. 94/599 is now under appeal in Cases T-305/94 *etc. NV Limburgse Vinyl Maatschappij v. Commission* (O.J. 1994 C 331/6). In the *LdPE* litigation, Dec. 89/191 (O.J. 1989 L 74/21) was annulled for procedural reasons, following the Court of Justice's attitude in the *PVC* litigation, in Cases T-80/89 *etc. BASF AG et al. v. Commission* [1995] ECR II-729. As to further illustrations of the difficulties in information exchanges and other collusive conduct, see the various judgments of 14 May 1998 (*e.g.* Case T-311/94 *BPB de Eendracht NV v. Commission* [1998] ECR II-nyr).
433. Case 32/65 *Italy v. Council and Commission* [1966] ECR 389 at 407. Third parties might be affected by *e.g.* a clause prohibiting parallel imports by third parties, or restrictions on third party access to technology or supplies, or restrictions on participation in trade fairs, or discriminatory tariffs.
434. [1966] ECR 299 at 342.
435. [1966] ECR 235 at 249.

first instance, therefore, an examination of the individual clauses of the agreement and of its scope as a whole will be sufficient. Moreover, the economic context of the implementation of the agreement must be taken into account. Agreements which do not significantly affect the competitive position of third parties, the marketing possibilities of suppliers or the market position of buyers will not be caught by Article 85 EC.[436] The *de minimis* rule applies even if absolute *territorial* protection is conferred. In the latest version of the Notice on Minor Agreements[437] the Commission, following the Court's indication, stated that agreements where the impact of the agreement on intra-Community trade or on competition is not appreciable, Article 85(1) EC will not be applicable. Thus agreements which are not capable of significantly affecting trade between Member States should be examined on the basis of, and within the framework of, national legislation alone. In order to fall within the terms of this Notice the maximum market share of the relevant product market in the relevant territorial part of the common market is 5% for horizontal agreements, 10% for vertical agreements, and 5% where it is difficult to classify the agreement as one type or the other. These market shares may be exceeded by no more than one-tenth during successive financial years without the Notice becoming inapplicable. However, the new version defines more precisely the relevant product market[438] and the relevant geographical market[439] than was the case in the earlier versions. The practical importance of the Notice has thus been increased (partly in response to criticisms received). The reference to market share rather than to turnover will simplify matters for larger undertakings active in many sectors. In point 6 of the Notice it is rightly pointed out that it is without prejudice to the powers of the Court of Justice or national courts. It can be seen as a sort of collective negative clearance to avoid the need for individual negative clearance and notifications.[440] As a rule the Commission will not commence proceedings in relation to these agreements, nor will it, in the absence of negligence, consider imposing fines.[441]

In its judgment in Case 56/65 *Société Technique Minière*[442] the Court added that if it does not appear from the examination of the content of the agreement that a restriction of competition was intended the effect of the agreement on competition still has to be examined. It then has to be

436. Case 5/69 *Völk v. Établissements J. Vervaecke* [199] ECR 295 at 302.
437. O.J. 1997 C 372/13.
438. Point 14. See also the Commission's Notice on the definition of the relevant market (OJ 1997 C 372/5).
439. Point 15.
440. See Point 4 of the Notice.
441. See point 5 of the Notice. Sometimes, though, reliance on the Notice will be to no avail, see *e.g.* Dec. 92/427 (O.J. 1992 L 235/9) *Quantel International Continuum/ Quantel SA* (para. 43).
442. [1966] ECR 235 at 249.

ascertained whether the competition is actually prevented, restricted, or distorted to an appreciable extent. For this purpose a comparison should be made with the competition that would exist without the agreement. Thus it is clearly the context of the agreement rather than the text of the agreement which is important.[443] In the case of an exclusive dealing agreement the nature and quantity of the products to which the agreement relates will have to be taken into account.[444] Furthermore the position the producer and the exclusive dealer occupy in the market for these products will have to be investigated, as will whether the agreement is an isolated one or whether it forms part of a complex of agreements, and whether the rules serving to protect the exclusive dealer are very radical, effectively preventing access to the relevant market, or on the contrary allow re-exportation and parallel importation of the products in question. It appears from the brewery judgments that the relationship with other agreements need not be a legal relationship.[445] If a great many agreements with similar or complementary competition-restricting effect merely exist side by side, the agreements may fall within Article 85, although the contracting parties to the individual agreements are in no way responsible for this relationship.[446]

It is submitted that this case-law of the Court contains something to go by in taking a view in the fierce dogmatic controversy raging in the literature on the concept of restriction of competition. The whole discussion as to whether competition is intended to mean perfect competition, or *funktionsfähiger Wettbewerb*, or 'workable competition' and what is to be understood by these terms, is cut off by the Court by the requirement that a comparison must be made with the competition that would exist without the agreement.[447] This will sometimes be a competition

443. Cases 29 and 30/83 *Compagnie Royale Asturienne des Mines SA et al. v. Commission* [1984] ECR 1679 at 1703–1704; Cases 142 and 156/84 *British American Tobacco Company Ltd. et al. v. Commission* [1987] ECR 4487 at 4577 and 4583.

444. 56/65 *Société Technique Minière* [1966] ECR 235 at 250.

445. Case 23/67 *SA Brasserie de Haecht v. Wilkin et al.* [1967] ECR 407 at 415; Case C-234/89 *Delimitis v. Henniger Bräu AG* [1991] ECR I-935 at 986–987, relating to the effect of a network of vertical agreements.

446. The key concept is the effect of the network of agreements as barriers to entry for third parties, see Case C-234/89 *Delimitis v. Henniger Bräu AG* [1991] ECR I-935 at 986–987. The degree of market saturation and customer brand loyalty may also be relevant barriers to entry. The Court's approach is not confined to brewery contracts, see *e.g.* Case C-393/92 *Gemeente Almelo et al. v. Energiebedrijf Ijsselmij NV* [1994] ECR I-1518–1519. As to the relationship between network agreements and the Commission's *de minimis* Notice (see note 437, *supra*), see Cases T-7/93 *Langnese-Iglo GmbH v. Commission* [1995] ECR II-1533 at 1572 *et seq.* (under appeal in Case C-279/95 P *Langnese-Iglo GmbH v. Commission* (O.J. 1995 C 286/3), and Case T-9/93 *Schöller Lebensmittel GmbH & Co. KG v. Commission* [1995] ECR II-1611 at 1642 *et seq.*

447. Case 56/65 *Société Technique Minière v. Maschinenbau Ulm GmbH* [1966] ECR 235 at 250; Case 172/80 *Züchner v. Bayerische Vereinsbank AG* [1981] ECR 2021 at 2033; Case 42/84 *Remia BV et al. v. Commission* [1985] ECR 2545 at 2571–2572 and Case

between many firms, sometimes one between few firms, sometimes competition between many or few firms with monopolistic elements. Typical of this last situation is the common form of competition where many or few producers have, by differentiation of their product, by trade marks, special packaging, advertising *etc.*, built up a limited monopolistic position for their product. This makes possible, *inter alia*, price differentials as compared with competing products (other brands) within certain limits. In view of this limited monopolistic position of a branded product it would seem that agreements for resale price maintenance for this product as well as exclusive dealing agreements which prevent or restrict competition in this product at trade level as a rule have to be considered as apt to restrict competition within the meaning of Article 85. This will specifically be so if there are marked price differentials between the various brands; in fact it is from the very possibility of maintaining price differentials that the comparative monopolistic position (or the existence of a relevant sectoral market) of a branded product will often become apparent.[448] With regard to more homogeneous products on the other hand (such as beer) as a rule only actual parallelism of the relevant market behaviour of the majority of producers will make it possible to speak of a competition-restricting *effect* of these types of agreement. This can also occur when the overwhelming proportion of producers apply selective distribution systems which through comparable effects exclude sales of the products concerned through certain channels of distribution.[449] In so far as individual agreements in such cases do not aim at or have the effect of already appreciable restrictions on competition a penetrating investigation of the market structure will often be necessary in order to ascertain the competition-restricting effects.

Quite generally speaking, a restriction of competition would seem to be involved if two requirements are met. In the first place, the agreement will have to restrict the free market behaviour or market policy of one or more of the parties on one point or another. In the second place, either an intended effect on third parties or an actual effect on the position of third parties (competitors, suppliers, or buyers) will have to be established. In the case of horizontal agreements an intended effect on third parties will generally follow simply from the content of the agreement, the number of parties to it, and their joint market position. Thus, a clause in a labour contract to the effect that the worker is not to establish, after termination

---

C-41/90 *Höfner and Elser v. Macrotron GmbH* [1991] ECR 2010 at 2017.

448. However, for an exception to this rule, see the judgment in Case 5/69 *Völk v. Établissements J. Vervaecke* [1969] ECR 295 at 302.

449. See Case 23/67 *SA Brasserie de Haecht v. Wilkin et al.* [1967] ECR 407, [1968] CMLR 26; Case 99/79 *SA Lancôme et al. v. Etos BV et al.* [1980] ECR 2511, [1981] 2 CMLR 164; Case 31/80 *L'Oréal NV et al. v. De Nieuwe AMCK PvbA* [1980] ECR 3775, [1981] 2 CMLR 235; Case 26/76 *Metro SB-Großmärkte GmbH & Co. KG v. Commission* [1977] ECR 1875, [1978] 2 CMLR 1 and Case 75/84 *Metro SB-Großmärkte GmbH & Co. KG v. Commission* [1986] ECR 3021, [1987] 1 CMLR 118.

of the contract, a competing business cannot as a rule be looked upon as a restriction of competition within the meaning of Article 85(1),[450] but a multilateral price agreement can. In order to be effective they must always embrace most market participants thus leaving buyers with very little room for manoeuvre. In the case of bilateral vertical agreements (exclusive dealing agreements, resale price maintenance, long-term selling contracts), on the other hand, as a rule a more detailed examination of the market position of the parties involved, the specific characteristics of the product, and the alternatives for competitors, suppliers, or buyers will have to take place. Unlike in classical forms of cartels which are probably primarily thought of in the examples quoted in Article 85(1)(a)–(d), market domination and the resulting influence on the position of third parties does not automatically result from the restriction of competition between the parties.[451] Often competition for third parties is not on the whole restricted. Whether the possibility of competition for third parties is significantly restricted will appear from extraneous circumstances.[452] Thus not all provisions of an agreement which have an effect on competition fall *per se* under the prohibition of Article 85(1) EC.[453] The above considerations make it plain that a thorough market analysis is always required, making the use of economists indispensable.

It should be noted that Article 85 EC is also concerned with agreements which prohibit unlawful or unfair competition, to the extent that it is not prohibited under Community or national legislation or case-law.[454] This point is relevant in particular for attempts to prevent parallel importers from benefitting for example from a 'free rider' on the back of advertising campaigns by official dealers in the product concerned. Here too, a parallel can be drawn with the case-law on Articles 30 and 34 EC.[455]

The effect on inter-state trade. As regards the second criterion, *i.e.* the possible[456] adverse effect of the agreement (or particular clauses there-

450. But *cf.* non-competition clauses on purchase of the goodwill of a business, Dec. 76/743 (O.J. 1976 L 254/40) *Reuter/BASF* and Dec. 83/670 (O.J. 1983 L 376/22) *Nutricia*, on appeal Case 42/84 *Remia BV et al. v. Commission* [1985] ECR 2545 (appeal dismissed).
451. There are also forms of horizontal cartels, such as specialization agreements and research cooperation in which market dominance is not always present, thus a closer investigation of the influence of the cartel on the position of third parties is necessary.
452. See *e.g.* Case 1/71 *SA Cadillon v. Firma Höss, Maschinenbau KG* [1971] ECR 351, [1971] CMLR 420 and Case 22/71 *Béguelin Import Co. et al. v. SAGL Import Export et al.* [1971] ECR 949, [1972] CMLR 81.
453. See Case 161/84 *Pronuptia de Paris GmbH v. Pronuptia de Paris Irmgard Schillgalis* [1986] ECR 353 at 380–384, see the different approach of VerLoren van Themaat, Adv. Gen. at 358 *et seq.*
454. Case 258/78 *L.C. Nungesser KG et al. v. Commission* [1982] ECR 2015 at 2068–2071.
455. *Cf.* Case 8/74 *Procureur du Roi v. Dassonville et al.* [1974] ECR 837 at 852.
456. Case 226/84 *British Leyland plc v. Commission* [1986] ECR 3263 at 3300–3302 (in relation to Art. 86 EC).

of)[457] on trade between two or more Member States, the Court observed in Case 56/65 *Société Technique Minière*[458] that 'it must be possible to foresee with a sufficient degree of probability on the basis of a set of objective factors of law or of fact that the agreement in question may have an influence, direct or indirect, actual or potential, on the pattern of trade between Member States.' The Court investigated in particular whether the agreement was 'capable of bringing about a partitioning of the market in certain products between Member States and thus rendering more difficult the interpenetration of trade which the Treaty is intended to create.'[459] This definition made it clear that the criterion of effect on trade between Member States is not only applicable to agreements concerning imports and exports.[460] Thus agreements which are confined to the territory of one Member State may, through acting as barriers to entry, hinder the interpenetration of national markets which the EC Treaty seeks to achieve. This is also true of agreements which have an indirect effect on trade between Member States, by, for example, prescribing minimum prices for semi-finished products which are not traded between Member States but which form the raw materials for a final product which is traded within between Member States.[461] The Court has expressly pointed out that even if as a result of the agreement there is an *increase* in intra-Community trade, the agreement may still be held to infringe Article 85(1) EC.[462] A clear example of such a circumstance is where a sales office charges higher prices for domestic sales in order to subsidize lower prices for products for export; such a practice has unfavourable effects on intra-Community trade in the same way as an export subsidy does for the purposes of Article 92 EC.

The formulation of the trade between Member States criterion appears, at least at first sight, to be the same as that in the classic definition of

---

457. Case 193/83 *Windsurfing International Inc. v. Commission* [1986] ECR 611 at 664 the Court held that Community law did not require that each individual clause in an agreement should be capable of affecting intra-Community trade. Community law applied to agreements between undertakings which may affect such trade; only if the agreement as a whole was capable of affecting trade would it be necessary to examine which clauses had as their object or effect a restriction or distortion of competition.

458. [1966] ECR 235 at 249. See also Cases 56 and 58/64 *Consten and Grundig* [1969] ECR 299 at 341, and Case 5/69 *Völk v. Vervaecke* [1969] ECR 295 at 302.

459. *Ibid.*

460. Case 43/69 *Brauerei A. Bilger Söhne GmbH v. Jehle et al.* [1970] ECR 127 at 135; Case 8/72 *Vereeniging van Cementhandelaren v. Commission* [1972] ECR 977 at 990–991; Case 126/80 *Salonia v. Poidomani et al.* [1981] ECR 1563 at 1578–1579; Cases 240/82 etc. *Stichting Sigarettenindustrie et al. v. Commission* [1985] ECR 3831 at 3783–3784; Case 65/86 *Bayer AG et al. v. Süllhöfer* [1988] ECR 5249 at 5286; Case 246/86 *Belasco et al. v. Commission* [1989] ECR 2117 at 2190–2191, and Case C-393/92 *gemeente Almelo et al. v. Energiebedrijf Ijsselmij NV* [1994] ECR I-1477 at 1518–1519.

461. Case 123/83 *Bureau national interprofessionnel du cognac v. Clair* [1985] ECR 391 at 425.

462. Cases 56 and 58/64 *Consten and Grundig* [1966] ECR 299 at 341.

measures having equivalent effect to quantitative restrictions on imports contained in Case 8/74 *Procureur du Roi v. Dassonville et al.*[463] This demonstrates again that Article 85 EC is to be seen as an extension of the first concept of freedom, explained in Chapter VII, above, which demonstrates that it does not merely concern agreements which hinder the establishment of a common market, but also agreements which hinder the functioning of that market as a market economy characterized by effective competition. A horizontal international price agreement, too, obstructs this instrumental function of the common market, although it is a matter for argument whether it erects trade barriers between Member States.[464] A word of caution is, however appropriate about the parallel interpretation of Articles 30 and 85 EC,[465] as in relation to the latter (and Article 86 EC), the Court speaks of affecting the pattern of trade between Member States, rather than affecting trade between Member States *simpliciter*. Thus, in Case 22/78 *Hugin Kassaregistr AB et al. v. Commission*,[466] the Court annulled the Commission's decision (relating to Article 86 EC) on the ground that there was no pattern of trade between Member States involved.[467]

The question also arises whether the criterion of effect on trade between Member States is of substantive importance or merely a jurisdictional criterion, drawing the dividing line between the competence of Community and national competition law. In Cases 56 and 58/64 *Consten and Grundig*[468] the Court clearly took the latter line. This is understandable, given that an agreement which prevents, restricts or distorts competition in the common market will always have an adverse effect on trade between Member States.[469] In Case 73/74 *Groupement des fabricants de papiers peints de Belgique et al. v. Commission*[470] the Court decided that the burden of proof of the possible effect on trade between Member States lay

463. [1974] ECR 837 at 852.
464. The Court also appears to be thinking in this direction in Case 48/69 *Imperial Chemical Industries Ltd. v. Commission* [1972] ECR 619, [1972] CMLR 557 and Case 8/72 *Vereeniging van Cementhandelaren v. Commission* [1972] ECR 977, [1973] CMLR 7.
465. See, generally, VerLoren van Themaat (1996) SEW 398.
466. [1979] ECR 1869 at 1989–1901.
467. The phrase 'patterns of trade' emerged early on, see Case 56/65 *Société Technique Minière* [1966] ECR 235 at 249; Case 5/69 *Völk v. Vervaecke* [1969] ECR 295 at 302; Case 61/80 *Coöperatieve Stremsel- en kleurselfabriek v. Commission* [1981] ECR 851 at 867, and Case 42/84 *Remia BV et al. v. Commission* [1985] ECR 2545 at 2572. Had the approach used in relation to Art. 30 EC been followed in *Hugin*, the result might well have been different (at least in relation to Liptons' attempts to obtain spare parts from Hugin dealers in other Member States).
468. [1966] ECR 299 at 341.
469. However, an example of a restriction of competition in the common market which has no effect on trade between Member States is a national common selling agency for exports to third countries, see Decs. 68/374 (O.J. 1968 L 276/13, corrigendum O.J. 1968 L 291/14) *Cobelaz I* and 68/375 (O.J. 1968 L 276/19) *Cobelaz II*.
470. [1975] ECR 1491 at 1514.

on the Commission (clearly, in national litigation it will be on the party seeking to challenge the agreement). It also held that the reasoning may be given in a summary manner and can refer to the grounds adduced in earlier decisions.

Extra-territorial effect. The fact that one of the undertakings participating in an agreement is established in a third country does not prevent the applicability of Article 85 if the agreement has effects within the territory of the common market.[471] This means that the effects doctrine applies, even if the Court does not itself use that term, so that it makes no difference to the applicability of Article 85 EC where the parties to an agreement are situated, or where the agreement is concluded: if an agreement has effects within the common market it falls within Community jurisdiction, assuming that it satisfies the trade between Member States test explained above. In any event the effects doctrine will often not need to be specifically applied as third country undertakings can be regarded as having themselves acted within the common market (for example by imputing the conduct of a subsidiary to the parent).[472]

The effects doctrine does not however solve all problems concerning the application of Community competition law to undertakings situated in third countries, particularly in relation to obtaining information and the enforcement of fines or daily penalties.[473] Thus it has been necessary to coordinate the application of Articles 85 and 86 EC through bilateral or multilateral agreements,[474] in particular concerning conflicts between Com-

471. Case 22/71 *Béguelin Import Co. et al. v. SAGL Import Export et al.* [1971] ECR 949 at 959; Cases 89/85 *etc. Wood Pulp* [1988] ECR 5193 at 5242–5244. See Torremans (1996) 21 ELRev. 280.
472. See Case 48/69 *Imperial Chemical Industries Ltd v. Commission* [1972] ECR 619 at 662–663 and Case 52/69 *J.R. Geigy AG v. Commission* [1972] ECR 787 at 835–837. See also Case 28/77 *Tepea BV v. Commission* [1988] ECR 1391 at 1416. The effects doctrine in Community competition law can be regarded an a logical extension of the general formula used in relation to Arts. 48 and 59 EC in Case 36/74 *Walrave and Koch v. Association Union Cycliste Internationale et al.* [1974] ECR 1405 at 1420.
473. Or even in relation to the enforcement of a third country's laws against disclosure of business secrets to punish 'whistle-blowers' such as Stanley Adams, see Case 145/83 *Adams v. Commission* [1985] ECR 3539, [1986] 1 CMLR 506. See also *Adams v. Staatsanwalt des Kantons Basel-Stadt* [1978] 3 CMLR 480.
474. In 1991 the Commission concluded an agreement with the United States providing for cooperation in competition matters, [1991] 4 CMLR 823, see Ham (1993) 30 CMLRev. 571, but this was annulled on the ground of lack of competence by the Court in Case C-327/91 *France v. Commission* [1994] ECR I-3641, [1994] 5 CMLR 517. As a result a new agreement was concluded between the Council and the Commission (for the Community) and the United States, see Dec. 95/145 (O.J. 1995 L 95/45) and the exchange of letters dealing with confidentiality questions (O.J. 1995 L 131/38); see the Commission's reports, COM (96) 479 Final and COM (97) 246 Final. Dec. 98/386 (O.J. 1998 L 173/26) deals with the agreement on the application of positive comity principles between the US and EC in respect of competition law. As to the

munity and American competition law.[475] This also applies in respect of export cartels agreed by undertakings based in the Community which may only fall within the scope of Community competition law through their possible side-effects within the common market. Provisions identical to Articles 85 and 86 EC are contained in countless association and free trade agreements which the Community has concluded with third countries,[476] and with the establishment of the EEA on 1 January 1994 an equivalent system has been established with an EFTA Surveillance Authority responsible for competition law policy and enforcement.[477]

Competition and Anti-dumping. International coordination of Community competition law and the competition law of third countries is desirable in order to permit effective action against individual or collective anti-dumping practices.[478] Thereby the phenomenon of anti-dumping measures leading to a reinforcement of the formation of cartels in the markets concerned can be avoided.[479]

4.2.1 Article 85(2) EC: the nullity of prohibited agreements

Article 85(2) EC provides that any agreements or decisions prohibited pursuant to Article 85(1) shall be automatically void;[480] this sanction is directly effective.[481]. With respect to the scope of the nullity, which makes enforcement impossible,[482] the Court has decided that only those parts of an agreement which fall within the prohibition are automatically void; the agreement as a whole is only void if these parts cannot be severed from

international dimension in general, see Cheng (ed.), *International Harmonization of Competition Laws* (London, 1995); Doern and Wilks (eds.), *Comparative Competition Policy: National Institutions in a Global Market* (Oxford, 1996) and De León (1997) ECLR 162.

475. *E.g.* Dec. 91/301 (O.J. 1991 L 152/54) *ANSAC*.
476. As to competition and the Europe Agreements, see Van den Bossche (1997) ECLR 24.
477. The equivalent provisions to Arts. 85 and 86 EC are Arts. 53 and 54 EEA. As to the EEA, see Blanchet *et al.*, *The Agreement on the European Economic Area (EEA)* (Oxford, 1994); Bright (ed.), *Business Law in the European Economic Area* (Oxford, 1994), Diem (1994) ECLR 263, and Norberg *et al.*, *EEA Law* (Stockholm, 1993).
478. See, generally, Marceau, *Anti-Dumping and Anti-Trust Issues in Free Trade Areas* (Oxford, 1994).
479. See Decs. 92/444 (O.J. 1992 L 246/37) *Scottish Salmon Board* (see Forrester and Norall (1992) 12 YBEL 547 at 582–584 and *XXIInd Report on Competition Policy 1992* (Brussels, Luxembourg, 1993) point 156) and Dec. 92/262 (O.J. 1992 L 134/1) *French–West African Shipowners' Committee*.
480. The consequences in national law of a breach of Art. 85(1) EC may include liability in tort, damages and restitution of sums paid but not due.
481. Case 127/73 *Belgische Radio en Televisie et al. v. SV SABAM et al.* [197] ECR 51 at 62–63.
482. Case 22/71 *Béguelin* [1971] ECR 949 at 961–962.

the other parts of the agreement,[483] as in the case of permissible parts which form a compensation for the prohibited parts, or where the agreements are daughter contracts implementing or supplementing a void agreement. In Case 319/82 *Société de Vente de Ciments et Betons de l'est SA* v. *Kerpen & Kerpen GmbH & Co. KG*[484] the Court made it clear that the consequences of the nullity of certain parts of an agreement for other parts of the agreement must be a matter for national law to decide. The application of the nullity sanction in terms of time is discussed briefly in section 4.2.3, below.[485]

4.2.2   Article 85(3) EC: exemptions

The prohibition of Article 85(1) EC may be declared inapplicable, either individually or generically, if two positive and two negative requirements are met.

Positive requirements. The *first* positive requirement is that the agreement or group of agreements must contribute to the improvement of the production or the distribution of the products or to the promotion of technical or economic progress. According to the judgment of the Court in Cases 56 and 58/64 *Grundig and Consten*[486] subjective advantages for the undertakings involved in the agreement are not sufficient. Distinct objective advantages must be involved, which tend to offset the disadvantages of the restriction of competition. Examples of such advantages include reduction of the undertaking's costs and improvement in quality. Reduction of costs and improvement of quality are also the first factors to be considered for the fulfillment of the *second* positive requirement, *viz.* that a fair share of the benefit resulting from the objective improvements must be passed on to the consumers. A specialization agreement, therefore, will have to lead, for instance, to lower prices or better qualities for buyers than might be expected without the agreement. If the agreement relates to secondary conditions of competition, such as conditions of supply and payment, supplementary supply of services, guarantees and warranties and the like, the positive effects for the buyers will naturally also have to flow to the

---

483. Cases 56 and 58/64 *Consten and Grundig* [1966] ECR 299 at 344; Case 56/65 *Société Technique Minière* [1966] ECR 235 at 250.
484. [1983] ECR 4173 at 4184.
485. At the beginning of that section.
486. [1966] ECR 299 at 348. As an example of an agreement which would otherwise satisfy the criteria of Art. 85(3) but was refused exemption because of action extrinsic to the agreement itself (a decision to cease supplying right-hand-drive cars in Germany, following complaints from dealers in the United Kingdom) see Dec. 83/560 (O.J. 1983 L 327/31), upheld on appeal as Cases 25 and 26/84 *Ford-Werke AG et al.* v. *Commission* [1985] ECR 2725, [1985] 3 CMLR 528.

users. The concept of consumers in Article 85(3) EC may well also embrace other buyers as end-users, not merely final consumers.[487]

Economic Policy objectives. It is not yet entirely clear to what extent the objectives of economic policy of the authorities which are favourably viewed at the Community level can or must play a role in these positive requirements.[488] It is not enough that the agreement conforms with objectives of national economic policy. In this respect account must be taken of the fact that the Member States have lost their powers in certain areas, such as the common commercial policy. In relation to other Community policies it may be that an agreement will have to be examined in the light of the objectives and means concerned.[489] But even if the Member States are free to act, the objectives concerned must be positively viewed also from the Community standpoint. This may be apparent because of the existence of specific Community action programmes for the achievement of the objectives involved (*e.g.* in the fields of scientific research and technological development,[490] energy-saving, environmental protection, health, transport,[491] and crisis management[492]). Indications can also be found in the (new) Treaty provisions on sectoral, horizontal and flanking competences, Community programmes on medium-term economic policy and other policy declarations at Community level.

487. *E.g.* in relation to specialization and cooperation agreements in the pharmaceutical sector, see Dec. 79/298 (O.J. 1979 L 19/32) *Beecham/Parke Davis*. See also WQ 307/84 (Welsh) (O.J. 1984 C 243/2). The interests of consumers mean that after-sales service and guarantees must be available throughout the Community, irrespective of where the product is purchased. The assessment of the alleged benefits of fixed book price agreements has led to considerable controversy (particularly as regards language areas covering more than one Member State), see, generally, Dec. 82/123 (O.J. 1982 L 54/36) *VBBB/VBVB*, upheld on appeal in Cases 43 and 63/82 *Vereniging ter Bevordering van het Vlaamse Boekwezen, VBVB et al. v. Commission* [1984] ECR 19, [1985] 1 CMLR 27, and Dec. 89/44 (O.J. 1989 L 22/12) *Publishers Association – Net Book Agreements*, annulled in part in Case C-360/92 P *Publishers Association v. Commission* [1995] ECR I-23, [1995] 5 CMLR 33 (quashing the decision in Case T-66/89 *Publishers Association v. Commission* [1992] ECR II-1995, [1992] 5 CMLR 120). The judgment in Case C-360/92 P makes it plain that the beneficial effects do not have to occur only on the territory of the Member States in which the parties are established, they may occur anywhere in the Community, [1985] ECR I-23 at 68. See Gormley (1997) 34 CMLRev. 401, and further, O.J. 1997 C 305/2.
488. *E.g.* employment, see Case 26/76 *Metro SB-Großmärkte GmbH & Co. KG v. Commission* [1977] ECR 1875 at 1916.
489. This principle is laid down in Reg. 26 (O.J. English Special Edition 1959–1962, p. 129 (as to which, see section 4.3, *post*), see Case 71/74 *Nederlandse Vereniging voor Fruit en Groentenimporthandel et al. v. Commission et al.* [1975] ECR 563, [1975] 2 CMLR 123 and Dec. 88/109 (O.J. 1988 L 59/25) *New Potatoes*. As an interesting example in the field of development cooperation, see Dec. 80/183 (O.J. 1980 L 39/64) *Cane Sugar*.
490. Dec. 76/248 (O.J. 1976 L 51/7) *United Reprocessors*.
491. Dec. 88/568 (O.J. 1988 L 311/36) *Eurotunnel*.
492. Dec. 83/671 (O.J. 1983 L 376/30) *International Energy Agency*.

Negative requirements. Cartel agreements in particular which have the effect of raising prices directly or indirectly, or which are intended to maintain separate national markets with separate market conditions, will as a rule naturally fail to qualify for exemption, falling at the initial hurdle of the two positive requirements.[493] For the forms of cooperation which are useful – and there are a great many of them – the *first* negative requirement, however, forms the principal barrier to be overcome.[494] This is that the agreement must not impose on the undertakings concerned any restrictions which are not indispensable to the attainment of the positive objectives (the requirement of indispensability).[495] Absolute territorial protection clauses will never get over this hurdle. The requirement of indispensability is by its nature an independent condition which stands apart from the balancing of objective advantages and restrictions of competition required by the first positive condition.

The *second* negative requirement, that the agreement must not enable the undertakings to eliminate competition in respect of a substantial part of the products in question, is a fundamental principle of the intended competition regime as well as an additional guarantee that the three other requirements will be met. While there is as yet scarcely any case-law on this requirement, which demands a precise definition of the relevant market in which competition is eliminated,[496] a guideline for its interpretation is to be found in the somewhat fuller description used in Article 65(2)(c) ECSC. This shows that exclusion of competition is primarily concerned with whether the cartel in question dominates the market as against a substantial proportion of the suppliers or buyers in respect of the principal aspects of competition (particularly quantity and price). Suppliers or buyers, therefore, must have an alternative, which ensures that there is still actual competition.[497] If substitute products exist which are fully comparable as to their useful value and price, competition of substitutes may be sufficient. Potential competition, too, may suffice,

---

493. This is primarily the problem area for the exemption of crisis cartels, see *Eleventh Report on Competition Policy 1981* (Brussels, Luxembourg, 1982) point 46. As examples of the Commission's attitude to crisis (or restructuring) cartels, see Dec. 84/380 (O.J. 1984 L 207/17) *Synthetic Fibres* and Dec. 84/387 O.J. 1984 L 212/1) *BPCL/ICI*.

494. Case 61/80 *Coöperatieve Stremsel- en Kleurselfabriek v. Commission* [1981] ECR 851 at 868; Case 45/85 *Verband der Sachversicherer e.V. v. Commission* [1987] ECR 405 at 462.

495. Cases 56 and 58/64 *Consten and Grundig* [1966] ECR 299 at 349–350. Arguments about indispensability played a major part in the *Net Book Agreement* saga (see note 485, *supra*).

496. See Cases 19 and 20/74 *Kali und Salz AG et al. v. Commission* [1975] ECR 499, [1975] 2 CMLR 154 and Cases 209–215 and 218/78 *Van Landewyck et al. v. Commission* [1980] ECR 3125, [1981] 3 CMLR 134.

497. See the extensive analysis in Case C-234/89 *Delimitis v. Henniger Bräu AG* [1991] ECR I-935, [1992] 5 CMLR 210. See also the Commission's Notice on the definition of the relevant market (O.J. 1997 C 372/5).

but in that case this must be a real possibility, capable of being realized at short notice.[498]

This requirement is referred to as an additional guarantee, because cooperation which brings economic or technical advantages as compared with competitors does not require a dominant position on the market. Conversely, in the absence of such a position the residual competition[499] will guarantee that the advantages of cooperation are passed on to purchasers.[500] When viewed in this light, the four requirements of Article 85(3) form a logical and coherent complex, which is in keeping with the dynamic objectives of Article 2 EC. In particular, dynamic forms of co-operation changing the *status quo* are made possible; attempts to protect existing market positions on the other hand as a rule are not.

4.2.3   The general mechanism of the application of Article 85 EC

Regulation 17. The most important provisions relating to the application of Articles 85 and 86 EC are contained in Regulation 17,[501] which was adopted by the Council under Article 87 EC.

Notification. For the principal competition-restricting agreements falling within Article 85(1), exemption under Article 85(3) can be claimed only for the period after they have been notified on the prescribed form,[502] and after they have been adapted, if necessary, to the four requirements of Article 85(3) discussed above.[503] These cartels 'subject to notification' can be roughly defined as including all agreements enumerated as examples in Article 85 as well as all other agreements which have as their object or

---

498. *Cf.* on this conclusion Case 13/60 *'Geitling' Ruhrkohlen- Verkaufsgesellschaft Bh et al. v. High Authority* [1962] ECR 83, [1962] CMLR 113 and Case 66/63 *Netherlands v. High Authority* [1964] ECR 533, [1964] CMLR 522, both concerning Art. 65 ECSC. In the case of industrial customers it may sometimes be demonstrated that they have the possibility of manufacturing the products concerned themselves. See also the facts in Case 6/72 *Continental Can v. Commission* [1973] ECR 215, [1973] CMLR 199 relating to Art. 86 EC. Because of the element of market domination, the case-law relating to Art. 86 EC forms a useful source of inspiration for the interpretation of Art. 85(3).

499. Case 43/85 *Associazione nazionale commercianti internazionali dentali e sanitari (Ancides) v. Commission* [1987] ECR 3131 at 3154.

500. Case 75/84 *Metro SB-Großmärkte GmbH & Co. KG v. Commission* [1986] ECR 3021 at 3089–3090.

501. O.J. English Special Edition 1959–62, p. 87, most recently amended by the Act of Austrian, Finnish and Swedish Accession.

502. See Reg. 17, Art. 24, and, for the new form A/B, Reg. 3385/94 (O.J. 1994 L 377/28). See Brown (1992) 17 ELRev. 323.

503. For agreements already in existence on the coming into force of Reg. 17 (as to which, see note 515, *infra*) and for accession agreements (those existing agreements which are affected by accession) special provisions applied for notification and adaptation (see Reg. 17, Arts. 5, 7 and 25 (as amended).

effect the prevention, restriction, or distortion of competition, if these agreements relate to trade between two or more Member States directly or apply to undertakings from two or more Member States.[504] National cartels which have only an indirect effect on trade between Member States do not need to be notified.[505] The same applies to individual resale price maintenance agreements, restrictions in bilateral agreements of the rights of the person acquiring or using rights of industrial property or know-how, agreements relating to the development or uniform application of standards and types, and joint research for technical development and specialization in the manufacture of products. For specialization agreements there is a ceiling on market share (15% of a significant area of the common market) and a turnover limit of 200 million ECU.[506] In relation to agreements which satisfy the conditions of the various block exemption regulations prior notification is also unnecessary.

Legal consequences of notification. An extensive body of case-law has arisen on the legal effects of the notification procedure in relation to 'new agreements.'[507] It can be summarized in four points as follows:

1. Agreements subject to notification because they infringe Article 85(1) EC which have not been notified are prohibited by law and are void.[508]
2. In the case of standard agreements with identical content the notification of one agreement also has the legal effects attached to notification with regard to the other agreements.[509]
3. Only notified agreements are eligible for an exemption under Article 85(3) EC.[510] This also applies to agreements not subject to notification.[511]

504. See Reg. 17, Arts. 4 and 5.
505. On direct and indirect effects, see Case 43/63 *Brauerei A. Bilger Söhne GmbH v. Jehle et al.* [1970] ECR 127 at 135; Case 63/75 *SA Fonderies Roubaix-Wattrelos v. Société nouvelle de Fonderies A Roux et al.* [1976] ECR 111, [1976] 1 CMLR 538, and Cases 96/82 etc. *NV IAZ International Belgium et al. v. Commission* [1983] ECR 3369 at 3413 which show that the concept must be interpreted as relating to the degree to which the agreement may isolate the markets.
506. Reg. 17, Art. 4(3). Reg. 417/85, Art. 3 (O.J. 1985 L 53/1, most recently amended by Reg. 2236/97 (O.J. 1997 306/12)) sets thresholds for the application of the block exemption for specialization agreements; agreements falling within block exemptions do not need to be notified.
507. New agreements are those entered into after the entry into force of Reg. 17 (13 March 1962), or after the date of accession of the relevant Member State.
508. Case 13/61 *De Geus v. Bosch* [1962] ECR 45, [1962] CMLR 1.
509. Case 56/65 *Société Technique Minière v. Maschinenbau Ulm GmbH* [1966] ECR 235, [1966] CMLR 357. See, though, the special circumstances in Cases 240/82 etc. *Stichting Sigarettenindustrie et al. v. Commission* [1985] ECR 3831 at 3877–3888.
510. Reg. 17, Art. 4(1); Case 126/80 *Salonia v. Poidomani et al.* [1981] ECR 1563 at 1581–1582.
511. There is no actual obligation to notify an agreement, even if it is subject to notifica-

4. Agreements which have been notified but which have not yet been granted exemption under Article 85(3) EC enjoy immunity from fines (if the notification has been full and frank)[512] unless the Commission has lifted that immunity by means of a so-called Article 15(6) letter.[513] This is a decision within the meaning of Article 189 EC and is thus open to judicial review.[514] The immunity from fines would imply that in cases of doubt about whether an agreement would benefit from Article 85(3) EC it is better to notify than not.

There are myriad judgments dealing with the legal consequences of the notification agreements which were in force at the date of entry into force of Regulation 17; these were known as 'old agreements' and were subject to transitional arrangements created by the Court.[515] In view of the ever diminishing importance of these agreements, it is sufficient for present purposes to note the main point that old agreements notified in good time and non-notified old agreements which were not subject to notification are fully effective until such time as the Commission has taken a decision under the powers conferred upon it.[516]

Negative clearance. After notification, the Commission may upon request issue not only an exemption, but also a so-called negative clearance, to the effect that 'according to the information it has received there are no grounds for it to intervene, under Article 85(1) or Article 86 of the Treaty, with respect to an agreement, decision or practice'.[517] This

tion: it is open to the parties to run the risk of a complaint to the Commission, or own-initiative proceedings being started by the latter, or indeed of civil proceedings in national courts, should they so wish. A decision not to notify may well result from a commercial assessment of the risk of discovery, the benefits of the agreement or conduct to the undertakings, and the likely fines or penalties.

512. A failure to make a full and frank notification may well be penalized, *e.g.* Case 28/77 *Tepea BV v. Commission* [1978] ECR 1391, [1978] 3 CMLR 392.

513. *I.e.* a decision under Reg. 17, Art. 15(6), informing the parties that after preliminary examination the Commission is of opinion that Art. 85(1) EC applies and that the application of Art. 85(3) EC is not justified. See Case 10/69 *Portelange* [1969] ECR 309, [1974] CMLR 426; Decs. 75/570 (O.J. 1975 L 249/27) *Bronbemaling/Heidemij*, 78/571 (O.J. 1978 L 191/41) *SNPE-LEL*, and Case T-19/91 *Société d'Hygiène Dermatologique de Vichy v. Commission* [1992] ECR II-415.

514. Cases 8-11/66 *SA Cimenteries CBR Cementbedrijven NV et al. v. Commission* [1967] ECR 75 at 92–93.

515. See the 2nd ed. of this work (1989), 523–526. The transitional regime is still of significance for maritime and air transport. In relation to accession agreements for the new Member States, see O.J. 1995 L 2/17.

516. Case 42/72 *Brasserie de Haecht* [1973] ECR 77 at 86–87. See also Case C-39/96 *Koninklijke Vereeniging ter bevordering van de Belangen des Boekhandels v. Free Record Shop BV et al.* [1997] ECR I-2303 at 2321–2323 which summarizes earlier case-law and deals with the effect of amendments to old agreements.

517. Reg. 17, Art. 2.

power is concerned particularly with those cases in which the interested parties wish to receive a declaration that Article 85(1) does not apply, so that no exemption is needed. Strictly speaking a national court is not bound by such a negative clearance. Unless, though, in the course of proceedings new information comes to light which leads to a different conclusion, a national court will be very likely to follow the Commission's decision.

Individual exemption. The Commission has exclusive competence, subject to review by the Court, to confer an exemption under Article 85(3) EC, in respect of a notified agreement,[518] from the prohibition in Article 85(1) EC.[519] If an agreement is exempted, the prohibition and the nullity sanctions are inapplicable, and the parties may enforce the agreement in national courts. Exemption decisions are granted for a specified period, frequently for 10 years, and may be subject to conditions and obligations.[520] Typically these might include reporting obligations of exclusions from networks or of further acquisitions, or the prohibition of the exchange of information or of the enforcement of certain conditions of an agreement. Individual exemptions in numerous areas preceded the adoption of block exemptions, as the Commission seeks to build up its experience. Given that there are now a number of block exemptions, as is explained below, individual exemptions are at present mostly used for those agreements which do not fall fair and square within an existing block exemption. In deciding whether to grant an exemption, and, if so, subject to what conditions, the Commission has a wide margin of discretion.[521] In the application of Article 85(3) EC the Commission may not take a merely passive role. In accordance with the principles of good administration it has to use the means available to it to contribute to ascertaining the relevant facts.[522] An exemption decision can only relate to conduct caught by Article 85(1) EC; it thus cannot affect the application of Article 86 EC.[523]

---

518. Case 31/80 *NV L'Oréal et al. v. PVBA DE Nieuwe AMCK* [1980] ECR 3775 at 3790. The Commission may also grant an exemption to an Art. 4(2) agreement, *i.e.* one which was not subject to notification, in which case the exemption may be retroactive to the date of the agreement.
519. Reg. 17, Art. 9(1).
520. *Ibid.*, Art. 8; they may be renewed, or in appropriate circumstances withdrawn, *ibid.* Exemptions will not normally be retroactive, so they run from the date of notification, Art. 6.
521. Cases 56 and 58/64 *Consten and Grundig* [1966] ECR 299 at 347; Case 17/74 *Transocean Marine Paint Association v. Commission* [1974] ECR 1063 at 1080. However, the review of whether the Commission's findings accord with the facts may well be detailed, particularly by the Court of First Instance.
522. Cases 56 and 58/64 *Consten and Grundig* [1966] ECR 299 at 347.
523. Case 85/76 *Hoffmann-La Roche & Co. AG v. Commission* [1979] ECR 461 at 550; Case T-51/89 *Tetra-Pak Rausing SA v. Commission* [1990] ECR II-309 at 356–361.

Informal Competition Policy (comfort letters). Formal decisions granting a negative clearance or exemption are in practice becoming acts of last resort. After notification of an agreement consultations take place between the Commission and the undertakings concerned, which result in adaptation of the agreement to meet the Commission's concerns, and may well also involve arrangements as to the undertakings' future conduct. The annual *Report on Competition Policy* is the most useful source of information on the evolution of the Commission's practice.[524] In view of the limited administrative resources at the Commission's disposal, it has long since made use of 'comfort letters' rather than take a formal decision. In such a letter, signed by a senior official of the Directorate General for competition, the Commission will express the view that the agreement is not prohibited under Article 85(1), or that it merits an individual exemption, or that it falls within a block exemption, and thus the file will be closed. In certain circumstances the value of such a letter is enhanced by the prior publication of an invitation of comments on the line of action proposed.[525] These letters do not have the formal status of a negative clearance or an exemption decision, nor are they binding on national courts,[526] although they may very well be of highly persuasive authority in such fora.[527] In appropriate cases the Commission may re-open its file where the circumstances which gave rise to the comfort letter have changed.[528]

Block exemptions. The second way in which Article 85(3) EC is applied is through means of block exemption regulations, which the Commission is entitled to lay down on the basis of powers conferred by the Council.[529]

---

524. Periodicals such as CMLRev., ELRev. and YBEL also contain annual or other regular surveys of competition law and policy.
525. See the Notice on procedures concerning notification pursuant to Reg. 17, Art. 4 (O.J. 1983 C 295/6), the Notice on procedures for negative clearance (O.J. 1982 C 343/4), and WQs. 813/82 (O.J. 1982 C 275/15) and 874/82 (O.J. 1982 C 287/11). See, further, Gyslen in Slot and McDonnell (eds.), *op. cit.* (see note 364, *supra*) 217; Stevens (1994) ECLR 81; Van Bael (1986) 23 CMLRev. 61; and Waelbroeck (D.) (1986) 11 ELRev. 268.
526. See the *perfumes* judgments, *e.g.* Cases 253/78 and 1–3/79 *Procureur de la République et al. v. Giry et al.* [1980] ECR I-2327 at 2373–2374; Case 31/80 *NV L'Oréal et al. v. PVBA De Nieuwe AMCK* [1980] ECR 3775 at 3789–3790. The problem of letters was also discussed in chapter V, section 1.4, *ante*.
527. See the discussion relating to national courts, *post*.
528. Case T-7/93 *Langnese-Iglo GmbH v. Commission* [1995] ECR II-1533 at 1553–1554 (under appeal in Case C-279/95 P *Langnese-Iglo GmbH v. Commission* (O.J. 1995 C 286/3); Case T-9/93 *Schöller Lebensmittel GmbH & Co. KG v. Commission* [1995] ECR II-1611 at 1653–1655.
529. See Regs. 19/65 (O.J. 1965–66, p. 35) bilateral exclusive dealing agreements and intellectual property licensing; 2821/71 (O.J. English Special Edition 1971 (III), p. 1032) uniform standards, specialization and research and development agreements; 3976/87 (O.J. 1987 L 374/9) air transport; 1534/91 (O.J. 1991 L 143/1) insurance, and 479/92 (O.J. 1992 L 55/3) liner shipping companies. These have been amended as appropriate to take account of the various accessions.

These regulations represent a significant relief of the Commission's administrative burden, at the same time offering considerable legal certainty to undertakings.[530] The national courts are bound by these regulations.[531] The normal structure of these regulations is that they closely define the agreements which fall under them and clearly indicate what clauses are permitted and what prohibited.[532] Agreements falling within the block exemptions do not have to be notified. The existence of the block exemption regulations does not, however, prevent the Commission from giving an individual exemption for a particular agreement.[533]

Prohibition decisions. The Commission may adopt a decision requiring undertakings to cease and desist from infringements of Articles 85 or 86 which it finds proved.[534] Such decisions may even be issued in respect of conduct which has ceased by the time the decision is adopted.[535] The decision may or may not include the imposition of fines.

---

530. Case T-51/89 *Tetra Pak Rausing SA v. Commission* [1990] ECR II-309 at 362. In a number of instances the block exemptions provide for an 'opposition procedure' for agreements which do not quite fall wholly within their terms. This gives the Commission a period within which to react to notification of the agreement, and in the absence of action the agreement is deemed approved, *e.g.* see, on technology transfer agreements, Reg. 240/96 (O.J. 1996 L 31/2), Art. 4 (the period in this case is four months). As to the merits and demerits of block exemptions, see Korah, *op. cit.* (see note 366, *supra*) 71–72.

531. Case C-234/89 *Delimitis v. Henniger Bräu AG* [1991] ECR I-935 at 992.

532. Block exemptions regulations (also amended where appropriate on by subsequent Acts of Accession) currently in force are: Regs. **1983/83** (O.J. 1983 L 173/1, corrigendum O.J. 1983 L 281/24) on *exclusive dealing agreements*, **1984/83** (O.J. 1983 L 173/5, corrigendum O.J. 1983 L 281/24) on *exclusive purchasing agreements* (the validity of both of these has been extended to the end of 1999, see Reg. 1582/97 (O.J. 1997 L 214/27)), see further on both of these regs., the Commission's Notice (O.J. 1984 C 101/2, amended O.J. 1992 C 121/2); **417/85** (O.J. 1985 L 53/1, most recently amended by Reg. 2236/97 (O.J. 1997 L 306/12, extending its validity until the end of 2000)) on *specialization agreements*; **418/85** (O.J. 1985 L 53/5, also so amended by Reg. 2236/97) on *research and development agreements*; **4087/88** (O.J. 1988 L 359/46) on *franchising agreements*; **3932/92** (O.J. 1992 L 398/7) on *insurance agreements*; **1475/95** (O.J. 1995 L 145/25) on *motor vehicle distribution and servicing agreements*, see also the Commission's Explanatory Brochure, *Distribution of Motor Vehicles* (Document IV/9509/95), and **240/96** (O.J. 1996 L 31/2) on *technology transfer agreements*. The regs. permit the Commission to withdraw in a particular case the benefits of a block exemption, but not in doing so to withhold the benefit of a block exemption from any future agreements, Case T-7/93 *Langnese-Iglo GmbH v. Commission* [1995] ECR II-1533 at 1606–1607, under appeal, Case C-279/95 P *Langnese-Iglo GmbH v. Commission* (O.J. 1995 C 286/3), and Case T-9/93 *Schöller Lebensmittel GmbH & Co. KG v. Commission* [1995] ECR II-1669–1671. Special block exemptions exist for various transport agreements, see section 4.3, *post*.

533. Either by a formal decision or by tacit acceptance under the opposition procedure (see note 530, *supra*).

534. Reg. 17, Art. 3.

535. Case 7/82 *Gesellschaft zur Vertretung von Leistungsschutzrechten mbH (GVL) v. Commission* [1983] ECR 483 at 502–503. There may well be a real danger of resumption of

Fines and periodic penalties. The commission is empowered under Article 15 of Regulation 17 to impose fines for incorrect or misleading notifications, the supply of incorrect information, refusal to submit to investigations ordered by way of decision, or to produce required books or other business records during an investigation, or infringement of Articles 85(1) or 86 EC, where the conduct concerned is ceither intentional or negligent.[536] Fines are tending nowadays to be larger, the Court observing that the general purpose of fines is to secure the   implementation of Community competition policy.[537] Thus fines are not meant to be merely punitive, they are also meant as deterrents.[538] The most important factors in fining policy are undoubtedly the nature of the infringement;[539] the market share and turnover; the effects of the infringement; the behaviour of the parties, and

the conduct, if the matters concerned are novel there may well be an interest in taking the decision in order that the issues may be tested on appeal.

536. As to the newly announced guidelines on the imposition of fines, see O.J. 1998 C9/3. As to negligence, see Case 28/77 *Tepea BV v. Commission* [1978] ECR 1391 at 1419–1420; Case 19/77 *Miller International Schallplatten GmbH v. Commission* [1978] ECR 131 at 152, Case 246/86 *Belasco et al. v. Commission* [1989] ECR 2117 at 2191–2192; Case T-66/92 *Herlitz AG v. Commission* [1994] ECR II-531 at 547, and Case T-77/92 *Parker Pen Ltd. v. Commission* [1994] ECR II-549 at 576. As to the determination of the amount of the fine, see in particular Cases 41/69 *ACF Chemiefarma NV v. Commission* [1970] ECR 661 at 701–703; Case 44/69 *Bucher & Co. v. Commission* [1970] ECR 733 at 760–762; Case 45/69 *Boehringer Mannheim GmbH v. Commission* [1970] ECR 769 at 805–807; Cases 6 and 7/73 *Instituto Chemioterapico Italiana SpA and Commercial Solvents Corporation v. Commission* [1974] ECR 223 at 257; Case 28/77 *Tepea, loc. cit.*; Cases 32 and 36–82/78 *BMW Belgium SA et al. v. Commission* [1979] ECR 2435 at 2478–2482; Cases 100–103/80 *SA Musique Diffusion Française et al. v. Commission* [1983] ECR 1825 at 1905–1911; Case 107/82 *Allgemeine Elektricitäts-Gesellschaft AEG-Telefunken AG v. Commission* [1983] ECR 3151 at 3220–3221; Case 322/81 *NV Nederlandsche Banden-Industrie Michelin v. Commission* [1983] ECR 3461 at 3523–3525; Case 193/83 *Windsurfing International Inc. v. Commission* [1986] ECR 611 at 667–668; Cases 240/82 etc. *Stichting Sigarettenindustrie et al. v. Commission* [1985] ECR 3831 at 3877; Case C-279/87 *Tipp-Ex GmbH & Co. KG v. Commission* [1990] ECR I-261 at 262 (summary publication), Case T-83/91 *Tetra Pak International SA v. Commission* [1994] ECR II-755 at 855–860, upheld on appeal in Case C-333/94 P *Tetra Pak International SA v. Commission* [1996] ECR I-5951 at 6013–6014, and Case T-29/92 *Vereniging van Samenwerkende Prijsregelende Organisaties in de Bouwnijverheid et al. v. Commission* [1995] ECR II-289 at 409–410 (appeal dismissed in Case C-237/95 P *Vereniging van Samenwerkende Prijsregelende Organisaties in de Bouwnijverheid et al. v. Commission* [1996] ECR I-1611 at 1628).

537. Cases 100–103/80 *Musique Diffusion* [1983] ECR 1825 at 1904–1905.

538. As to the Commission's fining policy, see Gyslen in Slot and McDonnell (eds.), *op. cit.* (see note 366, *supra*) 63; Kerse, *op. cit.* (see note 366, *supra*) 245–284 in the 3rd ed., London 1994); Van Bael (1995) ECLR 237; Wils (1995) 15 YBEL 17 and (1998) 23 ELRev. 252. The fixing of fines is scarcely an exact science, resembling more the proverbial Lord Chancellor's foot. See, referring to earlier case-law, Case T-49/95 *Van Mengen Sports Group BV v. Commission* [1996] ECR II-1799 at 1822–1824.

539. *E.g.* export bans will be viewed particularly seriously, as will price-fixing, market-sharing and predatory pricing. Non-notified agreements will also be hard hit.

the duration of the infringement.[540] The Commission may sometimes also take account of the profit made from an infringement.[541] In any event, ignorance of Community competition law is no defence.[542] The Commission does however reward and encourage cooperation or making a clean breast of past misdeeds.[543] A limitation period of five years from the date of the infringement applies, but in the case of continuing or repeated infringements time starts to run from the date on which the infringement ceases.[544] Periodic (daily) penalty payments may be imposed in order to compel compliance with certain procedural decisions or cease and desist decisions.[545] Fines and periodic penalties imposed by the Commission, unlike damages awarded by national courts, simply go to the Community budget. Undertakings may appeal against fines and periodic penalty payments to the Court of First Instance (subject to further appeal on a point of law only to the Court of Justice); as the Court has unlimited jurisdiction in relation to fines and periodic penalty payments, these may be raised or lowered on appeal.[546]

National proceedings and national authorities. The fact that proceedings have been initiated at Community level against undertakings for anti-competitive agreements or practices does not exclude the applicability of national provisions and the initiation of national proceedings in respect of the same conduct.[547] This is because they deal with different effects of the same conduct, the Community level with the effects on inter-State trade, the national level with the effects purely in the national market.[548]

---

540. See the discussion in Bellamy and Child, *op. cit.* (see note 232, *supra*) Chapter 12 and Kerse, *op. cit.* (see note 366, *supra*) Chapter 7.

541. *E.g.* Dec. 79/68 (O.J. 1979 L 16/9) *Kawasaki.*

542. *E.g.* Case 19/77 *Miller* [1978] ECR 131 at 152; Cases 32 and 36–82/78 *BMW* [1979] ECR 2435 at 2480, and Cases 96/82 *etc. NV IAZ International Belgium et al. v. Commission* [1983] ECR 3369 at 3415. If the Commission is breaking new ground in a decision, and the conduct was not obviously contrary to Community competition law as hitherto developed, the Commission may decide not to impose a fine. *E.g.* Decs. 78/252 (O.J. 1978 L 70/52) *Vegetable Parchment* and 79/934 (O.J. 1979 L 286/32) *BP Kemi/DDSF.*

543. See now the Commission's Notice on the non-imposition or reduction of fines in cartel cases (O.J. 1996 C 207/4), commonly called the whistle-blower's notice. See further, Hornsby and Hunter (1997) ECLR 38 and Wils (1997) 22 ELRev. 125.

544. Reg. 2988/74 (O.J. 1974 L 319/1), see Arts. 1(1)(b) and 1(2). As to interruptions of the limitation period, see Art. 2. Reg. 2988/74 was adopted as a result of the judgment in Case 41/69 *ACF Chemiefarma NV v. Commission* [1970] ECR 661 (and the other *Quinine* cartel judgments decided at the same time). As to the enforceability of a fine or periodic penalty payment, see section 4.6.3, *post.*

545. Reg. 17, Art. 16.

546. Reg. 17, Art. 17. See section 4.6.3, *post.*

547. Case 14/68 *Walt Wilhelm et al. v. Bundeskartellamt* [1969] ECR 1 at 13–14. Sanctions already imposed at one level should be taken into account by the authorities at the other level, *ibid.* at 15.

548. The distinction parallels that between federal offences and state offences in the US in

However, Community law takes precedence in the event of a conflict, and its useful effect may not be undermined by the national proceedings.[549] Cooperation between national competition authorities and the Community competition authorities is steadily improving,[550] not least as more Member States (and indeed numerous European non-Member States) are taking Articles 85 and 86 EC as the model for their revised competition laws.

National courts. It follows from the direct effect of Article 85(1) and (2) EC that national courts may themselves decide that agreements are prohibited and thus void, without it being necessary for the Commission to have first adopted a decision or initiated proceedings.[551] Thus competence in the application of Article 85(1) EC (and indeed of Article 86 EC) is shared between the Commission and the national courts.[552] This shared jurisdiction indeed runs the risk of the Commission and the national courts taking conflicting decisions, such as the national court concluding that an agreement is not incompatible with Article 85(1), whereas the Commission later adopts a decision prohibiting the agreement, or the national court concluding that an agreement would be unlikely to obtain an exemption and the Commission later granting one. If there is a risk of such a conflict the appropriate course for the national court is to stay the proceedings or adopt interim measures pursuant to its national rules of procedure.[553] The

respect of the same conduct (though EC law imposes administrative sanctions only; unlike in the US there are no criminal penalties). See, generally, the papers by Hawk and Veltrop, and Spratling in Slot and McDonnell (eds.), *op. cit.* (see note 366, *supra*) 21 and 76 respectively.

549. Case 14/68 *Walt Wilhelm* [1969] ECR 1 at 14. See Walz (1996) 21 ELRev. 449.
550. See Bos (1995) ECLR 410; Bourgeois in Gormley (ed.), *op. cit.* (see note 366, *supra*) 89 Ehlermann (1995) ECLR 454; (1996) ECLR 88; Kerse (1997) ECLR 17; Rodger (1994) ECLR 251, and Von Stoephasius in Slot and McDonnell (eds.), *op. cit.* (see note 366, *supra*) 32. See further, the Commission's Notice on cooperation with national authorities (O.J. 1997 C 39/6); Marsden (1997) ECLR 234 and Maitland-Walker (1998) ECLR 124. See alo the *Reports of the 18th FIDE Congress* (Stockholm, 1998) Vol. 2.
551. As to the application of Arts. 85 and 86 by national courts, see Bellamy and Child, *op. cit.* (see note 223, *supra*) Chapter 10; Goh (1993) ECLR 114; Hall in Slot and McDonnell (eds.), *op. cit.* (see note 366, *supra*) 41; Pijnacker Hordijk (1987) SEW 484; Van Bael (1994) ECLR 3; Van der Woude (1993) NJB 585; Whish (1994) 5 EBLR 3, (1994) ECLR 60, and in Gormley (ed.), *op. cit.* (see note 366, *supra*) 73. See also Cumming (1997) ECLR 368.
552. Case C-234/89 *Delimitis v. Henniger Bräu AG* [1991] ECR I-935 at 992, although the Commission is responsible for the implementation and orientation of Community competition policy, *ibid.* at 991. A national court is not entitled to exempt an agreement individually (Reg. 17, Art. 9(1) confers exclusive competence on the Commission), but it can find that an agreement falls within a block exemption, *ibid.* at 992. However national courts may not modify the scope of the block exemption regulations, as any extension of their sphere of application would impinge upon the Commission's competence, *ibid.*
553. Case C-234/89 *Delimitis* [1991] ECR I-935 at 993. The same applies if the national

national court may request the Commission to inform it of any procedure which may have been set in motion, and of the likelihood of an official ruling; it may also seek legal or economic information from the Commission in order to enable it to cope with particular difficulties in the application of Articles 85(1) and 86; the Commission is bound by the duty of sincere cooperation with national judicial authorities to assist the latter, subject to respecting the requirements of confidentiality.[554] Of course the possibility of asking the Commission for information is without prejudice to the national court's power, or, as appropriate, duty to make a reference under Article 177 EC to the Court of Justice.[555] The national court is entitled to look at both the case-law of the Court and the practice of the Commission (the latter being expressed in its decisions, the *Reports on Competition Policy* and its communications).[556] If it has any doubt it may, if appropriate and consistent with the national rules of procedure, obtain additional information from the Commission or allow the parties to seek a decision from the Commission.[557] It will be noticed that the Court has been most careful to phrase the national court's part in this aspect of cooperation in the application of Community competition law in terms of 'may' and 'consistent with national rules of procedure' rather than in terms of an obligation as such.

As a result of this judgment in *Delimitis* the Commission has published a Notice on cooperation between national courts and the Commission in applying Articles 85 and 86 EC.[558] This Notice also takes account of the express approval by the Court of First Instance[559] of the Commission's practice of determining priorities, in view of its scarce administrative

court considers that the agreement is caught by Article 85(1) but may be the subject of an exemption, *ibid.*
554. *Ibid.* at 994. The duty of sincere cooperation results from Art. 5 EC; the duty of confidentiality from Art. 214 EC and Reg. 17, Art. 20. Certainly this forced the Commission to review its approach to requests for assistance from national courts, previously they had invariably met with a dusty answer, saying that if the national court wanted to know the Commission's position it should make a reference under Art. 177 EC and the Commission would submit its observations to the Court of Justice in that context. As to confidentiality, see Case T-353/94 *Postbank NV v. Commission* [1996] ECR II-921 at 945–950 and 953–958.
555. Case C-234/89 *Delimitis, ibid.*
556. Cases C-319/93 *etc. Dijkstra et al. v. Friesland (Frico Domo) Coöperatie BA et al.* [1995] ECR I-4471 at 4510.
557. *Ibid.* at 4511 (in the context of the interpretation of Reg. 26 (O.J. English Special Edition 1959–62, p. 129) Art. 2(1) on agricultural cooperatives). See also Case C-399/93 *Oude Luttikhuis et al. v. Verenigde Coöperatieve Melkindustrie Coberco BA* [1995] ECR I-4515 at 4528–4529.
558. O.J. 1993 C 39/6. The Notice does not apply to the transport sector or to the ECSC competition rules (point 45 of the Notice). The EFTA Surveillance Authority has published a similar (but not wholly identical) Notice (O.J. 1995 C 112/7) relating to Arts. 53 and 54 EEA.
559. In Case T-24/90 *Automec srl v. Commission* [1992] ECR II-2250 at 2274 *et seq.*

resources, and referring complainants to seek their remedies in the national courts.[560] The Notice sketches various scenarios of possible conflicts between decisions of national courts and those of the Commission, particularly concerning the application of Article 85(3) EC. The apparent proposition that a national court would not be bound even by a Commission decision prohibiting an agreement seems, however, to be of extremely doubtful accuracy.[561] It may also be wondered whether the confidence in the effectiveness of compliance with Community competition law through national remedies as opposed to action by the Commission is not somewhat misplaced.[562]

4.2.4 The application of Article 85 EC in practice

Some 200 judgments of the Court and getting on for 400 decisions of the Commission handed down by the date at which this work states the law, relate to Article 85(1) or (3) EC alone.[563] This case-law and practice are discussed in summary form in this section. Attention turns first to horizontal and in certain instances vertical agreements which will virtually always fall foul of Article 85(1) EC and be incapable of exemption;[564] thereafter various types of permitted agreements are discussed.[565] The Commission's thinking on vertical restraints has recently been the subject of an important Green Paper, which, taking account of reactions received, will in due course form the basis of policy orientations for an important area of competition law.[566]

---

560. As to the duties of national courts, see *ibid.* at 2279–2280 (reflecting the national court's participation in pursuance of the duty of sincere cooperation with the Commission resulting from Art. 5 EC).

561. Point 20 of the Notice (the non-binding point should refer to opinions or other official statements, it is submitted, and not, as appears, also to Commission decisions). It will be remembered that in Case 314/85 *Foto-Frost v. Hauptzollamt Lübeck-Ost* [1987] ECR 4199 at 4231 the Court ruled that national courts were not entitled to declare acts of Community Institutions invalid.

562. The common complaint is that national courts are frankly ill-equipped to apply Community competition law, which often involves complex market assessments. The Commission (at point 16 of the Notice) makes no attempt to meet this criticism, but simply points to the advantages of the availability of damages, the speedier availability of interim measures, the combination of claims under Community competition law with claims under national law, and the power of national courts, in some Member States, to award costs to successful litigants.

563. As to the Court's contribution in the application and development of competition policy, see Koopmans (1987) SEW 424.

564. Art. 85(1) EC gives examples.

565. Detailed discussion of all the block exemption agreements is outside the scope of this work (Korah has written monographs on many of them). For discussion of individual decisions adopted prior to the adoption of block exemptions, as the Commission was gaining experience in the areas concerned, see the 2nd ed. of this work (1989) 529–549.

566. COM (96) 721 Final. See Schröter in Gormley (ed.), *op. cit.* (see note 366, *supra*) 15

Prohibited horizontal and vertical agreements. Multilateral horizontal agreements fixing prices or other selling conditions hinder the function of price competition, which is 'to keep prices down to the lowest possible level' and endanger 'one of the basic objectives of the Treaty' which is pursued by differences in rates, 'namely the interpenetration of national markets and, as a result, direct access by consumers to the sources of production of the whole Community.'[567] This is also true of agreements as to collective resale price maintenance;[568] credit terms;[569] consultation before quoting for work;[570] tariffs and costs;[571] minimum prices;[572] fixed prices;[573] rebates;[574] recommended prices;[575] exchanges of information;[576] and other parallel conduct which makes transparent the pricing policy of individual undertakings as a result of which coordination

(who also discusses earlier academic criticism of the Commission's approach). As to the situation in Member States, see Laudati *et al.*, *Survey of the Member State National laws governing Vertical Distribution Agreements* (Commission, Brussels, Luxembourg, 1996, ISBN 92-827-0366-5).

567. Case 48/69 *Imperial Chemical Industries Ltd. v. Commission* [1972] ECR 619 at 660 (see also the other *Dyestuffs* cartel cases decided on the same day). This builds on the first condemnation of horizontal price fixing in Case 41/69 *ACF Chemiefarma NV v. Commission* [1970] ECR 661 and the other *Quinine* cartel cases decided on the same day.

568. See Dec. 77/66 (O.J. 1977 L 16/8) *GERO-fabriek*, although the controversial evaluation in relation to book prices has been noted above (see note 487, *supra*), although the challenge to the infringement of Art. 85(1) was dropped by the Publishers Association before the Court of First Instance.

569. *E.g.* Cases 209/78 *etc. Van Landewyck Sàrl et al. v. Commission* [1980] ECR 3125 at 3269–3270. Extended credit is in fact a disguised price reduction if interest is not charged or charged at a preferential rate.

570. *E.g.* Case T-29/92 *Vereniging van Samenwerkende Prijsregelende organisaties in de Bouwnijverheid et al. v. Commission* [1995] ECR II-289 at 330–334, 340–345, and 350–353.

571. *E.g.* Dec. 92/212 (O.J. 1992 L 95/50) *Eurocheque – Helsinki Agreement*. The Court of First Instance agreed with the Commission that the French banks concerned were obliged to charge an extra commission by the agreement, but not that the amount was fixed by that agreement, Cases T-39 and 40/92 *Groupement des Cartes Bancaires 'CB' et al. v. Commission* [1995] ECR II-49 at 81–85. See also the Commission's Notice on the application of the EC competition rules to cross-border credit transfers (O.J. 1995 C 251/3).

572. *E.g.* Case 123/83 *Bureau national interprofessionnel du cognac v. Clair* [1985] ECR 391 at 423–424.

573. Case 73/74 *Groupement des fabricants de papiers peints de Belgique et al. v. Commission* [1975] ECR 1491 at 1511.

574. *E.g.* Cases 240/82 *etc. Stichting Sigarettenindustrie et al. v. Commission* [1985] ECR 3831 at 3870–3871 (bonus for certain specialist retailers).

575. *E.g.* Case 8/72 *Vereeniging van Cementhandelaren v. Commission* [1972] ECR 977 at 989–990, and Case T-13/89 *Imperial Chemical Industries plc v. Commission* [1992] ECR II-1021 at 1130–1131 (under appeal in Case C-200/92 P *Imperial Chemical Industries plc v. Commission* (O.J. 1992 C 167/8; Cosmas, Adv. Gen. gave his opinion on 15 July 1997).

576. See the Commission's general view expressed in the *7th Report on Competition Policy 1977* (Brussels, Luxembourg, 1978) points 5–8; and Decs. 77/592 (O.J. 1977 L 242/10)

can take place.[577] The Court has pointed out that collective vertical price-fixing systems deprive resellers of all freedom to determine their sales prices, right through to the level of the consumer.[578] In practice the case-law comes down to a *per se* prohibition of all horizontal price agreements.[579]

The extensive practice in Commission decisions demonstrates moreover that price agreements virtually always go hand-in-hand with market sharing.[580] This is always pro-hibited,[581] irrespective of the form which it may take.[582] Export bans will also not escape the ambit of Article 85(1)

COBELPA/VNP; 79/90 (O.J. 1979 L 21/16) *White Lead*; 87/1 (O.J. 1987 L 3/17) *Fatty Acids*; 92/157 (O.J. 1992 L 68/19) *UK Tractor*, and Cases 89/85 *etc. Wood Pulp* [1993] ECR I-1307 at 1614–1615 (but quarterly price announcements to users were not found to infringe Art. 85(1), *ibid.* at 1599). See also Dec. 94/601 (O.J. 1994 L 243/1) *Carton-board* (partially annulled in *inter alia* Case T-311/94 *BPB de Eenddracht BV v. Commission* [1998] ECR II-nyr (14 May 1998)), and Dec. 94/815 (O.J. 1994 L 343/1) *Cement* (under appeal in *inter alia* Case T-25/95 *SA Cimenteries CBR v. Commission* (O.J. 1995 C 101/10)). See also Kühn *et al.*, *Information Exchanges among Firms and their Impact on Competition* (Commission Document, Brussels, Luxembourg, revised 1995, ISBN 92-826-9705-3).

577. See Case 172/80 *Züchner v. Bayerische Vereinsbank AG* [1981] ECR 2021 at 2031–2033; Case 246/86 *Belasco et al. v. Commission* [1989] ECR 2117 at 2184–2189, and Cases 89/85 *etc. Wood Pulp* [1993] ECR I-1307 at 1620–1622.

578. Cases 43 and 63/82 *Vereniging ter Bevordering van het Vlaamse Boekwezen, VBVB et al. v. Commission* [1984] ECR 19 at 66.

579. To the extent that they have an appreciable effect. See, generally, Black (1997) ECLR 145 (reviewing much of the literature on *per se* and rule of reason analysis).

580. In addition to the decisions which led to the judgments referred to *supra*, see also Decs. 74/292 (O.J. 1974 L 160/1) *Glass containers*; 78/59 (O.J. 1978 L 20/18) *Centraal Bureau voor de Rijwielhandel*; 78/252 (O.J. 1978 L 70/54) *Vegetable Parchment*; 80/1334 (O.J. 1980 L 383/19) *Italian Cast Glass*; 81/881 (O.J. 1981 L 326/32) *Italian Flat Glass*; 83/546 (O.J. 1983 L 317/1) *Cast Iron and Steel Rolls*; 86/398 (O.J. 1986 L 230/1) *Polypropylene*, as to the appeals, see note 424, *supra*; 86/596 (O.J. 1986 L 348/50) *MELDOC*; 89/190 (O.J. 1989 L 74/1) *PVC*, annulled for procedural reasons in Case C-137/92 P *Commission v. BASF AG et al.* [1994] ECR I-2555, after which the Commission adopted Dec. 94/599 (O.J. 1994 L 239/14) *PVC II* which is under appeal in *inter alia* Case T-305/94 *NV Limburgse Vinyl Maatschappij v. Commission* (O.J. 1994 C 331/6), and 89/191 (O.J. 1989 L 74/21) *LdPE* (annulled in Cases T-80/89 *etc. BASF AG et al. v. Commission* [1995] ECR II-729).

581. See Dec. 69/240 (J.O. 1969 L 192/5) *Quinine*, mostly upheld on appeal: Case 41/69 *ACF Chemiefarma NV v. Commission* [1970] ECR 661, Case 44/69 *Buchler & Co. v. Commission* [1970] ECR 733, and Case 45/69 *Boehringer Mannheim GmbH v. Commission* [1970] ECR 769.

582. *E.g.* Decs. 74/432 (O.J. 1974 L 237/12) *Advocaat Zwarte Kip* (market partitioning through transfer of a trade mark); 75/297 (O.J. 1975 L 125/27) *Sirdar/Phildar* (agreement not to use the parties' respective trade marks in each other's 'home' markets); 78/571 (O.J. 1987 L 191/4) *SNPE-LEL* (cross-licensing and no manufacture or sale in each other's territory); 85/74 (O.J. 1985 L 35/1) *Peroxygen Products*, and 91/298 (O.J. 1991 L 152/16) *Soda-ash – Solvay, CFK*, annulled as regards Solvay, for procedural reasons in Case T-31/91 *Solvay SA v. Commission* [1995] ECR II-1821 (summary publication, see the other judgments relating to soda-ash handed down on the same day); the annulment is under appeal in Case C-297/95 P *Commission v. Solvay SA* (O.J. 1995 C 286/3). As to straightforward import bans, see Case 71/74 *Nederlandse Vereni-*

EC,[583] nor will obstacles to parallel imports.[584] The same applies in relation to market division of production or distribution.[585] A less stringent policy has been pursued since 1983 concerning temporary crisis cartels in sectors with overcapacity. The Commission's policy was outlined in the *Twelfth Report on Competition Policy*:[586] the Commission might be able 'to condone agreements in restraint of competition which relate to a sector as a whole, provided they are aimed solely at achieving a co-ordinated reduction of overcapacity and do not otherwise restrict free decision-making by the firms involved.'[587]

ging voor Fruit en Groentenimporthandel et al. v. Commission [1975] ECR 563, [1975] 2 CMLR 123 (*Frubo*), and Case T-16/91RV *Rendo NV v. Commission* [1996] ECR II-1827, which refers to earlier judgments in the saga). As to self-restraint agreements, see the Commission's Notice on Imports of Japanese Products (J.O. 1972 C 111/13) and Decs. 74/634 (O.J. 1974 L 343/19) *Franco–Japanese Ballbearings Agreement*, and 85/206 (O.J. 1985 L 92/1) *Aluminium Imports from Eastern Europe* (a quite extraordinary example of a notification in 1970, commencement of investigations in 1978 and a Decision taken in December 1984 after the period in which fines could be imposed had lapsed).

583. *E.g.* Case 19/77 *Miller International Schallplatten GmbH v. Commission* [1978] ECR 131 at 148; Cases 100–103/80 *Musique Diffusion Française et al. v. Commission* [1983] ECR 1825, [1983] 3 CMLR 221; Case 28/77 *Tepea BV v. Commission* [1978] ECR 1391, [1978] 3 CMLR 482; Cases 32 and 36–82/78 *BMW Belgium SA et al. v. Commission* [1979] ECR 2435, [1980] 1 CMLR 370; Case 136/79 *National Panasonic (UK) Ltd. v. Commission* [1980] ECR 2033, [1980] 3 CMLR 169; Case 86/82 *Hasselblad (GB) Ltd. v. Commission* [1984] ECR 883, [1984] 1 CMLR 559; Case C-277/87 *Sandoz prodotti farmaceutici SpA v. Commission* [1990] ECR I-45; Decs. 72/480 (J.O. 1972 L 303/52) *WEA-Fillipacchi Music SA*; 80/1283 (O.J. 1980 L 377/16) *Johnson & Johnson*; 85/79 (O.J. 1985 L 35/58) *John Deere*; 85/617 (O.J. 1985 L 376/21) *Sperry New Holland*; 88/86 (O.J. 1988 L 49/19) *Fisher Price/Quaker Oats Ltd.-Toyco*; 91/297–299 (O.J. 1991 L 152/1, 16 and 21) *Soda-ash – Solvay et al.* (annulled, but subject to some appeals, see note 582, *supra*); 91/335 (O.J. 1991 L 185/23) *Gosme/Martell-DMP*, and Dec. 91/532 (O.J. 1991 L 287/39) *Viho/Toshiba*.

584. *E.g.* Cases 56 and 58/64 *Consten and Grundig* [1966] ECR 299 at 343, and Dec. 92/426 (O.J. 1992 L 233/27) *Parker-Viho*, upheld on appeal in Case T-66/92 *Herlitz AG v. Commission* [1995] ECR II-531; Case T-77/92 *Parker Pen Ltd. v. Commission* [1995] ECR II-549 (fine reduced); and Dec. 98/273 (O.J. 1998 L 124/60) *VW*.

585. *E.g.* Cases 41/69 *ACF Chemiefarma NV v. Commission* [1970] ECR 661; Case 90/76 *Srl Ufficio Henry van Ameyde v. Srl Ufficio Centrale Italiano di Assistenza Assicurativa Automobilisti in Circolazione Internazionale (UCI)* [1977] ECR 1091, [1977] 2 CMLR 478; Cases 29 and 30/83 *Compagnie Royale Asturienne des Mines SA et al. v. Commission* [1984] ECR 1679, [1985] 1 CMLR 688; Decs. 78/156 (O.J. 1978 L 47/42) *Video Cassette Recorders*, and 90/45 (O.J. 1990 L 31/32) *Sugar Beet*.

586. Brussels, Luxembourg, 1983, 43 (points 38–41). See also the *Thirteenth Report (ibid.*, 1984) 53 (points 56–61). and formal decisions were first adopted in 1984 concerning capacity cutbacks in the sectors of synthetic fibres (Dec. 84/380 (O.J. 1984 L 207/17) and petrochemicals (Dec. 84/387 (O.J. 1984 L 212/1)). An example of economic difficulties in a sector mitigating the level of a fine but nevertheless not excusing long-term serious violations of Art. 85(1) can be seen in Dec. 84/405 (O.J. 1984 L 220/27) dealing with the antI-competitive behaviour of various zinc producers.

587. *Twelfth Report (ibid.)* point 39.

Collective exclusive dealing agreements between a substantial group of suppliers and a substantial group of professional buyers, such as wholesale dealers, large-scale consumers or processing firms also stand such a poor chance of benefiting from exemption from the prohibition of Article 85(1) EC that they can be said to be prohibited *per se*.[588] This type of arrangement appears to be a Belgian–Dutch specialty capable of entirely isolating a market from competition.[589]

Collective premium or rebate agreements will not benefit from exemption from the prohibition of Article 85(1) if the rebate on the total quantities purchased offered by producers to dealers only takes account of the quantities bought from the producers in the Member State concerned, thus leading to concentration of orders within the national territory to the detriment of undertakings from other Member States offering competing products.[590]

Joint selling agencies initially encountered difficulties if they also related to exportation to other Member States and involved production or selling quotas, uniform prices or other restrictions of competition between the parties which thus also inevitably restrict inter-state trade.[591] Negative clearances were only granted in these cases after any possibility of the selling agencies being involved in exportation had been excluded.[592] Since the judgment in Case 8/72 *Vereeniging van Cementhandelaren v. Commission*[593] the Commission's original view that national selling rules of a common selling agency were out of range for the time being was rather difficult to maintain.[594] Where, however, the activities of a small selling agency set up to promote exports or imports have no appreciable effect on competition in intra-Community trade a negative clearance can be

588. See, generally, the *Seventh, Eighth and Ninth General Reports* (Brussels, Luxembourg, 1965, 1966 and 1967 respectively) and *e.g.* Decs. 72/390 (J.O. 1972 L 264/22) concerning the central heating sector in Belgium; 72/478 (J.O. 1972 L 303/45) *GISA*; 75/497 (O.J. 1975 L 228/17) *IFTRA rules for producers of virgin aluminium*; 75/358 (O.J. 1975 L 159/22) *Stoves and Heaters* and 78/59 (O.J. 1978 L 20/18) *Central Bureau voor Rijwielhandel*.

589. See Case 8/72 *Vereeniging van Cementhandelaren v. Commission* [1972] ECR 977, [1973] CMLR 7 and Cases 43 and 63/82 *Vereniging ter Bevordering van het Vlaamse Boekwezen VBVB et al. v. Commission* [1984] ECR 19, [1982] 2 CMLR 344.

590. *E.g.* Decs. 71/23 (J.O. 1971 L 10/15) *German ceramic tiles*; 73/232 (O.J. 1973 L 217/34) *gas water heaters and bath heaters*; 80/1074 (O.J. 1980 L 318/32) *natural stone* and 82/506 (O.J. 1982 L 232/11) *SSI*, on appeal Cases 240/82 *etc. Stichting Sigarettenindustrie et al. v. Commission* [1985] ECR 3831, [1987] 3 CMLR 661.

591. *E.g.* Decs. 68/374 (J.O. 1968 L 276/13) *Cobelaz/Usines de Synthèse*; 68/375 (J.O. 1968 L 276(19) *Cobelaz/Cokeries*; 68/377 (J.O. 1968 L 276/29) *CFA*; 69/216 (J.0. 1969 L 173/8) *Seifa (fertilizers)*; 71/22 (J.O. 1971 L 10/12) *Supexie (fertilizers)*; 73/212 (O.J. 1973 L 217/3) *SCPA/Kali und Salz* and 80/182) O.J. 1980 L 39/51) *Floral*.

592. See *Supexie, ibid.*

593. [1972] ECR 977 at 991.

594. See *CSV* and *Flora* (which clearly overrule *Cobelaz, CFA* and *Seifa* on this point), see note 591, *supra*.

obtained.[595] The Commission's approach to joint purchasing agencies is well illustrated by Decision 79/182[596] *Intergroup*, which concerned Spar retailers: an appreciable effect on competition was not involved in view of the effective competition between a large number of undertakings, and without the co-operation envisaged inter-state trade would have been impossible. But the Commission's approach to joint purchasing by manufacturers of raw materials has not always been so sympathetic.[597]

Permitted restrictions of competition. First, exclusive dealing agreements. If they grant the exclusive dealer protection from parallel imports by competitors they will have scant chance of qualifying for an exemption from the prohibition of Article 85(1).[598] Unilateral or bilateral exclusive

595. Decs. 72/23 (J.O. 1972 L 13/44) *Safco* and 72/128 (J.O. 1972 L 61/27) *Wild/Leitz*. See also Case 43/85 *Associazione Nazionale Commercianti Internazionali Dentali e Sanitari (ANCIDES) v. Commission* [1987] ECR 3131, [1988] 4 CMLR 821.
596. O.J. 1975 L 212/23.
597. *E.g.* Dec. 80/917 (O.J. 1980 L 260/24) *National Sulphuric Acid Association* and Dec. 80/234 (O.J. 1980 L 51/19) *Rennet*, on appeal Case 61/80 *Coöperatieve Stremsel- en Kleurselfabriek v. Commission* [1981] ECR 851, [1982] 1 CMLR 240 (in the latter case exemption was refused and the refusal was upheld by the Court; in the former case an exemption was granted). See further, Case C-250/92 *Gøttrup-Klim Grovvareforening et al. v. Dansk Landbrugs Grovvareselkab* [1994] ECR I-5641 at 5687–5688 (prohibition of membership of competing cooperatives essential to enable combination of otherwise limited purchasing power in the face of powerful world suppliers). See also Dec. 93/403 (O.J. 1993 L 179/23) *EBU/Eurovision*, annulled in Cases T-528/93 *etc. Métropole télévision SA et al. v. Commission* [1996] ECR II-652 (under appeal in Case C-320/96 P *European Broadcasting Union v. Commission* (O.J. 1996 C 354/18), and the informal settlement in *BSB/Football Association* (*XXIIIrd Report on Competition Policy 1993* (Brussels, Luxembourg, 1994) Annex III, 459.
598. *E.g.* Cases 56 and 58/64 *Consten and Grundig* [1966] ECR 299, [1966] CMLR 18; Case 56/65 *Société Technique Minière v. Maschinenbau Ulm GmbH* [1966] ECR 235, [1966] CMLR 357; Case 32/65 *Italy v. Council et al.* [1966] ECR 389, [1966] CMLR 39; Case 1/71 *SA Cadillon v. Firma Höss, Maschinenbau KG* [1971] ECR 351, [1971] CMLR 420; Case 22/71 *Béguelin Import Co. et al. v. SAGL Import Export et al.* [1971] ECR 949, [1972] CMLR 81; Case 8/74 *Procureur du Roi v. Dassonville et al.* [1974] ECR 837, [1974] 2 CMLR 436; Case 25/75 *Van Vliet Kwasten- en Ladderfabriek NV v. Fratelli Dalle Crode* [1975] ECR 1103, [1975] 2 CMLR 549; Case 19/77 *Miller International Schallplatten GmbH v. Commission* [1978] ECR 131, [1978] 2 CMLR 334; Case 61/80 *Coöperatieve Stremsel- en Kleurselfabriek v. Commission* [1981] ECR 851, [1982] 1 CMLR 240; Case T-61/89 *Dansk Pelsdyravlerforening v. Commission* [1992] ECR II-1931, and Case T-43/92 *Dunlop Slazenger International Ltd. v. Commission* [1994] ECR II-441; Decs. 78/172 (O.J. 1978 L 53/20) *Spices*; 80/1333 (O.J. 1980 L 383/11) *Hennessy-Henkell*; 85/562 (O.J. 1985 L 369/11) *Distillers*; 85/618 (O.J. 1985 L 376/29) *Siemens-Fanuc*; 93/554 (O.J. 1993 L 272/28) *Zera/Montedison*, and 95/477 (O.J. 1995 L 272/16) *BASF Lacke + Farben AG/SA Accinauto*. The Commission has developed a distinction between active sales (actively seeking out-of-territory customers) and passive sales (simply meeting unsolicited orders from outside the contract territory), being often prepared to accept the former but not the latter, particularly in relation to exclusive distribution agreements and patent licensing, *e.g.* Dec. 87/100 (O.J. 1987 L 41/31) *Mitchell Cotts/Sofiltra*, a policy now reflected in various block exemption regulations.

dealing agreements between a producer in Member State A and exclusive dealer in Member State B which do not confer such absolute territorial protection benefit, originally under Regulation 67/67,[599] from a block exemption provided that certain express conditions specified in the appropriate regulation are satisfied, such as the absence of ancillary restrictions such as vertical price maintenance. As a result of developments in the case-law,[600] two separate block exemption regulations were adopted. Thus since July 1, 1983 the block exemption for exclusive distribution agreements is regulated by Regulation 1983/83[601] which covers short or medium-term exclusive distribution agreements (up to 5 years) in all sectors. Exclusive purchasing agreements for resale are dealt with by Regulation 1984/83[602] which also makes special provision for beer supply agreements (so-called brewery agreements)[603] and for service-station agreements.[604] In order to avoid perpetuating barriers to market entry which an exclusive purchasing network creates for suppliers outside the network, the block exemption only applies to agreements for a limited period of five years;[605] for brewery contracts and service station contracts it is generally ten years. If a brewery agreement relates to premises which the supplier lets to the reseller or allows the reseller to occupy on some other basis in law or in fact, the exclusive purchasing obligations and the bans on dealing in competing products specified in the regulation may be imposed on the reseller for the whole period for which he or she operates

599. O.J. English Special Edition 1967, p. 10.
600. In Case 63/75 *SA Fonderies Roubaix-Wattrelos v. Société nouvelle, des Fonderies A. Roux et al.* [1976] ECR 111, [1976] 1 CMLR 538 the Court held that, despite the wording of Reg. 67/67 to the contrary, even exclusive dealing agreements to which undertakings in only one Member State were party could benefit from the block exemption if they fulfilled all the other conditions for the grant of the block exemption. Furthermore, in Case 47/76 *De Norre et al. v. NV Brouwerij Concordia* [1977] ECR 65, [1977] 1 CMLR 378 the Court declared that the block exemption in principle also covered brewery contracts. Given that this judgment too did not accord with the wording of Reg. 67/67, the presently applicable regulations were adopted so as to accord with this case-law.
601. See note 532, *supra*. See, generally, Korah and Rothnie, *Exclusive Distribution and the EEC Competition Rules* (2nd ed., London, 1992).
602. *Ibid.*
603. See Case C-234/89 *Delimitis v. Henniger Bräu AG* [191] ECR I-935, [1992] 5 ECR 210.
604. See *Service station agreements in Spain* (*XXIIIrd Report on Competition Policy 1993* (Brussels, Luxembourg, 1994) point 226; *XXIVth Report 1994* (*ibid.*, 1995) Annex II 361); *Service station agreements in the Canary Islands* (*XXIIIrd Report* point 226(a)). See, further, Case C-39/92 *Petróleos de Portugal SA (Petrogal) v. Correia, Simões & Companhia Ld.ª et al.* [1993] ECR I-5659.
605. See, further, Case T-7/93 *Langnese-Iglo GmbH v. Commission* [1995] ECR II-1533, [1995] 5 CMLR 602, [1995] All ER (EC) 902, under appeal, Case C-279/95 P *Langnese-Iglo GmbH v. Commission* (O.J. 1995 C 286/3), and Case T-9/93 *Schöller Lebensmittel GmbH & Co. KG v. Commission* [1995] ECR II-1611, [1995] 5 CMLR 659, and Korah (1994) ECLR 171; Robertson and Williams (1995) ECLR 7; Sibree (1995) ECLR 203, and Maitland-Walker (1995) ECLR 451.

the premises. The regulation details further the restrictive conditions which may or may not be imposed. As is the case with all block exemption regulations, if an agreement falls outside its terms an individual exemption may still be sought.[606]

Selective distribution agreements are used to reserve the distribution of a particular product to a restricted circle of qualified traders. It is a topic which has given rise to extensive case-law as well as to a whole range of decision-making practice. These distribution systems are widespread in relation to numerous products, of which perhaps the most celebrated are motor vehicles, high quality watches and clocks,[607] cameras,[608] perfumes,[609] hi-fi, computers and other specialist electronic products,[610] jewellery and glass crystal,[611] ceramic tableware,[612] and dental protheses.[613] So far only the motor vehicle sector has been the subject of a block exemption.[614] The case-law on selective distribution can be summarized as

---

606. *E.g.* Dec. 84/381 (O.J. 1984 L 207/26) *Carlsberg*; see also the Commission's view in Dec. 78/172 (O.J. 1977 L 53/20) *spices.*

607. Decs. 70/488 (J.O. 1970 L 242/22) *Omega*; 77/100 (O.J. 1976 L 30/10) *Junghans*, and Case C-376/92 *Metro SB-Großmärkte & Co. KG v. Cartier SA* [1994] ECR I-15, [1994] 5 CMLR 331. But *cf.* Case 31/85 *ETA Fabriques d'Ébauches SA v. DK Investment SA et al.* [1985] ECR 3933, [1986] 2 CMLR 674 (mass-produced 'Swatch' watches).

608. Dec. 70/332 (J.O. 1970 L 147/24) *Kodak.*

609. Decs. 92/33 (O.J. 1992 L 12/24) *Yves Saint Laurent Parfums*, and 92/428 (O.J. 1992 L 236/11) *Parfums Givenchy.* These decisions were almost entirely upheld on appeal in Case T-19/92 *Groupement d'Achat Édouard Leclerc v. Commission* [1996] ECR II-1851 and Case T-88/92 *Groupement d'Achat Édouard Leclerc v. Commission* [1996] ECR II-1961, respectively. See also *Chanel* (O.J. 1994 C 334/1). Note the Court's attitude to a prohibition of re-importation into the Community of goods which were to be sold outside it, see Case C-306/96 *Javico International et al. v. Yves Saint Laurent Parfums SA (YSLP)* [1998] ECR I-nyr (28 April 1998).

610. *E.g.* Decs. 76/159 (O.J. 1976 L 28/19) *SABA I*, upheld on appeal in Case 26/76 *Metro SB-Großmärkte GmbH & Co. KG v. Commission* [1977] ECR 1875, [1978] 2 CMLR 1; 83/672 (O.J. 1983 L 376/41) *SABA II*, upheld on appeal in Case 75/84 *Metro SB-Großmärkte GmbH & Co. KG v. Commission* [1986] ECR 3021, [1987] 1 CMLR 118; 85/404 (O.J. 1985 L 233/1) *Grundig I*; and 94/29 (O.J. 1994 L 20/15) *Grundig II*, and *Sony Pan-European Dealer Agreement* (O.J. 1993 C 321/11; Commission Press Release IP (95) 736, [1995] 5 CMLR 126; *Sony España* (O.J. 1993 C 275/3), and *Kenwood Electronics Deutschland* (O.J. 1993 C 67/9). See also Case 210/81 *Schmidt, trading as Demo-Studio Schmidt v. Commission* [1983] ECR 3045, [1984] 1 CMLR 63. See further, Decs. 84/233 (O.J. 1984 L 118/24) *IBM Personal Computers*, and 87/407 (O.J. 1987 L 222/12) *Computerland.*

611. Decs. 83/610 (O.J. 1983 L 348/20) *Murat*, and 91/213 (O.J. 1991 L 97/16) *Baccarat* respectively.

612. Dec. 85/616 (O.J. 1985 L 376/15) *Villeroy & Boch.*

613. Dec. 85/559 (O.J. 1985 L 369/1) *Ivoclar.*

614. Reg. 1475/95 (see note 532, *supra*) replaces the old Reg. 123/85 (O.J. 1985 L 15/16), but the case-law on the old Reg. (which is important but too specialized to be included in the space available) is still relevant to the extent to which the provisions of the regs. are identical, see Bellamy and Child, *op. cit.* (see note 223, *supra*) 441–450 and Supp. 120–127. See also Dec. 91/39 (O.J. 1991 L 20/42) *D'Ieteren Motor Oils* and

finding that such systems fall outside Article 85(1) provided that resellers are chosen on the basis of objective criteria of a qualitative nature, such as criteria relating to the technical qualifications of the reseller and his or her staff and the suitability of the trading premises; such conditions must moreover be laid down uniformly for all potential resellers and are not applied in a discriminatory fashion.[615] However, this very generally formulated approach does not apply if all or many competing products are also sold through selective distribution systems, so that other distribution channels are excluded from the market place.[616] As the Commission rightly remarked in its *Twentieth General Report*[617] this makes it necessary for the Commission to analyze the market thoroughly before deciding whether a selective distribution system is compatible with Article 85 EC. Thus there is no question of a carte blanche for all selective distribution, as the judgment in Case 107/82 *Allgemeine Elektricitäts Gesellschaft AEG-Telefunken AG* v. *Commission*[618] well illustrates. In this case the Commission had imposed a fine of one million ECU because the supplier systematically imposed ancillary restrictions of competition on many resellers, containing in particular territorial protection of certain resellers, direct and indirect influence on resale prices and improperly refused admission to the selective system (which was based on qualitative criteria). The Court dismissed AEG's action against the Commission's condemnation of its system.[619] Various other cases show that selective distribution systems may not lead to the artificial maintenance of national frontiers within a common market; nor may they be used to maintain resulting price differentials.[620] Practice shows that selective distribution

Case C-41/96 *VAG-Händelerbeirat eV* v. *SYD-Consult* [1997] ECR I-3123 at 3138–3139: even if a selective distribution system meets the criteria for exemption, national law on unfair competition which means that such systems, even exempted ones, cannot be invoked against third parties unless they are watertight, remains unaffected by the provisions of Art. 85(3) EC or Reg. 123/85. See further, Case C-128/95 *Fontaine SA* v. *Acqueducs Automobiles SARL* [1997] ECR I-967 and Case C-230/95 *Cabour SA et al.* v. *Arnor 'SOCO' SARL* [1998] ECR I-nyr (30 April 1998).

615. Case 26/76 *Metro SB-Großmärkte GmbH & Co. KG* v. *Commission* [1977] ECR 1875 at 1907–1908.

616. See Case *ibid.* at 1904–1905 and Case 75/84 *Metro SB-Großmärkte GmbH & Co. KG* v. *Commission* [1986] ECR 3021 at 3085. The same is true if the existence of the systems results in an unduly rigid price structure not counterbalanced by other aspects of intra-brand competition and by effective inter-brand competition, *ibid.* See also the Opinion of VerLoren van Themaat, Adv. Gen., *ibid.* at 3059–3060. See further, Case 31/80 *L'Oréal NV et al.* v. *De Nieuwe AMCK PvbA* [1980] ECR 3775 at 3791–3792 and Decs. 85/44 (O.J. 1985 L 19/17) *Grohe* and 85/45 (O.J. 1985 L 20/38) *Ideal Standard, cf.* Dec. 88/84 (O.J. 1988 L 45/34, corrigendum O.J. 1988 L 212/62) *ARG/Unipart*.

617. (Brussels, Luxembourg, 1987), point 1025.

618. [1983] ECR 3151, [1984] 3 CMLR 413.

619. In Dec. 82/267 (O.J. 1982 L 117/15) *AEG*.

620. *E.g.* Cases 32 and 36–82/78 *BMW Belgium SA et al.* v. *Commission* [1979] ECR 2435, [1980] 1 CMLR 370; Case 126/80 *Salonia* v. *Poidomani et al.* [1981] ECR 1563, [1982]

systems for luxury goods and specialist goods are more likely to receive a favourable decision from the Commission than are mundane products or products the quality of which is already guaranteed by public law, for example through national or Community rules.[621]

Franchise agreements cover a form of distribution for goods and services (particularly but not only in the hotel, restaurant and fast food sectors), which had developed speedily in the Seventies in the distribution sector, but was initially scarcely noticed by the Commission.[622] Like exclusive purchasing and selective distribution agreements, franchise agreements are particularly prevalent at the retail sale stage. While parallel networks of exclusive purchasing agreements can significantly restrict market entry for new suppliers (particularly in brewery contracts and service station contracts for example), selective distribution agreements tend to exclude new forms of business in trade, such as warehouse and supermarkets, through their qualitative criteria. Franchise agreements, on the contrary, like exclusive dealing agreements at the wholesale stage, are also characterized by quantitative criteria. The franchisor undertakes, *inter alia*, not to grant a franchise to any other retailers in a certain area. Franchise agreements are also characterized by an extreme uniformity of trade-name, trademark, furnishing, and commercial and publicity management, purchasing obligations and an obligation on the franchisee to pay the franchisor a royalty. Attention was focused on this new method of distribution inn Case 161/84 *Pronuptia de Paris GmbH* v. *Pronuptia de Paris Irmgard Schillgalis.*[623] For the franchisor this method offers an inexpensive and – dependent on the royalty receipts – profitable method of penetrating new markets. It is inexpensive for the franchisor because the investment costs, save where the franchisor sets up its own subsidiary undertakings, are in principle borne by the franchisee. The consumer can

1 CMLR 64; Case 86/82 *Hasselblad (GB) Ltd.* v. *Commission* [1984] ECR 883, [1984] 1 CMLR 559; Case 243/83 *SA Binon and Cie* v. *SA Agence et messageries de la presse* [1985] ECR 2015, [1985] 3 CMLR 800; Cases 25 and 26/84 *Ford-Werke AG et al.* v. *Commission* [1985] ECR 2725, [1985] 3 CMLR 528; Case 31/85 *ETA Fabriques d'Ébauches SA* v. *DK Investment SA et al.* [1985] ECR 3933, [1986] 2 CMLR 674; Case 226/84 *British Leyland plc* v. *Commission* [1986] ECR 3263, [1987] 1 CMLR 184; Case T-19/91 *Société d'Hygiène Dermatologique de Vichy* v. *Commission* [1992] ECR II-415; Case T-43/92 *Dunlop Slazenger International Ltd.* v. *Commission* [1994] ECR II-441; Case T-77/92 *Parker Pen Ltd.* v. *Commission* [1994] ECR II-549; Case T-19/92 *Groupement d'Achat Édouard Leclerc* v. *Commission* [1996] ECR II-1851, and Case T-88/92 *Groupement d'Achat Édouard Leclerc* v. *Commission* [1996] ECR II-1961.

621. *E.g.* Case 31/80 *L'Oréal NV et al.* v. *De Nieuwe AMCK PvbA* [1980] ECR 3775, [1981] 2 CMLR 235; Dec. 91/153 (O.J. 1991 L 75/57 *Vichy*, upheld on appeal in Case T-19/91 *Société d'Hygiène Dermatologique de Vichy* v. *Commission* [1992] ECR II-415, and Dec. 90/33 (O.J. 1990 L 18/35) *APB*.

622. Koopmans notes the Commission's initial silence on the spread of franchising, (1987) SEW 32 *et seq.*

623. [1986] ECR 353, [1986] 1 CMLR 414. See the extensive analysis of VerLoren van Themaat, Adv. Gen., [1986] ECR 353 at 358–373.

also – if there are satisfactory alternatives – benefit from this quick method of marketing new quality products. As the *Pronuptia* case clearly demonstrates the new distribution methods involve risks primarily for the franchisee as the royalty obligations must also be met even where there is insufficient profitability. In the usually unlikely event of a lack of satisfactory alternatives for the consumer, though, the franchise system can also produce risks for the maintenance of sufficient competition.

The judgment in *Pronuptia* made the compatibility of franchise agreements for the distribution of goods with Article 85(1) EC dependent on the provisions in the agreements and the economic context.[624] As in the case of selective distribution agreements, in looking at the economic context both the market share of the system concerned and the structure of the relevant market in detail must be borne in mind. Provisions which are essential to ensure that the know-how communicated and assistance given to franchisees do not even indirectly benefit competitors, and provisions which are essential for maintaining the identity and reputation of the network are not regarded as restrictions on competition for the purposes of Article 85(1).[625] However, provisions which share markets between the franchisor and franchisees, or between the latter, or which prevent the latter from engaging in price competition with each other, are indeed regarded as restrictions on competition, but arguments can be advanced about their necessity for the purposes of deciding whether the conditions for the application of Article 85(3) are satisfied.[626] In due course the Commission adopted a block exemption for franchising agreements,[627] after some experience with individual exemptions.[628]

Constant case-law shows that the existence and defence of industrial property rights will not fall under the prohibition in Article 85(1) EC, but that the use that a right holder makes of rights conferred on him or her by

---

624. [1986] ECR 353 at 381–384.

625. *Ibid.* at 382.

626. *Ibid.* at 383–384. As has been observed, market sharing clauses are regarded as capable of hindering inter-state trade; the judgment in *Pronuptia* does not restrict this view to situations such as that *in casu* where the sales network is spread over various Member States. See, generally, Van Empel (1986) JWTL; 401 Korah (1986) ELR 99; Demaret (1986) *La Semaine Juridique* 729 and Venit (1986) 11 ELRev. 213.

627. Reg. 4087/88 (see note 532, *supra*). Since the adoption of Reg. 4087/88, see, in relation to franchised shops at petrol stations, *Texaco Ltd.*, *XXIIIrd Report on Competition Policy 1993* (Brussels, Luxembourg, 1994), point 225. See, further, the OECD Report *Competition Policy and Vertical Restraints: Franchising Agreements* (Paris, 1994, also in French as *Politique de la Concurrence et Restrictions Verticales: Les Accords de Franchise*). There have been no further individual exemptions since the entry into force of Reg. 4087/88, which suggests that the regulation was well-targeted.

628. Decs. 87/17 (O.J. 1987 L 13/39) *Pronuptia*; 87/14 (O.J. 1987 L 8/49) *Yves Rocher*; 87/407 (O.J. 1987 L 222/12) *Computerland*; 88/604 (O.J. 1988 L 332/38) *ServiceMaster*, and 89/94 (O.J. 1989 L 35/31) *Charles Jourdan*.

national law will be caught if it restricts competition.[629] Reliance on a national trade mark, patent or copyright in order to prevent imports from other Member States will no longer have any chance of success. In particular such attempts to restrict imports are prohibited if the product in question has been marketed in another Member State by the holder of the right or with his or her consent in a licensing agreement.[630] If, because of the absence of an agreement as one of the foundations of a claim seeking to restrain importation, Article 85 does not apply, Articles 36 or 86 EC may be relied upon to resist such a claim; the case-law in this context is discussed in more detail in section 3.2.3 of Chapter VII, above.

Licensing agreements relating to patents, trade marks, copyright, plant breeder's rights, or know-how rights, which permit the licensee, under certain limitations of time, space and scope defined in the agreement, to perform various production or distribution activities which fall within the legal or factual monopoly right, characterized by the intellectual property right, or the proprietorship of know-how, may fall under Article 85(1) EC. In Case 258/78 *L. C. Nungesser KG et al. v. Commission*[631] a distinction was drawn between open and closed exclusive licences. In an open exclusive licence the exclusivity of the licence relates solely to the contractual relationship between licensor and licensee. The licensor undertakes only to grant no other licences for the territory concerned and not to compete with the licensee on that territory. The Court concluded that, having regard to the specific nature of the products in question 'in a

---

629. *E.g.* Cases 56 and 58/64 *Consten and Grundig* [1966] ECR 299, [1966] CMLR 418; Case 16/74 *Centrafarm BV et al. v. Winthrop BV* [1974] ECR 1183, [1974] 2 CMLR 480 (both relating to the use of trade marks to hinder parallel imports); Case 24/67 *Parke, Davies & Co. v. Probel et al.* [1968] ECR 55, [1968] CMLR 47 and Case 15/74 *Centrafarm BV et al. v. Sterling Drug Inc.* [1974] ECR 1147, [1974] 2 CMLR 480 (relating to the use of patent rights to hinder parallel imports); Case 40/70 *Sirena Srl v. Eda Srl* [1971] ECR 69, [1971] CMLR 260 (relating to the use of transferred trade marks to restrain imports); Case 78/70 *Deutsche Grammophon Gesellschaft GmbH v. Metro SB-Großmärkte GmbH & Co. KG* [1971] ECR 487, [1971] CMLR 631; Case 51/75 *EMI Records Ltd. v. CBS United Kingdom Ltd.* [1976] ECR 811, [1976] 2 CMLR 235; Case 193/83 *Windsurfing International Inc. v. Commission* [1986] ECR 611, [1986] 3 CMLR 489, and Case 53/87 *Consorzio italiano della componentistica di ricambio per autoveicoli et al. v. Régie nationale des usines Renault* [1988] ECR 6039, [1990] 4 CMLR 265. On non-opposition clauses see Case 65/86 *Bayer AG et al. v. Süllhöfer* [1988] ECR 5249, [1990] 4 CMLR 182.
630. But note the Court's approach to licences of right and inter-state trade in Case 19/84 *Pharmon BV v. Hoechst AG* [1985] ECR 2281, [1985] 3 CMLR 775 and Case 434/85 *Allen and Hanburys Ltd. v. Generics (U.K.) Ltd.* [1988] ECR 1245, [1988] 1 CMLR 701. See also, as to the different effects of licensing to a licensee or affiliated undertaking (where quality control of the product can still be ensured) and assignment to an unrelated third party (where the assignor can no longer control the quality of the product), Case C-9/93 *IHT Internationale Heiztechnik GmbH et al. v. Ideal-Standard GmbH et al.* [1994] ECR I-2789.
631. [1982] ECR 2015, [1983] 1 CMLR 278.

case such as the present, the grant of an open exclusive licence, that is to say a licence which does not affect the position of third parties such as parallel importers and licensees for other territories, is not in itself incompatible with Article 85(1) of the Treaty.'[632] It is clear, therefore, that this approach does not apply to all open exclusive licences, given that the Court clearly took account of 'the specific nature of the products in question.'[633] In relation to exclusive licences which do affect third parties, particularly by conferring absolute territorial protection, the Court adopted a very different approach. These closed exclusive licences were roundly condemned; the Court noted that it had consistently held 'that absolute territorial protection granted to a licensee in order to enable parallel imports to be controlled and prevented results in the artificial maintenance of separate national markets, contrary to the Treaty.'[634] This clearly meant that closed exclusive licences could not benefit from an exemption under Article 85(3).[635] The Court did, of course, recognize that plant breeders' investment in developing new varieties required a certain protection from competition as without it there was a danger of prejudice to competition between the new product and similar existing products and a danger to the dissemination of new technology – those were the special factors which pleaded for a favourable view of open exclusive licences in *Nungesser*. Thus it was scarcely surprising that in Case 27/87 *Louis Erauw-Jacquery SPRL v. La Hesbignonne SC*[636] the Court found that a clause in an agreement on the sale and propagation of seeds between the proprietor of the production rights and a grower in which the latter was prohibited from selling and exporting basic seeds was compatible with Article 85(1) to the extent to which it was necessary to enable the breeder to select the growers to whom a licence is to be granted. This latter point was clearly a conclusion which had to be drawn by the national court; in any event it applied only in respect of the basic seeds and it cannot be seen as representing any general retreat from the Court's traditional attitude to export bans. The view that licences of plant breeders' rights generally fall within Article 85(1) EC has been confirmed in the Commission's practice.[637] As to the grant of Community-wide plant variety rights, see Regulation 2100/94.[638]

After the judgment in *Nungesser* and taking account of it, the

632. [1982] ECR 2015 at 2069.
633. *Ibid.*
634. *Ibid.* at 2070, referring to Cases 56 and 58/64 *Consten and Grundig* [1966] ECR 299, [1966] CMLR 418.
635. [1982] ECR 2015 at 2074.
636. [1988] ECR 1919, [1988] 4 CMLR 576.
637. See the Notices in O.J. 1990 C 6/3 *Standard Seed Production and Sales Agreements in France*; O.J. 1995 C 95/8 *SICASOV*, and O.J. 1995 C 211/11 *CRA*.
638. O.J. 1994 L 227/1 (amended by Reg. 2605/95 (O.J. 1995 L 258/3)), as to potatoes, see Reg. 2470/96 (O.J. 1996 L 333/10).

Commission – nearly twenty years after being so empowered by Council Regulation 19/65[639] – at last issued a block exemption for certain forms of patent licensing by Regulation 2349/84.[640] This was followed by Regulation 556/89 on know-how agreements.[641] After several prolongations, Regulation 2349/84 lapsed and Regulation 556/89 was repealed at the end of March 1996.[642] Their successor, Regulation 250/96 on technology transfer agreements,[643] contains in Articles 1 and 2 lists of permitted obligations, and in Article 3 a list of obligations which will take an agreement outside the scope of the block exemption, so that an individual exemption would be necessary for such obligations to be approved. Article 3 rightly makes it clear that even open exclusive licences may really have a disadvantaging influence on third parties through ancillary restrictions on competition. Article 7 of the regulation gives examples (not an exhaustive list) of instances in which the benefit of the block exemption may be withdrawn, according to Article 7 of Regulation 19/65, where the Commission finds that an exempted agreement 'nevertheless has certain effects which are incompatible with the conditions laid down in Article 85(3) of the Treaty.'[644] Article 4 of Regulation 240/96 provides for an accelerated opposition procedure, affording legal certainty: the exemption provided for in Articles 1 and 2 will apply to such restrictions not covered by those Articles and outside the scope of Article 3, provided that the agreements are notified with full and frank disclosure and the benefit of Article 4 is expressly claimed at the time of notification, and provided also that the Commission does not oppose the exemption within a period of four months. The opposition procedure is an extremely practical solution but given that it departs in various respects from the system of Article 85 it remains to be seen whether the Court will regard it as an acceptable process if the issue comes up for judgment. The block exemption will not normally apply to agreements between members of a patent or know-how pool relating to pooled technology between parties who compete with each other in the market for the products covered, or to reciprocal cross-licensing agreements between competitors holding interests in a joint venture or between one of them and the joint venture in so far as the

---

639. O.J. English Special Edition 1965–66, p. 35.
640. O.J. 1984 L 219/15, corrigendum O.J. 1985 L 113/24. (since replaced, as explained, *post*).
641. O.J. 1989 L 61/1, amended by Reg. 151/93 (O.J. 1993 L 21/8). See further, *e.g.* Decs. 72/25 (J.O. 1972 L 13/50) *Burroughs-Delphanque*; 72/26 (J.O. 1972 L 13/53) *Geha*; 83/622 (O.J. 1983 L 351/20) *Schlegel/CPIO*; 88/143 (O.J. 1988 L 69/21) *Rich Products/Jus-rol*; 88/563 (O.J. 1988 L 309/34) *Delta Chemie/DDD*, and 90/186 (O.J. 1990 L 100/32) *Moosehead/Whitbread*.
642. Reg. 240/96 (O.J. 1996 L 31/2), Art. 11.
643. O.J. 1996 L 31/2.
644. Note the importance of the provision relating to market share in Reg. 240/96, Art. 7(1), see *XXVth Report on Competition Policy 1995* (Brussels, Luxembourg, 1996), point 65.

agreements relate to the latter's activities (unless certain conditions are satisfied); nor does it apply to licensing agreements which contain provisions relating to intellectual property rights other than patents which are not ancillary to the agreement, it also does not extend to agreements contracted solely for the purpose of sale.[645] A good example of the Commission's policy on software licensing is provided by the undertaking given by *Microsoft*.[646]

In relation to trade mark licences besides the indicative judgment in Cases 56 and 58/64 *Consten and Grundig*,[647] the judgment in Case 35/83 *BAT Cigaretten-Fabriken GmbH* v. *Commission*[648] is also important. In this latter judgment the Court recognized that so-called delimitation agreements in which the parties delimit in their mutual interest the spheres in which their respective trade marks may be used, intending thereby to avoid confusion and conflict between them are in principle 'lawful and useful.' However, it went on to say that such agreements were not excluded from the application of Article 85 if (as was found in the instant case) they also had the aim of dividing up the market or restricting competition in other ways.[649]

In the evaluation of copyright licences the judgment in Case 262/81 *Coditel SA et al.* v. *Ciné-Vog Films SA et al.*[650] is of particular importance. In view of the characteristics of the cinematographic industry and of its markets in the Community, the Court found that an agreement conferring an exclusive exhibition licence for a certain period on the territory of another Member State did not in itself infringe Article 85(1) EC. None the less, the exercise of the exclusive right could fall within the prohibitions of Article 85(1) where, regard being had to the specific characteristics of the film market, there were economic or legal circumstances the effect of which was to restrict film distribution to a considerable extent or to distort competition on the cinematographic market. More generally, for the application of Article 85(1) it had to be established whether or not the exercise of the exclusive exhibition right created barriers which were

---

645. Reg. 240/96, Art. 5.
646. Bull. EU 7/8–1994, point 2.4.1. See also *XXIVth Report on Competition Policy 1994* (Brussels, Luxembourg, 1995) Annex II, p. 364.
647. [1966] ECR 299, [1966] CMLR 418.
648. [1985] ECR 363 at 385.
649. See *e.g.* Decs. 78/253 (O.J. 1978 L 70/69) *Campari* (see further, *Campari, Eighteenth Report on Competition Policy 1988* (Brussels, Luxembourg, 1989) point 69); 84/381 (O.J. 1984 L 207/26) *Carlsberg*, and 90/186 (O.J. 1990 L 100/32) *Moosehead/Whitbread*. See further, *Hershey-Herschi, XXth Report on Competition Policy 1990* (ibid., 1991) point 111, and Case C-9/93 *IHT Internationale Heiztechnik GmbH et al.* v. *Ideal-Standard GmbH et al.* [1994] ECR I-2789.
650. [1982] ECR 3381 at 3401–3402. See also the Commission's observations in a number of its *Reports on Competition Policy*: *Ninth Report 1979* point 116; *Eleventh Report 1981* point 98; *Twelfth Report 1982* points 88 and 90, and *Fifteenth Report 1985* point 81.

artificial and unjustifiable in terms of the needs of the industry, or the possibility of charging fees exceeding a fair return on investment or an exclusivity of disproportionate duration in relation to those requirements; it also had to be established whether the exercise of those rights within a given geographic area was such as to prevent, restrict or distort competition within the common market.[651] It had already been established that contractual export bans could not be justified by reliance on copyright protection.[652] With the explosion of the pan-European and worldwide television markets, the commercial importance of the Commission's regulatory role has been brought into ever sharper relief.[653]

As has already been observed in the general discussion of Article 85(1) EC, above, cooperation in the field of research will sometimes not entail any restriction of competition.[654] In other cases an exemption under Article

651. Case 395/87 *Ministère public v. Tournier* [1989] ECR 2521, [1991] 4 CMLR 248.
652. Cases 55 and 57/80 *Musik-Vertrieb membran GmbH v. GEMA* [1981] ECR 147, [1982] 2 CMLR 44. See also the *Fifteenth Report on Competition Policy* (Brussels, Luxembourg, 1986) point 81. See also, subsequently (on Art. 86) Case 402/85 *Basset v. Société des Auteurs, Compositeurs et Editeurs de Musique (SACEM)* [1987] ECR 1747, [1987] 3 CMLR 173. See further, Case 158/86 *Warner Bros. v. Christiansen* [1988] ECR 2605, [1990] 3 CMLR 684; Cases 110/88 *etc. Lucazeau et al. v. SACEM* [1989] ECR 2811, [1991] 4 CMLR 248; Case T-114/92 *Bureau Européen des Médias de l'Industrie Musicale (BEMIM) v. Commission* [1995] ECR II-147, [1996] 4 CMLR 305, and Case T-5/93 *Tremblay et al. v. Commission* [1995] ECR II-185 (appeal dismissed in Case C-91/95 P *Trembley et al. v. Commission* [1996] ECR I-5547).
653. The Commission's activity is not a new phenomenon, but it is assuming greater importance, see Decs. 89/536 (O.J. 1989 L 284/36) *Film Purchases by German Television Stations*; 93/403 (O.J. 1993 L 179/23), annulled in Cases T-528/93 *etc. Métropole télévision SA et al. v. Commission* [1996] ECR II-649 (under appeal in Case C-320/96 P *European Broadcasting Union v. Commission* (O.J. 1996 C 354/18)); 95/373 (O.J. 1995 L 221/34) *PMI-DSV*, and the informal settlements in *BSB/Football Association* (O.J. 1993 C 94/6) and *XXIIIrd Report on Competition Policy 1993* (Brussels, Luxembourg, 1994) Annex III, 459; *BBC Enterprises* (O. J. 1993 C 105/6 and *XXIIIrd Report, loc. cit.*), and *KNVB/Sport 7* (O.J. 1996 C 228/4). See, further (in relation to Art. 86 EC), Dec. 89/205 (O.J. 1989 L 78/43) *Magill TV Guide*, upheld on appeal in Case T-69/89 *Radio Telefis Eireann v. Commission* [1991] ECR II-485, [1991] 4 CMLR 586 (and in the other cases decided at the same time), which judgment was upheld in Cases C-241 and 242/91 P *Radio Telefis Eireann et al. v. Commission* [1995] ECR I-743, [1995] 4 CMLR 718. See also Dirs. 92/100 (O.J. 1992 L 346/1) and 93/83 (O.J. 1993 L 248/15). In the context of the Uruguay Round, see Dec. 94/824 (O.J. 1994 L 349/201).
654. *E.g.* Decs. 68/128 (J.O. 1968 L 57/9) *Eurogypsum*; 68/317 (J.O. 1968 L 201/1) *Alliance des Constructeurs Français*; 70/346 (J.O. 1970 L 153/14) *ASBL Pour la promotion du Tube d'Acier Soudé Électriquement*; 80/1074 (O.J. 1980 L 318/32) *Industrieverband Solnhofener Natursteinplatten*; 85/563 (O.J. 1985 L 369/25) *London Sugar Futures Market Ltd.*; 85/564 (O.J. 1985 L 369/28) *London Cocoa Terminal Market Association Ltd.*; 85/565 (O.J. 1985 L 369/31) *Coffee Terminal Market Association of London Ltd.*; 85/566 (O.J. 1985 L 369/34) *London Rubber Terminal Market Association Ltd.*; 87/2 (O.J. 1987 L 3/27) *International Petroleum Exchange of London Ltd.*; 87/44 (O.J. 1987 L 19/18) *GAFTA Soya Bean Meal Futures Association*; 87/45 (O.J. 1987 L 19/22) *London Grain Futures Market*; 87/46 (O.J. 1987 L 19/26) *London Potatoes Futures Association*; 87/47 (O.J. 1987 L 19/30) *London Meat Futures Exchange Ltd.*; 86/507 (O.J. 1986 L 295/28)

85(3) EC may well be possible.[655] Market sharing and similar practices remain unacceptable.[656]

A block exemption for specialization agreements is granted by Regulation 417/85,[657] which covers products which are the subject of the specialization together with the participating undertakings' other products which users consider to be equivalent in view of their characteristics, price and intended use and do not represent more than 20% of the market for such products in the common market or the aggregate annual turnover of all the participating undertakings does not exceed 1,000 million ECU (there are certain overrun provisions).[658] The block exemption principally interests small and medium-sized undertakings and enables them to achieve larger production runs which are important for their competitive position on the common market. For larger undertakings an opposition procedure (with a six month reaction period) is set up by Article 4 of the regulation. Specialization agreements between undertakings with high market shares quickly run the risk that the advantages will be outweighed by the restrictions on competition.[659]

A sister block exemption applies to research and development agreements under Regulation 418/85.[660] If (two or more of) the parties to the agreement are competing manufacturers the block exemption will only

Irish Banks' Standing Committee; 87/103 (O.J. 1987 L 43/51) *ABI*; 88/568 (O.J. 1988 L 311/36) *Eurotunnel*, and 89/95 (O.J. 1995 L 36/16) *Uniform Eurocheques*.

655. *E.g.* Decs. 68/319 (J.O. 1968 L 201/7) *ACEC/Berlinet*; 72/41 (J.O. 1972 L 14/14) *Henkel/Colgate* (a decision which was less than wholly convincing, see Baardman (1974) SEW 178, and which was not renewed, see the *Eighth Report on Competition Policy* (Brussels, Luxembourg, 1979) point 89); 78/251 (O.J. 1978 L 70/47) *Sopelem/Vickers*; 79/298 (O.J. 1979 L 70/11) *Beecham/Parke Davis*; 83/671 (O.J. 1983 L 376/30) *International Energy Agency* (allocation of supplies in time of shortages, renewed by Dec. 94/153 (O.J. 1994 L 68/35)); 84/191 (O.J. 1984 L 99/29) *Nuovo CEGAM*; 85/560 (O.J. 1985 L 369/6) *BP/Kellogg*; 85/615 (O.J. 1985 L 376/2) *P & I Clubs* (cooperation in insurance); 87/13 (O.J. 1987 L 7/27) *Belgische Vereniging der Banken / Association Belge des Banques*; 87/69 (O.J. 1987 L 35/36) *X/Open Group*; 87/3 (O.J. 1987 L 5/13) *ENI/Montedison* (restructuring); 88/84 (O.J. 1984 L 45/34) *ARG/Unipart*; 88/330 (O.J. 1988 L 150/53) *Bayer-BP Chemicals* (restructuring); 90/22 (O.J. 1990 L 13/34) *TEKO*, and 90/25 (O.J. 1990 L 15/25) *Concordato Incendio*.

656. *E.g.* Decs. 75/76 (O.J. 1975 L 29/20) *Rank/Sopelem* and 80/1334 (O.J. 1980 L 383/19) *Italian Cast Glass*.

657. See note 532, *supra*.

658. Reg. 417/85, Art. 3 (as substituted by Reg. 151/93 (O.J. 1993 L 21/8).

659. See Decs. 69/241 (J.O. 1969 L 195/1) *Clima-Chappée-Buderus*; 71/222 (J.O. 1971 L 134/6) *FN/CF*; 72/88 (J.O. 1972 L 31/29) *MAN/SAVIEM*; 72/291 (J.O. 1972 L 182/24) *Lightweight Paper*; and 76/172 (O.J. 1976 L 30/13) *Bayer/Gist-Brocades*. See also *Electrolux/AEG* (O.J. 1993 C 269/4).

660. See note 532, *supra*. See, generally, Korah, *R. & D. and the EEC Competition Rules: Regulation 418/85* (Oxford, 1986); Korah (1993) YBEL 39; Venit (1985) 10 ELRev. 151, White (1985) 16 IIC 663, and Elizalde (1992) 29 CMLRev. 309. See also *Cooperation Agreement between Peugeot and Fiat involving the Sevel joint venture*, *XXIIIrd Report on Competition Policy 1993* (Brussels, Luxembourg, 1994) point 227.

apply 'if, at the time the agreement is entered into, the parties' combined production of the products capable of being improved or replaced by the contract products does not exceed 20% of the market for such products in the common market or a substantial part thereof.'[661] The exemption runs for five years from the time the contract products are first put on the market within the common market, although there are certain provisions for extension of this period (relating to market share).[662] The block exemption contains a list of permitted restrictions in Articles 4 and 5 and a list of prohibited restrictions in Article 6. Again, the block exemption regulation provides for an opposition procedure (the period is six months) for agreements satisfying the conditions for exemption but which also contain restrictions on competition not classified by the regulation (often grey agreements).[663]

Although the enabling provisions contained in Council Regulation 2821/71[664] permit it, no block exemption has yet been created for standardization or normalization agreements. Article 4(2)(3)(a) of Regulation 17[665] provides that agreements having as their sole object 'the development or uniform application of standards or types' may be exempted from the notification requirement. As Advocate General VerLoren van Themaat put it in Case 188/84 Commission v. France,[666] despite the mutual acceptance and mutual recognition concepts developed in the Court's case-law on Article 30–36,[667] national standardization agreements can in fact lead to tangible barriers to trade.[668] A block exemption should at best relate to international arrangements (such as are concluded through the ISO or CEN, CENELEC or ETSI) and the Commission will need to pay particular attention to combating the negative effect of national standards by means of competition policy.[669] Given that Community standardization is still an interminable process, the Commission might usefully pay more attention to this point.

661. Reg. 418/85, Art. 3(2). See also Art. 3(a) (added by Reg. 151/93 (O.J. 1993 L 21/8)).
662. *Ibid.*, Art. 3(l) and (3), (4) and (5) (paras. (4) and (5) were amended by Reg. 151/93 (O.J. 1993 L 21/8)).
663. See in particular, Decs. 88/555 (O.J. 1988 L 305/33) *Continental/Michelin*; 90/46 (O.J. 1990 L 32/19) *Alcatel Espace/ANT Nachrichtentechnik*, and 91/38 (O.J. 1991 L 19/25) *KSB/Goulds/Lowara/ITT*. Two recent joint ventures which were notified to the Commission were exempted only after the importance of the non-R & D elements had been reduced: Decs. 94/770 (O.J. 1994 L 309/1) *Pasteur-Mérieux/Merck* and 94/896 (O.J. 1994 L 354/87) *Asahi/St. Gobain*.
664. J.O. 1971 L 285/46.
665. See note 501, *supra*. For an example of an exemption for a standardization agreement see Dec. 87/69 (O.J. 1987 L 35/36) *X/Open Group*. See also the *Seventeenth Report on Competition Policy* (Brussels, Luxembourg, 1988, point 75) *standardized bottles in Germany* (rejection of complaint).
666. [1986] ECR 419 at 420–421.
667. See Chapter VII, section 3, *ante*.
668. See further, Case 246/86 *S.C. Belasco et al. v. Commission* [1989] ECR 2117, [1991] 4 CMLR 96. and Dec. 87/69 (O.J. 1987 L 35/36) *X/Open Group*.
669. As to European standards and intellectual property licensing, see *ETSI Interim IPR*

The standpoint of the Commission as regards prohibited and permitted restrictions on participation in trade fairs and exhibitions has now become much clearer, particularly as regards bans on also exhibiting at exhibitions elsewhere.[670]

The block exemption for insurance agreements, contained in Regulation 3932/92,[671] covers common risk-premium tariffs based on collectively ascertained statistics or on the number of claims,[672] the establishment of standard policy conditions, the common coverage of certain types of risks, and the establishment of common rules on the testing and acceptance of security devices.

Concluding observations. From this brief survey of prohibited and permitted restrictions of competition, the following generalized observations may be made, with the necessary reserve:

(1) In relation to all forms of horizontal and vertical protection of national markets, quantitative market sharing, and absolute territorial protection, a *per se* prohibition applies, which means that the application of Article 85(3) EC is impossible. The same is true of horizontal price agreements and collective vertical resale price maintenance.

(2) Particularly through block exemptions, exclusive distribution and purchasing agreements, franchising and technology transfer agreements are exempt from the prohibition of Article 85(1) EC, provided that they satisfy the prescribed conditions. The same is true of limited forms of cooperation through specialization or research and development agreements.

(3) National cartel agreements and national resale price maintenance systems which cover the whole of national territory may also be caught by the prohibition of Article 85(1), even if they do not concern imports or exports. This has led particularly in the Netherlands to a

Policy, XXVth Report on Competition Policy 1995 (Brussels, Luxembourg, 1996), 131 (part of DG IV's *Report on the Application of Competition Rules in the European Union*, annexed to the formal Report).

670. See Decs. 71/337 (J.O. 1971 L 227/26) and 83/252 (O.J. 1983 L 140/27) *Cematex*; 69/90 (J.O. 1969 L 69/13), 79/37 (O.J. 1979 L 11/16), and 89/96 (O.J. 1989 L 37/11) *European Machine Tool Exhibitions (CECIMO)*; 77/722 (O.J. 1977 L 299/18) and 82/349 (O.J. 1982 L 156/16); 75/498 (O.J. 1975 L 228/14) and 84/588 (O.J. 1984 L 322/10) *UNIDI* (Dec. 84/588 was upheld on appeal, see Case 43/85 *Associazione nazionale commercianti internazionali dentali e sanitari (Ancides) v. Commission* [1987] ECR 3131, [1988] 4 CMLR 821); 83/666 (O.J. 1983 L 376/1) *SMM & T Exhibition Agreement*; 86/499 (O.J. 1986 L 291/46) *VIFKA*; 87/509 (O.J. 1987 L 293/58) *Internationale Dentalschau*, and 88/477 (O.J. 1988 L 233/15) *British Dental Trade Association*. See also the Commission's Interpretative Communication (O.J. 1998 C 143/2).

671. See note 532, *supra*.

672. This concerns the calculation of the average cost of risk cover (pure premiums) or the establishment and distribution of mortality or certain other actuarial tables.

change from the 'nod and a wink' approach which characterized the application of Dutch competition legislation for so long, so as to move to a more prohibition-based approach.[673]

4.3 Divergent rules for agriculture and transport[674]

Article 42 EC empowers the Council to determine whether, and if so, to what extent, Articles 85–90 EC shall apply to the conduct of undertakings engaged in the production of or trade in agricultural products.[675] On the basis of that provision the Council adopted Regulation 26[676] which made three exceptions to the application of Article 85(1) in the agricultural sector. In practice these three exceptions have a more general significance for agricultural cooperatives, the activities of which compensate for structural weaknesses in the production and trade of agricultural produce.[677] In many cases undertakings pray Regulation 26 in aid, but in vain do they seek to escape the ambit of Article 85(1).[678]

Separate competition rules apply to transport by rail, road and inland waterway,[679] these were followed much later by rules for maritime

673. See *par excellence* the Dutch building cartel, Dec. 92/204 (O.J. 1992 L 92/1) *Re: Building and Construction Industry in the Netherlands*, upheld on appeal, Case T-29/92 *Vereniging van Samenwerkende Prijsregelende Organisaties in de Bouwnijverheid et al. v. Commission* [1995] ECR II-289 and Case C-137/95 P *Vereniging van Samenwerkende Prijsregelende Organisaties in de Bouwnijverheid et al. v. Commission* [1996] ECR I-1611.
674. As to the ECSC competition regime, see Chapter X, *post*. The normal EC competition rules apply in relation to atomic energy.
675. See Case C-250/92 *Gøttrup-Klim Grovvareforening et al. v. Dansk Landbrugs Grovvareselskab AmbA (DLG)* [1994] ECR I-5641, [1996] 4 CMLR 191. There is a derogation, for certain producer groups for certain produce, in relation to no retroactive effect of a determination by the Commission that Art. 85(1) EC has been infringed, Reg. 1360/78 (O.J. 1978 L 166/1), Art. 17.
676. O.J. English Special Edition 1959–1962, p. 129.
677. See Cases C-319/93 *Dijkstra et al. v. Friesland (Frico Domo) Coöperatie BA et al.* [1995] ECR I-4471, [1996] 5 CMLR 178 and Case C-399/93 *Oude Luttikhuis et al. v. Verenigde Coöperatieve Melkindustrie Coberco BA* [1995] ECR I-4515. See also Dec. 92/444 (O.J. 1992 L 246/37) *Scottish Salmon Board*. See, further, Cases T-70 and 71/92 *Florimex BV et al. v. Commission* [1997] ECR II-693 and Case T-77/94 *Vereniging van Groothandelaren in Bloemkwekerijprodukten et al. v. Commission* [1997] ECR II-759.
678. See, in addition to the first two cases mentioned in note 677, *supra*, Cases 71/74 *Nederlandse Vereniging voor Fruit en Groentenimporthandel et al. v. Commission et al.* [1975] ECR 563, [1975] 2 CMLR 123; Case 61/80 *Coöperatieve Stremsel- en Kleurselfabriek v. Commission* [1981] ECR 851, [1982] 1 CMLR 240; Case 123/83 *Bureau national interprofessionnel du cognac v. Clair* [1985] ECR 391, [1985] 2 CMLR 430; Case 218/85 *Association comité économique agricole régional fruits et légumes de Bretagne v. Le Campion* [1986] ECR 3513, [1988] 1 CMLR 83, and Case T-61/89 *Dansk Pelsdyravlerforening v. Commission* [1992] ECR II-1931.
679. Reg. 1017/68 (O.J. English Special Edition 1959–62, p. 291). See *e.g.* Case T-14/93 *Union Internationale des Chemins de Fer v. Commission* [1995] ECR II-1503, [1996] 5

transport,[680] and air transport.[681] The procedural rules for the application of the competition provisions in the fields of maritime and air transport are mostly very similar to those applicable in other sectors. In respect of air transport the Commission is separately empowered[682] to adopt block exemptions.[683]

4.4   Article 86 EC

Article 86 EC declares incompatible with the common market, and thus prohibited, abuse of a dominant position within the common market or a significant part of it, in so far as it may affect trade between Member States. Each of these elements (with the prohibition there are four) is discussed in turn below. Attention is also paid to the illustrative list of abusive practices mentioned in Article 86; it is clear though from the wording of the Article that the list is not exhaustive.

4.4.1   Abuse of a dominant position

The most important element of this directly applicable prohibition concerns the abuse of a dominant position on the common market or a substantial part thereof.[684] There is a reciprocal relationship between the concept of 'abuse' and that of a 'dominant position.' On the one hand, a given practice (such as a refusal to sell or a price discrimination), which would be perfectly permissible, without an agreement so to act, for one or more undertakings having no dominant position, may constitute a prohibited abuse if it is carried out by one or more undertakings having a

CMLR 40, appeal dismissed in Case C-264/95 P *Commission v. Union Internationale des Chemins de Fer* [1997] ECR I-1287, and Dec. 94/894 (O.J. 1994 L 354/66) *Euro-tunnel III*, annulled in Cases T-79 and 80/95 *Société nationale des chemins de fer français et al. v. Commission* [1996] ECR II-1491.

680. Reg. 4056/86 (O.J. 1986 L 378/4). See *e.g.* Dec. 92/262 (O.J. 1992 L 134/1) *French–West African Shipowners' Committees*. A block exemption has been granted by Reg. 870/95 (O.J. 1995 L 89/7) for liner consortia.

681. Reg. 3975/87 (O.J. 1987 L 374/1), see *e.g.* Dec. 92/213 (O.J. 1992 L 96/34) *Aer Lingus*.

682. Reg. 3976/87 (O.J. 1987 L 374/9).

683. Regs. 1617/93 (O.J. 1993 L 155/18, amended by Reg. 1523/96 (O.J. 1996 L 190/11)) on capacity coordination in air transport, and 3652/93 (O.J. 1993 L 333/37) on air transport computer reservation systems.

684. Besides the literature cited in note 364, *supra*, see, *inter alia*, Dubois, *La position dominante et son abus dans l'article 86 du Traité CEE* (Paris, 1986); *Le problème de la concentration dans le Marché Commun* (CEE études, série concurrence, no. 3, Brussels, 1966); Joliet, *Monopolisation and abuse of dominant position* (The Hague, 1970), summarized in (1969) RTDE 645; Fejö, *Monopoly Law and Market* (Deventer, 1990); Enchelmaier, *Europäische Wettbewerbspolitik im Oligopol* (Baden-Baden, 1997); De Jong (1966–67) 4 CMLRev. 166 and *Ondernemingsconcentratie* (Leiden, 1971); VerLoren van Themaat (1968) SEW 162; Winter in Van Damme (ed.) *La réglementation du comportement des monopoles et enterprises dominante en droit communautaire* (Bruges,

dominant position. In these two examples, the buyer, who is faced with a dominant position within the common market or in a substantial part of it, has no alternatives and is thus placed at a competitive disadvantage by this practice. It is not required that there should be an intention to prejudice other parties.[685] Conversely, however, the concept of a dominant position is also dependent on the abuse in question. In the examples given, it will have to be clear that there is no reasonable alternative. This implies as a rule that the undertakings concerned, which thus abuse their dominant position, jointly or individually govern a substantial part of the market of the relevant products or services. In other cases, such as selective price-cutting, having as its object or effect the ousting of a competitor (predatory pricing), it is sufficient for the undertaking having the dominant position to possess enough financial strength to continue a price war longer than its competitor. No large market share is required for this. It must be stressed that the dominant position must exist in the common market as a whole, or in a substantial part thereof, so that even a localized price war against a producer who only distributes in a regional market may be prohibited: indeed, even an extremely small geographical area, such as a particular port, may be considered to be a significant part of the common market.[686]

From the mutual relation between the concepts of abuse and a dominant position it follows that ultimately the concept of abuse is the principal one. In fact, as has been shown, different forms of abuse are associated with

1977); Korah (1980) 17 CMLRev. 395; Baden Fuller (1979) 4 ELRev. 423; Verstrynge (1980) SEW 400; Gyselen and Kyriazas (1986) 11 ELRev. 134; Rodger (1994/2) LIEI 1; Ehlermann (1993) ECLR 61; Rodger (1995) ECLR 21, and Turnbull (1996) ECLR 96.

685. Case 85/76 *Hoffmann-La Roche & Co. AG v. Commission* [1979] ECR 461 at 554–555.

686. *E.g.* Case C-179/90 *Merci convenzionali porto di Genova SpA v. Siderurgica Gabrelli SpA* [1991] ECR I-5889 at 5928; Case C-18/93 *Corsica Ferries Italia Srl v. Corpo dei Piloti del Porto di Genova* [1994] ECR I-1783 at 1824–1825, and *Sealink/B & I* Commission Press Release IP (92) 478, [1992] 5 CMLR 255 (Holyhead harbour). These cases concern access to essential facilities, see Glasl (1994) ECLR 306; Temple Lang (1994) 18 Fordham Int'l. L.J. 437; Furse (1995) ECLR 469, and Ridyard (1996) ECLR 438. As Bellamy and Child, *op. cit.* (see note 223, *supra*) 616, rightly observe, what is a substantial part of the common market will thus be a matter of fact in each case. In Cases 40/73 *etc. Coöperatieve vereniging 'Suiker Unie' UA et al. v. Commission* [1975] ECR 1663 at 1977 the relevant market was found to be Belgium and Luxembourg and (at 1991) the southern part of Germany; in Case 322/81 *NV Nederlandsche Banden-Industrie Michelin v. Commission* [1983] ECR 3461 at 3501–3502 the Netherlands was found to be the relevant market. The Commission has found that a busy air route is a substantial part of the common market, see Dec. 92/213 (O.J. 1992 L 96/34) *British Midland/Aer Lingus*. In some circumstances the relevant geographic market may be the world market, see Dec. 91/619 (O.J. 1991 L 334/42) *Aerospatiale/de Haviland* and *Novell/Microsoft, XXIVth Report on Competition Policy (1994)* (Brussels, Luxembourg, 1995) point 200. Cf. *Carlsberg/Interbrew, ibid.*, point 201 (Belgium was the relevant market). As an *e.g.* of the Community as a whole being the relevant market, see Dec. 92/163 (O.J. 1992 L 72/1) *Tetra Pak II*, upheld in Case T-83/91 *Tetra Pak*

different interpretations of the concept of a dominant position. In other words, an undertaking in a specific case has a dominant position if it is able to commit the abuse in question exclusively owing to its market position.[687] This explains why it was considered necessary to make implicit or express mention of the element of prejudice to suppliers or buyers for each example in the illustrative[688] list mentioned in Article 86. If buyers have a real alternative of buying from other suppliers, they will not be prejudiced by the practices mentioned in the examples. In that case there is no question of abuse, and from the available alternatives it follows on the other hand that the undertakings engaging in such practices do not have a dominant position. In practice too, the Commission will usually act in response to an alleged abuse so the determination of a dominant position may to this extent be of a secondary character.

4.4.2   Aim and scope of the prohibition

In the light of the observations concerning the element of abuse of a dominant position, it is possible to define more closely the aim and scope of Article 86 EC. In section 4.1.1, above, it was noted that Articles 85 and 86 pursue the same aim on different levels, namely the maintenance of effective competition within the common market.[689] Restraint of competition, which is prohibited if it results from conduct prohibited by Article 85 EC, cannot be lawful if such behaviour results from the conduct of a single undertaking which is able so to act by reason of its market position. Also an undertaking possessing a dominant position may not act in such a way that the minimum of competition postulated in Article 85(3) is thereby affected.[690] In Case 6/72 Continental Can[691] the Court stressed that it was clear from the aim and scope of Article 86 EC that the concept of abuse also embraced exclusion of competition in a significant part of

International SA v. Commission [1994] ECR II-755 at 804–808 (further appeal rejected in Case C-333/94 P Tetra Pak International SA v. Commission [1996] ECR I-5951, [1997] 4 CMLR 662). See further, Cases C-68/94 and 30/95 France et al. v. Commission [1998] ECR I-1375 and the Commission's Notice on the definition of the relevant market (O.J. 1997 C 372/5).

687. See in particular the extensive analysis in Case 85/76 Hoffmann-La Roche [1979] ECR 461 at 520–524, and the definition (at 520) of a dominant position as relating 'to a position of economic strength enjoyed by an undertaking which enables it to prevent effective competition being maintained on the relevant market by affording it the power to behave to an appreciable extent independently of its competitors, customers and ultimately of the consumers.'

688. Case 6/72 Europemballage Corporation and Continental Can Company Inc. v. Commission [1973] ECR 215 at 245.

689. Case 40/70 Sirena Srl v. Eda Srl [1971] ECR 69 at 83.

690. Case 6/72 Continental Can [1973] ECR 215 at 244–245.

691. Ibid.

the relevant market through a merger or acquisition of a majority interest. Thus an answer was given to a heated discussion in early literature in this field,[692] particularly as to whether Article 86 only caught market behaviour of undertakings with a dominant position, which, it was argued, seemed to be indicated by the examples mentioned in Article 86 itself, or whether it also affected behaviour which changed the structure of competition on the relevant market. Apart from the fact that a distinction between market behaviour of an undertaking with a dominant position and market structure does not hold water, as even cut-throat price competition, boycotts, and other restrictions of competition by an undertaking with a dominant position may lead to structural changes in the market place,[693] the wording of Article 86 EC offers no support for the view that such a distinction lies behind that provision.[694] 'Abuse may therefore occur if an undertaking in a dominant position strengthens such position in such a way that the degree of dominance reached substantially fetters competition, *i.e.* that only undertakings remain in the market whose behaviour depends on the dominant one.'

Even though the this discussion about the interpretation of Article 86 has now been finally resolved, it is still worth examining this problem. What is at issue, according to the Court, 'is whether the word "abuse" in Article 86 refers only to practices of undertakings which may directly affect the market and are detrimental to production or sales, to purchasers or consumers, or whether this word also refers to changes in the structure of an undertaking, which lead to competition being seriously disturbed in a substantial part of the common market.'[695] From this reformulation of the problem by the Court, it is clear that the Court regarded the first type of behaviour (market behaviour injurious to third parties) as in any event an abuse in the sense of Article 86, without it being necessary to show as well that competition was thereby restricted. This, it is submitted, is correct and is of practical importance for the burden of proof on the Commission. It is correct because, particularly in the case of an undertaking which has such a strong dominant position that effective competition is already eliminated (an actual monopoly position), it is irrelevant whether the undertaking

---

692. Various arguments against the applicability of Art. 86 EC to mergers were advanced by Hefermehl and Dabin, and by Joliet in unpublished papers for the FIDE Congress in Rome in 1968. See also VerLoren van Themaat (1968) SEW 162. In Case 6/72 *Continental Can* [1973] ECR 215 at 243 the Court considered that a distinction between behaviour and structure was not decisive 'for any structural measure may influence market conditions, if it increases the size and the economic power of the undertakings.'

693. As is well illustrated in Cases 6 and 7/73 *Commercial Solvents* [1974] ECR 233, [1974] 1 CMLR 309.

694. Already in Cases 56 and 58/64 *Consten and Grundig* [1966] ECR 299 at 339 the Court had found that in principle 'no distinction can be made where the Treaty does not make a distinction.'

695. Case 6/72 *Continental Can* [1973] ECR 215 at 243.

restricts competition further by its behaviour. An undertaking with a dominant position in relation to its competitors in the market place 'has a special responsibility not to allow its conduct to impair genuine undistorted competition on the common market.'[696] There must in particular be no discrimination between customers or suppliers and no unfair contractual terms may be imposed; moreover a quantitatively and qualitatively reasonable supply must be ensured.[697] The influence of the condemned behaviour on the market structure in these cases does not need to be considered. It is felt necessary to stress this as a misunderstanding could arise from Case 85/76 *Hoffmann-La Roche*[698] to the effect that, unlike in Case 6/72 *Continental Can*, the Court considered that *only* the behaviour of an undertaking in a dominant position which is such as to influence the structure of a market by restricting the degree of competition still existing or its further development is caught by Article 86. It is clear that Article 86 is not confined to such behaviour.

4.4.3   One or more undertakings

Article 86 is applicable not only in the case of a dominant position of one undertaking, but also in that of a dominant position of several undertakings. It follows from the demarcation between Articles 85 and 86 EC that the latter does not cover agreements or concerted practices of the undertakings in question, or between undertakings forming an economic entity (belonging to one concern).[699] However, a cartel may well also produce a position of collective dominance, abuse of which may fall within Article 86 EC.[700] A collective dominance by several undertakings primarily involves an oligopolistic situation (a small number of undertakings are in

696. Case 322/81 *Michelin* [1983] ECR 3461 at 3511.
697. In determining the unfairness of sales or purchase prices either the profit margin or the prices may be compared with the situations on comparable other territorial or product markets, *cf.* the German concept of *als-ob-Wettbewerb*' and Case 27/76 *United Brands* [1978] ECR 207 at 299–303.
698. [1979] ECR 461 at 541.
699. Case 172/80 *Züchner v. Bayerische Vereinsbank AG* [1981] ECR 2021 at 20330–2031; as to parent company liability, see *e.g.* Case T-65/89 *BPB Industries plc et al. v. Commission* [1993] ECR II-389 at 440–442 (appeal dismissed in Case C-310/93 P *BPB Industries plc et al. v. Commission* [1995] ECR I-865, [1997] 4 CMLR 238).
700. See Cases T-68, 77 and 78/89 *Società Italiana Vetro SpA et al. v. Commission* [1992] ECR II-1403 at 1547–1548; Cases T-24–26 and 28/93 *Compagnie Maritime Belge SA et al. v. Commission* [1996] ECR II-1201, [1997] 4 CMLR 273, and Case C-393/92 *Gemeente Almelo et al. v. Energiebedrijf Ijsselmij NV* [1994] ECR I-1477 at 1519–1520. See also Dec. 92/262 (O.J. 1992 L 134/1) *French–West African Shipowners' Committees*. See also the somewhat hybrid situation where each undertaking (BBC, RTE and ITV) could prevent a listing magazine from publishing by refusing to supply information about its programmes, Cases C-241 and 242/91 P *Radio Telefis Eireann (RTE) et al. v. Commission* [1995] ECR I-743, [1995] 4 CMLR 718.

the market and there is significant collusive or parallel conduct between them)[701] where the applicability of Article 86 can be envisaged primarily in relation to measures designed to control prices.[702]

4.4.4 The application of Article 86 EC in practice

The practice of the Court and the Commission is first to establish the relevant product and geographical markets; then whether the undertaking(s) concerned have a dominant position in those markets, and, finally, whether there has been an abuse of that dominant position.[703] The most important element of Article 86 EC is that it is, unlike ancient Gaul, divided into four sub-parts, an approach which runs the risk of losing sight of the reciprocal relationship between abuse and a dominant position.

The relevant product market is usually defined by an analysis of the possibility of product substitutability on both the supply and the demand sides. This in effect looks at the possibilities available elsewhere to purchasers and suppliers (and the elasticity of supply and demand). Demand substitutability[704] depends not only on the actual interchangeability of a product, such as bananas and other types of fruit, but also on consumer preferences.[705] Depending on the possible

701. *Ibid.* See Stevens (1995) 15 YBEL 47 at 62 *et seq.* See also the Court's views on collective dominant position (in the merger context) in Cases C-68/94 and 30/95 *France et al. v. Commission* [1998] ECR I-1375 at 1501–1504.
702. See Dec. 92/262 (O.J. 1992 L 134/1) *French–West African Shipowners' Committee. Cf.* Case 13/60 *'Geitling' Ruhrkohlen-Verkaufsgesellschaft mbH et al. v. High Authority* [1962] ECR 83, [1962] CMLR 113 and Case 66/63 *Netherlands v. High Authority* [1964] ECR 533, [1964] CMLR 522 concerning Art. 65 ECSC (which parallels Art. 85 EC).
703. As to the fourth aspect, the question of the effect on trade between Member States, see section 4.2, *ante*; the approach is identical. As to the definition of the relevant Market, see the Commission's Notice (O.J. 1997 C 372/5).
704. The most important analysis of demand substitution is still to be found in Case 322/81 *Michelin* [1983] ECR 3461 at 3505–3507 (and see VerLoren van Themaat Adv. Gen. at 3532–3535); see also Case C-333/94 P *Tetra Pak International SA v. Commission* [1996] ECR I-5951 at 6004–6006 and Korah (1997) ECLR 98 (see further, Korah (1993) 46 CLP 148). Demand substitutability relates to the existence of an effective choice of reasonable substitutes for a purchaser.
705. Case 27/76 *United Brands Company et al. v. Commission* [1978] ECR 207 at 272–273: sufficient differentiation from other fruits as there are special features that render bananas only to a limited extent interchangeable with them and the competition from them was hardly perceptible; 'the banana has certain characteristics, appearance, taste, softness, seedlessness, easy handling, a constant level of production which enable it to satisfy the constant needs of an important section of the population consisting of the very young, the old and the sick.' As to the requirement of more than limited interchangeability, see also Case T-83/91 *Tetra Pak International SA v. Commission* [1994] ECR II-755 at 798–799 (on appeal from Dec. 92/163 (O.J. 1992 L 72/1) *Tetra Pak II*; see also the (dismissed) further appeal (see note 702, *supra*).

applications, a product may have several markets, as is the case for vitamins which may be used for bio-nutritional and industrial purposes.[706] It may even be that conduct intended to damage a competitor's activities on a separate market from that in which dominance is found will be held to infringe Article 86 EC.[707] Separate markets may exist for spare parts.[708] Whether supply substitutability exists will depend primarily whether suppliers of products which are not in specific cases demand substitutable can easily switch their resources in order to produce and supply demand substitutable products, *e.g.* shifting from producing aluminum cans to containers made of glass or plastic.[709] The relevant geographic market is determined largely as a function of the relevant product market and the area in which the abuse takes place, or in which the disadvantaged parties are located.[710] This shows once more the link between the concepts of dominant position and abuse.

The most important, but not the only criterion for the determination of the existence of a dominant position is still the market share.[711] Other

706. Case 85/76 *Hoffmann-La Roche* [1979] ECR 461 at 514–514–517.
707. Case C-62/86 *AKZO Chemie BV v. Commission* [1991] ECR I-3359 at 3448–3449.
708. Case 22/78 *Hugin Kassaregister AB et al. v. Commission* [1979] ECR 1869 at 1895–1896; Case C-53/92 P *Hilti AG v. Commission* [1994] ECR I-667 at 701–702 and Jacobs Adv. Gen. at 675–676). See also Case 238/87 *AB Volvo v. Erik Veng (UK) Ltd.* [1988] ECR 6211 at 6224–6225 (Mischo Adv. Gen.).
709. For the assessment of whether it is valid to choose a narrow relevant market, which may be the branded products of a particular supplier according to a particular technical specification (*e.g.* spare parts which are not interchangeable with other manufacturer's products), supply substitutability is a very appropriate criterion. See, further, *e.g.* Case 6/72 *Continental Can* [1973] ECR 215 at 247–248; Case 322/81 *Michelin* [1983] ECR 3461 at 3506–3507; Case 22/78 *Hugin* [1979] ECR 1869 at 1986–1987; Case C-62/86 *AKZO* [1991] ECR I-3359 at 3450–3451, and Case T-69/89 *Radio Telefis Eireann v. Commission* [1991] ECR II-485 at 516, upheld on appeal in Cases C-241 and 242/91 P *Radio Telefis Eireann (RTE) et al. v. Commission* [1995] ECR I-743 at 822.
710. See, further, note 686, *supra*, and text thereto.
711. Case 27/76 *United Brands* [1978] ECR 207 at 281–282 (although a 40–45% market share will not automatically demonstrate market dominance, regard must be had to the strength and number of competitors, but it is not necessary for an undertaking to have eliminated all opportunity for competition in order to be in a dominant position); Case 85/76 *Hoffmann-La Roche* [1979] ECR 461 at 520–521 (see also the additional factors discussed at 521–525). These judgments shed valuable light on the limits within which market share will form the basis of the dominant position. See also Case 322/81 *Michelin* [1983] ECR 3461 at 3509. *Hoffmann-La Roche* would indicate that a market share of more than 60% in itself indicates dominance, save in exceptional circumstances. In Case 62/86 *AKZO* [1991] ECR I-3359 at 3453 a market share of about 50% was again found to be evidence of a dominant position, see also Case T-30/89 *Hilti AG v. Commission* [1991] ECR II-1439 at 1480–1481 (70–80%; not challenged in the unsuccessful appeal in Case C-53/92 P *Hilti AG v. Commission* [1994] ECR I-667, [1994] 4 CMLR 614. However, particularly in relation to mergers (as to which, see section 4.5, *post*), where the test of dominance also plays a role, large market shares may not always create dominant positions: in Dec. 91/251 (O.J. 1991 L 122/48) *Alcatel/Telettra* even though the merged undertaking would have 81% of the

criteria which may play a part in interpreting market share for the purpose of determining dominance are the technological lead enjoyed over competitors, the existence or absence of potential competition, overall technical and economic strength, and whether the undertaking forms part of a European or worldwide concern.[712] Analysis of the relevant market and the existence of a dominant position will be superfluous, or in any event less important, if the undertaking concerned enjoys a factual or legal monopoly, such as the exclusive right to provide approvals or certificates,[713] or has a concession.[714] The mere possession of intellectual property rights cannot itself confer dominance, the question is rather whether the ownership of such rights enables the undertaking to impede effective competition in respect of the product (or service) concerned.[715]

As far as deciding that conduct of undertakings in a dominant position constitutes an abuse is concerned, in practice there is a striking parallel with the conduct which is prohibited under Article 85(1) EC. Horizontal and vertical price agreements find their parallel in Article 86 EC in the prohibition of unfair transactions.[716] When such prices are unfair is indeed

Spanish market for line transmission equipment, and 83% of the microwave equipment market, the Commission found that there was no dominant position created, as the market share of the merged undertaking would be depleted by the power of the national network operator which the Commission expected would continue to encourage competitors to enter the market and continue with its dual sourcing policy. See also the Court of Justice's criticism of the Commission's assessment of market share in the case of a collective dominant position in Cases C-68/94 and 30/95 *France et al. v. Commission* [1998] ECR I-1375 at 1519–1528.

712. See, generally, the judgments cited *ibid.*
713. Case 26/75 *General Motors Continental NV v. Commission* [1975] ECR 1367, [1976] 1 CMLR 95, and Case 226/84 *British Leyland plc v. Commission* [1986] ECR 3263, [1987] 1 CMLR 185.
714. *E.g.* Case 311/84 *Centre belge d'études de marché-Télémarketing (CBEM) SA v. Compagnie luxembourgeoise de télédiffusion SA et al.* [1985] ECR 3261 at 3275 (telemarketing); Case 155/73 *Sacchi* [1974] ECR 409, [1974] 2 CMLR 177 (television advertising); Case 311/84 *Centre belge d'études de marché-Télémarketing (CBEM) SA v. Compagnie luxembourgeoise de télédiffusion SA et al.* [1985] ECR 3261 at 3275; Case 30/87 *Bodson v. Pompes funèbres des régions libérées SA* [1988] ECR 2479, [1989] 4 CMLR 984 (local funerals monopoly); Case C-323/93 *Société Civile Agricole du Centre d'Insémination de la Crespelle v. Co-opérative d'Élevage et d'Insémination Artificielle du Département de la Mayenne* [1994] ECR 5077. *Cf.* the situation in cases of non-exclusivity, Case C-393/92 *Gemeente Almelo et al. v. Energiebedrijf Ijsselmij NV* [1994] ECR I-1477 at 1519–1520.
715. See *e.g.* Case 24/67 *Parke, Davis & Co.* [1968] ECR 55 at 62; Case 40/70 *Sirena v. Eda* [1971] ECR 69 at 83; Case 78/70 *Deutsche Grammophon* [1971] ECR 487 at 501; Case 51/75 *EMI v. CBS* [1976] ECR 811 at 849; Case T-51/89 *Tetra Pak Rausing SA v. Commission* [1990] ECR II-309 at 357,and Case T-69/89 *Radio Telefis Eireann v. Commission* [1991] ECR II-485 at 517 (upheld on appeal in Cases C-241 and 242/91 P *Radio Telefis Eireann (RTE) et al. v. Commission* [1995] ECR I-743 at 822).
716. Case 155/73 *Sacchi* [1974] ECR 409 at 430; Case 26/75 *General Motors* [1975] ECR 1367 at 1378–1379, and Case 247/86 *Société alsacienne et lorraine de télécommunications et de l'électronique (Alsatel) v. SA Novasam* [1988] ECR 5987 at 6008.

a complex question, but nevertheless the Court has established certain general criteria.[717] The question whether a price is unfair will be closely related with the power to impose unilaterally prices on customers or suppliers.[718] The same applies to predatory pricing[719] and also to price discrimination, the very existence of which is usually regarded as indicative that the dominant undertaking is dividing up the common market.[720] Rebate cartels find their parallel in the prohibition of abuse through a system of fidelity rebates and similar practices.[721] A close connection exists between collective exclusive dealing arrangements, and refusals to supply or boycott actions against unwilling purchasers or suppliers.[722] All such

717. *E.g.* Case 27/76 *United Brands* [1978] ECR 207 at 301–303 (cost price, profit margin and reference to economic theory); Case 66/86 *Ahmed Saeed Flugreisen et al. v. Zentrale zur Bekämpfung unlauteren Wettbewerbs e.V.* [1989] ECR 803 at 850–851 (criteria from community legislation in the air transport sector); Case 395/87 *Ministère public v. Tournier* [1989] ECR 2521 at 2577 and Cases 110, 241 and 242/88 *Lucazeau et al. v. Société des auteurs, compositeurs et éditeurs de musique (Sacem) et al.* [1989] ECR 811 at 2830–2833 (comparison with price levels in other Member States), and Case 26/75 *General Motors* [1975] ECR 1367 at 1379 (price excessive in relation to the economic value of the service provided).
718. Case 247/86 *Société alsacienne et lorraine de télécommunications et de l'électronique (Alsatel) v. SA Novasam* [1988] ECR 5987 at 6008.
719. Case 62/86 *AKZO* [1991] ECR I-3359 at 3455–3456, and Case T-83/91 *Tetra Pak International SA v. Commission* [1991] ECR II-755 at 826–828, upheld on appeal in Case C-333/94 P *Tetra Pak International SA v. Commission* [1996] ECR I-5951.
720. Case 27/76 *United Brands* [1978] ECR 207 at 301–303; Case C-62/86 *AKZO* [1991] ECR I-3359 at 3468–3471; Case T-83/91 *Tetra Pak* [1994] ECR II-755 at 831–835 (upheld on appeal, as noted, *supra*). See also Dec. 89/113 (O.J. 1989 L 43/27) *Decca Navigator System*.
721. *E.g.* Cases 40/73 *etc. Suiker Unie* [1975] ECR 1663 at 2003; Case 85/76 *Hoffmann-La Roche* [1979] ECR 461 at 539–546 (including a so-called English clause, allowing Hoffmann-La Roche the opportunity to match cheaper prices offered elsewhere); Case 322/81 *Michelin* [1983] ECR 3461 at 3514–3518; Case C-393/92 *Gemeente Almelo et al. v. Energiebedrijf Ijsselmij* [1994] ECR I-1477 at 1520; Dec. 88/518 (O.J. 1988 L 284/41) *Napier Brown/British Sugar*; Decs. 91/299 (O.J. 1991 L 152/21) *Soda Ash-Solvay* and 91/300 (O.J. 1991 L 152/40) *Soda Ash-ICI*, annulled in Case T-31/91 *Solvay SA v. Commission* [1995] ECR II-1825, [1996] 5 CMLR 91 and Case T-37/91 *Imperial Chemical Industries plc v. Commission* [1995] ECR II-1901, [1996] 5 CMLR 91 respectively, on procedural grounds (under appeal in Cases C-286/95 *etc.* P *Commission v. Imperial Chemical Industries plc et al.* (O.J. 1995 C 268/19 *et seq.*), and see also Case T-65/89 *BPB Industries plc et al. v. Commission* [1993] ECR II-389, [1993] 5 CMLR 32 (upheld on appeal in Case C-310/93 P *BPB Industries plc et al. v. Commission* [1995] ECR I-865, [1997] 4 CMLR 238). See further Dec. 97/624 (O.J. 1997 L 258/1) *Irish Sugar* (under appeal in Case T-228/97 *Irish Sugar plc v. Commission* (O.J. 1997 C 318/29).
722. *E.g.* Cases 6 and 7/73 *Commercial Solvents* [1974] ECR 223 at 250–251, and Case 27/76 *United Brands* [1978] ECR 207 at 292–294 (both in broadly defined markets); in relation to narrowly defined markets, see Case 22/78 *Hugin* [1979] ECR 1869 at 1900 (appeal allowed on other grounds) and Dec. 88/138 (O.J. 1988 L 65/19) *Eurofix-Bauco v. Hilti* (finding as to conduct not challenged on the unsuccessful appeal in Case T-30/89 *Hilti AG v. Commission* [1991] ECR II-1439, [1992] 4 CMLR 16). In relation to ancillary markets, see Case 311/84 *Centre belge d'études de marché-Télémarketing*

conduct can result in very heavily fines.[723] Tying clauses[724] and even inefficiency, mismanagement or failure adequately to meet demand[725] may also constitute abuses.

4.5 Merger control

Background. Although the Commission's intention to take steps to control mergers dates initially from 1973, it was only at the end of 1989 that political agreement permitted a Merger Regulation to see the light of day with the adoption of Regulation 4064/89.[726] The long history of the matter

(CBEM) SA v. Compagnie luxembourgeoise de télédiffusion SA et al. [1985] ECR 3261 at 3277–3278; see also *XXVth Report on Competition Policy 1995* (Brussels, Luxembourg, 1996) point 86. In relation to essential facilities, see the cases and literature cited at the beginning of note 686, *supra*. Note, though, the possibility of allocating priority to regular customers in times of shortage, Case 77/77 *Benzine en petroleum Handelsmaatschappij BV et al. v. Commission* [1978] ECR 1513 at 1527–1528, provided that the criteria are objective, objectively justified, and non-discriminatory, observing the rules governing fair competition between economic operators, Case T-65/89 *BPB Industries plc et al. v. Commission* [1993] ECR II-389 at 424–425 (appeal dismissed in Case C-310/93 P *BPB Industries plc et al. v. Commission* [1995] ECR 865, [1997] 4 CMLR 238).

723. *E.g.* Tetra Pak was fined 75 million ECU (upheld on appeal).
724. See Art. 86(d) and *e.g.* Dec. 88/138 (O.J. 1988 L 65/19) *Eurofix-Bauco/Hilti* (appeal dismissed, as noted, *supra*), and Dec. 92/163 (O.J. 1992 L 72/1) *Tetra Pak II*, upheld on appeal in Case T-83/91 *Tetra Pak International SA v. Commission* [1994] ECR II-755 at 821–824, and on further appeal in Case C-333/94 P *Tetra Pak International SA v. Commission* [1996] ECR I-5951 at 6010–6011). See also *Van den Bergh Foods* (O.J. 1995 C 211/4).
725. Case C-179/90 *Merci convenzionali porto di Genova SpA v. Siderurgica Gabrielli SpA* [1991] ECR I-5929 at 5889 (undertaking refusing to have recourse to modern technology, which involves an increase in the cost of operations and the time required for them to be performed), and Case C-41/90 *Höfner and Elser v. Macrotron GmbH* [1991] ECR I-1979 at 2018.
726. Integrally reproduced in the corrected version, O.J. 1990 L 257/14, amended by Reg. 1310/97 (O.J. 1997 L 180/1; Corrigendum O.J. 1998 L 40/17). Reg. 4064/89 has been implemented by Reg. 447/98 (O.J. 1998 L 61/1, Corrigendum O.J. 1998 L 66/25), which repeals and replaces the old implementing Reg. 3384/94 (O.J. 1994 L 377/1) with effect from 2 March 1998. A number of important Notices have been issued by the Commission: the Notice on full-function Joint Ventures (O.J. 1998 C 66/1, see also the Information on the assessment of full-function Joint Ventures pursuant to EC competition rules, O.J. 1998 C 66/38). the Concentration Notice (O.J. 1998 C 66/5); the Notice on Undertakings Concerned (O.J. 1998 C 66/14); the Notice on the concept of a concentration (O.J. 1998 C 66/5); the Notice on the Calculation of Turnover (O.J. 1998 C 66/25); the Notice on the alignment of procedures for processing mergers under the EC and the ECSC rules (O.J. 1998 C 66/36), and the Ancillary Restrictions Notice (O.J. 1990 C 203/5). See further, the Statements entered in the Council minutes at the time of adoption of Reg. 4064/89 (Bull. EC Supp. 2/90, p. 23). See also Bellamy and Child, *op. cit.* (see note 223, *supra*) Chapter 6; Bos *et al.*, *Concentration Control in the European Economic Community* (London, 1992); Cook

demonstrates its extremely sensitive nature, in relation to which the Member States have very divergent standpoints, against the background of their general views on questions of the power of undertakings and industrial policy in particular. Nevertheless, such preventive control is essential for the proper functioning of the common market, given that on the basis of Articles 85 and 86 EC only a partial control can be exercised over concentrations, in so far as there is an agreement,[727] or abuse of an already existing dominant position.[728]

Scope. According to Article 3(1) of Regulation 4064/89, concentrations can be generally defined as acts by which independent undertakings are merged to form a new economic entity,[729] or by which a controlling interest is acquired, directly or indirectly, in whole or in part. It makes no difference whether this occurs horizontally or vertically.[730] Not all concentrations fall within the scope of the regulation, only those which have a 'Community dimension.' Under Article 1(2) his will usually be the case if three tests are satisfied; taking these in the most simple order, the first question is:

(a) The two-thirds test: if there is no single Member State within which each of the undertakings concerned achieves more than two-thirds of its aggregate community-wide turnover.

If this negative text of a Community dimension has been overcome, does the concentration meet the primary thresholds:

and Kerse, *EC Merger Control* (2nd ed., London, 1996); Hawk and Huser, *European Community Merger Control: A Practitioner's Guide* (The Hague, 1996); Jones and González Díaz (ed. Overbury), *The EEC Merger Regulation* (London, 1992), and Van Bael and Bellis, *op. cit.* (see note 366, *supra*) Chapter 6.

Reg. 4064/89 is based on Art. 87 and, principally, on Art. 235 EC. Para. 8 of the Preamble states that this was in order to enable the Community to give itself the additional powers of action necessary for the attainment of its objectives, including in relation to concentrations in the markets for agricultural products. However, this latter point is not a justification for the addition of Art. 235 as a legal basis; it is irrelevant given that Art. 42 EC itself refers expressly to Arts. 85 and 86 EC. It is doubtful whether a preventive notification of concentrations by undertakings which were not as such dominant, could not have been compelled solely on the basis of Art. 87, given that the latter clearly refers to 'the principles set out in Articles 85 and 86.' Part of those principles is undoubtedly that expressed in Art. 3(g) EC. The addition of Art. 235 is rather to be explained by the requirement of unanimity in that provision, clothed in the (apparent) legal justification that Art. 87 affords an inadequate legal basis for the adoption of a Community control of concentrations.

727. Cases 142 and 156/84 *British–American Tobacco Company Ltd. et al. v. Commission* [1987] ECR 4487 at 4584 (in the context of a case in which there was no concentration on the facts).

728. Case 6/72 *Continental Can* [1973] ECR 215 at 245.

729. See the Concentration Notice (O.J. 1998 C 66/5).

730. Reg. 4064/89 also applies to the agricultural and transport sectors. As to joint ventures, see *post*.

(b) Worldwide turnover: the combined aggregate worldwide turnover of all the undertakings concerned is more than 5,000 million ECU; and

(c) Community turnover: each of at least two of the undertakings concerned must have an aggregate Com-munity-wide turnover of more than 250 million ECU.[731]

The first two recitals to Regulation 1310/97 (which amended the Merger Regulation with effect from 1 March 1998) make it clear that the amendments were designed to resolve the problems arising from the fact that concentrations with a significant impact in several Member States which fell below the primary thresholds could qualify for examination under a number of national merger control systems, and in particular to avoid the increased legal uncertainty, effort and cost for companies as well as the risk of conflicting assessments resulting from multiple notification of the same transaction. Extending the scope of Community merger control to concentrations with a significant impact in several Member States was thus designed to ensure that a 'one-stop shop' system applies, allowing an appreciation of the competition impact of such concentrations in the Community as a whole, in compliance with the principle of subsidiarity. Thus a concentration which does not meet the primary thresholds is still considered as having a Community dimension if the four, more frequently met, supplementary thresholds set out below are reached. Of these criteria, the second and third are clearly aimed at removing multinational undertakings with presence in at least three Member States from possibly divergent national merger control systems in order to permit Community-level assessment in accordance with the 'one-stop shop' principle. In order to achieve this it was necessary to replace the primary thresholds by the new ones, which are partially directed at the multinational nature of such undertakings. Given that most multinational concentrations within the Community already involved undertakings each of which has its head office in one of two Member States, it is to be regretted that those concentrations will not fall under the new thresholds without more ado. However, the new Article 1(4) and (5) of the Merger Regulation permit the Council, acting by qualified majority on a proposal from the Commission, and taking into account the report which the Commission is to present to it before 1 July 2000, to revise the thresholds further. It is to be hoped that

---

731. Reg. 4064/89, Art. 1(2). It was proposed (COM (96) 313 Final) to reduce the thresholds set out in (a) and (b) in the text to 3,000 million ECU and 150 million ECU respectively. However, below those levels, but above thresholds of 2,000 million ECU and 100 million ECU respectively, the Commission would have exclusive jurisdiction if the concentration would otherwise be subject to notification to three or more national competition authorities. The *XXXVIth Report on Competition Policy 1996* (Brussels, Luxembourg, 1997) point 139 states that the aggregate Community-wide turnover proposed was 200 million ECU. As is set out in the text, *post*, the final compromise revision, which applies from March 1, 1998, is a further compromise.

on that occasion the Council, on the basis of the experience which has been gained, will be prepared to adopt thresholds which are simpler to apply for commerce and industry, the Member States and the Commission alike. On that occasion it may be hoped that even concentrations involving undertakings in only two Member States which reach the lower aggregate turnover criteria will be brought within the ambit of the Merger Regulation.

These new supplementary thresholds are as follows:

(i)   Worldwide turnover: the combined aggregate worldwide turnover of all the undertakings concerned is more than 2,500 million ECU;

(ii)   Community turnover: in each of at least three Member States, the combined aggregate turnover of all the undertakings concerned is more than 100 million ECU;

(iii) In each of at least three Member States included for the purposes of (ii), the aggregate turnover of each of at least two of the undertakings concerned is more than 25 million ECU; and

(iv)   The aggregate Community-wide turnover of each of at least two of the undertakings concerned is more than 100 million ECU.

But, consistently with the initial approach, if each of the undertakings concerned achieves more than two-thirds of its aggregate Community-wide turnover within one and the same Member State, there is no Community dimension and the Merger Regulation does not apply.[732]

The approach seems complex, but can be simply expressed: if a concentration does not get beyond point (a) above, the Merger Regulation does not apply; if the primary thresholds are reached, it will apply; if they are not reached but the new supplementary ones are, it will apply.

In particular the thresholds of Article 1(2) are the result of numerous political compromises, and may well result in a large undertaking from a third country which has a low Community turnover being able to swallow up small Community undertakings without any regulatory problems at the Community level.[733] In most cases the new Article 1(3) will not solve this problem either; only an individual Member State might be able to prevent

732. Reg. 4064/89, Art. 1(3), as amended by Reg. 1310/97 (O.J. 1997 L 180/1). As is explained in the text, *post*, the amendments made by Reg. 1310/97 also bring cooperative Joint Ventures within the scope of the Merger Regulation, so that all structural ('full-function') Joint Ventures are now covered. The thresholds relating to financial institutions and insurance undertakings have also been revised, and a number of major procedural improvements have been made, in particular as regards the acceptance of commitments in order to obtain clearance, the possibility of waiving the suspension of a concentration pending a final decision, and referral of concentrations between the Commission and national authorities. See, further, Steenbergen (1998) SEW 192.

733. As to the calculation of turnover, see Reg. 4064/89, Art. 5. Special rules apply to the

such a hostile takeover by a foreign undertaking on the basis of its own system of merger control. Moreover, the two-thirds test can lead to different treatment of concentrations in smaller and larger Member States. Because of the absence of market share criteria in relation to the effect on inter-State trade, it really is questionable whether the regulation has established an effective preventive control system. Jacquemin *et al.* have demonstrated that there are at least 25 sectors in which total Community production is below the what are now the primary (but were then the only) thresholds of the regulation.[734] Thus it was regrettable that on the first review of the thresholds in 1993 the Commission decided not to seek a lowering of the thresholds at that time.[735]

Aim of the control. The purpose of the merger control system is to determine whether the concentration is compatible with the common market, and the Commission will have to take account of on the one hand the need to maintain and develop effective competition within the common market, in view of, *inter alia*, the structure of all the markets concerned and the actual or potential competition from undertakings located within or outside the Community,[736] and, on the other hand a number of factors which largely, but not entirely, accord with Article 85(3) EC.[737] In the light of these factors 'a concentration which does not create or strengthen a dominant position as a result of which effective competition would be significantly impeded in the common market or in a substantial part of it' is to be declared compatible with the common market;[738] if the reverse is the

calculation of turnover of credit institutions (such as banks) and other financial institutions, insurance companies and groups whose activities include those activities along with more general activities (*ibid.*, Art. 5(3) (as amended)). See further, the Turnover Notice (O.J. 1998 C 66/25). As to the practice in relation to which undertakings are concerned (particularly parent-subsidiary or group relationships), see the Undertakings Concerned Notice (O.J. 1998 C 14).

734. *European Economy* No. 40, May, 1989.
735. In accordance with Reg. 4064/89, Art. 1(3), see COM (93) 385 Final. As has been explained in note 731, *supra*, proposals were finally put forward, resulting in the introduction of the supplementary thresholds.
736. Reg. 4064/89, Art. 2(1)(a).
737. The market position of the undertakings concerned and their economic and financial power, the alternatives available to suppliers and users, their access to supplies and markets, any legal or other barriers to entry, supply and demand trends for the relevant goods and services, the interests of the immediate and ultimate consumers, and the development of technical and economic progress provided that it is to the consumers' advantage and does not form an obstacle to competition, *ibid.*, Art. 2(1)(b).
738. *Ibid.*, Art. 2(2). The term 'significantly' differs from the formulation in Art. 85(3) EC. But the term '*daadwerkelijk*' in the Dutch text of the regulation seems quite compatible with the concepts of 'effective' or 'workable' competition which, as explained in section 4.1.4, *ante*, underlie the system of Art. 85 EC.

case, a declaration of incompatibility is to result.[739] The primary approach for control is based on grounds of effective competition alone. But Paragraph 13 of the preamble to Regulation 4064/89 also makes it plain that 'the Commission must place its appraisal within the general framework of the achievement of the fundamental objectives referred to in Article 2 of the Treaty, including that of strengthening the Community's economic and social cohesion, referred to in Article 130a.' Depending on the circumstances a trade-off between competition considerations and other objectives, in particular of an industrial policy nature, is not excluded.[740] This results not merely from the regulation itself, but also from the system of the Treaty, according to which the competition regime is not only an instrument of market integration, but also of policy integration. The regime of Article 3(g) EC does however require the maintenance of the minimum of competition which is expressed in Article 85(3) EC, in the sense that in any event competition may not be totally eliminated in a substantial part of the common market. The addition of the word 'significantly'[741] indicates the grave danger that in the appraisal of concentrations this minimum standard will no longer be logically applied, but that the industrial policy[742] or other arguments which are advanced will gain the upper hand. The (perhaps inevitable) fierce political reactions which met the Commission after it had adopted its first decision prohibiting a merger on purely competition grounds[743] raises the question whether it possesses sufficient political weight and independence to ensure in the future that merger control policy is not simply derailed into an instrument of industrial policy.[744] So far, however, the practice of the Commission does not seem to justify such a fear.

739. *Ibid.*, Art. 2(3).
740. *E.g.* Dec. 94/449 (O.J. 1994 L 186/38) *Kali + Salz/MdK/Treuhand* (Case IV/M.308), annulled on appeal in Cases C-68/94 and 30/95 *France v. Commission* [1998] ECR I-1375. The decision was annulled on the ground that the Commission's analysis of the concentration and its effects was flawed as regards the economic assessment. On the other hand, the Court confirmed that collective dominant positions do not fall outside the scope of the Merger Regulation [1998] ECR I-1375 at 1501–1504. See also Case T-88/94 *Société Commerciale des Potasses et de l'Azote et al. v. Commission* [1995] ECR II-221 (disclaimer of jurisdiction in favour of the Court of Justice). The other objectives were: severe structural weakness of the eastern German regions affected by the proposed concentration; the likelihood of serious consequences of the closure of MdK; closure of MdK inevitable in the foreseeable future if not acquired by another undertaking.
741. Pointed out in note 738, *supra*.
742. See Art. 130 EC.
743. Dec. 91/619 (O.J. 1991 L 334/42) *Aérospatiale-Alenia/de Haviland* (IV/M.053).
744. The discussion about the establishment of a European cartel office, at more of a distance from political influence, was sharpened as a result. Because of the need for a well-coordinated implementation and interpretation of the five freedoms of the internal market and the rules on competition for undertakings, as the other main instruments for the establishment of a common internal market (economy) as required by Arts. 2, 3 and 3a EC, which should not be distorted by state aids and legislative

Procedure in merger control. Control is effected through the requirement of prior notification of concentrations.[745] This must take place not more than one week after the conclusion of the agreement, or the announcement of the public bid, or the acquisition of a controlling interest; the period runs from whichever of these events occurs first.[746] Normally no concentration may be put into effect before notification or until it has been declared compatible with the common market or deemed to be so, although the Commission may grant a derogation in appropriate circumstances.[747] Within one month of notification, the Commission either has to take a decision that the notified concentration does not fall under the regulation,[748] or it has to decide not to oppose it on the ground that although it falls under the regulation there are no serious doubts about its compatibility with the common market,[749] or it decides to initiate proceedings on the ground that the concentration falls within the scope of the regulation and that there are serious doubts as to its compatibility with the common market.[750] If the latter course of action is taken, the proceedings have to culminate within at the most four months[751] in a decision declaring the concentration compatible with the common market unconditionally or subject to conditions and obligations,[752] or declaring it incompatible with

distortion (Arts. 92, 100a and 101 EC), it seems quite justified that the Commission is strongly opposed to the creation of a European Cartel Office. It is understandable that those Member States which have a common domestic internal market in place often prefer an independent office for the application of competition rules to undertakings. It is because of the fundamental difference between the Community scene and the domestic scene that this Chapter has stressed the strong inter-relationship between the competition rules and the other EC policy areas. As to this discussion, see Ehlermann (1995) 32 CMLRev. 471, and literature referred to therein. See also Wolf (1994) EuZW 233.

745. Reg. 4064/89, Art. 4, see the detailed rules, and form CO, now in Reg. 447/98 (O.J. 1998 L 40/17).
746. *Ibid.*
747. *Ibid.*, Art. 7(1) and (4); as to the implementation of a public bid, see Art. 7(3); as to the validity of transactions carried out in breach of Art. 7(1), see Art. 7(5) (all as amended).
748. *Ibid*, Art. 6(1)(a).
749. *Ibid.*, Art. 6(1)(b) (as amended). The decision will now also cover restrictions directly related and necessary to the implementation of the concentration, *ibid.* This is effectively a negative clearance of the concentration.
750. Reg. 4064/89, Art. 6(1)(c) (as amended); this is without prejudice to the possibility of finding after all that the concentration does not fall within the scope of the regulation, *ibid.* As to the deadline, and the circumstances in which it is increased to six weeks, see *ibid.*, Art. 10(1) (as amended).
751. Reg. 4064/89, Art. 10(3). The time limit does not apply if the decision is revoked on the grounds that the declaration of compatibility was based on incorrect information for which one of the undertakings was responsible, or has been obtained by deceit, or that the undertakings have breached an obligation attached to a decision, *ibid.*, Art. 8(5) and (6). The four month period may exceptionally be extended, *ibid.*, Art. 10(4) (as amended), and if the Court annuls a decision under the regulation in whole or in part, time runs afresh from the date of the judgment, *ibid.*, Art. 10(5).
752. *Ibid.*, Art. 8(2) (as amended). See *e.g.* Decs. 91/251 (O.J. 1991 L 122/48) *Alcatel/Tele-*

the common market.[753] If this deadline is not met the concentration is deemed to be compatible with the common market.[754] If the concentration is not notified it is not automatically void.[755] Where a concentration has already been implemented, the Commission may however require the undertakings or assets brought together to be separated, or the cessation of joint control or any other action that may be appropriate for the restoration of conditions of effective competition.[756] The Commission is also empowered to obtain all necessary information,[757] to undertake the necessary investigations,[758] or require the competent authorities of the Member States to do so,[759] and to impose fines and periodic (daily) penalties.[760] These powers are comparable with those conferred on the Commission in normal competition proceedings. If a concentration which has been declared incompatible with the common market is nevertheless put into effect, or if the conditions or obligations prescribed by the Commission are not respected, the fine may be up to 10% of the aggregate turnover of the undertakings concerned. Appeal lies to the Court of First Instance, and

ttra (IV/M.042); 91/403 (O.J. 1991 L 222/38) *Magnetti Marelli/CEAc* (IV/M.043); 91/535 (O.J. L290/35) *Tetra Pak/Alfa-Laval* (IV/M.068); 91/595 (O.J. 1991 L 320/26) *Varta/Bosch* (IV/M.012); 92/385 (O.J 1992 L 204/1) *Accor/Wagons-Lits* (IV/M.126); 93/9 (O.J. 1993 L 7/13) *Du Pont/ICI* (IV/M.214); 94/449 (O.J. 1994 L 186/38) *Kali + Salz/MdK/Treuhand* (IV/M.308), annulled on appeal in Cases C-68/94 and 30/95 *France et al. v. Commission* [1998] ECR I-1375; 96/649 (O.J. 1996 L 294/14) *RTL/Veronica/Endemol* (IV/M.553). 97/469 (O.J. 1997 L 201/1) *Ciba-Geigy/Sandoz* (IV/M.737); 97/540 (O.J. 1997 L 218/15) *Coca-Cola/Amalgamated Beverages GB* (IV/M.794); 97/815 (O.J. 1997 L 336/1) *British Telecom/MCI (II)* (IV/M.856), and 97/540 (O.J. 1997 L218/15) *Coca-Cola/Amalgamated Beverages GB* (IV/M.877). This type of decision is comparable to Art. 85(3) exemptions, and the criteria of Art. 85(3) EC have now been specifically incorporated into the examination of cooperative Joint Ventures.

753. *Ibid.*, Art. 8(3) (as amended). See *e.g.* Decs. 97/26 (O.J. 1997 L 11/30) *Gencor/Lonhro* (IV/M.619) and 96/177 (O.J. 1996 L 53/20) *Nordic Satellite Distribution* (IV/M.490).

754. *Ibid.*, Art. 10(6). The very tight deadlines caused the Commission to establish the Merger Task Force (now also a normal Directorate within DG IV) in part in order to pursue an informal policy as much as possible. Thus most notifications have been cleared or found not to fall within the jurisdiction of the Commission by means of an informal decision. As to the role of the Advisory Committee see *ibid.* Art.19 and Case T-290/94 *Kaysersberg SA v. Commission* [1997] ECR II-2137.

755. Such an approach was expressly rejected during the procedure leading to the adoption of the Merger Regulation.

756. Reg. 4064/89, Art. 8(4). See Decs. 97/277 (O.J. 1997 L 110/53) and 97/409 (O.J. 1997 L 174/47) *Kesko/Tuko* (IV/M.784). See also the *Telefonica/Sogecable* saga, *XXVIth Report on Competition Policy 1996* (Brussels, Luxembourg, 1997) point 150, and Case T-52/96 R *Sogecable SA v. Commission* [1996] ECR II-797. See also Commission Press Release IP (98) 166 (18 February 1998) announcing a decision (not yet published) fining Samsung for putting a takeover into effect before notifying the Commission.

757. Reg. 4064/89, Art. 11.

758. *Ibid.*, Art. 13.

759. *Ibid.*, Art. 12.

760. *Ibid.*, Arts. 14 and 15.

thereafter on a point of law only to the Court of Justice,[761] the appellate jurisdiction in respect of fines and periodic penalty payments being unlimited; thus they may be cancelled, reduced, or even increased.[762]

Mergers and national law. The limited scope of the Merger Regulation means that the Member States remain competent to assess proposed mergers beneath the thresholds of the regulation. Nevertheless, a Member State, or two or more Member States jointly, may request the Commission to deal with such a concentration, even though effective competition would only be significantly impeded within the territory of the Member State concerned.[763] This clause, commonly referred to as the Dutch clause, has been retained even after the amendment of Article 1(3) of the Merger Regulation with regard to transnational concentrations beneath the normal thresholds of Article 1(2) which has been discussed above.[764] Member States have no

761. Minority shareholders have been held to have no standing to bring an appeal, see Case T-83/92 *Zunis Holding SA et al. v. Commission* [1993] ECR II-1169, [1994] 5 CMLR 154, result upheld on appeal on other grounds, Case C-480/93 P *Zunis Holding SA et al. v. Commission* [1996] ECR I-1, [1996] 5 CMLR 219 (but see Lenz Adv. Gen. [1996] ECR I-1 at 20–22). Competitors who played a part in the administrative proceedings have been allowed to challenge decisions, *e.g.* Case T-3/93 *Société Anonyme à Participation Ouvrière Compagnie Nationale Air France v. Commission* [1994] ECR II-121 and Case T-2/93 *Société Anonyme à Participation Ouvrière Compagnie Nationale Air France v. Commission* [1994] ECR II-323. The Commission or the competent authorities of the Member States may hear other natural or legal persons (than the undertakings concerned): 'Natural or legal persons showing a sufficient interest and especially members of the administrative or management bodies of the undertakings concerned or the recognized representatives of their employees shall be entitled, upon application, to be heard.' (Reg. 4064/89, Art. 18(4)), see Case T-96/92 *Comité Central d'Enterprise de la Société Générale des Grandes Sources et al. v. Commission* [1995] ECR II-1213 and Case T-12/93 *Comité Central d'Enterprise de la Société Anonyme Vittel et al. v. Commission* [1995] ECR II-1247 (non-intervention in the administrative procedure did not preclude challenge to the decision, but employees' representatives were not directly concerned within the meaning of Art. 173 EC and could not challenge an alleged breach of the substantive rules of the Merger Regulation; they could though challenge a refusal to hear them or otherwise respect their rights in the administrative procedure).
762. Reg. 4064/89, Art. 16.
763. *Ibid.*, Art. 22. The Commission may adopt decisions under *ibid.*, Art. 8(2), 2nd subpara. (3) and (4) in so far as the concentration affects trade between Member States, Art. 22(3) (as amended). The provision reflects concern that the initial thresholds were fixed so high that concentrations resulting in dominance in national markets would escape scrutiny because they were below the thresholds and the national authorities (at that time at least) had no suitable powers of investigation or enforcement. See *e.g.* Decs. 96/346 (O.J. 1996 L 134/32) and 96/649 (O.J. 1996 L 294/14) *RTL/Veronica/ Endemol*; *Blokker/Toys 'R'Us* (IV/M.801, decision of 22 August 1996); *British Airways/Dan Air* (IV/M.278, O.J. 1993 C 68/5) and Dec. 97/277 (O.J. 1997 L 110/53) *Keso/Tuko* (IV/M.784).
764. *Ibid.*, Art. 22(6) which would have terminated the effect of the Dutch clause on the threshold revision was repealed when the Merger Regulation was amended.

jurisdiction to apply their national legislation on competition to any concentration having a Community dimension,[765] but they may take appropriate measures to protect legitimate interests other than those taken into consideration by the Merger Regulation itself, provided that these interests are compatible with the general principles and other provisions of Community law.[766] The Joint Statement inserted in the Council's minutes on the adoption of the Merger Regulation, referring to Article 21(3) of the latter,[767] indicates that this provision is designed to permit the Member States to prohibit a concentration, or to subject it to additional conditions and requirements, even if the Commission has declared it compatible with the common market; the reverse is, however, not intended: if the Commission declares a concentration incompatible with the common market, a disgruntled party or Member State is left to its appeal. The fact that the regulation did not apply to any concentrations with insignificant cross-border effects meant, before the amendments of the Merger Regulation in 1997, that they were then exclusively subject to the concentration controls in the Member States concerned. These controls were then unable to afford sufficient guarantees against those concentrations having competition-restricting effects in other Member States. Moreover a cross-border merger or other concentration could lead to the simultaneous application of several national procedures with conflicting decisions resulting.[768] Given that the whole point of the Merger Regulation is to provide a one-stop shop, such a situation was indeed undesirable, and the deficiency has been repaired to a considerable extent by the amendments of the Merger Regulation in 1997. The German clause[769] makes it possible for the Commission to refer a concentration notified to it to the competent authorities of a Member State

765. *Ibid.*, Art. 21(2).
766. *Ibid.*, Art. 21(3). Public security, plurality of the media, and prudential rules are expressly regarded as legitimate interests, *ibid.* See *e.g.*, on public security, *IBM France/CGI* (IV/M.336, O.J. 1993 C 151/5, *XXIIIrd Report on Competition Policy 1993* (Brussels, Luxembourg, 1994) point 321) and *GEC/Thomson-CSF (II)* (IV/M.724) and *British Aerospace/Lagardère SCA* (IV/M.820), both in *XXVIth Report (ibid.*, 1997) point 157; on plurality of the media, *Newspaper Publishing* (IV/M.423, O.J. 1994 C 85/6); prudential rules relate to financial services, see *e.g.* *Sun Alliance/Royal Insurance* (IV/M. 759) in *XXVIth Report* point 156). As to other grounds claimed by Member States which the Commission is empowered to evaluate, see *e.g.* *Lyonnaise des Eaux/Northumbrian Water* (IV/M.567, O. J. 1995 C 322/19 and O.J. 1996 C 11/3).
767. See note 726, *supra.*
768. See VerLoren van Themaat and Ottervanger, *Concentraties en joint ventures in het mededingingsrecht* (Zwolle, 1992). The criticisms voiced therein may well have contributed to the solution formed to this problem in what is the new text of Art. 1(3) of the Merger Regulation.
769. As Reg. 4064/89, Art. 9 (as amended) has become known. See *e.g.* *GEHE/Lloyds Chemists* (IV/M.716, O.J. 1996 C 43/8), referral to the United Kingdom competition authorities; *RWE/Thyssengas* (IV/M.713) and *Bayernwerk/Isarwerke* (IV/M.808), referrals to the Bundeskartellamt, 25 November 1996. See *XXVIth Report on Competition Policy 1996* (Brussels, Luxembourg, 1997) points 153 and 154, respectively.

concerned, when effective competition would be significantly impeded on a market within that Member State, which presents all the characteristics of a distinct market, whether that market forms a substantial part of the common market or not. It will be apparent that the cat and mouse game between the Member States and the Commission in merger control has involved a considerable amount of compromise, which reflected much suspicion on the part of (some of) the Member States; in the light of the experience which has been gained since the regulation came into force, much of that suspicion has been allayed, but it has not yet wholly disappeared.

Applicability of Articles 85 and 86 EC to mergers. The Merger Regulation does not exclude the application of Articles 85 and 86 EC to concentrations.[770] In principle this means that anti-competitive effects of concentrations which do not fall under the Merger Regulation could still be examined by the Commission.[771] However, Regulation 17 is declared inapplicable to concentrations,[772] which means that Article 85 is not directly effective,[773] but Article 86 EC is[774] in respect of concentrations. In theory a national court could prohibit a concentration on the basis of Article 86 EC which the Commission had cleared on the basis of the Merger Regulation.[775] The fact that Regulation 17 is declared inapplicable excludes the possibility of third parties submitting complaints. A further problem is that only prohibitions or conditional clearances are actually published in the *Official Journal*.[776]

770. However, the Commission has declared that it will not apply these provisions to mergers, Bull. EC Supp. 2/90, p. 25.
771. See Dec. 93/252 (O.J. 1993 L 116/21) *Warner-Lambert/Gillette* and *Bic/Gillette*. What became Dec. 94/579 (O.J. 1994 L 223/36) *BT/MCI* was originally notified under the Merger Regulation but the Commission found that there was no concentration and treated the notification as an application for negative clearance or exemption under Reg. 17.
772. Reg. 4064/89, Art. 22(2) (as amended), thus except in relation to Joint Ventures that do not have a Community dimension and which have as their object or effect the coordination of the competitive behaviour of undertakings that remain independent.
773. Cases 209–213/84 *Ministère public v. Asjes et al.* [1986] ECR 1425 at 1469–1470 makes it evident that Art. 85 is not directly effective in the absence of measures adopted pursuant to Art. 87 EC.
774. Case 66/86 *Ahmed Saeed Flugreisen et al. v. Zentrale zur Bekämpfung unlauteren Wettbewerbs e.V.* [1989] ECR 803 at 848.
775. In such a case Art. 86 EC (as a Treaty provision) takes precedence over the scheme of the regulation, but only the Court of First Instance (or the Court of Justice on appeal) could annul the clearance decision; the Court of Justice could declare it invalid on a reference from a national court, and it would obviously be sensible for a national court which envisaged prohibiting a concentration which the Commission had cleared to make a reference.
776. Decisions declaring a concentration compatible with the common market, or concluding that there are no serious doubts about its compatibility are not so published, but a public version is available on Celex.

On the basis of its experience in the application of Articles 65 and 66 ECSC the Commission has also developed a policy towards Joint Ventures.[777] Such cooperation leads to a restriction of competition between the parent undertakings which in fact partially concentrate their activities in the Joint Venture. Such arrangements may fall outside Article 85(1) EC[778] and if the rationalization achieved does bring them within Article 85(1) they may well benefit from an exemption under Article 85(3).[779] If in addition arrangements are made about activities which fall outside the scope of the Joint Venture, Article 85(1) will certainly apply, albeit that exemption is not impossible even in these circumstances.[780] A Joint Venture may even function as the cartel organization for its parent undertakings. in a manner comparable with joint selling agencies. In its evaluation the Commission generally pays more attention to the substance of what is going on, rather than to the outward appearance of the form of the cooperation.[781]

Through the adoption of the Merger Regulation this policy has entered a new phase. Concentrative Joint Ventures have always fallen within the scope of the Merger Regulation, but cooperative Joint Ventures initially fell under the general system of Articles 85 and 86 EC. A concentrative Joint Venture is one which performs on a lasting basis all the functions of an autonomous economic entity, and does not give rise to coordination of the competitive behaviour of the parties amongst themselves or between them and the Joint Venture.[782] Although the Commission has explained the distinction between cooperative and concentrative Joint Ventures in a Notice,[783] the practical application of the distinction has not been problem-free. Joint Ventures not only take many shapes and forms, but

---

777. See the extensive discussion of various types of Joint Ventures in Bellamy and Child, *op. cit.* (see note 223, *supra*) Chapters 5 and (in relation to mergers) 6.

778. *E.g.* Decs. 75/95 (O.J. 1975 L 38/14) *SHV/Chevron*; 90/410 (O.J. 1990 L 209/15) *Elopak/Metal Box – Odin*, and 90/446 (O.J. 1990 L 228/31) *Konsortium*.

779. *E.g.* Decs. 77/543 (O.J. 1977 L 215/11) *De Laval/Stork* (exemption renewed by Dec. 88/110 (O.J. 1988 L 59/32); 77/81 (O.J. 1977 L 327/26 *GEC/Weir Sodium Circulators*; 78/251 (O.J. 1978 L 70/47) *Sopelem/Vickers*; 82/71 (O.J. 1982 L 39/25) *Langenscheidt*; 82/742 (O.J. 1982 L 314/34) *Amersham Buchler*; 83/390 (O.J. 1983 L 224/19) *Rockwell/Iveco*; 83/668 (O.J. 1983 L 376/11) *VW-MAN*; 83/669 (O.J. 1983 L 376/17) *Carbon Gas Technologie*; 88/87 (O.J. 1980 L 50/18) *ICI/Enichem*; 88/469 (O.J. 1988 L 230/39) *Iveco/Ford*, and 91/562 (O.J. 1991 L 306/22) *Eirpage*.

780. *E.g.* Decs. 76/172 (O.J. 1976 L 30/13) *Bayer/Gist-Brocades*; 78/921 (O.J. 1978 L 322/36) *WANO Schwarzpulver*; 90/535 (O.J. 1990 L 299/64) *Cekacan*, and 91/130 (O.J. 1991 L 63/32) *Screensport/EBU*.

781. The Commission's policy is extensively set out in the Notice on full-function Joint Ventures (O.J. 1998 C 66/1); as to the assessment of such Joint Ventures pursuant to EC competition rules, see O.J. 1998 C 66/38. See also the Notice on Ancillary Restrictions (O.J. 1990 C 203/5).

782. Reg. 4064/89, Art. 3(2), prior to amendment explained this distinction.

783. See now the Interface Notice (O.J. 1994 C 385/1). See also *XXIVth Report on Competition Policy 1994* (Brussels, Luxembourg, 1995) point 278.

because of the speedier procedures undertakings have been inclined to notify them as concentrative wherever possible. In order to redress this procedural imbalance, the Commission initially issued a Notice on the assessment of cooperative Joint Ventures under Article 85 EC[784] and amended a number of the block exemption regulations in order to clarify the position of cooperative Joint Ventures.[785] The amendments to the Merger Regulation in 1997 brought cooperative Joint Ventures too within the scope of that regulation (provided, of course, that they have a Community dimension), so that all structural ('full function') Joint Ventures are now covered.[786] However, the distinction between concentrative and cooperative Joint Ventures is still relevant, as the analysis of the latter is expressly based on the criteria of Article 85(3) EC, with particular account being taken, first, of whether two or more parent companies retain to a significant extent activities in the same market as the Joint Venture or in a market which is downstream or upstream from that of the Joint Venture or in a neighbouring market closely related to that market, and, secondly, of whether the coordination which is the direct result of the creation of the Joint Venture affords the undertakings concerned the possibility of eliminating competition in respect of a substantial part of the products or services in question.[787] This means that even if the creation of a Joint Venture does not lead to the creation or strengthening of a dominant position, it will be prohibited if it falls foul of the criteria of Article 85 itself.

4.6 Judicial protection in the application of the competition provisions

The formal regulation of judicial protection of private parties has been examined in sections 1.2 and 1.3. of Chapter VI, above. Because this judicial protection is of particular importance in the application of Articles 85 and 86 EC and displays certain specific features, it is appropriate to discuss briefly the specific aspects of judicial protection in the competition field. The principles laid down in the case-law of the Court of Justice and the Court of First Instance on the procedural aspects of the application of Articles 85 and 86 are of major importance in Community administrative law in general.

---

784. O.J. 1993 C 43/2. Notification of the creation of a cooperative Joint Venture which is structural in nature already resulted in accelerated examination (with a procedure analogous to that for mergers), see *XXIInd Report on Competition Policy 1992* (Brussels, Luxembourg, 1993), point 124.
785. See note 532, *supra* (the amendments were made by Reg. 151/93 (O.J. 1993 L 21/8)).
786. Reg. 4064/89, Art. 3(2) (as amended).
787. *Ibid.*, Art. 2(4) (added by the 1997 amendments). See also Steenbergen (1998) SEW 192.

4.6.1 The Commission's discretion

In the application of its decision-making powers under Regulation 17[788] the Commission has a certain margin of discretion, in the sense that it is not obliged to act against every infringement of Articles 85 and 86 EC, but is entitled to allocate priorities in the light on the one hand of the resources available to it, and on the other hand of the significance of the anti-competitive conduct concerned for the common market (the Community interest).[789] Article 3 of Regulation 17 makes it clear that the Commission *may* require the undertakings concerned to terminate infringements.[790] This approach is strengthened by the point that infringements of Articles 85(1) and 86 are prohibited, without the need for a prior decision to that effect.[791]

The Court of First Instance, and, on appeal on a point of law only, the Court of Justice, has unlimited jurisdiction under Article 172 EC in conjunction with Article 17 of Regulation 17 only in respect of fines and periodical penalty payments. Case-law shows that in relation to other decisions the control of the legality of the decision primarily relates to the questions whether the facts on which it is based are correct, whether all relevant factors have been taken into account, and whether the facts can support the conclusions drawn in relation to the constituent elements of Articles 85 and 86 EC.[792] In its judgment in Case 42/84 *Remia BV v. Commission*[793] the Court expressed these considerations succinctly and

---

788. O.J. English Special Edition 1959–62, p. 87, most recently amended by the Act of Austrian, Finnish and Portuguese Accession.
789. Case T-24/90 *Automec srl v. Commission* [1992] ECR II-2223 at 2275 and 2278 (hereafter '*Automec II*').
790. The power includes the possibility of ordering the parties to refrain from the prohibited conduct in the future (cease and desist), but not the power to deprive the parties of their freedom of contract by prescribing one particular course of conduct when there are other suitable means for forcing the termination of the conduct, Case T-24/90 *Automec II* [1992] ECR II-2223 at 2267–2268. Positive action may, though be ordered, in the sense of requiring that the undertaking provide advantages wrongfully withheld, or inform parties that the infringement has been terminated, or supply on request the information previously withheld, see *e.g.* Dec. 72/457 (J.O. 1972 L 299/51), upheld on appeal in Cases 6 and 7/73 *Commercial Solvents* [1974] ECR 223 (see at 255), and Dec. 89/205 (O.J. 1989 L 78/43) *Magill TV Guide/ITP, BBC and RTE*, upheld on appeal in Case T-69/89 *Radio Telefis Eireann v. Commission* [1991] ECR II-485, [1991] 4 CMLR 586 (and the other cases decided on the same day), further appeal dismissed in Cases C-241 and 242/91 P *Radio Telefis Eireann (RTE) et al. v. Commission* [1995] ECR I-743, [1995] 4 CMLR 718. The overwhelming majority of cases is resolved informally.
791. Reg. 17, Art. 1.
792. Long-standing case-law indicates that not all arguments and facts have to be addressed by the Commission; this applies in the competition field as well, Cases 43 and 63/82 *Vereniging ter Bevordering van het Vlaamse Boekwezen, VBVB et al. v. Commission* [1984] ECR 19 at 58–59.
793. [1985] ECR 2545 at 2575. The Court limited its examination 'to verifying whether the

noted that it could or would be more reticent in matters involving a complex economic assessment.[794] As far as the application of Article 85(3) is concerned, the Court tends to be satisfied with a more marginal examination.[795] Article 85(3) indeed clearly leaves a margin of discretion to the Commission, and it was precisely to permit this that the application of Article 85(3) was entrusted solely to the Commission.

4.6.2   Procedural Guarantees

The procedural provisions for the application of the competition provisions are set out in Regulation 17 and in the implementing provisions of Regulation 99/63[796] relating to the hearing of interested parties and third parties. These rules have been supplemented by the Court by a series of due process principles (proper administration), the requirements of which belong to the fundamental principles of Community law.[797]

General principles. The principles of proper administrative procedure[798] embrace: the right of parties concerned and other interested parties to be informed of the objections raised to their conduct;[799] the principle of *audi alteram partem*;[800] the right to confidentiality of the information communicated;[801] legal privilege,[802] and the right to remain

relevant procedural rules have been complied with, whether the statement of the reasons for the decision is adequate, whether the facts have been accurately stated and whether there has been any manifest error of appraisal or misuse of powers.' (*Ibid.*)

794. Although in general the review of the question whether or not the conditions for the application of Article 85(1) are met will be comprehensive, *ibid.* This is clearly also the case in respect of mergers, see Cases C-68/94 and 30/95 *France et al. v. Commission* [1998] ECR I-1375.

795. *E.g.* Cases 56 and 58/64 *Consten and Grundig* [1966] ECR 299 at 347; Case 17/74 *Transocean Marine Paint Association v. Commission* [1974] ECR 1063 at 1080, and Case 26/76 *Metro SB-Großmärkte GmbH & Co. KG v. Commission* [1977] ECR 1875 at 1916, 1918, and Reischl, Adv. Gen. at 1924.

796. O.J. English Special Edition 1963–64, p. 47.

797. *E.g.* Case 85/76 *Hoffmann-La Roche & Co. AG v. Commission* [1979] ECR 461 at 511.

798. Sometimes the Court speaks of the rights of the defence, the right of defence, or the right to be heard, without really specifying the precise content of these notions.

799. Reg. 99, Art. 2(1). This is done by means of a Statement of Objections (discussed *post*).

800. *Ibid.*, Art. 3. The parties may request an oral hearing, see *post*.

801. Reg. 17, Art. 20. See Cases 209/78 *etc. Van Landewyck Sàrl et al. v. Commission* [1980] ECR 3125 at 3239; Case 53/85 *AKZO Chemie BV v. Commission* [1986] ECR 1965 at 1991–1992; Case C-67/91 *Dirección General de la Competencia v. Associación Española de Banca Privada (AEB) et al.* [1992] ECR I-4785; Case C-36/92 P *Samenwerkende Elektriciteits-produktiebedrijven NV (SEP) v. Commission* [1994] ECR I-1911; Case T-353/94 R *Postbank NV v. Commission* [1994] ECR II-1141. See further *e.g.* Case T-17/93 *Matra Hachette SA v. Commission* [1994] ECR II-595 and Case T-66/94 *Auditel Srl v. Commission* [1995] ECR II-239.

802. Case 155/79 *AM & S Europe Ltd. v. Commission* [1982] ECR 1575, [1982] 2 CMLR

silent.[803] These principles (especially the second and the third ones) may not merely conflict,[804] they have to be balanced against the requirements of an effective procedure for ensuring compliance with the competition rules.[805] The Court has rejected the argument that as the Commission was at the same time investigator, prosecutor and judge there was a breach of due process, and, accordingly, a breach of Article 6 of the European Convention on Human Rights.[806]

Commencement of proceedings. The opening of proceedings, either on the Commission's own initiative, or at the request of a Member State or at the request of natural or legal persons who claim a legitimate interest[807] is a purely administrative act which does not need to be notified to the undertakings concerned or otherwise announced.[808] Nor is such a step an act capable of judicial review.[809]

Requests for information. In carrying out its duties ensuring the application of the Articles 85 and 86 EC, the Commission is entitled to obtain all necessary information from the Member States, undertakings and associations of undertakings.[810] It may also undertake general inquiries into particular sectors of the economy in which the trend of trade between Member States, price movements, inflexibility of prices or other circumstances suggest that

---

264. See, *inter alia*, Forrester (1983) 20 CMLRev. 75; Faull (1983) 8 ELRev. 11 and (1985) 10 ELRev. 119, and Christoforou (1985–1986) 9 Fordham Int'l. L.J. 1.
803. The privilege against self-incrimination: Case 374/87 *Orkem v. Commission* [1989] ECR 3283 at 3350–3351. See, though, the judgment of the European Court of Human Rights in *Funke et al. v. France* [1993] 1 CMLR 897. See, further, in relation to national courts, Case C-60/92 *Otto v. Postbank NV* [1993] ECR I-5683.
804. As in Case 85/76 *Hoffmann-La Roche & Co. AG v. Commission* [1979] ECR 461 at 511–513.
805. See *ibid.* and Cases 209/78 *etc. Van Landewyck* [1980] ECR 3125 at 3248; Cases 100–103/80 *SA Musique Diffusion Française et al. v. Commission* [1983] ECR 1825 at 1880–1882 (*Pioneer*), and Case 107/82 *Allgemeine Elektricitäts-Gesellschaft AEG-Telefunken AG v. Commission* [1983] ECR 3151 at 3192–3193.
806. In *Pioneer, ibid.* Given that judicial review is available that argument was always less than wholly meritorious. See the extensive discussion of Art. 6 ECHR in Cases T-213/95 and 18/96 *Stichting Certificatie Kraanverhuurbedrihf (SCK) et al. v. Commission* [1997] ECR II-1739 at 1763–1769.
807. Reg. 17, Art. 3(1) and (2).
808. Case 57/69 *Azienda Colori Nazionali – ACNA SpA v. Commission* [1972] ECR 933 at 947.
809. Case 60/81 *International Business Machines Corporation v. Commission* [1981] ECR 2369 at 2654. (The Court declined to consider any argument about exceptional circumstances in which the act lacked even the semblance of legality, finding that the circumstances did not warrant it.) See also Case T-64/89 *Automec Srl v. Commission* [1990] ECR II-367 at 381 (hereafter *Automec I*).
810. Reg. 17, Art. 11. This is done by means of a so-called Article 11 letter; if it is addressed to an undertaking or association of undertakings, a copy of which also goes to the competent authority in the Member State in which the addressee is situated, *ibid.*, Art. 11(2). See Joshua (1986) 11 ELRev. 409.

in the sector concerned competition is being restricted or distorted within the common market.[811] In both cases the ultimate sanction against undertakings and associations of undertakings for failure to supply information or for supplying incomplete information may take the form of a fine or periodic (daily) penalties.[812] The letter, and, if no reaction is forthcoming, any decision requiring the information to be produced, must state the legal basis and the purpose of the request as well as the consequences of failure to provide information or incomplete information; in the case of a decision requiring the information to be supplied, a deadline is specified, and the right to have the decision reviewed by the Court of First Instance (subject to appeal on a point of law only to the Court of Justice) must also be mentioned.[813] While undertakings and associations of undertakings are obliged to provide the required information,[814] they are not obliged to provide the Commission 'with answers which might involve an admission on [their] part of the existence of an infringement which it is incumbent on the Commission to prove.'[815]

Inspections, legal privilege, and confidentiality. The Commission (and at its request the Member States)[816] is entitled to undertake all necessary investigations into undertakings and associations of undertakings.[817] Its duly

811. *Ibid.*, Art. 12. In particular, the Commission may request all agreements, decisions and concerted practices which are exempt from notification to be communicated to it, as well as market structure and behaviour details relevant to the assessment of whether there is dominance.
812. *E.g.* Decs. 82/53 (O.J. 1982 L 27/31) *Comptoir Commercial d'Importation*; 82/124 (O.J. 1982 L 58/19) *Telos*; 82/260 (O.J. 1982 L 113/18) *National Panasonic*, and 91/55 (O.J. 1991 L 35/23) *Secrétema*. See also Dec. 91/213 (O.J. 1991 L 97/16) *Baccarat*. The sanction against non-cooperation by Member States is infringement proceedings (breach of the duty of cooperation under Art. 5 EC).
813. Reg. 17, Arts. 11(3), (5), 12(4), 15(1)(b), and 16(1)(c). See Case 374/87 *Orkem v. Commission* [1989] ECR 3283, [1991] 4 CMLR 502. There is an obligation on individuals to cooperate actively in the procedure, so a passive reaction may well justify the Commission adopting a formal decision, see Case T-46/92 *Scottish Football Association v. Commission* [1994] ECR II-1039 at 1056. As to the necessity of requests for information, see Case 374/87 *Orkem, supra*; Case 136/79 *National Panasonic (UK) Ltd. v. Commission* [1980] ECR 2033, [1980] 3 CMLR 169; Case C-36/92 P *Samenwerkende Elektriciteits-produktiebedrijven NV (SEP) v. Commission* [1994] ECR I-1911 at 1938 (approving Jacobs, Adv. Gen. at 1919–1923), and Case T-34/93 *Société Générale v. Commission* [1995] ECR II-545, [1996] 4 CMLR 665.
814. Reg. 17, Arts. 11(4), and 12(4). See Case 374/87 *Orkem* [1989] ECR 3283 at 3351.
815. Case 374/87 *Orkem, ibid.* See also Case 27/88 *Solvay & Cie v.Commission* [1989] ECR 3355.
816. Reg. 17, Art. 13.
817. *Ibid.*, Art. 14. See also the Commission's explanatory note on authorization to investigate, *Thirteenth Report on Competition Policy 1983* (Brussels, Luxembourg, 1984) 270–272. See, generally, Joshua (1983) 8 ELRev. 3, Kreis (1983) *Int. Lawyer* 19, and the House of Lords Select Committee on the European Communities, *Commission's Powers of Investigation and Inspection* Session 1983–84, 18th Report (HL 220), and

authorized officials are for this purpose entitled to examine the books and other business records and to take copies of or extracts therefrom, to ask for oral explanations on the spot, and to enter any premises, land, and means of transport of the undertakings concerned.[818] These powers are exercised on production of an authorization in writing, the identity of the inspectors being proved by their staff card. However, a mere authorization is not a search warrant, and an undertaking is entitled to refuse to submit voluntarily to investigation, although the likely result of a refusal will be the adoption of a decision requiring submission.[819] If, though, an undertaking does voluntarily submit to such an investigation, it must then cooperate and produce all the required books and records, on pain of a fine.[820] The Commission's officials are not entitled to use force or oblige the staff of an undertaking to give them access, nor may they carry out searches without the permission of the management of the undertaking, although that permission may be implied, particularly by the provision of assistance to the Commission's officials.[821] If the undertaking fails to cooperate, the Commission is entitled to require submission to an investigation, which is done by means of a decision.[822] Non-compliance may be sanctioned by fines and/or periodic (daily) penalties.[823] The Commission is not required to give advance notice to the undertaking of its intention to investigate it,[824] but it is required to inform the competent authorities of the Member State concerned,[825] and national officials will usually assist in the inspection.[826] The national authorities may in particular provide back-up in the

Enforcement of Community Competition Rules Session 1993–94, 1st Report (HL Paper 7).

818. Reg. 17, Art. 14(1).
819. *E.g.* Case 5/85 *AKZO Chemie BV et al.* v. *Commission* [1986] ECR 2585, [1987] 3 CMLR 716.
820. Reg. 17, Art. 15(1)(c).
821. Cases 46/87 and 227/88 *Hoechst AG* v. *Commission* [1989] ECR 2859 at 2927; Case 85/87 *Dow Benelux NV* v. *Commission* [1989] ECR 3137 at 3160, and Cases 97–99/87 *Dow Chemical Ibérica SA et al.* v. *Commission* [1989] ECR 3165 at 3189. These judgments contain many valuable observations about the limits of the Commission's powers in investigations, and on the cooperation with the national authorities in such investigations.
822. Reg. 17, Art. 14(3).
823. *Ibid.*, Arts. 15(1)(c) and 16(1)(d), respectively. See *e.g.* Decs. 80/334 (O.J. 1980 L 75/30) *Fabbrica Pisana and Fabbrica Sciara*; 92/237 (O.J. 1992 L 121/45) *Ukwal*, and 94/735 (O.J. 1994 L 294/31) *AKZO*.
824. In Case 136/79 *National Panasonic (UK) Ltd.* v. *Commission* [1980] ECR 2033 at 2057 the Court held that Article 8 of the European Convention on Human Rights was not infringed by the fact that the Commission had power to carry out investigations without prior notification.
825. Reg. 17, Art. 14(2), (4)–(6).
826. The importance of this can be seen in the notorious incidents in the PVC and Polyethylene investigations, see Cases 46/87 and 227/88 *Hoechst AG* v. *Commission* [1989] ECR 2859, [1991] 4 CMLR 410 (see also Case 46/87 R *Hoechst AG* v. *Commission* [1987] ECR 1549, [1988] 4 CMLR 430). In the United Kingdom the national officials

form of police assistance to obtain entry in execution of a decision.[827] The point clearly is that if an undertaking has prior warning of a 'dawn raid' inspection (and not all inspections are hostile by any means) the incriminating documents have a surprising tendency to disappear. Undertakings will be unable to rely on the right of respect for a person's home under Article 8(1) of the European Convention on Human Rights to resist inspections of their business premises.[828] Attempts to invoke the privilege against self-incrimination in respect of documents discovered in inspections have rightly not been the subject of wholesale acceptance by the Court.[829] The Commission is entitled to ask the national authorities to carry out investigations on its behalf, whether on the basis of an authorization or a decision, and those authorities may be assisted by the Commission in those investigations.[830] Appeal against decisions of the Commission ordering inspections or requiring the provision of information lies to the Court of First Instance.[831]

The Court considered the important issue of legal professional privilege in Case 155/79 *AM & S Europe Ltd. v. Commission.*[832] It achieved a careful balance between the principle of the protection of lawyer-client written communications on the one hand and the need to safeguard the

will usually be from the Office of Fair Trading, and are there to facilitate the investigation, and not to protect the interests of the undertaking concerned, Answer to a Question in the UK Parliament, 8 November 1979 (Hansard HL, Col. 1084). In Germany, the national officials will be from the Bundeskartellamt (as in the Hoechst saga, above). The Court has held that it follows from Reg. 17, Art. 14(6) that it is for each Member State to determine the conditions under which the national authorities will afford assistance to the Commission's officials. Thus the Member States are required to ensure that the Commission's action is effective, while respecting the general principles set out in the case-law (see the judgments cited in note 821, *supra*). Accordingly, within those limits, the appropriate procedural rules designed to ensure respect for the undertakings' rights are those laid down by national law, see *ibid.*

827. To this end, in the United Kingdom, where a hostile investigation is undertaken pursuant to a decision, an injunction from the duty Judge of the High Court can be speedily obtained, by telephone if necessary, and entry can be duly obtained.

828. Cases 46/87 and 227/88 *Hoechst AG et al. v. Commission* [1989] ECR 2859 at 2924. The Court also noted that the European Court of Human Rights had not pronounced on the point. See, though, *Chappell v. United Kingdom* [1989] ECHR Series A, Vol. 152, and Clapham (1990) 10 YBEL 309 at 337–338.

829. See Case 374/87 *Orkem v. Commission* [1989] ECR 3283 at 3350–3351; Decs. 76/593 (O.J. 1976 L 192/27) *C.S.V.* and 79/253 (O.J. 1979 L 57/33) *FIDES*, and Case C-60/92 *Otto BV v. Postbank NV* [1995] ECR I-5683 at 5712–5713. See also the decision of the European Court of Human Rights in *Funke* [1993] 1 CMLR 897. See, further, Waelbroeck and Fosselard (1994) 14 YBEL 111 at 136–138; Cumming (1995) ECLR 400 and Ortiz Blanco, *op cit.* (see note 366, *supra*) 121.

830. Reg. 17, Art. 13.

831. Reg. 17, Arts. 14(3) and 11(5), with a further appeal on a point of law only to the Court of Justice.

832. [1982] ECR 1575, [1982] 2 CMLR 264. See, as examples of the prolific writings on this case, Forrester (1983) 20 CMLRev. 75; Faull (1983) 8 ELRev. 11 and (1985) 10 ELRev. 119 and Christoforou (1985–1986) 9 Fordham Int'l. L.J. 1.

effectiveness of inspections. Privilege will not attach to written communications with in-house lawyers, nor to written communications between a client and an independent lawyer who is not entitled to practise his profession in one of the Member States (thus, for example, a member of the New York Bar who is not also a member of the Bar or a solicitor in a Member State entitled to practise there, irrespective of whether he or she lives in the Community, would not be a person in respect of communications with which a client could claim privilege).

An important issue in competition proceedings is the question of confidentiality. Already in Cases 209–215 and 218/78 *Van Landewyck Sàrl et al. v. Commission*[833] the Court found that the Commission should not have transmitted to a third party complainant certain tables (relating to the trend in receipts, purchases and payment terms) provided by an undertaking which was a party to an agreement.[834] In Case 53/85 *AKZO Chemie BV et al. v. Commission*[835] the Court confirmed this view. It found that the Commission's obligation of professional secrecy was indeed mitigated in relation to third parties who had a right to be heard (in particular, therefore, a third party who was a complainant) in so far as communication of information covered by professional secrecy was necessary for the proper conduct of the investigation. This could not, however, apply to business secrets; these are afforded very special protection and are thus not be disclosed. The assessment of whether a document contains business secrets is for the Commission to decide after having given the undertaking concerned an opportunity to state its views. A reasoned decision must then be adopted and communicated to the undertaking which must be given the opportunity to challenge it before the Court before the decision is implemented. The Court is only too well aware that if an undertaking had no means of preventing disclosure, the temptation for competitors to lodge complaints with the Commission solely to go fishing for business secrets would be severe indeed. The procedural requirements mean, though that there may be serious delays in the treatment of complaints. This is, however, a small price to pay to ensure that undertakings are treated fairly, irrespective of however unfairly they may have behaved towards competitors. Recent case-law demonstrates further just how sensitive the question of confidentiality can be, not only bearing competitors in mind, but also in relations between undertakings and national authorities.[836] The Commission and its officials

---

833. [1980] ECR 3125 at 3239.
834. The Court indicated though that this irregularity would involve the annulment in whole or in part of the contested decision only if it were shown that in the absence of the irregularity the contested decision might have been different. See also Case 85/76 *Hoffmann-La Roche & Co. AG v. Commission* [1979] ECR 461 at 510-513.
835. [1986] ECR 1965, [1987] 1 CMLR 231. See Vogelaar (1987) SEW 93, Joshua (1986) 11 ELRev. 409 and Shaw (1987) 12 ELRev. 199.
836. See the order in Case T-39/90 R *SEP v. Commission* [1990] ECR II-649, [1992] 5

are bound not to disclose information covered by the obligation of professional secrecy, or information obtained under Regulation 17,[837] and as the case-law referred to demonstrates, appeal against a decision as to confidential treatment is possible.

Statement of Objections. Before decisions finding an infringement of Articles 85 or 86 EC are adopted the undertakings concerned are presented with a Statement of Objections.[838] This contains the (provisional) findings of the Commission.[839] Under Regulation 99/63[840] the undertakings to which a statement of objections is addressed may reply in writing first of all and then also orally if necessary later. Interested third parties also have the right to be heard in accordance with Regulation 99/63, both orally and in writing if the Commission intends to give a favourable ruling on an agreement.[841] In its final decision the Commission may only rely on matters on which those concerned have been able to make their views known (and thus which have been included, albeit summarily, in the statement of objections or have otherwise been brought to the attention of the parties concerned).[842] From the judgment in Case 60/81 *International Business Machines Corporation* v. *Commission*[843] it appears that no action can be brought against a decision to open proceedings or against a statement of objections as such because they do not produce binding legal effects and

---

CMLR 27, and the judgments in Case C-67/91 *Dirección General de Defensa de la Competencia* v. *Associación Española de Banca Privada et al.* [1992] ECR I-4785 at 4830–4837; Case C-36/92 P *SEP* v. *Commission* [1994] ECR I-1911 at 1939–1943, Case T-353/94 R *Postbank NV* v. *Commission* [1994] ECR II-1141 at 1154–1147, and Case T-90/96 *Automobiles Peugeot SA* v. *Commission* [1997] ECR I-663. See also Case T-30/91 *Solvay SA* v. *Commission* [1995] ECR II-1775 at 1814–1816 and Case T-36/91 *Imperial Chemical Industries plc* v. *Commission* [1995] ECR II-1847 at 1892–1894. See further, the orders in Case T-57/91 *National Association of Licensed Opencast Operators* v. *Commission* [1993] 5 CMLR 124 (not published in the ECR); and the judgments in Case T-17/93 *Matra Hachette SA* v. *Commission* [1995] ECR II-595 at 609–610 and Case T-66/94 *Auditel Srl* v. *Commission* [1995] ECR II-239 at 249–250. See Joshua (1994) ECLR 68.

837. Art. 214 EC, with Reg. 17, Art. 20.
838. Reg. 17, Art. 19(1).
839. Case 48/69 *Imperial Chemical Industries Ltd.* v. *Commission* [1972] ECR 619 at 650–651; Cases 100–103/80 *SA Musique Diffusion Française et al.* v. *Commission* [1983] ECR 1825 at 1881–1882.
840. O.J. English Special Edition 1963–1964, p. 47, Art. 2(1).
841. Reg. 17, Art. 19(3) prescribes publication prior to the adoption of such a decision. The Commission used not to indicate in the publication (in the C series of the O.J.) whether it intended to grant a negative clearance or an exemption but now it generally does.
842. Reg. 99/63 (see note 840, *supra*), Art. 4. See, *inter alia*, Cases 100–103/80 *SA Musique Diffusion Française et al.* v. *Commission* [1983] ECR 1825, [1983] 3 CMLR 221.
843. [1981] ECR 2639 at 2654. (The Court declined to consider any argument about exceptional circumstances in which the measures lacked even the semblance of legality, finding that the circumstances did not warrant it.)

because such an action would anticipate the arguments on the substance of the case, confusing the administrative and judicial stages by making it necessary for the Court to arrive at a decision on questions on which the Commission had not yet had an opportunity to state its position.[844] The Commission is not obliged to give any indication of the amount of any likely fine.[845]

Hearing undertakings concerned, interested parties and third parties. Interested parties and even third parties may be heard during the proceedings,[846] and the undertakings or associations of undertakings concerned have a right to be heard.[847] If the Commission intends to issue a negative clearance or grant an exemption, a summary of the relevant application or notification is published in the 'C series' of the *Official Journal*, inviting all interested third parties to submit their observations within a certain period, which is not less than one month.[848] The hearing of the undertakings concerned, interested parties, and any other third parties, takes place in closed session[849] by the Commission's officials,[850] and is conducted by the Hearing Officer[851] who enjoys a certain independence within the relevant service (DG IV), in order to guarantee the objective character of the proceedings, thus contributing to the objectivity of the hearing itself and of any subsequent decision.[852]

---

844. But the Court did expressly leave open (*ibid.* at 2655) the possibility of challenging a Statement of Objections which lacked 'even the appearance of legality' and the Court of First Instance has noted in Cases T-10–12 and 15/92 *SA Cimenteries CBR et al. v. Commission* [1992] ECR II-2667 at 2683 that 'Only measures immediately and irreversibly affecting the legal situation of the undertakings concerned would be of such a nature as to justify, before completion of the administrative procedure, the admissibility of an action for annulment.' See also Case T-64/89 *Automec I* [1990] ECR II-367 at 382–383 and Case T-9/97 *Elf Altochem SA v. Commission* [1997] ECR II-909.

845. Cases 100–103/80 *SA Musique Diffusion Française v. Commission* [1983] ECR 1825 at 1883–1884.

846. Reg. 99/63 (see note 840, *supra*), Art. 7(2). The Commission has a discretion in this regard, Reg. 17, Art. 19(2), and Cases 209/78 *etc. Van Landewyck et al.* [1980] ECR 3125 at 3232–3234; Cases 43 and 63/82 *Vereniging ter Bevordering van het Vlaamse Boekwezen, VBVB et al. v. Commission* [1984] ECR 19 at 57–58.

847. Reg. 17, Art. 19(1). See also Reg. 99/63, *ibid.*

848. Reg. 17, Art. 19(3). Publication must respect the legitimate interest of the undertakings concerned in the protection of their business secrets, *ibid.*

849. Reg. 99/63 (see note 840, *supra*), Art. 9(3).

850. Reg. 99/63 (*ibid.*), Art. 9(1); Case 44/69 *Bucher & Co. v. Commission* [1970] ECR 733 at 753–754, and Cases 43 and 63/82 *Vereniging ter Bevordering van het Vlaamse Boekwezen, VBVB et al. v. Commission* [1984] ECR 19 at 57.

851. Who now acts under Dec. 94/810 (O.J. 1994 L 330/67). See Van der Woude (1996) 33 CMLRev. 531. See also *XXIIIrd Report on Competition Policy 1993* (Brussels, Luxembourg, 1994) points 203–206.

852. See, further, as to hearings, *e.g.* Case 44/69 *Buchler & Co. v. Commission* [1970] ECR 733 at 753–754; Case 51/69 *Farbenfabriken Bayer AG v. Commission* [1972] ECR 745 at 770–771; Case T-11/89 *Shell International Chemical Company Ltd. v. Commission* [1992]

Access to the file. Although there is no general right of access to the file,[853] the Commission has now made arrangements for the undertakings concerned to have access to the file upon submission of a request justified by the need for a better understanding of the file.[854] In principle undertakings concerned have access to the whole file, save in so far as documents are covered by the obligation to safeguard business secrets;[855] in this case a summary of the documents concerned can often be made available without breaching the obligation. Documents which are confidential for other reasons (such as the Commission's internal or working documents) will not be disclosed.[856] The principal objective of access to the file is to enable the right to be heard to be exercised effectively (ensuring that the undertaking knows the case it has to meet).[857] Sometimes lawyers are even known to request copies of letters they have sent to the Commission, hoping that someone may have scribbled something on the letter which might be useful to the client's case.

ECR II-757 at 779 (submissions) and 783 (rejection of submission), Case T-13/89 *Imperial Chemical Industries plc v. Commission* [1992] ECR II-1021 at 1045–1046, and Case T-90/96 *Automobiles Peugeot SA v. Commission* [1997] ECR II-663.

853. Cases 56 and 58/64 *Consten and Grundig* [1966] ECR 299 at 338; Case 54/69 *SA Française des Matières Colorantes (Francolor) v. Commission* [1972] ECR 851 at 872; Cases 43 and 63/82 *Vereniging ter Bevordering van het Vlaamse Boekwezen, VBVB et al. v. Commission* [1984] ECR 19 at 59, and Case 62/86 *AKZO Chemie BV v. Commission* [1991] ECR I-3359 at 3444.

854. The Commission's policy was initially stated in *Eleventh Report on Competition Policy 1981* (Brussels, Luxembourg, 1982) 30 (points 22–25); *Twelfth Report 1982* (*ibid.*, 1983) 40–41 (points 34 and 35); *Thirteenth Report 1983* (*ibid.*, 1984) 63–64 (point 74b), *Eighteenth Report 1988* (*ibid.*, 1989) point 44. In the light of numerous judgments, the Commission revised its policy in 1993, see the *XXXIIIrd Report 1993* (*ibid.*, 1994) points 201–202; see also the *XXVIth Report* (*ibid.*, 1997) points 40–45. The Commission has now issued a Notice on the internal rules of procedure for processing requests for access to the file (O.J. 1997 C 23/3). See Ehlermann and Drijber (1996) ECLR 375 and Levitt (1997) ECLR 187. For an overview of some of the cases, see the *XXIIIrd Report*, points 199–200. See, further, Case T-30/91 *Solvay SA v. Commission* [1995] ECR II-1775, [1995] All ER (EC) 600; Case T-36/91 *Imperial Chemical Industries plc v. Commission* [1995] ECR II-1847, and Case T-37/91 *Imperial Chemical Industries plc v. Commission* [1995] ECR II-1901. See also Case T-17/93 *Matra Hachette SA v. Commission* [1994] ECR II-595 at 609–610.

855. On the basis of Art. 214 EC and Reg. 17, Art. 20. See Case T-7/89 *SA Hercules Chemicals NV v. Commission* [1991] ECR II-1711, [1992] 4 CMLR 84, under appeal in Case C-51/92 P *SA Hercules Chemicals NV v. Commission* (O.J. 1992 C 77/5). See also the Commission's arguments in Case T-229/94 *Deutsche Bahn AG v. Commission* [1997] ECR II-1689 at 1728.

856. Case 212/86 R *Imperial Chemical Industries plc v. Commission* (Order of 11 December, 1986, unpublished, but referred to in Case T-13/89 *Imperial Chemical Industries plc v. Commission* [1992] ECR II-1021 at 1045) and Case T-65/89 *BPB Industries plc et al. v. Commission* [1993] ECR II-389 at 406.

857. Cases T-10–12 and 15/92 *SA Cimenteries CBR et al. v. Commission* [1992] ECR II-2667 at 2682.

4.6.3 Judicial protection in relation to fines

In relation to fines or periodical penalty payments imposed by the Commission, the Court has unlimited jurisdiction within the sense of Article 172 EC: it can cancel, increase or decrease them.[858] This means that the Court will not merely examine the correctness and evaluation of the facts and the application of Articles 85 or 86 to them, as in the case of an action for annulment under Article 173 EC. It can substitute its own view for that of the Commission. This is important because, as has been noted in section 4.6.2, above, the amount of the fine is never or never precisely mentioned in the statement of objections or in the administrative proceedings afterwards, and in the past there was little transparency in the manner in which the Commission arrived at an amount of a fine.[859] So far, the Court has not yet raised a fine and, as Advocate General VerLoren van Themaat pointed out in Cases 240/82 etc. *Stichting Sigarettenindustrie et al. v. Commission*,[860] if it were to do so there would be various procedural problems from the point of view of judicial protection. Reductions in fines have, however, regularly occurred. From Case 35/83 *BAT Cigaretten-Fabriken GmbH v. Commission*[861] it follows that in imposing a fine for infringement of Article 85 the Commission can only take account of those parts of an agreement from which the restriction of competition directly results. Myriad other judgments show also that the fact that the Court finds certain facts not proved may lead to a reduction in the fine.[862] Already in Case 45/69 *Boehringer Mannheim GmbH* v. *Commission*[863] the Court recalled that Article 15 of Regulation 17 showed that the sanctions provided for were not limited to cases in which the infringement was committed deliberately.[864] Nor is the power to fine limited to recidivist cases.[865] A

---

858. Reg. 17, Art. 17. This jurisdiction is now exercised by the Court of First Instance, subject to appeal, on a point of law only, to the Court of Justice.
859. See now the guidelines on the imposition of fines (O.J. 1998 C 9/3).
860. [1985] ECR 3831 at 3851.
861. [1985] ECR 363, [1985] 2 CMLR 470.
862. *E.g.* Cases 100–103/80 *SA Musique Diffusion Française et al. v. Commission* [1983] ECR 1825, [1983] 3 CMLR 221; Case 322/81 *Michelin* [1983] ECR 3461, [1985] 1 CMLR 282; Cases T-39 and 40/92 *Groupement des Cartes Bancaires 'CB' et al. v. Commission* [1994] ECR II-49; Case T-43/92 *Dunlop Slazenger International Ltd. v. Commission* [1994] ECR II-441; Case T-77/92 *Parker Pen Ltd. v. Commission* [1994] ECR II-549, and the judgments of 14 May 1998 in the cartonboard cartel, *e.g.* Case T-334/94 *Sarrió SA v. Commission* [1998] ECR II-nyr.
863. [1970] ECR 769 at 805.
864. See further, *e.g.* Case 19/77 *Miller International Schallplatten GmbH v. Commission* [1978] ECR 131 at 152 and Cases 240/82 *etc. Stichting Sigarettenindustrie et al. v. Commission* [1985] ECR 3831 at 3877.
865. Case 49/69 *Badische Anilin- und Soda-Fabrik AG (BASF) v. Commission* [1972] ECR 713 at 740.

decision imposing a fine or periodic payments is immediately executable, and, as an action for annulment of such a decision has no suspensory effect, the fine or periodic payments are due as specified in the decision, and default interest is due for late payment.[866] A practice has developed whereby the Commission and the Court will accept suspension of the payment of the fine or periodic payments when an action for annulment is lodged on provision of a bank guarantee in relation to the sum imposed and default interest up to the date of judgment (in case the imposition is not annulled or reduced). Various examples of this practice can be found in the case-law.[867] In principle neither the Commission nor the Court will take account of the precarious financial position of the undertaking being fined,[868] even in relation to the requirement of a bank guarantee as a condition for suspending payment during the proceedings before the Court. The Court of First Instance has shown itself sympathetic to the position of an undertaking which had not appealed against a decision imposing a fine but which sought review of that decision after the annulment of much of the decision as regards other addressees; the Commission had declined to review the decision as regards that undertaking.[869]

4.6.4 Position of complainants and informants

As has been noted at the end of section 4.6.2, above, interested third parties are informed of a proposal to grant negative clearance, or an exemption under Article 85(3) EC, by means of a Notice in the 'C series' of the *Official Journal*. While a complainant who sought a determination that an undertaking's conduct was incompatible with Community competition law[870] has no right to require from the Commission a final decision as regards the existence or non-existence of the alleged infringement,[871] he or she may appeal against the partial or total rejection

---

866. Case 107/82 *AEG-Telefunken v. Commission* [1983] ECR 3151 at 3221; see also Cases T-39 and 40/92 *Groupement des Cartes Bancaires 'CB' et al. v. Commission* [1995] ECR 2169 (2nd judgment, dealing with default interest).
867. *E.g.* Case 107/82 R *AEG-Telefunken v. Commission* [1982] ECR 1549; Case 861/82 R *Hasselblad (GB) Ltd. v. Commission* [1982] ECR 1555 and Case 213/86 R *Montedipe SpA v. Commission* [1986] ECR 2623.
868. Cases 96/82 etc. *NV IAZ International Belgium et al.* v.*Commission* [1983] ECR 3369, [1984] 3 CMLR 276.
869. Case T-227/95 *AssiDomän Kraft Products AB et al. v. Commission* [1997] ECR II-1185, under appeal in Case C-310/97 P *Commission v. Domän Kraft Products AB et al.* (O.J. 1997 C 318/11).
870. Reg. 17, Art. 3(2)(b). See Case T-114/92 *Bureau Européen des Médias de l'Industrie Musicale (BEMIM) v. Commission* [1995] ECR II-147.
871. Case 125/78 *GEMA v. Commission* [1979] ECR 3173 at 3189–3190.

of the complaint.[872] In *Automec I*[873] the Court of First Instance identified three successive stages in the complaint procedure. First, the collection of information, on the basis of which the Commission decides what decision to take on the complaint; the preliminary observations made by the Commission's officials in informal contacts will not be open to challenge. In the second stage, the Commission (if this is the line it intends to take) notifies the complainant of the reasons why it considers that there are insufficient grounds for granting the relief sought, and giving the complainant time to submit any further comments.[874] In the third stage, the Commission takes account of those further comments. The result may or may not be a final decision. If the complaint is rejected and the file closed, that decision can be challenged by the complainant.[875] Account has to be properly taken of their interests in that the Commission must examine carefully the factual and legal particulars brought to its notice, and the Commission is required to give a proper statement of reasons for closing the file, but the Court of First Instance has accepted that the Commission is entitled to fix priorities, in particular in view of the Community interest.[876] A complainant's rights are not as far-reaching as those of the undertaking which is the object of the investigation.[877]

872. Case 26/76 *Metro-SB Großmärkte GmbH & Co. KG v. Commission* [1977] ECR 1875 at 1901.
873. Case T-64/89 *Automec I* [1990] ECR II-367 at 382–383.
874. Reg. 99/63 (see note 840, *supra*), Art. 6. See Case C-282/95 P *Guérin Automobiles v. Commission* [1997] ECR I-1503.
875. Case 210/81 *Oswald Schmidt, trading as Demo-Studio Schmidt v. Commission* [1983] ECR 3045 at 3065 (duty to examine the complaint); Case 298/83 *Comité des industries cinématographiques des Communautés Européennes (CICCE) v. Commission* [[1985] ECR 1105 at 1122; Cases 142 and 156/84 *British-American Tobacco Company Ltd. et al. v. Commission* [1987] ECR 4487 at 4571; Case T-64/89 *Automec I* [1990] ECR 367 at 383. Case T-7/92 *Asia Motor France SA et al. v. Commission* [1993] ECR II-669 and Case T-387/94 *Asia Motor France SA et al. v. Commission* [1996] ECR II-961 well demonstrate the complexity and political sensitivity which are often involved in the assessment of complaints. See also Case T-16/91 RV *Rendo NV v. Commission* [1996] ECR II-1827 and Case T-504/93 *Tiercé Ladbroke SA v. Commission* [1997] ECR II-923 (under appeal in Case C-300/97 P *Tiercé Ladbroke SA v. Commission* (O.J. 1997 C 318/7).
876. Case T-24/90 *Automec II* [1992] ECR II-2223 at 2275–2276. In cases in which the Commission has sole power, such as to withdraw an exemption granted under Art. 85(3) EC, the Commission can be required to give a decision, *ibid.* at 2275. See, further, *e.g.* Case T-74/92 *Ladbroke Racing (Deutschland) GmbH v. Commission* [1995] ECR II-115; Case T-548/93 *Ladbroke Racing Ltd. v. Commission* [1995] ECR II-2565, [1996] 4 CMLR 459 (annulled on appeal in Cases C-359 and 379/95 *Commission et al. v. Ladbroke Racing Ltd.* [1997] ECR I-6265 and remitted to the Court of First Instance); Case T-575/93 *Koelman v. Commission* [1996] ECR II-1, [1996] 4 CMLR 637 (appeal dismissed in Case C-59/96 P *Koelman v. Commission* [1997] ECR I-4809), and Cases T-70 and 71/92 *Florimex BV et al. v. Commission* [1997] ECR II-693. See also Case T-77/94 *Vereniging van groothandelaren in Bloemkwekerijprodukten et al. v. Commission* [1997] ECR II-759.
877. *E.g.* Cases 142 and 156/84 *British–American Tobacco Company Ltd. et al. v. Commission* [1987] ECR 4487 at 4573; Case T-64/89 *Automec I* [1990] ECR 367 at 382–383.

A special duty of care is owed by the Commission to complainants and informers who draw its attention to infringements of Community competition law. This is brought home only too clearly by the whole Stanley Adams saga, from which very few emerge with a great deal of credit. In Case 145/83 *Adams* v. *Commission*[878] the Commission was ordered to pay a substantial sum by way of damages for breach of its duty of care to Adams (although he was held partly responsible).

4.6.5 Interim measures

Although, unlike Article 66 ECSC,[879] neither the EC Treaty itself nor any implementing measures expressly so provide, the Court held in Case 792/79 R *Camera Care Ltd.* v. *Commission*[880] that the Commission was entitled under Article 3(1) of Regulation 17 to adopt interim measures of a conservatory nature. A *lacuna* in the system of Regulation 17 was thereby closed. The reasoning behind this is essentially that of the doctrine of the useful effect ('*effet utile*') applied so as to ensure that the exercise of the power to adopt decisions does not become ineffectual or illusory. The Commission has to have regard to the legitimate interests of the undertaking concerned; interim measures may thus only be adopted 'in cases proved to be urgent so as to avoid a situation likely to cause serious and irreparable damage to the party seeking their adoption, or which is intolerable for the public interest.' Moreover, the measures must be of a temporary and conservative nature and not go beyond what is required in a given situation. The essential safeguards guaranteed to the parties concerned must be respected and it is clear that the application for interim measures must be accompanied by a complaint which appears *prima facie* justified. This parallels what the Court requires before it will consider granting interim relief. The measures are to be taken by the Commission in the form of a decision (which can, of course, be challenged before the Court). Subsequent cases show that these conditions must be strictly adhered to.[881] In the *Fourteenth Report on Competition Policy* the Commis-

---

878. [1985] ECR 3539, [1986] 1 CMLR 506. See also Dec. 76/642 (O.J. 1976 L 223/27) *Hoffmann-La Roche*, partially annulled on appeal in Case 85/76 *Hoffmann-La Roche & Co. AG v. Commission* [1979] ECR 461, [1979] 3 CMLR 211.
879. See Case 109/75 R *National Carbonising Company Ltd. v. Commission* [1975] ECR 1193, [1975] 2 CMLR 457.
880. [1980] ECR 119 at 131; see Baardman (1981) SEW 358; Gray (1979) 4 ELRev. 80; Ferry (1980) EIPR 30 and Temple Lang (1981) 18 CML Rev. 49.
881. *E.g.* Cases 228 and 229/82 R *Ford Werke AG et al. v. Commission* [1982] ECR 3091, [1982] 3 CMLR 649 (in which the scope of the interim measure was reduced); see also the final judgment in Cases 228 and 229/82 *Ford Werke AG et al. v. Commission* [1984] ECR 1129, [1984] 1 CMLR 649 in which the interim measures were finally struck down as they did not fall within the framework of a final decision which could be adopted.

sion served general notice that it could require undertakings to cease temporarily to apply certain restrictive clauses in an agreement, using a decision under Article 3 of Regulation 17; it could also issue an Article 15(6) decision under that regulation depriving an undertaking of the protection against fines conferred by notification.[882] The Commission has required undertakings to resume supplies,[883] cease predatory conduct,[884] issue an instruction to dealers,[885] and grant a competitor access to essential port facilities.[886] Sometimes the Commission has been able to accept a formal promise (confusingly, in the context of Community competition law, called an undertaking) which has removed the necessity for interim measures proceedings to be formally brought to fruition.[887] The Court of First Instance has now restated the criteria for the grant of interim measures in Case T-44/90 *La Cinq SA v. Commission*;[888] 'protective measures may be granted only where the practices of certain undertakings are prima facie such as to constitute a breach of the Community rules on competition in respect of which a penalty could be imposed by a decision of the Commission. Furthermore, such measures are to be taken only in cases of proven urgency, in order to prevent the occurrence of a situation likely to cause serious and irreparable damage to the party applying for their adoption or intolerable damage to the public interest.'[889]

4.7 Public undertakings: Article 90 EC[890]

It can be stated without exaggeration that Article 90 EC is probably the most difficult of all the competition provisions of the Treaty, given that the rules on public undertakings and undertakings which exercise public functions form a crossroads between the Treaty obligations imposed on

882. (Brussels, Luxembourg, 1985) 96 (point 124). The Commission based its view on the *Ford* judgment, *ibid.*
883. Dec. 87/500 (O.J. 1987 L 286/36) *BBI/Boosey & Hawkes*.
884. See Dec. 83/462 (O.J. 1983 L 252/13) *ECS/AKZO*.
885. Dec. 92/154 (O.J. 1992 L 66/1) *Eco System/ Peugeot*, see Case T-23/90 *Automobiles Peugeot SA v. Commission* [1991] ECR II-653 (appeal rejected).
886. In *Irish Continental v. CCI Morlaix* [1995] 5 CMLR 177 (not published in the *Official Journal*), see *XXVth Report on Competition Policy 1995* (Brussels, Luxembourg, 1996) Part 2, *Report on the application of competition rules in the United Kingdom* 120.
887. See the policy stated in *Fifteenth Report on Competition Policy 1985* (Brussels, Luxembourg, 1986) point 49; *Sixteenth Report 1986* (*ibid.*, 1987) point 74.
888. [1992] ECR II-1 at 13.
889. See Dec. 94/19 (O.J. 1994 L 15/8) *Sea Containers v. Stena Sealink* (claim for interim measures rejected), and Cases T-24 and 28/92 R *Langnese-Iglo GmbH et al. v. Commission* [1992] ECR II-1839.
890. See, generally, among more recent literature, Bright (1993) ECLR 263, Chung (1995) ECLR 87, Edward and Hoskins (1995) 32 CMLRev. 157, Ehricke (1990) *World Competition* 79, Fenger and Broberg (1995) ECLR 364, Gyslen (1989) 26 CMLRev. 33, Hoffman (1990) ECLR 11, and Joliet (1989) 12 Fordham Int'l. L.J. 163.

the Member States and those imposed on undertakings. Article 90 EC has in recent years developed into the most important weapon available to the Commission to open up the internal market in the utilities sectors such as energy supply, telecommunications and transport which had been closed off by public undertakings since time immemorial. Article 90 EC thus forms a means to set limits to the use of public and other undertakings as instruments of economic and fiscal policy[891] The case-law clearly places Article 90, like Articles 85 and 86 EC, in the perspective of the system of undistorted competition prescribed by Article 3(g) EC.[892]

Article 90 EC, like ancient Gaul, is divided into three parts. Article 90(1) and (2) are directly effective[893] and each contains a separate substantive rule. Article 90(1) confirms the applicability of the Treaty provisions to actions of the Member States in relation to public undertakings. Article 90(2) provides for an exception in respect of certain undertakings to this general rule which is already expressed in the other provisions of the Treaty. Article 90(3) contains an attribution of powers to the Commission for ensuring compliance with both of the first two limbs of Article 90.

4.7.1   Article 90(1) EC

At first sight it may be wondered what the directly effective Article 90(1) adds to the obligations incumbent on undertakings and the Member States in the present state of Community law. This is particularly so in relation to the category of undertakings mentioned in Article 90(1): public undertakings and undertakings to which Member States grant special or exclusive rights. In view of the wide interpretation given by the Court to the concept of an undertaking, Articles 85 and 86 EC already apply to such undertakings, irrespective of the precise meaning of the term 'special' rights.[894] The puzzlement is also appropriate in respect of the measures enacted or maintained in force by Member States in relation to these undertakings which could give rise to infringement of other provisions of

---

891. Case C-202/88 *France v. Commission* [1991] ECR I-1223 at 1263.

892. Cases C-46/90 and 93/91 *Procureur du Roi v. Lagauche et al.* [1993] ECR 5267 at 5331 (referring to the old Art. 3(f) EEC).

893. Case C-260/89 *Elliniki Radiophonia Tileorassi AE v. Dimotiki Etairia Pliroforissis et al.* [1991] ECR I-2925 at 2962 (hereafter: *ERT*); Case T-16/91 *Rendo NV et al. v. Commission* [1992] ECR II-2417 at 2448 (unaffected on this point by the judgment in Case C-19/93 P *Rendo NV et al. v. Commission* [1995] ECR I-3319, with rectification [1996] ECR I-1997).

894. The same is true for the provisions of Art. 6 EC (non-discrimination on ground of nationality). The versions of the Treaty published by the Community Institutions have (rightly) replaced the reference to Art. 7 [EEC] by a reference to Art. 6 [EC] even though this seems to have been overlooked in the text of the TEU itself.

the Treaty, in particular of Articles 6 and 85–94 EC. In relation to Articles 6, 85 and 86 EC the prohibition of such measures stems from the line of judgments that those provisions, in conjunction with Articles 3(g) and 5 EC, oblige the Member States to abstain from any measures which would undermine the competition provisions of the Treaty.[895] As far as the other provisions of the Treaty are concerned, it is not relevant whether the State acts through its own means, in law or in fact, or whether it acts through undertakings the market behaviour of which it has power to determine or the possibility of determining.[896]

The significance of Article 90(1) thus lies in the first instance in its declaratory character, in the sense that what already results from the other provisions of the Treaty is expressly confirmed in respect of public undertakings. This purpose also makes it plain that the interpretation of the concepts of 'public under-takings,'[897] 'special[898] or exclusive rights'[899] and 'measures' must be such as to ensure that the useful effect ('effet utile') of these other provisions is not undermined. The case-law noted above shows that the Court too adopts this approach. Secondly, the significance of Article 90(1) lies in the exception to its provisions contained in Article 90(2) and in the particular powers to ensure compliance contained in Article 90(3).

Accordingly, the prohibition in Article 90(1) can be summarized as follows: measures taken by the national authorities in relation to public undertakings or undertakings with special or exclusive rights, which infringe other provisions of the Treaty are only justified if the exceptions contained in those provisions are applicable. This means in particular the

895. *E.g.* Case 267/86 *Van Eycke v. ASPA NV* [1988] ECR 4769 at 4791.
896. Case 249/81 *Commission v. Ireland* [1982] ECR 4005, [1983] 2 CMLR 99 (relating to Art. 30 EC); Case C-302/88 *Hennen Olie BV v. Stichting Interim Centraal Orgaan Voorraadvorming Aardolieprodukten et al.* [1990] ECR I-4625 (Art. 34 EC); Case 78/76 *Firma Steinike und Weinlig v. Germany* [1977] ECR 595, [1977] 2 CMLR 688, Case 290/83 *Commission v. France* [1985] ECR 439, [1986] 2 CMLR 546, Case 57/86 *Greece v. Commission* [1988] ECR 2855, [1990] 1 CMLR 65, Cases 67, 68 and 70/85 *Kwekerij Gebroeders Van der Kooy BV et al. v. Commission* [1988] ECR 219, [1989] 2 CMLR 804 (state aids), and Case C-188/89 *Foster et al. v. British Gas plc* [1990] ECR 3313, [1990] 2 CMLR 833 (in relation to provisions in a directive).
897. Cases 188–190/80 *France, Italy and the United Kingdom v. Commission* [1982] ECR 2545 at 2579; Case 118/85 *Commission v. Italy* [1987] ECR 2599 at 2621–2622.
898. In Case C-202/88 *France v. Commission* [1991] ECR I-1223, [1992] 5 CMLR 552 and Cases C-271/90 *etc.* [1992] ECR I-5833, [1993] 4 CMLR 110 the Court partially annulled the Telecoms Terminals Equipment Directive (Dir. 88/301 (O.J. 1988 L 131/73)) and the Telecoms Services Directive (Dir. 90/388 (O.J. 1990 L 192/10)) on the ground that the definition of special rights was not adequate and the reasoning why such rights infringed the EC Treaty were insufficiently explained. In Dir. 94/46 (O.J. 1994 L 268/15) the Commission amended those directives to define special rights more precisely.
899. See Case 172/82 *Syndicat national des Fabricants Raffineurs d'Huile de Graissage et al. v. GIE 'Inter-Huiles' et al.* [1983] ECR 555 at 566–567.

exceptions specified in Articles 36,[900] 56[901] and 66 EC and in the case-law on the rule of reason in applied in respect of the free movement of goods and of services.[902] Moreover, Article 90(2) contains a supplementary exception for undertakings entrusted with the operation of services of general economic interest or having the character of a revenue-producing monopoly. Finally, Article 90 appears to be of significance for the health sector, in particular for particular sickness schemes.

As far as the applicability of the competition provisions to public sector is concerned, Article 90(1) EC and the case-law on these provisions draw a distinction between the public undertaking on the one hand and the relevant measure of the authorities on the other. To the extent that the undertaking acts autonomously on its own account and responsibility, so that its commercial conduct is not attributed, or not directly attributed to the Member State, it is possible that in addition to the applicability of Article 90(1), Articles 85 and 86 EC will also apply to such conduct of the undertaking.[903] This will frequently even be the case, given that the concept of an undertaking is widely interpreted. An independent application of Articles 85 and 86 or other Treaty provisions is excluded, if the action of the undertaking can be wholly attributed to the Member State.[904]

The controversial question whether the establishment or maintenance of statutory monopolies (through the grant or expansion of special or exclusive rights) may be *as such* incompatible with these provisions has been clarified by recent case-law. Constant case-law shows first that a statutory monopoly implies the existence of a dominant position,[905] and, secondly, that the existence of such a position and thus of the monopoly is not as such incompatible with Article 86 EC.[906] There may also be a

900. For a possibility under this heading, see Case 72/83 *Campus Oil Ltd. et al. v. Minister for Industry and Energy et al.* [1984] ECR 2727, [1984] 3 CMLR 544, but see Case C-347/88 *Commission v. Greece* [1990] ECR I-4747. Undertakings concerned with the collection and distribution of human blood and organs may also be covered by this heading.
901. Case C-260/89 *Elliniki Radiophona Tileorassi AE v. Dimotiki Etairia Pliroforissis et al.* [1991] ECR I-2925 at 2960–2961 (hereafter *ERT*) and Case C-353/89 *Commission v. The Netherlands* [1991] ECR I-4069 at 4097–4098.
902. Case C-202/88 *France v. Commission* [1992] ECR I-1223 at 1267–1269.
903. Case 41/83 *Italy v. Commission* [1985] ECR 873[1985] 2 CMLR 368.
904. This is particularly important in the application of Arts. 92 and 93 EC, see Case 78/76 *Firma Steinike und Weinlig v. Germany* [1977] ECR 595, [1977] 2 CMLR 688 and Cases 67, 68 and 70/85 *Kwekerij Gebroeders Van der Kooy BV et al. v. Commission* [1988] ECR 219, [1989] 2 CMLR 804.
905. Case 311/84 *Centre belge d'études de marché – Télémarketing (CBEM) SA v. Compagnie luxembourgeoise de télédiffusion SA et al.* [1985] ECR 3261, [1986] 2 CMLR 558; Case C-179/90 *Merci convenzionali porto di Genova SpA v. Siderurgica Gabrelli SpA* [1991] ECR 5889, [1994] 4 CMLR 422; Case C-18/88 *Régie des télégraphes et des téléphones v. GB-Inno-BM SA* [1991] ECR I-5941; Case C-320/91 *Corbeau* [1993] ECR I-2533, [1995] 4 CMLR 621.
906. Case 155/73 *Sacchi* [1974] ECR 409 at 430. The grant of exclusive rights within the

dominant position in the sense of Article 86 EC if there is a centrally run combination of local or regional monopolies, such as municipal concessions to one undertaking or a group of associated undertakings.[907] The abuse which is prohibited by Article 86 EC lies in the manner in which the monopoly is *exercized*. The establishment of a monopoly, or its extension, must not reduce competition in the relevant market to such a degree that it falls below the minimum degree of competition prescribed by Article 85(3) EC. This may very well occur through the grant of exclusive rights. A statutory monopoly through exclusive rights may be distinguished from a factual monopoly in that the former, unlike the latter, completely blocks off access to the market and thereby excludes potential competition. This leads to a situation in which goods and services from other Member States are discriminated against (as in the telecoms sector) or in which the supply governed by the exclusive rights does not correspond to the demand. In such a case the distinction between the existence and the exercise of the exclusive rights cannot be maintained. In so far as the grant of exclusive rights is not covered by the exceptions prescribed in the provisions referred to in Article 90(1) EC,[908] that grant or extension will infringe Article 86 EC. The Court thus takes an approach which parallels that in Case 6/72 *Continental Can*,[909] which takes place against the background of the realization that the system of Article 3(g) EC can only be maintained if the equality of competitive opportunities for the various market participants is guaranteed.[910]

4.7.2   Article 90(2) EC

For a special category of undertakings, Article 90(2) EC contains exceptions to the applicability of Articles 6, 85, 86 and 92 in particular, but also of

meaning of Art. 90(1) which create a dominant position is not incompatible with Art. 86; a Member State infringes those provisions only if the undertaking cannot avoid abusing that dominant position by exercising those rights, *e.g.* Case C-323/93 *Société Civile Agricole du Centre d'Insémination de la Crespelle v. Coopérative d'Élevage et d'Insémination Artificielle du Département de la Mayenne* [1994] ECR I-5077 at 5104. See also Case C-18/93 *Corsica Ferries Italia Srl v. Corpo dei Piloti del porto di Genova* [1994] ECR I-1783 and Case 242/95 *GT-Link A/s v. De Dansk Statsbaner (DSB)* [1997] ECR I-4449. *Cf.* Case C-387/93 *Banchero* [1995] ECR I-4663 at 4697–4700. There might well be an infringement of Art. 37 EC, if the appropriate conditions are fulfilled, see Chapter VII, section 3.4 *ante*.

907. Case 30/87 *Bodson v. Pompes funèbres des régions libérées SA* [1988] ECR 2479 at 2516–2517.

908. In Case 155/73 *Sacchi* [1974] ECR 409 at 429 the Court spoke of 'considerations of public interest, of a non-economic nature' – a phrase repeated in Case C-260/89 *ERT* [1991] ECR I-2925 at 2957.

909. [1973] ECR 215, [1973] CMLR 199.

910. This is clearly implied (although *not* expressly stated) in Case C-260/89 *ERT* [1991] ECR I-2925 at 2961; Case C-41/90 *Höfner and Elser v. Macrotron GmbH* [1991] ECR I-1979 at 2017–2018, and Case C-320/91 *Corbeau* [1993] ECR 2533 at 2567–2568.

other Treaty rules, including Article 90(1). These exceptions apply to undertakings entrusted with the operation of services of general economic interest or having the character of a revenue-producing monopoly.[911] The most important element for determining whether an undertaking falls within these exceptions is the word *entrusted*. This makes it clear that the tasks concerned must be imposed,[912] and not merely that there is a degree of general or specific supervision by the authorities.[913] This element explains further that the phrase 'services of general economic interest' must be interpreted primarily against the background of the national situation.[914] The mere possession of a special or exclusive right to operate certain economic services is not to say that they are services of general economic interest.[915] Examples of the latter include transport obligations for non-commercially viable routes,[916] radio and television,[917] postal and telecommunications services,[918] and certain forms of public employment agencies.[919] It may be deduced from the case-law cited above that Article 90(2) is primarily concerned with tasks of the authorities which in some Member States are performed by undertakings, and the aim is to avoid the performance of these general interest tasks of the authorities being hindered by the application of the EC Treaty. This leads to the conclusion that the group of undertakings mentioned in Article 90(2) may overlap with that referred to in Article 90(1), but not necessarily so. Both the objective and the scope of this exception and the undertakings affected by it make it clear

---

911. Revenue-producing monopolies embrace undertakings enjoying exclusive rights to produce and trade in products subject to specific taxes, such as alcohol and tobacco products. In many cases these monopolies infringed Art. 37 EC and have therefore been dismantled or adapted over the years.

912. Case 127/73 *Belgische Radio en Televisie et al. v. SV SABAM et al.* [1974] ECR 51 at 62–63; Case 7/82 *Gesellschaft zur Verwertung von Leistungsschutzrechten mbH (GVL) v. Commission* [1983] ECR 483 at 504.

913. As in the case of banking and insurance supervision, see Case 172/80 *Züchner v. Bayerische Vereinsbank AG* [1981] ECR 2021, [1982] 1 CMLR 313.

914. Case C-260/89 *ERT* [1989] ECR 2925 at 2960 and 2962. Note the terms of the new Art. 7d EC which will be introduced by the Treaty of Amsterdam (not yet in force). This reinforces the balance which must be struck between the rules on competition and the fulfilment of the missions of public services.

915. See as an interesting comparison the results in Case 10/71 *Ministère Public of Luxembourg v. Hein (née Muller) et al.* [1971] ECR 723 and Case C-179/90 *Merci convenzionali porto di Genova SpA v. Siderurgica Gabrelli SpA* [1991] ECR 5889, [1994] 4 CMLR 422. See also Case C-18/93 *Corsica Ferries Italia Srl v. Corpo dei Piloti del Porto di Genova* [1994] ECR I-1783.

916. Case 66/86 *Ahmed Saeed Flugreisen et al. v. Zentrale zur Bekämpfung unlauteren Wettbewerbs e.V.* [1989] ECR 803 at 853.

917. Case 155/73 *Sacchi* [1974] ECR 409 at 429–430; Case C-260/89 *ERT* [1991] ECR I-2925 at 2962–2963.

918. Case C-18/88 *Régie des télégraphes et des téléphones v. GB-Inno-BM SA* [1988] ECR I-5941 at 5979 (but the Court refused to accept that the production and sale of terminals could be restricted to the RTT, *ibid.* at 5980–5981).

919. Case C-41/90 *Höfner and Elser v. Macrotron GmbH* [1991] ECR I-1979 at 2017.

that Article 90(2) is a provision which is in fact entirely independent of Article 90(1).

The exception of Article 90(2) is applicable only if all the conditions are fulfilled. The first, and in practice the most important condition is that it must be shown, by the Commission, acting on the basis of Article 90(3), or by a litigant in a national court, that the competition rules or other provisions of the EC Treaty could obstruct the performance of the particular tasks concerned. The text of this clause, the decisions in practice,[920] and the case-law[921] all make it clear that this condition falls into two parts. The derogation from the competition provisions must be both necessary and proportionate. A practical consequence of this is that if the assignment by the authorities in relation to these special tasks does not or does not necessarily in itself restrict competition, it will be impossible for the undertaking concerned to rely on Article 90(2).[922] The second condition relates to the requirement that the development of trade is not affected to such an extent as would be contrary to the interests of the Community. The question is whether this condition has an independent significance. Given that Article 90(2) itself permits the restriction of competition subject to this condition, intra-Community trade may also as result inevitably be affected. From the requirements of necessity and proportionality in the first condition it must follow that the conduct of the undertaking which restricts competition and affects trade may not go further than is strictly necessary , and in any event may not wholly exclude competition for a significant part of the relevant products and services.[923] To this extent the minimum requirement of competition

---

920. See Decs. 90/16 (O.J. 1990 L 10/47) *Courier Services in the Netherlands*, on appeal, Cases C-48 and 66/90 *The Netherlands et al. v. Commission* [1992] ECR I-565; 90/456 (O.J. 1990 L 233/19) *Courier Services in Spain*, and 91/50 (O.J. 1991 L 28/32) *IJssel-centrale*, on appeal Case T-16/91 *Rendo NV et al. v. Commission* [1992] ECR II-2417, reversed in part and remitted in Case C-19/93 P *Rendo NV et al. v. Commission* [1995] ECR I-3319, [1997] 4 CMLR 392 (rectification [1996] ECR I-1997), see further Case T-16/91RV *Rendo NV et al. v. Commission* [1996] ECR II-1827.
921. Case C-18/88 *Régie des télégraphes et des téléphones v. GB-Inno-BM SA* [1988] ECR I-5941; Case C-41/90 *Höfner and Elser v. Macrotron GmbH* [1991] ECR I-1979, [1993] 4 CMLR 306.
922. See also the guidelines for the application of the competition rules in the telecommunications sector (O.J. 1991 C 233/2).
923. Case 202/88 *France v. Commission* [1991] ECR I-1223, [1992] 5 CMLR 552. In Case C-320/91 *Corbeau* [1993] ECR 2523 at 2568–2569 the Court accepted that the public service to all at a single tariff for basic postal deliveries was a service of general economic interest, but specific services which were dissociable from the traditional postal services could not be excluded from the wind of competition. See also Case T-106/95 *Fédération française des sociétés d'assurances (FFSA) et al. v. Commission* [1997] ECR II-229. In Case C-393/92 *Gemeente Almelo et al. v. Energiebedrijf Ijsselmij NV* [1994] ECR I-1477 at 1521 the Court regarded a ban on the importation of electricity by local distributors as acceptable if it was necessary to enable the regional distributor to perform its task of general interest, namely to ensure uninterrupted supply of elec-

prescribed by Article 85(3) EC also plays a role in the delimitation of the possibility of exemption afforded by Article 90(2) EC.

Article 90(2) is addressed to the category of undertakings specified therein, but also has consequences for the Member States. First, the Member States may not take any measures which would deviate from the scope of the exception and the conditions attached thereto. If they do then the measures fall under the prohibition in Article 90(1) and in the Treaty provisions referred to in that provision.[924] Secondly, such measures must not infringe the other provisions of the Treaty, even if the requirements of Article 90(2) are satisfied in relation to the service of general economic interest concerned.[925] This interpretation is in line with the objective of Article 90(2) which, as has been noted above, relates to the specific situation in which a general interest task of the authorities is performed by an undertaking, but does not amount to a general derogation enabling activities of the authorities to escape from the scope of the provisions of the EC Treaty by being performed in such a manner.

4.7.3   Article 90(3) EC

Since the last edition of this work (in 1989), the Court has considerably clarified the scope and content of the power conferred on the Commission by Article 90(3) EC to address appropriate directives or decisions to Member States for the purpose of applying Article 90(1) and (2). The case-law results from appeals by various Member States[926] against three directives adopted by the Commission under this provision: Directive 80/723 on the transparency of financial relations between Member States and public undertakings;[927] Directive 88/301 on competition in market for

tricity to all consumers in the territory it covered, the assessment having to take into consideration the economic conditions under which the latter operated, in particular the costs it had to bear, and the legislation – especially relating to the environment – to which it was subject.

924. Case 66/86 *Ahmed Saeed Flugreisen et al. v. Zentrale zur Bekämpfung unlauteren Wettbewerbs e.V.* [1989] ECR 803 at 851–852; Case C-41/90 *Höfner and Elser v. Macrotron GmbH* [1991] ECR I-1979 at 2017–2018.

925. Case 72/83 *Campus Oil Ltd. et al. v. Minister for Industry and Energy et al.* [1984] ECR 2727 at 2747.

926. Cases 188–190/80 *France, Italy and United Kingdom v. Commission* [1982] ECR 2545, [1982] 3 CMLR 144; Case C-202/88 *France v. Commission* [1991] ECR I-1223, [1992] 5 CMLR 552, and Cases C-271, 281 and 289/90 *Spain, Belgium and Italy v. Commission* [1992] ECR 5833, [1993] 4 CMLR 110. These cases concern in turn each of the directives referred to in the text. In the latter two judgments, it will be recalled that the Court partially annulled the directives on the grounds that special rights were not adequately defined and that it was not clearly explained why they were incompatible with the Treaty.

927. O.J. 1980 L 195/35, extended by Dirs. 85/412 (O.J. 1985 L 229/20) and 93/84 (O.J. 1993 L 254/16). In Case C-325/91 *France v. Commission* [1993] ECR I-3283 the Court annul-

telecommunications terminal equipment;[928] and Directive 90/388 on competition in the markets for telecommunications services.[929] In particular the telecommunications directives have demonstrated how effective an instrument Article 90(3) can be for obliging Member States to open up hitherto notoriously closed markets to competition. Directive 88/301 requires the withdrawal of special or exclusive rights of national telecoms companies concerning the importation, distribution, connection, bringing into service and maintenance of terminal equipment, and opened up the market for such activities to competitors, ensuring also that the tasks of drawing up and publishing the required specifications and indeed the certification of conformity thereto must be in the hands of a body independent of market participants.[930] Directive 90/388, as amended,[931]

led the Commission's Communication on the application of Arts. 92 and 93 EC and Art. 5 of Dir. 80/723 (O.J. 1991 C 273/2). The Communication was accordingly reissued, with the points which had caused the difficulty omitted (O.J. 1993 C 307/3) and Dir. 80/723 was amended by Dir. 93/84, *supra*. Dir. 80/273 is mainly designed to permit the Commission to verify that public undertakings do not receive state aids from the public authorities. They are obliged to keep the necessary information available for the Commission for five years and to supply such information to the Commission at its request. The original scope has been extended twice (as explained above) to include first the utilities and public sector credit institutions, and then annual reporting requirements for public undertakings in the manufacturing sectors with a turnover exceeding 250 million ECU per annum, including details of intra- and inter-group transactions and transactions between the Member States and those undertakings.

928. O.J. 1988 L 131/73, amended by Dir. 94/46 (O.J. 1994 L 286/25) in the light of the case-law noted above.
929. O.J. 1990 L 192/10 (amended by Dirs. 94/46 (O.J. 1994 L 286/25) on satellite communications; 95/51 (O.J. 1995 L 256/49) on cable television; 96/2 (O.J. 1996 L 20/59) on mobile telephony, and 96/19 (O.J. 1996 L 74/13) on full competition in telecommunications markets). See also Dir. 90/387 (O.J. 1990 L192/1) on Open Network Provision; Dir. 92/44 (O.J. 1992 L 165/27) on Open Network Provision for leased lines (a challenge to the validity of which was rejected in Case C-302/94 *R. v. Secretary of State for Trade and Industry, ex parte British Telecommunications plc* [1996] ECR I-6417 at 6468); Dir. 95/62 (O.J. 1995 L 321/6) on Open Network Provision in voice telephony; Dir. 97/33 (O.J. 1997 L 199/32) on interconnection, and Dir. 98/10 (O.J. 1998 L 101/24) on voice telephony and universal service, again in the context of Open Network Provision. Challenges have been mounted to the Commission's competence in relation to part of Dir. 95/51: Cases C-11 and 12/96 *Spain and Portugal v. Commission* (O.J. 1996 C 95/5). In the wider context of the Community's telecommunications policy, outside the framework of Art. 90(3) EC, see Council Dir. 97/13 (O.J. 1997 L 117/15) on a common framework for general authorizations and individual licences for telecommunications services. See also Dec. 1336/97 (O.J. 1997 L 183/12) and further policy statements in O.J. 1997 C 76/9 and O.J. 1998 C 71/4.
930. See also Cases C-46/90 and 93/91 *Procureur du Roi v. Lagauche et al.* [1993] ECR I-5267; Case C-69/91 *Gillon, née Decoster* [1993] ECR I-5335; Case C-92/91 *Neny, née Taillandier* [1993] ECR I-5383; Case C-314/93 *Rouffeteau and Badia* [1994] ECR I-3257, and Case C-91/94 *Tranchant et al.* [1995] ECR I-3911. It is permissible for Member States to prescribe that equipment must satisfy the essential requirements of Dir. 86/361 (O.J. 1986 L 271/21).
931. See note 929, *supra*.

requires the withdrawal of all exclusive rights for the supply of telecom-munications services, the last of which is to be public voice telephony.[932] It aimed to achieve an open internal market by not only requiring the abolition of monopolies for the provision of telecoms services, but also the introduction of objective, non-discriminatory and transparent criteria for the application for and grant of licences, the opening up to third parties according to published, objective and non-discriminatory criteria, of monopolies on setting up and exploiting telecommunications networks, and the transfer of various administrative, technical, controlling and supervisory functions, such as the grant of licences and approvals, to an independent body. The amendments to Directive 90/388 have considerably extended its scope, so that the Commission has now very nearly completely achieved its objective of telecommunications liberalization within the Community.[933]

The case-law noted above demonstrates that the Commission may prescribe general rules by means of directives in order to ensure that the conduct of undertakings covered by Article 90(1) and (2) conforms to the requirements of the EC Treaty. In concrete cases decisions may be adopted.[934] These directives and decisions are acts within the meaning of Article 189 EC,[935] which means that non-compliance has to be established through infringement proceedings under Article 169 EC, given that Article 90(3) does not permit the Commission to bring the matter directly to the Court.[936] Private parties can rely on these decisions and on any directly effective provisions of these directives. Although Article 90(3) is silent as to procedural guarantees, the Court has held that the Commission must

932. In most instances this had to take place by 1 January, 1998, but a few temporary transitional arrangements have been agreed for a number of Member States.
933. The Commission's strategy was initially set out in its Green Paper COM (87) 290 Final, and further in its Guidelines for the application of the competition provisions in the telecoms sector (O.J. 1991 C 233/2). See, further, COM (94) 492 Final and COM (95) 158 Final. For further details, see the most recent *Reports on Competition Policy* and the Green Paper COM (97) 623 Final. See also the Communications on voice communications on the Internet (O.J. 1998 C6/4) and on postal services (O.J. 1998 C39/2).
934. Cases C-48 and 66/90 *The Netherlands et al. v. Commission* [1992] ECR I-565 at 635. See, *e.g.* Decs. 95/489 (O.J. 1995 L 280/49) and 97/181 (O.J. 1997 L 76/19) on second GSM network licences in Italy and Spain, respectively. See also Decs. 97/606 (O.J. 1997 L 244/18) *VTM/VT4* on *TV advertising in Flanders*; 97/744 (O.J. 1997 L 301/17) *Italian Ports legislation on employment*, and 97/745 (O.J. 1997 L 301/27) *Piloting charges in the Port of Genoa*. For an unsuccessful attempt to force the Commission to take measures under Art. 90(3) EC, see Case C-107/95 P *Bundesverband der Bilanz-buchhalter eV v. Commission* [1997] ECR I-947.
935. Case 226/87 *Commission v. Greece* [1988] ECR 3611, [1989] 3 CMLR 569.
936. The Court also held that a Member State could not plead the unlawfulness of the decision addressed to it in defence to an infringement proceeding for non-compliance with the decision, [1988] ECR 3611 at 3623-3624. The Member State should have challenged the decision under Art. 173 EC.

respect fully the rights of the defence, so that the Member State concerned is entitled to a precise statement of the various elements alleged to infringe Community law, and is entitled to be heard, as is, where appropriate, the undertaking concerned.[937]

It follows that the scope of acts adopted on the basis of Article 90(3) is restricted to the undertakings of the types specified in Article 90(1) and (2) and to measures of the public authorities. Obligations may also only be imposed by means of decisions or directives.[938] Thus Article 90(3) affords no legal basis for general harmonization measures in the sense of Article 100a EC or regulations under Article 87 EC, nor does it afford a basis for 'soft law' obligations through communications.[939] Given that decisions and directives adopted by the Commission under Article 90(3) are independent instruments to ensure compliance with the rules of, and specified in, Article 90(1) and (2), it follows that the exercise of the Commission's powers is not affected by the exercise of the Council's powers on the basis of other provisions of the Treaty, such as Article 94 EC relating to state aids.[940] From this scope, it follows that the purpose of such decisions and directives adopted by the Commission is not restricted to merely ascertaining infringements of Article 90(1) and (2) and other provisions of the Treaty. Those acts may contain specific descriptions of certain obligations resulting from the Treaty and require that certain obstacles are removed.[941]

This specific character makes it plain that the relevant decisions and directives are declaratory in nature in so far as the obligations which they prescribe flow from the relevant treaty provisions themselves (such as Articles 30 and 59 EC), so that these obligations existed even before the adoption of the decisions or directives concerned.[942] These acts may be constitutive because, unlike reasoned opinions in the context of Article 169 EC proceedings, they can indicate in a concrete manner how certain infringements can or must be terminated and what the Commission regards as being compatible or incompatible with the relevant provisions.[943] There is to this extent a parallel between these decisions and

937. Cases C-48 and 66/90 *The Netherlands et al. v. Commission* [1992] ECR I-565 at 637 and 640.
938. Case C-325/91 *France v. Commission* [1993] ECR I-3283 at 3312.
939. *Ibid.* (as to communications) and Case C-202/88 *France v. Commission* [1991] ECR I-1223 at 1265–1266 (as to Arts. 100a and 87 EC).
940. Cases 188–190/80 *France, Italy and United Kingdom v. Commission* [1982] ECR 2545 at 2573–2575.
941. Case C-202/88 *France v. Commission* [1991] ECR I-1223 at 1264.
942. Case C-69/91 *Gillon, née Decoster* [1993] ECR I-5335 at 5380–5381.
943. It is an open question to what extent such directives and decisions may also deal with provisions of secondary Community law. Given that Art. 90(1) mentions 'the rules contained in this Treaty' it is unlikely that they may. Moreover, in such cases those acts would not aim to determine more precisely general obligations, given that the determination had already occurred in the secondary legislation concerned.

directives on the one hand and prohibition and exemption decisions and block exemption regulations under, as appropriate Articles 85 or 86 EC. In relation to the obligation to provide information, there is a parallel with Regulation 17.[944] However, Article 90(3) makes no provision for fines or sanctions in the form of nullity, although Member State could find a lump sum or penalty payment imposed on them under the procedure prescribed in Article 171(2) EC.

The parallel between Articles 85 and 86 EC on the one hand, and Article 90 EC on the other is, though, not complete. Unlike Article 85(3), Article 90(2) has full direct effect, so that the national courts may themselves determine whether the conditions for the application of Article 90(2) are satisfied.[945] They are, however, bound by decisions and directives adopted under Article 90(3) EC.

---

944. *E.g.* Reg. 80/723 (O.J. 1980) L 195/35). As to Reg. 17, see note 501, *supra*.
945. Case C-260/89 *ERT* [1991] ECR I-2925 at 2962.

CHAPTER IX

Economic, monetary and social policy*

1. INTRODUCTION

1.1 The link between negative and positive integration

As was seen in Chapter VIII, above, competition policy forms the transitional area between negative and positive integration.[1] On the one hand it is a necessary consequence of the liberalization of free movement of goods, persons, services and capital by the removal of internal frontiers resulting from differences in or systems of legislation and also by combating distortions of and interference with competition on the ever more liberalized market. On the other hand, competition policy, by combating disturbances and distortions of competition, seeks to guarantee the allocative operation of the liberalized market. All the aspects of competition policy involve policy choices at the Community level, which always inevitably implies *inter alia* policy integration.

Positive or policy integration is part of the task of the Community expressly mentioned in Article 2 EC and developed further in Articles 3 and 3a EC. The link between these provisions and the problems of interpretation which their present drafting causes have been discussed in Chapter III, above. The establishment of an Economic and Monetary Union is, moreover, in the long term inevitable (also from the national standpoint) because the effectiveness of purely national macro-economic and micro-economic steering measures – to the extent also that they are not incompatible with the EC Treaty – is in fact lessened as liberalization (or negative integration) progresses. This is clearly shown by the Zijlstra

---

* In the Dutch edition of this work, this Chapter was revised by L.A. Geelhoed. He produced a complete revision of that contribution for this edition in order to take account of important more recent developments since 1995. The editor has translated, edited and further revised that revision, taking additional account of literature, case-law and practice, including still more recent developments, particularly the decisions of May 1998 relating to the beginning of the third stage of Economic and Monetary Union on 1 January 1999.

1. These terms were defined in Chapter III, section 1.2.3, *ante*,

and WRR Reports[2] discussed in Chapter III, above. Since the last edition of this work in 1989 the completion of the internal market, including the liberalization of capital movements, has further accelerated the seepage of national ability to act in the monetary and socio-economic fields.[3] It is true that autonomously taking account of the policy of other Member States can contribute to national policy remaining effective, but the underlying tensions in the European Monetary System (EMS) in late 1992, the Summer of 1993 and early 1995 showed that such 'spontaneous policy imitation' has its limits.[4] A more or less far-reaching coordination of monetary and economic policies is not merely a legal obligation but an ever more pressing economic necessity.

In this Chapter the Economic and Monetary Union (EMU) set out in Title VI of Part Three of the EC Treaty occupies centre stage. The European Investment Bank is governed by Title IV of Part Ill of the Treaty but it is also discussed in this Chapter because of its increasing significance in the Community's economic policy. External economic policy is, however, discussed in Chapter XII below. The White Paper *Growth, Competitiveness and Employment*[5] adopted by the Commission in December 1993 confirmed again that a separation and even a sharp distinction between economic policy on the one hand and the social policy set out in Title VIII of Part Three of the EC Treaty on the other hand is as impossible at Community level as it is at national level. Economic growth and employment are the result of the general economic policy which is adopted: the functioning of the production, capital and primarily labour markets and the social security model. The disappointing development of employment in the European Union caused the European Council at Essen in December 1994 to establish what is known as the 'Essen procedure' which involves the Labour and Social Affairs and Ecofin Councils and the Commission keeping close track of employment trends, monitoring the relevant policies of the Member States, and presenting annually reports to the European Council on further progress on the employment market, starting in December 1995.[6] The first reports were used 'to examine on the one hand, the effects of tax and support systems on the readiness both to create and to take up jobs and, on the other, the inter-relationship between economic growth and the environment and the consequences this has for economic policy.'[7] The link between general economic policy, labour

2. Zijlstra, *Politique économique et problèmes de la concurrence dans la CEE et dans les pays membres de la CEE* (CEE études, série concurrence, no. 2. Brussels, 1966); WRR, *The Unfinished European Integration* (Report no. 28, The Hague, 1986).
3. Firstly through the adoption of Dir. 88/361 (O.J. 1998 L 178/5), now through the terms of Arts. 73a–73h EC.
4. See further, section 1.5, *post*.
5. COM (93) 700, Bull. EU Supp. 6/93.
6. Bull. EU 12–1994, point I.3.
7. *Ibid.*

market policy and social security policy has been at the forefront of these reports.[8] The new Title VIa which the Treaty of Amsterdam will, when it comes into force, insert into the EC Treaty, in fact codifies this Essen procedure.[9] These new provisions are discussed in section 4 of this Chapter, below.

Social policy and economic policy both influence the growth of employment, income generation and distribution, and developments on the labour market. Even if there are not often major tensions between both policy areas, separating them from each other is counterproductive. Thus social policy is also discussed in section 6 of this Chapter, below.

Economic and monetary policy integration implies at least centralization of monetary policy at Community level, as well as discipline in the financial-economic policy of the Member States. For the less prosperous Member States this means that they must renounce the 'easy' route to economic growth which lies in a combination of an expansive budgetary policy, an accommodating monetary policy, a relatively high level of inflation and a downward movement of exchange rates. A certain measure of financial equalization from the more prosperous Member States to the less prosperous Member States for the improvement of primarily the investment climate there is thus an almost unavoidable political condition which the formation of an EMU will have to satisfy.[10] Thus the discussion of economic and social cohesion, the subject of Title XIV of the EC Treaty, is also appropriate; as to this, see section 5 of this Chapter, below.

1.2 Market integration and monetary policy integration

With the achievement of the internal market and a common competition policy, the common market is not yet completed as a market having all the characteristics of a national market. Within a national market there are no internal monetary borders, unlike in the at present largely completed common market. The existence of diverse national currencies causes considerable transaction cost losses in intra-community traffic, which will only increase as such traffic intensifies. Moreover, the uncertainties connected to the existence of differences in parities within the common market form an important obstacle for taking investment decisions and entering into long-term contracts. Further, they may encourage speculative

---

8. See Bull. EU 12–1995, points I.50–I.54; Bull. EU 12–1996, points I.5, I.36 (The Jobs Challenge – The Dublin Declaration on Employment) and 1.3.210, and Bull. 11–1997, points I.2–I.10 (special European Council meeting at Luxembourg on employment).
9. See the new Arts. 109n–109s EC (and, as regards the reports, in particular Art. 109q).
10. Oort (1990) SEW 46 submits for good reasons that a horizontal equalization is strictly speaking not an economic condition for the formation of an EMU.

money and capital movements which have no 'real' economic rationale. In addition, the liberalization of money and capital movements in the internal market has made it more difficult to maintain the exchange rate arrangements of the EMS, as the national monetary authorities may no longer impose restriction on cross-border movements of money and capital.[11] Since the stabilizing power of the EMS had diminished, the allocative effect of the common market threatened to become intrinsically fragile. Exchange rate movements could thus seriously disturb competitive relationships within that market. There remained of course in such a situation the temptation for national authorities to have recourse to competitive realignment of exchange rates. The situation of monetary cooperation existing until recently within the Community may be sketched as a typical transitional phase, with its system of stable but adaptable exchange rates: a transitional period however, which, with the progress of market integration, became more fragile. Approached in this manner too, the step towards full monetary policy integration is the logical result of and the completion of market integration.

1.3 Market integration and economic policy integration[12]

For the economic policy of the Member States the establishment of a common market has far-reaching consequences. Various steering measures which act directly, such as national price-regulatory measures and other national intervention which affect or may affect inter-State movement of products and factors, have become unlawful, or to the extent to which they are still permitted they can be circumvented relatively easily within the common market. Within a liberalized capital market a relatively restrictive monetary policy may actually have an effect contrary to that intended, if an influx of capital is thereby stimulated.

Free movement of products and production factors also results in an increased national fragility in relation to external influences. In The Netherlands in 1990–1993 that was again evident with the sharp oscillation in the German economy after German unification. The major expenditure in the eastern part of Germany initially led to the economy in the western part of Germany overheating, which was followed by a sharp reaction in the Summer of 1992. Unilateral decisions by the larger Member States may thus occasion serious disturbances in the economic policy of smaller Member States. It was already clear that with the free movement of capital

11. See Hahn (1991) 28 CMLRev. 783 at 788; in the same sense, Gamble (1991) 28 CMLRev. 319.
12. See the WRR Report no. 28, *The Unfinished European Integration* (The Hague 1996); Geelhoed (1990) *International Spectator* 658, and De Grauwe *International Spectator* 665.

achieved, economic policy divergence between the Member States could be a major cause of disturbance in exchange rate parities.

The arguments in favour of economic policy integration so far summarized, mean that on the one hand the choice for such integration is more or less made by the integration of markets. On the other hand, it is becoming ever more evident that economic policy integration as a complement to the common market also has added value as such. Market integration leads the national economies associated therein to a certain regional specialization which is expressed in increased intra-Community trade. This economic interweaving is a positive development as long as the economic growth within the Community does not structurally lag behind that of the other major economic regions in the global economy. If the Community were to continue to have lower structural growth, this would form a handicap for the national economies which are strongly directed to the common market, the seriousness of which should not be underestimated.[13] If the German economy is unable to surmount its present, primarily structural, problems that would put a damper on the Dutch economy, which is so focused on the German market. From this perspective the Member States have a common interest in the economic performance of the Community remaining favourable measured by global standards.

General economic policy integration within the Community also has consequences for the Community policy in the sectors discussed in Chapter XI, below. This relationship became very evident for the Common Agricultural Policy in the problems concerning Monetary Compensatory Amounts (MCAs). When in the early Seventies the exchange rate parities within the Community fell apart, considerable consequences ensued for prices of agricultural produce expressed in national currencies. MCAs sought to compensate for such movements, although they were logically incompatible with the principle of the unity of the market.[14] More generally, the better in general economic policy the objectives of stability and growth are better united, the less the need to pursue sector-specific policies.

The relationship between economic policy integration and the external policy examined in Chapter XII is to a large extent determined by the principle of an open market economy mentioned in Article 3a EC. This principle, which is reaffirmed in Article 102a EC, implies that economic policy integration within the Community must respect the policy

13. See the White Paper (see note 5, *supra*), Chapter II.
14. But they were accepted by the Court as in effect being the lesser of two evils, see Case 5/73 *Balkan-Import–Export GmbH v. Hauptzollamt Berlin-Packhof* [1973] ECR 1091; Case 9/73 *Schlüter v. Hauptzollamt Lörrach* [1973] ECR 1135; Case 10/73 *Rewe-Zentral AG v. Hauptzollamt Kehl* [1973] ECR 1175, and Case 4/79 SC *'Providence Agricole de Champagne' v. Office National Interprofessionnel des Céréales (ONIC)* [1980] ECR 2823.

precondition of liberalized economic movement to be guaranteed in the context of the WTO. Of the matters discussed in Chapter X, below, as horizontal and flanking policies, it is primarily environment policy which is important for economic policy integration. That applies to the qualifying preconditions for economic growth which flow from environment policy, as well as to the shaping of the instruments of environment policy. Major disparities between the environment instruments of the Member States may lead to difficult problems in the coordination of economic policy, as is apparent from the discussions about the introduction of eco-taxes on energy use and on activities which are harmful to the environment, and at the same time reducing the burdens on the labour factor.

1.4 Market integration and social policy integration

Although the Member States' social policies are closely related to the manner in which the social constitution is developed both institutionally and substantively, social policy remains very closely related to general economic policy. There is a very sensitive interaction between the development of price levels in general and the development of labour costs: employment development is indeed determined in the short term by the course of economic growth, but in the longer term it is determined by the system of wage generation, the effect of the labour market, and the relationship between gross labour costs and labour productivity.

Because within a completed common market relative differences in prices and costs have a much quicker and deeper effect on the competitiveness of a national economy, market integration enforces a much more carefully guarded link to be maintained between general economic policy and social policy than hitherto. When monetary union is completed, the development of relative labour costs might well become the central variable for national economic policy.[15]

The relationship between economic growth, employment and price stability is also playing an increasingly important role at Community level. According to the analysis in the Commission's White Paper *Growth, Competitiveness and Employment* there are convincing causal links between the disappointing development in employment in the Community since the early Seventies and the manner in which the social constitution has been shaped at national level.[16] Because a high level of unemployment is reflected, through the need to finance it, in the level of labour costs of the still active professional population, the competitive position of the

---

15. Although the conclusions are diametrically opposed, this argument played a major part for Geelhoed in Amato *et al.*, *Is European Monetary Union Dead?* (Brussels, 1994) 40 and Hankel in *ibid.* 48.

16. See note 5, *supra*.

Community in the global context is placed under pressure.

If the maintenance and strengthening of the vitality of the West European economies is to be one of the central objectives of economic policy integration, also in terms of growth in employment, it is unimaginable not to involve social policy in such integration.

1.5 Forms of coordination in monetary, economic and social policy integration

Policy integration in the monetary, economic and social fields is considerably more difficult within the fairly light institutional construction of the Community than in more or less fully-grown federal state contexts.[17] First, because in classic federations such as the United States and Canada the federal authorities only started to play an active role in the social and economic spheres after the federal system had already established deep roots. As general economic policy is primarily aimed at influencing macro-variables in the national economy, it was also obvious that the pursuit of active general economic policy should primarily fall within the competence of the central, in these cases federal, authorities. As concerns social policy, which was strongly influenced by the principle of substantive equality, which laid a relatively large claim on collective expenditure, a dominant role for the federal authorities was also obvious. Thus in pretty well all federations the gradual establishment of a modern social constitution has resulted in a strengthening of the position of the federal authorities *vis-à-vis* the states.[18] This has not occurred without friction, and in some federations reactions are already visible against federal authorities which are perceived as being too dominant.

In the Community policy integration has to take place within a much lighter and significantly less well-rooted institutional order, which is not as such uncontroversial in some Member States. Moreover, this policy integration involves policy areas which are the subject of much constitutional discussion in all Member States. Finally, the Community has no powers of its own to raise taxes, and the relative weight of its budget is many times less than that of the Member States. Unlike in federal state contexts, policy integration in the economic and employment fields within

17. See the WRR Report (see note 12, *supra*) Chapter 3.
18. See Conlon, *New Federalism: Intergovernmental Reform from Nixon to Reagan* (Washington DC, 1988) 31–91 and Bullinger (1970) *Die Öffentliche Verwaltung* 761 and 785. This shift in the sphere of competence from state to federal level was the result of the *political* choice at federal level as to the content of the socio-economic policy pursued. No views about the desired allocation of competence between federal and state authorities lay behind this: thus the principle of subsidiarity played no role in this evolution, whether as a principle of policy or as a legal principle. See Geelhoed (1991) SEW 431.

the Community will remain primarily a question of *coordination* of the Member States' policies even in a complete EMU. This is confirmed in so many words in what will be the new Articles 3(1)(i) and 109o EC[19] as well as in the unchanged Article 103 EC. Although Articles 2 and 3 EC are silent as to this matter, social policy also involves only coordination or harmonization of the Member States' policies, as appears from the new Articles 118 and 118 EC.[20] This is understandable, as the most important instruments in this field, as in the field of economic policy, are in national hands and for the moment will remain there. For monetary policy in an EMU coordination of national powers is insufficient. In a completed monetary union complete unity of monetary policy will be necessary. Thus it cannot be determined elsewhere than at Community level.[21] Simply ascertaining that policy integration primarily implies coordination of the policy areas discussed here says nothing as to the nature and intensity of such coordination. Thus it is useful to develop the concept of coordination *in abstracto* somewhat further.[22] This enables the various coordination procedures which are dealt with later in this Chapter to be more closely characterized.

The concept of coordination set out in the new Article 3(1)(i) EC and in the present Article 3a(1) EC means that primary public competence to influence the economic development and the development of employment remains with the Member States. Conferring coordinating competence on the Community means that the Member States will or must take account of coordinating intervention by the central level concerned when they exercise their primary competences. The words 'will or must take account of' hide the fact that the degree of compulsion of Community intervention may vary enormously, from pure prognoses to obliging the Member States to comply with the policy prescribed. The concept of *intervention* embraces measures which are short-term as well as those which are medium or long-term or even those which are in principle permanent in nature. The *central level concerned* qualifies the substantive scope of the relevant Community competence, which may vary from the whole field affected by general economic policy to specific functionally or sectorally defined parts of that policy.

Thus the degree of compulsion of the broad economic policy guidelines mentioned in Article 103(2) EC is considerably lighter than the criteria for budgetary discipline set out in Article 104c(2) EC. The broad guidelines are determined annually, whereas the criteria for budgetary discipline are

19. When the Treaty of Amsterdam enters into force.
20. *Ibid.*
21. See Arts. 3a(2) with 105(2) EC. The Werner Committee Report (Bull. EC Supp. 11/70) already came to this conclusion, which was moreover confirmed by the conclusions of the Delors Report (*Report on Economic and Monetary Union in the European Community* (Brussels, Luxembourg, 1989)).
22. See the 2nd edition of this work (ed. Gormley, London, 1989) 588–600.

more or less permanent. On the other hand, the broad guidelines may encompass the entire socio-economic policy of the Member States, whereas the budgetary discipline criteria only relate to two aspects of national budgetary policy: the ratio of the planned or actual government deficit to GDP and the ratio of government debt to GDP.

In the last edition of this work the coordination procedures were characterized on the basis of Zijlstra's planning typology, to which reference has been made in particular in section 3.5.2 of Chapter III of this edition, above. Indeed, there is an unmistakable analogy between influence by the public authorities ('planning') of the conduct of market participants, and the influence which a public authority which is superior in the public law hierarchy has over decision-making by lower-level authorities. Forms of such a vertical coordinating influence are to be found in all individual constitutional structures. They always presuppose that the coordinating authority, in this case the Community, has the competence to coordinate, and that the primary competence lies with the units, in this case the Member States, whose exercise of competence is to be coordinated. As in the case of 'planning,' coordinating intervention may be classified according to the degree to which it has binding force, or according to its intensity, so that the lightest form is making prognoses available, and the heaviest form the imposition of precisely quantified obligatory tasks, compliance with which the coordinating authority may compel.[23]

Between the lightest form of prognoses and the heaviest form of precisely defined binding tasks there are various other forms which should be classified. In ascending order (of binding force or intensity) these are: information and compulsory consultation procedures; recommendations; indicative tasks; conditional loans and subsidies, and binding provisions. Unlike in previous editions, it is no longer considered appropriate to draw the analogy with Zijlstra's planning typology so far that the Community's coordinating intervention is fitted into his planning types, as the differences in principle between influencing conduct internally between authorities (coordination) and influencing conduct externally outside the sphere of authorities (planning) are too great. Thus the completed form of the heaviest *type of planning*, applied over the whole breadth of the economic order, is a centrally led economy. The completed form of the heaviest type of coordination, applied over the whole breadth of the public sector, establishes an extremely centralized unit state, the component parts of which are no more than deconcentrated parts of the central authority. The United Kingdom, which combines a strongly centralized administration with, by continental standards, an extensive and strongly liberalized market sector, demonstrates that a unit state in the constitutional sense does not have to lead to a centrally led economy in the economic-law

23. See further, VerLoren van Themaat, *The changing structure of International Economic Law* (The Hague, 1981) 157–184.

sense. The reverse is not the case. A centrally led economy will also in the constitutional aspect *de facto* lead to the centralization of public powers. The more an economic order leads to internal policy coordination, the more it will require centralization in the constitutional aspect. This is why at Community level there is a connection between the fairly restricted and light coordinating competence of the Community and the choice in Article 3a EC for an economic order 'conducted in accordance with the principle of an open market economy with free competition.'

For an analysis of the coordination problems in the Community, it is sensible also to draw a distinction according to the degree to which the constitutional units, whose policy is to be coordinated, are involved in the decision-making concerned. The coordinating decision-making may be the result of autonomous evaluation by the superior authority, producing a specification to which the inferior authority must conform (vertical subordinating coordination). Coordinating decision-making may also be the result of an evaluation involving consultation between the coordinating authority and the coordinee. The inferior authorities then comply with coordinating decisions in which they themselves are involved (vertical cooperative coordination). Finally, coordinating decision-making may be the result of – voluntary – consultation between authorities at the same level. This form of coordination often displays (quasi-)contractual traits, and sometimes it results from what has been described above as spontaneous policy imitation.[24]

The first form of coordination – vertical subordinating – primarily occurs in fully-grown federal systems, in which the exercise of competence at federal level and at state level is clearly delimited. It makes high demands of the democratic legitimacy of decision-making at federal level, as coordinating intervention from on high will not infrequently clash with the policy priorities chosen at state level. In the Community this form of coordination is rare. An example of such a form is to be found in Article 104c(13) EC in respect of measures or sanctions relating to deficit reduction; in such cases the Member State concerned has no vote.[25]

The second form of coordination – vertical cooperative – is the most frequently encountered in the Community structure. This is already contained in the institutional shape of decision-making, which generally guarantees an intensive involvement of (representatives of) the Member States, both in the preparatory phase and in the decision phase. Examples of this can be seen in the procedure for the establishment of the broad guidelines of economic policies of the Member States and of the

24. See section 1.1, *ante*, and Scharf (1988) Pub. Admin. 239.
25. At an earlier stage the Council will have made recommendations under Art. 104c(7) EC; they are adopted by qualified majority. The majority required for decisions under Art. 104c(13) is two-thirds of the votes weighted in accordance with Art. 148(2) EC, excluding the votes of the representative of the Member State concerned.

Community provided for in Article 103(2) EC, and for the annual guidelines which the Member States are to take into account in their employment policies in accordance with the new Article 109q(2) EC.[26]

The third form of coordination – spontaneous and (quasi-) contractual between the Member States – is not to be found in the EC Treaty in so many words. Nevertheless, it does occur on a large scale in policy practice. An example was the Dutch decision to maintain the Guilder's margin of fluctuation against the Deutschmark at 2.25% when the margins against other currencies were set at 15% in the Summer of 1993. For this 'spontaneous' horizontal coordination, arrangements were made between the German and the Dutch monetary authorities themselves. When the Treaty of Amsterdam enters into force the new Article 109o(2) EC will introduce into the EC Treaty itself a form of horizontal policy coordination, requiring Member States, having regard to national practices related to the responsibilities of management and labour, to regard promoting employment as a matter of common concern and to coordinate their action in that respect within the Council, in accordance with the provisions of the new Article 109q EC.

In the description in sections 3, 4, 5 and 6, below, of economic, monetary and social policy integration in the Community, particular attention will be paid to the characterization of the forms of cooperation, according to intensity, scope, permanence and type of decision-making. This enables the legal aspects and problems of the policy integration concerned to be analyzed more easily.

2. THE HISTORY OF ECONOMIC AND MONETARY UNION[27]

The coordination of economic and monetary policy was only summarily treated in the original EEC Treaty.[28] Among the policy provisions was the now repealed Article 6 EEC, which provided in general terms an obligation on the Member States to 'coordinate their respective economic policies to the extent necessary to attain the objectives of the Treaty.[29] This declaration of principle was developed further in Articles 103–105 and

---

26. The employment guidelines must be consistent with the broad guidelines adopted pursuant to Art. 103(2) EC, see the new Art. 109q(2) EC.
27. See, generally, Gros and Thygesen, *European Monetary Integration* (London, 1992) 3–56.
28. See the 2nd edition of this work, 598–600, 603–608 and 616–625, and literature cited there. It is remarkable that such a meagre and incomplete legal basis for economic and monetary policy integration should have led to so many thorough legal analyses. The incompleteness of the European integration process in the economic policy sense, which resulted from the fact that the rules in the then EEC Treaty demonstrated *lacunae* clearly formed a challenge in this respect.
29. Art. 6(1) EEC.

107–109 EEC. The first indent of Article 145 EEC (and still of Article 145 EC) endows the Council with responsibility to 'ensure coordination of the general economic policies of the Member States'. As far as policy practice is concerned, Article 103 EEC appeared to have the most importance. Although it was primarily meant for the coordination of short-term economic policy (conjunctural policy), it was used as the most important legal basis for the secondary legislation which in the Seventies was meant to lay the basis for the first moves towards an economic and monetary union. Article 103(4) indeed acquired a separate legal significance as the legal basis for Community action in case of problems in the supply of certain products, particularly during the first oil crisis in 1973. Article 104 EEC was primarily declaratory in nature: it set out the general objectives of economic policy which the Member States had to follow as members of the EEC. Article 105 EEC primarily dealt with the procedural aspects of the coordination of economic and monetary policy.

Article 107 EEC dealt with exchange rate policy of the Member States, which was a matter of common concern. It implied that exchange rate policy was not to be used in order to create artificial competitive advantages in the common market. The importance of this provision became steadily less after the final implosion in 1973 of the Bretton Woods system of fixed exchange rates. Articles 108 and 109 EEC provided for assistance and safeguard procedures respectively, for Member States faced with serious balance of payments difficulties from which – possibly – adaptation of their exchange rates could result. Since the end of the Sixties the practical importance of this provision too gradually diminished.[30]

The Single European Act inserted Article 102a EEC into the Treaty. The most important legal significance of that provision was that Article 102a(2) EEC expressly stated that insofar as further development in the field of economic and monetary policy (such as from monetary cooperation between the Member States towards a monetary union) necessitated institutional changes, amendment of the Treaty would be required.[31]

As early as 1962, in its memorandum on the working programme of the Community during the second stage of the transitional period, the Commission had argued that the customs union was bound to lead to an EMU if achievements so far attained were not to be jeopardized. In 1968 the Commission frankly propagated monetary unification, and this resulted in 1969 in the so-called Barre Memorandum. After the Summit in December 1969 at The Hague had given the first impulse for this, the

---

30. This does not diminish the great legal interest of these provisions, as they implied a considerably far-reaching limitation of national powers concerning exchange rate policy and related policies. See in this connection Cases 6 and 11/69 *Commission v. France* [1969] ECR 523 at 541–542.
31. There was a difference in views on this point prior to the adoption of the SEA, see the 2nd edition of this work 609.

Council on 6 March 1970 at last resolved to set up a special working group, which was to draw up a report. In this report, by reference to the various proposals, the fundamental options for a realization in stages of the economic and monetary union were to be laid down. This was the work of the so-called Werner Committee, whose members included, besides its President, Werner (the Prime Minister and Finance Minister of Luxembourg) the presidents of the Monetary Committee, the Committee of Governors of the Central Banks, the Committee for Medium-Term Economic Policy, the Committee on Short-Term Economic Policy, and the Budgetary Policy Committee, as well as a representative of the Commission. As early as May 1970 the Werner Committee presented an interim report, and on October 8, 1970 its final report.[32] Consultation of the Werner Committee Report shows that the arguments for economic, monetary and social policy integration leading to an economic and monetary union, summarized in sections 1.2 to 1.4, above, have essentially remained the same since the early Seventies: market integration presupposes a necessary complement to policy integration.

After the Commission had submitted the appropriate proposals towards the end of 1970, in February and March 1971 the time had grown ripe for a decision. On 22 March 1971 the relevant resolution of the Council and of the representatives of the Governments of Member States was finally adopted.[33] In this resolution the economic and monetary union, to be realized in the seventies, was defined in the sense '*that the principal decisions concerning economic policy will be taken at Community level, and that the powers required for this are therefore transferred from the national to the Community level. This process may result in the adoption of a single monetary unit, thus ensuring its irrevocability.*' According to the resolution these principles are to be applied in the following fields: internal monetary and credit policy; monetary policy with regard to the rest of the world; policy with respect to the unified capital market and the movement of capital with third countries; budgetary and taxation policy in the context of policy directed at stability and growth and, finally, structural and regional policy. It was expressly recognized that some of the necessary measures imply an amendment of the EEC Treaty. For the first three-year stage the resolution itself provided for a number of measures. Moreover the Council and, where necessary, the representatives of the Member States at the end of the resolution undertook to lay down before the end of the first stage on a proposal from the Commission, the measures which after the transition to the second stage were to lead to the full realization of an economic and monetary union, even as far as this required amendments of the Treaty.

The measures for the first stage included:

32. See note 21, *supra*.
33. O.J. English Special Edition (2nd Series) IX, p. 40.

(1) a strengthening of the co-ordination of short-term economic policies, taking into account the guiding principles for medium-term economic policy; measures for gradually harmonizing the instruments of economic policy and in particular for approximating the time-tables of the national budgetary procedures to each other;
(2) new harmonization measures in the field of turnover tax, excise duties, taxes on debenture interests and dividends, the structure of corporation taxes and the exemptions from taxes for private persons crossing frontiers;
(3) the promotion of free movement of capital;
(4) a regional and structural policy;
(5) co-ordination of the monetary and credit policies of Member States;
(6) monetary policy vis-à-vis third countries;
(7) a narrowing of the reciprocal fluctuation margins of exchange rates;
(8) the preparation of a European Monetary Co-operation Fund, destined in the future to form part of the Community system of central banks provided for in the resolution.

The period of euphoria about the importance of the steps that had been taken was unfortunately only short-lived. In May 1971 the Government of the German Federal Republic was compelled by the growing flow of dollars to allow the exchange rate of the German mark to fluctuate freely instead of narrowing the reciprocal fluctuation margins, as had been agreed upon in March of that year. This was the forerunner of further unrest in the international monetary system which in 1973 led to the final implosion of the Bretton Woods exchange rate system.

The first oil crisis at the end of 1973 introduced the end of the almost uninterrupted period of growth which the Community had enjoyed since 1958. Each national government attempted itself to limit as much as possible the damage caused by the threatening combination of inflation, stagnating economic growth and unemployment. In these efforts the absence of the exchange rate discipline was certainly not found to be a problem, as a lack of internal economic and monetary discipline could be as it were automatically corrected by a change in the now floating exchange rate parities. These global level disturbances form an important explanation for the fact that by three years into the first stage the Council had made only minimal progress towards meeting the obligations which it had undertaken in its resolution of 22 March 1971. External disturbances were an important factor, but not the only one.

Three elements are clear in the first stage of moves towards an economic and monetary union based on the Werner Committee Report:

– first, a sufficient degree of convergence of national economic and monetary policy and of national policy instruments would have to be

achieved before the process could result in a monetary union through the 'adoption of a single monetary unit';
- the catalogue of measures envisaged still embraced a number of actions which strictly speaking related to the further completion of the common market, such as the promotion of free movement of capital and far-reaching harmonization of turnover taxes;
- regional and structural policies were, as Community policies, not perceived as necessary elements of an economic and monetary union; they were at least as well founded in terms of flanking policies to market integration.[34]

Above all the priority in time given to convergence of national economic and monetary policy in general prior to the step towards a monetary union, must virtually inevitably lead to an unlimited postponement of the moment at which monetary union can become a reality. That is principally on account of the intrinsic restrictions of general economic policy coordination in the Community context. The strongly cooperative decision-making leads to coordinating intervention strongly characterized by compromise, and compliance at national level is very difficult for the Community to control, yet alone compel. That applies *a fortiori* as the context in which national economic policy has to be formulated and implemented is only partially susceptible to the influence of the national authorities: a higher exchange rate against the dollar or oil price can simply negate national action directed at price stability based on a Community recommendation. The same applies for wage rounds which well exceed the increase in productivity. In Member States in which the negotiating freedom of the social partners is constitutionally guaranteed, the authorities will look on powerlessly. If a monetary union is the final goal, it is recommended to direct policy convergence primarily towards those parts of national policy where their attuning is a necessary condition for such a union to function. The combination of free movement of products and factors of production (the internal market) and a centralized monetary policy aimed at price stability already has a disciplining effect and makes the necessary coordination of economic policy easier.[35] A clear parallel with market integration is evident: if this is made independent of prior harmonization of national legislation which is relevant to competitive relationships, the horizon for the necessary liberalization measures will immediately change.

34. See the WRR Report *De financiering van de Europese Gemeenschap* (The Hague, 1987) 44–47 and 60–62.
35. This assumes that the responsible authorities of the Member States are prepared to accept the restrictions for their social and economic policies which result from the combination of a completed internal market and a monetary union. See Wils (1992) SEW 475.

From the above it may be deduced that free movement of capital should preferably be achieved not as a measure forming part of the achievement of an economic and monetary union, but as an intervention prior to that step which strengthens the necessity for the national authorities to converge their policies and thus the formation of an economic and monetary union.

Market integration will always lead to reallocation of economic activities both geographically as well as sectorally. Regional and sectoral problems not infrequently coincide, as in the marginal Mediterranean agricultural areas and in Northern Ireland. Where such problems occur in the relatively economically weaker Member States there is reason *par excellence* for a certain financial reallocation between the more prosperous and the less prosperous parts of the Community. The relationship between market integration and geographical imbalances in levels of prosperity and development explains why, when in the second half of the Seventies and in the Eighties economic and monetary policy integration stalled, the Community's administration of funds still became important.[36]

Through the combination of a turbulent economic and political climate at global level and a not well-considered approach to deepening economic and monetary integration, the next step by the Council in February and March 1974 was decidedly small. The most important measures were Decision 74/120[37] on the attainment of a high degree of convergence of economic policies and Directive 74/121[38] on stability, full growth and employment in the Community. The practical significance of these instruments for the policy practice of the Member States always remained fairly limited. The convergence decisions based on the Decision 74/120, at least in The Netherlands, were never factors of any significance in macro-economic decision-making. In the monetary field the Council adopted two decisions on 22 March 1971, one concerning strengthening cooperation between central banks,[39] and the other creating a machinery for the grant of medium-term financial assistance.[40]

After the monetary unrest in the second half of 1971, agreement was reached on 18 December 1971 by the Ministers of the 'Group of Ten' on

---

36. See Padoa-Schioppa *et al. Efficiency, Stability and Equity, a strategy for the evolution of the Economic System of the European Community* (Oxford, 1987); Mortelmans (1989) SEW 766, and Scott and Mansell (1993) 18 ELRev. 87.
37. O.J. 1974 L 63/16, amended by Dec. 75/787 (O.J. 1987 L 330/52), supplemented by Dec. 79/136 (O.J. 1979 L 305/8) and repealed by Dec. 90/141 (O.J. 1990 L 78/23) on the attainment of progressive convergence of economic policies and performance in stage one of EMU.
38. O.J. 1974 L 63/19 (also repealed by Dec. 90/141, *ibid.*).
39. Dec. 71/142 (O.J. English Special Edition 1971 (I), p. 176).
40. Dec. 71/143 (O.J. English Special Edition 1971 (I), p. 177) which was revised on myriad occasions and finally replaced by Reg. 1969/88 (O.J. 1988 L 178/1) establishing a single medium-term facility for financial assistance.

new exchange rates with a simultaneous widening of the fluctuation margins to 2.25% in both directions. It then became possible again to make progress towards monetary union. On 21 March 1972, acting on proposals from the Commission, the Council adopted a new resolution on economic and monetary union.[41] This resolution strengthened the one of 22 March 1971 on the point of the coordination of the economic policies of Member States by providing for a coordination group at top level, in which the Commission was also represented.[42] This group existed somewhat vaguely for a number of years, being quickly eclipsed by the Economic Policy Committee established by Decision 74/122,[43] which is still in existence. Furthermore, the Commission was invited to propose at the earliest possible date a binding directive for promoting stability, growth, and full employment in the Community.[44] With regard to exchange rates, agreement was again reached on a gradual reduction of the currency fluctuations between Member States, the final object being the abolition of any fluctuation margin, although fluctuations *vis-à-vis* the external world only had to respect the wider fluctuation margins permitted by the International Monetary Fund. The Committee of Governors of the Central Banks[45] had to submit before 1 July 1972 a proposal on the organization, functions and statute of a European Monetary Cooperation Fund which was to form the prelude to a European central banking system; although the Council was due to decide on this proposal by the end of 1972, the relevant measure, Regulation 907/73 was in fact adopted only on 3 April 1973.[46] As far as the mutual parity maintenance was concerned the resolution of March 1972 did not weather subsequent monetary storms. Very quickly only the Benelux countries, Denmark and Germany adhered to the 'snake system' which was thus reduced to a mini-snake.

The European Monetary System (EMS) was finally introduced on 13 March 1979.[47] All the then Member States, save the United Kingdom, participated in a differently run, partially more flexible and partially more far-reaching exchange rate and intervention system set up under the EMS

41. O.J. English Special Edition 1972, 2nd Series IX, p. 65.
42. This coordination group was maintained in addition to the Economic Policy Committee set up by Dec. 74/122 (O.J. 1974 L 63/21).
43. O.J. 1974 L 63/21 (replacing earlier committees). This Committee now works closely with the new Employment and Labour Market Committee established by Dec. 97/16 (O.J. 1997 L 6/32).
44. This led to Dir. 74/121 (see note 38, *supra*).
45. Established by Dec. 64/300 (O.J. English Special Edition 1963–1964, p. 141, later amended by Dec. 90/300 (O.J. 1990 L 78/25)). This Committee ceased to exist at the start of the second stage of EMU on 1 January 1994 (Art. 109f(1) EC in conjunction with Art. 109e(1) EC).
46. O.J. 1973 L 89/2. See Louis (1973) CDE 277.
47. The intention had been to introduce it on 1 January 1979 but its introduction was delayed largely due to French attempts to reform the system of monetary compensatory amounts.

Resolution.[48] Despite the legal and substantive weaknesses already referred to, the system has worked not unsatisfactorily. With its grid of bilateral central rates and intervention obligations for the Central Banks whenever the actual exchange rates diverge more than 2.25% (for some participants 6%) from the central rate, the system has clearly contributed to a relatively large degree of stability of exchange rates within the Community, certainly when compared to the fluctuating exchange rates of the IMF system. Intervention credits in the form of very short-term facilities, short-term monetary support and the medium-term financial assistance mentioned above certainly played a part. However, more important than this mechanism is the real willingness of the monetary authorities of the Member States actively to use the interest rate mechanism at the right moment whenever a particular currency is placed under pressure. By this means possible speculative capital movements may be held at bay early enough.

In the meantime a system of stable but variable exchange rates like the EMS cannot avoid internal realignments of the central rates as long as inflation movements in the participating Member States diverge. That was the most important reason for the realignments in 1982, 1983, 1986 and 1992. The unmistakable convergence in real economic policy which has occurred in the Community since 1982 has undoubtedly contributed to the rather positive results of the EMS.[49]

Nevertheless, in the second edition of this work it was observed that the objective of complete economic and monetary union seemed to have slipped below the horizon.[50] It was, however, expressly maintained in the preamble to the SEA, although there was no attempt to set a deadline for its achievement and, in relation to the monetary aspects, Article 102a EEC made it clear that a real monetary union could only be completely achieved by amendment of the Treaty.

Looking back on the history of economic and monetary policy integration prior to the signature of the TEU, it must be stated that, apart from the political will for such a move, efforts to achieve an economic and monetary union in the legal and substantive sense foundered on the absence of a sufficiently well-anchored basis in the EEC Treaty for monetary union which would go further than the level of cooperation between the Member States. Thus Regulation 907/73 establishing the European Monetary Cooperation Fund[51] could not be much more than a framework for cooperation between the monetary authorities of the

---

48. As to the EMS Resolution, see Bull. EC 12–1978, point 1.1.11. See further, Reg. 3181/78 (O.J. 1978 L 379/2, amended by Reg. 3066/85 (O.J. 1985 L 290/95)). See also Louis (1979) SEW 441 and De Grauwe, *The EMS during 1979–1984* (Leuven, 1985).
49. In the same sense, Hahn (1991) 28 CMLRev. 783 at 786.
50. See p. 613.
51. See note 46, *supra.*

Member States, and the Fund as such largely remained a paper construction.[52] The same is true of EMS itself. Because neither Article 103 EEC nor Article 107 EEC provided powers for the Community to adopt binding measures concerning exchange rates and exchange rate stability, the EMS Resolution of December 1978, which required not merely consultation but also mutual agreement about the adjustment of central rates, could not be reflected in a legally binding instrument.

It has been submitted above that the instruments for the coordination of general economic policy in theory afforded sufficient possibilities for the achievement of the necessary policy integration. Instrumentally of particular importance appeared to be the power of the Council, set out in Article 103(2) and (3) EEC, to adopt by qualified majority directives needed to give effect to appropriate measures agreed upon unanimously, in order to oblige Member States to comply with those measures. It has already been noted, though, that the significance in reality of short-term economic policy or macro-economic steering measures lagged far behind the legal possibilities. Policy practice in the Seventies and Eighties confirmed this.

Since the beginning of the Seventies the arsenal of financial instruments at the Community's disposal has been considerably enlarged, both as regards scope and as regards means. The most important instruments for the coordination of *general* economic policy have been the machinery for medium-term financial assistance[53] and a system of loans for assistance in the event of balance of payments difficulties.[54] It is true that policy coordination conditions may be attached to the use of such instruments (now such a single facility with various possibilities), and that in practice they have indeed been used to a certain extent, but the importance of this instrument must not be overestimated. First, it can only be used selectively, *i.e.* primarily for the economically weaker Member States. As the economic policy of the stronger Member States is at the end of the day decisive for the economic development of the Community as a whole, this instrument does not appear so important seen from the Community level. Secondly, the scale of the single facility in the light of the relevant macro-variables which have to be influenced is scarcely imposing. Thirdly, it appears politically not to be a simple matter to compel compliance with the conditions attached to a loan if the Member State concerned fails to

---

52. See Gros and Thygesen, *op. cit.* (see note 27, *supra*) 21–22.
53. Originally set up by Dec. 71/143 (see note 40, *supra*). The available funds were increased to 11,000 million ECU by Dec. 78/1041 (O.J. 1978 L 379/3) and, with the adoption of Reg. 1969/88 (O.J. 1988 L 178/1) establishing a single facility, to 16,000 million ECU. See, further, *General Report 1995* (Brussels, Luxembourg, 1996) point 1015 and *General Report 1996* (Brussels, Luxembourg, 1997) point 1019.
54. Established by Dec. 397/75 (O.J. 1975 L 46/1, subsequently replaced by Reg. 626/81 (O.J. 1981 L 73/1, amended by Reg. 1131/85 (O.J. 1985 L 118/59), and replaced now by Reg. 1969/88 (O.J. 1988 L 178/1), see note 53, *supra*.

comply. Here too the practicalities of results of influence lag behind the theoretical legal possibilities. The cooperative slant of the decision-making about the use of the single facility and the obstacles in reality within the Community's political and institutional context facing compulsion, where necessary, of compliance with the conditions attached to loans, lead to particular caution in linking policy instrumental conclusions to legal powers of action. In this regard the history so far of economic and monetary policy integration presents a cautionary example. The provisions on EMU introduced into the EC Treaty by the TEU must thus also be interpreted in the light of the disappointing experiences so far.

3.   ECONOMIC AND MONETARY UNION (EMU)[55]

3.1   EMU as structured after the TEU

After the SEA entered into force, after a long period of little progress the liberalization of capital movements within the Community was finally readdressed. Liberalization of capital movements has major consequences for national policy options in the monetary field, and thus potentially also for the working of the EMS. It was thus no coincidence that during the decision-making on liberalization of capital movements the desirability of a fully-fledged EMU again became a live issue.[56] The basis of the negotiations about the EMU part of the contents of the TEU was the report on Economic and Monetary Union in the Community by the

---

55. See Alders *et al.* (eds.), *Begrotingsbeleid en financiering Nederlandse staatsschuld* (Amsterdam, 1992); Andenas *et al.* (eds.) *European Economic and Monetary Union: The Institutional Framework* (London, 1997); Cloos *et al. Le Traité de Maastricht, Genèse, Analyse, Commentaires* (Brussels, 1994) 31–36, 47–58, 94–101, and 176–286; De Grauwe, *The Economics of Monetary Integration* (2nd ed., Oxford, 1994); Gretschmann (ed.), *Economic and Monetary Union, Implications for National Policy Makers* (Dordrecht, 1993); Stuyck (ed.), *Financial and Monetary Integration in the European Economic Community: Legal, Institutional and Economic Aspects* (Deventer, 1993); Von der Groeben *et al.* (eds.), *Kommentar zum EU-/EG-Vertrag* (5th ed., Baden-Baden, 1997) Vol. 3 (not yet published, commentaries by various authors to Arts. 102a–109m EC); Gros and Thygesen, *op. cit.* (see note 27, *supra*) 229–480; Dunnett in O'Keeffe and Twomey (eds.), *Legal Issues of the Maastricht Treaty* (Chichester, 1994) 135; Gamble (1991) 28 CMLRev. 319; Hahn (1991) 28 CMLRev. 783 and (1998) 35 CMLRev. 77; Herdegen (1998) 35 CMLRev. 9; Louis (1989) 26 CMLRev. 301, (1992) CDE 251, (1998) 35 CMLRev. 33, and in Mégret *et al.* (eds.), *Commentaire Mégret Le Droit de la CEE* Vol. 6 (2nd ed., Brussels, 1995) 17–166; Oort (1990) SEW 46; Pipkorn (1994) 31 CMLRev. 263; Slot in Curtin and Heukels (eds.), *Institutional Dynamics of European Integration* (Essays in honour of Schermers, Vol. II, Dordrecht 1994) 229; Smits (1992) SEW 702, and VerLoren van Themaat (1991) 28 CMLRev. 291. The range of both legal and economic literature is now vast, but the above will give good indications for further reading.

56. See Cloos *et al., op. cit.* (see note 55, *supra*) 39–41.

Delors Committee.[57] This Committee, which had been set up in June 1988 by the European Council meeting at Hannover,[58] presented its report on 17 April 1989. This Report sketched out the main aspects of EMU, which are reflected in Title VI of Part Three of the EC Treaty.

In the negotiations leading to the present regime, four aspects played an important part:

(1) the German desire that at Community level the form, autonomy and mission of the central monetary authority should as far as possible mirror that of the Bundesbank in the German economic legal order;
(2) the fact that in view of the geographical inequalities in economic development the fairly ambitious timetable for full monetary union might prove too short for a number of Member States;
(3) the desire to express the practical connection between the budgetary policy of the Member States and the objective of monetary policy stability at Community level in binding obligations for the national budgetary authorities; and
(4) the British and later the Danish reticence about the formation of a monetary union as such, which found expression in separate national derogations for both countries in the transition to the final stage of EMU.[59]

The EMU as established by the amendments to the EC Treaty made by the TEU may be characterized as follows. The *economic union* embraces a fully achieved common market with free movement of products (goods and services) and factors of production (persons and capital) and free and undistorted competition. Within that framework the main features of economic policies are coordinated and stringent rules apply in respect of the budgetary policies of the Member States. Within the economic union as so described, Community and national policies may be implemented, for example for the strengthening of the Community's economic structure and competitive position, and to promote a balanced regional development. Only the global economic policy coordination and the binding rules concerning the budgetary policy of the Member States are included in the EMU provisions of the EC Treaty.[60] But that certainly does not mean that the other objectives mentioned in Article 2 EC could not play a role.[61] On

57. See note 21, *supra*.
58. Bull. EC 6–1988, point 3.4.1 (point 5 of the Presidency's Conclusions).
59. See Cloos *et al.*, *op. cit.* (see note 55, *supra*) 96–101.
60. Arts. 102a–104c EC.
61. See VerLoren van Themaat (1991) 28 CMLRev. 302. He rightly observes that given that an economic and monetary union also encompasses the common market the substantive scope of the union is much wider than the coordination of general or macro-economic policy alone. The concept of 'economic policies' in Art. 103(1) EC must not be interpreted restrictively as meaning only macro-economic policy. In the economic

the contrary, Articles 3a and 102a EC expressly refer to Article 2 EC, but the Treaty provides for the achievement of those other objectives by other means than those specified in the Economic Policy Chapter.

The *monetary union* can be described as a currency zone within which monetary policy is centrally determined with the objective of the maintenance of price stability, in order to contribute to the achievement of the objectives set out in Article 2 EC. Monetary union must satisfy three conditions:

(1) complete irreversible convertibility of currencies;
(2) complete liberalization of capital market transactions and complete integration of banking and other money and capital markets; and
(3) abolition of fluctuation margins and irrevocable coupling of exchange rate parities.

In its final stage monetary union is governed by Articles 105–109 EC as far as substantive provisions are concerned; the institutional provisions are contained in Articles 109a–109d EC. Liberalization of capital markets and of movement of payments is provided for in Chapter 4 of Title Three of part Three of the Treaty.[62] Although the description given here of a monetary union does not require the introduction of a single currency, practical arguments certainly militate in favour of such a move, which is accordingly provided for in Article 109l(4) EC.

EMU, as worked out in the amendments to the EC Treaty contained in the TEU and in the relevant Protocols, can be sketched as a system which combines a central monetary policy of an autonomous monetary authority at Community level with a vertical *cooperative* coordination of the economic policies of the Member States, a coordination which however has the traits for certain aspects of budgetary policy of a vertical *subordinating* coordination.[63] In this latter case coordination is compulsory depending on the degree of binding force involved for the Member States concerned, while the coordinating norms with which the Member States *must* comply are prescribed in the EC Treaty itself. If the old rules in Articles 102a–109 EEC were typical examples of a *traité-cadre* approach, which could be further filled-in and worked out by the Community Institutions and the Member States, the present Treaty rules for EMU, in combination with the relevant Protocols, display all the facets of a *traité-loi* which is in places worked out in considerable detail.

practice of the Member States economic policy is increasingly understood as embracing both macro-economic and micro-economic policy in general. This policy practice is reflected in the vocabulary in the policy documents such as the broad guidelines of economic policies discussed *post*.
62. Arts. 73a–73h EC. See Chapter VII, section 8, *ante*.
63. See Art. 104c EC.

3.2 Economic union: Articles 102a–104c EC

The Chapter dealing with the coordination of economic policy logically falls into five main segments:

(1) the objectives and principles of economic policy coordination within the Community, which are summed up in Article 102a EC, which refers back to Articles 2 and 3a EC;

(2) the actual coordination of the economic policies of the Member States and of the Community, which is regulated as a form of more or less permanent vertical cooperative coordination with multilateral surveillance in Article 103 EC;

(3) prohibitions of monetary financing, privileged access for the public sector to the financial markets, and liability for or assumption of public debt of other Member states by the Community and the Member States; these prohibitions are laid down in Articles 104, 104a and 104b EC respectively in order to ensure that national authorities at all levels, bodies governed by public law and public undertakings act in conformity with the financial market conditions;

(4) the excessive deficit procedure, which is provided for in Article 104c EC because authorities which are confronted with the requirement of coverage of their budgetary deficits in conformity with the market may still continue to make excessive calls on the capital markets, with all the interest-increasing effects which such action brings; and

(5) the special two provisions contained in Article 103a EC to deal with extraordinary circumstances.

Each of these five segments is now examined in turn.

A. The objectives and principles (Article 102a EC). As was already observed in Chapter III, above, in relation to Article 3a EC, the formulation of the objectives and principles of the coordination of economic policies raises some important legal questions. The express reference to the principle of an open market economy refers in particular to the relationship with the world market and thus supports the principle set out in Article 110 EC of a liberal commercial policy. Secondly, it contains a certain instruction norm for the Member States and for the Community in the formation, attuning and implementation of their policy, that they should opt as much as possible for solutions which leave the operation of the market intact at Community level.[64] Experiences in the past have

---

64. Louis in Stuyck (ed.), *op. cit.* (see note 55, *supra*) 18 suggests that the commitment to the principle of an open market economy with free competition appears to have been included in Arts. 3a and 102a EC for two reasons: first, in order to prevent the adoption of quantitative measures of limitation of credit allowed by financial institutions, a

demonstrated that disparities in the composition of the package of economic steering instruments and in their use may cause major specific or
generic distortions which could unnecessarily affect the functioning of the
common market. Thirdly, this reference implicitly indicates that the coordination of economic policies is *not* limited to macro-economic policy in
the narrow applied sense of steering influence of economic macro-variables. The institutional structure and operation of national economies is in
the long term at least as important for the economic development of the
Community as a whole as the question whether in a given phase of the
economic cycle a restrictive or an expansive budgetary policy should be
pursued. In this connection the Commission's celebrated White Paper is
illustrative.[65] The phrase 'favouring an efficient allocation of resources'
which is found in Article 102a EC but not in Article 3a EC can be interpreted in two ways. On one interpretation it sets out nothing more than an
adjunct to the principle of free competition. On the other hand it can be
read as an independent condition for the Member States and the Community in the conduct of their economic policies: the authorities should use
their – public – resources as efficiently as possible.[66]

The real coordination obligation process lies in the words 'Member
States shall conduct their economic policies ... and in the context of the
broad guidelines referred to in Article 103(2).' This is discussed in more
detail below.

The last phrase of Article 102a EC, which refers to the principles set out
in Article 3a EC, is scarcely precise. The reference concerns in particular
Article 3a(3) EC which incompletely summarizes the principles of economic
policy set out in Article 104 EC. The absence of reference to 'ensuring a
high level of employment' in these principles is a serious shortcoming
which can be traced back to the history of the drafting of the EMU part
of the TEU itself.

In the preparation and negotiation stages German views about the
conditions which the economic policy of the Member States should satisfy
with a view to monetary union were predominant. In those views the
primary and central element of financial, economic and monetary policy is
the maintenance of price stability. The realization of this objective is, in
the German view, one of the preconditions for economic growth and for

---

favourite instrument of French monetary policy in the past; and, secondly, to protect
against rescue operations by the ESCB as lender of last resort.

65. See note 5, *supra*.

66. Although on grammatical grounds the first interpretation appears to be more obvious,
there are also arguments in favour of the second view. Strictly speaking an efficient
allocation of resources is the consequence of an effective operation of the market.
Understood that way the addition would be superfluous. It can attain particular significance only if the desired efficient allocation is extended beyond the market sector.
The history of the origin of Arts. 3a and 102a would lend some support to this interpretation, see Cloos *et al.*, *op. cit.* (see note 55, *supra*) 234.

growth in employment. In the run-up to the Treaty of Amsterdam European employment problems attracted much political attention, the German government was willing to see the new Title VIa on employment inserted into the EC Treaty, which primarily relates to labour in the narrow sense, but the provisions on the coordinates of economic policy remained closed to any inclusion of an employment objective.

It is submitted that the absence of any express mention of the employment objective does not mean that employment could not be the subject of economic policy coordination at Community level. The express reference in Article 102a EC to the objectives of the Community in Article 2 EC which include 'a high level of employment' would not support the exclusion of employment. Thus it could be regarded as a shortcoming in the system of the Treaty which can be overcome by means of interpretation. But at least as important is the shortcoming in the policy system which could be caused by the absence of employment as an *objective of economic policy* in a completed EMU. Such an EMU would be characterized by a situation in which disturbances at national level of the internal economic balance, expressed *e.g.* in a relatively high level of inflation, would have to be absorbed by the least mobile factor of production, which is labour.[67] It is thus obvious that in the coordination of the economic policies of the Member States major attention is paid to the development of direct and indirect labour costs, to the operation of the labour market, to possible rigidities in the development of conditions of employment, and to qualitative discrepancies between labour supply and demand. This is already confirmed by the Community's present economic situation in which employment questions predominate. It is because in Western Europe employment has too long not been acknowledged as an objective of economic policy subject to strict economic analysis, but has instead been treated as a social problem to be tackled through social policy, that structural inactivity among the working population has reached such high levels. That already forms in itself a serious obstacle for a balanced economic development in the terms of Article 2 EC. In the broad guidelines of the economic policies of the Member States and of the Community which have been adopted annually since the entry into force of the TEU, attention is therefore systematically paid to the employment aspect. In the new Employment Title which the Treaty of Amsterdam will introduce into the EC Treaty there are two systematic references to these

---

67. See Geelhoed in Amato *et al.*, *op. cit.* (see note 15, *supra*) 43. Thus even the mention of the promotion of employment in the Agreement on Social Policy (which the Treaty of Amsterdam will, when it enters into force, repeal in favour of the new Employment Title (Title VIa in Part Three of the Treaty) does not compensate for the absence of this objective from Art. 102a EC. The mention of the employment objective first in the Agreement on Social Policy and now in the new Employment Title misunderstands the point that the achievement of a high degree of employment is primarily to be ensured through economic policy rather than social policy.

broad guidelines.[68] In the joint reports which are presented under the Essen procedure to the European Council, the analysis of the Ecofin Council tends to dominate that of the Labour and Social Affairs Council.[69] This makes the absence of a mention of employment in Articles 3a, 102a and 103 EC something of an anomaly.[70]

It is noticeable that neither in Article 102a EC nor in the following provisions on economic policy is there any mention of short-term economic policy. The fact that economic and administrative views as to the desirability and possibilities of conducting an active anti-cyclical policy have changed since the Fifties played a part in the removal of the old Article 103 EEC. Moreover, practical experiences of a demand-stimulating macro-economic policy in the Seventies, which had led to budgetary deficits in almost all Member States which were difficult to reverse, were not such that the remaining proponents of an active anti-cyclical policy could count on much spontaneous support in the drafting of the EMU provisions. But the consequences for the practice of economic policy coordination are not so great. Short-term macro-economic policy is also embraced by the concept of 'economic policies.' Given the present still too high level of budgetary deficits in most Member States the recommendations in the broad guidelines will not quickly incline towards anti-cyclical policy. Some Member States, such as France, during the recession in the second half of 1992, were advised to dampen down short-term pressure by permitting automatic stabilizers to have an effect on their economies. This concerns the scissor-movement which occurs during periods of low economic performance between lower fiscal revenue and increased expenditure on social security. The scissor-movement on the one hand has the effect of increasing the deficit, but on the other hand keeping expenditure level. The room for the application of automatic stabilizers in budgetary policy is determined by the *ex ante* budget balance.

B. Policy coordination, the broad guidelines and multilateral surveillance (Article 103 EC). The present Article 103 EC sets out the major traits of the policy coordination procedure set out in Decision 90/141 on the attainment of progressive convergence of economic policies and performance in the first stage of EMU.[71] Article 103(1) is to be read as bringing together the old Articles 6 and 103 EEC. The concept of economic policies must, as was noted above, be more widely interpreted than macro-economic policy or financial economic policy. The quality and competitive strength of the

---

68. See section 4, *post.*
69. See section 1.1, *ante.*
70. See the Council's Recommendations as to the broad guidelines: Recs. 94/7 (O.J. 1994 L 7/9); 94/480 (O.J. 1994 L 200/38); 95/326 (O.J. 1995 L 191/24); 96/431 (O.J. 1996 L 179/46), and 97/479 (O.J. 1997 L 209/12). See also the Commission's reflections in view of the 1998 broad guidelines, COM (98) 103 Final.
71. O.J. 1990 L 78/23, replacing earlier measures (see note 37, *supra*).

national economies and of the Community economy as a whole is only partly determined by the budgetary and monetary conditions which Article 109j prescribes for the transition to the third and final stage of EMU. Matters such as the quality of the working population, the performance of the labour and services markets, the scope of public investment, expenditure on research and development and so on are of major and increasing importance for the structural strength of Western economies. Thus they will also have to be increasingly involved in the coordination of economic policies. The broad guidelines referred to in Article 103(2) EC are the actual coordination instruments.[72] They are drawn up in draft form on the basis of a recommendation from the Commission by the Council.[73] The European Council then discusses the draft, and on the basis of the conclusion in that forum the Council, acting by a qualified majority, adopts a recommendation setting out the broad guidelines.[74] Although the broad guidelines are contained in recommendations which are, in accordance with Article 189 EC, non-binding, Article 103(3) and (4) provides for a procedure of multilateral surveillance of economic developments in each Member State and of the consistency of economic policies with the broad guidelines. The obligation on each Member State to forward information to the Commission 'about important measures taken by them in the field of their economic policy and such other information as they deem necessary' is important. If multilateral surveillance establishes that the economic policies of a Member State are not consistent with the broad guidelines, or that they risk jeopardizing the proper functioning of EMU, the Council may, acting by qualified majority on the basis of a recommendation from the Commission, make the necessary recommendations to the Member State concerned. Such recommendations are made privately unless the Council, acting by qualified majority on a proposal from the Commission, decides to make its recommendations public.[75]

After the disappointing experiences with the first convergence decision of

---

72. See note 69, *supra*.
73. This means the Ecofin Council, see the declaration in O.J. 1992 C 191/98 (Declaration No. 3 adopted on the occasion of signature of the Final Act of the TEU).
74. On the basis of Declaration No. 4, *ibid.*, the Ecofin Ministers are invited to participate in the discussion by the European Council of matters relating to EMU.
75. There is an interesting institutional point here: the recommendations to the Member State are adopted on the basis of a recommendation from the Commission (as opposed to a proposal which is required for the recommendations to be made public). On the basis of Art. 148(2) EC, the decision to adopt the recommendation to the Member State should be taken by the heavier qualified majority (with at least 10 Member States in favour), as the Council is not acting on a *proposal* from the Commission. If this is not the case then the distinction between a Commission proposal and a Commission recommendation would be meaningless, and it is submitted that the different phrasing has been carefully chosen. The ordinary qualified majority applies in relation to a decision to make the recommendations to the Member State public.

1974[76] it remains to be seen whether the present procedure of Article 103 EC will generate more coordinating effects. The Treaty status of the procedure, the permanent character of the multilateral surveillance, and the fact that the coordination procedure is supported, at least as far as the Member States' budgetary policies are concerned, by the excessive deficit procedure of Article 104c EC, provide positive indications. Moreover the sharply defined participation criteria for the final stage of EMU, set out in Article 109j can support the coordination of the economic policies of the Member States.[77] The wording of Article 103(2) does not prevent the broad guidelines from being targeted per Member State, without prejudice to the possibility of specific recommendations being made under Article 103(4) EC. In view of the diverse nature of the economic problems in the various Member States, such an approach seems even the most appropriate. Thus more precise evaluation criteria for the purpose of multilateral surveillance can be created.[78] For policy practice an important element is the timing of these broad guidelines; they tend to be discussed in the European Council meetings held at the beginning of the Summer each year, which permits them to be adopted at an appropriate time in the national budget cycle. So far no more detailed implementing provisions for multilateral surveillance have been adopted on the basis of Article 103(5) EC, although that provision has been used as the legal basis for part of the Stability and Growth Pact agreed at Amsterdam in June 1997, which is discussed below.[79]

C. The rules for deficit financing according to market principles (Articles 104, 104a and 104b EC. In most Member States – and The Netherlands is no exception – public authorities, bodies governed by public law and public undertakings have since time immemorial enjoyed a privileged position in the financing of their deficits. The most important route for an undisciplined budgetary policy is the so-called monetary deficit financing, through credit facilities afforded by the national central bank. Extensive monetary financing poses grave risks for internal price stability, and thus for the development of interest rates on the money market and the capital market. For this reason, Article 104 EC prescribes a general prohibition of monetary deficit financing by the public sector in the wide sense.[80] The

76. See note 37, *supra*.
77. See Dec. 98/317 (O.J. 1998 L 139/30).
78. The Commission makes a practice of adopting this approach in its recommendations to the Council relating to the broad guidelines, *e.g.* for 1994, O.J. 1994 L 200/8.
79. See Reg. 1466/97 (O.J. 1997 L 209/1), see, further, including as to its legal basis in Art. 103(5) EC, under point D, *post*, and, further, Herdegen (1998) 35 CMLRev. 9.
80. See Reg. 3604/93 (O.J. 1993 L 332/4) on definitions for the application of the provisions in Arts. 104 and 104b(1) EC. Art. 8 of this regulation adopts the definition of public undertakings used in Dir. 80/723 (O.J. 1980 L 195/35, most recently amended by Dir. 93/84 (O.J. 1993 L 254/16)) on the transparency of financial relations between

prohibition does not apply to publicly-owned credit institutions, but they must be treated in the same way as private credit institutions.[81]

Complementing the prohibition of monetary financing, Article 104a EC prohibits any measure not based on prudential considerations, establishing privileged access to financial institutions 'by the Community institutions or bodies, central governments, regional, local or other public authorities, other bodies governed by public law, or public undertakings.'[82] Practices such as privileging authorities in the provision of borrowing requirements, which also occurred until a short time ago in The Netherlands are thus forbidden.[83] Only if the privileged treatment results from normal business considerations of the relatively high creditworthiness of the authority concerned as a debtor will it be permissible.[84]

The rules for deficit financing on a strictly market conditions basis, contained in Articles 104 and 104a EC aim to confront national budgetary authorities with the financial consequences of a budgetary policy running in deficit. The financial markets will always reflect their confidence in the authority concerned in the terms under which they are prepared to provide the capital requirements concerned. This corrective operation of the market however stands or falls according to the certainty offered that the Community or other Member States will not be liable for or assume the commitments of Member States which pursue undisciplined budgetary behaviour. Article 104b is designed to afford such certainty. It should result in the weaker Member States having to offer higher interest rates on their securities.

No further implementing measures are required for Articles 104 and 104b to take effect, although the Council has taken advantage of the possibility, provided for in Article 104b(2) to adopt Regulation 3603/93 on

Member States and public undertakings. See Pipkorn (1994) 31 CMLRev. 263 at 277.
81. Art. 104(2).
82. See further, Reg. 3604/93 (O.J. 1993 L 332/4) specifying definitions for the prohibition of privileged access.
83. The Algemene Burgerlijke Pensioenwet (Stb. 1966, no. 6) envisaged the possibility of compulsory investment in public securities.
84. Reg. 3604/93 (O.J. 1993 L 332/4), Art. 2 defines prudential considerations as 'those which underlie national laws, regulations or administrative actions based on, or consistent with, EC law and designed to promote the soundness of financial institutions so as to strengthen the stability of the financial system as a whole and the protection of the customers of those institutions.' The first phrase of Art. 104a EC is not itself very clear, referring implicitly to the solvency rules established by Dir. 89/647 (O.J. 1989 L 386/14, most recently amended by Dir. 96/10 (O.J. 1996 L 85/17); a codification has been proposed, COM (97) 706 Final) on solvency ratios for credit institutions. These rules maintain a balance of banking activities according to the degree of risk. For the more risky the activities, more capital coverage is required than for less risky activities. According to these rules, loans to Member States are regarded in the evaluation as falling within the risk-free category. That makes it simpler and cheaper for the Member States to obtain their capital requirements. See Smits (1992) SEW 702 at 715.

definitions for the purposes of Articles 104 and 104b(1) EC.[85] The Council has also adopted the definitions which were essential for the operation of Article 104a(1) EC.[86]

D. The excessive deficit procedure (Article 104c EC). During the preparatory negotiations prior to the signature of the TEU, extensive discussion took place as to whether, in a completed EMU, the financial markets would be sufficiently able to correct excessive government deficits. The United Kingdom in particular, with its traditional aversion to forms of direct Community supervision of its internal policy, took the view that market forces would be able so to act. The drafters of the Treaty, however, rightly chose not to put their faith in this form of automatic correction through the reaction of the financial markets.

In his comments on the Delors Report, Oort has convincingly demonstrated the weaknesses in the British argument.[87] It is true that financial markets may express their view of the declining creditworthiness of undisciplined budgetary authorities through a risk premium in the form of higher interest rates, but it is very much an open question whether the authorities concerned would be sufficiently sensitive to interest rates to alter their conduct in the short term. The other correcting factor, the automatic upward effect on interest rates of large-scale calls by the authorities on the financial markets, works less directly in a completed EMU, although a major call on the Community capital market by different national authorities could cause interest rates to rise. But such a situation in which the good would suffer along with the bad, and in which the investment climate of the market sector would seriously deteriorate, would heavily mortgage EMU as such.

Article 104c provides for a monitoring procedure against the existence and continuation of excessive deficits. The core of this mechanism is formed by the main rule, namely that the Member States must avoid excessive government deficits,[88] and by the criteria set out in Article 104c(2) which are further worked out in the Protocol on the excessive deficit procedure.[89] These are:

85. Reg. 3603/93 (O.J. 1993 L 332/1).
86. Reg. 3604/93 (O.J. 1993 L 322/4).
87. (1990) SEW 46.
88. Art. 104c(1) EC. This obligation applies from the beginning of the third stage of EMU (*i.e.* from 1 January 1999), Art. 109e(3) EC. This date was the default date prescribed in Art. 109j(4) EC. Until that date the Member States are under an obligation to *endeavour to avoid* excessive deficits, Art. 109e(4) EC. The obligation to avoid excessive deficits does not apply to the United Kingdom, Protocol (No. 11, annexed to the EC Treaty) on certain provisions relating to the United Kingdom, Art. 5. However, the United Kingdom is under an obligation, in accordance with Art. 109e(4) EC to endeavour to avoid excessive deficits.
89. Attached to the EC Treaty (by the TEU), see O.J. 1992 C 191/84, and Art. 104c(14), 1st subpara. As to the definitions, see Reg. 3605/93 (O.J. 1993 L 332/7), adopted on

- whether the ratio of the planned or actual government deficit to GDP exceeds 3%;[90] and
- whether the ratio of government debt to GDP exceeds 60%.[91]

The Commission monitors compliance with these criteria. The evaluation is not mechanical in the sense of deviation from the criteria automatically leading to action. Article 104c(2) provides that the Commission may take account of trends and exceptional circumstances.[92] The composition of public expenditure, the relationship between interest expenditure and investment expenditure, as well as the economic and budgetary situation in the medium term may be taken into account. From the wording of the provisions concerned it can be deduced that the Commission may allow the credibility of the budgetary policy of the Member State concerned to weigh heavily in its assessment. One-off transactions for the reduction of the budget deficit, such as the sale of a public undertaking or the postponement of government debt in time may make the budgetary picture in the short term apparently more attractive, but they do not contribute to structurally healthy public finances. Thus Article 104c(3) EC expressly requires regard to be had *inter alia* to 'the medium-term economic and budgetary position of the Member State.'

The Commission tends to make vary careful use of the margins of discretion which it is permitted. In practice, failure to satisfy the criteria will always lead to the Commission drawing up a report on the basis of Article 104c(3) EC; it may also prepare a report on that basis if, even though the criteria are fulfilled, it is of opinion that there is a risk of an excessive deficit in a Member State. Any aggravating or mitigating factors are referred to in the reports This objective, and systematically correct, approach in the application of Article 104c(2) and (3) EC prevents discussions arising with Member States which do not satisfy the reference values concerned. The discussions in the Monetary Committee (from 1

the basis of Art. 104c(14), 3rd subpara. Art. 104c(14) EC, 2nd subpara. envisages the Protocol being replaced, and Reg. 1467/97 (O.J. 1997 L 209/6, corrigendum O.J. 1998 L 46/20) was adopted under that provision, but the first recital to that regulation makes it clear that it is designed to supplement, and not to replace the Protocol. Reg. 1467/97 makes no mention of the 2nd criterion set out, *post*. See Hahn (1998) 35 CMLRev. 77 at 95. See further, Italianer in Andenas *et al.* (eds.), *op. cit.* (see note 55, *supra*) 189.

90. Unless either the ratio has declined substantially and continuously and reached a level that comes close to 3%, or, alternatively, the excess over 3% is only exceptional and temporary and the ratio remains close to 3%. As to when a deficit is considered only exceptional and temporary, see Reg. 1467/97 (O.J. 1997 L 209/6, corrigendum O.J. 1998 L 46/20), Art. 2. Reg. 1467/97 applies from 1 January 1999, *ibid.*, Art. 18.

91. Unless the ratio is sufficiently diminishing and approaching the 60% level at a satisfactory pace.

92. See, further, Reg. 1467/97 (O.J. 1997 L 209/6, corrigendum O.J. 1998 L 46/20), which applies from 1 January 1999, *ibid.*, Art. 18.

January 1999 in the Economic and Financial Committee)[93] on the reports are considerably simplified by the Commission's strict approach, and its advisory opinion tends to support the Commission's report. The next step is that if the Commission considers that an excessive deficit in a Member State exists or may occur, it must address an opinion to the Council.[94] Such an opinion is based on a thorough monitoring of the budgetary policy concerned, which avoid much factual discussion in the Council. The Council, acting by qualified majority on the basis of the Commission's recommendation, and having considered any observations which the Member State concerned may wish to make, may, after an overall assessment, decide that an excessive deficit exists.[95] Since the entry into force of the TEU this matter has not caused tension in the Council.

Even though, as explained above, the obligation to avoid excessive deficits only applies from 1 January 1999, the obligation to endeavour to avoid them has applied since the beginning of the second stage of EMU on 1 January 1994.[96] If a decision that there is an excessive deficit is taken, the Council 'must make recommendations to the Member State concerned with a view to bringing that situation to an end within a given period.'[97] These recommendations are not made public.[98] If, however, the Council establishes that there has been no effective action in response to its recommendations, it may make them public.[99] However, the obligation looming on the now close horizon of 1 January 1999 remains an effective means of persuasion, as by that date the Member States are required to have their houses in order, irrespective of whether they participate in the

---

93. See Art. 109c(2) EC, referring also to Art. 109c(1) EC. See further, Reg. 1467/97 (O.J. 1997 L 209/6, corrigendum O.J. 1998 L 46/20), Art. 3(1), which applies from 1 January 1999, *ibid.*, Art. 18, and provides that the Economic and Financial Committee must present its report within two weeks.
94. Art. 104c(5) EC. See further, Reg. 1467/97 (O.J. 1997 L 209/6, corrigendum O.J. 1998 L 46/20), Art. 3(2), which applies from 1 January 1999, *ibid.*, Art. 18.
95. Art. 104c(6) EC. See further, Reg. 1467/97 (O.J. 1997 L 209/6, corrigendum O.J. 1998 L 46/20), Art. 3(3), which applies from 1 January 1999, *ibid.*, Art. 18.
96. Art. 109e(4) in conjunction with Art. 109e(1). As to the reasons for having a 'political' rather than a 'legal commitment to avoid excessive deficits during the 2nd stage, and as to the involvement of Member States not (yet) participating in the single currency during the 3rd stage, see Italianer in Andenas *et al.* (eds.), *op. cit.* (see note 55, *supra*) 196–199.
97. Art. 104c(7) EC. See further, Reg. 1467/97 (O.J. 1997 L 209/6, corrigendum O.J. 1998 L 46/20), Art. 3(3). As to the deadline, see *ibid.*, Art. 3(4). These provisions apply from 1 January 1999, *ibid.*, Art. 18.
98. *Ibid.* But the decision establishing that an excessive deficit is, see *e.g.* Dec. 96/421 (O.J. 1996 L 172/26, Germany). The date(s) on which recommendations were made is referred to in any subsequent decision withdrawing the earlier one, *e.g.* Dec. 96/420 (O.J. 1996 L 420/25, Denmark).
99. Art. 104c(8) EC. See further, Reg. 1467/97 (O.J. 1997 L 209/6, corrigendum O.J. 1998 L 46/20), Art. 4, which applies from 1 January 1999, *ibid.*, Art. 18.

single currency from the beginning.[100] This incentive has led to strong reductions in the budgetary deficits to under or about 3% of GDP in most Member States since 1994, so that in May 1998 nine earlier decisions establishing the existence of excessive deficits could be withdrawn.[101]

With effect from 1 January 1999, there is a further mechanism which only applies to those Member States which participate in the single currency.[102] Thus any participating Member State which persist in failing to put into practice the recommendations of the Council, may be given notice by the Council that it must take, within a specified time-limit, measures for the deficit reduction which the Council judges necessary in order to remedy the situation; the Council may in such cases request the Member States concerned to submit reports to it in accordance with a specific timetable in order to examine the adjustment efforts of that Member State.[103] Article 104c(11) EC permits the Council to apply, or as the case may be, intensify one or more of the following sanction measures:[104]

- it may require the Member State concerned to publish such additional information as the Council may specify before the Member State issues bonds and securities;
- it may invite the European Investment Bank to reconsider its lending policy towards the Member State concerned;

100. Art. 104c(1) is not one of the provisions which are declared inapplicable to Member States with a derogation, see Art. 109k(3). As to the meaning of that phrase, see Art. 109k(1) EC. The importance of the sustainability of the government financial position is emphasized in Art. 109j(1) EC, 2nd indent. Art. 104c(1) EC does not, however apply to the United Kingdom, Protocol (No. 11, annexed to the EC Treaty) on certain provisions relating to the United Kingdom, Art. 5. But, as was noted above, the United Kingdom still has to endeavour to avoid an excessive deficit.
101. Decs. 307–315/98 (O.J. 1998 L 139/9–20, Belgium, Germany, Austria, France, Italy, Spain, Portugal, Sweden and the United Kingdom). The earlier decisions involving The Netherlands and Finland had been withdrawn in 1997 (Decs. 97/416 (O.J. 1997 L 177/23) and 97/417 (O.J. 1997 L 177/23)), and that involving Denmark in 1996 (Dec. 96/420 (O.J. 1996 L 172/25)). Ireland and Luxembourg never had an excessive deficit decision made in respect of them.
102. Non-participants ('Member States with a derogation') are unaffected by *inter alia* Art. 104c(9) and (11) EC, by virtue of Art. 109k(3) EC; this means Greece, Sweden, and Denmark (the latter by virtue of Protocol (No. 12, annexed to the EC Treaty), Art. 2 (the Danish government having given notice of its intention not to participate); the United Kingdom is also unaffected, Protocol (No. 11, likewise so annexed) on certain provisions relating to the United Kingdom, Art. 5 (the United Kingdom government having notified the Council that it would not proceed to the third stage of EMU on 1 January 1999). As is explained in section 3.3.2, below, 11 Member States will participate in the single currency from the outset.
103. Art. 104c(9) EC. See further, Reg. 1467/97 (O.J. 1997 L 209/6, corrigendum O.J. 1998 L 46/20), Art. 5, which also applies from 1 January 1999, *ibid.*, Art. 18.
104. See further, Reg. 1467/97 (O.J. 1997 L 209/6, corrigendum O.J. 1998 L 46/20), Arts. 6–8, which apply from 1 January 1999, *ibid.*, Art. 18. Art. 104c(11) EC, 2nd subpara. provides that the President of the Council must inform the European Parliament of the decisions taken.

 – it may require the Member State concerned to make a non-interest-
   bearing deposit of an appropriate size with the Community until the
   excessive deficit has, in the Council's view, been corrected;[105]
 – it may impose fines of an appropriate size.[106]

If and to the extent that the excessive deficit in the Member State
concerned has, in the Council's view, corrected, the Council must then
abrogate some or all of its decisions referred to above,[107] and if it has made
public recommendations, it must, at the same time as it abrogates the
decision that there had been no effective response, make a public statement
that an excessive deficit in the Member State concerned no longer exists.[108]
The decisions making recommendations, on making them public, giving
notice, and applying or abrogating sanctions are taken by the Council,
acting on a recommendation from the Commission, by a majority of two-
thirds of the votes of its members, weighted as in the case of a qualified
majority, excluding the votes of the representative of the Member State
concerned.[109] Although Article 104c(10) EC excludes recourse to infringement proceedings under Articles 169 or 170 EC within the framework of
Article 104c(1)–(9) EC, that exclusion does not apply to any failure to
comply with decisions taken under Article 104c(11) EC. Article 104c(14)
EC refers to the Protocol on the excessive deficit procedure;[110] and the
third subparagraph of that provision, permits the Council to adopt, by
qualified majority on a proposal from the Commission, after consulting
the European Parliament, detailed rules and definitions for the application
of the provisions of that Protocol.[111]

This excessive deficit procedure has, as was observed above, the
characteristics of vertical subordinating coordination, with unequivocal
compulsory elements for the member States. This view is based on the

105. This sanction will as a rule be applied, although it may be supplemented by the first
     two set out above, see Reg. 1467/97 (O.J. 1997 L 209/6, corrigendum O.J. 1998 L 46/
     20), Art. 11. As to the mechanics, see, *ibid.*, Arts. 12 and 16. These provisions apply
     from 1 January 1999, *ibid.*, Art. 18.
106. A deposit will as a rule be converted into a fine if the Member State concerned has
     not, in the Council's view, corrected the excessive deficit within two years of the deci-
     sion requiring the deposit to be made, Reg. 1467/97, *ibid.*, Art. 13.
107. *I.e.* decisions taken under Art. 104c(6)–(9) and (11).
108. Art. 104c(12). See Reg. 1467/97, *ibid.*, Art. 15.
109. Art. 104c(13) EC. As was explained in note 75, *supra*, it still seems that there must be
     at least 10 Member States in favour.
110. Protocol (No. 5, annexed to the EC Treaty) on the excess deficit procedure. Art.
     104c(14) EC, 2nd subpara. envisages the Protocol being replaced, and Reg. 1467/97
     (O.J. 1997 L 209/6, corrigendum O.J. 1998 L 46/20) was adopted under that provi-
     sion, but the first recital to that regulation makes it clear that it is designed to supple-
     ment, and not to replace the Protocol. See Hahn (1998) 35 CMLRev. 77 at 95. See
     further, Italianer in Andenas *et al.* (eds.), *op. cit.* (see note 55, *supra*) 189.
111. See Reg. 3605/93 (O.J. 1993 L 332/7). Reg. 1467/97 (O.J. 1997 L 209/6, corrigendum
     O.J. 1998 L 46/20) was adopted on the basis of Art. 104c(14) EC, 2nd subpara.

clear evaluating role of the Commission, the fact that the criteria against which evaluation takes place are clearly both objective and permanent in nature, and the fact that a Member State, once it is found to have an excessive deficit, is no longer involved (at least in voting terms) in the decision-making process concerning the recommendations, the giving of notice and any sanctions which may be adopted.[112]

The excessive deficit procedure has, as indicated above, so far had a major effect on the budgetary policies of the Member States, including the United Kingdom and Denmark. Whether this result is primarily to be ascribed to the procedure as such or to the firm requirement of the second indent of Article 109j(1) EC of the absence of an excessive deficit before participation in the single currency is possible on the passage to the third stage[113] of EMU is still unclear. In any event, Germany and a number of other Member States remained apprehensive that not all Member States would continue to take the prohibition of an excessive deficit seriously once they had met the threshold requirement for participation in the single currency from the outset.

This apprehension was also caused by the experience in the mild economic recession which affected most of the European Union between mid-1992 and mid-1994. During that period most budgetary deficits actually increased quickly and without warning, at the cost of meeting the convergence criteria of Articles 104c and 109e EC. From this experience it could be deduced that the fact that the Member States met the criteria of Article 104c EC under normal economic conditions would afford no guarantee at all that they would continue to respect those criteria in a less favourable economic climate. In the West-European welfare states, the disappearance of economic growth immediately results in a major decline in public revenue and an increase in social expenditure through a larger share of the population being unemployed. If the Member States under normal economic conditions have budgetary deficits just under the 3% ceiling, in time of recession they will either immediately exceed that ceiling considerably or will feel themselves obliged to make cuts in their budgets which are socially or economically unattractive, and which may have internal political consequences.

These preoccupations lay behind the initiative of the German Finance Minister, Waigel, at the end of 1995 to supplement the excessive deficit procedure with what became known as a Stability Pact. The key elements in this proposal,[114] which can be traced in what was finally agreed, albeit in a somewhat modified form, were:

112. *Ibid.*
113. And indeed, before any derogation accorded to a Member States under Art. 109k EC should be abrogated.
114. *Stabilitätspakt für Europa in der dritten Stufe der VWU* (Press Release from the German Finance Ministry, Bonn, 10 November 1995). See, further, Hahn (1998) 35 CMLRev. 77 at 80 and Häde (1996) EuZW 138.

- a more ambitious budgetary criterion, thus in normal economic conditions a deficit of 1% was to be the medium term aim, with a balanced budget or a surplus preferred;
- a more stringent control of the progress of the Member States' budgetary policies, with half-yearly monitoring reports from the Commission which would make it possible to take action if the 3% ceiling threatened to be breached;
- a more stringent criterion even in adverse economic conditions, so that the 3% ceiling should not be breached save in extremely exceptional circumstances;
- the reduction of overall government debt should continue even below the 60% limit imposed when the TEU entered into force;[115]
- the imposition of firm deadlines within which the recommendations and notice provided for in Article 104c(7) and (9) EC had to be adopted;
- greater precision in the sanctions which could be imposed.

A closer economic analysis of the proposed Stability Pact demonstrates how appropriate its name was. First, it would force the Member States to maintain a balanced or nearly balanced budget in normal economic conditions; this could contribute to the maintenance of the price stability objective prescribed in Articles 3a, 102a and 105 EC. Secondly, it would create the necessary budgetary room for the so-called automatic stabilizers if economic growth were to disappear. Thirdly, both in times of economic prosperity and in times of economic adversity it would form an obstacle to pro-cyclical economic policy. A legal analysis of the original proposals confirms that in terms of scope and content they would fall fairly and squarely within the parameters of Article 104c EC. They were exclusively aimed at convergence and discipline of national budgetary policies. Initially these proposals encountered considerable opposition in the Member States, for which meeting the budgetary criteria of Article 104c EC on time was already a major effort. But gradually views came round to accepting that the Stability Pact in a completed monetary union would be a useful and logical complement to the provisions of Article 104c EC. Experience so far at that time in the second stage of EMU had shown that precise and far-reaching criteria of an objective nature could facilitate the necessary coordination of national budgetary policies through eliminating in advance possible political differences of views. Thus in the course of 1996 the Stability Pact gradually obtained sufficient support at the level of the European Council, and at its meeting in Dublin in December 1996 its members were substantially in agreement,[116] with the result that, as is explained

115. This criterion in particular did not survive in the final agreement.
116. Bull. EU 12–1996, point I.3.

below, agreement was reached at Amsterdam in June 1997 on what became known as the Stability and Growth Pact.

In the development of the original proposals into legal form, a legal complication was that Article 104c(14) EC affords an inadequate legal basis for the package: that provision is particularly designed for the application of the excessive deficit Protocol. Article 104c(14) does form the basis for rules relating to the description of the exceptional circumstances under which overshooting the 3% ceiling for the deficit and the 60% debt threshold would be permissible. A more precise description of the deadlines within which Member States which are in problems have to comply with the recommendations or the notice given by the Council, as well as the modalities of the sanctions provisions could certainly be based on Article 104c(14). But the development of permanent monitoring of national budgetary policies in the medium-term could not be based on that provision. As there was considerable political resistance to changing the Treaty provisions on EMU prior to the entry into force of the third stage of EMU, an impasse threatened. An attempt was made to solve this through basing the monitoring of national budgetary policies on Article 103(5) EC. That provision was intended to permit detailed rules to be adopted for the multilateral surveillance procedure of compliance with the broad guidelines of economic policies, which are certainly more extensive than budgetary policies. Despite the fact that there are serious objections to this approach from the point of view of the system of Community law, it was this route that was eventually followed.

Thus at the meeting of the European Council in Amsterdam in June 1997, the Stability Pact was adopted under the rather broader title of the Stability and Growth Pact. Its composition is tripartite: the European Council resolution on the Stability and Growth Pact;[117] Regulation 1466/97 on the strengthening of the surveillance of budgetary positions and the surveillance and coordination of economic policies,[118] and Regulation 1467/97 on speeding up and clarifying the implementation of the excessive deficit procedure.[119]

The European Council resolution contains various commitments by the Member States in relation in particular to the medium-term budgetary objective of being close to balance or in surplus set out in their stability or convergence programmes, taking corrective budgetary action and correcting excessive deficits as quickly as possible after their emergence. It also contains various guidelines for (and apparently records commitments by) the Commission as to its role in the in the early warning procedure

---

117. O.J. 1997 C 236/1, Bull. EU 6–1997, point I.27.
118. O.J. 1997 L 209/1. This regulation is based on Art. 103(5) EC.
119. O.J. 1997 L 209/6, corrigendum O.J. 1998 L 46/20. The mechanics of this regulation have been indicated in the notes to the discussion *ante*, and so are not substantively further discussed, *post*. This regulation is based on Art. 104c(14) EC, 2nd subpara.

and in the excessive deficit procedure. Finally, it notes the Council's commitment to a rigorous and timely implementation of all elements of the Stability and Growth Pact and makes various invitations to the Council and urges it to act in certain ways in relation to the excess deficit procedure and the surveillance procedure of budgetary positions.

With the adoption of Regulation 1466/97[120] on the strengthening of the surveillance of budgetary positions and the surveillance and coordination of budgetary policies, as the second limb of the Stability and Growth Pact, the Council sought to set out the framework for the operation of Article 103 EC: it sets out the rules covering the content, submission, examination and monitoring of stability programmes and convergence programmes as part of multilateral surveillance by the Council so as to prevent, at an early stage, the occurrence of excessive general government deficits and to promote the surveillance and coordination of economic policies.[121] Those Member States which will participate in the single currency *ab initio* must 'submit to the Council and Commission information necessary for the purpose of multilateral surveillance at regular intervals under Article 103 of the Treaty in the form of a stability programme, which provides an essential basis for price stability and for strong sustainable growth conducive to employment creation.'[122] The stability programmes must be submitted before 1 March 1999; thereafter, updated programmes must be submitted annually. A Member State which adopts the single currency at a later stage must submit a stability programme within six months of the Council Decision on its participation in the single currency. These programmes and updates must be made public.[123] The Commission and the Committee set up by Article 109c EC[124], make assessments on the basis of which the Council within the framework of multilateral surveillance, examines whether the medium-term budget objective in the stability programme provides for a safety margin to ensure the avoidance of an excessive deficit, whether the economic assumptions on which the programme is based are realistic and whether the measures being taken and/or proposed are sufficient to achieve the targeted adjustment path towards the medium-term budgetary objective.[125] The Council also examines whether the contents of the stability programme facilitate the closer coordination of economic policies, and whether the economic policies of the Member State concerned are consistent with the broad

120. O.J. 1997 L 209/1. This was adopted under Art. 103(5) EC . See, further, Herdegen (1998) 35 CMLRev. 9.
121. Reg. 1466/97, *ibid.*, Art. 1. It applies from 1 July 1998, Art. 13.
122. *Ibid.*, Art. 3(1). As to the required information, see Art. 3(2).
123. *Ibid.*, Art. 4.
124. As from 1 January 1999 this will be the Economic and Financial Committee established under Art. 109c(2) EC. Prior to that date it is the Monetary Committee provided for in Art. 109c(1) EC.
125. *Ibid.*, Art. 5(1), 1st subpara.

economic policy guidelines.[126] This examination must be carried out within at the most two months of the submission of the programme, and the Council, on a recommendation from the Commission and after consulting the Committee mentioned above, delivers an opinion on the programme. Where the Council, in accordance with Article 103 EC, considers that the objectives and contents of a programme should be strengthened, in its opinion it will invite the Member State concerned to adjust its programme.[127]

As part of multilateral surveillance, the Council will monitor the implementation of stability programmes, on the basis of information provided by participating Member States and of assessments by the Commission and the Committee mentioned above, in particular with a view to identifying actual or expected significant divergence of the budgetary position from the medium-term budgetary objective, or the adjustment path towards it, as set in the programme for the government surplus or deficit.[128] If the Council identifies significant divergence of the budgetary position from the medium-term budgetary objective, or the adjustment path towards it, then, with a view to giving early warning in order to prevent the occurrence of an excessive deficit, it will address, a recommendation to the Member State concerned to take the necessary adjustment measures.[129] If the Council in its subsequent monitoring judges that the divergence of the budgetary position from the medium-term budgetary objective, or the adjustment path towards it, is persisting or worsening, it will then make a recommendation to the Member State concerned to take prompt corrective measures and may make its recommendation public.[130]

Those Member States which are not (as yet) participating in the single currency must submit convergence programmes, the procedure in respect of which is similar to that set out above.[131] In addition, the Council

126. *Ibid.*, 2nd subpara.
127. *Ibid.*, Art. 5(2). Updated stability programmes are examined by the Committee on the basis of assessments by the Commission; if necessary, those programmes may also be examined by the Council in accordance with the procedure of *ibid.*, Art. 5(1) and (2).
128. *Ibid.*, Art. 6(1).
129. In accordance with Art. 103(4) EC (Reg. 1466/97, Art. 6(2).
130. *Ibid.* (Reg. 1466/97, Art. 6(3)).
131. Reg. 1466/97, Arts. 7–10. In view of the decisions taken at the beginning of May 1998, this means Greece and Sweden. Hahn (1998) 35 CMLRev. 77 at 89–90 states that the United Kingdom and Denmark do not for the time being have to submit convergence programmes. But Denmark is treated as if it had a derogation (Protocol (No. 12, annexed to the EC Treaty) on certain provisions relating to Denmark, Art. 2), which means that it is treated in the same way as Greece and Sweden, and Art. 103 EC is not one of the provisions declared inapplicable to the United Kingdom until such time as it decides to move to the third stage of EMU (Protocol (No. 11, likewise so annexed) on certain provisions relating to the United Kingdom, Art. 5. It is clear from the Commission's Report of 25 March 1998, *Euro 1999* (Brussels,

monitors the economic policies of non-participating Member States in the light of convergence programme objectives with a view to ensure that their policies are geared to stability and thus to avoid real exchange rate misalignments and excessive nominal exchange rate fluctuations.[132] As part of the multilateral surveillance under Regulation 1466/97, the Council carries out the overall assessment provided for in Article 103(3) EC. The results of the surveillance are included in the reports to the European Parliament in accordance with the second paragraph of Article 103(4) EC.

Regulation 1466/97 demonstrates the signs of its hybrid background. On the one hand, it pretty well literally refers to Article 104c EC, but on the other hand it seeks to align itself with the multilateral surveillance procedures of Article 103(3) and (4) EC. Strictly speaking it provides for two distinct procedures: the procedure for broad guidelines of economic policies and multilateral surveillance thereof,[133] and in addition the procedure for stability or convergence programmes, their evaluation and also the multilateral surveillance of their implementation.[134] As has been seen, the stability programmes of those Member States participating in the Single currency and the convergence programmes of the non-participating countries (Greece and Sweden) are substantively identical; the evaluation and supervision of their implementation is largely identical.

Regulation 1467/97, which is based on the second subparagraph of Article 104c(14) EC, is legally considerably less of a problem. In view of the high demands which it makes of the Commission, the Council and defaulting Member States through the strictness of the deadlines for decision-making, it remains to be seen whether in practice it will be as effective as its authors intended.

As a whole, Article 104c EC, including these implementing measures, is a most remarkable provision, as it confers on the Community powers giving it a far-reaching influence in the decision-making of the national budgetary legislator. The EC Treaty confers the central authority, in this case the Community authority, more far-reaching powers than the German Federal authorities have over the *Länder* under Article 109 of the German *Grundgesetz*. It is, though, to be recommended that at the first opportunity Article 104c(14) EC should be amended so that all implementing rules for the excessive deficit procedure may find their legal basis in that provision. The use of Article 103 EC as the legal basis for a measure implementing

---

Luxembourg, 1998) Part 2, 186 that the United Kingdom did submit a convergence programme for 1997, and it is evident from that report as a whole that the Danish government had supplied the necessary information. However, as is explained in section 3.3.2, *post*, there are differences between the convergence programmes required under Art. 103(3) EC and the reports required under Art. 109e(2) EC.

132. See *ibid.*, Art. 10(1).
133. Reg. 1466/97, Arts. 2–4.
134. Based on Art. 103(3) and (4) EC, but dealing in fact also with the objectives of Art. 104c EC, as does Reg. 1467/97.

Article 104 EC, which is a *lex specialis* in relation to Article 103 EC, is extremely confusing and legally impermissible from the point of view of the legal system of the EC Treaty.[135] An institutionally weak element in Art. 104c EC, the consequences of which have already been noted, is that the Council may take its decisions on the basis of *recommendations* from the Commission, which affords far too much room for purely political opportunism as the basis for decision-making in the Council.[136]

E. Powers in exceptional circumstances (Article 103a EC). In the old Article 103(4) EEC the Council was empowered to adopt 'appropriate measures' if any difficulty should arise in the supply of certain products.[137] This provision did not remain a dead letter. Particularly as a result of the two oil crises in the Seventies it was used as the legal basis for measures to ensure the Community's supplies of oil.[138] With the repeal of Article 103 EEC the basis for this power threatened to disappear; thus Article 103a(1) EC makes specific provision in this regard, ensuring that from the entry into force of the TEU this specific power continues to be available. It is submitted that the Council may, on the basis of this provision adopt any measures, including directly binding measures, which are possible in accordance with Article 189 EC.[139]

The tying of budgetary deficits to community criteria and the prohibition of monetary financing may make it difficult for the Member States to finance the consequences of events which cause severe economic shocks.

135. The clarity and uniformity of the definitions contained in Reg. 3605/93 (O.J. 1993 L 332/7) is important. This measure is based on Art. 104c(14), 3rd subpara.
136. This applies *a fortiori* in relation to the exclusion, by Art. 104c(10) EC of infringement proceedings in relation to the use of Art. 104c(1)–(9) EC. Thus the Commission has no opportunity to redress shortcomings in the Council's actions. Although there are certainly arguments why the application of Art. 104c(1)–(9), which is based on financial and economic analysis and evaluation, should not be brought within the judicial sphere, it is submitted that they are not decisive. There is a logical contradiction between the desire of the drafters of the treaty provisions that the excessive deficit procedure should as far as possible operate on the basis of hard objective criteria, and the prior exclusion of the judiciary which would in this situation conduct a marginal examination. Moreover, the Commission is in fact sidelined as far as supervision of this vital procedure in the establishment of EMU. See, in the same sense, though less explicitly, Slot in Curtin and Heukels (eds.), *op. cit.* (see note 55, *supra*) 229 at 242.
137. The words 'appropriate measures' were contained in the old Art. 103(2) EEC, which procedure, along with the possibility of adopting directives under the old Art. 103(3) EEC, was made applicable by the old Art. 103(4) EEC.
138. See Chapter XI, section 6.2, *post*.
139. This follows from the drafting of Art. 103a(1) EC, which is a combination of the old Art. 103(2) and (4) EEC. In Case 5/73 *Balkan-Import-Export GmbH v. Hauptzollamt Berlin-Packhof* [1973] ECR 1091 at 1110 the Court concluded that 'measures appropriate to the situation' meant 'that as regards form, too, the Council may choose whichever seems best suited to the case in hand.' See also Smits (1992) SEW 702 at 711.

With a view to such eventualities, the possibility of Community financial assistance to the Member State concerned is provided for in Article 103a(2) EC. In such cases the Council acts unanimously on a proposal from the Commission, and conditions may be attached to such assistance. If, however, the severe difficulties are caused by natural disasters, the Council acts by qualified majority.[140]

F. The structure of coordination. The coordination of economic policy may be characterized as an example of continual steering influence on the economic policies of the Member States, which is primarily in the executory sphere. Acts such as the preparation and establishment of the broad guidelines, multilateral surveillance, and monitoring the avoidance of excessive deficits are by nature not legislative acts. Just as at national level, parliamentary involvement is primarily in the nature of a political control of in this case coordinating conduct of policy. This is also visible in the at first sight scant role of the European Parliament in the coordination of economic policy.[141] It should, though, be added that there is nothing to prevent the European Parliament from calling the Commission to account in a political *ex ante* or *ex post* control of the policy objectives which the Commission seeks to attain for the Community in the exercise of its powers in the coordination processes of Articles 103 and 104c EC.[142] But

140. As a result of Art. 109e(3) EC, Art. 103a(2) EC may be invoked from the beginning of the third stage on 1 January 1999. In the Commission's original proposals there was to be a mechanism for financial assistance to Member States which had to make a particular effort to satisfy the conditions for proceeding to the third stage of EMU. The majority of Member States rejected this approach, without prejudice to measures to be adopted in the context of economic and social cohesion. In the majority view the budgetary and macro-economic discipline required to satisfy the EMU criteria should not be made dependent on further financial assistance. Although this view is objectively correct, the more prosperous Member States could not avoid establishing a new Cohesion Fund from which financial assistance would be granted for projects in the fields of environment and trans-European networks 'in Member States with a per capita GDP of less than 90% of the Community average *which have a programme leading to the fulfillment of the conditions of economic convergence as set out in Art. 104c EC.*' (Emphasis added.) This conditionality, which makes the connection between EMU and the Cohesion Fund, is not set out in the body of the EC Treaty itself, but in a Protocol (No. 15, annexed to the EC Treaty) on economic and social cohesion (see O.J. 1992 C 191/3). As to the Cohesion Fund, see section 5, *post*. As to the gestation, see Cloos *et al.*, *op. cit.* (see note 55, *supra*) 151–162 and Pipkorn (1994) 31 CMLRev. 263 at 274.

141. See Art. 103(2) and (4) EC.

142. It is thus a pity that in the multilateral surveillance procedure and in the excessive deficit procedure the Commission only has the power to make recommendations, in the face of which the Council is entirely free to chart its own course by qualified majority. *Ex post* supervision is thus somewhat left in an uncertain position. Pipkorn (1992) 29 CMLRev. 263 at 273 regards it as regrettable that the Parliament is only informed about events, but does not comment further. In Regulation 1466/97 (O.J. 1997 L 209/1) on the strengthening of the surveillance of budgetary positions and the

because this involves the attuning of policy for which the primary powers have remained with the Member States, the demarcation of the area in which the European Parliament can exercise its political control is a delicate matter.

The character of the policy coordination as a continual steering influence means that the Council is not the appropriate forum to serve as the permanent discussion partner with the Commission. Indeed, the drafters even of the original EEC Treaty recognized this when they established the Monetary Committee by the old Article 105 EEC. This Committee has continued to operate in the second stage of EMU, on the basis of Article 109c(1) EC, in the preparation of the coordination of economic policies. With effect from 1 January 1999 it is replaced by the Economic and Financial Committee,[143] by virtue of Article 109c(2) EC, and thenceforth the need to advise on the coordination of national monetary policy disappears, the matter being then uniformly run at Community level by the independent European System of Central Banks (ESCB). The Ecofin Committee will still be able to give opinions on the exercise of the Council's powers in the monetary field, particularly in relation to exchange rate policy.[144] It will also continue to play a major role in the context of the excessive deficit procedure. This role has received further emphasis, at the expense of that of the Commission, in the Stability and Growth Pact.

In the analysis of Articles 102a and 103 EC it already appeared that the powers of the Community encompass more than just the budgetary and monetary policies of the Member States. That was already the case with the old EEC Treaty. Already in the Seventies three committees has been established for the preparation of policy coordination in parts of economic policy as a whole; these were then merged into the Economic Policy Committee.[145] This committee played a major part in the preparation of the decision-making which led to the adoption of the convergence decision of 1974.[146] Its main task was 'to promote the coordination of Member States' short and medium-term economic policies.'[147] For the moment the Economic Policy Committee continues to exist, and there appears to be a demarcation of tasks between it and what is until 1 January 1999 the Monetary Committee: the former concentrates on actual economic developments within the Community, whereas the latter concentrates on the financial (budgetary) and monetary aspects of policy coordination. Once the new Title VIa of Part Three of the EC Treaty on employment comes into effect when the Treaty of Amsterdam enters into force, the

surveillance and coordination of economic policies, discussed *ante*, the Commission's role is reduced to one primarily of evaluation, see Reg. 1466/97, Arts. 5 and 6.
143. The Ecofin Committee.
144. *Cf.* Art. 109c(2) EC.
145. Dec. 74/122 (O.J. 1974 L 63/21). See also note 43, *supra*, and text thereto.
146. See note 37, *supra*.
147. Dec. 74/122 (O.J. 1974 L 63/21), Art. 1.

Economic Policy Committee will function as the counterpart of the new Employment Committee.[148]

3.3 Monetary union

3.3.1 In general

The Treaty provisions on the Monetary Union fall into two main groups. In Articles 105–109d EC and the Protocol on the Statute of the European System of Central Banks (ESCB) and the European Central Bank (ECB)[149] the substantive and the institutional aspects of the Monetary Union in its *final* stage are set out. The transition to the final stage is dealt with in Articles 109e–109m EC and in the Protocol on the Statute of the European Monetary Institute (EMI).[150] The transitional arrangements are complex. They had to take account of the possibility that not all Member States would satisfy the stringent criteria for movement to the third stage.[151] They also had to cope with the possibility, which turned out to be the reality, that the United Kingdom and Denmark would not wish to proceed to the third stage even if they satisfied the criteria.[152] One of the most important consequences of the establishment of EMU at different speeds is that for the relationship between participants in the single currency in stage three of EMU and non-participants therein is that special coordination structures will still be required. The Member States which remain behind (Greece and Sweden, in addition to the United Kingdom and Denmark[153]) will remain linked to the participating Member States in a new exchange rate mechanism, which has become known as ERM 2.[154] For these countries the special arrangements contained in Articles 109h and 109i EC, relating to balance of payments difficulties and precautionary measures to cope with sudden crises in the balance of payments, continue to apply until such time as they participate in the single currency.[155]

---

148. Which will be established by virtue of the new Art. 109s EC. See, further, section 4, *post*. See also the Employment and Labour Market Committee established by Dec. 97/16 (O.J. 1997 L 6/32).
149. Hereafter referred to as the ESCB/ECB Statute. This is to be found in O.J. 1992 C 191/68.
150. Hereafter referred to as the EMI Statute. This can be found in O.J. 1992 C 191/79.
151. Art. 109k EC.
152. See the relevant Protocols (Nos. 11 and 12, attached to the EC Treaty). These can be found in O.J. 1992 C 191/87 and 89 respectively.
153. Note that Denmark (see Protocol No. 12, Art. 2.) is treated on the same footing as Member States with a derogation (Greece and Sweden), whereas the United Kingdom remains in a separate situation.
154. See O.J. 1997 C 236/5; Bull. EU 6–1997, point I.29.
155. Art. 109k(6) EC; for the United Kingdom Protocol (No. 11, annexed to the EC

In the coming years the legal obligations which result from the provisions applicable to the transitional second stage of EMU will still be relevant because some Member States are not (yet) participating in the single currency. With the impending move to the third stage, with 11 of the 15 Member States participating in the single currency from the outset of the third stage on 1 January 1999, the legal complications of movement to a single currency at different speeds will become live issues. Given that it seems as if the multi-speed approach may well have a permanent character, or at least last for a number of years,[156] it is worthwhile considering the transitional arrangements in more detail than would otherwise be appropriate at the date at which this work states the law.

3.3.2 The transitional stage

A. Substantive coordination. Article 109e EC, which governs the move from the first to the second stage is interesting from the point of view of its system. It orchestrates the far-reaching coordination of economic and monetary policy during this stage.

The Member States have been obliged to 'endeavour to avoid excessive government deficits'[157] and already in the second stage have had to act according to market principles on the capital markets.[158] Moreover, they have been obliged to ensure the autonomy of their central banks.[159] As far as concerns substantive policy coordination which has to lead to a completed EMU, the convergence programmes of the Member States are of major importance.[160] They have to enable the Commission and the Council to 'assess the progress which has been made with regard to economic and monetary convergence, in particular with regard to price stability and sound public finances, and the progress made with the implementation of Community law concerning the internal market.'[161] This coupling of market integration and economic and monetary policy integration is noteworthy, as there can be no question of the convergence necessary for a completed EMU without market integration; they are thus seen as going hand-in-hand. The EC Treaty clearly requires progressivity here, as Article 109j(1) EC requires the examination of *inter alia* 'the

Treaty) on certain provisions relating to the United Kingdom, Art. 6. Arts. 109h and 109i EC reflect the old Arts. 108 and 109 EEC respectively.

156. Greece made it clear (during the 2089th meeting of the (Ecofin) Council in May 1998) that it hopes to move to the single currency by 1 January 2001.
157. Art. 109e(4) EC.
158. Art. 109e(3) EC.
159. Art. 109(5) EC. As to how this has been done, see the Commission's Report (see note 131, *supra*) Part 2, 43–82.
160. Art. 109e(2) EC. See the Commission's Report, *ibid.*, 17–42.
161. Art. 109e(2)(b) EC.

achievement of a high degree of sustainable convergence' by reference *inter alia* to 'the durability of the convergence achieved'.

Regulation 1466/97,[162] which has been discussed in the preceding section, does not, with respect, contribute to greater clarity in terms of the relationship with Art. 109e(2) EC, as both in the regulation and in that Treaty provision the Member States which are not (yet) participating in the single currency are obliged to draw up convergence programmes. Both as to substance and as to procedure there are considerable differences between the two types of programmes. The convergence programmes mentioned in Article 109e(2) EC tended in principle to be one-off programmes. They had to provide an overview of all the measures that the Member States had to take in order to be able to satisfy the criteria for movement to the third stage by participation in the single currency. The convergence programmes first submitted by the Member States were in most cases updated from time to time; thus they appeared to have attained a periodic rather than a one-off nature.[163] The convergence programmes referred to in Article 7 of Regulation 1466/97 are designed principally, but not exclusively, to give an insight into the medium-term budgetary policy of the Member States and the relevant economic indicators. These latter convergence reports are periodic in nature, having to be submitted first by 1 March 1999 and thereafter updated annually.[164] They are subject to the multilateral surveillance procedure of Article 103 EC. It would be desirable from a terminological standpoint to clarify the distinction between the two types of programmes.

B. The European Monetary Institute (EMI). Unlike in the final stage, monetary policy in the second stage expressly remains in the national hands. The coordination of policies and the preparation for a unified monetary policy and the introduction of what Article 109f(2) EC refers to as the ECU, but will be known as the euro,[165] has been entrusted to the EMI.

The idea of an EMI came into being very late in the negotiations on EMU. The fact that monetary policy would remain in national hands

162. O.J. 1997 L 209/1.
163. Italianer in Andenas *et al.* (eds.), *op. cit.* (see note 55, *supra*) 211 explains that Art. 109e(2)(a) EC only required convergence programmes to be adopted if necessary before the start of the 2nd stage (*i.e.* by 1 January 1994). In practice they continued to be presented by Member States in the context of multilateral surveillance under Art. 103 EC.
164. Reg. 1466/97, Art. 8(1). They must be published, *ibid.*, Art. 2.
165. This political decision was taken at the meeting of the European Council in Madrid in December 1995, Bull. EU 12–1995, points I.2 and I.3. As to the scenario agreed on that occasion, see point I.49. The legal instruments are noted in section 3.3.2, *post* (at the end of the discussion under point D).

during the second stage implied the continuation of the situation within the European Monetary System's existing exchange rate mechanism (ERM), in which the Bundesbank was able autonomously to decide on German monetary policy. Given that the Deutschmark functions as the fulcrum for exchange rate parities in the ERM, German monetary policy determined by the Bundesbank would continue to determine monetary policy in relation to the other currencies participating in the ERM.[166] In an attempt to break through this dominance by the Bundesbank, France in particular sought to strengthen the coordination of monetary policy during the second stage. The fundamental difference in the approaches of France and Germany about the division of accountability for monetary policy in the second stage was disguised but not resolved by the creation of the EMI. The in parts scarcely clear texts of the Treaty provisions on the EMI and its Statute are the result of this approach. The EMI's tasks are set out in Article 109f(2) and (3) EC. They fall into two principal categories. First, coordinating tasks which had been hitherto undertaken by the now dissolved Committee of Governors of the Central Banks of the Member States and the European Monetary Cooperation Fund.[167] Secondly, preparatory tasks relating to the activities designed to ensure a smooth transition to the third stage in which the autonomous ESCB will conduct a unified monetary policy. In the exercise of its coordinating tasks, the EMI is entitled to formulate or submit opinions and recommendations in the field of monetary and exchange rate policy in the second stage.[168] The terms of Article 109e(5) EC are particularly remarkable, as they permit the EMI to publish its opinions and recommendations if it unanimously so decides. An analogy may be drawn here with comparable provisions concerning multilateral surveillance and the excessive deficit procedure.[169] The rather heavier legal intensity of monetary coordination in the second stage is also expressed in Article 109f(6) EC which requires the Council to consult the EMI on any proposed Community act within its field of competence. Given that the life of the EMI will be only a few months by the time this work appears, the specific details of the operation of the EMI may be left aside.[170]

---

166. Hahn (1991) 28 CMLRev. 783 at 786.
167. As to the dissolution of the Committee, see Art. 109f(1) EC, final subpara.; as to the dissolution of the Fund, see Art. 109f(2) EC, 5th indent, and EMI Statute, Arts. 1.3 and 4.1.
168. Art. 109f(4) EC. It may also make recommendations to the monetary authorities of the Member States on the conduct of their monetary policy.
169. Arts. 103(4) and 104c(8) EC.
170. See Art. 109l(2) EC and EMI Statute, Art. 23. See further, EMI, *Role and Functions of the European Monetary Institute* (Frankfurt, 1996); Häde (1994) EuZW 685; Hahn (1995) 32 CMLRev. 1079, and Louis (1993) *Reflets et perspectives de la vie économique* 285. The EMI's annual reports also provide a good overview of its activities.

C. The criteria for transition to the third stage. The rules for transition to the third stage are complex, both in terms of substance and in the institutional sense. Those Member States which sought to qualify to move to the third stage had to satisfy five criteria, the first of which is clearly institutional in nature, the remaining four economic.[171] These criteria are now considered in turn.

(1) The compatibility of national legislation, including the statutes of the national central banks, with the requirements of Articles 107 and 108 EC and the Statute of the ESCB.[172] This concerns the independence of the national central banks, also in legislative terms, in their conduct of monetary policy.[173]

(2) The achievement of a high degree of price stability, apparent from a rate of inflation which is close to that of, at the most, the three best performing Member States in terms of price stability.[174] Although in the literature this condition attracted significantly less attention than the criteria relating to budgetary policy, the substantive significance of this criterion can scarcely be overestimated. The degree to which a Member State succeeds in achieving convergence in nominal price performance is the clearest measure of the adaptation capacity of its economy to the requirements of a completed EMU. An inflation level which is clearly out of step where exchange rate parities are linked together will certainly result in unemployment through a declining competitive position. Thus the ability of a Member State to achieve relative price stability is a reflection of its ability of the economy to achieve the discipline required by a completed EMU.[175]

(3) The sustainability of the government financial position: the absence of an excessive deficit.[176] The precise reference criteria for the application

---

171. See Art. 109j(1) EC. At the 2089th (Ecofin) Council meeting in May 1998 it was made clear that when Greece seeks to move to join the single currency (which it hopes to do by 1 January 2001), the evaluation of whether the derogation will be abrogated will take place according to the criteria of Art. 109j(1) EC, see also Art. 109k(2) EC. As to the evaluation, see the Commission's recommendation and report (see note 131, *supra*). As to the Council's assessment, see Rec. 98/316 (O.J. 1998 L 139/21), and Dec. 98/317 (O.J. 1998 L 139/30).

172. Art. 109j EC, 1st subpara.

173. In the Netherlands this required the repeal of Bankwet 1948, Art. 26, according to which the Minister of Finance could give instructions to the Nederlandsche Bank.

174. Art. 109j(1) EC, 1st subpara., 1st indent. See also the Protocol (No. 6, annexed to the EC Treaty) on the convergence criteria, Art. 1.

175. See Maggiuli (1993) RMC 620 and Hoek and Zalm in Alders *et al.* (eds.), *op. cit.* (see note 55, *supra*) 34.

176. Art. 109j(1), 1st subpara., 2nd indent. As to the determination, see Art. 104c(6) EC, the Excessive Deficit Protocol (No. 5, annexed to the EC Treaty), Art. 2, Regs. 3605/93 (O.J. 1993 L 332/7) and 1467/97 (O.J. 1997 L 209/6, corrigendum O.J. 1998 L 46/20).

of this criterion are those applied in the excessive deficit procedure of Article 104c EC itself, namely that the ratio of the planned or actual government deficit to GDP must not exceed 3% (subject to the suppleness expressly provided for), and the ratio of government debt to GDP must not exceed 60% or be sufficiently diminishing and approaching that level at a satisfactory pace.

The content of this criterion in particular has been controversial among economists.[177] It is pointed out that the sustainability of the government financial position is not only determined by a combination of the deficit and the debt ratio, but also by factors such as the level of national savings and forms of direct and indirect monetary financing. There is indeed a certain link between the 3% deficit criterion and the debt ration criterion of 60%. In the absence of monetary financing (prohibited under Article 104 EC), and with balanced economic growth the debt ratio will tend towards the relationship between government deficit and the growth level of nominal GDP. A maximum debt ratio of 60% is then compatible with a maximum deficit of 3% if the nominal growth in GDP is 5%. A nominal GDP growth of 5% is a reasonable and consistent hypothesis. On the basis of historical indices it may be assumed that actual GDP growth in the Community is about 2% structurally. Applying an inflation percentage of about 3% to that, a structural nominal GDP growth of 5% is attained.[178]

The twin parts of the budgetary transition criterion are clearly very ambitious. There was a serious risk that the majority of Member States would be able to meet the 3% deficit requirement but not the 60% debt ratio requirement. Thus the degree of suppleness set out in Article 104c(1)(b) in particular ('sufficiently diminishing and approaching the reference value at a satisfactory pace') is of considerable political and policy importance. It is submitted that a strict requirement of rapid achievement of far less than the 3% deficit by the end of 1997 is not required by the wording of article 104c(1)(a), nor is it economically desirable. The achievement of that level of deficit by then would under normal circumstances create the conditions for bringing the debt ratio under the 60% level.[179] A stricter interpretation would in periods of less favourable economic conditions lead to an unnecessarily deflationary budgetary policy in much of the Community, which could result in a nominal growth of GDP of much less than 5%. That would mean that despite their considerable political and economic sacrifices, the Member

177. See *e.g.* Buiter (1992) *Economisch Statistische Berichten* 268; Van Hoek and Zalm in Alders *et al.* (eds.), *op. cit.* (see note 55, *supra*) 34;
178. Italianer in Alders *et al.* (eds.), *op. cit.* (see note 55, *supra*) 14, particularly at 24–25; Van den Bempt in Gretschmann (ed.), *op. cit.* (see note 55, *supra*) 245.
179. As to what had been achieved by March 1998 (the date of preparation of the decisions on 1 and 2 May 1998), see Dec. 98/317 (O.J. 1998 L 139/30).

States would be confronted with a continually receding perspective as far as the 60% requirement was concerned.[180] In periods of more favourable economic conditions the Member States may indeed be required to pursue an ambitious budgetary policy.[181] Any mechanical application of the debt ratio requirement should be approached with a great deal of caution, as it could lead to countries which have pursued a disciplined budgetary policy throughout the swings of economic fortune in the first two stages being unable to meet the requirements for transition to the third stage. It might also be that a Member State in which the budget is not structurally in order could be tilted over the threshold to the third stage by a favourable economic climate.

(4) For at least two years a Member State must have observed the normal fluctuation margins provided for by the ERM of the EMS, without devaluing against the currency of any other Member State.[182] Taken literally this criterion was making impossible demands of the Member States at the time. The monetary unrest in September 1992 caused the United Kingdom and Italy to leave the ERM for a time (in the case of the United Kingdom, with little immediate prospect of re-entry), and Spain and Portugal were forced to devalue their currencies sharply. In itself, given the deadlines mentioned in Article 109j(4) EC, this would not be an absolute obstacle for those Member States. But far more serious was the disturbance in the Summer of 1993 which caused the margins of fluctuation within the ERM to be widened to 15%. In the new ERM 2 within which the currencies of the non-participating Member States will have central rates against the Euro, there will be one standard fluctuation band of 15% around the central rates.[183] In fact the Council was rightly more interested in whether there was a pattern of stability in the behaviour of a Member States's currency than whether the two-year period had been strictly met.[184]

---

180. If, *e.g.* a very ambitious restrictive budgetary policy were to result in a 1.5% of GDP deficit, then with a nominal growth in GDP of 2% the 60% debt ratio requirement remains unattainable (1.5% divided by 2% is 0.75, which is a 75% debt ratio).

181. Merely scraping past the 3% level would be insufficient to reduce the debt ratio below 60%.

182. Art. 109j(1) EC, 1st subpara., 3rd indent. See also the Convergence Criteria Protocol (No. 6, annexed to the EC Treaty), Art. 3.

183. O.J. 1997 C 236/5; Bull. EU 6–1997, point I.29 (point 2.1 of the European Council's ERM 2 resolution). This reflects the view that having regard to the intrinsic fragility of exchange rates, the original criteria were unrealistic and effectively hindered rather than assisted in compliance with the objectives of the EMS as a whole. Moreover, devaluation is not necessarily a unilateral act: it may be caused by revaluation by another member of the ERM (this is evident in the reasoning in relation to the revaluation of the Irish pound in March 1998, see Dec. 98/317 (O.J. 1998 L 139/30)). Case-by-case formally agreed fluctuation bands may be narrower than the standard 15% band, see point 2.4 of the European Council's ERM 2 resolution.

184. See Dec. 98/317 (O.J. 1998 L 139/30). Finland joined the ERM in October 1996 and

The requirement of participation in the ERM in order to proceed to the third stage does present a risk that a Member State which satisfies the other criteria but for domestic political reasons does not yet wish to participate in the single currency, would postpone its participation in the ERM.[185]

(5) A Member State had to have achieved durability of convergence and of its participation in the ERM; this has to be reflected in the long-term interest rate levels, so that the average nominal long-term interest rate has to be less than two percentage points in excess of that of, at most, the three best-performing Member States in terms of price stability.[186] This complements the second and third criteria. If in terms of price stability and budgetary policy a Member State is converging, that will also be apparent in the long term interest rate, given the freedom of capital movements. The confidence of the capital markets in the solidity of the Member State's policies is expressed in interest rate terms.[187]

Taking these criteria together, they make far-reaching demands of the national monetary and budgetary policies for transition to the third stage, and it is perhaps unsurprising that recourse was had to a certain degree of flexibility in Decision 98/317[188] in which the Council determined that 11 of the Member states satisfied the criteria. Despite the fact that, as Italianer has put it, there was a 'political' rather than a legal obligation to avoid excessive deficits during the second stage,[189] it has been felt to be none the less an obligation. The same has been true in relation to internal and external monetary policy. All this demonstrates the great coordinating effect of the in fact five criteria.[190] The final subparagraph of Article

its currency had been stable since, Italy only rejoined the ERM in November 1996 and had also been stable in terms of no unilateral devaluation; Greece joined only in March 1998 and was still under pressure. In view of the declaration made on the occasion of the 2089th meeting of the Council in May 1998, it appears that they will take a similar approach in relation to the Greek aspiration to participate in the single currency by 1 January 2001, as has been taken in relation to the evaluations in 1998.

185. Thus, although the two-year period was not (quite) strictly applied in May 1998, as is explained, *post*, as Sweden had never participated in the ERM, and Greece had only just joined it, the unintended escape route was used. See Cloos, *et al.*, *op. cit.* (see note 55, *supra*) 207.

186. Art. 109j(1), 1st subpara., 4th indent. See also the Convergence Criteria Protocol (No. 6, annexed to the EC Treaty), Art. 4. Interest rates are measures on the basis of long-term government bonds or comparable securities, taking into account differences in national definitions, Protocol, *ibid.*

187. Van Hoek and Zalm in Alders *et al.* (eds.), *op. cit.* (see note 55, *supra*) 37–38.

188. O.J. 1998 L 139/30.

189. Italianer in Andenas *et al.*, *op. cit.* (see note 55, *supra*) 196–199. He refers to Art. 109e(4) EC as a political obligation, contrasting it with the legal obligation in Art. 104c(1) EC.

190. Although Art. 109j(1) EC, 2nd subpara., speaks of the four criteria mentioned, it is

109j(1) EC refers, like Article 109e(2) EC, to market integration and to the situation and development of a number of economic factors in the Member States.[191] Thus the connection between monetary and economic policy strategy and market integration in this crucial step towards a completed monetary union is rightly emphasized yet again.

D. The procedure for transition to the third stage. Article 109j EC has in part already been overtaken by events. By 31 December 1996, in accordance with Article 109j(3) EC, the Council, meeting in the composition of the Heads of State or Government, was to decide, by qualified majority, whether a majority of the Member States fulfilled the necessary conditions for the adoption of the single currency, and whether it was appropriate for the Community to enter the third stage. On both points the decision of the Council, meeting in Dublin in December 1996 was negative.[192] The provisions of Article 109j(1), (2), and (4) remained operational. In accordance with Article 109j(1) the Commission and the EMI presented periodic reports on progress made by the Member States in the fulfillment of their obligations regarding the achievement of EMU, examining this by reference to the criteria discussed above.[193] On the basis of these reports the Ecofin Council, acting by a qualified majority on a recommendation from the Commission, assessed for each Member State,[194] whether it fulfilled the conditions for the adoption of the single currency, and whether a majority of the Member States did so. Given the results of the decision in Dublin in December 1996, Article 109j(4) came into operation and the date for the beginning of the third stage was set for 1 January 1999.[195] The Council,

clearly referring to the economic criteria in the four indents of the 1st subpara., ignoring the clear institutional criterion set out in the main body of that 1st subpara.

191. In the case of Art. 109j(1), 2nd subpara., balance of payments on current account, and the development of unit labour costs and other price indices.
192. Dec. 96/736 (O.J. 1996 L 335/48).
193. As to the Commission's recommendations and report in March 1998, see the two parts of *Euro 1999* (see note 131, *supra*). As to the EMI's report in March 1998, see its *Convergence Report* (Frankfurt, 1998).
194. In fact because the United Kingdom and Denmark were clearly not in contention for participation in the single currency from the outset, no evaluation was made in their cases in Rec. 98/316 (O.J. 1998 L 139/21) and in Dec. 98/317 (O.J. 1998 L 139/30).
195. Art. 109j(4) was added at the last minute, primarily at French insistence, during the gestation of the TEU, in order to avoid the procedure of Art. 109j(3) leading to a ever longer postponement of the transition to the third stage, see Cloos *et al.*, *op. cit.* (see note 55, *supra*) 203–205. The importance of Art. 109j(4) also lies in the obligation under the Protocol (No. 10, annexed to the EC Treaty) on the transition to the third stage, which was designed to ensure that those Member States which satisfied the conditions for participation did indeed participate (unless, like the United Kingdom and Denmark, other arrangements applied). Very carefully, Greece and Sweden were found not to satisfy the conditions (Greece was starting to make moves in the right direction, but Sweden very firmly sought to stay outside the single currency, and never participated in the ERM).

meeting in the composition of the Heads of State or Government thus only had to confirm which Member States fulfilled the necessary conditions for the adoption of the single currency. This provision is legally interesting as it creates an *obligation* to integrate monetary policy at variable speeds, even if the majority of the Member States did not meet the conditions for the highest speed. Previously decision-making as to variable-speed integration was always reserved to the political discretion of the Community Institutions. Given that the EC Treaty now no longer permitted the Council any margin of discretion, and the process of forming an EMU acquired an irreversible character, evaluation against the objective criteria for movement to the third stage became extremely important for the first time at Amsterdam in June 1997.[196] Member States which did not yet fulfill the criteria were almost bound to seek some suppleness in the application of the criteria. While Article 109j(4) EC permitted a certain degree of suppleness, it was clear that the margins were tight.[197] In order that the final preparations could be made in time, the decisions were required to be adopted before 1 July 1998.[198] Thus it was that on 1 May 1998 that the Ecofin Council was able to recommend to the Council meeting in the composition of the Heads of State or Government that 11 Member States fulfilled the conditions for the adoption of a single currency, that number also amounting to a majority of the Member States.[199] Accordingly, the Council in that latter composition adopted Decision 98/317[200] on the same day, having duly heard the opinion of the European Parliament.[201] That decision was that Belgium, Germany, Spain, France, Ireland, Italy, Luxembourg, The Netherlands, Austria, Portugal and Finland fulfilled the conditions to participate in the single currency, and thus those Member states will move to the third stage of EMU on 1 January 1999. The neces-

---

196. Pipkorn (1994) 31 CMLRev. 263 at 289–290 rightly observed that the so-called irreversible character of the formation of EMU did not automatically mean that EMU would automatically commence on 1 January 1999. If the Council had been forced to conclude that none or very few of the Member States fulfilled the criteria of Art. 109l(1) EC, transition to the third stage would not have gone ahead.

197. The judgment of the Bundesverfassungsgericht on the TEU in *Brunner* [1994] 1 CMLR 57, should not be forgotten. Of particular importance are the sections of that judgment dealing with the assurance of price stability, which made it plain that Germany should not move to the third stage of EMU if the assurance of price stability were not guaranteed. This was a factor which clearly was going to oblige the German representatives in the Council to evaluate strictly the question of compliance with Art. 109j(1) EC. Indeed, a commitment to price stability was made a precondition for the transfer of functions from the Bundesbank under Grundgesetz, Art. 88, 2nd sentence (as amended by the Law of 21 December, 1992 (BGBl. I S. 2086)).

198. Art. 109j(4) EC.

199. Rec. 98/316 (O.J. 1998 L 139/21).

200. O.J. 1998 L 139/30.

201. In accordance with Art. 109j(2) EC.

sary final regulations relating to the euro were accordingly adopted on 3 May, 1998.[202]

As has been noted above, the criteria permitted a degree of suppleness, but with a view to the possible national reactions, both in legal terms and in terms of market confidence, it was very clear that the degree of suppleness was very limited. The credibility of this decision-making was rightly seen as crucial to the credibility of the completed EMU as a whole. Rightly attention focused on the ability of the Member States to maintain price and exchange rate stability in the longer term, as that is at the end of the day a clearer indicator of the state of the economy than the precise attainment of the 3% deficit requirement, which could be met by shorter-term somewhat artificial techniques.

E. Derogations. The strict convergence criteria of Article 109j EC indeed made it unlikely that all Member States would be able to proceed to the third stage at the same time. For at present Greece and Sweden, and, as a result of the arrangements discussed under point F, below, Denmark, the following consequences result from their being 'Member States with a derogation'.[203]

(1) They must continue to make the necessary efforts to qualify for transition to the third stage.[204] Thus the provisions as to the coordination of economic policy, including the so-called 'political' obligation that they must endeavour to avoid excessive deficits apply with full force, save that they will not be subject to the notice regime of Article 104c(9) or the sanctions regime of Article 104c(11) EC. In view of the connection between the coordination of economic policies in general and the completed EMU, it must be assumed that those Member States which can adjust their economic policies and budgetary policies towards that coordination will in time be able to make the transition to the third stage as a matter of course.[205]

(2) At least once every two years, or at the request of at present Greece,

---

202. Regs. 974/98 on the introduction of the euro (O.J. 1998 L 139/1) and 975/98 (O.J. 1998 L 139/6) on the denominations and technical specifications for euro coins for circulation. Previously the Council had adopted Reg. 1103/97 (O.J. 1997 L 162/1) dealing with myriad aspects of the introduction of the euro.

203. Under Art. 109k(3) EC. In respect of Arts. 109c(4) and 109m EC (review by the Economic and Financial Committee and exchange rate policy continuing to be a matter of common concern, respectively) the United Kingdom is treated as if it were a Member State with a derogation, Protocol (No. 11, annexed to the EC Treaty) on certain provisions relating to the United Kingdom), Art. 6. See Cloos et al., op. cit. (see note 55, supra) 224–226 and Smits (1992) SEW 702 at 729–731.

204. This follows from Art. 3a(2) EC in conjunction with Art. 109k(2) and (3) EC and the Protocol (No. 10, annexed to the EC Treaty) on the transition to the third stage.

205. Van Hoek and Zalm, in Alders et al., (eds.), op. cit. (see note 55, supra) 37–38 point out that those Member States which miss the first boat could suffer a loss of reputa-

Sweden or Denmark,[206] the Commission and the ECB report to the Council on the progress made by those Member States in the fulfillment of their obligations regarding the achievement of EMU. The procedure for deciding whether the existing derogation in respect of any or all of them should be abrogated follows that applied in respect of the first wave in 1998.[207]

(3) The most important provisions of the third stage do not apply to those Member States with a derogation.[208] This means in particular that the notice and sanctions procedures do not apply to such Member States;[209] nor do various provisions relating to the tasks and powers of the ESCB and the ECB in the realm of internal and external monetary policy, and the provisions on external monetary and exchange rate policy set out in Article 109 EC.[210]

(4) Member States with a derogation are obliged to ensure that by 1 January 1999 their national legislation is compatible with the Treaty and the ESCB Statute, which means that the independence of their central banks must be ensured, both in terms of legislation and the bank's statutes.[211] The obligation to comply with the most important institutional provisions, which are set out in Articles 107 and 108 EC is designed to ensure that the final transition to the third stage can be made without difficulty at the desired time. It also has a certain budgetary discipline effect on the national budgetary authorities.

(5) Member States with a derogation have no voting rights in the Council when decisions have to be taken on the basis of Treaty provisions which are inapplicable to them. If a qualified majority is required, then by way of derogation from the normal requirements, it is deemed achieved with two-thirds of the votes of the representatives of the Member States without a derogation, weighted in the normal manner.

---

tion, which would make it more difficult to satisfy the criteria later on. This is undoubtedly what a number of Member States whose participation even in late 1997 might have seemed in doubt feared, hence there was some discussion about possibly postponing the transition to the third stage so that they would not more or less permanently be fixed with a derogation. In the event, the final decision that 11 Member States satisfied the criteria could be taken without undue stress.

206. Or if the United Kingdom gives notice that it intends to move to the third stage, see, further, point F, *post*.

207. *I.e.* that set out in Art. 109j(1) and (2) EC, see Art. 109k(2) EC. The abrogation procedure for Denmark will be initiated only at its request, Protocol (No. 12, annexed to the EC Treaty) on certain provisions relating to Denmark, Art. 4.

208. Art. 109k(3) EC.

209. *I.e.* Art. 104c(9) and (10) EC.

210. See Art. 109k(3) EC.

211. Arts. 107 and 108 EC. These are not provisions excluded by Art. 109k(3) EC, so they apply to all Member States (save the United Kingdom, although that Member State has in fact started the process of amending its legislation governing the Bank of England).

Mutatis mutandis, the same approach applies when unanimity is required.[212]

(6) The national central banks of Member States with a derogation do participate in the ESCB, but for obvious reasons the most important provisions of the ESCB Statute do not apply to them. Their shareholdings in the ECB are in effect frozen.[213]

(7) The situation in which most Member States will move to the third stage on 1 January 1999, but a few will not yet join them, means that substantive and institutional provisions have to be provided, in order to maintain the present level of coordination of monetary policy between the first wave Member States and the rest.

For this purpose a temporary third decision-making body of the ECB is established;[214] it will continue to exist as long as there is a Member States with a derogation.[215] This consists of the President and Vice-presidents of the ECB and the Governors of all the national central banks of the Member States.[216] It is entrusted with the coordinating tasks which the EMI carried out in the second stage,[217] although that coordination will be between on the one hand those Member States which have moved to the third stage, acting *en bloc*,[218] and on the other hand each of those Member States with a derogation separately. The latter still possess their monetary policy powers in accordance with their national legislation.[219] The coming into being of the single currency in these multi-speed circumstances has in fact made it necessary to create a new-style EMS, which is known as ERM 2.[220] In ERM 2 the non-participating Member States will have to regard their exchange rate policy as a matter of common interest.[221]

---

212. Art. 109k(5) EC.
213. ESCB and ECB Statute, Arts. 43–49 (their share subscribed capital only has to be paid up when the derogation in respect of their Member State has been abrogated, *ibid.*, Art. 49).
214. ESCB and ECB Statute, Art. 45.1.
215. See Art. 109l(3) EC.
216. ESCB and ECB Statute, Art. 45.2
217. *Ibid.*, Art. 44.
218. These Member States are becoming known as the euro area, see the European Council's ERM2 Resolution (O.J. 1997 C 236/5; Bull. EU 6–1997, point I.29).
219. See also Art. 109k(6) EC, which provides that Arts. 109h (balance of payments difficulties) and 109i EC (precautionary measures in sudden balance of payments crises) continue to apply for Member States with a derogation. Such difficulties could always cause those non-participating Member States to adopt particular measures, including exchange rate adjustments.
220. See the European Council's ERM2 Resolution, O.J. 1997 C 236/5; Bull. EU 6–1997, point I.29.
221. Art. 109m(2), which applies Art. 109m(1) by analogy. This obligation also applies to the United Kingdom, which for these purposes is treated as a Member States with a derogation, Protocol (No. 11, annexed to the EC Treaty) on certain provisions relating to the United Kingdom, Art. 6.

From this requirement, and from the requirement in the third indent of the first subparagraph of Article 109j(1) EC that, the normal fluctuation margins of the ERM (henceforth ERM 2) must be observed for at least two years without unilateral devaluation against the currency of any other Member State, it can be deduced that the non-participating Member States will have to endeavour to achieve exchange rate stability against the euro. It is submitted that this combination means that the Member States with a derogation will have to avoid competition-distorting devaluations.[222] The ERM 2 resolution does, however, make it plain that participation in ERM 2 is voluntary for the Member States outside the euro area.[223]

There can be no doubt that the complex institutional and substantive consequences of the establishment of a monetary union at varying speeds will make the functioning of the European Union as such more difficult. In such a situation those Member States with a derogation will be represented in the Council, but they will have no vote on important matters. They will also not be represented at all in the organs of the ECB (although the General Council of the ESCB will provide a forum for coordination and consultation), but in the Commission, the European Parliament, the Court of Justice and in the Court of Auditors, they will participate fully, even on matters relating to EMU. If the multi-speed approach lasts for a long time, this may well be a cause of tension between the ECB and the Community Institutions. The tension will certainly not be reduced by the French government's pressure during the meetings in Amsterdam in June 1997 for an 'economic government' in the form of strengthened coordination of policies between the participating Member States.[224] This would, in the French view, take place outside the normal institutional framework of the Community. Although there appeared to be serious reserves about the French proposal, it can indeed be seen in a weakened form in the Conclusions of the Presidency after the European Council meeting at Amsterdam in June 1997.[225] These political initiatives demonstrate yet again how regrettable it is that the United Kingdom and Denmark obtained at Maastricht the possibility of in effect a permanent derogation from participating in the single currency. It enabled other Member States to feel it legitimate to seek to create specific coordination mechanisms outside the framework of the EC Treaty itself.

---

222. The repeal of the old obligation in Art. 107(2) EEC which concerned such exchange rate alterations does not affect this legal duty. See, further, the ERM2 resolution (O.J. 1997 C 236/5; Bull. EU 6–1997, point I.29.
223. *Ibid.* (point 1.6 of the resolution).
224. See *European Economy* No. 64 (Brussels, Luxembourg, 1997) 37–40, particularly at 38.
225. Bull. EU 6–1997, point I.5 (at p. 10).

F. The exceptions for the United Kingdom and Denmark. By way of derogation from Article 109k(2) EC and the Protocol on the transition to the
third stage,[226] the United Kingdom negotiated at Maastricht a position in
which it is not obliged or required to move to the third stage without a
decision to do so by its government and parliament.[227] The United
Kingdom will notify the Council whether it intends to move to the third
stage before the Council makes its assessment under Article 109j(2) EC.[228]
Given that the United Kingdom notified the Council that it did not intend
to proceed to the third stage on 1 January 1999, some of the provisions
applicable to Member States with a derogation apply to it,[229] but the
exceptions in fact go further than those applicable to the other non-participating Member States. The most important further-reaching exceptions are
that the United Kingdom need not take steps to guarantee the independence of the Bank of England (although it is in fact doing so), it retains its
powers in the field of monetary policy according to national law, the prohibition of excessive deficits does not apply (although the so-called political
obligation to endeavour to avoid excessive deficits does), and the compulsory consultation of the ECB also does not apply.[230]

Although the origins of the special Protocol relating to the United
Kingdom were primarily determined by domestic considerations, both its
content and consequences are more than symbolic.[231] Thus the exemption
from the prohibitions of monetary financing and excessive deficits may in
theory seriously burden the coordination of the United Kingdom's
budgetary policy with a view to fulfillment of the conditions for transition
to the third stage. In practice the United Kingdom is endeavouring to
satisfy the substantive requirements in good time, so that the United
Kingdom government may use to the maximum the freedom of manoeuvre
which the Protocol accords it.

Denmark also has an special position, having an exemption from
participation in the third stage.[232] The Danish government notified the
Council that it would not participate in the third stage from 1 January
1999,[233] so (as in the case of the United Kingdom) no assessment was

---

226. Protocol (No. 10), annexed to the EC Treaty.
227. Protocol (No. 11, annexed to the EC Treaty) on certain provisions relating to the
   United Kingdom, Preamble, 1st recital.
228. *Ibid.*, Art. 1.
229. See *ibid.*, Art. 6.
230. *Ibid.*, Arts. 5, 8 and 11.
231. Cloos *et al.*, *op. cit.* (see note 55, *supra*) 211.
232. Protocol (No. 12, annexed to the EC Treaty) on certain provisions relating to
   Denmark. Arts. 2, 4 and 5 thereof speak of 'the exemption'.
233. This notification occurred during the European Council at Edinburgh in December
   1992 (Bull. EC 12–1992, point I.34). As a result of the compromise agreed on that
   occasion (see also point I.42), the Danish people in a second referendum finally ratified the TEU. This Edinburgh compromise implicitly left it open to Denmark to participate at a later stage, as no amendment was made to the Danish Protocol. See, in

made by the Council under Article 109j(2) EC in 1998. The effect of the exemption is 'that all Articles and provisions of this Treaty and the Statute of the ESCB referring to a derogation shall be applicable to Denmark.'[234]

3.3.3 The third stage: the single currency

A. Main features of the system. The transition from the second to the third stage means that the 11 Member States which are participating in the single currency[235] will lose their powers in the field of monetary policy on 1 January 1999. Likewise, the arrangements for the coordination of their national monetary policies discussed in section 2, above, will cease to apply. Instead there will be a uniform monetary policy for the single currency, the euro. In order to shape and implement such a policy the European System of Central Banks (ESCB) and the European Central Bank will come into being immediately after 1 July 1998, now that the Executive Board of the ECB has been appointed.[236] The ESCB is a system of finally 16 central banks: the 15 national central banks of the Member States and the new ECB.[237] The ECB has legal personality, but the ESCB as such does not.[238] The national central banks retain their own legal personality under national law. In case in which the EC Treaty or the ESCB Statute confer powers or place obligations on the ESCB, that means on all the legal persons forming part of the ESCB. Within the ESCB the policy-making powers are primarily in the hands of the ECB itself, although it has recourse as far as appropriate and possible to the national central banks to carry out operations which form part of the ESCB's tasks.[239] This latter point does not, though, form part of the application of the principle of subsidiarity. That principle, insofar as it can be enforced, deals with the allocation of competence among different autonomous administrative layers. This is not at all the case in relation to the ESCB, as the implementation of monetary policy operations by the national central banks is a form of geographically

---

the same sense, Curtin and Van Ooik (1993) SEW 675 at 684. The procedure under Art. 109k(2) EC for the abrogation of the exemption will only be initiated at Danish request, and if the exemption status is abrogated, the Protocol will cease to apply, Protocol, Arts. 4 and 5.

234. *Ibid.*, Art. 2. Thus Denmark was mentioned under point E, *ante*, dealing with Member States with a derogation.

235. See section 3.3.2, *ante*, under point E.

236. Art. 109l(1) EC. See Dec. 98/345 (O.J. 1998 L 154/33), adopted following Rec. 98/318 (O.J. 1998 L 139/36).

237. Art. 106(1) EC.

238. Art. 106(2) EC.

239. ESCB Statute, Art. 12.1.

deconcentrated administration, for which the system as a whole remains responsible.[240]

The substantive and institutional provisions in the EC Treaty on monetary policy and the ESCB are characterized by their great detail. They are in part reproduced and in part worked out further in the ESCB Statute.[241] The extensive nature of the rules in the EC Treaty in this area confirms the importance that the drafters of those provisions attached to the objectives of the common monetary policy, the autonomy of the ESCB and its component parts, as well as to the powers of the ECB.

Through the very detailed rules in the EC Treaty and in the ESCB Statute, the guarantees for the autonomy of the system are much more firmly anchored than those of the Bundesbank which are often regarded as sacrosanct. But the autonomy of the Bundesbank, like that of the Nederlandsche Bank are contained in an ordinary law, and thus are subject to the political views of the normal legislator.[242] The ECB and the other bodies which comprise the ESCB have their autonomy and their powers directly anchored in the EC Treaty and the ESCB Statute itself, which forms a very solid legislative basis, a hard constitution, in view of the strenuous requirements for an amendment of the EC Treaty laid down in Article N TEU.[243] This institutionally firmly anchored position has consequences which should not be underestimated for the autonomous exercise of its authority by the ECB. Member States which pursue insufficient discipline in their budgetary policies may count on the Community monetary authority being not very willing to facilitate such conduct. The ECB is well-protected against national political pressure through the institutional guarantees which the EC Treaty itself affords. It is not, however, entirely without risks. Experience in Member States which have a strongly autonomous central bank, such as Germany and The Netherlands, demonstrate that even an autonomous monetary authority must take account in its policy-making of the fact that the relationship between monetary policy and economic policy in general cannot be ignored without peril.[244] Major tensions in policy preferences between the monetary

240. In the same sense, Cloos et al., op. cit. (see note 55, supra) 221; Hahn (1991) 28 CMLRev. 783 at 799, contra, Smits (1992) SEW 702 at 717.
241. Protocol (No. 3, annexed to the EC Treaty) on the Statute of the ESCB and of the ECB.
242. Hahn (1991) 28 CMLRev. 783 at 803–810.
243. See Gormley and De Haan (1996) 21 CMLRev. 95 at 101. A simplified amendment procedure for certain provisions of the ESCB Statute is permitted, Art. 106(5) EC and Protocol, Art. 41.1.
244. National central bank autonomy used until recently to be more the exception than the rule in the Member States, see Louis (ed.), Vers un système européen des banques centrales (Brussels, 1989) 131–302. See, generally, Amtenbrink, The Democratic Account-ability of Central Banks (Diss, Groningen, 1998) and literature referred to therein; Goodhart, The Central Bank and the Financial System (Basingstoke, 1995), and Hasse, The European Central Bank: Perspectives for a Further Development of the European Monetary System (Gütersloh, 1990).

authority and the bodies which are politically responsible for general economic policy are undesirable in the national sphere, and this applies *a fortiori* for EMU, in which such tensions may easily take on the form of a conflict between the ECB, which will be responsible for monetary policy, and national governments. Those areas in which the ECB and the ESCB will have to defend their authority in fact embrace much less policy freedom than might be thought on a reading of the text of the Treaty.[245] Account must also be taken of the fact that the primary objective of price stability, set out in Articles 3a(2) and 105(1) EC, certainly does not correspond to the monetary traditions of *all* Member States.

B. The main objectives of the ESCB and the ECB.[246] The monetary policy of the ESCB has as its primary objective the maintenance of price stability.[247] In so far as such action is compatible with that primary objective, the ESCB is to support the general economic policies in the Community with a view to contributing to the achievement of the objectives of the Community as laid down in Article 2 EC.[248] This phrasing paraphrases Article 12 of the German Bundesbankgesetz 1957. Here more than anywhere else the central political exchange in the EMU part of the amendments made to the EC Treaty by the TEU is apparent. The German government was indeed prepared to surrender the Bundesbank's domination in monetary affairs, but required and obtained as counterpart that the hierarchy of objectives in the Bundesbankgesetz should be set out and guaranteed in the EC Treaty itself and in the ESCB Statute.[249] The commitment to 'the principle of an open market economy with free competition, favouring an efficient allocation of resources' in the last sentence of Article 105(1) EC repeats literally the last sentence of Article 102a EC. From the policy point of view this is not without significance, as major discrepancies in general policy orientation of an ordopolitical nature

245. The Bundesverfassungsgericht in *Brunner* [1994] 1 CMLR 57 made it clear that Germany would have to withdraw from EMU if the ECB did not hold on to its primary objective of maintaining price stability, see Herdegen (1994) 31 CMLRev. 235 at 247.
246. See Amtenbrink, *op. cit.* (see note 244, *supra*); Andenas *et al.* (eds.), *op. cit.* (see note 55, *supra*); Mehnert-Meland, *Central Bank to the European Union* (London, 1995); Smits, *The European Central Bank – Institutional Aspects* (The Hague, 1997); Brentford (1998) 47 ICLQ 75; De Beaufort Wijnholds and Hoogduin in De Beaufort Wijnholds *et al.* (eds.), *A framework for Monetary stability* (Dordrecht, 1994) 75; Gormley and De Haan (1996) 21 ELRev. 95; Harden in Gretschmann (ed.), *op. cit.* (see note 55, *supra*) 149; Heim (1994) 19 CMLRev. 48; Louis (1998) 35 CMLRev. 33; Slot in Curtin and Heukels (eds.), *op. cit.* (see note 55, *supra*) 229.
247. Art. 105(1) EC, ESCB Statute, Art. 2.
248. *Ibid.*
249. And, for good measure, it is also constitutionally guaranteed in Germany as a condition for the transfer of powers, see Grundgesetz, Art. 88, 2nd sentence, as amended by the Law of 21 December 1992 (BGBl. I S. 2086).

between monetary policy and economic policy are unsustainable in the long term. Thus a general economic policy which is more interventionist and protectionist in nature will almost inevitably result in flanking, protecting external monetary policy. In the history of French and Spanish monetary policy there are clear examples of this connection. The reverse is also imaginable. A monetary policy which uses strongly *dirigiste* instruments such as selective currency policy is over time incompatible with an open market economy.

The *tasks* of the ESCB and of the ECB may be divided into principal and ancillary tasks. The principal tasks are set out in Articles 105(2) and 105a EC. These are set out below.

(1) Defining and implementing the monetary policy of the Community.[250] In accordance with the principle set out in the final sentence of Article 105(1) EC, monetary policy must be market-oriented through open market and credit operations, and complementary thereto, the holding of minimum reserves.[251] For the use of other, non-market oriented, policy instruments which directly influence the creation of money by credit institutions, and fall within the limits permitted by the Council under the procedure of Article 106(6) EC, a majority of two-thirds of the Governing Council of the of the ECB is required.[252]

(2) Conducting foreign exchange operations consistent with Article 109 EC.[253] This task is closely linked with the powers of the ECB in external monetary policy, and is considered further, below.

(3) Holding and managing the official foreign reserves of the Member States.[254]

(4) The promotion of the smooth operation of payment systems.[255] The central banks have gradually started to act in relation to the quality and reliability of payment systems, and it was obvious that in a completed EMU this function should be entrusted to the ECB.

(5) The exclusive right to authorize the issue of banknotes within the Community; they are issued by the ECB and the national central banks, and will be the sole notes having the status of legal tender within the Member States participating in the single currency.[256] The

---

250. Art. 105(2) EC, 1st indent; ESCB Statute, Art. 3.1, 1st indent.
251. ESCB Statute, Arts. 18 and 19.
252. *Ibid.*, Art. 20.
253. Art. 105(2) EC, 2nd indent; ESCB Statute, Art. 3.1, 2nd indent.
254. Art. 105(2) EC, 3rd indent, ESCB Statute, Art. 3.1, 3rd indent. See, further, *ibid.*, Art. 30. This is without prejudice to the holding and management by the governments of Member States of foreign exchange working balances, Art. 105(3) EC, ESCB Statute, Art. 3.2.
255. Art. 105(1) EC, 4th indent; ESCB Statute, Art. 3.1, 4th indent. See further, *ibid.*, Art. 22.
256. Art. 105a(1) EC, ESCB Statute, Art. 16 (in conjunction with Art. 109k(3) EC). See

ECB also approves the volume of the coins which the Member States may issue.[257] This task is a direct result of the establishment of the single currency from the beginning of the third stage on 1 January 1999.[258] As a result of the first paragraph of Article 109g EC, the currency composition of the ECU basket was frozen with the entry into force of the TEU. On the transition to the third stage, the Council, acting by unanimity of the participating Member States, on a proposal from the Commission, will fix the conversion rates at which their currencies are to be irrevocably fixed and at which irrevocably fixed rate the euro will be substituted for those currencies; the euro will then become a currency in its own right.[259] A comparable procedure is followed for those Member States which move to join the single currency at a later date.[260]

The technical problems which may arise in the move to a single currency should not be underestimated, and account is taken of them in Article 109l(4) EC and Article 52 of the ESCB Statute, both of which envisage the Council taking such other measures as are necessary for the rapid introduction of the euro as the single currency of the participating Member States. Thus, as has been indicated above, preparations have started well ahead of the deadlines.[261] Technical problems could also arise if the definition of the euro used in private contracts were to be different from that chosen for the euro

---

Reg. 974/98 on the introduction of the euro (O.J. 1998 L 139/1). The euro will be legal tender from 1 January 2002. The Council had earlier adopted Reg. 1103/97 (O.J. 1997 L 162/1) dealing with the more urgent myriad aspects of the introduction of the euro.

257. Art. 105a(2) EC. As to the denominations and specifications, see Reg. 975/98 (O.J. 1998 L 139/6).

258. See Arts. 3a and 109l(4) EC. See also the declaration by the Ecofin Council and the Ministers on 1 May 1998 (O.J. 1998 L 139/28) and the Joint Communiqué of 3 may 1998 (O.J. 1998 C 160/1).

259. Art. 109l(4) EC, see also Art. 109 EC, 2nd para. The national currencies of the participating Member States will disappear on 1 January 2002, when the euro becomes legal tender. The operation fixing irrevocably the conversion rates may not itself modify the external value of the euro, Art. 109l(4) EC. There was an additional problem as Art. 109l(4) provides for measures to be adopted on the starting date of the third stage. From the viewpoint of legal certainty for existing financial contracts, it was essential that the necessary measures had to be adopted sooner; hence Reg. 1103/97 (O.J. 1997 L 162/1), based on Art. 235 EC, contained the necessary provisions. See, further, the Joint Communiqué of 3 May 1998 (O.J. 1998 C 160/1) and Dunnett (1996) 33 CMLRev. 1133. The risk of such a detailed regulation of monetary union in the EC Treaty itself possibly not offering solutions for all the practical problems to be solved had thus already materialized before monetary union started. In Case T-207/97 *Berthu v. Council* [1998] ECR II-nyr (12 March 1998) the Court of First Instance rejected as manifestly inadmissible a challenge to Reg. 1103/97 attacking the replacement of references to the ECU by references to the euro.

260. Art. 109l(5) EC.

261. See also Smits (1992) SEW 702 at 724–726.

at the start of the third stage.[262] Given that only the leading group of 11 Member States will actually make a start with the single currency, the composition of the euro basket will in any event be different from the weighted average of the currencies of all Member States.

The EC Treaty and the ESCB Statute also prescribe the following ancillary tasks for the ESCB and the ECB.

(1) In most Member States prudential supervision of credit institutions is entrusted to the national central bank (although the Bank of England is to lose that task). Although the Committee of Governors of Central banks has proposed that prudential supervision be included among the ESCB's principal tasks, the drafters of the TEU declined to follow this advice, as it could result in complications in those Member States in which supervision is entrusted to another authority.[263] Given that the activities of now 11 national supervisors within one market calls for a certain attuning, the ESCB contributes to the smooth conduct of prudential supervision policies pursued by the competent authorities of the participating Member States.[264] There is all the more reason for this complementary coordinating power for the ESCB, as the formal and substantive standards for prudential supervision are already substantially harmonized by the Second Banking Directive.[265] This complementary task may be extended and strengthened by the Council, acting unanimously.[266]

(2) The ECB also has advisory powers. It must be consulted on any proposed Community act within its fields of competence, and by national authorities regarding any draft legislative provision in its field of competence.[267]

(3) The collection of financial statistics is not expressly mentioned in the EC Treaty itself, but Article 5.1 of the ESCB Statute confers such

---

262. See Louis and De Lloneux (1991) 28 CMLRev. 335; hence the adoption of Reg. 1103/97 (O.J. 1997 L 162/1). See Wölker (1996) 33 CMLRev. 1117.
263. See De Swaan in Bakker *et al.* (eds.), *Monetary Stability through International Cooperation* (Dordrecht, 1994) 323, and the contributions by Andenas and Hadjiemmanuil, and by Schoenmaker in Andenas *et al.*, *op. cit.* (see note 55, *supra*) 375 and 421.
264. Art. 105(5) EC; ESCB Statute, Art. 25.1
265. Dir. 89/646 (O.J. 1989 L 386/1, as amended; codification proposed, COM (97) 706 Final).
266. Art. 105(6) EC; ESCB Statute, Art. 25.2.
267. Art. 105(4) EC. In the latter case this is subject to the limits and under the conditions laid down by the Council under Art. 106(6) EC; the consequence of this right to be consulted by the national authorities is that from 1 January 1999 the legislative authorities of *all* the Member States except the United Kingdom (Protocol (No. 11, annexed to the EC Treaty) on certain provisions relating to the United Kingdom, Art. 5) must consult the ECB on all national legislative initiatives which concern monetary policy, movement of payments, prudential supervision and financial statistics.

power. This is in most Member States a task of the central bank, which needs the information for conducting national monetary policy. Again, it was obvious that this power should pass to the ECB in respect of the participating Member States from the outset of the third stage; the ECB will be assisted in this by the relevant national central banks.

C. External monetary policy: exchange rate policy. Prior to the implosion of the Bretton Woods system of fixed exchange rates, it was customary at national level to make a clear division of powers between internal and external monetary policy.[268] For internal monetary policy the central bank was the primary competent authority, whereas for external monetary policy primacy lay in the hands of the political authorities. The system of fluctuating exchange rates put an end to this separation, at least after the introduction of the EMS, for exchange rate parities with third countries' currencies. A monetary policy aimed at national price stability will well nigh unavoidably lead to a relatively strong currency in the international monetary context. Conversely, fluctuations in international exchange rate parities may affect the objective of price stability in the national context. Moreover, in a system of floating exchange rates, formal decisions about fixing the exchange rate are no longer necessary, as the markets decide. It is against this background that the at first sight hardly clear provisions of Article 109 EC must be read.

Article 109(1) EC deals with the possibility that in the international context bilateral or multilateral exchange rate agreements may again be concluded. It is a *lex specialis* as far as Article 228 EC on the conclusion of international agreements is concerned. Article 109(1) EC deals with two distinct situations: first, decision-making with a view to the conclusion of 'formal agreements' on an exchange rate system for (now) the euro in relation to non-Community currencies; and secondly, decision-making on the central rates of the ECU within such an exchange rate system. It reflects its difficult gestation and leaves a number of questions of interpretation unresolved.[269] These are now examined in turn.

– Although the Council has competence to conclude the relevant agreements, the drafters of these provisions sought to establish the influence of the ECB in the matter; thus the Council may act unanimously either on a recommendation from the ECB, or on a recommendation from the Commission and after consulting the ECB in an endeavour to reach a consensus consistent with the objective of

---

268. In Dutch law this was expressed on the one hand in the Bankwet 1948 and the Wet toezicht kredietwezen for internal monetary policy, and on the other hand in the Wet inzake de wisselkoers van de gulden in respect of external monetary policy.
269. See Cloos *et al.*, *op. cit.* (see note 55, *supra*) 226–228.

price stability. This could be taken to mean that consultation of the ECB with a view to reaching that consensus is necessary only if the Council is deciding on a recommendation from the Commission.[270] It may also be read as meaning that such consultation is always necessary in order to ensure that the Council acts in accordance with the objective of price stability which the ECB is bound to maintain.[271]

– Although grammatical arguments support the first interpretation, it is submitted that on grounds of the system the second interpretation is to be preferred. If the Council, acting on a recommendation from the ECB, were simply to be able to ignore the content of the recommendation, without being obliged to seek a consensus with the ECB, the guarantee afforded by the ECB's involvement is devoid of purpose.

– On the basis that the Council must always consult the ECB, prior to concluding an agreement, the question of the nature of this obligation arises. At first sight it resembles a simple procedural requirement.[272] Yet, if the Council were to regard itself as free to conclude the agreements it wished, once it had consulted the ECB, the compatibility with the objective of price stability, which is expressly required, loses its purpose. Compatibility is required in order to protect the ECB in the exercise of its primary task. This compatibility leads, it is submitted, to the conclusion that the consensus requirement is a substantive requirement: where the objective of price stability is involved the Council may act only in consensus with the ECB.

– The use of the term 'formal agreements' may be traced back to the desire of the drafters of the provisions to delimit the scope of Article 109(1) EC more clearly from that of Article 109(2) EC. The agreements are ones which result in concrete legal obligations for the parties. Probably *ex abundanti cautela* a Declaration (No. 8), adopted by the Conference on the occasion of the signature of the TEU, on Article 109 EC, emphasizes that the use of the term 'formal agreements' in Article 109(1) EC is not intended to create a new category of international agreement within the meaning of Community law.[273]

– Although the term 'exchange rate system' in Article 109(1) EC gives a different impression, the legal history of this term of this provision shows that they may be bilateral or multilateral, so that, for example, an agreement between the United States and the Community on mutual fixed parities between the dollar and the euro would be in theory possible as a result of this provision.

270. *Ibid.* at 227.
271. Pipkorn (1994) 31 CMLRev. 263 at 285.
272. Cloos *et al., op. cit.* (see note 55, *supra*) 227.
273. The declaration may be found in O.J. 1992 C 191/99.

Article 109(2) EC concerns the present situation of floating exchange rates in the international sphere. The Council may formulate 'general orientations' for exchange rate policy in relation to these third currencies, which are without prejudice to the primary objective of the ESCB to maintain price stability. This time the Council acts by qualified majority, again with similar involvement of the Commission and the ECB to that applicable in Article 109(1) EC. It is certainly unclear what the concept of 'general orientations' embraces; it is also unclear what the degree of binding force is of the acts in which those orientations are set out.[274] Finally, it is also unclear who has to decide whether the 'general orientations' are compatible with the objective of price stability. It is no coincidence that Article 109(2) EC raises so many legal questions. It is based on a Franco-German compromise. German monetary policy tradition since exchange rates started to float, has been to leave monetary policy entirely in the hands of the Bundesbank, whereas in the more interventionist-oriented French policy tradition, influencing exchange rate parities has always remained an element of economic policy. The final compromise, it appears, will have few direct consequences policy practice. It is a reminder for the ECB to take into account the economic consequences of exchange rate movements, whereas the few concrete results of the heavy decision-making procedure will not tempt the Member States to entice the Commission to take an initiative leading to the formulation of 'general orientations.'

The difference in the Franco-German views over the respective powers of the Council and the ECB as to exchange rate policy in a system of floating exchange rates caused renewed discussions during the run-up to the European Council at Amsterdam in June 1997. Finally these discussions resulted in an invitation from the European Council to the Ecofin Council, the Commission and the EMI to investigate how Article 109 EC, and in particular Article 109(2) EC could be effectively implemented.[275] The requisite study, which was presented at the European Council's meeting in Luxembourg in December 1997, did not produce much: any more detailed text concerning the compromise contained in Article 109(2) EC is a more detailed compromise which leaves the initial standpoints carefully intact.[276]

Article 109(3) EC sets out a procedure, derogating from Article 228 EC, for decision-making with a view to the negotiation of agreements concerning monetary or foreign exchange matters in international fora. It

---

274. It is clear in any case that the legally binding force is less than the directives which the Council was entitled to give to the Board of Governors of the old European Monetary Cooperation Fund under Reg. 907/73 (O.J. 1973 L 89/2), Art. 2.
275. See (1997) *European Economy* No. 64, p. 38 and Bull. EU 6–1997, point I.5 (at p. 10).
276. See Bull. EU 12–1997, point I.9 (para. 45 of the Conclusions of the Presidency), which notes that 'it is understood that general exchange policy guidelines *vis-à-vis* one or more non-Community currencies will be formulated only in exceptional circumstances in the light of the principles and policies defined in the Treaty.'

also provides that any agreements resulting from such negotiations will be binding on the Community Institutions, on the ECB, and on the Member States.

Article 109(4) EC is designed to govern the division of powers between the Community and its Member States in international fora for issues which are of particular relevance for EMU. In so far as the conclusion of formal exchange rate agreements is concerned, unanimity is required;[277] the same applies to decisions as to representation of the Community. But the contents of positions to be adopted at international level are to be decided by the Council acting by qualified majority, on a proposal from the Commission and after consulting the ECB. In the completed EMU a complication arises as in the sphere of monetary policy competence (as regards participating Member States) is exclusively that of the Community, whereas as a result of Article 103 EC it is the Member States which are primarily competent for economic policy. Article 109(5) EC does oblige Member States to take account of Community competence and Community agreements as regards EMU when they negotiate in international bodies and conclude international agreements.[278]

On the basis of the Court's case-law, it can be argued that an intensive and effective coordination of national economic policies by the Community would confer exclusive competence upon it to act externally. In practice much will depend on the intensity of the coordinating involvement of the Community, whether it will *de facto* bring with it a transfer of national powers in the field of general economic policy to the Community. In view of the wording of Article 103(1) EC and the nature of the multilateral surveillance governed by Article 103 EC, it is submitted that there is unlikely to be any question of a speedy implied transfer of competence from the Member States to the Community.[279] The declaration that Article 109(5) EC does not affect the principles resulting from Case 22/70 *Commission v. Council*[280] thus appears superfluous.[281]

Even though it appears obvious that where actual monetary policy is involved, Community competence should be accepted, the questions how far such competence extends and which Institution(s) should represent the Community are certainly politically still very controversial, giving rise to a

277. Art. 109(4) EC in conjunction with Art. 109(1) EC.
278. Art. 109(4) hides myriad political complications, such as the question whether the Member States which participate in the G-7 (now G-8) discussions may continue to act in that forum, and, if so, what room they will give to the Community there. Questions of IMF membership and participation will also need to be resolved. As to the latter, see Martha (1993) 30 CMLRev. 749.
279. In the same sense, Slot in Curtin and Heukels (eds.), *op. cit.* (see note , *supra*) 240–241; *contra*, Smits (1992) SEW 702 at 734.
280. [1971] ECR 263 (the *ERTA* or *AETR* judgment).
281. Declaration (No. 11) adopted by the Conference on the occasion of the signature of the Final Act of the TEU. The declaration may be found in O.J. 1992 C 191/100.

separate request by the European Council meeting in Amsterdam in June 1997 to the Ecofin Council, the Commission and the EMI for a study.[282]

D. The autonomy of the ESCB.[283] In addition to Articles 105 and 106 EC, Article 107 EC is one of the cornerstones of monetary union. It anchors the autonomy of the ESCB by prohibiting the ECB, the national central banks,[284] and any member of their decision-making bodies from seeking or taking instructions from Community Institutions or bodies, from any government of a Member State, or from any other body. This level of independence parallels that applicable to the Commission and its members.[285] Thus unlike in the old European Monetary Cooperation Fund, in the completed EMU the ECB and the national central banks are not subject to political instructions in the formulation and implementation of the uniform monetary policy. This autonomy is taken through in the ESCB Statute into the internal organizational and financial spheres.[286] Article 108 EC, requiring the Member States to ensure that by 1 January 1999 their national legislation, including the statutes of their national central banks, is compatible with the EC Treaty and the ESCB Statute, applies to all Member States, save the United Kingdom.[287]

By virtue of Article 108a(1) EC the ECB is given the power to make regulations,[288] take decisions,[289] make recommendations and deliver opinions.[290] The effect of these is the same as those measures adopted under Article 189 EC,[291] and the ECB may decide to publish its decisions,

282. (1997) *European Economy* No. 64, p. 38; Bull. EU 6–1997, point I.5 (at p. 10). This produced a bland statement at Luxembourg in December 1997, see Bull. EU 12–1997, point I.9 (at para. 46 of the Conclusions of the Presidency).
283. See the bibliography cited in note 246, *supra*.
284. Other than the Bank of England, see Protocol (No. 11, annexed to the EC Treaty) on certain provisions relating to the United Kingdom, Art. 5. However, the independence of the Bank which now exists in practice is in the course of being put on a legislative footing through United Kingdom legislation.
285. See Art. 157(2) EC.
286. ESCB Statute, Art. 7 is in the terms of Art. 107 EC. As the ECB's income and expenditure do not fall under the Community budget, it has financial autonomy. As the Governing Council will adopt the ECB's rules of procedure, determining its internal organization and that of its decision-making bodies, the ECB has internal organizational autonomy, ESCB Statute, Art. 12.3.
287. The United Kingdom's new Bank of England Act (when adopted) will in fact meet this obligation, but it is a unilateral act, rather than an obligation flowing from the EC Treaty, Protocol (No. 11, annexed to the EC Treaty) on certain provisions relating to the United Kingdom, Art. 5.
288. To the extent necessary to implement certain specified tasks, and in such other cases as the Council may decide in accordance with Art. 106(6) EC, Art. 108a(1) EC, 1st indent.
289. Necessary for carrying out the tasks entrusted to the ESCB under the EC Treaty and the ESCB Statute, Art. 108a(1) EC, 2nd indent.
290. Art. 108a(1) EC, 3rd indent.
291. Art. 108a(2) EC.

recommendations and opinions.[292] It also has the power to impose fines or periodic penalty payments on undertakings for failure to comply with its regulations and decisions.[293] This power may be necessary in order to oblige credit institutions to comply with operational methods of monetary control.[294]

As has been observed, the Treaty and Statute-based protection of the ESCB, and of the ECB in particular, is much more firmly based than that of any national bank, but it was also essential that the protection should not make it virtually impossible to obtain agreement about changes to essentially operational details by obliging recourse to Article N TEU; hence the provision in Article 106(5) EC for a lighter procedure for amendment of certain specified provisions of the ESCB Statute. A remarkable feature of this system is that the Council will act by qualified majority after consulting the Commission if the recommendation for amendment emanates from the ECB,[295] but will act by unanimity after consulting the ECB if the proposal emanates from the Commission. In either event, the assent of the European Parliament is required. Article 106(6) EC permits the Council to adopt certain provisions envisaged in the ESCB Statute.[296]

E. **Political and institutional relationships.**[297] The political and institutional relationships within EMU are characterized by the far-reaching protection of the ESCB from political and policy influence, and by a strengthening of the position of the Ecofin Council at the expense of the Commission's position. The relationship between the ESCB and political decision-making can be divided into indirect and direct relations. The indirect relations are expressed in the appointment by the national political authorities of the governors of their national central banks, and in the appointment procedure for the Executive Board of the ECB.[298] The

292. Art. 108a(2) EC, last sentence. The previous sentence applies Arts. 190–192 EC to ECB regulations and decisions (thus ensuring that regulations are published as well).
293. Art. 108a(3) EC, the modalities will be established by an act of the Council, under Art. 106(6) EC.
294. See ESCB Statute, Art. 20.
295. Such a recommendation requires a unanimous decision by the Governing Council of the ECB, ESCB Statute, Art. 41.2.
296. As to the procedure, see Art. 106(6) EC. See *e.g.* COM (97) 725 Final (O.J. 1998 L 118/11 *et seq.*).
297. See the bibliography cited in note 246, *supra.*
298. Art. 109a(2)(b) sets out the procedure: the persons concerned must be persons of recognized standing and experience in monetary or banking matters; appointment is by common accord of the governments of the Member States at the level of Heads of State or Government, on a recommendation from the (Ecofin) Council, after it has consulted the European Parliament and the Governing Council of the ECB. As to the procedure the first time in 1998, see Art. 109l(1), 1st subpara., 2nd indent., and ESCB Statute, Art. 50. As to the first recommendation by the Ecofin Council, see Rec. 98/

members of the Executive Board and the governors of the national central banks constitute the Governing Council of the ECB.[299]

The right of political organs to appoint gives them at the most an *indirect* influence on the policy of the ESCB. The extent to which appointment policy may afford possibilities of influencing policy is in fact very light: the members of the Executive Board are appointed for a non-renewable period of eight years;[300] the conditions under which they may be removed from office are strict;[301] and appeal lies to the Court of Justice against dismissal by a Member State of the governor of its national central bank.[302]

The *direct* possibilities for influencing ECB policy are set out in Article 109b EC: the President of the Council and a member of the Commission may participate in meetings of the Governing Council of the ECB, but they have no vote;[303] the President of the Council may submit a motion for deliberation to the Governing Council;[304] the President of the ECB must be

318 (O.J. 1998 L 139/36). The combined effect of Arts. 109k(3) and 109l(1), 1st subpara., 2nd indent, is that the common accord and the Ecofin Council for these purposes refers to those Member States participating in the single currency, and their representatives in the Ecofin Council.

299. Art. 109a(1) EC; ESCB Statute, Art. 10(1); as to its functions, see *ibid.*, Art. 10. Art. 106(3) EC and ESCB Statute, Art. 9.3 state that the Governing Council and the Executive Board are the decision-making bodies of the ECB. As follows from the previous note, the Governing Council involves the governors of the national central banks of those Member States which are participating in the single currency. As was noted in section 3.3.2, in point E, *ante*, *ibid.* Art. 45 constitutes a third decision-making body, the General Council, for so long as there is a Member State with a derogation; this is the forum within which coordination and discussions with the governors of the central banks of non-participating Member States take place. As to the role of the United Kingdom (the Governor of the Bank of England will participate in the General Council), see Protocol (No. 11, attached to the EC Treaty) on certain provisions relating to the United Kingdom, Arts. 8 and 9.

300. Art. 109a(2)(b) EC, penultimate sentence. Gormley and De Haan (1996) 21 ELRev. 95 at 105 note that this term of office is longer than that of members of the Commission, the European Parliament, the Court of Justice, the Court of First Instance and the Court of Auditors; it is longer than the term of office of any national government. The absence of a possibility of reappointment removes any temptation for the members to adjust their policies accordingly.

301. ESCB Statute, Art. 11.4. They parallel the protection afforded to members of the Commission (Art. 160 EC) and members of the Court of Justice (Protocol on the Statute of the Court (No. B, attached to the EC Treaty), Art. 6).

302. ESCB Statute, Art. 14.2, 2nd subpara. The right of appeal lies for the Governor concerned or for the Governing Council of the ESCB. Interestingly the only grounds are infringement of the EC Treaty or of any rule of law relating to its application, see Gormley and De Haan (1996) 21 ELRev. 95 at 107.

303. Art. 109b(1) EC. They have no right to participate in meetings of the Executive Board (just as the Council has no right to participate in meetings of the Commission).

304. *Ibid.* But there is a distinction between a motion for deliberation and a proposal for a decision, as it is the Executive Board which prepares the meetings of the Governing Council, ESCB Statute, Art. 12.2.

invited to participate in Council meetings when it is discussing matters relating to the objectives and tasks of the ESCB;[305] the ECB has to present an annual report on the ESCB's activities and on the monetary policy of the previous and current year to the European Parliament, the Council and the Commission, and also to the European Council;[306] the President of the ECB presents this report to the Council and to the European Parliament, and the latter may hold a general debate on that basis;[307] finally, either at the request of the European Parliament or on their own initiative, the President of the ECB and the other members of the Executive Board may be heard by the competent committees of the European Parliament.[308] These direct possibilities for exerting influence are also very light, and do not affect the policy and administrative independence of the ESCB. As has been noted, the motions which the President of the Council may table for deliberation cannot create any substantive obligation for the ECB.

A particularly noticeable point is the specific role envisaged for the European Council, which appears in two instances in Articles 102a–109m EC: it discusses a conclusion on the broad guidelines of economic policies[309] and it receives the annual report on the ESCB's activities and monetary policy, as was noted above. There is also a specific role for the Council meeting in the composition of Heads of State or Government.[310]

The strengthening of the position of the (Ecofin) Council is primarily evident in the multilateral surveillance and excessive deficit procedures set out in Articles 103 and 104c EC, respectively. This type of controlling power has always been classically a matter for the Commission, as the Community's executive body. Compared with the situation under Article 113 EC for the common commercial policy, the Commission's role in relation to external monetary policy is considerably weakened in favour of the role of the Council.[311] The Commission exercises its right of initiative in the EMU provisions in three ways: in a number of instances it may only make recommendations rather than proposals, and the Council may decide otherwise at its pleasure, without any institutional safeguards;[312] in a number of cases the Commission's right of initiative is shared with the ECB;[313]

---

305. Art. 109b(2) EC.
306. Art. 109b(3) EC, 1st subpara.
307. *Ibid.*
308. *Ibid.*, 2nd subpara.
309. Art. 103(2) EC, 2nd subpara. On the basis of that conclusion they are then adopted by the Ecofin Council, *ibid.*, 3rd subpara.
310. Which, it will be recalled, is *not* the same as the European Council (*cf.* Art. D TEU, 2nd para.). The Council in this 'higher' composition acts under Arts. 109a(2)(b); 109f(1), 2nd subpara.; 109j(2)–(4), and 109k(2) EC.
311. See Art. 109 EC.
312. *E.g.* Arts. 109 and 109j EC.
313. *E.g.* Art. 106(5) and (6) EC.

and the Member States and the Council may even request the Commission to make a recommendation or proposal as appropriate, and the Commission must examine the request and submit its conclusions without delay.[314]

The combination of far-reaching autonomy for the ESCB, the strengthened position of the Council, and the weakened position of the Commission in the EMU provisions is not without problems. One of the most important conditions for effective policy coordination is the guarantee of the unity and equality of the guidelines by which the Member States are bound as a result of the coordination. The dominant position of the Council in the coordination of economic policies and in external monetary policy does not sufficiently assure that the conditions will be fulfilled. The firm anchoring of the ESCB's independence will tend to focus particular attention at *Community level* on the legitimacy of the actions of the ECB. It is certainly a weak spot that in Article 109b EC, which governs the relationship between the ECB and the Community's political organs, the Commission is assigned such a subordinate role. The subordinated formal role of the Commission might well be compensated by the quality of its contributions to the meetings of the Governing Council of the ECB. Those contributions may be based on a vaster and more detailed experience concerning all the relevant economic factors to be taken into account than that of the institutionalized short-term experience of the President-in-office of the Council.

As has already been observed above, the weakened position of the Commission also works through in the possibilities for the European Parliament to make its views on the desirable economic development of the Community visible in the political decision-making. This objection weighs even more heavily as in the field of monetary integration the powers of the European Parliament are mostly confined to rights to information and the right to advise; the assent of the European Parliament is only required in the relatively unimportant matters governed by Articles 105(6) and 106(5) EC. There are risks in the course of time for support for the Community's institutional system, as in EMU economic policy coordination has a strong intergovernmental slant which has to walk together with a strictly uniform monetary policy.

F. Judicial control. The EMU provisions introduced into the EC Treaty by the TEU bring no sensational changes in the Community system of judicial control. The drafters of the provisions were clearly conscious that, given the very weak political possibilities of influencing the ECB, which almost necessarily follow from its autonomy, it would be undesirable not to subject the Community's monetary authority to judicial supervision. Thus the ECB is fully bedded into the system of judicial supervision by the

---

314. Art. 109d EC. Of course, the conclusions *may* be that action is not appropriate.

Court of Justice and the Court of First Instance.[315] A number of observations may be made, however.

- The exclusion (in Article 104c(10) EC) of the possibility of bringing infringement proceedings under Articles 169 or 170 EC in the phases of the excessive deficit procedure contained in Article 104c(1)–(9) EC reflects the clear intention of the drafters that it should be the Council which decides on the existence of an excessive deficit. There are, it is submitted, good reasons for this, as the assessment of whether there is an excessive deficit, and of how it should be corrected, rests on a financial and economic analysis. But the restriction of the function of the Community judiciary must be narrowly interpreted, so that Article 173 EC remains applicable to decisions of the Council under Article 104c(1)–(9). The same applies if the Council were to fail to take a decision as to the existence of an excessive deficit, after a recommendation from the Commission that it should; in such a case Article 175 EC offers the necessary guarantee against a very much politically motivated application of Article 104c EC.
- The involvement of the Court in the procedures for removal of a member of the Executive Board of the ECB[316] and the right of appeal in the case of the dismissal of a governor of a national central bank[317] are not set out in the EC Treaty itself but in the ESCB Protocol.
- There is also no corresponding provision in the body of the EC Treaty itself to the provision in Article 35.6 of the ESCB Statute which sets out a procedure analogous to that of Article 169 EC, with the ECB able to bring proceedings if it considers that a national central bank has failed to fulfil an obligation under the ESCB Statute.[318]

315. As to which, see Chapter VI, *ante*. From the case-law of the Court of Justice on Monetary Compensatory Amounts (as to which, see Chapter XI, section 2.2, *post*), it may be concluded that the Community judiciary will accept that the monetary authority has a large margin of discretion in policy terms. It remains to be seen whether the Court will continue with this approach in view of the fact that Art. 105 EC contains a substantive normative criterion (maintenance of price stability).

316. Statute ESCB, Art. 11.4.

317. *Ibid.*, Art. 12.2, 2nd subpara.

318. This is logical, as the obligations are those under the Statute. This procedure may be seen as a type of *lex specialis* in relation to Art. 169 EC. Although the national authorities are responsible under Community law for acts of all types of public authorities, bodies governed by public law or publicly-owned undertakings, in terms of Art. 169 EC proceedings, it is clearly more appropriate that control over compliance by a national central bank with its obligations should be more in the hands of the ECB (under ESCB Statute, Art. 35.5 in the hands of the Governing Council) rather than in the (more political) hands of the Commission.

– The terms of Article 35.1 of the ESCB Statute refer to the general provisions of the EC Treaty.[319] This raises no particular questions as the ECB is mentioned where necessary in the appropriate provisions. For the EMI, which now has a limited shelf-life, Article 19.1 of its Statute contains a similar provision, but there is no express reference to the EMI in the relevant provisions of the EC Treaty. At first sight this might seem curious: although the obligations and powers of the EMI are considerably less than those of the ECB, it was not impossible that decisions addressed to national central banks[320] might be controversial enough to require judicial attention, or that compliance with the obligations flowing under Article 109e EC from the start of the second stage might cause the EMI to commence legal proceedings. The omission is of no importance, however, as Article 109f(9) EC expressly provides that during the second stage the term ECB used in those provisions is to be read as referring to the EMI.

– The Court will, it may be expected, be given unlimited jurisdiction in the implementing measures to be adopted under Article 106(6) EC relating to the power of the ECB to impose fines and periodic penalty payments for failure to comply with obligations under its regulations and decisions.[321]

4. EMPLOYMENT (THE NEW TITLE VIA)[322]

4.1 Between Maastricht and Amsterdam

The recession which large parts of the European Union experienced from mid-1992 to the beginning of 1994 led not merely to the decision not to move to the third stage of EMU before the default date of 1 January 1999, as the overwhelming majority of the Member States did not yet satisfy the criteria,[323] it also exposed how fragile the development of employment in Western Europe is. It is in itself a perfectly normal phenomenon that in times of economic recession unemployment will increase as a result of the cyclical movements. But if in a more favourable economic climate unemployment remains at a fairly high level, the unemployment is not cycle-related but structural in nature. Since the mid-Seventies it has been

319. '[I]n the cases and under the conditions laid down in this Treaty.'
320. Under EMI Statute, Art. 15.1, 3rd indent.
321. In accordance with ESCB Statute, Art. 34.3.
322. Title VIa of Part Three of the EC Treaty will have effect when the Treaty of Amsterdam enters into force. Given the political importance of the Community's employment strategy, this discussion is appropriate and, as will be shown, *post*, the Community Institutions and the Member States have in fact already anticipated the implementation of this new Title as far as possible.
323. See section 3.3.2, *ante*, Art. 109j(3) EC, and Dec. 96/736 (O.J. 1996 L 335/48).

apparent that job losses in times of cyclical recessions have not been regained when conditions improve. This has led to higher levels of unemployment at the end of the latest cycle than those which prevailed at the end of the previous one. This phenomenon of hysteresis, as economists now tend to call it, has been very evident after the last recession. In most Member States unemployment increased by several percentage points and then stayed pretty much at that level. The worrying developments in employment caused the European Council meeting in Essen in December 1994 to establish what has become known as the Essen procedure.[324] Under this procedure the European Council discusses employment issues annually on the basis of a joint report by the Ecofin and Social Affairs Councils, prepared by the Economic Policy Committee and now the new Employment and Labour Market Committee established by Decision 97/16.[325] These reports[326] are to focus on five areas, the so-called Essen priorities: improving employment opportunities for the labour force by promoting investment in vocational training; increasing the employment-intensiveness of growth; reducing non-wage labour costs sufficiently extensively to influence noticeably decisions to take on employees, particularly unqualified ones; improving the effectiveness of labour-market policy, and, finally, improving measures to help groups which are particularly hard-hit by unemployment.

Since the Essen European Council, each meeting of the European Council has paid separate attention to developments in employment, sometimes on the basis of an interim report. This intensive attention paid to employment issues at the highest political level of the European Union, has not yet led to significant improvements in employment developments. In fact this confirms that the issue is structural in nature, and that for its solution at national level measures for the adaptation of the national socio-economic system are necessary over a broad range of areas. The working out and implementation of such a strategy will take some time, and the results will be visible only in the medium term.

In this context, it was already explicable most governments were in favour of the idea of expanding the treatment of 'employment' in the EC Treaty. In the working out of this idea the problem arose that a whole range of public intervention measures can be covered by the term 'employment policy'. In the longer term the development of employment is determined by five economic factors:

(1) macro-economic developments (the structural basis of growth);

---

324. Bull. EU 12–1994, point I.3.
325. O.J. 1997 L 6/32.
326. See Bull. EU 12–1995, points I.50–I.54; Bull. EU 12–1996, points I.5, I.36 (The Jobs Challenge – The Dublin Declaration on Employment) and 1.3.210, and Bull. EU 11–1997, points I.2–I.10 (special European Council meeting at Luxembourg on employment).

(2) the dynamics of the markets for products and the factors of production (competitiveness);
(3) the performance of the labour market in particular;
(4) the incentive structure resulting from the national tax and social security system; and
(5) the quality of the public supply of skills and training, with particular attention to the unskilled, fragile groups in the labour market.

From this overview it is apparent that employment issues for the most part should fall within the ambit of general economic policy, which falls within the EMU provisions in Title VI of Part Three of the EC Treaty. As has been noted above, various Member States had major objections to reopening Title VI in the run-up to the final stage of EMU. Thus the drafters of the Treaty of Amsterdam finally opted to introduce into the EC Treaty a separate coordination procedure for those aspects of employment policy which fall outside the scope of the coordination of general economic policies provided for in Article 103 EC. This is contained in the new Articles 109n–109s EC. In the interpretation of these new provisions, it must continually be borne in mind that the coordination procedure provided for therein must *always* have a complement in the coordination of economic policies as provided for in Article 103 EC. In the field of employment policy the Ecofin Council, which is responsible for general economic policies, and the Social Affairs Council, which has specific labour market responsibilities, will be obliged to cooperate. That was clearly the objective of the Essen procedure, which has now in part, for the aspect of specific labour market policy, been worked out in the EC Treaty itself.

4.2 Coordination of employment policy

That the substantive scope of the new Title VIa is restricted to labour market policy is apparent from the new Article 109n EC, which does indeed speak of 'a coordinated strategy for employment', but which in the next breath indicates that what this really means is a coordinated strategy 'for promoting a skilled, trained and adaptable workforce and labour markets responsive to economic change'. The relationship with the coordination of economic policies is immediately established in the new Article 109o(1) EC, which will oblige the Member States to act 'in a way consistent with the broad guidelines of the economic policies of the Member States and of the Community adopted pursuant to Article 103(2) EC.' The new Article 109o(2) EC is the counterpart to Article 103(1) EC in that the Member States will be obliged to regard their employment policies as a matter of common concern and coordinate their action in the Council.

The new Article 109p EC is characterized by two inadequacies: there is no reference to the broad guidelines of Article 103(2) EC as far as the Community itself is concerned, and there is no indication of the activities of the Community which are of particular importance for employment. The latter is a deficiency, as it is submitted that the development of employment within the European Union is to a large extent determined by the design of the internal market and Community competition policy. The wording of the new Article 109p EC incorrectly creates the impression that the Community's complementary activities should be primarily financial. It is true, however, that the Structural Funds and the EIB are indeed increasingly acting with the express aim of promoting employment, particularly in small and medium-sized industries.

The new Article 109q EC is the key provision of this new Title VIa. The joint annual report to be presented by the Council and the Commission to the European Council involves both the Ecofin and Social Affairs Councils. The employment guidelines provided for in the new Article 109q(2) EC are again in their substantive scope more limited to labour market policy; the more economic policy aspects of employment will be dealt with in the broad guidelines under Article 103(2) EC, with which the employment guidelines must be consistent. From an institutional point of view it is remarkable that the Council will have to base the guidelines on the conclusions adopted by the European Council on the basis of the annual joint report; the Council will act on a proposal from the Commission after consulting the European Parliament, the Economic and Social Committee (ECOSOC), the Committee of the Regions, and the new Employment Committee.[327]

The reporting obligation contained in the new Article 109q(3) EC for the Member States about the principal measures taken to implement their employment policies in the light of the employment guidelines, goes further than the obligations incumbent on the Member States under Article 103 EC. The significance of the new Article 109q(3) EC in practice will only be apparent in time, as the development of employment is essentially the result of structural measures which only lead to results in the longer term. The experience with the Essen procedure so far has shown that there is the risk of an annual national report being strongly repetitive in nature, affording thus little further insight into what developments in the field really are.

The new Article 109q(4) EC is the counterpart to Article 103(4) EC. The most noticeable aspect is that the role of the new Employment Committee in the preparation of the examination by the Council of the implementation by the Member States of their employment policies in the light of the employment guidelines; the examination takes place on the

---

327. To be established by the new Art. 109s EC. This Committee will be the counterpart of the Economic and Financial Committee (which replaces the Monetary Committee from 1 January 1999, see Art. 109c(2) EC).

basis of the reports submitted by the Member States, and the Council receives the views of the new Employment Committee. If the Council considers it appropriate in the light of that examination, it may, acting by a qualified majority on the basis of a recommendation from the Commission, make recommendations to Member States. It is on the basis of this examination that the new Article 109q(5) EC requires the Council and the Commission to draw up their joint annual report to the European Council on the employment situation in the Community and on the implementation of the employment guidelines.

In the run-up to the special Employment Summit held in Luxembourg on 20 and 21 November 1997 the procedure of Title VIa was followed, even though, of course, those provisions were (and at the date at which this work states the law still are) not yet in force. In this period the following experience was encountered.

- the cooperation between the coordination of economic policies and employment policy is particularly essential, as the success of the latter is to a great extent determined by the results of the former. A method of working involving both the Ecofin and Social Affairs Councils has unmistakable advantages. It also avoids later friction between the various specialist Councils. These may occur simply because there can easily be overlaps between the broad economic guidelines and the specific employment guidelines, for example in the fiscal sphere.
- The necessary complementarity between the coordination under Article 103 EC and that under the new Articles 109q–109s EC makes it advisable to draw up the broad guidelines of economic policies an the employment guidelines simultaneously. That should preferably take place before the Summer, so that the national budgetary legislators may still work those guidelines into their budgets.
- In view of the major differences in the employment situations within the European Union, it would be unwise to formulate quantitative policy objectives in the guidelines. Insofar as the guidelines concern the set of instruments of employment policy, quantitative indications are certainly possible, provided that they relate to instruments which are equally relevant for all Member States.
  The careful formulation of the quantitative indications in the conclusions of the Employment Summit[328] should not be viewed as reflecting a lack of sufficient political will, but as a recognition of the great diversity in employment developments and employment policy within the European Union. This diversity will increase in an enlarged European Union.
- Compared with Article 103 EC, the reporting obligation and

328. Bull. EU 11–1997, points I.2–I.48.

examination procedure now set out in the new Article 109q seems to herald a considerable improvement. It will be essential for this to materialize, to avoid the reporting procedure becoming a mere ritual, with set-piece recitation of what each Member State's employment policy is, without a sharp analysis of the adequacy of that policy. In that case the examination by the Council, provided for in the new Article 109q(4) EC, would serve little purpose. Individual assessments on a Member State-by-Member State basis in the examination by the Council will be essential for the success of this procedure.

In the longer-term perspective the coordination of specific employment policy could lead to a geographic convergence of national objectives, arrangements and institutions, which, although not imposed, would result from a combination of information and indicative recommendations. In addition to geographic convergence, the substantive convergence which can flow from this coordination procedure is potentially of great importance. If the importance of the fiscal structure for employment is recognized, a convergence of fiscal systems may result, even without formal harmonization imposed by the Community mechanisms.[329] The same applies for matters such as the legal regulation of part-time employment, vocational training and so on. Guidelines on these matters invite Member States to try out the best practices of other Member States.

The new Article 109r EC describes, in terms intended to be restrictive, the incentive measures which the Community may adopt in the field of employment: these appear to be principally measures aimed at the labour market as such. This restrictive intention is however without prejudice to the powers of *e.g.* the EIB and the Structural Funds to use their financial instruments for economic investments creating new employment or for guaranteeing or facilitating loans in such a structural economic context; nor does it exclude employment aspects being taken into account in fiscal policy, as Commissioner Monti has made clear on myriad occasions in reports on this subject.

In the run-up to the Employment Summit in Luxembourg (which was a special meeting of the European Council), the Employment Committee conducted discussions with the social partners.[330] Although in the Conclusions of the Presidency after that meeting, great value was also attached to those discussions, a fruitful exchange of views presupposes a

---

329. It is proving notoriously difficult to achieve movement on the future direction of Community fiscal policy, not least because unanimity is required under Arts. 99 and 100 EC, without prejudice to Art. 101 EC (which permits acts to be adopted by qualified majority in cases of fiscal distortions), as explained in Chapter VIII, section 3.1, *ante*. See Wattel (1998) NTER 17.
330. See the new Art. 109s EC.

tighter organization of employees' and employers' organizations at Community level. The results of the new Employment Title will thus also in part depend on the necessary institutional convergence.

5. ECONOMIC AND SOCIAL COHESION[331]

5.1 Orientation and definition of the concept

The wording of Title XIV of Part Three of the EC Treaty is somewhat misleading. Articles 130a–130e EC, introduced by the SEA, do *not* relate to the cohesion between economic policies in general and social policy and only very partly to the cohesion between the development of the different sectors of the economy and the social consequences thereof. They mainly deal with the harmonious development of economic activity, and thus of employment and welfare, in the geographic sense. In view of the large differences in the geographical spread of prosperity both within and between the Member States, the question of a balanced economic development from the regional viewpoint forms one of the central subjects in economic policy formation by and within the Community. It plays a large, sometimes dominant role in all Community activities, both in the field of market integration and in the field of policy integration.

The scale of the geographic differences in prosperity within the Community is in the first place determined by the integration process as a *political* process. Through the accession of Ireland, Greece, Spain and Portugal, differences in prosperity within the Community have significantly increased since the beginning of the Seventies. German unification in 1990 has had a similar effect, as the level of prosperity of the new German *Länder* will in the coming years still lag far behind the Community average. The recent enlargement of the Community with the accession of Austria, Finland and Sweden has somewhat strengthened the share of the more prosperous Member States, which has somewhat increased the average level of prosperity. These differences in prosperity may have consequences for the distribution between the richer and poorer parts of the Community. The envisaged enlargement(s) to embrace the Central and Eastern European countries in particular will certainly drastically increase the geographic differences in prosperity. The consequences for the geographic distribution of prosperity of the integration process as a *market integration process* are not easily unequivocally stated. To the extent to

---

331. See Mortelmans *et al.*, *De Economische en Sociale Samenhang in de EG* (The Hague, 1989); Padoa-Schioppa *et al.*, *op. cit.* (see note 36, *supra*); Comijs (1997) SEW 281; Fraser (1995) 20 ELRev. 3; Fernández Martín and Stehmann (1991) 16 ELRev. 216; Van Ginderachter (1989) RMC 272; Mortelmans (1988) SEW 610 and (1989) SEW 766; Séché *et al.* in Mégret *et al.*, *op. cit.* (see note 55, *supra*) 167–248 and (1991) RMC 277, and Vaucher (1994) RTDE 525.

which market integration contributes to a raising of the general level of
prosperity, the economically weaker parts of the Community will also be
able to benefit therefrom. The reallocation of productive activities which is
a necessary and desirable consequence of the formation of a common
market, does not, as the experiences of past decades demonstrate,
necessarily need to work to the detriment of the initially weakest
economies. Thus Portugal and Ireland, in terms of relative growth in
prosperity, have been able to make up part of their initial disadvantage as
against the Community average.[332] Not only the formation of the common
market resulted in reallocation occurring, with the temporary frictions that
may cause, also the *operation* of that market will – have to – cause
symptoms of reallocation. These symptoms become apparent *inter alia* in
the decline and decay of old industrial centres, as has been evident in
places such as Alsace-Lorraine and Merseyside. It is thus wrong both in
principle and substantively to regard the question of regional differences in
levels of prosperity as a more or less invariable which is capable of solution
by mere income or capital transfers. Both the poorer and the richer parts
of the Community are sensitive to the geographic and sectoral reallocations
which a dynamic market process will occasion. The seriousness of the
resulting frictions, with all their undesirable social secondary symptoms, is
primarily determined by the degree to which the Community manages to
ensure a satisfactory economic growth over the whole field, with the
accompanying high level of investment and growth in employment. This
again involves the cohesion between *market integration* and *policy
integration* within the Community. The achievement of the objectives of
the coordination of economic policies regulated in Articles 102a and 103
EC is a necessary precondition for a harmonious development of economic
activities in the Community in geographical terms within the whole
Community. This does not exclusively mean macro-economic policy, but
embraces primarily the policy of the Member States pursue relating to the
public supply side of their economies: the availability of physical,
technological and educational infrastructure; the quality and mobility of
the labour force; the quality of the operation of the market place, and the
decision-making costs in socio-economic policy. The increasing significance
attached to these aspects is perhaps the most important reason for the
Community's action to reduce geographical differences in levels of
prosperity. Indeed, if the weaker Member States and regions do not have
sufficient resources to ensure the public supply side required by the ever
more demanding market sector, the dynamic differences in levels of
prosperity threaten to become permanent. Potentially attractive regions
would then remain permanently under-used in terms of natural conditions
of production. Both for the regions concerned which are confronted with
unnecessary losses of prosperity, and for the Community as a whole, which

332. See Molle *et al.* in Gretschmann (ed.), *op. cit.* (see note 55, *supra*) 217 at 220–222.

sees its potential being under-used, this is an undesirable situation. Particular policy coordination problems occur at Community level, in the relationship between Community sectoral policy, particularly the Common Agricultural Policy, and the policy for economic and social cohesion. Where marginal agricultural area in Western Europe are mostly situated in economically weaker regions, the spatial planning consequences of a reduction in the guaranteed price levels are considerable for the most important products. These consequences can only temporarily be compensated by income support for the producers concerned, as transfers of income which lead to economically non-viable firms remaining in being may finally result in serious disturbances of the market. A solution will at the end of the day have to be found in the improvement of the economic infrastructure of the agricultural areas concerned.[333]

Experiences with geographically relevant socio-economic policy in the Member States and in the Community have demonstrated that such policy is very sensitive to purely allocation-policy considerations, both on the income as well as the expenditure sides of the budget. Within the Community this was expressed in the so-called '*juste retour*' principle, according to which each Member State sought to attain a global or specific proportionality between its contributions to the Community or to a particular Community Fund, and the Community allocations.

The acceptance of the first Delors Package in 1988[334] has led to a departure from the principle of '*juste retour*' at least in the area of regional-economic policy. Since then the major part of expenditure from the Structural Funds has indeed been in the direction of the economically weaker regions. Taken globally, the effectiveness of Community regional policy has increased as a result, as more resources are now spent where they are most needed. But the much greater size of the intra-Community transfers (some 60,000 million ECU in the period 1989–93 and some 148,000 million ECU for the period 1993–1999) also creates policy and political risks. These are essentially fourfold.

First of all, the absorption capacity of the regions involved may be insufficient for the responsible expenditure of the available resources; there is little point in building cathedrals in the desert. Secondly, the public finances in the Member States with relatively many weaker regions may become too dependent on the Community transfers of funds. Thus the net balance between contributions to and receipts from the Community for Ireland is a good 6% of GDP, and for Greece a good 5% of GDP. This dependence may have the unintended side-effect of the Member State concerned becoming more fragile as far as its budgetary policy is

333. See the WRR Report *Grond voor keuzen* (The Hague, 1992).
334. See Franzmeyer *et al.*, *Die Reform der EG-Strukturfonds von 1988. Konzeption, Umsetzung, Weiterentwicklung aus deutscher Sicht* (Berlin, 1993); Lowe (1988) 25 CMLRev. 503, and Séché (1989) RMC 325.

concerned. Because the size and allocation of the Community transfers have to be flexible in time, from the point of view of expenditure efficiency, such a dependence places a heavy charge on the future policy flexibility of the Community. Thirdly, the preoccupation with allocation policy, which is virtually inseparable from spatial economic policy, tends to spread beyond the borders of that policy. This occurred on a grand scale in the run-up to the signature of the TEU, when the Southern Member States made their agreement to EMU more or less conditional upon an increase in the Community transfers in their direction.[335] From the point of the Community interest this approach may be counterproductive, as it leads to blockages in decision-making and cause an inefficient expenditure of Community resources. Finally, the political attention paid to differences in levels of prosperity between regions within the Community may lead to an introversion of policy which is risky for the future of the European integration process. This may over time be expressed in reserves on the part of those Member States which benefit considerably from the Structural Funds, about the enlargement of the European Union to embrace the Central and Eastern European candidate countries. This is already visible in the very distorted proportions of the intra-Community redistributing expenditure and the resources available for external measures which are in particular intended for future Member States in Central and Eastern Europe.[336] The discussions which are taking place on the Commission's Agenda 2000 proposals have confirmed the fears expressed above.[337]

Neither in the SEA, which brought Articles 130a–130e EC into the Treaty, nor in the amendments made by the TEU, is there any definition of the concept of economic and social cohesion. The nearest indicators which the EC Treaty gives are to be found in the second paragraph of Article 130a EC and the first two paragraphs of Article 130b EC. A definition could be deduced from the policy which is pursued on the basis of these two provisions, but that falters on the objection that the strongly broadened and intensified policy pursued since the entry into force of the SEA is not well-defined by reference to the Treaty provisions themselves. As will be apparent from the discussion in the following sections, below,

335. Indeed there was also much fluttering in the Southern dovecotes about the contribution of the EEA countries to Community cohesion, and even more so when Switzerland declined to join the EEA and the financial contribution had to be rejigged.

336. In 1994 some 20,000 million ECU was available for the Structural Funds, and for the Cohesion Fund some 1750 million ECU. In contrast, the external expenditure, primarily directed towards Central and Eastern Europe was only of the order of something more than 4,000 million ECU. The figures for expenditure directed at the Central and Eastern European countries in particular are increasing, and will increase still further as a result of the adoption of Reg. 622/98 (O.J. 1998 L 85/1) on assistance to the applicant countries in the framework of the pre-accession strategy.

337. As to Agenda 2000, see Bull EU Supp. 5/97.

the geographically relevant aspects of Community policy will still be in the process of rapid transformation in the coming years, Thus a functional description, which relates to the definitions which are in use for national regional economic policy, offers more solace: the Community policy is aimed at the optimization of the socio-economic potential of the parts of the Community which are lagging behind in prosperity and employment, and the promotion of necessary transformation in the sectoral or spatial reallocation of economic activities. This description expresses the fact that economic and social cohesion should not result in a mere reallocation of resources within the Community, nor can it take the place of the Member States' social and labour market policy and of the Community policy based on Articles 117–127 EC. Such a definition, it is submitted, also finds sufficient support in the wording of the first two paragraphs of Article 130b EC.

5.2 Legal basis

In their original version, Articles 130a–130e EC are scarcely models of clarity, as the drafters of those provisions sought to codify existing Community regional policy as well as to create a Treaty basis for its extension and intensification. The changes which were introduced through the TEU have not increased the transparency of those provisions.

Article 130a EC places the emphasis on regional policy in the more classical sense of that phrase, policy leading to the strengthening of the Community's least-favoured regions.[338] The emphasis was at the express behest of the Member States with relatively many weaker regions, as they wished to avoid Community expenditure fanning out too much had a wider terminology been employed. The present wording is a clear improvement on the original, now that it is stated that one of the objectives of Community action is to 'aim at reducing disparities between the levels of development of the various regions'. In the original wording only 'reducing disparities between the various regions' was mentioned, and the addition makes it clear that Community action has to be instrumental in the economic sense, and not primarily distributive.

Article 130b EC aims first of all to make a substantive demarcation between the objectives of Article 130a EC and the national economic policies which are to be coordinated in the Community context. The cohesion implicitly so created between Articles 102a and 103 EC on the one hand, and Article 130a EC on the other must be understood so that the strengthening of the macro-economic stability and growth and the increase in market dynamism can create the conditions in which the

338. The Treaty of Amsterdam will add to Art. 130a EC, 2nd para. the words 'or islands' after the words 'least-favoured regions'.

development potential of the weaker regions can be activated. The system of the EC Treaty requires that the specific regional-economic objectives of Article 130a EC be subordinated to the principles laid down in Articles 3a and 102a EC of the economic policies of the Member States and of the Community. If they were to be equally ranked, or, more strongly, if the relationship were the inverse, the operation of market allocation or the liberalization of trade would be (partly) made dependent on the possible consequences thereof for the allocation of regional prosperity within the Community. In other words, the tail, no matter how important, would wag the dog.

The second point about Article 130b EC is that it involves the obligation for the Community in the formation and execution of its policy, as well as in the establishment of the internal market, to take account of the objectives of Article 130a EC and to contribute to the achievement thereof. It is difficult to draw unequivocal conclusions from this two-part task. The application of the principles of market unity and equality in the internal market may in some cases lead to marginal activities relocating from weaker regions to elsewhere in the Community, although practice shows that with a favourable investment climate the weaker regions can actually attract investment. Moreover, in a completed EMU the mobility of investment will strongly increase, and the weaker regions should also benefit from this. It is in any event not really conceivable how these fundamental characteristics of market integration and of monetary policy integration could be subordinated to regional-economic policy objectives. This indeed leaves unaffected the possibility, in the formulation of the qualitative preconditions for market integration, of taking into account in competition policy and in sectoral policies such as the Common Agricultural Policy and transport policy, the consequences of those policies for the development of geographical prosperity and employment within the Community.

In the establishment of the internal market the balance of the package of liberalizing measures, in terms of composition and sequence in time, has been a wrongly neglected aspect of the market integration. The priority accorded to the achievement of the free movement of goods has to a certain degree been at the expense of those parts of the Community with a relatively strong service sector. The late development of the common transport policy has damaged the economic development of the peripheral Member States which have on account of their situation a relatively strong transport sector.

In competition policy the link between the application of Articles 92–94 EC and Article 130b EC is obvious. Where Community financial assistance is as a rule complementary to national financial assistance, the national aid should be permissible under Article 92(3) EC. Conversely, Community supervision of national aid measures should prevent Member States from thwarting Community structural policy through unilateral measures. The

Commission should be able to base reasons not only on Articles 92 and 93 EC, but also on the first two sentences of Article 130b EC.[339] More problematic may be the application of the instruction norms in those two sentences, if the Community action prescribed by the Treaty are irreconcilable or difficult to reconcile with economic and social cohesion. Thus Community policy in the field of research and technological development[340] may lead to a functionally necessary concentration of Community expenditure in that field in those areas of the Community where high-level technological research facilities are already available, or where advanced industries a re strongly represented. The spreading of these resources among the economically weaker areas in the Community would make the programmes considerably less effective. Nevertheless the interest of an as efficient as possible strengthening of the competitive power of European industry in the world market comes regularly under pressure from the cohesion argument. Other examples of erroneous invocation of the cohesion argument are to be found in environment policy, where economically weaker Member States require temporary or substantive exemptions from Community provisions in that field (witness the lingering discussion about a European energy tax), and in the common agricultural *market* policy.[341] Community activities in this Title should indeed be meant to conform to Community law and the other activities of the Community. This coordination requirement, which in a certain sense is the mirror image of the coordination principle of the first two sentences of Article 130b EC, is further, if incompletely worked out in Article 7 of the basic Regulation 2081/93.[342]

The third sentence of Article 130b EC summarizes the instruments at the Community's disposal in the realization of economic and social cohesion: the Structural Funds;[343] the European Investment Bank, and the other existing financial instruments. The drafting of this provision is somewhat unfortunate, as it appears to contain a limitative, rather than an illustrative, list of instruments. Thus for cases in which Articles 130a–130e EC create no general legal basis for the creation of new Funds, a specific legal basis must be found elsewhere in the EC Treaty, or, in the absence thereof, recourse must be had to Article 235 EC.

The legal basis for the Financial Instrument for Fisheries Guidance

339. See Hancher, *et al.*, *EC State Aids* (Chichester, 1993) 173 (2nd ed. in preparation) and Evans, *European Community Law of State Aid* (Oxford, 1997) 146–201.
340. Arts. 130f–130p EC.
341. There is indeed a direct connection between the evolution of the Community's agricultural market policy and the Community's agricultural structural policy which is conducted through the Guidance Section of the European Agricultural Guidance and Guarantee Fund, see Mortelmans (1989) SEW 766 at 774.
342. O.J. 1993 L 193/5.
343. The European Agricultural Guidance and Guarantee Fund, Guidance Section; the European Social Fund; the European Regional Development Fund.

(FIFG), established by Regulation 2080/93[344] was Article 43 EC rather than Article 130b EC. The legal basis for the European Agricultural Guidance and Guarantee Fund, Guidance Section is to be found in Art. 40(4) EC. Expenditure of the latter in 1997 amounted to some 3,649 million ECU. The legal basis for the European Social Fund (ESF) is the relevant provisions of the EC Treaty itself, presently Articles 123–125 EC. Prior to the entry into force of the SEA, the ESF was primarily an instrument for the purposes of Community social policy,[345] but all that changed with the SEA. Since 1988 the ESF's activities have formed part of Community policy for the strengthening of economic and social cohesion. Its activities do, though, remain within the context of its mission, set out in Article 123 EC: 'to improve employment opportunities for workers in the internal market and to contribute thereby to raising the standard of living, ... it shall aim to render the employment of workers easier and to increase their geographical and occupational mobility within the Community, and to facilitate their adaptation to industrial changes and to changes in productions systems, in particular through vocational training and retraining.' From this description it can be deduced that the activities of the ESF fit into the functional description of the policy for the promotion of economic and social cohesion set out above. The present activities of the ESF are set out in Regulation 2084/93.[346] In 1997 some 7.6,000 million ECU was spend on ESF projects, representing some 27% of expenditure on the Structural Funds and FIFG.[347]

The European Regional Development Fund (ERDF) was established in 1975, on the basis of Article 235 EC.[348] After an initially somewhat difficult existence, primarily caused by allocation policy reasons, since the beginning of the Eighties the ERDF has blossomed, with the introduction of the Integrated Mediterranean Programmes (IMPs)[349] and of Integrated Action Programmes (IAPs) in order to assist those regions of the Community which faced increased competition through Spanish and Portuguese accession.[350] But the instrumental policy effect of these instruments remained fairly limited, primarily through the modest amount of the available resources. With the entry into force of the SEA, the ERDF obtained a place in the EC Treaty itself, in Article 130c EC, albeit in the form of a description of its tasks, rather than a legal basis as such. The ERDF owes its present significance principally to the agreement

344. O.J. 1993 L 193/1, see further, Chapter XI, section 2.5.2, *post*.
345. See, as to that period, Keur (1982) SEW 267 at 270–272.
346. O.J. 1993 L 193/39 (which integrally replaces the previous text of Reg. 4255/88 (O.J. 1988 L 374/21)).
347. See *General Report 1997* ((Brussels, Luxembourg, 1998) points 392–407.
348. By Reg. 724/75 (O.J. 1975 L 73/1, most recently amended by Reg. 1987/84 (O.J. 1984 L 169/1).
349. Under Reg. 2088/85 (O.J. 1985 L 197/1).
350. See Keur (1982) SEW 267 at 272–276 and Mortelmans (1988) SEW 610 at 612–616.

reached by the European Council on the celebrated triptych in the Delors I package.[351] This also involved a substantial increase in the resources allocated to the Structural Funds and the use made of them.[352] The expenditure of the ERDF in 1997 amounted to some 13,000 million ECU, representing some 50% of the total expenditure on the Structural Funds and FIFG.

A new element in Article 130b is the three-yearly reporting obligation on the Commission to the European Parliament, ECOSOC, and the Committee of the Regions on the progress made towards achieving economic and social cohesion and the manner in which the various means provided for in Article 130b EC have contributed to it; the report may if necessary be accompanied by appropriate proposals. If specific actions appear necessary outside the Funds, they may be adopted by the Council, acting unanimously on a proposal from the Commission and after consulting the ECOSOC and the Committee of the Regions. A few observations are appropriate about this provision, which was added at a late stage in the negotiations leading to the TEU. First, for the evaluation of structural measures for these purposes, a three-year reporting cycle is far too much. Simply the decision-making process necessary for the execution of important measures strengthening structures takes more time. Secondly, such reports may certainly generate political pressure to make 'appropriate proposals.' Thirdly, the resulting specific measures must fit into the financial perspectives, which, for the most important categories of expenditure, have been agreed in the current Interinstitutional Agreement and the provisions relating to budgetary discipline.[353] Where the financial perspectives are set for a plan period of five years, a source of conflict between the Council and the European Parliament is laid, in which the cohesion countries will adopt their own position. Article 130c EC gives the ERDF now at least an implicit Treaty-based status.[354]

Article 130d EC, which was amended when the TEU came into force, envisages three types of instruments: the definition of the tasks, priority objectives and the organization of the Structural Funds, which may involve grouping them; the definition of the general rules applicable to them; and the adoption of the provisions necessary to ensure their effectiveness and the coordination of the Funds with one another and with the other existing

---

351. See Chapter V, section 2.1.2, particularly at point C, *ante*, and Mortelmans (1989) SEW 766 at 768–769.
352. See Chapter V, section 2.1.2, at point C, *ante*.
353. See Chapter V, section 2.2, *ante*.
354. In the 2nd edition of this work (at 643), it was submitted that the legal basis of any changing description of the ERDF's tasks would have to take place on the basis of either Arts. 130d or 235 EC. The combination of a basic regulation and the coordination regulation based on Art. 130d EC, with the implementing regulation based on Art. 130e EC covers pretty well all aspects of the ERDF's activities. This means that recourse to Art. 235 EC should no longer be necessary.

financial instruments.[355] These provisions are adopted by the Council, acting unanimously on a proposal from the Commission, after obtaining the assent of the European Parliament and consulting ECOSOC and the Committee of the Regions.[356] Implementing decisions relating to the ERDF are at present adopted by the Council under the cooperation procedure, and after consulting ECOSOC and the Committee of the Regions.[357]

The regulations dating from 1988 were last amended in 1993, with integral replacement of their texts, and thus are usually cited by reference to the new versions. The basic regulation, on the tasks of the Structural Funds and on coordination of their activities between themselves and with the operations of the EIB and the other existing financial instruments, is now set out in Regulation 2081/93.[358] That basic regulation is implemented by the coordinating regulation, now set out in Regulation 2082/93.[359] The basic regulation is then further implemented by a series of regulations dealing with particular Funds: thus Regulation 2083/93[360] deals with the ERDF; Regulation 2084/93[361] deals with the ESF; Regulation 2085/93[362] deals with the Guidance Section of the European Agricultural Guidance and Guarantee Fund (EAGGF), and Regulation 2080/93[363] deals with the Financial Instrument for Fisheries Guidance (FIFG).

As was noted above, in the run-up to the adoption of the TEU there was a major difference of opinion between the more prosperous Member States and the poorer Member States about the assistance which the latter should receive in order to be able to be ready to participate on time in moving to the third stage of EMU.[364] Initially the wish of Spain in particular for the addition of a separate transfer mechanism to the EMU provisions was rejected for reasons of principle by Germany and The Netherlands. At a late stage it was finally decided to supplement the range of instruments for

355. Art. 130d EC, 1st para.
356. *Ibid.*
357. Art. 130e EC, 1st para. The Treaty of Amsterdam (not yet in force) will instead prescribe the co-decision procedure (with the same additional consultations). Decisions regarding the European Agricultural Guidance and Guarantee Fund, Guidance Section, and the ESF continue to be taken under Arts. 43 and 125 EC respectively. Art. 125 EC is also revised under the Treaty of Amsterdam so as to use the co-decision procedure (rather than the present cooperation procedure), again with the additional consultations.
358. O.J. 1993 L 193/5 (amending integrally Reg. 2052/88 (O.J. 1988 L 185/9)). This regulation was further adjusted by Dec. 95/1 (O.J. 1995 L 1/1) which adjusted the Act of Austrian, Finnish and Swedish Accession (1994), and by Reg. 3193/94 (O.J. 1994 L 337/11).
359. O.J. 1993 L 193/20 (amending integrally Reg. 4253/88 (O.J. 1988 L 374/1)).
360. O.J. 1993 L 193/34 (amending integrally Reg. 4254/88 (O.J. 1988 L 374/15)).
361. O.J. 1993 L 193/39 (amending integrally Reg. 4255/88 (O.J. 1988 L 374/21)).
362. O.J. 1993 L 193/44 (amending integrally Reg. 4256/88 (O.J. 1988 L 374/25)).
363. O.J. 1993 L 193/1, see further, Chapter XI, section 2.5.2, *post*.
364. See Cloos *et al.*, *op. cit.* (see note 55, *supra*) 154–158.

economic and social cohesion with a separate Cohesion Fund. The legal basis for that Fund is now set out in the second paragraph of Article 130d EC. The different approach of the Cohesion Fund in terms of its structure, tasks and methods of application, when compared to the Structural Funds can be traced back to the Protocol on Economic and Social Cohesion.[365] The Cohesion Fund is dealt with in Regulation 1164/94.[366]

Unlike payments from the Structural Funds, those from the Cohesion Fund are targeted directly at the four cohesion countries, Spain, Greece, Portugal and Ireland, according to an indicative allocation system.[367] The resources are destined for investments in trans-European transport infrastructure and the improvement of the environment.[368] It is expressly provided that resources from the Cohesion Fund may not be used for projects which are already financed by the Structural Funds.[369] Article 2(1) of Regulation 1164/94 makes a certain link with EMU, in that the cohesion countries must have a programme leading to the fulfillment of the convergence criteria referred to in Article 104c EC. Article 6 of the regulation demonstrates further the conditional nature of the assistance: a decision (which is not abrogated within a year or within such other period as may be specified) that an excessive deficit exists, or a recommendation made with a view to bringing it to an end may lead to suspension of contributions from the Cohesion Fund to new projects or new stages of a project. Although the wording of the regulation is not unequivocal, the substantive connection with progress toward EMU logically seems to imply that the Cohesion Fund should disappear with as soon as the member States concerned have moved to the third stage of EMU. The Treaty itself is regrettably silent on the possible continuation of the Cohesion Fund, so that there was already a risk of its becoming a permanent instrument for horizontal financial equalization between the Member States: the regulation is to be re-examined before the end of 1999,[370] and the Commission has now proposed that it should indeed be

365. Protocol (No. 15) annexed to the EC Treaty (by the TEU). The Protocol can be found in O.J. 1992 C 191/93.
366. O.J. 1994 L 130/1. Prior to the entry into force of the TEU, a provisional Cohesion Financial Instrument was established by Reg. 792/93 (O.J. 1993 L 79/74), as the delay in the entry into force of the TEU made it impossible to establish the Cohesion Fund before 31 December 1993 on the basis of Art. 130d EC, 2nd para.
367. As to the system, see Reg. 1164/94, Art. 5 and Annex. As to the targeting, see *ibid.*, Art. 2(2). The criterion for assistance is a *per capita* GNP measured in purchasing power parities of less than 90% of the Community average, and (as explained in the text, *post*, the existence of a convergence programme), see *ibid.*, Art. 2(1). But the effect of Art. 2(2) is to grandfather the four Member States concerned until the end of 1999.
368. See Arts. 129c(1) EC, 1st subpara., 3rd indent and 130s(5) EC, 2nd indent; see further, Reg. 1164/94, Art. 2(1).
369. Reg. 1164/94, Art. 9(1).
370. Reg. 1164/94, Art. 16(1).

continued, although various modalities should be changed.[371] For the period up to 1999, some 2,600 million ECU per year has been set aside for the Cohesion Fund.

5.3   The implementation of economic and social cohesion

The regulations governing the Structural Funds as originally adopted in 1988[372] contained the first more or less coherently coordinated development of Articles 130a–130e EC. The doubling of the Structural Funds in real terms between 1994 and 1999 did not form a reason to revise the existing principles for the allocation and expenditure of these resources. The present versions of those measures do however represent a certain expansion of the scope of the Structural Funds, both in terms of territorial application and in terms of their substantive scope.

The process of simultaneous intensification through the increase in the available resources and extensification through an expansion of the territorial and substantive scope is not immune from criticism on budgetary policy and spatial economic grounds. The experiences with regional and structural administration of Funds in the Member States have demonstrated that this policy displays a high degree of asymmetrical political decision-making: decisions on intensification and extensification of policy are relatively easily arrived at, but decisions on reduction of expenditure and restrictions of its scope encounter major political and social objections. The risk of this occurring is greater according to the degree of influence on decision-making which the beneficiary entities (the economically weaker Member States) have.[373] This mechanism of cooperative vertical policy coordination led in Germany to the territorial scope of regional structural policy embracing on the eve of German unification about two-thirds of the then existing *Länder*. The same risk presents itself in the Community. The influence of the Member States on the final decision-making is certainly no less in the Community context than is that of the *Länder* in the German context. The probability of asymmetrical decision-making might be a major handicap for the Commission in its policy in relation to the candidate Central and Eastern European countries. If the existing allocation of expenditure among the present beneficiary Member States is regarded as being sacrosanct, any future enlargement(s) to the East might only be able to occur at the expense of a significant increase in the Community budget. Even if for the countries concerned a long transitional period were to be agreed, the

---

371. See COM (98) 130 Final (O.J. 1998 C 159/7).
372. The references in section 5.2, *ante*, to the current versions of these regulations give the references to the original versions as well.
373. See Scharf (1988) *Public Administration* 251.

maintenance of the present assumptions would, on the principle of substantive equality, require substantial transfers of income. If the European Union does not desire to deprive itself at the outset of the possibility of proceeding with the politically and economically desirable enlargement eastwards, the operation of cohesion set out below will have to acquire a degressive character. This will undoubtedly be one of the most difficult political issue for the European Union in the coming years.[374]

A. Objectives and means.[375] The objectives and means and the specific tasks of the various Structural Funds are set out in Articles 1–3 of the basic regulation, now contained in Regulation 1081/93.[376] They may be divided into *spatial-economic* objectives and *functional* objectives. The *spatial-economic* objectives are in fact now five-fold.

(1) Promotion of the development and structural adjustment of regions whose development is lagging behind. This is the celebrated Objective 1, to which the ERDF, the ESF, and the Guidance Section of the EAGGF contribute.

(2) Conversion of the regions, frontier regions or parts of regions (including employment regions and urban communities) seriously affected by industrial decline. This is known as Objective 2, to which the ERDF and the ESF both contribute.

(3) Promotion of rural development by speeding up the adjustment of agricultural structures in the framework of the reform of the Common Agricultural Policy. This is known as Objective 5(a), to which the Guidance Section of the EAGGF and FIFG both contribute.

(4) Promotion of rural development by facilitating the development and structural adjustment of rural areas. This is known as Objective 5b, to which the Guidance Section of the EAGGF, the ESF and the ERDF all contribute.

(5) Promotion of the development and structural adjustment of regions with an extremely low population density. This is known as Objective 6, to which all the structural Funds and the FIFG contribute. Objective 6 was added by the Act of Austrian, Finnish and Swedish Accession, as adjusted.

374. As to the Commission's proposals, see COM (98) 131 Final.
375. See, generally, the Commission's booklet, *Structural Funds and Cohesion Fund 1994– 1999 Regulations and Commentary* (Luxembourg, 1996). The Commission has now proposed that the present objectives be adjusted and reduced to three: promoting the development and structural adjustment of regions whose development is lagging behind; supporting the economic and social conversion of areas facing structural difficulties, and supporting the adaptation and modernization of policies and systems of education, training and employment (see COM (98) 131 Final (O.J. 1998 C 176/1)).
376. O.J. 1993 L 193/5.

The *functional* objectives are twofold.

(1) Combating long-term unemployment and facilitating the integration into working life of young people and of persons exposed to exclusion from the labour market. This is known as Objective 3, to which the ESF contributes.
(2) Facilitating the adaptation of workers of either sex to industrial changes and to changes in production systems. This is known as Objective 4, to which, again, the ESF contributes.

The EIB and other existing financial instruments also contribute in an appropriate fashion, each according to its own specific objectives, to the attainment of all these now six priority objectives (objective 5 is subdivided). The tasks and methods of operation of the EIB are considered in section 5.4, below. Examples of existing financial instruments include the Cohesion Fund, to which reference is made in the second paragraph of Article 130d EC,[377] and the financial instrument for trans-European networks, referred to in the third indent of the first subparagraph of Article 129c(1) EC.[378]

The financial and substantive policy core of these Objectives in undoubtedly Objective 1. Of the some 148,000 million ECU (at 1992 prices) available, some 96,000 million ECU is earmarked for Objective 1. Within Objective 1 a distinction is made between those regions in the cohesion countries (Spain, Greece, Ireland and Portugal) and other regions. Article 12(3) of Regulation 2081/93 prescribes that the increase in commitment appropriations for the Structural Funds must permit a doubling of commitments in real terms under Objective 1 and (now) the Cohesion Fund between 1992 and 1999. Thus, albeit implicitly, a substantive connection is made again between the establishment of EMU and economic and social cohesion. The Commission's proposals for revision of the Structural Funds and of the Cohesion Fund recognize the need to maintain the carrot-and-stick approach thereby implied.[379]

It is noticeable that the basic regulation,[380] and the coordinating regulation[381] pay considerable attention to the demarcation of Community intervention *within* the ambit of economic and social cohesion. The demarcation *vis-à-vis* other Community policies or with national policies coordinated by the Community receives in contrast far too

---

377. Because it replaces the Cohesion Financial Instrument which had been adopted prior to the entry into force of the TEU, as was explained in note 366, *supra*.
378. See Chapter XI, section 7.4, *post*.
379. See COM (98) 130 and 131 Final.
380. Now as contained in Reg. 2081/93 (O.J. 1993 L 193/5).
381. Now as contained in Reg. 2082/93 (O.J. 1993 L 193/20).

little attention.[382] The risk of decision-making on economic and social cohesion turning into an introverted reallocation mechanism, to which reference has already been made above, appears even greater.

Thus it is remarkable that in Objective 3 much attention is paid to the retraining of fragile, lower-educated and less productive employees, but there is scant mention of the conditions under which they may regain employment. If the demand for labour does not increase at macro-economic level, actions at the micro- and meso-economic levels will have little effect. The same applies to the connection between the spatial-economic Objectives 1, 2 and 5b, and the coordination of economic policies in general. It is true that Article 7 of Regulation 2081/93 provides that measures which are financed or supported must 'be in conformity with the provisions of the Treaties, with the instruments adopted pursuant thereto and with Community policies, including those concerning the rules on competition, the award of public contracts, and environmental protection and the application of the principle of equal opportunities for men and women.' But such a generally formulated coordination principle is administratively difficult to maintain. An example of inadequate attuning can be seen in the incongruity between the list of regions which are eligible for Community assistance under Objective 1 and the list of regions in which national state aids are regarded by the Commission as permissible.[383] The Commission has since promised to take the necessary steps to improve the coherence between Community policy concerning state aids and the Structural Funds.[384]

The objectives do not actually give an exhaustive overview of Community expenditure in the context of the Structural Funds: on the basis of Article 12(5) of Regulation 2081/93 and Article 11(1) and (2) of Regulation 2082/93 the Commission may reserve 9% of the commitment appropriations for the funding of Community Initiatives. These are measures which are of significant interest to the Community, and concern very diverse programmes in the regional-economic field and in the field of sectoral restructuring.[385] Some 1% of resources is reserved for Innovative measures, which are also taken on the initiative of the Commission, but they concentrate on exploring new ways of achieving the existing objectives. 90% of the assistance is undertaken at the initiative of a Member State.

382. Art. 130b, 1st para. should cause more attention to be given to this, see Mortelmans (1989) SEW 766 at 770–771.
383. Geelhoed, in the 5th Dutch edition (1995) of this work (at p. 603) based this comment on the Commission's Communication in O.J. 1988 C 212/2. As to the latest statement of the Commission's position, see O.J. 1998 C 74/9, and the Multisectoral Framework on regional aid for large investment projects (O.J. 1998 C 108/7).
384. See the latest views, *ibid.*
385. See COM (94) 46 Final and the Commission's booklet (see note 375, *supra*) 24–25.

B. General Principles. The basic regulation and the coordinating regulation are based on four operating principles: Concentration; Additionality; Programming, and Partnership. These are now considered in turn.

(1) Concentration

All financial instruments are open to political and social pressure to expand their scope. The principle of equality which is mostly wrongly adduced in support of such pressure thus prevails at the expense of the effectiveness of the range of policy instruments concerned. It is therefore correct that in the application of the Structural Funds the concentration principle should be applied: Community resources are principally concentrated on a limited number of priority objectives, namely where the areas and obstacles where the problems are greatest and the Community contribution is likely to be most effective. This substantively significant principle was formulated first in 1988, but, no matter how useful it may be, it is open to pressure to be watered down now that the scale of the Structural Funds has been virtually doubled as a result of the decisions taken at the European Council in Edinburgh in December 1992.[386]

From the *territorial* viewpoint there is a watering-down when the geographical scope of the Structural Funds is extended to new areas (such as the five new German *Länder* or various parts of the newest Member States) without that extension being compensated by removal of eligibility status from areas which have benefitted in the past (this is the asymmetry to which reference was made above). The increase in the Structural Funds causes the net-contributing Member States to propose regions which, on a strict application of the criteria, are not eligible for Community assistance (such as Flevoland in The Netherlands and Henegouwen in Belgium). From the *substantive* viewpoint there is a watering-down when the absorption capacity of the beneficiary Member States is insufficient and the scope of application of certain instruments is extended. Thus investments in the fields of health and education become eligible for ERDF assistance. If the description of the objectives is substantively extended there is also a watering-down of the concentration principle. By comparison with the original descriptions in 1988, the 1993 definitions of Objectives 3 and 4 demonstrate that this has occurred.

(2) Additionality (or complementarity)[387]

Community action through the Structural Funds and other financial instruments would remain largely ineffective if it were to take the place of existing national policies aimed at the same or comparable

---

386. Bull. EC 12–1992, point I.53.
387. The English text of Reg. 2081/93 refers to 'Complementarity', but the term 'Additionality' is more widely used in practice.

objectives, rather than bringing added value in terms of resources and results. Thus Article 4 of Regulation 2081/93 provides that 'Community operations shall be such as to complement or contribute to corresponding national operations.' This principle is developed further in Articles 9(1) and (2) of Regulation 2082/93. Thus Article 9(1) ensures that the Structural Funds and FIFG appropriations allocated in each Member State to each of the objectives 'may not replace public expenditure on structural or comparable expenditure undertaken by the Member State in the whole of the territory eligible under an objective' and Article 9(2) requires the Commission and the Member State concerned to 'ensure that the Member State concerned maintains, in the whole of the territory concerned, its public structural or comparable expenditure at least at the same level as in the previous programming period, taking into account, however, the macroeconomic circumstances in which funding takes place, as well as a number of specific economic circumstances, namely privatizations, an unusual level of public structural expenditure undertaken in the previous programming period and business cycles in the national economy.'[388]

There are still some practical difficulties in maintaining the additionality principle. As long as the total volume of Community transfers for a Member State remains relatively fairly limited, there are few co-financing problems in the national sphere. At the most national regional or structural programmes will have to be somewhat adapted in order to fulfil the conditions for Community financing. This will be different if the Community transfers for the beneficiary Member States become relatively greater: if the total collective expenditure of a member State amounts to about half of GDP, a positive financing percentage of 5% or more of GDP means a share of 10% or more of the total budget. Finding the then necessary national resources for co-financing would in such cases involve a substantive rearrangement of national collective expenditure. In order to avoid such alterations in priorities of national collective expenditure, the Community's regional programmes provide for a progressive Community contribution, in accordance with Article 13 of Regulation 2081/93, which may run to more than 80% of the total programme expenditure for the outermost regions and for the outlying Greek islands.

388. The additionality principle does *not* mean that Community assistance simply complements the expenditure of the Member States in the field concerned. The programming
principle requires that Community and national level efforts are brought together
coherently, which may mean that national policies may in some aspects have to be
adjusted in order to satisfy the conditions under which the Community may grant its
assistance, see Reg. 2082/93, Art. 5.

(3) **Programming**

Initially Community Funds financed mostly individual projects, but this did not assist the mutual coherence of Community actions and their coherence with national actions. With the introduction of the Integrated Mediterranean Programmes and the Integrated Action Programmes in the early Eighties the Commission for the first time attempted to give such actions a programmatic character, in order to strengthen their mutual coherence. With the reform of the Structural Funds this approach was also adopted there, and it is now expressed in Articles 5, 6 and 10 of the coordinating regulation, Regulation 2082/93.

There are three phases in the drawing up of programmes, as set out below.

- The Member States concerned first submit their development plans, drawn up at the geographical level they deem most appropriate, in which it sets out the current situation regarding the objective concerned, on the basis of which Community assistance on the basis of the objective concerned is requested, and the main steps which it has taken in that area. The plans should now also include quantified objectives, where appropriate, for the priorities and measures proposed for Community assistance (this is done with a view to *ex post* evaluation). For Objectives 1, 2, 5b and 6 the regional plans also have to contain an evaluation of the environmental impact of the strategy and operations proposed, as well as (for Objective 1) indicative financial details.
- The Commission establishes a Community Support Framework (CSF) in close consultation with the Member States and the regions concerned. The CSF sets out priorities, the extent of financial assistance, as well now as the additional information mentioned in the first indent, above.
- The implementation measures will usually be in the form of an Operational Programme (OP), but may take other forms. In OPs the Community and national and/or, as the case may be, regional activities are set out in substantive terms and their successive order is fixed. Implementing measures are submitted by the Member State in the form of a request for financing and are adopted by the Commission.

  Since the 1993 reforms the programming may be speeded up and simplified by the Member State submitting a Single Programming Document, consisting of the development plan and the financing request concerned. If this route is used, the Commission's single decision will include components of both the CSF and the OPs or other forms of assistance.[389]

389. See *e.g.* Dec. 97/711 (O.J. 1997 L 308/81) relating to structural assistance to the Gro-ningen-Drenthe region. Objective 5a programming displays some specific features, as to which, see the Commission's booklet (see note 375, *supra*) 23.

(4) **Partnership**

As the above three principles in fact confirm, Community action takes place through close consultation between the Commission and the competent national, regional or local authorities which are designated by each Member State. This partnership is worked out in Article 4 of Regulation 2081/93, which expressly requires the partnership to 'be conducted in full compliance with the respective institutional, legal and financial powers of each of the partners.' Thus the Commission does not have to become involved in questions of the administrative relationships within each Member State.

C. **Institutional coordination deficits.** The four principles set out above all aim to contribute to ensuring as well as possible the substantive internal coordination of the operations of the Community and the Member States. This is only partly reflected in the institutional working out of Articles 130a–130e EC. On the contrary, it is apparent that there is a fragmentation, like ancient Gaul, into three parts.

First, the four Funds (the ERDF, the ESF, the Guidance Section of the EAGGF, and the Cohesion Fund) and FIFG and the other Community financial instruments all remain separate. The first sentence of Article 130d EC does indeed open the possibility of merging the Funds, but this option is purely theoretical, at least for the ERDF, the ESF and the Guidance Section of the EAGGF, as the drafters of Article 130d EC failed to remove the consequences of such a step from the EC Treaty.[390]

Secondly, separate advisory or management committees continue to exist for all the Funds, for FIFG, and for Community Initiatives.[391] Thus the national division of competence in the different policy areas works through into Community decision-making, with all the attendant sensitivities and possible shortcomings.

Thirdly, this diversity in procedures for the adoption of implementing decisions in respect of the various Funds does not contribute to the substantive coherence of such decisions. Given the care which the drafters of these provisions ensured that different procedures applied for the ERDF, the ESF, and the Guidance Section of the EAGGF, the differences may be judged to have been intentional. In that context, it is remarkable that the drafters failed to provide for a procedure for the adoption of implementing decisions for the Cohesion Fund. In short, there is in the

---

390. This is very apparent in Art. 130e EC which provides for separate decision-making procedures in respect of the ERDF (cooperation procedure, which will be changed when the Treaty of Amsterdam enters into force, to substitute the co-decision procedure), with consultation of ECOSOC and the Committee of the Regions, whereas with regard to the Guidance Section of the EAGGF and the ESF, the relevant provisions of Arts. 43 and 125 EC apply (the latter requires the same procedure as applies in respect of the ERDF implementing decisions, and will likewise be changed).
391. Reg. 2081/93, Art. 17.

present text a clear discrepancy between the policy coordination required in Article 130b EC and the institutional and organizational shape of the decision-making procedures under Article 130e EC.[392]

D. Typology of the policy coordination in Articles 130a–130e EC. The objectives set out in section 5.1, above, of Articles 130a–130e EC require a substantive coordination between the operations of the Community and those of the Member States. Given the size of the resources at the Community's disposal up to the end of this Century, the potential instrumental effect of its operations is large, certainly if the additionality principle is taken into account, which requires co-financing by the Member States.

In a certain sense the comparison between Community financing and national linked subsidies is justified. With such subsidies in the Sixties and Seventies, the national central authorities sought unilaterally to influence the policy of the decentralized authorities in the direction which the former desired. The *vertical* coordinating effect of these operations was indeed great, but it led to a gradual undermining of the powers which the decentralized authorities possessed under their national constitutions or other normative arrangements. In the course of the Seventies a reaction occurred, which did lead to the maintenance of the financial streams from 'above' to 'below', but in the policy sense the expenditure of these streams more and more came to be based on agreements (covenants, public programme agreements, joint plans and so on) between the central and decentralized authorities concerned. Vertical coordination thus remained, but increasingly it acquired cooperative traits. In Germany in 1969 this vertical cooperative policy coordination even received constitutional status through the adoption of Article 91a of the Grundgesetz. In the shaping of Community regional policy, as conducted since the mid-Seventies by the ERDF, the German example has undeniably played a part.[393]

From this overview of the principles on which Community policy is based, and from the institutional shaping of the decision-making, it may be concluded that this policy does indeed have a *vertical* coordinating effect, but as far as its organization is concerned, it has extremely *cooperative* traits. The advantages of such an intensive involvement of the Member States, and of the competent decentralized authorities, in the preparation,

---

392. Nonetheless the Commission should at least seek to safeguard the necessary coherence in its policy preparation. It could most effectively fulfil this task by proposing the replacement of the present committees by one single committee. This has not, however, been proposed in the Commission's proposals of 18 March 1988 (COM (98) 131 Final).

393. See *inter alia* Marnitz, *Die Gemeinschaftsaufgaben des Artikel 91a GG als Versuch einer verfassungsrechtlichen Institutionalisierung der bundesstaatlichen Kooperation* (Berlin, 1974).

shaping and execution of the policy are evident. The objections thereto, particularly the domination of Community interests by national and regional particularism, and the risk that policy on Community Structural Funds might be unearthed into a rigid, asymmetrically working mechanism for allocation has already been noted above. In a future revision of the Treaty, Articles 130a–130e deserve thorough revision, both institutionally and substantively, in order to avoid the Community being imprisoned in the *status quo* of an allocation mechanism which becomes steadily more ineffective as time goes by.

5.4 The European Investment Bank (EIB)[394]

The old EEC Treaty provisions which originally governed the EIB[395] have been moved from Part three of the Treaty, dealing with Community policies, to Part Five, which contains the provisions dealing with the institutions, and are now to be found contained in Articles 198d and 198e EC. The present Article 198e EC has been enlarged to include a second paragraph which corresponds with the third sentence of Article 130b EC, in which the EIB is mentioned as one of the instruments for supporting the achievement of economic and social cohesion. Since the promotion of the development potential of the less-developed areas within the Community has grown into one of the Community's key tasks, the political and policy role which the EIB can play therein has increased strongly. This greater attention to the EIB is not only expressed in Articles 130b EC and in the basic and coordinating regulations envisaged in Article 130d EC, discussed in the preceding section, it also appears from the role assigned to the EIB in the decisions adopted during the meeting of the European Council at Edinburgh in December 1992 concerning the financing of major infrastructure projects of the Member States.[396] Although Article 129c(1) EC does not mention the EIB in so many words, the possible contribution which the EIB may make to the financing of trans-European networks for the transport of goods, energy and telecommunications seems to be of crucial importance.[397]

The description of the EIB's tasks in Article 198e EC is related on the one hand to the 'harmonious and balanced development of economic

---

394. See, generally, Currall (1988) CDE 39; Dunnett (1994) 31 CMLRev. 721, and Müller-Borle in Von der Groeben *et al.* (eds.), *op. cit.* (see note 55, *supra*) Vol. 4 1244.
395. Arts. 129 and 130 EEC.
396. Bull. EC 12–1992, point I.71.
397. See also the Conclusions of the Presidency after the European Council at Essen in December 1994, in which a major role is assigned to the EIB in the financing of trans-European networks. See Bull. EU 12–1994, point I.47. See, further, Chapter XI, section 7.4, *post*.

activities' mentioned in Article 2 EC, and, on the other hand, to Articles 130a–130e EC[398] and Articles 129b–129d EC.[399]

The means by which the EIB carries out its tasks are the granting of loans and the provision of guarantees. For these purposes it may have recourse to the capital market or utilize its own resources. After the last enlargement in 1995, the EIB's capital stood at some 62,000 million ECU, which is subscribed by the Member States,[400] although only a small percentage is actually paid-up (currently 4,652 million ECU). This capital permits an aggregate amount of loans and guarantees at any time of up to 155,000 million ECU;[401] but this is not an absolute upper limit for operations by the EIB. If necessary outstanding debts may be assigned in order to create extra room above this ceiling. The financial involvement of the EIB in investments in the Community is greater than that of all the Structural Funds together, and, with a view to the moves to increase employment, the EIB has recently started investing in health and education projects and, indirectly, in technology-related companies.

The first paragraph of Article 198d EC endows the EIB with legal personality, and it is autonomous within the limits prescribed in the EC Treaty itself and in the EIB Statute. This autonomy is a necessary condition for it to be able to function as a credit institution (it enjoys a Triple A rating), and only with autonomy is it in a position to operate under the most favourable conditions for borrowers. This financially-technical autonomy does impose functional limits on the degree to which involvement of the EIB can be coordinated with the involvement of other Community instruments in the context of Articles 129c and 130b EC.[402]

Although the EIB operates strictly according to banking requirements and rules, and evaluates accordingly all projects which it is asked to (co-) finance, it is attractive for most credit seekers in the economically weaker parts of the Community to seek its assistance. Because the EIB is a non-profit institution with an absolutely gilt-edged reputation as the rating implies, it is able to attract outside finance at relatively cheap rates, thus on the most favourable terms. This attractiveness has of course the other side of the coin, namely the danger of distortions of competition on the capital markets and an excessive call on its lending capacity. Thus Article 198e EC prescribes a two-part threshold:

398. See Art. 198e EC, 1st para., points (a) and (b), and 2nd para.
399. See Art. 198e EC, 1st para., point (c).
400. See the EIB Statute (No. A, annexed to the EC Treaty), Art. 4 (as amended). Under changes decided on 5 June 1998 this amount will increase to 100,000 million ECU on 1 January 1999.
401. See EIB Statute, Art. 18(4). This will rise to 250,000 million ECU on 1 January 1999.
402. See Case 85/86 *Commission v. Board of Governors of the European Investment Bank* [1988] ECR 1281, and Dunnett (1991) 31 CMLRev. 721 at 750–754.

(1) EIB financing is always partial financing, as its grants loans and guarantees which 'facilitate the financing' of projects;[403]
(2) a call may be made on the EIB only 'to the extent that funds are not available from other sources on reasonable terms'.[404]

From the principle that the EIB operates according to banking standards, it does not follow that it only finances *projects*. In the attuning of operations of the EIB and the Structural Funds, in the programmatic approach envisaged in Regulation 2081/93,[405] account must be taken of this fact.

Article 198e EC makes it plain that the EIB's financing activities embrace 'all sectors of the economy.' This phrase must be widely interpreted, as the public supply side of the market embraces more than purely 'economic' infrastructure. If it can be demonstrated that the investments concerned are macro-economically sufficiently cost-effective, environmental investments and investments in educational infrastructure will also be eligible for EIB finance.[406]

So far the major part of the activities of the EIB has been the grant of loans, although that appears to be changing. With the establishment of the European Investment Fund (EIF)[407] agreed at the European Council in Edinburgh[408] This Fund, which in addition to the EIB's involvement is also open to contributions by private capital lenders,[409] is designed to give guarantees for loans to small and medium-sized enterprises and for the development of trans-European networks in the fields of transport, telecommunications and energy infrastructure. With a gearing of 1:8, the capital of 2,000 million ECU permits 16,000 million ECU lending capacity to be generated on the ordinary capital markets. For guarantees its ratio of obligations to resources is limited to 1:3, so it may grant guarantees up to 5,397,000 million ECU.[410] The coming years will require

---

403. This applies 'as far as possible', see EIB Statute, Art. 18(2).
404. *Ibid.*, Art. 18(1). This applies even though the reference to projects being 'of such a size or nature that they cannot be entirely financed by the various means available in the individual Member States' is contained only in points (b) and (c) of Art. 198e, 1st para. (and thus not in *ibid.*, point (a)).
405. O.J. 1993 L 193/5.
406. Müller-Borle in Von der Groeben *et al.* (eds.), *op. cit.* (See note 55, *supra*) Vol. 4 1288.
407. Power to establish the EIF is conferred by EIB Protocol, Art. 30, inserted by the Act of 25 March 1993. The amendment entered into force on 1 May 1994 (see O.J. 1994 L 173/21). As to the Statute of the EIF, see O.J. 1994 L 173/1; as to Community participation in the EIF, see Dec. 94/375 (O.J. 1994 L 173/12). See, further, Dec. 97/761 (O.J. 1997 L 310/28) on transnational Joint Ventures for small and medium-sized enterprises and Dec. 98/347 (O.J. 1998 L 155/43).
408. Bull. EC 12–1992, point I.72.
409. At the end of 1997 the EIF had 79 shareholders 77 banks and financial institutions, the European Community, and the EIB, *General Report 1997* (Brussels, Luxembourg, 1998) point 127.
410. *General Report 1997, ibid.*

very extensive investment in infrastructure networks in the Community, in order to cope with increasing demands of transport and communications. The national budgets which must conform to the sharp requirements of Article 104c EC do not at present afford sufficient room, and so a growing role for the EIB in the financing of the required investments may be expected.

6. Social Policy[411]

6.1 Scope and history

The role of the Community in the field of social policy is still unclearly worked out, even after the changes which will result when the Treaty of Amsterdam enters into force. There are three factors which explain why. First, the EC Treaty provisions themselves are still unclear. The social provisions of Chapter 1 of Title VIII of Part Three of the EC Treaty do contain some powers for the Community to act in specific areas, but, unlike in the case of economic policy, there is no express policy-

---

411. For reasons set out at the beginning of this Chapter, *ante*, this discussion reflects the situation after the entry into force of the Treaty of Amsterdam. In view of the political developments since May 1997, this now reflects social policy in practice. The term 'the present Art. xxx' means that provision as it still is prior to the entry into force of the Treaty of Amsterdam, and the term 'the new Art. xxx' refers to the relevant provision as thus revised. This would appear to be the least confusing option.

The literature in this field is vast: see, *inter alia*, Barnard, *EC Employment Law* (Rev. ed., Chichester, 1996); Blanpain and Engels, *European Labour Law* (The Hague, 1997); Davies *et al.* (eds.), *European Community Labour Law* (*Liber Amicorum* Lord Wedderburn, Oxford, 1996); Ellis, *European Community Sex Equality Law* (2nd ed., Oxford, 1998); Hervey, *Justifications for Sex Discrimination in Employment* (London, 1993); and *European Social Law and Policy* (London, 1998); Hervey and O'Keeffe (eds.), *Sex Equality Law in the European Union* (Chichester, 1996); Lyon-Caen *et al. Droit social international et européen* (Paris, 1985); Nielsen and Szyszczak, *The Social Dimension of the European Community* (2nd ed., Copenhagen, 1993); Ribas, *La politique sociale des Communautés Européennes* (Paris, 1979); Vogel-Polsky *L'Europe sociale 1993 – Illusion, alibi au réalité?* (Brussels, 1991); Banks (1993) CDE 537 and in Curtin and O'Keeffe (eds.), *Constitutional Adjudication in European Community and National Law* (Essays for O'Higgins, Dublin, 1992) 107; Betten (1998) 23 ELRev. 20; Cloos *et al.*, *op. cit.* (see note 55, *supra*) 302–319; Davies (1997) 34 CMLRev. 571; Ellis (1994) 31 CMLRev. 47 and (1998) 35 CMLRev. 379; Fenwick and Hervey (1995) 32 CMLRev. 443; De Groot (1993) 30 CMLRev. 331; Laske (1993) 30 CMLRev. 515; More (1995) 15 YBEL 135; Moore (M.) (1998) 35 CMLRev. 409; Moore (S.) (1994) 19 ELRev. 425; Mosley (1990) RTDE 157; the contributions by Schulte and Willms in Von der Groeben *et al.* (eds.), *op. cit.* (see note 55, *supra*) Vol. 3 (commentary on Arts. 117–122 EC); Smitis (1996) ELJ 156; Van Raepenbusch *et al.* in Mégret *et al.*, *op. cit.* (see note 55, *supra*, Brussels, 1998) Vol. 7, 9–192; Watson (1991) 28 CMLRev. 37 and (1993) 30 CMLRev. 481; and Whiteford in Shaw and More (eds.), *New Legal Dynamics of European Union* (Oxford, 1995) 111 and (1995) 32 CMLRev. 801.

coordinating competence for the Community in the social policy field.[412]

In Articles 2 and 3 EEC there was no express reference to social policy. The TEU filled this *lacuna* by including in the objectives mentioned in Article 2 EC 'a high level of employment and of social protection' and by expressly mentioning in Article 3 EC, as one of the means specified there 'a policy in the social sphere comprising a European Social Fund'. This Article 3(i) EC (which will, confusingly, become Article 3(j) EC) demonstrates the unsure hand of the fathers of the revisions to the EC Treaty in this field: this provision offers no peg on which to hang anything about the nature of Community competence or over its scope.[413]

The second factor is that the content of the concept 'social policy' as such is very heterogeneous and open to changing interpretations. Thus there is no firm point to which to anchor the mutual demarcation between Community policies and national policies, unlike in the case of general economic policies. The complexity of the question of the division of competence becomes greater, if it is remembered that in the various Member States the mutual demarcation between public competence, the intermediate competence of the social partners, and the competence of individual employers and employees is extremely diverse and is subject to constant change. If social policy is described as the whole corpus of public arrangements which is applicable particularly to the protection of the labour factor and security of living of citizens, most of the elements of social policy in West European welfare states are caught by that description.[414]

Thirdly, there are major differences of views between the Member States about the objectives and shaping of social policy, and about the demarcation between the public, intermediate, and private sectors in that area. These differences in views find their reflection in fundamental conceptual differences as to the role which the Community should play in this area. This does not merely refer to the tensions between the British and continental views about the role of the public sector (and the

412. See the new Art. 118(1) EC: 'With a view to achieving the objectives of Art. 177, the Community shall support and complement the activities of the Member States in the following fields.' The new Art. 118c EC also does not provide a clear coordinating competence for the Community.

413. This does not detract from the point that the objective expressed in Art. 2 EC, which is further worked out in both the present Art. 117 EC, and in more detail in the new Art. 117 EC, may *not* be regarded as a mere declaration of intent without any obligation. As to earlier arguments on similar lines, see Case 149/77 *Defrenne v. SABENA* [1978] ECR 1365 at 1375–1377.

414. This description also embraces public law provisions regulating markets in which social risks are covered through means of private law, such as the legal provisions concerning employee pension funds, as well as the function, governed by public law, of the social partners in the primary pension funds, and also the likewise regulated role of the social partners in primary and secondary terms of employment and social security.

Community) in this area. Also the Member States which traditionally sought to attain a high level of public social protection have problems with conferring on the Community its own role in this area.[415] This is connected with the typical conflict of public and private powers which characterize this policy area in most continental Member States, where the social partners tend to play their own part in decision-making, and where it is not unusual for them to be endowed with their own responsibilities in the execution of policy. Thus the national social structure is the prime expression of national ideological, cultural and social traditions. It is thus extremely sensitive about external interventions, however small they may be. This was apparent *inter alia* in the implementation of Directive 79/7 on the application of the principle of equal treatment of men and women in the field of social security.[416] This fragility also exists in respect of exogenous developments at the macro- and meso-economic levels. The establishment and operation of the common market have increased this fragility.[417] The autonomous policy margin for national policies on employment, instruments influencing the general distribution of incomes, wages and other working conditions, and social security becomes squeezed. This two-part sensitivity for the existence and action of the Community as a framework of economic integration is expressed in the somewhat ambivalent attitude of most Member States towards the Community in the social field. On the one hand national primacy is jealously and not unegoistically guarded, yet on the other hand the criticism is voiced that the Community pays inadequate attention to the social consequences of the economic integration process.[418]

In order to determine correctly the scope of the Community's role in the social field, it is necessary to break through the highly artificial distinction between on the one part market integration and economic policy integration, and, on the other part, social policy and social integration. The welfare gains resulting from the combination of market integration and economic policy integration, for a large part bring direct benefits to the labour factor. Moreover, they increase the economic basis of support for social objectives.

---

415. Watson (1991) 28 CMLRev. 37 at 39–43.
416. O.J. 1979 L 6/24. As to implementation of directives in general, see Chapter VI, sections 2.2.2 and 2.2.4, *ante* This fragility is also particularly evident in the Member States' reaction to the judgment in Case C-262/88 *Barber v. Guardian Royal Exchange Group* [1990] ECR 1889, [1990] 2 CMLR 513 in the form of a Protocol (No. 2, annexed to the EC Treaty) concerning Art. 119 EC (the so-called *Barber* Protocol).
417. The fear of the results of exposure to these forces caused the French government in the negotiations leading to the EC Treaty in 1956 to seek harmonization in the social field which should precede the establishment of the common market, see Pipkorn in Von der Groeben *et al.* (eds.), *Kommentar zum EWG-Vertrag* (4th ed., Baden-Baden, 1991) Vol. 3, 3282–3286.
418. *E.g.* Steyger (1991) SEW 607.

Insofar as harmonization of national laws and policy in the social field is necessary for the achievement and proper functioning of the common market, the EC Treaty poses no obstacle to the choice *at Community level* for a responsible level of social protection. In addition to the present wording of Article 117 EC, also the present wording of Article 2 EC expressly points in the direction of this approach.[419] Thus it is certainly *not* the case that the social objectives set out in that latter provision ought to be achieved only by recourse to the provisions of the EC Treaty specifically devoted to social policy. This also follows implicitly from the wording of the beginning of the present Article 118 EC.[420] In the new Article 117 EC there is express reference to the significance of Community action in other areas for the achievement of the social objectives.[421]

As explained in the discussion of Articles 48–51 EC, above,[422] the free movement of workers cannot as such be achieved without coordination of the application of national social security systems to migrant workers In itself Article 51 EC leaves room to effect a certain convergence between national social security systems with a view to the free movement of workers. This is very necessary, as the reprivatization of parts of previously collective social security, whether or not it occurs under conditions imposed by public law, makes the mutual connection of national social security schemes as a result of Regulation 1408/71[423] more difficult. But up to now the Member States have been barely responsive to Commission proposals to adapt that regulation to the changes in the structure of national social security. Thus, through lack of maintenance, as it were, the regulation which should facilitate cross-border movement of workers forms a hindrance to such movement, the extent of which should not be underestimated.[424] The existing rules for free movement of workers are also outmoded in two other respects. The proportion of non-Community nationals among migrant workers has sharply increased in recent years. Given that Articles 48–51 EC are applicable only to nationals of the Member States, third-country nationals enjoy no rights on the basis of

419. In the same sense, Pipkorn in Von der Groeben *et al.* (eds.), *op. cit.* (see note 417, *supra*) 3278–3282.
420. 'Without prejudice to the other provisions of this Treaty and in conformity with its general objectives, the Commission shall....' A good example of a 'social' directive not based on the specific social provisions of the EC Treaty is Dir. 76/207 (O.J. 1976 L 39/40) on the implementation of the principle of equal treatment of men and women in access to employment, vocational training, promotion and working conditions.
421. See the new Art. 117 EC, 3rd para.
422. Chapter VII, section 5.4, *ante.*
423. In its original version, O.J. English Special Edition 1971 (II), p. 416; text most recently integrally replaced by Reg. 118/97 (O.J. 1997 L 28/1), and most recently amended by by Reg. 1223/98 (O.J. 1998 L 168/1). See Cornelissen (1996) 33 CMLRev. 439.
424. Watson (1991) 28 CMLRev. 37 at 54; Laske (1993) 30 CMLRev. 515 at 521–529.

those provisions.[425] To the extent that there is cross-border movement of nationals of Member States, the proportion of highly-educated persons in such movement appears to be increasing. Yet Regulation 1408/71 is oriented to the connection between *public* social security arrangements, and copes badly with the primarily *private* social protection arrangements which persons in that category frequently have.[426]

It was submitted in section 1.4 of this Chapter, above, that social policy cannot be uncoupled from general economic policy. A socio-economic system which even with economic growth exceeding 2% leads to greater inactivity of the working population becomes in time unsustainable.[427] Thus both coordination of economic policies in accordance with Article 103 EC and the coordination of employment policy under the new Articles 109n–109s EC will have positive social consequences. The social aspect also weighs heavily in the policy for the strengthening of economic and social cohesion discussed in section 5, above. The fact that the ESF is involved in this policy indicates this point convincingly.

The express emphasis which is placed in Articles 126 and 127 EC on the quality and availability of education and vocational training – one of the most important conditions for a socially vigilant working population – confirms once again that the possibilities for the Community to act in order to achieve social objectives are broader than those resulting from the 'social provisions' of the EC Treaty themselves. Viewed thus, in the achievement of its core objectives, the Community can also achieve its social objectives, without specific powers directed at social policy being necessary for this purpose.[428]

In the present state of the development of Community law in this field, as set out in the new Articles 117–118c EC, the Community will not be able to take over all the major tasks of the Member States relating to the regulation of their labour markets, the shaping of conditions of employment, the shaping and determination of the level of social security, and other forms of social protection. Apart from the major political differences in views on these aspects, the differences in policy strategy and policy culture within the Community, to which reference has been made, above, pose serious obstacles. Moreover, the still very considerable

425. This also appears to be confirmed by the Court in Case 118/75 *Watson and Belmann* [1976] ECR 1185, [1976] 2 CMLR 552 and Case 48/75 *Procureur du Roi v. Royer* [1975] ECR 497, [1976] 2 CMLR 619. See Hedemann-Robinson (1996) YBEL 321; Peers (1996) 33 CMLRev. 7, and Verschueren (1997) 34 CMLRev. 991. See now, however, the Commission's proposal to remedy this problem, COM (97) 561 Final (O.J. 1998 C 6/15).

426. Laske (1993) 30 CMLRev. 515 at 521.

427. See the Commission's White Paper, *Growth Competitiveness, Employment* (COM (93) 700), Bull. EU Supp. 6/93, Chapter II.

428. In the same sense, Centre for Economic Policy Research, *Making Sense of Subsidiarity* (London, 1993) 101–115.

differences in levels of prosperity, and the relatively small-scale Community budget, stand in the way of action by the Community itself.[429] The experiences in Germany with the social integration of the five new *Länder* provide a good example. The increase in the direct and indirect labour costs, which far exceeded labour productivity in the former DDR, led there to widespread open and disguised unemployment. For the restoration of the balance between labour costs and labour productivity, very high levels of investment are now necessary there, causing federal transfers of capital running into tens of thousands of million DM annually. And this apart from the consumer transfers for the benefit of the vastly increased reservoir of inactive persons.

The Community on the other hand cannot permit national interventions which, under the guise of employment policy, appear to be discriminatory or distortive of competition, without conflicting with its own key objectives of the unity of the market and equality.[430] Equally so, it is unable to dampen the reallocation symptoms which are inherent in the greater dynamism of an open common market, even if the sharper pressure of cross-frontier market competition would force adaptation of the social *acquis* in the national sphere. It can, on the other hand, act against economically unfounded policy competition by using its powers *inter alia* on the basis of Article 101 EC, although so far that particular provision has not been used.[431]

In the light of what has been observed above, the Community's own policies, specifically targeted at the social field will for the time being continue to be of a modest and complementary character. But before arriving at a judgment that the Treaty 'therefore' treats social policy ungenerously, the social elements in the other actions of the Community should be brought into the equation. *Grosso modo* the development of social policy in the Community may be divided into four phases.[432] The first phase runs from 1958–1972, during which period most attention was paid to the achievement of the free movement of persons. Regulation 1408/71[433] and its predecessors[434] on the coordination of national social security

---

429. The Community budget amounts to some 1.2% of the GDP of the Community, whereas the share of social security expenditure even in Member States with a relatively weakly developed social security structure, such as Portugal and the United Kingdom, accounts for more than 10 times that level.
430. See *inter alia* Case C-21/88 *Du Pont de Nemours Italiana SpA v. Unità sanitaria locale No 2 di Carrara* [1990] ECR I-889, [1991] 3 CMLR 25; Case 249/81 *Commission v. Ireland* [1982] ECR 4005, [1983] 2 CMLR 104, and Case 31/87 *Gebroeders Beentjes BV v. The Netherlands State* [1988] ECR 4635, [1990] 1 CMLR 287. See also Fernández Martín and Stehman (1991) 16 ELRev. 216.
431. See Chapters VII, section 5.4 and VIII, section 3.1, *ante*.
432. Watson (1991) 28 CMLRev. 37 at 43–45; Pipkorn in Von den Groeben *et al.*, *op. cit.*(see note 417, *supra*) 3286–3297.
433. See note 423, *supra*, and p. 692 (note 705) *supra*.
434. Regs. 3 and 4 (J.O. 1958, pp. 561 and 597 respectively).

schemes with a view to the free movement of workers were the most important results achieved. The second phase began at the Paris Summit in 1972, which, in addition to making efforts to achieve an EMU, also announced an active Community policy in the social field. That led to the adoption of the Social Action Programme in January 1974.[435] The main objectives of this programme were attainment of full and high value employment, the improvement of living and working conditions, and the strengthening of participation by employers' and employees' organizations in Community policy. The first of these objectives, as a primarily *economic* policy objective, remained in the Sixties and the Seventies largely beyond reach. Particularly in regard to the second objective, some important results were achieved, with the adoption of a trio of directives on protection of employees' rights in the event of collective redundancies,[436] the transfer of undertakings,[437] and the insolvency of their employer;[438] and a trio of directives to ensure the equal treatment of men and women in the application of the principle of equal pay,[439] access to employment, vocational training, promotion and working conditions,[440] and in matters of social security.[441] The first important Community initiatives in the field of working conditions and health and safety at work also date from this period, and include a directive on the provision of safety signs at places of work.[442] This second phase was concluded with the entry into force of the SEA. The introduction of Article 118a EC can be regarded as the creation of a specific legal basis for Community action, which had hitherto been based on the general harmonization powers contained in Article 100 EC. Article 118b EC is the renewed expression of the desirability of more active

---

435. O.J. 1974 C 13/1; Bull. EC Supp. 2/74.
436. Dir. 75/129 (O.J. 1975 L 48/29, amended by Dir. 92/56 (O.J. 1992 L 245/3)).
437. Dir. 77/187 (O.J. 1977 L 61/26).
438. Dir. 80/987 (O.J. 1980 L 283/23, amended by Dir. 87/164 (O.J. 1987 L 66/11)). This directive gave rise to celebrated case-law of more general application, see *e.g.* Cases C-6 and 9/90 *Francovich et al. v. Italy* [1991] ECR I-5357, [1993] 2 CMLR 66; Case C-479/93 *Francovich v. Italy* [1995] ECR I-3843; Cases C-94 and 95/95 *Bonifaci et al. v. Instituto nazionale della Previdenza Sociale (INPS)* [1997] ECR I-3969, and Case C-117/96 *Danmarks Aktive Handelsrejsende v. Lønmodtagernes Garantifond* [1997] ECR I-5017.
439. Dir. 75/117 (O.J. 1975 L 45/19).
440. Dir. 76/207 (O.J. 1976 L 39/40). This directive is discussed in more detail in section 6.2, *post*. Among more recent case-law, see Case C-450/93 *Kalanke v. Freie Hansestadt Bremen* [1995] ECR I-3051; Case C-139/95 *Balestra v. Instituto Nazionale della Previdenza Sociale (INPS)* [1997] ECR I-549; Case C-180/95 *Draehmpael v. Urania Immobilienservice ohG* [1997] ECR I-2195; Case C-1/95 *Gerster v. Freistaat Bayern* [1997] ECR I-5253; Case C-100/95 *Kording v. Senator für Finanzen* [1997] ECR I-5289; Case C-409/95 *Marschall v. Land Nordrhein-Westfalen* [1997] ECR I-6363, and Case C-249/96 *Grant v. South-West Trains Ltd.* [1998] ECR I-621. See, generally, Ellis (1994) 31 CMLRev. 43, (1998) 35 CMLRev. 379 and Ward (1998) 23 ELRev. 65.
441. Dir. 79/7 (O.J. 1979 L 6/24). This directive is also briefly discussed in section 6.2, *post*.
442. Dir. 77/576 (O.J. 1977 L 229/12, amended by Dir. 79/640 (O.J. 1979 L 183/11).

involvement on the part of employers' and employees' organizations in social policy at Community level. These provisions will be replaced by the new Articles 118 and 118a EC when the Treaty of Amsterdam enters into force.

The third phase commenced with the meeting of the European Council in Hannover in the Summer of 1988. On that occasion the European Council emphasized the importance of the social aspects of the internal market, and invited the Commission to make appropriate proposals.[443] This led in the first instance to the publication of a working paper, entitled *The Social Dimension of the Internal Market*[444] and later to a draft Community Social Charter.[445] This draft was largely based on the Council of Europe's existing European Social Charter,[446] to which most of the Member States were signatories. Although in various respects the Community Social Charter was weakened and shortened, it was accepted on 9 December 1989 by only 11 of the then 12 Member States.[447] The United Kingdom declined to agree, arguing that the matters contained therein fell within the competence of the Member States, rather than that of the Community.[448] The Community Charter of the Fundamental Social Rights of Workers (to give it its full title) does not itself impose binding obligations, it is merely declaratory.[449] In implementation of the Charter, an action programme was adopted by the Commission.[450] The proposals contained therein met little support in the Member States, some of which complained that the Commission was giving an extensive interpretation of Articles 100a and 118a EC, on the basis of which decision-making is possible by qualified majority. Although it might have been expected to be otherwise, the United Kingdom was not always in an isolated position in its opposition to the Commission's ideas. The equivocal attitude of the Member States, mentioned above, appeared here too: most were prepared to formulate ambitious objectives in the social field, but had major difficulties about Community action to implement those

---

443. Bull. EC 6–1988, point 3.4.1 (at p. 165).
444. Bull. EC 9–1988, points 1.1.1–1.1.7.
445. COM (89) 248 Final.
446. Turin, 18 October 1961 (ETS No. 35, with subsequent Protocols; revised at Strasbourg, 3 May 1996 (ETS No. 163)).
447. Bull. EC 12–1989, point 1.1.10. As to the Community Social Charter, see *Social Europe* 1/90 pp. 46–50 (that whole issue contains valuable articles and background documents).
448. Behind every argument as to competence there lurk substantive objections: the then United Kingdom government had pursued a policy of considerable deregulation and had effectively 'seen off the unions.' From its perspective, new rules coming from the Community level risked undoing much of what it felt it had achieved.
449. But that does not prevent it from being used as a guideline in the interpretation of national and Community level provisions, see Case C-106/89 *Marleasing v. La Comercial Internacional de Alimentación SA* [1990] ECR I-4135, [1992] 1 CMLR 305 and Case C-322/88 *Grimaldi v. Fonds des maladies professionnelles* [1989] ECR I-4407.
450. COM (89) 568 Final. See *Social Europe* 1/90 (Luxembourg, 1990) 51–76.

objectives. It is most regrettable that proposals for remedying the major *lacunae* in Regulation 1408/71 and for the expansion of its personal and substantive scope remained without result.[451] The same applied to the proposal[452] relating to posted workers, which followed in the footsteps of the Court's judgment in Case C-113/89 *Rush Portugesa Lda v. Office National d'Immigration*[453] and aimed to control the social abuse of the freedom to provide services by 'social dumping.' This equivocal stance did not, however, lead the vast majority of Member States to object to the inclusion of the objectives contained in the Community Social Charter in the EC Treaty, and to the extension of Community competence in this field.[454] Even after the original proposals had been watered down, the United Kingdom strenuously resisted any expansion of Community competence in this field. This finally resulted in the Protocol on Social Policy, to which was annexed the Agreement on Social Policy, which latter embodied arrangements agreed between the Member States other than the United Kingdom.[455] This multi-speed approach was in the event to have a relatively short life, but it caused interesting legal problems, resulting from social policy integration being based within the Community partly on the EC Treaty itself, and partly on a separate agreement: central in the discussion was the issue whether the Protocol, the Agreement, and legislation adopted thereunder, applicable to the then 11 Member States, formed part of the corpus of Community law, or whether it formed a *sui generis* international agreement.[456] In the event, the Agreement was only invoked as the legal basis for two measures prior to the signature of the Treaty of Amsterdam.[457]

The election of a Labour government in the United Kingdom in May 1997 heralded a major shift in that Member State's attitude to social policy, which meant that previous resistance to the integration of the

---

451. Laske (1993) 30 CMLRev. 515 at 518–519.

452. COM (91) 230 Final (O.J. 1991 C 225/6).

453. [1990] ECR I-1417, [1991] 2 CMLR 818.

454. Although a Luxembourg initiative to introduce decision-making by qualified majority in cooperation with the European Parliament into Art. 51 EC fell by the wayside at an early stage in the negotiations, see Laske (1993) 30 CMLRev. 515 at 519.

455. Protocol (No. 14, annexed to the EC Treaty). See Cloos *et al.*, *op. cit.* (See note 55, *supra*) 307–315.

456. Different views on this (now otiose) question were expressed in the literature, see *e.g.* Curtin (1993) 30 CMLRev. 17 at 53–61; Vogel-Polsky, *Evaluation of the Social Provisions of the Treaty on European Union* (Report for the Committee on Social Affairs, Employment and the Working Environment of the European Parliament, DOC EN (CM) 202155), and Watson (1993) 30 CMLRev. 481.

457. Dir. 94/45 on the establishment of a European Works Council or a procedure in Community-scale undertakings and Community-scale groups of undertakings for the purposes of informing and consulting employees (O.J. 1994 L 254/64) and Dir. 96/34 on the framework agreement on parental leave concluded by UNICE, CEEP and the ETUC (O.J. 1994 L 145/64).

Agreement on Social Policy into the EC Treaty disappeared immediately. Thus the Treaty of Amsterdam heralds the beginning of the fourth phase in the development of the Community's social policy. The provisions in the Protocol and the Agreement were adapted in various parts, and the present Articles 117–120 EC will be replaced by new Articles 117–120 EC. Even though the Treaty of Amsterdam is not yet in force at the date at which this work states the law, the United Kingdom government declared during the meeting of the European Council in Amsterdam in June 1997 that it wished to accept the directives which had been adopted under the Agreement.[458] This resulted in the United Kingdom being invited to express its views in discussions on acts which it was proposed to adopt on the basis of the Agreement, pending the entry into force of the Treaty of Amsterdam. In the meantime, the question arose as to how the existing directives might be extended to apply to the United Kingdom. It was concluded that Article 100 EC offered the best legal basis for this, and the Council adopted directives simply extending the scope of the earlier measures to the United Kingdom.[459] In the meantime, the Council adopted two more measures under the Agreement.[460]

The background history to the adoption of the Community Social Charter and the Protocol on Social Policy remains interesting simply because it sheds light on two completely different visions regarding the process of integration within Europe. The former Conservative government regarded as a matter of principle the Community as having absolutely no powers in the social field. It saw it as a matter for the Member States themselves to draw the consequences of the differences in their social legislation for the competitive position of their own industry. Thus a 'spontaneous' harmonization to the bottom, in the form of policy competition was entirely legitimate, as the logical result of market integration.[461] This view, in which competition of norms is a normal and acceptable consequence of market integration also extends to other flanking areas such as environmental policy and consumer policy. Certainly, in the resistance displayed by the previous British administrations, aversion as a matter of principle to any form of intermediary involvement of the

458. Bull. EU 6–1997, point I.8
459. See Dir. 97/74 (O.J. 1998 L 10/22) which extends the scope of Dir. 94/45 (O.J. 1994 L 254/64), and Dir. 97/75 (O.J. 1998 L 10/24) which extends the scope of Dir. 96/34 (O.J. 1996 L 145/4); both make consequential amendments as well.
460. There are two new measures Dir. 97/80 (O.J. 1998 L 14/6) on the burden of proof in sex discrimination cases (extension to the United Kingdom has been proposed (COM (98) 84 Final (O.J. 1998 C 123/6)) and is expected to be agreed very shortly), and Dir. 97/81 (O.J. 1998 L 14/9) concerning the framework agreement on part-time work concluded by UNICE, CEEP and the EUTC (amended and extended to apply to the United Kingdom by Dir. 98/23 (O.J. 1998 L 131/10)).
461. Cf. Case C-113/89 Rush Portugesa Lda v. Office National d'Immigration [1990] ECR I-1417, [1991] 2 CMLR 818.

social partners in the shaping and execution of social policy played a part. Moreover, they were convinced that against the background of increased competition on the world market level, the welfare state in the continental model was as such due for drastic slimming-down. The increase in the Community's social ambitions would be incompatible with that view.

The continental view that market integration requires harmonization of public legislation and public burdens in the interests of unity and its operation stood in marked contrast to the view of the former British administrations. In such harmonization, the continental approach seeks to balance economic interests against the interests involved in the legislation concerned. As has been noted above, the EC Treaty in certain places accords particular weight to certain specific non-economic interests, which the Community and the Member States must respect.[462]

It is submitted that it is impossible within the common market that an unrestrained competition of norms should force abolition of public law rules for the protection of public interests. Such a result would lead to major distortions of competition continuing within the common market, which could seriously damage its functioning. If, for example, major differences in environmental requirements for certain industrial activities could have far-reaching consequences for the allocation of such activities, that would be at the expense of the efficiency of the market mechanism as such. Moreover, forms of extremely low levels of protection in the social, environmental and health fields may have serious cross-border effects for other Member States. For this reason the original EEC Treaty envisaged from the outset powers for the Community to harmonize national legislation and coordinate national policies.[463] This view does *not* imply complete harmonization of public law rules within the Community in fields such as environmental protection and social policy. The major divergence of rules within the Community in these areas makes such a uniformization undesirable. Certainly in the social field, where, as has been noted above, national policy traditions play such an important role, a far-reaching harmonization of policy from on high is less desirable, also on economic grounds, certainly if considerable increases in gross labour costs would result. For this reason the new Articles 117–120 EC are timidly formulated, both as regards objectives and Community competence. In their application the cohesion with the coordination of economic policies under Article 103 EC and with policy coordination in the field of employment under the new Article 109q EC will have to be ensured.

---

462. *E.g.* Arts. 100a(3) EC; 129a EC (consumer protection), and 130a–130t EC (protection of the environment). As to the continental views, see, further, Cloos *et al.* (see note 55, *supra*) 306 (citing Delors).

463. See the general and specific harmonization provisions in the EC Treaty, particularly Arts. 100, 100a and 101 EC.

6.2 The new Articles 117–120 EC; Articles 121–122 and 126–127 EC

A. The new Articles 117 and 118 EC. The objectives of action by the Community and by the Member States are set out in the first paragraph of the new Article 117 EC. This expresses the continuity of legal developments in the Community in the social field by the express references to the European Social Charter of 1961 and the Community Social Charter of 1989. The catalogue of objectives set out embraces many matters, working out more precisely the objectives in the social field formulated in Article 2 EC. More particularly these are: the promotion of employment; improved living and working conditions; proper social protection; dialogue between management and labour; the development of human resources with a view to lasting high employment, and the combating of exclusion.[464] This clearly indicates that for the achievement of these objectives, action by the Community and the Member States will be required in a much broader range of areas than merely in the field of social policy in the narrow sense.

Thus for the promotion of employment Article 103 EC and the employment provisions in the new Articles 109n–109s EC will be of major importance. Improved living and working conditions require economic growth[465] For the convergence of living and working conditions, the unity and functioning of the common market and the policy on economic and social cohesion are of considerable importance. Particular Community competence for the development of human resources can be found in Articles 126 and 127 EC. Combating exclusion is best served by a high level of employment and a labour market policy directed at the weakest groups.[466]

The second paragraph of the new Article 117 EC confirms on the one hand the need to take account of the diverse forms of national practices in the social field, which was highlighted above. In mentioning the need to maintain the competitiveness of the Community economy, it reconfirms the connection between the economic and social policy objectives of the EC Treaty.[467] The important judgment in Case 126/86 *Zaera v. Instituto*

---

464. The importance of the promotion of improved working conditions and an improved standard of living for workers was already recognized in the present Art. 117 EC.
465. Art. 103 EC.
466. See the new Art. 109p EC.
467. An issue already addressed by the Court in Case 43/75 *Defrenne v. SABENA* [1976] ECR 455 at 472, from which it is apparent that the objectives of the present Art. 117 EC has an economic component (such as combating distortions of competition) as well as a social component, both of which are equally important. This was confirmed in Case 28/66 *The Netherlands v. Commission* [1968] ECR 1 at 12–13. This older case-law was confirmed and further developed in Case 149/77 *Defrenne* [1978] ECR 1365 at 1376–1379; Case 30/85 *Teuling v. Bedrijfsvereniging voor de Chemische Industrie* [1987] ECR 2497 at 2521–2523, and Case 71/85 *State of the Netherlands v. Federatie Nederlandse Vakbeweging*, [1986] ECR 3855 at 3875–3877 which cast further light on the interaction of economic policy and social policy. Attempts during the run-up to the

Nacional de la Seguridad Social et al.[468] is of interest for the interpretation of the first and third paragraphs of the new Article 117 EC.[469] The Court noted that the programmatic character of the objectives set out in the present Article 117 EC did not mean that they had no legal effect. They form elements for the interpretation and application of other provisions of the EC Treaty and secondary Community legislation in the social field. This view is most certainly also applicable in relation to the new Article 117 EC.

Three means are set out in the third paragraph of the new Article 117 EC: the functioning of the common market; the procedures provided for in the EC Treaty itself, and the approximation of provisions laid down by law, regulation or administrative action. These three means are the same as those contained in the second paragraph of the present Article 117 EC, and are now considered in turn because of the further elaboration of in particular the second and third means by the changes to be introduced by the Treaty of Amsterdam.

The functioning of the common market. The functioning of the common market in this context clearly refers primarily, but not exclusively, to the functioning of the common labour market which is created through the free movement of workers. In particular this common labour market concerns the intermediary forces which can influence it, such as employers' and employees' organizations. They may exercise such influence directly through the conclusion of cross-border collective labour agreements; they may also influence it indirectly through pressure on national and Community level legislators. In both cases a convergence of national social systems may result. So far the role of the social partners has been modest,[470]

Treaty of Amsterdam to alter this parity came to nothing. See also Watson (1993) 30 CMLRev. 481 at 487–498.

468. [1987] ECR 3697 at 3716.
469. The provisions of Art. 117 EC (both in its present and new forms) should not be interpreted so that an increasing social convergence could be attained without taking account of the economic development of the Community as a whole and with the development of the national economies. There is a close connection between economic growth, employment and the socio-economic system. The proportion of structural unemployment in the Community, which has steadily increased since 1971, was regarded by the Commission in its White Paper *Growth, Competitiveness and Employment* (COM (93) 700, Bull. EU Supp. 6/93) as the major threat to the maintenance of the European socio-economic model. Its recommendations essentially boil down to the need to increase the employment element in economic growth, even if that would require adaptation of the existing social systems. The maintenance in the new Art. 117 EC, 3rd para. of the phrasing found in the present Art. 117 EC, 2nd para. should also be seen in a wider context than simply that of social policy.
470. There are number of reasons for this, although the achievement of the frameworks which formed the basis of three of the directives adopted under the Agreement on Social Policy, noted above, should not be left out of the equation. Despite the formal achievement of the free movement of workers, cross-border mobility of the labour

despite the fact that both are represented in Community level organizations. The creation of a European trades union organization (paralleling UNICE which is the management body) contributed to the start of tripartite conferences in 1976. These conferences seek a broad consensus on a common approach to social problems, particularly relating to employment policy. They in turn have borne fruit in the social dialogue between the two sides of industry (the 'Val Duchesse' social dialogue so-called after the Chateau in Brussels so renowned in the Community and Belgian public circles) initiated under the present Article 118b EC. The establishment of the new Employment and Labour Market Committee by Decision 97/16[471] confirms the importance of the Community-level influence of the social partners; the importance of the dialogue is also recognized in the new Article 118b EC.[472]

The importance of market integration in the product and capital investment markets for the convergence of living conditions and conditions of employment should not be underestimated. The speed at which the *per capita* income in countries such as Spain, Portugal, and, above all, Ireland is approaching the European average is an important indicator of this. The welfare effects of a better and lower-priced supply of products must also not be underestimated. It has already been observed that the free movement of products and factors may not be misused for policy competition as to social norms and standards. Any such national policy is certainly incompatible with the new Article 117 EC and could, if necessary, be countered on the basis of Article 101 EC.

The procedures provided for in the EC Treaty. The procedures provided for in the EC Treaty means principally the procedures for the coordination of economic policies,[473] employment policy,[474] and for economic and social cohesion.[475] More specifically in the social field, the new Article 118 EC

---

factor is still relatively small. There has also been a shift in the type of workers who are more likely to move, with now more white-collar personnel moving, often within or for multinationals (in the past blue-collar personnel made up a larger proportion of those moving); until more recently the level of organization of white-collar highly-qualified employees has tended to be lower. As has been noted in the text, *ante*, the failure to modernize the Community coordination of social security rules has also been a disincentive to certain types of employees moving. Finally, while trade unions tend to take more account of the consequences of the common market (on occasions this has resulted in multinational strikes), even in discussions on conditions of employment in the national context, their conduct is at the end of the day still strongly determined by national traditions in their relationship with employers' organizations and government.

471. O.J. 1997 L 6/32.
472. See the Commission's Green Paper *Partnership for a new organization of work* COM (97) 128 Final.
473. Art. 103 EC.
474. See the new Arts. 109n–109s EC.
475. Arts. 130a–130e EC.

provides for a special procedure. The new Article 118(1) EC provides for Community action supporting and complementing that of the Member States in the following five fields.

(1) Improvement in particular of the working environment to protect workers' health and safety. This provision reflects concerns also expressed in the present Article 118a(1) EC.
(2) Working conditions. It is not entirely clear what this must cover, given that the new Article 118(6) EC excludes the application of the new Article 118 to pay, the right of association, the right to strike or the right to impose lock-outs.
(3) The information and consultation of workers. This power has already formed the basis for Directive 94/45.[476]
(4) The integration of persons excluded from the labour market. This will involve specific measures promoting the reintegration of fragile groups, such as the long-term unemployed and the handicapped.
(5) Equality between men and women with regard to labour market opportunities and treatment at work. This provision creates a specific legal basis for harmonization measures in this field, which had hitherto been based on Articles 100 and 235 EC.

The new Article 118(2) EC endows the Community with specific powers: the Council may adopt, using directives, *minimum requirements* for gradual implementation, having regard to the conditions and technical rules obtaining in each of the Member States, in the fields mentioned in the new Article 118a(1) EC. Those directives must avoid imposing administrative, financial and legal constraints in a way which would hold back the creation and development of small and medium-sized undertakings.[477] They will be adopted under the co-decision procedure of Article 189b EC, after consulting ECOSOC and the Committee of the Regions.[478] The third subparagraph of the new Article 118(2) EC permits the Council, acting by the same procedure, to 'adopt measures designed to encourage cooperation between Member States through initiatives aimed at improving knowledge, developing exchanges of information and best practices, promoting

476. On the establishment of a European Works Council or a procedure in Community-scale undertakings and Community-scale groups of undertakings for the purposes of informing and consulting employees (O.J. 1994 L 254/64, amended and extended to the United Kingdom by Dir. 97/74 (O.J. 1998 L 10/22)). This power was exercised under the identical provision of the Agreement on Social Policy.
477. Declaration (No. 26) adopted by the Conference on the occasion of signature of the Final Act of the Treaty of Amsterdam, states that 'the Community does not intend, in laying down minimum requirements for the protection of the safety and health of employees, to discriminate in a manner unjustified by the circumstances against employees in small and medium-sized undertakings.'
478. See the new Art. 118(2) EC, 2nd subpara.

innovative approaches and evaluating experiences in order to combat social exclusion.' This provision is the counterpart to the new Article 109r EC, which provides a similar power for employment policy.

The new Article 118(3) EC sets out a number of areas in which the Council is required to act unanimously, on a proposal from the Commission, after consulting the European Parliament, ECOSOC and the Committee of the Regions. These are: social security and social protection of workers; protection of workers where their employment contract is terminated; representation and collective defence of the interests of workers and employers, including co-determination;[479] conditions of employment for third-country nationals legally residing in Community territory, and financial contributions for promotion of employment and job creation.[480]

The new Article 118(4) EC permits a Member State to entrust management and labour, at their joint request, with the implementation of directives adopted under the new Article 118(2) and (3). The careful formulation of the second paragraph of the new Article 118(4) makes it clear that the ultimate responsibility for ensuring that the results imposed by directives so implemented are guaranteed rests with the Member State concerned.[481]

The new Article 118(5) EC, permitting Member States to maintain in force or introduce more stringent measures compatible with the EC Treaty, is strictly speaking superfluous, as it already follows from the above parts of the new Article 118 EC that Community action has a supporting and complementary nature, and that minimum requirements are to be prescribed at Community level. The effect of the new Article 118(6) EC had already been noted above. With the advent of the specific legal basis,

479. This is subject to the new Art. 118(6) EC, the effect of which has been noted in the text, *ante*. Dir. 94/45 (O.J. 1994 L 254/64, amended and extended to the United Kingdom by Dir. 97/74 (O.J. 1998 L 10/22)) does not embrace co-determination, but expressly concerns only information and consultation. Various old proposals in the field of co-determination have now been withdrawn, see Bull. EU 1/2–1998, points. 1.3.17–1.3.19. The relationship with the implementation of Art. 54(3)(g) EC might nevertheless continue to create problems (see Chapter VII, section 6.7, *ante*), particularly with regard to Germany (and, to a lesser extent, the Netherlands), where co-determination is partly a matter governed by company law, also in view of the wording of the wording of Art. 54(3)(g): 'protection of the interests of members [of companies or firms] and others'.

480. This overlaps with the new Art. 109r EC, and is without prejudice to the provisions relating to the ESF (Arts. 123–125 EC); as to which, see section 5, *ante*.

481. This in fact reflects the acceptance of such an approach by the Court in Case 143/83 *Commission v. Denmark* [1985] ECR 427 at 434–435, with the requirement (there concerning equal pay) that the 'State guarantee must cover all cases where effective protection is not ensured by other means, for whatever reason, and in particular cases where the workers in question are not union members, where the sector in question is not covered by a collective agreement or where such an agreement does not fully guarantee the principle of equal pay.'

recourse to other, more general legal bases for harmonization, such as Articles 100 or 235 EC will become less frequent.

Community action under the terms of the new Articles 118a–118c EC also falls within the ambit of procedures provided for in the EC Treaty. The new Article 118a EC contains extensive provisions governing contacts between the Commission and the social partners in the preparation of Community action in the social field. Compared with the present Article 118b EC, the new Article 118a EC is undoubtedly more prescriptive: the Commission is *required* to consult the social partners in a two-stage process about all its proposals 'in the social policy field.'[482] The first consultation takes place before it submits such proposals, and is as to 'the possible direction of Community action.'[483] If, after that consultation, the Commission considers Community action desirable, it must again consult the social partners, this time on the content of the envisaged proposal.[484] In response to this consultation, the social partners may present the Commission with their opinion or, if appropriate, with a recommendation.[485] Undoubtedly the most remarkable aspect of this procedure is the terms of the new Article 118a(4) EC, which permits the social partners to, as it were, take over the Commission's proposal and to flesh it out between themselves bilaterally, by initiating the procedure set out in Article 118b EC. This procedure is considered below.

The new Article 118a EC fits into the consensus-based socio-economic policy tradition of a number of the continental and Scandinavian Member States. However, the less than wholly precise drafting of that provision gives rise to a number of questions which may be important in its interpretation and application. The first question concerns the legal consequences of the Commission's obligation to consult under the new Article 118a. It is unclear whether this is a general norm of instruction to consult the social partners in the preparation and working out of its proposals in the social policy field, without any legal consequences flowing from it, or whether compliance with the obligation to consult is a constituent element for the legal validity of the Commission's proposals (and thus ultimately of any Community act which may result). The EC Treaty always prescribes exhaustively and specifically how legal acts affecting third parties must be adopted, which appears to indicate that it is unlikely that the manner in which the very generally formulated consultation obligation has been undertaken will have consequences for the legal validity of the Community acts concerned. Even in the Member States which have a tradition of consensual decision-making in the socio-economic field, there are no examples of a *general* norm of instruction

482. See the new Art. 118a EC.
483. *Ibid.*
484. See the new Art. 118a(3) EC.
485. *Ibid.*

requiring consultation and discussion with the social partners having consequences for the validity of *specific* decisions which have been adopted according to the constitutional provisions concerned. In some Member States there are examples in the case-law where compliance with a *specific* norm of instruction requiring consultation and discussion is indeed a precondition for the validity of a *specific* decision. On the basis of this analysis, it is submitted that the consultation requirement in the new Article 118a EC is a norm of instruction, compliance with which is primarily of political and/or policy relevance, but which does not involve direct legal consequences.

The second question is the scope of the new Article 118a EC *ratione materiae*. As has been explained above, the scope of action which is relevant to social policy is considerably wider than the field embraced by the new Articles 117–120 EC. It appears therefore that the norm of instruction requiring consultation embraces all Community initiatives and proposals which have a social or socio-economic significance, such as measures implementing the present Articles 51 and 130a–130e EC and the new Articles 109n–109s EC. This preference for a wide substantive sphere of operation of the new Article 118a EC is consistent with the view advanced above that it expresses a general norm of instruction, with no specific legal consequences.

The third question relates to whether, and, if so, to what extent, legal consequences are attached to compliance with the obligation to consult the social partners if, for example, they were either strongly in favour of the Commission's initiative, or strongly opposed to it. It is submitted that the standpoint adopted by the social partners is a matter of political and/or policy relevance, but not a matter which may detract from the Commission's own power to make up its own mind as to how it fulfils its tasks under the EC Treaty. Any other approach would be fundamentally inconsistent with the Commission's independence. This implies that if the social partners were to request, under the new Article 118a(4) EC, that the procedure of the new Article 118b EC be initiated, the Commission is entitled to make up its own mind whether or not to accede to that request. The social partners cannot take over the public law powers of the competent Community authorities; a point which also applies in the interpretation and application of the new Article 118b EC.

The terms of the new Article 118b EC are somewhat infelicitously drafted. The new Article 118b(1) EC is primarily declaratory in nature, because, as legal persons in private law both employers' and amplest were already competent to conclude agreements. It goes without saying that such agreements may not be incompatible with Community law and national law. Strictly speaking, the new Article 118b(2) EC is superfluous: by definition agreements concluded at Community level will have to fit within the rules and procedures applicable at national level to relations between the social partners, such as legal provisions relating to collective labour agreements. In this context, the Declaration on the new Article 118b EC[486] is somewhat curious. It is obvious that agreements concluded at national level will need to be worked out in collective negotiations under national law, and equally obvious that such national private law agreements cannot oust national legislation or oblige the Member States to amend existing national legislation to facilitate the implementation of those agreements.[487]

The provisions of the new Article 118b(2) EC are more important. Agreements concluded at Community level may be implemented by one of two routes. *Either* by the social partners themselves and the Member States: this may be done either via the non-legislative route, or through individual action by the national authorities where desired, or by a combination of these approaches. *Or*, at the joint request of the social partners signatory to such Community-level agreements, those agreements may, in matters covered by the new Article 118 EC, be 'grandfathered' by a Council decision on a proposal from the Commission.[488] Insofar as the agreement to be 'grandfathered' relates to the fields mentioned in the new Article 118(3) EC, the Council acts unanimously; otherwise it acts by qualified majority.[489]

The new Article 118b EC also gives rise to a number of legal questions. It looks, from the drafting of the new Article 118b(2) EC, as if the Council is obliged to act. However, it is submitted that this is a drafting slip: an agreement between the social partners cannot restrict the independent freedom of discretion which the Commission and the Council have under the EC Treaty. Both Institutions are, it is submitted, free to form their own views as to whether, and, if so, to what extent they wish to 'grandfather' a particular agreement concluded by the social partners. Any other interpretation would make nonsense of the distinct voting requirements set out in the second subparagraph of the new Article 118b(2) EC: there would be no point in maintaining that distinction if the Council *had* to act in only one manner

There is also another respect in which the drafting of the two subparagraphs of Article 118b(2) EC has not been entirely thought

---

486. Declaration (No. 27) adopted by the Conference on the occasion of signature of the Final Act of the Treaty of Amsterdam.
487. A similar declaration was made in relation to the Agreement on Social Policy, Art. 4(2), see O.J. 1992 C 191/92.
488. It will be recalled that two such framework agreements have so far been 'grand-fathered' under the equivalent procedure contained in the Agreement on Social Policy, Art. 4(2): Dir. 96/34 on the framework agreement on parental leave concluded by UNICE, CEEP and the ETUC (O.J. 1996 L 145/64), and Dir. 97/81 (O.J. 1998 L 14/9) concerning the framework agreement on part-time work concluded by UNICE, CEEP and the EUTC. Curiously, although both that provision of the Agreement and the new Art. 118b EC refer to 'a Council decision' the vehicle used is in fact a directive, as the above examples illustrate.
489. See the new Art. 118b(2) EC, 2nd subpara.

through. The impression is created that for the legal validity of the directives by which the agreements would be 'grandfathered' a proposal from the Commission and a decision by the Council are all that is required. This would clearly be a very different procedure from the co-decision and consultation procedures envisaged in the new Article 118a(2) or (3), which have been discussed above. It appears most unlikely that the intention should have been to bypass the rights of the European Parliament, ECOSOC and the Committee of the Regions to be involved in the decision-making process in this field, merely on the ground that the proposal for the directive involved is based on a framework agreement reached between the social partners. Indeed, given that in particular the Parliament's powers in Community decision-making have been very carefully set out and considered by the drafters of the EC Treaty and the successive amendments thereto, it is inconceivable that parliamentary control should be ousted in such a manner, which, moreover, would be without precedent in the constitutional laws of at least a number of Member States. Not surprisingly, practice hitherto under the equivalent provision of the Agreement on Social Policy confirms that the Parliament is indeed involved in the adoption of 'grandfathering' directives.[490]

The new Article 118c is almost literally a repetition of the present Article 118 EC, containing a general norm of instruction to the Commission to encourage (horizontal) cooperation between the Member States and to facilitate the coordination of their action in all social policy fields under the social provisions Chapter of Title VIII of Part Three of the EC Treaty. Unlike in the present provisions of that Chapter, in which there are very few real Community powers set out, the practical importance of this provision is small. Most of the various matters specifically mentioned,[491] fall either under the new Title VIa on Employment,[492] or under the new Art. 118 EC. Thus it is unclear what the added value of independent initiatives by the Commission may be in the field of employment, now that the new Articles 109n–109s EC provide for an apparently permanent coordination of the employment policies of the Member States. It would have been desirable to ensure rather more precise drafting, which took account of the new structure of competences which will apply once the Treaty of Amsterdam enters into force.

The history of the application of the present Article 118 EC remains of interest for the history and evolution of Community social policy. It demonstrates with how much difficulty the Member States have accepted

490. Thus it was involved in the adoption of the two directives so far 'grandfathered.'
491. Employment; labour law and working conditions; basic and advanced vocational training; social security; prevention of occupational accidents and diseases; occupational hygiene, and the right of association and collective bargaining between employers and employees.
492. See the new Arts. 109n–109s EC.

Community initiatives in the social field, even in periods in which they were still active with the further construction of their own welfare states. Initially the Commission primarily conducted studies and made recommendations to the Member States, acting on the basis of its powers under Article 155 EC. Since in accordance with the procedural rules of Article 118 EC elaborate consultation with representatives of Member States invariably preceded them, these recommendations were in practice largely complied with; they were modest in substance and uncontroversial. Although Article 118 expressly confers autonomous powers on the Commission, the latter's activities in this field have nevertheless led to tension with some Member States and even, between 1964 and 1966 to a complete halt in the Council's activities in the social field. A compromise put forward by the Dutch Minister Veldkamp at the end of 1966 led to the Commission working within the framework of programmes drawn up or approved by the Council. The somewhat counterproductive result was in fact that there was scarcely any room for independent, stimulating initiatives from the Commission.[493] Only with the adoption of the Social Action Programme of 21 January 1974 was this stagnation brought to an end.[494] Although various specific action programmes were adopted in the following years, including in the field of social equality for men and women,[495] until the signature of the SEA no further large-scale initiatives resulted. Subsequently, as has been noted above,[496] the initiative was taken to draw up the Community Social Charter, and later the political disagreement with the United Kingdom resulted in the Protocol and Agreement on Social Policy, the political shelf life of which has now expired.

Apart from the question of the *political* willingness of the Member States to accept autonomous Commission initiatives under Article 118 EC, there was also the *legal* question of the scope of the Commission's powers and the *policy* question of the content of the final action by the Community. The legal question was at the heart of the matter in Cases 281/85 *etc. Germany et al. v. Commission.*[497] In this judgment the Court found that as far as the substance was concerned the Commission's competence was strictly described by the matters mentioned in Article 118 EC itself, and that therefore cultural aspects were not covered by that provision. As to procedural matters, the Court found that the Commission's powers were restricted to the organization of a communication and discussion procedure. But this could not lead to the results of that procedure being binding. Thus Article 118 EC only permits purely procedural decisions by

493. See Pipkorn in Von den Groeben, *op. cit.* (see note 417, *supra*) 3287.
494. O.J. 1974 C 13/1 and Bull. EC Supp. 2/74.
495. O.J. 1982 C 186/3.
496. Under point A, *ante*.
497. [1987] ECR 3203, [1988] 1 CMLR 11.

the Commission; for substantive Community decisions another legal basis is necessary.[498] Given that substantively the new Article 118c EC is in the same terms as the present Article 118 EC, this case-law remains important, particularly since the amendments which the Treaty of Amsterdam will introduce create certain specific powers for Community acts in the field of employment and social policy.

The policy question relates to the subjects in respect of which the Commission's action under Article 118 EC has led to Community action. So far in practice the answer is varied.[499] In the fields of social security, collective bargaining and primary and secondary remuneration the Community has so far been somewhat reticent.[500] In the employment field initiatives have followed since the meeting of the European Council in Essen in December 1994 under the Essen procedure, involving the Commission and the Ecofin and Social Affairs Councils.[501] These have resulted in a light form of coordination, primarily based on mutual information. The Commission's role has been primarily a supporting one. The experiences with the Essen procedure, which had no explicit basis in the EC Treaty, have now resulted in the provisions contained in the new Articles 109n–109s EC.

The Community has however been more active in other areas of social policy: ensuring equality between men and women in the labour and social security markets;[502] the working environment and labour law;[503] vocational education and further training,[504] and protection against accidents at work and occupational illnesses, as well as the promotion of health and safety at work.[505]

---

498. Only two decisions have been based solely on Art. 118 EC: Decs. 88/383 (O.J. 1988 L 183/34) on providing for the improvement of information on safety hygiene and health at work and Dec. 88/384 (O.J. 1988 L 183/35) setting up a prior communication and consultation procedure on migration policies in relation to non-member countries (which replaced the measure annulled in Cases 281/85 etc. Germany et al. v. Commission [1988] ECR 3203, [1988] 1 CMLR 11).

499. Currall in Von der Groeben, op. cit. (See note 417, supra) 3347–3367, who gives an extensively documented overview of Community policy since 1990. The emphasis of the activities since has in fact not changed, even though various other measures have been adopted.

500. This reticence is also expressed in the new Arts. 51 (maintaining the unanimity requirement in social security matters) and 118(6) EC (excluding from the scope of Community action pay, the right of association, the right to strike and the right to impose lock-outs).

501. This shorthand (which is standard) is used, even though the Council is one Institution which may meet in different compositions.

502. Art. 119 EC and the case-law discussed under point B, post, have acted as catalysts.

503. Albeit not systematically. The addition of Art. 118a EC (by the SEA) strengthened Community action in this field.

504. Primarily through incentive measures and measures creating the conditions for action to take place.

505. Through a growing number of specific measures.

The approximation of provisions laid down by law, regulation or administrative action. Hitherto, this third means specified in the new Article 117 EC had to be based on Treaty provisions outside the Chapter on social provisions. This involved Articles 49 and 51 EC for social rights of migrant workers; 100 and 100a EC, as general harmonization provisions in the interest of the unity and proper functioning of the common and internal markets respectively, and 235 EC, as the fall-back provision in the absence of specific powers in cases where Community action was necessary, in the course of the operation of the common market, one of the objectives of the Community. Since the coming into force of the SEA, Article 118a EC has been an important legal basis for the adoption of Community directives in the field of the working environment and in particular health and safety at work. Although Articles 101 and 102 EC do offer a specific legal basis for Community action if differences in social legislation between the Member States result in distortions of competition, the question of such distortions suddenly burst into life when the United Kingdom resisted an extension of Community competence in the social field in what became the TEU. The Social Protocol and the Agreement on Social Policy created the possibility of active policy competition by the United Kingdom in the social field. Any resulting distortions of competition could have been tackled on the basis of Articles 101 or 102 EC, but in reality these provisions have remained just as much dead-letter provisions as before. That is not to say that if the economic importance of policy competition had been major, there would have been no pressure to activate those provisions. As has been indicated at various points elsewhere in this Chapter, an activation of Article 101 EC should indeed be seriously considered, in particular after the start of the third stage of EMU.

The replacement of the Agreement on Social Policy by the new provisions in the Chapter on social provisions marks a major watershed, as indeed does the political decision to extend to the United Kingdom, prior to the entry into force of the Treaty of Amsterdam, the directives which had been adopted under the Agreement. If still up to now a legal basis was used that was not primarily to do with the social field, from the entry into force of the Treaty of Amsterdam that will be different, as the new Article 118 EC supplies it. This legal basis appears broad enough at the moment for social policy integration, insofar as harmonization of laws is necessary for that purpose. Thus the legal significance of the Treaty of Amsterdam in the social field is greater than merely its actual political significance. There is indeed already Community legislation in almost all the fields mentioned in the new Article 118(1) EC, even though mostly on the basis of Treaty provisions not principally designed for that purpose. It is remarkable that in the field of the matters mentioned in the new Article 118(3) EC attempts at Community initiatives have been made in the past, particularly in matters such as codetermination, but with distinct lack of success.[506] The procedural requirement of unanimity for a Community act make it unlikely that Community action will become very important in this area in the foreseeable future. This view is supported by the distinct absence of any action under the terms of Article 2(3) of the Agreement on Social Policy, to which the new Article 118(3) EC is couched in corresponding terms.

Nevertheless, it remains interesting to see how the Community in the past was able to adopt legal acts in the social field, even in the absence of a specific legal basis in the EC Treaty. Prior to the entry into force of the SEA, Article 100 EC was the main legal basis for harmonizing action by the Community in the social field. It thus formed the basis for Directive 75/129[507] on collective redundancies; Directive 77/187[508] on safeguarding employees' rights in the event of transfers of undertakings; Directive 80/987[509] on protection of employees on the insolvency of their employer; Directive 91/533[510] on an employer's obligation to inform employees of the conditions applicable to the contract or employment relationship, and Directive 75/117[511] on the application of the principle of equal pay for men and women. Article 100 was also the legal basis for a number of health and safety at work directives.[512] After the coming into force of the

---

506. So much so that the old proposals have been dropped completely, see Bull. EU 1/2–1998, points 1.3.17–1.3.19.
507. O.J. 1975 L 48/29. See *e.g.* Case 284/83 *Dansk Metalarbejderforbund et al. v. H. Nielsen & Son, Maskinfabrik A/S* [1985] ECR 553, [1986] 1 CMLR 91.
508. O.J. 1977 L 61/26. See *e.g.* Case 135/83 *Abels v. The Administrative Board of the Bedrijfsvereniging voor de Metaalindustrie en de Electronische Industrie* [1985] ECR 469; Case 179/83 *Industriebond FNV et al. v. The Netherlands State* [1985] ECR 511; Case 186/83 *Botzen et al. v. Rotterdamche Droogdok Maatschappij BV* [1985] ECR 519; Case 24/85 *Spijkers v. Gebroeders Benedik Abbattoir CV et al.* [1986] ECR 1119; Case 237/84 *Commission v. Belgium* [1986] ECR 1247; Case 235/84 *Commission v. Italy* [1986] ECR 2291; Case 324/86 *Foreningen Arbejedsledere i Denmark v. Daddy's Dance Hall A/S* [1988] ECR 739; Cases 144 and 145/87 *Berg et al. v. Besselen et al.* [1988] ECR 2559; Case C-29/91 *Sophie Redmond Stichting v. Bartol* [1992] ECR I-3189, [1994] 3 CMLR 265; Case C-392/92 *Schmidt v. Spar- und Leihkasse der Frühren Ämter Bordesholm, Kiel und Cronshagen* [1994] ECR I-1311, [1995] 2 CMLR 331; Case C-472/93 *Spano et al. v. Fiat Geotech SpA et al.* [1995] ECR I-4321; Cases C-171 and 172/94 *Merckx et al. v. Ford Motors Company Belgium SA* [1996] ECR I-1253; Case C-298/94 *Henke v. Gemeinde Schierke et al.* [1996] ECR I-4989; Case C-13/95 *Süzen v. Gebäudereinigung GmbH Krankenhausservice* [1997] ECR I-1259, [1997] 1 CMLR 768; Case C-336/95 *Trevejo et al. v. Fondo Garantía Salaridad* [1997] ECR I-2115, and Case C-319/94 *Jules Dethier Equipment SA v. Dassy et al.* [1998] ECR I-1061. See also Bourn (1998) 23 ELRev. 59.
509. O.J. 1980 L 283/23, as amended by Dir. 87/164 (O.J. 1987 L 66/11).
510. O.J. 1991 L 288/32.
511. O.J. 1975 L 45/19.
512. *E.g.* Dirs. 77/576 (O.J. 1977 L 229/12, repealed and replaced by Dir. 92/58 (O.J. 1992 L 245/23)); Dir. 79/640 (O.J. 1979 L 183/11) on the provision of safety signs at places of work; Dir. 78/610 (O.J. 1978 L 197/12) on protection of the health of workers exposed to vinyl chloride monomer (which also no longer applies as a result of the

SEA, the situation became somewhat more complicated through the introduction of Articles 100a and 118a EC. Article 100a EC may be used as a general basis for harmonization, insofar as the unity and operation of the internal market is concerned. But for matters which *inter alia* relate to the free movement of persons and to the rights and interests of employees, Article 100a(2) EC provides that Article 100a may not be used . Thus Article 100a EC, which permits qualified majority voting, is primarily used as the legal basis for directives relating to materials, instruments and equipment as concerns safety at work. In addition, the Commission attempted systematically to use Article 100a EC to the maximum possible extent for harmonization in those matters related to working conditions which did not fall under Article 118a EC, by adopting as restrictive interpretation of Article 100a(2) EC as possible.

Article 118a EC offered a specific legal basis for minimum harmonization relating to health and safety at work within the Community. It gave rise to differences of opinion as to its scope as soon as it came into effect. The European Parliament defended the view that Article 118a EC could be used as the legal basis for any Community act which was particularly directed at employees.[513] This would have allowed Article 118a EC to be a legal basis for action over the whole field of Article 118 EC, but this view was untenable, both on the ground of the history leading to the adoption of Article 118a EC, and on the ground of a systematic approach.[514] The Commission's view, as may be deduced from the Action Programme for the implementation of the Community Social Charter,[515] was that the objectives of Article 118a(1) EC embraced the working environment and health and safety at work in the broad sense. Account would be taken of technological developments, the developments in employment relationships, and the desirability of involving employees in carrying out and controlling the necessary measures at the level of the firms concerned. In this view, Community acts relating to working time could not be based on Article 118a EC, unless they could objectively be linked with the protection of the health and safety of employees.[516] Some Member States, including until mid-1997, the United Kingdom, adopted a clearly more restrictive

adoption of Dir. 92/58), and Dir. 80/1107 (O.J. 1980 L 327/8, amended by Dir. 88/642 (O.J. 1988 L 356/74)) which is the framework directive on protection of workers from the risks related to exposure to chemical, physical and biological agents at work, and has been implemented by various directives dealing with particular risks.

513. See O.J. 1989 C 12/81.

514. It was also incompatible with clear case-law of the Court, which requires the choice of legal basis for a measure to be 'based on objective factors which are amenable to judicial review': see *e.g.* Case 45/86 *Commission v. Council* [1987] ECR 1493 at 1520 and Case 68/86 *United Kingdom v. Council* [1988] ECR 855 at 898. See also Case C-62/88 *Greece v. Council* [1990] ECR I-1527 at 1550–1551.

515. COM (89) 560 Final; *Social Europe* 1/90 (Luxembourg, 1990) 51–76.

516. See Pipkorn in Von der Groeben *et al.* (eds.), *op. cit.* (see note 417, *supra*) 3381–3383.

interpretation, namely that only measures which directly involved the health and safety of employees could be adopted on the specific basis of Article 118a EC. After the TEU came into force, this difference of views became particularly politically charged, as a wider interpretation would mean that the Commission and the majority of the Member States would have to have recourse to the Agreement on Social Policy far less frequently. Thus the adoption of the working time directive[517] on the basis of Article 118a EC occurred to the great dissatisfaction of the then United Kingdom government.[518]

The application of Article 118a EC by the Commission since 1987 has resulted in extensive legislative activity in the field of the working environment in the broad sense. Directive 89/391,[519] the framework directive on measures to encourage improvements in the safety and health of workers at work, has been of major importance. The specific interests of young people at work have also not been overlooked.[520] It is noticeable that various directives originally based on Article 100 EC, but which now fall *ratione materiae* within the scope of Article 118a EC, have been amended on the basis of that latter provision.[521] It may be expected that in the future this will also occur on the basis of the new Article 118(1) EC. The consequence of this legislative practice is that Article 100 EC has become a residual provision, which will only be used in relation to social policy in exceptional cases.

It may be anticipated that Article 235 EC will retain more significance than will Article 100 EC in this field. If the new Article 118 EC cannot be used, but Community action is thought necessary, and the establishment nor the functioning of the common (labour) market is involved, Article 235 EC may still be invoked.[522]

517. Dir. 93/104 (O.J. 1993 L 307/18).
518. In Case C-84/94 *United Kingdom v. Council* [1996] ECR I-5755 the Court dismissed the United Kingdom's appeal, save for the provision as to Sunday being in principle a day of rest (Dir. 93/104, Art. 5, 2nd sentence), which was annulled, as having been insufficiently reasoned. As the principal objective was the protection of health and safety of workers, the Council was entitled to act [1996] ECR I-5755 at 5806–5809, and the Court also noted that Community legislative action, particularly in the social field, could not be limited to circumstances where the justification for such action was scientifically demonstrated, *ibid.* at 5806.
519. O.J. 1989 L 183/1. This directive has been implemented by myriad individual directives. See Van der Heyden (1994) SEW 321 at 329–331 (also as the Dutch report in *Reports of the XVIth FIDE Congress* (Rome, 1994) Vol. II 399). See, further, the legally interesting and not uncontroversial Dir. 92/59 (O.J. 1992 L 228/24) on general product safety: the Court dismissed the appeal in Case C-359/92 *Germany v. Council* [1994] ECR I-3681, see Gormley (1996) 21 ELRev. 59 and Micklitz (1994) EuZW 631.
520. Dir. 94/33 (O.J. 1994 L 216/12).
521. *E.g.* Dir. 88/364 (O.J. 1988 L 179/44), implementing Dir. 80/1107 (O.J. 1980 L 327/8).
522. *E.g.* Dirs. 76/207 (O.J. 1976 L 39/40) and 79/7 (O.J. 1979 L 6/24) in the equal treatment field; Dec. 75/458 (O.J. 1975 L 199/34, as amended) on pilot schemes and studies to combat poverty (see, in relation to a subsequent programme, Case C-106/96

The introduction of the new Article 118 EC will mean that for the most part the Community acts mentioned above will have a specific legal basis in the EC Treaty. It follows from the new Article 118(2) EC that the Community's measures will mostly involve minimum requirements, and from the progressive nature of Community action, which is also evident from the new Article 117 EC, it follows that the new Article 118(5) EC permits the member States to maintain or introduce more stringent protective measures compatible with the EC Treaty. Thus such measures must not lead to infringements of the free movement of the factors of production, nor may they cause serious distortions of competition. The fact that the new Article 118(5) EC does not contain a notification obligation for those member States taking advantage of them is a clear drafting deficiency. It is all the more obvious given that Article 130t EC does provide for such a procedure in the environmental field and Article 100a EC, including in the form resulting from the amendments which the Treaty of Amsterdam will introduce, also provides for a notification procedure.

B. Articles 119–122 EC. The present Article 119 EC provides that each Member State during the first stage of the transitional period had to ensure and subsequently maintain the application of the principle that men and women should receive equal pay for equal work.[523] Views as to scope of this provision have developed so extensively over the years that the development is hardly likely to be concluded yet. The historical reason for including Article 119 in the Treaty was the French concern that France would be at a competitive disadvantage through applying this principle of equal pay for equal work better than it was applied in other Member States. This pointer to economic approximation by Article 119 has been treated by nobody else since as a basis of interpretation. With the development of the principle of equality as a fundamental principle in national constitutional law and in international law, such an approach rapidly became otiose. In the discussion of Article 119 considerations of equality are now to the fore. Because Article 119 EC is principally concerned with the labour market in the wide sense, the development of this

---

United Kingdom v. Commission [1998] ECR I-nyr (12 May 1998)); Reg. 337/75 establishing the European Centre for the Development of Vocational Training (CEDEFOP) (O.J. 1975 L 39/1, most recently amended by Reg. 354/95 (O.J. 1995 L 41/1)); Reg. 1365/75 (O.J. 1975 L 139/1, most recently amended by the Act of Accession (1994)) establishing the European Foundation for the Improvement of Living and Working Conditions; Rec. 86/379 (O.J. 1986 L 225/43) and the Council's Resolution on measures for the assistance of the long-term unemployed (O.J. 1990 C 157/4).

523. The literature on equal pay is extensive. See, generally, Ellis, *op. cit.* (see note 411, *supra*); Ellis (1994) 31 CMLRev. 43, (1998) 35 CMLRev. 379 and Prechal (1988) SEW 78. See also Pipkorn in Von der Groeben *et al.* (eds.), *op. cit.* (see note 417, *supra*) 3409–3484 and Wolfcarius and Margellos in Mégret *et al.* (eds.), *op. cit.* (see note 411, *supra*) 83–191.

legal principle in practice has a strongly, but not exclusively social tint.[524] This means that the initially very restrictive interpretation of the scope of the equality principle, advanced mainly by the Dutch government,[525] has gradually been replaced by the view that in substance Article 119 means that the sex of an employee may play no part in the fixing of salaries and all other benefits whether in cash or in kind, present or future, paid by the employer. This was made abundantly clear in Case 20/71 *Sabbatini, née Bertoni v. European Parliament*,[526] in which the Court found that the Community's Staff Regulations could not treat officials differently according to whether they are male or female, and in Case 129/79 *Macarthys Ltd. v. Smith*[527] in which the Court found that the equality principle was not confined to the *contemporaneous* execution of equal work for the same employer. The Court also held in Case 157/86 *Murphy et al. v. An Bord Telecom Eireann*[528] that Article 119 covers a worker seeking equal pay who is engaged in work of higher value than that of the person with whom a comparison is to be made. An excellent example of the broad interpretation of the concept of pay can be seen in Case 12/81 *Garland v. British Rail Engineering Ltd.*[529] In global terms, these judgments show that substantively Article 119 EC means the sex of a worker may play no part in the fixing of salaries or any other pecuniary or non-pecuniary advantages.

The Court, had already held in Case 43/75 *Defrenne v. SABENA*[530] that Article 119 could be relied upon before national courts in particular in cases in which unequal pay was received for equal work carried out in the same establishment or service, whether in the public or in the private sector.[531] This leading judgment raised immediately the question what the substantive scope of the concept of equal pay for equal work was, in particular what was meant by the concept of equal pay. Since the judgment in *Sabbatini*, extensive case-law has developed, which after the celebrated judgment in Case C-262/88 *Barber v. Guardian Royal Exchange Group*[532] may be summarized as follows.

Payments from a privately run social security scheme which directly or indirectly result from the employment relationship, including pension

---

524. In the same sense, Drijber and Prechal (1997) SEW 122.
525. That the rule in Art. 119 EC would only apply to professions and undertakings in which men and women performed the same activities, see Pipkorn in Von der Groeben *et al.* (eds.), *op. cit.* (see note 417, *supra*) 3420–2422.
526. [1972] ECR 345 at 351.
527. [1980] ECR 1275 at 1289. See also Case 96/80 *Jenkins v. Kingsgate (Clothing Productions) Ltd.* [1981] ECR 911.
528. [1988] ECR 673 at 689–690.
529. [1982] ECR 359, [1982] 1 CMLR 696.
530. [1976] ECR 455 at 473–476.
531. See also Case 58/81 *Commission v. Luxembourg* [1982] ECR 2175. Thus Art. 119 EC had both vertical and horizontal direct effect.
532. [1990] ECR 1889, [1990] 2 CMLR 513.

fund payments constitute pay; only payments which exclusively flow from legally prescribed social security systems do not amount to pay; future benefits, such as from private pension schemes constitute pay if the employer pays them on the basis of or in connection with the employment relationship; benefits which are extraneous to individual or collective employment contracts, such as bonuses do constitute pay if they are conferred in the context of the employment relationship, and payments on dismissal (golden handshakes and the like), on temporary lay-offs or short-time working and in the event of sickness are also pay within the meaning of Article 119 EC.[533] The significance of this broad definition of pay is immense in legal practice. But insofar as forms of direct or indirect discrimination cannot be brought under the substantive scope of Article 119 EC, a solution will have to be found on the basis of Article 235 EC. Directives 76/207[534] and 79/7,[535] which are discussed below, are based on Article 235 EC.

Although there was initially some doubt about this question, in its later case-law the Court held that the prohibition of discrimination in Article 119 EC was not restricted to cases of direct discrimination, but also embraced disguised and indirect discrimination. In Case 43/75 *Defrenne v. SABENA*[536] the Court had confined the scope of Article 119 EC to cases of direct discrimination. Gradually it retreated from this view.[537] First, it extended the scope of Article 119 EC to cover *disguised* discrimination: *i.e.* cases in which the reason for the discrimination as to pay lies in the sex of the person concerned, but in which another reason is advanced.[538] Then the Court also brought cases of indirect discrimination in pay within the ambit of Article 119 EC. These cases concerned differences in pay which result from the application of an apparently neutral criterion which in fact results in a group of employees being disadvantaged which is mainly composed of the same sex, such as part-time workers or workers on call-up contracts.[539] Thus all kinds of indirect discrimination are *per se* prohibited. The Court did leave open the possibility of a justification for an employer who can demonstrate

---

533. Pipkorn in Von der Groeben *et al.* (eds.), *op. cit.* (see note 417, *supra*) 3450–3464. As to travel concessions for same-sex partners, see Case C-249/96 *Grant v. South-West Trains Ltd.* [1998] ECR I-621.
534. O.J. 1976 L 39/40.
535. O.J. 1979 L 6/24.
536. [1976] ECR 455 at 473–476.
537. Prechal (1988) SEW 78.
538. Case 96/80 *Jenkins v. Kingsgate (Clothing Productions) Ltd.* [1981] ECR 911 at 925–926; Case 157/86 *Murphy et al. v. An Bord Telecom Eireann* [1988] ECR 673 at 689–690.
539. Case 170/84 *Bilka-Kaufhaus GmbH v. Weber von Hartz* [1986] ECR 1607, [1986] 2 CMLR 701; Case 171/88 *Rinner-Kühn v. FWW Spezial-Gebäudereinigung GmbH & Co. KG* [1989] ECR 2743, [1993] 2 CMLR 932; Case 109/88 *Handels-og Kontorfunktionær-ernes Forbund i Danmark v. Dansk Arbejdgiversforening, acting on behalf of Danfoss* [1989] ECR 3199, [1991] 1 CMLR 8; Case C-184/89 *Nimz v. Freie und Hansestadt*

that the measures chosen 'correspond to a real need on the part of the undertaking, are appropriate with a view to achieving the objectives pursued and are necessary to that end.'[540] But anyone seeking to do so will have to convince the national court of the genuineness of his or her case; it must be sufficiently specific and necessary and reasonable.[541] The Court has also safeguarded the dignity and freedom of transsexuals.[542]

No matter how widely the Court has cast the ambit of Article 119 EC, discrimination which has no connection with the labour market, such as differences in access to employment, vocational training, promotion chances and other conditions of employment which do not fall within the concept of pay are not covered by Article 119 EC itself. Benefits under legally compulsory statutory social security schemes are also not covered by that provision. The first *lacuna* is filled by Directive 76/207,[543] the second by Directive 79/7.[544] Both these directives have given rise to considerable case-law; they are now considered in turn below.

The Court has now decided that a number of the major provisions of Directive 76/207 may be relied upon against the State, even when acting as an employer rather than as a regulatory authority,[545] but in Case 152/84 *Marshall v. Southampton and South-West Hampshire Area Health Authority (Teaching)* the Court expressly held that these provisions were not horizontally directly effective, and could thus not be invoked in the private sector.[546] For the private sector the effects intended by the Community

---

Hamburg [1991] ECR I-297, [1992] 3 CMLR 699; Case C-360/90 *Arbeiterwohlfahrt der Stadt Berlin e. V v. Bötel* [1992] ECR I-3589, and Case C-127/92 *Enderby v. Fenchay Health Authority et al.* [1993] ECR I-5535, [1994] 1 CMLR 8. But see also the more recent cases discussed by Ellis (1998) 35 CMLRev. 380 at 382–386.

540. Case 170/84 *Bilka-Kaufhaus GmbH v. Weber von Hartz* [1986] ECR 1607, at 1628.

541. *Ibid.* and Case C-184/89 *Nimz v. Freie und Hansestadt Hamburg* [1991] ECR I-297 at 319. See also Case C-100/95 *Kording v. Senator für Finanzen* [1997] ECR I-5289 and Case C-243/95 *Hill et al. v. The Revenue Commissioners et al.* [1998] ECR I-nyr (17 June 1998).

542. Case C-13/94 *P v. S and Cornwall County Council* [1996] ECR I-2143 at 2165, see Flynn (1997) 34 CMLRev. 367 and Campbell and Lardy (1996) 21 ELRev. 412. But see, as to same-sex partners, Case C-249/96 *Grant v. South-West Trains Ltd.* [1998] ECR I-621. The new Art. 6a EC, introduced by the Treaty of Amsterdam, will make discrimination on the ground of sexual orientation a distinct question from discrimination on the ground of sex.

543. O.J. 1976 L 39/40.

544. O.J. 1979 L 6/24.

545. The relevant provisions of the directive are Arts. 3(1); 4(1) 5(1) and 6. See Case 152/84 *Marshall v. Southampton and South-West Hampshire Area Health Authority (Teaching)* [1986] ECR 723, [1986] 1 CMLR 688 and Case 222/84 *Johnston v. Chief Constable of the Royal Ulster Constabulary* [1986] ECR 1651, [1986] 3 CMLR 240.

546. [1986] ECR 723 at 749. The Court noted that any difference of treatment between

legislator required implementation of the directive by the national authorities.[547] In Case C-177/88 *Dekker v. Stichting Vormingscentrum voor Jong Volwassenen (VJV-Centrum)*[548] the Court held that as a result of Article 6 of Directive 76/207, any sanctions which the national legislation provided for unlawful discrimination had to be such as to guarantee real and effective protection and have a real deterrent effect on the employer concerned; thus infringement of the prohibition of discrimination sufficed in itself to make the employer liable.[549] Any remedy in damages clearly has to be adequate to make good the loss suffered.[550]

There are a number of exceptions to the equal treatment principle, contained in Article 2 of Directive 76/207, which are self-explanatory. In its case-law so far, the Court has been vigilant to ensure that these exceptions are strictly interpreted and that they are not extended in national implementing legislation.[551] In Case 152/84 *Marshall v. Southampton and South-West Hampshire Area Health Authority (Teaching)*[552] the Court found that permissible differentiation as to pensionable age under Article 7 of Directive 79/7[553] could not have any consequences for a general system of dismissal, in respect of which discrimination was prohibited under Article 5 of Directive 76/207.

Article 2(4) of Directive 76/207 permits measures to promote equal opportunity for men and women, in particular by removing existing inequalities which affect women's opportunities in the areas covered by the Directive. This provision has recently been considered in two celebrated

public sector and private sector employees could be rectified by proper compliance with the directive, *ibid.*

547. *Ibid.* See Prechal (1990) 27 CMLRev. 451. See further Case C-271/91 *Marshall v. Southampton and South-West Hampshire Area Health Authority* [1993] ECR I-4367, [1993] 3 CMLR 293.

548. [1990] ECR I-3941 at 3975–3976.

549. The idea is that although the directive left the choice of sanctions open to the Member States, if a Member State had opted for civil liability, infringement of the prohibition made the infringer liable, without regard to any grounds of exemption envisaged by national law, *ibid.*

550. See Ellis (1994) 31 CMLRev. 43 at 49–51. As to ceilings, see Case C-180/95 *Draehmpaehl v. Urania Immobilienservice ohG* [1997] ECR I-2195. See further, generally, Ellis (1998) 35 CMLRev. 379.

551. Case 165/82 *Commission v. United Kingdom* [1983] ECR 3431; Case 152/84 *Marshall v. Southampton and South-West Hampshire Area Health Authority (Teaching)* [1986] ECR 723, [1986] 1 CMLR 688 and Case 222/84 *Johnston v. Chief Constable of the Royal Ulster Constabulary* [1986] ECR 1651, [1986] 3 CMLR 240, and Case 318/86 *Commission v. France* [1988] ECR 3559.

552. [1986] ECR 723 at 746.

553. See further, Case C-139/95 *Balestra v. Instituto nazionale della Previdenza Sociale (INPS)* [1997] ECR I-549 and Cases C-377/96 etc. *De Vriendt et al. v. Rijksdienst voor Pensioenen et al.* [1998] ECR I-nyr (30 April 1998), referring to earlier case-law. As to pregnancy, see Case C-394/96 *Brown v. Rentokil Ltd.* [1998] ECR I-nyr (30 June 1998), also referring to earlier case-law.

judgments, in Case C-450/93 *Kalanke v. Freie Hansestadt Bremen*[554] and Case C-409/95 *Marschall v. Land Nordrhein-Westfalen.*[555] In *Kalanke* the Court held that a national rule which provided that where equally qualified men and women are candidates for the same promotion in fields where there are fewer women than men at the level of the relevant post, women are automatically to be given priority, constitutes discrimination on grounds of sex.[556] This conclusion in fact rhymes with earlier case-law in which the Court viewed the principle of equality in Article 119 EC as a *substantive* equality principle: an exception designed to compensate for the unequal starting position of women through expressly permitting positive action aimed at ensuring actual and substantive equality. A rule which gives women unconditional priority in appointment or promotion is incompatible with such an approach. In *Marschall* the Court clarified its stance, while maintaining it, to find that if, in each individual case the rules provided for a guarantee of objective assessment in the case of equally qualified male and female candidates, and that such assessment would take account of all criteria specific to the individual candidates, and override the priority accorded to female candidates where one or more of those criteria tilted the balance in favour of the male candidate, the rules would be acceptable, as long as the criteria were not such as to discriminate against female candidates.[557]

The introduction of the new Article 119(4) EC by the Treaty of Amsterdam, which permits the Member states to maintain or adopt measures providing for specific advantages in order to make it easier for the under-represented sex to pursue a vocational activity or to prevent or compensate for disadvantages in professional careers, is *not* a reaction to *Kalanke*, although the contrary is sometimes assumed. A comparable provision, albeit more summarily formulated, was already to be found in Article 6(3) of the Agreement on Social Policy. Moreover, the new Article 119(4) EC is compatible with the Court's approach in these two recent cases.

Directive 79/7 contains a prohibition of the application of any discrimination whatsoever on ground of sex, either directly or indirectly by reference in particular to marital or family status, in particular as concerns the scope of social security schemes and the conditions of access thereto; the obligation to contribute and the calculation of contributions, and the calculation of benefits, including increases due in respect of a spouse and for dependants, as well as the conditions as to duration and retention of entitlement to benefits.[558] In Case 71/85 *State of the Netherlands v.*

---

554. [1995] ECR I-3051, see Szyszczak (1996) MLR 876; Moore (1996) 21 ELRev. 156 and Schiek (1996) ILJ 239.
555. [1997] ECR I-6363.
556. [1995] ECR I-3051 at 3077.
557. [1997] ECR I-6363 at 6393.
558. Dir. 79/7, Art. 4(1).

Federatie Nederlandse Vakbeweging[559] the Court held that where Article 4(1) of this directive had not been implemented by the due date it could be relied upon so as to preclude the application of any national provision inconsistent with it. Although the term 'objective justification' is not mentioned in that directive, the Court has recognized that this may be possible in certain circumstances.[560] The personal scope of the directive has also given rise to a number of interesting judgments: the directive does not apply to persons who have not yet been employed,[561] or to persons whose working career has not been interrupted by one of the risks which the directive covers.[562]

Directive 86/378[563] deals with the principle of equal treatment of men and women in occupational social security schemes. The main problem in this directive is the question how far its scope has been limited by the celebrated judgment in Case C-262/88 *Barber v. Guardian Royal Exchange Group.*[564] Although in that judgment the Court stated expressly that the direct effect of Article 119 in this field applied from the date of the judgment (and to claims already actually pending at that date), the commotion surrounding that judgment caused a special Protocol to be annexed to the EC Treaty by the TEU, seeking to distinguish between Article 119 EC as applicable prior to the entry into force of the TEU, and Article 119 EC as interpreted by that Protocol. The Court in fact coped sensibly with the ensuing flood of cases.[565]

The new Article 119a EC is literally a repetition of the present Article

---

559. [1986] ECR 3855, [1987] 2 CMLR 767; see also Case 8/81 *Becker v. Finanzamt Münster-Innenstadt* [1982] ECR 53, [1982] 1 CMLR 499.
560. Case 30/85 *Teuling v. Bedrijfsvereniging voor de Chemische Industrie* [1987] ECR 2497; Case C-102/88 *Ruzius-Wilbrink v. Bedrijfsvereniging voor Overheidsdiensten* [1989] ECR 4311, and Case C-229/89 *Commission v. Belgium* [1991] ECR I-2205.
561. Cases 48/88 etc. *Achterberg-te Riele et al. v. Sociale Verzekeringsbank* [1988] ECR 7.
562. See Case C-31/90 *Johnson v. Chief Adjudication Officer* [1991] ECR I-3723 and Cases C-87–89/90 *Verholen et al. v. Sociale Verzekeringsbank* [1991] ECR I-3757.
563. O.J. 1986 L 225/40.
564. [1990] ECR 1889, [1990] 2 CMLR 513.
565. As to the effect of that Protocol (No. 2, annexed to the EC Treaty, as explained in the text), see Case C-7/93 *Bestuur van het Algemeen Burgerlijk Pensioenfonds v. Beune* [1994] ECR I-4471 at 4521–4524; Case C-57/93 *Vroege v. NCIV Instituut voor Volkshuisvesting BV et al.* [1994] ECR I-4541 at 4578–4580; Case C-128/93 *Fisscher v. Voorhuis Hengelo BV et al.* [1994] ECR I-4583 at 4600–4601; Case C-147/95 *Dimosia Epicheirisi Ilectrismou (DEI) v. Evrenopoulos* [1997] ECR I-2057 at 2085–2086, and Case C-246/96 *Magorrian v. Eastern Health and Social Services Board et al.* [1997] ECR I-7153 at 7183 and 7187–7188. As to the Court's view on the effect in time of the *Barber* judgment, see Case C-109/91 *Ten Oever v. Stichting Bedrijfspensioenfonds voor het Glazenwassers- en Schoonmaakbedrijf* [1993] ECR I-4879 at 4944–4945; Case C-200/91 *Coloroll Pension Trustees Ltd. v. Russell et al.* [1994] ECR I-4389 at 4417–4418; Case C-408/92 *Smith et al. v. Advel Systems Ltd.* [1994] ECR I-4435 at 4465–4466 and 4468; Case C-28/93 *Van den Akker et al. v. Stichting Shell Pensioenfonds* [1994] ECR I-4527 at 4537–4538; Case C-57/93 *Vroege* [1994] ECR I-4541 at 4574–4577, and Case C-128/93 *Fisscher* [1994] ECR I-4583 at 4594–4596. See also Curtin

120 EC and requires that Member States endeavour to maintain the existing equivalence between paid holiday schemes. Since the reference is merely to an endeavour, this Article in no circumstances has direct effect. The new Article 120 EC contains a specific reporting obligation for the Commission 'on progress in achieving the objectives of Article 117, including the demographic situation in the Community.' The report is to be presented annually to the European Parliament, the Council and ECOSOC. On the basis of the second paragraph of the new Article 120 EC, the Parliament may invite the Commission to draw up reports on particular problems concerning the social situation. The maintenance of the existing reporting obligation found in the present Article 122 EC, which is couched in very similar terms, is not an example of felicitous drafting in the preparation of the Treaty of Amsterdam. The present Article 122 EC, which was already in the original version of the EEC Treaty has remained a dead-letter provision to this day.

C. Articles 126 and 127 EC. The quality of the working population is increasingly one of the central areas of concern in current economic and social policy. From an economic standpoint it is primarily the ever-increasing intensity of knowledge in modern production processes which is relevant. Economies in which the supply of highly-qualified employees lags behind demand will inevitably have to struggle with lower levels of investment and economic growth. From the social viewpoint it is important that the major part of high long-term unemployment is to be found among the low-educated section of the working population. As there are no clear limits to the lowering of salary costs of the lowest-paid, the solution must be found as much as possible in attempts to raise the level of training among this group. As was observed in section 4, above, demand for vocational qualifications constantly changes under pressure from the dynamics of the market, both in terms of place and in terms of sector. It is obvious that the level of training of the working population must be a matter for coordination when coordinating the economic policies of the Member States and of the Community under Article 103 EC. It is also obvious that in Community action to strengthen economic and social cohesion in accordance with Articles 130a–130e EC, measures in the field of vocational training and retraining must play an important part. In the old EEC Treaty the Title on social policy contained a separate provision on vocational training,[566] which, in view of the importance of training for social policy was a natural complement to the other provisions of that Title.

On the basis of the old Article 128 EEC, the Council, acting on a proposal from the Commission and after consulting the Economic and

(1990) 27 CMLRev. 475; Barents (1992) SEW 684 at 690–691; Watson (1993) 30 CMLRev. 481 at 509–511, and Moore (1995) 20 ELRev. 159.
566. Art. 128 EEC.

Social Committee, was to lay down general principles for implementing a common vocational training policy, capable of contributing to the harmonious development both of the national economies and of the common market.[567] Because that provision regulated neither the legal character of the measures to be taken on the subject nor the way they are brought about, an extensive legal discussion arose on both points.[568] Two points were at the heart of this discussion.

1. What was to be understood by the concept of vocational training? This clearly went to the substantive scope of the old Article 128 EEC.
2. What was the nature of the Council's powers under the old Article 128 EEC? Could it only lay down general principles, or could it actually adopt measures implementing those principles on the basis of that provision?

The first question has been answered by the Court in the extensive sense: 'any form of education which prepares for a qualification for a particular profession, trade or employment or which provides the necessary training and skills for such a profession, trade or employment is vocational training, whatever the age and level of training of the pupils or students, and even if the training programme includes an element of general education.'[569] The second question was answered in two judgments on 30 May 1989 in Case 242/87 *Commission v. Council*[570] and case 56/88 *United Kingdom v. Council*.[571] The first case related to the Erasmus programme for student mobility, which was to be financed out of Community resources. The Commission's proposal was based solely on the old Article 128 EEC, but the Council added Article 235 EEC as a legal basis, according to which unanimity was required.[572] The second case concerned the Petra programme, which provided for Community co-financing for supplementary vocational training for early school leavers. The decision involved here was based exclusively on Article 128 EC.[573] In the first case the Commission argued that Article 235 EEC should not have been used

567. See, pretty exhaustively, Currall *et al.* in Von der Groeben *et al.*, *op. cit.* (see note 417, *supra*) 3521–3563.
568. As long as the Council restricted itself to laying down general principles these problems did not arise; thus already in Dec. 63/266 (O.J. English Special Edition 1963–64, p. 25) these principles were laid down. In 1991 the Commission presented a proposal to bring that decision up to date, COM (91) 397 Final. That proposal now appears overtaken by the changes in the EC Treaty made by the TEU.
569. Case 293/83 *Gravier v. City of Liège* [1985] ECR 593 at 614. See also Case 24/86 *Blaizot v. University of Liège et al.* [1988] ECR 379 at 403–404 and Case C-357/89 *Raulin v. Minister van Onderwijs en Wetenschappen* [1992] ECR I-1027 at 1064–1065.
570. [1989] ECR 1425, [1991] 1 CMLR 478.
571. [1989] ECR 1615, [1989] 2 CMLR 789.
572. Dec. 86/365 (O.J. 1986 L 222/17).
573. Dec. 87/569 (O.J. 1987 L 346/31, amended by Dec. 91/387 (O.J. 1991 L 214/69)).

as the joint legal basis; in the second case the United Kingdom argued that the old Article 128 EEC was the incorrect legal basis. The Court in both its judgments confirmed the view of the Commission, which meant that the Council would have the power to adopt legal acts establishing Community operations relating to vocational training and to oblige the Member States to cooperate.[574] The combination of a wide interpretation of the concept of vocational training and the possibility of being able to adopt implementing acts directly on the basis of the old Article 128 EEC opened up a potentially wide field for Community initiatives in this sphere.

It is against the background of these developments in Community policies and case-law that the present Articles 126 and 127 EC on education, vocational training and youth were adopted.[575] On the one hand they are based on the fear of far-reaching Community initiatives in the field of national – or regional – autonomy in the field of education. On the other hand they are based on the desire to create an unequivocal legal basis for Community activities both in the field of education and in the field of vocational training.[576]

Article 126 EC creates a very limited legal basis for Community action in the field of education as such. The Community contribution is essentially limited to encouraging cooperation between the Member States and 'if necessary' to supporting and supplementing their action, primarily through developing the European dimension in education, particularly through the teaching and dissemination of the languages of the Member States, and through the promotion of cooperation between educational institutions and the mobility of teachers and students.[577] Acting by the co-decision procedure, after consulting ECOSOC and the Committee of the Regions, the Council may adopt incentive measures. The involvement of the Committee of the Regions reflects the sensitivities as to education policy felt primarily by the German *Länder*.[578]

In the field of vocational education, the Article 127 EC as it will be amended by the Treaty of Amsterdam is somewhat more generous in its grant of competence to the Community. The Community is to implement a vocational training policy which is to fully support the action of the Member States, while fully respecting their responsibility for the content and organization of vocational training.[579] The legal uncertainties which

---

574. Subsequently, in Cases C-51/89 *etc. United Kingdom et al. v. Council* [1991] ECR I-2757, [1992] 1 CMLR 40 on the Comett II programme, the Court adopted an even wider definition of vocational training, so that training aimed at promoting research and technological development was also covered.

575. See Cloos *et al., op. cit.* (see note 55, *supra*) 317–319.

576. See Lane (1993) 30 CMLRev. 939 at 946–951.

577. See Art. 126(1) and (2) EC (Art. 126(2) sets out the full list of aims of Community action).

578. See Cloos *et al., op. cit.* (see note 55, *supra*) 317–319

579. Art. 127(1) EC.

surrounded the old Article 128 EEC now seem to be resolved by this wording. Implementing acts may also be based on Article 127 EC.[580] It is remarkable that both in Article 126(3) EC and in Article 127(3) EC the Community is conferred with powers to foster cooperation with third countries and with appropriate international organizations. Horizons towards the EEA States and the candidate central and Eastern European countries were clearly envisaged, although they are not restricted to those partners. The revised new Article 127(4) EC changes decision-making under Article 127 EC to use the co-decision procedure with consultation of ECOSOC and the Committee of the Regions.

6.3   The future of social policy integration

Like the coordination of economic policy, the coordination of social policy is founded on market integration, particularly here on the free movement of persons under Article 48–51 EC. The achievement of this is one of the core tasks of the Community. In this it has shortcomings in a number of respects. The restriction of free movement of workers to Community nationals is socially outdated, now that the reservoir of lower-educated persons in the Community is increasingly supplemented by workers coming from third countries who display as a rule a higher degree of mobility than Community nationals. The fact that they fall outside the Community coordination of national social security systems contributes to the fact that such third-country nationals often operate in the grayer or secondary circuits, with all the possible consequences of such a choice for the stability of labour relations within the Community. Legally too this remains an anomaly, now that third-country nationals lawfully resident in a Member State may work elsewhere in the Community if they are posted there to provide services by their employer in the Member State in which they are lawfully resident.

The coordination of social security systems, as worked out in the Community provisions adopted over the years, took place in a period in which the most important social security arrangements for the working population were wholly statutory in their basis and execution. Since the mid-Eighties in various Member States there has been a policy trend visible of moving various of these provisions into the hands of the private sector, albeit subject to statutory minimum and framework conditions. The consequences for the free movement of workers are perhaps recognized but so far the results of this trend for the Community provisions have not been worked through. Thus the latter loses its useful effect of ensuring that social security coverage is adequately maintained for migrant workers, which is a necessary precondition for free movement.

580. In the same sense, Lane (1993) 30 CMLRev. 939 at 949.

It is true that the theoretical and practical problems in regulating changes to private law-based contractual relationships are not small, but they are certainly not insoluble. If the tendency to public-law conditioned privatization of employees' insurance continues, then in time the public law conditioning must be coordinated at Community level, both from the viewpoint of the unity of the labour market and from the unity of *that* insurance market as a market for services.

In principle Article 51 EC offers a sufficient legal basis to achieve the necessary convergence of national rules in this field, although the requirement of unanimity in the application of Article 51 is a major practical obstacle. Nevertheless, a continued failure by the Community legislator to modernize the coordination system threatens to fragment the already fragile internal market for the labour factor. It is thus also to be regretted that the Treaty of Amsterdam did not extend the free movement of workers to embrace all lawful residents in the Community, instead of continuing its restriction to Community nationals and maintaining the unanimity requirement of Article 51 EC.[581] Another, although less pressing reason for a more active role of the Community legislator in the shaping – not the level – of social security in the Community lies in the challenges which the worldwide process of globalization poses for the West European welfare states. These are set out in the White Paper *Growth, Competitiveness and Employment*.[582] If each Member State separately were to remodel its social security system there would be a two-part risk: the existing systems would diverge so far that assuring transfer from one to the other would become impossible, and the Member States would find themselves in irresponsible policy competition. The avoidance of this has long been the core task of the Community in the system of Community law.

The substantive attuning of the coordination of economic policies and social policy will require ever more attention as EMU achieves its completion. Because in a completed EMU macro-economic and structural disturbances will primarily be expressed through the labour market, whether in the form of unemployment or in the form of wage cost inflation, the functioning of the labour market and the development of conditions of employment are central points for attention in the coordination of economic policies. As the international competitive position of Western Europe is to a large extent determined by the quality of its working population, vocational training and education can no longer be the monopoly domain of social policy. The same applies for the design and financing of social security, as they directly influence the development

581. The Commission has now presented a proposal to extend the ambit of Community legislation in the social security field (see note 423, *supra*) to embrace nationals of third countries COM (97) 561 Final (O.J. 1998 C 6/15).
582. COM (93) 700, Bull. EU Supp. 6/93.

of relative labour costs and thus the competitive power of the West
European economies.

For the solution of these questions some significant advances have been
made with the introduction of the new Title VIa on employment and the
substitution of the new Articles 117–120 EC for the contents of the
Agreement on Social policy. It is a pity that the changes both in terms of
system and in terms of drafting leave much to be desired in relation to the
quality of legislation. This means that the interaction between economic
and social policy integration is still not sufficiently expressed. In a
completed EMU disturbances in balance will primarily have to be absorbed
by the labour factor, and that makes a detailed substantive attunement of
the Community's coordinating actions at Community level in respect of
the policy areas discussed in this Chapter absolutely essential. On the next
revision of the EC Treaty this should be a priority issue.

CHAPTER X

Horizontal and flanking policies*

1. THE PLACE OF HORIZONTAL AND FLANKING POLICIES IN THE EC TREATY

The change of name from the European Economic Community to the European Community[1] is the culmination of a process which had already commenced in the Seventies. The Final communiqué of the Paris Summit in October 1972 and the Single European Act indicated that the Community was not merely an economic one. The Community was obliged to devote more attention to the social aspects of its policies and in due course to develop into an Economic and Monetary Union, as has been explained in Chapter IX, above. Moreover, the Heads of State and Government emphasized the importance of Community action in flanking policy areas, such as research and development, and environmental policy.[2]

The communitarization of the latter policy is exemplary as to the Community's approach. First the question whether the original EEC Treaty also sought to achieve environmental objectives was addressed.[3]

---

* In the Fifth Dutch edition of this work, this Chapter was written by K.J.M. Mortelmans. In this edition that structure has been retained, but the editor has, in addition to taking more account of case-law, literature and more recent developments, written in particular sections 3.2 and 4.2 (which in the Dutch edition are merely lists of measures), in order to give at least a brief overview of the policies concerned.

1. Art. G(1) TEU. See, generally, Lane (1993) 30 CMLRev. 939 and Mortelmans (1994) SEW 236.
2. Bull. EC 10–1972, pp. 17–19 (EMU) and 20–21 (R and D and environment).
3. Case 91/79 *Commission v. Italy* [1980] ECR 1099 at 1106. More precisely, the Court addressed the question whether provisions on the environment could be based on Art. 100 EEC. It replied affirmatively, *ibid.*, principally on the basis that the measure concerned had been adopted not only within the Community's Environmental Action Programme (O.J. 1973 C 112/1) but also under the General Programme for the elimination of technical barriers to trade (J.O. 1969 C 76/1). The Court further noted, *ibid.*, that it was by no means ruled out that provisions on the environment could be based on Art. 100 EEC. 'Provisions which are made necessary by considerations relating to the environment and health may be a burden on the undertakings to which they apply and if

Through a broad interpretation of Article 2 EEC, the two general provisions which formed the basis for Community action, Articles 100 and 235 EEC, were harnessed to enable concrete action to be taken, and subsequently, with the amendments to the EEC Treaty by the SEA, specific environmental objectives and legal bases were formulated. At the same time, Article 130r(4) EEC indicated that the principle of subsidiarity applied, and that the relevant requirements of environmental protection formed a component part of the other tasks of Community policy.[4]

In the amendments made to the EEC Treaty by the TEU, the same step was taken for various other flanking areas of Community policy which had been developed, such as consumer protection, education and culture: they were given a specific status and legal basis in the EC Treaty. Certain other flanking policies, such as civil protection and tourism were merely included in the catalogue of activities set out in Article 3 EC, finding their place in Article 3(t) EC. Culture, education, public health, consumer protection and environmental policy cover non-socio-economic subjects and interests, but they are subjects and interests which have socio-economic interfaces. In the EEA Agreement consumer protection and the environment are included in the areas described as 'horizontal provisions relevant to the four freedoms' all the flanking policies are included in the sphere of cooperation outside the four freedoms. Accordingly, the title of this Chapter refers to these policies by reflecting their dual vision.

Sectoral policy is discussed in Chapter XI, below. That Chapter is chiefly concerned with the question whether the specific economic provisions for the sectors concerned are applicable, or the general economic provisions of the Treaty. In the latter case the question of subsidiarity is far less relevant than is true in relation to the subjects discussed in this Chapter.

2. COMMON CHARACTERISTICS OF THE HORIZONTAL AND FLANKING POLICIES

If the various Titles of the EC Treaty which are devoted to horizontal and flanking policies are compared, it becomes clear that there is a common approach which is not always logically followed through. First of all the objectives are indicated which the Community is to pursue; secondly, the means by which these objectives are to be pursued are specified in the form of the legal bases available for Community action, and, thirdly, the legal instruments to be used are prescribed. The various Titles of the Treaty,

there is no harmonization of national provisions on the matter, competition may be appreciably distorted.'
4. Art. 130r(2) EEC.

save that dealing with consumer protection, contain a provision dealing with the promotion of cooperation between the Member States and the Community on the one hand, and the Community and third countries on the other. The cooperation between the Member States and the Community is also dealt with.

Those are the similarities. As far as the scope of Community action is concerned, a distinction may be drawn between two approaches. The Community is permitted to adopt harmonization mesures in the fields of the environment and consumer protection. This is excluded in the cases of public health, education and culture. The drafters of the Treaty have formulated these latter provisions with the policy-makers in the national 'caring' departments breathing down their necks: the provisions are conceived in a manner which at first sight appears to limit severely the possibilities for Community action. Thus the principle of subsidiarity, the exclusion of harmonization measures, the requirement of unanimity in decision-making, and the mechanism of non-binding instruments (recommendations) all seem have placed secure locks on the doors of the national departmental ministries.

It remains to be seen whether this vision is in fact correct. As has been explained, these are the caring, idealist and spending policy areas with economic interfaces. In Treaty terms the integration provisions which can be found in the various Titles function as switching provisions. The Community must in its action on the basis of other provisions of the EC Treaty also take account of cultural aspects;[5] requirements relating to health protection form a constituent part of the Community's other policies.[6] There is no such integrating provision in relation to education and vocational training, and consumer protection. From the absence of such a provision, it may be deduced that the Community may adopt measures affecting health and cultural matters on the basis of other Treaty provisions, such as those concerning the internal market and competition.[7] Article 130r(2) provides that environmental protection requirements must be integrated into the definition and implementation of other Community policies.

In the Conclusions of the Presidency at the Edinburgh European Council an interpretation of Articles 126–129 EC is advanced in the light of Article 3b EC that excludes harmonization measures.[8] That interpretation further purports to deduce that the use of Article 235 EC for harmonization measures in pursuit of the specific objectives laid down in Articles 126–129

---

5. Art. 128(4) EC.
6. Art. 129(1) EC, final para.
7. *E.g.* Dir. 89/552 (O.J. 1989 L 298/23) on television programmes is based on Arts. 57 and 66 EC but contains provisions relating to language and to the protection of minors, amended by Dir. 97/36 (O.J. 1997 L 202/60).
8. Bull. EC 12–1992, point I.16 (note to the final para. of the basic principles relating to subsidiarity).

is excluded. It remains to be seen whether that view will be shared by the Court of Justice.[9]

3. ENVIRONMENTAL POLICY

3.1 Legal basis of EC environmental policy

The SEA added a new Title VII to Part Three of the EEC Treaty[10] which dealt with the objectives and means of Community environmental policy. This was further developed by the TEU: Article B TEU states that one of the objectives of the European Union is 'to promote economic and social progress which is balanced and sustainable'. Article 2 EC itself speaks of 'sustainable and non-inflationary growth respecting the environment'.[11] Article 3(k) EC makes it clear that this objective must be achieved by means of 'a policy in the sphere of the environment' which effectively achieves a codification of the legal situation which had arisen through an extensive interpretation of the old Article 2 EEC.[12] For certain matters, such as nuclear safety and radioactive waste, the Euratom Treaty remains important. Article 1 Euratom specifies that it is the task of the Euratom Community 'to contribute to the raising of the standard of living'. By analogy with the legal situation in the EEC prior to the coming into force of the TEU, Article 1 Euratom is a proper environmental objective. Article B TEU is also of importance, so that in the development of its nuclear energy policy the Community must take account of the danger of environmental disasters. The absence of a specific provision in the Euratom Treaty means that in a number of instances the EC Treaty will be

9. *Cf.* the view of the Bundesverfassungsgericht in *Brunner et al.* [1994] 1 CMLR 57, points C.II.3.(b) and (c), and Koopmans (1994) NJB 248. However, the standpoint in the Presidency's Conclusions that this did not mean that the pursuit of other Community objectives through Treaty articles other than Arts. 126–129 might not produce effects in these areas is clearly correct.

10. See Behrens and Koch (eds.), *Umweltschutz in der Europäischen Gemeinschaft: Spannungsfelder zwischen nationalem Recht und europäischen Gemeinschaftsrecht* (Baden-Baden, 1991); Hannequart (1988) RMC 225; Jacobs in Schwarze and Schermers (eds.) *Structure and Dimensions of European Community Policy* (Baden-Baden, 1988) 117; Jacqué (1986) *Environmental Law and Policy* 115; Krämer (1987) 24 CMLRev. 659 and (1991) 11 YBEL 151, and Vandermeersch (1987) 12 ELRev. 407. See also the House of Lords Select Committee on the European Communities: *The Polluter Pays Principle* Session 1982–83 10th Report (HL 131). Many of Krämer's seminal articles have been collected in his *Focus on European Environmental Law* (2nd ed. London, 1997).

11. See Chapter III, section 1.2.1, *ante* and the Council Resolution on renewable energy sources (O.J. 1997 C 210/1).

12. Case 240/83 *Procureur de la République v. Association de défense des brûleurs d'huiles usagées* [1985] ECR 531 at 549. (The Court did not specifically mention Art. 2 EEC, but referred to environmental protection as 'one of the Community's essential objectives').

applicable.[13] The Environment Title was expanded in certain points by the amendments introduced by the TEU; these points are systematically discussed in the various sections below.[14] However, the principle of subsidiarity which was set out in Article 130r(4) EEC and had a spearhead function at that time is not discussed, as it was deleted in the amendments to the Environment Title made by the TEU, having been replaced by the general principle set out in Article 3b EC.[15]

3.1.1 Objectives

According to Article 130r(1) EC the Community policy on the environment is to contribute to the following four objectives: first, preserving, protecting and improving the quality of the environment; secondly, protecting human health; thirdly, a prudent and rational utilization of natural resources, and, finally, promoting measures at international level to deal with regional or worldwide environmental problems.[16] This final objective was added by the TEU. These objectives closely resemble or are inspired by Community practice developed since the United Nations Environmental Conferences in Stockholm in 1972 and Rio de Janeiro in

13. The myriad measures adopted after the Chernobyl disaster well illustrate this. See Case C-62/88 *Greece v. Council* [1990] ECR I-1527, [1991] 2 CMLR 649; Case C-70/88 *European Parliament v. Council* [1990] ECR I-2041, [1992] 1 CMLR 91, and Case C-146/91 *Koinopraxia Enoseon Georgikon Synetairismon Diacheiriseos Enchorion Proïonton Syn. PE (KYDEP) v. Council et al.* [1994] ECR I-4199.
14. See, generally, Behrens and Koch (ed.), *Umweltschutz in der Europäischen Gemeinschaft; Spannungfelder zwischen nationalem Recht und dem Europäischem Gemeinschaftsrecht* (Baden-Baden, 1991); Chalmers (1994) 14 YBEL 257; Cross (1995) 15 YBEL 107; Davies (1994) 14 YBEL 313; Hession and Macrory in O'Keeffe and Twomey (eds.), *Legal Issues of the Maastricht Treaty* (Chichester, 1994) 151; Kahl, *Umweltprinzip und Gemeinschaftsrecht* (Heidelberg, 1993); Krämer, *E.C. Treaty and Environmental Law* (2nd ed., London, 1995) and in Micklitz and Reich (eds.), *Public Interest Litigation before European Courts* (Baden-Baden, 1996) 297–318 (see also the contribution by Betlem, 319–341); Jans, *European Environmental Law* (London, 1995); Okowa (1995) 15 YBEL 169; Jarass and Neuman, *Umweltschutz und Europäische Gemeinschaften; rechts- und sozialwissenschafliche Probleme der umweltpolitischen Integration* (Heidelberg, 1992); Leefmans, *Externe milieubevoegdheden* (Deventer, 1998); Rengeling, *Umweltschutz und andere Politiken der EG* (Cologne, 1993); Robinson and Dunkley (eds.), *Public Interest Perspectives in Environmental Law* (Chichester, 1995); De Sadeleer, *Le droit communautaire et les déchets* (Brussels, 1995); Sevenster, *Milieubeleid en Gemeenschapsrecht* (Deventer, 1992) and (1993) *Milieu en Recht* 338; Wiggers-Rust et al. (eds.), *Waste Prevention in the EEC* (Zwolle, 1994), and Williams (1994) 14 YBEL 351. See further, Holder (ed.), *The Impact of European Community Environmental law in the United Kingdom* (Chichester, 1997) and Macrory and Hollins, *A Source Book of European Community Environmental Law* (Oxford, 1995). The *European Environmental Law Review*, *Journal of Environmental Law*, *Review of European Community and International Environmental Law* and *Tijdschrift voor Milieu en Recht* are regular sources of important articles.
15. See, further, Chapter III, section 5.1.1, *ante*.
16. See Case C-379/92 *Peralta* [1994] ECR I-3495 at 3504–3505.

1992. The term 'sustainable development', which played such a central role in the Rio Declaration[17] is not reflected in Article 130r(1) EC, although it is in Article 130u EC which deals with development cooperation. The principle also features – as 'sustainable growth' – in a Declaration on Assessment of the Environmental Impact of Community Measures, attached to the Final Act on the occasion of the TEU. Moreover, the Title of the Community's Fifth Environmental Action Programme is 'Towards Sustainability'.[18]

Article 130r(3) EC sets out certain matters which the Community must take account of in preparing its policy on the environment: available scientific and technical data; environmental conditions in the various regions of the Community; the potential benefits and costs of action or lack of action, and the economic and social development of the Community as a whole and the balanced development of its regions. These matters are further developed in the Fifth Environmental Action Programme, which, as Jans has put it, for the first time is much more a strategic programme and much less a list of concrete measures that ought to be taken in the short term.[19]

3.1.2 Principles

It is primarily in relation to the principles that the amendments made by the TEU have developed those made by the SEA. The central new element in Article 130r(2) EC is that 'Community policy on the environment shall aim at a high level of protection'. This principle had been included, in relation to the Commission's proposals as to harmonization measures, in Article 100a(3) EEC, but it now is more general in scope and development. But Article 130r(2) EC makes it clear that this high level must take 'into account the diversity of situations in the various regions of the Community.' This point is repeated in the second indent of Article 130r(3) EC, which provision, in its fourth indent, notes that the economic and social development of the Community as a whole must also be taken into account.

The precautionary principle is also new. It is not more fully defined in the Treaty but is developed in the Fifth Environmental Action programme. The preventive principle was already included in the Treaty by the amendments made by the SEA, having earlier featured in the second part of the First Environmental Action Programme.[20] The principle 'that environmental

17. 31 ILM 876 (1992). As to the balance between trade freedom and sustainable development, see Hession and Macrory in Emiliou and O'Keeffe (eds.), *The European Union and World Trade Law after the GATT Uruguay Round* (Chichester, 1996) 181–217.
18. O.J. 1993 C 138/1. Agreement on amendments was reached after conciliation; publication in the O.J. is awaited (July 1998).
19. Jans, *op. cit.* (see note 14, *supra*) 274–275.
20. O.J. 1973 C 112/1.

damage should as a priority be rectified at source' was already invoked before the entry into force of the TEU by the Court of Justice in Case C-2/ 90 *Commission v. Belgium*.[21] This principle is important in the matters in which tension exists between free movement and environmental policy.[22] The principle that the polluter pays was already established in 1975.[23] It can play a part in the working out of Community policy in two ways. First, the Commission applies the principle in the state aids field in the application of its powers under Articles 92 and 93 EC, which should mean here that in the future state aids will no longer be approved by the Commission.[24] This approach is supported by the fact that the principle is unchanged by the amendments made by the TEU. The drafters of the Treaty did not create an express exception for environmental aid, whereas in Article 92(3)(d) they did for aid for the promotion of culture and heritage conservation. It has been argued against that point that the absence of an express provision as to environmental aid can be explained that the interest of such aid was so obvious it was not thought necessary to make express provision for it.[25] The Commission's practice has in fact been to accept environmental aid, although this policy is subject to stringent conditions.[26]

21. [1992] ECR I-4431 at 4480. The Court referred to this in terms of 'the principles of self-sufficiency and proximity set out in the Basle Convention of 22 March 1989 on the control of transboundary movements of hazardous wastes and their disposal to which the Community is a signatory' (see Dec. 93/38 (O.J. 1993 L 39/1, corrigendum L 1994 L74/52; amendment approved by Dec. 97/640 (O.J. 1997 L 272/45)). The Convention was not even in force as regards the Community at the time of the judgment. See Hancher (1993) 30 CMLRev. 351; Von Wilmowsky (1993) 30 CMLRev. 541; Krämer (1993) 30 CMLRev. 111; Gormley in Holder (ed.), *op. cit.* (see note 14, *supra*) 289 at 299–301, and in Krämer *et al.* (eds.), *Law and Diffuse Interests in the European Legal Order* (*Liber Amicorum* Norbert Reich, Baden-Baden, 1997) 11 at 22–24.
22. See Krämer (1993) 30 CMLRev. 111; Gormley in Holder, *ibid.* 289 and Jans, *op. cit.* (see note 14, *supra*) 197–235.
23. Rec. 75/436 (O.J. 1975 L 194/1).
24. As to previous practice, see the *Fourth Report on Competition Policy 1974* (Brussels, Luxembourg, 1975) point 175, with the *Tenth Report 1980 ibid.*, 1981) points 222 *et seq.* and the *Sixteenth Report 1986* (*ibid.*, 1987) points 259 *et seq.* See also the Fourth Environmental Action Programme (O.J. 1987 C 328/5) point 2.3.15. In the Commission's proposal for a regulation permitting aids for certain horizontal purposes to be declared compatible with the common market and not subject to notification, environmental protection is one of the purposes covered, see COM (97) 396 Final (O.J. 1997 C 262/6).
25. Sevenster, *op. cit.* (see note 14, *supra*) 372.
26. See the new guidelines, O.J. 1994 C 72/3. As to the practice, see *e.g.* Dec. 92/316 (O.J. 1992 L 170/34) on aid for the recycling of manure surpluses in the Netherlands and WQ E-2746/94 (Van Dijk) O.J. 1995 C 103/33. See also Dec. 93/564 (O.J. 1993 L 273/ 51) *Cartiere del Garda*. The role of the common European interest exception in Art. 92(3)(b) in relation to environmental pollution, upheld by the Court in Case 62/87 *Exécutif régional wallon et al. v. Commission* [1988] ECR 1573 at 1595, will be modest under the new guidelines, as the primary evaluation takes place under Art. 92(3)(c) EC, see, further, Jans, *op. cit.* (see note 14, *supra*) 263–270 and Vogelaar in Hawk (ed.)

Secondly, the principle can also be used by the Community legislator in the adoption of directives, particularly in the determination of costs in the waste directives.[27] In this case Article 130s(5) EC permits the Council to lay down appropriate provisions in the form of temporary derogations and/or financial support from the Cohesion Fund[28] where the costs of a Community measure would involve costs deemed disproportionate for the public authorities of a Member State.

The wording of the integration principle has been changed,[29] so that the environmental protection requirements must be integrated into the definition and implementation of other Community policies.[30] Moreover, in appropriate cases a safeguard clause allowing the Member States to take provisional measures, for non-economic environmental reasons, subject to a Community inspection procedure, will now be included in harmonization measures meeting the requirements of Community environmental policy.[31] This provision bears considerable similarities to Article 100a(5) EC. Community policies in other areas covers not only the policy areas of agriculture, fisheries, economic and social cohesion, and research and technological development, it also embraces the policy for the achievement of the internal market, covering the five freedoms and competition.[32] As has been noted in section 3.1.1, above, the Final Act of the Intergovernmental Conference approving the TEU has a declaration attached to it on Assessment of the Environmental Impact of Community Measures, in which the Commission in is proposals, and the Member States in implementing them, undertook to take full account of their environmental impact and of the principle of sustainable growth.

International Antitrust Law and Policy 1994 (*1994 Fordham Corporate Law Institute*, Irvington-on-Hudson, 1995) 529. See also note 14, *supra*.

27. See section 3.2, *post*.
28. O.J. 1994 L 130/1.
29. See Zits, *Die Wertigheit des Umweltschutzes in Beziehung zu anderen Aufgaben der Europäischen Gemeinschaft* (Trier, 1993); Böhm and Breier (1992) EuZW 49, and Kamminga and Klatte (1994) *Milieurecht* 7.
30. Art. 130r(2) EC, 1st para. See *e.g. General Report 1997* (Brussels, Luxembourg 1998) points 538–540. The Treaty of Amsterdam (not yet in force) will amend Art. 130r(2) EC and move the integration provision into the new Art. 3c EC.
31. *Ibid.*, 2nd para.
32. See Barents (1993) SEW 5. As an example of the integration principle in action, see Reg. 2052/88 (O.J. 19988 L 185/9, as substituted by Reg. 2081/93 (O.J. 1993 L 193/5), Art. 7 (unaffected by subsequent further changes to Reg. 2052/88). See Case T-461/93 *An Taisce – The National Trust for Ireland et al. v. Commission* [1994] ECR II-733, appeal dismissed in Case C-325/94 P *An Taisce – The National Trust for Ireland et al. v. Commission* [1996] ECR I-3727 and Case T-585/93 *Stichting Greenpeace Council (Greenpeace International) et al. v. Commission* [1995] ECR II-2205, on appeal, Case C-321/95 *Stichting Greenpeace Council (Greenpeace International) et al. v. Commission* [1998] ECR I-nyr (2 April 1998). (The cases were found inadmissible by the Court of First instance (confirmed on appeal), so the substantive points were not reached). See also the Communication on Environment and Employment COM (97) 592 Final.

3.1.3 International cooperation

The first paragraph of Article 130r(4) provides that within their respective spheres of competence the Community and the Member States are to cooperate with third countries and with the relevant international organisations. Arrangements for Community cooperation may be the subject of agreements between the Community and the third parties concerned; these are to be negotiated and concluded in accordance with Article 228 EC. The phrase 'competent international organizations' at first sight means UNEP (the United Nations Environment Programme) but Halsbury's Laws[33] also rightly mentions other international organizations with which the Community cooperates in this and other fields, and these too must be covered by this provision: these include the International Union for the Conservation of Nature and National Resources (IUCN); the Economic Commission for Europe; the International Maritime Organisation (IMO – incidentally the only UN arm to be based in London); OECD and the Committee of International Development Institutions on the Environment, as well as the United Nations Food and Agriculture Organization (FAO) and now the World Trade Organization (WTO). Given that the Environment Title of the EC Treaty does not appear to derogate from the powers separately regulated by the Euratom Treaty, the International Atomic Energy Agency in Vienna would not appear to be covered by this provision.[34]

The second paragraph of Article 130r(4) EC provides that the first paragraph of that Article is without prejudice to the competence of the Member State to negotiate in international bodies and to conclude international agreements. The second part of the Declaration on Article 130r EEC annexed to the Final Act signed on the adoption of the SEA stated in relation to what was then Art. 130r(5) EEC that it did not affect the principles resulting from the judgment in Case 22/70 *Commission v. Council*.[35] That view is repeated, *inter alia* in relation to Article 130r(4) EC in a Declaration annexed to the Final Act on the occasion of signature of the TEU.[36] If there had been no such declaration, it would have been possible to argue that the second paragraph of Article 130r(4) consciously created a different approach from the doctrine expressed in that judgment. It was clearly not the intention to do this, so that doctrine must be applied to determine who is competent to act at international level.[37] The declaration does not however solve the problem of competence, as the first

33. 4th Ed. (London, 1986), Vol. 51, para. 8.02.
34. *Cf.* Case C-70/88 *European Parliament v. Council* [1991] ECR I-4529 at 4566–4567 (the judgment on the substance in that case).
35. [1971] ECR 263, [1971] CMLR 335.
36. Declaration No. 10. The other matters covered by the Declaration are monetary policy matters (Art. 109 EC) and development cooperation (Art. 130y EC).
37. Opinion 2/91 *ILO Convention No. 170 concerning safety in the use of chemicals at work*

paragraph of Article 130r(4) itself appears to indicate shared competence, whereas on the other hand, on the basis of internal Community instruments, such as those in the fisheries sector, exclusive Community competence can be argued in respect of various environmental measures.[38] If there is a dispute about the correct interpretation of the second paragraph of Article 130r(4) it will be for the Court of Justice to resolve the matter. In Case C-379/92 *Peralta*[39] it expressly refused to rule on the compatibility of a national provision adopted by a Member State with an international convention, it also refused to interpret Article 130r EC in the light of an international convention which was not binding on the Community and to which, moreover, not all the Member States were parties.

There are various important areas in which Community directives or regulations and international agreements with third countries in the environmental field are involved. These include air, sea and land pollution, noise pollution (caused by motor vehicles, aircraft, construction plant, lawnmowers *etc.*), major accident hazards and various measures in the conservation field such as Regulation 338/97 implementing the CITES Convention.[40] One major example of action in relation to marine pollution is the Convention for the Protection of the Mediterranean Sea against Pollution.[41]

3.1.4   Decision-making and legal bases

It can be deduced from Article 130s EC that Community environmental policy rests on two general legal bases, save where there is specific provision elsewhere in the Treaty.[42] The choice between Articles 100a and 113 EC on the one hand, and Article 130s on the other has been the subject of important case-law. Product-directed environmental policy will have to be harmonized largely on the basis of Article 100a EC.[43] But for waste Article 130s EC is also available.[44] The choice of legal basis is important because of the differences in decision-making procedure, voting

---

[1993] ECR I-1061 at 1077. See, critically, Hession and Macrory, in O'Keeffe and Twomey (eds.), *op. cit.* (see note 14, *supra*) 159–160.

38. See Sevenster, *op. cit.* (see note 14, *supra*) 148 *et seq.*, and Jans, *op. cit.* (see note 14, *supra*) 73 *et seq.*

39. [1994] ECR I-3453 at 3504.

40. O.J. 1997 L 61/1, which replaces Reg. 3626/82 (O.J. 1982 L 384/1, most recently amended by Reg. 2727/95 (O.J. 1995 L 284/3). CITES was signed at Washington on 3 March 1973.

41. The Barcelona Convention, O.J. 1977 L 240/3, approved by Dec. 77/585 (O.J. 1977 L 240/1).

42. *E.g.* Arts. 43, 75, 84(2), 213 EC, and Arts. 7 and 30–32 Euratom.

43. Case C-300/89 *Commission v. Council* [1991] ECR I-2867 at 2899–2900.

44. Case C-155/91 *Commission v. Council* [1993] ECR I-939 at 968–969; Case C-187/93 *European Parliament v. Council* [1994] ECR I-2857 at 2881–2882.

requirements, and conditions under which the provisions concerned may be relied upon. Article 130t EC permits the Member States to adopt or maintain in force more stringent preventive measures.[45] A procedure has been introduced by Article 100a(4) whereby even after the adoption of a harmonization measure national measures may be applied after being approved.[46]

Article 130s EC itself formulates a trio of legal bases. First, the Council, in accordance with the cooperation procedure, and after consulting the Economic and Social Committee (ECOSOC), decides what action is to be taken to achieve the objectives mentioned in Article 130r EC.[47] Secondly, the first paragraph of Article 130s(2) provides for unanimous decision-making by the Council, acting on a proposal from the Commission, with mere consultation of the European Parliament (and also ECOSOC) in respect of a number of types of measures;[48] in relation to these measures the Council may decide by this procedure that decisions on certain matters may be taken by a qualified majority. Thirdly, Article 130s(3) provides that in other areas general action programmes setting out priority objectives to be attained are to be adopted by the Council using the co-decision procedure (with again consultation of ECOSOC), and that the measures to implement those programmes are to be adopted under the procedure of Article 130s(1) or (2) as appropriate. This means that the Environmental Action Programmes will no longer have a hybrid structure (as a decision of the Council and of the Representatives of the Governments of the Member States meeting within the Council), but will be firmly embedded in the EC Treaty, just as is the case with research and technological development programmes under Article 130i EC.

3.1.5 Financing, implementation and enforcement

The Member States finance and implement Community environ-ment policy, without prejudice to certain measures of a Community

45. See section 2.1.6, *post*.
46. See Chapter VIII, section 2.2, *ante*. It will be recalled from that discussion that in case C-41/93 *France v. Commission* [1991] ECR I-2867 at 1849 the Court held that no Member State could apply national rules derogating from the harmonized Community rules without obtaining confirmation of the former from the Commission, which con-firmation had to be duly reasoned.
47. Art. 130s(1) EC. The Treaty of Amsterdam (not yet in force) will replace the coopera-tion procedure by the co-decision procedure, it will also compel consultation of the Committee of the Regions. The procedures set out in the text in relation to Art. 130s(2) and (3) will also change to involve consultation of that Committee.
48. These are: provisions primarily of a fiscal nature (which approach reflects that of Art. 99 EC); measures concerning town and country planning, land use (other than waste management and measures of a general nature), and management of water resources, and measures significantly affecting a member state's choice between different energy sources and the general structure of its energy supply.

nature.[49] This means that national environmental measures, such as infrastructure projects, are eligible for co-financing.[50] Community measures include assistance from the Cohesion Fund[51] and research and development funding from programmes such as LIFE.[52]

The implementation and enforcement is left to the Member States, under supervision of the Commission in accordance with Article 155 EC. In Chapter 9 of the Fifth Environmental Action programme the Commission noted that in the past there were problems in implementation and supervision of enforcement,[53] and proposed reforms such as improvement in the quality of legislation,[54] better integration of environmental policy in other Community policies, and an increased role for the European Environment Agency.[55] The Commission also stressed the importance of rules relating to liability for environmental damage. As always, questions of implementation still give rise to concern.[56]

3.1.6　More stringent national provisions

Article 130t EC provides that the protective measures adopted in common pursuant to Article 130s shall not prevent any Member State from maintaining in force or introducing more stringent protective measures compatible with the Treaty. Thus the harmonization level achieved is regarded as a minimum level, with the Member States free to strive to attain a higher level of protection.[57] These measures must, however, be compatible with the EC Treaty, and must be notified to the Commission.[58] Prior to the coming into force of the SEA, minimum harmonization

---

49. Art. 130s(4) EC. This wording is far clearer than the obligation to finance measures other than certain measures of a Community nature, contained in the old Art. 130r(4) EEC.
50. Sevenster, *op. cit.* (see note 14, *supra*) 144.
51. See Art. 130s(5); as to the Fund, see note 28, *supra*.
52. Reg. 1973/92 (O.J. 1992 L 206/1), amended by Reg. 1404/96 (O.J. 1996 L 181/1). See the Fifth Environmental Action Programme, point 7.7. (see note 18, *supra*) and Case T-117/94 *Associazione Agricoltori della Provincia di Rovigo et al. v. Commission* [1995] ECR II-455.
53. As a particularly notorious example, where the Agent of the Commission actually made the front page of various national newspapers in the United Kingdom by (during the hearing) invoking his Granny's holidays to demolish the United Kingdom government's absurd contention that Blackpool beaches were not bathing beaches, see Case C-56/90 *Commission v. United Kingdom* [1993] ECR I-4109 (see *e.g. The Times* 28 October, 1992).
54. See Jans (1990) SEW 503.
55. Established by Reg. 1210/90 (O.J. 1990 L 120/1).
56. See COM (96) 500 Final. As to the role of environmental agreements with industry, see COM (96) 561 Final and the Council's Resolution (O.J. 1997 C 321/6). See also Rec. 96/733 (O.J. 1996 C 333/59).
57. As to less stringent standards, see Jans, *op. cit.* (see note 14, *supra*) 114–118.
58. This latter requirement reflects the amendments introduced by the TEU.

provisions could be seen in various directives.[59] Given that there is no equivalent provision to Article 130t EC in the Euratom Treaty, measures based on that Treaty indicate whether they are minimum provisions.[60] The possibility of taking more stringent measures is not available in relation to acts which are based on other Treaty provisions than Article 130s EC, unless the act concerned expressly so permits. Depending on the legal basis of the act concerned there may[61] or may not[62] be safeguard clauses available.

The words 'maintaining or introducing' make it clear that existing as well as new national measures are covered. The protective measures concerned are exclusively those for the protection of the environment. Although words 'any Member State' are in the singular, it is submitted that if a number of Member States (such as the Benelux countries) wish to act together, such action is covered by Article 130t EC.[63] The words 'compatible with this Treaty' contain a double limitation, relating to primary as well as secondary Community law.[64] The sting of Article 130t EC lies in the tail of the provision. A more stringent national provision based on Article 130s EC may conflict with Articles 30–36 EC, without being justified under Articles 100a or 100b EC. It is also conceivable that a national provision may in some cases be incompatible with other articles of the Treaty, such as those concerning the Common Agricultural Policy. The other provisions of the Treaty then take precedence over the possibility of relying on Article 130t, unless the incompatibility[65] can be removed through an environmental exception.

3.2 European Community environmental policy: legislation

Since the First Environmental Action Programme in 1973,[66] myriad environmental protection measures have been adopted. While the space available does not permit a detailed discussion of all of these measures,[67] a flavour of the Community's approach can be given, albeit in the form of an indication of the major measures only.

59. See *e.g.* Case C-169/89 *Gourmetterie Van den Burg* [1990] ECR I-2143 at 2163–2164.
60. See Case C-376/90 *Commission v. Belgium* [1993] ECR I-6153 at 6181–6182.
61. Art. 100a EC.
62. *E.g.* Art. 43 EC.
63. *Cf.* Art. 233 EC.
64. See Temmink (1995) SEW 79.
65. *E.g.* with Arts. 30 or 92–93 EC.
66. See note 20, *supra*.
67. See in particular the books by Jans and Krämer (see note 14, *supra*), and Salter in Vaughan (ed.), *Law of the European Communities Service* (London, loose-leaf since 1990) Vol. 2, Part 8. See further, Dir. 96/61 on integrated pollution prevention and control (O.J. 1996 L 257/26) and the Council Resolution, O.J. 1997 C 321/1.

Water pollution.[68] The framework directive on pollution by certain dangerous substances discharged into the aquatic environment of the Community,[69] in part requires the Member States to take measures which are ultimately designed to eliminate water pollution by certain specified substances, but for the most part it demands that the Council adopt further directives prescribing limit values which emission values must not exceed, and establishing certain quality objectives. The Groundwater Directive[70] deals with the prevention or restriction of the discharge into groundwater of certain substances, establishing also various prior investigation and authorization requirements where substances are subject to discharge restriction; it also deals with the artificial recharge of groundwater. The Bathing Water Directive[71] lays down an obligation on the Member States to ensure that the quality of bathing water attains certain quality limit values, and to endeavour to observe certain other target values. The Court has made it clear the Member States are obliged to take steps to ensure that particular results are obtained.[72] Waters where protection or improvement is necessary for the support of shellfish life and growth[73] and freshwaters needing protection or improvement in order to support fish life[74] are also subject to quality requirements. Directive 75/440[75] establishes quality standards for surface water intended for the abstraction of drinking water, requiring also the drawing up of systematic plans of action and timetables to ensure continuing improvement.[76] In the case of transfrontier pollution, Member States are under an obligation at least to see how improvements can be made and to see whether the other country concerned would collaborate.[77] Water for

68. See the Framework for Community action in the field of Water Policy COM (97) 49 Final.
69. Dir. 76/464 (O.J. 1976 L 129/23), amended by Dir. 91/692 (O.J. 1991 L 377/48). See Case C-168/95 *Arcaro* [1996] ECR I-4705. See further, Dir. 86/280 (O.J. 1986 L 181/16), most recently amended by Dir. 91/692.
70. Dir. 80/68 (O.J. 1980 L 20/43), amended by Dir. 91/692 (O.J. 1991 L 377/48). See especially, Case 291/84 *Commission v. The Netherlands* [1987] ECR 3483, [1989] 1 CMLR 479 and Case C-131/88 *Commission v. Germany* [1991] ECR I-825.
71. Dir. 76/160 (O.J. 1976 L 31/1), most recently amended by Dir. 91/692 (O.J. 1991 L 377/48). See in particular Case 96/81 *Commission v. The Netherlands* [1982] ECR 1791 and Case C-56/90 *Commission v. United Kingdom* [1993] ECR I-4109, [1994] 1 CMLR 769.
72. Case C-56/90 *Commission v. United Kingdom* [1993] ECR I-4109 at 4144–4145.
73. Dir. 79/923 (O.J. 1979 L 281/47), amended by Dir. 91/692 (O.J. 1991 L 377/48). See Case C-298/95 *Commission v. Germany* [1996] ECR I-6747.
74. Dir. 78/659 (O.J. 1978 L 222/1), most recently amended by Dir. 91/692 (O.J. 1991 L 377/48). See Case 14/86 *Pretore di Salò v. Persons Unknown* [1987] ECR 2545, [1989] 1 CMLR 71; Case 322/86 *Commission v. Italy* [1988] ECR 3995, and Case C-298/95 *Commission v. Germany* [1996] ECR I-6747.
75. O.J. 1975 L 194/26, most recently amended by Dir. 91/692 (O.J. 1991 L 377/48). See Case C-58/89 *Commission v. Germany* [1991] ECR I-4983.
76. See also Dir. 79/869 (O.J. 1979 L 271/44), most recently amended by Dir. 91/692 (O.J. 1991 L 377/48).
77. Case C-58/89 *Commission v. Germany* [1991] ECR I-4983 at 5027. See for an analogous

human consumption is also subject to stringent quality standards,[78] but it applies only in respect of water supplied for human consumption or for use in foodstuffs by a food production undertaking, it does not cover water obtained from private wells.[79] Directive 91/271[80] deals *inter alia* with the collection, treatment and discharge of urban waste water, setting quality criteria, providing for cooperation in relation to discharges with cross-border effects, requiring authorizations for certain discharges of industrial waste water, and ensuring the re-use where possible of sludge from waste water. Nitrate pollution of water is tackled by Directive 91/676.[81] More generally, environmental safety at sea is the subject of Community action,[82] and the Community is signatory to various regional and international Conventions.[83]

Air pollution and energy. Three directives deal with air quality as such: Directive 80/779[84] deals with sulphur dioxide and suspended particles; Directive 82/884[85] sets out limit-values for lead particles in the air, and Directive 85/203[86] sets out limit-values and guide-values for nitrogen dioxide in the air. The lead content of petrol is subject to the provisions of Directive 85/210[87] and various directives deal with air pollution caused

approach in relation to air quality standards, Case C-361/88 *Commission v. Germany* [1991] ECR I-2567 at 2602.

78. Dir. 80/778 (O.J. 1980 L 229/11), most recently amended by Dir. 91/692 (O.J. 1991 L 377/48). See Case C-42/89 *Commission v. Belgium* [1990] ECR I-2821, [1990] 1 CMLR 716; Case 228/87 *Pretore di Torino v. Persons Unknown* [1988] ECR 5099; Case C-337/ 89 *Commission v. United Kingdom* [1992] ECR I-6103, and Case C-237/90 *Commission v. Germany* [1992] ECR I-5973. A new directive is under way, see the Common Position (O.J. 1998 C 91/1) and the re-examined proposal COM (98) 388 Final.

79. Case C-42/89 *Commission v. Belgium* [1990] ECR I-2821 at 2840.

80. O.J. 1991 L 135/40, see Dec. 93/481 (O.J. 1993 L 226/23).

81. O.J. 1991 L 375/1, corrigendum O.J. 1993 L 92/51.

82. See COM (93) 66 Final. See also Dir. 93/75 (O.J. 1993 L 247/19), amended by Dir. 97/ 34 (O.J. 1997 L 158/40) on minimum requirements for vessels bound for or leaving Community ports and carrying dangerous or polluted goods. See further, Dir. 95/21 (O.J. 1995 L 157/1, corrigendum O.J. 1996 L 291/42; amended by Dir. 98/42 (O.J. 1998 L 184/40)) on Port State Control.

83. Such as the Barcelona Convention (see note 41, *supra*). Jans, *op. cit.* (see note 14, *supra*) 311–312 lists the others; see also *General Report 1994* (Brussels, Luxembourg, 1995) points 514–517, *General Report 1995* (*ibid.*, 1996) point 495; *General report 1996* (*ibid.*, 1997) point 448 and *General Report 1997* (ibid., 1998) point 573. See also Dec. 97/825 (O.J. 1997 L 342/18).

84. O.J. 1980 L 229/30, most recently amended by Dir. 91/692 (O.J. 1991 L 377/48). See Case C-361/88 *Commission v. Germany* [1991] ECR 2567, [1993] 2 CMLR 821.

85. O.J. 1982 L 378/15, most recently amended by Dir. 91/692 (O.J. 1991 L 377/48); amendment proposed COM (97) 500 Final (O.J. 1998 C 9/6). See Case C-59/89 *Commission v. Germany* [1991] ECR I-2607.

86. O.J. 1985 L 87/1, most recently amended by Dir. 91/692 (O.J. 1991 L 377/48); amendment proposed COM (97) 500 Final (O.J. 1998 C 9/6). See Case C-186/91 *Commission v. Belgium* [1993] ECR I-851.

87. O.J. 1985 L 96/25, most recently amended by the Act of Austrian, Finnish and

by vehicles.[88] Air pollution from industrial plants[89] and emissions from large combustion plants have also been the subject of Community legislation.[90] Other provisions have been adopted for the protection of the ozone layer,[91] and the Community is party to various international conventions relating to air pollution.[92] The Community has also taken steps to protect forests against atmospheric pollution[93] and has set up a monitoring system for carbon dioxide and other greenhouse gas emissions.[94] Finally, Decision 96/737[95] establishes the SAVE II Programme which demands that the Member States establish and implement energy efficiency programmes to limit carbon dioxide emissions. The new framework directive on ambient air quality assessment and management[96] presages major improvements in air quality legislation.[97]

Swedish Accession (1994). See also Dir. 75/716 (O.J. 1975 L 307/22), most recently amended by Dir. 91/692 (O.J. 1991 L 377/48), on the sulphur content of certain liquid fuels.

88. For motor vehicles, Dir. 70/220 (O.J. English Special Edition 1970, I) p. 171), most recently amended by Dir. 96/69 (O.J. 1996 L 282/64); for diesel engines, Dirs 72/306 (O.J. English Special Edition 1972 (III) p. 889, most recently amended by Dir. 97/20 (O.J. 1997 L 125/21) and 88/77 (O.J. 1988 L 36/33), most recently amended by Dir. 96/1 (O.J. 1996 L 40/1). See Sevenster (1989) NJB 556; WQ E-127/93 (Metten) O.J. 1994 C 317/1; COM (95) 689, COM (96) 248 Final, and O.J. 1997 C 257/3.

89. Dir. 84/360 (O.J. 1984 L 188/20), most recently amended by Dir. 91/692 (O.J. 1991 L 377/48).

90. Dir. 88/609 (O.J. 1988 L 336/1), most recently amended by Dir. 94/66 (O.J. 1966 L 337/83). See also Dirs. 89/369 (O.J. 1989 L 163/32, corrigendum O.J. 1989 L 192/40) and 89/429 (O.J. 1989 L 203/50) on new and existing municipal waste incineration plants, and Dir. 94/67 on the incineration of hazardous waste (O.J. 1994 L 365/34, amendment proposed COM (97) 604 Final (O.J. 1998 C 13/6)..

91. Reg. 3093/94 (O.J. 1994 L 333/1), implementing the Vienna Convention for the Protection of the Ozone Layer (see O.J. 1988 L 297/10), with the Montreal Protocol on substances which deplete the ozone layer (O.J. 1988 L 297/21), which latter has been amended (O.J. 1991 L 377/30 and 1994 L 33/3).

92. E.g. the Vienna Convention, ibid.; the 1979 Geneva Convention on long-range transboundary air pollution and Protocols (O.J. 1981 L 171/13; O.J. 1986 L 181/2, and O.J. 1993 L 149/16), and the 1992 Rio Framework Convention on Climate Change (O.J. 1994 L 33/13). As to the energy dimension of climate change, see COM (97) 196 Final.

93. Reg. 3528/86 (O.J. 1986 L 326/2), amended by Reg. 307/97 (O.J. 1997 L 51/9). See also the EU strategy to combat acidification COM (97) 88 Final, and Reg. 2158/92 (O.J. 1992 L 217/3, amended by Reg. 308/97 (O.J. 1997 L 51/11).) on protection of the Community's forests from fires.

94. Dec. 93/389 (O.J. 1993 L 167/31). See also Dec. 98/352 (O.J. 1998 L 159/53 (Altener Programme II)).

95. O.J. 1996 L 335/50 (replacing Dec. 93/76 (O.J. 1993 L 237/28). See COM (97) 550 Final.

96. Dir. 96/62 (O.J. 1996 L 296/55). See Dec. 97/101 (O.J. 1997 L 35/14) and COM (97) 500 Final (O.J. 1998 C 9/6).

97. As to the reduction of methane emissions, see COM (96) 557 Final.

Noise pollution. While perhaps the most celebrated example in this field is Directive 84/538 on noise emissions from lawnmowers,[98] there is a vast amount of Community legislation in this field (particularly relating to motor vehicles, construction equipment, and exposure to noise at work). Another example is Directive 89/629 on noise emissions from subsonic civil jet aircraft.[99] A Green Paper has been issued on future noise policy.[100]

Dangerous substances. Again, a variety of substances are covered under this heading. Celebrated examples are the directives on waste oils;[101] fertilizers;[102] PCBs and PCTs;[103] pesticides;[104] the classification, packaging and labelling of dangerous substances;[105] asbestos pollution;[106] information on dangerous preparations;[107] titanium dioxide;[108] hazardous

98. O.J. 1984 L 300/171, most recently amended by Dir. 88/181 (O.J. 1988 L 81/71).
99. O.J. 1989 L 363/27.
100. COM (96) 540 Final. See also COM (96) 11 Final. As to noise emisssions from two-and three-wheeled vehicles, see Dir. 97/24 (O.J. 1997 L 226/1).
101. Dir. 75/439 (O.J. 1975 L 194/23, most recently amended by Dir. 91/692 (O.J. 1991 L 377/48). See Case 172/82 *Syndicat National des Fabricants Raffineurs d'Huile de Graissage et al. v. GIE 'Inter-Huiles' et al.* [1993] ECR 555, [1983] 3 CMLR 485; Case 295/82 *GIE 'Rhône Alpes-Huiles' et al. v. Syndicat National des Fabricants Raffineurs d'Huile de Graissage et al.* [1984] ECR 575; Case 240/83 *Procureur de la République v. Association de défense des brûleurs d'huiles usagées* [1985] ECR 531; Case C-366/89 *Commission v. Italy* [1993] ECR I-4201, and Case C-37/92 *Vanacker and Lesage* [1993] ECR I-4947.
102. Dir. 76/116 (O.J. 1976 L 24/21, most recently amended by Dir. 98/3 (O.J. 1998 L 18/25)).
103. Polychlorinated biphenyls and polychlorinated terphenyls respectively: Dir. 96/59 (O.J. 1996 L 243/31), replacing earlier legislation, under which see Case 380/87 *Enichem Base et al. v. Comune di Cinisello Balsamo* [1989] ECR 2491, [1991] 1 CMLR 313.
104. Dir. 79/117 (O.J. 1979 L 33/36), most recently amended by Dir. 96/28 (O.J. 1996 L 140/30). See Case 125/88 *Nijman* [1989] ECR 3533. See also Dirs. 76/895 (O.J. 1976 L 300/26, most recently amended by Dir. 97/41 (O.J. 1997 L 184/33)), as to which, see Case 94/83 *Albert Heijn BV* [1984] ECR 3263 and Case 54/85 *Ministère public v. Mirepoix* [1986] ECR 1067, [1987] 2 CMLR 44; 78/631 (O.J. 1978 L 206/13 most recently amended by Dir. 92/32 (O.J. 1992 L 154/1)), and 90/642 (O.J. 1990 L 350/71), most recently amended by Dir. 97/41, *supra*. See further, Dir. 91/414 (O.J. 1991 L 230/1), most recently amended by Dir. 97/73 (O.J. 1997 L 353/26).
105. Dir. 67/548 (O.J. English Special Edition 1967 p. 234, in the version of the last major amendment (the 7th.) by Dir. 92/32 (O.J. 1992 L 154/1), most recently amended by Dir. 97/69 (O.J. 1997 L 343/19). In the version of the 6th amendment (by Dir. 79/831 (O.J. 1979 L 259/10)), Dir. 67/548 was the subject of interesting case-law: see Case 187/84 *Caldana* [1985] ECR 3013; Case 208/85 *Commission v. Germany* [1987] ECR 4045; Case 278/85 *Commission v. Denmark* [1987] ECR 4069; Case 429/85 *Commission v. Italy* [1988] ECR 843, and Case C-43/90 *Commission v. Germany* [1992] ECR I-1909.
106. Dir. 87/217 (O.J. 1987 L 85/40), most recently amended by Dir. 91/692 (O.J. 1991 L 377/48).
107. Dir. 88/379 (O.J. 1988 L 187/14), most recently amended by Dir. 96/65 (O.J. 1996 L 265/15). See also Dir. 91/442 (O.J. 238/25), likewise so amended.
108. Dir. 92/112 (O.J. 1992 L 409/11, corrigendum O.J. 1993 L 48/68) which replaced the directive annulled by the Court in Case C-300/89 *Commission v. Council* [1991] ECR 2867, [1993] 1 CMLR 359.

waste;[109] and the incineration of hazardous waste.[110] The importation and exportation of certain dangerous chemicals is governed by Regulation 2455/92,[111] and vessels bound for or leaving Community ports and carrying dangerous or polluting goods must meet certain minimum requirements.[112] As examples of the many international or regional Conventions to which the Community is a party, see the Convention for the Protection of the Rhine against chemical pollution[113] and the Basle Convention.[114]

Waste. In addition to the two measures on hazardous waste just noted, the Community has adopted a series of provisions concerning waste in general. It should be observed that waste is a 'good' or 'product' and, as such, is subject to the free movement of goods principle just like other goods.[115] Directive 75/442[116] deals with waste, and Directive 94/62[117] covers packaging and packaging waste. Directive 86/278[118] deals with the use of sewage sludge in agriculture, and Directive 91/157[119] deals with batteries and accumulators containing certain dangerous substances. Regulation 259/93[120] deals with the supervision and control of shipments

---

109. Dir. 91/689 (O.J. 1991 L 377/20), amended by Dir. 94/31 (O.J. 1994 L 168/28). See Cases C-304/94 *etc. Tombesi et al.* [1997] ECR I-3561, [1997] 3 CMLR 673. See also Case 239/85 *Commission v. Belgium* [1986] ECR 3645.
110. Dir. 94/67 (O.J. 1994 L 365/34 corrigendum O.J. 1998 L 23/39; an amendment has been proposed COM (97) 604 Final (O.J. 1998 C 13/6)).
111. O.J. 1992 L 251/13, most recently amended by Reg. 1237/97 (O.J. 1997 L 173/37).
112. See also Dir. 93/75 (O.J. 1993 L 247/19), amended by 97/34 (O.J. 1997 L 158/40; see COM (97) 344 Final (O.J. 1997 C 264/4)).
113. And the Additional Agreement, Berne, 29 April 1963 (see Dec. 77/586 (O.J. 1977 L 240/35)), supplemented by Decs. 88/381 and 382 (O.J. 1988 L 183/27 and 30).
114. See note 21, *supra.*
115. Expressly in Case 2/90 *Commission v.Belgium* [1992] ECR I-4431 at 4478.
116. O.J. 1975 L 75/442, substantially amended by Dir. 91/156 (O.J. 1991 L 78/32) and most recently amended by Dec. 96/350 (O.J. 1996 L 135/32). See Cases 372–374/85 *Ministère public v. Traen et al.* [1987] ECR 2141; Case 380/87 *Enichem Base et al. v. Comune di Cinisello Balsamo* [1989] ECR 2491, [1991] 1 CMLR 313; Cases C-206 and 207/88 *Vessoso and Zanetti* [1990] ECR I-1461; Case C-359/88 *Zanetti et al.* [1990] ECR I-1509; Case C-2/90 *Commission v. Belgium* [1992] ECR I-4431, [1993] 1 CMLR 365; Case C-236/92 *Comitato di Coordinamento per la Difesa della Cava et al. v. regione Lombardia et al.* [1994] ECR I-483, Case C-422/92 *Commission v. Germany* [1995] ECR I-1097; Cases C-58/95 *etc. Galloti et al.* [1996] ECR I-4345; Cases C-304/94 *etc. Tombesi et al.* [1997] ECR I-3561, [1997] 3 CMLR 673. See also Case C-129/96 *Inter-Environnement Wallonie ASBL v. Walloon Region* [1997] ECR I-7411 and Case C-203/96 *Chemische Afvalstoffen Dusseldorp BV et al. v. Minister van Volkshuisvesting, Ruimtelijke Ordening en Milieubeheer* [1998] ECR I-nyr (25 June 1998).
117. O.J. 1994 L 365/10.
118. O.J. 1986 L 181/6, corrigendum O.J. 1986 L 191/23; amended by Dir. 91/692 (O.J. 1991 L 377/48) and by the Act of Austrian, Finnish and Swedish Accession (1994).
119. O.J. 1991 L 78/28, implemented by Dir. 93/86 (O.J. 1993 L 264/51).
120. O.J. 1993 L 30/1, corrigenda O.J. 1993 L 138/13 and 176/26, 1995 L 18/38, 1996 L 47/35 and L 59/64, amended by Reg. 120/97 (O.J. 1997 L 22/14) as regards certain shipments of waste to certain non-OECD countries. See Case C-187/93 *European Parlia-*

of waste within, into and out of the Community. The Council has also adopted a Resolution on a Community Strategy for Waste Management.[121]

Flora, fauna and conservation. The Community's implementation of the CITES Convention has already been noted.[122] The conservation of wild birds is the subject of Directive 79/409[123] which has given rise to a considerable amount of case-law.[124] Environmental impact assessments are required for major public and private projects, in accordance with Directive 85/337,[125] which again has been the subject of significant litigation.[126] The importance attached to the conservation of individual species may be gauged by Directive 83/129[127] on the importation of skins of certain seal pups and products derived from them, and the renowned Regulation 3254/91 on leghold traps.[128] Directive 92/43[129] deals with the conserva-

ment v. Council [1994] ECR I-2857; Case C-209/94 P *Buralux SA et al. v. Council* [1996] ECR I-615, and Cases C-304/94 *etc. Tombesi et al.* [1997] ECR I-3561, [1997] 3 CMLR 673. A number of other cases are currently pending.

121. O.J. 1997 C 76/1. As to landfill of waste, see COM (97) 105 Final (O.J. 1997 C 165/14); as to end of life vehicles, see COM (97) 358 Final (O.J. 1997 C 337/3).
122. See note 40, *supra*, and text thereto. See also Case C-182/89 *Commission v. France* [1990] ECR I-4337. The Community is also a party to the Bonn Convention on Migratory Species of Wild Animals (O.J. 1982 1210/11; see Dec. 82/461 (O.J. 1982 L 210/10, amended by Dec. 98/145 (O.J. 1998 L 46/6)).
123. O.J. 1979 L 103/1, most recently amended by Dir. 97/49 (O.J. 1997 L 223/9) and the Act of Austrian, Finnish and Swedish Accession (1994).
124. See in particular, Case 247/85 *Commission v. Belgium* [1987] ECR 3029; Case 262/85 *Commission v. Italy* [1987] ECR 3073; Case 412/85 *Commission v. Germany* [1987] ECR 3503; Case 236/85 *Commission v. The Netherlands* [1987] ECR 3989; Case 252/85 *Commission v. France* [1988] ECR 2243; Case C-339/87 *Commission v. The Netherlands* [1990] ECR I-851; Case C-169/89 *Gourmetterie Van den Burg* [1990] ECR I-2143; Case C-157/89 *Commission v. Italy* [1991] ECR I-57; Case C-334/89 *Commission v. Italy* [1991] ECR I-93; Case C-57/89 *Commission v. Germany* [1991] ECR I-883; Case C-355/90 *Commission v. Spain* [1993] ECR I-4221; Case C-435/92 *Association pour la Protection des Animaux Sauvages et al. v. Préfet de Maine-et-Loire et al.* [1994] ECR I-67; Case C-149/94 *Vergy* [1996] ECR I-299; Case C-202/94 *Van der Feesten* [1996] ECR I-355; Case C-118/94 *Associazione Italiana per il World Wildlife Fund et al. v. Regione Veneto* [1996] ECR I-1223; Case C-44/95 *R. v. Secretary of State for the Environment, ex parte The Royal Society for the Protection of Birds* [1996] ECR I-3805, and Case C-10/96 *Ligue royale belge pour la protection des oiseaux ASBL et al. v. Walloon Region* [1996] ECR I-6775.
125. O.J. 1985 L 175/40, amended by Dir. 97/11 (O.J. 1997 L 73/5).
126. Case C-396/92 *Bund Naturschutz in Bayern eV et al. v. Freistaat Bayern* [1994] ECR I-3717; Case C-431/92 *Commission v. Germany* [1995] ECR I-2189; Case C-133/94 *Commission v. Belgium* [1996] ECR I-2323; and Case C-72/95 *Aannemersbedrijf P.K. Kraaijeveld BV et al. v. Gedeputeerde Staten van Noord-Holland* [1996] ECR I-5403.
127. O.J. 1983 L 91/30, most recently amended by Dir. 89/370 (O.J. 1989 L 163/37).
128. O.J. 1991 L 308/1, implemented by Reg. 35/97 (O.J. 1997 L 8/2); see also Reg. 1771/94 (O.J. 1994 L 184/3). See also Dec. 97/602 (O.J. 1997 L 242/64 amended by Dec. 98/188 (O.J. 1998 L 70/28). International Agreements have been signed on humane trapping Council Press Releases Pres 97/403 and 98/105).
129. O.J. 1992 L 206/7, corrigendum O.J. 1993 L 176/29, amended by Dir. 97/62 (O.J.

tion of natural habitats and of wild flora and fauna, and the Commission has issued a Communication on wise use and conservation of wetlands.[130] Finally, Regulation 3062/95[131] sets out the objectives and forms of action to ensure the conservation and sustainable management of tropical forests and of their biological diversity.

Nuclear safety and radioactive materials. One of the earliest Community measures[132] on protection of the health of workers and the general public against the dangers of ionizing radiation has at long last been replaced by Directive 96/29,[133] but only with effect from 13 May 2000. The old Seveso Directive[134] on major-accident hazards of certain industrial activities has now been replaced by Directive 96/82.[135] In the wake of the Chernobyl nuclear disaster there was a flurry of legislative activity, of which a number of instruments have a permanent importance.[136] Further measures deal with the supervision and control of shipments of radioactive waste between Member States and into and out of the Community.[137] Finally, mention should be made of the G-24 Nuclear Assistance Coordination Secretariat, hosted by the Commission in DG XI in Brussels, which, with resources from a wider base than the Community alone, provides safety assistance in central and Eastern Europe, Russia and Eurasia.

Other measures. Directive 90/313[138] provides for free access to environmental information, and Regulation 880/92[139] establishes the scheme for

1997 L 305/42). See also the Berne Convention on the Conservation of European Wildlife and Natural Habitats (O.J. 1982 L 38/2; Dec. 82/71 (O.J. 1982 L 38/1).

130. COM (95) 189 Final, approved by the Council, *General Report 1996* (Brussels, Luxembourg, 1997) point 462.

131. O.J. 1995 L 327/9.

132. Dir. 59/221 (O.J. English Special Edition 1959–62, p. 7), most recently amended by Dir. 65/45 (O.J. English Special Edition 1965–66, p. 231. See also Dir. 80/836 (O.J. 1980 L 246/1), amended by Dir. 84/467 (O.J. 1984 L 265/4), likewise so replaced; see Case C-376/90 *Commission v. Belgium* [1992] ECR I-6153.

133. O.J. 1996 L 159/1, corrigendum O.J. 1996 L 314/20. See also Dir. 97/43 (O.J. 1997 L 180/22).

134. Dir. 82/501 (O.J. 1982 L 230/1), see Case C-190/90 *Commission v. The Netherlands* [1992] ECR I-3265.

135. O.J. 1997 L 10/13, corrigendum O.J. 1997 L 124/56.

136. *E.g.* Reg. 3954/87 (O.J. 1987 L 371/1 corrigendum O.J. 1988 L 18/74), amended by Reg. 2218/89 (O.J. 1989 L 211/1) on maximum permitted levels of radioactive contamination of foodstuffs and of feedingstuffs following a nuclear accident or other radiological emergency; Dec. 87/600 (O.J. 1987 L 371/76) on information exchange; Reg. 2219/89 (O.J. 1989 L 211/4) on the exportation of foodstuffs in such circumstances, and Dir. 89/618 (O.J. 1989 L357/31) on informing the public.

137. Dir. 92/3 (O.J. 1992 L 35/24). See also Reg. 1493/93 (O.J. 1993 L 148/1) and Dec. 93/552 (O.J. 1993 L 268/83).

138. O.J. 1990 L 158/56.

139. O.J. 1992 L 99/1. An amendment has been proposed, COM (96) 603 Final (O.J. 1997 C 114/9).

Eco-labels, by means of a market-based instrument, the aim of which is to stimulate supply and demand of products having a reduced environmental impact; this relies on the voluntary participation of manufacturers. Directive 91/692[140] has standardized and rationalized the information required to be presented by myriad directives, and Regulation 793/93[141] allows the systematic evaluation and control of the risks posed by the substances listed in the European Inventory of Existing Commercial Substances (Einces). Regulation 1836/93[142] establishes a Community eco-management and audit scheme, participation in which is also voluntary. There has been considerable interest in (and not a little resistance to) the idea of a Community environmental tax, with no immediate agreement in sight.[143] The adoption of Directive 96/61 represents an important advance in integrated pollution prevention and control.[144]

4. Consumer Protection

The Treaty provisions relating to consumer policy are discussed in section 4.1, below, and consumer policy itself is then briefly examined in section 4.2, below. As an initial observation, it might be noted that the EC Treaty is silent as to what is meant by the notion of a consumer, even though the word 'consumers' also features in Articles 39(1)(e), 40(3), 85(3), 86 and EC[145] and the words 'consumer protection' are also to be found in Article 100a EC. In Community secondary legislation, a consumer is defined as 'a natural person who, in transactions covered by this Directive, is acting for purposes which can be regarded as outside his trade or profession'.[146] Traders thus fall outside that definition.[147] In the

---

140. O.J. 1991 L 377/48.
141. O.J. 1993 L 84/1, corrigendum O.J. 1993 L 224/34.
142. O.J. 1993 L 168/1, corrigendum O.J. 1993 L 247/28, 1995 L 105/47 and L 205/17. See also the support programme for NGOs, Dec. 97/872 (O.J. 1997 L 354/25).
143. As to the Commission's latest thinking, see O.J. 1997 C 224/6.
144. O.J. 1996 L 257/26.
145. The French text of those provisions is 'consommateurs' in Arts. 39, 40, and 86 EC and 'utilisateurs' in Art. 85 EC, the Dutch, 'verbruikers' and 'gebruikers', respectively, whereas the German, like the English uses the term 'Verbraucher' in all these cases.
146. E.g. Dir. 85/577 (O.J. 1985 L 372/31) on contracts negotiated away from business premises., Art. 2.
147. Dir. 85/577, Art. 2, ibid. defines a trader as 'a natural or legal person who, for the transaction in question, acts in his commercial or professional capacity, and anyone acting in the name or on behalf of the trader'. See Case C-361/89 Di Pinto [1991] ECR I-1189 at 1211 (a trader canvassed with a view to the conclusion of an advertising contract concerning the sale of his or her business is not a consumer protected by the directive). As to the definition of a consumer in relation to the Judgments Convention (O.J. 1975 L 204/28; O.J. 1978 L 304/77), see Case 150/77 Société Bertrand v. Paul Ott KG [1978] ECR 1431 at 1446; Case C-89/91 Shearson Lehman Hutton v. TVB Treuhandgesellschaft für Vermögensverwaltung und Beteiligungen mbH [1993]

case-law of the Court on the rule of reason applied in relation to Article 30 EC (the so-called 'mandatory requirements') the concept of a consumer has a similar meaning.[148] The protection of non-end users is covered in the case-law by the term 'fairness of commercial transactions'.

The interests of the consumer as market participant are in the first instance protected by Community law on the free movement of goods, services and capital,[149] and competition.[150] Thus consumer policy as such is supplementary in nature. The concept of a consumer in the various consumer action programmes has a rather broader meaning, as it also refers to more social links, such as that between patient and care provider[151] and the consumer–tourist.[152] The Consumer Protection Title, in Article 129a(1)(b) EC, reflects this broader approach.

4.1 Treaty bases for consumer policy

In the original EEC Treaty there was no specific basis for consumer protection policy, an omission which was scarcely surprising in view of the virtual absence of pressure for recognition of consumers' interests as such at that time. Remarkably enough, in view of the political importance which government leaders regularly attach in the Community context to the idea of a people's Europe (and already at the Paris Summit in October 1972 to consumers in particular) the SEA did not add a separate Title to the EEC Treaty dealing with consumer protection: in Article 100a(3) EEC (now EC) it was provided that in its proposals for harmonization relating to the establishment and functioning of the internal market concerning, *inter alia*, consumer protection the Commission was to take as a base a high level of protection, but consumer protection was not included in the list of exceptions set out in Article 100a(4) EEC, and still is absent from Article 100a(4) EC. Not until the changes made by the TEU was there

---

ECR I-139 at 186–189, and Case C-269/95 *Benincasa v. Dentalkit Srl.* [1997] ECR I-3767. See also Mortelmans and Watson (1995) *Tijdschrift voor Consumentenrecht* 229.

148. See Chapter VII, section 3.3.3, *ante*.

149. See Chapter VII, *ante*. See, generally, Bourgoignie and Trubek, *Consumer Law, Common Markets and Federalism in Europe and the United States* (Berlin, 1987, part of the Integration through Law series); Bourgoignie, *Éléments pour une théorie du droit de la consommation au regards des développements du droit belge et du droit de la Communauté économique européenne* (Brussels, 1988); Kendall, *European Consumer Law* (Chichester, 1994); Reich, *Europäisches Verbraucherschutzrecht* (3rdEd., Baden-Baden, 1996), (1995) Eur.Rev.Priv. L. 285, and (1997) ELJ 131; and Reich and Woodroffe (eds.) *European Consumer Policy after Maastricht* (Dordrecht, 1994, reprint of (1993) Nos. 3–4 and (1994) No. 1 of the *Journal of Consumer Policy*).

150. See Chapter VIII, *ante*.

151. *E.g.* Council Resolution on consumer protection and information policy (O.J. 1975 C 92/1). See also COM (93) 378 Final and COM (95) 519 Final.

152. See section 8.1, *post*.

more attention paid at Treaty level to the interests of consumers. Thus Article 3(s) EC prescribes that Community action will include 'a contribution to the strengthening of consumer protection'; which is clearly a less far-reaching activity than the policy in the sphere of the environment prescribed by Article 3(k) EC.

The Community contributes in two ways to the achievement of a high level of consumer protection: first, through measures adopted pursuant to Article 100a EC in the context of the completion of the internal market,[153] which means that it is not just the Commission under Article 100a(3) EC, but also the Community which must strive for a high level of protection;[154] and, secondly, through the adoption, by the co-decision procedure, and after consulting ECOSOC, of specific action supporting and supplementing the policy pursued by Member States to protect the health, safety and economic interests of consumers, and to provide them with adequate information.[155] On the one hand, Article 129a(1)(b) EC mentions interests such as health and safety, which are also dealt with elsewhere in the Treaty,[156] and on the other hand, it offers an incomplete summary of consumers' rights. In particular, the rights to redress and to representation are not mentioned,[157] so it can be argued that those two matters will have to be the subject of action under Articles 100a or 235 EC. The term 'measures' in Article 129a(1)(a) EC demonstrates that, unlike in the Title on culture,[158] harmonization measures are possible. In this context the Commission has adopted Green Papers on consumer access to justice and the settlement of consumer disputes[159] and on guarantees for consumer goods and after-sales services.[160] The first of these Green Papers led to the action plan on consumer access to justice and the settlement of disputes,[161] and a proposal for a directive relating to injunctions for the protection of consumers' interests.[162] The second one led to the

153. Art. 129a(1)(a) EC.
154. Art. 129a(1) EC, introductory words.
155. Art. 129a(1)(b) with Art. 129a(2) EC.
156. Arts. 100a, 118a, and 129 EC.
157. These are two of the five fundamental rights of consumers, recognized by the Preliminary Programme (O.J. 1975 C 92/1); the others are: the right to the protection of economic interests; the right to information, and the right to education. As to the right to representation, see Dec. 95/260 (O.J. 1995 L 162/37), establishing a Consumer Committee (replacing the old Consumers' Consultative Council). As to the right to redress, see the Council Resolution on Consumer Redress (O.J. 1987 C 176/2). See also the new Art. 129a(1) EC in the form agreed by the Treaty of Amsterdam (not yet in force).
158. See section 6, *post*.
159. COM (93) 576 Final.
160. COM (93) 509 Final.
161. COM (96) 13 Final. See now Rec. 98/257 (O.J. 1998 L 115/31).
162. Which became Dir. 98/27 (O.J. 1998 L 166/51). See, generally, the contributions by

proposal for a directive on the sale of and guarantees for consumer goods.[163]

All the directives for the protection of the economic interests of consumers[164] which were adopted before the entry into force of the TEU were based on Articles 100 or 100a EEC. It still appears that Article 100a EC is the favourite legal basis for the Commission's proposals,[165] although Mortelmans is of opinion that this might possibly change.[166] This possibility arises from the judgment in Cases C-267 and 268/91 *Keck and Mithouard*,[167] in which a distinction was drawn between product requirements, which would in general be caught by Article 30 EC, and rules relating to 'certain selling arrangements' which would not be caught provided that certain conditions were fulfilled.[168] Such arrangements did not by nature prevent the access of foreign goods to the market or impede such access any more than they impeded the access of domestic products. Accordingly, it could be argued that measures relating to sales methods which protect the economic interests of consumers should be adopted on the basis of Article 129a(2)(b), rather than on the basis of Article 100a EC.[169] But, as has been noted above, most proposals to date have still been based on Article 100a EC.

The importance of Mortelmans's approach, however, lies not so much in the decision-making procedure (which is the usual ground for dispute as to the legal basis of Community legislation), as in both cases the cooperation procedure and consultation of ECOSOC apply, but in the degree of harmonization and the possibility for Member States to utilize the safeguard clause. Article 129a(3) provides that measures adopted pursuant to Article 129a(2) will not prevent a Member State from maintaining in force or introducing more stringent protective measures. The scope of this minimum harmonization provision has already been discussed in relation to environmental protection, and the wording of Article 129a(3) is identical.[170]

Christanos, Adamantopoulos. Wilhelmsson, Willett, Morin and Koch in Micklitz and Reich (eds.), *op. cit.* (see note 14, *supra*) 343 *et seq.*

163. COM (95) 276 Final (O.J. 1996 C 307/8), see the amended proposal COM (98) 217 Final.
164. See section 4.2, *post*.
165. *E.g.* the proposals just discussed in the text were based on Art. 100a EC, as is Dir. 97/7 (O.J. 1997 L 144/9) on consumer protection in respect of distance contracts. See also Case C-233/94 *Germany v. European Parliament and Council* [1997] ECR I-2405).
166. This view is defended in the Dutch edition of this work at p. 651. The following discussion repeats his explanation set out there.
167. [1993] ECR I-6907 at 6131 (para. 17). See, more generally, his views in (1994) SEW 236.
168. See Chapter VII, section 3.2.1, *ante*.
169. See Mortelmans, *ibid.* at 243–244.
170. See section 3.1.6, *ante*. See, further, Mortelmans (1994) *Tijdschrift voor Consumentenrecht* 290.

The words 'supports and supplements the policy pursued by the Member States' indicates that on the basis of Article 3b EC the Member States remain competent in certain cases, or that Community action has a supplementary character. This principle was clearly applied in relation to the liability of suppliers for services.[171] Finally, it is noticeable that, unlike in the other new Titles discussed in this chapter, there is no integration provision relating to consumer policy. This is a strange omission, given that the Council already adopted a resolution on this point in 1986.[172] In various other policy areas, such as agriculture, competition and the internal market, this omission is made good.[173]

4.2 EC consumer policy

Community policy is implemented on the basis of action plans.[174] Weatherill has traced the evolution of European consumer law from the informed consumer to the confident consumer,[175] noting the need to create a minimum common floor of EC consumer rights in order to invest consumers with the confidence in the operation of the market.[176] However, the case-law of the Court still seems to visualize national consumers whose interests are protected on a non-discriminatory basis, rather than a European consumer as such.[177] But certainly the European consumer is developing, as the wholesale increase in cross-border shopping demonstrates.[178] But, as has been stated in section 4.1, above, primary responsibility for consumer policy still rests with the Member States. Accordingly, legislative activity in the field of consumer policy falls into a trio of types of measures. The first type is at the national level: those national measures relating to goods and services which relate to consumers' interests.[179]

The second type is the Community directives which relate to specific matters which are important for the protection of consumers. These may

171. See COM (94) 260 Final, effectively withdrawing the proposal from 1990 (COM (90) 482 Final), after the Commission had initially announced it would be revised.
172. O.J. 1987 C 3/1.
173. Arts. 39 and 40 EC (agriculture), 85, 86 and 90(2) EC (competition), and 100a(3) EC (internal market).
174. The latest is for the period 1996–1998, COM (95) 919 Final.
175. In Micklitz (ed.), *Rechtseinheit oder Rechtsvielfalt in Europa?* (Baden-Baden, 1996) 423.
176. *Ibid.* at 463.
177. Gormley in *ibid.* 473 at 476 (comments on Weatherill's paper).
178. Perhaps the high water mark of the free, informed, and international consumer in the case-law of the Court is the judgment in Case C-362/88 *GB-INNO-BM v. Confédération du commerce luxembourgeois* [1990] ECR I-667 at 689 (which of course was decided well before *Keck and Mithouard* (see note 167, *supra*).
179. See Chapter VII, *ante*, in which the compatibility of such measures with Arts. 30 or 59 EC is discussed.

be seen against the background of the five fundamental rights of consumers.[180] The protection of economic interests for consumers covers matters such as the legal regulation of doorstep selling, consumer credit, misleading advertising, standard form contracts, distance selling and comparative advertising. Cartel policy and the common agricultural policy are also relevant.[181] Major examples of Community action in this field include Directive 84/450 on misleading advertising;[182] Directive 85/374 on product liability;[183] Directive 85/577 on contracts negotiated away from business premises[184] (which is also relevant to consumers' right to redress); Directive 87/102 on consumer credit;[185] Directive 90/314 on package travel, package holidays and package tours;[186] Directive 92/59 on general product safety;[187] Directive 92/13 on unfair terms in consumer contracts;[188] Directive 94/47 on time-sharing contracts;[189] and Directive 97/7 on distance contracts.[190] After recourse to a conciliation committee, Directive 97/55 on comparative advertising was finally adopted.[191] Also of

180. See note 156, *supra*, and text thereto.
181. See, generally, Bourgoignie *et al.*, *Protection du consommateur* (Paris, 1984); Salter in Vaughan (ed.), *Law of the European Communities Service* (London, loose-leaf since 1990) paras. 8.39–8.95; Woodroffe (ed.), *Consumer Law in the EEC* (London, 1984); Krämer, *Verbraucherschutz* (Baden-Baden, 1985) and *EEC Consumer Law* (Brussels, 1986); Bourgoignie and Trubek: *Consumer Law, Common Markets and Federalism in Europe* (Berlin, 1987, part of the *Integration through Law* series).
182. O.J. 1984 L 250/17, amended by Dir. 97/55 (O.J. 1997 L 290/18); see Case C-373/90 *Complaint against X* [1992] ECR I-131.
183. O.J. 1985 L 210/29. See Case C-339/89 *Alsthom Atlantique SA v. Compagnie de construction méchanique Sulzer SA* [1991] ECR I-107 (in relation to Arts. 2, 3(f), 34 and 85(1) EC), and, in relation to Dir. 85/374, Case C-293/91 *Commission v. France* [1993] ECR I-1 and Case C-300/95 *Commission v. United Kingdom* [1997] ECR I-2649. See, further (1995) ERPriv.L issue 3.
184. O.J. 1985 L 372/31. See, in relation to Art. 30 EC, Case 382/87 *Buet et al. v. Ministère public* [1989] ECR 1235, and, in relation to Dir. 85/577, Case C-361/89 *Di Pinto* [1991] ECR I-1189; Case C-91/92 *Faccini Dori v. Recreb Srl* [1994] ECR I-3325, [1995] 1 CMLR 665. Dir. 85/577 is not applicable to contracts for services concluded by telephone or contracts for securities, *ibid.* Art. 3(2)(e) and Case C-384/93 *Alpine Investments BV v. Minister van Financiën* [1994] ECR I-1141 at 1173. See also Case C-45/96 *Bayerische Hypotheken- en Wechselbank AG v. Dietzinger* [1998] ECR I-nyr (17 March 1998).
185. O.J. 1987 L 42/48, most recently amended by Dir. 98/7 (O.J. 1998 L 101/17). See Case C-192/94 *El Corte Inglés SA v. Blázquez Rivero* [1996] ECR I-1281. A proposal to amend this directive further has been presented, COM (96) 79 Final (O.J. 1996 C 235/8).
186. O.J. 1990 L 314/59. See Cases C-178, 179 and 188–190/94 *Dillenkofer et al. v. Germany* [1996] ECR I-4845.
187. O.J. 1992 L 228/24, see Case C-359/92 *Germany v. Council* [1994] ECR I-3681, and see Gormley (1996) 21 ELRev. 59.
188. O.J. 1993 L 95/29, see Hondius (1995) ERPriv.L 241.
189. O.J. 1994 L 280/83, see Mäsch (1995) EuZW 8.
190. O.J. 1997 L 144/9.
191. O.J. 1997 L 290/18. This in fact amends Dir. 84/450 (see note 182, *supra*). See (in relation to Art. 30 EC), Case C-126/91 *Schutzverband gegen Unwesen in der Wirtschaft*

interest in view of the fact that money does not grow on trees but comes out of holes in the wall or will soon be taken over by electronic point-of-sale transfer is Recommendation 87/598 on electronic payments.[192] The right to information is reflected in, *inter alia*, market transparency achieved by harmonisation of national provisions on packaging, labelling, presentation, composition, quantities and prices of products and harmonisation of national provisions governing weighing instruments. Examples (just three of many) may be seen in Directive 87/250 on the indication of alcoholic strength by volume in the labelling of alcoholic beverages for sale to the ultimate consumer;[193] Directive 79/581 on consumer protection in the indication of the price of foodstuffs,[194] and Directive 88/314 on the indication of the price of non-food products.[195] In the field of consumer education progress continues in implementing the resolution of June 9, 1986 of the Council and the Ministers of Education meeting within the Council on consumer education in primary and secondary schools.[196] Consumer protection also has, of course, a health and safety aspect, as the adoption of Directive 88/378 on toy safety;[197] Directive 89/662 on tobacco advertising,[198] and Directive 96/22 on hormones[199] illustrates.[200]

The third type of legislation is that for which Article 129a EC provides an express legal basis. It was on this legal basis that Decision 3092/94 on a Community system of information on home and leisure accidents (Ehlass) was established.[201] Directive 98/6 on indication of prices offered to consumers is also based on this provision.[202]

5. PUBLIC HEALTH

Article 3(o) EC proclaims that the Community shall make a contribution to the attainment of a high level of health protection.[203] In its policy in

Ev v. Yves Rocher GmbH [1993] ECR I-2361, and the case-law on Art. 30 EC, see Chapter VII, sections 3.2 and 3.3, *ante*.

192. O.J. 1987 L 365/72. See also Rec. 88/590 (O.J. 1988 L 317/55).
193. O.J. 1987 L 113/57.
194. O.J. 1979 L 158/19, most recently amended by Dir. 95/58 (O.J. 1995 L 299/11).
195. O.J. 1988 L 314/19, likewise most recently amended, corrigendum O.J. 1997 L 71/47.
196. O.J. 1986 C 184/21.
197. O.J. 1988 L 187/1, amended by Dir. 93/68 (O.J. 1993 L 220/1).
198. O.J. 2989 L 379/1, amended by Dir. 92/41 (O.J. 1992 L 158/30. See Case C-222/91 *ministero del Finanze et al. v. Philip Morris Belgium SA et al.* [1993] ECR I-3469 and Case C-11/92 *R. v. Secretary of State for Health, ex parte Gallaher Ltd. et al.* [1993] ECR I-3545.
199. O.J. 1996 L 125/3, replacing earlier legislation.
200. See also the resolution of December 5, 1986 (O.J. 1987 C 3/1).
201. O.J. 1994 L 331/1.
202. O.J. 1998 L 80/27.
203. See Casparie *et al. Competitive Health Care in Europe, Future Prospects* (Aldershot,

this field – as in others – the Community must respect the European Convention on Human Rights.[204] The inclusion in the EC Treaty of a Title on Public Health, containing Article 129 EC, means that the boundaries have to be drawn between that provision and the other provisions of the EC Treaty which deal *inter alia* with this subject. Articles 36, 48(3) and 56(1) EC permit the Member States to refuse admission (and/or residence for the first time as the case may be) to goods or persons on the ground of the protection of (public) health.[205] Article 56(2) EC permits the Council to adopt coordination directives; thus for example the Annex to Directive 64/221[206] encompasses a list of diseases which might endanger public health (as well as a list of diseases and disabilities which might threaten public policy or public security), and it is only such diseases or disabilities which may be invoked as grounds for refusal.[207] Myriad directives have been adopted on the basis of Articles 43(2), 100 and 100a EC relating to health aspects of agricultural products[208] and other products, such as pharmaceuticals for human use as well as those for animal use.[209] Article 57 EC gives the Council power to adopt directives for, *inter alia*, the medical profession.[210] Health insurance matters are coordinated in the context of social security by Regulation 1408/71.[211] Through the privatization of health insurance in many countries, Articles 85 and 86 EC also assume a more important dimension in relation to health care.[212] Article 118a deals with the healthand safety of workers, an area in which numerous directives havebeen adopted.[213] Articles 30–39 Euratom deal with health and safety. The Environment and Consumer Protection Titles, discussed in sections 3 and 4, above, also aim to play their part in health and safety issues. Article K.1 TEU also relates to health, in particular concerning the fight against drugs, which forms a key element in cooperation in Justice and Home Affairs.

1990); Hamilton (1989) *Tijdschrift voor Gezondheidsrecht* 315; Hancher (1991) 28 CMLRev. 821; Hermans, *Europese Unie en Gezondheidszorg – de gevolgen van de Europese eenwording voor de Nederlandse gezondheidszorg* (Deventer, 1994), and Du Pré and Sevinga (1990) SEW 350.
204. Case T-10/93 *A v. Commission* [1994] ECR II-179 at 200–201.
205. See Chapter VII, sections 3.3.2, 5.2 and 6.4, *ante*.
206. O.J. English Special Edition 1963–63, p. 117.
207. Dir. 64/221, Art. 4(1). See also Art. 4(2). The standstill provision in Art. 4(3) is also important.
208. See Chapter XI, section 2.2, *post*.
209. See Chapter VIII, section 2.7, *ante*.
210. *E.g.* Dirs. 93/116 (O.J. 1993 L 165/1) for medical doctors, and 85/584 (O.J. 1985 L 372/42) for pharmacists.
211. As codified, see Chapter VII, section 5.4, *ante*.
212. Cases C-159 and 160/91 *Poucet and Pistre v. Assurances Générales de France (AGF) et al.* [1993] ECR I-637; Case C-245/91 *Ohra Schadeverzekeringen NV* [1993] ECR I-5851.
213. *E.g.* Dirs. 89/391 (O.J. 1989 L 183/1, corrigenda O.J. 1989 L 347/37 and 1990 L 275/42) and 91/383 (O.J. 1991 L 206/19).

Whether the term 'health' in Article 3(o) EC has a wider meaning than the term 'public health' used in Title X of Part Three of the EC Treaty is unclear. In any event, just as in the case of culture and education, which are examined in the next two sections, below, a distinction may be drawn between individual measures and the global policy of a Member State. In the first case there are clear links to free movement issues and to competition policy; in the second case the link is weaker and the issues involved concern the system as such.[214] The first group of measures is linked to the Public Health Title by the integration provision.[215]

The Title on Public Health follows the structure set out in section 2, above, and aims to achieve a high level of health protection. The Community contributes towards the achievement of this aim by encouraging cooperation between the Member States, and, if necessary, lending support to their action. One example of this is the measures taken to prevent illegal trade in human organs.[216] The subsidiarity principle is emphasized by the prescription that Community action supports that of the Member States and is directed towards the protection of diseases, in particular the major health scourges, including drug dependence.[217] The methods by which the Community is to act are also prescribed: research into the causes of these diseases and scourges, and their transmission, as well as health information and education. Article 129(4) EC requires incentive measures to be adopted by the co-decision procedure, after consultation of ECOSOC and the Committee of the Regions, but excludes any harmonization measures. The integration provision in the third paragraph of Article 129(1) EC indicates that the influence of Community law on public health is greater than Article 129 EC itself would lead a reader to suspect.[218] Already in 1993 the Council adopted a resolution on future action in the field of public health,[219] and at the same time it decided to continue the Europe against cancer programme, the action plan for 1996–2000 being approved in March 1996 after a conciliation procedure.[220] That procedure was again necessary prior to the adoption of the Community action programme for the prevention of aids and other communicable diseases, also in March

214. Case 238/82 *Duphar BV et al. v. The Netherlands State* [1984] ECR 523, [1985] 1 CMLR 256; Cases C-159 and 160/91 *Poucet and Pistre v. Assurances Générales de France (AGF) et al.* [1993] ECR I-637.
215. Art. 129(1) EC, 3rd para. The Treaty of Amsterdam (not yet in force) will substantially improve the Community's scope for action with the new Art. 129 EC.
216. WQ E-3966/93 (Kostopoulos) O.J. 1994 C 340/60. See also, generally, the Resolution on the protection of Human Rights and Dignity with regard to the application of Biology and Medicine (O.J. 1996 C 320/268).
217. *Cf.* Art. K.1 TEU. See Dec. 102/97 (O.J. 1997 L 19/25) and O.J. 1997 C 241/7.
218. See the Second Report on the integration of requirements for the protection of health in Community policy measures, COM (96) 407 Final.
219. O.J. 1993 C 174/1.
220. Dec. 96/646 (O.J. 1996 L 95/9).

1996,[221] as yet again prior to the adoption of the Community programme on health monitoring in June 1997.[222] The frequent recourse to the conciliation procedure demonstrates the sensitivity of much Community action in this area, and the rather different wishes of the Council and the Parliament. Fortunately the interest in health protection is rather more important than many of these sensitivities. The Commission has adopted Communications with proposals for Community action programmes on rare illnesses;[223] pollution-related illnesses,[224] and injuries.[225]

Article 129(3) EC provides that the Community and the Member States are to foster cooperation with third countries and the competent international organizations in the sphere of public health. The logical international organizations are the WHO and the Council of Europe. The so-called ERTA Declaration attached to the TEU which applies to environmental policy, monetary policy and development cooperation does not apply to measures based on Article 129 EC. However, this does not affect the applicability of the ERTA doctrine to health measures taken on the basis of other provisions of the EC Treaty.[226]

6. CULTURE

For a long time national cultural bodies and their supporters have argued that their cultural policy must not be affected by Community law.[227] Judgments of the Court on related issues, such as sports policy,[228] media policy,[229] and cultural activities as such[230] have removed any doubt about the applicability of Community law in these areas. Now that it is clear that many cultural activities fall within the ambit of Community law

221. Dec. 96/269 (O.J. 1996 L 95/16).
222. Dec. 1400/97 (O.J. 1998 L 193/1). See further, the directive on tobacco advertising and sponsorship (Common Position O.J. 1998 C 91/34) awaiting publication.
223. COM (97) 225 Final (O.J. 1997 C 203/6).
224. COM (97) 266 Final (O.J. 1997 C 214/7).
225. COM (97) 178 Final (O.J. 1997 C 203/20).
226. See note 35, *supra*, and text thereto.
227. See Mourik, *Culturele coëxistentie in Europa* (Amsterdam, 1989) and Tomsen and Vossen (eds.), *Denken over Cultuur in Europa* (Houten/Zaventem, 1994).
228. Case 36/74 *Walrave and Koch v. Association Union Cycliste Internationale et al.* [1974] ECR 1405, [1975] 1 CMLR 320; Case 13/76 *Donà v. Mantero* [1976] ECR 1333, [1976] 2 CMLR 578; Case C-415/93 *Union Royale Belge des Sociétés de Football Association ASBL et al. v. Bosman et al.* [1995] ECR I-4921, [1996] 1 CMLR 645.
229. *E.g.* Case 352/85 *Bond van Adverteerders et al. v. The Netherlands State* [1988] ECR 2085, [1989] 3 CMLR 113; Case C-353/89 *Commission v. The Netherlands* [1991] ECR I-4069, and Case C-148/91 *Vereniging Veronica Omroep Organisatie v. Commissariaat voor de Media* [1993] ECR I-487.
230. *E.g.* Case 197/84 *Steinhauser v. City of Biarritz* [1985] ECR 1819, [1986] 1 CMLR 53; Case C-379/87 *Groener v. Minister for Education et al.* [1989] ECR 3967, [1990] 1 CMLR 401; Case C-154/89 *Commission v. France* [1991] ECR I-659; Case C-180/89

as economic activities, a cultural exception comes into sight. In the case of state aids, with the amendments made by the TEU, Article 92(3)(d) EC provides a Treaty basis for the promotion of culture and heritage conservation. The recent practice of the Commission demonstrates that culture will also be relevant in the application of Article 85 EC.[231]

With the coming into force of the TEU, a new Title on culture was inserted into the EC Treaty.[232] This Title deals with cultural policy globally, and has no effect on cultural activities and free movement; it follows the pattern of the other new Titles, and absolutely reeks of the principle of subsidiarity. It gives effect to Article 3(p) EC, according to which the Community contributes 'to the flowering of the cultures of the Member States'. This phrase is repeated in Article 128(1) EC and in that provision is filled out in a more balanced manner. The Community contributes to the flowering of the cultures of the Member States while respecting their national and regional diversity, and at the same time bringing the common cultural heritage to the fore. Community action in this field has a supporting and supplementary character, and is aimed at encouraging cooperation between the Member States: thus if necessary, Community action supports and supplements that of the Member States in the improvement of the knowledge and dissemination of the culture and history of the European peoples; conservation and safeguarding of cultural heritage of European significance; non-commercial cultural exchanges, and artistic and literary creation, including in the audio-visual sector. A number of programmes have been launched under the cultural heading.[233]

Commission v. Italy [1991] ECR I-709, and Case C-198/89 *Commission v. Greece* [1991] ECR I-727.

231. See the *XXIIIrd Report on Competition Policy 1994* (Brussels, Luxembourg, 1995) point 177. It remains to be seen whether the Commission will in this context respond to pressure to take a favourable view of book price agreements within common language areas which straddle national boundaries, see O.J. 1997 C 305/2.

232. Again, with a single provision: Art. 128 EC. See, generally, Bekemans (ed.), *Culture: Building Stone for Europe 2002* (Brussels, 1994); Blanke, *Europa auf dem Weg zu einer Bildungs- und Kulturgemeinschaft* (Cologne, 1994); De Witte in Schwarze and Schermers, *op. cit.* (see note 14, *supra*) 195, in Bieber and Ress (eds.), *Die Dynamik des Europäischen Gemeinschaftsrechts* (Baden-Baden, 1987), and in Cassese *et al.* (eds.), *Human Rights in the European Community: The Substantive Law* (Baden-Baden, 1991); FIDE, 13th Congress Report, *Legal Aspects of Community Action in the field of Culture* (Thessaloniki, 1988); Kuypers, *De Europese Gemeenschappen als vierde bestuurslaag op het terrein van onderwijs en cultuur* (The Hague, 1993); Lohman *et al.*, *Culture and Community Law, before and after Maastricht* (Deventer, 1992); Niedobitek, *Kultur und Europäisches Gemeinschaftsrecht* (Berlin, 1992); Ress (1992) Öff. Verv. 944.

233. See the Council's approval (Bull. EU 11–1994 point 1.2.223) of the Commission's Communication (COM (94) 356 Final), and the Kaleidoscope Programme (Dec. 719/96, O.J. 1996 L 99/20). Two other programmes have been started, the Ariane Programme (to promote knowledge and distribution of European literary works, Dec.

Article 128(4) EC is the integration provision,[234] and Article 128(3) obliges the Community and the Member States to foster cooperation with third countries and international organizations in the sphere of culture, particularly with the Council of Europe, although other fora such as UNESCO also spring to mind. The by now notorious ERTA Declaration attached to the TEU does not apply to the culture Title. As is the case with the public health sphere, this does not prevent the ERTA doctrine applying to the policy aspects which are regulated in other provisions of the EC Treaty.[235]

Article 128(5) EC makes it plain that the Community must restrict itself to incentive measures, and may not proceed to harmonization measures.[236] It remains to be seen whether this means that culture will remain a national and regional matter, or whether the Community will use other Treaty provisions, such as Article 100a or Article 57 EC[237] in order to adopt certain harmonization measures, in the film and audio-visual sector, for example, which have cultural consequences.

7. EDUCATION

A steady stream of case-law on students and teachers demonstrates that both these groups can be categorized in a number of cases as recipients or providers of services, or as employees.[238] The interpretation of Articles 48, 59 and 128 EC and associated measures[239] by the Court has resulted in the education authorities of the Member States being affected in areas in which they, however misconceived, felt that they were 'Community-proof'.[240] The case-law of the Court is far-reaching. If a measure, such as a bilateral agreement in the field of education and culture, does not fall

2085/97 (O.J. 1997 L 291/26)), and the Raphael programme (for the preservation of cultural heritage, Dec. 2228/97 (O.J. 1997 L 305/31)). See also Dec. 96/664 (O.J. 1996 L 306/40) on the promotion of linguistic diversity in the Community in the information society.

234. See COM (96) 160 Final. The Treaty of Amsterdam (not yet in force) will add the requirement that the diversity of the Community's cultures must be respected and promoted.

235. See note 35, *supra*. See also Reg. 3911/92 (O.J. 1992 L 395/1), amended by Reg. 2469/96 (O.J. 1996 L 335/9).

236. See the Commission's Communication COM (94) 356 Final. Even prior to 1992 assistance was granted to cultural projects, such as translations. This took place either through *ad-hoc* measures or through the European Social Fund or the European Regional Development Fund.

237. See Dir. 89/552 (O.J. 1989 L 298/33), amended by Dir. 97/36 (O.J. 1997 L 202/60)).

238. See Chapter VII, sections 4.1, 5.3.1 and 6.6, *ante*.

239. Such as Reg. 1612/68 (O.J. English Special Edition 1968 (II) p. 475, most recently amended by Reg. 2434/92 (O.J. 1992 L 245/1).

240. In Cases 389 and 390/87 *Echternach and Moritz v. Netherlands Minister for Education and Science* [1989] ECR 723, [1990] 2 CMLR 305 the Dutch government defended

within the scope of the EC Treaty, but hinders free movement because it discriminates, Article 5 EC means that the Member States must adopt measures to facilitate free movement.[241]

The Community status of students and teachers is further developed in secondary legislation,[242] such as Directive 93/36 on the right of residence for students,[243] Directive 89/48 on the general system of mutual recognition of higher education diplomas of at least three years' duration,[244] and Directive 92/51 on the second general system for mutual recognition of courses of shorter duration.[245]

The Chapter of Title VIII of Part Three of the Treaty dealing with education, vocational training and youth,[246] does not deal with individual free movement questions in the education sector, but with the broad thrust of education policy. It develops the reference in Article 3(p) EC to the Community contributing to education and training of quality. Through unambiguous drafting in the Treaty, the Member States have ensured that their responsibility for the content of teaching, the organization of education systems, and cultural and linguistic diversity is fully respected.[247] The Community contributes to the development of education of quality by encouraging cooperation between the Member States and, if necessary, by supporting and supplementing their action.[248] Community action is more concretely aimed at developing the European dimension in education, encouraging mobility of students and teachers, promoting cooperation between

standpoints already rejected by the Court more than 10 years earlier (this is in fact by no means uncommon, as any glance through infringement proceedings will show). See also Case C-357/89 *Raulin v. Minister van Onderwijs en Wetenschappen* [1992] ECR I-1027. As to the relationship between the Dutch constitution and EC cultural policy, see the Akkermans and Mentink Report (*Kamerstuk* 21 097, Dutch Parliamentary Session 1990–1991).

241. Case 235/87 *Matteucci v. Communauté française of Belgium et al.* [1988] ECR 5589 at 5611–5612. See, generally, Lenaerts (1994) 31 CMLRev. 7; Pertek (1992) 12 YBEL 293, and Van de Ven (1994) NTOR 140.
242. As to the problems which this legislation has given rise to, see WQs E-1689/94 (Van Velzen) O.J. 1995 C 306/6, and E-1754/94 (Ewing) O.J. 1995 C 30/13.
243. O.J. 1993 L 317/59.
244. O.J. 1989 L 19/16. See Case C-365/93 *Commission v. Greece* [1995] ECR I-499; Case C-216/94 *Commission v. Belgium* [1995] ECR I-2155; Case C-164/94 *Aranitis v. Land Berlin* [1996] ECR I-135, and Cases C-225–227/95 *Kapasakalis et al. v. Greece* (O.J. 1995 C 229/13).
245. Dir. 92/51 (O.J. 1992 L 209/25), most recently amended by Dir. 97/38 (O.J. 1997 L 184/31). See also Dec. 97/42 (O.J. 1997 L 17/38) granting a derogation to France concerning, *inter alia*, ski instructors.
246. Arts. 126 and 127 EC.
247. Art. 126(1) EC. See the Commission's White Paper COM (95) 590 Final; the Green Paper on obstacles to transnational mobility COM (97) 563 Final and COM (96) 471 Final. As to safety at school, see O.J. 1997 C 303/3.
248. *Ibid.* See O.J. 1998 C 1/4 and COM (97) 159 Final.

educational establishments, the development of exchanges of information and experience on issues common to the various systems of education, encouraging the development of youth exchanges and exchanges of socio-educational instructors, and encouraging the development of distance education.[249] For these purposes the Council is empowered to adopt incentive measures, but is prohibited from adopting harmonization measures.[250] The old Erasmus Programme[251] on the mobility of students, the old Comett Programme on cooperation between universities and industry in education and training for technology,[252] the old Lingua Programme promoting the knowledge of foreign languages,[253] and the Tempus Programme on trans-European mobility for university studies[254] are examples of this approach. Previously such activities were based on Articles 128 EEC or 235 EC. The current programmes, into which various earlier activities have migrated, are the Socrates Programme[255] and the Leonardo da Vinci Programme.[256]

Unlike the cultural objective which is also mentioned in Article 3(p) EC, Article 126 EC does not contain an integration provision. This is somewhat strange, as the relationship between education and free movement is much more clearly developed than is the case for culture, both in case-law and in secondary legislation. Education is also not mentioned in the ERTA Declaration.[257] Despite the absence of an integration provision, it is submitted that the ERTA doctrine also applies to educational activities which for not fall under the education Title.

Article 126(3) requires the Community and the Member States to foster cooperation with third countries and the competent international organizations in the field of education, particularly the Council of Europe.

---

249. Art. 126(2) EC.
250. Art. 126(4) EC, 1st indent (by the co-decision procedure, with consultation of ECOSOC and the Committee of the Regions). The Council may also adopt recommendations, by a qualified majority, on a proposal from the Commission, *ibid.*, 2nd indent.
251. Dec. 87/327 (O.J. 1987 L 166/20), amended by Dec. 89/663 (O.J. 1989 L 395/23). See Case 242/87 *Commission v. Council* [1989] ECR 1421. The programme was expanded to embrace Austria, Finland, Iceland, Norway, Sweden and Switzerland (see O.J. 1991 L 332/11 *et seq.*). Dutch students will be interested to read Van Ingen Scholten (1995) SEW 292.
252. Dec. 89/27 (O.J. 1989 L 13/28) on the Comett II Programme, see Cases C-51, 90 and 94/89 *United Kingdom et al. v. Council* [1991] ECR I-2757. The programme was similarly expanded (see O.J. 1990 L 102/1 *et seq.*).
253. Dec. 89/489 (O.J. 1989 L 239/24).
254. Dec. 93/246 (O.J. 1993 L 112/34), Tempus II, extended by Dec. 96/663 (O.J. 1996 L 306/36).
255. Dec. 819/95 (O.J. 1995 L 87/10, amended by Dec. 576/98 (O.J. 1998 L 77/1)). This embraces the European Union, the other countries of the EEA, the countries of Central and Eastern Europe, and Cyprus and Malta.
256. Dec. 94/819 (O.J. 1994 L 340/8).
257. See note 35, *supra*, and text thereto.

In this context, the recent agreements with the United States[258] and Canada[259] are but two examples.[260]

The provisions concerning vocational training, which are also included in the Education Title, are discussed in Chapter IX, above. Given that research and technology policy is closely related to industrial policy, it is discussed in Chapter XI, below.

8. OTHER HORIZONTAL AND FLANKING POLICIES

The horizontal and flanking activities of the European Union now embrace virtually every aspect of activity of the national authorities in these spheres, although some matters are dealt with only marginally or not at all. They nevertheless deserve brief mention.

8.1 Tourism

As a result of the Court's interpretation of the freedom to provide services as also embracing the freedom to receive services,[261] many tourists have been able to make use of that freedom. Article 3(t) EC permits the Community to take measures in the field of tourism, and the first Declaration annexed to the Final Act on the occasion of the signature of the TEU required a report to be submitted by the Commission by 1996 which would form the basis for consideration of introducing, inter alia, a Title on tourism into the EC Treaty.[262] In that Declaration the Commission stated that present Community action in, inter alia, the sphere of tourism would be pursued on the basis of the present provisions of the EC Treaty.

There are certainly certain pegs on which tourism policy may be hung: 1990 was proclaimed the year of tourism.[263] This led to various incentive measures, and to the adoption of Directive 90/314 on package travel, package holidays and package tours[264] and Directive 94/47 on time-sharing.[265] The Commission has adopted a Green Paper on tourism[266] and

---

258. Dec. 95/487 (O.J. 1995 L 279/11).
259. Dec. 95/523 (O.J. 1995 L 300/18).
260. See, further, the *General Reports 1995 and 1996* (Brussels, Luxembourg, 1996 and 1997 respectively), points 282–285 and 284–286 respectively.
261. Cases 286/82 and 26/83 *Luisi and Carbone v. Ministero del Tesoro* [1984] ECR 377, [1985] 3 CMLR 52; Case 186/87 *Cowan v. Trésor public* [1989] ECR 195, [1990] 2 CMLR 613.
262. In the Luxembourg draft of what became the TEU there were separate Titles dealing with civil protection and tourism, *Europe* Documents No. 1722/1723 (5 July 1991). See Bull. EU-4–1996, point 1.1. In the event the Treaty of Amsterdam failed to deal with this matter. See, generally, Dejemeppe (1994) JdT (Dr. Eur.) 97 and Wouters (1994) JdT (Dr. Eur.) 102.
263. Dec. 89/46 (O.J. 1989 L 17/53).
264. O.J. 1990 L 158/59.
265. O.J. 1994 L 280/93.
266. COM (95) 97 Final.

a multiannual programme supporting European tourism (Philoxenia) has been proposed.[267]

8.2 Civil protection

Tourism and civil protection are mentioned in the same breath in Article 3(t) EC and in the first Declaration.[268] A number of measures fall within the field of civil protection, such as those dealing with paging services[269] and mobile communications.[270] Moreover, the Community has signed the Convention on the Transboundary Impact of Industrial Accidents.[271] This type of Community action is closely linked to environmental policy[272] (and indeed in the General Reports, civil protection is included in the chapter on Environment). In 1997 the Council and representatives of the governments of the Member States adopted a decision establishing a Community Action programme on civil protection.[273] The value of Community cooperation was evident during the *Sea Empress* disaster at Milford Haven in 1996.[274]

8.3 Sport

The importance of sport for the development of European integration is regularly underestimated. There is frequent traffic in this context, both of sportsmen and women and of fans. Despite clear indications in the case-law of the Court,[275] the Community has still not really managed to use sport as a means of advancing integration; if anything the contrary was true at least until the celebrated judgment in *Bosman*.[276] The composition of teams was rife with discriminatory rules, and the settlement which the

267. See the amended proposal, COM (96) 635 Final (O.J. 1997 C 13/11).
268. See section 8.1, *ante*.
269. Rec. 90/543 (O.J. 1990 L 310/23).
270. *E.g.* Dir. 91/263 (O.J. 1991 L 128/1) on conformity of telecommunications terminal equipment (supplemented by Dir. 93/97 (O.J. 1993 L 290/1) in respect of earth station equipment), and Rec. 91/288 (O.J. 1991 L 144/47).
271. Helsinki, 18 March, 1992, under the auspices of the United Nations Economic Commission for Europe, *XXVIth General Report 1992* (Brussels, Luxembourg, 1993) point 611, see COM (97) 330 Final (O.J. 1997 C 267/60). That point also mentions that negotiations were under way concerning a Convention on the Prevention of Industrial Disasters, but, no further progress is reported under the civil protection heading in subsequent General Reports. See further SEC (91) 1736 Final.
272. *E.g.* the Seveso Directive, see note 134, *supra*.
273. Dec. 98/22 (O.J. 1998 L 8/20).
274. *General Report 1996* (Brussels, Luxembourg, 1997) point 459.
275. See the judgments cited in note 14, *supra*; Case 222/86 *Union nationale des entraîneurs et Cadres techniques professionnels du football (Unectef) v. Heylens et al.* [1987] ECR 4097, [1989] 1 CMLR 901, and Case T-46/92 *The Scottish Football Association v. Commission* [1994] ECR II-1039. See, generally, Kahlenberg (1994) Eur. W.St.R. 423; Klose, *Die Rolle des Sports bei der Europäische Einigung* (Berlin, 1989), and Weatherill (1989) YBEL 55.
276. Case C-415/93 *Union Royale Belge des Sociétés de Football Association ASBL et al. v. Bosman et al.* [1995] ECR I-4921, [1996] 1 CMLR 645.

Commission had reached with UEFA[277] was rightly shown to be
fundamentally misconceived in *Bosman*.[278] The Community has been
reticent in developing a sports policy as such, in view of the lack of specific
powers,[279] but it does have certain financial resources earmarked for
sporting activities,[280] and the Committee of the Regions has made
suggestions relating to youth and sport.[281]

8.4 Youth and senior citizens

Community policy on youth is embodied in the Chapter on education,
vocational training and youth. Unlike the first two of this trio of policy
areas, youth is not specifically mentioned in the catalogue of means
contained in Article 3 EC. Article 126(2) EC indicates that community
action is *inter alia* aimed at encouraging the development of youth
exchanges and exchanges of what the Treaty calls socio-economic
instructors, but most people refer to as youth workers. Article 127(2) EC
envisages various measures relating to vocational training, particularly of
young people. The Youth for Europe Programme[282] has now begun its
third phase.

Policy in relation to senior citizens was given a boost by the procla-
mation of 1993 as the European Year of Older People and Solidarity
between Generations,[283] which drew attention to the position of older
people in various policy areas, led to considerable subsidies being granted
to projects for older people,[284] and bore further fruit in the TIDE
initiative.[285]

8.5 Town and country planning

Planning policy is not yet actively pursued at Community level, although
various activities are fragmented and could well be brought together to
promote coherence and transparency. It is expressly referred to in Article
130s(2), but is also relevant in the Titles on Economic and Social
Cohesion (regional policy), Transport, Trans-European Networks, and
Industry. A report on *Town and Country Planning* was produced by the
Commission in July 1994.[286] On the basis of Article 222 EC and the

277. See WQs 610/90 (Ortega) O.J. 1990 C 233/35; 1880/91 (Di Rupo) O.J. 1991 C 327/25,
    and E-891/94 (Kostopoulos) O.J. 1994 C 349/48. See also WQ E-1987/94 (Ford) O.J.
    1995 C 24/52.
278. [1995] ECR I-4921 at 5078.
279. WQ 2810/92 (Banotti) O.J. 1994 C 25/6.
280. WQ E-1922/94 (Larive) O.J. 1995 C 30/34.
281. O.J. 1996 C 337/60. See also the Parliament's Resolution (O.J. 1997 C 200/252).
282. Dec. 95/818 (O.J. 1995 L 87/1). See also the amended proposal for a Community
    action programme for voluntary service by young people COM (98) 201 Final.
283. Dec. 92/440 (O.J. 1992 L 245/43).
284. WQ E-3357/92 (Lopéz) O.J. 1994 C 340/2.
285. Dec. 93/512 (O.J. 1993 L 240/42).
286. Commission Press Release IP/94/732, see (1995) EuZW 3. See, generally, Krautzberger

principle of subsidiarity, the Community will never be able to adopt such far-reaching measures as national, regional or local authorities. Thus the Community cannot force through compulsory purchase of land, but national property rules may be examined under the Treaty[287] or under Community policies, such as the market organization in wine and wine products, and in the light of the First Protocol to the European Convention on Human Rights.[288]

As a result of the widespread floods on the Continent in 1995, the Ministers of the Environment of the Benelux countries, France and Germany have declared their readiness to seek solutions to the flooding by the Rhine and the Meuse, which they envisage in the longer term as being an issue for Community action.[289]

8.6 Media policy

Media policies pursued at national level are in many cases at odds with the freedoms guaranteed by Community law, particularly with the freedom to provide services. The Netherlands,[290] Italy, [291] Belgium,[292] and Greece[293] have all found that in particular the application of the principle of proportionality means that compulsory truck systems, discriminatory advertising provisions, establishment requirements and other restrictions will not withstand Community scrutiny.[294] Articles 85

and Selke (1994) DöV 685; Pascallon (1990) RMC 514, and *1992, Pleisterplaats op weg naar 2015. Een verkenning naar de ruimtelijke consequenties van de voltooiing van de interne markt* (Studierapporten van de Rijksplanologische Dienst no. 46, The Hague, 1992).

287. Case 182/83 *Robert Fearon & Co. Ltd. v. The Irish Land Commission* [1984] ECR 3677, see Gormley (1985) 10 ELRev. 47.

288. Case 44/79 *Hauer v. Land Rheinland-Pfalz* [1979] ECR 3727, [1980] 3 CMLR 42.

289. *Staatscourant* 7 February 1995.

290. See the case-law mentioned in note 14, *supra*, and Case C-288/89 *Stichting Collectieve Anntennevoorziening Gouda et al. v. Commissariaat voor de Media* [1991] ECR I-4007. See further, generally, Case C-17/92 *Federación de Distribuidore Cinematográficos (FEDICINE) v. Spanish State* [1993] ECR I-2239; Case C-23/93 *TV 10 SA v. Commissariaat voor de Media* [1994] ECR I-4795; Case C-222/94 *Commisison v. United Kingdom* [1996] ECR I-4; Case 11/95 *Commission v. Belgium* [1996] ECR I-4115; Cases C-320/94 etc. *Reti Televisione Italiane SpA (RTI) et al. v. Ministero delle e Telcomunicazioni* [1996] ECR I-6471; Case C-14/96 *Denuit* [1997] ECR I-2785; Case C-56/96 *VTH Ltd. v. Vlaamse Gemeenschap* [1997] ECR I-3143, and Cases C-34–36/95 *Konsumentombudsman (KO) v. DeAgostini (Svenska) Förlag AB et al.* [1997] ECR I-3843.

291. Case 155/73 *Sacchi* [1974] ECR 409, [1974] 2 CMLR 177.

292. Case 52/79 *Procureur du Roi v. Debauve et al.* [1980] ECR 833, [1981] 2 CMLR 362, and Case C-211/91 *Commission v. Belgium* [1992] ECR I-6757.

293. Case C-260/89 *ERT* [1991] ECR I-2925, [1994] 4 CMLR 540.

294. See, further, Chapter VII, *ante*, and, see, generally, Barendt (1994) MJ 41; Bux, *EG-Kompetenz für den rundfunk* (Frankfurt, 1992); Van den Beukel, *Toegang tot de televisiemarkt* (Deventer, 1995), and Winn, *European Community and International Media Law* (London, 1994).

and 86 EC[295] and the Merger Regulation[296] have also been applied to media dossiers.

In 1984 the Commission published a celebrated White Paper on *Television without Frontiers*[297] which later led to Directive 89/552.[298] Those who favour an active cultural policy (with film quotas) are still not *ad idem* with the proponents of a free market.[299] Other, more technical measures, such as Directive 90/387[300] on telecommunication services and Open Network Provision, Directive 90/388[301] on competition in the markets for Telecommunications Services, and Directive 95/478 on HDTV[302] have given major incentives to (commercial) television without frontiers.

From the terms of Article 128 EC on culture and from the case-law of the Court, a genuine public service broadcaster may rely on the general interest exceptions (culture, pluriform nature of the media, and regional diversity) in order to broadcast its message. The policy of the Commission was further adapted in 1994 in the interest of strengthening the European programme industry.[303] In January 1996 the MEDIA II programmes got under way.[304] The Commission has also adopted a Green Paper on the protection of minors and human dignity in the context of audiovisual information services.[305]

295. Respectively, Case C-360/92 P *Publishers Association v. Commission* [1995] ECR I-23, see Gormley (1997) 34 CMLRev. 401, and Cases C-241 and 242/91 P *Radio Telefis Eireann (RTE) et al. v. Commission* [1995] ECR I-743, see Greaves (1995) ECLR 244.
296. *E.g.* Decs. 94/922 (O.J. 1994 L 364/1) *Media Service GmbH* and 96/649 (O.J. 1996 L 294/14) *RTL/Veronica/Endemol.*
297. COM (84) 300 Final, see Buckling (1987) EuGRZ 97, Roth (1985) ZHR 679 Schwarz (1986) 11 ELRev. 7, Tizzano (1986) *Il Foro Italiano* 464. See also Schwarze (ed.), *Rundfunk und Fernsehen im Lichte der Entwicklung des nationalen Grenzen* (Baden-Baden, 1986) and Bull. EC Supp. 5/86.
298. O.J. 1989 L 298/33, amended by Dir. 97/36 (O.J. 1997 L 202/60).
299. See *e.g. Europe* No. 6380, p. 9 (16 December 1994) and No. 6446 (23 March 1995).
300. O.J. 1990 L 192/1, corrigendum O.J. 1993 L 85/28, amended by Dir. 97/51 (O.J. 1997 L 295/23).
301. O.J. 1990 L 192/10, partly annulled in Cases C-271, 281 and 290/90 *Spain et al. v. Commission* [1992] ECR I-5833, [1993] 4 CMLR 110, most recently amended by Dir. 96/19 (O.J. 1996 L 74/13).
302. O.J. 1995 L 281/51.
303. COM (94) 96 Final.
304. Decs. 95/563 and 95/564 (O.J. 1995 L 321/25 and 33).
305. COM (96) 483 Final. See the Council's views, O.J. 1997 C 70/4.

CHAPTER XI

Sectoral policies[1]

1. GENERAL OBSERVATIONS

The three Community Treaties only make express provision for a sectoral policy for agriculture, transport, coal, steel, and atomic energy. To a lesser extent, since the amendments introduced by the TEU, industrial policy is also envisaged, as is, implicitly, energy policy in general. Although research and technological development policy and policy on trans-European networks are actually not sectoral policies but functional policies, they are also discussed in this chapter, as they are directly related to sectoral policy in the strict sense, particularly as concerns industry, transport and telecommunications. It will be seen that the market mechanism (competition) continues to perform an essential coordinating function for the attainment of the Community objectives. The evolution of the Common Agricultural Policy and transport policy demonstrate that the role of the market mechanism has become steadily more important.

In relation to sectors not covered by specific sectoral policy, the EC Treaty makes do with the degree of regulation resulting from the five freedoms, the competition provisions and harmonized provisions covering certain aspects of market behaviour. The Community directly influences market behaviour in terms of steering it only in regional policy, through the structural funds,[2] and in the very rarely used shortages policy interventions under Article 103a EC.[3]

It is submitted that this reserved attitude with regard to market-regulating measures is quite justified on various grounds. In the first place, at the national level, such measures for particular branches of

---

1. In the Dutch edition sections 1 and 2 of this chapter were revised by Barents, the other sections by Slot. The editor has further revised this chapter, taking account of still relevant additions from the last edition, and new case-law, literature and developments, and has considerably enlarged the discussion of fisheries.
2. See Chapter IX, section 4, *ante*.
3. See *ibid.*, section 3.2, point E.

industry (created often during the inter-wars depression period) have now declined in favour of broader measures, a tendency which was already more evident at the time the original EEC Treaty was drafted than it was at the time the ECSC Treaty was drafted. Regulating measures for particular sectors usually tend to check the dynamic adjustment of those sectors to the development of demand, are frequently detrimental to other sectors, and are obstructed by the creation of substitute products and the blurring out of demarcation lines between the branches, in industry as well as in trade. At the Community level there is further the problem that the members of the Council can hardly assume responsibility for regulating measures in consequence of which less efficient undertakings in their own country will lose ground to more efficient undertakings in other Member States. An optimum allocation of production factors is very difficult to achieve at supranational level by deliberate regulation, at all events so long as the Community Institutions taking the decisions have no really supranational character. If the relevant measures are not delegated to the Commission they therefore threaten to take on the character of an injurious cartel, which does not ensure optimum division of labour within the Community, but tends to keep alive inefficient undertakings. The experiences so far in all those sectors where Community regulation was considered inevitable are symptomatic in this respect. Thus agricultural policy must also take account of the 'highest cost of production' level within the Community. The annual battles over fixing the prices for cereals, dairy produce and sugar are good examples of this. The market organizations for wine, tobacco, olive oil and fruit and vegetables are examples of the danger of market-regulating measures going further than is economically justified, in order to ensure a uniform spread of the advantages of the agricultural policy. Furthermore, research in the nuclear power sector was for years subject to the notorious principle that each state desired to receive back in research orders what it had contributed financially to the joint research programmes. The dispute at the end of 1973 over the best procedure for uranium extraction and the long-running dispute about the site for the nuclear fusion JET project (now based at Culham in the United Kingdom) are but two examples of the priority which national interests enjoy over efforts to achieve an optimal solution from the Community point of view. Again, the difficulty in arriving at a common transport policy is largely due to widely divergent national interests which are opposed to optimum economic rationality of the common transport policy. The problems which arose particularly in the second half of the Seventies and in the early Eighties in a rational distribution of an organized reduction in overcapacity in the steel industry, in shipbuilding and in the textiles industry serve as more recent examples of the problems of a Community sectoral policy. Finally, it should be noted that the Community has not yet established a common energy policy. It is, therefore, fortunate that for most sectors the EC Treaty prescribes without restrictions the establishment of a common market, or in other words the possibility of undistorted competition free of artificial restrictions in the whole territory of the common market. Thus steps are at least taken to ensure that where there is overcapacity less efficient undertakings are not kept going at the expense of efficient undertakings, whilst new efficient undertakings immediately have a large market at their disposal. It has already been seen that this competition policy in the wide sense itself necessitates the adoption by the Community Institutions of numerous mandatory measures. In that context, however, the divergent national interests referred to above do not play so important a part. Where they do play an important part the relevant powers are as a rule vested in the Commission.

In the meantime, during the Seventies ever greater objections have been raised in many Member States to the shock reconstruction of sectors with overcapacity and to the allocation of new investment or scarcity solely on the basis of market forces. These objections arose particularly in the light of the recession after the oil crisis of 1973 in all the Member States, the collapse of the Bretton Woods exchange rate system and the economic rise of Japan. Economic growth, even during the upturn in the second half of the Eighties, never again reached the levels seen in the Sixties. In all Member States the recession led to significant unemployment which brought about calls for measures to protect existing (national) employment, for measures to be taken by the State to promote new employment and for stronger social measures for employees facing unemployment. Initially in the early Eighties this primarily defensive policy produced expensive subsidy competition between the Member States, which was able to postpone the inevitable adjustments, but could not prevent them taking place, but subsequently state aids became less intensive and more specific in nature. Under the influence of the OECD most Member States started to follow a policy of positive adjustment, so that on the one hand more importance was attached to a well-functioning market mechanism, and, on the other hand greater emphasis was placed on strengthening the so-called public supply side of the market: education, training, and infrastructure in the widest sense of the word. An example of this development can be seen in technology policy, which started to develop at Community and at national level in the early Eighties.

The unequal distribution of unemployment among the Member States, sectors and regions gave rise to Community level and national level measures intensifying three-dimensional economic policy. Community policy in this matter has been discussed in section 4 of Chapter IX, above. It will be recalled that concerns about tackling employment problems have been recognized in the Treaty of Amsterdam.

The structural unemployment confronting the Community also has structural causes. The increase in net salary costs has led to labour-intensive industries being transferred elsewhere, and indeed under the

Conservative governments the United Kingdom paraded its perceived ability to attract inward investment from outside the Community as a sign of the success of its deregulatory approach, leaving carefully to one side the question of whether real 'added value' jobs were in fact being created, and the effects of the second-class level of social protection in the United Kingdom during that period. The reallocation of primarily labour-intensive industries has accelerated since the beginning of the Nineties, through the economic liberalization of centrally-led economies. Moreover, the combination of the process of technological renewal and vigorous competition in the world market led to various capital and knowledge-intensive sectors, such as information technology and household electronic appliances, getting into difficulties. The pressure of increasing unemployment and the necessity to continue to play a part on the world stage in knowledge-intensive sectors has strengthened the call for the Community to pursue a more sector-oriented policy, not least in view of the failure of national protectionist approaches. This policy may take the form of typical market regulation of a particular sector, as in the case of steel, or as specific measures which create conditions, such as the improvement of technological and physical infrastructure. At the same time as sectoral policy measures are taken, regional differences in levels of employment and prosperity will also have to be taken into account. This plays a part in *inter alia* structural policy for agriculture.

The Community is still too greatly dependent on imported energy sources. This problem, and the need to safeguard the Community's energy provision in general obliges energy policy to be pursued at Community level. Finally, the increasing need to protect the environment means that the Member States can no longer leave the coordination of national policy in the matter purely to the common market mechanism. The introduction by the SEA of what are now Articles 100a and 130r–130t EC well illustrates this point. however, the development of sector-oriented measures at Community level is made none the easier by the fact that the objectives of environmental policy and sectoral policy still do not converge.

The possibilities of intervention in particular sectors, again, can be classified by means of the planning typology of Zijlstra, which has been repeatedly referred to.[4] It will then be found that the instrument of prognoses (type IA) is accepted for all sectors and is expressly supplemented by assignments for the sectors of coal and steel and nuclear research in accordance with the Treaties themselves (type IIIA). The planning types IVA and VA will be found to occupy a very important place for sectoral policy. Both these types are concerned with financial incentives, in the case of IVA with incentives without binding conditions for the industry with regard to market or investment behaviour, in the case of type VA with incentives which may involve binding conditions with

4. See Chapter III, sections 3.1. and 3.5.5, and Chapter IX, section 1.3., *ante*.

regard to market or investment behaviour. As will be seen, type VA plays a dominant role in agricultural policy, in coal and steel policy, and in nuclear power policy. The obligations on intervention agencies to purchase below a given market price within the framework of the agricultural policy belong to this type just as much as do the credit facilities for approved investments in the coal and steel sectors and the various forms of encouragement of nuclear research and dissemination of technical know-how as well as the facilitation of investments under the Euratom Treaty. Unconditional incentives for a particular investment policy play a part especially in the policy of the European Investment Bank. As was already demonstrated however in Chapters VIII and IX, above, in the supervision of national aid measures and in the development of Community financial incentives ever more express conditions are now attached to this type of intervention.

Although the ECSC Treaty also provides a number of possibilities for mandatory market-regulatory measures of the kind mentioned in Zijlstra's planning type VIA, in practice between 1960 and the end of the Seventies these hardly played a role. Only since the end of the Seventies with the onset of the steel crisis have binding provisions on prices and production played a decisive role in addition to a gradually tighter control on a gradual reduction of national aid measures temporarily permitted on condition that restructuring and a reduction in capacity are effected. The success of that policy subsequently permitted liberalization to be reintroduced. In the field of agricultural policy mandatory provisions initially played only a subsidiary part and even then only on relatively minor issues such as minimum quality and quality classification and authorization systems necessary for controls, although here too quota systems were later applied. Mandatory provisions play a greater role in the common transport policy (bracket tariffs, qualitative requirements for exercising the profession, harmonization of legal conditions of competition and also, in the transitional period, a quota system for international road transport). The Commission's ideas on energy policy, developed during the Seventies, likewise do not exclude compulsory measures, although mainly as an ultimate remedy, when the instruments of undistorted competition, prognoses and assignments (programmes), recommendations and financial incentives, have been exhausted. Had the energy crisis of the mid-Seventies been prolonged and intensified it might have compelled the establishment of Community distribution arrangements for crude oil and petroleum products, as happened in the past on the basis of the ECSC Treaty for coal. Certain steps in this direction were indeed taken. The most important mandatory provisions, though, concerned the formation of stocks and energy-saving. Since the Eighties the Commission has been pushing for a reorientation of the Community's energy policy, although this for many years met resistance from the Member States. Policy on trans-European networks has also latterly made considerable progress.

2. AGRICULTURE AND FISHERIES

2.1 The nature of the agricultural problems

Public authorities have since time immemorial been concerned about agriculture, and already in the Nineteenth Century there had developed the specialty presently known as agricultural law. It was principally concerned with the legal status of the farmer's land (title, mortgages and succession, *etc.*). Although the large-scale supply of cereals from Russia and Northern America, made possible by the fall in transport rates, had already caused a severe crisis in Western European agriculture on two occasions (first after the Napoleonic wars and then around 1880), it is only since the great world crisis of the Thirties that agriculture has become the subject of permanent government control, and that the more public-economic aspects of agricultural law developed. The illusion that this was merely a short-term economic phenomenon has had to be abandoned. The reasons for this are of a divergent, but especially of a structural nature. Some of the structural causes of the permanent problems, which are relevant to an understanding of European agricultural policy, will be briefly mentioned here.[5]

Neither the demand for nor the supply of agricultural products is very susceptible to rises or falls in prices (low price elasticity of supply and demand). This applies especially to short-term, but frequently also to long-term developments, particularly in case of falls in prices. A fall in prices tends to cause neither a corresponding short-term or long-term rise in demand nor a corresponding decrease in production. In the short term the volume of production depends rather on climatological factors and the biologically determined duration of the production cycle. In the long term it tends to increase in consequence of a rise of labour productivity, mechanization, more intensive use of fertilizers, improvements of seed strains, *etc.* This increase in production is not accompanied by a corresponding increase in outlets. At home this is due to the weak price elasticity (and for a number of products also to the weak income elasticity) of demand; on the export markets it is due either to the lack of purchasing power (developing countries) or to protection of those export markets where domestic agriculture is faced with the same problems. Since time

5. For a more extensive discussion see Van Lierde, *Europese landbouwproblemen en Europese landbouwproblematiek* (Antwerp, 1967). For more recent studies on European agricultural problems see Fennell, *The Common Agricultural Policy of the European Community* (2nd ed., Oxford, 1987); Neville-Rolfe, *The Politics of Agriculture in the European Community* (London, 1984); Priebe *et al.*, *Die agrarwirtschaftliche Integration Europas* (Baden-Baden, 1980); Ries, *Das ABC der europäischen Agrarpolitik* (Baden-Baden, 1970); Tracy and Hodac (eds.), *Les perspectives de l'agriculture dans la CEE* (Bruges, 1979), and the WRR Report no. 28, *The Unfinished European Integration* (The Hague, 1986).

immemorial the agricultural sector has been confronted by massive surpluses or sometimes massive shortages, resulting in unstable markets and price relationships. Many agricultural products are substitutable, both in terms of demand and supply, so that unstable situations for one product exercise a direct effect on the situation of other products. A surplus of milk, for example, may lead to the wholesale slaughter of milk cows, and thus an increase in the supply of beef, which results in a decrease in demand for pork and other pigmeat.

In the long term these problems stem from the structure of supply and demand. On the demand side problems may arise through a low or stagnating population growth, so that the improvements in mechanization, intensive farming and productivity cannot be fully absorbed: structural surpluses then result. In many countries, principally the Southern Member States, agricultural structures are relatively underdeveloped, primarily due to natural factors such as hill and mountain farming, climate, and inadequate infrastructure, and to the lack of organized processing (through agricultural cooperatives for example). These structural weaknesses often go hand in hand with social inequalities and economic development which is lagging behind. Although the average income position of farmers has improved, as a result of increased labour productivity and technological progress in agriculture, the average *per capita* earnings still remain lower than the average *per capita* earnings of those in comparable occupational groups. For small farmers they are lower than those of skilled workers. An important element in the problem is that production is relatively immobile. Farmers are tied to a given holding, which means that an agricultural producer, unlike most other producers, cannot as a rule increase the size of his undertaking by internal growth, but can do so exclusively by purchase of land from other farmers. However, such purchases are frequently restricted by rules of law. The differences between the earnings of farmers with small holdings and those with large holdings are thus largely maintained. If the rural area in question is insufficiently industrialized, the farmer with unsatisfactory earnings is also unable to switch to another branch of industry without migration, and the mobility of farmers in particular is usually small. The intensification of production acts as a further restraint on mobility. In some European countries agricultural land is particularly scarce and more economic production requires an active policy of land reallocation, infrastructural improvements and so on. It is still the case that most agricultural holdings are in the hands of marginal or almost marginal family enterprises, which, while economically of limited significance, have a social and electoral influence which is not to be underestimated (as any French Mayor or Prefect who has been faced with defenestration by a crowd of angry farmers will testify). Moreover, farmers are vitally important for management of the environment and natural surroundings.

This brief overview makes it clear that any form of intervention in the agricultural markets must deal not merely with short-term problems (market and price policies), it must also embrace the longer term (agricultural structures). Intervention in the context of market and price policies almost always aim to increase or stabilize producer incomes. Two types of short-term intervention should be distinguished: the first involves free price formation for agricultural products, so that farmers sell their products at market prices and receive 'deficiency payments' so as to assure them a reasonable income. This was long the system followed in the United Kingdom, but even before its accession to the Communities the United Kingdom government started to adapt this system to the Community system. The second type involves protecting national producers by stabilizing the internal market at a price level which assures a reasonable income, at least in efficiently managed standard undertakings. Thus surplus production is taken out of the national market through price intervention mechanisms. This of course requires effective prevention of the undermining of this price level by much cheaper imports from third countries; variable import levies have thus been imposed to bring third country imports up to the Community price level and export subsidies have been paid to compensate farmers for the lower prices on the world market.[6] In some cases this policy was accompanied by centralization of imports and exports. Price-stabilizers may also take the form of production quotas, which may be used in order to avoid cut-throat competition and the demise of many marginal producers. The choice for one method or the other depends on myriad political, economic and financial considerations, and has been a subject of constant debate primarily in economic literature.[7] Agricultural structural policy has not only to offer a long-term perspective for short-term interventions and their effects on the structure of supply and demand, it must also contribute to a harmonious development of the agricultural sector in public policy as a whole. Agricultural structural policy often relates to competition policy in the agricultural sector (the role of cooperatives), and production and processing structures, and is closely linked to regional and environmental policy.

6. Pressure in the Uruguay Round has led to a move from variable to fixed levies.
7. It is impossible to distill a *communis opinio*. In the same way as the agricultural community in many European countries, developing countries producing raw materials have
argued strongly against systems of deficiency payments or compensatory payments
related to export receipts, frequently proposed by the Western side, viewing them as a
form of charity. As a rule there is a preference for price intervention, given that this is
regarded as a deriving from the age-old principle of a 'just' price. Both the Baumgart-
ner–Pisani plan for the regulation of the world raw materials market, launched in 1963
but never implemented, and the integrated raw materials programme of UNCTAD from
1976 which was only realized to a limited extent were based on this approach.

2.2   The Agricultural Title in the EC Treaty

The Common Agricultural Policy (CAP)

It follows from Articles 7 and 7a EC that the agricultural sector also forms part of the common market. It is clear that this was not regarded as something which was obviously automatic, as the first sentence of Article 38(1) specifically extends the common market to agriculture and trade in agricultural products. Given that all Member States had for years and years regulated agricultural markets to a more or less far-reaching extent in the context of various types of market regulation, the application of the free movement of goods provisions after the transitional period would have irrevocably led to the undermining of these national market organizations which were primarily based on price interventions coupled with import and export regulation. The common market in the agricultural sector could only be established by specific measures involving the communitarization of the national regulatory policies, a principle which is already set out in Article 3(e) EC and developed in Articles 38–47 EC. What precisely 'a' or 'the' common policy measures should be is not specified in the Treaty itself. These provisions only sketch a framework consisting of a number of objectives,[8] some global indication of instruments[9], and a broad grant of powers.[10] Articles 3(e) and 38(2) and (4) EC do express the actually and legally indissoluble link between the CAP and the common market for agricultural products. The one is unimaginable without the other, as is confirmed by Article 43(3)(b) EC, which provides that the Community policy in this sector has the objective of creating a situation which is comparable to that of a national market. The CAP thus embodies the most far-reaching form of integration provided for in the EC Treaty, namely a total fusion of positive and negative integration.[11] It is

---

8.   Art. 39 EC.
9.   Arts. 40–42 EC.
10. Art. 43 EC.
11. In relation to the common organizations of the markets this principle means that after the end of the transitional period the free movement of goods provisions has become an integral part of these organizations. Before that date the terms of the free movement of goods provisions were repeated as part of the regulations establishing the common organizations of the markets concerned, so as to make the free movement principles apply by virtue of the regulations themselves, as Article 30 EC was at that stage not yet directly applicable and did not then have direct effect. Since the end of the transitional period the repetition is otiose, see Warner, Adv. Gen. in Case 5/79 *Procureur Général v. Buys et al.* [1979] ECR 3203 at 3243, confirmed by the Court in Case 251/78 *Denkavit Futtermittel GmbH v. Finanzamt Warendorf* [1979] ECR 3369 at 3384. See, further, Cases 3, 4 and 6/76 *Kramer et al.* [1976] ECR 1279, [1976] 2 CMLR 440; Case 83/78 *Pigs Marketing Board v. Redmond* [1978] ECR 2347, [1979] 1 CMLR 177, and Case 29/82 *Van Luipen en Zn. BV* [1983] ECR 151. This integral part

particularly on that point that the CAP has great economic and also legal significance for the whole integration process. The CAP not only serves to establish the common market, it is of essential importance for the whole of Community policy, in particular relating to the strengthening of economic and social cohesion, environmental policy, commercial policy and development cooperation. The Court has recognized in very clear terms this connection between the CAP and negative and positive integration aspects.[12]

Objectives

The connection between market integration and policy integration explained above appears from the objectives of the CAP[13] set out in Article 39(1) and the general guidelines expressed in Article 39(2) EC. By their nature these objectives, both as to the short-term and the long-term, and constituting an integral whole, can only be achieved in a completely communitarized agricultural market. The Court has drawn the important conclusion from this that the concept of a CAP, which is nowhere in the Agriculture Title clearly described, has an objective and indivisible character.[14] Thus all measures which relate to the realization of free movement of agricultural products contribute by their nature to these objectives, and as such constitute a matter falling within the competence of the Community under Article 43 EC. This is particularly true for the harmonization of national legislation relating to veterinary, health and phytosanitary matters, zootechnical and plant improvement questions, and the complex mass of legislation involving the production, composition,

principle is confusingly sometimes referred to as the 'open market' principle, see in particular Case 94/79 *Vriend* [1980] ECR 327 at 339, although such an approach is also implicit in Case 190/73 *Officier van Justitie v. Van Haaster* [1974] ECR 1123 at 1134, and Case 111/76 *Officier van Justitie v. Van den Hazel* [1977] ECR 901 at 910.

12. Cases 80 and 81/77 *Société Les Commissionnaires Réunis Sàrl et al. v. Receveur des Douanes* [1978] ECR 927 at 944–947 and Case 4/79 *Société Coopérative 'Providence Agricole de la Champagne' v. Office National Interprofessionnel des Céréales (ONIC)* [1980] ECR 2823 at 2844–2848.

13. See generally, Barents, *The Agricultural Law of the EC* (Deventer, 1994); Cardwell, *Milk Quotas* (Oxford, 1996); Druesne, *La Politique Agricole Commune devant la Cour de Justice des CE* (Paris, 1980); Korte and van Rhijn in Von der Groeben *et al.*, *Kommentar zum EWG-Vertrag* (5th ed., Baden-Baden, 1991) Vol. I 913–1011; McMahon, *Agricultural Trade, Protectionism and the Problems of Development* (Leicester, 1992); Olmi, *La Politique Agricole Commune* (Brussels, 1992); Snyder, *Law of the Common Agricultural Policy* (London, 1985), and Usher: *Legal Aspects of Agriculture in the European Community* (Oxford, 1988); 52 *Halsbury's Laws of England* (4th ed., London, 1986) Part 13; Druesne, *Droit matériel et politiques de la Communauté européenne* (Paris, 1986) 271-341; Bronkhorst (1987) SEW 27-51; and Götz (1986) EuR 29. On agricultural structures see Priebe (1988) CDE 3.

14. See Barents, *op. cit., ibid.* 65–66.

presentation of and trade in straight and compound animal feedingstuffs, as well as for commercial policy.[15]

As has been indicated above, these objectives cover all aspects of agricultural policy. The objectives specified in Article 39(1)(a) and (b) primarily deal with structural policy; those in Article 39(1)(c)–(e) primarily concern market and price policy. The achievement of these objectives, which conflict with each other, requires, according to long-established case-law, that the Community legislator should possess a wide margin of discretion so that account may be taken of, as appropriate, the political, economic and budgetary situation, and priorities established.[16] This choice of priorities means that in order to maintain the common market, it may even be split up, in principle on a temporary basis, by Community measures, if complete free movement is no longer possible because of serious reasons. Against this background, the Community was entitled to apply the monetary compensatory amounts which were necessary when the system of fixed exchange rates became untenable at the beginning of the Seventies.[17] The precise relationship between short-term and long-term policies is not clearly expressed in these objectives. On the one hand it can be deduced from the introductory word 'thus' in Article 39(1)(b) EC that increasing the individual earnings of persons engaged in agriculture should principally be achieved by structural measures.[18] On the other hand, an improvement of individual earnings can also be given a normative meaning in the sense that such an increase must occur, which implies a more or less permanent short-term intervention policy. The relationship between both components of the agricultural policy is a matter for the Council's discretionary power.[19] Individual rights relating to income (with as a

---

15. The delimitation between Art. 43 EC on the one hand and Arts. 100 and 100a EC on the other is set out in Case 68/86 *United Kingdom v. Council* [1988] ECR 855 at 895–897 (hormones); Case 131/86 *United Kingdom v. Council* [1988] ECR 905 at 930–933 (battery hens); Case C–131/87 *Commission v. Council* [1989] ECR 3743 at 3767–3771 (animal glands and organs), and Case C–11/88 *Commission v. Council* [1989] ECR 3799 (summary publication only), resolving a long-running dispute between the Commission and the Council about the legal basis of harmonization measures in the agricultural sector.

16. *E.g.* Cases 63–69/72 *Wilhelm Werhahn Hansamühle et al. v. Council* [1973] ECR 1229 at 1248–1249; Cases 197/80 *etc. Ludwigshafener Walzmühle Erling KG et al. v. Council et al.* [1981] ECR 3211 at 3251; Case 59/83 *Biovilac SA NV v. Commission* [1984] ECR 4057 at 4077–4078, and Case C–224/94 *Commission v. Council* [1996] ECR I-881 at 925–926.

17. *E.g.* Case 5/73 *Balkan Import–Export GmbH v. Hauptzollamt Berlin-Packhof* [1973] ECR 1091 at 1112; Cases 80 and 81/77 *Société Les Commissionnaires Réunis Sàrl et al. v. Receveur des Douanes* [1978] ECR 927 at 946–947.

18. Cases 36 and 71/80 *Irish Creamery Milk Suppliers Association et al. v. Government of Ireland et al.* [1981] ECR 735 at 752, and Case 297/82 *De Samvirkende Danske Landboforeninger v. Ministry of Fiscal Affairs* [1983] ECR 3299 at 3319.

19. Case 114/76 *Bela-Mühle Josef Bergmann KG v. Grows-Farm GmbH & Co. KG* [1977] ECR 1211 at 1220–1221. The Court annulled the contested regulation finding that

consequence certain intervention prices) or economic freedom (with as a consequence the absence or limitation of a certain intervention policy) have never been accepted by the Court.[20] Thus Article 39 forms an obligation for the Community and the Member States to take various steps, but it does not confer direct rights on operators in the agricultural sector.[21] In any event, both limbs of Article 39 EC make it plain that the CAP, in legal terms as in other terms, cannot only consist of a market and price policy. The factual accuracy of this legal statement has been confirmed in the over 30-year history of the CAP. If an improvement in producer incomes still remains only a matter of short-term policy, the inevitable consequence is that the price level to be achieved on the market through intervention will be fixed at the level of the marginal undertaking, with the result that a major incentive is created for primarily industrialized agricultural producers to increase production. The disregard of the structural component of agricultural policy has contributed to the fact that about 80% of agricultural production is accounted for by approximately 20% of agricultural firms, whereas there has scarcely been any change in agricultural structures through the years.

Scope

As has been noted above, the EC Treaty is silent as to what is meant by a or the 'Common Agricultural Policy.' Article 38(2) and (3) EC give a description of what are agricultural products, by referring to the list of products contained in Annex II to the EC Treaty. In conjunction with the case-law, the text of both these parts of Article 38 EC makes it clear that whether or not a product is on that list is decisive.[22] This limitative list, which could only be extended during the first two years of the Community's existence,[23] did not prevent products being brought within

there was a discriminatory distribution of the burden of costs between the various agricultural sectors, and that the obligation involved was not necessary to attain the objective in view, *ibid.* at 1221. See also *e.g.* Case 179/84 *Bozzetti v. Invernizzi SpA et al.* [1985] ECR 2301 at 2322; Case 265/87 *Hermann Schräder HS Kraftfutter GmbH & Co. KG v. Hauptzollamt Gronau* [1989] ECR 2237 at 2270; Cases C-267–285/88 *Wuidart et al. v. Laitière coopérative eupenoise et al.* [1990] ECR I-435 at 481, and Case C-311/90 *Hierl v. Hauptzollamt Regensburg* [1992] ECR I-2061 at 2081.

20. *E.g.* Case 139/79 *Maizena GmbH v. Council* [1980] ECR 3393 at 3422–3423; Case 281/84 *Zuckerfabrik Bedburg AG et al. v. Council* [1987] ECR 49 at 91, and Case C-311/90 *Heirl v. Hauptzollamt Regensburg* [1992] ECR I-2061 at 2081.
21. *Ibid.*
22. Case 61/80 *Coöperatieve Stremsel- en Kleurselfabriek v. Commission* [1981] ECR 851 at 869–870, and Case 77/83 *Srl CILFIT et al. v. Ministero della Sanità* [1984] ECR 1257 at 1265–1266.
23. Case 185/73 *Hauptzollamt Bielefeld v. OHG in Firma H.C. König* [1974] ECR 607 at 616–617.

the scope of application of the Title on Agriculture which are not specified therein, but which are economically or functionally of essential importance to the products which are mentioned therein.[24] A practical consequence of this demarcation of the Title on Agriculture by means of a list of agricultural products is that the EC Treaty does not make clear what should be understood by the concepts of agricultural holding or producers of agricultural products, which can lead to problems in measures which are not linked to products but to groups of people.[25] According to the text of Article 38 EC and the list of fish, crustaceans and molluscs in Annex II, the provisions of the Title on Agriculture also apply to saltwater and freshwater fishery.

Means

Article 38(2) and (4) EC make it plain that the means to achieve the objectives and guidelines set out in Article 39 EC concern the free movement of agricultural products (the common market) and a policy specifically relating to the agricultural sector (the common policy). The significance and connection of both instruments has been clarified in the case-law of the Court in two respects. First, after the end of the transitional period the Member States may not maintain in force any measures which conflict with the free movement of goods provisions.[26] This means in practical terms that national market organizations have become well nigh impossible, a principle which applies also if the Community has not taken or been able to take common measures in a particular sector.[27] In relation to the Member States the common market

24. Originally Art. 235 EC was used, later always Art. 43 EC.
25. As to this problem, see Case 85/77 *Società Santa Anna Azienda Avicola v. Instituto Nazionale della Previdenza Sociale (INPS) et al.* [1978] ECR 527 at 540–541; Case 139/77 *Denkavit Futtermittel GmbH v. Finanzamt Warendorf* [1978] ECR 1317 at 1332–1333; Case 312/85 *SpA Villa Banfi v. Regione Toscana et al.* [1986] ECR 4039 at 4054–4055, and Case C-162/91 *Tenuta il Bosco Srl v. Ministero delle Finanze* [1992] ECR I-5279 at 5295–5296.
26. In relation to Arts. 30-34 EC this means, *inter alia*, that the Member States may not apply quantitative restrictions on imports or exports or measures having equivalent effect even in the absence of or to supplement a common organization of the market, see Case 48/74 *Charmasson v. The Minister for Economic Affairs and Finance* [1974] ECR 1383, [1975] 2 CMLR 208. This doctrine was applied also in relation to the new Member States, see Case 118/78 *C.J. Meijer BV v. Department of Trade* [1979] ECR 1387, [1979] 2 CMLR 398; Case 231/78 *Commission v. United Kingdom* [1979] ECR 1447, [1979] 2 CMLR 427; Case 232/78 *Commission v. France* [1979] ECR 2729, [1980] 1 CMLR 418; Cases 194 and 241/85 *Commission v. Greece* [1988] ECR 1037, and Case 119/86 *Spain v. Council et al.* [1987] ECR 4121.
27. See Case 232/78 *Commission v. France* [1979] ECR 2729 at 2738–2739 concerning the importation of mutton and lamb into France after the expiry of the transitional period following United Kingdom accession. In non-regulated sectors Art. 46 EC, which envi-

takes precedence over national market organizations.[28] In relation to the Community itself, however, the situation is different, and is actually to be regarded as the mirror-image of the prohibition of unilateral intervention measures by the Member States. Although the Community is indeed bound by the free movement of goods provisions except to the extent expressly or implicitly authorized in the Treaty,[29] it is entitled, should the Community interest so require, to adopt measures which in principle could involve a temporary division of the common market.[30] A particularly interesting example of this is the acceptance of the division in fact on national lines by production quotas or dual market organizations established per Member State.[31] An example of this latter approach can be seen in the old sheepmeat market organization, which, as far as the United Kingdom was concerned, was based on a system of premiums 'per ewe' and in the other Member States on a system of price intervention. This meant that mutton and lamb exported from the United Kingdom to the other Member States was subject to an export levy equal to the ewe premium received (the clawback system). In these and other cases the Court regarded such measures as permissible, as long as they were based on Community action directed at the maintenance as much as possible of the common market, or at its completion at a later stage.[32]

sages the possibility of countervailing measures, retains some significance, see Case 337/82 *St. Nikolaus Brennerei und Likörfabrik, Gustav Kniepf-Melde GmbH v. Hauptzollamt Krefeld* [1984] ECR 1051 at 1062-1063; Case 114/83 *Société d'Initiatives de Coopération Agricoles et al. v. Commission* [1984] ECR 2589 at 2602, and Case 181/85 *v. Commission* [1987] ECR 689 at 711–712.

28. But the exception of Art. 36 EC remains applicable, as long as the measures based thereupon have not been superseded by harmonization of laws. As to the application of this provision in the agricultural sector, see particularly Case 251/78 *Firma Denkavit Futtermittel GmbH v. Minister für Ernährung, Landwirtschaft und Forsten des Landes Nordrhein-Westfalen* [1979] ECR 3369, [1980] 3 CMLR 513; Case 40/82 *Commission v. United Kingdom* [1982] ECR 2793, [1982] 3 CMLR 497 and [1984] ECR 283; Case 261/85 *Commission v. United Kingdom* [1988] ECR 547, [1988] 2 CMLR 11, and Case 29/87 *Dansk Denkavit ApS v. Danish Ministry of Agriculture* [1988] ECR 2965.

29. Cases 80 and 81/77 *Société Les Commissionnaires Réunis Sàrl et al. v. Receveur des Douanes* [1978] ECR 927 at 945–947; Case 218/82 *Commission v. Council* [1983] ECR 4063 at 4075; Case 37/83 *Rewe-Zentral AG v. Direktor der Landwirtschaftskammer Rheinland* [1984] ECR 1229 at 1248–1249, and Case 15/83 *Denkavit Nederland BV v. Hoofdproduktschap voor Akkerbouwprodukten* [1984] ECR 2171 at 2184. See also Case 199/84 *Procuratore della Repubblica v. Migliorini et al.* [1985] ECR 3317 at 3330–3331.

30. E.g. the acceptance of monetary compensatory amounts in *e.g.* Case 9/73 *Schlüter v. Hauptzollamt Lörrach* [1973] ECR 1135 at 1152, 1158 and 1159; they were deemed less damaging to Community interests than the diversion of trade caused by monetary interests.

31. E.g. Case 138/79 *SA Roquette Frères v. Council* [1980] ECR 3333 at 3358–3360, and Case 139/79 *Maizena GmbH v. Council* [1980] ECR 3393 at 3421–3423.

32. Case 106/81 *Julius Kind KG v. European Economic Community* [1982] ECR 2885 at 2921–2922; Case 61/86 *United Kingdom v. Commission* [1988] ECR 431 at 462–463,

Regulation of the market

Article 40(2) EC makes it plain that the core of the CAP is the common regulation of the agricultural markets, and that this may take three forms: either common rules on competition, or compulsory coordination of the various national market organizations, or a European market organization. From this summary it appears that the concept of a European market organization means nothing other than that the Community legislator should prescribe which of these models of regulation should be chosen in order to achieve the objectives specified in Article 39 EC.[33] The legal difference between the agricultural sector and other sectors of the economy is such that the choice of model for the coordination of supply and demand in the former requires an express decision by the Community.[34] As has been noted, the model to be chosen may range from the relatively liberal model of competition rules (dealing with cooperatives, quality rules for agricultural products, and external protection through the Common Customs Tariff) to a more interventionist model in the form of a real sectoral or other type of market regulation for the Community market as a whole.[35]

From the illustrative summary[36] of measures in the first and third sentences of Article 40(3) EC, it appears that the framers of the Treaty had a preference for price intervention policy, based on guarantees for the producer, and external protection, which is also indicated by the reference to guarantee funds in Article 40(4) EC. The decisive criterion for the measures to be applied is the necessity for them in the light of Article 39 EC,[37] which is also apparent from the wording of Articles 41 and 42 EC,

and (by reference to the latter judgment) Case 162/86 *Livestock Sales Transport Ltd. et al. v. Intervention Board for Agricultural Produce* [1988] ECR 489 at 523.

33. See Cases 6/71 *Rheinmühlen Düsseldorf v. Einfuhr- und Vorratsstelle für Getreide und Futtermittel* [1971] ECR 823 at 838; Case 153/73 *Holtz & Willemsen GmbH v. Council et al.* [1974] ECR 675 at 695, and Case 8/78 *Milac GmbH, Groß- und Aussenhandel v. Hauptzollamt Freiburg* [1978] ECR 1721 at 1732–1733.
34. Case 51/74 *P.J. Van der Hulst's Zonen v. Produktschap voor Siergewassen* [1975] ECR 79 at 93.
35. The terms 'a common organization of agricultural markets' and a 'European market organization' used in Art. 40(2) are in fact two distinct concepts, as is clear from the German version of the EC Treaty (*eine gemeinsame Organization der Agrarmärkte* and *eine Europäische Marktordnung*). Thus the former covers all three models specified in that provision, whereas the latter is a Community-wide common organization, see Cases 90 and 91/63 *Commission v. Luxembourg and Belgium* [1964] ECR 625 at 633–634; Case 48/74 *Charmasson v. Minister for Economic Affairs and Finance (Paris)* [1974] ECR 1383 at 1394–1395, and Cases 194 and 241/85 *Commission v. Greece* [1988] ECR 1037 at 1060–1061. The English and French versions of Art. 40(2) EC make this somewhat less clear, and are sometimes invoked to support the argument that 'a common organization' has to be 'a European market organization.'
36. Case C-240/90 *Germany v. Commission* [1992] ECR I-5383 at 5249.
37. *Ibid.*

relating respectively to a number of areas relating to the structure of agriculture and to competition. The powers conferred on the Community have always been broadly interpreted, so that although they are not enumerated in Article 40(3), many types of measures have been accepted which as a rule restrict economic freedom much more than the types of measures which are enumerated therein, such as production restrictions,[38] production prohibitions,[39] purchase and delivery obligations,[40] various types of import and production levies (such as the well-known co-responsibility levies and the super levies)[41] and various types of deposit obligations[42]. It should be observed that so far the Court has not condemned any category of intervention measures to be as such incompatible with the provisions of the EC Treaty or with general principles of law.

The market-regulatory action by the Community may have the objective of conserving certain natural resources, as is the case with catch quotas for sea fishing.[43] The term 'all measures' in Article 40(3) EC does not merely refer to the substantive provisions of the CAP, but also to their implementation (control and enforcement).[44] Depending on what is necessary in a concrete case, the Community may leave the implementation of its legislation in the hands of the Member States (which may be done on

38. Case 230/79 *SpA Eridania–Zuccherifici nazionali et al. v. Ministry of Agriculture and Forestry et al.* [1979] ECR 2749 at 2769–2771; Case 139/79 *Maizena GmbH v. Council* [1980] ECR 3393 at 3421–3422, and Case 84/87 *Erpelding v. Secrétaire d'État à l'Agriculture et à la Viticulture* [1988] ECR 2647 at 2673.

39. In order to reduce surpluses, Case C-331/88 *R. v. The Minister for Agriculture, Fisheries and Food et al., ex parte Fedesa et al.* [1990] ECR I-4023 at 4063 and 4065–66.

40. Case 114/76 *Bela-Mühle Josef Bergmann KG v. Grows-Farm GmbH & Co. KG* [1977] ECR 1211 at 1221 and Case 116/76 *Granaria BV v. Hoofdproduktschap voor Akkerbouwprodukten* [1977] ECR 1247 at 1265 (the compulsory purchase obligation was not the problem, but the obligation to purchase at a disproportionately high price was).

41. The basic criterion for levies is to be found in Case 17/67 *Firma Max Neumann v. Hauptzollamt Hof/Saale* [1967] ECR 441 at 452–453, which indicates that Art. 43 EC permits the imposition of financial burdens which pursue a market-regulatory objective. See also Case 108/81 *Amylum v. Council* [1982] ECR 3107 at 3136–3137 (production levies); Case 179/84 *Bozzetti v. Invernizzi SpA et al.* [1985] ECR 2301 at 2322–2323 (co-responsibility levies on milk producers); Case 265/87 *Hermann Schräder HS Kraftfutter GmbH & Co. KG v. Hauptzollamt Gronau* [1989] ECR 2237 at 2268–2271 (co-responsibility levy on cereals producers), and Case C-8/89 *Zardi v. Consorzio agrario provinciale di Ferrara* [1990] ECR I-2515 at 2532–2533 (additional co-responsibility for cereals, super levy). As examples of some of the problems surrounding additional levies on milk, see Case C-463/93 *Katholische Kirchengemeinde St. Martinus Elten v. Landwirtschaftskammer Rheinland* [1997] ECR I-255 and Case C-22/94 *The Irish Farmers Association et al. v. Minister for Agriculture, Food and Forestry, Ireland et al.* [1997] ECR I-1809.

42. Case 11/70 *Internationale Handelsgesellschaft mbH v. Einfuhr- und Vorratsstelle für Getreide und Futtermittel* [1970] ECR 1125 at 1135–1137.

43. Cases 3, 4 and 6/76 *Kramer et al.* [1976] ECR 1279 at 1309.

44. As to sanctions, see Case C-240/90 *Germany v. Commission* [1992] ECR I-5383.

the basis of specific instructions to take certain steps), or it may deal with implementing measures itself.

The regulation of the various markets is limited by the two standards of legality set out in the second sentence of Article 40(3) EC: proportionality and non-discrimination. The proportionality principle[45] restricts intervention in the market mechanism to that which is necessary in the light of the objectives of the CAP, with the evaluation of the necessity of measures being a matter for the Council's margin of discretion.[46] The non-discrimination principle refers, although the wording appears to suggest otherwise, to equal treatment of dissimilar cases, or unequal treatment of similar cases among producers, or among consumers (but not as between producers and consumers).[47] Both criteria have evolved in the Court's case-law as concrete expressions of the general legal principles of proportionality and equality.[48]

Competition

Article 42 EC is closely linked to Article 40 EC, which latter provision governs the extent to which the Community may affect competition in the common market through its regulatory action in order to achieve the objectives of Article 39 EC. In the case-law it has been expressly recognized that the CAP takes priority over the system of undistorted competition prescribed by Article 3(g) EC[49] and that such competition is only one of the interests which the Community may take into account in the framework of its discretionary powers.[50] Article 42 EC governs the interference with competition in the common market for agricultural products by undertakings (primarily cooperatives) and by the Member States (through state aids). Depending on the which of the three models is chosen for the CAP,[51] such private or national measures restricting competition may play a useful role, subject of course to this taking place on the basis of a Community law framework. Thus Article 42 EC permits

45. As to which, see, generally, Emiliou, *The Principle of Proportionality in European Law* (London, 1996).
46. *E.g.* Case C-306/93 *SMW Winzersekt GmbH v. Land Rheinland-Pfalz* [1994] ECR I-5555 at 5581.
47. Case 5/73 *Balkan-Import–Export GmbH v. Hauptzollamt Berlin–Packhof* [1973] ECR 1091 at 1113. The general proposition of the meaning of non-discrimination is well-formulated in Case C-217/91 *Spain v. Commission* [1993] ECR I-3923 at 3953 and in Case C-306/93 *SMW Winzersekt GmbH v. Land Rheinland–Pfalz* [1994] ECR I-5555 at 5583–5584.
48. See Bourgeois (1978) SEW 101.
49. Cases 41–44/70 *NV International Fruit Company et al. v. Commission* [1971] ECR 411 at 427, and Case 139/79 *Maizena GmbH v. Council* [1980] ECR 3393 at 3421–3422.
50. Case 68/86 *United Kingdom v. Council* [1988] ECR 855 at 896.
51. Art. 40(2) EC.

the establishment of a distinct competition regime for the agricultural sector.

As long as the Council has not decided on the matter, the application of the competition rules of the Treaty (Articles 85–94 EC) is suspended.[52] The decision concerned may involve applying those rules, or not, in whole or in part, conditionally or unconditionally, to certain sectors and activities. In Regulation 26/62[53] the Council used this power to permit, as far as the competition rules are for undertakings are concerned, three, somewhat unclear, exceptions to the prohibitions contained in Article 85(1) EC; the principal practical importance of these is for agricultural cooperatives.[54] As far as the rules on state aids are concerned, Article 4 of Regulation 26/62 declares the provisions of Article 93(1) EC and of the first sentence of Article 93(3) EC applicable to aids granted for the production of or trade in Annex II products.[55] The non-applicability of the other provisions of Articles 92–94 EC in Regulation 26/62 is in fact of scant practical importance, given that in various schemes of common organization of the market those provisions are specifically declared applicable.[56] The market organizations are thus also based on Article 42 EC as well as on Article 43 EC. The practical effect of the measures on the applicability of Articles 92–94 EC is that those provisions are inapplicable only in relation to sectors not covered by a scheme of common organization of the market. Article 46 EC makes it possible for a Member State to apply countervailing charges (at the level fixed by the Commission) on and, if authorized by the Commission, to adopt other measures to redress the competitive imbalance resulting from national aid measures for particular products.[57]

52. Case 337/82 *St. Nikolaus Brennerei und Likörfabrik, Gustav Kniepf–Melde GmbH v. Hauptzollamt Krefeld* [1984] ECR 1051 at 1062–1063.
53. O.J. English Special Edition 1959–62, p. 129.
54. See Case 71/74 *Nederlandse Vereniging voor Fruit en Groentenimporthandel et al. v. Commission et al.* [1975] ECR 563, [1975] 2 CMLR 123; Case 61/80 *Coöperatieve Stremsel- en Kleurselfabriek v. Commission* [1981] ECR 851, [1982] 1 CMLR 240; Case T-61/89 *Dansk Pelsdyravlerforening v. Commission* [1992] ECR II-1931; Case C-250/92 *Gttrup-Klim Grovvareforening et al. v. Dansk Landbrugs Grovvareselskab AmbA (DLG)* [1994] ECR I-5641, [1996] 4 CMLR 191; Cases C-319/93 *etc. Dijkstra et al. v. Friesland (Frico Domo) Coöperatie BA et al.* [1995] ECR I-4471, and Case 399/93 *Oude Luttikhuis et al. v. Verenigde Coöperatieve Melkindustrie Coberco BA* [1995] ECR I-4515. Of these, the last two are the most important, see Ackermann (1997) 34 CMLRev. 695 and Slot (1997) SEW 204.
55. As to state aids for advertising agricultural products, see the Commission's Guidelines O.J. 1986 C 272/4.
56. But even these clauses contain exceptions, as in the case of sugar and milk, see Case 105/76 *Interzuccheri SpA v. Ditta Rezzano e Cavassa* [1977] ECR 1029 at 1040 and Case 73/79 *Commission v. Italy* [1980] ECR 1533 at 1548.
57. The countervailing charge is applied to imports of the products concerned, unless the exporting Member State itself applies a countervailing charge on export. See note 27, *supra*. The Council is entitled, if Arts. 92–94 EC are applicable, on the basis of the

Article 42 EC applies only to the coordination of national aid measures by the application of Articles 92–94 EC.[58] National aid measures can be the subject of far-reaching coordination on the basis of Article 43 EC, for example by obliging or permitting the Member States to apply certain types of aid measures. Thus both on the basis of Article 42 and on the basis of Article 43 the Community has wide powers to coordinate national aid measures, a power which is of great importance, primarily for structural policy.

Allocation of powers

The real legal basis for the CAP is to be found in the very widely drafted Article 43(2) EC. This provision also applies to the conclusion of international agreements, a power which the Community used extensively in relation to agreements with third countries concerning reciprocal access to fishing grounds.[59] A constant line of case-law demonstrates that Article 43 EC confers wide discretionary powers on the basis of which the Community legislator may take all measures which it regards as appropriate and necessary for the priorities established in the light of the objectives set out in Article 39 EC.[60] Initially the consultation procedure provided for in Article 43 EC was the most demanding decision-making procedure contained in the Treaty, but at the present it is the most supple. Although Article 43 provides for qualified majority voting,[61] it is in this sector that the Luxembourg Accords of 1966[62] is of great importance. The Council still tends to take the most important decisions on the basis of unanimity, as is illustrated by the annual marathon sessions for the fixing of the common prices and other aspects of market and price policy. Only in exceptional cases has the Council decided on

---

third sentence of Art. 93(2) EC to declare in exceptional circumstances certain national aid measures compatible with the common market, see Case C-122/94 *Commission v. Council* [1996] ECR I-881 at 924.

58. Art. 42 EC clearly does not apply to Community aid measures, as they (and national measures allocating them) do not fall within Arts. 92–94 EC, see Cases 213–215/81 *Norddeutsches Vieh- und Fleischkantor Herbert Will et al. v. Bundesanstalt für landwirtschaftliche Marktordnung* [1982] ECR 3583 at 3602.

59. See Cases 3, 4 and 6/76 *Kramer et al.* [1976] ECR 1279, [1976] 2 CMLR 440.

60. *E.g.* Case 138/78 *Stölting v. Hauptzollamt Hamburg–Jonas* [1979] ECR 713 at 722; Case 166/78 *Italy v. Council* [1979] ECR 2575 at 2599; Cases 197/80 *etc. Ludwigshafener Walzmühle Erling KG et al. v. Council et al.* [1981] ECR 3211 at 3251 (see also the opinion of VerLoren van Themaat, Adv. Gen., *ibid.* at 3265–3267); Case C-306/93 *SMW Winzersekt GmbH v. Land Rheinland–Pfalz* [1994] ECR I-5555 at 5581, and Case C-122/94 *Commission v. Council* [1996] ECR I-881 at 924.

61. *I.e.* voting according to the weighting in Art. 148(2) EC, as most recently amended to take account of Austrian, Finnish and Swedish accession.

62. See Chapter V, section 3.2, *ante*.

such matters by qualified majority. The use of the 'right' of veto has meant that on a number of occasions the Council has been unable to reach decisions, so that it has been impossible to fix prices for the forthcoming agricultural year. In part on the basis of the case-law on the failure by the Council to fulfil its obligations in the fisheries sector,[63] the Commission has developed the practice of adopting itself the necessary measures, on the basis of Articles 5 and 155 EC,[64] to ensure the homogeneity and continuity of the CAP.[65]

As to the allocation of powers in the agricultural sector between the Community and the Member States, it appears from Article 40(2)(b) EC that the CAP does not as such mean that the Member States are *a priori* incompetent still to take measures in this sector.[66] Even the mere existence of common organizations of the market concerned will not make the Member States incompetent. But the model of organization chosen by the Community may well mean that the Member States may be unable to adopt any unilateral measures at all, or will be able to adopt only very few such measures.[67] Thus standing case-law indicates that the common organizations of the market mean that at the production and wholesale stages the Member States have scarcely any room for manoeuvre left in relation to the volume of production and prices, whereas the possibility to apply national aid measures concerning incomes, production or trading is expressly or impliedly excluded by the schemes of market organization.[68]

Implementation

As to the implementation of the CAP by the Community, standing case-law makes it plain that the Council is bound to prescribe the general rules of the measures concerned according to the procedure prescribed in Article 43(2) EC.[69] In cases in which the Council reserves to itself the right to adopt implementing powers, they can be adopted according to a simplified procedure, without consultation of the European

---

63. Case 804/79 *Commission v. United Kingdom* [1981] ECR 1045 at 1074.
64. Cases 47 and 48/83 *Pluimveeslachterij Midden-Nederland et al.* [1984] ECR 1721 at 1739
65. See Barents, *op. cit.* (see note 13, *supra*) 102–103.
66. Cases 141–143/81 *Holdijk et al.* [1982] ECR 1299 at 1314, and Case 237/82 *Jongeneel Kaas BV et al. v. State of the Netherlands et al.* [1984] ECR 483 at 502.
67. See *e.g.* Case 68/76 *Commission v. France* [1977] ECR 515 at 530–531 and Case 216/86 *Antonini v. Prefetto di Milano* [1987] ECR 2919 at 2931–2933 (citing earlier case-law).
68. *E.g.* Case 218/85 *Association comité économique agricole régional fruits et légumes de Bretagne v. Le Campion* [1986] ECR 3513 at 3532–3535 (citing earlier case-law).
69. Case 25/70 *Einfuhr- und Vorratsstelle für Getreide und Futtermittel v. Köster, Berodt & Co.* [1970] ECR 1161 at 1170, and Case 121/83 *Zuckerfabrik Franken GmbH v. Hauptzollamt Würzburg* [1984] ECR 1039 at 2057–2058.

Parliament.[70] More detailed implementation is left to the Commission, which may or may not have to act through a committee procedure.[71] On the basis of their general obligation to implement Community law, under Article 5 EC, the Member States are obliged to adopt all necessary measures to guarantee the application and effectiveness of Community law in general and of the acts concerned in particular.[72] This means for instance that they must specify which body is charged with the implementation and application. Initially it was usual for the regulation to use only general terms to oblige the Member States to take such measures. Gradually the Community legislation has come to contain more specific obligations concerning national implementation, particularly in relation to controls (especially financial irregularities and fraud), procedures, organizational matters and penalties.

2.3 Market and price policy

Common organizations of the market

The expression market and price policy covers the short-term regulation of agricultural markets, involving measures which may last as little as 1 day (such as certain import levies) or as long as 1 year (such as the common prices). Even after various reforms, this policy is still primarily a matter of price intervention in the context of European market organizations,[73] which aim to raise the price of the products concerned to a certain level (common prices) through the application of myriad levies and subsidies at virtually all stages between production and consumption. This Community-financed price intervention is based on the model of buffer stocks, so that the price fluctuations resulting from the seasonal cycles are reined in by buying up and storing temporary surpluses, which can then be released back into the market in periods of less supply (intervention purchasing). Price stability is maintained by the neutralization of the effects of price fluctuations in the generally lower world markets, traditionally through a system of variable import levies (Community preference), while exports from the Community are facilitated by the application of export refunds.[74]

70. 'According to the voting procedure of Art. 43(2) EC' is the way this is usually expressed, see Art. 145 EC, 3rd indent, 2nd and 3rd sentences.
71. As to comitology, see Chapter V, section 3.1, *ante*.
72. See Case 68/88 *Commission v. Greece* [1989] ECR 2965 at 2984–2985.
73. Art. 40(2)(c) EC.
74. In the rare event of world market prices being higher than Community prices, export levies may be imposed. This possibility was first used on a large scale in 1973. Variable levies are being or have been replaced by fixed levies as a result of the Uruguay Round.

The original model for market and price policy was thus based on a trio of principles: common prices; Community financing (via EAGGF)[75] and Community preference.[76] As a result of this sectoral approach based on price intervention, the structure of the common organizations of the market was initially very uniform. Each of these organizations is based on a basic Council regulation, adopted according to Article 43(2) EC, which forms the framework for implementing Council and Commission regulations in which the various mechanisms are worked out in more detail. The application of these rules is largely a matter for the Member States through the bodies which they designate for the purpose, such as the United Kingdom Intervention Board for Agricultural Produce, the Dutch *Voedsel In- en Verkoopbureau*, and the German *Bundesanstalt für landwirtschaftliche Marktordnung*, all of which have specific relationships with their respective Ministries for Agriculture. Presently there are 22 basic regulations,[77] which are further developed in some 350 Council regulations and some 900

75. The European Agriculture Guidance and Guarantee Fund, better known by its French acronym, *FEOGA*, is governed by Reg. 729/70 (O.J. English Special Edition 1970 (I), p. 218) and most recently amended by Reg. 1287/95 (O.J. 1995 L 125/1). See the Commission's proposals, COM (97) 607 Final and COM (98) 158 Final (O.J. 1998 C 170/85). As the name implies, it has two sections, the Guarantee section and the Guidance section. The former finances export refunds and interventions within the common market for products falling under a common organization of the market. The Guidance section is intended for aids towards improvement of agricultural structure.

76. The principle of Community preference has also given rise to case-law before the Court, see *e.g.* Case 55/75 *Balkan-Import–Export GmbH v. Hauptzollamt Berlin–Packhof* [1976] ECR 19 and Case 58/86 *Coopérative agricole d'approvisionnement des Avirons v. Receveur des Douanes de Saint Denis et al.* [1987] ECR 1525, [1988] 2 CMLR 30.

77. See **Regs. 136/66** (O.J. English Special Edition 1965–66, p. 221, most recently amended by Reg. 1581/96 (O.J. 1996 L 206/11)) on *Oils and fats;* **234/68** (O.J. English Special Edition 1968 (I), p. 26 (most recently amended by Reg. 3290/94 (O.J. 1994 L 349/105)) on *Live trees and other plants, bulbs, roots and the like, cut flowers and ornamental foliage;* **804/68** (O.J. English Special Edition 1968 (I), p. 176, most recently amended by Reg. 1587/96 (O.J. 1996 L 206/21)) on *Milk and milk products*; **805/68** (O.J. English Special Edition 1968 (I), p. 187, most recently amended by Reg. 2364/97 (O.J. 1997 L 356/13)) on *Beef and veal*; **1308/70** (O.J. English Special Edition 1970 (II), p. 411, most recently amended by Reg. 3290/94, *supra*) on *Flax and hemp*; **1696/71** (O.J. English Special Edition 1971 (II), p. 634, most recently amended by Reg. 1554/97 (O.J. 1997 L 208/1, corrig. O.J. 1997 L 230/19)) on *Hops*; **2358/71** (O.J. English Special Edition 1971 (III), p. 894, most recently amended by Reg. 192/98 (O.J. 1998 L 20/16)) on *Seeds*; **2759/75** (O.J. 1975 L 282/1, most recently amended by Reg. 3290/94, *supra*) on *Pigmeat*; **2771/75** (O.J. 1975 L 282/49, most recently amended by Reg. 1516/96 (O.J. 1996 L 189/1)) on *Eggs*; **2777/75** (O.J. 1975 L 282/77, most recently amended by Reg. 2916/95 (O.J. 1995 L 305/49)) on *Poultrymeat*; **1785/81** (O.J. 1981 L 177/4, most recently amended by Reg. 1148/98 (O.J. 1998 L 159/38)) on *Sugar*; **822/87** (O.J. 1987 L 84/1, most recently amended by Reg. 2087/97 (O.J. 1997 L 292/1)) on *Wine*; **3013/89** (O.J. 1989 L 289/1, most recently amended by Reg. 1589/96 (O.J. 1996 L 206/25)) on *Sheepmeat and goatmeat*; **3759/92** (O.J. 1992 L 388/1, most recently amended by Reg. 3318/94 (O.J. 1994 L 350/15)) on *Fish*; **1766/92** (O.J. 1992 L 181/21, most recently amended by Reg. 923/96 (O.J. 1996 L 126/37) on *Cereals*; **2075/92** (O.J. 1992 L 215/70,

Commission regulations. This whole structure is further put into operation through some 3500 Commission regulations annually, which are of limited duration, many of which fix the applicable levies and subsidies.

Common prices

Price intervention largely takes place by the establishment of common prices. For the most important products this Community price policy is based on the so-called three price model. This consists first of a *target price*, which reflects the level at which the Council considers the market price should be. In a certain sense the target price is an ideal, at which each producer is deemed to be able to obtain a sufficient income.[78] The *intervention price* is fixed at a certain level below the target price, at the level at which the national intervention body will or may buy products in order to support the market price. Given that for the most important products intervention buying was not limited as to quantities or in time, the intervention price in fact formed the guaranteed minimum price the producer would receive. Finally, a *threshold price* is fixed at such a level that imported products cannot be sold for less than the target price. The difference between the world market price and the threshold price is covered by a variable import levy. Variable levies are being transformed into fixed levies as a result of the Uruguay Round.

The three price model is the basis for all the market organizations which are based on price intervention, although because of the nature of the

most recently amended by Reg. 2595/97 (O.J. 1997 L 351/11) on *Raw tobacco*; **404/93** (O.J. 1993 L 47/1, most recently amended by Reg. 3290/94, *supra*) on *Bananas*; **603/95** (O.J. 1995 L 63/1, most recently amended by Reg. 1347/95 (O.J. 1995 L 131/1)) on *Dried fodder*; **3072/95** (O.J. 1995 L 329/18, amended by Reg. 192/98, *supra*) on *Rice*; **2200/96** (O.J. 1996 L 297/1) on *Fruit and Vegetables*; and **2201/96** (O.J. 1996 L 297/29, amended by Reg. 2199/97 (O.J. 1997 L 303/1)) on *Products processed from fruit and vegetables*. See also Reg. **827/68** (O.J. English Special Edition 1968 (I), p. 209, most recently amended by Reg. 195/96 (O.J. 1996 L 26/13) on *Certain products listed in Annex II to the EC Treaty*. See further the special measures in Regs. **845/72** (O.J. 1972 English Special Edition 1972 (II), p. 347, most recently amended by Reg. 2059/92 (O.J. 1992 L 215/19)) concerning *Silkworms*; a number of special measures for other sectors were abolished by Reg. 3290/94, *supra* (in the context of the results of the Uruguay Round) or 2800/95 (O.J. 1995 L 291/1) which amended the aid regime for certain producers established by Reg. 1765/92 (O.J. 1992 L 181/12, most recently amended by Reg. 2309/97 (O.J. 1997 L 321/3)). There are special 'trading arrangements' for certain goods obtained by processing of agricultural products (Reg. 3448/93 (O.J. 1993 L 318/18, amended by Reg. 1097/98 (O.J. 1998 L 157/1)), for albumens (Reg. 2783/75 (O.J. 1975 L 282/104, most recently amended by Reg. 2916/95 (O.J. 1995 L 305/49)), and a special scheme of aid for cotton is established by Reg. 1554/95 (O.J. 1995 L 148/48, amended by Reg. 1584/96 (O.J. 1996 L 206/16)).

78. See Case 60/75 *Russo v. Azienda di Stato per gli Interventi sul Mercato Agricolo (AIMA)* [1976] ECR 45 at 55–56.

products and the market conditions all sorts of differences are possible, which are also reflected in the different names attached to these prices in the various systems of common organization. These prices are not normative prices imposed on the Member States and economic operators, but they are prices at which certain mechanisms become operational or may become so (intervention buying, aid for private storage, import levies) in order to reach the level of the target price.[79] These prices are fixed annually by the Council, according to the procedure laid down in Article 43(2) EC.[80] The uniformity (common criteria and uniform methods of calculation) required by Article 40(3) EC is guaranteed by six standards: thus the prices are fixed for a certain standard product; for a certain product unit; for a certain time period; for a certain stage of trade; for the whole Community, and expressed in a common unit of account, since 1979 the ECU.

The level of the common prices, which indeed determines the intensity of the intervention in the market, is a matter for the discretion of the Council.[81] This is the reason that the prices are often referred to as political or institutional prices; they prescribe the level at which market prices should be. There is also another category of common prices which indicates how the real situation in the market is, for example the price level in the internal market for a certain type of wine, or the price level of imports of a certain type of cereal. These prices are very frequently calculated and established by the Commission (varying from a daily fixing to a quarterly fixing), and the difference between these market prices and the political prices determines whether for example an import levy must be charged, and, if so, how much. In total there are more than 100 common price concepts.

Regulation of the Internal Market

Initially intervention buying, unlimited in amount or in time, by the intervention bodies designated by the Member States, was the most important guarantee for producers.[82] This buying was of greatest importance in the two most important sectors of Community agriculture: cereals and dairy products. Given that in economic terms cereal feedstuffs are the most important component for pigmeat, poultry and eggs, the effect of price intervention in the cereals sector is felt in these sectors as

---

79. Case 49/79 *Pool v. Council* [1980] ECR 569 at 581.
80. Baudin has for many years written an extensive commentary in the *Revue du Marché Commun* on the annual price package.
81. Cases 197/80 *etc. Ludwigshafener Walzmühle Erling KG et al. v. Council et al.* [1980] ECR 3211 at 3251–3253.
82. Case 49/71 *Hagen OHG v. Einfuhr- und Vorratsstelle für Getreide und Futtermittel* [1972] ECR 23 at 36.

well. In the dairy sector intervention buying takes place for butter and milk powder, and such buying is also provided for in relation to sugar, beef and veal, and oils and fats. Intervention buying is limited to products harvested within the Community, although exceptions are made to permit intervention buying (of products exported to the Community) in accordance with obligations undertaken by the Community under the Lomé Convention[83] and under the annual agreement relating to cane sugar reached with India.[84] Although initially intended to smooth out primarily cyclical production patterns, public storage quickly expanded into an artificial distribution channel, so that sometimes more than 10% of annual production came into the hands of the intervention bodies. The limited cold storage capacity for beef meant that this development resulted in limits being placed already since the mid-Seventies on the quantity of intervention buying for beef. Presently all intervention operations and aid amounts are subject to restrictions or certain maximum amounts. For other products a number of mechanisms have been developed over the years in order to keep them off the market, such as deliveries at low prices or free of charge for consumption or industrial processing purposes. Extensive case-law exists in relation to this type of subsidies.[85] In the fruit and vegetable sectors surpluses are taken off the market by producers' organizations which pay certain minimum prices to producers for such produce. In the wine sector the technique of compulsory or voluntary distillation of wine into alcohol has been developed in order to restrain chronic surpluses. In all cases of intervention buying, the purchase by the body concerned at the intervention price or a price deduced from it forms a subsidy to the producer or trader for removing the product concerned from the market and delivering it to the intervention body. There is also the grant of a subsidy in the numerous actions and mechanisms for keeping products off the market. As a result of the derailing of the intervention system, the costs of maintaining it rose in the mid-Eighties to more than 25% of the guarantee expenditure.

In addition to intervention buying, aid is also granted by private storage, in which the warehouse keeper stores the products for a certain period under conditions imposed by the Community. The most important difference from the public storage system is that in the case of private storage the ownership of and liability for the produce remains with the warehouse keeper (which for the Community usually means lower costs and avoids the risks of quality depreciation and resulting depreciations in value). In the wine sector this used to be the only means of intervention.

The instrument of production aid demonstrates great variety. In a number of cases this is meant to supplement common prices. Given that

83. The latest is the Fourth (O.J. 1991 L 229/3, amended, O.J. 1998 L 156/3).
84. For the 1996–97 marketing year, see Dec. 98/7 (O.J. 1998 L 7/27).
85. See Barents, *op. cit.* (see note 13, *supra*) Chapter 5.

too high prices for high-cost durum wheat would undermine its position in relation to other types of wheat, production aid is granted for durum wheat in addition to the minimum price guarantee. The same applies to olive oil in relation to other oils and fats. Production aid instead of common prices may be applied either because the products concerned are of secondary importance in the totality of the CAP, or because international agreements mean that the protection of import and similar levies which is required for common prices cannot be applied. Production aid may be granted per unit product or per hectare; in the latter case the production incentive is less great than in the former; while regional differentiation may also be used.

There are also countless forms of processing subsidies in order to avoid or transform surpluses. Production rebates are a special form of subsidy, applied to enable the processing industry to compete with imports which have been manufactured using lower priced raw materials. The market organization for fish, which is also based on price intervention and implementation through producers' organizations, is largely comparable with the administrative law methods applied in other market organizations.

The instruments mentioned above all have as their objective the direct or indirect support of the common prices. In addition to common prices, in a number of cases rules relating to the quality of production and sale are applied, as in the case of the very technical oenological rules in the wine sector, and the quality requirements for fruit and vegetables. Initially direct production restriction through quotas was an exception to the market and price policy which was limited to the sugar sector. The restriction on production in that sector was designed to combat a too far-reaching removal of the sugar industry from high cost countries to low cost countries.[86] Direct restrictions on production were introduced in the dairy products sector in 1984[87] and in the tobacco sector in 1992, in both cases in order to combat chronic overproduction. Although quotas by their very nature lead to a certain compartmentalization of the market, the Court has always accepted this form of market regulation and has rejected allegations that these measures infringe fundamental rights.[88] The application of the super levy in the dairy sector led to myriad judgments concerning the division of the quotas among producers, and the consequences of that division for the economic, legal, social and fiscal position of landlords and tenants of the land concerned.[89] Since 1983 a system of maximum allowable catches has applied in relation to catches of fish.

86. As an illustration, see Case 106/83 *Sermide SpA v. Cassa Conguaglio Zucchero et al.* [1984] ECR 4209 at 4231–4234.
87. See Cardwell, *op. cit.* (see note 13, *supra*) Chapter 1.
88. Although see Case 120/86 *Mulder v. Minister voor Landbouw en Visserij* [1988] ECR 2321, [1989] 2 CMLR 1, and Cases 104/89 and 37/90 *Mulder et al. v. Council et al.* [1992] ECR I-3061.
89. See *e.g.* Case 5/88 *Wachauf v. Germany* [1989] ECR 2609, [1991] 1 CMLR 328 con-

Monetary Compensatory Amounts

As has been explained above, a common price policy in the absence of a common currency requires a common unit of account in order to express the prices and amounts which have to be translated into national currency with the help of a rate of conversion. This presupposes of course a system of fixed exchange rates. If these rates change, the prices expressed in national currencies go up or down with the all the consequences for producer incomes and prices to consumers. If devaluations and revaluations remain exceptions, these consequences can be absorbed by a degressive system of aid to or taxation on producer incomes (through the VAT system for example). If this is not the case, or if exchange rates start to fluctuate, then the solution lies in the application of levies and subsidies at the border, as otherwise intra-Community trade as well as the Community's external trade in general, and the intervention system in particular will be completely disrupted.[90] After the IMF (Bretton Woods) system of fixed exchange rates ended in 1971, these Monetary Compensatory Amounts (MCAs) became a permanent feature of the CAP, lasting until 1993,[91] with the result that the common agricultural market for agricultural products in reality remained a legal fiction, there being during that period a considerable renationalization of agricultural policy.[92] Apart from the actual barriers which MCAs caused to the movement of goods, this extremely labyrinthine system also had distortive effects on competition, which were at odds with the concept of comparative cost

cerning the relationship between the effects of the super levy and certain fundamental rights. Other celebrated cases include Case C-177/90 *Kühn v. Landwirtschaftskammer Weser-Ems* [1992] ECR I-35, [1992] 2 CMLR 242; C-63/93 *Duff et al. v. Minister for Agriculture and Food, Ireland et al.* [1996] ECR I-569 at 607–608; Case C-22/94 *The Irish Farmers Association et al. v. Minister for Agriculture and Food, Ireland et al.* [1997] ECR I-1809, and Case C-15/95 *EARL de Kerlast v. Union régionale de coopératives agricoles (Unicopa), Coopérative de Trieux* [1997] ECR I-1961.

90. Case 2/75 *Einfuhr- und Vorratsstelle für Getreide und Futtermittel v. Firma C. Mackprang* [1975] ECR 607 at 616.

91. See Heine, *Die agrarmonetären Regelen des Gemeinschaftsrechts – eine systematische Darstellung* (Regensburg, 1988) for a detailed discussion of all the technical aspects of MCAs. See also Barents, *op. cit.* (see note 13, *supra*) Chapter 6.

92. Although the MCAs were abolished in 1993, the practice of green currencies (special exchange rates in the agricultural sector) was not abolished. By creating a green ECU for the agricultural sector the positive MCAs were able to be transformed into negative MCAs and then dismantled over the latter years of the system. If exchange rate adjustments in the agricultural sector cannot be implemented immediately, provision is made for the possibility of applying degressive aid measures, see Reg. 3813/92 (O.J. 1992 L 387/1, most recently amended by Reg. 150/95 (O.J. 1995 L 22/1)). See also Reg. 724/97 (O.J. 1997 L 108/9). Nevertheless, in due course the green ECU will have to be replaced by the normal ECU in order to facilitate a complete integration of agriculture in the common market if the Member State concerned does not participate in the 3rd Stage of Economic and Monetary Union. See COM (98) 367 Final.

advantages which lies at the heart of the common market. The system of MCAs demonstrates that a far-reaching integration policy, as is found in the agricultural sector, is constantly exposed to the risk that when there are divergent economic and monetary developments the degree of integration already achieved has to be (at least partly) reversed. A CAP with real free movement of goods and without distortions of competition is really only safeguarded once Economic and Monetary Union is achieved.[93] In legal terms, MCAs (agri-monetary law) is interesting because they gave rise to extensive case-law , which apart from its relevance for the technical aspects of the system, is also important for general aspects of Community law, such as judicial control of the exercise of discretionary powers, the meaning of the principles of non-discrimination, proportionality and legal certainty, and the non-contractual liability of the Community.[94]

Regulation of external trade

The regulation of external trade in the context of common organizations of the market is largely based on a system of variable import levies and similar amounts which protect the Community's internal price level against lower-priced imports from third countries, although variable levies have been or are being replaced by fixed levies because of obligations resulting from the Uruguay Round. As such, import levies are an exception to the external protection afforded by the Common Customs Tariff. In a number of instances these levies are not applied because of GATT/WTO obligations, so that internal production aid has to be used in order still to afford an income guarantee to producers. The importance of import levies as one of the Community's own resources has dramatically decreased over the years. The importance of export refunds on the other hand has significantly increased. These subsidies are intended to facilitate exports to third countries at the world market price level, which in many cases is much lower than the price level within the Community. As a result of production surpluses this form of subsidy as developed over the years in a number of sectors (particularly cereals and beef) into a pure form of export subsidy and a commercial policy weapon, the use of which has already on many occasions lead to conflicts with a number of the Community's trading partners. Export refunds have been the most important type of subsidy in the market and price policy, a fact which has been reflected in extensive

93. As the Court already observed in Case 9/73 *Schlüter v. Hauptzollamt Lörrach* [1973] ECR 1135 at 1161.
94. See Barents (1983) SEW 239, who discusses this case-law, most of which is con-centrated in the period 1973–1979.

case-law on these amounts, in particular as concerns export refund nomenclature.[95]

The application of these levies and subsidies demands a close control of the stream of imports and exports, which takes place through a system of import and export certificates. The case-law on this system is of interest because of the so-called 'objective' nature of these mechanisms, in which the good faith or absence of guilt of the trader is irrelevant in relation to the forfeiture of the deposits which have to be paid as security that the obligations to import or export flowing from these certificates will be fulfilled.[96] Abnormal developments in imports and exports can be countered by the use of safeguard clauses, which are provided for in all the basic regulations. These measures too are commercial policy instruments which can be used to persuade weaker trading partners to adopt 'voluntary' export restraints. The case-law on these clauses forms a good illustration of the limited judicial control on these powers which, by their nature, are of a discretionary character.[97]

Financing of the CAP

The financing of the CAP takes place through the European Agricultural Guidance and Guarantee Fund,[98] which was first set up in 1962 and split into its two component parts in 1964. This Fund forms part of the Community budget and is thus financed from the Community's own resources, of which import levies on agricultural products and other production levies form part.[99] The basic regulation on the financing of the

95. See, generally, Rüsken and Sameluck (1993) ZzöVerbs 226 and 262; see also Barents, *op. cit.* (see note 13, *supra*) 149–152 and the Court of Auditors' Special Report 2/90 on the management and control of export refunds (O.J. 1990 C 133/1).The importance of export refunds has further diminished as a result of the Uruguay Round agreements, as is explained under *Reform of the CAP, post.*
96. See *e.g.* Case 158/73 *Firma E. Kampffmeyer v. Einfuhr- und Vorratsstelle für Gerteide und Futtermittel* [1974] ECR 101; Case 186/73 *Norddeutsches Vieh- und Fleischkontor GmbH v. Einfuhr- und Vorratsstelle für Schlachtvieh, Fleisch und Fleischerzeugnisse* [1974] ECR 533; Cases 44–51/77 *GIE 'Union Malt' et al. v. Commission* [1978] ECR 57; Case 54/81 *Firma Wilhelm Fromme v. Bundesanstalt für Landwirtschaftliche Marktordnung* [1982] ECR 1449; Case 109/83 *Interagra SA v. Fonds d'Orientation et de Régularisation des Marchés Agricoles (FORMA)* [1983] ECR 127, and Case 109/86 *Ioannis Theodorakis Biomichania Elaiou AE v. Greek State* [1987] ECR 4319.
97. See especially Case 112/80 *Firma Anton Dürbeck v. Hauptzollamt Frankfurt-am-Main Flughafen* [1981] ECR 1095; Case 345/82 *Wünsche Handelsgesellschaft GmbH & Co. v. Germany* [1984] ECR 1995, and Cases T-480 and 483/93 *Antillean Rice Mills NV et al. v. Commission* [1995] ECR II-2305 (under appeal as Case C-390/95 P *Antillean Rice Mills NV et al. v. Commission* (O.J. 1996 C 46/6).
98. See note 75, *supra.*
99. The revenue generated by the co-responsibility levies and other levies accrues to the EAGGF, although the own resources decision (Dec. 94/728 (O.J. 1994 L 293/9), see

CAP[100] governs the organization of expenditure and the annual clearance of accounts, a procedure which has led to much case-law.[101] In 1988 guarantee expenditure was first tied to an annual ceiling fixed for the medium-term,[102] an approach which has been continued in 1993 for the period to 1999.[103]

Evolution

In the Seventies and Eighties Community agricultural production increased by several per cent annually. This was partially caused by factors such as the increasing industrialization of agriculture, mechanization, and seed and animal improvements. Furthermore, through the open-ended price and income guarantees a favourable climate was created for investment, particularly as prices were fixed at the level of the marginal undertakings. At the same time, demand for agricultural products increased only slightly, particularly because of the high level of food already achieved, stagnating population growth, more conscious dietary patterns and better yield in the preparation of food products. As a result of these developments, Community agriculture has been characterized by structural surpluses since the Seventies, which required ever-increasing expenditure on taking products off the market through intervention buying, disposal, or subsidized disposal, and exportation with the help of export refunds. Thus in the mid-Eighties guarantee expenditure accounted for more than two-thirds of the entire Community budget. These developments illustrate that the CAP came more and more into conflict with itself, through on the one hand creating all the conditions for a continual increase in production, and on the other hand developing more and more mechanisms to control this growth in production. This all brought about a veritable mass of in complex and untransparent legislation, the implementation of which encountered great difficulties in the Member States, and which meant that fraud and combatting it have become constant parts of Community policy on subsidies and levies.[104] The general and special reports of the Court of

Chapter V, section 2.1.3, *ante*) does not mention them. This artifice is achieved by regarding this revenue as negative expenditure!

100. Reg. 729/70 (see note 75, *supra*).
101. *E.g.* Case 55/83 *Italy v. Commission* [1985] ECR 683; Case 133/84 *United Kingdom v. Commission* [1986] ECR 1259; Case 337/85 *Ireland v. Commission* [1987] ECR 4237; Case 347/85 *United Kingdom v. Commission* [1988] ECR 1749; Case C-48/91 *The Netherlands v. Commission* [1993] ECR I-5611, and Case C-50/94 *Greece v. Commission* [1996] ECR I-3331.
102. Dec. 88/739 (O.J. 1988 L 185/29) on budgetary discipline.
103. Dec. 94/729 (O.J. 1994 L 293/14). The share of guarantee expenditure (then 50%) has to be reduced to 45% by 1999.
104. See, generally, Vervaele, *Fraud against the Community: The Need for European Fraud Legislation* (Deventer, 1992).

Auditors illustrate this phenomenon in many ways.[105] Similar implementation problems arise in relation to the enforcement of restrictions on production, particularly in the dairy and fish sectors.[106]

Reform of the CAP and Agenda 2000

Attempts to turn around the strong income policy orientation of the open-ended price intervention system date from as long ago as the mid-Seventies. Because of inter-governmental decision-making, the income policy aspects continued to enjoy a strong priority, which finally led to an about-turn which was largely brought about by the looming budgetary disaster through the continually increasing guarantee expenditure. The first concrete measure which sounded the end of open-ended price intervention in due course was the introduction of the co-responsibility levy in the milk sector in 1977. This production levy constituted a legal confirmation of the already existing situation: in a sector characterized by surpluses a target price was an illusion. The initial philosophy of co-responsibility was based on a contribution by the producer towards the costs of the intervention system above certain production quantities. At the beginning of the Eighties an attempt was made to form an indirect link between the fixing of the common prices and the medium-term development in prices, through guarantee thresholds for cereals and milk. Exceeding these thresholds would result in a reduction in the annual price increases. However, these efforts too foundered, so that the extremely large increase in milk production in 1984 could only be brought under control through the introduction of the super levy, which was a prohibitive levy on individual production in excess of certain reference quantities. As in the sugar sector, this system of restrictions on production, which was meant to be temporary in order to balance the market, has in fact become a permanent feature of the market organization. The threat of the actual insolvency of the Community as a result of the ever-increasing guarantee expenditure, resulted in the introduction of a system of maximum guaranteed quantities, agreed at the European Council in Brussels in February 1988.[107] This introduced an automatic link between the fixing of prices and excess production above the prescribed limits; in certain cases this led to a reduction in the common prices.[108] This system, known as stabilizers, was

---

105. Year in, year out, the Court of Auditors draws attention to serious shortcomings, both on the part of the Commission and on the part of the national authorities. The laconic nature of the Commission's replies to these observations is striking (the replies are published with the reports).
106. See Ritsema, (1987) *Agrarisch Recht* 227.
107. See Bull. EC 2–1988, point 1.1.1. (p. 13 *et seq.*).
108. Community coordination mechanisms were also introduced concerning national aid to early retirement, conversion and diversification of production, and set-aside measures.

introduced into all the important market organizations. Although this system initially formed a clear disincentive to over-production, in the course of 1991 the problem of surpluses again reared its ugly head. This lead to a second reform operation (the McSharry Plan) which was agreed in June 1992.[109] This led reform covering about 75% of Community production, which reduced prices in the arable and beef sectors to levels much closer to those of the world market; granted compensatory payments on a historical basis to Community farmers to offset the reduction in Community support prices; made payment of compensation in the case of cereals and other arable crops generally dependent on land being set aside, as well as linking them to the respect of historical regional base areas and historical field, and, finally, introduced accompanying measures concerning agri-environment, afforestation and early retirement.

These reforms have started to have a major impact, with public stocks of cereals falling from around 30 million tonnes at the end of 1993 to less than 3 million tonnes at the end of the 1995/1996 marketing year.[110] Set-aside played an important role in this, although climatic conditions (droughts) also played a part. Reforms in the rice sector were agreed in December 1995, and in the fruit and vegetable sector in July 1996;[111] reform of the olive oil sector has been proposed.[112] The structural problems in the beef sector as a result of the BSE crisis[113] have given rise to the need for a restoration of a balance between supply and demand in view of the effects of the crisis on consumer confidence. As a result of the requirements of the GATT Uruguay Round Agreement, reductions of some 20% in domestic support for agriculture over six years, 36% in spending on export subsidies, and 21% in the quantity of subsidized exports are required.

Three major groups of challenges now face Community agriculture: the need internally for improvement in the long-term environmental sustainability of agricultural production, with the integration of agricultural policy into a coherent rural area policy[114] and a simpler CAP management; the adaptation of Community agriculture to the increasingly competitive conditions resulting from the further liberalization of world trade, and,

109. As to the Plan, see Bull. EC Supp. 5/91; as to the package of measures, see Bull. EC 6–1992, points 1.3.140–1.3.147.
110. Although in 1997 it appeared likely that without further action cereals intervention stocks might reach some 58 million tonnes by 2005. The trade deficit in oilseeds was also perceived as remaining a substantial problem (Commission Press Release July 16, 1997 (IP (97) 660)).
111. Bull. EU 12–1995, point 1.3.154 and Bull. EU 7/8–1996, point 1.3.198.
112. See COM (98) 171 (O.J. 1998 C 136/25).
113. See Case C-180/96 *United Kingdom v. Commission* (O.J. 1996 C 197/16) and the order in Case C-180/96 R *United Kingdom v. Commission* [1996] ECR I-3903. See also the *General Report 1996* (Brussels, Luxembourg, 1997) point 503.
114. See, generally, Chapter IX, section 4, *ante* (on economic and social cohesion) and the Cork Declaration – A Living Countryside (November, 1996) by the European Con-

finally, the prospect of coping with the potential doubling of the European Union's farm population and an increase of more than 40% in its agricultural area through enlargement to the East.

Particularly, but not solely in response to this latter challenge, Agenda 2000[115] addresses the need to take further steps to build on the 1992 reforms, with a more rational development of agricultural production through a greater market orientation of prices and continuing structural adjustments. This would involve further moves away from price support to direct payments subject to an individual ceiling governing all direct income payments granted under common organizations, with the Member States being permitted to introduce differentiation criteria according to commonly agreed rules, although renationalization of agricultural policy would be excluded. The addition of over a 100 million consumers with a purchasing power considerably lower than that of current consumers in the European Union, and the clear need for structural improvement in agriculture, bring with them additional problems, even more so if the existing support prices and direct payment instruments were to be applied by Central and Eastern European countries at their present levels. Income disparities and social distortions might result from excessive cash injections into farmers' pockets, and the already predicted surpluses in particular for sugar, milk and meat, after 2000 would be exacerbated. All in all, it may be expected that the reform of the CAP will be an ongoing item on the political agenda for some time to come.

Unity of the market

As has been explained above, price intervention policy lay at the heart of the common organizations of the market for nearly two decades. The dominant position of price intervention led to this instrument being, both legally and in fact, the only real instrument for achieving at the same time a trio of to a certain extent mutually incompatible objectives.

First, as the Court has emphasized, the common price policy is the essential instrument for the achievement and maintenance of the free movement of agricultural products in the sectors concerned.[116] In this light, the choice which at that time[117] was made for price intervention

ference on Rural Development (published in DG VI's pages on the Commission's internet site and referred to in brief in Bull. EU 11–1996, point 1.3.95).
115. Agenda 2000 – Volume I – Communication: *For a Stronger and Wider Union*, Bull. EU Supp. 5/97.
116. Case 31/74 *Galli* [1975] ECR 47 at 61, and Case 4/79 *Société Coopérative 'Providence Agricole de la Champagne' v. Office National Interprofessionnel des Céréales (ONIC)* [1980] ECR 2823 at 2845.
117. The choice is contained in the Stresa Resolution (J.O. 291/58) at the conclusion of the Stresa Conference in July 1958. The Commission's initial proposals (the First Man-

appears to have been a responsible one, given that is very much questionable whether another model, such as direct income support to farmers, would have afforded the same guarantee of market unity. Such a policy always requires a very close coordination and control of national aid measures. Yet the free movement objective was only achieved to a limited extent, given that the monetary union which was essential for the common price policy could not be maintained, as a result of the deficient coordination of economic and monetary policy.

Secondly, price intervention policy was the only instrument for the achievement of the income policy objective of a reasonable standard of living for agricultural producers.[118] Through the lack of a structural policy it was impossible to run the common price policy, in a climate of pure intergovernmental decision-making, as anything other than a political income guarantee for the many marginal farmers, which resulted in strong incentives to produce.[119] The resulting ever-increasing claim on the Community's available financial resources also contributed to the difficulties in establishing an effective structural policy, which is absolutely essential in the longer term for the maintenance of market unity. Thirdly, price intervention policy should also serve the economic function of allowing prices to find their level by an adaptation of supply and demand. However, this remained an illusion thanks to the strong income policy orientation. The final result was that in financial terms this policy became untenable.

It may thus be stated without exaggeration that the CAP, by raising price intervention to its most important instrument, already at the outset sowed the seeds of its own failure. The reform operations of 1988 and 1992 have further demonstrated the grave risks of an uncontrolled proliferation of national aid measures, to compensate primarily the marginal farmers for their reduced circumstances on account of the reduction in income and price guarantees. It was not without difficulty that in 1989 a Community framework for such income support could be developed.[120] These remarks indicate that the future development of market and price policy will have to be in the form of a mixture of sectoral price intervention in the shape of a safety net against large fluctuations in price, supplemented by regionally differentiated systems of direct income support. The question remains whether such non-production-linked income support will reduce the

---

sholt Plan) are to be found in COM (60) 105 Final, see Barents, *op. cit.* (see note 13, *supra*) 7–9.

118. See, as to the background to and derailment of this policy, Neville-Rolfe, *The Politics of Agriculture in the EC* (London, 1984).

119. The fact that already in 1964, when the common prices were first fixed, a high level was adopted, also played a part, see Weinstock in Von Urff (ed.), *Landwirtschaft, Umwelt und ländlicher Raum* (*Festschrift* for Priebe, Baden-Baden, 1987) 63.

120. See the *Nineteenth Report on Competition Policy 1989* (Brussels, Luxembourg, 1990) point 213 (see Reg. 768/89 (O.J. 1989 L 84/8) which applied until 31 March 1993).

problem of surpluses, given that marginal undertakings have no other option, in the absence of a comprehensive structural policy, than to increase their production as much as possible. As was seen at the end of the preceding section, surpluses, like the rich and the poor, are likely to be with us for some time to come.

2.4 Structural policy in agriculture[121]

There are a number of legally relevant causes for the fact that a real Community policy on agricultural structure was only developed at a much later stage. First, at the beginning of the Seventies priority was given to the market and price policy, which was necessary to achieve free movement of agricultural products at the end of the transitional period. Then in a number of Member States doubts arose about the competence of the Community to pursue a comprehensive structural policy on the basis of Article 43 EC, especially because of the regional policy implications of such measures.[122] During the transitional period Community activity in this area remained limited to an institutional facility in the form of a Standing Committee for Agricultural Structures[123] and a framework regulation on direct financial contributions for national measures for the improvement of production and trade.[124] Through Regulation 26/62 on competition in the agricultural sector[125] a provisional framework was created, according to the preamble to that regulation, for the role of agricultural cooperatives and for an inventory of national aid measures.[126]

A programme that was outstanding especially in relation to structural policy (but with consequences in the field of market policy as well) was laid down by the Commission on 18 December 1968 in the 'Memorandum

121. Diversity in all sorts of respects is a significant characteristic of Community agricultural production. The differences in *per capita* added value in the agricultural sector range from 2 to 5; 68% of working units earn less, and only 5% more than the average *per capita* income; productivity differences run from 1 to 5, and in the scale of undertakings from 1 to 30. More than 40% of all farming undertakings are located in hilly or mountainous regions.
122. See in particular the debate on this question between Götz (1971) *Agrarrecht* 33 and Ehlermann (1972) *Agrarrecht* 261. In the case-law competence was accepted without more ado, see Case 5/73 *Balkan-Import–Export GmbH v. Hauptzollamt Berlin–Packhof* [1973] ECR 1091 at 1108, and Case 114/76 *Bela-Mühle Josef Bergmann KG v. Grows-Farm GmbH & Co. KG* [1977] ECR 1211 at 1220–1221.
123. Decision of 4 December 1962, O.J. English Special Edition 1959–62, p. 295.
124. Reg. 17/64 (O.J. English Special Edition 1963–64, p. 135), no longer in force. A proposal for a separate fund for structural improvements in agriculture was not accepted by the Council; instead the EAGGF was split in two in 1964.
125. See note 53, *supra*.
126. A proposal for a definitive regime was rejected by the Council in 1967.

on the reform of agriculture in the European Community', with many annexes, also called the 'Agricultural Programme 1980' or the Second Mansholt Plan.[127] This appeared to be politically infeasible, and it was not until 1972 that three modest directives were adopted concerning the modernization of agricultural undertakings, the promotion of cessation of farming and incentives for the use of arable land for improvement of the agricultural structure, as well as socio-economic information and the training of persons employed in agriculture.[128] The adoption of Directive 75/268 made provision for assistance to mountain and hill farmers and to those farming in certain less-favoured areas;[129] this took the form of income supplements. After 1977 a number of measures were adopted primarily to improve the agricultural structures in the Southern part of the Community,[130] which began the so-called integrated approach through a coordinated use of Community financial resources and Funds. In 1985 the various Community and Member States' structural policy measures, whether co-financed or otherwise, were regrouped and strengthened by a general coordinating measure, Regulation 797/85,[131] covering investment aid, mountain farming, aid for afforestation and the environment. This was supplemented in 1987 by rules concerning conversion and extensification of production[132] and in 1988 by provisions on set-aside and early retirement.[133] These measures demonstrate that structural policy was primarily utilized to contribute to the diminution of structural over-production.

Structural policy in agriculture achieved greater status with the release of financial resources as a result of the decision at European Council's meeting in Brussels in February 1988 that on the one hand guarantee expenditure should be checked and in due course reduced, and on the other hand that expenditure in the context of the Structural Funds should

127. COM (68) 1000, Bull. CE 1969, No. 1, summarized in Mansholt (1969) RMC 587. The plan is still of interest, particularly as regards the inventory of possible measures in a structural policy.
128. Dirs. 72/159-161 (O.J. English Special Edition 1972 (II), p. 324 *et seq.*
129. O.J. 1975 L 128/1, amended on numerous occasions. See now Reg. 950/97 (O.J. 1997 L 142/1).
130. Particularly Reg. 355/77 (O.J. 1977 L 51/1) improving conditions for processing and marketing (replacing the old Reg. 17/64 (see note 124, *supra*), since repealed by Reg. 4256/88 (O.J. 1988 L 374/88), and Reg. 1360/78 (O.J. 1978 L 166/1, most recently amended by Reg. 3669/93 (O.J. 1993 L 338/26) making rudimentary rules concerning agricultural cooperatives. Reg. 1360/78 has now been replaced by Reg. 952/97 (O.J. 1997 L 142/30).
131. O.J. 1985 L 93/1, since replaced by Reg. 2328/91 (O.J. 1991 L 218/1, most recently amended by Reg. 409/97 (O.J. 1997 L 62/4)). The adoption of Reg. 2088/85 (O.J. 1985 L 197/1) on Integrated Mediterranean Programmes (which ran until the end of 1993) further intensified the regional orientation of agricultural structural policy.
132. This was done by amending Reg. 797/85, *ibid.*
133. *Ibid.*

be considerably increased.[134] The basic regulation on the coordinated approach is Regulation 2052/88,[135] which provided that aid in particular through the Guidance Section of the EAGGF is destined for Objectives 1 (development and structural adjustment of regions lagging behind); 5a (adjustment of agricultural structures in the framework of reform of the CAP) and 5b (facilitating the development and structural adjustment of rural areas). According to the current version of the implementing regulation,[136] Objective 5a contains six priority areas: adaptation of supply and demand (conversion and extensification, where their financing is not provided for under the EAGGF Guidance Section); farming in hill, mountain, and less-favoured regions; aid to the installation of young farmers of either sex; the improvement of efficiency of the structures of holdings (through assistance with matters such as investments to reduce production costs, the promotion of quality, improvement of the living and working conditions of farmers of either sex and their spouses who principally work on the farm, promoting diversification of activities, improved animal health and welfare, and care of the natural environment); improved marketing, processing and encouraging the establishment of producers' cooperatives, and, finally, encouragement of assistance to farmers of either sex and the creation of groupings to improve production conditions. These activities are further developed now in a quartet of regulations[137] which in effect amount to an extensive and detailed coordination of national and Community aid measures.

2.5 Fisheries[138]

2.5.1 Introduction

Although the sea is not, of course, part of the land and sea fish are not as a rule bred yet alone cultivated, the parties to the EC Treaty have used their sovereign power to include fish, crustacea, shell-fish and molluscs and

---

134. Bull. EU 2–1988, point I.1.1. (see especially pp. 8–12, 13–14, and 17).
135. O.J. 1988 L 185/9, integrally amended by Reg. 2081/93 (O.J. 1993 L 193/5) and adapted to take account of Austrian, Finnish and Swedish accession by Reg. 3193/94 (O.J. 1994 L 337/11).
136. Reg. 4256/88 (O.J. 1988 L 374/25, integrally amended by Reg. 2085/93 (O.J. 1993 L 193/44)).
137. Reg. 950/97 (O.J. 1997 L 142/1) on the effectiveness of agricultural structures; Reg. 951/97 (O.J. 1997 L 142/22) on the marketing and processing of agricultural products; Reg. 952/97 (O.J. 1997 L 142/30) on producers' groups, and Reg. 2079/92 (O.J. 1992 L 215/91, most recently amended by Reg. 2773/95 (O.J. 1995 L 288/37)) on early retirement. See further, COM (98) 158 Final.
138. See further: Booß (1983) RMC 269 and 404, and van Rhijn in Von der Groeben, op. cit. (see note 13, supra) Vol. I, 1012–1046; Churchill, EEC Fisheries Law (Dordrecht, etc., 1987) and (1988) 25 CMLRev. 369; Koers in Olmi et al., Thirty Years of Commu-

the first transformation of them under the provisions of the common agricultural policy in Annex II to the EC Treaty. Title II of Part Two of the EC Treaty thus also applies to fisheries and, in practice, particularly to sea fishing. However, legal and biological reality has operated so as to oblige the Council and the Commission, as well as the Court of Justice, to recognize certain specific characteristics of sea-fishing.

As far as the legal aspects are concerned, it should be particularly noted that, following the example of a large number of third countries, the Community extended its fisheries zone to 200 nautical miles with effect from 1 January 1977, pending the definitive results of the Third United Nations Conference on the Law of the Sea (UNCLOS III).[139] Thus the territorial scope of application of Community fisheries law was significantly extended.

As far as biological reality is concerned, this new legal reality brought about the need for the Community itself to develop a policy for the conservation of the biological resources of the sea (structural policy) and for the division of fishing rights in the enlarged Community waters among the Member States and with third countries. Indeed, already in Cases 3, 4 and 6/76 *Kramer et al.*[140] the Court had concluded 'that the Community has at its disposal, on the internal level, the power to take any measures for the conservation of the biological resources of the sea.' The Court went on to observe in the next breath that 'the rule-making authority of the Community *ratione materiae* also extends – in so far as the Member States have a similar authority under public international law – to fishing on the high seas.' The Court added that the 'only way to ensure the conservation of the biological resources of the sea both effectively and equitably is through a system of rules binding on all the States concerned, including non-member countries.' It concluded that the Community had authority to enter into international commitments for the conservation of the resources of the sea (although the Member States had temporary competence in the matter this has since expired).

Already in 1977 the Court was again concerned with fisheries after a unilateral prohibition on certain ships fishing in a particular sector off the West Coast of Ireland. At the Commission's request in Case 61/77 R *Commission v. Ireland*[141] the Court ordered the Irish government, as an interim measure, to suspend the contested measures, which discriminated against fishermen from other Member States, until the judgment in the main action. The judgment in Case 61/77 *Commission v. Ireland*[142]

nity Law (European Perspectives, Brussels, 1981) 529-537, and Sturt in Vaughan (ed.), *Law of the European Communities Service* (London, loose-leaf, since 1990) Part 14.

139. (1979) XV *International Legal Materials* 1425.
140. [1976] ECR 1279 at 1309.
141. [1977] ECR 1411.
142. [1978] ECR 417, [1978] 2 CMLR 466. See also Case 88/77 *Minister for Fisheries v. Schonenberg et al.* [1978] ECR 473, [1978] 2 CMLR 519.

condemned the measure concerned. Subsequent case-law of the Court – apart from that concerned specifically with Spanish fishermen[143] – principally concerned national measures which raised either the division of powers between the Community and the Member States,[144] or questions of discrimination against fishermen from other Member States (particularly in the light of the very real problems caused by 'quota-hopping'),[145] or indeed questions of alleged discrimination against a Member State's own nationals.[146] It has to be said that the United Kingdom's record in this respect is less than wholly exemplary.[147]

Various judgments have dealt with the temporary powers of the Member States in relation to fishing.[148] In its judgment in Case 804/79 *Commission v. United Kingdom*[149] the Court made what has become a famous statement and one which is also important in certain other areas in which one or more Member States block the compliance by the Council with its obligations: 'Thus in a situation characterized by the inaction of the Council and by the maintenance, in principle, of the conservation

143. *E.g.* Case 812/79 *Attorney-General v. Burgoa* [1980] ECR 2787, [1981] 2 CMLR 193; Case 181/80 *Procureur Général près la Cour d'Appel de Pau et al. v. Arbelaiz–Emazabel* [1981] ECR 2961; Case 138/81 *Directeur des affaires maritimes du Littoral du Sud-Ouest et al. v. Marticorena-Otazo et al.* [1982] ECR 3819. See, generally, Churchill and Foster (1987) 36 ICLQ 504 and (1987) 12 ELRev. 430 for a critical view of these cases. For more recent cases see *e.g.* Case 223/86 *Pesca Valentia Ltd. v. The Minister for Fisheries and Forestry, Ireland* [1988] ECR 83, [1988] 1 CMLR 888 and Case 207/86 *Asociacion profesional de empresarios de pesca comunitarios (APESCO) v. Commission* [1988] ECR 2151.
144. *E.g.* Case 804/79 *Commission v. United Kingdom* [1981] ECR 1045, [1982] 1 CMLR 543.
145. *E.g.* Case C-3/87 *R. v. Ministry of Agriculture, Fisheries and Food, ex parte Agegate Ltd.* [1989] ECR 4459, [1990] 1 CMLR 366; Case C-216/87 *R. v. Ministry of Agriculture, Fisheries and Food, ex parte Jaderow Ltd.* [1989] ECR 4509, [1991] 1 All ER 41; Case C-221/89 *R. v. Secretary of State for Transport, ex parte Factortame Ltd. et al.* [1991] ECR I-3905, [1991] 3 CMLR 589; Case C-93/89 *Commission v. Ireland* [1991] ECR 4569, [1991] 3 CMLR 697; Case C-246/89 *Commission v. United Kingdom* [1991] ECR I-4585, [1991] 3 CMLR 706; Case C-279/89 *Commission v. United Kingdom* [1992] ECR I-5785, [1993] 1 CMLR 564; Case T-493/93 *Hansa-Fisch GmbH v. Commission* [1995] ECR II-575, and Case C-334/94 *Commission v. France* [1996] ECR I-1307. See also Cases C-46 and 48/93 *Brasserie du Pêcheur SA et al. v. Germany et al.* [1996] ECR I-1029.
146. See *e.g.* Case C-370/88 *Procurator Fiscal, Stranraer v. Marshall* [1990] ECR I-4071, [1991] 1 CMLR 419 and Case C-251/90 *Procurator Fiscal, Elgin v. Wood and Cowie* [1992] ECR I-2873, [1992] 2 CMLR 493.
147. *E.g.* the cases against the United Kingdom and *Brasserie du Pêcheur*, referred to in note 145, *supra*; Case 269/80 *R. v. Tymen* [1981] ECR 3079, [1982] 2 CMLR 1111, and Case 141/78 *France v. United Kingdom* [1979] ECR 2923, [1980] 1 CMLR 6.
148. See Cases 185-204/78 *Firma J. van Dam en Zonen et al.* [1979] ECR 2345, [1980] 1 CMLR 350; Case 141/78 *France v. United Kingdom* [1979] ECR 2923, [1980] 1 CMLR 6; Case 32/79 *Commission v. United Kingdom* [1980] ECR 2403, [1981] 1 CMLR 219 and Case 804/79 *Commission v. United Kingdom* [1981] ECR 1045, [1982] 1 CMLR 543.
149. [1981] ECR 1045 at 1076.

measures in force at the expiration of the period laid down in Article 102 of the Act of Accession, the decision of 25 June 1979 and the parallel decisions, as well as the requirements inherent in the safeguard by the Community of the common interest and the integrity of its own powers, imposed upon Member States not only an obligation to undertake detailed consultations with the Commission and to seek its approval in good faith, but also a duty not to lay down national conservation measures in spite of objections, reservations or conditions which might be formulated by the Commission.'

In relation to the refusal to permit fishermen from other Member States to fish in zones to which conservation measures applied, a particularly vivid example of confrontation tactics can be seen in Case 63/83 *R. v. Kirk*[150] in which the Danish MEP challenged, in the swashbuckling style of the past, measures taken by the United Kingdom. In particular in this judgment the prohibition of discrimination contained in Article 2(1) of Regulation 101/76[151] was held to apply undiminished during the period in which the event leading to the prosecution of Kirk took place; it was also found that the retroactivity provided for in Article 6(1) of Regulation 170/83[152] could not validate *ex post facto* national measures imposing criminal penalties, at the time of the conduct at issue, if the national measures were not valid. The Court noted that the principle that penal provisions may not have retroactive effect is a fundamental right common to all the legal orders of the Member States and enshrined in Article 7 of the European Convention for the Protection of Human Rights and Fundamental Freedoms; it was thus one of the general principles of law the observance of which would be ensured by the Court of Justice. The importance of fisheries case-law for general principles of Community law is well-illustrated by the judgments on discrimination on ground of nationality mentioned above, as well as by the concern for the rights of the defence shown in Case C-135/92 *Fiskano AB v. Commission*.[153]

2.5.2 Fisheries policy

The common structural policy in this field is now governed by Regulation 101/76.[154] The Regulation provides for access to fishing waters (the non-discrimination principle for fishermen from all Member States) and empowers the Council to take the necessary conservation measures

---

150. [1984] ECR 2689, [1984] 3 CMLR 522, [1985] 1 All ER 453.
151. O.J. 1976 L 20/19.
152. O.J. 1983 L 24/1.
153. [1994] ECR I-2885.
154. O.J. 1976 L 20/19.

concerning fish stocks and the coordination of national structural policy measures, including research and scientific and technical assistance. The regulation also provides for the promotion of rational development (restructuring of the fishing fleet and development of processing installations) and an equitable standard of living in the fisheries sector.[155]

With the adoption of Regulation 2080/93,[156] establishing the financial instrument of fisheries guidance (FIFG), assistance for fisheries finally broke free of the general schemes of assistance for agriculture, although it is still brought under Objective 5(a) of the Structural Funds.[157] The Commission has issued Guidelines for the examination of state aids to fisheries and aquaculture.[158]

Conservation measures and associated catch quota arrangements were initially agreed in 1983, but were radically overhauled in the 1992 reforms.[159] Accordingly, Regulation 3760/92[160] establishes a Community regime for fisheries and aquaculture. This is based on three main approaches: binding programming of parameters likely to affect resource mortality due to fishing;[161] the establishment of a Community system of fishing licences[162] (nationally managed and implemented); and arrangements for monitoring the implementation of the common fisheries policy.[163] Exploitation of fisheries resources is controlled either through

---

155. See further, Sturt, *op. cit.* (see note 138, *supra*) paras. 14.09-14.10.

156. O.J. 1993 L 193/1. See also Reg. 3699/93 (O.J. 1993 L 346/1, most recently amended by Reg. 25/97 (O.J. 1997 L 6/7).

157. Reg. 2052/88 (O.J. 1988 L 185/9, as amended by Reg. 2081/93 (O.J. 1993 L 193/5), Art. 1 (final para.). See also the Pesca Initiative to assist coastal areas (O.J. 1994 C 180/1).

158. O.J. 1994 C 260/3. See, under the old guidelines, Case C-311/94 *IJssel-Vliet Combinatie BV v. Minister van Economische Zaken* [1996] ECR I-5023.

159. After the Commission's '1991 Report' (SEC (91) 2288 Final) on the mid-term review of the Common Fisheries Policy.

160. O.J. 1992 L 389/1 (most recently amended by Reg. 1181/98 (O.J. 1998 L 164/1). Under the predecessor regime, see Cases 6 and 7/88 *Spain and France v. Commission* [1989] ECR 3639, [1991] 1 CMLR 817.

161. See Dec. 97/413 (O.J. 1997 L 175/27) for 1997–2001, and the discussion below about TACs and controlling fishing effort. As to the Multiannual Guidance Programmes (MAGP IV) for this period see Decs. 98/119–131 (O.J. 1998 L 39/1 *et seq.*).

162. See Regs. 3690/93 (O.J. 1993 L 341/93) on the minimum information to be contained in fishing licences; 109/94 (O.J. 1994 L 19/5, amended by Reg. 493/96 (O.J. 1996 L 72/12)) on the Community fishing vessel register; 1627/94 (O.J. 1994 L 171/7) on special fishing permits implemented by Reg. 2943/95 (O.J. 1995 L 308/15), and 3317/94 (O.J. 1994 L 350/13) on authorization of fishing in the waters of a third country under a fisheries agreement. As to some of the problems which can occur in relation to Community licences under fishery agreements, see Case T-572/93 *Odigitria AAE v. Council et al.* [1995] ECR II-2025, on appeal, Case C-293/95 P *Odigitria AAE v. Council et al.* [1996] ECR I-6129 (appeal dismissed).

163. See the Commission's Report SEC (92) 394 on monitoring and implementation, which led to the adoption of Regs. 2847/93 (O.J. 1993 L 261/1, most recently amended by Reg. 2635/97 (O.J. 1997 L 356/14)) and 897/94 (O.J. 1994 L 104/18, amended by Reg.

restricting the volume of authorized catches through annual total allowable catches (TACs), which are allocated between the Member States as quotas, linked to the flag which vessels fly,[164] or by controlling fishing effort through limiting the number of days at sea in specific fisheries, through restrictions on the capacity of the fleet deployed there and the number of days spent fishing in the zone concerned,[165] or through a combination of these methods. Special arrangements apply to the Mediterranean[166] and to the Baltic Sea,[167] and there are various other technical conservation measures.[168] Fishing for certain types of fish by

376/96 (O.J. 1996 L 51/31)). See further, Regs. 1956/88 (O.J. 1988 L 175/1, most recently amended by Reg. 3067/95 (O.J. 1995 L 329/1)), 2868/88 (O.J. 1988 L 257/20, most recently amended by Reg. 494/97 (O.J. 1997 L 77/5)) and 1489/97 (O.J. 1997 L 202/18, amended by Reg. 435/98 (O.J. 1998 L 54/5)). See also Reg. 2807/83 (O.J. 1983 L 276/1, amended by Reg. 395/98 (O.J. 1998 L 50/17). See Case C-276/94 *Ohrt* [1996] ECR I-119.

164. See for 1998, Reg. 45/98 (O.J. 1998 L 12/1). See also Reg. 65/98 (O.J. 1998 L 12/145, most recently amended by Reg. 1283/98 (O.J. 1998 L 178/1)). See also the flexibility introduced by Reg. 847/96 (O.J. 1996 L 115/3) which permits precautionary TACs to be revised under certain conditions, permits quotas to be carried over and permitted landings to be exceeded within certain limits in respect of non-endangered stocks, applies deductions with penalties for landings exceeding the permitted quota for vulnerable stocks, and applies further penalties in the case of repeated overfishing of quotas. Although Reg. 3760/92 (O.J. 1992 L 389/1) permits TACs to be fixed on a multispecies basis and/or on a multiannual basis, these arrangements are not at present applied, see COM (93) 664 Final. As to the allocation of TACs, see Case C-70/90 *Spain v. Council* [1992] ECR I-5159; Case C-71/90 *Spain v. Council* [1992] ECR I-5175, and Case C-73/90 *Spain v. Council* [1992] ECR I-5191. As to the application of control measures to catches made outside the Community fishing zone of stocks subject to a TAC or quota, see Case C-258/89 *Commission v. Spain* [1991] ECR I-3977. As to the Antarctic, see Reg. 66/98 (O.J. 1998 L 6/1).

165. See Regs. 685/95 (O.J. 1995 L 71/5) and 2027/95 (O.J. 1995 L 199/1). This is the system applied in the Atlantic. See Case C-44/94 *R. v. Minister of Agriculture, Fisheries and Food, ex parte National Federation of Fishermen's Organizations et al.* [1995] ECR I-3115.

166. Reg. 1626/94 (O.J. 1994 L 171/1, most recently amended by Reg. 782/98 (O.J. 1998 L 113/6)).

167. Reg. 88/98 (O.J. 1998 L 9/1). See also Dec. 83/414 (O.J. 1983 L 237/4) on the Community's accession to the Gdansk Convention on Fishing and Conservation of the living Resources in the Baltic Sea and the Belts (O.J. 1983 L 237/5), as amended by the Warsaw Protocol (O.J. 1983 L 237/9).

168. Reg. 894/97 (O.J. 1997 L 132/1, most recently amended by Reg. 1239/98 (O.J. 1998 L 171/1) and largely repealed with effect from 1 January 2000 by Reg. 850/98 (O.J. 1998 L 125/1)). In relation to the method of determining the mesh size of nets, see *e.g.* Case C-348/88 *Hakvoort* [1990] ECR I-1647. As to driftnets, see Case C-131/92 *Arnaud et al. v. Commission* [1993] ECR I-2573, and Case C-405/92 *Éts. Armand Mondiet SA v. Armement Islais SARL* [1993] ECR I-6133. See, further, the Commission's Communication on the biological impact of fisheries, COM (95) 40 Final, and its Communication on the integrated management of coastal zones, COM (95) 511 Final.

vessels flying the flags of a particular Member State may be stopped for a particular period.[169]

2.5.3 The common organization of the market for fish

The common organization of the market in fishery products is currently to be found in Regulation 3759/92.[170] In comparison with the common organizations of the market for agricultural products properly so called, Regulation 3759/92 exhibits fewer specific characteristics than is the case with the structural policy for fisheries. It is characterized by guide prices, market standards (quality classification, size or weight, packaging, presentation and labelling), an arrangement for withdrawal from the market by producers' organizations of fishery products supplied by their members,[171] storage aid, Community producer prices for tuna products (and compensation for tuna for canning), a regime for trade with third countries, special commercial policy powers in the event of disturbance or threat of disturbance of the market, another arrangement for producers' organizations, and equal access for vessels flying the flag of a Member State to Community ports and first-stage marketing installations.[172]

Internationally, the Community has concluded a number of agreements with third countries, ranging from African and Indian ocean countries, North Atlantic, including Baltic countries, to Argentina. Since Finnish and Swedish accession in 1995 the Community manages the fisheries agreements concluded by those countries prior to accession. The origin of fish can bring its own problems,[173] as can the vexed question of access to stocks.[174]

2.6 The general significance of agricultural policy for integration

In many ways the Community agricultural law is of great importance for Community law as a whole. This position fully reflects the actual position

---

169. *E.g.* Reg. 1510/97 (O.J. 1997 L 204/10).
170. O.J. 1992 L 388/1, most recently amended by Reg. 3318/94 (O.J. 1994 L 350/15).
171. See, under previous legislation, Case C-301/88 *R. v. Intervention Board for Agricultural Produce, ex parte The Fish Producers' Organization Ltd. et al.* [1990] ECR I-3803.
172. For further details see Sturt, *op. cit.* (see note 138, *supra*) paras. 14.54–14.61.
173. Case 100/84 *Commission v. United Kingdom* [1985] ECR 1169.
174. Feeling in relations with Canada over fishing proved particularly problematic in 1992. For details of the considerable activity (as regards conservation and terms of access to stocks) undertaken in the context of numerous international fisheries organizations, see the Commission's annual *General Report*. See also Dec. 96/428 (O.J. 1996 L 177/24) relating to the conservation and management of straddling stocks and highly migratory species, and COM (95) 591 Final.

of the CAP in the whole integration process. The CAP is still the only real intervention policy of the Community, and it can be regarded as the backbone of that process because of its implications for the common market, the socio-economic position of agriculture in general, and its regional policy aspects in particular, its significance for external and commercial policy, the relationship between agriculture and the environment, and the consequences of the CAP for the Community budget.

Already in the early years of the Community the CAP played a crucial role in achieving agreement between France, as the principal exporting country, and the Federal Republic of Germany, as the principal importing country of agricultural products, but the principal exporting country of industrial products, resulting in regular package deals, which enabled simultaneous progress in different fields of Community policy. Thus, the cartel policy, the Kennedy Round, and the harmonization of turnover taxes were successively made conditions for the further development of the agricultural policy. The crucial position of agriculture was further demonstrated during the crisis concerning the future financing of the Community in 1966 with the French empty chair policy which was finally resolved by the Luxembourg Accords, and again during the struggle which lasted for nearly a decade over the division of budgetary burdens among the Member States, especially concerning the British share int the financing of the CAP. The implied threat by the French in the final months of 1993 to invoke the Luxembourg Accords in relation to the agreement reached between the Commission and the United States about agricultural exports in the framework of the GATT Uruguay Round again illustrates that the CAP still plays a key role in the corpus of intra-Community relations.

Against this background, the significance of Community agricultural law for Community law in general may be summarized as follows. *First*, agricultural law is qualitatively as well as quantitatively the most important component part of Community law. About 25% of Community legislation and a similar percentage of the court's case-law deals with the agricultural sector. Although at first sight agricultural law may be regarded as a special part of Community law in general, the relationship is in fact to a great extent the reverse, in view of the major influence which legislation and case-law in the agricultural sector have exercised on the other component parts of Community law.

From the constitutional viewpoint, agricultural law has set the standard for the development of general doctrines, such as the supremacy of Community law, especially in relation to regulations and their consequences for legal subjects in the Member States. Moreover, important doctrines such as the scope of judicial control of discretionary decision-making by the Community legislator, the non-contractual liability of the Community for unlawful legislative acts, and the general and particular implications of the implementation obligation incumbent on the Member

States have been largely developed in agricultural case-law. The same applies concerning the division of powers among the Community Institutions themselves, as is demonstrated by the case-law on the disputes between the Commission and the Council on the use of Article 43 EC as a legal basis[175] and on the possibility and limits of the Council's reserving to itself the right to adopt implementing legislation as opposed to delegating it to the Commission (comitology).[176] Of major importance also is the case-law on the delimitation of powers between the Community on the one hand and the Member States on the other in a sector which indeed potentially falls within the competence of the Community, but in practice is only partially brought within the scope of application of Community law.[177]

In substantive law terms agricultural law is of importance because of the development and application of general principles of law, such as legal certainty (protection of acquired rights and of legitimate expectation), equality, and proportionality, and, not least the potential, though in practice limited, importance of various fundamental rights for the policy freedom of the Community legislator. Further, Community agricultural law has seen the development of specific (but little-researched) substantive legal instruments, such as the integrated application of subsidies and levies in order to steer the behaviour of its economic subjects, and the development of its own specific enforcement instruments, especially the technique of guarantee deposits and the associated problems of the possibilities of and limits to administrative sanctions.

It may thus be stated that Community agricultural law occupies a unique position in the wider corpus of Community law, which is firmly linked to the fact that the CAP reflects the most far-reaching form of integration provided for in the EC Treaty. At the same time, and *secondly*, agricultural law is also extremely fragile through this exposed position. More than in any other area of Community activity, agricultural law has demonstrated that in the absence of an Economic and Monetary union, or at least a system of fixed exchange rates, there is always the risk that a level of integration which has once been achieved will in fact have to be reversed if the coordination of general economic and monetary policy is not in step. Through the introduction of MCAs the common market for agricultural products had already become to a large extent a legal fiction by the early Seventies. Agricultural law also shows the consequences of the lack of a link between on the one hand the far-reaching substantive law integration and on the other hand an institutional framework which in effect is based

175. See note 15, *supra*.
176. See Chapter V, section 3.1, *ante*.
177. See *e.g.* Cases 3, 4 and 6/76 *Officier van Justitie v. Kramer et al.* [1976] ECR 1279, [1976] 2 CMLR 440 and Case 804/79 *Commission v. United Kingdom* [1981] ECR 1045, [1982] 1 CMLR 543.

on intergovernmental decision-making. The unanimity policy of the Council and the consequent loss of authority for the Commission has led to the Council in fact operating as an intergovernmental price cartel, which assured the continued existence of even the most inefficient undertakings. This meant that the claim on the limited financial resources was an important factor in the tardiness in giving attention to the structural component of agricultural policy, which could contribute to the Community's economic and social cohesion. This decision-making, which was principally driven by short-term income policy aspects, has resulted in the CAP occupying a steadily more isolated position in Community policy as a whole, and finally being made subordinate to medium-term financial planning because of the looming budgetary catastrophe.

Thirdly, Community agricultural law contributes, albeit negatively, to the possible or impossible operationalization of the principle of subsidiarity. It may be recalled that a policy of price intervention leads by its very nature to a far-reaching centralization of legislation at the highest level. Given that in the framework of such a policy the competitive position of agricultural products is altered, particularly by the application of levies and subsidies, every actual or potential divergent application or interpretation of the rules concerned involves the possibility of distortions, which in turn may affect the proper functioning of the common organizations of the market and thus free movement. The principle of uniform application and interpretation which has long been recognized in the case-law,[178] means that the role of the Member States is largely limited to the strict application of these rules in individual cases. In addition to a large and continuing legislative production which does not benefit the accessibility and internal consistency of Community rules, this character trait of the common organizations of the market means that no account can be taken of regional differences in production and trade structures. Thus, as has already been noted, differences in for example common prices and amounts (such as import levies, export refunds, and various subsidies) may give rise to distortions of competition. This also demonstrates the inadequacy of price intervention as the only or most important instrument of the CAP, given that this policy, based on the formal principle of equality, does not do sufficient justice to the agricultural structure of the Community, characterized as it is by great diversity, which is indeed acknowledged in Article 39(2) EC.[179] Seen in this light, the 'U-turn' from price intervention to direct income support is of major importance, given that the unity of the common market in the long term cannot be maintained by price intervention alone. The CAP thus demonstrates that the centralization of legislation is a result of the chosen model of market

178. *E.g.* Case 93/71 *Leonesio v. Ministry for Agriculture and Forestry* [1972] ECR 287 at 295.
179. See Barents (1986) SEW 106.

intervention, which in its turn finds its essential justification in the need to maintain the free movement of goods. A policy of direct income support and structural policy instruments, based on regional differences, involves far greater possibilities for the Member States to apply Community legislation, within certain limits, and supplement it having regard to their own specific circumstances.

2.7 Some characteristics of Community agricultural administrative law

There are far too many interesting but also extremely complex aspects of Community administrative law in the agricultural sector to discuss them in detail here.[180] But this administrative law is largely concerned with steering the behaviour of economic subjects in such a way as to contribute to what the case-law usually refers to as the proper functioning of the common organization of the market concerned, which contributes to the achievement of the objectives specified in Article 39 EC.[181] For the most part this steering of conduct takes place by raising or lowering the costs or revenue of certain economic transactions. Thus, through the imposition of an import levy the costs of an import transaction are raised, and through the grant of an export refund the costs of an export transaction are lowered. The buying-in of agricultural produce by intervention agencies involves the grant of a subsidy, with the aim of taking off the market products which cannot be normally sold. Production levies are aimed at persuading the producer to adapt his or her production or even to limit it to certain pre-fixed amounts.

This approach demonstrates that the choice of the beneficiary or the person burdened largely rests on considerations of effectiveness. In order to combat overproduction, co-responsibility levies may for example be placed on producers, as occurred in the dairy and cereals sectors. Producer levies in the sugar sector are intended to finance the system of export refunds for sugar, through which the chronic surpluses will be partially remedied. These examples show that the attribution of rights and obligations under the price intervention system is heavily dependent on the objectives chosen, such as restraint of production or guaranteeing a certain price level. Although these rights and obligations are meant to act to the advantage or disadvantage of the producer, it is perfectly possible to impose those rights and obligations in other phases of the process between production and consumption.

Secondly, this administrative law illustrates a far-reaching integration of

---

180. See, generally, Barents, *op. cit.* (see note 13, *supra*).
181. *E.g.* Case 21/85 *A. Maas & Co. NV v. Bundesanstalt für landwirtschaftliche Marktordnung* [1986] ECR 3537 at 3556, and Case C-104/94 *Cereol Italia Srl v. Azienda Agricola Castello Sas* [1995] ECR I-2983 at 3018–3019.

the levies and subsidies instruments, so that it is possible to speak of just one category of administrative acts, the application of amounts. Depending on the objectives, structure of the market, budgetary considerations and the like, these amounts may be applied in the form of a subsidy or in the form of a levy. The application of MCAs is illustrative, for example: depending on the direction of the flow of goods, they are applied as levies or as subsidies. The extensive case-law on various subsidy and levy mechanisms demonstrates that the fixing of these amounts in concrete cases and the status of acquired rights rest upon a number of common principles.[182] In all this it is irrelevant whether the economic subject enjoys the benefit or bears the burden; what is relevant is that by the application of such an amount his or her conduct is steered in a direction which the Community legislator regards as necessary for the proper functioning of the common organizations of the market concerned.

Thirdly, the application of this combined levy and subsidy law is characterized by its so-called objective character. What is decisive for the existence of the rights or obligations is simply whether the conditions in the legislation concerned have been fulfilled, not whether the party concerned desired to bring about this legal result or not. The failure to fulfill the many and often extremely detailed conditions which are attached to many subsidies, means that the right to certain amounts is foregone, or that the party concerned is liable to repay the amounts involved, or that a deposit lodged as a security is declared forfeit, irrespective of whether the party was responsible for the failure to fulfill the conditions, or was guilty or negligent, or acted in good faith, and so on. The case-law shows that through this system the party concerned is confronted with a high risk of liability, from which he or she can only escape on ground of *force majeure*.[183] The Community's levy and subsidy policy demonstrates that individual freedom can be limited to a great extent through both levies and subsidies, by the simple lack of any possibility of escape. In many cases the undertaking can do nothing other than submit to these levies or subsidies, with the conditions attached to them, simply in order to exercise its economic activities.

---

182. See Barents (1986) SEW 710.
183. As to this administrative law concept, see *e.g.* Case 4/68 *Firma Schwarzwaldmilch GmbH v. Einfuhr- und Vorrratsstelle für Fette* [1968] ECR 377, [1969] CMLR 406; Case 42/79 *Milch-, Fett- und Eier-Kontor GmbH v. Bundesanstalt für landwirtschaftliche Marktordnung* [1979] ECR 3703; Case 266/84 *Denkavit France SARL v. Fonds d'orientation et de régularisation des marchés agricoles (FORMA)* [1986] ECR 149, [1987] 3 CMLR 202; Case 71/87 *Greek State v. SA Inter-Kom Emboriki kai Biomichaniki Epicheirisis Elaion, Liparon kai Trofimon AE* [1988] ECR 1979; Case 84/87 *Erpelding v. Secrétaire d'État à l'Agriculture et à la Viticulture* [1988] ECR 2647, Case C-299/94 *Anglo Irish Beef Processors International et al. v. Minister for Agriculture, Food and Forestry* [1996] ECR I-1925, and Case C-109/95 *Astir AE v. Elliniko Dimosio* [1997] ECR I-1385.

Fourthly, this instrumental position of the individual under Community agricultural law also has consequences for judicial protection. The case-law demonstrates, in global terms, that the principle of legal certainty primarily boils down to a prohibition of retroactive legislation, although this is not without exceptions,[184] and that the principle of the protection of legitimate expectations is very restrictively interpreted in order not to restrict the freedom of action of the Community legislator to adapt existing legislation to the economic reality at any time.[185] The principle of non-discrimination is also strongly dependent on the freedom which is left to the legislator to decide, in the context of its objectives and policy, what may or may not be regarded as like.[186] Furthermore, the case-law shows that the practical significance of the principle of proportionality depends on the fundamental rights enjoyed by the individual concerned. The significance of these fundamental rights is pretty small, given that constant case-law holds that they do not restrict the freedom of the Community legislator even to prescribe far-reaching limits to the exercise of the right to property, the freedom to pursue a trade or profession and the freedom of contract.[187] If the individual cannot lay claim to a right, but only to an interest, the failure to take account of that individual interest will only infringe the principle of proportionality if it can be shown that the measure involved is therefore to be regarded as not being appropriate or necessary in the light of the objectives of Article 39 EC. In general, the case-law on these legal principles confirms that the judicial control on the exercise of discretionary powers leans strongly in the direction of a prohibition of arbitrariness.[188]

184. See *e.g.* Case 98/78 *Firma A Racke v. Hauptzollamt Mainz* [1979] ECR 69, and Case C-368/89 *Crispoltoni v. Fattoria autonoma tabacchi di Città di Castello* [1991] ECR I-3695. See also Case C-337/88 *Società agricola fattoria alimentare SpA v. Amministrazione delle Finanze dello Stato* [1990] ECR I-1.
185. *E.g.* Case 84/78 *Angelo Tomadini Snc v. Amministrazione delle Finanze dello Stato* [1979] ECR 1801, [1980] 2 CMLR 573, and Cases C-143/88 and 92/89 *Zuckerfabrik Süderdithmarschen AG et al. v. Hauptzollamt Itzehoe et al.* [1991] ECR I-415, [1993] 3 CMLR 1.
186. See especially Case 166/78 *Italy v. Council* [1979] ECR 2575, [1981] 3 CMLR 770; Case 35/80 *Denkavit Nederland BV v. Produktschap voor Zuivel* [1981] ECR 45, and Cases 279/84 etc. *Walter Rau Lebensmittelwerke et al. v. Commission* [1987] ECR 1069, [1988] 2 CMLR 704. But see also the approach in Case C-309/88 *Codorniu SA v. Council* [1994] ECR I-1853 at 1888–1889.
187. *E.g.* Case 11/70 *Internationale Handelsgesellschaft mbH v. Einfuhr- und Vorratsstelle für Getreide und Futtermittel* [1971] ECR 1125, [1972] CMLR 255; Case 44/79 *Hauer v. Land Rheinland–Pfalz* [1979] ECR 3727, [1980] 3 CMLR 42, and Case 5/88 *Wachauf v. Germany* [1989] ECR 2609. See also Case C-22/94 *The Irish Farmers Association et al. v. Minister for Agriculture, Food and Forestry, Ireland et al.* [1997] ECR I-1809 and judgments cited there.
188. See especially Case 138/79 *SA Roquette Frères v. Council* [1980] ECR 3333; Case 167/88 *Association générale des producteurs de blé et al. v. Office national interprofessionnel des céréales (ONIC)* [1989] ECR 1653, and Case C-204/88 *Ministère public v. Paris* [1989] ECR 4361.

3. TRANSPORT POLICY

3.1 Introduction

The EC treaty deals with transport in a separate Title, and the ECSC
Treaty also contains a separate Chapter on transport.[189] For a number of
reasons the framers of the EC Treaty felt it necessary to establish a
common policy for the transport sector, and this is given expression in
Article 3(f) EC.[190] The special status of transport in the Treaty is in part
due to the fact that the transport sector was highly regulated in all the
original Member States. Moreover, it was seen as very important for the
establishment of a common market. The close link between the
establishment of the common market and transport was again emphasized
in the amendments introduced by the SEA. Article 7a EC explicitly refers
to Article 84 EC, thereby indicating that the internal market for transport
services also has to be achieved. Close has rightly pointed out for all
Member-States that transport represents a greater part of the gross
national product than agriculture.[191]

   A number of features of the transport sector deserve special attention.[192]
First, the great dependence on infrastructure and the associated problem of
cost allocation. This allocation does not take place in the same way in each
Member State individually, particularly in as far as road and rail transport
are concerned. Moreover, it does not take place in the same way in the
various Member States. This was one of the issues which came to the fore
in the discussion about the allocation of costs in road transport. The lack
of agreement in the Community about the allocation of these costs blocked
progress in the development of the common transport policy for years.
This was primarily the result of divergent views in Germany, which

189. The ECSC rules on transport are based on the premise that there must be no dis-
     crimination between users. Art. 70 ECSC prescribes extensive rules as to transport
     tariffs in the coal and steel sector, with the intention of preventing distortions of com-
     petition through differential transport tariffs. As a result of Art. 232 EC, the EC
     Treaty applies in so far as a matter is not governed by the ECSC Treaty. Thus the
     measures for a common transport policy in the coal and steel sector under Art. 75 EC
     have to respect the requirements of Art. 70 ECSC.
190. The Spaak Report (as to which, see Chapter I, section 4.1, *ante*) referred in Chapter
     III to transport services as being among the services the free provision of which would
     have to be achieved by the end of the transitional period at the latest. See further,
     Erdmenger in Von der Groeben *et al.* (eds.), *op. cit.* (see note 13, *supra*) Vol. I 1179 *et
     seq.*
191. Originally in 52 *Halsbury's Laws of England* (4th ed., London, 1986) para. 18.11, now
     in Vaughan (ed.), *op. cit.* (see note 138, *supra*) para. 18.11. See, generally, *ibid.* paras.
     18.01-18.433; Erdmenger in Von der Groeben, *op. cit.* (see note 13, *supra*) Vol. I
     1179–1295; Greaves, *Transport Law in the European Community* (London, 1991), and
     Tromm, *Juridische aspecten van het communautaire vervoersbeleid* (Tilburg, 1990).
192. For an extensive background discussion, see the 2nd ed. of this work ((ed. Gormley),
     Deventer, 1989) 705–711.

pursued a policy of fixing tariffs for road transport in such a way that the rail transport faced no real competition.[193] German seaport policy was also conducted for a long time with the assistance of low railway tariffs.[194] On the other hand the national railways were subsidized to a great extent in virtually all the Member States.[195] In inland waterway transport the allocation problem was far less significant; the problems in this sector were primarily caused by a relatively small sector, the small family firms. The second feature which also hindered the development of a common transport policy was the existence of strongly divergent national intervention systems.[196] Thirdly, it should be remembered that it is impossible to stock-pile transport services. Transport capacity, therefore, has to be adapted to peak demands, which leads to over-capacity during the other periods. When combined with high fixed charges, among which wages must now be included, it is feared that this may lead to disastrous price competition. Particularly in depressed areas, such as Southern Italy, but also elsewhere, there is over-capacity especially with regard to return freights. Since the transport charges as a rule are already defrayed on the outward journey, transport during the return journey will yield profit even if the price is very low. Fourthly, transport is characterized by small short-term elasticity of supply as well as demand, but it is doubtful whether the differences on this point as compared with other branches of industry are so great as to justify special interventions. A fifth feature which may justify intervention is the relatively low cost of investment required to engage in road transport (while labour costs are a high percentage of expenditure). By means of long driving periods particularly one-man undertakings, but frequently also larger undertakings, can keep down the cost even further at the expense of road safety. Social as well as safety considerations then, necessitate regulation. But since the low cost of investment stimulates the development of own-account transport by industrial undertakings, regulation must also take this into account. A sixth feature, but one which transport has in common with a number of other branches of industry, is its peculiar short-term economic sensitivity. When there is a slump in trade, and particularly in international trade, transport tends to decline as well. International transport is of course a particularly important aspect of maritime and air transport, but also plays a considerable role in road and inland waterway transport.

In the light of all the above peculiarities of the transport sector the

193. See Case C-185/91 *Bundesanstalt für den Güterfernverkehr v. Gebrüder Reiff GmbH & Co. KG* [1993] ECR I-5801, [1995] 5 CMLR 145. See also, in relation to inland waterway transport, Case C-155/93 *Germany v. Delta Schiffahrts- und Speditionsgesellschaft mbH* [1994] ECR I-2517, [1996] 4 CMLR 21.
194. As was confirmed in Dec. 94/210 (O.J. 1994 L 104/34) *HOV-SVZ/MCN*.
195. See Hancher *et al.*, *EC State Aids* (London, 1993) 140 *et seq.*
196. See Erdmenger, *op. cit.* (see note 190, *supra*) 1183.

development of a common transport policy was a long time in the making, although since the last edition of this work there have been such great strides forward that a common transport policy has finally largely become a reality. These developments were set in motion by the celebrated action brought by the European Parliament against the Council for failure to establish a common policy in the field of air transport,[197] by the changes introduced by the SEA,[198] by a couple of major judgments on Article 177 EC references,[199] and by the Commission's White Paper on *Completing the Internal Market*.[200] A coherent policy has been made possible principally through the adoption of the Third Aviation Package,[201] the acceptance of rules on cabotage in road transport,[202] and maritime transport[203] and the adoption of the directive on road tolls and infrastructure charges.[204] As will appear from the sector-by-sector description of the transport regime, there is a clear model which is based on a market economy orientation. In this model the price and capacity rules taken from the national regulatory systems have disappeared. Interference in prices is now restricted to only a very few precisely defined exceptional situations. The qualitative conditions for access to the profession are regulated for each sector. The requirements made of

197. Case 13/83 *European Parliament v. Council* [1985] ECR 1513, [1986] 1 CMLR 138.
198. In Art. 84 EEC (now Art. 84 EC) by altering the voting requirements to permit decision-making by qualified majority.
199. Cases 209–213/84 *Ministère public v. Asjes et al.* [1986] ECR 1425, [1986] 3 CMLR 173, and Case 66/86 *Ahmed Saeed Flugreisen et al. v. Zentrale zur Bekämpfung unlauteren Wettbewerbs eV* [1989] ECR 803, [1990] 4 CMLR 102.
200. COM (85) 310 Final.
201. This consists principally of Regs. 2407/92 (O.J. 1992 L 240/1) on licensing of air carriers; 2408/92 (O.J. 1992 L 240/8, amended by the Act of Austrian, Finnish and Swedish Accession, 1994) on access for Community air carriers to intra-Community air routes; 2409/92 (O.J. 1992 L 240/15) on fares and rates for air services; 2410/92 (O.J. 1992 L 240/18) and 2411/92 (O.J. 1992 L 240/19) which amend the competition rules in the air sector (Regs. 3975/87 (O.J. 1987 L 374/1) and 3976/87 (O.J. 1987 L 376/9) respectively), and 95/93 (O.J. 1993 L 14/1) on common rules for slot allocation at Community airports. The First Aviation Package was adopted in 1987, see Regs. 3975/87 (*supra*); 3976/87 (*supra*); Dir. 87/601 (O.J. 1987 L 374/12) on air fares for scheduled air services between Member States, and Dec. 87/602 (O.J. 1987 L 374/19) on sharing passenger capacity and on access to scheduled intra-Community routes. Both the latter have now been repealed. The Second Aviation Package was adopted in 1990, see Regs. 2342/90 (O.J. 1990 L 217/1) on fares for scheduled air services (now repealed by Reg. 2409/92, *supra*); 2343/90 (O.J. 1990 L 217/8) on access to scheduled intra-Community routes and passenger-sharing (almost entirely repealed by Reg. 2408/92, *supra*); and 2344/90 (O.J. 1990 L 217/15) amending Reg. 3976/87, *supra*, (now superseded by Reg. 2411/92, *supra*).
202. Reg. 3118/93 (O.J. 1993 L 279/1, most recently amended by Reg. 3315/94 (O.J. 1994 L 350/9)).
203. Reg. 3577/92 (O.J. 1992 L 364/7).
204. Dir. 93/89 (O.J. 1993 L 279/32, amended by the Act of Austrian, Finnish and Swedish Accession (1994)).

undertakings in the sector have only an indirect effect on market access. Furthermore, there are specific rules for each sector, such as the driving and rest hours provisions for road transport.[205]

The market economy model has come about for a number of reasons. First, it appeared impossible to achieve an internal market through an umbrella philosophy concerning intervention in prices and capacity. This was primarily because the national systems were based on specific policy objectives reflecting national political considerations. Moreover, in the course of the Eighties the intervention system was abandoned in various Member States.[206] This was particularly true in relation to road transport. In the field of air transport the market model was chosen as a result of external influences: deregulation in the United States which created strongly competitive airline companies, and competition from the Far East. Moreover the deregulation philosophy made its influence gradually felt in the Community as well.[207] In addition, the progressive development of the internal market certainly played a role. The liberalization in the rail transport sector is provided for in Directive 91/440[208] on the development of the Community's railways, which requires a separation of functions and makes provision concerning access to the rail network. Here too, external developments, particularly in the United States, played a role.

The market economy model is supplemented on a number of points. In road transport a crisis mechanism is provided for in emergency cases,[209] and in a public service obligation may be imposed in relation to road, rail, inland waterway and air transport.[210] These developments have not always been positively viewed. Particularly those who have always argued for harmonization of conditions of competition before liberalization submit that such harmonization is still insufficient.[211] Rules governing the application of Articles 85 and 86 EC in the maritime and air transport sectors have now at long last been adopted.[212]

The EC Treaty contains no definition of the concept of transport as such,[213] although it does indicate the scope of application of the transport Title. It can be deduced from Article 84 EC that in any event road, rail

---

205. Reg. 3820/85 (O.J. 1985 L 370/1). See also, as to tachographs, Reg. 3821/85 (O.J. 1985 L 370/8, most recently amended by Reg. 1056/97 (O.J. 1997 L 154/21)).
206. As to the changes in the Dutch approach, see Slot (1992) SEW 514.
207. Thus the United Kingdom and The Netherlands pursued a very clear open skies policy.
208. O.J. 1991 L 305/22. An amendment has been proposed, COM (97) 34 Final.
209. Reg. 3916/90 (O.J. 1990 L 375/10) for international transport; see also Reg. 3118/93 (see note 202, *supra*), Art. 7, for cabotage.
210. Such obligations are also found in other areas covered by Community law, see, in relation to energy, Slot in Gormley (ed.), *Current and Future Perspectives in EC Competition Law* (London, 1997) 109.
211. See Schmitt (1993) EuZW 305.
212. See sections 3.11 and 3.12, *post*, respectively.
213. Whereas a definition is given for agriculture, see Art. 38 EC.

and inland waterway transport fall within the ambit of transport, indicated
in Community jargon as inland transport. This term is used hereafter to
describe these three sectors collectively. 'Own transport', as defined in
Dutch transport legislation certainly falls within this definition. Maritime
and air transport also fall under the transport sectors regulated on the
basis of the EC Treaty, although Article 84 EC itself initially left that
open.[214] Article 84 EC is silent about transport by pipeline, although this
is treated as transport in practice, but it is an area which gives rise to
separate questions which are primarily addressed within the Community in
the context of a common energy policy.[215]

3.2   The relationship between the general principles of the EC Treaty and the special provisions of the transport Title

The relationship between the general principles to the special provisions
has given rise to much discussion. In contrast to the agriculture Title, the
transport Title contains no provisions which regulate this relationship. For
agriculture, Articles 38(2) and 42 EC determine the relationship with the
common market and competition respectively. Article 61(1) EC provides
that the free movement of services in the field of transport is governed by
the provisions in the title relating to transport. Article 74 EC provides that
the objectives of the Treaty in the field of transport are to be pursued by
Member States within the framework of a common transport policy. The
Court has pointed out that on the basis of Article 75(1)(a) and (b) EC the
Council is obliged to bring about the free movement of services in the
transport sector, and that the scope of those obligations is clearly laid
down in the Treaty.[216] For the rest the general rules of the Treaty are
applicable to transport, as various judgments make clear.[217] Although,
therefore, the free movement of services had to be achieved, it was for the
Council to take the measures it felt necessary to accompany the required
liberalization measures.[218] Thus the crisis mechanism for road transport,
for example, is just such an accompanying measure.[219] Such measures may

214. See section 3.2, *post.*
215. See, generally, section 6, *post.*
216. Case 13/83 *European Parliament v. Council* [1985] ECR 1513 at 1599.
217. See Case 167/73 *Commission v. France* [1974] ECR 359, [1974] 2 CMLR 216 (and, for
     interest, Case C-334/94 *Commission v. France* [1996] ECR I-1307); Case 156/77 *Com-
     mission v. Belgium* [1978] ECR 1881; Cases 209–213/84 *Ministère public v. Asjes et al.*
     [1986] ECR 1425, [1986] 3 CMLR 173, and Case 66/86 *Ahmed Saeed Flugreisen et al.
     v. Zentrale zur Bekämpfung unlauterer Wettbewerbs eV* [1989] ECR 803, [1990] 4
     CMLR 102. These last two judgments confirm the applicability of Arts. 85 and 86
     EC.
218. Case 13/83 *European Parliament v. Council* [1985] ECR 1513 at 1601.
219. See note 209, *supra.*

be based on Article 75 EC.[220] Articles 59 and 60 EC are however not directly applicable in the transport sector, specific measures were needed.[221] The question whether Article 75(1)(a) and (b) are directly applicable was side-stepped by the Court in Case C-17/90 *Pinaud Wieger GmbH Spedition v. Bundesanstalt für den Güterfernverkehr.*[222] The non-discrimination principle in Article 6 EC could also not be used as the legal basis for the achievement of the freedom to provide services in this area. While it is true that as a general rule of the Treaty,[223] Article 6 applies to transport,[224] questions of the freedom to provide services fall under Articles 74, 75 and 84(2) EC, by virtue of Article 61(1) EC.[225]

The wording of Article 84 EC has given rise to additional questions about the applicable Treaty regime for maritime and air transport,[226] but it is now clear that the general rules of the Treaty apply to these sectors as well.[227] The Court has held that on the basis of Article 84(2) EC the freedom to provide services in the areas covered by that provision had to

220. See Reg. 3916/90 (O.J. 1990 L 375/10).
221. Case 13/83 *European Parliament v. Council* [1985] ECR 1513 at 1599–1600.
222. [1991] ECR I-5253. In that case, Darmon, Adv. Gen. (at 5272–5273) was, like Jacobs, Adv. Gen in Case 4/88 *Lambregts Transportbedrijf v. Belgian State* [1989] ECR 2543 at 2601, of opinion that it was possible that the obligation to achieve the free movement of services had now to be directly effective. This can only mean, it is submitted, that Art. 75(1)(a) and (b) EC are now directly effective (the Court's ruling in *Lambregts* was expressly concerned with events which took place in 1982). In Cases C-184 and 221/91 *Oorburg et al. v. Wasser- und Schiffahrtsdirektion Nordwest* [1993] ECR I-1633 at 1649–1650 Gulman, Adv. Gen. came to a similar conclusion, pointing out (at 1649) that the reasoning of the Court in *Pinaud Wieger* did not apply to all fields of transport. According to *Pinaud Wieger* (at 5283) in view of the complexity of the cabotage sector, the Council was entitled to liberalize cabotage traffic gradually. Thus for some sectors direct effect is certainly possible. The further completion of the common transport policy reduces the importance of this discussion, as direct effect is really important for those areas where no secondary Community legislation has been adopted. The (Transport) Council adopted a resolution on 12 September 1985 (O.J. 1985 C 262/99) agreeing to establish a common transport policy by 1 January 1993. See further, the Commission's White Paper on the future development of the common transport policy (COM (92) 494 Final, Bull. EU Supp. 3/93); the Commission's Action programme for the period 1995–2000 (COM (95) 302 Final) and the Green Papers on *The Citizen's Network* (COM (95) 601, Bull. EU Supp. 5/95) and *Towards fair and efficient pricing in transport – Policy options for internalizing the external costs of transport in the European Union* (COM (95) 691 Final, Bull. EU Supp. 2/96).
223. Case 167/73 *Commission v. France* [1974] ECR 359 at 369.
224. Case C-18/93 *Corsica Ferries Italia Srl v. Corpo dei Piloti del Porto di Genova* [1994] ECR I-1783 at 1796 (Van Gerven, Adv. Gen.).
225. Case C-18/93 *Corsica Ferries Italia Srl v. Corpo dei Piloti del Porto di Genova* [1994] ECR I-1783 at 1820–1821.
226. See especially Erdmenger, *op. cit.* (see note 191, *supra*) 1262–1265.
227. Case 167/73 *Commission v. France* [1974] ECR 359, [1974] 2 CMLR 216; Cases 209–213/84 *Ministère public v. Asjes et al.* [1986] ECR 1425, [1986] 3 CMLR 173, and Case 66/86 *Ahmed Saeed Flugreisen et al. v. Zentrale zur Bekämpfung unlauteren Wettbewerbs eV* [1989] ECR 803, [1990] 4 CMLR 102.

be attained by the Council.[228] For these sectors too, the use of Article 6
EC as a legal basis for the application of the freedom to provide services is
excluded.[229] The Council finally got round to agreeing to the freedom to
provide services in the field of maritime transport both within the
Community and between the Community and third countries in 1986,[230]
and in the field of air transport within the Community in 1992.[231]

3.3 External relations in the transport field – general observations

The importance of relations with third countries in the transport field
cannot be under-emphasized: wider international arrangements concerning
transport may have an influence on transport within the Community or on
the autonomous regulation by the Community of transport with third
countries.

The judgment in Case 22/70 *Commission v. Council*[232] dealt with just
such an arrangement, even though the importance of the judgment reached
way beyond simply the transport sector. In that judgment the Court found
that if a particular matter was regulated by Community action within the
Community[233] only the Community itself was competent to regulate the
same matter in relation with third countries.

The Court went a step further in Opinion 1/76 on the *European Laying-
up Agreement for Inland Waterway Vessels*,[234] finding that the Community

228. Case C-49/89 *Corsica Ferries France v. Direction générale des douanes françaises* [1989]
     ECR 4441 at 4456. In Case C-381/93 *Commission v. France* [1994] ECR I-5145 at 5170
     the Court declared the rules which had already been the subject of Case C-49/89
     Corsica Ferries France to be incompatible with Art. 1 of Reg. 4055/86 (O.J. 1986 L
     378/1). The problem was a charge levied on embarkation and disembarkation of pas-
     sengers travelling to or from ports in other Member States whenever ships used
     harbour facilities (on the mainland or on an island), whereas in the case of transport
     between two French ports the charge was levied only on embarkation (on the main-
     land or on an island). The charge was moreover levied at a higher level for passengers
     travelling from and to another Member State than at that applicable to passengers
     whose journeys were only internal.
229. Case C-18/93 *Corsica Ferries Italia Srl v. Corpo dei Piloti del porto di Genova* [1994]
     ECR I-1783 at 1819–1820. The principle of Art. 6 EC can though be applied in rela-
     tion to other measures, such as environmental, safety and social measures.
230. Reg. 4055/86 (O.J. 1986 L 378/1, amended, so as to require adaptation by 1 January
     1995 of agreements concluded by the old German Democratic Republic, by Reg.
     3573/90 (O.J. 1990 L 353/16)).
231. Reg. 2408/92 (O.J. 1992 L 240/8, amended by the Act of Austrian, Finnish and
     Swedish Accession (1994)).
232. [1971] ECR 263, [1971] CMLR 335. The case concerned the ERTA, as to which, see
     note 318, *post*.
233. *In casu*, Reg. 543/69 (O.J. English Special Edition 1969 (I), p. 170), since replaced by
     Reg. 3820/85 (O.J. 1985 L 370/1).
234. [1977] ECR 741, [1977] 2 CMLR 779.

also had exclusive competence if the internal measures could only be adopted after the conclusion of the relevant international law arrangement with third countries, provided that such an arrangement was also necessary in order to achieve an internal Community objective. Thus the Community is competent to conclude international agreements implementing existing Community transport policy and establishing new policy. In Opinion 1/94 on *WTO – GATS and TRIPs*[235] the Court held that international agreements in the field of transport were excluded from Article 113 EC.[236]

A brief overview of existing external relations in the transport sector will give a flavour of the importance of the international dimension. In relation to road transport the Committee of European Ministers of Transport (CEMT) and the Economic Commission for Europe (ECE)[237] are the most important bodies. All the Member States participate, and the Community has observer status, in both fora. The ECE has undertaken much work in the field of technical provisions, and the CEMT plays an important role in the promotion of relations with third countries. In inland waterway transport matters the Central Commission for Rhine Navigation, in which the Community also has observer status, has long been an important forum.[238] For maritime transport the United Nations Conference on Trade and Development (UNCTAD) is a major forum: its maritime division has seen a number of conventions adopted, of which that laying down a code of conduct for Liner Conferences is the most important.[239] In the field of safety and the protection of the marine environment, the International Maritime Organization (IMO, based in London) is the relevant UN body. In both of these the Community has observer status. Furthermore, the Organization for Economic Cooperation and Development (OECD, based in Paris) plays an important role in the preparation of the decision-making by the Western countries (the so-called B Group) in the UNCTAD framework, as well as in the adoption of its own policies, as demonstrated

235. [1994] ECR I-5267 at 5402–5404.
236. Community competence is founded on Arts. 75 and 84 EC. These judgments are discussed further in Chapter XII, *post*.
237. Which is a regional commission of the United Nations Economic and Social Council.
238. Of the Member States, France, Germany, the Benelux countries and the United Kingdom are members. Switzerland is also a member. See Opinion 1/76, [1977] ECR 741, [1977] 2 CMLR 779. In an unpublished decision of 19 December 1978 (Bull. EC 11-1978, point 2.1.93; Bull. EC 12–1978 point 2.1.135) the Council took steps to ensure that the Member States concerned acted unanimously in the Central Commission for the Rhine. The Central Commission had been empowered under a Supplementary Protocol to the Revised Convention for Rhine Navigation to determine the conditions of access for vessels from third countries. The Convention was signed at Mannheim, 17 October 1868 (59 BFSP 470), and amended at Strasbourg, 20 November 1963 (TS 66(1967), Cmnd 3371).
239. UNCTAD Convention on a Code of Conduct for Liner Conferences (UKTS 45 (1987), Cm. 213). This is the only UNCTAD maritime transport convention to have entered into force.

by the Code of Liberalization of Current Invisible Operations.[240] In OECD, likewise, the Community has observer status. For the air transport field, the International Civil Aviation Organization is the worldwide forum responsible for economic and technical cooperation in civil aviation, and at European level the European Civil Aviation Conference exists to improve the coordination, better utilization and development of European air traffic. In both cases again, the Community has observer status. It also has such status with the Central Office for International Carriage by Rail. Close cooperation, of a more general nature also takes place with the relevant specialist committees of the Council of Europe, and cooperation also takes place with Eurocontrol (based in Brussels) in relation to air safety.

Concrete relations with third countries concerning maritime, air and road transport are usually set out in bilateral conventions, which means that there is an extensive set of rules, particularly in the aviation sector. Any incompatibility between these conventions and the EC Treaty has to be eliminated in accordance with the second paragraph of Article 234 EC. Particularly in the aviation sector steps to tackle these problems are still in their infancy.[241]

3.4 Competition in the transport sector: general observations

Article 1 of Regulation 141/62[242] expressly suspended the application of Regulation 17[243] (but not of Articles 85 and 86 EC themselves), and this exception did not cover all agreements embraced by Article 85 EC.[244]

240. OECD, Paris, 1992.
241. See the Commission's Communication on external relations in air transport (COM (92) 434 Final), although negotiations for a common airspace with the United States and various other arrangements are under way, see *General Report 1996* (Brussels, Luxembourg, 1997) point 405.
242. O.J. English Special Edition 1959–62, p. 291, most recently amended by Reg. 1002/67 (J.O. 1967 306/1).
243. O.J. English Special Edition 1959–62, p. 87 (most recently amended by the Act of Austrian, Finnish and Swedish Accession (1994)).
244. *E.g.* agreements to take over certain shareholdings (see, outside the transport sector, Cases 142 and 156/84 *British American Tobacco Company Ltd. et al. v. Commission* [1987] ECR 4487, [1988] 4 CMLR 24.
245. See Decs. 85/121 (O.J. 1985 L 46/51) *Olympic Airways* and 88/859 (O.J. 1988 L 317/24) *London European – Sabena*. As to ground handling services at airports, see now Dir. 96/67 (O.J. 1996 L 272/36).
246. Reg. 4064/89 (in its corrected version, O.J. 1989 L 257/14, amended by Reg. 1310/97 (O.J. 1997 L 180/1)). Art. 22(1) (as so amended) excludes the application of *inter alia* Regs. 4056/86 (O.J. 1986 L 378/4) and 3975/87 (O.J. 1987 L 374/1) to mergers, save for Joint Ventures not having a Community dimension and which have as their object or effect the coordination of competitive behaviour of undertakings remaining independent.

Moreover, it only covers transport itself, and thus not matters such as ground handling services.[245] At present each sector has been the subject of individual rules relating to competition. It should be noted that the Merger Regulation[246] applies in its entirety to the transport sector. Thus the air and maritime transport sectors are caught by the general regime of Regulation 4064/89, even where they are not yet covered by regulations implementing Article 85 EC.

3.5 The Treaty provisions on transport

Article 74 EC confirms the rule provided for in Article 61(1) EC that the freedom to provide services in the field of transport should be achieved in the context of the common transport policy. It also places that policy in the perspective of the general objectives of the EC Treaty. The Treaty itself gives no further indication of the concept of a common transport policy, unlike in the case of the CAP. In the absence of indications in the Treaty a considerable discussion ensued in the literature.[247] The Commission has produced various memoranda in which the common transport policy is discussed.[248] The concept was extensively discussed in Case 13/83 *European Parliament v. Council*[249] in which the common transport policy was described as coherent set of rules.[250] The importance of a correct definition of the concept was somewhat diminished by the conclusion that it was for the Council to determine the objectives and means of that policy.[251] As a result of that judgment the Council proceeded to draw up programmes for the achievement of a common policy in the various branches of transport.[252] In the discussion about a common transport policy there has long been a major debate between the proponents of liberalization and the supporters of harmonization. Now that the common transport policy has largely been achieved the importance of that discussion has receded, although more recent developments in the implementation of the new policy seem to indicate that this debate may be resurrected.

Article 75 EC is the core of the transport policy. It first of all indicates the procedural framework for the establishment of the policy. Then in Article 75(1)(a) and (b) prescribes that in any event common rules must be established for international transport to or from the territory of a Member State or passing across the territory of one or more Member

247. See the general discussion in Erdmenger, *loc. cit.* (see note 191, *supra*).
248. See Bull. EC Supp. 16/73; Bull. EC 11–1977 point 3.3.1, and O.J. 1980 C 294/6. As to more recent memoranda, see note 222, *supra*.
249. [1985] ECR 1513, [1986] 1 CMLR 138.
250. [1985] ECR 1513 at 1595.
251. *Ibid.* at 1596.
252. Resolution of 12 September 1985 (O.J. 1985 C 262/69).

States, and for the conditions under which non-resident carriers may operate transport services within a Member State (cabotage transport). The Court has decided[253] that the Council may adopt the measures it deems necessary to guide the required liberalization. Such measures may be based on Article 75(1)(d) EC, as well as on the words 'taking into account the distinctive features of transport' in the first sentence of Article 75(1) EC. The Council has a wide margin of discretion on this point.[254] In particular the Council may decide what degree of market intervention is necessary. On the basis of Article 75 EC the Council established a system to cope with any possible crisis in road transport.[255] The Commission collects data necessary to monitor the market and to detect a possible crisis.[256] If a Member State considers that there is a crisis it may request the Commission to investigate, and, if the Commission considers that there is a crisis, it may adopt measures to restrict the supply of capacity; such measures may last for up to six months and may be renewed once for up to six months more.[257] Article 75(1)(c) EC was added by the TEU, thereby conferring express competence on the Community to adopt measures to improve transport safety,[258] and Article 75(1)(d) permits the adoption of any other appropriate provisions.

Article 76 EC obliges the Member States, pending the adoption of the measures provided for in Article 75(1), not to introduce provisions which make the conditions of transport for transporters from other Member States less favourable, unless the Council unanimously agrees. In Case C-195/90 *Commission v. Germany*[259] the Court gave a broad interpretation of this obligation, so that measures designed to terminate the hitherto more favourable conditions for transporters from other Member States and place them on an equal footing with national undertakings also fell

253. Case 13/83 *European Parliament v. Council* [1985] ECR 1513 at 1596.
254. The Court confirmed this in Case C-17/90 *Pinaud Wieger GmbH Spedition v. Bundesanstalt für den Güterfernverkehr* [1994] ECR 5253 at 5283. At present measures are adopted under the cooperation procedure (Art. 189c EC) after ECOSOC has been consulted. The Treaty of Amsterdam will substitute the co-decision procedure and require consultation of the Committee of the Regions and ECOSOC.
255. Reg. 3916/90 (O.J. 1990 L 375/10).
256. *Ibid.*, Art. 3.
257. *Ibid.*, Art. 4. There is the possibility of a Member State bringing the matter before the Council, which may decide differently, *ibid.*, Art. 4(6), and the Commission may propose to the Council that the measures be extended (by the latter) for a longer period than that which the Commission may authorize, *ibid.* Art. 4(7).
258. Previously measures which had major safety justifications were adopted as social provisions, or as technical harmonization provisions under Arts. 100 or 100a EC. Specific competence in transport safety permits a much wider range of Community action in this important area. See *e.g.* the proposed action programme on traffic safety COM (97) 131 Final, the proposal for a decision on the promotion of a policy on sustainable and safe mobility in the transport sector, COM (96) 654 Final (O.J. 1997 C 28/21) and, earlier, COM (93) 246 Final and Dec. 93/704.
259. [1992] ECR I-3141 at 3182–3183.

foul of Article 76 EC. That provision ceases to have effect when the measures specified in Article 75(1) EC are adopted, and is thus for the moment still effective. In view of the drafting it can be accepted that Article 76 EC is directly effective.[260] This standstill clause may still be relevant for new accessions, even after the achievement of a common transport policy.

Article 77 EC provides that aid measures which meet the needs of coordination of transport or represent reimbursement for the discharge of certain obligations inherent in the concept of public service are compatible with the Treaty. This is generally regarded as supplementing the exceptions listed in Article 92(2) and (3) EC to the prohibition on state aids. Articles 92 and 93 EC are applicable to the transport sector in the normal way.[261] Article 77 EC is also to be seen as an exception to Article 90(2) EC,[262] and the provisions in the fields of public service and competition, discussed in section 3.6, below, are important for the interpretation of this provision.

Article 78 EC provides that measures taken within the framework of the Treaty in respect of transport rates and conditions must take account of the economic circumstances of carriers. This appears to confirm the rationale for a common transport policy discussed in section 3.1, above, and is a clear obligation which the Council has to take into account in the adoption of measures under Article 75 EC. Article 79 EC required the abolition at the latest before the end of the second stage of the transitional period of discriminatory carriage rates and conditions; it is a *lex specialis* in relation to Article 6 EC and has been directly effective since then. This obligation is worked out in more detail in Regulation 11/60.[263]

Article 80 EC contains a prohibition on Member States imposing, in respect of transport operations carried out within the Community, rates and conditions involving any element of support or protection in the interest of one or more particular undertakings or industries as from the beginning of the second stage of the transitional period, unless authorized by the Commission. It must be assumed that this prohibition too is directly effective.[264] To the extent that such support or protection constitutes aid in the sense of Article 92 EC, which, in view of the wide definition of state aid which the Court applies, is very likely, Articles 92 and 93 EC will apply in addition to Article 77 EC. A support tariff,

260. As appears from Cases C-184 and 221/91 *Oorburg et al. v. Wasser- und Schiffahrtsdirektion Nordwest* [1993] ECR I-1633 at 1660–1661.
261. See Case 156/77 *Commission v. Belgium* [1978] ECR 1881 at 1894–1895.
262. See also Case C-387/92 *Banco de Crédito Industrial SA, now Banco exterior de España SA v. Ayuntamiento de Valencia* [1994] ECR I-877 at 907–909.
263. O.J. English Special Edition 1959–62, p. 60, amended by Reg. 3626/84 (O.J. 1984 L 335/84).
264. See Gaudet & Bayens (1969) *European Transport Law* 42.

which is thus prohibited, may, however, be permitted by the Commission in exceptional cases.[265]

Article 81 EC prohibits the carriers from imposing charges or dues in respect of the crossing of frontiers (in addition to the transport rates) which are in excess of a reasonable level after taking the costs actually incurred thereby into account. The Member States are obliged to endeavour to reduce those costs progressively. This provision shows clear similarities with the prohibition of charges having equivalent effect to customs duties, and is clearly designed to ensure that inter-state traffic is not hindered by unreasonable charges imposed by the carriers themselves, which would in practice frustrate the liberalization achieved by the prohibition of state charges. If it can be shown in a particular case that the charges are disproportionate to the costs, it is submitted that shippers will be able to rely on Article 81 EC against carriers. Article 82 EC has lost its significance since German unification, but just like Article 92(2)(c) EC it may be of importance for industrial restructuring. Article 80(2) may also play a role in such circumstances. Article 83 EC establishes an Advisory committee for Transport, which is attached to the Commission.

The drafting of Article 84 EC has been revised by the SEA and a reference to that provision has been included in Article 7a EC. The drafting of Article 84(2) EC is decidedly infelicitous, as the first sentence still refers to the Council deciding 'by what procedure' appropriate provisions for sea and air transport are to be laid down, whereas the second sentence prescribes that of Article 75(1) and (3). Moreover, the word 'whether' in the first sentence is decidedly otiose. Keeping the present drafting still gives rise to doubt about the obligation to establish a common policy for maritime and air transport. The change in the decision-making process to permit qualified majority voting is though a clear improvement.

3.6 Inland transport – general observations

As was indicated in section 3.1, above, inland transport embraces transport by road, rail and inland waterway. Before looking at each of these sectors

---

265. Art. 80(2) EC. On the Commission's freedom of discretion here see Case 1/69 *Italy v. Commission* [1969] ECR 277, [1970] CMLR 17. See also Jeantet (1964) J.D. Int. 86 on the judgment of the French Cour de Cassation of 19 February 1964 on Art. 80 EEC and the further case-law cited by Close in Vaughan (ed.), *op. cit.* (see note 191, *supra*) para. 18.29 (note 1). The case-law shows that support tariffs are involved only if certain users are advantaged, not if they only advantage other transporters, which would, for example, be the case of railway tariffs which advantage national transporters in combined rail/road carriage. See also Case 2/84 *Commission v. Italy* [1985] ECR 1127.

individually, it is appropriate to give an overview of measures which apply in more than one sector.

Framework programmes

The EC Treaty suggests that transport policy should be more or less a coherent whole.[266] On various occasions the Council has adopted resolutions or decisions in which working programmes were set out;[267] subsequently these policy intentions have been laid down in the form of resolutions. An important example is the Council's Resolution of 12 September 1985[268] which can be seen as the Council's response to the judgment in Case 13/83 *European Parliament v. Council*.[269] Furthermore, the Commission has adopted a number of Communications in which it has proposed programmes for its future activities.[270] The Schaus Memorandum of 10 April 1961 formed the original basis for the Commission's activities, and gave the initial orientation for the development of a common transport policy.[271]

Public Services and State Aids

In Regulation 1191/69[272] the Council made provision for the removal of differences between the Member States legislation concerning the treatment of public service obligations in the transport sector.[273] Especially in that sector such differences are capable of significantly distorting competition. In order to attain the desired aim, common principles for the removal or

266. *Cf.* the discussion in Case 13/83 *European Parliament v. Council* [1985] ECR 1513, [1986] 1 CMLR 138.
267. The last one was on 14 December 1967 (Dec. 67/790 (O.J. English Special Edition 2nd Series IV, p. 23). A first step in the development of a common transport policy was the adoption of the decision establishing a procedure for prior examination and consultation of Member States' proposed transport measures (Decision of 21 March 1962 (O.J. English Special Edition 1969–62 p. 96, amended by Dec. 73/402 (O.J. 1973 L 347/48). That decision was intended to avoid divergent national transport policies. See *e.g.* Opinion 90/347 (O.J. 1990 L 170/49) to the Dutch government on a draft road transport law.
268. O.J. 1985 C 262/99.
269. [1985] ECR 1513, [1986] 1 CMLR 138.
270. See *e.g.* COM (83) 85 Final (O.J. 1983 154/1) and the Communications mentioned in note 222, *supra*.
271. Bull. EC 4–1961 p. 5, see Tromm, *op. cit.* (see note 191, *supra*) 125 *et seq*.
272. O.J. English Special Edition 1969 (I), p. 276, most recently amended by Reg. 1893/91 (O.J. 1991 L 169/1).
273. Separate rules govern such obligations in the field of air transport, see Reg. 2408/92 (O.J. 1992 L 240/8, amended by the Act of Austrian, Finnish and Swedish Accession (1994)), Art. 4.

treatment of public service obligations were established. Common rules and methods for the financial compensations arising from the normalization of railway accounts were laid down in Regulation 1192/69.[274]

As was noted in section 3.5, above, Articles 92–93 EC apply in the transport sector in the normal way, albeit supplemented by Article 77 EC.[275] In Decision 65/271[276] the Council adopted a programme for the harmonization of national provisions on competition affecting the inland transport sectors.[277] Regulation 1107/70[278] indicates in which cases and under what circumstances the Member States may adopt measures or impose public service obligations which on the basis of Article 77 EC will not be regarded as aid to the inland transport sectors. Article 3 of that regulation indicates when aid measures are permissible. Regulation 1108/ 70[279] lays down rules for an accounting system for expenditure on infrastructure in respect of transport by rail, road and inland waterways.

These regulations should be seen as a complement to the regulations mentioned above dealing with public service obligations and financial compensation. Until the *15th Report on Competition Policy*[280] no mention was made of aids in the transport sector, but since then many annual reports have noted the large-scale support granted to national railways.[281] 'The Commission's aim is gradually to arrive at a system where the only public financing of railways will be in the form of financing for infrastructure or compensation for public service obligations, or where it is part of an overall restructuring plan aimed at restoring the financial viability of the firm.'[282] Problems relating to inland waterway transport are also frequently encountered, and they have been countered with a

---

274. O.J. English Special Edition 1969 (I), p. 283, most recently amended by the Act of Austrian, Finnish and Swedish Accession (1994).

275. See extensively, Hancher *et al., EC State Aids* (Chichester, 1993) Chapter 10 (2nd ed. in preparation).

276. O.J. English Special Edition 1965–66, p. 67.

277. This decision was further developed in Regs. 1191/69 and 1192/69 (see notes 271 and 274, respectively).

278. O.J. English Special Edition 1970 (II), p. 360, most recently amended by Reg. 543/97 (O.J. 1997 L 84/6).

279. O.J. English Special Edition 1970 (II), p. 363, most recently amended by the Act of Austrian, Finnish and Swedish Accession (1994). This regulation has been further developed by the Commission in Regs. 2598/70 (O.J. English Special Edition 1970 (III), p. 899, amended by Reg. 2116/78 (O.J. 1978 L 246/7) and 281/71 (O.J. English Special Edition 1971 (I), p. 57, most recently amended by the Act of Austrian, Finnish and Swedish Accession (1994)). Note that Dir. 80/723 (O.J. 1980 L 195/35, amended by Dir. 93/84 (O.J. 1993 L 254/16)) on the transparency of financial relations between the Member States and public undertakings does not apply to the transport sector, *ibid.*, Art. 4.

280. For 1985 (Brussels, Luxembourg, 1986).

281. Thus in 1988–1990 some 6698 million ECU of aid was granted to the German railways.

282. *XXVIth Report on Competition Policy 1996* (Brussels, Luxembourg, 1997) point 201.

Community aid regime.[283] In other inland transport sectors only incidental problems are reported. In the air transport sector there have been considerable aid operations, which are discussed in section 3.12, below.

Competition

A separate system governs inland transport in accordance with Regulation 1017/68,[284] although Article 1 thereof makes it clear that it does not apply to all agreements, decisions and concerted practices in the transport sector. In addition to the legal exemption of technical agreements in Article 3 of that regulation, the most important departure from the normal competition procedural rules of Regulation 17[285] is that notification is not a prequisite for an individual exemption. There is provision in Article 12 of the regulation for an opposition procedure. The regulation also makes provision in Article 4 for a special exemption for groups of small and medium sized enterprises (SMEs). There is no provision for the grant of negative clearance. So far only one decision has been based on this regulation.[286] The system of the Community quota of authorizations for the carriage of goods by road has now been abolished.[287]

3.7   Road transport

As has been indicated in section 3.1, above, for professional freight transport by road a common transport policy has pretty well been established. Given that road freight transport forms a large part of the professional freight transport sector, the economic importance of this system is very great indeed. Regulation 881/92[288] establishes a system of Community licences, based on qualitative criteria.[289] Once a road haulage

283. Reg. 1101/89 (O.J. 1989 L 116/25, most recently amended by Reg. 2310/96 (O.J. 1996 L 313/8).
284. O.J. English Special Edition 1968 (I), p. 302, most recently amended by the Act of Austrian, Finnish and Swedish Accession (1994), and implemented by Regs. 1629/69 (O.J. English Special Edition 1969 (II), p. 344, most recently amended by Reg. 3666/93 (O.J. 1993 L 336/1) and the Act of Austrian, Finnish and Swedish Accession (1994)) and 1630/69 (O.J. English Special Edition 1969 (II), p. 381).
285. See note 243, *supra*.
286. Dec. 85/383 (O.J. 1985 L 219/35) *French Inland Waterway Transport – EATE*, upheld by the Court in Case 272/85 *Association nationale des travailleurs indépendants de la batellerie (Antib) v. Commission* [1985] ECR 2201, [1988] 4 CMLR 677.
287. By Reg. 881/92 (O.J. 1992 L 95/1, most recently amended by the Act of Austrian, Finnish and Swedish Accession (1994)). As to the predecessor regime, see Close in Vaughan (ed.), *op. cit.* (see note 191, *supra*) para. 18.111.
288. *Ibid.*
289. The Community authorizations are issued by the competent authorities in the Member

operator has a Community authorization, he or she may freely undertake international transport throughout the Community, as Regulation 881/92 has lifted all the earlier restrictions. Transport to third countries remains dependent on the agreements which have been concluded with those countries, many of which are now in the framework of the Europe Agreements. Important transit agreements have been concluded with Switzerland,[290] Austria (well prior to accession),[291] and Hungary.[292] Important general agreements relating to transport have also been reached with Slovenia[293] and with FYROM Macedonia[294] and negotiations have begun with Croatia.[295]

From 30 June 1998 the holder of a Community authorization is able to undertake cabotage transport throughout the Community.[296] Prior to that date there were rapidly increasing cabotage quotas.[297] The liberalization of cabotage transport was made possible after a solution was found to the very divergent fees for the use of infrastructure in the various Member States.[298] Motor vehicle taxation is thus now grouped in six minimum tariffs[299] and the Member States remain competent to introduce tolls or other road user charges, although they must not discriminate on the ground of carrier nationality or consignment origin or destination, nor

State of establishment, *ibid.*, Art. 5. The qualitative criteria for access to the occupation of road haulage operator are set out in Dir. 96/26 (O.J. 1996 L 124/1, to which an amendment has been proposed, COM (97) 25 Final (O.J. 1997 C 95/6)).

290. See Dec. 92/578 (O.J. 1992 L 373/1).

291. Dec. 92/577 (O.J. 1992 L 373/4 (the agreement is at L 373/6)). This involves the use of an Eco Points system (see Reg. 3637/92 (O.J. 1992 L 373/1) and Reg. 3298/94 (O.J. 1994 L 341/20, amended by Reg. 1524/96 (O.J. 1996 L 190/13))).

292. See the exchanges of letters, O.J. 1992 L 407/48; O.J. 1993 L 347/269, and Dec. 609/92 (O.J. 1992 L 407/47).

293. O.J. 1993 L 189/161 (see Dec. 93/409 (O.J. 1993 L 189/160)). For an Additional Protocol to ensure non-discriminatory treatment of all lorries, regardless of their country of origin, in haulage operations through Austria, see Dec. 97/863 (O.J. 1997 L 351/62).

294. See Dec. 97/832 (O.J. 1997 L 348/169).

295. *General Report 1995* (Brussels, Luxembourg, 1996), point 417. Negotiations with Hungary, Bulgaria and Romania designed to facilitate the transport of goods between Greece and the rest of the Community are also under way, *ibid.*, point 418.

296. Reg. 3118/93 (O.J. 1993 L 279/1, amended by Reg. 3315/94 (O.J. 1994 L 350/9) and implemented by Reg. 792/94 (O.J. 1994 L 92/13)). Art. 1(2) of Reg. 3118/93 empowers other carriers who are designated by national legislation to undertake such transport. Cabotage, it will be recalled, means a transport operation performed between two places in one country by a non-resident carrier.

297. See *e.g.*Case C-17/90 *Pinaud Wieger GmbH Spedition v. Bundesanstalt für den Güterfernverkehr* [1991] ECR I-5253.

298. With the adoption of Dir. 93/89 (see note 204, *supra*). This finally settled unrest over the introduction of road tax *vignets* for road haulage traffic from Denmark, Germany and Belgium. See also COM (96) 331 Final (O.J. 1997 C 59/9), and, more generally, in relation to telematics in the transport sector, COM (97) 223 Final.

299. *Ibid.*, Art. 6.

must they give rise to any undue hindrance.[300] If there are serious disturbances in relation to cabotage, safeguard measures may be invoked.[301] For cabotage transport, the rates and contractual conditions of the host state apply.[302] In a real internal market of course such a provision should not apply any more.[303] The Netherlands, the United Kingdom, and (since 1 January 1995) Germany no longer apply rate provisions; such provisions for domestic transport are only still found in Italy, Spain and Greece.

For international transport there are no common rules for rates and contractual conditions, thus Regulation 4058/89[304] prescribes that the rates for international carriage are to be freely fixed between the parties to the haulage contract[305] and the Member States have to establish a system whereby the rates charged are communicated to the national authorities, pending the introduction of a definitive system of market observation.[306] As from 1 January 1999, Regulation 1172/98 will govern statistical returns on the carriage of goods by road.[307]

As was observed in section 3.1, above, the completion of the common transport policy for road transport has been achieved in stages and has required a not inconsiderable amount of nimble political footwork, which has had the result of bringing the conditions of competition in the various Member States closer together, something which is also due to a number of the measures discussed below.

A number of measures concerning road transport are rather more general in scope. The first of these concerns the introduction of a Community driving licence.[308] The Community has also taken action relating to the technical control of motor vehicles and their trailers,[309] which ensures the mutual recognition of controls and establishes common rules. Thus lorries are assured of free movement. The formalities for the cross-frontier transport of goods have been adapted to the development of the internal market within the Community.[310]

A particular milestone in the achievement of the common transport policy in the road transport sector was the adoption of Directive 85/3 on weights, dimensions and certain other technical characteristics[311] which has

300. *Ibid.*, Art. 7. The directive also contains certain rules relating to uniform application.
301. See note 209, *supra*. This facilitated progress towards the liberalization of cabotage.
302. Reg. 3118/93 (see note 296, *supra*), Art. 6. *Cf.* Case C-17/90 *Pinaud Wieger GmbH Spedition v. Bundesanstalt für den Güterfernverkehr* [1991] ECR I-5253 at 5283.
303. *Cf.* Case C-113/89 *Rush Portugesa Lda v. Office national d'immigration* [1990] ECR I-1417, [1991] 2 CMLR 818. In a real internal market the rates of the land of establishment would apply, as in the case of the free movement of goods.
304. O.J. 1989 L 390/1.
305. Reg. 4058/89, *ibid.*, Art. 2.
306. *Ibid.*, Art. 3. Strangely the preamble to Reg. 3916/90 (see note 209, *supra*) makes no mention of this system.
307. O.J. 1998 L 163/1 which replaces Dir. 78/546 (O.J. 1978 L 168/29).

now been replaced by Directive 96/53.[312] The long-running debate particularly on axle weights which preceded the adoption of Directive 85/3 and again the adoption of Directive 96/53 well demonstrates the competing interests of transporters, who are anxious to transport goods as efficiently and cheaply as possible, freight vehicle manufacturers seeking to gain market domination through their own standards, safety considerations, and environmental interests. The interests of ensuring that adequate arrangements exist in relation to insurance have been taken care of by Directive 72/166.[313]

The Council has also taken steps to ensure the duty-free admission of fuel contained in commercial vehicle fuel tanks,[314] as differences in the duty-free exemptions lead to clear distortions of competition, especially where there are major differences in the level of diesel excise duty. Finally, Directive 84/647[315] makes provision concerning the use of vehicles hired without drivers for the carriage of goods by road.

One of the most important reasons why the transport sector has been subject to special rules in all the Member States and thus also at Community level is the social aspect. Many small firms operate in this sector and many measures were adopted with a view to protecting them against cut-throat competition. Thus questions of the social aspects of transport have always been considered important, and action in this area was already envisaged in 1965.[316] A first step was the establishment of what has now become the Joint Committee on Road Transport, which

308. See now Dir. 91/439 (O.J. 1991 L 237/1, most recently amended by Dir. 97/26 (O.J. 1997 L 150/41)). The national licences are drawn up according to a Community model.
309. See now Dir. 96/96 (O.J. 1996 L 46/1, corrig. O.J. 1998 L 93/22). Under the predecessor regime, see Case C-55/93 *Van Schaik* [1994] ECR I-4837.
310. The abolition of systematic frontier controls on the movement of goods between Member States has meant the repeal of earlier legislation. Dir. 83/643 (O.J. 1983 L 359/8, last amended by Dir. 91/342 (O.J. 1991 L 187/47)) was repealed with effect from 1 January 1993, which was the date when Reg. 2726/90 (O.J. 1990 L 262/1) on Community transit entered into force. That regulation was in turn repealed by *eg.* Reg. 2913/92 (O.J. 1992 L 302/1, most recently amended by Reg. 97/82 (O.J. 1997 L 17/1) establishing the Community Customs Code (implemented by Reg. 2454/93 (O.J. 1993 L 253/1, most recently amended by Reg. 75/98 (O.J. 1998 L 7/3)).
311. O.J. 1985 L 2/14 (amended on numerous occasions).
312. O.J. 1996 L 235/59, corrig. O.J. 1998 L 19/83.
313. O.J. English Special Edition 1972 (II), p. 360, most recently amended by Dir. 84/5 (O.J. 1984 L 8/17). The most important obligation is that the Member States cease to require production of a Green card at their borders; furthermore they are obliged to take all possible steps to ensure that vehicles registered in their countries have at least third party insurance.
314. Dir. 68/297 (English Special Edition 1968 (II), p. 313, most recently amended by Dir. 92/12 (O.J. 1992 L 76/1)). The latter has itself has been most recently amended by Dir. 96/99 (O.J. 1997 L 8/12).
315. O.J. 1984 L 335/72, amended by Dir. 90/398 (O.J. 1990 L 202/46)).
316. In Dec. 65/271 (O.J. English Special Edition 1965–66, p. 67.

assists the Commission in formulating and implementing Community social policy aimed at the improvement and harmonization of living and working conditions in road transport.[317] It was in this field that the celebrated litigation in Case 22/70 *Commission v. Council*[318] took place relating to the ERTA Agreement[319] to which all the Member States are contracting parties (but not yet the Community) and governs international road transport starting or finishing in, or transiting through third countries which are contracting parties to the agreement. Community provisions apply to journeys within the Community.[320] They deal with the age and number of crew members, driving time, breaks and rest periods (a tired driver is a dangerous driver), and also prohibit the payment of certain types of incentive payments (as these may encourage drivers not to comply with the safety provisions). These measures were designed at once to equalize conditions of competition as well as to take steps to promote safety and prevent the exploitation of crews. Similarly with the introduction of the tachograph,[321] initially so hated by United Kingdom lorry drivers (because it would stop them 'moonlighting' by bringing back a return load for their own profit on occasions when they should have returned unladen) that it was not until after the judgment of the Court that the United Kingdom government had the courage to comply with the then applicable regulation.[322] The real reasons for the introduction of the regulation (most welcomed by continental lorry drivers) were lost sight of in the United Kingdom with the tachograph being labelled as the 'spy in

317. The present Committee is set up by Dec. 85/516 (O.J. 1985 L 317/33, amended by Dec. 87/447 (O.J. 1987 L 240/37)) and replaces that originally established in 1965.
318. [1971] ECR 263, [1971] CMLR 335.
319. The European Agreement concerning the Work of Crews of Vehicles engaged in International Road Transport (Geneva, 1 July 1970 to 31 March 1971, TS 103 (1978); Cmnd 7401), frequently known by its acronym in French, AETR. Certain amendments came into force on 3 August 1983, see Close in Vaughan (ed.), *op. cit.* (see note 191, *supra*) para. 18.169.
320. The present provisions are contained in Reg. 3820/85 (O.J. 1985 L 370/1, corrig. O.J. 1986 L 206/36). A derogation has been granted to the United Kingdom, see Dec. 94/451 (O.J. 1994 L 187/9). As was noted in section 3.3, *ante*, the present provisions replace those applicable at the time of the dispute relating to the ERTA (see note 233, *supra*).
321. See now Reg. 3821/85 (O.J. 1985 L 370/8, most recently amended by Reg. 1056/97 (O.J. 1997 L 154/21)), which replaced the earlier Reg. 1463/70 (O.J. English Special Edition 1970 (II), p. 482) which was the measure which gave rise to the controversy described in the text, and was also one of the Community measures considered in the ERTA litigation mentioned in the text. The United Kingdom has been granted a derogation (see note 320, *supra*). See also Dir. 88/599 (O.J. 1988 L 325/55), to which an amendment has been proposed, see the amended proposal COM (95) 550 Final (O.J. 1996 C 25/5).
322. Case 128/78 *Commission v. United Kingdom* [1979] ECR 419, [1979] 2 CMLR 45. See also the bizarre spectacle in *Concorde Express Transport Ltd. v. Traffic Examiner Metropolitan Area* [1980] 2 CMLR 221.

the cab'. Vehicles intended to transport goods or persons by road have to be fitted with a tachograph, which must be used (although there are exemptions at Community level and exemptions may be granted at national level, sometimes after authorization by the Commission).[323] Perhaps predictably there has been considerable case-law concerning this social legislation.[324]

3.8   Carriage of passengers by road

The common system dealing with the carriage of passengers by road is also based on the one hand on controlling access to the occupation of passenger transport operator, through requirements as to good repute, appropriate financial standing and professional competence.[325] On the other hand international coach and bus transport is governed by Regulation 684/92.[326] By virtue of Article 3 of that regulation any passenger transport operator authorized in his or her Member State of establishment who satisfies the requirements as to access to the profession, and road safety requirements, may provide bus and coach services within the Community. Regular services and shuttle services without accommodation are subject to an authorization by the Member State in which the place of departure is situated, and authorizations are issued with the consent of the authorities of the other Member States concerned. Shuttle services with accommodation, certain occasional services and own-account services are possible on the basis of a control document or certificate issued by the competent authorities of the Member State in which the vehicle is registered.[327] Cabotage in coach and bus transport is governed by Regulation 12/98[328] which replaces earlier legislation annulled by the Court.[329] Since the beginning of January 1996 cabotage for certain

323. See, for further details, Close in Vaughan (ed.), *op. cit.* (see note 319, *supra*) paras. 18. 164–167 and 18.154). The exceptions parallel those applicable under Reg. 3820/85 (see note 320, *supra*).
324. See *e.g.* Case C-7/90 *Vandevenne et al.* [1991] ECR I-4371; Case C-116/92 *Charlton et al.* [1993] ECR I-6755; Case C-394/92 *Michielsen et al.* [1994] ECR I-2497, and Case C-39/95 *Mrozek et al.* [1996] ECR I-1573.
325. Dir. 96/26 (O.J. 1996 L 124/1) which replaces earlier legislation. An amendment has been proposed, COM (97) 25 Final (O.J. 1997 C 95/66).
326. O.J. 1992 L 74/1 amended by Reg. 11/98 (O.J. 1998 L 4/1), replacing earlier legislation. See also Reg. 1839/92 (O.J. 1992 L 187/5, most recently amended by the Act of Austrian, Finnish and Swedish Accession (1994).
327. The concept of shuttle services will be abolished from 11 December 1998 and all services (including special regular services under contract) other than regular services may be provided without the need for any form of authorization, see the amendments made by Reg. 11/98, *ibid.* Community licences will be introduced from 11 June 1999, *ibid.*
328. O.J. 1998 L 4/10.
329. In Case C-388/92 *European Parliament v. Council* [1994] ECR I-2067 the Court annulled Reg. 2454/92 (O.J. 1992 L 251/1) on the ground that the Parliament had not been

regular services was liberalized completely by virtue of the regulation which was annulled; the remaining liberalization means that all cabotage operations, whether national or international, will be subject to the legislation of the host Member State as regards the routes operated, and the regularity, continuity and frequency of services.[330]

3.9 Rail transport

The main objective of the policy in this sector has always been to promote the healthy financial position of the railways and to guarantee reasonable conditions of competition *vis-à-vis* transport by road and inland waterways. The fact that railways have been and for the most part still are public undertakings has been an important factor in this. The Member States have taken on an important part of the infrastructure costs, which makes the competitive relationship with other forms of transport very difficult, and it is unsurprising that for many years there was no agreement on the allocation of rail infrastructure costs. That has now changed with the adoption of Directive 95/19 on the allocation of railway infrastructural capacities and the charging of infrastructure fees.[331] The question of how to keep uneconomic services going is one which raises considerable questions of regional policy. The Commission has recently adopted a White Paper on *Revitalizing the Community's Railways*.[332]

Most secondary Community legislation in the field covers the transparency of the financial relations between the railways and the Member States.[333] Thus Regulation 1192/69[334] provides for common rules for the normalization of the accounts of railway undertakings; Regulation 2830/77[335] covers comparability of the accounting systems and annual accounts of such undertakings, and Regulation 2183/78[336] deals with uniform costing principles for railway undertakings. Decision 82/529[337]

reconsulted after substantial amendments to the original proposal which did not emanate from it, but the effects of that regulation were maintained in force until the adoption of Reg. 12/98.

330. Subject to the application of the Community provisions, Reg. 12/98, Act. 4. Regular urban and suburban services are excluded as they are of general interest, *ibid.*, Art 3.

331. O.J. 1995 L 143/75.

332. COM (96) 421 Final. See also the Communication on the development of the Community's railways COM (95) 337 Final (O.J. 1995 C 321/10).

333. As to the public service measures, see section 3.6, *ante*.

334. See note 274, *supra*.

335. O.J. 1977 L 334/13, most recently amended by the Act of Austrian, Finnish and Swedish Accession (1994).

336. O.J. 1978 L 258/1, most recently amended by the Act of Austrian, Finnish and Swedish Accession (1994).

337. O.J. 1982 L 234/5, most recently amended by the Act of Austrian, Finnish and Swedish Accession (1994).

deals with the fixing of rates for the international carriage of goods by rail and Decision 83/418[338] covers the commercial independence of the railways in the management of their international passenger and freight traffic. The adoption of Directive 91/440 on the development of the Community's railways[339] has ensured that a clear separation is made between the management and accounts concerning on the one hand the provision of transport services, and on the other hand the management of railway infrastructure. Access and transit rights are ensured for third parties, and the infrastructure manager has to levy a fee for use of the infrastructure for which it is responsible. That fee must not discriminate between railway undertakings. Agreements relating to international combined transport of goods and the use of the infrastructure by international groupings are concluded with the infrastructure manager, again on non-discriminatory terms.[340]

Directive 95/18 on the licensing of railway undertakings[341] establishes the criteria and procedures for the grant of licences. Finally, Directive 96/49 deals with the transport of dangerous goods by rail,[342] and Directive 80/1177 deals with statistical returns in respect of the carriage of goods by inter alia rail.[343]

3.10 Inland waterway transport

Inland waterway transport in the Community occupies a special position in that it really only concerns Belgium, France, Germany and The Netherlands. The most important inland waterway route in the Community, the Rhine and its tributaries are governed by the Mannheim Convention.[344] This Convention guarantee free navigation of the Rhine

---

338. O.J. 1983 L 237/32, most recently amended by the Act of Austrian, Finnish and Swedish Accession (1994).
339. O.J. 1991 L 305/22. An amendment has been proposed, see the amended proposal COM (97) 34 Final.
340. As to competition aspects of agreements in the rail sector, see *e.g.* Decs. 94/174 (O.J. 1994 L 73/38) *Tariffs for combined goods transport*; 94/210 (O.J. 1994 L 104/34) *HOV/SVZ/MCN*; and 94/663 (O.J. 1994 L 259/20) *Night Services*. See also the exemption in Dec. 94/894 (O.J. 1994 L 354/66) *Eurotunnel*, annulled on appeal in Cases T-79 and 80/95 *Société nationale des chemins de fer français et al. v. Commission* [1996] ECR II-1491. In relation to ticket distribution, see Case T-14/93 *Union Internationale des Chemins de Fer v. Commission* [1995] ECR II-1503, upheld on appeal in Case C-264/95 P *Commission v. Union Internationale des Chemins de Fer v. Commission* [1997] ECR I-1287.
341. O.J. 1995 L 143/70.
342. O.J. 1996 L 235/25, amended by Dir. 96/87 (O.J. 1996 L 335/45).
343. O.J. 1980 L 350/23, most recently amended by the Act of Austrian, Finnish and Swedish Accession (1994).
344. See note 238, *supra*.

not simply for the riparian States but also for other countries, but the prospect of the opening of the Rhine–Main–Danube canal and thus of access of East European inland waterway fleets to the Community's inland waterway network led to the Member States which were party to the Convention being obliged to adopt two protocols to the Revised Mannheim Convention dealing with access to the Rhine and its associated waterways.[345] Thus access is confined to vessels having a real connection with one of the contracting parties to the Convention. At Community level this is ensured by Regulation 2919/85 which makes provision for certification that a vessel belongs to the Rhine navigation.[346]

Cabotage is permitted under Regulation 3921/91[347] for those carriers of goods or passengers by inland waterway established in a Member State in accordance with its legislation and, where appropriate, entitled there to carry out the international transport of goods or persons by inland waterway.[348] Cabotage operations are carried out under various national provisions of the host Member State, subject to the application of Community rules.[349] Regulation 1356/96[350] prohibits discrimination on grounds of nationality or place of establishment in the carriage of goods or persons by inland waterway between and through Member States against carriers of goods or passengers by inland waterway established in a Member State in accordance with its legislation and entitled there to carry out the international transport of goods or persons by inland waterway.[351] Directive 96/75 on systems of chartering and pricing in national and international waterway transport[352] provides for the gradual abolition by 1 January 2000 of the system of minimum compulsory tariffs and the rotation system.

Here too there are rules governing access to the occupation of carrier of goods by waterway[353] and the mutual recognition of certificates of professional competence.[354] Unlike in the equivalent directives in other

---

345. As to the Revised Convention, see *ibid.* The Council decisions of 19 December 1978 and 24 July 1979 were not published. See Close in Vaughan (ed.), *op. cit.* (see note 191, *supra*) para. 18.215.
346. O.J. 1985 L 280/4.
347. O.J. 1991 L 373/1.
348. *Ibid.*, Art. 1. As to the vessels which may be used for cabotage, see Art. 2.
349. *Ibid.*, Art. 3. The national rules as to rates and conditions governing transport contracts and chartering and operating procedures apply, as do those on technical specifications (which are those applicable to vessels authorized to carry out international transport operations); navigation and police regulations; navigation time and rest periods, and VAT on transport services.
350. O.J. 1996 L 175/7.
351. *Ibid.*, Art. 2. As to the vessels which must be used in order to benefit from this provision, see *ibid.*
352. O.J. 1996 L 304/12.
353. Dir. 87/540 (O.J. 1987 L 322/20).
354. *Ibid.*, Art. 7. The requirements are set out in the Annex.

transport sectors, professional competence is the sole Community criterion for access to the occupation.[355] The mutual recognition of national boatmaster's certificates has also been ensured,[356] such certificates must be issued according to a uniform Community model from early April 1998 at the latest.[357] Directive 82/714 establishes a system of Community inland waterway certificates.[358]

The inland waterway transport sector has for years been characterized by problems of structural overcapacity.[359] Regulation 2255/96[360] provides for the implementation until the end of 1999 of a system of national aid to support investment in certain types of inland waterway infrastructure. Finally, Directive 80/1177 deals with statistical returns in respect of the carriage of goods by *inter alia* inland waterway.[361]

3.11 Maritime transport

The Commission has recently adopted a Communication entitled *Towards a New Maritime Strategy*[362] which sets out three themes for the development of the Community's maritime policy: safety at sea, maintaining open markets, and the improvement of the competitiveness of Community shipping.

The core of the Community's policy in relation to maritime transport

355. *Ibid.*, Art. 3. If a Member State imposes on its own nationals requirements of good repute or absence of bankruptcy, or as to financial standing it must accept the appropriate certificates or documents issued in other Member States, see *ibid.*, Arts. 8 and 9.
356. Dir. 91/672 (O.J. 1991 L 373/29, most recently amended by the Act of Austrian, Finnish and Swedish Accession (1994)).
357. Dir. 96/50 (O.J. 1996 L 235/31), Art. 13 (18 months after notification, *viz.* by April 7, 1998).
358. O.J. 1982 L 301/1, amended by the Act of Austrian, Finnish and Swedish Accession (1994). This largely replaces the navigability licence system of Dir. 76/135 (O.J. 1976 L 21/10), but that system remains in place for certain vessels (including passenger vessels), see Close in Vaughan (ed.), *op. cit.* (see note 191, *supra*) para. 18.216. As to the system of Dir. 82/714, see Close, *ibid.* paras. 18.219 *et seq.* As to the transport of dangerous goods, see Dir. 82/714, Art. 6.
359. See the Commission's Communication COM (95) 199. Reg. 1101/89 (O.J. 1989 L 116/25, most recently amended by Regs. 2254/96 (O.J. 1996 L 304/1) providing for new measures for 1996–1998 and 2310/96 (O.J. 1996 L 313/8) dealing with new capacity in pusher boats). The scrapping scheme is designed to limit overcapacity, and through the 'old for new' rule restricts investment in new vessels. See Cases C-248 and 249/95 *SAM Schiffahrt GmbH et al. v. Germany* [1997] ECR I-4475.
360. O.J. 1996 L 304/3. It amends Reg. 1107/70 (see note 278, *supra*).
361. O.J. 1980 L 350/23, most recently amended by the Act of Austrian, Finnish and Swedish Accession (1994).
362. COM (96) 81 Final. The Council agreed with the strategy, see Bull. EU 12–1996, point 1.3.139. As to coastal shipping, see COM (95) 317 Final; as to short sea shipping, see COM (95) 317 Final and Bull. EU 12–1995, point 1.3.117.

(or sea transport as Article 84(2) EC calls it)[363] is to be found in Regulation 954/79,[364] in the implementation of the UNCTAD Convention on a Code of Conduct for Liner Conferences,[365] and the package of measures adopted in December 1986. This package comprises: Regulation 4055/86 on the application of the principle of the freedom to provide services;[366] Regulation 4056/86 on the application of the competition rules to this field;[367] Regulation 4057/86 on unfair pricing practices in the maritime sector,[368] and Regulation 4058/86 on free access to cargoes.[369] These measures together form the system applicable to liner traffic, which is of major economic importance.[370] This system is characterized by the principle of free access to the market: there are no rules relating to access to the occupation or to cargoes, although there are now minimum training requirements for seafarers.[371]

Access to liner conferences is restricted on the basis of Articles 1 and 2 of the UNCTAD Code of Conduct.[372] Article 2 of Regulation 954/79 in fact sets aside Article 1 of the Code as regards shipping lines established in Member States.[373] Special provision is made for the redistribution of any pooled cargo arrangements.[374] The other provisions of that regulation aim to guarantee and safeguard the market economy system. However, in practice the UNCTAD Code does not play

363. See, generally, Power, *EC Shipping Law* (London, 1992) and Bull and Stemshaug (eds.), *EC Shipping Policy* (Oslo, 1997).
364. O.J. 1979 L 121/1. It can be deduced from Case 355/87 *Commission v. Council* [1989] ECR 1517 that Art. 1 of Reg. 954/79 does not oblige the Member States to accede to the UNCTAD Liner Conferences Convention.
365. See note 239, *supra*. Liner traffic is traffic by merchant ships providing a regular service on particular routes.
366. O.J. 1986 L 378/1, amended by Reg. 3573/90 (O.J. 1990 L 353/13). This aims to apply this principle to maritime transport between the Member States and between them and third countries (thus Art. 1 of Reg. 4055/86 does not embrace cabotage; that has now been the subject of a separate measure, as is explained, *post*.) The abolition of unilateral national restrictions occurred in stages (it is now complete). Reg. 4055/86 also governs the conditions under which Member States may conclude cargo-sharing arrangements with third countries. In Case 355/87 *Commission v. Council* [1989] ECR 157 the Commission unsuccessfully challenged Dec. 87/475 (O.J. 1987 L 272/37) in which the Council authorized Italy to conclude such an agreement with Algeria.
367. O.J. 1986 L 378/4, amended by the Act of Austrian, Finnish and Swedish Accession (1994).
368. O.J. 1986 L 378/14.
369. O.J. 1986 L 378/21.
370. Regs. 954/79, 4056/86 and 4057/86 do not cover tramp vessel services.
371. Dir. 94/58 (O.J. 1994 L 319/28), amended by Dir. 98/35 (O.J. 1998 L 172/1)).
372. See in detail, Close in Vaughan (ed.), *op. cit.* (see note 191, *supra*) paras. 18.262 *et seq.*
373. *Ibid.*, para. 12.265.
374. Reg. 954/79 (see note 364, *supra*), Art. 3.

an important role, as it is not applied on numerous important sea routes.[375] Cabotage traffic has now also been liberalized.[376]

Various measures have been taken in relation to problems encountered or feared with third country shipping.[377] Decision 77/587 established a consultation procedure on relations between the Member States and third countries in shipping matters and on action on such matters in international organizations.[378] Dec. 78/774[379] requires the Member States to establish an information collection system on the activities of third country fleets whose practices are harmful to the shipping interests of Member States. As a result of experience in the collection of such information, the Council adopted Decision 83/573 requiring Member States which have adopted or intend to adopt counter-measures against third countries relating to international merchant shipping to consult the Commission and the other Member States.[380] Dumped freight rates by shipping companies of third countries have found a response in Regulation 4057/86,[381] and Regulation 4058/86 on free access to cargoes[382] provides for coordinated action against restrictions of free access for shipping companies of Member States or for ships registered in Member States, or threats thereof.

Ever more attention is rightly focused on safety and environmental issues, although Close notes that it has not been Community policy to substitute internal measures for the many international conventions covering shipping safety, but rather the Community has encouraged

---

375. It does apply on the Community–West Africa routes, see *e.g.* Dec. 92/262 (O.J. 1992 L 134/1). As to those routes, see COM (97) 41 Final. See, further, the observations on competition, below.

376. Reg. 3577/92 (O.J. 1992 L 364/7). Art. 6 provides for a number of transitional periods, the longest (for Greece) expires at the end of 2003. Temporary exemptions are possible: see, as to problems with Spain, Decs. 93/125 (O.J. 1993 L 49/88) and 93/396 (O.J. 1993 L 178/33). Reg. 3577/92 prescribes that Community shipowners having their ships registered in or flying the flag of a Member State may undertake cabotage operations if they comply with all the conditions for cabotage in that State. For vessels undertaking mainland cabotage operations and cruise liners, matters relating to manning are the responsibility of the State of registration, unless the vessel is less than 650 gross tons, in which case the host State may apply its conditions. Except for such smaller vessels, all matters relating to manning are the responsibility of the host State for vessels carrying out island cabotage.

377. See, generally, Close in Vaughan (ed.), *op. cit.* (see note 191, *supra*) paras. 18.256 and 18.284–18.294. Draft agreements on sea transport between the Community and India and between the Community and China have been recommended for adoption (Bull. EU 1/2–1997, points 1.2.143 and 1.2.144).

378. O.J. 1997 L 239/23.

379. O.J. 1978 L 258/35, amended by Dec. 89/242 (O.J. 1989 L 97/47).

380. O.J. 1983 L 332/37.

381. See note 368, *supra*. So far a redressive duty has been impose in only one case, relating to container traffic between the Community and Australia, against the South Korean company Hyundai (Reg. 15/89 (O.J. 1989 L 4/1)).

382. See note 369, *supra*.

Member States to ratify or accede to existing conventions.[383] However, Community legislative action in this field is now considerable, not least in the wake of the shipping disasters, both human and environmental, in or near Member States' waters within the past decade or so.[384] Directive 79/ 115 deals with the pilotage of vessels by deep-sea pilots in the North Sea and the English Channel,[385] and Directive 93/75 establishes minimum requirements for ships entering or leaving Community seaports and carrying dangerous or polluting goods.[386] Directive 96/98 on marine equipment[387] seeks to improve the safety performance of equipment carried on board and strengthen the powers of the authorized inspection bodies. It thus ensures the uniform application of international testing standards and facilitates the free movement of marine equipment within the Community. Directive 94/57 had already established common rules and standards for ship inspection and survey organizations.[388] Regulation 3051/95 establishes safety procedures for ro/ro passenger vessels[389] and Directive 95/21 ensures the enforcement of international standards for ship safety, pollution prevention and shipboard living and working conditions in respect of shipping using Community ports and sailing in the waters under the jurisdiction of the Member States.[390] Recently measures have been adopted dealing with safety rules and standards for passenger ships,[391] the registration of persons sailing on board passenger ships,[392] and a harmonized safety regime for fishing vessels of 24 metres in length and over.[393] Finally, Decision 92/143 recommends, without prejudice to the

383. Close in Vaughan (ed.), *op. cit.* (see note 191, *supra*) para. 12.295. He lists numerous Council recommendations which the Council adopted in pursuance of even major International Conventions.
384. See, generally, the action programme relating to safety at sea, COM (93) 66 Final.
385. O.J. 1979 L 33/32.
386. O.J. 1993 L 247/19, most recently amended by Dir. 97/34 (O.J. 1997 L 158/40). A further amendment has been proposed, COM (96) 455 Final (O.J. 1996 C 334/11). See note 389, *infra*. See also the Council Resolution of 19 June 1990 on the prevention of accidents causing marine pollution (O.J. 1990 C 206/1).
387. O.J. 1997 L 46/25, corrig. O.J. 1997 L 246/7.
388. O.J. 1994 L 319/20, amended by Dir. 97/58 (O.J. 1997 L 274/8).
389. O.J. 1995 L 320/14, amended by Reg. 179/98 (O.J. 1998 L 19/35). Ro/ro vessels are 'roll on, roll-off' vessels.
390. O.J. 1995 L 157/1, most recently amended by Dir. 98/42 (O.J. 1998 L 184/40). See Dir. 96/40 (O.J. 1996 L 196/8). Dir. 95/21 reflects the experience gained in the application of the Memorandum of Understanding on Port State Control (Paris, January 26, 1982), which involved cooperation between the maritime authorities of all the (present) Member States (except Luxembourg) and Norway. Ships are controlled as to compliance with safety and environmental standards. These subjects have long been the subject of considerable work within the International Maritime Organization. See also, as to medical treatment on board vessels, Dir. 92/29 (O.J. 1992 L 113/19).
391. Dir. 98/18 (O.J. 1998 L 144/1).
392. Dir. 98/41 (O.J. 1998 L 188/35).
393. Dir. 97/70 (O.J. 1998 L 34/1).

development of satellite-based systems, the development of the Loran C (radio location) system as a radio navigation system for Europe.[394]

Compared with the competition rules applicable to other sectors of the economy, Regulation 4056/86[395] affords shipping companies a very favourable regime indeed. Thus price agreements are possible,[396] and the Commission may grant an exemption at any time even if the agreement has not been notified.[397] This favourable regime is in fact heavily influenced by the UNCTAD Code of Conduct.[398] For the rest the Regulation follows a similar pattern to Regulation 1017/68.[399] Regulation 4056/86 applies only to international maritime services from or to one or more Community ports, and excludes tramp vessel services.[400] Certain types of technical agreements are held to fall outside Article 85(1) EC,[401] and Article 3 of the regulation grants a block exemption for certain agreements between members of liner conferences[402] and Article 6 does the same for certain agreements between transport users and liner conferences or transport users *inter se*. Article 12 makes individual exemptions possible, using an opposition procedure.[403] Article 9 is an interesting provision

394. O.J. 1992 L 59/17.
395. See note 367, *supra*. See further, the contributions by Rakosky and Forwood in Hawk (ed.), *1992 Fordham Corporate Law Institute* (Irvington-on-Hudson, 1993) 845 *et seq.*
396. Reg. 4056/86, *ibid.*, Art. 3.
397. *Ibid.*, Art. 11(4). The exemption may be retroactive, *ibid.*, Art. 12(4).
398. See Slot (1987) SEW 774.
399. See note 284, *supra*. As to procedural provisions, see Reg. 4260/88 (O.J. 1988 1 376/1, most recently amended by the Act of Austrian, Finnish and Swedish Accession (1994)). As to failure to provide complete and accurate answers to the Commission's inquiries, see Decs. 91/55 (O.J. 1991 L 35/23) *Secrétema*; 92/237 (O.J. 1992 L 121/45) *Ukwal*, and 93/47 (O.J. 1993 L 20/6) *Mewac*.
400. Reg. 4056/86, Art. 1(2) as rates for tramp service vessels are freely negotiated. Cabotage and other maritime services, such as tug services and offshore supplies services, are also excluded. These fall under the so-called *Asjes-Saeed* regime, named after Cases 209–213/84 *Ministère public v. Asjes et al.* [1986] ECR 1425, [1986] 3 CMLR 173, and Case 66/86 *Ahmed Saeed Flugreisen et al. v. Zentrale zur Bekämpfung unlauteren Wettbewerbs eV* [1989] ECR 803, [1990] 4 CMLR 102. This means that Art. 85 EC is not directly effective in relation to these matters, it can only be applied through Arts. 88 and 89 EC. Art. 86 EC on the other hand is directly effective in this as in other areas. However, the Commission does not possess the normal powers of investigation, imposition of fines or periodic penalties, or of granting individual exemptions. See also Dec. 94/985 (O.J. 1994 L 378/17) *Far Eastern Freight Conference*. As to cross-Channel services, see Dec. 97/84 (O.J. 1997 L 26/23) *Ferry Services – Currency Surcharges*.
401. *Ibid.*, Art. 2.
402. The conditions and obligations largely reflect those of the UNCTAD Code of Conduct. One of the conditions (Art. 7(2)(i)) requires that remaining competition should not be wholly excluded. In its submissions in Case 355/87 *Commission v. Council* [1989] ECR 1517 at 1524 the Commission explained this obligation as an obligation to ensure that Community-registered companies which do not belong to any conference have access to part of the cargoes allocated under bilateral agreements.
403. As an *e.g.* of a refusal to exempt, see Dec. 94/980 (O.J. 1994 L 376/1) *Trans-Atlantic*

which deals with the resolution of conflicts through the application of international law; these are to be discussed with the competent authorities of the third countries concerned, and the Council may authorize the Commission to enter into the necessary negotiations if agreements need to be reached. Like Regulation 1017/68, Regulation 4056/86 does not make any provision for negative clearance of agreements. In Regulation 479/92[404] the Council empowered the Commission to grant a block exemption for liner consortia, a power which has now been exercised by Regulation 870/95.[405]

A number of decisions have been adopted penalizing infringements of Article 86 EC in the sea transport sector.[406] Articles 92 and 93 EC have been applied on myriad occasions in the shipping sector since 1985.[407]

Finally, it might be noted that although the Member States still have power to determine the conditions for registering a ship and the right to fly the appropriate flag, that power must be exercise in accordance with Community law, which means in particular that there must be no discrimination on ground of nationality, or any obstacle to the free movement of goods, workers, the exercise of the right of establishment, or the freedom to provide services save where permitted by Community law itself.[408] In this context, Regulation 613/91[409] deals with the transfer certain types of cargo ships from one register to another within the Community.

Agreement, on appeal Case T-395/94 *Atlantic Container Line AB et al. v. Commission* (O.J. 1997 C 392/15). See, as to interim measures, Case T-395/94 R *Atlantic Container Line AB et al. v. Commission* [1995] ECR II-595, upheld on appeal in Case C-149/95 P(R) *Commission v. Atlantic Container Line AB et al.* [1995] ECR I-2165 and Case T-395/94 RII *Atlantic Container Line AB v. Commission* [1995] ECR II-2893. See further, Case T-18/97 *Atlantic Container Line AB et al. v. Commission* [1998] ECR II-nyr (23 March 1998).

404. O.J. 1992 L 55/3.
405. O.J. 1995 L 89/7. See Commission Press Release IP (96) 400, [1996] 5 CMLR 6 and Clough (1995) ECLR 417.
406. See *e.g.* Dec. 92/262 (O.J. 1992 L 134/1) *French–West African Shipowners' Committees* (also based on Art. 85 EC); Dec. 93/82 (O.J. 1993 L 34/20) *Cewal, Cowac and Ukwal,* upheld on appeal in Cases T-24/93 *etc. Compagnie Maritime Belge SA et al. v. Commission* [1996] ECR II-1201, [1997] 4 CMLR 273, under further appeal in Case C-395/96 P *Compagnie Maritime Belge SA v. Commission* (O.J. 1997 C 54/10) and Case C-396/95 P *Dafra Lines A/S v. Commission* (O.J. 1997 C 54/12), and 94/119 (O.J. 1994 L 55/92) *Rødby – access to harbour.*
407. As to the present guidelines for aid to shipping companies, see O.J. 1997 C 205/5. See also *e.g. General Report 1994* (Brussels, Luxembourg, 1995), point 392.
408. See *e.g.* Case C-221/89 *R. v. Secretary of State for Transport, ex parte Factortame Ltd. et al.* [1991] ECR I-3905, [1991] 3 CMLR 589; Case C-93/89 *Commission v. Ireland* [1991] ECR I-4569, [1991] 3 CMLR 697; Case C-246/89 *Commission v. United Kingdom* [1991] ECR I-4585, [1991] 3 CMLR 706; Case C-334/94 *Commission v. France* [1996] ECR I-1307, and Case C-151/96 *Commission v. Ireland* [1997] ECR I-3327.
409. O.J. 1991 L 68/1.

3.12 Air transport

As was indicated in section 3.1, above, the developments in this field have been truly spectacular.[410] Since April 1, 1997 there has been an internal market within the Community for air transport.[411] Any Community airline company which possesses an authorization issued by a Member State[412] is free to fly both national and international routes within the Community.[413] The application of this principle in practice has not been without problems, as was seen in early 1994 concerning access to Paris Orly.[414] Member States are entitled to impose public service obligations.[415] The notorious capacity and price restrictions which had long existed are in principle as dead as the dodo, although it is possible for safeguard measures to be adopted if cut-throat competition emerges.[416] The competition rules in the air transport sector have also been extensively developed and indeed applied, as is explained below.

Economic and financial requirements are prescribed before an authorization will be granted.[417] The most controversial point in the system is the definition of effective control and ownership, and it is clearly the intention to refuse authorization to third country airlines, in derogation from Article 58 EC.[418] It is significant that no reciprocity clause has been

410. See, generally, Adkins, *Air Transport and EC Competition Law* (London, 1994) and Balfour, *European Community Air Law* (London, 1995). See also Close in Vaughan (ed.), *op. cit.* (see note 191, *supra*) paras. 18.304–18.422. As to state aids in this field, see Soames and Ryan (1995) ECLR 290, and as to predatory pricing, see Soames and Ryan (1994) ECLR 151.

411. By virtue of Reg. 2408/92 (O.J. 1992 L 240/8, amended by the Act of Austrian, Finnish and Swedish Accession (1994)). Free access to international intra-Community routes was achieved by January 1, 1993, and full cabotage rights by April 1, 1997. The internal market system was extended to the Scandinavian countries by a separate agreement (see Dec. 92/384 (O.J. 1992 L 200/20, amended by Dec. 93/453 (O.J. 1993 L 212/17)) which has been superseded by the EEA Agreement and then in turn by Swedish accession (see the adaptation decision, Dec. 95/1 (O.J. 1995 L 1/1)).

412. Reg. 2407/92 (O.J. 1992 L 240/1).

413. Reg. 2408/92, Art. 3(1).

414. See Dec. 94/290 (O.J. 1990 L 127/22) *TAT – Paris (Orly)-London*, and Dec. 94/291 (O.J. 1994 L 127/32) *TAT – Paris-(Orly)- Marseille and Paris-(Orly)-Toulouse*. The latter decision was upheld on appeal in Case T-260/94 *Air Inter SA v. Commission* [1997] ECR II-997. The challenge by France was dropped (O.J. 1996 C 210/11). See, further, Dec. 95/259 (O.J. 1995 L 162/25) on the air traffic system in the Paris area. See also *e.g.* Dec. 93/347 (O.J. 1993 L 140/51) *Viva Air – Paris Charles de Gaulle–Madrid*.

415. Reg. 2408/92, Art. 4.

416. Reg. 2409/92 (O.J. 1992 L 240/15), Art. 6.

417. Reg. 2407/92, Art. 5.

418. See Slot in Dagtoglou (ed.), *European Air Law Conference Papers* (No. 5, Deventer, 1993) 21. But see Dec. 95/404 (O.J. 1995 L 239/19) *Swissair/Sabena* which found that the requirements of Reg. 2407/92, Art. 4 were satisfied.

included.[419] The problem of effective control and ownership is particularly more difficult in relation to air transport as bilateral aviation agreements link landing rights to this criterion.

Air transport between the Community and third countries is not yet subject to Community rules, and the way ahead is clearly perceived as being through the negotiation of bilateral agreements between the Community and third countries,[420] With the achievement of the internal market the power of the Member States to enter into agreements with third countries which jeopardize or are at odds with the Community system has disappeared.[421] Thus the most important problems for the further development of Community policy lie in the realm of external aspects of air transport.

Internally, the most pressing problem is one of air traffic management, requiring a solution to problems of take-off and landing slots.[422] Directive 96/67 deals with access to ground handling at Community airports,[423] and

419. In the field of maritime transport a precedent exists, see Reg. 954/79 (see note 239, *supra*), Art. 4, relating to the UN Liner Conference Code.
420. The Commission did make a proposal in 1992 (COM (92) 434 Final (amending an earlier proposal in COM (90) 17 Final) which was based on Art. 113 EC. However, this legal basis proved controversial (see O.J. 1993 C 112/8) as the Member States preferred Art. 84 EC to be the legal basis, in order to exclude sole Community competence. In Opinion 1/94 *WTO – GATS and TRIPs* [1994] ECR I-5267 at 5402–5404 the Court held that international agreements on transport did not fall within the ambit of Art. 113 EC, which leaves Art. 84 EC as the sole legal basis. The most recent *General Reports* note that the Commission has been given negotiating mandates to seek air transport agreements with a number of third countries, including the United States.
421. On the basis of Case 22/70 *Commission v. Council* [1971] ECR 263, [1971] CMLR 335 (*ERTA*). While Reg. 2408/92 itself does not expressly exclude the grant of fifth freedom rights to airlines from third countries, this would appear to be excluded on the basis of the *ERTA* judgment. Thus the Open Skies Agreements concluded between some Member States and the USA would appear to be incompatible with Community law. Fifth freedom rights permit, for example, KLM to fly on from New York (having arrived from Amsterdam) to Mexico City, picking up passengers for this additional leg of the journey in New York. Inside the Community an example would be an American airline landing from New York at Schiphol, picking up passengers there and flying on to Copenhagen. The latter example clearly affects traffic on Community airlines on that last leg.
422. See Reg. 95/93 (O.J. 1993 L 14/1). See further COM (95) 318 Final and the Commission's White Paper *Freeing Europe's airspace* COM (96) 57 Final. Heathrow Airport is a particularly notorious congestion spot. As slots are allocated on the basis of previous services, it is difficult for market entrants to obtain attractive slot allocations, which reduces the very competitive ability which the new legislation created for them. Thus slot allocation is probably one of the most important elements in the future development of air transport policy within the Community. Airlines which merge or form alliances are often forced to surrender certain lucrative slots as a condition for regulatory approval, precisely to remove strangleholds on competition. See, *e.g.* Commission Press Release IP (98) 641 8 July 1998, *BA/American Airlines*.
423. O.J. 1996 L 272/36.

the Commission has presented a proposal for a directive on airport charges.[424] Measures will certainly have to be taken to tackle the fragmented organization of air traffic control within Europe, and indeed these have now been proposed.[425] In order to facilitate the elimination of operational incompatibilities, Directive 93/65 makes certain Eurocontrol standards mandatory at Community level for the procurement of air navigation equipment.[426] But problems of competence still abound, as the Community does not yet have clear and adequate powers. Regulation 2027/97 now governs on air carrier liability for air accidents,[427] and Directive 94/56 establishes fundamental principles governing the investigation of civil aviation accidents and incidents, based on the standards published by the International Civil Aviation Organization.[428] Regulation 3922/91 harmonizes many technical requirements and administrative procedures in the field of civil aviation,[429] and the Commission has proposed the adoption of a directive establishing a safety assessment of third countries aircraft using Community airports.[430]

Regulation 3925/91 deals with the controls and formalities relating to the baggage of persons taking an intra-Community flight,[431] and Regulation 295/91 makes most welcome provision for denied boarding compensation.[432] At present the qualifications for aviation cockpit personnel are not laid down at Community level, so Directive 91/670 makes provision for the mutual recognition of national licences for such persons.[433] Given that aircraft noise problems are a matter of considerable concern, several directives have been adopted with a view to reducing these problems.[434]

---

424. COM (97) 154 Final (O.J. 1997 C 257/2). See also Dec. 95/364 (O.J. 1995 L 216/8) *Zaventem*.
425. The Commission has proposed that the Community should accede to Eurocontrol, Bull. EU 11–1996, point 1.3.126, and a negotiating mandate has been proposed for the creation of a European organization responsible for civil aviation safety, Bull. EU 12–1996, point 1.3.141 (see also COM (94) 218 Final).
426. O.J. 1993 L 187/52, amended by Dir. 97/15 (O.J. 1997 L 95/16).
427. O.J. 1997 L 285/1.
428. O.J. 1994 L 319/14.
429. O.J. 1991 L 373/4, amended by Reg. 2176/96 (O.J. 1996 L 291/15). A further amendment has been proposed, COM (96) 186 Final (O.J. 1996 C 179/96).
430. COM (97) 55 Final (O.J. 1997 C 124/39), amended by COM (98) 123 Final (O.J. 1998 C 122/10).
431. O.J. 1991 L 374/4, now implemented by Reg. 2454/93 (O.J. 1993 L 253/1, most recently amended by Reg. 75/98 (O.J. 1998 L 7/3)).
432. O.J. 1991 L 36/5. Proposed amendment COM (98) 41 Final (O.J. 1998 C 120/18).
433. O.J. 1991 L 373/21.
434. Dirs. 80/51 (O.J. 1980 L 18/26, amended by Dir. 206/83 (O.J. 1983 L 117/15) on subsonic aircraft; 89/629 (O.J. 1989 L 363/27) on civil subsonic jets; and 92/14 (O.J. 1992 L 76/21, amended by Dir. 98/20 (O.J. 1998 L 107/4)) on the gradual withdrawal from the registers of Member States of aircraft not meeting the prescribed stricter standards. See also the Green Paper on combating noise nuisance, COM (96) 540 Final.

The application of Articles 85 and 86 in the air transport sector is of major importance. Regulation 3975/87 governs the application of those provisions to the air transport sector.[435] It applies solely to air transport within the Community,[436] but the Commission has now proposed that its scope should be extended to embrace air transport between the Community and third countries.[437] At the same time it has proposed that the Council adopt a regulation empowering the Commission to adopt a block exemption regulation dealing with air transport between the Community and third countries.[438]

Regulation 3975/87 in fact follows a different approach than that in Regulations 1017/68[439] and 4056/86.[440] It does exempt technical agreements, but the most important block exemptions are in fact granted by the Commission on the basis of Regulation 3976/87.[441] Regulation 3975/87 sets out the customary procedural provisions in the transport sector, relating to the obtaining of an individual exemption, with an opposition procedure, the Commission's powers of investigation and its powers to impose fines and daily penalties. However, unlike in the other transport sectors, provision is made for the grant of negative clearance.[442]

Regulation 3976/87[443] empowers the Commission to grant block exemptions in respect of: joint planning and coordination of airline schedules; consultations on tariffs for the carriage of passengers and baggage and of freight on scheduled services; joint operations on new less busy scheduled air services; slot allocation at airports and airport scheduling, and common purchase, development and operation of computer reservation systems. In this context the presently applicable block exemptions are Regulation 1617/93 on capacity coordination,[444] and Regulation 3652/93 on computer reservation systems.[445] It would perhaps

435. O.J. 1987 L 374/1, most recently amended by Reg. 2410/92 (O.J. 1992 L 240/18).
436. *Ibid.*, art. 1(2). It now covers not just international air transport but also purely national air transport.
437. COM (97) 218 Final (O.J. 1997 C 165/13). The proposal includes a provision permitting the Commission to deal with any conflict arising in the international law field concerning the application of the regulation. This would put an end to the situation in which transport between the Community and third countries falls under the *Asjes–Saeed* regime (as to which, see note 400, *supra*).
438. COM (97) 218 Final (O.J. 1997 C 165/13).
439. See note 284, *supra*.
440. See note 367, *supra*.
441. See note 443, *infra*.
442. Reg. 3975/87, Art. 3(2).
443. O.J. 1987 L 374/9, most recently amended by the Act of Austrian, Finnish and Swedish Accession (1994) (as, adapted by Dec. 95/1 (O.J. 1995 L 1/1)). Procedural matters are governed by Reg. 4261/88 (O.J. 1988 L 376/10, likewise most recently amended).
444. O.J. 1993 L 155/18, amended by Reg. 1523/96 (O.J. 1996 L 190/11). This was due to expire on 30 June 1998 (see Art. 7) but had not been extended by the date at which this work states the law.
445. O.J. 1993 L 333/37, the remarks as to expiry, *ibid.* apply here too (see Art. 15). See

be an understatement to say that Articles 85 and 86 EC have been actively applied in the air transport sector.[446]

Finally, Articles 92 and 93 EC have been actively applied in the air transport sector, occasioning not a little controversy on occasions, and a great deal of suspicion of undue political influence with the concept of one time last time being rendered on occasions meaningless.[447] National measures are subject to thorough review, and approval may well be subjected to stringent conditions.[448]

3.13   Infrastructure and combined transport

As was emphasized in section 3.1, above, transport is strongly dependent on an adequate infrastructure. Thus it is scarcely surprising that the Community has adopted a number of measures in this matter, which largely relate to the allocation of costs and to access to infrastructure, whether in terms of tolls, access to harbour facilities or take-off and landing slots. Reference has been made to various measures at the appropriate points in the preceding sections.[449] The Commission's Green

also the explanatory memorandum, O.J. 1990 C 184/2 and Reg. 2299/89 (O.J. 1989 L 220/1, amended by Reg. 3089/93 (O.J. 1993 L 278/1, corrigendum O.J. 1995 L 17/18)) on the Code of Conduct for computerized reservations systems. See also the undertakings given in *Amadeus/Sabre* (Commission Press release IP (91) 784); *Global Logistics System* (O.J. 1993 C 76/5) and *Galileo and Covia CRSs* (O.J. 1993 C 107/4).

446. *E.g.* Decs. 88/589 (O.J. 1988 L 317/47) *London European/Sabena*; 91/480 and 91/481 (O.J. 1991 L 258/18 and 29) *IATA Passenger and Cargo Agency Programmes*; 92/213 (O.J. 1992 L 96/34) *British Midland/Aer Lingus*, and 96/180 (O.J. 1996 L 54/28) *LH/SAS* (appeal withdrawn (O.J. 1996 C 354/36)). The most recent *Reports on Competition Policy* give other examples of Commission action in this field. Similarly, they are good sources of information relating to (proposed) mergers, see also *e.g.* Dec. 95/404 (O.J. 1995 L 239/19 *Swissair/Sabena* and the decision in IV/M.806 (O.J. 1996 C 316/11) *British Airways/TAT (II)*. It was noted at the end of section 3.4, *ante*, that the Community merger control regime also applies to the transport sector (see Chapter VIII, section 4.5, *ante*).

447. See WQ 809/93 (Van der Waal) O.J. 1993 C 350/8 and Decs. 92/8 (O.J. 1992 L 5/26) *Air France* and 94/662 (O.J. 1994 L 258/26, amended by Dec. 95/367 (O.J. 1995 L 219/34)) *Air France*. In the first decision the Commission took the view that the huge loan to Air France was acceptable from a market viewpoint. Several airlines appealed against that decision, see *e.g.* Cases T-374 and 394/94 *British Airways Plc et al. v. Commission* [1998] ECR II-nyr (25 June 1998). The second decision approved further support in the form of issues of securities, see Case T-358/94 *Compagnie nationale Air France v. Commission* [1996] ECR II-2109 and Case C-282/94 *France v. Commission* (O.J. 1994 C 351/7). See also *e.g.* Decs. 94/666 (O.J. 1994 L 260/27) *TAP*; 94/696 (O.J. 1994 L 273/22) *Olympic Airways*; 94/698 (O.J. 1994 L 279/29) *TAP*; and 96/278 (O.J. 1996 L 104/25) *Iberia*.

448. See Decs. 91/555 (O.J. 1991 L 300/48) *Sabena*, and 94/118 (O.J. 1994 L 54/30) *Aer Lingus* (see as to approval of revised capacity figures, Dec. 94/997 (O.J. 1994 L 379/21)).

449. See, generally, Close in Vaughan (ed.), *op. cit.* (see note 191, *supra*) paras. 18.423 *et seq.*

Paper *The Citizens' Network: fulfilling the potential of public passenger transport in Europe* is designed to lay the groundwork for the promotion of a sustainable public transport network within the Community.[450] Trans-European networks are discussed in section 7.4, below.

The principal Community provisions on combined transport are to be found in Directive 92/106.[451] Future policy of the Commission has now been set out in a Communication on Intermodal Goods Transport.[452]

4. THE EUROPEAN COAL AND STEEL COMMUNITY[453]

4.1 Objectives and the system of co-ordination

The oldest European Community is based, for coal and steel, on principles of market economy to an even higher degree than the agricultural and transport policies. However, the possibilities of intervention in the sense of market regulation and in the social sphere go much further than the possibilities of intervention within the EC for sectors other than agriculture and transport. Also, the degree of supranationality of the Community Institutions is higher, and the High Authority from the outset possessed an autonomous power to levy taxes and contract loans.[454] The objectives are defined in Article 2 ECSC and especially in Article 3, in a much more 'dirigistic' way than in Articles 2 and 3 EC. Thus, in Article 3 ECSC the following are among the tasks of the Institutions: assuring that the common market is regularly supplied; assuring to all consumers in comparable positions in the common market equal access to the sources of production; seeking the establishment of the lowest possible prices; ensuring conditions which will encourage undertakings to expand and improve their ability to produce, promoting the improvement of the living and working conditions of the labour force and their gradual equalization; and promoting the regular expansion and the modernization of production. While Article 4 broadly lays down the principles of a market economy, Article 5 sets out the principles on which the Community is to base its intervention policy.

450. COM (95) 601 Final.
451. O.J. 1992 L 368/38, amended by the Act of Austrian, Finnish and Swedish Accession (1994).
452. COM (97) 243 Final.
453. See Quadri *et al.*, *Commentario C.E.C.A.: Trattato instutivo della Communità europea del carbone e dell'acciaco. Commentario* (Milan, 1970) and, more recent but shorter, Byrne *et al.* in Vaughan (ed.), *op. cit.* (see note 138, *supra*) Part 9. On the steel crisis policy see, in addition to specific literature cited *post*, Barents (1984) SEW 255 and Benyon (1986) CDE 251. See also Hosman (1987) SEW 267 and Hyden (1991) ECLR 160.
454. Arts. 49, 50 and 51 ECSC.

In this context it is established at the outset that the Community is to intervene directly as little as possible. As will be seen below, though, in case of need (crisis or shortage) the Community possesses very drastic powers to intervene directly in production, distribution, and prices. The principles of Articles 2–5 ECSC also play a considerable role as coordinating principles for interpretation of other parts of the Treaty by the Court. Particularly in respect of Articles 2, 3, and 4 ECSC the Court decided in Case 1/54 *France v. High Authority*[455] that they must be borne in mind in the application of all other Articles of the ECSC Treaty, precisely because they set out the fundamental objectives of that Treaty. Some years after the steel crisis which developed at the end of 1974 and lasted certainly until nearly the end of the Eighties, the Court considered the relationship between the market mechanism and powers of intervention as means for achieving the objectives set out in Articles 2 and 3 ECSC again in great detail in Cases 154/78 etc. *SpA Ferriera Valsabbia et al. v. Commission.*[456] The Court here considered, in addition to Articles 2–5 and 57 ECSC, pretty well all the powers of the Commission to intervene in the market, although the specific matter under consideration was General Decision 962/77[457] fixing minimum prices under Article 61 ECSC.[458] In Case 36/83 *Mabanaft GmbH v. Hauptzollamt Emmerich*[459] the Court noted that the principle of a customs union (with free movement for products from third countries which are in free circulation within the Community) also applies to the ECSC on the basis of Article 4(a) ECSC, subject to the provisions of the that Treaty.

4.2　The principles of market economy

The system of competition of the ECSC departs form the EC system on the following points:

(a) no common external tariff and common commercial policy are ensured, although the Community does possess considerable co-ordinating powers in this matter;[460]

(b) subsidies or state assistance or special charges imposed by the state, in any form whatsoever, are absolutely prohibited under Article

---

455. [1954-56] ECR 1 at 9 and 16.
456. [1980] ECR 907.
457. O.J. 1977 L 114/1.
458. As Barents (1984) SEW 255 indicates, in accordance with the priority principle laid down in Art. 5 ECSC the minimum price provisions of 1977 were preceded by market monitoring measures in 1975 and a system of voluntary supply undertakings in 1976.
459. [1984] ECR 2497 at 2523.
460. Arts. 4 and 71–75 ECSC. In practice the new Combined Nomenclature also covers ECSC products.

4(c) ECSC, and this rigorous prohibition could be mitigated only to a limited degree for unforeseen cases on the strength of Article 95 ECSC, which is comparable with Article 235 EC.[461] The concept of special charges was considered in Case 30/59 *De Gezamenlijke Steenkolenmijnen in Limburg v. High Authority*.[462] An Article which is comparable with Article 101 EC, on the other hand, is Article 67 ECSC. Unlike Article 101 EC, Article 67 ECSC has repeatedly been applied and has given rise to some case-law of the Court.[463]

(c) Articles 4(b) and 60 contain a prohibition of price discrimination and an obligation to publish prices, both of which had the effect of making prices rather rigid, partly by the way they were implemented by the High Authority. Ultimately, however, the rules issued were found incapable of resisting the pressure of competition, and the Commission in the course of 1972 adopted new decisions on the

461. As examples of earlier decisions relating to coal see Decs. 71/121 (J.O. 1971 L 57/19), 72/65 (J.O. 1972 L 20/30) on aid to the coal mining industry, 73/287 (O.J. 1973 L 259/36) on coal and coke for the iron and steel industry, and 528/76 (O.J. 1976 L 63/1) on a Community rules for state aid to the coal industry. Current rules for state aids to the coal industry are set out in Dec. 3632/93 (O.J. 1993 L 329/12) which is implemented by Dec. 341/94 (O.J. 1994 L 49/1). These apply until 23 July 2002. On state aids in the initial period of the steel crisis of the late Seventies and early Eighties see Heusdens and De Horn (1980) 17 CMLRev. 31 (in Dutch (1979) SEW 299). After the steel crisis worsened precise rules on the grant of state aids were set out by the Commission in Dec. 257/80 (O.J. 1980 L 29/5), subsequently changed by Dec. 2320/81 (O.J. 1981 L 228/14) and by Dec. 1018/85 (O.J. 1985 L 110/5) before being replaced by Dec. 3484/85 (O.J. 1985 L 340/1) which applied until the end of 1988. There then followed a number of successor regimes: Decs. 322/89 (O.J. 1989 L 38/8); 3855/91 (O.J. 1991 L 362/57), and the present regime, Dec. 2496/96 (O.J. 1996 L 338/42), which also applies until the lapse of the ECSC Treaty. On the system of aid see in particular Case 119/81 *Klöckner Werke AG v. Commission* [1982] ECR 2627; Case 222/83 *Commune de Differdange v. Commission* [1984] ECR 2889; Case 63/84 *Finsider SpA v. Commission* [1985] ECR 2857; Case 214/83 *Germany v. Commission* [1985] ECR 3053; Case 211/83 *Krupp Stahl AG et al. v. Commission* [1985] ECR 3409; Case 304/85 *Acciaiere e Ferriere Lombarde Falck v. Commission* [1987] ECR 871; Case T-26/90 *Società Finanziaria Siderurgica Finsider SpA v. Commission* [1992] ECR II-1789, upheld on appeal in Case C-320/92 P *Finanziaria Siderurgica Finsider SpA v. Commission* [1994] ECR I-5697; Case C-99/92 *Terni SpA et al. v. Cassa Conguaglio per il Settore Elettrico* [1994] ECR I-541; Case C-100/92 *Fonderia A. SpA v. Cassa Conguaglio per il Settore Elettrico* [1994] ECR I-561; and Case C-399/95 *Germany v. Commission* (O.J. 1996 C 77/5), see the order in Case C-399/95 R *Germany v. Commission* [1996] ECR I-2441. Whilst a number of aids granted earlier have remained in being, new aid will be authorized only in very limited circumstances indeed, and the conditions have become stricter over the years.
462. [1961] ECR 1.
463. Cases 27-29/58 *Compagnie des Hauts Fourneaux et Fonderies de Givors et al. v. High Authority* [1960] ECR 241; Case 30/59 *De Gezamenlijke Steenkolenmijnen in Limburg v. High Authority* [1961] ECR 1, and Cases 6 and 11/69 *Commission v. France* [1969] ECR 523, [1970] CMLR 43.

matter which were more in conformity with the market.[464] The judgment and the opinion of the Advocate General in Case 8/83 *Officine Fratelli Bertoli SpA v. Commission*[465] give a good overview of the background to, the temporary slack maintenance and present significance of Article 60 ECSC which is a remarkable provision from the viewpoint of competition policy.

(d) Under Article 53 and 62 ECSC systems of price equalization and price compensation may be introduced or adopted, which was done in particular for scrap metal.[466]

(e) Article 65 ECSC contains for cartel agreements a system which is broadly comparable with Article 85 EC, but one which is also applicable to agreements having effects exclusively within one Member State. Various judgments of the Court on Article 65 ECSC are also of interest for the interpretation of Article 85 EC. Thus the ideas at the root of the judgment in Case 1/58 *Friedrich Stork & Co. v. High Authority*[467] pointed in the direction of Case 13/61 *Kledingverkoopbedrijf de Geus en Uitdenbogerd v. Robert Bosch GmbH et al.*[468] concerning related problems in Article 85 EC. The judgment in Case 66/63 *Netherlands v. High Authority*[469] is also of interest for the conditions which can be attached to an exemption under Article 85(3) EC and for the interpretation of point (b) of Article 85(3). In Case 36/64 *Société Rhenane d'Exploitation et de Manutention (SOREMA) v. High Authority*[470] the Court indicated that an authorization of an agreement must be revoked if the actual results of the agreement or of its application are found to be contrary to the requirements for its authorization. Case 13/60 *'Geitling' Ruhrkolen-Verkaufsgesellschaft GmbH et al. v. High Authority*[471] and Opinion 1/61 *On the proposed amendment to*

---

464. See Decs. 72/440–443 (J.O. 1972 L 297/39 *et seq.*) and the Commission's Communications (O.J. 1973 C 29/26 *et seq.*). See also Dec. 18/72 (J.O. 1972 L 4/1) prolonging the validity of Rec. 1/64 (J.O. English Special Edition 1963-64, p. 91, now most recently amended by Dec. 457/92 (O.J. 1992 L 257/42)) concerning an increase in the protective duty on iron and steel products at the external frontiers of the Community (there have been over 160 derogations from this recommendation over the years); Dec. 73/152 (O.J. 1973 L 172/20) obliging undertakings of the steel industry to publish schedules of transport charges for routes involving intra-Community sea links and Dec. 3073/73 (O.J. 1973 L 314/1, amended by the Act of Spanish and Portuguese Accession (1985)) on the sale of iron and steel products in certain EFTA countries.
465. [1984] ECR 1649.
466. See Valentine, *The Court of Justice of the European Communities* (London, 1965) Vol. II 419 *et seq.*
467. [1959] ECR 17.
468. [1961] ECR 271, [1962] CMLR 1.
469. [1964] ECR 533, [1964] CMLR 522.
470. [1965] ECR 329 at 339.
471. [1962] ECR 83, [1962] ECR 113.

Article 65 ECSC[472] appear to be of importance for the interpretation of point (b) of Article 85(3) EC as well as for an evaluation of the possibility of using Article 235 EC to derogate from Articles 85 and 86 EC.[473] Article 66 ECSC provides that any form of concentration of undertakings which have not been exempted by the High Authority in view of their small importance shall be submitted to prior authorization. As conditions for such authorization Article 66(2) mentions that the concentration in question must not give the power to determine prices, control or restrict production or distribution, or prevent the maintenance of effective competition in a substantial part of the market for the products concerned. Nor must the concentration give the power to evade the rules of competition as they result from the execution of the ECSC Treaty, in particular by establishing an artificially privileged position involving a substantial advantage in access to supplies or markets. The criteria for judging these matters are, therefore, purely negative. Positive effects of a concentration are not required, but neither can they help to ignore the negative criteria.

The *Journal Officiel* of 30 January 1970[474] contains an interesting Communication from the Commission on the broad lines of the competition policy concerning the structures of the steel industry. This gives evidence in particular of a favourable attitude with regard to regroupings of undertakings by mergers, participation, and joint management, so long as effective competition is not endangered. The Commission deems that the danger zone has been reached when the share of the biggest groups exceeds 12 to 13% of the production of crude steel. On account of the numerous financial and staff relations existing between different groups it would further appear important that the Commission announced that it would see to it that relations and competition-restricting agreements of this kind between groups do not jeopardize the independence of the individual groups. The Commission will also look after the independence of the individual markets of the different groups. With regard to small and medium-sized undertakings, on the other hand, different forms of co-operation in production (exchange of capacity and specialization) and sales will be judged favourably.

Article 66 is also applicable if only one of the undertakings wishing to concentrate is a producer or wholesale dealer or middle-

---

472. [1961] ECR 243.
473. See further Cases 36–38 and 40/59 *President Ruhrkohlen-Verkaufsgeselischaft mbH et al. v. High Authority* [1960] ECR 423 and Case 67/63 *Société Rhenane d'Exploitation et Manutention 'SOREMA' v. High Authority* [1964] ECR 151, [1964] CMLR 350.
474. J.O. 1970 C 12/5.

man for coal or steel.[475] This is quite logical, since a coal producer may, for instance, obtain a privileged position *vis-à-vis* competitors by vertical concentration with transport undertakings, and a steel producer may do so by concentration with important consumers, such as shipbuilding yards or motorcar industries. Article 66(5) provides for fines if no prior authorization has been requested for a concentration which does satisfy the conditions for approval. On the other hand, according to the same paragraph of the Article the undertakings can be ordered to be separated if a concentration not satisfying the conditions for approval has been established.

Over undertakings which already had a dominant position in the market before the Treaty entered into force, or which acquired such a position after it had entered into force through internal growth or any other circumstances falling outside the supervision of concentrations, the Commission will exercise supervision in order to prevent this position being used for purposes contrary to the objectives of the Treaty. The Commission may address relevant binding recommendations to the undertakings, and if such recommendations are not carried out satisfactorily, it may fix the prices and conditions of sale to be applied by the undertaking in question or draw up production or delivery programmes which it must fulfil.[476] It has been laid down explicitly that this provision also applies to public enterprises.

The great emphasis laid by Article 66 ECSC on supervision of concentrations as such can be accounted for, not only by the previous political history of the Allied policy of separation of concentrated enterprises in Germany, but also by the high degree of concentration which the coal and steel industry had reached in other Member States as well by the time at which the Treaty was being prepared. The dangers of a further concentration from the outset were greater in these two sectors than in most of the sectors coming within the (then) EEC Treaty. Given that, as was observed in Chapter VIII, above, preventive control of concentrations has been introduced for other sectors as well, the global scheme is pretty much in line with the ECSC system.

In Case 13/60 *'Geitling'*[477] the Court developed a theory of effective oligopolistic competition which may also be of importance for oligopolistic markets in the EC, as has already been observed in the discussion of Articles 85 and 86 EC in Chapter VIII, above. In Case C-128/92 *H.J. Banks & Co. Ltd. v. British Coal Board*[478] the

475. Art. 60 ECSC with Art. 80 ECSC.
476. Art. 66(7) ECSC.
477. See note 470, *supra*.
478. [1994] ECR I-1209, [1994] 5 CMLR 30. Van Gerven, Adv. Gen. arrived at the

Court found on the basis of the wording of Article 65(4) ECSC that Articles 65 and 66 ECSC were not directly effective. With respect, it seems that, having regard to the first paragraph of Article 65(4), a question mark should be placed against the unnuanced statement that Article 65 does not create rights on which individuals may rely before national courts. That first paragraph states unequivocally that prohibited agreements are automatically void and may not be relied upon before national courts or tribunals. This is meaningless if it cannot be relied upon before national courts. It would appear much better if the national court were to ask the Commission to pronounce on the nullity involved.

(f) Article 70 ECSC contains a ban on discrimination as to rates and conditions of any kind in the field of transport, which are based on the country of origin or of destination of the products. Further the Article contains an obligation to publish these rates and conditions or to bring them to the knowledge of the High Authority. Special domestic tariff measures in the interest of one or several coal- or steel-producing undertakings shall be subject to the prior agreement of the High Authority, now the Commission which ensures that such measures are in accordance with the principles of the Treaty.[479]

4.3 The powers of intervention

The principal positive powers of the Commission enabling it to direct the development of the coal and steel market are the following:

(a) drawing up programmes giving forecasts, for guidance of production, consumption, exports, and imports, and setting out general objectives with regard to modernization, the long-term planning of production, and the expansion of productive capacity.[480]

opposite conclusion, also finding (contrary to the Court's judgment) that Community law obliged the national courts to make award damages for infringement of the ECSC Treaty provisions involved. See also Case C-18/94 *Hopkins et al. v. National Power plc et al.* [1996] ECR I-2281, [1996] 4 CMLR 745 and Case T-57/91 *National Association of Licensed Opencast Operators v. Commission* [1996] ECR II-1019.

479. As examples of the application of this important Article see Decs. 78/975 (O.J. 1975 L 330/34); 79/411 (O.J. 1979 L 103/25); 82/445 (O.J. 1982 L 206/38) and 84/89 (O.J. 1984 L 50/9). See also Case 3/58 *etc. Barbara Erzbergbau AG et al. v. High Authority* [1960] ECR 173; Case 27–29/58 *Compagnie des Hauts Fourneaux de Givors et al. v. High Authority* [1960] ECR 241; Cases 24 and 34/58 *Chambre Syndicale de la Sidérurgie de l'Est de la France v. High Authority* [1960] ECR 281; Case 20/59 *Italy v. High Authority* [1960] ECR 325; Case 9/61 *Netherlands v. High Authority* [1962] ECR 213; [1962] ECR 59; and Case 28/66 *Netherlands v. High Authority* [1968] ECR 1, [1969] CMLR 377.

480. Art. 46 ECSC, points 2 and 3.

(b) facilitating the carrying out of investment programmes by granting loans to undertakings or by giving a guarantee to other loans which they obtain elsewhere, or giving financial contributions for investments which contribute to an increase of production, lower production costs, or facilitate marketing.[481]

(c) issuing opinions on individual investment programmes where an unfavourable opinion on the ground of subsidies, assistance, protection, or discriminations connected with the proposed programme has the effect of prohibiting the undertakings concerned from financing the investments in question from resources other than its own funds.[482] However, an unfavourable opinion based on the economic merits of an investment project will in practice also render external financing very difficult.[483]

(d) encouraging – by means even including financial contributions – technical and economic research.[484]

(e) facilitating the financing of such programmes as the Commission may approve for the provision of re-employment in case of an exceptionally large reduction in labour requirements in special areas, due to the realization of the general objectives for the coal and steel industries mentioned under (a), as well as direct financial contributions to the payment of compensation to tide the workers over until they can obtain new employment, the granting of resettlement allowances, and the financing of retraining for workers.[485] After the deepening of the crisis Article 56 ECSC was regularly applied, and it has even been applied after the quota scheme came to an end in 1988.

(f) establishing a system of production quotas in a period of manifest crisis.[486] The first implementation of Article 58 ECSC was by

481. Art. 54 ECSC, 1st and 2nd paras.
482. *Ibid.*, 3rd–6th paras.
483. See Theunissen (1977) SEW 499. He notes that already in 1968 the European Parliament complained that because of its reticent policy in applying Arts. 46 and 54 ECSC the High Authority was scarcely able to achieve anything relating to the longer-term development of the steel industry. After the merger of the Institutions for years the Commission too did not use to the full extent the opportunities for a far-seeing investment policy with the aid of the instruments at its disposal. Only under pressure as a result of the steel crisis which started in 1975 did its policy on this matter sharpen. On the policy pursued thereafter see Heusdens and De Hom, *op. cit.* (see note 460, *supra*). Theunissen feels that this aside the investment policy pursued between 1952 and 1975 achieved clearly positive results. Without this policy the 1975 crisis would have undoubtedly been even worse. Notification of investment programmes was more closely regulated by the action which the Commission took in 1981 and 1985 (see note 461, *supra*).
484. Art. 55 ECSC.
485. Art. 56 ECSC and Convention on the Transitional Provisions, Art. 23.
486. Art. 58 ECSC.

Commission Decision 2794/80[487] which was later replaced by Decision 1831/81[488] and was then changed annually. Only at the end of 1986 was it possible to hack out a path towards liberalization which has now measured sufficient success that the production quota system came to an end on June 30, 1988.[489] For certain products system of surveillance was introduced by Decision 2448/88[490] and lasted until the end of June 1990.[491] The Community steel market is thus increasingly having to face up to foreign competition on a more liberalized basis. There is, though, abundant case-law stemming from the Eighties, first on the scope and prior conditions for declaring a period of manifest crisis[492] and then a whole spate of attacks on individual quota decisions.[493] Later there followed a mass of appeals against fines imposed for exceeding the quotas fixed (in principle 75 ECU per tonne in excess).[494]

487. O.J. 1980 L 291/1.
488. O.J. 1981 L 180/1.
489. The last decision, Dec. 194/88 (O.J. 1988 L 25/1) expired on 30 June 1988.
490. O.J. 1988 L 212/1.
491. Steel production continued to be closely monitored through a system of quarterly guidelines until the end of 1994. Forward programmes for each half-year still maintain a certain monitoring of developments within the Community, and this has been accompanied by varying degrees of prior statistical monitoring of imports from Central and Eastern Europe. Various measures supporting the restructuring of the Community steel industry have been withdrawn, given that the industry's own proposals on capacity-shedding were deemed inadequate in late 1994. Much assistance has been granted towards the restructuring of the iron and steel industry in Central and Eastern Europe and in the former Soviet Union. See, generally, COM (90) 201 *General objectives for steel – 1995*; SEC (92) 2160 Final on greater competitiveness in the steel industry and the need for further restructuring; COM (94) 265 Final; COM (94) 466 Final, and *e.g.* the *General Reports 1994 and 1995* (Brussels, Luxembourg, 1995 and 1996), points 210 and 183 respectively.
492. In Case 276/80 *Ferriera Padana SpA v. Commission* [1982] ECR 517 the scope of the prior conditions for declaring a period of manifest crisis was defined.
493. Many of the fundamental questions arising here were discussed in the opinion in Case 119/81 *Klöckner-Werke AG v. Commission* [1982] ECR 2627 at 2658. See also Cases 244/81 *Klöckner-Werke AG v. Commission* [1983] ECR 1451, [1984] 2 CMLR 43; Cases 303 and 312/81 *Klöckner-Werke AG v. Commission* [1983] ECR 1507, [1984] 2 CMLR 714; Cases 311/81 and 30/82 *Klöckner-Werke AG v. Commission* [1983] ECR 1549, [1984] 2 CMLR 752; 136/82 *Klöckner-Werke AG v. Commission* [1983] ECR 1599; and Case 263/82 *Klöckner-Werke AG v. Commission* [1983] ECR 4143.
494. See *e.g.* Case 179/82 *Lucchini Siderurgica SpA v. Commission* [1983] ECR 3083; Case 188/82 *Thyssen AG v. Commission* [1983] ECR 3721; Case 64/84 *Queenborough Rolling Mill Company Ltd. v. Commission* [1985] ECR 1829, [1986] 2 CMLR 211; and Case 268/84 *Ferriera Valsabbia SpA v. Commission* [1987] ECR 353. The opinions in the first three of these cases discuss the principle questions arising on the Commission's fining policy in more detail. On the quota system see, generally, the literature cited in notes 453 and 461, *supra* and the *General Reports* for the periods involved. Barents (1984) SEW 255 makes some interesting comparisons with the case-law on agriculture.

(g) establishment of a system of allocations in case of serious short-ages.[495] It follows, however, from Article 57 ECSC that Articles 58[496] and 59 ECSC can only be applied if indirect means are not sufficient. Article 57 gives a few examples of this, from which it appears that also price regulations, as mentioned below, are included among the indirect means.

(h) fixing maximum or minimum prices both for sales within the common market and for export.[497]

(i) binding recommendations for the termination of 'social dumping'.[498]

(j) measures for promoting the free movement of workers.[499]

(k) ensuring non-discriminatory rates and other conditions of transport for coal and steel.[500]

As appears from this enumeration, intervention is possible on grounds of short-term economic, or anti-cyclical, policy and structural policy, and on social grounds, while there are also great possibilities for promoting economic and technical research. The financial autonomy of the ECSC reinforces these possibilities. In accordance with the opening words of Article 5 ECSC, the powers of direct intervention mentioned above under (f) and (g) as well as the slightly less direct powers referred to under (h) have only played a part in accordance with the principle that the more direct interventions should be applied if the less direct interventions appear insufficient and only in exceptional circumstances.[501]

The Community's own resources,[502] in conjunction with the wide

495. Art. 59 ECSC.
496. In Cases 32/87 etc. Industrie Siderurgische Associate (ISA) et al. v. Commission [1988] ECR 3305 at 3329–3330 the Court decided that the Commission should have used the flexible system of Art. 58(3) ECSC for the partial termination of quotas.
497. Art. 61 ECSC. On the minimum prices laid down in the context of steel crisis policy see Heusdens and De Hom, op. cit. (see note 461, supra) 318 et seq. As to the means by which the Commission sought to give a certain binding force to indicative production programmes even before Art. 58 ECSC was applied see ibid. 328–329. The application of Arts. 54 and 55 ECSC can also be a pretty effective way of controlling the restructuring of the steel industry, see ibid. 331. Nevertheless the state aid systems discussed above have appeared more effective. In accordance with a suggestion made by VerLoren van Themaat, Adv. Gen. in Case 119/81 Klöckner-Werke AG v. Commission [1982] ECR 2627 at 2672, a quota sanction was introduced into later quota arrangements to ensure compliance with the aid codes.
498. Reduction of wages or social security burdens to obtain price reductions (Art. 68 ECSC).
499. Art. 69 ECSC.
500. Art. 70 ECSC.
501. In 1953 Art. 59 played a role in the division of coal which was then in short supply, see Dec. 5/52 (J.O. 10 February 1953, p. 3). Art. 59 ECSC and this application of it have a certain significance as a precedent for a Community distribution system for other scarce energy sources. For a good commentary on Art. 59 ECSC see Quadri, op. cit. (see note 453, supra) 759–775.
502. Arts. 49 and 50 ECSC.

definition of its task under Article 3(e) ECSC and the interpretation given to the second paragraph of Article 54 ECSC, have made possible, even apart from the powers of intervention referred to above, a policy for improving the living and working conditions of workers, particularly as regards vocational training, harmonization of working conditions, social security, industrial health and industrial medicine, industrial safety in the pits, and the building of workers' dwellings. The experience of the ECSC has undoubtedly shown to what extent the Community's own resources tend to promote the development of a Community policy. In the field of coal policy the High Authority was handicapped more and more by the circumstance that the development of the coal market was increasingly determined by competition from other sources of energy, particularly oil products, natural gas, and potentially also the nuclear power stations.

An unusual situation relating to the position of an ECSC production levy (as an own resource) in a liquidation was considered by the Court in Case 168/82 *European Coal and Steel Community (ECSC) v. The Liquidator of Ferriere Sant' Anna SpA*[503] which was referred under Article 41 ECSC. The Court found that in the absence of a provision adopted by the Community legislature within the bounds envisaged by the Treaty ECSC levies could not be considered as preferential debts ranking with similar debts owed to the State. The judgment and the opinion of the learned Advocate General are also incidentally of significance for fiscal privileges in favour of the Community concerning EC levies. In 1986 the Commission adopted a binding ECSC recommendation, Recommendation 86/198[504] as a result of that judgment, dealing with the establishment of preferential treatment for debts in respect of levies on the production of coal and steel. In that recommendation (which is comparable to a directive under the EEC Treaty) the Member States in which the state's fiscal claims have special priority (all the then Member States save Denmark) were obliged to accord a general or special priority of the same rank as their legislation accorded to claims relating to VAT to claims arising from the imposition of ECSC levies.

5. THE EUROPEAN ATOMIC ENERGY COMMUNITY[505]

5.1 Aims and means

As appears at once from Articles 1 and 2 Euratom, the character of Euratom is quite different from that of the two other Communities.

503. [1983] ECR 1681 at 1696.
504. O.J. 1986 L 144/40. See Case C-221/88 *European Coal and Steel Community v. Acciaiere e ferriere Busseni SpA (in liquidation)* [1990] ECR I-495.
505. See, generally, Grazebrook *et al.* in Vaughan (ed), *op. cit.* (see note 138, *supra*) Part 10 (to be published, updating the contribution to 51 *Halsbury's laws of England* (4th ed.,

The centre of gravity of its task is the development of research and the dissemination of technical knowledge.[506] In addition, Article 2 refers to the establishment of uniform safety standards,[507] the facilitation of investments, the ensuring of regular and equitable supplies of ores and nuclear fuels, the guaranteeing by appropriate measures of control that nuclear materials are not diverted for purposes other than those for which they are intended, the exercise of property rights in respect of special fissionable materials, the establishment of a common market for specialized materials and equipment, free movement of capital for nuclear investment, and freedom of employment for specialists within the Community, and finally the establishment with other countries and with international organizations of any contacts likely to promote progress in the peaceful uses of nuclear energy. The Community has no powers in respect of the use of ores and nuclear fuels for military purposes.

As appears from the definition of the task in Article 2, Euratom, unlike the other Communities, has certain powers for the independent development and dissemination of research and knowledge. In the period of the development of atomic energy, the establishment achieved within one year – of a common market[508] was and remains of less importance than this task of independent management. It is principally the research agreements and the patent property of Euratom which have attracted the attention of lawyers in this context. Further original features which have received attention from lawyers and, particularly since the Chernobyl disaster, of others, are the tasks of ensuring safety control, the common ownership of fissionable materials, the common enterprises, and the regulation of civil liability for nuclear risks. A brief outline of the principal original points from this Treaty is given below.

As is well-known, in the last decade nuclear energy policy has become the subject of increasing controversy on the grounds of fears about environmental pollution, danger to population, the risk of proliferation of nuclear weapons and the uncertainty of supplies of raw materials. The wording of the Treaty appears to have had an eye to all these dangers

London, 1986) paras. 10.14–10.65, and Grünwald (1990) EuZW 209. As to border installations see Lenaerts (1988) 13 ELRev. 159, and on the beginnings of Euratom see Weilemann, *Die Anfänge der Europäischen Atomgemeinschaft* (Baden-Baden, 1983).
506. Arts. 2(a) and 4–29 Euratom.
507. The wording of Art. 2 Euratom corresponds badly in this respect with the further working-out of the Treaty itself. The safety standards for the protection of the health of workers and the general population are worked out in Chapter III under the title Health and Safety (these have been further developed since COM (86) 434 Final). The term 'safeguards' is correctly used in Chapter VII for control against the misuse of nuclear energy for military purposes.
508. Arts. 92–100 Euratom.

and on each of the points the Euratom Treaty already contains a number of guarantees and provides for powers to develop those guarantees. It should be noted, moreover, that so far the objection referred to above principally relate to the process of nuclear *fission*; they do not apply to the same degree or in the same way to the process of nuclear fusion which is now being developed. The wording of Article 1 Euratom – which speaks of the Community's task being 'to contribute to raising of the standard of living in the Member States and to the development of relations with other countries by creating the conditions necessary for the speedy establishment and growth of nuclear industries' – would not be so easily ratified in all Member States now as it was in 1957. As far as positive law is concerned the fears expressed above have not as yet had any clearly visible effect on this area of Community law. It seems sure that these fears would not be allayed simply by terminating the Euratom Treaty or making it in practice a dead letter. Both of these solutions would merely mean that the development of nuclear energy would thenceforth continue without control or co-ordination at the Community level. The risks feared would if anything increase rather than decrease. For critics as well as for proponents of nuclear energy, the best perspective would appear to lie in managing at the Community level and in broader international co-operation (particularly in the framework of the International Atomic Energy Agency in Vienna) the movement of emphasis, differentiated between the Member States, from existing nuclear energy technology to other energy sources and energy-saving measures. Various attempts after the Chernobyl disaster to strengthen Community co-operation for the prevention and control of accidents have led to the adoption of Decision 87/600 on Community arrangements for the early exchange of information in the event of a radiological emergency.[509] Various measures were taken also in the aftermath of the Chernobyl disaster relating to foodstuffs, feeding-stuffs and agricultural products.[510] Moreover, other measures concern civil protection;[511] information for the

---

509. O.J. 1987 L 371/76.
510. Some measures were temporary. See, though, Regs. 3954/87 (O.J. 1987 L 317/11, amended by Reg. 2218/89 (O.J. 1989 L 211/1)) on foodstuffs; 944/89 (O.J. 1989 L 101/17) on less important foodstuffs; 2219/89 (O.J. 1989 L 211/4) on the export of foodstuffs and feeding-stuffs; 770/90 (O.J. 1990 L 83/78) on feeding-stuffs, and 737/90 (O.J. 1990 L 82/1, amended by Reg. 686/95 (O.J. 1995 L 71/15) on imports of agricultural products from third countries. More generally, see COM (86) 327, 434/3 and 607 final; the Schmid Report of 1987 on the Community's reaction (EP Doc. 112.005 Final) and the Von Blottnitz Report of 1987 on foodstuffs contamination (EP Doc. 112.007 Final). See Chabannes and Lecocq (1988) RMC 389.
511. Council Resolutions of 25 June 1987 (O.J. 1987 C 176/1); 23 November 1990 (O.J. 1990 C 315/1), and 31 October 1994 (O.J. 1994 C 313/1).

public;[512] international cooperation,[513] and assistance in the event of nuclear accidents.[514]

5.2 Research

The struggle for the delimitation between a joint research programme and national research programmes must be viewed against the background of Articles 4–7, 10, and 215 Euratom. It appears already from Article 4 that the joint research programme, the carrying out of which has been entrusted to the Commission, has a supplementary character, and that the Commission is primarily responsible for promoting nuclear research in Member States. On the basis of Article 72 Euratom the Commission may issue loans for this purpose.[515] Articles 5 and 6 provide for a fairly weak form of co-ordination of national research programmes. In this context, research contracts and expert assistance can constitute financial incentives; subsidies are not allowed. For the first five years the joint research programme was laid down during the negotiations on the Treaty[516] and it must subsequently be laid down for a period not exceeding five years by the Council, acting by unanimity on a proposal from the Commission, which must consult on the subject a Scientific and Technical Committee set up for this purpose.[517] After the third programme, which should have already been established in 1967, was blocked for years by French resistance a certain measure of progress was achieved in 1971. In that year two small five-year programmes for research and training programmes were set up in the fields of biology and health physics[518] and fusion and plasma physics.[519] Various programmes were adopted after 1972 which also dealt with non-nuclear matters such as informatics, in part reflecting the trend after the

512. Dir. 89/618 (O.J. 1989 L 357/31).
513. See the Commission's programme (O.J. 1992 C 142/5) and the proposal (COM (94) 362 Final) that the Community should accede to the IAEA Convention on Nuclear Safety (Vienna, 19–23 September 1994), which entered into force on 24 October 1996 (*General Report 1996*, Brussels, Luxembourg, 1997) point 480) but no reaction appears to have followed the proposal. See further, on East–West cooperation, O.J. 1996 C 320/45. See also *General Report 1996* (Brussels, Luxembourg, 1997) points 485–490 and Chapter X, section 3.2, *ante* (as to nuclear safety and radioactive materials).
514. The Council has approved the IAEA Convention (26 September 1986) on assistance in the case of a nuclear accident or radiological emergency, see Bull. EC 11–1989, point 2.1.136. See also COM (89) 25 Final on Community cooperation in such circumstances, approved by the Council, Bull. EC 11–1989, point 2.1.134. The IAEA Convention on Early Notification of a Nuclear Accident (Vienna, 26 Sesptember 1986) has also been approved by the Council, Bull. EC 12–1987, point 2.1.294.
515. Dec. 77/271 (O.J. 1977 L 88/11, most recently amended by Dec. 90/212 (O.J. 1990 L 112/26) to raise the maximum to 4,000 million ECU.
516. Art. 215 and Annex V Euratom.
517. Art. 7 Euratom.
518. Dec. 71/236 (J.O. 1971 L 143/31).
519. Dec. 71/237 (O.J. 1991 L 143/33).

Paris Summit in 1972 to adopt multiannual research programmes outside the Euratom area; initially these were based on the old Article 235 EEC.[520] Title VI of Part Three of the EC Treaty (introduced by the SEA) offers an independent legal basis for such Community multiannual programmes in addition to that provided by the Euratom Treaty. Indeed, the idea in drafting that Title was to make a link with the relevant Articles of the Euratom Treaty.[521]

The current framework programme for 1994–1998 is set out in Decision 94/268[522] and runs until the end of 1998. In view of the French and later Dutch opposition to an extensive joint programme, it is interesting to mention that Article 6 Euratom permits the Commission to place facilities, equipment, or expert assistance of the Community at the disposal of Member States, persons, or undertakings, either for payment or free of charge. Examples of the facilities referred to in Article 6 are the Joint Nuclear Research Centre, set up under Article 8, and its establishments at Ispra, Geel, Karlsruhe, and Petten. In 1978 after a long period of courtship concerning its place of establishment the 'Joint European Torus' (JET) Joint Undertakings[523] was set up to conduct research into thermonuclear fusion at Culham in Oxfordshire (United Kingdom) Article 10 Euratom provides for the possibility of entrusting Member States, persons, or undertakings, third countries, international organizations or nationals of third countries with the implementation of certain parts of the Community's research programme. This possibility has often been made use of by means of the conclusion of research or association contracts.[524]

520. See the *Sixth General Report* (Brussels, Luxembourg, 1973) point 318.
521. As was pointed out in the explanatory memorandum to the proposal for approval of the SEA by the Dutch Parliament (Kamerstukken 1985-86, 10626, no. 3, p. 7).
522. O.J. 1994 L 115/31, amended by Dec. 96/253 (O.J. 1996 L 86/72). A second amendment has been proposed, COM (96) 12 Final (O.J. 1996 C 115/13), amended COM (96) 453 Final (O.J. 1997 C 70/25).
523. Dec. 78/471 (O.J. 1978 L 151/10), most recently amended by Dec. 96/305 (O.J. 1996 L 117/9). A further amendment proposed COM (98) 13 Final (O.J. 1998 C 108/3).
524. Mathijsen in Ganshof van der Meersch (ed.), *Droit des Communautés européennes; Les novelles* (Brussels, 1969) 1098 mentions that the number of agreements concluded annually rose constantly and reached a (then) record 120 in 1967. In 1972 some sixty association contracts had been concluded in the fields of nuclear fusion, biology and health protection. In 1978 over 600 research and development contracts had been concluded in connection with energy saving, new energy sources and systems analysis. In 1980 the Council established a new four-year programme, in which research into nuclear safety (the Super-Sara project) was the cornerstone but in which new energy sources such as solar energy as well as environmental problems played a part. The Super-Sara project was later abandoned; this gave a new impetus to the integration of nuclear research in a broader programme of scientific and technical activities. The change of emphasis in fields of attention which has been mentioned above clearly continues and thus general frameworks now tend to be set. The financing of the JET plays a major part, although there are many other activities. The relevant sections of the *General Reports* give further details.

As a curiosity it should finally be mentioned that Article 9 Euratom lays down, amongst other things, the obligation to set up an institution at university level. The particulars of its operation has to be settled by the Council, acting by a qualified majority on a proposal from the Commission. Unfortunately no time-limit has been set for the implementation of this duty to set up a 'European University' which need by no means be confined to the science of nuclear energy. The European University Institute (EUI) which was founded from scratch in 1973 can be regarded as a somewhat meagre substitute for this Community university institution. The EUI is not in fact based on Article 9 Euratom but on a separate convention[525] and is now having increasing success in the fields of historical, economic, legal and political science research, rather than working in the field of the natural or applied sciences.

5.3 Dissemination of knowledge

The Community may acquire patents both by means of its own research programme and by purchase. Thus already in 1968 patent applications were filed for 107 inventions. Article 12 imposes on the Commission the obligation to grant to Member States, persons, and undertakings, at their request, non-exclusive licenses under these patents, provided that the applicants are in a position effectively to exploit the inventions to which they relate. *Mutatis mutandis* the same applies to applications for sub-licenses of licenses held by the Community. The Commission may indeed attach conditions to such licenses and sub-licenses, in order thus to contribute to the achievement of the tasks of the Community referred to in Articles 1 and 2 Euratom.[526] Articles 14, 15 and 16 Euratom provide for other means available to the Community to obtain and disseminate (under carefully developed guarantees as to exclusive dissemination among interested parties within the Community) confidential information in the field of atomic energy. Article 16 contains an important obligation to communicate information relating to national patent applications to the Commission. Another item to be added to the list of means is the unique semi-automatic system for nuclear documentation of non-confidential information which has been developed by the 'Information and Documentation Centre' and which already by the end of 1968 had computerized about 850,000 scientific and technical documents from all over the world.

Articles 17–23 contain an original, but complicated procedure for the

---

525. O.J. 1976 C 29/1.
526. The non-exclusive character of the licenses and sub-licenses was found to diminish their attractiveness in practice. For the way in which this problem and other problems in the patent field were solved see Mathijsen, *op. cit.* (see note 524, *supra*) 1104–1106.

grant of compulsory licenses of a non-exclusive character to the Community or to the joint undertakings to be discussed below, or under certain conditions also to others. In practice, however, these articles have not yet appeared to be of any importance.

Article 23 formed the basis of the important Security Regulation in the matter of secrecy.[527] Articles 24-28 themselves contain already important rules concerning secrecy for the protection of defence interests which are also of interest to industry.

5.4 Health protection

With a view to the protection of the health of the general public and of workers, Articles 30-39 Euratom provide for the establishment of basic standards within the Community and compulsory compliance with these basic standards and additional measures by Member States. Particularly after the judgment in Case 187/87 *Saarland et al. v. Minister for Industry, Post, and Telecommunications and Tourism et al.*[528] in which the Court held that Member States were required to provide the Commission with general data relating to any plans for the disposal of radioactive waste *before* authorization of the disposal is granted, Article 37 EC has really come into its own.[529] The Commission also makes recommendations under Article 33 Euratom[530] and carries out inspections under Article 35 Euratom.

The basic safety standards for the protection of the health of the general public and workers against the dangers of ionizing radiation are now laid down in Directive 96/29,[531] and protection against ionizing radiation in connection with medical exposures is the subject of Directive 97/43.[532] Reference has already been made to various measures adopted in the wake of the Chernobyl disaster.[533]

5.5 Safety control

Rules to be distinguished from the provisions for health protection are the rules of Articles 77-85 concerning safety control, which are important in

527. Reg. 3/58 (O.J. English Special Edition 1952-58, p. 63). See *51 Halsbury's Laws* (see note 505, *supra*) paras. 10.28–10.29
528. [1989] ECR 5013 at 5041–5042.
529. *E.g.* Opinions 92/236 (O.J. 1992 L 121/44) *Corva NV, Sloe*; 92/269 (O.J. 1992 L 138/36) *Thorp, Sellafield*; 94/747 (O.J. 1994 L 297/39) *Konrad, Salzgitter*; 95/172 (O.J. 1995 L 114/28) *TU5, Pierrelatte*, and 96/171 (O.J. 1996 L 48/13) *UKAEA, Windscale*.
530. *E.g. General Report 1996* (Brussels, Luxembourg, 1997) point 475. But see Rec. 90/143 (O.J. 1990 L 80/26) which appears to be the only published recommendation.
531. O.J. 1996 L 159/1 corrig. O.J. 1996 L 314/20.
532. O.J. 1997 L 180/22. This replaces in due course Dir. 84/466 (O.J. 1984 L 265/1), having to be implemented by 2000.
533. See the end of section 5.1, *ante*.

connection with the non-proliferation treaty. The controlling task with which the Commission is entrusted in this context serves to ensure that ores, source materials, and special fissionable materials are not diverted from their intended uses as formulated by the users, and to ensure the observance of the provisions of any agreements on the subject between the Community and third States or an international organization. In this context the important co-operation agreement with the United States[534] and the agreement with the International Atomic Energy Agency (IAEA)[535] are of particular importance. In implementation of the provisions of the Treaty on Non-proliferation of Nuclear Weapons[536] a separate agreement was concluded between Belgium, Denmark, Germany, Ireland, Italy, Luxembourg and the Netherlands and the IAEA.[537]

In order to ensure the observance of these provisions, Article 83 provides for purely administrative penalties, among which the temporary placing of the undertaking under the administration of a person or board and the complete or partial withdrawal of source materials or special fissionable materials go furthest.[538] With regard to France and the United Kingdom it is of interest that under Article 84 the control may not extend to materials used for purposes of defence. The application of the Treaty provisions relating to safeguards is now ensured by Regulation 3227/76[539] In relation to non-military materials and equipment the United Kingdom, Euratom and the IAEA concluded a separate co-operation agreement in 1976 and France, Euratom and the IAEA concluded such an agreement in 1978.[540]

5.6   Investments

Just as for coal and steel, the Commission must periodically publish programmes indicating, in particular, the production targets for nuclear energy and the various types of investment required to attain them.[541] Article 41 Euratom imposes an obligation on persons and undertakings to

---

534. The old agreement dating from 1960 expired at the end of 1995 and the new agreement applies from April 12, 1996 (see Dec. 96/314 (O.J. 1996 L 120/1)).

535. O.J. 1975 L 329/28.

536. London, Moscow and Washington, July 1, 1968 (TS 88 (1970)).

537. O.J. 1978 L 51/1.

538. See Case C-308/90 *Advanced Nuclear Fuels GmbH v. Commission* [1993] ECR I-309. By Decs. 90/413 (O.J. 1990 L 209/270) and 90/465 (O.J. 1990 L 241/14) the company concerned was placed under administration on the basis of Art. 83(1) Euratom. In an unpublished decision the Court granted the immediate enforcement of these decisions, later rejecting the substantive appeal (*supra*).

539. O.J. 1976 L 363/1, most recently amended by Reg. 2130/93 (O.J. 1993 L 191/75). See Hibert (1977) RTDE 282.

540. For that concluded by Euratom see note 535, *supra*.

541. Art. 40 Euratom.

communicate certain types of investment projects to the Commission.[542] The Commision's powers of co-ordination on the subject are, though, less far-reaching than those relating to investments in the coal and steel industry and in fact only imply the giving of an opinion.[543]

It is far more important that the Community may, by virtue of Articles 6, 47, 171, 172 and 174 Euratom, directly participate in investments. The first programme for this purpose provided in particular for a considerable amount of participation in the construction of reactors for electric power stations. Since 1977 the Commission has been empowered to issue Euratom loans for the purpose of contributing to the financing of nuclear power stations.[544]

5.7 Joint undertakings

Undertakings of fundamental importance to the development of the nuclear industry in the Community can be established under Article 45 Euratom as Joint Undertakings in accordance with Articles 46–51. Since the Treaty by no means requires that these must be 'joint ventures' from two or more Member States, while in practice only one really international enterprise (in this case a joint Belgian and French one) was established under this regime before 1978[545] the name is somewhat misleading. The Commission has rightly observed that the JET Joint Undertaking is the first real joint undertaking within the meaning of the Euratom Treaty.[546] However, although the Court in 1987 found that the Community character of JET did not stretch to the conditions of employment there for personnel of British nationality,[547] in 1996 the Court of First Instance decided the contrary (following the opinions of Advocates General VerLoren van Themaat and Mischo in the earlier judgment).[548] The legal position of

542. See Euratom Council Reg. 4/58 (O.J. English Special Edition 1952–58, p. 71 and Euratom Commission Reg. 5/58 (O.J. English Special Edition 1952–58, p. 74).
543. Art. 43 Euratom.
544. See note 515, *supra*.
545. Originally by Dec. 66/31 (O.J. English Special Edition 1965–66, p. 175, revised and implicitly repealed by Dec. 87/297 (O.J. 1987 L 148/1) *SENA*). See also *e.g.* Dec. 63/27 (O.J. English Special Edition 1963–64, p. 32, amended by Dec. 88/446 (O.J. 1988 L 222/3) *RWE–Bayerwerk*) (statutes last amended by Dec. 96/243 (O.J. 1996 L 80/62)).
546. *Twelfth General Report* (Brussels, Luxembourg, 1979) point 397 and note 523, *supra*.
547. See Cases 271/83 etc. *Ainsworth et al. v. Council et al.* [1987] ECR 167.
548. Cases T-177 and 377/94 *Altmann et al. v. Commission* [1996] ECR-SC IA-533; II-1471. This was possible because of changes in the nature of the JET from a short-term project into a more permanent project. The short-term nature had been crucial to the Court's earlier judgment. Formally, the Court of First Instance could depart from the earlier judgment of the Court of Justice as the identity of the litigants and their arguments were different. Significantly this new judgment has not been the subject of an appeal: it was very well documented and reasoned. The new judgment is of impor-

joint undertakings is hybrid. Legal personality is conferred by the Council decision which establishes a joint undertaking and this decision also lays down its Statutes (articles of association). The latter may diverge from national law which is otherwise applicable. Furthermore, Article 49 Euratom provides that not only shall joint undertakings have legal personality; they shall also enjoy the most extensive legal capacity accorded to legal persons under the respective national laws of each of the Member States. From the possibility of the Community's participation in financing laid down in Article 47, a power to take part in the management has also been derived. Finally, the advantages mentioned in Annex III to the Treaty may be granted to a Joint Undertaking. The most important of these advantages are the very far-reaching tax exemptions that may be granted.

5.8 Supply of ores, source materials and special fissile materials

On the basis of the procedure of confirmation and revision which was laid down in Article 76 at the end of a period of seven years, but which came to a deadlock in the Council, a difference of opinion arose on the question whether Articles 52–75 still are or are not any more in force. This question, however, was answered in the affirmative by the Court of Justice in its important judgment in Case 7/71 *Commission v. France*.[549] Various proposals for modification of these provisions have been made,[550] but so far to no avail. The Court has held that the Commission is obliged to give a decision under the procedure of the second paragraph of Article 53 Euratom on request.[551] The chief principles on which the Articles in question are based are those of equal access to resources and of a common supply policy.[552] In connection with the first principle all practices designed to ensure a privileged position for certain users are prohibited. In connection with the second principle an agency was constituted, which has, amongst other things, the exclusive right of concluding contracts relating to the supply of ores, source materials, or special fissile materials coming from inside or from outside the Community, and further a right of option on the materials in question produced in the territory of the Community.[553] In Articles 59-76 the two tasks are worked out further. To the right of monopoly of the agency in respect of imports from third

tance not merely in relation to staff cases as such, but also in relation to the JET structure and its history.
549. [1971] ECR 1003, [1972] 2 CMLR 453.
550. That put forward in 1982 (O.J. 1982 C 330/4) envisaged the abolition of the European Supply Agency.
551. Case C-107/91 *Empresa Nacional de Urânio SA (ENU) v. Commission* [1993] ECR I-599 at 633–634.
552. Art. 52 Euratom. See, generally, Allen (1983) 20 CMLRev. 473.

countries an exception has been made in Regulation 17/66,[554] in conformity with Article 74, for small quantities, but this exception does not apply to special fissile materials. A 'supervised exception' applies if the agency is unable, within a reasonable period, to fulfil an order for supplies or is able to fulfil it only at an excessive price.[555] In practice the liberalization of the supply policy for materials other than special fissile materials went even further. Under the Rules of the Euratom Supply Agency determining the manner in which demand is to be balanced against the supply of ores, source materials and special fissile materials[556] transactions relating to these materials can be concluded directly between producers and consumers, such contracts are to be communicated to the Agency, which has a right of veto.[557] With regard to the imports and exports of special fissile materials the intervention of the Agency is found to be necessary, partly in view of the existing international co-operation agreements. For intra-Community transactions in this case on the other hand the necessity of active intervention of the Agency would appear doubtful.[558] Appropriate amendments to the Statutes of the Euratom Supply Agency have been made on the accession of new Member States.

5.9 The regulation of the right of ownership of special fissile materials

A legal curiosity which has attracted a good deal of attention in the literature is the provision of Article 86, according to which all the special fissile materials defined in Article 197 are the property of the Community. Exceptions exist only for materials processed for foreign owners[559] and for materials held on lease from the United States under the cooperation agreement.[560] Under Article 87 the Member States, persons, or undertakings only have the right – which is extremely wide – of use and consumption of special fissile materials properly in their possession, subject to their obligations resulting from the provisions of the Treaty. The property right of the Community arises at the moment of production or import of the special fissile materials. If they have been produced or

---

553. Arts. 57 and 58 Euratom.
554. O.J. English Special Edition 1965–66, p. 297, amended by Reg. 313/74 (O.J. 1974 L 333/27).
555. Art. 66 Euratom.
556. O.J. English Special Edition 1950–62, p. 46, amended (O.J. 1975 L 193/37).
557. See Cases T-149 and 181/94 *Kernkraftwerke Lippe-Ems GmbH v. Commission* [1997] ECR II-161.
558. For the numerous interesting legal problems in the field of supply policy see Mathijsen, *op. cit.* (see note 523, *supra*) 1138–1148 and literature cited there. See also, more extensively, *51 Halsbury's Laws* (see note 505, *supra*) paras. 10.38–10.52.
559. Art. 75 Euratom.
560. See note 534, *supra*.

imported for the account of a Member State, a person, or an undertaking, the price is refunded by the Community. In this context Articles 88–89 provide for a special account. Fluctuations of value are to be borne by the owner, so that the Community cannot grow any poorer or richer on account of this property right.

5.10   The common market in the field of nuclear energy

On the basis of Article 232(2) EC it must be assumed that the provisions of that Treaty are applicable to the extent that the Euratom Treaty does not diverge from them. This is important, for instance, with regard to the right of establishment, the movement of capital, the rules of competition, the harmonization of laws, the power laid down in Article 235 EC to regulate unforeseen problems, the common commercial policy, and (last but not least) a common market regulation for energy. The latter will have to be brought about on the basis of the ECSC and EC Treaties, since the Euratom Treaty – except with regard to the supply of source materials – gives no powers in this respect. As will be seen in the next section, the powers conferred by the EC Treaty are also limited, although they are not altogether lacking. The applicability of Article 85 EC in the atomic energy sector was confirmed by the Commission in a reply to a parliamentary question[561] concerning a British–French–German agreement on the recycling of nuclear fuels. It appears from the Commission's reply that this agreement was also notified to it in accordance with Regulation 17/62.[562]

Concerning the establishment of a common market for the source materials and other goods and products playing a part in the use of nuclear energy and enumerated in Euratom lists Al and A2 of Annex IV to the Treaty, Article 93 provides for an abolition of customs duties, charges with equivalent effect, and quantitative restrictions in imports and exports in internal trade before 1 January 1959. For these source materials and auxiliary materials, machines, equipment, vehicles, packaging materials, and tools mentioned in lists Al and A2, which by their nature are specially intended for the field of nuclear energy, the common customs tariff was also established at an earlier date.[563] A possibility of an earlier application of the common customs tariff was also provided for by Article 95 for the products from list B (which can also be used for other purposes), but this power was not made use of. In view of this, it was equally impossible to abolish under Article 93 the internal tariffs for these products at an earlier date. Article 96 provides for free movement of workers for specialized em-

561. WQ 169/71 (Vredeling) J.O. 1972 C 5/1.
562. O.J. English Special Edition 1959–62, p. 87, most recently modified by the Act of Austrian, Finnish and Swedish Accession (1994).
563. By agreements on 22 December 1958 (J.O. 406/59 and 410/59).

ployment in the nuclear field.[564] With regard to the social security of the workers concerned, the previously discussed '*droit commun*' of the EC applies again.

Article 97 Euratom contains a directly applicable prohibition on the application of restrictions based on nationality to natural or legal persons, whether public or private, coming within the jurisdiction of a Member State and desiring to participate in the construction within the Community of nuclear facilities of a scientific or an industrial character.

Article 98 Euratom provides for an obligation on the part of Member States to take all necessary measures to facilitate the conclusion of insurance contracts covering atomic risks. The directives required in this Article were, however, considered unnecessary in view of the Treaty on third-party liability in the nuclear field concluded on 29 July 1960 within the framework of the OEEC and supplemented on 31 January 1963 on the initiative of the Community.[565] The Commission has indeed addressed recommendations to the Member States on the implementation of these treaties and has drawn up, in co-operation with producers and insurers, a skeleton policy for the insurance of third-party liability in the. permanent nuclear facilities of Member States. However, partly with a view to Article 85 of the EC Treaty, the Commission was opposed to giving a binding character to this skeleton policy. The parties are free to agree on different conditions. This whole problem of third-party liability for atomic risks again has received much attention in the legal literature.[566]

Articles 99 and 100 Euratom on the liberalization of capital and payments have lost their significance since the coming into force of Article 73b EC.[567]

5.11 External relations under the Euratom Treaty

On the basis of Article 101 and 102 Euratom numerous agreements and conventions have been concluded by the Community with third countries (including the United States of America, Argentina, Australia, Brazil, Canada and, with reference to the JET project, Sweden and Switzerland) as well as with the OECD (the 'Dragon Agreement') and with the International Atomic Energy Agency.[568]

---

564. Implemented by a directive of 5 March 1962 (O.J. English Special Edition 1959--62, p. 229). See Plender in Vaughan (ed.), *op. cit.* (see note 138, *supra*) paras. 15.43 and 15.46–47.

565. Tractatenblad (NL) 1964, 175 and 176. Various additional Protocols were con-cluded in 1982.

566. See, for an overview Schrans, *Inleiding tot het Europees Economisch Recht* (2nd ed., Ghent, Leuven, 1972) 568–569.

567. See, further, Chapter VII, section 8, *ante*.

568. See 51 *Halsbury's Laws* (see note 138, *supra*) paras. 10.58–10.65. Recent *General*

Article 103 provides for supervision and the possibility of intervention by the Commission in the matter of the conclusion of agreements or conventions between Member States themselves and third countries, to the extent that they are concerned with the field of application of the Euratom Treaty. This provision has become of great political importance in connection with the non-proliferation Treaty.[569] Articles 104–106 regulate the relation between old and new agreements or conventions with third countries, international organizations, or nationals of third countries on the one hand and the Euratom Treaty on the other hand in a general way. These Articles are also of interest for private agreements with the external world.

6. ENERGY POLICY[570]

6.1 Introduction

Just like agriculture and transport, energy is usually considered a sensitive sector of the economy.[571] But the EC Treaty does not provide for special powers in this area, although Article 3(t) EC now specifically envisages measures in this sphere.[572] The Declaration on civil protection, energy and tourism annexed to the Final Act on the occasion of signature of the TEU envisages the possibility of a separate Title on energy being included in the revisions resulting from the 1996 Intergovernmental Conference.[573] Energy is also mentioned as one of the sectors for which trans-European networks should be developed.[574]

In a Declaration on Article 130r EC (as it now is) attached to the Final Act on the occasion of signature of the SEA, the then Intergovernmental Conference confirmed that the Community's activities in the sphere of the

    Reports give further details. As to the new agreement with the United States, see note 534, *supra*.

569. See note 536, *supra*. As to the relationship between the powers of the Member States and those of the Community concerning the external relations of Euratom see section 5.5 of this Chapter, *supra*. See also in the field of atomic energy the important Ruling 1/78 *Draft IAEA Convention on the Physical protection of Nuclear Materials, Facilities and Transports* [1978] ECR 2151, [1979] 1 CMLR 131.

570. See Daintith and Hancher, *Energy Strategy in Europe: The Legal Framework* (Berlin, etc., 1986); Daintith and Williams, *The Legal Integration of Energy Markets* (Berlin, etc., 1987) Scholz in Von der Groeben, *op. cit.* (see note 13, *supra*) Vol. 4, 6241 and Vaughan (ed.), *op. cit.* (see note 138, *supra*) Parts 9 and 10.

571. The Spaak Report already earmarked energy as a sector requiring urgent action.

572. While it is unclear what sort of measures are meant, it may be assumed on the basis of the general principles of the Treaty that they may not derogate from the fundamental rules, save where specifically permitted.

573. But this was not included in the Treaty of Amsterdam (1997), not yet in force. The Commission stated in the same declaration that it would pursue its action on the basis of the present provisions.

574. See section 7.4, *post*.

environment may not interfere with national policies regarding the exploitation of energy resources, a declaration which the national governments regarded as confirming their sovereignty over mineral resources. This still influences the willingness of the Member States to agree a common energy policy.[575] It is interesting to draw the parallel with the development of the common transport policy, outlined in section 3.1, above. In the energy market – save for coal and nuclear energy – the general provisions of the EC Treaty apply, so for that part of the energy market there is in principle no other regulatory regime than the liberal market regime of the Treaty itself. It would be possible to introduce a specific regime in any new energy Title, but that would require unity of approach among the Member States as to the type of regime involved. As long as this is lacking, the sole option for the Community appears to be the formation of a strongly liberalized energy market, which in fact means that the same choice has been made as in the case of transport policy.

The fact that the EC Treaty has to take account of the existence of the ECSC Treaty (until mid-2002) and the Euratom Treaty is also important for the development of energy policy. The scope of application of the three treaties was discussed in section 1 of Chapter II, above. The divided approach has scarcely assisted the development of energy policy.

6.2 Energy policy prior to 1988 – a brief overview

At the start of the European integration process with the establishment of the ECSC, King Coal played a dominant role in the provision of energy. The availability of cheap oil, and, from 1961, natural gas, meant that the importance of the coal sector declined rapidly. The reduction in coal production did not go smoothly: social considerations and the desire that the Community should not become wholly dependent on imports of oil and coal led to massive aid programmes in the Member States. But EC policy was initially very liberally oriented, influenced by cheap oil. After the oil crisis in 1973 particular attention was paid to reducing external dependency. Directives based on the old Article 103(4) EEC established a crisis mechanism.[576] The second oil crisis led to an extension

---

575. This became clear in the discussion on the Commission's proposal on upstream licensing, which has now become Dir. 94/3 (O.J. 1994 L 164/3). Norway was particularly opposed to the proposal. A similar standpoint was evident in the negotiations on the European Energy Charter, discussed in section 6.3, *post*.
576. Dir. 73/238 (O.J. 1973 L 228/1), which was not yet operational during the crisis in Autumn 1973, had been preceded by Dir. 68/414 (O.J. English Special Edition 1968 (II), p. 586, amended by Dir. 72/435 (O.J. English Special Edition 1972 (28–30 Dec.), p. 69)) establishes minimum stocking obligations (90 days' supplies, which can be held in another Member States). The 2nd ed. of this work (1989) gives an extensive discussion of the development of energy policy prior to 1989 (pp. 755–764).

of these measures[577] and also to various measures concerned with energy-saving.[578]

In 1981 the Commission developed a new policy strategy and a certain number of conclusions were drawn by the Council on November 3, 1981 as a result.[579] In its communication the Commission said, in as many words, that as a result of the very divergent situations in the Member States[580] while Community objectives were required, neither a common (centralized) policy nor uniformity in the diversification of energy sources pursued was necessary. A common policy would be necessary only in areas in which the Community itself possessed specific or even exclusive powers.

6.3   Energy policy since 1988

Objectives

Community energy policy has for a long time been strongly influenced by the fact that the objectives were difficult to reconcile. First, especially since

577. The crisis measures implement the International Energy Agency's rules (Dir. 73/238, *ibid.*). They are supplemented by an agreement between the major oil companies which has been the subject of exemption under Art. 85(3) EC (Dec. 83/671 (O.J. 1983 L 376/30) *International Energy Agency*, renewed by Dec. 94/153 (O.J. 1994 L 68/35)). The obligation on oil companies to maintain emergency stocks has in some countries been restrictively applied in a manner incompatible with the internal market, thus the companies have been obliged to keep stocks on national territory, without being allowed to count stocks elsewhere, see CEPS, *Relaunching the Debate on Energy Policy* (Brussels, 1993) 16. The judgment in Case 72/83 *Campus Oil Ltd. et al. v. The Minister for Industry and Energy et al.* [1984] ECR 2727, [1984] 3 CMLR 544 demonstrates that the system is not regarded as affording complete guarantees of security of supply. In Case C-347/88 *Commission v. Greece* [1990] ECR I-4747 the Court did not take such a lenient view of the Greek rules. The Commission has proposed a revision of the system (COM (92) 145 Final), but withdrew its proposal on December 14, 1993. Dec. 77/186 (O.J. 1977 L 61/23, amended by Dec. 79/879 (O.J. 1979 L 270/58)) on exports from one Member State to another in the event of supply difficulties has now been repealed by Dec. 97/37 (O.J. 1997 L 158/4).
578. Dec. 77/706 (O.J. 1977 L 292/9), implemented by Dec. 79/639 (O.J. 1979 L 183/1), provides for the setting of a Community target for the reduction in energy consumption in the case of supply difficulties for crude oil and petroleum products. Two measures restricting the use of natural gas and petroleum products in power stations have been repealed, see Decs. 91/148 (O.J. 1991 L 75/52) and 97/8 (O.J. 1997 L 3/7).
579. The text is annexed to Daintith and Hancher, *op. cit.* (see note 570, *supra*).
580. One of the most important objectives of the study by Daintith and Hancher *(ibid.)* is to make clear that these differences do not only concern the strongly divergent weight of the different energy sources and the structure of the market but also the objectives, principles and instruments of the legal regulation of energy supplies (*ibid.* 33–128). Particularly the different ways in which the states partici-pate in production do not lend themselves, on the basis of Art. 222 EC, to a transfer of powers to the Community. The competition rules of the EC Treaty have long since not been not been applied to oligopolistic market structures or even monopolistic market structures in sectors of the market, see Slot (1994) 31 CMLRev. 511.

the publication of the Commission's working document *The Internal Energy Market*,[581] the objective of an internal market for energy has to be achieved. This means in practice that normal, healthy conditions of competition are created in the markets for the separate sources of energy: coal, gas, oil, and electricity. It also means healthy competition between the different forms of energy. In that working document the Commission did not make it clear whether it was concerned with competition in the individual energy markets or between them.[582] It is submitted, though, that there should be no contradiction between intra-fuel and inter-fuel competition.

There are still many obstacles to the internal market in energy, of which the working document gives an overview[583] and only a few are highlighted in the present discussion. Various Member States maintain exclusive import and export rights for gas and electricity. The Commission's attempts to tackle these using infringement proceedings have been distinctly unsuccessful.[584] Other obstacles include those resulting from exclusive rights to produce, transport and distribute gas and electricity. The effect of these rights is often strengthened through long-term contracts concluded by the companies concerned. The application of Articles 85 and 86 EC to these contracts is still in its infancy.[585] In the oil sector production monopolies form particular obstacles: in *Commission v. Greece*[586] the Commission failed to contest this, and thus the import monopoly for crude oil was accepted by the Court.[587] Extensive aid measures, particularly in the coal sector also constitute major obstacles, the stream of which the Commission has attempted to bring under control.[588]

581. COM (88) 238 Final.
582. See Hancher (1991) SEW 350.
583. See, for more details of policy and measures in the energy field, COM (97) 167 Final.
584. Case C-157/94 *Commission v. The Netherlands* [1997] ECR I-5669; Case C-1594/94 *Commission v. France* [1997] ECR I-5815, and Case C-160/94 *Commission v. Spain* [1997] ECR I-5851.
585. See Slot (1994) 31 CMLRev. 511 and Ritter in Hawk (ed.) 1993 Fordham Corporate Law Institute (Irvington-on-Hudson, 1993) 511 and, as to public service obligations in the energy sector, Slot in Gormley (ed.), *op. cit.* (see note 210, *supra*) 109.
586. Case C-347/88 [1990] ECR I-4747.
587. The Commission confirmed this approach in COM (92) 152 Final. The import regime for petroleum products was found incompatible with Art. 37 EC, which indicates a sharpening of the approach adopted in Campus Oil (see note 577, *supra*). The judgment in Case 231/83 *Cullet et al. v. Centre Leclerc Toulouse et al.* [1985] ECR 305, [1985] 2 CMLR 524 also had a liberalizing effect; as the French price system for fuel was found incompatible with Art. 30 EC, imports became worthwhile again.
588. See now Dec. 3632/93 (O.J. 1993 L 329/12), implemented by Dec. 341/94 (O.J. 1994 L 49/1), which applies until the end of the ECSC regime. Aid will only be compatible with the common market if it contributes to at least one of the following objectives: making further progress towards economic viability, in the light of coal prices on the international markets, with the aim of reducing aid progressively; solving the social and regional problems created by total or partial reduction in the activity of

However, at least under the predecessor regime the Commission was still willing to accept large-scale aid.[589]

The establishment of the internal market was also negatively affected by differences in national taxation, which distort competition between sources of energy. A high tax on energy within the Community may also competitively disadvantage Community industry *vis-à-vis* third countries.[590]

The internal market for electricity has at long last been achieved with the adoption of Directive 96/92,[591] and has now also been achieved for natural gas by Dir. 98/30.[592] The internal market for electricity is based on: the opening up of electricity production to competition, either based on a transparent and objective authorization procedure, or on a system of calls for tender with an authorization system for independent producers and autoproducers; and the gradual opening up at least one-third of the market in all Member States; the right of access to the network (with a right to construct direct lines). Moreover, the Member States may impose, within a Community framework, public service obligations, which will be monitored by the Commission, and must be transparent, non-discriminatory and verifiable. There are also temporary provisions for safeguards, failed investments and small isolated systems.

The second objective is security of supplies. It is useful for analytical purposes to distinguish between security of supplies as a geopolitical concept and as an operational concept. In the former concept it manifested itself heavily in the development of energy policy after the oil crises. In this context the emphasis lies on measures to reduce dependency on external energy sources, particularly oil, but also, increasingly, gas. The second concept is often invoked to justify exclusive rights to produce, transport and distribute energy. In the latter two of these activities the concept is particularly involved in the network-lined forms of energy: gas and electricity. In some instances the one concept follows the other, and both can be seen in the energy objectives set for 1995.[593]

production units; helping the coal industry adjust to environmental protection standards.

589. As to the predecessor regime, see Dec. 2064/86 (O.J. 1986 L 177/1). See e.g. Decs. 126/93 (O.J. 1993 L 50/16) Jahrhundertvertrag (Germany); 135/93 (O.J. 1993 L 55/65) (Portugal); 93/145 (O.J. 1993 L 57/93) (Spain), and 93/151 (O.J. 1993 L 59/33) (Germany). Recent examples of approvals under the present system include Decs. 94/995 (O.J. 1995 L 379/6) (United Kingdom) and 95/519 (O.J. 1995 L 299/18) France).

590. See CEPS, *op. cit.* (see note 577, *supra*) 28, and the Commission's proposal COM (97) 30 Final (O.J. 1997 C 139/14).

591. O.J. 1997 L 27/20.

592. O.J. 1998 L 204/1 (too late for discussion here).

593. Council Resolution of 16 September 1986 (O.J. 1986 C 241/1), see also COM (88) 238 Final. For further objectives, see Commission's proposal COM (96) Final (O.J. 1997 C 27/9), amended COM (97) 436 Final (O.J. 1997 C 305/7).

The case-law on Articles 30, 37 and 90(2) EC and Commission policy in the application of Articles 85, 86 and 90(2) EC leads to the conclusion that a satisfactory definition of the possibility of exceptions for security of supplies has not yet been found. For many years the not uncontroversial judgment in *Campus Oil* set the tone: in particular the observations that in the case of interests of security of supply the fact that other, in fact economic, objectives could be achieved would not exclude the application of Article 36 EC, and the Court's view of the proportionality of the measures concerned, so that the prices fixed by the Minister were accepted by the Court, gave the Member States the feeling that the exception was far-reaching.[594] As has been demonstrated, that view has now been somewhat nuanced.[595]

In the meantime the Court has recognized that restrictions of competition for energy utilities are permitted on the basis of Article 90(2) EC: account must be taken of the economic conditions under which the undertaking operates, in particular the costs it has to bear and the rules, particularly as to environmental policy, to which it is subject.[596]

The Commission has never really fulfilled its intention to clarify the concept of security of supply. Its communication of 1990 was unsatisfactory[597] and it cannot really be said that the new White Paper *An Energy Policy for the European Union*[598] exactly meets this need, although it is littered with references to the concept, develops considerable attention to it, and, along with ensuring competitiveness, and environmental protection, security of supplies is one of the objectives of this policy.[599] The Commission has applied the concept in the context of national rules prescribing the use of a fixed quota of nationally produced fuel for electricity generation.[600] The Commission did give further useful indications in its proceedings on the oil monopoly in Case C-347/88 *Commission v. Greece*.[601] In the context of applying Article 85 EC the Commission has on

594. Case 72/83 *Campus Oil Ltd. et al. v. Minister for Industry and Energy et al.* [1984] ECR 2727 at 2752 *et seq.*
595. See note 577, *supra.*
596. Case C-393/92 *Gemeente Almelo et al. v. Energiebedrijf Ijsselmij NV* [1994] ECR I-1477 at 1520–1521. This judgment builds on that in Case C-320/91 *Corbeau* [1993] ECR I-2533, see Hancher (1994) 31 CMLRev. 105 and (1995) 32 CMLRev. 305. See also Case T-16/91 RV *Rendo NV v. Commission* [1996] ECR II-1827, and note 584, *supra.*
597. SEC (90) 1248, of 14 September 1990.
598. COM (95) 682 Final.
599. See, though, the report on the situation of oil supply, refining and markets, COM (96) 143 Final, and the Council's conclusions (Bull. EU 12–1996, point 1.3.132).
600. The Commission accepted a maximum of 20% in the case of the United Kingdom non-fossil fuel obligation, see *XXth Report on Competition Policy 1990* (Brussels, Luxembourg, 1991) point 293. In the case of the *Jahrhundertvertrag* (Dec. 93/126 (O.J. 1993 L 50/14) the Commission permitted a higher figure than that as a temporary measure. Dir. 96/92 (O.J. 1997 L 27/20), Art. 8(4) prescribes a maximum of 15%.
601. [1990] 1 ECR 4747.

a number of occasions discussed security of supplies as an argument for
granting or refusing an exemption under Article 85(3), but the decision in
Ijsselcentrale did not.[602]

Another objective is that energy policy must contribute to the fulfillment of environmental requirements.[603] Article 130r(2) EC appears to
give the integration principle more weight than it had hitherto.[604] As
the discussion about the introduction of a carbon dioxide tax[605]
demonstrates, the environmental component of energy policy has increased
sharply in the last years.[606] This has been yet further reason for the
Community to develop energy policy further.[607] Many environmental
questions have a pronounced cross-border effect, which would suggest that
they should be tackled at Community level.[608] An objective which is clearly
related to this is energy saving, which in part involves increased energy
efficiency.[609]

Other influences

The development of an energy policy in the Community is also influenced
by a number of factors which are to only a slight degree susceptible to
control. First, the price of crude oil. The significance of this factor for the
whole energy sector is enormous, as the policy of all other energy providers
(gas, coal, nuclear energy, hydro-electric power and alternative energy

602. Dec. 91/50 (O.J. 1991 L 28/32), annulled in part, see Case T-16/91 RV *Rendo NV et al. v. Commission* [1996] ECR II-1827.
603. Thus it is not surprising that this is one of the highlights of the new White Paper, COM (95) 682 Final. See, further, the Commission's proposal for a decision on coop-eration over agreed objectives, COM (96) 431 Final (O.J. 1997 C 27/9), amended COM (97) 436 Final (O.J. 1997 C 305/7).
604. *Cf.* Sevenster, *Milieubeleid en Gemeenschapsrecht* (Deventer, 1992) 208 and 116. This is also emphasized by the Declaration on the assessment of the environmental impact of Community measures attached to the Final Act on the signature of the TEU.
605. As to the proposal, see COM (92) 226 Final (O.J. 1992 C196/1), amended COM (95) 172 Final.
606. See the Commission's proposal, COM (97) 30 Final (O.J. 1997 C 139/14).
607. See the Commission's Communication on Energy and the Environment, COM (89) 369 Final and the Fifth Environmental Action Programme (O.J. 1993 C 138/1), section 4.2 (p. 31 *et seq.*).
608. A clear example is Dir. 88/609 (O.J. 1988 L 336/1, most recently amended by Dir. 94/66 (O.J. 1994 L 337/83)) on emissions from large combustion installations. In a sepa-rate declaration attached to the Final Act on the occasion of signature of the TEU, Spain and Portugal claimed an exemption until 1 January 2000. See also Hancher, (1989) 26 CMLRev. 457.
609. This is clearly evident in the new White Paper COM (95) 682 Final. See also the pro-posal for a directive introducing rational planning techniques in the gas and electricity distribution sectors COM (95) 369 Final, amended by COM (97) 69 Final (O.J. 1997 C 180/37). The 1986 resolution on objectives for 1995 (see note 593, *supra*) set con-crete objectives for reduced consumption and environmental improvements.

sources such as wind farms) is ultimately determined by the price of oil. The Community's influence on the price of oil is pretty well in inverse proportion to the importance of that price. Thus Community policy has been aimed at facilitating a reduction in the risk of price movements.

The possibility of turning to nuclear energy has been pretty well blocked in most Member States, save France.[610] The possibility of using coal produced in the Community for energy production is strongly hindered by the fact that its production price ia about twice the world market price. Moreover, environmental requirements pose ever-increasing restrictions on coal, even though new technology has made major reductions in emissions possible. The development of combined heat and power stations has led to a major increase in energy efficiency. As these power stations run on gas, this has caused an increase[611] in the use of gas.

Finally, the network-bound nature of gas and electricity should not be forgotten. This has frequently led to exclusive rights to transport and distribution. As has been noted above, the existence of these exclusive rights has rendered the application of the competition rules very difficult.

The production of gas and oil, which are activities linked to concessions also gives rise to problems in relation to procurement. While the utilities were not originally embraced by the initial public procurement regime, they are now covered by a specific procurement regime.[612] Directive 94/22 ensures that the conditions for the award of contracts for the exploration and exploitation of hydrocarbons are brought into line with Community law.[613]

The geopolitical aspect of security of supplies has also led to major attention being focused on external policy. This has translated into an active policy in relation to the major oil-producing countries in the framework of the Gulf Cooperation Council. The same purpose is served by the European

610. Which produces some 77% of its electricity requirements from nuclear energy (*Power in Europe* 22 October 1993, no. 160).

611. See Wiersema (1991) Util. LRev. 170.

612. Dir. 93/38 (O.J. 1993 L 199/84, most recently amended by Dir. 98/4 (O.J. 1998 L 101/1) to take account of the results of the Uruguay Round. Dir. 93/38, Art. 2 sets out the relevant activities subject to the procurement regime. Art. 3 permits exemptions from the application of that regime to be granted in relation to the exploration for and exploitation of oil, gas coal, or other solid fuels, where *inter alia* the award of contracts occurs on a non-discriminatory basis. So far three Member States have been granted such an exemption in relation to oil and natural gas: France (Dec. 93/18 (O.J. 1993 L 12/19); the United Kingdom (Decs. 93/425 (O.J. 1993 L 196/55) and 97/367 (O.J. 1997 L 156/55, and The Netherlands (Dec. 93/676 (O.J. 1993 L 316/41). The general criteria for the grant of an exemption by the Commission are set out in Dec. 93/327 (O.J. 1993 L 129/25), which remarkably, in para. 17 of the preamble, argued that a directive was not the appropriate instrument to abolish obstacles to inter-state trade in electricity. However, a directive was in fact used: see Dir. 96/92 (O.J. 1996 L 27/20) on the internal market for electricity.

613. O.J. 1994 L 164/3, corrig. O.J. 1996 L 79/30.

Energy Charter Treaty and its protocol on energy efficiency and related environmental aspects.[614] It seeks to develop new relations between Canada, the United States, Japan, most of the Independent States of the former Soviet Union and Central and Eastern Europe, and the main European countries dealing with trade, investment and energy cooperation. At the same time it seeks to improve the Community's security of supplies and develop the energy potential of the Independent states of the former Soviet Union and the Eastern European countries. A strategy for energy cooperation with Asia has also been developed.[615]

Legislation

The Commission in its working document of 1988[616] envisaged concrete measure concerning the transparency of prices for gas and electricity, and Directive 90/377 on price transparency for industrial end-users[617] has made a first step in this direction. Transit rights through international electricity and gas networks have also been assured.[618] As has been noted above, the internal market for electricity has now been achieved, and the thorny subject of third party access has been dealt with in a manner which provides some leeway, even in the presence of exclusive rights.[619] It was also noted above that the problems with the proposals as to gas have now at last been resolved. Myriad other legislation has been adopted in the energy field,[620] but mention might be made of Directive 96/57 which relates to energy efficiency requirements for household electric refrigerators, freezers and their combinations[621] which is a major part of Community

614. The Charter was signed at The Hague on December 17, 1991 (the text is reproduced in Wlde and Nidi, *International Oil and Gas Investment: Moving Eastward?* (London, 1994) 367); it was translated into a Treaty after detailed negotiations, which was signed at Lisbon on December 17, 1994. See Dec. 98/181 (O.J. 1998 L 69/1). The Charter was provisionally applied by Decs. 94/998 (O.J. 1994 L 380/1) and 94/1067 (O.J. 1994 L 380/113). (O.J. 1994 L 380 contains all the relevant documents, see also 33 ILM 360 at 373 (1995)). See also Beazell (1994) JE&NRL 299 and Van den Oosterkamp (1992) SEW 623 and COM (98) 267 Final.
615. COM (96) 308 Final, see Bull. EU 5–1997, points 1.3.107–1.3.108.
616. See note 581, *supra.*
617. O.J. 1990 L 185/16, most recently amended by the Act of Austrian, Finnish and Swedish Accession (1994).
618. Dirs. 90/547 (O.J. 1990 L 33/30, most recently amended by Dec. 95/162 (O.J. 1995 L 107/53)) for electricity, and 91/296 (O.J. 1991 L 147/37, most recently amended by Dir. 95/49 (O.J. 1995 L 233/86)) for gas. They do not deal with third party access to these networks which has long been on the Commission's agenda. The European Energy Charter Treaty also expressly excludes this in a Ministerial declaration. As to electricity, see Dir. 96/92 (O.J. 1996 L 27/20), Arts. 16–18, and gas see note 592, *supra.*
619. See Dir. 96/92, *ibid.* As to the earlier proposals, see Ehlermann (1991) *Oil and Gas Taxation Review* 295 and (1994) JE&NRL 342, and Hancher and Trepte (1992) ECLR 149.
620. As to which, see the literature cited in note 570, *supra.*
621. O.J. 1996 L 236/36).

efforts to reduce carbon dioxide emissions by the year 2000 to their 1990 levels.

Other important documents include the Communication on the energy dimension of climate change;[622] the Green Paper for a Community Strategy *Energy for the future: renewable sources of energy*,[623] and the Commission's Communication *An overall view of energy policy and actions*.[624]

6.4 State aids

Articles 92 and 93 EC have had important application in the energy sector.[625] The judgment in Cases 67, 68 and 70/85 *Kwekerij Gebroeders Van der Kooy BV et al. v. Commission*[626] had important implications for the Dutch government's policy regarding energy tariffs, as the Court found that the fixing of the contested tariff could be imputed to the Dutch government.[627] Furthermore, in both that judgment and in Case 169/84 *Compagnie française de l'azote (Cofaz) SA v. Commission*[628] the Court examined extensively the tariffs of the Gasunie. As a result of these judgments and the Commision's decision after *Cofaz*[629] the following conclusions may be drawn: differences in the level of energy tariffs are justified, first, to the extent that they result from reductions in costs; secondly, to the extent that they form part of a general system applicable to the industry as a whole; thirdly, to the extent that there is a commercial reason for them, and, fourthly, to the extent that they serve an objective recognized by Community law, are necessary for that purpose, and are reasonably proportionate to that objective.[630] As the energy sector is one where many public sector undertakings are active, this case-law has led to stringent Community control of tariffs, a Commission policy which is in stark contrast to its action under Articles 85 and 86 EC.

622. COM (97) 196 Final, and the Council's conclusions thereon (see Bull. EU 5–1997, points 1.3.101–1.3.102.)
623. COM (96) 576 Final, approved by the Council (O.J. 1997 C 167/160), see also the Council's Resolutions O.J. 1997 C 210/1 and O.J. 1998 C 198/1.
624. COM (97) 167 Final.
625. See Slot (1994) 31 CMLRev. 511. See also the forthcoming 2nd ed. of Hancher *et al.*, *EC State Aids* (London, 1998).
626. [1988] ECR 219, [1989] 2 CMLR 804.
627. [1988] ECR 219 at 271–272. See also Case 213/85 *Commission v. The Netherlands* [1988] ECR 281, [1988] 2 CMLR 287.
628. [1986] ECR 391, [1986] 3 CMLR 385.
629. See O.J. 1992 C 344/4. This contains a useful summary of the Commission's views on when an undertaking's conduct is objectively justified. The Commission applies the market investor principle. See also the decision on tariffs for gas used as a raw material by industry, O.J. 1994 C 35/6.
630. *Cf. Van der Kooy, supra.* The objective recognized by Community law was environmental protection, and both the Commission and the court were of opinion that the

7. INDUSTRIAL POLICY, RESEARCH AND TECHNOLOGICAL
DEVELOPMENT, AND TRANS-EUROPEAN NETWORKS

7.1 Introduction

Of the matters discussed here, industrial policy and trans-European
networks were added to the EC Treaty as Titles XIII and XII of Part
Three of the Treaty respectively. Research and Technological development
had already been added by the SEA, but was extended as Title XV of Part
Three by the TEU. In addition to the objective of strengthening the
research and technological foundations of Community industry and
promoting the Community's international competitive position, research
activities are now provided for in the activities falling under other Chapters
of the Treaty. This expansion is the logical complement of the Treaty
developments in these areas and the widening of the objectives of the
Community.

The provisions on trans-European networks are new, as are the ideas
contained therein. This Title is in the first place to be regarded as a
supplement to the achievement of the internal market for transport,
telecommunications[631] and energy.[632] It is also intended to create a
framework for measures to open up regional and local communities,
particularly in peripheral and insular regions of the Community, and to
promote economic and social cohesion. The provisions on trans-European
networks thus have a wider, functional ambit than sectoral policy as such.

Although the industry Title is new, the problems with which it deals are
certainly not. Industrial policy has been the subject of discussion pretty
well since the beginning of the Community. Already in 1970 the
Commission published an extensive memorandum on this subject.[633]

Of the policies discussed here, research and technological development
can be seen as a horizontal and flanking policy, and for that reason the
observations made in sections 1 and 2 of Chapter X, above, are also
relevant here. Given that research and technological development is so
closely linked to industrial policy, it is discussed here rather than in
Chapter X. However, unlike the Treaty's provisions on horizontal and
flanking policies, there is no common approach in the subjects examined
here. Both trans-European networks and industrial policy are somewhat

---

reduction in the gas tariffs went beyond what was necessary to ensure that the greenhouse growers would not switch from gas to coal.
631. Particularly in view of the communications superhighway ideas launched in the last
few years in the United States and in Europe.
632. Particularly in view of the internal market achieved for electricity and now agreed for
gas, referred to in section 6.3, *ante*. See also Dec. 96/391 (O.J. 1996 L 161/154) and
Dec. 1254/96 (O.J. 1996 L 161/147)).
633. Often called the Colonna memorandum: *La Politique industrielle de la Communauté*
(Brussels, 1970).

extraneous to the system of the Treaty. This is particularly so for industrial policy. The provisions of the Industry Title are not really couched in terms of obligations and contain hardly any concrete instruments. The Titles on research and development and trans-European networks do clearly confer competence on the Community, and are thus important in the light of Article 3b EC.

Section 1 of Chapter X, above, examined the place of horizontal and flanking policies in the EC Treaty. It should also be noted that research and technological development has found a place as an objective in Article 3(m) EC, and that industrial policy and trans-European networks are mentioned in Article 3(l) and (n) respectively.

7.2 Industrial policy

The text of Article 130 EC clearly bears the traces of a compromise between the age-old differences of views about the need for an industrial policy. The conflict was principally between the more *dirigiste* approach based on Southern European thinking, and the liberal non-interventionist approach.[634] The original draft was much more *dirigiste* in nature, but resistance from the Northern, more market-oriented Member States led to the present text.

A number of points stand out on reading Article 130 EC. Article 130(1) sets out the guidelines for promoting greater competitiveness:

- speeding up the adjustment of industry to structural changes;
- encouraging an environment favourable to initiative, particularly for small and medium-sized undertakings;
- encouraging a climate favourable to competition between undertakings, and
- fostering better exploitation of the industrial potential of innovation, research and development policies.

It is very important that all this takes place in accordance with a system of open and competitive markets, a point which is emphasized by the last paragraph of Article 130(3). Thus the Community measures must not on the basis of these industrial policy considerations introduce measures which could lead to a distortion of competition. This would appear to be a clear confirmation of the free-market philosophy of the more liberally- minded Member States.

634. See, generally, Cloos *et al.*, *Le Traité de Maastricht Genèse, analyse, commentaires* (2nd ed., Brussels, 1994) 288 *et seq.*, and Hellmann in Von der Groeben *et al.*, *op. cit.* (see note 13, *supra*) 6269. Both works give an extensive summary of Community policy.

For the interventionist-minded Member States, Article 130 EC merely offers an instrument for consultation and coordination. The first paragraph of Article 130(3) provides that the objectives of Article 130(1) are to be achieved – as far as the Community's contribution to their achievement is concerned – through the policies and activities which the Community pursues under other provisions of the EC Treaty. This appears on the one hand to confirm the approach that industrial policy can be pursued without the need for common steering measures, other than policy coordination. This corresponds to the theory and practice of the old Article 103 EEC, which was used for measures in case of actual or threatened shortages, and offered the possibility of adopting market-regulatory measures.[635] As has been demonstrated in Chapter IX, above, the first measures implementing the White Paper *Growth, Competitiveness and Employment*[636] have shown that coordination may also be based on Article 103 EC. On the other hand, Article 130 EC also offers the possibility of using other instruments of the Treaty in a manner which does not always indicate a liberal trading policy. Use of the anti-dumping regulation is a clear example of this.[637] Remarkable cases can also be seen in the sphere of competition law.[638] The importance of the practical application of Article 92 EC in this connection is discussed below.

Article 130 EC does afford Community competence on one point: on the basis of Article 130(3), the Council may unanimously adopt specific measures supporting the action taken by the Member States.[639] It remains to be seen to what extent these heavy procedural requirements will really make an active policy possible, especially towards SMEs, as the White Paper recommends.

Much of the activity of the European Investment Bank in recent years has been directed at a strengthening of Community initiatives for economic growth, competitiveness and employment. In this connection a particularly significant development is the establishment of the European Investment Fund, which provides guarantees for and participates in funds or other instruments for investment in small and medium-sized undertakings and in trans-European networks.[640] As the successive annual reports of the EIB

635. See the 2nd ed. of this work (1989) 605–608.
636. Bull. EU Supp. 6/93.
637. See Case C-358/89 *Extramet Industrie SA v. Council* [1992] ECR I-3813. Péchiney succeeded in persuading the Community to take action against imports of raw materials by Extramet, a competitor of Péchiney, whereas Extramet had been forced to import raw materials because of Péchiney's refusal to supply Extramet with them (they competed in respect of a product of the raw material).
638. Case T-28/90 *Asia Motor France SA et al. v. Commission* [1992] ECR II-2285 and Case T-7/92 *Asia Motor France SA et al. v. Commission* [1993] ECR II-669.
639. The European Parliament and Economic and Social Committee need only be consulted. This is similar to the procedures of Arts. 99, 100 and 235 EC (but the ECOSOC is not consulted in the latter case).
640. The EIF was established as part of the growth initiative agreed at the Edinburgh

demonstrate, considerable financial resources have been pumped into accelerated financing for trans-European networks in the field of transport, telecommunications and energy.[641] A special window has also been created at the EIB for the financing of trans-European networks, a development which the European Council at Essen particularly welcomed.[642] That the policy is not without difficulties is demonstrated by the Council's unwillingness to support, at least in present circumstances, the Commission's proposal for a European Loan Insurance scheme for Employment.[643]

Industrial policy in the Community was initially pursued through negative integration, by removing technical, administrative, fiscal and other barriers to trade.[644] Even the harmonization programme in many fields necessary to achieve such a market contained in the Commission's White Paper on *Completing the Internal Market*[645] and the SEA, which was principally inspired by that White Paper, were primarily aimed at removing the many remaining technical, administrative, fiscal and other obstacles to trade. But in addition to this approach, the positive integration method has become increasingly important. The Bangemann Memorandum on the competitiveness and prospects of the Community automobile industry is an interesting example of Community industrial policy.[646] The basic approach in that memorandum is that by increasing the competitive strength of European industry its future will be safeguarded. The Community's task is thus to create a supporting framework in the form of a free market based on competition. This supporting framework would be achieved through horizontal structural policy instruments. These would in particularly take the form of improved education and training of workers, as envisaged in

European Council in December 1992. As to the Statute of the EIF, see O.J. 1994 L 173/1; as to Community participation, see Dec. 94/375 (O.J. 1994 L 173/12). The Board of Governors of the EIB was empowered to establish the EIF by an amendment to the Statute of the EIB, which came into force on 1 May 1994, following ratification in accordance with the various national procedures (see further, Chapter IX, section 5.4, *ante*).

641. This again reflects the temporary lending facility agreed at Edinburgh, see Bull. EC 12–1992, point I.30 (p. 21).
642. Bull. EU 12–1994, points I.6 and I.38.
643. See *General Report 1996* (Brussels, Luxembourg, 1997) point 79.
644. See the assessment in Bull. EC Supp. 3/91 *European Industrial Policy for the 1990s*.
645. COM (85) 310 Final.
646. COM (94) 49 Final. The Community had earlier argued, in the framework for aid to the automobile industry, that it did not seek to prescribe an industrial policy for that sector, and that decisions on that were best left in the hands of industry itself. In the light of the massive amount of aid which had been granted to that sector in the past and of the improved general position of Community manufacturers, the Commission's aim was to ensure that Community automobile manufacturers could 'in the future' operate in a climate of fair competition by removing the distortions to trade resulting from state aids and by creating a general climate of competition in which productivity and competitiveness of the industry would flourish. See O.J. 1989 C 123/3 at 4.

Article 123 EC, and research and technological development. In addition external measures were envisaged, such as the extension of the voluntary export restraint agreement with Japan.[647]

In less important industries, a similar strategy has been followed, but of an offensive (rather than defensive) nature. Thus the Green Paper on mobile telecommunications[648] was aimed at opening up the markets and research and development. Competition policy also plays an important part in industrial policy, and the policy in relation to Joint Ventures can be seen as a horizontal instrument for industrial policy purposes.[649] In the context of merger control the Commission has so far examined almost all mergers notified to it on competition criteria, which is a very positive approach,[650] indicating resistance to the temptation to allow industrial policy arguments to prevail. The Commission's competition policy has on numerous occasions been influenced by industrial policy considerations, mostly in the context of exemptions under Article 85(3) EC, often when considering whether a fair share of the benefit enures to consumers.[651] The Commission's policy on state aids leaves the Member States a relatively large room for the promotion of national industry.[652]

The Commission's White Paper *Growth, Competitiveness and Employment* has much to say about industrial policy. Restoration of the competitiveness of European industry is perceived as requiring competitive labour costs, a better functioning labour market, education and training, the promotion of structural adjustment, and infrastructure, knowledge and technology.[653] As far as actual Community level action was concerned, new stimuli or new approaches in five directions were proposed: maximization of the advantages of the single market; supporting development and adaptation of small and medium-sized undertakings; continuation of the social dialogue in which the social partners had so far had fruitful consultations and been able to adopt common positions which had been very useful for the Community's work; the creation of major European infrastructure networks, and immediate preparation of and laying of the foundations for the information society.[654] The importance of commitment

---

647. A similar approach can be seen in the Commission's policy for the steel industry, see COM (94) 125 Final.
648. COM (94) 145 Final. See also the Commission's outlines of an industrial policy for the pharmaceutical sector, COM (93) 718 Final.
649. See Van den Bossche, *Gemeenschappelijke ondernemingen in het Europees mededingingsrecht* (Ghent, 1994).
650. In Dec. 94/209 (O.J. 1994 L 102/15) *Mannesmann/Vallourec/Ilva* the potential competition of East European suppliers was expressly taken into account in the evaluation of a merger. See Halverson (1992/2) LIEI 49.
651. *E.g.* Dec. 93/49 (O.J. 1993 L 20/14) *Ford/Volkswagen*.
652. See Hancher *et al.*, *op. cit.* (see note 623, *supra*).
653. As to the reaction of the Dutch government, see Tweede Kamer 1993–1994, Kamerstuk 23 639, no. 1.
654. As to the follow up to the White Paper, see Bull. EU Supp. 2/94.

to quality was also not overlooked, as if Europe cannot compete on price, it must compete on matters such as quality and reliability.

The last two of these five points are in fact the key to improved competitiveness and will put Europe in a position to apply technical progress in order to improve employment and welfare in the Community.[655] The Council set out in a resolution on 21 November 1994 its position on strengthening the competitiveness of Community industry,[656] which was in line with the approach of the White Paper. By the time of the European Council in Florence in June 1996, the major strategy had taken further shape in the Commission's *Action for Employment in Europe – A confidence pact*.[657] The importance of the issues of employment and Community competitiveness can also be measured by the hasty inclusion of provisions on employment in the new Treaty of Amsterdam.

Research and technological development policy is also an important instrument in an active industrial policy, and, as will be evident from the following section, the Community possesses wider powers in this sphere. The same is true of trans-European networks, albeit to a lesser degree.

7.3   Research and technological development

Title XV of Part Three of the EC Treaty contains the provisions relating to Community research and technological development. The need for Community activities in the field of research and technological development arises in part by the greatly increased importance of such activities for the economic development and competitiveness of industry. Important product markets such as telematics, chips and pharmaceuticals are characterized by the increasingly shorter life-cycles of their products. Thus the time within which new generations of chips can be profitably produced has been reduced to a very few years indeed.[658] There has also been an enormous increase in the scale of investment for new products, so that millions of pounds go into the development of, for instance, a new model range of cars or aircraft designs. It was thus inevitable that because of this trend there should be an increasing number of joint ventures among the major players.[659]

---

655. See the conclusions of the Council in the composition of the Industry Ministers, April 22, 1994 (Bull. EU 4–1994, point 2.2.1).
656. O.J. 1994 C 343/1, Bull. EU 11–1994, point 2.2.1.
657. Bull. EU Supp. 4/96. See also the conclusions of the Presidency at Florence, Bull. EU 6–1996, point I.3; the Conclusions by the Chairman of the Tripartite Conference on Growth and Employment, *ibid.*, points I.29 *et seq.*, and the further details in *ibid.*, points 1.3.1–1.3.6. See, further, Bull. EC 11–1997, points I.2 *et seq.*
658. See *inter alia* De Jong, *Dynamic Market Theory* (Leiden, 1989).
659. *E.g.* Volvo Car and Mitsubishi, the take-over of Fokker by DASA, and even the cooperation announced in 1997 between the Microsoft and Apple Corporations.

Barriers to market entry such as high promotion costs, have also greatly increased.

But these developments do not in themselves lead to the conclusion that Community action is necessary. Rather, such a conclusion follows from the evidence that research and technological development policy fragmented along national lines results in fewer patents and less technological innovation than in the United States and Japan. The technological harvest is less in Europe than in those countries, not least due to a lack of expenditure on research and technological development.[660]

The legally relevant horizontal character of this Community policy is clear from Article 130f EC. While Article 130f(1) states the vertical objective of strengthening the scientific and technological bases of Community industry and encouraging it to become more competitive at international level, Article 130f(2) demonstrates that it is not enough to 'encourage undertakings, including small and medium-sized undertakings, research centres and universities in their research and technological development activities': cooperation is also necessary.[661] It was also necessary to open up matters such as procurement practices, particularly of the post and telecommunications monopolies, which are already being tackled, and to encourage the development of common standards. The fragmentation caused by the protection of national champions through national standards frustrates not only the internal market as such but also the real competitiveness of Community industry in the long term and its the development of its technological potential. Furthermore, legal and fiscal barriers had to be abolished. These include divergent public law technical regulations, the legal monopolies accorded in the field of telecommunications, and, despite the various Patent Conventions, divergent national patent protection.

As was indicated in section 7.1, above, the provisions of Title XV were introduced by the TEU. They appear to lay more accent on the Community's activities than was hitherto the case, as is expressed in Article 130f(3) EC. Compared with the provisions in the form introduced by the SEA, it is primarily the procedural provisions which have been adapted. The new rules are designed to facilitate a more coherent and a more global approach, and they should facilitate a better institutional balance in

---

660. See André, *Research and Technological Development Policy* (3rd ed., Luxembourg, 1988). Expenditure on research and technological development in the United States is not only significantly higher, the fragmentation there is much less. See Hellmann, *op. cit.* (see note 634, supra).

661. See the block exemptions for specialization agreements, Reg. 417/85 (O.J. 1985 L 53/1, amended by Reg, 151/93 (O.J. 1993 L 21/8)); research and development agreements, Reg. 418/85 (O.J. 1985 L 53/5, likewise so amended), and technology transfer agreements, Reg. 240/96 (O.J. 1996 L 31/2). The stimulus to innovation is also essential, see the Green Paper on innovation, COM ((95) 688 Final, Bull. EU Supp. 5/95.

decision-making.[662] The Council's major voice in the form of unanimity, until the Treaty of Amsterdam enters into force, is retained in Article 130i EC. The European Parliament has obtained a greater say: under Article 130i(1) the co-decision procedure of Article 189b EC for the adoption of the multiannual framework programme; Article 130o EC provides that the cooperation procedure of Article 189c EC is used for supplementary programmes but this is due to change to the co-decision procedure, and Article 130i(4) requires the consultation procedure to be used for the specific programmes. The co-decision procedure has led to long-running blockades between the Council and the Parliament, and it may be wondered whether it is suitable for programmatic decision-making. For the specific programmes the Council decides by qualified majority, under Article 130i(4), and supplementary programmes require the consent of the Member States concerned.[663] Article 130g EC makes it plain that the Community's actual research and development activities are solely complementary to those of the Member States. This does not exclude very expensive research in certain areas being promoted exclusively at Community level, whether or not in cooperation with third countries or international organizations. Indeed this happens for projects such as the JET project in Culham, and express provision for such research, technological development and demonstration is made in Article 130g(b) EC. Nevertheless, the large Member States in particular still seem to persist in the illusion that in the most important areas research and technological development of sufficient scale and quality can be undertaken exclusively or largely at national level. This misconception is evident not merely from practice concerning standards and procurement in highly technologically developed sectors, but also from their attempts to reduce the Community research budget to below the minimum which Community level industrial organizations such as UNICE regard as necessary. Thus the link between technological development and the achievement of the internal market as a large domestic market for technologically advanced industries, an achievement which is essential for the very viability of undertakings in those large Member States themselves, risks being forgotten.

Typical of the fact that Community policy is seen as supplementing national policy is the fact that in Article 130h EC the coordination of national policy by the Member States is clearly given pride of place in the implementation of this Title. Cooperation and specialization may be promoted, and Article 130h(2) permits the Commission too to take the initiative in this regard. The Commission's supervision of state aids may also contribute to this. Without the Community's own activities and financial support, this coordination of national policies will probably have insufficient effect, if experience in other areas is any guide. In general the

662. See Cloos, et al., op. cit. (see note 634, supra) 293 et seq.
663. Art. 130o EC (final sentence).

Commission adopts a positive stance towards aid measures for research and technological development.[664] Article 130f EC has been used as an extra justification for national aid measures.[665] Aids which clearly are designed to foster research and technological developments, such as fundamental research, will be accepted, but aids for normal modernization and improvement of production facilities will not be considered to be compatible with the common market.

The way Community activities are to function is set out in Articles 130i–130o EC. The modalities of adoption have been mentioned above. The multiannual framework programme[666] drawn up by the Council establishes the scientific and technological objectives to be achieved, indicates the broad lines of the activities to be undertaken, and fixes the maximum overall amount and detailed rules for Community financial participation in the framework programme, as well as the respective shares in each of the activities provided for. This is then implemented by specific programmes which are developed within each activity, which also make the necessary financial provision within the constraints fixed for the framework programme overall and for each activity. The Council determines under Article 130j EC the rules for the participation of undertakings, research centres and universities,[667] and the dissemination of research results.[668] Thus matters such as the conditions for the grant of patents and patent licences are dealt with.[669] As a result of Articles 130k and 130l EC provision may be made in the framework programme for the adoption of supplementary programmes, in which only some Member States participate and finance, subject to possible Community participation. Under Article 130m EC, which permits the Community to make provision for cooperation with third countries or international organizations in research, development and demonstration, several agreements have been adopted.[670]

The Community is permitted to establish joint undertakings or any other structure necessary for the efficient execution of Community research, technological development and demonstration programmes.[671] As far as joint undertakings are concerned, the analogy would seem to be with

---

664. See the current framework, O.J. 1996 C 45/5.
665. See O.J. 1994 C 244/2 *Bull.*
666. For 1994–1998, see Dec. 1110/94 (O.J. 1994 L 126/1, most recently amended by Dec. 2535/97 (O.J. 1997 L 347/1)).
667. Dec. 94/762 (O.J. 1994 L 306/5).
668. Dec. 94/763 (O.J. 1994 L 306/8).
669. *Cf.* Arts. 12–23 Euratom.
670. Decs. 94/457 (O.J. 1994 L 188/17) with Australia; 96/219 (O.J. 1996 L 74/26) with Canada; and Dec. 96/505 (O.J. 1996 L 209/23) with Israel.
671. Art. 130n EC. The Council acts unanimously, on a proposal from the Commission, after consulting the Parliament and ECOSOC, Art. 130o, 1st para. The Treaty of Amsterdam will replace the unanimity requirement by that of a qualified majority.

Articles 45–51 Euratom,[672] but those provisions are not expressly declared applicable. Again, JET in Culham is the obvious example (joint nuclear fusion research).[673] It also appears that more generally an effort has been made in this Title to ensure coherence with similar provisions of the Euratom Treaty.

Prior to competence in this field being based on a separate Title in the Treaty, recourse was primarily had to Article 235 EC.[674] Since then a number of important decisions have been taken on the basis of this Title.[675] The Fourth Framework Programme was adopted in 1994,[676] and the Commission has submitted its proposal for a Fifth Framework Programme covering the period 1998–2002.[677] The financial resources of the Fourth Framework Programme now stand at 11,897 million ECU for the 1994–1998 period.[678]

Although the EC Treaty no longer refers to the link between research and technological development, the establishment of the internal market and competition policy,[679] it is still important to emphasize that link. As has been explained above, competition law provides for three block exemptions which relate to important issues for the promotion of research and technological development. The Commission's policy in applying Articles 85 and 86 EC is heavily influenced by the promotion of research and technological development, and the same is true of the case-law of the Court of Justice and the Court of First Instance.[680]

672. See section 5.7, *ante.*
673. See, generally, *General Report 1996* (Brussels, Luxembourg, 1997), points 239–240.
674. See TMC Asser Institute, *Technical Development and Cooperation in Europe, Legal Aspects* (The Hague, 1987) and André, *op. cit.* (see note 660, *supra*). Celebrated examples were the ESPRIT, BRITE and RACE programmes and the Biotechnology programmes, all dating from 1984 or 1985. In the latter year the EUREKA programme brought together 18 European countries and the Commission, concentrating on the advanced technology in non-military fields, the development of common standards, the removal of existing technical barriers to trade and the opening up of public procurement in the advanced technology field for firms from the participating countries. See *Nineteenth General Report 1985* (Brussels, Luxembourg, 1986), points 318–353.
675. E.g. the specific programmes adopted in 1991 and again in 1995 (see the *General Reports* for those years). A number of agreements have also been concluded in specific areas with third countries, and cooperation is also extended in the context of the European Economic Area. Again, the *General Reports* give details. The *General Report 1996* gives particularly useful information on international cooperation in this field.
676. See note 664, *supra.*
677. See the Council's Common Position (O.J. 1998 C 178/49). See also COM (97) 587 Final (O.J. 1998 C 40/14).
678. See Dec. 2535/97 (O.J. 1997 L 347/1).
679. The text inserted by the SEA was Art. 130f(3) EEC.
680. See Ritter *et al.*, *EEC Competition Law* (Deventer, 1991) 453–560, and Bellamy and Child, *Common Market Law of Competition* (4th ed., London, 1993, and 1st Supp., London, 1996), Chapter 8.

7.4 Trans-European networks

The idea for trans-European networks was born in the late Eighties and early Nineties.[681] The Commission perceived the design and stimulation of trans-European networks as an important component in the completion of the internal market. Later economic and social cohesion in particular was linked to this concept. Portugal in particular was seen as having a major interest in good transit links,[682] and the same undoubtedly applies to Greece and the three new Member States, Austria, Finland and Sweden.

The basic concept is set out in Article 129b(1) EC: the Community contributes to the achievement of the objectives concerned, which means that, as in the case of research and development policy, its action is complementary. On the one hand the aim is to achieve the objectives of the internal market set out in Article 7a EC and the strengthening of economic and social cohesion in accordance with Article 130a EC; on the other hand to enable citizens of the Union, economic operators and regional and local communities to derive full benefit from the setting up of an area without internal frontiers. The trans-European networks are to be established in the areas of transport, telecommunications and energy infrastructures. Attempts during the Intergovernmental Conference preceding the TEU to extend the ambit of these networks did not succeed.

Article 129b(2) EC emphasizes that within the framework of a system of open and competitive markets Community action is aimed at promoting both the interconnection and interoperability of these networks and also access to them.[683] All this has been powerfully brought together in the White Paper *Growth, Competitiveness and Employment*.[684] Trans-European networks must create better, safer and cheaper transport, telecommunications and energy; they must make planning of European territory possible and also promote relations with Eastern Europe.[685] These objectives are to be achieved by removing legal obstacles, awakening the interest of private investors for projects of European interest, and a selection of projects from among those already agreed (such as transport infrastructure projects) or to be approved (such as energy structure projects).[686]

681. See Vinois (1993) RMUE 99.
682. Cloos *et al.*, *op. cit.* (see note 634, *supra*) 299 mention Portuguese access via Spain to the French electricity grid.
683. This tailpiece demonstrates again that the Commission's efforts to open up the gas and electricity markets to assure third-party access rhyme with this general approach as well, see section 6.3, *ante*.
684. See note 636, *supra* (at p. 15). See also COM (98) 356 Final and Chapter IX, section 4, *ante*.
685. The parallel with the objectives of the European Energy Charter Treaty is clear, see note 614, *supra*.
686. As to the practical difficulties, see the interim report on trans-European networks, Bull. EU Supp. 2/94, p. 56 *et seq*. The White Paper itself also discussed these problems.

Article 129c EC specifies as instruments the establishment of a series of guidelines covering the objectives, priorities and broad lines of the measures envisaged, which identify projects of common interest. Further, the Community is to implement any measures that may prove necessary to ensure the interoperability of the networks, particularly as regards standardization; it may also support the Member States' financial efforts (which will change to permit support of projects of common interest when the Treaty of Amsterdam enters into force). A contribution may be made through the Cohesion Fund.[687] The first experiences in this field have shown that finding finance is not a simple matter.[688] The guidelines are adopted under the first paragraph of Article 129d EC by the Council in accordance with the co-decision procedure of Article 198b EC, after consulting ECOSOC and the Committee of the Regions. Guidelines have now been adopted for the development in the telecommunications field of Euro-ISDN,[689] for the development of energy networks;[690] for the development of transport networks,[691] and for the development of telecommunications networks.[692] Where guidelines and projects of common interest relate to the territory of a Member State, they require the approval of the Member State concerned.[693] A list of projects specified as being of common interest in the energy sector has been adopted by the Commission.[694] Other measures are adopted by the Council under the cooperation procedure of Article 189c EC, again after consultation of the two committees (the changes made by the Treaty of Amsterdam will permit the other measures to be adopted in the same way as the guidelines). Thus Regulation 2236/95 sets out the general rules for the grant of Community financial assistance for trans-European networks;[695] Decision 96/391 is designed to create a more favourable climate for the development of trans-European networks in the energy sector;[696] Decision 96/715 deals with the Edicom telematic network between national

---

687. As to the Fund, see Reg. 1164/94 (O.J. 1994 L 130/1), see also Reg. 1831/94 (O.J. 1994 L 191/9). As to proposals for changes, see COM (98) 130 Final.
688. See the interim report on trans-European networks (by the Christophersen group), Bull. EU Suppl 2/94, 58–59. What that report does not mention is that the experience of those who invested in the Channel Tunnel was not as rosy as they might have wished, and that this, along with other factors, may have affected the willingness of the private sector to find the desired resources.
689. Dec. 95/489 (O.J. 1989 L 282/16).
690. Dec. 1254/96 (O.J. 1996 L 161/147, amended by Dec. 1047/97 (O.J. 1997 L 152/2)).
691. Dec. 1692/96 (O.J. 1996 L 228/1).
692. Dec. 1336/97 (O.J. 1997 L 183/12).
693. Art. 129d EC, 2nd para.
694. Decs. 96/537 (O.J. 1996 L 230/16) and 97/548 (O.J. 1997 L 225/25), in accordance with Dec. 1254/96, *supra*, Art. 6(4).
695. O.J. 1995 L 228/1. For proposed amendment, see COM (98) 172 Final (O.J. 1998 C 175/7).
696. O.J. 1996 L 161/154.

administrations on goods transport between Member States;[697] and Directive 96/48 concerns the interoperability of trans-European high speed rail links.[698] Among the instruments available, the activities of the European Investment Bank and the European Investment Fund in promoting trans-European networks should not be overlooked.[699]

Article 129c(2) EC obliges the Member States to coordinate among themselves the policies which they pursue at national level which may have a significant impact on the development of trans-European networks; the Commission may take any useful initiative, in close cooperation with the Member State concerned, to promote such coordination. Finally, Article 129c(3) EC permits the Community to cooperate with third countries to promote projects of mutual interest and ensure the interoperability of networks.[700] This is particularly important for the Central and East European countries in the context of the various Europe Agreements.

The development of trans-European networks is now beginning to take shape, although it is one thing to have the legislative framework in place, and quite another to make a success of its implementation. This is demonstrated by the sometimes conflicting planning interests involved. Once agreement has been reached at European level, having taken account of opposition and sometimes mutually inconsistent views in the Member States, then that agreement should form the basis of national planning. This does of course require a far-reaching national contribution in the European decision-making process (which is a very good reason for the involvement of the Committee of the Regions). But once, for example, the cross-frontier part of the Betuwe Line (the proposed new goods traffic link from Rotterdam to the German industrial heartland and net) has been agreed in Brussels after negotiations between Germany and the Netherlands, the Dutch should no longer seek to impose unilateral changes to the plan. Thus at the later stage of working the trans-European networks out in detail, it would be sensible to streamline as far as possible the procedure for authorizations and consents.[701] Article 129c would appear to afford possibilities for such a policy to be drafted and adopted.

697. O.J. 1996 L 327/34. It replaces Dec. 94/445 (O.J. 1994 L 183/42) which was annulled by the Court of Justice in Case C-271/94 *European Parliament v. Council* [1996] ECR I-1689 (although the effects of that decision were maintained pending the adoption of Dec. 96/715).
698. O.J. 1996 L 235/6.
699. See section 7.2, *ante* and Dunnett (1994) 31 CMLRev. 721. See also Chapter IX, section 5.4, *ante*.
700. See COM (97) 172 Final.
701. See Roggenkamp (1992) Util.L.Rev. 127.

CHAPTER XII

External relations*¹

I. INTRODUCTION

It was clear that a common market such as that created by the three Treaties would manifest itself externally, towards third countries, as one unit. The establishment of a customs union resulted in the creation of a common customs tariff. Moreover 'other trade regulations' *vis-à-vis* third countries had to be made uniform.² The concept of other trade regulations is discussed further in section 3 of this Chapter, below. For the present, it should be remembered that the internal market and the advantages which it brings need a certain external protection and that such protection must in principle be based on uniform measures: an external policy as a complement to internal policies becomes necessary in order to protect the attainments of the integration process and to promote its objectives. There are also exogenous factors which contribute to the need to pursue a common external policy. The establishment of a common market of now 15 European States has

---

* In the Dutch edition this chapter was revised by P.J. Kuyper. The editor has further revised this chapter, taking on board those revisions, and taking account of still relevant additions from the last edition, and new case-law, literature and developments.
1. See, generally, Groux and Manin, *The European Communities in the International Legal Order* (European Perspectives, Brussels, Luxembourg, 1985); Jacot-Guillarmod, *Droit communautaire et droit international public* (Geneva, 1979); Kruck, *Völkerrechtliche Verträge im Recht der Europäischen Gemeinschaften* (Berlin, 1977); Leenen, *Gemeenschapsrecht en Volkenrecht* (Deventer, 1984); Macleod *et al.*, *The External Relations of the European Communities* (Oxford, 1996); McGoldrick, *International Relations Law of the European Union* (London, 1997), with a most useful bibliography; O'Keeffe and Schermers (eds.), *Mixed Agreements* (Deventer, 1983); Timmermans and Völker (eds.), *Division of powers between the Communities and their Member States in the field of external relations* (Deventer, 1981), and TMC Asser Instituut (ed.), *Externe bevoegdheden van de Europese Unie* (The Hague, 1994). See also Flaesch-Mougin (1993) CDE 351; Neuwahl (1996) 33 CMLRev. 667, and Steenbergen (1992) SEW 741.
2. These terms come from Art. XXIV GATT, which maintains an exception for customs unions and free trade areas, on which the Communities rely in order not to be obliged to grant the advantages of the Community system to third countries in accordance with the most-favoured nation principle which underlies GATT/WTO system. See generally, Scott (1996) Int.TLR 219 and literature cited there.

indeed had a major effect on the world economy, which involves for the European Community (and now the Union) a heavy responsibility for the functioning of the international economic system. It appears from Article 110 EC, which prescribes the programme of the Community contributing to a harmonious development of world trade and to a reduction in barriers to trade, that the founding fathers of the Community were conscious of this responsibility from the very beginning. Article 73b EC, introduced by the TEU, and Article J.1(2) TEU also confirm that external openness, also with regard to monetary union and Common Foreign and Security Policy, remains a fundamental characteristic of the European Union.

Since the very beginning European integration has also had political objectives, which are expressed along with other objectives in the first paragraph of the Preamble to the EC Treaty. Economic integration also gave rise to expectations in third countries concerning a common political stance by the Member States. As regards external matters, the possibility of a common political stance was initially created in the context of European Political Cooperation.[3] This loose intergovernmental cooperation framework has found a more solid form in the so-called Second Pillar of the TEU, the provisions concerning Common Foreign and Security Policy (CFSP). These provisions are also largely intergovernmental in nature, so that in external relations the Union has two sets of instruments at its disposal: the Community instruments provided for in the EC, ECSC and Euratom Treaties; and the intergovernmental instruments set out in Article J.11 TEU.

When looking at the European Union's external relations, it is essential to bear in mind that the Union itself, which does not as such have legal personality, can only act on the international stage as a concerted body of its Member States, and thus is not in a position to conclude international agreements as a Union. Only the Communities are in a position to conclude such agreements, as they are all equipped with (international) legal personality and the competence to conclude treaties.

CFSP is based on the general guidelines of the European Council, and it is on the basis of those guidelines that the Council decides that any given matter shall be the subject of joint action.[4] It is also possible for the Council to define a common position in the field of CFSP.[5] This trio of instruments: guidelines, joint action and common positions are the instruments which the TEU provides for the execution of CFSP.[6]

The EC Treaty expressly provides for two types of instruments for giving form to the Community's external relations: autonomous (unilateral) measures, and agreements with third countries. Initially as far as the latter

---

3. See Chapter I, section 6, *ante*.
4. Art. J.3(1) TEU.
5. Art. J.2(2) TEU.
6. See section 2.6, *post*, which also examines Art. 228a EC.

was concerned, specific mention of them was to be found only in the areas of commercial policy[7] and associations.[8] The SEA in 1986 and the TEU in 1992 led to express mention of competence to conclude agreements in the field of monetary policy,[9] research and technology,[10] environment,[11] and development cooperation.[12] The old provision on common action in international organizations[13] was deleted from the EC Treaty by the TEU and has been only partly replaced by Article J.2(3) TEU. The TEU has also introduced a whole Title devoted to development cooperation, which, like commercial policy, can take the form of autonomous measures and agreements with third countries and international organizations.[14] The amendments made by the TEU have also set out in greater detail than was the case in the old EEC Treaty the different arrangements for concluding such agreements.[15] Finally, already since the beginning account has been taken of the desirability in general of maintaining all appropriate relations or, as the case may be, developing cooperation with other international organizations.[16] Using these instruments the Community has given form and substance to its relations with the outside world on an extensive scale and sometimes in a very intensive way.

The new article in the EC Treaty brought in by the SEA and the TEU mean that the development of a simple commercial policy, primarily embracing free movement of goods, into a much more extensive external economic policy through the doctrine of implied powers accepted by the Court of Justice,[17] and the use of Article 235 EC has as it were been codified. This creates clarity, but also removes a certain dynamic from the development of the law, which does not wholly exclude a possible stagnation in the development of the Community's external powers.

Section 2 of this Chapter deals with the basis, scope and nature of the Union's external competence, and with that of the European Community in particular. Legal aspects of external relations involving the ECSC and Euratom will be discussed only incidentally in the treatment of the external competence of the EC, as these matters have already been discussed as far as necessary.[18] A distinction will be drawn between the real Community competence in the external sphere and that of CFSP, with the former being discussed first on the basis that CFSP has developed out of the

7. Art. 113 EC.
8. Art. 238 EC.
9. Art. 109 EC.
10. Art. 130m EC.
11. Art. 130r(4) EC.
12. Art. 130y EC.
13. Art. 116 EEC.
14. Art. 130u–130y EC.
15. Art. 228 EC.
16. Arts. 229–231 EC.
17. See Chapter IV, section 6.3., *ante,* and section 2.1, *post.*
18. See Chapter XI, sections 4 and 5, *ante.*

Community. In discussing Community competence other distinctions are drawn: between express and implied external competence,[19] and between exclusive Community competence and competence shared between the Community and its Member States.[20] In relation to the latter, the discussion then turns to mixed agreements and to Community membership of international organizations.[21] Then the manner in which the external powers of the Community are exercised is examined, particularly as regards the power to conclude agreements.[22] The exercise of powers within CFSP is also discussed in outline.[23] Section 3 of this chapter then examines in detail the Community's common commercial policy, turning first to the concept of commercial policy and to the exclusive nature of that policy.[24] The principles of the Community's commercial policy are then examined in the framework of the GATT/WTO and in conjunction with the completion of the internal market and the developments in Central and Eastern Europe.[25] Attention then turns to a brief description of the most important commercial policy instruments at the Community's disposal for the pursuit of autonomous commercial policy, and to practice concerning trade and cooperation agreements concluded by the Community Member States.[26] Finally, the system of Community agreements is examined.[27] These agreements can be seen as being constructed in a series of concentric circles, in which the European Economic Area (EEA) is the innermost and the various cooperation agreements with countries in Asia and Latin America form the outermost circle.[28] In this context the so-called development associations and the new Treaty provisions on development are also examined. Finally, in section 4.4, below, the Community agreements are also examined from a sectoral viewpoint and briefly related to autonomous external policy in the various sectors concerned.

2.   EXTERNAL COMPETENCE OF THE EUROPEAN UNION

2.1   Express and implied external competence of the European Community

Unlike the ECSC and EC Treaties, the Euratom Treaty, in Article 101, expressly provides that the Community 'may, within the limits of its

19. In section 2.1, *post.*.
20. In section 2.2, *post.*
21. In sections 2.3 and 2.4 respectively, *post.*
22. In section 2.5, *post.*
23. See section 2.6, *post.*
24. Section 3.1, *post.*
25. See section 3.2, *post.*
26. See section 3.3, *post.*
27. In section 4, *post*
28. This system is discussed in section 4.1, *post.*

powers and jurisdiction, enter into obligations by concluding agreements or contracts with a third State, an international organization or a national of a third State.' In the Court's interpretation the phrase 'within the limits of its powers and jurisdiction' means within the limits of its external as well as internal powers.[29] This appears to anchor the parallel between internal and external competence (*in foro interno, in foro externo*) firmly in Community law for Euratom matters. The EC Treaty makes do with conferring specific powers in the external field.[30] As a result of the Court's case-law, particularly the judgments in Case 22/70 *Commission v. Council*[31] and Cases 3, 4 and 6/76 *Kramer et al.*[32] and the findings in Opinion 1/75 *OECD Understanding on a Low Cost Standard*[33] and Opinion 1/76 *European Laying-up Fund for Inland Waterway Vessels*[34] a similar situation prevails in relation to non-Euratom matters to that provided for in the Euratom Treaty.[35]

The Court bases the *capacity* of the Community to enter into binding agreements with other subjects of international law over the whole field of objectives set out in Part One of the Treaty on Article 210 EC which confers legal personality on the Community.[36] Whether the Community has the *competence* to enter into agreements in a particular case depends on the question whether a Treaty provision expressly[37] or impliedly provides the power. Such an implied power may also result from the actions performed by the Community Institutions in the context of the provisions concerned.

However, such a power cannot be derived from the existence of an internal power linked to a general provision such as that contained in Article 101 Euratom; it must be derived using the *effet utile* principle (the principle of effectiveness) from the interpretation of specific provisions or, as the case may be, the Community implementation of them, which relate to the Community's internal powers. There must always be an examination of whether the powers expressly conferred to adopt measures internal to

---

29. See Van Dijk (1979) SEW 191.
30. Arts. 109, 113, 130m, 130r(4), 130y, 229–231 and 238 EC.
31. [1971] ECR 263, [1971] CMLR 335 (the *ERTA* (in French, *AETR*) judgment).
32. [1976] ECR 1279, [1976] 2 CMLR 440.
33. [1975] ECR 1355, [1976] 1 CMLR 85.
34. [1977] ECR 741, [1977] 2 CMLR 279.
35. *Cf.* Ruling 1/78 *IAEA Convention on the physical Protection of Nuclear Materials, Facilities and Transports* [1978] ECR 2151 at 2180–2181 where the Court spoke of 'the necessity for harmony between international action by the Community and the distribution of jurisdiction and powers within the Community which the Court of Justice had occasion to emphasise in its case-law originating with the judgment of 31 March 1971 (Case 22/70 *Commission* v. *Council* [1971] 1 ECR 263 on the European agreement on road transport).'
36. Case 22/70 *Commission v. Council* [1971] ECR 263 at 274; Case 3, 4 and 6/76 *Kramer et al.* [1976] ECR 1279 at 1308. See Chapter II, section 5.1, *ante.*
37. As in the provisions mentioned in note 30, *supra.*

the Community necessarily include in any particular case the power to enter into international commitments.[38] 'The Court has concluded *inter alia* that whenever Community law has created for the institutions of the Community powers within its internal system for the purpose of attaining a specific objective, the Community has authority to enter into the international commitments necessary for the attainment of that objective even in the absence of an express provision in that connexion.'[39] Thus it appears justified to speak of *derived* or *implied* external powers in the sense of the theory of implied powers discussed in section 6.3 of Chapter IV, above.

Such derived powers appear to have been avoided in the parts of the EC Treaty introduced by the SEA and the TEU by expressly including the power to conclude agreements in the relevant provisions.[40] On the other hand, Declaration No. 10 attached to the Final Act on the occasion of signature of the TEU states that the ERTA doctrine is unaffected by these provisions.

The discussion above, like the case-law cited, has spoken of entering into international *commitments*. The external competence of the Community is, though, as this phrase expressly makes clear, not confined to the conclusion of agreements. It also covers the power, with deference to the Treaty,[41] to set up international organizations[42] or to accede to them[43] and to cooperate in the elaboration of decisions of international bodies and in that context to enter into international commitments.[44] The Court has opined that 'when a question of powers is to be determined it is clearly in the interests of all the States concerned, including non-member countries, for such a question to be clarified as soon as any particular negotiations are commenced.'[45]

---

38. This is the *ERTA* doctrine: Case 22/70 *Commission v. Council* [1971] ECR 263 at 275; Cases 3, 4 and 6/76 *Kramer et al.* [1976] ECR 1279 at 1309.
39. Opinion 1/76 [1977] ECR 741 at 755. See, generally, Tridimas and Eekhout (1994) 14 YBEL 143.
40. See Arts. 109, 130m, 130r(4) and 130y EC.
41. For the difficulties which may arise see Opinion 1/76 [1977] ECR 741 at 755–756 and Kapteyn (1978) SEW 360.
42. Opinion 1/76, *ibid.*
43. Cases 3, 4 and 6/76 *Kramer et al.* [1976] ECR 1279 at 1311.
44. *Ibid.* at 1307. See also Case 61/77 *Commission v. Ireland* [1978] ECR 417 at 449 and Opinion 1/75 [1975] ECR 1355 at 1360 on the concept of an 'agreement' within the meaning of Art. 228(1) EC.
45. Ruling 1/78 [1979] ECR 2871 at 2909. But if the agreement has already been concluded, the Court will refuse to give an opinion, see Opinion 3/94 *GATT – WTO Framework Agreement on Bananas* [1995] ECR I-4577 at 4596. If Member States or other Community Institutions wished to challenge the Council's decision concluding the agreement, they could do so under the normal procedures of Art. 173 EC, and seek interim measures if appropriate, *ibid.*

2.2 When is external competence exclusive?

The mere existence of an expressly conferred or derived external competence need not mean that this competence is also *exclusive*, *i.e.* that only the Community has the right to exercise this competence in relation to the outside world to the exclusion of the Member States. The question of exclusivity depends on whether a transfer of powers to the Community flows from the Treaty or its application. Thus the exclusive character of the external competence of the Community which is expressly conferred by the Treaty in the field of the common commercial policy has been confirmed by the Court: after the end of the transitional period the Member States have transferred their competence in this field to the Community.[46]

A derived external competence will have an exclusive character if competence has also been ceded in the internal sphere. There are two possibilities here. Treaty provisions may confer an exclusive character on internal competence with effect from a particular time and thereby also form the hallmark of exclusivity for external powers derived from them.[47] The exercise of internal competence may also lead to the exclusivity of the derived external competence linked to it, *viz.* if and in so far as the internal measures taken contain a cession of competence to the Community in the matter concerned.[48] In Opinion 2/91 *ILO Convention No. 170 on Safety in the Use of Chemicals at Work*[49] the Court held that there is no question of complete cession of competence to the Community, whether internal or external, if internal Community competence is exercised through the adoption of provisions laying down minimum requirements. This is the case in the fields of social policy;[50] consumer protection,[51] and environmental protection,[52] and in practice is quite often the case in harmonization of laws in the technical field.[53]

---

46. See para. 3.1.2, *post*.
47. As in the case of the Act of Accession (1972), Art. 102 which gave the Council the task of determining, at the latest from the sixth year after accession, 'conditions for fishing with a view to ensuring protection of the fishing grounds and conservation of the bio-logical resources of the sea.' See Cases 3, 4 and 6/76 *Kramer et al.* [1976] ECR 1279 at 1309.
48. Case 22/70 *Commission v. Council* [1971] ECR 263 at 275 and, *a contrario*, Cases 3, 4 and 6/76 *Kramer et al.* [1976] ECR 1279 at 1309.
49. [1993] ECR I-1061 at 1079.
50. Art. 118a EC.
51. Art. 129a EC.
52. Art. 130t EC.
53. Under Art. 100a EC. Opinion 2/91 concerned the question whether the Community had exclusive competence as far as Community law was concerned, to conclude the relevant ILO Convention. The objective of that convention overlapped that of a number of directives based on Art. 118a EC which established minimum requirements concerning safety in the use of chemicals at work.

Opinion 2/91 did however confirm what had already been concluded in academic literature,[54] namely that the application of the *ERTA* doctrine is not simply limited to Community rules in the framework of common policies, such as transport policy.[55] What matters is whether the intensity of the arrangement, whatever its denomination, is such as to involve a cession of national powers in favour of Community competence in the field of application of the rules concerned.[56]

If the subject-matter of the external commitment to be entered into falls within this field of application then only the Community may enter into it.[57] More generally, it should be noted that, to the extent to which Community rules are adopted for the attainment of the objectives of the Treaty, the Member States may not, outside the framework of the Community Institutions, assume obligations (whether mutually or with third countries) which could affect those rules or could alter their scope.[58] Given that both the ILO Convention No. 170 and the relevant Community measures contained minimum requirements, the Court considered in Opinion 2/91 that it was unlikely that the Member States would infringe Community rules by ratifying the Convention: if the Community rules afforded a lower level of protection than that of the ILO Convention the Member States could respect the latter's requirements without infringing the Community rules; but if the converse were the case the Member States could respect the Community rules without being in breach of the Convention.[59] It was also inconceivable that an agreement such as the ILO Convention, which was also intended to regulate relations between the Member States, but which clearly covered matters also falling within the Community's internal legislative competence under Article 118a EC, should be concluded only by the Member States.[60] Such internal competence meant that the Member States could only act in the Community context, thus not outside the framework of the Community Institutions.[61] Accordingly, the Convention would have to be concluded as a mixed agreement by the Member States and the Community.[62] The mixed nature of the agreement was clearly not a result of the simultaneous exercise of different external powers by the Community and

54. See Kapteyn (1978) SEW 360. See also Timmermans in Timmermans and Völker, *op. cit.* (see note 1, *supra*) 15–28 and Bourgeois in *ibid.*, 97–110.
55. [1993] ECR I-1061 at 1077.
56. *Ibid.*
57. Case 22/70 *Commission v. Council* [1971] ECR 263 at 275.
58. *Ibid.* and Opinion 2/91 [1993] ECR I-1061 at 1077. This results from the obligations of Art. 5 EC, as to which, see Chapter III, section 5.2, *ante*.
59. [1993] ECR I-1061 at 1079.
60. Case 22/70 *Commission v. Council* [1971] ECR 263 at 275; Opinion 2/91 [1993] ECR I-1061 at 1081.
61. *Ibid.*
62. See section 2.3, *post*.

the Member States, but of the simultaneous exercise of parallel internal powers.

The mere existence of derived competence does not, or so it appears, lead to exclusivity as long as and in so far as no transfer of powers in the internal sphere has yet taken place by or by virtue of the Treaty.[63] Except where internal powers can only be effectively exercised at the same time as external powers, internal competence may give rise to external competence only if it is exercised.[64] If, however, the Community exercises its derived external competence this is done to the exclusion of the competence of the Member States and it is also exclusively competent to adopt measures implementing the agreement concluded, either in the Community context or together with other parties to the agreement. The exclusivity does not in this case result from internal competence but from the exercise of the external competence derived from it.[65]

On the other hand, it is not evident that if the Member States are obliged or called upon to implement provisions of an international agreement, that such an agreement would (also) fall within the competence of the Member States and thus at least have to be concluded as a mixed agreement. If an agreement falls within the exclusive competence of the Community, that is unaffected by the fact that the Member States have to adopt implementing measures or have to adapt their legislative or other provisions; the Community remains competent to act at the international level.[66]

---

63. Cases 3, 4 and 76 *Kramer et al.* [1976] ECR 1279 at 1309. Confirmation of this view can also be deduced from Ruling 1/78 [1978] ECR 2151, [1979] 1 CMLR 131: see Van Dijk (1979) SEW 191 at 192. Declaration No. 10 annexed to the Final Act on the occasion of signature of the TEU also shows that the existence of parallel external powers of the Community and the Member States and the exclusivity of external competence stemming from the *ERTA* judgment are two distinct concepts.

64. Opinion 2/92 *Third Revised OECD Decision on National Treatment* [1995] ECR I-521 at 560. Thus the Community's external competence does not automatically result from its power to prescribe rules at internal level and it is the adoption of common rules which effects the transfer of competence, see *e.g.* Opinion 1/94 *WTO-GATS and TRIPs* [1994] ECR I-5267 at 5411. Although the Community's exclusive competence may arise without prior adoption of internal common measures, this will only be the case if the conclusion of an international agreement is necessary to achieve Treaty objectives which cannot be attained by the adoption of autonomous Community rules, see *e.g.* Opinion 2/92 [1995] ECR I-521 at 559; Opinion 1/94 [1994] ECR I-5267 at 5413–5414. Art. 235 EC does not itself vest exclusive competence in the Community at international level, Opinion 1/94 at 5414; Opinion 2/92 at 560.

65. *Cf.* Opinion 1/76 [1977] ECR 741 at 756 from which it appears that the Court rejects a parallel exercise of derived external competence by the Member States in addition to the Community. *Cf.* also, on the necessary harmony between the Community's international powers, the point made in note 35, *supra*.

66. Opinion 2/91 [1993] ECR I-1061 at 1082.

2.3 Mixed agreements

As long as and in so far as no internal transfer of powers has occurred and no use has been made of derived external competence, each of the Member States remain competent to enter into international commitments in the areas concerned, subject in any event to respecting the obligations flowing from Community law. In doing so the Member States might hinder the Community's use at a later stage of the internal competence and the external competence derived therefrom. It is true that the Community itself is not bound by such arrangements or legally obliged to respect them but it may well be in fact forced to take account of them in the exercise of its powers. Only an application by analogy of the second paragraph of Article 234 EC (which is not applicable to obligations entered into by Member States after the coming into force of the EEC Treaty)[67] could perhaps offer a solution.

If, though, the Treaty obliges the Community to fulfil a task of regulating a matter by a particular date the Member States may not enter into any commitments which hinder the Community in the execution of its task. The Court bases this obligation on the provisions of Article 5 EC.[68] It appears justified to regard such an obligation as being also present if there is no such set date but the Community is preparing to exercise its powers as, for example, in cases in which the Council itself has asked the Commission to make proposals by a certain date or in which the Commission has itself taken steps to prepare the decision-making process in the Council.

The Court has also drawn a strict distinction between the external competence of the Community on the one hand and that of the Member States on the other in relation to mixed agreements. These are permitted only if the agreements also cover subjects in relation to which the Community has no express or implied external powers.[69] As regards other parties to an international convention, the Court has pointed out that 'it is not necessary to set out and determine, as regards [them], the division of powers ... between the Community and the Member States, particularly as it may change in the course of time. It is sufficient to state to the other contracting parties that the matter gives rise to a division of powers within the Community, it being understood that the exact nature of that question is a domestic question in which third parties have no need to intervene.'[70]

---

67. Or in the case of Member States acceding subsequently, after accession, see *e.g.* Act of Accession (1972), Art. 5.
68. Cases 3, 4 and 6/76 *Kramer et al.* [1976] ECR 1279 at 1310.
69. *Cf.* Opinion 1/76 [1977] ECR 741 at 756. See, generally, O'Keeffe and Schermers (eds.), *op. cit.* (see note 1, *supra*); Bourgeois *et al.* (eds.), *La Communauté européenne et les accords mixtes Quelles perspectives?* (Brussels, 1997), and Neuwahl (1991) 28 CMLRev. 717.
70. Ruling 1/78 [1978] ECR 2151 at 2180.

This is a nice theory put forward by the Court, but in practice, though, third countries who are parties to mixed agreements are not content with such a manifest lack of clarity. It is understandable that they should wish to know who is competent in respect of the various elements in a mixed agreement, and whom, the Community or the Member States, they should hold responsible in case of breach or inadequate implementation of the agreement. The Community often cannot avoid giving some explanation about the division of competence between the Community and its Member States. Given that it is inherent in the *ERTA* doctrine that this division is not fixed for all time, but may well develop, considerable problems may result. Annex IX to the United Nations Convention on the Law of the Sea[71] illustrates the complicated arrangements which may in certain circumstances arise from the participation of the Community and the Member States in multilateral agreements. The Annex sets out the conditions under which international organizations such as the European Community may become parties to the Convention in accordance with Articles 305(1)(f) and 306 of the Convention.[72] Despite these practical difficulties, more and more mixed agreements are being concluded, even though on a broader interpretation of the Community's relevant external competence[73] this would be unnecessary. Thus, despite the broad interpretation of Article 238 EC by the Court,[74] almost all Association Agreements[75] are concluded in the form of mixed agreements, and the Tokyo Round agreements relating to technical barriers to trade and civil aircraft were also ratified by the Member States even though they were based on Article 113 EC.[76] Sometimes such recourse to mixed agreements is unavoidable, particularly if it is desired to embrace aspects of political cooperation in the same agreement alongside matters falling within Community competence. This was the case in the Europe Agreements with the countries of Central and Eastern Europe.[77] In fact this tendency will only increase in the future, as CFSP takes greater shape. Given that the Union as such is not yet empowered to conclude international agreements, agreements covering at the same time matters falling within CFSP and within Community competence will necessarily have to be mixed agreements, rather than Union agreements.

71. Montego Bay, December 10, 1982 – December 9, 1984 (Cmnd. 8941).
72. See the critical discussion by Simmonds (1986) 23 CMLRev. 521.
73. *E.g.* Arts. 113 and 238 EC.
74. See Case 12/86 *Demirel v. Stadt Schwäbisch Gmünd* [1987] ECR 3719 at 3751 and the Commission's comments in the *Twenty-first General Report* (Brussels, Luxembourg, 1988), point 953. See also Temple Lang (1986) 23 CMLRev. 157.
75. See section 4.2, *post*.
76. See Steenbergen (1980) SEW 752 at 763–765, and the reply by Bourgeois (1982) 19 CMLRev. 5 at 21–22.
77. See section 4.2.3, *post*.

2.4   Membership of international organizations[78]

It is obvious that if the Community has the power to enter into agreements it may also accede to international organizations which are concerned with subjects which fall within the competence of the Community. International organizations are always established by agreements, most of which also contain specific provisions on membership, accession and voting. Even if accession is an obvious step from the perspective of the Community and its powers, both they and those provisions of the treaties establishing the organizations concerned pose problems for Community accession. Thus most international organizations accept only States as members, relegating other international organizations such as the Community to the status of observers. This is particularly so in the case of the United Nations and its specialized organizations, in which the Community has long had observer status.[79]

In those international organizations that do provide for the possibility of other international organizations acceding, and which are active in the areas of exclusive Community competence, there is no obstacle to Community accession. The international fisheries organizations are celebrated examples of such bodies,[80] and the Community enjoys one vote in such circumstances.

Most international organizations would need to adapt their statutes if the Community were to be able to participate as a full member.[81] This is often a far from simple matter: even with an international organization such as the UN Food and agriculture Organization (FAO), which works in fields – agriculture and fisheries – which fall to an overwhelming degree within Community competence, and even the Community's exclusive competence, it required an enormous effort to obtain acceptance of the

---

78. See Frid, *The Relations between the EC and International Organizations* (The Hague, 1995) and Sack (1995) 32 CMLRev. 1227.

79. See Sybesma-Knol, *The Status of Observers in the United Nations* (Leiden, 1981), Chapter VI-I. As a result of the UN General Assembly's Resolution 3208 (XXIX) of October 1, 1984, the Community participates in the sessions and work of the General Assembly with observer status. Macleod *et al.*, *op. cit.* (see note 1, *supra*) 195 *et seq.* give a useful table of the Community's participation in international organizations, including those of the UN family.

80. *E.g.* Reg. 3179/78 (O.J. 1978 L 378/1) on the Convention on Future Multilateral Cooperation in the Northwest Atlantic Fisheries (NAFO); Dec. 81/608 (O.J. 1981 L 227/21) on the Convention on Future Multilateral Cooperation in the North-East Atlantic Fisheries (NEAFC), and Dec. 81/691 (O.J. 1981 L 252/26) on the Convention on the Conservation of Antarctic Marine Living Resources (CCAMLR).

81. This would also be the case for accession to the European Convention on Human Rights, to which, in the present state of Community law, the Community has no competence to accede in the absence of an amendment of the Community Treaties, see Opinion 2/94 *Accession to the European Convention on Human Rights* [1996] ECR I-1759 at 1789.

Community as a member. In order for this to take place Article II of the FAO constitution had to be amended. To this end, in 1991 a number of specific provisions concerning regional economic integration organizations (REIOs) were approved. A REIO may only accede to the FAO if the majority of its member states is a member of the FAO, and if those member states have transferred competence in the areas of activity of the FAO to the REIO concerned, which on that basis may adopt decisions binding those member states. Although these provisions are cast in general terms, it is clear that they primarily envisage the Community, and that as yet no other international organization satisfies those criteria. The Community was unable to avoid the FAO involving itself to a considerable extent in the division of powers between a REIO and its member states. On application for FAO membership, a REIO must submit a declaration as to the division of competence, and the FAO has to be informed of any change therein. The REIO and its member states exercise their votes alternatively: thus if the REIO votes, the member states may not, and vice-versa. If the REIO votes, it enjoys the number of votes equal to the number of its member states who are members of the FAO. On the one hand, accession to the FAO has been an important step forward; on the other hand the conditions are very onerous. In particular the exercise by the Community of the right to speak and vote in the various FAO organs gives rise to great difficulties in practice: here too declarations of competence are often necessary, and at short notice, which frequently gives rise to difficult debates within the Council.[82] In the World Trade Organization (WTO) which has been established as a result of the successful GATT Uruguay Round negotiations, the Community enjoys the number of votes equal to the number of its Member States who are members of the WTO.[83]

2.5   Exercise of external competence

2.5.1   Treaty-making power

Under Article 101 Euratom the Commission negotiates and concludes agreements or contracts with third countries and international organizations. The Council's role is limited to giving directives for the negotiations and to approving by a qualified majority the conclusion of the agreements or contracts. If the implementation of the agreements or contracts does not require action by the Council and can be effected within

---

82. See Frid (1993) EJIL 239. See also Case C-25/94 *Commission v. Council* [1996] ECR I-1469 at 1508–1511. See also the end of section 4.4, *post*.
83. WTO Agreement (Marrakesh, 15 April 1994, Cmnd. 2571), Art. IX(1). As to the Final Act of the Uruguay Round negotiations, see Cmnd. 2570.

the limits of the relevant budget, their negotiation and conclusion is a matter for the Commission alone, subject to the Council being kept informed. The analogous provision of the EC Treaty[84] is significantly less clear about the Commission's powers to conclude treaties. The Commission had developed a practice in the context of the EC Treaty of concluding independently so-called administrative agreements, and effectively applying, albeit on a modest scale, the criteria of Article 101 Euratom. However, practices which have grown up are no substitute for legal powers, and the Court has now held that this analogous application of Article 101 Euratom is unjustified,[85] declaring void an agreement between the Commission and the United States government on cooperation in the field of anti-trust policy.[86]

For the rest, Article 228 EC has been heavily reshaped by the amendments made by the TEU, so as to comprise a number of provisions which systematically bring together all the procedures for negotiating and concluding agreements. Before negotiations are formally opened, the Commission makes recommendations to the Council, which authorizes the Commission to open the necessary negotiations. This authorization is usually referred to as a negotiating mandate. Frequently the Commission will already have conducted informal exploratory discussions. The Commission then conducts the formal negotiations, in consultation with a special committee appointed by the Council. In the area of commercial policy there is a special committee constituted on the basis of Article 113 EC.[87] The Commission follows the directives given to it by the Council,[88] although these are not always given and they are not as such binding. The Commission may thus stray from its negotiating mandate, but will need the cooperation of the Council if the negotiations are to result in the conclusion of an agreement. In practice, therefore, the committee concerned plays a key role: on the one hand it watches the Commission like a hawk; on the other hand, it may be very difficult indeed for the Commission to persuade the Council to conclude an agreement which the committee does not support. For the authorization to open negotiations, the issue of directives, and the final conclusion of the agreement the Council acts by qualified majority, save where the agreement concerned covers a field for which unanimity is required for

---

84. Art. 228(2) EC, 1st sentence.
85. Case C-327/91 *France v. Commission* [1994] ECR I-3641 at 3677.
86. An agreement was subsequently signed by the Council and the Commission jointly with the United States government, see Dec. 95/145 (O.J. 1995 L 95/45).
87. This is the Article 113 Committee, see section 3.1.3, *post.*
88. Art. 228(1) EC (like Art. 113(3) EC) speaks of the Commission acting within the framework of such directives as the Council may issue to it, but this does not refer to directives in the normal sense of Art. 189 EC, as these are addressed to Member States. The word 'directives' here means instructions or guidelines expressed in the negotiating mandate.

the adoption of internal rules or is an Association Agreement based on Article 238 EC.[89]

The provisions of Article 228(3) EC, introduced by the TEU, dealing with the powers of the European Parliament are hardly beacons of clarity, but practice is now making it clear that Parliament is willing to use its powers at the very least to delay matters and draw attention to its political objectives.[90] In principle the Parliament has to have been consulted (and thus to have delivered its opinion) on all agreements before they are concluded by the Council. In the case of commercial policy agreements under Article 113(3) EC, the opinion of Parliament does not have to be obtained. But certain specific types of agreement do need the assent of Parliament before they may be concluded: association agreements concluded under Article 238 EC; other agreements establishing a specific institutional framework by organizing cooperation procedures; agreements having important budgetary implications for the Community, and agreements entailing amendment of an act adopted under the co-decision procedure of Article 189b EC.

Two views of the assent procedure are possible. A strict interpretation in the light of the history of the negotiations leading to the adoption of the TEU would indicate that this procedure is simply a recognition of a right of assent already conferred by the SEA (in what is now Article 238 EC), supplemented by provisions designed to counteract the undermining of the powers of the Parliament through the conclusion of agreements.[91] On the other hand, if these provisions are regarded in the light of the Court's judgments on the democratic legitimacy of the legal acts of the Community,[92] a rather broader interpretation is justified. In particular, the concept of 'other agreements establishing a specific institutional framework' can be understood as embracing pretty well all international

---

89. Art. 228(1) and (2) EC. The Treaty of Amsterdam, not yet in force, will amend Art. 228(2), so as to permit agreements to be provisionally applied pending entry into force. The present text, so amended, will become the 1st sub-para. of Art. 228(2). A new 2nd sub-para. will also make express provision for the adoption of a decision to suspend the application of an international agreement or for the establishment of the Community position in a body set up under an agreement concluded under Art. 238 EC, when that body is to adopt decisions having legal effects other than decisions supplementing or amending the institutional framework of the agreement (the rules of the first sub-para. will apply, by way of derogation from Art. 228(3) EC). The European Parliament will have to be immediately and fully informed of any decision on the provisional application or suspension of agreements, or on the establishment of the Community position in a body set up by an agreement.

90. See the examples quoted by Bradley and Feeney in (1993) 13 YBEL 383 at 403 and 406–407; (1994) 14 YBEL 401 at 420–421 and (1995) 15 YBEL 283 at 308–309.

91. Agreements which though not based on Art. 238 EC are comparable to such agreements, and agreements which would affect Parliament's right of co-decision on budgetary matters or on certain Community decisions.

92. See *e.g.* Case C-300/89 *Commission v. Council* [1991] ECR I-2867 at 2900.

organizations; it will also be more readily accepted that an agreement has 'important budgetary implications for the Community'.[93] Such an approach also has consequences for the manner in which the powers of the European Parliament are interpreted concerning the conclusion of commercial agreements: if democratic legitimacy is placed in the foreground, it must be accepted that certain commercial agreements also need the assent of the European Parliament, as they fall under one of the three categories of agreements requiring assent, specified in the second paragraph of Article 228(3) EC, even though under the first paragraph of Article 228(3) EC commercial agreements as such do not even need to be submitted for the opinion of Parliament. Practice would seem to indicate that this second approach is in fact more appropriate.[94]

Of course the time factor may well be important in seeking the opinion or the assent of the Parliament. If the former is sought, the Council may, according to the urgency of the matter, prescribe a time-limit for the delivery of Parliament's opinion, and in the absence of the opinion within that period the Council may act.[95] If Parliament's assent is required, the Council and the Parliament may, in an urgent situation, agree upon a time-limit for the assent.[96]

A practical addition, which was introduced by an amendment made by the TEU, is the possibility for the Council to authorize the Commission to approve modifications to agreements (largely of subsidiary importance) on behalf of the Community, where the agreement being modified provides for modifications to be adopted by a simplified procedure or by a body set up by the agreement.[97] The Council may attach specific conditions to such

93. The first difference of opinion over this concept occurred shortly after the TEU came into force, and related to the approval of the third EC-UNRWA Convention which involved budgetary consequences amounting to some 90 million ECU. Parliament gave its assent, but in its decision concluding the agreement on behalf of the Community, the Council referred only to the Parliament's opinion, and based its decision on the 1st para. of Art. 228(3) EC, rather than on the 2nd para. of that Article, see Dec. 94/13 (O.J. 1994 L 9/16).

94. See note 90, *supra*. The view as to whether assent shoudl be obtained on the basis of democratic legitimacy depends on whether a wide or narrow view of commercial policy is adopted. Given that in Opinion 1/94 *WTO-GATS and TRIPS* [1994] ECR I-5267 the Court took a narrow view of what constituted commercial policy, it is difficult to imagine trade agreements making charges necessary to Community acts adopted by co-decision (such as in the fields of free movement of persons and service and harmonization of laws), thus there is hardly likely to be a contradiction between the beginning of the first paragraph of Article 228(3) EC and the second paragraph of that provision.

95. Art. 228(3) EC, 1st para. Although the Parliament is perfectly capable of going slow on the consideration of a request for assent in order to make its dissatisfaction about a time-limit imposed for delivery of an opinion on another matter very plain, see Bradley and Feeney (1994) 14 YBEL 401 at 420–421.

96. Art. 228(3) EC, 3rd para.

97. Art. 228(4) EC.

authorization.[98] It is unclear whether this addition should be read in conjunction with the opening words of Article 228(2) EC,[99] so that in fact it would lead to a restriction of the powers left to the Commission by those opening words. In any event, the procedure is designed to stop minor and uncontroversial amendments to international agreements being held up by the Commission having to go through the whole procedure of seeking prior approval of the Council, with a negotiating mandate and all the rest.[100]

It is evident where the Council envisages concluding an international agreement which involves amendments to the TEU or to the EC Treaty, it will have to follow the procedure prescribed by Article N TEU,[101] although this has not yet come to pass. If there is doubt about the compatibility of a proposed international agreement with the EC Treaty, the Council, the Commission or a Member State may obtain the opinion of the Court of Justice.[102] When in the past the Court has given a negative opinion, the agreement has been adapted, not the EC Treaty,[103] although as a result of Opinion 2/94 *Community Accession to the European Convention on Human Rights*[104] any future Community accession to that Convention will require a Treaty amendment, as well as amendment of the Convention itself to permit Community accession.

Finally, Article 228(7) EC contains the useful guarantee also for third countries that not just the Community and its Institutions, but also the Member States are bound by agreements concluded by the Community. If necessary the Commission or a Member State could react to a breach by one of the Member States of an agreement concluded by the Community by bringing infringement proceedings under, as appropriate, Articles 169 or 170 EC. In practice little has occurred in this direction. The liability of the Community for infringements of community agreements by Member States is however recognized by third countries. Thus the Community has been subject to GATT panels if one of the Member States does not meet its obligations under the GATT.[105]

The Council's power to conclude agreements is, by virtue of Article 228(2) EC, subject to the powers vested in the Commission in this field.

98. *Ibid.*
99. 'Subject to the powers vested in the Commission in this field....'
100. Cloos *et al.*, *Le Traité de Maastricht: Genèse, Analyse, Commentaires* (2nd ed., Brussels, 1994) 358.
101. Art. 228(5) EC.
102. Art. 228(6) EC. See Christianos (1994) RMCUE 37; Gray (1983) 8 ELRev. 24, and Diez de Velsaco in Capotorti *et al.* (eds.), *Du droit international au droit de l'intégration* (*Liber Amicorum* Pescatore, Baden-Baden, 1987) 177.
103. *E.g.* Opinion 1/92 *EEA II* [1992] ECR I-2821, [1992] 2 CMLR 217.
104. [1996] ECR I-1759, [1996] 2 CMLR 265.
105. See the Panel Report (which was never accepted) on the German system of exchange rate guarantees for Deutsche Airbus aircraft (DOC. SCM/142, 4 March 1992). The same is now true in relation to WTO Panels.

Thus in Article 229 EC the Commission is charged with the maintenance of all appropriate relations with the organs of the United Nations, of its specialized agencies and of the GATT and with the maintenance of such relations as are appropriate with all international organizations. Special provision is made in relation to the Council of Europe and what is now the OECD: thus the Community as such is obliged under Article 230 EC to establish all appropriate forms of cooperation with the Council of Europe and under Article 231 EC the Community was obliged to establish close co-operation with the Organization for European Economic Co-operation which was the predecessor of what is now the OECD. In numerous cases the Commission itself may conclude the agreements for the maintenance of such relations.[106]

Derogations from the procedure of Article 228 EC are provided for in the context of the provisions on Economic and Monetary Union.[107] If any agreements concerning monetary or foreign exchange regime matters need to be negotiated by the Community with one or more third countries or international organizations, the Council, acting by a qualified majority, on a recommendation from the Commission and after consulting the ECB, is to decide on the appropriate arrangements for the negotiation and conclusion of such agreements.[108] These arrangements must ensure that the Community expresses a single position.[109] While Article 109(3) EC is silent on who actually conducts the negotiations (the possibilities are the Commission, the ECB, the Council secretariat on behalf of the Council, or by or on behalf of the Member States, of which the first two are the most obvious), the fact that the Commission is to be fully associated with the negotiations would suggest that it will have a subsidiary role, with the ECB being given the lead role.[110] Such agreements bind the Community Institutions, the ECB and the Member States.[111] The competence to *conclude* formal agreements on an exchange-rate system for the euro (as

---

106. See *e.g.* the Agreement of Relations between the International Labour Organization and the EEC (J.0. 521/59). The Luxembourg Accords of January 1966 (see Chapter V, section 3.2, *ante*) envisaged establishing a consultation between the Council and the Commission on the way in which the Commission would implement this Article (point (a)(5) of the Accords). See further *e.g.* the exchange of letters between the World Health Organisation and the European Communities (O.J. 1982 L 300/20) and the cooperation agreement with the Council of Arab Economic Unity (O.J. 1982 L 300/23). The Office for Official Publications of the European Communities publishes a collection of the international agreements concluded by the Communities, reissued from time to time. However, relations with OECD are covered by the OECD Convention (Paris, 14 December 1960, 888 UNTS (1973) 179), Art. 13 2 Supp. Protocol No. 1.
107. See Chapter IX, section 3.4.3, point C, *ante*.
108. Art. 109(3) EC, 1st para.
109. *Ibid.*
110. See the discussion in Gormley and De Haan (1996) 21 ELRev. 95 at 102 (note 55).
111. Art. 109(3) EC, 2nd para.

the ECU will be known) in relation to non-Community currencies lies with the Council, acting unanimously on a recommendation from the ECB, or on a recommendation from the Commission and after consulting the ECB.[112] The European Parliament is consulted.[113]

2.5.2 *Autonomous external action by the Community*

The Community does not only exercise its external powers in a contractual manner through the conclusion of agreements; it may also act autonomously in external matters. This is clearest in the exercise of autonomous commercial policy competence.[114] But the Community also acts autonomously in external matters in all sorts of other areas of international relations: it performs unilateral public international law acts, reacts to such acts of States and other international legal persons, and issues letters of protest and the like.

The first and most well-known example of this type of action is investigations followed by decisions in the competition field against undertakings established outside the Community; these involve the unilateral exercise of Community legal authority over those undertakings, in relation to conduct the effects of which are felt on inter-State trade within the common market.[115] On the other hand the Community has protested strongly at what it regarded as excessive exercise of legal powers by the United States.[116] Moreover, it is unavoidable that the Community from time to time becomes entangled in questions of recognition of other States and regimes. It is often said that the Community cannot recognize States or regimes, as this is reserved to the Member States, but Institutions such as the Commission are naturally enough often in practice confronted with questions of (implicit) recognition whenever there are revolutions or secessions in States in which the Commission has opened delegations. Thus the Commission, on behalf of the Community, declined to recognize Northern Cyprus.[117] Subsequently, in the context of European Political Cooperation, the Community and the

---

112. Art. 109(1) EC.
113. *Ibid.*
114. See section 3.3.1, *post.*
115. See as to the extra-territorial effect of Community competition law, Cases 89/85 *etc.* A. Ahlström Osakeyhtiö et al. v. Commission [1988] ECR 5193, [1988] 4 CMLR 901. The decision (Dec. 85/202 (O.J. 1985 L 85/1) *Wood Pulp*) was largely annulled, see the final judgment in those cases [1993] ECR 1307, [1993] 4 CMLR 407. The freedom to provide services also has extraterritorial effects in that contracts signed or to be performed in the Community are covered, see Case 36/74 *Walrave and Koch v. Association Union Cycliste Internationale et al.* [1974] ECR 1405 at 1420.
116. *E.g.* the pipeline protest (1982) ILM 891–904. See also the reaction to the Helms-Burton and D'Amato Acts (see note 141, *post*).
117. Bull. EC 11–1983, points 2.2.33–34. That the commercial consequences of non-recognition can be dramatic is evident from the judgment in Case C-432/92 *R. v. Minister*

Member States developed criteria for the recognition of the States which emerged from the former Soviet Union.[118] In the context of CFSP such a joint approach to recognition questions is the obvious way forward. The Community must also from time to time adopt standpoints on the international law of treaties. The Community even participated in the conference on the law of treaties between States and international organizations and between international organizations,[119] although in treaty law questions the Commission prefers to rely on the Vienna Convention on the Law of Treaties[120] rather than on the Convention resulting from that conference.[121] The Community is bound by the rules of the Vienna Convention in so far as they are an expression of customary international law.[122] As a result of German unification and the great tumult in Eastern Europe and the former Soviet Union, the Community has also had to determine its position in relation to questions of State succession.[123]

The exercise of these autonomous external powers, through which the Community and its Institutions also contribute to international legal practice and thus to the formation or confirmation of international customary law, in practice occurs according to procedures which are to a large extent the same as those applicable to the exercise of the power to conclude agreements. Given that the emphasis in this type of instance is placed on policy questions, it is primarily the Commission which acts externally, albeit normally in consultation with the Article 113 Committee if the matter is one of commercial policy, or other appropriate bodies or committees under the Council. Given that the European Parliament now possesses increased responsibilities in the field of external affairs, it is not unnatural that it will wish to be involved in these consultations on the exercise of autonomous external competence as well.

2.6 Common Foreign and Security Policy

CFSP has already been briefly discussed in section 1.3.1 of Chapter II, above. The present discussion focuses on the instruments of CFSP and

of Agriculture, Fisheries and Food, ex parte S.P. Anastasiou (Pissouri) Ltd. et al. [1994] ECR I-3087 (impossibility of accepting certificates of origin or phytosanitary certificates not issued by the competent authorities of the Republic of Cyprus).
118. Bull. EC 12–1991, point 1.4.5.
119. See Manin (1987) 24 CMLRev. 457.
120. 1969 UKTS 58 (1980), Cmnd. 7964.
121. 1986 Misc. 11 (1987), Cm. 244.
122. See Case T-115/94 Opel Austria GmbH v. Council [1997] ECR II-39 at 70–71. In that judgment the Court of First Instance effectively condemned the Council for breaching Art. 18 of the Vienna Convention, by adopting a regulation contrary to the EEA Treaty after it had been signed but a few weeks before it entered into force.
123. See Kuyper in Curtin and Heukels (eds.), The Institutional Dynamics of European Integration (Essays in honour of Schermers Vol. II, Dordrecht 1994) 619.

their connection with Community law. It has already been noted in section 1 of this Chapter, above, that CFSP has a trio of instruments at its disposal: general guidelines from the European Council;[124] joint action,[125] and common positions.[126] The latter two are adopted by the Council. While the European Council still has not actually adopted formal guidelines stated to be such within the meaning of Article J.8 TEU, the guidelines adopted shortly before the entry into force of the TEU and shortly afterwards at two meetings of the European Council in Brussels in October and December 1993 appear to be treated as if they were such guidelines.[127] Indeed the practice appears to be that the statements in the Conclusions of the Presidency at the various European Council meetings are treated as guidelines for the Council.[128]

Given the now increasing number of decisions taken in the context of CFSP, a number of illustrations must suffice to indicate the scope of the Union's activities in this field.[129] Joint Action has covered matters such as assistance in the preparation of supervision of free and democratic elections in Russia[130] and South Africa;[131] support for the convoying of humanitarian aid in Bosnia–Herzegovina;[132] the administration of Mostar;[133] the Stability Pact Conference;[134] the process of democratization in Zaire;[135] and the nomination of special representatives for the peace process in the Middle East[136] and for the African Great Lakes region.[137]

124. Art. J.8 TEU.
125. Art. J.3 TEU.
126. Art. J.2 TEU.
127. See Bull. EC 10–1993, point I.4 and 12–1993, points I.9–I.12. See *e.g.* Decs. 93/603 (O.J. 1993 L 286/1) and 94/276 (O.J. 1994 L 119/1). See also *General Report 1994* (Brussels, Luxembourg, 1995) point 730.
128. *E.g.* Dec. 96/476 (O.J. 1996 L 195/1) referred to the guidelines adopted at the European Council in Corfu in June 1994 (Bull. EU 6–1994, point I.22).
129. For a more detailed overview, see the annual *General Report* since 1994. Further details are always given in the issues of Bull. EU. See also Tietje (1997) 2 EFARev. 211.
130. Dec. 93/604 (O.J. 1993 L 286/3).
131. Dec. 93/687 (O.J. 1993 L 316/45).
132. Initially through Dec. 93/603 (O.J. 1993 L 286/1), as amended and extended.
133. In former Yugoslavia, originally through Dec. 94/790 (O.J. 1994 L 326/2), subsequently extended through to mid-1996.
134. Dec. 93/728 (O.J. 1993 L 339/1), subsequently extended. The Stability Pact was Mitterand's initiative aimed at promoting stability in Europe through settling the question of minorities and confirming the inviolability of frontiers. The Pact on Stability in Europe was signed in Paris on March 21, 1995, see Bull. EU 3–1995, point 1.4.4 and *General Report 1995* (Brussels, Luxembourg, 1996) point 696.
135. JA 96/656 (O.J. 1996 L 300/1). Initially the decisions on Joint Action were classified as decisions (sector 3 in the Celex database), but they are nowadays listed under sector 4, supplementary instruments. The nomenclature used here reflects the Celex approach, which makes it clear that these are not Community decisions.
136. JA 96/676 (O.J. 1996 L 315/1).
137. JA 96/250 (O.J. 1996 L 87/1), subsequently extended and supplemented.

The first Joint Action to be taken in under the security component of CFSP concerned the 1995 Conference on the Non-Proliferation of Nuclear Weapons Treaty.[138] The wide ambit of the Union's support for security questions is also evidenced by the Joint action in relation to the Korean Peninsula Energy Development Organization (KEDO).[139] Use has also been made of the possibility afforded by Article J.3(3) TEU to adapt Joint Action to changed circumstances, and of the provisions of Article J.11 TEU which permit the expenses of such Joint Action to be billed in whole or in part not to the Community budget but to the budgets of the Member States.[140] No use has yet been made of the possibility provided for in Article J.3(2) TEU for the Council to adopt implementing decisions by qualified majority.[141] A noteworthy example of how action in CFSP can come together with that in JHA and that under the Community system can be seen in the Joint Action concerning measures protecting against the extra-territorial effects of legislation adopted by a third country and actions based thereon or resulting therefrom.[142]

Common positions under Article J.2 TEU were initially only adopted in connection with politically motivated restrictions on trade, but their scope has since broadened considerably to embrace the Union's objectives and priorities on matters as diverse as problems in Rwanda;[143] the Ukraine;[144]

---

138. Dec. 94/509 (O.J. 1994 L 205/1). The Review and Extension Conference was held in New York from April 17 to May 12, 1995, see Bull. EU 5–1995, point 1.4.4. and *General Report 1995* (Brussels, Luxembourg, 1996) point 699. See also JA 97/288 (O.J. 1997 L 120/1) on the promotion of transparency in nuclear-related export controls.

139. JA 96/195 (O.J. 1996 L 63/1). KEDO is designed to seek a solution to the proliferation of nuclear weapons on the Korean Peninsula.

140. *E.g.* Dec. 94/308 (O.J. 1994 L 134/1). See Monar (1997) JCMS 57.

141. The political problems have not yet been surmounted. However, in relation to the Joint Action concerning land mines, in Dec. 95/170 (O.J. 1995 L 115/11), Art. 6(3) provision is in fact made for qualified majority decisions.

142. JA 96/668 (O.J. 1996 L 309/7) is based on Arts. J.3 and K.3 TEU. This forms part of the EU's response to the Helms-Burton Act in the USA. In the Community system, see Reg. 2271/96 (O.J. 1996 L 309/1), which also responds to the D'Amato Act in the USA. These American measures concern penalties to be imposed on those having assets in the USA who conduct business with certain countries (Cuba, and Iran and Libya respectively). It was perceived that these Acts could be used to force European companies not to deal with those countries. The EU initiated a WTO special group procedure in respect of this legislation, but its work was suspended in April 1997 after various American concessions, see Bull. EU 4–1997, point 1.4.90. Negotiations between the EU and the USA resumed in October 1997 after a hiatus and culminated in agreement in May 1998.

143. Dec. 94/697 (O.J. 1994 L 283/1).

144. CP 94/779 (O.J. 1994 L 313/1). Although the Common Position speaks of the Council deciding, this type of measure is no longer listed as a decision (Celex sector 3, but as supplementary legislation, sector 4), but the Council always refers to such Common Positions as decisions. The nomenclature used here reflects the Celex approach, which makes clear that these are not Community decisions.

the situation in East Timor,[145] and in Myanmar (Burma).[146] The political decision to execute the United Nations sanctions against Libya and Haiti in the Community framework was taken in this manner[147] and was immediately accompanied by the necessary Council regulations and ECSC decisions based on Article 228a EC.[148] Even where there is no resolution of the United Nations Security Council, an arms embargo can be imposed through a Common Position on the basis of Article J.2 TEU.[149] The general rule of Community law that Member States may exercise their retained powers only in a manner which is in conformity with Community law also applies to the powers under the old European Political Cooperation and now CFSP, thus national measures adopted in the exercise of national competence in foreign and security policy must respect the Community rules adopted under the common commercial policy.[150]

3. THE COMMON COMMERCIAL POLICY[151]

3.1 The commercial policy competence of the Community

3.1.1 The concept of commercial policy

The power to regulate commercial policy relations by unilateral measures concerning imports and exports (autonomous commercial policy) or by agreements with third countries (conventional commercial policy) is expressly included in the EC Treaty in Article 113. The power includes the power to adopt autonomous measures relating to the common customs tariff under Articles 18, 25 and 27–29 EC and to regulate commercial traffic in agricultural products between the Community and the rest of the world by means, for example, of levies and refunds under

---

145. CP 96/407 (O.J. 1996 L 168/2).
146. CP 96/635 (O.J. 1996 L 287/1), since extended.
147. See Decs. 93/614 (O.J. 1993 L 295/7) Libya, and 94/315 (O.J. 1994 L 139/10) Haiti. Sanctions against Haiti were lifted by Dec. 94/681 (O.J. 1994 L 271/3).
148. See section 3.3.5, *post*. The sanctions against Haiti have been lifted (see Bull. EU 10–1994, point 1.3.3).
149. Dec. 94/165 (O.J. 1994 L 75/1). This demonstrates that the Member States continue to take the view that arms do not fall under Community law by virtue of Art. 223 EC. The Commission's view is, though, that if the Council desired to remove disparities in trade in arms it could do so in the same manner as obstacles to trade permitted under Art. 36 EC are removed, namely by harmonization. Some progress has been made in this, see Dir. 91/477 (O.J. 1991 L 256/51).
150. Case C-124/95 *R. ex parte Centro-Com Srl v. H.M. Treasury et al.* [1997] ECR I-81 at 123–124.
151. See, generally, Emiliou and O'Keeffe (eds.), *The European Union and World Trade Law* (Chichester, 1996) and Maresceau (ed.), *The European Community's Commercial Policy after 1992: The Legal Dimension* (Dordrecht, 1993).

common organizations of the market (in accordance with Articles 40 and 43 EC).

Article 113 EC does not contain a definition of commercial policy but provides a non-exhaustive[152] list of uniform principles on which it is to be based, 'particularly in regard to changes in tariff rates, the conclusion of tariff and trade agreements, the achievement of uniformity in measures of liberalization, export policy and measures to protect trade such as those to be taken in case of dumping or subsidies.' The Council has advanced the view that only measures relating to the volume or flow of trade fall within the scope of commercial policy (a subjective doctrine, looking at the content to identify the objective) whereas the Commission has taken the view that the assessment must primarily be made by reference to the specific character of a measure as an instrument regulating international trade (an objective or instrumental doctrine).[153] On this controversy the Court did not expressly take a position, although elements of both views have been reflected in its case-law.[154] The case-law has, though, contributed to further detailing the scope of the field covered by the common commercial policy.

The starting-point is that the concept of commercial policy has 'the same content whether it is applied in the context of the international action of a State or to that of the Community'[155] There is therefore no reason for interpreting the concept more narrowly in the case of the Community. On the contrary, the proper functioning of the customs union justifies a wide interpretation of inter alia Article 113 and of the powers thereby conferred on the Community Institutions 'to allow them thoroughly to control external trade by measures taken both independently and by agreement'.[156] Thus the Court concluded that aids for exports to third countries,

152. Opinion 1/78 [1979] ECR 2871 at 2913.
153. Cf. the explanation of these views fully set out in Opinion 1/78, ibid. at 2880–2894. See also the opinion of Lenz, Adv. Gen. in Case 45/86 Commission v. Council [1987] ECR 1493 at 1508–1511. Here the Commission presented a more nuanced argument based on the direct and specific regulation of trade with third countries. See also Bourgeois in Völker (ed.), Protectionism and the European Community (2nd ed., Deventer etc., 1987) 1 at 4–6 (and literature cited there).
154. Case C-62/88 Greece v. Council [1990] ECR I-1527 at 1549–1550. This controversy has since diminished in importance. It seems that the respective standpoints are politically less attractive, as the subjective doctrine would cause certain measures or agreements to fall within the commercial policy competence of the Community, such as agreements on intellectual property protection aimed at encouraging trade in high technology goods, which would not fall within such competence if the objective doctrine were applied. Thus both Institutions have retreated somewhat from their extreme positions. The legal content of these two doctrines also appears on closer examination to be thin.
155. Opinion 1/75 OECD Understanding on a Local Cost Standard [1975] ECR 1355 at 1362.
156. Case 8/73 Hauptzollamt Bremerhaven v. Massey-Ferguson GmbH [1973] ECR 897 at 908.

mentioned in Article 112 EC, and in particular measures concerning export credits necessarily fell within the scope of 'export policy' mentioned in Article 113.[157] The definition of the uniform principles prescribed in Article 113 included 'the elimination of national disparities', whether in the field of taxation or of commerce, affecting trade with third countries.[158]

The Court has also held that it is 'not possible to lay down, for Article 113 of the Treaty, an interpretation the effect of which would be to restrict the common commercial policy to the use of instruments intended to have an effect only on the traditional aspects of external trade to the exclusion of more highly developed mechanisms'[159] such as the more recent international commodity agreements which are associated with United Nations resolutions concerning the development of a new international economic order. If it were otherwise, observed the Court, the common commercial policy 'would be destined to become nugatory in the course of time'. Although it may be thought that at the time when the Treaty was drafted liberalization of trade was the dominant idea, the Treaty nevertheless does not form a barrier to the possibility of the Community's developing a commercial policy aiming at a regulation of the world market for certain products rather than at a mere liberalization of trade.[160]

Development policy and environmental policy are integral aspects of a modern concept of commercial policy. Thus the Court has stated that the Community system of generalized tariff preferences for developing countries (the GSP) 'reflects a new concept of international trade relations in which development aims to play a major role'.[161] Thus the regulations applying the GSP, or restrictions of patterns of trade in the aftermath of an environmental disaster (such as that at Chernobyl) need no legal base in the Treaty other than Article 113 itself as the GSP falls within the sphere of the common commercial policy; a general reference to the EC Treaty is insufficient nor is recourse to Article 235 EC permitted.[162] In Opinion 1/78[163] which concerned the Community's competence relating to an international rubber agreement to be concluded under the auspices of UNCTAD, the Court saw no reason to exclude the agreement from the domain of the common commercial policy because of its possible repercussions on certain sectors of economic policy such as the supply of

157. Opinion 1/75 [1975] ECR 1355 at 1362.
158. Cases 37 and 38/73 *Sociaal Fonds voor de Diamantarbeiders* v. *NV Indiamex et al.* [1973] ECR 1609 at 1623.
159. Opinion 1/78 [1979] ECR 2871 at 2913.
160. *Ibid.*
161. Case 45/86 *Commission* v. *Council* [1987] ECR 1493 at 1521; Case C-62/88 *Greece* v. *Council* [1990] ECR I-1527 at 1550–1551.
162. *Ibid.*, [1987] ECR 1493 at 1520 and 1522; [1990] ECR I-1527 at 1550–1551. It is questionable to what extent this case-law retains the same value after the introduction of Arts. 130r EC *et seq.*
163. [1979] ECR 2871 at 2915.

certain raw materials to the Community or price policy or because the building up of stocks of a product might have a political importance. It also appears from the same opinion that the description of an agreement 'must be assessed having regard to its essential objective rather than in terms of individual clauses of an altogether subsidiary or ancillary nature' such as technological assistance, research programmes, labour conditions in the industry concerned or consultations relating to national tax policies which could have an effect on the price of the product concerned.[164]

The most important controversy in recent times on the concept of the common commercial policy concerns its scope: whether it only concerns the external aspects of the customs union, and thus only tariff and non-tariff barriers to trade in goods, or whether it also embraces other aspects of the common market, such as international trade in services and certain external aspects of the right of establishment. External aspects of the free movement of capital are regulated in Article 73c EC and are normally in general economic usage not considered as falling under commercial policy. The Commission has long taken the view that trade in services falls under the common commercial policy, and also those aspects of the right of establishment and of the free movement of persons which are directly linked to the liberalization of trade in services. It is evident that for the effective provision of services over international borders it is sometimes necessary to be established on the spot, while it is sometimes also necessary that persons may temporarily move to another country in connection with the provision of services.[165] The Commission based its view on the increasing intermingling of traffic in services with traffic in goods and the increasing importance of international traffic in services as such; accordingly, it made a link with the evolutionary approach of the Court to the concept of the common commercial policy in order to reach the conclusion that international trade in services formed part of the common commercial policy. The Council and pretty well all the Member States rejected this view. They remained firmly attached to the narrow view of the concept of the common commercial policy, restricting its scope to the movement of goods and some services directly linked thereto. They approached international trade in services on the basis of the *ERTA* doctrine, so that a case-by-case approach should be taken in deciding whether autonomous measures should be taken or agreements concluded on the basis of the relevant provision on which internal Community competence is founded, or whether the Member States could still exercise their own powers. It is plain that this view scarcely

164. *Ibid.* at 2917. Again, it may well be that the introduction of Arts. 130u EC *et seq.* has changed this situation.
165. In so far as the provision of services inside the Community is concerned, such free movement of persons linked to the freedom to provide services was recognized by the Court in Case C-113/89 *Rush Portugesa Lda v. Office national d'immigration* [1990] ECR I-1417 at 1444–1445.

simplifies the promotion of a coherent external policy on trade in services. The practice of the Community Institutions has varied: on occasions it is clear that the *ERTA* doctrine is being applied, but on other occasions reliance is placed on Article 113 EC.[166]

In Opinion 1/94 *WTO – GATS and TRIPs*[167] the Court sought to give something of a judgment of Solomon on the scope of the Community's commercial policy competence, but in practice the result will largely favour the Council's approach. The Court recognized that developments in the practice of international trade indicate that trade in services and the trade aspects of intellectual property are playing an increasingly important role. Thus the common commercial policy had an open nature[168] and thus could evolve with practice. But in view of the structure of the EC Treaty the Court was unwilling to draw the full consequences of this approach. It found that the cross-frontier provision of services involving no movement of persons was not unlike trade in goods and, as the latter was unquestionably within the scope of the common commercial policy, so was the former. But the other forms of provision of services dealt with in the definition of trade in services under Article I(2) GATS[169] were, the Court concluded, very closely linked to the free movement of persons, the freedom of undertakings to establish themselves, and the specific EC Treaty provisions on transport. Thus for these modes of providing services and for transport any exclusive Community competence had to be established on the basis of the *ERTA* doctrine or on the basis of the existence of specific clauses in Community legislation relating to the treatment of persons or undertakings from third countries or dealing with negotiations with third countries. The same view was taken in relation to the international aspects of intellectual property rights: here too determination of external competence depended on the doctrine of implied powers, save in relation to frontier measures against counterfeit goods, which clearly fell under Article 113 EC.[170]

---

166. *E.g.* the Agreement with Switzerland on direct insurance other than life assurance (see Dec. 91/370 (O.J. 1991 L 205/2) is based on Arts. 57(2) and 235 EC; whereas the Agreement with the United States on government procurement (see Dec. 93/323 (O.J. 1993 L 125/1) which also covers the procurement of services, was based on Art. 113 EC. That decision approving the agreement was duly annulled by the Court in Case C-360/94 *European Parliament v. Council* [1996] ECR I-1195. This result followed in the light of Opinion 1/94, discussed next in the text, see also section 4.4, *post.*
167. [1994] ECR I-5267 at 5400–5403 and 5404–5406.
168. *Ibid.* at 5401.
169. *I.e.* consumption abroad (movement into the country where the supplier is established); commercial presence through a branch or subsidiary in the host country, and the presence of natural persons actually enabling the supplier from the home country to supply services in the host country.
170. [1994] ECR I-5267 at 5404. The measures were contained in Reg. 3842/86 (O.J. 1986 L 357/1), since replaced by Reg. 3295/94 (O.J. 1994 L 341/8), implemented by Reg. 1367/95 (O.J. 1995 L 133/2).

Thus although the Court in theory did not exclude a further evolution of the common commercial policy, it seems that the concept is clearly restricted to trade in goods, in the direct provision of cross-frontier services without movement of persons, and measures at the Community frontier to combat counterfeit goods and other infringements of intellectual property rights.

The concept of a common commercial policy means that Member States may not restrict its scope by freely deciding, in the light of their own foreign policy or security requirements, whether a measure is covered by Article 113 EC.[171]

3.1.2 The exclusivity of Community competence in the field of commercial policy

The case-law demonstrates that the Community has exclusive competence in relation to conventional as well as autonomous measures; indeed after the end of the transitional period national commercial policy measures are only permissible by virtue of specific authorization by the Community.[172] In Opinion 1/75[173] the Court based this exclusivity on the ground that the common commercial policy was conceived 'in the context of the operation of the Common Market, for the defence of the common interests of the Community, within which the particular interests of the Member States must endeavour to adapt to each other.' 'Quite clearly,' continued the Court, 'this conception is incompatible with the freedom to which the Member States could lay claim by invoking a concurrent power, so as to ensure that their own interests were separately satisfied in external relations, at the risk of compromising the effective defence of the common interests of the Community.'[174] If such a parallel competence were to be accepted that 'would amount to recognizing that, in relations with third countries, Member States may adopt positions which differ from those which the Community intends to adopt, and which would thereby distort the institutional framework, call into question the mutual trust within the Community and prevent the latter from fulfilling its task in the defence of the common interest.'[175]

---

171. Case C-70/94 *Fritz Werner Industrie-Ausrüstungen GmbH v. Germany* [1995] ECR I-3189 at 3224. Nor may the nature of goods as dual-use foods be invoked to take them outside the scope of the common commercial policy, Case C-83/94 *Leifer et al* [1995] ECR I-3231 at 3244. See further, Govare (1997) 34 CMLRev. 1019 at 1032, See also Govare and Eeckhout (1992) 29 CMLRev. 941 and Schroeder and Köhncke (1995) Int. TLR 101.

172. Case 41/76 *Criel, née Donckerwolcke et al. v. Procureur de la République au Tribunal de Grande Instance Lille et al.* [1976] ECR 1921 at 1937.

173. [1975] ECR 1355 at 1363–1364.

174. *Ibid.* at 1364.

175. *Ibid.*

No obstacle to the Community's common commercial policy competence arises from the fact that the obligations and financial burdens inherent in the execution of an envisaged agreement are borne directly by the Member States; such obligations and burdens do not necessarily have to be transferred to the Community Institutions,[176] nor does the implementation of the obligations have to be completely the task of the Community Institutions.[177] The Community does though have the power to enter into financial obligations arising from an instrument of commercial policy which fall on the Community budget (even if they are not incidental or subsidiary obligations but are an essential part of the system set up, as, for example, in the case of a buffer stock mechanism which has to be financed as part of the regulatory system of an international commodity agreement).[178]

It appears from Opinion 1/78[179] that in certain circumstances[180] it will do if the financial burdens arising from an agreement fall on the Member States. In the case of the financing of buffer stocks in the framework of the international rubber agreement, considered in Opinion 1/78, the Court felt that if the financing was to be by the Member States the exclusive competence of the Community could not be envisaged. Two arguments led the Court to this conclusion. First, the extent of and the detailed arrangements for the financial undertakings which the Member States would be required to satisfy would directly condition the possibilities and degree of efficiency of intervention by the buffer mechanism. Secondly, the Court pointed out that price decisions to be taken by the International Rubber Council which was to be set up would have immediate repercussions on the use of the financial means put at that Council's disposal. The Court observed that if the financing was to be by participating Member States that would imply their participation in the decision-making machinery or at least their agreement with regard to the financing envisaged; this consequently implied their participation with the Community in the agreement.[181] The Court did not draw the resulting conclusion that the, in principle, exclusive Community competence to conclude an agreement which provided for the introduction of a buffer stock mechanism should, in these circumstances, necessarily lead to the financing of the mechanism by the community budget; it merely noted that if the financing of the agreement were a matter for the Community the necessary decisions would be taken according to the appropriate Community procedures. However, the approach in Opinion 1/78 must not

176. *Ibid.*
177. Opinion 2/91 *ILO Convention No. 170* [1993] ECR I-1061 at 1082.
178. Opinion 1/78 [1979] ECR 2871 at 2918.
179. *Ibid.*
180. *Cf.* Opinion 1/94 [1994] ECR I-5267, [1995] 1 CMLR 205, discussed in section 3.1.1, *ante.*
181. Opinion 1/78 [1979] ECR 2871 at 2918.

be misused: thus where an international organization has an operating budget rather than a financial policy instrument, the fact that the Member Sates would bear some of its expenses would not itself justify participation in the conclusion of an agreement.[182]

3.1.3 Procedure in the exercise of the commercial policy

Despite the fact that, as was demonstrated in section 2.5, above, the new version of Article 228 EC prescribes a general procedure for the exercise of external competence which is largely inspired by the procedure under Article 113 EC, the latter still sets out in a separate provision the manner in which commercial negotiations have to be opened and conducted. Article 113(3) EC is thus now virtually identical to Article 228(1) EC.

The importance of the Article 113 Committee in the conduct of commercial policy is crucial.[183] This committee meets monthly at the level of the national Directors General for commercial policy and weekly at the level of their deputies. Further, the Article 113 Committee meets at least weekly in Geneva, the seat of the WTO. It may also meet in various compositions anywhere in the world where the Commission is conducting negotiations on behalf of the Community. The negotiations are opened after the Council has authorized this, acting by a qualified majority on the basis of a recommendation from the Commission.[184] The resulting negotiation mandate may well be accompanied by directives issued to the Commission by the Council and it is the Article 113 Committee which ensures that these instructions or guidelines are adhered to by the Commission during the negotiations.

In fact only in very formal negotiations sessions are the Commission's representatives actually accompanied by members of the Article 113 Committee as observers. In certain important informal negotiating situations the Commission is accompanied by the representative of the Member State currently holding the Presidency of the Council, and thus of the Article 113 Committee.[185] In other cases the Commission negotiates independently, but has to report regularly to the Article 113 Committee. The committee thus functions as a permanent sounding-board for the Commission, not only during negotiations, but also continually, in the conception and execution of the common commercial policy. While the committee is an advisory committee having no power of decision of its

182. Opinion 1/94 *WTO – GATS and TRIPs* [1994] ECR I-5267 at 5395.
183. This is the 'special committee appointed by the Council to assist the Commission' in its negotiating task, Art. 113(3) EC, 2nd para.
184. Art. 113 (3) and (4).
185. This occurred for example during the so-called Green Room sessions in which the Director General of the GATT met leaders of delegations during the Uruguay Round negotiations.

own, it is evident that the Commission will attempt to achieve if not a consensus, at least a qualified majority support for its intended stance. This latter is at the end of the day the majority by which the Council is to approve commercial agreements or adopt autonomous commercial policy measures. Although, as was noted in section 2.5, above, Article 228(3) EC appears scarcely to accord powers to the European Parliament in the approval of commercial policy agreements, it cannot be excluded that such agreements may establish 'a specific institutional framework' or have 'important budgetary implications for the Community' or require the amendment of Community measures adopted under the co-decision procedure of Article 189b EC, and thus require the assent of the European Parliament before they may be adopted by the Council. Apart from these instances, there is no obligation on the Council to consult the European Parliament on agreements in the field of the common commercial policy, but since 1973 the Parliament has in fact been consulted as a rule.[186] While the European Parliament does not yet seem to go as far as the American Congress does in respect of United States commercial policy, by seeking to determine the content of Community commercial policy, there have been problems with lack of cooperation motivated by political objectives unrelated to the agreement under consideration, an approach which has been clearly disapproved by the Court.[187]

If the Community and the Member States are participating in the negotiations (for so-called mixed agreements) then there is a dual leadership of the Community delegation. The mixed delegation is led by a representative of the Commission and of the Member State holding the Presidency of the Council, and includes one civil servant from each Member State. This style of delegation – the so-called UNCTAD formula – is also used without the participation in the negotiations of separate delegations from each Member State. The Commission tends to be entrusted with the role of common spokesman.

At the close of negotiations the draft agreement is initialed by the Commission in the name of the Community. Signature by the President of the Council and/or the responsible Commissioner will only occur after conclusion of the agreement has been approved by the Council on the basis of the mandate which it had given to the Commission.[188] If, though, the agreement contains a ratification clause then the agreement is signed on behalf of the Community (by the representative of the Commission)

---

186. Here the so-called Luns/Westerterp procedure is applied. This is a slightly watered-down version of the Luns procedure which was the practice in concluding association agreements. Cf. Bull. EC 1973–10 p. 89 at 90 (point 2427 (11)). See also Quintin (1975) RTDE 211.
187. See Case C-65/93 European Parliament v. Council [1995] ECR I-643 at 669.
188. The decision approving the conclusion of the agreement empowers the Presidency of the Council to designate the persons who will actually sign on behalf of the Community.

and then the approval procedure begins. Approval by the Council is then transmitted either to the other parties to the agreement or to the deposit-holder in accordance with the provisions of the agreement.

3.2 Principles and development of the common commercial policy

3.2.1 GATT/WTO rules and generalized preferences (GSP)

In regulating commercial policy relations by means of autonomous measures such as modifications to the common customs tariff or the adoption of import regulation (autonomous commercial policy) or by means of agreements with third countries (conventional commercial policy) the Community is bound to respect the international commercial policy rules which bound the Member States before the entry into force of the EEC Treaty.[189] The most important of these rules are those contained in the General Agreement on Tariffs and Trade (the GATT)[190] which has largely governed international trade since 1947. This agreement has now been subsumed in the form of GATT 1994 into the new World Trade Organization which came into being on 1 January 1995.[191] In Cases 21–24/72 *International Fruit Company NV et al.* v. *Produktschap voor Groenten en Fruit*[192] the Court held that the Community as such was bound by the provisions of the GATT 'in so far as under the EEC Treaty the Community has assumed the powers previously exercised by the Member States in the area covered by the General Agreement'. In this respect the binding effect of the GATT on the Community no longer resulted from Article 234 EC but from the Community's succession as an international legal person to the rights and obligations of the Member States under the GATT, which, as the Court acknowledged, had been recognized by the other contracting parties to the GATT. The establishment of the

189. *Cf.* the various Acts of Accession (1972, 1979, 1985 and 1994), Art. 5 (in each case) concerning the position of new Member States. Art. 234 EC applies to all agreements concluded by them with third countries prior to accession, see Case 812/79 *Attorney-General v. Burgoa* [1980] ECR 2787 at 2802.
190. Geneva, October 30, 1947 (55–61 UNTS 194). See Hilf *et al.* (eds.), *The European Community and GATT* (2nd ed., Deventer, 1989); McGovern, *International Trade Regulation* (2nd ed., Exeter, 1986); Dam, *The GATT* (Chicago and London, 1970), and Jackson, *World Trade and the Law of GATT* (Indianapolis, 1969). See also Simmonds (1988) 25 CMLRev. 95 and Tarullo (1987) 24 CMLRev. 411.
191. See note 83, *supra*. See also Dennin (ed.), *Law and Practice of the World Trade Organisation (WTO)* (New York, loose-leaf, since 1995); Jackson, *Implementing the Uruguay Round* (Oxford, 1997); Petersmann, *The GATT/WTO Dispute Settlement System* (London, 1997) and *International Trade Law and the GATT/WTO Dispute Settlement System* (London, 1997); Quershi, *The World Trade Organization* (Manchester, 1996), and Stoll (1997) ZaöRV 83.
192. [1972] ECR 1219 at 1227, see also Kapteyn (1973) SEW 491.

Community's Common Customs Tariff occurred largely in tandem with two rounds of tariff negotiations on the basis of the most-favoured-nation principle in the GATT: the Dillon Round (1961–1962) and the Kennedy Round (1964–1967). In these Rounds the Commission acted as representative of the Community and thus strengthened the confidence of the GATT partners in the Community as such. In this manner the Community also clearly indicated that in the GATT framework it was inspired by the liberal bases of the common commercial policy.[193] In total tariff reductions of some 40% were achieved in the Common Customs Tariff. Thus in the GATT a situation arose in which the Member States remained contracting parties to the GATT but the Community became in effect also a contracting party which spoke for the Member States in nearly all areas covered by the GATT.[194]

When in the Seventies attention in the GATT began to move towards non-tariff barriers to trade, and the Tokyo Round (1973–1979) dealt not only with further tariff reductions (an average reduction in tariffs of around 30% and in the case of the EEC's common customs tariff of around 26% was achieved), but also with the drafting of Codes, covering matters such as technical barriers to trade; customs valuation; subsidies and anti-dumping, the Community became a party to these Codes which were linked to the GATT.[195] Despite this the Member States remained contracting parties to the GATT itself and they even acceded as such, most probably for symbolic reasons, to two of these Codes, the Code on Technical barriers to Trade and the Code on Trade in Civil Aircraft.[196] Those two Codes were in practice never treated as mixed agreements; the Member States left the management of those Codes to the Community in the same manner as for the GATT and the other Tokyo Round agreements.

In the framework of the Uruguay Round (1986–1993) the GATT was transformed into the World Trade Organization, which covers pretty well all aspects of international trade. In addition to the matters dealt with in the Tokyo Round, the WTO Agreement also covers trade in services (the General Agreement on Trade in Services – GATS) and the trade aspects of intellectual property rights (Trade-Related Intellectual Property Rights – TRIPs). Given that competence in these two latter areas is mixed,[197] the

---

193. See Arts. 18, 29(a) and 110 EC.
194. This was so far-reaching that if occasionally a Member State put forward a view different from that of the Community the president of the GATT Council ruled that only the representative of the Community could bind the Community in a GATT Council decision, see Kuyper, *Het GATT en het Volkenrecht* (Mededelingen NVIR [Dutch International Law Association] No. 107) 26.
195. See Dec. 80/271 (O.J. 1980 L 71/1), implemented by Regs. 1224/80 (O.J. 1980 L 134/1) and 1494/80 (O.J. 1980 L 154/3).
196. See Steenbergen (1980) SEW 752 and Bourgeois (1982) 19 CMLRev. 5.
197. See Opinion 1/94 [1994] ECR I-5267, [1995] 1 CMLR 205.

Community and the Member States will participate together in the activities of the WTO, although in practice the Commission will tend to act as their representative. When the WTO Agreement was signed at Marrakesh on 15 April 1994, the Community and the Member States signed it and all have ratified it.[198]

At the heart of the GATT 1947 and also of the GATT 1994 lie the core standards of the most-favoured nation principle and the national treatment principle. The former obliges the contracting parties to grant the advantages, of whatever kind, which they grant to any other country relating to the import or export of goods, and now also of services, to all other members of the WTO. Thus, tariff concessions or agreed treatment of providers of services do not merely benefit the contracting party to which they are accorded, but all members of the WTO. The national treatment principle requires each WTO member to grant national treatment to its partners in the fields of internal taxation and legislation. In such a manner trade advantages which have been accorded cannot be in fact rendered nugatory through discriminatory national taxation or legislation. The national treatment clause in Article XVII GATS means that this principle is conditional as far as services are concerned.

An extremely important exception as far as the Community is concerned is the exception in Article XXIV(4)–(8) GATT and Articles V and 5a GATS, relating to the formation of customs unions and free trade areas which satisfy certain conditions. On the establishment and later expansions of the Community, the Member States relied on the provision concerning customs unions as against their GATT partners. Thus they are not obliged to grant the advantages which they accord each other in the Community framework to all their GATT and now WTO partners. The Community itself has also relied on this exception, although it is questionable, now that the Community itself is formally a member of the WTO, whether it still needs to rely on that exception. Community legislation in the internal market field does not necessarily any longer need to be seen as advantages which the Member States confer on each other, but purely as legislation of one member of the WTO.

Nevertheless, the exception for customs unions and free trade areas remains and will in the future remain important for the Community, as it has concluded many such agreements with its neighbouring countries and with developing countries. The old agreements with the EFTA countries (of which only that with Switzerland still applies) were free trade agreements; the EEA Agreement establishes a free trade area in goods and a common market in other sectors of the economy between the Community and the remaining EFTA members other than Switzerland, called the European Economic Area; the Europe Agreements concluded

---

198. See, generally, Paemen and Bensch, *From the GATT to the WTO The European Community in the Uruguay Round* (Leuven, 1995).

with Central and Eastern European countries also aim to create a free trade area between the Community and each individual country; only the older agreements with Turkey and Cyprus and the agreement with Malta provide for a customs union with the Community. It is not always clear, though, that these agreements satisfy the requirements of Article XXIV GATT. First, the requirement that 'substantially all the trade' in products originating in the constituent territories must be free is not met, as trade in agricultural products is to a great degree excluded in connection with the Common Agricultural Policy. Secondly, the requirement that the free trade area shall be formed, according to a plan and schedule set out in advance, within a reasonable length of time does not appear to have been observed. Thus the agreement with Turkey was in force for a good 30 years before the customs union between the Community and Turkey finally came into being.[199] Various GATT working groups have criticized these Community agreements, but so far they have not been clearly rejected. Thus these agreements have long operated in a legally uncertain situation as far as the GATT is concerned.

Another important exception to the core principles of the GATT is the Community's Generalized System of Preferences (GSP). This concept, developed and accepted in the United Nations Conference on Trade and Development (UNCTAD), seeks to raise the export revenue of developing countries, to promote their industrialization and to accelerate their economic growth. These tariff preferences were to be introduced autonomously by all industrialized countries on a non-reciprocal basis and on the basis of non-discrimination concerning finished and semi-finished products from all developing countries (this was the GSP). The GATT accepted this clear derogation from the most-favoured-nation principle initially for a period of ten years by a waiver of GATT obligations under Article XXV(5) GATT, and subsequently through accepting a more general exception for differentiated and more favourable treatment of developing countries.[200] The idea of generalized preferences also found acceptance in the Community, even though it had already established association agreements with developing countries in Africa, granting them specific preferences, and these countries would not readily wish to see the preferences disappear. In 1971 the Council decided to introduce a GSP, taking the interests of the associated countries into account as far as possible; in taking this step the Community was one of the first developed economies to offer a GSP system. This system, which is revised annually in regulations has gradually been extended and improved. When the systems of the Member States which acceded to the Community in 1973 were

---

199. See Dec. 1/95 of the EC-Turkey Association Council (O.J. 1996 L 35/1) and *General Reports 1995 and 1996* (Brussels, Luxembourg, 1996 and 1997 respectively), points 844 and 818 respectively.
200. GATT *Basic Instruments and Selected Documents* (BISD) 26S/203.

integrated into the Community system in 1974 there was a particular improvement in the GSP.

The GSP preferential rules are established by regulations favouring the importation of products from almost 150 non-European developing countries, which include certain Eastern European countries and countries of the former Soviet Union as they are economies in transition. Of all these countries, nearly 50 are treated as being the least developed and accordingly benefit from an even more favourable treatment than the other countries which benefit from the GSP system.[201] Certain South American countries which risk becoming particularly dependent on the harvest of and trade in drugs also benefit in the same way as the least developed countries.[202] Such privileges within the GSP have been regarded as controversial, as was the grant of GSP status to Eastern European countries: it is regarded as being incompatible with the non-discriminatory nature of the GSP which is laid down in the GATT decision on the differentiated and preferential treatment of developing countries. Despite ferocious discussions in the responsible GATT working group, the controversy was unresolved, with the result that both the Community and the United States have continued their differentiation policy within their GSP systems.

The Commission announced in June 1994 that it was proposing to the Council that the GSP system should be reformed.[203] In the past there was a complicated system which involved the suspension of the otherwise applicable tariff in respect of a certain quota or up to a certain ceiling; this had not always functioned satisfactorily.[204] In the new GSP the products covered by the system are divided according to different degrees of sensitivity, so that the amount of the duty suspended varies, from only 85% suspended for the most sensitive products (textiles and clothing) to complete suspension for non-sensitive products. This modulation does not apply to the least developed countries and countries treated on a similar basis; they benefit from complete suspension for all products.[205]

---

201. The list of such countries can be found in Annexes III, IV and V to Reg. 3281/94 (O.J. 1994 L 348/1, most recently amended by Reg. 998/97 (O.J. 1997 L 144/13)). As to the revised scheme applicable to agricultural products, see Reg. 1256/96 (O.J. 1996 L 160/1, amended by Reg. 2448/96 (O.J. 1996 L 333/12)).

202. Bolivia, Columbia, Guatemala, Ecuador, Peru and Venezuela, see now Reg. 1256/96, *ibid.*, Annex V.

203. COM (94) 212 Final.

204. Frequently the ceilings for certain Member States were exhausted, so that full import duties had to be paid there, while that was not the case in other Member States. This unequal tariff treatment in different Member States (apportionment into national shares) was found to be unacceptable by the Court, see Case 51/87 *Commission v. Council* [1988] ECR 5459.

205. Reg. 3281/94 (O.J. 1994 L 348/1, as amended), Arts. 2 and 3. A similar approach is taken in Reg. 2448/96 (O.J. 996 L 333/12, as amended) in relation to agricultural products.

A graduation mechanism operates for imports from the most developed of the developing countries and for countries which have large shares of the exports to the Community of certain products, so that their preferences are gradually lost.[206] The Community has also announced incentive measures, so that instead of removing GSP advantages if requirements relating to social conditions and to the environment are not respected, there is the prospect of extra preferences if such requirements are complied with. Thus the stick is transformed into a carrot. In the course of 1997 the Council was to reconsider the system in order to introduce such extra advantages on the basis of internationally accepted objective criteria.[207] A mechanism has now clearly been established for the temporary, total or partial withdrawal of GSP preferences.[208]

The GATT scheme also contains a number of provisions which have a special character, those in part IV relating to trade and development. This Part was added to the GATT system in 1964 in order to take account of the demands of developing countries, and entered into force in 1966. Article XXXVI(8) GATT is of particular importance for the Community, as it provides that the developed countries will not expect reciprocity from developing countries in the granting of mutual tariff concessions. On the basis of this provision, and under strong political pressure from the United States, the Community transformed its preferential cooperation system with ex-colonies of various of its Member States in Africa, the Caribbean and the Pacific Ocean (the ACP States) from a reciprocal into a non-reciprocal system, in the Lomé Convention, which is now in its Fourth version.[209] A GATT Panel decided some time ago that the non-reciprocal advantages afforded to a limited group of developing countries could not be based on Part IV of the GATT, and that the GATT decision on differentiated and preferential treatment for developing countries only permitted non-discriminatory treatment of those countries.[210] While the Panel's decision was never definitively adopted, the system of non-reciprocal preferential agreements which the Community had concluded was called into question, not merely in the context of the Lomé Convention, but also in the context of the Community's Mediterranean policy, unless the Community could obtain a specific waiver in accordance with Article XXV(5) GATT from its GATT

---

206. Reg. 3281/94, *ibid.*, Arts. 4 and 6 and Annex II. Again, there is an equivalent approach in relation to agricultural products. This system might more appropriately be known as a promotions system, and demands complicated calculations.
207. *Ibid.*, Arts. 7 and 8. Account will also be taken of such reconsideration for the system applicable to agricultural products.
208. *Ibid.*, Arts. 12 *et seq.*. Similar provisions are made in relation to agricultural products.
209. See section 4.2.5, *post.*
210. See GATT Panel reports DS 32/R (3 June 1993) and DS 38/R (18 January 1994), both unadopted.

partners. Accordingly, the Community sought and on December 9, 1994 obtained a waiver for that Convention.[211]

3.2.2 The completion of the internal market and the common commercial policy

There is an inseparable link between the internal free movement of goods within the Community and the commercial policy of Member States towards third countries. As a matter of fact, products from third countries are in free circulation within this market on the same footing as those originating from Member States as soon as the import formalities have been complied with and any customs duties and charges which are due have been paid in respect of them in one Member State.[212] A free movement of these goods as well as of those originating from Member States can be fully maintained only if the import as well as the export regime of Member States is broadly identical not only in the matter of customs tariffs (the Common Customs Tariff), but on other points as well. If there are clear differences, this results in a deflection of trade to the countries whose regime is least restrictive, with all the harmful consequences this entails. After the completion of the internal market within the Community this is no longer acceptable.[213]

How common must the common commercial policy be? This question must be distinguished from that of whether or not the Community has exclusive competence in this field. The exclusivity which the Court has conferred on this competence after the end of the transitional period involves the Member States being unable to derive from their national law the competence to take national commercial policy measures. Community exclusivity, however, does not prevent Community law conferring such competence on them, although it is clear since the judgment in Case 41/76 *Criel, nee Donckerwolcke et al. v. Procureur de la République au Tribunal de Grande Instance, Lille*[214] that 'measures of commercial policy of a national character are only permissible after the end of the transitional period by virtue of specific authorization by the Community.'[215] It can be deduced

---

211. Extended on 14 October 1996 until 29 February 2000. See, *inter alia* on the interpretation of this Lomé Waiver, WTO Appellate Body Report (Bananas) WT/DS27/AB/R of 9 September 1997.
212. Arts. 9 and 10 EC.
213. See, generally, Demaret (ed.), *Relations extérieurs de la CE et marché intérieur; aspects juridiques et fonctionnels* (Bruges, 1986); Eekhout, *The European Internal Market and International Trade: A Legal Analysis* (Oxford, 1994), and Hilf and Tomuschat (eds.), *EG und Drittstaatsbeziehungen nach 1992* (Baden-Baden, 1992).
214. [1976] ECR 921 at 1937. *Cf.* on this Kapteyn (1976) Texas Int'l. L.J. 487–489.
215. In Case 174/84 *Bulk Oil (Zug) A G v. Sun International Ltd et al.* [1986] ECR 559 at 586–587 the Court stretched the meaning of the phrase 'special authorization' in what was, with respect, a manner not immune from criticism. It regarded Art. 10 of Reg.

from this that Article 113 EC does prevent the Community from limiting itself to establishing uniform principles and conferring on the Member States a *general* authorization to apply those principles in their autonomous or conventional commercial policies. The Community should itself adopt measures applying these principles, thus itself taking autonomous measures and entering into agreements with third countries and international organizations. Article 113 does not prevent the Community in well-defined cases and subject to well-defined conditions from granting the Member States powers of execution (decentralization) or making differences in the extent of these measures from Member State to Member State (differentiation).

Decentralization of the common commercial policy occurs regularly. In particular all customs aspects of commercial policy are decentralized. Although the Community has a Customs Code,[216] it does not have its own customs service as such. It uses the customs authorities of the Member States in the implementation of many aspects of its commercial policy. In particular autonomous commercial policy, considered in the following sections, below, is executed by the competent authorities of the Member States, which means not just the customs administrations but also the departments responsible for the grant of import and export authorizations (such as the Dutch Centrale Dienst In- en Uitvoer, or the British Department of Trade and Industry). The common provisions that these administrations have to follow ensure that decentralization does not affect the unity of the commercial policy. However, the various regimes have been tightened over the years, first by improving the early directives, then by substituting regulations for directives, and finally by bringing policy much more tightly together in the Community Customs Code. Thus holes or leaks in the application of commercial policy in practice have been plugged and the discretionary freedom of the Member States to weaken the common market concept (through for example an excessive use of zones under customs control for processing of goods under favourable regimes) has been considerably tightened.[217]

Differentiation is a rather more difficult matter, as it means that per Member State a certain adaptation of the common commercial policy is possible. Such differentiation may be the result of remaining aspects of

---

2603/69 (O.J. English Special Edition 1969 (II), p. 590, as amended, on common rules for exports) as such a special authorization, but that provision merely stated that for the time being the common rules did not apply to, *inter alia*, crude oils and petroleum oils. *Cf.* Feenstra (1987) SEW 145 and Slot (1987) 24 CMLRev. 99.

216. Reg. 2913/92 (O.J. 1992 L 302/1, most recently amended by Reg. 82/97 (O.J. 1997 L 17/1)), implemented by Reg. 2454/93 (O.J. 1993 L 1993 L 253/1, most recently amended by Reg. 75/98 (O.J. 1998 L 7/3)). See, generally, Gormley in Emiliou and O'Keeffe (eds.), *op. cit.* (see note 151, *supra*) 124 and in Vaughan (ed.) *Law of the European Communities Service* (London, loose-leaf since 1990) paras. 12.1–12.323.

217. See Gormley in Emiliou and O'Keeffe (eds.), *ibid.*

national commercial policies which could not immediately be completely removed on 1 January 1970 or on the day following accession to the Community or the Union (as the case may be), even if this was only because a number of national trade agreements remain in force or national trade restrictions continue to remain. As has been noted above, a specific authorization from the Community is necessary for such differentiation. As will become apparent below, as far as autonomous commercial policy measures were concerned, such an authorization for far-reaching maintenance of national quantitative restrictions was until recently built into the common system for imports. Since the completion of the internal market at the end of 1992 and also in conjunction with the conclusion of the Uruguay Round this has drastically diminished. As far as conventional commercial policy is concerned, there is a duo of decisions addressed to the Member States which permit them to maintain national trade agreements and to conclude national cooperation agreements, provided that these satisfy certain conditions. These are discussed below.

Thus in the present situation, after the completion of the internal market, it is not entirely excluded that disparities between the Member States in the field of commercial policy continue to exist. That is the reason why Article 115 EC was not removed from the EC Treaty by the TEU. That provision enables the Commission, if there are such disparities which lead to economic difficulties, to make recommendations 'as to the methods for the requisite cooperation between Member States' or to authorize Member States to take the necessary protective measures. When the Community still had effective internal frontiers, these were continually restrictions on the free transit of goods from third countries placed in free circulation in a Member State.[218] Given that systematic border controls on the movement of goods within the Community have now been abolished, the Commission can do little else than authorize a Member States still to refuse goods having a certain origin when they carry out internal fiscal or other controls.[219] In the years leading up to 1992 the Commission systematically discouraged use of Article 115, with the result that the number of applications for authorizations and decisions granting them fell dramatically.[220] Since the coming into force of the TEU this provision has effectively become redundant.

Contrary to what has been briefly set out above, the Court's case-law confirms that the degree of centralization and uniformity of the common

218. The goods were thus denied Community treatment.
219. The appropriate decisions, addressed to an individual Member State are not published, but they do contain a prohibition on border controls.
220. At the height of the popularity of Art. 115, in 1980, there were 356 applications (of which 269 related to the textiles sector), and the Commission granted 222 authorizations. In 1990 these figures had sunk to 112 applications, with 69 in the textile sector, and 79 authorizations. In 1992 19 applications were submitted, of which eight were in the textile sector; eight applications were granted.

commercial policy is not a matter left to the complete discretion of the Council. In Opinion 1/75 *OECD Understanding on a local cost standard for export credits*[221] the Court indicated that the common commercial policy was conceived in Article 113 'in the context of the operation of the Common Market, for the defence of the common interests of the Community within which the particular interests of the Member States must endeavour to adapt to each other.' This means *inter alia* that it is not permitted to promote national undertakings on export markets through excessive export credits, and that strict uniformity in that field has to be maintained.[222] Similarly, in Cases 37 and 38/73 *Sociaal Fonds voor de Diamantarbeiders v. NV Indiamex et al.*[223] the Court held that the definition of the uniform principles of the common commercial policy 'involves, as does the common customs tariff itself, the elimination of national disparities, whether in the field of taxation or of commerce, affecting trade with third countries.' The next step is thus that distortions of competition too, caused by ordinary market participants, are combated in international trade.

If the functioning of the common market is indeed decisive for the common commercial policy, then the question again arises, both before and, with still more force, after the completion of the internal market, of the scope of the latter. A common market, and also an internal market, embrace more than merely a customs union, and if they are decisive for the commercial policy of the Community this must reach further than only the external aspects of movement of goods, and should embrace the external aspects of all facets of the common market, albeit that the TEU has introduced specific provisions dealing with the external aspects of capital movements and of monetary policy. As was noted in section 3.1, the Court was unwilling to go so far in Opinion 1/94 *WTO – GATS and TRIPs*[224] This problem has now been addressed to some extent by the Member States.[225]

The external aspects of the customs union were always the most simple to visualize, as the customs union has a naturally uniform external barrier: the Common Customs Tariff. This simply had to be complemented by uniform quantitative barriers and common commercial policy instruments. Most other aspects of the internal market lack such an obvious uniform external barrier. Of these other aspects, the free movement of persons has an obvious external barrier in theory: the external frontier of the

---

221. [1975] ECR 1355 at 1363–1364.
222. *Ibid.* at 1364.
223. [1973] ECR 1606 at 1623.
224. [1994] ECR I-5267, [1995] 1 CMLR 205.
225. Thus the Treaty of Amsterdam, not yet in force, adds a new Art. 113(5) EC, which will permit the Council to extend the application of Art. 113(1)–(4) to embrace international negotiations and agreements on services and intellectual property insofar as they are not covered by those provisions.

Community, where all control of persons should take place according to uniform principles. But the access of persons from third countries is such a sensitive matter that merely the first steps have been ventured, and that has mostly been in an intergovernmental context.[226] As far as the external aspects of freedom of establishment within the Community is concerned, there has always been the so-called gap in Article 58 EC: thus each Member State could independently determine which companies were established in accordance with its own law, even if they were daughter companies of non-Community undertakings. Thus the question whether undertakings linked to third countries may benefit from the freedom of establishment was and indeed still is a question of the national law of the individual Member States and of their bilateral investment treaties with third countries.[227] There is virtually no Community law on the right of establishment in relation to third countries. In relation to international trade in services, where the external barriers are in part based on those in the two last-mentioned areas, establishment of companies and access for personal providers of services, it is even more difficult to draw a clear border. A first step in this direction was taken with the introduction of reciprocity clauses, such as those in the Second Banking Directive: the advantages of the directive are granted to third country banks only if Community banks enjoy comparable access to the market for banking services in the third country concerned.[228] Virtually identical provisions are to be found in two directives in the insurance field[229] and in Directive 94/

226. See the Agreement on the Gradual Abolition of Controls at the Common Frontiers (Schengen, 14 June 1985, HL Paper 90 (1989) *1992: Border Controls of people*, HL Select Committee on the European Communities, Session 1988–89, 22nd Report, 35. See further, the Convention implementing the Schengen Agreement (Schengen, 19 June 1990 (1991) CLE 33, (1991) 30 ILM 73). As to these, see O'Keeffe (1992) 18 ELRev. 3 and (1995) 20 ELRev. 20, and Heilbronner and Thiery (1997) 34 CMLRev. 957. See also Plender in Vaughan (ed.), *op. cit.* (see note 216, *supra*) Part 15, paras. 4 and 381 *et seq.*, and Bieber and Monar (eds.), *Justice and Home Affairs in the European Union* (Brussels, 1995). The Schengen *acquis* will be integrated into the framework of the European Union if the Treaty of Amsterdam enters into force. The Dublin Convention on Asylum Matters (Dublin, 15 June 1990, O.J. 1997 C 254/1) entered into force on 1 September 1997. The proposed External Frontiers Convention (see COM (93) 684 Final) has not yet been adopted.

227. In the GATS the Community attempted to give effect to certain criteria from the liberalization programme of late 1961 (the General Programme for the abolition of restrictions on freedom of establishment (O.J. English Special Edition (2nd Series) IX, p. 7)) *inter alia* through the definition of the concept of a 'juridical person of another Member' which is linked to being 'engaged in substantive business operations in the territory of that Member State or of any other Member,' GATS, Art. XXVIII(m). Work is taking place within OECD on the preparation of a multilateral investment agreement.

228. Dir. 89/646 (O.J. 1989 L 386/1), see Art. 9 in particular.

229. See Dirs. 90/618 (O.J. 1990 L 330/44) and 90/619 (O.J. 1990 L 330/50), see in particular Arts. 4 (adding a new Art. 29(b) to Dir. 73/329 (O.J. 1973 L 228/3, most recently amended by Dir. 95/26 (O.J. 1995 L 168/7)) and Art. 32(b), respectively.

22 on the conditions for granting and using authorizations for the prospection, exploration and production of hydrocarbons.[230] So far these are the only examples of autonomous measures in the field of commercial policy in the services sector, although a similar reciprocity provision was included in Directive 93/38 on procurement procedures of the utilities.[231] Autonomous commercial policy in the field of services is thus clearly still in its infancy, thus the main emphasis in the following discussion is placed on commercial policy measures governing trade in goods.[232]

3.3 Commercial policy arrangements

3.3.1   Autonomous commercial policy; regulation of imports and exports

As a result of the completion of the single internal market within the Community on 1 January 1993, and as a result of the negotiations in the Uruguay Round, the Community's import regime has been considerably simplified. The transformation in Central and Eastern Europe, which saw numerous countries depart from communist planned economies, also contributed to a more liberal regime for imports into the Community. In principle imports into the Community are wholly free from quantitative restrictions. Although in the early Eighties Community legislation still permitted numerous Member States to restrict the quantity of various imports from certain third countries, including certain market economy countries, and although until recently trade with state trading countries was largely a question of quota restrictions, the general import regime for industrial products as a whole no longer contains quantitative restrictions.[233] Even for the few countries which still have not introduced a complete market economy, there are almost no more restrictions: only in the case of China is the import of certain sensitive products permanently

---

230. O.J. 1994 L 164/3, see in particular Art. 8.
231. O.J. 1993 L 199/84, Art. 36. See Dec. 95/215 (O.J. 1995 L 134/25) on the Agreement with the United States.
232. Generally on trade in services, with particular emphasis on GATS, see the various contributions in Bourgeois *et al.* (eds.), *The Uruguay Round Results* (Brussels, 1995) 361 *et seq.*; Kampf (1995) Int. TLR 157; Kennedy (1995) Int. TLR 11; Metzger, *GATS and the European Union: Free Trade in Banking* (Brussels, 1995), and Weiss (1994) 32 CMLRev. 1177. It should be noted that the reciprocity provisions in the banking and insurance directives also served as bargaining counters in the negotiations on financial services in the framework of the WTO. Now that these negotiations have resulted in agreement, see Dec. 96/412 (O.J. 1996 L 167/23), their remaining usefulness is limited.
233. Reg. 3285/94 (O.J. 1994 L 349/53, most recently amended by Reg. 2315/96 (O.J. 1996 L 314/1)), Art. 1(2). *Cf.* previously, Reg. 288/82 (O.J. 1982 L 35/1), Annex I. The latter regulation was repealed by Reg. 518/94 (O.J. 1994 L 67/77), which was then in turn repealed by Reg. 3285/94.

subject to quotas or placed under supervision.[234] In contrast, textile products are still subject to far-reaching quantitative restrictions. In addition to the continuing regulation of trade in these products through the Multi-Fibre Textile Arrangement,[235] which was concluded in the framework of the GATT, and on the basis of which the Community concluded a large number of bilateral agreements, certain textile products,[236] particularly those originating from the countries of the Commonwealth of Independent States and other State trading countries, are subject to autonomous quantitative restrictions To the extent to which such restrictions are maintained in relation to market economy countries, they are suspended until the goods covered by the Multi-Fibre Arrangement have been integrated into the normal GATT system. This takes place through the Agreement on Textiles and Clothing (ATC), which is part of the Uruguay Round Final Act and provides for a phased integration over 10 years from the date of establishment of the WTO (1 January 1995) in three stages, so that full integration of the textiles and clothing sectors into the normal GATT system will occur by 1 January 2005 at the earliest. The maintenance in the meantime of quotas is clearly partly symbolic, as a negotiating matter.[237] Moreover, only these restrictions not covered by the ATC can still be regarded as being in fact a coordinated system of national protection measures;[238] otherwise such quantitative restrictions as remain are fixed at Community level, which represents an important step forward.

Long before this uniformization of external policy in relation to quantitative restrictions, the Common Customs Tariff was established, much earlier than envisaged in the EC Treaty, on 1 July 1968. Furthermore, harmonized or common rules have been adopted in the field of customs legislation, and the myriad instruments have now been codified in the Community Customs Code, the coming into force of which paralleled the completion of the Community's internal market.[239]

234. See Reg. 519/94 (O.J. 1994 L 67/89, Annexes II and III, most recently amended by Reg. 1138/98 (O.J. 1998 L 59/1).
235. Geneva, 20 December 1973 (Cmnd. 6205; O.J. 1974 L 118/2) as adapted subsequently, see Perlow (1981) Am.J.Int'l. L. 93 and in Van Dijk (ed.), *Supervisory Mechanisms in International Economic Organization in the perspective of a restructuring of the International Economic Order* (Deventer, 1984); Ying-Pik Choi *et al.*, *The Multi-Fibre Arrangement in Theory and Practice* (London, 1985), and Blokker, *International Regulation of World Trade in Textiles* (Dordrecht, 1989).
236. See Dec. 92/625 (O.J. 1995 L 410/1) (the agreements are also in that issue of the O.J.), which applied until the end of 1997 (changes were made in 1994, see Dec. 94/216 (O.J. 1994 L 110/1)).
237. The Community's common rules for imports of certain textile products from third countries are set out in Reg. 3030/93 (O.J. 1993 L 275/1), most recently amended by Reg. 1053/98 (O.J. 1998 L 151/10).
238. See Timmermans in Völker (ed.), *Protectionism and the European Community* (2nd ed., Deventer, 1987) 167, referring to an earlier regime.
239. See Chapter VII, section 2.7, *ante*.

The Community's export regime has long been based on the principle that exports to third countries are unrestricted. This was already ensured in Regulation 2603/69.[240] Until recently it was possible for the Member States to maintain unilateral export restrictions for a small number of products, including petroleum, but that possibility has now lapsed.[241]

However, the common rules on exports do contain a number of exceptions which are also to be found in Article XX GATT. First, there is the exception on the ground of a 'critical shortage' of certain products in the Community: in such cases quantitative restrictions may be introduced. At the moment no use is being made of this provision, which is an exception which has to be invoked at the Community level. There are also exceptions which do not merely run parallel to Article XX GATT but also to Articles 36 and 224 EC, in that they may be unilaterally invoked by the Member States.[242] The common export regime and also the various common regimes for imports contain a national safeguard measures clause which permits each of the Member States to apply quantitative restrictions or supervisory measures justified on the grounds of public policy, public morality, public security; the health and life of humans, animals and plants; the protection of national treasures possessing artistic, historic or archaeological value; or the protection of industrial and commercial property. Furthermore, Member States may also impose restrictions on imports or exports in connection with special formalities for the export of currency or which, in conformity with the EC Treaty, are introduced on the ground of international agreements.[243] This latter category embraces in particular matters such as trade restrictions applying to certain endangered species and hazardous waste.

It is clear that the general regulations on the import and export regimes play only a supplementary role as far as imports and exports of agricultural products are concerned. They are governed in the first instance by the relevant provisions of the rules for the common organization of the agricultural markets involved.[244] The rules for processed agricultural products also establish a special regime for those products. For both types of product this system has been based on a so-called Community

---

240. O.J. English Special Edition 1969 (II), p. 590, most recently amended by Reg. 3918/91 (O.J. 1991 L 372/31). As to the export of dual-use goods, see sesction 3.3.5 *post.*

241. See Reg. 3918/91, *ibid.* The Member States retain only the limited possibilities in the framework of the International Energy Agency's sharing system to adopt restrictive measures for exports.

242. See Case C-124/95 *R. v. H.M. Treasury et al., ex parte Centro-Com Srl* [1997] ECR I-81.

243. Reg. 3285/94 (see note 230, *supra*), Art. 24. See, under the predecessor regime, Case C-124/95 *R. v. H.M. Treasury et al., ex parte Centro-Com Srl* [1997] ECR I-81.

244. See Reg. 3285/94, *ibid.*, Art. 25.

preference for products in the common market, the subsidized export of Community surpluses, and specific protective measures against imports from third countries, provided certain conditions are fulfilled.[245] Given the requirements of the GATT Uruguay Round, the latter types of measures have been adapted to the new climate;[246] the system of Community preference has long been difficult to reconcile with GATT requirements. The special regime which the Community has established for bananas[247] has been the subject of, to say the least, considerable controversy,[248] and has now been condemned within the WTO dispute settlement mechanism.[249]

In relation to the manner in which the Member States promote exports to third countries relatively little has been done in the way of introducing uniform principles in the sense of Article 113 EC. Pure

245. See Chapter X, section 2.1, *ante.*

246. By Reg. 3290/94 (O.J. 1994 L 349/105, most recently amended by Reg. 1340/98 (O.J. 1998 L 84/1)).

247. As to imports, see Reg. 2947/94 (O.J. 1994 L 310/62, most recently amended by Reg. 1869/95 (O.J. 1995 L 179/38)). As to the common organization, see Reg. 404/93 (O.J. 1993 L 47/1, most recently amended by Reg. 3290/94 (O.J. 1994 L 349/105, most recently amended by Reg. 1161/97 (O.J. 1997 L 169/1)). See also Dec. 94/800 (O.J. 1994 L 336/1) partially annulled in Case C-122/95 *Germany v. Council* [1998] ECR I-973 and Cases C-364 and 365/95 *T. Port GmbH & Co. v. Hauptzollamt Hamburg-Jonas* [1998] ECR I-1023.

248. See *e.g.* Everling (1996) 33 CMLRev. 401; Kuschel (1995) EuZW 689 and (1996) EuZW 645; Weber (1997) EuZW 165; Petersmann (1997) EuZW 325, and Huber (1997) EuZW 517. The banana litigation has been enormous, see Case C-280/93 *Germany v. Council* [1994] ECR I-4973; Case C-389/93 *Firma Anton Dürbeck GmbH v. Bundesamt für Ernährung und Forstwirtschaft* [1995] ECR I-1509; Case C-478/93 *The Netherlands v. Commission* [1995] ECR I-3081; Case C-465/93 *Atlanta Fruchthandelsgesellschaft mbH et al. (I) v. Bundesamt für Ernährung und Forstwirtschaft* [1995] ECR I-3761; Case C-466/93 *Atlanta Fruchthandelsgesellschaft mbH et al. (II) v. Bundesamt für Ernährung und Forstwirtschaft* [1995] ECR I-3799; Case C-68/95 *T. Port GmbH & Co. KG v. Bundesanstalt für Landwirtschaft und Ernährung* [1996] ECR I-6065; Cases C-9, 23 and 156/95 *Belgium et al. v. Commission* [1997] ECR I-645; Cases C-71, 155 and 271/95 *Belgium v. Council* [1997] ECR I-687; Case T-571/93 *Lefebvre Fères et Soeurs et al. v. Commission* [1995] ECR II-2379; Case T-18/95 *Atlanta Handelsgesellschaft Harder & Co. GmbH et al. v. Commission* [1996] ECR II-1669; Case T-521/93 *Atlanta AG et al. v. European Community* [1996] ECR II-1707; Case T-70/94 *Comafrica SpA et al. v. Commission* [1996] ECR II-1741; Case T-6/97 R *Comafrica SpA et al. v. Commission* [1997] ECR II-291; Case T-79/96 R *Camar Srl v. Commission* [1997] ECR II-403; Case T-47/95 *Terres rouges consultant SA et al. v. Commission* [1997] ECR II-481; and Case C-369/95 *Somalfruit SpA et al. v. Ministero delle Finanze et al.* [1977] ECR I-6619. In Opinion 3/94 *WTO – Framework Agreement on Bananas* [1995] ECR I-4577 the Court declined to pronounce, on the basis that the agreement had already entered into force. See also Case C-257/93 *Van Parijs et al. v. Council* [1993] ECR I-3335 and Case C-276/93 *Chiquita Banana Company BV et al. v. Council* [1993] ECR I-3345.

249. See WTO Appellate Body Report (Bananas) WT/DS27/AB/R of 9 September 1997, adopted on 25 September 1997. See COM (98) 5 Final (O.J. 1998 C 108/91).

export promotion, in the sense of propaganda for national products is probably still permissible for the Member States.[250] But once propaganda for a Member State's own products develops into their substantive promotion, the realm of distortion of competition between Community undertakings is reached, and, in accordance with Article 112 EC the national aid measures for exports to third countries[251] should be harmonized. It also cannot be excluded that the competitive relationships within the Community are distorted by national aids to exports, and thus Articles 92–94 EC may be brought into play.[252] There has been pretty well no harmonization under Article 112(1) EC.[253] Myriad proposals from the Commission have been resoundingly buried by the Council. In the closely related field of export credits, guarantees and insurance,[254] a group of officials is entrusted with the co-ordination of Member States' policies in these matters and an information and consultation procedure is prescribed.[255] The Council has also adopted a number of directives in this

250. In the United States, where competence in relation to foreign commerce is a federal matter, the states are permitted to promote their exports in this manner. Thus *e.g.* Georgia and Michigan have their own offices abroad.

251. The linking of bilateral (development) aid to purchases being made in the donor Member State falls under this heading, but the Commission's initiative to disassociate aid at Community level was not discussed by the Council, see SEC (91) 2273. Member States were not interested in giving aid which might fund purchases from another Member State. The following is an example of how such a problem might arise. A Ghanaian Health Authority decides to buy medicines from a British company, because this is required by the U.K. government as a condition of development aid. An Irish company which has supplied the Ghanaians for years thus loses the contract. It could not even continue to supply via a British intermediary, as the goods had to be made in the U.K. *Quaere* whether such a measure also affects trade between Member States and is prohibited under Art. 30 EC as it prevents an Irish manufacturer selling to a British wholesaler (albeit for resale (or supply) outside the Community). See, in relation to agricultural products, Case 177/78 *Pigs and Bacon Commission v. McCarren and Co. Ltd.* [1979] ECR 2161 at 2189 (additional export bonuses).

252. Case C-142/87 *Belgium v. Commission* [1990] ECR I-959 at 1013. This is an alternative approach to the question raised in note 51, *supra.*

253. On 28 July 1969 the Council adopted for the first time a directive based on Arts. 112 and 92 EEC concerning the grant of aid to shipbuilding to correct distortions of competition on the international market. This has since been replaced by directives based on Arts. 113 and 92 EC. See, most recently, the 7th directive on aid to shipbuilding, Dir. 90/684 (O.J. 1990 L 380/27 most recently amended by Dir. 94/73 (O.J. 1994 L 351/10)) which is due to be replaced on the entry into force of the OECD Agreement on aid to shipbuilding by Reg. 3094/95 (O.J. 1995 L 332/1), the entry into force of which has been postponed until then (and at the latest 31 December 1998) by Reg. 2600/97 (O.J. 1997 L 351/18). See also Reg. 1013/97 (O.J. 1997 L 148/1).

254. These instruments too may fall within Arts. 92–94 EC, see Case C-63/89 *Les Assurances du crédit et al. v. Council et al.* [1991] ECR I-1799 at 1849.

255. See the decision of 27 September 1960 setting up a Policy Co-ordination Group on Credit Insurance, Credit Guarantees and Financial Credit (O.J. English Special

field[256] although it has not yet proved possible to bring them into force in the absence of agreement on a common premium system. The Council did adopt by a decision on 4 April 1978 on behalf of the Community the OECD consensus reached as an Arrangement on Guidelines for Officially Supported Export Credits.[257] The Commission negotiated the adoption of these Guidelines on the basis of the Community's exclusive competence recognized by the Court's Opinion 1/75.[258] Financial instruments relating to the development of commercial traffic with particular countries or territories remain in the hands of the Member States.[259] This can only tally with the Community's exclusive competence in the field of export policy as long as the rules governing the use of such instruments provide for 'a strict uniformity of credit conditions granted to undertakings in the Community whatever their nationality' as required by the Court in Opinion 1/75.[260] It can be seriously doubted whether they do in fact satisfy this condition.

3.3.2   *Autonomous commercial policy; safeguard measures*

The basic regulation on the common rules regime for imports[261] provides for the possibility of keeping a weather eye on the importation of certain products which has been liberalized in the Community context. There are provisions concerning an information and consultation procedure, which forms the first step towards the adoption of surveillance or safeguard measures. In the context of this procedure the Member States may provide information to the Commission and request that such measures be adopted. Such a request is discussed in the Advisory Committee, which consists of representatives of the Member States, and is chaired by a representative of the Commission. If the discussion in the committee gives

---

Edition 1959–62, p. 67) and Dec. 73/391 (O.J. 1973 L 346/1, most recently amended by Dec. 76/641 (O.J. 1976 L 223/25)).

256. See now Dir. 98/29 (O.J. 1998 L 148/22). See also Dir. 71/86 (O.J. English Special Edition 1971 (I), p. 71). See, further Dec. 82/854 (O.J. 1982 L 357/20) on export guarantees and finance for export for certain sub-contracts with parties in other Member States or in non-member countries and Dir. 84/568 (O.J. 1984 L 314/24) on certain insured transactions in co-operation between export credit insurance organizations.

257. The original decision does not seem to have been published in the O.J., although the revised version of the OECD Consensus was reflected in the changes made by Dec. 93/112 (O.J. 1993 L 44/1); the Consensus in its current form is reflected in the most recently amendments of the 1978 decision (as so revised) by Dec. 97/173 (O.J. 1997 L 69/19). The Consensus now applies for an indefinite period.

258. [1975] ECR 1355, [1976] 1 CMLR 85.

259. A proposal made in 1976 to establish a European Export Bank was withdrawn in 1981.

260. [1975] ECR 1355 at 1364.

261. Reg. 3285/94 (O.J. 1994 L 349/53, most recently amended by Reg. 2315/96 (O.J. 1996 L 314/1)).

cause, and if the Commission is of opinion that there is sufficient evidence, a Community investigation procedure may be initiated. The Commission is charged with undertaking this investigation, and is bound to follow the rules laid down in Regulation 3285/94.[262] These rules guarantee a certain transparency of the investigation and permit the Commission to gather information and to undertake verification inspections on the premises of the parties concerned. Interested parties (primarily exporters, importers and producers) may have access to the information collected and can be heard by the Commission. The investigation should be aimed at the importation of the products concerned, particularly looking at the quantities imported (the circumstances under which, and the prices at which goods are imported) and any damage which there may be for Community industry. Within nine months at the most from the opening of the investigation, the Commission has to decide whether Community surveillance measures or safeguard measures should be adopted, or whether the file should be closed without further action. Only in exceptional cases may this deadline be extended by up to two months at the most.[263]

The measures which the Commission may decide to adopt may take one of two forms: Community retrospective surveillance or Community prior surveillance. The latter form of supervisory measures is clearly more restrictive, requiring the presentation of an import document in order to place the goods in free circulation within a Member State, even though the document is to be endorsed free of charge and within five days of request by the importer. In certain cases the Commission may decide to impose regional surveillance measures, which are limited to one or two regions (often Member States) of the Community. The Commission adopts Community and regional surveillance measures according to a special procedure for safeguard measures, laid down in the Comitology decision.[264] This procedure enables a Member State to bring a Commission decision before the Council, which may confirm, amend or revoke the decision, acting by a qualified majority. If the Council takes no decision within three months of the matter being laid before it, the Commission's decision is deemed to be revoked.[265] Such surveillance measures may only be adopted if the developments on the market for a product originating in a third country cause or threaten to cause serious injury to Community producers of like or directly competing products *and* the interests of the Community require such action to be taken. This last condition permits the Commission a certain freedom of discretion, but there is scarcely a

---

262. *Ibid.*
263. *Ibid.*, Title III. The conditions under which safeguard measures may be adopted, and the mechanism for their adoption are based on the GATT Agreement on Safeguards (O.J. 1994 L 336/184).
264. *Ibid.*, Title IV, especially Arts. 14(5) and (6); Dec. 87/373 (O.J. 1987 L 197/33), Art. 3.
265. See *e.g.* Reg. 2914/95 (O.J. 1995 L 305/23, rectified by Reg. 494/96 (O.J. 1996 L 65/4)), confirmed by Dec. 96/208 (O.J. 1996 L 68/29).

sufficiently significant number of instances in which the power to impose measures has been used under the present instrument to permit a detailed evaluation of the way in which this discretion is exercised.[266]

Safeguard measures may be adopted by the Commission for protection of the interests of the Community if a product is imported into the Community in such increased quantities and/or[267] under such conditions that Community producers of like or directly competing products are serious injured or if such serious injury threatens to occur. Such measures are adopted by the Commission according to the safeguard measures procedure outlined above, and may be of two types: the period of validity of import documents to be endorsed may be limited after the entry into force of a prior Community surveillance measure, and the import rules for the product in question may be altered by making its release for free circulation conditional on production of an import authorization, the granting of which is governed by such provisions and subject to such limits as the Commission lays down. The measures may be of a Community or regional nature. In addition, the Council may, on a proposal from the Commission, decide by a qualified majority to adopt appropriate safeguard measures and measures to allow the exercise of international rights (such as the right of retaliation flowing from certain WTO procedures) or the fulfilment of international obligations of the Community or its Member States, particularly those relating to trade in commodities.[268]

In the regulation on common rules for imports from State trading countries,[269] the conditions for the instituting surveillance measures and for the application of safeguard measures are less stringently formulated. The countries to which that regulation applies are not yet members of the WTO.[270] Community surveillance may be instituted simply whenever the

266. The term 'Community interests' is a major discretionary element (which is scarcely capable of detailed judicial review as such, in the absence of clear factual errors of assessment). Under the predecessor regime the question of Community interests was extensively discussed in Reg. 1830/84 (O.J. 1984 L 172/1) *Quartz Watches*, confirming Reg. 1087/84 (O.J. 1984 L 106/31).
267. The text of Reg. 3285/94, Art. 16(1) is largely based on Art. XIX GATT, which makes it clear that both these conditions have to be satisfied; see also Art. 16(2) of the regulation. Measures against other WTO members may only be taken if both conditions are satisfied; see Art. XIX (1) GATT. As to the GATT Agreement on Safeguards, see O.J. 1994 L 336/184.
268. See Reg. 3285/94, Arts. 17 and 23. See, generally, Brakeland and Turner (1997) RMC 454 and literature cited there.
269. Reg. 519/94 (O.J. 1994 L 67/89, most recently amended by Reg. 1138/98 (O.J. 1998 L 59/1)). Special quantitative quotas are established (and from time to time revised) in relation to imports of certain products from the People's Republic of China.
270. Although negotiations for WTO membership are under way, and for some, such as China, accession may not be too far in the future. In that case for such countries a safeguard clause conforming to the GATT would have to apply, unless a special safeguard clause is negotiated as part of their accession protocol to the GATT or now to the WTO, as was formerly the case with *inter alia* Poland.

interests of the Community so require.[271] The Commission may institute such Community or regional surveillance entirely independently, and, if necessary, may strengthen it by restricting the period of validity of import documents or subjecting their endorsement to certain conditions.[272] In the conditions for the adoption of safeguard measures there is a clear choice between importation under such conditions *or* in such increased quantities that the adoption of such measures is justified. The Commission is entitled to make release of the products concerned for free circulation subject to import authorizations, under such conditions and subject to such limits as it may determine, again under the scheme applicable to safeguard measures set out in accordance with the Comitology decision explained above. The Council may in such circumstances adopt appropriate measures by qualified majority, on a proposal from the Commission. The regulation is itself silent as to what 'appropriate measures' may be, and practical use of this provision is scarcely frequent as yet. Regional surveillance or safeguard measures are probably possible under this regulation as well.[273]

In the framework of the common rules for imports of textile products, surveillance is pretty well permanent. The Member States have to provide the Commission with monthly reports of the quantities and origin of imports of textiles covered by Regulation 517/94,[274] and with annual information about the export of textile products.[275] In this manner the Commission can evaluate at any given moment whether a Community investigation procedure should be initiated; a Member State may also request that this occur. Such a procedure runs in a broadly similar manner to that provided for in the general rules on imports.[276]

In this investigation and in the adoption of any measures which may follow, the Commission is assisted by a committee. The investigation proceedings may be terminated without any measures, or it may lead to surveillance or safeguard measures. Again, supervision may be prior or retrospective in nature. The safeguard measures consist of the introduction of an authorization system, under which authorizations are granted under the conditions prescribed by the Commission and within the limits it establishes. In certain cases urgent measures or regional safeguards are possible. Again, measures against textile imports from non-market economy countries may be adopted under less stringent conditions than those applicable to imports from market economy countries. The surveillance or safeguard procedures are adopted according to various procedures. Normally the management committee procedure is used;[277] in

271. Reg. 519/94, Art. 9.
272. *Ibid.*, Art. 11.
273. *Ibid.* Arts. 15–17.
274. O.J. 1994 L 67/1, most recently amended by Reg. 1457 (O.J. 1997 L 199/6).
275. Reg. 517/94, *ibid.*, Art. 6(1) and (2).
276. *Cf.* Reg. 517/94, Arts. 8–10 with Reg. 3285/94 (see note 261, *supra*), Arts. 5–10.
277. Type II(a) in the Comitology decision (Dec. 87/373 (O.J. 1987 L 197/33)).

the case of urgent procedures this procedure is also followed, unless the Council can muster a simple majority against the decision if the committee has delivered a negative opinion or failed to deliver an opinion. In the case of normal safeguard measures the special procedure for safeguard measures is followed.

As has been noted above, the lion's share of import restrictions of textile products now take the form of Community (as opposed to national) measures; the management of these import restrictions is now also regulated at Community level. Thus the Member States inform the Commission of the quantities for which they have received applications for import authorizations; the authorizations are granted centrally by the Commission on a first-come, first-served basis.[278] An advanced data processing system has been set up in the Community for this purpose. The authorizations granted have a limited period of validity, and if they are not used within that period they must be returned to the Member State concerned, which returns them to the pool of available central authorizations. Thus, after the Court on grounds of principle had found against the division of quotas among Member States,[279] even in one of the most sensitive sectors of the economy, for which the Court had originally been prepared to countenance an exception it has proved possible to introduce a real Community system of quota management.

More generally, the management of quantitative quotas is governed by Regulation 520/94.[280] In addition to the first-come, first-served technique, two other methods of quota management are prescribed in this regulation, the method chosen depending on the circumstances. The method of allocation of quotas according to traditional trading patterns is used for quotas imposed as a result of safeguard measures adopted against imports from other WTO members. Within the GATT it had become customary that in such cases quotas would be established on the basis of the average trading patterns in the last three representative years, a custom which has been codified in the new Agreement on Safeguards.[281] The final method is division in relation to the quantities requested. This method is primarily applied in cases in which the quota will probably be quickly exhausted. In order to ensure that the quotas are in fact used up as much as possible, Regulation 520/94 permits a combination of methods to be used (limited period of validity of authorizations; return of unused authorizations, and return to the Community pool) so that unused authorizations may be reissued by the Commission.

278. Reg. 3030/93 (O.J. 1993 L 275/1, most recently amended by Reg. 1053/98 (O.J. 1998 L 151/10)), Art. 12.
279. Case 51/87 *Commission v. Council* [1988] ECR 5459 at 5479.
280. O.J. 1994 L 66/1, most recently amended by Reg. 138/96 (O.J. 1996 L 21/6).
281. *Cf.* Reg. 520/94, *ibid.*, Arts. 6–11 with the Agreement on Safeguards (O.J. 1994 L 336/184), Art. 5. The regulation also takes account of individual traditional importers, and not simply of traditional trading patterns as a whole.

Despite the increased communitarization of the surveillance and safeguards regimes in the Community, it remains possible to adopt regional measures, *viz.* measures limited to one Member State. This may in some cases probably be economically justified[282] and the Community was able to negotiate this right under the Agreement on Safeguards,[283] but it can be wondered whether this right makes sense and whether in practice it will now be very much used, given that it is nowadays so much more difficult to apply Article 115 EC (following the abolition of systematic controls on the movement of goods at the Community's internal borders with the result that it is effectively impossible to control the further destination of a product within the Community).

It should be noted, finally, that unlike in the case of the commercial policy instruments which are discussed below, there is no provision in the current version of the basic regulations on imports for individuals or Community industry to complain and thus persuade the Commission to initiate proceedings, although they may be heard if they can demonstrate an interest in the matter. This is partly due to the fact that safeguards remain within the realms of 'fair trade' (as opposed to unfair trading practices), and that any complaint can best be left as a matter for the decision of the authorities. The anti-dumping and anti-subsidies measures discussed in the next section are designed to combat unfair trading practices, and in such circumstances the initiative in the form of a complaint is best left in the hands of the industry concerned.

3.3.3 Anti-dumping duties and countervailing duties[284]

Dumping and subsidization are regarded as unfair trading practices because a company or a country does not, unlike in the case of safeguards, simply use its comparative advantage to export large quantities of products at low prices, but in fact artificially changes its comparative costs. In the case of subsidization this occurs through state subsidies; in the case of

282. *E.g.* measures to counter dumping affecting only a particular region of the Community, see Reg. 384/96 (O.J. 1996 L 56/1, most recently amended by Reg. 905/98 (O.J. 1998 L 128/18)), Art. 4(1)(b).
283. See the footnote to Art. 2 of that Agreement.
284. The literature on anti-dumping is extensive. The leading recent practitioner works are Khan *et al.*, *EC Anti-Dumping Trade Laws* (Chichester, 1997); Stanbrook and Bentley, *Dumping and Subsidies* (3rd ed., London, 1996); Van Bael and Bellis, *Anti-Dumping and other Trade Protection Laws of the EC* (3rd ed., Bicester, 1996), and Vermulst and Waer, *E.C. Anti-Dumping law and Practice* (London, 1996). See also Jackson and Vermulst (eds.), *Anti-Dumping law and Practice: A Comparative Study* (New York, 1990); Vander Scheuren (1996) 33 CMLRev. 271 and, in relation to recent practice involving China, see Coppieters (1997) SEW 272 and Case T-170/94 *Shanghai Bicycle Corporation (Group) v. Council* [1997] ECR II-1383. Among the older literature see Beseler and Williams. *Anti-Dumping and Anti-Subsidy Law* (London, 1986).

dumping this occurs because a company is prepared to export a product for a long period at a lower price than the sales price applicable on its domestic market, and sometimes even at a lower price than the cost price.[285] It will be evident that this is only possible if the products cannot flow back onto the company's domestic market, and that dumping assumes a certain division of markets, which in international trade is frequently present in the form of tariffs.[286]

With a view to the accelerated introduction of the common customs tariff, the Council already before the end of the transitional period supplemented it by adopting a regulation enabling the Community to defend itself against dumping and against the grant of export premiums and subsidies by third countries. Between 1968 and 1988 the measures were revised on a number of occasions until the adoption of Regulation 2423/88.[287] Initially after the revision of the GATT Anti-Dumping Code and the GATT Agreement on Subsidies and Countervailing Duties during the Uruguay Round negotiations the deadlines laid down in Regulation 2423/88 were tightened and the decision-making procedures were simplified.[288] Subsequently, in the implementing package after the conclusion of the Uruguay Round, the provisions relating to anti-dumping and anti-subsidies were split into two separate regulations: Regulation 3283/94 on anti-dumping[289] and Regulation 3284/94 on anti-subsidies.[290] However, the former was quickly amended twice and it became clear that it also contained significant errors. Accordingly, Regulation 3283/94 was repealed and replaced by the current provisions which are set out in Regulation 384/96.[291] Drafting problems also became apparent with Regulation 3284/94 which has now been repealed and replaced by the current provisions set out in Regulation 2026/97.[292] As is evident from the preamble to Regulations 384/96 and 2026/97, they are designed to give effect to the results of the Uruguay Round negotiations in the fields concerned. The obligations flowing from these agreements lay down strict requirements with which Community action in both areas must comply.[293]

285. For a certain period sales at less than the cost price or below marginal costs may constitute a legitimate market strategy. For this reason the basis of anti-dumping duties has been subject to criticism, see Deardorff in Jackson and Vermulst (eds.), *ibid.*, 23–39. See further, Marceau, *Anti-Dumping and Anti-Trust issues in Free Trade Areas* (Oxford, 1994).
286. Within a common market such as the EC dumping was thus only a problem during the transitional period, see Art. 91 EC.
287. O.J. 1988 L 209/1; for ECSC products, in similar terms, Dec. 2424/88 (O.J. 1988 L 209/18, corrigendum O.J. 1988 L 273/19).
288. By Regs. 521/94 (O.J. 1994 L 66/7) and 522/94 (O.J. 1994 L 66/10).
289. O.J. 1994 L 349/1.
290. O.J. 1994 L 349/22, amended by Reg. 1252/95 (O.J. 1995 L 122/2)..
291. O.J. 1996 L 56/1, most recently amended by Reg. 905/98 (O.J. 1998 L 128/18). The new regime for ECSC products is contained in Dec. 2277/96 (O.J. 1996 L 308/11).
292. O.J. 1997 L 288/1.
293. Thus Reg. 2423/88, Art. 13(10), the 'screwdriver' anti-circumvention provision, was

Anti-dumping duties may be applied 'to any dumped product whose release for free circulation in the Community causes injury.' [294] The concepts of dumping and injury are thus the crucial concepts in the regulation. Under Article 1(2) of Regulation 384/96 a product is considered to have been dumped 'if its export price to the Community is less than a comparable price for the like product, in the ordinary course of trade, as established for the exporting country.' This is called the 'normal value' of the product, and is normally 'based on the prices paid or payable, in the ordinary course of trade, by independent customers in the exporting country'.[295] The export price is 'the price actually paid or payable for the product when sold for export from the exporting country to the Community.'[296] The methods of calculating the export price and the normal value and the comparison between them are thus all set out in Article 2 of Regulation 384/96. The determination of normal value in particular is a complex question because sometimes there is no comparable price actually paid or payable in the ordinary course of domestic trade in the exporting country or the country of origin available (or the comparable price cannot be regarded as sufficiently normal). The regulation provides for methods of calculating the normal price in these circumstances. Special criteria are applied for imports from non-market economy countries as prices in such countries cannot be regarded as market prices.[297] A comparison between the normal value and the export price gives what is called the dumping margin, *i.e.* the amount by which the normal value

declared incompatible with Art. III GATT and unjustifiable under Art. XX(d) GATT by a GATT Panel which was adopted by the GATT Council on 16 May 1990 (*EEC Regulation on Imports of Parts and Components* BISD 37S 132), see Torremans (1993) 18 ELRev. 288 and Willemen (1993) SEW 187. However, this did not remove the issue of anti-circumvention from the Uruguay Round agenda, and although it proved impossible to reach agreement during the negotiations in that Round on the wording of a circumvention provision, the EC included such a provision in its anti-dumping regulation (Reg. 384/96, Art. 13). The screwdriver provision covers imports of parts (for assembly in the Community) as well as imports of finished products where circumvention of measures in force is taking place. The industrial policy aspects of encouraging assembly in the Community have been the subject of continuing controversy (as French efforts to keep out the Nissan Bluebird cars, assembled in the United Kingdom, demonstrated in the Eighties). In any national 'local content' agreements it must be made clear that the term local content means Community content and not merely national content, otherwise Art. 30 EC will be infringed. In any event, local content requirements for investments are contrary to GATT, Article III and the Agreement on Trade-Related Investment Measures, see the *FIRA* Panel report, BISD 30S 140.

294. Reg. 384/96, Art. 1(1).
295. *Ibid.*, Art. 2(1), 1st para. Art. 2 also explains *inter alia* in what circumstances alternative normal value tests may be used and when sales are considered not to be 'in the ordinary course of trade'.
296. *Ibid.*, Art. 2(8). The export price may in certain cases be a constructed price, see Art. 2(9).
297. *Ibid.*, Art. 2(7).

exceeds the export price.[298] Where dumping margins vary, weighted averages may be established.[299] Any anti-dumping duty is subject to a double proportionality limit: it may never be higher than the dumping margin,[300] 'but it should be less than that margin if such lesser duty would be adequate to remove the injury to Community industry.'[301] This latter element reflects a Community practice which is in sharp distinction to that followed in the United States. The second crucial concept, injury, means, in the terms of Article 3(1) of the regulation 'material injury to the Community industry, threat of material injury to the Community industry or material retardation of the establishment of such an industry.' This involves determination of both on the one hand the volume of the dumped imports and their effect on prices on the Community market for like products, and on the other hand the consequent impact of those imports on the Community industry.[302] In determining whether there is material injury various factors, no one or several of which can necessarily give decisive guidance, are examined: the volume of dumped imports, in particular whether there has been a significant increase, either in absolute terms or relative to production or consumption in the Community; the prices of dumped imports, in particular whether there has been a significant price undercutting as compared with the price of a like product in the Community; and the consequent impact on the industry concerned as indicated by actual or potential trends in the relevant economic factors such as production, utilization of capacity, stocks, sales, market share prices, (i.e. depression of prices or prevention of price increases which otherwise would have occurred), profits, return or investment, cash flow, employment and the magnitude of the actual margin of dumping. A determination of threat of injury may only be made where a particular situation is likely imminently to develop into actual injury. There has to be a causal link shown between the dumping or subsidy and the injury. Injuries caused by other factors, such as volume and prices of imports which are not sold at dumping prices, or contraction in demand or changes in the patterns of consumption, restrictive trade practices of or competition between third country producers and Community producers, technological developments, and the export performance and productivity of Community industry, which, individually or in combination, also adversely affect the Community industry concerned may not be attributed to the dumped imports. The term 'Community industry' is defined in Article 4(1) of the regulation as referring to 'the Community producers as a whole of the like products or those of them whose collective output of the products

---

298. *Ibid.*, Art. 2(12). As to the means of comparison, see Art. 2(10) and (11).
299. *Ibid.*, Art. 2(12).
300. *Ibid.*, Art. 7(2), provisional duties; Art. 9(4) final sentence, definitive duties.
301. *Ibid.*
302. *Ibid.*, Art. 3(2).

constitutes a major proportion of the total Community production of those products'.[303] Besides the presence of dumping and industry, it must also be in 'the Community interest' to impose anti-dumping duties; this concept is now extensively defined in Article 21 of Regulation 384/96.

Anti-dumping law as set out above might appear deceptively simple, but it is in reality extremely complex, as the establishment of the normal value and the export price is usually far from being a straightforward matter, particularly in the case of large multinationals. On their domestic markets they may distribute their products through subsidiaries rather than to independent buyers directly, and on their export markets this also often occurs. In non-market economy countries both domestic prices and costs are of relatively little value. In these circumstances recourse is had to a constructed normal value, which is calculated on the basis of production costs plus a reasonable amount for selling, general and administrative costs and for profits, or to an export price which is calculated on the basis of data for a third country, called the analogue country[304] or the export price is constructed on the basis of the sale to the first independent buyer.[305] Furthermore, in order to achieve a valid comparison at the same level of trade between the normal value and the export price, adjustments are often necessary for differences in physical characteristics of the product concerned between products sold on the domestic market and products sold to the Community market; import charges and indirect taxes; discounts, rebates and quantities; the level of trade (including any differences which may arise in OEM (Original Equipment Manufacturer) sales); transport, insurance, handling, loading and ancillary costs; packing; credit; after-sales costs; commissions; currency conversions, and other factors.[306] It will be apparent that in a comparison between two prices, of which frequently one and sometimes both are constructed, and in the calculation of which adjustments are so often necessary, the question easily arises as to how far there is actually dumping, and just how far the result of the investigation is in reality an artifice.

Both in the old Agreement on Subsidies and Countervailing Duties concluded as a result of the Tokyo Round, and in Regulation 2423/88 there was no definition of the concept of a subsidy. This brought about considerable conflict, particularly in relations between the Community and the United States. The current version of the Agreement on Subsidies and Countervailing Measures,[307] which forms part of the Uruguay Round

---

303. As to what constitutes a major proportion, see *ibid.*, Art. 5(4). As to the approach in the case of producers who are related to the exporters or importers, or who are themselves importers, see Art. 4(1)(a) and (2), and as to defining Community industry in relation to a regional problem, see Art. 4(1)(b) and (3).
304. Reg. 384/96, Art. 2(3).
305. *Ibid.*, Art. 2(9). Otherwise any reasonable basis may be used, *ibid.*
306. *Ibid.*, Art. 2(10), as amended by Reg. 2331/96 (O.J. 1996 L 317/1).
307. O.J. 1994 L 336/156.

package now embraces a large number of improvements. For this reason it was decided to adopt a separate Community regulation dealing with anti-subsidies measures, permitting countervailing duties to be imposed. Thus Articles 2 and 3 of Regulation 2026/97[308] largely reflect the definition of a subsidy in the new Agreement, and the conditions under which a subsidy is or is not countervailable. A subsidy is deemed to exist whenever there is 'a financial contribution[309] by a government'[310] in the country of origin or export[311] 'and a benefit is thereby conferred'[312] on the subsidized enterprise or body. Subsidies will only lead to the imposition of countervailing duties if they are specific.[313] Certain types of subsidies, such as those contingent upon export performance or on the use of domestic rather than imported goods are *ipso facto* specific.[314] On the other hand there is a so-called 'green list' of subsidies which, even though they are specific, are exempt from retaliation in the form of countervailing duties: subsidies for research and technological development up to certain levels and subject to stringent conditions; subsidies to disadvantaged regions under a general framework of regional development, again provided that stringent criteria are satisfied'; subsidies to promote adaptation of existing facilities to new environmental requirements imposed by law and/or regulations which result in greater constraints and financial burdens on firms, again provided that certain conditions are met, and certain types of domestic support to agriculture.[315] It will not go unnoticed that these very much take account of the system of Community assistance in particular, and also (particularly in relation to environment) of the needs of developing countries. By the

308. O.J. 1997 L 288/1.
309. This means not just obvious financial benefits such as direct transfers of revenue or non-collection of taxes or levies (tax holidays and the like), but also the provision of goods or services other than general infrastructure, or the purchase of goods, or financial contributions through intermediaries or funding mechanisms, see Reg. 2026/97, Art. 2(1)(a)(i)–(iv). It also embraces any form of income or price support within the meaning of GATT 1994, Art. XVI, Art. 2(1)(b).
310. Which means ' a government or any public body within the territory of the country of origin or export', see *ibid.*, Art. 1(3).
311. *Ibid.*, Art. 2(1).
312. *Ibid.*, Art. 2(2).
313. Ibid., Art. 3(1). Under Art. 3(2) a subsidy is specific to an enterprise or an industry or group thereof if the granting authority or the legislation under which it operates explicitly limits access to a subsidy to certain enterprises and there are no objective criteria or conditions governing the eligibility for and the amount of a subsidy. Objective criteria or conditions are those which are neutral and do not favour certain enterprises over others, and which are economic in nature and horizontal in application, such as the number of employees or the size of enterprise. There are provisions enabling the Community to look behind an appearance of non-specificity in certain circumstances. Regional subsidies are specific save as regards the setting of generally applicable tax rates by all levels of government entitled to do so, Art. 3(3).
314. *Ibid.*, Art. 3(4).
315. *Ibid.*, Art. 4(1) sets out the principle, Art. 4(2)–(4) and Annex IV the details.

end of 1997 the Community still seemed to be more sinned against (in its view) than sinning in terms of disputes on subsidies pending within the WTO. Regulation 2026/97 also contains detailed criteria as to the calculation of the amount of the countervailable subsidy.[316] The determination of injury, the description of the concept of the Community industry affected and the procedures leading to the imposition of countervailing duties follow largely those applicable in the anti-dumping field.[317] The considerations relating to material injury set out above in relation to anti-dumping apply equally in the case of efforts to countervail subsidies.

The Commission plays a central part in the procedures which can lead to anti-dumping duties and countervailing duties being imposed even though at many stages it is obliged to consult an advisory committee, consisting of representatives of each Member State with a representative of the Commission as its chairman.[318] Consultation may where necessary be carried out in writing. Only if the Commission proposes to close the proceeding in its consultation of the Advisory Committee does the result of the consultation have legal effects. If there are objections within the committee from one or more Member States to the proposal to close the proceeding the Commission must forthwith submit to the Council a report on the results of the consultation together with a proposal that the proceeding be terminated. If within one month the Council, acting by a qualified majority, has not decided otherwise the proceeding shall stand terminated. This procedure, laid down in Article 9(2) of Regulation 348/96 and Article 14(2) of Regulation 2026/97, also applies if there are objections in the committee to a proposal to accept an undertaking (as to price revision) offered during the course of an investigation.[319]

Anti-dumping or anti-subsidy proceedings may be opened *inter alia* on the basis of a complaint by an undertaking or an association of undertakings.[320] In this case the so-called sector or representative requirement applies: thus while any natural or legal person or any association not having legal personality may lodge a written complaint, it must be acting on behalf of a Community industry which considers itself injured or threatened by dumped or subsidized imports.[321] The complaint

---

316. *Ibid.*, Art. 5 sets out the principle, Arts. 6 and 7 set out the rules for calculation of the benefit. The terms of Arts. 6 and 7 are taken directly from Art.14 of the current GATT Agreement on Subsidies and Countervailing Measures.
317. For anti-dumping, Reg. 384/96, Arts. 5–21; for subsidies, Reg. 2026/97, Arts. 8–32.
318. *Ibid.*, Arts. 15 and 25 respectively.
319. *Ibid.*, Arts. 8(5) and 13(5) respectively.
320. *Ibid.*, Arts. 5(1) and 10(1) respectively. See, generally, the views of Bronckers, Ter Kuile and Steenbergen (1985) SEW 599 *et seq.*
321. *Ibid.* See Ter Kuile's critical observations on the representative requirement (1985) SEW 641 *et seq.* Clear thresholds now apply in the determination of whether a complaint is submitted by or on behalf of Community industry, see Reg. 384/96, Art. 5(4)

must contain sufficient evidence of the existence of dumping or
subsidization and the injury resulting therefrom; it may be submitted to
the Commission directly or to a Member State and in the latter case it is
forwarded to the Commission; copies of complaints received by the
Commission are sent to the Member States. If there is no complaint but a
Member State is in possession of sufficient evidence both of dumping or
subsidization and of injury resulting therefrom for a Community industry,
it must communicate that evidence to the Commission. If after
consultation it appears that there is sufficient evidence to justify initiating
a proceeding the Commission announces the initiation of proceedings in
the *Official Journal*, invites interested parties to make their views known
and advises the exporters and importers which it knows to be concerned as
well as representatives of the exporting country and the complainants.[322]
The Commission commences the investigation at Community level and
may request the Member States to carry out checks and inspections for it.
Investigations may also be carried out in third countries by the
Commission or, at its request, by Member States, provided that the firms
concerned given their consent and the government of the country
concerned has been officially notified and raises no objection.

  Interested parties have the right to provide the Commission with
information; to inspect on written request information which the Commission has collected, apart from internal documents and confidential
information; to be heard (again on written request), and on request to be
given an opportunity to meet the other parties to the proceedings.
Exporters and importers of the product subject to investigation and the
representatives of the country of origin have the right to be informed, if
they so request, of the essential facts and considerations on the basis of
which it is intended to recommend the imposition of provisional measures,
definitive duties or the termination of an investigation or proceedings
without the imposition of measures. These various rights are set out in
detail in Article 20 of Regulation 384/96 and Article 30 of Regulation
2026/97. The obligation to maintain the confidentiality of certain
information[323] must be interpreted in such a way that the rights which are
designed to ensure that interest parties can make their views known are
not deprived of their substance. Thus the Commission ought to make
every effort, as far as is compatible with the obligation not to disclose
business secrets, to provide interested parties with information relevant to
the defence of their interests.[324]

---

and Reg. 2026/97, Art. 10(8). See, generally, the contributions by Depayre and Wenig
in Micklitz and Reich (eds.), *Public Interest Litigation before European Courts* (Baden-
Baden, 1996) 209 and 213.
322. *Ibid.*, Arts. 5(9)–(11) and 10(13)–(15) respectively.
323. *Ibid.*, Arts. 19 and 29 respectively, see also Art. 214 EC.
324. Case 264/82 *Timex Corporation* v. *Council et al.* [1985] ECR 849 at 870 and 868.

If the (provisional) investigation shows that the conditions laid down for the imposition of duties are satisfied a provisional anti-dumping or countervailing duty is imposed by the Commission within nine months of the initiation of the proceedings.[325] These provisional measures (which in fact take the form of provision of a security, usually in the form of a bank guarantee) may be imposed only for a limited period.[326] If further investigation shows that the necessary conditions are satisfied, the Commission submits to the Council a proposal for a definitive anti-dumping or countervailing duty, having consulted the Advisory Committee. The Council now decides by a simple majority.[327]

However, it is not enough that the facts as finally established show that there is dumping or subsidization during the period under investigation and that injury is caused thereby; it is also required that 'the Community interest calls for intervention'.[328] In the balancing of interests, besides the interests of the complainant, consumers and importers and the like, more general considerations of a commercial policy and external relations policy nature may play a part. The decision to impose duties thus has a purely discretionary character and, more generally on the basis of these regulations the Commission 'has a very wide discretion to decide, in terms of the interests of the Community, any measures needed to deal with the situation which it has established.'[329]

If it becomes apparent after consultation of the Advisory Committee that protective measures are unnecessary or if the firms or governments causing the injury are prepared to enter into undertakings acceptable to the Commission under which the injury is eliminated the proceedings or

---

325. Reg. 384/96, Art. 7(1); Reg. 2026/97, Art. 12(1). The earliest that provisional measures may be imposed is 60 days from the initiation of the proceedings.
326. In the case of provisional anti-dumping duties for six months with the possibility of extension for three months, or for nine months (the extension or longer period requires in effect the consent of exporters representing a significant percentage of the trade involved), Reg. 384/96, Art. 7(7). In the case of provisional countervailing measures the maximum period of validity is four months, Reg. 2026/97, Art. 12(6).
327. *Ibid.*, Arts. 9(4) and 15(1) respectively. This is in fact quite remarkable, a substantive decision under a measure based on Art. 113 EC can be adopted by a less stringent majority than that provided for in the parent Treaty provision.
328. *Ibid.*, Arts. 7(1) and 12(1)(d) respectively (provisional measures); Arts. 9(4) and 15(6) respectively (definitive duties). As to the Community interest, see Arts. 21 and 31 respectively.
329. Case 19/82 *EEC Seed Crushers' and Oil Processors' Federation (Fediol) v.* Commission [1983] ECR 2913 at 2934–2935; see also Case 188/85 *EEC Seed Crushers' and Oil Processors' Federation (Fediol) v.* Commission [1988] ECR 4193 at 4231 (referring to a predecessor regime). Judicial review will verify whether or not the Commission or the Council, as the case may be, has observed the procedural guarantees granted to complainants or defendants by the Community provisions in question, has committed manifest errors in the assessment of the facts, has omitted to take into consideration any essential matters or has based the reasons for its decision on considerations amounting to a misuse of powers, see *e.g. ibid.* at 4223–4224.

the investigation respectively are terminated; the role of the Advisory Committee has been discussed above. The Commission informs any representatives of the country of origin or export and the parties known to be concerned and the termination is announced in appropriate form in the *Official Journal*.[330]

Anti-dumping and countervailing duties are imposed by means of a regulation.[331] The case-law shows that this does not prevent complainants from bringing an action before the Court.[332] In particular all producers or exporters mentioned in the regulation or involved in the investigation may challenge the measures taken. They are regarded as directly and individually concerned by the provisions of the regulation relating to the duties imposed on their products.[333] This is not the case for importers unless dumping is established on the basis of their price. Independent importers have virtually always been left to seek redress in the national courts.[334] In the present state of the case-law, complainants at least have a right of action if they feel that the specific rights, discussed above, which (now) Regulations 384/96 and 2026/97 confer upon them relating to the administrative proceeding have been infringed.[335] OEM (Original Equipment Manufacturer) buyers have been held to have standing,[336] and standing is also now available to consumer organizations in relation to inspection of the non-confidential file,[337] although the standing of the

330. See *e.g.* Dec. 97/634 (O.J. 1997 L 267/81) acceptance of undertakings in relation to anti-dumping and anti-subsidy proceedings concerning *Farmed Norwegian Atlantic Salmon*.

331. See *e.g.* Regs. 1890/97 (O.J. 1997 L 267/1) and 1891/97 (O.J. 1997 L 267/19) dealing respectively with anti-dumping and countervailing duties in relation to imports of *Farmed Norwegian Atlantic Salmon*.

332. The same applies for undertakings whose objections to dumping are central to the proceeding, see Case 264/82 *Timex Corporation v. Council et al.* [1985] ECR 849 at 866–867. See, generally, Chapter VI, section 1.3.1, *ante*.

333. Thus it appears that unlike, for example, in its judgment in Case 45/81 *Alexander Moksel Import–Export GmbH & Co. Handels KG v. Commission* [1982] ECR 1129 at 1144, the Court now accepts that a provision may be a measure of general application but yet as against a particular party have the character of an individual measure. *Cf.* VerLoren van Themaat, Adv. Gen. in Cases 239 and 275/82 *Allied Corporation et al. v. Commission* [1984] ECR 1005 at 1041. See also Case 258/84 *Nippon Seiko KK v. Council* [1987] ECR 1923 at 1961–1962.

334. *E.g.* Case 307/81 *Alusuisse Italia SpA v. Council et al.*[1982] ECR 3463 at 3472–3473. A spectacular exception to this can be seen in Case C-358/89 *Extramet Industrie SA v. Council* [1991] ECR I-2501 (in which an equitable rabbit appeared to be pulled out of the remedies hat; *cf.* the approach of Jacobs, Adv. Gen., *ibid.* at 2510 *et seq.*).

335. Case 19/82 *EEC Seed Crushers' and Oil Processors' Federation (Fediol) v. Commission* [1983] ECR 2913 at 2935–2936.

336. Cases 133 and 150/87 *Nashua Corporation v. Commission et al.* [1990] ECR I-719 at 772–773; Case 156/87 *Gestetner Holdings plc v. Council et al.* [1990] ECR I-781 at 833–834.

337. *Cf.* Reg. 384/96, Art. 6(7) and Reg. 2026/97, Art. 11(7). See earlier, Case C-170/89 *Bureau Européen des Unions de Consommateurs (BEUC) v. Commission* [1991] ECR I-5709 at 5742–5743.

latter in relation to other acts in this field is still open to question. Since the judgment in Case 19/82 *EEC Seed Crushers' and Oil Processors' Federation (Fediol) v. Commission*[338] it appears that in answering questions of admissibility the Court attaches much weight to the system of (now) Regulations 384/96 and 2026/97 in addition to the nature of the measures in connection with the second paragraph of Article 173 EC. Litigants sometimes allege that anti-dumping measures are incompatible with the GATT Anti-Dumping Code, and will undoubtedly do the same in respect of the present Agreement. This leads to the question whether that Agreement is directly effective, a question which so far the Court has always answered negatively in relation to the GATT itself.[339] In one judgment the Court was willing to examine the anti-dumping regulation in the light of the then GATT Anti-Dumping Code, in the context of reliance on the plea of illegality under Article 184 EC.[340] The Court did not on that occasion find that there was an incompatibility, but that although that judgment demonstrated how the Code could be indirectly brought into play, there is still no clear verdict on whether the Code was or the new Agreement is as such directly effective.[341]

Each year quite a substantial number of anti-dumping proceedings are opened, principally against imports from certain state trading countries, the United States and Japan. In many instance definitive or provisional anti-dumping duties are imposed, or undertakings are accepted under which the injurious effects are removed or reduced. The length of a proceeding usually stays well within the 'normal' period of one year of initiation, although an absolute limit of 15 months is now prescribed for in relation to anti-dumping investigations, and 13 months in respect of anti-subsidy investigations.[342] The manner in which anti-dumping procedures in particular are applied by the Community (and by the United States[343]) has been a matter of increasing controversy.[344] The application sometimes

---

338. [1983] ECR 2913 at 2935. See also Cases 239 and 275/82 *Allied Corporation et al. v. Commission* [1984] ECR 1005 at 1029–1030 and Case 264/82 *Timex Corporation v. Council et al.* [1985] ECR 849 at 865.

339. Cases 21–24/72 *International Fruit Company NV et al. v. Produktschap voor Groenten en Fruit* [1972] ECR 1219 at 1227–1228; Cases 267–269/81 *Amministrazione delle Finanze dello Stato v. Società Petrolifera Italiana SpA (SPI) et al.* [1983] ECR 801 at 830–831. See, generally, Eeckhout (1997) 34 CMLRev. 11 and Zonnekeyn (1996) Int. TLR 63.

340. Case C-69/89 *Nakajima All Precision Co. Ltd. v. Council* [1991] ECR I-2069 at 2178–2181.

341. See Meng in Beyerlin *et al.* (eds.), *Recht zwischen Umbruch und Bewahrung: Völkerrecht, Europarecht und Staatsrecht (Festschrift* for Bernhardt, Berlin, 1995) 1063.

342. Reg. 384/96, Art. 6(9); Reg. 2026/97, Art. 11(9).

343. As to recent changes, see Holec and Weigel (1997) Int.TLR 124.

344. See, for the Commission's practice since 1984, successive *General Reports*, and the Annual Report on Anti-Dumping and Anti-Subsidies Measures. See also Dielmann (1985) 22 CMLRev. 697 and the regular reports on 'Commercial Defense Actions and

simply could find no justification in the then GATT Anti-Dumping Code, and both the Community and the United States have had their proverbial knuckles rapped by various GATT panels. Some disputes relating to anti-dumping and countervailing duties have been the subject of proceedings within the new WTO dispute settlement mechanism (and prior to that being established, within the GATT dispute settlement mechanism).[345] But even the new Agreement resulting from the Uruguay Round has not been immune from criticism.[346] Now that the Court of First Instance has jurisdiction to hear appeals in anti-dumping cases (and in all appeals by private parties) the actions of the Council and the Commission are under much closer scrutiny than was often the case in the past.

3.3.4   The Trade Barriers Regulation[347]

On 20 September 1984 the so-called new commercial policy instrument was introduced,[348] designed to strengthen the Community's common commercial policy with regard in particular to protection against illicit commercial practices. The immediate cause for the adoption of this regulation was the deterioration in international trade relations with *inter alia* the unilateral measures adopted by the Reagan administration[349] on steel imports and against American firms working under American licences who wished to supply the Soviet Union with materials and services for the Siberian pipeline project. The European Council in June 1982 considered that it was of the highest importance to defend vigorously the legitimate interests of the Community in the appropriate bodies (in particular in the

other International Trade Developments in the European Communities' by Vermulst and Graafsma in EJIL. See further, Pescatore *et al.*, *Handbook of WTO/GATT Dispute Settlement* (Irvington-on-Hudson, loose-leaf, since 1991); Cameron and Campbell (eds.), *Dispute Resolution in the World Trade Organisation* (London, 1997) and the regular notes and comments in Int.TLR.

345. The WTO's internet home page (www.wto.org) gives a regularly updated overview of disputes and panel and appellate body reports. See also the GATT Panel Report on *EEC Regulation of Imports of Parts and Components* BISD 37S 132, and the unadopted Panel report on EC Anti-Dumping Duties on Audio Cassettes originating in Japan (Doc. ADP/136 & Corr., 1 June 1995)

346. See Horlick (1993) JWT 5, and Vermulst and Waer (1994) JWT 5.

347. See Stewart (1996) Int.TLR 121 and Bronkers (1997) Int.TLR 76. See also van Bael and Bellis, *op. cit.* (see note 284, *supra*) 469.

348. Reg. 2641/84 (O.J. 1984 L 252/1, amended by Reg. 522/94 (O.J. 1994 L 66/10)). See Steenbergen (1985) 22 CMLRev. 421; Denton (1988) 13 ELRev. 3; Bourgeois and Laurent (1985) RTDE 41; Bronckers (1985) SEW 599 and literature cited in note 12 thereto (619); Bourgeois in Hawk (ed.) *1989 Fordham Corporate Law Institute* (Irvington-on-Hudson, 1990) Ch. 6, and Arnold *et al.* (1988) JWTL 19. See also *EEG-Handelspolitiek* (Asser Institute Colloquium on European Law, 13th session, 1983, The Hague, 1984).

349. Under section 301 of the Trade Act 1974.

GATT) and to make sure that the Community, in managing trade policy acts with as much speed and efficiency as its trading partners.[350]

As a result of the Uruguay Round negotiations, the Community's measures are now contained in Regulation 3286/94,[351] which has become known as the Trade Barriers Regulation (TBR). The TBR is, like its predecessor, based on Article 113 EC and thus only covers rights in the field of trade in goods and trade in direct cross-frontier services.[352] It is intended to permit the exercise of the Community's rights, particularly within the WTO, and to this end two procedures are established. First, a procedure aimed at 'responding to obstacles to trade that have an effect on the market of the Community, with a view to removing the injury resulting therefrom';[353] secondly a procedure aimed at 'responding to obstacles to trade that have an effect on the market of a third country, with a view to removing the adverse trade effects resulting therefrom'.[354] Article 15 of the TBR provides that the regulation does not apply in cases covered by other existing rules in the common commercial policy field and that it is without prejudice to other measures which may be taken pursuant to Article 113 EC.

The TBR defines 'obstacles to trade' as 'any trade practice adopted or maintained by a third country in respect of which international trade rules establish a right of action.'[355] 'Such a right of action exists when international trade rules either prohibit a practice outright, or give another party affected by the practice a right to seek elimination of the effects of the practice in question.'[356] The consequences of such obstacles to trade may be felt directly on the Community market[357] or indirectly through the effects of such measures felt by Community undertakings on the market in third countries.[358] The new instrument in 1984 added a new dimension to the arsenal of the Community's commercial policy protective measures

350. Bull. EC 6–1982, point 1.5.2.
351. O.J. 1994 L 349/71, amended by Reg. 356/95 (O.J. 1995 L 41/3). The regulation does not apply to products falling within the scope of the ECSC Treaty, and there is no ECSC equivalent measure.
352. See Opinion 1/94 *WTO – GATS and TRIPs* [1994] ECR I-5267 at 5399 and 5401–5402. It is not impossible to interpret Opinion 1/94 so that for the TBR it is only important that the final Community retaliatory measures can be based on Art. 113 EC, and not that the interests to be protected are covered by that provision, see *ibid.* at 5406–5407. See, though, Reg. 3286/94, Art. 2(8).
353. Reg. 3286/94, Art. 1(a).
354. *Ibid.*, Art. 1(b). The concept of 'adverse trade effects' is defined in Art. 2(4); it comes from the GATT Agreement on Subsidies and Countervailing Measures, Art. 5. A 'right of action' is specified in relation to the 'non-violation' complaints under Art. XXIII(1)(b) GATT.
355. Reg. 3286/94, Art. 2(1).
356. *Ibid.* International trade agreements are the WTO Agreement itself (and the specific agreements reached in or subsequent to the conclusion of the Uruguay Round), and the bilateral or multilateral agreements to which the Community is a partner.
357. Reg. 3286/94, Art. 2(3).

which had hitherto only been aimed at avoiding or limiting injury caused by importation into the Community. Like its predecessor, the TBR deals with illicit commercial practices of States, not with unfair commercial practices of private undertakings, at least in so far as the latter practices are not to be imputed to states. The dispute settlement procedures of the appropriate trade agreements, particularly those of the WTO, must be respected.[359]

Proceedings may be initiated in one of three ways: a complaint may be submitted on behalf of Community industry as a result of injury within the Community;[360] or on behalf of Community enterprises, alleging the existence of adverse trade effects in a third country;[361] or a Member State may refer either type of matter to the Commission.[362] The Commission conducts the Community examination procedure,[363] and is assisted by a committee. The latter is purely consultative as regards the initiation of the procedure: if after consultation, it appears that an examination procedure is justified as a result of a complaint or referral under the three procedures outlined above, the Commission initiates the procedure. In essence the examination follows similar lines to those applicable in relation to imports of subsidized products, as under the TBR like with subsidies, it is practices of states which are the subject of the investigation. Article 10 of the TBR explains in detail what constitutes evidence of injury or adverse trade effects. The examination procedure is terminated or suspended under Article 11 of the TBR if the interests of the Community do not require any action to be taken, or if the third country adopts satisfactory measures or if negotiations with that country about a solution are possible. Such a decision is adopted by means of the committee procedure set out in Article 14 of the TBR,[364] and any Member State may refer the Commission's decision to the Council within 10 days; if there is such a reference, the Council may revise the decision, acting by a qualified majority, but if it

---

358. *Ibid.*, Art. 2(4).
359. *Ibid.*, Art. 12(2).
360. *Ibid.*, Art. 3.
361. *Ibid.*, Art. 4. This was new in the TBR. It is understandable that individual under-takings should be able to complain about obstacles to exports from the Community, as they are often individually hindered, without a whole branch or sector of industry being affected. Moreover, they may in many countries not be able to seek relief from the national courts, as the WTO or other trade agreements may not always be found to be directly effective in those countries. See Bronckers (1996) 33 CMLRev. 299. In Case 70/87 *Fédération de l'industrie de l'huilerie de la CEE (Fediol) v. Commission* [1989] ECR 1781 at 1831 the Court indicated that it will interpret a measure which is based on an instrument that refers to the GATT provisions in the light of those pro-visions. That does not, though, amount to giving those provisions real direct effect. See, generally, Zonnekeyn (1996) Int.TLR 63.
362. *Ibid.*, Art. 6.
363. *Ibid.*, Art. 8. It acts in cooperation with the Member States, Art. 8(1)(c).
364. *Ibid.*, Art. 13(1).

has not so acted within 30 days of the reference to it, the Commission's decision stands. If no reference is made within the 10 day period, the Commission's decision applies without more ado. The same procedure applies if the Community decides to follow formal international consultation or dispute settlement procedures, for decisions relating to the initiation, conduct or termination of such procedures, before resorting to any retaliatory measures.[365] Such retaliatory commercial policy measures, consisting of the suspension or revocation of trade concessions, the raising or introduction of customs duties or levies, or the imposition of quantitative restrictions,[366] may only be adopted under the normal procedure of Article 113 EC by the Council, acting by a qualified majority, within 30 days of receiving the proposal.[367]

The predecessor new commercial policy instrument of 1984 was not intensively used during its lifetime of about a decade, with some ten disputes being examined. On the other hand, it was certainly not superfluous or harmful, as the Dutch government had initially feared.[368] It was largely used for its intended purpose, namely the removal of barriers to trade or unfair trading practices in other countries. Thus, for instance, it was used to counter subsidy practices in Latin American countries;[369] to counter the absence of minimum protection of intellectual property rights in Korea;[370] to counter very inadequate enforcement of intellectual property rights in Indonesia and Thailand;[371] to counter alleged illicit licensing practices concerning pharmaceuticals in Jordan;[372] to counter disputed Japanese harbour fees which were incompatible with the GATT;[373] and, ironically in view of the Dutch government's initial fears, the very first complaint came from a Dutch company, AKZO NV, because of its exclusion from the United States market by the application of section 337 of the United States Tariff Act 1930 to exclude unlicensed

365. *Ibid.*, Art. 13(2).
366. *Ibid.*, Art. 12(3) makes it clear that these are examples; any commercial policy measures compatible with existing international obligations may be taken.
367. *Ibid.*, Art. 13(3). The Community must have acted in accordance with Art. 12(2): thus any consultation or dispute settlement procedures required under the Community's international obligations must have been terminated, and any measures taken must accord with the recommendations of the international dispute settlement body concerned, or must take account of the results of the procedure.
368. See Bolkestein's answer to a question from Mateman in the Dutch Parliament, *Aanh. Hand. Tweede Kamer* II 1984–1985, no. 70.
369. These gave rise to the judgment in Case 70/87 *Fediol*, see note 365, *supra*.
370. Reg. 3912/87 (O.J. 1987 L 369/1) withdrew the benefit of the GSP from Korea.
371. See O.J. 1991 C 189/26. The procedure against Thailand was opened, but never brought to a definitive conclusion; the procedure against Indonesia was first suspended and then closed, see Decs. 87/553 (O.J. 1987 L 335/22) and 88/287 (O.J. 1988 L 123/51).
372. Dec. 89/74 (O.J. 1989 L 30/67) rejected the complaint.
373. Dec. 92/169 (O.J. 1992 L 74/47).

importations of certain forms of aramid fibre manufactured outside the
United States by AKZO NV[374] or its affiliated companies.[375] Some of
these procedures were closed without measures being adopted, such as
those involving the Latin American countries, Japan and Jordan; others
resulted in international dispute settlement procedures being activated.
Whatever the formal result, virtually all the procedures led to an
improvement in the situation of Community exporters. The predecessor
new commercial policy instrument thus appeared to be a reasonably
successful, even if not intensively used, means of promoting the
Community interest in international trade in accordance with international
law. The new TBR has (by July 1998) given rise to a small number of
procedures which have resulted in formal decisions.[376] Given the strategic
importance which the Commission now attaches to its market access
strategy,[377] and the development of an interactive database accessible to all
via the Europa internet server, it may well be that more frequent use will
be made of the TBR in the future, although recourse to retaliatory
measures is an ultimate rather than a first strategy.

3.3.5   Community economic sanctions

Since the beginning of the Eighties, the developments have caused the
Community to adopt, or rather implement economic sanctions against
third countries.[378] The practice was that a decision was first taken in the
framework of European Political Cooperation and then sanctions were
adopted in a Council regulation based on Article 113 EC, in which
reference was made to that decision. This practice commenced with the
unilateral sanctions adopted against Argentina in connection with the
Falklands, an instance of military self-defence by a Member State (the
United Kingdom) accompanied by self-defence by economic means by the
Community.[379] Unilateral economic sanctions were also adopted for

374. See *e.g.* Dec. 97/162 (O.J. 1997 L 62/43) and Bull. EU 1/2–1997, points 1.3.53 and
   1.3.54.
375. The Commission took the matter to the GATT and the American measures were
   eventually condemned by a GATT Panel, see BISD 36S 345.
376. Decs. 96/40 (O.J. 1996 L 11/7) *Thailand, Sound Recordings* (suspension); 96/714 (O.J.
   1996 L 326/71) *Turkey, Mass Housing Fund Levy and increased polymer fibres duty*
   (termination); 97/162 (O.J. 1997 L 62/43) *U.S.A – rules of origin for textiles processed
   in the Community* (opening an international dispute settlement procedure), and 98/277
   (O.J. 1998 L 126/36 *U.S.A. – failure to repeal legislation.*
377. COM (96) 53.
378. See Kuyper in Meessen (ed.), *The International Law of Export Control* (London, 1992)
   57.
379. Reg. 877/82 (O.J. 1982 L 102/1) was twice extended; sanctions were lifted by Reg.
   1577/82 (O.J. 1982 L 177/1). See Kuyper in O'Keeffe and Schermers (eds.), *Essays in
   European law and Integration* (Deventer, 1982) 141.

political reasons against the then USSR to express rejection of the latter's interference in the crisis in Poland in 1981–82.[380] The sanctions adopted against South Africa, long since lifted as a result of the changes there, had a more targeted political aim: a reaction to the widespread breaches of human rights and democratic principles.[381]

Starting with the sanctions against Iraq, the implementation of binding economic sanctions, adopted by the UN Security Council, was also undertaken by the Community. This implementation is often extremely detailed, as the Security Council resolutions are becoming ever more detailed. The Community is then often much less bothered than normal about what the Council in particular continually regards as the boundaries of the common commercial policy. Thus the implementation of the sanctions against Iraq[382] included measures in the field of international sea and air transport; sanctions against Libya[383] consisted mainly of such measures. One aspect of sanctions against Iraq, the implementation of which was primarily undertaken by the Community in order to prevent distortions in competition in the banking sector in the Community, was finally based on Article 235 EC.[384]

There are also categories of economic sanctions which are not reactions to a particular event or circumstance, but are the consequence of longer term security policy considerations. In the new situation without internal frontiers in the Community's internal market, a Member State can no longer itself effectively control the export of sensitive products. This was one of the causes for the extension of the practice concerning economic sanctions to embrace precursors of chemical weapons.[385] The Council has also now adopted Regulation 3381/94 on dual-use products.[386] This

380. Reg. 596/82 (O.J. 1982 L 72/15); this was extended until the end of 1983, when it lapsed.
381. Reg. 3302/86 (O.J. 1986 L 304/11) suspending the importation of gold coins from South Africa was repealed by Reg. 219/92 (O.J. 1992 L 24/86). By a decision of the representatives of the governments of the Member States meeting within the Council, adopted on the same day as Reg. 3302/86 (Dec. 86/517 (O.J. 1986 L 305/45)), the governments were obliged to take measures to suspend new direct investment in South Africa. That decision was repealed by Dec. 91/114 (O.J. 1991 L 59/18).
382. Reg. 2340/90 (O.J. 1990 L 213/1) was revised on several occasions until its repeal and replacement by Reg. 2465/90 (O.J. 1996 L 337/1). See also Dec. 90/414 (O.J. 1990 L 213/3), which was amended once and then repealed and replaced by Dec. 96/740 (O.J. 1996 L 337/4).
383. Reg. 945/92 (O.J. 1992 L 101/53) was repealed and replaced by Reg. 3274/93 (O.J. 1993 L 295/3). See also Dec. 93/614 (O.J. 1993 L 295/7).
384. Reg. 3541/92 (O.J. 1992 L 361/1).
385. Reg. 428/89 (O.J. 1989 L 50/1). This measure was silently repealed by Reg. 3381/94 (O.J. 1994 L 367/1). A somewhat comparable regulation on measures to discourage diversion of substances to the illicit manufacture of narcotic drugs and psychotropic substances was simply based on Art. 113, see Reg. 3677/90 (O.J. 1990 L 357/1, most recently amended by Reg. 3769/92 (O.J. 1992 L 383/17)).
386. O.J. 1994 L 367/1, amended by Reg. 837/95 (O.J. 1995 L 90/1). See Dec. 94/942 (O.J.

restricts the export of goods which can be used not merely for peaceful purposes, but also for military purposes. The export of such products used to be regulated informally by the western countries within the Co-Com framework. Regulation 3381/94 is based on Article 113 EC and really should have been in place by January 1, 1993, but its adoption, along with a decision on a joint action, based on Article J.3 TEU[387] was somewhat delayed.

After the introduction of Article 228a EC by the TEU, that provision is the logical future basis for economic sanctions,[388] as is Article 73g EC for financial sanctions. Article 228a in fact codifies the previous practice set out above. Thus it is unsurprising that the actual decision to implement sanctions under that provision is based upon a prior decision in a common position or joint action in the framework of CFSP.[389] Since the break-up of the former Yugoslavia there have been numerous sanctions adopted from time to time in respect of various countries which have emanated from that former State.[390]

3.3.6 Trade agreements

Traditional agreements. In the Treaty system after the end of the transitional period competence to conclude trade agreements was transferred exclusively to the Community. Thus the Member States are no longer free

1994 L 367/8, most recently amended by Dec. 97/633 (O.J. 1997 L 266/1). See, generally, Govaere and Eeckhout (1992) 29 CMLRev. 941 Shcroeder and Köhncke (1995) Int. TLR 101; Govare (1997) 34 CMLRev. 1019, and Jestaedt and von Behr (1995) EuZW 137. See also Case C-367/89 *Richardt et al.* [1991] ECR I-4621 [1992] 1 CMLR 61; Case 70/94 *Fritz Werns Industrie-Ausrüstungen GmbH v. Germany* [1995] ECRR I-318 and Case C-83/94 *Leifer et al.* [1995] ECR I-3231.

387. Dec. 94/942 (O.J. 1994 L 367/8, most recently amended by Dec. 98/232 (O.J. 1998 L 92/1).

388. *Contra*, Govaere and Eekhout (1992) 29 CMLRev. 941 and Gilsdorf (1994) RMC 17. However, practice supports the view advanced in the text, *e.g.* Reg. 2465/96 (O.J. 1996 L 337/1) was based on Arts. 228a and 73g EC.

389. *E.g.* the UN sanctions against Haiti: for the relevant CFSP decisions, EC regulations, decisions of the representatives of the governments of the Member States meeting within the Council, and even a Council recommendation which demonstrated that at that stage the Council was unwilling to use the new powers of Art. 73g EC to the full extent, see O.J. 1994 L 139.

390. *E.g.* Regs. 1432/92 (O.J. 1992 L 151/4), 2655/92 (O.J. 1992 L 266/26) and 2656/92 (O.J. 1992 L 266/26), which, after amendment, were then repealed and replaced by Reg. 990/93 (O.J. 1993 L 102/14), which was suspended on many occasions, amended, and finally repealed by Reg. 2382/96 (O.J. 1996 L 328/1) following CP 708/96 (O.J. 1996 L 328/5). Reg. 2471/94 (O.J. 1994 L 266/1), adopted in the wake of Decs 94/672 (O.J. 1994 L 266/10) and 94/673 (O.J. 1994 L 266/11), and comparable to the sanctions against Iraq discussed earlier in the text, was also repealed by Reg. 2382/96. Various ECSC measures were also adopted; they were later repealed by Dec. 96/707 (O.J. 1996 L 328/3). See Case C-84/95 *Bosphorus Hava Yollari Turizim ve Ticaret As*

to conclude such agreements unless they have been specifically authorized to do so by the Community. As a rule it will not be possible to make such an authorization compatible with the requirements which the functioning of the common market makes of the uniformity of a Community conventional commercial policy.

In the first years after the entry into force of the EEC Treaty, the Council adopted a number of measures which were intended to prevent the establishment of the common commercial policy being delayed or obstructed by bilateral agreements between Member States and third countries. On 20 July 1960 it was decided that Member States would seek to incorporate in bilateral treaties an EEC clause providing for negotiations on the modification of such an agreement if the development of the common commercial policy should require it.[391] One year later it was laid down in two Council decisions of 9 October 1961 that the duration of trade agreements was not to extend beyond the transitional period. Further, a procedure of prior consultation concerning negotiations on trade agreements and modifications of the liberalization arrangements with respect to third countries was provided for.[392]

An investigation made by the Commission in 1969[393] showed that there were some 128 treaties of friendship, trade and navigation and some 196 trade agreements (in the narrower sense) between Member States and third countries. In addition there were a great many agreements relating to economic, industrial, scientific and technical co-operation, which could also be relevant on certain points to the commercial policy of the Community. It appeared neither necessary nor possible to replace all these agreements by Community agreements. That was necessary only to the extent that provisions of these agreements directly affected the commercial policy of the Community which had to be applied. The agreements of primary importance in this context were the 196 trade agreements in the narrower sense – and particularly the agreements with the State trading countries and Japan – which then formed the basis for trade between Member States and these countries.

The difficulty involved in the case of the countries of Eastern Europe and the then Soviet Union, however, was that they refused to recognize the Community as a subject of international law and wished to negotiate only

---

v. *Minister for Transport, Energy and Communications, Ireland et al.* [1996] ECR I-3953; Case C-124/95 *R. v. H.M. Treasury et al., ex parte Centro-Com Srl* [1997] ECR I-81, and Case C-177/95 *Ebone Maritime SA et al. v. Prefetto della Provincia di Brindisi et al.* [1997] ECR I-1111.

391. *Fourth General Report* (EEC) (Brussels, Luxembourg, 1961), point 192.

392. The decision on prior consultation on trade agreements (O.J. English Special Edition 1959–1962, p. 84) was considered in Case 174/84 *Bulk Oil (Zug) AG v. Sun International Ltd. et al.* [1986] ECR 559 at 593–594. The decision limiting the duration of trade agreements can be found in O.J. English Special Edition 1959–1962, p. 86.

393. SEC (69) 1175 Final, March 28, 1969.

with individual Member States. As will be seen below, this attitude changed even before the implosion of the Soviet Union. Given that most of the Member States, for political and economic reasons, were reluctant to lose their freedom to conduct commercial policy relations with state trading countries as they saw fit, it was only after laborious consultations that the Council adopted Decision 69/494[394] on the progressive standardization of agreements concerning commercial relations between Member States and third countries and on the negotiation of Community agreements. This decision provides in Title I for a Community procedure of prior information and consultation with respect to the express of tacit renewal, after the end of the transitional period, of any bilateral agreements in the matter of the trade relations between Member States and third countries. An extension of agreements whose provisions fall under the common commercial policy is permitted only if the Council has authorized it. Even then it is permitted for a period not exceeding one year, unless such agreements contain an EC clause or can be terminated by the end of every year. Such authorization can be granted only if the provisions of an agreement do not obstruct the application of the common commercial policy. If they do, the Commission submits to the Council a detailed report, along with appropriate suggestions and, if necessary, recommendations to the Council to grant an authorization for opening Community negotiations with the third country concerned.

Title II of Decision 69/494 lays down the general rule that as from 1 January 1970 only Community negotiations are to be carried on in the sphere of trade agreements. The Commission takes the initiative for making suggestions and recommendations for this purpose to the Council whenever it considers this opportune, or at the request of a Member State or a third country or even without such a request. If the Commission thinks, in the light of a request, that the conditions for opening Community negotiations have not been fulfilled or that these negotiations are not opportune, it has to find out whether a coordination of the commercial relations of Member States with third countries by means of autonomous Community measures is desirable.

In view of the attitude of the then Soviet Union and the East European countries at that time, but principally under pressure from France in particular, which had more or less presented the Community with a *fait accompli* by concluding a framework agreement with the Soviet Union for the period 1970–1974, Title III of Decision 69/494 provided for a transitional arrangement.[395] The last agreement with a state trading country renewed under this arrangement expired in 1975. Although the particular problems with the former Soviet Union and the other countries of the old

394. O.J. English Special Edition 1969 (II), p. 603.
395. See the 1st edition of this work (London, 1973) 368.

Warsaw Pact and COMECON no longer exist,[396] Decision 69/494 still plays a role, as it reminds the Member States that there must be prior consultation at Community level about trade agreements if they could form an obstacle to the common commercial policy. It also reminds the Member States that even though third countries may invoke the first paragraph of Article 234 EC in relation to agreements they have concluded with Member States, the latter are obliged, as a result of the second paragraph of that provision, to take all appropriate steps to eliminate any incompatibilities with Community law in such agreements. This is certainly not a superfluous provision: the Commission in more recent years has campaigned together with the Member States to remove all the commercial policy provisions from their agreements with the EFTA countries. It has also appeared that the treaties of friendship, trade and navigation which the United States has concluded on a large scale with Member States may sometimes give rise to considerable complications, as they embrace many national treatment clauses which may be incompatible with Community law and with the obligations incumbent on WTO members.[397]

It is important to note that classic trade agreements are being steadily less and less used. Even the title of the agreements concluded with the United States demonstrates that even classic trade agreements embraced far more than simply trade. More and more in the Sixties and Seventies parties began to include, in addition to trade provisions, provisions dealing with industrial cooperation – in agreements with the old Eastern bloc countries – and on technical and development cooperation – in agreements with developing countries. Initially cooperation agreements appeared to be primarily used by the Member States to conclude semi-trade agreements with the old Eastern bloc countries, at the same time getting round the exclusive commercial policy competence of the Community. Later not only the Member States but also the Community itself uses the instrument of cooperation agreements. Classic trade agreements, *viz.* those dealing solely with trade in goods, are almost never concluded nowadays, even by the Community.

Cooperation agreements. As has just been noted, cooperation agreements were primarily concluded by the Member States with the former Eastern

---

396. The gradual changes in relations with these countries up to the end of 1988 were discussed in the 2nd edition of this work (London, 1989) 823–824.

397. In late 1993 the Commission declined to propose that these agreements be extended under Dec. 69/494, Art. 3 unless the Member States declared that they would not interpret the national treatment clauses in such agreements in a manner incompatible with Community law. This followed an incident in which Germany declined to apply the Community preference provisions concerning in the public procurement field against the USA, as that country allegedly invoked the provisions of a treaty of friendship, trade and navigation with Germany. See Dec. 93/67 (O.J. 1993 L 317/61) and Abbot (1994) ZaöRV 756.. The current authorization for tacit renewal is set out in Dec. 97/351 (O.J. 1997 L 151/24) which runs until 30 April 2001.

bloc countries. This was caused by the fact that more and more the latter were becoming contracting parties to the GATT and thus an exchange of elementary trade concessions, such as most-favoured and national treatment was no longer necessary in bilateral agreements. Moreover, the Eastern European countries were attempting to modernize their economies while at the same time retaining elements of a communist planned economy. This meant that they grasped the opportunity of the instrument of cooperation agreements, which enabled them, within the framework of pretty vague and general provisions concerning industrial, technological and financial cooperation, to develop concrete projects in specific industrial sectors which enabled them to attract Western investment and technical knowledge in exchange for guaranteed markets for their products. Such a concrete exchange of advantages could then be integrated into their national plans. The Member States were willing participants in this construction, as it meant employment and export markets for their industries. Moreover, these agreements also involved extensive credits repaid over a long period by means of supplies of the goods to be produced and/or out of the proceeds of the sale of these goods in third countries, the financing of which was only possible by means of state participation or guarantees.[398] Similar cooperation agreements have also played a part in relations between the EC countries and Arabian oil-producing countries and other fast-growing developing countries.

It cannot be denied that these agreements have in part clear commercial policy aspects. Frequently they contain most favoured nation treatment clauses, clauses promoting long-term contracts, the exchange of licences and know-how, compensating transactions for the supply of complete factories, favourable credit terms and so on.[399] The question then arises whether the Member States are still competent to conclude such agreements and to enter into more defined commitments or to take further measures in execution of them.

So far the Council has limited itself to the adoption of Decision 74/393,[400] establishing a consultation procedure for cooperation agreements between Member States and third countries; thus prior notification and, if necessary, consultation is required. The consultation has in particular the aim of avoiding interference with the common commercial policy, promoting the co-ordination of cooperation activities with third countries and investigating the desirability of supporting these activities through autonomous commercial policy measures.

398. See Pinder (1984) Eur. Arch. 105 and Jolivet (1977) RMC 361.
399. See Sasse (1975) Eur. Arch. 700; see also, on cooperation agreements, Bot (1976) 13 CMLRev. 335 and literature cited there. The question of the relationship between the Community and COMECON is now of only historical interest (there was a short-lived agreement between the two organizations).
400. O.J. 1974 L 208/23.

It may, with respect, be doubted whether Decision 74/393 is reconcilable with the case-law of the Court on the division of competence between the Community and the Member States.[401] The case-law justifies a claim by the Community to the exclusive competence to conclude such agreements if, as is the case with most of these agreements, their most important subject-matter is of a commercial policy nature in the wide sense in which that term must be used. Community commercial policy is not restricted to the use of traditional commercial policy instruments, such as trade agreements, but also embraces new instruments which are developed to promote and support external trade. The reasoning of the Court in Case 45/86 *Commission v. Council*[402] appears to apply appropriately in relation to cooperation agreements.

Recognition of exclusive Community competence in this field would have to lead to rules analogous to those in Decision 69/494[403] on the progressive standardization of policy relating to traditional trade agreements.[404] The willingness on the part of the Member States to adopt such rules has so far been minimal. The Council still considers that such matters are outside the sphere of operation of Article 113 EC. Thus Decision 74/393 itself and the framework agreements for commercial and economic co-operation which the Community concluded with Canada (1976); the ASEAN countries (1979); India (1980); Brazil (1982); the Andean Pact countries (1983); China and the Yemen Arab Republic (1985); with Pakistan (1986) and with the Gulf Cooperation Council (1989) were based on Articles 113 and 235.[405] With some countries in South America (*e.g.* Brazil in 1982 and 1992) and in Asia (*e.g.* India in 1981 and 1994) such development agreements have been concluded a second time.

The question arises whether in particular cooperation agreements with the major developing countries should not now be concluded on the basis of Article 113 EC and on the basis of Article 130y EC. That latter provision provides that arrangements for Community development cooperation which are the subject of agreements between the Community

---

401. Opinion 1/75 [1975] ECR 1355, [1976] 1 CMLR 85; Opinion 1/78 [1979] ECR 2871, [19791 3 CMLR 639, and particularly Case 45/86 *Commission* v. *Council* [1987] ECR 1493, [1988] 2 CMLR 131 (see sections 2.1.1 and 2.1.3, *ante*).
402. [1987] ECR 1493 at 1521–1522.
403. O.J. English Special Edition 1969 (II), p. 603.
404. In the same sense Bot (1976) 13 CMLRev. 335 at 362 *et seq.*
405. These framework agreements include a so-called 'Canada Clause', named after the first agreement in which it was used, which states that they do not affect the powers of the Member States to pursue bilateral activities in the field of economic co-operation with these countries and if necessary to conclude new agreements on such matters with these countries without prejudice to the relevant provisions of the Treaties establishing the European Communities. This provision can actually be regarded as superfluous, as Art. 235 EC does not confer exclusive powers in the external field on the Member States, but clearly there is felt to be a need to make the situation explicit for the third country concerned.

and third countries are to be negotiated and concluded on the basis of Article 228 EC. It is striking that the second paragraph of Article 130y EC expressly reserves the Member States' competence to negotiate in international bodies and to conclude international agreements. It seems that the Member States, as Community constitutional legislators have effectively enshrined the Canada Clause in the EC Treaty, and thus established parallel competence in the field of development cooperation.[406] In practice all the cooperation agreements which cite Article 130y EC among their legal bases are also based on Article 113 EC.[407]

4. THE SYSTEM OF COMMUNITY AGREEMENTS

4.1 The system viewed geographically

The system of agreements that the Community has concluded over the years is constructed in concentric circles, which are discussed in more detail in sections 4.2.2–4.2.5, below. The innermost circle consists of the European Economic Area (EEA) Agreement. This establishes a free trade area for the movement of goods and a common market in the area of the other freedoms: workers, establishment, and the provision of services. This most far-reaching form of cooperation with the economies of a number of the Community's immediate neighbours has been established with (now) Iceland, Liechtenstein, and Norway; Austria, Finland and Sweden were originally EEA members, but acceded to the European Union on 1 January 1995. Switzerland, the remaining fourth member of EFTA remained outside the EEA as a result of a referendum, and its old free trade agreement with the Community remains in force.[408]

The next circle outwards embraces the Europe Agreements with Poland; the Czech Republic; Slovakia; Hungary; Romania; Bulgaria; the Baltic States and Slovenia. The eventual conclusion of such agreements with

---

406. As to the Canada Clause, see *ibid.* In this way the Member States probably wanted to side-step the Court's Opinion 1/78 *International Rubber Agreement* [1979] ECR 2781, [1979] 3 CMLR 639, in which it noted that development objectives could form part of a modern commercial policy. On the other hand, Art. 130w EC expressly states that it applies without prejudice to the other provisions of the Treaty, which must include Art. 113 EC. It is in fact doubtful whether Art. 130y EC can serve as a legal basis for cooperation agreements with developed countries. See, on parallel competence, Cases C-181 and 248/91 *European Parliament v. Council et al.* [1993] ECR I-3685, [1994] 3 CMLR 317 and Case C-316/91 *European Parliament v. Council* [1994] ECR I-625, [1994] 3 CMLR 149.

407. *E.g.* the Agreements with South Africa and India (1994); Brazil (1995); Nepal and Vietnam (1996) and the Euro-Mediterranean Interim Agreement on trade and cooperation with the PLO (Dec. 97/430 (O.J.1997 L 187/1; Agreement L 187/3)). See Case C-268/94 *Portugal v. Council* [1996] ECR I-6177, [1997] 3 CMLR 331.

408. See Chapter I, section 5, *ante.*

other Central and East European countries will depend on political developments in those countries. The Europe Agreements are intended to establish a free trade area over a period, to make progress on the way to the achievement of the other economic freedoms between the partners, to establish broad cooperation in myriad fields, and to create a framework for political dialogue between the partners. In effect they can be seen as pre-accession agreements.

Such pre-accession agreements had already been concluded in the early Sixties with Greece and Turkey (the former acceding to the Communities in 1981) and later with Malta and Cyprus. They were intended to establish in the long term a common market based on the Community's five freedoms, with a view to paving the way for accession by the partners to the Communities, now to the Union. While Turkey, Malta and Cyprus have in the meantime applied to accede, political problems mean that the accession of these countries in the short term presently appears less likely.

The next circle outwards comprises development associations. The Lomé Convention (presently in its Fourth version) is a multilateral association agreement between on the one hand the Communities and Member States, and on the other hand some 80 countries from Africa, the Caribbean and the Pacific Ocean regions (the ACP countries); it is undoubtedly the best-known example of such associations. Similar, but bilateral, agreements have been concluded with the Maghreb countries (Algeria, Morocco and Tunisia) and the Mashreq countries (Egypt, Jordan, Syria and Lebanon). There are also agreements with Israel and with the PLO in relation to the Palestinian Territories. These are agreements which confer free trade concessions (in the case of Lomé one-sided) and extensive cooperation provisions in diverse areas. The policy behind the agreements with the Maghreb and Mashreq countries, Israel, the Palestinian Territories, Cyprus, Malta and Turkey is often referred to as the Community's Mediterranean Policy.[409]

All of the above categories of agreement are based on Article 238 EC, which regulates association with the Community, and is discussed in section 4.2.1, below. Moreover, they are usually mixed agreements. The Partnership and Cooperation Agreements with Russia and numerous other states of the former Soviet Union, and the Community's Central Asia Strategy are not based on Article 238 EC, but they still represent a far-reaching level of cooperation. These agreements are examined in section 4.3.1, below.

Finally, the outermost circle of the Community's agreements, both geographically, politically and legally, consists of the diverse forms of trade and cooperation agreements with countries of the Americas, the Arabian

---

409. See, generally, Bull. EU Supp. 2/95, the Barcelona Euro-Mediterranean Conference, Bull. EU 11–1995, points 1.4.56 and 2.3.1, and the follow-up (COM (97) 68 Final) and Bull. EU 4–1997, point 1.4.63.

Peninsula, Asia and the Far East. These agreements are usually based on Articles 113 and 235 EC, and, to the extent that they concern development, now also on Article 130y EC.

4.2 Agreements based on Article 238 EC

4.2.1 Article 238 EC

The characteristics of an association agreement under Article 238 EC lie in the reciprocal rights and obligations – although that is true of all agreements – and in joint action and special procedures. Given the pluriformity of agreements concluded on the basis of Article 238, it is difficult to point out specific characteristics which these agreements have in common as against other forms of cooperation agreements, and indeed the distinction between association agreements and those other forms has always been a problem for the Community Institutions. The following is based on the practice followed and on case-law. Association agreements are concluded with countries with which the Community has or wishes to establish particularly close links. These links may have historic roots, as in the case of the ACP, the Maghreb and the Mashreq countries; they may be geographical or political in nature, as in the case of the EEA countries and the countries with which there are, or may in the future be, Europe Agreements. Association agreements may involve the whole gamut of Community competence, and thus often embrace broad fields.[410] Nevertheless, they are in practice mostly concluded as mixed agreements; only those with Cyprus and Malta were concluded solely by the Community. As the Court has put it, association agreements presuppose participation in the Community system; thus certain fundamental rules of Community law, even if sometimes only in the form of free trade, are extended to the association partner. That does not mean, though, that such rules have to be interpreted in the framework of the association in the same manner as in the framework of the Community itself.[411] Finally, association agreements are characterized by their strong institutional structure: they are often equipped with several bodies, including an association council at ministerial level and an association committee at the level of senior civil servants. The association council is often endowed with decision-making powers, and its decisions are binding on the participants

---

410. Case 181/73 *Haegeman v. Belgian State* [1974] ECR 449, [1975] 1 CMLR 515; Case 12/86 *Demirel v. Stadt Schwäbisch Gmünd* [1987] ECR 3719, [1989] 1 CMLR 421.
411. Case 270/80 *Polydor Ltd. et al. v. Harlequin Record Shops Ltd. et al.* [1982] ECR 329 at 348; Case 104/81 *Hauptzollamt Mainz v. Kupferberg & Cie. KG a.A.* [1982] ECR 3461 at 3666, but see the useful effect argument of the Court in Case C-207/91 *Eurim-Pharm GmbH v. Bundesgesundheitsamt* [1993] ECR I-3723 at 3748.

in the association. The decisions of the association council form an integral part of Community law, without having to be transposed; they can thus be interpreted by the Court of Justice.[412]

Since the entry into force of the SEA the assent of the European Parliament has been required for the conclusion of association agreements.[413] In urgent situations a time-limit for the assent may be agreed by the Council and the Parliament.[414] If and when the Treaty of Amsterdam comes into force, specific provisions will apply regarding the provisional application or the suspension of the application of agreements, and for the establishing of Community positions in bodies established by association agreements , where the bodies are called upon to adopt decisions having legal effects.[415]

4.2.2 The EEA Agreement[416]

Initially the Community had simple free trade agreements with its non-communist neighbours in Europe, which were members of the EFTA. The EEA Agreement, however, is designed to create 'a homogeneous European Economic Area'[417] and to this end creates an association which provides for the same five freedoms as are found in the EC Treaty, although the free movement of goods remains limited to a free trade area as opposed to a customs union.[418] There is as yet no complete free trade in agricultural products. A system is established whereby undistorted competition and equal compliance with the rules on competition is guaranteed.[419] There is

---

412. Case 181/73 *Haegeman v. Belgian State* [1974] ECR 449 at 460; Case C-192/89 *Sevince v. Staatssecretaris van Justitie* [1990] ECR I-3461 at 3501.
413. Art. 228(3) EC, 2nd para.
414. *Ibid.*, 3rd para. So far this provision has not been used.
415. Except for decisions supplementing or amending the institutional framework of the agreement. The European Parliament will have to be immediately and fully informed about the provisional application or suspension of agreements, or the establishment of Community positions, see the new Art. 228(2) EC.
416. Oporto, May 2, 1992 (O.J. 1994 L1/3), as amended by the Adjusting Protocol of March 17, 1993 (O.J. 1994 L 1/572), see Decs. 94/1 and 94/2 (O.J. 1994 L 1/1 and 571). See, generally, Norberg *et al.*, *EEA Law* (Stockholm, 1993); Blanchet *et al.*, *The Agreement on the European Economic Area (EEA)* (Oxford, 1994); Bright (ed.), *Business Law in the European Economic Area* (Oxford, 1994), and Stuyck and Looijestijn-Clearie (eds.), *The European Economic Area EC-EFTA* (Deventer, 1994). See also Cremona (1994) 19 ELRev. 508; Norberg (1992) 29 CMLRev. 1171; Reymond (1993) 30 CMLRev. 449; Toledano-Laredo (1992) 29 CMLRev. 1199 and Weiss (1992) 12 YBEL 385.
417. Art. 1(1) EEA.
418. Thus a common market as such is not created, even though Art. 1(1) EEA does refer to 'equal conditions of competition,' as the common external element (common commercial policy with a common external tariff) is not present.
419. Arts. 53–59 and Annex XIV EEA (undertakings); Arts. 61–64 and Annex XV EEA

also provision for close cooperation in fields such as research and technological development, environment, education and social policy.

In order to achieve all this, the EEA Agreement contains a great many provisions which are identical or virtually so to the fundamental provisions on the five freedoms in the EC Treaty, as well as to its competition provisions and the provisions on state aids. The EEA partners also take on board almost the whole *acquis communautaire*. For this purpose myriad Protocols and Annexes to the Agreement contain long lists with references to Community secondary legislation in all sorts of areas, which has force in the EEA partner states. Sometimes the references are accompanied by minor notes on the conditions under which this will occur, or with textual adaptations for this purpose.

From the institutional viewpoint, the EEA is extremely well-equipped. There is an EEA Council, consisting of the members of the Council of the European Union,[420] members of the Commission of the European communities, and one member of the government of each of the EFTA States which are parties to the EEA Agreement.[421] The EEA Council meets twice a year,[422] and is 'in particular responsible for giving the general political impetus' in the implementation of the EEA Agreement and for laying down general guidelines for the Joint Committee.[423] The Joint Committee consists of representatives of the contracting parties, with the Commission representing the Community; it meets in principle at least once a month.[424] Its task is to 'ensure the effective implementation and operation of the agreement'[425] and this largely takes the form of keeping track of legislative developments within the Community and continually adapting EEA law to developments in secondary Community law. The relevant Protocols and Annexes to the EEA Agreement are revised accordingly. There is also a Joint Parliamentary Committee, which consists of equal numbers of MEPs on the one hand and MPs of the EFTA States which are parties to the EEA on the other.[426]

The EEA Agreement also creates bodies which are competent only in relation to the EFTA States which are parties to the EEA Agreement. Thus the EFTA Surveillance Authority has a role which is somewhat

---

(state aids). Enforcement is through the EFTA Surveillance Authority as regards those EFTA members who are party to the EEA.

420. Substituting that Council's name for the term 'Council of the European Communities' used in Art. 90(1) EEA (see Dec. 93/591 (O.J. 1993 L 281/18)).

421. Art. 90 (1) EEA.

422. *Ibid.*, Art. 91(2). The presidency alternates between a member of the Council of the European Union and a member of the government of an EFTA State which is a party to the EEA Agreement, Art. 91(1).

423. *Ibid.*, Art. 89(1).

424. *Ibid.*, Arts. 93(1) and 94(1) and (2).

425. *Ibid.*, Art. 92(1).

426. *Ibid.*, Art. 95(1) and Protocol 36.

similar to that of the Commission in the Community, namely supervision of the implementation and fulfilment of EEA law by the EFTA States which are parties to the EEA Agreement.[427] This role is particularly developed in respect of competition law. The EFTA Court deals with appeals against the surveillance procedure regarding the EFTA States concerned, appeals concerning decisions in the competition field taken by the EFTA Surveillance Authority, and the settlement of disputes between two or more of the EFTA States concerned.[428]

Given that the intention is to maintain a homogeneous interpretation of Community law and EEA law which is identical to it, a special procedure for this purpose has been established. Accordingly, the Joint Committee is charged with keeping the development of the case-law of the Court of Justice and of the EFTA Court under constant review, and with acting 'so as to preserve the homogeneous interpretation of the Agreement.'[429] If it is unable to preserve such homogeneous interpretation within two months of a difference in the case-law of the two courts being brought before it, the Contracting Parties may, if the dispute concerns provisions of the EEA Agreement which are identical in substance to those of the EC or ECSC Treaties and secondary legislation adopted thereunder,[430] place the matter before the Court of Justice for a ruling on the interpretation of the relevant rules.[431] If, within six months, the Joint Committee has not resolved the dispute, or if, by then the Contracting Parties have not referred the matter to the Court of Justice, safeguard measures may be taken or provisional suspension of the provision concerned may follow.[432]

This dispute settlement procedure was set up in this form only after the Court of Justice had found the dispute settlement procedure originally proposed to be incompatible with the EC Treaty.[433] The initial proposal was to establish an EEA Court, which would draw the majority of its members from the Court of Justice, and which would have had to interpret EEA law in the light of the case-law of the Court of Justice as it stood

---

427. *Ibid.*, Art. 108(1). The Agreement establishing the EFTA Surveillance Authority and the EFTA Court was signed at the same time as the EEA Agreement and was likewise adjusted, see O.J. 1994 L 344/1.
428. Art. 108(2) EEA and see the Agreement establishing the EFTA Surveillance Authority and the EFTA Court (O.J. 1994 L 344/1).
429. Art. 105(2) EEA.
430. It should be noted that on the Community side the EEA Agreement was concluded in respect of the EC and ECSC; it does not cover Euratom matters.
431. Art. 111(3) EEA, 1st para. This may be done if the Joint Committee has not settled the matter within three months of being seized of it, *ibid.*
432. *Ibid.*, 2nd para. Safeguard measures are applied in accordance with Art. 112(2), by the procedure set out in Art. 113; provisional suspension may occur in accordance with Art. 102(5).
433. Opinion 1/91 *EEA Agreement I* [1991] ECR 6079, [1992] 1 CMLR 245. As to the Court's favourable view of the revised draft, see Opinion 1/92 *EEA Agreement II* [1992] ECR I-2821, [1992] 2 CMLR 217.

prior to the signature of the EEA Agreement. Thus that body of case-law would have been effectively frozen in time as far as the EEA was concerned. The Court of Justice found that this was incompatible with the EC Treaty, as in this manner Community law, particularly the provisions on free movement and competition, would be interpreted by a body other than the Court of Justice itself; this was found to be incompatible with Article 164 EC. The fact that judges of the Court of Justice would form the majority of judges of the proposed EEA Court made no difference, because as judges in the EEA Court they would sometimes have to interpret essentially identical provisions in different ways, as the objective of the EEA Agreement was substantially different from the objectives of the EC Treaty. Then, in the Community context, they could not later decide on identical provisions with the necessary independence.[434]

Although the practical importance of the EEA Agreement has undoubtedly diminished as a result of Austrian, Finnish and Swedish accession to the European Union, the EEA phase undoubtedly facilitated the accession negotiations (as much work on alignment by the candidate countries had already been undertaken, thus the *acquis communautaire* had been already accepted). The EEA model also remains an interesting model for close integration in a brief pre-accession period.[435]

4.2.3   The Europe Agreements[436]

Very shortly after the first signs of reform appeared in Central and Eastern Europe the Community concluded trade and cooperation agreements with

434. [1991] ECR I-6079 at 6106–6108. Moreover, the original draft of the EEA Agreement proposed that the EFTA States could authorize their courts to make references for preliminary rulings to the Court of Justice, but with no obligation to make a reference obligatory from courts of last instance, and no obligation to ensure that referring courts treated judgments on such references as binding. It was this latter point that the Court of Justice also found objectionable, *ibid.* at 6109–6110.

435. It could also form a halfway house for countries which wished to have many of the benefits of Community membership but were not yet ready (or politically not yet in a position) to accede to the Union as such. It could also form a possible vehicle for a Member State which felt unable to participate further in the development of the Union to seek to negotiate continued mutual benefits in a less far-reaching form of integration (assuming that the remaining Member States felt inclined to such an arrangement).

436. See Evans (1996) 21 ELRev. 263 and (1997) 22 ELRev. 201; Govare (1997) SEW 42; Kennedy and Webb (1993) 30 CMLRev. 1095; Maresceau and Montaguti (1995) 32 CMLRev. 1327, Peers (1995) 32 CMLRev. 187, and Scott and Mansell (1993) 64 BYIL 391. The Europe Agreements set out below have been amended or supplemented on various occasions. In order that the trade benefits of the agreements could start to flow without waiting for the agreements to be ratified (they were mixed agreements), interim agreements, based on Art. 113 EC were also concluded to bridge the gap; they could be adopted quickly (*e.g.* the Interim Agreement with Bulgaria (O.J. 1993 L 323/2, see Dec. 93/690 (O.J. 1993 L 323/1)).

countries such as Hungary, Poland, Czechoslovakia, Bulgaria and Romania.[437] An autonomous system of economic assistance to promote economic reforms in Poland and Hungary was established in the form of the PHARE programme, which now assists all the Central European countries, including the Baltic States.[438] Once the political reforms took on a permanent character, relations with these countries have been gradually transformed into what are known as the Europe Agreements. So far 10 such agreements have been concluded, of which six have so far been ratified.[439]

If the Europe Agreement with Poland is taken as an example, it is clear that the agreement has the long-term objective of creating a framework for the gradual integration of Poland into the Community, and that Poland will take steps to fulfil the necessary conditions. The Agreements open with provisions concerning the political dialogue between both parties, viz. Poland on the one hand and the Community and its Member States on the other. It is primarily for this reason that the Europe Agreements were concluded as mixed agreements.

The association has a transitional period of 10 years, for the establishment of a free trade area, which comes about on the Community side in two stages within two years, and on the Polish side in five stages over the full 10-year period, resulting in the abolition of all customs duties between the parties. There is, though, a specific safeguard clause which is

437. The first of these was with Hungary (O.J. 1988 L 327/2, see Dec. 88/595 (O.J. 1988 L 327/1)). These were still based on Arts. 113 and 235 EC. Similar agreements were also concluded with the Baltic States in 1992 (see O.J. 1992 L 403 (whole issue)).

438. Reg. 3906/89 (O.J. 1989 L 375/11, most recently amended by Reg. 753/96 (O.J. 1996 L 103/5)). The Commission has proposed new guidelines for the PHARE programme, concerning pre-accession assistance (COM (97) 112 Final), principally directed at addressing the two major difficulties facing the beneficiary countries which are preparing for accession, viz. their capacity in fact to implement the acquis communautaire, and the upgrading of enterprises and major infrastructure to Community standards. See also O.J. 1998 C 202. These guidelines will not affect programmes for other PHARE countries (Albania, Bosnia-Herzegovina and the Former Yugoslav Republic of Macedonia). In the wider context of G-24, the Community also acts as coordinator for assistance granted by those 24 countries to Central and Eastern Europe.

439. Agreements are presently in force with Hungary (O.J. 1993 L 347/2, see Dec. 93/742 (O.J. 1993 L 347/1)); Poland (O.J. 1993 L 348/2, see Dec. 93/743 (O.J. 1993 L 348/1)); the Czech Republic (O.J. 1994 L 360/2, see Dec. 94/910 (O.J. 1994 L 360/1)); Slovakia (O.J. 1994 L 359/2; see Dec. 94/909 (O.J. 1994 L 359/1)); Bulgaria (O.J. 1994 L 358/2, see Dec. 94/908 (O.J. 1994 L 358/1)); Romania (O.J. 1994 L 357/2, see Dec. 94/907 (O.J. 1994 L 357/1)); Latvia (O.J. 1998 L 26/3; see Dec. 98/98 (O.J. 1998 L 26/1)); Lithuania (O.J. 1998 L 51/3; see Dec. 98/150 (O.J. 1998 L 51/1)), and Estonia (O.J. 1998 L 68/3; see Dec. 98/180 (O.J. 1998 L 68/1)). The agreement with Slovenia is in the process of ratification. The agreements with Hungary, Poland, and the Czech Republic and the Slovak Republic replace first wave Europe Agreements concluded with the Visegrad countries on 16 December 1991 (the original agreement with the then Czechoslovakia never entered into force as that country dissolved into the Czech Republic and Slovakia before the ratification process was completed).

easier to apply than Article XIX GATT.[440] As far as the other Community freedoms are concerned, the transitional period consists of two five-year stages. In the fields of free movement of workers, freedom of establishment, the freedom to provide services and the free movement of capital, the agreement also contains certain principles such as non-discrimination as regards workers legally employed in the territory of the other party, which apply on both sides.[441] A number of other objectives in related fields (such as coordination of social security systems) are also set out in the agreements; these are to be achieved by decisions of the Association Council.

The Europe Agreements also contain extensive provisions on economic cooperation in myriad areas, such as industrial cooperation, promotion and protection of investments, energy (including nuclear energy), the environment, transport *etc.*, even embracing money-laundering. A separate Title in the Agreements concerns financial cooperation, and this is designed to permit the beneficiary countries to obtain loans from the European Investment Bank.

The institutional structure follows the customary pattern for association agreements, with an Association Council at ministerial level and a Joint Committee, as well as a Joint Parliamentary Committee. If everything proceeds according to the plans set out in the Agreements, the Association Councils will make significantly greater use of their decision-making powers than has traditionally been done in the case of older associations: at the end of the day the establishment of a common market with Poland and the other partner countries will depend on the capability of these councils to adopt decisions which will achieve the objectives in the fields of free movement of workers, establishment, the provision of services and the free movement of capital, bringing them gradually fully into line with the freedoms enjoyed by Community citizens and nationals of the EFTA States which are parties to the EEA.

The adoption of Agenda 2000[442] has concentrated political minds on the development of the partnership into real accession negotiations, and the first wave of accession negotiations commenced with Hungary, Poland, Estonia, the Czech Republic and Slovenia on 31 March 1998.[443]

440. Europe Agreement with Poland, Arts. 30–33, see Reg. 3491/93 (O.J. 1993 L 319/1).
441. Note that unlike the EEA Agreement (which effectively applies to nationals of the EFTA States which are parties to the EEA Agreement the provisions of Community secondary legislation on the free movement of workers), the Europe Agreements confer on the non-Community workers concerned who are lawfully employed in a Member State the right to non-discrimination, but they do not confer upon them the right to go and look for work for a period. Thus the treatment is significantly less favourable than that afforded to Community or EEA workers until a Europe Agreement worker has gone through the hoops of obtaining the necessary permits to take up a job offer.
442. COM (97) 2000 (in 2 Vols.).
443. Bull. EU 12–1997, point I.5 (at point 27); 3–1998, point 1.3.32.

4.2.4 Association as a preliminary to accession

It was observed above that the Europe Agreements are a type of pre-accession association. The earliest examples of such associations were with Greece (1961) and Turkey (1963). Greece acceded to the Community on 1 January 1981 as the tenth Member State. The association with Turkey has in many respects a similar structure to that of the Europe Agreements, in the sense that the agreement, albeit in a much more simple manner, only sketches the objectives in the field of the four freedoms which have to be achieved through decisions of the Association Council; moreover, it contains similar asymmetrical obligations concerning tariff concessions. The original Agreement with Turkey was however too simple, and a protocol was signed in 1970 which brought a transitional phase into being, designed to lead to a customs union over 20 years.[444] But the Agreement remained essentially unaltered in its objectives: a customs union, with free movement of workers, services and capital, as well as freedom of establishment, modeled on the EC Treaty. When a military regime came to power in Turkey in 1981 financial assistance was frozen until there was an improvement in respect for human rights and in democratic institutions. Relations were thus effectively frozen, and it was only in 1986 that the Association Council met again (involving ministerial level contact). Because of this long freeze and because the Association Council could not always arrive at decisions, the establishment of the customs union took rather longer than originally envisaged. The limited degree of liberalization for Turkish workers lawfully employed in a Member State has also caused such problems[445] that full free movement of workers does not seem to be a realistic proposition for the foreseeable future.

In the meantime, Turkey has applied to accede;[446] the Commission delivered an opinion stating that while accession is in principle possible, 'Turkey would find it hard to cope with the adjustment constraints with which it would be confronted in the medium term if it acceded to the Community.'[447] Only at the beginning of 1996 was the customs union

---

444. See O.J. 1973 L 293/68.
445. A number of judgments of the Court which endowed decisions of the Association Council on right of access to other work within the Community with direct effect met with unprecedented criticism from the German authorities, *e.g.* Case C-192/89 *Sevince v. Staatssecretaris van Justitie* [1990] ECR I-3461, [1992] 2 CMLR 57, and Case C-237/91 *Kus v. Landeshauptstadt Wiesbaden* [1992] ECR I-6781; [1993] 2 CMLR 887. See, generally, Lichtenberg *et al.* (eds.), *Gastarbeiter – Einwanderer – Bürger?* (Baden-Baden, 1996); and, further, *e.g.* Case C-36/96 *Günaydin et al. v. Freistaat Bayern* [1997] ECR I-5143; and Case C-98/96 *Ertanir v. Land Hessen* [1997] ECR I-5179.
446. Bull. EC 4–1987, points 1.3.1 and 1.3.2.
447. Bull. EC 12–1989, point 2.2.37.

between the Community and Turkey finally fully established.[448] The most difficult problem was the necessity of establishing a common commercial policy, which is a *sine qua non* for a customs union. It was scarcely conceivable that a country with such increasing economic importance as Turkey would completely adopt the Community's common commercial policy, without exercising any influence upon it, yet this was precisely what was required within the framework of association. In this respect, the Europe Agreements, which as yet do not go beyond the creation of a free trade area, have been somewhat more realistic, and thus easier to facilitate. There are still, though, formidable obstacles of a political nature in the path of Turkish accession.[449]

The associations with Malta (1970) and Cyprus (1972) were originally associations as substitutes for accession, later supplemented by financial protocols in 1976 and 1973 respectively. Both of these countries have since applied to accede. In respect of Cyprus, the transformation into a pre-accession association was already started by the adaptation of the association agreement and the creation of a customs union was proclaimed as the ultimate objective (1986). However, accession will certainly depend on a peaceful, balanced and lasting resolution of the conflict between the two Cypriot communities, as the Commission's opinion on the application recognized.[450] Nevertheless, accession negotiations began on 31 March 1998.[451] Because of political difficulties there was no similar adaptation of the agreement with Malta, which desired to proceed straight to accession. However, although the Commission was broadly positive in its opinion on the Maltese application,[452] the Maltese government suspended Malta's application in October 1996.[453]

4.2.5 Development association

The classic examples of development association are the successive Yaoundé and Lomé Conventions. After the independence of the French–African states it was felt necessary to continue the association provided for in Article 131 EC in a different manner. This took the form of a

---

448. Dec. 1/95 of the EC-Turkey Association Council (O.J. 1996 L 35/1). The European Parliament gave its assent on 13 December 1995 (Bull. EU 12–1995, points 1.4.67 and 1.10.1.
449. See Bull. EU 10–1996, point 1.4.69 and 4–1997, point 1.4.74 and it is now generally recognized that this is unlikely in the near future. See Epilogue, section 8.5.2, *post*.
450. COM (93) 313 Final, see Bull. EU 6–1993, point 1.3.6 and Supp. 5/93; see also *XXXVIIth General Report 1993* (Brussels, Luxembourg, 1994) points 642–645 (especially at 643).
451. Bull. EU 12–1997 point I.5 (at point 27); 3–1998, point 1.3.32.
452. COM (93) 312 Final, see Bull. EU 6–1993, point 1.3.7 and Supp. 4/93.
453. Bull. EU 5–1997, point 1.4.65, as corrected Bull. EU 6–1997, point 2.5.1.

combination of a free trade area and the grant of financial and technical assistance, initially contained in the Yaoundé Conventions. Currently this is governed by the Fourth Lomé Convention,[454] concluded between the Community and its Member States on the one part and now some 80 developing countries in Africa, the Carribean and the Pacific Ocean (the ACP States) on the other, which lasts until 28 February 2000, and has flowered into an extremely wide-ranging and complex agreement.

As to free trade, the agreement is non-reciprocal: the Community permits free access to ACP products (except for agricultural products, in respect of which a system of preferential treatment applies), while the ACP countries only grant Community products most-favoured nation treatment. The cooperation provisions of the Convention cover a multitude of areas which are important for development, such as agriculture, fisheries, industrial development, mining, energy, the environment and so on. In the sphere of financial development the European Development Fund has been created in order to support development activities under soft conditions.[455] The Convention also establishes a number of instruments such as a stabilization mechanism for exports of agricultural commodities (STABEX) and a special financing mechanism for countries which are particularly dependent on mining activities (SYSMIN), as well as special importation and sales conditions and guarantees for rum, bananas and sugar from the ACP States. Particularly the implementation of the obligations for access for ACP bananas to the Community market, after the establishment of the Community's internal market, has given rise to major controversy, both within and outside the Community, and brought the compatibility of the Lomé Convention with the GATT into problems.[456]

The most important institutions of cooperation are the Council of Ministers, the Committee of Ambassadors and the Joint Assembly. The members of the Council of the European Union and the members of the Commission on the one hand, and a member of the government on each of the ACP States on the other, comprise the Council of Ministers, it acts by agreement between the Community on the one hand and the ACP States on the other.[457] The Committee of Ambassadors consists on the one hand of the permanent representatives of the Member States to the Communites and a representative of the Commission, and on the other hand of the head of each ACP State's mission to the Communites.[458] An internal agreement governs the procedure by which the Community arrives at its position. The Joint Assembly is set up on a fifty-fifty basis and is composed of Members

454. O.J. 1991 L 229/3 (see Dec. 91/400 (O.J. 1991 L 229/1)). See Dec. 98/344 (O.J. 1998 L 156/1) on the mid-term review. South Africa has now acceded (O.J. 1997 L 220/2).
455. As to the 8th EDF, see Dec. 95/581 (O.J. 1995 L 327/16) of the Representatives of the governments of the Member States meeting within the Council.
456. See the end of section 3.2.1, *ante.*
457. Fourth Lomé Convention, Arts. 30 and 338, see also Arts. 339–345.
458. *Ibid.*, Art. 31, see also Arts. 346 and 347.

of the European Parliament on the one side and members of parliament or other designated representatives of the ACP States.[459] Dispute settlement is regulated by Articles 352 and 353 of the Fourth Lomé Convention.

Similar associations, with a clear development character, primarily characterized by one-sided free trade[460] have been concluded with the Maghreb and Mashreq countries, but they are called cooperation agreements. A particular aspect of the agreements with Morocco and Algeria is that they contain specific provisions concerning migrant workers, particularly non-discrimination provisions in relation to social security. These provisions have been endowed with direct effect by the Court of Justice.[461] New agreements with the Mediterranean countries now take the form of Euro-Mediterranean agreements, in pursuit of the Community's Mediterranean policy, now known as the Euro-Mediterranean partnership.[462] This involves gradual reciprocity in free trade, a political dialogue, and financial, economic and social and cultural cooperation.

In the past the Community had an agreement with Yugoslavia, similar to those with the other Mediterranean countries, but with the disintegration of Yugoslavia and the introduction of sanctions against Serbia and Montenegro, an end came to the old arrangements.[463]

4.3 Other cooperation agreements

4.3.1 Partnership agreements

The meeting of the European Council on Corfu in June 1994 saw the signature of the Partnership and Cooperation Agreement with Russia

459. *Ibid.*, Art. 32., see also Arts. 350–351.
460. Save for products in respect of which these countries enjoy a comparative advantage, but also form a threat for the agricultural sectors in the more 'Southern' Member States, such as vegetables, fruit and subtropical fruits.
461. See Case C-18/90 *Office national de l'emploi (Onem) v. Kziber* [1991] ECR I-199; Case C-58/93 *Yousfi v. Belgian State* [1993] ECR 1353; Case C-103/94 *Krid v. Caisse Nationale d'Assurance Vieillesse des Travailleurs Salariés (CNAVTS)* [1995] ECR I-719, and Case C-126/95 *Hallouzi-Choho v. Bestuur van de Sociale Verzekeringsbank* [1996] ECR I-4807. These judgments caused certain negative reactions on the part of the French government, just as those cited in note 445, *supra* brought forth such reactions on the part of the German government.
462. These agreements have been concluded with Tunisia (1995) and Morocco (1996), and negotiations have been opened with Algeria. Euro-Mediterranean Agreements have also been concluded with Israel (1996), the PLO for the benefit of the Palestinian Authority of the West Bank and the Gaza Strip (1997); an Agreement was initialed with Jordan in April 1997 (Bull. EU 4–1997, point 1.4.75, see COM (97) 554 Final), and negotiations on a new Agreement are still ongoing with Egypt (replacing the old Agreement from 1978).
463. See Lucron (1992) RMC 7 see, subsequently Dec. 93/407 (O.J. 1993 L 189/1) concerning Croatia; Dec. 93/408 (O.J. 1993 L 188/152) concerning Slovenia. See also General Report 1996 (Brussels, Luxembourg 1997) point 788.

which was followed later that year by Agreements with the Ukraine and Moldova, in 1995 by Agreements with Kyrgyzstan, Belarus, and Kazakhstan, and in 1996 by Agreements with Armenia, Azerbaijan, Georgia and Uzbekistan.[464] Initially, after the first internal reforms in the old Soviet Union a Trade and Cooperation Agreement was concluded with that country.[465] After the disintegration of the former Soviet Union, that agreement continued to be applied in relations with Russia and the New Independent States, although it has now been supplanted by the interim agreements pending the entry into force of the PCAs. The PCAs are mixed agreements, which, after Opinion 1/94 *WTO – GATS and TRIPS*[466] will require legal bases in several substantive articles of the EC Treaty as well as Articles 113 and 235 EC.[467] The agreement with Russia is perhaps understandably the most extensive, and it is that agreement which is the model for the approach discussed below.

One of the initial provisions notes expressly that respect for democratic principles and human rights form the basis of the domestic and foreign policies of the partners and for their cooperation. Reference is made to the Final Act of the Helsinki Conference and to the Charter of Paris for a New Europe.[468] The agreement establishes a political dialogue between the partners and also contains a large number of provisions concerning trade in the wide sense of the word: trade in goods, services, and establishment, as well as movement of capital and payments, competition and intellectual property. The fact that Russia is as yet not a member of the WTO and is

---

464. The various Partnership and Cooperation Agreements (PCAs) are being applied provisionally, through interim agreements, pending their ratification by all the contracting parties (although the interim agreement for Kazakhstan was made contingent on the holding of democratic elections, a condition which has since been satisfied); additional Protocols have also been signed in view of Austrian, Finnish and Swedish accession to the European Union.

465. O.J. 1990 L 68/3. This was an agreement between the EC and Euratom on the one hand and the USSR on the other. Shortly afterwards the TACIS programme was established (effectively a PHARE-type programme for the USSR) in order to offer technical assistance to restructuring efforts and economic recovery, see Reg. 2157/91 (O.J. 1991 L 201/2) which applied until the end of 1992. Later the TACIS programme was extended to all the New Independent States and to Mongolia by Reg. 2053/93 (O.J. 1993 L 187/1). The present programme is governed by Reg. 1276/96 (O.J. 1996 L 165/1) which applies until the end of 1999.

466. [1994] ECR I-5267, [1995] 1 CMLR 205.

467. Arts. 54(2), 57(2), 73c(2), 75 and 84(2) EC, as well as Art. 228(2) and (3). The interim agreements were concluded on the basis of Art. 113 EC.

468. As to the Charter of Paris, see Bull. EC 11–1990, point 2.2.1; 30 ILM 190 (1991). As to the Helsinki Final Act (1 August 1975), see 14 ILM 1292 (1975). See, generally, McGoldrick (1992) 12 YBEL 433 and extensive literature cited there. Such clauses do not occur in the Europe Agreements, although they can be traced in the preambles to those agreements. Membership of the Council of Europe and of the European Convention on Human Rights are usually given as the reasons for the absence of specific human rights and democracy provisions in the Europe Agreements.

still in the midst of the transition to a market economy played an important role in the drafting of this part of the agreement in particular. Thus a most-favoured-nation clause is introduced for trade in goods and for establishment, while at the same time exceptions are possible for special advantages which Russia may grant to the New Independent States. Current payments are liberalized, as are capital payments linked to direct investments. The agreement also contains a Title on economic cooperation, which envisages cooperation in the most diverse areas. In addition to the customary industrial cooperation, the fields of cooperation specified include transport, science and technology, nuclear matters, mining and the like. As in the Europe Agreements, drugs and money-laundering also feature. There is also a Title on financial cooperation.

The institutional structure of the agreement resembles that of association agreements, with a Cooperation Council at ministerial level, and a Cooperation Committee at the level of senior civil servants, and a Parliamentary Cooperation Committee. Although the Cooperation Council may make recommendations, it has no power, unlike most association councils, to adopt binding decisions. As has been indicated above, these PCAs are in the process of being ratified, but the partner countries are mostly already seeing the benefits through the interim agreements.

4.3.2   Diverse cooperation agreements

Since the mid-Seventies the Community has hardly signed any more classic trade agreements with non-European States which do not fall under development association, but only cooperation agreements based on Articles 113 and 235 EC. One of the first examples was the Cooperation Agreement with Canada (1976), but that remained an exception in the sense that the Community has not concluded any more general agreements with countries relations with which fall under the GATT and are not developing countries.[469] Transatlantic Declarations have been adopted with the United States and Canada, and a comparable agreement was reached with Japan, but these are political documents which fell more within the ambit of the then European Political Cooperation, now under CFSP, than within the ambit of Community law.[470]

---

469. *E.g.* the United States, Japan, Australia, New Zealand and South Korea.
470. See Bull. EC 11–1990, point 1.5.3 (United States), in the context of which a new
     transatlantic agenda and joint action plan was agreed in December 1995, see Bull. EU
     12–1995, points I.71–I.75 and 1.4.104; Bull. EC 11–1990, point 1.5.4, in the context
     of which a joint political declaration and action plan was agreed, see Bull. 12–1996,
     points 1.4.80 and 2.3.1 (Canada), and Bull. EC 7/8–1991, points 1.3.33 and 1.4.8
     (Japan), see the Commission's Communication *Europe and Japan: the next steps.*
     (COM (95) 73 Final). These Declarations are paved with good intentions in the form
     of consultation clauses and plans for cooperation, but it would unfortunately be exag-

If this outermost circle of the Community's agreements is analyzed, it is noticeable first that the Community renewed its agreements with Latin America. After 1990 the Community concluded agreements with Argentina, Chile, Uruguay and Brazil in rapid succession.[471] The Community also renewed its agreements with the countries of two regional economic organizations, the Andean Pact (Cartagena Agreement) countries (Bolivia, Ecuador, Columbia, Peru and Venezuela), and with the countries of the Central American Common Market (CACM).[472] In 1995 an interregional framework and cooperation agreement was negotiated with Mercosur, designed to strengthen existing ties and prepare for eventual association.[473] All these agreements follow the same global pattern: they contain a clause concerning most-favoured nation treatment (which was sometimes superfluous, sometimes not, as not all the Latin American countries involved were at that time parties to the GATT). The agreements also contain very wide provisions on economic, industrial and trade cooperation, and sometimes provisions concerning investments and cooperation in the field of the environment. The agreements each establish a Joint Committee for the cooperation, but it does not have real decision-making powers, unlike in the case of associations. It is also striking that nearly all these agreements open with a provision concerning the basis of democracy and human rights on which these mutual relations are founded.[474] Further political and economic dialogue takes place with the Rio Group,[475] and with the San José Group.[476]

As far as relations with Asian countries are concerned, the Community has had a cooperation agreement with the five ASEAN countries (Indonesia, Malaysia, the Philippines, Singapore and Thailand) since 1979, which corresponds to the agreements with the regional economic organizations in Latin America. The Community's relations with the South

gerating to say that they were more than expressions of pious hopes, as they have not really brought about a less confrontational conduct in (trade) policy, particularly between the United States and the Community.

471. *E.g.* the Framework Agreement with Chile (O.J. 1991 L 79/2, see Dec. 91/158 (O.J. 1991 L 79/1)).

472. Costa Rica, El Salvador, Guatemala, Honduras, Nicaragua and Panama.

473. The Southern Cone Common Market: Argentina, Brazil, Paraguay and Uruguay, see COM (95) 495 Final and Bull. EU 12–1995, point 1.4.111.

474. This provision in different from was also added to other agreements, such as those with the Baltic States and with Asian countries; the Lomé Convention also currently refers to the importance of human rights for development, see Kuyper in Maresceau (ed.), *op. cit.* (see note 151, *supra*) 401.

475. The permanent members of which are Argentina, Bolivia, Brazil, Chile, Colombia, Ecuador, Mexico, Panama, Paraguay, Peru, Uruguay and Venezuela; the dialogue was institutionalized in the Rome Declaration in 1990, Bull. EC 12–1990, points 1.4.39 and 2.4.1.

476. This embraces the Central American countries with Columbia, Mexico and Venezuela as cooperating countries, and Belize as an observer; the dialogue was established in San José in September 1984, Bull. EC 9–1984, points 1.3.1 *et seq.*

Asian countries (India, Pakistan, and Sri Lanka) have been revised in the light of the Commission's Communication *Towards a new strategy for Asia*[477] which adopts a similar approach, with a view to partnership, particularly in terms of emphasis on human rights, to that adopted in relations with Latin America. Thus the Community has concluded new partnership and development agreements with India (1993),[478] and Sri Lanka (1994) and a cooperation agreement with Nepal (1995); negotiations are also under way for cooperation agreements with Pakistan and Bangladesh; non-preferential agreements without financial protocols seem to be largely the order of the day. Although it has been argued that the decisions approving these agreements on behalf of the Community should refer to Article 130w EC rather than Article 130y EC, on the somewhat strange notion that Article 130y is simply procedural in nature, the practice is indeed to refer to Article 130y rather than Article 130w.[479] Similar agreements were signed with Vietnam in 1995, and Cambodia and Laos in 1997. Relations with China are also governed by a cooperation agreement dating from 1985, and there has been a structured political dialogue with China since 1994.[480] Commercial relations with Taiwan are formally conducted on the basis of autonomous Community measures, even though they are often preceded by unofficial negotiations. In this manner the Community takes account of China's sensitivities, but at the same time it can seek a *modus vivendi* with Taiwan, which is of particularly great importance in matters such as trade in textile products. The Community also played a role in enabling 'China–Taipei' to commence negotiations for future membership of the WTO.[481] A Framework Agreement on trade and cooperation was signed with South Korea in 1996, which envisages intensified cooperation between the parties in myriad fields. 1996 also saw the first ASEM (Asia–Europe dialogue) Summit in Bangkok; the second is due to take place in London in April 1998.

Relations between the Community and the countries of the Middle East have not yet been highly developed in contractual terms. A Euro–Arab dialogue has existed since 1976 in the context first of European political cooperation, now of CFSP. One of the objectives of this dialogue is to contribute to the Middle Eastern peace process. The old cooperation

---

477. COM (94) 314 Final; Bull. 7/8–1994, point 1.3.55.
478. Which it is intended to strengthen, see COM (96) 275 Final; Bull. 6–1996, point 1.4.94.
479. Although the proposal for the decision on the Sri Lankan agreement (O.J. 1994 C 86/5) mentioned Art. 130w, the final decision mentioned Art. 130y EC instead, see Dec. 95/129 (O.J. 1995 L 85/32). This is in addition to Article 113 EC; Article 235 EC is no longer invoked in such agreements. See the end of section 3.3.6, *ante*.
480. See the Commission's Communication, COM (95) 279; Bull. EU 7/8–1995, point 1.4.98.
481. Both China and 'China–Taipei' (Taiwan) enjoy observer status at the WTO (all observers are currently negotiating WTO membership).

agreement with North Yemen, dating from 1984, was extended with effect from 1995 to embrace the new unified Republic of Yemen, reflecting the stabilization since the original exchange of letters in 1993.[482] Since 1989 the Community has had a cooperation agreement with the Gulf Cooperation Council countries[483] which in the longer term should lead to the establishment of a free trade area. The realization of this goal has caused considerable problems.[484]

A number of autonomous measures relating to development assistance and humanitarian aid should also be noted. In 1992 the Council adopted Regulation 443/92 on financial and technical assistance to and economic cooperation with the non-associated developing countries in Asia and Latin America.[485] Here too strong emphasis was placed on the basis of the Community's development policy being democracy and human rights. The Community is also a large-scale provider of food aid, in part on the basis of the World Food Programme[486] and obligations undertaken towards UNRWA. Current food aid is governed by Regulation 1292/96.[487] While some assistance is in the form of standard aid, much takes the form of emergency aid. For these purposes the Community has established ECHO, which is a semi-independent service and is in a position to make money and goods available at short notice to assist in coping with the consequences of disasters, whether natural or otherwise; this now operates on a firm legal basis.[488] These latter two instruments are based on Article 130w EC.

4.4 The system of agreements viewed by sectors

This section gives a brief overview of the Community's system of agreements on a sector-by sector basis; reference is also made from time to time to autonomous external measures in the sectors concerned.

The first paragraph of Article 71 ECSC provides that save as otherwise provided therein the powers of the governments of the Member States in matters of commercial policy are unaffected by the ECSC Treaty: thus

---

482. See now Dec. 98/189 (O.J. 1998 L 72/17).
483. Bahrein, Oman, Qatar, Kuwait, Saudi Arabia and the United Arab Emirates.
484. As to the agreement, see O.J. 1989 L 54/3 (and Dec. 89/147 (O.J. 1989 L 54/1). See also COM (95) 541 Final.
485. O.J. 1992 L 54/1.
486. Which is a joint UN–FAO Programme under the Food Aid Convention which forms part of the International Grains Agreement (the latest dates from 1995, published by the International Grains Council, London), see Dec. 96/88 (O.J. 1996 L 21/47), and the package (O.J. 1996 L 21/49).
487. O.J. 1996 L 166/1. See also Reg. 2200/87 (O.J. 1987 L 204/1, amended by Reg. 790/91 (O.J. 1991 L 81/108).
488. Reg. 1257/96 (O.J. 1996 L 163/1).

their competence to conclude trade agreements relating to products falling under the ECSC Treaty is unaffected. Only to counter 'dumping or other practices condemned by the Havana Charter', international distortions of competition, or vastly increased imports was the ECSC entitled to take measures in the commercial policy field.[489] It may be wondered whether these provisions really deserve to continue to exist in a situation in which commercial policy competence for all other products has in principle been transferred to the Community, and there is no longer a situation in which such transfer had not occurred (as was the case between 1952 and 1970) and it made little sense to adopt a common commercial policy in respect of two products. Article 232(1) EC provides that Treaty does not affect the provisions of the ECSC Treaty and in particular the rights and obligations of the Member States thereunder. It may rightly be wondered whether the 'notwithstanding' provision of Article 71 ECSC is actually a right of the Member States. In the light of the above, it could very well be concluded that with the coming into force of the common commercial policy in 1970 the Member States no longer have commercial policy competence in relation to coal and steel products. All the more so since the Court of Justice has held that the principle of free movement of goods within the Community also applies to coal and steel products from third countries, and that the residual powers of the Member States in the part of the ECSC Treaty concerned must be strictly interpreted.[490] In practice trade agreements concerning ECSC products are sometimes partially governed by Acts of the Representatives of the governments of the Member States meeting within the Council and partially implicitly based on Article 113 EC, on other occasions they are effected by the so-called minor revision procedure of Article 95 ECSC.[491] The Court has accepted conclusion of agreements on the basis of Article 113 EC if the agreement to be concluded does not specifically relate to ECSC products.[492]

In relation to products falling under the Euratom Treaty, the situation is even less clear. On the one hand Articles 64–66 Euratom confer far-reaching powers on the Euratom Supply Agency and the Commission in the context of supply contracts or contracts for the supply of ores, source materials and special fissile materials coming from outside the Community, yet on the other hand the Euratom Treaty contains no commercial policy provisions. It is submitted that the better view is that trade in Euratom

---

489. Art. 74 ECSC.
490. See Case 36/83 *Mabanaft GmbH v. Hauptzollamt Emmerich* [1984] ECR 24972523–2524 and Case 328/85 *Deutsche Babcock Handel GmbH v. Hauptzollamt Lübeck-Ost* [1987] ECR 5119 at 5139.
491. The former approach was taken in relation to the results of the GATT Tokyo Round, see Benyon and Bourgeois (1982) 19 CMLRev. 23. The latter approach was adopted for the agreements with the United States over export restrictions for steel products, see Dec. 2871/82 (O.J. 1982 L 307/11) and Dec. 3724/89 (O.J. 1989 L 368/21).
492. Opinion 1/94 *WTO – GATS and TRIPs* [1994] ECR I-5267 at 5396–5397.

products in falls principle under the common commercial policy,[493] save as far as concerns supplies of products specified in Article 64 Euratom to the Community from third countries.[494] In the other areas covered by the Euratom Treaty, such as nuclear safety and nuclear research the Community has concluded myriad agreements with third countries on the basis of Article 101 Euratom.

In section 3.1.1 above the question was raised whether international trade in services and establishment fell within the concept of the common commercial policy.[495] Sometimes Article 59 EC is seen as a provision which could support an external policy in relation to trade in services, but it is submitted that Article 59 is too limited in nature to be capable of doing so. It is rather a provision which enables internal provisions relating to free movement to be declared also applicable to subjects of third countries who have established themselves in the Community. The admission of persons or undertakings established outside the Community to provision of services within the Community or to the provision of services over the Community's external frontiers cannot be based on this provision. This would have to occur through an *ERTA* approach, as in the case of the agreement with Switzerland on insurance, which was based on Articles 57 and 66 EC.[496] This approach has now been endorsed by the Court in Opinion 1/94.[497] It has already been observed in section 3.2.2 above that autonomous policy in this field has so far been limited to reciprocity requirements in banking and insurance directives. Such provisions involve the grant of exclusive external competence in the fields which they cover,[498] as long as no use has been made of the power in Article K.9 TEU to communitarize policy in relation to third country nationals.

The question of free movement of workers for the benefit of workers from third countries, insofar as it is not limited to what is necessary for the international provision of services, but represents an independent value, has two facets. The first is free movement of such workers within the

493. See Art. 234 EC, 2nd para.
494. Opinion 1/94 [1994] ECR I-5267 at 5396 would appear to confirm this view.
495. It will be recalled that the Treaty of Amsterdam (not yet in force) would add a new Art. 113(5) expressly permitting the Council to extend the application of Art. 113(1)–(4) to international negotiations and agreements on services and intellectual property insofar as they are not covered by those provisions. Art. 2, point 20 TA.
496. See Reg. 2155/91 (O.J. 1991 L 205/1); Dec. 91/370 (O.J. 1991 L 305/2); the Agreement itself (O.J. 1991 L 205/3), and Dir. 91/371 (O.J. 1991 L 205/48). On the other hand, the Agreement with the United States on public procurement, which also embraced services, was concluded on the basis of Art. 113 EC, see Dec. 93/323 (O.J. 1993 L 125/1) and the Agreement itself (O.J. 1993 L 125/1), a matter which caused the decision to be annulled, see Case C-360/93 *European Parliament v. Council* [1996] ECR I-1195, although its effects were preserved.
497. [1994] ECR I-5267 at 5402–5403.
498. *Ibid.* at 5416.

Community. This clearly falls under Community competence, as only the Community may extend the preferential treatment granted to nationals of other Member States so as to benefit third country nationals.[499] The second aspect, free movement between the Community and third countries, which embraces the problem of first admission onto the territory of a Member State, is still regarded as falling within the powers of the Member States, and at best what may be expected is coordination under the intergovernmental Article K TEU.[500]

The EC Treaty contains fundamental rules on the movement of capital and of payments with third countries, and makes it clear that these are separate from the common commercial policy as such. In principle capital movements and payments to and from third countries are totally liberalized.[501] Only to the extent to which restrictions on capital movements with third countries are directly linked to policy concerning direct investment (including investment in real estate), establishment, the provision of financial services, or the admission of securities to capital markets may existing restrictions be maintained or may the Council adopt measures by a qualified majority, on a proposal from the Commission.[502] Given that this area involves the interaction of commercial policy on services with external policy on capital movements, there may well be complications in the exercise of this provision in the future.

As far as international transport policy is concerned, in Opinion 1/94 the Court expressly stated in clear terms that the whole of transport policy should be based on the *ERTA* doctrine, and thus access to the market for transport services was not a matter falling within the common commercial policy.[503] It is remarkable that it is only now, more than 20 years after the judgment dealing with the ERTA that the Community is actually considering acceding to it. The Community concluded its first civil air transport agreements, with Norway and Sweden, in 1992.[504]

On the borders of international maritime policy and competition policy, the Community has bound itself in a unique and indirect manner to the UNCTAD Convention on a Code of Conduct for Liner Shipping Conferences, by prescribing that on ratification of or accession to that Convention the Member States must enter certain reserves which are designed to ensure that the Code will be compatible with Community law

---

499. Reg. 1612/68 (O.J. 1968 English Special Edition 1968 (II), p. 475, most recently amended by Reg. 2434/92 (O.J. 1992 L 245/1), Arts. 16(2) and 19(2).
500. The Treaty of Amsterdam (not yet in force) will bring first admission of third country nationals into the EC Treaty itself, see the new Arts. 73i–73k EC.
501. Art. 73b EC.
502. Art. 73c EC. Unanimity is required for measures under Art. 73c(2) which constitute a step back in Community law as regards the liberalization of capital movements to or from third countries.
503. [1994] ECR I-5267 at 5402–5404.
504. Since superceded, see Chapter XI, section 3.12, *ante*.

and the legal requirements of OECD.[505] Many Community agreements, particularly association and free trade agreements with European countries contain provisions, often analogous to Articles 85, 86 and 90 EC, relating to guaranteeing competition in trade between the parties. The procedures laid down in those agreements for this purpose are in fact rarely or never applied; distortions of competition in trade between the contracting parties always involved distortions of competition in trade between Member States as well, so Articles 85 and 86 EC could be applied directly without objection.[506] There is no doubt that the Community may be a party to agreements of the soft law variety, such as that established in the framework of OECD, concerning notification, information exchange and cooperation in the field of application of the competition laws of the parties involved. The Court answered in the negative the question whether the Commission, as the competition authority, could conclude such agreements on its own account.[507]

The field of public procurement has undergone a stormy Community evolution in recent years, not only due to internal pressures but also in response to external pressures. The Utilities Directive[508] contained a similar reciprocity provision to that used in the banking and insurance sectors.[509] This was in reality an invitation to other countries to open up their markets in advance of the conclusion of the GATT Agreement on Government Procurement (GAPA) at the end of the Uruguay Round.[510] Agreements concerning public procurement were originally seen as trade agreements, but their extension in some cases to embrace procurement of services and to public works contracts caused Article 113 EC alone to be a controversial and ultimately unacceptable legal basis.[511]

External aspects of Community fisheries policy are also important, as was stressed in section 2.5 of Chapter XI, above. International agreements are an absolute necessity in order to permit the Community's fishing fleet to fish in the exclusive economic zones of third countries. After the judgment in Cases 3, 4 and 6/76 *Kramer et al.*[512] there is no doubt as to the Community's exclusive competence to deal with fisheries and the conservation of the biological resources of the sea. The Community has

---

505. See *ibid.*, section 3.11, *ante*. See Kuyper (1981) XII NYBIL 73 (and in relation to the competition aspects at 80–81).
506. See Cases 89/85 *etc. A. Åhlström Osakeyhtiö et al.* v. *Commission* [1988] ECR 5193 at 5246–5247.
507. Case C-327/91 *France* v. *Commission* [1994] ECR I-3641.
508. Now Dir. 93/38 (O.J. 1993 L 199/84).
509. *Ibid.*, Art. 36.
510. See Dec. 93/323 (O.J. 1993 L 125/1), the agreement with the United States (O.J. 1993 L 125/2) and Dec. 93/324 (O.J. 1993 L 125/54). Both decisions were annulled, see note 496, *supra*, but the effects were preserved (although replacement measures have not been adopted, as the agreement expired on 30 May 1995).
511. See Case C-360/93 *European Parliament* v. *Council* [1996] ECR I-1195 at 1218–1219.
512. [1976] ECR 1279 at 1309.

concluded countless bilateral agreements concerning fishing with the Scandinavian, African (including north African) and South American countries. These grant reciprocal access to fishing rights in the parties' exclusive economic zones, or obtain access for Community fishing boats in return for payments. The Community is also a party to many agreements concerning fishing or conservation on the High Seas, such as the North Atlantic Fisheries Organization (NAFO). When the Council sought to grant the Member States (as opposed to the Community itself) the right to vote in the FAO on a draft agreement relating to the promotion of conservation and management measures by fishing vessels on the High Seas, the Court made it very clear that this was not an acceptable course of action.[513]

The Community's international environmental policy is characterized by the conclusion of regional or global multilateral environmental agreements, initially on the basis of Article 235 EC, nowadays on the basis of Article 130r(4) EC. Almost all of these agreements have been concluded in the form of mixed agreements, an approach which is effectively pre-programmed by the text of Article 130r(4), particularly its second paragraph. The subsidiarity principle, which was initially specifically laid down in this provision, has disappeared from it now that it has become a general principle in Article 3b EC.

As far as international aspects of Community research and technology policy are concerned, the amendments made by the TEU have continued those introduced by the SEA. The exercise of the power to conclude agreements in this field[514] is directly linked to the execution of the multiannual framework programmes which, in accordance with Article 130i EC, embraces all Community activities in the area of research and technological development. These framework programmes have been established, as have various specific programmes, as was seen in section 7.3 of Chapter XI, above. A whole host of agreements have now been concluded on the basis of Article 130m EC. It is still true that there has been a certain variable geometry in the Community's activities in research and technological development: internally, supplementary programmes to the multiannual framework programmes could only be carried out by the Member States; externally, a flexible cooperation with the European member countries of the OECD was possible in the context of COST or the EUREKA programme.[515]

The development of the Community's international energy policy has been a difficult process. It was always possible for the Community to accede to the International Energy Agency in Paris, but it was never taken up. As was seen in section 6 of Chapter XI, above, the Community was

---

513. Case C-25/94 *Commission v. Council* [1996] ECR I-1469 at 1508–1511.
514. Art. 130m EC.
515. The annual *General Report* gives further details.

heavily involved in the drawing up of the European Energy Charter, the initiative for which owed much to the former Dutch Prime Minister, Lubbers. The Community and the Member States signed the non-binding Charter together, and the accompanying European Energy Charter Treaty contains rules on trade, investment, technological cooperation and the like concerning energy generation and raw materials for that purpose. Again, the format of a mixed agreement is adopted.[516]

---

516. See COM (94) 405 Final (O.J. 1994 C 334/1) and Dec. 98/181 (O.J. 1998 L 69/1).

EPILOGUE

The horizon 2000*

1. INTRODUCTION

The major tasks identified in the final Chapter of the second edition[1] for the period 1989–1993 have been largely achieved on schedule. It is still less clear to what extent the same will be able to be said of the new challenges facing the Community within the European Union during the coming years. Although it has too frequently been suggested in the discussions surrounding the Intergovernmental Conference of 1996 programmed by Article N TEU that these challenges are exclusively institutional in nature, this is incorrect: institutional solutions must always be adapted to the substantive challenges. Indeed, as was shown in Chapter I, above, a major reason for the convincing success of the Spaak Report was that it deduced the institutional structure from the problems to be solved.

This epilogue discusses therefore a number of major and interlinked substantive challenges as perceived at the end of 1995; challenges which at least for the next years at both sides of the millennium require an indicative beginning of a response. They are all linked to the TEU and more recent developments.

First, attention turns in section 2 to the development of programmes in the field of economic and social cohesion after the expiry of the present programmes in 1999. This point is linked to the further development of the social dimension of the Communities and, partly on budgetary grounds, with the answer to be given to the accession applications of the various Central and Eastern European countries. By virtue of Article 130b EC the objective of economic and social cohesion plays a role in the coordination of economic policy and in the establishment of the internal market; it is in

---

* In the Dutch edition this Epilogue was written by VerLoren van Themaat. The editor has translated and edited that contribution (which forms sections 1–7, post), also adding some points, particularly in the notes; VerLoren van Themaat and the editor have collaborated in writing the additional material in section 8, post, in order to take further account of developments, particularly with a view to enlargement, and the results of the European Council in Amsterdam in June 1997, to the beginning of May 1998.

1. Deventer and London, 1989 (ed. Gormley).

any event also mentioned in Article 2 EC as a general objective of the Community. In turn, Article 130v EC provides that the execution of that objective must also take account of the objectives of the new Title on Development Cooperation.

Secondly, Article 2 EC already contains the important new objective of achieving sustainable and non-inflationary growth, respecting the environment. Article 130r(2) EC requires the requirements set out in Article 130r(1) EC to be integrated into the determination and execution of Community policy in all other (relevant) areas. It thus appears that this new objective will necessitate more far-reaching internal coordination by all the policy-making Institutions than that required by the objective of economic and social cohesion, particularly in relation to the Community's external policies. Section 3, below, examines some of the important links in these matters.

Thirdly, section 4 deals separately with the achievement of Economic and Monetary Union, as this will also involve some problems beyond the year 2000 which have been confronting the 1996 Intergovernmental Conference.[2]

Fourthly, under the heading 'the external stance of the European Union' the external aspects of the first three matters are discussed, in section 5, below, along with the external aspects of other areas, and the substantive problems confronting the Community in the prospect of further enlargement, particularly involving the Central and Eastern European countries. In addition to external Community policy and the problems of enlargement, the second pillar (CFSP) is also briefly discussed, bearing in mind that the IGC has in any event been obliged to discuss it on the basis of Article J.4(6) TEU. The provisions on CFSP are also decisive for the future of the Union, including of the Community itself. The substantive problems of the third pillar, JHA, have such an individual character that they are only briefly discussed in section 6, below, insofar as they are of importance for the IGC.

The institutional changes, which have in fact played a major role in the discussions in the IGC will primarily have to enable the Union, with the Community as its central pillar, to accomplish its tasks effectively. This requires fundamental institutional changes, apart from those which were necessitated on the enlargement at the beginning of 1995, with Austrian, Finnish and Swedish accession, and those which will result from the expected enlargements to nineteen, twenty-five or more Member States.[3] But before dealing with those matters, in section 7.1 attention turns to the probably too great a role played by divergent conceptions of the

---

2. Hereafter, IGC.
3. In particular the applications of Cyprus, the Czech Republic, Hungary and Poland come to mind, and the later applications of the other Central and East European countries and Slovenia.

future of European integration in present discussions. Section 7.2 deals with the institutional changes necessary on the basis of the substantive analysis, also taking account of the conclusions from the strongly divergent conceptions as to the future; it is submitted that the proposed changes should be defensible in all Member States. Some possible variants are, however, also mentioned, taking account of the already evident need on the part of some Member States for differentiated integration (multiple-speed or variable geometry), a need which may well increase with the envisaged enlargement eastwards. Section 7.3 examines the possibilities of making the unnecessarily complex European Treaties more transparent, and, section 7.4 makes some observations about the preparations for the IGC. Section 8 presents a brief overview of the perspectives resulting from the Treaty of Amsterdam, in particular with regard to the challenges perceived a year before the start of the 1996 IGC.

2. ECONOMIC AND SOCIAL COHESION AND SOME ALLIED PROBLEM AREAS

In view of the expiry of present programmes in 1999, a timely and thorough evaluation of the results of the structural funds coordinated under Title XIV of the EC Treaty with a view to economic and social cohesion will be essential.[4] The point of departure will have to be, as was noted in Chapter IX, that the set of instruments of the basic and coordination regulations seeks to strengthen the development potential of the economically weaker areas of the Community, and improve the adaptation of the labour factor to the process of reallocation of the market. Just like the assistance which Germany accords to the new Länder, the cohesion programmes are by their very nature temporary and they will tail off over the years. In the evaluation of the current programmes, attention will thus first have to focus on the extent to which the results achieved – also through the other policy instruments specified in Article 130b EC – justify the continuation of the financial programmes in a modified form. In this evaluation attention must also be paid to the so far very critical reports of the Court of Auditors, as well as the adaptations of policy resulting from them and the organizational structure of supervision of the implementation of the programmes.

Secondly, during the course of the IGC the results and prospects of the Protocol on Social Policy, which is also important for economic and social cohesion, came up for evaluation. For the reasons set out in Chapter IX,

---

4. See now, generally, *Agenda 2000* (Bull. EU Supp. 5/97) and COM (98) 131 Final. See also the Communication on the link between regional and competition policy (O.J. 1998 C 90/3), and, as to financial aspects, COM (98) 158 Final.

above, thought had to be given to the connection between social policy and the coordination of economic policy. The key connector is above all employment opportunities. This connection had to lead to a thorough revision of the place and fleshing out of all the Treaty provisions on social policy.[5] As indicated in Chapter IX, above, such a revision of the Treaty provisions and integration into the Treaty itself of the Agreement annexed to the Protocol on Social Policy have now indeed been achieved by the Treaty of Amsterdam.[6]

Thirdly, already during the IGC it was necessary to take account of the budgetary need to adapt the scope of the internal Structural Funds to take account of the policy objectives concerning Central and Eastern Europe and developing countries. This subject is revisited in section 5, below. However, it is appropriate to note here that, in view of the financial aspects of present and future external policy objectives, the present approximately 5:1 ratio between the costs of internal and external financial assistance will have to be drastically altered in the coming years.[7]

3. THE NEW OBJECTIVE OF SUSTAINABLE GROWTH

As was explained in Chapter III, above, the old objective of a 'constant and balanced expansion' in Article 2 EEC was replaced in the TEU by a reference to 'a sustainable and non-inflationary growth respecting the environment' in Article 2 EC.[8] From Article 130r(1) EC it appears that the italicized parts of the new objective embraces not merely 'preserving, protecting and improving the quality of the environment' but also 'prudent and rational utilization of natural resources.' Moreover, the last sentence of the first paragraph of Article 130r(2) EC requires

5. Apart from the implications for the promotion of employment opportunities, matters considered in the Fifth Dutch edition of this work included the desirability of expanding the scope of Articles 48 *et seq.* to embrace employees from third countries, lawfully resident in a Member State; an adaptation of the implementing regulations, and, if necessary, an adaptation of the text of Art. 51 EC to the development of privatized public-law orientated social security rules and other new developments in the field of social security, which undermine the coordination approach which forms the present basis of Art. 51; and the desirability of creating a legal basis in the Treaty for cross-border collective labour agreements and the rights and duties of the social partners. These important problem areas have however been left open by the Treaty of Amsterdam.
6. This is not yet in force at the date at which this work states the law.
7. See the realistic estimates of the Independent Experts' Report for the Commission, *Stable Money – Sound Finances* (European Economy, No. 53, Luxembourg, 1993), and Van Wersch (1991) *Internationale Spectator* 442.
8. Emphasis added. The new version of Art. 2 EC which the Treaty of Amsterdam (not yet in force) will introduce the new overriding concept of promoting sustainable development into the objectives of the European Community.

environmental protection requirements to be integrated into the definition and implementation of other Community policies. Article 130r(1) and (4) make it plain that this applies in respect of the Community's external as well as internal policies. The major importance of the common commercial policy in this connection was further emphasized with the conclusion of the Uruguay Round in Marrakesh in 1994. The connection is further stressed in relation to development cooperation in Article 130u(1) EC, which mentions 'the sustainable economic and social development of the developing countries, and more particularly the most disadvantaged among them' as one of the objectives of such cooperation. The terms 'sustainable growth' and 'sustainable development' which were used at the UNCED Conference in 1992, clarify more precisely what is involved: guaranteeing for future generations not only environmental protection but also the continued availability of sufficient natural resources. Thus this objective is of unlimited long-term significance, and something which will have to be integrated not merely into world environmental policy, the common commercial policy and development cooperation, but also in agricultural policy, industrial policy, Economic and Monetary Union, and social policy. The environmental policy objective will also have to be clearly integrated into the policy on the achievement and maintenance of the common market, as Article 130r(2) EC makes clear, in addition to the other policy areas involving positive integration just mentioned. This will involve both the primary freedoms of movement of goods and establishment, as well as the proper functioning of the internal market. Leaving policy on sustainable growth respecting the environment too much in the hands of the Member States on the basis of the principle of subsidiarity would not only endanger the objectives of this policy themselves, it would also endanger the maintenance of the internal market. Chapter 10 of the Commission's White Paper on *Growth, Competitiveness and Employment*[9] summarizes only some of the implications of these new objectives, which have been fleshed out in somewhat greater detail in earlier parts and are directly linked with the subject-matter of the White Paper.[10] The few considerations mentioned above must suffice to make it clear that this new objective, like that of economic and social cohesion will make high institutional demands of the Community in bringing this linkage to fruition. Section 7, below, deals further with this point.

9. Bull. EU, Supp. 6/93, p. 161 *et seq.*
10. See, further, Wolfson in Kremers (ed.), *Inspelen op Europa* (Schoonhoven, 1993) 321. The theoretical and practical implications and the political implementation of this objective will require considerable thought and political action, see Tims and De la Rive Box, in *De toekomst van de nederlandse buitenlandse politiek* (Clingendael, The Hague, 1993) 89. See also the WRR Report, *Duurzame risico's: een blijvend gegeven* (The Hague, 1994), and the reactions to that Report in *WRR Mededelingen* No. 56 (The Hague, 1994).

4. ECONOMIC AND MONETARY UNION

The achievement of Economic and Monetary Union is in the first instance
a medium-term project, although one which is concentrating minds more
and more in the short term. Article 109j(4) EC prescribes that monetary
union, which is politically and legally the most spectacular element of
EMU, will commence at the latest in 1999. Given that it is not expected
that all the Member States will be ready to participate at the outset,
entirely new problems, also of an institutional nature, will arise in view of
a differentiated, two-speed policy. These problems, along with others
facing the IGC, have been carefully analyzed before the IGC began, and
have been the focus of considerable discussion, both in political and
negotiating circles. Two of the other problems deserve brief mention. First,
as has been pointed out in Chapter IX and as follows from the preceding
sections in this Chapter, the coordination of economic policy governed in
Articles 102a–104c EC will have to embrace more than merely macro-
economic policy, budgetary policy and the other matters expressly
mentioned in those provisions. It is evident from the absence in Article
3a(3) EC of mention of the objective of a high degree of employment,
which is mentioned in Article 104 EC, and also from the institutional
provisions concerning EMU, that the drafting of that part of the TEU was
left too much in the hands of the Finance Ministers and the Governors of
the Central Banks. The reference in Articles 3a and 102a EC to all the
objectives mentioned in Article 2 EC as such leaves room for a wider
interpretation of the concept of economic policy, but from an institutional
perspective it will not be easy to involve all the relevant departmental
ministers in the coordination of the economic policy of the Member States
(even though they may be involved in national economic policy-making),
and to avoid the specialist Councils taking decisions which are at odds
with the global guidelines for economic policy. As was explained in
Chapter IX, above, the EMU provisions themselves offer no clear solution
to the institutional and procedural questions which arise, although in
practice efforts in that direction are indeed made, as with the discussion of
the Commission's White Paper on *Growth, Competitiveness and
Employment*.[11] One of the possibilities which might be envisaged is a rather
broader composition of the Economic and Financial Committee provided
for in Article 109c(2) EC.

Secondly, the manner in which the EMU provisions were drafted has
resulted in their having much more the character of a *Traité-Loi*, like the
ECSC Treaty, than of a *Traité-Cadre*, to be fleshed out in the form of
subsequent secondary legislation. Thus these provisions stand out from the
approach of the rest of the EC Treaty. From the point of view of economic
actors this has clear medium-term advantages. Nevertheless, experience

11. See note 9, *supra*.

with the ECSC Treaty shows that the circumstances and viewpoints which led to the drafting of a *Traité-Loi* can change over the course of time. The question thus arises whether it might not be desirable to include a provision permitting amendment of the EMU provisions, including the Protocol on the Statute of the ESCB and the ECB, on the basis of experience, maintaining the central elements of monetary union, but without requiring that such amendments be ratified by each Member State in accordance with its respective constitutional requirements.[12] It could be prescribed that such an amendment could be made by co-decision by the Council and the European Parliament, acting by a qualified majority, embracing all participants in the third stage of EMU, with serious weight given to the views of the ECB, as in the case of Article 106(5) EC. The legitimate expectation of economic actors that the third stage of EMU would start on 1 January 1999 in accordance with Article 109j(4) EC would remain intact, and the coordination of economic policy, particularly of the Member States which already participate in the third stage of monetary union by that date, could be strengthened also after 1999. Germany already argued in the IGC on Economic and Monetary Union which preceded the TEU that such a strengthening of the coordination of economic policy was an essential guarantee for the proper functioning of monetary union. Moreover, the view is also gaining ground in wider circles that, in part for the reasons advanced earlier in this Chapter, a strengthening of (socio-) economic policy after 1999 will be essential. A Treaty amendment along the lines suggested above could, in the first instance, be used particularly for the coordination of economic policy between the (first) participants in the third stage of monetary union. The mandate of the 1996 IGC did not however allow such an amendment of the EMU provisions by the Treaty of Amsterdam.

5. THE EXTERNAL STANCE OF THE EUROPEAN UNION AS REGARDS THIRD COUNTRIES AND INTERNATIONAL ORGANIZATIONS

5.1 External aspects of Community policy areas

All the policies discussed in the preceding sections, which are intertwined with many other policy areas, also have external aspects which are clearly indicated in the relevant provisions. The same applies to the common market, which is mentioned in Article 2 EC, along with EMU as a principal means through which the objectives mentioned in that provision

12. It will be recalled that 'small' revisions of the ECSC Treaty are permitted, and that the Treaties have on two occasions been amended by Council decision to take account of the non-accession of Norway to the Communities (in 1973) and to the Union (in 1995), see Case C-259/95 *European Parliament v. Council* [1997] ECR I-5303.

are to be achieved. As was indicated in Chapter III, above, the concept of a common market lies behind the establishment of the internal market, as well as behind Community competition policy and the common commercial policy. Certainly after the conclusion of the Uruguay Round it is clear that the open, and thus not protectionist stance of the common market vis-à-vis the world market, in accordance with Articles 3a and 110 EC, will require ever more attention. This is rightly pointed out in Chapter 3 of the White Paper.[13] In the WTO, which succeeded the old GATT as a result of the successful completion of the Uruguay Round, similar problems from a legal standpoint will arise as occurred with the realization of free movement of goods and services, and to a lesser extent with foreign investment, within the Community. The WTO will also have to cope with legal policy problems similar to those which have arisen in relation to the application of Community internal and external competition policy. Despite, or even precisely through the conceptual differences to be taken into account, an institutionally assured mutual policy determination will be required, and new requirements will be made of the case-law of the Court of Justice, in view of the binding dispute settlement system at world level. It may be expected that the WTO will also have to deal with social, cultural and environmental aspects, as well as other non-economic aspects of international policy.

In Chapter XII above, and in other chapters, it has already been mentioned which external aspects of other policy areas than those discussed in this Epilogue will demand attention, and which legal questions may arise which are already partly answered in the case-law of the Court. In the previous chapters mention has also been made of a large number of international economic organizations, other than the GATT and the ILO, with which the Community already cooperates or, as in the case of external monetary policy, will have to deal. In the political and economic relations with certain third countries or with other regional organizations in the world new institutional problems may also arise.

5.2   The external stance of the European Union

5.2.1   The new challenges for the Community's general external policy

The successful completion of the GATT Uruguay Round at Marrakesh demands a new stance from the common market, and thus of the Community, in the increasingly important world market and the WTO which has been established. The discussion about the substantive aspects of this has already begun on the basis of the White Paper,[14] which was

---

13. See note 9, *supra*.
14. *Ibid.*

examined in Chapter IX, above. As a result of the integration of the coal
and steel markets into the common market, by 2002 at the latest (with the
expiry of the ECSC Treaty), in addition to the internal aspects of free
movement of goods and competition, external trade in these sectors will
also be completely integrated into Community policy. In all these three
policy areas this integration may lead to a simplification and
rationalization of present policy. It might have been thought sensible for
transitional problems concerning the integration of coal and steel policy to
be placed on the agenda of the 1996 Intergovernmental Conference,[15] but
this did not happen.

The objectives of internal economic and social cohesion of the
Community will, as was noted in section 2, above, have to be reconsidered, not merely on their internal merits and for budgetary reasons,
but also in the light of the problems of enlargement, which are considered in section 5.2.2, below, and of the objective of 'the smooth and
gradual integration of the developing countries into the world economy'.[16]
This will be in the context of a coherent Community external economic
policy.

The new objectives of sustainable growth and sustainable development, will, as was noted in section 3, above, also have important
consequences for the Community's external economic policy. In the
closing session of the Uruguay Round in Marrakesh the environment question in particular was already placed on the agenda of the new
WTO.

As has been demonstrated in Chapter IX, above, the third phase of
Economic and Monetary Union will bring its own new external challenges
in the relationship to the most important other currencies in the world and
to the IMF. The coordination of economic policy will before then already
have to take account of the strongly evolving new world market
relationships. The great importance of world market relationships for
sectoral policy, particularly for the Community's common agricultural,
fisheries and transport policies was noted in Chapter XI. Community
social policy will also have to be brought into line with that of the ILO,
but in view of the conclusions at Marrakesh it may also have certain
repercussions within the WTO.

The increasing importance of the external aspects of significant parts of
Community policies which has been briefly summarized here will also have
its consequences for the internal policy coordination within the
Commission, the Council and the European Parliament. Section 7, below,
examines this point further.

---

15. Attention would then also have to be paid to the elements of the ECSC Treaty summarized briefly in Chapter XI, above, apart from those noted in the text above, which
might, with the necessary adaptations, be taken over into the EC Treaty.
16. Art. 130u(1) EC, 2nd indent.

5.2.2   The problems of enlargement

The accession application of Cyprus will have to be examined also in the light of the relationship to countries outside Europe, including Turkey (of which but a small part forms part of the European continent), the Middle East and the North African countries. The complications in relation to the northern part of Cyprus are particularly important.[17] The political and economic relationship of the European Union with all the countries bordering the Mediterranean will have to be taken into account. Without measures for the benefit of those countries the increasing divide in prosperity between the Member States of the Union and those countries will lead to continual pressure from emigration from the latter to the former. Thus as hitherto, these countries will in the future have to continue to enjoy a certain preferential treatment, in proportion to the stronger degree of interdependence which they have with the Community than do other developing countries, to the extent that the requirements of the WTO do not prevent such treatment. This latter point may be a powerful argument for seeking to create a free trade area between the European Union and the Mediterranean non-Member States concerned. Substantial financial assistance to those countries will necessitate conditions as to sound government and administration there, as happened with the Marshall Plan.

To a much greater extent than the application to accede from Cyprus, the applications by the countries of Central and Eastern Europe will require a general strategy: this time concerning the successor States to the old USSR on the one hand, and the other former COMECON countries on the other. In the course of history prior to 1940, for example, Hungary, Poland, and the now Czech and Slovak Republics maintained much closer political, cultural and economic ties with Western Europe than did the successor states to the old USSR. The successor states had never even known a parliamentary democracy and political and civil freedoms on the Western model, and during most of the last two centuries they also had no social and economic system on the Western model. The generations which above all in the four Central and East European countries just mentioned came to adulthood prior to 1940 or could become aware in their education at the latest after the transformation of 1989 of the soon again very dominant Western political, cultural, social and economic approaches, had better opportunities to orientate themselves again towards West European values. Nevertheless, it is difficult to overestimate the scale of the cultural,

17. As to the consequences of the Cyprus problem in relation to official certificates, see Case C-432/92 *R. v. Minister of Agriculture, Fisheries and Food, ex parte S.P. Anastasiou (Pissouri) Ltd. et al.* [1994] ECR I-3087, and Emiliou (1995) 20 ELRev. 202. As another example of political sensitivities, see Case 204/86 *Greece v. Council* [1988] ECR 5323.

administrative, social, political and economic transformation which was still needed. A transitional period of some twenty years or more was thought by many from Eastern and Western Europe alike to be necessary for these four countries and probably also for the Baltic States in order to satisfy most of the requirements which the Community makes of its Member States. In the event, accession negotiations with Cyprus, the Czech Republic, Estonia, Hungary, Poland and Slovenia in the first wave began pretty quickly after the signature of the Treaty of Amsterdam and political agreement on phasing at the European Council meeting in Luxembourg in December 1997.[18] It was also agreed on that occasion that the preparation of negotiations with Bulgaria, Romania, Latvia, Lithuania, and Slovakia would be speeded up. The accession of these second wave countries may probably be envisaged only after the turn of the century, given that in many areas they are running considerably behind the other applicant countries. In this context the respect for the rights of the numerous minority groups in these countries will play an important part. For that matter, for all the Central and East European countries other than the successor states, including therefore the other Balkan states, accession will only be a possibility if it is ascertained that they actually satisfy the criteria of the principles mentioned in the Preamble to the TEU, namely freedom, democracy, and respect for human rights, fundamental freedoms and the rule of law. That rule of law will certainly have to include the necessary institutional framework for the socio-economic order resulting from Community law. In relation to the successor states, on the contrary, besides political cooperation and accession to the WTO, there does not seem to be as yet any thought of closer cooperation with the European Union than in the form of a free trade association along the lines of NAFTA. Such a gradation in relations with the European Union appears proportionate to the fundamental differences in the points of departure, and conforms to the practice of concentric circles in foreign relations of the Union, to which reference has been made in Chapter XII, above.

For good reasons, therefore, the prospect of future membership of the Union has only been offered to a number of Central and Eastern European countries outside the former USSR, linked with a second generation of association and cooperation agreements, commonly referred to as the Europe Agreements. Even Hungary and Poland in their applications for accession set out from the premise that as a result of the conclusions of the 1996 IGC, the conditions for the negotiations to be conducted would require prior substantive and institutional Treaty amendments, so that the negotiations would not get off the ground before 1998, leading to accession not before 2000. A logical date for accession would be the year in which

18. Bull. EU 12–1997, point I.5 (at point 27). See Bull. EU 3–1998, points 1.3.51 and 1.3.52.

the end of the transitional period in the present Europe Agreements is provided for, viz. 2003.

The following points of departure are, it is submitted, important for the strategy to be developed by the Union. First, already prior to accession there must be an increase in the aid granted to the countries concerned, as well as in their possibilities to export goods to the Community. Institutional and economic conditions could be linked to such developments. In accordance with the studies which have already been referred to above,[19] the assistance (in particular for infrastructure, education and environmental investment, where the Central and Eastern European countries are still seriously lagging behind the Member States of the Union) could very well follow the objectives and principles which were so successful in the Marshall Plan. These studies indicate that the burden for the Community as a whole would be a mere fraction of the GDP percentage amounts that the German government has spent annually on the integration of the new Länder. The estimate of probable costs is now in the region of 6,000 million ECU annually for the Central and Eastern European countries outside the former USSR. Of that, in accordance with present arrangements, a part could be financed by other countries in the G–24 Group. After accession the new Member States would of course then have to receive assistance according finally to the same criteria as the present poorest countries and regions of the Community.

Secondly, there is no reason to suppose that there should be any change in the traditional approach, maintained also in the negotiations which led to Austrian, Finnish and Swedish accession (and Norwegian non-accession), that acceding Member States must adjust to the *acquis communautaire* by the end of the agreed transitional period.[20] In the context of the possibilities of differentiation and different speeds the 1996 IGC would have the possibility of extending the already existing possibilities for differentiation in policy areas. This question is further examined in general in section 7.1, below, and various other observations are made in the light of the Treaty of Amsterdam in section 8, below.

Thirdly, it seems desirable, not only because of the break in historic development between 1940 and 1990, that longer transitional periods should be permitted for the Central and Eastern European countries on accession than has been the case hitherto. Even the original Member States needed in practice 35 years to adapt to the requirements of what is now Article 7(7) EC,[21] as the common market required by that provision was in reality only largely achieved by the beginning of 1993, even though the transitional period came to an end at the end of 1969. The point of

---

19. See note 10, *supra*.
20. In fact with that last accession the process had been much eased by the adaptations which had already taken place in the context of the EEA Agreement.
21. Previously Art. 8(7) EEC.

departure of the Central and Eastern European countries is more comparable to the situation of the founding Member States themselves in 1958, rather than to that of those newer Member States that have acceded since 1973. At that time the original Member States still had to uproot themselves from the tradition of a strong level of central regulation of the economy, which had developed in the crisis period of the Thirties and the shortages which characterized the period from 1940–1950, a tradition which continued even in Germany into the Sixties and Seventies in a different form in certain sectors of the economy.[22] Following the example of Article 7 EC, in addition to this practical experience of the founding Member States, the stage system set out in that provision could be a source of inspiration during the accession negotiations. Article 7 EC provided for three stages, with each successive transition from one to the other not being automatic, but expressly conditional upon a Council decision. The new Member States would of course participate in such a Council decision, according to the weighted voting agreed upon. Article 7(2) EC assigned to each stage 'a set of actions to be initiated and carried through concurrently.' On the accession of the Central and Eastern European countries they could for example accede to the Second and Third Pillars of the TEU, if necessary with the differentiation which already exists. Further, complete liberalization of most movement of goods (with a temporary transitional regime for agricultural products), application of the competition rules and liberalization of the relevant rules concerning transport, could be dealt with in the first stage. So also harmonization directives for goods would already become effective and be implemented in the national laws of the new Member States. A programme of adaptation of laws is already under way,[23] although equal legal guarantees to those already existing in the Community would indeed have to await accession. In the second stage, in accordance with the practical experience with the original Member States, there could follow the liberalization of other movement in services (save financial services linked to free movement of capital), the application of the right of establishment, the liberalization of direct investments and continuation of the necessary harmonization of laws (such as emission standards, employment conditions, turnover tax and excise duties). Remaining for the third stage for diverse reasons would be, in addition to complete liberalization of movement of goods, persons, services and capital, in particular complete participation in the two remaining major common policies (agricultural policy and commercial

22. See the Report by the German Ministry of Economics, *Bericht über den Stand der Deregulierungspolitik* (Bonn, 1993). It appears that even a country as heavily committed to the market economy as Germany still needed a substantial degree of internal deregulation, largely concerning legislation which was adopted or strengthened during the Sixties and Seventies.
23. See, generally, COM (94) 320 Final; COM (94) 361 Final; Bull. EU 12–1994, points I.39–I.54, and COM (95) 163 Final.

policy), social policy, gradual integration into Economic and Monetary Union, complete application of policy on economic and social cohesion, and environmental policy. The complete participation in these policies would, as was the case with the founding Member States, not exclude already making a start on these matters in the earlier stages. Thus, linked to the gradual liberalization of movement of goods, a gradual start could be made into the common commercial policy. In May 1994 Dankert pointed out that the quick participation of Hungary, Poland and two other Central European countries in the Common Agricultural Policy and in the present structural policy for the development of backward regions would cost the European Union between 150,000 and 200,000 million Guilders.[24] Moreover, these policy areas in their present form make such high demands of the implementing bodies in the Member States that for the moment the Central European countries mentioned simply could not meet the requirements. Simply in order to make the burdens bearable for the Union and for the countries concerned, these policy areas will have to undergo drastic revision, as Dankert observed. A number of years appear to be necessary to achieve this. The maximum length of the transitional period for the countries concerned should preferably not be specified in advance in a staged approach, such as that suggested above. In order to maintain sufficient pressure for the process of adaptation, a period of 20 years could be prescribed for Hungary and Poland, with the possibility of it being lengthened or shortened by the Council.[25] For various other East European countries a longer accession period may well have to be considered in due course. Discussion by the 1996 IGC of other models for the gradual integration of the Central and Eastern European countries appeared very likely, although it is submitted that the model tentatively suggested above is that which best corresponds to the expectations to which the European Union has so far given rise. Certainly, there seems to be now no serious discussion of an expansion of the EEA as a sort of halfway house to full membership: the only talk is of accession itself.

5.3   The necessary reform of the Second Pillar

Because of their Community character, the institutional facilities in the field of the common commercial policy have so far been sufficient to permit the Community to play a useful major role in regulating world

24. Some £50–70,000 million (at 1998 rates of exchange), see Dankert, *Vrij Nederland*, 21 May 1994, p. 11. Subsequent estimates, based on a more gradual enlargement process, are much lower, as indicated above.
25. A relatively recent example of the shortening of a transitional period can be seen in relation to the free movement of workers after Spanish and Portuguese accession, see Reg. 2194/91 (O.J. 1991 L 206/1).

trade, as the world's most important trading power, alongside the United States of America and Japan. The same cannot be said of the European Union's record in general foreign and security policy. In particular the crisis in former Yugoslavia has shown that in this field, even after the coming into force of the TEU, the European Union is not only less skilled in negotiations and in action than the United States and Russia, even in relation to its European neighbours, it is also less skilled than the UN Security council and NATO. If, in accordance with Article B TEU the European Union wishes to confirm its identity in this area as well, and really arrive at a common foreign and security policy, then there will have to be reforms on at least the following points. First, the Commission will have to play a full role in the analyses of the most important problems in this area, on the basis of a common vision. The Commission is particularly well-suited to this task, in part through its composition and its specific institutional role set out in Article 157 EC, its Community relations with the most important third countries, and its experience in external economic relations. This would not necessarily require a formal amendment of the Treaty concerning the Commission's role in the decision-making process. Its influence will principally depend on the quality of its contribution. The analyses of the Commission and the proposals based on them, which are by definition on the basis of Article 157 EC based on the general Community interest, will also be able to contribute to bridging the gap between the still existing major differences of opinion between the Member States in this area. To the extent that the 1996 IGC envisaged sticking to the main lines of the present intergovernmental model for actual decision-making on foreign policy, the replacement of the principle of unanimity in the Council for decisions on joint action by the possibility of decisions by qualified majority became a realistic scenario. As it appeared desirable to maintain the fundamental principle that the sovereignty of each Member State must be respected in this field, the possibility for the outvoted Member States to declare themselves not bound by the decision to take joint action in certain areas also became feasible. In the field of security policy, in the WEU, this possibility of opting out had already been accepted in practice in a different form.

Thirdly, the IGC had to examine more closely the question of integrating the WEU into the Union.[26] The fourth matter was the necessity of strengthening the influence of the European Parliament in relation to decisions within the meaning of Article J.3(1) TEU. Fifth, the manner in which the Union is represented in the United Nations was an obvious area for reconsideration (although this is obviously something for a wider forum than merely the IGC): so far there has principally been discussion about an additional permanent seat in the Security Council for Germany. Creation of the possibility for the Union itself to conclude treaties or to

---

26. See, as to four of the possible options, Bal et al., (1995) *Atlantisch Perspectief* No. 1.

adopt other measures with external legal consequences would make more fundamental Treaty revisions inevitable.

6. REFORM OF THE THIRD PILLAR

While in the context of CFSP no measures are taken which affect legal or natural persons,[27] Title VI of the TEU does involve such measures in the context of the cooperation in the nine areas specified in Article K.1 TEU. This requires in the first place either the realization of fully-fledged control by the European Parliament, or fully-fledged control by the national parliaments supplementing the powers of the European Parliament. Secondly, to the extent that the TEU makes no provision for judicial protection,[28] it must be conferred in respect of decisions affecting natural and legal persons, particularly asylum seekers and immigrants from third countries. If recourse is had to national judicial protection, this must go hand-in-hand with guarantees of the uniform interpretation of such decisions. Thus it is unacceptable that Article K.2 TEU offers no real fully-fledged judicial protection, even though it provides that the matters referred to in Article K.1 TEU must be dealt with 'in compliance with the European Convention for the Protection of Human Rights and Fundamental Freedoms' and of 'the Convention relating to the Status of Refugees of 28 July 1951'. The most that is offered is the reference in Article K.2(1) to 'the protection offered by Member States to persons persecuted on political grounds.' As protection by the Court of Justice and by the European Court of Human Rights is not really guaranteed, the degree of judicial protection for natural and legal persons concerning the implementation of this Title of the TEU will largely depend on the divergent national legislation and case-law. A far-reaching communitarization of Title VI TEU, or at least fully-fledged parliamentary control and more harmonized judicial protection than is presently available was thus a prime issue for resolution during the 1996 IGC. In relation to sanctions for infringement of Community law and movement of persons with third countries, a real communitarization had to be considered, instead of the Conventions envisaged in Article K.3(2) TEU with the possible competence for the Court envisaged in the third subparagraph of point (c) of the second indent of that provision. Particularly when cross-border facts or the interests of the Community as such are in issue, it is inadequate to make the Member States and their citizens dependent on very diverse legal guarantees. In addition to a harmonized judicial protection, guaranteed by the Court, in these other cases too fully-fledged

27. Any measures having such an effect are taken within the Community framework.
28. *E.g.* the provisions of Art. K.3(2)(c) TEU permit jurisdiction to be conferred on the Court of Justice, but do not compel this.

parliamentary control was necessary, as was a clearer role for the Commission. Finally, the 1996 IGC needed to take account of the lessons and the experience with the anticipating policy in this area of the Member States which participate in the Schengen Agreement.

7. THE NECESSARY INSTITUTIONAL REVISION

7.1 The different existing conceptions at the beginning of 1995

There are very diverse conceptions about the future development of the European Union, in part linked to the coming enlargements of the number of Member States. At one extreme stand the federalists, to the extent to which they seek in due course to unite the Member States in a sovereign federal European State. Apart from the fact that in many Member States, including the Netherlands, an amendment of the Constitution would be required, it is clear that at least two of the larger Member States and a number of the smaller Member States would lend no support to such a development. Further, it cannot be expected of the Central and Eastern European countries that they should surrender their sovereignty – which they have in reality only just regained – in exchange for the principle of subsidiarity as a guarantee for an – even then incomplete – national autonomy in a number of fields. The other extreme is represented by the type of vision proclaimed by the then British Prime Minister Major, as set out in inter alia his well-known article in The Economist.[29] Further in this line is the Report of the European Constitutional Group.[30] Although these two visions may be correct in perceiving that a federal state is not a realistic option, it is submitted neither of these visions is itself realistic. Major's rejection of Economic and Monetary Union is simply illogical, for the reasons set out in Chapter IX, above, in view of his commitment to the optimal further development of the common market. His far-reaching ideas on deregulation are perfectly open to discussion precisely in the context of EMU, as appeared in the discussions leading to the adoption of the Commission's White Paper on Growth, Competitiveness and Employment,[31] but not without measures of adjustment such as those discussed in earlier chapters of this work, various points of which have been summarized in the preceding sections of this chapter. His plea for integration of the EFTA States (which has in the meantime largely occurred) and the Central and Eastern European countries can in itself be supported. But neither the results of the negotiations with the various EFTA States nor the needs of

---

29. 25 September 1993 (p. 23 in the U.K. edition; 19 in the EU edition, and 27 in the U.S. edition).
30. *A Proposal for a European Constitution* (London, 1993).
31. See note 9, *supra*.

the Central and Eastern European countries justify his conclusion that an enlargement of the Community requires a strengthening of the intergovernmental character of the decision-making process, and of the legislative competence of the national parliaments, with full restoration of the sovereignty of the Member States. This conclusion appears so broadly formulated, to be itself inconsistent with his agreement to an optimal further development of the common market without EMU. The experiences up to 1985 have consistently shown that a purely intergovernmental decision-making process, even with a much smaller number of Member States, made the completion and maintenance of the common market impossible (including in the sectors of financial services and transport which are so important for the United Kingdom). Only after more far-reaching communitarization of the decision-making process through the SEA was it possible to complete, at least for the most part, the internal market within the Community. Even the most die-hard defender of national sovereignty among the list leaders of the Dutch parties for the last elections to the European Parliament, recognized that parliamentary sovereignty in the present day is not absolute in nature.[32] If the experiences of the European Communities have made anything clear, also in their external relations, it is that a solution to trans-frontier problems and a defence of common interests and standpoints against the rest of the world and in international organizations and conferences does not rhyme with a purely intergovernmental form of decision-making with unlimited national sovereignty. Even the suggestion awakened in the final paragraphs of Major's article that a completed common market, strengthened free trade with the outside world, and an intergovernmental common security policy would be sufficient for an optimal satisfaction of the needs of European nations will not be shared by most of the other Member States of an enlarged European Union. But nevertheless, the visions of Major and a large number of his supporters were of great practical importance, as they automatically might threaten to become reality with a further increase in the number of Member States without fundamental institutional amendments to the Treaties. Without such amendments, neither the Commission nor the Council would any longer be in a position to adopt the mutually coherent decisions, particularly in the area of positive integration, which are necessary in the common interest. Already with the present number of Member States it appears difficult to do justice to the links between the various policy areas using present working methods. Moreover, other Member States, according to Major's intentions, would be confronted with detailed proposals for Treaty amendments, developed by a task force set up for the purpose. Some British observers argue that the Report of the European Constitutional Group mentioned above was in part influenced by that task force.

32. Van der Waal, *Europa van Morgen*, 19 May 1994, p. 161.

Between these two radical streams, and perhaps partly in reaction to them, radical proposals were submitted at the end of August and the beginning of September 1994 by authoritative sources in Germany and France.[33] The German proposal, which did not deny its federalist source of inspiration, in fact pleaded for the formation of a hard core group of states, capable of expansion; the French proposal pleaded for a Europe of three different circles, which encompasses a greater or lesser number of Member States and policy areas. These proposals appear important primarily because they make it clear that in all discussions over the further institutional development of the Union, a substantive distinction should be drawn between five points.

First, the substantive hard core of the Community: this embraces the common market, and everything which is directly linked to it – the five freedoms, and the harmonization directives necessary for the completion of the internal market; the common competition policy and the common agricultural, fisheries and transport policies. Further, it embraces the EMU, which, as was demonstrated in Chapters III and IX, above, is both a necessary complement to the internal market (abolition of exchange rate frontiers) and required as supplementary policy complement for the Community (coordination of national economic policies).

Secondly, complementary measures to enable the common market to function as much as possible without exceptions: in particular reference should be made here to the policy areas in the third pillar (JHA) of the TEU which relate to internal and external movement of persons, or sanctions for infringement of Community law, or for the protection of the Community's financial interests, which, in connection with the realization of the internal free movement of persons will have to provide for a common policy concerning the movement of third country nationals. Such a complement is just as necessary in relation to the free movement of persons within the Community as the common commercial policy is necessary as a complement to the free movement of goods.

Thirdly, complementary policy on positive integration is necessary to deal with the regulation of wholly or partial cross-border developments, in areas such as environmental policy, social policy, research and technology policy, Trans-European Networks, and countering cross-border 'ordinary' crime. The arguments for complementary policies in these areas are essentially derived from the negative and positive spill-overs of national policy in a situation of free movement of goods and persons. In the case of negative spill-overs, the Member States will be inclined to pass the buck, as where a state situated upstream releases untreated waste water into a river. In the case of positive spill-overs, policy which is in itself useful is not

33. Reflections on European Policy (CDU/CSU parliamentary party in the *Bundestag*, 1 September, 1994), and Balladur (then French Prime Minister) in an interview in *Le Figaro*, 30 August 1994.

pursued on the ground that others would also profit from it, as with macro-economic financial measures favouring in the first place imports, the development of new infrastructure, and support of research and development. In modern economic game theory these phenomena are advanced as important arguments for policy strategy formation at a higher than national level. The concept of 'complementary policy' is itself somewhat misleading here, as it gives the impression of being of less importance. In political reality though, it appears sometimes to be indeed regarded as a less necessary complement to the common market.

Fourth is a specific policy in favour of certain Member States or third countries, such as policy programmes to accelerate the process of making up the development deficit of certain Member States, developing countries or Central and Eastern European countries.

Fifth is the new policy areas of culture and public health, which have a strongly subsidiary character at the Community level in relation to national policy in these areas. In particular foreign and security policy fall also into this category.

All Member States will have to participate in the first two of these groups of policy areas, insofar as there is no clear basis for exceptions in the Treaties.[34] Within the third pillar the Schengen countries form a hard core group, as long as a far-reaching communitarization of that pillar has not yet occurred, although that core is not without its frayed edges when it comes to the abolition of systematic frontier controls. The third group of policy areas set out above actually provides in part for minimum provisions which do not exclude more far-reaching national policies, to the extent that no infringement of provisions which form part of the first two core areas thereby occurs. The fourth group of policy areas is not so much substantively as politically linked with the first two core areas, and is thus largely dependent on political agreement being reached.

In the fifth group of policy areas in particular, it is foreign and security policy which, in part due to its far-reaching or wholly intergovernmental nature, is so very dependent on the political will to cooperate, which here makes the formation of more institutionalized core groups not impossible, although they must be open to all Member States who desire to join them. The link which Balladur made in the interview cited above between foreign and security policy and participation in EMU appears at first sight still somewhat artificial. He was correct to observe, though, in relation to the future relationship with the Central and Eastern European countries, that a core group in the field of foreign policy envisaged by him would have a

34. Such as Art. 36 EC in relation to the free movement of goods; the monetary provisions, which, like the special opt-out arrangements for Denmark and the United Kingdom, expressly envisage some Member States pressing on ahead; Arts. 7c and 100a(4) EC; transitional arrangements or other specific provisions in Treaties or Acts of Accession.

large degree of political freedom to force through a certain way of shaping that relationship in a specific form. More concretely, as he suggested, to accept accession of those countries, with the necessary transitional arrangements, or to strive for a new sui generis relationship with them in the context of the Conference on Security and Cooperation in Europe. The argument advanced by the German Report mentioned above, however, is outspoken in its advocacy of integration of the Central and Eastern European neighbours into the Union, following on from German unification. Balladur's linkage of foreign and security policy to monetary union would appear in fact to have a more bilateral background to it (exchanging agreement to enlargement for a guarantee of German cooperation over EMU), rather than to be an attempt to make a logical connection between policy areas which are not logically related to each other. In the line of this analysis, the German plea for an institutionalized hard core appears to be particularly directed at the new policy areas, but as in the interpretation of Balladur's vision outlined here, a political link is being made also from the German side between EMU and foreign policy as other important elements of a political union. In the German proposal the core group would have to cooperate more strongly in relation to monetary, fiscal, budgetary, economic and social policy. Combined, these two proposals appeared to pave the way for Franco-German agreement in relation to the 1996 IGC.

How the voting rules would be in the case of different speeds or concentric circles has largely been resolved in the TEU in relation to EMU. As was observed above in relation to the coordination of economic policy, this probably requires strengthening after the start of the third phase of EMU, which could be enabled by a Treaty amendment. This problem, like those regarding the second and third pillars, would have to be dealt with during the 1996 IGC.

On the basis of developments to the beginning of 1995, including the enlargement on 1 January 1995 of the Union from 12 to 15 Member States, it seemed more realistic to expect that the *acquis communautaire* rather than radical reform plans would characterize the 1996 IGC. Substantively this acquis, certainly with enlargement to the South and the East, and with the increasing importance of worldwide problems of negative and positive integration, will require definite adaptation and often more austere rules of positive integration. It will have to be ensured that in those areas in which the Union will be able to tackle cross-border problems more effectively than worldwide organizations, because of its stronger interdependence and greater homogeneity of views, the institutional structure remains sufficiently adapted to the tasks. (It will be remembered that one of the great strengths of the Spaak report was that it first identified the tasks to be achieved, and then looked at the institutional structure which would be best suited to achieving them.) In external relations, CFSP and external policy on the movement of persons will have to be as effectively prepared and implemented as is the common commercial policy. In the terminology of Article 92 of the Dutch constitution, the Union must remain in legal terms an (advanced) international organization with its own powers of legislation, administration of policies and administration of justice. These attributed powers will by their very nature also in the future continue to restrict to a larger degree the exercise of national sovereignty by the Member States than do the existing worldwide international organizations, or than does an organization such as OECD.[35] In the following section, brief observations are made about the possibility of strengthening the effectiveness of the policy-making institutions of the Community, and briefer observations are made with regard to the second and third pillars of the TEU. The need to adapt the structure and working methods of the Court as a result of future enlargement is also very briefly mentioned.

7.2 Some possibilities for making the institutional structure more effective

(A) The composition and working methods of the Commission

Deviating from the order of the Treaties, it seems appropriate to commence with the Commission, as its policy proposals are still the most important point of departure for decision-making by the Council and the European Parliament. The point of departure for all proposals in this area must be that already the composition and working method of the Commission are no longer appropriate to its tasks, and that they will be even less so after the next enlargements. Moreover, the TEU and the experience of the last few years, inter alia in the context of the Uruguay Round, have shown the need for a strengthening of the coherence between internal and external aspects of policies individually, as well as between internal and external Commission policy. Two conclusions may be drawn. First, the number of tasks of the existing Directorates general and other services are insufficient to provide members of the Commission from more than 20 Member States with portfolios which are of equal value. Secondly, the necessary endeavour to achieve greater coherence between the diverse policy areas seems to make cluster formation necessary among the myriad Directorates General and probably a number of other services, both within and outside the Secretariat General.

In order to concentrate minds, the following 10 clusters might be thought of in general terms; they in part reflect the original organization

---

35. See VerLoren van Themaat in Curtin and Heukels (eds.), *Institutional Dynamics of European Integration* (Essays in honour of Schermers, Vol. II, Dordrecht, 1994) 3.

chart, and in part result from new tasks, added later and linked to each other. **Cluster I** would embrace external relations (external economic relations, other external relations, enlargement negotiations and development cooperation, including ACP policy). **Cluster II** would take the new objectives of sustainable growth, with the present DG IX (environment) as its core; it would also embrace Trans-European networks and all other Community activities in the area of physical infrastructure and spatial planning. Treatment as a separate cluster would be justified on the ground of the important external as well as internal aspects involved, as well as their fundamental importance for almost all other policy areas. **Cluster III** would tackle EMU and economic structural policy (embracing economic, monetary and financial affairs; the economic aspects of employment policy; regional policy and economic and social cohesion, and more general aspects of structural policy, such as horizontal policy on small and medium-sized enterprises, as well as coordinating responsibility for the Statistical office). **Cluster IV** would cover the common market economy, embracing competition policy; the internal market; harmonization of laws, and customs and indirect taxation, as well as the consumer policy service. **Cluster V** would deal with agriculture and fisheries. **Cluster VI** would be responsible for other sectoral policy, embracing inter alia transport policy, the energy sector, industry, research and technological development, telecommunications, the information technology market, and the exploitation of research results. **Cluster VII** would deal with social aspects of employment policy; modernization of the provisions on the free movement of persons; industrial relations; other aspects of social policy, public health, cultural policy and education. **Cluster VIII** would embrace home affairs, justice and coordination of prevention of fraud. **Cluster IX** would look after internal organization; budgetary policy; ensuring that there were effective and necessary changes to internal organization; financial and personnel efficiency in that context, and coordination of relations with other Institutions, in conjunction with the Secretariat General. Finally, **Cluster X** would ensure general coordination of policy, press and information towards the outside and look after the Secretariat General, the Spokesman's Service, and the Legal Service.

For the future composition of the Commission, such a cluster formation, which would could be filled in after closer examination, could lead to there being one responsible coordinating member of the Commission per cluster (for Clusters I, IX and X respectively two responsible Vice-Presidents and the President responsible for the general lead). Particularly in Clusters I, III, and IV, the member of the Commission responsible for coordination could be assisted by two specialist members, and for Clusters II, IV, V, and VI by one specialized member, who could take on prime responsibility for certain parts of the cluster. In a manner analogous to that for Dutch Secretaries of State (confusingly equivalent to Ministers of State in the United Kingdom) in relation to the Dutch Cabinet, the specialist members could then participate in meetings of the Commission, with or without the right to vote, on matters falling within their portfolios. In this structure the Commission would have at the most 10 coordinating members (an inner cabinet) and 10 specialized members. Certainly, if there is an enlargement to more than 20 Member States, it seems unlikely that the Commission would still be able to fulfil its tasks effectively and with sufficient power of decision, and possess sufficient fully-fledged portfolios to be able to offer all Member States a permanent seat in the Commission. The choice for a coordinating or specialist function could be made either in the appointment procedure, or, according to regional criteria, with sufficiently objective guarantees for equal chances of appointment for qualified candidates from all Member States involved being offered. Permanent contact points for Member States without a member of the Commission could also be guaranteed in the composition of the President's cabinet. On the basis that the composition of the Commission would require the approval of the governments of the Member States by common accord, and of the European Parliament, there should be no need to fear that there will be an over-representation of either the larger or the smaller Member States. The Parliament will undoubtedly also guarantee a balanced party-political composition of the Commission.

The basis of these conclusions is that the specific role of the Commission in the institutional system of the European Communities must be the starting point in the search for a satisfactory solution to the problem of the composition of the Commission. On the basis of Article 157 EC the members of the Commission exercise their office in complete independence in the general interest of the Communities. This objective task is certainly the most important guarantee in the institutional system, particularly for the smaller countries, that also the specific interests of all the Member States are objectively taken into account in the decision-making process. The influence of the Commission and thus the value of this guarantee for the Member States depends on its ability to make high-quality policy proposals which are well thought-out, on the basis of expert and objective analyzes by its services of economic, financial, social, cultural, political and legal data from all Member States and from the Community as a whole. In this task there will often have to be a compromise between the various Community (not national) political options. In view of the political nature of the latter, they must also take account of the party-political set-up in the European Parliament. The necessary technical and political quality and coherence of its policy proposals – and of its own implementing policy – certainly demand that account is taken of the interests of all Member States in the analyzes by the Commission's services on which its decision-making rests. Thus it is more important that all of its services are composed of specialists from all Member States than that the Commission itself should be composed of members from every Member State each time. Decision-making in the Commission as a collegiate decision-making body, its ability to pursue a policy which is coherent in its constituent parts and also balances objectively all relevant interests, and its external authority depend in particular on a limited number of coordinating members, who have a dominant influence and who should in principle – unlike the specialist members – be present at all meetings of the Commission. It is not the institutional task of members of the Commission, but that of members of the Council, to regard the interests of their own country as the starting point for their position. A Commission which does not adequately fulfil its role as an objective evaluator, synthesizer of diverse interests, and independent body will see its external authority diminish and thus eventually dig its own grave. The Executive Board of the future European Central Bank will rightly not consist of more members than is necessary for an optimal fulfilment of its tasks; other international organizations with many members also have bodies of limited size to perform their supranational or trans-national tasks. But the Parliament and the governments of the Member States will have to leave the possibility open of candidacies from all Member States. It is submitted that in the future the European Council will be the ideal forum in which to select 10 coordinating and an appropriate number of specialist members of the Commission, in consultation with a President chosen by the Parliament and the Council together, and probably with a strengthened involvement of the Parliament, which can be worked out in due course.[36] These candidates, proposed by common accord of the Member States and/or by the Parliament should be deemed to be best placed to pursue a coherent policy over the 10 groups of policy clusters identified above. It appeared at the beginning of 1995 that for some of the coordination questions the Commission had found a solution through the introduction of five working groups of six to 10 participants, three of which groups are chaired by the President personally.[37] But far from all the central coordination questions identified in the preceding analysis can be solved in this manner, and the problems of too many participants at meetings of

36. It is not merely the Parliament which desires this, see the CDU/CSU Report (see note 33, *supra*), as well as the far-reaching changes suggested in Weidenfeld (ed.), *Europa '96, Reformprogramm für die Europäische Union* (Gütersloh, 1994), in which authoritative German lawyers and political scientists cooperated, alongside aides of Kohl and Delors.
37. These three are external relations; growth, competitiveness and employment, and equal opportunities for men and women, with women's rights, see Europe Documents No. 1921 of 27 January 1995. The Commission's Rules of Procedure (Dec. 93/492 (O.J. 1993 L 230/15, amended, but not on this point, by Dec. 95/148 (O.J. 1995 L 97/82)), Art. 13 makes provision for such working groups.

the Commission and of its working methods can also not be solved without an amendment of the Treaties.

(B)   The working methods of the Council

In accordance with the principle of 'sovereign equality of states' in public international law,[38] and on the basis of the institutional structure of the Treaties, all Member Sates will have to continue to be represented in the Council. In order to avoid a repetition of painful discussions about qualified majority voting prior to each enlargement, as occurred particularly notoriously prior to Austrian, Finnish and Swedish accession at Ioannina, and to promote a more transparent system which citizens can more easily understand, a simple formula should be found during the 1996 IGC, which could simply be applied mechanically without having to be changed on each enlargement. Because it is the task of the Union, and thus also of the Council, 'to organize, in a manner demonstrating consistency and solidarity, relations between the Member States and between their peoples'[39] account must be taken of both elements of this task, and thus of the size of the different populations, as happens at present in the weighting of votes per Member State, although the system is as yet inscrutable for the man on the Clapham omnibus or Madame Dupont. The most simple and thus attractive and balanced formula which has been proposed so far, is one which sets out from the premiss that decisions should be taken by a simple majority, or in appropriate cases by a qualified majority of both the number of Member States and of the size of the population of the Union represented by those states.[40] The rotation of the presidency of the Council will again inevitably be the subject of discussion in the light of further enlargement. There has been discussion prior to the IGC of two formulae for this: one would have the most competent presidency (Member State as President-in-office) being chosen in good time by the European Council, with the troika system being

38. Charter of the United Nations, Art. 2(1). Even in the example of the UN itself, this principle does not exclude structures in treaties permitting decision-making bodies to decide by majority vote (General Assembly) or establishing bodies in which not all members are represented, and not all votes have an equal weight (Security Council). Other examples outside the European Union where the latter two of these three points apply include the IMF and the World Bank.

39. Art. A TEU, 3rd para., final sentence.

40. This proposal was advanced by Lamers (of the Bundestag) and Bourlanges (a French MEP). See Lamers, *Deutschlands aussenpolitische Verantwortung und seine Interessen* (CDU/CSU Pressedienst, 25 August 1993). Bourlanges' views (in an internal European Parliament document from around the same time) ran pretty well parallel to those of Lamers. Both also pleaded for a limitation of the number of members of the Commission to 10, as did (giving more extensive reasons) Leon Brittan in his *The Europe We Need* (London, 1994).

maintained, so that one of the large Member States would always have a seat in the troika; the other would extend the period of each presidency to one year, but have the Council in its myriad compositions presided over by a president and two vice-presidents (presidency countries), so that each of the three countries would chair the Council in certain compositions, and one of the three would always have to come from a large Member State. Whichever formula is chosen, discrimination on ground of nationality would have to be avoided, and each Member State with sufficient ability to exercise this increasingly demanding role should have an equal opportunity. A neutral, technical chairman, as is found in other international organizations, would seem to be inappropriate in view of the presidency's political tasks in international relations and its political role in the European Parliament. Finally, each enlargement of the present number of members of the Council will have to lead to changes in its working methods, and will make it inevitable that implementing rules building on basic regulations and, where necessary, basic directives, might have to be left more and more to be dealt with by the Commission. The IGC will thus have to review the question of introducing a hierarchy of norms which was left open by the TEU.

(C)   The European Parliament

In any event the co-decision procedure will have to be extended, so as to embrace in principle all legislative decisions taken by the Council by qualified majority. Moreover, there will have to be an effort to achieve a clearer and simpler system in the various forms of involvement of the Parliament. In relation to the composition of the Parliament after further enlargement, proposals from the Parliament itself will have to be awaited, but a further expansion of the number of members will have to be avoided, and indeed there are calls from many quarters for the number of MEPs to be reduced. European political parties, as mentioned in Article 138a EC, must have a real chance of being represented, even in the smallest Member States. Whether or not this is institutionalized, many suggestions have been made that there should be more contact between MEPs and the members of their national parliaments, in order to avoid tension through lack of communication. The experience after the signature of the TEU has clearly and unmistakably demonstrated the risks of a great gap between European and national opinion-forming. If this gap cannot be satisfactorily bridged by the European Parliament, the existing pressure for the formation of a second chamber, composed of members of the national parliaments, might become irresistible. In principle, this latter solution appears constitutionally incorrect, as the members of the Council already have the task of representing their people in the decision-making process, which itself can scarcely withstand further complication.

(D) The Court of Justice

The Court of Justice presented its proposals to the IGC,[41] and a considerable amount of academic effort has been expended on suggestions,[42] but it remained (in 1995) to be seen whether reforms in this Institution would be regarded as having any political priority.

7.3 The problem of transparency

The referenda in Denmark, France and Ireland and the discussions in national parliaments on the ratification of the TEU demonstrate that the transparency of the development of the process of European integration is not only hindered by the insufficient openness of the decision-making process in the Council and in the intergovernmental conferences. Transparency and thus less distance from the citizens would be greatly served by greater clarity and as much simplification as possible of the system and working out of Community law. In the Weidenfeld Report first of all a merger is thus suggested of the three Community Treaties into one single Community Treaty. Secondly, the EC Treaty itself should be simplified, so that provisions which have become obsolete, such as the original transitional period arrangements for the five freedoms of the common market and other policy areas linked to the establishment of the common market, would be removed. The other provisions of the Treaty would be more rationally arranged and more clearly formulated so that citizens can understand what they mean. Moreover the confusing number of diverse legislative procedures and the sometimes overlapping legal bases for harmonization measures could be cut back.

Provided that such an operation was, from the substantive political viewpoint, simply a neutral technical matter, prepared by competent lawyers, without endangering the *acquis communautaire*, it appears at first sight an attractive proposition. But one obstacle that is difficult to overcome through such a substantively neutral and purely technical simplification operation lies in the traité-loi parts of the three Community Treaties. A particular example can be seen in the consciously very detailed and moreover very technically complex provisions relating to monetary union. In order to reduce the distance from the citizens and increase the

41. See Arnull (1995) 20 ELRev. 599. The Court's Report and the contribution of the Court of First Instance were published in the *Weekly Proceedings*, No. 5/95.
42. See *e.g.* Slynn et al. *The Role and Future of the European Court of Justice* (London, 1996); Everling (1997) EuR 398; Howe of Aberavon (1996) 21 ELRev. 187; Kapteyn in Curtin and Heukels (eds.), *op. cit.* (see note 35, *supra*) 135 at 138 *et seq.*; Scorey (1996) 21 ELRev. 224; Van Gerven (1996) 21 ELRev. 211 and in Winter *et al.* (eds.), *Reforming the Treaty on European Union – The Legal Debate* (The Hague, 1996) 221 at 229 *et seq.*, and the Weidenfeld Report (see note 36, *supra*), in which Everling was involved.

transparency of the Treaty, it might be better to start by transforming Parts One and Two of the EC Treaty to a fundamental part embracing all substantive and institutional major principles of the EC Treaty (and possibly also Title I of the TEU which is excluded from judicial protection in front of the Court), which would have at the most 50 Articles of a constitution-type nature. This Part would then precede the more technical and detailed Treaty provisions, shorn of obsolete provisions, but would, like the present Part I of the EC Treaty, be relevant for the legal and political interpretation of those technical and detailed provisions. The Weidenfeld Report envisages such a solution as a longer term solution, but for the reasons advanced above it should indeed be seen as a priority matter, if a small group of lawyers from a number of Member States can demonstrate before the IGC starts that it is feasible.

7.4 The preparation of the 1996 IGC

As appears from the above, the 1996 IGC, unlike its predecessor of 1991, has already been preceded by the publication of myriad points of view and discussions.[43] Leading politicians in Germany, France and the United Kingdom have been active in those discussions, as have many other politicians, academics and journalists. Many more official standpoints were expected prior to the start of the Reflection Group of personal representatives of the Foreign Ministers of the Member States, in the workings of which some MEPs and representatives of the Commission participate. When the Dutch version of this epilogue was concluded, the texts of the European Parliament and of many political parties and national parliaments were at advanced stages of preparation. Analytical reports were promised by the Commission and the Council on the problems which had to be solved in the light of the experiences since the coming into force of the TEU. Detailed suggestions for solutions could certainly be expected from the Commission and the European Parliament. All these reports had to be published in good time to permit discussion in the European Parliament and national parliaments, so that the IGC itself could take account of reactions to those reports and of discussions going on elsewhere. It was already clear, after the delay of a year in the coming into force of the TEU, that the 1996 IGC would not commence at the beginning of that year. By taking sufficient account of public opinion in the Member States prior to the IGC itself, unpleasant surprises during the ratification process, such as occurred with the TEU, could be avoided this time round.

43. See, generally, Dashwood (ed.), *Reviewing Maastricht, Issues for the 1996 IGC* (London, 1996) and Winter *et al.* (eds.), *op. cit.* (See note 42, *supra*).

8. THE PERSPECTIVES AFTER AMSTERDAM

8.1   Introduction

After political agreement was reached by the IGC in the composition of
the Heads of State or Government in Amsterdam in June 1997, the text of
the Treaty of Amsterdam was finalized, in terms of polishing the drafting,
integrating it into the existing text of the TEU and ensuring the necessary
linguistic coherence, and the Treaty was duly signed in Amsterdam on 2
October 1997.[44] The unprecedented discussions and publicity – with
discussion pages on the Internet, and most key documents being available
on the Europa Home Page – have certainly been a vast improvement
compared with the goings on prior to past revisions of the Treaties. In
view of the still uncertain fate of the Treaty (even though a few Member
States are expected to have completed the ratification process while this
work is being printed), the following observations are more general in
nature, although they are followed by mostly brief observations of a more
specific nature; they should be read in the light of the challenges and the
various options for their resolution set out in the preceding sections.[45]
Those challenges correspond to the interpretation of Article N(2) TEU
which formed the starting point for the IGC 'convened in 1996 to examine
those provisions of this Treaty for which revision is provided, in
accordance with the objectives of Articles A and B.'[46] A brief comparison
of the outcome of the IGC (which formally opened on 29 March 1996 in
Turin and ended in June 1997), with the relevant questions, general ideas,
proposals and expectations identified in 1995 may in its own way
contribute to the appraisal of both the positive achievements and those
most sensitive institutional questions, the resolution of which has been left
to a later Intergovernmental Conference dealing exclusively with such
questions. This new IGC will have to be organized in due time before the
next potential enlargement of the Union; in order to deal in particular with
the relevant final adaptations of the composition of the Commission, the
voting system and other working mechanisms of the Council 'with the aim
of ensuring the effectiveness of the mechanisms and the institutions of the

---

44. Between the drafting of these observations and publication the first commentaries on
    the Treaty of Amsterdam began to appear. See Barents, *Het Verdrag van Amsterdam*
    (Deventer, 1998); Duff (ed.), *The Treaty of Amsterdam* (London, 1997); Barents (1998)
    SEW 2, and Langrish (1998) 23 ELRev. 3. Duff's commentary (which is more political
    than legal) is particularly useful for insights into what actually went on in the final
    negotiations at Amsterdam. See also Dehousse (F.) (1997) *Courrier hebdomadaire* Nos.
    1565–1566 (CRISP, Brussels) Dehousse (R.) (1998) 35 CMLRev. 595; Shaw (1998)
    ELJ 63, and the bibliography cited on p. 44, *ante*.
45. Those have been factually updated (as far as the applicant countries are concerned)
    and linguistically revised, but remain valid.
46. Art. N(2) TEU.

Community.'[47] On the one hand this follow-up IGC should take place as early as possible now that negotiations have started with a view to the next enlargement, so that the applicant countries are not faced with uncertainty as to the institutional conditions of membership, which could otherwise complicate the negotiations. But on the other hand the ratification process of the Treaty of Amsterdam should not be complicated by too early a start of the follow-up IGC, the results of which would also require separate ratification in due course. Accordingly, it is submitted that this follow-up IGC should be scheduled for the year 2000.

The discussion in following sections is solely intended to deal with the response in and in the margins of the Treaty of Amsterdam to the matters raised in the preceding sections of this epilogue, but first a few general observations are appropriate about the arrangement of the Treaty of Amsterdam in the draft form resulting from the political agreement in June 1997.[48] That arrangement appeared to have been chosen in the first place to respond to the proximity desires at the level of ordinary citizens, so as to ensure optimal transparency of the text and thus to reduce the growing lack of understanding, if not scepticism, with regard to the activities in 'Brussels.' The arrangement differed in any case significantly from the order of the existing TEU, and from the arrangement in the final form of the Treaty as signed, as well as from the priority concerns of the political debates and expectations as they were in 1995 reflected in the preceding sections of this epilogue, even though they were certainly addressed in the results. The draft Treaty presented six sections: the first three contained provisions on freedom, security and justice; the Union and the citizen; an effective and coherent external policy; attention then turned to the Union's institutions, closer cooperation (flexibility), and simplification and consolidation of the Treaties. From the point of view of presentation, this certainly facilitated debate, but it was not surprising that when the political agreement was transformed into legal form, a presentation more clearly related to the order of the TEU was followed.

A number of general themes stand out from the Treaty of Amsterdam. First, the change in power in a number of Member States, particularly France and the United Kingdom, just before the meetings of the IGC in the composition of the Heads of State and Government and of the European Council on 16 and 17 June 1997[49] has been reflected in a

---

47. Art. B TEU (this is retained in the new Art. B TEU which will be substituted on the entry into force of the Treaty of Amsterdam).
48. IGC Doc. CONF/4001/97. The proposals to the IGC in the composition of the Heads of State or Government meeting at Amsterdam are contained in IGC Doc. CONF/4000/97.
49. It should be noted that the two meetings were logically separate (as is evident from Bull. EU 6–1997, points I.3 and II), even though the Conclusions of the Presidency (point I.2) state that '[t]he European Council meeting in Amsterdam ... successfully concluded the IGC with full agreement on a draft Treaty.'

number of interesting ways which signal a change of emphasis from what might have been expected had the predecessors been at the table. The increased profile of human and fundamental rights in the Union is important. This is in general reflected in the revision of Article F TEU, with the recognition in Article F(1) of 'the principles of liberty, democracy, respect for human rights and fundamental freedoms, and the rule of law, principles which are common to the Member States.' It is further worked out in the revision of Article O TEU, which confirms that respect for the principles set out in Article F(1) are a precondition for applicant countries to accede to the Union. Concerns about respect for national identities of the Member States have been addressed in the new Article F(3) TEU by obliging the Union to respect those identities. More concretely, the new Article 6a EC will permit the Council, acting unanimously on a proposal from the Commission, and after consulting the European Parliament, to take appropriate action to combat discrimination based on sex, racial or ethnic origin, religion or belief, disability, age or sexual orientation. The emphasis on the equality of men and women in the new Article 3(2) EC is also particularly significant. The concern for individual protection in relation to the processing and free movement of personal data is a further sign that politicians are listening to concerns about the role of national authorities in an area in which national boundaries are seeming increasingly irrelevant.[50] The possibility of suspending certain of the rights, but not the obligations of a Member State which is seriously and persistently in breach of the principles set out in the new Article F(1) TEU is a major innovation, which is taken clearly not simply with a view to the possibility of a totalitarian regime (of the left or the right) being elected in any new Member State, but also in case that should occur in any existing Member State. Furthermore, the clear commitment to equality of opportunity and to the development of a Community strategy for employment, with a skilled, trained and adaptable workforce and labour markets responsive to change, marks a clear recognition that the Community must play its part in supporting the efforts of the Member States to improve employment opportunities for their citizens.[51] In line with this commitment, the Agreement on Social Policy established at Maastricht becomes integrated into the main Treaty provisions,[52] and thereby the second-class level of social protection in the United Kingdom comes to an end.

Secondly, the influence and power of the European Parliament has again undoubtedly increased. In particular, the extension of the co-decision procedure and its simplification, so that a failure to agree a joint text in a Conciliation Committee will lead to the proposed text being deemed not to

---

50. See the new Art. 213b EC.
51. See the new Arts. 109o–109s EC.
52. See the new Arts. 117–120 EC.

have been adopted represent major steps forward.[53] This means that the Council cannot attempt to bludgeon through a text despite opposition in the Parliament, hoping that the Parliament would be unable to muster sufficient votes to block it. Thirdly, there has been at least a modest extension of qualified majority voting in the Council. These two points are also mentioned further in section 8.7, below.

There are, though, a number of developments which can perhaps be viewed as mixed blessings. Clear measures are now envisaged to deal with the question of third country nationals and the promotion of what is starting to become a European judicial area, although it is clear that internal law and order and security will remain the preserve of the individual Member States. The position of the United Kingdom and Ireland on the one hand (which have long had a common travel area) and Denmark on the other has had to be catered for in the form of protocols.[54] The Schengen *acquis* will be taken up as between 13 of the 15 Member States,[55] so that the variable geometry approach continues in this field too, although the door has been left open for a future change of heart by Ireland and/or the United Kingdom. No role is envisaged for the European Parliament in the measures implementing the applicability of that *acquis* although it is implied in the determination of the legal basis of each of the provisions or decisions constituting that acquis, if provision for its involvement is made in the relevant provisions of the Treaties. The questions of institutional reform of the Commission and the Council have largely been side-stepped until the next enlargement, although the authority of the President of the Commission has undoubtedly been strengthened vis-à-vis his or her colleagues, given that their nomination now involves the common accord of him or her and the governments of the Member States,[56] and the consent of the European Parliament, and that the Commission will work under the political guidance of its President.[57]

8.2 Economic and social cohesion and some allied problem areas

The evaluation of the current programmes on economic and social cohesion and the financial perspectives of the structural funds is now under way, with, in the first instance the presentation of Agenda 2000 by the Commission; the concrete proposals for reform have also now been

53. See the revised Art. 189b EC.
54. The curious formulation of the Protocol on the position of the United Kingdom and Ireland, Art. 3(1) reflects the problems between Spain and the United Kingdom relating to Gibraltar.
55. See the Protocol integrating the Schengen *acquis* into the framework of the European Union, annexed to the TEU and the EC Treaty.
56. See the amended Art. 158(2) EC.
57. See the amended Art. 163 EC.

presented,[58] and contributed to the need for a complete revision of Chapter IX of this work. The integration of the Agreement on Social Policy which formed part of the relevant Protocol to the TEU into the EC Treaty, and the link between economic and social cohesion on the one hand and the coordination of economic policy on the other, particularly as regards the Treaty objective of a high level of employment have already been examined in Chapter IX, above. The issues involved had to be dealt with in Amsterdam, partly within and partly outside the new Treaty framework. They were of such current importance and so intertwined with the topics covered in Chapter IX that they had to be included in that discussion. In particular, the experiences of France and Germany during 1996 and the first half of 1997 made it clear that their programmes for meeting the EC Treaty's convergence criteria for participation in the third stage of Economic and Monetary Union risked being thwarted by the budgetary and macro-economic consequences of the rapid rise in unemployment. Moreover, for the same reason the participants in the final session of the IGC in Amsterdam had to repair the failure of the original TEU agreed at Maastricht to make the employment objective in Article 2 EC operational; this took place partly within and partly outside the new Treaty structure. It was necessary to clarify that the coordination of economic policy would also have to take into account the employment objective and to pave the way for the special meeting of the European Council held in Luxembourg in November 1997, devoted to employment issues.[59] This was of course well before any ratification instrument of the Treaty of Amsterdam had been deposited.

8.3 The new objective of sustainable development

The clarifications of this fundamental new objective which were set out in section 3, above have been overtaken by amendments to the TEU in the Preamble and the new version of Article B, the new version of Article 2 EC, the new Article 3c EC, the replacement of the old Article 100a(3)–(5) EC, and a Declaration (No. 12) adopted by the IGC, annexed to the Final Act on the occasion of the signature of the Treaty of Amsterdam, which noted the Commission's undertaking to prepare environmental impact assessment studies when making proposals which might have significant environmental implications. By virtue of these amendments, the objective of sustainable development will also become an objective of the internal policies of the Community. By these various amendments to the EC Treaty the integration of environmental protection into the definition and

58. This section responds to the topics considered in section 2, above. See COM (98) 131 Final, building on Agenda 2000 (Bull. EU Suppl. 5/97), and O.J. 1998 C 202.
59. Bull. EU 11–1997, points I.1–2 *et seq.*

implementation of all Community policies and activities referred to in Article 3 EC has been strengthened considerably.

8.4 Economic and Monetary Union

Because, at the beginning of the IGC's work, agreement was reached that the text of the EMU provisions themselves should not be amended on this occasion, the necessary clarifications on the manner of their interpretation have been effected by other means which could be used for the implementation of the EMU provisions without waiting for the ratification of the Treaty of Amsterdam. Those means, outside the scope of that Treaty, include the Resolutions and Regulations concerning the Stability and Growth Pact[60] and have been examined in section 3.2 of Chapter IX, above. The suggested amendments to the EMU provisions set out in section 4 of this epilogue have, however, not materialized.

8.5 The external stance of the European Union as regards third countries and international organizations

In relation to the new challenges facing the external relations of the European Union, it follows from what has been stated in sections 5.1 and 5.2, above, that these in the first place concern the European Community as such. Yet already the problems of the envisaged enlargement(s) of the membership of the European Union embrace important political problems falling under the Second Pillar of the TEU; these have been more specifically discussed in section 5.3, above.

8.5.1 External economic relations

In response to the new challenges in external economic relations arising from the expansion of the areas covered by the WTO compared to those previously falling under the GATT, noted in section 5.1, above, and not least dealing with the view of the Community's external competence in commercial policy taken by the Court in Opinion 1/94 WTO-GATS and TRIPs,[61] the new Article 113(5) EC empowers the Council, acting unanimously on a proposal from the Commission and after consulting the European Parliament, to extend the application of the existing Article 113(1)–(4) EC to international negotiations and agreements on services and intellectual property insofar as they are not covered by the those

---

60. Bull. EU 6–1997, points I.5 and I.27, see also point I.29.
61. [1994] ECR I–5267.

provisions. Even if it might have been better to extend this possibility to all areas covered by the WTO, including rules of competition and the regulation of foreign investment, and to adopt the Commission's suggestion that the extension be authorized in the amendments introduced by the Treaty of Amsterdam itself, the solution found will probably lead to an analogous result. Indeed, the possibility for the Community to obtain optimal results in multilateral WTO negotiations covering as well its new areas of competence would be considerably weakened if the Commission were unable as negotiator to exchange concessions in one area against concessions by other parties in other areas, or to use its unique experience in the field of international rules of competition as negotiator for the Community as a whole.

The general amendments to Article 228(3) EC are significant in three respects: first, there is now express authorization of the practice of provisional application of international agreements;[62] secondly, there is the possibility of suspending the application of an agreement, and, thirdly, there is a mechanism for establishing the Community position in a body set up by an agreement based on Article 238 EC, when that body is called upon to adopt decisions having legal effects (other than decisions amending the legal framework of the agreement concerned).

As to the other challenges identified in section 5.2.1, above, facing the Community's economic relations, they were not addressed in the Treaty of Amsterdam but nevertheless remain important for the future.

8.5.2   The problems of enlargement

Directly after political agreement was reached on what became the Treaty of Amsterdam, the Commission submitted its proposals for the commencement of negotiations for accession to the European Union by various applicant countries,[63] and the decisions were taken at the European Council meeting in Luxembourg in December 1997.[64] Thus accession negotiations have begun with Cyprus, the Czech Republic, Estonia, Hungary, Poland and Slovenia in the first wave, and the preparation of negotiations with Bulgaria, Romania, Latvia, Lithuania, and Slovakia is

---

62. This practice is already well-known: GATT 1947 only entered into force provisionally and functioned for nearly 50 years; the various Europe Agreements were accompanied by interim agreements which covered the areas of exclusive Community competence, permitting many benefits to start flowing immediately, pending ratification of the Europe Agreements themselves (which were mixed agreements, as is explained in sections 2.3 and 4.2.3 of Chapter XII, *ante*).

63. See *Agenda 2000*, Bull. EU Supp. 5/97, and the Commission's Opinions, Bull. EU Supp. 6/97–15/97.

64. Bull. EU 12–1997, point I.5 (at point 27).

being speeded up. The prospect of Turkish accession in the foreseeable future seems if anything to have receded.[65] From the end of 1998 the Commission is to make regular reports to the Council, based on implementation of the accession partnerships and progress in adopting the Union acquis, together with any necessary recommendations for opening bilateral intergovernmental conferences. These reports will review progress of the Central and Eastern European applicant countries in the light of the Copenhagen criteria.[66]

8.5.3 The necessary reform of the Second Pillar

The main challenges resulting from the experiences of the past few years for the institutional reform of the Second Pillar of the TEU on CFSP were briefly summarized in section 5.3, above. It was noted there that unlike in the field of external commercial policy, the crisis in former Yugoslavia in particular has shown that in the field of general foreign and security policy the European Union has been not only less skilled in negotiations and in action than the United States of America, but also less skilled than the UN Security Council and NATO.[67] The approach to the inspections crisis with Iraq in late 1997 and early 1998 has not given grounds for reviewing this conclusion.

There are a considerable number of reforms which will be introduced by or in consequence of the Treaty of Amsterdam. First, there is a completely new text of the provisions governing CFSP in the new Articles J.1–J.18 TEU. Secondly, an Interinstitutional Agreement between the European Parliament, the Council and the Commission has been adopted on provisions regarding the financing of CFSP,[68] which accepts that CFSP expenditure is non-compulsory expenditure, but establishes the methods of dealing with it, including an ad hoc concertation procedure with a view to reaching an agreement between the two arms of the budgetary authority in relation to the amount of operational CFSP expenditure and the distribution of that amount over the relevant articles of the CFSP budget chapter.[69] Thirdly, there is a Declaration (No. 6) adopted by the IGC,

---

65. Turkey (alone of all the applicant countries) was not present at the European Conference held in London on 12 March 1998, perceiving it as something of a window-dressing exercise. As to the purpose of the European Conference, see Bull. EU 12–1997, point I.4.
66. As to which, see Bull. EU 6–1993, point I.13.
67. See, further, section 5.3, ante.
68. Bull. EU 7/8–1997, point 7.3.1.
69. The draft agreement uses the French term 'concertation' which has found its way into English, as distinct from the term 'conciliation' used in English in the early days, so that there is no confusion with the Article 189b EC procedure; see Chapter V, section 3.4.2, ante.

annexed to the Final Act on the occasion of signature of the Treaty of Amsterdam, on the establishment of a policy planning and early warning unit in the general secretariat of the Council under the responsibility of the Secretary-General, whom the revised Article 151 EC proclaims High Representative for CFSP. This will, however, establish appropriate cooperation with the Commission in order to ensure full coherence with the Union's external economic and developments policies. Among the units' tasks is monitoring and analyzing developments in areas relevant to CFSP. This important unit will consist of personnel drawn from the general secretariat of the Council, the Member States, the Commission and the WEU and 'any Member State or the Commission may make suggestions to the unit for work to be undertaken.' Fourthly, although a new Title VIa is inserted into the TEU, containing provisions on closer cooperation,[70] those provisions apply only to the First and Third Pillars (as is evident from the new Article K.15(1)(h) TEU); for the Second Pillar the device of constructive abstention fulfils an analogous function. This procedure, set out in the second subparagraph of the new Article J.13(1) TEU permits a Member State which abstains to qualify its abstention by making a formal declaration. While abstention does not prevent the Council from acting in cases in which unanimity is required, the effect of a declaration here is that while the Member State concerned accepts that the decision commits the Union, it is not itself obliged to apply the decision.[71] Nevertheless, the new Article J.13(1) TEU requires the Member State concerned to refrain from any action likely to conflict with or impede Union action based on the decision, and the other Member States are obliged to respect its position. In those areas in which the new Article J.13(2) TEU permits actions by qualified majority,[72] a member of the Council who declares that 'for important and stated reasons of national policy' it intends to oppose the adoption of a decision by such a majority, it can prevent a vote being taken. However, the Council may, by qualified majority request that the matter be referred to the European Council for decision by unanimity.[73]

70. See section 8.6, post.

71. If the members of the Council who qualify their abstentions in this way represent more than one-third of the votes weighted in accordance with Article 148(2) EC (*i.e.* 29 votes), the decision concerned will not be adopted, new Art. J.13(1) TEU.

72. The qualified majority required is that for action not taken on the basis of a Commission proposal, even if the Commission is actually the driving force behind the proposal concerned.

73. The reference up is not to the Council meeting at the level of Heads of State or Government, but to the European Council: the requirement of unanimity means that action may only be taken if the President of the Commission also agrees. This is perhaps less surprising than it may seem, given that it will still be the European Council which gives the leading and strategic direction to CFSP; in those fields too the President of the Commission meets on equal terms with the other members of that body.

This Epilogue is not the place for detailed analysis of these changes,[74] so the following comments are brief and related to the discussion in section 5.3, above.

The provisions adopted in Amsterdam with regard to the Second Pillar cover the matter, dealt with by the final four conclusions set out in section 5.3; they could not cover of course the fifth conclusion on the composition of the Security Council, and they did not provide for a legal personality of the Union, which would permit it to conclude itself treaties with third countries and international organizations in the area of the CFSP. The solution found for the establishment of an analytical and planning unit and the strengthening of the influence of the European Parliament at least as regards budgetary aspects[75] might compensate for weaknesses of the decision-making rules. The possibilities of 'constructive abstention' may compensate in part for the rigidity of the general unanimity rule. If the analytical and planning unit fully exploits the lessons from the experiences of Jean Monnet during the two last world wars (in the supply of the allied forces), in the League of Nations shortly after the First World War (with his way of finding a peaceful solution for a most dangerous conflict between Germany and Poland) and decades later with the preparation of the ECSC Treaty (for which the solution of the previous German–Polish conflict seemed to have been a valuable pilot-project), the result of this 'method of Jean Monnet'[76] might well be to reduce enormously the impact of the differences of opinions and national interests which has so far blocked effective results in CFSP. The budgetary powers which will be attributed to the European Parliament in the field of CFSP may also result in wider effects: experience on its part might strengthen its influence in this field, as has occurred as a result of experience with the use of budgetary powers in other policy fields.

Of the other innovations to be found in the revised provisions of the Second Pillar, the new Article J.8 merits special attention. The new Article J.8(1) provides that the Presidency will represent the Union in matters coming within CFSP; thus Article J.8(2) makes it responsible for the implementation of decisions taken under the CFSP Title and confers upon it the duty of in principle expressing the Union's position in international organizations and international conferences. In its tasks, the Presidency will be assisted by the Secretary-General of the Council as High Representative for CFSP. By virtue of Article J.8(4) the Commission is fully associated with the tasks referred to in Article J.8(1) and (2), and if

74. As to which, see Barents, *op. cit.* (see note 44, *supra*) and works which will no doubt appear in other languages in due course (including the forthcoming collections of papers resulting from the various conferences held since October 1997).
75. *Cf.* the first and fourth points identified in section 5.3, *ante*.
76. See VerLoren van Themaat in Curtin and Heukels (eds.), *op. cit.* (See note 35, *supra*) 3 at 6–9. See also Klip (1997) NJB 663. See also Monnet's own account in the early part of his *Memoirs* (London, 1978).

need be the Presidency is to be assisted by the next member State to hold the Presidency. It is unclear whether this means a replacement of the present 'troika' approach whereby the Presidency is assisted by the immediate past Member State having performed that function as well as the Member State next in line, with a 'duet' approach. The new Article J.8(5) TEU permits the Council, wherever it deems it necessary, to appoint a special representative with a mandate in relation to particular policy issues.

8.6   Reform of the Third Pillar

All the challenges mentioned in section 6 above, which corresponded to the main criticisms of the existing provisions of Title VI of the TEU and their implementation in practice, have been responded to in ways which may bring enormous improvements in comparison with those existing provisions. But these ways are very complicated, insofar as they are different in character from the various parts of the existing Title VI. Of the areas dealt with in the existing Title VI on JHA only provisions on police and judicial cooperation in criminal matters remain in the new Title VI, which is renamed accordingly. The objective is 'to provide citizens with a high level of safety within an area of freedom, security and justice by developing cooperation among the Member States in the fields of police and judicial cooperation in criminal matters and by preventing and combating racism and xenophobia.' The nature of the legally binding instruments that can be used for its implementation has now been clarified in the new Article K.6(2) TEU: framework decisions for the approximation of laws and regulations in the Member States are clearly inspired by directives within the Community framework, but direct effect is expressly excluded; decisions for any other purpose consistent with the objectives of the new Title VI will exclude such approximation, but will be binding, even though they too will not have direct effect;[77] finally, conventions may be established by the Council which it recommends to the Member States for adoption in accordance with their respective constitutional requirements.[78]

77. The Council may by qualified majority adopt measures to implement those decisions at the level of the Union. The qualified majority required is that for action not taken on the basis of a Commission proposal, even if the Commission is actually the driving force behind the proposal concerned, see the new Art. K.6(3) TEU. But in procedural questions throughout the new Title VI TEU the Council acts by simple majority, see the new Art. K.6(4) TEU.

78. The Council may set a time-limit for the start of such procedures, and unless they otherwise so provide, the conventions will enter into force, as among those Member States which have adopted them, once at least half of the Member States have adopted the necessary provisions, see the new Art. K.6(2) TEU. The conventions may be compared with the conventions adopted under Art. 220 EC, but it is significant that the

A Declaration (No. 7) adopted by the IGC, annexed to the Final Act on the occasion of signature of the Treaty of Amsterdam, on the new Article K.2 TEU makes it clear that action in the field of police cooperation under that provision, including activities of Europol, shall be subject to appropriate judicial review by the competent national authorities in accordance with rules applicable in each Member State.

The new Article K.7 TEU ensures a very minimum guarantee of the possibility of requesting preliminary rulings from the Court of Justice on the validity and interpretation of framework decisions and decisions, on the interpretation of conventions established under the new Title VI, and on the validity and interpretation of the measures implementing them. Whether in fact any (and if so, which) national courts will be permitted to make a reference will depend on whether the Member State has by declaration accepted the jurisdiction of the Court to give such rulings, and the choice of courts permitted to make references made by the Member State concerned.[79] This means that the possibility of obtaining rulings may vary from Member State to Member State, which runs the danger of encouraging forum-shopping. It also means that where the more restrictive option has been applied, litigants seeking a reference will have to exhaust local remedies until they reach the relevant court of final jurisdiction before they even have a chance of getting to the Court of Justice. For those who are in countries in which litigation is expensive this is not a happy state of affairs. However, the Court will have jurisdiction to review the legality of framework decisions and decisions in actions brought by a Member State or the Commission on grounds which are in fact identical to those applicable under Article 173 EC; it will also have jurisdiction to rule on any dispute between Member States regarding the interpretation or the application of acts adopted under the new Article K.6.(2) TEU, if such a dispute cannot be settled within the Council within six months of its being referred to the Council by one of its members.[80] Finally, the Court will also be able to rule on any dispute between Member States and the Commission regarding the interpretation or application of conventions

new proposal for a Judgments Convention COM (97) 609 Final (O.J. 1998 C 33/20) is based on the existing Art. K.3(2)(c) TEU (the corresponding, but not identical provision is the new Art. K.6(2)(d) TEU), and not on Art. 220 EC.

79. The choice is either any court or tribunal, or only those against whose decisions there is no judicial remedy under national law. The Court of Justice will have no jurisdiction to review the validity or proportionality of operations carried out by the police or other law enforcement services of a Member State or the exercise of the responsibilities incumbent on Member States with regard to the maintenance of law and order and the safeguarding of internal security, see the new Art. K.7(5) TEU. Clearly national courts are the appropriate forum for review of such operations.

80. This is particularly interesting: the clear desire is for a political opportunity to resolve the dispute, but if it is resolved with an interpretation which as a result of a later judgment of the Court is shown to be misconceived, the potential legal weakness of political fora for dispute settlement will be clearly exposed.

established under the new Article K.6(2)(d) TEU. While the criticisms as to the lack of legal certainty and legal protection have been met to an extent, the absence of direct effect and the optional jurisdiction for preliminary rulings are clearly designed to limit or discourage the opportunities for challenge by individuals; the intergovernmental approach dies hard.

The role of the European Parliament is certainly considerably strengthened in the new Title VI TEU. Thus Article K.11 requires consultation of the European Parliament before the adoption by the Council of any measure referred to in the new Article K.6(2)(b), (c) and (d) TEU.[81] The existing powers of the Parliament to question or make recommendations to the Council, and to hold an annual debate are continued in the new provisions. It should also not be forgotten that the intergovernmental character of this Title implies the possibility of parliamentary control by the national parliaments in conformity with their own rules of procedure.

The 'flexibility' provisions permitting closer cooperation between at least a majority of Member States on an inclusive basis, without affecting either the acquis communautaire or measures adopted under the other provisions of the TEU or the EC Treaty, or the competence, rights, obligations or interests of non-participating Member States clearly confirm the concept of permissible multi-speed integration within the Third Pillar of the European Union;[82] such a concept is also provided for in the new Article 5a EC in respect of the First Pillar.

The other parts of the old Title VI TEU, as well as the Schengen *acquis*, have been transferred in various ways into the ambit of the First Pillar. Thus free movement of persons, asylum and immigration have now found their place in a new Title IIIa in Part Three of the EC Treaty under that joint designation.[83] After a transitional period of five years from the date of entry into force of the Treaty of Amsterdam in which unanimity is the general rule (although the new Article 73o(3) EC does make some exceptions), the new Article 73o(2) EC provides that the Council must, by unanimity and after consulting the European Parliament, take a decision providing that all or some of the matters covered by that Title shall be governed by the co-decision procedure; as a result of the new Article 73o(4) EC, some of the measures concerned will in any event after the expiry of that five-year period be adopted using the co-decision procedure. The new Article 73p makes special provision regarding the applicability of Article 177 EC in the fields falling under this Title and permits the

---

81. *I.e.* framework decisions, decisions or conventions. The Council may fix a time-limit for the Parliament to deliver its opinion, which must be no less than three months, and in default of the delivery of an opinion within that time-limit, the Council may act without more ado.

82. As to the detailed conditions, see the new Art. K.15 TEU; the criteria of the new Arts. 5a EC or K.12 TEU as appropriate must be respected. As to the mechanics of decision-making, see the new Art. K.16 TEU.

Council, the Commission or a Member State to request a ruling from the Court of Justice on the interpretation of this Title or of acts adopted on the basis of it; these latter rulings will not apply to national judgments which have become res judicata.[84] At the end of the same five-year period, the Council may, under the new Article 73o(2) EC, acting unanimously after consulting the European Parliament, adapt the provisions of the new Article 73p on the Court of Justice's powers under this Title.

Powers to adopt measures to combat fraud affecting the Community's financial interests will also be transferred from the Third Pillar to the First Pillar when the Treaty of Amsterdam enters into force. Thus the new Article 209a EC obliges both the Community and the Member States to take the necessary steps which will act as a deterrent and afford effective protection in the Member States. The Council, acting under the co-decision procedure, and after consulting the Court of Auditors, will adopt 'the necessary measures in the fields of the prevention of and fight against fraud affecting the financial interests of the Community with a view to affording effective and equivalent protection in the member States' However, the measures may not concern the application of national criminal law or the national administration of justice. Powers for strengthening customs cooperation between Member States and between them and the Commission will also be transferred from the old Title VI of the TEU to the new Article 116 EC; the co-decision procedure applies, and again, the measures may not concern the application of national criminal law or the national administration of justice. The reason in these instances for excluding the latter type of measures is that they remain firmly within the ambit of the new Title VI TEU.

The existing provisions of Article K.1.(4) TEU on combating drug addiction, as far as this is not covered by the powers concerning police and judicial cooperation in criminal matters, have been replaced by the new Article 129 EC. In this way the current partial overlap between the powers of the Ministers of Home Affairs and Justice, acting under the old Title VI of the TEU who appeared to abuse their power sometimes by getting round the prohibition of any harmonization of the laws and regulations of the Member States in Article 129 EC, and the power of the Ministers of Health, acting under Article 129 EC, has now been excluded.

83. The new Arts. 73i–73q EC.
84. Although the Court of Justice's powers under the new Article 73p EC are perhaps comparable to its powers under the new Title VI TEU, they are very clearly distinct. Under the new Article 73p EC jurisdiction is not optional, and references for preliminary rulings may only be made by a national court or tribunal against whose decisions there is no judicial remedy under national law; the Court of Justice will have no jurisdiction to rule on any decisions taken pursuant to the new Article 73j(1) EC relating to the maintenance of law and order and the safeguarding of internal security. Clearly national courts are the appropriate forum for review of such operations.

8.7 The necessary institutional revisions

There is no doubt that the Treaty of Amsterdam contains a great number of measures contributing to ensuring 'the effectiveness of the mechanisms and the institutions of the Community' which the 1996 IGC was required to consider by virtue of Article N.(2) TEU in accordance with the fifth indent of the first paragraph of Article B TEU.

There has been a major improvement in Community decision-making through a number of changes. First, the previous great variety of ways of involving the European Parliament in decision-making has been streamlined, to in principle three forms: the assent procedure, the co-decision procedure, and the cooperation procedure. The latter is now only retained in the area of EMU provisions. In a few cases the only involvement of the Parliament will be in the form of consultation. The clearly more far-reaching acceptance of the Parliament as a legislative partner by the Council is also manifest in the changes made to the co-decision procedure in the new Article 189b EC, which not only considerably simplify that procedure but also strengthen the Parliament's role considerably. It is however to be regretted that the suggestions made before the IGC to provide for a 'hierarchy of norms' found no response. Had these been taken up, it might have been possible to extend the co-decision procedure at least to the basic regulations in the very important area of the Common Agricultural Policy. Secondly, the modest extension of qualified majority voting in the Council, both in relation to new and existing Treaty provisions,[85] continues, albeit now slowly, a trend which was already envisaged in the old EEC Treaty when at various points movement from unanimity to qualified majority voting was triggered, and which has continued with every major amendment of the EC Treaty.

The third improvement is in the new Article 151 EC. This is two-fold in nature: the power of procedural decision conferred on Coreper permits it in particular to adapt to the objective of the more effective functioning of the Second Pillar;[86] the raising of the right of access to Council documents to Treaty level is a major step in improving the perception of improved transparency in the operation of the Council. In this context, the new Article 191a EC recognizes the right of access of any citizen of the Union and any natural or legal person residing in or having its registered office in a Member State to European Parliament, Council and Commission

85. Santer recognized that the extension was more modest than had been hoped, see his speech to the European Parliament on 26 June 1997 (Bull. EU 6–1997, point 2.2.1 (at p. 164)).
86. This goes hand-in-hand with the revision of the provision concerning PoCo (the Political Committee which will be governed by the new Art. J.15 TEU); this is no longer to be specifically composed of the Political Directors of the national Foreign Ministries, and it would seem that this will firmly signal that PoCo is in practice as well as legally indeed inferior to *Coreper* (see Chapter IV, section 3.4, *ante*).

documents.[87] This solution to the 'transparency problem' seems quite satisfactory.

The fourth notable improvement is that the first steps have been taken or announced to strengthen the position of the Commission and to improve the effective exercise of its institutional function as laid down in Article 157 EC and explained in section 7.2, above. The strengthened hand of the nominee for President of the Commission and his or her stronger position once in office have already been noted in section 8.1, above. In a Declaration (No. 32) adopted by the IGC, annexed to the Final Act on the occasion of signature of the Treaty of Amsterdam, on the organization and functioning of the Commission, the IGC noted that the Commission intended to prepare a reorganization of tasks within the college in good time for the Commission which will take up office in 2000, in order to ensure an optimum division between conventional portfolios and specific tasks. Moreover, the IGC noted that the Commission intended to undertake in parallel a corresponding reorganization of its departments, and in particular the desirability of bringing external relations under the responsibility of a Vice-President. This Declaration to some extent actually paves the way for a more effectively functioning Commission, even after the intended enlargements of the number of Member-States. In particular it could indeed contribute to finding a rational compromise between the position of France on the one hand (with its initial proposal to have only 10 members in the Commission) and most of the smaller Member States on the other as to the maximum number of members of the Commission which would be acceptable to ensure the effective exercise of its constitutional function, laid down in Article 157(2) of the EC, even after the intended enlargement of the EU to some 26 Member-States. This is particularly important in view of the stated opinion of the current President of the Commission (Santer) that the number of 'conventional portfolios' in the terms of the first paragraph of the Declaration, should

87. The principles and conditions of access (including limits on grounds of public or private interest governing the right of access to documents) are to be determined by the Council, acting under the co-decision procedure, within two years of the entry into force of the Treaty of Amsterdam. At the moment, as has been noted at the relevant places in Chapter IV, *ante*, the European Parliament, the Council, and the Commission all have rules in place on this subject (as do various other organs, as set out there). The major difference will be that for the three named Institutions the Council will have to prescribe, using the co-decision procedure, the general principles and limits, but each of these three will draw up (or continue to apply) its own Rules of Procedure on the matter, with existing rules being adapted if necessary to conform to the new general principles and limits. In a Declaration (No. 35) adopted by the IGC, annexed to the Final Act on the occasion of signature of the Treaty of Amsterdam, on the new Article 191a EC, the IGC agreed that the principles and conditions referred to in that provision 'will allow a Member State to request the Commission or the Council not to communicate to third parties a document originating from that State without its agreement.'

not exceed 12, although he carefully left open the number of 'specific tasks' to be exercised by other members of the Commission.[88] The desirability of bringing external relations under the responsibility of a Vice-President, also seems to pave the way to a better coordinated composition and functioning Commission in power areas which are now spread over several of its members (turf wars always distract from the achievement of substantive goals).

In view of the failure of the IGC, in the composition of the Heads of State or Government in the protracted negotiations in Dutch Central Bank's headquarters at Amsterdam during the night and into the early hours, to agree on the future composition of the Commission, it annexed to the TEU and to the EC, ECSC and Euratom Treaties a Protocol on the Institutions with the prospect of enlargement of the European Union. This provides that at the date of entry into force of the first enlargement, the relevant EC, ECSC and Euratom Treaty provisions notwithstanding, the Commission will comprise one national of each of the Member States. This is, however, subject to the weighting of the votes in the Council having been modified, whether by re-weighting of the votes or by dual majority, in a manner acceptable to all Member States, taking into account all relevant elements, notably compensating those Member States which give up the possibility of nominating a second member of the Commission.[89] The second Article of the Protocol makes clear that, at least one year before the membership of the European Union exceeds 20, an IGC of the Member States will be convened to carry out a comprehensive review of the provisions of the Treaties on the composition and functioning of the Institutions. As Santer stressed in his speech to the European Parliament on 26 June 1997, that means all the Institutions, not merely the Commission.[90] This text seems to suggest, or at least leaves open the possibility, that a compromise on that occasion could fix the maximum number of members of the Commission at 20. In combination with the Declaration on the organization and functioning of the Commission, already discussed above, a compromise could also be found in a provision which leaves the fixing of the optional numbers of conventional portfolios

---

88. In his speech to the European Parliament on 26 June 1997, Santer indicated the present Commission's view that there should be one member of the Commission from each Member State, and that there should be in the future a mechanism for changing the system if the number of Member States rises above 20 (Bull. EU 6–1997, point 2.2.1 (at p. 164). He did not on that occasion address the question of division between conventional portfolios and specific tasks.
89. As to the background to this, see Duff (ed.), *op. cit.* (see note 44, *supra*) 132–133. Duff explains that two possible types of dual majority were discussed at Amsterdam: one comprising qualified majority voting plus a certain proportion of the population of the Union; the other comprising both a certain population and a certain majority of Member States.
90. Bull. EU 6–1997, point 2.2.1 (at p. 164).

on the one hand and specific tasks (each of which sufficiently important to require a specialized Member of the Commission) on the other to the common accord of the governments of the Member States and the nominee for President of the Commission (approved by the European Parliament), a system which will apply for nomination of the other members of the Commission in the amended Article 158(2) EC. This last form of compromise solution would, however, risk leading to a deadlock in the nomination procedure. It would certainly be better therefore to fix the maximum number of coordinating and specialized Commission members at 20, without prejudice to the already existing provisions of Article 157(1) EC (and the corresponding ECSC and Euratom provisions), enabling the Council acting unanimously, to alter the number of members of the Commission. As indicated in the Declaration on the organization and functioning of the Commission, it is essential that the President of the Commission enjoy broad discretion in the allocation of tasks within the college, as well as in any reshuffling of those tasks during a Commission's term of office. The decision-making procedure on this point should be laid down in the Commission's Rules of Procedure, as provided for in Article 162 EC (and equivalent provisions).

In section 7.2 , above, it was illustrated in some detail how, on the basis of the state of the relevant discussions in 1995, these various aspects of the composition and working methods of the Commission could be worked out. The views expressed by Santer which have been quoted above, and the tone of the Declaration would seem to point, albeit in less elaborate detail, in a similar direction. Without repeating the comments already advanced in section 7.2, above, it should be noted that Santer appears to prefer 12 conventional (in the terminology of section 7.2, 'coordinating') portfolios rather than the 10 which were suggested in that section on the basis of the present organization of the Commission and its administration.[91]

The Protocol on the Institutions referred to above has undoubtedly complicated the task of reaching a compromise regarding the composition of the Commission by linking it to the other unsolved problem of the modification of the weighting of the votes in the Council and expressing this in such crucial terms, particularly as regards compensating those five Member States who would each be giving up 'their' second member of the Commission. This concept of compensation seems fundamentally incompatible with the institutional independence of the Commission. It may be recalled that Article 157(2) EC (and the equivalent provisions) provides that 'members of the Commission shall, in the general interest of the Community, be *completely independent* in the performance of their duties'[92] and that in such 'they shall neither seek nor take instructions

91. See also Timmermans in Winter et al. (eds.), op. cit. (see note 42, supra) 133 at 143–144 in a similar vein.
92. Emphasis added.

from any government or from any other body.' The concept of compensation is clearly incompatible with the fundamental constitutional differences between the position of the Commission and that of the Council (whose members of course may and do seek or take instructions from their governments) within the balance of power between the various Institutions of the European Union, both as ensured by the TEU itself and by the Community Treaties of the First Pillar of the Union.

The possible loss of members of the Commission should be seen exclusively as one element in the process of ensuring its efficient and coherent functioning as an independent institution. To take an example from the Court, no Member State has ever argued that the fact that not all the Member States have an Advocate General of their nationality in the Court should be compensated by a greater number of votes in the Council, while the efficient functioning of the Court only required a smaller number of Advocates General than the number of judges. It should be recalled in this context also, that France, in its proposal to limit the number of members of the Commission to 10 in the interest of efficient functioning, even accepted as a logical consequence that the larger Member-States also should then participate in a system of rotation of their membership.[93]

In relation to the Council, as the Declaration (No. 50) adopted by the IGC, annexed to the Final Act on the occasion of signature of the Treaty of Amsterdam, on the Protocol on the Institutions confirms, it was at Spain's insistence that the Ioannina Compromise on qualified majority voting is extended until the next enlargement, by which date 'a solution for the special case of Spain will be found' This special case reflects the difficulties in the discussion on re-weighting or some form of dual majority which it was impossible to resolve at Amsterdam. The questions involved choices such as: re-weighting votes in the Council in a manner which is in adequate proportion to population; a more arbitrary reallocation of votes according to bands; the adoption of a form of dual majority of qualified majority voting plus a certain proportion of the population of the Union, or the adoption of a dual majority reflecting both a certain population and a certain majority of the Member States. These problems result from having Member States with such differing sizes and populations, particularly with the prospect of a large increase in the number of smaller Member States following future enlargements. The failure to settle re-weighting at Amsterdam probably indicates that such an approach will lead nowhere; accordingly, the arguments for choosing a type of dual majority should in the end prevail. These issues have already been addressed in section 7.2, above. In view of Duff's account, it is not surprising that the issue was quickly postponed at Amsterdam.[94]

It is submitted that the new IGC to be concerned with finding solutions

93. See Duff, op. cit. (see note 44, *supra*) 132.
94. *Ibid.*, at 133.

for the questions regarding the institutions (in particular the Commission and the Council) left open at Amsterdam should be convened as soon as practicable, probably around the year 2000, which was also the horizon of the preceding sections. The main reason for such a timetable, as the Czech government has also made clear,[95] is that any unnecessary delay in completing the institutional framework to be offered to the applicant countries would complicate the negotiations with them. It should be recalled that the relevant institutional questions are of course just as much vital issues for the applicant countries as they proved to be in Amsterdam for the existing Member States. Therefore the risk of the absence of a clear solution constituting a severe handicap for the negotiation process, is also valid for a European Union with perhaps more than 25 Member States.

Finally, with regard to the Court of Justice, the competence of which for judicial protection has been extended to new areas as above, it is to be regretted that the Treaty of Amsterdam does not also provide a procedure for adapting the working methods of this other independent Institution to the coming increase of the number of its judges. A plenary court with over 20 judges will not, it is respectfully submitted, be able to deliberate efficiently and coherently on the cases submitted to it. The text of Article 2 of the Protocol on the Institutions with the prospect of enlargement would, however, certainly permit this issue to be addressed by the IGC which will be convened by virtue of that provision.

95. See *Europe*, 27 August 1997, p. 3. The Czech Foreign Minister expressed his concern, during a visit to Prague by the Presidency of the European Union, that the institutional questions left open at Amsterdam risked delaying the negotiation process.

Index